C0-DVZ-869

A LEARNER'S
ARABIC - ENGLISH DICTIONARY

A LEARNER'S
ARABIC - ENGLISH
DICTIONARY

BY

F. STEINGASS, Ph. D.,

LIBRAIRIE DU LIBAN
Riad Solh Square
BEIRUT

Riverside Community College
'00 Library
MAY 4800 Magnolia Avenue
Riverside, CA 92506

REF PJ 6640 .S8 1989

Steingass, Francis Joseph,
1825-1903.

A learner's Arabic-English
dictionary

LIBRAIRIE DU LIBAN
Riad Solh Square - Beirut

Associated companies, branches and representatives throughout the world.

New Impression, 1989

Printed in Lebanon *by* A . J

PREFACE

We are now going to set forth, as briefly as can be done compatibly with clearness, the general plan on which this Dictionary is worked out. The Arabic words are given in their crude form, *i.e.* the form in which they appear before the grammatical terminations are added, and in Arabic type only as far as they are represented by the letters of the alphabet, leaving the rendering of the diacritical signs, *Hamzah* included, to the transliteration.* Thus each word forms, as it were, a skeleton, dead and meaningless in itself, but *moved* into life by the *Ḥarakât* (vowel-points), and further to be individualized, as of *Arab kin* by the *I'râb* (grammatical inflection). To every *male*, if I may be allowed to continue the metaphor, its *consort* is allotted, that is to say, under each heading the form or forms with the feminine termination ة are subjoined to those without it, if both are in use. This has been done, because frequently the two forms stand mutually in the relationship of singular and plural, and therefore, by bringing them together in the same article, many cross-references could be spared.† In a similar way derivatives with a final ى, especially when forming the so-called

---

* The student, when about to make use of this Dictionary, is of course supposed to be well acquainted with these signs from his Grammar, and should his text be pointed, he will have no difficulty in finding the equivalent in transliteration, for any word he may look out, by referring to the heading in Arabic type. If, on the contrary, these signs are omitted from the text, as is always done in editions printed in the East (for instance, in the *Arabian Nights*, which he is particularly expected to read), it would be decidedly more bewildering for him to pick out, from perhaps half-a-dozen or more repetitions of the *same group* of Arabic letters, *variously marked*, that special combination which he wants; while, by using the *one* heading, which represents the letters in his book, as a master-key for the different meanings, his eye has simply to run over the article in order to ascertain that particular form which gives an appropriate sense to the passage in hand.

† If in the first part of an article ة is placed *after* a generic noun, it indicates either the female or the noun of unity; if *after* an adjective, it stands for the feminine. In the second part, the various forms are given in which a word has a feminine termination without such reference to sex or gender, and here the ة *heads* the transliteration. (Compare e.g. the articles اسد *asad*, ة, "lion," &c., p. 41; ثمر *s̱amar*, ة, "fruit," &c., p. 209; حار *ḥârr*, ة, "hot," &c., p. 258; خلف *h̤alf*, "behind," &c.;—ة *h̤ilfa-t*, "difference of opinion," &c., p. 337.)

Nisbah or noun of relation (in يّ), are, as a natural *offspring*, joined under the same heading to the *parent*-form, but only, if the alphabetical order would already bring them in immediate contact with it (see e.g. article خيال *ḥayâl*, &c., p. 347).

Roots, whether triliteral or quadriliteral, are found under two headings. One, placed in parentheses, gives the primitive verbs in the third person singular masculine, together with their Infinitives, and the Infinitives of the derived conjugations. In triliteral verbs the medial vowel of the Aorist is added, *if it differs* from that of the Preterite. Where therefore no such vowel is mentioned, the vowel of the Preterite is retained in the Aorist, which is frequently the case if it is *a*, rarely if it is *i*, but *always* if it is *u*. The second heading comprises those simple Derivatives, either nouns or adjectives, which do not exceed in number the original letters of the root.*

Derivatives which are formed by the introduction of so-called servile or additional letters, and the various measures of the broken Plural, are to be looked for in their natural alphabetical order, where their meanings or reference to the singular is given, unless they can be readily traced back to their respective origin by eliminating such additional letters according to a few simple rules of easy application. In order to impress these rules more effectively on the mind of the student, and to facilitate reference to them in case of need, we will divide the words in question into four classes, namely: — I. Words containing a letter of prolongation (ا — *â*, و — *û*, ى — *î*) or a doubled consonant; II. Words beginning with the letter ا; III. Words beginning with the letter ت *t*; IV. Words beginning with the letter م *m*.

I.—Words containing a letter of prolongation or a doubled consonant. In Derivatives or Plurals of this description, not found in the Dictionary, or only rendered by meanings which do not fully meet the requirements

---

* It is true that, by the arrangement explained in this and the previous paragraph, sometimes different roots or their derivatives are thrown together under the same heading: under the heading عد for instance, we give, besides *'add* and *'idd*, belonging to the root (عدّ), also the word *'udd*, "pustule," apparently itself a root, and under the feminine form عدة we include *'ida-t*, "promise, threat," derived from the root (وعد). But this very juxtaposition of disparate meanings will strike the attention of a thoughtful student, and continually remind him, that in Arabic, more than in any other language, very similar forms may have a vastly distinct origin.

of the case, these letters are to be thrown out, to obtain the root, or the singular, if it is a plural noun; thus:—

1. ا — in words of the measures

فاعل *fâ'il*, the well-known form of the Agent or active participle, "who does."

فعّال *fa''âl*, where also the double consonant is to be rejected, or in other words, the *Taśdîd* to be removed, intensive of the former, "who does frequently, habitually, by way of trade."

فعال *fi'âl*, Infinitive, exceptionally of the primitive verb (in which case, however, it will be found as a reference in its alphabetical place), regularly of the third conjugation, along with the more frequently used measure مفاعلة *mufâ'ala-t*, "doing with regard to another, doing reciprocally on the part of two or more." Also Plural of nouns of the measure فعل *fa'l*, *fi'l*, *fu'l*, and its feminine form in ة.

فعلاء *fa'lâ'*, feminine of the measure افعل *af'al*, forming adjectives of defect and colour (see Class II.).

Lastly, in Plurals of words which consist of four or more letters, either originally, or through the introduction of servile letters into triliteral roots. These plurals are trisyllabic, with *a* (—) after the first, *â* (ا —) after the second, and *i* (—) after the penultimate consonant. If all the letters of the singular are radical, the measure is—

فعالل *fa'âlil*, where the second *l* corresponds to the fourth and following consonants of the singular; and if the singular is quadriliteral, it will be obtained by dropping the of prolongation of the plural; otherwise it will be referred to in the alphabetical place of the latter.*

The plural measures of words of four and more letters, reducible to triliteral roots, are

افاعل *afâ'il*, plural of nouns, or of certain other plurals beginning with ا, or of adjectives of the measure افعل *af'al* used substan-

* The plural دراهم *dirâhim*, for instance, is not mentioned, in the alphabetical order, because the elimination of the ا points to the singular درهم *dirham*, name of the well-known coin; but سفارج *safârij* is quoted as plural of سفرجل *safarjal*, "quince," عنادل *'anâdil* as plural of عندليب *'andalîb*, "nightingale," because they do not contain all the letters of their respective singulars.

tively (see Class II.).†

تفاعل *tafâ'il*, plural of تفعلة *taf'ila-t*, Infinitive of the second conjugation, mostly of verbs terminating in a weak consonant (see Class III.).

فعائل *fa'â'il*, not given in the Dictionary amongst the alphabetical references when it is plural of فعيل *fa'îl* or فعيلة *fa'îla-t* (the elimination of the ا leading to the singular), but inserted as a reference if the singular has *â* (ا —) or *û* (و —) after the second radical.*

فواعل *fawâ'il*, plural of فاعل *fâ'il*, and much more frequently of its feminine form فاعلة *fâ'ila-t*. Here the ا of the singular has been changed into و before the ا of prolongation of the plural, and would have to be restored after throwing out the latter; practically, therefore the rule takes this shape: Suppress the و of such a plural, instead of the ا, to find the singular as given in the Dictionary; or as to be further derived from the verbal root according to the direction in the beginning of this Section.†

All these plurals, except فعائل *fa'â'il*, have parallel forms with *î* (ى —) instead of *i* (—) in the third syllable, corresponding to a long vowel in the second syllable of the singular. If the latter be *â* or *û*,

---

† For instance: اصابع *aṣâbi'*, plural of اصبع *aṣba'*, *'iṣba'*, "finger"; اكالب *akâlib*, plural of اكلب *aklub*, plural of paucity of كلب *kalb*, "dog"; اداهم *adâhim*, plural of ادهم *adham*, "very black," used substantively for a black horse, or for the chains of a prisoner. Throwing out the *Alif* of prolongation you obtain the heading under which the wished-for information will be found.

* We omit, for instance, the plural قصائد *qaṣâ'id*, as a reference to the singular قصيدة *qaṣîda-t*, "poem," but we give رسائل *rasâ'il* as plural of رسالة *risâla-t*, "mission," &c., and حلائب *ḥalâ'ib* as plural of حلوبة *ḥalûba-t*, "milch-camel." for the reason stated in the text.

† In the opening lines of al-Ḥarîrî's first Assembly we meet with the expression طوائح الزمن *ṭawâ'iḥu 'z-zamani*, which the Commentators explain by حوادثه وقواذفه *ḥawâdiṣu-hu wa qawâẓifu-hu*. Dropping the و in these three forms we obtain the Agents or participles طائح *ṭâ'iḥ*, "perishing," حادث *ḥâdiṣ*, "happening, befalling," and قاذف *qâẓif*, "flinging, casting," of whose feminines the said forms would be the regular plurals. But the native dictionaries, speaking of the term طوائح, tell us that it belongs to the نوادر *nawâdir*, or rare exceptions (plural, on the same principle, of نادرة *nâdira-t*, "anything rare"), its singular not being طائحة *ṭâ'iḥa-t*, according to rule, but مطوحة *muṭawwiḥa-t*, feminine of the Agent of the second conjugation, "that which casts about." Hence we give it in its alphabetical place, with the meaning resulting from the explanation of the Commentators, "impelling calamities," or, as Chenery translates it in the quoted passage, "*the shocks* of the time," while the forms *ḥawâdiṣ*, *qawâẓif*, and *nawâdir* could be passed over, as easily re-traced to their singular.

the plural is given as a reference in its alphabetical place; if it is *î*, such reference could be dispensed with, as here again the simple rejection of the ا leads to the singular.

2. و as letter of prolongation is to be thrown out in words of the measures

فعول *fa'ûl*, intensive of the Patient, rarely of the Agent, and

فعول *fu'ûl*, Infinitive of neuter verbs (also فعولة *fu'ûla-t*), or plural form of nouns.

3. ى as letter of prolongation is to be thrown out in words of the measures

فعيل *fa'îl*, intensive of the Agent, rarely of the Patient, and—

فعّيل *fi''îl*, where also the *Taśdîd* is to be removed, with the same meaning more forcibly expressed.

In this place may further be mentioned the final ىَ (*a*) of the measure

فعلى *ful'a*, fem. of the comparative form افعل *af'al* (see Class II.).

II.—Words beginning with the letter ا. This class comprises words of the measures

أفعل *af'al*, f. فعلاء *fa'lâ'*, forming adjectives of intransitive verbs, particularly expressive of defect or colour.

أفعل *af'al*, f. فعلى *fu'la*, which forms the comparatives and superlatives of any adjective, not belonging to the previously mentioned measure.

أفعل *af'ul*, one of the so-called plurals of paucity.

افعال *af'âl*, another plural of paucity, but common to plurals of multitude also, and therefore of very frequent occurrence.

If any word of this kind is not found in the Dictionary, the dropping of the initial ا (in the last-named measure, together with the rejection of the *Alif* of prolongation), will lead at once to the verbal root, from which the meaning may be gathered, if it is an adjective, or to the singular, if it is a plural noun. The two plurals of paucity (*af'ul* and *af'âl*) may form a new plural of their own of the measures افاعل *afâ'il* (also occasionally plural of the comparative), and افاعيل *afâ'îl* respectively, as has been mentioned under Class I.

To this Class belong further the Infinitives of the derived conjugations from the fourth upwards, except the fifth and sixth, all beginning with ا *i*, and having an *Alif* of prolongation after the last letter but one. The root of such an Infinitive will most easily be found by changing it

into a so-called Infinitive in *Mîm*, and applying to it the rules for words beginning with that letter, as will be explained under Class IV.

III.—Words beginning with the letter ت. This Class contains the measures

تفعلل *taf'alul*, Infinitive of the second conjugation of quadriliterals.

تفعيل *taf'îl*, تفعلة *taf'ila-t*, with their respective plurals, تفاعيل *tafâ'îl* and تفاعل *tafâ'il* (see Class I.), Infinitive of the second conjugation of triliterals.

تفعّل *tafa''ul*, Infinitive of the fifth, and—

تفاعل *tafâ'ul*, Infinitive of the sixth conjugations of the same.

By cutting off the initial ت *ta*, and throwing out a letter of prolongation or a double consonant, where such appear, the root is obtained, under which the Infinitive in question, with its different meanings, will be found.

IV.—Words beginning with the letter م *m*. The initial, not radical, م of words belonging to this Class may be read with *a* (*Fatḥah*) or *i* (*Kasrah*), in which case it is followed by a triliteral root, frequently with a letter of prolongation in the second syllable, or it may be pronounced with *u* (*Ḍammah*), when it forms participles and verbal nouns of quadriliterals, and is mostly accompanied by one or several more servile letters. We will therefore consider them under two heads, making henceforth use of dots to indicate the number of radical letters occurring in a word, as has been done all through the letter *M* in the Dictionary. It must, however, be remarked, with regard to the transliteration in Roman character, that only consonants and *long* vowels—which in Arabic contain a quiescent weak consonant—are reckoned to be *letters*, while the short vowels, as merely represented by orthographical signs, do not count as such; قال *qâl*, for instance, would consist of three letters, but قُل *qul* only of two in the eyes of an Arabic grammarian.

1. The measures of the form . . . مْ, *i.e.* consisting of a triliteral root, preceded by initial *ma* or *mi*, are—

مَفْعَل *maf'al*, Infinitive or noun of Action (in certain cases *maf'il*), and noun of Place or Time.

مِفْعَل *mif'al* and مِفْعَلة *mif'ala-t*, noun of Instrument.

These form their plural in مفاعل *mafâ'il*, which could be omitted from amongst the alphabetical references, as simply the elimination of the ا would lead to the singular. The noun of Instrument, however, takes more frequently the measure مفعال *mif'âl* (. ا . . مْ), with the plural مفاعيل *mafâ'îl*, and if such a singular is given in the Dictionary, the

plural will also be found with a reference to it, as here the dropping of the ا in the plural form would leave it still undecided whether it belongs to the singular مفعال *mif'âl*, or to either of the last two measures to be mentioned in this Section, viz.:

مفعيل *mif'îl*, a rare form of the intensive Agent, and—

مفعول *maf'ûl*, the regular form of the *nomen patientis* (Patient) of the transitive triliteral verb.

The plural of the latter (of the measure مفاعيل *mafâ'îl*) is quoted in its alphabetical place, for the reason stated above, but not that of the former, because here the removal of the ا suffices to find the singular.

2. The second category of words belonging to this Class are all Participles, nouns of Place or Time, and nouns of Action or so-called Infinitives in *Mîm*, and have the general form — مُ, *i.e.* the initial syllable *mu* is followed by an indefinite number of letters, from three to five, which, if not quiescent, are pronounced with *a* (*Fathah*), except the penultimate, which takes *i* (*Kasrah*), if the word is an active participle (Agent). At least three, frequently four, of these letters, are radical, as will be seen by comparing the different measures with the more general symbols included in parentheses. These measures are—

مفعل (. . . م) *muf'il*, Agent, *muf'al*, Patient, noun of Place or Time, and Infinitive in *mîm* of the fourth conjugation of a triliteral.

مفعلل (. . . . م) *mufa'lil*, Agent, *mufa'lal*, Patient, &c. of a quadriliteral.

مفعّل (. . . م) *mufa''il*, Agent, *mufa''al*, Patient, &c. of the second conjugation of a triliteral.

مفاعل (. . ا . م) *mufâ'il*, Agent, *mufâ'al*, Patient, noun of Place or Time, and in its feminine form مفاعلة *mufâ'ala-t*, Infinitive of the third conjugation of a triliteral.

مفعلّ (. . . م) *muf'all* (for *muf'alil*), Agent, and (for *muf'alal*) Infinitive in *Mîm* of the ninth conjugation of a triliteral.

In these five measures the root is obtained by simply cutting off the initial *mu*, and, where such occur, throwing out the ا of prolongation or doubled consonant, according to the rule given for Class I.

متفعلل (. . . . مت) *mutafa'lil*, Agent, *mutafa'lal*, Patient, &c. of a quadriliteral.

متفعّل (. . . مت) *mutafa''il*, Agent, *mutafa''al*, Patient, &c. of the fifth conjugation of a triliteral.

متفاعل (. . ا . مت) *mutafâ'il*, Agent, *mutafâ'al*, Patient, &c. of the sixth conjugation of a triliteral.

In these three measures the root is obtained by combining with the previous direction the rule given for Class III., in other words, by cutting off the initial *mu-ta*, besides removing the *Alif* or *Taśdîd*, if there should be any.

منفعل (. . . منْ) *munfa'il*, Agent, *munfa'al*, Patient, &c. of the seventh conjugation of a triliteral.

مستفعل (. . . مست) *mustaf'il*, Agent, *mustaf'al*, Patient, &c. of the tenth conjugation of a triliteral.

In these measures the root is obtained at once by cutting off the initial *musta* or *mun* respectively.

Most troublesome for beginners will be the measure

مفتعل (. . تْ . م) *mufta'il*, Agent, *muftā'al*, Patient, &c. of the eighth conjugation of a triliteral, where the first radical of the root appears between two servile letters.

If the initial letter of such a root is *n* or *s*, he will be liable to confound this form with the two previous ones, as it would begin with *munta* (possibly belonging to the seventh conjugation of a verb with initial *t*) in the first case, and with *musta* in the second case. Here he must consider whether *musta* is followed by three letters, when the word belongs to the tenth conjugation of a root composed of these three letters; or by two, when it appertains to the eighth conjugation of a root composed of these two letters preceded by *s*.* He must bear in mind, however, that in these measures of the eighth and tenth conjugations, as in the corresponding ones of the fourth and seventh, the *Alif* of prolongation, represented in the Roman character by *â*, counts as a full letter, and points to a so-called hollow root, *i.e.* a root with a weak consonant for its second radical. With regard to words beginning with *munta*, it will be a comfort for him to learn that the roots with *t* as a first radical are few in number, and very rarely form the seventh conjugation, so that he may in all safety turn at once to a root beginning

---

* Verbal forms may, in this case, sometimes be perplexing at first sight: استبقوا for instance, may stand for "they allowed to live" (tenth form of بقى *baqiya*), or for "they vied to be first" (eight of سبق *sabaqa*). But the vocalisation of the former would be *istabqau* (استبْقَوا where the *Fatḥah* is remainder of the ـَى — of the singular استبْقى *istabqa*), that of the latter, *istabaqû* (استبقُوا).

with *n.* Still, to help him over the difficulties which undoubtedly will beset his path, we have placed, as it were, road-marks on it, by freely interspersing the letter م of the Dictionary with general leading-forms, like those given above, the purport and use of which he will now easily understand.

We have here to add a word more about the usual Infinitives with initial ا of the derived conjugations of a triliteral, other than the second, third, fifth, and sixth. Their measures are: fourth, افعال *if'âl;* seventh, انفعال *infi'âl;* eighth, افتعال *ifti'âl;* ninth, افعلال *if'ilâl*; and tenth, استفعال *istif'âl.* When, by attending to the rules laid down in the previous pages, some practice has been acquired in separating the radical from the servile letters, the student will, of course, turn from such Infinitives directly to the root. But in the earlier stage of his reading he will find it safer mentally to transform them into the corresponding Infinitives in *Mîm* by substituting the syllable *mu* for the initial ا (*Hamzah*), throwing out the ا (*Alif*) of prolongation, and pronouncing the letters not quiescent with *a* (*Fathah*). So fourth, افعال *if'âl* changes into مفعل *muf'al;* seventh, انفعال *infi'âl* into منفعل *munfa'al;* eighth, افتعال *ifti'âl* into مفتعل *mufta'al;* ninth, افعلال *if'ilâl* into مفعل *muf'all;* and tenth, استفعال *istif'âl* into مستفعل *mustaf'al*, with which measures of the present Class he will by this time have become familiar. It must, however, be observed that a great number of the Infinitives with initial ا have been given in their alphabetical order, especially such of frequent occurrence or of more or less irregular formation.

By adhering, as we hope, judiciously, if not with slavish rigour, to a system of arrangement with regard to cross-references based on the foregoing rules, it was possible not only to reduce our German model to nearly half its size without omitting anything essential, but even to gain room for several important additions, which we will now shortly point out. Firstly, wherever a referenee is given, we did not confine ourselves to quoting the word referred to, unless it occurs in closest proximity, but we accompanied the reference with one or two of the principal significations, so as to spare the student as much as possible time and trouble. Secondly, the number of meanings has frequently been increased. Here we are indebted for many of the English renderings to Chenery's translation of the first 26 *Assemblies of Al Ḥarîri*, Rodwell's *Korân*, Palmer's *El Baha Zoheir*, and Lane's *Arabian Nights.* Thirdly, the stock of words itself has been not inconsiderably enlarged from the

Standard Works of Arabic Literature, particularly those mentioned in the beginning of this Preface, and, to quote a distinguished modern writer of Arabic, from the *Maqâmât* of Naṣîf al-Yazaji, on which remarkable work compare Chenery's Introduction to Al Ḥarîri, p. 99. Fourthly, the last and most comprehensive addition is the introduction of the Infinitives of the derived conjugations of all verbal roots. In a book of this kind, we did not think it sufficient to designate them merely by their numbers, for to put unerringly the right number upon the right form requires a certain amount of practice which can scarcely be expected from a learner at the outset of his studies; so we thought it incumbent upon us to give either the third person singular masculine of the Preterite or the Infinitive, and as the former course would have frequently necessitated the additional introduction of the *Fâ'il* or Agent, we decided for the second plan.* Some inconsistency in this and other respects will be noticed in the early part of the Dictionary, namely, with regard to roots beginning with ا, whose derived Infinitives, however, will be mostly found in their alphabetical place, and in the beginning of the letter ب *b*, when our views on this point were not quite settled. This is a blemish which we must beg to excuse, and reserve ourselves to efface in any later edition.

* These Infinitives may frequently be merely theoretical, not actually used as مفعول مطلق *maf'ûl muṭlaq*, i.e. corroborative or adverbial *maṣdar*. Nevertheless, they are fit representatives of their conjugation, as their formal relation to the conjugated verb remains always the same.

CORRIGENDA ET ADDENDA.

Page 333, *read* under the heading خفيف after the words "a metre:" *fâ'ilâtun mustaf'i-lun fâ'ilâtun* — ⏑ — — | — — ⏑ — | — ⏑ — — twice.

Page 492, *add* under سريع: a metre, *mustaf'ilun mustaf'ilun maf'û-lâtu* — — ⏑ — | — — ⏑ — | — — — ⏑ twice.

Page 958, *add* after مجتبا the heading: مجتث *mujtaṣṣ*, a metre, *mus-taf'i-lun fâ'ilâtun fâ'ilâtun* — — ⏑ — | — ⏑ — — | — ⏑ — — twice.

Page 1015, *add* under مضارع: a metre, *mafâ'ilun fâ'ilâtun mafâ'ilun* ⏑ — — — | — ⏑ — — | ⏑ — — — twice.

TRANSLITERATION.

The Arabic letters have, in this volume, been transliterated as follows :—

ا *a*, *i u*, at the beginning of a word (see the remark on the Hamzah below).

ب *b*.

ت *t*.

ث *s̱*. Pronounced like the English *th* in *thing*.

ج *j*.

ح *ḥ*. A guttural aspirate, stronger than *h*.

خ *ḫ*. Pronounced like the Scotch *ch* in *loch*.

د *d*.

ذ *ẕ*. Pronounced like the English *th* in *that*, *with*.

س *s*.

ش *ś*. Pronounced like the English *sh* in *shut*.

ص *ṣ*. Strongly articulated *s*.

ض *ḍ*. Similar to the English *th* in *this*.

ط *ṭ*. Strongly articulated palatal *t*.

ظ *ẓ*. Strongly articulated *z*.

ع *'*. Strong guttural, the pronunciation of which must be learnt by the ear.

غ *g*.

ف *f*.

ق *q*.

ك *k*.

ل *l*.

م *m*.

ن *n*.

ه *h*.

و *w*.

ى *y*.

The Hamzah has not been marked at the beginning of a word, where it has always the Alif for a prop, and is pronounced as *a, i, u,* preceded by a very slight aspiration, like *h* in the English word “honour.”

The vowel signs have been rendered by *a* for ـَ, *i* for ـِ, *u* for ـُ; the long vowels by *â* for ـَا, ـٰ, or آ, *î* for ـِي, *ai* for ـَيْ, *û* for ـُو, *au* for ـَوْ, all to be pronounced as in Italian or German. Final ـَى is rendered by *a*, ـٰى by *ā*.

The feminine termination ـَة is represented by *a-t*, where the final letter is joined to the body of the word by a hyphen, to show that in modern Arabic it is not to be pronounced, unless the noun is placed in a state of construction with a pronominal suffix, or another noun preceded by the article.

In addition to the Abbreviations in common use the following are employed:—

Ag. for Agent (active participle).
Pat. „ Patient (passive participle).
(m.) „ modern form or expression.
n.u. „ noun of unity.

Where an asterisk (*) is inserted in an article, it means that, besides the forms or meanings given under the heading, others may be looked for in accordance with the indications set forth in the Preface.

ARABIC-ENGLISH DICTIONARY.

ا

ا (الف *alif*), **as a numeral sign = 1; also abbreviation for** اول *awwal*, as: ربيع الاول = را *rabî'u-'l-awwal*, جمادى الاول = جا *jumâẓiyu-'l-awwal*, ذو القعدة الاول = ذا *ẓû-'l-qa'datu-'l-awwal*; — *a*, particle of interrogation placed at the beginning of the first word of a sentence; followed by ام = whether ... or.

اب *ab*, father, patriarch; الاب *al-ab*, our Heavenly Father; — *ab, âb*, month of August; — آب *âb-in*, see آبى *âbî*.

(اب) *abb*, I and U, INF.; اب *abb*, اباب *abâb*, اباية *abâba-t*, *ibâba-t*, put the hand to (as to the sword); move, agitate; long for (one's country); prepare (for a journey); intend; be straight, upright (as a road, conduct); defeat; II. cry out; V., VIII. wonder, be astonished (with ب *bi*); — *abb*, pl. اوب *a'ubb*, intention; travelling plan; fodder, grass, meadow.

(ابا) *abâ* (for ابو *abaw-a*) U, INF. اباوة *ibâwa-t*, become father; II. call a person father; V. take for a father, consider as a father; — *aba'*, A, INF. ابا *ab'*, throw, shoot, hit.

ابا *abâ'* reeds, rushes; — *ibâ'*, refusal, rejection, disobedience, abhorrence, disgust; unwillingness; — *ubâ'*, pl. of آبى *âbî*; — — *âbâ'*, pl. of ابو *abû*, fathers, forefathers, ancestors; — ة *abâ'a-t*, reed; — *ibâ'a-t*, INF. of ابى; — *ubât*, pl. of ابى *âbî*, q.v.

اباب *ubâb*, great bulk of water, billow, wave; — *abâb*, luggage; also ة *abâba-t*, *ibâba-t*, way, conduct, manner of living; longing for; INF. of (اب) q.v.

ابابيل *abâbîl*, some fabulous birds; for اباويل *abâwîl*, pl. of ابول *ibbaul*, troops of camels.

ابابين *abâbîn*, pl. of ابان *ibbân*, q.v.

اباتر *ubâtir*, without children, solitary.

اباتة *ibâta-t*, passing the night, giving a night's lodging, doing anything at night time; IV. of (بيت) q.v.

اباثة *ibâsa-t*, examining; ploughing; IV. of (بوث) q.v.

اباجر *abâjir*, اباجير *abâjîr*, pl. of بجر *bujr*, q.v.

اباجل *abâjil*, sinews of the foot, pl. of ابجل *abjal*.

اباحة *ibâḥa-t*, making public; revealing, disclosing; giving full permission; license, licentiousness; IV. of (بوح) q.v.

اباحس *abâḥis*, pl. finger-tops.

اباخة *ibâḫa-t*, extinguishing; IV. of (بوخ) q.v.

اباد *âbâd*, eternities, pl. of ابد *abad*; — ة *ibâda-t*, annihilation; IV. of (بيد) q.v.

اباديد *abâdîd*, scattered animals, birds, etc.

ابار *ab'âr*, *âbâr*, pl. of بئر q.v.; —

abâr, lead ;—*ibâr*, ة *ibâra-t*, fructification of the palm tree, s. ابر ;—*ibâr*, needles, pl. of ابرة *ibra-t* ;—*abbâr*, maker or seller of needles ; flea.

ابارق *abâriq*, pl. of ابرق *abraq*, q.v.—ة *abâriqa-t*, اباريق *abârîq*, pl. of ابريق *abrîq*, q.v.

ابارمة *abârima-t*, ابارهة *abâriha-t*, pl. of ابرهيم *ibrahîm*.

اباز *abbâz*, who jumps, leaps (as a gazelle).

ابازير *abâzir*, herbs for seasoning, pl. of ابزار *abzâr*.

ابازيم *abâzîm*, buckles, &c., pl. of ابزيم *ibzîm*.

اباس *ubâs*, shrew.

اباشة *ubâśa-t*, rabble, vagabonds ; impurities.

اباض *ibâḍ*, vein, sinew ; pl. ابض *ubuḍ*, rope for tying up the forefoot of a camel ;—*âbâḍ*, pl. of ابض *ubḍ*, q.v.

اباط *âbâṭ*, shoulders, armpits, pl. of ابط *ibṭ* ;—*ibâṭ*, what is carried under the armpits.

اباطلة *abâṭila-t*, pl. اباطيل *abâṭîl*, thing of no value ; nothingness ; trifle.

اباعد *abâ'id*, strangers, not related, pl. of ابعد *ab'ad*.

اباعة *ibâ'a-t*, sale, traffic ; IV. of (بيع) q.v.

اباق *ibâq*, ة *ibâqa-t*, escape ; INF. of (ابق) q.v. ;—*ubbâq*, pl. of آبق *âbiq*.

ابال *âbâl*, camels, pl. of ابل *ibl*, *ibil* ;—ابال *abbâl*, camel-herd ;—ابال *ubbâl*, pl. of آبل *âbil* ;—ة *ibâla-t*, administration of property ; economy ; police ; clientship ; tribe.

ابالسة *abâlisa-t*, اباليس *abâlîs*, devils, pl. of ابليس *iblîs*.

آبان *abân*=ابوان du. of ابو father and mother ;—*ibbân*, pl. ابابين *abâbîn*, opportunity, favourable moment ; beginning ;—ة *ibâna-t*, distinction, separation ; explanation ; publication ; IV. of (بين).

اباهم *abâhim*, thumbs, pl. of ابهام *ibhâm*.

اباوة *ibâwa-t*, paternity.

اباويل *abâwîl*, pl. of ابول *ibbaul*.

(ابت) *abat*, U, INF. *abt*, *ubût*, be hot ; *abit*, A, the same ; swell (with drink) ; — V. INF. *ta'abbut*, kindle, n.

ابت *abt*, *abit*, *âbit*, hot ;—*abati*, for ابتى *abatî*, O my father ; — ة *abta-t*, heat ; violent anger.

ابتات *ibtât*, cutting off, plucking off ; accomplishing ; IV. of (بت).

ابتحاث *ibtiḥâs̱*, examination ; investigation ; scrutiny ; inquest ; disputation ; VIII. of (بحث) q.v.

ابتجاح *ibtiḥâḥ*, rich harvest ; abundance, plenty.

ابتدا *ibtidâ'*, beginning, commencement, noviciate ; — *ibtidâ'an*, in the beginning, at first.

ابتدار *ibtidâr*, pushing on, setting about any work, running in advance, hastening (to arms, &c.).

ابتداع *ibtidâ'*, invention, discovery, innovation.

ابتداه *ibtidâh*, improvisation.

ابتداى *ibtidâ'iyy*, incipient, beginning, original.

ابتذال *ibtizâl*, continual use, wearing out, wasting ; disdain, contempt.

ابتر *abtar*, f. بترا *batrâ'*, curtailed, crippled ; bereft of children ; useless, vile ; — du. *al-abtarân*, one's slave and ass.

ابتراد *ibtirâd*, refrigeration, cooling.

ابتزاز *ibtizâz*, robbery, abduction.

ابتسال *ibtisâl*, defiance of danger, contempt of death.

ابتسام *ibtisâm*, smiling, smile ; gladness, cheerfulness.

ابتع *abta'*, pl. ابتعون *abta'ûn*, f. بتعا *bat'â*, pl. بتع *buta'*, entire, whole, all.

ابتعاد *ibti'âd*, departure, abandoning ; absence.

ابتغا *ibtiqâ'*, longing, desire.

ابتكار *ibtikâr*, rising early, coming soon in the morning ; ripeness ; first-fruit ; first enjoyment.

ابتلا *ibtilâ'*, trial, visitation, temptation; passion, inclination, propensity; calamity, distress.
ابتلاش *ibtilâś*, (m). beginning, undertaking.
ابتلاع *ibtilâ'*, swallowing, absorption.
ابتلال *ibtilâl*, being wet; recovery.
ابتنا *ibtinâ'*, building, construction, foundation.
ابتهاج *ibtihâj*, joy, gladness, cheerfulness, alacrity.
ابتهال *ibtihâl*, supplication, fervent prayer, deprecation.
ابتياع *ibtiyâ'*, purchase.
(ابث) *abas*, I, calumniate, accuse (acc. or على 'ala); — *abis*, pert, impudent.
ابثاث *ibsâs*, spreading.
ابج *abaj*, eternity; ابجا *abajan*, for ever.
ابجال *ibjâl*, honouring, rendering honour.
ابجد *abjad*, ancient arrangement of the alphabet, in which the letters denote the numbers from 1 to 1000.
ابجل *abjal*, pl. اباجل *abâjil*, sinew of the foot; واهى الاباجل *wâhi-'l-abâjil*, swift-footed.
ابحار *ibhâr*, sea-voyage; salt taste; — *abhâr*, and
ابحر *abhur*, seas, pl. of بحر *bahr*.
ابخرة *abhira-t*, pl. of بخور *bahûr*.
ابخق *abhaq*, f. بخقا *bahqâ'*, one-eyed; f. blind (eye).
ابخل *abhal*, more or most avaricious, comp. of بخيل *bahîl*.
(ابد) *abad*, U, I, INF. *ubûd*, grow wild, savage; I, stop, halt; continue; — *abid*, A, grow wild; be waste; grow angry; redden in the face; — II. INF. *ta'bîd*, scare, frighten; cause to continue; — V. INF. *ta'abbud*, grow waste, empty; keep aloof from women; immortalize one's self.
ابد *abad*, pl. *âbâd*, *ubûd*, eternity; *abad-an*, ever; never; — ة *âbida-t*, pl. *ubbad*, an animal grown wild; pl. اوابد *awâbid*, the same; misfortune; anything extraordinary; riddle, fable, funny tale.
ابدا *ibdâ'*, beginning, creation; communication; revelation.
ابداد *ibdâd*, distribution.
ابدار *ibdâr*, light of the full moon.
ابداع *ibdâ'*, invention; innovation; lie; original thought, originality.
ابدال *abdâl*, pl. of بدل *badal*, *bidl*, and بديل *badîl*; — *ibdâl*, exchanging, exchange.
ابدع *abda'*, extraordinary, original and beautiful, comp. of بديع *badî'*.
ابدى *abadiyy*, eternal, everlasting; — ة *abadiyya-t*, eternity.
(ابر) *abar*, I, U, INF. *abr*, prick; make a dog swallow a needle; calumniate; annihilate; kill; — INF. *abr*, *ibâr*, *ibâra-t*, fructify the palm-tree; — II. fructify the palm-tree; — VIII. dig a well.
ابر *abarr*, more, most, or very pious, upright; internal; — ة *ibra-t*, pl. *ibar*, ابار *ibâr*, needle, needle of the compass; hand of a watch; string; malice; fruit of the sycamore tree; — ابرة الراعى *ibratu-'r-râ'i*, geranium.
ابرا *ibrâ'*, liberating, delivery, cure, discharge from debt; absolution; acquittal, quittance.
ابراح *abrâh*, pl. of برح *barh*; — *ibrâh*, honouring, &c.; IV. of (برح) q.v.
ابراد *ibrâd*, cooling, refreshing, refrigeration.
ابرار *abrâr*, pl. of بار *bârr* and بر *barr*; — *ibrâr*, state of being well pleased, satisfaction; attestation by witnesses.
ابراز *ibrâz*, publication; production of proof or evidence.
ابراق *ibrâq*, lightening, shining, glittering.
ابرام *ibrâm*, importunity, molestation; cross-examination.
ابراه *ibrâh*, convincing proof, evidence.

ابرج *abraj*, f. *barjâ'*, having beautiful eyes; — ة *abrija-t*, towers, &c., pl. of برج *burj*.

ابرد *abrad*, f. ة, pl. ابارد *abârid*, very cold; الابردان *al-abradân*, morning and evening; — ة *ibrada-t*, coolness; impotence; — ى *abradiyy*, papyrus.

ابرسيم *ibrisim*, s. ابريسم *abrîsam*.

ابرش *abraś*, f. برشا *barśâ'*, pl. برش *burś*, spotted, dappled.

ابرشاش *ibriśâś*, being dappled.

ابرشية *abarśiyya-t* (m.), diocese.

ابرص *abraṣ*, f. برصا *barṣâ*, pl. برص *burṣ*, leprous; الابرص *al-abraṣ*, the moon; more excellent, comp. of بريص *bariṣ*.

ابرغشاس *ibrigśâs*, recovery.

ابرق *abraq*, f. برقا *barqâ* = ابلق *ablaq*, spotted (white and black); pl. ابارق *abâriq*, stony and sandy ground.

ابرك *abrak*, more or very much blessed.

ابره *abrah*, f. برها *barhâ'*, recovered; having a white skin.

ابرهيم *ibrahîm*, pl. ابارمة *abârima-t*, ابارهة *abâriha-t*, Abraham.

ابرى *ibriyy*, seller of needles; — *ibariyy*, in the shape of a needle, pointed, sharp; — ة *ibriyya-t*, scurf.

ابريا *abri'yâ'*, pl. of برى *bari'*.

ابريز *abrîz*, pure gold (also ذهب ابريزى *zahab abrîziyy*).

ابريسم *ibrîsam*, *ibraisam* (Pers. ابريشم *abrîśam*), vulg. ابرسيم *ibrisîm*, silk; — ابريسمى *ibrîsamiyy*, silk-merchant.

ابريق *ibrîq*, pl. اباريق *abârîq*, ابارقة *abâriqa-t*, ewer; water-jug; brig, brigantine, sloop of war.

(ابز) *abaz*, U, INF. *abz*, *ubûz*, leap; rush against; offend; die.

ابز *abiz*, leaping (as a gazelle).

ابزار *abzâr*, pl. of بزر *bazr*; pl. اباذير *abâzîr*, aromatic herb for seasoning.

ابزاز *abzâz*, nipples, teats, pl. of بز *bizz*.

ابزخ *abzaḫ*, with a hump on his breast.

ابزن *abzan*, water-basin of copper.

ابزيم *ibzîm*, pl. ابازيم *abâzîm*, buckle, clasp, agraffe.

(ابس) *abas*, U, INF. *abs*, scold, frighten, humiliate, subdue; revile, despise; imprison; receive badly; — INF. *ta'bîs*, despise; — V. INF. *ta'abbus*, be despised.

ابس *abs*, famine; also *ibs*, rugged ground; tortoise; — *ibs*, low descent.

ابسان *ibsân*, beauty.

(ابش) *abaś*, U, INF. *abś*, gather hastily, grasp up; — II. INF. *ta'bîś*, the same: talk confusedly; dote.

ابش *abaśś*, f. بشا *baśśâ'*, friendly and talkative, affable; (m.) smiling.

ابشار *ibśâr*, good tidings; good humour.

ابشع *abśa'*, uglier, very ugly, comp. of بشيع *baśî'*.

(ابص) *abiṣ*, A, INF. *abaṣ*, be quick, swift, alert.

ابصار *abṣâr*, pl. of بصر *baṣar*; — *ibṣâr*, IV. of (بصر) q.v.

ابصع *abṣa'*, f. بصا *baṣâ'*, pl. بصع *buṣ'*, stupid; whole, all.

(ابض) *abaḍ*, I, INF. *abḍ*, tie up the forefoot of a camel; — V. INF. *ta'abbuḍ*, have the forefoot tied up; — *abiḍ*, A, INF. *abaḍ*, abstain from one's wife; stand quiet, and, in opposition, move, stir; — V. = I.

ابض *ubḍ*, pl. *âbâḍ*, eternity; — *ubuḍ*, pl. of اباض *ibâḍ*, q.v.

ابط *ibṭ*, pl. *âbâṭ*, shoulder, arm-pit.

(ابط) *abaṭ*, A, INF. *abṭ*, throw down, throw to the ground; — V. INF. *ta'abbuṭ*, carry under one's arm (تابط شرا *ta'abbaṭa śarran*, proper name); throw (a garment) over the left shoulder; — VIII. INF. *it'ibâṭ*, stand quiet and in equilibrium, and, in opposition, be agitated; — X. INF. *isti'bâṭ*, dig a trench so as to be narrow at the top and wide at the bottom.

ابطال *abṭâl*, heroes, pl. of بطل *baṭal*; — *ibṭâl*, abolishing, abrogating annulling, repealing.

ابطح *abṭaḥ*, f. بطحا *baṭḥâ'*, flat, flattened.

ابطن *abṭun*, bellies, pl. of بطن *baṭn*; — ة *abṭina-t*, pl. of باطن *bâṭin*.

ابطى *ibṭiyy*, what is carried under the arm-pit.

ابظر *abẓar*, f. بظرا *baẓrâ'*, not circumcised.

ابعاد *ib'âd*, removing to a distance.

ابعد *ab'ad*, more remote, far distant; bad; perishing; pl. الاباعد *al-abâ'id*, strangers, no relatives.

ابعرة *ab'ira-t*, camels, pl. of بعير *ba'îr*.

ابغاض *ibgâḍ*, hatred, grudge, inveterate enmity.

ابغث *abgas*, f. بغثا *bagsâ'*, with dark spots; lion; f. a sandy place; rabble.

ابغض *abgaḍ*, more or very much hated.

(ابق) I, INF. *abq*, *abaq*, *ibâq*, run away, escape (as a slave); — V. INF. *ta'abbuq*, hide one's self; abstain (عن *'an*); refuse; sin.

ابق *abaq*, a kind of hemp; — *âbiq*, pl. ابق *ubbaq*, اباق *ubbâq*, escaped (slave).

ابقا *ibqâ'*, preserving, reserving, keeping alive, rendering permanent.

ابقع *abqa'*, f. بقعا *baq'â'*, spotted (white and black); f. year, partly fertile, partly not.

ابقور *ubqûr*, cows, pl. of بقرة baqara-t.

ابقى *abqa*, more durable, comp. of باقى *bâqî*; may God preserve him! IV. of بقى.

(ابك) *abik*, A, INF. *abak*, be fleshy.

ابك *abbak*, pl. بكان *bukkân*, active, severe and active; destructive to cattle (as a season); cruel.

ابكا *ibkâ'*, causing to weep.

ابكار *abkâr*, pl. of بكر *bikr*, q.v.; — *ibkâr*, early morning.

ابكم *abkam*, f. بكما *bakmâ'*, pl. بكم *bukm*, dumb.

(ابل) *abal*, U, I, *abil*, I, be numerous, rove and pasture freely; — *abil*, INF. *abal*, *abâla-t*, have many camels, breed camels; — INF. *abl*, *ubûl* and V. INF. *ta'abbul*, eat herbs from thirst; I. and II. keep aloof from; I. and V. abstain from women; devote one's self entirely to God; — *abal*, conquer; beat; dig a well; — II. INF. *ta'bîl*, lament and praise the dead; also V. have or acquire many camels.

ابل *ibl*, *ibil*, (f.) pl. آبال *âbâl*, camel; ابل ابل *ibl ubbal*, roving camels; ابل اوابل *ibl awâbil*, numerous camels; a large, fructifying cloud; — *aball*, f. بلا *ballâ'*, pl. بل *ball*, strong; not to be shaken; unjust; who pays badly; smooth; wetter.

ابلا *iblâ'*, trial, visitation; wearing out of clothing.

ابلاس *iblâs*, being struck dumb with grief, despair, astonishment.

ابلاغ *iblâg*, conveying, sending, informing; consummating, accomplishing; arriving at the age of puberty.

ابلام *iblâm*, being silent, silence.

ابلج *ablaj*, f. بلجا *baljâ'*, pl. بلج *bulj*, shining, serene, bright-faced; clear and distinct; with separated eye-brows.

ابلخ *ablaḫ*, f. بلخا *balḫâ'*, stupid.

ابلد *ablad*, with separated eyebrows; stout; stupid.

ابلغ *ablag*, more or most effectual; more eloquent; (m.) more than.

ابلق *ablaq*, f. بلقا *balqâ'*, pl. بلق *bulq*, spotted (white and black), piebald.

ابلالاج *iblîlâj*, distinctness.

ابله *ablah*, f. بلها *balhâ'*, pl. بله *bulh*, foolish, stupid; careless, easy going; simple, bashful; arrogant; bearing hard work and thirst (camel).

ابلوج *ablûj*, sugar-loaf, sugar-candy.

ابليس *iblîs*, pl. اباليس *abâlîs*, ابالسة *abâlisa-t*, Satan, the Devil.

ابليم *iblîm*, ambergris; honey.

(ابن) *aban*, A. I, U, suspect; — I. and II. INF. *ta'bîn*, blame; — *abin*, coagulate and become black

(blood of a wound); II. blame; watch; lament and praise the dead; — II. and V. INF. *ta'abbun*, follow one's track.

ابن *ibn*, *abn*, between two proper names بن *bin*, pl. *banûn*, in statu constr. *banû*, vulg. *banî*, son. Frequently used in composition, as: بنو آدم *banû âdam*, men; ابن السبيل *ibn as-sabîl*, wanderer, wayfarer; ابن كم سنة *ibn kam sana-t*, son of how many years, how old? ابن الغمد *ibn al-gimd*, son of the scabbard, sword, &c.; — ة *ibna-t*, pl. ابنات *ibnât*, daughter; — *ubna-t*, pl. ابن *uban*, *ubanât*, knot; larynx; hatred; disgrace; unnatural vice.

ابنم *ibnam*, son.

ابنوس *abnûs*, *abanûs*, ebony.

ابنية *abniya-t*, buildings, pl. of بنا *binâ'*, بنى *baniyy*.

(ابه) *abah*, *abih*, INF. *abh*, remember, pay attention to; II. remind; exhort, call one's attention to; suspect; V. show pride, turn from proudly; — ة *abha-t*, *ubbaha-t*, splendour; beauty; pride.

ابهات *abahât*, fathers, mothers, pl. of ابو *abû*; — *ibhât*, astonishment; perplexity.

أبهار *ibhâr*, (m.) blinding, deprivation of light.

ابهال *ibhâl*, license; flattery; sprinkling.

ابهام *ibhâm*, pl. اباهم *abâhim*, اباهيم *abâhîm*, thumb, big toe; — IV. of (بهم), ambiguity.

ابهم *abham*, pl. بهم *buhm*, *buhum*, who cannot speak; stranger, barbarian.

ابو *abû*, gen. ابى *abî*, acc. ابا *abâ*, pl. ابون *abûn*, آبا *âbâ'*, ابهات *abahât*, du. ابوان *abwân*, ابان *abân*, father, parent, ancestor; in composition, master, possessor, as: ابو الحصين *abû-'l-ḥuṣain* (small castle), fox; ابو اليقظان *abû-'l-yaqẓân* (awakening), cock; ابو ايوب *abû ayyûb* (patience), camel; ابو جعدة *abû ja'da-t* (curled hair), wolf, fox; ابو حنبس *abû ḥambas* (stratagems), fox; ابو ذنب *abû ẓanab* (tail), comet, &c.; — ة *abuwwa-t*, paternity.

ابواب *abwâb*, doors, pl. of باب *bâb*.

ابواع *abwâ'*, cubits, ells, pl. of باع *bâ'*.

ابوبة *abwiba-t*, doors, pl. of باب *bâb*.

ابوت *ubût*, heat.

ابود *ubûd*, continuance, duration.

ابوص *abûṣ*, swift (horse).

ابوق *abûq*, escaped (slave).

ابول *abûl*, troop, swarm; — *ibbaul*, pl. اباويل *abâwîl*, troop of camels.

ابوى *abawiyy*, paternal, fatherly; — ة *ubuwiyya-t*, (m.) paternity.

(ابى) *aba*, A, I, INF. ابا *ibâ'*, *ibâ'a-t*, have aversion for, refuse, reject; — *abî*, and its pass. *ubî*, suffer from indigestion; — IV. INF. *i'bâ'*, refuse (with two acc.); — V. INF. *ta'abbi*, the same (علية هيا *ale-hi śai'-an*).

ابى *abiyy*, who refuses from pride fastidious; haughty; — *âbî* (آب *âbin*), pl. *âbûn*, اباة *ubât*, ابا *ubâ'*, *ubiyy*, the same; الابى *al-âbî*, lion; — *ubayy*, little father; — ة *abiyya-t*, she-camel, who refuses water or food; — *ibya-t*, retention of the milk; — *ubiyya-t*, pride.

ابيات *abyât*, verses, distichs, pl. of بيت *bait*.

ابيان *abyân*, refusing from disgust.

ابيب *abîb*, month of July

ابيد *abîd*, eternal.

ابيرة *ubairih*, little Abraham.

ابيص *abîṣ*, swift (horse).

ابيض *abyaḍ*, f. بيضا *baiḍâ'*, pl. بيض *bîḍ*, white; pure; sword; silver; ابو الابيض *abû-'l-abyaḍ*, milk; الموت الابيض *al-maut al-abyaḍ*, sudden death; اليد البيضا *al-yad al-baiḍâ'*, benefit, power; البيض *al-bîḍ*, the fair (women); الابيضان *al-abyaḍân*, milk and water; water and bread.

ابيعا *abyi'â'*, buyers, pl. of بيع *bayyi'*.

ابيل *abîl*, sad; monk; ابيل الابيلين *abîl al-abîlîn*, Christ; pl. ابل *ubul*, heavy stick; — ة *ubaila-t*, small camel; — *abîla-t*, green food.

ابين *abyan*, more distinct, clear, evident.

(ات) *att*, U, get the better of (in a law-suit); break the skull.

اتا ام *it'am*, giving birth to twins; being double-barrelled.

اتاحة *itâḥa-t*, decree of fate.

اتان *atân*, *itân*, pl. اتن *utn*, *utun*, *âtun*, ماتونا *ma'tûnâ'*, she-ass.

اتاوة *itâwa-t*, pl. اتاوى *atâwî*, crops; tribute; present; bribe.

اتاويه *atâwih*, deserts, pl. of تيه *tîh*.

اتاى *atâî*, (m.) tea.

(اتب) *itb*, pl. آتاب *âtâb*, اتوب *utûb*, chemise without sleeves.

اتب *atab*, put on such a chemise; — II. *ta'bît*, dress a person with it; pass., being made in shape of it (dress); — V. INF. *ta'attub* and VIII. INF. *it'itâb*, put on the chemise.

اتباع *atbâ'*, pl. of تبع q.v.; — *itbâ'*, following or causing to follow; attaining; — *ittibâ'*, following, obeying.

اتجاج *ittijâj*, conflagration, heat.

اتجار *itjâr*, *ittijâr*, traffic, commerce.

اتحاد *ittiḥâd*, union, concord; unanimity; identity.

اتحاف *itḥâf*, presenting with.

اتحم *atḥam*=ادهم *adham*, black; — ى *atḥamiyy*, a striped material.

اتخاذ *ittiḫâẕ*, taking, accepting, election; adoption.

اتر *attar*, for وتر *wattar*, see وتر.

اتراك *atrâk*, Turks, pl. of ترك *turk*.

اتربة *atriba-t*, pl. of تراب *turâb*, earth, dust.

اترج *utruj*, *utrujj*; اترنج *atrunj*, citron.

اتساع *ittisâ'*, extension; commodiousness; capacity (of a place); amplitude of meaning.

اتسام *ittisâm*, token, sign; seal.

اتصاف *ittiṣâf*, quality; description; praise.

اتصال *ittiṣâl*, union; adhesion; being connected; attachment, neighbourhood.

اتضاع *ittiḍâ'*, humiliation, abasement.

اتعاب *at'âb*, vexations, pl. of تعب *ta'b*; — *it'âb*, causing fatigue, lassitude, vexation.

اتعاس *it'âs*, ruining, causing perdition.

اتعاظ *itti'âẕ*, yielding to remonstrances.

اتفاق *ittifâq*, agreement, union, concord, harmony; compact, league, alliance; conspiracy; fortune, chance, accident; — ى *ittifâqiyy*, accidental, casual, fortuitous.

اتقا *ittiqâ'*, piety, fear of God; fear; avoidance; abstraction.

اتقان *itqân*, fixing; perfecting; skilful arrangement; — *ittiqân*, disquisition; certifying.

اتقيا *atqiyâ'*, pious men, devotees, pl. of تقى *taqiyy*.

اتكا *itkâ'*, propping; — *ittikâ'*, leaning against, reclining upon.

اتكال *ittikâl*, confidence, reliance.

(اتل) *atal*, I, INF. *atl*, *atalân*, *itlâl*, approach in anger; من *min*, be full of food and drink.

اتل *utul*, for وتل *wutul*, pl. of اوتل *autal*, full of food and drink.

اتلا *itlâ'* causing to follow one another; continuation.

اتلاد *atlâd*, inherited goods, pl. of تلد *talad*; — *itlâd*, property under the law of prescription.

اتلاف *itlâf*, causing ruin, destruction, waste; squandering.

(اتم) *atam*, *atim*, INF. *atm*, burst; cut; remain behind or standing.

اتم *atam*, slowness, laziness; procrastination; — *utm*, *utum*, wild

olive-tree ; — *atamm*, more perfect.

اتمام *itmâm*, completion, perfection ; conclusion.

(اتن) *atan*, I, halt, stop ; approach, step up to ; I. and IV., give birth, so that the child's feet come first ; buy a she-ass ; to come down from a horse to an ass.

اتن *utn*, *utun*, pl. of اتان *atân*, she-ass ; — *utun*, stoves, pl. of اتون *atûn*.

اته *atah*, اتوه *atûh*, panting of one who carries a burden.

اتهام *ithâm*, causing to be suspected ; accusation.

(اتو) *atâ*, U, INF. *atw*, *itw*, *atwa-t*, *itâ'*, arrive (after a prosperous journey) ; visit ; meet ; come plentifully ; — INF. *itâwa-t*, bribe.

اتو *atw*, ة *atwa-t*, station ; gift, present ; calamity, death ; quickness.

اتوا *itwâ'*, ruin.

اتوان *atwân*, eager for presents.

اتون *atûn*, *attûn*, pl. اتونات *atûnât*, اتن *utun*, اتاتين *atâtîn*, stove, oven, furnace.

(اتى) *ata*, I, INF. *ity*, *uty*, *ityân*, *utyân*, *ityâna-t*, *utyâna-t*, *ma'tât*, *itiyy*, *utiyy*, come ; with ب *bi*, come with, bring, give, give birth ; — with acc., approach (a woman) ; punish ; begin, undertake ; — with ل *li*, happen ; — على *'ala*, come over, destroy ; pass., be surprised or killed by one's enemy ;—II. INF. *ta'tiya-t*, smooth the way ; — III. agree with a person (acc.) about a matter (على *'ala*) ; be agreeable, favourable ; — IV. drive towards, bring, give as a present ; reward ; — V. succeed ; be ready, in good order ; — VI. associate, prove one's self a good companion ; — X. wish for someone's arrival ; rut (she-camel).

آتى *âtî*, (آت *ât-in*), coming next ; الآتية *al-âtiya-t*, الآتى *al-âtî*, the future ; — *atiyy*, new comer ; sudden irruption (of water, &c.).

اتيان *ityân*, arrival.

اتيس *atyas*, goatish ; stubborn ; stupid.

اتيه *atyah*, wandering, straying.

(اث) *a<u>ss</u>*, A, I, U, INF. *a<u>s</u>a<u>s</u>*, *a<u>s</u>â<u>s</u>a-t*, *u<u>s</u>û<u>s</u>*, grow luxuriantly (grass, hair) ; have large thighs and hips (a woman) ; — II. spread carpets, furnish (m.) ; — V. be furnished ; be lodged conveniently.

اثا *i<u>s</u>â'*, stone.

اثابة *i<u>s</u>âba-t*, retribution ; requital ; recovery.

اثاث *a<u>s</u>â<u>s</u>*, household furniture ; goods (comprising herds, slaves, &c.).

اثار *i<u>s</u>'âr*, *a<u>s</u>'âr*, pl. of ثار *<u>s</u>a'r*, vengeance ; retribution ; — *â<u>s</u>âr*, tracks, traces, pl. of اثر *a<u>s</u>ar*.

اثاف *a<u>s</u>âf-in*, اثافى *a<u>s</u>âfî*, pl. of اثفية *u<u>s</u>fiyya-t*.

اثال *a<u>s</u>âl*, noble origin ; authority and respect ; — *â<u>s</u>âl*, pl. of اثل *a<u>s</u>l*, tamarisk ; — *i<u>s</u>âl*, pl. of اثلة *a<u>s</u>la-t*, root, &c.

اثام *a<u>s</u>âm*, *i<u>s</u>âm*, sin, guilt, punishment ; — *â<u>s</u>âm*, sins, pl. of اثم *i<u>s</u>m* ; — *a<u>ss</u>âm*, sinner.

اثانين *a<u>s</u>ânîn*, Monday.

اثاوة *i<u>s</u>âwa-t*, اثاية *i<u>s</u>âya-t*, information (to the judge).

اثبات *a<u>s</u>bât*, pl. of ثبت *<u>s</u>abat*, truthful man, &c. ; — *i<u>s</u>bât*, pl. *i<u>s</u>bâtât*, proof, demonstration ; reason ; confirmation.

(اثج), X. استاثج *ista'<u>s</u>aj*, grow luxuriantly ; entwine.

اثجل *a<u>s</u>jal*, f. *<u>s</u>ajlâ'*, big-bellied.

اثد *a<u>s</u>d-in*, اثدا *a<u>s</u>dâ'*, اثدى *a<u>s</u>dî*, breasts, pl. of ثدى *<u>s</u>ady*, *<u>s</u>idy*, *<u>s</u>adan*.

(اثر) *a<u>s</u>ar*, U, I, INF. *a<u>s</u>r*, take or choose for one's self ; cover frequently (camel) ; excite ; forge (a sword) ; quote, cite ; — *a<u>s</u>ir*, A, excel (على 'ala), decide on ; begin (with aor. or ان an ;) — II. INF. *ta'<u>s</u>îr*, leave

traces, impress, make an impression (فى fî);—III. INF. *mu'âsara-t*, prefer; — IV. INF. *i'sâr*, prefer, give precedence; — V. INF. *ta'assur*, also VIII. INF. *it'isâr*, follow one's tracks; — VI. INF. *ta'âsur*, not admit of doubt; — X. INF. *isti'sâr*, claim for one's self.

اثر *asr*, pl. *usûr*, undulating ground; splendour; — *asar*, trace, sign, impression, remains; monument; memoirs, sayings, tradition; deeds; — *isr*, trace, اثر *isr-a*, prep. after, close behind; — ة *asara-t*, choice, preference; egotism; — *isra-t*, selfishness; — *usra-t*, pl. اثر *usar*, exploit; hereditary merit; mention; remainder.

اثرا *isrâ'*, being rich; riches.

اثرم *asram*, f. ثرما *sarmâ*, toothless; full of notches, blunt; shortened (foot in poetry).

اثعل *as'al*, f. *sa'lâ'*, having overgrown teeth.

اثف *asaf*, I. follow, pursue; seek, look for; — II. support, prop; pursue incessantly.

اثفيا *asfiyâ*, اثفية *usfiyya-t*, pl. *asâf-in*, *asafî*, prop of the pot.

(اثل) *asal*, I. INF. *usûl*; —*asul*, INF. *asâla-t*, be firmly rooted; be of noble origin; — II. INF. *ta'sîl*, increase (a.); confer benefits and distinctions; — V. INF. *ta'assul*, be firmly rooted; increase (n.); acquire; make provisions; dig (a well).

اثل *asl*, pl. اثول *usûl*, آثال *âsâl*, tamarisk; — ة *asla-t*, pl. اثال *isâl*, root, origin; family; authority; livelihood; provisions; utensils.

اثلاج *islâj*, snowing.

اثلم *aslam*, notchy, blunt; shortened foot in poetry.

(اثم) *asam*, A, U, INF. *ism*, *ma'asm*, deem guilty; impute as a sin; — *asim*, sin; — II. accuse of sin, sin; — IV. cause to fall into sin; — V. sin, and, by opposition, renounce sin, do penance.

اثم *ism*, pl. آثام *âsâm*, sin, state of sin; — *âsim*, sinner; — ة *isama-t*, pl. of اثيم *asîm*, sinner.

اثمار *asmâr*, fruits, pl. of *samar*.

اثمان *asmân*, prices, pl. of *saman*; — eighth parts, pl. of *sumn*; — *ismân*, being precious; value.

اثمد *ismid*, *usmud*, antimony.

اثمن *asman*, more, most, or very precious, dear.

اثن *usun*, for *wusun*, statues, idols.

اثنا *asnâ'*, fold; middle; interval;— فى اثنا ذلك *fî asnâ' zalik*, meanwhile; — *isnâ'*, praise, eulogy.

اثنان *isnâni*, f. *isnatâni*, *sintâni*, two; in composition, *isnâ*, vulg. *isne*, as: اثنا (اثنى) عشر *isnâ* (*isne*) *'aśara*, f. *isnatâ 'aśrata*, twelve; — يوم الاثنين *yaumu-'l-isnaini*, Monday.

اثنية *asniya-t*, praises, pl. of *sanâ'*.

(اثو) اثا *asâ*, U, INF. *asw*, *isâwa-t*, also اثى *asa*, I, INF. *asy*, *isâya-t*, accuse, calumniate (عليه او به عند احد *'ale-hi* or *bi-hi 'inda ahad-in*).

اثواب *aswâb*, اثوب *aswub*, cloths, &c., pl. of *saub*.

اثوار *aswâr*, pl. of *saur*, large piece of the cream-cheese اقط *aqt*, *iqt*.

اثور *usûr*, traces, pl. of *asar*.

اثول *aswal*, giddy (sheep); slow; stupid; mad.

اثوم *asûm*, sinner, liar.

اثون *asûn*=*atûn*, furnace.

اثى *âsî*, informer, spy.

اثيث *asîs*, luxuriant, large; pl. *asâyis*, woman with large thighs and hips; see (اث) *ass*.

اثير *asîr*, what bears traces, signs; exquisite, excellent; intimate friend; sky, ether.

اثيل *asîl*, belonging to the root, original; firm; of noble birth.

اثيم *asîm*, pl. *isama-t*, sinner, liar; —ة *asîma-t*, great criminal; great sinfulness.

اثين *asîn*=*asîl*.

(اج) *ajj*, U, INF. *ajij*, burn, blaze;— U, I, INF. *ajj*, run; charge, attack

(an enemy); — INF. *ajûj*, be bitter, salt; — II. INF. *ta'jîj*, kindle, inflame; — IV. INF. *îjâj*, make bitter or salt; — V. INF. *ta'ajjuj*, and VIII. INF. *it'ijâj*, blaze; — V., VI. INF. *ta'âjuj*, and VIII. be hot (day, weather); — ة *ajja-t*, heat, fire; rebellion.

اجا *aja'*, flee, take to flight; — ة *ijâ'a-t*, bringing, procuring (s.).

اجاب *ijâb*, ة *ijâba-t*, (favourable) reply; approval; consenting; complying with.

اجاج *ujâj*, bitter, salt; heat (of war); — *ajjâj*, burning.

اجاجرة *ajâjira-t*, اجاجير *ajâjîr*, roofs, pl. of اجار *ijjâr*.

اجاجين *ajajin*, pl. of اجانة *ijjâna-t*, q.v.

اجاح *ajâḥ*, *ijâḥ*, *ujâḥ*, veil; — ة *ijâḥa-t*, annihilation.

اجادل *ajâdil*, pl. of اجدل *ajdal*, q.v.

اجادة *ijâda-t*, giving generously; acting or speaking well; excellence (IV. of جود).

اجار *ijjâr*, pl. *ajâjîr*, *ajâjira-t*, roof; — *âjâr*, rewards, pl. of اجر *ajr*; — ة *ijâra-t* (IV. جور), protection, patronage; — *ijâra-t*, *ajâra-t*, *ujâra-t*, reward; rent, hire, contract.

اجازة *ijâza-t*, permission, leave; venia docendi; diploma for it; present; completion of a verse.

اجاص *ajâṣ*, cotton; — *ijjâṣ*, plum; — ية *ijjâṣiyya-t*, soup of plums.

اجاعة *ijâ'a-t*, causing to hunger, starving.

اجال *âjâl*, terms, &c., pl. of اجل *ajal*, q.v.; — ة *ijâla-t*, causing to make a round; distribution all around.

اجام *âjâm*, *ijâm*, bushes, &c., pl. of اجم *ajam*; — *âjâm*, frogs.

اجانب *ajânib*, pl. of اجنب *ajnab*, q.v.

اجانة *ijjâna-t*, pl. *ajâjîn*, urn; amphora; washing-tub.

اجاود *ajâwid*, اجاويد *ajâwîd*, pl. of جواد *jawâd*, q.v.

اجباب *ajbâb*, wells, &c., pl. of جب *jubb*.

اجبار *ijbâr*, compulsion, force, violence.

اجبال *ajbâl*, mountains, pl. of جبل *jabal*.

اجبس *ajbas*, weak, stupid.

اجبن *ajbun*, ة *ajbina-t*, foreheads, pl. of جبين *jabîn*.

اجبه *ajbah*, f. *jabhâ'*, pl. *jubh*, having a broad, fine forehead; *al-ajbah*, lion.

اجبو *ajbû'*, pl. of جب *jab'*, q.v.

اجتبا *ijtibâ'*, choice, election, selection.

اجتثاث *ijtiṡâṡ*, cutting off, tearing out, rooting up.

اجتدار *ijtidâr*, surrounding with a wall.

اجتذاب *ijtizâb*, attraction.

اجترا *ijtirâ'*, daring, boldness.

اجتراح *ijtirâḥ*, striving to get; (m.) doing wonders.

اجترار *ijtirâr*, drawing, drawing up; chewing the cud.

اجتراف *ijtirâf*, shovelling away, digging.

اجترام *ijtirâm*, guilt, transgression, offence (على 'ala, الى ila).

اجتزا *ijtizâ'*, being contented with (ب bi).

اجتزاز *ijtizâz*, mowing, math, swath; harvest; shearing.

اجتساس *ijtisâs*, spying.

اجتلاب *ijtilâb*, import (of slaves, goods).

اجتماع *ijtimâ'*, gathering, assembly, concourse, meeting; social intercourse; accumulation.

اجتنا *ijtinâ'*, gathering fruit; fruition.

اجتناب *ijtinâb*, avoiding, shunning, turning aside, flight.

اجتهاد *ijtihâd*, zeal; solicitude, diligence, effort, exertion; perfection in the knowledge of law.

اجتياب *ijtiyâb*, roaming about a country.

اجتياح *ijtiyâḥ*, annihilation, destruction; eradication.

اجتياز *ijtiyâz*, passing on, passage; journey to a distance.

اجحافات *ijḥâfât*, injuries; insults.

اجحد *ajḥad*, poor; barren; avaricious.

اجد *ajadd*, new; du. *ajaddân*, day and night; — *ajd-in*, *ajdi*, he-goats, pl. of جدى *jady*.

اجدا *ijdâ'*, profiting, procuring of advantages (s.).

اجداب *ijdâb*, sterility, barrenness; dryness.

اجداد *ajdâd*, grandfathers, ancestors, pl. of جد *jadd*.

اجدار *ijdâr*, growing, budding.

اجدب *ajdab*, barren, waste; f. *jadbâ'*, desert; — *ajdub*, vices, pl. of جدب *jadab*.

اجدر *ajdar*, worthier, fitter, more appropriate; f. جدرا *jadrâ*, scabby; marked by small-pox.

اجدع *ajda'*, f. *jadâ'*, mutilated; *al-ajda'*, the devil.

اجدل *ajdal*, pl. *ajâdil*, f. *jadlâ'*, pl. *judl*, lovely, handsome; a kind of falcon; — *jadlâ'*, beautiful woman; fine, strong coat of mail; bitch.

اجذال *ajẕâl*, stems, roots, pl. of جذل *jiẕl*; — *ijẕâl*, cheering up.

(اجر) *ajar*, I, U, INF. *ajr*, *ijâra-t*, reward, pay; hire, work for hire; let for money; — INF. *ajr*, *ajâr*, *ujûr*, be set and heal (broken bone); set a broken bone; pass. اجر فى ولده *ujira fî waladi-hi*, his son has died; — II. INF. *ta'jîr*, burn bricks; — III. INF. *mu'âjara-t*, hire slaves; pay; stipulate wages; prostitute one's self (a woman); — IV. INF. *î'jâr*, reward; let for hire; — VIII. INF. *it'ijâr*, ask for reward, wages, presents, alms; — X. INF. *isti'jâr*, hire; burn bricks; . (m.) let.

اجر *ajr*, pl. *ujûr*, *âjâr*, wages; hire; reward; recompense, requital; gift, morning gift; — *ajur*, *ujur*, *âjur*, pl. *ajurûn*, brick; — *âjar*, Hagar; — *ajr-in*, *ajrî*, pl. of جرو *jarw*, q.v.; — ة *ujra-t*, wages, salary; — *ajirra-t*, straps, reins, pl. of جرير *jarîr*; — *âjura-t*, *âjira-t*, brick.

اجرا *ujarâ'*, servants, pl. of اجير *ajîr*; — *ajrâ'*, bolder; pl. of جرى *jarî'*, bold, and of جرو *jarw*, young beast of prey; — *ijrâ'*, bringing into circulation; execution of an order.

اجراس *ajrâs*, bells, pl. of جرس *jars*; — *ijrâs*, producing a sound, a noise.

اجرام *ajrâm*, pl. of جرم *jirm* and *jaram*, q.v.; — *ijrâm*, crime, fault.

اجران *ajarrâni*, men and genii; — *ajrân*, basins, &c., pl. of جرن *jurn*.

اجرب *ajrab*, pl. *jurb*, scabious; kind of cucumber; — f. *jarbâ'*, sky; barren land; beautiful girl; — ة *ajriba-t*, pl. of جراب *jarâb* and جريب *jarib*, q.v.

اجرد *ajrad*, f. *jardâ'*, pl. *jurd*, naked, smooth; without vegetation; hairless; pure (wine); complete (day, month).

اجرنشم *ijranšam*, fall head over heels; adhere, stick to.

اجرنة *ajrina-t*, fore-necks, pl. of جران *jirân*.

اجرودى *ajrûdi*, beardless.

اجرى *ajri*, ة *ajriya-t*, pl. of جرو *jarw*, young beast of prey; — *ijriyy*, run, course; — ة *ijriyya-t*, form, shape; natural disposition.

اجريا *ajriyâ'*, pl. جرى youthful; — *ijriyâ'*, run, course; proceeding; custom, habit; form, shape; natural disposition.

(اجز) X. استاجز *ista'jaz*, lean with one's side against a cushion.

اجزا *ajzâ'*, parts, &c., pl. of جز *jaz'*.

اجزاجى *ajzâjiyy*, اجزاى *ajzâ'i* (m.) pl. ة, apothecary, chemist, druggist.

اجزال *ijzâl*, giving abundantly.

اجزل *ajzal*, greater, more considerable; sore (beast of burden); of great intellect.

اجزم *ajzam*, more cutting; more effectual; more decided.

اجساد *ajsâd*, bodies, pl. of جسد *jasad*.

اجسام *ajsâm*, bodies, pl. of جسم *jism*.

اجش *ajaśś*, of a harsh sound.

اجشا *ajśâ'*, pl. of جش *jaś'*, q.v.

اجشر *ajśar*, hoarse, coughing.

اجعال *aj'âl*, salaries, pensions, pl. of جعل *ju'l*.

اجفال *ijfâl*, taking fright, running away.

اجفان *ajfân*, eyelids, pl. of جفن *jafn*.

اجفلة *ajfala-t*, اجفلى *ajfala*, numerous troop.

اجفيل *ijfîl*, shy; male ostrich; old woman; far-carrying bow.

اجكار *ijkâr*, (m.) obtruding one's merchandise on a buyer.

(اجل) *ajal*, I, U, fix a term; delay, tarry; prevent (cattle from pasturing); bring distress upon (على *'ala*); bring good luck to (ل *li*) one's people; cure of a sore throat; — *ajil*, I, have a sore throat; — II. INF. *ta'jîl*, fix a term to a person (acc.), grant him a delay; — II., III. INF. *mu'âjala-t*, prevent from; cure of a sore throat; collect water in a pond; — V. INF. *ta'ajjul*, have or attain a term; assemble in due time; gather in a herd; collect (n.), as water; ask for a term or delay; — X. INF. *isti'jâl*, ask for a delay.

اجل *ajal*, pl. *âjâl*, appointed time, term; fate, destiny; death; *al-âjâl*, hour of death; — *ajal*, indeed, no doubt, undoubtedly; — *ajl*, troop of buffaloes; — *ajl*, *ijl*, cause, reason, motive, sake: *min ajlak*, *li-ajlak*, for thy sake; *min ajl an*, because; — *ijl*, pl. *âjâl*, sore throat; — *âjil*, who grants a delay, who delays, what is postponed; *al-âjil*, ة *al-âjila-t*, the future life; — *ujjal*, *ijjal*, chamois; — *ajall*, f. *julla*, greater, more illustrious, more important; — ة *ajilla-t*, pl. of جليل *jalîl* and جل *jall*, sublime, &c.

اجلا *ajillâ*, *ijlâ'*, emigration; expulsion; — pl. of جليل *jalîl*, sublime, &c.

اجلاب *ajlâb*, pl., camel-dealers.

اجلاس *ijlâs*, causing, ordering, requesting one to sit down; being seated or enthroned.

اجلال *ajlâl*, housings, &c., pl. of جل *jull*; — *ijlâl*, magnificence, majesty, grandeur, splendour, sublimeness, loftiness; honour; reverence.

اجلح *ajlaḥ*, bald on the forehead; without horns; camel-litter.

اجلس *ajlas*, (m.) straighter, more direct.

اجلل *ajlal*=اجل *ajall*.

اجلنفع *ijlanfa'* (جلفع), be stout.

اجلة *ajlah*, without horns; with a high, bald fore-head.

اجلى *ajla*, f. *jalwâ'*, *jalyâ'*, brighter, more resplendent; smoother; serene; beautiful; with a high forehead.

(اجم) *ajam*, INF. *ajm*, *ajîm*, be burning hot; — *ajim*, loathe; get corrupted (as water); force one against his will; — IV. INF. *i'jâm*, disgust, inspire with aversion; — V. *ta'ajjum*, be excessively hot; blaze; be angry with (على 'ala); enter a thicket (lion).

اجم *ajam*, ة *ajma-t*, pl. *ujm*, *ujum*, *ijâm*, *âjâm*, bush, thicket, wood; refuge; asylum; — *ujum*, pl. *âjâm*, castle, little fortress; — *ajm*, heat, anger; square house with roof; — *ajamm*, f. *jammâ'*, fleshy; smooth; without horns; without battlements; without a lance (horseman); unadorned (women); pudenda (of a woman).

اجماع *ijmâ'*, assembly, collection; unanimity, accordance in religious teaching; shortening of a vowel.

اجمال *ijmâl*, collection, abridgment, compendium, summary, synopsis; treating a matter in a

general way, opposed to تفصيل *tafṣîl*, treating in detail.

اجمع *ajma'*, pl. *ajma'ûn*, f. *jam'â'*, pl. *jum'*, all, universal, the whole.

اجمل *ajmal*, more beautiful, handsomer, better.

اجمى *ajamiyy*, swampy, bushy.

(اجن) *ajan*, I, U, *ajin*, A, INF. *ajn*, *ajan*, *ujûn*, change its taste and colour, get corrupted (as water);—*ajan*, cleanse dirty linen, cloth, &c.; — *âjin*, corrupted water; — ة *ajinna-t*, pl. of جنين *janîn*, embryo; — *ajna-t*, *ijna-t*, *ujna-t*, fullest part of the cheek.

اجناس *ajnâs*, kinds, sorts, pl. of جنس *jins*.

اجنب *ajnab*, pl. *ajânib*, indocile, disobedient; also ى *ajnabiyy*, foreign, outlandish; belonging to another; — ة *ajniba-t*, pl. of جناب *janâb*, q.v.

اجنح *ajnuḥ*, ة *ajniḥa-t*, wings, pl. of جناح *janâḥ*.

اجنف *ajnaf*, declining from the right way; unjust; humpbacked.

اجنن *ajnun*, pl. of جنين *janîn*, embryo.

اجهاد *ijhâd*, stimulation.

اجهار *ijhâr*, making public, publication.

اجهر *ajhar*, day-blind; well made, of handsome form; white above nose and forehead (horse), f. *jahrâ'*, flat, treeless ground; troop; elite of a tribe.

اجهزة *ajhiza-t*, pl. of جهاز *jahâz*, q.v.

اجهل *ajhal*, more, most or very ignorant.

اجهى *ajha*, bald, uncovered; f. *jahwâ'*, serene sky.

اجواخ *ajwâḥ*, pl. of جوخ *jûḥ*, cloth.

اجواد *ajwâd*, pl. of جواد *jawâd*, noble.

اجوار *ajwâr*, neighbours, pl. of جار *jâr*.

اجوب *ajwab*, more effective; more to the purpose; more advantageous; — ة *ajwiba-t*, answers, replies, pl. of جواب *jawâb*.

اجود *ajwad*, f. *jaudâ'*, pl. *jûd*, more generous, more distinguished.

اجور *ajûr*, *âjûr*, brick;—*ujûr*, setting of a broken bone; rewards, &c., pl. of اجر *ajr*.

اجوز *ajwaz*, ة *ajwiza-t*, pl. of جائز *jâ'iz*, q.v.

اجوف *ajwaf*, f. *jaufâ'*, pl. *júf*, concave, hollow (verb); spacious; *al-ajwaf*, lion; *al-ajwafân*, belly and vagina.

اجول *ajwal*, turning round more frequently; dusty.

اجوم *aj'um*, cups, pl. of جام *jâm*; — *ajûm*, causing horror; abhorred, hateful.

اجون *ajûn*, corrupted, foul (water); — *ajwan*, white, and, by opposition, black; red; f. *jaunâ'*, sun; blackened pot; black camel.

اجياد *ajyâd*, necks, pl. of جيد *jîd*.

اجياف *ajyâf*, dead bodies, carcasses, pl. of جيفة *jîfa-t*.

اجيال *ajyâl*, generations, pl. of جيل *jîl*.

اجيج *ajîj*, fire, flame.

اجيد *ajyad*, f. *jaidâ'*, pl. *jûd*, *jîd*, with a long, well-shaped neck.

اجير *ajîr*, pl. *ujarâ'*, servant; day labourer; workman.

اجيل *ajîl*, who grants delay, who delays;—assembled.

اجيم *ajîm*, heat, fire; zeal.

(اح) *aḥḥ*, U, INF. *aḥḥ*, cough; II. cough repeatedly, frequently.

احابش *aḥâbiś*, Abyssinians, pl. of احبش *aḥbaś*.

احاثة *iḥâsa-t*, digging up and exploration of the ground.

احاح *uḥâḥ*, inner heat, thirst; anger; grief; — alas!

احاجى *aḥâjî*, *aḥâjiyy*, riddles, pl. of احجوة *uḥjuwwa-t*.

احاد *uḥâda*, احاد احاد *uḥâda uḥâda*, by ones, single; — *âḥûd*, pl. of احد *aḥad*, one; — ة *iḥâda-t*, alienation; causing estrangement.

احاديث *aḥâdîs*, pl. of حديث *ḥadîs* and حدوثة *ḥadûsa-t*, q.v.

احاذة *iḥâẕa-t*, quick driving, urging.
احارر *aḥârir*, pl. of حر *ḥarr*, heat.
احارة *iḥâra-t*, answer.
احاسن *aḥâsin*, pl. of احسن *aḥsan*, handsomer, better.
احاسى *aḥâsî*, draughts, pl. of حسوة *ḥaswa-t*.
احاشة *iḥâśa-t*, chase.
احاطة *iḥâṭa-t*, surrounding; investing; comprehension, conception.
احاظ *aḥâẕẕ*, pl. of حظ *ḥaẕẕ*, q.v.
احافير *aḥâfîr*, wells, pl. of حفر *ḥafr*, *ḥafar*.
احاكة *iḥâka-t*, weaving; impression (made by a speech, &c.).
احالة *iḥâla-t*, change; conversion to Islam; transfer (of a bill of change); bill of change; cheque; improbability; absurdity.
احاليل *aḥâlîl*, pl. of احليل *iḥlîl*, penis.
احامر *aḥâmir*, pl. of احمر *aḥmar*, q.v.
احان *aḥḥân*, hater, hateful; furious.
احايين *aḥâyîn*, pl. of حين *ḥîn*, moment, &c.
احب *aḥabb*, dearer, more agreeable, comp. of حبيب *ḥabîb*.
احبا *aḥbâ'*, favourites, pl. of حبا *ḥaba'*;—*aḥibbâ*, ة *aḥibba-t*, and
احباب *aḥbâb*, pl. of حبيب *ḥabîb*, friend.
احبار *aḥbâr*, Hebrew doctors, pontiffs, scribes, pl. of حبر *ḥabr*.
احبش *aḥbâś*, loud; —*aḥbaś*, *uḥbuś*, pl. احابش *aḥâbiś*, Abyssinian.
احبل *aḥbal*, *iḥbil*, *uḥbul*, bean.
احبن *aḥban*, dropsical.
احبوش *aḥbuś*, pl. *aḥâbîs*, troop composed of members of different tribes.
احبول *uḥbûl*, ة *uḥbûla-t*, hunting-net, snare.
احتا *iḥtâ'*, sowing; fastening.
احتات *aḥtât*, pl. of حت *ḥatt*, q.v.
احتباس *iḥtibâs*, retaining; confining; imprisoning; keeping captive.

احتجاب *iḥtijâb*, seclusion; retreat; taking the veil.
احتجاج *iḥtijâj*, documentary proof; litigating.
احتدام *iḥtidâm*, great heat.
احتذا *iḥtiẕâ'*, putting on shoes.
احتذار *iḥtiẕâr*, احتراز *iḥtirâz*, احتراس *iḥtirâs* } cautiousness, being on one's guard.
احتراق *iḥtirâq*, conflagration, burning; being consumed; tarnishing; strong desire.
احترام *iḥtirâm*, veneration, reverence.
احتزان *iḥtizân*, sadness, sorrowfulness.
احتساب *iḥtisâb*, computation, reckoning; estimating; opinion; supposition.
احتشام *iḥtiśâm*, bashfulness; modesty; reverence.
احتصاد *iḥtiṣâd*, harvest, crops.
احتضان *iḥtiḍân*, embrace.
احتطاط *iḥtiṭâṭ*, degradation, abasement; contempt; abatement of price.
احتفا *iḥtifâ'*, being bare-foot.
احتفاد *iḥtifâd*, zeal, quickness.
احتفار *iḥtifâr*, digging out, excavation.
احتفاظ *iḥtifâẕ*, preserving; guarding against.
احتفال *iḥtifâl*, solemnity; pomp.
احتقار *iḥtiqâr*, being despised.
احتقان *iḥtiqân*, dysury; administering a clyster, syringing.
احتكار *iḥtikâr*, hoarding grain, to sell it at high prices; monopoly.
احتكام *iḥtikâm*, authority over (على *'ala*).
احتلاب *iḥtilâb*, milking.
احتلام *iḥtilâm*, dreaming; wet dreams; getting of full age.
احتما *iḥtimâ'*, taking refuge with (ب *bi*); abstaining from (من *min*).
احتمال *iḥtimâl*, patience, suffering patiently; possibility; probability; supposition; danger.

احتوا *iḥtiwâ'*, collection; contents; comprising.

احتياج *iḥtiyâj*, want; having need of; indigence.

احتياط *iḥtiyâṭ*, investing, siege, blockade; caution; circumspection.

احتيال *iḥtiyâl*, stratagem; fraud; sagacity; art of living.

احثاث *iḥsâs*, instigation, spurring on, urging.

احجار *aḥjâr*, stones, pl. of حجر *ḥajar*.

احجام *iḥjâm*, cupping.

احجة *aḥijja-t*, pl. of حجاج *ḥajâj*, q.v.

احجوة *uḥjuwwa-t*, احجية *uḥjiyya-t*, pl. *aḥâj-in*, *aḥâjî*, *aḥâjiyy*, riddle, enigma.

(احد) *aḥad*, f. *iḥda*, pl. *âḥâd*, *uḥdân*, *aḥâdûn*, one; someone, somebody; *al-âḥâd*, the units (1 to 9); يوم الاحد *yaum al-aḥad*, Sunday; — II. *aḥḥad*, INF. *ta'ḥîd*, profess that there is one God; —make one out of two; add one; — V. INF. *ta'aḥḥud*, separate one's self, seclude; — VIII. INF. *it'iḥâd*, the same; (m.) unite; be identical; — X. INF. *isti'ḥâd*, seclude one's self; devote one's self entirely to (ب *bi*); — *aḥadd*, more, most or very acute, sharp, cutting, vehement; fierce; with sharp teeth (wolf).

احداث *aḥdâs*, pl. of حدث *ḥadas* and حديث *ḥadîs*, q.v.; — *iḥdâs*, creation; invention; innovation.

احداق *aḥdâq*, pupils, eye-balls, pl. of حدقة *ḥadaqa-t*; — *iḥdâq*, blockade.

احدان *uḥdân*, see احد *aḥad*.

احدب *aḥdab*, hump-backed; arched; f. *ḥadbâ'*, pl. *ḥudb*, misfortune; difficulty; she-camel.

احدر *aḥdar*, squinting; with slender hips (horse).

احدل *aḥdal*, f. *ḥadlâ'*, pl. *ḥudul*, wry, oblique; left-handed (ambidexter).

احدوثة *uḥdûsa-t*, pl. احاديث *aḥâdis*, rumour, news, information; tale, narrative.

احدودب *iḥdaudab*, XII. of حدب q.v.

احدودق *iḥdaudaq*, XII. of حدق q.v.

احدور *uḥdûr*, steep precipice.

احدوة *uḥduwwa-t*, melody of a camel-driver.

احدى *aḥadiyy*, unique; — *iḥda*, f. of احد *aḥad*; — ة *aḥadiyya-t*, oneness, unity; uniqueness; — *uḥdiyya-t*, melody of a camel-driver.

احديباب *iḥdîbâb*, being hump-backed.

احذية *aḥziya-t*, shoes, pl. of حذا *ḥizâ'*.

احر *aḥarr*, hotter, hottest, very hot.

احرا *aḥrâ'*, pl. of حر *ḥar-in*, حرى *ḥarî*, worthy, fit.

احرار *aḥrâr*, pl. of حر *ḥurr*, free, &c.

احراز *aḥrâz*, pl. of حرز *ḥirz*, q.v.; — *iḥrâz*, watching over, surveillance; solicitude.

احراق *iḥrâq*, kindling, setting on fire.

احرام *aḥrâm*, pl. of حرم *ḥaram*, and حريم *ḥarîm*, q.v.; — احرام *iḥrâm*; time during which certain things are forbidden; excommunication, anathema, interdiction; (m.) disinheriting.

احرج *aḥraj*, narrower, comp. of حرج *ḥarij*.

احرس *aḥras*, very old.

احرش *aḥraś*, rough to the touch; a coin; a kind of lizard.

احرف *aḥruf*, letters, pl. of حرف *ḥarf*.

احرنجام *iḥrinjâm*, crowd, see حرجم *ḥarjam*.

احرنشف *iḥranśaf*, be ready to anger, to do evil.

احرنفز *iḥranfaz*, gather, assemble (n.).

احرى *aḥra*, more appropriate; more worthy; better, best; كم احرى *kam aḥra*, how much the more.

احريا *aḥriyâ'*, pl. of حرى *ḥarî-y*, q.v.

احزاب *aḥzâb*, troops, &c., pl. of حزب *ḥizb*.

احزام *aḥzâm*, companions; — *iḥzâm*, bridling, loading a beast of burden.

احزان *aḥzân*, sorrows, &c., pl. of

حزن *ḥuzn*; — *iḥzân*, grieving, causing to be sad.

احزر *aḥzir*, f. *ḥazrâ'*, sour (milk, wine).

احساس *iḥsâs*, perception by the senses.

احسان *iḥsân*, benefit, beneficence; favour; present; kindness; courtesy.

احسب *aḥsab*, more, most or very much esteemed; a good substitute; leprous.

احسن *aḥsan*, pl. احاسن *aḥâsin*, more, most or very beautiful, handsome; better, best.

احسية *aḥsiya-t*, draughts, pl. of حسوة *ḥaswa-t*.

احشا *aḥśâ'*, intestines, pl. of حشا *haś-an*.

احشاش *iḥśâś*, mowing of grass.

احشام *aḥśâm*, retinue.

احشم *aḥśam*, very timid, bashful.

احصا *iḥṣâ'*, counting, reckoning; comprehending, expressing, describing; skill.

احصرة *aḥṣira-t*; pl. of حصير *ḥaṣîr*, q.v.

احصن *aḥṣan*, f. *ḥaṣnâ'*, chaste; — ة *aḥṣina-t*, horses, pl. of حصان *ḥiṣân*; arrow-heads, lances.

احضار *iḥḍâr*, producing, causing to be present; summoning; calling; preparing, making ready.

احضان *aḥḍân*, sides, pl. of حضن *ḥiḍn*.

احضة *aḥiḍḍa-t*, lowest parts, &c., pl. of حضيض *ḥaḍîḍ*, q.v.

احطب *aḥṭab*, f. *ḥaṭbâ'*, very thin; miserable.

احظ *aḥuẓẓ*, pl. of حظ *ḥaẓẓ*, q.v.

احظا *iḥẓâ'*, protection.

احفة *aḥiffa-t*, pl. of حفاف *ḥifâf*, q.v.

احق *aḥaqq*, worthier, worthiest; fitter for (ب *bi*); — *aḥq-in*, for

احقى *aḥqi*, pl. of حقو *ḥaqw*, q.v.

احقا *aḥiqqâ'*, pl. of حقيق *ḥaqîq*; — *aḥqâ'*, pl. of حقو *ḥaqw*, q.v.

احقاد *aḥqâd*, pl. of حقد *ḥaqad*, hatred, rancour; deep grudge; — *iḥqâd*, instigation to hatred.

احقار *iḥqâr*, contempt.

احقاق *aḥqâq*, pl. of حقة *ḥuqqa-t*, q.v.; — *iḥqâq*, getting the better of an adversary in a law-suit; certainty, knowing for certain.

احقال *aḥqâl*, pl. of حقلة *ḥaqla-t*, colic.

احقر *aḥqar*, more, most, or very much despised, viler, meaner, lower; poorer, humbler.

احكال *iḥkâl*, abstruseness, confusion.

احكام *aḥkâm*, judgments, &c., pl. of حكم *ḥukm*; — *iḥkâm*, ordaining, arrangement, institution.

احكم *aḥkam*, wiser, wisest; احكم الحاكمين *aḥkam al-ḥâkimîn*, lord chief justice; God.

احكومة *uḥkûma-t*, judges.

احلابة *iḥlâba-t*, milk.

احلال *iḥlâl*, causing to stop, to halt; permission.

احلام *aḥlâm*, bodies; also pl. of حلم *ḥilm*, mildness, حلم *ḥulm*, dream, and حليم *ḥalîm*, mild, gentle.

احلوفة *uḥlûfa-t*, oath.

احلى *aḥla*, f. *ḥalwâ'*, sweeter; (m.) handsomer, better.

احليل *iḥlîl*, pl. *aḥâlîl*, penis.

احم *aḥamm*, f. *ḥammâ'*, pl. *ḥumm*, white, and, by opposition, black; nearer related; shaft of an arrow.

احما *aḥmâ'*, pl. of حم *ḥam*, حمو *ḥamû*, father-in-law; — *iḥmâ'*, annealing, causing iron to glow; — *aḥimmâ'*, pl. of حميم *ḥamîm*, q.v.

احماس *iḥmâs*, roasting meat in a stove; irritating.

احمال *aḥmâl*, pl. of حمل *ḥaml*, *ḥiml*, *ḥamal*, q.v.

احمام *iḥmâm*, heating of water, heating.

احمد *aḥmad*, more, most or very praiseworthy.

احمر *aḥmar*, f. *ḥamrâ'*, red; pl. *aḥâmir*, red by nature; pl. *ḥumr*, *ḥumrân*, painted red; *al-aḥmarân*, flesh and wine; الموت الاحمر *al-maut al-aḥmar*, violent death; *ḥamrâ'*, heat of mid-day; — ة *aḥmira-t*, asses, pl. of حمار *ḥimâr*.

احمرار *iḥmirâr*, reddening, blushing (s.).

احمرى *aḥmarî-y*, red.

احمز *aḥmaz*, firmer, stronger.

احمس *aḥmas*, f. *ḥamsâ'*, pl. *ḥums*, *aḥâmis*, strong, firm; persevering; hard; — *al-aḥâmis*, calamity.

احمق *aḥmaq*, f. *ḥamqâ'*, pl. *ḥumuq*, *ḥimăq*, *ḥamqa*, *ḥamâqa*, *ḥumâqa*, stupid, foolish, dull, ignorant; (m.) easily provoked anger.

احموقة *uḥmûqa-t*, very foolish, very stupid.

(احن) *aḥin*, A, grow angry; hate (على *'ala*); — ة *iḥna-t*, pl. *iḥan*, anger, inveterate grudge; — *aḥinna-t*, pl. of حنين *ḥanîn*, *ḥinnîn*, q.v.

احنا *aḥnâ*, vulg. we; — *aḥnâ'*, pl. of حنو *ḥinw*, q.v.

احناط *iḥnâṭ*, being ripe (corn); embalming; death.

احنف *aḥnaf*, f. *ḥanfâ'*, having the feet turned inside; — *al-ḥanfâ'*, sea-tortoise; bow; razor; a kind of fish; chameleon; name of a celebrated mare.

احواض *aḥwâḍ*, cisterns, &c., pl. of حوض *ḥauḍ*.

احوال *aḥwâl*, pl. of حال *ḥâl*, state, &c., and of حول *ḥaul*, year; — احواله *aḥwâla-hu*, all around him.

احوب *aḥwab*, sinner, criminal.

احوج *aḥwaj*, more in want of (الى *ila*).

احور *aḥwar*, f. *ḥaura*, pl. *ḥûr*, with large eyes of intense white and black; — حور العيون *ḥûru-'l-'uyûn*, persons with beautiful eyes; houris; — prudence; the planet Jupiter.

احوز *aḥwaz*, f. *ḥauzâ'*, also ى *aḥwaziyy*, active, acting prudently, always ready; black.

احوس *aḥwas*, bold, brave; wolf.

احوص *aḥwaṣ*, with one eye smaller than the other.

احول *aḥwal*, f. *ḥaulâ'*, squint-eyed.

احولال *iḥwilâl*, squinting.

احوى *aḥwa*, f. *ḥawwâ'*, pl. *ḥuww*, dark green, black; ruddy-lipped; — ة *aḥwiya-t*, tents, pl. of حوا *ḥiwâ'*.

(احى) *aḥḥa*, II. cough, see اح.

احى *aḥayy*, more alive.

احيا *aḥyâ'*, pl. of حى *ḥayy*, living, &c., and of حيا *ḥayâ*, parts of a woman; womb; — *iḥyâ*, bringing to life, recalling to life, saving the life; refreshing, animating.

احيان *aḥyân*, times, epochs, pl. of حين *ḥîn*.

احيل *aḥyal*, more cunning.

احيية *aḥyiya-t*, wombs, pl. of حيا *ḥayâ'*.

اخ *aḫ*, brother; — *aḫ*, *aḫḫu*, interjection of disgust; — *aḫ*, *iḫ*, call for the camel to kneel down; — *aḫḫ*, *iḫḫ*, dirt.

اخا *iḫâ'*, brotherhood; friendship.

اخابة *iḫâba-t*, fraud, deceit.

اخابير *aḫâbîr*, informations, &c., pl. of خبر *ḫabar*.

اخادع *aḫâdi'*, pl. of اخدع *aḫda'*, carotid.

اخاديد *aḫâdîd*, pl. of أخدود *aḫdûd*, q.v.

اخادير *aḫâdîr*, curtains, &c., pl. of خدر *ḫidr*, q.v.

اخاذ *aḫâẕ*, اخاذة *iḫâẕa-t*, pl. *uḫuẕ*, pond, fish-pond, horse-pond; handle; land taken possession of; feudal tenure.

اخاريج *aḫârîj*, revenues, expenses, &c., pl. of خرج *ḫarj*, *ḫurj*, q.v.

اخاسى *aḫâsî*, odds, pl. of خساً *ḫas-an*.

اخاضر *aḫâḍir*, pl. of اخضر *aḫḍar*, green, &c., q.v.

اخاقيق *aḫâqîq*, clefts, pl. of اخقوق *uḫqûq*, اخقيق *iḫqîq*.

اخالة *iḫâla-t*, imagination.

اخاليط *aḫâliṭ*, complicated matters or things, pl. of اخلوطة *uḫlûṭa-t*.

اخاوة *iḫâwa-t*, brotherhood.

اخاوى *aḫâwî*, اخايا *aḫâyâ*, pl. of اخية *aḫya-t*, q.v.

اخاير *aḫâyir*, pl. of خير *ḫair*, good, excellent.

اخايل *aḫâyil*, pl. of اخيل *aḫyal*, q.v.

اخبا iḫbâ', extinguishing (a.); pitching a tent.

اخبار aḫbâr, information, &c., pl. of خبر ḫabar; — iḫbâr, giving news, giving information.

اخباری aḫbâriyy, chronicler, who hands down traditions.

اخبث aḫbas, more or most impure; — al-aḫbasân, urine and faeces; sleeplessness; foul breath.

اخبر aḫbar, better or best informed; more experienced.

اخبل aḫbal, mad, possessed (by a demon).

اخبية aḫbiya-t, small tents of camel-hair, &c., pl. of خبا ḫibâ', q.v.

اخت uḫt (for uḫwa-t), pl. aḫawât, sister.

اختبا iḫtibâ', concealment; hiding one's self.

اختبار iḫtibâr, experience.

اختباط iḫtibâṭ, confusion; strife.

اختتام iḫtitâm, completion, end, conclusion.

اختتان iḫtitân, being circumcised.

اختداع iḫtidâ', fraud, deceit.

اختراع iḫtirâ', invention, discovery; contrivance, artifice.

اختشا iḫtišâ', fear.

اختصا iḫtiṣâ, being gelded, castrated.

اختصار iḫtiṣâr, abridgement, compendium.

اختصاص iḫtiṣâṣ, particular calling; distinction; close attachment; devotedness.

اختصام iḫtiṣâm, dispute, quarrel.

اختطاب iḫtiṭâb, preaching, sermon; betrothal.

اختطاف iḫtiṭâf, carrying off, abduction; violence.

اختفا iḫtifâ', concealing one's self; absconding.

اختلا iḫtilâ', retirement, seclusion.

اختلاج iḫtilâj, confusion, agitation, excitement; trembling.

اختلاس iḫtilâs, snatching off, pickpocketing.

اختلاط iḫtilâṭ, mixture; confusion; commerce, intercourse.

اختلاف iḫtilâf, discord; difference; discrepancy; resistance; contradiction.

اختلال iḫtilâl, confusion, disorder; disturbance, tumult.

اختمار iḫtimâr, fermentation.

اختناق iḫtinâq, choking, suffocation.

اختوا iḫtiwâ', emptiness.

اختی uḫtiyy, sisterly.

اختيار iḫtiyâr, choice, election; free will; aged; — ی iḫtiyâriyy, of free will, voluntary; with premeditation; — ة al-iḫtiyâriyya-t, the ancients, people of old.

اختياض iḫtiyâḍ, dipping, diving.

اختيال iḫtiyâl, walking with a proud step, strutting; haughtiness.

اختيان iḫtiyân, treason, treachery.

اخشم aḫšam, with a flat nose; without smell; lion; broad sword.

اخدان aḫdân, friends, comrades, pl. of خدن ḫidn.

اخدب aḫdab, big and stupid; obstinate; inflicting large wounds.

اخدر aḫdar, dark, obscure; — ی aḫdariyy, wild ass.

اخدع aḫda', more or most deceitful, crafty, cunning; more concealed; pl. aḫâdi', carotid.

اخدة aḫidda-t, pl. of خد ḫadd, track, &c., q.v.

اخدود uḫdûd, pl. aḫâdîd, furrow; mark of a blow; (m.) a heavy blow.

(اخذ) aḫaz, U, INF. aḫz, ta'ḫâz, receive, accept, take, seize; derive (grammatically); hear or learn from (من min); yield to remonstrances (ب bi); come suddenly upon, surprise; punish; begin, set out; lead to (a road); — aḫiz, INF. aḫaz, suffer from indigestion; become furious (camel); water (eyes); — aḫuz, INF. uḫûza-t, turn sour (milk); — II. INF. ta'ḫîz, seize, take; cause milk to turn sour; — III. INF. mu'âḫaza-t, chastise, punish; — VIII. INF. it'iḫâz, choose for one's self and take possession of; associate with; prepare for one's use

(food); come to close quarters; — X. INF. *isti'ḫâẕ*, take possession of; drop one's head; submit to the will of God.

اخذ *aḫẕ*, taking, اخذ وقبض *aḫẕ wa qabḍ*, receivings, revenue; اخذ ومصرف *aḫẕ wa maṣraf*, revenue and expenditure; punishment; custom, habit; — *iḫẕ*, mark made by branding (for an amulet); — *âḫiẕ*, with watering eyes, blear-eyed; — *uḫuẕ*, watering of the eyes, being blear-eyed; pl. of اخاذة *iḫâẕa-t*, pond, &c.; — ة *uḫẕa-t*, stratagem; love-charm, elixir, amulet; — *âḫiẕa-t*, torpor, torpidity.

(اخر) *uḫur*, end, what is last; — *uḫur-an, min uḫur-in*, behind, from behind; lastly; — *âḫar*, f. *uḫrâ'*, *uḫrât* (اخراة), pl. *uḫar*, vulg. *aḫarîn, aḫâra*, other, another, second; — تارة واخرى *târat-an wa uḫra*, at one time and another; *al-uḫra*, life eternal; pl. *uḫar*, *uḫrayât*, last parts, last rows; — *âḫir*, f. ة last, remotest; absent; concealed; pl. اواخر *awâḫir*, end, termination (gram.); الى اخره *ila âḫiri-hi*, abbreviated الخ, to the end, and so on, &c.; *al-âḫira-t*, the future life; day of judgment; — *aḫḫar*, II. INF. *ta'ḫîr*, cause a delay; also V. INF. *ta'aḫḫur* and X. INF. *isti'ḫâr*, remain behind, delay, come last; — III. INF. *mu'âḫara-t*, delay, postpone, adjourn.

اخراب *iḫrâb*, destruction, ruin.

اخراد *iḫrâd*, bashful silence.

اخراج *iḫrâj*, producing, drawing forth, bringing out; sally.

اخرب *aḫrab*, f. *ḫurbâ'*, more devastated; pierced (ear); — ة *aḫriba-t*, ruins, pl. of خراب *ḫarâb*.

اخرج *aḫraj*, f. *ḫurjâ'*, black and white; — ة *aḫrija-t*, pl. of خرج *ḫarj*, q.v.

اخرس *aḫras*, f. *ḫarsâ'*, pl. *ḫurs*, *ḫursân*, dumb; soundless, noiseless, echoless; *al-ḫarsâ*, misfortune; cloud without thunder and lightning.

اخرشة *aḫriśa-t*, pl. of خراش *ḫarâś*, mark (by branding) of a camel.

اخرفة *aḫrifa-t*, sheep, pl. of خروف *ḫurûf*.

اخرق *aḫraq*, f. *ḫarqâ'*, pl. *ḫurq*, awkward, stupid; f. violent wind, plain exposed to the wind.

اخرماس *iḫrimmâs*, silence, see خرمس *ḫarmas*, خرمص *ḫarmaṣ*.

اخرنبق *iḫrimbaq*, اخرمفق *iḫrimfaq*, see خربق *ḫarbaq*.

اخروى *uḫrawiyy*, referring to the future life.

اخرى *âḫiriyy*, *iḫiriyy*, *uḫriyy*, last; — *uḫra*, f. of اخر *âḫar*, another.

اخزم *aḫzam*, male snake.

اخزة *aḫizza-t*, hares, pl. of خزز *ḫazaz*.

اخس *aḫass*, viler, vilest; meaner, meanest, comp. of خسيس *ḫasîs*.

اخسر *aḫsar*, who loses or spends much.

اخشب *aḫśab*, f. *ḫaśbâ'*, hard, rough to the touch; severe.

اخشن *aḫśan*, f. *ḫaśnâ'*, pl. *ḫuśn*, *ḫuśun*, hard, rough, rude; difficult of approach or attack; lean.

اخشة *aḫiśśa-t*, pl. of خشاش *ḫaśâś*, wooden ring for the nose of a camel.

اخشى *aḫśa*, more or most timid; a dangerous place.

اخص *aḫaṣṣ*, more particular, more private, comp. of خصيص *ḫaṣîṣ*.

اخصن *aḫṣun*, small axes, pl. of خصين *ḫaṣîn*.

اخضر *aḫḍar*, f. *ḫaḍrâ'*, pl. *ḫuḍr*, green; of dark colour, grey, black; (m.) fresh, vigorous; palm-tree; *al-aḫḍar*, the dark night; f. sky; crowd of men, army; — pl. *al-aḫâḍir*, gold, wine and flesh (meat).

اخضع *aḫḍa'*, more, most or very submissive.

اخضف *aḫḍaf*, a kind of snake.

اخطا *iḫṭâ'*, erring, committing a fault.

أخطار *aḫṭâr*, pl. of خطر *ḫaṭar*, danger, risk, and of خطر *ḫiṭr*, large troop of camels; — *iḫṭâr*, remind, causing to recollect.

أخطاط *aḫṭâṭ*, lines, strokes, &c., pl. of خط *ḫaṭṭ*.

أخطب *aḫṭab*, of dirt colour; striped; tattooed.

أخطف *aḫṭaf*, with a slender waist.

أخطل *aḫṭal*, f. *ḫaṭlâ'*, pl. *ḫuṭul*, with flabby ears, breasts; vulgar talker; ابو الاخطل *abû-'l-aḫṭal*, horse, mule.

أخطم *aḫṭam*, with a long nose, trunk, beak.

أخفا *iḫfâ'*, hiding, concealing, suppressing.

أخفار *iḫfâr*, protection, escort.

اخفاف *aḫfâf*, pl. of خف *ḫuff*, hoof of the camel; foot of the ostrich.

أخفاق *iḫfâq*, failure; distress.

أخفش *aḫfaś*, day-blind.

أخفية *aḫfiya-t*, coverings, veils, hidden things, pl. of خفا *ḫifâ'*.

أخقاق *aḫqâq*, clefts, rents in the ground, pl. of خق *ḫaqq*.

أخقوق *uḫqûq*, أخقيق *iḫqîq*, pl. *aḫâqîq*, cleft, rent in the ground.

أخل *aḫall*, poorer, very poor; — ة *aḫilla-t*, pl. of خلة *ḫilla-t*, scabbard, and of خلال *ḫilâl*, toothpick, &c., q.v.

أخلا *aḫlâ'*, pl. of خلو *ḫilw*, q.v.; — *aḫillâ'*, friends, pl. of خليل *ḫalîl*.

أخلاب *aḫlâb*, claws, pl. of خلب *ḫilb*.

أخلاص *iḫlâṣ*, candour, sincerity, probity, true friendship; correction; emendation.

أخلاط *aḫlâṭ*, mixtures, humours, &c., pl. of خلط *ḫilṭ*.

أخلاف *aḫlâf*, a breach of contract, &c., pl. of خلف *ḫulf*.

أخلاق *aḫlâq*, qualities, manners, &c., pl. of خلق *ḫulq*; — *iḫlâq*, being worn out; shame.

أخلال *aḫlâl*, friends, pl. of خل *ḫill*.

أخلج *aḫlaj*, rope.

أخلص *aḫlaṣ*, more or most sincere; purer, purest.

أخلف *aḫlaf*, left-handed; walking with difficulty; stupid; squint-eyed; more deceitful; stream; snake.

أخلق *aḫlaq*, even, smooth; poor, fitter, worthier (comp. of خليق *ḫalîq*).

أخلوطة *uḫlûṭa-t*, pl. *aḫâlîṭ*, complication, anything complicated.

أخليا *aḫliyâ*, pl. of خلى *ḫaliyy*, empty, free, &c., q.v.

أخليج *iḫlîj*, fine, swift horse; rhubarb.

أخماس *aḫmâs*, fifth parts, pl. of خمس *ḫums*.

أخمرة *aḫmira-t*, veils, head-gears, pl. of خمار *ḫimâr*.

أخمسا *aḫmisâ'*, fifth parts, pl. of خميس *ḫamîs*.

أخمص *aḫmaṣ*, pl. *aḫâmiṣ*, middle of the sole; foot; waist; with a slim waist.

أخن *aḫann*, pl. خن *ḫunn*, who speaks through the nose.

أخنس *aḫnas*, flat-nosed; *al-aḫnas*, lion; — f. *al-ḫansâ*, wild cow.

أخنى *aḫinna*, striped material; coarse linen.

أخو *aḫw*, *aḫû*, pl. *aḫûn*, *aḫâ'*, *âḫâ'*, *aḫwa-t*, *iḫwa-t*, *uḫwa-t*, *uḫuww*, *uḫuwwa-t*, *iḫwân*, *uḫwân*, brother; companion; the like of; أخو الموت *aḫû-'l-maut*, sleep; أخو الخير *aḫû-'l-ḫair*, evil; — ة *uḫuwwa-t*, brotherhood.

(أخو) أخا *aḫâ*, U, (1 pret. *aḫau-tu*, *aḫai-tu*) INF. *uḫuwwa-t*, be brother or as a brother; — III. *iḫâ'*, *iḫâwa-t*, *mu'âḫât*, become one's brother; fraternise, make friends with (acc.); be fit for (ل *li*); V. prove one's self a brother to, fit for; VI. establish brotherhood between one another.

أخوات *aḫawât*, sisters, pl. of أخت *uḫt*.

أخوال *aḫwâl*, pl. of خال *ḫâl*, maternal uncle.

احوان *aḥwân*, brothers, pl. of احو *aḥû*; — *iḥwân*, table, tray.

احوت *aḥwat*, (m.) pl. *ḥûtân*, *ḥût*, stupid; mad.

احور *aḥûr*, stable; مير احور *mîr aḥûr*, equerry, master of the horse.

احوف *aḥwaf*, more, most, very timorous.

احولة *aḥwila-t*, pl. of خال *ḥâl*, maternal uncle.

احونة *aḥwina-t*, tables, trays, pl. of خوان *ḥiwân*, *ḥuwân*.

احوى *aḥawiyy*, brotherly; — ة *uḥuwiyya-t*, fraternity, congregation.

احى *aḥḥa*, II. make a noose; — ة *aḥiyya-t*, pl. *aḥâwî*, *aḥâyâ*, peg or line to tie up a horse.

اخيار *aḥyâr*, pl. of خير *ḥair*, good.

اخياش *aḥyâś*, pl. of خيش *ḥaiś*, canvas.

اخياف *aḥyâf*, people of different lineage; of the same mother, but another father.

اخيال *aḥyâl*, horses, pl. of خيل *ḥail*.

اخيب *aḥyab*, wrong (way).

اخيذ *aḥîẕ*, prisoner.

اخير *aḥyar*, better, best; — *aḥîr*, last.

اخيرى *uḥaira*, never, dim. of آخر *âḥar*.

اخيس *aḥyas*, numerous.

اخيف *aḥyaf*, pl. *ḥûf*, *ḥîf*, f. *ḥaifâ*, having one eye black, the other blue; — *ḥaifâ'*, a composition in which all the letters of each alternate word are pointed, the other words being without points.

اخيل *aḥyal*, with moles on the face; pl. *aḥâyil*, white falcon; vain, haughty; haughtiness; pl. *ḥîl*, a bird of evil omen; — ة *aḥyila-t*, fancies, ideas, &c., pl. of خيال *ḥayâl*, q.v.

اد *ad*=يد *yad*, hand.

(اد) *add*, A, I, U, INF. *add*, roar (camel); fondle (she camel); offer, present; rove; come upon suddenly; — V. INF. *ta'addud*, become violent, get worse.

اد *add*, *idd*, pl. *idâd*, ة *idda-t*, pl. *idad*, power, victory; calamity; — *udd*, power, victory.

ادا *adâ*, paying, requital; fulfilling a duty; manner, tone; — ة *adât*, pl. *adawât*, tool, utensil; particle (gram.)

آداب *âdâb*, civilities, &c., pl. of ادب *adab*.

ادابر *udâbir*, who turns away and will not listen.

اداد *adâd*, power, victory; — *idâd*, pl. of اد *add*, see above.

ادار *adâr*, March; — ة *idâra-t*, revolving (a. and n.); circuit of a magistrate, &c.; administration; prefecture; district.

اداف *udâf*, penis; ear.

اداله *idâla-t*, victory.

ادام *adâm*, reconcilement; — *idâm*, pl. *udum*, *âdâm*, *âdima-t*, by-dish, as vegetables, &c.; leader; consenting; — *âdâm*, pl. of اديم *adîm*, skin; — *addâm*, manufacturer of leather; — ة *idâma-t*, perseverance; remaining, staying.

ادان *adân-in*, pl. of دنى *daniyy*, low, etc.

(ادب) *adab*, I, prepare a banquet, invite to a meal; wonder; — *adub*, INF. *adab*, be well educated and of refined manners; — II. INF. *ta'dîb*, educate; correct, chastise; — IV. INF. *idâb*, make justice prevail in a country; invite to a meal; — V. INF. *ta'addub* and X, INF. *isti'dâb*, receive education, be refined.

ادب *adab*, pl. *âdâb*, refined manners; politeness; literary persuits; liberal education; — *al-âdâb*, literature; — ة *udba-t*, entertainment; wonderful things.

ادبا *udabâ*, pl. of اديب *adîb*, well bred, &c., q.v.

ادباب *adbâb*, pl. of دب *dabb*, bear.

ادبار *adbâr*, the last or hindmost

parts or persons; backs; — *idbâr*, turning one's back; adversity; — *iddibâr*, retreat.
ادبح *adbaḥ*, worthless things.
ادبخانه *adab-ḫâna-h*, water-closet.
ادبس *adbas*, dark red, brown.
ادبى *adabiyy*, polite, well-educated; العلم الادبى *al-'ilm al-adabiyy*, morals, moral philosophy; — ة *adabiyya-t*, pl. *adabiyyât*, literature, pl. what promotes civilisation and refinement, accomplishments.
ادثر *adsar*, lazy, negligent.
ادجن *adjan*, f. *dajnâ'*, of a deep black; cloudy.
ادحى *udḥiyy*, *idḥiyy*, ة *udḥiyya-t*, ادحوة *udḥuwwa-t*, ostrich nest.
ادخال *idḫâl*, introducing; causing to enter; enclosing.
ادخر *idḫir*, rush (plant).
ادخل *adḫal*, entering more deeply into; more familiar.
ادخن *adḫan*, f. *daḫnâ'*, of the colour of smoke; — ة *adḫina-t*, fumes of smoke, &c., pl. of دخان *duḫân*, *daḫḫân*.
ادد *idad*, powers, victories, pl. of ادة *idda-t*.
(ادر) *adir*, A, INF. *adar*, be afflicted with a rupture.
ادر *a'dar*, pl. *udr*, f. *adrâ'*, afflicted with a rupture; — *udur*, majesty; — *adarr*, f. درا *darrâ'*, yielding abundant milk; — ة *adara-t*, *udra-t*, rupture.
ادراج *idrâj*, march; folding; insertion.
ادرارة *idrâra-t*, pl. *-ât*, wages, military pay.
ادراع *iddirâ'*, putting on a coat of mail.
ادراك *idrâk*, comprehension; intelligence; genius.
ادرجة *udrujja-t*, ladder, stairs; step, degree.
ادرد *adrad*, toothless.
ادرع *adru'*, coat of mail, &c., pl. of درع *dir'*, q.v.
ادرم *adram*, f. *darmâ*,' pl. *durm*, uniform; fleshy, well rounded; toothless; big-headed; f. *darmâ'*, hare.
ادرنة *adrana-t*, Adrianople.
ادرون *idraun*, manger; stable; dwelling; home; origin.
ادريس *idrîs*, Enoch (prophet); ابو ادريس *abû idrîs*, penis.
ادسق *adsaq*, with a large mouth.
ادسم *adsam*, pl. *dusm*, *dusum*, very fat; dark grey; mean.
ادعا *iddi'â'*, claim, pretension; arrogance; law-suit; inviting, calling to.
ادعب *ad'ab*, stupid.
ادعج *ad'aj*, f. *da'jâ'*, pl. *du'j*, black; with large black eyes; dark; — f. *da'jâ'*, moonless nights; last day of the lunar month; raving; hill.
ادعيا *ad'iyâ*, pl. of دعى *da'iyy*, q.v.
ادعية *ad'iya-t*, calls, prayers, &c., pl. of دعا *du'â'*, q.v.; — *ud'iyya-t* and ادعوة *ud'uwwa-t*, dark question of dispute; riddle.
ادغال *adgâl*, faults, defects, &c., pl. of دغل *dagal*; — *idgâl*, fraud, deceit.
ادغام *idgâm*, contraction, assimilation of letters by *taśdîd*.
ادفا *adfâ'*, pl. of دف *dif'*, heat, &c., q.v.
ادق *adaqq*, thinner, more delicate, more accurate, comp. of دقيق *daqîq*; — ة *adiqqa-t*, pl. of دقيق *daqîq*, thin, &c., q.v.
ادقى *adqa*, violent hunger.
(ادل) *adal*, I, heal (n.), also II.; — A, shake the milk in the leather pipe for buttering; drag along under a burden.
ادل *idl*, sore throat; — sour milk; object of litigation; — *adl-in*, buckets, &c., pl. of دلو *dalw*; — ة *adilla-t*, pl. of دليل *dalîl*, proof, &c.
ادلا *adillâ'*, pl. of دليل *dalîl*, guide.
ادلال *idlâl*, arrogance; wantonness.
ادلص *adlaṣ*, hairless; growing fresh hair.

ادلم *adlam*, black; dark brown, f. *ad-dalmâ'*, last night of the lunar moon.

ادلى *adli*, buckets, &c., pl. of دلو *dalw*.

(ادم) *adam*, U, I, INF. *adm*, unite two things, join together, reconcile; give a by-dish with bread; lead; — *adim*, A, INF. *adam*, also *adum*, INF. *udûma-t*, be reddish, brownish, blackish; — IV. reconcile; give a by-dish with bread; turn the inside of the skin outside; — VIII. eat a by-dish with bread; be full of sap.

ادم *adam*, human skin; leathern pipe; date; tomb; pl. of اديم *adîm*, earth; — *adm*, concord, union; — *udm*, skin; leader; example for imitation; (m.) ration; — *udum*, pl. of اديم *adîm*, q.v., and ادام *adâm*, by-dish; — *âdam*, pl. *udm*, *udmân*, f. *admâ'*, *adam*, pl. *awâdim*, reddish; of the colour of human flesh; browned; white (camel); Adam; بنو ادم *banû* (*bani*) *âdam*, mankind; — ة *adma-t*, *adama-t*, leader; — *udma-t*, reddishness; whitish colour of the (camel) skin; conjunction; — *udma-t*, *adama-t*, relationship.

ادمان *idmân*, exercise; experience; perseverance; — *udmân*, white, pl. of. آدم *âdam*.

ادمغة *admiga-t*, brains, pl. of دماغ *dimâg*.

ادموس *idmûs*, dark.

ادمى *adamiyy*, man; human; — ة *adamiyya-t*, humanity; politeness.

ادنا *adnâ*, nearer; viler, meaner; — *adnâ'*, pl. of دنى *danî*, vile, worthless, &c.

ادهان *adhân*, pl. of دهن *dahn*, fat, &c.

ادهر *adhur*, ages, &c., pl. of دهر *dahr*.

ادهس *adhas*, f. *dahsâ*, pl. *duhs*, of rust-colour; soft, gentle.

ادهم *adham*, black, blackish (horse); dark green; old, and, by opposition, fresh; — f. *dahmâ'*, pot, kettle; what appears black in the distance (crowd of people); — pl. *duhm*, the moonless nights.

ادهية *adhiya-t*, pl. of دهى *dahiyy*, sly, cunning.

(ادو) *adâ*, U, assist; — INF. ادو *aduww*, ripen; — INF. *adw*, waylay; deceive; provide with, fit out; — VI. INF. *ta'âdî*, provide one's self with; — IV. INF. *îdâ*, and X. INF. *isti'dâ'*, see (ادى).

ادوا *adwâ'*, illness, pl. of دا *dâ'*.

ادوار *adwâr*, houses, &c., pl. of دار *dâr*, and revolutions, &c., pl. of دور *daur*.

ادوب *ad'ub*, pl. of داب *da'b*, custom, habit.

ادور *ad'ur*, *adwur*, ادورة *adwira-t*, houses, &c., pl. of دار *dâr*.

ادوم *adwam*, more or most durable.

ادوية *adwiya-t*, medicines, pl. of دوا *dawâ'*.

(ادى) *ada*, I, INF. *udiyy*, coagulate (milk); be many, abundant; — INF. *ady*, lay snares for; waylay; — II. INF. *ta'diya-t*, cause to reach a place, bring to; pay a person; — IV. INF. *îdâ'*, assist; be strong, powerful; be numerous and well off (people); grow too much or many; prepare for; — V. INF. *ta'addî*, pay one's debts; — X. INF. *isti'dâ'*, ask for help; take one's fortune by force; — VI. see (ادو).

ادى *âda*, better paying; conscientious; — *adiyy*, equipment, outfit; preparation; — *idan*, vessel, leather bag; nimble, agile.

اديان *adyân*, beliefs, &c., pl. of دين *dîn*.

اديب *adîb*, pl. *udabâ'*, of polite manners, well bred; literary, learned, scholar; teacher, tutor.

اديد *adîd*, hard to bear, violent; — *idîd*, shouting, scream; roar.

اديم *adîm*, entire; brightness of the day; time before midday;

origin; authority; — pl. *adam*, earth; — pl. *udum*, what can be seen from heaven and earth; — pl. *udum*, *âdâm*, *âdima-t*, skin of the face; skin of an animal.

ادين *adyan*, more pious, more religious.

اذ *iẓ*, behold! when; as; since; if; اذما *iẓmâ*, when, at the time when; اذاك , اذذاك *iẓẓâk*, at that time, then; — اذ *iẓ-in*, then; affixed, as: يومئذ *yaumi'ẓ-in*, on that day; حينئذ *ḥînai'ẓ-in*, وقتئذ *waqtai'ẓ-in*, at that time; — *âẓ-in*, see اذى .

(اذ) *aẓẓ*, INF. *aẓẓ*, cut.

اذا *iẓâ*, behold! when (in the sense of future), followed by the pret.; اذا ما *iẓâ mâ*, when, as soon as; — *iẓan*, well then! in this case then; — ة *aẓât*, injury, damage; evil; pain.

اذابة *iẓâba-t*, melting.

اذاخر *aẓâḥir*, rushes, pl. of *iẓḥir*.

اذاعة *iẓâ'a-t*, publication.

اذان *âẓân*, ears, pl. of اذن *uẓn*.

اذانى *aẓâniyy*, long-eared.

اذب *aẓabb*, wild bull; — ة *aẓibba-t*, flies, pl. of ذباب *ẓubâb*.

اذبل *aẓbal*, f. *ẓablâ'*, thirsty, with dry lips.

(اذج) *aẓaj*, drink much wine.

اذخر *iẓḥir*, pl. *aẓâḥir*, a fragrant kind of rush.

اذرع *aẓra'*, cross born from a freeman and a slave; eloquent; quick, swift; — *aẓru'*, pl. of ذراع *ẓirâ'*.

اذرة *aẓirra-t*, powders, pl. of ذرور *ẓarûr*.

اذعاج *aẓ'âj*, worrying, teazing, urging.

اذعان *aẓ'ân*, obedience, submission.

اذفر *aẓfar*, strongly scented; — f. *aẓ-ẓafrâ'*, wild rue.

اذقن *aẓqan*, f. *ẓaqnâ'*, pl. ذقن *ẓuqn*, having a long or hanging chin.

اذكر *aẓkar*, more pointed, sharper.

اذكى *aẓka*, more acute; more sagacious; more vivid.

اذكيا *aẓkiyâ*, pl. *ẓakî*, acute; sharp; ingenious.

(اذل) *aẓal*, I, INF. *aẓl*, lie.

اذلا *aẓillâ'*, pl. of ذليل *ẓalîl*, abject, mean, vile.

(اذلعب) *iẓla'abb*, hasten away.

اذلق *aẓlaq*, f. *ẓalqâ'*, sharp; ready of speech.

اذلولى *iẓlaula*, depart, go away, XII. of (ذلى).

اذم *aẓamm*, more or most blameworthy; — ة *aẓimma-t*, duties, &c., pl. of ذمام *ẓimâm*.

(اذن) *aẓan* INF. *aẓan*, listen to (ل *li* and الى *ila*); get appetite for (acc.); — INF. *aẓn*, strike on the ear, box the ears; (pass.) suffer from ear-ache; — INF. *âẓân* and *aẓẓân*, announce, especially the time for prayer; — *aẓin*, listen to; — INF. *iẓn*, *aẓan*, *aẓân*, *aẓâna-t*, know; — INF. *iẓn*, *aẓîn*, communicate, impart; II. impart, communicate frequently; rubb the ears; prevent from drinking or from entering; be door-keeper; call out the hour of prayer; — IV. inform of (ب *bi*); astonish; prevent; box the ears; call out the hour for prayer; begin to fade; — V. swear, take an oath; make known; shout at threateningly; venture; — X. ask for permission

اذن *iẓn*, permission; leave; farewell; adieu; furlough; — *uẓn*, *uẓun*, pl. *âẓân*, ear, handle; — ة *aẓana-t*, cotyledon.

اذناب *aẓnâb*, tails, &c., pl. of ذنب *ẓanab*.

اذهان *aẓhân*, intellects, pl. of ذهن *ẓihn*.

اذهل *aẓhal*, more distracted.

اذوب *aẓ'ub*, wolves, pl. of ذئب *ẓi'b*.

اذوذ *aẓûẓ*, cutting, sharp.

اذوط *aẓwa-t*, with a short chin.

(اذى) *aẓi*, A, INF. اذى *iẓan*, *aẓâ'* suffer a damage, an injury; — — II, IV. injure, damage; — V. = I,

الذى *âẕî* (اذ *âẕ-in*), hurtful; offensive; — *aẕan*, also ة *aẕẕiyya-t*, injury, damage; — *âẕiyy*, wave, billow.

اذيال *aẕyâl*, trains of garments, &c., pl. of ذيل *ẕail*.

اذيب *aẕyab*, mass of water; terror; swiftness.

اذين *aẕîn*, call to prayer; caller, Muazzin; prince; bail; knowledge; ear; — *uẕain*, little ear.

(ار) *arr*, U, INF. *arr*, drive; drive away; throw away; have connexion with a woman (acc.); kindle; — IV. INF. *i'rār*, cause to grow lean, thin; — VIII. INF. *it'irâr*, hasten.

ار *âr*, shame, disgrace; — ة *ira-t*, pl. *irûn*, fire; hearth, chimney; provisions of roast meat; — *âra-t*, chimney, stove; difficulty in pronouncing the letter ر.

ارا *arâ'*, *ârâ'*, opinions, &c., pl. of راى *ra'y*.

اراب *ârâb*, pl. of ارب *irb*, member, and of اربة *irba-t*, *urba-t*, need; — ة *irâba-t*, prudence.

اراث *irâs̱*, tinder; fire.

اراج *arrâj*, intriguer.

اراجل *arâjil*, اراجيل *arâjîl*, hunters, pl. of رجل *rajil*, راجل *râjil*.

اراجيح *arâjîḥ*, deserts; pl. of ارجوحة *arjûḥa-t*, swing, rocking-board.

اراجيز *arâjîz*, poems in the metre *rajaz*, pl. of ارجوزة *arjûza-t*.

اراجيف *arâjîf*, false rumours, scandals, pl. of ارجاف *irjâf*.

اراحة *irâḥa-t*, resting, reposing; granting; alleviating; refreshing.

اراخنة *arâḫina-t*, archons, chiefs, pl. of ارخون *arḫon*.

اراخى *arâḫi*, veils, curtains, pl. of ارخية *urḫiyya-t*.

ارادة *irâda-t*, will, intention, desire, decree; high-priest of the Druses.

ارادى *irâdiyy*, who acts according to his own will.

اراذل *arâẕil*, rabble, pl. of ارذل *arẕal*.

ارارس *arâris*, ة *arârisa-t*, peasants countrymen, pl. of اريس *arîs*.

اراض *ârâḍ*, اراضى *arâḍî*, lands, &c., pl. of ارض *arḍ*.

اراعيل *arâ'îl*, herds, troops, etc., pl. of رعلة *ra'la-t*.

اراغن *arâgin*, organs, pl. of ارغن *argun*.

اراقم *arâqim*, poisonous snakes, pl. of ارقم *arqam*.

اراقة *irâqa-t*, pouring out.

اراك *arâk*, a thorny tree; its berries; bitter herb; field.

اراكين *arâkin*, props, supports, &c., pl. of ركن *rukn*.

آرام *ârâm*, stones to indicate the road in the desert, &c., pl. of ارم *iram*; — *ar'âm*, *ârâm*, gazelles, pl. of رئم *ri'm*; — *arâm*, crown of the head.

ارامل *arâmil*, pl. of ارمل *armal*, widowed; poor.

ارامن *arâmin*, ة *arâmina-t*, Armenians, pl. of ارمن *arman*.

اران *irân*, hearse; pl. *urun*, lair of a wild animal; sword; — *arân-in*, and

ارانب *arânib*, hares, pl. of ارنب arnab.

اراوى *arâwiyy*, mountain-goats, pl. of اروية *urwiyya-t*.

ارای *ar'a*, fitter, more appropriate.

ارايك *arâyik*, pl. of اريك *arîk*, divan for a bride, throne.

(ارب) *arab*, I, make tight (a knot); strike on a member of the body; — *arib*, A, need; be poor and needy; have flaccid members; be out of order (stomach); be bad and hard (times); be strongly attached; be versed in (ب *bi*); — *arub*, be wise, prudent; — II. INF. *ta'rîb*, make fast, tight; sharpen; increase and perfect; — IV. INF. *i'râb*, overcome, conquer; — V. INF. *ta'arrub*, raise difficulties; take affected airs; affect slyness.

ارب *arab*, need; — *arb*, fore-finger; — *arib*, prudent, sly; — *irb*, cun-

ning; malice; pl. *ârâb*, *ar'âb*, limb, member; need; aim; piece; — *urb*, misfortune, religious scruple; — ة *irba-t*, misfortune; cunning; also *urba-t*, chain, necklace; pl. *ârâb*, necessaries, need; — *urba-t*, pl. *urab*, strong knot; — *aribba-t*, allies, pl. of رباب *ribâb*.

اربا *arbâ'*, pl. of ربو *rabw*, troop; — *urubbâ*, Europe.

ارباب *arbâb*, masters, lords, &c., pl. of رب *rabb*.

ارباع *arbâ'*, pl. of ربع *rab'*, *rub'*, *ruba'*, *rubu'*, q.v.

اربان *urbân*, pledges, pl. of ربون *rabûn*.

اربط *arbaṭ*, childless; — *arbuṭ*, pl. of رباط *ribâṭ*, q.v.

اربع *arba'*, f., ة *arba'a-t*, m., four; ذوات الاربع *zawât al-arba'*, quadrupeds; — *arbu'*, vernal habitations, &c., pl. of ربع *rab'*; — ة *arbi'a-t*, spring-seasons, pl. of ربيع *rabî'*.

اربعا *arbi'â'*, *arba'â'*, *arbu'â'*, pl. اربعا ات *arbi'â'ât*, Wednesday; — *arbi'â'*, springs, pl. of ربيع *rabî'*; — *arbu'â'*, pillars, columns.

اربعاوا *arbu'âwâ'*, temple with columns.

اربل *arbal*, Arbela; flourishing again.

اربى *arba*, more numerous, more.

ارت *aratt*, f. *ruttâ'*, pl. *rutt*, stammerer; chatterer; — ة *urta-t*, crest of the chameleon.

ارتاع *artâ'*, crowd.

ارتباط *irtibâṭ*, ligament, connexion; tie; friendship.

ارتجاج *irtijâj*, trembling.

ارتجاع *irtijâ'*, return; recollection; conversion.

ارتجال *irtijâl*, improvisation; — *irtijâl-an*, ex tempore; inconsiderately.

ارتحال *irtiḥâl*, departure, emigration.

ارتخا *irtiḥâ'*, relaxation.

ارتداد *irtidâd* (عن *'an*), apostacy; (الى *ila*), return, conversion.

ارتسام *irtisâm*, being marked; consecration of a priest.

ارتشا *irtiśâ'*, corruption, bribery.

ارتضا *irtiḍâ'*, contentment; consent; approval.

ارتعا *irti'â'*, pasturing (s.).

ارتعاب *irti'âb*, being frightened, alarmed.

ارتعاد *irti'âd*, trembling, being frightened.

ارتعاش *irti'âś*, trepidation.

ارتغاب *irtigâb*, desire, longing.

ارتفاع *irtifâ'*, pl. ات, elevation, exaltation, high dignity; removing; disappearance; apogee; yield of crops.

ارتفاق *irtifâq*, supporting one's self; leaning against.

ارتقا *irtiqâ'*, ascension, promotion; increase.

ارتقاب *irtiqâb*, observation from a watch-tower.

ارتكاب *irtikâb*, committing a sin; undertaking; riding on horseback.

ارتكاض *irtikâḍ*, movement of a child in the womb; agony; anxiety.

ارتكام *irtikâm*, accumulation.

ارتهاب *irtihâb*, fear, terror.

ارتهاط *irtihâṭ*, assembly.

ارتهاف *irtihâf*, (m.) friendly reception.

ارتهاك *irtihâk*, weakness of limbs.

ارتهان *irtihân*, mortgaging, pawning; seizure.

ارتيا *irtiyâ'*, consideration, taking of thought.

ارتياب *irtiyâb*, doubt, hesitation, uncertainty.

ارتياح *irtiyâḥ*, rest; repose; vivacity; cheerfulness; zeal; endeavour; mercy of God.

ارتياض *irtiyâḍ*, training, dressing (an animal); exercise.

ارتياع *irtiyâ'*, fear, fright.

(ارث) *araṡ*, INF. *arṡ*, kindle; — II. the same; sow discord; — V. being kindled.

ارث *irṡ* (for ورث *wirṡ*), inheritance; ashes, remains; old custom; root; — *urṡ*, thorn; — *araṡṡ*,

worn out, tattered ; — ة *ursa-t*, pl. *uras*, red soil ; tinder ; boundary.

(ارثعن) *irsa'ann*, fall plentifully (rain) ; fall down in abundance (hair) ; be weak.

ارثومة *ursûma-t*, soil, ground, territory.

ارثى *arsa*, untiring, indefatigable, unremitting.

(ارج) *araj*, INF. *arj*, sow discord ; — INF. *arjan*, the same ; spread calumnies ; — *arij*, A, INF. *araj*, *arîj*, *arîja-t*, be fragrant ; — II. sow discord ; spread strong scents, perfume, fumigate, incense ; — ة *arja-t*, scent, perfume.

ارجا *arjâ'*, sides, &c., pl. of رجا raj-an.

ارجاف *irjâf*, disturbance, alarm ; pl. *arâjif*, alarming rumours.

ارجان *arajân*, disturbance ; — *arjân*, wild almond tree.

ارجح *arjah*, more probable, comp. of راجح *râjih*.

(ارجحن) *irjahann*, swing up and down (balance).

ارجعة *arji'a-t*, pl. of رجاع *rijâ'*, halter of a camel.

ارجل *arjal*, more manly ; with large feet ; stony (road) ; — ة *arjila-t*, pedestrians, &c., pl. of رجيل *rajil*.

ارجوان *arjawân*, *urjuwân* (Pers.), purple ; a shrub with red blossoms ; — ى *arjawâniyy*, purple (colour).

ارجوجة *arjûja-t*, *urjûja-t*, and

ارجوحة *arjûha-t*, *urjûha-t*, pl. *arâjîh*, swing, hammock.

إرجوزة *arjûza-t*, poem in the metre رجز *rajaz* (six times مستفعلن *mustaf'ilun*).

ارجى *arja*, from whom is more to be hoped for ; — ة *urjiyya-t*, a thing delayed.

ارحا *arhâ'*, mills, pl. of رحا *rahan*, رحى *raha*.

ارحام *arhâm*, wombs, pl. of رحم *rahm*.

ارحم *arham*, more or most merciful, compassionate.

ارحى *arhiyy*, ة *arhiya-t*, mills, pl. of رحا *rahan*, رحى *raha*.

(ارخ) *arah*, also II. and IV., date, fix the date.

ارخ *irh*, *urh*, bullock ; young cow, heifer ; — ة *urha-t*, date, epoch.

ارخا *irhâ'*, relaxing ; giving the reins ; quick riding.

ارخص *arhas*, cheaper, comp. of رخيص *rahîs*.

ارخل *arhul*, lambs, pl. of رخل *rihl*.

ارخون *arhôn*, *arhûn*, pl. *arâhina-t*, archon ; chief ; high - priest ; abbot ; patriarch.

ارخى *arha*, laxer, looser ; more yielding ; thinner (fluid) ; — ة *urhiyya-t*, pl. اراخى *arâhî*, what is to be let down, veil, curtain ; calf of a buffalo.

ارد *aradd*, more useful, more nearly concerning (على *'ala*) ; f. *ruddâ'*, divorced wife.

اردا *ardâ'*, worse, comp. of ردى *radî'* ;— *ardi'â*, pl. of the same.

ارداج *ardâj*, black leather.

اردب *ardabb*, *irdabb*, corn measure =five bushels ; — *irdabb*, ة *irdabba-t*, canal.

اردمة *ardama-t*, root of a tree.

اردن *ardan*, Jordan ; silk ; — *urdunn*, sleepiness ; Jordan.

اردية *ardiya-t*, cloaks, robes, pl. of ردا *ridâ'*.

ارذل *arzal*, pl. ون and *arâzil*, more or most vile, mean ; abject ; decrepit.

(ارز) *araz*, *ariz*, A, I, U, INF. *'urûz*, contract (n.), stand firm, be firmly rooted ; be cold (night) ; retreat to her hole (snake).

ارز *âriz*, firm, firmly rooted, strong ; cold ; chief of a clan ; — *arz*, *urz*, ة, cedar, pine-tree ; — *aruz*, *âruz*, *aruzz*, *uruz*, *uruzz*, *urz*=رز *ruzz*, rice.

ارزاق *arzâq*, riches, &c., pl. of رزق *rizq*.

ارزبة *irzabba-t*, iron bar or mace.

ارزع *arza'*, cowardly, more or most cowardly.

ارزيز *irzîz*, shudder, trembling; hailstorm; push, thrust.

(ارس) *aras*, I, INF. *ars*, carry on agriculture as a peasant or farmer; — II. the same; hire one's services.

ارسا *irsâ'*, fixing, rendering firm; casting anchor in a port; landing.

ارسال *irsâl*, sending, mission; quotation of a tradition of Muhammad without mentioning an authority.

ارسان *arsân*, halters, &c., pl. of رسن *rasan*.

ارسخ *arsaḫ*, firmer, comp. of راسخ *râsiḫ*.

ارسل *arsul*, messengers, &c., pl. of رسول *rasûl*, and رسيل *rasîl*.

ارسوسة *arsûsa-t*, a high cap.

ارش *arś*, men, creatures; gift, compensation, blood-money; bribe; dispute, law-suit; instigation to quarrelling.

(ارش) *araś*, INF. *arś*, scratch one's face in sign of mourning; incite to enmity; give (2 acc.); pass. be claimed for extradition, in order to atone for bloodshed; — II. INF. *ta'rîs*, kindle; — VIII. INF. *it'irâś*, take revenge or blood-money; be delivered up for atonement.

ارشاد *irśâd*, direction in the right way; spiritual remonstrance.

ارشح *arśaḥ*, more perspiring.

ارشد *arśad*, straight, straighter; more or most upright.

ارشية *arśiya-t*, ropes, pl. of رشا *riśâ'*.

ارص *araṣṣ*, f. رصا *raṣṣâ*, with well set teeth; closely joining.

ارصاد *irṣâd*, astronomical, observation.

ارض *arḍ*, f. pl. *arḍûn*, *araḍûn*, *araḍât*, *ârâd*, *arâḍî*, earth; ground; land; sole, lowest part of anything; ابن ارض *ibn arḍ*, wanderer, wayfarer, stranger; — *araḍ*, ة, wood-worm; — *âra* worthier, worthiest; — *ara ḍ*, not stirring from the place; — ة *irḍa-t*, *urḍa-t*, luxuriant grass.

(أرض) *araḍ*, INF. *arḍ*, consume into dust; — *ariḍ*, INF. *araḍ*, cover itself with pustules and get bad (wound); — *aruḍ*, INF. *arḍ*, abound with food; — INF. *arâḍa-t*, be well overgrown with plants; be worthy of, fit for (ل *li*); — pass. have a cold; — II. INF. *ta'rîḍ*, graze all the herbs of a place and look for fresh pasture; prepare for fasting; embellish a speech; reconcile; molest, detain, prevent; — IV. INF. *i'râḍ*, give a cold; — V. INF. *ta'arrûḍ*, bend to the earth from heaviness; be ripe for mowing; hinder, thwart; — VI. INF. *ta'â-ruḍ*, settle in a place; — X. INF. *isti'râḍ*, cover itself with pustules; push forth roots.

ارضا *irḍâ'*, satisfying, consenting, complying with.

ارضاع *irḍâ'*, giving the suck, suckling.

ارضى *arḍiyy*, earthly, terrestrial; — ارضى شوكى *arḍiyy śokiyy*, artichoke; — ة *arḍiyya-t*, ground; floor; bottom of a vessel; grounding colour of a stuff.

ارطال *arṭâl*, pounds (of 12 ounces), pl. of رطل *raṭl*, *riṭl*.

ارعا *ar'â'*, pastures, pl. of رعى *ri'y*.

ارعاوية *ar'âwiyya-t*, pasturing cattle.

ارعن *ar'an*, f. *ra'nâ'*, talkative; stupid; flabby; demoralised (army); mild (air); mountain.

ارعوة *ur'uwwa-t*, yoke (pair) of oxen.

ارغاد *irġâd*, cable; living in affluence.

ارغب *arġab*, more or most greedy, covetous; more desirable.

ارغد *arġad*, more or most commodious, pleasant, affluent.

ارغفة *arġifa-t*, loaves, rolls, cakes, pl. of رغيف *raġîf*.

ارغل *arġal*, commodious, comfortable (life); uncircumcised.

ارغن *arġun*, pl. *arâġin*, *arġanûn*, organ (instrument).

ارغول *argûl*, oboe.
(ارف) *araf*, II. *arraf*, make a knot; pass. be delimited; III. confine with; — ة *urfa-t*, pl. *uraf*, boundary; knot.
ارفاق *irfâq*, supply, IV. of (رفق).
ارفضاض *irfiḍâḍ*, dispersing, disappearing.
ارفع *arfa'*, more elated, higher.
ارفل *arfal*, f. *raflâ'*, awkward, slovenly; flab-eared (ass).
ارفى *urfiyy*, pure milk.
(ارق) *ariq*, INF. *araq*, and VIII. INF. *i'tirâq*, wake, be awake, sleepless; — II. INF. *ta'riq*, and IV. INF. *i'râq*, cause to wake.
ارق *arq*, *araq*, *uraq*, disease in the corn; jaundice;—*araqq*, thinner, &c., comp. of رقيق *raqîq*.
ارقام *arqâm*, written characters, &c., pl. رقم *raqam*.
ارقان *irqân*, henna; saffron.
ارقم *arqam*, spotted; *al-arqam*, a poisonous snake, viper.
ارقط *arqa-ṭ*, f. *raqṭâ'*, spotted.
(ارك) *irk*, a thorn tree; — *arak*, *arik*, also pass. *urik*, have stomach-ache from feeding on its fruit; stop and feed on it; insist; tarry; — II. INF. *ta'rîk*, place the bride on the throne (اريكة *arîka-t*).
ارك *arakk*, stupid, imbecile, weak-minded, N.B. ارك II.
اركاك *arkâk*, slight showers, pl. of رك *rakk*.
اركان *arkân*, pillars, props, &c., pl. of ركن *rukn*; — *irkân*, (m.) confidence.
اركب *arkub*, cavalcades, troops of horsemen, pl. of ركب *rakb*.
اركوب *arkûb*, troop of travellers on camels.
اركون *arkûn*, pl. *arâkina-t*, archon, &c., see ارخون *arḫûn*.
اركى *arka*, weaker, comp. of ركى *rakiyy*.
(ارم) *aram*, I, INF. *arm*, bite; eat all; decimate (famine); tie up; twist tight; soften, pacify.
ارم *arm*, stature, form of the body; — *arim*, *iram*, pl. *ârâm*, large stone to indicate the way in a desert; mountain-peak (pl. also *urûm*); crown of the head; — *uram*, *urram*, molar teeth; finger-tips; pebbles; — ة *âri-ma-t*, tooth.
ارما *urmâ*, such a one, so and l. a-certain person; — *armâ'*, p رمى *ramiyy*, hit, thrown at.
ارماث *armâs̱*, old rope.
ارماح *armâḥ*, lances, pl. of رمح *rumḥ*.
ارمد *armad*, ashy grey, f. *ar-ramdâ'*, ostrich; pl. رمد *rumd*, flies; very small; numerous; with watering (running) eyes.
ارمض *armaḍ*, burnt (ground); pebbled; pebbles;—*armuḍ*, ة *armi-ḍa-t*, pl. of رمضان *ramaḍân*, the month of fasting.
ارمل *armal*, pl. *arâmil*, *arâmîl*, *arâmila-t*, single; widowed; poor; f. *armala-t*, poor widow; *al-armala-t*, the needy and desolate.
ارمن *arman*, ى *armaniyy*, Armenian; ية *armaniyya-t*, Armenia.
ارمولة *armûla-t*, pl. *arâmil*, poor; unmarried.
ارمى *urma*=ارما *urmâ*; —ة *armiya-t*, pl. of رمى *ramiyy*, thrown, hit.
(ارن) *aran*, INF. *arn*, bite; — *arin*, A, INF. *aran*, *arîn*, *irân*, be quick, agile, brisk; — III. vie in beauty, elegance, &c.; long for the cow (bull).
ارناوط *arnauṭ*, Arnaut.
ارنب *arnab*, pl. *arânib*, *arân-in*, hare.
ارنمة *arnama-t*, (m.) *arnaba-t*, groin.
ارهاص *irhâṣ*, premeditation.
ارهاط *arhâṭ*, families, pl. of رهط *rahṭ*, *rahaṭ*.
ارهان *irhân*, pledging, pawning.
ارو *arw*, deceit, cunning.
ارواء *irwâ'*, watering, quenching of the thirst; wetting.
ارواح *arwâḥ*, pl. of روح *rûḥ*, breath, &c., and of ريح *rîḥ*, wind, &c.; evening; — *irwâḥ*, bad smell.
ارواع *arwâ'*, pl. of رائع *râ'i'*, q.v.

ارواق *arwâq*, tents, &c., pl. of روق *rauq*.

اروام *arwâm*, Greeks, Romans, pl. of روم *rûm*.

اروح *arwah*, f. *rauḥâ'*, pl. *rûḥ*, wide, spacious; more airy, thinner; more pleasant; quiet.

ارود *arwad*, slow, deliberate.

اروس *ar'us*, heads, &c., pl. of راس *ra's*, *râs*.

اروع *arwa'*, f. روعا *rau'â'*, causing pleasure and admiration by beauty, bravery, &c.; noble; prudent, cunning.

اروغ *arwag*, more or most cunning.

اروقة *arwiqa-t*, tents, &c., pl. of رواق *riwâq*, *ruwâq*.

اروم *arûm*, ة, root; — *urûm*, mountain peaks, pl. of ارم *aram*.

ارون *irûn*, hearths, &c., pl. of ارة *ira-t*.

اروية *urwiyya-t*, pl. (3 to 10) *arâwiyy*, (above 10) *arwa*, chamois, mountain-goat.

(ارى) *ary*, honey; dew; manna; shining cloud; squall; — *iry*, *ariy*, pl. *awâr-in*, *awâiyy*, manger; stable; peg or rope for tying up.

(أرى) *ara*, I, INF. *ary*, I., V., VIII., make honey; drive the clouds and bring rain; to eat from the same manger with another animal; — II. INF. *ta'riya-t*, make an animal eat from the same manger with another; tie up, fasten; conceal; — IV. INF. *i'râ'*, accustom one animal to another; — V. INF. *ta'arri*, remain behind; — V. and VIII. INF. *it'irâ'*, be kept back; look out for what is fit, appropriate; — *ara*, *arî*, I, burn with anger; — II. blow the fire.

ارياح *aryâḥ*, winds, pl. of ريح *rîḥ*.

ارياش *aryâś*, feathers, pl. of ريش *rîś*, ة *rîśa-t*.

ارياف *aryâf*, fertile tracts, &c., pl. of ريف *rîf*.

اريب *arîb*, clever, skilful, prudent, cunning; arrow; winner in the game of arrows; f. ة *arîba-t*, large and wide (kettle).

اريج *arîj*, ة *arîja-t*, INF. of (ارج) q.v.; — *arîj*, fragrance; fragrant.

اريح *aryaḥ*, spacious, airy; — ى *aryaḥiyy*, *arîḥiyy*, high-minded and liberal; vivacious, quick; — ية *aryaḥiyya-t*, liberality, generosity.

اريز *arîz*, very cold; hoar-frost; prince.

اريس *arîs*, *irrîs*, pl. *ûn* and *arâris*, *arâris*, *arârisa-t*, peasant; — *irrîs*, leader, prince.

اريش *aryaś*, with a strong beard.

اريض *arîḍ*, very rich; well overgrown; clever, fit; modest; pure.

اريك *arîk*, ة pl. *arâyik*, divan for the bride; throne.

اريم *arîm*, a certain person.

ارين *aryan*, what is beyond anybody's strength.

(از) *azz*, I, U, INF. *azz*, *azâz*, *azîz*, thunder; bubble; — I. and II. beat (pulse); agitate, excite; make boil; kindle; make eager; pain; pour out; have sexual intercourse with; — V., VIII. boil; be agitated; — VIII. hasten.

از *azz*, pulsation; sexual intercourse; pressing of a crowd; — ة *azza-t*, confusion, throng.

(ازا) *aza'*, satiate; flinch.

ازا *izâ'*, vis à vis; site; ازاوهم *izâ'uhum*, their comrades; ازا العيش *izâ' al-'aiś*, livelihood.

ازابى *azâbiyy*, difficult and important matters, &c., pl. of ازبى *uzbiyy*.

ازاتة *izâta-t*, abundance of olives and oil.

ازاج *âzâj*, colonnades, pl. of ازج *azaj*.

ازاحة *izâḥa-t*, removing, taking away; conclusion.

ازار *izâr*, veil = ازر *izr*, q.v.

ازاز *azâz*, INF. of (از) *azz*.

ازالة *izâla-t*, abolition, annulling, annihilation.

ازام *azâm*, year of famine.

ازاند *azânid*, fire-staves, pl. of زند *zand*.

ازاهير *azâhîr*, flowers, pl. of زهرة *zahra-t*.

(ازب) *azab*, I, flow; — V. INF. *ta'azzub*, divide a fortune between each other.

ازب *azzab*, f. *zabbâ'*, hairy, shaggy, downy, woolly; fertile; dreadful; — ة *azba-t*, misfortune; famine; — ى *azban*, excessive; — *uzbiyy*, pl. *azâbiyy*, matter of importance and difficulty; great calamity; quickness; manner, way, method.

(ازج) *azaj*, U, *azij*, A, INF. *uzûj*, hasten; forsake in need, leave in the lurch; — II. build a colonnade.

ازج *azaj*, pl. *âzâj*, *âzuj*, *izaja-t*, colonnade, oblong hall with columns; arch of a door; — *azajj*, with long eye-lashes; walking with quick long strides; — ى *azja*, who manages skilfully and executes well.

(ازح) *azaḥ*, I, INF. *uzûḥ*, contract (n.); approach one another; tarry, remain behind; slip; beat (artery); — V., VI. be slow, remain behind.

ازدحام *izdiḥâm*, crowd, throng, multitude.

ازدرا *izdirâ'*, contempt, disdain, insult.

ازدها *izdihâ*, pride; contempt.

ازدواج *izdiwâj*, copulation, pairing.

ازدياد *izdiyâd*, growth, increase.

(ازر) *azar*, INF. *azr*, be vigorous; surround (for protection); strengthen; — II. cover, veil; strengthen; — III. grow close together and entwine; assist; console; correspond; — IV. strengthen, invigorate; — V. grow strong; — V., VIII. cover one's self with the veil ازار *izâr*.

ازر *azr*, strength, and, by opposition, weakness; back; — *izr* (more frequently *izâr*), pl. *uzr*, *uzur*, *azira-t*, a long wrapper, veil; women; chastity; — *izr*, ة *izra-t*, manner of wearing the *izâr*; — *izr*, root; — *uzr*, waist.

ازرار *azrâr*, buttons, &c., pl. of زر *zirr*.

ازرق *azraq*, f. *zarqâ'*, pl. *zurq*, blue, light blue, pale; عدو ازرق *'aduww azraq*, mortal enemy; *zarqâ'*, wine.

ازرم *azram*, cat.

ازز *azaz*, crowd, thronged assembly.

ازعكى *az'akiyy*, small, bad.

ازعيل *iz'il*, lively, cheerful.

(ازف) *azif*, A, INF. *azf*, *uzûf*, approach, come suddenly; be insignificant; — *azaf*, *azif*; *azuf*, close (as a wound); — II., IV., V. the same; — VI. approach one another.

ازف *azaf*, poverty, misery; — ة *uzfa-t*, pl. *uzaf*, boundary, limit; — *âzifa-t*, day of the last judgment.

ازفل *azfal*, anger, burst of anger; — ة *azfala-t*, ى *azfala*, troop, crowd; — *izfalla-t*, vivacity.

ازفى *azfa*, hurry, haste, speed.

ازقاق *azqâq*, leather pipes, pl. of زق *ziqq*.

ازقة *aziqqa-t*, lanes, &c., pl. of زقاق *zuqâq*.

ازكيا *azkiyâ'*, pl. of زكى *zakiyy*, good, upright, &c.

(ازل) *azal*, I, INF. *azl*, be in need, misery; suffer from hunger; shorten a horse's tether, and allow it to graze; not allow the cattle to pasture (from fear or scarcity of food); — V. be in anxiety.

ازل *azal*, time without beginning, eternity; — *izl*, falseness, lie; great calamity; extraordinary occurrence; — ى *azaliyy*, eternal, God; — ية *azaliyya-t*, eternity.

(ازم) *azam*, I, INF. *azm*, adhere, be firmly attached; carry on assiduously; watch; — INF. *azm*, *uzûm*, bite with all the teeth; bite the bridle; bite into pieces,

cut; annihilate; overcome, conquer (على *'ala*); lock; twist tight; oppress; abstain from (عن *'an*); — *azim*, A, INF. *azam*, contract and unite (n.); alight; — V. stay long in a place; be oppressed (by famine, &c.).

ازم *azm*, manner of plaiting the hair; meal; bite; silence; — *âzim*, pl. *uzzam*, *uzûm*, tooth; — ة *azma-t*, *azama-t*, pl. *azm*, *izam*, one daily meal; famine, poverty, distress; — *âzima-t*, pl. *awâzim*, tooth; — *azimma-t*, pl. *zimâm*, strap; leading cord.

ازماع *azmâ'*, rivulets; valleys, pl. of زمعة *zam'a-t*.

ازمت *azma-t*, graver, more dignified, &c., comp. of زميت *zamît*.

ازمع *azma'*, pl. *azâmi'*, calamity.

ازمل *azmal*, pl. *azâmil*, *azâmîl*, indistinct sound, noise; family, household; — *uzmal*, *azmul*, luggage —; *izmall*, weak-minded; — ة *azmala-t*, numerous; sound of the bow; luggage, household furniture; family comprising slaves.

ازمنة *azmina-t*, times, pl. of زمن *zaman* and زمان *zamân*.

ازميل *izmîl*, knife for scraping; spear, spit; chisel; engraving-needle; scissors; hammer; strong, and, by opposition, weak.

ازهر *azhar*, f. *zahrâ*, pl. *zuhr*, shining white, fresh, resplendent; moon; star; lion; milk fresh from the udder; Friday; *al-azharân*, sun and moon; *az-zahrawân*, the second and third chapters of the Qur'ân: البقرة *al-baqra-t* (the cow) and آل عمران *âl 'imrân* (the family of Imrân, father of Moses).

ازهى *azha*, shining; yellowish red; ripe.

(ازو) *azâ*, U, INF. *azw*, grow short (shadow when the sun is high).

ازواد *azwâd*, ازودة *azwida-t*, travelling provisions, pl. of زاد *zâd*.

ازوار *azwâr*, pl. of زوار *ziwâr* and زيار *ziyâr*, q.v.

ازور *azwar*, f. *zaurâ'*, pl. *zûr*, inclined; oblique; squinting; deep well; tomb; army; *az-zaurâ'*, Bagdad.

ازوش *azwaś*, proud boaster.

ازوم *azûm*, pl. *uzum*, tooth; biting with all teeth; sterile; — *azûm*, f. ة, addicted to (ب *bi*).

(ازى) *aza*, I, INF. *azy*, *uziyy*, be added; add; grow shorter (shadow); play a confidence trick; come suddenly upon; torment; waste one's fortune; — III. INF. *mu'âzât*, keep pace with, accompany; — IV. INF. *i'zâ'*, repay a benefit twice over; fear; stand in fear of, correspond; keep pace with; torment; — V. INF. *ta'azzî*, crowd together, assemble (n.); tremble (an arrow which has hit the mark); make a canal.

ازياف *azyâf*, pl. of زائف *zâ'if* and زيف *zaif*, clipped coin.

ازيان *izyân*, *izziyân*, adorning, &c., IV. and VIII. of (زين).

ازيب *azyab*, liveliness, nimbleness; nimble, brisk, alert; insignificant; calamity; enmity; fear; Satan; bastard; adopted son; hedgehog; east wind; — *izyabb*, great, violent.

ازيد *azyad*, greater, more.

ازيز *azîz*, violent motion; cold (s. and adj.).

(اس) *ass*, INF. *ass*, *iss*, *uss*, ruin; cause discord; secrete honey; build a house; — II. INF. *ta'sîs*, mark out and lay the foundations of a building.

اس *ass*, *iss*, *uss*, pl. *âsâs*, *âsâsât*, *isâs*, foundation; beginning; cause; trace; remainder; excrements; — *âs*, ة, myrtle; remainder, trace; tomb; companion; — *âs-in*, see اسى *âsî*.

اسا *asâ*, grief; — ة *usât*, physicians, pl. of اسى *âsî*.

اسابيع *asâbî'*, weeks, pl. of اسبوعة *asbû'a-t*.

اساتيذ *asâtîz*, ة *asâtiza-t*, masters, &c., pl. of استاذ *ustâz*.

اساتير *asâtîr*, pl. of استار *istâr*, q.v.

اساتين *asâtîn*, columns.

اساجيع *asâjî'*, cadences, &c., pl. of سجع *saj'*.

أساد *âsâd*, lions, pl. of اسد *asad*; — ة *isâda-t*, *usâda-t*, cushion.

اسار *as'âr*, remainders, rests, pl. of سور, سؤر *su'r*; — *isâr*, *isâra-t*, pl. *usur*, strong strap; captivity; left side.

اسارى *usâra*, captives, pl. of اسير *asîr*.

اسارير *asârîr*, pl. of سر *sirr*, line in the palm of the hand.

اساس *asâs*, pl. *usus*, foundation; base; — *âsâs*, *isâs*, see اس *iss*; — ى *asâsiyy*, fundamental; foundation stone.

اساطم *asâṭim*, middles, &c., pl. of اسطما *usṭummâ'*.

اساطير *asâṭîr*, stories, fables, pl. of اسطور *asṭûr*, ة *asṭûra-t*.

اساطيل *asâṭîl*, fleets, pl. of استول *usṭûl*.

اساطين *asâṭîn*, columns, &c., pl. of اسطوانة *usṭuwâna-t*.

اسافل *asâfil*, rabble, &c., pl. of اسفل *asfal*.

اساقف *asâqif*, ة *asâqifa-t*, bishops, pl. of اسقف *usquf*.

اساقى *asâqî*, leather bags for water or milk, pl. of سقا *saqâ'*.

اسال *âsâl*, pl. resemblance, similitude; signs; — *is'âl*, complying with a request, IV. of (سال); — ة *asâla-t*, being oral; — *isâla-t*, causing to flow, IV. of (سيل).

اساليب *asâlîb*, manners, ways, pl. of اسلوب *uslûb*.

اساليق *asâlîq*, glands of the palate.

اسام *âsâm*, *âsâm-in*, اسامى *asâmî*, names, pl. of اسم *ism*, *usm*; — ة *asâma-t*, *usâma-t*, lion; — ى *asâmiyy*, (m.) client; debtor; tenant; counsel in a law-suit; office

اسان *âsîn*, characters, pl. of اسن *usun*.

اسانيد *asânîd*, quotations, &c., pl. of اسناد *isnâd*.

اساود *asâwid*, pl. of اسود *aswad*, black.

اساور *asâwir*, ة *asâwira-t*, bracelets, pl. of سوار *siwâr*.

اساوة *usâwa-t*, art of the physician; medicine; cure.

اسايا *asâyâ*, pl. of اسوان *aswân*, اسيان *asyân*, sad, sorrowful.

اسباب *asbâb*, causes, &c., pl. of سبب *sabab*.

اسباط *asbâṭ*, tribes of Israel, &c., pl. of سبط *sibṭ*.

اسباع *asbâ'*, seventh parts, pl. of سبع *sub'*; — *isbâ'*, be or become seven, IV. of (سبع).

اسبانج *isbânaj*, spinach.

اسبع *asbu'*, seventh parts, pl. of سبع *sub'*.

اسبق *asbaq*, first comer; ovetraking the others; prior, superior.

اسبل *asbal*, with long moustaches; f. *sablâ*, with long eye-lashes.

اسبوبة *usbûba-t*, quarrel, dispute.

اسبوع *usbû'*, ة *usbû'a-t*, pl. اسابيع *asâbî'*, week; *usbû'an*, in the seventh place.

اسبيداج *isbîdâj*, white lead.

است *ist*, pl. *istât*, back part, buttock; anus; foundation.

استاج *istâj*, shuttle.

استاذ *ustâz* (استاد *ustâd*), pl. *-ûn*, *asâtîz*, *asâtiza-t*, master; teacher; artisan; celebrated doctor; prefect.

استار *astâr*, veils, &c., pl. of ستر *sitr*; — *istâr*, pl. *asâtîr*, a coin, worth about a florin; four; — *istâra-t*, the same; covering; veiling.

استباحة *istibâḥa-t*, giving leave, permission; giving up, abandoning.

استباعة *istibâ'a-t*, exhibition for sale; wish to sell.

استباق *istibâq*, contest for superiority, striving to be first.

استبانة *istibâna-t*, wish to know accurately; distinctness.
استبداد *istibdâd*, absolute power; exclusive possession; usurpation; obstinacy; being reduced to one's own resources.
استبداع *istibdâ'*, innovation.
استبدال *istibdâl*, change, exchange.
استبرا *istibrâ'*, getting free; menses.
استبراز *istibrâz*, challenging for a combat.
استبرق *istabraq*, shot silk, brocade; dress of it.
استبسال *istibsâl*, defying danger.
استبشار *istibśâr*, good news, or rejoicing at such; teaching (the Gospel).
استبصار *istibṣâr*, looking closely, examining; sagacity.
استبضاع *istibḍâ'*, sorting goods for sale.
استبطا *istibṭâ*, delaying; being slow, late, or deeming anyone to be so; waiting with impatience.
استبطان *istibṭân*, concealing.
استبعاد *istib'âd*, removing to a distance, departure.
استبعال *istib'âl*, taking a husband, marrying.
استبغا *istibġâ'*, desire, longing for.
استبقا *istibqâ'*, keeping alive.
استبلال *istiblâl*, wetness; recovery.
استبهاج *istibhâj*, joy, cheerfulness, merriment.
استبهام *istibhâm*, obscurity, abstruseness.
استتار *istitâr*, hiding one's self.
استتام *istitâm*, completion, wish to complete.
استثبات *istis̱bât*, perseverance.
استثقال *istis̱qâl*, molestation, deeming anyone a bore.
استثنا *istis̱nâ'*, exception; exclusion; praise.
استجابة *istijâba-t*, listening favourably, complying with a request.
استجادة *istijâda-t*, finding good, choosing the best.
استجارة *istijâra-t*, asking for protection or assistance; hiring, renting.
استجازة *istijâza-t*, asking leave.
استجبار *istijbâr*, compulsion; violence; making firm, strong.
استجداد *istijdâd*, renovation; innovation.
استجزاز *istijzâz*, being ripe for harvest.
استجعال *istij'âl*, conflagration; lust; rut.
استجلاب *istijlâb*, attraction; driving cattle, &c., to market.
استجماع *istijmâ'*, assembling, assembly; career (swiftest running of a horse).
استجمام *istijmâm*, recreation; resting.
استحاثة *istiḥâs̱a-t*, digging and exploring of the ground; export.
استحار *istiḥâr*, crowing of the cock in the morning; early departure; — ة *istiḥâra-t*, disquisition, x. of (حور); — astonishment, x. of (حير).
استحالة *istiḥâla-t*, change, transformation; being undulated; being impossible or absurd.
استحباب *istiḥbâb*, loving, longing for; supererogation.
استحثاث *istiḥs̱âs̱*, spurring on, urging.
استحداث *istiḥdâs̱*, receiving of news; deeming new or fresh.
استحداد *istiḥdâd*, sharpening.
استحسان *istiḥsân*, approval; praise; admiration; taking as a favour.
استحصاد *istiḥṣâd*, being ripe for harvest.
استحصال *istiḥṣâl*, acquiring, obtaining; gathering.
استحصان *istiḥṣân*, retiring to a fortress; intrenching.
استحضار *istiḥḍâr*, summoning before.
استحفاظ *istiḥfâẓ*, preserving in memory, recollection.
استحقار *istiḥqâr*, treating with contempt; scorning; vilifying.
استحكام *istiḥkâm*, strengthening, fortifying; corroboration; promoting; securing.
استحلاف *istiḥlâf*, demanding an

oath; adjuring; swearing solemnly.

استحلال *istiḥlâl*, deeming or making lawful; prescription (of property).

استحمال *istiḥmâl*, patience; toleration; resignation.

استحمام *istiḥmâm*, bathing; taking a warm bath.

استحيا *istiḥyâ'*, being ashamed or bashful; remaining alive.

استخارة *istiḫâra-t*, prayer for good things, blessings, &c.; desire for good.

استخبا *istiḫbâ'*, pitching a tent; hiding one's self.

استخبار *istiḫbâr*, inquiring.

استخدام *istiḫdâm*, making use of or hiring one's services; looking out for work or service.

استخذا *istiḫẓâ'*, self-humiliation.

استخراج *istiḫrâj*, extraction; derivation; choosing.

استخفا *istiḫfâ'*, hiding one's self; absconding.

استخفاف *istiḫfâf*, slighting, despising; making light of.

استخلاص *istiḫlâṣ*, setting at liberty, desire to liberate.

استخلاف *istiḫlâf*, leaving descendants; succession.

استدارة *istidâra-t*, surrounding; being circular or globular.

استدامة *istidâma-t*, perseverance; endurance.

استدانة *istidâna-t*, borrowing.

استدبار *istidbâr*, returning, turning one's back to; tardy wisdom.

استدخال *istidḫâl*, desire to enter; intermeddling.

استدراج *istidrâj*, advancing by steps or degrees.

استدراك *istidrâk*, comprehending, understanding; acquiring; reaching, overtaking; improving, mending.

استدعا *istid'â'*, humble request; soliciting.

استدفاع *istidfâ'*, prayer for the averting of evil.

استدقاق *istidqâq*, accuracy; punctiliousness.

استدلال *istidlâl*, bringing forth proofs, demonstration; asking for reasons.

استذكار *istiẕkâr*, reminding, recalling to memory, recollection.

استذلال *istiẕlâl*, contempt; vilifying.

استذمام *istiẕmâm*, deserving blame; asking protection.

استذناب *istiẕnâb*, following closely; being terminated; suspecting.

استرابة *istirâba-t*, doubting, suspecting.

استراحة *istirâḥa-t*, smelling; reposing, resting; tranquillity; pausing.

استراق *istirâq*, theft.

استرتاج *istirtâj*, giving way of the voice.

استرجا *istirjâ'*, petitioning, supplicating.

استرجاع *istirjâ'*, asking or taking back; reclamation; wish to return.

استرخا *istirḫâ'*, relaxation.

استرخاص *istirḫâṣ*, cheap bargain; wish for cheapness; bartering.

استرداد *istirdâd*, asking or taking back, demanding restitution; remonstrance.

استرديا *istiridiyâ*, oyster.

استرذال *istirẕâl*, contempt, disdain.

استرشا *istirśâ'*, demanding a bribe.

استرشاد *istirśâd*, being rightly directed.

استرضا *istirḍâ'*, striving to please.

استرعا *istir'â'*, committing to another's care.

استرقاق *istirqâq*, enslaving.

استرفاد *istirfâd*, seeking help.

استرك *istarak*, storax.

استرموك *astarmûk*, ostrich.

استرهاب *istirhâb*, frightening.

استرهان *istirhân*, taking a pledge.

استرواح *istirwâḥ*, resting; smelling.

استزادة *istizâda-t*, asking for more.

استزارة *istizâra-t*, asking for a visit.

استزلال *istizlâl*, slipping.

استسخار *istisḫâr*, mocking at, making sport of.

استسداد *istisdâd*, stopping, locking up.
استسرا *istisrâ'*, travelling at night-time.
استسرار *istisrâr*, being covered by clouds (moon); hiding one's self.
استسعا *istis'â'*, effort; haste.
استسعاد *istis'âd*, wish for happiness; happiness; wishing joy; demand for help.
استسقا *istisqâ'*, desire for drink; taking drink; dropsy.
استسلاف *istislâf*, prepayment; advance of money.
استسلام *istislâm*, submission, obedience; conversion to Islâm.
استسناد *istisnâd*, reclining against, leaning on.
استسهال *istishâl*, commodiousness; ease.
استشارة *istiśâra-t*, consulting, asking for advice.
استشانة *istiśâna-t*, disapproval.
استشعار *istiś'âr*, conception of fear.
استشفا *istiśfâ'*, wish for recovery; indulging one's desires.
استشفاع *istiśfâ'*, asking for intercession.
استشفاف *istiśfâf*, transparency.
استشمام *istiśmâm*, smelling (a.), snuffling.
استشهاد *istiśhâd*, taking or demanding evidence; martyrdom.
استشهار *istiśhâr*, eagerness for glory, ambition.
استصابة *istiṣâba-t*, approval.
استصبا *istiṣbâ'*, childishness, childish manners.
استصحاب *istiṣḥâb*, associating, wishing for one's company.
استصحاح *istiṣḥâḥ*, soundness, health.
استصعاب *istiṣ'âb*, difficulty.
استصغار *istiṣgâr*, holding in small estimation, despising, slighting.
استصفا *istiṣfâ'*, choice of the best.
استصلاح *istiṣlâḥ*, petition for peace.
استصواب *istiṣwâb*, approval, deeming right.
استضاءة *istiḍâ'a-t*, desire to be enlightened.
استضافة *istiḍâfa-t*, request for help, for hospitality.
استضحاك *istiḍḥâk*, laughing or mocking at.
استطابة *istiṭâba-t*, approbation; liking, finding agreeable; ablution.
استطار *istiṭâr*, drawing, delineation; description.
استطاعة *istiṭâ'a-t*, possibility; being capable of, able to; obedience.
استطالة *istiṭâla-t*, length; victory.
استطباب *istiṭbâb*, wish for a physician or a medicine.
استطراد *istiṭrâd*, digression.
استطعام *istiṭ'âm*, desire for food.
استطلاع *istiṭlâ'*, inquiry; trying to fathom one's mind.
استطلاق *istiṭlâq*, delivery, setting free; stool.
استطلس *istaṭlas*, asphalt.
استظلال *istiẕlâl*, sitting in the shade.
استظهار *istiẕhâr*, seeking for protection; protection.
استعاذة *isti'âẕa-t*, refuge to God.
استعارة *isti'âra-t*, borrowing; metaphor; — ى *isti'âriyy*, borrowed; falsified; metaphorical.
استعادة *isti'âda-t*, wish for exchange
استعباد *isti'bâd*, reducing to slavery.
استعبار *isti'bâr*, taking an example.
استعجال *isti'jâl*, hastening, accelerating.
استعجام *isti'jâm*, stammering, speaking in a barbaric or unintelligible manner, deeming one to speak so.
استعدا *isti'dâ'*, asking for help or vengeance against an enemy.
استعداد *isti'dâd*, readiness; skill; merit; tendency.
استعذار *isti'ẕâr*, asking excuse.
استعصا *isti'ṣâ'*, rebellion.
استعطا *isti'ṭâ'*, asking for a gift.
استعطاف *isti'ṭâf*, courting favour with, insinuating one's self into another's good graces; soliciting.
استعظام *isti'ẕâm*, striving for greatness; considering as great; esteemi

استعفا *isti'fâ'*, asking pardon or absolution; resignation (of an office); deposition.
استعفاف *isti'fâf*, abstinence; abstemiousness.
استعقاد *isti'qâd*, credulity.
استعلا *isti'lâ*, elevation.
استعلاج *isti'lâj*, medical treatment, cure.
استعلام *isti'lâm*, asking for information, inquiry.
استعلان *isti'lân*, publication.
استعمار *isti'mâr*, cultivation, colonisation.
استعمال *isti'mâl*, employment, use.
استعهاد *isti'hâd*, stipulation, contract.
استعوا *isti'wâ'*, call for help.
استغاثة *istigâṡa-t*, asking for help, for one's right; appeal.
استغراب *istigrâb*, wonder, astonishment, amazement.
استغراق *istigrâq*, being submerged; exaggeration.
استغشا *istigśâ'*, covering, veiling one's self.
استغفار *istigfâr*, asking forgiveness, repentance, deprecation.
استغلاق *istiglâq*, being bound to do; obscurity.
استغنا *istignâ'*, being satisfied; not being in want of a thing, therefore contemning it; superciliousness.
استغنام *istignâm*, exploiting.
استغوا *istigwâ'*, fraud, deceit.
استفادة *istifâda-t*, advantage, gain.
استفاضة *istifâḍa-t*, publication; overflowing; abundance.
استفاقة *istifâqa-t*, recovering consciousness; superiority.
استفاهة *istifâha-t*, eating one's fill.
استفتا *istiftâ'*, consulting the Mufti, a lawyer.
استفتاح *istiftâḥ*, asking for help; summons to open, to surrender; demanding an explanation.
استفراخ *istifrâḥ*, breeding poultry, pigeons, &c.
استفرار *istifrâr*, running away, flight.

استفراغ *istifrâg*, vomiting; rejecting.
استفساد *istifsâd*, tendency to injure.
استفسار *istifsâr*, request for explanation, information; question.
استفلاح *istiflâḥ*, well-being.
استفنان *istifnâm*, classification.
استفهام *istifhâm*, wish to comprehend; desire for instruction; inquiry; question.
استقا *istiqâ'*, drawing water.
استقاتة *istiqâta-t*, requiring provisions; provisioning.
استقامة *istiqâma-t*, uprightness; rectitude; sincerity; rising; dwelling; fortitude; estimating the value of goods; (m.) pregnancy.
استقباح *istiqbâḥ*, detesting, abhorring.
استقبال *istiqbâl*, going to meet; reception; future; — ى *istiqbâliyy*, future, impending.
استقتال *istiqtâl*, murderous disposition, blood-thirstiness.
استقدام *istiqdâm*, going in advance; surpassing; wish to surpass.
استقرار *istiqrâr*, confirmation, ratification; settling down.
استقراض *istiqrâḍ*, borrowing; asking for a loan.
استقصا *istiqṣâ'*, desire for knowledge; disquisition; investigation.
استقصاص *istiqṣâṣ*, thirst for revenge; requital.
استقضا *istiqḍâ'*, demand for payment.
استقطار *istiqṭâr*, dropping, dripping.
استقفال *istiqfâl*, covetousness, avarice.
استقلال *istiqlâl*, absolute power, full powers, proxy.
استكانة *istikâna-t*, submission, submissiveness.
استكبار *istikbâr*, arrogance, pride; choosing the largest.
استكتام *istiktâm*, keeping secrets, secrecy; taciturnity.
استكثار *istikṡâr*, increasing the quan-

tity; wanting more; wanting or using a large amount.

استكرا *istikrâ'*, hiring, renting.

استكراه *istikrâh*, detesting, aversion, abhorrence, contempt.

استكساب *istiksâb*, gain, earnings.

استكشاف *istikśâf*, uncovering, elucidation; close observation.

استكلاب *istiklâb*, hydrophobia; raving madness; rage.

استكمال *istikmâl*, completion; bringing to perfection; wishing to complete or make perfect.

استلا *istilâ'*, melting.

استلاب *istilâb*, plundering.

استلام *istilâm*, submission; veneration; kissing with reverence, VIII. of (سلم); — *istil'âm*, misalliance, x. of (لام).

استلجاج *istiljâj*, claiming for one's self.

استلحاق *istilḥâq*, accompanying.

استلحام *istilḥâm*, pursuing, persecution.

استلذاذ *istilẕâẕ*, relishing, delighting in, delight.

استلزام *istilzâm*, deeming necessary; forcing from.

استلقا *istilqâ'*, meeting; catching what has been thrown; falling on one's back.

استماحة *istimâḥa-t*, begging, asking for pardon.

استماع *ístimâ'*, hearing, listening.

استمالة *istimâla-t*, caressing, gaining or courting favour with.

استمتاع *istimtâ'*, enjoying; usufruct; celebration of a feast in Mekka.

استمداد *istimdâd*, asking for supplies, subsidies, aid; extension; reach; prolongation.

استمرا *istimrâ'*, digestibility.

استمرار *istimrâr*, persisting, persevering, continuation; proceeding; finding bitter.

استمزاج *istimzâj*, inquiring for one's health.

استمساك *istimsâk*, holding fast, retaining.

استمكات *istimkât*, suppuration.

استمكان *istimkân*, capability; taking hold of; consolidation.

استملاك *istimlâk*, taking possession.

استملال *istimlâl*, disgust, bad humour.

استمنان *istimnân*, asking a favour.

استمهال *istimhâl*, asking for delay.

استناد *istinâd*, reclining on, leaning against, standing firm.

استنارة *istinâra-t*, seeking light, illumination, enlightening the heart.

استنامة *istinâma-t*, sleepiness; dreaminess.

استنان *istinân*, VIII. of (سن), cleansing the teeth; friskiness; gallop.

استنبا *istimbâ'*, seeking instruction, information.

استنباط *istimbâṭ*, discovery, invention; deducing from or referring to an authority.

استنتاج *istintâj*, logical inference, conclusion; result.

استنجا *istinjâ'*, getting free, desire for liberty; asking for relief or forgiveness; obtaining; ablution.

استنجاح *istinjâḥ*, desire for success; fulfilment, happy issue.

استنجاد *istinjâd*, asking for help or protection; recovery.

استنجاز *istinjâz*, despatch of business.

استنجاس *istinjâs*, soiling, polluting, defiling.

استنداه *istindâh*, success.

استنزال *istinzâl*, hospitable reception; dismissal from office.

استنسا *istinsâ'*, asking for delay of payment; begging to forget.

استنساب *istinsâb*, claiming or deriving descent from; approving.

استنساخ *istinsâḥ*, copying; correcting; effacing; abolishing.

استنشا *istinśâ'*, smelling, snuffling; examining.

استنشاط *istinśâṭ*, shrinking, shrivelling.

استنشاف *istinśâf*, breathing through the nose, inhaling.

استنصاح *istinṣâh*, asking advice.

استنصار *istinṣâr*, asking help; victory.

استنظار *istinẓâr*, wish to see; expectation; asking for a delay, respite.

استنغاص *istingâṣ*, (m.) pity, mercy, compassion.

استنفاد *istinfâd*, emptying, voiding.

استنفار *istinfâr*, flight; refuge; (m.) aversion.

استنفاق *istinfâq*, spending money.

استنقاذ *istinqâẓ*, rescue, escape, salvation.

استنقاش *istinqâś*, painting, engraving.

استنقاص *istinqâṣ*, demanding an abatement of price; disapproval.

استنقاع *istinqâ'*, stagnation.

استنقام *istinqâm*, revenge (m.).

استنكاح *istinkâh*, marrying.

استنكاد *istinkâd*, aversion.

استنكار *istinkâr*, denying, refusing; not knowing; abhorrence (m.).

استنكاف *istinkâf*, declining, refusing, rejecting; disdaining; horror.

استنهاض *istinhâḍ*, rousing, inciting, ordering to do anything.

استهام *istihâm*, throwing lots by means of arrows.

استهانة *istihâna-t*, contempt.

استهدا *istihdâ'*, desire for direction; attaining one's end.

استهزا *istihzâ'*, derision, mocking at.

استهلاك *istihlâk*, destruction, annihilation; consumption; dilapidation; mortal enmity.

استهلال *istihlâl*, appearance of the new moon; beginning of a lunar month; exordium (m.); cheerfulness.

استهمام *istihmâm*, zeal and carefulness in doing anything; instigation; stimulation.

استهنا *istihnâ'*, asking help.

استهوا *istihwâ'*, enchantment; seduction; making fall in love.

استوا *istiwâ'*, being equal, parallel; uniformity; equanimity; (m.) patience; being well done (cooked); ripeness; getting of full age; خط الاستوا *ḥaṭṭu-'l-istiwâ'*, equator.

استوتاه *ustautâh*, alas! woe!

استى *istiyy*, fundamental.

استيا *istiyâ'*, VIII. of (سا), toleration of an evil or a sin.

استيار *istiyâr*, VIII. of (سير), making provision for a journey; — *isti'âr*, X. of (وار), running away, flight.

استياس *isti'âs*, (تئس), despair.

استياق *istiyâq*, driving along, urging on.

استياك *istiyâk*, pick the teeth with the مسواك *miswâk*.

استيال *isti'âl* (وال), assemblage.

استيبال *istîbâl* (وبل), unwholesome condition of the air.

استيثاج *istîs̱âj* (وثج), dense growth.

استئثار *isti's̱âr* (اثر), preference, distinction; claiming for one's self; solitude; — *istîs̱âr* (وثر), molestation; astonishment.

استيثاق *istîs̱âq* (وثق), firmness; standing firm.

استيثان *istîs̱ân* (وثن), being or growing fat; increase, plenty.

استيج *istîj*, shuttle.

استيجاب *istîjâb*, worthiness; approval; deeming necessary.

استئجار *isti'jâr* (اجر), hiring, renting.

استئجال *isti'jâl* (اجل), asking a delay, a respite; reaching a term.

استيجاف *istîjâf* (وجف), being in love.

استيحاد *istîḥâd* (وحد), being alone, solitariness.

استئخاذ *isti'ḥâẓ* (اخذ), stumbling from near-sightedness.

استئخار *isti'ḥâr* (اخر), remaining behind; delaying; procrastination.

استئدا *isti'dâ'* (ادى), asking help; importunity.

استيداع *istîdâ'* (ودع), trusting with a deposit; recommendation.

استئذان *isti'ẓân* (اذن), asking leave, permission.

استملا *istîlâ'* (ولى), victory; conquest; dominion; authority.
استيلاد *istîlâd* (ولد), acknowledgment of a child; desire to beget.
استئمار *isti'mâr* (امر), consultation.
استئمان *isti'mân* (امن), confidence; imploring for protection.
استئنا *isti'nâ'* (انى), expectation.
استئناس *isti'nâs* (انس), familiarity, sociability; approving (s.).
استئناف *isti'nâf* (انف), beginning.
استيهاب *istîhâb* (وهب) asking a gift.
استئهال *isti'hâl* (اهل), worthiness.
اسجاد *asjâd*, tribute; capitation-tax; tributary Jews and Christians; — *isjâd*, adoration.
اسجاع *asjâ'*, rhymes, cadences, pl. of سجع *saj'*.
اسجح *asjaḥ*, f. *sajḥâ'*, well proportioned.
اسجوعة *usjû'a-t*, pl. *asâjî'*, rhymed prose.
اسحار *asḥâr*, mornings, pl. of سحر *saḥar*; — *isḥâr*, early sunrise; coming early in the morning.
اسحاق *isḥâq*, Isaac; removal, &c., IV. of (سحق).
اسحلانية *isḥilâniyya-t*, tall, handsome woman.
اسحم *asḥam*, f. *saḥmâ*, black; pl. *asâḥim*, horn; cloud; leathern bag for wine; raven; blood.
اسحنفار *isḥinfâr*, swiftness; talkativeness.
اسحوان *usḥuwân*, اسحوب *usḥûb*, voracious.
اسحية *asḥiya-t*, membranes of papyrus, &c., pl. of سحا *saḥâ* and سحاية *saḥâya-t*, q.v.; — *usḥiyya-t*, parchment.
اسخاف *isḫâf*, imbecility.
اسخم *isḫam*=اسحم *asḥam*.
اسخنة *isḫina-t*, hot fever.
اسخى *asḫa*, more or most liberal.
اسخيا *asḫiyâ'*, pl. of سخى *saḫiyy*, liberal.
(اسد) *asad*, I, (also II.) cause discord, rebellion; scold, abuse; — *asid*, be frightened at the sight of a lion; have the

استمراح *istîrâḥ* (ورح), watering, irrigation.
استيراد *istîrâd* (ورد), invitation; (m.) gain.
استيزار *istîzâr* (وزر), appointment as a vizier.
استيزاع *istîzâ'* (وزع), praying for divine inspiration.
استئسا *isti'sâ'* (اسو), consolation.
استئسار *isti'sâr* (اسر), taking captive; — *istîsâr* (يسر), being easy, commodious, in good order.
استيساع *istîsâ'* (وسع), great extent; abundance; opportunity.
استيسان *istîsân* (وسن), sleep.
استيصا *istîṣâ'* (وصى), wish to make a will; commission.
استئصال *isti'ṣâl* (اصل), taking root; eradicating, extirpating, destroying.
استيضاح *istîḍâḥ* (وضح), strict inquiry, asking exact information.
استيضام *istîḍâm* (وضم), offence.
استيطان *istîṭân* (وطن), dwelling, settling down in a place.
استيفا *istîfâ'* (وفى), full payment, entire satisfaction; exhaustive treatment of a matter; (m.) indemnity, damages; revenge.
استيفار *istîfâr* (وفر), receiving or granting full payment.
استيفاز *istîfâz* (وفز), being on the wing; being always in readiness.
استيفاض *istîfâḍ* (وفض), haste; pursuit; banishment.
استيفاق *istîfâq* (وفق), imploring the grace of God; assistance.
استيقاد *istîqâd* (وقد), shining of the fire.
استيقاظ *istîqâẓ* (يقظ), waking, being awake; attention, being on one's guard.
استيقاع *istîqâ'* (وقع), anxiety; expectation; sharpening.
استيقاف *istîqâf* (وقف), standing, waiting.
استيقان *istîqân* (يقن), knowing for certain, making certain of.
استيقاه *istîqâh* (وقه), obedience.

courage of a lion; — II. and IV. set a dog at another animal; — V. be angry, be like a lion; — X. be as a lion; show courage against anybody; (pass.) be irritated against (على *'ala*); grow vigorously in all directions (plant).

اسد *asad*, f. ة, pl. *usd*, *âsud*, *âsâd*, *usûd*, *usdân*, *ma'sadat*, lion; — *asadd*, who hits on the right thing, goes straight on; — ة *asida-t*, (sheep-)fold; — *asidda-t*, pl. of سد *sadd*, bodily defect, impediment.

اسدال *asdâl*, curtains, &c., pl. of سديل *sadîl*.

اسدران *isdarân*, the shoulders.

اسدف *asdaf*, black.

اسدل *asdal*, pl. *sudul*, hanging down; — *asdul*, veils, pl. of سدل *sidl*, *sudl*.

اسدى *asadiyy*, like a lion; — *asdiyy*, *usdiyy*, warp; — ة *asdiya-t*, warps, &c., pl. of سداة *sadât*, q.v.

(اسر) *asar*, I, INF. *asr*, tie, bind; take captive; create strong and powerful; — pass. suffer from dysury; — II. tie up; — V. inquire for the reasons of anything; — X. take captive; become a prisoner; addict one's self entirely.

اسر *asr*, strap, rope; sinew; باسره, lit. (the camel) with its rope, i.e. all, the whole of; — *usr*, detention; اسر البول *usr al-bûl*, dysury; — *usur*, straps, &c., pl. of اسار *isâr*; — *asarr*, hollow; excellent; familiar friend; f. *sarrâ'*, joy, prosperous condition; — ة *usra-t*, pl. *usar*, strong coat of mail; fortress; relationship; kin; — *asirra-t*, pl. of سر *sirr*, *surr*, line in the palm of the hand; *surr*, umbilical cord; سرار *sirâr*, line in the palm of the hand or on the forehead; سرير *sarîr*, throne, sofa, &c.

اسرا *usarâ'*, captives, pl. of اسير *asîr*; — *isrâ'*, travelling by night, &c., IV. of (سرى).

اسرار *asrâr*, secrets, &c., pl. of سر *sirr*; — *isrâr*, keeping secret, &c., IV. of (سر).

اسراع *isrâ'*, haste, acceleration.

اسراف *isrâf*, dissipation, squandering.

اسرافيل *asrâfîl*, the angel of death.

اسرايل, اسرائيل *isrâ'îl*, اسرائين *isrâ'în*, Israel.

اسرب *usrub*, *asrub* (Pers.), lead; — ى *usrubiyy*, leaden.

اسرع *asra'*, swifter, swiftest, comp. of سريع *sarî'*.

اسرى *asra*, nobler, more generous; pl. of اسير *asîr*, captive.

اسريا *asriyâ'*, liberal men; — اسرية *asriya-t*, canals for irrigation, pl. of سرى *sariyy*, q.v.

اسس *asas*, foundation; — *usus*, pl. of اساس *asâs*, id.

اسط *asaṭṭ*, long-footed.

اسطار *asṭâr*, lines, &c., pl. of سطر *saṭr*, *saṭar*; — *isṭâr*, *isṭâra-t*, story, fable, see اسطور *asṭûr*.

اسطبل *istabl*=اصطبل *iṣṭabl*, stable, q.v.

اسطبة *usṭubba-t*, oakum.

اسطر *asṭur*, lines, &c. pl. of سطر *saṭr*, *saṭar*.

اسطرلاب *asṭarlâb*, *usṭurlâb*, astrolabe.

اسطع *asṭa'*, f. *saṭ'â'*, long-necked.

اسطقس *istuqis*, pl. *-ât*, element (στοιχεῖον).

اسطم *usṭumm*, waving of the sea; place where bees are swarming, middle; nobler; right, just.

اسطما *usṭummâ'*, اسطمة *usṭumma-t*, pl. *asâṭim*, middle, core, kernel; the best; assembly.

اسطوان *usṭuwân*, high; long-necked; — ة *usṭuwâna-t*, pl. *asâṭîn*, column, pillar; cylinder; penis of an animal; اهل الاسطونة *ahlu-'l-ustuwâna-t*, Stoics; — ى *usṭuwâniyy*, cylindrical.

اسطور *usṭûr*, ة *usṭûra-t*, also *isṭâr*, *isṭâra-t*, pl. *asâṭîr*, story, tale, fable, romance.

اسطول *usṭûl* (στόλος), pl. *asâṭîl*, fleet.
اسعاد *is'âd*, making happy or prosperous.
اسعار *as'âr*, prices, &c., pl. of سعر *si'r*.
اسعاطة *is'âṭa-t*, imbibing by the nose, inhaling; causing to do so.
اسعاف *is'âf*, help, assistance.
اسعد *as'ad*, more fortunate, happier, comp. of سعيد *sa'îd*; scab; mange.
اسعر *as'ar*, lean, thin, meagre.
اسغان *asgân*, bad food, bad victuals.
(اسف) *asif*, A, INF. *asaf*, be very sad, be angry; — IV. render sad, irritate; — V. grieve; sigh.
اسف *asaf*, grief, sorrow; — *âsif*, *asif*, sorrowful, angry; f. *asifa-t*, bad soil.
اسفا *usafâ'*, pl. of *asîf*, sad, &c.
اسفار *asfâr*, travellers, pl. of سافر *sâfir*; journeys, pl. of سفر *safar*; books, pl. of سفر *sifr*; — *isfâr*, splendour; twilight; dawn of the morning.
اسفراج *asfarâj*, asparagus.
اسفع *asfa'*, reddish black; *al-asfa'*, buffalo; hawk; f. *saf'â'*, pl. سفع *suf'*, a kind of ring-dove; tripod.
اسفل *asfal*, f. *sufla*, pl. *asâfil*, low, lower, inferior; *al-asâfil*, rabble; *asfal as-sâfilin*, the damned; f. *sufla*, diabolic magic.
اسفن *asfan*, (m.) wedge.
اسفناج *isfanâj*, spinage.
اسفنج *isfunj* (σπογγος), sponge; a kind of pastry; — ى *isfunjiyy*, spongy.
اسفنط *isfanṭ*, aromatic wine.
اسفهان *isfahân*, Ispahan.
اسفى *asfa*, f. *safwâ'*, *safyâ*, good ambler; stupid; having a few hairs falling over the forehead.
اسفيداج *isfîdâj*, white lead, ceruse (used as paint by women).
اسقاط *isqâṭ*, causing to fall; miscarriage; subtraction; discount.

اسقح *asqaḥ*, bald.
اسقف *asqaf*, *asquf*, f. *saqfâ'*, long and crooked; long-necked (ostrich); bony; hairless; — *usquf*, pl. *asâqif*, *asaqifa-t*, bishop (ἐπίσκοπος); — ية *usqufiyya-t*, dignity of a bishop; bishopric.
اسقنقور *isqanqûr*, Egyptian lizard.
اسقية *asqiya-t*, leathern vessels, pl. of سقا *siqâ'*; waters, pl. of سقى *siqy*; abundantly raining clouds, pl. of سقى *saqiyy*.
اسكاب *iskâb*, shoe-maker; — ة *iskâba-t*, stopper, cork.
اسكات *askât*, remainders; rabble; moderately warm days after heat; — *iskât*, bidding silence, silence.
اسكاف *iskâf*, اسكف *askaf*, pl. *asâkifa-t*, shoe-maker, cobbler; blacksmith; carpenter; artisan.
اسكان *iskân*, causing to stay; continuing to dwell.
اسكبة *uskubba-t*, اسكفة *uskuffa-t*, lintel.
اسكلة *iskala-t*, pl. *asâkil*, (m.) stairs; ladder; harbour; scale of taxes, &c.
اسكملة *iskamla-t*, (m.) stool, chair.
اسكن *askan*, more quiet, more secure.
اسكوب *uskûb*, flowing; poured out; shed; full stream; — ة *uskûba-t*, stopper, cork.
اسكوف *uskûf*=اسكاف *askâf*, shoemaker, &c.
اسكيم *iskîm*, hood, capouche, cowl.
(اسل) *asul*, *asil*, INF. *asal*, *asâla-t*, be oval; — II. INF. *ta'sîl*, come up to the finger-tops; sharpen; — V. INF. *ta'assul*, resemble.
اسل *asal*, rush; a tree with long thorns, thorn; top of a lance, lance; — ة *asala-t*, finger-top; funny-bone; tip of the tongue; penis.
اسلاف *aslâf*, ancestors, pl. of سلف *salaf*; brothers-in-law (sister's husbands), pl. of سلف *silf*; — *islâf*, paying in advance.

اسلام *islâm*, submission to the will of God; humbling one's self; Islamism.

اسلت *aslat*, f. *saltâ'*, having the nose cut off; f. a woman who has not painted her finger-tops.

اسلحة *asliḥa-t*, arms, weapons, pl. of سلاح *silâḥ*.

اسلط *aslaṭ*, more eloquent; pert.

اسلم *aslam*, f. *sulma*, more secure, safer; in better condition; more regular.

اسلوب *uslûb*, pl. *asâlîb*, way; course; manner, style, method; length.

اسلوفة *uslûfa-t*, affinity by marriage of sisters and brothers.

اسم *ism*, pl. *asmâ'*, *asâm-in*, *asâmiyy*, *asmâwât*, name, noun.

اسمال *asmâl*, pl. rags.

اسمر *asmar*, f. *samrâ'*, pl. *sumr*, brown, tawny, deep yellow; *al-asmar*, lance; *al-asmarân*, wheat and water, the lance and water; *as-samrâ*, wheat; cake.

اسمن *asman*, fatter; plump; lusty.

اسمى *asma*, more honourable; — *ismiyy*, referring to a name, to a noun; — ة *asmiya-t*, heavens, pl. of سما *samâ'*.

(اسن) *asan*, U, I, *asin*, A, INF. *asan*, *usûn*, change colour and taste; — V. INF. *ta'assun*, remember things past; tarry, delay; take after one's father; change colour and taste.

اسن *usun*, pl. *âsân*, character; — *âsin*, corrupted (water).

اسن *asann*, with more or stronger teeth; older; — *asunn*, teeth, pl. of سن *sinn*; — ة *asinna-t*, id.; arrow-heads, pl. of سنن *sanan*.

اسناد *asnâd*, props, supports, pl. of سند *sanad*; — *isnâd*, *iswâda-t*, pl. *asânîd*, quotation; referring to an authority; relation between subject and predicate; imputing; ascending; causing to ascend.

اسناط *asnâṭ*, pl. of سناط *sanâṭ*, beardless.

اسنان *asnân*, teeth, &c., pl. of سن *sinn*.

اسنع *asna'*, great, greater; more beautiful.

اسنمة *asnima-t*, humps of camels, pl. of سنام *sanâm*.

اسنى *asna*, higher, highest; sublime.

اسها *ashâ'*, pl. colours.

اسهاب *ishâb*, prolixity; garrulity.

اسهال *ishâl*, facilitating; loosening; purging.

اسهام *ashâm*, arrows, pl. of سهم *sahm*.

اسهان *ashân*; pl. soft sand.

اسهد *ashad*, more vigilant, wider awake.

(اسو) *asâ*, U, INF. *asw*, اسى *asan*, nurse, cure; make peace; — II. exhort to patience; console, and V. be consoled; — III. assist out of one's fortune, not out of one's superfluities; — III. console, and VI. console each other; — IV. and VIII. afford consolation by anything.

اسوا *aswa'*, f. *sau'â'*, bad; abominable; worse; — *aswâ'*, evils, pl. of سو *sau'*; pl. of سوا *sawâ'*, equal, &c.

اسوار *iswâr*, *uswâr*, pl. *asâwir*, *asâwira-t* (Pers. سوار *sawâr*), horseman; — *uswâr*, bracelet; walls, pl. of سور *sûr*.

اسواق *aswâq*, markets, &c., pl. of سوق *sûq*.

اسوان *aswân*, sad, sorrowful.

اسود *aswad*, f. *saudâ'*, pl. *sûd*, black; blacker, very black; سودا (اسود) القلب *saudâ' (aswad) al-qalb*, the innermost heart; f. *saudâ'*, gall; melancholy; original sin; *al-aswadân*, dates and water; — f. ة pl. *asâwid*, black snake; اساود الدار *asâwid ad-dâr*, household furniture or utensils; — pl. *sûdân*, negro; — *usawwid* (dim.), blackish; — *usûd*, lions, pl. of اسد *asad*; — ة *aswida-t*, dark objects in the distance, &c., pl. of سواد *sawâd*.

اسودانى *aswadânî-y*, blackish.

اسودى *aswadiyy*, black.

اسورة *aswira-t*, bracelets, rings, pl. of سوار *siwâr*, *suwâr*.
اسوف *asûf*, sad; touchy.
اسوق *as'uq*, legs, pl. of ساق *sâq*; — *aswaq*, f. *sauqâ'*, long-legged, long-shank.
اسويا *aswiyâ'*, pl. of سوى *sawiyy*, equal, &c.
(أسى) *asa*, INF. *asy*, reserve; — *asî*, A, INF. اسى *asan*, be sad, sorrowful.
اسى *âsî*, f. ة, sad; — *âsî*, اس *âs-in*, physician; — اسى *asan*, sadness; art of the physician; — *usan*, patience; — *usiyy*, remaining; traces of old dwellings; small pieces of furniture or utensils; — ة *âsiya-t*, woman who circumcises girls, undertakes cures; support; pillar; firm building.
أسياف *asyâf*, swords, pl. of سيف *saif*; banks, shores, pl. of سيف *sîf*; — pl. crowds of people.
اسيان *asyân*, pl. *-ûn*, *asyânât*, *asâyâ*, sad, sorrowful.
اسيد *usayyid*, dim. of اسود *aswad*, blackish.
اسير *asîr*, pl. *asra*, *usâra*, *usarâ'*, bound; captive; slave.
اسيس *asîs*, foundation.
اسيف *asîf*, sad; touchy, susceptible; barren, sterile; old man; slave; client; mercenary.
اسيل *asîl*, having an oval cheek or face; smooth; — also ة *asîla-t*, flux of water.
اسينة *asîna-t*, pl. *asâyin*, character.
اش *aś*, *eś*, from ايش *eś*, for اى شى *ayyu śay-in*, how? what? — *aśś*, dry bread.
(اش) *aśś*, I, INF. *aśś*, rise and bestir one's self; = هش *haśś*, beat down leaves.
اشابانى *aśâbâniyy*, crimson.
اشابة *uśâba-t*, pl. *aśâyib*, rabble; ill-acquired wealth.
اشاجع *aśâji'*, pl. of اشجع *aśja'*, brave, &c.
اشاح *iśâḥ*, *uśâḥ*, leathern belt.
اشادة *iśâda-t*, raising one's voice; announcement; building.

اشارة *iśâra-t*, pointing to; sign, signal; advice; command; allusion.
اشاش *aśâś*, ة *aśâśa-t*, merriment.
اشاعة *iśâ'a-t*, making public, divulging.
اشافى *aśâfî*, awls, pl. of اشفى *aśfan*.
اشام *aś'am*, ill-omened; pl. *aśâ'im*, the unfortunate; f. *śu'ma*, the left hand.
اشاوات *aśâwât*, things, &c., pl. of شى *śai'*, *śe*.
اشاوز *aśâwiz*, form, figure.
اشاوة *aśâwa-t*, اشاوى *aśâwî*, اشايا *aśâyâ*, things, &c., pl. of شى *śai'*.
(اشب) *aśab*, I, U, INF. *aśb*, blame; — I, mix, entwine; — *aśib*, A, INF. *aśab*, be thickly grown (tree); — II. entwine; set people one against another; — V. VIII. be thickly grown; be mixed up, mingled.
اشب *aśab*, complication; discord; — *aśib*, complicated; thickly grown; يوم اشب *yaum aśib*, day of battle; — ة *uśba-t*, wolf.
اشباح *aśbâḥ*, indistinct objects in a distance, &c., pl. of شبح *śabḥ*.
اشبار *aśbâr*, spans, pl. of شبر *śibr*.
اشباع *iśbâ'*, satiating, satisfying; insertion of a letter of prolongation.
اشبانى *uśbâniyy*, with red cheeks, moustaches.
اشباه *aśbâh*, similitudes, &c. pl. of شبه *śibh*, *śabah*; — *iśbâh*, resembling, resemblance, IV. of (شبه).
اشبه *aśbah*, more alike, more similar.
اشتات *aśtât*, pl. of شت *śatt*, dispersed, &c.
اشتباك *iśtibâk*, being entwined, complicated; confusion, mixture.
اشتباه *iśtibâh*, resemblance, similitude; ambiguity; doubt; scruple.

اهتداد *iśtidâd*, violence; strength; making compact, tight.
اهترا *iśtirâ'*, buying.
اهترار *iśtirâr*, chewing the cud.
اهتراع *iśtirâ'*, legislation.
اهتراك *iśtirâk*, companionship; reception into a society.
اهترغاز *uśturgâz*, thistle.
اهتعال *iśti'âl*, inflammation; conflagration; grey-headedness.
اهتغال *iśtigâl*, occupation.
اهتفا *iśtifâ'*, recovery.
اهتقاق *iśtiqâq*, derivation of a word from another word or a root.
اهتكا *iśtikâ'*, complaint, lamentation; reproach.
اهتلاق *iśtilâq*, (m.) surmise, supposition.
اهتمال *iśtimâl*, containing, comprising.
اهتها *iśtihâ'*, appetite; desire.
اهتهادة *iśtihâda-t*, testimony.
اهتهار *iśtihâr*, being known, renowned, fame; publication; divulging.
اهتياق *iśtiyâq*, longing for, yearning, desire.
اهتية *iśtiya-t*, winters, pl. of هتا *śitâ'*.
اهج *aśajj*, with a broken skull; with a scar on the forehead.
اهجار *aśjâr*, trees, pl. of هجر *śajar*.
اهجر *aśjar*, f. *śajrâ'*, abundant; f. (s.) plant with a stalk, tree.
اهجع *aśja'*, f. *śajâ'*, pl. *śujû'*, *śijâ'*, *śajâyi'*, brave, courageous; lion; swift, quick; very long; time; a poisonous snake.
اهجى *aśja*, more sorrowful.
(اهح) *aśiḥ*, A, INF. *aśaḥ*, be angry.
اهحا *aśiḥḥâ'*, اهحة *aśiḥḥa-t*, pl. of هحيح *śaḥîḥ*, miserly, avaricious, &c.
اهخاص *aśḥâṣ*, persons, &c., pl. of هخص *śaḥṣ*.
اهخم *aśḥam*, getting grey (hair); without vegetation.
اهد *aśadd*, more violent, stronger harder, used to form comparatives; — *aśudd*, *uśudd*, strength; vigour of life.

اهدا *aśiddâ'*, pl. of هديد *śadîd*, strong, &c.
اهداق *aśdâq*, corners of the mouth, &c., pl. of هدق *śidq*, *śadq*.
اهدح *aśdaḥ*, vast, spacious.
اهدف *aśdaf*, f. *śadfâ'*, left-handed; maimed of hand or arm; leaning to one side; strongly bent (bow).
اهدق *aśdaq*, f. *śadqâ*, pl. *śudq*, with large corners of the mouth; glib, fluent, eloquent.
(اهر) *aśar*, U, INF. *aśr*, saw; — I, INF. *aśr*, file old teeth so as to become sharp; — *aśir*, A, INF. *aśar*, be merry, jolly; shine (lightning); — II. file the teeth; — IV. saw; — VIII., X. have one's teeth filed.
اهر *aśr*, *aśar*, boisterous merriment; wantonness; — *aśar*, *uśur*, pl. *uśûr*, sharpness and polish of the teeth; — *aśir*, *aśur*, pl. *-ûn* and *uśur*, jolly, boisterously merry; — *iśr*, *uśra-t*, pl. *uśar*, a toothed blade (saw); — *aśarr*, f. *surra*, worse, more or most wicked (comp. of هرير *śarîr*); — ة *aśira-t*, woman with filed teeth.
اهرا *aśirrâ'*, pl. of هرير *śarîr*, bad, wicked; — pl. of اهرى *aśran*, region; district.
اهراب *iśrâb*, admixture of a different colour; impregnating; watering.
اهرار *aśrâr*, pl. of هر *śarr* and هرير *śarîr*, wicked, &c.; — ة *iśrâra-t*, large herd of camels.
اهراع *aśrâ'*, sails, &c., pl. of هراع *śarâ'*; divine laws, pl. of هرعة *śir'a-t*.
اهراف *aśrâf*, pl. of هريف *śarîf*, noble, &c.; projecting parts of the body (ear, nose).
اهراق *iśrâq*, rising of the sun; shining, flashing, resplendent.
اهراك *aśrâk*, companionships, &c., pl. of هرك *śirk*; companions, &c. pl. of هريك *śarîk*; — *iśrâk*, giving companions to God.

اشران *aśrân*, pl. *aśârî*, brisk, sprightly.

اشربة *aśriba-t*, drinks, &c., pl. of شراب *śarâb*.

اشرس *aśras*, bad, evil; quarrelsome; lion; hard, difficult; f. *śarsâ*, hard ground; bright cloud.

اشرط *aśraṭ*, very contemptible, vile.

اشرع *aśra'*, prolonged, lengthened; more excellent.

اشرف *aśraf*, f. *śarfâ'*, pl. *śurf*, high, sublime; nobler, of nobler origin; prolonged; with battlements; bat; f. long ear; — ى *aśrafiyy*, a gold coin.

اشرك *aśruk*, straps, bootlaces, pl. of شراك *sirâk*.

اشرم *aśram*, with a maimed nose; (m.) blunt; اشرم الاسنان *aśram al-aśnân*, gap-toothed.

اشرى *aśra*, more impetuous; — ة *aśriya-t*, pl. of شرى *śir-an*, bargain.

اشزر *aśzar*, f. *śazrâ'*, red, reddish; looking askance.

اشعار *aś'âr*, hair, pl. of شعر *śa'r*, *śa'ar*; poems, &c., pl. of شعر *śi'r*.

اشعاع *iś'â'*, shining, resplendent.

اشعال *iś'âl*, setting on fire, kindling.

اشعب *aś'ab*, broad in the shoulders; having the horns distant from one another.

اشعث *aś'as̱*, f. *śa'ṡâ'*, pl. *śu's̱*, dishevelled; dispersed; pole.

اشعر *aś'ar*, f. *śa'râ'*, pl. *śu'r*, hairy, woolly; well overgrown; more intelligent, judicious; more poetical; f. ugly; bad; fur; crowd; — ة *aś'ira-t*, pl. of شعار *śi'âr*, underclothing, &c.

اشعن *aś'an*, dishevelled.

اشعة *aśi''a-t*, rays, &c., pl. of شع *śu''* and شعاع *śu'â'*.

اشغال *aśgâl*, affairs, &c., pl. of شغل *śugl*.

اشغولة *uśgûla-t*, work, occupation.

اشغى *aśga*, f. *śagwâ'*, *śagyâ'*, pl. *śugw*, unequal, splay (teeth), crooked; f. eagle.

اشفار *aśfâr*, edges, &c., pl. of شفر *śufr*, *śafr*.

اشفاق *aśfâq*, twilights, &c., pl. of شفق *śafaq*; — *iśfâq*, being on one's guard; fearing and shunning; having compassion with.

اشفه *aśfah*, with a large mouth, large lips.

اشفى *aśfa*, more salutary, more efficacious; — *iśf-an*, pl. *aśâfiyy*, *aśâfî*, awl; punch; — ة *aśfiya-t*, pl. of شفا *śifâ'*, medicine.

اشق *aśaqq*, f. *śaqqâ*, pl. *śuqq*, balancing in walking; long-footed; long;—*uśśaq*, ammoniac (Pers.).

اشقر *aśqar*, f. *śaqrâ'*, of a bright red; f. fire.

اشقرانى *asqarâniyy*, (m.) reddish.

اشقيا *aśqiyâ'*, pl. of شقى *śaqiyy*, miserable, wretched.

اشكا *iśkâ'*, complaining, lamenting.

اشكال *aśkâl*, shapes, figures, &c., pl. of شكل *śakl*.

اشكز *uśkuzz*, saddle-strap; a sea animal.

اشكل *aśkal*, f. *śaklâ'*, pl. *śukl*, of mixed colour; more alike, more similar; more doubtful, obscurer, more difficult; more handsome; mountain lotus; f. want, need; — ة *aśkala-t*, difficulty; want, need; prettiness; similarity, resemblance; manner; mountain lotus.

اشل *aśall*, f. *śallâ*, with a maimed hand; blind;—ة *aśilla-t*, clothes worn under coats of mail, &c., pl. of شليل *śalîl*.

اشلا *aślâ'*, limbs, &c., pl. of شلو *śilw*.

(اشم) *aśim*, A, INF. *aśam*, cause pain.

اشم *aśamm*, f. *śammâ'*, pl. *śumm*, with a straight nose; proud, haughty; f. highest mountain ridge; wind from above.

اشمات *iśmât*, rejoicing at another's misfortune.

اشمط *aśmaṭ*, f. *śamṭâ'*, pl. *śumṭ*, *śumṭân*, turning grey.

اشمق *aśmaq*, bloody foam.

اهمل *aśmul*, pl. of شمال *śamâl*, left hand or side.
اشمئزاز *iśmi'zâz*, shudder; cramp; disgust.
(اشن); — II. INF. *ta'śîn*, wash one's hands with اشنان *iśnân*, *uśnân*, alkali; — ة *uśna-t*, moss of trees.
اشنب *aśnab*, f. *śambâ'*, with fine, fresh teeth; f. pomegranate without grains.
اشنع *aśna'*, f. *śan'â'*, horrid, hideous; disastrous; more or most vile, shocking, comp. of شنيع *śanî'*.
اشهاد *aśhâd*, witnesses, pl. of شاهد *śâhid*; — *iśhâd*, taking to witness; attesting; bringing proof.
اشهب *aśhab*, f. *śahbâ*, white and black, grey; glittering; barren; misfortune; *al-aśhab*, lion; pig; — *aśhub*, brilliant stars, &c., pl. of شهاب *śihâb*.
اشهر *aśhar*, more renowned; *al-aśharân*, drum and flag; — *aśhur*, months, pl. of شهر *śahr*.
اشهى *aśha*, more or most desirable; more or most desirous.
اشواق *aśwâq*, desires, &c., pl. of شوق *śauq*.
اشوز *aśwaz*, haughty.
اشوس *aśwas*, pl. *śûs*, اشوص *aśwaṣ*, f. *śauṣâ'*, blinking, squinting.
اشوع *aśwa'*, f. *śaw'â'*, pl. *śû'*, rough, rugged, shaggy.
اشوق *aśwaq*, pl. *śûq*, desirous.
اشوك *aśwak*, f. *śaukâ'*, hard, stiff.
اشوه *aśwah*, f. *śauhâ'*, ugly, and, by opposition, handsome; proud; with the evil eye; long and swift (horse), fiery.
(اشى) *aśa*, I, INF. *aśy*, invent (lies); — *aśî*, A, INF. *aś-an*, want, be in need of (الى *ala*); — IV. cure (a broken bone).
اشى *aśiyy*, white spot on the forehead (of a horse).
اشيا *aśyâ'*, اشيايا *aśyâyâ*, اشياوات *aśyâwât*, things, pl. of شى *śay'*.
اشياع *aśyâ'*, amounts, &c., pl. of شيع *śai'*, *śi'*; — troops of followers, &c., pl. of شيعة *śî'a-t*.
اشيام *aśyâm*, f. *śaimâ'*, pl. *śîm*, with a mole; with a black spot; black.
اشيب *aśyab*, f. *śaibâ'*, pl. *śîb*, *śuyub*, white-haired, white; *aś-śîb*, the days of hoar-frost; ليلة شيبا *lailat śaibâ*, last night of the lunar month.
اشيه *aśyah*, injuring by the evil eye.
(اص) *aṣṣ*, I, U, INF. *aṣṣ*, break into pieces; press flat and smooth; be strong, have firm flesh; yield much milk; throng; — I, shine, flash; — II. strengthen, make firm; — V., VIII. gather, assemble (n.).
اص *iṣṣ*, *aṣṣ*, *uṣṣ*, pl. *aṣûṣ*, root, foundation.
اصا *aṣâ*, see (اصو), (اصى).
اصابع *aṣâbi'*, اصابيع *aṣâbî'*, fingers, pl. of اصبع *aṣba'*, &c.
اصابة *iṣâba-t*, a hitting shot; right aiming; sound judgment; rectitude.
اصاحيب *aṣâḥîb*, companions, &c., pl. of صاحب *ṣâḥib*.
اصاد *iṣâd*, low ground with stagnating water between mountains.
اصادق *aṣâdiq*, true friends, pl. of صديق *ṣadîq*.
اصار *âṣâr*, compacts, &c., pl. of اصر *iṣr*, *uṣr*; — *iṣâr*, pl. *uṣur*, *âṣira-t*, tent-rope; tent-peg.
اصارم *aṣârim*, اصاريم *aṣârîm*, crowds, &c., pl. of صرم *ṣirm*.
اصاص *aṣâṣ*, foundations, &c., pl. of اص *iṣṣ*.
اصاطب *aṣâṭib*, اصاطل *aṣâṭil*, stables, pl. of اصطبل *iṣṭabl*.
اصاغر *aṣâgir*, ة *aṣâgira-t*, pl. of اصغر *aṣgar*, smaller, &c.
اصال *âṣâl*, evenings, pl. of اصيل *aṣîl*; — ة *iṣâla-t*, firmness; what is original; high lineage; real tenure of an office (not as a substitute).
اصالف *aṣâlif*, pl. of اصلف *aṣlaf*, hard and barren.

اصالق *aṣâliq*, plain fields, pl. of صلق *ṣalaq*.

اصائل *aṣâ'il*, evenings, pl. of اصيل *aṣîl*, ة *aṣîla-t*.

اصب *aṣb-in*, اصبى *aṣbî*, youths, pl. of صبى *ṣabiyy*.

اصبا *aṣbâ'*, east winds, pl. of صبا *ṣab-an*.

اصباح *aṣbâḥ*, mornings, pl. of صبح *ṣubḥ*; — *iṣbâḥ*, dawning; dawn.

اصبر *aṣbar*, more patient (على *'ala*).

اصبع *aṣba'*, *aṣbi'*, *aṣbu'*; *iṣba'*, *iṣbi'*, *iṣbu'*; *uṣba'*, *uṣbi'*, *uṣbu'*, pl. *aṣâbi'*, *aṣâbî'*, finger; digit; benefit.

اصبغ *aṣbag*, f. *ṣabgâ*, with a white top of the ear, the tail, &c.; wetted and soiled; violent torrent.

اصبوحة *aṣbûḥa-t*, dawn of the morning, early morning.

اصبوع *uṣbû'*, pl. *aṣâbi'*, *aṣâbî'*, finger; digit.

اصبية *aṣbiya-t*, youths, pl. of صبى *ṣabiyy*.

(اصت) *aṣat*, I, INF. *aṣt*, be without vegetation.

اصح *aṣaḥḥ*, truer; more genuine, &c., pl. of صحيح *ṣaḥîḥ*; — ة *aṣiḥḥa-t*, pl. of صحاح *ṣaḥâḥ*, whole, complete.

اصحا *aṣiḥḥâ'*, pl. of صحيح *ṣaḥîḥ*, true, &c.

اصحاب *aṣḥâb*, companions, &c., pl. of صاحب *ṣâḥib*; — *iṣḥâb*, following.

اصحاح *iṣḥâḥ*, pl. *-ât*, chapter (m.); — making sound, &c., IV. of صح *ṣaḥḥ*.

اصحر *aṣḥar*, f. *ṣaḥrâ'*, white mingled with red; yellow; *al-aṣḥar*, lion; f. *ṣaḥrâ*, pl. *ṣaḥâra*, *ṣaḥârî*, *ṣaḥrâwât*, *ṣuḥar*, desert, wilderness.

اصحل *aṣḥal*, hoarse, with a rough voice.

(اصد) *aṣad*; — II. cloth with the اصدة *uṣda-t*, q.v.; — IV. lock.

اصد *aṣadd*, pl. *ṣudad*, turned enemy; — ة *iṣda-t*, pl. *iṣad*, place of assembly; — *uṣda-t*, short chemise for a girl.

اصدار *iṣdâr*, issuing (an order, &c.); leading back from the watering place.

اصداغ *aṣdâg*, temples and hair thereon, pl. of صدغ *ṣudg*.

اصداف *aṣdâf*, shells, shell-fish, &c., pl. of صدف *ṣadaf*.

اصدح *aṣdaḥ*, screamer, brawler; lion.

اصدر *aṣdar*, with a broad, strong chest.

اصدغ *aṣdag*, du. *aṣdagân*, the arteries of the temples.

اصدق *aṣdaq*, truer, &c., comp. of صديق *ṣadîq*.

اصدقا *aṣdiqâ'*, true friends, pl. of صديق *ṣadîq*.

اصدم *aṣdam*, bald.

(اصر) *aṣar*, I, INF. *aṣr*, tie up with the rope اصار *iṣâr*; shut up and retain; break into pieces; make one well disposed to another; — III. be a neighbour; — VI. be each other's neighbour; — VIII. be abundant and grow high (plants); be thickly overgrown; be numerous.

اصر *iṣr*, *uṣr*, pl. *âṣâr*, *iṣrân*, compact; league; obligation by oath; piercing the ear; burden; sin; — *uṣur*, ropes, pl. of اصار *iṣâr*; — *aṣarr*, f. *ṣarrâ'*, hard; — ة *âṣira-t*, pl. *awâṣir*, womb; consanguinity; favour; claim; ropes, pl. of اصار *iṣâr*;—*aṣirra-t*, pl. of صرار *ṣirâr*, q.v.

اصرار *iṣrâr*, perseverance, &c., IV. of (صر).

اصرد *aṣrad*, colder; sharper (eyesight).

اصرم *aṣram*, poor with a large family; *al-aṣmarân*, day and night; wolf and raven; f. *ṣarmâ'*, waterless desert; milkless camel; cooking-vessel.

اصرى *iṣirra*, *aṣirrî*, firm resolution.

اصطبار *iṣṭibâr*, patience, toleration.

اصطبل *iṣṭabl*, pl. *aṣâṭib*, *aṣâṭil*, *aṣâbil*, *iṣṭablât*, stable.

اصطبة *uṣṭubba-t*, oakum.

اصطرك *iṣṭurak*, *iṣṭraq*, storax.

اصطرلاب *iṣṭarlâb*, astrolabe.

اصطفا *iṣṭifâ'*, choice, selection.

اصطلاح *iṣṭilâḥ*, ة *iṣṭilâla-t*, pl. *-ât*, reconciliation; emendation; technical meaning of a word, idiom;—ى *iṣṭilâḥiyy*, in a technical sense.

اصطلاق *iṣṭilâq*, clamour, noise.

اصطمة *uṣṭumma-t* (also *ustumma-t*, *usṭumma-t*, *uṣṭumma-t*), (stagnating) sea water.

اصطناع *iṣṭinâ'*, artificiality; affectation; invention.

اصطياد *iṣṭiyâd*, hunting, fishing.

اصعب *aṣ'ab*, more or most difficult.

اصغا *iṣgâ'*, friendly reception; consent; attention.

اصغر *aṣgar*, pl. *aṣâgir*, *aṣâgira-t*, *aṣgarûn*, smaller, very small; younger son; *al-aṣgarân*, heart and tongue;—f. صغرى *ṣugra*, pl. *ṣugar*; *aṣ-ṣugra*, the minor term in a logical proposition.

اصف *aṣaf*, Asaph, Solomon's vizier; the grand vizier; a pasha having rank of such.

اصفا *aṣfâ'*, large rocks, pl. of صفاة *ṣafât*.

اصفر *aṣfar*, f. *ṣafrâ'*, yellow, black; *al-aṣfarân*, gold and saffron; *al-aṣfar*, the Byzantines; *aṣ-ṣufrâ'*, gold; gall; bee;—*aṣfar*, emptier; more whistling or singing.

اصفرار *iṣfirâr*, yellowness; pallor.

اصفى *aṣfa*, f. *ṣafwâ'*, purer, clearer; f. rock.

اصفيا *aṣfiyâ*, pl. of صفى *ṣafiyy*, pure, clear.

اصقح *aṣqaḥ*, f. *ṣaqḥâ'*, bald.

اصقر *aṣqar*, containing more sugar.

اصقع *aṣqa'*, f. *ṣaq'â'*, with a white spot on the head; f. the sun.

(اصل) *aṣl*, pl. *uṣûl*, *âṣul*, root, origin; material; اصل المال *aṣl al-mâl*, capital, stock of trade; *al-uṣûl*, the elements, rudiments, principal parts; *aṣl-an*, with negative, not at all;—*aṣal*, snake with a venomous breath;—*aṣil*, uprooted; rooted firmly;—*uṣul*, evenings, pl. of اصيل *aṣîl*;—ة *aṣala-t*, root; snake;—also *iṣla-t*, totality;—*aṣla-t*, the whole of a property.

اصل *aṣal*, INF. *aṣl*, touch or injure the root; kill; rush upon;—*aṣil*, INF. *aṣal*, get corrupted, foul (water, meat);—*aṣul*, INF. *aṣâla-t*, be firmly rooted, stand firm; be excellent; have a firm character, a noble origin;—II. INF. *ta'ṣîl*, root firmly (a.); consider as firm of character and of noble origin;—IV. INF. *îṣâl*, come in the evening;—IV., V. INF. *ta'aṣṣul*, be firmly rooted;—X. INF. *isti'ṣâl*, *istîṣâl*, root; uproot; extirpate, destroy.

اصلاح *iṣlâḥ*, correction, emendation; rectitude.

اصلال *aṣlâl*, rains, &c. pl. of صل *ṣill*, q.v.

اصلان *uslân*, evenings, pl. of اصيل *aṣîl*.

اصلتى *aṣlatiyy*, energetic.

اصلج *aṣlaj*, hard and smooth; deaf.

اصلح *aṣlaḥ*, better, best.

اصلخ *aṣlaḫ*, deaf, f. *ṣalḫâ'*, mangy (camel).

اصلد *aṣlad*, hard, miserly.

اصلع *aṣla'*, f. *ṣal'â'*, pl. *ṣu'l*, *ṣul'ân*, bald; bare (ground);, shining (weapon); f. misfortune, calamity.

اصلف *aṣlaf*, pl. *aṣâlif*, *ṣalâfi*, hard and barren; more fruitless, to less purpose.

اصلم *aṣlam*, whose ears have been cut off, maimed; *al-aṣlam*, flea.

اصلى *aṣliyy*, noble; original; radical;—ة *aṣliyya-t*, root (of words).

اصليت *iṣlît*, polished and sharp.

اصم *aṣamm*, f. *ṣammâ'*, pl. *ṣumm*, *ṣummân*, deaf; inexpressible; massive, solid, not resounding; فعل اصم *fi'l aṣamm*, verb whose

second and third radicals are the same; f. hard ground; calamity.

اصمت *iṣmit*, ة *iṣmita-t*, silent and waste (desert).

اصمح *aṣmaḥ*, brave, bold.

اصمخة *aṣmiḫa-t*, ears (their cavities), pl. of صماخ *ṣamâḫ*, *ṣimâḫ*.

اصمع *aṣma'*, f. *ṣam'â'*, pl. *ṣum'*, ascending; vivacious; bold; insolent, and, by opposition, dumbfounded; sword; small and delicate; pl. *ṣum'ân*, the longest feather in the wing.

اصموخ *uṣmûḫ*, canal of the ear; ear.

اصن *uṣun*, pl. ropes of a tent.

اصنا *aṣnâ*, equals, brothers of the same mother, &c., pl. of صنو *ṣinw*, *ṣunw*.

اصناف *aṣnâf*, forms, kinds, pl. of صنف *ṣanf*, *ṣinf*.

اصنام *aṣnâm*, idols, statues, pl. of صنم *ṣanam*.

اصنان *iṣnân*, IV. of (صن), q.v.

اصهب *aṣhab*, f. *ṣahbâ*, pl. *ṣuhb*, red, bay (camel, horse); blond: صهب السبال *ṣuhbu-'s-sibâl*, with yellow moustaches, the Greeks; *al-aṣhab*, lion; *aṣ-ṣahbâ'*, white wine.

(اصو) *aṣâ*, U, INF. *aṣw*, grow plentiful and close together.

اصوا *aṣwâ'*, hills, &c., pl. of صوة *ṣuwwa-t*.

اصوات *aṣwât*, voices, &c., pl. of صوت *ṣaut*.

اصواع *aṣwâ'*, pl. of صاع *ṣâ'*, q.v.

اصواف *aṣwâf*, fleeces, &c., pl. of صوف *ṣûf*.

اصور *aṣwar*, inclined; — ة *aṣwira-t*, pl. of صوار *ṣiwâr*, &c., grain of musk; perfume.

اصوع *aṣwu'*, pl. of صاع *ṣâ'*, q.v.

اصوف *aṣwaf*, woolly.

اصول *uṣûl*, roots, &c., pl. of اصل *aṣl*; — ى *uṣûliyy*, original; radical; fundamental; erudite.

اصون *aṣwan*, who preserves better; — ة *aṣwina-t*, cloth-presses, wardrobes, &c., pl. of صوان *ṣawân*, &c.

(اصى) *aṣâ*, I, INF. *aṣy*, be very fat; — II. pass. be difficult; — ة *âṣiya-t*, syrup of dates; relationship; favour; continual misfortune.

اصيد *aṣyad*, better for hunting; bearing one's head high, proud; king; lion; f. *ṣaidâ'*, hard, rugged ground; Sidon.

اصيل *aṣîl*, pl. *uṣul*, *âṣâl*, *aṣâ'il*, *uṣlân*, evening (between عصر *'aṣr*, q.v., and sunset); — *aṣîl*, firmly rooted; firm of character and energetic; hereditary; noble; death; — ة *aṣîla-t*, pl. *aṣâ'il*, evening; death; totality; the whole of the property.

اصيلال *uṣailâl*, اصيلان *uṣailân*, short evening, dim. of اصيل *aṣîl*.

اصيهب *uṣaihib*, dim. of اصهب *aṣhab*, stupid.

(اض) *aḍḍ*, INF. *aḍḍ*, vex, torment, grieve; force to take refuge with (الى *ila*); break into pieces; — I., III. run to its nest (ostrich); — VIII. seek; beat; be forced, obliged; force, oblige.

(اض) *iḍḍ*, origin; root.

اضا *aḍâ'*, field of pebble ground; — ة *aḍât*, pl. *aḍûn*, *aḍwât*, *aḍyât*, *iḍâ'*, pond, swamp; — *iḍâ'a-t*, lighting up, illumination.

اضابير *aḍâbîr*, pl. of ضبارة *ḍibâra-t*, troop, company.

اضاحى *aḍâḥî*, lambs for sacrifice, pl. of اضحية *uḍḥiyya-t*.

اضاحيك *aḍâḥîk*, jests, witty sayings, pl. of اضحوكة *uḍḥûka-t*.

اضاض *iḍâḍ*, refuge.

اضافة *iḍâfa-t*, addition; junction; reference; attribute.

اضافى *iḍâfiyy*, additional; relative; dependent on.

اضالع *aḍâli'*, ribs, sides (as of a triangle), &c., pl. of ضلع *ḍil'*, *ḍila'*.

اضاليل *aḍâlîl*, errors, pl. of اضلولة *uḍlûla-t*.

اضامة *iḍâma-t*, injury.

اضاميم *aḍâmîm*, leaves (stitched

together); troops (of people, &c.), pl. of اضمامة *iḍmâma-t*.

اضائف *aḍâ'if*, guests, pl. of ضيف *ḍaif*.

اضب *aḍubb*, pl. of ضب *ḍabb*, lizard.

اضباث *aḍbâs̱*, pl. hands, paws.

اضبارة *aḍbâra-t*, *iḍbâra-t*, leaves stitched together, pamphlet.

اضجاع *iḍjâ'*, inclining, reclining, lying down.

اضجم *aḍjam*, wry, awry (nose, mouth).

اضحاة *aḍḥât*, pl. اضحى *aḍḥā*, lamb sacrificed at the hour ضحى *ḍuḥân*.

اضحوكة *uḍḥûka-t*, pl. *aḍâḥîk*, jest, witty saying; ridiculous thing.

اضحى *aḍḥa*, later; — *aḍḥā*, see اضحاة *aḍḥât* above; — ة *uḍḥiyya-t*, pl. *aḍâḥiyy*, lamb for a sacrifice; — ليلة اضحية (اضحيانة) *laila-t iḍḥiyyà-t* (*iḍḥiyâna-t*), serene night.

اضخم *aḍḥam*, larger, bulkier; very large, bulky, comp. of ضخيم *ḍaḥîm*.

اضخومة *uḍḥûma-t*, artificial buttocks, hip-improvers.

اضداد *aḍdâd*, contraries, opposites, pl. of ضد *ḍidd*, *ḍudd*.

اضر *aḍurr*, misfortunes, losses, &c., pl. of ضرا *ḍarrâ'*;—*aḍr-in*, see اضرى *aḍrî*.

اضرا *aḍirrâ'*, pl. of ضرير *ḍarîr*, who has become blind, &c.

اضراب *aḍrâb*, pl. of ضرب *ḍarb*, contemporary; equal; — *iḍrâb*, taking back.

اضرار *aḍrâr*, injuries, hurts, pl. of ضرر *ḍarar*.

اضرام *iḍrâm*, setting on fire, conflagration.

اضرس *aḍras*, dumb.

اضرع *aḍra'*, submissive; f. *ḍar'â'*, with large udders.

اضرى *aḍrî* (اضر *aḍr-in*), sporting dogs, pl. of ضرو *ḍirw*, ضرى *ḍar-an*.

اضريج *iḍrîj*, red colour; red silk; yellow garment; courser.

اضز *aḍazz*, malicious, prone to anger.

اضطراب *iḍṭirâb*, disquieting, disquietude; violent emotion of any kind; perplexity.

اضطرار *iḍṭirâr*, necessity; force, constraint, violence; extreme misery; despair; — ى *iḍṭirâriyy*, forced to.

اضطرام *iḍṭirâm*, inflammation, conflagration.

اضطناك *iḍṭinâk*, misfortune, calamity.

اضطهاد *iḍṭihâd*, bad treatment, persecution, oppression.

اضعاف *aḍ'âf*, double quantities, &c., pl. of ضعف *ḍi'f*, q.v.

اضعف *aḍ'af*, weaker, weakest; most humble, comp. of ضعيف *ḍa'îf*.

اضكل *aḍkal*, poor and naked.

اضل *aḍall*, more erring, more wandering out of one's way.

اضلاع *aḍlâ'*, ribs, &c., pl. of ضلع *ḍil'*, *ḍila'*.

اضلال *aḍlâl*, pl. of ضل *ḍill*, abject, reprobate, worthless.

اضلع *aḍla'*, pl. ضلع *ḍul'*, big and strong; with large teeth;—*aḍlu'*, ribs, pl. of ضلع *ḍil'*, *ḍila'*.

اضلولة *uḍlûla-t*, pl. اضاليل *aḍâlîl*, erring, error.

(اضم) *aḍim*, A, INF. *aḍam*, be angry; practice malice against (ب *bi*); bite and kick.

اضم *aḍam*, pl. *aḍamât*, anger, envy.

اضمار *iḍmâr*, thought, idea; plotting; concealing in one's mind; what is left understood; rendering the second letter of a foot quiescent, when it has a vowel.

اضمامة *iḍmâma-t*, pl. *aḍâmîm*, leaves stitched together, copy-book, pamphlet; troop (of people, horses, &c.).

اضمحلال *iḍmiḥlâl*, disappearing, dispersion; fainting fit, swoon.

اضمن *aḍman*, who is a better security.

اضها *aḍhâ'*, ponds, pl. of ضهوة *ḍahwa-t*.

اضوا *aḍwâ'*, lights, pl. of ضو *ḍau'*, *ḍû'*.

اضوات *aḍwât*, ponds, pl. of اضاة *aḍât*.

اضوط *aḍwaṭ*, stupid.

امون ***aḍûn,*** **امياض** ***aḍyât,*** **ponds, pl. of** **اضاة** ***aḍât.***

اضياف ***aḍyâf,*** **guests, pl. of** **ضيف** ***ḍaif.***

اضيق ***aḍyaq,*** **f.** ***ḍîqâ', ḍûqa,*** **narrower; more pressed, thronged; more severe.**

(اط) *aṭṭ*, I, INF. *aṭîṭ*, crack, creak; scream, roar; feel compassion with (ل *li*).

اطار *aṭṭâr*, maker of hoops; — *iṭâr*, pl. *uṭur*, inclosure; circumference; outline; belt, strap; hoop.

اطاط *aṭṭâṭ*, screamer; — ة *iṭâṭa-t*, crack, creaking noise; sound; hunger.

اطاعة *iṭâ'a-t*, obedience; submission; resignation.

اطاقة *iṭâqa-t*, power; ability; capacity; power of endurance; reach.

اطال *âṭâl*, sides, hypochondres, pl. of اطل *iṭl, iṭil*; — ة *iṭâla-t*, prolonging, extending; delay.

اطام *âṭâm*, castles, &c., pl. of اطم *uṭm, uṭum*;—*iṭâm*, constipation; dysury.

اطاميم *aṭâmîm*, pl. feet.

اطاول *aṭâwil*, pl. of اطول *aṭwal*, taller, &c.

اطايب *aṭâyib*, pl. of اطيب *aṭyab*, better.

اطبا *aṭbâ'*, udders, pl. of طبى *ṭiby*; — *aṭibbâ'*, physicians, pl. of طبيب *ṭabîb*.

اطباع *aṭbâ'*, rivers, canals, &c., pl. of طبع *ṭib'*.

اطبخ *aṭbaḥ*, very stupid.

اطبع *aṭba'*, very dirty.

اطبقة *aṭbiqa-t*, lids, &c., pl. of طبق *ṭabaq*.

اطبة *aṭibba-t*, physicians, pl. of طبيب *ṭabîb*.

اطحل *aṭḥal*, f. *ṭaḥlâ'*, turbid, muddy; blackish grey, blackish green.

اطد *aṭad*, blackthorn, sloe; — II. *aṭṭad*, INF. *ta'ṭîd*, strengthen.

(اطر) *aṭar*, I, U, INF. *aṭr*, enclose; protect against (على *'ala*); — I., II. bend; fold; — II. live for a time with the parents; — V. being bent; be detained; stay always indoors; — V., VII. be crooked.

اطر *uṭur*, enclosures, &c., pl. of اطار *iṭâr*.

اطرا *iṭrâ'*, excessive praise, panegyric; seasoning.

اطراب *aṭrâb*, fragrant nosegay.

اطراد *iṭrâd*, expelling, banishing; — *iṭṭirâd*, following closely one another; being well connected, in good order.

اطرار *aṭrâr*, edges, boundaries, &c., pl. of طرة *ṭurra-t*.

اطراف *aṭrâf*, sides, &c., pl. of طرف *ṭaraf*; — *iṭṭirâf*, acquiring or purchasing new and beautiful things.

اطرش *aṭraś*, f. *ṭarśâ'*, pl. *ṭurś*, deaf.

اطرط *aṭraṭ*, f. *ṭarṭâ'*, with scanty or no eye-brows.

اطرق *aṭraq*, with crooked or weak legs; peaceable, submissive; — *aṭruq*, ة *aṭriqa-t*, and

اطرقا *aṭriqâ'*, roads, pl. of طريق *ṭarîq*.

اطروان *uṭruwân*, freshness; honeymoon; bloom of youth.

اطروش *uṭrûś*, deaf.

اطروفة *uṭrûfa-t*, new merchandise; curiosity, novelty.

اطسمة *uṭsumma-t*, the best of a tribe; assembly.

اطعام *iṭ'âm*, feeding.

اطعمة *aṭ'ima-t*, اطعمات *aṭ'amât*, victuals, &c. pl. of طعام *ṭa'âm*.

اطغا *iṭgâ'*, seducing, leading into error.

اطفا *iṭfâ'*, extinguishing.

اطفال *aṭfâl*, infants, children, pl. of طفل *ṭifl*.

اطفل *aṭfal*, more childish; more importunate.

اطل *iṭl, iṭil*, pl. *âṭâl*, side of the body, hypochondre; — *uṭl*, something, anything.

اطلا *aṭlâ'*, children, young ones, &c., pl. of طلا *ṭal-an, ṭalâ*, and طلو *ṭalw*.

اطلاع *iṭṭilâ'*, study; strict examination; sight, insight.
اطلاق *iṭlâq*, general meaning; generalisation.
اطلال *aṭlâl*, objects, persons, &c., pl. of طلل *ṭalal*.
اطلح *aṭlaḥ*, f. *ṭalḥâ*, stupid.
اطلس *aṭlas*, smooth; satin; worn out, shabby; dirty, black; suspicious; dog, wolf; thief.
اطلط *aṭlaṭ*, unhappy, unfortunate.
اطلى *aṭla*, f. *ṭalyâ'*, smeared with tar; mangy (camel); mange, itch; tumour.
(اطم) *aṭam*, I, INF. *aṭm*, bite into (ب *bi*); throw; narrow the mouth of a well; hang a house or tent with curtains, &c.; — *aṭim*, A, INF. *aṭam*, be angry; be added, joined; suffer from constipation; — II. INF. *ta'ṭîm*, cover; — IV. INF. *i'ṭâm*, lock; — V. INF. *ta'aṭṭum*, be in violent anger; be agitated with waves; be very dark; snore; conceal one's thoughts.
اطم *uṭm*, *uṭum*, pl. *âṭâm*, *uṭûm*, castle, small fortress, stone building with a flat roof.
اطماع *aṭmâ'*, pl. of طمع *ṭam'*, wages, &c.; pl. of طامع *ṭâmi'*, greedy, &c.; *iṭmâ'*, exciting to cupidity.
اطمع *aṭma'*, greedier, &c., comp. of طامع *ṭâmi'*.
اطمئنان *iṭmi'nân*, quietude, security.
اطناب *aṭnâb*, ropes of a tent, &c., pl. of طنب *ṭunub*; — *iṭnâb*, prolixity; sublimeness of style; — ة *iṭnâba-t*, roof to protect against the sun; sun-shade; umbrella; tent.
اطنان *aṭnân*, human bodies, &c., pl. of طن *ṭunn*, q.v.
اطهار *aṭhâr*, pl. of طهر *ṭahir*, طاهر *ṭâhir*, pure, &c.
اطوار *aṭwâr*, pl. of طور *ṭaur*, measures, manners, &c., q.v.
اطواق *aṭwâq*, juice of the cocoa-nut; — pl. of طوق *ṭauq*, necklace, &c. q.v.
اطور *aṭwar*, end, extremity; *al-aṭwarân*, the extremes, extremities; calamity.
اطول *aṭwal*, pl. *aṭâwil*, f. *ṭûla*, pl. *ṭuwal*, longer, taller.
اطوم *aṭûm*, sea-tortoise; sea-urchin; — *uṭûm*, castles, &c., pl. of اطم *uṭm*, *uṭum*.
اطياب *aṭyâb*, perfumes, &c., pl. of طيب *ṭîb*.
اطيب *aṭyab*, f. *ṭûba*, better, more pleasant, pl. *al-aṭâyib*, the best of any thing; f. pleasantness, happiness; a tree of Paradise.
اطير *aṭîr*, sin; guilt; gossiping talk.
اطيط *aṭîṭ*, cracking, creaking; cry of the camel; murmuring of empty bowels.
اطيفال *uṭaifâl*, pl. little children.
اطيمة *aṭîma-t*, hearth, fire-place, chimney.
اظار *aẕâr*, nurses, &c., pl. of ظئر *ẕi'r*; — *aẕẕâr*, nurse.
اظافير *aẕâfir*, cloves, pl. of اظفار *aẕfâr*; — nails, claws, &c., pl. of اظفور *aẕfûr*.
اظانين *aẕânîn*, opinions, &c., pl. of ظن *ẕann*.
اظب *aẕb-in*, اظبى *aẕbî*, gazelles, &c., pl. of ظبى *ẕaby*.
اظراب *aẕrâb*, the anterior molar teeth; roots of the teeth.
اظرف *aẕraf*, more elegant, &c., comp. of ظريف *ẕarîf*.
اظعان *aẕ'ân*, litters, sedan-chairs, pl. of ظعينة *ẕa'îna-t*.
اظفار *aẕfâr*, ة *aẕfâra-t*, pl. *aẕâfîr*, clove (spice).
اظفر *aẕfar*, with long nails, claws.
اظفور *aẕfûr*, pl. *aẕâfir*, nail (of the finger), claw, talon, clutch; vine-branch.
اظلال *aẕlâl*, shadows, shades, &c., pl. of ظل *ẕill*.
اظلم *aẕlam*, more cruel, unjust, oppressive; f. *ẕalmâ'*, dark; darkness.
اظما *aẕmâ'*, pl. of ظم *ẕim'*, thirst, &c.

المى *azma*, f. *zamyâ*, brown; bloodless; fleshless; blackish; with small eye-lids.

اظهار *izhâr*, publication; explanation; pretending; outward show; dissimulation.

اظهر *azhar*, clearer, more distinct, more evident.

اعابد *a'âbid*, slaves, &c., pl. of عبد *'abd*.

اعاتيب *a'âtîb*, subjects of blame, quarrel, &c., pl. of اعتوبة *u'tûba-t*.

اعاجل *a'âjil*, pl. young ones.

اعاجم *a'âjim*, pl. of اعجم, not Arab, foreign, &c., q.v.

اعاجيب *a'âjîb*, miracles, &c., pl. of اعجوبة *u'jûba-t*.

أعادة *i'âda-t*, repetition; return; extradition.

اعادى *a'âdî*, enemies, pl. of عدو *'aduww*.

اعارة *i'âra-t*, lending, loan.

اعاريب *a'ârîb*, nomadic Arabs, Bedouins, pl. of اعراب *a'râb*.

اعاريض *a'ârîḍ*, poems, metres, &c., pl. of عروض *'arûḍ*.

اعاصر *a'âṣir*, اعاصير *a'âṣîr*, hurricanes, pl. of اعصار *a'ṣâr*.

اعاقة *i'âqa-t*, obstacle, hindrance.

اعالة *i'âla-t*, poverty while encumbered with a numerous family.

اعالى *a'âlî*, pl. of اعلى *a'la*, higher, most high, &c.

اعاليم *a'âlîm*, signs, secret communications, pl. of اعلومة *u'lûma-t*.

اعانة *i'âna-t*, help, assistance.

اعب *a'abb*, poor; having a big nose.

اعبا *a'bâ'*, loads, luggage, pl. of عب *'ib'*; — *i'bâ'*, filling to the brim; planting densely.

اعبش *a'baś*, with running eyes.

اعبل *a'bal*, big and strong; a thick rope; granite; f. عبلا *'ablâ'*, a white rock visible from a distance.

اعبئة *a'bi'a-t*, coarse clothes, cloaks, pl. of عبا *'abâ'*, ة *'abât*.

اعتاب *i'tâb*, thresholds, pl. of عتبة *'ataba-t*.

اعتاق *i'tâq*, setting at liberty; giving leave.

اعتام *i'tâm*, getting dark.

اعتبار *i'tibâr*, steem; honour; respect; consideration; comparison; — ى *i'tibâriyy*, relative.

اعتجان *i'tijân*, kneading.

اعتد *a'tud*, preparations for a journey, &c., pl. of عتاد *'atâd* and عتدة *'utda-t*.

اعتدا *i'tidâ'*, enmity; injustice; iniquity; transgression.

اعتداد *i'tidâd*, (m.) self-complacency; pride.

اعتدال *i'tidâl*, equilibrium between two things; اعتدال الليل و النهار *i'tidâlu-'l-lail-i wa-'n-nahâr-i*, equinox; symmetry; due proportion; moderate state or temperature; (m.) corpulence; — ى *i'tidâliyy*, equinoctial.

اعتذار *i'tizâr*, excuse, apology.

اعترا *i'tirâ'*, coming suddenly (of a calamity, &c.).

اعتراض *i'tirâḍ*, encounter; obstacle; opposition; contradiction; animosity.

اعتراف *i'tirâf*, confession.

اعتراك *i'tirâk*, throng; (m.) kneading; brushing.

اعتزا *i'tizâ'*, deriving one's descent.

اعتزاز *i'tizâz*, becoming powerful or important.

اعتزال *i'tizâl*, abdication.

اعتزام *i'tizâm*, firm resolution; perseverance.

اعتساف *i'tisâf*, oppression; violence.

اعتصام *i'tiṣâm*, seeking refuge; innocence.

اعتطاب *i'tiṭâb*, ruin; (m.) hurt; injury.

اعتفا *i'tifâ'*, abdication, apology; justification.

اعتقاد *i'tiqâd*, confidence; trust; belief; article of faith.

اعتقال *i'tiqâl*, seizing; binding; imprisoning; being bound, &c.

اعتكار *i'tikâr*, darkness; clouds of dust.

اعتكاف *i'tikâf*, spiritual retirement, retreat.

اعتلا *i'tilâ'*, ascending, height.
اعتلال *i'tilâl*, pretext.
اعتماد *i'timâd*, confidence, reliance; firm resolution; (I L.) baptism.
اعتمام *i'timâm*, wearing the turban.
اعتنا *i'tinâ'*, great care, taking pains.
اعتناف *i'tinâf*, beginning; taking by force; abhorrence.
اعتناق *i'tinâq*, embracing, embrace.
اعتوبة *u'tûba-t*, subject of reproach, of a quarrel.
اعتياد *i'tiyâd*, custom; — ى *i'tiyâdiyy*, customary, usual.
اعتياز *i'tiyâz*, being in want, neediness.
اعتياش *i'tiyâś*, living on anything; livelihood.
اعتياض *i'tiyâḍ*, exchange.
اعتياق *i'tiyâq*, being prevented.
اعثك *i'sak*, left-handed; more difficult.
اعثى *a'sa*, f. *'aswâ'*, blackish; hairy; stupid; hyena; f. old woman.
اعجاب *i'jâb*, wondering, causing wonder.
اعجاز *a'jâz*, roots of palm-trees; — *i'jâz*, power of persuasion; — ة *i'jâza-t*, artificial thighs, hip-improvers.
اعجال *i'jâl*, hastening, accelerating; ripening.
اعجب *a'jab*, more wonderful, surprising.
اعجر *a'jar*, stout and fat; knotty, f. *'ajrâ'*, knotty stick.
اعجس *a'jas*, full in the waist.
اعجف *a'jaf*, thin, lean.
اعجل *a'jal*, quicker, quickest; the first.
اعجم *a'jam*, f. *'ajmâ'*, pl. *-ûn*, *a'âjim*, not an Arab; who speaks Arabic badly; foreigner; Persian; dumb; deaf; see عجما *'ajmâ'*; — ى *a'jamiyy*, not Arabian, foreign; a Persian.
اعجوبة *u'jûba-t*, anything wonderful, marvel, miracle, prodigy, phenomenon.
اعدا *a'dâ'*, enemies, pl. of عدو *'aduww*; — regions, &c., pl. of عدى *'id-an*.
اعداد *a'dâd*, numbers, &c., pl. of عد *'idd* and عدد *'adad*; — *i'dâd*, preparation; equipment.
اعدال *a'dâl*, pl. of عدل *'idl* and عديل *'adîl*, equal, &c., q.v.
اعدام *i'dâm*, annihilating; ruining.
اعدل *a'dal*, more or most equitable, just, comp. of عادل *'âdil*.
اعدى *a'dâ*, more or most hostile.
اعذار *a'ẓâr*, excuses, pl. of عذر *uẓr*; — *i'ẓâr*, banquet, festival; making excuses, excuse, IV. of (عذر), q.v.
اعذب *a'ẓab*, sweeter; — ة *a'ẓiba-t*, chastisements, &c., pl. of عذاب *'aẓâb*.
اعذر *a'ẓar*, excused.
اعر *a'arr*, f. *'arrâ'*, mangy; strong of neck and chest; f. a young girl.
اعرا *a'râ'*, open spaces, &c., pl. of عرا *'arâ'*; — pl. of عرو *'irw*, side; negligent.
اعراب *a'râb*, pl. nomadic Arabs, Bedouins, pl. *a'ârîb*; sing. *a'râbiyy*; — *i'râb*, grammatical inflection; syntax; grammatical analysis.
اعراش *a'râś*, thrones, &c., pl. of عرش *'arś*.
اعراص *a'râṣ*, open spaces, yards, &c., pl. of عرصة *'arṣa-t*.
اعراض *a'râḍ*, pl. of عرض *'arḍ*, *'irḍ*, *'araḍ*, and عرضة *'arḍa-t*, *'urḍa-t*, q.v.; — *i'râḍ*, petitioning, soliciting; exposition; turning one's back; return.
اعراف *a'râf*, pl. of عرف *'urf*, height, &c., q.v.; the wall between heaven and hell; purgatory.
اعرج *'araj*, f. *'arjâ'*, pl. *'urj*, *'urjân*, lame, halting; raven; f. hyena.
اعرف *a'raf*, f. *'urfâ'*, pl. *'urf*, having a mane, crested; with a long and strong neck; f. *al-'urfâ'*, hyena.
اعرق *a'raq*, deeply or more deeply rooted.
اعرم *a'ram*, f. *'armâ'*, pl. *'urm*, spotted white and black; herd

of sheep and goats mingled; spotted egg; pl. *'urmân*, pl. *'arâmîn*, not circumcised; f. a spotted snake.

اعز *a'azz*, f. عزى *'uzza*, dearer; more powerful, more important, &c., comp. of عزيز *'azîz*, q.v.; f. mistress, lady-love; name of an idol; — f. عزا *'azzâ'*, calamitous; calamity; — ة *a'izza-t* and—

اعزا *a'izzâ'*, pl. of عزيز *'azîz*, excellent, &c., q.v.

اعزاز *i'zâz*, magnificence, honour, reverence.

اعزال *a'zâl*, pl. of اعزل *a'zal*, q.v.

اعزب *a'zab*, f. *'azbâ'*, single, unmarried; bachelor; spinster.

اعزل *a'zal*, pl. *'uzl*, *'uzzal*, *'uzlân*, *a'zâl*, *ma'âzîl*, f. *'azlâ'*, pl. *'azâlî*, *'azâla*, who secludes himself; singled out; without arms, without a lance; السمك الاعزل *as-samak al-'azal*, spica virginis (a constellation).

اعساج *i'sâj*, stooping walk.

اعسام *a'sâm*, pl. forms of the body.

اعسان *a'sân*, pl. traces, remainders.

اعسر *a'sar*, f. *'asrâ'*, left-handed; more difficult, harder; disastrous.

اعسم *a'sam*, f. *'asmâ'*, pl. *'usm*, having a withered arm or leg.

اعشاب *i'sâb*, covering itself with green herbage; finding herbs for food.

اعشار *a'šâr*, pl. of عاشرة, gain in play; tenth parts, pl. of عشر *'ušr*; — ى *a'šâriyy*, decimal.

اعشاش *a'šâš*, nests on trees, pl. of عش *'ušš*.

اعشر *a'šar*, stupid.

اعشرا *a'širâ'*, pl. of عشير *'ašîr*, tenth part; cry of the hyena.

اعشم *a'šam*, f. *'ašmâ'*, of a mixed colour; dried up in dust; dim-sighted; f. dusty ground.

اعشى *a'ša*, f. *'ašwâ*, dim-sighted; blind; f. darkness; — ة *a'šiya-t*, evening meals, suppers, pl. of عشا *'ašâ'*.

اعص *a'ṣ-in*, اعصى *a'ṣî*, اعصا *a'ṣâ'*, staves, &c., pl. of عصا *'aṣ-an*, *'aṣâ*, q.v.

اعصاب *a'ṣâb*, nerves, sinews, &c., pl. of عصب *'aṣab*.

اعصار *a'ṣâr*, ages, &c., pl. of عصر *'aṣr*, *'iṣr*, &c.; — *i'ṣâr*, pl. *a'âṣîr*, *a'âṣir*, hurricane; — *i'ṣâr*, IV. of (عصر), q.v.

اعصج *a'ṣaj*, bald.

اعصل *a'ṣal*, pl. *'uṣl*, *'iṣâl*, crooked, not straight; having crooked legs; assiduous; f. *'aṣlâ*, thin, lean.

اعصم *a'ṣam*, f. *'aṣmâ'*, pl. *'uṣm*, having a red beak and red feet; having a white spot on the fore-foot; f. mountain goat.

اعضا *a'ḍâ'*, members, pl. of عضو *'uḍw*, *'iḍw*.

اعضاد *i'ḍâd*, help, assistance.

اعضب *a'ḍab*, f. *'aḍbâ'*, having one horn broken; having one hand short; who has lost his only brother; shortened (foot of a verse); weak.

اعطا *a'ṭâ'*, who gives much or more; — *i'ṭâ*, giving, bestowing.

اعطر *a'ṭar*, more or very much perfumed.

اعطيات *a'ṭiyât*, gifts, pl. of عطا *'aṭ-an*, *'aṭâ*.

اعطياة *i'ṭiyâ-t*, wages, pay.

اعطية *a'ṭiya-t*, gifts, pl. of عطا *'aṭ-an*, *'aṭâ*.

اعظامة *i'ẓâma-t*, greatness.

اعظم *a'ẓam*, f. *'uẓma*, greater; more powerful; more important; better; الصدر الاعظم *aṣ-ṣadru-'l-a'ẓam*, prime minister; — (adv.) more; — *a'ẓum*, bones, pl. of عظم *'aẓm*.

اعفا *i'fâ'*, cure; deliverance; excuse; — *a'iffâ'*, pl. of عفيف *'afîf*, chaste.

اعفت *a'fat*, stupid; awkward; clumsy.

اعفص *a'faṣ*, who shows his nakedness; who talks ribaldry or foolish things.

اعفش *a'faš*, with running eyes.

اعفك *a'fak*, f. *'afkâ'*, very stupid; flighty and fickle; left-handed; f. restive she-camel.

اعق *a'aqq*, disobedient;—ة *a'iqqa-t*, pl. of عاق *'âqq*, disobedient and of عقيق *'aqîq*, mountain torrent, &c.

اعقاب *a'qâb*, sons, &c., pl. of عقب *'aqb* and عقب *'aqib*; ends, issues, &c., pl. of عقب *'uqb*.

اعقار *a'qâr*, pl. trees.

اعقب *a'qub*, black eagles, pl. of عقاب *'uqâb*.

اعقد *a'qad*, f. *'aqdâ'*, pl. *'uqd*, knotty; stammering; having a flexible tail, therefore: dog, wolf, goat; f. maid-servant.

اعقر *a'qar*, f. *'aqrâ'*, toothless; f. sand-hill.

اعقف *a'qaf*, f. *'aqfâ*, crooked; boorish; poor; f. an iron hook on a stick; cramp-iron.

اعقل *a'qal*, f. *'aqlâ'*, more intelligent.

اعلال *a'lâl*, indispositions, &c., pl. of علة *'illa-t*; — *i'lâl*, interchange of the so-called weak letters, ا, و, ى.

اعلام *a'lâm*, signs, flags, mountains, &c., pl. of علم *'alam*; — *i'lâm*, instruction; information; communication; placard.

اعلان *i'lân*, publication; advertisement.

اعلطة *a'liṭa-t*, pl. of علاط *'ilâṭ*, q.v.

اعلم *a'lam*, f. *'almâ'*, more learned; knowing better; والله اعلم *wa-'l-lâh a'lam*, God knows best; f. cuirass.

اعلومة *u'lûma-t*, pl. *a'âlîm*, sign, (m.) secret communication.

اعلى *a'la*, pl. علی *'ul-an*, *a'âlî*; f. *'ulyâ'*, pl. *'ul-an*, *'ulyayât*, higher, nobler, sublime; f. the tribe Koreish; — f. *'alyâ'* and *'alwâ'*, height, summit; Heaven; noble deed, exploit.

اعم *a'amm*, f. *'ammâ'*, pl. *'umm*, high; great; more general; multitude; — *a'umm*, ة *a'imma-t*, uncles (on father's side), &c., pl. of عم *'amm*.

اعما *a'mâ'*, errors, pl. of عمو *'amw*; — ignorants, &c., pl. of اعمى *a'mî*.

اعمار *a'mâr*, lives, lifetimes, &c., pl. of عمر *'umr*; — *i'mâr*, cultivating, rendering habitable.

اعمال *a'mâl*, deeds, actions, &c., pl. of عمل 'amal.

اعمام *a'mâm*, (paternal) uncles, pl. of عم *'amm*.

اعمتة *a'mita-t*, clews of wool, pl. of عميتة *'amîta-t*.

اعمدة *a'mida-t*, columns, &c., pl. of عمود *'amûd*.

اعمر *a'mar*, better populated, more cultivated.

اعمش *a'maś*, f. *'amśâ'*, blear-eyed, with running eyes.

اعمص *a'maṣ*, (m.) the same.

اعممون *a'mumûn*, paternal uncles, pl. of عم *'amm*.

اعمه *a'mah*, f. *'amhâ*, without signs to mark the road (desert).

اعموى *a'mawiyy*, referring to the blind.

اعمى *a'ma*, f. *'amyâ'*, pl. *'umy*, *'umyân*, blind; dark; *al-'amayân*, inundation and conflagration; — pl. اعما *a'mâ'*, ignorant men; fools; deserts.

اعنا *a'nâ'*, sides, pl. of عنا *'anân*; — *i'nâ'*, allusion, IV. of (عنى).

اعنات *i'nât*, insertion of a letter in a rhyme; (m.) torment; vexation.

اعناق *a'nâq*, necks, &c., pl. of عنق *'unq*, *'unuq*, *'unaq*.

اعنان *a'nân*, objects coming into view, apparitions, pl. of عنن *'anan*;—*i'nân*, bridling, checking with the reins.

اعنجة *a'nija-t*, ropes, connections, &c., pl. of عناج *'inâj*, q.v.

اعنق *a'naq*, long-necked; name of a celebrated stallion; f. *'anqâ'*, fabulous bird, griffin, phœnix; mountain-peak; calamity; — *a'nuq*, kids, &c., pl. of عناق *'anâq*.

اعنة *a'inna-t*, pl. of عنان *'inân*, bridle, &c.

اعوار *i'wâr*, suspicion.

اعواز *i'wâz*, neediness, indigence, destitution.

اعوام *i'wâm*, years, pl. of عام *'âm*.

اعوان *a'wân*, pl. of عون *'aun*, helper, servant, &c.

اعوج *a'waj*, crooked, malicious; f. *'aujâ'*, bow; lean, slender.

اعوجاج *i'wijâj*, crookedness; falseness, perfidy, malice.

اعود *a'wad*, more advantageous (على *'ala*).

اعور *a'war*, f. *'aurâ'*, pl. *'ûr*, *'ûrân*, *'îrân*, one-eyed; corrupted, perverse, bad; deceived; bad guide, wrong road; effaced writing; pl. *a'âwir*, nits, see عورا *'aurâ'*.

اعوس *a'was*, f. *'ausâ'*, who draws in the corners of the mouth; furbisher of knives or swords.

اعوص *a'waṣ*, f. *'auṣâ'*, pl. *'ûṣ*, unintelligible, difficult to understand; unusual; see عوصا.

اعون *a'wan*, more helping.

اعيا *a'yâ'*, pl. of عي *'ayy*, incapable, &c., and عيا *'ayâ'*, difficult, &c.; — *i'yâ'*, fatigue.

اعياد *a'yâd*, feasts, &c., pl. of عيد *'îd*.

اعيان *a'yân*, great men, grandees, pl. of عين *'ain*.

اعيس *a'îs*, f. *a'îsâ'*, pl. *'îs*, whitish-yellow (camel).

اعيط *a'yaṭ*, f. *'aiṭâ'*, pl. *'îṭ*, long-necked; high; proud; stiff-necked, obdurate.

اعين *a'yan*, f. *'ainâ'*, pl. *'în*; having a large black pupil; wild bull; visible, in view, evident; perforated; who has many servants; green; — *a'yun*, *a'yunât*, eyes, pl. of عين *'ain*; — ة *a'yina-t*, plough-shares, pl. of عيان *'iyân*.

اعيى *a'ya*, more stammering; more obdurate; — ة *u'yiyya-t*, stammering (s.); — *a'yiya-t*, اعييا *a'yiyâ*, pl. of عيى *'ayiyy*, stammering (adj.).

اغا *âgâ*, pl. *agâwat*, Aga, eunuch (Turk.).

اغاثة *igâsa-t*, help, assistance.

اغارة *igâra-t*, raid.

اغاريد *agârîd*, warblings of birds, pl. of اغرود *ugrûd*.

اغاظة *igâẓa-t*, rousing to anger, irritating.

اغاليج *agâlîj*, tender branches, pl. of اغلوج *uglûj*.

اغاليط *agâlîṭ*, misemployed or misleading words, pl. of اغلوطة *uglûṭa-t*.

اغاليق *agâlîq*, bolts, &c., pl. of غلق *galaq*.

اغان *agân-in*, اغاني *agânî*, songs, melodies, pl. of اغنية *ugniya-t*, &c.

اغاوي *agâwî*, snares, &c., pl. of اغوية *ugwiyya-t*.

اغبث *agbaṡ*, ash-coloured; lion.

اغبر *agbar*, f. *gabrâ'*, pl. *gubr*, dusty; dust-coloured; dark; عام اغبر *'âm agbar*, barren year; quickly passing; soon effaced; *al-agbar*, wolf; *al-gabrâ'*, the earth; بنو الغبرا *banû-'l-gabrâ'*, poor people, travellers; tomb.

اغبرار *igbirâr*, dust-colour; becoming dusty; secret hatred, grudge.

اغبس *agbas*, dark.

اغبى *agba*, f. *gabyâ'*, having dense foliage; more stupid, comp. of غبى *gabiyy*.

اغتام *agtâm*, pl. of اغتم *agtam*, q.v.

اغتباط *igtibâṭ*, contentment in prosperity.

اغتباق *igtibâq*, evening cup.

اغتراب *igtirâb*, travelling into foreign countries, becoming a stranger to one's own.

اغترار *igtirâr*, infatuation; ambition; being deceived; being inattentive.

اغتراز *igtirâz*, being ready for departure.

اغتراف *igtirâf*, drawing water.

اغتسال *igtisâl*, ablution.

اغتشاش *igtiśâś*, revolt, rebellion.

اغتصاب *igtiṣâb*, open violence; seizing violently.

اغتصاص *igtiṣâṣ*, great anxiety; suffocation.
اغتم *agtam*, pl. *gutm*, pl. pl. *agtâm*, speaking unintelligibly or barbarously; — ى *agtamiyy*, not Arab; foreigner; barbarian.
اغتمار *igtimâr*, submersion; sinking.
اغتماض *igtimâḍ*, closing or blinking one's eyes.
اغتمام *igtimâm*, sadness, sorrow, melancholy.
اغتنام *igtinâm*, getting spoil; seizing an opportunity.
اغتياب *igtiyâb*, calumniating the absent; back-biting.
اغتيار *igtiyâr*, vying, competing with each other.
اغتياظ *igtiyâẕ*, burst of anger.
اغتيال *igtiyâl*, assaulting, rushing against; seizing suddenly.
اغثا *agṡâ'*, scums. &c., pl. of غثا *guṡâ'*, *guṡṡâ'*.
اغثر *agṡar*, f. *gaṡrâ*, pl. *guṡr*, dark reddish brown; dirty green; woolly; moss; common or vulgar man; lion; f. crowd, rabble; threats; hyena; pl. populace.
اغثى *agṡa*, lion (robber).
اغدرة *agdira-t*, ponds, pl. of غدير *gadîr*.
اغدية *agdiya-t*, breakfasts, luncheons, pl. of غدا *gadâ'*.
اغر *agarr*, f. *garrâ'*, pl. *gurr*, having a white spot on the forehead (horse); white; shining brightly; very hot; eminent, distinguished; f. *al-garrâ'*, Mecca; first night of the full moon; hottest part of the day; pl. the worthies; water-bubbles; — ة *agirra-t*, pl. of غرار *girâr*, head of an arrow or lance; also—
اغرا *agirrâ'*, pl. of غرير *garîr*, easily deceived, inexperienced; — *igrâ'*, instigation.
اغرار *agrâr*, pl. of غر *girr*, unexperienced, easily deceived.
اغراس *agrâs*, grafts, proselytes, pl. of غرس *gars*.
اغراض *agrâḍ*, designs, intentions, &c., pl. of غرض *garaḍ*, q.v.
اغراق *igrâq*, drowning, plunging; exaggeration.
اغرب *agrub*, ة *agriba-t*, pl. of غراب *garâb*, raven, crow, &c., q.v.
اغرل *agral*, uncircumcised; commodious; abundant; — long (= غرل *garil*).
اغرود *agrûd*, ة *ugrûda-t*, pl. *ugârîd*, warbling of birds.
اغريض *igrîḍ*, fresh and tender; palm-blossom.
اغريقى *igrîqiyy*, Greek, Grecian.
اغزل *agzal*, erotic poet; frequently recurring.
اغسان *agsân*, pl. worn-out clothes; manners, morals, character.
اغشى *agśa*, f. *gaśwâ*, having the head entirely white (horse, &c.).
اغصان *agṣân*, branches, &c., pl. of غصن *guṣn*.
اغضا *igḍâ'*, knitting the brows; averting the face.
اغضاب *igḍâb*, moving to anger, irritating.
اغضف *agḍaf*, pl. *guḍf*, having flabby ears; with lowered eye-lids (lion); sinking, falling down (night), dark; densely feathered (arrow); luxurious (life).
اغط *agaṭṭ*, rich, abundant, luxurious.
اغطش *agṭaś*, f. *gaṭśâ'*, dim-sighted; dark; f. pathless desert.
اغطف *agṭaf*, easy, luxurious; having heavy eyebrows or lashes.
اغطية *agṭiya-t*, coverings, veils, pl. of غطا *giṭâ'*.
اغفا *agfâ'*, chaff, pl. of غفى *gafan*.
اغفال *igfâl*, causing to forget or neglect.
اغفر *agfar*, not susceptible.
اغلا *iglâ'*, being dear, costly; making dear; — also ة *iglâ'a-t*, boiling, bubbling, ebullition.
اغلاق *aglâq*, bolts, &c., pl. of غلق *galaq*; — *iglâq*, locking, shutting, fastening a door.
اغلال *aglâl*, pl. of غل *gull*, chains,

manacles, &c.; — *iglâl*, deceit, fraud.

اغلب *aglab*, f. *galbâ'*, pl. *gulb*, having a high and thick-set neck: lion; high; powerful; numerous; *al-aglab*, the highest number, the most probable case; *fi-'l-aglab*, mostly, pre-eminently; f. with rich vegetation.

اغلف *aglaf*, f. *galfâ*, pl. *gulf*, sheathed, encased, under envelope; uncircumcised; rough, untamed; عيش اغلف *'aiś aglaf*, *al-galfâ'*, easy and comfortable life.

اغلمة *aglima-t*, boys, servants, &c., pl. of غلام *gulâm*.

اغلوج *uglûj*, pl. *agâlîj*, tender, flexible branch.

اغلوطة *uglûṭa-t*, pl. *agâlîṭ*, a wrong or misleading word.

اغلى *agla*, dearer, more expensive.

اغم *agamm*, f. *gammâ'*, covering all; more grievous; see غما.

اغما *agmâ*, pl. of غمى *gaman*, in a swoon, fainting, and of غمى *gaman*, roof; visor.

اغماد *agmâd*, sheaths, scabbards, &c., pl. of غمد *gimd*; — *igmâd*, sheathing, putting one thing in another.

اغماض *igmâḍ*, shutting the eyes, conniving.

اغمرا *agmirâ'*, masses of water, pl. of غمير *gamîr*.

اغمص *agmaṣ*, with watering eyes.

اغمض *agmaḍ*, more unintelligible.

اغمية *agmiya-t*, roofs, visors, pl. of غمى *gaman*.

اغن *agann*, f. *gannâ'*, speaking through the nose; screaming; singing; well populated; richly overgrown.

اغنا *agnâ'*, pl. things, outfit; — *ignâ'*, enriching.

اغنام *agnâm*, sheep, &c., pl. of غنم *ganam*.

اغنيا *agniyâ'*, pl. of غنى *ganiyy*, rich.

اغنية *ugniya-t*, *igniya-t*, *igniyya-t*, *ugniyya-t*, song, air, melody.

اغوا *igwâ'*, seduction, temptation; deceit.

اغوار *agwâr*, caves, &c., pl. of غار *gâr*, q.v.

اغواط *agwâṭ*, plains, &c., pl. of غائط *gâ'iṭ*, *gâyiṭ*.

اغوسطوس *agûsṭûs*, (m.) month of August.

اغول *agwal*, commodious, easy (life); rushing along, coming over suddenly.

اغوى *agwa*, more erring, more easily led astray; — ة *ugwiyya-t*, pl. *agâwî*, what leads astray and into perdition; snare; pitfall; danger.

اغيد *agyad*, f. *gaidâ'*, pl. غيدى *gaidâ*, *gîd*, young, delicate and supple; having one's head bent; richly overgrown.

اغيف *agyaf*, nodding (before falling asleep); luxurious.

اغين *agyan*, f. *gainâ'*, pl. *gîn*, dark green, see غينا.

اف *âf*, ة *âfa-t*, pl. *âfât*, damage, loss; calamity; harm; bane; — *aff*, little, small quantity; — *iff*, pusillanimity; — *uff*, parings or dirt of the nails; chip; small quantity; — *uff-i*, *uff-a*, *uff-u*, *uff-un*, *uff-in*, افا *uff-an*, oh! alas! woe! fie! — ة *uffa-t*, weakling; poor.

(اف) *aff*, U, INF. *aff*, call out اف *uffa* from pain or grief; — II. INF. *ta'fîf*, V. INF. *ta'affuf*, the same.

افات *âfât*, damages, &c., pl. of اف *âf*; — *ifât*, transitoriness, perishableness; — ة *ifâta-t*, frustration; making disappear.

افاتيح *afâtîḥ*, seed-lobes, pl. of افتوحة *uftûḥa-t*.

افاحة *ifâḥa-t*, diffusing odour, fragrance.

افاحيص *afâḥîṣ*, holes in the ground, &c., pl. of افحوص *ufḥûṣ*.

افادة *ifâda-t*, advantage, gain.

افارقة *afâriqa-t*, افاريق *afârîq*, troops of people, &c., pl. of فرقة *firqa-t*.

افاضل *afâḍil*, pl. of افضل *afḍal*, more excellent, &c.

افاضة *ifâḍa-t*, giving abundantly; clear delivery; heaving to and fro.

افاطير *afâṭîr*, splits, &c., pl. of افطور *ufṭûr*.

افاعى *afâ'î*, serpents, vipers, pl. of افعى *af'an*.

افاعيل *afâ'îl*, actions, deeds, verbs, &c., pl. of فعل *fi'l*.

افاف *affâf*, who sighs and groans much; — *ifâf*, pusillanimity; cowardice; moment, epoch.

افاق *âfâq*, regions, &c., pl. of افق *ufq*; — *affâq*, great traveller; adventurer; — ة *ifâqa-t*, re-animation; recovery; (m.) awakening; rest, pause; — ى *afâqiyy*, horizontal; universal.

افاك *affâk*, great liar.

افاكل *afâkil*, افاكيل *afâkîl*, pl. of افكل *afkal*, *ifkil*, troop.

افاكيه *afâkîh*, things which cause wonder or merriment, pl. of افكوهة *ufkûha-t*.

افان *iffân*, *affân*, time.

افانين *afânîn*, branches; manners, ways, varieties, pl. of فنن *fanan* and افنون *afnûn*.

افاوج *afâwij*, افاويج *afâwîj*, troops, &c., pl. of فوج *fauj*, q.v.

افاويق *afâwîq*, milk-flows, pl. of فيقة *faiqa-t* (m.).

افاويه *afâwîh*, mouths, &c., pl. of فوه *fûh*.

افائك *afâ'ik*, lies, pl. of افيكة *afîka-t*.

(افت) *afat*, INF., *aft*, alienate, prevent, restrain from.

افت *aft*, patient, enduring and swift (camel); — *ift*, the same; lie; — *âfat*=افة *âfa-t*, damage, loss, calamity.

افتا *iftâ'*, solving a question of law or conscience; judicial decision.

افتتاح *iftitâḥ*, opening, beginning; consecrating; inauguration; introduction; conquest; — ى *iftitâḥiyy*, introductory, preliminary.

افتتان *iftitân*, instigating to revolt or discord; seduction; temptation.

افتجا *iftijâ'*, robbery by sudden invasion.

افتحاص *iftiḥâṣ*, disquisition, examination.

افتح *aftaḥ*, f. *fatḥâ'*, having weak joints or limbs; with soft soles; with large feet or paws; blear-eyed; see فتخا.

افتخار *iftiḫâr*, boasting; glory.

افتدا *iftidâ'*, ransom.

افترا *iftirâ'*, lie; (m.) insult, offence; calumny.

افترار *iftirâr*, flashing; showing the teeth.

افتراص *iftirâṣ*, availing one's self of an opportunity.

افتراض *iftirâḍ*, precept; (m.) supposition, hypothesis.

افتراق *iftirâq*, separation.

افتراك *iftirâk*, (m.) grinding to pieces; agitation (of a sick person).

افتصال *iftiṣâl*, disjunction, separation; weaning.

افتضاح *iftiḍâḥ*, being dishonoured; exposure.

افتضاض *iftiḍâḍ*, defloration.

افتعال *ifti'âl*, action.

افتق *aftaq*, f. *fatqâ'*, afflicted with a rupture, see فتقا.

افتقاد *iftiqâd*, visitation, visit; trial, probing.

افتقار *iftiqâr*, poverty.

افتك *aftak*, more daring, more venturesome; readier to shed blood.

افتكار *iftikâr*, thought, contemplation, meditation.

افتل *aftal*, pl. *fatl*, f. *fatlâ'*, having the legs wide apart; distorted.

افتهام *iftihâm*, comprehension, understanding.

افتوخة *uftûḫa-t*, pl. *afâtîḫ*, seed-lobe; what is germinating.

افتى *afta*, later born, younger; manlier, more courageous.

افجيج *ifjîj*, valley, mountain-cleft, bed of a river.

افحا *afḥâ'*, seasonings, &c., pl. of فحا *faḥan, faḥa, fiḥa.*

افحش *afḥaś*, more shameful, baser, comp. of فاحش *fâḥiś.*

افحوص *ufḥûṣ*, pl. افاحيص *afâḥîṣ*, hole in the ground; nest of the bird Qaṭâ'.

(افح) *afaḥ*, INF. *afḥ*, hit on the crown of the head.

افخرة *afḫira-t*, rich garments.

افخم *afḫam*, more powerful, more respected.

(افد) *afid*, A, INF. *afad*, hasten, and, by opposition, tarry; approach; come up.

افد *afad*, term, end, death; — *afid*, who hastens; who tarries; — ة *afada-t*, delay.

افدا *ifdâ'*, exacting a ransom from a prisoner.

افدع *afda'*, f. *fadâ'*, having a distorted limb; distorted; see فدعا.

افدنة *afdina-t*, yokes of oxen, &c., pl. of فدان *fadân*, q.v.

افذ *afazz*, not feathered (arrow).

افذاذ *afẕâẕ*, pl. of فذ *faẕẕ*, single, isolated, &c.

(افر) *afar*, I, INF. *afr, ufûr*, cross (على *'ala*); run, jump; attack; be very hot, boil; get fat; be zealous and quick in serving; drive away; — *afir*, A, INF. *afar*, be very hot and boil violently; grow fat.

افر *afarr*, f. *farrâ'*, showing beautiful teeth in laughing or smiling; — ة *ufurra-t*, troop; mixture; adversity.

افرا *afrâ'*, wild asses, pl. of فرا *farâ'*.

افراخ *afrâḫ*, young birds, &c., pl. of فرخ *farḫ*.

افراد *afrâd*, pl. of فرد *fard*, individual, &c., q.v.; — *ifrâd*, separating; making unequal; reducing to the simplest expression; isolation.

افراز *ifrâz*, separating, distinguishing, sequestering.

افراس *afrâs*, horses, mares, pl. of فرس *faras*.

افراض *ifrâḍ*, precept; assignment; present.

افراط *ifrâṭ*, excess; extreme; exaggeration; superfluity.

افراغ *ifrâg*, emptying; casting metals; putting into shape.

افراق *ifrâq*, recovery.

افرخ *afruḫ*, ة *afriḫa-t*, young birds, &c., pl. of فرخ *farḫ*.

افرس *afras*, clever horseman.

افرض *afraḍ*, very learned in divine law.

افرغ *afrag*, f. *fargâ'*, free of cares; making large wounds; — ة *afriga-t*, vacancies, &c., pl. of فراغ *firâg*, q.v.

افرقا *afriqâ'*, افرقة *afriqa-t*, compartments, &c., pl. of فريق *farîq*, q.v.

افرنج *afranj, ifranj*, Frank, French, European; — ى *afranjiyy*, European.

افرنسة *afransa-t*, France; — ى *afransiyy*, Frenchman, French.

افريز *ifrîz*, roof for protection against rain; frieze; cornice.

افريقى *afrîqiyy*, African; — ة *afrîqiyya-t*, Africa.

افزاز *afzâz*, pl. of فز *fazz*, excitable, fickle, &c.

افزاع *ifzâ'*, frightening, terrifying.

افساد *ifsâd*, corrupting, adulterating; instigation to mischief or revolt; oppression.

افسق *afsaq*, more or most perverse, wicked, vile.

افسنتين *afsintîn* (*absintîn*), wormwood.

افشا *ifśâ'*, divulging a secret.

افشغ *afśag*, with a protruding tooth, having the teeth separated.

افشل *afśal*, (m.) left-handed; f. *faślâ'*, the left hand.

افشين *ifśîn*, (m.) formula of prayer.

افصاح *ifṣâḥ*, speech, IV. (فصح).

افصال *ifṣâl*, death.

افصح *afṣaḥ*, more eloquent, clearer; more abundant, comp. of فصح *faṣḥ*, فصيح *faṣîḥ*.

افصم *afṣam*, broken, torn.
افضال *afḍâl*, superfluities, excellencies, &c., pl. of فضل *faḍl*; — *ifḍâl*, superiority; eminence.
افضل *afḍal*, more or most excellent; better deserving; more learned.
افط *afaṭṭ*, having a flat nose.
افطار *ifṭâr*, break of fasting; breakfast.
افطس *afṭas*, f. *faṭsâ'*, flat-nosed.
افطور *ufṭûr*, pl. *afâṭîr*, split, fissure, crevice; scratch, scar.
افظع *afẓa'*, more shameful, comp. of فظيع.
افعا *af'â'*, perfumes, scents.
افعوان *uf'uwân*, male viper.
افعى *af'an*, pl. *afâ'î*, viper, serpent.
افف *afaf*, a little, small quantity, trifles.
(افق) *afaq*, I, INF. *afq*, travel to distant parts, all over the world; give more to the one than the other; deceive; conquer; circumcise; — *afiq*, A, INF. *afaq*, attain to the highest distinction; — V. INF. *ta'affuq*, come from distant climates.
افق *ufq*, *ufuq*, *afaq*, pl. *âfâq*, climate, region, country; horizon; the wide world; — *âfaq*, uncircumcised; — *âfiq*, *afiq*, far superior; — *âfiq*, *ufuq*, quick, swift; — ة *afaqa-t*, hypochondre; — *ufqa-t*, prepuce; — ى *ufuqiyy*, *afaqiyy*, horizontal.
افقار *ifqâr*, impoverishing (s.).
افقر *afqar*, poorer, more wretched.
(افك) *afak*, I, *afik*, A, INF. *ifk*, *afk*, *afak*, *ufûk*, lie; — INF. *ifk*, cause to change one's purpose or opinion; cause to tell a lie; thwart one's wishes, declare them to be unlawful; — pass. *ufiq*, INF. *afk*, produce nothing from want of rain; have little understanding; — II. INF. *ta'fâk*, lie; — VIII. INF. *it'ifâk*, be turned topsy-turvy, overthrown.
افك *afik*, liar; — *ifk*, ة *ifka-t*, lie; — *ufuk*, great liars, pl. of افوك *afûk*.
افكار *afkâr*, thoughts, &c., pl. of فكر *fikr*.
افكل *afkal*, *ifkil*, fright; a kind of wood-pecker; pl. *afâkil*, *afâkîl*, troop; *bi-afâkili-hum*, all of them.
افكوهة *ufkûha-t*, pl. *afâkîh*, what causes wonder or merriment.
(افل) *afal*, I, U, *afil*, A, INF. *ufûl*, vanish, disappear (moon); — INF. *ufûl*, *afal*, dry up (milk of a suckling woman); — *afil*, INF. *afal*, be alert, quick; — II. INF. *ta'fîl*, procure honour, respect to anybody; — V. INF. *ta'afful*, be proud.
افل *âfil*, ة *âfila-t*, big with young (lioness).
افلا *aflâ'*, wide waterless deserts, pl. of فلاة *falât*; foals, pl. of فلو *filw*.
افلات *iflât*, help to escape; escape.
افلاح *iflâḥ*, good fortune, prosperity.
افلاس *iflâs*, poverty; (m.) bankruptcy.
افلاطون *aflâṭûn*, Plato.
افلاق *aflâq*, mountain-clefts, &c., pl. of فلق *falaq*, q.v.
افلاك *aflâk*, spheres, heavenly bodies, &c., pl. of فلك *falak*, q.v.
افلال *aflâl*, breaks, rents; fugitives, &c., pl. of فل *fall*; — deserts without rain, pl. of فل *full*, fill.
افلج *aflaj*, f. *faljâ'*, having fingers or teeth far apart; (m.) gouty, paralysed.
افلح *aflaḥ*, having the nether lip split.
(افن) *afan*, I, INF. *afn*, milk out of the proper time; exhaust all milk in the udder; have little milk; give little understanding to anybody (God); — pass. be spoiled (food).
افن *afn*, *afan*, weakness of intellect.
افنا *ifnâ'*, annihilation.
افناق *afnâq*, high-bred stallions, pl. of فنيق *fanîq*.

افنان *afnân*, branches, pl. of فنن *fanan*.

افند *afnud*, silliness;—ى *afandî*, pl. *afandiyya-t*, master, sir, gentleman, monsieur (Turk. from the Greek αὐθέντης).

افنون *afnûn*, pl. *afânîn*, class, category; manner, way; — *ufnûn*, snake; bent; obscure speech; calamity; beginning.

افنى *afna*, rich, full; f. *fanwâ'*, having a rich head of hair; densely branched (also *afann*); more perishable, comp. of فانى *fânî*; — ة *afniya-t*, enclosures in front of houses, pl. of فنا *finâ'*.

افها *afhâ'*, mouths, pl. of فوه *fûh*.

افهام *ifhâm*, making understand.

افواج *afwâj*, troops, crowds, flocks, &c., pl. of فوج *fauj*.

افواق *afwâq*, pl. of فوق *fûq*, lank, &c.; awakenings, remembrances, pl. of فيقة *faiqa-t* (m.).

افواه *afwâh*, mouths, &c., pl. of فوه *fûh*.

افوس *af'us*, axes, &c., pl. of فاس *fa's*.

افوغ *afwag*, having thick lips.

افوف *afûf*, in great haste.

افوق *afwaq*, f. *fauqâ'*, broken at the notch; see فوقا.

افوك *afûk*, pl. *ufuk*, great liar; — *ufûk*, INF. of (افك).

افول *af'ul*, omens, &c., pl. of فال *fa'l*.

افوه *afwah*, f. *fauhâ'*, *fahwâ'*, having a large mouth, a wide opening.

افيا *afyâ'*, pl. of فى *fai'*, shadow, &c., q.v.

افيال *afyâl*, elephants, pl. of فيل *fîl*.

افيح *afyaḥ*, f. *faiḥâ'*, pl. *fîḥ*, extensive, spacious; see فيحا.

افئدة *af'ida-t*, the intestines; heart, lungs and liver, pl. of فواد *fu'âd*.

افيق *afîq*, f. ة, excellent; misfortune.

افيكة *afîkat*, pl. افائك *'afâ'ik*, liar.

افين *afîn*, stupid; corrupted, spoiled.

افيون *afyûn*, *ifyaun*, opium; روح الافيون *rûhu-'l-'afyûn*, laudanum.

اقاتة *iqâta-t*, nutrition, feeding; power.

اقاح *aqâḥ-in*, اقاحى *aqâḥî*, camomiles, pl. of اقحوان *uqḥuwân*.

اقاديح *aqâdîḥ*, arrows without feathers and head, satires, &c., pl. of قدح *qidḥ*.

اقارب *aqârib*, near relations, pl. of اقرب *aqrab*.

اقارع *aqâri'*, pl. of اقرع *aqra'*, very hard; cutting, sharp, &c.

اقازل *aqâzil*, pl. of اقزل *aqzal*, halting, limping.

اقاسيم *aqâsîm*, parts, &c., pl. of قسم *qism* and اقسومة *uqsûma-t*.

اقاصر *aqâṣir*, pl. of اقصر *aqṣar*, shorter.

اقاصى *aqâṣî*, pl. of اقصى, extreme, farthest.

اقاصير *aqâṣîr*, pl. fords.

اقاصيص *aqâṣîṣ*, tales, stories, pl. of اقصوصة *aqṣûṣa-t*.

اقاطع *aqâṭi'*, cut off branches, &c., pl. of قطيع *qaṭî'*.

اقاطيع *aqâṭî'*, objects sent to indicate the break of friendship, pl. of اقطوعة *uqṭû'a-t*.

اقالة *iqâla-t*, legal annullation of a bargain; pardon; watering (beasts) at noon; (m.) deliverance, release.

اقاليم *aqâlîm*, climates, &c., pl. of اقليم *iqlîm*.

اقامة *iqâma-t*, staying, remaining, stopping; establishing; performing; raising of the dead; the second and last call for prayer.

اقانيم *aqânîm*, roots, &c., pl. of اقنوم *uqnûm*, q.v.

اقاوم *aqâwim*, اقاويم *aqâwîm*=اقايم q.v.

اقاويل *aqâwîl*, speeches, sayings, &c., pl. of قول *qaul*.

اقايم *aqâyim*, peoples, tribes, &c., pl. of قوم *qaum*.

اقب *aqabb*, f. *qabbâ'*, pl. قب *qabb*, having a very slender waist.

اقبال *iqbâl*, approach; arrival;

coming first; favouring; prosperity.
اقبح *aqbaḥ*, viler, vilest; more or most infamous, comp. of قبيح *qabîḥ*.
اقبية *aqbiya-t*, overcoats, &c., pl. of قبا *qabâ'*.
(اقت)=وقت *waqt*, time, epoch; — II. اقت *aqqat*, fix a time.
اقتباس *iqtibâs*, fetching fire from another's hearth; borrowing; acquiring; borrowed thoughts.
اقتبال *iqtibâl*, accepting; reception; consent.
اقتحام *iqtiḥâm*, rashness, temerity.
اقتدا *iqtidâ'*, imitation, emulation.
اقتدار *iqtidâr*, power; wealth.
اقتراب *iqtirâb*, approaching.
اقتراح *iqtirâḥ*, improvisation; (m.) invention.
اقتراض *iqtirâḍ*, borrowing money.
اقتراع *iqtirâ'*, casting lots; (m.) scuffle.
اقتران *iqtirân*, joining, coupling, pairing.
اقتصاد *iqtiṣâd*, moderation, economy; علم الاقتصاد فى المصاريف *'ilmu-'l-iqtiṣâd-i fi-'l-maṣârîf-i*, book-keeping.
اقتصار *iqtiṣâr*, abbreviation, abridgement; restriction.
اقتصاص *iqtiṣâṣ*, report; revenge.
اقتضا *iqtiḍâ'*, exigency; requisite; necessary consequence; demand.
اقتطاف *iqtiṭâf*, plucking, gathering, selecting.
اقتع *aqta'*, more contemptible.
اقتفا *iqtifâ'*, following upon one's heels; imitation; giving the preference; friendly reception.
اقتنا *iqtinâ'*, acquiring, receiving, possessing.
اقتناص *iqtinâṣ*, hunting.
اقتناع *iqtinâ'*, being satisfied.
اقحاح *aqḥâḥ*, pl. of قح *quḥḥ*, pure, &c.
اقحمة *aqḥama-t*, severe cold.
اقحوان *uqḥuwân*, pl. *aqâḥ-in*, *aqâḥiyy*, camomile; اقاحى الامر *aqâḥiyyu-'l-amr-i*, first beginnings.
اقد *aqudd*, ة *aqidda-t*, statures, &c., pl. of قد *qadd*.
اقدام *aqdâm*, feet, &c., pl. of قدم *qadam*; — *iqdâm*, advancing; boldness; endeavour; diligence.
اقداح *aqdâḥ*, cups, pl. of قدح *qadaḥ*.
اقدح *aqdaḥ*, fly.
اقدر *aqdar*, f. *qadrâ'*, more powerful, wealthier.
اقدم *aqdam*, foremost, boldest; older.
اقرا *aqrâ'*, canals, acqueducts, pl. of قرى *qariyy*; — pl. rhymes.
اقراح *aqrâḥ*, ulcerating.
اقرار *iqrâr*, confirmation, affirmation; confession; acknowledgment of a duty or debt; bond;— ى *iqrâriyy*, truthful; confirmed.
اقراض *iqrâḍ*, lending money; sum lent.
اقراع *iqrâ'*, faulty rhyme.
اقران *aqrân*, peers, equals, &c., pl. of قرين *qarîn*.
اقرب *aqrab*, nearer; more probable; pl. *aqrabûn*, *aqârib*, near relations.
اقرع *aqra'*, f. *qar'â'*, pl. *qur'*, *qur'ân*, bald (in consequence of illness); naked; peeled; grazed off; empty; complete (number); pl. *aqâri'*, very hard; cutting, sharp; clever; *al-qarâ'*, yard; calamity.
اقرف *aqraf*, crimson.
اقرم *aqram*, stallion (for breeding).
اقرية *aqriya-t*, canals, aqueducts, pl. of قرى *qariyy*.
اقزل *aqzal*, pl. *aqâzil*, halting, limping; having thin legs; wolf.
اقسام *aqsâm*, parts, portions, pl. of قسم *qism*; — oaths, pl. of قسم *qasam*.
اقسما *aqsimâ'*, parts, portions, pl. of قسم *qism*;—pl. of قسيم *qasîm*, sharer, co-heir.
اقسة *aqissa-t*, priests, pl. of قسيس *qasîs*.
اقسومة *uqsûma-t*, pl. *aqâsîm*, portion, lot; destiny, fate.
اقشع *aqśa'*, more elevated; of higher rank or birth.

اقصا *aqṣâ'*, pl. of قصى *qaṣiyy* and قاص *qâṣ-in*, far distant.

اقصر *aqṣar*, f. *qaṣrâ*, pl. *aqâṣir*, shorter; having an emaciated neck.

اقصوصة (*uqṣûṣa-t*), pl. *aqâṣîṣ*, stories, tales.

اقصى *aqṣa*, f. *qaṣwâ*, *qaṣyâ*, pl. *aqâṣî*, more or most distant; last; extreme.

اقض *aqaḍḍ*, f. *qaḍḍâ'*, hard, pebbled; not flexible (coat of mail); جماعة قضا *jamâ'a-t qaḍḍâ'*, troop of people armed to the teeth.

اقضى *aqḍa*, more or most judicious; — ة *aqḍiya-t*, fates, decrees, judgments, &c., pl. of قضا *qaḍâ*.

(اقط) *aqṭ*, *iqṭ*, *uqṭ*, *aqiṭ*, pl. *aqṭân*, a friable cheese of congelated cream; — *aqiṭ*, indigestible; — *aqaṭ*, I, INF. *aqṭ*, prepare a dish with the said cheese, give a person to eat of it; throw the adversary to the ground; mix; — IV. INF. *i'qṭâ'*, have plenty of cheese.

اقطار *aqṭâr*, tracts (of land), &c., pl. of قطر *quṭr*.

اقطاع *aqṭâ'*, pl. of قطع *qiṭ'* and قطيع *qaṭî'*, q.v.; — *iqṭâ'*, cutting, lopping; assigning lands on tenure; — ة *iqṭâ'a-t*, feudal tenure, assigned for military service.

اقطان *aqṭân*, cottons, pl. of قطن *quṭn*, *quṭun*, *quṭunn*.

اقطع *aqṭa'*, f. *qaṭ'â'*. pl. *quṭ'*, *quṭ'ân*, having his hand cut off; cut off; interrupted; dumb; sharper, more cutting; *al-aqṭa'ân*, sword and pen; (m.) worse, more wicked; — *aqṭu'*, ة *aqṭi'a-t*, cut off branches, pl. of قطيع *qaṭî'*.

اقطف *aqṭaf*, who gathers more; what itches more.

اقطوعة *uqṭû'a-t*, pl. *aqâṭî'*, object sent to cut a person's friendship.

اقعاد *iq'âd*, causing to sit; disease which compels to a sitting position; weakness of the hips; halting, limping.

اقعد *aq'ad*, juster, more legal (m.); — ة *aq'ida-t*, young camels, pl. of قعود *qu'ûd*.

اقعس *aq'as*, f. *qas'â'*, pl. *qu's*, having the back drawn in and the chest protruded; having a high croup; ant; firmly grounded; powerful; long.

اقف *aqf-in*, see اقفى *aqfî*.

اقفا *aqfâ'*, the same; — *iqfâ'*, preference, IV. of (قفو).

اقفار *iqfâr*, being ruined, deserted; finding a town destroyed and desolate.

اقفاص *aqfâṣ*, cages, &c., pl. of قفص *qafaṣ*.

اقفاف *aqfâf*, stony hills, &c., pl. of قف *quff*.

اقفال *aqfâl*, locks, bolts, &c., pl. of قفل *qufl*, q.v.

اقفر *aqfar*, uncultivated, f. *qufra*, desert.

اقفس *aqfas*, f. *qafsâ'*, born from a free woman by a slave; long and making folds; f. intestines, bowels.

اقفى *aqfî* (اقف *aqf-in*), ة *aqfiya-t*, occiputs, &c., pl. of قفا *qaf-an*, *qafâ*.

اقل *aqall*, less, least; smaller; rarer; poor; f. *qullâ*, the little one; *aqall-an*, at least.

اقلا *aqillâ'*, pl. of قليل *qalîl*, little, few, &c.

اقلاد *aqlâd*, pl. of اقليد *iqlîd*, neck.

اقلاع *iqlâ'*, intermission of a fever; eradicating, pulling out.

اقلال *iqlâl*, poverty.

اقلام *aqlâm*, pens, &c., pl. of قلم *qalam*.

اقلب *aqlab*, f. *qalbâ'*, turned over, overthrown; having turned-up lips.

اقلح *aqlaḥ*, f. *qalḥâ*, pl. *qulḥ*, having yellow teeth; dung-fly.

أقلط *aqlaṭ*, hopeless, despairing.

اقلف *aqlaf*, f. *qalfâ'*, pl. *qulf*, uncircumcised; fertile; luxurious; full of notches.

اقلوم *uqlûm*, hunting-hut (m.).
اقليد *iqlîd*, key ; ring for the nose (of a camel) ; wire ; rope of palm-leaves ; pl. *aqlâd*, neck.
اقليدس *iqlîdas*, Euclid.
اقليلى *iqlîlan*, the whole of anything.
اقليم *iqlîm*, pl. *aqâlîm*, climate ; zone ; region, tract, province.
اقليميا *iqlîmîyâ'*, scum and vapour of melting metals.
اقمار *aqmâr*, moons, pl. of قمر *qamar* ; —adversaries in a game of chance, pl. of قمير *qamîr*.
اقماع *iqmâ'*, taming; subduing; submission.
اقمر *aqmar*, f. *qamrâ'*, pl. *qumr*, shining white ; shining like the moon; moonlit ; *al-qamrâ'*, moonlit night; moonlight.
اقمشة *aqmiśa-t*, stuffs, &c., pl. of قماش *qumâś*.
اقمصة *aqmiṣa-t*, shirts, &c., pl. of قميص *qamîṣ*.
اقمطة *aqmiṭa-t*, swaddling clothes, &c., pl. of قماط *qimâṭ*.
اقنا *aqnâ'*, bright red ; — *iqnâ'*, enriching ; — ة *aqnâ'a-t*, shady side.
اقناع *iqnâ'*, satisfying, rendering content, persuading.
اقنة *aqinna-t*, slaves, &c., pl. of قن *qinn*.
اقنوم *uqnûm*, pl. *aqânîm*, root ; person (of the Holy Trinity).
اقنى *aqna*, f. *qanwâ'*, having an aquiline nose ; — ة *aqniya-t*, canals, &c., pl. of قنى *qaniyy*.
اقنيز *iqnîz*, small cup.
اقهب *aqhab*, f. *qahbâ'*, grey ; *al-aqhabân*, elephant and buffalo.
اقوا *iqwâ'*, faulty rhyme.
اقوات *aqwât*, victuals, &c., pl. of قوت *qût*.
اقواس *aqwâs*, bows, pl. of قوس *qaus*.
اقواع *aqwâ'*, plains, pl. of قاع *qâ'*.
اقوال *aqwâl*, sayings, &c., pl. of قول *qaul*.
اقوام *aqwâm*, peoples, tribes, &c., pl. of قوم *qaum*.
اقود *aqwad*, f. *qaudâ'*, pl. *qûd*, guidable ; long-necked ; high ; lengthy ; miserly ; skilful as a go-between ; f. high summit.
اقور *aqwar*, f. *qaurâ'*, spacious, roomy ; — *al-aqwarûn*, *al-aqwariyyât*, great calamities.
اقوس *aqwas*, hard, cruel ; vaulted, arched ; far off ; long.
اقوع *aqwu'*, plains, pl. of قاع *qâ'*.
اقوف *aqwaf*, clever physiognomist.
اقوم *aqwam*, more or most upright, &c., comp. of قويم *qawîm*.
اقوى *aqwa*, stronger, richer.
اقويا *aqwiyâ'*, pl. of قوى *qawiyy*, strong, vigorous, powerful, &c.
(اقى) *aqa*, INF. *aqy*, feel nauseous in consequence of illness.
اقياد *aqyâd*, fetters, &c., pl. of قيد *qaid*.
اقير *aqyar*, more bitter.
اقيسة *aqyisa-t*, measures, &c., pl. of قياس *qiyâs*, q.v.
اقيط *aqîṭ*, indigestible.
(اك) *akk*, U, INF. *akk*, be very hot ; push back ; press ; be oppressed, contracted with anxiety ; — VIII. INF. *i'tikâk*, be very hot ; throng ; be pressed (by business, &c.) ; knock against each other (feet) ; — ة *akka-t*, suffocating heat ; plight ; tumult ; hatred, envy ; death.
اكابر *akâbir*, the great ones, grandees, pl. of اكبر *akbar*.
اكاد *ikâd*, pl. *akâyid*, saddle-strap, girth-leather.
اكاذيب *akâẕîb*, lies, pl. of اكذوبة *ukẕûba-t*.
اكار *akkâr*, pl. اكرة *akara-t*, digger, peasant.
اكارس *akâris*, اكاريس *akârîs*, neighbouring houses, &c., pl. of كرس *kirs*.
اكاريم *akârîm*, noble deeds, pl. of اكرومة *ukrûma-t*.
اكاسر *akâsir*, ة *akâsira-t*, the Chosroes, pl. of كسرى *kisra*.
اكاسفة *akâsifa-t* = اساكفة *asâkifa-t*, shoe-makers.
اكاف *ukâf*, *ikâf*, pl. *ukuf*, saddle for

horses or asses ; — *akkâf*, maker of such saddles.

اكال *akâl*, food ; — *ukâl*, *ikâl*, itch ; —*akkâl*, voracious ; glutton.

اكاليل *akâlîl*, diadems, crowns, garlands, &c., pl. of اكليل *iklîl*.

اكام *âkâm*, *ikâm*, chains of hills, pl. of اكم *akam*.

اكاميم *akâmîm*, sleeves, &c., pl. of كم *kimm*.

اكايد *akâyid*, girth-leathers, pl. of اكاد *ikâd*.

اكباد *akbâd*, livers, hearts, pl. of كبد *kabd*, *kibd*, *kabıd*.

اكبد *akbad*, f. *kabdâ'*, stout, fat ; slow ; see كبدا.

اكبر *akbar*, pl. *-ûn*, f. *kubra*, pl. *kubar*, greater ; older ; more important ; *al-akbarân*, the two first Caliphs ; *al-akbar*, *al-kubra*, the major term in a proposition ; pl. *al-akâbir*, the great ones, grandees ;—ة *akbirra-t*, *ikbirra-t*, nearest related to the first ancestor.

اكتاف *aktâf*, shoulders, pl. of كتف *kitf*, *kataf*, *katif*.

اكتحال *iktiḥâl*, anointing the eyes with collyrium.

اكترا *iktirâ'*, hiring, renting.

اكتراث *iktirâs̱*, sorrow, anxiety.

اكتسا *iktisâ'*, dressing, putting on clothes.

اكتساب *iktisâb*, acquiring, earning, gain.

اكتف *aktaf*, having broad shoulders ; having a lame shoulder (horse).

اكتفا *iktifâ'*, having enough ; being satisfied.

اكتناف *iktinâf*, help, protection.

اكتناه *iktinâh*, endeavour to understand a thing thoroughly.

اكث *akas̱s̱*, f. *kas̱s̱â*, pl. كث *kus̱s̱*, dense ; with a dense beard.

اكثر *aks̱ar*, more numerous, more ; — ى *aks̱ariyy*, frequent ; *aks̱ariyy-an*, mostly ; — ية *aks̱ariyya-t*, plurality, generality.

اكثم *aks̱am*, stout, fleshy ; with a big belly ; satiated ; broad, wide.

اكحت *akḥat*, short.

اكحل *akḥal*, having the eye-lashes black by nature or blackened with collyrium ; black-eyed ; black.

(اكد) *akad*, INF. *akd*, thresh corn ; — II. INF. *ta'kîd*, strengthen, fortify ; — V. INF. *ta'akkud*, be strengthened, fortified.

اكدار *akdâr*, troubles, pl. of كدر *kadar*.

اكدر *akdar*, f. *kadrâ'*, pl. *kudr*, troubled, turbid ; *al-akdar*, torrent.

اكذاب *ikẕâb*, detecting a lie, causing to lie ; proving one to be a liar.

اكذب *akẕab*, more lying, falser, more deceitful.

اكذوبة *ukẕûba-t*, pl. *akâẕib*, lie.

(اكر) *akar*, INF. *akr*, also V. INF. *ta'akkur*, dig the ground ; — ة *ukra-t*, pl. *ukar*, well.

اكرا *ikrâ'*, hiring, renting, letting.

اكراب *ikrâb*, haste, hurry ; afflicting, troubling.

اكرام *ikrâm*, honouring ; hospitable reception ; respect, reverence.

اكرامية *ikrâmiya-t*, a present in cash given to one in office.

اكراه *ikrâh*, disgust, aversion, horror, hatred.

اكرب *akrab*, more sorrowful, in greater anxiety.

اكسا *aksâ'*, back parts, pl. of كس *kus'*.

اكساد *iksâd*, being dull, languid.

اكسح *aksaḥ*, pl. *kuḥsân*, lame.

اكسد *aksad*, dull (market).

اكسع *aksa'*, having a white spot on the forehead (horse, &c.).

اكسى *aksa*, better dressed or dressing (others) ;—ة *aksiya-t*, dresses, pl. of كسا *kisâ'*.

اكسيد *uksîd*, oxyde (m.).

اكسير *iksîr*, elixir, philosopher's stone.

اكشر *akśar*, who shows his teeth.

اكشف *akśaf*, f. *kaśfâ'*, pl. *kuśfân*, uncovered ; open ; (fighting)

without shield or helmet ; avoiding the combat.

اكشم *akśam*, lynx ; injured.

اكعا *ak'â'*, pl., boasting and cowardly.

(اكف) II. *akkaf*, saddle ; — *ukuf*, saddles, pl. of اكاف *ukâf, ikâf*; — *akuff*, pl. of كف *kaff*, palm of the hand ; — ة *akiffa-t*, livings, livelihoods, &c., pl. of كفاف *kafâf*.

اكفا *akfâ'*, pl. of كفو *kafw*, equal, &c., q.v. ;—*ikfâ'*, dissonance of vowels in a rhyme.

اكفح *akfaḥ*, black.

اكفهرار *ikfihrâr*, shining of the stars, and, by opposition, darkness.

(اكل) *akal*, U, INF. *akl, ma'kal*, IMP. *kul*, eat, consume ; — INF. *ikla-t, ukâl, akâl*, scratch ; gain ; — *akil*, INF. *akâl*, be eaten, corroded ; be scratched ; have an itching ; — II. INF. *ta'kil*, ask one to eat ; to give much to eat, eat much ;—III. INF. *mu'âkala-t, ikâl*, eat together with another, share in another's meal ; — IV. INF. *i'kâl*, give to eat, invite to eat ; sow discord ; bring forth fruit ; bring one in another's power ; — V. INF. *ta'akkul*, shine brightly ; — V., VIII. INF. *i'tikâl*, get corroded ; burst into a rage, fly into a passion ; — X. INF. *isti'kâl*, ask for something to eat ; ruin.

اكل *akil*, eating, corroding ; also *âkil*. pl. *âkâl*, tyrant, king ; pl. *akala-t*, eating ;—*ukl, ukul*, food, victuals, 'livelihood ; pasture ; fruit ; goods of the world ;—*ukl*, prudence, intelligence ; solidity (of materials) ;—ة *akila-t, ikla-t*, itching ; cancer, gangrene ; — *akla-t*, meal ; — *akla-t, ukla-t, ikla-t*, calumny ; — *ukla-t*, pl. *ukal*, morsel, mouthful ; — *ukala-t*, hearty eater, glutton ; — *âkila-t*, herd ; cancer ;—*akilla-t*, diadems, &c., pl. of اكليم *iklîm*.

اكلب *aklab*, more like a dog.

اكلط *aklaṭ*, limping, halting.

اكلف *aklaf*, f. *kalfâ'*, pl. *kulf*, dark yellow, brown ; *al-aklaf*, lion ; *al-kalfâ'*, wine.

اكليل *iklîl*, pl. *akâlîl, akilla-t*, frontlet, circlet, diadem, crown ; the white of the eyes ; the flesh round the root of a nail ; the 27th station of the moon ; — ى *iklîliyy*, the seam of the skull.

(اكم) *akam*, pl. *ikâm, âkâm, ukum, âkum*, chain of hills ; — ة *akama-t*, pl. *akm*, rising ground, hill, heap of stones ; — *ukim*, pass. be quite eaten up (pasture ground) ; — X. INF. *isti'kâm*, be hilly ; find a place soft (for sitting upon).

اكما *akmâ'*, pl. of كمى *kamiyy*, armed from head to foot ; brave.

اكمال *ikmâl*, completion, perfection.

اكمام *akmâm*, flower-sheaths, &c., pl. of كم *kimm* ; — sleeves, pl. of كم *kumm*.

اكمل *akmal*, more or most perfect.

اكمه *akmah*, born blind ; rich of herbs.

اكمو *akmu'*, mushrooms, truffles, pl. of كم *kam'*.

اكناف *aknâf*, sides, tracts, &c., pl. of كنف *kanaf*.

اكنان *aknân*, veils, &c., pl. of كن *kinn*.

اكنة *akinna-t*, veils, coverings, &c., pl. of كنان *kinân* ; — *ukna-t*, nest.

اكواخ *akwâḫ*, huts, &c., pl. of كاخ *kâḫ* and كوخ *kûḫ*.

اكواد *akwâd*, troops, squadrons, &c., pl. of كود *kaud* ; — heaps of earth, pl. of كودة *kauda-t*.

اكواز *akwâz*, cups, &c., pl. of كوز *kûz*.

اكواع *akwâ'*, wrists, pl. of كاع *kâ'* and كوع *kû'*.

اكوام *akwâm*, heaps of earth, &c., pl. of كومة *kûma-t*, q.v.

اكوس *aku's*, cups, &c., pl. of كاس *ka's* ; — *akwas*, prettier, comp. of كويس *kuwayyis*.

اكوع *akwa'*, f. *kau'â'*, having a

sprained wrist; having big ankles or knuckles.

اكول *akûl*, gluttonous, voracious; — *akwal*, elevated; *al-akwal*, rising of the ground; — ة *akûla-t*, fatted beast; — *ukûla-t*, bait.

اكوم *akwam*, f. *kaumâ'*, pl. *kûm*, high, elevated; *al-akwamân*, the nipples; كوما *kûma'*, having a high hump (camel).

اكياح *akyâḥ*, mountain slopes or ridges, pl. of كاح *kâḥ* and كيح *kîḥ*.

اكياس *akyâs*, purses, &c., pl. of كيس *kîs*; — pl. of كيس *kayyis*, cunning, intelligent, &c.

اكيال *akyâl*, measures, &c., pl. of كيل *kail*.

اكيد *akîd*, firm, strong; certain, positive, true.

اكيس *akyas*, f. *kisâ'*, *kûsâ'*, prudent, cunning; — prettier, comp. of كويس *kuwayyis*.

اكيك *akîk*, very hot.

اكيل *akîl*, f. ة, eating, devouring; eatable (adj., s.); bait; table-companion.

(ال) *all*, U, INF. *all*, be agitated, moved, hurry in agitation; hasten anywhere; tremble, quiver; shine, glitter; drive away; irritate against; pierce; sew, stitch; — INF. *all*, *alal*, *alîl*, sigh; cry out aloud imploringly or from pain; murmur (water); dress the ears (horse); refuse to chase (falcon); — *alil*, A, INF. *alal*, be corrupted, have a nasty smell; — II. INF. *ta'lîl*, sharpen into a point.

ال *al*, Arabic definite article, joined in writing to the following word, and in pronunciation (by *wasla-t*) to the previous one, as: العبد *al-'abdu*, the slave; عبد الملك *'abdu-'l-malik-i*, the slave of the king; — *âl* (v.), see (اول); — *âl*, pl. *awâl*, family, race, dynasty; vapour round the sun; mirage; object, person, thing; prop; — *âl-in*, see الى *âlî*; — *all*, sigh, call, cry; — *ill*, covenant; oath; relationship; neighbour; origin; hatred; God; religion; — *ull*, the first; — ة *âla-t*, pl. *âlât*, tool, instrument (also musical); engine; member; bier, hearse; prop, support; *âla-t*, a family or tribe; steam, vapour; condition; — *alla-t*, pl. *all*, *alal*, *ilâl*, short lance with a broad iron; — *illa-t*, pl. *ilal*, relationship; groaning; — *ulla-t*, pl. *ulal*, a herd on a distant pasture.

الا *a-lâ*, nonne? is it not so? halloa! — *alâ'*, wild bullocks; — *âlâ'*, benefits, boons, pl. of الى *ily*; — *al-lâ*=ان لا *an lâ*, that not, lest; — *il-lâ*=ان لا *in lâ*, if not, unless, except; less, e.g. الف الا ثلاثين *alf illâ salâsîn*, one thousand less thirty, 970; — *ullâ*=اولى *ûla*, these.

الأم *al'âm*, pl. of لئيم *la'îm*, equal, similar.

الات *âlât*, instruments, &c., pl. of آلة *âla-t*; — *ulât*, female possessors, see اولو *ûlû* and ذو *zû*.

الاتى *âlâtiyy*, musician.

الادة *ilâda-t*, birth.

الاس *ulâs*, madness.

الاف *al'af*, friends, &c., pl. of الف *ilf*; — *âlâf* and الافات *alâfât*, thousands, pl. of الف *alf*; — *ullâf*, companions, pl. of الف *âlif*.

الاقى *alâqiyy*, riddles, &c., pl. of القية *ulqiyya-t*.

الاك *ullâk*, those.

الال *alâl*, lie; — *ilâl*, lances, pl. of الة *alla-t*.

الأم *al'am*, rejoined (what was broken); — more to be blamed; — *âlâm*, pains, sorrows, pl. of الم *alam*; — *ilâma*=الى ما *ila mâ*, until when; until.

الان *al-ân*, now, at present.

الاه *ilâh*, God, see اله *ilâh*; — ة *ulâha-t*, divinity; — ى *ilâhiyy*, f. ة, divine.

الائف *alâ'if*, pl. of اليف *alif*, familiar, intimate.

(الب) *alab*, I, U, INF. *alb*, assemble, gather together from all sides; drive together; be driven together; collect; hasten; return; rain continually;—II. INF. *ta'lib*, drive speedily along; incite to enmity; — V. INF. *ta'allub*, assemble (n.), gather together.

الب *alb*, urging; instigating; vivid affection, sympathy; violent heat; fever-heat; thirst; first membrane of a healing wound; skin; poison; stratagem; — *ilb*, span between thumb and forefinger; assembly; a poisonous tree; — ة *ulba-t*, hunger.

البا *alibbâ'*, pl. of لبيب *labîb*, clever, &c.

الباب *albâb*, pl. of لب *lubb*, heart, mind, intellect; — throats, &c., pl. of لبب *labab*.

الباط *albâṭ*, pl. skins.

البب *albub*, vessels of the heart, heart; pl. of لب *lubb*.

البتة *al-battat-an*, certainly, by all means, altogether, on the whole.

البس *albas*, f. لبسا *labsâ'*, enveloping everything; داهية لبسا *dâhiya-t labsâ'*, immense calamity; — ة *albisa-t*, garments, pl. of لباس *libâs*.

البوب *albûb*, *ulbûb*, kernel of the lotus-fruit.

(الت) *alat*, I, INF. *alt*, injure anyone in his right; restrain; ward off; compel one to an oath or to give evidence; calumniate;—IV. INF. *i'lât*, injure.

الت *alt*, false accusation, calumny; — *allat*, *allati*=التى *allatî*, f. of الذى *allaẕî*, which, who.

التباس *iltibâs*, ambiguity, doubt; confusion, chaos; disquietude; epilepsy.

التثام *iltis̱âm*, kiss, kissing.

التجا *iltijâ'*, seeking refuge with.

التجاج *iltijâj*, heaving of waves.

التح *altaḥ*, more sagacious in interpreting.

التحا *iltiḥâ'*, becoming bearded.

التحام *iltiḥâm*, union, alliance; attachment; healing (wound); growing fierce (battle).

التذاذ *iltiẕâẕ*, tasting, enjoying, relishing.

التزام *iltizâm*, necessity; obligation; dependence; adhesion; renting; taking the public revenues on farm.

التفات *iltifât*, turning round; attention; solicitude; favour; sudden transition in a speech.

التقا *iltiqâ'*, interview, meeting, encounter, mingling together.

التقاط *iltiqâṭ*, chance, hazard, accident.

التماس *iltimâs*, petition, prayer, supplication.

التهاب *iltihâb*, conflagration, inflammation.

التوا *iltiwâ'*, complication, involution.

التى *allatî*, f. of الذى *allaẕî*, which, who;—*allatî* and dim. *allatayyâ'*, calamity.

التياح *iltiyâḥ*, thirst; glittering, sparkling.

التئام *ilti'âm*, reuniting (n.); rejoining (n.); agreement; (m.) council.

الثع *als̱a'*, who pronounces badly the letters ث and ع.

الثغ *als̱ag*, who pronounces badly, stammerer, lisper.

الجا *iljâ'*, compulsion.

الجاج *iljâj*, (m.) molestation, importunity.

الجام *iljâm*, bridling.

الجمة *aljima-t*, bridles, pl. of لجام *lijâm*.

الجى *aljiyy*, musician; — *ilchî* (Turk.), ambassador; plenipotentiary; legate.

الحاح *ilḥâḥ*, importunity.

الحاد *ilḥâd*, impiety; apostasy; heresy.

الحاق *ilḥâq*, reaching; adding; annexing; affiliation; aggregation; codicil.

الحان *alḥân*, notes, modulations, pl. of لحن *laḥn* ; — *ilḥân*, song.
الحق *al-ḥaqq*, truly, really, in fact.
الحم *alḥum*, kinds or pieces of flesh, pl. of لحم *laḥm*.
الحن *alḥan*, having an agreeable enunciation ; good singer.
الحى *alḥa*, having a long beard.
(الخ) *alaḥ*, VIII. ائتلخ *i'talaḥ*, become complicated, getting difficult ; grow high and luxuriantly ; mingle together ; turn sour.
الخ, abbreviation for الى اخره *ila âḥiri-hi*, to the end of it, i.e. etc.
الخن *alḥan*, pl. *luḥn*, f. *laḥnâ*, uncircumcised ; smelling badly.
الخى *alḥa*, f. *laḥwâ'*, garrulous, talkative ; see لخوا .
(الد), pass. *ulid*, be born ; — v. become confused.
الد *aladd*, pl. *ludd*, *lidâd*, very quarrelsome ; contentious ; long-necked (camel) ; — ة *ilda-t*=ولدة, *wilda-t*, children, sons, &c., pl. of ولد *walad* and وليد *walîd*.
الداس *aldâs*, pl. of لديس *ladîs*, fleshy.
الذ *allaẕ*, *allaẕi*, الذى *allaẕî*, f. الت *allat*, *allati*, التى *allatî*, du. الذان *allaẕâni*, f. التانى *allatâni*, pl. الذين *allaẕîna*, f. اللاتى *allâtî*, which, who ; — *alaẕẕ*, sweeter, more pleasant, more delightful ; — ة *aliẕẕa-t*, people who live in enjoyment.
(الز) *alaz*, I, INF. *alz*, firmly adhere to (ب *bi*) ; — *aliz*, INF. *alaz*, be agitated, disquieted.
الزاق *ilzâq*, making to adhere, cementing, glueing ; attaching.
الزام *ilzâm*, compulsion ; necessitating.
الزم *alzam*, more or most necessary.
الزن *alzan*, difficult, hard.
(الس) *alas*, I, INF. *als*, betray ; deceive ; lie ; steal ; err, be of a wrong opinion ; — pass. be violently agitated, in emotion ; — III. INF. موالسة *mu'âlasa-t*, deceive ; betray ; — v. INF. *ta'allus*, feel pain ; be agitated.
الس *als*, deceit, treachery, lie ; theft ; bad race ; corrupted state ; madness.
السن *alsan*, pl. *lusn*, eloquent ; — *alsun*, ة *alsina-t*, tongues, &c., pl. of لسان *lisân*.
الص *alaṣṣ*, f. *laṣṣâ'*, having some parts of the body (shoulders, teeth, &c.) too close together ; having a narrow forehead ; more thievish.
الصاص *alṣâṣ*, robbers, pl. of لص *laṣṣ*, *liṣṣ*, *luṣṣ*.
الصاق *ilṣâq*, adhesion, IV. (لصق).
الط *alaṭṭ*, toothless, having bad teeth.
الطف *alṭaf*, more lovely ; kinder, comp. of لطيف *laṭîf*.
العا *al'â'*, bones of the fingers.
العبان *ul'ubân*, who is fond of play, of game.
العث *al'as*, slow, heavy, ponderous.
العوبة *ul'ûba-t*, play, pleasantry.
الغ *ulug* (Turk.), great, powerful.
الغا *ilgâ'*, omission ; abolishing ; annulling.
الغاز *algâz*, riddles, pl. of لغز *lugz*.
الغوزة *ulgûza-t*, riddle.
(الف) *alif*, first letter of the Arabic alphabet ; hence : II. *allaf*, INF. *ta'lîf*, write an alif ; — *alf*, pl. *ulûf*, *âlâf*, *alâfât*, thousand ; hence : *alaf*, I, give a thousand pieces ; II., IV. INF. *i'lâf*, make the thousand full ; — become raised to a thousand.
(الف) *alif*, A, INF. *ilf*, *alf*, accustom one's self to (acc.) ; grow tame ; hence II. unite, establish friendship (between others) ; compose a book ; — IV. accustom anyone to, become accustomed to ; gain one's confidence and favour by intercourse ; — v., VIII. assemble (n.) ; — VIII. have familiar intercourse.
الف *ilf*, pl. *al'âf*, friend, companion, confidant (also female) ; — *alif*, bachelor ; friend, companion ;

— *uluf*, pl. of الوف *alûf*, very familiar ; — *âlaf*, tamer, more familiar ; — *âlif*, pl. الاف *ullâf*, f. ة *âlifa-t*, pl. ات *-ât* and *awâlif*, friend, companion ; — *alaff*, f. *laffâ'*, pl. *luff*, implicated in difficult business, not equal to such ; awkward ; slow ; with a heavy pronunciation ; densely populated ; thronged ; f. fleshy thigh ;— ة *ilfa-t*, female companion ; — *ulfa-t*, familiar intercourse.

الفاظ *alfâẓ*, words, &c., pl. of لفظ *lafẓ*.

الفاف *alfâf*, densely grown trees, gardens with luxuriant vegetation, pl. of لف *liff*, *laff*.

الفت *alfat*, f. *laftâ'*, awkward ; stupid.

الفث *alfas*, stupid ; foolish.

الفك *alfak*, awkward, stupid.

(الق) *aliq*, A, INF. *alq*, *ilâq*, deceive ; shine, glitter, flash ; — pass. be mad ; — V. INF. *ta'alluq*, sparkle ; gleam ; shine (with jewelry) ; raise the head and be ready for quarrel (a woman) ; — VIII. INF. *i'tilâq*, flash (lightning).

الق *illaq*, flashing ; — *ilq*, f. ة pl. *ilaq*, wolf ; female ape ; — ة *ulqa-t*, flash, glitter.

القا *alqâ'*, pl. of لقوة *laqwa-t*, *liqwa-t*, female eagle, alert woman ; — pl. of لقى *laqan*, what is thrown away as worthless ; — *ilqâ'*, throwing away, &c., IV. of (لقى), q.v.

القاب *alqâb*, titles of honour, &c., pl. of لقب *laqab*.

القى *alaqa*, irascible woman ; shrew ; — ة *ulqiyya-t*, pl. *alâqiyy*, riddle, problem ; *al-alâqiyy*, calamities.

(الك) *alak*, INF. *alk*, bite the bridle ; send ; — pass. be mad ; — X. INF. *isti'lâk*, bring a message, a letter.

الكد *alkad*, who never leaves home ; cowardly.

الكن, ى, *alkaniyy*, who speaks with difficulty, with an impediment.

الل *alal*, the shoulders ; side of a blade ; — *alal*, lances, pl. of الة *alla-t* ; — *ilal*, relationships, pl. of الة *illa-t* ; — *ulal*, herds on a distant pasture, pl. of الة *ulla-t*.

اللا *allâ'*, اللائى *allâ'î*, اللاوون *allâwûn*, اللايين *allâyîn*, pl. of الذى *allaẕî*, which, who.

اللاتى, pl. f. which, who.

اللتت , اللتان , اللذ=الت , &c., q.v. under الذ .

اللتيا *allatayyâ*, calamity ; dim. of اللاتى *allâtî*, f. which, who.

الله *allâh*, God, see اله *ilâh*.

الم=الم *a-lam*, interrogative, nonne? (also الما *a-lammâ*) ; — *alam*, pl. *âlâm*, pain, grief ; (m.) irritation ; passion ; — *alim*, *âlim*, feeling pain.

(الم) *alim*, A, INF. *alam*, feel pain, ache ; — IV. INF. *i'lâm*, pain, cause pain ; — V. INF. *ta'allum*, feel pain ; be irritated ; be revengeful ; grudge.

الماس *almâs*, diamond.

الماع *ilmâ'*, shining ; cracking the fingers ; stealing.

المع *alma'*, having a vivid mind ; vivacious.

المعى *alma'iyy*, vivacious ; liar ; — ة *alma'iyya-t*, vivacity.

المى *alma*, f. *lamyâ*, having dark red lips ; shady ; cold of spittle.

النجج *alanjaj*, النجوج *alanjûj*, aloe.

الندد *alandad*, quarreller ; screamer.

(اله) *alah*, INF. *ilâha-t*, *ulûha-t*, *ulûhiyya-t*, adore ; — *alih*, INF. *alah*, be perplexed, confused ; be very much afraid of (على *'ala*) ; seek help or refuge with (الى *ila*) ; — INF. *alh*, grant shelter or security to (acc.) ; — II. INF. *ta'lîh*, deify a being ; make one a slave ; — IV. INF. *i'lâh*, help, rescue ; — V. INF. *ta'alluh*, adore.

اله, الاه *ilâh*, pl. *âliha-t*, god, divinity ; with art. اللاه *allâh*, the one true

God; بالله *bi-'llâhi*, تالله *ta'llâhi*, والله *wa'llâhi*, by God; لله *li-'llâhi*, for God's sake, to God; — *âlih*, perplexed; — ة *ilâha-t*, goddess; coll. deities, false gods, idols; adoration; passionate love; half moon; sun; snake.

الهاب *ilhâb*, inflaming, kindling (s.).

الهام *ilhâm*, divine inspiration, revelation; instinct.

الهانية *ulhâniyya-t*, deity; adoration.

الهم *allahumma*, O God! by God!

الهوب *ulhûb*, mettle of a steed, of a race-horse; heat.

الهوة *ulhuwwa-t*, الهية *ulhiyya-t*, toy, pastime, amusement; funny question.

الهى *ilâhiyy*, f. ة, divine; علم الالهيات *'ilm al-ilâhiyyât*, theology, divinity; metaphysics.

(الو) *alâ*, U, INF. *alw*, *uluww*, *aliyy*, *alan*, be not equal to a thing or person, therefore hesitate, desist; with negative: be not afraid of; —be haughty, proud;—IV. swear, take an oath;—V. swear; be not equal to a thing; be haughty;—VIII. INF. *i'tilâ'*, be not equal to and desist, fail; swear; — X. desist from a thing on account of its difficulty.

الو *alw*, benefit, favour, present; excrement of sheep; — *uluww*, wood for fumigation; (distance of a) bow-shot; race-course; abundance; — ة *alwa-t*, arrow-shot; — *alwa-t*, *ilwa-t*, *ulwa-t*, *aluwwa-t*, *iluwwa-t*, *uluwwa-t*, oath;—*alwa-t*, *uluwwa-t*, riches, plenty, large number; fragrant wood for fumigation.

الواح *alwâḥ*, planks, &c., pl. of لوح *lauḥ*.

الواد *alwâd*, pl. ill-wishers, ill-disposed persons.

الواع *alwâ'*, pl. of لاع *lâ'*, timorous, &c.

الوان *alwân*, colours, shades, kinds, &c., pl. of لون *laun*.

الوث *alwas̱*, f. *laus̱â*, soft, flabby, and, by opposition, vigorous, energetic; foolish.

الود *alwad*, pl. *alwâd*, unjust; refractory.

الوس *alûs*, something (with negative, nothing).

الوف *alûf*, pl. *uluf*, very familiar; — *ulûf*, thousands, pl. of الف *alf*.

الوق *alwaq*, stupid.

الوقة *alûqa-t*, cream with dates; butter.

الوك *alûk*, messenger; — *ulûk*, ة *ulûka-t*, message.

الوم *alwam*, more to be blamed; — ة *alûma-t*, vice; abominations.

الوهة *ulûha-t*, الوهية *ulûhiyya-t*, divinity, divine essence.

الى *ila*, to, unto, until; — *ily*, *ilan*, pl. *âlâ'*, benefit; — *âlî* (ال *âl-in*), f. ة, too weak, insufficient; — *aliyy*, who takes many oaths, swears frequently; — ة *alya-t*, pl. *alyât*, *alâyâ'*, sheep with a rich tail; calf (of the leg); fleshy part of the hips; — *aliyya-t*, oath.

الياط *alyâṭ*, reeds, spears, &c., pl. of ليطة *lîṭa-t*.

اليث *alyas̱*, pl. *lîs̱*, strong, courageous.

اليس *a-laisa*, is not? — *alyas*, pl. *lîs*, courageous; noble; generous; lion; strong and willing; by opposition, cowardly; not jealous.

اليغ *alyag*, who pronounces badly; stupid.

اليف *alîf*, pl. *alâ'if*, intimate, familiar; friend, companion.

اليق *alyaq*, more appropriate, fitter.

اليل *alîl*, grief of a mother at the loss of children; ague, shivering from fever; murmuring of water, &c.; — *alyal*, f. *lailâ*, long and dark (night, lit. more of a night than another).

اليم *alîm*, painful, aching.

الين *alyan*, softer, more delicate.

اليناء *alyinâ'*, pl. of **لين** *layyin*, soft, &c.

ام *am*, or? (in the second part of a question), or not? yes, certainly.

(ام) *amm*, U, INF. *amm*, intend, strive after; go towards a place; repair to; visit; strike on the middle of the skull; — INF. *amm*, *imâm*, *imâma-t*, go in front, lead, give an example to others; command; — *amm*, for *amim*, INF. *umûma-t*, be or become mother; — INF. *amam*, be close together; — II. INF. *ta'mîm*, ordain; — II., V. INF. *ta'ammum*, intend; — III. INF. *mu'âmma*, be clear, evident; be near; approach; find fit, convenient; — V. consider as one's mother, take for a mother; make one's ablutions with earth instead of water; — VIII. INF. *i'timâm*, intend; imitate; take for an example; — X. INF. *isti'mâm*, consider as one's mother, take for a mother; take for a guide.

ام *am*, or? **ام هل** *am hal*, or not? yes, certainly; — *amm*, intention; — *umm*, pl. *ummât*, *ummahât*, mother; du. *ummân*, mother and mother-in-law; origin, first principle, prototype; *ummahât*, elements of created things; nation; species; frequently in composition with other words, as: **ام عامر** *umm 'âmir*, hyena; **ام القرآن** *ummu-'l-qur'ân*, first chapter of the Koran; **ام القرى** *ummu-'l-qura*, Mecca, &c.; — *âm*, see **(اوم)**; — **ة** *ama-t*, pl. *a'm-in*, *âmî*, *imâ'*, *amawât*, *amwân*, *imwân*, *umwân*, female slave; — *âma-t*, rich harvest; grass; rain; placenta; — *imma-t*, favour, benefit; rule of conduct; kind; form; religion; leadership; — *umma-t*, pl. *umum*, assembly, crowd; nation, tribe, family; partisans; creatures; Imam; form, figure; mother; time, term; obedience; — *âmma-t*, broken skull.

اما *a-mâ*, is it not? or not? — certainly, undoubtedly; — *ammâ*, but, but as to; — *immâ*, if; *immâ-immâ*, whether or; — *imâ'*, female slaves, pl. of *ama-t*.

اماتة *imâta-t*, killing, causing one's death.

اماثل *imâsil*, pl. of **امثل** *amsal*, most like the model, exemplary; *al-amâsil*, the great ones.

اماجد *amâjid*, pl. of **امجد** *amjad*, nobler.

اماديح *amâdîh*, praises, noble deeds, pl. of **امدوحة** *umdûha-t*.

امار *amâr*, time or place of an appointment, sign; — *imâr*, order, decree, edict; — *ammâr*, inclined; commanding; dictatorial; — **ة** *amara-t*, power; sign; — *imâra-t*, government, power, dominion; prefecture; pl. *imârât*, *amâ'ir*, signs, indications, way-marks.

امارد *amârid*, pl. of **امرد** *amrad*, beardless.

امازر *amâzir*, pl. of **مزير** *mazîr*, brave, &c.

اماس *âmâs*, yesterdays, pl. of **امس** *ams*.

اماعز *amâ'iz*, **اماعيز** *amâ'îz*, goats, &c., pl. of **امعوز** *am'ûz*.

اماق *am'âq*, *âmâq*, inner corners of the eyes, pl. of **موق** *mu'q*, *mûq*; — *âmâq*, the same, pl. of **امق** *amq*, *umq*.

اماكن *amâkin*, places, habitations, &c., pl. of **مكان** *makân*.

امال *âmâl*, hopes, thoughts, pl. of **امل** *amal*; — *amâl-in*, dictations, &c., pl. of **املا** *imlâ'*; — **ة** *imâla-t*, causing to incline; pronunciation of *â* like *e* or *î*.

امالس *amâlis* (*amâlîs*), deserts, pl. of **امليس** *imlîs*.

اماليت *amâlît*, pl. swift camels.

امام *amâm*, before, in front; — *imâm*, pl. *a'imma-t*, leader, president; title of the first Caliphs;

antistes ; sacred book ; high road ; road to Mecca ; direction towards Mecca; example, model ; command of God ; plumb-line ; moderator ; school-task ; — ة *imâma-t*, leadership, dignity of an Imâm ; — *umâma-t*, herd of 300 camels ; — ية *imâmiyya-t*, the Shiites.

امان *amân*, ة *amâna-t*, security, protection ; safe-guard ; escort ; faith ; — *amân*, pardon, mercy ; — *ummân*=امى *ummiyy* ; confiding ; stupid ; peasant, farmer ; — *amân-in*, ى *amânî*, desires, fancies, pl. of امنية *umniyya-t* ; —*umâniyy*, deposit ;—ة *amâna-t*, deposit, truss.

(امت) *amat*, I, INF. *amt*, guess or try to determine the number or quantity ; intend ; be crooked ; slope ; be elevated ; — II. INF. *ta'mîn*, determine the number or quantity.

امت *amt*, pl. *umût*, *âmât*, uneven, crooked ; rising of the ground ; difference of opinion, doubt.

امتثال *imtisâl*, obedience, complying with.

امتحان *imtiḥân*, examination.

امتداد *imtidâd*, extension, protraction, prolongation; ductility.

امتزاج *imtizâj*, mixture, conjunction, intercourse ; constitution of body and mind.

امتعة *amti'a-t*, goods, &c., pl. of متاع *matâ'*.

امتلا *imtilâ'*, fill, indigestion, oppression of the stomach.

امتناع *imtinâ'*, hindrance, refusal, abstinence.

امتنان *imtinân*, obligation, favour received.

امتياز *imtiyâz*, distinguishing, distinction ; preference ; pre-eminence ; privilege.

امثال *amsâl*, fables, proverbs, &c., pl. of مثل *masal*.

امثل *amsal*, f. *musla*, pl. *amâsil*, more closely approaching the original, more like the model ; exemplary ; *al-amâsil*, the great ones ; grandees ; — ة *amsila-t*, similitudes, types, models, &c., pl. of مثال *misâl*.

امثولة *umsûla-t*, example, quotation, sentence ; school-task.

(امج) *amaj*, I, INF. *amj*, walk very quickly ; — *amij*, A, INF. *amaj*, be very hot ; be thirsty.

امج *amaj*, very hot ; heat ; thirst.

امجد *amjad*, pl. اماجد *amâjid*, nobler ; more illustrious ; more celebrated.

(امح) *amaḥ*, INF. *amaḥân*, cause a throbbing pain.

امحا *immiḥḥâ*, getting effaced.

امحاق *immiḥâq*, calamity.

امحص *amḥaṣ*, easily pacified.

امحق *amḥaq*, who has no good luck ; small.

امحوضة *umḥûḍa-t*, unselfish advice ; admonition of a true friend.

(امد) *amad*, be finished, be determinated ; — *amid*, A, INF. *amad*, be angry with (على *'ala*) ; — II. fix a term ; — VIII. agree with each other about a term.

امد *amad*, anger ; end, term ; limit ; death ; goal of a race-course ; — *âmid*, full, loaded (ship) ; — *amadd*, more extended.

امداد *imdâd*, help, succour (in troops, money, &c.) ; subsidies.

امدوحة *umdûḥa-t*, pl. *amâdiḥ*, praise ; praiseworthy deed.

امدود *umdûd*, habit ; custom ; manner.

امدية *amdiya-t*, watering-places, pl. of مدى *madiyy*.

(امر) *amar*, U, INF. *amr*, *imâr*, *âmira-t*, IMP. *mur*, *âmur*, order, command ; — *amir*, A, INF. *imâra-t*, be or become a leader, prince ; — *amir*, A, INF. *amar*, *amara-t*, be plentiful and perfect ; have many cattle ; be hard, difficult ; — II. INF. *ta'mîr*, make one a prince ; mark (by branding) ; mark out the boundaries ; place the iron on a lance ;

— III. INF. *mu'âmara-t*, X. INF. *isti'mâr*, consult;—IV. INF. *i'mâr*, order, command; increase one's children and cattle (God); — V. INF. *ta'ammur*, consult; exercise dominion; — VI. INF. *ta'âmur*, consult each other; — VIII. INF. *i'timâr*, receive an order.

امر *amr*, pl. *awâmir*, order, edict; IMP. power, dominion; — pl. *umûr*, matter, business, case, affair; — *imr*, very difficult, important; wonderful case; — *âmir*, commander; God; Mahomet; numerous, complete; Muḥarram; — *amarr*, f. *murra*, more bitter, comp. of مر *murr*; *al-amarrân*, old age and poverty; f. *al-murrayân*, wormwood and coloquintida;—*amarr*, firmer, comp. of مرير *marîr*; — *imra'*, *imru'*, f. ة *imra'a-t*, *imru'a-t*, man; wolf; — ة *amara-t*, stone to mark the road; — *amra-t*, command, power, dominion; — *imra-t*, dominion by a substitute; increase of fortune; administration of a fortune; expenditure; — *âmira-t*, pl. *awâmir*, order, command.

امرا *umarâ'*, chiefs, princes, &c., pl. of امير *amîr*; — ة *imra'a-t*, *imrât*, woman.

امرار *amrâr*, pl. of مر *murr*, bitter, &c.; — pl. of مرة *mirra-t*, vigour, power, intelligence, &c.

امراض *amrâḍ*, diseases, &c., pl. of مرض *maraḍ*; — *immirâḍ*, weakness.

امراع *amrâ'*, pl. of مريع *marî'*, abounding in herbs and water.

امراق *amrâq*, spikes (of corn).

امرد *amrad*, f. *mardâ'*, pl. *murd*, beardless; covered with down; hairless; leafless.

امرط *amraṭ*, pl. *murṭ*, *miraṭa-t*, hairless; featherless (arrow); thief.

امرع *amru'*, pl. of مريع *marî'*, abounding in herbs and water.

امرو *imru'*, man.

امروعة *umrû'a-t*, pl. *amârî'*, land yielding abundant fruit and pastures.

امرى *imra'iyy*, manly, manful; — ة *amri'a-t*, pl. of مرى *mari'*, alimentary canal.

امزاجة *imzâja-t*, bodily constitution; temper.

امزجة *amzija-t*, mixtures, constitutions, &c., pl. of مزاج *mizâj*.

امس *ams*, pl. *âmus*, *âmûs*, *âmûs*, yesterday; time just past; *ams-in*, *bi-'l-ams-i*, *al-ams-a*, yesterday, just now; مسى امس *musya ams-in*, last night; — *amass*, more; principal.

امساك *imsâk*, parsimony, avarice; (m.) withholding; abstinence; abstemiousness.

امسخ *amsaḥ*, more stupid; more tasteless.

امسلة *amsila-t*, channels, gutters, pl. of مسل *masal*.

امسوح *umsûḥ*, plank, board.

امسى *imsiyy*, of yesterday; — ة *umsiyya-t*, yesterday's evening.

امشاج *amśâj*, mixtures, pl. of مشج *maśaj*, *maśij*; — pl. of مشيج *maśîj*, mixed, mixtures.

امشاط *amśâṭ*, combs, pl. of مشط *muśṭ*, &c.

امصاخ *immiṣâḥ*, weaning of a child; — *imṣâḥ*, pushing forth leaves.

امصار *amṣâr*, large cities, &c., pl. of مصر *miṣr*.

امصح *amṣaḥ*, declining and disappearing (shadow).

امصدة *amṣida-t*, highest summits, pl. مصاد *maṣâd*.

امصرة *amṣira-t*, pl. of مصير *maṣîr*, gut, intestine.

(امض) *amiḍ*, A, INF. *amaḍ*, persist in spite of objections, remonstrances, &c.; talk otherwise than one thinks; dissimulate.

امضا *imḍâ'*, sealing; execution; (m.) signature; subscription.

امضى *amḍa*, passing more quickly; more penetrating; more acute; more effectual.

امطا *amṭâ'*, beasts of burden, &c., pl. of مطية *maṭiyya-t*; — pl. of مطا *mat-an, maṭâ*, and مطو *maṭw*, q.v.

امطار *amṭâr*, rains, pl. of مطر *maṭar*; — *imṭâr*, causing to rain.

(امع) *amma'*, *immâ'*, ة *imma'-t*, stupid, dull; weak of character and without opinion of one's own; parasite; — v., x. be or become stupid, &c.

امعا *am'â'*, intestines, bowels, pl. of معى *ma'y, mi'an*.

امعاق *am'âq*, pl. اماعق *amâ'iq* (*amâ'îq*), borders of the desert.

امعان *im'ân*, guarding carefully; looking intently.

امعط *am'aṭ*, f. *ma'ṭâ'*, pl. *m'uṭ*, hairless (wolf); bare (ground); thief.

امعوظ *am'ûẓ*, pl. *amâ'iẓ*, *amâ'îẓ*, goat; troop of gazelles.

امق *amq*, *umq*, pl. *âmâq*, inner corner of the eye.

امكا *amkâ'*, burrows of hares or foxes, pl. of مكو *makw*.

امكان *imkân*, possibility; — ى *imkâniyy*, possible; — ية *imkâniyya-t*, possibility.

امكر *amkar*, more cunning.

امكنة *amkina-t*, places, dwellings, &c., pl. of مكان *makân*.

(امل) *amal*, U, INF. *aml*, hope, hope for; — *amul*, INF. *amâla-t*, have an oval face; — II. INF. *ta'mîl*, hope greatly; cause to hope; — v. INF. *ta'ammul*, look long and attentively; meditate; think of (من *min*).

امل *amal*, pl. *âmâl*, hope; pl. thoughts; — *aml*, *iml*, hope; — *umul*, sand-hills, pl. of اميل *amîl*; — ة *amala-t*, pl. defenders; *imla-t*, hope; — *amîla-t*, tears, lamentations.

املا *amlâ'*, quantities which fill up, &c., pl. of ملا *malâ'*, *mil'*; — *imlâ'*, pl. *amâl-in*, *amâlî*, dictation, writing; orthography; filling up; completing.

املاج *imlâj*, ة *imlâja-t*, sucking.

املاح *amlâḥ*, salts, &c., pl. of ملح *milḥ*; — pl. of مليح *malîḥ*, handsome, fine, good, &c.

املاس *immilâs*, escaping; being rescued; VII. of (ملس); — *imlâs*, twilight of the morning.

املاق *imlâq*, poverty.

املاك *amlâk*, goods, riches, &c., pl. of ملك *milk*, *mulk*; — *imlâk*, giving in marriage.

املال *imlâl*, dictation; annoying; annoyance.

املج *amlaj*, yellow, fading; bare desert; poor.

املح *amlaḥ*, f. *malḥâ'*, spotted black and white; blue-eyed; steel-coloured (f. troop of armed men seen from a distance); white (with snow, hoar frost); — handsomer, &c., comp. of مليح *malîḥ*.

املد *amlad*, f. *maldâ'*, tender, supple, flexible; — *umlud*, ان *umludân*, انى *umludâniyy*, same meaning.

املذ *amlaẕ*, insincere.

املس *amlas*, f. *malsâ*, smooth; short-haired; without knots; flowing down easily (wine); by opposition, toilsome; see ملسا.

املص *amlaṣ*, smooth and slippery; short-haired; bald.

املغ *amlag*, lascivious (speech).

املك *amlak*, who or what possesses most, holds fastest, binds strongest.

املوت (*umlût*), pl. امالیت *amâlît*, swift camels.

املوحة *umlûḥa-t*, pl. *amâlîḥ*, wit, elegance.

املوك *umlûk*, pl. possessors; kings of Himyar.

امليجاج *imlîjâj*, pushing teeth.

امليد *imlîd* = املد *amlad*; = امليس *imlîs*, bare desert.

امليص *imlîṣ*, swift, speedy.

امم *amam*, in moderate distance; small, unimportant; middle; — *umam*, nations, &c., pl. of امة *umma-t*.

(امن) *aman*, trust (على *'ala*); — *amin*, A, INF. *amn*, *amân*, *aman*, *amana-t*, *imn*, be safe, fearless (من *min*); consider one's self safe; repair to (الى *ila*) for protection; trust a person (acc.) with anything (على *'ala*, ب *bi*); — II., VIII., X. confide in (acc.); trust with; II. say "Amen"; — IV. believe a person; believe in God, accept His law; trust; trust with; encourage, afford security, protect against (على *'ala*, من *min*); show submission to (ل *li*); — V. entirely rely upon (على *'ala*); — X., II. ask for protection.

امن *amn*, *aman*, security, safety; trustworthiness, fidelity;—*amin*, safe; seeking security; — *âman*, what is best; — *âmin*, safe; trustworthy; — *imn*, INF. of (امن); — *amn-in*, see امنى *amnî*; — ة *amana-t*, trustworthiness, fidelity;—also *amina-t*, *umana-t*, *âmina-t*, faithful, trustworthy person.

امنا *amnâ'*, pl. of منا *man-an*, *manâ*, weight of about two pounds; — *umanâ*, pl. of امين *amîn*, faithful, &c., q.v.

امنان *amnân*, pl. of من *mann*, weight of two pounds;—*imnân*, weakening, IV. of (من).

امنع *amna'*, inaccessible, impregnable.

امنى *amnî*, pl. of منا *man-an*, *manâ*, weight of two pounds; — ة *umniyya-t*, pl. *amân-in*, *amânî*, desire, fancy.

(امه) *amah*, U, INF. *amh*, promise by contract, stipulate; prescribe; recommend; pass. be mad, foolish; — *amih*, A, INF. *amah*, forget; avow, confess; have an eruption (of the skin); — II. madden; — V. make a compact; take for a wife.

امه *amah*, oblivion; the created things; — ة *ummaha-t*, mother.

امهات *ummahât*, mothers, &c., pl. of ام *umm*.

امهال *imhâl*, delay, respite; prolongation; prorogation.

امهج *umhuj*, امهجان *umhujân*, thin (of a liquid).

امهدة *amhida-t*, beds, &c., pl. of مهاد *mihâd*.

امهر *amhar*, more clever, comp. of ماهر *mâhir*.

امهود *umhûd*, hole in the ground, pit.

(امو) *amâ*, U, INF. *imâ'*, mew;—*amâ* and امى *amî*, امو *amû*, INF. *umuwwa-t*, become a (female) slave;— II. make a (female) slave; — V., X. buy a (female) slave; — ة *amwa-t*=امة *ama-t*, female slave.

اموات *amawât*, female slaves, pl. of امة *ama-t*;—*amwât*, dead bodies, &c., pl. of ميت *mait*, *mayyit*; ancestors.

امواج *amwâj*, waves, pl. of موج *mauj*.

اموال *amwâl*, riches, possessions, &c., pl. of مال *mâl*.

اموان *amwân*, &c., female slaves, pl. of امة *ama-t*.

امواه *amwâh*, waters, pl. of ما *mâ'*; — *imwâh*, having much water; raining heavily, IV. of (موه).

اموت *umût*, pl. of امت *amt*, uneven, &c., q.v.

امور *amûr*, commanding; — *umûr*, pl. of امر *amr*, thing, affair, &c.

اموس *âmûs*, yesterdays, pl. of امس *ams*.

امومة *umûma-t*, maternity, motherhood.

امون *amûn*, pl. *umun*, trustworthy.

اموه *amwah*, better provided with water.

اموى *amawiyy*, referring or belonging to a female slave.

اموية *amûya-t*, drink, beverage; — river Oxus.

امى *âmî*, female slaves, pl. of امة *ama-t*; — *ummiyy*, motherly, maternal; uncultivated, uneducated, ignorant; idle; idiot; — ة *umayya-t*, little (female) slave;

the family *Umayya-t*; — *um-miyya-t*, maternity, motherhood.

امير *amîr*, pl. *umarâ'*, leader, prince, Emîr; — امير المومنين *amîru-'l-mûminîn-a*, commander of the faithful, Caliph; امير البحر *amîru-'l-bahr-i*, admiral; امير اخور *amîr ahor, mîr ahor*, equerry; امير سلاح *amîr silâh*, arm-bearer of the king; — ة *amîra-t*, princess, mistress; — ى *amîriyy*, princely; — abbreviated ميرى *mîriyy*, fisc; public exchequer.

أمير *amyaz*, more or most distinguished.

اميل *amîl*, pl. *umul*, sand-mountain a mile broad and a day's journey long; — *amyal*, inclined.

اميلح *umailih*, very pretty.

اميمة *umaima-t*, little mother, mother dear.

امين *amîn*, pl. *umanâ'*, faithful; trustworthy; confident; minister; safe, secure; proper name; — *amîn, âmîn*, be it so! Amen! — official, prefect.

اميه *amyah*, better provided with water.

ان *an*, that, lest; الى ان *ila an*, until; على ان *'ala an*, under condition that, providing that; لما ان *lammâ an*, after; also for ان *anna*: كان *ka-an*, as if, لان *li-an*, because; — *in*, if; ان لم *in lam*, if not; unless; except; — *in*=ما *mâ*, not; — *ân*, pl. *âwân*, time, moment; *al-ân*, now, at present; — *ân-in*, see انى *ânî*; — *anna*, that, because, since; على ان *'ala anna*, so that; لان *li-anna*, for, since; ان . . . او, whether...or; — *inna*, فان *fa-inna*, انه *inna-hu*, فانه *fa-inna-hu*, truly, indeed, certainly; with suffixes: انني *inna-nî*, انى *innî*, truly, I; انا *innâ*, truly, we, &c.; — *inna-hu*, so it is; yes; — *inna-mâ*, however, yet; only that; — ة *anna-t*, sigh; — *ânna-t*, sighing.

(ان) *ann*, I, INF. *ann, anîn, unân, ta'nân*, groan; — INF. *ann*, pour out; = عن *'ann*, appear, be visible; — II., V. be pleased with anything (acc.).

انا *anâ*, I; — *innâ*, see under ان; — *annâ* = انى *anna*, wherever? where? how? — *an-an, inan*, highest degree, completion, ripeness, maturity; — *anâ'*, time; ripeness, maturity; completion; hindrance; — *inâ'*, pl. *âniya-t*, pl. pl. اوان *awân-in*, اوانى *awânî*, vessel; — *ânâ'*, proper times, &c., pl. of انى *anan*; — ة *anât*, expectation; delay; patience; modesty; awkward woman.

اناب *anâb*, jujube; — *inâb*, substitution; repentance, &c., IV. of (نوب).

انابشة *anâbiśa-t*, sergeants, pl. of انباشى *on-bâśî* (Turk.).

انابيب *anâbîb*, knots in a cane, &c., pl. of انبوب *ambûb*, q.v.

انابير *anâbîr*, magazines, &c., pl. of انبار *ambâr*.

انابيش *anâbîś*, torn out (roots or trees), pl. of انبوش *ambûś*.

اناث *inâs*, اناثى *anâsa*, women, pl. of انثى *unsa*.

اناجر *anâjir*, anchors, &c., pl. of انجر *anjar*.

اناجير *anâjîr*, roofs, pl. of انجار *anjâr*.

اناجيل *anâjîl*, gospels, pl. of انجيل *anjîl*.

انادر *anâdir*, threshing-floors, &c., pl. of اندر *andar*, q.v.

اناديد *anâdîd*, pl. scattered persons.

انارة *inâra-t*, enlightening, illumining.

اناس *unâs*, men, pl. of انسان *insân*; — *ânâs* and اناسى *anâsiyy*, men, &c., pl. of انسى *insiyy*, q.v.

اناسم *anâsim*, pl. men, mankind.

اناشيد *anâśîd*, poetical recitals, &c., pl. of انشودة *unśûda-t*.

اناص *anâs-in*, اناصى *anâsî*, the most select parts, &c., pl. of نصية *nasiyya-t*.

اناصيب *anâsîb*, pl. road- or land-marks.

اناطولى *anâṭûlî*, Anatolia, Asia Minor.
اناظيم *anâẓîm*, pl. of نظام *niẓâm*, constitution, &c., q.v.
اناعيم *anâ'îm*, herds of cattle, &c., pl. of نعم *na'am*.
اناف *ânâf*, noses, &c., pl. of انف *anf*.
انافح *anâfiḥ*, stomachs of sheep or goats, &c., pl. of انفحة *infaḥa-t*.
انافى *unâfiyy*, having a large nose.
انافيض *anâfîḍ*, leaves beaten from the trees for food, pl. of انفوضة *unfûḍa-t*.
اناقة *anâqa-t*, *inâqa-t*, beauty.
انالة *inâla-t*, giving, bestowing; causing to attain.
انام *anâm*, *ânâm*, pl. men, mankind; created beings.
انامل *anâmil*, fingers, &c., pl. of انملة *anmula-t*.
انان *unân*, sighing, groaning; — *annân*, who sighs frequently.
انانية *anâniyya-t*, egotism, arrogance.
انايب *anâyîb*, canine teeth, pl. of ناب *nâb*.
(انب) II. *annab*, scold, treat roughly; repel.
انبا *ambâ'*, news, tidings, &c., pl. of نبا *naba'*; — prophets, pl. of نبى *nabiyy*; — *imbâ'*, communicating, giving intelligence.
انبار *ambâr*, pl. *anâbîr*, magazine; granary; deck of a ship (Pers.).
انباشى *on-bâśî*, pl. *anâbiśa-t*, sergeant (Turk.).
انباط *ambâṭ*, the Nabatheans.
انبب *umbub*=انبوب *umbûb*.
انبتات *imbitât*, break, cut.
انبجات *ambajât*, pl. jams; sweet medicines.
انبخ *ambaḥ*, rough, hard; cruel; impure (colour); heaped up; f. *nabḥâ'*, pl. *nabâḥa*, heap of earth.
انبخان *ambaḥân*, dough of bad flour.
انبذة *ambiẕa-t*, pl. of نبيذ *nabîẕ*, wine.
انبس *ambas*, severe.
انبساط *imbisâṭ*, joy, gladness; recreation; unreserve.
انبعاث *imbi'âs*, sending, mission.
انبل *ambal*, a better arrow-shooter; more clever.
انبوب *ambûb*, ة *ambûba-t*, pl. *anâbîb*, knot in a cane, part of a cane between two knots; pipe, tube; flute.
انبوش *umbûś*, pl. *anâbîś*, torn out root or tree.
انبيا *ambiyâ'*, prophets, &c., pl. of نبى *nabiyy*.
انبيق *ambîq*, انبيك *ambîk*, alembic.
(انت) *anat*, I, INF. *anît*, groan, sigh; envy; determine the quantity, measure; be blunt.
انت *anta*, f. *anti*, thou.
انتاج *intâj*, the time of giving birth; producing as a consequence; drawing an inference.
انتان *intân*, stench.
انتباه *intibâh*, awakening; vigilance; attention; circumspection.
انتثار *intisâr*, being scattered, dispersed; falling of the leaves.
انتجاب *intijâb*, choice, election.
انتجاس *intijâs*, soiling, polluting.
انتحاب *intiḥâb*, lamentation.
انتحار *intiḥâr*, suicide.
انتحال *intiḥâl*, plagiarism, literary theft.
انتخا *intiḥâ'*, haughtiness; (m.) defiance.
انتخاب *intiḥâb*, choice; high calling; selection; predestination.
انتخاص *intiḥâṣ*, dwindling away.
انتخال *intiḥâl*, filtering, percolating.
انتدا *intidâ'*, appointment; interview; rendezvous.
انتداب *intidâb*, call, calling upon, summoning; invitation; giving the preference.
انتذار *intiẕâr*, vow.
انترا *intizâ'*, wish, desire.
انتزاع *intizâ'*, putting off; pulling out; taking away; (m.) being spoiled (engine, watch).
انتسا *intisâ'*, being forgotten;

retreat, migrating to other pastures.

انتساب *intisâb*, derivation of descent, genealogy; reference.

انتساخ *intisâḥ*, being copied; being abolished, annulled, effaced.

انتسار *intisâr*, reopening of a wound; being torn to pieces.

انتشا *intiśâ'*, beginning; growing; smelling.

انتشاب *intiśâb*, being taken hold of, taken prisoner; being implicated.

انتشار *intiśâr*, spreading; publishing; divulging; انتشار الايمان *intiśâru-'l-îmân-i*, propaganda.

انتصاب *intiṣâb*, being planted, raised; pronouncing a word with *fatḥa* (accusative, subjunctive).

انتصاح *intiṣâḥ*, accepting an advice.

انتصار *intiṣâr*, victory; triumph; revenge.

انتصاف *intiṣâf*, equity; claiming or obtaining justice.

انتضاح *intiḍâḥ*, sprinkling; baptism.

انتظار *intiẕâr*, waiting for, expectation.

انتظام *intiẕâm*, order; arrangement.

انتعات *inti'ât*, qualification by an attribute.

انتعاش *inti'âś*, revival.

انتعال *inti'âl*, being shoed.

انتفا *intifâ'*, banishment; ruin; destruction.

انتفاخ *intifâḥ*, being or becoming inflated; pride; swelling.

انتفاش *intifâś*, standing on end (of the hair), ruffling (feathers); (m.) being swollen.

انتفاع *intifâ'*, deriving a profit; advantage.

انتقا *intiqâ'*, choice, election.

انتقاب *intiqâb*, veiling.

انتقاذ *intiqâẕ*, rescue, delivery.

انتقاص *intiqâṣ*, diminution; decrease; decay; loss of one's honour.

انتقاض *intiqâḍ*, overthrow; downfall; abolition; (m.) being copied.

انتقاع *intiqâ'*, solution, dissolving by a fluid; maceration.

انتقال *intiqâl*, removal; emigration; death; transport; being copied; (m.) assumption of the Holy Virgin.

انتقام *intiqâm*, revenge; vindictiveness.

انتقاه *intiqâh*, recovery.

انتكا *intikâ'*, receiving payment of a debt; (m.) violent rage.

انتكاس *intikâs*, turning upside-down; relapse.

انتلاف *intilâf*, ruin, perdition, destruction.

انتم *antum*, you; انتما *antumâ*, both of you.

انتما *intimâ'*, being related with, claiming relationship with.

انتها *intihâ'*, end, termination, the last.

انتهاب *intihâb*, plundering, pillaging, spoil.

انتهار *intihâr*, driving away with scolding; scolding, reproach; — bleeding; diarrhœa.

انتهاز *intihâz*, watching and seizing an opportunity.

انتياب *intiyâb*, concerning; (one's) turn; repetition; succession.

انتياش *intiyâś*, touching, feeling or seizing with the hand.

انتياق *intiyâq*, choice, election.

(انث) *anus̱*, be soft; — II. put into the feminine gender; effeminate; — II., V. flatter or caress in the fashion of women; — IV. bring forth a female; — V. be feminine; flatter or caress.

انث *ânis̱*, soft, delicate; feminine; —*unus̱*, women, pl. of انثى *uns̱a*.

انثا *ins̱â'*, abuse, invective.

انثاع *ins̱â'*, vomiting; bleeding.

انثمام *ins̱imâm*, recovery; weakness; melting (n.), consuming (n.).

انثى *uns̱a*, pl. *unus̱*, *inâs̱*, *anâs̱â*, woman; female; inanimate object.

(انج) *anaj*, I, enter.
انجا *injâ'*, rescue; salvation; delivery.
انجاب *anjâb*, pl. of نجيب *najîb*, of noble descent, &c.; — *injâb*, being noble, high-minded, generous; begetting an excellent son.
انجاح *injâḥ*, succeeding; accomplishing.
انجاد *anjâd*, helps, victories, pl. of نجد *najd*; — *injâd*, assistance.
انجار *injâr*, roof.
انجاز *injâz*, despatching; fulfilling; keeping a promise.
انجاس *anjâs*, pl. of نجس *najs*, *najis*, &c., impure, polluted; — *injâs*, polluting; desecration.
انجاف *anjâf*, pl. threshold; lintel.
انجام *anjâm*, heavenly bodies, stars, &c., pl. of نجم *najm*; — *injâm*, rise, apparition.
انجبار *injibâr*, setting a broken bone.
انجبارى *injibâriyy*, of small means or talents (m.).
انجح *injaḥ*, more successful, comp. of ناجح *najiḥ* and نجيح *najîḥ*.
انجذاب *injizâb*, attraction; allurement; inclination; affection.
انجر *anjar*, pl. *anâjir*, anchor; a flat dish; — ة *anjura-t*, nettle (Pers.).
انجرار *injirâr*, extension; extent; wearisomeness, ennui.
انجس *anjas*, very dirty, impure, more polluted.
انجع *anja'*, more salutary, comp. of نجيع *najî'*.
انجفال *injifâl*, emigration, disappearance.
انجل *anjal*, f. *najlâ'*, pl. *nujl*, *nijâl*, with large well-split eyes; causing a large wound; broad; spacious.
انجلا *injilâ'*, appearance; splendour; revelation; disappearance.
انجم *anjam*, having a spot on the forehead (horse); — *anjum*, heavenly bodies, &c., pl. of نجم *najm*.
انجماد *injimâd*, freezing, curdling, congelation.
انجماع *injimâ'*, assembling, assembly.
انجوج *anjûj*, aloe-wood.
انجورى *anjûriyy*, from Angora.
انجوك *anjûk*, marjoram.
انجوية *anjûya-t*, anchovy.
انجيل *anjîl*, pl. *anâjîl*, gospel; — ى *anjîliyy*, evangelical; evangelist.
انجية *anjiya-t*, pl. of نجى *najiyy*, who has knowledge of a thing, accessory; mystery.
(انح) *anaḥ*, I, INF. *anḥ*, *unâḥ*, *anîḥ*, breathe heavily; sigh.
انح *âniḥ*, pl. *unnaḥ*, breathing heavily; sighing; miserly, avaricious.
انحا *anḥâ'*, sides, directions, tendencies, purposes, &c., pl. of نحو *naḥw*, q.v.
انحدار *inḥidâr*, descending, alighting; the rolling of a ship.
انحراف *inḥirâf*, inclination, declination (astron.); deflexion; change; distemper.
انحصار *inḥiṣâr*, being besieged, blockaded.
انحطاط *inḥiṭâṭ*, descending.
انحف *anḥaf*, thinner, comp. of نحيف *naḥîf*.
انحلال *inḥilâl*, solution; chemical analysis; unbinding.
انحنا *inḥinâ'*, bending, inflection; bow, obeisance.
انخب *anḥab*, more timorous.
انخع *anḥa'*, more contemptible.
انخفا *inḥifâ'*, hiding, concealing one's self.
انخفاض *inḥifâḍ*, putting in the oblique case, pronouncing with *kasra-t*.
انخفة *anḥifa-t*, boots, pl. of نخاف *niḥâf*.
انخلاع *inḥilâ'*, being removed; uprooting; abdication; (m.) relaxation of the joints.
انخناث *inḥinâs*, flexibility.
اند *anadd*, who flies, escapes more frequently.

اندا *andâ'*, humidities, &c., pl. of ندى *nad-an, nada.*
انداد *andâd*, antitypes, counterparts, &c., pl. of ند *nidd*, q.v.; — *indâd*, dispersing, separating.
اندباغ *indibâg*, being tanned.
اندخ *andaḫ*, stupid; who does not talk.
اندر *andar*, pl. *anâdir*, threshing-floor; melody accompanying the threshing of corn, &c.; heap of corn; name of a town in Syria; — rarer, rarest, comp. of نادر *nâdir.*
اندراس *indirâs*, obliteration, erasing.
اندرون *andarûn*, young folks.
اندرى *andariyy*, thick rope; from *Andar.*
اندعا *indi'â'*, accepting an invitation.
اندفاع *indifâ'*, being refused, repelled.
اندفان *indifân*, being interred.
اندلال *indilâl*, being led, guided.
اندلس *andalus*, Spain; — ى *andalusiyy*, Spain, Spanish.
اندم *andam*, more or most repenting.
اندمال *indimâl*, scarification; suppuration.
اندى *anda*, more liberal; carrying farther; — ة *andiya-t*, humidities, &c., pl. of ندى *nad-an, nada*; — pl. of ندى *nadiyy*, humid, fresh, &c.
انديشة *andiśa-t*, lace, galloon (m.).
انذار *inzâr*, warning, admonition; hint.
انزال *inzâl*, divine revelation.
انزلاق *inzilâq*, gliding, slipping.
انزع *anza'*, bald on the temples.
انزعاج *inzi'âj*, agitation, emotion, fear.
انزوال *inziwâl*, being separated.
(انس) *anis*, A, INF. *anas, anasa-t*; — *anas*, INF. *ans, uns*, be accustomed, become familiar with (الى *ila*); have familiar intercourse with (ب *bi*); — II. INF. *ta'nîs*, accustom (a.), render familiar; tame; see; — III. INF. *mu'ânasa-t*, have familiar intercourse with (acc.), be accustomed to; be social, polite; — IV. INF. *înâs*, render familiar, social; see; perceive, contemplate; know, learn; feel, experience, hear; (m.) cheer by society, entertain pleasantly; — V. INF. *ta'annus*, become familiar, accustomed (ب *bi*); be social; grow tame; become acquainted; become man (God); — X. INF. *isti'nâs*, become social, familiar, tame, accustomed; be social, converse familiarly; become aware of the presence of man (wild beast); see accurately, regard attentively; inquire; ask permission.
انس *anas*, pl. *ânâs*, familiar, joined in friendship; society of people living together; mankind; intercourse; — *ins*, mankind; man in his social state, a social person; companion; friend; — *unus*, pl. of انوس *anûs*, tame; — *uns*, social life, sociability; familiarity, affability, politeness; — *ânas*, more familiar, dearer; more cheerful; — ة *ânisa-t*, f. compatible; good-natured.
انسا *ansâ'*, nerves or sinews of the hips, &c., pl. of نسا *nas-an, nasa*; — *insâ'*, prolongation, respite.
انساب *ansâb*, origins, &c., pl. of نسب *nasab.*
انسان *insân*, pl. *unâs, nâs*, man (انسان العين *insânu-'l-'ain-i*, the pupil of the eye, pl. *anâsiyy*); human shadow; flesh of the finger-tips; summit, elevation; unsown land; — ة *insâna-t*, woman; — ى *insâniyy*, human; — ية *insâniyya-t*, human nature; humanity; humaneness; urbanity; politeness.
انسب *ansab*, fitter, more appropriate; more convenient, agreeable; f. *nasbâ'*, a very near female relative.

انسبا *ansibâ'*, pl. of نسيب *nasîb*, related by blood, &c.
انسباك *insibâk*, melting (n.).
انسحال *insiḥâl*, richness of style.
انسداج *insidâj*, lying on one's belly or face.
انسداح *insidâḥ*, lying on the back.
انسداد *insidâd*, being locked, shut, stopped.
انسراق *insirâq*, weakness of the limbs.
انسكاب *iksikâb*, being shed, spilt, poured out.
انسلاخ *insilâḫ*, being skinned, flayed; ending of the month.
انسى *insiyy*, pl. *ânâs*, *anâsiyy*, man; what is turned towards man, the inner side; any double member.
انشا *inśâ'*, creating, inventing; composing a letter, &c.; wording; diction; letter-writer (book).
انشاد *inśâd*, recital, recitation.
انشار *inśâr*, resuscitation of the dead.
انشائى *inśâ'iyy*, productive; referring to the wording.
انشتات *inśitât*, dispersion, separation.
انشراح *inśirâḥ*, gladness, cheerfulness.
انشعاب *inśi'âb*, splitting, ramification.
انشقاق *inśiqâq*, being divided, split; schism.
انشودة *unśûda-t*, pl. *anâśîd*, poetical recital; poem, hymn.
انشوطة *unśûṭa-t*, noose.
انصا *anṣâ'*, the most select parts, &c., pl. of نصية *naṣiyya-t*.
انصات *inṣât*, silence; listening.
انصار *anṣâr*, helpers, &c., pl. of ناصر *nâṣir*, نصير *naṣîr*.
انصاف *inṣaf*, equity, justice.
انصبا *anṣibâ'*, انصبة *anṣiba-t*, portions, &c., pl. of نصيب *naṣîb*.
انصباب *inṣibâb*, being poured out; flowing into the sea; running, careering.
انصباغ *inṣibâg*, being dyed; baptism.

انصر *anṣar*, uncircumcised.
انصراح *inṣirâḥ*, clearness; openness; open declaration.
انصرار *inṣirâr*, packing up.
انصراف *inṣirâf*, departure; leave; declension and conjugation.
انصع *anṣa'*, purer.
انصف *anṣaf*, more equitable; juster.
انصلاح *inṣilâḥ*, reconciliation; pacification; emendation.
انصياغ *inṣiyâg*, fashioning.
(انض) *anaḍ*, I, INF. *anîd*, be foul, corrupt (meat); — *anuḍ*, INF. *anâḍa-t*, be badly done (in cooking), be half raw; — IV. underdo (the meat).
انض *anaḍḍ*, less; leaner, comp. of نضيض *naḍîḍ*; — very rich; — ة *aniḍḍa-t*, pl. of نضيضة *naḍîḍa-t*, little rain, thirst, &c.
انضا *anḍâ'*, pl. of نضو *niḍw*, emaciated and weak, &c.; — *inḍâ'*, emaciating and weakening.
انضاج *inḍâj*, digestion; over-cooking.
انضاد *anḍâd*, carpets placed one on the top of the other, &c., pl. of نضد *naḍad*, q.v.
انضر *anḍar*, beautiful and splendid; more splendid; purest gold or silver; — *anḍur*, pl. of نضر *naḍr*, gold, silver; greening, blooming.
انضرا *inḍirâ'*, being slaughtered, killed; dying off.
انضمام *inḍimâm*, uniting, conjunction; meeting; addition; collection; coercing.
انضية *anḍiya-t*, pl. of نضى *naḍiyy*, arrow without head or feathers.
انط *anaṭṭ*, f. *naṭṭâ'*, pl. *nuṭuṭ*, long; far distant.
انطاكى *anṭâkiyy*, from Antioch.
انطباخ *inṭibâḫ*, being cooked.
انطباع *inṭibâ'*, being sealed, impressed, printed upon; tameness, obedience.
انطباق *inṭibâq*, accordance; conformity.
انطفا *inṭifâ'*, being extinguished, going out.

انطلاق *inṭilâq*, dismissal; divorce; going away.
أنطلة *anṭila-t*, pl. calamities.
انطوا *inṭiwâ'*, folding up.
انطياع *inṭiyâ'*, obedience.
انظام *inẓâm*, putting in order; composing poetry.
انظمة *anẓima-t*, constitutions, &c., pl. of نظام *niẓâm*.
انعاث *in'âs*, setting out; setting to work.
انعال *in'âl*, putting on shoes; shoeing (a horse).
انعام *in'âm*, cattle, &c., pl. of نعم *na'am*; — *in'âm*, granting a favour; present, largess, benefit.
انعراج *in'irâj*, being bent, inflected, inclined.
انعزال *in'izâl*, dismissal.
انعصاب *in'iṣâb*, harshness; hardness; severity.
انعطاف *in'iṭâf*, being inclined, inverted, folded, bent.
انعقاد *in'iqâd*, being tied; contract, covenant; curdling.
انعكاس *in'ikâs*, being reversed; reflection; reverberation; refraction; recoiling.
انعم *an'am*, softer, more pleasant; —*an'um*, prosperities, &c., pl. of نعم *nu'm*.
انغسال *ingisâl*, washing, ablution.
انغلاق *ingilâq*, locking up.
انغماس *ingimâs*, diving, sinking.
انغماض *ingimâḍ*, wink, sign with the eyes.
انغمام *ingimâm*, sorrowing; being covered.
انغيا *ingiyâ'*, being deceived, seduced; allured.
انغياض *ingiyâḍ*, sinking of the water.
انغياظ *ingiyâẓ*, rage, fury, violent anger.
(انف) *anf*, pl. *ânuf*, *ânâf*, *anûf*, *ânûf*, nose; beak; projection; cape, promontory, peak; beginning; مات حتف انفه *mât-a hatf-a anfi-hi*, he died a natural death; — ة *anafa-t*, contempt, indignation; sense of honour; — *ânifa-t*, first walking of children; — *anfa-t*, beginning; omen' fore-token.
انف *anaf*, U, I, INF. *anf*, hit on the nose; reach up to the nose (water); come to untouched pasture-ground; — *anif*, A, INF. *anaf*, *anafa-t*, despise and refuse from high-mindedness or haughtiness; have no appetite and feel nauseous; have pain in the nose; find anything troublesome and complain of it; advance; — II., IV. lead the camels to fresh pastures; cause one to despise a thing; — II. sharpen; — IV. cause the nose to ache; hasten; reach up to the nose; — V. try and dismiss one thing after another; hurry; — VIII. arrive; happen; — VIII., X. begin, be the first to do a thing.
انفاد *infâd*, dissipation.
انفاذ *infâẓ*, performing a business, executing; message; piercing, penetrating.
أنفار *anfâr*, persons, individuals, &c., pl. of نفر *nafar*; — troop, &c., pl. of نفير *nafîr*.
انفاس *anfâs*, breathings, &c., pl. of نفس *nafas*; — *anfâs-an*, in intervals.
انفاع *infâ'*, profiting; gaining; being profitable.
انفان *anfân*, supercilious, haughty.
انفتات *infitât*, being crumbled, broken into pieces.
انفتاح *infitâh*, being wide open.
انفجانى *anfajâniyy*, inflated.
انفحة *infaha-t*, *infihha-t*, pl. *anâfih*, stomach of a goat or sheep; acid in the stomach; heartburn.
انفخ *anfah*, afflicted with a rupture of the testicles.
انفخان *infihân*, *unfuhân*, ى *infihâniyy*, fattened; battened.
انفدا *infidâ'*, being ransomed.
انفذ *anfaẓ*, more piercing, more penetrating.
انفراج *infirâj*, recreation; rest; pause.

انفراد *infirâd*, being alone, single; singularity; doing a thing by one's self.
انفراق *infirâq*, being separated.
انفس *anfas*, more precious; more exquisite; — *anfus*, breaths of life, &c., pl. of نفس *nafs*.
انفساح *infisâḥ*, spaciousness; recreation; cheerfulness.
انفساخ *infisâḥ*, getting into disorder, abolition of a contract or bargain; abolition.
انفساد *infisâd*, corrupted state; corruption.
انفصاد *infiṣâd*, bleeding, letting of blood.
انفصال *infiṣâl*, separation, division; termination; final decision.
انفصام *infiṣâm*, being broken in two; bursting.
انفضاح *infiḍâḥ*, ignominy.
انفطار *infiṭâr*, being split.
انفعال *infi'âl*, feasibility, practicableness; evil impression; bad humour; — ى *infi'âliyy*, passive (gram.).
انفق *anfaq*, more saleable.
انفقاق *infiqâq*, separation, division; split.
انفلاج *infilâj*, apoplexy.
انفلاط *infilâṭ*, flattening.
انفهام *infihâm*, understanding.
انفوضة (*unfûḍa-t*), pl. *anâfiḍ*, beaten off leaves for food.
(انق) *aniq*, INF. *anaq*, rejoice at (ب *bi*); like; be agreeably surprised; — II. INF. *ta'nîq*, astonish; — IV. INF. *înâq*, *nîq*, astonish; eagerly long for (فى *fî*); — V. INF. *ta'annuq*, devote one's self assiduously to a thing; perform a thing intelligently and well; like; rejoice in (فى *fî*).
انق *anaq*, pleasure, admiration; — *aniq*, beautiful, pleasing; — *ânaq*, more or most pleasant.
انقا *anqâ'*, heaps of sand, &c., pl. of نقى *naq-an*, *naqa*; — pl. of *naqy*, marrow of the bones, &c.
انقاذ *inqâẓ*, rescue, setting at liberty; saving.
انقاع *inqâ'*, macerating, dissolving.
انقاص *înqâṣ*, diminution; injury; offence.
انقاض *inqâḍ*, roaring of a young camel; cracking a whip, the fingers, &c.; calling.
انقباض *inqibâḍ*, preventing; impediment; contraction; oppression of the heart; constipation.
انقد *anqad*, hedge-hog; tortoise.
انقدار *inqidâr*, fate.
انقذ *anqaẓ* = انقد *anqad*, hedge-hog.
انقراض *inqirâḍ*, lapse of time; extinction of a dynasty.
انقراع *inqirâ'*, casting lots; (m.) itch, mange.
انقس *anqas*, slave born in the house; — *anqus*, pl. of نقس *niqs*, ink.
انقسام *inqisâm*, being divided; division; discord.
انقصار *inqiṣâr*, (m.) washing, bleaching.
انقصاف *inqiṣâf*, being broken; defeat, flight.
انقضا *inqiḍâ'*, end; fulfilment, completion; expiration of any term or respite; death.
انقطاع *inqiṭâ'*, separation; break; interruption; end; cessation.
انقع *anqa'*, better quenching the thirst; — *anqu'*, pl. of نقع *naq'*, stagnating water; — ة *anqi'a-t*, pl. of نقيع *naqî'*, overflowing well; scream.
انقطاف *inqiṭâf*, being culled, plucked, gathered; crops, harvest.
انقلاب *inqilâb*, revolution; overthrow; vicissitude; change; solstice.
انقلاع *inqilâ'*, being up-rooted, torn out; (m.) departure.
انقليس *anqalîs*, eel.
انقهار *inqihâr*, succumbing, being compelled; irritation; bad humour.
انقور *unqûr*, notch of the date-stone.
انقوعة *unqû'a-t*, cavity where water or fat gathers.
انقى *anqa*, f. *naqwâ'*, having thin

fingers; — purer, comp. of نقى *naqiyy*.

انقيا *anqiyâ'*, pl. of نقى *naqiyy*, pure, clean, holy; the Saints.

انقياد *inqiyâd*, submission; submissiveness; obedience.

انقيض *inqîḍ*, a perfume.

(انك) *anak*, INF. *ank*, be large and stout; be long, lengthy; feel pain; list, long for.

آنك *ânuk*, lead, tin.

انكاح *inkâḥ*, sexual intercourse; marriage.

انكار *inkâr*, denying; rejecting; disavowing; — ى *inkâriyy*, negative.

انكاف *inkâf*, abhorring false gods; praising the one God.

انكتار *inkitâr*, name given by the Arabian historians to Richard Cœur de Lion.

انكح *ankaḥ*, given to sexual intercourse; — ة *ankiḥa-t*, dowries, &c., pl. of نكاح *nikâḥ*.

انكد *ankad*, not serviceable, useless, wretched.

انكسار *inkisâr*, being broken, rupture; contrition; despondency; defeat; bankruptcy.

انكساف *inkisâf*, eclipse; being darkened, eclipsed.

انكشاف *inkiśâf*, being unveiled, discovered, laid open.

انكع *anka'*, having a red nose.

انكلاث *inkilâs*, superiority.

انكليس *ankalîs*, eel.

انكماش *inkimâś*, hurry, haste.

انكى *anka*, who does more mischief.

انكيرة *ankîra-t*, tobacco-pipe.

انكيس *inkis*, magic figure.

انم *anam*, creatures, created things.

انما *innamâ*, only; yet, however; since, because; then, therefore; certainly; — *inmâ'*, growing; causing to grow; increasing, &c., IV. of (نمى); — *animmâ'*, pl. of نم *namm*, slanderer, tell-tale.

انماش *inmâś*, calumny.

انماطى *anmâṭiyy*, seller of blankets, pillows, &c.

انمحا *inmiḥâ'*, being effaced, erased.

انمحاق *inmiḥâk*, annihilation, destruction, ruin.

انمر *anmar*, f. *namrâ'*, pl. *numr*, spotted like a panther; dapple-grey horse.

انمس *anmas*, f. *namsâ'*, dusky grey; pl. *nums*, the birds *qaṭa*.

انمش *anmaś*, variegated, party-coloured.

انمص *anmaṣ*, having thin hair; downy; — ة *anmiṣa-t*, pl. of نماص *numâṣ*, month.

انملة *anmila-t*, *inmila-t*, *unmula-t*, pl. *anâmil*, *anmulât*, the fleshy tip of the finger; (m.) hand.

انمهلال *inmihlâl*, leisure; delay.

انموذج *unmûdaj*, sample, pattern (Pers.).

انمى *anma*, more prospering.

(انه) *anah*, I, INF. *anh*, *unûh*, *anîh*, breathe heavily; sigh, groan; envy; — v. show foolishness.

انه *anh-in*, see انهى *anhî*; — *anna-hu* (ان *anna*, q.v., with pron. of the 3rd person), because, that; perchance, peradventure; since; how! why! — *inna-hu*, certainly, indeed; to be sure; yes.

انها *anhâ'*, pl. of نهى *nahy*, rain-pit, pond; — *inhâ'*, bringing news, announcing, &c., IV. of (نهى), q.v.

انهار *anhâr*, rivers, &c., pl. of نهر *nahr*, *nahar*.

انهاض *inhâḍ*, raising; encouraging; instigating; calling out.

انهدام *inhidâm*, destruction; ruin; overthrow.

انهر *anhar*, bright, serene; — *anhur*, rivers, pl. of نهر *nahr*, *nahar*; — days, pl. of نهار *nahâr*.

انهزاز *inhizâz*, being shaken; wavering.

انهزام *inhizâm*, being routed; defeat; flight.

انهش *anhaś*, more given to biting; worse.

انهضام *inhiḍâm*, digestion.

انهلاك *inhilâk*, self-destruction.

انهماز *inhimâz*, marking with *hamza-t*.
انهماك *inhimâk*, entirely devoting one's self to a thing; zeal; diligence.
انهمال *inhimâl*, delaying; neglecting; being neglected; raining gently but incessantly.
انهى *anhî* (انه *anh-in*), pl. of نهى *nahy*, rain-pit, pond.
انهيا *anhiyâ*, pl. of نهى *nahiyy*, prudent, wise; forbidden.
انهيار *inhiyâr*, downfall, overthrow.
انهيان *inhiyân*, contempt; (m.) insult (offered).
(انو) *inw*, pl. *ânâ*, time; night.
انوا *anwa'*, having knowledge of the stars, skilled in astronomy.
انوار *anwâr*, fires, lights, &c., pl. of نار *nâr*, نور *nûr*.
انواع *anwâ'*, sorts, kinds, &c., pl. of نوع *nau'*.
انواق *anwâq*, she-camels, pl. of ناقة *nâqa-t*.
انوال *anwâl*, gifts; looms, &c., pl. of نول *naul*, q.v.
انوح *anûḥ*, breathing heavily; sighing; avaricious; — *unûḥ*, sighing, INF. of (انح).
انور *anwar*, brighter, more shining, more luminous; — ة *anwira-t*, fires, &c., pl. of نار *nâr*.
انوس *anûs*, fame; pl. *unus*, not given to biting (dog); — ة *unûsa-t*, human society.
انوف *anûf*, chaste (woman); — *unûf*, *ânûf*, noses, pl. of انف *anf*.
انوق *anûq*, a carrion-kite; pelican; — *anwuq* = انواق *anwâq*.
انوك *anwak*, stupid.
(انى) *ana*, I, INF. *any*, *an-an*, *anâ'*, *an*, *in*, be opportune; be or come in time; be nearly ripe; reach boiling heat; — INF. *iny*, *uniyy*, tarry, cause delay; — *anî*, A, INF. *inan*, not to be in a hurry; — II. tarry, hesitate; — IV. INF. *înâ'*, delay anybody; — V., X. treat a matter diligently and considerately; treat a person with patience; wait patiently for.

انى *an-an*, pl. *ânâ'*, *uniyy*, the proper time; highest degree; the whole of the day; — *any*, modesty, staidness; — *iny*, *any*, night-time; — *aniyy*, ripe, mature; — *ânî* (آن *ân-in*), f. ة boiling; overflowing; mild, gentle, and patient; — *anna*, wherever, anywhere; where? how? — ة *âniya-t*, vessels, pl. of انا *anâ'*.
انياب *anyâb*, canine teeth, &c., pl. of ناب *nâb*.
انيب *anyab*, provided with canine teeth, a tusk, &c.; — *anyub*, canine teeth, pl. of ناب *nâb*.
انيت *anît*, envied; envy; groaning.
انيث *anîs̱*, soft iron; — ة *anîs̱a-t*, luxuriant (pasture).
انيح *anîḥ*, heavy breathing; sighing.
انير *anyar*, brighter, clearer, more luminous.
انيس *anîs*, of equal disposition; familiar; confidant; companion; cock; — *anîs*, ة *anîsa-t*, magpie; — *anîsa-t*, fire; — ية *anîsiyya-t*, familiarity.
انيض *anîḍ*, half raw or corrupted (meat); fright.
انيق *anîq*, pleasing, pretty; — *anyuq*, she-camels, pl. of ناقة *nâqa-t*.
انيم *anîm*, creatures, created things = انام *anâm* and انم *anam*.
انين *anîn*, sighing (s.).
انيه *anîh*, weak.
اه *ah*, *ah-i*, *âh*, *âh-i*, oh! alas! — ة *âha-t*, measles; lamentation.
(اه) *ahh*, INF. *ahh*, *ahha-t*, *ihha-t*, be grieved and sigh; — II., V. same meaning.
اهاب *ihâb*, pl. *ahab*, *uhub*, *âhiba-t*, skin; complexion; raw leather.
اهاجى *ahâjiyy*, satires, lampoons, pl. of اهجوة *uhjuwwa-t*.
اهاضب *ahâḍib*, اهاضيب *ahâḍîb*, rain-showers in heavy drops, mountain masses, pl. of هضبة *haḍba-t*.
اهال *ahâl*, *âhâl*, pl. of اهل *ahl*, q.v.; — ة *ihâla-t*, fat, grease; sheep with a fat tail; — ى *ahâlî*, pl. of اهل *ahl*, q.v.

اهاليب *ahâlîb*, kinds, manners, ways, pl. of اهلوب *uhlûb*, ة *ahlûba-t*.
اهاليل *ahâlîl*, new moons, &c., pl. of هلال *hilâl*.
اهان *ihân*, bunch of green dates; trunk of a tree; — ة *ihâna-t*, contempt; treachery.
اهانيد *ahânîd*, pl. of هند *hind*, Hindoo.
(اهب), II. *ahhab*, get ready, be prepared; — V. INF. *ta'ahhub*, get ready; prepare for war; equip one's self.
اهب *ahab*, *uhub*, skins, pl. of اهاب *ihâb*; — ة *âhiba-t*, skins, pl. of اهاب *ihâb*; — *uhba-t*, pl. *uhab*, war material; ammunition; gear; what is necessary.
اهبا *ahbâ'*, atoms, f. pl. of هبا *hibâ'*; — *ihbâ'*, raising dust.
اهبرة *ahbira-t*, lowlands, pl. of هبير *habîr*.
اهتا *ahta'*, hump-backed.
اهتزاز *ihtizâz*, becoming agitated; wavering, tottering; exulting, rejoicing.
اهتزام *ihtizâm*, haste; noise.
اهتمام *ihtimâm*, pl. *-ât*, zeal, diligence; care, solicitude.
اهجر *ahjar*, longer and thicker; better; f. *hajrâ'*, unbecoming (speech).
اهجورة *uhjûra-t*, habit, custom.
اهجوة *uhjuwwa-t*, اهجية *uhjiyya-t*, pl. *ahâjiyy*, satire, lampoon.
اهجيج *ihjîj*, deep valley.
اهجيرى *ihjîra*, اهجيرا *ihjîrâ'*, custom, habit.
اهد *ahadd*, cowardly.
اهدا *ahda'*, hump-backed; — *ihdâ'*, offering; giving for a present; conducting in the right way.
اهدب *ahdab*, with long eye-lashes; with long branches.
اهدل *ahdal*, f. *hadlâ'*, flabby.
اهدى *ahda*, better guide.
اهذاب *ihẕâb*, swiftness.
(اهر) *ahar*, coll., noun of unity; — ة *ahara-t*, pl. *aharât*, furniture of a room; good condition; shape, form.
اهرا *ahrâ'*, granaries, pl. of هرى *hury*.
اهراق *ihrâq*, pouring out, shedding.
اهرام *ahrâm*, pl. of هرم *haram*, pyramid.
اهرت *ahrat*, اهرد *ahrad*, having a large mouth (lion).
اهزع *ahza'*, only left, last.
اهصا *ahṣâ'*, strong valiant men.
اهضا *ahḍâ'*, troops of people.
اهضم *ahḍam*, f. *haḍmâ'*, thin, lean; having strong front teeth.
اهطل *ahṭal*, f. *haṭlâ'*, falling in heavy drops.
اهكا *ahkâ'*, pl. perplexed people.
اهكومة *uhkûma-t*, jest, mockery.
اهل *ahl*, pl. *ahlûn*, *ahâl-in*, *ahâlî*, *ahâl*, *âhâl*, *ahlât*, *ahalât*, family; house, tent; master of the house; wife; people, men, man; fit for; inhabitants; *al-ahâlî* (m.) peasants; vagabonds; adventurers; — *ahil*, tame; — *âhil*, populated; — ة *ahla-t*, pl. *ahlât*, family, race; wife; — *ahila-t*, wealth; — *ahilla-t*, new moons, pl. of هلال *hilâl*.
(اهل) *ahal*, I, U, INF. *uhûl*, take a wife; — *ahil*, A, INF. *ahal*, become familiar with (ب *bi*); become accustomed to a place (acc.); — II. INF. *ta'hîl*, welcome; deem fit for or worthy of (ل *li*); IV. INF. *i'hâl*, same meaning; make one master and father of a family; give a wife; — V. INF. *ta'ahhul*, VIII. INF. *i'tihâl*, take a wife; V. be worthy of (ل *li*); — X. INF. *isti'hâl*, deem worthy; take the fat for one's self.
اهلا *ahl-an*, welcome! اهلا و سهلا *ahl-an wa sahl-an*, be welcome and at your ease.
اهلاك *ihlâk*, annihilation; destruction.
اهلال *ihlâl*, beginning of the lunar month; (m.) exordium; shouting of pilgrims or of those who perceive the new moon.

اهلب *ahlab*, f. *halbâ'*, hairy, bristly, and, by opposition, hairless, plucked; rainy; very fertile.

اهلوب *uhlûb*, ة *uhlûba-t*, pl. *ahâlîb*, kind, species; manner, way of doing a thing.

اهلول *uhlûl*, vain; vanities.

اهلى *ahliyy*, tame, domesticated; accustomed to a place; — ة *ahliyya-t*, being fit for; skill; ability; duty; sociability; relationship; possession; (m.) wife.

اهليلج *ihlîlij*, myrobalan tree.

اهم *ahamm*, graver, more important, more distressing.

اهما *ahmâ'*, worn out clothes, pl. of هم *him'*; — *ihmâ'*, wearing out.

اهمال *ihmâl*, leaving in the lurch; neglecting; negligence.

اهمام *ahmâm*, pl. of هم *himm*, decrepit; — *ihmâm*, grieving, causing sorrow.

اهن *'âhan*, iron (Pers.); — اهن المال *âhinu-'l-mâl-i*, hereditary property; ready money.

اهنع *ahna'*, slipping, sliding to and fro; son of a high-born Arabian woman; small.

اهو *âhû*, gazelle (Pers.).

اهوا *ahwâ'*, passions, loves, desires, &c., pl. of هوى *hawa*; — *ihwâ'*, falling down, &c., IV. of (هوى) q.v.

اهوال *ahwâl*, terrors, &c., pl. of هول *haul*.

اهوج *ahwaj*, f. *haujâ'*, pl. *hûj*, lengthy; fiery; precipitate; fleet; fool-hardy, rash; violent.

اهود *ahwad*, Monday.

اهوس *ahwas*, f. *hausâ'*, *hausā*, greedy; voracious.

اهوعة *ahwi'a-t*, pl. of هواع *hawâ'*, the month ذو القعدة *zû-'l-qa'dat-i*.

اهول *uhûl*, taking a wife, INF. of اهل *ahal*; — *ahwal*, more or most formidable.

اهوم *ahwam*, having a large head.

اهون *ahwan*, easier, easiest; toilless; unimportant; Monday.

اهونا *ahwinâ'*, pl. of هين *hayyin*, *hain*, easy to be done or borne, &c.

اهوى *ahwa*, more wished for, more desirable; dearer; — ة *uhwiyya-t*, deep valley; atmosphere.

(اهى) *ahâ*, INF. *ahy*, laugh aloud.

اهيب *ahyab*, more or very much revered.

اهيجنة *uhaijina-t*, youths married to girls before either have attained to puberty.

اهيس *ahyas*, courageous; fiery.

اهيغ *ahyag*, plentiful, abundant; *al-ahyagân*, eating and drinking; food and sexual enjoyment.

اهيف *ahyaf*, f. *haifâ'*, pl. *hîf*, thin, slender; not bulked out.

اهيق *ahyaq*, long-necked.

اهيل *ahîl*, well populated; — *uhail*, folks; common people.

اهيم *ahyam*, dark; — f. *haimâ'*, pl. *hîm*, wandering (diseased camel); thirsty, languishing; pl. *hiyâm*, waterless desert.

اهينا *ahyinâ'*, pl. of هين *hayyin*, *hain*, easy to be done or borne, &c., q.v.

او *au*, or, unless; — *a-wa*, interrogative; — *aww*, the conjunction او *au* (used as a substantive); — *aww*, oh; — ة *uwwa-t*, pl. *uwaw*, calamity.

اوا *iwâ'*, receiving hospitably, IV. of (اوى); — calamity, misfortune.

اواب *âwâb*, pl. of اوب *aub*, region, &c., q.v.; — *awwâb*, who returns to God; penitent.

اوابد *awâbid*, pl. of ابدة *âbida-t*, disaster, calamity.

اوابل *awâbil*, camels, pl. of ابل *ibl*, *ibil*.

اواخر *awâḥir*, pl. of اخرة *âḥira-t*, end, extreme, termination (gram.).

اواخى *awâḥî*, pl. of اخية *âḥiyya-t*, need, distress; ties.

اوادم *awâdim*, pl. of ادم *âdam*, Adam.

اواذى *awâẕî*, waves, pl. of اذى *âẕiyy*.

اوار *uwâr*, pl. اور *ûr*, heat; ardour; flame; thirst; smoke; south-

wind; — ى *awâr-in, awârî*, mangers, stables, pl. of ارى *iry, ariy.*

اوارج *awârij*, ة *awârija-t*, journal, a diary, a memorandum-book (Pers.).

اواز *awâz*, time before the spring equinox (Pers.).

اوازم *awâzim*, teeth, pl. of آزمة *âzima-t.*

اواسط *awâsiṭ*, middles, &c., pl. of اوسط *ausaṭ* and وسيط *wasîṭ.*

اواسى *awâsî*, women who circumcise girls, &c., pl. of آسية *âsiya-t*, q.v.

اواصر *awâṣir*, wombs, &c., pl. of آصرة *âṣira-t.*

اواضح *awâḍiḥ*, moonlit nights (13th to 15th of the month); pl. of اوضح *audaḥ*, more or most evident, clear, distinct.

اواطب *awâṭib*, leathern bags for milk, &c., pl. of وطب *waṭb*, q.v.

اواق *awâq-in*, اواقى *awâqî*, pounds, pl. of اوقية *ûqiyya-t*; — *awâqiyy*, shuttle.

اوالف *awâlif*, (female) companions, pl. of آلفة *âlifa-t.*

اوالى *awâlî*, pl. of اولى *aula*, nearer, worthier, fitter, &c.; — pl. of اول *awwal*, first, best, &c.; — pl. of آل *âl-in*, too weak, insufficient.

اوام *uwâm*, violent thirst; heat; smoke; giddiness; sinew.

اوامر *awâmir*, pl. of امر *amr*, order, command.

اوان *awân, iwân*, pl. *âwina-t*, time, season; *âwinat-an* (*a'inat-an*), sometimes; اوانئذ *awâna'ẓ-in*, at that time, then; — *iwân*, pl. اون *ûn*=ايوان *îwân*, palace, &c., q.v.; — *âwân*, times, moments, pl. of آن *ân*; — ى *uwânî*, vessels, vases, pl. of اناء *inâ'.*

اواه *awwâh*, who sighs frequently; merciful; learned in law; secure, certain; Abraham; prayer; — *uwwâh*, oh! alas!

اواهد *awâhid*, Mondays, pl. of اوهد *auhad.*

اواوين *awâwîn*, palaces, &c., pl. of ايوان *îwân*, q.v.

اوائل *awâ'il*, the first, &c., pl. of اول *awwal.*

اوائن *awâ'in*, pl. f. of آئن *â'in*, quiet.

(اوب) *âb*, U, INF. *aub, iyâb, auba-t, aiba-t, îba-t, iyyâb*, return; — INF. *aub*, intend; come to the water at night-time; keep away; — INF. *iyâb, uyûb*, set (sun); — *awib*, A, INF. *awab*, be angry; — II. INF. *ta'wîb, ta'yîb*, return; intonate again; travel the whole day; II., III. (INF. *mu'âwaba-t, mu'waba-t*), vie in walking (camels); — IV. INF. *î'âb* (ايئاب), provoke to anger; — V. INF. *ta'awwub*, return; INF. *ta'wwub, ta'yubb*, come to the water at night-time; VIII. INF. *i'tâb, ittâb*, same meaning; return.

اوب *aub*, return; repentance; pl. *âwâb*, region; quick walking; custom, habit; intention; way, road; cloud; wind; — ة *auba-t*, quick walking; return; coming homeward; (m.) set of friends; tent; — pl. *aubât*, foot.

اوبا *aubâ'*, catching diseases, plagues, &c., pl. of وبا *waba'*, q.v.

اوباش *aubâś*, rabble, populace, &c., pl. of وبش *wabaś.*

اوبر *aubar*, very hairy (camel).

اوتاد *auttâd*, pegs, &c., pl. of وتد *watad*, q.v.

اوتار *autâr*, strings, &c., pl. of وتر *watar.*

اوتل *autal*, pl. *wutul, utul*, who gorges himself with food and drink.

اوثان *ausân*, idols, pl. of وثن *wasan.*

اوثر *ausar*, enmity.

اوثق *ausaq*, f. *wusqa*, trustworthy; firm, strong.

اوج *auj*, height, summit, culmination.

اوجاع *aujâ'*, ailings, &c., pl. of وجع *waja'.*

اوجاق *ûjâq*, fire-place; hearth; chimney; the corps of janissaries (Turk.).

اوجال *aujâl*, fears, tender feelings, pl. of وجل *wajl*.

اوجب *aujab*, more or most necessary.

اوجر *aujar*, f. *wajrâ'*, very cautious; timid, timorous; — ة *aujira-t*, dens, &c., pl. of وجار *wajâr*, *wijâr*.

اوجس *aujas*, a little, something; time.

اوجع *auja'*, more painful.

اوجل *aujal*, who is afraid of (من *min*)

اوجم *aujam*, more or much extended.

اوجن *aujan*, strong, firm; *al-aujan*, strong rope.

اوجه *aujah*, more sightly, handsome; more esteemed; clearer; — *aujuh*, faces, &c., pl. وجه *wajh*, q.v.

اوجى *auja*, having a sore hoof; — ة *aujiya-t*, bundles of clothes, portmanteaus, pl. of وجا *wijâ'*.

اوحاج *auḥâj*, loop-holes, holes, pl. of وحجة *waḥja-t*.

اوحال *auḥâl*, puddles, &c., pl. of وحل *waḥl*.

اوحد *auḥad*, pl. *uḥdân*, *wuḥdân*, unique, incomparable.

اوحى *auḥa*, happening sooner.

(أود) *âd*, U, INF. *aud*, bend (a.); incline to one side (n.); return; —INF. *aud*, *uwûd*, importune;—*awid*, A, INF. *awad*, grow crooked; crouch; — II. make crooked; fold; make one's speech obscure; — V. grow crooked; bend (n.); — V., VI. importune, molest; — VII., VIII. grow crooked; bend (n.).

اود *awad*, hard work; molestation; bother; — crookedness, INF. of (اود);—*âwad*, f. *audâ'*, crooked;—*awadd*, dearer, more agreeable; — *awidd*, *awudd*, pl. of ود *wadd*, *wudd*, *widd*, lover, friend; — ة *auda-t*, load, weight.

اودا *audâ'*, f. of اود *awad*, crooked; also ة *audât*, ية *audâya-t*, valleys, &c., pl. of واد *wâd-in*, وادى *wâdî*; —*awiddâ'*, lovers, friends, pl. of وديد *wadîd*.

اوداد *audâd*, friends, lovers, pl. of ود *wadd*, *wudd*, *widd*.

اودع *auda'*, with a white throat (pigeon); field-mouse; shrew-mouse.

اودك *audak*, f. *wadkâ'*, sand-hill; بنات اودك *banât audak*, calamities.

اودن *audan*, soft, supple, flexible.

اودية *audiya-t*, valleys, &c., pl. of واد *wâd-in*, وادى *wâdî*.

اودح *auẓaḥ*, contemptible.

(اور) *âr*, U, I, have sexual intercourse with a woman; — II. inflame, ignite; — X. be afraid; flee and disperse in a plain; hasten in the darkness; be in violent anger; prepare for a leap.

اور *aur*, north-wind; motion of the clouds;—*ûr*, south-wind; pl. of اوار *awâr*, heat, etc., q.v.; — *awir*, stony.

اوراق *aurâq*, leaves, &c., pl. of ورق *waraq*, q.v.

اوردة *aurida-t*, jugular veins, pl. of وريد *warîd*.

اورس *awiras*, *auras*, cypress.

اورق *auraq*, f. *warqâ'*, pl. *wurq*, dark grey; ashes; rainless year; milk with two parts of water; f. *warqâ'*, pl. وراقى *warâqî*, *warâqā*, she-wolf; dove.

اورك *aurak*, f. *warkâ'*, having full hips.

اورم *auram*, people; troop.

اوره *aurah*, f. *warhâ'*, stupid; bluff; violent; raining abundantly.

(اوز) *auz*, *awaz*, computation.

اوز *iwazz*, pl. *iwazzûn*, goose; fat dwarf; mobile, agile.

اوزار *auzâr*, heavy burdens, crimes, sins, pl. of وزر *wizr*.

اوزان *auzân*, weights, measures, &c., pl. of وزن *wazn*.

اوزن *auzan*, weightier.

اوزى *iwazza*, waddling (s.); — *iwazziyy*, belonging or referring to a goose.

(اوس) *âs*, U, INF. *aus*, *iyâs*, present with, retribute; — X. get retribution, company, a present, help.

اوس *aus*, present; loan; opportunity; wolf; — *aus-an*, in the stead of.

اوساخ *ausâẖ*, impurities, &c., pl. of وسخ *wasaẖ*.

اوساط *ausâṭ*, middles, &c., pl. of وسط *wasaṭ*.

اوسخ *ausaẖ*, dirtier, more polluted.

اوسط *ausaṭ*, pl. *awâsiṭ*, f. *wusṭâ'*, middle part; medium; moderate; — ى *ausaṭiyy*, same meaning.

اوسع *ausa'*, wider, more spacious.

اوشحة *auśiḥa-t*, jewelled belts of women, &c., pl. of وشاح *wiśâḥ*, q.v.

اوشن *auśan*, parasite.

اوصاف *auṣâf*, pl. of وصف *waṣf*, quality, &c.

اوصر *auṣar*, elevated (ground).

اوصيا *auṣiyâ'*, testators, &c., pl. of وصى *waṣiyy*, q.v.

اوضاع *auḍâ'*, pl. of وضع *waḍ'*, q.v.

أوضح *auḍaḥ*, pl. اواضح *awâḍiḥ*, more or very distinct, clear, evident.

اوضع *auḍa'*, lower.

اوضة *oḍa-t*, pl. *oḍât*, *uwaḍ*, room; company of soldiers (Turk. اوطه).

اوضيا *auḍiyâ'*, pl. of وضى *waḍî'*, shining with purity and whiteness; pure, neat; handsome of face.

اوطان *auṭân*, native countries, homes, &c., pl. of وطن *waṭn*, *waṭan*.

اوطة *oṭa-t*, see اوضة *oḍa-t*, above.

اوظفة *auẕifa-t*, pl. of وظيف *waẕîf*, thinnest part of a horse's leg.

اوعب *au'ab*, more fit, to grant or exhaust the whole of a thing.

اوعر *au'ar*, rough, rugged; complicated; — *au'ur*, pl. of وعر *wa'r*, rough, rugged, difficult.

اوعية *au'iya-t*, vessels, vases, &c., pl. of وعا *wi'â'*, q.v.

اوغا *auġâ'*, wind, air.

(اوف) *âf*, U, injure; hurt; afflict.

اوفر *aufar*, f. *wafrâ'*, very capacious; full; large; richly grown.

اوفق *aufaq*, more or most appropriate.

اوفى *aufa*, more abundant, more sufficient.

(اوق) *âq*, U, INF. *auq*, be higher than; incline towards; bring misfortune upon (all with على *'ala*); — II. INF. *ta'fîq*, vex, torment; bring into difficulties; humble; prevent; — V. INF. *ta'affuq*, be prevented.

اوق *auq*, burden, load, weight; difficulty; bother; sewer; — ة *auqa-t*, troop; — *ûqa-t*, pl. *ûq*, *ûqât*, cistern; eyrie; — *uqa-t*, *uqqa-t*, pl. *uqaq*, okka=3 lbs. 4 oz. Engl.

اوقات *auqât*, times, seasons, &c., pl. of وقت *waqt*.

اوقاف *auqâf*, pl. of وقف *waqf*, bequest, pious foundation, &c.

اوقر *auqar*, graver, steadier.

اوقص *auqaṣ*, short-necked; nearest (way).

اوقية *ûqiyya-t*, وقية *waqiyya-t*, pl. *awâq-in*, *awâqî*, *waqâyâ*, a weight of about a pound.

اوقيانوس *oqiyânus*, ocean.

اوكح *aukaḥ*, earth, sand and stones.

اوكد *aukad*, firmer; more secure; more certain.

اوكس *aukas*, vulgar, common man.

اوكع *auka'*, contemptible; big and stupid.

اوكن *aukun*, nests, pl. of وكن *wakn*.

اوكة *auka-t*, anger, malice; calamity.

اوكية *aukiya-t*, pl. of وكا *wikâ'*, q.v.

(اول) *âl*, U, INF. *aul*, *ma'âl*, return; be reduced; come to a pass; renounce; separate from (عن *'an*); — INF. *ma'âl*, diminish (a.); — INF. *aul*, *iyâl*, coagulate, condense; — INF. *aul*, *iyâl*, *iyâla-t*, superintend; govern; keep in good order or condition; escape; take to flight; waste, grow thin; — INF. *iyâl*, govern well; —*awil*, A, go in front; — II. cause to return; explain, make clear; interpret (dreams); determine the number, measure, or quantity; — V. explain; expose; — VIII. keep in good order.

اول *awwal*, pl. *awâ'il*, *awâlî*, f. اولى

ûla, vulg. *awwala-t*, pl. *ûlayât*, first, foremost; beginning; *al-awwalûn*, *al-awâ'il*, the ancient, ancestors; — ة *awwala-t*, beginning; the first.

اولا *ulâ'i*, pl. of اذا *ẓâ*, ذه *ẓih*, this.

اولات *ulât*, see اولو *ulû*, اولى *ûla*.

اولاد *aulâd*, sons, children, pl. of ولد *walad*.

اولائك *ulâ'ika*, comm., and f. اولاك *ulâk*, pl. of ذاك *ẓâk*, تاك *tâk*, that.

اولائلك *ulâ'ilika*, pl. of ذلك *ẓalik*, that.

اولع *aula'*, foolishness; infatuation.

اولق *aulaq*, foolishness; fool.

أولم *a-wa-lam*, is it not so?

اولو *ulû*, f. اولات *ulât*, possessors, owners, pl. of ذو *ẓû*, frequent in composition.

اولون *aulauna*, pl. of اولى *aula*, nearer; — *awwalûn*, pl. of اول *awwal*, the first, ancestors.

اولوية *ulûwiyya-t*, majority, priority, superiority.

اولى *aula*, pl. *aulaun*, *awâlî*, du. *aulayân*, f. *wulyâ'*, du. *wulyayân*, pl. *wulâ*, *wulyayât*, nearer; worthier; more appropriate; — *ula*=اولا *ulâ'i*, these; in poetry= الذين *allaẓîn*, pl. which, who, اولاك *ulâk*, f. those, اولائك *ulâ'ika*, comm. those, اولائلك *ulâ'ilikâ*, those; — *ûla*, f. of اول *awwal*, the first; — *ulî*=اولو *ulû*, f. اولات *ulât*, possessors; in poetry= الذين *allaẓin*, pl. which, who; — *awwaliyy*, f. ة, the first, foremost; previous; an evident proposition; major term of a proposition; *awwaliyya-t*, priority, superiority, precedence.

اوليا *auliyâ'*, friends, patrons, &c., pl. of ولى *waliyy*, q.v.

اوليات *ûlayât*, pl. of اول *awwal*, first, &c.

(اوم) *âm*, U, INF. *aum*, be very thirsty; cry out from thirst; keep in good condition, govern well; —INF. *aum*, *iyâm*, fumigate, drive the bees out by smoke; — II. INF. *ta'wîm*, make thirsty; render tall and stout.

اوم *uwam*, pl. disastrous; — *awamm*, a better prefect or Imâm.

(اون) *ân*, U, INF. *aun*, be in easy circumstances; rest; — II. eat his fill (ass); easily accommodate one's self to circumstances.

اون *aun*, ease, and, by opposition, fatigue; rest; gentleness; equal walk; the two equal parts of a burden; pack-saddle; — *ûn*, palaces, &c., pl. of ايوان *iwân*; — *âwin*, at ease, quiet, at rest; — ة *âwina-t*, pl. tortoises; times, pl. of اوان *awân*.

اونق *aunuq*, she-camels, &c., pl. of ناقة *nâqa-t*.

(اوه) آه *âh*, *âh-i*, *âh-in*, آها *âh-an*, اوه *auh-a*, *auh-u*, اوه *awwah*, *awwuh*, *âw-in*, *âw-i*, *âww-i*, آو اوتاه *awatâh-u*, oh! alas! — آه *âh*, INF. *auh*, II. INF. *ta'wîh*, V. INF. *ta'awwuh*, call out oh! lament; feel pain.

اوهاط *auhâṭ*, pl. quarrels, contentions, disputes.

اوهام *auhâm*, opinions, fancies, suspicions, &c., pl. of وهم *wahm*.

اوهد *auhad*, pl. *awâhid*, Monday.

اوهز *auhaz*, having a graceful walk.

اوهن *auhan*, weaker.

اوهية *auhiya-t*, rents, clefts, pl. of وهى *wahy*.

اوور *awûr*, east-wind.

اووه *awûh*, oh! alas!

اووى *awawiyy*, corporeal; wonderful, miraculous (derived from آية *âya-t*).

(اوى) *awa*, I, INF. *iwiyy*, *uwiyy*, *iwâ'*, look for shelter, put up, alight (with الى *ila* or acc. of place); receive hospitably; — *awi*, A, INF. *auya-t*, *ayya-t*, *ma'wât*, *ma'wiyat*, have mercy upon (ل *li*), compassionate; — II. INF. *ta'wiyat*, alight; receive hospitably; — IV. receive hospitably; V., VI. alight; gather together; — VIII. INF. *ittiwâ'*, *i'tiwâ'*,

alight; rest, repose; have mercy upon (ل *li*).

اوى *âwî*, pl. *uwiyy*, alighting, having command of; compassionate; — *uwiyy*, flocks of birds.

اويجه *uwaijih*, dim. of وجه *wajh*, face, &c.

اويد *awîd*, noise of a crowd, tumult.

اويس *uwais*, dim. of اوس *aus*, wolf.

اويل *uwail*, dim. of آل *âl*=اهل *ahl*, people.

اى *ai*, viz., namely, that is, i.e.; — *î*, well, yes! — *ayyu*, O! O thou! — ة *âya-t*, pl. *âi*, *âyâ*, *âyât*, sign, wonder, miracle; verse of the Koran; tomb-stone; anything existing; body; pl. *âi*, example for imitation; characteristic; assembly; — *aya-t*, embassy; missive.

(اى) *ayy*, comm. and f. ة *ayya-t*, whoever, whichever; which? what? followed by a noun in the oblique case, as اى رجل *ayy-u rajul-in*, what man; or by an affixed personal pron., as ايكم *ayyu-kum*, which of you, &c.;—vulg. *e*, *eh*, *enâ*, with شى *śayy*, *śê*, contracted into ايش *êś*, what? ليش *leś* (for لاى شى *li-ayy-i śayyin*), for what reason? for what purpose? why? عليش *'aleś*, why? بايش *beś*, wherewith?

ايا *ayâ*, ha! ho! holla! — *iyyâ*, a prop for the pronominal affixes, when any personal pronoun is to be expressed emphatically, mostly in the accusative, and especially when two affixes depend on the same verb in a sentence, as, اعطيتك اياه *aṭaitu-ka iyyâ-hu*, I have given it to thee; *iyyâ-ka*, *f. iyyâ-ki* (supply احذر *iḥẕar*), be on thy guard! — وايا *wa-iyyâ*, ويا *wayyâ*, with, together with, as, وياكم *wayyâ-kum*, together with you, &c.; — ة *ayât*, *iyyât*, light; splendour, radiance; — *ai'a-t*, form; sight; aspect.

اياب *iyâb*, return, sunset (اوب); — *i'ab*, IV. of (واب), q.v.; —*ayyâb*, seller of water;—*iyyâb*, leathern bag, leathern pipe.

ايابس *ayâbis*, pl. of ايبس *aibas*, dry, &c.

ايات *âyât*, signs, miracles, &c., pl. of آية *âya-t*.

اياد *iyâd*, protection; refuge; entrenchment; rampart; rind; wing of an army; sand-hill; — *ayâd-in* and ايادى *ayâdi*, hands, &c., pl. of يد *yad*.

اياديم *ayâdim*, surface of the earth, &c., pl. of أئدامة *i'dâma-t*.

ايار *ayâr*, brass, latten; — *iyâr*, air; — IV. of (وار), q.v.; — *ayyâr*, month of May; — *âyâr*, pudenda of a man, pl. of اير *air*.

ايارج *iyârij*, ة, laxative (medicine).

اياس *iyâs*, despair; softness.

اياسين *ayâsîn*, men, pl. of انسان *i'sân*.

اياصر *ayâṣir* (اياصى *ayâṣî*), pl. of ايصر *aiṣar*, q.v.

اياطل *ayâṭil*, hypochondres, pl. of ايطل *aiṭal*.

اياغ *ayâg*, cup; glory; dignity; present; compassion (Pers.).

اياك *iyyâka*, *iyyâki*, see ايا *iyyâ*.

ايال *iyâl*, ة, see (اول), (وال); — ة *iyâla-t*, pl. *iyâlât*, district; government, province; — *iyâlât*, pl. river-dales.

ايام *iyâm*, driving out bees by smoke; — *uyâm*, *iyâm*, pl. *uyâm*, smoke; — *ayyâm*, days, pl. of يوم *yaum*.

ايامن *ayâmin* (ايامين *ayâmîn*), right hands, &c., pl. of ايمن *aiman* and يمين *yamîn*.

ايامى *ayâmā*, pl. of ايم *ayyim*, husbandless, widowed.

ايانق *ayâniq*, she-camels, &c., pl. of ناقة *nâqa-t*.

اياوم *ayâwim*, days (especially of calamity), pl. of يوم *yaum*.

اياوين *ayâwîn*, palaces, &c., pl. of ايوان *îwân*.

ايايا *ayâyâ*, along with you! go on!

ايائل *ayâ'il*, mountain-goats, deer, stags, pl. of ايل *ayyal*, &c.

ايائم *ayâ'im*, pl. of ايم *ayyim*, husbandless, widowed.

اتبا *i'bâ*, refusing (ابى); — *ibâ'*, being visited by the plague (وبا).
ایباد *ibâd*, singling out (وبد).
ایباس *ibâs*, drying, drying up, parching (يبس).
ایباش *ibâś*, hastening (وبش).
ایباط *ibâṭ*, weakening, making powerless (وبط).
ایباق *ibâq*, throwing into prison, ruining, annihilating (وبق).
ائبال *i'bâl*, being rich in camels.
ایباه *ibâh*, not caring for (وبه).
ايبس *aibas*, pl. *ayâbis*, dry, parched; fleshless; anything hard, to try upon the sharpness of a blade, &c.; — *aibis*, be silent! IMP. of (يبس).
ایبل *îbal*, *aibal*, *aibul*, ى *aibaliyy*, Christian monk; — ة *îbala-t*, fagot.
ايبة *aiba-t*, return; fodder, food; — *â'iba-t*, *îba-t*, watering at night-time.
ائتا *i'tâ'*, making a present; liberality; gift, present.
ایتاح *îtâḥ*, giving or possessing but little, living in strait circumstances; dunning (وتح).
ایتاد *îtâd*, fastening a peg, &c., in the ground (وتد).
ایتار *îtâr*, IV. of (وتر), q.v.
ایتاغ *îtâg*, ruining, destroying, &c. (وتغ).
ایتام *aitâm*, orphans, &c., pl. of يتيم *yatîm*; — *îtâm*, making an orphan; having fatherless children (يتم).
ائتباب *i'tibâb*, being prepared for a journey.
ائتبار *i'tibâr*, digging a well.
ائتباط *i'tibât*, standing quiet, and, by opposition, being agitated.
ائتثار *i'tisâr*, following the traces.
ائتجار *i'tijâr*, asking for wages, presents, alms.
ائتخاذ *i'tiḥâẓ*, choosing and taking for one's self, &c., VIII. (اخذ).
ائترار *i'tirâr*, hastening.
ائتزاز *i'tizâẓ*, boiling, becoming agitated.
ائتسا *i'tisâ*, affording consolation by anything.
ایتسار *îtisâr*, deciding by casting lots (يسر).
ایتساع *îtisâ'*, extending far, being spacious, &c. (وسع).
ایتشا *îtisâ'*, being embroidered (وشى).
ائتشا *i'tiśâ'*, being healed (broken bone), (اشى).
ائتصار *i'tiṣâr*, growing high and abundantly, &c. (أصر).
ائتصاص *i'tiṣâṣ*, assembling.
ایتصاف *îtisâf*, being described, &c. (وصف).
ائتضاض *i'tiḍâḍ*, seeking, &c. (اض).
ایتطا *îtiṭâ'*, being levelled and softened, &c. (وطا).
ائتفاك *i'tifâk*, being overthrown.
ائتكاك *i'tikâk*, being very hot, &c. (اك).
ائتلاف *i'tilâf*, concord.
ائتمام *i'timâm*, intending, taking for a model (ام).
ایثا *îsâ'*, suffering shipwreck, &c. (وثى).
ائثار *i'sâr*, preferring, giving precedence.
ایثاق *îsâq*, fastening, confirming, &c. (وثق).
ائثام *i'sâm*, causing to sin, throwing into sin.
ایجا *îjâ'*, preventing, being disappointed (وجا).
ایجاب *îjâb*, answering, affirming, granting, affirmation (وجب); — ى *îjâbiyy*, affirmative; positive.
ایجاد *îjâd*, invention; discovery; creation; becoming an author, publisher (وجد).
ائجار *i'jâr*, hire, rent (اجر); — *îjâr*, giving medicine to a child (وجر).
ایجاز *i'jâz*, brevity; abbreviation (وجز).
ایجاس *îjâs*, conceiving an idea; imagining; sense (وجس).
ایجاع *îjâ'*, causing pain (وجع).
ایجاه *îjâh*, making respected and honoured, &c. (وجه).
ایجانة *îjâna-t*, stone jug.
ایحا *îḥâ'*, sending, inspiring (وحى).

ايحاد *îḥâd*, rendering unique, incomparable; leaving in the lurch (وحد).

(ايد) *âd*, A, INF. *aid*, grow hard and firm; grow strong and powerful; — II. INF. *ta'yîd*, make firm, strengthen; confirm; — III. INF. *mu'âyada-t*, same meaning; help, assist; — IV. INF. *i'yâd*, same meaning; — V. INF. *ta'ayyud*, be strengthened, helped, assisted.

ايد *aid*, strength; vigour; power; authority; — *ayyid*, strong, powerful; — *â'id*, onerous, troublesome; — *aid-in*, see ايدى *aidî*.

ائدا *i'dâ*, help, &c. (ادى); — *îdâ'*, ruin (ودى).

ائداب *i'dâb*, spreading justice in the land; inviting to an entertainment.

ايداح *îdâḥ*, obeying, yielding (ودح).

ايداع *îdâ'*, depositing; taking leave, &c. (ودع).

ائدامة *i'dâma-t*, pl. *ayâdim*, hard ground without stones; pl. surface of the earth.

ايدع *aida'*, dragon's blood; saffron; basil.

ايدى *aidî*, pl. of يد *yad*, benefits; — *aida*, more or very clever.

ائذا *a-iẓâ*, whether? if? — *i'ẓâ'*, injuring (اذى).

ايذام *îẓâm*, putting a strap to the bucket (وذم).

ائذان *i'ẓân*, *îẓân*, call for prayer.

(اير) *âr*, I, INF, *aur*, *air*, have sexual intercourse with a woman; — II. have frequent sexual intercourse.

اير *air*, pl. *âyur*, *âyâr*, *uyûr*, penis; —*air*, *îr*, north-wind; east-wind; hot wind; — *îr*, cotton; — *ayyir* (*ayar*), a very hard stone; — *â'ir*, strong in sexual intercourse; — *ayarr*, f. *yarrâ'*, pl. *yurr*, hard as stone.

ايرا *îrâ'*, striking fire; showing (وري).

ائراب *i'râb*, conquering; prospering.

ايراث *îrâs*, making one an heir; inheriting (ورث).

ائراخ *i'râḥ*, *îrâḥ*, dating, fixing the date.

ايراد *îrâd*, revenues; objection; argument; exposition; address; intention; IV. (ورد).

ائرار *i'râr*, emaciating, jading.

ايراط *îrâṭ*, overthrowing, ruining (ورط).

ايرمى *airamiyy*, a stone as waymark in the desert; — *airamiyy*, *îramiyy*, somebody, anybody.

ايريداد *îrîdâd*, rose-colour, XI. (ورد).

ائزا *i'zâ'*, IV. of (ازى), q.v.; — *îzâ'*, leaning upon, rest upon; limewashing a house (وزى).

ائزار *i'zâr*, strengthening (ازر); — *îzâr*, preserving, guarding; carrying off, taking away (وزر).

ايزان *îzân*, pondering over a matter (وزن).

(ايس) *ayas*, despair of (acc.); — *ayis*, A, INF. *iyâs*, be without hope, despair of (من *min*); — *âs*, I, INF. *ais*, do violence, compel, force; soften; —II. INF. *ta'yîs*, IV. INF. *i'yâs*, rendering desperate; making an impression upon (فى *fi*); disdain, make little of; soften; — V. INF. *ta'ayyus*, be soft.

ايس *ais*, what exists; — *aisa*, there is, there are, with negative ليس *laisa*, there is not, there are not; — *âyis*, *â'is*, despairing, desperate; — *âyas*, more desperate.

ايسا *aisâ'*, ائسة *aisa-t*, a woman who no longer has her menses; —*îsâ'*, shaving (the head); cutting (وسى).

ايساخ *îsâḥ*, soiling, polluting (وسخ).

ايسار *aisâr*, pl. of يسر *yasar*, easy, &c.; pl. of يسرة *yasara-t*, lines of the hand; pl. of ياسر *yâsir*, who kills and divides a camel; — *îsâr*, easy birth; prosperity; getting rich (يسر).

ائساف *i'sâf*, saddening, embittering (اسف).

ايساق *îsâq*, loading a camel, a ship (وسق).

ائسان *i'sân*, pl. *ayâsîn*, man; — *îsân*, render insensible (gas); sleeping, slumbering (وسن).

ايسر *aisar*, easier to be done; more convenient; more fortunate; favourable; left, left hand.

ايش *eś* (for اى شى *ayy-u śay-in*), what? how? why?

ائشا *i'śâ*, healing (اشى); — *îśâ*, slandering, tale-telling, &c. (وشى).

ايشاك *iśâk*, walking quickly, accelerating, being on the point (وشك).

ايشام *îśâm*, flashing lightly, beginning of anything to appear, as hair, breasts, &c. (وشم).

ايصا *îṣâ'*, making a will, &c. (وصى).

ايصاب *îṣâb*, being ill, making ill (وصب).

ايصاف *îṣâf*, being fit to become a servant (وصف).

ايصال *îṣâl*, bringing, uniting (وصل); — *i'ṣâl*, coming at evening time; being rooted (اصل).

ايصر *aiṣar*, pl. *ayâṣir*, hay, grass; a short tent-rope (pl. also *ayâṣî*).

(ايض) *âḍ*, I, INF. *aiḍ*, return to a former state, do again or repeatedly; become; return to one's people.

ايضا *aiḍan*, again; also; likewise.

ايضاح *îḍâḥ*, clear explanation; making evident; evidence (وضح).

ايضاع *îḍâ'*, hastening, causing to go quicker (وضع).

ايطان *îṭân*, choosing for a dwelling, &c. (وطن).

ايطب *aiṭab*=اطيب *aṭyab*, better, &c.; — ة *aiṭaba-t*, *aiṭabba-t*, rut.

ايطل *aiṭul*, pl. *ayâṭil*, side, hypochondrium.

ايعا *i'â'*, putting a thing in any receptacle; keeping secret (وعى).

ايعاب *î'âb*, taking all, &c. (وعب).

ايعاد *î'âd*, promising; threatening (وعد).

ايغار *îġâr*, making water or milk to boil; provoking to anger; taking the custom taxes in farm (وغر).

ايغال *îġâl*, stepping quickly, entering suddenly, &c.; adorning one's speech (وغل).

ايفا *îfâ'*, fulfilment; satisfaction; payment (وفى).

ايفاد *îfâd*, sending; very quick walk (وفد).

ايفاز *îfâz*, causing to hasten; hastening (وفز).

ايقاد *îqâd*, lighting, burning (وقد).

ايقار *îqâr*, loading, burdening, &c. (وقر).

ايقاظ *îqâẕ*, awakening (a.), (يقظ).

ايقاع *îqâ'*, causing to fall, assaulting; bringing into harmony (وقع).

ايقان *îqân*, certitude, firm belief (يقن).

ايقونة *aiqûna-t*, image, picture (εἰκών).

(ايك) *aik*, ة, thicket; — *ayik*, INF. *ayak*, being closely entwined, grown together; — x. same meaning.

ايكا *îkâ'*, causing to lean, to recline (وكا) and (وكى).

ايكاد *îkâd*, making firm (وكد).

ائكال *i'kâl*, giving to eat, &c. (اكل); — *îkâl*, confiding in God (وكل).

ايل *îl* (ال *il*), God; — *ayyal*, *iyyal*, *ayyul*, *ayyil*, pl. *ayâyil*, mountain-goat; deer; stag; — *uyyal*, curdled milk; water.

ايلا *îlâ'*, making one governor of a province, &c. (ولى).

ايلاج *îlâj*, inserting, placing one thing into another (ولج).

ايلاد *îlâd*, giving birth (ولد).

ايلاع *îlâ'*, making eager for anything, causing to desire; instigating (ولع).

ائلاف *i'lâf*, accustoming to a place; making the thousand full.

ائلام *i'lâm*, causing pain.

ايلچى *ilchiyy*, pl. *ilchiyya-t*, ambassador, envoy (Turk.).

ايلمة *ailama-t*, anxiety; stir; sound; tone.

ايلول *ailûl*, month of September.

ايليا *îliyâ'*, *îliyyâ'*, Elias; Jerusalem.

(ايم) *âm*, I, INF. *aim*, *aima-t*, *îma-t*, *uyûm*, be without a husband or

wife (single, divorced, widowed); — INF. *iyâm*, drive out bees by smoke, to get at the honey;—II. INF. *ta'yîm*, cause to become widowed;—IV. marry a widowed person; — V. be deprived of a husband, &c.

ايم *aim*, *îm*, serpent; — ايم الله *aimu* (*îmu*) *'l-lâh*, by God! — *ayyim*, pl. *ayâ'im*, *ayâma*, comm., without a husband or wife, widowed; pl. *ûyûm*, a serpent; — *ayamm*, a better foreman or Imâm; — ة *aima-t*, widowhood; — also *ayimma-t*, feudal estate, land held in tenure; — *a'imma-t*, Imâms, priests, &c., pl. of امام *imâm*.

ايما *îmâ'*, sign, hint; signal; symbol (وما); — *ayyu-mâ*, f. ايتما *ayyatu-mâ*, whosoever, whatsoever; who? what?

ائمار *i'mâr*, order; increase, augmentation.

ايماض *îmâḍ*, glimmer, glitter; glance; wink (ومض).

ايمان *aimân*, f. *aima*, deprived of wife or husband, longing for (الى *ila*) either; — pl. of يمين *yamîn*, right, right-hand side, &c.; — *îmân*, creed, belief, religion.

ايمن *aiman*, f. *yamnâ'*, pl. *ayâmin*, *ayâmîn*, fortunate, propitious; secure; right hand, right; — *aimun*, pl. of يمين *yamîn*, right, right hand, right side, &c.; — *ayyu-man*, whoever.

ايمى *aima*, f. of ايمان *aimân*, see above.

(اين) *a'an*, *ân*, I, INF. *ain*, happen at the proper time, be in time; draw near; be tired.

اين *ain*, the proper time; fatigue, tiredness; — *în*=حين *ḥîn*, time; —*â'in*, quiet;—*ain-a*, *en*, where? whither? اين هذا واين هذاك *en hazâ wa-en hazâk*, what difference between this and that; — ة *â'inat*, pl. *â'inât*, easy, commodious; — times, pl. of اوان *awân*.

ائنا *i'nâ'*, causing delay (انى); — *înâ'*, relaxing, tiring (n. and a.), weakening (ونى).

ائناث *i'nâs̱*, giving birth to a female.

ائناس *i'nâs*, rendering familiar, sociable, &c. (انس).

ايناع *înâ'*, ripening (s.), INF. IV. of (ينع).

اينق *ainuq*, she-camels, pl. of ناقة *nâqa-t*.

اينكشارية *înkiśâriyya-t*, janissary.

لينما *aina-mâ*, wherever; everywhere.

ايه *îh-a*, *îh-i*, *âh-in*, well! —*ayyahu*, O! O thou! — *ayyah*, II., call out to (ب *bi*).

ايها *ayyuhâ*, O! O thou! — *aih-an*, be off with you! — *îh-an*, be silent! — *îhâ'*, rendering weak, lax, &c. (وهى).

ايهاب *îhâb*, gift; concession (وهب).

ائهال *i'hâl*, welcoming, &c. (اهل).

ايهام *îhâm*, making believe or suppose; ambiguity; (m.) intimidation.

ايهان *aihân*, away with you! — *îhân*, weakening, unnerving (وهن).

ايهم *aiham*, f. *yahmâ'*, stupid; dumb; brave; smooth; steep; desert; *al-aihamân*, torrent and mad camel, danger from water and fire.

ائوا *i'wâ'*, hospitality, shelter.

ايوان *îwân*, pl. *îwânât*, *awânîn*, *ayâwîn*, palace; portico; gallery; saloon, hall; balcony, belvedere.

ايوب *ayyub*, Job;—*uyûb*, setting of the sun (اوب).

ايور *uyûr*, membra virilia, pl. of اير *air*.

ايوم *aiwam*, bright day, lit. more of a day than another, comp. of يوم *yaum*.

(ابى), V., تايى *ta'ayya*, تايا *ta'ayyâ*, remain; proceed slowly; — V., VI. walk straight up to (acc.).

ب

ب *b*; as a numerical sign=2, expressing also Monday as the second day of the week; abbreviation for the month of Rajab; — *bi*, inseparable preposition, with, by, at, in, to, towards; also denoting the object of a transitive verb, as مررت به *marartu bi-hi*, I met him, passed him; used after اذا *izâ*, as: اذا برجل *izâ bi-rajul-in*, behold, there was (or came) a man.

با *bâ'*, *be'*, name of the letter ب; — *bâ'*, matrimonial intercourse; wedlock; — ة *bâ'a-t*, matrimonial intercourse; night's lodging; hotel; wild-bee hives.

(باب) *bâb*, pl. *abwâb*, *bîbân*, *abwiba-t*, door; باب الابواب *bâbu-'l-abwâb-i*, Darband (portae Caspiae); باب المالدب *bâbu-'l-mândab-i*, gate of tears, Babelmandel; باب العالي *bâbu-'l-'âlî*, Sublime Porte; — also ة *bâba-t*, pl. *bâbât*, chapter; class; species; category; object; conjugation; limit of a calculation; *al-abwâb*, repentance (gate of heaven); *bâbât*, verses, alineas.

بابا *bâbâ*, pl. *bâbâwât*, pope; father, grandfather, eldest (m.); — *ba'ba'*, knowing, conversant with.

(بابا) *ba'ba'*, INF. *ba'ba'a-t*, call father or consider as such; — II. run fast.

باباری *bâbâriyy*, black pepper.

باباوی *bâbâwiyy*, papal (m.).

بابل *bâbil*, Babylon; — ی *bâbiliyy*, Babylonian; enchanting; poison; ية *bâbiliyyat*, wine (the two latter significations poetical).

بابوج *bâbûj* (بابوش *bâbûś*), pl. *bawâbîj*, slipper (Pers.).

بابوس *bâbûs*, child, young of an animal, foal.

بابونج *bâbûnaj*, camomile (Pers.).

بابية *bâbiyya-t*, miraculous things.

باتت *bâtt*, cutting, breaking, weakening; foolish, drunk; lean, thin; completed, put into order.

باتر *bâtir*, cutting, sharp; pl. *bawâtir*, sword.

باتك *bâtik*, cutting, sharp.

باتور *bâtûr*, pl. *bawâtîr*, mat of rushes for silk-worms.

باثر *bâsir*, showing itself spontaneously; envious.

باثق *bâsiq*, overflowing.

(باج) *ba'aj*, A, INF. *ba'j*, turn, change; cry out; — II. cry out.

باج *ba'j*, *bâj*, ة, species; manner, way, method; — *bâj*, best head of a flock; entrance custom, tribute (m. Pers.).

باجس *bâjis*, pl. *bujjas*, pouring in torrents.

باحث *bâhis*, examiner.

باحر *bâhir*, stupid; liar; meddling; perplexed.

باحة *bâha-t*, mass of water; depth of the sea; gulf; palm-grove; pl. *bûh*, passage; courtyard.

باحور *bâhûr*, hottest days of July; month; يوم باحوری *yaum bâhûriyy*, critical day; باحورا *bâhûrâ'*, dog-days.

باخس *bâhis*, cunning; malicious; cheat.

باخق *bâhiq*, one-eyed; blind.

باخل *bâhil*, pl. *buhhal*, miserly, avaricious.

باداة *bâdât*, desert.

بادر *bâdir*, shining in full; f. ة, hastening, hurried; *bâdira-t*, pl. *bawâdir*, first movement or impulse; impetuosity; sharpness of a sword.

بادروج *bâdarûj*, basil.

بادلان *bâdalân*, oyster.

بادن *bâdin*, pl. *budun*, *buddan*, stout, corpulent; old, aged.

بادنجان *bâdinjân*, love-apple (Melongena).

بادهنج *bâdhanj* (باداهنج *bâzâhanj*), ventilator, chimney.

بادوان *bâduwân*, Bedouins (m.).

بادى *bâdî* (باد *bâd-in*), pl. *bâdûn*, *budd-an*, *buddâ*, externally visible, distinct; living in the desert; — *bâdi'*, who begins, sets to work first; f. ة *bâdi'a-t*, first cause, reason; — ة *bâdiya-t*, inhabitants of the desert; nomads; desert.

باذ *bâẓẓ*, old, ragged.

باذخة *bâẓiḥa-t*, pl. *bawâẓiḥ*, very high mountains.

باذل *bâẓil*, liberal, generous.

باذلة *bâẓana-t*, recognition, submission; knowledge.

باذى *bâẓiyy*, indecent speech, ribaldry.

(بار) *ba'ar*, A, INF. *ba'r*, dig a well; hide, conceal; send good deeds before one's self, do good in secret; — IV. INF. *ib'âr*, dig a well for another; — VIII. INF. *ibti'âr*, dig a well; conceal.

بار *bâr*, the first emanation of the Divinity; — *bârr*, pl. *abrâr*, *bararat-t*, innocent, pious; liberal, beneficent.

بارج *bârij*, a good sailor; — ة *bârija-t*, man of war; pl. *bawârij*, hotel, inn.

بارح *bâriḥ*, pl. *bawâriḥ*, living in the plain; turning the left side towards; hot wind; *al-bâriḥ*, ة *al-bâriḥa-t*, yesterday; البارحة الاولى *al-bâriḥatu-'l-'ula*, the day before yesterday.

بارد *bârid*, cold, cooling, agreeable; dull, slow; poor (wit, poetry); incontestable (right); safely placed (money); غنيمة باردة *ganîma-t bârida-t*, easy booty (obtained without bloodshed); pl. *bawârid*, sharp sword.

بارز *bâriz*, f. ة, projecting; external; the pronominal affix of a verb.

بارض *bâriḍ*, first cotyledon.

بارع *bâri'*, ة, exceedingly beautiful; excelling in knowledge; excelling; *bâri'a-t*, excellence, merit.

بارق *bâriq*, f. *bâriqa-t* (pl. *bâriqât*, *bawâriq*), shining, flashing.

بارك *bârik*, ة, kneeling; (m.) blessing; — ة *bârika-t*, pl. *bawârik*, knee.

بارنج *bâranj*, cocoa-nut.

بارود *bârûd*, powder; بارود ابيض *bârud abyaḍ*, nitre; — ة *barûda-t*, pl. *bawârîd*, gun (m); — ية *barûdiyya-t*, powder-bag.

باروق *bârûq*, white lead.

باروك *bârûk*, timid, lazy.

بارى *bârî'*, *bârî*, creator, God; pl. *birâ'*, healed; — who planes, smoothes, &c.; — ة *bâri'ya-t*, pl. *bawârî*, mat of bulrushes.

باز *ba'z*, *bâz*, pl. *bu'uz*, *bi'zân*, *bîzân*, *ab'uz*, *buz'ân*, falcon, hawk.

بازار *bâzâr*, market, market-place, emporium; traffic; a bargain (Pers.).

بازارگان *bâzârgân* (بازرکان *bazirgân*), merchant (Pers.).

بازدار *bâzdâr*, pl. *bazâdira-t*, *bâzdâriyya-t*, falconer (Pers.).

بازل *bâzil*, experienced.

بازى *bâziyy*, pl. *buzât*, *bawâzî*, falcon, hawk.

باس *ba's*, *bâs*, courage, boldness; power, strength; calamity, adversity, misfortune; damage; punishment; لا باس *lâ bâs*, there is no harm in it.

باسا *bâsâ'*, pain, sorrow; misfortune; poverty.

باسابورط *bâsâborṭ*, passport (m.).

باسره *bi-asri-hi*, the whole of it, and so on, &c., see اسر *asr*.

باسرة *bâsira-t*, stern countenances.

باسط *bâsiṭ*, distant; thirsting; spreading; embracing; *al-bâsiṭ*, God; — ة *bâsiṭa-t*, ell, cubit.

باسق *bâsiq*, high; — ة *bâsiqa-t*, pl. *bawâsiq*, high palm-tree; white cloud; danger; a fruit.

باسل *bâsil*, pl. *busl*, *bussal*, *busalâ'*, having a stern countenance; pl. *bawâsil*, lion; brave; terrible; strong, and, by opposition, in-

sipid (beverage); blunt, bluff; sour milk.

باسم *bâsim,* smiling.

باسن *bâsin,* ة, plough-share; tool; coarse sack.

باسور *bâsûr,* pl. *bawâsîr,* emerods, piles.

باسليق *bâsilîq,* vena basilica.

(باش) *ba'aś,* A, INF. *ba'ś,* throw down unawares; ما باش *mâ ba'aś,* it is not forbidden;— III. seize and throw down, without resistance on the part of the assaulted.

باش *bâś*=باى شى *bi-ayy-i śay-in, bi-eś,* why? in order that;—*bâś,* chief (Turk.);—*bâśś,* friendly, amiable, smiling.

باشا *bâśâ,* pl. *bâśâwât, bâśât,* pasha (Turk.).

باشر *bâśir,* propitious, auspicious; prudent.

باشق *bâśiq,* pl. *bawâśiq,* sparrow-hawk.

باصر *bâṣir,* who looks at; sagacious; intelligent;—ة *bâṣira-t,* sight, eye.

باضع *bâḍi',* pl. *baḍa'a-t,* cutting, sharp; good; broker; pedlar; camel-dealer;—ة *bâḍi'a-t,* pl. *bawâḍi',* herd; wound from which blood is dropping.

باضوض *bâḍûḍ,* humidity.

(باط) *ba'aṭ;*—V. lie on one's side; be of a careless mind; not trouble about a matter.

باطح *bâṭiḥ,* fallen on the face.

باطل *bâṭil,* pl. *buṭul,* vain, foolish; useless; false; lie; play: ذو باطل *zû bâṭil,* jester; devil; pl. *baṭala-t,* sorcerer.

باطن *bâṭin,* pl. *bawâṭin,* inner, interior; concealed, secret; mystical; who penetrates the heart (God); pl. *abṭina-t, buṭnân,* lowlands; fissures of the ground caused by water;—ية *bâṭiniyya-t,* the Batanians or assassins.

باطية *bâṭiya-t,* pl. *bawâṭî,* deep dish; vat.

باع *bâ',* fathom (measure);—ة *bâ'a-t,* courtyard;—sellers, &c., pl. of بائع *bâ'i'.*

باعث *bâ'is,* who sends; who causes; author; cause; subject;—ة *bâ'isa-t,* pl. *bawâ'is,* motive, reason; charm;—ية *bâ'isiyya-t,* causality.

باعد *bâ'id,* far, distant; perishing; contemptible.

باعق *bâ'iq,* stream; waterspout; crash, peal.

باعك *bâ'ik,* stupid.

باعوث *bâ'ûs,* Easter-feast.

باغ *bâg,* pl. *bâgât,* garden (Pers.); —*bâg-in,* see باغى *bâgî.*

باغبان *bâgbân,* gardener (Pers.).

باغز *bâgiz,* ribald; swiftness;—ية *bâgiziyya-t,* a coarse silk-stuff; dress made of it.

باغض *bâgiḍ,* who hates.

باغمة *bâgima-t,* low and modest or tender talk.

باغوث *bâgûs,* Easter.

باغى *bâgî* (باغ *bâg-in*), f. ة *bâgiya-t,* pl. *bugât, bugyân,* who seeks or desires passionately; rebellious; unjust; tyrant; *bâgiya-t,* adulteress.

(باق) *ba'aq,* INF. *ba'ûq,* befall;— VII. befall suddenly.

باق *bâq-in,* see باقى *bâqî;*—ة *bâqa-t,* pl. *bâqât,* batch of flowers, nosegay; bouquet.

باقر *bâqir,* herd of cattle; rich in goods and pastures; great; pl. *bawâqir,* ox; lion;—ة *bâqira-t,* sharp.

باقع *bâqi',* spotted like a tiger; hyena;—ة *bâqi'a-t,* prudent, cautious; calamity.

باقل *bâqil,* greengrocer; name of a certain lazy blockhead.

باقلا *bâqilâ',* باقلى *bâqilâ,* باقلاة *bâqilât,* Egyptian bean.

باقور *bâqûr,* ة *bâqûra-t,* herd of cattle; *bâqûra-t,* cow.

باقول *bâqûl,* pl. *bawâqîl,* cup; earthen inkstand (m.).

باقى *bâqî* (باق *bâq-in*), pl. *bâqîn,* f. ة, pl. *bâqiyât,* who remains, survives; remaining, lasting;

eternal ; God ; *al-bâqî*, rest, balance of an account ; *al-bâqiya-t*, duration ; pl. remainders ; good actions.

باك *bâk-in*, see باكى *bâkî*.

باكر *bâkir*, early in the morning ; — ة *bâkira-t*, virgin ; bearing early fruit (palm-tree).

باكور *bâkûr*, first spring shower ; f. ة, premature.

باكى *bâkî* (باك *bâk-in*), pl. *bukât*, *bukiyy*, f. ة *bâkiya-t*, pl. *bawâkî*, weeping, lamenting ; *bâkiya-t*, female mourner.

بال *bâl*, heart, mind ; attention ; solicitude ; — *bâl-in*, see بالى *bâlî*, mouldering ; shabby garb ; — ة *bâla-t*, bale ; perfume-bag ; scent-bottle ; grief, sorrow ; whale ; — *bâlla-t*, humidity ; drop ; advantage.

بالح *bâliḥ*, dry, bare.

بالد *bâlid*, inhabitant of the country or town.

بالغ *bâlig*, who reaches, penetrates ; f. ة, of age ; having attained to puberty ; excellent.

بالوع *bâlû'*, wide open, gaping abyss ; — ة *bâlû'a-t*, pl. *bawâlî'*, sink, sewer, cloaca.

بالول *bâlûl*, a little water ; drop.

بالى *bâlî* (بال *bâl-in*), worn-out (clothes).

(بان) *bân*, ة, the Egyptian willow ; حب البان *ḥabbu-'l-bân-i*, nutmeg.

بان *bân-in*, بانى *bânî*, f. *bâniya-t*, pl. *bunnât*, *bawânî*, who builds, founds ; architect ; composer ; author ; — *bâniyy*, straight and slender (like the willow-tree).

(باه) *ba'ah*, INF. *ba'h*, notice, comprehend quickly (ل *li*, ب *bi*).

باه *bâh*, sexual intercourse ;—*bâh-in*, see باهى *bâhî*.

باهت *bâhit*, liar ; slanderer ; (m.) languid, pale ; astonished, perplexed.

باهر *bâhir*, ة, handsome ; shining ; admirable ; clear, distinct ; *bâhirât*, ships.

باهظ *bâhiz̤*, oppressive, difficult ; important ; *al-bâhiz̤*, calamity ; ة *bâhiz̤a-t*, adversity.

باهج *bâhig*, sleeping, sleepy.

باهل *bâhil*, pl. *buhl*, *buhhal*, free ; at leisure ; idler ; *bâhil*, and ة *bâhila-t*, unmarried woman.

باهم *bâhim*, pl. *bawâhim*, thumb ; big toe (m.).

باهى *bâhî* (باه *bâh-in*) ; f. ة, empty ; having a wide cavity ; — *bâhiyy*, aphrodisiac.

(باو , باى) *ba'â*, A, U, INF. *ba'w*, *ba'wâ'*, rise high and exert one's self in running (camel) ; surpass in glory ; glory, boast.

باو *ba'w*, glory, pride.

باى *bai*=بك *beg* (Turk.), Bey, prince, chief.

بائت *bâ'it*, passing the night ; a night old ; of yesterday ; stale.

بائجة *bâ'ija-t*, pl. *bawâ'ij*, misfortune.

بائح *bâ'iḥ*, who promulgates a secret ; (m.) traitor ; shameless.

بائخ *bâ'iḫ*, tired.

بائد *bâ'id*, perishable.

بائس *bâ'is*, poor, miserable.

بائض *bâ'iḍ*, laying eggs.

بائع *bâ'i'*, pl. *bâ'a-t*, seller ; informer ; traitor ; a woman who has many suitors (pl. also *bâwâ'i'*).

بائق *bâ'iq*, of little value ; — ة *bâ'iqa-t*, pl. *bawâ'iq*, misfortune, calamity ; wrong.

بايلك *bailik*, government ; fisc (Turk.).

بائن *bâ'in*, ة, distinct, evident, notorious ; f. a divorced woman ; f. pl. *bawâ'in*, proof by four witnesses.

بايية *bâyiya-t*, Palm-feast.

بب *babb*, sort, kind ; — ة *babba-t*, saying "papa," prattle of children.

ببان *babân*, *babbân*, kind ; manner ; way of living.

ببغا *babagâ'*, *babbagâ'*, *babgâ'*, ببغاة *babagât*, ببغال *babagâl*, parrot ; nightingale.

(بت) *batt*, U, I, INF. *batt*, cut, lop ;

be cut or lopped; perform, accomplish; decide; over-drive an animal and be unable to complete one's journey; — INF. *batta-t, batât*, divorce a wife for once and all; — INF. *batût*, grow thin; make and sell the head-dress بت *batt*; — cut off; perform quickly, despatch; provide with provender; — IV. cut off; complete; — V. get provided with provender; furnish a house to live in; — VII. be cut off, decided, finished; grow impotent.

بت *batt*, pl. *butût, bitât*, a coarse piece of dress to cover the head; hood, wrapper; rope; (m.) skein; — ة *bita-t*, stay, remaining, INF. of (وبت); — *batta-t*, cut, separation; *battat-an, al-batta-t*, بتة بتلة *battat-an batlat-an*, irrevocably; (m.) not at all.

(بتا) *bata'*, INF. *bat'*, remain, stay.

بتات *batât*, pl. *abitta-t*, travelling requisites; supplies; household things, furniture; outfit; hood; anything separated from a whole; divorce; performance; *batât-an*, irrevocably; — *battât*, maker and seller of the head-dress *batt*; — ى *batâtî*, small casks, pl. of بتية *batiyya-t*.

بتار *battâr, butâr*, sharp.

بتاع *batâ'* (Eg.)=متاع *matâ'*, goods, property; followed by pronominal affixes it is used as a possessive adjective, f. *batâ'a-t*, pl. *butû'*.

بتاك *battâk*, sharp.

بتائل *batâ'il*, palm-shoots, &c., pl. of بتيلة *batîla-t*.

(بتر) *batar*, U, INF. *batr*, maim, curtail; cut off; outroot; — *batir*, A, INF. *batar*, have lost the tail; be childless, useless; — II. annihilate; — IV. curtail; deprive of posterity; give, and, by opposition, refuse; perform the morning prayer only at sunrise; — VIII. be cut off, lopped; run.

بترا *batrâ'*, Mahomet's coat of mail.

بترة *batra-t*, she-ass.

(بتع) *bata'*, I, INF. *bat'*, prepare the wine بتع *bit'*; INF. *butû'*, remove to a distance; be cut off, separated; — *bati'*, A, INF. *bata'*, have a long neck, strong limbs; follow one's head; — VII. be cut off, separated.

بتع *bit', bita'*, strong wine, mead; — *but'*, pl. of ابتع *abta'*, whole, all.

بتعا *bat'â'*, f. of ابتع *abta'*, whole, all; strong of joints.

(بتك) *batak*, I, U, INF. *batk*, cut, cut off; seize and draw towards one's self, offer violence; — II. cut; — V., VII. be cut, cut off; — ة *bitka-t, batka-t*, pl. *bitak*, part, piece, portion; night.

(بتل) *batal*, U, INF. *batl*, cut off; separate, sever; — II. cut off; separate from (عن *'an*); devote one's self entirely to (ل *li*); — IV. sever; — V., VII. be separated, severed; — V. devote one's self entirely to God; — X. be severed.

بتل *batl*, ة, things separated; separation.

(بتو) *batâ*, U, INF. *batw*, remain, stay.

بتوت *batût*, INF. of (بت); — *butût*, pl. of بت *batt*, q.v.

بتوع *batû'*, pl. of بتاع *batâ'*, q.v.

بتوك *batûk*, sharp.

بتول *batûl* (بتيل *batîl*), virgin; nun; vestal; *al-butûl, al-butûla-t*, the Holy Virgin; Fatimah; palm-shoot; — ية *batûliyya-t*, virginity.

بتى *batiyy*, table-cloth; towel; = بتات *battât*, maker and seller of hoods; — ة *battiyya-t*, pl. *batâtî*, small cask (m).

بتيرة *bataira-t*, sun.

بتيلة *batîla-t*, pl. *batâ'il*, palm-shoot; fleshy limb; buttock; nun.

(بث) *bass*, I, U, INF. *bass*, disperse, blow away; publish; communicate, impart, bestow; spread a doctrine; — II. disperse; spread about, publish; — III., IV. impart a secret to (acc.); — VI. impart secrets to each other; — VII. be dispersed, dissolved, published; — VIII. demand information.

بث *bass*, things spread about, dispersed; publication; state, condition; need; grief, sorrow; — ة *bisa-t*, pl. بثى *bisa*, ashes.

بثاث *bisâs*, communication (of a secret).

(بثار) ابثار *ibsa'arr*, INF. *ibsîrâr*, leap.

(بثبث) *basbas*, INF. *basbasa-t*, raise dust; spread about news.

(بثر) *basar*, *basur*, U, INF. *basr*, *basar*, *busûr*, get covered with pustules; — V. same meaning.

بثر *basr*, much, and, by opposition, little; — *basir*, covered with pustules; — ة, pl. *busûr*, pustule, efflorescence

(بثط) *basit*, A, INF. *basat*, swell.

(بثع) *basi'*, A, INF. *basa'*, *busû'*, be full, curl (lips).

(بثعر) ابثعر *ibsa'ar*=ابثار *ibsa'ar*, q.v. under (بثار).

(بثق) *basaq*, U, INF. *basq*, *basaq*, *tabsâk*, overflow and break the banks; overflow with tears; — INF. *busuq*, be brimful; — II. break the banks; — VII. break forth; inveigh against (على *'ala*); proceed from the father and the son (m.).

بثق *basq*, *bisq*, pl. *busûq*, place where the water breaks through.

بثلة *busla-t*, celebrity.

بثن *busun*, pl. gardens; — *bisan*, soft sand; — ة *basna-t*, soft level ground; fine woman with a soft skin; butter; best wheat; abundance of wealth; Bethania; — *bisna-t*, pl. *bisan*, soft level ground.

(بثو) *basâ*, U, INF. *basw*, sweat, perspire.

بثير *basîr*, much, many; covered with pustules.

(بج) *bajj*, U, INF. *bajj*, prick open (a tumour); pierce; fatten; conquer; — VIII. almost burst with fat.

بج *bujj*, a young bird.

بجاج *bujâj*, stout, fat; — ة *bujâja-t*, contemptible fellow.

بجاد *bajâd*, pl. *bujud*, a striped upper garment.

بجارم *bajârim*, pl. calamities.

بجارى *bajâriyy*, calamities, pl. of بجرى *bujriyy*.

بجال *bajâl*, *bajjâl*, stately old man, prince; — ة *bajâla-t*, tall handsome woman.

بجاوة *bujâwa-t*, Nubia.

بجباج *bajbâj*, ة, fat man with shaking flesh; fool; babbler; heap of sand.

(بجبج) *bajbaj*; — II. INF. *tabajbuj*, be fat and loose; (m.) be swollen (in the face); — ة *bajbaja-t*, lullaby.

(بجح) *bajih*, A, INF. *bajah*, rejoice (n.); — II. rejoice (a.); — V. rejoice (n.); be delighted.

بجح *bajah*, joy; high rank, dignity.

(بجد) *bajad*, I, *bujûd*, remain, stay; remain on the pasture; — II. same meanings.

بجد *bajd*, troop of people, of horses (100 and more); — *bujud*, striped upper garments, pl. of بجاد *bijâd*; — ة *bajda-t*, root, origin; essence of a thing; desert; — *bajda-t*, *bujda-t*, *bujuda-t*, deep and solid knowledge; skill; who adheres to his word.

(بجر) *bajir*, A, INF. *bajar*, be afflicted with a rupture of the navel; have a big belly; be full of water or milk without being satiated; be tired of a thing and desist from it (عن *'an*); — V. indulge in wine; — XI. desist; — ة *bujra-t*, pl. *bujar*, navel; — ى *bujriyy*, *bujriyya-t*, pl. *bajâriyy*, misfortune, calamity.

(بجس) *bajas*, I, U, INF. *bajs*, open

a wound and let flow out the water; gush forth; — INF. *bujûs*, scold; — II. make the water flow; — V., VII. break through; flow out; gush forth.

بجس. *bajs*, running water; — *bujs*, *bujjas*, raining cloud.

(بجع) *baja'*, A, INF. *baj'*, cut off, lop.

بجع *baja'*, pelican; swan.

(بجل) *bajal*, INF. *bajl*, *bujûl*, be in easy circumstances, good condition; — *bajil*, A, INF. *bajal*, same meaning; — *bajul*, INF. *bajâla-t*, *bujûl*, be great and respected; — II. honour and praise; applaud; say it is enough for you; — IV. be sufficient for (acc.).

بجل. *bajal*, indeed! verily! yes! ثم بجل. it is enough now! that will do! ذو بجل *ẕû bajal*, a dispirited man without ambition; — *bajal*, *bujal*, *bujul*, great calumny; lie; anything wonderful; — ة *bajla-t*, small tree; of graceful figure.

(بجم) *bajam*, I, INF. *bajm*, *bujûm*, be silent; hesitate; contract (n.); — II. hesitate; contract; give a sharp look.

(بجن) II. *bajjan*, impress (upon the mind).

بجوم. *bajwam*, full of water.

بجير. *bajîr*, a great many, very numerous.

بجيس. *bajîs*, overflowing.

بجيل. *bajîl*, respected old man; honoured; leader; prince; big, stout, coarse, rude.

(بح) *baḥḥ*, A, INF. *baḥḥ*, *baḥaḥ*, *baḥâḥ*, *buḥûḥ*, *baḥâḥa-t*, *buḥûḥa-t*, be hoarse; — say "pooh! pooh!" — II., IV. render hoarse; — VII. be hoarse (m.); — VIII. have plenty and above.

بح *buḥḥ*, pl. of ابح *abaḥḥ*, hoarse, &c.; gold coins; gross timber; — ة *baḥḥa-t*, woman with a rough voice; — *buḥḥa-t*, hoarseness.

بحا *baḥḥâ'*, f. of ابح *abaḥḥ*, hoarse, &c., hill in the desert.

بحابح. *baḥâbiḥ*, middles of houses, courtyards, &c., pl. of بحبوحة. *baḥbûḥa-t*.

بحاث. *biḥâs̱*, disquisition; disputation; — *baḥḥâs̱*, disputant.

بحاح. *buḥâḥ*, hoarseness.

بحار. *biḥâr*, seas, &c., pl. of بحر. *baḥr*; — lands, countries, &c., pl. of بحرة. *baḥra-t*; — *baḥḥâr*, pl. ة *baḥḥâra-t*, mariner.

بحارين. *baḥârîn*, days of crisis, &c., pl. of بحران. *baḥrân*.

بحباح. *baḥbâḥ*, as long as broad; — *baḥbâḥ-i*, what a pity! — ة *baḥbâḥa-t*, shrew.

(بحبح.) *baḥbaḥ*, INF. *baḥbaḥa-t*, abide in a place; (m.) give abundantly; enrich; — II. INF. *tabaḥbuḥ*, abide in a place; be in the middle of the premises; (m.) live in abundance; — ة *baḥbaḥa-t*, crowd, troop; — ى *baḥbaḥiyy*, living in plenty and happiness.

(بحبش.) *baḥbaś*, INF. *baḥbaśat*, gather together, assemble (n.).

بحبوح. *buḥbûḥ*, root; middle; kernel; marrow; — ة *buḥbûḥa-t*, pl. *baḥâbiḥ*, middle of the house; courtyard; open square; (m.) middle, centre.

بحبور. *baḥbûr*, young bustard.

(بحت.) *baḥut*, INF. *baḥûta-t*, be pure and unmixed; — III. INF. *mubâḥata-t*, love with pure and sincere affection; be open with (acc.); give unmixed food to the cattle.

بحت. *baḥt*, ة, pure, unmixed, unalloyed.

بحتر. *buḥtur*, short and stout; great; — ى *buḥturiyy*, same meaning.

(بحث.) *baḥas̱*, A, INF. *baḥs̱*, seek; inquire; examine, try, discuss; — III. INF. *mubâḥas̱a-t*, examine; discuss; dispute; — V., VII., VIII., X. seek for, inquire, investigate; — VI. try to fathom (فى *fî* or عن *'an*).

بحث. *baḥs̱*, pl. *abḥâs̱*, examination; discussion; disputation; contro-

versy; pl. *buḥûs̱*, mine; a large snake; wager, bet.

(بحثر) *baḥs̱ar*, INF. *baḥs̱ara-t*, pick out and separate; take out and uncover; examine; separate (milk) from the butter (n.); disperse; squander; — II. INF. *tabaḥs̱ur*, be picked out and separated; — ة *baḥs̱ara-t*, dissipation.

(بحثن) *baḥs̱an*, INF. *baḥs̱ana-t*, be lazy, negligent.

بحح *baḥaḥ*, hoarseness.

بحدرى *buḥduriyy*, badly fed and not growing.

(بحدل) *baḥdal*, INF. *baḥdala-t*, having a crooked shoulder; walk fast; — ة *baḥdala-t*, swiftness.

(بحر) *baḥar*, INF. *baḥr*, split wide; — *baḥir*, A, INF. *baḥar*, be confused, perplexed (with fear); be overjoyed; be very thirsty; waste in flesh; — IV. go to sea; find the water salt; be consumptive; meet accidentally; have a red nose; have many pools of stagnating water; — V., X. swim in riches, knowledge, &c., as in a sea; meditate profoundly; travel towards the sea; — X. be large as a sea; walk about; have full command of the language.

بحر *baḥr*, pl. *abḥur*, *baḥûr*, *biḥâr*, sea; البحر المحيط *al-baḥru-'l-muḥîṭ-u*, Pacific; بحر الظلمات *baḥru-'z-zulmât-i*, Atlantic; البحر الوسطانى *al-baḥru-'l-wasṭâniyyu* (المتوسط *'l-mutawassiṭ-u*), بحر الروم *baḥru-'l-rûm-i*, البحر الابيض *al-baḥru-'l-abyaḍ-u*, the Mediterranean; — بحر بنطس *baḥr bonṭus*, البحر الاسود *al-baḥru-'l-aswad*, the Black Sea; بحر الخزر *baḥru-'l-ḥazar-i*, the Caspian Sea; بحر القلزم *baḥru-'l-qulzum*, بحر سويس *baḥr suwais*, البحر الاحمر *al-baḥru-'l-aḥmar-u*, the Red Sea; large river (Nile); title of large works; liberal man; generous; wide-stepping horse; metre; split; — *baḥar*, consumption; confusion, &c., see (بحر); —*baḥir*, confused, frightened; very thirsty; consumptive; — ة *baḥra-t*, pl. *buḥr*, *biḥâr*, land, district; low-lands; park; place or town with water; Medina; pond, basin.

بحران *baḥrân*, the Bahrein Islands; — *buḥrân*, pl. *baḥârîn*, critical day; delirium; — ى *buḥrâniyy*, pure and red (blood); foolish, mad.

(بحرن) *baḥran*, INF. *baḥrana-t*, have a crisis; be delirious.

بحرى *baḥriyy*, referring or belonging to the sea; sea-green; from Bahrein; — ة *baḥriyya-t*, mariners, sailors; ship.

بحرين *baḥrain*, the two seas, the White and Black, Mediterranean and Euxine; the Bahrein Islands.

(بحز) *baḥaz*, A, INF. *baḥz*, box the ears.

بحزج *baḥzaj*, calf; foal of a camel; dwarf; short and stout.

(بحش) for (بحث), dig and search the ground.

بحل *baḥl*, violent impulse.

(بحلس) II. *tabaḥlas*, have the hands empty, have nothing to do.

بحنا *baḥnâ'*, large basket for dates; large village or camp.

بحنانة *baḥnâna-t*, large spark; large basket for dates.

بحوثة *buḥûta-t*, purity, &c., see (بحث).

بحوث *baḥḥûs̱*, mighty disputant; the Sura توبة *tauba-t* of the *Qur'ân*; — *buḥûs̱*, pl. of بحث *baḥs̱*, mine, &c.

بحوحة *buḥûḥa-t*, hoarseness, &c., see (بح).

بحور *baḥûr*, wide-stepping courser; — *buḥûr*, seas, &c., pl. of بحر *baḥr*.

(بحى), IV. INF. ابحا *ibḥâ'*, give way, refuse further service (beast of burden).

بحيح *baḥîḥ*, greedy.

بحير *baḥîr*, consumptive ; — ة *buḥaira-t*, small lake ; Medina.

بخ بخ *baḫ-in baḫ-in! baḫ-i baḫ-i! baḫ baḫ!* well done! bravo! — *baḫḫ*, high-minded ; prince.

(بخ) *baḫḫ*, U, INF. *baḫḫ*, be important ; calm down (from anger) ; snore ; (m.) sprinkle tobacco with water ; drizzle.

بخار *buḫâr*, pl. *abḫira-t*, *buḫûr*, vapour, steam ; smoke ; fog ; bad smell ; foul breath ; miasma ; fever ; — ى *buḫâriyy*, from Bokhara ; fumigator.

بخارا *buḫârâ'*, Bokhara.

بخاشيش *buḫâśîś*, presents, pl. of بخشيش *baḫśîś*.

بخاعة *baḫâ'a-t*, submission, &c., INF. of (بخع), q.v.

بخاق *buḫâq*, wolf.

بخال *baḫḫâl*, great miser.

بخاند *baḫânid*, fine women, pl. of بخنداة *baḫandât*.

(بخبخ) *baḫbaḫ*, INF. *baḫbaḫa-t*, call out *baḫ baḫ*, well done! bravo! rejoice ; be satisfied, pleased ; cry out (camel) ; grow cool ; resound ; snore ; subside (anger, &c.) ;—II. same meanings ; rest ; (m.) drizzle.

بخبوحة *buḫbûḫa-t*, drizzling rain.

(بخت) *baḫat*, INF. *baḫt*, beat ; pass. be desponding.

بخت *baḫt*, destiny, fortune, luck, especially good luck ; بخت اسود *baḫt aswad*, bad luck, misfortune ; — *buḫt*, Bactrian camel ; بخت نصر *buḫt Naṣar*, Nabuchodonossor.

بختج *buḫtaj*, pl. *baḫâtij*, cooked, boiled (Pers.).

(بختر) *baḫtar*, I. and II. have a graceful gait, balance in walking, walk wantonly, swagger ; II. grow proud : — ة *baḫtara-t*, graceful gait ; — ى *baḫtariyy*, and—

بختير *biḫtîr*, having a graceful gait.

(بخثر) *baḫṯar*, INF. *baḫṯara-t*, separate, disperse ;—V. be separated, disperse (n.) ; — ة *baḫṯara-t*, stain.

(بخثن)=(بخثن), q.v.

بخدن *baḫdan*, delicate girl.

(بخر) *baḫar*, U, INF. *baḫr*, steam ; — *baḫir*, A, INF. *baḫar*, stink, have a bad smell, foul breath ; II. fumigate ; smoke ; perfume ; — IV. cause the breath to be foul ; — V. perfume one's self, be perfumed.

بخر *baḫar*, stench, foul breath ; — *baḫir*, strong smell.

(بخز) *baḫaz*, INF. *baḫz*, gouge an eye.

(بخس) *baḫas*, A, INF. *baḫs*, diminish ; injure ; wrong ; — II., V. waste away ; — VI. deceive and injure each other.

بخس *baḫs*, excessive taxes or tribute ; defect, injury ; defective measure, low price ; the gouging of an eye.

(بخش) *baḫś*, make a hole, pierce ; — II. give a gratuity (m.) ; — ة *buḫśa-t*, pl. *buḫûś*, *abḫâś*, hole.

بخشش *baḫśaś*, give a gratuity (m.).

بخشيش *baḫśîś*, pl. *baḫâśîś*, (m.) gratuity, present, bribe ; pin-money (Pers.).

(بخص) *baḫaṣ*, A, INF. *baḫṣ*, gouge ; — V. stare at with wonder.

(بخع) *baḫa'*, INF. *baḫ'*, cut the throat ; commit suicide from despair ; dig a well until water comes ; give sincere advice ; carry on with zeal ; believe the news ; (m.) blame publicly ; — *baḫi'*, INF. *buḫû'*, *baḫâ'a-t*, submit to (ل *li*), plead guilty ; — ة *baḫ'a-t*, public blame ; shame, putting to shame.

(بخق) *baḫaq*, blind a person of one eye ; — *baḫaq*, U, *baḫiq*, A, grow blind ; — IV. knock out an eye.

بخق *baḫuq*, kerchief.

(بخل) *baḫul*, INF. *buḫl*, *baḫal*, be miserly, avaricious ; — II. reproach with avarice ; — IV. find miserly.

بخل *baḫal*, very miserly ; — *buḫul*,

pl. of بخيل. *baḥîl*, miserly;—*buḥl*, *buḥûl*, *baḥl*, *baḥal*, avarice;—*buḥḥal*, pl. of باخل *bâḥil*, miserly.

بخلا. *buḥalâ'*, pl. of بخيل. *baḥîl*, miserly.

بخم. *baḥm*, any plant without a stalk.

(بخن.) *baḥn*, tall, long;—ابخن *ibḥann*, INF. ابخنان *ibḥinân*, sleep; take an upright position;—*ibḥânn*, *ibḥa'ann*, INF. *ibḥînân*, *ibḥi'nân*, die.

بخنداة. *baḥandâ-t*, بخندى. *baḥandā*, pl. *baḥânîd*, well-made woman with delicate knuckles;—*ibḥanda*, be such.

بخنق. *buḥnaq* (بخنك. *buḥnak*), kerchief, veil; snail-shell.

(بخو.) *baḥâ*, INF. *baḥw*, subside, calm down.

بخو. *baḥw*, bad date; soft.

بخور. *baḥûr*, pl. *baḥûrât*, scent, perfume; fragrant wood for fumigation.

بخول. *buḥûl*, avarice.

بخيت. *baḥît*, fortunate, happy, lucky.

بخيق. *baḥîq*, one-eyed, blind.

بخيل. *baḥîl*, pl. *buḥul*, *buḥalâ'*, miserly, avaricious.

(بد) بد بد *bad bad*, well done! bravo!—*badd*, fatigue, tiredness;—*bidd*, similar, equal;—*budd*, pl. *bidada-t*, *abdâd*, idol; separation; part, portion; equivalent; flight, escape; لا بد من *lâ budd min*, there is no help from, one must; *lâ budd*, by all means, necessarily;—*bad'*, pl. بدو *budu'*, *abdâ'*, beginning; master; pl. بدو *budû'*, *abdâ'*, first portion of a slaughtered camel; new well;—ة *bidda-t*, *budda-t*, power; pl. *bidad*, *budad*, portion, share;—*budda-t*, extreme.

(بد) *badd*, U, INF. *badd*, separate; remove, keep separate; injure; place a cloth under the saddle;—II. separate, disperse; (m.) squander; be drowsy with fatigue;—III. INF. *bidâd*, *mubâdda-t*, exchange goods;—IV. distribute; stretch the hand towards the ground;—V. separate (n.); get separated, dispersed; distribute between each other; cover entirely;—VI. fight man to man; take as an equal;—VIII. two attack one on both sides; two children suck one mother;—X. treat a thing by or claim it for one's self; usurp; follow one's own head.

(بدا) *badâ'*, A, INF. بد *bad'*, begin, commence; do a thing the first; bring the first news; emigrate; pass. get the small-pox;—II. (m.) accept for a novice (in a convent); do one thing before (على *'ala*) another;—IV. make a beginning; be the first to do; create; emigrate;—V. begin;—VIII. begin; do first before anything else; (m.) be a novice.

بدا *bad-an*, first; before all;—*buddâ*, inhabitants of the desert, &c., pl. of بادى *bâdî*;—ة *bad'a-t*, a mushroom; first portion of a slaughtered camel; portion;—*bad'a-t*, *bid'a-t*, *bud'a-t*, beginning;—*bud'a-t*, prince;—*badâ'a-t*, *budâ'a-t*, beginning; anything unexpected; done or said ex tempore.

بداح *badâḥ*, pl. *buduḥ*, extensive and good land;—*bidâḥ*, plains, pl. of بدح *bidḥ*.

بداد *badâd*, challenge for combat;—*bidâd*, saddle-cloth;—exchange of goods, INF. III. of (بد);—*bidâd*, *badâd*, portion, share; contribution; comrades.

بدار *bidâr*, INF. III. of بدر, q.v.;—*bidâr-an*, *badâr-i*, make haste! look sharp! be quick!

بدال *bidâl*, exchange, III. of (بدل);—*baddâl*, dealer in victuals.

بدان *badân*, ة *badâna-t*, corpulence.

بداهة *badâha-t, budâha-t*, pl. *badâ'ih*, beginning; anything unexpected; improvisation; readiness.

بداوة *badâwa-t*, first appearance; beginning; a mushroom; — *badâwa-t, bidâwa-t*, desert life; — pl. *badâwât*, efforts.

بداوى *badâwiyy, bidâwiyy*, referring to the desert; inhabitant of the desert.

بدائد *badâ'id*, saddle-cloths, pl. of بداد *bidâd*.

بدائع *badâ'i'*, new things, &c., pl. of بديعة *badî'a-t*.

بدائه *badâ'ih*, unheard-of things, pl. of بداهة *badâha-t*.

بداية *badâya-t*=بداوة *badâwa-t*, q.v.

(بدح) *badah*, INF. *badh*, cut down, fell; cleave; beat; do or say ex tempore, improvise; communicate a secret (ب *bi*); not be able to carry the burden; press upon, be hard upon; have an affected walk; — V. have an affected walk; — VI. throw at each other anything not hard.

بدح *bidh*, pl. *bidâh*, plain, spacious place, square; — *buduh*, extensive and good lands, pl. of بداح *badâh*; — بدحا *badah-an* (adv.), openly, distinctly; — ة *badha-t*, courtyard.

(بدخ) *badah, badih, baduh*, INF. *badh, badâha-t*, be in a high position; (m.) be proud; squander; — V. boast, be proud.

بدخ *badh*, pride; (m.) dissipation.

بدخا *budahâ'*, pl. of بديخ *badîh*, eminent, &c.

بدد *badad*, need, want; exchange; power, ability; *badad-an*, singly, dispersedly; by way of exchange; — *bidad*, portions, pl. of بدة *bidda-t*; *bidad-an*, in portions; — ة *bidada-t*, idols, &c., pl. of بد *budd*.

(بدر) *badar*, U, INF. *badûr, badr*, come quickly or unexpectedly upon (الى *ila*); surprise; break forth suddenly; — III. INF. *mubâdara-t, bidâr*, hasten; overtake, anticipate; break forth suddenly; improvise; — IV. rise over one and light his journey (sun, moon); administer with full powers (guardian the fortune of a ward); — VI. hasten together, hasten up (الى *ila*); — VIII. hasten; surprise; overtake, anticipate.

بدر *badr*, perfect state or condition; pl. *budûr*, full moon; disc; mature youth; prince; — ة *badra-t*, pl. *bidar*, full, fresh eye; a weight (20 raṭl); pl. *budûr, bidar*, milk-bucket of lamb's skin.

(بدرق) *badraq*, INF. *badraqa-t*, waste, squander; V. be squandered.

بدرى *badriyy*, rain before winter time; fat; partaker in the battle of Badr.

(بدع) *bada'*, INF. *bad'*, produce, originate, begin; dig a well till water comes; — *badi'*, A, INF. *bada'*, grow fat; — *badu'*, INF. *badâ'a-t, budû'a-t*, be perfect, incomparable; — II. impute a new invention, an innovation, a heresy to (acc.) anybody; (m.) do anything extraordinary; — IV. be the first to do a thing; be original (poet); cause a heresy; excel in doing a thing; leave in the lurch, abandon in need; — *ubdi'*, his camel has become disabled; — V. turn towards new things; — VIII. produce new things; — X. consider as new.

بدع *badi'*, new; — *bid'*, new, original; invention; eminent man; fleshy body; pl. *abdâ', budu'*, wonderful, incomparable; — *bud'*, pl. of بديع *badî'*, wonderful, &c.; — ة *bid'a-t*, pl. *bida'*, anything new, innovation, heresy, schism; oppression; pig; *bida'*, pl. incomparable women.

بدعتى *bid'atiyy*, tyrant; heretic.

بدعى *bid'iyy*, heretical.

(بدغ) *badig*, A, INF. *badag*, pollute

one's self with a crime; INF. *badg*, crack nuts and almonds.

بدغ *badg*, shells of nuts or almonds; — *badig*, polluted; pl. *badigûn*, fat, strong.

(بدل) *badal*, U, INF. *badl*, change, exchange, interchange; mistake one thing for another; — *badil*, A, INF. *badal*, have pains in the hands and joints; — II. take or give in exchange; change; invert; do one thing instead of another; — III. INF. *mubâdala-t bidâl*, give in exchange; — IV. take in exchange; change against (ب *bi*); place a word in apposition; — V. accept in exchange; get exchanged, mistaken, altered; (m.) alternate, relieve one another; change dress; — have pains in the hands or joints; wander; — VI. interchange; — VII. be interchanged; — X. demand an exchange; accept in exchange.

بدل *badal*, *bidl*, pl. *abdâl*, compensation; substitution; equivalent; exchange; apposition; requital; generous, magnanimous; حروف البدل *harûfu-'l-badal-i*, letters which are interchanged; — *badal*, gout in the hand; — *badil*, gouty; — ة *badla-t*, (m.) complete suit of clothes; vestment; — *bidla-t*, change of dress.

بدلا *budalâ'*, substitutes, pl. of بديل *badîl*.

(بدن) *badan*, U, INF. *badn*, *budn*, — *badun*, INF. *badn*, *badân*, *badâna-t*, grow corpulent, fat; — II. grow old and weak; be very rich; clothe one with a coat of mail.

بدن *badan*, pl. *abdân*, body, trunk; member; entrenchment, rampart, wall; short coat of mail; relationship, race, family; dignity; pl. *abdun*, old mountain goat; a lady's belt; pl. *budûn*, old; — *badin*, old; stout, fat; — *budun* and *buddan*, pl. of بدين, q.v.; — ة *badana-t*, pl. *budun*, animal to be sacrificed in Mecca according to a vow; — ى *badaniyy*, bodily; corpulent; — ية *badaniyya-t*, corpulence.

(بده) *badah*, A, INF. *badh*, come unexpectedly, surprise; answer or speak ex tempore; — III. INF. *mubâdaha-t*, come unexpectedly; — VI. practise improvisation together; — VIII. speak ex tempore, improvise.

بده *badh*, *budh*, beginning.

(بدو) *badâ*, U, commence, begin; INF. *badâ'*, go into the desert; — INF. *badâwa-t*, living in the desert; — INF. *badw*, *buduww*, *badî'*, *badâ'a-t*, appear; — INF. *badw*, *badâ'*, *badâ'a-t*, occur suddenly; — *badî*, A, INF. *bada*, abound in mushrooms; — III. INF. *mubâdât*, transgress; act unjustly; show openly; — IV. show or do openly; do for the first time; go beyond measure; show; — V. live in the desert; show one's self, appear; — VI. imitate or resemble the inhabitants of the desert; show openly mutual hatred.

بدو *badw*, desert; beginning; — *budû'*, pl. of بد *bad'*; INF. of (بدو), q.v.

بدوات *badawât*, pl. new opinions; innovations; ذو بدوات *zû badawât*, fertile in new ideas, inventive; tyrant.

بدوح *badûḥ*, mystical word written under the address of a letter, as an invocation for its safe arrival.

بدور *budûr*, full moons, &c., pl. of بدر *badr*, milk-buckets of lamb's skin, pl. of بدرة *badra-t*.

(بدى) *badâ*, INF. *bady*, *badî*, begin; — IV. go beyond measure; — V., VIII. begin; appear.

بدى *badiyy*, new; first.

بديح *badîḥ*, pl. *budaḥâ'*, eminent in rank and dignity.

بديد *badîd*, open plain; portmanteau; pl. *badâ'id*, *abidda-t*, saddle-cloth; equal, similar; — ة *badîda-t*, calamity; desert; equal.

بديع *badî'*, pl. *bad'*, wonderful, astonishing, rare; incompatible; inventor, discoverer; creator; بديع صنيع *badî' ṣanî'*, the Holy Ghost; invention, discovery; علم البديع *'alam albadî'*, art of fine style, rhetoric; the human frame; doubly twisted rope; new leathern flask; fat; — ة *badî'a-t*, pl. *badâ'i'*, anything wonderful, new, unheard-of.

بديل *badîl*, pl. *abdâl*, *budalâ'*, substitute; an upright, pious man; pl. the seventy just ones.

بدين *badîn*, pl. *budun*, *buddan*, fat and strong.

بديها *badîh-an*, على بدية *'ala badîh-in*, unexpectedly; ex tempore; — ة *badîha-t*, anything unexpected; occurring thought, sally; ex tempore speech; improvisation; (m.) beginning; principle; — ى *badîhiyy*, ة, ex tempore, improvised; unexpected; (m.) from principle, essential; pl. *badîhiyyât*, unforeseen occurrences.

(بذ) *baẕẕ*, U, INF. *baẕẕ*, *baẕîẕa-t*, conquer, overcome, overtake; — *baẕiẕ*, A, INF. *baẕaẕa-t*, *baẕâẕ*, *biẕâẕ*, *buẕûẕa-t*, be in a bad condition, be badly off; be old and dirty; — III. INF. *mubâẕẕa-t*, try to overtake; — VIII. INF. *ibtiẕâẕ*, receive one's due from another; cut off; — X. INF. *istibẕâẕ*, treat a thing by or claim it for one's self; usurp; possess exclusively; follow one's own head.

بذ *baẕẕ*, victory, conquest; old, worn out; dirty; f. ة, bad, equal; — *biẕẕ*, equal; — ة *biẕẕa-t*, portion, share.

(بذا) *baẕa'*, A, INF. *baẕ'*, find abominable; contemn, despise; blame; — *baẕi'*, offer no food (pasture ground); *baẕa'*, *baẕi'*, *baẕu'*, INF. *baẕâ'*, *baẕâ'a-t*, be impudent; — III. INF. *mubâẕât*, *biẕâ'*, talk or act impudently, commit fornication, adultery.

بذاذ *baẕâẕ*, ة *baẕâẕa-t*, bad condition; dirt (بذ).

بذار *biẕâr*, pl. of بذر *biẕr*, seed; — ة *baẕâra-t*, *baẕârra-t*, dissipation, squandering; — *buẕâra-t*, abundance; descendants.

(بذح) *baẕaḥ*, A, INF. *baẕḥ*, split, wound; peel, skin; — *baẕiḥ*, INF. *baẕaḥ*, be sore; be of no use; — V. rain.

بذح *baẕḥ*, pl. *buẕûḥ*, split; — *biẕḥ*, wound or scar in the hand.

(بذخ) *baẕiḫ*, *biẕiḫ* = بخ *baḫḫ*, well done! bravo! — *baẕaḫ*, INF. *buẕûḫ*, be high, proud; — *baẕiḫ*, A, INF. *baẕaḫ*, same meanings; — V. id.

بذخ *baẕaḫ*, pride.

(بذر) *baẕar*, U, INF. *baẕr*, sow, scatter seed; spread, preach; push forth the seed (ground); — II. sow, scatter; spread about, promulgate; squander; try, tempt one; — V. get foul and yellow (water).

بذر *baẕir*, sower, winnower; chatterer; abundant; — *baẕr*, grain of seed; descendants; pl. *buẕûr*, *biẕâr*, seed, grain of seed; — *buẕur*, blabbers, pl. of بذور *baẕûr*; — ة *baẕra-t*, grain of seed; child, son.

(بذرق) *baẕraq*, INF. *baẕraqa-t*, protect, escort; — protector, who escorts; — *baẕraqa-t*, protection, escort.

بذرى *buẕurrā*, vain; dissipated, squandering.

(بذع) *baẕa'*, A, INF. *baẕ'*, I., IV. frighten; — I. drop, fall in drops.

(بذعر), ابذعر *ibẕa'arr*, INF. *ibẕi'râr*, flee and disperse; try to reach a thing first.

بذق *bazq*, pl. *buzûq*, guide; small.
(بذقر), ابذقر *ibzaqarr* = ابذعر *ibza'ar*; remain separate (blood in water).
(بذقط) *bazqat*, INF. *bazqata-t*, waste (a.).
(بذل) *bazal*, I, U, INF. *bazl*, give abundantly; give with one's own hands; take pains, make efforts; — V. do a thing one's self; be not sparing with one's own; waste; dissipate; — VI. give to each other; — VIII. = V.; use a thing daily.
بذل *bazl*, giving for a present; generous gift; — ة *bizla-t*, every day dress.
بذلاخ *bizlâḥ*, who promises without keeping his word.
بذلخ *bazlaḥ*, INF. *bazlaḥa-t*, promise without giving effect to the promise.
(بذم) *bazum*, INF. *bazâma-t*, keep one's senses in anger.
بذم *buzm*, full senses; intellect; perseverance; strength; skin; fattiness; thickness.
(بذو) *bazu'*, U, INF. *bazâ'*, *bazâ't*, *bazw*, talk ribaldry; — IV. same meaning.
بذوذة *buzûza-t*, bad condition.
بذور *bazûr*, pl. *buzur*, who blabs out secrets; — *buzûr*, pl. of بذر *bazr*, seed, &c.
بذول *bazwal*, liberal, generous.
(بذى) = (بذو), (بذا).
بذى *baz-an*, impudence, ribaldry; — *baziyy*, f. ة, pl. *abziyân*, impudent, talking ribaldry; — *bazi'*, id.; without food.
بذيذ *baziz*, equal; — ة *baziza-t*, portion, share; bad portion, bad clothing; victory.
بذير *bazîr*, blabber; slanderer; كثير بذير *kasîr bazîr*, much, many.
بذيم *bazim*, self-possessed; powerful; foul (breath).
(بر) *barr*, I; *barir*, A, INF. *birr*, act well towards God, parents, children; make a pilgrimage; be agreeable to God; obey God; — INF. *barr*, *birr*, *burûr*, be truthful; keep one's word or oath; — II. consider pious, just, truthful, or proclaim any-one to be so; justify; — III. benefit; live on a continent, in the country, in the desert; — IV. accept as duly performed; confirm another's oath, subscribe to it; live or travel in the country; have many children; be numerous; conquer; — V. be pious, obey God; justify one's self; — VI. benefit each other, act with piety towards each other; — VIII. be separated from one's companions; deprive.
بر *barr*, continent, shore, bank; pl. *barara-t*, *abrâr*, beneficent, pious, charitable; just; truthful; God; faithfulness to one's oath; — *birr*, loving conduct, piety; good action; present; truthfulnesss; pilgrimage to Mecca; paradise; heart; young fox; — *birr*, *burr*, INF. of (بر); — *burr*, pl. *abrâr*, wheat; — *bar'*, creation, creating; — *bur'*, liberation; recovery; cure; — ة *bura-t*, pl. برى *buran*, *birîn*, *burîn*, *burât*, ring for the nose of a camel; anklet.
(برا) *bara'*, A, INF. *bar'*, *burû'*, create; — *bari'*, A, U, INF. *barâ'*, *barâ'a-t*, *burû'*, be free from guilt; — *bara'*, INF. *bur'*, *burû'*; *bari'*, INF. *bar'*,; *buru'*, INF. *bur'*, *burû'*, recover; — II. INF. *tabri'a-t*, acquit; remit a debt; cause to recover; — III. INF. *mubârât*, dismiss in a friendly and peaceable way (a companion, a wife); — IV. = III.; enter on the first or last day of the month; — V. get acquitted of a debt or guilt; take refuge to (الى *ila*) for the sake of acquittal; — VI. declare each other free from any obligation; — X. demand acquittal; abstain from one's wife; abstain; enter on the

the first or last day of the month.

برا *bira'*, pl. of برى *barî'*, recovered; — *barâ'*, *burâ'*, free, guiltless; INF. of (برا); first or last day of a month; — *birâ'*, *burâ'*, pl. of برى *barî'*, pure, innocent, free; — *burâ'*, shavings, &c., pl. of براية *burâya-t*; — *barr-an*, abroad, in foreign countries; outdoors, outside; — *barrâ'*, maker of bows; — ة *barât*, knife for shaving; pen-knife; — *bur'ât*, pl. *burâ'*, hiding-place of a hunter; — *barâ'a-t*, innocence; recovery; *barâ'a-t zimma-t*, receipt.

برابيك *barâbik*, tales, stories, lies, pl. of بربكة *barbaka-t*.

برات *barât*, letter; diploma; patent; edict; privilege; assignment; receipt; — *burât*, rings for the noses of camels; anklets, pl. of برة *bura-t*; — *burrâ-t*, *birrâ-t*, pl. good actions.

براتك *barâtik*, pl. low hills.

براح *barâḥ*, clear, distinct; evil; large desert; حبيل براح *ḥabil barâḥ*, lion, hero; لا براح *lâ barâḥ*, certainly, at once, immediately; — *barâḥ-i* (*birâḥ-i*), sun.

براد *burâd*, cold; INF. of (برد); — ة *burâda-t*, chips, shavings, filings; — *barrâda-t*, vessel for cooling water; watering-place.

براذين *barâẕin*, slow beasts of burden, &c., pl. of برذون *barẕûn*.

برارة *barâra-t*, innocence.

برارى *barârî*, deserts, pl. of برية *barriyya-t*.

براز *barâz*, vast plain; — *birâz*, human excrements; stool; sallying forth; — ة *barâza-t*, INF. of (برز).

برازق *barâziq*, برازيق *barâzîq*, assemblies; by-paths, pl. of برزيق *barzîq*.

براسا *barâsâ'*, troop of people, people, number of men.

براسم *burâsim*, sharp-sighted.

براسن *burâsin*, staring at.

براص *birâṣ*, deserts, pl. of برصة *barṣa-t*.

براطم *burâṭim*, having thick lips.

براعة *barâ'a-t*, distinction; elegance.

براعيم *barâ'im*, mountain-heights.

براغ *barrâg*, cupper.

براغيث *barâgis*, fleas, pl. of برغوث *bargûs*.

براغيس *barâgis*, pl. generous animals (camels).

براق *burâq*, the animal on which Mahomet ascended to heaven; — *barrâq*, flashing, shining; f. ة, beautiful, handsome; — ية *barrâqiyya-t*, splendour, brilliancy.

براك *birâk*, pl. *burk*, sword-fish; — blessing; — *barâk-i barâk-i*, courage! take courage! — (m.) *barrâk*, miller; — ية *burâkiyya-t*, a kind of ship.

براكا *barâkâ'*, pl. *barâ'ik*, endurance in battle; kneeling down.

(برال) *bur'al*, INF. *bar'ala-t*, bristle up the feathers of the neck (cock in fighting); — II., IX. the same.

برام *birâm*, kettles, pl. of برمة *burma-t*; — *burâm*, pl. *abrima-t*, sheep-louse.

برامكة *barâmika-t*, the Barmakides, pl. of برمكى *barmakiyy*.

برانك *barânik*, a kind of black dresses, pl. of برنكان *barnakân*, *barankân*.

برانى *barâniyy*, pots, &c., pl. of برنية *barniyya-t*; — *barrâniyy*, external; foreign; forged (coin).

براهم *barâhim*, براهيم *barâhîm*, ة *barâhima-t*, pl. of ابراهيم *ibrâhîm*, Abraham.

براهمن *barâhman*, pl. *barâhima-t*, Brahmin.

براهين *barâhîn*, arguments, &c., pl. of برهان *burhân*.

برايا *barâyâ'*, creatures, pl. of برية *bariyya-t*.

برائك *barâ'ik*, pl. of براكا *barâkâ'*, q.v.

برائل *burâ'il*, برائلى *burâ'ila*, small feathers of the neck; plants;

— ابو *abû-burâ'il*, ى *burâ'iliyy*, cock.

براية *burâya-t*, pl. *burâ'*, shaving, chip, paring; fat; endurance on a long journey.

بربار *barbâr*, murmuring, clattering, crying out; lion.

برباس *birbâs*, deep well.

(بربخ) *barbaḥ*, pl. *barâbiḥ*, earthen water-pipe; water-duct; urinary canal from the kidneys; sink, sewer.

برختى *barbaḥtiyy*, chameleon.

(بربر) *barbar*, INF. *barbara-t*, bleat; be clamorous, noisy; (m.) murmur, grumble.

بربر *barbar*, pl. *barâbir*, *barâbira-t*, native of Barbary; — *birbir*, ة, bleating of sheep; — *burbur*, ة, clamorous, noisy; — ى *barbariyy*, the same; — ية *barbariyya-t*, Barbary.

(بربس) *barbas*, INF. *barbasa-t*, seek, look for; — II. walk like a dog; walk lightly, softly; pass quickly.

(بربص) *barbaṣ*, INF. ة, water the ground abundantly.

(بربط) *barbaṭ*, pl. *barâbiṭ*, lute, harp.

(بربك) *barbak*, INF. ة, cheat; tell stories (m.); — ة *barbaka-t*, pl. *barâbik*, deceit; fable, story.

بربور *burbûr*, pearl-wheat.

(برت) *barat*, A, INF. *bart*, cut; — *barit*, A, INF. *barat*, be astonished, perplexed, confused; — ة *burta-t*, skill, cunning.

برتقان *bortuqân*, orange.

(برتك) *bartak*, firmly insist.

برتكال *bortukâl*, orange.

(برث) *baris*, A, INF. *baras*, live in ease and enjoyment.

برث *bars*, pl. *birâs*, *abrâs*, *burûs*, *barâris*, good soft ground; sand-hill; good guide.

(برشط) *barsat*, INF. ة, stay at home; ascend a mountain; sit with crossed legs (in Oriental fashion), squat.

برثن *bursun*, pl. *barâsin*, fleshy part of the paws; paw; hand.

برثوطة *bursût-at*, dangerous place.

(برج) *barij*, A, INF. *baraj*, have eyes, the white of which is visible all round the black; have food and drink in abundance; look well; — II., IV. build a tower; II. predict from the stars; — V. display one's self in adornment (woman to men).

برج *baraj*, pl. *abrâj*, of a handsome face; INF. of (برج); — *burj*, pl. *burûj*, *abrâj*, *abrija-t*, tower, castle; stations of the zodiac; angle; support; supreme power.

برجا *barjâ'*, f. of ابرج *abraj*, having beautiful eyes.

برجد *burjud*, pl. *barâjid*, garment of a coarse material, or, by opposition, a fine garment.

(برجم) *barjam*, INF. ة, speak rudely.

(برجم) *burjum*, *burjuma-t*, pl. *barâjim*, middle joint of a finger; middle finger; knuckle.

برجيس *birjis*, planet Jupiter.

(برح) *baraḥ*, INF. *burûḥ*, show the left side coming from the right; — U, INF. *barḥ*, be angry; — *bariḥ*, A, INF. *barâḥ*, leave, discontinue; sojourn in the desert; come to light; become manifest; — II. cause pain and trouble; — IV. astonish, please; do marvels; honour; injure; — V. be grieved.

برح *barḥ*, misfortune, evil; — ة *burḥa-t*, pl. *buraḥ*, excellent she-camel.

برحا *buraḥâ'*, greatest calamity; paroxysm; disorder; grief.

برحى *barḥa*, well hit!

برخ *barḫ*, increase; abundance; cheapness; power; thinness, weakness; cut of a sword; — II. *barraḫ*, submit humbly.

برخاش *barḫâš*, confusion.

برخداة *buraḫdâ-t*, delicate, fleshy woman.

(برد) *barad*, U, INF. *bard*, be cold, freeze, make cold or freeze; die; sleep; — INF. *burâd*, *burûd*,

be weak, ill; dry up, get lean, thin; be blunt; cool with water; put collyrium on the eye; file; beat; kill; send as a messenger; be incontestable; hail; — *barud*, INF. *burûda-t*, be cold; be incontestable; abate (n.) (pain); — II. cool, refresh; assuage; abate (a.); — III. treat one coldly; — IV. bring anything refreshing; give anything cold to drink; enter into the coolness of evening; weaken; send as a messenger; — V. refresh one's self; take a cold bath; abate (n.); — VI. treat each other coldly; — VIII. pour cold water upon one's self; refresh one's self by a cold drink; — X. find cold.

برد *barad*, pl. *burûd*, hail; — *barid*, cold, hailing (cloud); — *bard*, cold (s. and adj.); sleep, rest; spittle; *al-bardân*, morning and evening; — *burd*, ة, pl. *burûd*, *abrud*, *abrâd*, striped garment, upper garment; wing (of a locust, &c.); برد فاخر *burd fâhir*, war; — *burud*, messengers, &c., pl. of بريد *barîd*; — ة *barada-t*, *barda-t*, indigestion; — *barada-t*, hail-stone; middle of the eye; — *burda-t*, pl. *burad*, striped upper garment; curtain; cloak of a dervish.

بردا *buradâ'*, shiver of an ague.

برداخ *birdâh*, polish, finish, completion (m.).

بردان *bardân*, cold, freezing.

بردایة *burdâya-t*, curtain.

بردج *bardaj*, prisoner (Pers.)

(بردس) *birdis*, haughty; repugnant, ugly.

بردعة *barda'a-t*, pl. *barâdi'*, saddle-cloth, pack-saddle; — بردعی *barda'iyy*, maker of such.

بردی *bardiyy*, papyrus; branch; wing of the locust; — *burdiyy*, a kind of dates; — ة *bardiyya-t*, cold fever, ague.

بردیس *birdis*=بردس *birdis*.

(بردخ) *bardah*, I, ة, smooth, polish; complete; — II. get smoothed, polished; be refined, civilised.

برذج *burzaj*, roar of a lion.

(برذع), *ibranza*, be ready.

برذعة *barza'a-t*=بردعة *barda'a-t*.

(برذن) *barzan*, INF. ة, overcome, conquer; not be able to answer from exhaustion; walk as a beast of burden.

برذون *birzaun* (*burzûn*), pl. براذين *barâzîn*, slow beast of burden; pack-horse; Turkish horse.

بررة *barara-t*, pl. of بار *bârr*, innocent, &c.

(برز) *baraz*, INF. *burûz*; *bariz*, A, INF. *baraz*, go into the open plain; appear; show forth (n.); issue; — *baruz*, INF. *barâza-t*, be abstemious, virtuous; — II. make come forward; make known; surpass others in virtue and bravery, in swiftness; save his master by his swiftness (horse); go to stool; — III. INF. *mubâraza-t*, step forward for a single combat; fight a duel; provoke; — IV. make come forward, publish; intend a journey; take pure gold; — V. go out; — VI. come forward against each other for a single combat; separate from the crowd to seek one's companion (mutually); — X. cause or wish anyone to come forward, anything to appear.

برز *barz*, intelligent; venerable; moderate; one who goes forth; open tract of land; — ة *barza-t*, respectable matron; mountain summit; steepness; — *birza-t*, look, aspect.

برزاغ *birzâg*=برزغ *burzug*, q.v.

(برزخ) *barzah*, pl. *barâzih*, interval; barrier; medium; isthmus; time between death and resurrection; tomb; abyss, depth; the Holy Ghost.

(برزعة) *barza'a-t*, bed, couch.

(برزغ) *burzug*, liveliness, sprightliness; well-grown fellow.

(برزل) *burzul*, heavy man.
برزوغ *burzûg*=برزغ *burzug*.
برزى *barziyy*, venerable.
برزيق *birziq*, pl. *barâziq*, assembly; by-path.
برزين *birzin*, cup of palm-tree wood.
(برس) *baris*, A, INF. *baras*, be hard on a debtor; — II. level and soften the ground.
برس *bars*, opiate; — *birs*, *bars*, skill of a guide.
برسا *barsâ'*, troop, number of people.
برسام *birsâm*, pleurisy; headache.
(برسم), pass. *bursim*, suffer from pleurisy.
(برش) *baraś*, spot on the nail; — *burś*, pl. *abraś*, piebald; — IX. *ibraśś*, INF. *ibriśâś*, be piebald; — ة *burśa-t*, spot (of a horse).
(برش) *baraś*, INF. *barś*, fade (colour).
برشاع *birśâ'*=برشع *birśi'*.
برشام *birśâm*, sharp-sighted eye.
برشان *barśân*, people of the same creed; — *burśân*, wafer, holy wafer, host.
برشت *biriśt*, soft-boiled egg (Pers.).
(برشط) *barśaṭ*, INF. ة, tear with the teeth.
(برشع) *birśi'*, tall and stout; head-strong; malicious; stupid, foolish.
(برشق) *barśaq*, INF. ة, cut into pieces; beat with a whip; — III. INF. *ibrinśâq*, rejoice (n.); blossom; expand (flower).
برشك *barśak*, INF. ة, divide and place separately.
(برشم) *barśam*, INF. ة, show one's grief in the face; frown; mark with dots of different colours; — INF. ة, and *birśâm*, fix one's look at a thing (الى *ila*).
(برشم) *barśam*, INF. ة, brush (m.).
برشم *burśum*, veil for the face.
برشوم *barśûm*, a high kind of palm-tree.
برشيمة *barśima-t*, brush (m.).
(برص) *bariṣ*, A, INF. *baraṣ* (also used in the pass.), be a leper; — II. render similar to a leper; shave the head; water the ground before tilling it; — IV. render a leper; have a leprous child; cure from leprosy; — V. graze entirely off.
برص *baraṣ*, white leprosy; — *barṣ*, camel-louse; — *burṣ*, pl. of ابرص *abraṣ*, leprous; — ة *biraṣa-t*, pl. poisonous lizards; — *burṣa-t*, pl. *biraṣ*, dwelling-place of the demons, genii.
برصا *barṣâ'*, grazed off; shining white; f. of ابرص *abraṣ*, leprous; — *buraṣâ'*, pl. of بريص *bariṣ*, shining; leprous.
برصوم *barṣûm*, leathern case for flasks, &c.
(برض) *baraḍ*, U, INF. *barḍ*, be little or few; flow scantily; — I, U, INF. *barḍ*, give little; — INF. *burûḍ*, just sprout forth, so that the species cannot yet be recognised; — II., IV. produce such sprouts in quantity; — V. be satisfied with little; receive anything piecemeal; sip with the edges of the lips.
برض *barḍ*, pl. *birâḍ*, *burûḍ*, *abrâḍ*, a little, driblet; — ة *barḍa-t*, a little water.
برطاش *barṭâś*, pl. *barâṭiś*, sill (m.).
(برطس) *barṭas*, INF. ة, let beasts of burden.
(برطع) *barṭa'*, INF. ة, be agitated, moved, in emotion.
(برطل) *barṭal*, INF. ة, give a present to the judge, bribe; — II. accept a bribe; allow one's self to be bribed.
برطل *barṭul*, high cap; — ة *barṭala-t*, under-cap; — *barṭulla-t*, small sun-shade.
(برطم) *barṭam*, INF. ة, stammer; swell with anger; provoke to anger; be very dark; — II. get angry at a speech.
برطم *barṭam*, stammerer.
برطوم *birṭûm*, trunk (of an elephant, &c., m.).
برطيخ *barṭîḥ*, melon.
(برع) *bara'*, INF. *burû'*, *bari'* and

baru', INF. *barâ'a-t*, surpass others in knowledge, virtue, beauty, &c.; be perfect; conquer, vanquish; ascend a mountain; — V. give as a present, bestow benefits of free will.

(برعل) *bur'ul*, the young of the hyena or jackal.

(برعم) *bar'am*, INF. ة, I., II. bud forth.

برعم *bur'um*, ة, pl. *barâ'im*, برعوم *bar'ûm*, ة, bud, chalice of a flower; rose; — pl. *barâ'îm*, mountain heights.

برعيس *bir'îs*=برغيس *bargîs*.

(برغ) *barg*, spittle, drivel.

برغ *barig*, A, INF. *barag*, live in ease and enjoyment.

برغث *bargas*, INF. ة, have fleas, be full of fleas; — ة *bargasa-t*, ash-colour.

برغز *barguz*, malicious.

(برغش) *bargaś*, fly; — *ibragaśś*, INF. *ibrigśâś*, recover from an illness or wound and be able to walk again.

(برغل) *burgul*, pearl-wheat.

برغل *bargal*, INF. ة, live in a place near water, or between cultivated land and the desert.

(برغوث) *burgûs*, pl. *barâgîs*, flea.

برغى *bargiyy*, pl. *barâgi*, screw.

(برغيس) *birgis*, patient; not losing one's head; — pl. *barâgis*, generous camels.

برغيل *birgil*, pl. *barâgîl*, country near water or between cultivated ground and desert.

برفير *birfîr*, purple.

(برق) *baraq*, U, INF. *barq*, *burûq*, *burqân*, flash, lighten; wink, threaten; — INF. *barq*, *bariq*, *burqân*, shine, glitter; be brilliant; rise (star); adorn one's self; — INF. *barq*, *burûq*; *bariq*, A, INF. *baraq*, stare from fear; burst through the heat (leathern pipe); — II. adorn one's self or one's house; open the eyes wide and look sharp; undertake a long journey; persist in rebellion; be too difficult for (ب *bi*); — IV. lighten; threaten; be struck by lightning; cause to flash; adorn one's self; desist; unveil the face; track a wild animal.

برق *baraq*, pl. *abrâq*, *birqân*, *burqân*, lamb, ram; fear, fright; — *barq*, pl. *burûq*, lightning; brilliancy, flash; — *buraq*, necessary business, pl. of برقة *burqa-t*; — *burq*, pl. African lizards; — ة *barqa-t*, confusion; (m.) pain in the loins; — *burqa-t*, pl. *buraq*, urgent business; bad ground.

برقحة *barqaḥa-t*, ugliness.

برقروق *birqarûq*, plum (m.).

(برقش) *barqaś*, INF. ة, be variegated; separate (n.); paint gaudily, adorn; bungle; set to (على *'ala*); — II. be gaudily adorned; (m.) be piebald.

برقش *birqiś*, ابو براقش *abû barâqiś*, finch; — ة *barqaśa-t*, confusion; being piebald.

(برقط) *barqaṭ*, INF. ة, make short steps; turn round in running; disperse (a.); speak without order; ascend a mountain; sit in Oriental fashion; — II. fall on the back of the head; get mingled in pasturing.

برقطة *barqaṭa-t*, short step.

(برقع) *barqa'*, INF. ة, veil; cover one's animal; hit on the ears; — II. veil one's self.

برقع *birqi'*, *burqu'*, seventh heaven; — *burqa'*, *burqu'*, pl. *barâqi'*, a lady's veil, which allows only the eyes to be seen; curtain; — ة *burqu'a-t*, mark by branding (camel).

(برقل) *barqal*, INF. ة, lie; lighten without raining.

برقوش *barqûś*, pl. *barâqîś*, worn-out shoe.

برقوع *barqû'*, *burqû'*, violent; — *burqû'*=برقع *burqa'*, veil.

برقوق *burqûq*, *birqûq*, apricot, yellow plum.

برقيل *birqîl*, ballista, cross-bow.

(برك) *barak*, U, INF. *burûk*, *tabrûk*, kneel; stand firm; (m.) be obliged to remain, not be able to get away; sit down; rain continuously; exert one's self; — II. kneel down; make kneel down; (m.) cause to remain; be miller; — say a blessing; — III. INF. *mubâraka-t*, carry on a thing (على *'ala*) assiduously; bless, make happy; pray for (على *'ala*); — IV. make the camel kneel down; — V. be blessed, happy; hope for blessing, happiness, or good luck; congratulate one's self; insist on (ب *bi*); — VI. be praised and hallowed (God); accept as a good omen; be blessed, fortunate; — VIII. place the chest on the ground for the rider to mount (camel); fight on one's knees; rush forward; lean over one's work; carry on assiduously; pour out much water; rain continuously; insult; — X. be blessed, find blessed; — ة *baraka-t*, pl. *barakât*, blessing, happiness; abundance; fertility; — *birka-t*, kneeling down; upper part of the chest; a striped stuff; pl. *birak*, pond, fountain-basin; milk-pail; milking; — *burka-t*, pl. *burak*, *abrâk*, *birkan*, *burkân*, duck; frogs; persons of rank; tax; tax-gatherers.

بركان *birkân*, pl. of بركة *burka-t*, q.v.; — *burkân*, volcano (m.).

(بركع) *barka'*, INF. ة, cut, cut off; throw on the ground; — II. fall down.

(برم) *baram*, INF. *barm*, fix, make firm; twist a rope tight; (m.) turn round, roam about; — *barim*, A, INF. *baram*, be ill-tempered, peevish; be embarrassed; — II. turn to and fro (a.); make ill-tempered; — IV. twist the rope doubly; make firm; render ill-tempered; importune by questions; — V. be ill-tempered; — VII. be firmly twisted; be fixed.

برم *baram*, pl. *abrâm*, toil, grief; miser; trouble-feast; unripe grapes; mountain summits; — *barim*, unbearable (person); — *burm*, rope; — ة *barma-t*, turn, twist; — *burma-t*, pl. *burm*, *buram*, *birâm*, stone vessel for cooking; kettle.

برمكي *barmakiyy*, pl. *barâmika-t*, Barmakide.

برميل *barmîl*, pl. *barâmîl*, cask (m).

برناسا *barnâsâ'*, man.

برنتى *baranta*, ill-tempered, peevish.

برنجك *baranjik*, gauze, crape (Turk.).

برند *birand*, *birind*, old sword; glitter of a sword.

(برنس) *burnus*, pl. *barânis*, a kind of hood; prince; — II. *tabarnas*, put on a *burnus*.

برنسا *barnasâ* (برنشا *barnaśâ*), man.

برنكان *barnakân*, *barankân*, pl. *barânik*, a black garment (Pers.).

برنى *barraniyy*, external, foreign; — ة *barniyya-t*, pl. *barâniyy*, pot, vessel of earth or glass, jar; young cock.

برنيطة *burnaiṭa-t*, pl. *barânîṭ*, hat (m.).

برنيق *barniq*, hippopotamus; — *birniq*, mud; a mushroom.

(بره) *barih*, A, INF. *barah*, *burhân*, recover, regain strength; have a white body; — IV. proffer convincing proofs or arguments, get the better by arguments.

بره *barah*, delicacy of the skin; fat; — ة *barha-t*, *burha-t*, length of time.

برها *barhâ*, f. of ابره *abrah*, white of skin.

برهان *burhân*, pl. *barâhîn*, argument, demonstration, proof, evidence; clear sign; decision; prince, leader; — INF. of (بره); — ى *burhâniyy*, demonstrative; decisive; convincing.

(برهرهة) *barahraha-t*, handsome and lively, bright.

(برهم) *barham*, INF. ة, stare at (الى *ila*); — ة *barhama-t*, *burhuma-t*, flower-bud.

برهمن *barahman*, برهمند *barahmand*, pl. *barâhima-t*, Brahman.

(برهن) *barhan*, INF. ة, bring forth strong arguments, convincing proof; testify; — II. demonstrate, argue; be proved, demonstrated; — ة *barhana-t*, demonstration.

برهوت *barahût*, *burhût*, pit of the damned souls.

(برو) *barâ*, U, INF. *barw*, smoothe, plane, shave; create; put a ring through the nose of a camel.

برو *burû'*, recovery; deliverance, rescue.

بروات *barawât*, diplomas, &c., pl. of برات *barât*.

بروج *burûj*, towers, &c., pl. of برج *burj*.

بروح *barûḥ*, passing from the right to the left.

برود *barûd*, cold; cooling; — *burûd*, striped garments, &c., pl. of برد *burd*; INF. of (برد), q.v.; dulness; — ة *burûda-t*, coolness; coldness; dulness.

برور *burûr*, faithfulness to one's oath.

بروز *burûz*, getting known, becoming evident, INF. of (برز).

بروض *burûḍ*, pl. of برض *barḍ*, a little; INF. of (برض).

بروع *burû'*, perfection.

بروق *burûq*, lightnings, &c., pl. of برق *barq*; INF. of (برق), q.v.

بروك *burûk*, kneeling, INF. of (برك); sweetmeat made of dates and butter; — troops of camels, &c., pl. of برك *bark*; — ة *barwaka-t*, female hedge-hog.

بروكا *barûkâ'*, endurance; kneeling.

(برى) *bara*, I, INF. برى *bar-an*, *bary*, plane, shave; make or mend a pen; emaciate (a.); (m.) tear by use; — III. INF. *mubârât*, imitate; compete; separate in a peaceable way from a partner or wife; cover with dust; soil; find sugar canes; — V. present one's self; free one's self; — VI. imitate each other, emulate; — VII. be smoothed (arrow, &c.); be made or mended (pen); be emaciated; present one's self; be ready; — VIII. smooth; be smoothed; — X. examine, spy out; reconnoitre.

برى *bar-an*, earth, dust; — *buran*, rings for the noses of camels, pl. of برة *bura-t*; — *bariyy*, smoothed, planed; acquitted, free; — *bari'*, pl. *bari'ûn*, *bura'â'*, *birâ'*, *abrâ'*, *ibri'â*, *burâ'*, f. *bari-'a-t*, pl. *bari'â-t*, *bariyyât*, *barâyâ*, pure, guiltless, innocent, free; pl. *birâ'*, recovered, cured; — *burra*, friendly word; — *barriyy*, rustic, wild; continental; countryman, native; external, foreign; level; — ة *barya-t*, making of a pen; — *bariyya-t*, pl. *bariyyât*, *barâyâ*, creature, people; — *barriyya-t*, pl. *barârî*, desert.

برئات *bari'ât*, *bariyyât*, see برى *bari'*.

بريت *barrît*, pl. *barârît*, desert; — *birrît*, prudent guide or leader; plain.

بريح *barîḥ*, bad omen; — ام بريح *umm barîḥ*, crow; calamity.

بريد *barîd*, pl. *burud*, ready; messenger; courier; express; خيل البريد *ḥailu-'l-barîd*, relay horses; صاحب البريد *ṣâḥibu-'l-barîd*, post-master; a measure = 16 English miles.

بريش *barîś*, piebald.

بريص *barîṣ*, pl. *buraṣâ'*, shining; leprous; — *buraiṣ*, ابو بريص *abû buraiṣ*, lizard.

بريع *barî'*, excellent, f. *barî'a-t*, handsome and witty (woman).

بريق *barîq*, brilliancy; INF. of (برق); — brig (m.); — ة *barîqa-t*, pl. *barâ'iq*, milk with butter; lightning, flash; brilliancy.

بريك *barîk*, pl. *burk*, blessed with abundance; *barîk* and *barîka-t*, dates with butter; — brig (m.).

برم *barîm*, twisted; string of pearls, &c.; amulet; motley crowd; army; mixed herd; dawn; suspicious; *al-barîmân*, liver and hump of the camel as a dish; — ة *barîma-t, barrîma-t*, borer; cork-screw; screw.

برين *burîn*, pl. of برة *bura-t*; — ة *barrîna-t, birrîna-t*=بريمة *barîma-t*.

بريه *buraih*, بريهم *buraihim*, little Abraham.

(بز) *bazz*, U, capture, rob, plunder; INF. *bazz, bizzîzâ*, conquer, vanquish; — VIII. INF. *ibtizâz*, take from by violence, rob.

بز *bazz*, fine linen; silk; clothing; armour; drapery; superiority; victory; end; INF. of (بز); — *bizz*, pl. *bizâz, abzâz*, nipple; bosom; (m.) mouth-piece of a pipe; — ة *bizza-t*, rich robe of honour; garb; arms, armour; form, figure.

برابز *buzâbiz*, agile, active; strong but not brave.

براج *bizâj*, boast, swagger.

برادرة *bazâdira-t*, falconers, pl. of بازدار *bâzdâr*.

برار *bazzâr*, seller of linseed, of grain.

براز *bazzâz*, linen-draper, draper; merchant; — ة *bizâza-t*, linen trade.

براع *buzâ'*, active servant; — ة *bazâ'a-t*, good breeding, being well brought up.

براق *buzâq*, spittle, saliva.

برال *bizâl, buzâl*, bung; bung-hole.

براة *buzâ-t*, falcons, hawks, pl. of باز *bâz*.

(برزب) *bazbaz*, INF. ة, urge on; walk fast; take to flight; move about much and quickly; conciliate; disquiet; steal, rob; throw away.

برزبز *buzbuz*, agile, active.

(برج) *bazaj*, U, INF. *bazj*, boast; irritate against (على *'ala*); — II. adorn; — III. INF. *mubâzaja-t*, *bizâj*, boast; — VI. contest fo glory.

(برح) *bazaḥ*, I, INF. *bazḥ*, take the merchandise without weighing or measuring; — II. show one's self submissive; — VI. desist.

برح *bazaḥ*, hump on the chest.

برد *bazd*, scabbard.

(برر) *bazar*, I, INF. *bazr*, beat; sow (a field); blow the nose; fill; — II. sprout; make ears (corn); grow grain (ear); lay eggs (silk-worm); — V. descend from the Banu Bazra.

برر *bazr, bizr*, ة, pl. *buzûr*, seed, grain of seed; egg of the silk-worm; pl. *abzâr, abâzir*, herbs for seasoning; descendant; mucus.

برا *bazrâ'*, woman who has many children.

برز *bazaz*, arms, armour.

(برع) *bazu'*, INF. *bazâ'a-t*, be handsome, witty, and well bred; be pert, saucy; — INF. *baz'*, increase; — V. be handsome, well bred; be rife, rampant; threaten (danger).

(برغ) *bazag*, U, INF. *bazg*, bleed with a lancet; — INF. *bazg*, *buzûg*, be on the point of rising; push (tooth of a camel); peep forth.

برغ *bazg*, lancet.

(برغر) *buzgur*, malicious.

(برق) *bazaq*, U, INF. *bazq*, sow the ground; spit; throw out; rise (sun); — ة *bazqa-t*, spittle, saliva.

برقى *bazaqâ*, quick walk.

(برل) *bazal*, U, INF. *bazl*, split; tap a cask; clarify the wine; cut off; decide; — II. split; tap; clarify; — V. split (n.); tap; — VII. split (n.), get split; — VIII. open (n.); tap; bid to broach; clarify.

برل *buzl*, goat.

برلا *bazlâ'*, good idea or advice; misfortune; خطة برلا *ḥaṭṭa-t bazlâ'*, the line between good and evil.

(بزم) *bazam*, I, U, INF. *bazm*, bite with the fore-teeth; carry a burden for a long time; milk a camel; draw the bow-string with fore-finger and thumb; rob; resolve firmly; speak rudely; break into pieces; — IV. give; — VIII. pass the day in (participle or aorist).

بزم *bazm*, firm resolution; harsh word; break, rupture; — ة *baz-ma-t*, meal; weight of 10 *dirham*.

(بزمخ) *bazmah*, INF. ة, be proud.

(بزو) *bazâ*, بزى *baza*, U, INF. *bazw*, be in equilibrium, be one's equal; raise one's self above (على *'ala*) another; accustom one's self to, become familiar with (ب *bi*); overcome by force and carry off; — *bazâ*, U, *bazi*, INF. *baz-an*, be hump-chested; — IV. be one's equal in (ب *bi*); overcome by force and carry off; wrong; give the suck; — VI. make long strides; boast of things one has not got.

بزو *bazw*, in equilibrium with others, equal to others.

بزوان *bazawân*, attack; impulsiveness, impetuosity.

بزورى *bazûriyy*, greengrocer; seed-merchant.

بزوغ *bazûg*, sunrise.

بزول *bazul*, pl. *buzul*, camel 9 years of age (pushing its corner-tooth).

بزى *baziyy*, foster-brother.

بزيج *baziy*, thankful.

بزيزى *bizziza*, victory, conquest.

بزيع *bazî'*, wide awake; eloquent; agile; impudent.

(بس) *bass*, U, INF. *bass*, drive the camels slowly on by the call *bas! bas!* prepare or eat the dish بسيسة *basisa-t*; — send out cattle, goods, scouts, to different countries; demand; exert one's self; pass. be crushed, sink, become dust (the mountains); — IV. drive on or decoy camels by the call *bas! bas!* decoy goats to the water; — VII. be sent out; dissolve (n.).

بس *bass*, demand, request; power; strength; work, labour; zeal; sufficiency, enough; — *bass*, *biss*, ة *bissa-t*, pl. *bisas*, domestic cat.

(بسا) *basâ'*, *basi'*, A, INF. *bas'*, *basa'*, *basâ'*, *busû'*, become familiar, intimate with (ب *bi*); — I, INF. *bas'*, *busû'*, get accustomed to (ب *bi*); despise; — IV. make familiar, accustom.

بساتيق *basâtiq*, pottery, &c., pl. of بستوقة *bastuqa-t*.

بساتين *basâtin*, gardens, pl. of بستان *bustân*.

بساتينى *basâtiniyy*, gardener.

بسارة *bisâra-t*, summer-rain.

بساسة *bassâsa-t*, Mecca.

بساط *basât*, vast plain; open country; surface; large pot; — *bisât*, pl. *busut*, covering, carpet, mat, cushion; pl. *bist*, *bust*, *busut*, she-camels with sucking foals; — ة *basâta-t*, free talk, ingenuousness; simplicity; — ى *bisâtiyy*, pedlar, shopkeeper (m.).

بساق *busâq*, spittle.

بسال *basâl*, *bisâl*, see (بسل); — ة *basâla-t*, bravery, prowess, heroism; contempt of death.

بسام *bassâm*, who smiles much.

بسباس *basbâs*, fennel.

(بسبس) *basbas*, INF. ة, walk very fast; set quickly to; decoy by the call *bas! bas!* endure; — II. flow.

بسبس *basbas*, desert; silly behaviour or talk.

بستان *bustân*, pl. *basâtin*, garden (Pers.); — *bustâniyy*, gardener.

بستج *bastaj*, frankincense.

(بسترط) *bistart*, she-camel with foal.

(بستق) *bastaq*, servant.

بستقان *bustaqân*, gardener; field-watch.

بستنجى *bustanjiyy*, pl. *bustanjiyya-t*, gardener.

بستوقة *bastûqa-t*, pl. *basâtîq*, earthenware; water-jug.

بسذ *bussaz*, coral (Pers.).

(بسر) *basar*, U, INF. *basr*, do hastily, precipitately; do or demand anything before the proper time (also IV., V., VIII.); begin, commence (ب *bi*); subdue, offer violence; — INF. *basr*, *basûr*, show a severe face, frown; pass. have piles; — IV. see I.; press unripe dates; stop, stick fast (ship); — V. see I.; get benumbed; be cold; — VIII. see I.; begin, commence (ب *bi*); get benumbed; subdue; oppress; pass. change (colour).

بسر *basr*, cold water; first beginning; — *busr*, dates beginning to ripen; pl. *bisâr*, refreshing rain; fresh and tender; — ة *busra-t*, *busura-t*, pl. *busur*, *busurât*, date beginning to ripen; rising sun; first germ; glass beads.

(بسط) *basaṭ*, U, INF. *basṭ*, spread; stretch out or open the hand; cheer, rejoice (a.); hold (as a room); be large enough; render more excellent, bolder; accept an excuse; — *basuṭ*, overcome one's own timidity, get bolder; — II. spread; — *mubâsaṭa-t*, be without timidity; speak out freely; receive anybody with joy; — V., VII. be extended, long; wander far, travel; be without timidity, put off restraint; — VII. be cheerful, merry, rejoice, divert one's self; make too free with (على *'ala*).

بسط *basṭ*, spreading, &c., INF. of (بسط); joy; cheerfulness; amusement; intoxicating paste of hemp and tobacco;—*bisṭ*, ة *bisṭat*, *busṭ*, *busuṭ*, pl. *absâṭ*, *busuṭ*, *bisâṭ*, *busâṭ*, camel with sucking foal on the pasture; open; liberal; — *busuṭ*, pl. of بسيط *basîṭ*, wide, extensive, &c.; — ة *basṭa-t*, *busṭa-t*, deep knowledge; distinction; largeness and abundance; extension; (m.) pedestal; — ى *basṭiyy*, seller of بسط *basṭ*, q.v.; — ية *basṭiyya-t*, pleasure, amusement.

(بسق) *basaq*, U, INF. *basq*, spit; — INF. *busûq*, be high; surpass; — II. make long; keep waiting a long time; importune; molest.

بسكل *buskul*, the hindmost horse in a race.

(بسل) *basal*, U, INF. basl, blame, reproach; hasten, urge on; take piecemeal and by degrees; shut up; allow; — INF. *busûl*, be forbidden; grow thick (milk, &c.); — *basul*, INF. *basâla-t*, *basâl*, be of severe looks, courageous, brave, terrible; — II. loathe; — III. INF. *mubâsala-t*, attack with fury; outflank an enemy; — IV. forbid; offer as a pledge; give a commission, charge with (ل *li* or ب *bi*); devote one's self to death or destruction; cook or dry unripe dates; — V. frown; be avoided, shunned; defy danger; — VIII. receive one's fee; devote one's self to death (also X.).

بسل *basal*, yes, so it is; — *basil*, severe-looking; bold; — *basl*, forbidden, and, by opposition, lawful; repulsive; haste; violence, severity; blame; imprisonment, prison; torture; بسلا بسلا *basl-an basl-an*, Amen! Amen! بسلا له *basl-an la-hu*, بسلا و اسلا *basl-an wa asl-an*, woe to him! — *busl*, *busul*, pl. of باسل *bâsil*, bold, &c.; — ة *busla-t*, fee of the snake-charmer.

بسلا *busalâ'*, pl. of باسل *bâsil*, bold, &c.

(بسم) *basam*, I, INF. *basm* (also V. and VIII.), smile.

بسم *bism*, for بسم الله *bi'smi-'l-lâh-i*, in the name of God.

بسمل *basmal*, INF. ة, pronounce the above words; — *basmala-t*, invocation of God.

(بسن) *basan*, beautiful; hence IV. *absam*, be beautiful.

بسور *basûr*, severe-looking, grim; lion; — *busûr*, INF. of (بسر).

بسوق *busûq*, growth; INF. of (بسق).

بسيس *basîs*, a little; — ة *basîsa-t*, flour roasted in butter; scraped cheese; tale-bearing; spying, INF. of (بس).

بسيط *basîṭ*, pl. *busuṭ*, wide, extensive, level; superficial; pl. *busaṭâ*, *basâ'iṭ*, simple, not compound; single; naïve, artless, open, free; liberal; name of a metre: *mustaf'ilun fâ'ilun mustaf'ilun fâ'ilun* twice repeated; — ة *basîṭa-t*, open country; surface of the earth; sun-dial; quadrant; she-camel with her foal; clear and simple matter; pl. *basâ'iṭ*, element.

بسيل *basîl*, severe-looking; repulsive; — ة *basîla-t*, bitter taste.

بسيم *basîm*, smiling; sprightly.

بسين *busain*, ة, cat, kitten.

(بش) *baśś*, A, INF. *baśś*, *baśâśa-t*, show an open, friendly face; receive with friendliness; rejoice at seeing again; rejoice at (ب *bi*); — IV. be densely overgrown, produce the first plants.

بش *baśś*, open, friendly; joyful reception; joy at seeing again.

بشا *buśâr*, pl. vilest of men; — ة *baśâra-t*, *biśâra-t*, *buśâra-t*, news, happy tidings, gospel; — *baśâra-t*, pl. *baśâ'ir*, beauty; — *buśâra-t*, guerdon for good news; scurf; — *baśśâra-t*, butterfly.

بشاش *baśâś*, friendly, humane; — ة *baśâśa-t* = بش *baśś*, INF. of (بش).

بشاع *baśâ'*, indigestion; — ة *baśâ'a-t*, ugliness.

بشاق *baśśâk*, great liar.

بشائر *baśâ'ir*, messengers of joyful news; — pl. of *baśâra-t*, beauty.

بشتخته *baśtaḥta-t*, writing-table, portfolio (Pers.).

بشخانة *baśḫâna-t*, ante-room; vestibule (Pers.).

(بشر) *baśar*, U, INF. *baśr*, peel, pare, shave so as to render the skin visible; eat the ground bare (locusts); take a business into one's own hands; — U, INF. *baśr*, *buśûr*, bring good news; report; receive; have sexual intercourse; — I, *baśir*, A, INF. *baśar*, rejoice at; — II. gladden by good news; — III. INF. *mubâśara-t*, id.; take a matter into one's own hands; exercise a profession; have sexual intercourse; — IV. shave to the skin; bring good news or rejoice at it; rejoice; get covered with plants; adorn; — VI. receive good news from each other; — X. gladden by good news; rejoice at such, expect it.

بشر *baśar*, pl. *abśâr*, human skin; man, mankind; ابو البشر *abû-'l-baśar-i*, Adam; *abû baśar-in*, dessert, sweetmeats; — *biśr*, open, joyful countenance; joy; cheerful welcome; — *buśr*, good tidings; *buśr* and بشرا *buśarâ'*, messengers of good news, &c., pl. of بشير *baśîr*; — ة *baśara-t*, pl. *baśar*, epidermis; surface; human frame; humanity, mankind; — ى *buśrâ*, pl. *buśrawât*, happy tidings, gospel; — *baśariyy*, human, referring to mankind, mortal; — ية *baśariyya-t*, human nature, humanity.

(بشط) II. and IV. hasten (n. and a.).

(بشع) *baśi'*, A, INF. *baśa'*, *baśâ'a-t*, have a foul breath, bad or insipid taste; be ugly, disgusting, hateful; be too narrow (bed of a river); be not equal to (ب *bi*) a thing; have horror or disgust of (من *min*); — II. disfigure; blacken, calumniate; commit evil; — V. be ugly, repulsive; — X. find ugly, disgusting, &c.; be unsuccessful.

بشع *baśi'*, ugly; having a bad taste; stale and insipid; smelling badly; objectionable, shocking;

who eats or does bad things; knotty, f. ة; — ة *baśa'at*, pelican.

(بشغ) pass. *buśig*, INF. *baśg*, be watered by a drizzling rain; — IV. water by a drizzling rain.

بشغ *baśg*, drizzling rain.

(بشق) *baśaq*, I, INF. *baśq*; — *baśiq*, A, INF. *baśaq*, beat with a stick; strain one's look; — *baśaq*, not be able to proceed any further.

(بشك) *baśak*, U, INF. *baśk*, do badly or precipitately, bungle; sow with large stitches; lie; cut; loosen the tether of a camel; mix; urge on; walk fast; step lightly; — VIII. lie; be cut off; disparage; run fast.

بشك *baśk*, precipitation; lie; cutting off; — *baśk*, *baśak*, swiftness; see (بشك).

بشكانى *buśkâniyy*, stupid; gibbering; not knowing Arabic.

بشكى *baśaka*, swift, agile.

(بشلل) *baślal*, INF. ة, bring a thing or a person into confusion; — II. be in confusion (m.); — ة *baślala-t*, confusion.

(بشم) *baśim*, A, INF. *baśam*, suffer from indigestion; loathe; — IV. cause indigestion; — VII. (m.) =I.

بشم *baśam*, indigestion, oppression of the stomach; — *baśim*, suffering from indigestion, loathing, over-eaten.

بشماط *biśmâṭ*, biscuit, rusk.

(بشو) *baśâ*, U, INF. *baśw*, be of excellent disposition.

بشور *buśûr*, joyful tidings, INF. of (بشر).

بشوش *baśûś*, friendly, smiling.

بشير *baśîr*, ة, pl. *buśarâ'*, *buśr*, messenger of good news; beautiful, handsome.

بشيش *baśîś*, brisk and sprightly; — ة *baśîśa-t*, one's own money; one's own things.

بشيع *baśî'*, ugly; smelling badly; repulsive; reprobate, abject, &c.

(بص) *baṣṣ*, I, INF. *baṣîṣ*, shine, glitter; give (little); exude; — II. show the first vegetation; open the eyes for the first time; caress, coax; — IV. INF. *baṣâṣ*, exude; show the first vegetation.

بصا *biṣ-an*, *biṣâ'*, castration.

بصار *biṣâr*, INF. III. of (بصر); — *baṣṣâr*, who looks sharply; soothsayer; — ة *biṣâra-t*, insight.

بصاص *baṣṣâṣ*, having flashing eyes; — ة *baṣṣâṣa-t*, eye; (m.) spy, watch, sentinel, vedette.

بصاق *baṣâq*, spittle; a species of the palm-tree; a kind of camel.

بصال *baṣṣâl*, seller of onions.

(بصان) *buṣân*, *buṣṣân*, pl. *-ât* and *abṣina-t*, month of Rabi' II.

بصباص *baṣbâṣ*, ة, quick, swift; agile; little water; bread; grass-fibre; *al-baṣbâṣ*, milk.

(بصبص) *baṣbaṣ*, INF. ة, reflect, reverberate; show the first vegetation; walk fast; wag the tail; caress; open the eyes for the first time; (m.) wink with (فى *fî*) the eyes.

بصبوص *baṣbûṣ*, pupil of the eye (m.).

(بصر) *baṣir*, A, INF. *baṣar*; — *baṣur*, INF. *baṣâra-t*, *biṣâra-t*, perceive, see, recognise (ب *bi*); — II. cause to see or recognise, show; reveal secrets; instruct; open the eyes; cut; dissect and loosen from the bones; cut off the head; go to Bassorah; — III. vie, who sees, perceives, recognises first; look out from on high; — IV. look, whether one can perceive or recognise; perceive (ب *bi*); be distinct, recognisable; have anything cut into pieces; go to Bassorah; — V. look, whether one can perceive; see distinctly, recognise; look at, contemplate, reflect; understand; see through secrets; — VI. see or try to see each other; pretend to see or recognise; — X. observe attentively, try to recognise, recognise; be seen, recognised.

بصر *baṣar*, seeing, sight; pl. *abṣâr*, what appears to the eye, spectacle, sight; eye; discernment; intelligence; صلوة البصر *ṣalautu-'l-baṣar-i*, prayer of morning and evening, dusk; — *baṣr*, skin; INF. of (بصر); — *buṣr*, skin; rind, crust; edge, border; cotton; — ة *baṣra-t*, *biṣra-t*, *baṣara-t*, *biṣara-t*, Bassorah; *al-baṣratân*, Bassorah and Koufah; — ى *baṣriyy*, of or from Bassorah.

بصرا *buṣarâ*, pl. of بصير *baṣîr*, q.v.

(بصط) = (بسط).

(بصع) *baṣa'*, A, INF. *baṣ'*, gather, take with one's self; flow, stream; — II. come forth in drops.

بصع *baṣ'*, small crevice; span between thumb and middle finger; thick cloth; — *biṣ'*, beginning of the night; — *buṣ'*, pl. of *abṣa'*, whole, all; stupid; — drops of perspiration, pl. of بصيع *baṣî'*.

بصعا *baṣ'â'*, f. of ابصع *abṣa'*, stupid; whole, all.

(بصق) *baṣaq*, U, INF. *baṣq*, spit.

(بصل) *baṣal*, ة, onion, bulb.

بصل *baṣṣal*, and V. *tabaṣṣal*, skin, peel; undress, rob of the clothes; V. question, cross-examine.

بصم *baṣm*, interval, span between the third and little finger.

بصم *baṣam*, INF. ة, print upon (m. from Turk.); ساعة بصم *sâ'a-t baṣam*, repeating watch; — ة *baṣma-t*, printing-mark; printed pattern (on stuffs).

(بصو) *baṣâ*, U, INF. *baṣw*, press a debtor, dun; — ة *baṣwa-t*, live coal, spark.

بصير *baṣîr*, pl. *buṣarâ'*, seeing, sharp-sighted, discerning, intelligent; God; connoisseur; — ة *baṣîra-t*, pl. *baṣâ'ir*, look, sight; sagacity, penetration; cautiousness, prudence; opinion; tenet; demonstration; evidence; meditation; armour; shield.

بصيص *baṣîṣ*, shining, brilliant; splendour; fright; INF. of (بص).

بصيع *baṣî'*, pl. *buṣ*, drops of perspiration.

(بض) *baḍḍ* (*baḍaḍ*, *baḍiḍ*), I, A, INF. *buḍûḍa-t*, be plump with delicate skin; — I, INF. *baḍḍ*, *baḍûḍ*, *baḍîḍ*, flow slowly out, drip, ooze; give sparingly; tune the strings of an instrument; — II. be soft and delicate; — IV. give sparingly; — V. receive a debt by small instalments; take everything from (acc.); — VIII. sell one's self from need; totally annihilate.

بض *baḍḍ*, ة, plump with delicate skin; small gift; — also ة *baḍḍa-t*, sour milk.

بضابض *buḍâbiḍ*, strong, brave.

بضاض *biḍâḍ*, wells or leathern bags with little water, pl. of بضوض *baḍûḍ*; — ة *baḍâḍa-t*, plump with a delicate skin (girl); — *buḍâḍa-t*, little water.

بضاع *biḍâ'*, sexual intercourse; — parts, portions, &c., pl. of بضعة *baḍ'a-t*; — ة *biḍâ'a-t*, pl. *baḍâ'i'*, capital; stock or share in trade; merchandise; price; present to the judge.

بضان *buḍân*, month of Rabî' II.

بضباض *baḍbâḍ*, coll. mushrooms.

بضرا مضرا *biḍr-an miḍr-an*, shed unavenged (blood).

بضرة *baḍra-t*, vanities.

بضض *baḍaḍ*, little water.

(بضع) *baḍa'*, A, INF. *baḍ'*, cut off; split, cleave; shred, dissect, cut into pieces; marry; have sexual intercourse; explain; be clear, intelligible; stick to the eyelashes (tears); — INF. *buḍû'*, understand; be foiled; — INF. *baḍ'*, *baḍâ'*, *buḍû'*, be impregnated with water; — II. cut off; — III. *mubâḍa'a-t*, lie with a woman; — IV. explain; (two acc.); give in marriage; invest a capital; quench another's

thirst; pledge with wine; ex-plain or answer satisfactorily; —v. perspire; (m.) buy goods, make purchases; —vii. be cut off; —viii. be clear, intelligible; x. invest a capital; traffic.

بضع *baḍ'*, pl. of بضيع *baḍî'*; —*biḍ'*, *baḍ'*, part of the night; part; small number of people, less than 20 (m. *baḍ'a-t*, f. *baḍ'*); the numeral 7; —*buḍ'*, pudenda of a woman; marriage-contract; sexual intercourse; divorce; —ة *baḍ'a-t*, *biḍ'a-t*, pl. *baḍ'*, *biḍa'*, *biḍâ'*, part, portion; piece, slice; —*baḍa'a-t*, pl. of بضيع *baḍî'*, cutting, sharp, &c., q.v.

(بضك) *baḍak*, I, INF. *baḍk*, cut off, lop.

(بضم) *baḍam*, U, INF. *baḍm*, grow thick in grain; swell by degrees.

بضم *baḍm*, soul, self.

بضوض *baḍûḍ*, pl. *biḍâḍ*, well or leathern bags with little water.

بضوك *baḍûk*, sharp, cutting.

بضيض *baḍîḍ*, INF. of (بض); —ة *baḍî-ḍa-t*, little water; drizzling rain; plump and with a delicate skin; property.

بضيع *baḍî'*, pl. *baḍ'*, partner, associate; flesh; perspiration; sea; good water; island.

(بط) *baṭṭ*, U, INF. *baṭṭ*, cut open; —II. trade with ducks and geese; be enfeebled, low in health or circumstances; —IV. buy a small jug of oil.

بط *baṭ*, for *bâṭil*, false, vain, delusive; —*baṭṭ*, ة, pl. *buṭûṭ*, duck; goose; —ة *baṭṭa-t*, she-bear; low bottle, flask, cup, pot; calf of the leg.

بطا *buṭ'an*, بطاى *buṭ'â*, never; —*buṭâ'*, *biṭâ'*, slowness; —pl. of بطى *baṭî'*, slow, lazy.

بطاح *buṭâḥ*, pleurisy; —*biṭâḥ*, pl. of بطحا *baṭḥâ'*, q.v.; —ى *buṭâḥiyy*, suffering from pleurisy.

بطاحى *buṭâḥiyy*, stout, corpulent.

بطارق *buṭâriq*, tall, long.

بطاش *baṭṭâś*, brave, strong.

بطاطى *baṭâṭî*, small casks, pl. of بطية *baṭiyya-t*.

بطاقة *biṭâqa-t*, pupil of the eye; price-mark; pl. *baṭâ'iq*, letter.

بطال *baṭṭâl*, lazy, idle; trifling, toying; vain; obsolete, abolished; valiant hero; —ة *baṭâla-t*, idleness; trifling (s.); (m.) holidays; furlough, leave of absence; day of rest; feast-day; —*biṭâla-t*, bravery; see (بطل).

بطان *biṭân*, pl. *abṭina-t*, *buṭan*, girth; pl. *baṭâ'in*, small ship; —pl. of بطن *baṭin*, q.v.; —ة *biṭâna-t*, pl. *baṭâ'in*, inner side; lining; centre of a town, a country; true friend; fidelity; secret.

بطائق *baṭâ'iq*, pl. of بطاقة *baṭâqa-t*.

بطائن *baṭâ'in*, pl. of بطان *biṭân*, بطانة *biṭâna-t*.

(بطبط) *baṭbaṭ*, INF. ة, gabble, cackle; dive; have a weak judgment; —ة *baṭbaṭa-t*, weak intellect.

(بطح) *baṭaḥ*, throw one upon his face; —II. strew with pebbles; —III. floor in wrestling; —v. extend; overflow; —VI. wrestle; —VII. be thrown upon one's face; lie down on one's face; extend wide and far; —X.=V.; —ة *baṭḥa-t*, human frame; —*buṭḥa-t*, true state or condition.

بطحا *baṭḥâ'*, pl. *biṭâḥ*, broad pebble-bed; open field; valley of Mecca.

(بطخ) *baṭaḫ*, U, INF. *baṭḫ*, lick, lick at; —IV. (see بطيخ), have many melons.

(بطر) *baṭar*, U, INF. *baṭr*, split, cleave, cut open (tumours); —*baṭir*, A, INF. *baṭar*, be wanton; go beyond measure, do evil; be intoxicated with good fortune; despise; —IV. perplex, put to confusion; render overbearing; (m.) be overbearing or insolent.

بطر *baṭar*, insolence; —*baṭir*, insolent, overbearing; careless; —*biṭr-an*, shed with impunity (blood).

بطراكة *baṭrâka-t*, patriarchate.

بطران *baṭrân*, overbearing, insolent.

(بطرق), II. *tabaṭraq*, be stupid, insolent; walk like a prancing horse; — ة *baṭruqa-t*, pl. *baṭâriq*, melon.

بطرك *biṭrak*, *baṭrak*, *biṭark*, patriarch; — *baṭrak*, INF. ة, be patriarch.

بطرير *biṭrîr*, boisterous, impudent; persevering in error.

بطريق *biṭrîq*, pl. *baṭâriq*, *baṭâriqa-t*, *baṭâriq*, leader of 10,000; patriarch (also بطريك *baṭrîk*, بطريرك *baṭrairik*, pl. *baṭârîk*, *baṭârika-t*); proud, fat; — بطريق *bi-ṭarîq-i*, by way of, in the manner, for the sake of.

بطريكية *baṭrîkiyya-t*, patriarchate.

بطس *baṭas*, ة (also بطشة *baṭśa-t*), war-vessel.

(بطش) *baṭaś*, I, U, INF. *baṭś*, seize, attack; carry off by force; recover from a fit of ague, although in a weak state; (m.) act courageously; — III. INF. *mubâṭaśa-t*, seize by force; undertake, manage; come to close quarters; — IV. seize by force; — V. drag one's self along with difficulty under a burden.

بطش *baṭiś*, strong, brave; — *baṭś*, power; violence; anger; — ة *baṭśa-t*, power; superior power; violence; battle; day of judgment.

(بطغ) *baṭig*, INF. *baṭag*, be stained.

(بطل) *baṭal*, U, INF. *buṭl*, *buṭûl*, *buṭlân*, happen in vain, fail; be repealed, abolished; — INF. *baṭala-t*, jest; be idle; — *baṭul*, INF. *biṭâla-t*, *buṭâl*, *buṭûla-t*, be brave, be a hero; — II. render useless, repeal, abolish; — IV. id.; jest; tell falsehoods; — V. tell each other falsehoods; be lazy; be brave, be a hero; (m.) be celebrated (feast-day).

بطل *baṭal*, ة, pl. *abṭâl*, brave, a hero; given to jesting; — *buṭul*, vanities, &c., pl. of باطل *bâṭil*; — *buṭl*, idleness; being in vain; lie; anything unfounded; — ة *baṭala-t*, pl. sorcerers.

بطلات *baṭṭalât*, buffooneries; vanities.

بطلان *buṭlân* = بطل *buṭl*; INF. of (بطل).

(بطم) *buṭm*, *buṭum*, turpentine tree; granulous tumour.

(بطن) *baṭan*, U, enter, penetrate, fathom; — INF. *baṭn*, strike on the belly; — INF. *baṭn*, *baṭûn*, be hidden, secret; know; be an intimate friend; — INF. *biṭna-t*, indulge the belly, be a glutton; pass. *buṭin*, have a belly-ache; — *baṭin*, INF. *baṭan*, *baṭana-t*, have a full belly; — *baṭun*, be big-bellied; — II. strike on the belly; (also IV.) line (clothes); tighten the girth of a camel; — IV. hide, conceal; choose for a confidant; — V. put under one's belly; penetrate; go right through; be the inner part; — VI. be distant; — VIII. give birth; — X. put anything under one's belly; keep secret; know accurately; penetrate into, try to fathom anything.

بطن *baṭan*, corpulence; surfeit; belly-ache; — *baṭin*, pl. *biṭân*, big-bellied; gluttonous; rich; low; — *baṭn*, pl. *baṭûn*, *buṭnân*, *abṭun*, belly; contents of the belly; inner side of the sky; river-bed; esoteric meaning; relations; small tribe; second degree of relationship; — *buṭun*, girth-leathers, pl. of بطان *biṭân*; — ة *biṭna-t*, boisterous merriment; overbearingness; surfeit.

بطنان *buṭnân*, bellies, &c., pl. of بطن *baṭn*; — pl. of باطن *bâṭin*, interior, &c.

(بطو) *baṭu'*, U, INF. *buṭ'*, *biṭâ'*, move slowly or lazily; detain; — II. render slow, delay (a.); — III. delay (n.), tarry; — IV. tarry; have slow beasts of burden;

remain behind; detain, delay (a. ب *bi*); — V., VI. tarry, delay (n.); — consider slow or lazy; find tardy.

بطو *buṭu'*, slowness, laziness.

بطول *buṭûl*, foolery; INF. of (بطل); — ة *buṭûla-t*, bravery, heroism; INF. of (بطل).

بطى *baṭi'*, *baṭiyy*, pl. *biṭâ'*, slow, lazy, tardy; — ة *biṭya-t*, delay; — *baṭiyya-t*, pl. *baṭâṭi*, jug; small cask.

بطيحة *baṭîḥa-t*, pl. *baṭâ'iḥ*, swamped pebble-ground; large sheet of stagnating water.

بطيخ *biṭṭîḥ*, ة, pl. *baṭâṭîḥ*, melon, pumpkin; — ى *biṭṭîḥiyy*, melon-seller.

بطير *baṭîr*, split; veterinary surgeon.

بطيش *baṭîš*, mighty, powerful.

بطيط *baṭîṭ*, miracle; lie; calamity; — ة *baṭîṭa-t*, *buṭayyiṭa-t*, white ant, termite; worm (in wood, &c.).

بطين *baṭîn*, bellied; spacious; rich; full; distant; nick-name of Ali; — *buṭain*, little belly; second moon station.

(بظ) *bazz*, U, INF. *bazz*, tune and touch the strings of an instrument; exert one's self zealously; excel; — IV. grow fat.

بظا *buz-an*, *buzâ*, fleshy parts.

بظارة *bizâra-t*, smack of a kiss.

بظاظة *bazâza-t*, queer fellow.

(بظر) *bazir*, A, INF. *bazar*, have a protuberance on the lips; — II. circumcise (a girl).

بظر *bazr*, pl. *buzûr*, clitoris; finger-ring; sealing-ring.

بظرا *bizr-an*, unavenged (blood).

بظرم *bazram*, sealing-ring; — II. *tabazram*, INF. ة, show the rings by moving about the hand.

بظريرة *bizrîra-t*, boisterous woman.

(بظو) *bazâ*, U, INF. *buzuww*, be dense, solid, massy; — *bazî*, *bazâ*, INF. *baz*, be fleshy.

بظيظ *bazîz*, fat and soft.

(بع) *ba"*, I, INF. *ba"*, pour out in abundance; — INF. *ba"*, *ba'â'*, remain in the same spot and rain (cloud); be importunate.

بع *ba"*, abundant outpour.

بعابعة *ba'âbi'a-t*, poor people.

بعاد *bi'âd*, INF. III. of (بعد); — *bu'âd*, distant, far off.

بعار *bi'âr*, INF. III. of (بعر); — *bu'âr*, lotus.

بعاس *bi'âs*, lean camels, pl. of بعوس *ba'ûs*.

بعاع *ba'â'*, household things, furniture; travelling requisites; outfit of a bride; INF. of (بع).

بعاق *bu'âq*, *ba'âq*, *bi'âq*, raining cloud; waterspout; first shower; noise of a torrent.

بعال *bi'âl*, husbands, &c., pl. of بعل *bu'l*; INF. III. of (بعل).

بعائس *ba'â'is*, lean camels, pl. of بعوس *ba'ûs*.

(بعبع) *ba'ba'*, INF. ة, follow quickly; flee from battle.

بعبع *ba'ba'*, gurgling of water; prime of youth; — ة *ba'ba'a-t*, glibness of tongue; flight from the battle-field.

(بعث) *ba'as*, A, INF. *ba's*, send; loosen; urge on; awaken; raise the dead; follow on one's heels; — *ba'is*, A, INF. *ba'as*, be awake, wake; — V. proceed from; — VII. id.; be sent; be awakened; issue, proceed from; spread (n.); depart; — VIII. send.

بعث *ba'as*, army; — *ba'is*, vigilant; — *ba's*, pl. بعوث *bu'ûs*, detached army; يوم البعث *yaumu-'l-ba's*, day of resurrection; INF. of (بعث); — ة *ba'sa-t*, message; — *bi'sa-t*, mission (of a prophet); detachment.

(بعثر) *ba'sar*, INF. ة, throw topsy-turvy, rummage, overturn; take out, uncover and examine; look for, seek; put goods into order; — ة *ba'sara-t*, confusion; dirt-colour; dirt.

بعثط *bu'sut*, *bu'sutt*; بعثوط *bu'sût*, pl. *ba'âsit*, middle, centre; navel.

(بعشق) *ba'ṡaq*, INF. ة, flow out; — V. break through.

(بعج) *ba'aj*, A, INF. *ba'j*, split, slit; torment; (m.) emboss, cover with raised ornamental work; — II. split, slit; furrow; (m.) break into pieces; — V.=VII.; — VI. be distant, far off; — VII. split (n.), be split; burst, (m.) be embossed; — X. be distant (n.), consider far.

بعج *ba'ij*, walking slowly or with difficulty.

(بعد) *ba'ud*, INF. *bu'd*, be far, distant; die; — *ba'id*, A, INF. *ba'ad*, be distant; perish; — II. remove to a distance (a.); keep far, distant; — III. INF. *bi'âd*, *mubâ'ada-t*, remove (a.), render distant; be distant, far; keep distant; remove (n.); be far away; — IV. render or be distant; be extreme; destroy; — VI. be far from each other; abandon each other; — VIII. remove (n.); abandon; — X. consider far, find too far; remove to a distance.

بعد *ba'd*, after, afterwards, later; بعد بكرة *ba'da bukrat-in*, the day after to-morrow; اما بعد *ammâ ba'd*, but then, phrase of transition from the beginning of a letter, &c., to the chief matter; — *bu'd*, distance; absence; death; interval; بعدا له *bu'd-an la-hu*, away with him! ذو بعد *ẕû bu'd*, seeing far, cautious, prudent; — *ba'ad*, distant; valueless; distance, going to a distance; death; — *ba'id*, distant; dying; — *bu'ad*, utility; غير بعد *gair bu'ad*, useless; — *bu'ud*, and بعدا *bu'adâ*, بعدان *bu'dân*, pl. of بعيد *ba'îd*, far distant; — ة *bu'da-t*, pl. *bu'ad*, distance; not being related.

(بعذر) *ba'ẓar*, INF. *biẓâra-t*, move; shake; damage one's honour, disparage.

(بعر) *ba'ar*, A, INF. بعر *ba'r*, drop excrement; — *ba'ir*, A, INF. *ba'ar*, grow five years old (camel); — II., IV. empty the bowels.

بعر *ba'r*, *ba'ar*, ة, pl. *ab'âr*, globular dung of animals; — *ba'r*, deepest poverty; bait; — ة *ba'ra-t*, wrath (of God); — *ba'ra-t* and *ba'ara-t*, globular excrement; — *ba'ara-t*, gland of the penis.

بعران *bu'rân*, camels, &c., pl. of بعير *ba'îr*.

(بعرص), II. *taba'raṣ*, quiver (lopped limb).

(بعزق) *ba'zaq*, INF. ة, disperse; dissipate; — ة *ba'zaqa-t*, dissipation.

(بعص) *ba'ṣ*, leanness, thinness; movement, motion; — V. *taba'aṣ*, move (n.).

(بعصص), II. *taba'ṣaṣ*, move (n.).

بعصوص *ba'aṣûṣ*, *bu'ṣûṣ*, thin, mobile; hip-bone.

(بعض), pass. *bu'iḍ*, be molested by flies; — II. dissect, divide; — IV. abound in flies; — V. be dissected, divided.

بعض *ba'ḍ*, pl. *ab'âḍ*, part, portion; some; sundry, a certain; in repetition; each other, reciprocal; — ة *ba'iḍa-t*, abounding in flies.

(بعضض), II. *taba'ḍaḍ*, try to catch one another.

بعضوضة *ba'ḍûḍa-t*, an insect.

(بعط) *ba'aṭ*, A, INF. *ba'ṭ*, slaughter, kill; exceed all bounds in disgraceful behaviour; — IV. id.; speak otherwise than intended, blunder in speech; exceed one's power; cause one to spend beyond his means; go far; remove to a distance (a.); escape (slave).

بعط *ba'ṭ*, infamy.

(بعق) *ba'aq*, U, INF. *bu'ûq*, groove, furrow; — INF. *ba'q*, slaughter; uncover; dig a well; (m.) emboss; — II. split; slaughter; — V. be slaughtered; — V., VII. empty itself with violent rain

(cloud); — VII. surprise, attack suddenly; speak precipitately; (m.) be embossed.

(بعقط) *bu'quṭ*, small; dwarf.

بعقوط *bu'qûṭ*, dwarfish.

(بعك) *ba'ak*, U, INF. *ba'k*, strike arm or leg with the sword.

بعك *ba'ak*, thickness; roughness; spasm.

(بعكر) *ba'kar*, INF. ة, cut off.

بعكوك *bu'kûk*, ة, impression from sitting or lying; place of assembly; *bu'kûka-t*, heat; middle; crowd.

بعكوكا *ba'kûkâ'*, calamity; noise, tumult.

(بعل) *ba'al*, A, INF. *bu'ûla-t* (*ba'ul*, INF. *ba'âla-t*), be a husband or a wife; refuse; — *ba'il*, A, INF. *ba'al*, not know what one is doing from confusion; — INF. *bi'âl*, *mubâ'ala-t*, lie or sport with one's wife; take a husband; intermarry; sit down by the side of another; — V. be obedient to one's husband, adorn one's self for him; take a husband; — VI. sport with one's wives; — VIII.=V.; — X. take for a wife (ل *li*); be situated on high; suffice to one's self.

بعل *ba'al*, INF. of (بعل); — *ba'il*, ة, distracted in mind; (m.) dry; — *ba'l*, pl. *bi'âl*, *bu'ûl*, *bu'ûla-t*, husband; wife; master, lord; the idol Baal; burden; rising ground; palm-tree; — ة *ba'la-t*, wife, mistress (of the house, &c.).

بعلبك *ba'labakk*, *ba'albakk*, Balbek in Syria.

بعلزبوب *ba'alzabûb*, Belzebub.

بعلى *ba'liyy*, watered by rain only; (m.) dry; weak.

(بعنس) *ba'nas*, INF. ة, grow mean (by serving, &c.).

بعنس *ba'nas*, a stupid female slave.

بعنقاة *ba'naqât*, having sharp claws.

(بعو) *ba'â*, A, I, U, INF. *ba'w*, act unjustly, sin; borrow or lend each other; win in the game of dice; injure by the evil eye; cause misfortune to anybody; — IV. lend one's horse to another; — X. lend mutually.

بعو *ba'w*, transgression; anything borrowed.

بعوس *ba'ûs*, pl. *bi'âs*, *ba'â'is*, lean milkless she-camel.

بعوض *ba'ûḍ*, ة, fly, gnat.

بعيث *ba'îs̱*, sent.

بعيج *ba'ij*, woman with many children; flowing abundantly.

بعيد *ba'îd*, pl. *bu'ud*, *bu'adâ'*, *bu'dân*, far, distant; scarcely related; بعيد الغور *ba'îdu-'l-gaur-i*, unfathomably deep; — *bu'aid*, in a little distance, soon after.

بعير *ba'îr*, *bi'îr*, pl. *ab'ira-t*, *abâ'ir*, *abâ'ir*, *bu'rân*, *bi'rân*, camel nine (or four) years old; beast of burden; ass.

بعيق *bâ'iq*, cry; cracking.

بعيم *ba'îm*, false god, idol.

(بغ) *bagg*, U, INF. *bagg*, heave, swell; become agitated.

بغ *bugg*, ة, small camel.

بغا *bigâ'*, *bugâ'*, see (بغى); — ة *bugâ-t*, pl. of باغى *bâgî*, passionate, rebellious, &c.

بغاث *bagâs̱*, *bigâs̱*, *bugâs̱*, pl. *bigs̱ân*, a kind of vulture; chough; small birds.

بغاددة *bagâdida-t*, people of Bagdad, pl. of بغدادى *bagdâdiyy*.

بغاضة *bagâḍa-t*, hatred.

بغال *bigâl*, mules, pl. of بغل *bagl*; — *baggâl*, muleteer.

بغاوة *bagâwa-t*, rebellion, insurrection.

بغايا *bagâyâ*, pl. of بغى *bagiyy*, ة *bagiyya-t*, q.v.

بغاية *bugâya-t*, desired things; — *bi-gâya-t*, in the extreme; extremely; very much; exceedingly.

(بغبغ) *bugbug*, full well.

بغبغ *bagbag*, INF. ة, roar; snore; tread, tread down.

بغبور *bugbûr*, *bagbûr*, altar for sacrifice; emperor of China.

(بغت) *bagat*, A, INF. *bagt*, happen unexpectedly; fall upon; — III. fall upon suddenly.

بغت *bagt*, what happens unexpectedly; — ة *bagta-t*, unexpected occurrence; surprise, sudden attack, invasion; *bagtat-an*, suddenly.

(بغث) *bagis*, A, INF. *bagas*, have black spots (white bird); — IV. come on soft ground; make lavish expenditure; — IX. ابغث *ibgass*, INF. *ibgisâs*=I.; — ة *bagsa-t*, slight rain; — *bugsa-t*, black spotted with white, or vice versa.

بغثا *bagsâ'*, white with black spots; mixed multitude.

بغثان *bigsân*, pl. of بغاث *bagâs*.

(بغثر) *bagsar*, INF. ة, be wickedly and passionately disposed; be agitated; separate; =(بعثر); — II. *tabagsar*, be wickedly disposed.

بغثر *bagsar*, stupid; troublesome; unwholesome; big and awkward (camel); weak; — ة *bagsara-t*, commotion, confusion; villany, vileness; separation, dispersion.

بغداد *bagdâd* (بغذاذ *bagzâz*, بغداذ *bagdâz*), Bagdad; — II. *tabagdad*, go to Bagdad; — ى *bagdâdiyy*, of or from Bagdad; pl. *bagâdida-t*, native or inhabitant of Bagdad.

بغدان *bagdân*, بغدين *bagdîn*, Bagdad.

(بغر) *bagar*, A, INF. *bugûr*, set and cause rain (constellation); — INF. *bagr*, rain heavily, water the ground with rain; also *bagir*, A, INF. *bagar*, drink and not become satiated, but ill (camel).

بغر *bagr*, *bagar*, ة, violent downpour; INF. of (بغر); — ة *bagra-t*, what has been sown after rain; annual gift.

(بغز) *bagaz*, A, INF. *bagz*, beat, kick; put into lively motion.

بغز *bagz*, lively motion; vivacity; vehemence.

(بغش) *bagaś*, A, INF. *bagś*, drop a slight rain (sky); run crying up to his mother (child); penetrate.

بغش *bagś*, ة, fine rain.

(بغض) *bagaḍ*, U, *bagiḍ*, A, *baguḍ*, U, INF. *bagaḍa-t*, be hateful; (m.) hate; — *bagiḍ*, look at with anger; — II. INF. *tabgîḍ*, render hateful; hated; — IV. INF. *ibgâḍ*, hate; — V. INF. *tabagguḍ*, show hatred; — VI. INF. *tabâguḍ*, hate one another; — VII. INF. *imbigâḍ*, be hated.

بغض *bugḍ*, hatred; — ا *bagḍâ'*, ة *bigḍa-t*, violent hatred, wrath.

(بغل) *bagl*, f. ة, pl. *bigâl*, *mabgûlâ'*, mule; — ة *bagla-t*, (m.) counterfort, buttress.

بغل *bagal*, A, INF. *bagl*, insult other people's children; — II. INF. *tabgîl*, id.; walk slowly; have the walk of a mule.

(بغم) *bagam*, A, I, U, INF. *bugâm*, *bugûm*, call fondly for her young ones (gazelle, &c.); cry out, call; express one's meaning indistinctly; — III. INF. *mubâgama-t*, speak in a soft tone; — V. INF. *tabaggum*=I.

بغم *bagam*, secret talk; — ة *bagma-t*, soft call of a camel; — *bugma-t*, pl. *bugam*, pearl necklace (m.).

(بغنج), II. INF. *tabagnuj*, coquettishness.

(بغو) *bagâ*, U, INF. *bagw*, look at, regard, contemplate.

بغو *bagw*, observation; — *baguww* =بغى *bagiyy*, q.v.; — ة *bagwa-t*, unripe date; opening palm-blossom.

بغور *bugûr*, setting (of the stars).

بغوم *bagûm*, crying out, calling.

(بغى) *bagâ*, I, INF. *bagy*, transgress; exercise violence and injustice; commit fornication; walk proudly and swiftly; rain heavily; swell and suppurate; look at, regard, observe and expect; — INF. *bagâ*, *bag-an*, *bugya-t*, *bigya-t*, seek, wish

for, desire ; — III. INF. *bigâ'*, *mubâgât*, treat unjustly ; oppress ; contend ; fornicate ; seek, desire ; — IV. INF. *ibgâ'*, seek for another, help to seek ; — V. INF. *tabaggî*, seek, desire ; observe and expect ; — VI. INF. *tabâgî*, transgress against each other ; — VII. INF. *imbigâ'*, VIII. INF. *ibtigâ'*, be easy, desirable, convenient ; VIII. and X. INF. *istibgâ'*, seek, desire ; X. cause to demand or desire.

بغى *bagy*, transgression, injustice, outrage, injury ; heavy rain ; — *bagiyy*, unjust ; striving eagerly, observing strictly ; pl. *bagâyâ*, whore, adultress ; — ة *bigya-t*, *bugya-t*, wish, desire ; anything wished for or sought ; — *bagiyya-t*, pl. *bagâyâ*, id. ; outpost, van-guard.

بغيان *bugyân*, pl. of باغى *bâgî*, desirous, &c.

بغيبغ *bugaibig*, little well.

بغيث *bagîs*, wheat.

بغير *bagîr*, ill from thirst (camel).

بغيض *bagîd*, hateful ; enemy.

(بق) *baqq*, U, INF. *baqq*, give abundantly ; rain abundantly ; show pride ; spread, strew out ; dissipate ; split, tear ; begin to bloom ; give birth to many children ; — INF. *baqq*, *baqâq*, importune by talk ; — (m.) blot (as paper) ; — II. INF. *tabaqbuq*, disperse, dissipate ; — IV. INF. *ibqâq*, have many children ; importune by talk ; do abundantly good or evil to anybody ; produce grass or food ; bring forth weak young ones.

بق *baqq*, ة, fly ; bug ; — *baqq*, woman with many children ; لق بق *laqq baqq*, talkative, garrulous ; — بالبق *bi'l-buqq*, in vain (m.).

بقا *baqâ'*, continuance, duration (بقى).

بقار *baqqâr*, breeder of oxen ; blacksmith ; — *buqqâr*, cows, pl. of بقرة *baqra-t* ; — ى *buqqârā*, lie ; calamity ; — *baqqâriyy*, cudgel.

بقاع *biqâ'*, places, &c., pl. of بقعة *buq'a-t*, *baq'a-t*.

بقاق *baqâq*, things of little value, sweepings ; INF. of (بق) ; also ة *baqâqa-t*, talkative, garrulous.

بقال *baqâl*, ة, bringing forth plenty of vegetables ; — *baqqâl*, green-grocer, grocer, oil-merchant ; inn-keeper ; — ة *baqâla-t*, green or kitchen garden.

بقامة *baqâma-t*, of weak intellect ; coarse wool or flax ; offal.

بقاوة *baqâwa-t*, INF. of (بقى).

بقايا *baqâyâ*, remains, &c., pl. of بقية *baqiyya-t*.

بقباق *baqbâq*, mouth.

(بقبق) *baqbaq*, INF. ة, gurgle, water flowing out from a narrow-mouthed vessel, or boiling ; coo (dove) ; chatter ; (m.) swell ; bubble ; have blisters ; — ة *baqbaqa-t*, gurgling of water ; blister.

بقبوقة *baqbûqa-t*, bubble ; blister (m.).

(بقت) *baqat*, U, INF. *baqt*, stir up.

(بقث) *baqas*, U, INF. *baqs*, stir up, bring into confusion.

بقجة *buqja-t*, bundle, parcel ; knapsack.

(بقح) *baqah*=(بقع) (m.) ; — II. INF. *tabqîh*, soil ; — V. INF. *tabaqquh*, be soiled ; — ة *baqha-t*, stain.

بقدونس *baqdûnas*, parsley.

(بقر) *baqar*, A, INF. *baqr*, split, cleave ; enlarge ; seek knowledge ; look out for water and find it ; know another's circumstances, try to know them ; — *baqir*, A, INF. *baqr*, *baqar*, be scarcely able to see ; be tired ; rejoice at the sight of ; — V. INF. *tabaqqur*, be extensive, rich ; stay in a town or village while one's people are outside ; — VIII. INF. *ibtiqâr*, get split, cleft ; split (n.).

بقر *baqar*, pl. *buqûr*, *abâqir*, ox, head of cattle ; — *buqar*, lie ; calamity ;

— ة *baqara-t*, pl. *baqar, buqur, baqarât, bawâqir, buqqâr, ubqûr*, cow; ox; — ى *baqariyy*, of cattle, referring to cattle.

بقراط *baqrâṭ*, Hippocrates.

بقس *baqs*, بقسيس *baqsîs*, box-tree.

بقسماط *baqsimâṭ*, biscuit, rusk.

(بقط) *baqṭ*, furniture; diversion, amusement; tenure for a part of the produce.

(بقط), II. INF. *tabqîṭ*, ascend a mountain; walk swiftly; talk quickly; silence by scolding; disperse; (m.) hasten; give to eat in small quantities; — V. INF. *tabaqquṭ*, receive news piecemeal; take food in small quantities.

بقطرية *buqṭuriyya-t*, an ample white garment.

(بقع) *baqa'*, INF. *baq'*, go; pass. be abused; — *baqi'*, A. INF. *baqa'*, be spotted (white and black); be satisfied with little; be void of (من *min*); be wet in some places and stained; — II. INF. *tabqî'*, go anywhere; spot white and black; stain; — V. INF. *tabaqqu'*, be wetted, sprinkled in some places; be spotted; — VII. INF. *imbiqâ'*, walk fast; — VIII. INF. *ibtiqâ'*, change (colours, n.).

بقع *baqa'*, spottedness; — ة *baq'a-t*, pl. *buqa'*, spot, stain; — *buq'a-t*, *baq'a-t*, pl. *buqa'*, *biqâ'*, place; spot; low ground with water; building.

بقعا *baq'â'*, spotted, f. of ابقع *abqa'*.

بقعان *buq'ân*, pl. Ethiopian slaves.

(بقل) *baqal*, U, INF. *baql*, appear, push (as a plant, a tooth); make to sprout; get green; gather food; — INF. *buqûl*, begin to grow a beard; — II. INF. *tabqîl*, cause to sprout, to push; keep one's animals well; — IV. INF. *ibqâl*, push forth (a.); get green; begin to grow a beard; bring to light, show openly; pasture (a.); — V. INF. *tabaqqul*, fetch food; pasture (n.); — VII. INF. *imbiqâl*, pasture (n.); — VIII. INF. *ibtiqâl*, pasture (n. and a.).

بقل *baql*, ة, pl. *buqûl*, vegetables, cabbage, greens, beans, &c.; بقلة الانصار *baqlatu-'l-anṣâr-i*, cauliflower; البقلة المباركة *al-baqlatu-'l-mubâraka-t*, endive; — *buql*, spring herbs.

بقلاوة *baqlâwa-t*, almond cake (m.).

(بقلش) *baqlaś*, INF. ة, and II. INF. *tabaqluś*, be covered with blisters; form (into blisters).

(بقم) *baqim*, A, INF. *baqam*, get ill from eating the plant *'unzuwân*.

بقم *baqqam*, Brasil wood; a tree with a red colouring wood; — II. INF. *tabqîm*, dye red.

(بقو) *baqâ*, U, INF. *baqâwa-t*, look upon, regard; expect; INF. *baqw, baqwa-t, baqâwa-t*, protect, preserve; — ة *baqwa-t*, INF. of (بقى); — ى *baqwa, buqwa*, remainder; what has been left or preserved; what remains alive; life.

(بقى) *baqî*, A, INF. *baqâ', baq-an, baqy*, remain, endure, survive; continue; — INF. *baqy*, look at or upon, regard; observe; — INF. *baqwa-t*, protect, preserve; — II. INF. *tabqiya-t*, render lasting, cause to remain; leave; preserve alive; — III. INF. *mubâqiya-t*, fight another for the preservation of one's life; — IV. INF. *ibqâ'*, let remain, cause to last, preserve alive; spare; fail to destroy entirely; — V. INF. *tabaqqî*, preserve alive; remain alive; be left; — VI. INF. *tabâqî*, remain alive one and the other; — VII. INF. *imbiqâ'*, be left, preserved; — X. INF. *istibqâ*, preserve alive; spare; leave part of a thing (من *min*); — ة *baqiyya-t*, pl. *baqâyâ*, remainder, rest, surplus; life; sparing, preservation.

بقيا *baqyâ* = بقوى *baqwa, buqwa*, q.v.

بقير *baqîr*, ة *baqîra-t*, under-garment without sleeves.

بقيع *baqî'*, place with roots of trees; — ة *baqî'a-t*, fields.
بقيل *baqîl*, ة, producing greens; — ة *baqîla-t*, soup of vegetables; — *buqaila-t*, small cabbage-plant.
(بك) *bakk*, U, INF. *bakk*, *bakka-t*, tear, break into pieces; separate; spoil; press, urge; break one's head; humiliate; grow poor; (m.) vomit; — VI. INF. *tabâkk*, be pressed upon each other, press one another in a throng.
بكا *bikâ'*, she-camels with little milk, pl. of بكى *bakî'*; — *bukâ*, crying, INF. of (بكى); — *bakkâ'*, who cries much; having little milk; — ة *bukât*, pl. of باكى *bâkî*, crying, weeping.
بكابك *bukâbik*, lively, sprightly.
بكار *bikâr*, young she-camels, pl. of بكرة *bakra-t*; — ة *bakâra-t*, *bikâra-t*, virginity; — young camels, pl. of بكر *bakr*.
بكامة *bukâma-t*, dumbness.
بكان *bukkân*, pl. of ابك *abakk*, strenuous, &c.
بكاوير *bakâwîr*, pl. of بكيرة, bearing early fruit, &c.
بكايا *bakâyâ*, she-camels with little milk, pl. of بكيئة *bakî'a-t*.
(بكبك) *bakbak*, INF. ة, throw one thing upon another; turn topsy-turvy; press (n.); come and go; move, shake; lick.
(بكت) *bakat*, U, INF. *bakt*, beat, strike; receive with anything unpleasant; — II. INF. *tabkît*, scold; reproach; chide; upbraid; silence by arguments; — V. INF. *tabakkut*, be scolded; have qualms of conscience, remorses.
(بكر) *bakar*, U, INF. *bukûr*, happen early in the morning; rise early; do anything or come early in the morning; — *bakir*, A, INF. *bakar*, hasten; — II. INF. *tabkîr*, rise, set out, do anything, come early in the morning; anticipate; come in time for the beginning of prayer; do anything too early; cause to rise or to come early; — III. INF. *mubâkara-t*, come early in the morning; — IV. INF. *ibkâr*, id.; hasten to come early; cause to come early; anticipate; water the cattle early in the morning; — V. INF. *tabakkur*, anticipate; — VIII. INF. *ibtikâr*, rise early; come early; come at the beginning of the sermon; eat the first fruit; be the first to do anything; deflower; give first birth to a boy.
بكر *bakar*, morning; haste, hurry; — *bakir*, *bakur*, who rises or does anything early; — *bakr*, *bukr*, ة, pl. *abkur*, *bukrân*, *bikâr*, *bikâra-t*, *bakâra-t*, young camel; — *bikr*, pl. *akbâr*, virgin, maiden; first-born; having given birth or produced fruit for the first time; what has never been before; spring-cloud heavy with rain; ضربة بكر *ḍarbat bikr*, deadly stroke; — *bukr*, pl. of بكور *bakûr*, بكير *bakîr*, bearing early fruit; — ة *bakra-t*, pl. *bikâr*, young she-camel; troop, number of people; — *bakra-t*, *bakara-t*, pl. *bakar*, *bakarât*, pulley; water-wheel; wheel; troop; *bakarât*, rings of a dagger-belt; — *bikra-t*, virgin; — *bukra-t*, pl. *bukar*, early morning; *bukrat-an*, early in the morning; (m.) to-morrow; *ba'da bukrat-in*, the day after to-morrow.
بكرج *bakraj* (بقرج *baqraj*), can, tankard (Turk).
بكرى *bikriyy*, virginal.
(بكس) *bakas*, U, INF. *baks*, overcome, vanquish an enemy.
بكش *bakaś*, U, INF. *bakś*, loosen the tethers of a camel.
(بكع) *baka'*, A, INF. *bak'*, receive with anything unpleasant; scold into silence; beat violently and repeatedly in different places; cut; give the whole; go any-

where ; — II. INF. *tabkî'*, scold into silence; cut into pieces.

بكك *bukuk*, pl. vigorous fellows; frisky donkeys.

(بكل) *bakal*, U, INF. *bakl*, mix; prepare the dish *bakîlat*; speak confusedly ; — II. INF. *tabkîl*, mix; pass. *bukkil bi-hi*, he is hand and glove with him; (m.) buckle; button; — V. INF. *tabakkul*, conquer and make booty; offer one thing for sale against another; get the better of (acc. or على *'ala*) by scolding and beating; get confused in speaking; walk haughtily; — VIII. INF. *ibtikâl*, carry off as a booty.

بكل *bakal*, *bakl*, booty, plunder; *bakl*, mixture, confusion; — ة *bikla-t*, nature, form, site; — *bikla-t*, *bukla-t*, pl. *bikal*, *bukal*, *biklât*, buckle (m.).

(بكم) *bakim*, A, INF. *bakam*, *bakâma-t*, be dumb; — *bakum*, INF. *bakâma-t*, be obstinately silent; abstain from sexual intercourse; — V. تبكم عليه الكلام *tabakkam 'ale-hi al-kalâm*, he speaks with difficulty.

بكم *bakam*, dumbness; — *bukm*, pl. of ابكم *abkam*, dumb.

بكمان *bukmân*, pl. of بكيم *bakîm*, dumb.

بكور *bakûr*, pl. *bukr*, bearing early fruit (date-tree); early fruit; first spring-rain; — *bukûr*, INF. of (بكر).

بكورية *bukûriyya-t*, primogeniture.

(بكى) *baka*, I, INF. *buk-an*, *bukâ'*, weep; INF. *bukâ'*, weep over, lament (acc.); sing; — II. INF. *tabkâ'*, *tibkâ'*, weep violently; INF. *tabkiyat*, cause to weep; weep, lament; — III. vie in weeping; — IV. INF. *ibkâ'*, cause to weep; push to extremes; — VI. force one's self to weep; — VII. be induced to weep; — VIII. cause to weep.

بكى *bakiyy*, who weeps easily; a little; — *bukiyy*, pl. of باكى *bâkî*, weeping; — *bakî'*, ة, *bakî'a-t*, pl. *bikâ'*, *bakâyâ*, she-camel with little milk.

بكير *bakîr*, ة *bakîra-t*, pl. *bukr*, *bukâwîr*=بكور *bakûr*, q.v.; — *bikkîr*, very early.

بكيل *bakîl*, neat; careful; — ة *bakîla-t* (بكالة *bakâla-t*), dish of flour, dates, &c.; mixed herd; plunder, booty; nature, condition, state.

بكيم *bakîm*, pl. *bukmân*, deaf; dumb, silent.

(بل) *ball*, U, INF. *ball*, *billa-t*, wet, sprinkle; — INF. *ball*, *bilâl*, benefit one's relatives, be on good terms with them; bless anyone (acc.) with (acc. or ب *bi*); drop; sow (the ground); — INF. *ball*, *bulûl*, *balal*, recover; — INF. *ball*, be given to, infatuated with (ب *bi*); go, travel; — INF. *bulûl*, blow damp and cold; escape; — *balil*, A, INF. *balal*, vanquish, conquer; know; be quarrelsome, oppressive, impious; undergo great calamity; be always by one's side; — *balil*, INF. *balal*, *balâla-t*, *bulûl*, and *balal*, INF. *bulûl*, be infatuated, in love with (ب *bi*); INF. also *billa-t*, *balla-t*, be wet, moist; — disperse (n.); — II. INF. *tablîl*, wet through, water; — IV. INF. *iblâl*, escape; recover; bear fruit; wander in the desert; drop, drip; go; travel; be malicious and mischievous; vanquish; refuse; be unwilling; be absent, hidden; — V. INF. *taballul*, scratch the ground; — V., VII. (INF. *imbilâl*), VIII. (INF. *ibtilâl*), get wetted, moistened; — V., VIII. recover; get better; — X. INF. *istiblâl*, id.

بل *bal*, or rather, on the contrary; no; nay; certainly; sometimes; — *ball*, strong desire; who frees himself from an obligation by perjury; unjust; quarreller; able, doughty; — *bill*, common

property; remedy; — *bull*, pl. of ابل *aball*, q.v.; — ة *bula-t*, bunch of grass; — *balla-t*, drop; moisture; wetting; — *billa-t*, moisture; eloquence; distinct pronunciation; INF. of (بل); — *bulla-t*, sap; pl. *bilâl*, last touches of love; wickedness.

بلا *balâ'*, visitation, affliction, calamity; sorrow; trouble; bravery; wear of clothing = بلى *bil-an*; — *bi-lâ*, without, beyond; — *ballâ'*, adultress; f. of ابل, q.v.

بلابل *balâbil*, nightingales, pl. of بلبل *bulbul*; — pl. of بلبلة *balbala-t*, sorrow; — *bulâbil*, pl. *balâbil*, agile, active; *balâbil*, vigour and zeal.

بلاتة *balâta-t*, prudence; INF. of (بلت).

بلاثيق *balâṡiq*, extensive sheets of stagnating water, pl. of بلثوق *bulṡûq*.

بلاخ *bilâḫ*, having heavy hips (woman); — *bulâḫ*, holm-oak.

بلاد *bilâd*, cities, &c., pl. of بلدة *balda-t*; — INF. III. of (بلد); — ة *balâda-t*, stupidity, silliness, folly.

بلارج *balâraj*, stork.

(بلاز) *bal'az*, INF. ة, flee; jump, run; eat one's fill.

بلاز *bul'az*, short, strong and hardened; Satan.

بلاس *balâs*, pl. *bulus*, coarse cloth; mattress.

بلاش *bilâś* (for بلا شي *bi-lâ śay-in*), gratis; in vain; without reason.

(بلاص) *bal'aṣ*, INF. ة, flee.

بلاط *balâṭ*, level ground; smooth pavement; bricks or flats for paving; palace.

بلاطح *bulâṭiḥ*, broad, wide.

بلاعق *balâ'iq*, pl. spacious.

بلاعة *ballâ'a-t*, pl. *balâli'*, sewer.

بلاغ *balâg*, arrival; delivery (of a message, &c.); sufficiency; enough; — *bilâg*, III. (بلغ); — ة *balâga-t*, eloquence; pl. *balâgât*, talk; (بلغ); — ى *balâga*, *bulâga*, eloquent, clear.

بلال *balâl*, *bulâl*, *bilâl*, moisture; freshness; water, milk, &c., refreshment; benefit; union with relatives; — *bilâl*, pl. last touches of love; — *ballâl*, linseed; seeds of vegetables; who waters; — *balâla-t*, INF. of (بل); — *bulâla-t*, moisture; driblet.

بلالير *balâlîr*, crystals, pl. of بلور *bilaur*, *ballûr*.

بلاليط *balâliṭ*, level ground; broad pavement.

بلاليع *balâlî'*, sewers, pl. of بلاعة *balâ'a-t*, بلوعة *balû'a-t*.

بلان *ballân*, f. ة, waiter in a public bath; *ballâna-t*, pl. *-ât*, warm bath.

بلاهة *balâha-t*, utter stupidity, idiotcy.

بلاهن *balâhin*, بلاهى *balâhî*, lives passed in ease and enjoyment, pl. of بلهنية *bulahniya-t*.

بلايا *balâyâ*, pl. of بلية *baliyya-t*, q.v.

بلبال *balbâl*, ة *balbâla-t*, pl. *balâbil*, emotion, anxiety, sorrow; wolf; — ة *balbâla-t*, vigour and zeal; see the following.

(بلبل) *balbal*, INF. ة, mix, throw together or into confusion; bring about difference of opinion, differ in views; squander; disquiet or irritate by innuendoes; — INF. *balbâla-t*, *bilbâl*, irritate, incite; = II. INF. *bilbâl*, be confused (speech); — II. INF. *tabalbul*, be agitated, disquieted, confused; have grazed off all the herbs of a pasture-ground.

بلبل *bulbul*, pl. *balâbil*, nightingale (Pers.); — *bulbul*, pipe, channel, groove; agile and helping; — ة *balbala-t*, emotion, anxiety, sorrow; confusion, confusion of languages; pearl; pl. *balâbil*, sorrows; — *bulbula-t*, can with a pipe; travelling litter; — ى *bulbuliyy*, agile, nimble, ready (as a helper, &c.).

(بلت) *balat*, I, INF. *balt*, cut, cut into pieces; — *balat*, U, INF. *balt*, also *balit*, A, INF. *balat*, be cut,

separate (n.); — *balut*, INF. *balâta-t*, be reserved and prudent; — IV. INF. *iblât*, urge to take an oath; — VII. INF. *inbilât*, be cut, separated.

بلتاة *baltât*, cutting, severing, splitting.

(بلتع) *balta'*, sly, cunning; f. ة *balta'a-t*, talkative woman; — II. INF. *tabaltu'*, whet one's tongue for abuse; part. *mutabalti'*.

بلتعانى *balta'âniyy*, who affects wit and elegance.

بلتعى *balta'iyy*, eloquent; bold, courageous.

(بلتم) *baltam*, people, number of men; stammerer.

(بلتى) *balta*, INF. *baltât*, cut.

بلثوق *bulṯûq*, extensive sheet of stagnating water.

(بلج) *balaj*, U, INF. *bulûj*, glitter, shine; — I, INF. *balj*, open; — *balij*, A, INF. *balâj*, have the eye-brows separated; rejoice; — IV. INF. *iblâj*, shine; light up, make clear, unveil; distinguish, separate; rejoice; — V. INF. *taballuj*, VII. INF. *inbilâj*, VIII. INF. *ibtilâj*, shine, dawn, brighten; — V. rejoice, laugh; be open, outspoken; — XI. INF. *iblijâj*, be cleared up, unveiled, revealed.

بلج *balaj*, بلجة *bulja-t*, space between the eye-brows; — *balja-t*, *bulja-t*, light, brightness; twilight, dawn; — *balj*, pl. of ابلج *ablaj*, shining; having the eye-brows separated, &c.; — *baluj*, pl. who have smooth beardless cheeks.

(بلح) *balaḥ*, A, INF. *balḥ*, dry up; — INF. *bulûḥ*, be tired, weak; flow off; be lost (as labour, &c.); — II. INF. *tabliḥ*, be tired; — IV. INF. *iblâḥ*, bear unripe dates; — V. INF. *taballuḥ*=II.; — VI. INF. *tabâluḥ*, give the lie to each other.

بلح *balaḥ*, ة, unripe date; greenness.

(بلخ) *baliḫ*, A, INF. *balaḫ*, and V. INF. *taballuḫ*, be proud, haughty.

بلخ *balḫ*, oak-tree of some kind; height, greatness; — *balḫ*, *bilḫ*, haughty, proud; high, elevated, sublime.

بلخا *balḫâ'*, f. of ابلخ *ablaḫ*, stupid.

بلخش *balaḫš*, hyacinth (precious stone); ruby.

(بلخص), II. INF. *tabalḫuṣ*, be big and large, be much of a thing.

بلخص *balḫaṣ*, thick, coarse.

بلخية *balaḫiyya-t*, pomegranate tree of some kind.

(بلد) *balad*, A, INF. *bulûd*, reside, take a place for a dwelling and defend it by arms; — *balid*, A, INF. *balad*, id.; — INF. *balad*, *balda-t*, have the eye-brows separated; — *balid* and *balud*, INF. *balâda-t*, be impudent, shameless, stupid, lazy; — II. INF. *tablid*, naturalise; acclimatise; not care for anything; be miserly without getting rich; throw one's self on the ground; not rain; remain behind; — III. INF. *bilâd*, *mubâlada-t*, fight any-one with a sword or stick; — IV. INF. *iblâd*, cause one to settle in a place (two acc.); stick to a place (from poverty); have stupid and lazy beasts of burden; — V. INF. *taballud*, be acclimatised, or naturalised; occupy a deserted country, take possession; fall to the ground; show or pretend to be stupid; be lazy; be confused, perplexed; be moved with passion; sigh with grief; clap the hands; turn the palms outside; — XIV. INF. *iblindâ'*, be strongly built and of firm flesh.

بلد *balad*, ة, pl. *bilâd*, *buldân*, city, district, province, country; house, domicile, dwelling; Mecca; ground where no fire has been burning nor a well been dug; pl. *ablâd*, ostrich-nest, ostrich; burial-place,

tomb; sign, trace; twenty-first station of the moon; space between the eye-brows and the root of the nose; fore-neck, chest; palm of the hand; principle, element; — *balad*, *buld*, plummet; — ة *bulda-t*, space between the eye-brows; shape of the face.

بلدام *bildâm*, *bildâma-t*, loosely built.

بلدان *buldân*, pl. of بلد *balad*.

(بلدح) *baldaḥ*, INF. ة, throw one's self on the ground; I. and II. INF. *tabalduḥ*, promise and not keep the promise; — III. INF. *iblindâḥ*, stretch far and wide; decay, get destroyed.

(بلدم) *baldam*, INF. ة, be afraid and keep silent.

بلدم *baldam*, larynx; — *buldum*, indigestible; peevish; blunt (also بلذم).

بلدى *baladiyy*, countryman, native.

(بلز), III. INF. *mubâlaza-t*, and VIII. INF. *ibtilâz*, take, receive.

(بلز) *biliz*, *bilizz*, short and stout (woman).

(بلس) *bils*, soda.

(بلس), II. INF. *tablîs*, drive desperate; — IV. INF. *iblâs*, despair; be perplexed; confound; be silent with grief; be prevented from the pilgrimage.

بلس *balas*, reprobate, wicked; a kind of fig; — *balis*, wrapped up in grief; — *bulus*, *buls*, lentil; — *bulus*, pl. of بلاس *balâs*.

بلسام *bilsâm*, pleurisy.

بلسان *balasân*, balsam, balsam-tree.

بلسك *balsak*, bur.

(بلسم) *balsam*, INF. ة, put balsam on a wound; embalm; — be silent from fear; look sour; — II. INF. *tabalsum*, id.

بلسمة *balsama-t*, embalming (m.).

بلسمين *balsamîn*, balsam-tree.

بلسن *bulsun*, ة, lentil.

(بلش) *balaś*, (m.) embarrass, entangle; — II. INF. *tabliś*, begin, undertake; — VII. INF. *inbilâś*, get embarrassed, entangled; be in a plight; — VIII. INF. *ibtilâś*, undertake.

بلشة *balaśa-t*, embarrassment.

بلشوم *balaśûm*, بلشون *balaśûn*, heron.

(بلص), II. *ballaṣ*, INF. *tabliṣ*, take all one's property; I., II. (m.) oppress with taxes; have little milk (sheep); — III. INF. *mubâlaṣa-t*, rush upon or against; — V. INF. *taballuṣ*, graze the pasture bare; look for in secret; long or strive for (ل *li*); — VII. (m.) INF. *inbilâṣ*, be oppressed with taxes; — XIV. INF. *iblinṣâ'*, depart, go away; undress; put off one's clothes.

بلص *balṣ*, ة *balṣa-t*, oppression; heavy taxation.

(بلصق), II. INF. *tabalṣuq*, look for in secret; enter into relationship.

(بلصم) *balṣam*, INF. ة, flee.

(بلط) *balaṭ*, U, INF. *balṭ*, pave; — II. INF. *tablîṭ*, id.; fillip the ear; get tired and weak with walking; — III. INF. *mubâlaṭa-t*, flee; make efforts, exert one's self; descend into the plain for combat; fight anyone with the sword; — IV. INF. *iblâṭ*, pave; fall on the pavement (rain); get poor and therefore bound to a place; pass. id.; take everything from (acc.); make ill-tempered by begging or asking questions; — V. INF. *taballuṭ*, get paved; — VI. INF. *tabâluṭ*, fight each other with the sword; be foolhardy, hector; — VII. INF. *inbilâṭ*, remove to a great distance; be far away.

بلط *balṭ*, *bulṭ*, turning-lathe; — *buluṭ*, pl. deserters; impudent fellows (Soufis); (m.) foolhardy; swaggerer; — ة *balṭa-t*, axe of a sapper, executioner (m.); — *balṭa-t*, hour; space of time;

anything unexpected; destiny; hill; (m.) causeway, high road; poor, moneyless.

بلطجى *baltajiyy*, pl. *baltajiyya-t*, sapper; executioner (Turk.).

(بلطح) *baltah*=بلدح *baldah*; — (m.) flatten anything convex; — II. INF. *tabaltuh*, be flattened.

(بلع) *bali'*, *bala'*, A, INF. *bala'*, swallow; pierce; — II. INF. *tabli'*, give to swallow, make swallow; begin to appear (white hair); — IV. INF. *iblâ'*, make swallow, allow to swallow (one's spittle, i.e., grant him a delay, a respite); — VII. INF. *inbilâ'*, get swallowed; — VIII. INF. *ibtilâ'*, swallow, especially without chewing; feed on (ب *bi*).

بلع *bala'*, swallowing; — *bula'*, glutton; twenty-third station of the moon; — ة *bala'a-t*, gulp, mouthful; — *bula'a-t*, glutton; — *bal'a-t*, pl. *bula'*, hole of a pulley, a mill-stone, &c.

بلعبيس *bala'bîs*, pl. miracles, marvels.

بلعث *bal'as*, fat and flabby; — ة *bal'asa-t*, fat, ill-tempered (woman).

بلعس *bal'as*, fat and flabby.

بلعق *bal'aq*, best kind of dates.

(بلعك) *bal'ak*, INF. ة, cut (with the sword).

بلعك *bal'ak*, old and with loose flesh; stupid, contemptible; a kind of date.

(بلعم) *bal'am*, INF. ة, swallow greedily.

بلعم *bal'am*, glutton; who swallows greedily; — *bul'um*, pl. *balâ'im*, alimentary canal, gullet.

بلعوس *bil'aus*, foolish woman.

بلعوم *bul'ûm*, pl. *balâ'im*, alimentary canal; gullet; cave, groove.

(بلغ) *balag*, U, INF. *bulûg*, reach, be about to reach; attain to puberty; grow of age; come to (الى *ila*, ب *bi*); conquer, overcome, get the better of (acc.); occupy entirely; — *balug*, INF. *balâga-t*, be eloquent; bestow pains on (فى *fi*) anything; — II. INF. *tablig*, cause to obtain; send; inform; report upon (عن *'an*); give with outstretched arms the reins to a horse; — III. INF. *mubâlaga-t*, *bilâg*, exert one's self zealously in a matter (فى *fi*); do a thing to perfection, accomplish; get the better in a dispute; exaggerate; — IV. INF. *iblâg*, send or bring news; — V. INF. *taballug*, be satisfied with (ب *bi*); not give in until the place is reached; fall upon with violence; increase (illness, &c.); — VI. INF. *tabâlug*, oppress; — VIII. pass. *ubtulig*, it is enough.

بلغ *balg*, *bilg*, *bilag*, eloquent; distinct, clear; superior in strength (army); penetrating, irresistible; — ة *bulga-t*, coll. *bulag*, what is sufficient to live upon; sufficiency.

بلغا *bulagâ'*, pl. of بليغ *balîg*, eloquent, &c.

بلغار *bulgâr*, Bulgaria; perfumed leather.

بلغث *balgas*, fat and flabby; — ة *balgasa-t*, flabbiness; flaccidness.

بلغم *balgam*, pl. *balâgim*, phlegm; — *balgamiyy*, phlegmatic.

بلغن *bilagn*, pl. *balâgin*, eloquent.

بلغين *bilagîn*, *bulagin*, misfortune; danger; completion, end.

(بلق) *balaq*, U, INF. *bulûq*, hasten, walk fast; — INF. *balq*, carry off, wash away; open a door entirely or with violence, and, by opposition, close the door; assault, commit a rape (on a slave-girl); — *baliq*, A, INF. *balaq*; *baluq*, INF. *balk*, be spotted (white and black); have white legs (horse); — *baliq*, A, INF. *balaq*, be stunned, perplexed; — IV. INF. *iblâq*, be piebald, spotted (white and black); beget piebald foals;

open a door with violence ; — v.
INF. *taballuq*, shine, flash ; —
VII. INF. *inbilâq*, be opened
entirely or with violence ;—VIII.
INF. *ibtilâq*, shine, flash ; — IX.
INF. *ibliqâq*, XI. INF. *ibliqâq*, be
piebald ; — XIV. INF. *iblinqâq*, be
clearly distinguished from others
(road).

بلق *balaq*, being piebald (white and
black) ; tent of camel-hair ;
door ; a kind of marble ; madness ; dense crowd ; —بلق *bulq*,
snakes ; pl. of ابلق *ablaq*, piebald ; — ة *bulqa-t*, spottedness.

بلقا *balqâ*, f. of ابلق *ablaq*, piebald.

(بلقط) *bulqut*, short ; dwarfish.

(بلقع) *balqa'*, INF. ة, be uncultivated and uninhabited ; — III.
INF. *iblinqâ'*, subside, pass away
(grief) ; shine.

بلقع *balqa'*, ة *balqa'a-t*, pl. *balâqi'*,
uncultivated and uninhabited
country ; lonely ; thoroughly
bad woman ; — ى *balqa'iyy*, with
a broad head (arrow).

بلقوط *bulqût*, short.

(بلك) *balak*, U, INF. *balk*, mix.

(بلكثة) *balkaṣa-t*, a large mouse.

(بلكع) *balka'*, INF. ة, cut, cut off.

بلل *balal*, moisture ; freshness of
youth ; health ; well-being ;
wealth (after poverty) ; banquet ; endurance in sufferings ;
remains of food ; trifle ; — *bulal*,
seed, crop ; — *ballal*, moist,
damp ; — ة *balala-t*, *bulula-t*,
moisture ; remainder, rest ;
misfortune ; pl. *balalât*, last
touches of love ; — *bulala-t*,
form, state, condition.

(بلم) *balam*, U, INF. *balm*, long for
the stallion ; — II. INF. *tablîm*,
spoil, mar ; — IV. INF. *iblâm*=
I. and II. ; be silent ; — VII. INF.
inbilâm, (m.) be silent ; — ة
balama-t, rut (of a she-camel).

بلما *balmâ*, 14th night of the month.

بلنتع *balanta'*, clever, cunning, sly ;
— ة *balanta'a-t*, talkative woman.

بلندح *balandaḥ*, short and plump.

(بلندك) *balandak*, INF. *iblindâk*, be
spacious ; be level with the
ground.

بلندم *balandam*, loosely built.

بلندى *balanda*, broad, wide.

بلنزى *balanza*, stout and strong.

بلنسم *balansam*, tar, pitch.

بلنط *balnat*, a coarse kind of
marble.

بلنقع *balanqa'*, distinct, trodden
(road).

(بله) *balih*, A, INF. *balah*, *balâha-t*,
be careless, thoughtless, stupid ;
be simple and good-natured
not be able to state one's reasons ; — III. INF. *mubâlaha-t*,
act stupidly towards ; — IV. INF.
iblâh, find stupid ; — V. INF.
taballuh, be stupid ; show stupidity or simplicity ; look for a
stray animal ; walk carelessly on
a wrong road without asking ; —
VI. INF. *tabâluh*, show stupidity,
pretend to be stupid.

بله *balah*, stupidity, idiotcy, lout-
ishness ; — *balha*, leave off !
have done ! ما بله *balha mâ*, not
considering that, without regard
to ; — *bulh*, pl. of ابله *ablah*,
stupid.

بلها *balhâ*, of high rank or birth ;
f. of ابله *ablah*, stupid, &c.

(بلهس) *balhas*, INF. ة, walk fast.

(بلهص) *balhaṣ*, INF. ة, flee from
fear ; — II. INF. *tabalhuṣ*, put
off one's clothes.

(بلهق) *bilhiq*, talking much and
blushing frequently (woman).

بلهنية *bulahniya-t*, pl. *balâhi*, *balâhin*,
life without cares, abundance of
wealth.

بلهور *balahwar*, spacious.

(بلو) *balâ*, U, INF. *balw*, *balâ'*, try,
probe, test, put to severe trials,
grieve (a.) ; make public ; —
bali, A, INF. بلى *bil-an*, *balâ'*,
be old and worn ; be clad or
covered ; be seized with sorrow
and fear ; be rotten ; — pass.
INF. *baly*, be tied up at her

master's tomb to die from hunger (she-camel); — INF. *tabliya-t*, wear out a garment; cause one to put on an old garment; — III. INF. *bilâ'*, *mubâlât* (also *bâl*, *bâla-t*), pay regard, show attendance; boast; vie in boasting; — IV. *iblâ'*, wear out; inform, give news or intelligence; bestow a benefit or an advantage on (acc.); cause to take an. oath; take an oath; be satisfied; try, put to the test; cleanse; show zeal; show prowess in combat; publish; — VI. INF. *tabâl-in*, *tabâlî*, VIII. INF. *ibtilâ'*, question, cross-examine; put to the test, try; be visited by (ب *bi*) calamities; exact an oath.

بلو *bilw*, pl. *ablâ'*, administrator; manager; camel emaciated by the journey; down in the world; equal to calamities, inured, experienced; — ة *bilwa-t*, trial, experiment; temptation; visitation, affliction; punishment; grief; (m.) leprosy.

بلوح *balûḥ*, emptied well; without relations, friendless.

بلور *bilaur*, *billaur*, *ballûr*, pl. *balâlîr*, crystal, beryl; — *billaur*, tall and stout; brave.

(بلوز) *balwaz*, INF. ة, frame (a picture, m.).

بلوس *balûs*, something, a little; *mâ balûs*, nothing.

بلوط *ballûṭ*, oak-tree; acorn; — شاه بلوط *śâh ballûṭ*, hazel-nut tree, chestnut-tree.

بلوع *balû'*, wide.

بلوعة *ballû'a-t*, pl. *balâlî'*, sewer, sink.

بلوغ *balûg*, who has arrived; highest (m.); — *bulûg*, puberty, maturity; full age, majority; execution, accomplishment, completion (بلغ).

بلوغية *bulûgiyya-t*, puberty, maturity.

بلوك *bulûk*, division; company of soldiers; squadron (Turk.).

بلول *bulûl*, ة *bulûla-t*=بللة *bulala-t*, q.v.; see (بل).

بلوى *balw-an*=بلوة *bilwa-t*, q.v.

بلى *bala*, yes, indeed, in answer to a negative question; — *bil-an*, *bal-an* (بلو), threadbareness; (m.) putrifaction; — *bily*, pl. *ablâ'*=بلو *bilw*; — *baliyy*, f. ة, worn, threadbare=بالى *bâlî*; (m.) putrid; — *bulla*, wealth after poverty; — ة *baliyya-t*, pl. *balâyâ*, *baliyyât*, visitation; calamity; state, condition; camel tied up at the tomb of her master.

بليان *balayân*, people without order or leader; gone nobody knows whither.

بليت *billît*, taciturn; wise.

بليج *balîj*, resplendent, shining; clear, distinct, open; — *billîj*, oar (m.).

بليد *balîd*, stupid, idiotic; — ة *bulaida-t*, little village, hamlet.

بلئز *bil'iz*, short and strong.

بليق *balîq*, pl. *bulaqâ'*, eloquent, mature, complete; efficacious, effective, forcible; considerable, numerous, innumerable.

بليل *balîl*, sound, noise, tumult; *balîl*, ة *balîla-t*, cold damp wind; *balîl*, preceded by قليل *qalîl*, little, small quantity; — *bulail*, open road.

بم *bi-ma*, for بما *bi-mâ*, whereby, &c.; — *bamm*, pl. *bumûm*, bass-string, bass; — *bumm* (for بوم *bûm*), owl.

بما *bi-mâ*, whereby, so that; nevertheless; whereby? how? why? what for?

بن *ban*=بل *bal*, rather, &c.; — *bun*, *ban*, for ابن *ibn*, between two proper names; — *binn*, fat; bad-smelling place; — *bunn*, coffee-berry; coffee-tree; — ة *banna-t*, pl. *binân*, smell, odour.

(بن) *bann*, I, INF. *bann*, stand,

remain, stay, settle; — II. INF. *tabnîn*, tie up animals in order to fatten them; — IV. INF. *ibnân*=I.

بنا *bi-nâ*, by us, with us, &c.

(بنا) *binâ'*, INF. (بنى); pl. *abniya-t*, pl. pl. *abniyât*, building, structure; vault; form; conjugation; — *bannâ'*, pl. *bannâ'ûn*, builder; architect.

بنات *banât*, daughters, &c., pl. of بنت *bint*; بنات النعش *banâtu-'n-na'ś-i*, constellation of the bear; بنات البحر *banâtu-'l-baḥr-i*, syrens, mermaids, dolphins; بنات الاربعة *banâtu-'t-arba't-i*, word of four consonants.

بنادرة *banâdira-t*, pl. of بندار *bundâr*.

بناديق *banâdîq*, pl. of بندوق *bundûq*.

بنام *banâm*, for—

بنان *banân*, ة, finger, finger-top; — *binân*, smells, scents, pl. of بنة *banna-t*; — *bunâna-t*, magnificent garden, rich meadow.

بناية *binâya-t*, lofty building.

(بنت), II. *bannat*, INF. *tabnît*, ask many questions; communicate everything; blame, scold.

بنت *bint*, pl. *banât*, daughter; girl; puppet; frequent in composition, as: ب الشفة *bintu-'ś-śafat-i*, daughter of the lip, speech; ب الجبل *bintu-'l-jabal-i*, daughter of the mountain, echo; ب العين *bintu-'l-'ain-i*, daughter of the eye, tear; ب العنب *bintu-'l-'inab-i*, daughter of the grape, wine; — ى *bintiyy*, daughterly, filial.

(بنج) *banj*, henbane, a soporific herb; — *binj*, root, origin; family.

بنج *banaj*, U, INF. *banj*, return to the original or former state; — II. INF. *tabnîj*, drug by the plant بنج *banj*; peep, cluck; — IV. INF. *ibnâj*, claim or arrogate a noble origin.

بنجرة *banjara-t*, pl. *banâjir*, window-hole (Pers.).

(بنح) *banaḥ*, A, INF. *banḥ*, cut into slices.

بنح *bunuḥ*, pl. gifts, presents.

بند *band*, pl. *bunûd* (Pers.), banner, flag; legion of 10,000 men; pawn in chess; band; sword-belt; noose; division, chapter; oblong flat stone; (m.) gut; — II. *bannad*, INF. *tabnîd*, array in battle-order; cut flat-stones, cut in stone.

بندار *bundâr*, pl. *banâdira-t*, forestaller, who buys up, buyer on speculation.

بندر *bandar*, pl. *banâdir*, harbour, port; emporium; (m.) workshop; شاه بندر *śâh bandar*, syndic of the merchants.

(بندق) *bandaq*, INF. ة, give a globular form to (acc.); fix one's look sharply at (الى *ila*); (m.) cause to degenerate; cause to beget bastards.

بندق *bunduq*, ة, pl. *banâdiq*, hazel-nut, nut; sling-stone; ball (m.); — ى *bunduqiyy*, dress of finest linen; — ية *bunduqiyya-t*, gun, musket.

بندوق *bundûq*, pl. *banâdîq*, bastard; gun, musket (m.).

بنديرة *bandaira-t*, banner, flag, banderol, pennon, streamer (m.).

(بنس) *banis*, A, INF. *banas*, shun or escape an evil; — II. INF. *tabnîs*, remain behind, tarry; — IV. INF. *ibnâs*=I.

(بنش) *banaś*, U, INF. *banś*, slacken, relax, be remiss in anything; — II. INF. *tabnîś*, id.

بنش *baniś*, cloak with sleeves (Turk.)

بنصر *binṣir*, pl. *banâṣir*, ring-finger.

بنظر *bunẓur*, clitoris.

بنفسج *banafsaj*, violet (Pers.); — ى *banafsajiyy*, violet colour.

(بنق) *banaq*, U, INF. *banq*, arrive; plant palms on part of a valley; — II. INF. *tabnîq*, IV. INF. *ibnâq*, id.; II. remain in a place; speak tersely and concisely; forge a lie; cut one's back by

lashing ; put round one's neck ; put a gore into a shift or shirt (see بنيقة *banîqa-t*) ; make a quiver wide at the top and narrow at the bottom.

بنقة *binaqa-t*, opening of a shirt or shift at the breast.

(بنك), II. INF. *tabnîk*, go a-gossiping ; tell, narrate ; perform ; — V. INF. *tabannuk*, stand firm ; remain.

بنك *bank*, pl. *bunûk*, bank (m.) ; — *bunk*, root ; essence or best part of a thing.

بنو *banû*, sons, pl. of ابن *ibn* ; — ة *bunuwwa-t*, sonship, filiation.

بنودة *bannûda-t*, back ; buttocks.

بنور *banûr*, tried, experienced.

بنون *banûn*, sons, pl. of ابن *ibn*.

بنوى *banawiyy*, filial, referring to or becoming a son.

(بنى) *banâ*, I, INF. *bany*, *binâ'*, *bunyân*, *binya-t*, *binâya-t*, build, construct, raise ; INF. *binâ'*, inflect a word grammatically, construe ; strengthen, fatten ; assist by benefits ; lead a bride in procession to her new home ; lie with a woman ; — II. INF. *tabniya-t*, build ; — IV. INF. *ibnâ'*, give materials for building, cause to build ; batten ; report, relate ; — V. INF. *tabannî*, call one's son, adopt ; have full thighs ; — VIII. INF. *ibtinâ'*, build ; have built ; give building materials ; lead the bride home ; pitch a tent for one's wife ; lie with ; beget, give birth.

بنى *banî*, sons, pl. of ابن *ibn* ; — *baniyy*, pl. *abniya-t*, building ; — *bunayy*, little son ; pl. f. *bunayyât*, small cups ; بنيات الطريق *bunayyâtu-'t-tarîqi*, ramifications of a road ; — ة *binya-t*, *bunya-t*, pl. بنى *binan*, *bunan*, edifice ; structure of the body ; — *baniyya-t*, the Caaba ; — *buniyya-t*, coffee (as drink).

بنيان *banyân*, work, deed, action ; corrupt (language) ; — *bunyân*, building, edifice ; wall, rampart ; foundation ; ب صالح *bunyân sâliḥ*, edifying example.

بنيقة *banîqa-t*, pl. *banâ'iq*, shoot of a vine ; tuft of hair ; gore of a dress or shirt ; opening of a shirt or shift at the breast.

بنين *banîn*, firmly built or founded ; wise.

به *bah*, well done ! bravo ! — *bi-hi*, by him, with him, &c.

(بهّ) *bahh*, U, INF. *bahh*, rise in honour and authority with the sovereign.

(بها) *baha'*, *bahi'*, *bahu'*, INF. *bah'*, *bahâ'*, *buhû'*, get accustomed to (ب *bi*) ; *baha'*, understand ; A, INF. *bah'*, empty or destroy the tent or house ; — IV. INF. *ibhâ'*, id. ; — VIII. INF. *ibtihâ'*, get accustomed.

بها *bahâ'*, beauty, brilliance, elegance ; — *bi-hâ*, with her.

بهات *bahhât*, calumniator, slanderer.

بهاجة *bahâja-t*, INF. of (بهج).

بهار *bahâr*, beautiful, resplendent ; beauty ; pimento ; ox-eye ; custom tax ; excise ; — *buhâr*, an idol ; swallow ; fresh cotton ; tacking of a ship ; a weight (400–1000 *ratl*).

بهاليل *bahâlîl*, pl. of بهلول *buhlûl*, laugher, &c.

بهالين *bahâlîn*, pl. of بهلوان *bahluwân*, pugilist, &c.

بهانس *buhânis*, tame ; lion.

بهباه *bahbâh*, hoarse roar.

(بهبه) *bahbah*, INF. ة, *bahbâh*, roar low and in a muffled manner, as if hoarse ; — II. INF. *tabahbuh*, get honoured and elevated ; — ى *bahbahiyy*, great, tall, strong.

(بهت) *bahat*, U, INF. *baht*, surprise and seize ; — INF. *baht*, *bahat*, *buhtân*, accuse wrongly ; lie ; — *bahat*, *bahit*, *bahut*, INF. *baht*, *bahat* (also pass.), lose one's head, be perplexed, stunned, astonished ; (m.) be of a faint colour, be dimmed ; — II. INF.

tabhît, bewilder, astonish and perplex; — IV. INF. *ibhât*, be perplexed; be of a faint colour.
بهت *buht*, lie, calumny; — great liars, pl. of بهوت *buhût*; — ة *bahta-t*, astonishment, bewilderment.
بهتان *buhtân*, calumny; falsehood; INF. of (بهت).
(بهتر) *bahtar*, lie; — *buhtur*, *buhtura-t*, pl. *bahâtir*, short of stature.
(بهتن) *bahtan*, INF. ة, calumniate, lie.
(بهث) *bahas*, A, INF. *bahs*, receive with joy; — VI. INF. *tabâhus*, id.
بهثة *buhsa-t*, wild cow; son of a whore.
(بهج) *bahaj*, A, INF. *bahj*, rejoice (a.), cheer; — *bahij*, A, INF. *bahaj*, rejoice (n.), be cheerful; — *bahuj*, INF. *bahâja-t*, be handsome, elegant, lovely; — II. INF. *tabhîj*, embellish, adorn; cheer up (a.); — III. INF. *mubâhaja-t*, boast of greater beauty; — IV. INF. *ibhâj*, cheer, rejoice (a.); show beautiful vegitation; — V. INF. *tabahhuj*, be glad, cheerful; — VI. INF. *tabâhuj*, be adorned with flowers; — VII. INF. *inbihâj*, rejoice (n.), wonder; — VIII. INF. *ibtihâj*, rejoice at (ب *bi*); — X. INF. *istibhâj*, id.
بهج *bahaj*, joy, gladness, INF. of (بهج); — *bahij*, glad, cheerful; handsome; — ة *bahja-t*, joy, rejoicing; beauty, loveliness, splendour, elegance.
(بهدر) *bahdar*, INF. ة, squander, dissipate (m.).
بهدری *buhduriyy*, child which does not thrive.
(بهدل) *bahdal*, INF. ة, walk quickly and with a light step; (m.) insult; slight; despise, condemn.
بهدل *bahdal*, the young of a hyena; — ة *bahdala-t*, insult; treating with contempt.
(بهر) *bahar*, A, INF. *bahr*, *buhûr*, shine, be brilliant; outshine, surpass; be far; be unsuccessful, unlucky, unfortunate; importune, molest, overburden; calumniate, abuse; utter the phrase بهر الله *bahar âla-hu*, may God destroy his people, either in earnest or in jest to express wonder; — pass. be tired so as to be out of breath; be blunted (sword); be dazzled (by the sun); — II. INF. *tabhîr*, season, pepper (m.); — IV. INF. *ibhâr*, relate something wonderful; grow rich after poverty; be scorched by the mid-day sun; behave one time well, another badly; marry a handsome woman; (m.) dazzle; — V. INF. *tabahhur*, shine, be resplendent; be full; be out of breath; — VII. INF. *inbihâr*, be out of breath; fall into ruins; wonder; — VIII. INF. *ibtihâr*, boast falsely of a crime; be talked about on account of attentions shown to a woman; reproach, put to shame; pray and invoke God continually; fall asleep over one's day dreams; not slacken in one's zeal for or against (ل *li*, فی *fî*); break asunder; — XI. INF. *ibhîrâr*, be half spent or more, be dark (night).
بهر *bahr*, distinction; superiority; victory; filling, completing; removal; friendship, love; sorrow; calumny; overburdening; astonishment; — *buhr*, shortness of breath; town, province; middle of a valley; — ة *buhra-t*, pl. *buhar*, middle part; centre; extensive tract of good land.
بهرا *bahr-an*, a curse on him!
بهرام *bahrâm*, planet Mars (Pers.).
(بهرج) *bahraj*, INF. ة, mislead travellers (guide); cause one's blood to be shed unavenged.
بهرج *bahraj*, vain, in vain; lie; corrupt, bad; forged, counterfeit; in everybody's reach;

valueless; nothingness;—*bahraj* and بهرجان *hahrajân*, tinsel; — ة *bahraja-t*, deviation.

(بهر), II. INF. *tabahrur*, be dazzled by the sun.

(بهرس), II. INF. *tabahrus*, walk along proudly.

(بهرم) *bahram*, INF. ة, dye one's beard with hennah;—II. INF. *tabahrum*, be red.

بهرم *bahram*, ة *bahrama-t*, saffron; hennah.

(بهز) *bahaz*, A, INF. *bahz*, push back violently.

بهزر *bahzar*, active and prudent; noble, generous; — ة *bahzura-t*, *bahzara-t*, pl. *bahâzir*, *bahâzira-t*, big she-camel; tall palm-tree.

بهس *bahs*, boldness.

(بهش) *bahaś*, A, INF. *bahś*, examine, investigate into (عن *'an*); be taken up with (الى *ila*); stretch out the hand for (الى *ila*) anything, whether taking it or not; be ready to cry or to laugh; assemble (n.); — V. INF. *tabahhuś*, assemble, gather together (n.); — VI. INF. *tabâhuś*, reach or throw to each other anything.

بهش *bahś*, willingly; friendly.

(بهص) *bahiṣ*, A, INF. *bahaṣ*, be thirsty;—IV. INF. *ibhâṣ*, prevent, hinder.

بهص *bahaṣ*, thirst.

(بهصل) *bahṣal*, INF. ة, play at dice for one's coat; eat the meat to the bones; oust.

بهصل *buhṣul*, stout; white; f. small.

(بهصم) *buhṣum*, firm, hard; brave.

بهصوص *buhṣûṣ*, something; ما ب *mâ buhṣûṣ*, nothing.

(بهض) *bahaḍ*, A, INF. *bahḍ*, molest, cause difficulty; — IV. INF. *ibhaḍ*, id.

بهط *bahaṭṭ*, rice cooked with milk and butter (Pers.).

(بهظ) *bahaẓ*, A, INF. *bahẓ*, molest, overwhelm (work); overburden; seize at the beard.

بهظ *bahẓ*, burden, weight; importance.

(بهغ) *bahag*, U, INF. *buhûg*, sleep.

(بهق) *bahaq*, leprosy, white scab; ringworm;—*bahiq*, afflicted with such.

(بهكثة) *bahkaṣa-t*, swiftness.

(بهكل), ة, full of sap and healthy; smooth and exuberant; sleek.

(بهكن) *bahkan*=(بهكل); — II. INF. *tabahkun*, trip, take short steps.

(بهل) *bahal*, A, INF. *bahl*, curse; leave one to his own will; — *bahil*, A, INF. *bahal*, (m.) be stupid; — III. INF. *mubâhala-t*, curse one another; — IV. INF. *ibhâl*, leave, leave alone, leave to one's own will; set free; coax; water the crops; (m.) render stupid; blunt; — V. INF. *tabahhul*, look for a thing with anxiety; — V., VI. INF. *tabâhul*, VIII. INF. *ibtihâl*, curse one another; — VII. INF. *inbihâl*, get stupid; — VIII. humiliate one's self before God and call to Him; exert one's self; — X. INF. *istibhâl*, milk; leave the subjects to their own will; secure the freedom of a people or tribe; (m.) find a person stupid.

بهل *bahl*, curse; a little of anything; *bahl*, *bahal*, INF. of (بهل); — *buhl*, *buhhal*, pl. of باهل *bâhil*, free, &c.

بهلا *bahl-an*, gently! patience!

(بهلس), II. INF. *tabahlus*, return from foreign parts unexpectedly and empty-handed.

(بهلص), II. INF. *tabahluṣ*, undress.

(بهلق) *bahlaq*, pl. *bahâliq*, calamity; — *bahlaq*, *buhluq*, woman with a red complexion; talkative woman; — ة *bahlaqa-t*, pride, lie; scolding, insulting; pl. *bahâlîq*, vanities; — II. INF. *tabahluq*, lie.

بهللة *bahlala-t*, بهلة *bahala-t*, stupidity (m.); — *bahla-t*, *buhla-t*, curse.

بهلوان *bahluwân*, pl. *bahâlîn*, pugi-

list ; rope-dancer ; merry Andrew (Pers.).

بهلول *buhlûl*, laughing, smiling ; prince endowed with every accomplishment ; — pl. *bahâlîl*, laugher ; blockhead ; merry Andrew.

بهم *bahm*, *baham*, lambs, kids and calves in one flock ; — *buhm*, *buhum*, pl. naked, bare ; healthy and faultless ; — ة *bahma-t*, pl. *bihâm*, *bihâmât*, kid, lamb, calf, foal of a camel ; — *buhma-t*, pl. *buham*, stone, rock ; inconquerable combatant ; very arduous matter ; army ; squadron of horse.

(بهم), II. INF. *tabhîm*, separate young cattle from their mothers ; abide in a place ; — IV. INF. *ibhâm*, shut or lock a door ; leave doubtful or ambiguous ; be so ; conceal ; avert ; — V. INF. *tabahhum*, be doubtful, ambiguous, obscure ; be covered, concealed ; — X. INF. *istibhâm*, be doubtful, &c., talk unintelligibly or barbarously ; not be able to speak, keep silent ; appear as a stranger or barbarian ; find anything obscure.

(بهنانة) *bahnâna-t*, having a sweet breath ; friendly, smiling.

(بهنس) *bahnas*, tame docile camel ; heavy and fat ; lion ; — II. INF. *tabahnus*, walk along proudly (part. *mutabahnis*, lion).

(بهو) *bahâ*, *bahû*, *bahî*, INF. *bahâ'*, be beautiful, shine with beauty ; — *baha*, surpass in beauty ; — *bahî*, INF. *bahy*, be empty ; — II. INF. *tabhiya-t*, enlarge and furnish ; — III. INF. *mubâhât*, vie or surpass in beauty ; boast ; — IV. INF. *ibhâ'*, empty ; tear ; let loose or free, leave unemployed (a horse, &c.) ; — VI. INF. *tabâhî*=III. ; be proud, glory.

بهو *bahw*, pl. *abhâ'*, *buhuww*, *buhiyy*, advanced house or tent ; lair of the wild buffalo ; apartment for the women ; hold of a ship ; large stable ; — pl. *abhâ'*, *abhî*, *bihiyy*, *buhiyy*, large, extensive ; wide tract of land ; cavity of the chest or belly ; — *buhû'*, INF. of (بها).

بهوت *bahût*, pl. *buht*, *buhût*, great liar.

بهور *bahwar*, lion.

بهوع *buhûg*, going to sleep.

بهى *baha*, *bahî*, see (بهو) ; — *bahî'*, see (بها) ; — *bahiyy*, handsome, beautiful, elegant, shining, resplendent ; — *bihiyy*, *buhiyy*, pl. of بهو *bahw*.

بهير *bahîr*, adj. breathing heavily, panting ; — ة *bahîra-t*, pl. بهائر *bahâ'ir*, handsome, delicate (woman).

بهيصل *buhaiṣil*, weak, small, insignificant.

بهيلة *bahîla-t*, free woman with rich dowry.

بهيم *bahîm*, pl. *buhum*, *buhm*, one-coloured horse ; black ; unknown ; soundless, without an echo ; pure, unmixed ; faultless ; excellent ; — ة *bahîma-t*, pl. *bahâ'im*, quadruped ; brute, in opposition to a rational being ; — ى *bahîmiyy*, referring to beasts, bestial, brutal ; — ية *bahîmiyya-t*, bestiality.

بهينس *buhainis*, lion.

بو *bû*, in comp. for ابو *abû*, father ; — *baww*, foal of a camel ; ashes ; — f. ة, stupid, foolish, mad.

(بو) *bâ'*, U, INF. *bau'*, return, come back ; bring back (acc. or ب *bi*) ; draw upon one's self ; agree with, suit (acc. or ب *bi*) ; — INF. *bau'*, *bawâ'*, acknowledge (debt, &c.) ; atone, retaliate ; be killed in retaliation ; — II. INF. *tabwî'*, bring or lead back ; take for a wife, lie with (acc.) ; invite into one's house, receive hospitably ; alight and stay ; point the lance against (نحو *naḥw-a*) ; — III. INF. *mubâwa'a-t*, retaliate, kill

by way of retaliation; — IV. INF. *ibâ'a-t*, bring or lead back; =III.; put the hand to the sword, get ready for combat; receive in one's house; alight; follow in succession; flee; — V. INF. *tabawwu'*, alight, choose a house for a lodging, take possession of or possess a house; take possession of a wife and her dowry; — VI. INF. *tabâwu'*, resemble each other, be able to pass one for another; — X. INF. *istibâ'a-t*, take or furnish a place for a lodging; retaliate, kill in retaliation; return to each other or to one's people.

بوا *bawâ'*, equality, similarity; atonement, retaliation.

بواب *bawwâb*, door-keeper, porter; — ة *biwâba-t*, office of door-keeper; — *bawwâba-t*, litter, sedan-chair.

بواتر *bawâtir*, swords, pl. of باتر *bâtir*.

بواحا *bawâḥ-an*, openly, publicly.

بواد *bawâd*, INF. of (بيد).

بوادر *bawâdir*, fleshy parts between neck and shoulders; pl. of بادرة *bâdira-t*.

بوادى *bawâdî*, inhabitants of the desert, deserts, pl. of بادية *bâdiya-t*.

بواذخ *bawâẕiḫ*, high mountain-chains, pl. of باذخة *bâẕiḫa-t*.

بوار *bawâr*, destruction, ruin, perdition; bad affairs; INF. of (بور); woman whom no one sues; pl. بور *bûr*, uncultivated fields.

بوارح *bawâriḥ*, pl. of بارح *bâriḥ*, living in the plain, &c., q.v.

بوارد *bawârid*, sharp swords; pl. of بارد, q.v.

بوارق *bawâriq*, pl. of بارق *bâriq*, ة, flashing, &c.

بوارى *bawârî*, reed mats, mats of bulrushes, pl. of بارية *bâriya-t*, بورى *bûriyy*, &c.; — *bawâriyy*, maker of such.

بوازل *bawâzil*, pl. of بازل *bâzil*, experienced.

بوازى *bawâzî*, falcons, pl. of بازى *bâziyy*.

بواسق *bawâsiq*, high palm-trees, &c., pl. of باسق *bâsiq*.

بواسير *bawâsîr*, piles, pl. of باسور *bâsûr*; بوسير *bausîr*.

بواشق *bawâšiq*, sparrow-hawks, pl. of باشق *bâšiq*.

بواضع *bawâḍi'*, herds, &c., pl. of باضعة *bâḍi'a-t*, q.v.

بواطن *bawâṭin*, pl. of باطن *bâṭin*, interior, &c.

بواطى *bawâṭî*, vats, pl. of باطية *bâṭiya-t*.

بواعث *bawâ'is̱*, reasons, motives, pl. of باعثة *bâ'is̱a-t*.

بواق *bawwâq*, trumpeter.

بواقر *bawâqir*, cows, pl. of بقرة *baqra-t*.

بواكر *bawâkir*, virgins, pl. of باكرة *bâkira-t*.

بواكى *bawâkî*, mourning women, pl. of باكية *bâkiya-t*.

بوال *buwâl*, diabetes; — *bawwâl*, who makes water frequently; piss-a-bed.

بواليع *bawâlî'*, sewers, sinks, pl. of بالوعة *bâlû'a-t*.

بوان *biwân*, *buwân*, pl. *abwina-t*, *bûn*, *buwan*, peg or pole of a tent; door-post.

بوانى *bawânî*, pl. ribs of the chest; legs of quadrupeds; pl. of بانية *bâniya-t*, see بان *bân-in*, بانى *bânî*.

بواهد *bawâhid*, pl. calamities.

بوائج *bawâ'ij*, misfortunes, calamities, pl. of بائجة *bâ'ija-t*.

بوائع *bawâ'i'*, pl. of بائع *bâ'i'*, woman with many suitors.

بوائق *bawâ'iq*, calamities, pl. of بائقة *bâ'iqa-t*.

(بوب) *bâb*, U, be door-keeper to (ل *li*); make an opening or door; — II. INF. *tabwîb*, divide into chapters; (m.) guide; — V. INF. *tabawwub*, take as a door-keeper; pass. become such.

بوباة *baubât*, desert, waste.

بوبو *bu'bu'*, pupil of the eye; middle or principal part; root; eminent

genius, scholar, &c.,; body of a locust.

بوتاتى *bûtâtiyy*, referring to household expenditure.

بوتقة *bûtaqa-t*, crucible (Pers.).

(بوث) *bâs̱*, U, INF. *baus̱*, reject, disperse, squander; examine, try, investigate; — IV. INF. *ibâs̱a-t*, id.; tear up the ground, plough; — VIII. INF. *ibtiyâs̱*, examine, investigate; — X. INF. *istibâs̱a-t*, excite, raise (dust); extract, draw out.

(بوج) *bûj*, U, INF. *bauj*, *bawajân*, be tired; shine, flash; cry out, call; befall; — II. INF. *tabwîj*, V. INF. *tabawwuj*, VII. INF. *inbiyâj*, shine, flash; — VII. befall (على *'ala*).

بوج *bauj*, بوجان *bawajân*, flash of lightning; clamour; tiredness.

(بوح) *bâḥ*, U, INF. *bauḥ*, *bu'ûḥ*, *bu'ûḥa-t*, be known, public; make known, publish, divulge, show clearly; boast in public; — IV. INF. *ibâḥa-t*, communicate; escape, abscond; betray a client; profess publicly; make anything public property; allow; offer; — X. INF. *istibâḥa-t*, make public property; allow; prostitute; squander or lose one's property; consider lawful; do or take what is lawful; annihilate.

بوح *bûḥ*, root, origin; pudenda; sexual intercourse; soul; sun; confusion of affairs; — *bauḥ*, see (بوح); — *ba'uḥ*, who betrays his secrets.

بوحى *bauḥa*, thrown down, prostrate

(بوخ) *bâḥ*, U, INF. *bauḥ*, subside, become extinct; be tired; — INF. *bu'ûḥ*, turn bad, smell badly (meat); — IV. INF. *ibâḥa-t*, extinguish.

بوخ *bûḥ*, confusion.

(بود), see (بيد).

بود *baud*, well; departure (بيد).

بودقة *bûdaqa-t*, crucible.

(بوذ) *bâẕ*, U, INF. *bauẕ*, transgress, encroach; grow poor, needy; humble one's self.

بوذ *bauẕ*, encroachment, transgression; poverty; humiliation.

(بور) *bâr*, U, INF. *baur*, *bawâr*, perish; be dull (market), not sell (merchandise); lie uncultivated or fallow; be lazy; be spoiled; be in vain; devastate; — INF. *baur*, explore, spy out; — IV. INF. *ibâra-t*, destroy, annihilate; — V. INF. *tabawwur*, complain of impending ruin; — VIII. INF. *ibtiyâr*, explore, spy out; lie with a woman.

بور *baur*, ruin, perdition, destruction; knowledge from experience; INF. of (بور); — *baur*, *bûr*, uncultivated or fallow land; — *bûr* (du. and pl. m. and f.), reprobates, people doomed to perdition; — *baur*, *bûr*, pl. of بائر *bâ'ir*, q.v.; — ة *bu'ra-t*, hole in the ground to make fire in; treasure; provisions; — *bûra-t*, a fallow.

بورق *bûraq*, بورك *bûrak*, borax; saltpetre.

بورى *bûriyy*, ة *bûriyya-t*, بوريا *bûriyâ*, pl. *bawârî*, reed mat, mat of bulrushes; street (Pers.).

(بوز) *bûz*, snout (m.); — II. INF. *tabawwuz*, make a sour face.

بوز *bu'uz*, falcons, pl. of باز *bâz*; — ة *bûza-t*, ى *bûza*, beer.

(بوس) *bâs*, U, INF. *baus*, be rough; kiss; kiss the ground before (ل *li*); mix with (ب *bi*).

بوس *bûs*, calamity, poverty; mixture; kiss; — *bu's*, pl. *ab'us*, evil, calamity, misery; empoverishment; INF. of (بئس); — ة *bûsa-t*, kiss.

بوستان *bûstân* = بستان *bustân*, garden.

بوسطة *bûsṭa-t*, post (m.).

بوسى *bu'sa*, misery, INF. of (بئس).

بوسير *bausîr*, pl. *bawâsîr*, emerods, piles.

(بوش) *bâś*, U, INF. *bauś*, clamour, be boisterous (crowd); reach

over to (acc.); — II. INF. *tabwiś*, V. INF. *tabawwuś*, be crowded in confusion; — VI. INF. *tabâwuś*, stretch out the arms against each other (for combat); — VII. INF. *inbiyâś*, turn aside from a thing.

بوش *bauś*, *bûś*, crowd; troop, gang; for *abwâś*, rabble, vagabonds; clamour, tumult; a dish of flour and lentils;—*bauś*, vain, useless, in vain (m.).

بوشاد *bûśâd*, turnip.

بوشى *bauśiyy*, pauper with many children; vulgar or vile fellow; — *bûśiyy*, stuff from *Bûś*, in Egypt.

(بوص) *bâṣ*, U, INF. *bauṣ*, remain, stay; walk fast; get tired; urge to haste; flee and hide; importune by questions or demands; — II. INF. *tabwîṣ*, head in a horse-race; have a pure complexion; have full hips (woman).

بوص *bauṣ*, *bûṣ*, colour, complexion; hips of a woman; their softness; — *bauṣ*, quick walk; tiredness; pl. *abwâṣ*, species, race of animals.

بوصا *bauṣâ'*, f. having full hips.

بوصى *bûṣiyy*, boat.

بوصير *bauṣîr*, piles.

بوضة *bûḍa-t*=بوزة *bûza-t*, beer.

(بوط) *bâṭ*, U, INF. *bauṭ*, grow poor after being rich; be despised after enjoying honours; — ة *buṭa-t*, crucible.

بوطاقة *bû-ṭâqa-t*, Maria Theresa dollar (possessor of a window, the Hungarian coat of arms).

بوطانية *bûṭâniya-t*, wild vine plant.

بوطقة *bûṭaqa-t*, crucible.

(بوظ) *bâẓ*, U, INF. *bauẓ*, grow thin after being stout.

(بوع) *bâ'*, U, INF. *bau'*, stretch out the arms and measure by them; reach with outstretched hand; make long strides; — V. INF. *tabawwu'*, measure; be measured; be long; make long strides; keep up with (acc.);— VII. INF. *inbiyâ'*, be measured; uncoil in order to spring; spring (snake); stretch one's self; depart; run, flow (perspiration); give the merchandise cheaper.

بوع *bau'*, *bû'*, باع *bâ'*, cubit, ell; stride; loftiness; nobility; honour; قصير (ضيق) الباع *qaṣîr-u* (*dayyiq-u*) *'l-bâ-i*, miserly, avaricious; — *bau'*, mountain slip.

(بوغ) *bâg*, U, INF. *baug*, conquer, vanquish, surpass; — V. INF. *tabawwug*, boil, be agitated; conquer.

بوغا *baugâ'*, soft, friable earth; flighty, frivolous people; confusion; scent, fragrance.

(بوق) *bâq*, U, INF. *bauq*, cause mischief or quarrel; befall; fall upon from an ambush; gird, surround; rush together upon a person and kill him; perish; surprise or intrude upon (على *'ala*); steal from (acc.); blow the trumpet.

بوق *bauq*, trumpet; talkative fellow, babbler, chatterer; — *bûq*, pl. *bûqât*, *abwâq*, *bîqân*, trumpet; shell, flute, pipe; rattle; talker; vain, false, unjust; — ة *bûqa-t*, pl. *buwaq*, heavy shower.

بوقات *bûqât*, pl. of بوق *bûq*, (m.) rattle.

بوقال *bûqâl*, tankard without handle, drinking-vessel.

بوقلمون *bû-qalamûn*, chameleon; tortoise; turkey; anything gaudy; changing colour, fickle, capricious; fickleness; caprice of fortune.

بوقيصا *bûqîṣâ*, elm-tree.

(بوك) *bâk*, U, INF. *bauk*, cover (as a stallion); lie with a woman; form into a ball between one's palms; sell or buy; stir up a spring with a stick to make it

flow more abundantly; be complicated, confused, entangled; be perplexed, at one's wits' end; — INF. *bu'ûk*, get fat; — VII. INF. *inbiyâk*, be perplexed.

(بوك) اول بوك *awwal-a bauk-in*, the first time; before all others.

بوكا *baukâ'*, confusion.

بوكر *baukar*=بيكر *baikar*, measure with the compasses (m.)

(بول) *bâl*, U, INF. *baul*, make water; break forth, flow; melt (n.); — *ba'ul*, INF. *ba'âla-t*, *bu'ûla-t*, be small and weak; — II. INF. *tabwîl*, make water; — IV. INF. *ibâla-t*, cause to make water; — X. INF. *istibâla-t*, want to make water; cause to make water.

بول *baul*, pl. *abwâl*, urine; wedlock; children; son; large number; great liberality; بول العجوز *baulu-'l-'ajûz*, cow-milk; — ة *baula-t*, daughter.

بولاد *bûlâd* (Pers.), steel; (m.) razor.

بولس *bûlas*, dungeon in hell.

بولصة *bûlṣa-t*=بوليصة *bûlîṣa-t*.

بولع *baula'*, glutton.

بوليصة *bûlîṣa-t*, pl. بواليص *bawâlîṣ*, money-letter, draft, bill of exchange; cheque, circular note (Ital. *polizza*).

بوم *bûm*, ة, owl.

(بون) *bân*, U, INF. *baun*=(بين).

بون *baun*, *bûn*, interval, interstice; difference; — *bûn*, *buwan*, tent-poles, door-posts, pl. of بوان *biwân*, *buwân*; — ة *bauna-t*, little daughter.

بونافع *bû-nâfi'*, wine.

(بوه) *bâh*, U, INF. *bauh*, lie with one's wife; — U and A, INF. *bauh*, *baih*, fix one's thoughts upon (ل *li*), understand, animadvert.

بوه *bauh*, curse, imprecation; — *bûh*, ة *bûha-t*, owl; moulting hawk; feather in the wind; dry wool in the ink-bottle; thin of bones; lean; stupid, dull, insipid.

بووح *ba'ûḥ*, who cannot keep his secrets; — *bu'ûḥ*, see (بوح).

بووخ *bu'ûḫ*, see (بوخ).

بووز *bu'ûz*, falcons, pl. of باز *bâz*.

بووس *bu'ûs*, see (بئس); بووق *bu'ûq*, see (باق).

بوى *bawa*, INF. *bayy*, be similar to another in speech and manners; — *bawan*, hope; desire; emulation; malice; trouble, vexation, molestation; talents; — *bawiyy*, stupid, foolish, mad.

بويحيا *bû-yaḥyâ*, angel of death.

(بى) *bâ'*, salute anyone with the words بياك الله *bayyâ-ka 'l-lâh-u*, "May God prosper thee!" &c.; — II. INF. *tabyî*, explain, comment upon, elucidate; take a firm purpose, intend earnestly.

بى *bay*, prince (Turk. بك); — *bayy*, vile person; ابن بى *abn-u bayy-in*, stranger, one unknown; — ة *bi'a-t*, epidemic; plague.

بياب *bayyâb*, seller of water.

بيات *bayât*, night attack; night-time; INF. of (بيت).

بياحة *bayyâḥa-t*, net for fishing.

بياد *bayâd*, INF. of (بيد).

بيادر *bayâdir*, threshing-floors, pl. of بيدر *baidar*.

بيادقة *bayâdiqa-t*, بياذق *bayâẓiq*, ة *bayâẓiqa-t*, see بيدق *baidaq*.

بيادى *bayâdiyy*, foot-soldier (Pers. m.).

بئار *bi'âr*, wells, pl. of بئر *bi'r*.

بيارق *bayâriq*, standards, pl. of بيرق *bairaq*.

بيازر *bayâzir*, ة *bayâzira-t*, cudgels, &c., pl. of بيزر *baizar*; — *bayâzira-t*, pl. of بيزار *baizâr*, penis.

بيازير *bayâzîr*, maces, pl. of بيزارة *baizâra-t*.

بياس *bai'as*, strong, bold; hard, severe; lion.

بياض *bayâḍ*, whiteness; brightness; milk; (m.) anything made of milk (butter, cheese); eggs; white paper; leprosy; بياض الوجه

bayâḍu-'l-wajh-i, observance of good manners; generosity; — *bayyâḍ*, white earth; — ة *bayâḍa-t*, whiteness; brightness; white spot in the eye; — *bayyâḍa-t*, hen which lays many eggs; — ى *bayâḍiyy*, elegant poem.

بياطرة *bayâṭira-t*, veterinary surgeons, pl. of بيطار *baiṭâr*.

بيازير *bayâzîr*, maces, pl. of بيزارة *baizâra-t*.

بياع *bayyâ'*, pl. *bayyâ'ûn*, seller; appraiser; — ة *biyâ'a-t*, pl. *biyâ'â-t*, merchandise.

بياكر *bayâkir*, pl. of بيكار *baikâr*, compasses.

بيان *bayân*, explanation; commentary; evident meaning; demonstration; eloquence, rhetoric; division; — *bayyân*, thing; = بى *bayy*; — ى *bayâniyy*, explaining, commenting.

بيب *bîb*, pipe, drain.

بيبان *bîbân*, doors, &c., pl. of باب *bâb*.

(بيت) *bât*, I, A, INF. *bait*, *bayât*, *mabît*, *baitûta-t*, do anything at night-time; pass the night; — II. INF. *tabyît*, perform at night; attack at night; give a night's lodging; consult, resolve at night; leave a thing in the same condition during the night; prevent from (عن *'an*); — III. INF. *mubâyata-t*, pass the night with anyone; — IV. INF. *ibâta-t*, give a night's lodging, cause to do anything at night; — X. INF. *istibâta-t*, seek or have a night's food, provide one's self; have no place for passing the night; be poor, a beggar.

بيت *bait*, pl. *buyût*, *buyûtât*, tent; house, building; Caaba; palace, castle; house-floor; apartment, room; case, compartment; tomb; ب ما *bait-u mâ'-in*, ب الفراغ *baitu-'l-firâg-i*, ب الخلا *baitu-'l-ḥalâ-i*, water-closet; ب اللطف *baitu-'l-luṭf-i*, wine-house; — family; wedlock; members of the household, servants; — pl. *abyât*, distich, couplet, strophe; noble, nobility; — INF. of (بيت); — *bît*, ة *bîta-t*, provisions, victuals (for a night); passing the night (s.), night's lodging.

بيتوتة *baitûta-t*, see (بيت).

بيتى *baitiyy*, domestic, belonging or referring to the house.

بيث *baiṡa*, see (حيث).

بيجادق *baijâdaq*, a kind of ruby (Pers.).

(بيح), II. INF. *tabyîḥ*, cut into pieces and distribute; let out a secret to (ب *bi*).

بيحان *baiḥân*, *bayyaḥân*, who betrays his secret; name of a tribe.

(بيد) *bâd*, I, INF. *baud*, *baid*, *buyûd*, *bawâd*, *bayâd*, *baidûda-t*, depart, separate entirely from one's people; — INF. *buyûd*, set (sun), disappear; — INF. *baid*, *buyûd*, perish; — IV. INF. *ibâda-t*, destroy, annihilate, ruin.

بيد *baid*, ruin, perdition; loss; injurious; — *baid-a*, بيد ان *baid-a an*, except that; however, yet; because; — *bîd*, pl. of بيدا *baidâ'*.

بيدا *baidâ'*, pl. *bîd*, *baidâwât*, dangerous desert.

بيدانة *baidâna-t*, wild she-ass.

بيدح *baidaḥ*, بيداحة *baidâḥa-t*, fleshy (woman).

بيدر *baidar*, pl. *bayâdir*, threshing-floor, barn; quantity of grain piled up in a barn; — *baidar*, INF. ة, pile up, gather into heaps; — ى *baidara*, glib.

بيدستر *baidastar*, beaver (Pers.).

بيدق *baidaq* (also بيذق *baiẕaq*), pl. *bayâdiq*, *bayâdiqa-t*, pawn in chess; foot-soldier; leader, guide; single, not married.

بيدودة *baidûda-t*, see (بيد).

بيذار *baiẕâr*, ة, talker, babbler.

بيذخ *baiẕaḥ*, fleshy, plump.

بيذرانى *baiẕarâniyy*, talker, babbler.

بئر *bi'r*, f. pl. *ab'âr*, *ab'ur*, *âb'ur*, *bi'âr*, well; — ة *bi'ra-t*, anything

hidden in the ground, treasure; provender, provisions; — *bîra-t*, beer (m.).

بيراق *bairâq*=بيرق *bairaq*.

بيرام *bairâm*, Bairam-feast.

بيرق *bairaq*, pl. *bayâriq*, standard, flag; troop of soldiers (Pers.).

بيرقدار *bairaqdâr*, standard-bearer, ensign.

بيرم *bairam*, borer; axe, hatchet; liquid collyrium.

بيرمون *bairamûn*, eve of a festival, vigil (m.).

بيروزج *bairûzaj*, turquoise.

(بيز) *bâz*, INF. *baiz*, *buyûz*, perish, and, by opposition, live, live on, escape.

بيزار *baizâr*, pl. *bayâzira-t*, penis; — *bîzâr*, falconer; peasant; — ة *baizâra-t*, pl. *bayâzîr*, big mace.

بئزان *bi'zân*, *bîzân*, falcons, pl. of باز *bâz*, بازى *bâziyy*.

بيزر *baizar*, beater of a fuller; cudgel, mace.

(بيس) *bâs*, I, INF. *bais*, hurt in a haughty manner; — *ba'is*, A, INF. *bu's*, *bu'ûs*, *ba's*, *bu'sa*, *bî'isa*, be very needy, indigent; — *ba'us*, INF. *ba's*, be courageous and brave in battle; be very destitute; — IV. INF. *ib'âs*, bring on calamity or a defeat; injure; — VI. INF. *tabâ'us*, show one's poverty with self-humiliation; — VIII. INF. *ibti'âs*, be sorrowful, grieved at (ب *bi*); complain.

بئس *bi's*, hard, severe; — *bi's-a*, fie!—*ba'is*, violent, hard, severe; bold; indigent, destitute.

بيش *bîś*, ة, aconite; — *bîś*, pl. *abyâś*, hole in the ground for a tree (m.).

(بيش), II. *bayyaś*, INF. *tabyîś*=*bayyaḍ*, render the face of a man shining and beautiful; (m.) dig a hole in the ground to plant a tree; — IV. INF. *ibâśa-t*, cause to spring forth.

(بيص) *bais*, *bîṣ*, misfortune, calamity; difficulty.

(بيض) *bâḍ*, I, INF. *baiḍ*, surpass in whiteness; lay eggs; have an egg-like tumour on the fore-foot (horse); be very violent (heat); — lose its moisture (wood); remain, stay; rain; be entirely destroyed; — (m.) INF. *bayâḍ*, be white; — II. INF. *tabyîḍ*, whiten, white-wash; bleach; tin; make a clean copy; fill, and, by opposition, empty; call forth fine hopes and fulfil them; dazzle; — III. INF. *mubâyada-t*, vie and surpass in whiteness; — IV. INF. *ibâḍa-t*, give birth to white children; — V. INF. *tabayyud*, be made a clean copy of; — VIII. INF. *ibtiyâḍ*, put on the helmet; destroy entirely, annihilate; — IX. INF. *ibyiḍâḍ*, and XI. INF. *ibyîḍâḍ*, grow white; observe good manners; be generous.

بيض *baiḍ*, surpassing splendour; violent heat; tumour on the fore-foot of a horse; eggs (coll.); — *bîḍ*, hens, pl. of بيوض *bayûḍ*; — pl. of ابيض *abyaḍ*, white; beauties; — *buyuḍ*, pl. of بائض *bâ'iḍ*, oviparous, and بيوض *bayûḍ*, hen; — ة *baiḍa-t*, pl. *buyûḍ*, *baiḍât*, coll. *baiḍ*, egg; testicle; fluor albus; small number of men; place surrounded by tents; middle, centre; helmet; head-ache; beauty; virgin; ب الديك *baiḍat-u-'d-dîk* (egg of the cock), anything that cannot be got.

بيضا *baiḍâ'*, f. of ابيض *abyaḍ*, pl. *bîḍ*, white, shining; the sun; white paper; wheat; pearl-barley; untrodden ground; sally; misfortune; leathern bag; pot; snare; name given to Aleppo and other cities; اليد البيضا *al-yad-u-'l-baiḍâ'-u*, beneficence, merit, glory, power.

بيضان *bîḍân*, white men (in opposition to سودان *sûdân*, negroes).

بيضوى *baiḍawiyy*, oval, elliptical; native of Baiḍâ'.
بيضى *baiḍiyy*, whiteness, purity; oval, elliptical; oval (s.), ellipsis.
بيطار *baiṭâr*, pl. *bayâṭira-t*, veterinary surgeon; blacksmith.
بيطر *baiṭar*, *biyaṭr*=بيطار *baiṭâr*;—*biyaṭr*, tailor;—*baiṭar*, INF. ة, be a veterinary surgeon; open veins or tumours;—ة *baiṭara-t*, profession of a veterinary surgeon.
(بيظ)=(بوظ).
بيظ *baiẓ*, sperm; ovum of an ant; uterus, womb.
بيظر *baiẓar*, clitoris.
(بيع) *bâ'*, I, INF. *bai'*, *mabî'*, sell (two acc. or من *min*, ل *li*, with regard to the person); pass. be for sale; sell, figuratively, in the sense of the English word;—buy;—III. INF. *mubâya'a-t*, sell to; do business or make a contract with another; bet; swear lealty, acknowledge as a sovereign; do homage;—IV. INF. *ibâ'a-t*, exhibit or offer for sale;—VI. INF. *tabâyu'*, conclude a sale or make a contract between each other;—VII. INF. *inbiyâ'*, get sold, sell well;—VIII. INF. *ibtiyâ'*, buy;—X. INF. *istibâ'a-t*, wish to sell; wish to be sold (slave).
بيع *bai'*, pl. *buyû'*, sale, exchange; merchandise; acknowledgment and inauguration; cheerfulness;—*bayyi'*, pl. *biya'â'*, *abyi'â'*, seller; merchant; buyer; who offers more; du. *bayyi'ân*, seller and buyer; horse with a wide step;—ة *bai'a-t*, contract of sale; commercial transaction; acknowledgment, recognition; oath of lealty;—*ḅî'a-t*, pl. *biya'*, Christian church; synagogue; buying and selling.
(بيغ) *bâg*, I, INF. *baig*, perish; boil;—II. INF. *tabyîg*, devote one's self entirely to one thing, renouncing everything else; pass. get confused, embarrassed;—V. INF. *tabayyug*, get confused; boil; carry away (as passion); be in abundance.
بيغ *baig*, ebullition.
بيقان *bîqân*, trumpets, &c., pl. of بوق *bûq*.
(بيقر) *baiqar*, INF. ة, live in a village or town while one's people are in the desert; alight and stay in a place; emigrate; travel from land to land; go from Syria to Iraq; step along proudly; walk quickly with the head bent down; raise the forefoot (horse), be tired; perish; get spoiled; be doubtful in a matter; try to gather riches; be rich;—II. INF. *tabaiqur*, be in abundanee; have rich pastures.
بيقر *baiqar*, weaver;—ة *baiqara-t*, abundance of household furniture; INF. of (بيقر).
بيقور *baiqûr*, cattle.
بيك *baik*, prince (Turk. بك).
بيكار *baikâr*, pl. *bayâkir*, *bawâkir*, pair of compasses (Pers. بركار *barkâr*);—combat (Pers. پيكار *paikâr*).
بيكر *baikar*, INF. ة, measure with compasses.
بيلسان *bailasân*, elder, lilac.
بيلسة *bailasa-t*, devilry.
بيلم *bailam*, pl. *bayâlim*, bud of cotton; wool of the Egyptian papyrus; pennant, streamer, banderol.
بيلة *bîla-t*, making water.
بيمارستان *bîmâristân*, hospital (Pers.).
(بين) *bân*, I, INF. *bain*, *buyûn*, *bainûna-t*, be separate, distinct, far distant;—INF. *bain*, *bainûna-t*, separate (n.); depart; divorce; be joined to each other;—INF. *baun*, be eminent, distinguish one's self; I, INF. *bayân*, be distinct, appear distinctly; (m.) appear, seem;—render clear, explain; be elo-

quent and persuasive; — II. INF. *tabyîn*, separate (a.), distinguish; render clear, propound, explain, show; bring; be distinctly perceptible; show the first leaves; spring forth; divorce; give one's daughter in marriage; allow some time to pass, tarry; — III. INF. *mubâyana-t*, separate from another; intercede; — IV. INF. *ibâna-t*, sever, separate (a.); explain; speak distinctly; make known, publish; be clear, evident; marry one's daughter; — V. INF. *tabayyun*, be evident or easily understood; become evident; render clear, reveal; publish; understand, apprehend; — VI. INF. *tabâyun*, separate from each other; be clear, become evident; — X. INF. *istibâna-t*=V.; find clear, understand; acknowledge.

بين *bain*, separation; interstice, interval; difference, distinction; absence; desert; relation, reference, union; — *bîn*, pl. *buyûn*, horizon, reach of sight; region; boundaries; rising of rugged ground; — *bain-a*, between, among; بين يديه *bain-a yadai-hi*, before him, in his presence; بين بين *bain bain*, so so, middling, indifferent; — *bayyin*, pl. *abyinâ'*, *bîna-t*, distinct, clear, evident; — pl. *abyinâ'*, *abyân*, *buyanâ'*, eloquent; — ة *bîna-t*, pl. of بين *bayyin*; — *bayyina-t*, pl. *bayyinât*, evident demonstration, clear proof; evidence; witness.

بينب *bainab*, evergreen (plant).

بينط *biyanṭ*, weaver.

بينما *baina-mâ*, whilst; meanwhile.

بينونة *bainûna-t*, separation, INF. of (بين).

(بيه) *bâh*, A, INF. *baih*, notice, understand, apprehend.

بيهس *baihas*, lion; brave; — II. INF. *tabaihus*, walk along proudly.

بيهن *baihan*, narcissus; dog-rose.

بيهوج *baihûj*, scarecrow.

بيوت *buyût*, pl. of بيت *bait*, house; — *bayyût*, stale (bread); cold water; night-work.

بيوتات *buyûtât*, many houses; outbuildings; household expenses; inventory.

بيود *buyûd*, INF. of (بيد); بيوز *buyûz*, INF. of (بيز).

بيوردى *buyurdu*, بيورلدى *buyuruldu*, imperial edict; firman, passport (Turk.).

بيوض *bayûḍ*, pl. *bîḍ*, *buyuḍ*, hen who lays many eggs; — *buyûḍ*, pl. of بيضة *baiḍa-t*.

بيوع *buyû'*, commercial transactions, &c., pl. of بيع *bai'*.

بيون *bayûn*, deep and full; — *buyûn*, horizons, &c., pl. of بين *bîn*; INF. of (بين).

بييت *buyait* (بويت *buwait*), small house.

بئيرة *ba'îra-t*, what lies in the treasury or storehouse.

بئيس *ba'îs*, bold; hard, severe.

بييضة *buyaiḍa-t*, a sexagonal house, or one decorated with paintings.

بئيل *ba'îl*, small and weak.

بيئة *bî'a-t*, site, state; habitation; hospitable reception.

ت

ت *t*, as a numeral sign=400; — *ta*, particle of conjuration.

تا *tâ*, f. of ذا *ẓâ*, this; — that, in order that; — *tâ'*, name of the letter ت.

تاب *tâbb*, pl. *atbâb*, tall but weak; sore on the back; — ة *tâba-t*, repentance.

تاباق *tâbâq*, stick.

تأبب *ta'abbub*, astonishment, v. (اب).

تابع *tâbi'*, plur. ون *-ûn*, *taba'*, *taba'a-t*, *tawâbi'*, follower; dependent on a person or thing; partisan; fond of women; companion of Mohamet; spiritus familiaris; guardian, guard; servant; adept; — ة *tâbi'a-t*, pl. *tawâbi'*, female companion; consequence, succession; — ى *tâbi'iyy*, ة, pl. *-ûn*, *-ât*, companion; follower of Mahomet.

تابل *tâbal*, *tâbil*, (m.) ة *tâbila-t*, pl. *tawâbil*, herbs for seasoning; — *ta'abbul*, INF. V. of (ابل), q.v.

تابه *tâbah*, frying-pan (Pers.); *ta'abuh*, pride, haughtiness, V. (ابه).

تابوت *tâbût* (تابوه *tâbûh*), pl. *tawâbît*, shrine; chest; bier, coffin; Ark of the Covenant.

تابول *tâbûl*, betel leaf.

تابى *ta'abbî*, refusal, V. (ابى); — ة *ta'biya-t*, disgust, II. (ابو).

تابيب *ta'bîb*, clamour, II. (اب).

تابيد *ta'bîd*, scaring away, &c., II. (ابد).

تابير *ta'bîr*, fructification of the palm-tree, II. (ابر).

تابيه *ta'bîh*, exhortation, &c., II. (ابه).

تاتا *ta'ta'*, INF. ة, have difficulty in pronouncing the letter *t*; — INF. *ta'tât*, *ta'tâ'*, walk (as a child); walk along proudly.

تاتار *tâtâr*, Tartar, Scythian.

تاتب *ta'attub*, INF. V. of (اتب), q.v.

تاته *ta'attuh*, delirium, V. (اته).

تاتى *ta'tiyy*, INF. II. of (اتى); — *ta'attî*, INF. V. of (اتى); derivation, origin; — ة *ta'tiya-t*, making a way, INF. II. of (اتى).

تاتيب *ta'tîb*, INF. II. of (اتب).

تاثث *ta'assus*, furnishing, furniture, INF. V. of (اث).

تاثر *ta'assur*, following one's tracks; INF. V. of (اثر).

تاثل *ta'assul*, being firmly rooted, &c., INF. V. of (اثل).

تاثيث *ta'sîs*, furnishing a house, II. (اث).

تاثير *ta'sîr*, impression, influence, II. (اثر); — *ta'âsîr*, beadles, &c., pl. of توثور *tu'sûr*.

تاثيف *tâsîf*, support, &c., II. (اثف).

تاثيم *ta'sîm*, accusation, sin, II. (اثم).

تاج *tâj*, pl. *tîjân*, crown, diadem; comb; mane; *at-tâj*, lion.

تاجج *ta'ajjuj*, conflagration, V. (اج).

تاجر *tâjir*, pl. *tijâr*, *tujjâr*, *tajr*, *tujr*, merchant; wine-seller; — f. ة, clever, skilful; looked for, selling well.

تاجل *ta'ajjul*, term, &c., V. (اجل).

تاجيج *ta'jîj*, inflammation, inflaming, II. (اج).

تاجير *ta'jîr*, baking bricks, II. (اجر).

تاجيل *ta'jîl*, fixing a term; delay, prolongation, respite, &c., II. (اجل).

تاحد *ta'ahhud*, isolation, &c., V. (احد).

تاحم *tâhim*, weaver.

(تاحى) *tâhî*, gardener, watchman.

تاحيد *ta'hîd*, profession of one God, &c., II. (احد).

تاخ *tâhh*, having no appetite.

تاخاذ *ta'hâz*, acceptation; receiving.

تاخر *ta'ahhur*, delay, remaining behind, coming late, &c., V. (اخر).

تاخى *ta'ahhî*, INF. V. of (اخو); — *ta'âhî*, being brotherly; concord, agreement, VI. of the same.

تاخير *ta'hîr*, delay, procrastination, postponing, II. (اخر).

تادب *ta'addub*, good breeding, literary education; V. (ادب).

تادى *ta'addî*, INF. of V., *ta'âdî*, INF. of VI. (ادو), q.v.; — ة *ta'diya-t*, causing to arrive, sending, payment, &c., II. (ادى).

تاديب *ta'dîb*, good education, politeness, cultivation; chastisement; pl. *-ât*, admonitions.

تاذن *ta'azzun*, publication, &c., V. (اذن).

تاذى *ta'aẓẓî*, injury, insult, v.
(اذى).

تاذین *ta'ẕin*, permission; exhortation; call to prayer, II. (اذن).

تار (تار) *ta'ar*, A, INF. *ta'r*, molest, plague, hinder; — IV. INF. *it'âr*, follow with the eyes; look sharply at; beat.

تار *târ*, pl. تئر *ti'ar*, turn, time; — *târr*, ة, juicy; fleshy; weak from hunger; far from home; — ة *târa-t*, pl. *ti'ar*, *târât*, turn, time; — *târat-an*, once; *târat-an târat-an*, now . . . then, at one time . . . at another.

تارات *târât*, malice; pl. of تارة *târa-t*, q.v.

تارب *ta'arrub*, raising difficulties, affectation, v. (ارب).

تارث *ta'arruṣ*, conflagration, being lit, v. (ارث).

تارج *ta'arruj*, fragrance, scent, v. (ارج).

تارخ *ta'arruḥ*, putting the date, v. (ارخ).

تارز *târiz*, hard; dry; dead.

تارس *târis*, armed with a shield.

تارش *târiš*, light, flighty, fickle.

تارص *târiṣ*, strongly-built (horse, &c.).

تارك *târik*, leaving, renouncing.

تاریب *ta'rîb*, fastening, making firm, &c., II. (ارب).

تاریث *ta'rîs*, sowing discord, II. (ارث).

تارخ *ta'rîḥ*, pl. *tawârîḥ*, putting the date, date; history, chronicle; chronology, era; end, extreme limit; II. (ارخ); — ى *ta'rîḥiyy*, historian; chronologist.

تاریس *ta'rîs*, agriculture; taking in service, II. (ارس).

تاریض *ta'rîḍ*, INF. II. of (ارض), q.v.

تاریف *ta'rîf*, limitation, II. (ارف).

تاریة *ta'riya-t*, INF. II. of (ارى), q.v.

تاز *ta'az*, A, INF. *ta'z*, close (n.), come to close quarters.

تازر *ta'azzar*, put on the *izâr*, v. (ازر).

تازز *ta'azzuz*, boiling, agitation, v. (از).

تازة *tâzah*, fresh, young, green, tender (Pers.).

تازى *tâziyy*, of Arabian origin; sporting dog (Pers.); — *ta'azzî*, assembling, &c., v. (ازى).

تازیر *ta'zîr*, veiling, II. (ازر).

تاسس *ta'assus*, having a firm foundation, foundation, v. (اس).

تاسع *tâsi'*, f. ة, ninth.

تاسف *ta'assuf*, sighing, groaning, lamenting, &c., v. (اسف).

تاسوعا *tâsû'â*, the ninth day of the month *Muḥarram*.

تاسوم *tâsûm*, ة, pl. *tawâsim*, sandal, shoe.

تاسى *ta'assî*, INF. v.; *ta'âsî*, INF. VI.; — ة *ta'siya-t*, INF. II. of (اسو, اسى); consolation; taking example.

تاسیر *ta'sîr*, tying up, II. (اسر); — *ta'âsîr*, girth-leathers.

تاسیس *ta'sîs*, laying the foundation, foundation; confirmation, the fundamental letter of a rhyme.

تاشب *ta'aššub*, dense growth, crowd, v. (اشب).

تاشن *ta'aššun*, washing with *ušnân*, v. (اشن).

تاشیب *ta'šîb*, INF. II. of (اشب).

تاشیر *ta'šîr*, filing of the teeth, II. (اشر).

تاصص *ta'ṣṣuṣ*, assembling, v. (اص).

تاصل *ta'aṣṣul*, being firmly rooted, v. (اصل).

تاصیص *ta'ṣîṣ*, making firm, II. (اص).

تاصیل *ta'ṣîl*, rooting firmly, considering noble, II. (اصل).

تاطر *ta'aṭṭur*, INF. v. of (اطر), q.v.

تاطید *ta'ṭîd*, making firm, consolidation, II. (اطد).

تاطیر *ta'ṭîr*, INF. II. of (اطر), q.v.

تاعس *tâ'is*, dying (تعس).

تاعة *tâ'a-t*, lump.

تافر *tâfir*, dirty.

تافف *ta'affuf*, INF. v. of (اف).

تافق *ta'affuq*, coming from distant parts, v. (افق).

تافیف *ta'fîf*, INF. II. of (اف).

تافیل *ta'fîl*, procuring honour, II. (افل).

تافه *tâfih*, a little; insignificant.

تافة **tâfa-t**, defect, fault, vice; need, want; excess; delay.
تاقة *ta'aqa-t*, burst of anger; passionateness.
تاك *tâk*, f. of ذاك *ẓâk*, that; — *tâkk*, pl. *tâkkûn*, *takaka-t*, *tukâk*, *tukak*, foolish, stupid; emaciated; on the verge of ruin.
تاكل *ta'akkul*, INF. V. of (اكل); (m.) itching.
تاكيد *ta'kîd*, consolidation; confirmation; attestation; perseverance; emphasis; security; certainty; enjoining; — *ta'âkîd*, pl. girth-leathers.
تاكيف *ta'kîf*, saddling, II. (اكف).
تاكيل *ta'kîl*, inviting to eat, &c., II. (اكل).
تال *tâl*, ة, shoots of the palm-tree; — *tâl-in*, see تالى *tâlî*; — *tâll*, wandering.
تالب *ta'lab*, strong; name of a tree.
تالد *tâlid*, inherited property; home-bred cattle; — *ta'allud*, getting confused, confusion, V. (الد).
تالف *ta'alluf*, INF. V. of (الف).
تالق *ta'alluq*, shining, &c., V. (الق).
تالك *tâlika*, f. of ذالك *ẓâlika*, that.
تالم *ta'allum*, suffering pain, pain, grief; irritation; thirst for vengeance, vindictiveness, V. (الم).
تاله *ta'alluh*, adoration, V. (اله); — تاله العقل *tâlihu-'l-'aql-i*, mad.
تالى *tâlî*, following, subsequent; reader; the fourth horse in a race; — *ta'allî*, INF. V. of (الى=الو); — ة *tâliya-t*, pl. *tawâlî*, extremity (foot, &c.); subsequent part.
تاليد *ta'âlîd*, pl. generations.
تاليف *ta'lîf*, pl. *ta'lîfât*, *ta'âlîf*, literary composition, work, publication, II. (الف).
تاليل *ta'lîl*, sharpening into a point, II. (ال).
تاليم *ta'lîm*, causing pain, II. (الم).
تاليه *ta'lîh*, apotheosis, II. (اله).
(تام) *ta'am*, be born as a twin; — III. INF. *mutâ'ama-t*, id.; be a twin; weave with a double warp; race again immediately after a race; — IV. INF. *it'âm*, give birth to twins; (m.) be double-barrelled; — VIII. INF. *ittiʻâm*, kill a milch sheep.
تام *tâmm*, whole, complete, perfect.
تامر *tâmir*, rich in dates; — *ta'ammur*, mutual consultation, VI. (امر); — ى *ta'muriyy*, somebody.
تامك *tâmik*, hump of a camel; camel with a large hump.
تامل *ta'ammul*, pl. *-ât*, thought; contemplation; meditation; reflection, V. (امل).
تامم *ta'ammum*, considering as or taking for a mother, V. (ام); washing with sand, for تيمم *tayammum*.
تامور *ta'mûr*, *tâmur*, somebody, anybody; something, anything; soul; breath; spirits of life; blood; — *tâmûr*, ة *tâmûra-t*, heart; wine; water; saffron; monastic life; monastery; lion's den; prime minister, vizier; embryo; puppet, doll; purse; box; jug; — ى *ta'mûriyy*, somebody.
تامى *ta'ammî*, buying a female slave, V. (امو=امى).
تاميت *ta'mît*, defining the number or quantity of anything, II. (امت).
تاميد *ta'mîd*, fix the end or term, II. (امد).
تامير *ta'mîr*, raising to the dignity of a prince, II. (امر); — *ta'âmîr*, pl. of تومور *tu'mûr*, stone as road-sign in the desert.
تاميل *ta'mîl*, hoping strongly, making hope, II. (امل).
تاميم *ta'mîm*, causing to do, ordaining, II. (ام).
تامين *ta'mîn*, confiding, inspiring confidence, II. (امن).
تان *tân*, thread; — *tâni*, these two, f. du. of ذا *ẓâ*; — *ta'ann-in*, see تانى *ta'annî*.
تانان *ta'nân*, finding pleasure with, II. (أن).

تانبول *tâmbûl*, betel-leaf (Pers.).
تانث *ta'annus*, emolliating, effeminacy, v. (انث).
تانس *ta'annus*, becoming man (of Christ); humane or familiar treatment, v. (انس).
تانف *ta'annuf*, aversion, disgust, v. (انف).
تانق *ta'annuq*, carefulness, solicitude, daintiness, v. (انق).
تانك *tânika*, *tânnika*, those two, f. du. of ذا *zâ*.
تانن *ta'annun*, INF. v. of (ان)=تانان *ta'nân*.
تانی *tâni'*, peasant, countryman; — *ta'annî* (تان *ta'ann-in*), slowness, gentleness, considerateness, v. (انی); — ة *ta'niya-t*, the same, II. (انی).
تانيب *ta'nîb*, expostulation, reproof, II. (انب).
تانيث *ta'nîs*, give a feminine termination; feminine gender; effeminacy, II. (انث).
تانيس *ta'nîs*, taming, accustoming, making familiar; being friendly, II. (انس).
تانيف *ta'nîf*, INF. II. of (انف).
تانين *ta'nîn*, INF. II. of (ان)=تانان *ta'nân*.
تاهب *ta'ahhub*, readiness, preparation, v. (اهب).
(تاهل) *ta'ahhul*, marriage, v. (اهل).
تاهم *ta'ahhum*, INF. v. of تهم, q.v.
تاهه *ta'ahhuh*, sighing, v. (اه).
تاهور *tâhûr*, cloud.
تاهيب *ta'hîb*, getting ready, preparation, II. (اهب).
تاهيل *ta'hîl*, welcome; considering worthy, II. (اهل).
تاوب *ta'awwub*, return; coming at night-time, v. (اوب).
تاورية *tawûriyyat*, theory (m.).
تاول *ta'awwul*, explanation, v. (اول).
تاوه *ta'awwuh*, sighing, sigh, v. (اوه).
تاوی *tâwî*, falling, dying; — *ta'awwî*, v., *ta'âwî*, VI. (اوی), alighting, gathering together; — *tâwiyy*, terminating in the letter ت; — ة *ta'wiya-t*, alighting, hospitable reception, II. (اوی).
تاويب *ta'wîb*, repetition, return, II. (اوب).
تاويد *ta'wîd*, folding, &c., II. (اود).
تاويق *ta'wîq*, vexing, &c., II. (اوق).
تاويل *ta'wîl*, explanation, commentary; analysis; interpretation of a dream, II. (اول); — ی *ta'wîliyy*, explanatory, &c.
تاويم *ta'wîm*, causing thirst, &c., II. (اوم).
تاويه *ta'wîh*, groaning, lamenting, II. (اوه).
(تای) *ta'a*, A, INF. *ta'y*, go in advance, precede, overtake.
تای *tâi*, tea; — ة *tâya-t*=طاية *ṭâya-t*, flat roof, &c.
تائب *tâ'ib*, repenting, penitent.
تايب *ta'ayyub*, return, v. (ايب=اوب).
تائج *tâ'ij*, crowned.
تايد *ta'ayyud*, strengthening, security, v. (ايد).
تائر *tâ'ir*, beginning afresh earnestly.
تايس *ta'ayyus*, despair, v. (ايس).
تائق *tâ'iq*, desirous, intent upon.
تائك *tâ'ik*, malicious fool.
تايم *ta'ayyum*, widowhood, v. (ايم).
تائه *tâ'ih*, haughty; gone astray, lost; (m.) dispersed.
تايی *ta'ayyî*, slowness, v. *ta'âwî*, going straight towards, VI. (ايی). — *tâ'iyy*, terminating with the letter ت.
تاييب *ta'yîb*, return, II. (اوب=ايب).
تاييد *ta'yîd*, pl. *-ât*, assistance, help; support; proof; authorisation, II. (ايد).
تاييس *ta'yîs*, bringing to despair, &c., II. (ايس).
تاييم *ta'yîm*, making a widow, II. (ايم).
(تب) *tabb*, INF. *tabb*, *tabâb*, *tabîb*, cut off; destroy; be always at loss; — *tubb*, id.; perish; — II. INF. *tatbîb*, injure, ruin; imprecate, wish ruin to anyone; — IV. INF. *itbâb*, weaken; abstain from (عن *'an*); — X. INF. *istitbâb*, be

in good order, be perfected, completed.

تب *tabb*, ة, loss, ruin; — ة *tibba-t*, distress.

تبابعة *tabâbi'a-t*, تبابيع *tabâbî'*, } pl. of تبع *tubba'*, q.v.

تبابيل *tabâbîl*, hatreds, pl. of تبل *tabl*.

تبابين *tabâbîn*, breeches, pl. of تبان *tubbân*.

تباد *tabâdd*, hand to hand fight, VI. (بد).

تبادل *tabâdul*, exchange, interchange; permutation, transposition; reciprocity, VI. (بدل).

تباديد *tabâdîd*, pl. dispersed (birds).

تبار *tabâr*, ruin, destruction.

تباريح *tabârîḥ*, pl. passionate desires.

تباريق *tabârîq*, pl. anything moderately spiced or seasoned.

تباطى *tabâṭî*, slowness, VI. (بطو).

تباع *tibâ'*, succession of things, continuation; INF. III. of (تبع); pl. of تبيع *tabî'*, q.v.; — تباع العسكر *tubbâ'u-'l-'askar-i*, military train; — ة *tabâ'a-t*, punishment; INF. of تبع *tabi'*, q.v.; — *tibâ'a-t*, consequence; bad end; — ية *tabâ'iyya-t*, obedience; dependence; retainership.

تبال *tabbâl*, who spices, seasons.

تبان *tabbân*, seller of straw; (m.) straw magazine; — *tubbân*, pl. *tabâbîn*, short trowsers of a sailor; — ة *tabâna-t*, sagacity, INF. of (تبن).

تباو *tabâwu'*, INF. VI. of (بو), q.v.

تباين *tabâyun*, difference; contradiction; contrast; incommensurability; departure, VI. (بين).

تبب *tabab*, ruin, perdition, death.

(تبتب) *tabtab*, INF. ة, grow old.

تبتل *tabattul*, celibacy, V. (بتل).

(تبث), INF. *tabs*, grieve, sorrow.

تبجبج *tabajbuj*, swelling, tumour.

تبجج *tabajjuj*, great rejoicing.

تبجيلات *tabjîlât*, pl. of تبجيل *tabjîl*, II. of (بجل), ceremonies, compliments, applause.

تبدرق *tabadruq*, dissipation (m.).

تبدل *tabaddul*, INF. V. of (بدل); holiday-clothes; pl. *tabaddulât*, changes of persons; permutations.

تبديع *tabdî'*, INF. II. of (بدع); pl. *tabâdî'*, unheard-of things, anything extraordinary.

تبديل *tabdîl*, INF. II. of (بدل); pl. *-ât*, transposition; substitution; compensation; pl. changes in ministry; *tabdîl-an*, in a disguised manner, with dissimulation.

تبدية *tabdiya-t*, receiving as a novice, II. (بدا).

تبذار *tibẕâr*, talker, babbler; — ة *tibẕâra-t*, spendthrift.

(تبر) *tabar*, I, INF. *tabr*, break into pieces; destroy; annihilate; — *tabir*, A, INF. *tabar*, perish; separate (n.); — II. INF. *tatbîr*, break into pieces; annihilate; — IV. *itbâr*, abstain from (عن *'an*).

تبر *tabr*, destruction (a.); *tabr*, *tabar*, ruin; — *tibr*, pl. *tubûr*, gold or silver from the mine; fragments of metal, glass, &c.; ة *tibra-t*, lump of gold, &c.

تبراك *tabrâk*, kneeling, INF. II. of (برك).

تبرال *tabar'ul*, ruffling of the feathers.

تبردخ *tabarduḫ*, smoothness; polish; good breeding, culture (m.).

تبرع *tabarru'*, pl. *-ât*, free gift or vow; pious foundation; *tabarru'-an*, gratis.

تبرعم *tabar'um*, budding.

تبرغص *tabarguṣ*, quivering, convulsion.

تبرق *tabarruq*, adorning one's self.

تبرك *tabarruk*, pl. *-ât*, blessing; good omen; abundance, wealth; relics; gifts, presents, leavings of the great; honours, dignities; — ى *tabarrukiyy*, compliment (m.).

تبرو *tabarru'*, تبرى *tabarrî*, justification, absolution (pass.).

تبريح *tabrîḥ*, pl. *tabârîḥ*, vexation, grief.

تبريز *tabrîz*, INF. II. of (برز), q.v.; town Tebris; — *tibrîz*, table (Pers.).

تبرئة *tabri'a-t*, absolution; setting free; cure, II. (برا); — *tibriya-t*, dandriff.

تبزق *tabazzuq*, spitting.

تبزلة *tibzila-t*, *tibzilla-t*, dwarfish.

تبزيغ *tabzîg*, bleeding, venesection.

تبسط *tabassuṭ*, vast extent; roaming, wandering about.

تبسم *tabassum*, smile.

تبشبش *tubaśbuś*, joyfulness, gladness.

تبشش *tabaśśuś*, friendliness.

تبشير *tabśîr*, II. (بشر), pl. *tabâśîr*, good news; preaching of the Gospel; Angelus in the Mass; announcement; first light of the morning.

تبصبص *tabaṣbuṣ*, flatteries.

تبصرة *tabṣira-t*, what renders prudent; a caution.

تبصية *tabṣiya-t*, castration.

تبطرق *tabaṭruq*, graceful walk.

تبطئة *tabṭi'a-t*, delay.

(تبع) *tabi'*, A, INF. *taba'*, *tibâ'*, *tabâ'a-t*, follow, join a person, obey, serve; follow a doctrine; — II. *tatbî'*, seek or strive for zealously; cause one to follow another; — III. INF. *tibâ'*, cause one thing to succeed another immediately; INF. *tibâ'*, *mutâba'a-t*, make equally firm and strong in every part; render fat; pursue with zeal and gain a solid knowledge of; write books continually; follow a person's tracks; follow and emulate; — IV. INF. *itbâ'*, follow and overtake; cause one to follow and overtake another; send after; cause to succeed, give in addition; — V. INF. *tatabbu'*, seek or strive for zealously; follow up the development of a thing; dwell upon; — VI. INF. *tatâbu'*, happen repeatedly, do repeatedly or in quick succession; arrive one after another; succeed to each other; — VIII. INF. *ittibâ'*, follow; reach; seek zealously; pursue; — X. INF. *istitbâ'*, ask or wish one to follow; lead.

تبع *taba'*, pl. *atbâ'*, successor, companion; emulator, disciple; intent on a thing; (m.) belonging to, property; foot of a quadruped; pl. of تابع *tâbi'*, follower, &c.; INF. of (تبع); — *tabi'*, emulator; intent on; — *tib'*, suitor; lover; — *tubba'*, pl. *tabâbi'a-t*, title of the Himyarite kings; Aldabaran (star); pl. *tabâbî'*, mother bee; — *tubba'*, *tubbu'*, shadow; — ة *tabi'a-t*, consequence; punishment; bad end; continual effort.

تبعد *taba''ud*, removal.

تبعزق *taba'zuq*, dissipation.

تبعى *taba'iyy*, dependent; — ة *taba-'iyya-t*, dependence; imitation; — *tab'iyya-t*, consequence, succession; dependence; retainership.

تبغ *tabg*, tobacco.

تبغثر *tabagsur*, confusion.

تبغنج *tabagnuj*, coquettishness, amorous allurements.

تبقى *tabaqqî* (تبقية *tabqiya-t*), preservation, II.; *tabaqqî*, remaining, remaining alive, v. of (بقى).

تبكا *tabkâ'*, *tibkâ'*, violent weeping.

تبكيت *tabkît*, reproach, reproof; remorse; qualms of conscience.

تبكية *tabkiya-t*, causing to weep, weeping, lamenting, INF. II. of (بكى).

(تبل) *tabal*, U, INF. *tabl*, consume, drive out of one's senses; confuse a man's mind (woman); destroy, annihilate; — I., II. INF. *tatbîl*, III. INF. *mutâbala-t*, spice, season; — IV. INF. *itbâl*, drive out of one's senses; hate; inflict a calamity; destroy, annihilate.

تبل *tabl*, pl. *tubûl*, *tabâbîl*, hatred; pl. *atbâl*, illness; — *tabil*, destructive

تبلغة *tabliga-t*, pl. *tabâlig*, rope for pulling a water-wheel.
تبليط *tablîṭ*, paving, II. (بلط); (m.) altar-stone.
تبن *tabin*, intelligent; penetrating, sagacious; — *tabn*, *taban*, see (تبن); — *tibn*, pl. *atbân*, *tubûn*, straw; generous lord; a large dish.
(تبن) *taban*, I, INF. *tabn*, feed the cattle with straw; sell straw; — *tabin*, A, INF. *taban*, *tabâna-t*, be penetrating, sagacious, intelligent; — II. id.; bring the straw into the barn; — VIII. INF. *ittibân*, put on the short trowsers *tubbân*; — ة *tibna-t*, stalk of straw; — ية *tabniya-t*, solid building; adoption, II. (بنى).
تبهلل *tabahlul*, laughing.
(تبو) *tabâ*, U, INF. *tabw*, invade and make booty.
تبو *tabawwu'*, taking possession of; inhabiting, V. (بو).
تبوب *tabbûb*, place of perdition; desert; — *tabawwub*, taking for a door-keeper, V. (بوب).
تبوت *tabût*, bier; chest.
تبورد *tabaurud*, taking fresh air (m.).
تبوط *taba''uṭ*, lying on the side.
تبويب *tabwîb*, division into chapters; (m.) guidance.
تبوير *tabwîr*, leaving land fallow.
تبويس *tabwîs*, kissing.
تبويق *tabwîq*, a blast of the trumpet.
تبوية *tabwiya-t*, INF. II. of (بو), q.v.
تبيان *tabyân*, *tibyân*, explanation; comment; expounding; manifestation, INF. of (بين).
تبيب *tabîb*, damage, loss, ruin.
تبيزلة *tubaizila-t*, little dwarf.
تبيطر *tabaiṭur*, being shod, cure of a horse, &c.
تبيع *tabî'*, ة, follower; *tabî'a-t*, suit; pl. *tibâ'*, *tabâ'i'*, calf following its mother; companion, helper; debtor; who searches, strives zealously.
تبيو *tabayyu'*, تبيى *tabayyî*, intention, purpose.

تتار *tatâr*, Tartar.
تتالى *tatâlî*, uninterrupted succession, VI. (تلو).
تتبع *tatabbu'*, zealous study.
تتر *tatar*, Tartar; — ى *tatra*, one after the other; — *tatariyy*, foot-soldier (m.).
تتعتع *tata'tu'*, hesitating, stammering; (m.) idle talk.
تتفل *tatfal*, *titfil*, *tutful*, pl. *tatâfil*, fox; whelp of a fox.
تتلى *tatallî*, INF. V. ة *tatliya-t*, II. of (تلو), following; dunning, pressing for payment.
تتماج *tutmâj*, vermicelli.
تتمة *tatimma-t*, pl. *-ât*, supplement, appendix, integration.
تتن *tutun*, tobacco (m.).
تتو *tatw*, tassel of a cap.
تتوبة *tatwîba-t*, repentance.
تتويب *tatwîb*, calling to repentance.
تثخين *tas̱ẖîn*, rudeness.
تثريد *tas̱rîd*, INF. II. of (ثرد), breaking bread, &c.; slight rain.
تثل *tas̱al*, an aroma.
تثليث *tas̱lîs̱*, INF. II. of (ثلث); trinity.
تثليج *tas̱lîj*, being icy cold; icy cold.
تثنية *tas̱niya-t*, INF. II. of (ثنى); dual; تثنية الاشتراع *tas̱niyatu'l-istirâ'-i*, Deuteronomy.
تثوب *tas̱a''ub*, yawning, V. (ثاب).
تثوية *tas̱wiya-t*, detaining, hospitable reception; death; II. (ثوى).
تثى *tas̱y*, wild date.
تجاب *tijâb*, silver obtained at the first melting of the ore.
تجار *tujjâr*, merchants, pl. of تاجر *tâjir*; — ة *tijâra-t*, commerce; traffic.
تجارب *tajârib*, experiments, trials, pl. of تجربة *tajriba-t*.
تجارى *tajârî*, commerce, intercourse; VI. (جرى); — *tujjâriyy*, commercial, mercantile.
تجاريد *tajârîd*, detached troops; military expeditions.
تجازى *tajâzî*, pressing demand.
تجافيف *tajâfîf*, pl. of تجفاف *tijfâf*.
تجال *tajâll*, exalting one's self, VI. (جل).

تجالس *tajâlus*, sitting, session.
تجاليد *tajâlîd*, person; figure, shape.
تجان *tajânn*, تجانن *tajânun*, VI. (جن) madness.
تجاه *tajâh*, *tijâh*, *tujâh*, opposite, in front of, vis à vis.
تجاويد *tajâwîd*, rain.
تجاويز *tajâwîz*, pl. of تجواز *tajwâz*.
تجاويف *tajâwîf*, holes, cavities, pl. of تجويف *tajwîf*.
تجباب *tijbâb*, vein of silver.
تجبار *tajbâr*, haughtiness.
تجبية *tajbiya-t*, bow, obeisance.
تجديف *tajdîf*, pl. *tajâdîf*, blasphemy.
تجذير *tajẕîr*, extraction of a root; eradication.
تجذيم *tajẕîm*, amputation.
(تجر) *tajar*, U, INF. *tajr*, *tijâra-t*, carry on commerce, traffic; — III. INF. *mutâjara-t*, IV. INF. *itjâr*, VIII. INF. *ittijâr*, id.
تجر *tujur*, merchants, pl. of تاجر *tâjir*.
تجربة *tajriba-t*, pl. *tajârib*, *tajârîb*, trial, essay, experiment; experience.
تجرد *tajarrud*, INF. V. of (جرد), q.v.; (m.) impartiality.
تجريد *tajrîd*, INF. II. of (جرد), q.v.; ascetic life; pl. *tajârîd*, military expeditions; sending of a detachment; — ة *tajrîda-t*, detachment.
تجريم *tajrîm*, fine, mulct.
تجرئة *tajri'a-t*, تجريء *tajrî'*, encouraging, II. (جرو); — تجرية *tajriya-t*, INF. II. of (جرى), q.v.
تجزو *tajazzu'*, being satisfied, v. (جزأ).
تجزى *tajazzî*, تجزئة *tajziya-t*, dividing.
تجسد *tajassud*, incarnation, incorporation, V. (جسد).
تجسس *tajassus*, exploring, spying out, &c., V. (جس).
تجشو *tajaśśu'*, V. تجشئة *tajśi'a-t*, II. of (جشا), belching.
تجفاف *tijfâf*, pl. تجافيف *tajâfîf*, armour of a horseman and his horse; housing, saddle-cloth.

تجفية *tajfiya-t*, lopping of trees, II. (جفى).
تجلة *tajilla-t*, respect, esteem, reverence.
تجلى *tajallî*, V. (جلو), pl. *-ât*, revelation; apparition; transfiguration; epiphany; splendour; — V. (جلى), preference, pre-eminence; — ة *tajliya-t*, polishing, making smooth; revealing; explaining, II. (جلو), (جلى).
تجمل *tajammul*, V. of جمل *jamal*, q.v.; pomp; pl. *tajammulât*, ornaments, pieces of furniture, articles of luxury.
تجمم *tajammum*, V. (جم); (m.) full measure.
تجنزر *tajanzur*, concatination (m.)
تجنيس *tajnîs*, INF. II. of (جنس); alliteration; play on words; figure of speech.
تجنيك *tajnîk*, heat of battle (m.).
(تجه) *tajah*, A, originating from اتجه *ittajah*, VIII. of وجه *wajah*, turn the faces towards each other.
تجهية *tajhiya-t*, widening, II. (جهى).
تجواب *tajwâb*, INF. of (جوب), q.v.
تجواز *tijwâz*, pl. *tajâwîz*, a striped garment.
تجوال *tajwâl*, INF. II. of (جول), roaming about in distant parts.
تجوز *tajawwuz*, INF. of جوز; vulg. for تزوج *tazawwuj*, marriage.
تجوع *tajawwu'*, starving one's self; abstaining from food.
تجويد *tajwîd*, doing or speaking right; swift running of a horse, II. (جود).
تجويز *tajwîz*, INF. II. of (جوز); (m.) for تزويج *tazwîj*, giving in marriage.
تجويف *tajwîf*, hollowing, II. (جوف); pl. *tajwîfât*, *tajâwîf*, cavities, hollows, holes.
تجوية *tajwiya-t*, taming, domestication.
تجير *tajîr*, pressed olive-seed; residue.
تجيش *tajayyuś*, great excitement;

assembling of the troops under their colours.
تجيف *tajayyuf*, putrefaction.
تجييف *taj'îf*, frightening, II. of (جاف) ;—putrefaction, II. (جيف).
تحاب *taḥâbb*, تحابب *taḥâbub*, mutual love, VI. (حب).
تحاشى *taḥâśî*, shunning, being on one's guard against (من *min*).
تحالز *taḥâluz*, dialogue.
تحالم *taḥâlim*, pl. of تحلمة *taḥlama-t*; — *taḥâlum*, VI. of (حلم).
تحان *taḥânn*, strong emotion, violent desire.
تحانى *taḥânî*, leaning against.
تحاور *taḥâwur*, dialogue.
تحاوش *taḥâwuś*, ensnaring, surrounding with nets.
تحاويل *taḥâwîl*, alternately fertile and sterile years.
تحائف *taḥâ'if*, presents; jewellery.
تحبب *taḥabbub*, showing love; granulating, V. (حب).
تحبس *taḥabbus*, being imprisoned; detention.
تحبير *taḥbîr*, INF. II. of (حبر); elegant style.
تحبيس *taḥbîs*, imprisonment; detention; reservation, proviso.
تحبيك *taḥbîk*, II. (حبك), q.v.; (m.) indentation; twisting, plaiting.
تحبية *taḥbiya-t*, defence, protection.
(تحت) *taḥt*, the lower part; under, below; — hence: *taḥat*, sit down at the lower end, occupy a low place; — *tuḥut*, pl. the lower classes.
تحتانى *taḥtâniyy*, inferior; low; marked with dots beneath (letter); lowly placed.
(تحتح) *taḥtaḥ*, INF. ة, move, stir (with a noise); — II. INF. *tataḥtuḥ*, id.
تحتحة *taḥtaḥa-t*, noise in moving.
تحتم *taḥattum*, benevolence, V. (حتم).
تحتى *taḥtiyy*, low, inferior.
تحتيث *taḥtîs̱*, weakness.
تحثيث *taḥs̱îs̱*, spurring on, urging.
تحجج *taḥajjuj*, pretext, subterfuge, excuse.
تحجم *taḥajjum*, great avarice.
تحدث *taḥaddus̱*, INF. V. of (حدث); conversation; recent event; result.
تحدم *taḥaddum*, rage; boiling.
تحذل *taḥazzul*, compassion.
تحرش *taḥarruś*, تحرحش *taḥarḥuś*, challenge.
تحرمز *taḥarmuz*, INF. II. of حرمز *ḥarmaz*; illegitimate birth.
تحرير *taḥrîr*, INF. II. (حر); devoting one's self to God; تحرير اقليدس *taḥrîr iqlîdas*, Euclid's elements; pl. *taḥrîrât*, letter, note, notice; pl. documents, despatches.
تحريف *taḥrîf*, INF. II. of (حرف); permutation of letters; anagram.
تحريم *taḥrîm*, INF. II. of (حرم); donning the dress of pilgrimage;— *taḥrîmiyy*, unlawful.
تحزب *taḥazzub*, II. حزب; party; confederation; set of persons.
تحزو *taḥazzû*, تحزى *taḥazzî*, soothsaying.
تحزين *taḥzîn*, grieving; reading the Koran in public.
تحسف *taḥassuf*, falling of the hair.
تحسين *taḥsîn*, II. (حسن); pl. *taḥâsîn*, good action, benefit; approval.
تحشية *taḥśiya-t*, trimming the edge of a garment; marginal notes.
تحصل *taḥaṣṣul*, V. (حصل); produce.
تحصن *taḥaṣṣun*, V. (حصن); chastity.
تحصيلدار *taḥṣîldâr*, tax-gatherer.
تحصين *taḥṣîn*, II. (حصن); thoroughbredness of a stallion.
(تحف) *tuḥaf*, pl. of تحفة *tuḥfa-t*; — II. INF. *tatḥîf*, adorn; — IV. INF. *itḥâf*, bestow costly presents; present with; — ة *tuḥfa-t*, *tuḥafa-t*, pl. *tuḥaf*, *taḥâ'if*, present; favour; tribute; anything precious, beautiful, rare and fit

object for a present; masterpiece.

تحفاية *taḥfâya-t*, respectful treatment, INF. (حفى).

تحفظ *taḥaffuẓ*, v. (حفظ); (m.) quarantine.

تحفل *taḥafful*, v. (حفل); numerous assembly.

تحفى *taḥaffî*, v. (حفى); humanity, humane proceedings.

تحقد *taḥaqqud*, grudge, inveterate hatred.

تحقيق *taḥqîq*, II. (حق); pl. *taḥqîqât*, certain truths; — ى *taḥqîqiyy*, certain; affirmative.

تحكم *taḥakkum*, v. (حكم); usurpation, disposal.

تحل *taḥill*, redeeming one's oath; — ة *taḥilla-t*, permission, dispensation; absolution; redeeming of an oath.

تحلاق *taḥlâq*, shaving.

تحليل *taḥlîl*, INF. II. of (حل); cure; — ة *taḥlîla-t*, permission; dispensation; absolution.

(تحم) *taḥam*, U, INF. *taḥm*, weave a variegated or striped garment; — IX. *itḥamm*, INF. *itḥimâm*, be black; — ة *taḥama-t*, yellow-striped stuffs; — *taḥimma-t*, dresses which a divorced wife receives; — *tuḥma-t*, deep black colour.

تحمال *tiḥimmâl*, bearing, suffering.

تحمى *taḥammî*, abstinence; protecting one's self; — ة *taḥmiya-t*, make to glow.

تحناذ *taḥnâẓ*, roasting by means of stones.

تحنف *taḥannuf*, profession of the true faith.

تحنو *taḥannu'*, being coloured with hannâh, v. (حنا).

تحنى *taḥannî*, v. (حنو=حنى), bent; inclination; — *taḥni'*, ة *taḥni'a-t*, colouring with henna, II. (حنا); — *taḥniya-t*, bending, II. (حنى =حنو).

تحوت *tuḥût*, pl. the lower classes.

تحوط *taḥûṭ*, dry year; — *taḥaiwwuṭ*; v. (حوط), vigilance.

تحول *taḥawwul*, v. (حول); cunning; power; removal.

تحون *taḥawwun*, meanness, lowness; ruin.

تحويل *taḥwîl*, II. (حول); pl. *-ât*, transformation; revolution; transport; cheque.

تحيت *tuḥait*, rather low, dim. of تحت *taḥt*.

تحيط *tuḥîṭ*, *taḥîṭ*, *tiḥîṭ*, dry year.

تحيل *taḥayyul*, cunning, stratagem; power.

تحين *taḥîn*, space of time; — *taḥayyun*, v. (حين); expectation; arrival.

تحية *taḥiyya-t*, pl. *-ât*, *taḥâyâ*, welcome, salutation; congratulation, II. (حى).

تحيين *taḥyîn*, fixing a term; death.

(تخ) *taḫḫ*, U, INF. *tuḫûḫa-t*, get sour; — IV. INF. *itḫâḫ*, leaven the dough well.

تخ *taḫḫ*, sesame-oil; leavened dough.

تخاريب *taḫârîb*, pl. of تخروب *taḫrûb* and تخريب *taḫrîb*.

تخاريم *taḫârîm*, pl. of تخريم *taḫrîm*.

تخاويف *taḫâwîf*, pl. of تخويف *taḫwîf*.

تخبث *taḫabbuṯ*, filth, dirt.

تخبى *taḫabbî*, being concealed, concealment; — ة *taḫbiya-t*, pitching a tent; — *taḫbi'a-t*, concealment.

تخت *taḫt*, ة, pl. *tuḫût*, seat, bench; sofa; throne; saddle; bed, couch; cloth-press; تخت روان *taḫt rawân*, litter, sedan-chair (Pers.); — ة *taḫta-t*, sheet of metal; board on which a corpse is washed.

تختاخ *taḫtâḫ*, تختاخانى *taḫtâḫâniyy*, stammerer; foreigner.

تختج *taḫtaj*, pl. *taḫâtij*, board, plank; table (Pers.)

(تختخ), تختخة *taḫtaḫa-t*, unarticulated sound.

تختمة *taḫtima-t*, dissimulation.

تخثر *taḫaṯṯur*, getting thick; curdling.

تخذ *taḫaẕ*, *yatḫaẕ*, take, for اتخذ *ittaḫaẕ*, VIII. of (اخذ).

تخربش *taharbuś*, scribbling, scrawling.
تخرص *tahris*, ة, *tahrisa-t*, jutting part of a dress or shirt.
تخربوب *tahrabûb*, a superior kind of camel.
تخروب *tuhrûb*, pl. *tahârîb*, wasp-nest.
تخرور *tuhrûr*, neither strong nor stout.
تخريب *tahrîb*, pl. *tahârîb*, devastation, injury.
تخريص *tahrîs*=تخرص *tahris*.
تخريم *tahrîm*, II. (خرم); pl. *-ât*, *tahârîm*, embroidery; laces; chased work.
تخس *tuhas*, dolphin.
تخشخش *tahaśhuś*, rustling.
تخشية *tahśiya-t*, frightening.
تخصة *tahissa-t*, specification, particular distinction (a.).
تخصص *tahassus*, peculiar quality; distinction; V. (خص).
تخصيص *tahsîs*, II. (خص); pl. *-ât*, special funds.
تخطية *tahtiya-t*, seduction; accusation.
تخفى *tahaffî*, hiding one's self; — ة *tahfiya-t*, concealing.
تخفيف *tahfîf*, INF. II. of (خف); dropping of the *tasdîd*.
تخلخل *tahalhul*, clattering; wavering; want of firmness; adorning one's self with an ankle-ring.
تخلف *tahalluf*, INF. V. of خلف; difference.
تخلى *tihli'*, *tahli'*, world; food and drink; — ة *tahliya-t*, leaving empty; leaving alone; abandoning.
(تخم) *taham*, I, INF. *tahm*, confine, limit; — *tahim*, A, suffer from indigestion; — III. INF. *mutâhama-t*, adjoin, border upon; — IV. INF. *ithâm*, suffer from indigestion, have a stomach-ache.
تخم *tahm*, indigestion; — *tahm*, *tuhm*, pl. *tuhum*, *tuhûm*, boundary, boundary-stone; — *tuhama-t*, pl. *-ât*, *tuham*, indigestion.
تخمين *tahmîn*, supposition, estimation, conjecture; — *tahmîniyy*, approximate, conjectural.
تخورق *tahauruq*, getting impaled (m.).
تخومة *tuhûma-t*, pl. *tuhûm*, *tuhum*, boundary; district; — *tuhûm*, desirable condition, prosperous state.
تخويف *tahwîf*, INF. II. of (خوف); pl. *tahâwîf*, terrible phantom; scarecrow.
تخيب *tahayyub*, fraud, deceit, deception.
تخيف *tahayyuf*, variegation, various shades of colour (خيف).
تخيل *tahayyul*, INF. V. of (خيل); pl. *-ât*, conception; imagination, fancy; supposition.
تخيلى *tahyîliyy*, imaginary.
تدابير *tadâbîr*, pl. of تدبير *tadbîr*.
تداخل *tadâhul*, INF. VI. of (دخل); arrears.
تدارج *tadârij*, pl. of تدرج *tadruj*=تذرج *tazruj*.
تدارك *tadâruk*, INF. VI. of (درك); atonement; remedy; legal remedy; pl. *-ât*, preparations, provisions.
تداعة *tadâ'a-t*, repose, rest, ease.
تدامير *tadâmîr*, pl. of تدمير.
تدانى *tadânî*, neighbourhood; mutual approach, VI. (دنو).
تداهى *tadâhî*, cunning, craft; skill, VI. (دهو).
تداوك *tadâwuk*, throng of battle.
تداوير *tadâwîr*, pl. of تدوير *tadwîr*.
تدبيج *tadbîj*, adornment.
تدبير *tadbîr*, pl. *-ât*, *tadâbîr*, order; arrangement; administration; government; politics, policy; consideration; opinion, II. (دبر).
تدبية *tadbiya-t*, profession, trade, II. (دبى); — *tadbi'a-t*, concealment, II. (دبا).
تدجيل *tadjîl*, pitching; gilding; lie.

تدرا *tudrâ*, ة, *tudrâ-t*, might, power, strength.
تدره *tudrih*, protection.
تدرة *tadirra-t*, abundant flow of milk.
تدرج *tadruj* = تذرج *taẕruj*.
تدريك *tadrîk*, INF. II. (درك); (m.) foresight; prudence.
تدعة *tud'a-t*, easy life.
تدقيق *tadqîq*, exactness, precision, subtilty; pounding to powder, II. (دق).
تدلق *tadalluq*, inundation.
تدمر *tadmur*, Palmyra;—*tadammur*, discontent; murmuring, grumbling; ruin, v. (دمر);—ى *tadmuriyy*, a small field-mouse; unworthy; mean; somebody, anybody.
تدمية *tadmiya-t*, wounding so as to cause the blood to flow, II. (دمى).
تدنى *tadannî*, approach, v. (دنو).
تدنيق *tadnîq*, INF. II. (دنق); (m.) freezing to death.
تدهور *tadahwur*, ruin; overthrow.
تدورة *tadwira-t*, round sand-hill.
تدوير *tadwîr*, INF. II. (دور); circle; circumference; epicycle; — ة *tadwîra-t*, small turban.
تذارج *taẕârij*, pl. of تذرج *taẕruj*.
تذاكر *taẕâkir*, pl. of تذكرة *taẕkira-t*; — *taẕâkur*, INF. VI. of (ذكر).
تذبذب *taẕabẕub*, palpitation; agitation; doubt; uncertainty.
تذرج *taẕruj*, pl. *taẕârij*, *taẕruja-t*, pheasant (Pers.).
تذكار *taẕkâr*, remembrance; mention; keepsake; present.
تذكر *taẕakkur*, remembrance; conference, conversation; private night-study; — ة *taẕkira-t*, pl. *taẕâkir*, remembrance; keepsake; memorandum, memoir; note; testimonial; receipt; passport; — *taẕkara-t*, id.; biography.
تذنوب *taẕnûb*, ripening on the stalk (date).
تذييل *taẕyîl*, INF. II. of (ذيل); appendix, supplement; adding a quiescent letter to a *watad majmû'* at the end of a foot.
(تر) *tarr*, U, INF. *tarr*, *turûr*, appear and be cut out (bone); be cut off; remove, depart; cut off; resound; — INF. *tarr*, *turûr*, *tarâra-t*, be full in flesh and bones; — IV. INF. *itrâr*, amputate; remove (a.), send away; throw away; fling; make resound.
تر *tarr*, good stepper (horse); — *tarr*, root, origin; plummet; — ة *tira-t*, INF. of (وتر), hatred, &c.; — *turra-t*, handsome; delicate and coquettish.
تراب *turâb*, pl. *atriba-t*, *tirbân*, earth, ground, dust; — ة, *turâba-t*, clod of earth; — ى *tarâbiyy*, earthly, earthy, earthen.
تراتور *tarâtûr*, sweetmeat made of nuts.
تراتر *tarâtir*, pl. calamities.
تراتير *tarâtîr*, pl. handsome but stupid girls.
تراتيل *tarâtîl*, pl. of ترتيل *tartîl*.
تراث *turâs̱*, inheritance (ورث).
تراجم *tarâjim*, pl. of ترجمان *tarjamân* and ترجمة *tarjama-t*; — *tarâjum*, INF. V. of رجم, throwing stones at each other.
تراجيل *tarâjîl*, parsley.
تراح *tarâḥ*, beaver.
ترارة *tarâra-t*, being juicy, full of sap or marrow.
ترارية *tarârîh*, pl. of ترهة *turraha-t*.
تراز *turâz*, dying suddenly.
تراس *tirâs*, shields, pl. of ترس *turs*; —*tarrâs*, shield-bearer; —*tara''us*, INF. V. of (راس); — *tarâss*, INF. VI. of (رس); — ة *tirâsa-t*, making shields.
تراش *tarâś*, razor; قلم تراش *qalam tarâś*, pen-knife.
تراع *tarrâ'*, filling the basin or channel; door-keeper.
تراغيف *tarâgîf*, loaves, &c., pl. of رغيف *ragîf*.

ترأف *tarâ'uf*, benevolence; kindness.

تراقى *tarâqî*, collar-bones, pl. of ترقوة *tarquwa-t*; loftiness, INF. VI. of (رقى).

تراك *tarâk*, leave it alone! do not interfere!

تراكم *tarâkum*, condensation; accumulation; increasing;—ة *tarâkima-t*, Turcomans, pl. of تركمان *turkmân*.

تراكيب *tarâkîb*, pl. of تركيب *tarkîb*.

(ترامز) *tarâmiz*, strong and fine camel; full grown.

ترامس *tarâmis*, pl. silver-beads.

تراوض *tarâwuḍ*, drill, exercise.

تراويح *tarâwîḥ*, the twenty-two genuflections after the last prayer of Ramadan.

ترائب *tarâ'ib*, ribs, &c., pl. of تريبة *tarîba-t*.

ترائق *tarâ'iq*, collar-bones, pl. of ترقوة *tarquwa-t*.

ترائك *tarâ'ik*, helmets, &c., pl. of تريكة *tarîka-t*, q.v.

(ترب) *tarib*, A, INF. *tarab*, abound in earth, ground, dust (place); cling to the ground or dust; be covered with earth or dust;—INF. *tarab*, *matrab*, be hopeless, desperate, despair; be poor, miserable;—INF. *tarb*, cover with earth or dust;—II. INF. *tatrîb*, id.; cling to the ground; be rich, and, by opposition, poor; turn into dust, decay, putrify; grow dust-coloured;—III. INF. *mutâraba-t*, be of the same age; become familiar with; be a comrade;—IV. INF. *itrâb*, cover or pelt with earth or dust; be rich, poor; possess a female slave who had already three masters before;—V. INF. *tatarrub*, be covered with earth or dust.

ترب *tarb*, *turb*, earth, ground, dust;—*tirb*, f. pl. *atrâb*, of the same age, companion, friend;—*tarib*, earthy; poor;—ة *tarba-t*, weakness;—*turba-t*, pl. *turab*, earth, ground, dust; tomb; tombstone or memorial to the dead; cemetery;—*tariba-t*, pl. *-ât*, finger-top; raising dust (wind);—*taribba-t*, education; rearing, INF. II. of (رب).

تربا *tarbâ'*, *turabâ'*, earth; ground.

ترباض *tirbâḍ*, saffron in bloom.

تربان *tirbân*, pl. of تراب *turâb*.

تربتى *turbatiyy*, earthy; referring to the tomb.

تربد *tirbid*, *turbid*, laxative.

تربوت *tarabût*, docile (camel).

تربى *tarabbî*, education, rearing; making conserves, INF. V. of (ربو=ربى).

تربيع *tarbî'*, INF. II. of (ربع); right angle;—ى *tarbî'iyy*, quadratic square;—ت مختلف *tarbî'iyy muḥtalif*, trapezium.

تربيق *tarbîq*, INF. II. (ربق);—*tirbîq*, rope for tying up sheep.

تربية *tarbiya-t*, education; rearing of plants or animals; pupil, foster-child, ward; emendation, expostulation; good manners; progress; increase; composition, II. (ربو).

ترتار *tartâr*, whirlpool; abyss.

ترتب *turtab*, everlastingness; bad slave;—*turtab*, *turtub*, firm; well-managed; earth, dust;—*turtub-an*, altogether;—*tarattub*, INF. V. of (رتب); getting into shape; appearing; resulting.

ترتبة *tartubba-t*, trodden path.

(ترتر) *tartar*, INF. ة, move, shake (a.); talk much; (m.) chatter;—II. be shaken, tremble;—ة *tartara-t*, shaking; motion; talkativeness; languidness; dulness of speech.

ترتم *turtam*, *turtum*, lasting.

ترتة *turta-t*, stammering.

ترتور *turtûr*, turtle-dove; tax-gatherer; body-guardsman; pl. *tarâtîr*, handsome but stupid girls.

ترتيب *tartîb*, INF. II. of (رتب); method, plan, system; precept, prescription; layer, row.

ترتيل *tartîl*, INF. II. of (رتل); pl. *tarâtîl*, chant, chorale; anthem.
ترتية *tartiya-t*, (m.) restoration, emendation, II. (رتو).
ترج *taraj*, U, INF. *tarj*, be veiled and hidden; — *tarij*, A, INF. *taraj*, be in the dark about a difficult matter; — ة *turujja-t*, citron, lemon.
ترجح *tarajjuḥ*, shaking, swinging, rocking, v. (رجح).
(ترجم) *tarjam*, INF. ة, translate from one language into another; — ة *tarjama-t*, *tarjuma-t*, pl. *tarâjim*, translation.
ترجمان *tarjamân*, *tarjumân*, *turjumân*, pl. *tarâjim*, (m.) *tarâjima-t*, *tarâjamîn*, interpreter, translator.
ترجى *tarajjî*, hoping, INF. v. (رجى = رجو); — ة *tarjiya-t*, hope; desire.
ترجيح *tarjîḥ*, INF. II. (رجح); preference; overweight.
ترجيع *tarjî'*, INF. II. (رجع); repetition; burden (of a song); echo; compensation.
ترجيل *tarjîl*, INF. II. (رجل); white spot on the hind foot of a horse; shadow.
(ترح) *tariḥ*, A, INF. *taraḥ*, be sad; descend; — II. INF. *tatrîḥ*, grieve; IV. INF. *itrâḥ*, id.; — v. INF. *tatarruḥ*, be grieved.
ترحاب *tarḥâb*, welcome.
ترحال *tirḥâl*, departure; travelling.
ترحيل *tarḥîl*, INF. II. (رحل); patience.
(ترخ) *taraḥ*, A, INF. *tarḥ*, make slight incisions in the skin; scarify.
ترخ *tarḥ*, scarification; cupping.
ترخم *turḥam*, *turḥum*, ة, *tarḥama-t*, *tarḥuma-t*, man, individual.
ترخية *tarḥiya-t*, softening, loosening; relaxation; yielding.
ترداد *tardâd*, INF. II. of (رد).
تردب *taraddub*, INF. v. of (ردب); gracefulness; affection.
تردد *taraddud*, INF. v. of (رد); hesitation, irresolution; refusal; conversation; correspondence; effort; endeavour; emendation; progress.
ترديد *tardîd*, INF. II. of (رد); discord; disjunction.
ترديف *tardîf*, escort.
(ترز) *taraz*, I, INF. *tarz*; — *tariz*, A, INF. *taraz*, be hard, dry, arid; wither; die; be hungry; throw on the ground; — *tariz*, A, INF. *taraz*, freeze; — IV. INF. *itrâz*, render hard and dry; knead hard.
ترز *tarz*, hunger; colic (of cattle); epilepsy; — *taraz*, freezing; hunger.
(ترس) *turs*, pl. ة, *tirasa-t*, *atrâs*, *tirâs*, *turûs*, shield; hard piece of ground; — hence: II. *tarras*, INF. *tarsîs*, cover one's self with a shield, arm with a shield; — v. INF. *tatarrus*, cover one's self with a shield; — ة *tirsa-t*, tortoise.
ترسانة *tarsâna-t*, and—
ترسخانة *tarsḥâna-t*, arsenal (Pers.).
ترسى *tursiyy*, shield-like, of the shape of a shield.
ترسيم *tarsîm*, INF. II. of (رسم); calligraphy; painting; drawing; printing upon.
(ترش) *tariś*, A, INF. *taraś*, be flighty, of a bad disposition, miserly.
ترش *tarś*, *taraś*, lightness, levity; bad disposition; avarice.
ترشا *tirśâ'*, rope to draw a bucket.
ترشاش *tarśâś*, sprinkling, II. (رش).
ترشية *tarśiya-t*, bribing, II. (رشى).
(ترص) *taruṣ*, INF. *tarâṣa-t*, be strong, firm; — II. INF. *tartîṣ*, tare, correct the weight; — IV. id.; make strong and firm.
ترص *tariṣ*, ة, strong.
ترصد *taraṣṣud*, observing; expecting; hoping, v. (رصد).
ترصيص *tarṣîṣ*, INF. II. of (رص); tinning; glazing; soldering.
ترضيض *tarḍîḍ*, INF. II. of (رض;) (m.) push; bruise, contusion.
ترضية *tarḍiya-t*, satisfaction, render-

ing content; apology, deprecation, II. (رضى).

(ترع) tara', A, INF. tar', keep off, keep at a distance; — tari', A, INF. tara', be prone to evil; cheerfully and confidently engage in a business; be full; — II. INF. tatrî', lock; — IV. INF. itrâ', fill; — V. INF. tatarru', be prone to evil towards (ب bi) anybody; — VIII. INF. ittirâ', get full.

ترع tara', full; — tari', full; prone to evil; — ة tur'a-t, pl. tura', door; terraced garden; step, degree; open place; apparition, vision; mouth of a well; spring; basin of a fountain; tank, reservoir; fall of a river.

ترعاب tar'âb, frightening, threatening, II. (رعب); ة, tir'âba-t, timorous.

ترعى tir'iyy, ة, tar'iyya-t, tir'iyya-t, tur'iyya-t and tar'iya-t, tir'iya-t, tur'iya-t, who takes good care of camels, tends them well; — tara''î, INF. V. of (رعى).

ترعيبة tir'îba-t, slice of a camel's hump.

ترغلة targalla-t, turtle-dove (m.).

ترغيب targîb, II. INF. of (رغب); temptation.

(ترف) tarif, A, INF. taraf, live in abundance; — II. INF. tatrîf, effeminating, seduce into wantonness, render overbearing; — IV. INF. itrâf, id.; afford ease and comfort; persist in wantonness or arrogance; — V. INF. tatarruf, live in affluence; — X. istitrâf, be wanton, overbearing, unjust.

ترف taraf, effeminacy; delicacy; softness; ease; — tarif, thin; commodious, easy-going; effeminate; — ة turfa-t, ease, comfort; dainty; anything beautiful or rare as a present.

ترفاس turfâs, poisonous mushroom.

ترفل tarafful, ة tarfala-t, strutting along, walking in jerks (from old age).

ترفيل tarfîl, addition of a sabab hafîf to a watad majmû' at the end of a foot.

ترفية tarfiya-t, II. (رفى), ترفئة tarfi'a-t, ترفيى tarfî', II. (رفا), congratulation to a newly-married couple.

ترفيق tarfîq, INF. II. of (رفق); (m.) assistance, aid, subsidy.

ترقاة tarqât, injury to the collar-bone.

ترقوة tarquwa-t, turquwa-t, pl. tarâqî, tarâ'iq, collar-bone.

ترقى taraqqî, INF. V. (رقى); pl. taraqqiyât, progress; increase; advancement; — ة tarqiya-t, progress, II. (رقى).

ترقيم tarqîm, INF. II. of (رقم), vocalisation; furnishing with a list of prices; embroidering; dashes to fill up, asterisks.

(ترك) tarak, U, INF. tark, tirkân, leave, abandon, desist, neglect; do, put, arrange; — tarik, A, INF. tarak, marry a deserted woman; — III. INF. tirâk, mutâraka-t, leave one alone, at rest; leave a business to another; accord a truce, grant an amnesty; — VI. INF. tatâruk, let a business drop between one another; — VI. INF. intirâk, be abandoned; be left behind (inheritance); — VIII. INF. ittirâk, abandon, leave.

ترك tark, abandoning, leaving; doing, putting; — turk, Turk, Tartar; rude or brutal fellow; — ة tarka-t, thick-set, stubby (woman); pl. tark, iron helmet; — tirka-t, tarika-t, anything left behind, legacy, inheritance.

تركان tirkân, INF. of (ترك).

تركمان turkmân, pl. tarâkima-t, Turcoman.

تركى turkiyy, Turk; f. ة, Turkish; pl. turkiyyât, anything Turkish.

تركيب tarkîb, INF. II. (ركب); composition; mechanism; the human body; musical note; — ى tarkî-

biyy, compound; skilful, ingenious.

ترلك *tarlik*, ترليك *tarlîk*, shoes of Morocco-leather (m.).

ترم *tirm*, term (m.); — hence: II. *tarram*, INF. *tatrîm*, fix a term.

ترمبجى *turumbaji*, fireman (m.).

ترمبة *turumba-t*, fire-engine (m.).

(ترمس) *tarmas*, INF. ة, withdraw from the turmoil, from battle.

ترمس *turmus*, *tarmus*, bramble; (Egyptian) bean; — ة *tarmasa-t*, INF. of ترمس *tarmas*;—*turmusa-t*, hole in the ground (for preserving fruit, cooling, &c.).

ترميق *tarmîq*, INF. II. of (رمق); sketch, first outline.

(ترن) *taran*, dirt.

ترنج *turunj*, ة, orange (Pers.).

ترنجان *turunjân*, melissa, balm-mint.

ترنجبين *taranjabîn*, manna.

ترنجى *turunjiyy*, orange-coloured.

ترنم *tarannum*, INF. V. of (رنم); reading of the Koran with a singing voice; song; psalmody; chirping.

ترنموت *tarnamût*, sound; clank; tinkle; sounding, clinking, tinkling.

ترنوق *tarnûq*, *turnûq*, ترنوقا *turnûqâ*, mire.

ترنوك *turnûk*, contemptible; lean, weakly.

ترنومة *tarnûma-t*, melodious voice; melody; rhythm.

(ترنى) *turna*, female slave; strumpet; — ة *tarniya-t*, enchanting, delighting, cheering, II. (رنو).

ترنيمة روحية *tarnîma-t rûḥiyya-t*, ejaculatory prayer.

(ترة) *tarih*, A, INF. *tarah*, indulge in frivolities or vanities.

ترة *turrah*, pl. *tarârîh*, lie, anything frivolous; — ة *turraha-t*, pl. ات *-ât*, *tarârîh*, the same; buffoonery; empty talk; trifle; calamity; wind; cloud; side-path; broad lowland; small animal in the sand.

ترهوط *tarhûṭ*, who swallows large morsels.

تروبص *taraubuṣ*, purifying (of gold, m.).

ترور *turûr*, INF. of (تر).

تروز *turûz*, thickness and firmness.

تروس *tarawwus*, sharpening into a point, V. (راس).

تروعة *tarwi'a-t*, blast of a trumpet.

تروم *tara''um*, compassion, love, V. (رام); — *tarawwum*, mockery, V. (روم).

تروى *tarawwî*, INF. V. of (روى); — تروى *tarwî'*, INF. II. of (روا).

ترويس *tarwîs*, sharpening into a point, II. (راس).

ترويقة *tarwîqa-t*, breakfast (m.).

تروئة *tarwi'a-t*, INF. II. of (روا); — تروية *tarwiya-t*, INF. II. of (روى).

(ترى) *tara*, A, INF. *tary*, relax; — be cheerful, in good humour; be numerous; — IV. INF. *itrâ'*, perform one work after another with intervals of rest between.

ترى *turra*, cut off hand; enfeebled strength.

ترياق *tiryâq*, theriac; antidote; panacea; — ة *tiryâqa-t*, wine; — ى *tiryâqîyy*, inebriated; drunkard; opium-eater.

تريب *tiryab*, *tarîb*, earth, ground; — ة *tarîba-t*, pl. *tarâ'ib*, the four upper ribs; ribs; chest, breast, bosom; place above the collar-bone; neck; hands; feet; eyes.

تريج *tarîj*, violent (wind); strongly-built and sinewy.

تريص *tarîṣ*, strong; well-poised balance; twisted, plaited.

تريع *tarî'*, cheery for work, light-minded; — *tarayyu'*, V. (ريع), assembly.

تريف *tarîf*, commodious, easy-going; effeminate.

تريك *tarîk*, empty stalks of a grape; — ة *tarîka-t*, pl. *tarâ'ik*, *tarîk*, helmet; abandoned; left property without an heir; stagnating water after a flood.

ترىم *tarîm*, resigned to the will of God; dirtied; sinful.

ترييح *taryîḥ*, setting at rest, tranquillising, quieting (m.).

ترئية *tar'iya-t*, beautiful look; hypocrisy; II. (رأى); — *taryi'a-t*, INF. II. of (ريا).

تزايد *tazâyud*, increase, VI. (زيد).

تزبرة *tazbira-t*, own hand-writing, autograph; *tazbira-t* and تزبير *tazbîr*, INF. II. of (زبر).

تزحر *tazaḥḥur*, colic; travail; labour of child-birth.

تزحل *tazaḥḥul*, تزحول *tazaḥwul*, being set in motion, sliding, slipping.

تزخرف *tazaḥruf*, false ornaments, trumpery.

تزعيم *taz'îm*, INF. II. of (زعم); claim.

تزقيب *tazqîb*, twitter of birds.

تزكى *tazakkî*, sanctification; almsgiving, V. (زكو); — ة *tazkiya-t*, sanctifying, consecrating; justification; character; giving and also receiving alms, II. (زكو).

تزكيم *tazkîm*, cold, rheum, II. (زكم).

تزلزل *tazalzul*, INF. II. of (زلزل); earthquake.

تزليق *tazlîq*, shaving, anointing, II. (زلق).

تزمت *tazammut*, gravity, steadiness; authority.

ترمير *tazmîr*, INF. II. of (زمر); psalm.

تزندق *tazanduq*, Parseeism.

تزنتر *tazantur*, تزنطر *tazanṭur*, INF. II. of (زنتر , زنطر); anger, rage; caprice.

تزواج *tazwâj*, pairing, coupling, copulation.

تزيدى *tazîdiyy*, red-striped garment.

تزيى *tazayyî*, costume, dress, garb.

تزييح *tazyîḥ*, INF. II. of (زيح); procession.

تسابغ *tasâbug*, ornament of the neck-part of a helmet.

تسابيح *tasâbîḥ*, pl. of تسبيحة *tasbîḥa-t*.

تساخين *tasâḥîn*, pl. of تسخان *tasḥân*.

تسافح *tasâfuḥ*, dissoluteness.

تسافد *tasâfud*, copulation,. sexual intercourse.

تسافه *tasâfuh*, INF. VI. of (سفه); levity; foolishness.

تسال *tasâl*, تسئال *tas'âl*, question, request.

تسامع *tasâmu'*, hearing, listening.

تسامى *tasâmî*, emulation, VI. (سمو).

تساند *tasânud*, INF. VI. of (سند); mutual help.

تساوى *tasâwî*, INF. VI. of (سوى); equality, similarity; indifference; neutrality; levelness; level (s.).

تسايف *tasâyuf*, fight with the sword, fencing.

تسبب *tasabbub*, INF. VI. of (سب); retail trade.

تسبغ *tasbig*, *tasbug*, ة, *tasbiga-t*, pl. *tasâbig*=تسابغ *tasâbug*.

تسبيب *tasbîb*, INF. II. of (سب); motive, reason; reproach; curse.

تسبيح *tasbîḥ*, INF. II. of (سبح); praise of God; hymn; rosary; purity; — ة *tasbîḥa-t*, pl. *tasâbîḥ*, song, hymn.

تسبيغ *tasbîg*, adding a quiescent letter to a *sabab ḥafîf* at the end of a foot.

تسبيق *tasbîq*, INF. II. of (سبق); stake at a race.

تستوق *tustûq*, bad money, dipped in a solution of silver.

تسجية *tasjiya-t*, shrouding of a corpse, II. (سجو).

تسجيع *tasjî'*, rhythmical and rhymed prose.

تسحر *tasaḥḥur*, INF. V. (سحر); early departure.

تسخان *tasḥân*, pl. *tasâḥîn*, greaves; boots; hood.

تسخر *tasḥar*, jest, irony; — INF. V. of (سخر); compelled service; socage.

تسدية *tasdiya-t*, weaving, weaving the warp, II. (سدى).

تسديس *tasdîs*, INF. II. of (سدس); hexagon.

تسرر *tasarrur*, concubinage, V. (سر).

تسرع *tasarru'*, haste, hurry, v. (سرع).

تسرق *tasarruq*, INF. v. of (سرق); systematic robbery, system of rapine.

تسرة *tasirra-t*, cheering up, gladdening.

تسرى *tasarrî*, INF. v. of (سرى); concubinage.

تسس *tusus*, people of low extraction.

(تسع), f. *tis'*, m. تسعة *tis'a-t*, nine; — hence: *tasa'*, A, I, INF. *tas'*, take the ninth part; — come as the ninth to a company of eight; — II. INF. *tatsî'*, III. *mutâsa'a-t*, id.; — IV. INF. *itsâ'*, complete the number of nine; become nine of them; take the ninth part of people's property.

تسع *tus'*, pl. *atsâ'*, ninth part; — *tusa'*, the 7th, 8th, and 9th night of a month; — *tasa'*, for *ittasa'*, VIII. of (وسع).

تسعون *tis'ûn*, (m.) تسعين *tis'în*, ninety; ninetieth.

تسقف *tasaqquf*, INF. v. of (سقف); consecration of a bishop.

تسقية *tasqiya-t*, giving to drink, watering; saying سقاك الله *saqâ-ka 'l-lâh-u*, may God quench thy thirst.

تسكين *taskîn*, INF. II. of (سكن); being without a vowel.

تسلخ *tasalluḥ*, skinning, casting off the skin.

تسلسل *tasalsul*, INF. II. of (سلسل); concatenation; degrees of relationship; advancement by degrees.

تسلط *tasalluṭ*, INF. v. of (سلط); usurpation; arbitrariness; oppression.

تسلم *taslam*, thou art alive and in good health (i.e., the person whom you inquire after is dead); indeed! certainly! — *tasallum*, INF. v. of (سلم).

تسليف *taslîf*, INF. II. of (سلف); payment in advance; borrowing; breakfast.

تسليم *taslîm*, INF. II. of (سلم); salutation; salvation, rescue; preservation; delivery, surrender; transmission; resignation; consent; well-being, safety, peace.

تسلية *tasliya-t*, consolation; tranquillisation.

تسمعة *tasmi'a-t*, making to be heard.

تسمن *tasammun*, growing fat.

تسمى *tasammî*, INF. v. of (سمو); denomination; — ة *tasmiya-t*, giving a name; denomination; II. of the same.

تسميت *tasmît*, INF. II. (سمت); orthodoxy, professing the true faith.

تسميط *tasmîṭ*, INF. II. of (سمط); receipt, acquittance.

تسميع *tasmî'*, INF. II. of (سمع); speech.

تسهر *tasahhur*, waking, keeping awake.

تسهيل *tashîl*, INF. II. of (سهل); marking with *hamza-t*.

تسوك *tasawwuk*, cleaning the teeth with a toothpick.

تسومة *tasûma-t*, sandal.

تسويد *taswîd*, INF. II. of (سود); rough copy; dung.

تسويغ *taswîg*, INF. II. of (سوغ); pl. *-ât*, magnificent present to a sovereign.

تسويق *taswîq*, cattle-driving.

تسويل *taswîl*, pl. *-ât*, adornment; deceit; fiction, II. (سول).

(تسوئة) *taswi'a-t*, تسوى *taswî'*, reproach, II. (سو).

تسيار *tasyâr*, walk; journey; message; expedition.

تسيب *tasayyub*, neglect.

تسير *tasayyur*, conduct of life.

تسيع *tasî'*, ninth part.

تسيح *tasyîḥ*, weaving.

تشارك *taśâruk*, INF. VI. of (شرك); partnership.

تشامخ *taśâmuḥ*, INF. VI. of (شمخ); haughtiness.

تشانو *taśânu'*, mutal hatred.

تشاهير *taśâhîr*, pl. of تشهير *taśhîr*.

تشايع *taśâyu'*, INF. V. of (هيع); professing the Shi'ite faith; partnership.

تشبت *taśabbut*=تشبث *taśabbus*, INF. V. of (هبث).

تشبير *taśbîr*, INF. II. of (هبر); pl. *taśâbîr*, gesticulation, gesture.

تشبيك *taśbîk*, INF. II. of (هبك); net-work; complication; (m.) rheumatism in a horse's legs.

تشبيه *taśbîh*, INF. II. of (هبه); pl. *-ât*, comparison; allegory; metaphor; similitude; anthropomorphism.

تشتى *taśattî*, v. تشتية *taśtiya-t*, II. of (هتو), passing the winter; hibernation.

تشجع *taśajju'*, INF. V. of (هجع); bravado.

(تشح), IV. INF. *itśâh*, pelt, shoot at (acc.) with (ب *bi*); — ة *tuśha-t*, boldness in defending one's right; covetousness; anger; perversity; cowardice.

تشخيص *taśhîs*, INF. II. of (هخص); individualisation; diagnosis; taxation; census.

تشديد *taśdîd*, INF. II. of (هد); violent pressure; hardness, severity; the sign ـ and its application.

تشذب *taśazzub*, breaking into splinters, shivering to pieces.

تشراب *taśrâb*, drinking; draught.

تشرف *taśarruf*, honour, glory; pride, II. (هرف).

تشريج *taśrîj*, contraction, embroidering; hem sewn with large stitches.

تشريح *taśrîh*, INF. II. of (هرح); commentary; dissection; anatomy.

تشريف *taśrîf*, INF. II. of (هرف); His Grace (title); pl. *-ât*, *taśârîf*, honours, distinctions, ceremonies, robe of honour.

تشريفاتجى *taśrîfâtji*, تشريفاتى *taśrîfâtiyy*, master of ceremonies, Grand Chamberlain.

تشرين *taśrîn*, October (ت اول *taśrîn awwal*) and November (ت ثانى *taśrîn sânî*).

تشرية *taśriya-t*, drying (fruit, &c.) in the air.

تشعب *taśa''ub*, INF. V. of (هعب); ramification; separation; death.

تشعيث *taś'îs*, suppression of one of the movable letters of a *watad majmû'*.

تشغية *taśgiya-t*, gonorrhœa.

تشفية *taśfiya-t*, advantage; growth.

تشقيع *taśqî'*, INF. II. of (هقع); pl. *taśâqî'*, insult, abuse.

تشكل *taśakkul*, INF. V. of (هكل); beauty; appearance; representation in painting, &c.

تشكيك *taśkîk*, INF. II. of (هك); offence, scandal; doubt; suspicion.

تشكيل *taśkîl*, INF. II. of (هكل); difficulty; complication; — ة, *taśkîla-t*, (m.) many-coloured nosegay.

تشميس *taśmîs*, INF. II. of (همس); worship of the sun.

تشنج *taśannuj*, INF. V. of (هنج); spasm.

تشنن *taśannun*, INF. V. of (هن); shrinking, shrivelling, getting wrinkled.

تشنيج *taśnîj*, cramp in the throat; stiff neck, II. (هنج).

تشنيط *taśnît*, roasting, broiling.

تشهاق *taśhâq*, sigh; whine.

تشهد *taśahhud*, profession of the Mohametan faith.

تشهى *taśahhî*, passionate desire, II. (ههو).

تشود *taśawwud* (تشوذ *taśawwuz*), culmination of the sun.

تشويد *taświd* (تشويذ *taświz*), id.

تشوية *taświya-t*, roasting, broiling.

تشيع *taśayyu'*, INF. V. of (هيع); profession of Shi'ism.

تصابى *taṣâbî*, childishness, v. (صبو).

تصادف *taṣâduf*, unexpected occurrence, sudden emergency; accident, chance.

تصاديع *taṣâdî'*, pl. of تصديع *taṣdî'*.

تصارف *taṣârif*, تصارفة *taṣârifa-t*, sovereign commands.

تصاريف *taṣârîf*, pl. of تصريف *taṣrîf*.
تصاف *taṣâff*, array in battle order.
تصافى *taṣâfî*, acting sincerely towards each other, VI. (صفو).
تصاليب *taṣâlîb*, images of the cross.
تصانيف *taṣânîf*, pl. of تصنيف *taṣnîf*.
تصاول *taṣâwul*, fierce attack, VI. (صول).
تصاوير *taṣâwîr*, pl. of تصوير *taṣwîr*.
تصبيح *taṣbîḥ*, INF. II. of (صبح); morning draught; breakfast.
تصبير *taṣbîr*, INF. II. of (صبر); ballast.
تصحيح *taṣḥîḥ*, INF. II. of (صح); correction; verification; liquidation; legalisation.
تصدى *taṣadî*, setting to work, &c., V. (صدو).
تصدير *taṣdîr*, INF. II. of (صدر); issuing, publishing.
تصديع *taṣdî'*, INF. II. of (صدع); pl. *taṣâdî'*, head-ache; confusion.
تصديق *taṣdîq*, INF. II. of (صدق); receiving alms; — ى *taṣdîqiyy*, confirming.
تصرف *taṣarruf*, INF. V. of (صرف); control; influence; skill; art; domestic expenditure; coition; pl. *-ât*, possessions; behaviour; relations; expenses; — ى *taṣarrufiyy*, household expenditure.
تصريف *taṣrîf*, INF. II. of (صرف); pl. *taṣarîf*, inflection, declension, conjugation; etymology.
تصعاق *taṣ'âq*, fainting-fit.
تصعد *taṣa''ud*, INF. V. of (صعد); evaporation, sublimation (n.).
تصعرر *taṣa'rur*, globular form.
تصعلك *taṣa'luk*, poverty.
تصعيد *taṣ'îd*, INF. II. of (صعد); melting; distillation, sublimation (a.).
تصغير *taṣgîr*, INF. II. of (صغر); diminutive.
تصفية *taṣfiya-t*, purification; clearing; straining the wine.
تصقير *taṣqîr*, INF. II. of (صقر); hunting with the falcon.
تصلب *taṣallub*, INF. V. of (صلب); hardness; inflexibility.
تصلق *taṣalluq*, labour of child-birth, colic, V. (صلق).
تصليب *taṣlîb*, INF. II. of (صلب); hanging; impaling; sign of the cross.
تصلية *taṣliya-t*, roasting; singeing.
تصميم *taṣmîm*, INF. II. of (صم) firm resolution.
تصنيف *taṣnîf*, INF. II. of (صنف); pl. *taṣânîf*, invention; literary composition, work, record.
تصنيم *taṣnîm*, INF. II. of (صنم); idolatry.
تصور *taṣawwur*, INF. V. of (صور); representation by image, &c.; portrait; picture; conception, idea, imagination; — ى *taṣawwuriyy*, imaginary.
تصوف *taṣawwuf*, INF. V. of (صوف); obscure mystical speech; mysticism; Sufiism; contemplation; gibberish.
تصويب *taṣwîb*, approval.
تصويت *taṣwît*, exclamation, resounding, echo.
تصوير *taṣwîr*, INF. II. of (صور); pl. *taṣâwîr*, representation, &c.= تصور *taṣawwur*.
تصيت *taṣayyut*, renown, celebrity.
تضاد *taḍâdd*, INF. VI. of (ضد); hostility; contrast; contradiction; opposition; absurdity.
تضارب *taḍârub*, INF. VI. of (ضرب); excitement, agitation.
تضاعيف *taḍâ'îf*, pl. of تضعيف *taḍ'îf*.
تضاف *taḍâff*, throng, VI. (ضف).
تضامم *taḍâmum*, accumulation.
تضحضح *taḍaḥḍuḥ*, modulation.
تضرة *taḍirra-t*, *taḍurra-t*, need, want.
تضع *tuḍ'*, *tuḍu'*, INF. of (وضع), give birth, produce, &c.
تضعيف *taḍ'îf*, pl. *taḍâ'îf*, INF. II. of (ضعف); reduplication; chemical adulteration; lining clothes.
تضلال *taḍlâl*, misleading, seduction, II. (ضل).
تضلل *tuḍallil*, *tuḍullil*, false.
تضمن *taḍammun*, INF. V. of (ضمن); contents; security, bail; tenure as a farmer; — ى *taḍammuniyy*, elliptical; understood (thought not expressed).

تضميد *taḍmîd*, dressing of a wound; bandage, ligature.

تضمين *taḍmîn*, INF. II. of (ضمن); inclosure; elliptical speech; pl. *-ât*, damages, compensation; farming out.

تضوية *taḍwiya-t*, lighting up, illumination.

تضييع *taḍyî'*, INF. II. of (ضيع); loss, ruin.

تطاريف *taṭârîf*, pl. finger-tops.

تطاول *taṭâwul*, INF. VI. of (طول); robbery, plunder, oppression.

تطبيق *taṭbîq*, INF. II. of (طبق); trying whether two things fit each other, as a seal and its impression, &c.

تطرية *taṭriya-t*, freshening up; refreshing.

تطفل *taṭafful*, parasitism.

تطفئة *taṭfi'a-t*, extinguishing (a.).

تطهر *taṭahhur*, INF. V. of (طهر); sanctification.

(تطو) *taṭâ*, U, INF. *taṭw*, wrong a person, injure, tyrannise.

تطواف *taṭwâf*, *tiṭwâf*, garment worn during the procession round the Ka'aba.

تطوع *taṭawwu'*, supererogatory work, good action of free will.

تطول *tiṭwal*, long rope, chain; — *taṭawwul*, INF. V. of (طول).

تطويب *taṭwîb*, pl. *-ât*, beatification; beatitude.

تطويل *taṭwîl*, INF. II. of (طول); prolixity.

تظلل *taẓallul*, seeking the shade, v. (ظل).

تع *ta'*, for تعالى *ta'âla*, let him be praised!

تع *ta''*, U, INF. *ta''*, ة *ta''a-t*, be weak, languid; vomit.

تعاتع *ta'âti'*, idle talk.

تعاجيب *ta'âjîb*, wonders, marvels.

تعادى *ta'âdî*, INF. VI. of (عدو); rugged places.

تعارف *ta'âruf*, mutual acquaintance; rule; manner, method, VI. (عرف).

تعاسة *ta'âsa-t*, ruin, perdition.

تعاشيب *ta'âśîb*, herbs, shrubs.

تعافى *ta'âfî*, recovery.

تعاقب *ta'âqub*, INF. VI. of (عقب); pursuit; overtaking; punishment.

تعاقد *ta'âqud*, confederacy, alliance.

تعال *ta'âl*, be praised! come here! come along! IMP. VI. of (على).

تعالى *ta'âla*, let him be praised!

تعاليف *ta'âlîf*, pl. of تعليفة *ta'lîfa-t*.

تعاليم *ta'âlîm*, pl. of تعليم *ta'lîm*.

تعامل *ta'âmul*, management of business.

تعانيق *ta'ânîq*, pl. of تعنوق *ta'nûq*.

تعاويذ *ta'âwîẕ*, pl. of تعويذ *ta'wîẕ*.

تعاهد *ta'âhud*, INF. VI. of (عهد); pl. *-ât*, agreement; alliance; conspiracy.

(تعب) *ta'ib*, A, INF. *ta'ab*, be tired, fatigued; toil; lose one's labour; — IV. INF. *it'âb*, give trouble; tire, vex, torment; have overworked beasts; fill; break again a bone which had been healed.

تعب *ta'ab*, tiredness, fatigue; vexation; hard work, toil; — *ta'ab*, *ta'ib*, tired.

تعبان *ta'bân*, tired.

تعبير *ta'bîr*, INF. II. of (عبر); explanation, interpretation; denomination; expression; word.

(تعتع) *ta'ta'*, INF. ة, stick (in the sand, &c.); get entangled, confused (in speech); shake (a.), push; disquiet, confound; (m.) talk idly, chatter; — II. INF. *tata'tu'*, get confused (in speech).

تعتع *ta'ta'*, pl. *ta'âti'*, stammered words; foolish or idle talk; confusion.

تعثير *ta'ṡîr*, INF. II. of (عثر); misery.

تعجابة *ti'jâba-t*, worker of miracles.

تعجرف *ta'ajruf*, haste, precipitation.

تعجيز *ta'jîz*, INF. II. of (عجز); importunity, molestation.

تعداد *ta'dâd*, counting, reckoning, calculating.
تعدد *ta'addud*, equipment.
تعدى *ta'addî*, INF. V. of (عدو); transgression, excess; — ية *ta'diya-t*, INF. II. of (عدو); transitive meaning of a verb; entrance.
تعذر *ta'azzur*, INF. V. of (عذر); difficulty; impossibility.
(تعر) *ta'ar*, A, INF. *ta'r*, cry out, call.
تعر *ta'ar*, battle-cry.
تعرج *ta'arruj*, declination, deviation.
تعرض *ta'arruḍ*, INF. V. of (عرض); meddling; arbitrary interference.
تعريب *ta'rîb*, INF. II. of (عرب); speaking pure Arabic.
تعريض *ta'rîḍ*, INF. II. of (عرض); blame, reproach.
تعريف *ta'rîf*, INF. II. of (عرف); pl. *-ât*, *ta'ârîf*, instruction; description; tariff; definition; assertion; guessing; حرف التعريف *ḥarfu-'l-ta'rîf*, definite article;— ى *ta'rîfiyy*, remarkable; worthy of notice.
تعزوة *ta'zuwa-t*, patience.
تعزى *ta'azzî*, INF. V. of (عزو , عزى); condoling; — ة *ta'ziya-t*, consolation; mourning for the dead; letter of condolence; mimic representation of the death of Hasan and Husain.
(تعس) *ta'as*, *ta'is*, A, INF. *ta's*, *ta'as*, perish; fall on one's face; ruin, cause to perish; stumble and fall; be dismissed, deposed; be far; — IV. INF. *it'âs*, ruin, cause to perish; make miserable.
تعس *ta's*, fall, ruin, overthrow; misfortune, calamity; — *ta'is*, perishing; unhappy, miserable; — ة *ta'sa-t*, stumbling, falling.
تعسف *ta'assuf*, tyranny, oppression; pervert the meaning of a word.
تعشم *ta'aśśum*, INF. V. of (عشم); (m.) hope; interestedness, avidity.
تعشى *ta'aśśî*, taking an evening's meal; supper, V. (عشو); — ة *ta'śiya-t*, invitation to supper.
تعشير *ta'śîr*, INF. II. of (عشر); division by ten; decimating.
(تعص) *ta'iṣ*, A, INF. *ta'aṣ*, feel pain in the sinews of the foot from walking.
تعصب *ta'aṣṣub*, INF. V. of (عصب); partiality; bigotry; fanaticism; (m.) plot; conspiracy.
تعصرن *ta'aṣrun*, afternoon luncheon (m.).
تعضية *ta'ḍiya-t*, separation, division.
تعطف *ta'aṭṭuf*, INF. V. of (عطف); affection; sympathy; tenderness, fondness.
تعطى *ta'aṭṭî*, INF. V. of (عطو); demand for a present.
تعطيل *ta'ṭîl*, INF. II. of (عطل); loss, damage; (m.) interest (for a loan).
تعظم *ta'azzum*, INF. V. of (عظم); false pomp.
تعظيم *ta'zîm*, INF. II. of (عظم); pomp, magnificence.
تعفن *ta'affun*, INF. V. of (عفن); stench; putrefaction.
تعفير *ta'fîr*, INF. II. of (عفر); (m.) gleaning.
تعفية *ta'fiya-t*, effacing, blotting out, extinguishing, &c., INF. II. of (عفو).
تعقب *ta'aqqub*, INF. V. of (عقب); considering the issue or consequences; punishment.
تعقل *ta'aqqul*, understanding; foresight, prudence; device, contrivance.
تعقيب *ta'qîb*, INF. II. of (عقب); delay.
تعقيد *ta'qîd*, INF. II. of (عقد); difficulty; obscurity.
(تعل) *ta'al*, heat in the throat; — ة *ta'illa-t*, what draws off attention; subterfuge, pretext.
تعلامة *ti'lâma-t*, great scholar; genealogist.
تعلق *ta'alluq*, INF. V. of (علق);

dependence; attachment; relationship; property; (landed) estate; dependants; appurtenance; — ة ta'alluqa-t, id.

تعلل ta'allul, INF. V. of (عل); delay; excuse; subterfuge; pretext.

تعلمة ti'lima-t = تعلامة ti'lâma-t.

تعليق ta'lîq, INF. II. of (علق); Persian handwriting or character; — ة ta'lîqa-t, pl. ta'âlîq, marginal note, gloss; (m.) burning tinder; necklace.

تعليل ta'lîl, INF. II. of (عل); causality.

تعليم ta'lîm, pl. -ât, ta'âlîm, INF. II. of (علم); instruction; marking; mark, sign; catechism; military drill; copy-writing of pupils.

تعمد ta'ammud, full consideration; firm resolution, v. (عمد).

تعمم ta'ammum, INF. V. of (عمم); (m.) great bulk.

تعميد ta'mîd, INF. II. of (عمد); (m.) baptism.

تعمير ta'mîr, INF. II. of (عمر); emendation, restoration; civilisation; prosperity of the country.

تعميم ta'mîm, INF. II. of (عم); generalisation.

تعمية ta'miya-t, blinding; blindness; darkness; obscure meaning.

تعنت ta'annut, criticism; fault-finding; making difficulties, v. (عنت).

تعنوق tu'nûq, pl. ta'ânîq, level ground, field.

تعنيف ta'nîf, INF. II. of (عنف); importunity, molestation; rebuke.

تعنين ta'nîn, INF. II. of (عن); title, superscription; impotence; bridling a horse; — ة ta'nîna-t, impotence.

تعوكر ta'aukur, turbidness; disquietude.

تعويذ ta'wîẕ, INF. II. of (عوذ); ta'wîẕ and ة ta'wîẕa-t, talisman.

تعويل ta'wîl, INF. II. of (عول); cry for help; wailing; resolution; reliance.

(تعى) ta'â, INF. a'y, jump, run.

تعيس ta'îs, unhappy, miserable; perishing.

تعين ta'ayyun, INF. V. of (عين); pl. -ât, essential qualities; fixed salary; office; recruiting, levy.

تعييب ta'yîb, INF. II. of (عيب); blame, reproach; putting to shame, exposure.

تعيين ta'yîn, INF. II. of (عين); pl. -ât, fixed daily salary, ration.

تغ تغ tig tig, sound produced by laughing.

تغابن tagâbun, mutual deceit, fraud (يوم التـ yaumu-'t-tagâbun-i, Day of Judgment); irritability; v. (غبن).

تغار tagârr, violently bleeding (adj.); — ة, foaming and running straight onward (camel).

تغاريد tagârîd, pl. of تغريد tagrîd.

تغاريز tagârîz, pl. of تغريز tagrîz.

تغاز tagazz, quarrel, VI. (غز).

تغاضى tagâḍî, inattention; neglect, VI. (غضو).

تغالى tagâlî, INF. VI. of (غلو); dearness, scarcity, dearth.

تغايب tagâyub, absence.

(تغب) tagib, A, INF. tagab, perish; — IV. INF. itgâb, ruin.

تغب tagab, ruin; want, dearth, famine; vice; — tagb, infamy, vice; — ة tagibba-t, false testimony.

(تغتغ) tagtag, INF. ة, deliver a speech in a confused and indistinct manner.

تغدى tagaddî, meal, breakfast, v. (غدو).

تغذى tagazzî, taking food; meal, v. (غذو).

(تغر) tagar, A, tagir, A, INF. tagarân, boil; — INF. tugûr, pour down; make water (dog); burst and let out water or any fluid; spirt; fall abundantly (rain);

— VII. INF. *intigâr*, rain heavily (cloud); — ة *tagirra-t*, risk of life, staking one's life.

تغران *tagarân*, boiling (adj.); INF. of (تغر).

تغرى *tugra*, imperial signature (Pers.); — ة *tagriya-t*, INF. II. of (غرو); adhesion.

تغريم *tagrîm*, INF. II. of (غرم); enforced payment; fine, mulct.

تغس *tags*, small cloud.

تغشية *tagśiya-t*, INF. II. of (غشو); whipping.

تغضوض *tagḍûḍ*, sweet kind of dates.

تغطية *tagṭiya-t*, covering, veiling, v. (غطو).

تغلب *tagallub*, INF. V. of (غلب); victory; superiority; oppression.

تغلس *tagallus*, misfortune; evil; calamity.

تغليل *taglîl*, INF. II. of (غل); (m.) gagging.

(تغم), IV. INF. *itgâm*, suffer from indigestion.

تغماض *tagmâḍ*, falling asleep.

تغميض *tagmîḍ*, INF. II. of (غمض); indulgence.

تغور *tugûr*, INF. of (تغر).

تغوية *tagwiya-t*, seduction, deceit.

(تغى) *taga*, A, INF. *tagy*, burst out laughing; — perish; — *tig-an*, loud laughter.

تغير *tagayyur*, INF. V. of (غير); change, transformation, alteration.

(تف) *tuff*, pl. *tifafa-t*, dirt or parings of the nails; — pl. *atfâf*, *tufûf*, what sticks between the teeth; — *tuff-in*, fie!

(تف) *taff*, U, INF. *taff*, spit (blood, &c.); — II. *taffaf*, INF. *tatfiya-t*, say fie!

تفا *tuff-an*, fie!

تفاتيف *tafâtîf*, pl. of تفتاف *taftâf*.

تفاح *tuffâḥ*, ة, apple; apple-tree; ت أرمنى *tuffâḥ armaniyy*, apricot; ت فارسى *tuffâḥ fârisiyy*, pear; ت ماهى *tuffâḥ mâhiyy*, orange; ت برى *tuffâḥ barriyy*, medlar; — ية *tuffâḥiyya-t*, apple sauce; fruiterer.

تفاريج *tafârîj*, pl. openings, interstices.

تفاريق *tafârîq*, pl. of تفريق *tafrîq*.

تفاسير *tafâsîr*, pl. of تفسير *tafsîr*.

تفاصيل *tafâṣîl*, pl. of تفصيل *tafṣîl*.

تفاضل *tafâḍul*, INF. VI. of (فضل); superiority; surplus; remainder; — ى *tafâḍuliyy*, see تمامى *tamâmiyy*.

تفال *tafâl*, spittle; foam; —*tafa''ul*, good omen, v. (فال).

تفان *tiffân*, proper time, nick of time.

تفاوت *tafâwut*, INF. VI. of (فوت); also *tafâwit*, *tafâwat*, interval of space or time; difference, discrepancy; want; blame; absence.

تفاول *tafâ'ul*, omen, VI. (فال).

تفائف *tafâ'if*, pl. dirt, offal, parings, trifles.

تفتاف *taftâf*, pl. *-ûn*, *tafâtîf*, blabber, tell-tale; go-between.

تفتر *taftar*=دفتر *daftar*, book, &c.

تفتيشى *taftîśiyy*, investigator, examiner.

(تفث) *tafis̱*, A, INF. *tafas̱*, trim the nails, hair, beard (for the sake of the pilgrimage to Mecca); clean one's self.

تفث *tafas̱*, dirt and parings of the pilgrims to Mecca; squalor; — *tafis̱*, having one's hair and beard neglected.

(تفر) *tafr*, تفران *tafrân*, dirty; — *tafar*, bud; — IV. INF. *itfâr*, id.; — ة *tifra-t*, *tufra-t*, *tafira-t*, *tufara-t*, dimple between the nose and upper lip.

تفراجة *tifrâja-t*, coward.

تفراق *tafrâq*, separation.

تفرجا *tifrijâ'*, coward.

تفرجة *tifrija-t*, pl. *tafârij*, interval, interstice, chink; pleasant sight, fine view; coward.

تفرد *tafarrud*, INF. V. of (فرد); obduracy; restiveness, refractoriness, insubordination; rebellion.

تفرقة *tafriqa-t*, separation; diffusion; distribution; distinction; dispersion; discord.

(تفروق) *tufrûq*, pedicle of the date.

تفريط *tafrîṭ*, INF. II. of (فرط); excess; too little; exaggeration; (m.) dissipation.

تفريق *tafrîq*, INF. II. of (فرق); pl. *tafârîq*, division, distribution; department; distinction; schism; subtraction; suspicion; jealousy.

تفرية *tafriya-t*, cutting into pieces, II. (فرى); — lining with fur, see (فرو).

تفسح *tafassuḥ*, INF. V. of (فسح); spaciousness; commodiousness; recreation in the open air; dispensation.

تفسرة *tafsira-t*, diagnosis from the urine; symptom; prescription.

تفسير *tafsîr*, INF. II. of (فسر); pl. *tafâsîr*, commentary; paraphrase; gloss.

تفشى *tafaśśî*, ة *tafśiya-t*, spreading of a contageous disease.

تفصيد *tafṣîd*, INF. II. of (فصد); incision; groove.

تفصيل *tafṣîl*, INF. II. of (فصل); pl. *tafâṣîl*, division into chapters; analysis; detail, narrating in detail; inventory; explicitness; sketch, plan of a building; cut of a dress; pl. *-ât*, details; — ة *tafṣîla-t*, pl. *tafâṣîl*, piece of cloth cut off for a dress.

تفضيل *tafḍîl*, INF. II. of (فضل); اسم ت *ism tafḍîl*, comparative and superlative.

تفضية *tafḍiya-t*, emptying, II. (فضى).

تفطينة *tafṭîna-t*, memorandum-book.

تففة *tifafa-t*, pl. of تف *tuff*.

تفقد *tafaqqud*, INF. V. of (فقد); inquiries after an absent person.

تفقع *tafaqqu'*, bursting (n.).

تفقئة *tafqi'a-t*, INF. II. of (فقا); (m.) peeling.

(تفل) *tafal*, U, I, INF. *tafl*, spit out; — *tafil*, A, INF. *tafal*, smell badly; — IV. INF. *itfâl*, cause to smell badly.

تفل *tafal*, bad smell, stench; — *tafil*, ة, having a foul breath; — *tufl*, thin spittle; saliva; foam; — *tuffal*, fox; whelp of a fox; — ة *tafala-t*, foul breath.

تفلدان *tufldân*, spittoon.

تفليح *taflîḥ*, INF. II. of (فلح); agriculture.

تفلية *tafliya-t*, hunting for lice or fleas.

تفن *tafan*, dirt.

تفنك *tufank*, ة *tufanka-t*, gun, musket (Pers.).

تفنكجى *tufankji*, pl. *tufankjiyya-t*, musketeer.

تفنين *tafnîn*, INF. II. of (فن); invention; inequality in the thread of cloth; mixture.

(تفه) *tafih*, A, INF. *tafâh*, *tufûh*, be in small number or quantity and worthless; — INF. *tufûh*, grow stupid, become a fool; — *tafih*, *tafah*, INF. *tafh*, *tufûh*, emaciate (n.), grow thin, decrease; — INF. *tafh*, be insipid, tasteless.

تفه *tafih*, ة, tasteless, insipid; — *tufah*, lynx.

تفوت *tafawwut*, INF. V. of (فوت); exceeding; going beyond.

تفوف *tufûf*, pl. of تف *tuff*, impure matter between the teeth.

تفوق *tafawwuq*, INF. V. of (فوق); superiority; pre-eminence.

تفول *tafa''ul*, *tafawwul*, prediction, V. (فال).

تفون *tafawwun*, abundance, profusion.

تفويف *tafwîf*, printing on stuffs; striping white.

تفيد *tafayyud*, INF. V. of (فيد); advantage, profit.

تفيئة *tafyi'a-t*, proper time; immediately after; casting a shadow, shadow; II. (فى).

تفئيل *taf'îl*, prediction, II. (فال.

تقا *tiqâ'*, fear; — ة *taqâ-t*, piety; fear of God.

تقاتل *taqâtul*, INF. VI. of (قتل); fight, combat; murder.

تقادم *taqâdim*, pl. of تقدمة *taqdima-t*.
تقادير *taqâdîr*, pl. of تقدير *taqdîr*.
تقار *taqârr*, standing firm, VI. (قر).
تقارش *taqâruś*, dint of battle.
تقارير *taqârîr*, pl. of تقرير *taqrîr*.
تقازيح *taqâzîḥ*, spices; herbs for seasoning.
تقاص *taqâṣṣ*, mutual requital or assistance, VI. (قص).
تقاصير *taqâṣîr*, pl. of تقصار *taqṣâr* and تقصير *taqṣîr*.
تقاضا *taqâḍâ*, تقاضى *taqâḍî*, money claim, dunning, pressing for payment; want, need; VI. (قضى).
تقاطع *taqâṭu'*, intersection; VI. (قطع).
تقاطيع *taqâṭî'*, pl. of تقطيع *taqṭî'*.
تقاعد *taqâ'ud*, INF. VI. of (قعد); retirement from active service with a pension.
تقاليب *taqâlîb*, pl. of تقليب *taqlîb*.
تقاليد *taqâlîd*, pl. of تقليد *taqlîd*.
تقامر *taqâmur*, INF. VI. of (قمر); game of chance; bet.
تقانة *taqâna-t*, completion.
تقاود *taqâwud*, guidance.
تقاوه *taqâwuh*, INF. VI. of (قوه); watchword; parole.
تقاوة *taqâwa-t*, piety.
تقاوى *taqâwî*, INF. VI. of (قوى); advance for seed to a farmer.
تقاويم *taqâwîm*, pl. of تقويم *taqwîm*.
تقايى *taqâyî*, vomiting, VI. (قيا)
تقتال *taqtâl*, killing; murder.
تقتيت *taqtît*, INF. II. of (قت); talebearing; slander.
تقتير *taqtîr*, INF. II. of (قتر); avarice; niggardliness.
تقدم *taqaddum*, INF. VI. of (قدم); pl. *-ât*, pre-eminence; priority; premise; — ة *taqdima-t*, pl. *taqâdim*, present; dedication; premise, proposition of a syllogism; lieutenancy.
تقدة *taqda-t*, *tiqda-t*, coriander; cumin.
تقدير *taqdîr*, INF. II. of (قدر); pl. *-ât*, *taqâdîr*, predestination, fate; hypothesis, case; measuring; evaluation; virtual (implicit) meaning;—ى *taqdîriyy*, virtual, implicit; decreed by fate; supposed.
(تقر) *taqir*, spice; herb for seasoning; greens; — ة *taqira-t*, cumin; — *taqirra-t*=تقرار *taqrâr*.
تقرار *taqrâr*, firmness.
(تقرد) *tiqrid*, greens; cumin.
تقرو *taqarru'*, study of the Holy Scriptures; intelligence; V. (قرا).
تقريب *taqrîb*, INF. II. of (قرب); present; approximation; probability; pretext; — *taqrîb-an*, *bi-'t-taqrîb*, approximately; — ى *taqrîbiyy*, approximate; presumable, probable.
تقرير *taqrîr*, INF. II. of (قر); pl. *taqârîr*, official report; diploma; notice, memorandum; narrative; pleasure; — ى *taqrîriyy*, justificative; vouching.
تقريض *taqrîḍ*, INF. II. of (قرض); approbatory criticism.
تقريظ *taqrîẓ*, eulogy on a living person, II. (قرظ).
تقسيم *taqsîm*, INF. II. of (قسم); division; land census; land-tax-roll; conjuration;—ى *taqsîmiyy*, land-tax.
تقشيب *taqśîb*, INF. II. of (قشب); scratch on the skin.
تقشيط *taqśîṭ*, robbing (m.).
تقصار *tiqṣâr*, ة *tiqṣâra-t*, pl. *taqâṣîr*, a short collar.
تقصبة *taqṣiba-t*, تقصيبة *taqṣîba-t*, pl. *-ât*, plaited lock of hair.
تقصير *taqṣîr*, INF. II. of (قصر); pl. *taqâṣîr*, abbreviation; defect, fault; negligence, neglect; stigma; pl. *-ât*, faults.
تقصية *taqṣiya-t*, paring the nails; cropping the ears.
تقضية *taqḍiya-t*, INF. II. of (قضى); decree of God; sufficiency.
تقطير *taqṭîr*, INF. II. of (قطر); diabetes; gonorrhœa.
تقطيع *taqṭî'*, INF. II. of (قطع); pl. *taqâṭî'*, draft; stature; feature; colic; cesura of a verse.

تقطيف *taqṭîf*, sifting of flour; gathering grapes.

(تقع) *taqa'*, hunger;—*taqi'*, violent hunger.

تقفى *taqaffî*, rhyming (m.).

تقليب *taqlîb*, INF. II. of (قلب); pl. *taqâlîb*, rotations, revolutions.

تقليد *taqlîd*, INF. II. of (قلد); pl. *taqâlîd*, *taqâlîdât*, imitation; spectacle, theatrical representation; investiture, diploma of such; *at-taqlîdât*, oral traditions (m.);— ى *taqlîdiyy*, imitated.

تقليل *taqlîl*, INF. II. of (قل); scarceness.

تقمقم *taqamqum*, murmuring.

(تقن) *tiqn*, ة *tiqna-t*, nature, natural disposition;—*tiqn*, skilful; mire; — hence II. *taqqan*, INF. *tatqîn*, irrigate with miry water; — II. and IV. INF. *itqân*, arrange skilfully; build solidly; make fast, fortify; improve.

تقنو *taqannu'*, V. تقنئة *taqni'a-t*, II. of (قنا); crimson; colouring red; dying the beard.

تقوا *taqwâ*, piety, fear of God; — *tuqawâ'*, pl. of تقى *taqiyy*.

تقواد *taqwâd*, leading, driving.

تقوالة *tiqwâla-t*, talkative.

تقوح *taqawwuḥ*, suppuration.

تقولة *tiqwila-t*, talkative.

تقوى *taqwa*, piety; fear of God; abstemiousness; — ة *taqwiya-t*, strengthening; encouraging.

تقى *taqa*, for اتقى *ittaqa*, VIII. of (وقى), INF. تقى *tuq-an*, *tiqâ'*, *taqiyya-t*, fear, fear God; — *taqiyy*, pl. *tuqawâ'*, *atqiyâ'*, pious, God-fearing; — ة *taqiyya-t*, piety; fear; caution, prudence.

تقييف *taqyîf*, INF. II. of (قيف); criticism; (m.) libel.

تقيو *taqayyu'*, تقيى *taqayyî*, vomiting.

تقييح *taqyîḥ*, making purulent; II. (قيح).

تقييد *taqyîd*, INF. II. of (قيد); تقييد عقلى *taqyîd 'aqliyy*, mental reservation.

تقيئة *taqyi'a-t*, causing to vomit, II. (قيا).

(تك) *takk*, I, INF. *tukûk*, be stupid, absent-minded; — U, INF. *takk*, *takka-t*, cut; tread under the feet, crush by stamping; inebriate; — X. INF. *istitkâk*, tie up the trowsers with the *tikka-t*; — ة *tikka-t*, pl. *tikak*, string for tying up the trowsers, belt.

(تكا), IV. INF. *itkâ'*, cause to lean upon; throw down; pierce with the sword; — VIII. INF. *ittikâ'*, lean upon or against (على *'ala*); — ة *tuka'a-t*, support, back of a chair, &c.; cushion; stick; one-sided.

تكاتع *takâtu'*, INF. VI. of (كتع); consequence.

تكاثر *takâsur*, INF. VI. of (كثر); frequency; *bi-'t-takâsur*, frequently.

تكارى *takârî*, hiring, renting, farming.

تكافو *takâfu'*, equality, VI. (كفا).

تكاك *takâk*, pl. of تاك *tâkk*, stupid, foolish, &c.

تكاكرة *takâkira-t*, pl. of تكرى *takkarî*.

تكاك *takkâk*, maker of the string تكة *tikka-t*.

تكاليف *takâlîf*, pl. of تكليف *taklîf*.

تكايا *takâyâ*, pl. of تكية *takya-t*.

تكبرانية *takbirâniyya-t*, summit of greatness, or glory.

تكبير *takbîr*, INF. II. of (كبر); praise; pronouncing the words الله اكبر *allâh akbar*; magnifying word.

(تكتك) *taktak*, INF. ة=(تك).

تكتم *tuktam*, the well Zemzem.

تكدر *takaddur*, INF V. of (كدر); dregs, sediment.

تكدير *takdîr*, INF. II. of (كدر); blame, reproach.

تكذاب *tikizzâb*, liar.

تكرار *takrâr*, repetition; tautology; objection; dispute, quarrel; purification; refining.

تكرمة *takrima-t*, cushion of honour.

تكرى *takkariyy*, *tukkariyy*, pl. *takâ-*

kira-t, leader, general;—*takarrî*, sleeping, sleep, v. (كرو).

تكرير *takrîr*, INF. II. of (كر); revision; reply.

تكريس *takrîs*, INF. II. of (كرس); pl. *takrîsât*, dedication.

تكريشة *takrîśa-t*, surfeited stomach; sausage.

تكريم *takrîm*, INF. II. of (كرم); pl. *-ât*, honour, cushion of honour.

تكسير *taksîr*, INF. II. of (كسر); fraction (of numbers); approximate measuring; جمع التـ *jam-'u-'t-taksîr-i*, broken plural.

(تكش) *tikś*, old hawk.

تكشيف *takśîf*, INF. of (كشف); uncovering, &c.; apocalypse.

تكعب *taka''ub*, cubic form, cube.

تكعيبة *tak'îba-t*, trellis-work (m.).

تكفور *takfûr*, Greek Emperor.

تكفير *takfîr*, INF. II. of (كفر); covering, &c.; atonement.

تكك *tikak*, pl. of تكة *tikka-t*;— *takak*, *takaka-t*, pl. of تاك *tâkk*, foolish, &c.

(تكل) *takil*, A, *takul*, INF. *tuklân*, from اتكل *ittakal*, VIII. (وكل), rely upon (على *'ala*);—X. INF. *istitkâl*, consider skilful, reliable;— ة *tukla-t*, trust in God; — *takala-t*, who relies or is obliged to rely on others; (m.) trustworthy; skilful, experienced, proved.

تكلام *taklâm*, *taklâmm* and ة, eloquent, talkative; — *tikillâm*, conversation.

تكلان *takalân*, who relies upon others;—*tuklân*, trust in God.

تكلف *takalluf*, INF. V. of (كلف); taking trouble, &c.; expenditure; ceremonies, compliments; affectation;— ة *taklifa-t*, toilsome work.

تكلم *takallum*, INF. V. of (كلم); talking, &c.; speech, language; word.

تكليف *taklîf*, INF. II. of (كلف); imposing trouble, &c.; pl. *takâlîf*, trouble, vexation; (m.) imposts, taxes; proposal, motion; ceremonies, compliments.

تكنبش *takambuś*, motley crowd.

تكنى *takannî* v. تكنية, II. of (كنو); giving a nickname; using metaphoric language.

تكوين *takwîn*, INF. II. of (كون); causing to be, &c.; book of Genesis.

تكوية *takwiya-t*, cauterisation; (m.) ironing of linen, II. (كوى).

تكى *takkiyy*, maker of the string تكة *tikka-t*; — ة *takya-t*, pl. *takâyâ*, asylum; convent (Pers.).

(تل) *tall*, U, INF. *tall*, throw one down on his neck, cheek or forehead; throw into difficulties; throw or push a thing into one's hand; — U, I, humble one's self, fawn; fall down; pour out; drop with perspiration; let down; (m.) take by the hand; lead a beast of burden;—III. INF. *mutâlla-t*, seek a stallion to cover one's mare; — IV. INF. *itlâl*, render fluid; tie up and lead a horse.

تل *tall*, pl. *tilâl*, *tulûl*, small hill; sand-hill; pl. *atlâl*, pillow; a garment; — ة *talla-t*, drinking-vessel of palm-leaves;—*tilla-t*, laziness; reclining posture; state, condition; humidity.

تلا *talâ*, see (تلو); — *talâ'*, compact; protection; share, lot;—*tallâ*, (public) reader of the Koran.

تلابيبة *tula'bîba-t*, well-managed business.

تلات *talât*, (m.) for ثلاث *s̱alâs̱*, three.

تلاتف *talâtuf*, تلاتوف *talâtûf*, dirty, squalid; sordid; detested; tumult, quarrel.

تلاتل *talâtil*, pl. of تلتل *taltal* and تليل *talîl*;—*tulâtil*, strong and fat.

تلاتين *talâtîn*, (m.) for ثلاثين *s̱alâs̱în*, thirty; Russian leather (Turk.).

تلاحق *talâḥuq*, following successively, succession.

تلاد *tilâd*, hereditary property, heirloom; — ى *tilâdiyy*, hereditary, inherited, domestic.

تلاشى *talâšî*, INF. VI. of (لشو); getting destroyed, &c.; utter perplexity, bewilderment.

تلاع *tilâ'*, pl. of تلعة *tal'a-t*; — ة *talâ'a-t*, length of the neck.

تلاف *tallâf*, who spoils everything; bungler; — ى *talâfî*, recovering from a loss; amendment, VI. (لفى).

تلافيف *talâfîf*, densely-grown grass.

تلاق *talâq-in*, تلاقى *talâqî*, INF. VI. of (لقى), meeting; يوم التلاقى *yaumu-'t-talâqî*, Day of Judgment.

تلالة *talâla-t*, error.

تلالو *talâlu'*, glimmering, flashing, II. (لالا).

تلاليس *talâlîs*, pl. of تليس *tillîs*.

تلامذة *talâmiza-t*, تلاميذ *talâmîz*, pupils, disciples, pl. of تلميذ *tilmîz*.

تلاميح *talâmîḥ*, pl. of تلميح *talmîḥ*.

تلاميع *talâmî'*, pl. of تلميع *talmî'*.

تلان *talân*, now, at present.

تلاهى *talâhî*, sporting, toying, amusement.

تلاوة *tilâwa-t*, reading, rehearsal, praying; lecture; recital, INF. of (تلو); — *tulâwa-t*, balance (of an account); rest.

تلاوى *talâwî*, consent, agreement.

(تلب) *talab*, damage, loss; — hence *itla'abb*, INF. *itli'bâb*, be well managed (business); be (placed) upright; be straight and level (road); lift up the neck and head.

تلبيس *talbîs*, INF. II. of (لبس); decking, dressing, &c.; mixture; lie, deceit; impostor, knave; investiture; incognito.

تلبينة *talbîna-t*, soup of bran, milk and honey.

(تلتل) *taltal*, INF. ة, move, shake (a. and n.); walk fast and with violent movements; urge on with violence.

تلتل *taltal*, hard trot; pl. *talâtil*, harshness; calamity; drinking-vessel of palm-leaves.

تلج *tulaj*, eaglet.

(تلج), IV. *atlaj*, INF. *itlâj*, cause to enter, put into, insert.

تلجئة *talji'a-t*, compulsion; violence, II. (لجا).

تلحين *talḥîn*, INF. II. of (لحن); pronouncing badly, modulating, &c.; psalmody.

تلخيص *talḫîṣ*, INF. II. of (لخص), cleaning, extracting the purest part, &c.; quintessence; abstract, report of a minister; publication; explanation.

(تلد) *talad*, U, I, INF. *tulûd*, be inherited, hereditary; — U, INF. *tulûd*, also *talid*, A, INF. *talad*, remain, to stay in a place (new comer); — II. INF. *tatlîd*, grasp with avidity and prevent others getting; — IV. INF. *itlâd*, possess or succeed to hereditary property; accumulate property to the inherited one.

تلد *talad*, born in a foreign country but brought as a child to Muslims; — *talad*, *tald*, *tuld*, born in the house; hereditary property; — *tuld*, eaglet.

تلداغ *taldâg*, stinging, sting, II. (لدغ).

تلسى *tulsiyy*, sweet basil.

تلطط *talaṭṭuṭ*, denying a debt, V. (لط).

تلطع *tilṭi'*, toothless (camel).

(تلع) *tala'*, A, INF. *tal'*, rise; spread; stretch forth the head; — *tali'*, A, INF. *tala'*, be full; — *tali'*, *talu'*, INF. *tala'*, be long, have a long neck; — IV. INF. *itlâ'*, stretch forth the head; stretch the neck; — VI. INF. *tatâlu'*, stretch the neck and raise the head in walking.

تلع *tal'*, hill; — *tala'*, length of the neck; — *tali'*, who looks much about or round; full; — ة *tal'a-t* pl. *tilâ'*, *tala'ât*, mountain-slope with currents; torrent; river-

head; سيل تلعتى *sail-u tal'atî*, my own relations; (m.) hill, glebe.

تلعاب *tal'âb*, play; *tal'âb*, *til'âb*, *tili''âb*, ة *tili''âba-t*, too much given to playing and sporting.

تلعوس *talau'us*, chewing.

تلعيب *til'ib*, ة = تلعاب *tal'âb*, ة.

(تلف) *talif*, A, INF. *talaf*, perish; — IV. INF. *itlâf*, ruin, make disappear; render destructive or recognise anything to be so; — VII. INF. *intilâf*, perish.

تلف *talaf*, ruin, perdition; loss; dissipation; *talaf-an*, unavenged (blood); — *talif*, perishing.

تلفاق *tilfâq*, two pieces of cloth or dresses sewn together.

تلفان *talfân*, on the point of dying; worn out by use.

تلفظ *talaffuz*, pronunciation, v. (لفظ).

تلفيت *talfît*, turning one's head towards another, II. (لفت).

تلفيظ *talfîz*, pronouncing, II. (لفظ).

تلفيق *talfîq*, INF. II. of (لفق), sewing together, &c.; fabrication, falsification; (m.) medley, ragout; calumny; — ة *talfîqa-t*, collection; miscellany (tales, sayings, &c.).

تلقا *tilqâ'*, meeting, encounter; side; vis-à-vis; on the part of; towards.

تلقاع *tiliqqâ'*, ة *tiliqqâ'a-t*, talker.

تلقام *tilqâm*, ة *tilqâma-t*, who swallows large morsels.

تلقين *talqîn*, INF. II. of (لقن), instructing, &c.; addressing the dead; (m.) insinuation, innuendo, tale-bearing, goading up against; dictation.

تلك *tilka*, f. of ذالك *zâlik*, that one.

تلل *talal*, humidity; — *tulul*, pl. of تليل *talîl*.

تلم *talam*, pl. *atlâm*, furrow; cleft; — hence II. *tallam*, INF. *tatlîm*, furrow; — *tilm*, pl. *tilâm*, lad, youth, servant; ploughman; goldsmith; windpipe; bellows.

تلماح *talmâḥ*, flashing, shining, II. (لمح).

تلماظ *tilimmâz*, fickle; f. ة; talkative; a boisterous woman.

(تلمذ) *talmaz*, INF. ة, be a pupil to (ل *li*); (m.) teach; have for a pupil; — II. INF. *tatalmuz*, be a pupil, disciple.

تلميح *talmîḥ*, INF. II. of (لمح), speaking obscurely; allusion; pl. *talâmîḥ*, features which remind of the father.

تلميذ *tilmîz*, pl. *talâmîz*, *talâmiza-t*, *talâm-in*, *talâmî*, pupil, disciple; student; (m.) confessor (who goes to confession).

تلميع *talmî'*, INF. II. of (لمع), glittering, &c.; pl. *talâmî'*, glitter of arms, flashing of swords; bright stripes.

تلنة *talunna-t*, *tulunna-t*, delay; necessaries.

(تله) *talih*, A. INF. *talah*, perish; be sad, perplexed; forget.

تله *talah*, ruin, perdition; confusion, perplexity.

تلهية *talhiya-t*, diversion, unbending the mind, amusement; toy.

(تلو) *talâ*, U, *tala*, I, INF. *tuluww*, follow, walk behind another; abandon, leave in the lurch; despise; — INF. *tilâwa-t*, read; recite; meditate; — INF. *talw*, buy (the foal of) a mule; — *talî*, A, INF. تلى *til-an*, remain, rest; — II. INF. *tatliya-t*, follow; press for payment, dun; follow up the prayers prescribed by others; redeem one's vow; lie in agony; — III. INF. *mutâlât*, follow; accompany (in music); — IV. INF. *itlâ'*, cause one to follow another; press by the bailiff for payment; overtake; entrust with (على *'ala*), commission; leave the remainder of a debt outstanding; give, bestow on; grant protection; hand an arrow as a sign of protection;

be followed by her foals (camel, &c.); — v. INF. *tatallî*, follow unceasingly; press by the bailiff; — VI. INF. *tatâlî*, follow each other in uninterrupted succession; — X. INF. *istitlâ'*, desire one to follow, to espouse a cause; lead; continue.

تلو *tilw*, pl. *atlâ'*, following (adj.); ة *tilwa-t*, foal; summer-lambs; a goat above four months old; trace; sublime, noble;—*talaww*, who follows continually; — *tuluww*, INF. of (تلو); — ة *tilwa-t*, remainder of a debt.

تلواذ *talwâz*, seeking refuge.

تلوط *talawwuṭ*, sodomy.

تلوع *tulû'*, day-break.

تلول *talûl*, lazy, restive (camel).

تلون *tulûn*, ة *tulûna-t*, delay; necessaries.

تلوه *talawwuh*, glitter, glimmer.

تلوى *talawwa*, small ship;—*talawwî*, INF. V. of (لوى), getting twisted, &c.; — ة *talwiya-t*, bending, folding, II. (لوى).

تلويج *talwîj*, INF. II. of (لوج), turning aside, &c.; bend of the road.

تلويح *talwîḥ*, pl. *talâwîḥ*, INF. II. of (لوح), causing to flash, &c.; metonymy; pl. fruit which begins to ripen.

تلى *tala*, remainder of the month; — *tily*, who swears much; rich; — *talla*, pl. of تليل *talîl*; — *tulla*, slaughtered sheep; — ة *taliyya-t*, remainder of a debt; remainder, rest.

تليد *talîd*=تلد *talad*, hereditary, &c.

(تليس) *tillîs*, ة *tillîsa-t*, pl. *talâlîs*, testicle; little basket made of leaves.

تليع *talî'*, long-necked; long, tall.

تليفة *talîfa-t*, anything lost or spoiled.

تليل *talîl*, pl. *talla*, thrown down, prostrate; pl. *atilla-t*, *tulul*, *talâtil*, neck.

(تم) *tamm*, I, INF. *tamm*, *timm*, *tumm*, *tamâm*, *timâm*, *tumâm*, *tamâma-t*, *timâma-t*, be complete, whole, perfect; complete, finish (ب *bi* or على *'ala*); go to (الى *ila*); — II. INF. *tatmîm*, *tatimma-t*, improve, make perfect; be complete; finish off (a wounded man); annihilate, ruin; give to anyone his gain in the game of arrows; belong to or side with the tribe of Tamîm; suspend a talisman round one's neck; — III. INF. *mutâmamat*, vie with another in completing a thing; — IV. INF. *itmâm*, complete, finish; improve, make perfect; be on the point of giving birth; be in full growth; be full (moon); obtain one's wish; give the axe تم *timm* to anyone; go to; — V. INF. *tatammum*, be complete (fracture); walk with a broken leg until the fracture is complete; — VI. INF. *tatâmm*, come in full numbers, reach the full number; — X. INF. *istitmâm*, wish for, demand or bring about the completion of a thing; ask for anything necessary to the completion of a work; ask for the axe تم *timm*.

تم *tamm*, *timm*, *tumm*, completion; end, finish; a kind of goose; لتم *li-timm-in*, mature; — *timm*, axe, hatchet; anything complete; — *tumm*, mouth (m.); — ة *tamma-t*, talisman of camel-hair; — *timma-t*, *tumma-t*, pl. *tumam*, the same; — *tumma-t*, gift, present.

تماتين *tamâtîn*, pl. of تمتان *timtân*.

تماثيل *tamâsîl*, pl. of تمثال *timsâl*.

تمار *tammâr*, seller of dates.

تماريد *tamârîd*, pl. of تمراد *timrâd*.

تماسى *tamâsî*, INF. VI. of (مسى), being cut; gangrene.

تماسيح *tamâsîḥ*, pl. of تمساح *timsâḥ*.

تماشا *tamâšâ*, pleasure-walk, promenade; sight, spectacle; amusement.

تمام *tamâm*, *timâm*, completed;

perfect; whole, entire; full (moon); completion, end; — *tammâm*, troop, crowd; — ة *tamâma-t*, completion; end; — *tumâma-t*, remainder, rest; — ى *tamâmî*, complete, entire; حساب تمامى و تفاضلى *ḥisâb tamâmî wa tafâḍulî*, integral and differential calculus;—*timâmiyy*, the longest (night).

تمائم *tamâ'im*, pl. of تميمة *tamîma-t*.

تمتام *tamtâm*, stammerer; — ة *tamtâma-t*, stammering.

تمتان *timtân*, pl. *tamâtîn*, tent-rope.

(تمتم) *tamtam*, INF. ة, pronounce badly the ت and م; speak with an impediment.

تمته *tamattuh*, error; v. (مته).

تمتين *tamtîn*, pl. *tamâtîn*, tent-rope.

تمثال *tamṣâl*, comparison, resemblance; — *timṣâl*, pl. *tamâṣîl*, resemblance; image, likeness, portrait.

تمثيل *tamṣîl*, INF. II. of (مثل), representing by an image, &c.; making an example of; pl. *-ât*, example; allegory.

تمجيد *tamjîd*, INF. II. of (مجد), praising, &c.; eulogy; hymn.

تمحية *tamḥiya-t*, erasing, blotting out.

تمدن *tamaddun*, INF. V. of (مدن), uniting in civic society, &c.; polite manners; civilisation, refinement.

تمر *tamr*, ة, pl. *tumûr*, *tumrân*, full ripe date; تمر هندى *tamr hindiyy*, tamarind; — hence: *tamar*, U, INF. *tamr*, feed with dates; — II. INF. *tatmîr*, enter the last stage of ripening; bear ripe or ripening dates; feed with dates; dry, make dry (fruit); mince and dry meat; — IV. INF. *itmâr*, abound in dates; enter the last stage of ripening; bear dates; feed with dates; — ة *tamara-t*, knot in a whip.

تمراد *timrâd*, pl. *tamârîd*, dove-cot; bird's-nest; — *tamrâd*, INF II. of (مرد), building high.

تمران *tumrân*, pl. of تمر *tamr*.

تمردى *tamarrudiyy*, refractory, rebellious.

(تمرز) *tumariz*, *tummariz*, dwarfish.

تمرض *tammarruḍ*, weakness, insufficiency.

تمرى *tamriyy*, fond of dates.

تمريش *tamriś*, a little rain.

تمريغ *tamrîg*, INF. II. of (مرغ); anointing, smearing.

تمزية *tamziya-t*, high praise, eulogy; II. (مزى).

تمساح *timsâḥ* (تمسح *timsaḥ*), pl. *tamâsîḥ*, crocodile; liar; malicious; — *tamsâḥ*, lie.

تمسخر *tamasḫur*, jest; masquerade.

تمسك *tamassuk*, INF. V. of (مسك), seizing, &c.; attachment; pl. *-ât*, written obligation; note of hand, bond, bonus; receipt.

تمسيحا *tamsîḥâ*, a prayer.

تمسية *tamsiya-t*, wishing good evening, II. (مسو).

(تمش) *tamaś*, U, INF. *tamś*, gather, assemble.

تمشا *timśâ'*, walk, gait; step.

تمشك *tumśak*, sandal of Bagdad.

تمشيق *tamśîq*, dying red.

تمشية *tamśiya-t*, causing to walk; putting into motion; purging; giving the preference; II. (مشى).

تمطى *tamaṭṭî*, stretching one's self and yawning, II. (مطو).

تمقيت *tamqît*, hatred.

(تمك) *tamak*, U, I, INF. *tamk*, *tumûk*, be long and high, juicy and firm (hump of a camel); — IV. INF. *itmâk*, fatten.

تمكن *tamakkun*, INF. V. of (مكن), having authority and influence, &c.; power, wealth; taking up an abode; settling in a place.

تمكين *tamkîn*, INF. II. of (مكن), giving authority, &c.; making

possible; investiture; declension.

تملاق *tamlâq*, *timillâq*, declaration of love, caressing, fondling.

تملان *timlân*, pl. of تملية *tamliya-t*.

تملق *tamalluq*, blandishment, flattery, v. of (ملق).

تملو *tamallu'*, being full, II. (ملا).

تملوك *tumlûk*, wild olive.

تمليكى *tamlîkiyy*, one's own, hereditary; — ة *tamlîkiyya-t*, right of property, of inheritance.

تملية *tamliya-t*, pl. *timlân*, long life, II. (ملو);—*tamli'a-t*, filling; fetching water, II. (ملا).

تمم *tamam*, perfect, complete; — *tumam*, *timam*, pl. of تمة *timma-t*, تمى *tumma*.

تمنا *tamannâ*, wish, desire; saluting by kissing one's fingers and placing them on the forehead.

تمنى *tamannî*, pl. *-ât*, wish; request, petition, v. (منى).

(تمه) *tamih*, A, INF. *tamah*, *tamâha-t*, deteriorate in taste and smell; smell badly, be rancid.

(تمهل) *itmahall*, INF. *itmihlâl*, be long, hard, straight and strong.

تمهيد *tamhîd*, INF. II. of (مهد), spreading out, &c.; removing difficulties; laying a broad, sound foundation.

تمهير *tamhîr*, INF. II. of (مهر), demanding or taking a dowry, &c.; — sealing, from Pers. مهر *muhr*, seal.

تمهيك *tamhîk*, reducing to powder.

تمور *tamawwur*, INF. V. of (مور), oscillating, &c.; — *tumûr*, pl. of تمر *tamr*.

تموز *tamûz*, month of July.

تمون *tamawwun*, domestic expenditure, taking in provisions, v. (مون).

تمويل *tamwîl*, enriching, II. (مول).

تمى *tumma*=تمة *timma-t*, *tumma-t*.

تميلة *tumaila-t*, pl. *-ât*, *timlân*, a kind of cat.

تميم *tamîm*, perfect, complete; name of a tribe; — ة *tamîma-t*, pl. *tamîm*, *tamâ'im*, talisman, amulet; — ى *tumîmiyy*, belonging to the tribe Tamîm.

تمييت *tamyît*, killing, murder.

تمييز *tamyîz*, INF. II. of (ميز), separating, discerning; discrimination, discernment, judgment, discretion.

(تن) *tinn*, pl. *atnân*, equal, similar; one's equal, companion, comrade; — hence III. INF. متانة *mutânna-t*, compare; — IV. *itnân*, be far, absent; weaken and prevent from growing.

تن *tunn*, ة, tunny-fish; — ة *tina-t*, endurance; continual flow; INF. of (وتن).

(تنا) *tana'*, A, INF. *tunû'*, stay, dwell, inhabit (ب *bi*, فى *fî*).

تنا *tunnâ'*, peasants, countrymen, pl. of تانى *tânî'*; — ة *tinâ'a-t*, dwelling, living in a place, fixed residence.

تنابيل *tanâbîl*, pl. of تنبال *timbâl*, تنبول *tambûl*.

تنادى *tanâdî*, INF. VI. of (ندو), calling to each other, &c.; يوم التنادى *yaumu-'t-tanâdî*, Day of Judgment.

تناديد *tanâdîd*, pl. stray birds; stray fugitives.

تنار *tannâr*, maker of stoves, &c.

تناسب *tanâsub*, INF. V. of (نسب), claiming relationship; symmetry; gracefulness of proportion; conformity.

تناسخ *tanâsuḥ*, ية *tanâsuḥiyya-t*, metempsychosis; — *tanâsuḥiyy*, believer in such.

تناسل *tanâsul*, begetting, generation; descent, VI. (نسل).

تناسى *tanâsî*, real or pretended forgetfulness, VI. (نسى).

تناشير *tanâšîr*, exercises in calligraphy.

تناصيب *tanâṣîb*, mile-stones, stones to mark out the road.

تناعس *tana'us*, drowsiness; pretending to be asleep, VI. (نعس).

تنافيج *tanâfîj*, pl. wedge-like pieces inserted in a dress.

تناقيص *tanâqîṣ*, pl. defects, shortcomings.

تناكح *tanâkuḥ*, intermarriage, VI. (نكح).

تنانير *tanânîr*, pl. of تنور *tannûr*.

تنانين *tanânîn*, pl. of تنين *tinnîn*.

تناهى *tanâhî*, INF. VI. of (نهى), arriving, &c.; — pl. of تنهية *tanhiya-t*.

تناوب *tanâwub*, doing alternately, VI. (نوب).

تناول *tanâwul*, INF. VI. of (نول), taking, seizing, &c.; Holy Communion.

تناوة *tinâwa-t*, تناية *tinâya-t*, neglect of study and discussion (between scholars).

تناويح *tanâwîḥ*, pl. of تنويح *tanwîḥ*.

تنائف *tanâ'if*, pl. of تنوفة *tanûfa-t*.

تنبال *timbâl*, pl. *tanâbîl*, *tanâbila-t*, dwarf;—ة *timbâla-t*, id.; dwarfish figure.

تنبج *tanabbuj*, swelling of a bone.

تنبك *tumbak*, tobacco (Pers.).

تنبل *timbal*=تنبال *timbâl*; (m.) pl. *tanâbil*, weak, soft; lazy; idler; — *tanabbul*, INF. V. of (نبل), excelling by birth, skill, &c.

تنبو *tanabbu'*, office of a prophet, V. (نبا).

تنبور *tambûr*, small; dwarf.

تنبول *tumbûl*, pl. *tanâbîl*, dwarf.

تنبيت *tambît*, INF. II. of (نبت), causing to grow, &c.; *tambît*, *timbît*, anything sprouting; (m.) trees, bushes, shrubs; projection of a sill, of ornaments; stitches of a seam.

تنبئة *tambi'a-t*, prophesying, prophecy, II. (نبا).

تنبيه *tambîh*, INF. II. of (نبه), awakening, &c.; pl. *-ât*, admonition; aviso; decree, edict; notice.

تنتاش *tantâś*, calumny.

تنتالة *tintâla-t*, تنتل *tintal*, dwarf.

تنتن *tantan*, INF. ة, leave one's friends for other people's company.

تنتيل *tantîl*, dwarfish, dwarf.

تنجرة *tanjara-t*=طنجرة *ṭanjara-t*, frying-pan; kettle; pot.

تنجى *tanajji*, INF. V. of (نجو), saving one's self, escaping; salvation, eternal bliss; — ة *tanjiya-t*, rescue, deliverance, II. (نجو); city of Tangier.

تنجيس *tanjîs*, INF. II. of (نجس), polluting, &c.; amulet against the evil eye.

تنحيت *tanḥît*, planing; cutting the hoof.

(تنخ) *tanaḫ*, U, INF. *tunûḫ*, stay, dwell; — *taniḫ*, A, INF. *tanaḫ*, suffer from indigestion; — II. INF. *tatnîḫ*, stay, remain, abide (ب *bi*); — III. INF. *mutânaḫa-t*, make a stand in battle; — IV. INF. *itnâḫ*, cause indigestion; — V. INF. *tatannuḫ*, stay, abide (ب *bi*).

تنخذ *tanaḫḫuẕ*, command of a ship, captainship.

تنخير *tanḫîr*, speech.

تنزه *tanazzuh*, INF. V. of (نزه), being far from water and pasture-ground, &c.; purity, chastity; elevation of the mind; recreation; amusement; walk in the open air; entertainment.

تنزيل *tanzîl*, INF. II. of (نزل), sending down, &c., revelation; Koran; hospitable reception; diminishing, subtracting; humiliation; deposition: insertion.

تنساس *tansâs*, swiftness.

تنسم *tanassum*, pleasant breeze.

تنسيب *tansîb*, praise, approval.

تنسيق *tansîq*, INF. II. of (نسق), arranging in good order, &c.; pl. *-ât*, ordinance, regulation.

تنشق *tanaśśuq*, snuffing, II. (نشق).

تنشئة *tanśi'at*, bringing up, education, II. (نشا).

تنضاح *tanḍâḥ*, exuding, perspiration; dew.

تنظار *tanẓâr*, perceiving, INF. of (نظر).

تنظيم *tanẓîm*, INF. II. of (نظم),

putting in order, &c.; ordinance, regulation.

تنعيم *tan'im*, INF. II. of (نعم), procuring a happy life, &c.; pampering, effeminating.

تنفر *tanaffur*, abhorrence, detestation.

تنفس *tanaffus*, INF. V. of (نفس); breathing, sighing, &c.; recreation.

تنفيذ *tanfîz*, transmission; execution; enforcing.

تنفيس *tanfîs*, cheering, refreshing, consoling; حرف الت *ḥarfu-'t-tanfîs-i*, particle of wishing.

تنقاد *tanqâd*, separating, sifting.

تنقاص *tanqâṣ*, diminishing, damaging, injuring.

تنقام *tiniqqâm*, vengeance, punishment.

تنقص *tanaqquṣ*, diminution; injury, damage, V. (نقص).

تنقيب *tanqîb*, INF. II. of (نقب), examining, &c.; criticism; mining.

تنقيح *tanqîḥ*, INF. II. of (نقح), sucking the marrow out of the bones, &c.; concise and hitting speech; correction of style, &c.; revision.

تنقية *tanqiya-t*, purification; cleaning; selecting; winnowing; taking out the intestines, II. (نقى).

تنك *tanak*, sheet metal, tin plates (m.).

تنكجى *tanakjî*, pl. ية *iyya-t*, tinman, tinker.

تنكر *tanakkur*, disguise, incognito; transformation into a lower state, indefiniteness, V. (نكر).

تنكيت *tankît*, INF. II. of (نكت), cavilling, &c., (m.) criticism; censure; vexation.

تنكير *tankîr*, INF. II. of (نكر), altering, disfiguring, &c.; disguise; generalisation.

(تنم) *tanam*, U, INF. *tanm*, browse on the tree *tannûm*.

تنميق *tanmîq*, INF. II. of (نمق), writing with large letters, &c.; choice handwriting, exquisite penmanship.

تنمية *tanmiya-t*, causing to grow, to increase, to flourish, II. (نمو); — adulteration; lie; calumny; quotation; growth, increase, II. (نمو).

تنها *tanhâ*, alone, solitary (Pers.); —*tanhâ'*, highest point of rising water.

تنهكة *tanhika-t*, punishment, torture.

تنهية *tanhiya-t*, prohibition, forbiddance; termination; attaining to the extreme limits; pl. تناهى *tanâhî*, highest point of rising water.

تنوا *tanwâ'*, rising with difficulty (under a burden); INF. of (نو).

تنواط *tanwâṭ*, decoration of a sedan-chair.

(تنوب) *tannûb*, fir-tree.

تنور *tannûr*, pl. *tanânîr*, stove, oven, furnace; pit for baking; surface of the earth; source; — *tanawwur*, INF. V. of (نور), shining, &c.; — ى *tannûriyy*, maker of stoves, &c.

تنوفة *tanûfa-t*, ية *tanûfiyya-t*, pl. *tanâ'if*, vast desert.

تنوم *tannûm*, name of a tree; hemp-seed; — hence: V. INF. *tanawwum*, browse on the tree *tannûm*; — *tanawwum*, INF. V. of (نوم), sleeping.

تنويح *tanwîḥ*, pl. *tanâwîḥ*, lamentation, mourning for the dead, II. (نوح).

تنوين *tanwîn*, nunnation (marking with ـٌ, ـٍ, ـً).

تنوية *tanwiya-t*, INF. II. of (نوى), accomplishing a purpose; (m.) mewing.

تنين *tinîn*, equal, similar;—*tinnîn*, pl. *tanânîn*, large serpent; dragon (constellation); shark.

ته *tih*, for ذه *ẓih*, this, f. s.

تهاتر *tahâtir*, pl. of تهتر *tahtar*; — *tahâtur*, INF. VI. of (هتر), being arrogant towards each other.

تهاته *tahâtih*, pl. vanities.

تهام *tahâm*, pl. *-ûn*, native of Mecca ; — ة *tihâma-t*, Tihâma ; Mecca ; — ى *tihâmiyy*, from Tihâma.

تهانى *tahânî*, pl. of تهنئة *tahni'a-t*.

تهاوش *tahâwiś*, تهاويش *tahâwîś*, pl. of تهواش *tahwâś* ; — تهاوش *tahâwuś*, INF. VI. of (هوش), being mixed up together, set against each other.

تهاويل *tahâwîl*, pl. of تهويل *tahwîl*.

تهايو *tahâyu'*, consent, VI. (هيا).

تهبيل *tahbîl*, ة, (m.) steam-bath ; fomentation.

تهتار *tahtâr*, stupid insolence.

تهتال *tahtâl*, continual rain.

تهتان *tahtân*, continual light rain.

تهتر *tahtar*, pl. *tahâtir*, contradictory and on either part false evidence ; mutual false accusation.

(تهته) *tahtah*, INF. ة, indulge in idle doings.

تهجا *tahjâ'*, satire, libel, pasquinade.

تهجاع *tahjâ'*, light slumber.

تهجع *tahja'*, broad.

تهجو *tahajju'*, تهجى *tahajjî*, تهجية *tahjiya-t*, spelling ; حروف التهجى *ḥurûfu-'t-tahjî*, alphabet.

تهدى *tahaddî*, right guidance, v. (هدى) ; — *tahaddi'*, alleviation, mitigation ; abatement of price, v. (هدا) ; — ة *tahdiya-t*, offering, giving for a present ; II. (هدى) ; —*tahdi'a-t*, soothing, quieting, &c., II. (هدا).

تهذار *tahẕâr*, talking nonsense, absurd talk.

تهذو *tahazẕu'*, bursting (of a tumour).

تهرو *taharru'*, over-cooking, v. (هرا).

تهرئة *tahri'a-t*, dissolving by boiling, II. (هرا).

تهزل *tahazzul*, facetiousness, jocoseness.

تهطل *tahṭal*, lasting rain.

تهلكة *tahlika-t*, *tahlaka-t*, *tahluka-t*, ruin ; danger ; what leads to ruin.

تهلل *tahallal*, vain, idle ; — *tahallul*, rejoicing, delight, v. (هل).

تهلوك *tuhlûk*, ruin, INF. of (هلك).

(تهم) *tahim*, A, INF. *taham*, *tahâma-t*, get deteriorated and smell badly (meat) ; stink ; perceive one's insufficiency for a thing and get confused at it ; refuse the pasture ; be very hot, while the air is calm ; — *tahum*, be suspected, for اتهم *ittaham*, VIII. (وهم) ; (m.) *taham*, suspect, accuse ; — III. INF. *mutahâma-t* =V. ; — IV. INF. *ithâm*, go to Tahâma or live there ; find the air of a country oppressive and unwholesome ; suspect and accuse falsely ; suppose, doubt ; suggest an opinion or suspicion ; — III. and V. INF. *tatahhum*, go to Tahâma, or live there ; — VII. INF. *intihâm*, (m.) be suspected, accused ; — VIII. INF. *ittihâm*, suspect.

تهم *taham*, calm (of the air) ; excessive heat ; sea-shore ;—*tahim*, smelling badly, stinking ; — *tahm*, Tahâma ; sea-shore ; — ة *tahama-t*, stench ; pl. *tahâ'im*, shore ;—*tahma-t*, Tahâma ; town, city ; — *tuhma-t*, suspicion, bad opinion.

تهمتى *tuhmatiyy*, suspicious, suspected (m.).

(تهن) *tahin*, A, INF. *tahan*, sleep.

تهن *tahin*, sleeping (adj.).

تهنئة *tahni'a-t*, تهنيى *tahnî'*, congratulation ; saying هنيا *haniyy-an*, may it do you good ! ungrudgingness.

(تهو) *tahâ*, U, INF. *tahw*, being negligent.

تهوا *tahwâ'*, part of the night.

تهواد *tahwâd*, speaking low and gently (s.).

تهواش *tahwâś*, pl. *tahâwiś*, *tahâwîś*, crowd of people ; tumult.

تهود *tahawwud*, INF. V. of (هود), being gentle in speech, becoming a Jew, &c. ; conversion ; repentance ; conciliation.

تهويع *tahwî'*, violent agitation; vomiting, II. (هوع).

تهويل *tahwîl*, INF. II. of (هول), frightening, &c.; pl. *tahâwîl*, terrific sight; goblin; phantom; calumny.

تهى *tihî*, this, f. sing. of ذا *zâ*; — *tahiyy*, void, vacant (Pers.).

تهيم *tahîm*, suspect, suspicious; — *tahayyum*, elegant gait, v. (هيم).

تهيو *tahayyu'*, being prepared, &c., v. (هيا).

تهيى *tahyî'*, تهيئة *tahyi'a-t*, pl. *-ât*, preparation; good guidance, II. (هيا).

تو *taww*, pl. *atwâ'*, alone; single; simple, not compound; finished; 1000 horses; — ة *tawwa-t*, hour; *tawwat-an*, just now, this very moment.

توا *tawâ'*, sign of the cross.

تواب *tawwâb*, repenting, penitent; long-suffering; — ة *tu'âba-t*, disgrace, ignominy.

توابع *tawâbi'*, dependencies, pl. of تابعة *tâbi'a-t*.

توابل *tawâbil*, spices, pl. of تابل *tâbil*.

توابيت *tawâbît*, biers, &c., pl. of تابوت *tâbût*.

تواتر *tawâtur*, INF. VI. of (وتر), following each other in short intervals, &c.; uninterrupted tradition; frequency; publicity.

تواثير *tawâsîr*, pl. of تؤثور *tu'sûr*.

تواج *tuwâj*, bleating.

تواد *tau'ad*, considerateness; deliberation; — *tawâdd*, mutual love, VI. (ود); — ى *tawâdî*, pl. of تودية *taudiya-t*.

توارد *tawârud*, INF. VI. of (ورد), coming together to the watering-place, &c.; in rhetoric: chance agreement between two poets.

تواريخ *tawârîh*, historical dates, &c., pl. of تاريخ *târîh*.

تواضع *tawâdu'*, INF. VI. of (وضع), deporting one's self with humility; false politeness; cringing.

تواطو *tawâtu'*, agreement; self-humiliation, VI. (وطا).

توافق *tawâfuq*, INF. VI. of (وفق), agreeing one with another, &c.; league; leaving no remainder in division; commensurability.

تواق *tawwâq*, longingly attached.

تواقيع *tawâqî'*, pl. of توقيع *tauqî'*.

تواكظ *tawâkuz*, complication; entanglement.

تواكيد *tawâkîd*, pl. of توكيد *taukîd*.

توالى *tawâlî*, succession, VI. (ولى); — pl. of تالية *tâliya-t*, the extremities of the body.

توام *tau'am*, pl. توائم *tawâ'im*, *tu'âm*, twin-brother; the second best cast of the dice, arrow or lot; constellation of the Twins; — *tu'âm*, (m.) twin-like, double; — ة *tau'ama-t*, pl. *tawâ'im*, twin-sister; a litter or sedan-chair open at the top for women; — ية *tu'âmiyya-t*, a pearl.

توان *tawân-in*, توانى *tawânî*, slowness; tiredness; delay; negligence; VI. (ونى).

توائم *tawâ'im*, by-paths; — pl. of توام *tau'am*.

(توب) *tâb*, U, INF. *taub*, *tauba-t*, *matâb*, *tâba-t*, *tatwiba-t*, return penitently to God; admit the penitent to His mercy (God); draw back; —X. INF. *istitâb*, call or move to repentance.

توب *tob*, *top*, cannon (Turk.); — ة *tauba-t*, repentance; confession of sins.

(توبل) *taubal*, INF. ة, put seasoning into the cooking-pot.

توبل *taubal*, pl. *tawâbil*, herbs for seasoning.

توت *tût*, mulberry; mulberry-tree.

توتر *tawattur*, tension; stiffness.

توتماج *tûtmâj*, a dish of vermicelli (Pers.).

توتن *tûtun*, tobacco (Turk.).

توتيا *tûtiyâ'*, philosopher's stone; smoke of huts; zinc.

توتيد *tautîd*, INF. II. of (وتد), ramming in pegs; priäpism.
توث *tûs̱*=توت *tût*, mulberry.
توثب *tawas̱s̱ub*, assault, v. (وثب).
توثور *tu'ṡûr*, pl. *tawâs̱îr*, *ta'âs̱îr*, military escort of the tax-gatherer; beadle; iron for branding the soles of a camel.
(توج) *tâj*, U, INF. *tauj*, get crowned;—II. INF. *tawîj*, crown;—V. INF. *tatawwuj*, get crowned.
توج *tûj*, quince (Pers.); bronze, brass (Turk.).
توجه *tawajjuh*, INF. V. of (وجه), turning towards, &c.; kind attention, favour, pl. *-ât*, marks of favour.
توجيه *taujîh*, INF. II. of (وجه), turning towards, &c.; pl. *-ât*, new nominations (to office); census; tax-roll; last consonant but one of a verse with *u* or *a* for a vowel.
(توح) *tâḥ*, U, INF. *tauḥ*, be broad.
توحش *tawaḥḥuś*, INF. V. of (وحش), growing desolate, savage, &c.; abhorrence, aversion.
(توخ) *tâḫ*, U, INF. *tauḫ* (also تاج *tâj*), touch anything swollen or dip into anything soft (finger).
توخم *tawaḫḫum*, being unwholesome, v. (وخم).
توخيم *tauḫîm*, soiling, polluting, II. (وخم).
توخية *tauḫiya-t*, message, transmission.
تودة *tu'ada-t*, *tu'da-t*, sedateness, steadiness; deliberateness; quiet deportment.
تودية *taudiya-t*, pl. *tawâdî*, dwarf; sending; guidance, II. of (ودى).
(تور) *târ*, U, INF. *taur*, flow; roam about;—IV. INF. *itâra-t*, do a thing repeatedly; for اتار *at'ar*, fix the look sharply at (الى *ila*).
تور *taur*, pl. *atwâr*, mediator, envoy; a vessel for water; course; wax-cake;—ة *taura-t*, messenger of love.
توراب *taurâb*, earth, dust.
توراة *taurât*, Thora, Pentateuch.
تورنج *tûrunj*, orange (Pers.).
تورور *tu'rûr*, pl. *tawârîr*=ثورور *s̱u'rûr*.
توريت *taurît*, Pentateuch (m.).
توريخ *taurîḫ*, putting the date, II. (ارخ).
تورية *tauriya-t*, INF. II. of (ورى), lighting a fire, &c.; notion, conception, idea; riddle, word in its rarest signification; alliteration of final consonants; (m.) theory;—تورئة *tauri'a-t*, perspective (m.).
(توز) *tûz*, U, INF. *tauz*, be thick, coarse, rude.
توز *tûz*, natural disposition; origin; bat (of wood); paling.
توزان *tiwzân*, ة *tiwzâna-t*, contrary, opposed.
توزلا *tauzalâ'*, توزلى *tauzalā*, *tauzala*, misfortune, calamity.
توزى *tauzî'*, ة *tauzi'a-t*, throwing off the rider, II. (وزا).
(توس) *tûs*, natural disposition; origin.
توسط *tawassuṭ*, INF. V. of (وسط), placing one's self in the middle; penetrating deeply into a matter, fathoming.
توسع *tawassu'*, INF. II. of (وسع), getting extended, enlarged, widened, &c.; extensive knowledge.
توسوس *tawaswus*, disquietude; scruple; temptations of the devil.
توشيح *tauśîḥ*, INF. II. of (وشح), girding with a sash, &c.; paraphrase; adornment; vignette; acrostic.
توشية *tauśiya-t*, painting, embroidering, &c., II. (وشى).
توصيفى *tauṣîfiyy*, descriptive; attributive.
توصية *tauṣiya-t*, INF. II. of (وصى), enjoining, &c.; recommendation; admonition; commission; testament, will; banns.
توضو *tawaḍḍu'*, ablution before prayer, v. (وضا).
توظيف *tauẓîf*, nomination to an

office; assigning a salary; impost on transactions.

(توع) *tâʻ*, U, INF. *tauʻ*, dip bread into butter, milk, &c., to suck them up;—ية *tauʼiya-t*, awakening (a.), II. (وعى).

(توف) *tâf*, U, INF. *tauf*, be dimmed; —INF. *taufa-t*, relax from weariness; — ة *taufa-t*, deception of the senses, delusion; error; transgression; — *tûfa-t*, fault, vice; want; excess; hesitation, delay.

توفاق *taufâq*, توفق *taufaq*, time; first appearance.

توفيق *taufîq*, INF. II. of (وفق), fitting, &c.; guidance and grace of God; fulfilment of one's wishes, success, prospering (s.); adjustment, agreement; time.

توفية *taufiya-t*, full payment, II. (وفى).

(توق) *tâq*, U, INF. *tauq*, *tuʼûq*, *tawaqân*, *tiqâya-t*, long for, desire; favour; be eagerly set on doing; be quick and vigilant; come out with a prize (arrow in the game); bend the bow by tension; — INF. *tauq*, *tawaqân*, sacrifice one's self from generosity; — IV. INF. *itʼâq*, bend the bow strongly.

توق *tauq*, longing, desire; passion; concupiscence; — *tûq*, bend, incurvation; — *tuʼuq*, fervent desire.

توقان *tawaqân*, INF. of (توق).

توقف *tawaqquf*, INF. V. of (وقف), stopping (n.), hesitating, &c.; perseverance; expectation, dependency.

توقلة *tauqala-t*, horse walking safely over rocks and stones.

توقيت *tauqît*, fixing a time, II. (وقت).

توقيع *tauqîʻ*, INF. II. of (وقع), dropping, &c.; pl. *tawâqîʻ*, royal signet; seal; notion, idea.

توقية *tauqiya-t*, protection, guard, II. (وقى).

توكاف *taukâf*, eaves.

توكيد *taukîd*, INF. II. of (وكد), making firm, &c.; pl. *tawâkîd*, confirmation; ratification; emphasis; girths.

(تول) *tâl*, U, INF. *taul*, practice sorcery; — ة *taula-t*, *tûla-t*, *tuwala-t*, calamity; — *tuwala-t*, *tiwala-t*, love-spell; magic.

تولا *tûlâ*, تولات *tûlât*, misfortune, calamities.

تولب *taulab*, pl. *tawâlib*, foal of an ass; calf; ام ت *umm taulab*, she-ass.

تولج *taulaj*, lair of a wild beast, den.

تولدن *tawaldun*, childishness, childish tricks.

توليج *taulîj*, INF. II. of (ولج), making enter, &c.; transmission of property during lifetime.

توليد *taulîd*, INF. II. of (ولد), assisting at a birth, &c.; begetting; education.

تولية *tauliya-t*, INF. II. of (ولى), turning the back, &c.; nomination as a governor, prefect, &c.; administration of pious foundations.

توم *taʼum*, *tauʼam* = توأم *tauʼam*, twin; — *tûm*, garlic; — ة *tûma-t*, pl. *tûm*, *tuʼam*, pearl; ear-ring with a large pearl; egg of the ostrich; ام ت *umm tûma-t*, mother of pearl; ostrich; — *tauʼama-t*, open vehicle for women.

تومار *tûmâr*, roll, book, volume (Pers.).

تومان *tûmân*, a Persian gold coin; 10,000 men.

تومرى *tuʼmuriyy*, somebody, anybody.

تومن *tawammun*, number of children.

تومور *tuʼmûr*, somebody, anybody; pl. تامير *taʼâmîr*, stone to mark the road in the desert.

تومى *tûma*, Thomas; — ة *taumiʼa-t*, wink, sign (وما).

(تون) *tûn*, leathern game-board; — ية *tuniyya-t*, tunic.

(تون), VI. INF. *tatâwun*, surround the game.

(توه) *tâh*, U, INF. *tauh*, perish; depart and disappear; wander; wander in mind; (m.) be absent-minded; be proud, haughty, supercilious; — II. INF. *tatwîh*, cause to perish; render confused, perplexed; — IV. INF. *itâh*, perplex, confound.

توه *tuwah*, pl. *tûh*, *atwâh*, *atâwîh*, thunderstruck, utterly perplexed, bewildered; — *tauh*, *tûh*, ruin.

توهان *tauhân*, perplexity, bewilderment; (m.) absent-mindedness.

توهد *tauhad*, perfect of form.

توهرى *tauhariyy*, long hump of a camel.

(توى) *tawî*, A, INF. *taw-an*, perish; be spent (money); — IV. INF. اتوا *itwâ*, ruin, cause to perish.

توى *taw-an*, ruin;—*tawî*, perishing, falling, lost;—*tawiyy*, stationary, dwelling.

تويبع *tuwaibi'*, Aldabaran.

تى *tî*, she, this, f. of ذا *zâ*; — *tî*, (m.) tea; — *tayy*, write a ت *t*.

تيا *tayyâ*, the little one, f. dim. of تا *tâ*.

تياح *tayyâḥ*, a lively horse, walking sideways.

تيار *tayyâr*, pl. *-ât*, wave which breaks and dissolves; the deep; bleeding vein; astonished; pompously dressed up.

تياز *tayyâz*, short and thick-set; dwarf; strong; sower.

تياس *tayyâs*, who keeps he-goats; du. *tayyâsân*, name of two stars; — *tiyâs*, INF. III. of (تيس).

تياقة *tiyâqa-t*, longing, desire, INF. of (توق).

تياك *tayyâk*, تيالك *tayyâlik*=تيا *tayyâ*.

تئام *tai'am*, twin-brother.

تيان *tayyân*, seller of figs.

تياه *tayyâh*, proud; gone astray, lost.

تياهر *tayâhir*, تياهير *tayâhîr*, pl. of تيهور *taihûr*.

تيتل *taital*=ثيتل *saital*, ثيثل *saisal*, old male chamois.

تيجان *tîjân*, crowns, pl. of تاج *tâj*.

(تيح) *tâḥ*, I, INF. *taiḥ*, be ready; move to and fro in walking; go astray, wander; — IV. INF. *itâḥa-t*, make ready, set on foot; decree, measure out to (ل *li*), destine, appoint, allot.

تيحان *tayyaḥân*, who talks about things which do not concern him; =تياح *tayyâḥ*.

(تيخ) *tâḫ*, I, INF. *taiḫ*, cudgel.

(تيد) *taid*, gentleness, mildness, kindness; تيدك *taida-ka*, gently!

(تير) *târ*, I, swell, billow.

تير *tîr*, pride; haughtiness; head-beam; desert, wilderness; — *tiyar*, تئر *ti'ar*, pl. of تارة *târa-t*; *tiyar-an*, often, many times.

تيراب *tairâb*, تيرب *tairab*, earth, ground.

(تيز) *tâz*, I, INF. *tayazân*, die; — INF. *taiz*, contend for victory; — III. INF. *mutâyaza-t*, id.; — V. INF. *tatayyuz*, make high steps in walking, have a longing affection for (الى *ila*).

تيز *tiyyaz*, broad-shouldered; — *ta'iz*, with strong sinews.

تيزان *tayazân*, dying, death, INF. of (تيز).

(تيس) *tais*, pl. *tuyûs*, *atyâs*, *tiyasa-t*, *matyûsâ'*, he-goat; obstinate, restive, refractory; blockhead; name of a star; — *tayas*, shape of horns like those of a he-goat; — hence: II. *tayyas*, INF. *tatyîs*, tame, break in; — III. INF. *tiyâs*, *mutâyasa-t*, exercise one's self in a thing; — X. INF. *istitâsa-t*, turn into a he-goat; figuratively, a low-born person attains to a high office; imitate the voice of a he-goat.

تيسا *taisâ'*, goat with horns like those of a he-goat.

تيسنة *taisana-t*, (m.)=تيسوسية *taisûsiyya-t*.

تيسور *taisûr*, light step; fatness.

تيسوسية *taisûsiyya-t*, goat-like, goatish manners; stubborn stiffness.

تيسى *tîsa*, fie! hyena;—ة *taisiyya-t* =تيسوسية *taisûsiyya-t*;—*tîsiyya-t*, lie.

تيسير *taisîr*, INF. II. of (يسر), rendering easy, &c.; light step (of a horse).

تيسيق *taisîq*, good guard; confinement; consignation to the barracks, sequestration.

(تيع) *tâ'*, I, INF. *tai'*, *taya'*, *taya'ân*, come or flow out; be fluid, flow; melt (n.); go, depart; hasten up; long for; infest the roads; take away; dip bread into butter, milk, &c., and suck them up;—II. INF. *tatyî'*, id.;—IV. INF. *itâ'a-t*, vomit; vomit repeatedly;—V. INF. *tatayyu'*, be prone to evil; —VI. INF. *tatâyu'*, id.; persist in evil; persist in a thing against general opinion; importune; rise and stand upright; move the shoulders in walking; raise and blow about dust or dry leaves;—X. INF. *istitâ'a-t*, be able.

تيع *tayyi'*, تيعان *tayya'ân*, prone to evil; quick, swift;—ة *tî'a-t*, herd of 40 heads and above, of which one is to be sacrificed.

تيعيط *tai'îṭ*, alarm-cry.

تيغار *tîġâr*, water-jug; freely-bleeding wound.

تيفاق *taifâq*, *tîfâq*, opposite;—*tîfâq*, time=توفاق *taufâq*.

تئفة *ta'iffa-t*, time and opportunity.

(تئق) *ta'iq*, A, INF. *ta'q*, be full; be full of grief or anger;—IV. INF. *it'âq*, fill; bend the bow to the full length of the arrow.

تئق *ta'iq*, hasty, passionate, rash; bold, sharp; lively; malicious; irascible.

تيقان *tayyiqân*, impetuous, impulsive.

تيقظ *tayaqquẓ*, waking, lucubration, V. (يقظ).

تيقور *taiqûr*, modest; prudent.

(تيك) *tâk*, I, INF. *tuyûk*, be very stupid, be an idiot;—IV. INF. *itâka-t*, pull out the hair.

تيك *tîka*, that one, f. sing. for تلك *tilka*.

(تيم) *tâm*, I, INF. *taim*, enslave; degrade; inspire with love;—II. INF. *tatyîm*, id.;—VIII. slaughter a sheep تيمة *tîma-t*.

تيم *taim*, slave; name of a tribe;—*ta'im*, twin-brother;—ة *ti'ma-t*, *tîma-t*, a sheep kept at home for time of need; a sheep belonging to a herd of 40 or above; talisman.

تيما *taimâ'*, desert; *at-taimâ'*, constellation of the Twins.

تيمن *taiman*, the south;—ى *taimaniyy*, Arabia felix, Yaman;—*tayammun*, INF. V. of (يمن), belonging to Yaman, &c.; blessing of God; success; felicitation.

تين *tîn*, ة, fig;—ة *tîna-t*, the buttocks.

تينا *tînâ'* (preceded by طور *ṭûr*), Mount Sinai.

تينان *tînân*, wolf.

(تيه) *tâh*, I, INF. *taih*, *tîh*, be lost in the desert, wander in bewilderment; be proud, haughty; extend far and rise high; relax, grow dim;—II. INF. *tatyîh*, lead astray, destroy, ruin; (m.) cause one to be absent-minded, divert one's attention.

تيه *taih*, *tîh*, pl. *atyâh*, *atâwîh*, *atâwiha-t*, desert in which one is wandering; *at-tîh*, the wilderness of the Israelites;—*tîh*, pride, haughtiness.

تيها *taihâ'*, desert.

تيهان *taihân*, wandering in the desert;—*tayahân*, INF. of (تيه);—*tayyahân*, *tayyihân*, haughty.

تيهوج *taihûj*, grey variety of partridge.

تيهور *taihûr*, pl. *tayâhîr*, *tayâhir*, dangerous desert; vast plain;

low ground; quicksand, river-sand; haughty, arrogant; out of senses; — ة taihûra-t, plain, field.

تيهوة taihuwa-t, whirlpool.

تيوى taiwiyy, terminating in ت.

تيئم tai'am, twin-brother.

ث

ث s̱; as a numerical sign=500.

ثاّج s̱a''âj, (roarer) lion.

ثادة s̱a'âda-t, fatness, plumpness; clumsiness.

ثابت s̱âbit, ة, standing firm; constant, persevering; certain, sure; stiff, rigid; of a strong intellect; safe (animal in walking); — ة s̱âbita-t, pl. s̱awâbit, fixed star.

ثابت s̱âbba-t=شابة śâbba-t, girl, damsel.

ثابق s̱âbiq, overflowing; liberal, generous.

(ثاثا) s̱a's̱a', INF. ة, allow to drink its fill (a camel), and, by opposition, allow to be thirsty; drink, and, by opposition, be thirsty; prevent, detain, repel; get appeased, subside; remove, take away; extinguish (a.); — II. INF. تثاثو tas̱a's̱u', fear; intend a journey and then prefer staying at home.

(ثاج) s̱a'aj, U, INF. s̱a'j, bleat; roar.

ثاد s̱a'd, moisture, dew, wet ground; cold; s̱a'ad, abominations; inconvenient place; — ة s̱a'ada-t, plump (woman); — s̱a'âda-t, plumpness, fatness.

ثادا s̱a'dâ', maid-servant; stupid girl; ابن ث ibn s̱a'dâ', weakling.

(ثار) s̱a'ar, A, INF. s̱a'r, take revenge upon or for (acc. or ب bi); take revenge upon (acc.) or for (ب bi); seek revenge upon; — IV. INF. is̱'âr, and VIII. INF. is̱s̱i'âr, obtain revenge; — X. INF. isti̱'âr, seek assistance for the purpose of taking revenge.

ثار s̱a'r, pl. as̱'âr, âs̱âr, s̱a'â'ir, s̱u'ûr, s̱a'rât, revenge for murder; murderer of him who is to be revenged; s̱a'rât, يالث yâ as̱-s̱a'rât, يالث yâ li's̱-s̱a'rât, revenge! let us take revenge! — ة s̱ârra-t, talkative woman.

ثاط s̱a't, INF. of (ثط); — ة s̱a'ṭa-t, pl. s̱a'ṭ, thin black mud; a stinging insect.

ثاطا s̱a'ṭâ'=ثادا s̱a'dâ'.

ثاع s̱â'-in (ثاعى s̱â'î), who pelts with stones, accuses, reveals a crime or profits by it; — ة s̱â'a-t, vomiting.

ثاغم s̱âgim, white, whitish.

ثاغى s̱âgî (ثاغ s̱âg-in), part. a. of (ثغو); — ة s̱âgiya-t, sheep.

ثافل s̱âfil, dregs, sediment; excrements; anything stinking.

ثاقب s̱âqib, p. a. of (ثقب); planet Saturn; beggar; a she-camel abounding in milk.

ثاقل s̱âqil, pl. s̱awâqil, heavy, weighty; over-burdened, oppressed, molested.

ثاكل s̱âkil, pl. s̱awâkil, without friends or children, bereaved.

ثالث s̱âlis̱, ة, third; a third (unconcerned) person, mediator, arbitrator; — s̱âlis̱-an, in the third place; — ة s̱âlis̱a-t, tierce.

ثالثون s̱âlis̱ûn, thirtieth.

ثالج s̱âlij, icy cold.

(ثالل) s̱u'lil, pass. and II. tas̱a'lal, INF. tas̱a'lul, be disfigured by warts.

ثالوث s̱âlûs̱, trinity.

ثالى s̲âlî, third.
ثاليل s̲a'âlîl, warts, pl. of ثؤلول s̲u'lûl.
ثامر s̲âmir, fruit-bearing; pea; blossom of the sorrel.
ثامل s̲âmil, rusty sword; delightful habitation.
ثامن s̲âmin, eighth; ثامنا s̲âmin-an, in the eighth place.
(ثان), VI. tas̲â'an, tas̲âwan, INF. tas̲â'un, surround the game with nets; overcome by stratagem, outwit.
ثان s̲ân-in, ثانى s̲ânî, ة, second, double; ثانيا s̲âniy-an, in the second place; ثانى الحال s̲ânî 'l-ḥâl, in future, henceforth; ثانى عطف s̲ânî 'atf, proud; s̲âniya-t, pl. s̲awânî, a second — s̲ânî, p. a. of (ثنى).
ثاهت s̲âhit, gullet; diaphragm.
ثاو s̲a'w, weakness; leanness; — ة s̲a'wa-t, old lean sheep; small rest; — s̲âwa-t, sheep-fold.
(ثاى) s̲a'a, A, INF. s̲a'y, ثئى s̲a'an, spoil, deteriorate; bring about mischief; break or deteriorate the seams of a leathern bag; — IV. INF. is̲'â', wound and kill savagely.
ثاى s̲a'y, s̲a'an, destruction; crime; wounding; murder; — s̲a'-an, scars; — also ة s̲âya-t, pl. s̲ây, sheep-fold; road-mark.
ثائجة s̲â'ija-t, pl. -ât, s̲awâ'ij, bleating; roaring.
ثائر s̲â'ir, vengeance, revenge; anger; malice; revenging; vindictive; — p. a. of (ثور), dusty.
ثب s̲ib, jump! &c., IMP. of (وثب); — ة s̲uba-t, middle of a well or pond; pl. s̲abât, s̲ubûn, as̲biya-t, as̲âbî, herd; troop of men (up to eleven).
(ثب) s̲abb, INF. s̲abâb, sit firm; be completed.
ثبات s̲abât, firmness; durability; perseverance; proof, demonstration; INF. of (ثبت); — s̲ibât, string or girth for fastening; INF. III. of (ثبت); — s̲ubât, disease impeding the movements; pl. of ثبة s̲uba-t.
ثبار s̲ibâr, persevering, diligence, III. (ثبر); على الث 'ala's-s̲ibâr, nearly finished.
ثبان s̲ibân, INF. of (ثبن); = ثبنة s̲ubna-t.
(ثبت) s̲abat, U, INF. s̲abât, s̲ubût, stand firm and permanently; persist; not allow of elision (grammatical letter); — s̲abut, INF. s̲abâta-t, s̲ubâta-t, be firm of character and courageous; — II. INF. tas̲bît, make firm, strong; be very persevering and enduring; exhort to perseverance; keep in confinement; register, note down; prove, demonstrate; (m.) confirm (in the religious sense); — III. INF. mus̲âbata-t, s̲ibât, know for a certainty; — IV. INF. is̲bât, make firm and strong; know for certain; confirm, attest; inform accurately, give a precise answer; write down; register one's name; prove; wound severely, keep in confinement; — V. INF. tas̲abbut, take a fixed residence; be strengthened, fortified; persevere; hesitate; oppose persistently; complete, achieve, carry through; (m.) receive the confirmation; — VIII. INF. is̲tibât, be strengthened, fortified; — X. INF. istis̲bât, be kept confined; persevere; behave with patience and mildness; hesitate; do gradually; ask for reliable information or safe advice; find true; verify; make firm and strong.
ثبت s̲abt, firm; resolute; persevering; brave, hero; — s̲abat, endurance, perseverance; proof, demonstration; a trustworthy man; list, register.
(ثبثب) s̲abs̲ab, INF. ة, sit firm.
(ثبج) s̲abaj, U, INF. s̲abj, speak or

write indistinctly ; — I, INF. s̱abj, sit on one's toes with the buttocks on the heels ; — II. INF. tas̱bîj, speak or write indistinctly ; — XI. INF. is̱bîjâj, be full ; be fat and flabby.

ثبج s̱abaj, pl. as̱bâj, space between the shoulders ; middle and larger part ; indistinctness of speech or writing ; a bird ; — ة s̱abaja-t, moderate ; indifferent.

(ثبجر), اثبجر is̱bajarr, INF. is̱bijrâr, desist from fear ; slacken in an undertaking and not carry it out ; be perplexed, confused ; run away and fart (ass) ; turn back, retreat ; flow.

(ثبر) s̱abar, U, INF. s̱abr, keep one to a thing ; retain, prevent, turn from ; disappoint ; curse ; drive away ; ebb : — INF. s̱ubûr, perish ; ruin ; — s̱abir, A, INF. s̱abar, burst (tumour) ; — II. INF. tas̱bîr, keep one to a thing ; prevent from (عن 'an) ; — III. INF. mus̱âbara-t, s̱ibâr, persevere with diligence ; — VI. INF. tas̱âbur, rush against each other ; — XI. INF. is̱bîrâr, find a thing difficult and desist.

ثبر s̱abr, ebbing of the sea ; — ة s̱abra-t, level ground ; a kind of chalk ; ditch, water-ditch ; — s̱ubra-t, a heap of corn on the threshing-floor.

(ثبط) s̱abaṭ, U, INF. s̱abṭ, prevent, delay ; — INF. s̱abṭ, s̱abaṭ, swell ; — INF. s̱abaṭ, direct another's mind to a thing ; — s̱abiṭ, A, INF. s̱abaṭ, be weak, slack, indolent, stupid ; — II. INF. tas̱bîṭ, prevent ; weaken and relax ; — IV. INF. is̱bâṭ, keep in continual confinement ; — V. INF. tas̱abbuṭ, fix one's mind continually on a thing ; hesitate.

(ثبق) s̱abaq, I, INF. s̱abq, shed tears ; — INF. s̱abq, tas̱bâq, flow fast and with masses of water ; pour out ; — INF. s̱ubûq, be full ; — VII. INF. ins̱ibâq, break suddenly upon ; pour out a flood of words.

ثبق s̱abq, s̱ibq, pl. s̱ubûq, what has been torn off.

(ثبل) s̱ubl, s̱abal, small remainder of a fluid in a vessel.

(ثبن) s̱aban, I, INF. s̱abn, s̱ibân, stitch together, sow a seam ; put into the bosom of a dress and carry along ; — IV. INF. is̱bân, make a bosom in the dress for carrying ; — V. INF. tabas̱s̱un = I. ; — ة s̱ubna-t, pl. s̱uban ; sack, bag ; bosom in a dress.

ثبوت s̱ubût, firmness ; proof ; incontestability.

(ثج) s̱ajj, U, INF. s̱ajj, s̱ujûj, flow abundantly ; pour out, spill ; — VII. INF. ins̱ijâj, flow ; be poured out.

ثج s̱ajj, blood flowing from a victim ; — ة s̱ajja-t, fine garden or park with ponds.

ثجاج s̱ajjâj, who pours out or spills much ; pouring heavy rain ; torrent.

(ثجثج), II. tas̱ajs̱aj, INF. tas̱ajs̱uj, flow ; be poured out ; spilt.

(ثجر) s̱ajar, U, INF. s̱ajr, mix anything with the fermenting juice of a fruit ; — II. INF. تثجير tas̱jîr, widen ; be weak, relaxed ; — VII. INF. ins̱ijâr, break forth (water, blood) ; flow over copiously.

ثجر s̱ajr, s̱ajir, broad and thick ; — s̱ujar, pl. stray troops of men, &c. ; arrow with a broad head ; — ثجرة s̱ujra-t, widest part of a valley ; deepening of the ground ; group.

(ثجل) s̱ajil, A, INF. s̱ajal, be fat and flabby ; — ة s̱ajla-t, corpulence.

ثجلا s̱ajlâ', f. of اثجل as̱jal, big-bellied ; wide (pocket).

(ثجم) s̱ajam, A, INF. s̱ajm (also II.), detach easily ; — s̱ajim, A, INF. s̱ajam, be easily detached ; —

II. INF. *tasjîm*, and IV. INF. *isjâm*, rain fast and continuously; — IV. last.

(ثجن) *sajn*, *sajan*, rugged road.

(ثجو) *sajâ*, U, INF. *sajw*, be silent; disperse, squander; — IV. INF. *isjâ'*, silence.

ثجوج *sajûj*, ثجيج *sajîj*, water from above; wild mountain-torrent.

ثجير *sajîr*, dregs, thick pressed juice.

(ثحثاح) *saḥsâḥ*, night-journey for getting water.

ثحج *saḥaj*, A, INF. *saḥj*, drag along.

ثحف *sahf*, guts of animals, tripes.

ثخانة *saḥâna-t*, (m.) ثخانية *saḥâniyya-t*, thickness and hardness; coarseness; rudeness.

ثخن *saḥun*, INF. *siḥan*, *saḥâna-t*, *suḥûna-t*, be thick, hard and firm; — II. INF. *tasḥîn*, make so; talk rudely to; — IV. INF. *isḥân*, make thick, hard and firm; inflict severe wounds on an enemy, vanquish him; inflict a severe defeat; weaken; handle roughly; — VIII. INF. *issiḥân*, be weakened by wounds; — X. INF. *istisḥân*, overcome.

ثخونة *suḥûna-t*, thickness; hardness.

ثخين *saḥîn*, thick and hard; firm of character.

ثدام *sidâm*, strainer; filtering-vessel; straining-cloth.

(ثدغ) *sadag*, A, INF. *sadg*, break another's head; — VII. INF. *insidâg*, get broken.

(ثدق) *sadaq*, U, INF. *sadq*, be copious, abundant; flow; pour out; desmiss, dispatch; open the bowels (of a victim); — VII. INF. *insidâq*, be flabby; rush upon (على *'ala*).

ثدقم *sidqim*, stammerer.

(ثدم) *sadm*, having a heavy tongue, stammerer; corpulent, stout, fat; stupid.

(ثدن) *sadin*, A, INF. *sadan*, smell badly, stink; be fleshy and clumsy; — II. INF. *tasdîn*, pass. *suddin*, id.

ثدن *sadin*, corpulent; heavy; f. ة *sadina-t*, afflicted with a bodily infirmity (woman).

(ثدو) *sadâ*, U, INF. *sadw*, moisten, wet.

(ثدى) *sadî*, A, INF. *sad-an*, be moistened, wetted; — II. INF. *tasdiya-t*, feed, bring up.

ثدى *sady*, *sidy*, *sad-an*, pl. اثد *asd-in*, *asdî*, *sudiyy*, *sidiyy*, breast; — *sad-an*, thick-breastedness; — ة *sudayya-t*, little breast; box with the necessaries for cleaning the bow and the arrows.

ثديا *sadyâ*, f. having large breasts.

(ثر) *sarr*, A, I, U, INF. *sarr*, *sarâr*, *surûr*, *surûra-t*, abound in water, milk, &c.; have full udders; shed much blood or rain; make many words; move the feet quickly; — I, INF. *sarr*, disperse, divide; — II. INF. *tasrîr*, wet, moisten; water, irrigate.

ثر *sarr*, ة, pl. *sirâr*, *surur*, abounding in water, in milk, &c.; gaping (wound); talkative; swift-footed; — ة *sarra-t*, heavy shower; pouring out a torrent of words (angry woman).

ثرا *sarâ'*, riches, wealth, abundance; = ثرى *saran*, earth.

ثراب *sarâb*, clay-pit.

ثرارة *sarrâra-t*, overflowing well.

(ثرب) *sarab*, I, INF. *sarb*, rebuke, fall foul upon (على *'ala*); undress a sick person; — II. INF. *tasrîb*, rebuke, fall foul upon; chide; fold, wrap up; — IV. INF. *isrâb*, rebuke; be very fat.

ثرب *sarb*, pl. *surûb*, *asrub*, *asârib*, fat of the bowels; caul of the bowels; ruin; — ة *sarba-t*, pl. *sarb*, *sirâb*, tail; fat of the tail.

ثربا *sarbâ'*, f. fat.

ثربات *sarabât*, pl. fingers.

(ثرتم) *surtum*, pl. *sarâtim*, remainders of food in a dish.

ثرثار s̱arṡâr, ة, garrulous ; — ة s̱arṡâra-t, garrulous woman ; overflowing, gushing.

(ثرثر) s̱arṡar, INF. ة, disperse, divide ; be talkative, garrulous ; eat much ; mingle together ; — ة s̱arṡara-t, garrulity.

ثرثورة s̱urṡûra-t, overflowing.

(ثرد) s̱arad, U, INF. s̱ard, break bread to dip it into the broth, &c. ; dip the cloth into the dye ; castrate by squashing the testicles ; kill the victim without cutting its throat ; — II. INF. tas̱rîd, id. ; pass. be carried from the battle-field with broken limbs ; — XV. INF. is̱rindâ', be fleshy on the chest (also is̱rintâ').

ثرد s̱ard, light rain ; — s̱arad, rent, cleft ;—s̱urud, pl. of ثريد s̱arîd ;— ة s̱urda-t, pieces of bread steeped in broth, &c. ; mess.

(ثرط) s̱araṭ, I, U, INF. s̱arṭ, scold, rebuke.

ثرط s̱arṭ, fluid manure ; paste, glue ; stupidity.

(ثرطلة) s̱arṭala-t, flaccidity ; relaxedness ; slackness.

(ثرطم) s̱arṭam, INF. ة, be silent while in company ; be exceedingly fat.

ثرطئة s̱irṭi'a-t, short and thick-set.

(ثرع) s̱ari', A, INF. s̱arâ', importune, intrude.

(ثرعط) s̱ur'uṭ, thin and fluid.

(ثرعلة) s̱ur'ula-t, feathers on the throat of a cock.

(ثرغامة) s̱irġâma-t, woman ; wife.

(ثرم) s̱arim, A, INF. s̱aram, have broken or decayed teeth, suffer from the falling out of teeth ; — s̱aram, I, INF. s̱arm, break another's teeth ; — IV. INF. is̱râm, cause the teeth to fall out (illness) ; — VII. INF. ins̱irâm, have broken or decayed teeth, be gap-toothed ; be broken out (tooth).

ثرم s̱arm, suppression of the first and fifth letters of a foot in poetry.

ثرما s̱armâ', f. of اثرم as̱ram, toothless, gap-toothed.

(ثرمد) s̱armad, INF. ة, under-do the meat, or soil it with ashes.

ثرمط s̱irmiṭ, big sheep ; — s̱uramiṭ and ة s̱urmuṭa-t, thin mud or clay.

(ثرمط) s̱armaṭ, INF. ة, be muddy or composed of thin clay (ground) ; chew audibly ; — IV. is̱rimâṭ, be inflated (leathern pipe) ; be overcome and swell with anger.

(ثرمل) s̱armal, INF. ة, ease the bowels ; eat meat ; under-do the meat, &c., or not clean it from the ashes ; eat in an untidy manner ; bungle, huddle up ; — ة s̱urmula-t, she-fox, fox ; dimple between the upper-lip and nose ; remains of food or a fluid in a vessel.

(ثرن) s̱arin, A, INF. s̱aran, vex or injure friends and neighbours.

(ثرنبج), IV. is̱rambaj, INF. is̱rimbâj, be roasted and dried up on the surface (skin of a sheep).

(ثرو) s̱arâ, U, INF. s̱arâ', be numerous, multiply ; (n.) possess a greater number of cattle ; — INF. s̱arw, make numerous, multiply (a.) ; be lit by the Pleiades and the moon as well (night) ; — s̱arî, A, INF. s̱aran, be rich in cattle, be wealthy ; have a sufficiency ; rejoice ; — IV. INF. is̱râ, be rich in cattle, be wealthy ; — ة s̱arwa-t, plenty ; wealth, riches.

ثروا s̱arwâ', f. of اثرى as̱ra, rich.

ثروان s̱arwân, f. s̱arwa, very rich ; — s̱arawân, du. of ثرى s̱aran.

ثرودة s̱arûda-t, bread to be steeped in broth, &c.

ثرور s̱urûr, abounding in milk ; — INF. of (ثر) ; — pl. of ثر s̱arr.

ثروى s̱arwa, f. of ثروان s̱arwân.

(ثرى) s̱arî, A, INF. s̱aran, be moist and softened ; — II. INF. tas̱riya-t, moisten ; sprinkle ; put

the nands into moist ground; — IV. INF. *isrâ'*, be very moist; contain much water; thoroughly wet the ground.

ثری *saran*, du. *sarawân*, *sarayân*, pl. *asrâ*, moisture (du. of the air and the ground); earth, ground, humus; anything good or pleasant; — *sariyy*, ة, moist; rich, abundant; — *sariyya-t*, ground, humus.

ثریا *saryâ*, moist ground; f. of اثری *asra*, rich; — *surayyâ*, the Pleiades; chandelier, lustre.

ثریاطة *siryâṭa-t*, watery mud.

ثریان *saryân*, moist; — *sarayân*, du. of ثری *saran*.

ثرید *sarîd*, ة *sarîda-t*, pl. *sarâ'id*, *su-rud*, pieces of bread to be steeped in broth, &c.; bread-soup.

(ثش) *saśś*, INF. *saśś*, compress a leathern bag or pipe to expel the air.

(ثط) *saṭṭ*, I, U, INF. *saṭṭ*, *saṭaṭ*, *saṭâṭa-t*, *suṭûṭa-t*, have little hair on the chin, cheeks and brows; — U, ease the bowels.

ثط *saṭṭ*, ة, pl. *siṭâṭ*, *siṭaṭa-t*, *suṭṭân*, *asṭâṭ* (*aṭṭâṭ*), having little hair on the chin, the cheeks, or the brows.

(ثطا) *saṭa'*, A, INF. *saṭ'*, tread down; — *saṭi'*, A, INF. *saṭâ'*, be very stupid; — ة *saṭât*, stupidity.

ثطاط *saṭâṭ*, pl. of ثط *saṭṭ*; — ة, *saṭâṭa-t*, INF. of (ثط).

ثطاع *suṭâ'*, cold, catarrh; — ی *suṭâ-'iyy*, having a cold.

ثطان *suṭṭân*, pl. of ثط *saṭṭ*.

ثطط *saṭaṭ*, INF. of (ثط); — ة *siṭaṭa-t*, pl. of ثط *saṭṭ*.

(ثطع) *saṭa'*, A, INF. *saṭa'a-t*, ease the bowels; be polluted by blood or excrements, so as to render the prayer ineffectual; appear, become visible; pass. have a cold; — II. INF. *tasṭî'*, break into pieces.

(ثطعم), ة *saṭ'ama-t*, eminent gift of speech, highest eloquence; — II. INF. *tasaṭ'um*, surpass in eloquence.

(ثطف) *saṭaf*, abundance and ease in consequence of a plentiful year.

(ثطو) *saṭâ*, U, INF. *saṭw*, place the foot on the ground, make a step; ease the bowels; — VIII. INF. *isṭiṭâ'*, be relaxed.

ثطوطة *suṭûṭa-t*, INF. of (ثط).

(ثطی) *saṭî*, A, INF. *saṭy*, be very stupid.

ثطی *saṭî* (ثط *saṭ-in*), very stupid; — *saṭy*, great stupidity; — *suṭa*, pl. spiders.

(ثع) *sa''*, I, INF. *sa''*, vomit; — VII. INF. *insi'â'*, break forth.

ثعابیب *sa'âbîb*, pl. streams of pure water.

ثعابین *sa'âbîn*, pl. of ثعبان *sa'bân*.

ثعال *su'âl*, she-fox; a small worm; — ة *su'âla-t*, she-fox; fox, like Reynard; hay; nightshade (plant); — ی *su'âli*, pl. of ثعلب *sa'lab*.

ثعامة *su'âma-t*, adulteress.

(ثعب) *sa'ab*, A, INF. *sa'b*, make flow; shed; — VII. INF. *insi'ab*, be shed; flow; — VIII. INF. *is-si'âb*, flow.

ثعب *sa'b*, *sa'ab*, flowing, fluid; pl. ثعبان *su'bân*, watercourse of a valley; — ة *su'ba-t*, *su'aba-t*, pl. *su'ab*, a venomous lizard; mouse; rat; name of a tree.

ثعبان *subân*, pl. ثعابین *sa'âbîn*, large serpent; boa; dragon; basilisk; — pl. of ثعب *sa'b*, *sa'ab*.

(ثعثع) *sa'sa'*, pearl; mother of pearl; — ة *sa'sa'a-t*, stammering; vomiting.

(ثعج) *sa'aj*, troop of travellers.

(ثعجر) *sa'jar*, INF. ة, pour out; — IV. INF. *is'injâr*, be poured out.

(ثعجج), IV. INF. *is'injâh*, flow copiously and continuously.

ثعد *sa'd*, soft dates of a bad quality; soft, fresh.

(ثعر), IV. INF. *is'âr*, spy, spy out

(ثعرر) *sa'rar*, INF. ة, be split.

ثعرور s̱u'rûr, short thick-set man; wart; a small cucumber.
(ثعط) s̱a'iṭ, A, INF. s̱a'aṭ, get corrupted and smell badly (water, &c.); have a bad smell; decay, putrify; swell and be split (lips); — II. INF. tas̱'îṭ, pound, crush.
ثعط s̱a'ṭ, corrupted meat;— ة s̱a'ṭa-t, bad egg.
(ثعل) s̱a'il, A, INF. s̱a'al, grow one over another (teeth); — IV. INF. is̱'âl, be numerous, throng; obstruct, oppose; be high (wages); be a matter of importance and perplexing.
ثعل s̱u'l, s̱a'al, overgrown tooth; — s̱u'l, contemptible; a worm.
ثعلا s̱a'lâ', f. of اثعل as̱'al, having overgrown teeth.
ثعلب s̱a'lab, pl. s̱a'âlib, s̱a'âlî, fox (ث الما s̱a'labu-'l-mâ-i, otter); head-piece of a spear; alimentary canal; outlet (of water); root of the palm-tree; — ة s̱a'laba-t, she-fox; the buttocks, rump.
ثعلول s̱a'lûl, overgrown tooth; angry.
(ثعم) s̱a'am, A, lift up, take away; — V. tas̱a''um, please, be agreeable.
ثعو s̱a'w, soft unripe dates.
ثعوب s̱u'ûb, gall, bitterness.
ثعول s̱a'ûl, equipped (army).
ثعيط s̱a'îṭ, moving sand, quicksand.
ثعية s̱a'ya-t, famine.
ثعيلبة s̱u'ailiba-t, baldness (m.).
ثغ s̱ug, name of an idiot.
ثغا s̱ugâ', division of the lips; cries of a woman in child-birth.
(ثغب) s̱agab, A, INF. s̱agb, pierce; slaughter; — s̱a'ib, A, INF. s̱agab, melt (n.); —V. INF. tas̱aggub, bleed (n.).
ثغب s̱agb, pl. s̱igâb, as̱gâb, cold running water in a valley; shaded water; mountain-lake; — s̱agab, pl. s̱igbân, s̱ugbân, id.; thaw.
ثغثاغ s̱ags̱âg, stammerer.
(ثغثغ) s̱ags̱ag, INF. ة, utter a confused speech, stammer; bite (toothless child); examine, investigate.
ثغثغ s̱ags̱ag, stammering (adj.).
(ثغر) s̱agar, A, INF. s̱agr, break, blunt; (m.) make a breach; by opposition, stop a rent or hole; occupy a mountain-pass against (على 'ala) the enemy; break another's front teeth; — pass. lose the teeth; be hit on the mouth; — IV. INF. is̱gâr, lose, or, by opposition, get the front teeth (child); pass. be hit on the mouth; — VIII. INF. is̱s̱igâr, ittigâr, iddigâr, get the front teeth.
ثغر s̱agr, pl. s̱ugûr, separated, dispersed; mouth; lips; row of teeth; front tooth; mountain-cleft, pass; stronghold; boundary; name of a tree; best grass; — ة s̱ugra-t, pl. s̱ugar, cavity of the throat; cleft; mountain-pass; plain road; breach in a wall.
ثغرب s̱igrib, yellow teeth.
ثغرور s̱ugrûr, boundaries (against an enemy).
ثغم s̱agim, sporting dog.
(ثغو) s̱agâ, U, INF. s̱ugâ', bleat; — IV. INF. is̱gâ', cause to bleat; give a sheep to another, or slaughter it in his honour.
(ثفا) s̱afa', A, INF. s̱af', diminish the boiling of a kettle.
ثفا s̱uffâ', mustard-seed; mustard; cress.
ثفاجة مفاجة s̱afâja-t mafâja-t, very stupid.
ثفاريق s̱afârîq, pl. of ثفروق s̱ufrûq.
ثفافيد s̱afâfîd, piles of white clouds; underclothing; secrets.
ثفال s̱afâl, slow; — s̱ifâl, ة s̱ifâla-t, bolting cloth; water-pot; — s̱ifâl, s̱ufâl, the lower millstone.
(ثفج) s̱afaj, U, INF. s̱afj, be stupid, foolish.

(ثفد), II. s̱affad, INF. tas̱fîd, line (clothes).

(ثفر) s̱afr, s̱ufr, womb of an animal; — s̱afr, s̱afar, pl. as̱fâr, crupper, hindmost strap of the saddle; — hence: II. s̱affar, INF. tas̱fîr, drive from behind; — IV. INF. is̱fâr, id.; put the hindmost strap to a saddle or tighten it; show to be near giving birth (goat); — X. INF. istis̱fâr, be breeched; put the tail between the legs (dog); — ة s̱ufra-t, hair of the armpits.

(ثفرق), II. INF. tas̱afruq, not curdle (milk).

ثفروق s̱ufrûq, pl. s̱afâriq, pedicle of a date or grapes.

(ثفل) s̱afal, U, INF. s̱afl, settle, sink, have a sediment; put a bolting-cloth under the millstone; disperse; — II. INF. tas̱fîl, eat anything in milk; have much sediment; — III. INF. mus̱âfala-t, eat solid food (corn, &c.) without milk; be continually at a person's apron-strings; — IV. INF. is̱fâl, have a sediment; — V. INF. tas̱afful, hold back from what is good (wicked disposition).

ثفل s̱ufl, dregs, sediment; solid food (without milk; s̱afil, who eats such); — s̱ufl, s̱ifl, bolting-cloth, bolter; — s̱afal, slow.

(ثفن) s̱afan, I, INF. s̱afn, push, push back; follow, overtake; — s̱afin, A, INF. s̱afan, get callous; — III. INF. mus̱âfana-t, be always at a person's apron strings; help, assist; — IV. INF. is̱fân, make callous; — ة s̱afina-t, pl. -ât, s̱afun, callous parts of the chest, knees, hind legs (of a camel); lower edge or seam; plenty, heap, crowd.

(ثفو) s̱afâ, U, INF. s̱afw, ثفى s̱afa, I, INF. s̱afy, follow; chase, drive away (also II. and IV.); — II. INF. tas̱fiya-t, and IV. INF. is̱fâ', prop the kettle, &c., with three stones, put it on a tripod; — IV. marry three wives; — V. INF. tas̱affi, hold back from what is good (wicked disposition); — ة s̱ufwa-t, small bowl or basin, pan.

ثفى s̱afa, see (ثفو).

ثق s̱iq, IMP. of وثق, was̱iq, trust, rely, &c.; — ة s̱iqa-t, confidence, trust; tie; — ثقة نقة s̱iqa-t niqa-t, trustworthy; pl. as-s̱iqât, the familiar companions of Muhammad; INF. of (وثق).

ثقاب s̱iqâb, pl. s̱uqub, chips, dry twigs, stubble, dung (for making fire); plane; — ة s̱aqâba-t, s̱iqâba-t = ثقافة s̱aqâfa-t.

ثقاف s̱aqâf, very prudent; — s̱iqâf, contest, emulation, III. (ثقف); — pl. s̱uquf, instrument for straightening lances and polishing; plane; — ة s̱aqâfa-t, sagacity, intelligence, wit, refinement.

ثقال s̱aqâl, heavy; grave, serious, sedate; slow; — s̱uqâl, clumsy; shunned, avoided, & pl.; — s̱iqâl, pl. of ثقيل s̱aqîl; — ة s̱aqâla-t, heaviness, clumsiness, ponderousness; morosity; molestation, trouble, grief; sultriness; INF. of (ثقل).

(ثقب) s̱aqab, U, INF. s̱aqb, pierce, bore, make holes; penetrate; seize with the mind; — INF. s̱uqûb, burn; shine; rise, spread; abound in milk; penetrate; — s̱aqub, INF. s̱aqâba-t, be intensely red; — II. INF. tas̱qîb, pierce repeatedly, riddle; light a fire; show itself (grey hair); — IV. INF. is̱qâb, light a fire; render shining, resplendent; — V. INF. tas̱aqqub, get pierced, torn, corroded, lit; pierce, light; — VII. INF. ins̱iqâb, get pierced, torn.

ثقب s̱aqb, s̱uqb, ة, pl. as̱qub, s̱uqûb, as̱qâb, perforation, hole;

— s̲uqub, pl. of ثقاب s̲iqâb ; — ة s̲uqba-t, pl. s̲uqub, s̲uqb, canal.
(ثقثق) s̲aqs̲aq, INF. ة, talk stupidly or foolishly.
(ثقر), V. tas̲aqqar, INF. tas̲aqqur, be shaken, shake (n.), tremble.
(ثقف) s̲aqif, A, INF. s̲aqf, s̲aqaf ; s̲aquf, INF. s̲aqâfa-t, have a sharp penetrating intellect ; be clever and successful ; surpass in intellect ; — s̲aqif, A, INF. s̲aqaf, meet, reach, seize, take hold of ; understand ; obtain, find ; — II. INF. tas̲qîf, straighten a lance, make straight again ; educate, refine ; correct ; — III. INF. mus̲âqafa-t, vie and surpass in penetration ; INF. s̲iqâf, dispute in a haughty manner ; — IV. INF. is̲qâf, pass. get into one's own power ; — VI. INF. tas̲âquf, quarrel with each other.
ثقف s̲aqf, s̲iqf, s̲aqif, s̲aquf, sharp, penetrating, active.
(ثقل) s̲aqal, U, INF. s̲aql, estimate the weight, weigh, make two things equal in weight ; put a weight on ; — s̲aqul, INF. s̲aqâla-t, s̲iqal, be heavy, weighty ; molest (على 'ala) ; be troubled in body and mind ; be hard of hearing ; feel pregnant ; be full of sap ; — II. INF. tas̲qîl, deem or declare a thing to be difficult ; make heavy, lay a weight on ; surfeit the stomach ; burden, molest, annoy ; weigh to ; — IV. INF. is̲qâl, make one carry a heavy burden ; press upon, oppress ; grieve ; feel pregnant ; — VI. INF. tas̲âqul, be heavy, ponderous ; be a burden ; bend from heaviness to the earth ; gravitate ; find a thing too difficult and desist ; refuse help ; — X. INF. istis̲qâl, find or be heavy, ponderous, troublesome.
ثقل s̲aql, luggage, baggage ; — s̲iql, pl. as̲qâl, weight, burden ; heaviness ; weightiness ; troublesomeness ; — s̲aqal, pl. as̲qâl, luggage, baggage ; retinue, servants, family ; overload ; of great value ; du. as-s̲aqalân, men and demons ; — s̲iqal, heaviness, ponderousness, INF. of (ثقل) ; — s̲uql (also ثقلا s̲uqalâ'), pl. of ثقيل s̲aqîl ; — ة s̲aqla-t, s̲aqala-t, heaviness, trouble ; indigestion, surfeit ; — s̲aqla-t, tiredness ; heaviness in the limbs ; molestation ; الثقلة الذاتية as-s̲aqla-t az-z̤âtiyya-t, the specific weight ; — s̲aqila-t, s̲iqala-t, s̲aqala-t, luggage, baggage.
ثقوب s̲aqûb, pl. s̲uqub, fuel ; — s̲uqûb, pl. of ثقب s̲aqb ; INF. of (ثقب).
ثقوة s̲uqwa-t, pl. -ât, earthen dish.
ثقيب s̲aqîb, abounding in milk ; intensely red.
ثقيف s̲aqîf, very sour (ابو ثقيف abû s̲aqîf, vinegar) ; sagacious, penetrating, intelligent ; — s̲iqqîf, id.
ثقيل s̲aqîl, ة, pl. s̲uql, s̲iqâl, s̲uqalâ', heavy ; burdensome ; indigestible ; morose ; tiresome ; troublesome, disagreeable ; ponderous, clumsy ; lazy ; troubled in body or mind ; harsh ; severe ; weighty.
(ثك) s̲akk, U, INF. s̲akk, travel, roam about.
(ثكثك) s̲aks̲ak, INF. ة, be stupid and malicious ; — ة s̲aks̲aka-t, stupid woman.
(ثكل) s̲akil, A, INF. s̲akal, be bereft ; mourn for ; — IV. INF. is̲kâl, bereave ; be bereft.
ثكل s̲akl, s̲akal, death ; destruction, ruin ; bereavement ; — s̲akil, ثكلان s̲aklân, f. ة, s̲akla, pl. s̲akâla, bereft.
(ثكم) s̲akam, U, INF. s̲akm, follow the tracks ; persevere in a matter ; dwell, abide, stay ; — s̲akim, A, INF. s̲akam, id.

ثكم *sakam*, middle of the road; guidance.

(ثكن) *sukn*, levelness of the road; — ة *sukna-t*, pl. *sukan*, adornment for the neck; ditch for a fire, ditch, grave; religious zeal; standard, flag; military gathering-place; bevy of birds.

ثكول *sakûl*, bereft; pathless.

(ثل) *sall*, INF. *sall*, *salal*, annihilate, destroy from the foundations; kill; overthrow; throw earth into a well; make coins; drop excrements; — U, INF. *sall*, remove earth out of a well; — IV. INF. *islâl*, have plenty of sheep and wool; cause to restore, to rebuild; restore; beat out another's teeth; — V. INF. *tasallul*, be annihilated, destroyed; — VII. INF. *insilâl*, run together from all sides and fall upon; break down upon; — ة *salla-t*, pl. *silal*, *silâl*, large flock; gap, breach; wool mixed with camel-hair; also pl. *tulal*, mud from a well; great quantity of money; watering-places; — *silla-t*, death, destruction; — *sulla-t*, pl. *sulal*, troop of people; great quantity of money.

ثلاب *sallâb*, calumniator, slanderer; devil.

ثلاث *salâs*, f., ة *salâsa-t*, m., three; — *sulâs*, by threes, triple.

ثلاثا *salâsâ'*, *sulâsâ'*, pl. *salâsâwât*, Tuesday; *salâs-an*, thrice, three times.

ثلاثون *salâsûn*, (m.) ثلاثين *salâsîn*, thirty; thirtieth.

ثلاثى *salâsiyy*, referring to three; — *sulâsiyy*, ة, having three radical letters; — ة *sulâsiyya-t*, person of highest rank, vizier, &c.

ثلاج *sallâj*, seller of ice; — ة *salâja-t*, avalanche of snow; — ى *sulâjiyy*, white as snow; shining, bright.

ثلال *salâl*, destruction; — *silâl*, pl. of ثلة *salla-t*.

(ثلب) *salab*, I, INF. *salb*, rebuke, scold, inveigh against; slander, calumniate; repel, drive away; turn back, turn round; blunt; spoil; destroy; — *salib*, A, INF. *salab*, contract (n.), get soiled; get blunted or spoiled; — II. INF. *taslîb*, grow old, toothless, and bald.

ثلب *silb*, *salb*, insult; calumny; — *silb*, ة, pl. *aslâb*, *silaba-t*, old, toothless, and bald; pl. *silâb*, fault, vice; — *silb*, *salib*, vicious; dirty; broken; — *salab*, dirt; colic; — *sulub*, pl. of ثلوب *salûb*.

(ثلث) *salas*, U, INF. *sals*, divide into three parts; take the third part of one's property; — I, INF. *sals*, come as the third one to two, or as the thirtieth to twenty-nine; — II. INF. *taslîs*, triple; declare to be three, do thrice; make triangular; divide by three; touch the third string of the lute; reach the goal as the third; become three.

ثلث *sils*, watering (of a field, &c.) on the third day; the third foal; — *suls*, *sulus*, pl. *aslâs*, third part; — *salas*, f. three; — *salas-an*, thrice.

ثلثل *sulsul*, destruction; — ثلثلان *sulsulân*, *silsilân*, nightshade (plant); hay.

ثلثماية *sulsmâya-t*, three hundred (m.).

ثلثى *sulusiyy*, a large ornamental hand-writing.

(ثلج) *salaj*, U, INF. *salj*, snow; macerate; — INF. *sulûj*, also *salij*, A, INF. *salaj*, recover, refresh one's self, be at rest again (after fatigue, &c.); — *salij*, A, INF. *salaj*, be cheerful, rejoice; snow; — II. INF. *taslîj*, be icy cold, frozen; — IV. INF. *islâj*, snow, cover with snow; be snowy (day); get into snow; get quieted; rejoice (a.); subside; come in digging upon clay.

ثلج salj, pl. sulûj, snow;—salj and salij, icy cold, cold.

(ثلخ) saliḫ, A, INF. salaḫ, be soiled, dirtied; — II. INF. tasliḫ, soil, dirty.

(ثلط) salaṭ, I, INF. salṭ, throw dirt at, soil.

ثلط salṭ, thin excrements.

(ثلع) sala', A, INF. sal', (ثلغ) salag, A, INF. salg, break a person's head; sala', (m.) harrow;—salag, VII. INF. insilâg, get broken; have soft and ripe dates.

ثلل salal, destruction; — silal, pl. of ثلة salla-t; — sulal, pl. of ثلة sulla-t.

(ثلم) salam, I, INF. salm, blunt the edge of a vessel, sword, &c.; make a breach in a wall; disparage; — salim, A, INF. salam, be blunted; broken in; also used actively; — II. INF. taslîm, blunt much; — V. INF. tasallum and VII. INF. insilâm, passive of the previous.

ثلم salm, notch, gap; suppression of the first letter of a wata-t mafrûq, at the beginning of a foot otherwise perfect;—salam, breaking of a river-bank; — ة sulma-t, pl. sulam, notch, gap; breach; split, cleft.

(ثلمط) salma-t, INF. ة, be flabby, relaxed.

ثلمط salmaṭ, ثلموط salmûṭ=ثلط salṭ.

ثلوب salûb, pl. sulub, cavilling, finding fault, criticising (adj.).

ثلى sulla, fallen greatness.

ثليث salîs, third part.

ثليجى sulaijiyy, a kind of finch (m.).

ثليل salîl, gurgling or purling of water.

(ثم) samm, U, INF. samm, tread down; restore, amend; corroborate; put into order; gather; contain; wipe with grass; pull out with the mouth; eat or gather pell-mell the good and bad; sweep a room; — II. INF. tasmîm, tread down; break a dressed bone; — VIII. INF. insimâm, fall from all sides upon; melt and blend; waste away; grow old and weak.

ثم samm-a, yonder; =summ-a, then, after that, thereupon; — summ, household vessels; ما له ثم ولا رم mâ la-hu summ wa-lâ rumm, he has nothing whatever; — ة samma-t, there, yonder; — simma-t, old man; — summa-t, handful of grass.

(ثما) sama', A, INF. sam', offer fat food; throw truffles into the fat; break bread and steep it with broth; dye the beard with henna; break a person's head; ease the bowels; — VII. INF. insimâ', be broken.

ثمار samâr, fruit; possessions; — simâr, pl. of ثمر samar.

ثمال simâl, helper, avenger; — sumâl, deadly poison; hole; — ة sumâla-t, pl. sumâl, foam, froth; rest, remainder.

ثمانون samânûn (m. ثمانين samanîn), eighty.

ثمانى samânî, f., ة samâniya-t, m. eight.

ثمت summat, in poetry=ثم summ, then, thereupon.

(ثمثم) samsam, INF. ة, cover or stop up a vessel; desist; leave time for rest; do a thing not well; tie up the leathern bag for buttering; not bend in striking (sword); — II. INF. tasamsum, desist.

ثمثم samsam, sporting-dog.

(ثمج) samj, confusion; medley.

(ثمد) samad, U, find water in a ditch and preserve it there for the time of need; take everything from, exhaust; give, and, by opposition, demand; — IV. INF. ismâd, preserve water for the time of need; — VIII. INF. istimâd, issimâd, drink of such water; — X. INF. istismâd, pre-

serve water; ask for a little; — XI. INF. *ismîdâd*, grow fat.

ثمد *samd*, *samad*, water in a ditch preserved for the time of need; remainder of water; spring which disappears in summer.

(ثمر) *samar*, U, INF. *sumûr*, bear fruit; get rich; gather brushwood; — II. INF. *tasmîr*, cause to bear fruit; increase, heap up riches; form buds; — IV. INF. *ismâr*, bear fruit; be fertile; be or get rich; purpose; — X. *istismâr*, endeavour to make a thing bear fruit or bring advantage; consider fertile or advantageous; have the usufruct or profit; gather.

ثمر *samar*, ة, pl. *simâr*, *sumur*, *asmâr*, fruit; produce, gain, advantage, profit; possessions, riches; gold, silver; knot at the top of a whip; — *samir*, plentiful, much, many; — *sumr*, *sumur*, plenty of riches; — ة *samara-t*, *samura-t*, pl. *-ât*, fruit-tree; descendant; consequence, result; tip of the tongue; — *samira-t*, sweetness; friendship.

(ثمط) *samṭ*, thin excrements, mud.

(ثمعد) *sam'ad*, handsome; مثمعد *musma'idd*, handsome of face.

(ثمغ) *samag*, U, INF. *samg*, mingle white with black; dye deep red; dip the head repeatedly into henna; grease the head with oil; — II. INF. *tasmîg*, rub a person's head with grease, &c.; — VII. *insimâg*, get squashed (falling fruit); get moist; — ة *samga-t*, mountain-summit.

(ثمل) *samal*, I, U, INF. *saml*, *sumûl*, stay, remain staying; help, assist, stand by a person; give food and drink; eat; — *samil*, A, INF. *samal*, get or be drunk; stay, remain staying; II. INF. *tasmîl*, leave (water, &c.); raise foam; trouble the water; — IV. INF. *ismâl*, leave water; have much foam or froth; have pure milk; — V. INF. *tasammul*, drink out entirely; protect, help; eat.

ثمل *saml*, delay, stay; — *samal*, id.; drunkenness; means of subsistence; shadow; — *samil*, drunk, intoxicated; in love; — *suml*, ة, a certain amount of intellect and firmness; — ة *sumla-t* (*samla-t*), pl. *sumal*, grains and legumes; oatmeal porridge; also *samala-t*, pl. *samal*, remainder of water; mud of a well.

(ثملط) *samlaṭ*, INF. ة=(ثلمط).

(ثمن) *saman*, U, INF. *samn*, take the eighth part of a man's property; levy every eighth man; — I, be the eighth, come as the eighth to others; — II. INF. *tasmîn*, make or be eightfold, octangular; (m.) value, estimate, esteem; — IV. INF. *ismân*, consist of eight; water the camels on the eighth day; pay the price of goods; (m.) be precious, costly, valuable.

(ثمن) *saman*, pl. *asmân*, *asmun*, *asmina-t*, price, value; — *simn*, eight days' thirst of a camel; — *sumn*, *sumun*, pl. *asmân*, eighth part.

ثمود *samûd*, *sumûd*, tribe Samûd (Thamûd).

ثمول *samûl*, delay, stay.

ثمير *samîr*, ة *samîra-t*, butter-milk; — ابن ث *ibn samîr*, moon-lit night; — ة *samîra-t*, fertile ground.

ثميغة *samîga-t*, fluid food with the fat of meat; moist ground; wound on the head.

ثميل *samîl*, sour milk with bread; watering-place; also ة *samîla-t*, pl. *samâ'il*, remainder of water; rest, remainder; house with furniture and beds; water-reservoir of stone; = ثملة *sumla-t*.

ثمين *samîn*, pl. *asmân*, valuable, precious, costly; eighth part.

(ثن) *sinn*, dry hay; blackish and

friable parts of wood; — ة sunna-t, pl. sunan, hair on a horse's hoof; abdomen; pudenda.

ثنا sana', abbreviation for حدثنا hadasa-nâ, he told us, related to us; — sanâ', pl. asniya-t, salutation, felicitation; rendering the salutation; praise, and, by opposition, blame; — sinâ', song, melody; rope, string; courtyard; pl. of ثنى saniyy; — sunâ', sunâ' sunâ', two and two, in twos.

ثنان sinân, densely-grown plants.

ثنايا sanâyâ, pl. of ثنية saniyya-t.

ثناية sinâya-t=ثنا sinâ'.

ثنائى sunâ'iyy, having two radical letters.

(ثنت) sanit, A, INF. sanat, smell badly, stink; be relaxed and bleed.

ثنت sanit, ة, faded; relaxed and bleeding.

ثنتان sintân, f. two.

(ثنتاية) sintâya-t, ribald.

(ثنتل) santal, INF. ة, get soiled.

ثنتل santal, ة santala-t, bad egg; — sintil, short; soiled; impotent.

ثندوة sundu'a-t, sunduwa-t, pl. sanâdî', nipple; teat.

(ثنط) sant, cleft, rent.

ثنوى sanwa, exception; head and feet of sacrificed animals; — sanawiyy, professing two principles of creation; fire-worshipper; — ة sanawiyya-t, sect of such.

ثنى sana, I, A, INF. sany, fold; double; be the second; repeat, do a second time; prevent, avert; — II. INF. tasniya-t, double; bend, turn; put a word into the dual; point a letter with two dots; eat a second time of a dish; touch the second string of the lute; praise or blame; render thanks; — IV. INF. isnâ', praise or blame; lose the front teeth; — V. INF. tasannî, become six years old (camel); — VII. INF. insinâ', turn aside, desist; come off; — VIII. INF. issinâ', become six years old; — V., VII., VIII., be bent, folded; doubled up; walk with a bent body, or swinging to and fro; undulate; — X. INF. istisnâ', make an exception or proviso; swear with a reservation; — XII. isnauna, INF. isnînâ', be bent, folded, doubled up.

ثنى sany, folding (s.); — siny, pl. asnâ, bend, fold, doubling; double; second child or foal; giving birth for the second time (also tinan); an hour of the night; asnâ, qualities; — siny, sun-an, sin-an, pl. sinya-t, the second person in the kingdom; governor; — sinan, pl. ة sinya-t, anything doubled, repeated; repetition; pl. asnâ, asânîn, Monday; — saniyy, ة, pl. sunyân, asnâ, sinâ', losing the first teeth (adj.), becoming respectively six, four, three, or two years of age (camel, horse, cattle, sheep); — ة sinya-t, utterly contemptible; pl. of ثنيان sunyân; — saniya-t, second (moment of time); — saniyya-t, pl. ات -ât, sanâyâ, front tooth; mountain-slope; rugged mountain-path; narrow pass; mountain-chain; exploit; martyr; leader of men; = ثنوى sanwa; praise, eulogy, panegyric.

ثنيا sunyâ = ثنوى sanwa.

ثنيان sunyân, pl. sinya-t, second in the kingdom, in rank; governor; head of the family; unreasonable; pl. of ثنى saniyy.

(ثهت) sahit, A, INF. sahat, saht, suhat, call, call out to.

(ثهثه) sahsah, INF. ة, melt (n.).

(ثهل) sahil, A, INF. sahal, be spread on the floor.

ثهمد sahmad, tall and stout (woman).

(ثهو) s̲aha͡, u, inf. s̲ahw, be stupid; — iii. inf. مثاهاة mus̲âhât, talk to (acc.).

(ثهود) s̲ahwad = ثوهد s̲auhad.

(ثو), iv. is̲â', inf. is̲â't, throw, pelt, shoot; — ة s̲awwa-t, s̲uwwa-t, heap of stones as a road-mark in the desert; — s̲uwwa-t, pl. s̲uwa-n, household furniture.

ثوا s̲awâ', inf. of (ثوى).

ثواب s̲awâb, reward, recompense; requital; punishment; good work; honey; bee; — s̲awwâb, dealer in clothes; keeper of the wardrobe; — ة s̲awâba-t, work (of charity); — s̲uwâba-t, shooting-star, planet.

ثوابت s̲awâbit, pl. of ثابتة s̲âbita-t.

ثواج s̲u'âj, bleating of cattle.

ثوار s̲awwâr, herdsman; — s̲iwâr, inf. of (ثور).

ثواط s̲u'âṭ, cold, catarrh.

ثوالث s̲awâlis̲, of the third generation.

ثوالة s̲awwâla-t, swarm of locusts.

ثوام s̲awwâm, seller of garlic.

ثوانى s̲awânî, pl. of ثانية s̲âniya-t.

ثوايا s̲awâyâ, pl. of ثوية s̲awiyya-t.

ثوائج s̲awâ'ij, pl. of ثائجة s̲â'ija-t.

(ثوب) s̲âb, u, inf. s̲aub, s̲u'ûb, ثوب s̲ûb, return; be full or almost full; — inf. s̲u'b, assemble, gather; — inf. s̲awabân, recover; — ii. inf. tas̲wîb, return; reward; retaliate; call to prayer or repeat the call; assume the posture of prayer; increase the number of one's prayers of free will; — iv. inf. is̲âba-t, reward; recover; fill; — v. inf. tas̲awwub, say after the prescribed prayer a second one; — x. inf. istis̲âba-t, demand a reward; ask back.

ثوب s̲aub, pl. s̲iyâb, as̲wub, as̲'ub, as̲wâb, dress, garment, cloth (ث اهباب s̲aub ahbâb, ث هبابيب s̲aub habâbîb, tattered clothes); armour; coat of the horse; actions, deeds; heart; protection; clientship; ث الما s̲aubu-'l-mâ'i, placenta.

ثوبا s̲u'abâ', yawning (s.).

ثوبان s̲awabân, recovery, inf. of (ثوب).

(ثوج) s̲âj, bleat, for (ثاج).

ثوج s̲auj, basket made of leaves of the palm-tree.

(ثوخ) s̲âḥ, u, inf. s̲auḥ, and—

(ثيخ) s̲âḥ, i, inf. s̲aiḥ, touch anything soft or swollen; sink in mud.

(ثور) s̲âr, u, inf. s̲aur, s̲u'ûr, s̲awarân, stir and rise; rise and spread; leap up; rush against, attack; break out, appear; flow; — ii. inf. tas̲wîr, stir up and rouse; study the meaning of the Koran; — iii. inf. mus̲âwara-t, s̲iwâr, spring or rush against; — iv. inf. is̲âra-t, excite, rouse; provoke a tumult or quarrel; urge on; drive the clouds; frighten; plough; pass. rise, grow; — v. inf. tas̲awwur, stir and rise; ascend; appear; attack; — viii. inf. is̲s̲iyâr, id.; — x. inf. istis̲âra-t, raise dust, hunt up animals; provoke war or tumult, or incite to do so; be excited; appear; call to revenge.

ثور s̲aur, pl. s̲iyâr, s̲iwara-t, s̲iyara-t, s̲îra-t, s̲îrân, bull; sign of the Bull; lord, master; morning, dawn; white of the nail; pl. as̲wâr, s̲iwara-t, large piece of the cream-cheese اقط aqṭ; water-moss; madness; stupid; — s̲u'ur, pl. of ثار s̲a'r, revenge, &c.; — ة s̲u'ra-t, s̲u'ura-t, thirst for vengeance, vindictiveness; inf. of (ثار); — s̲aura-t, large troop; wealth; passionateness.

ثوران s̲awarân, cloud of dust; inf. of (ثور).

ثورور s̲u'rûr, policeman; beadle.

(ثوع) s̲â', u, inf. s̲au', flow.

(ثول) s̱âl, U, INF. s̱aul, show signs of incipient madness; pour out; gather (n.); — s̱awil, A, INF. s̱awal, (m.) be giddy, hare-brained; — V. INF. tas̱awwul, form clusters (swarming bees); insult and offer violence; — VII. INF. ins̱i'âl, pour upon (n.); fall upon from all sides; crowd together; (m.) be giddy, act foolishly.

ثول s̱aul, swarm of bees; crowd; male bee; — s̱awal, St. Vitus's dance; — s̱aul, s̱awal, ة s̱aula-t, (m.) giddiness; — s̱ûl, pl. of اثول as̱wal, giddy, &c.

ثولا s̱aulâ', f. of اثول as̱wal, giddy, &c.

ثولول s̱u'lûl, pl. s̱a'âlîl, wart.

ثوم s̱ûm, ة, garlic; — ة s̱ûma-t, pommel of a sword.

(ثوهد) s̱auhad, ة, full and fat and close to puberty.

ثووب s̱u'ûb, INF. of (ثوب).

ثوور s̱u'ûr, INF. of (ثور); — ة s̱u'ûra-t, vindictiveness.

(ثوى) s̱awâ, I, INF. s̱awâ', s̱uwiyy, make a halt, stop, remain, stay for a permanency; receive hospitably; pass. be interred; — II. INF. tas̱wiya-t, cause to remain, retain; receive hospitably; die; — IV. INF. is̱wâ', live, dwell; cause to remain; receive hospitably; shoot arrows.

ثوى s̱awiyy, pl. as̱wiyâ, guest; inhabitant; ready for a guest; — s̱uwan, pl. of ثوة s̱uwwa-t; — ة s̱awiyya-t, pl. s̱awâyâ, (sheep-) fold; stone as a road-mark; woman, wife.

ثويلة s̱awîla-t, bundle of herbs; crowd.

ثياب s̱iyâb, pl. of ثوب s̱aub.

ثيابى s̱iyâbiyy, keeper of the wardrobe.

ثيار s̱iyâr, pl. of ثور s̱aur, bull.

(ثيب) II. s̱ayyab, INF. tas̱yîb, have sexual intercourse; — V. INF. tas̱ayyub, separate from the husband after the first coition.

(ثئب) s̱a'ib, yawn; pass. s̱u'ib, INF. s̱a'b, grow lazy, sleepy; — V. INF. tas̱a''ub, yawn; — VI. INF. tas̱â'ub, id.; go to spy out.

ثيب s̱ayyib, who divorces from wife or husband after the first coition; f. no longer a virgin.

(ثيتل) s̱aital (also ثيثل s̱ais̱al), old chamois; antelope; impotent; — INF. ة, prove foolish.

(ثيخ) see (ثوخ).

(ثئد) s̱a'id, A, INF. s̱a'ad, be moist; freeze, be chilled.

ثئد s̱a'id, moist; frozen; — ة s̱a'ida-t, fleshy.

ثير s̱îr, pellicle upon the eye; — ة s̱iyara-t, ثيران s̱îrân, pl. of ثور s̱aur, bull.

(ثئط) s̱a'iṭ, A, INF. s̱a'aṭ, be putrid; — pass. s̱u'iṭ, catch a cold.

ثيموم s̱aimûm, a kind of wheat.

(ثين) s̱în, place for pearl-fishing; tool for piercing pearls.

ثية s̱iyya-t, fold; stable.

ثيوبة s̱iyûba-t, widowhood.

(ثئى) see (ثاى).

ج

ج j, as a numerical sign=3; abbreviation for: Tuesday, as third day of the week; جمع jam', plural; the constellation Cancer, as the third sign of the zodiac; and the month جمادى الاخر jumâda al-âḫir, 2nd J. (جا being abbreviation for جمادى الاول jamâda al-awwal, 1st J.).

جا jâ'in, coming=جاى jâ'i, (m.) جاى jâi, ag. of (جى).

(جاب) jâb, aor. yajib, IMP. jib,

bring (m. for original جا ب *jâ'a bi*, come with); —*ja'ab*, A, INF. *ja'b*, gain, earn; sell red clay.

جاب *jâb*, see جابى; —*ja'b*, *jâb*, pl. *ju'ûb*, *jûb*, strong ass; red clay; navel; f. ة, stout and strong; savage; over-bearing, haughty; — ة *ja'ba-t*, hypochondres; — *jâba-t*, answer, reply.

جابر *jâbir*, who sets broken bones; forcing, compelling; powerful, tyrannical;—ة *jâbira-t*, Medina.

جابى *jâbi'*, *jâbî*, locust; —*jâbî* (جاب *jâb-in*), tax-gatherer, collector of revenue; — ة *jâbiya-t*, pl. *jawâbî*, water-reservoir.

(جاث) *ja'as̱*, A, INF. *ja's̱*, walk along with a heavy load; relate, narrate; — جئث *ja'is̱*, A, INF. *ja'as̱*, rise or walk with difficulty (on account of a burden); pass. INF. *ju'ûs̱*, get frightened; — IV. INF. *ijâs̱a-t*, burden, put a load on; — VII. INF. *inji'âs̱*, id.; be overthrown.

جاث *ja''âs̱*, of a bad disposition.

جاثوم *jâs̱ûm*, nightmare, incubus; sleeper, lazy.

جاثى *jâs̱iyy*, pl. *jus̱iyy*, *jis̱iyy*, kneeling (adj.); the sign of Hercules;—ة *jâs̱iya-t*, kneeling (s.); name of the 45th chapter of the Koran.

(جاج) *ja'aj*, A, INF. *ja'j*, stand as a coward; — ة *jâja-t*, glass bead; string of pearls.

(جاجا) *ja'ja'*, INF. ة, call the camels to the watering-place; — II. INF. *taja'ju'*, desist; fear.

جاجا *ja'ja'*, flight; dispersion.

جاجى *ja'âjî'*, pl. of جوجو *ju'ju'*, breast, &c.

جاح *jâḥ*, veil.

جاحد *jâḥid*, denying; refractory; adversary, opponent; apostate.

جاحظ *jâḥiẓ*, pl. *juḥḥaẓ*, goggle-eyed; du. *aj-jâḥiẓân*, the pupils of the eyes.

جاحم *jâḥim*, battle; ة, glowing.

جاد *jâd*, in vain, ineffectual;— *jâdd*, zealous; quick; — ة *jâdda-t*, pl. *jawâd*, causeway; high-road.

جادس *jâdis*, ة, effaced, obliterated; uncultivated; hard, firm, strong.

جادل *jâdil*, grown up; brawler.

جادى *jâdî*, pl. *judât*, asking for a gift (adj.); saffron; wine.

جاديا *jâdiyâ'*, saffron.

(جاذ) *ja'aẕ*, A, INF. *ja'ẕ*, drink without sipping or pausing.

جاذب *jâẕib*, ة, pl. *jawâẕib*, ag. of (جذب); *jâẕiba-t*, charm, attraction, grace, loveliness.

جاذر *ja'âẕir*, buffaloes, pl. of جوذر *ju'ẕar*.

جاذى *jâẕî*, pl. *jiẕâ'*, f. ة, pl. *jawâẕî*, standing on tip-toe; having short arms.

(جار) *ja'ar*, A, INF. *ja'r*, *ju'âr*, low; raise one's voice in prayer; — INF. *ja'r*, be high (plants); bear high plants;—*ja'ir*, A, INF. *ja'ar*, have a fit of suffocation.

جار *jâr*, pl. *jîrân*, *jîra-t*, *ajwâr*, neighbourhood; neighbour; client; confederate; friend; companion; husband; pudenda of a woman; buttocks; —*jâr'in* = جارى *jârî*; —*jârr*, ag. of (جر), draw, &c.; governing the oblique case; — ة *jâra-t*, pl. *-ât*, female neighbour; woman; second wife; protection; buttocks; pl. of جائر *jâ'ir*; —*jârra-t*, camels led by the halters; way to the watering-place.

جارح *jâriḥ*, ag. of (جرح), wound; — ة *jâriḥa-t*, pl. *jawâriḥ*, wild beast; pl. limbs.

جارش *jâriś*, pl. *jurrâś*, criminal.

جارف *jârif*, ag. of (جرف), shovel; sweep (who cleans the streets); epidemic amongst animals; plague.

جارم *jârim*, pl. *jurram*, *jurrâm*, who gathers dates; sinner.

جارود *jârûd*, very dry.

جارور *jârûr*, torrent; brook; hinge of a door.

جاروش *jârûś*, hand-mill.

جاروفة *jârûfa-t*, shovel; (m.) mattock, hoe, rake.

جارى *jârî*, flowing, running, current; passing, happening;—ة *jâriya-t*, pl. *jawârî*, slave-girl; girl; mercy of God; ship; sun.

جاز *ja'az*, INF. of (جئز); *ja'z*, fit of suffocation.

جازر *jâzir*, killer of camels.

جازع *jâzi'*, prop; quarrelsome.

جازم *jâzim*, pl. *jawâzim*, ag. of (جزم).

جازى *jâzî*, sufficient, equivalent;—ة *jâziya-t*, reward; compensation;—*jâzi'a-t*, pl. *jawâzî*, wild beast.

جاسر *jâsir*, pl. *jawâsir*, bold, venturesome, daring.

جاسوس *jâsûs*, pl. *jawâsîs*, scout, spy; white poppy;—ية *jâsûsiyya-t*, spying (s.).

جاسى *jâsî*, hard.

جاسيا *jâsiyâ'*, hardness.

(جاش) *ja'aś*, A, INF. *ja'ś*, come up to, approach; be deeply moved.

جاش *jâś*, pl. *ju'ûś*, heart; senses; bosom, breast, chest.

(جاص) *ja'aṣ*, A, INF. *ja'ṣ*, drink.

جاعة *jâ'a-t*, pl. hungry people.

(جاف) *ja'af*, A, INF. *ja'f*, throw on the ground; frighten; uproot;—*ja'if*, A, INF. *ja'af*, be hungry; be terrified; shrink.

جاف *jâff*, dry, withered;—*ja''âf*, who calls;—*jâf-in*=جافى *jâfî*.

جافل *jâfil*, pl. *juffâl*, running, &c., ag. of (جفل); confused, in disorder; agile;—ة *jâfila-t*, high wind.

جافى *jâfî* (جاف *jâf-in*), cruel, savage; tyrannical; coarse, rude; stupid.

(جال) *ja'al*, A, INF. *ja'l*, come and go; gather (a. and n.);—*ja'il*, A, INF. *ja'alân*, limp, halt;—IX. INF. *ij'ilâl*, fear.

جال *jâl*, wall, parapet; river; mountain slope; (m.) forged, adulterated;—ة *jâlla-t*, *jâla-t*, pl. *jawâl*, exiles, fugitives.

جالب *jâlib*, attracting, &c., ag. of (جلب); importer (of cattle, goods, &c.), pl. *jawâlib*, *jullab*, curing, healing.

جالبية *jâlibiyya-t*, attractiveness, attraction, charm; import and export.

جالس *jâlis*, pl. *jalûs*, sitting, &c., ag. of (جلس); comrade, companion.

جالوت *jâlût*, Goliath.

جالينوس *jâlînûs*, Galen.

جالية *jâliya-t*, exile; exiles; tribute; tributaries.

جام *jâm*, pl. *aj'um*, *ajwâm*, *jâmât*, *jaum*, cup, goblet; tumbler;—*jâmm*, abundant; rested, recovered from fatigue.

جامح *jâmiḥ*, pl. *jummaḥ*, proud.

جامد *jâmid*, pl. *jamad*, *jawâmid*, growing hard, &c., ag. of (جمد); tearless; stilling the blood; inorganic; fossil; radical word; *al-jawâmid*, solid bodies, minerals, fossils.

جامع *jâmi'*, pl. *jum'*, assembling, &c., ag. of (جمع); all, the whole of; encyclopædia; collector; compiler; large kettle; pl. *jawâmi'*, great mosque; cathedral;—ة *jâmi'a-t*, pl. *jawâmi'*, large kettle; necklace, chain, neck-tie; pillory;—ية *jâmi'yya-t*, generality.

جامكية *jâmakiyya-t*, pl. *jawâmik*, salary, pay.

جامل *jâmil*, gathering, melting, ag. of (جمل); troop of camels, pl. of جمل *jaml*, *jamal*.

جاموس *jâmûs*, pl. *jawâmîs*, buffalo.

جان *jânn*, pl. *jinân*, genie, demon; serpent;—*jân-in*=جانى *jânî*.

جانب *jânib*, deflecting, &c., ag. of (جنب); pl. *jawânib*, side, part, direction; tract of land; mountain-slope; disposition; dignity; majesty; pl. *junnâb*, strange, foreign, foreigner; shunned,

despised; avoiding, shunning; — ة *jâniba-t*, side.

جانباز *jâmbâz*, rope-dancer; horse-dealer, jockey (Pers.).

جانحة *jâniḥa-t*, pl. *jawâniḥ*, last rib.

جاندار *jândâr*, pl. *jandâriyya-t*, guardsman, one of the body-guard (Pers.).

جانش *jâniś*, near, close, confining with; ag. of (جنش).

جانى *jânî* (جان *jân-in*), pl. *junât*, *junnâ'*, *ajnâ'*, gathering, &c.; sinner, criminal.

جاه *jâh*, ة *jâha-t*, place, rank, dignity; honour, glory; prosperity (Pers.).

جاهبا *jâhiban*, publicly.

جاهشة *jâhiśa-t*, troop of men.

جاهضة *jâhiḍa-t*, pl. *jawâhiḍ*, foal (a year old).

جاهل *jâhil*, pl. *juhl*, *juhul*, *juhhal*, *juhhâl*, *juhalâ'*, *ajhâl*, *jahala-t*, ignorant, &c., ag. of (جهل); idiot; barbarian; — ى *jâhiliyy*, heathen; — ية *jâhiliyya-t*, state of ignorance; heathenism of the Arabs before Muḥammad.

جاهى *jâhî*, destroyed; open, public.

جاو *ja'w*, INF. of (جاى).

جاورس *jâwars*, millet (Pers.).

(جاى) *ja'a*, A, INF. *ja'y*, bite upon (على *'ala*); — INF. *ja'w*, mend; tend; cover, hide, conceal; prevent; wipe; — also *ja'î*, A, INF. *ja'an*, *ji'a-t*, *ju'wa-t*, be of a chestnut brown.

جاى *jâ'î*, ة, coming, ag. of (جى).

جائبة *jâ'iba-t*, pl. *jawâ'ib*, news.

جائد *jâ'id*, pl. *jaud*, abundant, plentiful; liberal, beneficent.

جائر *jâ'ir*, pl. *-ûn*, *jawara-t*, *jûra-t*, unjust, tyrannical; heart-burn, acidity in the stomach; sycophant, parasite.

جائز *jâ'iz*, passing, &c., ag. of (جوز); metaphorical; pl. *ajwuz*, *ajwiza-t*, *jûzân*, *jîzân*, *jawâ'iz*, cross-beam; lever of a printing-press; garden; — ة *jâ'iza-t*, kindness; pl. *jawâ'iz*, present, gratuity; honorific gift; provender; review; certificate; signature; pl. verses; current sayings.

جائشة *jâ'iśat*, soul, mind.

جائع *ja'i'*, pl. *jiyâ'*, *juwwa'*, hungry, starving.

جائف *jâ'if*, penetrating, ag. of (جوف);— ة *jâ'ifa-t*, thrust, deep wound; pl. *jawâ'if*, hill.

جائل *jâ'il*, turning round, &c.; ag. of (جول); roaming about; loose; — ة *jâ'ila-t*, business, affair.

جائى=جاى;— ة *jâji'a-t*, pus; blood.

(جب) *jabb*, INF. *jabb*, *jibâb*, lop, cut off or out; beat down the leaves; fructify the female palm; surpass, overcome, vanquish :— II. INF. *tajbîb*, have the lower part of the front-feet white; fear; flee; water the cattle until satisfied; — III. INF. *jibâb*, *mujâbba*, vie in riches or beauty; cut off; — IV. INF. *ijbâb*, be covered with foam; — V. INF. *tajabbub*, put on the جبة *jubba-t*; — VI. INF. *tajâbb*, marry one another's sister; — VIII. INF. *ijtibâb*, cut off; wander through the cities; put on the جبة *jubba-t*.

جب *jubb*, pl. *ajbâb*, *jibâb*, *jibaba-t*, deep well; cistern; water-bag; ditch, hole; (m.) shrub, shrubbery; — *jab'*, pl. *ajbu'*, *jiba'a-t*, *jaba'*, a kind of mushroom; hill; cistern, hole for holding water; — ة *jiba-t*, INF. of (وجب), be necessary, &c.; — *jubba-t*, pl. *jabab*, *jibâb*, vest or jacket with wide sleeves; armour, coat of mail, cuirass; ankle, instep; eye-bones.

(جبا) *jabâ'*, A, INF. *jab'*, *jubû'*, also *jabi'*, A, INF. *jaba'*, desist; detest, abhor; come out; hide; remain behind; sell red clay; incline the neck; be blunt or dim; — INF. *ijbâ'*, abound in truffles; sell the crops before they are reaped; conceal; fall upon.

جبا *jiban*, water in a cistern; — *jibâ'*, pl. of جباية *jibâya-t*, tribute, impost; — *jabbâ'*, point of a horn; — *jubbâ'*, cowardly; a kind of arrow; — ة *jiba'a-t*, pl. of جب *jab'*; — *jabbâ'a-t*, point of a horn.

جباب *jabâb*, *jubâb*, year of famine; — *jubâb*, lawful shedding of blood; froth of the milk; — *jibâb*, pl. of جب *jubb*; INF. of (جب); — *jabbâb*, ى *jabbâbiyy*, maker or seller of the جبة *jubba-t*.

جبابرة *jabâbira-t*, pl. of جبار *jabbâr*, ة.

جبابين *jabâbîn*, pl. of جبان *jabbân*.

جبار *jubâr*, lawful shedding of blood; war; free; also *jibâr*, Tuesday; — *jabbâr*, ة, pl. *-ûn*, *jabâbira-t*, strong, powerful, omnipotent; God; tyrant; proud, cruel; great, giant; Orion; high; also *jubbâr*, high palm-tree; — ة *jibâra-t*, setting of broken bones, INF. of (جبر); pl. *jibâr*, bandage, splint.

جباش *jabbâś*, barber.

جبال *jibâl*, body; — pl. of جبل *jabal*.

جبان *jabân*, ة, pl. *jubanâ'*, coward, cowardly; — *jabbân*, ة, pl. *jabâbîn*, cheese-monger; coward; cemetery, burial-place; desert; — ة *jabâna-t*, cowardice, INF. of (جبن); — ية *jabâniyya-t*, id.

جباه *jibâh*, pl. of جبهة *jabha-t*.

جباوة *jibâwa-t*, water in a cistern; INF. of (جبو).

جباى *jab'a*, having full breasts (adj.); — ة *jibâya-t*, gathering, gathering of taxes; collection; pl. *jibâ'*, tribute, impost, tax.

جبب *jabab*, whiteness of the lower part of the front feet of a horse; — *jubab*, pl. of جبة *jubba-t*; — ة *jibaba-t*, pl. of جب.

(جبت) *jibt*, idol; magician; magic.

(جبج) *jabaj*, U, INF. *jabj*, recover from weakness and get strong again.

(جبجب) *jabjab*, INF. ة, travel, wander, roam about; stuff the intestines of a camel with meat, &c.; — ة *jabjaba-t*, *jubjuba-t*, intestines stuffed in this manner; *jubjuba-t*, leathern basket; drum; — ى *jubjubiyy*, maker or seller of sausages; — ية *jubjubiyya-t*, soup with sausages.

(جبح) *jabaḥ*, U, INF. *jabḥ*, cast the dice to see who will be victorious.

جبح *jabḥ*, *jibḥ*, *jubḥ*, pl. *ajbuḥ*, *ajbaḥ*, bee-hive.

(جبخ) *jabaḫ*, I, INF. *jabḫ*, turn the dice.

جبخانة *jabḫâna-t*, store-house for powder; ammunition (Pers.).

(جبذ) *jabaẕ*, I, INF. *jabẕ*, draw, pull; — VII. INF. *injibâẕ*, be drawn, pulled; — VIII. INF. *ijtibâẕ*, draw, pull.

(جبر) *jabar*, U, INF. *jabr*, *jubûr*, *jibâra-t*, set a broken bone; contract (n.); do good to or enrich the poor; help, assist, put under obligation; force, compel; (m.) curry a horse; — I, INF. *jabr*, *jubûr*, get healed, restored; — II. INF. *tajbîr*, set a broken bone; mend anything broken; help or enrich the poor; compel; — III. INF. *mujâbara-t*, give pleasure by anything; — IV. INF. *ijbâr*, compel; consider as healed or restored; — V. INF. *tajabbur*, get set; receive a gift or become enriched; be haughty, overbearing; push leaves; grow again; recover in health; recover anything lost; — VII. INF. *injibâr*, get set; be compelled; — VIII. INF. *ijtibâr*, set a bone; enrich; gain riches; — X. INF. *istijbâr*, get set; gain riches.

جبر *jabr*, force, compulsion, violence; setting of broken bones; bandage; reunion of what has

been separated; reduction of fractures; *al-jabr*, algebra; predestination; man; youth; hero; king; slave; — ة *jabra-t*, currycomb (m.).

جبراعل *jabrâ'il*, جبراعيل *jabrâ'îl*, جبرائل *jabrâ'il*, and several other similar forms, archangel Gabriel.

جبروت *jabrût, jubrût, jabarût*, جبروتى *jabarûta, jabarûtî*, جبروة *jabaruwwa-t, jubaruwwa-t, jabruwwa-t*, pomp, pride; —*jabarût*, power; omnipotence; highest heaven.

جبرى *jabriyy*, compelled (m.); — ة *jibriyya-t, jabriyya-t, jibiriyya-t, jabiriyya-t*, pomp, pride; also جبريان *jabariyyân*, sect of fatalists; جبريات *jabariyyât*, algebraic exercises.

جبريا *jibriyâ'*, pride, haughtiness.

جبريل *jibrîl, jabrîl*, جبرين *jabrîn*; archangel Gabriel.

(جبز) *jabuz*, INF. *jabâza-t*, be dry, unleavened (bread); give part of one's own to another.

جبز *jibz*, hard and dry; miserly, avaricious; mean; cowardly; — ة *jabza-t*, piece, portion.

(جبس) *jibs*, pl. *ajbâs, jubûs*=جبز; also جبسين, cement, gypsum; —*jabas*, water-melon; — hence v. *tajabbas*, INF. *tajabbus*, strut along proudly.

(جبش) *jabaś*, I, INF. *jabś*, shave.

جبصين *jibṣîn*, gypsum.

(جبل) *jabal*, I, U, INF. *jabl*, form, create; shape after a model; knead; mix chalk with sand; compel; — II. INF. *tajbîl*, cut in pieces; — IV. INF. *ijbâl*, form, shape, create; go into the mountains; find miserly; handle the language with difficulty; hit on anything hard in digging; stamp the ground; have blunted weapons; — V. INF. *tajabbub*, go into the mountains; take everything away; — VII. INF. *injibâl*, get formed, shaped, kneaded, mixed.

جبل *jabl, jibl, jubl, jubul, jibill, jubull*, ة *jabla-t*, &c., troop of men; numerous; —*jabl*, creation; formation; kneading (s.); — *jabal*, pl. *ajbâl, jibâl, ajbul*, mountain, mountain-chain; prince; avaricious; — ة *jabla-t, jibla-t, jubla-t, jabala-t, jibilla-t*, natural form or disposition; constitution; temper; —*jibala-t, jabala-t*, face; creature; hardness of the ground; strength; fault, vice; —*jibla-t, jubla-t, jubulla-t*, the created things; descendants; — *jubla-t*, hump of the camel.

جبلقوم *jaballaqûm*, amethyst.

جبلى *jabaliyy*, mountainous; mountaineer; — *jibilliyy*, natural, inborn; constitutional.

(جبن) *jabun*, INF. *jabâna-t, jubn, jubun*, be timid, cowardly; — II. INF. *tajbîn*, accuse of cowardice, deem or find one to be a coward; impute to cowardice; render a coward; effeminate; cause the milk to curdle; — IV. INF. *ijbân*, deem or find one to be a coward; curdle, coagulate; — V. INF. *tajabbun*, coagulate into cheese; — VIII. INF. *ijtibân*, deem a coward; prepare cheese.

جبن *jubn, jubun, jubunn*, cheese; cowardice; —*jubun*, pl. of جبين *jabîn*; — ة *jubna-t, jubunna-t*, cheese.

جبنا *jubanâ'*, pl. of جبان *jabân*.

جبنان *jabnân*, coward.

جبنى *jubniyy*, maker of cheese, cheesemonger.

(جبه) *jabah*, A, INF. *jabh*, hit or strike on the forehead, say disagreeable things in one's face, receive or refuse in an insulting manner; see water without being able to reach it; come upon unexpectedly; — II. INF. *tajbîh*, receive in an offensive manner; cause one to bend his head, put to shame; — VIII.

INF. *ijtibâh*, refuse as injurious to the health.

جبة *jabah*, breadth of the forehead; — *jubbah*, coward; — ة *jabha-t*, pl. *-ât*, *jibâh*, forehead, brow; troop; chief, prince; highly esteemed; moon; an idol; contempt.

(جبو) *jabâ* (I. p. *jabau-tu*, *jabai-tu*), I, U, INF. *jibâwa-t*, *jibâya-t*, gather taxes, tribute; — جبى *jabâ*, INF. *jab-an*, *jib-an*, *jub-an*, *jaby*, id.; collect water in a pond; — II. INF. *tajbiya-t*, lean the hands on the knees or the ground; prostrate one's self for prayer; — IV. INF. *ijbâ'*, sell the crops before they are ripe; conceal one's camels from the tax-gatherer; — VIII. INF. *ijtibâ'*, select; — ة *jabwa-t*, (m.) collection of taxes; collect; — *jibwa-t* = جبارة *jibâwa-t*.

جبوب *jabûb*, hard ground; — ة *jabûba-t*, clod.

جبورة *jubûra-t*, *jabbûra-t*, haughtiness, pride.

جبوس *jabûs*, mean person; vine-branch; — *jubûs*, pl. of جبس *jabs*.

(جبى), see (جبو) and (جبا).

جبى *jib-an*, collected water or money.

جبير *jibbîr*, haughty, overbearing; — ة *jabîra-t*, pl. *jabâ'ir*, splint for setting bones; bracelet; (m.) leathern sack; portfolio.

جبيز *jabîz*, dry or stale bread.

جبيس *jabîs*, mean person; cub of the bear.

جبيل *jabîl*, troop of men; ugly; — *jibîl*, the ancient Byblus; — *jubail*, small mountain; — ة *jabîla-t*, a tribe.

جبين *jabîn*, pl. *ajbun*, *ajbina-t*, *jubun*, temple, brow, forehead.

(جت) *jatt* = (جس), feel, &c.

(جث) *jass*, U, INF. *jass*, cut off or down, up-root; fear; beat; hum; — VIII. INF. *ijtisâs*, cut off or down, up-root.

جث *juss*, watch, guard; shell or skin of a fruit; high ground, hill; impurity in the honey; — ة *jussa-t*, pl. *jusas*, body, corpse; human frame; stature; — *jissa-t*, calamity.

جثا *jasâ'*, reward; number, amount; also *jusâ'*, figure, form, person.

جثال *jusâl*, lark; — ة *jusâla-t*, fallen leaves.

(جثال), III. *ijsa'all*, INF. *ijsi'lâl*, pluck out its feathers; prepare in anger for combat or evil.

جثام *jusâm*, nightmare, incubus, phantom, ghost; — ة *jasâma-t*, dull, sleepy person; sluggard; indolent, foolish.

جثث *jusas*, pl. of جثة *jussa-t*.

(جثجث) *jasjas*, INF. ة, serpentine; — II. INF. *tajasjus*, be dense; shake itself (as a bird, &c.).

جثف *jasif*, belly.

(جثل) *jasal*, drive on fast; — *jasil*, A, INF. *jasal*; also *jasul*, INF. *jasâla-t*, *jusûla-t*, be dense; be dense, short and black (hair, &c.).

جثل *jasl*, *jisl*, dense, densely grown; abundant; — *jasl*, ة, large ant; — *jasal*, mother; wife; — ة *jasla-t*, overhanging hair, foliage, &c.

(جثم) *jasam*, I, U, INF. *jasm*, *jusum*, sit quiet with its breast on the ground, roost; cover the young ones with the wings; brood; — INF. *jusûm*, be half passed (night); rise just above the ground; gather clay, earth, ashes; perish; — II. INF. *tajsîm*, cause a bird to roost or brood.

جثم *jasm*, *jasam*, sprouting crops; — *jusam* = جثامة *jasâma-t*; — ة *jasama-t*, hill; — *jusama-t*, sleeper, sluggard.

جثمان *jusmân*, body; form, resembling a human body, but indistinct; — ية *jusmaniyya-t*, corporality; essence, what is essential; heart, core.

(جثو) *jasâ*, U, I, INF. *jusuww, jussiyy, jissiyy*, sit with the knees upon the ground; stand on tip-toe; gather; — III. INF. *mujâsât*, sit knee against knee with another; sit cross-legged; — IV. INF. *ijsâ'*, make one kneel or stand on tip-toe; — VI. INF. *tajâsî*, sit knee against knee with another; — ة *jaswa-t, jiswa-t*, heap of stones; body; live coal; — *juswa-t*, pl. جثا *jusan*, heap of stones; pl. جثى *jusan*, tomb.

جثولة *jusûla-t*, density, denseness; INF. of (جثل).

جثوم *jasûm*, squatting, crouching; hill; — *jusûm*, INF. of (جثم).

جثيث *jasîs*, ة, shoot of a palm-tree.

جثيل *jasîl*, densely grown.

(جح) *jaḥḥ*, U, INF. *jaḥḥ*, spread; eat melon; — IV. INF. *ijḥâḥ*, be on the point of giving birth.

جح *juḥḥ*, a small kind of melon.

جحاجح *jaḥâjiḥ*, ة *jaḥâjiḥa-t*, pl. of جحجح *jaḥjaḥ*.

جحاجيح *jaḥâjîḥ*, pl. of جحجاح *jaḥjâḥ*.

جحاد *jaḥḥâd*, who denies everything; ungrateful person; — ى *juḥadiyy*, ة, full, stout.

جحاس *jiḥâs*, INF. III. of (جحس); crowd, throng.

جحاظ *jiḥâz*, socket of the eye.

جحاف *juḥâf*, great mortality; death; inundation; diarrhœa; — *jiḥâf*, combat.

جحال *juḥâl*, poison.

جحامر *jaḥâmir*, pl. of جحمرش *jaḥmariś*.

جحجاح *jaḥjâḥ*, pl. *jaḥâjîḥ*, prince, chief; man of great authority, and, by opposition, a worthless person, wretch.

(جحجب) *jaḥjab*, INF. ة, ruin, destroy, annihilate; act repeatedly in a matter; come and go.

(جحجح) *jaḥjaḥ*, INF. ة, examine a thing and bring it speedily to a conclusion; desist.

جحجح *jaḥjaḥ*, pl. *jaḥâjiḥ*, ة *jaḥâjiḥa-t*, big ram; = جحجاح *jaḥjâḥ*.

(جحد) *jaḥad*, A, INF. *jaḥd, juḥûd*, know better and deny; refuse one's right; apostatize; find miserly; — *jaḥid*, A, INF. *jaḥad*, be scarce; be not thriving; be not well off; do little good; — IV. INF. *ijḥâd*, be not thriving; — VI. INF. *tajâḥud*, deny to one another.

جحد *jaḥd, juḥd, jaḥad*, of little good; — *jaḥd*, negation; denying, refusing; — *jaḥd, jaḥid*, scanty; poor, penurious; niggardly.

(جحدر) *jaḥdar*, INF. ة, throw on the ground; roll; — II. INF. *tajaḥdur*, stir and fly up.

جحدر *jaḥdar*, dwarf; short.

(جحدل) *jaḥdal*, INF. ة, gather camels, to let them on hire; become a *jammâl*; gather riches, grow rich; throw on the ground; bind; fill.

جحدل *jaḥdal, juḥdul*, fat and strong.

(جحر) *jaḥar*, A, INF. *jaḥr*, burrow; creep into a hole; drive into a burrow; be deep-set (eye); rise on high; be sparing or behind with anything; remain behind; — IV. INF. *ijḥâr*, drive into the hole or burrow; conceal; compel to flight; compel, force; not bring any rain; be threatened by scarcity or famine; — V. INF. *tajaḥḥur*, VII. INF. *injiḥâr*, burrow, flee to its hole; — VIII. INF. *ijtiḥâr*, seek or dig a hole, burrow.

جحر *jaḥr*, deep hole; — *juḥr*, pl. *jiḥara-t, ajḥâr, juḥrân, ajḥira-t*, den, hole, burrow.

جحرا *jaḥrâ*, f. deep-set.

جحران *juḥrân*, pudenda of a woman; hole, burrow; hiding-place.

(جحرم) *jaḥram*, wicked or malicious

man; — ة *jaḥrama-t*, wickedness, malice; poverty.

(جحس) *jaḥas*, A, INF. *jaḥs*, enter; scratch the skin; kill; — II. INF. *jiḥâs*, repel, ward off; press.

جحس *jaḥs*, cunning, stratagem.

(جحش) *jaḥaś*, A, INF. *jaḥś*, scratch the skin; — III. INF. *jiḥâś*, *mujâḥaśa-t*, repel, ward off; press.

جحش *jaḥś*, f. ة, pl. *jiḥâś*, *jiḥśân*, foal of an ass; foal; he-goat; blockhead; (m.) stand, trestle, horse (for towels, &c.); thickness, hardness, cruelty; war against infidels; effort, endeavour.

(جحشل) *jaḥśal*, *juḥśul*, جحاشل *jaḥâśil*, swift, fleet, agile.

(جحظ) *jaḥaẕ*, A, INF. *juḥûẕ*, have a large or protruding pupil or eye; — II. INF. *ijḥâẕ*, look sharply at (الى *ila*).

جحظ *juḥḥaẕ*, pl. of جاحظ *jâḥiẕ*.

(جحظم) *jaḥẕam*, having large eyes (adj.).

(جحف) *jaḥaf*, A, INF. *jaḥf*, peel, shell, pare; sweep away; dig up and cast away; gather; lean towards (مع *ma'*); take out; catch the ball; — INF. *jaḥf*, *jaḥfa-t*, play at balls; — III. INF. *mujâḥafa-t*, press one in a crowd, come quite close to (acc.); — IV. INF. *ijḥâf*, injure; take; render poor; oppress, press; come close up to (ب *bi*); — VI. INF. *tajâḥuf*, fight each other; play at balls together; — VIII. INF. *ijtiḥâf*, take away, rob; draw out the water.

جحف *jaḥf*, peeling, &c.; game at balls; — ة *jaḥfa-t*, id.; slice of butter; colic; — *juḥfa-t*, remains of water in a well, of food in a vessel.

(جحفل) *jaḥfal*, INF. ة, throw to the ground; blame, scold, rebuke; — II. INF. *tajaḥful*, assemble.

جحفل *jaḥfal*, pl. *jaḥâfil*, great army; great, powerful.

(جحل) *jaḥal*, A, INF. *jaḥl*, throw on the ground; — II. INF. *tajḥîl*, id.

جحل *jaḥl*, pl. *jiḥâl*, large water-bag; pl. *juḥûl*, *juḥlân*, mother-bee; a beetle; chameleon; lizard; lord, prince; small camels.

جحلا *jaḥlâ*, f. big, stout.

(جحلم) *jaḥlam*, INF. ة, throw to the ground.

(جحم) *jaḥam*, A, INF. *jaḥm*, kindle; open the eyes and fix them upon anything; — *jaḥim*, A, INF. *jaḥam*, *juḥûm*, also *jaḥum*, INF. *juḥm*, burn; — II. INF. *tajḥîm*, look at sharply and fixedly; — IV. INF. *ijḥâm*, abstain, desist; approach anyone for the purpose of killing him; — V. INF. *tajaḥḥum*, burn with rage, passion, desire, &c.; be narrow, be oppressed.

جحم *jaḥm*, ة, burning; — ة *jaḥma-t*, eye; — *juḥma-t*, large fire.

جحمر *jaḥmar*, جحمرش *jaḥmariś*, pl. *jaḥâmir*, decrepit old woman; suckling hare; a kind of snake.

جحمش *jaḥmaś*, decrepit old woman.

(جحمظ) *jaḥmaẕ*, INF. ة, wind round; wrap up, swaddle; tie one's hands below his knees; run fast; make short steps.

جحمظة *jaḥmaẕa-t*, swaddle-cloth; rope.

جحموش *juḥmûś*, decrepit old woman.

(جحن) *jaḥin*, A, INF. *jaḥan*, be starved; — *jaḥan*, A, INF. *jaḥn* = II. INF. *tajḥîn*, and IV. INF. *ijḥân*, starve a child or one's family.

جحن *jaḥin*, starved; — also ة *juḥna-t*, louse, tick.

(جحنب) *jaḥnab*, *jaḥannab*, dwarfish.

جحنبار *jiḥimbâr, juḥumbâr,* ة *jiḥimbâra-t, juḥumbâra-t,* short and thick-set.
جحنبرة *jaḥambara-t,* female dwarf.
(جحنش) *jaḥnaś,* INF. ة, also احجنشش *ijḥanśaś,* INF. *ijḥinśâś,* be large and thick.
جحنش *jaḥnaś,* having a big belly; thick, stout.
(جحنفل) *jaḥanfal,* having thick lips.
(جحو) *jaḥâ,* U, INF. *jaḥw,* uproot; stay, remain; walk, step; pass; — VIII. INF. *ijtiḥâ',* uproot; — ة *jaḥwa-t,* step; face; kind, sort.
جحوف *juḥûf,* bucket.
جحيش *jaḥîś,* side, region, tract of land; living in solitude; — *juḥaiś,* little ass.
جحيم *jaḥîm,* large fire; hell.
جحيمى *jaḥîmiyy,* hellish.
جحينا *juḥainâ',* longing desire.
(جخ) *jaḫ,* well done! bravo!
(جخ) *jaḫḫ,* wander from place to place; take the position of prayer; squirt water, &c.; throw up the ground with the foot; lie on the side; lie with a woman; (m.) be pompously adorned.
جخ *jaḫḫ,* جخابة *jaḫâba-t,* stupid; lazy; thick, stout; — ة *jaḫḫa-t,* luxury, luxuriousness.
جخادب *juḫâdib,* ابو ج *abû juḫâdib,* ابو جخاد *abû juḫâd,* جخادبا *juḫâdibâ',* جخادبة *juḫâdiba-t,* جخادبى *juḫâdiba,* paunch-bellied; a locust; a beetle.
جخادر *juḫâdir,* stout, corpulent.
جخادى *juḫâdiyy,* milk-pail; stout.
جخاف *jaḫḫâf,* proud, boasting.
(جخب) *jaḫb,* lean; thin; hollow; —*jiḫabb,* large, big; leader; weak.
(جخجخ) *jaḫjaḫ,* INF. ة, lie with a woman; throw to the ground; conceal one's thoughts; call, cry out to; applaud, call bravo! come to the best of a thing; enter a large assembly; lie prostrate with fatigue; — II. INF. *tajaḫjuḫ,* lie prostrate with fatigue; lie with; be very dark.
جخدب *juḫdub,* pl. *jaḫâdib,* stout; a kind of locust; lion.
(جخدل) *jaḫdal,* strong and fat.
(جخدم) *jaḫdam,* INF. ة, be quick, swift.
(جخذر) *jaḫẕar,* ى *jaḫẕariyy,* stout.
(جخذف) *jaḫẕaf,* great, large, stout; excellent.
(جخر) *jaḫir,* A, INF. *jaḫar,* be putrid; be wide; be empty; — II. INF. *tajḫîr,* widen the mouth of a well; — IV. INF. *ijḫâr,* id.; cause water to gush out.
جخر *jaḫir,* ة, who eats much, is soon hungry; thin, lean; weak in the loins or in the head; cowardly; ugly; putrid.
(جخف) *jaḫaf,* I, U, INF. *jaḫf, jaḫîf,* also *jaḫif,* A, boast; sleep; intimidate.
جخف *jaḫf,* snoring (s.); levity; boasting (s.); جخفا *jaḫfâ,* boasting (adj.); —*juḫuf,* pl. of جخيف *jaḫîf.*
(جخو) *jaḫâ,* U, INF. *jaḫw,* hold upside down; — II. INF. *tajḫiya-t,* draw in the belly leaning with the hands on the ground (in prayer); be bent; draw to an end; be turned upside down.
جخو *jaḫw,* looseness of the skin; thinness of the hips.
جخوذة *jaḫwaẕa-t,* run, trot.
جخيف *jaḫîf,* proud and boasting; snoring (s.); levity; pl. *juḫuf,* soul, mind; large army; dwarfish.
(جد) *jadd,* I, INF. *jadd,* be great, honoured, rich; pass. be rich and happy; be hard, difficult, troublesome; afflict; be serious or of importance; — U, INF. *jadd,* cut, lop; prune; — INF. *jidd,* exert one's self in a

matter, take it seriously; be truthful; — I, INF. *jidda-t*, be new; — II. INF. *tajdîd*, renew, restore; interweave with variegated stripes; clip the camel's udder; (m.) repeat; return in a worse degree (illness); — III. INF. *mujâdda-t*, deal with according to strict law; vie earnestly; — IV. INF. *ijdâd*, renew, restore, mend; act with earnestness and zeal; be in earnest; hasten; be hard and level; travel on such ground; — V. INF. *tajaddud*, be renewed, restored, mended; be milkless; — X. INF. *istijdâd*, renew, &c.; deem or take for new; take afresh; (m.) put again into good condition.

جد *jadd*, pl. *ajdâd*, *judûd*, *judûda-t*, grandfather, ancestor (صحيح *ṣaḥîḥ*, on father's, فاسد *fâsid*, on mother's side); riches, wealth, good fortune; greatness, honour; rich; bank of a river; — *jidd*, exertion, diligence, zeal; earnestness, serious matter; serious, in earnest; haste; high degree; جدا *jidd-an*, much, earnestly, with zeal; — *judd*, well, cistern; fatness; side; coast of Mecca; — ة *jida-t*, wealth, INF. of (وجد); — *jadda-t*, grandmother; — *jidda-t*, novelty, freshness; wealth; surface of the ground; also *judda-t*, coast; port of Mecca; — *judda-t*, pl. *judad*, stripe; tract; path, road; manner, method, system; sign.

جدا *jaddâ'*, f. of اجد *ajadd*, waterless; desert; milkless; — *jiddâ'*, evident; — ة *judât*, pl. of جادى *jâdî*.

جداد *jidâd*, pruning of the palm-tree; — *jaddâd*, wine-merchant; — *juddâd*, old clothes.

جدار *jidâr*, pl. *judr*, *judur*, wall; (m.) dung-hill.

جدافا *judâfâ'*, plunder, booty.

جدال *jadâl*, ة, unripe; — *jidâl*, quarrel, altercation, dispute, contention, combat, III. (جدل); — *jaddâl*, quarrelsome; disputant.

جدامة *judâma-t*, chaff.

(جدب) *jadab*, U, I, INF. *jadb*, blame, rebuke; — *jadub*, INF. *jadûba-t*, be dry; — II. INF. *tajdîb*, dry up; — III. INF. *mujâdaba-t*, have a dry year; — IV. INF. *ijdâb*, find the ground dry; — IV. and V. INF. *tajaddub*, have a dry year; suffer from drought; be rainless (sky).

جدب *jadb*, *jidab*, sterility; drought; dearth; bad season; f. ة, sterile, dry, dried up; (m.) dull, stupid; — ة *jadba-t*, dulness, stupidity (m.).

(جدث) *jadas̱*, pl. *ajdus̱*, *ajdâs̱*, tomb; — hence VIII. *ijtidâs̱*, adorn the tomb; — ة *jads̱a-t*, sound of the hoof; chewing (s.)

جدجد *jadjad*, hard level ground; *judjud*, pl. *jadâjid*, cricket.

(جدح) *jadaḥ*, A, INF. *jadḥ*, stir up, shake, mix; — II. INF. *tajdîḥ*, soil; smear, anoint; — IV. INF. *ijdâḥ*, VIII. INF. *ijtidâḥ*=I.

جدد *jadad*, hard level ground; fine sand; — *judad*, pl. of جدة *judda-t*; — *judud*, pl. of جديد *jadîd*.

(جدر) *jadar*, INF. *jadr*, break out (small-pox, &c.); pass. be seized with the small-pox; — U, INF. *jadr*, bud; sprout forth; get callous; render fit or worthy; wall in; keep within one's walls; — *jadir*, A, INF. *jadar*, bud; be seized with the small-pox; — *jadur*, INF. *jadâra-t*, be worthy; bud; sprout; — II. INF. *tajdîr*, be seized with the small-pox; — II. and IV. INF. *ijdâr*, bud, sprout; — IV. swell; — VIII. INF. *ijtidâr*, make walls, enclosures.

جدر *jadr*, pl. *judr*, *judur*, *judrân*, wall, enclosure; eruption of the

small-pox ; —(m. for جذر *jazr*) root; origin; root of a number; exponent; —*jadar*, ة *jadara-t*, pustule, pock; also *judar*, pl. *ajdâr*, callosity; scar; —*jadir*, worthy, fit, proper.

جدرا *jadrâ'*, f. of اجدر *ajdar*, marked by the small-pox, &c.

جدرى *jadariyy*, *jadriyy*, *judariyy*, small-pox.

(جدش) *jadaś*, I, INF. *jadś*, turn round anything to seize it.

(جدع) *jada'*, A, INF. *jad'*, cut off the ears, the nose, the lips, hands, &c.; maim, mutilate; imprison; starve; — *jadi'*, A, INF. *jada'*, be mutilated; be starved; — II. INF. *tajdî'*, maim badly; wish one to be maimed; starve; injure; — III. INF. *mujâda'a-t*, quarrel with (acc.); scold; — IV. INF. *ijdâ'*, starve; keep back; — VI. INF. *tajâdu'*, quarrel with, scold each other; — VIII. *ijtidâ'*, get maimed; shear the camel.

جدع *jad'*, mutilation; — *jadi'*, starved; — ة *jada'a-t*, stump of a maimed limb, &c.

جدعا *jad'â'*, f. of اجدع *ajda'*, mutilated.

(جدف) *jadaf*, I, INF. *jadf*, cut off; throw; move the hands about in walking fast; walk fast; mark the tact; run in short leaps; — U, INF. *judûf*, fly with clipped wings; — II. INF. *tajdîf*, make slight of or not believe in God's kindness and mercy; blaspheme; — IV. INF. *ijdâf*, raise a cry, clamour.

جدف *jadaf*, pl. *ajdâf*, tomb; wine; foam, dregs, dirt; — ة *jadafa-t*, noise, clamour.

(جدل) *jadal*, I, U, INF. *jadl*, make firm, twist tight; twist ropes; grow and thrive vigorously; get full and bend to the ground (ears); throw on the ground; melt fat; — II. INF. *tajdîl*, throw to the ground; — III. INF. *mujâdala-t*, *jidâl*, quarrel, dispute; — IV. INF. *ijdâl*, have a young one able to follow its mother; cheer up; — V. INF. *tajaddul*, be tightly twisted; fall on the ground; stretch one's self on the ground; — VI. INF. *tajâdul*, quarrel, dispute amongst each other; — VII. INF. *injidâl*, be twisted, plaited; be thrown down.

جدل *jadl*, tomb; twisting, plaiting (s.); syllogism, logic conclusion; also *jidl*, pl. *ajdâl*, *judûl*, bone; sinew; limb, member; —*jadal*, quarrel, dispute; demonstration; dialectics; —*jadil*, quarrelsome; disputant; —*judul*, pl. of جديل *jadîl*; — *judl*, pl. and —

جدلا *jadlâ'*, f. of اجدل *ajdal*, graceful, handsome, &c.

جدلى *jadaliyy*, quarrelsome; disputant; object of quarrel or litigation.

(جدم) *jadam*, U, INF. *jadm*, wither after producing good fruit; cut off; — IV. INF. *ijdâm*, urge on a horse; — VII. INF. *injidâm*, be cut off.

(جدن) *jadan*, pleasantness of voice; — IV. INF. *ijdân*, get rich.

(جدو) *jadâ*, U, INF. *jadw*, be useful, good for, fit; give; demand; — IV. *ijdâ'*, give; be useful, profitable to (acc.); — VIII. INF. *ijtidâ'*, X. INF. *istijdâ'*, demand.

جدو *jadw*, ة, herd; cattle.

جدوب *jadûb*, dry, sterile, arid; — ة *judûba-t*, sterility, aridity; dearth, scarcity.

جدول *jadwal*, *jidwal*, pl. *jadâwil*, brook, streamlet, canal; rubric; column of a page; astronomical, statistical, &c., tablets; paradigm; model; almanac.

جدوم *jaddûm*, pl. *jadâdîm*, hammer (m.).

جدوى *jadwa*, gift, present; profit, advantage; abundant rain.

(جدى) *jada*, A, INF. *jady*, demand; — IV. INF. *ijdâ'*, flow.

جدى *jadan*, gift, bounty; — *jady*, pl. اجد *ajd-in, ajdî, jidâ', jidyân, jadâya-t*, kid; he-goat; Capricorn; — *judayy*, polar star; — *jaddiyy*, of or by a grandfather; — *juddiyy*, fortunate, prosperous, rich; — ة *jadya-t*, pl. *jadyât*, also *jadiyya-t*, pl. *jadâyâ*, stuffing of a saddle, cloth placed under the saddle; blood.

جديب *jadîb*, arid, sterile.

جديد *jadîd*, ة, pl. *judud*, new; fresh; modern; prosperous, rich; surface of the ground; death; du. *al-jadîdân*, day and night; — ة *jadîda-t*=جدية *jadya-t*.

جدير *jadîr*, ة, pl. *-ûn, judarâ'*, fit, worthy, proper; becoming; afflicted with small-pox; walled in; — ة *jadîra-t*, enclosure of stone; nature.

جديل *jadîl*, pl. *judul*, rein, bridle; girdle; — ة *jadîla-t*, pl. *jadâ'il*, plait, tress, braid of hair; anything plaited or twisted; bird's cage; manner, state, condition; region; a garment.

(جذ) *jaẕẕ*, U, INF. *jaẕẕ*, hasten; cut off at the root; pluck; destroy; — II. INF. *tajẕîẕ*, invite in vain to follow; — VII. INF. *injiẕâẕ*, VIII. INF. *ijtiẕâẕ*, get cut or plucked off.

جذ *jaẕẕ*, pl. *ajẕâẕ*, piece, morsel; — ة *juẕẕa-t*, strip of cloth, patch.

جذا *jaẕẕâ'*, broken; interrupted; separated; — *jiẕâ'*, pl. of جاذى *jâẕî* and جذوة *jaẕwa-t*; — ة *jaẕât*, pl. *jiẕâ'*, root of a tree.

جذاب *jaẕâb*, death; — *jaẕẕâb*, attracting powerfully, attractive.

جذاذ *jaẕâẕ*, cutting off, extirpating (s.); also ة *jaẕâẕa-t*, superiority; — also *jiẕâẕ, juẕâẕ*, ة *jaẕâẕa-t*, &c., pl. *-ât*, particle, portion; pl. gold-dust.

جذام *juẕâm*, elephantiasis, leprosy; — ة *juẕâma-t*, stubble; chaff.

(جذامر) *juẕâmir*, breaking a contract.

جذامير *jaẕâmîr*, pl. of جذمور *juẕmûr*.

(جذب) *jaẕab*, I, INF. *jaẕb*, stretch, extend; attract, draw off, take away; win, captivate; drag along; draw (a sword); cause to change place; take the young from its dam; sip water; make eager; have little milk; be passed for the greater part; — U, get the better in pulling one another; — III. INF. *jiẕâb*, *mujâẕaba-t*, contend, combat, vie in pulling; try to wrest from; cause to change places; — V. INF. *tajaẕẕub*, sip, drink; (m.) stretch one's self; be annoyed, wearied; — VI. INF. *tajâẕub*, pull alternately or vie in pulling; contend, combat, vie; be drawn off, transferred; — VII. INF. *injiẕâb*, be drawn off, taken away, carried away, transferred; tear one's self away from (عن *'an*); walk fast; — VIII. INF. *ijtiẕâb*, attract, draw, draw out; take greedily; strive for; rob; transfer from one place to another.

جذب *jaẕb*, attraction; fast walking; — ة *jaẕba-t*, pl. *jaẕabât*, long stretch of road; attraction; passion; pl. charms, allurements.

جذبان *jiẕibbân*, string of a sandal between the big toe and the second one.

(جذجذ) *jaẕjaẕ*, INF. ة, cut off at the root.

(جذر) *jaẕar*, U, INF. *jaẕr*, lop, cut off; up-root; — II. INF. *tajẕîr*, IV. INF. *ijẕâr*, id.; II. extract the quadratic or cubic root; — VII. INF. *injiẕâr*, be cut off, up-rooted.

جذر *jaẕr*, *jiẕr*, pl. *juẕûr*, root, origin; quadratic or cubic root; ebb.

(جذع) *jaẕa'*, A, INF. *jaẕ'*, shut up the cattle without food; tie

together two camels; pass or surmount quickly, finish a journey; cut off; — IV. INF. *ijẓâ'*, shut up; keep off, prevent.

جذع *jiẓ'*, pl. *juẓû'*, trunk or stump of a palm-tree; — *jaẓa'*, pl. *jiẓâ'*, *juẓ'ân*, ة, pl. *-ât*, young; young cattle; lad, youth; recruit; — جذع مذع *jiẓa' miẓa'*, in all directions.

(جذف) *jaẓaf*, I, INF. *jaẓf*, cut off; impel, row; — II. INF. *tajẓîf*, IV. INF. *ijẓâf*, fly fast; make short steps; hasten; — VII. INF. *injiẓâf*, fly fast.

(جذل) *jaẓal*, U, INF. *juẓûl*, stand firm, be firmly planted; — *jaẓil*, A, INF. *jaẓal*, rejoice (n.), be glad, be merry; — IV. INF. *ijẓâl*, gladden, rejoice (a.); — VI. INF. *tajâẓul*, be hostile to each other; — VIII. *ijtiẓâl*, be merry, joyful.

جذل *jiẓl*, pl. *jiẓâl*, *juẓûl*, *juẓûla-t*, *ajẓâl*, root, trunk or stump of a tree; — *jaẓil*, pl. *juẓlân*, merry, joyful; — ة *jaẓila-t*, luxuriant; — جذلان *jaẓlân*, id.

(جذم) *jaẓam*, I, U, INF. *jaẓm*, cut off, maim, mutilate; pierce; — *jaẓim*, A, INF. *jaẓam*, be maimed, especially of hand or fingers; — *jaẓum* (also pass. *juẓim*), be afflicted with elephantiasis or leprosy; — II. INF. *tajẓîm*, cut off, maim; — IV. INF. *ijẓâm*, id.; hasten one's walk; run fast; abstain; resolve upon (على *'ala*); — V. INF. *tajaẓẓum* (m.), be afflicted with leprosy; — V. and VII. INF. *injiẓâm*, be cut off.

جذم *jaẓm*, *jiẓm*, pl. *juẓûm*, *ajẓâm*, root; trunk or stump of a tree; branch; root of a tooth; — *jaẓim*, nimble, agile; — ة *jiẓma-t*, pl. *jiẓam*, fragment, splinter; — *juẓma-t*, mutilation; leprosy.

جذما *juẓmâ'*, f. جذمى *jaẓma*, pl. of اجذم *ajẓam*, maimed, mutilated; leprous.

جذمور *juẓmûr*, pl. *jaẓâmîr*, trunk of a palm-tree; root; principal part.

جذن *jiẓn*=جذل *jiẓl*.

(جذو) *jaẓâ*, U, INF. *jaẓw*, *juẓuww*, stand firm; stand on tip-toe; sit firm; be fat; — IV. INF. *ijẓâ'*, stand firm; get a fat hump; be fat; fix the look at; — VI. INF. *tajâẓî*, sit knee against knee with one another; — ة *jaẓwa-t*, *jiẓwa-t*, *juẓwa-t*, pl. جذى *jiẓa-an*, *juẓ-an*, *jiẓâ'*, firebrand; half-burnt log.

جذوب *jaẓûb*, attractive, charming, alluring.

(جذى) *jaẓa*, I, INF. *jaẓy*, and IV. INF. *ijẓâ'*, hinder, prevent; — VI. INF. *tajâẓî*, slip from the hand.

جذى *jiẓy*, ة, root; — *jiẓ-an*, pl. of جذوة *jaẓwa-t*.

جذيذ *jaẓîẓ*, ة *jaẓîẓa-t*, coarse flour.

جذيم *jaẓîm*, cut off, maimed.

(جر) *jarr*, U, INF. *jarr*, draw, drag, attract; acquire; abstract, rob; drive slowly; pasture freely; wean the foal of a camel (by splitting its tongue); bear beyond the usual time (pregnant woman, &c.); put a word in the oblique case; use the rein جرير *jarîr*; — for *jarir*, U, A, INF. *jarr*, impute falsely a crime to (على *'ala*); — II. INF. *tajrîr*, pull or draw strongly; — III. INF. *mujârra-t*, ask for a delay or respite; pay by instalments; — IV. INF. *ijrâr*, wean the foal of a camel; give the reins to one's beast; grant a further delay; imitate; pierce one with the lance and draw him towards one's self; be deep; — VII. INF. *injirâr*, be pulled, drawn, attracted; pasture freely; be put in the oblique case; trail (n.); — VIII. INF. *ijtirâr*, *ijdirâr*, attract, draw towards one's self;

chew the cud; — x. INF. *istijrâr*, draw or take to one's self; submit; pay by instalments.

جر *jarr*, foot of a mountain; valley; cave; basket; oblique case; pulling (s.), pull; stretching, lengthening, extending (s.); — ة *jarra-t*, pl. *jarr*, *jirâr*, water-jug; bread baked in the ashes; — *jirra-t*, pull; expedition, migration; pl. *ajirra-t*, cut; — *jur'a-t*, boldness, courage.

جرا *jarâ'*, *jirâ'*, bloom or pride of youth; youth; gherkins; — *jirâ'*, INF. III. of (جرى); pl. of (جرو); — *jarrâ'*, good courser, racer; very swift; crime, transgression; — ة *jur'a-t*, *jara'a-t*, boldness, courage.

جراب *jirâb*, pl. *jurub*, *jurb*, *ajriba-t*, leathern sack, knapsack; scrotum; — pl. of جرب *jarib*; — *jurâb*, empty ship; — ة *jirâba-t*, pl. *-ât*, stocking, sock.

جراح *jarrâḥ*, surgeon; — ة *jarâḥa-t*, art of a surgeon; — *jirâḥa-t*, pl. *jirâḥ*, wound; pus; — ى *jarrâḥiyy*, surgical.

جراد *jarâd*, ة, locusts; — *jarrâd*, polisher of copper-ware; — ة *jurâda-t*, rind, skin; leaf.

جرادين *jarâdîn*, pl. of جردان *jardân*.

جرار *jarrâr*, who pulls, draws, or drags anything; numerous; bold robber or warrior; impudent beggar; seller of buckets; (m.) drawer (of a chest, &c.); — ة *jarrâra-t*, large army; scorpion.

جراز *jurâz*, sharp; voracious.

جراش *jurrâś*, pl. of جارش *jâriś*.

جراضم *jurâḍim*, glutton, great eater.

جراف *jurâf*, *jirâf*, a measure for solids; *jurâf*, carrying everything along; voracious; — *jarrâf*, sweeper.

من جراك *min jarâka* (*jarrâka*), for your sake.

جرام *jarâm*, harvest of dates; stones of dates; dry dates; — *jirâm*, pl. of جريم *jarîm*; — *jurrâm*, pl. of جارم *jârim*, name of a fish.

جرامز *jarâmiz*, pl. trunk of the body and feet.

جرامض *jurâmiḍ*, unhealthy, unwholesome.

جراميز *jarâmîz*, pl. of جرموز *jurmûz*.

جراميق *jarâmîq*, pl. of جرموق *jarmûq*.

جران *jirân*, pl. *jurun*, *ajrina-t*, foreneck, neck.

(جراهم) *jurâhim*, bulky, massy.

جراهية *jarâhiya-t*, shrill voice; noise; important; excellent.

جرايا *jarâyâ*, pl. of جريئة *jarî'a-t*.

جرائحى *jarâ'iḥiyy*, surgeon.

من جرائك *min jarâ'ika* = من جراك *min jarâka*.

جراية *jarâya-t*, course, run; also *jirâya-t*, representation, deputation; — *jirâya-t*, salary; — *jarâya-t*, *jirâya-t*, جرائية *jarâ'iya-t*, boldness, audacity; tire of youth.

(جرب) *jarib*, A, INF. *jarab*, have the mange; be rusty; have mangy camels; have a devastated country; — II. INF. *tajrîb*, experience, test, put to the test, probe; get wise by experience; — IV. INF. *ijrâb*, have mangy cattle; — V. INF. *tajarrub*, be put to the test, probed, tried.

جرب *jarab*, mange, scab, itch; rust; blame; rebuke; — *jarib*, pl. *jirâb*, *jurb*, mangy, scabious; — *jurb*, pl. of اجرب *ajrab*, mangy, &c.; pl. of جراب *jirâb*; — *jarrab*, short, little, small; flatterer; cheat; — ة *jirba-t*, pl. *jirab*, sown field; leathern cover for protection of a well; — *jarabba-t*, troop.

جربا *jarbâ'*, heaven; f. of اجرب *ajrab*, mangy, &c.; — *jiribbâ'*, *jaribbâ'*, front of a shirt.

جربان *jarbân*, pl. *jarba*, mangy, scabious; — *jirbân*, *jurubbân*, scabbard; sword-belt; — *jurubbân*, front of a shirt; — ة *jiribbâna-t*, boisterous woman.

(جربز) *jarbaz*, INF. ة, walk; contract (n.); fall; become a cheat.

جربز *jurbuz*, sly, cunning; cheat; — ة *jarbaza-t*, slyness; ready wit.
جربوع *jarbû'*, jerboa = يربوع *yarbû'*.
جربى *jarba*, pl. of جربان *jarbân*.
جربيا *jirbiyâ'*, south-east; north (wind).
(جرثل) *jarṡal*, INF. ة, scatter.
(جرثم), II. INF. *tajarṡum*, take the largest part; — II. and IV. INF. *ijrinṡâm*, fall (from on high); assemble and cling to the place; shrink.
جرثوم *jurṡûm*, ة *jurṡûma-t*, pl. *jarâṡîm*, root, origin; root of the tongue; noble extraction; seat of the passions; earth round the root of a tree; pl. grandees, lords; *jurṡûma-t*, ant-nest.
جرثئة *jirṡi'a-t*, wind-pipe; throat, larynx.
(جرج) *jarij*, A, INF. *jaraj*, be loose; walk on hard ground; — II. INF. *tajrîj*, make loose, rickety.
جرج *juraj*, ة *jaraja-t*, hard ground; causeway;—*jarij*, loose, rickety; — ة *jurja-t*, pl. *jurj*, *juruj*, travelling-bag; knapsack.
جرجار *jarjâr*, roaring; — *jurjâr*, ripe olives (m.); — ة *jarjâra-t*, mill.
(جرجب) *jarjab*, INF. ة, eat; empty.
جرجب *jurjubb*, جرجبان *jurjubbân*, belly; inside.
جرجر *jarjar*, INF. ة, gurgle; quaff; roar with a gurgling noise; — II. INF. *tajarjur*, drink with a gurgling noise.
جرجس *jirjis*, wax; sealing-wax; book, leaf; gnats, flies.
(جرجم) *jarjam*, INF. ة drink, eat; throw down; destroy; — II. INF. *tajarjum*, fall in ruins; let one's self down; crouch; get destroyed; eat and drink much.
جرجمان *jurjumân*, glutton, great eater.
جرجور *jurjûr*, pl. *jarâjîr*, tall, generous camel; troop; thunder, peal, roaring; pl. grandees.

جرجيس *jirjîs*, Georges.
(جرح) *jaraḥ*, A, INF. *jarḥ*, wound; injure, hurt; make sick, ill; accuse a witness of telling a lie; seize; strive to obtain, obtain; —*jariḥ*, A, INF. *jaraḥ*, be wounded; be rejected; — II. INF. *tajrîḥ*, inflict many and severe wounds; be on one's guard against being wounded; —VII. INF. *injirâḥ*, be wounded; — VIII. INF. *ijtirâḥ*, try to obtain; commit evil or draw it on one's self; (m.) perform miracles; — X. INF. *istijrâḥ*, be deteriorated, corrupted.
جرح *jurḥ*, ة, pl. *jurûḥ*, *ajrâḥ*, wound; — ى *jarḥa*, pl. of جريح *jarîḥ*.
(جرخ) *jarḫ*, wheel; pl. of جروخ *jurûḫ*, catapult (m. from Pers.).
(جرد) *jarad*, U, INF. *jard*, strip; peel; shave; card; draw the sword; eat up the grass; eat locusts; receive nothing or grudgingly after asking; — *jarid*, A, INF. *jarad*, be naked, bare, hairless; have little hair; lose the hair; wear out; fade; get spoiled; be eaten up by locusts; have eruptions or (pass.) colic after eating locusts; — II. INF. *tajrîd*, peel, pare; strip; draw the sword; loose the flesh from the bones; prune; wear threadbare clothes; abstract, subtract; separate, isolate; detach, send detached troops; — V. INF. *tajarrud*, be peeled, pared, shelled, stripped; undress; free one's self from (من *min*); loose itself; renounce worldly things; devote one's self entirely to (ل *li*); be taken in abstract sense; be separated, isolated; resemble; cease to ferment; — VII. INF. *injirâd*, be stripped, peeled, shaved, worn out; have lost the hair; be separated, isolated; last long; depart; — VIII. INF. *ijti-*

rûd, draw the swords against each other and fight.

جرد *jard*, shield; f. ة, pl. *ajrâd*, worn out, threadbare; —*jarad*, baldness; bare field, threadbare garment; — *jarid*, ة, without any vegetation; — *jurd*, pl. *jurûd*, high bare mountains; — *jard*, pl. جرداء *jardâ'*, f. of اجرد *ajrad*, bare, naked, &c.; — ة *jarda-t*, detachment, detached troops; military expedition, campaign; escort; — *jurda-t*, nakedness, bareness, baldness.

جردان *jurdân*, pl. *jarâdîn*, penis of hoofed animals.

(جردب) *jardab*, INF. ة, eat greedily; eat bread with one hand and push others back with the other hand.

جردبان *jardabân*, جردبى *jardabiyy*, eating greedily (adj.).

(جردح) *jardaḥ*, INF. ة, stretch.

جردحل *jirdaḥl*, stout camel; valley; river-bed.

جردق *jardaq*, ة *jardaqa-t*, pl. *jarâdiq*, a thin cake.

(جردل) *jardal*, INF. ة, stumble, fall.

(جردم) *jardam*, INF. ة, eat, eat up; gnaw, nibble; talk much and fast; be above sixty years old.

جردى *jardiyy*, belonging to a high mountain-chain.

(جرض) *jaraẓ*, U, INF. *jarẓ*, harden in tumour form; — IV. INF. *ijrâẓ*, lead out, take out; separate; compel.

جرض *jaraẓ*, tumour; — *juraẓ*, pl. *jurẓân*, *jirẓân*, also جرذون *jirẓaun*, pl. *jarâẓîn*, field-mouse; rat; — *jariẓ*, ة, full of mice.

(جرز) *jaraz*, U, INF. *jarz*, cut off, lop; annihilate, kill; kick; sting, injure; hurt by epigrams, &c.; eat quickly; — *jaruz*, INF. *jarâza-t*, be voracious; — IV. INF. *ijrâz*, have barren, rainless land; be emaciated; — VI. INF. *tajâruz*, hurt, insult, inveigh against each other; talk and act badly.

جرز *jarz*, pl. *ajrâz*, without vegetation, dry, barren; — *jirz*, pl. *jurûz*, *ajrâz*, a coarse garment; — *jurz*, pl. *ajrâz*, *jiraza-t*, club, staff, sceptre (Pers.); — ة *jarza-t*, *jaraza-t*, destruction, annihilation; — *jurza-t*, pl. *juraz*, bundle of hay, &c.; sheave; parcel, packet.

(جرزم) *jarzam*, dry bread.

جرزون *jarzûn*, vine-branch, vine (m.).

(جرس) *jaras*, I, U, INF. *jars*, produce a low sound; speak in a low voice; lick; suck; — II. INF. *tajrîs*, speak in a low voice; dishonour, put to shame; disgrace one's self; lead the criminal through the streets before execution; render one experienced and well versed in a thing; — IV. INF. *ijrâs*, produce a low sound or noise, hum; sing to the camels; hear a low sound or noise; — V. INF. *tajarrus*, speak in a low voice; — VIII. INF. *ijtirâs*, strive for.

جرس *jars*, *jirs*, low sound, undertone; — *jirs*, root, origin; — *jaras*, pl. *ajrâs*, bell; — ة *jarsa-t*, little bell, hand-bell; — *jirsa-t*, disgrace, ignominy; dishonouring (s.).

جرسام *jirsâm*, pleurisy (?).

(جرش) *jaraś*, I, U, INF. *jarś*, rub, rub and knead; comb; peel, pare; grind; run slowly; — VII. INF. *injirâś*, be coarsely ground; — VIII. INF. *ijtirâś*, strive for, endeavour to earn; take, snatch, steal.

(جرشب) *jarśab*, INF. ة, recover from an emaciating disease; have reached the turning age (woman).

(جرشم) *jarśam*, INF. ة=(جرشب); also =(برشم).

جرشى *jiriśśa*, soul; anything animate.

(جرض) *jaraḍ*, U, INF. *jarḍ*, strangle, suffocate, smother; —*jariḍ*, A, INF. *jaraḍ*, not be able to swallow one's spittle from anxiety, grief, &c.; be in an agony of grief, &c.;—IV. INF. *ijrâḍ*, cause one to feel the greatest anxiety, &c.

(جرضم) *jarḍam*, emaciated tottering old man; —*jurḍum*, *jirḍamm*, glutton, voracious eater.

جرضى *jurḍa*, pl. of جريض *jariḍ*.

(جرط) *jariṭ*, A, INF. *jaraṭ*, almost choke with a morsel.

(جرع) *jara'*, A, INF. *jar'*; —*jari'*, A, INF. *jara'*, sip and swallow water; —*jari'*, A, INF. *jara'*, be bold, daring, courageous; —II. INF. *tajrî'*, make one to eat or swallow a thing against his will; encourage; —IV. INF. *ijrâ'*, submit; incline; fall; —V. INF. *tajarru'*, swallow, calm down, get tranquil; show prowess; —VIII. INF. *ijtirâ'*, swallow with one gulp; break by one effort; —ة *jar'a-t*, *jir'a-t*, *jur'a-t*, draught of water; draught; drink.

(جرف) *jaraf*, U, INF. *jarf*, *jarfa-t*, take up and remove; shovel or sweep away; scour; hew, hoe; —II. INF. *tajrîf*, carry away; dig out; —IV. INF. *ijrâf*, reach and wash against (flood); —V. INF. *tajarruf*, take much or all, take away, carry off; —VII. INF. *injirâf*, be shovelled off; —VIII. INF. *ijtirâf*, take away, carry away.

جرف *jarf*, INF. of (جرف); —*jirf*, corner of the mouth; —*jirf*, *jurf*, place not reached by a flood; —*jurf*, pl. *ajrâf*, *jirafa-t*, what is carried away by the water; torn off or broken by a flood.

(جرفس) *jarfas*, INF. ة, throw on the ground; take away everything; eat much.

(جركش) *jarkaś*, INF. ة, embroider; adorn, embellish (m.).

(جرل) *jaril*, A, INF. *jaral*, be hard; stony; —IV. INF. *ijrâl*, hit on stones in digging.

جرل *jaral*, pl. *ajrâl*, stone; stony ground; —*jaril*, ة, stony.

(جرم) *jaram*, I, INF. *jarm*, commit a crime; sin; sin against; cut off, take away; —INF. *jarm*, *jirâm*, *jarâm*, reap dates; —INF. *jarm*, estimate the produce of the date-crop; shear; gain, earn; deserve; urge; —II. INF. *tajrîm*, lop off, cut out; emigrate; —IV. INF. *ijrâm*, commit a crime, be guilty; be great; be pure; have a pure voice; stick, adhere; —V. INF. *tajarrum*, be completed, passed; impute falsely a guilt to (على *'ala*); —VIII. INF. *ijtirâm*, commit a crime; cut off; take away; gather dates or estimate their produce; gain, earn.

جرم *jarm*, INF. of (جرم), cutting off, &c.; pl. *jurûm*, boat, barque (m.); —*jaram*, pl. *ajrâm*, sin, crime; لا جرم *lâ jaram-a* (*lâ jurma*), undoubtedly; of course; accordingly; —*jirm*, pl. *jurum*, *jurûm*, *ajrâm*, body, bulk; colour; sound; —*jurram*, pl. of جارم *jârim*.

جرمان *jirmân*, body.

(جرمز) *jarmaz*, INF. ة, contract (n.), close (n.), unite (n.); flee; —II. INF. *tajarmuz*, happen to, fall to the share of, devolve upon (على *'ala*); —III. *ijramazz*, INF. *ijrimzâz*, contract, &c.=I.

جرمشق *jurmaśaq*, maple-tree.

جرموز *jurmûz*, pl. *jarâmîz*, cistern; fountain-basin; small house; members of the body, see جرامز *jarâmiz*.

جرموق *jarmûq*, galoche (Turk.).

(جرن) *jaran*, U, INF. *jurûn*, grind; be steady and zealous in anything, practise it; be smoothed, polished; —IV. INF. *ijrân*, gather

dates from the drying-floor; — VIII. INF. *ijtizân*, prepare a drying-floor.

جرن *jurn*, pl. *ajrân*, drying-place, drying-floor; mortar; basin, font; — *jurun*, pl. of جران *jarân* and جرين *jarîn*.

(جره) *jarah*, several dates on the same stalk; — II. INF. *tajrîh*, make public, publish; — V. INF. *tajarruh*, become public.

(جرهاس) *jirhâs*, tall, strong.

(جرهد) *jarhad*, *jurhud*, cheerful wanderer; — III. *ijrahadd*, INF. *ijrihdâd*, hasten; stretch (n.), be long; last; be hard.

(جرو) *jarw*, *jirw*, *jurw*, pl. *jirâ'*, *ajr-in*, *ajrî*, *ajrâ'*, pl. *ajriya-t*, whelp, cub; small fruit; anything little.

(جرو) *jaru'*, INF. *jur'a-t*, *jura-t*, *jarâ'a-t*, *jarâ'iya-t*, *jarâya-t*, be bold, courageous; — II. INF. *tajrî'*, embolden, encourage; — V. INF. *tajarrî*, prove bold, courageous; dare, venture; — VIII. INF. *ijtirâ'*, take courage and venture upon (على *'ala*); — ة *jirwa-t*, small cucumbers, gherkins; coloquintida.

جروان *jirwân*, wine.

جرود *jarûd*, worn, worn out (clothes).

جرور *jarûr*, restive, refractory; deep.

جروز *jarûz*, voracious.

(جروهق) *jarauhaq*, clew.

(جرى) *jara*, I, INF. *jary*, *jarayân*, *jirya-t*, flow; — INF. *jirâ'*, *jary*, run; issue and take force (edict, &c.); be current; happen, come to pass, take place; fall to the share of (ل *li* or على *'ala*); for (جرا), be bold; — II. INF. *tajriya-t*, urge to run; send or appoint as one's envoy, plenipotentiary, governor; — II. and IV. render current, cause to circulate; execute; order the salary to be paid; settle an account; — III. INF. *jirâ'*, *mujârât*, vie in running, walk or run with another; concur; agree; — INF. *ijrâ'*, to appoint (a salary, &c.); introduce (a custom, &c.); have full-grown fruit; — VI. INF. *tajârî*, vie in running, run or walk together; concur; agree; — X. INF. *istijrâ'*, beg another to be one's deputy, &c.; show one's self bold against (acc.).

جرى *jary*, course, run; water-course; diarrhœa, dysentery; من جراك *min jarâk*, من جرايك *min jarâik*, for your sake, on your account; — *jar-an*, *jara*, youthfulness; — *jarî'*, *jarî*, pl. *jur'ât*, *ajrâ'*, who advances boldly, venturesome; — *jariyy*, pl. *ajriyâ'*, youthful; — *jirriyy*, pl. *jarârî*, eel; — ة *jirya-t*, INF. of (جرى); — *jirriyya-t*, crop of a bird.

جريا *jirriyâ'*, course of events.

جريال *jiryâl*, ة *jiryâla-t*, colour of gold; wine.

جريان *jiryân*, id.; — *jarayân*, INF. of (جرى).

جريب *jarîb*, pl. *ajriba-t*, *jarâ'ib*, *jurbân*, a measure of corn; a field-measure; acre; large river; produce of a field, garden, &c.

جريث *jirrîs*, eel.

جريح *jarîḥ*, pl. *jarḥa*, wounded.

جريد *jarîd*, branch of a palm-tree stripped of the leaves; staff, lance, spear; full; — ة *jarîda-t*, pl. *jarâ'id*, squadron, company of horse; scroll, register; diploma; rest.

جرير *jarîr*, pl. *ajirra-t*, leading-rope, rein; strap; — ة *jarîra-t*, pl. *jarâ'ir*, sin, crime.

جريش *jarîś*, coarsely ground or pounded; (m.) peeled grain or barley.

جريض *jarîḍ*, suffocation, agony; grief; pl. *jarḍa*, grieved; — *jura'iḍ*, ة, big.

جريعة *jurai'a-t*, little draught, sip; — ج الذقن *jurai'atu-'ẓ-ẓaqani*, last gasp.

جريف *jarîf*, dry, withered.

جريم *jarîm*, dry dates; date-stones; ة, pl. *jirâm*, bulky, voluminous; criminal, guilty; — ة *jarîma-t*, pl. *jarâ'im*, sin, guilt, crime; usurer; punishment; fine, mulct; — *jirrîma-t*, tail.

جرين *jarîn*, pl. *juran*, drying-place, drying or threshing-floor; ground (adj.).

جريئة *jarî'a-t*, pl. *jarâyâ*, *jarâ'î*, ambush or watching-place of a hunter; — *jirrî'a-t*, crop of a bird.

(جز) *jazz*, U, INF. *jazz*, *jazza-t*, *jizza-t*, shear, shave; cut, mow; reap, gather; — INF. *juzûz*, begin to dry (n.); — IV. INF. *ijzâz*, have corn to be reaped, sheep to be shorn; be ripe for harvest; begin to dry (n.); give to anyone (acc.) the produce of the shearing; — VII. INF. *injizâz*, get shorn; — VIII. INF. *ijtizâz*, *ijdizâz*, cut off, shear, mow, reap; — X. INF. *istijzâz*, be fit to be shorn, mown, reaped.

جز *juz'*, pl. *ajzâ'*, portion, part, particle, atom; piece; ingredient; division, section, volume of a work; quire of paper; foot of a verse; female slaves; — ة *jizza-t*, pl. *jizaz*, *jizâ'iz*, shorn off wool, fleece; shearing of the year; — *jizza-t*, *jazza-t*, pl. *-ât*, shearing; wool; dates of the year; (m.) clippings; remainder of mulberry-leaves.

(جزا) *jaza'*, A, INF. *jaz'*, take a part of (acc.); divide; be content with (ب *bi*) one thing instead of (عن *'an*) another; tie up, fix, fasten; — جزى *jazî*, A, INF. *jaz-an*, be content with one thing instead of another; — II. INF. *tajzî'*, *tajziya-t*, divide; cause to be content with . . . instead of . . .; suffice to (acc.); — IV. INF. *ijzâ'*, content (a.); cause one to be content, &c.; put the ring on (ل *li*, فى *fî*) the finger; have dense grass; give birth to girls; put a handle to a knife; — V. INF. *tajazzî*, be divided; — V. and VIII. *ijtizzâ'*, be content with (ب *bi*) instead of (عن *'an*).

جزا *jazâ'*, requital, reward; consequent proposition in a conditional sentence; part, portion; — *jizâ'*, INF. III. of (جزى); — ة *juz'a-t*, handle; pole.

(جزاجز) *jazâjiz*, pl. the testicles.

جزار *jazzâr*, butcher; slaughterer; cut-throat; tyrant; — ة *jazâra-t*, head and feet of a sacrificed animal; — *jizâra-t*, trade of a butcher; butchery, slaughter, massacre.

جزاز *jazâz*, *jizâz*, harvest; — *jizâz*, shearing (s.); — *juzâz*, ة *juzâza-t*, pl. *jazâ'ir*, gleanings, clippings, shavings, &c.; — *jazzâz*, shearer.

جزاع *juzâ'*, impatient.

جزاف *jazâf*, *jizâf*, *juzâf*, ة *jazâfa-t*, &c., approximate estimation; buying in the lump; surmise, supposition; by way of supposition; — *jazzâf*, fisherman.

جزال *jizâl*, *jazâl*, gathering of the dates; — pl. of جزل *jazl* and جزيل *jazîl*; — ة *jazâla-t*, plenty, abundance; eloquence; magnificence; high rank; sharp intellect, penetration; firmness; energy.

جزاية *jizâya-t*, taxation, tax.

جزائر *jazâ'ir*, pl. of جزيرة *jazîra-t* and جزور *jazûr*.

جزائز *jazâ'iz*, pl. of جزازة *juzâza-t*.

(جزب) *jizb*, share, portion; — *juzb*, pl. servants.

(جزح) *jazaḥ*, A, INF. *jazḥ*, set to work; go to its lair; beat the tree to make the leaves fall; give a handsome present; give part of one's fortune to another.

جزح *jazḥ*, gift, present; — *jaziḥ*, *jazaḥ*, sharp, intelligent, prudent.

(جزر) *jazar*, I, U, INF. *jazr*, *jazâr*, *jizâr*, cut, cut off ;—U, slaughter, kill, massacre ; — I, U, INF. *jazr*, subside, fall, ebb ; — IV. INF. *ijzâr*, give to kill ; be proper to be killed ; be near death ; be ripe for harvest ; — V. see VIII. ; — VI. INF. *tajâzur*, inveigh against each other ; — V. INF. *tajazzur*, VIII. INF. *ijtizâr*, be left on the battle-field.

جزر *jazr*, *juzr*, ebb ; sea ; —*jazar*, land exposed to floods ; also ة *jazara-t*, sheep to be slaughtered ; —*jazar*, *jazir*, ة, turnip ; parsnip ; —*juzur* and—

جزرات *juzurât*, pl. of جزور *jazûr*.

جزرى *jazariyy*, insular ; islander ; Mesopotamian.

جزز *jazaz*, anything cut ; —*jizaz*, pl. of جزة *jizza-t*.

(جزع) *jaza'*, A, INF. *jaz'*, cross, traverse ; cut off ; give part of one's fortune to another ; — *jazi'*, A, INF. *jaza'*, *juzû'*, grow impatient under sufferings ; be sad, grieved, seized by fear ; be importunate, molest ; — II. INF. *tajzî'*, cut into slices or pieces ; exhaust one's patience ; be ripe by two-thirds ; mark with black and white dots ; — IV. INF. *ijzâ'*, render impatient ; leave part ; — V. INF. *tajazzu'*, get broken ; — VII. INF. *injizâ'*, get broken, torn ; — VIII. INF. *ijtizâ'*, break, cut, tear.

جزع *jaz'*, *jiz'*, ة, a shell ; glass bead ; onyx ; pl. *ajzâ'*, winding of valley, width of valley ; bee-hive ; — *juz'*, saffron ; — *juz'*, *jazi'*, axis of a pulley ; — *jaza'*, impatience ; fear ; — *jazi'*, *jazu'*, impatient ; — ة *jiz'a-t*, small number or quantity ; a little water ; also *jaz'a-t*, part of the night ; — *juz'a-t*, handle of a knife.

(جزف) *jazaf*, estimate approximately, surmise ; — III. INF. *mujâzafa-t*, buy or sell in a lump ; — V. INF. *tajazzuf*, select ; — VIII. INF. *ijtizâf*, buy in a lump.

(جزل) *jazal*, I, INF. *jazl*, cut, cut through, cut off ; distribute ; cut asunder ; make sore ; — *jazil*, A, INF. *jazal*, be sore ; — *jazul*, be considerable, numerous, abundant ; be very prudent ; — IV. INF. *ijzâl*, make sore ; be liberal to (ل *li*) ; give in addition.

جزل *jazl*, liberal, generous ; intelligent, prudent ; = جزيل *jazîl* ; pl. *juzûl*, *ajzâl*, *jizâl*, thick wood for burning ; — *jizl*, ة *jizla-t*, bunch of dates ; — ة *jazla-t*, leathern bag for milk ; basket.

جزم *jazam*, I, INF. *jazm*, cut off, lop ; break off ; fulfil a vow or oath ; mark a consonant with *jazm* ; pronounce or read slowly and distinctly ; fill ; impose ; estimate the produce of a palm-tree ; be discouraged and incapable ; conceal, keep silent about a matter ; — II. INF. *tajzîm*, fill ; be discouraged and incapable ; conceal ; — V. INF. *tajazzum*, be broken ; — VII. INF. *injizâm*, be cut off ; be interrupted, left undone ; be broken ; be marked with *jazm* ; be solved ; — VIII. INF. *ijtizâm*, estimate the produce of a palm-tree ; receive part of a fortune ; buy.

جزم *jazm*, cutting off (s.) ; also *jazma-t*, absence of a vowel and sign thereof ـْ ; shortened aorist ; equality of the characters in writing ; pen with a broad nib ; decision ; apodictical proposition ; — *jizm*, ة *jizma-t*, part, portion, share ; *jizma-t*, herd ; (m.) boot ; — ة *jazma-t*, a single meal.

(جزن) *jazn*, pl. *ajzun*, thick wood for burning.

(جزو) *jazâ*, U, INF. *jazw*, subdue, subjugate ; — I, INF. *jazâ'*, requite, reward, punish ; suffice ; pay ; — III. INF. *jizâ'*, *mujâzât*,

requite; wish to anybody that God may reward him; — IV. INF. *ijzâ'*, suffice; satisfy; supply another's place insufficiently; put a handle to a knife; — VI. INF. *tajâzî*, requite or satisfy one another; get rewarded or punished; press one to do a thing; demand the payment of a debt; — VIII. INF. *ijtizâ'*, ask for a reward or requital; do what is agreeable to another; requite; be zealous and persevering in a matter.

جزور *jazûr*, pl. *jazâ'ir*, *juzur*, *juzurât*, animal to be slaughtered, camel for a sacrifice.

جزوز *jazûz*, ة *jazûza-t*, shorn or to be shorn.

جزوع *jazû'*, impatient.

جزوى *juzwiyy*, pl. *juzwiyya-t*, small portion, trifle; a little of; unimportant.

(جزى) *jaza*, I, INF. *jazâ'* = (جزو).

جزى *jazi'*, sufficient;—*juzy* and جزئى *juz'iyy*, particle, small quantity, a little; f. ة, partly, in a small quantity; special, particular; pl. *juziyyât*, particles, trifles, details; — ة *jizya-t*, pl. *jizy*, *jiza*, *jizâ'*, capitation-tax; custom-tax; produce of the ground.

جزير *jizzîr*, butcher; slaughterer; tyrant; — ة *jazîra-t*, pl. *jazâ'ir*, island; peninsula; land exposed to floods; *al-jazîra-t*, Mesopotamia; *al-jazâ'ir*, Algiers; الجزائر الخالدات *al-jazâ'iru 'l-ḥâlidâtu*, the Canary Islands.

جزيز *jazîz*, cut, shorn; — ة *jazîza-t*, tuft of wool.

جزيعة *jazî'a-t*, separate part; — *juzai'a-t*, small flock of sheep.

جزيف *jazîf*, fishing-net; buying in a lump.

جزيل *jazîl*, pl. *jizâl*, much, many, numerous, abundant; great; eloquent; energetic.

(جس) *jass*, feel, touch; investigate, spy out; — V. INF. *tajassus*, VIII. INF. *ijtisâs*, id.; touch or seize with the lips.

جس *jas'*, rough skin; ice.

(جسا) *jasa'*, A, INF. *jus'a-t*, *jusu'*, be hard; get dry and callous.

جسا *jas'â'*, callous; — ة *jus'a-t*, callousness.

جساد *jisâd*, saffron; —*jusâd*, bellyache.

جسارة *jasâra-t*, foolhardiness.

جساس *jassâs*, prying inquirer; spy.

جسام *jisâm*, pl. of جسيم *jasîm*; — *jasâm*, corpulent, bulky; — ة *jasâma-t*, corpulence; bulk, bulkiness; importance.

جسان *jussân*, pl. players on the tambourine.

(جسد) *jasid*, A, INF. *jasad*, stick, adhere; — II. INF. *tajsîd*, IV. *ijsâd*, cause to adhere, glue; pass. be impregnated; — V. INF. *tajassud*, embody one's self, take flesh and blood.

جسد *jasad*, pl. *ajsâd*, *jusûd*, body, flesh; blood; saffron; the golden calf; — *jasad*, *jasid*, coagulated.

جسدانى *jasadâniyy*, جسدى *jasdiyy*, bodily, corporeal; carnal, material.

(جسر) *jasar*, U, INF. *jasâra-t*, dare, venture boldly; be foolhardy; INF. *jusûr*, *jasâra-t*, leave off covering (stallion); walk; travel over or through; build a bridge; — II. INF. *tajsîr*, render bold, brave;—VI. INF. *tajâsur*, venture boldly, be foolhardy; vie in boldness; stretch one's self, lift up the head; brandish a stick; — VIII. INF. *ijtisâr*, travel over, across; sail.

جسر *jasr*, *jisr*, pl. *ajsur*, *jusûr*, bridge; dam; causeway; (m.) supporting-beam; —*jasr*, ة, big and strong; brave;—*jusr*, *jusur*, pl. of جسور *jasûr*.

(جسرب) *jasrab*, long.

(جسع) *jasa'*, A, INF. *jas'*, chew the

cud; vomit; — VIII. INF. *ijtisâ'*, id.

(جسم) *jasam*, INF. *jasâma-t*, be bulky, big, corpulent; — II. INF. *tajsîm*, make big, corpulent, bulky; increase; exaggerate; bring into bodily shape, incorporate, embody; — V. INF. *tajassum*, be or grow corpulent, bulky; be incorporated, embodied, incarnate; assault; travel to; elect; undertake anything great; begin a thing at the principal and most difficult part; ascend a mountain on the steepest side.

جسم *jism*, pl. *ajsâm*, *jusûm*, body; substance; bulk, mass.

جسمان *jusmân*, body; bulk; mass; — ى *jasmâniyy*, bodily; material; — ة *jismâniyya-t*, corporality; materiality.

جسمية *jismiyya-t*, corporality; materiality.

(جسو) *jasâ*, U, INF. *jusuww*, *jasw*, be hard; — INF. جسا *jasan*, *jusuww*; get dry, wither; — INF. *jusuww*, grow decrepit; freeze; — III. INF. *mujâsât*, be hostile to (acc.).

جسور *jasûr*, pl. *jusr*, *jusur*, bold, courageous, brave.

جسوع *jusû'*, niggardliness.

جسيد *jasîd*, coagulated.

جسيس *jasîs*, spy.

جسيم *jasîm*, pl. *jisâm*, bulky, corpulent; important, difficult; highly esteemed.

(جش) *jaśś*, U, INF. *jaśś*, pound, grind coarsely; beat; clean, sweep; shed; — IV. INF. *ijśâś*, pound, grind; be covered with densely grown plants.

جش *jaśś*, middle of the desert; middle of the body; stony ground; — *juśś*, pl. *jiśâś*, mountain-chain; an hour of the night; — *jaś'*, pl. *jaś'ât*, *ajśâ'*, light bough, branch; much, many; — ة *jaśśa-t*, brothers, relations; servants; also *juśśa-t*, troop of travellers; departure; — *juśśa-t*, loud noise, tumult; violent sneezing.

(جشا) *jaśa'*, A, INF. *juśû'*, جشو *juś'*, *jaśa'*, be deeply moved; belch; emigrate; darken (n.), threaten, lurk, impend; — II. INF. *tajśi'a-t*, V. *tajaśśu'*, belch; — VIII. INF. *ijtiśâ'*, not suit, not feel comfortable in a place (acc.).

جشا *juśâ'*, ة *juśâ'a-t*, belching; irruption.

جشار *juśâr*, cough; — *jaśśâr*, owner, possessor; — ى *jaśśâriyy*, menial taking care of the cattle.

جشامة *jaśâma-t*, heavy work.

(جشب) *jaśab*, INF. *jaśb*, grind coarsely; break; spoil, render vile, humiliate; — U, also *jaśib*, A, INF. *jaśab*, be coarse and without a by-dish (food); — *jaśub*, INF. *juśûba-t*, be coarse and bad.

جشب *jaśb*, coarse food; — *juśb*, skin of an orange.

(جشجش) *jaśjaś*, INF. ة, clean.

(جشر) *jaśar*, U, INF. *jaśr*, drive the cattle to the pasture and leave it there all night; let the horses graze in front of the house; leave, leave behind; — INF. *juśûr*, break forth, shine; — *jaśir*, A, INF. *jaśar*, be hard and rugged; also pass. have a cough or hoarseness; — II. INF. *tajśîr*, drive the cattle to the pasture.

جشر *jaśar*, herds on the pasture-ground; spring-herbs; bachelor; hoarseness; — *juśr*, pl. جشرا *jaśrâ'*, f. of اجشر *ajśar*, hoarse coughing; — ة *juśra-t*, hoarseness.

(جشع) *jaśi'*, A, INF. *jaśa'*, be greedy; covet violently and want to take from another; — V. INF. *tajaśśu'*, id.; — VI. INF. *tajâśu'*, quarrel about the water.

جشع *jaśa'*, envious greed; — *jaśi'*, greedy.

(جشم) *jaśim*, A, INF. *jaśm*, *jaśâma-t*, toil at (acc.); — II. INF. *tajśîm*,

IV. INF. *ijśâm*, put a heavy burden or hard work upon (two acc.); — V. INF. *tajaśśum*=I; undertake anything toilsome or dangerous.

جشم *jaśm, jaśam, juśam*, burden; grief;—*jaśam*, fatness;—*juśam*, basket; belly; heaviness; — *juśum*, pl. fat people.

جشيش *jaśîś*, coarsely ground; — also ة *jaśîśa-t*, groats.

(جص) *jaṣṣ*, I, INF. *jaṣṣ*, sigh and lament; — II. INF. *tajṣîṣ*, cover with mortar, cement, gypsum, plaster; parquet; open the eyes; sprout, spring up; fill up; attack; — VIII. INF. *ijtiṣâṣ*, live close to each other.

جص *jaṣṣ, jiṣṣ*, gypsum; chalk, mortar, cement.

جصاص *jaṣṣâṣ*, mason, parqueter, plasterer; seller of gypsum, chalk, cement.

(جض) *jaḍḍ*, U, I, *jaḍḍ*, swagger in walking; (m.) clamour, cry out; — also II. *tajḍîd*, attack with a sword or lance; run very fast; — ة *jaḍḍa-t*, clamour, noise (m.).

(جضم) *juḍum*, glutton, voracious eater; — hence V. INF. *tajaḍḍum*, seize with the mouth.

(جظ) *jazz*, U, INF. *jazz*, push back, drive away; throw to the ground; lie with a woman; be short and fat; run fast; render anxious, sorrowful; — IV. INF. *ijzâz*, be proud.

(جع) *ja''*, U, INF. *ja''*, eat earth, clay; pelt with clay; — ة *ji'a-t*, beer.

جعاب *ja''âb*, ى *ja''âbiyy*, maker of quivers; — ة *ji''âba-t*, his trade.

جعار *ja'âr*, hyena; — *ji'âr*, rope.

جعاف *ju'âf*, torrent.

جعال *ji'âl*, pl. *ju'ul*, also ة *ja'âla-t*, *ji'âla-t*, *ju'âla-t*, pl. *ja'â'il*, payment, pay, wages; bribe; (m.) pension.

جعانس *ja'ânis*, pl. beetles.

(جعب) *ja'ab*, I, INF. *ja'b*, throw down; make quivers; gather; turn, turn round (a.); — II. INF. *taj'îb*, throw down; — V. INF. *taja''ub*, VII. INF. *inji'âb*, pass. of the last; — ة *ja'ba-t*, pl. *ji'âb*, quiver; (m.) barrel of a gun.

(جعبر) *ja'bar*, INF. ة, throw down.

جعبس *ju'bus*, جعبوس *ju'bûs*, stupid.

جعبلة *ja'bala-t*, haste, hurry.

جعبوب *ju'bûb*, pl. *ja'bâbîb*, the black part of a wick.

جعتبة *ja'taba-t*, greed, avidity, covetousness.

(جعثم) *ja'ṡam*, lean; weak; — II. INF. *taja'ṡum*, contract (n.), shrink, draw in.

جعجاع *ja'jâ'*, narrow, uncomfortable place; prison; battle-field.

(جعجع) *ja'ja'*, INF. ة, bring to a narrow uncomfortable place, confine, shut up; hold fast; be in such a place; slaughter; make the camels kneel down or rise; clapper; — II. INF. *tajaju'*, throw one's self on the ground from pain.

(جعد) *ja'ud*, INF. *ja'âda-t*, *ju'ûda-t*, be curly; — II. INF. *taj'îd*, curl (a.), frizzle; dress the hair; wrinkle, rumple; have projecting muscles or bones; — V. INF. *taja''ud*, be curly, frizzled, wrinkled; be contracted.

جعد *ja'd*, ة, pl. *ji'âd*, curly, curly-haired; curl, lock of hair; crooked; liberal, and, by opposition, miserly; — ة *ja'da-t*, curl, lock of hair; curly-haired (f.); ابو جعدة *abû ja'da-t*, wolf.

جعدبة *ju'daba-t*, water-bubbles; spider's web.

(جعدر) *ja'dar*, short, small.

(جعدل) *ja'dal*, strong, brave.

جعذرى *ja'ẓariyy*, voracious.

(جعر) *ja'ar*, A, INF. *ja'r*, drop excrement; (m.) low, bellow; — V. INF. *taja''ur*, tie a rope

round the waist; — VII. INF. *injiʻâr*=I.

(جعس) *jaʻas*, ease the bowels; — V. INF. *tajaʻʻus*, consider impure; talk ribaldry to (ل *li*).

جعس *jaʻs*, excrement, dung; place where it falls.

جعسوس *juʻsûs*, pl. *jaʻâsîs*, little, small, contemptible.

جعشب *jaʻśab*, long and thick.

جعشم *jaʻśam*, middle, placed in the middle.

(جعظ) *jaʻaẓ*, A, INF. *jaʻẓ*, repel; — IV. INF. *ijʻâẓ*, id.; flee.

جعظار *jiʻẓâr*, ة *jiʻẓâra-t*, dwarf; boaster.

(جعظر) *jaʻẓar*, INF. ة, run clumsily; flee.

جعظرى *jaʻẓariyy*=جعظار *jiʻẓâr*.

(جعف) *jaʻaf*, A, INF. *jaʻf*, throw to the ground; cut down; tear or pluck out; — IV. INF. *ijʻâf*, throw to the ground; — VII. INF. *injiʻâf*, be torn out; — VIII. INF. *ijtiʻâf*, tear out.

(جعفر) *jaʻfar*, brook, rivulet; river, stream; ابو ج *abû jaʻfar*, fly.

جعفرية *jaʻfariyya-t*, art of a soothsayer.

(جعفل) *jaʻfal*, INF. ة, strike one dead from his horse.

(جعل) *jaʻal*, A, INF. *jaʻl*, put, place, pile; put upon (على *ʻala*, ل *li*); give; — INF. *jaʻl*, *juʻl*, *jaʻâla-t*, *jiʻâla-t*, make, do; effect, prepare, produce; instal, name; take for, consider, deem; invest (capital, &c.); fix (as payment, wages, a pension); make a condition for (على *ʻala*); undertake, begin; — II. INF. *tajʻîl*, assemble (a.); gather (n.); — III. INF. *mujâʻala-t*, give a bribe; — IV. make, effect; fix and pay wages; drop young ones; be hot; abound in dung-flies; — VI. INF. *tajâʻul*, agree for wages or a payment; — VII. INF. *injiʻâl*, be placed, put; — VIII. INF. *ijtiʻâl*, place, put, pile; make, do; be done, effected; receive wages; — X. INF. *istijʻâl*, be hot (bitch).

جعل *jaʻl*, ة, small palm-tree; palm-shoot; adulteration; — *juʻl*, pl. *ajʻâl*, pay; pension; present; — *juʻal*, pl. *jiʻlân*, dung-fly; scarabæus; common, mean; watchman; — *juʻul*, pl. of جعال *jiʻâl*.

(جعلك) *jaʻlak*, INF. ة, crumple (m.).

جعلى *jaʻliyy*, adulterated, false, not genuine.

(جعم) *jaʻam*, have an appetite; muzzle; — *jaʻim*, A, INF. *jaʻm*, *jaʻam*, desire strongly, have great appetite, and, by opposition, have no appetite; have a thick voice; lose the teeth from old age; — IV. INF. *ijʻâm*, up-root; be bare, grazed off; — V. INF. *tajaʻʻum*, desire.

(جعمظ) *juʻmuẓ*, old miser.

(جعن) *jaʻan*, INF. *jaʻn*, contract (n.), get wrinkled; relax or be relaxed; — IV. INF. *ijʻân*, be hard and fat.

(جعنب) *jaʻnab*, small, dwarfish.

(جعو) *jaʻâ*, U, INF. *jaʻw*, gather dung in a heap; — *jaʻw*, heap, dung-hill.

جعودة *juʻuda-t*, curliness.

جعول *juʻûl*, pay; pension.

جعيدى *juʻaiddiyy*, men of the populace (m.).

جعيلة *jaʻîla-t*, pl. *jaʻâʼil*, pay; (m.) flock of sheep; company of herdsmen.

جغرافية *jagrâfiyya-t*, geography (m.).

(جف) *jaff*, I, A, also for *jafif*, A, INF. *jafâf*, *jufûf*, dry, get dry, wither; — U, INF. *jaff*, collect and take away; — II. INF. *tajfâf*, *tajfîf*, dry thoroughly (a.); put the war-armour on a horse; move the wings; — V. INF. *tajaffuf*, be dry; — VIII. INF. *ijtifâf*, eat up, drink out.

جف *juff*, calyx of the palm; large number, crowd; anything hollow, hollow tooth; case; bucket;

— ة *jaffa-t*, *juffa-t*, numerous cavalcade, crowd;—*juffa-t*, large bucket.

(جفا) *jafa'*, A, INF. *jaf'*, throw up mud, foam, &c.; scum; empty the pot into a plate; lock, and, by opposition, open the door; eradicate; throw to the ground; — IV. INF. *ijfâ'*, V. *tajaffî*, throw up mud, foam, &c.; lock or open; wear out and starve a beast of burden; throw down; — VIII. INF. *ijtifâ'*, tear out by the root and throw away.

جفا *jafâ'*, tyranny, cruelty, oppression; boorishness; misuse; —*jufâ'*, what is carried away by the stream; foam; empty ship; what is in vain; *jufâ'an*, in vain.

جفاخ *jaffâh*, proud boaster.

جفاسة *jafâsa-t*, stomach-ache.

جفال *jufâl*, also ة *jufâla-t*, foam, scum; what is carried away by a stream; *jufâla-t*, fleeing crowd;—*jufâl*, thick hair;—*juffâl*, pl. of *jâfil*.

جفاية *jufâya-t*, empty ship.

(جفت), VIII. INF. *ijtifât*, take everything away, carry off, remove.

جفت *juft*, a pair.

(جفجف) *jafjaf*, INF. ة, hold firm, retain, seize, gather and keep together; — II. INF. *tajafjuf*, ruffle the feathers, covering the eggs with the wings; be half dry.

جفجف *jafjaf*, low ground; plain; violent; raving, in delirium.

(جفخ) *jafah*, A, INF. *jafh*, boast; be proud; hasten, hurry; — III. INF. *mujâfaha-t*, boast to.

(جفر) *jafar*, U, INF. *jafr*, also V., X., be full grown, four months old (lamb); — U, INF. *jufûr*, be wide, spacious; be inflated; recover; — IV. INF. *ijfâr*=I.; keep apart from one's wife; be concealed; neglect; leave off; — X. INF. *istijfâr*=I.; blow.

جفر *jafr*, art of soothsaying; — also ة *jafra-t*, pl. *jifâr*, *jafara-t*, *jufûr*, *ajfâr*, spacious and half-full well; full-grown lamb; f. ة, pl. *jafara-t*, child beginning to eat; — ة *jufra-t*, pl. *jufur*, *jifâr*, middle; inside; hollow, hole; belly; bulk; large district; — ى *jafriyy*, spathe of the palm (also *jufurra*); soothsayer; maker of amulets.

(جفز) *jafz*, quick step.

(جفس) *jafis*, A, INF. *jafas*, *jifâsa-t*, suffer from indigestion, have a stomach-ache.

جفس *jifs*, *jafis*, degenerate; stupid.

(جفص) *jafuṣ*, INF. *jufûṣa-t*, be sour, acid (m.).

جفص *jafiṣ*, sour, acid; refractory, obstinate (m.).

(جفظ) *jafẓ*, filling up, being full, fulness; cable.

(جفع) *jafa'*, A, INF. *jaf'*, throw to the ground.

(جفل) *jafal*, U, INF. *jufûl*, walk along with a light and swift step; run; flee; shy and run away; blow violently; put to flight; be dishevelled; — I, INF. *jafl*, peel, skin, loose the flesh from the bones; shovel away; throw out; throw to the ground; chase, carry along; burn (a.); — II. INF. *tajfîl*, put to flight, frighten; peel; remove; — IV. INF. *ijfâl*, run away, flee, speed off; urge to speed; put to flight; frighten; — V. INF. *tajafful*, ruffle the feathers of the neck; flee; tremble with fear; — VII. INF. *injifâl*, hasten away; hurry by; be carried along swiftly; disappear.

جفل *jafl*, fear; alarm; flight; timid; rain-cloud; pl. *jufûl*, black ant; ship.

جفلان *jaflân*, timid, timorous.

جفلقة *jaflaqa-t*, hypocrisy; dissimulation.

جفلى *jafla*, commonalty; general (invitation), opposed to نقرى *naqra.*

(جفن) *jafan*, U, INF. *jafn*, keep aloof from anything vile or impure; slaughter a camel and place it in dishes before the guests; — II. INF. *tajfîn*, place the dish on the table; — IV. INF. *ijfân*, indulge in sexual intercourse.

جفن *jafn*, pl. *jufûn, ajfun, ajfân*, eye-lid; also *jifn*, scabbard; vine-shoot; vine; — ة *jafna-t*, pl. *-ât, jifân*, large and deep dish or plate of wood; small well; a noble, generous man; man-of-war;—*jufna-t*, pl. *jufan*, vine-branch.

(جفو) *jafâ*, U, I, INF. *jafw, jafan, jafâ*, oppress, treat cruelly, tyrannise; be insolent; troublesome; molest; — INF. *jafwa-t* (also VI.), neglect; — take off the saddle; — U, INF. *jafâ'*, *jafâ'a-t* (also VI.); be restless, swerve, shrink from; — III. INF. *mujâfât*, maltreat; remove, take away; — IV. INF. *ijfâ'*, treat cruelly and unjustly, injure; take off the saddle; — VI. INF. *tajâfî*, see I.; (m.) abuse one another; — VIII. INF. *ijtifâ'*, move, remove; — X. INF. *istijfâ'*, deem cruel and unjust.

جفو *jafw*, ة *jafwa-t, jifwa-t*, cruelty, oppression, injustice.

جفول *jafûl*, pl. *jufûl*, fleet; pl. *jafl*, bringing clouds.

(جفى) *jafy*, I, INF. *jafy*, throw down; — II. INF. *tajfiya-t*, prune (m.); — V. INF. *tajaffî*, be pruned (m.); — ة *jifya-t*=جفو *jafw*, ة.

جفير *jafîr*, quiver; case, scabbard; — ة *jafîra-t*, portfolio (m.).

جفيس *jafîs*, weak; stupid.

جفيظ *jafîz*, swollen.

جفيف *jafîf*, dry.

جفيل *jafîl, jaffîl*, timid, timorous.

(جق) *jaqq*, U, INF. *jaqq*, drop excrement.

جق *juqq*, pl. *jiqâq*, rectum.

(جقم) *jaqim*, arrogant, insolent; — hence: VI. INF. *tajâqum*, be insolent towards (على *'ala*).

جكجكة *jakjaka-t*, clash, clinking.

(جكر) *jakir*, INF. *jakar*, be importunate; (m.) be offended, nettled, angry; — III. INF. *mujâkara-t*, (m.) offend, irritate, spite; — IV. INF. *ijkâr*, press to buy; — ة *jakra-t*, anything necessary; business, affair.

جكران *jakrân*, offended, nettled (m.).

(جل) *jall*, I, INF. *jalâl, julâl*, shine out, be great, powerful, sublime; be terrible; — INF. *jalâl, jalâla-t*, be old and experienced; — INF. *julûl, jall*, migrate, emigrate; — U, INF. *jall, jalla-t* (also VIII.), gather dung; — INF. *jall*, cover an animal with a cloth; — II. INF. *tajlîl*, be general; honour; cover a horse with a cloth, saddle a mule; — IV. INF. *ijlâl*, deem great, powerful, &c.; honour; give much; take off the covering; be strong, and, by opposition, weak; — V. INF. *tajallul*, surpass in greatness, &c.; be honoured; receive the best part; be covered, clad; sit on horseback; — VI. INF. *tajâll*, scorn; — VII. INF. *injilâl*, be honoured; —VIII. INF. *ijtilâl*, see I.; take the best part to one's self.

جل *jall, jill*, great, glorious, sublime; rough, rude; — *jall, jull*, pl. *julûl*, sail; — *jull*, pl. *jilâl*, *ajlâl, julûl*, covering, saddle-cloth, pack-saddle; veil; principal part, the whole; rose, jessamine (Pers. گل); (m.) avenue of trees; — ة *jilla-t*, old, old woman; grandees, pl. of *jalîl*; — *julla-t*, pl. *jilâl*, basket of dry dates.

(جلا) *jala'*, A, INF. *jal'*, *jalâ'*, *jalâ'at*, throw down, throw away, pelt.

جلا *jalan*, *jalâ*, emigration; exile; —*jalâ'*, splendour, brightness, polish; —*jilâ'*, a kind of collyrium; a honorary title; INF. III. of (جلو); —*jallâ'*, pl. *-ûn*, who wipes, smoothes, polishes.

جلاب *jilâb*, wallet; case, scabbard; —*jallâb*, pl. *-ûn*, importer of goods, cattle, slaves; —*jullâb*, rose-water; a kind of sherbet; —ة *jallâba-t*, boisterous woman.

جلابيب *jalâbîb*, pl. of جلباب *jilbâb*.

جلاد *jallâd*, skinner; executioner; —ة *jalâda-t*, hardness; activity; perseverance, patience; firmness; prompt justice.

(جلادح) *julâdiḥ*, pl. *jalâdiḥ*, long.

جلاذى *julâẕiyy*, strong and stout; artisan; monk; sacristan.

جلافة *jalâfa-t*, hardness, roughness, rudeness.

جلال *jalâl*, splendour, majesty, glory, power; —*jilâl*, sail; (m.) pack-saddle; —*julâl*, *jullâl*, f. ة, great, glorious; —ة *jalâla-t*, human greatness; majesty (title).

جلالاتى *jilâlâtiyy*, maker of pack-saddles.

جلاميد *jalâmîd*, pl. of جلمود *julmûd*.

جلاه *jilâh*, pl. banks (of rivers).

جلاهق *julâhiq*, bullet; stone to be thrown by a sling; weaver.

جلاوزة *jalâwiza-t*, pl. of جلواز *jilwâz*.

جلائب *jalâ'ib*, imported female slaves.

(جلب) *jalab*, I, U, INF. *jalb*, *jalab*, pull, draw, drag, bring; import; seek gain by business transactions; plan a stratagem; cry out, call to; urge on; be bound for a place; assemble; incite; dry up; INF. *julûb*, cover itself with a thin skin (healing wound); — U, sin, transgress; — *jalib*, A, INF. *jalab*, gather (n.) from all sides against (على *'ala*); — II. INF. *tajlîb*, raise a cry, cry out at, urge on; collect from everywhere, import; gain the good will of a person; draw upon one's self; — III. INF. *mujâlaba-t*, help; — IV. INF. *ijlâb*, cry out, raise a clamour or tumult; urge on; be bound for a place; plan a stratagem; threaten; be dried up; heal (n.); cover the saddle with fresh leather; help; call together, collect; gather (n.); — V. INF. *tajallub*, raise a clamour or tumult; — VII. INF. *injilâb*, be imported; — VIII. INF. *ijtilâb*, collect and export cattle, &c.; draw upon one's self; earn, acquire; — X. INF. *istijlâb*, have anything imported, order a thing; try to attract or gain the favour of anybody.

جلب *jalb*, importation, import; crime, transgression; —*jilb*, a small saddle; —*julb*, darkness of night; anything stripped; booty; cloud; —*jalab*, pl. *ajlâb*, clamour, noise, tumult; imported goods, cattle, slaves; cattle- or slave-dealer; —*jullab*, pl. of *jâlib*, healing; —ة *julba-t*, skin of a healing wound; leather; pl. *jalab*, hoop; year of famine; need; —*jalaba-t*, clamour, tumult, sudden invasion.

جلبا *julabâ'*, pl. of جليب *jalîb*.

جلباب *jilbâb*, *jilibbâb*, pl. *jalâbîb*, wide shirt, wrapper, long veil, tunic; pl. slaves; mosquito-net; fillet.

جلبارة *jalbâra-t*, cast a net (m.).

جلبان *jullubân*, pea, vetch (m. *julbân*); boisterous person; —ة *julubbâna-t*, boisterous woman.

(جلبب) *jalbab*, INF. ة, dress with a *jilbâb*; — II. INF. *tajalbub*, be dressed with it.

جلبح *jilbiḥ*, disaster, calamity; decrepit old woman.
جلبدة *jalbada-t*, neigh.
(جلبز) *julabiz*, hard, brave.
جلبقة *jalbaqa-t*, clamour, noise, tumult.
جلبى *jalba*, pl. of جليب *jalîb*.
(جلت) *jalat*, I, INF. *jalt*, beat; — VIII. INF. *ijtilât*, id.; eat up.
جلج *jalaj*, beginning of dawn; — *jalaj*, ة, pl. *jalâj*, *jilâj*, skull; bubble; — ة *jalaja-t*, Calvary.
(جلجل) *jaljal*, INF. ة, shake, move (a.); mix (a.); frighten, confuse; twist tightly; touch and make to sound; cry out, call aloud; clap, thunder; neigh; — II. INF. *tajaljul*, be dipped into, sink; be beaten, shaken, fall in ruins.
جلجل *juljul*, pl. *jalâjil*, little bell; strings of such to adorn the necks of cattle, &c.; — ة *jaljala-t*, skull.
جلجلان *juljulân*, coriander-seed; sesame; core, bottom of the heart.
(جلح) *jalaḥ*, A, INF. *jalḥ*, browse; — *jaliḥ*, A, INF. *jalaḥ*, be bald on the sides of the forehead, grow bald; — II. INF. *tajlîḥ*, browse entirely off; attack; be bold, courageous; set to work, continue, perpetrate; — III. INF. *mujâlaḥa-t*, make known; publish; show one's self proud, empassioned, hostile.
جلح *jalaḥ*, baldness; — *julḥ*, pl. of اجلح *ajlaḥ*, bald; — ة *jalaḥa-t*, front part of the head; baldness.
جلحا *jilḥâ'*, ة *jilḥâ'a-t*, barren, sterile.
(جلحز) *jalḥaz*, miserly, mean.
(جلحم) *jalḥam*, INF. ة, twist a rope; — II. INF. *tajalḥum*, assemble (n.).
(جلخ) *jalaḫ*, A, INF. *jalḫ*, fill up; cut off a piece of flesh; skin; throw to the ground; lie with a woman; stretch, lengthen, extend; — IX. INF. *ijliḫâḫ*, be weak and soft of bones; stretch out the arms in prayer; — XV. INF. *ijlinḫâ'*, fall in ruins.
(جلخب), III. INF. *ijliḫbâb*, fall down.
(جلخم), III. INF. *ijliḫmâm*, be numerous, assembled in a crowd; be proud.
(جلد) *jalad*, I, INF. *jald*, *jalda-t*, beat, hit, scourge, whip; skin, flay; compel; throw down; sting; lie with a woman; commit onanism; — *jalid*, A, INF. *jalad*, be damaged by hoar frost; =*jalud*, INF. *jalad*, *jalâda-t*, *julûda-t*, *majlûd*, be hard, tough, strong; be prudent and active; pass. be injured by hoar frost; — II. INF. *tajlîd*, skin, flay; have whipped, scourged; bind (a book); cause to freeze, freeze; — III. INF. *jilâd*, *mujâlada-t*, show one's self hard, energetic, persevering towards; fight with; — IV. INF. *ijlâd*, be covered with hoar frost; be injured by it; cause one to take refuge with another; — V. INF. *tajallud*, show one's self hard, energetic, persevering, patient; be bound (book); — VI. INF. *tajâlud*, fight, whip each other; — VII. INF. *injilâd*, be whipped, scourged; — VIII. INF. *ijtilâd*, id.; drink out.
جلد *jald*, pl. *jalda*, hard, prudent; active and strong; flogging, whipping, scourging (s.); pl. *ajlâd*, *jilâd*, *julud*, energetic, active; — *jild*, ة, pl. *julûd*, skin, hide; leather; binding (of a book); volume; price; — *juld*, pl. of اجلد *ajlad*, hard; — *jalad*, hardness, perseverance; endurance, patience; firmament; hard ground; — *julud*, see above; pl. of جليد *jalîd*.
(جلدب) *jaldab*, hard, severe.
(جلذ) *julẓ*, pl. *manâjiẓ*, mole.
جلذى *julẓiyy*=جلاذى *julâẓiyy*.

(جلز) *jalaz*, I, INF. *jalz*, fold and wrap up; twist firmly together; (also II.), tie round with the sinew of the camel's neck; extend, stretch; pull out; — II. INF. *tajlîz*, see I.; depart quickly; — V. INF. *tajalluz*, be ready for action.

جلز *jalz*, sinew of a camel's neck for tying.

(جلس) *jalas*, I, INF. *julûs*, *majlas*, sit, sit down; hold a session, grant an audience; (m.) be placed upright; travel to Najd, the Arabian highlands; — II. INF. *tajlîs*, place upright; cause to sit; — III. INF. *mujâlasa-t*, sit down by, sit in company with (acc.); — IV. INF. *ijlâs*, order or beg to sit down; — V. INF. *tajallus*, sit down, hold a session or conference; — VI. INF. *tajâlus*, sit down together.

جلس *jals*, high land; the country of Najd; lady; strong camel; member of an assembly, guest; pond; time; wine; thick; — *jils*=جليس *jalîs*; — ة *jalsa-t*, pl. *jalasât*, session; assembly, company; state, condition; — *jilsa-t*, way of sitting; — *julasa-t*, person who always sits at home.

جلسا *julasâ'*, pl. of جليس *jalîs*.

جلسام *jilsâm*, pleurisy.

(جلط) *jalaṭ*, I, INF. *jalṭ*, lie, tell a lie; swear, take an oath; draw (a sword); shave; skin, flay; drop excrement; — V. INF. *tajalluṭ*, fight against by stratagem; — VII. INF. *injilâṭ*, fall down; — VIII. INF. *ijtilâṭ*, steal secretly; drink out; — ة *julṭa-t*, thick milk.

جلطا *jalṭâ'*, loose.

(جلع) *jala'*, A, INF. *julû'*, be naked; strip; — *jali'*, A, INF. *jala'*, be open; be impudent, talk ribaldry; quarrel in a game, over the wine, in dividing the booty; — VII. INF. *injilâ'*, be uncovered, bared, stripped.

جلع *jali'*, ة, impudent, shameless.

(جلعب) *jal'ab*, ة, malignant, malicious; — hence: III. *ijla'abb*, INF. *ijli'bâb*, lie down on one's side and stretch one's self out; depart; exert one's self in walking; be numerous; be dispersed.

(جلعد) *jal'ad*, INF. ة, stretch lengthways on the ground (a.); — *ijla'add*, INF. *ijli'dâd*, be thrown down, stretched out.

جلعد *jal'ad*, hard; strong; brave.

(جلعم) *jal'am*, impudent, shameless.

(جلغ) *jalag*, U, INF. *jalg*, cut one another with swords; (m.) whet, sharpen.

(جلف) *jalaf*, U, INF. *jalf*, tear, scrape or scratch off; peel, shell; shovel away; cut down, up-root; annihilate; cut with the sword; — *jalif*, A, INF. *jalaf*, *jalâfa-t*, be hard, rough, rude; — II. INF. *tajlîf*, destroy; blunt; break off the edge of a vessel; — IV. INF. *ijlâf*, scrape or scratch off; — VIII. INF. *ijtilâf*, destroy.

جلف *jilf*, pl. *ajlâf*, *julûf*, hard, unjust; stupid and rude, brutal; pl. *julûf*, pot, vessel; — *jilf*, also ة *julfa-t*, a small piece of skin; scratch; chip; — ة *jilfa-t*, slice of dry bread; piece; cut of a pen.

جلفدة *jalfada-t*, idle clamour.

(جلفز) *jalfaz*, strong and stout.

(جلفط) *jalfaṭ*, INF. ة, caulk, repair a ship.

(جلق) *jalaq*, I, INF. *jalq*, shave; shoot, pelt at; uncover, bare; =V. INF. *tajalluq*, open the mouth in laughing, so that the back teeth can be seen; — VII. INF. *injilâq*, be shot, pelted at.

جلق *jalq*, peace; — *jilliq*, a kind of wheat; Damascus; — ة *jilliqa-t*, old woman.

جلل *jalal*, important matter; with من *min* and a pronominal suffix: for the sake of.

(جلم) *jalam*, U, INF. *jalm*, lop; loose the flesh from the bones of a slaughtered animal; shear.

(جلم) *jilm*, sheep's tallow;—*jalam* and du. *jalamân*, scissors; pl. *jilâm*, a kind of sheep; he-goat; tick (insect); the new moon; a kind of hawk;—ة *jalma-t*, trunk of a slaughtered animal.

(جلمح) *jalmaḥ*, INF. ة, shave.

(جلمد) *jalmad*, large rock;—also ة *jalmada-t*, a brave warrior, hero; herd;—*jalmada-t*, stony ground.

(جلمط) *jalmaṭ*, INF. ة, shave.

جلمود *julmûd*, *jalmûd*, pl. *jalâmîd*, *jalâmid*, large rock; brave warrior.

جلنار *jullanâr*, blossom of the pomegranate (Pers.).

(جلنبط) *jalambaṭ*, lion.

جلنجبين *julanjubîn*, conserve of roses (Pers.).

(جلنظى) *jalanẓa*, broad-shouldered;—hence IV. *ijlanẓa*, INF. *ijlinẓa'*, be enraged.

(جلنفع) *jalanfa'*, stupid; ة, stout;—hence IV. *ijlanfa'*, INF. *ijlinfâ'*, be stout.

(جله) *jalah*, A, INF. *jalh*, remove; prevent, divert, dissuade; put away; uncover;—*jalih*, A, INF. *jalah*, lose the front hair.

(جلهز) *jalhaz*, INF. ة, keep silent about a matter known.

(جلهم) *julhum*, a large mouse;—ة *julhuma-t*, *jalhama-t*, bank of a river; side of a valley; anything important; misfortune, calamity.

(جلو) *jalâ*, U, INF. *jalw*, *jalâ'*, disclose, reveal, communicate; polish, smooth, clean; wash, rinse; wipe away; dispel grief; throw away; be high;—INF. *jilâ'*, *jalwa-t*, *jilwa-t*, *julwa-t*, unveil the bride to the bridegroom; make presents to the bride on this occasion; see the bride adorned; be shown to the bridegroom; be evident, known, public; migrate, emigrate; compel to emigrate;—INF. *jalâ'*, drive the bees out of the hive by smoke;—II. INF. *tajliyy*, *tajliya-t*, polish, smooth, make bright; disclose, publish; explain; give presents to a bride; throw food to the cattle; cast a glance at; lift up the head and look out;—III. INF. *mujâlât*, confront as an enemy, fight against;—IV. INF. *ijlâ'*, emigrate; force to emigrate, expel; be freed from grief; be far distant; hasten;—V. INF. *tajallî*, be unveiled, uncovered, made known; appear; reveal himself (God); lift up the head and look out; look at;—VI. INF. *tajâlî*, communicate each other's circumstances to one another;—VII. INF. *injilâ'*, be disclosed; reveal himself (God); clear up; disperse (clouds, n.); be bright, polished; disappear, subside;—VIII. INF. *ijtilâ'*, see the bride unveiled; show her to the bridegroom; force to emigrate; take off the turban; glance at, observe, have regard to;—X. INF. *istijlâ'*, present the bride unveiled; migrate;—ة *jalwa-t*, *jilwa-t*, *julwa-t*, splendour, brightness, brilliancy; a thing of beauty; beauty of things; unveiling of the bride; bride-gift; coquettishness; shining garments; submersion of a man in God.

جلوا *jalwâ*, f. of اجلى *ajla*, brighter, more shining, &c.

جلواز *jilwâz*, pl. *jalâwiza-t*, taxgatherer; executor; guard.

جلوبة *jalûba-t*, anything imported.

جلودة *julûda-t*, hardness; aptness.

جلودى *julûdiyy*, seller of hides or leather.

جلوز *jillauz*, hazel nut.

جلوس *julûs*, sitting, session; assembly; ascension to the throne; — pl. of جالس *jâlis*; — ى *julûsiyy*, dating from, referring to the beginning of the reign.

(جلى) *jala*, I, INF. *jaly*, polish; — *jalî*, A, INF. *jalan*, lose the front hair; — II. INF. *tajliya-t*, cause to appear; show forth; — V. INF. *tajallî*, see V. (جلو); mount, ascend; look at anything on high.

جلى *jaly*, polishing (s.), polish; — *jily*, small window in the roof; — *jaliyy*, ة, bright, polished; evident, clear; light; loud; a character of handwriting; — ة *jaliyya-t*, clear matter or news; clearness.

جليان *jalayân*, revelation; apocalypse.

جليب *jalîb*, pl. *jalabâ'*, *jalba*, also ة *jalîba-t*, pl. *jalâ'ib*, imported slave, merchandise, cattle.

جليد *jalîd*, pl. *juladâ'*, *ajlâd*, *jilâd*, *julud*, hard, strong, apt, active; hoar-frost, frost, ice; — ة *julaida-t*, thin skin, membrane; — *jalîdiyya-t*, moisture of the eye.

جليس *jalîs*, pl. *julasâ'*, *jullâs*, companion; intimate; confidant; assessor.

جليف *jalîf*, ة, peeled; blunt, notchy; scraped off; — ة *jalîfa-t*, pl. *jalâ'if*, *juluf*, *julf*, severe, fatal season; ruin, destruction.

جليل *jalîl*, ة, pl. *ajillâ*, *jilla-t*, *ajilla-t*, magnificent, glorious, great; venerable; strong, stout, rough; — pl. *jilla-t*, *ajilla-t*, old, experienced; — ة *jalîla-t*, pl. *jalâ'il*, matter of importance.

(جم) *jamam* (also V.), spread luxuriantly; — *jamm*, I, U, INF. *jumûm*, be abundant; get full; INF. *jamm*, *jumûm*, be or get brimful; be fleshy; impend; approach; leave water; — I, INF. *jamm*, *jamâm*, fill to the brim or above; (m.) cut off the tree at the surface of the ground; — INF. *jamâm* (also I, INF. *jimâm*), rest after covering (stallion); — INF. *jamm*, *jamâm*, be left without work to rest; — A, INF. *jamam*, be hornless (ram); — II. INF. *tajmîm*, fill to the brim or above; — IV. INF. *ijmâm*, id.; leave water; allow to rest; impend; — V. INF. *tajammum*, see I.; be full (to the brim), heaped up; — X. INF. *istijmâm*, be plentiful; have gathered; leave water in (acc.) the well; rest; refresh one's self; be covered with vegetation.

جم *jamm*, plenty, abundance; heap; heaped up measure; exceeding; numerous; mass of water; (m.) water-line, level; pl. *jimâm*, *jumûm*, abundant, inexhaustible; — *jimm*, devil; — ة *jamma-t*, pl. *jumûm*, overflowing well or pond; pl. *jumam*, hold of a ship; — also *jumma-t*, troop, crowd; — *jumma-t*, rich hair falling on the shoulders; tuft of hair; bud.

جما *jama'*, INF. of (جمى); also *jamâ'*, ة *jamâ'a-t*, somebody; individual; — *jammâ*, f. of اجم *ajamm*, fleshy, &c., q.v.

جماح *jimâḥ*, refractoriness; INF. of (جمح); — *jummâḥ*, pl. fugitives.

جماد *jamâd*, dry year or season; pl. *-ât*, *jumud*, dried up ground; anything inanimate; inorganic; fossil; pl. *jamâdât*, minerals, fossils; — *jimâd*, pl. of جمد *jumd*; — *jammâd*, sharp; seller of ice; — ى *jumâda*, pl. *jumâdayât*, name of a month; — *jamâdiyy*, inorganic.

جمار *jamâr*, crowd, people; — *jummâr*, ة *jummâra-t*, pl. *-ât*, marrow in the top of the palm-tree.

جماز *jammâz*, swift; jumping, leaping; also ة *jammâza-t*, fleet camel.

جماش *jammâś*, dandy; lady's man.

جماع *jimâ'*, coition; whole, entire, all; sum, total, the whole, plenty; pl. *jum'*, large kettle, cauldron; —*jammâ'*, given to sexual intercourse; — ة *jamâ'a-t*, troop; crowd; assembly; party; community; the believers; pl. *-ât*, tax-roll, registers.

جمال *jamâl*, beauty, grace, gracefulness; elegance; purity of life, good conduct, refined manners; beneficence; —*jimâl*, pl. of جمل *jamal*; — *jammâl*, pl. *jammâla-t*, *jammâlûn*, camel-driver; —*jummâl*, very beautiful; — ة *jumâla-t*, pl. of جمل *jamal*.

جمام *jamâm*, heaped up measure; superabundance; level.

جمان *jumân*, ة, pearl, jewel; silver beads; — *jammân*, measured full.

جماهير *jamâhîr*, pl. of جمهور *jumhûr*.

جمجم *jamjam*, INF. ة, speak indistinctly; conceal in one's heart; — II. INF. *tajamjum*, speak indistinctly; not dare to (عن *'an*); — ة *jumjuma-t*, pl. *jumjum*, *jamâjim*, skull; plough-staff; drinking-cup; a measure.

(جمح) *jamaḥ*, A, INF. *jamḥ*, *jimâḥ*, *jumûḥ*, be restive and run away; act capriciously; be headstrong; run fast, hurry; throw at, hit.

(جمخ) *jamaḫ*, U, INF. *jamḫ*, be proud; — III. INF. *mujâmaḫa-t*, boast.

جمخ *jamḫ*, pride; glory;—*jummaḫ*, pl. of جامخ *jâmiḫ*.

(جمد) *jamad*, U, INF. *jamd*, *jumûd*, harden; stiffen, coagulate, freeze (n.); grow tranquil, calm down; be hard, miserly; insist on one's right; cut, cut off; — *jamud*, get rigid, freeze (n.); — II. INF. *tajmîd*, condense, coagulate, freeze (a.); — IV. INF. *ijmâd*, id.; make stand to right; not be of any more good; — V. INF. *tajammud*, VII. INF. *injimâd*, coagulate, freeze (n.).

جمد *jamd*, condensation, coagulation, congelation; frozen hard; ice; —*jumd*, *jumud*, *jamad*, pl. *ajmâd*, high ground; pl. strongholds; —*jamad*, ice, snow; pl. of جامد *jâmid*; —*jumud*, pl. of جماد *jamâd*.

(جمر) *jamar*, I, INF. *jamr* (also II. and IV.), unite for a purpose (n. and a.); give live coal; jump with the feet tied together; turn off, keep off; — II. INF. *tajmîr*, see I.; — gather, unite; tie together the back hair (also IV.); retain an army on the soil of the enemy; take the marrow out of the top of a palm-tree; pelt with stones (m.); cover with coal; change into coal, carbonise; get carbonised; — IV. INF. *ijmâr*, see I. and II.; hasten; fumigate clothes; — INF. *majmar*, poke the fire; estimate the produce of a palm-tree; jump with the feet tied together; have an uncloven hoof; have the new moon covered; refer to all, concern all; emaciate; — V. INF. *tajammur*, unite (n.) or keep together (a.); be retained on hostile soil; — VIII. INF. *ijtimâr*, fumigate; — X. INF. *istijmâr*=V.; use a pebble instead of curl-paper for the sake of cleanliness.

جمر *jamr*, ة, pl. *jamr*, *jamarât*, live coal; pebble; an Arabic tribe; stoning of the devil in the valley of Mîna; new infusion of vital heat in spring-time, &c.

(جمز) *jamaz*, I, INF. *jamz*, جمزى *jamzâ*, hurry with long steps:

leap; go abroad; — ة jamza-t, pl. jamazât, leap, jump.

(جمزر) jamzar, INF. ة, run away; flee.

جمزى jamza, quick pace.

(جمس) jamas, U, INF. jumûs, harden, coagulate (n.); — ة jamsa-t, fire; — jumsa-t, pl. jums, half-ripe dates.

(جمست) jamast, a kind of turquoise.

(جمش) jamaś, U, INF. jamś, shave; smooth; milk only with finger-tops; make love to (acc.); — II. INF. tajmîś, make love; help, assist.

جمش jamś, low sound.

(جمع) jama', A, INF. jam', gather, assemble, keep together (a.); unite, reconcile; collect one's self, recollect; lie with (ب bi); add; form the plural; contain; be full grown; — II. INF. tajmî', gather, collect, assemble from all sides; heap up; count; attend to the Friday's service; — III. INF. mujâma'a-t, jimâ', agree with (acc.); yield; have sexual intercourse, lie with (acc.); — IV. INF. ijmâ', gather, assemble (a.); take all; drive all of them (camels); make familiar; agree in (على 'ala); resolve; prepare, make ready; dry (a.); — V. INF. tajammu', assemble (n.), flock together; hold an assembly, a Friday's service; resolve; — VIII. INF. ijtimâ', ijdimâ', assemble (n.); meet (ب bi); agree in (على 'ala); conspire; attain to puberty; — X. INF. istijmâ', be willing to assemble, assemble (n.), gather (n.); happen according to one's wish; collect all strength; levy troops.

جمع jam', pl. jumû', troop, crowd; assembly; pl. troops, an army; sum, total, majority; plural; produce, rent, interest; rent-roll, rent-book; price, value; addition; coition; INF. of (جمع); يوم الجمع yaumu 'l-jam'i, Day of Judgment, day of the gathering on Mount 'Arafat; — jum', pl. ajmâ', fist; بجمع bi-jum', entire, all of it; secret, pregnant; — jum', pl. of جامع jâmi'; — ة jum'a-t, pl. -ât, juma', union, gathering, concourse; friendship; handful; week; — also jumu'a-t, juma'a-t, pl. -ât, Friday; — jama'a-t, pl. -at, troop, company; sum.

جمعا jamâ', pl. جمع jum', f. of اجمع ajma', entire, all.

(جمعد) jam'ad, heap of stones.

(جمعر) jam'ar, INF. ة, make a top spin; turn in a circle; be given to biting.

جمعور jum'ûr, large troop, crowd; — ة jum'ûra-t, potter's wheel; spinning-top.

جمعى jam'iyy, total; — ة jam'iyya-t, assembly; conference; small party, company; committee; congregation; collection of mind.

(جمل) jamal, U, INF. jaml, gather, assemble (a.); make fluid, melt (a.); — jamul, INF. jamâl, be handsome, elegant, of good manners; — II. INF. tajmîl, make handsome, embellish, adorn; do anything in a pleasant way; melt much; give much fat to eat; offer a camel for food; keep an army long in the field; — III. INF. mujâmala-t, treat with benevolence, show courtesy, be obliging; — IV. INF. ijmâl, act in a handsome, decent, moderate manner; make pleasant; deserve well of (عند 'inda); gather, assemble (a.); add, count up, resume; melt fat; have many camels; —V. tajammul, behave decently; be embellished, adorned; eat fat; — VIII. INF. ijtimâl, melt

or eat fat; eat a camel; — x. INF. *istijmâl*, find handsome, decent; be full grown.

جمل *jaml, jamal*, pl. *jimâl, jimâla-t, jamâla-t, jumâla-t, jimâlât*, &c.; *juml, jâmil*, pl. *jamâ'il, ajâmil, ajmal*, he-camel; ج اليهود *jamalu 'l-yarhûdi*, chameleon; — *juml, jamal, jumal, jumul, jummal*, cable; — *jumal, jummal*, addition; — *jumal*, troop; — ة *jumla-t*, pl. *jumal*, sum, total, totality; troop, number; class, category; sentence, phrase, period; paragraph.

جملا *jamlâ'*, f. of perfect beauty.

جملان *jimlân*, pl. of جميل *jumail*; — ة *jumlâna-t*, nightingale.

جملون *jamlûn*, gable, cupola, dome; roof which is not flat.

(جمهر) *jamhar*, INF. ة, assemble (a.), heap up; raise a tomb; keep most and the best to one's self; — II. INF. *tajamhur*, assemble (n.); be hostile.

جمهور *jumhûr*, pl. *jamâhîr*, the principal part or majority, totality, all; troop, crowd; people, public; community, commonwealth, republic; constitutional assembly, parliament, &c.; noble woman; high sand-hill; — ى *jumhûriyy*, ة, referring to the community; popular; vulgar; — ية *jumhûriyya-t*, republican government, republic.

جموح *jamûḥ*, refractory.

جمود *jamûd*, dry; — *jumûd*, INF. of (جمد); indifference; severity; — ة *jumûda-t*, hardness; harshness.

جموع *jamû'*, grasping (adj.).

جمول *jamûl*, fat-boiler.

جموم *jamûm*, overflowing.

(جمى) *jama*, gather; — V. INF. *tajammî*, be gathered, assembled.

(جمى) *jamî*, A, INF. *jama*, be angry; — V. INF. *tajammuww*, be gathered, assembled; wrap one's self up in one's clothes; take and conceal anything.

جمير *jamîr*, place of assembly; ابن ج *ibn jamîr*, dark night; — ابنا ج *ibnâ jamîr*, day and night; — ة *jamîra-t*, tress of hair.

جميز *jamîz*, intelligent, considerate; — also *jummaiz*, ى *jummaiza*, wild fig, sycamore.

جميش *jamîś*, shaved smooth; hair-remover.

جميع *jamî'*, collected, assembled; crowd, army; all (جميعا *jamî'an*, altogether; all at once); mature and having a beard; — ة *jamî'a-t*, assembly.

جميل *jamîl*, ة, handsome, fair, elegant; well-bred, of good manners; good, excellent; pl. *jamîlât*, good deed, favour, benefit; good qualities; molten; fat; — *jumail, jummail*, pl. *jimlân*, nightingale.

جميلانة *jumailâna-t*, nightingale.

جميلى *jamîliyy*, dealer in fat.

جميم *jamîm*, pl. *ajimmâ'*, luxuriant plant; much, many.

جن *jann*, I, INF. *jann*, be concealed; — INF. *jann, junûn*, cover, veil, conceal; pass. جن *junn*=act.; — INF. *jinn, junûn, jinnân*, be dark; be covered with verdure or vegetation; be concealed from (عن *'an*); shroud and bury the dead; INF. *junûn*, grow luxuriantly; — INF. *jann, junûn*, pass. be possessed by a demon, be mad; be out of one's senses by rage, joy, &c; be enthusiastic for (على *'ala*); — II. INF. *tajnîn*, madden; (m.) cover, conceal; — IV. INF. *ijnân*, be concealed; cover, conceal, veil in darkness; shroud, bury the dead; madden; — V. INF. *tajannun*, be covered with plants; be mad, out of senses; — VI. INF. *tajânn*, feign madness, show symptoms of it; — VIII. INF. *ijtinân*, be covered, concealed;

cover one's self; bury; — x. INF. *istijnân*, be covered, concealed, protected; cover, protect one's self; excite; pass. be possessed by demons.

جن *jinn*, pl. جنة *jinna-t*, demon, genie, fairy; heat of youth; beginning; concealment; dark; blossom; — ة *janna-t*, pl. *jinân*, *jannât*, orchard, garden; paradise; —*jinna-t*, fairy; madness; —*junna-t*, pl. *junan*, covering (s.); veil; shield; protection.

(جنا) *ja'na'*, جنى *jani'*, A, INF. *janâ'*, *junû'* (also III. INF. *mujânât*, IV. INF. *ijnâ'*), fall on the face; bend over (على *'ala*).

جنا *janâ'*, plucked fruit; fruit of trees; harvest, crops; —*junnâ'*, ة *junât*, pl. of جانى *jânî*, who gathers; sinner; — ة *janât*, newly gathered; pl. *jana*, such fruit.

جناب *janâb*, pl. *ajniba-t*, side; edge; threshold; enclosure or surrounding of a house; courtyard; region; place, spot; rank, title, as Excellency, Highness, Majesty, &c.; —*jinâb*, gentle (horse); pl. of جنيب *janîb*; INF. III. of (جنب); —*junâb*, pleurisy; —*junnâb*, travelling companion; — ة *janâba-t*, pollution; impure one; life with strangers.

جناح *janâḥ*, pl. *ajniḥa-t*, *ajnuḥ*, wing; shoulder, arm, hand; side, edge; wing of an army, window, building; fin; projecting roof; protection, refuge; — *junâḥ*, sin, crime.

جنادرة *janâdira-t*, body-guard.

جنار *jinâr*, plane-tree; —*junnâr*, blossom of the pomegranate.

جنازة *jinâza-t*, *janâza-t*, pl. *janâ'iz*, bier; corpse; — also جناز *jannâz*, pl. *janânîz*, funeral.

جناس *jinâs*, homogeneousness; play on words; assonance.

جناف *jinâf*, transgression.

جنافى *junâfiyy*, oppressive, tyrannical, haughty.

جنافير *janâfîr*, pl. of جنفور *junfûr*.

جنان *janân*, pl. *ajnân*, veil; darkness, night; sanctuary, harem; pl. *ajinna-t*, heart, mind, soul; beloved one, f. ة; INF. of (جن); —*jinnîn*, pl. of جنة *jinna-t*, garden; —*junân*, darkness; also ة *junâna-t*, shield; —*jinnân*, pl. of جان, demon.

جنانيز *janânîz*, pl. of جناز *jannâz*.

جنائب *janâ'ib*, pl. of جنبة *jamba-t*, جنوب *janûb*, جنيب *janîb*.

جنائز *janâ'iz*, pl. جنازة *jinâza-t*.

جناية *jinâya-t*, transgression, offence; fine, mulct; extortion; taxation, taxes.

(جنب) *janab*, I, INF. *jamb*, turn aside, decline; refuse, turn off; remove; shun, flee from; hit sideways; — INF. *janab*, *majnab*, lead by the side, place a horse as leader beside another; — INF. *jinâb*, be far off; keep far; shun, avoid; cause to avoid; miss, long for; U, be a stranger, reside amongst strangers;—INF. *junûb*, blow from the south, towards the south; — pass. *junib*, suffer from pleurisy; be exposed to the south-wind; — II. INF. *tajnîb*, keep far, remove to a distance (a.); cause one to avoid another; put aside; lead walking by the side; be distant from (acc.); — III. INF. *mujânaba-t*, *jinâb*, be or remain by the side of (acc.); avoid; — IV. INF. *ijnâb*, keep distant (a. and n.); avoid; cause to avoid; be or come as a stranger; be exposed to the south-wind; be polluted; — V. INF. *tajannub*, be far from (acc.); turn aside (n.); shun, avoid; keep from (عن *'an*, a.); — VI. INF. *tajânub*, keep distant (n.), avoid; — VIII. INF. *ijtinâb*, turn aside from (n.), shun, avoid; feel aversion

against (acc.); — X. INF. *istijnâb*, be polluted (by sperm).

جنب *jamb*, pl. *junûb*, *ajnâb*, side, flank, half of the body; boundary; coast; tract, region; principal part; combat, battle; reproach; ذاة الج *zâtu 'l-jambi*, pleurisy, ذو الج *zû 'l-jambi*, afflicted with it; — *janab*, short; pl. of جنيب *janîb*; — *janib*, leaning on one side, keeping aloof (adj.); — *junub*, pl. *ajnâb*, stranger, guest; restive, refractory; polluted; — ة *jamba-t*, pl. *janabât*, *janâ'ib*, side; tract, region; turning aside (s.); apostacy; — *junaba-t*, anything avoided.

جنباظ *jambâz*, pl. ة *janâbiza-t*, quack, charlatan; who overcharges in selling (Pers.).

جنبذ *jumbuz*, bad; also ة *jumbuza-t*, pl. *janâbiz*, cupola, dome; arch, flying buttress (Pers.).

جنبش *jumbuś*, gymnastics; game; amusement (Pers.).

جنبظ *jambaz*, INF. ة, also II. INF. *tajanbuz*, behave as a quack or in a haughty manner; over-sell.

جنبى *jambiyy*, side (adj.).

جنتى *junnatiyy*, paradisiacal.

جنث *jins*, origin; genus, species, kind; — hence: V. INF. *tajannus*, claim an origin to which one is not entitled; incline in love towards (على *'ala*); wrap up anything in one's clothes; spread the wings.

جنثى *jinsiyy*, a superior kind of iron; — *junsiyy*, maker of coats of mail; sword.

(جنجل) *junjul*, asparagus.

(جنجن) *janjan*, *jinjin*, also ة *janjana-t*, pl. *janâjin*, breast-bone; rib of the chest.

(جنح) *janah*, A, I, U, INF. *junûh*, incline towards (ل *li*, الى *ila*); break (a.) a shoulder, arm, hand, wing, rib; pass. be injured in those parts; walk fast; — II. INF. *tajnîh*, provide with wings; — IV. INF. *ijnâh*, cause to incline towards; incline; — V. INF. *tajannuh*, incline towards one side; — VIII. INF. *ijtinâh*, bend, incline towards (n.); walk apace; — X. INF. *istijnâh*, bend (a.), cause to incline towards.

جنح *jinh*, side, edge; shore, bank; also *junh*, darkness; part of the night; night; — ة *junha-t*, transgression, crime.

(جند) *jund*, pl. *junûd*, *ajnâd*, army, corps of troops; fellow-combatants; soldiers; fixed camp; military capital; species; — *janad*, pebbled ground; — II. *jannad*, INF. *tajnîd*, levy troops, enlist sailors, &c.; — V. INF. *tajannud*, enlist (n.).

جندب *jindab*, *jundab*, *jundub*, pl. *janâdib*, a black locust; ام ج *umm jundub*, calamity.

جند بدستر *jund badastar*, جند بيدستر *jund bîdastar*, castoreum.

(جندر) *jandar*, INF. ة, restore old writing or embroidery.

(جندع) *janda'*, pl. *janâdi'*, black locust; a kind of lizard; — ة *jundu'a-t*, pl. *janâdi'*, id.; bubble; جنادع الشر *janâdi' aś-śarr*, beginnings of an evil.

(جندل) *jandal*, INF. ة, throw on the ground.

جندل *jandal*, pl. *janâdil*, large round stone; waterfall; cataracts of the Nile; — *junadil*, ة *junadila-t*, stony tract of land.

جندى *jundiyy*, soldier, trooper.

(جنز) *janaz*, I, INF. *janz*, cover, veil; gather (a.); pass. be placed on the bier; be dead; — II. INF. *tajnîz*, place the corpse on the bier; arrange the burial.

جنز *janz*, clay hut.

جنزار *jinzâr*, verdigris.

جنزر *janzar*, INF. ة, put into chains; get covered with verdigris; —

II. INF. *tajanzur*, be put into chains.

جنزير *janzîr*, pl. *janâzîr*, chain.

(جنس) *janas*, U, INF. *jans*, ripen fully; —*janis*, A, INF. *janas*, freeze (n.); — II. INF. *tajnîs*, be fully ripe; make homogeneous; specify, classify; — III. INF. *mujânasa-t*, be or appear homogeneous; be similar.

جنس *jins*, pl. *ajnâs*, *junûs*, genus, species, kind, family, race; gender; category, class; nationality; — ى *jinsiyy*, referring to genus, gender, sex, &c.; — ية *jinsiyya-t*, common genus, gender, or origin.

(جنش) *janaś*, U, INF. *janś*, exhaust; move towards or against; desire; fear; — I, INF. *janś*, lack corn; be deeply moved, highly agitated.

(جنص), II. *jannâṣ*, INF. *tajnîṣ*, die; flee in fear; open the eyes wide, stare from fear; ease the bowels.

جنع *jana'*, small plants.

(جنف) *janaf*, I, *janif*, A, INF. *junûf*, *janaf*, turn aside, decline; be unjust; overcharge in selling; — IV. INF. *ijnâf*, V. INF. *tajannuf*, deflect from what is right; finding one to do so; — VI. INF. *tajânuf*, turn aside; incline to injustice.

جنف *janaf*, *janf*, deflection from what is right; iniquity of fate; wrong; ruggedness; — *janif*, unjust, iniquitous.

جنفاص *janfâṣ*, coarse linen, canvas.

جنفور *junfûr*, pl. *janâfîr*, ancient tomb.

(جنق) *janaq*, I, and II. INF. *tajnîq*, throw projectiles by catapults, &c.

(جنك) *junk*, pl. *junûk*, large Chinese ship; harp; —*jank*, war, combat; — hence: II. *jannak*, INF. *tajnîk*, get heated (in battle); — ى *junkiyy*, f. ة, player on the harp.

جنمة *janma-t*, plenty, abundance; the whole.

جنن *janan*, pl. *ajnân*, tomb; shroud; corpse; —*junan*, pl. of جنة *junna-t*; —*junun*, madness.

جنهى *jannahiyy*, Indian cane.

جنو *junnû'*, INF. of (جنا).

جنوب *janûb*, pl. *janâ'ib*, south; south wind; — ى *janûbiyy*, ة, southern; sultry.

جنوح *junûḥ*, pl. of جانح *jâniḥ*, ag. of (جنح); INF. of the same.

جنور *jannûr*, thrashing-floor.

جنون *janûn*, demon; a kind of harmless snake; —*junûn*, madness; darkness.

(جنى) *jana*, I, INF. *jan-an*, *jany*, *janâya-t*, pluck, gather; use up, wear out, draw advantage from (acc.); — INF. *jinâya-t*, sin, commit a crime; accuse falsely of a crime; — INF. *janwa-t*, wrong; be froward to; prove false against (على *'ala*, ب *bi*); — IV. INF. *ijnâ'*, pluck, gather; bear ripe fruit; abound in plants, herbs, &c.; be ripe for harvest; — V. INF. *tajannî*, pluck; accuse falsely; find fault; seek a false pretext or excuse; — VIII. pluck, cull, gather; draw advantage from (من *min*); find rain-water and drink it.

جنى *janan*, *jana*, pl. *ajnâ'*, freshly plucked fruit, dates; honey; gold; a kind of shell; pl. of جناة *janât*; —*janiyy*, ة, freshly plucked; —*jinniyy*, demoniacal; demon; — ة *janniyya-t*, silken robe; falsely-imputed crime; (m.) fine for bloodshed; —*jinniyya-t*, pl. demons.

جنيب *janîb*, ة *janîba-t*, pl. *janâ'ib*, *jinâb*, *janab*, *janaba-t*, leading horse, camel, &c.

جنيس *janîs*, of the same kind, homogeneous; of pure descent.

جنيص *janîṣ*, dead, deceased.

جنين *janîn*, embryo; concealed, covered.

(جه) *jahh*, U, INF. *jahh*, turn off ignominiously;—ة *jiha-t*, *juha-t*, pl. *-ât*, side; front, surface; shape; manner; regard (من ج, with regard to); cause, reason; direction.

جهاد *jahâd*, hard ground;—*jihâd*, INF. III. of (جهد); invitation to profess the Islâm; war against the infidels; war; effort, zeal.

جهار *jihâr*, open hostility; INF. of (جهر); جهارا *jihâran*, openly, publicly, aloud;—ة *jahâra-t*, loud voice; grace, loveliness.

جهاز *jahâz*, *jihâz*, pl. *ajhiza-t*, utensil, tool, anything necessary, requisite, equipment; furniture; trousseau, outfit of a bride; provender; rigging of a ship; ship; camel-saddle.

جهال *juhhâl*, pl. of جاهل, ignorant, &c.;—ة *jahâla-t*, ignorance; folly; rudeness.

جهام *jahâm*, rainless cloud.

جهانة *juhâna-t*, young maid-servant.

(جهب) *jahb*, repulsive face.

(جهبذ) *jahbaz*, *jihbiz*, pl. *jahâbiza-t*, sagacious, penetrating, skilful; clever money-changer; expert in coins and money matters (Pers.).

(جهش) *jahas*, A, INF. *jahs*, be easily agitated; be excitable.

(جهجه) *jahjah*, INF. ة, cry out at; cry out; (m.) shine, be resplendent;—II. INF. *tajahjuh*, desist, abstain.

(جهد) *jahad*, A, INF. *jahd*, exert one's self in anything, endeavour, make efforts; overload or overwork a beast; put to the test; emaciate; pain, vex, molest; want food; eat much; turn the milk entirely into butter;—*jahid*, A, INF. *jahad*, be toilsome;—III. INF. *jihâd*, *mujâhada-t*, struggle against difficulties; wage war against the infidels;—IV. INF. *ijhâd*, cause one to exert himself, to make efforts; molest; injure; overwork; set to a thing zealously; go far in a thing; demand food; lavish, squander; be on one's guard; appear; come to light; be mixed up; be or live close to (ل *li*); be possible;—VI. INF. *tajâhud*, exert one's self;—VIII. INF. *ijtihâd*, make efforts; be diligent; consider well.

جهد *jahd*, effort, exertion, zeal, diligence; affliction, misery;—also *juhd*, power, resources.

(جهدم) *jahdam*, INF. ة, hasten.

(جهر) *jahar*, A, INF. *jahr*, *jihâr*, be public; publish, divulge; disclose; speak loud; neigh; see without a veil; admire; dazzle; clean a well, hit on water; estimate approximately, guess at; surprise by an early attack; deem numerous; value highly, honour; shake the milk-bag to make butter; travel over;—*jahir*, A, INF. *jahar*, be dazzled by the sun; not be able to see in sunlight;—*jahur*, INF. *juhûra-t*, have a clear and loud voice; call, speak, read aloud; publish; show open hostility; surpass, overcome, vanquish;—IV. INF. *ijhâr*, publish, promulgate; divulge; have handsome sons;—V. INF. *tajahhur*, VI. INF. *tajâhur*, appear in public;—VII. INF. *injihâr*, be published;—VIII. INF. *ijtihâr*, clean a well; consider numerous; see unveiled, uncovered.

جهر *jahr*, ة *jahra-t*, publicity (جهرا *jahran*, جهرة *jahratan*, publicly, evidently, aloud); loud voice; a space of time;—*juhr*, graceful figure, lovely face;—*jahir*, public, manifest; loud;—ة *jahra-t*, what is known, evident, manifest;—*juhra-t*, a yellow berry used for dyeing.

جهرا *jahrâ*, plain, treeless ground;

troop, &c., f. of اجهر *ajhar*; — *juharâ'*, pl. of جهير *jahîr*.

(جهرم), II. INF. *tajahrum*, defy (على *'ala*).

(جهز) *jahaz*, A, INF. *jahz* (also IV.), finish off a wounded man; — II. INF. *tajhîz*, equip, fit out; set up a bridal procession, a burial; organise; put in order; address to; — IV. INF. *ijhâz*, see I.; — V. INF. *tajahhuz*, equip, prepare one's self; adorn; be provided, ready, prepared; — XI. INF. *ijhîzâz*, be ready.

جهزا *jahzâ'*, f. high; prominent; projecting.

(جهش) *jahaś*, *jahiś*, A, INF. *jahś*, *jahûś*, *jahaśân* (also IV.), be on the point of crying and run to its mother (child from fear); — INF. *jahaśân*, fear, flee; be on the point of crying; jump up, rise; — IV. INF. *ijhâś*, see I.; be on the point of crying; bid one to make haste.

(جهض) *jahaḍ*, A, INF. *jahḍ*, surpass, get the better of. (acc.), forestall in (عن *'an*); — III. prevent and forestall; urge to haste; — IV. INF. *ijhâḍ*, surpass, be superior, overcome, vanquish; cause one to desist and flee; urge to haste; make a miscarriage.

جهض *jahiḍ*, miscarriage.

(جهضم) *jahḍam*, having a broad head and chest; — hence: II. INF. *tajahḍum*, behave proudly; tower above, excel.

(جهل) *jahil*, A, INF. *jahl*, *jahâla-t*, ignore, be ignorant, stupid, brutal; show one's self ignorant in (على *'ala*); be indifferent, listless; — II. INF. *tajhîl*, call or deem one ignorant; impute anything to ignorance; — III. INF. *mujâhala-t*, act towards anyone with levity or carelessness; — VI. INF. *tajâhul*, affect ignorance; — X. INF. *istijhâl*, deem ignorant; disdain, make light of; move (a.).

جهل *jahl*, ignorance; stupidity; — *juhl*, ة *jahala-t*, pl. of جاهل *jâhil*, ignorant, &c.

جهلا *jahlâ*, f. time of gnorance, heathendom; — *juhalâ'*, pl. of جهول *jahûl*.

(جهم) *jaham*, A, *jahim*, A (also V.), frown at; — *jahum*, INF. *jahâma-t*, *juhûma-t*, be harsh and repulsive; have harsh and repulsive features; — IV. INF. *ijhâm*, have rainless clouds; — V. INF. *tajahhum*=I.; — VIII. INF. *ijtihâm*, enter on the last part of the night.

جهم *jahm*, weak; — also *jahim*, morose; — ة *juhma-t*, troop of camels (80); — also *jahma-t*, last part of the night.

(جهن) *jahan*, U, INF. *juhûn*, be near, close at hand.

جهن *jahn*, moroseness; — *juhn*, current near the sea-coast; — ة *juhna-t*, beginning of night.

جهنم *jahannam*, hell; — ى *jahannamiyy*, hellish.

جهوا *jahwâ'*, f. cloudless; bare, naked.

جهود *jahûd*, zealous, eager, diligent.

(جهور) *jahwar*, INF. ة, deliver in a loud voice.

جهور *jahûr*, loud, having a clear voice; — *jahwar*, bold; — ة *juhûra-t*, loudness of voice; prettiness; — ى *jahwariyy*, spoken aloud; having a loud voice; pretty.

جهوضة *jahûḍa-t*, slyness, cunningness, archness.

جهول *jahûl*, pl. *juhalâ'*, very ignorant; crude, brutal; — ية *juhûliyya-t*, ignorance.

(جهى) *jahî*, A, INF. *jahan*, get devastated, fall in ruins; — II. INF. *tajhiya-t*, widen a wound; — III. INF. *mujâhât*, boast to, try to surpass in glory; — IV. INF. *ijhâ'*, be distinct, open; be

clear; enjoy the bright weather; be niggardly; bring no child to the husband; — VI. INF. *tajâhî*, boast to each other, vie for glory.

جهيد *jahîd*, toilsome; frequented by cattle.

جهير *jahîr*, of a loud voice; loud; pl. *juharâ'*, of a handsome face.

جهيز *jahîz*, nimble, agile, swift.

جهيض *jahîḍ*, miscarriage; abortive.

جهين *jahîn*, rust of a mirror.

جو *jaw-in*=جوى *jawan*; — *jaww*, pl. *ajwâ'*, *jiwâ'*, atmosphere; air; sky; wide valley; open pasture-ground; interior of a house; hall; Yamâma;—ة *ju'a-t*, reddish brown;—*juwwa-t*, id.; cavity; rugged ground.

جوا *jawwan*, inside, within; — *jiwâ'*, pl. *ajwiya-t*, wide valley; wallet; — pl. of جو *jaww*.

جواب *jawâb*, pl. *ajwiba-t*, answer; speech, assertion; — *jawwâb*, ة *jawwâba-t*, traveller through the deserts; wanderer.

جوائى *ju'aṡa*, tripe, guts.

جواد *jawâd*, pl. *ajwâd*, *ajâwid*, *juwadâ'*, *jûd*, *juwada-t*, liberal, generous, kind; pl. *jiyâd*, *ajyâd*, *ajâwid*, generous horse, excellent steed; — *juwâd*, violent thirst; — *jawwâd*, highroads, causeways, pl. of جادة *jâda-t*.

جوادس *jawâdis*, pl. f. of جادس *jâdis*, effaced, uncultivated, &c.

جوار *jawâr*, deep water; area of a house; ships; — *jiwâr*, neighbourhood; protection, INF. III. of (جور); — *jawwâr*, farmer, peasant.

جوارب *jawârib*, ة *jawâriba-t*, pl. of جورب *jaurab*; — ى *jawâribiyy*, maker of stockings, hosier.

جوارح *jawâriḥ*, wild beasts; limbs of the body, pl. of جارحة *jâriḥa-t*.

جوارس *jawâris*, pl. f. of جارس *jâris*, ag. of (جرس).

جوارش *jawâriś*, pl. *-ât*, cordial (s.); spice (Pers.).

جوارى *jawârî*, female slaves, &c., pl. of جارية *jâriya-t*.

جواز *jawâz*, lawfulness; allowableness; passage; transit; passport; — *jiwâz*, INF. III. of (جوز); — *juwâz*, thirst;—*jawwâz*, seller of nuts.

جوازل *jawâzil*, pl. of جوزل *jauzal*.

جوازم *jawâzim*, pl. of جازم *jâzim*, cutting off, &c.

جوازى *jawâzi'*, waste, wild; wild animals, game.

جواس *jawwâs*, spy; lion; — *jawâss*, pl. senses.

جواسق *jawâsiq*, pl. of جوسق *jausaq*.

جواسيس *jawâsîs*, spies, &c., pl. of جاسوس *jâsûs*.

جواشن *jawâśin*, pl. of جوشن *jauśan*.

جواظ *juwâẓ*, impatience; — *jawwaẓ*, melancholic; — ة *juwwâẓa-t*, melancholy.

جوال *jawwâl*, who travels to and fro; — *jawâll*, exiles, pl. of جالة *jâlla-t*; — ة *jawâla-t*, the best part of a thing; — pl. of جول *jûl*.

جوالب *jawâlib*, pl. of جالب *jâlib*, curative.

جوالح *jawâliḥ*, gossamer.

جوالق *jiwâliq*, *juwâliq*, pl. *jawâliq*, *jawâlîq*, *jawâliqât*, large corn-sack.

جوامك *jawâmik*, salary, wages, pl. of جامكية *jâmikiyya-t*.

جواميس *jawâmîs*, buffaloes, pl. of جاموس *jâmûs*.

جوانة *jawânna-t*, the buttocks.

جوانى *jawânî*, pl. sides; — *jawwâniyy*, interior; concealed; the inside, interior (s.).

جواهر *jawâhir*, pl. of جوهر *jauhar*; — ى *jawâhiriyy*, jeweller.

جواهض *jawâhiḍ*, foals, pl. of جاهضة *jâhiḍa-t*.

جوائب *jawâ'ib*, pl. rumours.

جوائز *jawâ'iz*, pl. of جائز *jâ'iz*, ة *jâ'iza-t*, q.v.

(جوب) *jâb*, U, INF. *jaub*, *tajwâb*, split, tear, cut through; break stones; — U, I, travel over, wander through; pass; bring;

give birth; — U, I, INF. *jaub* (also II. and VIII.), put a front or a slit to a shirt; — II. INF. *tajwîb*, id.; — III. INF. *mujâwaba-t*, answer; respond, return; (m.) resound; — IV. INF. *ijâb*, *ijâba-t*, answer, respond; reply to (acc.); come at call; grant a request, consent; bring forth fruit, plants, &c.; — V. INF. *tajawwub* (also VII.), be torn; — VI. INF. *tajâwub*, answer to one another; — VII. INF. *injiyâb*=V.; stretch out the neck; — VIII. *ijtiyâb*, see I.; split; travel over, pass through; dig a well; — X. INF. *istijâba-t*, answer; listen to, grant a prayer; consent, approve.

جوب *jaub*, journey, travelling over; pl. *ajwâb*, shield; strap; shirt without sleeves; hearth; — ة *jauba-t*, pl. *juwab*, opening, interstice; breach; hole.

جوث *jauṡ*, tripe, guts; —*jauṡâ'*, id.; — f. of *ajwaṡ*, arched.

جوجو *ju'ju'*, pl. جاجى *ja'âji'*, breast, chest; fore-part of a ship.

(جوح) *jâḥ*, U, INF. *jauḥ*, destroy, annihilate; turn aside from the right way; — II. INF. *tajwîḥ*, pull off the shoes; — IV. INF. *ijâḥa-t*, VIII. INF. *ijtiyâḥ*, annihilate.

(جوحم) *jauḥam*, centifoliate rose.

(جوخ) *jâḫ*, U, INF. *jauḫ*, undermine and break the banks; — II. INF. *tajwîḫ*, id.; throw down; — V. INF. *tajawwuḫ*, fall in ruins; burst.

جوخ *jûḫ*, pl. *ajwâḫ*, cloth (m.); — ة *jûḫa-t*, hole in the earth; (m.) overcoat with long sleeves; — ى *jauḫa*, f. weak.

(جود) *jâd*, U, INF. *jauda-t*, excel, be of the best quality; benefit, do good; — INF. *jûd*, be liberal; expose one's self to deadly danger; be quick, fleet; —*jaud*, *juwûd*, be plentiful; water abundantly; INF. *jûda-t*, be on the point of dying from thirst; pass. long ardently for (الى *ila*); sleep, slumber; — INF. *jaud*, *ju'ud*, shed tears abundantly; — II. INF. *tajwîd*, render good, excellent, liberal; mend; be a good race-horse; —III. INF. *mujâwada-t*, vie with another in liberality and beneficence; — IV. INF. *ijâda-t*, *ijwâd*, give abundantly; do or say anything excellent; have an exquisite race-horse; generate an excellent son; — V. INF. *tajawwud*, take the best part for one's self; — X. INF. *istijâda-t*, make claims on anybody's liberality; deem or find anything excellent; demand the best.

جود *jaud*, abundant rain; pl. of جائد *jâ'id*, abundant; beneficent; —*jûd*, liberality; liberal; pl. of جواد *jawâd*, and اجيد *ajyad*, having a long and beautiful neck; — ة *jûda-t*, *jauda-t*, goodness, excellence; best quality; superior qualifications; INF. of (جود); —*juwada-t*, pl. of جواد *jawâd*.

جوداء *juwadâ'*, pl. of جواد *jawâd*.

جودى *jaudiyy*, liberal; abundant.

جوذر *ju'ẓar*, pl. *ja'âẓir*, buffalo-calf.

(جور) *jâr*, U, INF. *jaur*, wander astray from (عن *'an*); be unjust; — INF. *jiwâr*, *jawâr*, supplicate for protection; — II. INF. *tajwîr*, deem unjust, accuse of tyranny; (m.) hollow out; — III. INF. *jiwâr*, *juwâr*, *mujâwara-t*, be one's neighbour; to be neighbourly; take into protection or clientship; INF. *mujâwara-t*, stay in the temple and pray; — IV. INF. *jâra-t*, *ijâra-t*, take into protection, protect; free from tyranny; cause one to turn aside from; — VI. INF. *tajâwur*, VIII. INF. *ijtiwâr*, to act neighbourly and

protect each other; — X. INF. *istijâra-t*, sue for protection.

جور *jaur*, violence, oppression, tyranny; tyrant; (m.) stranger; —*ju'ar*, abundant rain; — ة *jûra-t*, pl. *juwar*, hollow, cavity, hole; —*jawara-t*, tyrants, pl. of جائر *jâ'ir*, unjust.

(جورب) *jaurab*, ة, pl. *jawârib*, *jawâriba-t*, shoe; stocking; — hence: *jaurab*, INF. ة, wear stockings; put stockings on a person.

جوری *jûriyy*, rose of Bengal.

(جوز) *jâz*, U, INF. *jauz*, *jawâz*, *ju'ûz*, *majâz*, pass, pass by; travel over, through, or on; disappear; be passable, allowable, a matter of indifference; be possible, happen; INF. *jawâz*, irrigate; — II. INF. *tajwîz*, cause to travel over, pass through, perform; carry through one's views; present in detail; declare allowable, permit; water; (m.)=*tajwîz*, give in marriage, marry; — III. INF. *jiwâz*, pass a place; leave a thing and pass on to another; cross a river; cause to pass, to cross; INF. *mujâwaza-t*, close the eyes to, pass over, be indulgent; exceed the bounds, go beyond measure, make an excess; — IV. INF. *ijâza-t*, pass through and leave behind; cause to pass through; allow to pass; carry over; provide with money for a journey, make a present; carry through one's views; allow, approve, confirm, ratify, sign; authorise; benefit; give in return; — V. INF. *tajawwuz*, suffer, permit; pass over, be indulgent; speak figuratively; abbreviate; — VI. INF. *tajâwuz*, travel over, pass through; exceed the bounds, commit excesses; pass over, forgive, forbear with; — VII. INF. *injiyâz*, desist from, leave; desert to the enemy; — VIII. INF. *ijtiyâz*, pass, pass by; travel over; depart; — X. INF. *istijâza-t*, ask for permission, for a gift; deem lawful.

جوز *jauz*, ة, pl. *-ât*, *ajwâz*, nut; kernel, stone (of a fruit), middle (ج رومی *jauz rûmiyy*, walnut; ج بوا *jauz bawwâ'*, ج الطيب *jauzu 't-ṭîb*, nutmeg; ج هندی *jauz hindiyy*, cocoa-nut); passage.

جوزا *jauzâ'*, constellation of the Twins; Orion.

جوزان *jûzân*, pl. of جائز *jâ'iz*, cross-beam, &c.

جوزق *jauzaq*, ة, fruit of the cotton-tree; —ی *jauzaqiyy*, seller of the fruit of the cotton-tree.

جوزل *jauzal*, pl. *jawâzil*, the young of a dove.

جوزينج *jauzînaj*, جوزينق *jauzînaq*, confection of nuts.

(جوس) *jâs*, U, INF. *jaus*, *jawasân*, VIII. INF. *ijtiyâs*, look for eagerly, search.

جوسق *jausaq*, pl. *jawâsiq*, palace; zodiac.

(جوش) *jauś*, breast; middle; night-journey; — hence V. INF. *tajawwuś*, be partly over; enter the middle of a country.

جوشن *jauśan*, pl. *jawâśin*, armour, coat of mail; breast; midnight; — ی *jauśaniyy*, armour-maker, armourer.

(جوظ) *jâẓ*, U, INF. *jauẓ*, *jawaẓân*, step along proudly; strut; grieve, render sorrowful; — II. INF. *tajwîẓ*, and V. INF. *tajawwuẓ*, hasten, run.

(جوع) *jâ'*, INF. *jau'*, *jau'a-t*, *majâ'a-t*, be hungry; thirst for; wish for eagerly; — II. INF. *tajwî'*, IV. INF. *ijwâ'*, starve; — V. INF. *tajawwu'*, master one's hunger; — X. INF. *istijâ'a-t*, show one's self always hungry.

جوع *jû'*, hunger (ج الكلب *jû'u 'l-kalbi*, ravenous hunger); —*juwwa'*, pl. of جائع *jâ'i'*, hungry; — ة *jau'a-t*, fit of hunger.

جوعان *jau'ân*, f. جوعى *jau'a*, pl. *jiyâ'*, hungry.

(جوف) *jâf*, U, INF. *jauf*, be hollow, concave, bulging; penetrate, pierce; — II. INF. *tajwîf*, hollow, render concave; — IV. INF. *ijâfa-t*, penetrate; shut; — V. INF. *tajawwuf*, be hollow inside; be concave; be concealed in the hollow interior, penetrate to it, pierce; — VIII. INF. *ijtiyâf*=V.; be spacious.

جوف *jauf*, last third of the night; pl. *ajwâf*, belly, intestines; cavity; inside; middle, heart, core, principal part; vast plain; — *jûf*, pl. of اجوف *ajwaf*, hollow; — *jawaf*, spaciousness of a cave.

جوفا *jaufâ'*, f. of اجوف *ajwaf*, hollow.

جوفى *jaufiyy*, ة, hollow, spacious; internal; — ة *jaufiyya-t*, hole, cavity.

(جوق) *jawiq*, A, INF. *jawaq*, be contorted; — II. INF. *tajwîq*, cry out at; assemble (a.); — V. INF. *tajawwuq*, be gathered, assembled.

جوق *jauq*, ة *jauqa-t*, pl. *ajwâq*, troop, legion; — *jawiq*, contorted.

(جول) *jâl*, U, INF. *jaul*, *jûl*, *juwûl*, *jawalân*, *jîlân*, step around, revolve; pass through, travel over; rise; lead about; — INF. *jaula-t*, turn round in combat, vault; flee and turn to attack again; choose; — II. INF. *tajwâl*, roam about; — III. INF. *mujâwala-t*, turn around in a combat, try to attack in the flank; — IV. INF. *ijâla-t*, turn, cause to turn around; cause to circulate; make roam; — VI. INF. *tajâwul*, turn around one another in a combat; — VIII. INF. *ijtiyâl*, seduce; cause to desert the true faith.

جول *jaul*, herd, troop; — *jûl*, pl. *ajwâl*, *jiwâl*, *jiwâla-t*, coating of a well; wall of a tomb; coast, side; pl. *jawâl*, herd, flock; — *jaul*, ة *jaula-t*, INF. of (جول).

جولان *jaulân*, dust and sand; — *jawalân*, revolving (s.), revolution, circulation; vaulting (s.); drill, exercise; travelling through or over (s.); first movement; emotion; INF. of (جول).

(جوم) *jâm*, U, INF. *jaum*, seek, crave for, demand.

جوم *jaum*, allied herdsmen; — cups, pl. of جام *jâm*.

(جون) *jaun*, pl. *jûn*, red; white, and, by opposition, black; day; — *jûn*, bay, gulf; — ة *jauna-t*, disc of the sun; coal; red; — *jûna-t*=*jûn*; blackness; pl. *juwan*, also *ju'na-t*, pl. *ju'an*, leathern box for spices; — hence V. INF. *tajawwun*, paint white (bridal chamber); paint black (door of the dead); اهل الت *ahlu 't-tajawwuni*, voluptuaries.

جونا *jaunâ'*, sun; kettle.

(جوه) *jâh*, U, INF. *jauh*, receive gruffly; prevent, hinder.

جوه *jûh*, face, look, features.

جوهر *jauhar*, ة, pl. *jawâhir*, jewel, pearl; precious ore; essence, substance, matter, nature; element; soul; marrow; worth, excellence; lines of a Damascene blade; veins of marmor, &c.; diacritical point; ج فرد *jauhar fard*, atom (Pers.).

جوهرجى *jauharjiyy*, jeweller.

جوهرى *jauhariyy*, jeweller; essential, natural; elementary.

جووب *ju'ûb*, pl. of جاب, q.v.

جووة *ju'wa-t*, reddish-brown.

جووث *ju'ûs*, being frightened (s.); INF. pass. of (جاث).

(جوى) *jawî*, A, INF. *jawan*, be passionately moved; be afflicted with a consuming chest fever; suffer from indigestion; have disgust or aversion; find unhealthy, inconvenient; get corrupted; putrify; — II. INF.

tajwiya-t, tame, grow tame (m.); — VIII. INF. *ijtiwâ*, be seized with passionate grief, &c.; consider unhealthy.

جوى *jawan*, *jawa*, fervour; passionate love; consumptive fever; stench; foul water; — *jawî* (جو *jaw-in*), aching; — *jawiyy*, having indigestion; unhealthy, unwholesome; f. ة *jawiyya-t*, unhealthy country.

جويد *juwayyid*, liberal; yielding much milk.

(جى) *jâ'*, I, INF. *jai'*, *jai'a-t*, *majî'*, *majiyy*, come, come up suddenly; come with, bring; — III. INF. *jiyâ'*, *mujâya'a-t*, confront face to face; agree; — IV. INF. *ijâ'a-t*, bring or lead up; urge on; compel to take refuge with (الى *ilâ*); mend; — ة *ji'a-t*, *jîya-t*, *jiyya-t*, stagnating water; large cistern; — *jayya-t*, putrefaction, stench.

جئا *ji'â*, pl. of جئاوة *ji'âwa-t*; — *jiyâ'*, INF. III. of (جى); — *jayyâ'*, approaching (adj.); — ة *jai'a-t*, pus; blood; arrival; INF. of (جى); — *ji'a-t*, stagnating water.

جياحة *jiyâḥa-t*, annihilation.

جياد *jiyâd*, جيادات *jiyâdât*, pl. of جواد *jawâd* and جيد *jaid*.

جيار *jayyâr*, heat in the stomach; rage; quicklime.

جياع *jiyâ'*, pl. of جائع *jâ'i'*, hungry.

جياف *jayyâf*, despoiler of dead bodies.

جيال *jai'al*, pl. *jayâ'il*, hyena; — ة *jai'ala-t*, pus.

جئاوة *ji'âwa-t*, *jiyâwa-t*, pl. جئا *ji'â'*, leathern case for kettles, &c.

جيائد *jayâ'id*, pl. of جيد *jayyid*.

جيائل *jayâ'il*, pl. of جيال *jai'al*.

(جيب) *jâb*, I, INF. *jaib*, cut a bosom to a shirt or garment; split, cut; widen; travel over, wander through; — II. INF. *tajyîb*, put a bosom or collar to a shirt or garment.

جيب *jaib*, ة *jaiba-t*, pl. *juyûb*, bosom of a garment; breast-pocket; pocket, purse; sine (in trigonometry); — ة *jîba-t*, answer; — ى *jaibiyy*, ة, referring to the sine, of the sine.

(جيتر) *jaitar*, short of stature.

(جثث), see (جاث).

(جيخ) = (جوخ).

(جيد) *jayid*, A, INF. *jayad*, have a long and graceful neck; — *jîd*, pass. of (جود).

جيد *jîd*, pl. *juyûd*, *ajyâd*, long and graceful neck; pl. of اجيد *ajyad*, having such (adj.); — *jayyid*, pl. *jiyâd*, *jiyâdât*, *jayâ'id*, good, excellent; beautiful, handsome; of best quality; جيدا *jayyid-an*, very well.

(جيدار) *jaidâr*, short, dwarfish; — *jîdâr*, holm-oak.

جيدانة *jaidâna-t*, f. having a graceful neck.

جيدران *jaidarân*, جيدرى *jaidara*, short, dwarfish.

جيذر *jaiẕar*, id.; calf of a wild cow.

(جير) *jair*, quicklime; — *jairin*, *jairi*, *jaira*, certainly; — *jayar*, shortness, smallness.

جئر *ja'ir*, see (جار); — *ja'ir*, stout; — *ji'arr*, abundant; — ة *jîra-t*, neighbourhood; also—

جيران *jîrân*, pl. of جار, neighbourhood, &c.

جيز *jîz*, cricket (insect); — ة *jîza-t*, pl. *jîz*, *jiyaz*, side of a valley, side, coast, region; — *jîza-t* = زيجة *zîja-t*, marriage.

(جئز) *ja'iz*, A, INF. *ja'az*, have fits of suffocation.

جيزان *jîzân*, pl. of جائز *jâ'iz*, cross-beam, &c.

(جيش) *jâś*, I, INF. *jaiś*, *juyûś*, *jayaśân*, be agitated, billow, boil; flow over; — II. INF. *tajyîś*, raise an army; — V. INF. *tajayyuś*, gather, assemble; — X. INF. *istijâśa-t*, ask for troops, gather troops.

جيش *jaiś*, pl. *juyûś*, army; legion;

—*jaiś*, جيشان *jayaśân*, INF. of (جيش); — ة *jîśa-t*, ebullition.
(جيض) *jâḍ*, I, INF. *jaiḍ*, turn aside, decline; flee; desist from fatigue; — II. INF. *tajyîḍ*, id.
جيض *jiyaḍḍ*, جيضى *jiyiḍḍa*, proud gait; — ة *jaiḍa-t*, fatigue.
(جيظ) *jâẓ*, I, INF. *jayaẓân*, drag along under a heavy burden; = (جوظ).
جيعان *jai'ân*, hungry.
جيعر *jai'ar*, hyena.
(جيف) *jâf*, I, II. INF. *tajyîf*, putrify; — ة *jîfa-t*, pl. *jiyâf*, *ajyâf*, corpse, dead body, carcase, carrion; — ى *jîfiyy*, carrion (adj.).
(جيل) *jail*, side, coast; — *jîl*, troop of men; tribe; people, nation; century, age; pl. *ajyâl*, generations, races.
جيلان *jailân*, dust; — also ى *jailâniyy*, dusty.
(جيلم) *jailam*, new moon.
(جيم) *jîm*, letter ج; — hence II. INF. *tajyîm*, write such.
جيه *jîh*, face, look, features.
جيهابوق *jaihâbûq*, excrement of mice.
جيهمان *jaihumân*, saffron.
جئوة *ji'awa-t*, famine.
جيئة *jai'a-t* = جياة; — *jî'a-t* = جئة *ji'a-t*.

ح

ح *ḥ*, as a numerical sign = 8; abbreviation for the 2nd Jumâda; as the *sixth* month of the Arabic year; also for حين *ḥîn*, حينئذ *ḥîna'iẓ-in*, when; — حا = جمادى الاول *jumâdá al-awwal*.
حاب *ḥâb*, ة *ḥâba-t*, sin.
حابل *ḥâbil*, woof; setting nets (adj.); — ة *ḥâbila-t*, pl. *ḥabala-t*, big with child; pregnant.
حابى *ḥâbî*, who gives; near.
حاتم *ḥâtim*, pl. *ḥutûm*, who imposes, makes it a duty; judge; raven; name of a liberal man of the tribe Tâi; hence: حاتمى *ḥâtimiyy*, very liberal.
حاج *ḥâj*, pl. of حاجة *ḥâja-t*; — *ḥâjj*, pl. *ḥujjâj*, *ḥajîj*, *ḥujj*, pilgrim, especially to Mecca; — ة *ḥâja-t*, pl. *ḥâj*, *ḥâjât*, *ḥiwaj*, *ḥawâyij*, anything necessary, requisite; want, need; necessity; object; utensil; desire, wish; a plant; pl. *ḥawâyij*, things; — *ḥâjja-t*, pl. *ḥawwâj*, woman who has performed the pilgrimage.
حاجب *ḥâjib*, pl. *ḥajaba-t*, *ḥujjâb*, ag. of حجب *ḥajab*, chamberlain; door-keeper; attendant; edge; pl. *ḥawajib*, eye-brows, lashes.
حاجج *ḥâjij*, Mecca-pilgrim.
حاجر *ḥâjir*, partition, wall; dam; high road, causeway.
حاجز *ḥâjiz*, pl. *ḥajaza-t*, *ḥawâjiz*, ag. of (حجز); partition; bar, list; curtain; dam; diaphragm.
حاجم *ḥâjim*, bath-keeper; cupper.
حاجى *ḥâjiyy*, = حاج *ḥâjj*, pilgrim.
حاد *ḥâd-in*, see حادى *ḥâdî*; — *ḥâdd*, ة, sharp, pointed; hot, strong (as spices); wearing mourning apparel (adj.); — ة *ḥâdda-t*, instrument for making wire; roller.
حادث *ḥâdis̱*, happening for the first time or recently; new, fresh; young; event; — ة *ḥâdis̱a-t*, pl. *ḥawâdis̱*, recent event; news; accident, calamity; (m.) scruple of conscience.
حادق *ḥâdiq*, looking sharply at; penetrating; clever, sharp.
حادى *ḥâdî* (حاد *ḥâd-in*), pl. *ḥudât*, camel-driver; — *ḥâdî'*; who defends; — حادى عشر *ḥâdî 'aśar*, the eleventh.

حاذ *ḥâẕ*, back; du. *ḥâẕân*, the buttocks.

حاذق *ḥâẕiq*, sharp, penetrating; hot, piquant; intelligent, clever; حاذق باذق *ḥâẕiq bâẕiq*, skilful; subtle.

حاذلة *ḥâẕila-t*, f. inflamed.

حار *ḥârr*, ة, hot; glowing; sharp, piquant; difficult; ح يار *ḥârr yârr*, very hot; — ة *ḥâra-t*, *ḥârra-t*, street; quarter; house.

حارث *ḥâriṯ*, pl. *ḥurrâṯ*, ploughman; peasant; lion.

حارد *ḥârid*, angry; grudging; pl. *ḥawârid*, solitary; lonely.

حارس *ḥâris*, pl. *ḥaras*, *aḥrâs*, *ḥurrâs*, guard, watchman; defender; governor; vigilant; الملاك الح *al-mal'aku-'l-ḥârisu*, guardian angel.

حارص *ḥâriṣ*, greedy; ambitious.

حارق *ḥâriq*, ة, burning, glowing; hot-tempered; — ة *ḥâriqa-t*, fire.

حارك *ḥârik*, moving; withers.

حازب *ḥâzib*, pl. *ḥuzb*, *ḥawâzib*, difficult; grave, serious.

حازر *ḥâzir*, bitter, sour; morose.

حازم *ḥâzim*, pl. *ḥazama-t*, prudent; resolute.

حازة *ḥâzza-t*, pl. *ḥawâzz*, what oppresses the mind.

حاس *ḥâss*, ة, perceiving by the senses; — ة *ḥâssa-t*, pl. *ḥawwâs*, sense, perception by the senses.

حاسب *ḥâsib*, pl. *ḥasaba-t*, *ḥussâb*, paymaster; accountant.

حاسد *ḥâsid*, pl. *ḥussad*, *ḥussâd*, *ḥasada-t*, envious; envier.

حاسر *ḥâsir*, pl. *ḥussar*, free, empty, bare; without weapon of defence.

حاسم *ḥâsim*, destructive.

حاسى *ḥâsiyy*, ة, perceiving by the senses; sensitive; — ة *ḥâsiyya-t*, sensibility, sensitiveness.

حاش *ḥâś*, حاشا *ḥâśâ*, حاشى *ḥâśâ*, except; God forbid! without offence!

حاشية *ḥâśiya-t*, pl. *ḥawâśi*, edge, rim, border; hem; marginal note; appendix; supplement; postscript; (m.) digression; region, tract; shade, protection; attendants.

حاصب *ḥâṣib*, pl. *ḥawâṣib*, storm, such as to throw up pebbles.

حاصد *ḥâṣid*, pl. *ḥaṣada-t*, *ḥuṣṣâd*, mower; reaper.

حاصر *ḥâṣir*, who besieges, blockades; astringent; accountant; mat.

حاصل *ḥâṣil*, pl. *ḥawâṣil*, what happens, results, remains finally; produce; sum, product, quotient in arithmetic; advantage, gain; tax, custom; (m.) corn-magazine, store-house, store-room, pantry.

حاصن *ḥâṣin*, ة *ḥâṣina-t*, pl. *ḥawâṣin*, chaste (woman).

حاضر *ḥâḍir*, ة, pl. *ḥuḍḍar*, *ḥuḍûr*, present, before the eyes, ready (also applied to money); the present tense; second person; pl. *ḥuḍḍâr*, *ḥaḍara-t*, settled, domiciled; inhabitant of a village or town; family; tribe; — ة *ḥâḍira-t*, fixed residence, village, town.

حاضن *ḥâḍin*, pl. *ḥuḍḍân*, who embraces, caresses; — ة *ḥâḍina-t*, pl. *ḥawâḍin*, nurse; midwife.

حاطب *ḥâṭib*, gathering wood; in rhetorical parlance: one who picks up phrases carelessly.

حاطوم *ḥâṭûm*, pl. *ḥawâṭîm*, what promotes digestion; want, lack; crushing.

حاف *ḥâf-in*, see حافى *ḥâfî*; — *ḥâff*, surrounding, ag. of (حف); — ة *ḥâfa-t*, edge, rim, border; coast; need; adversity; — pl. of حائب.

حافد *ḥâfid*, pl. *ḥafad*, *ḥafada-t*, *ḥawâfid*, *aḥfâd*, grandson; active servant; helper, assistant.

حافر *ḥâfir*, ag. of (حفر); pl. *ḥawâfir*, hoof, claw; hoof-print; foot; — ة *ḥâfira-t*, beginning; original state; road, trace, track.

حافشة *ḥâfiśa-t*, watercourse.

حافظ *ḥâfiẓ*, ة, pl. *ḥuffâẓ*, *ḥafaẓa-t*, ag. of (حفظ); God; guardian, watcher; governor; who knows the Koran by heart; — ة *ḥâfiẓa-t*, memory.

حافل *ḥâfil*, pl. *ḥuffal*, entirely full.

حافى *ḥâfî* (حاف *ḥâf-in*), pl. *ḥufât*, bare-foot; unshod (hoof); judge; benevolent; merry.

حاق *ḥâqq*, perfect; truthful; middle; — ة *ḥâqqa-t*, pl. *ḥawâqq*, what is sure to come; Day of Judgment; perfect, truthful, zeal.

حاقن *ḥâqin*, suffering from dysury; — ة *ḥâqina-t*, pl. *ḥawâqin*, stomach; abdomen.

حاك *ḥâk-in*, see *ḥâkî*; — ة *ḥâka-t*, pl. of حائك *ḥâ'ik*; — *ḥâkka-t*, tooth.

حاكم *ḥâkim*, pl. *ḥukkâm*, judge; governor.

حاكورة *ḥâkûra-t*, pl. *ḥawâkîr*, vegetable-field; enclosure (m.).

حاكى *ḥâkî* (حاك *ḥâk-in*), pl. *ḥukât*, narrator.

حال *ḥâl*, pl. *aḥwâl*, *aḥwila-t*, state, condition, circumstance; position; rank, profession; present time; لسان الح *lisân al-ḥâl*, language befitting the circumstances; — *ḥâll*, pl. *ḥulûl*, *ḥullâl*, *ḥullal*, descending, impending, due; — ة *ḥâla-t*, pl. *ḥâlât*, *ḥâl*, state, condition.

حالب *ḥâlib*, pl. *ḥalaba-t*, milker; pl. *ḥawâlib*, groin (m.).

حالق *ḥâliq*, f. ة, pl. *ḥalaqa-t*, barber; epilatory; — *ḥâliq*, ة *ḥâliqa-t*, one who is unfortunate, miserable; — *ḥâliq*, pl. *ḥawâliq*, full udder; hill; night.

حالك *ḥâlik*, pitch dark, black as a raven.

حالم *ḥâlim*, ag. of (حلم); mature (youth); cress.

حالوس *ḥâlûs*, sickle (m.).

حالى *ḥâliyy* (حال *ḥâl-in*), referring to the present time or state; modern; in present currency; ة *ḥâliyya-t*, present participle; conditionality; — *ḥâlî*, ة, pl. *ḥawâlî*, adorning one's self; adorned; ornamental; handsome, lovely, graceful; (m.) small peas; — ة *ḥâlî'a-t*, a poisonous snake.

حام *ḥâm*, Ham; — ة *ḥâmma-t*, grandees, noblemen, gentry.

حامز *ḥâmiz*, strong; sharp, piquant; wide awake, witty.

حامض *ḥâmiḍ*, ة, sour; bitter; salt; embittered.

حامل *ḥâmil*, pl. *ḥamala-t*, porter; الوحى ح *ḥâmil al-waḥy*, Gabriel; — also ة *ḥâmila-t*, big with young, pregnant; laden with fruit; overflowing; — *ḥâmila-t*, pl. *ḥawâmil*, river-bed; handbasket.

حامى *ḥâmî* (حام *ḥâm-in*), ة, glowing, burning hot; pl. *ḥumât*, f. ة, pl. *ḥawâmî*, protector; clientship, defensive alliance; — *ḥâmiyy*, Hamite, descendant of Ham.

حان *ḥânn*, greedy; agitated, moved; f. ة *ḥânna-t*, calling for her foal or young one; — ة *ḥâna-t*, wine-house, tavern.

حانط *ḥâniṭ*, crimson.

حانك *ḥânik*=حالك *ḥâlik*.

حانوت *ḥânût*, pl. *ḥawânît*, wine-house; shop, office.

حانوى *ḥânawiyy*, inn-keeper; shopkeeper; official.

حاوى *ḥâwî* (حاو *ḥâw-in*), ة, comprising, encompassing, containing; collector; ledger; snake-charmer; — ة *ḥawiya-t*, and—

حاويا *ḥâwiyâ'*, pl. *ḥawâwî*, gut, intestine.

حائب *ḥâ'ib*, sinner, criminal (حوب).

حائج *ḥâ'ij*, wanting (حوج).

حائد *ḥâ'id*, deviating; wanderer (حيد).

حائر *ḥâ'ir*, ة, confused, perplexed (بائر ح *ḥâ'ir bâ'ir*, who has entirely lost his head); lean, thin; low-land, garden; pl.

ḥûrân, *ḥîrân*, place where water gathers.

حائز *ḥâ'iz*, who obtains, possesses (حوز).

حائض *ḥâ'iḍ*, pl. *ḥuyyaḍ*, ة *ḥâ'iḍa-t*, pl. *ḥawâ'iḍ*, having the menses.

حائط *ḥâ'iṭ*, pl. *ḥîṭân*, *ḥiyâṭ*, wall; enclosure; garden.

حائف *ḥâ'if*, pl. *ḥâfa-t*, *ḥuyyaf*, edge, border, side; cruel.

حائك *ḥâ'ik*, pl. *ḥâka-t*, *ḥuyyak*, f. ة *ḥâ'ika-t*, pl. *ḥawâ'ik*, weaver.

حائل *ḥâ'il*, pl. *ḥiyâl*, *ḥûl*, *ḥuwwal*, *ḥûlal*, ag. of (حول), q.v.

حائم *ḥâ'im*, pl. *ḥuwwam*, thirsty, eager for, desirous; flying around (حوم).

حايى *ḥâyî* (حاى *ḥây-in*), alive, living.

(حب) *ḥabb*, I, INF. *ḥibb*, *ḥubb*, love, be in love, like; desire, wish for; pass. be tired; — *ḥabib*, A, *ḥabub*, INF. *ḥabab*, make friends with (الى *ila*); — II. INF. *taḥbîb*, render dear, endear; run to seed; make pills; — III. INF. *ḥibâb*, *muḥâbaba-t*, *muḥâbba-t*, cultivate one's friendship; show love to (acc.); — IV. INF. *iḥbâb*, love; desire, crave for; prefer; be run to seed; kneel down without stirring any more (camel); — V. INF. *taḥabbub*, show love; — VI. INF. *taḥâbb*, love one another; — X. INF. *istiḥbâb*, find amiable, beautiful, agreeable; love; prefer to (على *'ala*).

حب *ḥabb*, pl. *ḥubûb*, *ḥubbân*, grain; corn; seed; berry; nut; pill; bud; ح الملوك *ḥabb al-mulûk*, cherry; ح الغمام *ḥabb al-gamâm*, hail-stone; — *ḥibb*, *ḥubb*, love, friendship, benevolence; — *ḥibb*, pl. *aḥbâb*, *ḥibbân*, lover, beloved one, friend; — *ḥubb*, pl. *aḥbâb*, *ḥibaba-t*, *ḥibâb*, grape-stone; wine-jug; — *ḥabb-a*, حب به *ḥabb-a bi-hi*, how nice! how beautiful! — ة *ḥabba-t*, pl. *ḥabbât*, grain, corn, berry; globule; blister, pustule; grain (measure); morsel, trifle, a little; ح القلب *ḥabba-t al-qalb*, bottom of the heart; original sin; — *ḥibba-t*, pl. *ḥibab*, berry; — *ḥubba-t*, pl. *ḥubab*, beloved; love, friendship; also *ḥuba-t*, pl. *ḥuba*, grape-stone.

حبا *ḥaba'*, pl. *aḥbâ'*, favourite; — *ḥibâ'*, gift, present; — *ḥubâ*, pl. of حبوة *ḥubwa-t*.

حباب *ḥabâb*, *ḥubâb*, ة, bubble, drop; the deep; — *ḥibâb*, INF. III. of (حب); pl. of حب *ḥubb*; — *ḥubâb*, love; loved, beloved one; serpent; — *ḥabbâb*, seller of jugs.

حبار *ḥabâr*, *ḥibâr*, pl. *ḥabârât*, *ḥibârât*, sign; trace.

حبارج *ḥubârij*, حبارى *ḥubâra*, pl. *ḥubârâyât*, *ḥabârî*, *ḥabâ'ir*, bustard.

حباشة *ḥvbâśa-t*, medley, crowd.

حباك *ḥibâk*, pl. *ḥubuk*, strap; girdle, belt; path, course; orbit of a star; — *ḥabbâk*, lacemaker.

حبال *ḥibâl*, pl. of حبل *ḥabl*; — *ḥubâl*, pregnancy; fulness; — *ḥabbâl*, rope-maker; — ة *ḥabâla-t*, rope-making; — *ḥibâla-t*, pl. *ḥabâ'il*, net, snare, noose; string; vine-shoot.

حبان *ḥibbân*, *ḥubbân*, pl. of حب *ḥabb*, *ḥibb*.

حبائر *ḥabâ'ir*, pl. of حبارى *ḥubâra*.

حبائل *ḥabâ'il*, pl. of حبالة *ḥibâla-t*.

حبب *ḥabab*, *ḥibab*, bubble; row of pearl-like teeth; fine set of teeth; — *ḥibab*, *ḥubab*, pl. of حبة *ḥibba-t*, *ḥubba-t* respectively; — ة *ḥubaba-t*, pl. of حب *ḥubb*.

(حبتر) *ḥubtar*, short of stature; — *al-ḥabtar*, fox.

(حبج) *ḥabaj*, I, INF. *ḥabj*, appear suddenly; walk fast; approach; — INF. *ḥabja-t*, beat with a stick; (m.) thrash; — *ḥabij*, A, INF. *ḥabaj*, be puffed up with food.

حبحب *ḥabḥab*, ة, melon.

حبذا *ḥabbaẕâ*, well done! bravo! hence: II. *ḥabbaẕ*, INF. *taḥbîẕ*, call bravo, applaud, praise.

(حبر) *ḥabar*, U, INF. *ḥabr*, embellish, adorn; benefit; (m.) meditate; — INF. *ḥabr*, *ḥabra-t*, rejoice (a.), amuse, divert; — *ḥabir*, A, INF. *ḥabar*, have a luxuriant vegetation; be yellow; be healed, pass. id.; also INF. *ḥubûr*, rejoice (n.), be glad and content; — II. INF. *taḥbîr*, embellish, adorn; (m.) provide the ink-bottle with ink; make striped garments; — VI. INF. *taḥâbur*, lend one another oxen for ploughing.

حبر *ḥabr*, *ḥabar*, gladness, cheerfulness, contentment; benefit; — *ḥabr*, *ḥibr*, a Jewish doctor, scribe, pontiff (الح الاعظم *al-ḥabr al-a'ẕam*, the Pope); — *ḥibr*, pl. *aḥbâr*, beauty; ink; — ة *ḥabra-t*, amusement, music and dance; — *ḥabara-t*, *hibara-t*, a striped stuff made in Yaman.

حبرج *ḥubruj*, pl. *ḥabârij*, *ḥabârîj*, bustard.

حبرى *ḥabra*, Hebron; — *ḥabriyy*, (m.) حبروى *ḥabrawiyy*, pontifical; solemn; — *ḥibriyy*, maker of ink; — *ḥibariyy*, seller of striped cloth of Yaman.

(حبس) *ḥabas*, I, INF. *ḥabs*, *maḥbas*, hold, hold back, retain, prevent; confine, imprison; devote to pious use; envelop, wrap up; — II. INF. *taḥbîs*, imprison, wrap up; — III. INF. *muḥâbasa-t*, try to hold back or prevent, prohibit, prevent; — IV. INF. *iḥbâs*, imprison, keep prisoner; consecrate to pious use; — VIII. INF. *inḥibâs*, be prohibited, kept back, imprisoned; restrain one's self; — X. INF. *istiḥbâs*, retire from the world; live as a hermit.

حبس *ḥabs*, imprisonment; retention; pl. *ḥubûs*, prison; — *ḥabs*, *ḥibs*, pl. *aḥbâs*, weir, dam; pond; — *ḥubs*, *ḥubus*, pl. *aḥbâs*, pious endowment; — ة *ḥubsa-t*, retention; self-restraint; silence; impediment of speech; difficulty in expressing one's self.

حبسا *ḥubasâ'*, pl. of حبيس *ḥabîs*.

(حبش) *ḥabaś*, U, INF. *ḥabś*, also II. INF. *taḥbîś*, collect; — V. INF. *taḥabbuś*, be collected, assembled.

حبش *ḥabaś* (also coll.), pl. *ḥubśân*, Abyssinian, Ethiopian; — ة *ḥabaśa-t*, Abyssinia; — ى *ḥabaśiyy*, an Abyssinian.

(حبض) *ḥabaḍ*, I, INF. *ḥabḍ*, beat, throb; die; — also *ḥabiḍ*, I, INF. *ḥabaḍ*, make resound the string of a bow; fall down before the shooter; — U, INF. *ḥubûḍ*, decrease; lessen; be not valid; — IV. INF. *iḥbâḍ*, invalidate, abolish; make efforts, exert one's self.

حبض *ḥabaḍ*, motion; pulsation, throbbing; sound, noise.

(حبط) *ḥabaṭ*, I, INF. *ḥabṭ*, *ḥubûṭ*; also *ḥabiṭ*, A, INF. *ḥabaṭ*, come to nought; be useless; be spilt unavenged; — *ḥabiṭ*, have the belly puffed up with food; break up again; — IV. INF. *iḥbâṭ*, nullify.

(حبق) *ḥabaq*, I, INF. *ḥabq*, *ḥabiq*, *ḥubâq*, break wind; — II. INF. *taḥbîq*, gather one's things for departure, put them in good order.

حبقر *ḥabqar*, *ḥabaqurr*, hail.

حبقى *ḥibiqqa*, quick travelling or walking.

(حبك) *ḥabak*, weave skilfully; unite firmly; lop, cut off; — II. INF. *taḥbîk*, unite firmly, fasten tightly; (m.) interweave; twist a thread; — V. INF. *taḥabbuk*, be firmly united, tightened; be girdled; work well together (parts of a machine, &c.); — VIII. INF. *iḥtibâk*, weave well; arrange and carry out well; be well woven; be full.

حبك *ḥubuk*, part, morsel; coat of mail; pl. of حباك *ḥibâk* and حبيكة *ḥabîka-t*; — *ḥubukk*, firm, strong; — ة *ḥabka-t*, texture; — *ḥubka-t*, pl. *ḥubak*, strap; girdle; — *ḥabaka-t*, vine-root.

(حبكر) *ḥabkar*, INF. ة, gather, assemble; — II. INF. *taḥabkur*, be perplexed, confused.

(حبل) *ḥabal*, U, INF. *ḥabl*, set nets or snares, catch with such; fasten with ropes; make a covenant; — *ḥabil*, U, INF. *ḥabal*, be full; be pregnant; conceive (woman); be angry; — II. INF. *taḥbîl*, IV. INF. *iḥbâl*, get with child; — VIII. INF. *iḥtibâl*, catch game with a net or noose.

حبل *ḥabl*, pl. *ḥibâl*, *ḥubûl*, *aḥbâl*, *aḥbul*, string, rope, cable (ح المساكين *ḥabl al-masâkîn*, ivy); fetter; far-stretching sand-hill; vein, sinew; covenant, compact; friendship, protection; — *ḥibl*, skilful, clever, prudent; also *ḥabl*, pl. *ḥubûl*, evil; — *ḥabal*, pregnancy, conception; replenishing (s.); anger; — ة *ḥabla-t*, *ḥabala-t*, *ḥubla-t*, vine-root, shoot; — *ḥubla-t*, pl. *ḥubal*, neck-tie; — *ḥabala-t*, pl. of حابلة *ḥâbila-t*; — ى *ḥubla*, pl. *ḥublayât*, *ḥabâla*, pregnant; big with young.

حبلان *ḥablân*, ة, full; enraged; f. pregnant, big with child.

(حبن) *ḥabin*, A, also pass. *ḥubin*, INF. *ḥabn*, *ḥaban*, be afflicted with dropsy; be enraged against (على *'ala*).

حبن *ḥabn*, rose-laurel; — *ḥibn*, monkey; also ة *ḥibna-t*, pl. *ḥubûn*, blister; boil; — *ḥaban*, dropsy.

حبنا *ḥabnâ'*, f. of احنب *aḥnab*, dropsical.

(حبو) *ḥabâ*, U, INF. *ḥabw*, crawl (as a child); not be able to move from weakness; appear; give, present with; prevent, detain, keep from; — INF. *ḥubuww*, be near; be close together; — III. INF. *ḥibâ'*, *muḥâbât*, show regard; show preference, favour; abate from the price; — VIII. INF. *iḥtibâ'*, gather the clothes behind or tie them up to the hips; — ة *ḥabwa-t*, *ḥibwa-t*, *ḥubwa-t*, gift, present; — *ḥubwa-t*, *ḥibwa-t*, pl. *ḥuba*, *ḥiba*, gathering and tucking up of a garment; loop or girdle for that purpose.

حبوب *ḥubûb*, pl. of حب *ḥabb*; hence a new sing.: ة *ḥubûba-t*, grain; plague-blister; pl. *ḥubûbat*, corn-fruit; fruit with shells.

حبور *ḥubûr*, indolence, laziness; — *ḥabbûr*, pl. *ḥabâbîr*, the young of a bustard; — ة *ḥubûra-t*, knowledge of the Jewish law.

حبول *ḥabûl*, evil.

حبى *ḥuba*, pl. of حبة *ḥuba-t* and of حبوة *ḥabwa-t*.

حبيب *ḥabîb*, f. ة, pl. *aḥbâb*, *aḥibbâ'*, *aḥibba-t*, *ḥabâ'ib*, beloved one; lover; sweetheart, darling; ح الله *ḥabîb allâh*, Muḥammad; — ة *ḥabîba-t*, anything loved; Medina; — *ḥubayyib*, little darling.

حبيس *ḥabîs*, consecrated to pious use; hermit.

حبيكة *ḥabîka-t*, pl. *ḥubuk*, *ḥabîk*, *ḥabâ'ik*, path in the sand; orbit of a star.

حبين *ḥabîn*, dropsical.

(حت) *ḥatt*, U, INF. *ḥatt*, wipe, rub off; peel, shell; strip the leaves from a branch; fall off; — VI. INF. *taḥâtt*, VII. INF. *inḥitât*, fall off or out.

حت *ḥatt*, pl. *aḥtât*, making quick and long steps; ostrich; what has fallen off, anything dry, withered.

(حتا) *ḥata'*, A, INF. *ḥat'*, beat; lie

with; twist; fix; sew, stitch; unload.

حتات *ḥatât*, noise, tumult; — *ḥutât*, chips, shavings.

حتار *ḥitâr*, pl. *ḥutur*, edge, border; circumference; shell of the ear, prepuce.

حتام *ḥattâma*=حتى ما *ḥatta mâ*, until when? how long?

(حتام), III. *iḥta'amm*, INF. *iḥti'mâm*, cut or break off.

(حتحت) *ḥatḥat*, INF. ة, fall off.

(حتد) *ḥatad*, I, INF. *ḥutûd*, remain, stay; — *ḥatid*, A, INF. *ḥatad*, be of pure descent.

حتد *ḥatid*, of pure descent;—*ḥutud*, root, essence, origin.

(حتر) *ḥatar*, I, U, INF. *ḥatr*, fasten, tie; fix one's look at (acc.); — INF. *ḥatr*, *ḥutûr*, present food, give to eat; give little to one's people, prove niggardly; taste food, eat.

حتر *ḥitr*, present, gift; — *ḥutur*, pl. of حتار *ḥitâr*.

حترب *ḥatrab*, short, small.

(حترش) *ḥitriś*, short, small, dwarfish; — hence II. INF. *taḥrâś*, assemble (m.); try to catch in running.

(حترف) *ḥatraf*, INF. ة, remove, push aside.

(حتش) *ḥataś*, U, INF. *ḥatś*, come together; fix one's look long upon; pass. be seized with merriment.

(حتف) *ḥatf*, pl. *ḥutûf*, death; followed by انف *anf* or فم *fam*, as a complement: natural death.

(حتك) *ḥatak*, I, INF. *ḥatk*, *ḥatakân*, walk fast and with short steps; cut off, scrape or shave off.

(حتل) *ḥatl*, gift, present; resemblance, similarity; the worse of two things.

(حتم) *ḥatm*, I, INF. *ḥatm*, inspire; indicate; impose as necessity or duty; order, decree; decide finally; fix, confirm; — II. INF. *taḥtîm*, finish.

حتم *ḥatm*, pl. *ḥutûm*, final decision; order, decree.

(حتن) *ḥatin*, A, INF. *ḥatan*, be violent (as heat, &c.);—VI. INF. *taḥâtun*, equal one another.

حتن *ḥatn*, *ḥitn*, pl. *aḥtân*, similar, equal; comrade; du. two equals in anything.

(حتو) *ḥatâ*, U, INF. *ḥatw*, run fast; twist tightly.

حتوم *ḥutûm*, pl. of حاتم *ḥâtim* and حتم *ḥatm*.

(حتى) *ḥata*, I, INF. *ḥaty*, also IV. INF. *iḥtâ'*, sew together; twist together; fix, fasten.

حتى *ḥatta*, until, as far as; ح متى *ḥatta mata*, ح ما *ḥatta mâ*, حتام *ḥattâma*, until when? how long? *ḥatta* and ح ان *ḥatta ann*, until, so that; in order that; nay even; as well; except.

(حث) *ḥaṯṯ*, U, INF. *ḥaṯṯ*, also II. INF. *taḥṯîṯ* and IV. INF. *iḥṯâṯ*, instigate, incite, encourage; speed onward; — VI. INF. *taḥâṯṯ*, do so mutually; — VII. INF. *inḥiṯâṯ*, pass. of I.; — VIII. INF. *iḥtiṯâṯ*= I. and also its pass.

حث *ḥaṯṯ*, instigation, incitement.

حثاث *ḥaṯâṯ*, *ḥiṯâṯ*, sleep; a black collyrium; — *ḥiṯâṯ*, pl. of حثيث *ḥaṯîṯ*.

حثحث *ḥaṯḥaṯ*, INF. ة = (حث); urge, hasten (a.); flash; move the pencil with collyrium to the eye.

(حثر) *ḥaṯir*, A, INF. *ḥaṯar*, be covered with pustules; be running (eye).

(حثل) *ḥaṯil*, A, INF. *ḥaṯal*, be badly fed; — IV. INF. *iḥṯâl*, feed badly; make the condition of anyone worse.

(حثلب) *ḥiṯlib*, dregs, sediment.

(حثم) *ḥaṯam*, U, INF. *ḥaṯm*, give; rub, rub off.

(حثو) *ḥaṯâ*, U, INF. *ḥaṯw*, give little; — also حثى *ḥaṯa*, I, INF. *ḥaṯy*, *taḥṯâ'*, strew; be strewn upon the head, on a dead body, &c. (dust).

حثوث *ḥaṣûṣ*, حثيث *ḥaṣîṣ*, pl. *ḥiṣâṣ*, instigated, incited; quick.

(حشى) see (حشو).

(حج) *ḥajj*, U, INF. *ḥajj*, go or wander to, especially in pilgrimage to Mecca; desist; get the better of in a lawsuit or by legal means; — III. INF. *ḥijâj*, *muḥâjja-t*, dispute, argue, demonstrate; plead one's case; — V. INF. *taḥajjuj*, proffer as a proof, reason, or pretext; — VI. INF. *taḥâjj*, argue against one another; — VIII. INF. *iḥtijâj*= V.; excuse one's self.

حج *ḥijj*, pilgrimage to Mecca; — *ḥujj*, pl. of حاج *ḥâjj*; — ة *ḥijja-t*, pl. *-ât*, *ḥijaj*, a pilgrimage to Mecca; a year; ذو الح *zû 'l-ḥijja-t*, pl. ذوات الح *zawât al-ḥijja-t*, the last month of the Muḥammadan year; — *ḥujja-t*, pl. *ḥujaj*, proof, argument, demonstration; certificate; document, deed, legal papers; sentence (of a judge); law-suit; pretext, excuse, subterfuge.

(حجا) *ḥaja'*, A, INF. *ḥaj'*, rejoice at; retain, keep back; flee, take refuge; — حجى *ḥajî'*, *ḥajî*, also V. INF. *taḥajjî*, rejoice at, be greedy for or sparing with (ب *bi*).

حجاب *ḥijâb*, pl. *ḥujub*, partition; veil; curtain; bashfulness, modesty; amulet; — *ḥujjâb*, pl. of *ḥâjib*; — ة *ḥijâba-t*, office of a door-keeper or chamberlain.

حجاج *ḥajâj*, *ḥijâj*, pl. *aḥijja-t*; eye-bone; eye-brow; side, edge, border; — *ḥijâj*, INF. III. of (حج), arguing (s.); dispute; — *ḥajjâj*, quarrelsome, litigious; dogmatical person; tyrant; who makes frequent pilgrimages; — *ḥujjâj*, pl. of حاج *ḥâjj*.

حجار *ḥajjâr*, stone-cutter; mason; — ة *ḥijâra-t*, pl. of حجر *ḥajar*.

حجاز *ḥijâz*, rope; region surrounded by mountains; Hijâz; — ة *ḥijâza-t*, hindrance; — ى *ḥijâziyy*, of Hijâz.

حجال *ḥajjâl*, splendour, brightness.

حجام *ḥijâm*, set of teeth; muzzle; — *ḥajjâm*, cupper; bath-keeper; — ة *ḥijâma-t*, *ḥajâma-t*, cupping (s.).

(حجب) *ḥajab*, U, I, INF. *ḥajb*, *ḥijâb*, cover, veil; separate by stepping between; shut off, inclose, wall; (m.) cup; — II. INF. *taḥjîb*, veil entirely; put out of sight; shut off; — V. INF. *taḥajjub*, VII. INF. *inḥijâb*, VIII. INF. *iḥtijâb*, pass. of II.; conceal one's self; sit behind a curtain; — X. INF. *istiḥjâb*, make anybody one's door-keeper or chamberlain.

حجب *ḥujub*, pl. of حجاب *ḥijâb*; — ة *ḥajaba-t*, pl. of حاجب *ḥâjib*.

حجج *ḥijaj*, *ḥujaj*, pl. of حجة *ḥijja-t*, *ḥujja-t* respectively.

(حجحج) *ḥajḥaj*, INF. ة, recede; be on the point of speaking, but abstain; stop, stay.

(حجدم) *ḥajdam*, pl. *ḥajâdim*, sown field.

(حجر) *ḥajar*, U, INF. *ḥajr*, *ḥijr*, *ḥujr*, *ḥijrân*, *ḥujrân*, hinder, refuse admission or the use of a thing; place under curatorship; — II. INF. *taḥjîr*, pelt or cover with stones; stone; turn into stone; — V. INF. *taḥajjur*, harden (n.), turn into stone, petrify; be very stony; — X. INF. *istiḥjâr*=V.; make a room or stable for one's use.

حجر *ḥajr*, *ḥijr*, hindrance, prohibition, defence; placing under curatorship; bosom; — *ḥijr*, *ḥujr*, unlawful, forbidden; pl. *aḥjâr*, *ḥijâr*, wall, inclosure; dam; northern wall of the Ka'aba; bosom; gathered seam of a garment; seam of a shirt; intellect; pl. *aḥjâr*, hole of a mouse, snake, &c.; pl. *aḥjâr*, *ḥujûr*, *ḥujûra-t*, mare; the ancient dwellings of the Thamûd-

ites ; — *ḥujr*, bosom ; embrace ; — *ḥajar*, pl. *aḥjâr*, *aḥjur*, *ḥijâr*, *ḥijâra-t*, stone ; ح ارمنى *ḥajar armaniyy*, azure-stone, lazuli ; du. *al-ḥajarân*, gold and silver ; — ة *ḥajra-t*, pl. *ḥajr*, *ḥajarât*, *ḥiwâjir*, side of a house, courtyard ; stony, f. (*ḥajratan*, separately, by one's self) ; bosom ; understanding, intellect ; — *ḥijra-t*, mare ; — *ḥujra-t*, pl. *ḥujar*, *ḥujrât*, *ḥujarât*, *ḥujurât*, stable, fold ; room, chamber ; sepulchre ; wall-niche.

حجران *ḥijrân*, *ḥujrân*, INF. of (حجر) ; — *ḥujrân*, pl. of حاجر *ḥâjir*.

حجرى *ḥajariyy*, ة , stony, of stone ; — ة *ḥajariyya-t*, stoniness ; (m.) macadam.

(حجز) *ḥajaz*, U, I, INF. *ḥajz*, *ḥajîz*, *ḥijâza-t*, *ḥijjîza*, shut off, cover, conceal ; prevent from approaching, hinder ; step between, keep asunder ; — *ḥajiz*, A, INF. *ḥajaz*, have heat in the intestines and feel thirsty ; — III. INF. *muḥâjaza-t*, oppose, try to prevent ; — IV. INF. *ijḥâz*, come or travel to Hijâz ; — VII. INF. *inḥijâz*, be prevented, hindered ; — VIII. INF. *iḥtijâz*, id. ; gird one's self round the waist ; carry anything in one's bosom ; be gathered, assemble (n.).

حجز *ḥajz*, prevention, hindrance ; — *ḥijz*, *ḥujz*, origin ; relations ; — ة *ḥujza-t*, pl. *ḥujaz*, girt, girdle ; waist ; شدة الح *śidda-t al-ḥujza-t*, patience, endurance ; — *ḥajaza-t*, pl. of حاجز *ḥâjiz*.

(حجف), III. *ḥâjaf*, INF. *muḥâjafa-t*, oppose, hinder ; — VII. INF. *inḥijâf*, humble one's self ; — VIII. INF. *iḥtijâf*, abstain, desist ; appropriate ; — ة *ḥajafa-t*, leathern shield ; breast.

(حجل) *ḥajal*, U, I, INF. *ḥajl*, *ḥajalân*, hop ; run in leaps ; — I, INF. *ḥujûl*, be sunk in its socket (eye) ; — pass. INF. *ḥajl*, step between ; — II. INF. *taḥjîl*, have all four or three feet white or white-spotted.

حجل *ḥajl*, *ḥijl*, *ḥijil*, *ḥijill*, pl. *ḥujûl*, *aḥjâl*, fetter, ring on the foot (also for ornament) ; white spot on a horse's hoof ; — *ḥijl*, pl. *ḥujûl*, horse with three or four white feet ; — *ḥajal*, pl. *aḥjâl*, حجلى *ḥijla*, noun of unity ة *ḥajala-t*, pl. *ḥujlân*, male partridge ; — *ḥajala-t*, pl. *ḥajal*, *ḥijâl*, bridal chamber ; bridal throne.

حجلا *ḥajlâ'*, f. of احجل *aḥjal*, white-footed.

حجلان *ḥajalân*, INF. of (حجل).

(حجم) *ḥajam*, U, A, INF. *ḥajm*, *ḥajâma-t*, cup ; — U, I, INF. *ḥajm*, suck ; be high (breasts) ; muzzle ; prevent ; — II. INF. *taḥjîm*, look at sharply, with passion ; — IV. INF. *iḥjâm*, cup ; desist from fear ; show one's self cowardly ; forbear ; shrink back ; refuse respect, help ; be high (breasts) ; — VII. INF. *inḥijâm*, get cupped ; — VIII. INF. *iḥtijâm*, get one's self cupped ; cup.

حجم *ḥajm*, pl. *ḥujûm*, swelling ; thickness ; bulk.

(حجن) *ḥajin*, A, INF. *ḥajan*, adhere to ; act miserly ; stop, remain ; be crooked ; — *ḥajan*, U, bend, make crooked ; divert, dissuade ; also VIII. INF. *iḥtijân*, draw to one's self by a hooked stick ; hold fast ; — II. INF. *taḥjîn*, bend, make hooked or crooked.

حجن *ḥajan*, ة *ḥujna-t*, crook, bend ; — *ḥajan*, *ḥajin*, tick (insect).

(حجو) *ḥajâ*, U, INF. *ḥajw*, suppose, be of opinion, assert without sufficient foundation ; judge of a person ; remain, stay, stop ; adhere to a thing, be sparing with it ; keep (a secret) ; reward, requite ; urge on ; pre-

vent; surpass in solving riddles; — حجى *ḥajî*, A, INF. *ḥajan*, be addicted to, infatuated with (ب *bi*); — III. INF. *ḥijâ'*, *muḥâjât*, surpass in solving riddles; propose a riddle.

حجى *ḥijan*, *ḥija*, pl. *aḥjâ'*, considerateness; prudence; cunning; riddle; — *ḥajî*, worthy; — *ḥajî*, *ḥajiyy*, intelligent, considerate.

حجيا *ḥujayyâ*, riddle.

حجيج *ḥajîj*, ة *ḥajîja-t*, pl. of حاج *ḥâjj*.

حجير *ḥajîr*, stony.

حجيزى *ḥajjîza*, hindrance, INF. of (حجز).

حجيل *ḥajîl*, having three or four white feet.

(حد) *ḥadd*, U, and (m.) A, INF. *ḥadd*, sharpen; sharpen one's look; confine, define, distinguish; restrain, prevent, hinder; chastise; refuse; — U, I, INF. *ḥadd*, *ḥidâd*, put off all ornaments; wear mourning apparel; — I, INF. *ḥidda-t*, be sharp, cutting; — U, and (m.) I, INF. *ḥadd*, *ḥidda-t*, be violent, empassioned, enraged; fly into a passion against (على *'ala*); pass. *ḥudd*, be unhappy, unfortunate, miserable; — II. INF. *taḥdîd*, sharpen; confine; define; forge iron; be a blacksmith; — III. INF. *muḥâda-t*, prevent, hinder, restrain; oppose as an enemy; grow passionate against; — IV. INF. *iḥdâd*, put off all ornaments, wear mourning; — V. INF. *taḥaddud*, be limited, defined; — VIII. INF. *iḥtidâd*, be sharp; be empassioned, enraged; fly into a passion; — X. INF. *istiḥdâd*, shave off the hair of the pubes.

حد *ḥida'*, pl. of حداة *ḥidât*; — *ḥadd*, pl. *ḥudûd*, limit, boundary; term; end, goal, aim; district; reach, sphere of action; difference; definition; rule; punishment; edge, point; passion; intoxicating strength of liquors; strength, bravery; energy; manner, way; hindrance; (m.) side; violent, passionate; — ة *ḥida-t*, INF. of وحد *waḥid*, being alone, solitariness; — *ḥidda-t*, edge of a sword, &c.; sharpness; passionateness; impulsiveness; impetuosity; anger; intoxicating strength (of wine, &c.).

(حدا) *ḥada'*, A, INF. *ḥad'*, turn; divert (a.), dissuade; — حدى *ḥadi'*, A, INF. *ḥada'*, take refuge with (الى *ila*); take into clientship, protect; be angry with (على *'ala*).

حدا *ḥaddâ*, camel-driver; — ة *ḥada'a-t*, pl. *ḥada'*, *ḥadâ'*, double-edged axe, hatchet; — *ḥidât*, *ḥida'a-t*, pl. حد *ḥida'*, *ḥidâ'*, *ḥid'ân*, vulture; hawk.

حداب *ḥadâb*, time of famine; — *ḥidâb*, pl. of حدب *ḥadab*.

حداث *ḥidâs*, talk, chat; — *ḥuddâs*, pl. of حادث *ḥâdis*, ag. of (حدث); — ة *ḥadâsa-t*, newness; youth; — *ḥidâsa-t*, freshness; beginning.

حداجة *ḥidâja-t*, pl. *ḥadâ'ij*, camel-saddle or litter.

حداد *ḥidâd*, mourning, mourning-apparel; INF. of (حد); pl. of حديد *ḥadîd*; — *ḥudâd*, sharp, pl. *aḥiddâ'*, *aḥidda-t*, of a sharp intellect, of fluent speech; passionate; — *ḥaddâd*, pl. *-ûn*, who limits, confines, hinders; blacksmith; tinker; — ة *ḥidâda-t*, occupation of a blacksmith.

حداشة *ḥidâśa-t*=حداجة *ḥidâja-t*.

حداية *ḥidâya-t*, vulture.

(حدب) *ḥadib*, A, INF. *ḥadab*, bulge, be convex, be hump-backed; be devoted, benevolent, kind, compassionate; not marry again; — II. INF. *taḥdîb*, make convex; — XII. *iḥdaudab*, INF. *iḥdîdâb*,

be hump-backed; extend in a crooked line.

حدب *ḥadab*, pl. *ḥidâb*, rugged rising ground; back of a wave; — *ḥadib*, kind, compassionate; hump-backed; — *ḥudb*, pl. of احدب *aḥdab*, hump-backed; — ة *ḥadaba-t*, hump; being crooked, hump-backed; convexity.

حدبا *ḥadbâ'*, f. of احدب *aḥdab*, hump-backed.

(حدث) *ḥadas̱*, I, INF. *ḥudûs̱*, *ḥadâs̱a-t*, happen for the first time, happen, happen to (الى *ila*); — *ḥadus̱*, INF. *ḥadâs̱â-t*, be new, fresh, young; — II. INF. *taḥdîs̱*, tell (something new); address, talk to (الى *ila* or ب *bi*); explain a text; — III. INF. *muḥâdas̱a-t*, converse with (acc.); — IV. INF. *iḥdâs̱*, produce anything fresh, cause to exist; drop excrement and get polluted thereby; happen; — V. INF. *taḥaddus̱*, tell, converse; — VI. INF. *taḥâdus̱*, tell to one another, converse together; — X. INF. *istiḥdâs̱*, find new.

حدث *ḥads̱*, anything new; recent event; event, accident; *ḥids̱*, *ḥadis̱*, who narrates well; — *ḥadas̱*, pl. *aḥdâs̱*, id., pl. *aḥdas̱ât*, events, accidents; youth, young man; f. ة; beginning; pollution by excrement.

حدثان *ḥids̱ân*, novelty, freshness; pl. events, accidents; young people.

(حدج) *ḥadaj*, I, f. *ḥadj*, saddle and load the camel, especially with the litter for women; accuse, calumniate; cheat; shoot; look sharply at; strike, hit; — IV. INF. *idḥâj*, put the load or the litter on the camel.

حدج *ḥidj*, pl. *ḥudûj*, *aḥdâj*, load of a camel; camel-litter for women.

(حدر) *ḥadar*, U, I, INF. *ḥadr*, *ḥudûr*, descend; let down; swell and get hard; cause to do so; purge; surround; be assembled; — U, INF. *ḥadr*, hasten, do anything in a hurry; INF. *ḥadr*, *ḥadâra-t*, be fat and thick-set; — U, I, INF. *ḥadr*, flow over with tears; — IV. INF. *iḥdâr*, cause to descend; throw down; hasten through the sea; — V. INF. *taḥaddur*, descend gradually; let one's self down, glide down; swim down, flow — VII. INF. *inḥidâr*, be let down; descend; swell.

حدر *ḥadar*, declivity; — *ḥudurr*, thick, swollen.

حدرا *ḥadrâ'*, f. of احدر *aḥdar*, squint-eyed; having thin flanks.

حدرج *ḥadraj*, INF. ة, twist firmly.

(خدس) *ḥadas*, U, I, INF. *ḥads*, wander about without a guide; wander; err about; hasten; surmise, conjecture; intend; purpose; conquer in wrestling; tread down; — V. INF. *taḥaddus*, inquire after the truth of anything.

حدس *ḥads*, quick understanding; foresight; guess.

حدسية *ḥadsiyya-t*, supposition, surmise.

(حدق) *ḥadaq*, I, INF. *ḥadq*, surround, encompass, enclose, wall in; look at; — II. INF. *taḥdîq*, surround, look sharply at; — IV. INF. *iḥdâq*, XII. *iḥdaudaq*, INF. *iḥdîdâq*, surround; — ة *ḥadaqa-t*, pl. *ḥadaq*, *ḥidâq*, *aḥdâq*, the black of the eye, pupil.

(حدل) *ḥadal*, I, INF. *ḥadl*, *ḥudûl*, also *ḥadil*, A, INF. *ḥadal*, be unjust against (على *'ala*); have one shoulder higher than the other; — (m.) I, INF. *ḥadâla-t*, smooth a flat roof with a roller and make it impermeable.

حدل *ḥadl*, flat, smooth (m.); — *ḥadil*, unjust; partial.

(حدم) *ḥadm*, glow of a fire; —

hence: IV. *aḥdam*, INF. *iḥdâm*, burn, glow; — V. INF. *taḥaddum*, be glowing, burn with anger.

(حدو) *ḥadâ*, U, INF. *ḥadw*, *ḥidâ'*, *ḥudâ'*, urge on; drive camels by singing to them; incite, spur; follow;—VIII. INF. *iḥtidâ'*, urge on; follow.

حدوث *ḥudûs*, novelty, freshness; originality; happening of anything; appearance; invention; — ة *ḥudûsa-t*, youthfulness.

حدور *ḥadûr*, steep declivity, precipice; — *ḥudûr*, descent, INF. of (حدر); — ة *ḥadûra-t*, *ḥudûra-t*, flood of tears.

(حدى) *ḥadî*, A, INF. حدا *ḥadan*, stick to a place; — IV. INF. *iḥdâ'*, do on purpose; — ة *ḥiddiyya-t*=حدة *ḥidda-t*.

حدى الدهر *ḥada 'd-dahr*, never.

حديا *ḥudayyâ*, being an adversary, antagonism.

حديث *ḥadîs*, pl. *aḥdâs*, new, recent, fresh; pl. *ḥidsân*, youth, young man; pl. *aḥâdîs*, *ḥidsân*, *ḥadsân*, recent event, fresh news; tradition of Muḥammad; story, tale; conversation, chat; — *ḥiddîs*, talkative; — ى *ḥiddîsa*, tale, narrative.

حديد *ḥadîd*, confining with, bordering upon; — pl. *ḥidâd*, of quick understanding, of fluent speech; passionate; — pl. *ḥadâ'id*, iron; armour, helmet; — ة *ḥadîda-t*, pl. *ḥadâ'id*, piece of iron; sharp sword; weapon; iron tool; — ى *ḥadîdiyy*, ة, of iron.

حديقة *ḥadîqa-t*, pl. *ḥadâ'iq*, enclosed garden or vineyard.

(حذ) *ḥazz*, U, INF. *ḥazz*, cut off entirely.

حذ *ḥazz*, cutting off, lopping (s.); — ة *ḥuzza-t*, slice of meat; — *ḥizat-an*, opposite.

حذا *ḥizâ'*, opposite; — *ḥizâ'-a*, vis-à-vis; pl. *aḥziya-t*, shoe, sandal; sole of the foot; — *ḥazzâ'*, shoemaker.

حذار حذار *ḥazâr-i ḥazâr-i*, take care! be on your guard! beware!

حذارى *ḥazâra*, pl. of حذر *ḥazir*; — *ḥazâra*, *ḥazârî*, pl. of حذرية *ḥizriya-t*.

حذاق *ḥazâq*, INF. of (حذق); — *ḥizâq*, *ḥuzâq*, pl. of حذقة *ḥizqa-t*; — *ḥuzzâq*, pl. of حاذق *ḥâziq*; — ة *ḥizâqa-t*, penetration; sagacity; skill; learning the Koran by heart; — *ḥuzâqa-t*, mouthful.

حذال *ḥuzâl*, ة *ḥuzâla-t*, a red resin; — *ḥuzâla-t*, seam of a shirt; chaff.

بحذاميره *bi-ḥazâmîr-i-hi*, the whole of it, all.

حذذ *ḥazaz*, mobility; wagging of the tail; suppression of a *watad majmû'* at the end of a foot of verse.

(حذر) *ḥazir*, A, INF. *ḥazr*, *ḥazar*, *maḥzûra-t*, be on one's guard; fear for a person (على *'ala*) from (من *min*); — II. INF. *taḥzîr*, inspire with fear from (two acc.); frighten by threats; warn, bid to be careful; — III. INF. *ḥizâr*, *muḥâzara-t*, fear from, be on one's guard against (من *min*); be afraid lest (ان *an*); — V. INF. *taḥazzur*, be on one's guard; — VIII. INF. *iḥtizâr*, id.; shun, avoid (acc. or من *min*).

حذر *ḥizr*, *ḥazar*, caution; distrust; — *ḥazir*, *ḥazur*, pl. *-ûn*, *ḥazâra*, cautious, on one's guard.

حذريان *ḥizriyân*, very cautious.

حذرية *ḥizriya-t*, pl. *ḥazâra*, *ḥazârî*, comb of a cock; also حذريا *ḥizriyâ*, rugged hill.

(حذف) *ḥazaf*, I, INF. *ḥazf*, take away, cut off, suppress; cut off part of one's hair; throw, fling; move the shoulders and hips in walking; bestow; despatch (business, &c.); (m.) adjourn, delay; — II. INF. *taḥzîf*, make, prepare; — III. INF. *muḥâzafa-t*, delay, adjourn (m.).

حذف *ḥaẕf*, elision; apocopy; suppression of a *sabab ḥafîf* at the end of a foot of verse.

حذفر *ḥaẕfar*, INF. ة, fill up.

(حذق) *ḥaẕaq*, I, *ḥaẕiq*, A, INF. *ḥiẕq*, *ḥiẕâq*, *ḥiẕâqa-t* (*ḥaẕq*, *ḥaẕâq*, *ḥaẕâqa-t*), be skilful, well versed in anything (acc.); learn the Koran by heart; — I, INF. *ḥiẕq*, *ḥiẕâqa-t*, cut, stretch out anything in order to cut it through, cut by tying too tight; — INF. *ḥaẕq*, *ḥuẕûq*, be sour; — INF. *ḥaẕq*, *ḥiẕq*, burn on the tongue; — V. INF. *taḥaẕẕuq*, understand a thing thoroughly.

حذق *ḥiẕq*, sharpness; penetration; skill; — ة *ḥiẕqa-t*, pl. *ḥiẕâq*, *ḥuẕâq*, piece; cut; portion, part.

(حذل) *ḥaẕil*, A, INF. *ḥaẕal*, suffer with the falling out of the eye-lashes; be red and water (eyes).

(حذلق) *ḥaẕlaq*, INF. ة, II. INF. *taḥaẕluq*, show one's skill; boast.

(حذلم) *ḥaẕlam*, INF. ة, walk fast; train; shave and sharpen into a point; — II. INF. *taḥaẕlum*, walk fast; cultivate one's mind and attain to excellence.

(حذم) *ḥaẕam*, I, INF. *ḥaẕm*, cut off; hurry; INF. *ḥaẕamân*, walk fast.

حذم *ḥaẕim*, cutting.

حذمر *ḥiẕmir*, short-bodied.

(حذن) *ḥuẕn*, room, apartment.

(حذو) *ḥaẕâ*, U, INF. *ḥaẕw*, *ḥiẕâ'*, put the shoes on to a person; measure one shoe by another; do the same thing; sit opposite; burn the tongue; give; — III. INF. *ḥiẕâ'*, *muḥâẕât*, be opposite to one another; emulate, imitate; — IV. INF. *iḥẕâ'*, put the shoes on to; share with (two acc.); — VI. INF. *taḥâẕî*, divide equally between each other; share; match; — VIII. INF. *iḥtiẕâ'*, use for a shoe; put on the shoes; be shod; imitate; pattern by; — X. INF. *istiḥẕâ'*, put on shoes.

حذو *ḥaẕw*, حذوة *ḥiẕwat-a*, opposite, vis-à-vis.

(حذى) *ḥaẕa*, I, INF. *ḥaẕy*, burn the tongue.

حذيا *ḥuẕyâ*, gift, present.

(حر) *ḥarr*, for *ḥarir*, A, INF. *ḥarâr*, become or be free; be born as a freeman, be of noble birth; — for *ḥarir*, *ḥarar*, A, I, U, INF. *ḥarr*, *ḥurûr*, *ḥarâra-t*, be hot; be thirsty; burn the tongue; — U, INF. *ḥarr*, make hot; — I, INF. *ḥarr*, make silk garments; II. INF. *taḥrîr*, examine minutely; verify; compose carefully; write; adjust; — V. INF. *taḥarrur*, be set free, freed; grow hot or hotter; be carefully composed or written; — X. INF. *istaḥrâr*, grow hotter; be embittered.

حر *ḥar-in*, see حرى *ḥarî*; — *ḥarr*, pl. *ḥurûr*, *aḥârir*, heat; — *ḥir*, *ḥirr*, pudenda of a woman; — *ḥurr*, pl. *ḥirâr*, *aḥrâr*, free; set free, freeman; born free and noble; virtuous, genuine, true, pure, good; unmixed; — ة *ḥira-t*, pl. *ḥirûn*, pudenda of a woman; — *ḥarra-t*, pl. *ḥarr*, *ḥirâr*, *ḥarrât*, *aḥarrûn*, stony volcanic tract of land; thirst; pain; punishment; — *ḥirra-t*, violent thirst; — *ḥurra-t*, pl. *ḥarâ'ir*, free-born, noble lady; the first night of the month; freehold.

حرا *ḥarâ*, ة *ḥarât*, open place, courtyard; nest; lair; crackling of a fire, flame.

حراب *ḥirâb*, ة *ḥirâba-t*, pl. *ḥirâbât*, warfare; pl. of حربة *ḥarba-t*; INF. III. of (حرب).

حرابى *ḥarâba*, *ḥarâbiyy*, pl. of حربا *ḥirbâ*.

حراث *ḥarâs*, notch of the bow; —

ḥarrâs̱, ploughman, peasant; — *ḥurrâs̱*, pl. of حارث *ḥâris̱*; — ة *ḥirâs̱a-t*, agriculture; tilling of the ground.

حراج *ḥarâj*, selling out (s.); cry of a seller.

حراد *ḥirâd*, pl. of حريد *ḥarîd*.

حرار *ḥirâr*, pl. of حر *ḥurr* and حران *ḥarrân*; — ة *ḥarâra-t*, heat, warmth; passionateness; fanaticism; thirst.

حراس *ḥurrâs*, pl. of حارس *ḥâris*; — ة *ḥirâsa-t*, watch, guard.

حراص *ḥurrâṣ*, pl. of حريص *ḥarîṣ*.

حراض *ḥarrâḍ*, maker of potash, of mortar; — ة *ḥarâḍa-t*, love-sickness.

حرافة *ḥarâfa-t*, piquancy, sharpness of taste, pungency of spices.

حرافيش *ḥarâfîś*, pl. of حرفوش *ḥurfûś*.

حراق *ḥurâq*, very salt; — also *ḥurrâq*, tinder; fiery horse; maker of mischief; — *ḥarrâq*, incendiary; fire-brand; fire-ship; — ة *ḥurâqa-t*, *ḥurrâqa-t*, tinder; — *ḥarrâqa-t*, id.; fire-ship; fire-place; glowing ball, bomb; (m.) blistering.

(حراقم) *ḥarâqim*, reddish-brown.

حراقيص *ḥarâqîṣ*, pl. of حرقوص *ḥurqûṣ*.

(حرام) *ḥarâm*, unlawful, forbidden; sacred; pl. *ḥurum*, venerable, hallowed; ابن ح *ibn ḥarâm*, son of a prostitute, bastard;—*ḥirâm*, (m.) woollen blanket; INF. III. of (حرم); pl. of حرمى *ḥarma*; — ى *ḥarâmiyy*, pl. *ḥarâmiyya-t*, robber; vagabond; — *ḥarâma*, pl. of حرمى *ḥarma*.

حران *ḥirân*, restiveness; — *ḥarrân*, stony ground; f. *ḥarra*, pl. *ḥirâr*, thirsty; strict.

حراوة *ḥarâwa-t*, heat; piquancy; acidity.

حرايا *ḥarâyâ*, pl. f. of حرى *ḥariyy*.

حرائر *ḥarâ'ir*, pl. of حرة *ḥurra-t* and حرير *ḥarîr*.

(حرب) *ḥarab*, U, INF. *ḥarb*, *ḥarab*, rob, plunder; wage war; sharpen; — *ḥarib*, A, INF. *ḥarab*, be seized with anger, have a fit of rage; be taken with hydrophobia; — II. INF. *taḥrîb*, provoke to anger; irritate; incite; sharpen; — III. INF. *ḥirâb*, *muḥâraba-t*, wage war against, fight (acc.); — VI. INF. *taḥârub*, wage war against, fight one another; — VIII. INF. *iḥtirâb*, id.; be robbed entirely; — X. INF. *istiḥrâb*, prepare for war.

حرب *ḥarb*, f. and m., pl. *ḥurûb*, war, combat, battle; a brave one; enemy; — *ḥarab*, rage; — *ḥarib*, pl. *ḥarba*, warlike; enraged; — ة *ḥarba-t*, pl. *ḥirâb*, lance, spear, head of a spear; bayonet; pl. *ḥarabât*, Friday.

حربا *ḥirbâ*, f. ة, pl. *ḥarâbiyy*, chameleon; — pl. *ḥarâba*, sunflower; — *ḥurabâ'*, pl. of حريب *ḥarîb*.

(حربج) *ḥurbuj*, big.

حربش *ḥirbiś*, ة *ḥirbiśa-t*, *ḥirribiś*, *ḥirribiśa-t*, poisonous snake.

(حربص) *ḥarbaṣ*, INF. ة, irrigate.

حربى *ḥarba*, pl. of حرب *ḥarib*; — *ḥarbiyy*, ة, warlike, hostile.

(حرت) *ḥarat*, U, INF. *ḥart*, rub hard; cut round; — *ḥarit*, A, INF. *ḥarat*, be malicious, mischievous.

(حرث) *ḥaras̱*, I, U, INF. *ḥars̱*, till and sow the ground; gain, earn a fortune; study carefully, especially the Koran; study law; investigate into the truth; poke the fire; overwork and emaciate the camel; marry four wives; have frequent sexual intercourse; make a notch to the bow; — II. INF. *taḥrîs̱*, make the oxen plough; suffer shipwreck; — VIII. INF. *iḥtirâs̱*, gain a fortune.

حرث *ḥars̱*, agriculture, husbandry; pl. *ḥurûs̱*, tilled ground; high road; — *ḥaris̱*, lion; — ى *ḥars̱iyy*, ة, referring to agriculture.

(حرج) *ḥarij*, A, INF. *ḥaraj*, be oppressed, straitened; be for-

bidden; be kept aloof from the stallion; be bewildered with fear; commit a crime; be dense; —II. INF. *taḥrîj*, straiten; forbid, defend; restrain one's self by a vow; call to a public sale; sell out, sell by auction; (m.) molest by repeated demands or questions; set upon; — IV. INF. *iḥrâj*, straiten; defend; reduce to poverty; compel; — V. INF. *taḥarruj*, restrain one's self, abstain.

حرج *ḥirj*, *ḥaraj*, narrowness; narrowed place; anything forbidden; crime; — *ḥirj*, pl. *aḥrâj*, a small white shell worn as an amulet, &c.; pl. *ḥirâj*, trap for game; — *ḥaraj*, bier; litter; — *ḥarij*, narrow, straitened; criminal; — ة *ḥurja-t*, small bucket; — *ḥaraja-t*, pl. *ḥaraj*, *ḥarajât*, *ḥirâj*, troop of camels; thicket.

(حرجف) *ḥarjaf*, pl. *ḥarâjif*, cold wind; blast of wind.

(حرجل) *ḥarjal*, INF. ة, be long; complete a good part of anything; run to and fro.

(حرجم) *ḥarjam*, ة, drive back towards each other; — III. INF. *iḥrinjâm*, press one another.

(حرح) *ḥaraḥ*, A, INF. *ḥarḥ*, touch the pudenda of a woman.

حرح *ḥirḥ*, pl. *aḥrâḥ*, pudenda of a woman; — *ḥariḥ*, given to fornication.

(حرحر) *ḥarḥar*, INF. ة, burn the tongue (as spices).

(حرد) *ḥarad*, I, INF. *ḥard*, pierce, bore through; hinder, prevent; intend, propose, be willing; — INF. *ḥurûd*, withdraw from one's people, I, also *ḥarid*, A, INF. *ḥarad*, be angry; pout, be sulky, bear a grudge; — II. INF. *taḥrîd*, provoke to anger; irritate.

حرد *ḥarad*, anger, grudge, hatred; — *ḥarid*, bearing a grudge in solitude (adj.).

حرداء *ḥuradâ'*, pl. of حريد *ḥarîd*.

حردان *ḥardân*, angry; bearing a grudge.

حرذون *ḥirẓaun*, pl. *ḥarâẓîn*, Libyan lizard; crocodile.

(حرز) *ḥaraz*, U, INF. *ḥarz*, guard; — *ḥariz*, A, INF. *ḥaraz*, be cautious, on one's guard; be worth the while; — *ḥaruz*, INF. *ḥarâza-t*, be strong, fortified; — II. INF. *taḥriz*, warn one to be on his guard, be very cautious in a mattter (acc.); — IV. INF. *iḥrâz*, guard carefully; secure; be on one's guard; serve as a refuge; accumulate one's wages; — V. INF. *taḥarruz*, guard against (من *min*); protect one's self with the help of another; — VIII. INF. *iḥtirâz*, be on one's guard against; — XV. INF. *iḥrinzâ'*, be afraid; be on one's guard.

حرز *ḥarz*, protection, guard; — *ḥirz*, pl. *aḥrâz*, caution, cautiousness; protection, guard; means of protection; amulet; stronghold, castle, fortification, garrisoned town; — *ḥaraz*, nut; also ة *ḥaraza-t*, what is to be guarded carefully.

(حرزق) *ḥarzaq*, INF. ة, shut up, confine, straiten.

(حرس) *ḥaras*, U, I, INF. *ḥars*, guard, watch; — I, INF. *ḥars*, steal from the pasture-ground; — *ḥaris*, A, INF. *ḥaras*, live long; — V. INF. *taḥarrus*, be on one's guard; be well guarded or protected; — VIII. INF. *iḥtirâs*, guard, protect, watch over; be cautious, on one's guard; steal by night.

حرس *ḥars*, *ḥirs*, guard, watch, surveillance; — *ḥars*, pl. *aḥrus*, century; opportunity, favourable time; du. *al-ḥarsan*, day and night; — *ḥaras*, watchman; body-guard, pl. of حارس *ḥâris*; — ى *ḥarasiyy*, pl. *ḥarasiyya-t*,

guardsman, satellite; pl. body-guard.

(حرش) *ḥaraś*, I. INF. *ḥaraś*, *taḥrâś*, hunt for lizards; — INF. *ḥarś*, wound with the claws; — *ḥariś*, A, INF. *ḥaraś*, be hard and rough to the touch; — II. INF. *taḥrîś*, make rough; set against one another; — III. INF. *ḥirâś*, id.; — V. INF. *taḥarruś*, (m.) seek a quarrel, challenge, attack; — VIII. INF. *iḥtirâs*, hunt for lizards.

حرش *ḥarś*, pl. *ḥirâś*, sign, trace; — *ḥurś*, pl. *aḥrâś*, wood, thicket; — *ḥuruś*, pl. of حريش *ḥarîś*; — ة *ḥurśa-t*, roughness.

حرشا *ḥarśâ'*, f. of احرش *aḥraś*, rough; wild mustard.

(حرشف) *ḥarśaf*, scales of a fish, a coat of mail, &c.; a kind of thistle; troop, crowd; — hence: III. INF. *iḥrinśâf*, be prone to anger, to evil.

(حرص) *ḥaraṣ*, I, INF. *ḥirṣ*, crave for; be covetous; pass. be entirely grazed off; — II. INF. *taḥrîṣ*, make eager, incite.

حرص *ḥirṣ*, greed, craving, eagerness; (m.) fruit-stone, pulp round the stone; — *ḥuruṣ*, pl. of حارص *ḥâriṣ*, ag. of (حرص).

حرصا *ḥuraṣâ'*, pl. of حريص *ḥarîṣ*.

(حرض) *ḥaraḍ*, I, INF. *ḥarḍ*, ruin one's self; — I, U, INF. *ḥurûḍ*, be emaciated by illness; — *ḥariḍ*, A, INF. *ḥaraḍ*, be low in body and mind; not be able to rise on account of weakness; — *ḥaruḍ*, INF. *ḥarâḍa-t*, be on the point of death; pine away; INF. *ḥarâḍa-t*, *ḥurûḍ*, *ḥurûḍa-t*, be low in the world, despised; — II. INF. *taḥrîḍ*, incite, instigate, encourage; dye with saffron; — IV. INF. *iḥrâḍ*, make to pine away.

حرض *ḥaraḍ*, bodily and moral ruin; — *ḥariḍ*, sickly, pining away; pl. *aḥrâḍ*, *ḥurḍân*, *ḥaraḍa-t*, from whom one may neither fear nor hope anything; — ة *ḥirḍa-t*, emaciated; sickly.

(حرف) *ḥaraf*, I, INF. *ḥarf*, turn round; change; carry on, traffic, gain, provide for one's people; — INF. *ḥarfa-t*, lay on collyrium; pass. lose part of (في *fî*); — II. INF. *taḥrîf*, turn about, transpose; alter, change, falsify; move or bend a thing aside; sharpen; cut in an angle; mend a reed pen; — III. pass. *ḥûrif*, have nothing to live upon; — IV. INF. *iḥrâf*, exert one's self for the sustenance of one's family; grow wealthy; overdrive, emaciate; requite, reward, punish; — V. INF. *taḥarruf*, be changed, turned, transposed, falsified; deviate; be edged, angled; — VI. INF. *taḥâruf*, exert one's self; think of means; use stratagem against (على *'ala*); — VII. INF. *inḥirâf*, decline, deviate, turn aside to the right or left; make a roundabout way; be changed, turned, transposed; — VIII. INF. *iḥtirâf*, carry on a trade; — XII. *iḥrauraf*, INF. *iḥrîrâf*, deviate altogether, lean to extremities.

حرف *ḥarf*, watercourse, canal; pl. *ḥiraf*, edge, border, extremity, end, point; mountain-ridge; edge of any cutting instrument; angle, margin; pl. *ḥurûf*, *ḥurûfât*, *aḥruf*, letter; word; particle (in grammar); lean camel; pl. *aḥruf*, dialect; — *ḥurf*, cress; calamity; — ة *ḥirfa-t*, pl. *ḥiraf*, trade, profession; guild, corporation; industry; skill; stratagem, expedient; — also *ḥurfa-t*, misfortune, calamity; — *ḥarfa-t*, INF. of (حرف).

حرفش *ḥirfiś*, pl. *ḥarâfiś*, viper.

(حرفص), II. *taḥarfaṣ*, INF. *taḥarfuṣ*, contract (n.).

حرفوش *ḥurfûś*, pl. *ḥarâfîś*, man of the lowest class.

حرفي *ḥarfiyy*, ة, referring to a

particle; literal; — ة *ḥarfiyya-t*, the state of being a particle; — ى *ḥurfiyy*, seller of cress.

حرق *ḥaraq*, I, INF. *ḥarq*, kindle, ignite, burn; — I, U, rub two things against each other; gnash the teeth with rage; file; — *ḥariq*, A, INF. *ḥaraq*, burn (n.), be burnt; fall out; — II. INF. *taḥrîq*, burn (a.) by a large fire; burn with anger; make thirsty; — III. INF. *muḥâraqa-t*, burn (a.); — IV. INF. *iḥrâq*, kindle, burn (a.); — V. INF. *taḥarruq*, burn with anger, grief, &c.; be burnt; kindle, burn (a.); — VIII. INF. *iḥtirâq*, be kindled; burn (n.), be consumed by the flames, &c.; — ة *ḥurqa-t*, pl. *ḥuraq*, flame, heat in the intestines.

حرقد *ḥirqid*, ة *ḥarqada-t*, root of the tongue; larynx; Adam's apple.

(حرقص) *ḥarqaṣ*, INF. ة, take short steps; talk very quick (m.); roast; vex, enrage; — II. INF. *taḥarquṣ*, be roasted; get enraged; be disquieted, agitated.

حرقفة *ḥarqafa-t*, pl. *ḥarâqîf*, hip; hip-bone.

حرقوص *ḥurqûṣ*, pl. *ḥarâqîṣ*, a stinging fly.

حرقوة *ḥarquwa-t*=حرقدة *ḥarqada-t*.

حرقى *ḥurqa*, pl. of حريق *ḥarîq*.

(حرك) *ḥarak*, U, INF. *ḥark*, refuse payment of a debt; beat on the back; — *ḥarik*, A, INF. *ḥarak*, be impotent; — *ḥaruk*, INF. *ḥark*, *ḥaraka-t*, move (n. and a.), shake, stir up; intrigue; — II. INF. *taḥrîk*, move (a.), put into motion; excite; instigate, encourage; put the vowel-points; — V. INF. *taḥarruk*, move, stir (n.); be vocalised.

حرك *ḥarak*, impotence; — *ḥarik*, mobile, nimble, active; — ة *ḥaraka-t*, movement, motion; gesture; behaviour, bearing, proceeding; insurrection, tumult; short vowel.

(حركث) *ḥarkaṯ*, INF. ة, move violently.

(حركش) *ḥarkaś*, INF. ة, move, stir up; grub; poke, rake (the fire).

حرككة *ḥarkaka-t*, pl. *ḥarâkik*, hip-bone.

(حركل) *ḥarkal*, INF. ة, walk pompously; return from hunting without a prey; — ة *ḥarkala-t*, pedestrian.

حركوشة *ḥarkûśa-t*, rebellion, insurrection (m.).

(حرم) *ḥaram*, I, *ḥarim*, A, INF. *ḥirm*, *ḥarim*, *ḥirma-t*, *ḥarîm*, *ḥarima-t*, *ḥarîma-t*, *ḥirmân*, turn off, refuse, defend, forbid; (m.) expel, banish, excommunicate, disinherit; pass. *ḥurim*, be deprived, robbed of (acc.); — *ḥaram*, proclaim unlawful; — *ḥarim*, A, INF. *ḥaram*, *ḥarâm*, be unlawful, forbidden; be sacred, inappraochable; be invalid; — INF. *ḥirâm*, be hot, rutting; — *ḥarum*, INF. *ḥurm*, *ḥaram*, be unlawful; — INF. *ḥurm*, *ḥurum*, id.; be invalid; — II. INF. *taḥrîm*, proclaim unlawful, forbid; proclaim sacred and inapproachable; — IV. INF. *iḥrâm*, exclude, expel, excommunicate, anathematise; disinherit; refuse; enter on a holy month into the sacred precinct of Mecca and put on the garment of a pilgrim (*iḥrâm*); enter any inviolable place; — V. INF. *taḥarrum*, be forbidden; be proclaimed sacred or inapproachable; be venerated; abstain; be absorbed in prayer; — VII. INF. *inḥirâm*, be banished, excluded, excommunicated; be forbidden; — VIII. INF. *iḥtirâm*, honour, venerate; be venerable; —X. INF. *istiḥrâm*, rut.

حرم *ḥirm*, defence, prohibition,

anathema, excommunication; pl. *ḥurum*, unlawful, forbidden; — *ḥurm*, anything sacred; woman; also *ḥirm*, pilgrim's cloak; — *ḥaram*, pl. *aḥrâm*, *ḥurum*, unlawful, forbidden; anything sacred; family, woman, wife, harem; sanctuary; sacred precinct of Mecca; — ة *ḥurma-t*, pl. *ḥuram*, *ḥuramât*, anything forbidden, sacred; wife, daughter, family; clientship; portion, share; sacred claim; veneration; sanctity; honour, dignity, good name; chastity;— *ḥirma-t*, rut; deception.

حرمان *ḥirmân*, deception, thwarted plan, frustrated hope.

(حرمد) *ḥarmad*, *ḥirmid*, black putrid mud.

(حرمز) *ḥarmaz*, INF. ة, curse; — II. INF. *taḥarmuz*, and IV. INF. *iḥrimmâz*, be sagacious, cunning.

(حرمس) *ḥirmis*, pl. *ḥarâmis*, sterile year.

(حرمل) *ḥarmal*, wild rue.

حرمى *ḥarma*, pl. *ḥirâm*, *ḥarâma*, rutting; — *ḥaramiyy*, made or worn in Mecca.

حرمين *ḥaramîn*, vulg. du., Mecca and Medina.

(حرن) *ḥaran*, U, *ḥarun*, INF. *ḥirân*, *ḥurân*, stop suddenly in running; rear and kick; be restive; — *ḥaran*, ask a moderate price in selling; card cotton.

حرور *ḥarûr*, hot night-wind; heat of the sun; *ḥurûr*, heat; — ة *ḥarûra-t*, piquancy, acidity; heat; — *ḥurûra-t*, also ية *ḥurûriyya-t*, freedom.

حروض *ḥurûḍ*, ة *ḥurûḍa-t*, sickness, INF. of (حرض).

حروق *ḥarûq*, *ḥurûq*, pollen of the male palm-tree;' hoof; — also *ḥarrûq*, and—

حروقا *ḥarûqâ'*, tinder.

حروك *ḥarûk*, nimble, mobile, agile.

حرون *ḥarûn*, restive.

حروة *ḥarwa-t*, heat in the chest, &c.; piquancy, acidity.

(حرى) *ḥara*, I, INF. *ḥary*, decrease; — *ḥarî*, A, INF. *ḥar-an*, be worthy of (ب *bi*); — V. INF. *taḥarrî*, do on purpose; select the best, the most suitable, strive for; stay, abide.

حرى *ḥarî* (حر *ḥar-in*), pl. *aḥrâ'*, worthy, suitable; — *ḥariyy*, pl. *aḥriyâ'*, f. *ḥariyya-t*, pl. *ḥarâyâ*, id.; — *ḥar-an*, *ḥar-a*, court-yard; nest of an ostrich; — *ḥarra*, f. of حران *ḥarrân*; — ة *ḥariyya-t*, liberty, freedom.

حريب *ḥarîb*, pl. *ḥarba*, *ḥurabâ'*, robbed, plundered; — ة *ḥarîba-t*, pl. *ḥarâ'ib*, robbed goods.

حريثة *ḥarîs̱a-t*, pl. *ḥarâ'is̱*, gain; emaciated she-camel.

حريد *ḥarîd*, pl. *ḥirâd*, *ḥuradâ'*, solitary, isolated; pouting, bearing a grudge.

حرير *ḥarîr*, pl. *ḥarâ'is*, silk, silkware; f. ة, hot-blooded, choleric; — ة *ḥarîra-t*, silk garment; — ى *ḥarîriyy*, silk-merchant; silklike.

حريز *ḥarîz*, fortified, guarded, garrisoned; valued; an antidote.

حريس *ḥarîs*, ة, watchful, vigilant; — ة *ḥarîsa-t*, sheep-fold; stolen sheep.

حريش *ḥarîś*, pl. *ḥuruś*, rough to the touch; rhinoceros; a snake; ear-wig.

حريص *ḥarîṣ*, ة, pl. *ḥurrâṣ*, *ḥuraṣâ'*, eager, greedy; covetous; taken up with; torn.

حريف *ḥarîf*, fellow, comrade; partner; adversary; sly; — *ḥirrif*, sharp, piquant, hot (as spices).

حريفية *ḥirîfiyya-t*, piquancy, acidity.

حريق *ḥarîq*, pl. *ḥarqa*, burning, burnt; flame; conflagration; hell; nettle.

حريك *ḥarîk*, lame in the hips; impotent.

حريم *ḥarîm*, pl. *aḥrâm*, *ḥurum*, anything forbidden, sacred; women; apartments of women; sanctuary; precinct; pilgrim's cloak; companion; friend.

(حز) *ḥazz*, U, INF. *ḥazz*, cut, make incisions, carve; — II. INF. *taḥzîz*, id.; sharpen; — III. INF. *ḥizâz*, *muḥâzza-t*, investigate; — V. INF. *taḥazzuz*, get indented, have incisions made; — VIII. INF. *iḥtizâz* = I.

حز *ḥazz*, ة *ḥazza-t*, pl. *ḥuzûz*, incision, notch; proper time.

(حزا) *ḥaza'*, A, INF. *ḥaz'*, show in the air (mirage); — II. INF. تحزئة *taḥzi'a-t*, drive together; lie with a woman.

حزا *ḥazâ'*, ة, wild anise seed; — *ḥazzâ'*, soothsayer.

حزار *ḥazzâr*, who guesses easily.

حزاز *ḥazâz*, ة *ḥazâza-t*, dandruff; dry scab; lichen; — *ḥazzâz*, bestirring one's self, active.

حزام *ḥizâm*, ة, pl. *ḥuzm*, belt, girth; swaddling bands; — ة *ḥizâma-t*, prudence and firm resolution.

حزان *ḥizân*, pl. of حزن *ḥazin*, *ḥazun*; — *ḥizzân*, *ḥuzzân*, pl. of حزيز *ḥazîz*.

حزانى *ḥazânî*, pl. of حزنان *ḥaznân*.

حزاور *ḥazâwir*, ة *ḥazâwira-t*, pl. of حزورة *ḥazwara-t*.

حزاوير *ḥazâwîr*, pl. of حزوارة *ḥizwâra-t*.

(حزب) *ḥuzb*, U, INF. *ḥazb*, happen unexpectedly, cause anxiety; — II. INF. *taḥzîb*, assemble (a.); form a party; divide into parts (especially the Koran into 60 chapters); — III. INF. *muḥâzaba-t*, belong to one's party, make common cause with; be assembled; — V. INF. *taḥazzub*, gather in troops, confederate, form a league or party; attack in troops.

حزب *ḥizb*, pl. *aḥzâb*, troop, number of men; party, partisans; confederates; sect; part; division of the Koran; — *ḥuzb*, pl. of حازب *ḥâzib*; — *ḥuzub*, pl. of حزيب *ḥazîb*.

(حزر) *ḥazar*, U, I, INF. *ḥazr*, *maḥzara-t*, estimate; (m.) guess, surmise; — INF. *ḥazr*, get sour; frown; — V. INF. *taḥazzur*, try to guess; make suppositions, surmise; — IV. INF. *taḥâzur*, give to one another anything to guess at.

حزر *ḥazr*, (m.) guess, conjecture, supposition; — *ḥazar*, pea; — ة *ḥazra-t*, best part of a property.

حزز *ḥazaz*, violence; severity; swathes; — *ḥuzuz*, pl. of حزيز *ḥazîz*.

(حزفر) *ḥazfar*, INF. ة, fill; tie up, strap; get ready, prepare for battle.

(حزق) *ḥazaq*, I, INF. *ḥazaq*, fasten with strings; twist firmly round; strain, press; break wind; — IV. INF. *iḥrâq*, hinder.

حزق *ḥizq*, small pack-saddle; — also ة *ḥizqa-t*, pl. *ḥizaq*, crowd; swarm; troop; — *ḥazaq*, avarice; — *ḥuzuq*, pl. of حزيقة *ḥazîqa-t*.

(حزك) *ḥazak*, I, INF. *ḥazk*, tie round; fasten; press, compress; — VIII. INF. *iḥtizâk*, gird one's self round the waist.

(حزم) *ḥazm*, I, INF. *ḥazm*, tie together; pack up; make a bundle; gird; — *ḥazim*, A, INF. *ḥazam*, have the chest oppressed; — *ḥazum*, INF. *ḥazm*, *ḥazâma-t*, *ḥuzûma-t*, be prudent and resolute; — IV. INF. *iḥzâm*, gird; embale, make packets or bundles; — V. INF. *taḥazzum*, be girt; gird one's self; — VII. INF. *inḥizâm*, be tied together, embaled, packeted; — VIII. INF. *iḥtizâm*, gird one's self.

حزم *ḥazm*, prudence and resolution; caution; pl. *ḥuzum*, rough elevated ground; — *ḥuzm*, pl. of حزام *ḥizâm*; — *ḥuzum* and حزما *ḥuzamâ'*, pl. of حزيم *ḥazîm*; — ة

ḥuzma-t, pl. *ḥuzam*, bundle; armful; packet, parcel, bale; sheaf; — *ḥazama-t*, pl. of حزيم *ḥazîm*.

(حزن) *ḥazan*, U, INF. *ḥuzn*, grieve (a.); — *ḥazin*, A, INF. *ḥazan*, be grieved; — II. INF. *taḥzîn*, grieve (a.), sadden; — IV. INF. *iḥzân*, id.; — V. INF. *taḥazzun*, grieve (n.), be sad; — VI. INF. *taḥâzun*, show or feign sadness, grief; — VIII. INF. *iḥtizân*=V.

حزن *ḥazn*, ة, pl. *ḥuzûn*, *ḥuzûna-t*, rough elevated ground; — *ḥuzn*, *ḥazan*, pl. *aḥzân*, sadness, grief; — *ḥazin*, *ḥazun*, pl. *ḥizân*, *ḥuzanâ'*, sad, sorrowful, grieved; — ة *ḥuzna-t*, pl. *ḥuzan*, rugged mountains.

حزنا *ḥuzanâ'*, pl. of حزن *ḥazin*, *ḥazun*, and of حزين *ḥazîn*.

حزنان *ḥaznân*, pl. *ḥazâna*, very sad.

حزنى *ḥazna*, pl. of حزين *ḥazîn*.

(حزو) *ḥazâ*, U, INF. *ḥazw*, and V. INF. *taḥazzuww*, *taḥazzî*, predict, soothsay.

حزوارة *ḥizwâra-t*, pl. *ḥazâwîr*, hillock.

حزور *ḥazwar*, *ḥazawwar*, pl. *ḥazâwira-t*, doughty fellow; — ة *ḥazwara-t*, pl. *ḥazâwir*, *ḥazâwira-t*, hillock; — *ḥazzûra-t*, riddle (m.).

حزوز *ḥuzûz*, pl. of حز *ḥazz*.

حزومة *ḥuzûma-t*, prudence and resolution.

حزونة *ḥuzûna-t*, ruggedness.

(حزى) *ḥaza*, I, INF. *ḥazy*, stir up birds to take omen from their flight; — II. INF. *taḥziya-t*, id.; estimate the produce of a palm-tree; show the image of a person in the air (mirage); — IV. INF. *iḥzâ'*, fear, be afraid of a person; overcharge in selling; be expert, know; be near; tower, rise.

حزيب *ḥazîb*, pl. *ḥuzub*, difficult.

حزيران *ḥazîrân*, month of July.

حزيز *ḥazîz*, pl. *ḥuzuz*, *aḥizza-t*, *ḥizzân*, *ḥuzzân*, rugged place; very active man.

حزيقة *ḥazîqa-t*, pl. *ḥazîq*, *ḥazâ'iq*, *ḥuzuq*, orchard; troop, crowd; part, division.

حزيم *ḥazîm*, pl. *ḥuzamâ'*, prudent and resolute; pl. *ḥuzum*, *aḥzima-t*, breast, chest.

حزين *ḥazîn*, pl. *ḥuzanâ'*, *ḥazna*, sorrowful, grieved, sad.

(حس) *ḥass*, U, INF. *ḥass*, freeze (a.); kill; annihilate; curry; — I, INF. *ḥass*, be moved with compassion; — for *ḥasis*, A, INF. *ḥass*, *ḥiss*, id.; feel; have sensation, perceive by the senses; listen; notice, know, understand; know for certain; (m.) awake (n.); — II. *ḥassas*, *ḥassa*, INF. *taḥsîs*, perceive, feel; cause to feel, make feel; put meat on the coals; awake (a.); — IV. INF. *iḥsâs*, feel, perceive, see; hear a low sound; know, think (believe); curry; — V. INF. *taḥassus*, listen to, be attentive; try to obtain information; — VII. be extracted, fall out, decay (teeth); — X. INF. have a sensation or perception.

حس *ḥass*, *ḥiss*, perception, sensation; instinct; compassion; low sound; the currying of a horse; (m.) voice; — *ḥiss*, blast (by the frost); — *ḥass-i*, exclamation of pain; — ة *ḥassa-t*, *ḥissa-t*, sensation; state, condition.

حسا *ḥasâ'*, soup, broth; draught; — pl. of حسى *ḥisy*.

حساب *ḥisâb*, pl. *ḥusbân*, account, calculation, arithmetic; ح الجمل *ḥisâb al-jummal*, use of the letters as numerical signs; يوم الح *yaum al-ḥisâb*, Day of Judgment; — *ḥassâb*, accountant, calculator, arithmetician; — *ḥussâb*, pl. of حاسب *ḥâsib*; — ة *ḥisâba-t*, office of an accountant; estimation, valuation.

حساد *ḥussâd*, pl. of حاسد *ḥâsid*, envious; — ة *ḥasâda-t*, envy.

حسار *ḥussâr*, pl. of حاسر *ḥâsir*, free, bare.

حساس *ḥassâs*, endowed with senses, sensitiveness ; living being ; cunning.

حسافة *ḥusâfa-t*, offal, remains; populace ; hatred, rage.

حسالة *ḥusâla-t*, offal.

حسام *ḥusâm*, sharp sword ; edge of a sword ; blade.

حسان *ḥisân*, pl. of حسن *ḥasan*, ة, and of حسين *ḥasîn* ; — *ḥusân*, ة, very beautiful.

(حسب) *ḥasab*, U, and (m.) A, INF. *ḥasb*, *ḥisâb*, *ḥisba-t*, *ḥisâba-t*, *ḥisbân*, *ḥusbân*, count, count together, calculate ; — INF. *ḥasb*, suffice ; — *ḥasib*, I, A, INF. *ḥisbân*, *maḥsaba-t*, *maḥsiba-t*, opine, surmise, think, consider ; — *ḥasub*, INF. *ḥasab*, *ḥasâba-t*, be esteemed ; be of a noble family ; — II. INF. *taḥsîb*, satisfy, content ; place a cushion beneath a person ; — III. INF. *muḥâsaba-t*, settle an account with, ask an account from (acc.) ; — IV. INF. *iḥsâb*, satisfy, content ; — V. INF. *taḥassub*, investigate into one's circumstances ; lie down on a cushion ; — VI. INF. *taḥâsub*, settle an account with one another ; — VIII. INF. *iḥtisâb*, take into account ; calculate, count together ; estimate ; surmise ; think, believe ; deem ; impute ; reckon upon.

حسب *ḥasb*, reckoning, counting (s.) ; what is sufficient, sufficiency ; lot, portion, share ; equivalent ; according to, with regard to ; — *ḥasab*, *ḥasb*, pl. *aḥsâb*, measure, quantity, amount, value ; honour, distinction ; merits or nobility of the ancestors ; pedigree ; paternal relations ; one's own merits and consideration ; good action ; religion ; riches ; heart, soul ; — ة *ḥisba-t*, pl. *ḥisab*, account ; pay of wages ; divine requital ; hope for a reward ; office of overseer in the market (*muḥtasib*) ; management of public affairs, administration ; — *ḥusba-t*, leprosy ; — *ḥasaba-t*, accountants, pl. of حاسب *ḥâsib*.

حسبا *ḥusabâ'*, pl. of حسيب *ḥasîb*.

حسبان *ḥisbân*, *ḥusbân*, pl. *ḥisbânât*, *ḥusbânât*, counting, reckoning (s.) ; supposition, surmise ; esteem, estimation ; *ḥusbân*, coll. ; ة, small arrows ; thunderbolt ; punishment, affliction ; small cushion ; — *ḥusbân*, pl. of حساب *ḥisâb*.

(حسبل) *ḥasbal*, INF. ة, utter the words حسبنا الله *ḥasbunâ allâh-u*, God is what suffices us.

حسبى *ḥasabiyy*, referring to nobility.

(حسحس) *ḥasḥas*, INF. ة, place meat on the coals ; complain of pain ; — II. INF. *taḥasḥus*, move to and fro (n.) ; fall out.

(حسد) *ḥasad*, I, U, INF. *ḥasd*, *ḥusûd*, *ḥasâda-t*, *ḥasîda-t*, envy ; punish for envy ; — II. INF. *taḥsîd*, envy ; — VI. INF. *taḥâsud*, envy one another ; — VII. INF. *inḥisâb*, be seized with envy (m.).

حسد *ḥasad*, envy, grudge ; — *ḥusûd*, pl. of حسود *ḥasûd* ; — *ḥussad*, ة *ḥasada-t*, pl. of حاسد *ḥâsid*.

(حسدل) *ḥasdal*, tick (insect) ; louse.

(حسر) *ḥasar*, I, U, INF. *ḥasr*, uncover, lift the veil, bare ; peel, pare, shell ; sweep ; jade, fatigue ; — INF. *ḥusûr*, be uncovered ; — I, INF. *ḥusûr*, get tired, fatigued, fall short ; — *ḥasir*, A, INF. *ḥasar*, *ḥasra-t*, be pained, anxious, sigh at (على *'ala*) ; be fatigued, weary ; — V. be fatigued, sigh for (على *'ala*) ; — VII. INF. *inḥisâr*, be uncovered, bared ; fall out ; — X. INF. *istiḥsâr*, be fatigued.

حسر *ḥasir*, purblind ; — ة *ḥasra-t*, pl. *ḥasarât*, sigh ; regret ; anxiety ; grief.

حسران *ḥusrân*, sighing.

حسرى *ḥasra*, f. fatigued, weary ; pl. of حسير *ḥasîr*.

(حسف) *ḥasaf*, I, INF. *ḥasf*, clean,

select; drive; pass quickly by; — INF. *ḥasf*, *ḥasîf*, rustle, rattle (as a snake); — INF. *ḥasf*, *ḥusâf*, mow, reap; — *ḥasif*, bear a grudge against, treat roughly; pass. be despised; — II. INF. *taḥsîf*, shave off the moustache; — V. INF. *taḥassuf*, hang loose and be dishevelled.

(حسك) *ḥasik*, A, INF. *ḥasak*, be angry with (على *'ala*); eat, nibble; — II. INF. *taḥsîk*, save, put by; choke with a fish-bone.

حسك *ḥasik*, hostile; — ة *ḥasaka-t*, fish-bone; beard of an ear; prickles of a thistle; thorn-bush.

حسكل *ḥaskal*, slaughter of young camels; — *ḥiskil*, ة, small young animal; trifle.

(حسل) *ḥasal*, U, INF. *ḥasl*, despise; grow mean; leave the worst part; drive violently.

(حسم) *ḥasam*, I, INF. *ḥasm*, cut, cut off; lance and then cauterise a vein; cure by medicine; prevent (2 acc.); subtract, deduct.

(حسن) *ḥasan*, U, *ḥasun*, INF. *ḥusn*, be handsome, beautiful, seem good; — II. INF. *taḥsîn*, make or create handsome and good; — III. INF. *muḥâsana-t*, treat handsomely or well; vie in beauty or goodness; — IV. INF. *iḥsân*, act well or right; do or say anything well or in a handsome manner; benefit; give for a present; be favourable; embellish, adorn; be well versed in (acc. or ب *bi*); — X. INF. *istiḥsân*, find beautiful or good, approve of.

حسن *ḥusn*, pl. *maḥâsin*, beauty; goodness; praiseworthy qualities; skill; ح تعبير *ḥusn ta'bîr*, beautiful style; ح اختيار *ḥusn iḥtiyâr*, freedom of will; — *ḥasan*, f. *ḥasana-t*, *ḥasnâ'*, beautiful, fair, elegant; good, excellent (also حسن بسن *ḥasan basan*); high sand-hill; — *ḥusan*, pl. of حسنى *ḥusna*; — ة *ḥasana-t*, pl. *ḥasanât*, a fair one (f. of حسن *ḥasan*); pl. *ḥasanât* and *ḥisân*, good action, benefit, bounty, alms; pl. *ḥasanât*, pious endowments; — *ḥisna-t*, pl. *ḥisan*, projecting part of a mountain; — ى *ḥusna*, f. of احسن *aḥsan*, more beautiful, better; *al-ḥusna*, what is good, handsome, best; beneficence; fair treatment; virtue; Islâm; Paradise; pl. *ḥusan*, death of a martyr; du. victory and death of a martyr; — ية *ḥasaniyya-t*, beauty.

(حسو) *ḥasâ*, U, INF. *ḥasw*, drink, sip, lap; — III. INF. *muḥâsât*, IV. INF. *iḥsâ'*, give to sip; — V. INF. *taḥassî*, sip; — VIII. INF. *iḥtisâ'* = III. and IV.

حسو *ḥasw*, pl. *aḥsuwa-t*, *aḥsiya-t*, soup, broth; — ة *ḥaswa-t*, *ḥuswa-t*, pl. *aḥâsî*, draught, gulp.

حسود *ḥasûd*, pl. *ḥusud*, envious; — *ḥusûd*, envy, INF. of (حسد).

حسوم *ḥusûm*, disastrous days or nights; calamity; diligence; حسوما *ḥusûm-an*, consecutively.

حسون *ḥassûn*, goldfinch.

(حسى) *ḥasa*, I, INF. *ḥasy* (also II. and VIII.), dig for water in saturated ground; sip; — *ḥasî*, A, INF. *has-an* (also VIII.), try to find out another's intentions; — II. INF. *taḥsiya-t*, VIII. INF. *iḥtisâ'*, see I.

حسى *ḥisy*, *ḥasy*, *ḥis-an*, pl. *ḥisâ'*, *aḥsâ'*, flat saturated ground; well; — *ḥasiyy*, *ḥissiyy*, sensual; perceiving or perceptible by the senses; referring to the senses; material.

حسيب *ḥasîb*, pl. *ḥusabâ'*, esteemed, valued; avenger.

حسير *ḥasîr*, pl. *ḥasra*, sad; weary; fatigued; sighing; purblind.

حسيس *ḥasîs*, slight noise, low sound.

حسيكة *ḥasîka-t*, grudge, inveterate hatred; hedge-hog; . oats.

حسيل *ḥasîl*, f. ة, calf; pl. *ḥusul*, offal, remains; — *ḥusail*, little lizard.

حسين *ḥasîn*, pl. *ḥisân*, beautiful; — *ḥusain*, dim. of حسن *ḥasan*, beautiful; proper name.

(حش) *ḥaśś*, U, INF. *ḥaśś*, light, kindle; get dry, wither; run fast; mow; feed on hay; promote one's wealth; increase one's fortune; give to (acc); — look out for grass or hay, mow.

حش *ḥaśś*, *ḥiśś*, *ḥuśś*, pl. *-ûn*, *ḥuśûś*, garden; privy, sewer; — *ḥaśś*, pl. *ḥiśśân*, garden; fire; — *ḥiśś*, something, anything; — ة *ḥuśśa-t*, pl. *ḥuśaś*, cupola, dome.

(حشا) *ḥaśa'*, A, INF. *ḥaś'*, strike on the belly, in the sides; injure interior parts; lie with; kindle, light.

حشا *ḥaśâ'*, pl. of حشية *ḥaśiyya-t*; — *ḥaś-an*, pl. *aḥśâ'*, intestines, bowels, heart.

حشاش *ḥiśâś*, fodder-bag; — *ḥuśâś*, ة *ḥuśâśa-t*, last spark of life, last breath, throb; — *ḥaśśâś*, pl. *-ûn*, mower, seller of hay; smoker or seller of *ḥaśiś*.

حشاف *ḥiśâf*, pl. of حشفة *ḥaśafa-t*.

حشان *ḥiśân*, pl. of حش *ḥaśś*, *ḥuśś*.

حشايا *ḥaśâyâ*, pl. of حشية *ḥaśiyya-t*.

حشائشى *ḥaśâ'iśiyy*, seller of hay; gatherer of herbs, botanist.

(حشحش) *ḥaśḥaś*, INF. ة, set out, depart; — II. INF. *taḥaśḥuś*, id.; disperse (n.).

(حشد) *ḥaśad*, I, INF. *ḥaśd*, gather, assemble (a.); come forth in its entirety (seed); espouse one's party, defend; (m.) be partial; — V. INF. *taḥaśśud*, assemble for help; — VI. INF. *taḥâśud*, assemble to help one another; act in common against an enemy; — VIII. INF. *iḥtiśâd*= V.; be ready for help; — X. INF. *istiḥśâd*, assemble (n.).

حشد *ḥaśad*, pl. *ḥuśûd*, troop; — *ḥaśid*, ready for help.

(حشر) *ḥaśar*, U, I, INF. *ḥaśr*, assemble, unite; raise for the last judgment; expel, banish; destroy; work out elaborately; (m.) press, compress, pile or heap up (also V.); intermeddle, intrigue; pass. be dead; — V. INF. *taḥaśśur*, see I.

حشر *ḥaśr*, pl. *ḥuśr*, assembly, crowd, throng (يوم الح *yaum al-ḥaśr*, Day of Judgment); the public treasury, fisc; exile, banishment; sharp; — ة *ḥaśara-t*, pl. *ḥaśar*, husk; chaff; — *ḥaśara-t*, pl. *ḥaśarât*, small creeping animals, reptiles; (m.) insects; — *ḥuśra-t*, inquisitiveness, intermeddling; — ى *ḥaśriyy*, intermeddler; intriguer.

(حشرج) *ḥaśraj*, INF. ة, emit the death-rattle; roar with a rattling noise; — ة *ḥaśraja-t*, death-rattle; a wine-vessel.

حشش *ḥuśaś*, pl. of حشة *ḥuśśa-t*.

(حشط) *ḥaśaṭ*, INF. *ḥaśṭ*, take away; uncover, unveil.

(حشف), II. INF. *taḥśîf*, look with compressed eye-lids.

حشف *ḥaśf*, dry bread; — *ḥaśaf*, bad pulpless dates; — ة *ḥaśafa-t*, pl. *-ât*, *ḥaśaf*, *ḥiśâf*, rock; cliff; ulcer in the throat; stubble; gland of the penis.

(حشك) *ḥaśak*, I, INF. *ḥaśk*, collect the milk in the udder; leave the camels unmilked; abound in water; bear plenty of fruit; (m.) fill up; — II. INF. *taḥkîś*, fill up, stuff; — VIII. INF. *iḥtiśâk*, be full of milk; be filled up, stuffed.

حشك *ḥaśak*, plenty of milk in the udder.

(حشل) *ḥaśal*, INF. *ḥaśl*, despise, contemn.

(حشم) *ḥaśam*, U, I, INF. *ḥaśm*, tell unpleasant things; — I, put to shame; — *ḥaśim*, A, INF. *ḥaśam*, grow irritated, angry; become

ashamed, blush; — II. INF. *taḥśîm*, make angry, irritate; — V. INF. *taḥaśśum*, be ashamed; — VIII. INF. *iḥtiśâm*, be awed; revere; bear one's self with reverence towards; be abashed.

حشم *ḥaśam*, ة *ḥaśama-t*, family with attendance or retinue; great pomp; — ة *ḥiśma-t*, fear, awe, reverence; shame, bashfulfulness, blush; modesty; (m.) ceremonies, compliments.

(حشن) *ḥaśin*, A, INF. *ḥaśan*, smell badly from remains of milk.

(حشو) *ḥaśâ*, U, INF. *ḥaśw*, stuff, cram; injure the intestines; — V. INF. *taḥaśśî*, VIII. INF. *iḥtiśâ'*, be stuffed, crammed.

حشو *ḥaśw*, INF. of (حشو); any material for stuffing; wadding, wad; intestines; superfluous phrase; part of a half-verse preceding the *'arûḍ* or *ḍarb*; — ة *ḥuśwa-t*, *ḥiśwa-t*, intestines; — *ḥiśwa-t*, rabble.

حشودة *ḥuśûda-t*, assistance; (m.) partiality.

حشورة *ḥaśwara-t*, avaricious old woman; having full flanks.

حشوى *ḥaświyy*, pl. *ḥaświyya-t*, who talks stuff or nonsense; pl. *ḥaświyyât*, stuff, rubbish; stuffing.

(حشى) *ḥaśî*, A, INF. *ḥaśan*, breathe with difficulty, suffer from asthma; smell badly from remains of milk; — INF. *taḥśiya-t*, put trimmings, &c., to a garment; — III. INF. *muḥâśât*, except, spare, heed a person; pass. *ḥuśi*, God forbid (followed by ان *an*, that); — V. INF. *taḥaśśî* = III.; exclaim حاشا *ḥâśâ*, God forbid! be ashamed; abstain, recede from; heed, be on the guard.

حشى *ḥaśan*, intestines; asthma; — *ḥaśî*, ة, asthmatic; — *ḥaśiyy*, dried up, withered; rotten in the root; — ة *ḥaśiyya-t*, pl. *ḥaśâyâ*, *ḥaśâ'*, bolster; mattress; padded garment; false breasts or hips.

حشيا *ḥaśyâ'*, f., and—

حشيان *ḥaśyân*, asthmatic.

حشيش *ḥaśîś*, ة, pl. *ḥaśâ'iś*, grass; hay; herb; intoxicating extract of hemp.

حشيف *ḥaśîf*, worn-out cloth.

حشيم *ḥaśîm*, feared, revered; full of reverence; timid, shy.

(حص) *ḥaṣṣ*, U, INF. *ḥaṣṣ*, shave; rub off the hair; strip; fall to the lot of (acc.); give a share in; refuse protection; — III. INF. *ḥiṣâṣ*, *muḥâṣṣa-t*, IV. INF. *iḥṣâṣ*, allot or give for a share; — VI. INF. *taḥâṣṣ*, divide between each other by lot, &c.; — VII. INF. *inḥiṣâṣ*, fall off; be lopped off.

حص *ḥuṣṣ*, pearl; pl. *ḥuṣûṣ*, saffron; — *ḥuṣṣ*, pl. and حصا *ḥaṣâ*, f. of احص *aḥaṣṣ*, having little hair or few feathers; miserable; — ة *ḥiṣṣa-t*, pl. *ḥiṣaṣ*, part, portion, share, lot; inheritance; division.

(حصا) *ḥaṣ'*, A, INF. *ḥaṣ'*; also حصى *ḥaṣî*, A, INF. *ḥaṣ-an*, suck or drink one's fill; eat or drink greedily; break wind; — INF. *iḥṣâ'*, water to the fill.

حصاد *ḥaṣâd*, ة *ḥaṣâda-t*, harvest, harvest-time; — *ḥaṣṣâd*, reaper; — *ḥuṣṣâd*, pl. of حاصد *ḥâṣid*, who reaps.

حصار *ḥaṣâr*, *ḥiṣâr*, saddle-cushion; — *ḥiṣâr*, siege, blocade; surrounding wall; fortress, fortification; — *ḥuṣṣâr*, pl. of حاصر *ḥâṣir*, besieger, &c.

حصاص *ḥiṣâṣ*, allotment, INF. III. of (حص); — *ḥuṣâṣ*, swiftness in running; breaking of wind; — ة *ḥuṣâṣa-t*, grapes left on the stem in gathering the harvest.

حصافة *ḥaṣâfa-t*, sound judgment.

حصان *ḥaṣân*, ة, pl. *-ât*, *ḥuṣun*, chaste woman; lawful wife; matron; — *ḥiṣân*, pl. *ḥuṣun*, *aḥṣina-t*, horse; a thorough-

bred; stallion; — ة ḥaṣâna-t, chastity; steadfastness, firmness that cannot be shaken; impregnability.

حصاة ḥaṣât, pl. حصى ḥaṣan, ḥaṣa, ḥaṣayât, ḥuṣiyy, pebble; calculus in the bladder; particle; intelligence.

(حصب) ḥaṣab, U, I, INF. ḥaṣb, strew with pebbles or gravel; pelt with pebbles; pelt, throw at; set out on a journey, travel about; turn away, leave in the lurch; — ḥaṣib, A, INF. ḥaṣab, have the small-pox; (m.) suffer from typhus; pass. id.; — II. INF. taḥṣîb, strew with gravel;— IV. INF. iḥṣâb, raise gravel; turn aside, leave in the lurch.

حصب ḥaṣab, pebble, stone; small wood fuel; — ḥaṣib, abounding in pebbles or gravel;—ة ḥaṣba-t, gravel; ḥaṣaba-t, a pebble-stone; ḥaṣba-t, ḥaṣaba-t, ḥaṣiba-t, small-pox; measles; (m.) typhus; pl. -ât, marks of small-pox, &c.

(حصحص) ḥaṣḥaṣ, INF. ة, come to light, become public, evident.

(حصد) ḥaṣad, U, I, INF. ḥaṣd, ḥaṣad, ḥiṣâd, mow, reap; die; (also II. INF. taḥṣîd) twist firmly;—ḥaṣid, A, INF. ḥaṣad, be firmly twisted, strongly made;—IV. INF. iḥṣâd, be ripe for harvest; — VIII. INF. iḥtiṣâd, mow, reap; — X. INF. istiḥṣâd=IV; be firmly twisted, strongly made.

حصد ḥaṣd, mowing, reaping (s.); — ḥaṣad, mown corn; — ḥaṣid, firmly twisted, strongly made; — ة ḥaṣada-t, pl. of حاصد ḥâṣid, who reaps.

حصداء ḥaṣdâ', strong coat of mail.

(حصر) ḥaṣar, U, I, INF. ḥaṣr, press, oppress; shut in, besiege, blockade; restrain, restrict; surround; prevent; take and keep the whole; put the saddle-cushion on the camel's back; — ḥaṣir, A, INF. ḥaṣar, have the heart oppressed; be avaricious; keep strict secrecy; speak with great difficulty; pass. ḥuṣir, INF. ḥuṣr, suffer from strangury or constipation; — III. INF. ḥiṣâr, muḥâṣara-t, besiege; blockade; — IV. iḥṣâr, drive into a corner; cause anxiety; prevent, hinder; pass. suffer from strangury or constipation; — VII. INF. inḥiṣâr, be driven into a corner, besieged, blockaded; be straitened, feel a natural want; (m.) live in solitude.

حصر ḥuṣr, strangury, constipation; — ḥaṣar, anxiety; oppression of the heart; impediment of speech; melancholy of solitary life; restriction; avarice; — ḥaṣir, having the heart oppressed; confounded; avaricious; keeping strict secrecy; — ḥuṣur, pl. of حصير ḥaṣîr.

(حصرم) ḥaṣram, INF. ة, draw the bow strongly; twist tightly; mend a pen.

حصرم ḥiṣrim, ة, green sour fruit, especially grapes; their juice; — ة ḥaṣrama-t, avarice; — يّة ḥiṣrimiyya-t, dish of unripe dates.

حصص ḥaṣaṣ, thinness of the hair; — ḥiṣaṣ, pl. of حصّة ḥiṣṣa-t.

(حصف) ḥaṣaf, U, INF. ḥaṣf, remove to a great distance (a.); — ḥaṣif, A, INF. ḥaṣaf, be afflicted with dry scab; — ḥaṣuf, INF. ḥaṣâfa-t, have a sound judgment and a strong mind; — IV. INF. iḥṣâf, remove far (a.); establish well and solidly; twist tightly; run fast; — X. INF. istiḥṣâf, be established well and solidly.

(حصل) ḥaṣal, A, INF. ḥuṣûl, maḥṣûl, result, remain; appear; happen, take place; be produced; reach; cash a sum or debt; draw an advantage, obtain; — ḥaṣil, A, INF. ḥaṣal, swallow earth or gravel and have the gripes therefrom; have calculus in the bladder; — II. INF. taḥṣîl,

cause to result; obtain; acquire; (m.) reach at last and with difficulty; select; have unripe dates; resume, recapitulate; — V. INF. *taḥaṣṣul*, result; get realised; take place; be obtained; be paid in.

حصل *ḥuṣl*, unripe dates; — *ḥaṣal*, partition between two rooms.

(حصم) *ḥaṣam*, I, INF. *ḥaṣm*, break wind; — VII. INF. *inḥiṣâm*, get broken.

(حصن) *ḥaṣan*, *ḥaṣun*, be strong by nature or fortified by art; — *ḥaṣun*, INF. *ḥaṣn*, *ḥiṣn*, *ḥuṣn*, keep at home and be chaste; — II. INF. *taḥṣîn*, fortify; wall in; entrench; — IV. INF. *iḥṣân*, id.; keep the wife at home; keep at home and be chaste; — V. INF. *taḥaṣṣun*, protect one's self by fortifications; entrench one's self, retire to a fortress; lead a chaste life.

حصن *ḥiṣn*, pl. *ḥuṣûn*, *ḥiṣana-t*, *aḥṣân*, stronghold, fortress, entrenchment; (ابو الح *abû 'l-ḥiṣn*, fox); armour; weapons; destruction, annihilation; — *ḥiṣn*, *ḥuṣn*, chastity; — *ḥuṣun*, pl. of حصان *ḥuṣân* and *ḥiṣân*.

حصنا *ḥaṣnâ'*, chaste woman.

(حصو) *ḥaṣâ*, U, INF. *ḥaṣw*, prevent, hinder.

حصور *ḥuṣûr*, asthmatic; having the heart oppressed; avaricious; chaste; castrated; timid; who always sits at home; *al-ḥuṣur*, St. John Baptist.

حصول *ḥuṣûl*, happening of an event; taking place of a thing; realisation.

(حصى) *ḥaṣa*, I, INF. *ḥaṣy*, pelt with pebbles; — *ḥaṣî*, A, INF. *ḥas-an*, make an impression, leave a mark; designate; abound in pebbles; pass. suffer from calculus; — IV. INF. *iḥṣâ'*, count, count up; impress on the memory; know; write, narrate; put into order.

حصى *ḥaṣan*, number; gravel, small pebbles; calculus, gravel of the kidneys (noun of unity حصاة *ḥaṣât*); — *ḥaṣiyy*, very prudent; — *ḥuṣiyy* and—

حصيات *ḥaṣayât*, pl. of حصاة *ḥaṣât*.

حصيد *ḥaṣîd*, mown off, reaped; destroyed; firmly twisted, strongly made; — ة *ḥaṣîda-t*, pl. *ḥaṣâ'id*, moth; harvest, crops; stalks of reaped corn.

حصير *ḥaṣîr*, oppressed of heart, asthmatic; avaricious; timorous; — pl. *ḥuṣur*, *aḥṣira-t*, also ة *ḥaṣîra-t*, pl. *ḥaṣâ'ir*, mat of reeds or bulrushes; — *ḥaṣîr*, side of the body; side muscle or sinew; king; prison; — ى *ḥaṣîriyy*, seller of mats.

حصيف *ḥaṣîf*, of sound judgment, firm; strong of tissue.

حصيلة *ḥaṣîla-t*, pl. *ḥaṣâ'il*, rest, remainder.

حصين *ḥaṣîn*, ة, well fortified; fortress; strongly made; ة *ḥaṣîna-t*, armour; — *ḥuṣain*, little castle; ابو الح *abû 'l-ḥuṣain*, fox.

(حض) *ḥaḍḍ*, U, INF. *ḥaḍḍ*, *ḥuḍḍ*, *ḥiḍḍîda*, *ḥuḍḍîda*, stimulate, spur on, investigate, incite; — II. INF. *taḥḍîḍ*, make eager; — III. INF. *muḥâḍḍa-t*, id.; — VI. INF. *taḥâḍḍ*, stimulate one another.

حض *ḥaḍḍ*, stimulation.

(حضا) *ḥaḍa'*, A, INF. *ḥaḍ'*, kindle, light; poke the fire; burn (n.); — VIII. INF. *iḥtiḍâ'*, poke the fire.

حضار *ḥaḍâr-i*, make haste! look sharp! come! — *ḥiḍâr*, running of a horse; — *ḥuḍâr*, rheumatism; — *ḥuḍḍâr*, pl. of حاضر *ḥâḍir*, present, &c.; — ة *ḥaḍâra-t*, *ḥiḍâra-t*, place with settled inhabitants; INF. of (حضر).

حضارمة *ḥaḍârima-t*, natives of Hadramaut.

حضان *ḥiḍân*, brooding, hatching (s.); — ة *ḥiḍâna-t*, id.; embrace, caress; nursing and bringing up of children.

حضايا *ḥaḍâyâ*, pl. of حضية *ḥaḍiyya-t*.

(حضب) *ḥaḍab*, I, INF. *ḥaḍb*, make a fire blaze, put on wood; fall down; catch.

حضب *ḥiḍb*, *ḥuḍb*, pl. *aḥḍâb*, whizzing of the bow-string.

(حضج) *ḥaḍaj*, U, INF. *ḥaḍj*, kindle; beat; stamp; dip into water; run; replenish.

(حضجر) *ḥaḍjar*, INF. ة, fill.

(حضر) *ḥaḍar*, U, INF. *ḥuḍûr*, be present; come into the presence of; remove from (n. عن *'an*); fetch or bring; occupy; damage, injure; — INF. *ḥuḍr*, stepping high in running; — *ḥaḍir*, A, INF. *ḥaḍâra-t*, be present, in the presence of; appear before; assist at an assembly, &c.; happen; be ready; — II. INF. *taḥḍîr*, lead up, bring; cause to come, call or send for; bring; place ready; prepare and present; — III. INF. *muḥâḍara-t*, be present; present one's self; have a ready answer; converse with; vie in running; plead a cause; scourge, whip, beat; dispute for a thing and carry it off; — IV. INF. *iḥḍâr*=II.; run fast; trot; — V. INF. *taḥaḍḍur*, be present; present one's self; keep ready; — VIII. INF. *iḥtiḍâr*=V.; assist at; pre-occupy; come to a place with settled inhabitants; pass. *uḥtuḍir*, be approached by death; — X. INF. *istiḥḍâr*, wish for one's presence; represent; represent to one's self as present; represent to one's self, call back to memory, remember; imagine to be in the presence of God; come into the presence of God; urge on to run.

حضر *ḥaḍr*, place with settled inhabitants; habitation, house, vestibule of the house; staying at home; — *ḥuḍr*, running with highly raised feet; race; — *ḥaḍar*, presence; permanently inhabited place; — *ḥaḍir*, fixed, settled; — *ḥaḍur*, eloquent; learned in law; — *ḥuḍur*, uninvited guest, intruder; — *ḥuḍḍur*, pl. of حاضر *ḥâḍir*, present, &c.; —ة *ḥaḍra-t*, presence; place with settled inhabitants; residence; title of honour: Majesty, Highness, Excellency, Eminence; — *ḥiḍra-t*, *ḥuḍra-t*, *ḥaḍara-t*, presence; — *ḥaḍara-t*, pl. of حاضر *ḥâḍir*, present, ready, &c.

(حضرب) *ḥaḍrab*, INF. ة, strain the bow-string; twist tightly.

(حضرم) *ḥaḍram*, INF. ة, have a faulty pronunciation; strain the bow; peel.

حضرموت *ḥaḍramaut*, *ḥaḍramût*, Hadramaut.

حضرمي *ḥaḍramiyy*, pl. *ḥaḍârima-t*, native of Hadramaut; — ة *ḥaḍramiyya-t*, long-pointed shoe; faulty pronunciation.

حضري *ḥaḍriyy*, *ḥaḍariyy*, settled, domiciled; inhabitant of a town.

ما حضض *mâ ḥaḍaḍ*, nothing whatever; — *ḥuḍuḍ*, pl. of حضيض *ḥaḍîḍ*.

(حضل) *ḥaḍal*, A, INF. *ḥaḍal*, be rotten at the place where the branches shoot.

(حضن) *ḥaḍan*, U, INF. *ḥaḍn*, *ḥiḍân*, *ḥiḍâna-t*, *ḥuḍûn*, brood, hatch; — INF. *ḥaḍn*, *ḥiḍâna-t*, embrace, take into, carry in one's arms; bring up; — INF. *ḥuḍn*, *ḥiḍâna-t*, embrace, take into, carry in one's arms; bring up; — INF. *ḥaḍn*, refuse a service to a neighbour; — INF. *ḥiḍân*, have one breast or udder larger than the other; — VI. INF. *taḥâḍun*, embrace each other; — VIII. INF. *iḥtiḍân*, embrace; press to one's bosom; carry in arms; bring up.

حضن *ḥiḍn*, pl. *ḥuḍun*, *aḥḍân*, bosom; pl. *aḥḍân*, side; also *ḥuḍn*, foot of a mountain.

(حضو) *ḥaḍâ*, U, INF. *ḥaḍw*, stir up the fire.

حضور *ḥuḍûr*, presence; appearance, approach; waiting, attendance, ceremonious call; royal presence, court, government; quietude, tranquility of mind, ease; pl. of حاضر *ḥâḍir*, present, ready, &c.; — ى *ḥuḍûriyy*, waiter (m.).

حضيرة *ḥaḍîra-t*, pl. *ḥaḍîr*, *ḥaḍâ'ir*, small body of men for a sudden attack; vanguard.

حضيض *ḥaḍîḍ*, pl. *aḥiḍḍa-t*, *ḥuḍuḍ*, the lowest part; basement; foot of a mountain; aphelion, apogee; precipice.

حضية *ḥaḍiyya-t*, pl. *ḥaḍâyâ*, favourite.

(حط) *ḥaṭṭ*, U, INF. *ḥaṭṭ*, put, place, lay down; remit; abate; depose, degrade, humiliate; despise; descend, alight; — INF. *ḥaṭṭ*, fall, go down (price); polish and mark leather; — VII. INF. *inḥiṭâṭ*, be put, taken, let down; descend, alight; fall; be deposed, degraded, humbled; humble one's self; decrease; — VIII. INF. *iḥtiṭâṭ*=I.; — X. INF. *istiḥṭâṭ*, wish for an abatement; deserve abatement.

حط *ḥaṭṭ*, putting down (s.); deposition, degradation; slope, declivity; falling of the prices; cheapness of corn; — ة *ḥiṭṭa-t*, remission; month of Ramaḍân.

(حطا) *ḥaṭa'*, A, INF. *ḥaṭ'*, throw to the ground; beat with the palm of the hand on the back; beat; lie with; throw; throw up foam or scum; bring one round from his opinion; — A, I, ease the bowels.

حطاب *ḥaṭṭâb*, pl. *ḥaṭṭâba-t*, woodcutter; seller of fuel.

حطام *ḥuṭâm*, ة, anything dry or crumbling (ح الدنيا *ḥuṭâm ad-dunyâ*, perishable goods of the world); dry fruit; household furniture; ة *ḥuṭûma-t*, morsel, crumb; — *al-ḥaṭṭâm*, lion.

(حطب) *ḥaṭab*, I, INF. *ḥaṭb*, abound in wood; cut or look for wood; help; calumniate; — II. INF. *taḥṭîb*, VIII. INF. *iḥtiṭâb*, look for wood; gather firing.

حطب *ḥaṭab*, pl. *aḥṭâb*, wood for burning, fuel; — *ḥaṭib*, lank.

حطبا *ḥaṭbâ'*, f. of احطب *aḥṭab*, very thin, miserable.

(حطحط) *ḥaṭḥaṭ*, INF. ة, let one's self down; descend; hasten.

(حطر) *ḥaṭar*, U, INF. *ḥaṭr*, lie with; put a string to or draw the bow; pass. be thrown on the ground.

(حطل) *ḥiṭl*, pl. *aḥṭal*, wolf.

(حطم) *ḥaṭam*, I, INF. *ḥaṭm*, break (a.); weaken; make digestible; — *ḥaṭim*, A, INF. *ḥaṭam*, be broken with old age; — II. INF. *taḥṭîm*, break to pieces; — V. INF. *taḥaṭṭum*, VII. INF. *inḥiṭâm*, get broken; break, crumble (n.).

حطم *ḥaṭim*, broken with old age; — *ḥuṭam*, cruel; — *ḥuṭum*, pl. of حطوم *ḥaṭûm*; — ة *ḥaṭma-t*, dryness, aridity, drought; — *ḥiṭma-t*, pl. *ḥiṭam*, morsel, crumb; — *ḥuṭama-t*, hell-fire; glutton; cruel herdsman.

(حطمر) *ḥaṭmar*, INF. ة, fill; draw the bow.

(حطو) *ḥaṭâ*, U, INF. *ḥaṭw*, shake.

حطوبة *ḥuṭûba-t*, armful of wood.

حطوط *ḥaṭûṭ*, steep, precipitous; low; swift, fleet; — *ḥuṭûṭ*, abatement of price.

حطوم *ḥaṭûm*, pl. *ḥuṭum*, breaker; lion.

حطيب *ḥaṭîb*, ة, abounding in wood; — ة *ḥaṭîba-t*, wood, forest.

حطيط *ḥaṭîṭ*, dwarf; — ة *ḥaṭîṭa-t*, abatement of price.

(حظ) *ḥaẓẓ*, obtain one's wish; have luck; receive one's share; — IV. INF. *iḥẓâẓ*, id.; — VII. INF. *inḥiẓâẓ*, have luck; obtain one's wish.

حظ *ḥaẕẕ*, pl. *aḥuẕẕ*, *ḥuẕûẕ*, *ḥiẕâẕ*, *ḥiẕẕâ'*, *ḥuẕẕ*, *ḥuẕûẕa-t*, *aḥâẕẕ*, share, portion, lot; luck, good fortune, enjoyment, pleasure; —*ḥaẕẕ*, lucky, fortunate, happy; — ة *ḥiẕa-t*, enjoyment of good fortune, of consideration.

حظا *ḥiẕâ'*, pl. of حظوة *ḥiẕwa-t*, *ḥaẕwa-t*; —*ḥiẕẕâ'*, and حظاظ *ḥiẕâẕ*, pl. of حظ *ḥaẕẕ*; — ة *ḥaẕât*, louse.

حظايا *ḥaẕâyâ*, pl. of حظية *ḥaẕiyya-t*.

(حظب) *ḥaẕab*, I, INF. *ḥuẕûb*; — *ḥaẕib*, A, INF. *ḥaẕab*, be fat; have the belly full.

(حظر) *ḥaẕar*, U, INF. *ḥaẕr*, prevent, hinder, prohibit; render inaccessible; surround with a wall; make a fold; enclose cattle in a fold; take all for one's self; — VIII. *iḥtiẕâr*, make a fold.

حظر *ḥaẕr*, defence, forbidding.

(حظرب) *ḥaẕrab*, INF. ة, strain the bow; fill and extend.

(حظل) *ḥaẕal*, U, I, INF. *ḥaẕl*, *ḥiẕlân*, *ḥaẕalân*, hinder in spending money, in freedom of motion; — INF. *ḥaẕalân*, walk with short abrupt steps, like a .man in anger.

حظلان *ḥiẕlân*, thrift, domestic economy.

(حظو) *ḥaẕâ*, U, INF. *ḥaẕw*, go a slow pace; — حظى *ḥaẕî*, A, INF. *ḥaẕwa-t*, *ḥiẕwa-t*, *ḥiẕa-t*, enjoy the consideration of the husband, the prince; obtain; be favoured with; — IV. INF. *iḥẕâ'*, cause to obtain; favour, prefer; — VIII. INF. *iḥtiẕâ'*, enjoy consideration and favour; — ة *ḥiẕwa-t*, *ḥuẕwa-t*, pl. حظى *ḥiẕan*, حظا *ḥiẕâ'*, share of luck; abundance; consideration, honour, favour;— *ḥaẕwa-t*, *ḥuẕwa-t*, pl. *ḥiẕâ'*, *ḥaẕawât*, small arrow for gaming.

حظول *ḥaẕûl*, thrifty, economical.

(حظى) see (حظو).

حظى *ḥaẕan*, *ḥaẕa*, noun of unity حظاة *ḥaẕât*, louse; —*ḥiẕan*, share of luck; pl. of حظوة *ḥiẕwa-t*; — *ḥaẕiyy*, ة, honoured, esteemed, considered; name of the eighth horse in a race; — ة *ḥaẕiyya-t*, pl. *ḥaẕâyâ*, concubine of a married man; share, lot; — *ḥuẕayya-t*, pl. *-ât*, small gaming-arrow.

حظيا *ḥuẕayyâ*, slow pace.

حظيرة *ḥaẕîra-t*, pl. *ḥaẕâ'ir*, fold for cattle; wall for protection; fence; ح القدس *ḥaẕîrat al-quds*, Paradise.

حظيظ *ḥaẕîẕ*, who obtains his wish or share; fortunate.

(حف) *ḥaff*, I, INF.. *ḥufûf*, be dishevelled; bear dry herbs; vanish entirely; — U, INF. *ḥaff*, shave; — I, INF. *ḥaff*, *ḥifâf*, clean the face from hair, pluck out the hair; shave; (m.) rub or scrape off, erase; — INF. *ḥaff*, turn around, surround from all sides; enclose, encompass, cover; —I, INF. *ḥafîf*, rumble (bowels); snort; hiss (snake); — II. INF. *taḥfîf*, surround, enclose, cover; beat, fall; — IV. INF. *iḥfâf*, id.; — VIII. INF. *iḥtifâf*, pull out the hair; pluck herbs; surround from all sides; turn around; cover, wrap up; be surrounded.

حف *ḥaff*, loom; trace; — ة *ḥaffa-t*, edge, border, rim, side; wall of support to terraces, &c.; loom.

(حفا) *ḥafa'*, A, INF. *ḥaf'*, throw on the ground.

حفا *ḥafa'*, papyrus; its fresh root; — *ḥaf-an*, حفا *ḥafâ'*, going barefoot (s.), INF. of (حفى); — ة *ḥufât*, pl. of حافى *ḥâfî*, bare-foot, &c.

حفاث *ḥuffâs*, a harmless snake.

حفار *ḥaffâr*, digger.

حفاصة *ḥufâṣa-t*, collection.

حفاظ *ḥifâẕ*, protection; sentiment of honour; — *ḥuffâẕ*, pl. of حافظ *ḥâfiẕ*, watcher, &c.; — ة *ḥifâẕa-t*, careful guard; memory.

حفاف *ḥifâf*, pl. *aḥiffa-t*, curling lock on the top of a bald head; side;

trace ; INF. of (حف) ;—ة ḥufâfa-t, stubble.

حفاوة ḥafâwa-t, ḥifâwa-t, and—

حفاية ḥifâya-t, molestation by questioning ; joyful reception ; courtesy ; INF. of (حفى).

(حفت) ḥafat, U, INF. ḥaft, annihilate, destroy ; pound, grind ; thrash, flog.

حفت ḥafit, and—

(حفث) ḥifs̱, ḥafis̱, ة ḥafis̱a-t, pl. afḥâs̱, tripe, guts ; belly ; a large snake.

(حفحف) ḥafḥaf, INF. ة, have little to live upon ; produce the sound of a revolving top, purr, buzz.

(حفد) ḥafad, I, INF. ḥafd, ḥafadân, be active and nimble in one's work ; speed ; — IV. INF. iḥfâd, urge to haste, hasten ; — VIII. INF. iḥtifâd=I.

حفد ḥafad, حفدان ḥafadân, a pace of the horse ; — ḥafad and ة ḥafada-t, daughters, sons, grandchildren, sons-in-law, nephews, &c., pl. of حافد ḥâfid and حفيد ḥafîd.

حفدلس ḥafadlas, black woman ; melancholy.

(حفر) ḥafar, I, INF. ḥafr, dig, dig out, hollow ; dig or clean a well ; investigate ; lie with ; emaciate by milking frequently ; — also ḥafir, A, INF. ḥafar, and pass. ḥufir, have decayed teeth ; lose the milk teeth ; — IV. INF. iḥfâr, help another to dig a well (2 acc.) ; lose the milk-teeth ; — VIII. INF. iḥtifâr, dig, dig out ; — X. INF. istiḥfâr, be willing to dig ; be time for digging.

حفر ḥafr, digging (s.) ; — also ة ḥafara-t, pl. aḥfâr, aḥâfîr, spacious well ; ditch, pit ; dug out ground ; — ḥafar, decayedness of the teeth ; — ة ḥufra-t, pl. ḥufar, ditch, pit, hole, cave ; grave.

(حفز) ḥafaz, I, INF. ḥafz, push away from behind ; hurry a person and thereby cause him to desist from a thing ; follow immediately ; pierce ; lie with ; — V. INF. taḥaffuz, VIII. INF. iḥtifâz, keep ready to leap, be watchful, vigilant, attentive ; devote care and zeal to (ب bi).

حفز ḥafaz, end, limit.

(حفس) ḥafis, I, INF. ḥafas, eat.

(حفش) ḥafaś, I, INF. ḥafś, gather, grasp ; assemble (n.) ; come or stream together ; carry off the ground ; remove with a shovel ; peel ; extract ; draw ; expel, banish ; run again immediately after running ; devote zeal to (فى fî) ; — ḥafiś, A, INF. ḥafaś, show love to the husband ; be consumed by an ulcer ; rain abundantly.

حفش ḥifś, pl. aḥfâś, rubbish, rags, lumber, old bottles, &c. ; tent ; little house ; case, box, trunk, chest.

(حفص) ḥafaṣ, I, INF. ḥafṣ, collect, gather (a.) ; throw away ; drop.

حفص ḥafṣ, pl. aḥfâṣ, ḥufûṣ, leathern bag for earth ; whelp of a lion ; — ة ḥafṣa-t, hyena ; ام ح umm ḥafṣa-t, hen.

(حفض) ḥafaḍ, U, INF. ḥafḍ, bend, crook ; throw away ; let fall, drop ; — II. INF. taḥfîḍ, id. ; allow another to get behind one.

حفض ḥafaḍ, pl. ḥifâḍ, aḥfâḍ, household furniture ready for removal ; camel to carry it ; tent ; tent-pole.

حفضاج ḥifḍâj, حفاضج ḥufâḍij, fat and flabby.

(حفضج), pass. ḥafḍij, INF. ة ḥafḍaja-t, grow fat ;—ḥifḍij, fat and flabby.

(حفظ) ḥafiẕ, A, INF. ḥifẕ, guard, preserve, preserve from ; tend (cattle) ; learn or know by heart ; (m.) reserve the absolution from a sin (bishop) ; — II. INF. taḥfîẕ, make to learn by heart (2 acc.) ; — III. INF. ḥifâẕ, muḥâfaẕa-t, defend one's own,

protect; be a guardian; give careful attendance; observe and fulfil a duty; — IV. INF. *iḥfâẕ*, provoke to anger; — V. INF. *taḥaffuẕ*, be on one's guard; be watchful; observe; keep carefully, be sparing with; — VIII. INF. *iḥtifâẕ*, watch over, guard, preserve; observe; burn with anger; — X. INF. *istiḥfâẕ*, require one to learn by heart or keep in remembrance (2 acc.).

حفظ *ḥifẕ*, guard, preservation; vigilance; caution; careful watch; observance; memory; — ة *ḥifẕa-t*, zeal in defending; anger; — *ḥafaẕa-t*, guardians, garrison, pl. of حافظ *ḥâfiẕ*.

(حفل) *ḥafal*, I, INF. *ḥafl*, *ḥufûl*, *ḥafîl*, gather, assemble (n.); rain violently; flow or stream in abundance; collect (a.); smooth, polish; be afraid; give care and attention; — II. INF. *taḥfîl*, collect, gather (a.); adorn; — V. INF. *taḥafful*, gather in large numbers (n.); adorn one's self, get adorned; — VIII. INF. *iḥtifâl*, collect, gather (n.); stream in fulness; hurry up from all sides; throng; receive with pomp, show or give attention; care for; show itself distinctly.

حفل *ḥafl*, numerous, plentiful; crowd, large assembly; zeal; — *ḥuffal*, pl. of حافل *ḥâfil*, quite full; — ة *ḥafla-t*, all, everything; diligence, zeal; — *ḥufla-t*, general assembly; council.

(حفلج) *ḥaflaj*, who moves his body in walking; — *ḥafallaj*, pl. *ḥafâlij*, young camel.

(حفلق) *ḥaflaq*, *ḥafallaq*, enervated, weak, stupid.

(حفن) *ḥafan*, U, INF. *ḥafn*, take a handful; give little; — VIII. INF. *iḥtifân*, take for one's self; eradicate, uproot; carry a child by its knees; — ة *ḥafna-t*, *ḥufna-t*, pl. *ḥufan*, handful; hollow of the hand; small gift.

(حفنج) *ḥafannaj*, small, short.

(حفو) *ḥafâ*, U, INF. *ḥafw*, make a present, or, by opposition, turn off without a gift; be benevolent to; render honoured or esteemed; keep one aloof from all that is good; shave off the moustache; — حفى *ḥafî*, A, INF. *ḥaf-an*, go bare-foot; be foot-sore; — INF. *ḥafâwa-t*, *ḥifâwa-t*, *ḥifâya-t*, *taḥfâya-t* (also V. and VIII.), receive with great joy and courteous inquiries; inquire repeatedly for (عن *'an*); — III. INF. *muḥâfât*, dispute, quarrel with (acc.); — IV. INF. *iḥfâ'*, allow one to go bare-foot, to get foot-sore; inquire repeatedly for (acc.); molest, importune; shave off the moustache; — V. INF. *taḥaffî*, see I.; rejoice; give attention (also VIII.); put on stockings and shoes; lose the shoes (horse); go bare-foot; — VIII. INF. *iḥtifâ'*, see I. and V.; — ة *ḥafwa-t*, *ḥifwa-t*, going bare-foot (s.).

حفواء *ḥufawâ'*, pl. of حفى *ḥafiyy*.

حفوف *ḥufûf*, INF. of (حف); poverty.

حفول *ḥafûl*, abounding in milk; — *ḥufûl*, plenty, fulness, abundance, wealth; INF. of (حفل).

(حفى) see (حفو).

حفى *ḥafî*, foot- or hoof-sore; — *ḥafiyy*, pl. *ḥufawâ'*, well-instructed; receiving joyfully, benevolent, compassionate; — ة *ḥifya-t*=حفوة *ḥafwa-t*.

حفيد *ḥafîd*, pl. *ḥafada-t*, grandson.

حفير *ḥafîr*, ة *ḥafîra-t*, pl. *ḥafâ'ir*, pit, cavity; — ة *ḥufaira-t*, small cavity.

حفيظ *ḥafîẕ*, watcher, guardian; administrator, manager; governor; God; who knows by heart (particularly the Koran); — ة *ḥafîẕa-t*, pl. *ḥafâ'iẕ*, zeal in defending; anger.

حفيف *ḥafîf*, INF. of (حف); noise, sound.

حفيل *ḥafîl*, zealous, diligent, industrious; numerous; — ة *ḥafîla-t*, troop; totality.

(حق) *ḥaqq*, U, I, INF. *ḥaqq*, *ḥaqqa-t*, be unavoidable, happen undoubtedly; be real, a fact; be true, right, just; be a duty; befit, be worthy of; be incumbent upon; have a right to; fall due; — U, put down as true or real; know for certain; impose as a duty, render indispensable; fulfil one's duty; act rightly; keep the middle of the road; hit on the middle of the head; visit, meet; get the better of an adversary in a law-suit; — II. INF. *taḥqîq*, act according to truth and right; verify; confirm; prove by argument; deem true, believe; impose as a necessity or duty; help another to the obtainment of his wish; — III. INF. *muḥâqqa-t*, *ḥiqâq*, contend for a right; dispute a thing with another; — IV. INF. *iḥqâq*, get the better of an adversary in a law-suit; impose as a necessity or duty; deem necessary, consider worthy; make clear; hit upon; hit the game so as to kill it; — V. INF. *taḥaqquq*, learn or know for a certainty; prove true, be doubtless; appear true; assure one's self of a thing; — VI. INF. *taḥâquq*, contend for a right; — VII. INF. *inḥiqâq*, be firmly tied; — VIII. INF. *iḥtiqâq*, have a law-suit against each other; hit so as to kill; get emaciated; — X. INF. *istiḥqâq*, be worthy of, deserve; deem necessary, consider worthy; fall due.

حق *ḥaqq*, pl. *ḥuqûq*, right, claim; privilege; perquisite; duty; obligation, debt; what is as it ought to be; true, truthful, certain; necessary; real; good, just; firm, persevering; truth; reason; certainty; evident proof; perseverance; sincerity; justice; law; God; the Koran; Islâm; worth, price, payment, reward; honour; — *ḥiqq*, m. and f. (f. also ة *ḥiqqa-t*), pl. *ḥiqaq*, *ḥiqâq*, *ḥuquq*, *ḥaqâ'iq*, camel of three years; truth; certain proof; — *ḥuqq*, cavity of the hip- or arm-bone; upper part of the arm; hip; pix; — ة *ḥaqqa-t*, truth, certainty; INF. of (حق); — *ḥiqqa-t*, incontestable right; indispensable duty; mature she-camel; INF. of (حق); — *ḥuqqa-t*, pl. *ḥuqq*, *ḥuqûq*, *ḥuqaq*, *aḥqâq*, *ḥiqâq*, case, box, casket; ink-bottle; cup of a juggler; compass; vessel of water through which the tobacco-smoke passes; pix; cavity of the hip-bone, &c. (see حق *ḥuqq*); woman.

حقا *ḥaqâ'*, trowsers; — *ḥiqâ'*, pl. of حقو *ḥaqw*; — *ḥaqqan*, truly, indeed, certainly.

حقاب *ḥiqâb*, pl. *ḥuqub*, belt set with jewels; the white of the nail.

حقارة *ḥaqâra-t*, *ḥiqâra-t*, *ḥuqâra-t*, contempt, disdain; contemptibleness; lowness, vileness.

حقاق *ḥiqâq*, litigation, law-suit; hostility; INF. III. of (حق); pl. of حق *ḥiqq* and حقة *ḥuqqa-t*; — *ḥaqqâq*, maker or seller of boxes, &c.

حقال *ḥiqâl*, sale of the crops before they are reaped; tenure of a farm against part of the harvest.

حقالى *ḥaqâlî*, pl. of حقلة *ḥaqla-t*.

حقانى *ḥaqqâniyy*, truthful; just; sincere; divine; — ة *ḥaqqâniyya-t*, justice.

حقائق *ḥaqâ'iq*, pl. of حق *ḥiqq* and حقيقة *ḥaqîqa-t*.

(حقب) *ḥaqib*, A, INF. *ḥaqab*, be unproductive; fail, be in default; — IV. INF. *iḥqâb*, id.; — VIII. INF. *iḥtiqâb*, allow another to sit behind one's self on a horse, &c.; tie another behind

one's self; put by for later use; take a crime upon one's self.

حقب *ḥuqb*, *ḥuqab*, pl. *aḥqub*, *aḥqâb*, time of eighty years, space of time; year; — *ḥaqab*, belt set with jewels; hind strap of a camel's girth; — *ḥuqub*, pl. of *ḥiqâb*; — ة *ḥiqba-t*, pl. *ḥiqab*, *ḥuqûb*, space of time; many years; year; — *ḥuqba-t*, calm (in the air); — *ḥaqiba-t*, portmanteau.

حقبا *ḥaqbâ'*, galaxy; wild she-ass.

(حقحق) *ḥaqḥaq*, INF. ة, step high (horse); travel (on horseback, at night) with difficulty; override one's horse.

(حقد) *ḥaqad*, I, INF. *ḥiqd*, *ḥuqd*, *ḥaqad*, *ḥaqîda-t*, bear a grudge or hatred (على *'ala*); be very fat; — *ḥaqid*, A, INF. *ḥaqad*, be full of hatred; fail, be in default; be unproductive; — IV. INF. *iḥqâd*, instigate to hatred; — VIII. INF. *iḥtiqâd*, bear a grudge; fail, be in default.

حقد *ḥiqd*, pl. *ḥuqûd*, *ḥaqâ'id*, *aḥqâd*, hatred, grudge; — *ḥaqad*, id.

(حقر) *ḥaqar*, I, INF. *ḥaqr*, *ḥuqriyya-t*, *maḥqara-t*, also *ḥaqur*, INF. *ḥaqâra-t*, be contemptible, mean, vile; — I, INF. *ḥaqr*, despise, treat with contempt; — *ḥaqir*, A, INF. *ḥaqar*, become contemptible; — II. INF. *taḥqîr*, deem contemptible; despise; abase, disparage; call contemptuously by the diminutive; — VIII. INF. *iḥtiqâr*, despise; — X. INF. *istiḥqâr*, deem contemptible; despise.

حقر *ḥaqr*, حقرية *ḥuqriyya-t*, contempt; contemptibleness.

حقدا *ḥaqd-an*, in rapid course.

(حقط) *ḥaqaṭ*, agility; — ة *ḥaqṭa-t*, little, nimble, f.

حقطان *ḥiqiṭṭân*, ة, short; dwarfish.

(حقف) *ḥaqaf*, INF. *ḥuqûf*, sleep on a sandhill (see the following); sleep with the head between the legs; — XII. *iḥqauqaf*, INF. *iḥqîqâf*, form long winding hills (sand); bow together, crouch.

حقف *ḥiqf*, pl. *aḥqâf*, *ḥiqâf*, *ḥuqûf*, pl. pl. *ḥaqâ'if*, *ḥiqafa-t*, long winding sandhill.

(حقل) *ḥaqil*, A, INF. *ḥaqal*, *ḥaqla-t*, *ḥuqûl*, eat earth with the herb and get the gripes from it; — III. INF. *maḥâqala-t*, sell the crops before they are reaped; let a field for half or a third of the harvest; — IV.

حقل *ḥaql*, pl. *ḥuqûl*, seed pushing leaves; sown field; column (in a book); — *ḥiql*, camel-litter; colic; — ة *ḥaqla-t*, pl. *aḥqâl*, colic; pl. *ḥaqâlî*, arable land, orchard, garden.

(حقلد) *ḥiqlid*, malicious, unsociable.

(حقم) *ḥaqm*, pigeon.

(حقن) *ḥaqan*, U, I, INF. *ḥaqn*, put milk into the leathern bag for churning; let water into a reservoir; stop, retain, keep back; prevent a man's blood being shed; administer a clyster; — VII. INF. *inḥiqân*, have a clyster administered; — VIII. INF. *iḥtiqân*, suffer from strangury; be laid out in form of an amphitheatre (garden); — ة *ḥaqna-t*, pl. *aḥqân*, colic; — *ḥuqna-t*, pl. *ḥuqan*, clyster; (m.) clyster-pipe.

(حقو) *ḥaqâ*, U, INF. *ḥaqw*, hit in the side; pass. حقى *ḥuqî*, have the colic from eating meat.

حقو *ḥaqw*, pl. *ḥiqâ'*, *ḥuqiyy*, احق *aḥq-in*, *aḥqî*, *aḥqâ'*, side, hypochondres, loins; also ة *ḥaqwa-t*, trowsers, trowser-belt; colic; pl. *ḥiqâ'*, mountain-slope, steep river-bank.

حقود *ḥaqûd*, full of hatred.

حقى *ḥuqî*, see (حقو); — *ḥuqiyy*, pl. of حقو *ḥaqw*; — ة *ḥaqqiyya-t*, truth, reality.

حقيب *ḥaqîb*, who sits behind another on horseback or lags

behind ;—ة *ḥaqîba-t*, pl. *ḥaqâ'ib*, what is put behind on the saddle; portmanteau; post-bag; saddle-bag.

حقيدة *ḥaqîda-t*, hatred, grudge.

حقير *ḥaqîr*, ة, despised; contemptible; mean, vile, paltry; "your humble servant," in letters, &c.

حقيق *ḥaqîq*, pl. *aḥiqqâ'*, deserving, worthy of (ب *bi*);—ة *ḥaqîqa-t*, pl. *ḥaqâ'iq*, reality, truth, essence; true statement of a case; genuineness; maxim;—ى *ḥaqîqiyy*, ة, real, true, genuine.

حقيم *ḥaqîm*, the outer corner of the eye.

حقين *ḥaqîn*, stopped, kept back, spared.

(حك) *ḥakk*, U, A, INF. *ḥakk*, rub; shave or scrape off; erase; engrave; probe by the touchstone; scratch, have one's self scratched;—for *ḥakik*, INF. *ḥakak*, be hoof-sore;—II. INF. *taḥkîk*, rub violently;—III. INF. *ḥikâk*, *muḥâkka-t*, rub against each other; produce electricity; flatter; resist;—V. INF. *taḥakkuk*, rub one's self against;—VI. *taḥâkk*, scratch one another;—VIII. INF. *iḥtikâk*=V.

حك *ḥakk*, rubbing, engraving, erasing (s.); pl. *ḥukûk*, erasures;—*ḥikk*, doubt, agitation, disquietude; (m.) compass;—ة *ḥikka-t*, pl. *ḥikak*, scab, itch; itching (s.).

(حكا) *ḥakâ*, A, INF. *ḥak'*, tie tight;—ة *ḥukât*, narrators, pl. of حاكى *ḥâkî*.

حكاك *ḥikâk*, refractoriness, INF. III. (حك);—*ḥukâk*, scratching (s.); sugar; borax;—*ḥakkâk*, polisher of precious stones; borer of pearls; engraver; itching, scratching (adj.); pl. *ḥakkâkât*, temptations;—ة *ḥukâka-t*, scrapings, &c.

حكام *ḥikâm*, summons;—*ḥukkâm*, judges, &c., pl. of حاكم *ḥâkim*;—ة *ḥakâma-t*, scholarship, wisdom.

حكاية *ḥikâya-t*, pl. *ḥakâyâ*, tale, narrative, story, anecdote, historical account; resemblance; simile.

(حكد) *ḥakad*, I, INF. *ḥakd*, return to the beginning.

(حكر) *ḥakar*, I, INF. *ḥakr*, wrong, oppress; be a bad comrade; be quarrelsome; store corn for the time of famine, carry on a usurious trade in corn;—*ḥakir*, A, INF. *ḥakar*, quarrel continually; be headstrong;—II. INF. *taḥkîr*, hinder;—III. INF. *muḥâkara-t*, quarrel with (acc.);—V. INF. *taḥakkur*, VIII. INF. *iḥtikâr*, buy up corn for usurious purposes; exercise a monopoly.

حكر *ḥakr*, injustice;—*ḥakar*, great stores of corn; quarrel, dispute;—*ḥakir*, who carries on a usurious corn trade;—also ة *ḥukra-t*, usurious corn-trade;—ى *ḥakriyy*, bad comrade; quarrelsome; fault-finding, cavilling.

(حكش) *ḥakaś*, I, INF. *ḥakś*, gather (a); shrink; (m.) rummage, stir up.

(حكف) *ḥakaf*, U, INF. *ḥukûf*, relax, slacken, grow tired and get remiss.

حكك *ḥakak*, INF. of (حك);—*ḥikak*, pl. of حكة *ḥikka-t*.

(حكل) *ḥakal*, U, INF. *ḥakl*, be obscure, doubtful; place the lance on one foot; bet; press hard;—IV. INF. *iḥkâl*, be obscure, doubtful;—VII. INF. *inḥikâl*, be pressed by want;—VIII. INF. *iḥtikâl*=IV.;—ة *ḥikla-t*, pressure, oppression, want, need;—*ḥukla-t*, stammering (s.).

(حكم) *ḥakam*, U, INF. *ḥukm*, exercise authority, command, bid; protect; (m.) hit upon, obtain;

happen; — U, INF. *ḥukm, ḥukûma-t,* deliver sentence, judge between; — INF. *ḥakm,* bridle; put the bit to a bridle; restrain, keep back from evil; — INF. *ḥikma-t,* be learned, wise, a philosopher, a physician; establish solidly; — II. INF. *taḥkîm,* appoint as a judge or governor; bid to give judgment; give full powers; be a physician; treat medically; — III. INF. *muḥâkama-t,* summon another or go with him before the judge; — IV. INF. *iḥkâm,* manage well, confirm, consolidate; protect; bridle; restrain; — V. INF. *taḥakkum,* possess and exercise power; treat one's self or be treated medically; — VI. INF. *taḥâkum,* summon each other or go together before the judge; — VIII. INF. *iḥtikâm,* exercise authority; deliver justice in the name of a superior; have full power over another's property; — X. INF. *istiḥkâm,* be well established, consolidated; try to consolidate, to improve; (m.) be able to reach, to obtain, to hit.

حكم *ḥukm,* pl. *aḥkâm,* sentence, judgment; jurisdiction; power; authority; magistrate; government; decree, command, precept; rule of life; prediction from the stars; fate, predestination; knowledge, wisdom; reason; category; regard; — *ḥakam,* judge, arbitrator; commander; — ة *ḥikma-t,* pl. *ḥikam*; wisdom; knowledge; medical art; philosophy; justice, equity; reason; secret decree of God; prophecy; the Koran; (m.) the Gospel; — *ḥakama-t,* bridle, bit; power; rank.

حكما *ḥukamâ',* pl. of حكيم *ḥakîm.*

(حكو) *ḥakâ,* U, INF. *ḥakw,* and حكى *ḥaka,* I, INF. *ḥikâya-t,* speak, tell, relate; resemble; imitate; tie a knot firmly; — III. INF. *muḥâkât,* resemble, be like; imitate; converse with another; — IV. INF. *iḥkâ',* tie tight; overcome, surpass; — VIII. INF. *iḥtikâ',* be firm, solid.

حكومة *ḥukûma-t,* authority, dominion; government; empire, state; jurisdiction; sentence, judgment.

(حكى) see (حكو).

حكى *ḥaky,* speaking, talking (s.); — *ḥakiyy,* talking, chattering; — *ḥakkiyy,* erasing-knife.

حكيك *ḥakîk,* smooth, polished.

حكيم *ḥakîm,* pl. *ḥukamâ',* wise; a sage, scholar, physician, naturalist, philosopher; acting with prudence and successfully; solid; — ة *ḥakîma-t,* learned woman; female judge.

(حل) *ḥall,* U, INF. *ḥall,* solve; dissolve; loosen; absolve; unfold; unbend; reel off; pass. *ḥull,* dissolve (n.), melt, thaw; — INF. *ḥulûl,* fall due; be a duty; come to the place of sacrifice (sheep, &c.); — INF. *maḥill,* fall or be due; — I, U, INF. *ḥall, ḥulûl, ḥalal,* alight, rest, put up; settle on; grant a place for doing so; come upon, befall; pass. be inhabited; — I, INF. *ḥill,* be lawful; put off the pilgrim's cloak; — I, INF. *ḥilla-t,* come to the place of sacrifice; have passed the days of impurity (woman); — for *ḥalil,* A, INF. *ḥalal,* have pains in the hips or knees; — II. INF. *taḥlîl,* solve, dissolve, analyse; redeem an oath; bid or allow to alight, put up, make a halt, stay; permit, proclaim lawful; legitimise; make a mental reservation in taking an oath; — IV. INF. *iḥlâl,* bid to alight and make a halt; allow, permit, impose as a duty; draw divine punishment upon one's self; put off the pilgrim's

cloak; have passed the time of pilgrimage, fasting, &c.; — V. INF. *taḥallul*, dissolve (n.); vanish; not keep one's oath on account of a mental reservation; — VII. INF. *inḥilâl*, get solved, dissolved, unfolded, unbent, reeled off, absolved; get weakened; — VIII. INF. *iḥtilâl*, alight, put up; — X. INF. *istiḥlâl*, deem lawful; beg one to allow a thing (2 acc.); acquire by right of prescription.

حل *ḥall*, solving, dissolving (s.), solution, absolution; sesame-oil; — *ḥill*, anything lawful; who alights, puts up, a sojourner; — also *ḥull*, redeeming of an oath or vow; — ة *ḥilla-t*, alighting-place; quarter, street; large basket; kettle; permission, dispensation, absolution; — *ḥilla-t*, pl. *ḥilâl*, alighting-place; village of a hundred tents; assembly, place of assembly; weakness; — *ḥulla-t*, pl. *ḥulal*, *ḥilâl*, underclothing; garment; cloak; garb; armour; (m.) cooking-pot, kettle.

(حلا) *ḥala'*, A, INF. *ḥal'*, make collyrium and put it to another's eye; beat; throw on the ground; bribe; — II. INF. *taḥli'*, *taḥli'æ-t*, give; keep the camels away from the water; — ة *ḥalât*, adornment of a sword.

حلاب *ḥilâb*, fresh milk; INF. III. of (حلب); — *ḥallâb*, milker; — ة *ḥallâba-t*, milch cow; fig. a person from whom advantages are drawn.

حلاج *ḥallâj*, cotton-carder; — ة *ḥilâja-t*, profession of such.

حلاحل *ḥulâḥil*, pl. *ḥalâḥil*, prince; chieftain; of high rank.

حلاس *ḥallâs*, seller of coarse carpets.

حلاشة *ḥalâśa-t*, mowing with a sickle.

حلاف *ḥilâf*, oath, obligation by oath; — *ḥallâf*, who takes frequent oaths.

حلاق *ḥalâq*, death; — *ḥilâq*, shaving (s.); — *ḥulâq*, sore throat; — *ḥallâq*, barber; — ة *ḥilâqa-t*, profession of a barber; — *ḥulâqa-t*, cuttings of hair.

حلال *ḥalâl*, lawful; indifferent; legitimate; lawful wife; mastic; — *ḥilâl*, anything lawful; vehicle for women; goods; furniture; pl. of حلة *ḥilla-t*; INF. III. of (حل); — *ḥallâl*, who solves, dissolves; — *ḥullâl*, pl. of حال *ḥâll*, descending, due; — ة *ḥalâla-t*, hut where the cocoons are reeled off; spinning-house, cotton-mill; divorced woman who, after the dissolution of the second marriage, returns to her first husband.

حلاواتي *ḥalâwâtiyy*, confectioner.

حلاوة *ḥalâwa-t*, sweetness.

حلاوى *ḥalâwa*, sweets, sweetmeats, pl. of حلوى *ḥalwa*.

حلائب *ḥalâ'ib*, pl. of حلبة *ḥalba-t* and حلوبة *ḥalûba-t*.

(حلب) *ḥalab*, I, U, (m.) A, INF. *ḥalb*, *ḥilâb*, milk; yield milk; bid to milk (2 acc.); — *ḥalib*, A, INF. *ḥalab*, be black; — IV. INF. *iḥlâb*, assist in milking; assist; — V. INF. *taḥallub*, get milked; fall in drops; perspire, shed tears, salivate; flow; — VIII. INF. *iḥtilâb*, X. INF. *istiḥlâb*, milk; — X. press out juice.

حلب *ḥalb*, milking (s.); — *ḥalab*, fresh milk; Aleppo; — *ḥulub*, pl. of حلوبة *ḥalûba-t*; — *ḥullab*, plant with milky juice; — حلب قلب *ḥullab qullab*, versatile, cunning; — ة *ḥalba-t*, pl. *ḥalâ'ib*, race-horses; horse-race; milking (s.); — *ḥulba-t*, fennel, tragacanth; clover; — *ḥalaba-t*, horse-race; pl. of حالب *ḥâlib*, milking (adj.).

حلبانة *ḥalbâna-t*, milch camel.

(حلبد) *ḥilbid*, f. ة, small camel.

(حلبس) *ḥalbas*, INF. ة, go, go away;

— *ḥalbas*, lion; devoted; also *ḥulabis*, a brave one, hero.
حلبوت *ḥalabût*, حلبى *ḥalba*, milch camel.
حلبى *ḥalabiyy*, native of Aleppo.
(حلت) *ḥalat*, I, INF. *ḥalt*, shave off, pull out.
حلتيت *ḥiltît*, حلتيث *ḥiltîs̱*, asafœtida.
(حلج) *ḥalaj*, U, I, INF. *ḥalj*, card cotton; round, roll; travel all night; walk short distances; beat; break wind; (m.) halt with one foot.
(حلحل) *ḥalḥal*, INF. ة, push from one's place; shake; — II. INF. *taḥalḥul*, be pushed, shaken.
(حلز) *ḥalaz*, U, INF. *ḥalz*, remove the hair from a skin, the bark from wood, &c.; — V. INF. *taḥalluz*, gird one's self; make ready for.
حلز *ḥilliz*, ة, short; avaricious; malicious; owl.
حلزون *ḥalazûn*, snail; — ى *ḥalazûniyy*, snail-shaped, spiral; spiral staircase; spiral shell.
(حلس) *ḥalas*, I, INF. *ḥals*, cover a camel with the saddle-cloth; rain continuously; — *ḥalis*, A, INF. *ḥalas*, attend continually, be continually at a place; — IX. INF. *iḥlisâs*, be chestnut coloured; — X. INF. *istiḥlâs*, use for a saddle-cloth; cover the ground entirely.
حلس *ḥils*, *ḥalas*, pl. *aḥlâs*, *ḥulûs*, *ḥalasa-t*, woollen covering placed beneath a camel's saddle; — *ḥils*, *ḥals*, covenant, alliance; — *ḥils*, *ḥalis*, fourth arrow in the game of arrows; *ḥalis*, apt, strong, brave; avaricious.
حلسا *ḥalsâ*, f. of احلس *aḥlas*, chestnut coloured.
(حلسم) *ḥilsamm*, avaricious.
(حلش) *ḥalaś*, INF. *ḥalś*, reap with a sickle.
(حلط) *ḥalaṭ*, U, INF. *ḥalṭ*, be rash, hasty, angry, obstinate; swear, take an oath; — *ḥaliṭ*, A, INF. *ḥalaṭ*, be hasty, angry; — VIII. INF. *iḥtilâṭ*=I.; separate in enmity from (عن *'an*).
(حلف) *ḥalaf*, I, INF. *ḥalf*, *ḥilf*, *ḥalif*, *maḥlûf*, *maḥlûfa-t*, swear, take an oath; conjure; — II. INF. *taḥlîf*, exact an oath from (acc.); — III. INF. *muḥâlafa-t*, take an oath of covenant with another; — IV. INF. *iḥlâf*=II.; — VI. INF. *taḥâluf*, bind one another by an oath of covenant; — X. INF. *istiḥlâf*, conjure, exact an oath from (acc.); renounce by oath.
حلف *ḥalf*, *ḥilf*, *ḥalif*, taking an oath, swearing (s.); — *ḥilf*, pl. *aḥlâf*, oath; sworn covenant; pl. who have sworn a covenant, confederates; friendship; partisanship, party; — *ḥalif*, covenant, confederacy.
حلفا *ḥalfâ'*, pl. *ḥaluf*, a shameless and boisterous woman; bulrushes for making baskets; — *ḥulafâ'*, pl. of حليف *ḥalîf*.
حلفان *ḥalfân*, oath.
(حلفس) *ḥilfas*, fat.
(حلق) *ḥalaq*, I, INF. *ḥalq*, *taḥlâq*, shave; shear; — U, injure in the throat, the palate; fill a cistern; determine approximately; — II. INF. *taḥlîq*, shave smooth; soar into the air, fly in circles; rise; have a halo; be three-quarters ripe; — V. INF. *taḥalluq*, be surrounded by a circle; have a halo; form a circle, sit in a circle; describe circles in the air.
حلق *ḥalaq*, throat, palate; — *ḥilq*, seal-ring; — *ḥullaq*, pl. of حالق *ḥâliq*, full udder, hillock; — ة *ḥalqa-t*, *ḥilqa-t*, pl. *ḥalaq*, *ḥaliq*, *ḥilaq*, ring; round clamp; buckle; lock of hair, ringlet; ear-ring; twist (pastry); circle; halo; fold, enclosure, fence; assembly, troop; armour; rope; empty vessel; mark of a camel

by branding; — *ḥalaqa-t*, pl. of حالق *ḥâliq*, barber.

حلقان *ḥulqân*, ة *ḥulqâna-t*, three-quarters ripe.

(حلقم) *ḥalqam*, INF. ة, sever one's throat.

(حلقن) *ḥalqan*, INF. ة, be three-quarters ripe.

حلقوم *ḥulqûm*, pl. *ḥalâqîm*, throat; gullet.

حلقى *ḥalqiyy*, guttural.

حلك *ḥalik*, A, INF. *ḥalak*, *ḥulûka-t*, also XII. *iḥlaulaq*, INF. *iḥlîlâq*, be black as a raven; — ة *ḥulka-t*, thorough blackness.

(حلكم) *ḥalkam*, *ḥulkum*, entirely black.

حلل *ḥalal*, lameness of the hips; INF. of (حل); — *ḥilal*, *ḥulal*, pl. of حلة *ḥilla-t*, *ḥulla-t*, respectively; — *ḥullal*, pl. of حال *ḥâll*, impending, due.

(حلم) *ḥalam*, A, *ḥalum*, INF. *ḥalm*, dream; have a wet dream; *ḥalam*, louse; — *ḥalum*, INF. *ḥilm*, be gentle, mild; — *ḥalim*, A, INF. *ḥalam*, swarm with worms or lice; — II. INF. *taḥlîm*, render gentle, mild; rid of worms or lice; — IV. INF. *iḥlâm*, have gentle and good children; — V. INF. *taḥallum*, show one's self gentle and considerate; dream; tell false dreams; — VII. INF. *inḥilâm*, VIII. INF. *iḥtilâm*, dream; VIII. attain to puberty.

حلم *ḥilm*, pl. *ḥulûm*, *aḥlâm*, gentleness combined with considerateness, mildness, urbanity;—*ḥulm*, *ḥulum*, pl. *aḥlâm*, dream, vision; maturity, puberty; — *ḥalam*, ة, small worm or louse; — *ḥalim*, swarming with lice; — ة *ḥalama-t*, teat, nipple; (m.) mouthpiece of a pipe.

حلما *ḥalamâ'*, pl. of حليم *ḥalîm*

حلمية *ḥilmiyya-t*, gentleness, mildness.

(حلو) *ḥalâ*, U, INF. *ḥalw*, *ḥulwân*, be sweet, pleasant to the taste, sugared; be agreeable, pleasing to the eye or mind; — INF. *ḥalw*, make sweet, pleasant; give; — حلى *ḥalî*, A, INF. *ḥalâwa-t*, be sweet, pleasant; deem or find sweet; receive anything pleasant; — حلو *ḥalû*, INF. *ḥalâwa-t*, be sweet, pleasant; — II. *ḥalla'*, (m.) حلى *ḥalla*, INF. *taḥliya-t*, sweeten; sugar; make pleasant; — III. INF. *muḥâlât*, show one's self amiable to (acc.), treat kindly, caress, flatter; — V. INF. *taḥallî*, deem or find sweet; — VI. INF. *taḥâlî*, show one's self amiable; — X. INF. *istiḥwâ*, find sweet, agreeable; be sweet; — XII. *iḥlaula*, INF. *iḥlîlâ*, be sweet, agreeable.

حلو *ḥulw* (also *ḥuluww*), ة, sweet, agreeable, lovely, amiable; — *ḥalû'*, collyrium.

حلوا *ḥalwâ'*, f. sweet, pleasant, agreeable; aything sugared, confectionery, confitures; *ḥalwâ'*, f. of احلى, sweeter.

حلوان *ḥulwân*, INF. of (حلو); — also ة *ḥulwâna-t*, portion, dowry; compensation to a divorced woman; gratification, present, gratuity; fee;—ى *ḥalwâniyy*, confectioner;—*ḥulwâniyy*, sweet.

حلوائى *ḥalwâ'iyy*, confectioner.

حلوب *ḥalûb*, milking (adj.); milked; — ة *ḥalûba-t*, pl. *ḥalâ'ib*, *ḥulub*, animal that yields milk, milch.

حلول *ḥulûl*, INF. of (حل); incorporation, incarnation, penetration; — pl. of حال *ḥâll*, descending, impending, due; — ى *ḥalûliyy*, believer in the incarnation of God.

حلوى *ḥalwa*, pl. *ḥalâwa*, sweets, confectionery; — *ḥalwa*, sweet; — ات *ḥalwiyyât*, sweetmeats, sweets.

(حلى) *ḥala*, I, INF. *ḥaly*, adorn; — *ḥalî*, A, INF. *ḥaly*, be adorned; adorn one's self; — II. INF. *taḥliya-t*, adorn; describe a

person ; — v. INF. *taḥallî*, be adorned.

حلى *ḥali'*, v. see (حلا) ; — *ḥaly*, pl. *ḥuliyy*, *ḥiliyy*, ornaments of a woman, jewellery ; — *ḥaliyy*, ة, pl. *aḥliya-t*, white thistle ; adorned ; — ة *ḥalya-t*, adornment, jewel ; — *ḥilya-t*, pl. *ḥila*, adornment, jewellery ; distinguishing quality ; consonance.

حليب *ḥalîb*, milk.

حليت *ḥalît*, frost ; — *ḥillît*, asafœtida.

حليج *ḥalîj*, carded ; — ة *ḥalîja-t*, dates in milk ; cream.

حليف *ḥalîf*, pl. *ḥulafâ'*, confederate ; fellow conspirator ; sharp ; nettled.

حليق *ḥalîq*, shaved.

حليل *ḥalîl*, pl. *aḥillâ'*, husband, wife ; anything lawful ; — ة *ḥalîla-t*, pl. *ḥalâ'il*, wife.

حليم *ḥalîm*, pl. *ḥulamâ*, *aḥlâm*, gentle and considerate, mild ; gracious.

(حم) *ḥamm*, U, (m.) A, INF. *ḥamm*, make hot, heat ; melt ; hasten the pace of an animal ; make it hot for, cause anxiety ; pass. *ḥumm*, have a hot fever ; be troubled, put to anxiety ; — INF. *ḥumûm*, decree ; intend ; determine according to weight or measure ; — for *ḥamim*, A, INF. *ḥamam*, have ceased to glow ; be black as coal ; be very hot ; — IV. INF. *iḥmâm*, warm, heat ; cause anxiety ; afflict with a fever ; be at hand, present, near ; — V. INF. *taḥammum*, take a warm bath ; — VII. INF. *inḥimâm*, be heated, grow anxious, heated with passion ; have a fever ; — VIII. INF. *iḥtimâm*, be caused anxiety ; be prevented from sleep by sorrow or anxiety ; X. INF. *istiḥmâm*, take a warm bath.

حم *ḥam*, *ḥam'*, *ḥama'* (حما *ḥam-an*), pl. *aḥmâ'*, father-in-law ; — *ḥamm*, anxiety ; flight, escape ; — *ḥumm*, pl. *ḥamâ'im*, the best part ; heat of mid-day ; pl. of احم *aḥamm*, white, &c. ; — ة *ḥamma-t*, thermal spring ;—*ḥimma-t*, sweat, perspiration ; death ; —*ḥumma-t*, heat ; fervour ; fever ; blackish brown ; pigeon-colour ; pl. *ḥumam*, *ḥimâm*, destiny ; ح الفراق *ḥumma-t al-firâq*, fate, death ; also *ḥuma-t*, poison of a scorpion.

(حما) *ḥama'*, A, INF. *ḥam'*, cleanse from mud ; — حمى *ḥami'*, A, INF. *ḥam'*, *ḥama'*, be muddy ; be angry.

حما *ḥamâ'*, حماة *ḥam'a-t*, pl. حما *ḥam-an*, thin mud, filth, dung ; — *ḥimâ'*, INF. III. of (حمى) ; defence ; anything forbidden ; precinct ; — *ḥammâ'*, pl. *ḥumm*, the buttocks ; — *ḥummâ'*, pl. *ḥummayâ-t*, hot fever ; — ة *ḥamât*, mother-in-law ; pl. *ḥamawât*, calf of the leg ; Hama ; — *ḥumât*, pl. of حامى *ḥâmî*, protector.

حماد *ḥamâd-i*, well done ! bravo !— *ḥammâd*, who praises much ; — ى *ḥumâda*, pl. *ḥumâdayât*, end, extremity, what is last.

حمار *ḥimâr*, pl. *ḥamîr*, *aḥmira-t*, *ḥumur*, *ḥumûr*, *ḥumurât*, *maḥmûrâ'*, ass, wild ass ; ة *ḥimâra-t*, pl. *ḥamâ'ir*, she-ass ; upper part of the foot ; instep ; *ḥimâr*, *ḥimâra-t*, wooden fore-part of a camel's saddle ; wood for sharpening knives ; — *ḥammâr*, pl. *ḥammâra-t*, ass-driver, muleteer ; — ة *ḥammâra-t*, lazy beast ; highest heat of summer.

حمارس *ḥumâris*, strong, bold ; lion.

حمارى *ḥimâriyy*, ة, ass-like ; — ة *ḥimâriyya-t*, agreement for equal division.

حمازة *ḥamâza-t*, strength ; sharpness.

حماسة *ḥamâsa-t*, bravery ; energy ;

title of an ancient collection of poetry.

حماض *ḥummâḍ*, sorrel.

حماط *ḥamâṭ*, ة, a herb; rice-straw; —ة *ḥamâṭa-t*, secret of the heart; pl. *ḥimâṭ*, mountain-fig.

حماق *ḥamâq*, *ḥumâq*, small-pox; — *ḥimâq*, حماقى *ḥamâqâ*, *ḥumâqâ*, pl. of احمق *aḥmaq*, stupid, foolish; — ة *ḥamâqa-t*, stupidity, foolishness.

حماقيس *ḥamâqîs*, pl. calamities.

حمال *ḥammâl*, porter; — ة *ḥamâla-t*, undertaking, carrying, suffering (s.), INF. of (حمل); mulct for bloodshed; — *ḥimâla-t*, pl. *ḥumul*, tribute; fine; pl. *ḥamâ'il*, sword-belt; trade of a porter.

حماليج *ḥamâlîj*, pl. of حملوج *ḥamlûj*.

حماليق *ḥamâlîq*, pl. of حملاق *ḥimlâq*.

حمام *ḥamâm*, ة, pl. *-ât*, *ḥamâ'im*, turtle-dove; dove, pigeon; any bird with a neck-ring;—*ḥimâm*, fate, death; — *ḥumâm*, fever of a beast of burden; nobleman, lord;—*ḥammâm*, pl. *ḥammâmât*, warm bath; — ى *ḥammâmiyy*, bath-keeper.

حمائر *ḥamâ'ir*, pl. of حمارة *ḥimâra-t*.

حمائل *ḥamâ'il*, pl. of حمالة *ḥimâla-t*.

حمائم *ḥamâ'im*, pl. of حم *ḥumm*, حامة *ḥamâma-t*, and حميمة *ḥamîma-t*.

حماية *ḥimâya-t*, protection; (m.) protégé, client; fuel.

(حمت) *ḥamat*, I, INF. *ḥamt*, set over and fill with love for; — *ḥamit*, A, INF. *ḥamat*, be rank, spoiled, deteriorated; — *ḥamut*, INF. *ḥumûta-t*, be very hot, sultry.

(حمج), II. *ḥammaj*, INF. *taḥmîj*, compress the eye-lids to see better; look sharply at (الى *ila*); be sunk; be defaced by anger.

(حمحم) *ḥamḥam*, INF. ة, and II. INF. *taḥamḥum*, neigh, roar; — *ḥimḥim*, entirely black; a bird; — ة *ḥimḥima-t*, ox-tongue (plant).

(حمد) *ḥamid*, A, INF. *ḥamd*, *maḥmad*, *maḥmid*, *maḥmida-t*, praise; reward, thank; find praiseworthy, good; be angry; — II. INF. *taḥmîd*, praise highly, glorify God; — IV. INF. *iḥmâd*, show one's self praiseworthy; find good, praiseworthy; approve, be pleased with; deserve thanks from (على *'ala*); be kind.

حمد *ḥamd*, praise; kindness, favour, grace; reward, thank; — ة *ḥamda-t*, praiseworthy (f.); — *ḥumada-t*, who always praises, flatterer.

حمدل *ḥamdal*, INF. ة, say الحمد لله *al-ḥamd-u li-'l-lâh-i*.

(حمر) *ḥamar*, U, INF. *ḥamr*, scrape off; skin; shave; — *ḥamir*, A, INF. *ḥamar*, suffer from indigestion; grow stupid, like an ass; burn with anger; — II. INF. *taḥmîr*, call or treat as an ass; dye red, rubricate; speak as a Himyarite; — V. INF. *taḥammur*, id.; rouge (n.); — IX. INF. *iḥmirâr*, be red, redden, blush; — XI. INF. *iḥmîrâr*, be very red.

حمر *ḥamr*, skinning, flaying (s.); —*ḥumr*, pl. of احمر *aḥmar*, red; — *ḥumar*, tamarind; bitumen, asphalt; — *ḥumur*, pl. of حمار *ḥimâr*; — *ḥummâr*, ة, a finch with a red head;—ة *ḥumra-t*, pl. *ḥumar*, redness; blush; rough; dust of red brick; plague-blister, anthrax; erysipelas.

حمرا *ḥamrâ*, f. حمران *ḥumrân*, pl. of احمر *aḥmar*, red.

حمرات *ḥumurât*, pl. of حمار *ḥimâr*.

(حمز) *ḥamaz*, I, INF. *ḥamz*, burn on the tongue; sharpen, point; seize; — *ḥamuz*, INF. *ḥamâza-t*, be strong, hard.

حمز *ḥamz*, sharpness, acidity; — ة *ḥamza-t*, lion; a herb.

(حمس) *ḥamas*, U, INF. *ḥams*, stew meat; provoke to anger; —

ḥamis, A, INF. ḥamas, be firm in one's belief, brave in battle; — ḥamus, INF. ḥamâsa-t, id.; — II. INF. taḥmîs, IV. INF. iḥmâs, stew meat; irritate; — v. show one's self unshakeable in belief, brave in battle; grow angry, fly into a passion.

حمس ḥums, pl. of احمس aḥmas, strong, firm, &c.; — ḥamas, unshaken firmness; ة ḥamasa-t, tortoise; — ḥamis, unshakeable, brave, energetic; — ḥumsa-t, honour, consideration.

حمسا ، ḥamsâ, f. of احمس aḥmas, strong, firm.

(حمش) ḥamaś, I, INF. ḥumûśa-t, be thin; — U, INF. ḥamś, gather, assemble (a.); provoke to anger; pursue in anger, chase; — ḥamiś, A, INF. ḥamś, ḥamśa-t, be angry; be violent, oppressive; — INF. ḥamś, ḥamaś, have thin thighs or legs; — ḥamuś, INF. ḥumûśa-t, be thin; — II. INF. taḥmîś, itch, burn; be granulous, coagulate and become granulous; — VIII. INF. iḥtimâś, grow inflamed with anger; fight.

حمش ḥamś, ḥamiś, having thin thighs; thin; fleshless; ḥamś, pl. ḥimâś, thin; — ة ḥimśa-t, anger, rage, indignation, vexation.

(حمص) ḥamaṣ, U, INF. ḥamṣ, ḥumûṣ, subside, abate; cease to be swollen; take a mote out of the eye; perspire violently; — INF. ḥamṣ, rock gently to and fro (n.) — II. INF. taḥmîṣ, roast; —V. INF. taḥammuṣ, get roasted; shrink; — VII. INF. inḥimâṣ, subside, abate.

(حمض) ḥamaḍ, U, INF. ḥamḍ, be sour, acid; have aversion for (عن 'an); desire; — INF. ḥamḍ, ḥumûḍ, browse on bitter herbs; — ḥamiḍ, A, be or turn sour; — ḥamuḍ, INF. ḥumûḍa-t, id.; — II. INF. taḥmîḍ, IV. INF. iḥmâḍ, make sour, acidulate, leaven.

حمض ḥamḍ, pl. ḥumûḍ, a bitter plant; sorrel (also حمضيض ḥamḍîḍ); — ḥumuḍ, pl. of حميض ḥamîḍ; — ة ḥamḍa-t, desire, craving.

(حمط) ḥamaṭ, I, INF. ḥamṭ, peel, pare.

(حمطر) ḥamṭar, INF. ة, fill; put a string to the bow.

(حمظ) ḥamaẓ, U, INF. ḥamẓ, spur, urge on.

(حمظل) ḥamẓal, coloquintida; — INF. ة, gather coloquintida.

(حمق) ḥamiq, A, INF. ḥumq, ḥumuq, be stupid, imbecile, foolish; (m.) be vexed, angry; — ḥamuq, INF. ḥamâqa-t, be stupid, an idiot; be dull (market); — II. INF. taḥmîq, call or deem stupid, treat as a fool; declare to be foolishness; pass. drink wine; — IV. INF. iḥmâq, find stupid; — VI. INF. taḥâmuq, feign stupidity; — X. INF. istiḥmâq, find stupid; be stupid; act foolishly.

حمق ḥumq, stupidity, idiotcy, foolishness; wine; — ḥamaq, fluor albus; anger, vexation; — ḥamiq, pl. ḥumaqâ', حمقى ḥamqa, blockhead; ḥumuq, pl. and—

حمقا ḥamqâ', f. of احمق aḥmaq, stupid, foolish.

حمقان ḥamqân, angry; vexed.

(حمك) ḥamik, A, INF. ḥamk, step along.

حمك ḥamak, ة, anything small; small lice, ants; children; low people; leader; ة, small, low (f.).

(حمل) ḥamal, I, INF. ḥaml, ḥumlân, carry; support, endure; import; send; impose, impute; treat kindly; attack, charge; instigate, incite, excite against; bear great hardships in travelling; refer a word to or make it agree with another; show one's self angry; know a book by heart; give over to destruction; — I, INF. ḥaml, be

pregnant; bear fruit; swell, over-flow; — INF. *ḥamâla-t*, be at one's service, ready for; pass. be covered (mare); — II. INF. *taḥmîl*, burden with (2 acc.); cause, bid, or ask to carry, deliver, &c.; impute to (2 acc.); — IV. INF. *iḥmâl*, impose a burden; help to carry (2 acc.); — V. INF. *taḥammul*, take up a burden; carry, support, bear, suffer; make debts; break up a camp and depart; — VI. INF. *taḥâmul*, impose anything hard, treat harshly; oppress; — VII. INF. *inḥimâl*, be carried; be bearable; — VIII. INF. *iḥtimâl*, carry; bear, support, suffer; permit, allow; overlook an offence; acknowledge a benefit, be thankful (also pass. *uḥtumil*, be allowable, possible; pass. with على *'ala*, grow angry); impose a burden; break up the camp and depart; — X. INF. *istiḥmâl*, charge one's self with one's own affairs, perform them one's self; ask or demand to carry.

حمل *ḥaml*, carrying (s.); pregnancy; pl. *ḥimâl, aḥmâl*, embryo (in the womb); pl. *ḥimâl, ḥumûl, aḥmâl*, fruit of a tree; — *ḥiml*, pl. *aḥmâl*, burden, load; pl. *ḥumûl*, camel-litter, camels bearing litters; — *ḥamal*, pl. *ḥumlân, aḥmâl*, lamb, ram, wether; sign of the Ram; — *ḥuml*, pl. of حمالة *ḥimâla-t*; — ة *ḥamla-t*, attack; charge of horse; push; effort; — *ḥimla-t*, load, burden; — *ḥamala-t*, bearers, pl. of حامل *ḥâmil*.

حملاج *ḥimlâj*=حملوج *ḥumlûj*.

حملاق *ḥimlâq, ḥumlâq*, pl. *ḥamâlîq*, the inner side of the eye-lid; edge of the eye coloured with collyrium.

حملان *ḥumlân*, INF. of (حمل); pl. of حمل *ḥamal*; hospitable gift.

(حملج) *ḥamlaj*, INF. ة, twist a rope very firm.

(حملق) *ḥamlaq*, INF. ة, open the eyes wide and stare at, gaze.

حملوج *ḥumlûj*, pl. *ḥamâlîj*, bellows of a goldsmith.

حملوق *ḥumlûq*=حملاق *ḥimlâq*.

حملى *ḥamliyy*, categorical.

حمم *ḥamam*, blackness; — *ḥimam*, INF. of (حم); — *ḥumam*, pl. of حمة *ḥumma-t*; — ة *ḥumama-t*, coal.

(حمن) *ḥamn*, small lice (also حمنانة *ḥamnâna-t*); ticks (insects).

(حمو) see (حمى).

حمو *ḥamw*, heat; also ة *ḥamwa-t*, first heat of the morning; prime; — *ḥamû, ḥamw, ḥam'*, father-in-law, brother-in-law; — *ḥumaw*, poison of a scorpion; — *ḥumawât*, pl. of حماة *ḥamât*.

حمود *ḥamûd*, praised, praiseworthy.

حمور *ḥumûr*, pl. of حمار *ḥimâr*.

حموشة *ḥumûśa-t*, thinness of the legs.

حموضة *ḥumûḍa-t*, acidity; acid taste, INF. of (حمض).

حمول *ḥamûl*, porter; bearer, sufferer; gentle, mild; — ة *ḥamûla-t*, beast of burden; load, burden, freight, cargo; — *ḥumûla-t*, camel-loads; fee of a porter; carriage, costs of transport.

(حمى) *ḥamâ*, I, INF. *ḥamy, ḥimâya-t, maḥmiya-t*, protect, defend, ward off, forbid to touch or enter (acc. or من *min*); not be ridden or loaded; — INF. *ḥamy, ḥamwa-t, ḥimâya-t, ḥamiyya-t*, forbid, bid one (acc. or ل *li*) to abstain from (acc. or عن *'an* respectively); — *ḥamî*, A, INF. *ḥamiyya-t, maḥmiyya-t*, be in awe of, abstain with awe or reverence; — INF. *ḥamy, ḥumiyy, ḥumuww*, glow, be hot, perspire; — INF. *ḥamy, ḥumuww*, glow, be heated; be angry against (على *'ala*); — II. INF. *taḥmiya-t*, make hot or to glow; heat; — III. INF.

muḥâmât, *ḥimâ'*, defend; plead for; — IV. INF. *iḥmâ'*, make hot or to glow; brand; declare a place prohibited to others, declare one's determination to defend a place; meet such a place: — V. INF. *taḥammî*, get hot, be heated; rush upon with impetuosity; — VI. INF. *taḥâmî*, be on one's guard against, set guard on; go aside from, refrain from (acc.); — VIII. INF. *iḥtimâ'*, abstain from (من *min*); fast; defend one's self; call for protection or help; — XII. *iḥmauma*, INF. *iḥmîmâ'*, be black.

حمى *ḥamî'*, see (حما); — *ḥamî'*, muddy; — *ḥim-an*, *ḥima*, du. *ḥimawân*, pl. *aḥmâ'*, well guarded and prohibited to others; precinct; domain; sanctuary; anything forbidden; — *ḥumma*, pl. *ḥummayât*, hot fever; — *ḥamiyy*, pl. *ḥamiyya-t*, protected, prohibited=*ḥim-an*; hot, glowing; —ة *ḥimya-t*, anything defended or to be defended; anything forbidden; diet; — *ḥamiyya-t*, feeling of honour and shame; dignity joined to modesty; abstinence, diet; zeal; — *ḥammiyya-t*, intense heat.

حميا *ḥumayyâ*, *ḥumayy-an*, ardour of passion; fire of youth, of wine; wine; — *ḥammayâ*, anything that must be defended.

حميت *ḥamît*, extreme rage; pl. *ḥumut*, leathern flask.

حميد *ḥamîd*, ة, praised, praiseworthy; — ة *ḥamîda-t*, pl. *ḥamâ'id*, praiseworthy quality or action.

حمير *ḥamîr*, pl. of حمار *ḥimâr*; also ة *ḥamîra-t*, strap, girth; — *ḥimyar*, name of the first ancestor of a tribe; — ة *ḥumaira-t*, erysipelas; — ى *ḥimyariyy*, ة, belonging to the tribe of Himyar; — ية *ḥimyariyya-t*, language of the Himyarites.

حميز *ḥamîz*, firm, vigorous.

حميس *ḥamîs*, ة, brave; impetuous, vehement; stove; — ة *ḥamîsa-t*, stew.

حميصة *ḥamîṣa-t*, pl. *ḥamâ'iṣ*, stolen sheep.

حميض *ḥamîḍ*, pl. *ḥumuḍ*, tract of land abounding in bitter herbs.

حميقا *ḥumaiqâ'*, حميقى *ḥumaiqa*, small-pox.

حميل *ḥamîl*, carried, carried off; imported when young (slave); stranger; foundling; bastard; — ة *ḥamîla-t*, people of the house; pl. *ḥamâ'il*, sword-belt.

حميم *ḥamîm*, hot water; thermal spring, hot bath; summer-heat; afflicted with fever; pl. *aḥimmâ'*, fever; relation, relative, friend; — ة *ḥamîma-t*, pl. *ḥamâ'im*, hot water or milk; best part of one's property; — ات *ḥumaimât*, live coal.

(حن) *ḥann*, I, INF. *ḥanîn*, call tenderly, cry, sigh, complain; be moved with a longing desire; resound; — INF. *ḥann*, *ḥanân*, have compassion on (على *'ala*); — II. INF. *taḥnîn*, bloom; — IV. INF. *iḥnân*, make the bow resound; err, transgress; — V. INF. *taḥannun*, be moved with love and compassion; — VI. INF. *taḥânn*, X. INF. *istiḥnân*, long for; — ة *ḥanna-t*, sister-in-law; wife; folly.

(حنا) *ḥana'*, A, INF. *han'*, be densely covered with vegetation; lie with; — II. INF. *taḥnî'*, *taḥni'a-t*, dye red with henna; — V. INF. *taḥannî*, be dyed red.

حنا *ḥinnâ*, ة, pl. *ḥun'ân*, the plant henna (*Lawsonia inermis*).

حنابلة *ḥanâbila-t*, pl. of حنبلى *ḥambaliyy*.

حناجر *ḥanâjir*, pl. of حنجرة *ḥanjira-t* and (also حناجير *ḥanâjîr*) of حنجور *ḥunjûr*.

حناجيف *ḥanâjîf*, pl. of حنجوف *ḥunjûf*.

حناط *ḥannâṭ*, corn-merchant ; — *ḥinâṭ*, materials for embalming ; — ة *ḥinâṭa-t*, art of embalming ; corn-trade ;— ى *ḥannâṭiyy*, pl. ة, corn-merchant.

حنان *ḥanân*, compassion, mercy ; tenderness ; abundance ; wages, pay ; — *ḥannân*, moved with compassion or tenderness ; merciful ; resounding ; open ; — *ḥun'ân*, pl. of حنا *ḥinnâ'*.

حنايا *ḥanâyâ*, pl. of حنية *ḥaniyya-t*.

حناية *ḥinâya-t*, bending (s.).

حنائى *ḥinnâ'iyy*, seller of henna ; henna-coloured.

(حنب) *ḥanib*, A, INF. *ḥanab* ; — II. INF. *taḥnîb*, be gracefully bent in the loins ;— II. INF. *taḥannub*, be bent.

(حنبش) *ḥambaś*, INF. ة, jump, leap ; clap the hands ; play, laugh, amuse by telling stories.

حنبص *ḥimbiṣ*, ة *ḥimbaṣa-t*, stratagem in warfare ; ابو الح *abû 'l-ḥimbiṣ*, fox.

(حنبل) *ḥambal*, INF. ة, eat of the bean *ḥumbul* ; put on a fur coat ; — II. INF. *taḥambul*, hang down the head.

حنبل *ḥambal*, short, dwarfish ; fur coat ; worn boot ; fleshy, paunch-bellied ; sea ; name of the founder of one of the four law-schools ; — *ḥumbul*, French bean ; — ى *ḥambaliyy*, pl. *ḥanâbila-t*, follower of Hambal.

(حنتف) *ḥantaf*, locusts as a dish

(حنتم) *ḥantam*, ة, pl. *ḥanâtim*, green water-jug ; coloquintida.

(حنث) *ḥaniṡ*, be a blasphemer and perjurer ; break one's oath ; waver between good and evil ;— IV. INF. *iḥnâṡ*, induce to perjury ; — V. INF. *taḥannuṡ*, shun false gods and sin.

حنث *ḥinṡ*, sin, crime, perjury.

(حنثر) *ḥanṡar*, حنثرى *ḥanṡariyy*, stupid.

حنثل *ḥanṡal*, weak.

(حنج) *ḥanaj*, I, INF. *ḥanj*, bend, cause to bend ; twist strongly ; present itself, happen, occur.

حنج *ḥinj*, pl. *ḥinâj*, root, origin.

(حنجب) *ḥunjub*, dry, withered.

(حنجد) *ḥunjud*, long, lengthy.

(حنجر) *ḥanjar*, ة *ḥanjara-t*, pl. *ḥanâjir*, throat, gullet ;— *ḥanjar*, INF. ة, slaughter (by cutting the throat).

(حنجف) *ḥanjaf*, *ḥinjif*, *ḥunjuf*, ة *ḥanjafa-t*, &c., upper edge of the hip.

حنجور *ḥunjûr*, pl. *ḥanâjir*, gullet ; throat ; (m.) phial, small bottle.

حنجوف *ḥunjûf*, part of the ribs which joins the spine.

(حنحن) *ḥanḥan*, INF. ة, be moved with compassion or tenderness.

(حندج) *ḥunduj*, pl. *ḥanâdîj*, long sand-hill.

(حندر) *ḥundur*, حندور *ḥundûr*, pl. *ḥanâdir*, pupil of the eye.

(حندس) *ḥindis*, pl. *ḥanâdis*, dark night ; darkness ; — *ḥandas*, INF. ة, II. INF. *taḥandus*, be very dark.

حندقوق *ḥandaqûq*, *ḥindaqûq*, lotus ; clover.

حندوجة *ḥundûja-t*=حندج *ḥunduj*.

حندورة *ḥundûra-t*=حندر *ḥundur*.

(حنذ) *ḥanaẓ*, I, INF. *ḥanẓ*, *taḥnâẓ*, roast beneath heated stones.

(حنر) *ḥanar*, INF. *ḥanr*, construct a vault or arch.

(حنزاب) *ḥinzâb*, strong ass ; parsnip ; a bird ; strong dwarf.

(حنس) *ḥanis*, A, INF. *ḥanas*, be always in the midst of the battle.

(حنش) *ḥanaś*, sting ; — II. INF. *taḥnîś*, chase ; avert from, cause to desist ; — IV. INF. *iḥnâś*, avert, cause to desist ; urge to speed.

حنش *ḥanaś*, pl. *aḥnâś*, male snake, reptile ; fly.

(حنص) *ḥanaṣ*, U, INF. *ḥanṣ*, die.

حنصا *ḥinṣa'*, weak.

حنظل *ḥandal*, ة *ḥandala-t*, pond, water-ditch.

(حنط) *ḥanaṭ*, I, INF. *ḥanṭ*, sigh with grief; be red; — U, INF. *ḥunûṭ*, be ripe for harvest; — II. INF. *taḥnîṭ*, embalm; — IV. INF. *iḥnâṭ*, id.; die; be ripe for harvest; — V. INF. *taḥannuṭ*, get embalmed; be irritated against (ل *li*); — X. INF. *istiḥnâṭ*, id.; seek death, rush into the din of battle; — ة *ḥinṭa-t*, pl. *ḥinaṭ*, wheat.

(حنطب) *ḥanṭab*, goat.

(حنطر), II. *taḥanṭar*, INF. *taḥanṭur*, turn and twist about, be irresolute in a matter.

(حنظل) *ḥanẓal*, ة, coloquintida.

(حنظى) *ḥanẓa*, INF. حنظاة *ḥanẓâ'a-t*, talk ribaldry (woman).

حنظيان *ḥinẓiyân*, shameless, impudent (woman).

(حنف) *ḥanaf*, I, INF. *ḥanf*, bend; — *ḥanif*, A, INF. *ḥanaf*, have the feet turned inwards; — *ḥanuf*, INF. *ḥanâfa-t*, id.; — V. INF. *taḥannuf*, turn from idolatry to the true religion.

حنفا *ḥanfâ'*, f. of احنف *aḥnaf*, turned inwards; tortoise; bow; razor; — *ḥunafâ'*, pl. of حنيف *ḥanîf*.

(حنفس) *ḥinfis*, shameless, impudent (woman).

(حنفش) *ḥinfiś*, viper.

حنفى *ḥanafiyy*, follower of Abû Hanîfa; orthodox; — ة *ḥanafiyya-t*, sect of Hanîfites; orthodoxy; reservoir with taps; tap.

(حنق) *ḥaniq*, A, INF. *ḥanaq*, *ḥaniq*, be enraged; hate, bear a deep grudge; — IV. INF. *iḥnâq*, hate with irreconcilable hatred.

حنق *ḥanaq*, pl. *ḥinâq*, violent anger, rage; — *ḥaniq*, enraged; spiteful.

(حنك) *ḥanak*, I, U, INF. *ḥank*, bridle; make wise; understand well; chew; — II. INF. *taḥnîk*, make wise; chew; — IV. INF. *iḥnâk*, make wise; — VIII. INF. *iḥtinâk*, id.; bridle.

حنك *ḥanak*, pl. *aḥnâk*, palate; lower part of the chin; — *ḥunk*, experience; firmness and prudence; — *ḥunuk*, ة, experienced; prudent; — ة *ḥanaka-t*, rugged ground.

(حنكل) *ḥankal*, INF. ة, walk clumsily and heavily.

(حنم) *ḥanam*, ة, owl.

(حنو) *ḥanâ*, U, INF. *ḥanw*, *ḥanâ'*, bend, crook; contort; bend the head; — INF. *ḥanw*, make a bow; — INF. *ḥunuww*, lean towards, incline, have an inclination for (على *'ala*); — II. INF. *taḥniya-t*, bend, crook; — IV. INF. *iḥnâ'*, incline towards; — V. INF. *taḥannî*, be bent, crooked; — VII. INF. *inḥinâ'*, id.; be flexible; incline towards.

حنو *ḥunuww*, inclination, affection, tenderness, compassion; — *ḥinw*, pl. *ḥaniyy*, *ḥuniyy*, *aḥnâ'*, bend, inflection; saddle-bridge; bending outlines of the body, &c.; chin; ribs; mountain-slope.

حنوط *ḥanûṭ*, fragrant herbs; materials for embalming.

حنون *ḥanûn*, tender, fond, affectionate, compassionate; — *ḥunûn*, pl. of حنين *ḥanîn*, *ḥinnîn*.

(حنى) *ḥana*, I, INF. *ḥinâya-t*, bend, crook, contort, incline; peel.

حنى *ḥin-an*, *ḥina*, henna; — *ḥaniyy*, pl. of حنو *ḥinw*; — ة *ḥaniyya-t*, pl. *ḥaniyy*, *ḥanâyâ*, bow.

حنيا *ḥanyâ'*, f. of احنى *aḥna*, crooked.

حنيث *ḥanîṡ*, impious, blasphemous, perjured.

حنيذ *ḥanîẕ*, roasted on heated stones; perspiring.

حنيرة *ḥanîra-t*, pl. *ḥanâ'ir*, arch, vault; key-stone of an arch or vault; bow without string.

حنيف *ḥanîf*, pl. *ḥunafâ*, professor of the true faith; orthodox; circumcised; — ابو حنيفة *abû ḥanîfa-t*, founder of one of the

four law-schools; — ية *ḥanîfiyya-t*, his sect; orthodoxy.
حنيق *ḥanîq*, enraged.
حنيك *ḥanîk*, experienced; prudent.
حنين *ḥanîn*, emotion, cry or sigh of tenderness or compassion; fond affection; sound of the bow; also *ḥinnîn*, pl. *aḥinna-t*, *ḥunûn*, *ḥanâ'in*, the two months of *jumâda*.
حو *ḥuww*, pl. of احوى *aḥwa*, black; — ة *ḥuwwa-t*, dark red.
حوا *ḥawâ'*, حواة *ḥawât*, voice, noise, sound; — *ḥiwâ'*, pl. *aḥwiya-t*, hair-tent; village of tents; — *ḥawwâ'*, Eve; f. of احوى *aḥwa*, black.
حواج *ḥawâjj*, pilgrimesses to Mecca, pl. of حاجة *ḥâjja-t*.
حواجب *ḥawâjib*, pl. of حاجب *ḥâjib*, eye-brows, eye-lashes.
حواجر *ḥawâjir*, yards, &c., pl. of حجرة *ḥajra-t*.
حواجل *ḥawâjil*, pl. of حوجلة *ḥaujala-t*.
حوادث *ḥawâdis*, pl. of حادث *ḥâdis*, ة, new, fresh, event, &c.
حوادر *ḥawâdir*, pl. of حادر *ḥâdir*, ag. of (حدر).
حوار *ḥawâr*, answer; speech, conversation, dialogue; — *ḥuwâr*, *ḥiwâr*, pl. *ḥûrân*, *ḥîrân*, *aḥwira-t*, foal of a camel not yet weaned; — ة *ḥawwâra-t*, chalk; — ى *ḥawwâra*, white earth; very white flour or bread; — *ḥawâriyy*, ة, shining white; fuller; bleacher, washerman; helper, true friend; disciple of Christ, apostle; disciple of a prophet.
حواز *ḥawwâz*, instigating, inciting (adj.).
حوازب *ḥawâzib*, pl. of حازب *ḥâzib*, difficult, grave, serious.
حواس *ḥawâs*, senses, pl. of حاسة *ḥâssa-t*; *ḥawwâs*, night-watchman.
حواشى *ḥawâšî*, pl. of حاشية *ḥâšiya-t*, q.v.; retinue, attendance, camp-followers; throng.

حواصب *ḥawâṣib*, storms, pl. of حاصب *ḥâṣib*.
حواصل *ḥawâṣil*, results, &c., pl. of حاصل *ḥâṣil*; pl. of حوصلة *ḥauṣala-t*.
حواصن *ḥawâṣin*, pl. of حاصن *ḥâṣin*, chaste.
حواضر *ḥawâḍir*, fixed residences, &c., pl. of حاضرة *ḥâḍira-t*.
حواضن *ḥawâḍin*, nurses, &c., pl. of حاضنة *ḥâḍina-t*.
حواط *ḥawwâṭ*, superior, pre-eminent; (m.) tax-gatherer; furnisher, purveyor; — ة *ḥuwâṭa-t*, corn-magazine, granary.
حواطيم *ḥawâṭîm*, pl. of حاطوم *ḥâṭûm*, promoting digestion, &c.
حواق *ḥawâqq*, things that are certain to happen, &c., pl. of حاقة *ḥâqqa-t*.
حواقل *ḥawâqil*, pl. of حوقلة *ḥauqala-t*.
حواقة *ḥawâqa-t*, sweepings.
حوال *ḥawâl*, circumference, circle (*ḥawâl-a*, all around; again); change, revolution; — ة *ḥawâla-t*, turn; commission, security, bail, note of hand; transfer of a debt; letter of exchange; cheque; — ى *ḥawala*, all around; — *ḥawâlî*, surroundings; pl. of حالية *ḥâliya-t*, adorned; — *ḥawâliyy*, very cunning; pl. ة *ḥawâliyya-t*, soldier of a garrison, policeman, satellite, usher; pl. of حولى *ḥauliyy*.
حوالق *ḥawâliq*, pl. of حالق *ḥâliq*, udder; hill.
حوانى *ḥawânî*, the long ribs.
حوانيت *ḥawânît*, wine-houses, &c., pl. of حانوت *ḥânût*.
حواوى *ḥawâwî*, pl. of حاوية *ḥâwiya-t*, gut, intestine.
حوايا *ḥawâyâ*, pl. of حاوية *ḥâwiya-t*, gut, intestine, and of حوية *ḥawiyya-t*.
حوائم *ḥawâ'im*, pl. thirsty camels.
(حوب) *ḥâb*, U, INF. *ḥaub*, *ḥauba-t*, *ḥiyâba-t*, sin, transgress; — II. INF. *taḥwîb*, call to the camels; — V. INF. *taḥawwub*, be sorrow-

ful, grieved; abstain from what is unlawful; — x. INF. *istiḥâba-t*, be sorrowful.

حوب *ḥaub*, *ḥûb*, ة *ḥauba-t*, *ḥûba-t*, sin, transgression; — ة *ḥauba-t*, relationship on mother's side; love of a mother; — *ḥûba-t*, mother, wife.

حوبا *ḥaubâ'*, body, person, individual; somebody; soul, heart.

(حوت) *ḥât*, U, INF. *ḥaut*, *ḥawatân*, run or fly round.

حوت *ḥût*, pl. *ḥiwata-t*, *ḥîtân*, *aḥwât*, large fish; sign of the Fishes; صاحب الح *ṣâḥib al-ḥût*, Jonas.

(حوث), IV. INF. *iḥâsa-t*, X. INF. *istiḥâsa-t*, search the ground; stir up, disperse; throw about; harass.

حوث *ḥaus*, wherever, whenever; حوث بوث *ḥaus baus*, dispersed.

حوثا *ḥausâ*, liver and gall; fat (f.).

(حوج) *ḥâj*, U, INF. *ḥauj*, want, be in need of (الى *ila*, ان *an*); — II. INF. *taḥwîj*, lead astray; — IV. INF. *iḥwâj*, want, be in need of (الى *ila*); cause to want; compel; — V. INF. *taḥawwuj*, demand for a thing wanted; provide one's self with the necessary goods, make purchases; — VIII. INF. *iḥtiyâj*, want, be in need of (الى *ila*); be in want, poor; long for.

حوجا *ḥaujâ'*, want, need; business, affair; desire; answer.

حوجلة *ḥaujala-t*, *ḥaujalla-t*, pl. *ḥawâjil*, *ḥawâjîl*, bottle large at the bottom.

حوجمة *ḥaujama-t*, pl. *ḥaujam*, red rose.

(حود) *ḥâd*, U=(حيد); — III. INF. *muḥâwada-t*, cause continual pain.

(حوذ) *ḥâẓ*, U, INF. *ḥauẓ*, drive the camels fast; guard, keep watch over; preserve carefully, attend to; — IV. INF. *iḥwâẓ*, drive fast; cause to turn round quickly; gather the garments; — X. INF. *istiḥyâẓ*, overcome.

(حور) *ḥâr*, U, INF. *ḥaur*, *ḥu'ûr*, *maḥâr*, *maḥâra-t*, return, come back; be too little of, run short; be bewildered, stunned, perplexed; — INF. *ḥaur*, bleach, wash clean; — *ḥawir*, A, INF. *ḥawar*, be shining white, be of intense white and black (eye), have such eyes, have delicate brows, together with a white complexion; — II. INF. *taḥwîr*, whitewash; cover a flat roof with earth; — III. INF. *ḥiwâr*, *muḥâwara-t*, give an account, answer, converse; — IV. INF. *iḥâra-t*, answer; give for an answer; yield flour; — VI. INF. *taḥâwur*, converse; — IX. INF. *iḥwirâr*=*ḥawir*, be white.

حور *ḥaur*, want; — *ḥûr*, decrease; destruction, annihilation; pl. of احور *aḥwar* and حورا *ḥaurâ'*, houris; — *ḥawar*, pl., also ة *ḥawara-t*, pl. *ḥûrân*, red leather; white cordovan; *ḥawar*, pl. *aḥwâr*, cow; a paint made of lead; — *ḥawar*, also *ḥawwar*, (m.) *ḥaur*, ة, poplar-tree.

حورا *ḥaurâ'*, f. of احور *aḥwar*, having eyes of intense white and black.

حوران *ḥûrân*, pl. of حائر *ḥâ'ir*, place where water gathers; pl. of حوار *ḥuwâr* and حور *ḥawar*, ة.

(حوز) *ḥâz*, U, INF. *ḥauz*, *ḥiyâza-t*, collect, gather, grasp, get; possess; lie with; strain the bow; drive camels quickly, and, by opposition, slowly; walk slowly; — III. INF. *muḥâwaza-t*, have to deal with; occupy one's self with; tread down, subdue; — V. INF. *taḥawwuz*, be coiled up; — VI. INF. *taḥâwuz*, separate, sever one's self from; — VII. INF. *inḥiyâz*, break up the camp and depart; leave; retire; go over from one (عن *'an*) to (الى *ila*) the other; incline towards; draw aside to; flee; — VIII. INF. *iḥtiyâz*, take all for one's self; grasp.

حوز *ḥauz*, taking possession, possession; district; surroundings; —ة *ḥauza-t*, region, tract, coast, side; centre of the empire; court; precinct, domain, territory; troop; taking possession, possession.

حوزا *ḥauzâ'*, general war.

(حوس) *ḥâs*, U, INF. *ḥaus*, enter and search for booty; walk among the people and seek; trail on the ground; skin; — V. INF. *taḥâwus*, show boldness and bravery; be seized with pain; be about to depart and remain.

(حوش) *ḥâś*, U, INF. *ḥauś*, surround the game and drive it into the net; stir up tumult, disorder, &c.; gather camels and drive them along; (m.) surround, envelop; — II. INF. *taḥwiś*, gather, assemble (a.); — VII. INF. *inḥiyâś*, be surrounded and driven into the net; flee in fright; — VIII. *iḥtawaś* and *iḥtâś*, INF. *iḥtiyâś*, surround the game and start it from its lair, chase; place one in the middle, form a circle around, surround.

حوش *ḥûś*, desert inhabited by demons; cattle grown savage (and possessed by demons); demons; — *ḥauś*, pl. *aḥwâś*, enclosure for cattle; fold; farm; (m.) reclusion; —ى *ḥûśiyy*, grown wild; wild, unmanageable; misanthrope; dark; obscure; —ية *ḥûśiyya-t*, growing wild (s.); misanthropy.

(حوص) *ḥâṣ*, U, INF. *ḥauṣ*, sew, stitch together; unite closely; fly around; cover the eyes of the hawk.

حوص *ḥûṣ*, pl. حوصا *ḥauṣâ'*, f. of أحوص *aḥwaṣ*, having one eye smaller than the other; narrow-eyed; — *ḥawaṣ*, night; narrowness of the eye.

حوصل *ḥauṣal*, crop of a bird; حوصلا *ḥauṣalâ'*, id.; حوصلة *ḥauṣala-t*, *ḥauṣalla-t*, id.; pl. *ḥawâṣil*, id.; stomach; power of comprehension, faculty; ambition; — *ḥauṣal*, INF. ة, fill its crop.

(حوض) *ḥâḍ*, U, INF. *ḥauḍ*, collect water; make a water-reservoir; — II. INF. *taḥwîḍ*, fly around; —X. INF. *istiḥâḍa-t*, collect water in a reservoir.

حوض *ḥauḍ*, pl. *ḥiyâḍ*, *aḥwâḍ*, reservoir; cistern; watering-place for cattle.

(حوط) *ḥâṭ*, U, INF. *ḥauṭ*, *ḥîṭa-t*, *ḥiyâṭa-t*, watch, guard, attend to; withdraw; cover (stallion); — II. INF. *taḥwîṭ*, guard; surround; enclose, wall in; build a wall; — IV. INF. *iḥâṭa-t*, surround, encompass, enclose; invest, besiege; be fully master of a science, art, or profession; —V. INF. *taḥawwuṭ*, guard, watch over; — VIII. INF. *inḥiyâṭ*, surround; invest, besiege; be on one's guard, be cautious, be wary.

حوط *ḥauṭ*, moat; circumvallation; amulet; — ة *ḥauṭa-t*, caution, guard.

(حوف), II. *ḥawwaf*, INF. *taḥwîf*, place on the edge; — V. INF. *taḥawwuf*, trim at the edges.

(حوق) *ḥâq*, U, INF. *ḥauq*, surround, encompass, embrace; also II. INF. *taḥwîq*, sweep; polish; sharpen; erase, efface.

حوق *ḥauq*, ة *ḥauqa-t*, great quantity.

(حوقل) *ḥauqal*, INF. ة, be very old, impotent from old age; zigzag in walking; pronounce the phrase لا حول الخ *lâ ḥaul-a*, &c.

حوقل *ḥauqal*, ة, decrepit.

(حوك) *ḥâk*, U, INF. *ḥauk*, *ḥiyâk*, *ḥiyâka-t*, weave; compose poetry; be firmly impressed on the mind.

حوك *ḥauk*, parsley.

(حول) *ḥâl*, U, INF. *ḥaul*, *ḥu'ûl*, pass from one condition to another, change, alter, deteriorate; be crooked; deviate; emigrate;

come upon, come to; jump on horseback; pass, be passed, be over; intervene, separate; hinder; — INF. *ḥu'ûl, ḥiyâl, hiyâla-t,* fail to conceive when covered; remain barren; rut; — *ḥâl, ḥawil,* A, INF. *ḥawal,* be contorted, squint; — II. INF. *taḥwîl,* change, alter (a.); transport, transfer; give a letter of change, &c.; force by execution to payment; turn the eyes from; alight; attempt foolish or impossible things; — III. INF. *ḥiwâl, muḥâwala-t,* wish, desire; visit (God, punishment); (m.) make subterfuges, defer payment; act or speak ambiguously; change colour; — IV. INF. *iḥâla-t,* change (a. & n.); transfer payment, draw a bill upon, &c.; utter untruth or absurdities; be a year old, have lasted for a year, live through the year, &c.; assault with a whip; pour water from one's own bucket to another; — V. INF. *taḥawwul,* change, alter (n.), pass from one state or place to another; remove; be a double-dealer (m.); be served with an execution, have soldiers billeted in one's house; — VIII. INF. *iḥtiyâl,* be sly, cunning, subtle; scheme, use stratagem, lay traps; beguile; be a year old, &c.; INF. *iḥtiwâl,* surround; — IX. *iḥwilâl* (also XI. INF. *iḥwîlâl*), squint; — X. INF. *istiḥâla-t,* change (n.); get crooked; be rugged; be stupid, absurd, or deem to be so; become absurd.

حول *ḥaul,* pl. *aḥwâl,* power; strength; stratagem; change, exchange; pl. *ḥuwûl, ḥu'ûl, aḥwâl,* year; partition; *ḥaul-a,* all round; — *ḥawal,* squint; — *ḥawil,* squinting (adj.); very cunning; — *ḥiwal,* squint; change, removal; transport; prudence, power; miracle; — *ḥûl, ḥuwwal,* very cautious and cunning, wily; pl. of حائل *ḥâ'il,* severing, &c.; — ة *ḥaula-t,* power; cunning (s.); — *ḥûla-t,* pl. *ḥûl,* very cunning; calamity; miracle; — *ḥuwala-t,* very cunning.

حولا *ḥaulâ',* f. of احول *aḥwal,* squinting.

حولان *ḥûlân, ḥawalân,* vicissitude.

حولق *ḥaulaq,* INF. ة, pronounce the phrase لا حول الخ *lâ ḥaul-a,* &c. (there is no strength nor power but in God).

حولل *ḥûlal,* pl. of حائل *ḥâ'il,* severing, separating, &c.

حولى *ḥaula,* all around, again; — *ḥauliyy,* ة, pl. *ḥawâliyy,* a year old; — *ḥuwwaliyy,* very cunning.

(حوم) *ḥâm,* U, INF. *ḥaum, ḥawamân,* fly or run around; describe circles in the air; — INF. *ḥaum, ḥawamân, ḥiyâm, ḥu'ûm,* desire, long for.

حوم *ḥûm,* pl. of حوئم *ḥâ'im,* severing, separating, &c.; — ة *ḥauma-t,* pl. *ḥaum,* bulk and power, depth (as of the sea, &c.); din of battle; — *ḥûma-t,* beryl.

حومان *ḥaumân,* a plant; — ة *ḥaumâna-t,* pl. *ḥamân, ḥawâmîn,* rugged ground; a plant; — *ḥawamân,* INF. of (حوم).

(حومل) *ḥaumal,* INF. ة, carry water, be a water-carrier; (m.) pour down abundant rain; throng and throw down everything (crowd).

حومل *ḥaumal,* dark rain-cloud; limpid stream.

(حوى) *ḥawa,* I, INF. *ḥayy, ḥawâya-t,* gather, assemble, accumulate, gain; preserve, guard; contain (من *min*); occupy; — V. INF. *taḥawwi,* contract (n.), shrink, coil itself (snake); — VIII. INF. *iḥtiwâ',* collect, accumulate, preserve; contain; take possession of (على *'ala*).

(حوى) *ḥawî*, A, INF. *ḥaw-an*, be of dark green or dark red colour; have nearly black eyes; — IX. INF. *iḥwiwâ*, XI. INF. *iḥwîwâ*, id.; green, be verdant.

حوى *ḥawwa*, Eve; — *ḥawiyy*, who takes possession of; small reservoir or cistern; — ة *ḥawiyya-t*, pl. *ḥawâyâ*, gut, intestine; fat or caul of the intestines; small reservoir; bulk, circumference; thick cloth placed under the load of a camel.

حويجا *ḥuwaijâ*, want; desire.

خويذ *ḥawîẓ*, able and active.

حوير *ḥawîr*, hostility; — also ة *ḥawîra-t*, answer.

حويل *ḥawîl*, anything desired; intention; aim; change of place, transport; security, bail; testimony; versatility; — ة *ḥawîla-t*, cunning; power.

(حى) *ḥayy*, A, (حيى) *ḥayî*, A, INF. *ḥayâ'*, live, be alive; — *ḥayî*, A, INF. *ḥayâ'*, be distinct; turn in repentance; be ashamed; — II. INF. *taḥiyya-t*, bring to life, keep alive; say to a person حياك الله *ḥayyâka Allah-u*, may God spare your life! greet, salute; — III. INF. *muḥâyât*, cause to blush; — IV. INF. *iḥyâ'*, bring to life, keep alive, restore to life, cultivate; wake all night; — X. INF. *istiḥyâ'*, spare one's life; be ashamed; blush.

حى *ḥayy*, ة, pl. *aḥyâ'*, alive, living; ashamed, blushing, bashful; large division of a tribe; class; (m.) neighbours of the same tribe; — distinct, open, good; pudenda of a woman; — *ḥayy*, INF. of (حوى); — *ḥayy*, *ḥiyy*, pl. of حيا *ḥayâ'*, womb; — *ḥayya*, حى هلا *ḥayya halâ*, here! come here! — ة *ḥayya-t*, pl. *ḥayyât*, *ḥayawât*, snake.

حيا *ḥay-an*, abundant produce of a year; rain; pudenda of a woman; — *ḥayâ'*, shame, bashfulness, blush; bashful avoidance of a thing; fear of blame; rich produce; rain; pl. *aḥyâ'*, *aḥyiya-t*, *ḥayy*, *ḥiyy*, pudenda of a woman, womb; — ة *ḥayât*, life, life-time; shame, bashfulness.

حيابة *ḥiyâba-t*, INF. of (حوب).

حيارى *ḥayâra*, pl. of حيران *ḥairân*.

حيازة *ḥiyâza-t*, INF. of (حوز).

حياض *ḥiyâḍ*, pl. of حوض *ḥauḍ*.

حياط *ḥiyâṭ*, walls, pl. of حائط *ḥâ'iṭ*; — ة *ḥiyâṭa-t*, INF. of (حوط); enclosure; circumvallation, line of fortification.

حياك *ḥiyâk*, weaving (s.); — *ḥayyâk*, weaver; — ة *ḥiyâka-t*, profession of a weaver.

حيال *ḥiyâl*, ة, INF. of (حول); — *ḥiyâl*, pl. of حائل *ḥâ'il*, severing, separating.

حيتان *ḥîtân*, pl. of حوت *ḥût*.

(حيث) *ḥais* (*ḥais-u*); حيثما *ḥaisumâ*, wherever; من ح *min ḥais*, بح ان *bi-ḥais an*, as far as, because, since; بح ان *bi-ḥais an*, in a measure as, in a manner that, so that; ح بيث *ḥais-a bais-a*, dispersed.

حيثية *ḥaisiyya-t*, locality; ubiquity; universality; personal qualities, qualification; reference, regard; consideration, dignity, rank.

(حيد) *ḥâd*, I, INF. *ḥaid*, *ḥuyûd*, *ḥaida-t*, *ḥayadân*, *maḥîd*, *ḥaidûda-t*, deviate, remove; abstract from, disregard; shun; — III. INF. *muḥâyada-t*, avoid, shun; — IV. INF. *iḥâda-t*, avert from; — VI. INF. *taḥâyud*, avoid one another.

حيد *ḥaid*, pl. *ḥuyûd*, *aḥyâd*, *ḥiyad*, side towards the looker on; projection; anything strongly bent; — *ḥaid*, *ḥîd*, similar.

حيدر *ḥaidar*, ة *ḥaidara-t*, lion, sobriquet of the Caliph Ali; — ة *ḥaidara-t*, destruction.

حيدودة *ḥaidûda-t*, INF. of (حيد)

حيذوان *ḥaiẕuwân*, ring-dove.

(حير) *ḥâr*, A, INF. *ḥair*, *haira-t*, *ḥayar*, *ḥayarân*, be bewildered.

perplexed, stunned; be gone astray; surge, billow; — II. INF. *taḥyîr*, perplex, confuse, bewilder; astonish; embarrass; —V. INF. *taḥayyur*, be perplexed, &c.; form eddies or whirlpools; be full of water; — X. INF. *istiḥâra-t*, be perplexed, embarrassed.

حير *ḥair*, enclosure, fold; garden; asylum, place of refuge; — ة *ḥaira-t*, INF. of (حير), bewilderment, embarrassment, &c.; — *ḥîra-t*, Hira; du. *ḥîratân*, Hira and Kufa.

حيرا *ḥairâ'*, f. bewildered.

حيران *ḥairân*, f. *ḥaira*, pl. *ḥayâra*, *ḥuyâra*, stunned, bewildered, embarrassed; — *ḥîrân*, pl. of حائر *ḥâ'ir*, place where water gathers; and of حوار *ḥuwâr*, camel's foal; — *ḥayarân*, and—

حيرى *ḥaira*, f. of حيران *ḥairân*; — *ḥîriyy*, native of Hira.

(حيز) *ḥâz*, I, INF. *ḥaiz*, drive cattle; — V. INF. *taḥayyuz*, coil itself; be entirely taken possession of; incline, lean sideways; be at the side of.

حيز *ḥaiz*, *ḥayyiz*, pl. *aḥyâz*, side; region, district; courtyard; — *ḥîz*, pl. *aḥyâz*, trace; stripe, stroke, line.

حيزبون *ḥaizabûn*, old and cunning.

(حيس) *ḥâs*, I, INF. *ḥais*, mix; twist; — *ḥayis*, A, INF. *ḥayas*, approach.

حيس *ḥais*, dish of mashed dates with milk and butter.

(حيش) *ḥâś*, I, INF. *ḥaiś*, be horror-stricken; frighten; walk fast, hasten; swell, overflow; — V. INF. *taḥayyuś*, flee; be terrified.

(حيص) *ḥâṣ*, I, INF. *ḥaiṣ*, *ḥaiṣa-t*, *ḥuyûṣ*, *ḥayaṣân*, *maḥûṣ*, *maḥîṣ*, deviate, turn aside, flee, shun.

حيص بيص *ḥaiṣ baiṣ*, complicated matter; calamity.

(حيض) *ḥâḍ*, I, INF. *ḥaiḍ*, *maḥâḍ*, *maḥîḍ*, have the menses; — INF. *ḥaiḍ*, ooze out a blood-like sap (tree).

حيض *ḥaiḍ*, ة, menses; — *ḥuyyaḍ*, pl. of حائض *ḥâ'iḍ*, having the menses.

حيطان *ḥîṭân*, walls, pl. of حائط *ḥâ'iṭ*.

حيطة *ḥaiṭa-t*, *ḥîṭa-t*, prudence; — *ḥîṭa-t*, guard, custody, care, attendance; enclosure; fold; court-yard; open place; inclination, INF. of (حوط).

(حيعل) *ḥai'al*, INF. ة, call to prayer.

(حيف) *ḥâf*, I, INF. *ḥaif*, be unjust against (على *'ala*), wrong.

حيف *ḥaif*, injustice, violence, oppression; exclamation of rebuke or pity; — *ḥuyyaf*, pl. of حائف *ḥâ'if*, edge, &c.; — ة *ḥîfa-t*, pl. *ḥiyaf*, side, edge, angle.

(حيق) *ḥâq*, I, INF. *ḥaiq*, *ḥuyûq*, *ḥayaqân*, surround and take hold of; be unavoidable; penetrate; — III. INF. *muḥâyaqa-t*, envy; — IV. INF. *iḥâqa-t*, surround; bring home a crime or artifice to its author.

حيق *ḥaiq*, consequence of a wicked action falling back on the perpetrator.

حيقط *ḥaiquṭ*, حيقطان *ḥaiquṭân*, snipe.

(حيك) *ḥâk*, I, INF. *ḥaik*, *ḥayakân*, weave; strut, swagger; — INF. *ḥaik*, penetrate; make an impression; — II. INF. *taḥyîk*, weave; — IV. INF. *iḥâka-t*, id.; make an impression.

(حيل) *ḥâl*, I, INF. *ḥuyûl*, get changed, transformed; — V. INF. *taḥayyul*, VI. INF. *taḥâyul*, use stratagem; beguile.

حيل *ḥail*, strength, power, might; pl. *ḥuyûl*, *aḥyâl*, stagnating water in a ravine; — ة *ḥaila-t*, flock of small cattle; — *ḥîla-t*, pl. *ḥiyal*, *ḥîlât*, *ḥiyalât*, stratagem; expedient, device, pretext, subterfuge; invention, art (علم الحيل *'ilm al-ḥiyal*, mechanics); resource.

حيلاز *ḥailâz*, idler.
حيلولة *ḥailûla-t*, INF. of (حول).
(حين) *ḥân*, I. INF. *ḥîn*, *ḥainûna-t*, be the proper time, be opportune; perish; dry up, wither; — II. INF. *taḥyîn*, III. INF. *muḥâyanat*, V. INF. *taḥayyun*, fix a time or term; V. watch one's time; be the proper time; reach one's term, perish, die.
حين *ḥain*, calamity, visitation, affliction; ruin, perdition, death; — *ḥîn*, pl. *aḥyân*, pl. pl. *aḥâyin*, term, nick of time; season; epoch; *ḥîn-an*, some day, once; *aḥyân-an*, from time to time; *li'l-ḥîn*, instantaneously, at once; — ة *ḥaina-t*, *ḥînat*, appointed time.
حينونة *ḥainûna-t*, INF. of (حين).
حينئذ *ḥîna'iẓ-in*, at that very time; then.
حيهل *ḥaihal*, *ḥayyahal*, a salt-plant; — *ḥayyahal*, here! come here!
حيوات *ḥayawât*, pl. of حية *ḥayya-t*.
حيوان *ḥaiwân*, pl. *ḥaiwânât*, animal; cattle; beast of burden; blockhead; ح ناطق *ḥaiwân nâṭiq*, rational being; — *ḥayawân*, anything living, life, INF. of (حيى); ى *ḥaiwâniyy*, ة, animal (adj.); — ية *ḥaiwâniyya-t*, animality; stupidity.
حيوص *ḥayûṣ*, frightened.
حيوة *ḥayat*=حياة *ḥayât*, life.
حيوى *ḥayawiyy*, ة, referring to life; vital; snake-like; belonging to the tribe of Hayy.
حيى *ḥayî*, see (حى); — *ḥayiyy*, bashful, chaste; — ة *ḥuyayya-t*, small snake; — ى *ḥaiyiyy*, belonging to the tribe Hayy.

خ

خ *ḥ*, as a numeral sign=600; abbreviation for اخر *âḥar*, and so on, etc.; and for خميس *ḥamîs*, Thursday.
خابث *ḥâbis*, ة, impure, vile; — ة *ḥâbisa-t*, vileness.
خابز *ḥâbiz*, who has bread.
خابس *ḥâbis*, lion.
خابط *ḥâbiṭ*, who strides along; somebody; خ الليل *ḥâbiṭ al-lail*, ghost, spectre, phantom.
خابل *ḥâbil*, disastrous; being possessed by demons (s.); devil, seducer.
خابة *ḥâbba-t*, pl. *ḥawâbb*, relationship, relations, relatives.
خابى *ḥâbi'*, ة, frustrated, without success; — ة *ḥâbi'a-t*, pl. *ḥawâbi'*, large jug, jar, cask.
خاتام *ḥâtâm*, pl. *ḥawâtîm*, seal.
خاتر *ḥâtir*, impostor, cheat; perfidious.
خاتم *ḥâtam*, end, conclusion; — *ḥâtim*, pl. *ḥawâtim*, sealing-ring, seal; end; the last one; — ة *ḥâtima-t*, end, conclusion; epilogue; — ى *ḥâtamiyy*, maker of seals.
خاتون *ḥâtûn*, pl. *ḥawâtîn*, noble lady, matron; princess; queen (Tart.).
خاتية *ḥâtiya-t*, eagle.
خادر *ḥâdir*, hidden, veiled; lion.
خادع *ḥâdi'*, pl. *ḥada'a-t*, impostor; deceiving, deceitful; clipped (coin).
خادم *ḥâdim*, pl. *ḥuddâm*, *ḥadam*, *ḥadama-t*, servant, slave, eunuch; — ة *ḥâdima-t*, maid-servant, &c.; — ية *ḥâdimiyya-t*, servitude, service.
خاذر *ḥâẓir*, who evades justice or a creditor.
خاذل *ḥâẓil*, pl. *ḥuẓẓâl*, *ḥawâẓil*, who

forsakes his friend, renounces his religion; separated from the flock.

خارب *ḥârib*, pl. *ḥurrâb*, *ḥurrâba-t*, thief, robber; devastator.

خارج *ḥârij*, ة, exterior, external; rebel; enemy; — ة *ḥârija-t*, last word of a page; cue; — ى *ḥârijiyy*, ة, exterior, external; provincial; pl. *ḥawârij*, rebel, enemy; usurper; apostate; heretic; upstart.

خارص *ḥâriṣ*, pl. *ḥurrâṣ*, who estimates the produce of fruit.

خارق *ḥâriq*, ة, tearing; piercing through; liar; pl. *ḥawâriq*, anything extraordinary, unheard of, wonderful.

خازق *ḥâziq*, piercing, tearing; hitting the mark; head of a spear.

خازن *ḥâzin*, pl. *ḥazuna-t*, treasurer, cashier.

خازندار *ḥâzindâr*, pl. *ḥazindâra-t*, *ḥâzindâriyya-t*, treasurer (Pers.).

خازوق *ḥâzûq*, pl. *ḥawâzîq*, pole, stake (for empaling).

خاسف *ḥâsif*, pl. *ḥusuf*, thin, lean; light.

خاسى *ḥâsi'*, *ḥâsî*, remote from men (خسا).

خاش *ḥâśś*, pl. *ḥaśś*, pedestrian; — *ḥâś-in*=خاشى *ḥâśî*.

خاشع *ḥâśi'*, ة, pl. *ḥuśśa'*, humble, modest; low; quiet; moved, touched.

خاشى *ḥâśî* (خاش *ḥâś-in*), timid, timorous.

خاص *ḥâṣṣ*, ة, peculiar, particular, special; private; noteworthy; pure, unmixed, of a fine quality; attached to or attending on a prince, &c.; public (as buildings); pl. *ḥawwâṣ*, favourite of a prince, person of rank (الخاص و العام, *al-ḥâṣṣ wa 'l-'âm*, high and low); domain, royal revenue; — ة *ḥâṣṣa-t*, peculiar quality, peculiarity; essence; — *ḥâṣṣat-an*, in particular, particularly.

خاصرة *ḥâṣira-t*, pl. *ḥawâṣir*, hypochondres.

خاصية *ḥâṣṣiya-t*, pl. *ḥaṣâyiṣ*, peculiarity; principle; particular efficacy; power, energy.

خاط *ḥâṭ*, tailor.

خاطب *ḥâṭib*, pl. *ḥuṭṭâb*, *ḥuṭabâ'*, public speaker; preacher; — II. person in grammar; who promises his child in marriage; betrothed.

خاطر *ḥâṭir*, pl. *ḥawâṭir*, mind, soul, consciousness; also ة, *ḥâṭira-t*, thought, idea, notion; remembrance; inclination, choice, will; — pl. *ḥuṭṭâr*, visitor, guest.

خاطف *ḥâṭif*, pl. *ḥawâṭif*, robbing, seizing with violence; wolf; striking, blinding (lightning).

خاطى *ḥâṭi'*, f. ة, pl. *ḥuṭât*, sinner.

خافض *ḥâfiḍ*, ة, pressing down; who humbles, humiliates; governing the oblique case; convenient, commodious, comfortable; — ة *ḥafiḍa-t*, woman who circumcises girls.

خافق *ḥâfiq*, ة, beating, throbbing, having palpitations, trembling; glittering; horizon, du. *al-ḥâfiqân*, east and west; pl. *al-ḥawâfiq*, the four points of the compass; — ة *ḥâfiqa-t*, setting star.

خافل *ḥâfil*, fugitive.

خافة *ḥâfa-t*, leathern bag for honey or to serve as a table-cloth.

خافى *ḥâfî* (خاف *ḥâf-in*), pl. *ḥawâfî*, hidden; — ة *ḥâfiya-t*, same pl., who does everything in secret; hidden; pl. demons.

خاقان *ḥâqân*, pl. *ḥawâqîn*, Emperor of Tartary, emperor, king.

خال *ḥâl*, pl. *aḥwâl*, *aḥwila-t*, *ḥu'ul*, *ḥuwwal*, *ḥu'ula-t*, maternal uncle; cousin; — pl. *ḥîlân*, mole, beauty-spot, patch; supposition; infatuation, pride, arrogance; a cloud promising rain; — *ḥâl-in*, see خالى *ḥâlî*; — *ḥâll*, dispersed, routed; — ة *ḥâla-t*, paternal aunt; pl. of خائل *ḥâ'il*, proud.

خالد *ḥâlid*, ة, eternal, everlasting; adhering to the spot.

خالص *ḥâliṣ*, ة, pl. *ḥullaṣ*, pure, unmixed; sincere; the best of a thing, essence, extract; (m.) liberated, free; — ة *ḥâliṣa-t*, friendship; true friend; supreme court of accounts; fief, feudal tenure.

خالف *ḥâlif*, successor; the last; stupid; bad wine; — ة *ḥâlifa-t*, refractory; pl. *ḥawâlif*, tent-pole.

خالق *ḥâliq*, creator; worker in leather; — يّة *ḥâliqiyya-t*, creative power.

خالون *ḥâlûn*, pl. of خالى *ḥâlî*, mower.

خالى *ḥâlî* (خال *ḥâl-in*), ة, pl. *ḥuluw*, empty; free, vacant, at leisure; pure, unmixed; alone; single; uncultivated, uninhabited; past (adj. and s.); pl. *ḥâlûn*, mower.

خام *ḥâm*, raw; stallion; — *ḥâmm*, putrid, deteriorated; — ة *ḥâma-t*, unhealthy place.

خامد *ḥâmid*, expiring; dead.

خامس *ḥâmis*, fifth.

خامط *ḥâmiṭ*, bitter; of agreeably sourish smell.

خامعة *ḥâmi'a-t*, pl. *ḥawâmi'*, hyena.

خامل *ḥâmil*, pl. *ḥamal*, nameless, unrenowned; weak.

خان *ḥân*, pl. *ḥânât*, inn, alighting-place; shop; prince (Pers.); — ة *ḥâna-t*, sound; house; — INF. of (خون); pl. of خائن *ḥâ'in*.

خانر *ḥânir*, pl. *ḥunnar*, true friend.

خانع *ḥâni'*, pl. *ḥunu'*, *ḥana'a-t*, fornicator; impious.

خانق *ḥâniq*, pl. *ḥawâniq*, ag. of (خنق); narrow street, lane, mountain-path.

خانوق *ḥânûq*, pl. *ḥawâniq*, angina, croup, diphtheria.

خاو *ḥâw-in*, خاوى *ḥâwî*, ة, empty, hollow; uncultivated, uninhabited, deserted; — يّة *ḥâwiya-t*, desert; wilderness.

خائر *ḥâ'ir*, weak, cowardly; soft.

خائط *ḥâ'iṭ*, tailor.

خائف *ḥâ'if*, pl. *ḥuwwaf*, *ḥuyyaf*, *ḥiyyaf*, *ḥauf*, ag. of (خوف); fugitive.

خائل *ḥâ'il*, pl. *ḥawal*, good economist; husbandman, keeper, herdsman; servant; who fancies or imagines; pl. *ḥâla-t*, proud.

خائن *ḥâ'in*, ة *ḥâ'ina-t*, pl. *ḥâna-t*, *ḥawana-t*, *ḥuwwân*, betrayer, impostor; perfidious; خائن العين *ḥâ'in al-'ain*, lion; خائنة العين *ḥâ'ina-t al-'ain*, furtive glance.

(خب) *ḥabb*, for *ḥabib*, A, INF. *ḥibb*, be an impostor, cheat; — INF. *ḥabb*, *ḥabab*, *ḥabîb*, amble, trot, run; course along; — U, INF. *ḥâbb*, *ḥibâb*, be agitated, surge; be long and high; — II. INF. *taḥbîb*, deceive, seduce; — IV. INF. *iḥbâb*, put to an ambling pace; — VIII. INF. *iḥtibâb*, amble; tear off a strip of cloth.

خب *ḥab'*, concealment; anything concealed; خ السما *ḥab' as-samâ'*, rain; خ الارض *ḥab' al-arḍ*, plants; — *ḥabb*, pl. *ḥubûb*, billow, wave; sandhill; cunning cheat; — *ḥibb*, deceit; treachery; billowing of the sea; — *ḥubb*, pl. *aḥbâb*, *ḥubûb*, bark of a tree; — ة *ḥabba-t*, *ḥibba-t*, *ḥubba-t*, pl. *ḥubab*, long strip.

(خبا) *ḥaba'*, A, INF. *ḥab'*, II. *taḥbi'a-t*, conceal, hide (a.); — V. hide (n.), be concealed; — VIII. INF. *iḥtibâ'*, hide (a. and n.).

خبا *ḥibâ'*, pl. *aḥbiya-t*, small tent of wool or camel-hair; curtain, veil; case, box; — pl. *aḥbi'a-t*, secret brand-mark of a camel; — ة *ḥub'a-t*, hidden treasure; — *ḥuba'a-t*, hiding low.

يا خباث *yâ ḥabâs-i*, you wretch! (speaking to a woman).

خباثة *ḥabâsa-t*, خباثية *ḥabâsiyya-t*, infamy, depravity, vileness.

خبار *ḥabâr*, soft loose ground; — *ḥibâr*, pl. of خبرا *ḥabrâ'*; — ة *ḥabâra-t*, knowledge; information; — ى *ḥabâra*, pl. of خبرا *ḥabrâ'*.

خباز *ḥabbâz*, pl. *ḥabbâza-t*, *ḥabbâzûn*,

baker; — ḥubbâz, ة ḥubbâza-t, and ى ḥubâza, ḥubbâza, mallows; — ة ḥibâza-t, baking (s.); trade of a baker.

خباس ḥabbâs, خبسا ḥubasâ, خباسة ḥubâsa-t, plunder, booty.

خباط ḥabâṭ, plunder; — ḥibâṭ, pl. ḥubuṭ, brand-mark of cattle; — ḥubâṭ, madness.

خبا ḥibâ', tent.

خبال ḥabâl, ruin; madness; fault, deformity; weakness; deadly poison; purulent matter flowing from the damned; fatigue, toil; family cares; encumbrances.

خبايا ḥabâyâ, pl. of خبيئة ḥabî'a-t.

خبب ḥabab, amble, pace, trot; swiftness.

(خبت) ḥabt, pl. ḥubût, aḥbât, wide plain, field; sandy low-land; — ḥabat, INF. ḥabt, and IV. INF. iḥbât, humble one's self before God; enjoy quiet and peace; — ة ḥabta-t, humility.

(خبتل) ḥabtal, nimble little woman.

(خبث) ḥabus, INF. ḥabs, ḥabâsa-t, ḥabâsiya-t, be rotten, depraved; — INF. ḥubs, be impure, vile, perfidious, impious; be disagreeable; commit fornication with (ب bi); — IV. INF. iḥbâs, act infamously; induce to do so, seduce, deprave; — IV. INF. tabâḥus, show one's self vile, perfidious; beguile, cheat, outwit; — X. INF. istiḥbâs, act infamously; find depraved, vile, treacherous, malicious.

خبث ḥubs, fornication; depravity; foulness; malice; deceit; — ḥabas, dross, scoria; rust; — ḥubus, خبثا ḥubasâ, pl. of خبيث ḥabis; — ة ḥibsa-t, foulness.

(خبج) ḥabaj, U, INF. ḥabj, beat, flog; break wind; lie with.

(خبجر) ḥabjar, having a big flabby paunch.

(خبخب) ḥabḥab, INF. ة, deceive, cheat.

خبدع ḥabda', frog.

(خبر) ḥabar, U, INF. ḥubr, ḥibra-t, probe, test, learn to know by experience; — ḥibr, ḥubr, ḥibra-t, ḥubra-t, maḥbara-t, maḥbura-t, know by experience, learn, know; (also IV.) make food fat or greasy; — ḥabir, A, know; abound in mouse-holes; — ḥabur, INF. ḥubr, be well informed, well versed, know; — II. INF. taḥbîr, IV. INF. iḥbâr, inform, make known to, acquaint, report; — V. INF. taḥabbur, know; ask for information; question; — VIII. INF. iḥtibâr, learn by experience, probe, test; learn from (من min); — X. INF. istiḥbâr, ask for information; question, make inquiries; try to instruct one's self.

خبر ḥabr, pl. ḥubûr, large travelling-bag for provender; milch camels; — ḥibr, large travelling-bag; also ḥubr, knowledge, information; — ḥabar, pl. aḥbâr, pl. pl. aḥâbîr, news, intelligence, rumour; history; prophecy; attribute, predicate; something, anything; — ḥabir, ة, knowing, well informed; f. producing lotus; lotus-tree; — ة ḥibra-t, ḥubra-t, knowledge, information; experience; probation.

خبرا ḥabrâ', large travelling-bag for provender; pl. ḥibâr, ḥabâra, ḥabârî, ḥabrâwât, field with lotus-trees; pool of water round the lotus-tree.

(خبربج) ḥabarbaj, soft and delicate.

(خبرجل) ḥabarjal, crane (bird).

(خبرع) ḥabra', INF. ة, calumniate, slander, tell tales about.

(خبرق) ḥabraq, INF. ة, split, tear.

خبرى ḥabariyy, reporter; historian; attributive, predicative; — ة ḥabariyya-t, report; story; history.

(خبز) ḥabaz, I, INF. ḥabz, bake bread; feed on bread (a.); beat; drive with violence; — VIII. INF. iḥtibâz, bake bread.

خبز ḥubz, bread; — ة ḥubza-t, pl. aḥbâz, loaf.

(خبس) *ḥabas*, U, INF. *ḥabs*, seize with the hand; wrong, oppress; — V. INF. *taḥabbus*, take as a booty.

(خبش) *ḥabaś*, U, INF. *ḥabś*, V. INF. *taḥabbuś*, gather up from here and there.

(خبص) *ḥabaṣ*, I, INF. *ḥabṣ*, II. INF. *taḥbîṣ*, mix together, bring into confusion; spoil, bungle; prepare the dish خبيص *ḥabîṣ*; — ة *ḥabṣa-t*, bungling, bringing into confusion; anything spoiled by bungling work; confusion; hurly-burly.

(خبط) *ḥabaṭ*, I, INF. *ḥabṭ* (also V. and VIII.), beat the ground with the fore-foot; beat about; stumble; make to stumble (ب *bi*); tread down; beat off leaves; (also V.) injure, render mad, ruin; rush blindly into; sprawl; travel at night without a secure road; make a mistake; catch a cold at the beginning of winter; — II. INF. *taḥbîṭ*, beat vehemently; — V. INF. *taḥabbuṭ*, see I.; — VI. INF. *taḥâbuṭ*, beat one another; — VII. INF. *inḥibâṭ*, be disordered, disturbed (mind); — VIII. INF. *iḥtibâṭ*, see I.; beat violently; be shaken, broken, agitated; feel one's way with hand and foot; sprawl; ask for a favour.

خبط *ḥabṭ*, blow; — *ḥabaṭ*, beaten off leaves; — *ḥubuṭ*, pl. of خباط *ḥibâṭ* and خبيط *ḥabîṭ*; — ة *ḥabṭa-t*, error, mistake; — *ḥibṭa-t*, remains of milk or food; pl. *ḥibaṭ*, a number of houses.

(خبع) *ḥaba'*, A, INF. *ḥab'*, conceal; — INF. *ḥubû'*, not to be able to speak from crying.

(خبعث) *iḥba'aṣṣ*, INF. *iḥbi'ṣâṣ*, step along like a lion.

خبعثن *ḥaba'ṣan*, *ḥaba'ṣin*, ة, big and strong; lion.

(خبعج) *ḥab'aj*, INF. ة, walk with short steps.

(خبق) *ḥabaq*, I, INF. *ḥabq*, break wind; deem another lower than one's self, despise.

(خبك), VIII. *iḥtabak*, INF. *iḥtibâk*, tighten th belt or girdle.

(خبل) *ḥabal*, INF. *ḥabl*, drive out of one's senses, madden; maim; — U, bind, fetter, imprison; weaken; — I, INF. *ḥabl*, hinder, prevent; — *ḥabil*, A, INF. *ḥabâl*, be mad, out of mind; be maimed or lamed; — II. INF. *taḥbîl*, madden; maim, lame, weaken; — V. INF. *taḥabbul*, be mad, maimed, weakened; — VIII. INF. *iḥtibâl*, madden.

خبل *ḥabl*, borrowed money; suppression of the second and fourth letters of a foot when both are quiescent; pl. *ḥubûl*, palsy, hemiplexy; utter weakness of the limbs; also *ḥubl*, madness; — *ḥubl*, mind, heart, thought; — *ḥabal*, palsy; epilepsy; madness; — *ḥabil*, mad.

(خبن) *ḥuban*, I, INF. *ḥabn*, *ḥibân*, sew in a garment; store secretly corn or provender for a time of want; — VIII. INF. *iḥtibân*, hide in one's bosom.

خبن *ḥabn*, suppression of the second letter of a foot when it is quiescent; — ة *ḥubna-t*, pl. *ḥuban*, armful; trowser-belt.

خبندى *ḥabanda*, pl. *ḥabânid*, f. خبنداة *ḥabandât*, pl. *ḥabandayât*, having strong sinews; — *iḥbanda*, INF. *iḥbindâ'*, have strong sinews.

(خبو) *ḥabâ*, U, INF. *ḥabw*, *ḥubuww*, be extinguished, put out, expire, subside; — IV. INF. *iḥbâ'*, extinguish; calm, terminate.

خبورة *ḥubûra-t*, information, communication.

خبول *ḥubûl*, maiming (s.); amputation.

(خبى), II. *ḥabba*, INF. *taḥbiya-t*, pitch a small tent.

خبى *ḥabî'*, hidden, concealed; — ة *ḥabiyya-t*, hidden treasure; hiding-place, ambush.

خبيب *ḫabîb*, cleft in the ground; — ة *ḫabîba-t*, strip, slice.

خبيث *ḫabîs̱*, ة, pl. *ḫubus̱*, *ḫubas̱â'*, impure, vile, malicious, perfidious; — ة *ḫabîs̱a-t*, pl. *ḫabâ'is̱*, prostitute; pl. *ḫabâ'is̱*, infamous actions; ام الخ *umm al-ḫabâ'is̱*, wine; — *ḫibbîs̱*, very vile, &c.; — ى *ḫibbîs̱a*, impurity, vileness, malice.

خبير *ḫabîr*, ة, knowing, well informed; experienced, skilful; farmer; ploughman.

خبيز *ḫabîz*, bread; mallow.

خبيسة *ḫabîsa-t*, plunder, booty.

خبيص *ḫabîṣ*, ة *ḫabîṣa-t*, dish of dates with flour and butter.

خبيط *ḫabîṭ*, stamping the fore-foot; pl. *ḫubuṭ*, blow; trodden, stamped upon; thick milk.

خبيئة *ḫabî'a-t*, anything hidden.

(خت) *ḫatt*, vigorous lance-thrust; dispatching thrust; — IV. INF. *iḫtât*, give to anyone less than his due; blush, be ashamed.

(ختا) *ḫata'*, A, INF. *ḫat'*, prevent, hinder; — VIII. INF. *inḫitâ'*, deceive; be afraid or ashamed and conceal one's self.

ختا *ḫattâr*, great impostor, deceiver, cheat.

ختاع *ḫitâ'*, glove.

ختام *ḫatâm*, sealing (s.); — *ḫitâm*, sealing-wax; conclusion; pl. *ḫutum*, joint of a horse.

ختان *ḫitân*, circumcision; feast of circumcision; wedding; — *ḫattân*, who circumcises; — ة *ḫitâna-t*, profession of such.

(ختر) *ḫatar*, I, U, INF. *ḫatr*, *ḫutûr*, deceive villainously, betray; be disordered in mind or drunk; — V. INF. *taḫattur*, id.; be lax, lazy, weak; walk lazily.

ختر *ḫatr*, perfidy, treachery, guile.

(خترب) *ḫatrab*, INF. ة, cut into pieces.

(خترف) *ḫatraf*, INF. ة, cut or beat off.

(خترق) *ḫutraq*, wormwood.

(خترم) *ḫatram*, INF. ة, be silent.

(ختع) *ḫata'*, A, INF. *ḫat'*, *ḫutû'*, travel, depart, set out; travel at night on the straight road; fall upon; flee, escape; hasten; limp; disappear.

ختع *ḫuta'*, hyena; also *ḫati'*, skilful guide.

ختعر *ḫat'ar*, INF. ة, disappear.

ختل *ḫatal*, U, I, INF. *ḫatl*, *ḫatalân*, deceive, cheat, outwit; hide (n.) for an attack; — III. INF. *muḫâtala-t*, treat insidiously, deceive; — VI. INF. *taḫâtul*, deceive one another; — ة *ḫatla-t*, covered position; corner of a wall.

(ختلم) *ḫatlam*, INF. ة; take clandestinely.

(ختم) *ḫatam*, I, INF. *ḫatm*, *ḫitâm*, seal, put one's seal beneath; obstruct the mind; — INF. *ḫatm*, conclude, terminate; read the Koran all through; close (n.); — II. INF. *taḫtîm*, seal; — III. INF. *muḫâtama-t*, bring to a conclusion, terminate; — IV. INF. *iḫtâm*, lock, shut up; — V. INF. *taḫattum*, put the seal-ring on one's finger; — VII. INF. *inḫitâm*, be finished, concluded; — VIII. INF. *iḫtitâm*, conclude, finish, read the Koran to the end.

ختم *ḫatm*, sealing (s.); honey; pl. *ḫutûm*, seal, impression of a seal; — *ḫatam*, sealing-wax; sealing-ring; pl. *ḫatamât*, end, termination, conclusion; — *ḫutum*, pl. of ختام *ḫitâm*; — ة *ḫatma-t*, pl. *ḫatamât*, sealing (s.); epilogue; — ى *ḫatmiyy*, concluding, conclusive.

(ختن) *ḫatan*, I, U, INF. *ḫatn*, circumcise; cut off; — III. INF. *muḫâtana-t*, become related with another by one's wife; — VIII. INF. *iḫtinân*, get circumcised.

ختن *ḫatn*, circumcision; — *ḫatan*, pl. *aḫtân*, nearest relative of one's wife; father-in-law, brother-in-law, son-in-law; — ة *ḫutna-t*, feast or present on the

occasion-of circumcision — *ḫata-na-t*, mother- or sister-in-law.

(ختو) *ḫatâ*, U, INF. *ḫatw*, VIII. INF. *iḫtitâ'*, hang down one's head.

ختور *ḫatûr*, deceiver, betrayer; — *ḫutûr*, deceit; betrayal.

ختول *ḫatûl*, perfidious, treacherous.

ختون *ḫatûn*, relationship on the wife's side.

ختيت *ḫatît*, bad, spoiled, faulty; deteriorated goods.

ختير *ḫatîr*, deceiver.

ختيعة *ḫatî'a-t*, pl. *ḫatâ'i'*, thimble; thumb-stall of an archer.

ختين *ḫatîn*, circumcised.

(خث), II. *ḫassas*, INF. *taḫsîs*, gather; mend, fit; — ة *ḫussa-t*, *ḫassa-t*, bundle of sticks.

خثار *ḫusâr*, ة *ḫusâra-t*, remains of food; rest.

(خثارم) *ḫusârim*, who perceives bad omens; thick-lipped.

(خثر) *ḫasar*, INF. *ḫasr*, *ḫusûr*, coagulate, curdle; be troubled, confused; — *ḫasir*, A, curdle; be put to shame; — *ḫasur*, INF. *ḫasâra-t*, *ḫusûra-t*, curdle; — II. INF. *taḫsîr*, coagulate (a.), cause to curdle; thicken; — IV. INF. *iḫsâr*, coagulate (a.).

(خثل) *ḫasl*, ة, paunch-bellied; — ة *ḫasla-t*, *ḫasala-t*, abdomen.

(خثلم) *ḫaslam*, be mixed up, brought into confusion; take away clandestinely.

(خثم) *ḫasam*, U, INF. *ḫasm*, beat flat; — *ḫasim*, A, INF. *ḫasam*, have a flat nose and a broad root of the ear; be broad, large; be blunted; — II. INF. *taḫsîm*, flatten.

خثم *ḫasim*, having a flat nose, broad ears.

(خثى) *ḫasa*, I, INF. *ḫasy*, drop excrement; — VIII. INF. *iḫtisâ'*, turn pale (with fear).

(خج) *ḫajj*, INF. *ḫajj*, drive away, repel, turn off; split, tear; be contorted; lie with; ease the bowels; (also VIII.) raise dust; — VIII. INF. *iḫtijâj*, speed along with a curved body (camel).

(خجا) *ḫaja'*, A, INF. *ḫaj'*, beat; draw to an end; lie with; be vanquished, tamed; — خجى *ḫaji'*, A, INF. *ḫaja'*, grow ashamed; talk wantonly; — VI. be thick; hesitate in walking; — ة *ḫajât*, pl. *ḫaja*, dirt; vileness; dirty; vile.

خجاجة *ḫajjâja-t*, blockhead.

خجاف *ḫijâf*, pl. of خجيف *ḫajîf*.

خجالة *ḫijâla-t*, putting to shame, shame, bashfulness, modesty.

(خجر) *ḫajar*, foul breath; — *ḫijirr*. voracious; cowardly.

(خجف) *ḫajf*, levity; pride.

(خجل) *ḫajil*, A, INF. *ḫajal*, be silent from shame or confusion; be ashamed, blush; be luxuriant, complicated, overcharged, overbearing; — II. INF. *taḫjîl*, IV. INF. *iḫjâl*, put to shame and confusion; — VII. INF. *inḫijâl*, pass. of the previous.

خجل *ḫajal*, ة *ḫajla-t*, shame, confusion; — *ḫajil*, bashful, modest; luxuriant; worn out.

خجلان *ḫajlân*, ashamed, confused.

خجوج *ḫujûj*, whirlwind.

خجى *ḫaji'*, see (خجا); — *ḫaja*, pl. of خجاة *ḫajât*.

خجيف *ḫajîf*, pl. خجاف *ḫijâf*, thin, slim.

(خد) *ḫadd*, U, INF. *ḫadd*, split, cut; furrow; impress; — II. INF. *taḫdîd*, split, cut, tear; (also V.) grow thin, shrink, be wrinkled; — V. INF. *taḫaddud*, see II.; be split.

خد *ḫadd*, pl. *ḫudûd*, cheek; pl. *ḫidâd*, *aḫidda-t*, *ḫiddân*, furrow, track; road; trace; troop; broad side of a camel's litter; — ة *ḫudda-t*, pl. *ḫudad*, cheek; furrow.

خداب *ḫaddâb*, liar.

خداد *ḫidâd*, brand-mark on the cheek.

خدارن *ḫadârin*, pl. of خدرنق *ḫadar-naq*.

خدارة *ḥadâra-t*, chastity.
خداری *ḥudâriyy*, ة, black, dark; — ة *ḥudâriyya-t*, an eagle.
خداش *ḥidâś*, scratching (s.).
خداع *ḥaddâ'*, impostor, cheat; ة, deceptive; — *.
خدافر *ḥadâfir*, خدافل *ḥadâfil*, worn-out clothes.
خدام *ḥaddâm*, ة, skilful in serving; servant; — *ḥuddâm*, servants, pl of خادم; — *.
خدان *ḥidân*, good comeradeship; — *ḥiddân*, pl. of خد *ḥadd*.
(خدب) *ḥadab*, U, INF. *ḥadb*, wound the flesh; bite; tell a lie; milk frequently; — V. INF. *taḥaddub*, be forward and talkative.
خدد *ḥudad*, pl. of خدة *ḥudda-t*.
(خدج) *ḥadaj*, U, I, INF. *ḥidâj*, miscarry.
(خدر) *ḥadar*, U, INF. *ḥadr*, keep a girl continually in seclusion; remain, stay, abide; remain behind; get confused; — *ḥadir*, A, INF. *ḥadar*, be or get benumbed; be secluded; remain in the thicket; — II. INF. *taḥdîr*, benumb; keep secluded; drug into sleep with opium; — IV. INF. *iḥdâr*, keep secluded; — V. INF. *taḥaddur* (also VII. INF. *inḥidâr*, VIII. INF. *iḥtidâr*, IX. INF. *inḥidrâr*), be benumbed; — V. and VIII., keep secluded, hidden.
خدر *ḥidr*, pl. *ḥudûr*, *aḥdâr*, pl. pl. *aḥâdîr*, curtain, veil; women's apartment; alcove, closet; den, lair; back of a saddle; — *ḥadar*, numbness; stupefaction; indifference; rain; — *ḥadir*, ة, benumbed; wet; dark; — ة *ḥudra-t*, darkness.
خدران *ḥadrân*, benumbed.
(خدرع) *ḥadra'*, INF. ة, hasten.
خدرنق *ḥadarnaq*, pl. *ḥadârin*, male spider.
خدری *ḥudariyy*, ة, very black.
(خدش) *ḥadaś*, I, INF. *ḥadś*, *ḥuduś*, scratch, scrape; — II. INF. *taḥdiś*, do so violently.
خدش *ḥadś*, ة, pl. *ḥudûś*, scratch; rebuke; — *ḥadiś*, alarm.
(خدع) *ḥada'*, A, INF. *ḥad'*, *ḥid'*, cover, hide; deceive, outwit; not be plentiful; refuse a gift; be dull (market); be sunk; set; dry up; creep or slip into the hole; differ, be in contradiction; fold up; — III. INF. *ḥidâ'*, *muḥâda'a-t*, outwit or try to outwit; leave in the lurch; — V. INF. *taḥaddu'*, contemplate deceit; hide (n.); — VI. INF. *taḥâdu'*, try to outwit one another; pretend to be outwitted; — VII. INF. *inḥidâ'*, be or allow one's self to be outwitted; — VIII. INF. *iḥtidâ'*, deceive, outwit.
خدع *ḥad'*, *ḥid'*, ة, deceit; — *ḥadi'*, deceiver; — *ḥudu'*, pl. of خدوع *ḥadû'*; — ة *ḥuda'a-t*, pl. *ḥuda'*, deceiver, cheat; time; destiny.
(خدف) *ḥadaf*, I, INF. *ḥadf*, walk with short quick steps; live in affluence; cut; snow.
خدف *ḥadf*, oar, rudder, helm; — ة *ḥidfa-t*, pl. *ḥidaf*, rent in a garment.
(خدفل) *ḥadfal*, INF. ة, put on a worn-out garment.
(خدل) *ḥadil*, A, INF. *ḥadal*, *ḥadâla-t*, *ḥudûla-t*, be plump and round, have plump and round limbs.
خدل *ḥadl*, ة, plump and round.
خدلا *ḥadlâ'*, خدلجة *ḥadallaja-t*, خدلم *ḥidlim*, خدلة *ḥadla-t*, *ḥidla-t* (pl. *ḥidâl*), having plump and round limbs (f.).
(خدم) *ḥadam*, U, I, INF. *ḥadma-t*, *ḥidma-t*, serve; — II. INF. *taḥdîm*, make one's servant, have one's self served by (acc.); have white legs (horse, sheep); — IV. INF. *iḥdâm*, give for a servant, have one served; take as a servant; — VIII. INF. *iḥtidâm*, serve one's self; — X. INF. *istiḥdâm*, have one's self served; take into service; ask for a servant.
خدم *ḥadam*, servants, pl. of خادم

ḫâdim ; — ة ḫadma-t, an hour ; ḫidma-t, pl. ḫidam, service ; office ; official duty ; work ; present to a king or superior, gift of homage ; — ḫadama-t, pl. ḫadam, ḫidam, ḫidâm, ḫadamât, bracelet ; strap of a camel's shoe ; leg ; assembly ; pl. of خادم ḫâdim.

(خدن) ḫidn, خدين ḫadîn, pl. aḫdân, of equal age, coeval ; friend, comrade ; — III. ḫâdan, INF. muḫâdana-t, treat as a friend ; — ة ḫudana-t, friend of everybody.

خدوع ḫadû', pl. ḫuda', deceitful, deceptive.

خدوم ḫadûm, servant (m. f.).

(خدى) ḫada, I, INF. ḫady, ḫadayân, walk apace.

خديدية ḫudaidiyya-t, small cushion.

خديرة ḫadîra-t, leading a chaste and secluded life (f.).

خديعة ḫadî'a-t, pl. ḫadâ'i', deceit, treachery.

خديم ḫadîm, ḫiddîm, f. ة, servant.

خدين ḫadîn, see (خدن).

خديو ḫidîw, prince (Khedive, Pers.) ; — ى ḫidîwiyy, princely.

خذ ḫuẕ, take ! IMP. of (اخذ).

(خذ) ḫaẕẕ, U, INF. ḫaẕîẕ, suppurate, fester.

(خذا) ḫaẕa', A, INF. ḫaẕ', ḫuẕû', humble one's self, submit, obey ; — خذى ḫaẕi', A, INF. ḫaẕa', id. ; — X. INF. istiḫẕâ', submit, obey.

خذارق ḫuẕâriq, purgative water.

خذاريف ḫaẕârîf, pl. of خذروف ḫuẕrûf.

خذاريم ḫaẕârîm, pl. rags, tatters.

خذال ḫuẕẕâl, pl. of خاذل ḫâẕil, who forsakes his friend, &c.

خذامة ḫuẕâma-t, slice, morsel.

(خذرف) ḫaẕraf, INF. ة, walk apace, speed, hurry ; stir up the gravel ; fill ; sharpen ; maim.

(خذرنق) ḫaẕarnaq, pl. ḫaẕârin= خدرنق ḫadarnaq ; penis.

خذروف ḫuẕrûf, pl. ḫaẕârîf, running fast ; spinning-top.

(خذع) ḫaẕa', A, INF. ḫaẕ', cut, shred, hash.

خذع مذع ḫiẕa' miẕa', dispersing in all directions, helter-skelter.

(خذعب) ḫaẕ'ab, INF. ة, cut, shred.

(خذعل) ḫiẕ'il, stupid woman ; — ḫaẕ'al, INF. ة, cut into small slices.

(خذف) ḫaẕaf, I, INF. ḫaẕf, fling away.

(خذق) ḫaẕaq, I, U, INF. ḫaẕq, drop excrement ; urge on ; spur.

خذق ḫaẕq, excrement, dung.

(خذل) ḫaẕal, U, INF. ḫaẕl, ḫiẕlân, leave in the lurch, forsake ; remain behind ;—II. INF. taḫẕîl, cause to forsake ; — III. INF. muḫâẕala-t, leave helpless in the lurch ; — VI. INF. taḫâẕul, leave one another in the lurch ; —VII. INF. inḫiẕâl, find one's self helplessly forsaken and flee.

خذل ḫaẕl, abandonment ; — ة ḫaẕala-t, pl. forsaken ones ; — ḫuẕala-t, who leaves frequently in the lurch.

خذلان ḫiẕlân, forsaking, leaving in the lurch (s.) ; desertion ; cowardice.

(خذلم) ḫaẕlam, INF. ة, hasten (n.).

(خذم) ḫaẕam, I, INF. ḫaẕm, cut, cut into pieces ; clutch ;—ḫaẕim, A, INF. ḫaẕam, be cut off, lopped ; be drunk ; hasten (n.) ;—II. INF. taḫẕîm, cut well ;—IV. INF. iḫẕâm, intoxicate ; — V. INF. taḫaẕẕum, cut ; be cut off.

خذم ḫaẕim, cutting, sharp ; swift ; worn-out ; liberal.

(خذو) ḫaẕâ, U, INF. ḫaẕw, be flaccid, flabby, pendulous ; be fat.

خذو ḫuẕû, submissiveness.

خذوم ḫaẕûm, sharp ; swift.

(خذى) ḫaẕî, A, INF. ḫaẕ-an, hang down flabbily ; — X. INF. istiḫẕâ', humble one's self ; treat kindly.

خذى ḫuẕayy, donkey.

خذيذ ḫaẕîẕ, suppuration.

خذيعة ḫaẕî'a-t, hashed meat.

خذيم ḫaẕîm, cut off ; drunk.

(خر) ḫarr, I, U, INF. ḫarîr, ripple ; roar ; buzz ; snore ; — I, U, INF. ḫarr, ḫurûr, fall, fall from on

high; prostrate one's self in adoration; split, cut; attack from an ambush; die.

خر *ḥurr*, hole in the millstone to put the corn in; pl. *ḥirara-t*, channel; gutter; — *ḥur'*, pl. *ḥurû'*, *ḥur'ân*, also—

خرا *ḥirâ'*, excrement.

خراب *ḥarâb*, pl. *aḥriba-t*, *ḥirab*, noun of unity ة *ḥarâba-t*, pl. *ḥarâbât*, devastation; ruin, destruction; wilderness; robbed, devastated, deserted; — ة *ḥurâba-t*, rope of palm-leaves; —also *ḥarrâba-t*, *ḥurrâba-t*, eye of a needle;—ية *ḥarâbiyya-t*, devastation.

خراج *ḥarâj*, *ḥurâj*, pl. *aḥrija-t*, poll-tax; land-tax; tax; tribute; public revenue; — *ḥurâj*, *ḥurrâj*, eruption of the skin; tumour, abscess; — *ḥarrâj*, rich in expedients; prudent, cunning.

خراجي *ḥarâjjiyy*, pl. ة, tax-gatherer.

خرار *ḥarrâr*, murmuring, rippling; — ة *ḥarrâra-t*, spinning-top; waterfall, cascade; (m.) sink.

خراريت *ḥarârît*, pl. of خريت *ḥirrît*.

خراز *ḥarrâz*, cobbler; shoe-maker; belt-maker.

خراس *ḥarrâs*, maker of jugs.

خراسان *ḥurâsân*, Khorasan; — ى *ḥurâsâniyy*, خراسى *ḥurâsiyy*, of Khorasan.

خراش *ḥirâś*, irritation; pl. *aḥriśa-t*, brand-mark of a camel; — *ḥurâś*, scar; — ة *ḥurâśa-t*, filings; — ى *ḥarâśiyy*, pl. of خرشا *ḥirśâ'*.

خراص *ḥarrâṣ*, liar; — *ḥurrâṣ*, pl. of خارص *ḥâriṣ*, who estimates the produce of fruit; — ة *ḥirâṣa-t*, emendation, reparation.

خراط *ḥarrâṭ*, tumour; maker of boxes, spindles, &c.; who puts a false construction on another's speech, liar; — *; — ة *ḥirâṭa-t*, trade of a turner; (m.) sill.

خراطيم *ḥarâṭîm*, pl. of خرطوم *ḥurṭûm*.

خراطين *ḥarâṭîn*, pl. earth-worms.

خراف *ḥarâf*, *ḥirâf*, gathering of fruit; — ة *ḥurâfa-t*, gathered fruit; wonderful tale, fairy tale, funny story; witticism.

خرام *ḥurrâm*, pl. obdurate sinners; — ة *ḥarâma-t*, INF. of (خرم).

خرامل *ḥarâmil*, pl. old clothes.

(خرب) *ḥarab*, I, INF. *ḥarb*, devastate, destroy, demolish, depopulate; turn a robber; strike on or wound the ear; pierce; split, tear; — INF. *ḥarb*, *ḥurûb*, *ḥarâba-t*, *ḥirâba-t*, steal camels; — *ḥarib*, A, INF. *ḥarâb*, be devastated, &c.; INF. *ḥarab*, have the ear split; — II. INF. *taḥrîb*, devastate, destroy, ruin; (m.) injure, spoil; — IV. INF. *iḥrâb*, id.; — V. INF. *taḥarrub*, VII. INF. *inḥirâb*, get devastated, destroyed; — X. INF. *istiḥrâb*, wish to destroy.

خرب *ḥarb*, round hole; eye of a needle; — *ḥarab*, devastation, ruin; degeneration of religion; pl. *aḥrâb*, *ḥirâb*, *ḥirbân*, male bustard; — *ḥarib*, devastated, depopulated; — ة *ḥarba-t*, pl. *ḥarabât*, sieve; also *ḥurba-t*, any round hole; eye of a needle; hollow of the ear; handle of a travelling-bag, travelling-bag; — *ḥirba-t*, pl. *ḥirab*, devastated place, ruin; — *ḥaraba-t*, fault, default, want; vileness; — *ḥariba-t*, pl. -*ât*, *ḥarib*, *ḥarâ'ib*, devastated place.

خربا *ḥarbâ'*, split, slit (adj. f.).

خربان *ḥirbân*, pl. of خرب *ḥarab*; — *ḥiribbân*, cowardly.

(خربد) *ḥurabid*, sour milk.

(خربز) *ḥirbiz*, water-melon.

(خربش) *ḥarbaś*, INF. ة, spoil, ruin; (also II. INF. *taḥarbuś*), write badly, scribble; (m.) scratch; — ة *ḥarbaśa-t*, scribble, scrawl.

خربص *ḥarbaṣ*, INF. ة, eat off all the herbage; carry off everything; distinguish between; separate from one another.

(خربط) *ḥarbaṭ*, INF. put out of order,

spoil; put into bad humour; — II. INF. *taḥarbuṭ*, pass. of the previous.

(خربق) *ḥarbaq*, INF. ة, *ḥirbâq*, bring out of order, spoil; cut, tear; walk fast; break wind; — III. INF. *iḥrinbâq*, sneak in; steal; (m.) crouch, sit on the hind legs.

خربق *ḥarbuq*, hellebore.

خربندى *ḥarbandiyy*, pl. ة, ass-driver, muleteer (Pers.).

(خرت) *ḥarat*, U, INF. *ḥart*, pierce, make holes; — *ḥarit*, A, INF. *ḥarat*, know the roads well to serve as a guide.

خرت *ḥurt*, pl. *ḥurût*, *aḥrât*, hole; eye of a needle; hollow of the ear.

خرثا *ḥarsâ'*, woman with loose flesh and big hips.

خرثمة *ḥarsama-t*, tip of a toe; top of a shoe.

خرثى *ḥarsiyy*, lumber; booty.

(خرج) *ḥaraj*, U, INF. *ḥurûj*, *maḥraj*, come out, come forth, issue (n.), go aside; terminate, come to an issue; revolt; be an exception to a rule; — INF. *ḥurûj*, get informed, instructed; — II. INF. *taḥrîj*, cause to come out, &c.; instruct, educate; (m.) subtract; — III. INF. *muḥâraja-t*, divide by lot; — IV. INF. *iḥrâj*, *muḥraj*, make come out; take or draw out; expel; translate; demand or pay tribute; subtract; — V. INF. *taḥarruj*, be educated, educate one's self; — VIII. INF. *iḥtirâj*, bring out, produce, derive; — IX. INF. *iḥrijâj*, be spotted black and white; — X. INF. *istiḥrâj*, make come out, make to spring from, ask one to bring out; draw out; derive; extract, distil; get as result of a calculation; translate; require tribute; — XI. INF. *iḥrîjâj*=IX.

خرج *ḥarj*, *ḥurj*, pl. *aḥrâj*, *aḥrija-t*, *aḥârîj*, produce, income; expenditure, costs; tribute; (m.) assistance, subsidies; requisites of a workman; mortar; cement; fit, convenient; — *ḥurj*, pl. *ḥiraja-t*, portmanteau, large travelling-bag; — *ḥaraj*, mixture of white and black; — *ḥuruj*, pl. of خروج *ḥarûj*; — ة *ḥuraja-t*, who goes frequently in and out.

خرجا *ḥarjâ'*, f. of اخرج *aḥraj*, spotted white and black.

خرجية *ḥarjiyya-t*, means of subsistance; what one is able to spend.

خرخار *ḥarḥâr*, running water.

(خرخر) *ḥarḥar*, INF. ة, produce a rattling noise; — II. INF. *taḥarḥur*, id.; waddle.

خرخر *ḥirḥir*, خرخور *ḥarḥûr*, yielding much milk; effeminate; — ى *ḥirḥiriyy*, thin, weak.

(خرد) *ḥarid*, A, INF. *ḥarad*, be intact; be very chaste; behave bashfully, keep a modest silence or speak with modesty; — IV. INF. *iḥrâd*, be bashful, and, by opposition, be inclined to sport and jest.

خرد *ḥarad*, bashful silence; — *ḥurud*, *ḥurad*, *ḥurrad*, pl. of خريد *ḥarîd*; — ة *ḥurda-t*, small goods (Pers.).

(خرداذى) *ḥardâziyy*, wine.

خردجى *ḥurdajiyy*, pl. ة, haberdasher.

(خردق) *ḥardaq*, broth; — *ḥurduq*, small shot; — hence *ḥardaq*, INF. ة, disperse (a.); — II. INF. *taḥarduq*, disperse (n.).

(خردل) *ḥardal*, mustard, mustard-seed; cress; — ة *ḥardala-t*, grain of mustard-seed.

خردل *ḥardal*, INF. ة, hash meat; eat the best of a dish.

خررة *ḥirara-t*, pl. river-beds.

(خرز) *ḥaraz*, U, I, INF. *ḥarz*, sew with the awl; stitch together; mend, patch, cobble; — *ḥariz*, A, INF. *ḥaraz*, do one's work well, establish solidly.

خرز *ḥaraz*, small shells or beads for ornament; خ الظهر *ḥaraz az-zahr*, spine; — ة *ḥurza-t*, pl. *ḥuraz*, stitch of an awl; — *ḥaraza-t*, jewel, pearl; خ البئر *ḥaraza-t al-bi'r*, parapet of a well.

خرزاف *ḥirzâf*, ة *ḥirzâfa-t*, who sits in company in an improper manner; great talker.

(خرزف) *ḥarzaf*, INF. ة, tremble in walking.

(خرس) *ḥaris*, A, INF. *ḥaras*, drink from the cask; be dumb; — II. INF. *taḥrîs*, make dumb, create dumb; prepare food for a confined woman; — IV. INF. *iḥrâs*, make dumb, strike dumb; — V. INF. *taḥarrud*, prepare for one's self food fit for a confined woman.

خرس *ḥars*, *ḥirs*, pl. *ḥurûs*, wine-cask; — *ḥurs*, ة *ḥursa-t*, food for a confined woman; banquet on account of the birth of a child; *ḥurs*, pl. of اخرس *aḥras*, dumb; — *ḥaras*, dumbness; — ة *ḥursa-t*, confined woman.

خرسا *ḥarsâ'*, f. خرسان *ḥursân*, pl. of اخرس *aḥras*, dumb.

خرستان *ḥuristân*, cupboard in a wall.

(خرش) *ḥaraś*, I, INF. *ḥarś*, also VIII. INF. *iḥtirâś*, scrape, scrape off; draw the camel towards one's self; earn a sustenance for one's family.

خرش *ḥaraś*, pl. *ḥuruś*, lumber; — ة *ḥaraśa-t*, a fly.

خرشا *ḥirśâ*, pl. *ḥarâśiyy*, spittle; foam; phlegm; thin skin on the milk; slough; broken egg-shell.

(خرشاف) *ḥirśâf*, very rough, impassable ground.

(خرشب) *ḥarśab*, INF. ة, perform negligently, bungle, daub.

خرشب *ḥurśub*, big, stout, fat; hard, rough.

خرشعة *ḥarśa'a-t*, pl. *ḥarśa'*, *ḥarâśi'*, small mountain-top.

خرشف *ḥarśuf*, خرشوف *ḥarśûf*, artichoke.

(خرشوم) *ḥurśûm*, rocky mountains; high mountain; very rugged ground; (m.) groove in upper lip between mouth and nose.

(خرص) *ḥaraṣ*, I, INF. *ḥarṣ*, estimate the produce of a palm-tree, &c.; rate a number approximately; give one's opinion; lie, speak untruth; dam in a river; — INF. *ḥirâṣa-t*, mend, put to rights again; — *ḥariṣ*, A, INF. *ḥaraṣ*, starve; — III. INF. *muḥâraṣa-t*, give in exchange; — V. INF. *taḥarruṣ*, calumniate; — VIII. INF. *iḥtirâṣ*, forge lies; put into a bag, pocket.

(خرص) *ḥarṣ*, *ḥirṣ*, *ḥurṣ*, lance of reed or its head; — *ḥirṣ*, estimation of the produce; supposition, surmise, opinion; — *ḥirṣ*, *ḥurṣ*, leafless palm-branch; travelling-bag, basket; pl. *ḥirṣân*, ring; wooden stopple; — *ḥurṣ*, *ḥuraṣ*, *ḥuruṣ*, pl. *aḥrâṣ*, piece of wood for taking out the honey; — *ḥariṣ*, starving.

خرضة *ḥurḍa-t*=خردة *ḥurda-t*, small goods.

(خرط) *ḥaraṭ*, U, I, INF. *ḥarṭ*, shell, strip off bark, leaves, berries; deflower; lie with; turn (on a lathe); send, let loose, let down; purge; break wind; (m.) forge lies, invent stories, chatter; be restive and run away; yield turned or watery milk on account of sickness; — II. INF. *taḥrîṭ*, purge; — VIII. INF. *inḥirâṭ*, be turned (on a lathe); be strung up; be slender, slim, light; walk fast; travel far; sttempt a thing without sufficient knowledge; insult in words or deeds; — VIII. INF. *iḥtirâṭ*, unsheathe; strip a bunch of grapes by drawing it through the mouth; — X. INF. *istiḥrâṭ*, cry violently and unceasingly; — XIII. INF. *iḥriwwâṭ*,

get entangled; be long; extend (n.); walk or travel fast.

(خرط) *ḫarṭ*, turning (on a lathe, s.); — *ḫirṭ*, male partridge; — *ḫurṭ*, pl. of خروط *ḫarûṭ*.

(خرطل) *ḫarṭal*, oats.

(خرطش) *ḫarṭaś*, INF. ة, scribble.

(خرطم) *ḫurṭum*, pl. *ḫarâṭim*, nose, snout; — *ḫarṭam*, INF. ة, strike on or take by the nose; — III. INF. *iḫrinṭâm*, be proud; be angry.

خرطوم *ḫurṭûm*, pl. *ḫarâṭim*, trunk, snout, muzzle, nose; ugly face; sucking pipe of a pump, &c.; spout.

(خرع) *ḫara'*, A, INF. *ḫar'*, split, break; — *ḫari'*, A, INF. *ḫara'*, be weak, relaxed, split, broken, sprained; — *ḫaru'*, INF. *ḫur'*, *ḫurû'*, *ḫarâ'a-t*, have weak or relaxed limbs, be weak; — II. INF. *taḫrî'*, relax (a.), lame; discourage; — VII. INF. *inḫirâ'*, be split, broken, relaxed, weak, sprained; — VIII. INF. *iḫtirâ'*, split (a.); derive; invent; produce, frame, create; perform anything new.

خرع *ḫar'*, incision; relaxation, weakness; — *ḫari'*, weak, relaxed.

(خرعب) *ḫar'ab*, also خرعوب *ḫur'ûb*, ة *ḫur'ûba-t*, fresh branch; delicate, slim, and at the same time full girl.

(خرف) *ḫaraf*, U, INF. *ḫarf*, *ḫarâf*, *ḫirâf*, *maḫraf*, cull or gather fruit; pass. be moistened with autumn rains; — *ḫarif*, A, INF. *ḫaraf*, be out of mind, delirious, dote; — *ḫaruf*, INF. *ḫarûfa-t*, id.; — II. INF. *taḫrîf*, deem or declare weak-minded or imbecile; — IV. INF. *iḫrâf*, spoil; have ripe dates; — VIII. INF. *iḫtirâf*, cull.

خرف *ḫarf*, slender she-camel; — *ḫaraf*, delirium; dotage; a bad kind of date; — *ḫarif*, imbecile, idiotic, doting, delirious; — ة *ḫurfa-t*, autumn fruit; — *ḫurafa-t*, fairy tale, funny story, &c.

خرفان *ḫarfân*, dotard; — *ḫirfân*, pl. of خروف *ḫurûf*.

(خرفج) *ḫarfaj*, INF. ة, take or contain much; — *ḫurfaj*, خرفيج *ḫirfîj*, abundance; — *ḫurafij*, fat.

(خرفش) *ḫarfaś*, INF. ة, mix, mix up, confuse; speak confusedly.

(خرفق) *ḫarfaq*, mustard seed; cress.

خرفى *ḫarfa*, peas; — *ḫarfiy*, *ḫirfiyy*, autumnal.

(خرق) *ḫaraq*, U, I, INF. *ḫarq*, tear; to fill; open a way, travel over; permeate, forge lies, lie; INF. *ḫurûq*, stop indoors; — *ḫariq*, A, INF. *ḫaraq*, stop indoors; act awkwardly or foolishly; cower; — *ḫaruq*, INF. *ḫarâqa-t*, manage badly; be stupid, foolish; — II. INF. *taḫrîq*, tear violently; lie with impudence; (m.) stop indoors; cower; — V. INF. *taḫarruq*, be torn, pierced, crippled; have rents; spend all one has; forge lies; — VII. INF. *inḫirâq*, get torn, get impregnated, drenched, &c.; — VIII. INF. *iḫtirâq*, make one's self a way; blow through; pierce through; forge lies; — XII. INF. *iḫrîqâq*, be torn.

خرق *ḫarq*, rent, cleft, split; خ العادة *ḫarq al-'âda-t*, anything out of the way, extraordinary; pl. *ḫurûq*, tract exposed to the winds, desert; — *ḫirq*, pl. *aḫrâq*, *ḫurrâq*, *ḫurûq*, very liberal, open handed; a handsome noble youth; — *ḫurq*, awkwardness, stupidity; misplaced harshness; pl. of اخرق *aḫraq*, awkward, &c.; — *ḫaraq*, being out of one's senses with fear or shame; apathy; — *ḫariq*, ة, out of one's senses with fear or shame; senseless, apathetic; awkward, clumsy; — *ḫuruq*, pl. of خريق

ḫarîq ; — ḫurraq, pl. ḫarâriq, sparrow ; — ة ḫirqa-t, pl. ḫiraq, rag, tatter ; strip of cloth ; garment made of patches ; garment of a penitent.

خرقاهة ḫarqâha-t, tent.

(خرقل) ḫarqal, INF. ة, aim well and hit.

خركاه ḫarkâh, ة ḫarkâha-t, tent (Pers.).

(خرم) ḫaram, I, INF. ḫarm, unsew ; cut off ; pierce the partition of the nose ; deviate ; — ḫarim, A, INF. ḫaram, have the partition of the nose or the ear pierced ; — ḫarum, INF. ḫarâma-t, talk or act at random ; live extravagantly ; — II. INF. taḫrîm, unsew ; embroider ; enchase ; — V. INF. taḫarrum, be unsewn ; be torn ; eradicate ; rush into extravagance and follies ; (m.) be embroidered, enchased ; — VII. INF. inḫirâm, be torn ; break (n.) ; — VIII. INF. iḫtirâm, carry off ; cut off.

خرم ḫarm, ḫurm, pl. ḫurûm, towering mountain-top ; suppression of a short syllable in the beginning of a verse ; — ḫurm, pl. ḫurûm, (m.) eye of a needle ; ḫurm, pl. (خرما ḫarmâ', f.) of اخرم aḫram, having the partition of the nose or the ear pierced ; — ة ḫarama-t, pierced partition of the nose ; — ḫurrama-t, bean.

(خرمس) ḫirmis, dark night ; — III. اخرمس iḫrammas, INF. iḫrimmâs, iḫrinmâs, humble one's self, submit, cringe ; keep silent.

(خرمش) ḫarmaś, INF. ة, scribble over, spoil ; efface ; (m.) scratch.

(خرمص), اخرمص iḫramaṣṣ, INF. iḫrimṣâṣ, keep silent.

(خرمل) ḫirmil, stupid woman ; decrepit old woman ; — II. INF. taḫarmul, be torn.

خرمية ḫurramiyya-t, believers in metempsychosis and leaders of a loose life.

(خرنف) ḫarnaf, INF. ة, strike.

(خرنق) ḫirniq, pl. ḫarâniq, young hare, rabbit.

خرنوب ḫarnûb, ḫurnûb, خروب ḫarrûb, carob-tree.

(خرنوص) ḫirnauṣ, sucking-pig.

خرو ḫurû', excrement ; — ḫurwa-t, pl. ḫurât, hole of the iron of an axe, &c. ; — ḫuru'a-t, stool, easing of the bowels.

خروج ḫarûj, going out ; pl. ḫuruj, long-necked ; — ḫurûj, INF. of (خرج), coming out, issue, &c. ; apostacy ; rebellion ; Day of Judgment.

خرود ḫarûd, virtuous woman, matron.

خروط ḫarûṭ, pl. ḫurṭ, restive.

خروع ḫirwa', palma Christi, ricinus ; — *.

خروف ḫarûf, pl. aḫrifa-t, ḫirfân, ḫirâf, lamb, sheep.

خرى ḫary, written document ; — ḫurriyy, hole in the mill-stone for putting in the corn.

(خرى) ḫari', A, INF. ḫar', ḫir', ḫarâ'a-t, ḫurû', ease the bowels.

خريان ḫirriyân, coward.

خريت ḫirrît, pl. ḫarârît, experienced guide.

خريج ḫirrîj, refined ; pupil, disciple.

خريد ḫarîd, ة ḫarîda-t, pl. ḫarâ'id, ḫurud, ḫurad, ḫurrad, ḫirâd, virgin ; bashful, modest, virtuous woman ; — ة ḫarîda-t, unbored pearl.

خرير ḫarîr, ripple, murmur of flowing water ; snoring ; rumbling noise.

خريص ḫarîṣ, spices ; cold water ; starving (adj.) ; bay, gulf ; — ة ḫarîṣa-t, also خريضة ḫarîḍa-t, handsome girl.

خريطة ḫarîṭa-t, pl. ḫarâ'iṭ, leathern bag ; satchel of a schoolboy ; post-bag ; letter.

خريطى ḫarîṭiyy, maker of leathern bags ; — ḫurraiṭa, bitter tears.

خريع ḫarî', ة, weak, flabby ; — ḫirrî', saffron in bloom ; — ة

ḥarî'a-t, delicately reared woman; adultress.

خريف *ḥarîf*, autumn; autumn rain; culled, reaped; ivy; doting; — ة *ḥarîfa-t*, palm-tree whose fruit is rented; — ى *ḥarîfiyy*, autumnal.

حريق *ḥarîq*, ة, torn, injured; crippled, pierced through; furrow; ditch; pl. *ḥuruq*, plain with vegetation; violent cold wind; pl. *ḥarâ'iq*, *ḥurûq*, continuously blowing wind; — *ḥirrîq*, exceedingly liberal.

حريم *ḥarîm*, dissolute, licentious.

(حز) *ḥazz*, INF. *ḥazz*, also VIII. INF. *iḥtizâz*, pierce and nail; protect a wall with pikes, &c.

حز *ḥazz*, pl. *ḥuzûz*, silk; silk-ware; beaver-hair.

حزاز *ḥazzâz*, silk-merchant.

حزاع *ḥazâ'*, death; — ة *ḥazâ'a-t*, slice, piece.

حزاف *ḥazzâf*, potter; dealer in earthenware.

حزام *ḥazâm*, ة *ḥazâma-t*, ring for the nose; — *ḥazzâm*, maker and seller of bast-ropes; — ة *ḥizâma-t*, pl. *ḥazâ'im*, *ḥizâm*, nose-ring of a camel; strap; — ى *ḥuzâma*, lavender.

حزان *ḥazzân*, collector; — *ḥizzân*, pl. of حزز *ḥuzaz*; — *ḥuzzân*, pl. of حازن *ḥâzin*, ag. of (حزن); — ة *ḥizâna-t*, pl. *ḥazâ'in*, treasure; collection; magazine; barn; chamber of a gun; INF. of (حزن).

حزايا *ḥazâyâ*, pl. of حزيان *ḥazyân*.

حزائم *ḥazâ'im*, pl. of حزامة *ḥizâma-t* and حزومة *ḥazûma-t*.

حزائن *ḥazâ'in*, pl. of حزانة *ḥizâna-t*.

حزاية *ḥazâya-t*, putting to shame (s.); shame, disgrace.

(حزب) *ḥazib*, A, INF. *ḥazab*, be or seem to be swollen.

(حزبر), II. *taḥazbar*, INF. *taḥazbur*, be proud; frown; kick with the fore feet.

(حزحز) *ḥuzḥuz*, firm of muscle, muscular.

(حزر) *ḥazar*, U, INF. *ḥazr*, look with compressed eyelids; look askance; be sly; flee; — *ḥazir*, A, INF. *ḥazar*, be narrow and small; be awry; — VI. INF. *taḥâzur*, compress the eyelids in order to see sharper.

حزر *ḥazr*, looking askance (s.); — *ḥazar*, narrowness and wryness of the eyes; fat broth; بحر الخ *baḥr al-ḥazar*, Caspian Sea.

حزران *ḥazurân*, bamboo.

حزربة *ḥazraba-t*, confusion of speech.

(حزرج) *ḥazraj*, INF. ة, limp.

(حزرف) *ḥazraf*, INF. ة, walk along proudly.

(حزرنق) *ḥazarnaq*, male spider.

حزز *ḥuzaz*, pl. *ḥizzân*, *aḥizza-t*, male hare.

(حزع) *ḥaza'*, A, INF. *ḥaz'*, cut off; retain, remain behind, abandon one's people; — II. INF. *taḥzî'*, cut off; retain, keep back; — V. INF. *taḥazzu'*, cut off; remain behind and forsake one's people; carve and distribute between each other; — VII. INF. *inḥizâ'*, break in the middle (n.); — VIII. INF. *iḥtizâ'*, separate one from his people and retain him.

(حزعبل) *ḥuza'bal*, ة *ḥuza'bala-t*, حزعبيل *ḥuza'bîl*, ة *ḥuza'bîla-t*, invented story, idle tale; fable; anything untrue, ridiculous.

(حزعل) *ḥaz'al*, INF. ة, limp, throw the feet about in walking.

حزعل *ḥaz'al*, hyena.

(حزف) *ḥazaf*, I, INF. *ḥazf*, walk proudly along with swinging arms.

حزف *ḥazaf*, earthenware; — ى *ḥazafiyy*, earthen; brittle; potter; dealer in earthenware.

(حزق) *ḥazaq*, I, INF. *ḥazq*, hit and pierce; penetrate, permeate; (m.) tear; drop excrement; — II. INF. *taḥzîq*, tear; — V. INF. *taḥazzuq*, VII. INF. *inḥizâq*, get pierced; get torn; — VIII. INF. *iḥtizâq*, be drawn (sword).

خرق *ḥazq*, rent, hole.

(خزك) *ḥazik*, A, INF. *ḥazak*, persist.

(خزل) *ḥazal*, A, INF. *ḥazal*, walk heavily; cut, lop; prevent, hinder; — *ḥazil*, A, INF. *ḥazal*, have a broken back; walk heavily; — VII. INF. *inḥizâl*, walk heavily; cease to speak; abstain from answering; be torn off, loosened; separate from (n.), forsake; — VIII. INF. *inḥizâl*, cut or tear off; separate another from his people; separate from one's people.

خزل *ḥazl*, making quiescent the second letter of a foot when it has a vowel, and suppressing the fourth when it is quiescent.

(خزلب) *ḥazlab*, cut off quickly.

(خزلج), II. تخزلج *taḥazlaj*, INF. *taḥazluj*, hurry, speed along.

(خزم) *ḥazam*, I, INF. *ḥazm*, split; pierce; pierce the partition of a camel's nose; string pearls; spit locusts; — II. INF. *taḥzîm*, put a ring in the camel's nose.

خزم *ḥazm*, suppression of the first letter of a *watad mafrûq* at the beginning of a verse; — *ḥazam*, tree with abundance of bast.

(خزن) *ḥazan*, U, I, INF. *ḥazn*, store, hoard; restrain one's tongue; keep secret, conceal; — INF. *ḥuzn*, *ḥuzûn*, be deteriorated, putrid; — *ḥazin*, A, INF. *ḥazan*, also *ḥazun*, INF. *ḥazâna-t*, id.; — IV. INF. *iḥzân*, VIII. INF. *iḥtizân*, hoard treasures; enrich one's self; — ة *ḥazna-t*, treasure, treasury; store-room, for valuable furniture; — *ḥazana-t*, pl. of خازن *ḥâzin*, treasurer, cashier.

خزندار *ḥazandâr*, *ḥaznadâr*, treasurer.

خزنزر *ḥazanzar*, mischievous, malicious, of a wicked disposition.

(خزو) *ḥazâ*, U, INF. *ḥazw*, subdue, tame, lead, rule, dominate; possess; turn aside from (a.); be hostile to (acc.); slit the tongue of a camel's foal.

خزوم *ḥazûm*, ة, pl. *ḥazâ'im*, cow.

(خزى) *ḥaza*, I, put to shame, abash, make to blush, disgrace;—*ḥaza*, A, INF. *ḥizy*, *ḥaz-an*, fall into misery or disgrace, be despised; — INF. *ḥaz-an*, *ḥazâya-t*, be ashamed, blush; — III. INF. *muḥâzât*, disgrace, put to shame; — IV. INF. *iḥzâ'*, bring into misery and disgrace, abase; visit, afflict; destroy; — X. INF. *istiḥzâ*, be ashamed, blush.

خزى *ḥazy*, *ḥizy*, shame, disgrace, foul thing; — *ḥazî* (خز *ḥaz-in*), ashamed; — ة *ḥazya-t*, visitation, affliction; disgrace, abasement.

خزيان *ḥazyân*, f. *ḥazyâ'*, pl. *ḥazâyâ*, ashamed, abashed.

خزيبة *ḥuzaiba-t*, gold mine.

خزيز *ḥazîz*, thorn hedge.

خزينة *ḥazîna-t*, treasure, treasury, collection.

خزيى *ḥazya*, f. bashful.

(خس) *ḥass*, INF. *ḥissa-t*, *ḥasâsa-t*, be ignoble, mean, low-minded; be miserly, avaricious; (m.) injure, damage; — U, make one's share small; — IV. INF. *iḥsâs*, act meanly; find mean; — X. INF. *iḥtisâs*, deem or find mean, vile, miserly.

خس *ḥass*, lettuce, salad;—ة *ḥissa-t*, meanness, avarice.

(خسا) *ḥasa'*, A, INF. *ḥas'*, *ḥusû'*, drive or scare away; be driven away, removed; be blunt, dim; — *ḥasi'*, A. INF. *ḥasa'*, be driven away.

خسا *ḥas-an*, pl. *aḥâsî*, odd (number).

خسار *ḥasâr*, ة *ḥasâra-t*, loss, damage.

خساس *ḥisâs*, pl. of خسيس; — ة *ḥasâsa-t*, meanness, vileness; avarice; small share, a little; — *ḥusâsa-t*, horse-race.

خساق *ḥassâq*, liar.

خسال *ḥisâl*, pl. of خسيل *ḥasîl*; — *ḥussâl*, reprobate (s.); — ة

ḥusâla-t, metallic splinters; silver.

خسر *ḥasar*, I, INF. *ḥasr*, *ḥusr*, *ḥusur*, *ḥasâr*, *ḥusrân*, *ḥasâra-t*, lose one's way, go astray; — INF. *ḥusr*, *ḥusrân*, also *ḥasir*, A, INF. *ḥasar*, have a loss, suffer damage, get cheated; — INF. *ḥasr*, *ḥusrân*, diminish; — II. INF. *taḥsîr*, damage, cause a loss to (acc.); — IV. INF. *iḥsâr*, diminish; falsify the weight; fall short.

خسر *ḥasr*, *ḥusr*, and—

خسران *ḥasrân*, loss, damage.

(خسع) *ḥusi'* (pass.), INF. *ḥas'*, be turned off, refused.

(خسف) *ḥasaf*, I, INF. *ḥusûf*, sink, disappear, vanish; get eclipsed; lose the milk; — INF. *ḥasf*, diminish (a. and n.); cause to lose the milk; — VII. INF. *in-ḥisâf*, get eclipsed.

خسف *ḥasf*, diminution, decrease; abasement; place where water appears; walnut; على الخ *'ala 'l-ḥasf*, fasting; شرب على الخ *śarib 'ala 'l-ḥasf*, drink without eating; — *ḥusuf*, pl. of خاسف *ḥâsif*, lean, &c., خسوف *ḥasuf* and خسيف *ḥasîf*.

(خسق) *ḥasaq*, I, INF. *ḥasq*, hit and pierce.

(خسل) *ḥasal*, U, INF. *ḥasl*, refuse, reject.

(خسم) *ḥasam*, subtract; cut through a bone; remove a difficulty; — VII. INF. *inḥisâm*, get removed; get finished.

خسو *ḥusû'*, INF. of (خسا).

خسوف *ḥasûf*, pl. *aḥfisa-t*, *ḥusaf*, perennial well in a rock; — *ḥusûf*, eclipse of the moon; sinking (s.), decline, decay, ruin.

(خسى), II. *ḥassa*, INF. *taḥsiya-t*, play at odds and evens with nuts; — VI. INF. *taḥâsî*, pelt each other with stones.

خسى *ḥasi'*, see (خسا); — *ḥasiyy*, also—

خسيج *ḥasîj*, woollen blanket; coat of a woollen cloth; tent.

خسير *ḥasîr*, suffering a loss (adj.); gone astray.

خسيس *ḥasîs*, ة, f. *ḥisâs*, *aḥissâ'*, vile, mean, miserly; — ة *ḥasî-sa-t*, pl. *ḥasâ'is*, low extraction or position; vileness, meanness, avarice.

خسيعة *ḥasî'a-t*, dregs of the populace.

خسيف *ḥasîf*, ة, blinded by pressure; well almost dried up; shallow; pl. *ḥusuf* = خسوف *ḥasûf*.

خسيل *ḥasîl*, pl. *ḥasâ'il*, *ḥisâl*, very mean, vile, bad.

(خش) *ḥaśś*, U, INF. *ḥaśś*, put a wooden ring in the camel's nose; enter on; revile; call forth a noise, &c.; — IV. INF. *iḥśâś*, put on the nose-ring; — VII. INF. *inḥiśâś*, enter on; mix with the people.

خشا *ḥaś-an*, *ḥiś-an*, fear; — *ḥaśśâ'*, gravel and clay ground; hornet's nest; — *ḥiśśâ'*, scarecrow; — ة *ḥaśât*, fear.

خشاب *ḥaśśâb*, wood-seller.

خشار *ḥuśâr*, ة *ḥuśâra-t*, husks of oats; remains, crumbs; dregs of the populace; worst parts.

خشاش *ḥaśâś*, *ḥiśâś*, *ḥuśâś*, insects, reptiles, birds; sparrows; bold, active, penetrating; — *ḥiśâś*, pl. *aḥiśśa-t*, wooden nose-ring of a camel.

خشاف *ḥuśâf*, sherbet of raisin-juice (m.); — *ḥuśśâf*, bat (animal).

خشام *ḥuśâm*, broad; lion; — *ḥaśśâm*, broad-nosed.

خشايا *ḥaśâyâ*, pl. of خشيا *ḥaśyâ'*.

خشب *ḥaśab*, I, INF. *ḥaśb*, mix together; choose, select; smooth, polish; forge; — II. INF. *taḥśîb*, wainscot, floor with wood; put wooden handcuffs on a prisoner (acc.); — V. INF. *taḥaśśub*, chew and eat wood; — VIII. INF. *iḥtiśâb*, sketch roughly out a

poetical composition; — XII. *iḥśauśab*, INF. *iḥśîśâb*, be long, lean, and bony.

خشب *ḥaśab*, pl. *ḥuśb*, *ḥaśab*, *ḥuśub*, *ḥuśbân*, *aḥśâb*, hard wood, timber-wood; ة *ḥaśaba-t*, piece of wood; (gun-) stock, (gun-) carriage; (weaver's) loom; — *ḥuśub*, pl. of خشيب *ḥaśîb*.

خشبا *ḥaśbâ*, f. of اخشب *aḥśab*, rough to the touch, &c.

(خشتق) *ḥastaq*, hemp; silk (Pers.).

خشخاش *ḥaśḥâś*, poppy; troop of armed men; also ة *ḥaśḥâśa-t*, charnel-house.

(خشخش) *ḥaśḥaś*, INF. ة, make a noise, clatter, &c.; — II. INF. *taḥaśḥuś*, id.; hide (n.).

خشخشة *ḥaśḥaśa-t*, noise, clatter, &c.

(خشر) *ḥaśar*, INF. *ḥaśr*, clean from the worse parts; leave the worse part of food; — *ḥaśir*, A, INF. *ḥaśar*, flee cowardly.

(خشرب) *ḥaśrab*, INF. ة, do anything negligently.

(خشرم) *ḥaśram*, INF. ة, make a noise in eating.

(خشرم) *ḥaśram*, pl. *ḥaśârima-t*, swarm of bees or wasps; wasp-nest; mother-bee; — *ḥuśrum*, noise; big.

(خشع) *ḥaśa'*, INF. *ḥuśû'*, be submissive, humble; humble one's self; be near setting; have almost disappeared; grow silent; repent; expectorate, be expectorated; — II. INF. *taḥśî'*, IV. INF. *iḥśâ'*, humble, humiliate; move to repentance; touch, soften; — V. INF. *taḥaśśu'*, humble one's self, submit; get humbled, humiliated; be moved, touched; — VIII. INF. *iḥtiśâ'*, id.; hang down the head.

خشع *ḥuśśa'*, pl. of خاشع *ḥâśi'*, humble, &c.; — ة *ḥiśa'a-t*, child cut out of the womb; — *ḥuś'a-t*, pl. *ḥuśa'*, low hill.

(خشف) *ḥaśaf*, I, INF. *ḥaśf*, *ḥaśfa-t*, creak; dash the head to pieces; drop the child quickly; — INF. *ḥuśûf*, *ḥaśafân*, roam through; disappear, vanish; enter, enter on; be violent; freeze (n.); — U, INF. *ḥaśafa-t*, show the way, guide; — *ḥaśif*, A, INF. *ḥaśaf*, be scabby all over; — III. INF. *muḥâśafa-t*, break a covenant or clientship quickly; drive on the camels all night; — VII. INF. *inḥiśâf*, enter, enter on.

خشف *ḥaśf*, *ḥuśf*, bad wool; — *ḥiśf*, *ḥuśaf*, a green fly; — *ḥiśf*, *ḥaśf*, *ḥuśf*, f. ة, pl. *ḥiśafa-t*, the young of a gazelle; — *ḥuśf*, pl. of اخشف *aḥśaf*, scabby; — ة *ḥaśafa-t*, low noise; creaking, crackling; movement.

خشكار *ḥuśkâr*, bran; bran-bread (Pers.).

خشكر *ḥuśkur*, bran and flour mixed; — ية *ḥuśkuriyya-t*, bran-bread.

(خشل) *ḥaśal*, U, INF. *ḥaśl*, reject as base and worthless; — *ḥaśil*, A, INF. *ḥaśal*, be worn out; — V. INF. *taḥaśśul*, be mean, bad, worthless.

خشل فشل *ḥaśil faśil*, weak.

(خشم) *ḥaśam*, I, INF. *ḥaśm*, break or injure the cartilage of the nose; — *ḥaśim*, A, INF. *ḥaśm*, *ḥuśûm*, have a broad nose; smell badly; — INF. *ḥaśm*, *ḥuśâm*, not be able to smell on account of the loss of the cartilage of the nose.

خشم *ḥaśm*, cartilage of the nose; كسر خشمه *kasar ḥaśma-hu*, abash, humble, humiliate.

(خشن) *ḥaśun*, *ḥaśin*, A, INF. *ḥaśn*, *ḥuśna-t*, *ḥaśâna-t*, *ḥuśûna-t*, *maḥśana-t*, be hard and rough to the touch; be rough, rude; — II. INF. *taḥśîn*, make rough, hard, rude, coarse; take the stiffness out of a garment by wearing it once; — III. INF. *muḥâśana-t*, treat one roughly, harshly; — V. INF. *taḥaśśun*, show one's self very harsh,

rough, rude; be rough, rugged; lead a hard, rough life; wear stiff garments; be unstiffened; — VIII. INF. *iḥtiśân*, be rough, hard, rude; — X. INF. *istiḥśân*, find rough, &c.; — XII. *iḥśauśan*, INF. *iḥśîśan*, be very rough and hard to the touch.

خشن *ḥaśn*, roughness; — *ḥuśn*, pl. of اخشن *aḥśan*, hard, rough; — *ḥaśin*, ة, pl. *ḥiśân*, rough, hard to the touch; rude, rough of manners; — ة *ḥuśna-t*=خشونة *ḥuśûna-t*.

(خشو) *ḥaśâ*, U, INF. *ḥaśw*, *ḥuśuww*, produce small and bad dates.

خشوع *ḥuśû'*, submission, submissiveness; humility, humiliation; (m.) emotion, repentance.

خشوعى *ḥuśû'iyy*, humiliating; (m.) touching, sentimental.

خشونة *ḥuśûna-t*, roughness, hardness; rudeness; severity, sharpness.

(خشى) *ḥaśî*, A, INF. *ḥaś-an*, *ḥiś-an*, *ḥaśy*, *ḥiśy*, *ḥaśât*, *ḥaśya-t*, *ḥaśayân*, *maḥśât*, *maḥśiya-t*, fear; fear for (على *'ala*); surpass in fear or timidity; — II. INF. *taḥśiya-t*, frighten, terrify; — V. INF. *taḥaśśî*, VIII. INF. *iḥtiśâ'*, fear.

خشى *ḥaśî*, *ḥaśiyy* (خش *ḥaś-in*), ة, timid, timorous; — ة *ḥaśya-t*, fear.

خشيان *ḥaśyân*, f. ة, خشيا *ḥaśyâ*, pl. *ḥaśâyâ*, timid, timorous; — *ḥiśyân*, *ḥaśayân*, fear.

خشيب *ḥaśîb*, pl. *ḥuśub*, *ḥaśâ'ib*, rough, unsmooth; hard of bone; big.

خشين *ḥasîn*, ة, rough, rude, hard, severe.

(خص) *ḥaṣṣ*, U, INF. *ḥaṣṣ*, *ḥuṣûṣ*, *ḥiṣṣiya-t*, *ḥiṣṣîṣâ'*, *ḥiṣṣîṣa*, *ḥaṣûṣiyya-t*, *taḥiṣṣa-t*, impart or impute as particular to (acc.); assign; be one's property or peculiarity, concern especially; — for *ḥaṣiṣ*, A, INF. *ḥaṣâṣ*, *ḥaṣâṣa-t*, also pass., be poor, needy; — II. INF. *taḥṣiṣ*, impart or impute as particular quality or property; — IV. INF. *iḥṣâṣ*, do less than one ought to do; — V. INF. *taḥaṣṣuṣ*, be one's private property, be peculiar to, concern particularly (ل *li*); — VIII. INF. *iḥtiṣâṣ*, be one's particular property or quality; be a particular friend to (ب *bi*); impute as a peculiarity; destine to a particular use; distinguish one's self by (ب *bi*); — X. INF. *istiḥṣâṣ*, claim as a particular property or quality; claim exclusively for one's self.

خص *ḥiṣṣ*, defective; — *ḥuṣṣ*, pl. *ḥiṣâṣ*, *ḥuṣûṣ*, *aḥṣâṣ*, hut, cottage; wine-house; good wine.

خصا *ḥiṣâ'*, castration.

خصاص *ḥaṣâṣ*, ة *ḥaṣâṣa-t*, poverty, penury, straitness; split, rent, chink, hole;—*ḥuṣâṣa-t*, pl. *ḥuṣâṣ*, grapes left in harvesting.

خصاف *ḥaṣṣâf*, liar; shoemaker.

خصالة *ḥuṣâla-t*, offal, sweepings.

خصام *ḥiṣâm*, dispute, INF. III. of (خصم).

خصان *ḥiṣṣân*, *ḥuṣṣân*, grandees; royal favourites.

(خصب) *ḥaṣab*, I, INF. *ḥiṣb*, abound in plants and fruit; — *ḥaṣib*, A, INF. *ḥaṣab*, id.; — IV. INF. *iḥṣâb*, id.; fertilise.

خصب *ḥiṣb*, abundance, plenty, fertility; — *ḥaṣib*, ة, fertile.

(خصر) *ḥaṣir*, A, INF. *ḥaṣar*, be frozen; be very cold; — V. INF. *taḥaṣṣur*, take one by the hand and walk at the side of him; rest one's hands on the hips; lean on; — VI. INF. *taḥâṣur*, take one another by the hands; — VIII. INF. *iḥtiṣâr*, cut off or remove superfluities; abbreviate, abridge, resume; take the shortest way; take a stick.

خصر *ḥaṣr*, pl. *ḥuṣûr*, middle of the body, waist; — *ḥaṣar*, cold (s.);

— *ḫaṣir*, cold (adj.);—ة *ḫuṣra-t*, shortness, brevity.

(خصف) *ḫaṣaf*, I, INF. *ḫaṣf*, sole; cover one's nakedness with leaves; — INF. *ḫiṣâf*, miscarry in the ninth month; pass. have others behind one's self; — II. INF. *taḫṣîf*, mingle white hair with the black; show ill will; claim without a right; — IV. INF. *iḫṣâf*, hasten; (also VIII. INF. *iḫtiṣâf*) cover one's nakedness with leaves.

خصف *ḫaṣf*, double sole; — ة *ḫaṣafa-t*, pl. *ḫaṣaf*, *ḫiṣâf*, basket of palm-leaves; very coarse garment; — *ḫuṣfa-t*, stitch of an awl.

(خصل) *ḫaṣal*, INF. *ḫaṣl*, *ḫiṣâl*, surpass in shooting; cut off, sever; — II. INF. *taḫṣîl*, cut off; implant a bad habit, spoil; — III. INF. *ḫiṣâl*, enter with another (acc.) a contest in shooting.

خصل *ḫaṣl*, contest and victory in shooting; stake in such; — ة *ḫaṣla-t*, pl. *ḫiṣâl*, peculiarity, particular quality; whim, hobby-horse, crotchet; fault, vice; division, paragraph; — *ḫuṣla-t*, dishevelled hair; tuft; cluster or bunch of grapes.

(خصم) *ḫaṣam*, I, INF. *ḫaṣm*, conquer an avdersary; subtract; — III. INF. *ḫiṣâm*, *muḫâṣama-t*, *ḫuṣûma-t*, dispute, have a law-suit against (acc.); — VI. INF. *taḫâṣum*, dispute with one another, contest in a law-suit; — VIII. INF. *iḫtiṣâm*, consider as one's adversary; dispute.

خصم *ḫaṣm* (sing. du. and pl.), pl. also *ḫuṣûm*, *ḫuṣmân*, (m.) *aḫṣâm*, adversary, competition; — *ḫuṣm*, pl. *ḫuṣûm*, *aḫṣâm*, side, edge, border; corner; — *ḫaṣam*, husband; — *ḫaṣim*, engaged in a dispute; quarrelsome.

خصما *ḫuṣamâ'*, and—

خصمان *ḫuṣmân*, pl. of خصيم *ḫaṣîm*; — *ḫuṣmân*, also pl. of خصم *ḫaṣm*.

خصن *ḫuṣun*, pl. of خصين *ḫaṣîn*.

خصوص *ḫuṣûṣ*, particular circumstance, speciality, peculiarity; particular attachment, friendship, affection; *ḫuṣûṣ-an*, especially, in particular; — *.

خصوصى *ḫuṣûṣiyy*, ة, concerning particularly, peculiar; — ة *ḫuṣûṣiyya-t*, peculiarity.

خصومة *ḫuṣûma-t*, object of litigation, litigation, law-suit; enmity.

(خصى) *ḫaṣa*, I, INF. *ḫiṣâ'*, geld, castrate; — IV. INF. *iḫṣâ'*, learn only one art or science; — VIII. INF. *iḫtiṣâ'*, get castrated, castrate one's self; be castrated.

خصى *ḫaṣiyy*, pl. *ḫiṣya-t*, *ḫiṣyân*, one castrated, eunuch; — ة *ḫaṣya-t*, pl. *ḫuṣa*, testicle; — *ḫiṣṣîyya-t*, INF. of (خص).

خصيب *ḫaṣîb*, abundant.

خصيص *ḫaṣîṣ*, particular, peculiar, private.

خصيصا *ḫiṣṣîṣâ'*, خصيصى *ḫiṣṣîṣa*, INF. of (خص).

خصيف *ḫaṣîf*, double-soled; sweet and sour milk mixed together; ashes; comm. and f. ة, spotted white and black; armed.

خصيلة *ḫaṣîla-t*, pl. *ḫaṣîl*, *ḫaṣâ'il*, piece of meat, joint; thick muscle.

خصيم *ḫaṣîm*, pl. *ḫuṣamâ'*, *ḫuṣmân*, quarrelsome; adversary in a law-suit; enemy.

خصين *ḫaṣîn*, pl. *ḫuṣun*, *aḫṣun*, hatchet.

(خض), II. *ḫaḍḍad*, INF. *taḫḍîd*, adorn with shells; shake; rinse; — III. INF. *muḫâḍḍa-t*, sell on credit to (acc.), give in exchange; — VII. INF. *inḫiḍâḍ*, get shaken; — ة *ḫaḍḍa-t*, shaking (s.), agitation.

خضاب *ḫiḍâb*, dye, colour.

خضار *ḫaḍâr*, watered milk; first green, first vegetables;—*ḫuḍḍâr*, a bird; — ة *ḫuḍâra-t*, verdure; sea.

خضارع *ḥuḍâri‘*, miserly, avaricious.

خضارى *ḥaḍâra*, pl. of *ḥuḍriyy*; — *ḥuḍâriyy*, a bird; maritime.

خضاض *ḥaḍâḍ*, *ḥiḍâḍ*, ink; — *ḥaḍâḍ*, trumpery, tinsel-finery.

(خضب) *ḥaḍab*, I, INF. *ḥaḍb*, dye (especially red); green, be green, have green shoots; — *ḥaḍib*, and pass., INF. *ḥuḍûb*, green, be verdant; — II. INF. *taḥḍîb*, dye richly; — IV. INF. *iḥḍâb*, be covered with green; — VIII. INF. *iḥtiḍâb*, be dyed; dye one's self; — XII. *iḥḍauḍab*, INF. *iḥḍîḍâb*, be covered with green, be verdant.

(خضج), IV. *aḥḍaj*, INF. *iḥḍâj*, dissolve; — V. INF. *taḥaḍḍuj*, limp; — VII. INF. *inḥiḍâj*, be trodden down; burn with anger.

(خضخض) *ḥaḍḥaḍ*, INF. ة, shake; rinse; — II. INF. *taḥaḍḥuḍ*, be shaken; — ة *ḥaḍḥaḍa-t*, shake; agitation.

(خضد) *ḥaḍad*, I, INF. *ḥaḍd*, break; cut, cut off; eat greedily and with a noise; eat anything soft and smack; — V. INF. *taḥaḍḍud*, VII. INF. *inḥiḍâd*, get broken but not severed; — VIII. INF. *iḥtiḍâd*, bridle the camel and ride on it.

(خضر) *ḥaḍar*, U, INF. *ḥaḍr*, cut off, cut down; — *ḥaḍir*, green, be green; be soft and tender; — II. INF. *taḥḍîr*, dye green; — III. INF. *muḥâḍara-t*, buy the fruit while yet green; — IV. INF. *iḥḍâr*, green, be green; — VIII. INF. *iḥtiḍâr*, carry; cut green food; pass. die when young; — IX. *iḥḍarr*, INF. *iḥḍirâr*, be green; be dark, XI. *iḥḍârr*, INF. *iḥḍîrâr*, XII. *iḥḍauḍar*, INF. *iḥḍîḍâr*, be green; be dark.

خضر *ḥiḍr*, the prophet Khedr, Moses's companion; Elias; the wandering Jew; St. George; — *ḥaḍar*, verdure, freshness, youthfulness; — *ḥaḍir*, ة, green, verdant, pleasant to the eye; — ة *ḥuḍra-t*, pl. *ḥuḍar*, *ḥuḍr*, green (s.), verdure; dark grey; blackish; herbs, greens, vegetables.

خضرا *ḥaḍrâ’*, f. of اخضر *aḥḍar*, green; firmament; terebinth; pl. *ḥiḍrâwât*, greens.

(خضرب) *ḥaḍrab*, INF. ة, be agitated.

خضرم *ḥiḍrim*, pl. *-ûn*, *ḥaḍârim*, *ḥaḍârima-t*, abundant, plentiful; abounding with water; large; very liberal.

خضرمى *ḥiḍrimiyy*, pl. *ḥaḍârima-t*, stranger, Persian, Syrian.

خضروات *ḥaḍrawât*, greens, vegetables; fruit.

خضرى *ḥuḍriyy*, pl. *ḥaḍâriyy*, wild duck.

خضض *ḥaḍaḍ*, small shells.

(خضع) *ḥaḍa‘*, INF. *ḥuḍû‘*, be submissive, humble; submit; be near setting; rest; bring to rest, quiet; bend; incite to anything bad; walk along vigorously; — II. humble, tame, subdue; cut meat into pieces; — III. INF. *muḥâḍâ‘a-t*, address one's wife softly and imploringly; — IV. INF. *iḥḍâ‘*, id.; humble, subdue; — V. INF. *taḥaḍḍu‘*, humble one's self, submit; — VIII. INF. *iḥtiḍâ‘*, behave humbly, submissively; get humbled; — XII. *iḥḍauḍa‘*, INF. *iḥḍîḍâ‘*, be humble, submissive.

خضع *ḥuḍu‘*, pl. of خضوع *ḥaḍû‘*; — *ḥuḍ‘*, pl. and خضعا *ḥaḍ‘â’*, f. of اخضع *aḥḍa‘*, submissive; — ة *ḥuḍa‘a-t*, submissive to everybody.

(خضعب), II. تخضعب *taḥaḍ‘ab*, INF. *taḥaḍ‘ub*, be confused, complicated, intricate; — ة *ḥaḍ‘aba-t*, fat and helpless woman.

(خضف) *ḥaḍaf*, I, INF. *ḥaḍf*, *ḥuḍûf*, break wind; eat.

(خضل) *ḥaḍil*, A, INF. *ḥaḍal*, be moist, wet; get moistened; —

II. INF. *taḫḍîl*; — IV. INF. *iḫḍâl*, moisten, wet; — IX. *iḫḍall*, INF. *iḫḍilâl*, be moist, moistened, wetted; have dense branches and foliage; be dark.

خضل *ḫaḍil*, ة, moist, wet; fresh and tender; plenteous; — ة *ḫudulla-t*, affluence and enjoyment of life; delicate pleasing woman; wife.

(خضلف) *ḫaḍlaf*, INF. ة, bear only few dates.

(خضم) *ḫaḍam*, I, INF. *ḫaḍm*; *ḫaḍim*, A, INF. *ḫaḍam*, eat, chew; — *ḫaḍam*, I, INF. *ḫaḍm*, cut, cut off; give to anybody part of one's property.

خضم *ḫiḍamm*, sea (of bounty, knowledge, &c.); a great and liberal lord; large assembly; heavy horse; sharp sword; whetstone; — ة *ḫaḍma-t*, amulet; — *ḫuḍama-t*, great eater, glutton; — *ḫuḍumma-t*, the thickest part, principal part, middle.

خضن *ḫaḍan*, U, INF. *ḫaḍn*, rush furiously at the she-camel and bite her (he-camel); pass. be wanting; — III. INF. *muḫâḍana-t*, jest amorously with one's wife; talk ribaldry to one another.

خضوع *ḫaḍû'*, pl. *ḫuḍu'*, humble, submissive; — *.

خضيب *ḫaḍîb*, dyed; dyed red; bloody, gory, sanguinary.

خضير *ḫaḍîr*, ة, green, greening; green food.

خضيعة *ḫaḍî'a-t*, rumbling in the belly of a horse; murmuring of a stream.

خضيلة *ḫaḍîla-t*, garden; flower-bed; meadow.

خضيمة *ḫaḍîma-t*, boiled wheat; soft, delicate.

(خط) *ḫaṭṭ*, U, INF. *ḫaṭṭ*, draw lines; make stripes or furrows; form letters, write; lie with; taste of a meal; mark as one's exclusive property; — INF. *ḫiṭṭ*, *ḫiṭṭa-t*, mark out and take possession of uninhabited land; — II. INF. *taḫṭîṭ*, mark with lines, &c.; stripe, weave in stripes, furrow; — IV. INF. *iḫṭâṭ*, be marked with lines, &c.; be tattooed; — VIII. INF. *iḫṭiṭât*= IV.; draw lines; show the first down; mark out and take possession of a tract of land.

خط *ḫaṭṭ*, pl. *ḫuṭûṭ*, *aḫṭâṭ*, stroke, line, stripe; stroke of the pen, handwriting; boundary-line; road, street, lane; furrow; down (of a beard); coast; خ الاستوا *ḫaṭṭ al-istiwâ'*, equator; خ نصف نهار *ḫaṭṭ nisf-i nahâr*, meridian; خ هريف *ḫaṭṭ-i-śarîf*, خ همايون *ḫaṭṭ-i-ḫumâyûn*, imperial edict; — *ḫiṭ'*, error; transgression; — ة *ḫiṭṭa-t*, pl. *ḫiṭaṭ*, land for the first time taken possession of; place marked out for building; district, tract, region; town; pl. precinct, neighbourhood of a town; — *ḫuṭṭa-t*, pl. *ḫuṭuṭ*, circumstance; affair; state; performance; difficult undertaking; firm purpose and resolute execution.

(خطا) *ḫaṭa'*, A, INF. *ḫaṭ'*, throw up foam; — خطى *ḫaṭi'*, A, INF. *ḫiṭ'*, *ḫiṭ'a-t*, err, transgress, sin; — INF. *taḫṭi'a-t*, accuse of error or sin; lead into error or sin; — IV. INF. *iḫṭâ'*, err, transgress, sin; miss one's aim; lead into error or sin; — V. INF. *taḫaṭṭu'*, err, transgress; lead into error or sin; — VI. INF. *taḫâṭu'*, lead into error or sin.

خطا *ḫaṭa'*, *ḫaṭâ'*, error, mistake, transgression, sin; missing of an aim or end; — *ḫiṭâ'*, *ḫuṭâ'*, pl. of خطوة *ḫaṭwa-t* and *ḫuṭwa-t*, respectively; — *ḫaṭṭâ'*, who always errs or transgresses; — ة *ḫuṭât*, sinews, pl. of خاطى *ḫâṭi'*.

خطاب *ḫiṭâb*, address, speech; *ḫiṭâban*, entering *in medias res*, directly; — *ḫaṭṭâb*, mediator in

marriage transactions, match-maker; very eloquent;—*ḥuṭṭâb*, orators, &c., pl. of خاطب *ḥâṭib*; —*; — ة *ḥaṭâba-t*, preaching (s.); — *ḥiṭâba-t*, office of a preacher.

خطار *ḥaṭṭâr*, ة, trembling; brandishing a spear; wagging the tail; catapult, shooting engine; a perfume; perfumer; — *ḥuṭṭâr*, minds, &c., pl. of خاطر *ḥâṭir*; —*

خطاط *ḥaṭṭâṭ*, calligraphist; drawer of maps.

خطاطيف *ḥaṭâṭîf*, see the following.

خطاف *ḥaṭṭâf*, robber; Satan; — *ḥuṭṭâf*, pl. *ḥaṭâṭîf*, swallow; hook, cramp, harpoon; pl. claws.

خطال *ḥaṭṭâl*, economical; — ة *ḥaṭṭâla-t*, shameless woman.

خطام *ḥiṭâm*, pl. *ḥuṭum*, bridle; halter; string of a bow; — *ḥaṭṭâm*, strong musk; — *.

خطايا *ḥaṭâyâ*, خطائى *ḥaṭâ'i*, pl. of خطيئة *ḥaṭî'a-t*.

(خطب) *ḥaṭab*, U, INF. *ḥuṭba-t*, *ḥaṭaba-t*, preach; have the public prayers said for one's self, i.e. seize the reins of dominion; — U, INF. *ḥaṭb*, *ḥiṭba-t*, *ḥiṭṭîba*, sue in marriage, court; betroth one's self; give one's daughter in betrothal; — *ḥaṭib*, INF. *ḥaṭab*, be dirt-coloured; — *ḥaṭub*, INF. *ḥaṭâba-t*, become a preacher, preach; — III. INF. *ḥiṭâb*, *muḥâṭaba-t*, address; deliver a speech; — IV. INF. *iḥṭâb*, offer the side to the hunter at a short distance; — VIII. INF. *iḥtiṭâb*, deliver the (Friday) sermon; ask in marriage; betroth one's self; celebrate the betrothal.

خطب *ḥaṭb*, pl. *ḥuṭûb*, difficult affair, important business; calamity; — *ḥiṭb*, f. ة, pl. *aḥṭâb*, suitor; sued woman; betrothed; — ة *ḥiṭba-t*, betrothal; — *ḥuṭba-t*, impure colour, dirt-colour; pl. *ḥuṭab*, the Friday sermon; harangue.

خطبا *ḥaṭbâ'*, f. of اخطب *aḥṭab*, tattooed; — *ḥuṭabâ'*, orators, &c., pl. of خاطب *ḥâṭib*.

خطبانى *ḥuṭbâniyy*, dark brown.

(خطخط) *ḥaṭḥaṭ*, INF. ة, stoop in walking.

(خطر) *ḥaṭar*, I, INF. *ḥaṭr*, *ḥaṭîr*, *ḥaṭarân*, swing the tail to and fro, beat the loins with it; INF. *ḥaṭarân*, brandish the sword or spear; tremble; step along proudly with a swinging body; (m.) step along, travel, visit; — I, A, INF. *ḥuṭûr*, occur, come back to one's mind; — *ḥaṭur*, INF. *ḥuṭûra-t*, be eminent; — III. INF. *muḥâṭara-t*, expose one's self (ب *bi*) to danger, risk; make a wager with (acc.) another; — IV. INF. *iḥṭâr*, cause to remember; move in one's mind (two acc.); — V. INF. *taḥaṭṭur*, step along proudly; — VI. INF. *taḥâṭur*, make a wager against one another; beat each other with the tail.

خطر *ḥaṭr*, thought, what occurs to the mind; a large measure; consideration, dignity; — *ḥiṭr*, indigo; pl. *aḥṭûr*, large number of camels; — *ḥuṭr*, pl. of خطير *ḥaṭîr*; — *ḥaṭar*, pl. *ḥiṭâr*, *aḥṭâr*, danger, risk; wager; calamity; pl. *ḥiṭâr*, *ḥuṭur*, stake; high authority, rank; importance; equal, similar; — *ḥaṭir*, dangerous; risky; of high authority, highly considered; — ة *ḥaṭra-t*, time, turn; *ḥaṭrat-an*, sometimes; (m.) march; travel; — *ḥaṭira-t*, what occurs to the mind, fancy, idea.

خطط *ḥiṭaṭ*, *ḥuṭaṭ*, pl. of خطة *ḥiṭṭa-t*, *ḥuṭṭa-t*, respectively.

(خطف) *ḥaṭif*, A, INF. *ḥaṭaf*; *ḥaṭaf*, I, INF. *ḥaṭafân*, step apace; — *ḥaṭif*, A, *ḥaṭaf*, I, INF. *ḥaṭf*, snatch away, rob, steal, abduct; — II. INF. *taḥṭîf*, rob with vio-

lence; — IV. INF. *iḥṭâf*, miss the aim; — V. INF. *taḥaṭṭuf*, snatch away, rob; — VII. INF. *inḥiṭâf*, be snatched away, carried off, robbed; (m.) be transported (by emotion, &c.), fall in ecstacy; — VIII. INF. *iḥtiṭâf*, snatch away, rob.

خطف *ḥaṭf*, snatching away (s.); abduction, robbery; theft; rapaciousness; — ة *ḥaṭfa-t*, limb torn off by a wild beast.

(خطل) *ḥaṭil*, A, INF. *ḥaṭal*, indulge in idle or unseemly talk.

خطل *ḥaṭal*, lightness, swiftness; idle or indecent talk; — *ḥaṭil*, idle talker; — *ḥuṭul*, pl. and—

خطلا *ḥaṭlâ'*, f. of اخطل *aḥṭal*, having flabby ears, &c.

خطلبة *ḥaṭlaba-t*, shallow and confused talk.

(خطم) *ḥaṭam*, I, INF. *ḥaṭm*, hit on the nose, bridle the nose, bridle; silence; — INF. *ḥaṭm*, *ḥiṭâm*, put a string to the bow; — II. INF. *taḥṭîm*, VIII. INF. *iḥtiṭâm*, bridle, muzzle.

خطم *ḥaṭm*, nose, muzzle; beak; mouth of a wild animal; important matter; — *ḥuṭum*, pl. of خطام *ḥiṭâm*; — ة *ḥuṭma-t*, mountain peak.

خطمى *ḥiṭmiyy*, *ḥaṭmiyy*, marsh-mallow.

(خطو) *ḥaṭâ*, U, INF. *ḥaṭw*, take a step, step, walk; — V. INF. *taḥaṭṭî*, put one's foot upon; tread on; follow in one's steps, step or pass by, overtake; (m.) overstep the bounds, encroach; — VIII. INF. *iḥtiṭâ'*, step along, walk; overtake; — ة *ḥaṭwa-t*, pl. *ḥaṭawât*, *ḥiṭâ'*, stepping, walking (s.); step; — *ḥuṭwa-t*, pl. *ḥuṭâ'*, خطى *ḥuṭ-an*, *ḥuṭa*, *ḥuṭwât*, *ḥuṭawât*, *ḥuṭuwât*, step, width of a step.

خطوطى *ḥuṭûṭiyy*, linear.

خطى *ḥuṭ-an*, pl. of خطوة *ḥuṭwa-t*; — *ḥaṭi'*, see (خطا); — *ḥaṭṭiyy*, pl. ة, lance, spear; — ة *ḥaṭi'a-t*, *ḥaṭiyya-t*, خطيئة *ḥaṭi'a-t*, pl. *ḥaṭâyâ*, *ḥaṭâ'i*, transgression, offence, sin.

خطيب *ḥaṭîb*, preacher; reciter of the public prayers; — *ḥiṭṭîb*, *ḥaṭîb*, f. ة, betrothed.

خطيبى *ḥiṭṭîba*, INF. of (خطب).

خطير *ḥaṭîr*, pl. *ḥuṭr*, great; high; powerful and respected; of high rank; important, weighty; dangerous, risky; — ة *ḥaṭîra-t*, pl. *ḥaṭâ'ir*, important matter.

(خظ) *ḥaẓẓ*, U, INF. *ḥaẓẓ*, suffer from diarrhœa.

خظا بظا *ḥaẓ-an baẓ-an*, firm, compact; — *ḥaẓâ'*, firmness, compactness.

خظارة *ḥuẓâra-t*, valerian.

(خظو) *ḥaẓâ*, U, INF. *ḥuẓuww*, be firm, compact.

خظوان *ḥaẓawân*, who is getting corpulent.

(خظى) *ḥaẓî*, A, INF. *ḥaẓ-an*, be firm, compact.

خظى *ḥaẓẓiyy*, lance, spear.

(خع) *ḥa''*, I, INF. *ḥa''*, pant.

(خف) *ḥaff*, I, INF. *ḥaff*, *ḥiff*, *ḥiffa-t*, be light (of weight); be of no consequence, unimportant; be slight; get lighter, decrease; be accomodating, tractable; cry out; depart in haste, emigrate; go briskly to; — INF. *ḥufûf*, be few in number; — INF. *ḥiffa-t*, be active, nimble; — II. INF. *taḥfîf*, make light, alleviate, ease; — IV. INF. *iḥfâf*, induce to levity; — V. INF. *taḥaffuf*, get alleviated; put on a boot; — VI. INF. *taḥâff*, show one's self active, nimble; — X. INF. *istiḥfâf*, deem or find light; make light of, slight, disdain; enliven.

خف *ḥiff*, light; light-minded, frivolous; agile, nimble; small troop; inconsiderable, insignificant; lightness; insignificance; INF. of (خف); — *ḥuff*, pl. *ḥifâf*, short boot; shoe; sole; pl. *aḥfâf*, camel's hoof; foot of the ostrich; — ة *ḥiffa-t*, lightness;

agility, nimbleness; levity, frivolity, fickleness; inconsiderableness, insignificance.

(خفا) *ḥafa'*, A, INF. *ḥaf'*, tear out and fling on the ground; demolish; empty, pour out.

خفا *ḥaf-an*, *ḥafa*, secret; — *ḥafâ'*, concealment;—*ḥifâ'*, pl. *aḥfiya-t*, covering; veil; curtain; anything covered, concealed.

(خفاجل) *ḥufâjil*, stupid; stammering.

خفادد *ḥafâdid*, خفاديد *ḥafâdîd*, pl. of خفيدد *ḥafaidad*.

خفار *ḥufâr*, fee of a guide or escort; — ة *ḥifâra-t*, *ḥafâra-t*, deep shame; — *ḥufâra-t*, protection; clientship; escort and its reward; safe conduct (also *ḥafâra-t*, *ḥifâra-t*).

خفاش *ḥuffâś*, pl. *ḥafâfîś*, bat (animal).

خفاف *ḥufâf*, light; light-minded, frivolous; agile, nimble; — *ḥaffâf*, shoe or boot maker; — *.

خفافيش *ḥafâfîś*, pl. of خفاش *ḥuffâś*.

خفايا *ḥafâyâ*, pl. of خفى *ḥafiyy*.

(خفت) *ḥafat*, U, INF. *ḥufût*, become or be silent; cease to speak; be low (voice); INF. *ḥaft*, speak secretly and in an undertone; INF. *ḥufât*, die suddenly; — III. INF. *muḥâfata-t*, address secretly and in a low voice; read in a low voice;—IV. INF. *taḥâfut*, talk to one another secretly and in an undertone.

خفت *ḥaft*, slow speech, whisper; — also *ḥuft*, rue (plant).

خفتان *ḥaftân*, quilted armour; padded overcoat (Pers.).

(خفثل) *ḥafṣal*, خفائل *ḥufâṣil*, pl. *ḥafâṣil*, weak in body and mind.

(خفج) *ḥafij*, A, INF. *ḥafaj*, suffering from a trembling of the fore-feet; — *ḥafij*, have pains in the legs from tiredness; lie with.

خفخفة *ḥafḥafa-t*, noise made in eating; rustling of new clothes.

(خفد) *ḥafad*, U, INF. *ḥafd*, *ḥafadân*, stride apace; — *ḥafid*, A, INF. *ḥafad*, id.; — IV. INF. *iḥfâd*, miscarry, seem big with young without being so.

(خفر) *ḥafar*, I, U, INF. *ḥafr*, *ḥufâra-t*, protect, escort; take a fee for escort or protection; INF. *ḥifâra-t*, protect a sown field, palms, &c., against injury; keep a compact; — INF. *ḥafar*, *ḥufûr*, break a compact; — *ḥafir*, A, INF. *ḥafar*, *ḥafâra-t*, be greatly ashamed, blush deeply; — II. INF. *taḥfîr*, protect, defend, escort, give an escort; — IV. INF. *iḥfâr*, grant a safe conduct, an escort, and, by opposition, abandon treacherously one escorted or placed in safe conduct; break a compact; — V. INF. *taḥaffur*, place one's self under one's protection; grant protection; be bashful, blush.

خفر *ḥafr*, safe conduct, escort; — *ḥafar*, escort; violent shame; modesty; — *ḥafir*, f., also ة *ḥafira-t*, very bashful; — ة *ḥufra-t*, protection; — *ḥufara-t*, protector.

خفرا *ḥufarâ'*, pl. of خفير *ḥafîr*.

خفرجة *ḥufraja-t*, excellence or daintiness of food.

خفرنج *ḥafarnaj*, delicate, dainty.

(خفس) *ḥafas*, U, INF. *ḥafs*, mock at, ridicule; talk ribaldry; vanquish in wrestling; demolish; eat or drink little of a thing; break in the bottom of a cask; fall down; — VII. INF. *inḥifâs*, lose the bottom.

(خفش) *ḥafaś*, U, INF. *ḥafś*, pelt with; —*ḥafiś*, A, INF. *ḥafaś*, have small purblind eyes; be weak, imbecile.

خفش *ḥafaś*, purblind sight.

خفشا *ḥafśâ'*, f. of اخفش *aḥfaś*, purblind.

(خفض) *ḥafaḍ*, I, INF. *ḥafḍ*, remain, abide, stay; sink (a.), let down, place lower; humble, humiliate;

lower the voice; bend wood; walk slowly; put a word in the oblique case; — *ḫafuḍ*, be easy and comfortable; pass. get circumcised (girl); — II. INF. *taḫfîḍ*, sink (a.), lower; do or say anything gently or with moderation; lower the voice; — VII. INF. *inḫifâḍ*, be thrown down, sunk; sit in a low place; be humble; — VIII. INF. *iḫtifâḍ*, get circumcised.

خفض *ḫafḍ*, quiet, comfortable life; ease and comfort, affluence; humiliation; low tone or voice; measured walk; oblique case.

(خفع) *ḫafa'*, INF. *ḫaf'*, fall down in a fit of giddiness; beat, hit with the sword; — INF. *ḫafa'*, *ḫafa'ân*, be put in motion; be relaxed; pass. *ḫufi'*, be tormented with hunger.

(خفق) *ḫafaq*, I, U, INF. *ḫafq*, *ḫafaqân*, move gently, wave to and fro; beat, throb; be moved; nod; INF. *ḫafq*, flash; give a light tap; INF. *ḫafaqân*, produce a whistling, hissing, clattering, creaking, &c., noise; fly; be for the greatest part passed; — I, INF. *ḫufûq*, set (star, &c.); wave; — II. INF. *taḫfîq*, talk confusedly, dote; (m.) do in a desultory way, sketch hurriedly; — IV. INF. *iḫfâq*, not obtain one's wish, miss one's end; fail; return without prey or booty; throw down in wrestling; nod; flap the wings; be near setting.

خفق *ḫafiq*, ة *ḫafiqa-t*, pl. *ḫifâq*, having thin flanks; — ة *ḫafqa-t*, throb of the pulse or heart; — *ḫifqa-t*, plain with a mirage.

خفقان *ḫafaqân*, gentle motion; tremble; palpitation; — ى *ḫafaqâniyy*, suffering from palpitations.

(خفو) *ḫafâ*, U, INF. *ḫafw*, *ḫufuww*, shine far; appear; — ة *ḫifwa-t*, secret.

خفوف *ḫaffûf*, hyena; — *

(خفى) *ḫafa*, I, INF. *ḫafy*, *ḫufiyy*, bring to light, reveal, and, by opposition, conceal, keep secret; INF. *ḫafy*, shine sideways; — *ḫafî*, A, INF. *ḫafâ'*, be secret, concealed from (على *'ala*); INF. *ḫiffa-t*, *ḫufya-t*, conceal one's self from (ل *li*), withdraw from sight; — II. INF. *taḫfiya-t*, IV. INF. *iḫfâ'*, keep secret, conceal; — VIII. INF. *iḫtifâ'*, pass. of the previous; disappear, vanish; publish, make known; — X. INF. *istiḫfâ'*, be concealed.

خفى *ḫafiyy*, ة, pl. *ḫafâyâ*, concealed, secret; thin, fine; of a low or feeble sound; — *ḫafy*, *ḫufiyy*, INF. of (خفى); — ة *ḫifya-t*, *ḫufya-t*, hiding one's self (s.), concealment; — *ḫafiyya-t*, pl. *-ât*, *ḫafâyâ*, what is hidden, secret; thicket; madness.

خفيدد *ḫafaidad*, pl. *ḫâfâdid*, *ḫafâdîd*, *ḫafaidadât*, swift, quick; male ostrich.

خفير *ḫafîr*, pl. *ḫufarâ*, protector; escort; protected; escorted; faithful to a compact; fee for escorting; gate-toll.

خفيض *ḫafîḍ*, sunk, lowered, low; oppressed; subdued; humiliated.

خفيف *ḫafîf*, ة, pl. *ḫifâf*, *aḫfâf*, *aḫiffâ'*, light; nimble, agile, skilful; insignificant; weak, feeble; light-minded, frivolous, fickle; imbecile; a metre: *fâ'ilâtun mustaf'ilun mustaf'ilun*, twice.

(خق) *ḫaqq*, I, INF. *ḫaqîq*, rattle; clatter; buzz; seethe.

خق *ḫaqq*, pl. *aḫqâq*, *ḫuqûq*, cleft or rent in the ground.

خقان *ḫaqân*, pl. *ḫuquna-t*=خاقان *ḫâqân*, emperor (Turk.).

خقن *ḫaqqan*, INF. *taḫqîq*, invest as emperor.

(خل) *ḫall*, U, I, INF. *ḫall*, *ḫulûl*, be emaciated, wasted; — INF. *ḫalal*, be in disorder confusion;

be disturbed (mind); — INF. *hulûla-t*, become poor, needy; want; do anything by one's self; — INF. *hall*, pierce, penetrate; clean the teeth with the tooth-pick; fix with a peg; split the tongue of a camel's foal; draw a seton; — pass. *hull*, become poor, needy, be in need of; — II. INF. *tahlîl*, turn into vinegar (a.); clean the teeth; acidulate, make sour; be or turn sour; turn into vinegar (n.); — III. INF. *hilâl*, *halâl*, *muhâlla-t*, keep up a true friendship, cultivate one's friendship; — IV. INF. *ihlâl*, cause to want a thing; pass. want, be in need of, lack; forsake, leave in the lurch, fail, deceive; bring in disorder and confusion; exceed the bounds; — V. INF. *tahallul*, engage in, enter on, step in the middle of the people; clean the teeth with the tooth-pick; comb one's beard with the fingers; — VI. INF. *tahâlul*, keep up a true friendship between one another; — VIII. INF. *ihtilâl*, turn into vinegar (n.); take vinegar; be put in disorder or confusion; be disturbed; have splits, interstices, pores, &c.; pierce; want; grow thin, waste away (n.).

خل *hall*, pl. *ahull*, *hilâl*, vinegar; evil, ill; path through sandy ground; a vein of the neck and back; worn garment; camel in the second year; *hill*, close friendship; needy; — *hill*, *hull*, pl. *ahlâl*, true friend; — ة *halla-t*, pl. *hilâl*, nature, natural disposition or qualification; need, poverty, misery; pl. *halal*, interstice, interval, breach, rent, opening, hole; vacancy; camel in the second year (m. and f.); — *hilla-t*, pl. *hilal*, *hilâl*, pl. pl. *ahilla-t*, case for precious scabbards; pl. *hilal*, *hilâl*, remains of food between the teeth; true friendship; — *hulla-t*, a thorny tree; any plant with a sweet juice; pl. *hulal*, sincere friendship, friend (m. and f.).

(خلا) *hala'*, INF. *hal'*, *hilâ'*, *hulû'*, fall on the knees, be restive; INF. *hulû'*, not stir from the place; desist from one thing and take up another.

خلا *halâ*, خلا ما *halâ mâ*, except, excepting that; — *halâ'*, free, independent; empty; empty space, void (s.); privy; INF. of (خلو).

خلاب *hallâb*, ة, very deceptive, very deceitful; beguiling; given to telling lies; — *hilâb*, ة *hilâba-t*, deceit; beguilement; blandishment; — *hilâba-t*, pincers.

خلابس *hulâbis*, pl. *halâbîs*, beguiling words; lie, swindle, fiction.

خلاس *hallâs*, robber, plunderer; — ى *hilâsiyy*, ة, born from a white mother by a black father, mulatto.

خلاص *halâs*, deliverance, rescue, salvation; — *hilâs*, sincerity; what is best and purest; pure ore; clarified butter; placenta; — *hallâs*, deliverer, saviour; — *hullâs*, rent, cleft, chink; — ة *hilâsa-t*, *hulasa-t*, what is best and purest, cream, essence; clarified butter; final moral; principal contents, résumé, extract; — ى *halâsiyy*, saving, salutary.

خلاط *hilât*, mixture; medley crowd; fundamental humour of the body; — *; — ة *halâta-t*, a folly.

خلاع *hulâ'*, ة *hulâ'a-t*, epilepsy; palsy; — ة *halâ'a-t*, disorderly life.

خلاف *hilâf*, contradiction; contrast; reverse, the contrary; what is against or in contradiction with; untruth; falseness; a false person; oriental poplar; — *; —

ḥallâf, who contradicts; disputant, quarrelsome; — ة *ḥalâfa-t*, degeneration; fault, vice; stupidity, folly, foolishness; — *ḥilâfa-t*, vicegerency, substitution, succession; dignity of a caliph, caliphate.

خلاق *ḥalâq*, full share of happiness, abundance; — *ḥilâq*, a cosmetic; — *ḥallâq*, creator; — ة *ḥalâqa-t*, INF. of (خلق).

خلال *ḥalâl*, sour dates; — *ḥilâl*, pl. *aḥilla-t*, tooth-pick; seton; borer; interval, interstice, intermission; middle; term; paradigm; — *ḥallâl*, seller of vinegar; — *; — ة *ḥalâla-t*, *ḥilâla-t*, *ḥulâla-t*, true friendship; — *ḥulâla-t*, impurity between the teeth.

خلان *ḥullân*, pl. of خليل *ḥalîl*.

خلاوى *ḥalâwî*, pl. of خلوة *ḥalwa-t*; — *ḥalâwiyy*, referring to a forest.

خلايا *ḥalâyâ*, pl. of خلية *ḥaliyya-t*.

(خلب) *ḥalab*, U, I, INF. *ḥalb*, wound, scratch; clutch and tear; split, tear; bite; beguile; captivate; — INF. *ḥalb*, *ḥilâb*, *ḥilâba-t*, deceive, beguile; — *ḥalib*, A, INF. *ḥalab*, be stupid, imbecile; — II. INF. *taḥlîb*, III. INF. *muḥâlaba-t*, beguile, deceive; — VIII. INF. *iḥtilâb*, be cut off with a sickle; deceive, beguile; allow one's self to be beguiled; — X. INF. *istiḥlâb*, scratch, wound; cut, mow.

خلب *ḥilb*, pl. *aḥlâb*, claw, clutches; nail; liver, lobe of the liver; flesh between the ribs; diaphragm; pl. *ḥulabâ'*, fond of women, lady's man; — *ḥulb*, *ḥulub*, bast of the palm-tree or rope of it; — *ḥullab*, cloud or lightning without rain.

خلبا *ḥalbâ*, silly, foolish (f.).

(خلبس) *ḥalbas*, INF. ة, beguile.

(خلبص) *ḥalbaṣ*, INF. ة, flee.

(خلج) *ḥalaj*, I, INF. *ḥalj*, draw, attract; tear out; move, shake; wean; occupy, engross; wink; nod, beckon, invite by nodding or beckoning; lie with; — I, U, INF. *ḥulûj*, tremble, quiver; — INF. *ḥalajân*, tremble, be agitated; — *ḥalij*, A, INF. *ḥalaj*, have pain in the bones; be deteriorated or corrupted; — III. INF. *muḥâlaja-t*, engross, fill with anxiety; — VI. INF. *taḥâluj*, engross the mind (فى *fî*); — VIII. INF. *iḥtilâj*, draw, attract; be agitated, tremble; wink; quiver; — XII. INF. *iḥlaulaj*, INF. *iḥlîlâj*, be complicated.

خلج *ḥuluj*, pl. of خليج *ḥalîj*; — *ḥillîj*, far, remote; — ة *ḥalija-t*, quivering, winking (adj.).

خلجان *ḥalajân*, trembling (s.); motion, emotion, agitation; curiosity; INF. of (خلج); — *ḥuljân*, pl. of خليج *ḥalîj*.

(خلجم) *ḥaljam*, tall and corpulent.

خلخال *ḥalḥâl*, pl. *ḥalâḥîl* = خلخل *ḥalḥal*.

(خلخل) *ḥalḥal*, INF. ة, bare the bones of the flesh; shake, agitate, bring out of order; — II. INF. *taḥalḥul*, get shaken, agitated; be rickety, out of order (m.).

خلخل *ḥalḥal*, *ḥulḥal*, pl. *ḥalâḥil*, *ḥalâḥîl*, ankle-ring; fine dresses; — hence II. *taḥalḥal*, INF. *taḥalḥul*, adorn the ankle with a ring.

(خلد) *ḥalad*, U, INF. *ḥald*, *ḥulûd*, last for ever, be eternal; enjoy lasting wealth; remain, abide; be still vigorous in advanced age; age late; — II. INF. *taḥlîd*, make eternal, render lasting, remain, abide; age late; — IV. INF. *iḥlâd* = II.; incline towards; be attached to one's companion, &c.

خلد *ḥuld*, everlastingness, eternity; paradise; vigorous old age; pl. *ḥilada-t*, ear-ring, bracelet; — *ḥuld*, *ḥald*, ة, pl. *manâjiz*, mole (animal); — *ḥalad*, mind, heart,

thought; — ة *ḫalada-t*, pl. *ḫalad*, ear-ring, bracelet.

(خلس) *ḫalas*, I, INF. *ḫals*, *ḫillîsa*, snatch away clandestinely, rob by surprise, steal; — III. INF. *muḫâlasa-t*, snatch from (acc.); do anything furtively; dodge; —IV. INF. *iḫlâs*, be half withered and half green; be half grey;— V. INF. *taḫallus*, rob;—VIII. INF. *iḫtilâs*, snatch, rob.

خلس *ḫuls*, pl. of *ḫalsâ'*; — ة *ḫulsa-t*, pl. *ḫulas*, sudden robbery; secret theft; stolen good.

خلسا *ḫalsâ'*, pl. *ḫuls*, half grey (f.); aged woman.

(خلص) *ḫalaṣ*, U, INF. *ḫulûṣ*, *ḫâlîṣa-t*, be pure, genuine; INF. *ḫulûṣ*, happen, happen to; protect, preserve; save one's self, escape safely; finish, complete; — also *ḫaliṣ*, A, INF. *ḫalaṣ*, be broken in several places; — II. INF. *taḫlîṣ*, purify, clean; love sincerely; deliver, rescue, save; extricate one's self out of a plight; take the best part; — III. INF. *muḫâlaṣa-t*, act with faithfulness and sincerity towards (acc.); — IV. INF. *iḫlâṣ*, purify, clean; be sincere; — V. INF. *taḫalluṣ*, get freed, saved, rescued; free one's self, &c.; escape; — X. INF. *istiḫlâṣ*, wish for sincerely; demand a thing pure, unadulterated, in best quality; appropriate; rescue, free, loosen.

خلص *ḫilṣ*, pl. *ḫulaṣâ'*, *ḫulṣân*, sincere friend; — *ḫullaṣ*, pl. of خالص *ḫâliṣ*, pure, &c.

(خلط) *ḫalaṭ*, I, INF. *ḫalṭ*, mix; tell every secret to, initiate in everything; — II. INF. *taḫlîṭ*, mix well; confuse; — III. INF. *ḫilâṭ*, *muḫâlaṭa-t*, mix with people; have intercourse with, visit frequently; meet; lie with; — IV. INF. *iḫlâṭ*, cover (a mare); mix with (ب *bi*); — VIII. INF. *iḫtilâṭ*, be mixed, mingled; be in confusion; get confused, grow passionate.

خلط *ḫalṭ*, *ḫaliṭ*, everybody's friend; stupid; fool; — *ḫalṭ*, mixing (s.), mixture; confusion, mistake, misunderstanding; خ • ملط *ḫalṭ malṭ*, hurly-burly; — *ḫilṭ*, pl. *aḫlâṭ*, mixture; the four fundamental humours of the body; chyme; خ • ملط *ḫilṭ milṭ*, of mixed blood; mixed fodder; medley; — *ḫuluṭ*, pl. of خليط *ḫalîṭ*; — ة *ḫilṭa-t*, *ḫulṭa-t*, social intercourse, friendship; (m.) share in a business, &c.

خلطا *ḫulaṭâ'*, pl. of خليط *ḫalîṭ*.

خلطى *ḫilṭiyy*, humorous.

(خلع) *ḫala'*, INF. *ḫal'*, draw out slowly, take from beneath; pull off, strip; depose, dethrone, abdicate; repudiate; rebel, revolt; lead a self-willed life; unhinge a door; — INF. *ḫal'*, dismiss a wife renouncing her dowry; invest with a robe of honour; — *ḫalu'*, INF. *ḫalâ'a-t*, lead a dissolute life and be given up by one's people; — II. INF. *taḫlî'*, draw out, extract; remove; (m.) sprain, put out of joint, unhinge; — III. INF. *muḫâla'a-t*, ask for a divorce; play at dice; — V. INF. *taḫallu'*, be taken out, taken away, removed; be sprained, relaxed, contorted; get unhinged; be given to drink; — VI. INF. *taḫâlu'*, divorce from one another; break a contract mutually; — VII. INF. *inḫilâ'*, get extracted, drawn out, removed; abdicate, resign; be sprained, relaxed; — VIII. INF. *iḫtilâ'*, obtain a divorce by renouncing the dowry; deprive one of his property.

خلع *ḫal'*, dethronement, deposition, abdication, dismissal; revolt, rebellion; — *ḫul'*, divorce; — ة *ḫil'a-t*, pl. *ḫila'*, robe of honour; — *ḫul'a-t*, divorce at

the wife's wish; also *hil'a-t*, the best part of a property.

خلعا *hal'â'*, hyena; — *hula'â'*, pl. of خليع *halî'*.

(خلعلع) *hala'la'*, female hyena.

(خلف) *halaf*, U, (A), INF. *hilâfa-t*, *hillîfa*, come after, follow, succeed; remain behind of (عن 'an), not equal, survive; seize from behind; flee; compensate; — INF. *hilâfa-t*, *hulûf*, be stupid; degenerate; — INF. *halfa-t*, patch up; compensate, restore; marry a woman (على 'ala) after her husband's death; — INF. *hulûf*, *hulûfa-t*, have foul breath (from fasting); be deteriorated, putrid; — *halif*, A, INF. *halaf*, lean towards one side in walking; be big with young; be left-handed; have only one eye; — II. INF. *tahlîf*, allow another to get behind one's self; choose for a successor; leave descendants, beget children, give birth, drop young ones; — III. INF. *hilâf*, *muhâlafa-t*, disagree, contradict, thwart; transgress the law; caper in walking, &c.; — IV. INF. *ihlâf*, break a promise; compensate for a loss; patch up; — V. INF. *tahalluf*, lag behind; follow, succeed; — VI. INF. *tahâluf*, be of an opposite opinion, contradict one another, oppose one another; — VIII. INF. *ihtilâf*, disagree; be heterogeneous, vary; turn to one to adopt his opinions, to learn from him; be a successor or substitute; — X. INF. *istihlâf*, wish or appoint for one's successor or substitute.

خلف *half*, behind, after; back; successor, descendant; descendants; posterity; خ الباب *half al-bâb*, bolt; — pl. *hulûf*, short rib; descendant; absent from the tribe or just returned; — *hilf*, contradictory, different; discord; pl. *ahlâf*, short rib; udder or teat of a camel; — *hulf*, pl. *ahlâf*, contradictory; deceptive; not according to promise; breach of word; discord; fault; — *halaf*, pl. *ahlâf*, coming after, successor, descendant, offspring; apprentice; consequence, requital; recompense; — ة *hilfa-t*, difference of opinion; disagreement; contradiction; coming after or behind, successor; succession; relapse, return of an illness; diarrhœa; — *hulfa-t*, difference of opinion; difference; contradiction, contrast; refractoriness; vice, fault; stupidity, foolishness; pl. *hulaf*, after-taste; loss of appetite; — *halifa-t*, camel big with young.

خلفا *hulafâ'*, pl. of خليفة *halîfa-t*.

خلفانى *halfâniyy*, coming behind or after; back part.

(خلفف) *hulfuf* (m. and f.), f. also ة, stupid.

خلفنة *hilafna-t*, خلفنات *hilafnât* (m. and f., sing. and pl.), who is of a totally different opinion; strong divergence of opinion.

خلفى *halafiyy*, following each other, successive.

(خلق) *halaq*, U, INF. *halq*, create; invent; determine according to weight and measure; polish a speech; smoothe, level; fit to one another, adapt; sew together; — INF. *halq*, *halqa-t*, measure out leather, &c., before cutting it; — *haliq*, A, INF. *halaq*, be worn out, threadbare; be smooth, level; — *haluq*, INF. *hulûqa-t*, *halâqa-t*, be smooth, level; be suitable, fit; INF. *halâqa-t*, be of a good disposition; INF. *hulûqa-t*, *halaq*, be worn out, threadbare; — II. INF. *tahlîq*, create; form beautiful; level, smoothe; invent lies; perfume; — III. INF. *muhâlaqa-t*, show a handsome disposition towards

(acc.); — IV. INF. *iḫlâq*, wear out, use up, fray; be worn out, threadbare; — V. INF. *taḫalluq*, invent; form one's self after another; take after his character or manners; change one's character; be impregnated with perfumes; grow angry against (على *'ala*); — VIII. INF. *iḫtilâq*, invent, feign, forge lies; be suited to (ب *bi*); — XII. *iḫlaulaq*, INF. *iḫlîlâq*, be level and smooth; be very much worn out.

خلق *ḫalq*, creation; creatures; mankind; people; — *ḫulq*, *ḫuluq*, pl. *aḫlâq*, natural disposition; inborn quality; manners; (m.) anger, irritation; bravery; religion; humanity, refinement; — *ḫalaq* (m. and f.), f. also ة, pl. *ḫulqân*, *aḫlâq*, worn, threadbare; rags; old age; men, people; — *ḫaliq*, having good endowments or natural disposition; — ة *ḫilqa-t*, pl. *ḫilaq*, natural shape, inborn quality; make; face; *ḫalqat-an*, by nature; — *ḫulqa-t*, creation; character; — *ḫalaqa-t*, pl. *ḫalaq*, rags, tatters.

خلقا *ḫalqâ'*, f. of اخلق *aḫlaq*, smooth, level, &c.; — *ḫulaqâ'*, pl. of خليق *ḫalîq*.

خلقى *ḫalqiyy*, ة, produced by nature, natural; — *ḫulqiyy*, natural, inborn; — ة *ḫalqiyya-t*, creation.

خلقين *ḫalqîn*, pl. *ḫalâqîn*, kettle.

خلل *ḫalal*, pl. *ḫilâl*, break of continuity, intermission; laxity; breach; rent, split, interstice, interval; gap; hiatus; cavity; cell; disorder; disturbance (of the mind); fault, defect, injury, damage; pl. of خلة *ḫalla-t*; — *ḫilal*, pl. of خلة *ḫilla-t*; — *ḫulal*, pl. of خلة *ḫulla-t*.

(خلم), II. *ḫallam*, INF. *taḫlîm*, choose, elect, select; — III. INF. *muḫâlama-t*, contract a friendship with (acc.); — VIII. INF. *iḫtilâm*, choose, select.

خلم *ḫilm*, pl. *ḫulamâ'*, *aḫlâm*, friend, comrade.

خلنبوس *ḫalambûs*, marcasite; flint-stone.

خلنج *ḫalanj*, a tree of whose wood vessels were made; (m.) quite new.

(خلو) *ḫalâ*, U, INF. *ḫalâ'*, *ḫuluww*, be void, empty, vacant; be free, at leisure, have time for; desist from; fail; keep to one dish; come to an empty, solitary, or secret place; be one's exclusive property; pass. have passed; mock at; — INF. *ḫalw*, be alone with in private; retire to or be in a private place; retire alone; admit without a witness; — II. INF. *taḫliya-t*, empty, void; leave, let; keep alive, spare; dismiss, set free; — III. INF. *muḫâlât*, leave, leave off, let; — IV. INF. *iḫlâ'*, empty or have emptied; set apart; find a place empty; find a secret place; be empty, secret, private; be with one or find one with another alone in a private place; admit without a witness; — V. INF. *taḫallî*, be alone with, have commerce only with, make use of one's exclusive service; have nothing to do with, withdraw one's hand from, renounce, repudiate; be weakened, depressed; — VIII. INF. *iḫtilâ'*, retire into solitude, lead a solitary life; be empty, void, free, vacant; ask for admission without a witness.

خلو *ḫilw*, pl. *aḫlâ'*, alone in a private place; empty, free, vacant; rid of; — *ḫuluww*, emptiness; vacuum, empty space; being without occupation, at leisure; unconcern; *ḫuluww-an min*, without, except; INF. of (خلو); — *ḫalû'*, restive; — *ḫulû'*, INF. of (خلا); — ة *ḫalwa-t*, pl.

ḫalawât, secret or private place;
temple of the Druses; solitude,
solitary life; pl. *ḫalâwî*, private
room, closet; private audience;
— *ḫilwa-t*, free, vacant, single
(f.).

خلوب *ḫalûb*, who beguiles, tells lies
(f.).

خلود *ḫulûd*, eternity; everlasting
happiness; vigorous old age.

خلوص *ḫalûṣ*, sincere friendship; sincerity; true devotion, genuine
piety.

خلوصات *ḫulûṣât*, purest extract.

خلوصية *ḫulûṣiyya-t*, sincerity; purity.

خلوف *ḫulûf*, degeneracy, corruption;
absent.

خلوق *ḫalûq*, an aroma; — *

خلول *ḫulûl*, emaciation.

خلولة *ḫulûla-t*, friendship.

(خلى) *ḫala'*, I, INF. *ḫaly*, cut or
tear out greens or herbs for
the cattle; — IV. let herbs grow
for the cattle; abound in herbs;
— VIII. INF. *iḫtilâ'* = I.

خلى *ḫal-an*, *ḫal-a*, greens, herbs;
— *ḫaliyy*, ة, pl. -ûn, *aḫliyâ'*,
empty, free, vacant, single (not
married); bee-hive; honey-jar;
— ة *ḫaliyya-t*, freely pasturing
milch-camel; pl. *ḫalâyâ*, bee-
hive; large ship.

خليج *ḫalij*, pl. *ḫuluj*, *ḫuljân*, bay;
gulf; strait; river, canal; bank,
shore; small ship.

خليس *ḫalîs*, half-grey; withered.

خليسى *ḫillîsa*, INF. of (خلس).

خليط *ḫalîṭ*, pl. *ḫuluṭ*, *ḫulaṭâ'*, mixed;
mixture; mixed crowd, medley;
caravan; companionship, partnership; partner; mate, husband; neighbour; cousin; — ة
ḫalîṭa-t, mixed milk; — ى *ḫillîṭa*,
who mixes; — *ḫulaiṭa*, disorder,
confusion; rabble.

خليع *ḫalî'*, pl. *ḫula'â'*, taken from
its place; given up, repudiated;
worn out; wolf; العذر خ *ḫalî'
al-'iẕr*, empty, free, headstrong,
refractory, shameless.

خليف *ḫalîf*, pl. *ḫalaf*, *ḫuluf*, *ḫulf*,
channel, canal; valley; sharp
arrow; — ة *ḫalîfa-t*, pl. *ḫalâ'if*,
successor; vicegerent, substitute; caliph; deputy; assistant,
lieutenant; — *ḫillîfa-t*, refractory; — ى *ḫillîfa*, successor; vicegerency, lieutenancy; dominion;
INF. of (خلف).

خليق *ḫalîq*, pl. *ḫulaqâ'*, *ḫuluq*, fit,
suitable, appropriate; accus-
tomed; — *ḫulaiq*, slightly worn;
— ة *ḫalîqa-t*, pl. *ḫalâ'iq*, nature,
natural disposition; creature;
mankind; the animal world; pl.
character, manners.

خليقا *ḫulaiqâ'*, tip of a horse's
nose; soft parts of the head.

خليل *ḫalîl*, pl. *aḫillâ'*, *ḫullân*, f. ة,
pl. -ât, *ḫalâ'il*, familiar friend
(الله خ *ḫalîl al-lâh-i*, Abraham);
beloved one; f. friendship.

(خم) *ḫamm*, I, U, INF. *ḫamm*,
ḫumûm, be deteriorated, putrid;
cut into pieces; cry violently;
— U, INF. *ḫamm*, sweep, clean,
brush; — V. INF. *taḫammum*,
make a clean dish of it.

خم *ḫimm*, empty garden; — *ḫumm*,
pl. *ḫimama-t*, manger, basket
for hens, &c.

خمار *ḫimâr*, pl. *aḫmira-t*, *ḫumur*,
ḫumur, veil, head-gear of women;
covering; — *ḫumâr*, headache,
seediness; — *ḫammâr*, wine-
merchant; tavern-keeper; — ة
ḫammâra-t, *ḫamâra-t*, tavern,
wine-house.

خماس *ḫumâs-a*, by fives; — ى *ḫu-
mâsiyy*, consisting of five letters
(foot of verse); five spans long.

خماس *ḫimâs*, خماص *ḫamâ'iṣ*, pl. of
خميص *ḫamîṣ*, ة *ḫamîṣa-t* resp.; —
ة, خماصة *ḫamâṣa-t*, hunger; INF.
of (خمص).

خماض *ḫummâḍ*, sorrel.

خماط *ḫammâṭ*, roaster of meat.

خمال *ḫumâl*, sincere friend; a
disease of the joints causing to
limp.

خمالات *ḥimâlât*, pl. of خملة *ḥimla-t*.
خمالى *ḥumâliyy*, sincere friend.
خماما *ḥamâmâ*, elder (tree).
خمامة *ḥumâma-t*, sweepings, offal; crumbs.
خمان *ḥumân*, elder (tree); — *ḥammân*, *ḥimmân*, *ḥummân*, rabble; anything worthless.
خمبرجى *ḥumbarajiyy*, pl. ة, bombardier.
خمبرة *ḥumbara-t*, bomb, shell (m., Pers.).
(خمج) *ḥamij*, A, INF. *ḥamaj*, be tired or weakened by illness; be deteriorated, putrid; be corrupted; mention with blame.
(خمجر) *ḥamjar*, *ḥumajir*, brackish water, brine.
خمجرير *ḥamjarîr*, bitter, briny, brackish; — ة *ḥamjarîra-t*, turmoil, tumult.
(خمخم) *ḥamḥam*, INF. ة, speak through the nose; drawl; eat in an improper manner.
خمخم *ḥimḥim*, a thorn-bush.
(خمد) *ḥamad*, U, INF. *ḥamd*, *ḥumûd*, cease to flicker without going out entirely; smoulder; subside; calm down; swoon, die; get disheartened; — *ḥamid*, A, INF. *ḥamad*, cease to flicker; — II. INF. *taḥmîd*, extinguish (a.); cover the fire; cool; discourage; —IV. INF. *iḥmâd*=II.; be quiet; silent.
(خمر) *ḥamar*, I, U, INF. *ḥamr*, cover, conceal; withhold one's evidence; be ashamed; give intoxicating drink; leaven; pass. *ḥumir*, have a headache, be seedy; — *ḥamir*, A, INF. *ḥamar*, conceal or veil one's self, be hidden; change completely; — II. INF. *taḥmîr*, cover; veil; leaven; — III. INF. *muḥâmara-t*, hide one's self from (ب *bi*); be close to; abide in a place; blend with, pervade, permeate; disturb the mind; sell a free man as a slave; (m.) cheat, conspire against; — IV. INF. *iḥmâr*, be hidden behind; hide one's self; withhold one's evidence; leaven; carry in one's mind; neglect; — V. INF. *taḥammur*, veil head and face; ferment; rise (dough); — VI. INF. *taḥâmur*, conspire; — VIII. INF. *iḥtimâr*=V.; — X. INF. *istiḥmâr*, take as a slave.
خمر *ḥamr*, pl. *ḥumûr*, wine; any fermented or intoxicating drink; — *ḥimr*, hatred; — *ḥamar*, what covers, conceals; — *ḥamir*, abounding in wine; intoxicated; — *ḥumur*, *ḥumr*, pl. of خمار *ḥimâr*; — *ḥimirr*, veil; — ة *ḥamra-t*, wine; intoxicating drink; leaven; — *ḥamra-t*, *ḥamara-t*, great crowd; — *ḥimra-t*, way of wearing a veil; shell; — *ḥumra-t*, leaven; dregs, lees of wine; rouge; headache; pl. *ḥumar*, small prayer-carpet; — *ḥumra-t*, *ḥamara-t*, perfumes; — *ḥamara-t*, *ḥimara-t*, *ḥumara-t*, scent, fragrance; — ى *ḥamriyy*, purple-coloured; wine-like.
(خمس) *ḥamas*, U, INF. *ḥams*, take the fifth part of one's property; be or come as the fifth; — II. INF. *taḥmîs*, construct a pentagon, make pentagonal, divide by five; — IV. INF. *iḥmâs*, become five; water a camel on the fifth day.
خمس *ḥams*, f. five; hand; — *ḥims*, watering the camel on the fifth day (s.); — *ḥums*, *ḥumus*, pl. *aḥmâs*, fifth part; — ة *ḥamsa-t*, m. five.
خمسون *ḥamsûn*, (m.) خمسين *ḥamsîn*, fifty; the fifty days before the spring equinox; fifty days hot wind; fiftieth.
(خمش) *ḥamaś*, U, INF. *ḥamś*, *ḥumûś*, scratch, wound with the claws or nails; give a box on the ear; cut off a limb, amputate.
(خمشتر) *ḥamaśtar*, mean, miserly, avaricious.

(خمص) *ḥamaṣ*, U, INF. *ḥamṣ*, *ḥumûṣ*, subside, decrease; — INF. *ḥamṣ*, *ḥumûṣ*, *maḥmaṣa-t*, empty; be empty and hungry; be thin; — *ḥamiṣ*, be empty, thin in the waist; — *ḥamuṣ*, INF. *ḥamâṣa-t*, id.; — VI. INF. *taḥâmuṣ*, be close by without touching; be near the morning; — VII. INF. *inḥimâṣ*, decrease, subside; — ة *ḥamṣa-t*, hunger.

خمصان *ḥumṣân*, ة=خميص *ḥamîṣ*.

(خمط) *ḥamaṭ*, I, INF. *ḥamṭ*, roast meat; skin and roast a kid; — U, I, put milk into the bag; — U, INF. *ḥamṭ*, *ḥumûṭ*, smell nice, and, by opposition, smell badly; — *ḥamiṭ*, A, INF. *ḥamaṭ*, id.; be proud; be angry; — V. INF. *taḥammuṭ*, be proud; be agitated; be angry; roar.

خمط *ḥamṭ*, sour, bitter; a tree of which tooth-picks are made; — *ḥamiṭ*, agitated; — ة *ḥamṭa-t*, smell of the milk of the vine-blossom; sourish wine.

(خمطرير) *ḥamṭarîr*, salt water, brine.

(خمع) *ḥama'*, INF. *ḥam'*, *ḥumû'*, *ḥama'ân*, limp, halt.

خمع *ḥim'*, pl. *aḥmâ'*, wolf.

(خمل) *ḥamal*, U, INF. *ḥumûl*, be unknown and count for nothing; be powerless, in a fainting fit, weak; pass. *ḥumil*, limp in consequence of a disease of the joints; — IV. INF. *iḥmâl*, leave in obscurity; fringe a garment.

خمل *ḥaml*, long-haired carpet; down of plush or velvet; fringes; noun of unity, ة, plumage of an ostrich; — *ḥiml*, *ḥuml*, sincere friend; — *ḥamal*, pl. of خامل *ḥâmil*, nameless, &c.; — ة *ḥamla-t*, thicket; plumage of an ostrich; fringe; — *ḥimla-t*, stuff of camel's hair, silk, plush, camelot; — *ḥimla-t*, pl. *ḥimâlât*, secret.

خممة *ḥimama-t*, pl. of خم *ḥumm*.

(خمن) *ḥaman*, U, INF. *ḥamn*, say by way of surmise, surmise, suppose, think; estimate approximately; — II. INF. *taḥmîn*, id.

(خمو) *ḥamâ*, U, INF. *ḥamw*, be thick and consistent.

خمود *ḥumûd*, going out (s.); cooling (s.); decrease, subsiding (s.); discouragement; — *; — *ḥammûd*, place where fire is covered up and preserved.

خمور *ḥamûr*, leaven; — *

خموش *ḥamûš*, pl. flies.

خمول *ḥumûl*, obscure station; abandonment; weakness; — *

خميت *ḥamît*, big, stout, fat.

خمير *ḥamîr*, leavened; also ة *ḥamîra-t*, leaven; plastic material; — *ḥimmîr*, drunkard.

خميرجى *ḥamîrjiyy*, pastry-cook.

خميس *ḥamîs*, pl. *aḥmisâ'*, *aḥmisa-t*, fifth part; Thursday; army (as consisting of five parts).

خميص *ḥamîṣ*, pl. *ḥimâṣ*, f. ة, pl. *ḥamâ'iṣ*, empty; having an empty stomach; hungry; thin of waist; — ة *ḥamîṣa-t*, a black square garment.

خميط *ḥamîṭ*, roasted; sour milk.

خميل *ḥamîl*, soft, tender; with long and soft hair; — ة *ḥamîla-t*, pl. *ḥamâ'il*, soft sand, soft ground with luxuriant vegetation, woodland; soft long-haired carpets or stuffs, plush, velvet, camelot; plumage of an ostrich.

خميم *ḥamîm*, praised; high-minded.

(خن) *ḥann*, U, INF. *ḥann*, cut down the trunk of a palm-tree; take one's property; empty by degrees; tread under foot one's honour or rights; — I, INF. *ḥanîn*, speak, cry, or laugh through the nose; — X. INF. *istiḥnân*, smell badly.

(خنا) *ḥana'*, A, INF. *ḥan'*, cut down the trunk of a palm-tree.

خنا *ḥan-an*, *ḥan-a*, indecent talk

or actions ; debauchery ; calamity.

خناب *ḥinnâb*, long ; stupid ; thick-nosed ; — ة *ḥinnâba-t*, thick top of the nose.

خنابس *ḥunâbis*, pl. *ḥanâbis*, dwarfish ; very dark ; old ; strong ; lion.

خناث *ḥanâs-i*, fie on you! (speaking to a woman).

خنادر *ḥanâdir*, pl. of خندريس *handarîs*.

خنادل *ḥanâdil*, cataracts of the Nile.

خناس *ḥannâs*, devil ;—ى *ḥannâsiyy*, devilish, diabolical.

خناطيط *ḥanâṭîṭ*, dispersed troops of men.

خناطيل *ḥanâṭîl*, pl. of خنطولة *ḥunṭûla-t*.

خنافس *ḥunâfis*, lion.

خناق *ḥinâq*, *ḥunâq*, string for strangling ; throat ; (m.) collar ; — * ; — *ḥunâq*, strangulation ; also ة *ḥunâqa-t*, angina, croup ; — *ḥannâq*, hangman, executioner.

خنان *ḥanân*, joys of life ; — *ḥinân*, circumcision ; — *ḥunân*, cold, rheum, mucus.

خنانيص *ḥanânîṣ*, pl. of خنوص *ḥinnauṣ*.

(خنب) *ḥanib*, A, INF. *ḥanab*, suffer from a rheum ; be weak ; limp ; perish ; — IV. INF. *iḥnâb*, perish ; ruin, destroy, annihilate ; cut off ; weaken ; — V. INF. *taḥannub*, be proud.

خنب *ḥimb*, pl. *aḥnâb*, inner side of the knees and thighs ; — *ḥanab*, weakness of the joints ; — ة *ḥamba-t*, destruction, ruin ; — *ḥaniba-t*, charming and sweet of voice (f.).

(خنبس) *ḥambas*, INF. ة, divide the booty.

(خنبق) *ḥumbuq*, avaricious.

(خنبوص) *ḥumbûṣ*, spark.

(خنتار) *ḥintâr*, خنتور *ḥuntûr*, ravenous hunger.

خنتب *ḥuntab*, uncircumcised ; weak, dwarfish.

(خنتعة) *ḥuntu'a-t*, female fox.

(خنتف) *ḥuntuf*, rue (plant).

(خنث) *ḥanas*, I, INF. *ḥans*, bend outwards ; laugh at, mock ; — *ḥanis*, A, INF. *ḥanas*, be bent, inclined ; be soft ; be weak, impotent ; (m.) be effeminate, spoiled ; — II. INF. *taḥnis*, effeminate, spoil ; — V. INF. *taḥannus*, be soft, weak, impotent ; speak like a woman and submissively ; (m.) be effeminate, spoiled ; — V. INF. *inḥinâs*, id.

خنث *ḥins*, inner back part of the cheek ; — *ḥuns*, pl. *ḥinâs*, fold, bend ; — *ḥanis*, flexible ; weak, powerless, impotent ; (m.) spoiled.

خنثاة *ḥansât*, INF. of (خنثى).

خنثبة *ḥinsaba-t*, milch camel.

خنثر *ḥansar*, offal, rubbish, &c., remains of a camp.

خنثعبة *ḥansa'ba-t*, *ḥinsa'ba-t*, *ḥunsa'ba-t*, milch camel.

(خنثعة) *ḥunsu'a-t*, female fox.

(خنثل) *ḥansal*, fat and with a flabby belly (f.).

(خنثى) *ḥansa*, INF. *ḥansât*, make impotent.

خنثى *ḥunsa*, asphodel ; pl. *ḥanâsî*, *ḥanâsa*, *ḥinâs*, hermaphrodite.

(خنجر) *ḥanjar*, pl. *ḥanâjir*, large dagger ; poniard.

خنجل *ḥinjil*, stupid and boisterous woman ; — *ḥanjal*, INF. ة, marry such.

(خنخن) *ḥanḥan*, INF. ة, speak through the nose.

(خندب) *ḥundub*, malignant.

خندريس *ḥandarîs*, pl. *ḥanâdir*, old wine ; wheat.

(خندع) *ḥunda'*, small locusts ; — *ḥundu'*, frog.

(خندف) *ḥandaf*, INF. ة, walk fast ; step along proudly.

(خندق) *ḥandaq*, INF. ة, make a ditch, surround with a ditch or trench.

خندق *ḫandaq*, pl. *ḫanâdiq*, ditch, trench, moat.

خنذلة *ḫanẕala-t*, fulness of body.

خنذى *ḫanẕa*, INF. *ḫanẕât*, talk ribaldry.

خنذيذ *ḫinẕîẕ*, pl. *ḫanâẕîẕ*, good poet and reciter of older poems; mountain summit; long and thick; able, apt; heroic; stallion, and, by opposition, gelding, eunuch.

خنر *ḫunnar*, pl. of خانر, true friend.

(خنز) *ḫaniz*, A, INF. *ḫanaz*, be putrid.

(خنزب) *ḫanzab*, Satan; reprobate.

خنزجة *ḫanzaja-t*, haughtiness, pride.

خنززة *ḫanzaza-t*, iron tool for breaking stones; thickness.

(خنزوان) *ḫanzuwân*, boar; ape; — *ḫunzuwân*, ة *ḫunzuwâna-t*, ية *ḫunzuwâniyya-t*, haughtiness, pride.

خنزير *ḫinzîr*, f. ة, pl. *ḫanâzir*, *ḫanâzîr*, pig; خ برى *ḫinzîr barriyy*, wild boar; — ة *ḫinzîra-t*, goiter.

(خنس) *ḫanas*, I, U, INF. *ḫans*, *ḫunûs*, remain behind, lag; allow to get behind one's self; leave behind; seize by the thumb; speak evil of the absent; — *ḫanis*, A, INF. *ḫanas*, have an up-turned nose; — IV. INF. *iḫnâs*, let get behind one's self; — V. INF. *taḫannus*, calumniate, slander; — VII. INF. *inḫinâs*, remain behind.

خنس *ḫuns*, pl. of اخنس *aḫnas*, flat-nosed, &c.; — *ḫunus*, deer and their haunts; — *ḫunnas*, declining stars; planets (especially Venus and Mercury).

خنسا *ḫansâ'*, f. of اخنس *aḫnas*, having a flat or up-turned nose, &c.

(خنسر) *ḫansar*, pl. *ḫanâsira-t*, walking on the road to perdition.

خنسرى *ḫansariyy*, id.

خنشار *ḫanśâr*, fern.

(خنشل) *ḫanśal*, INF. ة, totter and tremble.

(خنصر) *ḫinṣir*, *ḫinṣar*, pl. *ḫanâṣir*, little finger or toe.

(خنط) *ḫanaṭ*, I, INF. *ḫanṭ*, grieve (a.), render sorrowful.

خنطول *ḫunṭûl*, long horn or penis; — ة *ḫanṭûla-t*, part of a cloud; — *ḫunṭûla-t*, pl. *ḫanâṭîl*, herd of cattle or camels separate from others.

(خنظى) *ḫanẓa*, INF. *ḫanẓât*, *ḫanẓâya-t*, talk ribaldry; expose to public shame, disgrace; mock at; excite hatred and enmity.

خنظيان *ḫinẓiyân*, obscene; shameless.

(خنع) *ḫana'*, INF. *ḫan'*, fornicate; sport with women; — A, INF. *ḫunû'*, submit to (n.); — II. INF. *taḫnî'*, cut down; — IV. INF. *iḫnâ'*, submit (a.), subdue, make submissive.

خنع *ḫunu'*, pl. of خانع *ḫâni'*, fornicator; — ة *ḫan'a-t*, pl. *ḫunu'*, suspicion; obscene story; fornication; — *ḫana'a-t*, pl. of خانع *ḫâni'*.

(خنعب) *ḫan'ab*, long hair.

(خنعس) *ḫan'as*, hyena.

(خنف) *ḫanaf*, I, INF. *ḫinâf*, have tender soles; turn the mouth from the bridle, turn the neck towards the rider; cut into slices; beat one's breast; — INF. *ḫunûf*, be angry; — *ḫanif*, A, INF. *ḫanaf*, have a broken rib on one side.

خنف *ḫunuf*, traces; pl. of خنوف *ḫanûf* and خنيف *ḫanîf*; — ة *ḫanafa-t*, slice of orange.

(خنفس) *ḫanfas*, INF. ة, detest and turn from.

خنفسا *ḫunfusâ'*, *ḫunfasâ'*, خنفسة *ḫunfasa-t*, *ḫunfusa-t*, pl. *ḫanâfis*, *ḫanâfîs*, black beetle (scarabæus).

خنفع *ḫunfu'*, stupid.

(خنفقيق) *ḫanfaqîq*, misfortune, calamity.

(خنق) *ḫanaq*, U, INF. *ḫanq*, strangle, choke (a.); — II. INF. *taḫnîq*, id.; be close to; — III. INF.

ḥinâq, (m.) scold, rebuke and beat; — VI. INF. *taḥânuq*, beat one another and quarrel; — VII. INF. *inḥinâq*, get strangled, choke (n.).

خنق *ḥanq*, strangulation, suffocation; — *ḥaniq*, strangled; — *ḥunuq*, narrow clefts; — ة *ḥanqa-t*, base (of the hand).

خنة *ḥunna-t*, tone uttered through the nose; prepuce.

(خنو) *ḥanâ*, U, INF. *ḥanw*, talk ribaldry, act indecently, commit obscenities.

خنوت *ḥinnaut*, able and persevering.

خنوخ *ḥanûḥ*, Enoch.

خنور *ḥinnaur*, *ḥanawwar*, world; ام خ *umm ḥinnaur*, hyena, cow; good or bad fortune; Egypt; Balsorah; — *ḥannûr*, *ḥanawwar*, a reed; good fortune, luck.

خنوص *ḥinnauṣ*, pl. *ḥanânîṣ*, sucking pig; also ة *ḥinnauṣa-t*, the young of an animal; small.

خنوع *ḥanû'*, deceiver; who breaks his word; — *ḥunû'*, submissiveness.

خنوف *ḥanûf*, pl. *ḥunuf*, having the soles tender; — *ḥunûf*, anger.

(خنى) *ḥanî*, A, INF. *ḥan-an*, talk obscenely; cut down the trunk of a palm-tree; — IV. INF. *iḥnâ'*, talk ribaldry, talk obscenely; ruin, mar, destroy, annihilate (على *'ala*).

خنى *ḥan-an*, INF. of (خنى); misfortune, calamity.

خنيز *ḥanîz*, unleavened bread.

خنيف *ḥanîf*, pl. *ḥunuf*, coarse hemp, garments of hemp.

خنيق *ḥanîq*, strangled; choked.

خنين *ḥanîn*, crying or laughing through the nose, INF. of (خن).

(خو) *ḥaww*, hunger; — *ḥuww*, honey; — *ḥaw-in*=خوى *ḥawî*; — ة *ḥuwwa-t*, adversity; large plain.

خوا *ḥawâ'*, empty belly or stomach; empty space; interval, interstice; bleeding of the nose.

خواب *ḥawâbb*, pl. of خابة *ḥâbba-t*, relationship, relations.

خوات *ḥawât*, rustling of wings; low sound; (m.) folly; — *ḥawwât*, intrepid.

خواتم *ḥawâtim*, seals, &c., pl. of خاتم *ḥâtim*.

خواتين *ḥawâtîn*, princesses, matrons, &c., pl. of خاتون *ḥâtûn*.

خواجه *ḥawâja-h*, *ḥâja-h*, *ḥôja-h*, sir, master, doctor, &c., used in addressing gentlemen, especially Europeans.

خوار *ḥuwâr*, bellowing of cattle, bleating; — *ḥuwwâr*, ة, pl. *ḥûr*, very weak; sensitive, touchy; — ة *ḥawwâra-t*, hips.

خوارج *ḥawârij*, pl. of خارجى *ḥârijiyy*, rebel, &c.

خوارق *ḥawâriq*, pl. of خارق *ḥâriq*, extraordinary occurrence, &c.

خوارنة *ḥawârina-t*, pl. of خورى *ḥûriyy*.

خواص *ḥawwâṣ*, seller of palm-leaves; — *ḥawâṣṣ*, pl. of خاص *ḥâṣṣ* and خاصة *ḥâṣṣa-t*, favourite, &c.

خواصر *ḥawâṣir*, hypochondres, pl. of خاصرة *ḥâṣira-t*.

خواض *ḥawwâḍ*, a bold diver; enterprising.

خواطر *ḥawâṭir*, minds, &c., pl. of خاطر *ḥâṭir*.

خواطف *ḥawâṭif*, pl. of خاطف *ḥâṭif*, who seizes, &c.

خواطى *ḥawâṭi'*, sinners (f.), pl. of خاطئة *ḥâṭi'a-t*.

خواف *ḥawâf*, rumour, noise.

خوافق *ḥawâqif*, the four climates or quarters of the world, pl. of خافق *ḥâfiq*.

خوافى *ḥawâfî*, pl. of خافى *ḥâfî*, ة, concealed, &c.

خواقين *ḥawâqîn*, great moguls, pl. of خاقان *ḥâqân*.

خوالف *ḥawâlif*, pl. of خالفة *ḥâlifa-t*, tent-pole.

خوامع *ḥawâmi'*, hyenas, pl. of خامعة *ḥâmi'a-t*.

خوان *ḥiwân*, *ḥuwân*, pl. *aḥwina-t*, pl. pl. *ḥûn*, table; — *ḥawwân*, traitor; — *ḥawwân*, *ḥuwwân*, pl.

aḫwina-t, ḫaun, ḫûn, third month of the pagan Arabs; — ḫuwwân, pl. of خائن ḫâ'in, traitor, &c.; — ة ḫawwâna-t, back part, reverse.

خوانق ḫawâniq, pl. of خانق ḫâniq, strangling, &c.

خوانيق ḫawâniq, pl. of خانوق ḫânûq and خناق ḫunâq, angina.

خواية ḫawâya-t, emptiness; hollow (s.).

(خوب) ḫâb, U, INF. ḫaub, fall into poverty; — ة ḫauba-t, hunger.

(خوت) ḫât, U, INF. ḫaut, ḫawatân, pounce upon, seize; chase; break faith or one's word; suffer damage; age; — INF. ḫawât, rustle with the wings; (m.) be or become a fool; — V. INF. taḫawwut, seize, clutch; desist; — VII. INF. inḫiyât, VIII. INF. iḫtiyât, pounce upon.

خوت ḫût, خوتان ḫûtân, pl. of اخوت aḫwat, stupid, foolish, mad; — ḫaut, see above.

خوتع ḫauta', skilful guide.

(خوث) ḫawis̱, A, INF. ḫawas̱, be flabby, relaxed; be full of food and drink; have a flabby belly; associate with.

(خوخ) ḫauḫ, ة, peach; plum; — IV. INF. iḫâḫa-t, be small and hidden; — ة ḫauḫa-t, small skylight; peep-hole; bolt.

خوخا ḫauḫâ, ة, stupid, foolish.

خود ḫaud, pl. ḫûd, ḫaudât, handsome and delicate girl; — II. ḫawwad, INF. taḫwîd, walk apace; admit the stallion to the she-camels; take a little of a dish; — V. INF. taḫawwud, bend down (n.).

(خوذ), III. INF. muḫâwaẓa-t, dissent from, and, by opposition, agree with; — IV. INF. iḫâẓa-t, urge on; — VI. INF. taḫâwuẓ, make a compact or covenant; — ة ḫûẓa-t, pl. ḫuwaẓ, helmet (Pers.).

خوذان ḫauẓân, pl. servants.

(خور) ḫâr, U, INF. ḫuwâr, bellow, low, bleat; U, INF. ḫu'ur, ḫu'ûra-t, be weak; subside; melt (n.); — INF. ḫaur, beat or prick animals in their hind parts; — ḫawir, A, INF. ḫawar, be weak; — II. INF. taḫwîr, be enfeebled by hunger; be empty, starved; — IV. INF. iḫâra-t, turn, twist, bend (a.); — X. INF. istiḫâra-t, try to conciliate; clean.

خور ḫaur, pl. aḫwâr, valley; mountain-ridge; bay, gulf; river-mouth; — ḫûr, women of ill fame; pl. of خوار ḫawwâr, ة; — ḫawar, great weakness; futility; — ة ḫûra-t, what is best, most exquisite.

خورانة ḫûrâna-t, priesthood (m.).

خورانية ḫûrâniyya-t, parish (m.).

خوری ḫûriyy, pl. ḫawârina-t, parson (m.).

(خوز) ḫauz, enmity, hostility.

(خوزق) ḫauzaq, INF. ة, impale.

(خوس) ḫâs, U, INF. ḫaus, deceive; break one's word; be putrid; be unsaleable; — II. INF. taḫwîs, admit the camels singly to the water.

(خوش) ḫâś, U, INF. ḫauś, pierce; lie with; take; fill by small quantities; — II. INF. taḫwîś, diminish, lessen.

خوش ḫauś, hypochondres, side.

(خوص) ḫawiṣ, A, INF. ḫawaṣ, have deep-set eyes; — II. taḫwîṣ, adorn with thin plates of gold; take a little; begin to appear; — III. INF. muḫâwaṣa-t, offer an exchange; exchange; ponder over, consider; — IV. INF. iḫâṣa-t, bear leaves; — V. INF. taḫawwuṣ, take a little; — VI. INF. taḫâwuṣ, exchange between one another.

خوص ḫûṣ, ة, leaf; tender branch.

(خوض) ḫâḍ, U, INF. ḫauḍ, ḫiyâḍ, enter or drive into the water; engage hastily in, rush into danger; begin with (فی fi); penetrate deeply; turn the sword in a wound; shake, stir up, mix

— II. INF. *taḥwîḍ*, enter the water; shake violently; mix; — III. INF. *muḥâwaḍa-t*, IV. INF. *iḥâḍa-t*, lead into the water; — VIII. INF. *iḥtiyâḍ*, go into the water; wade.

خوضة *ḥauḍa-t*, pearl.

(خوط), V. INF. *taḥawwuṭ*, come repeatedly to (acc.).

خوط *ḥûṭ*, pl. *ḥîṭân*, *aḥwâṭ*, tender branch; man in his prime.

خوطانة *ḥûṭâna-t*, خوطانية *ḥûṭâniyya-t*, slender, m. and f.

(خوطر), II. *taḥauṭar*, INF. *taḥauṭur*, change one's mind (m.).

(خوع), II. *ḥawwa'*, INF. *taḥwî'*, diminish, subtract from; break its bed; enfeeble by beating; pay a debt.

خوعم *ḥau'am*, stupid.

(خوف) *ḥâf* (I. Pers. *ḥiftu*), A, INF. *ḥauf*, *ḥaif*, *ḥîfa-t*, *maḥâfa-t*, fear, be afraid of (عن *'an*, من *min*); know; — U, surpass in fear; — II. INF. *taḥwîf*, frighten, cause to fear; render formidable, feared; — III. INF. *muḥâwafa-t*, surpass in fear; — IV. INF. *iḥâfa-t*, frighten, terrify; make unsafe; — V. INF. *taḥawwuf*, fear; diminish, lessen.

خوف *ḥauf*, fear; — خوف *ḥûf*, pl. of اخيف *aḥyaf*, having one eye blue, the other black, &c.; — خوف *ḥuwwaf*, pl. of خائف *ḥâ'if*, ag. of (خوف).

(خوق) *ḥâq*, U, INF. *ḥauq*, adorn with ear-rings; lie with; — II. INF. *taḥwîq*, widen; — IV. INF. *iḥâqa-t*, set out, travel; — V. INF. *taḥawwuq*, be wide, widened; be far; — VII. INF. *inḥiyâq*, be wide.

خوق *ḥauq*, ring for the ear or nose; — *ḥawaq*, scab; width, spaciousness.

(خول) *ḥâl*, U, INF. *ḥaul*, protect, govern, take care of one's people; — INF. *ḥaul*, *ḥiyâl*, administer well a fortune, &c.; — II. INF. *taḥwîl*, put into possession; enrich; endow with, bestow on (2 acc.); take as a manager or administrator; — IV. INF. *iḥwâl* (act. and pass.), have many uncles; judge well of a person by external signs; — V. INF. *taḥawwul*, id.; be another's manager; — X. *istiḥwal*, *istiḥâl*, have for an uncle; take as a slave.

خول *ḥawal*, possessions, property; bit of a bridle; — *ḥawal*, good economists, &c., pl. of خائل *ḥâ'il* and خولى *ḥauliyy*; — *ḥu'ul*, *ḥuwwal*, uncles, pl. of خال *ḥâl*; — ى *ḥauliyy*, pl. *ḥawal*, good economist, manager, steward, herdsman, gardener.

(خون) *ḥân*, I, INF. *ḥaun*, *ḥâna-t*, *ḥiyâna-t*, *maḥâna-t*, deceive, betray; break one's word or compact with (2 acc.); — II. INF. *taḥwîn*, deem or declare one to be a traitor; — V. INF. *taḥawwun*, VIII. INF. *iḥtiyân*, deceive, betray; — X. INF. *istiḥâna-t*, try to deceive or betray; mistrust.

خون *ḥaun*, (m.) *ḥawan*, deceit; treachery; abuse of confidence; breach of promise; (m.) adultery; — ة *ḥawana-t*, pl. of خائن *ḥâ'in*, traitor.

خوور *ḥu'ûr*, ة *ḥu'ûra-t*, great weakness.

خوولة *ḥu'ûla-t*, being a maternal uncle (s.); pl. of خال *ḥâl*, uncle.

خوون *ḥu'ûn*, treacherous; perfidious.

(خوى) *ḥawa*, I, INF. *ḥawâ'*, be waste and deserted; — INF. *ḥaw-an*, *ḥawâ'*, have repeated fits of hunger; have an empty stomach; be not pregnant or have just borne; give no fire; — I, INF. *ḥayan*, deceive by not bringing rain (stars); set; — INF. *ḥayy*, intend, undertake; INF. *ḥawa-n*, *ḥawâya-t*, seize, rob, snatch away; — *ḥawî*, A, INF. *ḥayan*, *ḥuwiyy*, *ḥawâ'*, *ḥawâya-t*, be empty and deserted; be

empty; be not pregnant; — II. INF. *taḥwiya-t*, grow very fat; give suitable food to a confined woman; deceive; decline towards setting (star); draw in the body in the position of prayer; — IV. INF. *iḥwâ'*, be waste and deserted; be empty, be hungry; be very fat; give no fire; deceive; — VIII. INF. *iḥtiwâ'*, be empty; take everything from (من *min*); become a dotard; rob and devour; take possession of a piece of land.

خوى' *ḥawî* (خو *ḥaw-in*), having an empty stomach, empty, hungry; — *ḥawan*, emptiness of the stomach, hunger; — ة *ḥawiya-t*, food suitable for a confined woman.

خويف *ḥawîf*, timid, timorous.

خويل *ḥuwail*, patch of beauty.

خى *ḥayy*, intention, aim, end; INF. of (خوى); — ة *ḥiyya-t*, noose; rope.

خياب *ḥayyâb*, deceptive.

خيار *ḥiyâr*, choice; selection; conditional purchase; — also ة *ḥiyâra-t*, what is best, select; cucumber; water-melon; — *.

خيازر *ḥayâzir*, pl. of خيزران *ḥaizurân*.

خياشيم *ḥayâśîm*, pl. of خيشوم *ḥaiśûm*.

خياض *ḥiyâḍ*, INF. of (خوض).

خياط *ḥiyâṭ*, needle; path, road; — *ḥayyâṭ*, tailor; Enoch; — ة *ḥiyâṭa-t*, profession of a tailor.

خيال *ḥayâl*, pl. *aḥyala-t*, conception, idea; imagination, fancy; phantom, apparition, spectre, ghost; hallucination; human shape, person, object seen in the distance; terrible sight; scarecrow; — *ḥiyâl*, imagination, fancy; shadow; good administration; — *ḥayyâl*, horseman, cavalry-man; — ة *ḥayâla-t*, pl. -*ât*, *aḥyila-t*, imagination, phantasm, phantom, spectre; form; — *ḥayyâla-t*, troop of horsemen; cavalry; — ى *ḥayâliyy*, ة, imaginary, ideal; قوة خيالية *quwwa-t ḥayâliyya-t*, imagination, imaginative power.

خيام *ḥiyâm*, pl. of خيم *ḥaim* and خيمة *ḥaima-t*; — *ḥayyâm*, inhabitant of a tent; nomad; maker of tents.

خيانة *ḥiyâna-t*, deceit, treachery, abuse of confidence.

(خيب) *ḥâb*, I, INF. *ḥaiba-t*, be excluded, expelled, repudiated; be deluded in one's hope, disappointed; suffer a loss or damage; — II. INF. *taḥyîb*, IV. INF. *iḥâba-t*, delude, disappoint; — ة *ḥaiba-t*, deception, disappointment; mischance, miscarriage.

خيت *ḥât*, I, INF. *ḥait*, damage one's property, diminish; — INF. *ḥait*, *ḥuyût*, produce a sound.

خيتعور *ḥaita'ûr*, mirage; wolf; lion; demon; Satan; death, calamity.

(خير) *ḥâr*, I, INF. *ḥair*, have or possess anything good; — INF. *ḥîra-t*, be good, merciful; — INF. *ḥiyar*, *ḥîra-t*, *ḥiyara-t*, prefer, choose, select; surpass in goodness; — II. INF. *taḥyîr*, deem better, prefer; choose in preference; leave the choice to (acc.); — III. INF. *muḥâyara-t*, contest for preference, emulate, vie; — V. INF. *taḥayyur*, choose in preference; — VIII. INF. *iḥtiyâr*, id.; select; prefer; desire; — X. INF. *istiḥâra-t*, demand anything good from (2 acc.); want the best of a thing for one's self.

خير *ḥair*, ة, pl. *ḥiyâr*, *aḥyâr*, pl. pl. *aḥâyir*, good, excellent; better; pl. *ḥuyûr*, anything good, desirable; good (s.); pl. wealth, good fortune; good action; — *ḥîr*, liberality; generosity; — *ḥiyar*, INF. of (خير); — *ḥayyir*, ة, pl.

ḥâra-t, good, pious person; generous, high-minded, liberal; ة *ḥayyira-t*, Medina; — ة *ḥaira-t*, anything good, select, exquisite; best; good action; pious foundation.; good disposition; — *ḥîra-t*, mercy and blessing of God;—*ḥîra-t*, *ḥiyara-t*, anything select, exquisite; choice; preference, preferment; — ية *ḥairiyya-t*, goodness; weal, welfare, luck, good fortune; advantage, source of advantage.

خيزران *ḥaizurân*, ة, pl. *ḥayâzir*, reed; bamboo; stick; spear; oar.

خيزور *ḥaizûr*, reed.

(خيس) *ḥâs*, I, INF. *ḥais*, be putrid; be deteriorated, smell badly; lie; — I, INF. *ḥais*, *ḥayasân*, break one's word or faith; abide in a place; fall in price; suffer damage.

خيس *ḥîs*, pl. *aḥyâs*, thicket; reed-bank; lair of a lion; — ة *ḥisa-t*, pl. *ḥiyas*, id.

(خيش) *ḥaiś*, pl. *ḥuyûś*, *aḥyûś*, tissue of linen, canvas; — ى *ḥaiśiyy*, maker of such stuff.

خيشوم *ḥaiśûm*, pl. *ḥayâśîm*, nose and its inside; promontory.

(خيص) *ḥâṣ*, I, INF. *ḥaiṣ*, be few or little; diminish in value; suffer loss or damage; — *ḥayiṣ*, A, INF. *ḥayaṣ*, have one eye smaller than the other.

(خيط) *ḥâṭ*, I, INF. *ḥaiṭ*, sew, stitch together; creep; — V. INF. *taḥayyuṭ*, be sewn, stitched together; — VIII. INF. *iḥtiyâṭ*, pass by with a leap, hurry by.

خيط *ḥaiṭ*, pl. *ḥuyûṭ*, *ḥuyûṭa-t*, *aḥyâṭ*, *ḥîṭân*, thread; الخ الاسود *al-ḥaiṭ al-aswad*, darkness preceding the dawn; الخ الابيض *al-ḥaiṭ al-abyaḍ*, light of dawn; خ باطل *ḥaiṭ bâṭil*, gossamer; pl. *ḥîṭân*, also sing. *ḥîṭ*, swarm of locusts, or ostriches; — *ḥayaṭ*, length of the neck; — ة *ḥaiṭa-t*, passed; thread.

خيطان *ḥîṭân*, pl. of خوط *ḥûṭ* and خيط *ḥaiṭ*.

(خيف) *ḥayif*, A, INF. *ḥayaf*, have eyes of different colour; — II. INF. *taḥyîf*, settle, settle down; — IV. INF. *iḥyâf* (also VIII.), come to *al-ḥaif* (see below); — V. INF. *taḥayyuf*, be of different colour, change from one colour into another;—VIII. INF. *iḥtiyâf* = II.

خيف *ḥaif*, pl. *ḥuyûf*, mountain-slope; side, region; *al-ḥaif*, a temple on mount Mina near Mecca; fear; pl. *aḥyâf*, kind, species; اولاد اخياف *aulâd aḥyâf*, children of the same mother by different fathers; — *ḥîf*, pl. of اخيف *aḥyaf*, having eyes of different colours; — *ḥiyyaf*, *ḥuyyaf*, pl. of خائف *ḥâ'if*, timid; — ة *ḥaifa-t*, knife; lair of a lion; — *ḥîfa-t*, pl. *ḥîf*, fear, fright; INF. of (خوف).

(خيل) *ḥâl*, A, INF. *ḥâl*, *ḥail*, *ḥiyal*, *ḥaila-t*, *ḥîla-t*, *ḥayalân*, *ḥailûla-t*, *maḥâla-t*, *maḥîla-t*, conceive, imagine; consider, take for; take untruth for truth; — II. INF. *taḥyîl*, imagine falsely, delude one's self; judge well of by outward signs; throw a suspicion upon (على *'ala*); look rainy; (m.) ride on horseback; gallop; put a horse into gallop; — III. INF. *muḥâyala-t*, be vain, proud; surpass in haughtiness; promise rain; (m.) inspire with a suspicion; (m.) yield shade; — IV. *aḥâl*, *aḥyal*, INF. *iḥâla-t*, appear probable; imagine falsely; promise rain, augur rain; set up a scarecrow, &c.; — V. INF. *taḥayyul*, imagine, take into one's head; be conceived, imagined; appear probable; suppose good or evil of a person; be haughty; be variegated; — VI. INF. *taḥâyul*, fancy, imagine; pretend, feign; — VIII. INF. *iḥtiyâl*, be haughty; walk

proudly; fancy, imagine; be thought, imagined, believed.

خيل *ḥail*, pl. *ḥuyûl*, *aḥyâl*, horses; horsemen, cavalry; also *ḥîyal*, INF. of (خيل); — *ḥîl*, asafœtida; rue; pl. of اخيل, q.v.; — *ḥayal*, ة *ḥayala-t*, haughtiness; — ة *ḥaila-t*, *ḥîla-t*, imagination.

خيلا *ḥailâ'*, f. of اخيل *aḥyal*, having many patches of beauty or moles; — *ḥuyalâ'*, haughtiness, pride, vanity.

خيلان *ḥîlân*, pl. of خال *ḥâl*, mole, &c.; (m.) siren, mermaid; — *ḥayalân*, INF. of (خيل).

خيلولة *ḥailûla-t*, imagination; haughtiness; INF. of (خيل).

(خيم) *ḥâm*, I, INF. *ḥaim*, *ḥiyâm*, *ḥuyûm*, *ḥuyûma-t*, *ḥayamân*, desist through cowardice and afterwards use stratagem; lift up the foot; — II. INF. *taḥyîm*, enter the tent; pitch a tent; settle, abide; form an arbour; — IV. *aḥâm*, *aḥyam*, INF. *iḥâma-t*, pitch a tent; — V. INF. *taḥayyum*, enter the tent, live in the tent; dwell.

خيم *ḥaim*, pl. *ḥiyâm*, hut of clay; — *ḥîm*, natural disposition, character; — ة *ḥaima-t*, pl. *-ât*, *ḥaim*, *ḥiyam*, *ḥiyâm*, tent; pavilion; arbour; arbour-walk; — ى *ḥaimiyy*, maker of tents.

خيهفعى *ḥaihaf'a*, خيهفعا *ḥaihaf'â'*, bastard of a dog and she-wolf.

خيور *ḥuyûr*, pl. of خير *ḥair*.

خيوش *ḥuyûš*, pl. of خيش *ḥaiš*.

خيوط *ḥuyûṭ*, ة *ḥuyûṭa-t*, pl. of خيط *ḥaiṭ*.

خيول *ḥuyûl*, pl. of خيل *ḥail*; — ة *ḥiyûla-t*, horsemanship.

خيوم *ḥuyûm*, ة *ḥuyûma-t*, fear; INF. of (خيم).

خييل *ḥuyail*, patch of beauty.

د

د *d*, as a numerical sign=4; abbreviation for Wednesday, fourth day of the week; for the planet Mercury, and for the sign of the Lion in the zodiac.

د *da'*, IMP. of (ودا), leave! let! — *dâ'*, pl. *adwâ'*, illness, disease; د الثعلب *dâ' as-sa'lab*, loss of the hair; د الذئب *dâ' az-zi'b*, hunger; د الفيل *dâ' al-fîl*, elephantiasis, leprosy; د الكلب *dâ' al-kalb*, hydrophobia.

(داب) *da'ab*, A, U, INF. *da'b*, *da'ab*, *du'ûb*, be zealous and diligent in a matter, exert one's self in it; repeat frequently; — INF. *da'b*, urge on violently; drive away; — IV. INF. *id'âb*, do anything with zeal and diligence.

داب *da'b*, matter, object of exertion; state, condition; — ة *dâbba-t*, pl. *dawâbb*, slowly moving, crawling animal; beast of burden; ass; sumpter.

دابر *dâbir*, past; extreme or last part; follower; root, foundation, reason; vault.

دابوغ *dâbûg*, water-melon.

دابوق *dâbûq*, bird-lime.

(داث) *da'as*, INF. *da's*, eat; be heavy; be soiled; soil.

داثا *da'sâ*, *da'asâ*, pl. *da'âs*, maid-servant, female slave.

داج *dâjj*, pl. *dâjja-t*, walking slowly; assistants, companions, partners; — *dâj-in*, see داجى *dâjî*.

داجن *dâjin*, ة, pl. *dawâjin*, tame; raining fast.

داجى *dâjî* (داج *dâj-in*), ة, enveloping, covering; dark; — ة *dâjiya-t*, pl. *dawâjî*, night.

داحس *dâhis*, داحوس *dâḥûs*, whitlow, abscess in the finger; — *dâḥis*, name of a celebrated horse.

داخل *dâḥil*, ة, ag. of (دخل); interior, inside; — ة *dâḥila-t*, pl. *dawâḥil*, mind, way of thinking; intention; custom; income; — ى *dâḥiliyy*, ة, interior; ناظر الداخلية *nâẓir ad-dâḥiliyya-t*, minister of the interior, home secretary.

(دادا) *da'da'*, INF. دئداء *di'dâ'*, *da'dât*, run very fast, hurry; move (a.), and, by opposition, set to rest, stop; cover; — II. INF. *tada'du'*, be moved, rolled, revolved.

دادا *dâdâ'*, pl. دادى *da'âdi'*, the last three or five days of the month; end of the month; broad canal; — *dâdâ*, pl. *dâdâwât*, chief of the dervishes; — ة *da'da'a-t*, rocking noise of a cradle.

(دادد) *da'dad*, INF. ة, play, toy, dally.

دار *dâr*, m. and f. pl. *diyâr*, *âdur*, *adwur*, *ad'ur*, pl. pl. *dûr*, *dûrât*, *diyârât*, *dîrân*, *adwâr*, *adwira-t*, house surrounding a yard, house; vestibule, yard; habitation, dwelling, residence; du. *ad-dâran*, this world and the world to come; د البقا *dâr al-baqâ'*, life eternal; د السلام *dâr as-salâm*, Paradise; Bagdad; د البوار *dâr al-bawâr*, hell; د الضرب *dâr aḍ-ḍarb*, mint; — *dârr*, pl. *durrâr*, bright; abounding in milk; abundant; — ة *dâra-t*, pl. *-ât*, *dûr*, house; halo; circle; circular inclosure.

دارابذين *dârâbzîn*, sofa; gallery; parapet; trellis-work.

دارب *dârib*, ة, exercised in hunting; well-drilled, clever.

دارج *dârij*, ة, ag. of (درج); spreading in all directions; vulgar; العربية الدارجة *al-'aribiyya-t ad-dârija-t*, vulgar Arabic.

دارس *dâris*, effaced, illegible.

دارش *dâriś*, black leather (Pers.).

دارع *dâri'*, armoured; cuirassier.

داركة *dârika-t*, understanding; intelligence, intellectual power.

دارمة *dârima-t*, porcupine.

داروس *dârûs*, pl. *dawârîs*, who treads out corn; thresher.

دارى *dârî* (دار *dâr-in*), knowing, having knowledge of, aware.

داسم *dâsim*, friend, comrade.

داسوس *dâsûs*, pl. *dawâsîs*, spy.

داشر *dâśir*, pl. *duśśâr*, pasturing freely (m.).

داصة *dâṣa-t*, pl. of دائص *dâ'iṣ*.

(داض) *da'aḍ*, fatness; plenty.

(داظ) *da'aẓ*, INF. *da'ẓ*, fill; worry, strangle, choke (a.); press out a tumour; grow fat; provoke to anger.

داعر *dâ'ir*, ة, pl. *du''âr*, impure; fornicator; whore; — ة *dâ'ira-t*, pl. *madâ'ir*, *madâ'ir*, fertile palm-tree.

داعى *dâ'î* (داع *dâ'-in*), pl. *du'ât*, ag. of (دعو), who calls, &c.; muezzin; preacher; supplicant; pretender, claimant; dey;—also ة *dâ'iya-t*, pl. *dawâ'î*, forcible cause, cause, pressing occasion, emergency; motive; claim; summoning; intention; petition.

داغ *dâg*, mark; stigma; impression (Pers.).

داغصة *dâgiṣa-t*, knee-pan.

داغم *dâgim*, black.

دافرة *dâfira-t*, curtain of a door.

دافعة *dâfi'a-t*, pl. *dawâfi'*, hindrance; stream; كوة دافعة *kuwwa-t dâfi'a-t*, power of repulsion.

دافة *dâffa-t*, army approaching the enemy.

داق *dâqq*, pl. *daqaqa-t*, who knocks.

(دال) *da'al*, INF. *da'l*, *da'al*, دالى *da'ala*, run with short steps, walk fast; INF. *da'al*, *da'alân*, deceive, lay snares for, waylay.

دال *da'l*, deceit; wolf; weasel; — *dâl*, name of the letter د *d*; crooked; — *dâl-in*, see دالى *dâlî*; — *dâll*, indicating, pointing to, demonstrating (adj.); leader, guide; significative; typical;

— ة *dâla-t*, pl. *dâl*, rumour; publicity; — *dâlla-t*, love-making; procuress; bravery.
دالب *dâlib*, live coal.
دالح *dâliḥ*, pl. *dullaḥ*, *dawâliḥ*, pregnant with rain.
دالف *dâlif*, pl. *dullaf*, *duluf*, heavily burdened.
داله *dâlih*, ة *dâliha-t*, weak-minded, imbecile.
دالى *dâlî* (دال *dâl-in*), pl. *dulât*, who draws water; — ة *dâliya-t*, pl. *dawâli*, water-wheel put in motion by oxen; vine; vein.
(دام) *da'am*, INF. *da'm*, prop up; — V. INF. *tada''um*, cover; — VI. INF. *tadâ'um*, cover entirely; — ة *dâma-t*, convent-soup; game of draughts (m.).
داما *da'mâ'*, *dâmâ'*, *dâmmâ'*, pl. *dawwâm*, sea; mouse-hole.
دامجانة *dâmjâna-t*, large bottle.
دامعة *dâmi'a-t*, wound which easily bleeds.
دامغة *dâmiga-t*, brain-wound.
دامكة *dâmika-t*, pl. *dawâmik*, calamity.
داموغ *damûg*, wounding the brain.
دامى *dâmî*, ة, bleeding; — ة *dâmiya-t*, wound from which blood is dropping.
دانق *dânaq*, *dâniq*, داناق *dânâq*, pl. *dawâniq*, sixth (or fourth) part of a drachm; small coin; — *dâniq*, contemptible; stupid.
دانى *dâni* (دان *dân-in*), approaching; near, close at hand; neighbouring; — also *dâni'*, contemptible, mean, low.
داهر *dâhir*, ever, never.
داهن *dâhin*, greased, anointed.
داهى *dâhî* (داه *dâh-in*), pl. *duhât*, *duhûn*, sagacious; prudent, cunning; *ad-dâhî*, lion; — ة *dâhiya-t*, pl. *dawâhî*, calamity; danger; very prudent.
داو *da'w*, INF. of (داى); — *dâw*, a kind of ship.
داود *dâwud*, داوود *dâwûd*, David.
داور *dâwar*, prince (Pers.); — ى *dâwariyy*, princely.
داوى *dâwî*, creamy; abundant; — *dâwiyy*, pl. *dâwiyya-t*, templar; — ة *dâwiyya-t*, *dâwiya-t*, desert.
(داى) *da'a*, INF. *da'w*, *da'y*, waylay, hunt after; take in, outwit.
داى *da'y*, ة *da'ya-t*, pl. دئى *da'iyy*, *da'yât*, place of the camel's hump where it is touched by the wood of the saddle; pl. *dâyât*, the six ribs of the shoulders; — ة *dâya-t*, nurse (Pers.).
دائب *dâ'ib*, diligent; tired; du. *ad-da'ibân*, day and night.
دائث *da'â'is*, pl. origins.
دائحة *dâ'iḥa-t*, pl. *dawâ'iḥ*, tree which spreads its shadow far.
دائخ *dâ'iḫ*, giddy; dark.
دائر *dâ'ir*, revolving, forming a circle; encompassing; roaming about; circle, roundness; round; — ة *dâ'ira-t*, pl. *dawâ'ir*, circle, periphery; disc; compass; cycle; revolution, rotation; orbit of a planet; reverse, vicissitude, calamity; defeat; suit of apartments; division, department, compartment; convent; retinue, attendants.
دائش *dâ'iś*, Christian.
دائص *dâ'iṣ*, pl. *dâṣa-t*, robber; beadle, bailiff, usher, summoner.
دائق *dâ'iq*, stupid; worthless.
دائم *dâ'im*, ة, pl. *dawâ'im*, lasting, eternal; quiet; stagnating.
دائمية *dâ'imiyya-t*, eternity.
دائن *dâ'in*, debtor; creditor.
دائى *dâ'i*, *dâ'iyy*, ة, ill, sick.
(دب) *dabb*, I, INF. *dabb*, *dabîb*, walking along slowly; crawl, creep.
دب *dibb*, ة *dibba-t*, slow walk; creeping, crawling (s.); — *dubb*, state, condition; inborn peculiarity; constitution; also ة *dubba-t*, mode, manner, method; — *dubb*, pl. *dibaba-t*, *adbâb*, f. ة, bear; — ة *dabba-t*, pl. *dibâb*, skin bag; tumbler; pumpkin.
(دبا) *daba'*, INF. *dab'*, rest; beat,

cudgel; — II. INF. *tadbî'*, cover, conceal.

دبا *dabbâ'*, f. hairy; — *dubbâ'*, ة, pumpkin; cucumber;—ة *dab'a-t*, flight; — *dabât*, pl. دبى *dab'an*, small wingless locust.

دباب *dibâb*, pl. of دبة *dabba-t*; — *dubâb*, fly (m.); — *dabbâb*, ة, what crawls, creeps; quadruped; — ة *dabbâba-t*, a war-engine used in a siege.

دبابيج *dabâbîj*, pl. of ديباج *dîbâj*.

دبابيز *dabâbîz*, pl. of دبوز *dabûz*.

دبابيس *dabâbîs*, pl. of دبوس *dabbûs*.

دباج *dabbâj*, seller of brocade.

دبادب *dabâdib*, pl. of دبداب *dabdâb*; — *dubâdib*, stout man with a loud voice.

دبار *dibâr*, *dubâr*, Wednesday; — *dibâr*, ة *dibâra-t*, piece of a sown field; — *dabbâr*, pl. *dabbârât*, expedient; — *; — ة *dubâra-t*, string, pack-thread, cord.

دباس *dabbâs*, maker of date-honey; — ى *dabâsî*, pl. of دبسى *dubsiyy*, *dubsa*.

دباغ *dibâg*, tanning (s.); — *dabbâg*, tanner; — ة *dibâga-t*, trade of a tanner.

دبال *dubâl*, dung.

دبان *dibbân*, ة, fly; د هندى *dibbân hindiyy*, Spanish flies.

دببة *dibaba-t*, pl. of دب *dubb*.

(دبج) *dabaj*, U, INF. *dabaj*, *dabaja-t*, paint with figures, embroider; — II. INF. *tadbîj*, id.; dress in brocade.

(دبح), II. *dabbaḥ*, INF. *tadbîḥ*, stretch the neck and bend down the head; sit always at home.

دبحس *dubbaḥs*, big and stout; lion.

(دبخ), II. *dabbaḥ*, INF. *tadbîḥ*=دبح *dabbaḥ*.

دبداب *dabdâb*, pl. *dabâdib*, drum.

(دبدب) *dabdab*, INF. ة, tread, step; walk slowly; crawl.

دبدب *dabdab*, ة *dabdaba-t*, drum; — ة *dabdaba-t*, trampling of hoofs.

(دبر) *dabar*, U, INF. *dubûr*, be hindmost, come behind, follow; INF. *dabr*, *dubûr*, turn the back; pass; grow old, age; veer to the west; be turned backwards; commemorate a deed or saying after one's death; fall behind the aim; take away; — INF. *dabr*, write; compose; die; — *dabir*, A, INF. *dabar*, be sore or ulcerated on the back; be rich in treasures; pass. be exposed to a west wind; — II. INF. *tabîr*, arrange, direct, dispose, plan; set free;—IV. INF. *idbâr*, turn the back; turn aside; desist; yield, flee; decline towards setting (star); come behind, follow; make the back sore; — V. INF. *tadabbur*, plan prudently and execute well; be well planned and executed; read attentively, study; pay attention; — VI. INF. *tadâbur*, leave one another in the lurch; — X. INF. *istidbâr*, turn aside; turn one's back to Mecca; recede; drive back; see at last and when it is too late.

دبر *dabr*, *dibr*, pl. *dibâr*, *dubûr*, *adbur*, swarm of bees; bee; great wealth; — *dubr*, *dubur*, pl. *adbâr*, back, back side, reverse; the buttocks; — *dabar*, turning one's back (s.); flight; —*dabir*, sore on the back (adj.); — ة *dabra-t*, pl. *dibâr*, flight; defeat; calamity; piece of sown field; — *dibra-t*, what one turns the back to, what is behind; — *dabara-t*, flight; pl. *dabar*, *adbâr*, soreness of the back.

دبران *dabarân*, fourth station of the moon; name of a star (bull's eye).

دبرى *dabariyy*, *dabriyy*, coming behind; coming or happening too late; *dabariyy-an*, too late; after one's death.

دبزة *dabza-t*, fist.

(دبس), II. *dabbas*, INF. *tadbîs*, conceal; be concealed; mend; boil must into syrup;—IV. INF. *idbâs*,

produce plants;—IX. INF. *idbisâs*, get black.

دبس *dibs*, honey; date-honey; syrup; — *dibs*, *dabs*, crowd of people; — *dubs*, pl. of *adbas*, dark-red; brown.

دبسى *dubsiyy*, *dubsa*, f. ة, pl. *dabâsî*, a dark bird; wild pigeon.

(دبش) *dabaś*, U, INF. *dabś*, peel; eat.

دبش *dabś*, ة, quarry-stone (m.); — *dabaś*, lumber; — ة *dabśa-t*, bush; thicket.

(دبغ) *dabag*, U, A, I, INF. *dabg*, *dibâg*, *dibâga-t*, tan; — VII. INF. *indibâg*, be tanned.

دبغ *dibg*, ة *dibga-t*, tanning-bark.

(دبق) *dabiq*, A, INF. *dabaq*, adhere, stick to (ب *bi*); smear with lime; — II. INF. *tadbîq*, catch birds with lime-rods; — IV. INF. *idbâq*, glue, lime; — V. INF. *tadabbuq*, get caught with lime-rods.

دبق *dibq*, glue, lime; bird-lime.

(دبك), II. *dabbak*, INF. *tadbîk*, stamp, trample, sprawl.

(دبكل) *dabkal*, INF. ة, drive together dispersed cattle.

(دبل) *dabal*, U, INF. *dabl*, *dubûl*, manure and improve the ground; —U, I, INF. *dabl*, bring together, gather; beat repeatedly; make a large morsel; — *dabil*, A, INF. *dabal*, be fat; — II. INF. *tadbîl*, make a large morsel.

دبل *dabl*, pl. *dubûl*, ulcer; plague-blister; brook;—*dibl*, pl. *dubûl*, calamity; robbery;—*dubal*, id.; robbed; bereaved, orphaned (f.); — *dubul*, pl. of دبيل *dabîl*; — ة *dabla-t*, *dubla-t*, ulcer, abscess; — *dubla-t*, pl. *dubul*, *dubal*, large round morsel; confection, confiture, &c.; belly-ache, colic; hole of the iron of an axe.

دبن *dibn*, sheep-fold.

(دبه) *dabah*, sandy tract; — II. *dabbah*, INF. *tadbîh*, get into sand.

دبوب *dabûb*, slanderer; walking slowly (adj.);, bleeding violently.

دبوز *dabûz*, double-warped cloth; variegated (Pers.).

دبور *dabûr*, west wind; — *; — *dabbûr*, custom; kind, species; party; sect; — *dubbûr*, pl. *dabâbîr*, hornet (m.); — ة *dabbûra-t*, mason's mallet.

دبوس *dabûs*, dates in butter; — *dabbûs*, pl. *dabâbîs*, iron mace; pin.

دبوق *dabûq*, bird-lime; lime-rods.

دبوقا *dabûqâ'*, bird-lime.

دبول *dabûl*, bereft of a son (f.); calamity; — *.

(دبى) *daba*, I, INF. *dab-an*, creep; walk slowly;—II. INF. *tadbiya-t*, make; — IV. INF. *idbâ'*, get covered with lice (leaves of a plant).

دبى *dab-an*, slow walk; lice on plants; — *dibbiy*, *dubbiyy*, someone, anyone, no one; — ة *dabiyya-t*, flight.

دبيب *dabîb*, creeping; reptile; animal; — *.

دبيج *dibbîj*, somebody, anybody, nobody.

دبير *dabîr*, thread drawn out in spinning.

دبيغ *dabîg*, tanned.

دبيل *dabîl*, heavy; — ة *dabaila-t*, calamity; ulcer, abscess.

(دث) *da<u>ss</u>*, U, INF. *da<u>ss</u>*, shoot from near and beneath one's clothes; beat severely; drive back, ward off; pass. have distorted limbs.

دث *da<u>ss</u>*, دثاث *di<u>s</u>â<u>s</u>*, slight rain; *da<u>ss</u>â<u>s</u>*, bird-catcher, fowler; — ة *da<u>ss</u>a-t*, slight cold.

دثار *di<u>s</u>âr*, pl. *du<u>s</u>ur*, upper garment; overcoat; destruction, ruin.

دثاى *da<u>s</u>â'iyy*, rain after heat.

(دثر) *da<u>s</u>ar*, U, INF. *du<u>s</u>ûr*, be effaced; be old; have fallen into oblivion; be abolished; be

dirty, rusty ; forget quickly ;
push forth leaves ; — II. INF.
tads̱îr, build a nest ; — V. INF.
tadas̱s̱ur, mount a horse ; — VI.
INF. tadâs̱ur, wrap one's self in
one's clothes ; vanquish the
enemy ; — VII. INF. indis̱âr, be
effaced, destroyed ; — VIII. INF.
iddis̱âr, gain riches.

دثر das̱r, great riches ; abundant ;
— dis̱r, good economist ; —
das̱ar, dirt, dregs, sediment ; —
dus̱ur, pl. of دثار dis̱âr.

(دظ) das̱at, U, INF. das̱t, open and
void a tumour.

(دع). das̱a', INF. das̱', kick violently.

(دثق) das̱aq, U, INF. das̱q, pour
out.

(دثن), II. das̱s̱an, INF. tads̱în,
pounce ; build a nest in a
tree.

دثور das̱ûr, sleepy, slow, lazy ; —
dus̱ûr, oblivion.

دثيمة das̱îma-t, mouse.

(دج) dajj, I, INF. dajîj, dajajân,
walk along slowly ; creep ; drop
the curtain ; INF. dajj, drop,
drip ; — II. INF. tadjîj, arm or
be armed to the teeth ; — V.
INF. tadajjuj, arm one's self to
the teeth ; — ة duja-t, pl. -ât,
دجى duja, button ; thumb, fore-
finger and middle finger ; —
dujja-t, deep darkness ; thick
fog.

دجا duj-an, dujâ, darkness.

دجاج dajâj, ة, pl. -ât, dujuj, dajâ'ij,
poultry ; cock, hen ; دجاج هندى dajâj
hindiyy, turkey.

دجارى dajâra, pl. of دجران dajrân.

دجال dajâl, dung ; — dajjâl, liar,
impostor, cheat ; Anti-Christ ;
— also ة dajjâla-t, large travelling company ; — dujâla-t, pitch.

دجانة dajâna-t, laden with goods.

دجائج dajâ'ij, pl. of دجاجة dajâja-t.

دجج dujuj, deep darkness ; pl. of
دجاج dajâj.

دجمان dajajân, INF. of (دج).

دجداج dajdâj, دجدج dujduj, pitch
dark.

(دجدج) dajdaj, INF. ة, decoy
poultry ; also II. INF. tadajduj,
be dark.

(دجر) dajir, A, INF. dajar, be dumbfounded, perplexed, confused in
one's speech, drunk ; — III. INF.
mudâjara-t, flee.

دجر dajr, dijr, dujr, dujur, bean ;
— dajar, astonishment, bewilderment ; drunkenness ; — dajir,
and—

دجران dajrân, pl. دجرى dajra, dajâra, dumbfounded, astonished,
bewildered ; drunk ; talking
confusedly.

(دجل) dajal, U, INF. dajl, smear
with pitch ; lie, deceive, cheat ;
lie with ; travel over a country ;
— II. INF. tadjîl, smear with
pitch, &c. ; gild, plate with
silver ; — ة dijla-t, Tigris.

(دجم) dajam, U, INF. dajm, be
dark ; — dajim, A, INF. dajam
and pass. dujim, be sad, sorrowful ; — ة dajma-t, word ; —
dijma-t, pl. dijam, friend, acquaintance ;—dujma-t, pl. dujam,
darkness ; love-sickness.

(دجن) dajan, U, INF. dujûn, remain,
stay, abide ; be tame ; — INF.
dajn, dujûn, be cloudy, dark,
rainy ; deceive, cheat, make
sport of (acc.) ; — IV. INF. idjân,
rain continuously ; last ; be dark,
rainy.

دجن dajn, pl. dujun, dijân, adjân,
plenteous rain ; cloudy sky ;
mist ; — dujunn, dijinn, ة du-
junna-t, pl. dujunn, dujunnât,
dark cloud without rain ; darkness ; gloomy weather.

دجنا dajnâ', f. of ادجن adjan, black ;
cloudy.

(دجه), II. dajjah, INF. tadjîh, pass
the night in a hunter's ambush
or hunting-hut.

(دجو) dajâ, U, INF. dajw, dujuww,

cover, wrap up; cover with darkness; be wide and long; spread far; — III. INF. *mudâjât*, flatter with concealed enmity; dissimulate; — IV. INF. *idjâ*, V. INF. *tadajjî*, XII. *idjauja*, INF. *idjijâ'*, be dark.

دجو *dajw*, darkness.

دجوجى *dajûjiyy*, dark, black.

دجى *dujan*, darkness; — ة *dujya-t*, darkness; pl. دجى *duj-an*, ambush of a hunter, hunting-hut.

دجيل *dujail*, pitch; little Tigris.

(دح) *daḥḥ*, U, INF. *daḥḥ*, hide, conceal in the ground; lie with; — VII. INF. *indiḥâḥ*, be wide, extensive.

دحاس *duḥâs*, chilblain; corn.

دحاق *diḥâq*, bearing down of the womb.

دحامس *daḥâmis*, pl. moonless nights.

(دحب) *daḥab*, I, INF. *daḥb*, drive back, turn off; INF. *daḥb* and *duḥûb*, lie with.

(دحبا) *daḥba'*, INF. ة, lie with.

(دحث) *daḥs*, eloquent, of elegant diction.

(دحج) *daḥaj*, INF. *daḥj*, drag on the ground; lie with.

دحجاب *dihjâb*, دحجبان *duḥjubân*, rising ground; hill.

دحدح *daḥdaḥ*, دحداح *daḥdâḥ*, ة *daḥdaha-t*, *daḥdâḥa-t*, short, small, little.

(دحدر) *daḥdar*, INF. ة, roll (a.); — II. INF. *tadaḥdur*, roll (n.), be rolled.

(دحر) *daḥar*, INF. *daḥr*, *duḥûr*, drive back, chase away, remove, turn off.

(دحرج) *daḥraj*, INF. ة, *diḥrâj*, roll down, roll (a.); — II. INF. *tadaḥruj*, roll, roll down (n.), be rolled.

(دحز) *daḥaz*, INF. *daḥz*, sleep with.

(دحس) *daḥas*, INF. *daḥs*, excite enmity, bring on mischief; conceal from (عن *'an*); skin; fill; be full; seek by groping with the foot.

(دحسم) *duḥsum*, دحسمان *duḥsumân*, ى *duḥsumâniyy*, corpulent, stout, fat and strong; dark brown; mischief-maker.

(دحص) *daḥaṣ*, INF. *daḥṣ*, beat the ground with the feet; sprawl; examine.

(دحض) *daḥaḍ*, INF. *daḥḍ*, sprawl; stir up the ground to seek; examine; — IV. INF. *idḥâḍ*, refute; annul, destroy; condemn.

دحض *daḥḍ*, *daḥaḍ*, pl. *diḥâḍ*, slippery place.

(دحق) *daḥaq*, INF. *daḥq*, drive away, remove, refuse; — IV. INF. *idḥâq*, id.; — VII. INF. *indiḥâq*, bear down after giving birth (womb).

(دحقب) *daḥqab*, INF. ة, push from behind.

(دحقل) *daḥqal*, INF. ة, swell.

(دحل) *daḥal*, INF. *daḥl*, dig into a well sideways; creep in; remove (n.); — *daḥil*, A, INF. *daḥal*, hide one's self; — III. INF. *mudâḥala-t*, use stratagem against, try to deceive; — IV. INF. *idḥâl*, creep in; hide one's self in a corner.

دحل *daḥl*, *duḥl*, pl. *diḥâl*, *duḥûl*, *duḥlân*, *adḥul*, *adḥâl*, burrow; side-hole; corner of a tent; — *daḥil*, impostor, cheat.

دحلا *daḥlâ'*, f. well narrow at the top.

(دحلط) *daḥlaṭ*, INF. ة, talk confusedly.

(دحلم) *daḥlam*, INF. ة, throw down from a mountain into a ravine; throw into a well.

(دحم) *daḥam*, INF. *daḥm*, push violently; lie with.

دحم *diḥm*, origin.

(دحمر) *daḥmar*, INF. ة, fill.

(دحمس) *daḥmas*, ة, black, dark; fat.

(دحمل) *daḥmal*, INF. ة, roll over the ground (a.); stretch on the ground to be trodden upon.

(دحن) *daḥin*, A, INF. *daḥan*, be short and paunch-bellied.

(دحو) *daḥâ*, U, A, INF. *daḥw*, extend, spread (a.); push; throw down; lie with; be big and flabby; — V. INF. *tadaḥḥî*, be spread; — *idḥawa*, INF. *idḥiwâ'*, id.

دحوق *daḥûq*, be afflicted with a bearing down of the womb.

(دحى) *daḥa*, INF. *daḥy*, spread; urge on; — ة *daḥya-t*, female ape; — *diḥya-t*, leader, general.

دحيق *daḥîq*, expelled, repudiated; removed; purblind.

دخ *daḫḫ*, *duḫḫ*, smoke.

دخا *daḫ-an*, darkness.

دخاخيل *daḫâḫîl*, pl. of دخل *duḫḫal*.

دخال *diḫâl*, mind, intention; insertion of a joint; religious custom; — *daḫḫâl*, who enters, interferes; mediator; د الاذن *daḫḫâl al-uẕn*, ear-wig.

دخان *duḫân*, *duḫḫân*, pl. *adḫina-t*, *dawâḫin*, *dawâḫîn*, smoke, steam.

دخانى *duḫḫâniyy*, smoky; smoke-coloured.

(دخج) *daḫaj*, blackness.

دخدبة *daḫdaba-t*, *diḫdiba-t*, having firm flesh (f.).

(دخدخ) *daḫdaḫ*, INF. ة, curb, tame, humble; hinder, prevent; make short steps; be tired, weary.

(دخدر) *daḫdar*, INF. ة, gild.

(دخر) *daḫar*, *daḫir*, A, INF. *duḫr*, *duḫûr*, be small, mean and contemptible.

(دخرص) *daḫraṣ*, INF. ة, make clear, explain.

دخرص *diḫriṣ*, who sees through and knows a thing.

(دخس), pass. *duḫis*, INF. *daḫs*, be concealed or buried in the ground.

دخس *duḫas*, dolphin.

(دخش) *daḫiś*, A, INF. *daḫaś*, be fleshy.

(دخص) *daḫaṣ*, A, INF. *duḫûṣ*, be fat.

(دخل) *daḫal*, U, INF. *duḫûl*, *madḫal*, enter; visit and lie with one's wife; perform the marriage rites; be included, enclosed; introduce; mediate between (بين *bain*); interfere, intermeddle; yield an advantage or rent; fall to one's share; pass. *duḫil*, INF. *daḫl*, also *daḫil*, A, INF. *daḫal*, suffer from an internal complaint, particularly from a disturbed mind; — II. INF. *tadḫîl*, cause to enter, introduce; inclose; insert; — III. INF. *mudâḫala-t*, frequent, be intimate with (acc.); intrude; seek an agreement with (acc.) in a matter (فى *fî*); — IV. INF. *idḫâl*, *mudḫal*, id.; — V. INF. *tadaḫḫul*, obtain admission by degrees; insinuate one's self; ask as a favour; — VI. INF. *tadâḫul*, steal in, intrude; intermeddle; intrigue; — VIII. INF. *iddiḫâl*, enter, enter upon, engage zealously in.

دخل *daḫl*, entrance; interference; intrusion, disturbance; mediation; income, rent, revenue; — *daḫl*, *diḫl*, mind, intention; custom, habit; — *daḫl*, *daḫal*, internal complaint; disturbance of mind; doubt, surmise, suspicion; dissimulation, stratagem; *daḫal*, (m.) *daḫl*, client, protégé; proselyte; intruder; — *duḫḫal*, secret intentions; pl. *daḫâḫîl*, wren; — ة *daḫla-t*, entrance; interior, core, best part of; bee-hive; — also *diḫla-t*, *duḫla-t*, what is innermost, core, secret; mind, heart, intention; law, rule.

دخلا *duḫalâ*, pl. of دخيل *daḫîl*.

دخلل *duḫlul*=دخيل *daḫîl*.

(دخم) *daḫam*, INF. *daḫm*, push back, repel, turn off; lie with.

(دخمر) *daḫmar*, INF. ة, fill; cover, veil.

(دخمس) *daḥmas*, INF. ة, conceal one's mind from (على *'ala*).

(دخن) *daḥan*, U, A, INF. *daḥn*, *duḥûn*, smoke, steam; — INF. *duḥûn*, rise like smoke; — *daḥin*, A, INF. *daḥan*, smoke strongly; taste of smoke; — *daḥun*, INF. *duḥna-t*, be smoke-coloured, blackish; — II. INF. *tadḥîn*, smoke, steam; impregnate with smoke, fumigate; smoke tobacco; — IV. INF. *idḥân*=II.; — V. INF. *tadaḥḥun*, be impregnated with smoke, spoiled by smoke.

دخن *daḥn*, smoking (s.); — *duḥn*, millet; — *daḥan*, smoke; smoky taste; smoke-colour; malice, grudge; — *daḥin*, malicious; — ة *daḥna-t*, smoke; malice, grudge; — *duḥna-t*, smoke-colour; incense; fumigation.

دخنا *daḥnâ'*, f. of ادخن *adḥan*, smoke-coloured.

(دخنس) *daḥnas*, strong, muscular.

دخول *duḥûl*, entrance, admission; intrusion; coition, performance of the marriage act; income.

دخى *daḥ-an*, *daḥa*, darkness.

دخيا *daḥyâ'*, f. dark.

دخيل *daḥîl*, pl. *duḥalâ*, interior, internal; intimate, familiar; stranger living with a tribe or community; foreigner; intruder; proselyte; foreign word; mind, intention; — ة *daḥîla-t*, also—

دخيلا *duḥailâ'*, دخيلى *duḥḥaila*, mind, heart, secret intention; secret.

(دد) *dad*, game, sport, jest; space of time; — *dadd*, and—

ددا *dad-an*, ددن *dadan*, id.

(در) *darr*, I, U, INF. *darr*, abound, yield in abundance; — INF. *darr*, *durûr*, yield plenteous rain; purl abundantly; be plentiful; come in profusedly; have a good sale; grow luxuriantly; shine brightly; recover colour (convalescent); — IV. INF. *idrâr*, yield abundant milk; cause to rain copiously; rain abundantly; provoke urine; — X. INF. *istidrâr*, be copious; yield abundant milk; seek the milk-flow (*e.g.* of eloquence); cause to rain copiously.

در *darr*, copious flow of milk; milk; nature, natural disposition; soul, mind, intellect; لله دره *li'l-lâh-i darru-hu*, how exquisite! — *durr*, ة, pearl; musicians; — ة *darra-t*, copious flow of milk; pl. *-ât*, *dirâr*, teat; female breast; — *dirra-t*, pl. *dirar*, id.; abundance of milk; milk; plenteous rain; liveliness of the market; — *durra-t*, pl. *durr*, *durar*, *durrât*, a large pearl; parrot.

(درا) *dara'*, INF. *dar'*, *dar'a-t*, push back, repel, drive from; stray; receive a fresh impulse; shine, flicker, sparkle; spread (a.); have an ulcer on the back; — III. INF. *mudârât*, treat with kindness, courtesy; flatter, cajole, and, by opposition, repel, push back; — V. INF. *tadarru'*, conceal one's self, lie in ambush; be haughty towards (على *'ala*); — VI. INF. *tadâru'* (also VIII.), push one another back in a quarrel; quarrel, scuffle; — VII. INF. *indirâ'*, be repelled, pushed back, driven from; receive a fresh impulse; come unexpectedly upon; — VIII. INF. *iddirâ'*=VI.

درا *dar'*, sudden invasion, surprise; pl. *durû'*, cleft, rent; — *darrâ'*, yielding plenty of milk; — *durrâ'*, millet (m.).

دراب *darrâb*, door-keeper, porter; — ة *durâba-t*, great practice in, familiarity with a thing; courage, boldness; — *darrâba-t*, clever woman; — *

درابزين *darâbzîn*, parapet, balustrade, trellis-work (Pers.).

درابكة *darâbukka-t*, tambourine.

درابنة *darâbina-t*, درابين *darâbîn*, pl. of دربان *darbân*.

دراج *darrâj*, tell-tale, tale-bearer; porcupine; — *durrâj*, pl. *darârij*, partridge; pheasant; — ة *darrâja-t*, siege-engine.

درار *durrâr*, pl. of دار *dârr*; — ة *darrâra-t*, spindle.

دراريج *darârîj*, pl. of دراج *durrâj*.

دراريع *darâri'*, pl. of دراعة *durrâ'a-t*.

دراس *dirâs*, ة *dirâsa-t*, the treading out of corn, threshing;—*darrâs*, who treads out corn, threshes; studied, learned; effaced; — ة *dirâsa-t*, study.

دراعة *durrâ'a-t*, pl. *darârî'*, coarse upper garment; cuirass.

دراق *durâq*, earthen vessel with a narrow neck; — *darrâq*, theriac; wine; also—

دراقن *durrâqin*, peach.

دراك *darâki*, after him! stop him! seize him; — *dirâk*, intellect, intellectual power, comprehension; — *;—*darrâk*, who obtains his end, reaches his goal; — ة *darrâka-t*, understanding, intellect.

درام *darrâm*, ة *darrâma-t*, porcupine.

دران *darân*, fox; — *.

درانى *dar'âniyy*, very white.

درانيك *darânîk*, pl. of درنوك *durnûk*.

دراهس *darâhis*, pl. calamities.

دراية *dirâya-t*, knowledge; peculiarity; temper.

(درب) *darib*, A, INF. *darab*, *darba-t*, accustom one's self to a thing, make one's self familiar with, practice in (acc. or ب *bi*); be badly off; — II. INF. *tadrîb*, accustom, make familiar with, exercise, drill; show one's self enduring; guide, direct; — V. INF. *tadarrub*, be accustomed to, drilled; practice.

درب *darb*, pl. *dirâb*, *durûb*, mountain-path; path, road; street; gate; custom; method;—*darib*, ة, practised, exercised, drilled; — ة *darba-t*, great practice or familiarity; courage, boldness; —*darîba-t*, practised in hunting.

درباس *dirbâs*, lion; mordacious dog.

دربان *darbân*, pl. *darâbina-t*, *darâbîn*, door-keeper, porter (Pers.).

(دربج) *darbaj*, INF. ة, become meek after being restless; walk slowly.

(دربح) *darbaḥ*, INF. ة, run from fear; bend the neck, hang down the head; humble one's self.

(دربخ) *darbaḫ*, INF. ة, stoop.

(دربس), II. *tadarbas*, INF. *tadarbus*, go in advance, precede.

(دربص) *darbaṣ*, INF. ة, be silent from fear.

دربكة *darabukka-t*, tambourine.

(دربل) *darbal*, INF. ة, beat the drum; — ة *darbala-t*, pace of a horse; drum.

(درثا) *darsâ'*, old camel.

(درج) *daraj*, U, INF. *durûj*, step, step onward, walk; proceed or ascend gradually; be or become customary; be a custom, the fashion; be current, have currency; pass, depart, disappear, get destroyed; die; roll up or close a book; — U, INF. *daraj*, cause the gravel to fly; — *darij*, A, INF. *daraj*, ascend gradually; die; be fond of partridges; — II. INF. *tadrîj*, cause to proceed or ascend gradually; let advance, promote; consecrate as a priest; introduce a custom; give currency to; roll or fold up paper or cloth; wrap up; walk much; — IV. INF. *idrâj*, roll or fold up; wrap up; have not yet dropped young ones at the end of the year; — V. proceed or ascend gradually; approach by degrees; — VII. INF. *indirâj*, get destroyed; — X. INF. *istidrâj*, cause to proceed or mount gradually; bring or lead up by degrees.

درج *darj*, pl. *durûj*, roll of paper; volume; fold; entering into a book or register; putting in (s.); — *durj*, pl. *diraja-t*, *adrâj*, box, casket, case; — *daraj*, pl. *dirâj*, *adrâj*, road, path; staircase, ladder; mediator; copy-book; — *durraj*, complicated matters; — ة *durja-t*, *duraja-t*, *daraja-t*, pl. *duraj*, stair-case, flight of steps, ladder; step, degree, round of a ladder; rank, dignity; degree in Paradise.

(درجب) *darjab*, INF. ة, be fond of her young (camel).

(درجع) *durju'*, herbs for cattle.

(درجل) *darjal*, INF. ة, twist a string (*darjala-t*) round the bow.

(درح) *daraḥ*, INF. *darḥ*, push back, turn off, repel; — *dariḥ*, A, INF. *daraḥ*, be old and decrepit.

درحبيل *dùraḥbîl*, درحبين *duraḥbîn*, calamity.

(درد) *darad*, the decaying and falling out of teeth.

دردا *dardâ'*, f. toothless old woman.

دردار *dardâr*, elm-tree.

(دردب) *dardab*, INF. ة, be accustomed to, practised in.

(دردبيس) *dardabîs*, calamity; old man or woman; glass bead as an amulet.

(دردح) *dirdiḥ*, pl. *darâdiḥ*, zealous, eager, greedy for; old man or woman.

(دردر) *dardar*, INF. ة, chew; (m.) disperse, scatter, throw about.

دردر *durdur*, pl. *darâdir*, tooth-socket; young sharp teeth.

(دردق) *dardaq*, ة, pl. *darâdiq*, child; young of an animal; a wine-measure.

دردور *durdûr*, whirlpool, eddy.

دردی *durdiyy*, dregs, sediment.

درر *dirar*, pl. of درة *darra-t*, *dirra-t*.

(درز) *dariz*, A, INF. *daraz*, grasp and enjoy the pleasures of the world; — II. INF. *tadrîz*, sew, stitch, embroider; speak with a Druzian accent.

درز *darz*, pl. *durûz*, stitch, seam; joint of a wall; seam of bones; — ة *darza-t*, tailors, weavers; اولاد د *aulâd darza-t*, poverty-stricken rabble.

درزی *durziyy*, pl. *durûz*, Druze.

(درس) *daras*, U, INF. *durûs*, be effaced; be decayed, in ruins; efface; wear out a garment; jade; destroy, annihilate; INF. *dars*, *durûs*, have the menses; — U, I, INF. *dars*, *dirâsa-t*, read, peruse, study, repeat; lie with; INF. *dars*, *dirâs*, tread out the corn, thresh; — II. INF. *tadrîs*, read, study; cause to read or study; teach, lecture; — III. INF. *mudârasa-t*, study with; — VI. INF. *tadârus*, read, study; study together; — VII. INF. *indirâs*, be effaced, obliterated.

درس *dars*, pl. *durûs*, lesson, school-hour; — *dirs*, pl. *dirsân*, *adrâs*, worn-out garment.

درسية *darsiyya-t*, teacher's fee.

درشة *durśa-t*, obtrusiveness; litigiousness.

(درص) *dariṣ*, A, INF. *daraṣ*, have broken teeth.

درص *darṣ*, *dirṣ*, pl. *durûṣ*, *dirașa-t*, *dirṣân*, *adruṣ*, *adrâṣ*, young of an animal; ام ادراص *umm adrâṣ*, calamity.

(درع) *dara'*, INF. *dar'*, skin; cut off the neck; be partly eaten; — II. INF. *tadrî'*, clothe with a breast-plate, cuirass; put a chemise on a woman; strangle, choke (a.); step forward, go in advance; — V. INF. *tadarru'*, be clad in armour or a cuirass; wear a woollen chemise; take courage, arm one's self, strengthen one's self.

درع *dir'*, m. and f., pl. *adru'*, *adrâ'* *durû'*, breast-plate, cuirass, coat of mail; m. pl. *adrâ'*, woollen chemise; smock; — *dur'*, *dura'*,

16th, 17th, and 18th nights of the month; pith of the palm-tree; — *dari'*, tender, delicate; — ة *dur'a-t*, pith of the palm-tree; — *dur'a-t*, *durr'a-t*, coat of mail, cuirass, armour.

(درعش), III. *idra'aśś*, INF. *idri'śâś*, recover from an illness.

درف *darf*, shadow, shade; protection; protector; side, flank; (m.) = ة *darfa-t*, door-wing; shutter.

(درفس) *darfas*, INF. ة, ride on a big camel; carry the imperial flag.

درفس *dirafs*, big, stout; corpulent; the imperial flag.

(درق) *daraq*, hurry, hasten; — II. INF. *tadrîq*, soften.

درق *darq*, hard; — ة *daraqa-t*, pl. *daraq*, *dirâq*, *adrâq*, leathern shield; shield.

(درقل) *darqal*, INF. ة, hasten by, hurry past; leap, dance; step along proudly; listen to, obey.

(درك) *darak*, I, INF. *darak*, follow, pursue, reach; seize, take hold of; conceive, perceive; reach maturity; — II. INF. *tadrîk*, follow up one thing with another; last, continue; — III. INF. *dirâk*, *mudâraka-t*, reach; let part of a thing follow another; (m.) foresee and try to meet evil; watch over, guard, heed; — IV. INF. *idrâk*, pursue; reach; comprehend, conceive, perceive; attain to puberty, reach maturity; waste away, disappear; — VI. INF. *tadâruk*, reach and seize; reach one another; comprehend; bestow on; put into order; mend; compensate for; — VIII. INF. *iddirâk*, reach and seize; — X. INF. *istidrâk*, try to reach; reach; comprehend; try to put into order, to compensate for; mend; blame; recant; foresee an evil and try to obviate it.

درك *dark*, supervision, superintendence, inspection; police; reaching, overtaking (s.); — *darak*, pl. *adrâk*, consequence of an action; punishment; compensation, damages; dispute in a commercial transaction; depth, bettom, pit (of hell); — *darak*, (m.) *dark*, reaching, comprehending (s.); — ة *daraka-t*, lowest degree; the eight degrees of hell; pit.

دركاه *darkâh*, royal or imperial court (Pers.).

(دركب) *darkab*, INF. ة, throw into a precipice; — II. INF. *tadarkub*, throw one's self down.

(درم) *daram*, I, *darim*, A, INF. *darm*, *daram*, *darim*, *daramân*, *darâma-t*, run fast and with short steps or leaps; step gracefully; — *darim*, A, INF. *daram*, be equally rounded and therefore not projecting (ankle, &c.); fall out.

درم *durm*, pl. and—

درما *darmâ'*, f. of ادرم, well rounded, fleshy, &c.

(درمق) *darmaq*, very white flour; grit.

(درمك) *darmak*, id.; bread made of it.

(درن) *darin*, A, INF. *daran*, be dirty.

درن *daran*, pl. *adrân*, dirt, impurity; ام د *umm daran*, the world; — *darin*, ة, pl. *dirân*, dirty; f. beneficent.

درناس *dirnâs*, lion.

(درنفق) *daranfaq-an*, quickly, hastily; — IV. *idranfaq*, INF. *idrinfâq*, hasten, overtake, take the lead.

درنك *dirnik*, درنوك *durnûk*, درنيك *dirnîk*, pl. *darânîk*, coarse long-haired carpet or garment.

(دره) *darah*, INF. *darh*, ward off; protect; attack, fall upon.

درهام *dirhâm*, pl. *darâhîm*, and—

درهم *dirham*, *dirhim*, pl. *darâhim*, silver drachm (20=a dinâr); silver coin, money; a weight

(8th part of an ounce); — hence: *darham*, INF. ة, weigh with a *dirham* or any small weight.

درو *durû'*, INF. of (درأ); pl. of در *dar'*.

درواس *dirwâs*, mastiff; lion.

دروان *darwân*, flake of snow (m.); — *darawân*, hybrid of a hyena and a she-wolf.

دروب *darûb*, well-drilled; obedient; — *.

دروج *darûj*, swift.

درور *darûr*, yielding much milk; abundance of milk; affluence; — *.

دروس *durûs*, threadbareness; — *

درومس *daraumas*, a snake.

درويش *darwîś*, pl. *darâwîś*, dervish, mendicant.

(دری) *darâ*, I, INF. *dary*, *diry*, *darya-t*, *dirya-t*, *diryân*, *darayân*, *dirâya-t*, *duriyy*, know, know by experience; see through; learn; comprehend;—INF. *dary*, surround and ensnare the game; lie in ambush; use stratagem; turn the corn with a pitch-fork; comb, curry; — II. INF. *tadriya-t*, part the hair; — III. INF. *mudârât*, surround or ensnare game; treat kindly, courteously, cajole; dissimulate; — IV. INF. *idrâ'*, teach, instruct, inform, communicate;—V. INF. *tadarrî*, ensnare the game; — VI. INF. *tadârî*, hide one's self; seek protection, shelter; shelter one's self.

دری *dirri'*, *durri'*, *dirriy*, *durriyy*, glittering, sparkling (adj.); — *durrî*, glittering, sparkling (s.); — ة *darya-t*, *dirya-t*, knowing (s.), knowledge; — *dariyya-t*, ring to run at in a tilting-match; hiding-place of a hunter.

درياق *diryâq*, *daryâq*, ة *diryâqa-t*, *daryâqa-t*, theriac; wine.

دريان *diryân*, *darayân*, INF. of (دری).

دريس *darîs*, worn out, threadbare.

دريص *durais*, little mouse.

دريكة *darîka-t*, game; hunting-prey.

درين *darîn*, worn out; dry, arid.

(دزر) *dazar*, U, INF. *dazr*, repel, drive away.

دزكين *dazkîn*, bridle.

(دس) *dass*, U, INF. *dass*, *dassîsa*, hide one thing beneath another; bury in the sand, the ground; grope for, feel for; spy out; smear the camel with pitch; intrigue, plot against (على *'ala*); tell one a secret that he may tell it to others; send a secret messenger; — II. INF. *tadsîs*, hide, conceal; — VII. INF. *indisâs*, be hidden under; steal in; intrigue against; try to injure a person in the estimation of others.

دساتير *dasâtîr*, pl. of دستور *dustûr*.

دساتين *dasâtîn*, pl. of دستان *dastân*.

دسار *disâr*, pl. *dusr*, *dusur*, strong bast of a palm-tree; oakum; rivet.

دساس *dassâs*, ة *dassâsa-t*, earth-worm; a snake.

دسافى *dusâfa*, دسافين *dasâfîn*, pl. of دسفان *disfân*.

دسام *disâm*, stopper, cork.

دست *dast*, pl. *dusût*, plain, desert; uppermost seat at the table; hand; lead (in a game at cards), victory; quire of paper; cushion; clothing, suit of clothes; assembly, company (Pers.).

دستجة *dastaja-t*, pl. *dasâtîj*, bundle, handful, armful (Pers.).

دستور *dustûr*, *dastûr*, pl. *dasâtîr*, army-list, register; ledger; sample, model; support; senator; minister; permission; pl. religious books of the Parsees.

(دسج), VII. *indasaj*, INF. *indisâj*, fall on one's face.

(دسدس) *dasdas*, INF. ة, touch, finger, feel at; grope one's way.

(دسر) *dasar*, U, INF. *dasr*, push,

push back; pierce; lie with; **caulk, repair a ship;** rivet boards **or staves.**

دسر *dusr*, pl. of دسار *disâr*, and of—
دسرا *dasrâ'*, ship.

دسس *dusus*, pl. of دسيس *dasîs.*

(دسع) *dasa'*, INF. *das'*, push back; belch, vomit; fill; stop; recede; bestow a handsome present.

دسفان *disfân*, pl. *dusâfa*, *dasâfîn*, pander; procurer, go-between; spy; — *dusfân*, id.; guidance.

(دسف), IV. *adsaf*, INF. *idsâf*, gain one's living as a procurer.

دسفة *dasfa-t*, bawding, procuring (s.); guidance.

(دسق) *dasiq*, A, INF. *dasaq*, be full to overflowing; be clear and shining; — IV. INF. *idsâq*, fill.

دسكرة *daskara-t*, pl. *dasâkir*, *dasâkira-t*, town with a castle on a mountain; village; canton; cell of a hermit; inn, wine-hall (Pers.).

(دسم) *dasam*, U, INF. *dasm*, stop up, cork; shut, lock; lie with; wet slightly; efface; — I, smear the camel with pitch; — *dasim*, A, INF. *dasam*, be fat, greasy; be slightly wetted; — II. INF. *tadsîm*, make fat, grease; — IV. INF. *idsâm*, cork a bottle, stop up.

دسم *dasam*, fatness, greasiness; fat, grease; — *dasim*, fat, greasy; — *dusm*, pl. of ادسم *adsam*, fat, greasy; dirty clothes; — ة *dusma-t*, ash-colour; mean person; — *dasama-t*, atom.

دسما *dasmâ'*, ash-coloured, dark grey, f. of ادسم *adsam*.

(دسو) *dasâ*, U, INF. *daswa-t*, not grow, not increase; hide one's self.

دسومة *dusûma-t*, grease, dirt.

(دسى) *dasa*, I, INF. *dasy*, be impure, unclean; not grow, not increase; — II. INF. *tadsiya-t*, seduce, corrupt.

دسيس *dasîs*, pl. *dusus*, spy; secret agent; false brother; roasted; — ة *dasîsa-t*, pl. *dasâ'is*, secret, intrigue; innuendo, suggestion.

دسيسى *dissîsa*, concealment, secrecy, INF. of (دس).

دسيع *dasî'*, place where the neck joins the shoulders; — ة *dasî'a-t*, pl. *dasâ'i'*, natural disposition; present; power; table-slab; rich ornamental table.

(دش) *daśś*, U, INF. *daśś*, travel; prepare the dish دشيشة *daśîśa-t*; pound, grind; — ة *daśśa-t*, push, thrust, bruise, contusion.

دشار *duśśâr*, pl. of داشر *dâśir*, pasturing freely.

دشأة *daś'a-t*, belching (s.).

دشت *daśt*, desert plain (Pers.).

(دشر), II. *daśśar*, INF. *tadśîr*, let, leave; dismiss, discharge (m.).

(دشن) *daśan*, U, INF. *daśn*, give, hand over, present.

(دشو) *daśâ*, U, INF. *daśw*, rush into battle.

(دشى), V. INF. *tadaśśî*, belch.

دشيشة *daśîśa-t*, broth of wheat to be sipped; (m.) measles.

(دص) *daṣṣ*, U, INF. *daṣṣ*, wait on, serve.

(دصدص) *daṣdaṣ*, INF. ة, shake the sieve.

(دصق) *daṣaq*, U, INF. *daṣq*, break.

(دض) *daḍḍ*, U, INF. *daḍḍ*=(دص).

(دظ) *dazz*, U, INF. *dazz*, push aside; tear; doubt.

دع *da'*, leave off! IMP. of (ودع); — ة *da'a-t*, quiet, peaceful; rest, repose.

(دع) *da''*, U, INF. *da''*, push violently, push aside; repudiate an orphan.

دعا *da'-an*, pay attention! — *du'â'*, pl. *ad'iya-t*, call, acclamation; prayer for blessing, felicitation, salutation; deprecation, curse; prayer, request; invitation; invocation; — ة *du'ât*, pl. of داعى *dâ'î*, who calls, &c.; — *da''â'a-t*, fore-finger, index.

دعاب *di'âb*, ة *du'âba-t*, play, game, sport, jest, joke; — *da''âb*, ة

da‘‘âba-t, who is fond of play, &c.; jester.

دعات *du‘ât*, invocations, prayers.

دعار *du‘‘âr*, pl. of داعر *dâ‘ir*, fornicator; — ة *da‘âra-t*, *di‘âra-t*, fornication, unchastity, lewdness.

دعاع *du‘â‘*, ة *du‘â‘a-t*, winged ant.

دعام *di‘âm*, ة *di‘âma-t*, pl. *da‘â’im*, support, pillar; prop of a vine-tree; *di‘ama-t*, copula in a sentence; دعائم الابواب *da‘â’im al-abwâb*, principal forms of a verb; — ة *da‘âma-t*, condition.

دعاميص *da‘âmîṣ*, pl. of دعموص *du‘mûṣ*.

دعانة *da‘âna-t*, carelessness, thoughtlessness.

دعاوة *da‘âwa-t*, *di‘âwa-t*, claim, pretension, arrogance.

دعائم *da‘â’im*, pl. of دعام *di‘âm*, ة, and of دعمة *di‘ma-t*.

(دعب) *da‘ab*, INF. *da‘b*, push back, repudiate, expel; play, sport, jest with (acc.); lie with; — III. INF. *mudâ‘abat*, play, sport, jest with; make impatient, vex, annoy; — VI. INF. *tadâ‘ub*, play, sport, jest with one another.

دعب *da‘b*, play, game, sport, jest; — *da‘ib*, who is fond of play, &c.

(دعبل) *da‘bal*, INF. ة, round off by the hand (m.).

(دعبوب) *du‘bûb*, black-winged ant; black corn; night.

(دعبوث) *du‘bûs̱*, who prostitutes himself to unnatural vice; suspicious person.

دعبوس *du‘bûs*, mad, foolish, stupid.

(دعت) *da‘at*, INF. *da‘t*, push violently; drive away.

(دعث) *da‘as̱*, INF. *da‘s̱*, stir up dust; pass. be seized with a shudder.

دعث *di‘s̱*, rests of water; pl. *ad‘âs̱*, *di‘âs̱*, hatred, inveterate grudge.

(دعثر) *da‘s̱ar*, INF. ة, break, destroy.

دعثور *du‘s̱ûr*, cracked cistern.

(دعج) *da‘ij*, A, INF. *da‘aj*, be large and of a dark black.

دعج *du‘j*, pl. of ادعج *ad‘aj*, black-eyed, &c.; — ة *du‘ja-t*, largeness and darkness of the eye.

دعجا *da‘jâ’*, f. of ادعج *ad‘aj*, black-eyed.

(دعد) *da‘d*, chameleon; pl. *du‘ûd*, *da‘dât*, *ad‘ud*, female proper name.

دعداع *da‘dâ‘*, dwarf.

(دعدع) *da‘da‘*, INF. ة, *da‘dâ‘*, run slowly and with short steps to and fro; INF. ة, call to be on one's guard, call to the cattle; fill the dish; shake the measure; — II. INF. *tada‘du‘*, walk like a decrepit old man.

(دعر) *da‘ir*, A, INF. *da‘ar*, be corrupt, impure; smoke violently without igniting; give no fire; — V. INF. *tada‘‘ur*, be disfigured, gloomy; be wicked, corrupt.

دعر *da‘ar*, corruption, wickedness; putrefaction; dissolute life; — *da‘ir*, bad, corrupt; dissolute; impure; dirty; not igniting.

(دعز) *da‘az*, INF. *da‘z*, push, push back; lie with.

(دعس) *da‘as*, INF. *da‘s*, tread under foot; treat with contempt; pierce; fill; skin; — II. INF. *tad‘îs*, pierce; — III. INF. *mudâ‘asa-t*, fight one with a lance; — V. INF. *tada‘‘us*, VII. INF. *indi‘âs*, be trodden under foot; be contemned.

دعس *da‘s*, ة, foot-print, trace, track; — *di‘s*, cotton; — ة *da‘sa-t*, treading under foot (s.).

(دعسق) *da‘saq*, INF. ة, rush against (على *‘ala*); destroy a cistern by trampling upon; advance and recede again; chase away.

(دعص) *da‘aṣ*, U, INF. *da‘ṣ*, kill; lift up the foot; — IV. INF. *id‘âṣ*, kill.

دعص *di‘ṣ*, ة, pl. *di‘aṣ*, *di‘aṣa-t*, *ad‘âṣ*, sand-hill.

(دعق) *da‘aq*, INF. *da‘q*, trample

upon, destroy a cistern by trampling upon; urge on; allow an army to plunder the enemy's country; frighten, excite; put to flight.

(دعك) *da'ak*, INF. *da'k*, rub, smooth; unstiffen a garment by wearing it; pacify an enemy; allow a beast of burden, &c., to roll on the ground; (m.) practise (a.), drill, exercise; — *da'ik*, A, INF. *da'ak*, be stupid, a fool, mad; — III. INF. *mudâ'aka-t*, rub one's self against, dispute with, fight; (m.) get practised in, carry on a business.

دعك *da'ak*, stupidity, foolishness, folly; — *da'ik*, quarrelsome; — *du'ak*, weak; — ة *da'ka-t*, the trodden part of a road.

(دعكس) *da'kas*, INF. ة, dance with the hands entwined.

(دعكن) *da'kan*, gentle, obedient.

(دعل) *da'al*, I, INF. *da'al*, deceive, cheat, outwit; — III. INF. *mudâ'ala-t*, try to deceive.

(دعلق) *da'laq*, INF. ة, go deep into the water; seek perseveringly, pursue.

(دعم) *da'am*, INF. *da'm*, support what is on the point of falling; lie with; — VIII. INF. *iddi'âm*, be supported, propped up.

دعم *da'm*, support, pillar, prop; — *da'am*, firmness, strength; — ة *di'ma-t*, pl. *di'am*, *da'â'im*, support, pillar, prop of a vine-tree.

دعمص *da'maṣ*, INF. ة, be full of worms.

(دعموص) *du'mûṣ*, pl. *da'âmîṣ*, *da'âmiṣ*, a black worm bred in drying up water; tadpole; a court favourite who has access everywhere; sagacious, penetrating.

دعمى *du'miyy*, carpenter; middle of the road; firmly supported.

(دعنكر) *da'ankar*, دعنكران *da'ankarân*, who disgraces others; — ادعنكر *id'ankar*, INF. *id'inkâr*, disgrace; rush suddenly up.

(دعو) *da'â*, U, دعى *da'a*, I, INF. *du'â'*, call aloud; call to; call up, send for, summon; call together; call upon, urge, instigate; give a calling; invite; name, denominate; — INF. *da'wân*, *du'â'*, invoke, pray; invoke a blessing upon (ل *li*), a curse upon (على *'ala*); visit, afflict; leave a little milk in the udder; — II. INF. *tad'iya-t*, call upon, summon; — III. INF. *mudâ'â-t*, claim; propose riddles; call to God; demolish a wall; — IV. INF. *id'â'*, cause to make false claims on a man as one's father; — V. INF. *tada''î*, raise claims; exact a right; — VI. INF. *tadâ'î*, call to one another; dispute one another's claim, have a law-suit against one another; challenge each other; be on the point of falling in ruins; be almost worn out; — VII. INF. *indi'â*, accept an invitation; follow a call; — VIII. INF. *iddi'â'*, raise claims against (على *'ala*); claim; desire; pray for a blessing; be plaintiff or defendant; summon before the judge; call up, send for; confess, state, maintain a statement; call one's self; boast of a descent, deny a descent; — X. INF. *istid'â'*, call pu, invite; call to, ask for help; demand, solicit; — ة *da'wa-t*, call; (also *du'wa-t*) invitation to a banquet; banquet; appeal; pl. *da'wât*, *da'âwî*, invocation of God, prayer for a blessing; deprecation; claim; request; desire; legal summons; invitation to adopt Islâm; affair, matter; — also *di'wa-t*, claim of kinship, especially false one.

دعوا *da'wâ'* = دعوى *da'w-an*, *da'wa*.

(دعوس) *da'was*, INF. ة = (دعس).

دعوس *da'ûs*, eager for combat.

دعوى *da'w-an*, *da'wa*, assertion; claim; legal title; process, law-

suit; — *du'wiyy*, someone, anyone; ما د *mâ du'wiyy*, no one.

دعى *da'a*, see (دعو); — *da'iyy*, pl. *ad'iyâ'*, whose claims of a certain descent are doubtful; bastard; son of adoption.

دعيميص *du'aimîṣ*, sagacious, sharp of intellect.

(دغت) *dagat*, INF. *dagt*, worry to death, strangle, throttle.

(دغدغ) *dagdag*, state a thing in an unintelligible manner; tickle; taunt, gibe; (m.) begin to ripen; — ة *dagdaga-t*, tickling (s.); tumult, noise.

(دغر) *dagar*, INF. *dagr*, *dagar*, fall upon an enemy in a disorderly manner; intrude; push, push away; rob by force; throttle; mix.

دغرى *dagr-an*, *dagar-an* (also دغرا *dagrâ'*), disorderly attack; surprise; rashness, foolhardiness; — *dugriyy*, straightforward (Turk.).

(دغش) *dagaś*, INF. *dagś*, attack; (also IV.) enter on the darkness of night; grow dark, become night; — III. INF. *mudâgaśa-t*, press one another, throng; — IV. INF. *idgâś*, see I.; — VI. INF. *tadâguś*, get mixed (in a battle, &c.).

دغش *dagaś*, darkness; nightfall.

(دغص) *dagiṣ*, A, INF. *dagaṣ*, surfeit; be enraged.

(دغف) *dagaf*, INF. *dagf*, take much of a thing.

(دغفر) *dagfar*, big lion.

(دغفل) *dagfal*, the young of an elephant; abundant, plentiful; fertile.

(دغل) *dagal*, surmise, doubt; — *dagil*, A, INF. *dagal*, be covered with a thicket; lie in ambush; steal in; be full of passion or hatred; — IV. INF. *idgâl*, lie in ambush; fall upon from an ambush; outwit, take in, deceive; spoil an affair.

دغل *dagal*, ة *dagala-t*, thicket, dense copse; — *dagal*, pl. *digâl*, *adgâl*, defect, flaw; false coin; — *dagil*, secret, concealed; spoiled; full of passion or hatred.

(دغم) *dagam*, INF. *dagm* (also *dagim*, A, INF. *dagam*, and IV.), overpower, overwhelm; — INF. *dagm*, break one's nose-bone; cover a vessel; — IV. INF. *idgâm*, see I.; assimilate two consonants and join them by *taśdîd* put the bit into a horse's mouth; (m.) insert; (m.) slur over words in talking; — VIII. INF. *iddigâm*, assimilate; insert; slur over; — XI. *idgâmm*, INF. *idgîmâm*, be dark about the nose and mouth, with an otherwise clear complexion; — ة *dugma-t*, darkness about the nose and mouth, with an otherwise clear complexion.

(دغمر) *dagmar*, INF. ة, mix; confuse; blame.

(دغن) *dagan*, INF. *dagn*, be gloomy and rainy.

(دغوش) *dagwaś*, INF. ة, come to close quarters.

دغوة *dagwa-t*, pl. *dagawât*, and—

دغية *dagya-t*, pl. *dagayât*, bad disposition.

(دف) *daff*, I, INF. *daff*, *dafîf*, move on slowly; try to approach an enemy cautiously; INF. *dafîf*, (also IV.) skim the ground; flap the wings and leap; swing, winnow; — INF. *daff*, tear out and throw into the air; — II. INF. *tadfîf*, despatch a wounded man; — IV. INF. *idfâf*, see I.; = II.; — X. INF. *istidfâf*, be easily performed or despatched.

دف *dif'*, pl. *adfâ'*, heat, warmth; warming (s.); warm garment of wool or hair; warmest corner; produce of a camel, as milk, hair, foals; present; — *daff*, pl. *dufûf*, side; broadside; mountain-slope in front; door-

wing; board, ḍeal, plank; — also *duff*, tambourine, hand-drum; — ة *daffa-t*, side; door-wing; cover of a book; rudder, helm.

(دفا) دفى *dafi'*, A, INF. *dafa'*, also دفو *dafu'*; INF. *dafâ'a-t*, preserve the heat (be a bad conductor of heat), keep warm, be warm; — II. INF. *tadfi'a-t*, keep warm; warm; — IV. INF. *idfâ'*=II.; clothe with a warm garment; — V. INF. *tadaffu'*, keep one's self warm, warm one's self; — VIII. INF. *iddifâ'*, be warm; — X. INF. *istidfâ'*=V.

دفا *dafa'*, warmth; tent; — *difâ'*, warm garment; branches and twigs of a tree; — *daf'â'*, f. warmly dressed; — ة *dafa'a-t*, *dafâ'a-t*, great warmth.

دفار *dafâr*, wench, strumpet; putrid (f.); ام د *umm-u dafâr-in*, the world.

دفاش *daffâś*, who pushes, pushes back; مركب د *markab daffâś*, screw-steamer (m.).

دفاع *difâ'*, warding off, driving away (s.); INF. III. of (دفع); —*daffâ'*, who pushes back, wards off, defends; — *duffâ'*, water-flood, surge, billow.

دفاف *dafâf*, who plays on the tambourine.

دفاق *dufâq*, powerful stream; swift.

دفان *daf'ân*, f. دفاى *daf'a*, kept warm, dressed warmly.

دفتر *daftar*, pl. *dafâtir*, book, writing-book; list, register, roll, matricula; catalogue; diary; album; fascicule of legal papers (Pers.).

دفتردار *daftardâr*, minister of finances, lord of the exchequer.

(دفدف) *dafdaf*, INF. ة, skim the ground in flying; hasten.

دفدف *dafdaf*, pl. *dafâdif*, slope of a hill.

(دفر) *dafar*, U, INF. *dafr*, push back, drive away; — *dafir*, A, INF. *dafar*, be full of mites; INF. *dafar* and *dafr*, be putrid, stink; be despised.

دفر *dafr*, stench; ام دفر *umm-u dafr-in*, the world; دفرا له *dafr-an la-hu*, fie on him! — *dafir*, ة, putrid.

دفرا *dafrâ'*, f. of ادفر *adfar*, putrid, &c.

(دفس), IX. *idfass*, INF. *idfisâs*, be black in the face.

(دفش) *dafaś*, U, INF. *dafś*, push with the hand, push back, buffet; — VII. INF. *indifâś*, be pushed, pushed back.

(دفض) *dafaḍ*, I, INF. *dafḍ*, break.

(دفطس) *dafṭas*, INF. ة, lose one's cattle or fortune.

(دفع) *dafa'*, INF. *daf'*, *madfa'*, push back, keep off, remove, drive or scare away; ward off evil, preserve from (عن *'an*); push towards, hand over, give, pay; grow luxuriantly; — III. INF. *difâ'*, *mudâfa'a-t*, ward or keep off, defend; put off, delay, hinder; — VI. INF. *tadâfu'*, push one another back; — VII. INF. *indifâ'*, be pushed back, kept off, removed; rush along in full career; break forth; be handed over, paid; — X. INF. *istidfâ'*, pray to God to ward off calamity, deprecate.

دفع *daf'*, pushing back, warding off, removing (s.); payment; —ة *daf'a-t*, pl. *-ât*, *dufû'*, thrust, push; time, turn, moment; payment; *daf'at-an*, once, at once, suddenly; — *duf'a-t*, pl. *dufa'*, push, rebound; downpour, shower; career; — ى *daf'iyy*, sudden, happening once.

(دفغ) *dafg*, millet-straw.

(دفق) *dafaq*, U, I, INF. *dafq*, pour out; be poured out; flow over; — II. INF. *tadfîq*, IV. INF. *idfâq*, pour out; — V. INF. *tadaffuq*, VII. INF. *indifâq*, flow over; be poured out, shed.

دفق *dafq*, pouring out, flowing over (s.); — ة *dufqa-t*, one outpouring or overflowing; *dufqat-an*, at once, suddenly; — ى *diffaqa, diffiqa*, quick pace.

دفل *difl*, pitch.

دفلى *difl-an, difla*, rose-laurel, rhododendron, oleander.

(دفن) *dafan*, I, INF. *dafn*, cover, shroud, conceal, bury; — INF. *dafn*, walk straight on; — V. INF. *tadaffun*, VII. INF. *indifân*, bury, be buried; — VIII. INF. *iddifân*, cover, conceal; flee, escape.

دفن *dafn*, burying, burial; — *difn*, latent.

دفنا *dufanâ'*, دفنى *dafna*, pl. of دفين *dafîn*, ة *dafîna-t*.

دفناس *difnâs*, lazy, negligent.

دفنس *difnis*, (m. f.) stupid; heavy, clumsy; useless.

دفو *dafu'*, see (دفا).

دفوا *dafwâ*, eagle; high tree; hill.

دفوع *dafû'*, who or what pushes back, propels; gun, cannon.

دفى *dafi'*, see (دفا); — *dafi'*, ة *dafiyy*, warm; — also—

دفيان *dafyân*, warmly dressed.

دفين *dafîn*, pl. *adfân*, *dufanâ'*, buried; concealed, latent; — ة *dafîna-t*, pl. *dafna*, *dafâ'in*, retired, secluded (f.); pl. *dafâ'in*, buried treasure.

(دق) *daqq*, I, INF. *diqqa-t*, be thin, fine, ground to powder; — U, INF. *daqq*, grind, pound; beat out, thresh; knock, rap; shoot at a wall; ring a bell; publish, announce; tattoo; pass. *duqq*, have a hectic fever; — II. INF. *taqdîq*, grind to powder; make thin, fine; make precise, accurate; be precise, accurate; — III. INF. *madâqqa-t*, reckon closely with (acc.); — IV. INF. *idqâq*, grind very finely, make very thin; look closely into, examine; give little; — VII. INF. *indiqâq*, be ground, pounded; be beaten; — X. INF. *istidqâq*, grow thin, lean.

دق *daqq*, ة, grinding, pounding (s.); rapping, knocking (s.); begging (s.); tattooing; — *diqq*, thin, fine, subtle, lean; any consumptive illness, hectic fever; — ة *diqqa-t*, thinness, fineness, leanness; exactness, accuracy, precision; subtlety; littleness, scarceness, paucity; nearness, niggardliness, avarice; — *duqqa-t*, pl. *duqaq*, *duqq*, fine dust; salt, &c., in powder; beauty, elegance.

دقارير *daqârîr*, pl. of دقرارة *diqrâra-t*, دقرورة *duqrûra-t*.

دقاريس *daqârîs*, pl. foxes.

دقاق *diqâq*, *duqâq*, chips, shavings, &c.; *diqâq*, pl. of دقيق *daqîq*; — *duqâq*, finely ground, reduced to powder; crumb, grain; — *daqqâq*, flour-merchant; fuller; — ة *daqqâqa-t*, pestle.

(دقدق) *daqdaq*, INF. ة, make a noise, trample; — ة *daqdaqa-t*, noise; trampling (s.).

(دقر) *daqir*, A, INF. *daqar*, be surfeited, vomit; be well watered, abound in vegetation; grow luxuriantly; — *daqar*, U, INF. *daqr*, touch slightly; hurt, offend (m.); — VII. INF. *indiqâr*, pass. of the previous (m.); — ة *daqra-t*, garden in bloom; (m.) slight touch; offence.

دقرار *diqrâr*, short trowsers of a sailor; — ة *diqrâra-t*, دقرورة *duqrûra-t*, pl. *daqârîr*, id.; calumny, slander; slanderer; contradiction; calamity.

(دقس) *daqas*, U, INF. *duqûs*, travel through; penetrate into the ground; fall into the rear of an enemy; fill; — ة *duqsa-t*, millet.

دقش *daqś* = نقش *naqś*, graving, engraving (s.).

(دقع) *daqi'*, A, INF. *daqa'*, live in misery, and therefore adhere to

a place; bear misery cowardly; — IV. INF. *idqâ'*, throw into misery.

دقق *duqaq*, pl. of دقة *duqqa-t*; — ة *daqaqa-t*, pl. of داق *dâqq*, who knocks.

(دقل) *daqal*, U, INF. *daql*, prevent, hinder, forbid; strike on the mouth, nose, neck or beard; — INF. *duqûl*, be hidden; enter.

(دقم) *daqam*, U, I, INF. *daqm*, break another's front teeth; push or thrust suddenly; blow in; — *daqim*, A, INF. *daqam*, lose the front teeth.

(دقن) *daqan*, U, INF. *daqn*, hit on the beard; hinder, forbid.

دقوق *daqûq*, a collyrium; — ة *daqûqa-t*, oxen employed in treading out the corn.

(دقى) *daqî*, A, INF. *daqa-n*, have the stomach surfeited with milk (camel's foal).

دقيرة *daqîra-t*, garden in bloom.

دقيق *daqîq*, pl. *diqâq*, *adiqqa-t*, fine, thin; brittle; subtle, difficult to comprehend; fine flour; pl. *adiqqa-t*, good-for-nothing fellow; — ة *daqîqa-t*, pl. *daqâ'iq*, subtlety, difficult question; small thing, trifle; minute, moment; a kind of sheep; — ى *daqîqiyy*, flour-merchant.

(دك) *dakk*, U, INF. *dukk*, grind, pound, pulverise, crumble; beat flat, level; make a way; bring low, pass. be ill; destroy; mix, confuse; fill a well with earth; (m.) charge a gun or cannon; be ground, pounded, pulverised, beaten flat, levelled; — II. INF. *tadkîk*, mix, mingle; — VII. INF. *indikâk*, be pounded, &c.; be charged.

دك *dakk*, pl. *dikâk*, level sand, pl. *dukûk*, plain (s.); — *dukk*, pl. *dikaka-t*, low hill, hillock; — ة *dakka-t*, charge of a fire-arm; pl. *dikâk*, bench or seat in front of a house; small shop; — *dikka-t*, trowser-belt or string.

(دكا) *daka'*, INF. *dak'*, push back; — VI. INF. *tadâku'*, push one another back.

دكا *dakkâ'*, flat hill; pl. *dakkâwât*, having a broad back (f.).

دكاع *dukâ'*, complaint of the chest.

دكاكين *dakâkîn*, pl. of دكان *dukkân*.

دكالى *dakâla*, *dukâla*, Satan.

دكان *dukkân*, (m. f.) pl. *dakâkîn*, shop.

دكدك *dakdak*, INF. ة, fill a well with earth.

(دكز) *dakaz*, I, spur (m.).

(دكس) *dakas*, U, INF. *daks*, heap up a great quantity of earth; — *dakis*, A INF. *dakas*, be piled up; — IV. INF. *idkâs*, produce plants; — VI. INF. *tadâkus*, accumulate (n.); grow difficult; — VII. INF. *indikâs*, have a relapse (m.); — ة *daksa-t*, relapse.

(دكش), III. *dakaś*, INF. *tadâkuś*, exchange with (acc.).

(دكع), pass. *daki'*, suffer from a complaint of the chest.

(دكل) *dakal*, I, U, INF. *dakl*, knead clay; tread, tread down; — II. INF. *tadkîl*, allow a beast of burden to roll on the ground; — V. INF. *tadâkul*, jest or sport with a lover; treat haughtily; rebel through pride; be vain, arrogant; delay, desist; — ة *dakala-t*, thin clay or loam.

(دكم) *dakam*, U, INF. *dakm*, knock on the chest; knock one hard thing against another; pound; — II. INF. *tadkîm*, insert one thing into another; thrust one's head against another's throat.

(دكن) *dakan*, U, INF. *dakn* (also II.), place things one on the top of the other, pile up; — *dakin*, A, INF. *dakan*, be smoke-coloured, blackish; — II. INF. *tadkîn*, see I.; — ة *dukna-t*, blackish-colour, smoke-colour.

(دكه) *dakah*, INF. *dakh*, breathe or blow into another's face.

دكيش *dakîś*, exchange, trade by exchange (m.); — ة *dakîśa-t*, troop.

(دل) *dall*, U, INF. *dalâla-t*, *dilâlat*, *dulâlat*, *dulûlat*, *dillîla*, show the right way; lead; give a hint, point out, furnish with an argument; — I, INF. *dall*, *dalâl* (also V.), provoke by coquettishness to love-making; — II. INF. *tadlîl*, spoil (a child); cry out for sale, sell by auction; — IV. INF. *idlâl*, be over bold from trust in one's affection; be arrogant; seize the prey from above; be old and shabby; — V. INF. *tadallul*, see I.; be familiar with, live on friendly and pleasant terms with; spoil a child; — X. INF. *istidlâl*, have a thing shown to one's self; ask for a hint, sign, argument, &c.; make a thing an argument against; — ة *dalla-t*, amorousness, coquetry.

دلاص *dilâṣ*, polished, shining; armour; — *; — *dallâṣ*, polisher; shining, smooth, polished; — ة *dalâṣa-t*, polish, brightness.

دلاك *dallâk*, attendant in a bath; bath-keeper.

دلال *dalâl*, lascivious and provoking coquetry; boldness, pertness; great intimacy; spoiling a child (s.); — *dallâl*, go-between, procurer; broker; auctioneer, public crier; road-sign; — ة *dalâla-t*, indication, hint, argument, guidance; — also *dilâla-t*, trade or fee of a guide, a broker, procurer, public crier; (m.) sale by auction; — *dallâla-t*, procuress.

دلام *dalâm*, black; blackness.

دلاة *dalât*, pl. دلى *dal-an*, small vessel, urn; — *dulât*, pl. of دالى *dâli*, who draws water.

دلب *dulb*, ة, pl. *dulab*, plane-tree; — ة *dulba-t*, blackness.

(دلبح) *dalbaḥ*, INF. ة, bend back and head forward.

(دلث) *dalaṡ*, I, INF. *dalîṡ*, walk with short steps; — V. INF. *tadalluṡ*, rush against; — VII. INF. *indilâṡ*, inveigh against (على *'ala*); — VIII. INF. *iddilâṡ*, cover and wrap up.

(دلثع) *dalṡa'*, level road.

(دلثم) *dalṡam*, *dulaṡim*, quick, swift.

(دلج) *dalaj*, U, INF. *dulûj*, draw water from the well and carry it into the cistern; — IV. INF. *idlâj*, set out at nightfall; — VIII. INF. *iddilâj*, travel towards the end of the night; go by night.

دلج *dalaj*, departure at nightfall.

(دلح) *dalaḥ*, INF. *dalḥ*, walk bending under a burden with short steps; — VI. INF. *tadâluḥ*, carry between one another upon a litter.

(دلخ) *dalih̲*, A, INF. *dalah̲*, be fat.

(دلدل) *daldal*, INF. ة, *dildâl*, swing the head and arms in walking; — II. INF. *tadaldul*, swing to and fro.

دلدل *duldul*, pl. *dalâdil*, hedgehog; difficult matter.

(دلس), II. *dallas*, INF. *tadlîs*, cheat in selling; quote apocryphical or doubtful authorities; — III. INF. *mudâlasa-t*, deceive, cheat; — IV. INF. *idlâs*, be covered with late summer-plants, or to find such; — V. INF. *tadallus*, hide one's self.

دلس *dalas*, pl. *adlâs*, darkness, deceit; pl. plants growing at the end of summer; — ة *dulsa-t*, darkness.

(دلص) *dalaṣ*, U, INF. *daliṣ*, be polished, be smooth, shine; — *daluṣ*, INF. *dalâṣa-t*, shine, be bright, resplendent; be smooth; — II. INF. *tadlîṣ*, polish, smooth; — VII. INF. *indilâṣ*, pass. of the previous; slip from the hand and fall.

دلص *daliṣ*, pl. *dilâṣ*, slipping or stumbling frequently; closely shaved, smooth, bald; — *duluṣ*,

pl. of دليص *dalîṣ*; — ة *dalîṣa-t*, level ground.

(دلظ) *dalaz̤*, I, INF. *dalz̤*, knock on the chest; run swiftly past; — VII. INF. *indilâz̤*, surge, billow, be violently agitated; — XV. *idlanz̤a*, INF. *idlinz̤â'*, hurry past.

(دلظم) *dalz̤am*, *dilz̤im*, *dilz̤amm*, *dilaz̤m*, decrepit camel.

دلظى *dalaz̤â*, hero whom nobody dares to combat.

(دلع) *dala'*, A, U, INF. *dal'*, pull out the tongue; — INF. *dal'*, *dulû'*, hang out from the mouth; — II. INF. *tadlî'*, spoil a child (m.); — VII. INF. *indilâ'*, be pulled out.

دلع *dali'*, stupid; insipid; flat (of taste).

دلغام *dilgâm*, clay (m.).

(دلغف), III. *idlagaff*, INF. *idligfâf*, sneak into a place for the purpose of stealing.

(دلف) *dalaf*, I, INF. *dalf*, *dalaf*, *dalafân*, *dalîf*, *dalûf*, walk heavily as if with tied feet, creep; rise with its burden; march quickly, advance in battle; overtake, get the lead of (acc.); (m.) trickle through the roof; — IV. INF. *idlâf*, address harshly, snap at; — V. INF. *tadalluf*, approach; — VII. INF. *indilâf*, be poured out over (على *'ala*).

دلف *dilf*, bold, brave, warlike; (m.) trickling of the rain through a roof; eaves-trough, gutter; — *dulf*, pl. of دلوف *dalûf*; — *duluf*, *dullaf*, pl. of دالف *dâlif*, laden heavily.

(دلفق) *dalfaq*, دلفاق *dilfâq*, open road, thoroughfare.

دلفين *dilfîn*, *dulfîn*, pl. *dalâfîn*, dolphin.

(دلق) *dalaq*, U, INF. *dalq*, draw the sword; pour out; come out of the scabbard; INF. *dulûq*, command the horse (cavalry) to advance; — VII. INF. *indilâq*, glide from the scabbard; rush up furiously; be poured out, shed; come forth, issue; — X. INF. *istidlâq*, pull out, draw.

دلق *daliq*, gliding from the scabbard; — *dalaq*, weasel, marten; frock of a dervish; — *duluq*, pl. of دلوق *dalûq*.

(دلك) *dalak*, INF. *dalk*, rub off and smooth; rub and press the joints (in a bath); render prudent and experienced; INF. *dulûk*, decline towards setting, set; — II. INF. *tadlîk*, rub strongly, smooth; put off a creditor; — V. INF. *tadalluk*, have one's self rubbed; get accustomed to (ب *bi*).

دلك *dalak*, smoothness; weakness.

(دلم) *dalim*, A, INF. *dalam*, be black, soft and smooth; hang down.

دلم *dalam*, wood-pigeon; — *dulam*, elephant; — *dulum*, swelling of the skin.

دلما *dalmâ'*, f. of *adlam*, very black, dark.

(دلمس) *dilmis*, *dulamis*, pl. *dalâmis*, calamity; deep darkness; — IV. *idlammas*, INF. *idlimmâs*, be very dark.

(دلمص) *dulamiṣ*, polished, bright; — II. *tadalmaṣ*, INF. *tadalmuṣ*, be bald.

(دلنظى) *dalanz̤a*, f. دلنظاة *dalanz̤ât*, fat, strong and swift.

(دلنع) *dalanna'*, pl. *dalâni'*, smooth and level.

(دله) *dalih*, A, INF. *dalah*, be stunned, perplexed; — INF. *dalah*, *dalh*, *dulûh* (also V.), be maddened with love, grief, &c.; — *dalah*, INF. *dalh*, be not concerned about, not care for; — V. INF. *tadalluh*, see I.

دلها *dalh-an*, with impunity.

دلهاث *dilhâs̱*, lion.

(دلهث) *dalhas̱*, INF. ة, walk fast, overtake.

دلهم *dalham*, dark; mad with love; wolf; — III. *idlahamm*, INF. *id-*

lihmâm, be very thick, dense, dark.

(دلو) *dalâ*, U, I, INF. *dalw*, let the bucket into the well; draw it out of the well; INF. *dalw*, drive the camel slowly; treat kindly; — II. INF. *tadliya-t*, let down; put into; take in by deceit;—III. INF. *mudâlât*, treat kindly, with flattery; court; — IV. INF. *idlâ'*, let the bucket into the well; try to enter into relationship with; produce a proof; try to bribe; — V. INF. *tadallî*, be suspended and swing to and fro; let one's self down; approach.

دلو *dalw*, pl. *adl-in*, *adlî*, *dilâ'*, *daliyy*, *dala*, bucket; jar; mill-hopper; the sign Aquarius.

دلوح *dalûḥ*, pl. *duluḥ*, heavy with rain; a name of the Sun.

دلوخ *dalûḫ*, pl. *dullaḫ*, *dawâliḫ*, fat; loaded with fruit.

دلوف *dalûf*, pl. *dulf*, swift eagle.

دلوق *dalûq*, pl. *duluq*, gliding from the scabbard; pl. quickly advancing troop.

دلوك *dalûk*, remedy to be rubbed in.

دلول *dalûl*, dromedary; — ة *dulûla-t*, INF. of (دل).

(دلى) *dalî*, A, INF. *dalan*, be stunned, perplexed, bewildered; — V. INF. *tadallî*, be near; be submissive.

دلى *dulla*, high road; — ة *dulayya-t*, small bucket.

دليص *dalîṣ*, pl. *duluṣ*, smooth; shining, bright, polished.

دليع *dalî'*, broad even road.

دليف *dalîf*, slow walk.

دليق *dalîq*, dust raised by the wind; dish of dates and milk; pl. *duluk*, well versed in affairs.

دليل *dalîl*, pl. *adillat*, *dalâ'il*, sign, indication, proof, demonstration; syllogism; road-sign; road, street; pl. *adillâ'*, guide.

دليلى *dillîla*, INF. of (دل).

(دم) *damm*, U, INF. *damm*, smear, cover; colour, dye; level; make a hole level with the ground; punish severely; knock in the head; beat; destroy; hasten; — for *damim*, I, A, also *damum*, INF. *damâma-t*, act infamously; be small, ill-shaped and despised; be ugly; — II. INF. *tadmîm*, anoint the outer eye; — IV. *admam*, *adamm*, INF. *idmâm*, act infamously; beget ugly children.

دم *dam*, pl. *dimâ'*, *dumiyy*, blood; ebullition of the blood; life; — *damm*, salve, ointment; blood; — *dimm*, rupture; — ة *dama-t*, a little blood; — *dimma-t*, ball of camel-dung; — *dumma-t*, pl. *dumam*, hole of a field-mouse; manner, method.

دما *dimâ'*, pl. of دم *dam*.

دماثة *damâṯa-t*, gentleness, mildness; softness, delicacy.

دماج *dimâj*, *dumâj*, firm, solid; well wrought; adorned.

(دماحس) *dumâḥis*, lion.

دمار *damâr*, ة *damâra-t*, destruction, annihilation; — *.

دماع *dimâ'*, furrow of tears; — *dammâ'*, who cries much; always running.

دماغ *dimâg*, pl. *admiga-t*, brain; — ام دماغ *umm-u dimâg-in*, dura mater.

دمال *damâl*, dung; expectoration.

دمالص *dumâliṣ*, shining, bright.

دماليج *damâlîj*, pl. of دملوج *dumlûj*.

دمام *dimâm*, salve, ointment; pl. of دميم *damîm*;—*dammâm*, tinker; — ة *damâma-t*, infamy, INF. of (دم).

دماميس *damâmîs*, pl. of ديماس *daimâs*.

دمان *damân*, rottenness of a palm-tree; callosity.

(دمث) *damiṯ*, A, INF. *damaṯ*, be soft and level; be gentle, mild; — II. INF. *tadmîṯ*, make soft and level, smooth.

دمث *damiṯ*, pl. *dimâṯ*, soft and

level; smooth, polished; gentle, mild.

(دمج) *damaj*, U, INF. *dumûj*, be inserted, joined; work one into the other (teeth of a wheel); (m.) make a thing good and solid; — III. INF. *mudâmaja-t*, flatter; — IV. INF. *idmâj*, wrap into one's cloth, hide beneath it; roll up a garment; twist firmly; make solid, consolidate; (m.) adorn; complete, carry out well; — VI. INF. *tadâmuj*, help; — VII. INF. *indimâj* (also VIII.), be inserted into one another and cohere strongly; VII. be well and solidly made, be adorned; — VIII. INF. *iddimâj*, see VII.

دمج *damj*, twisted curl; — *dimj*, friend.

(دمح), II. *dammaḥ*, INF. *tadmîḥ*, bend the head.

(دمحق) *damḥaq*, thick milk; — INF. ة, starch linen.

دمحل *damḥal*, INF. ة, roll.

(دمحمح) *damaḥmaḥ*, glomerated; strongly built.

(دمخ) *damaḫ*, INF. *damḫ*, tower, be high; knock in the skull.

(دمدم) *damdam*, INF. ة, fix in the ground; smear carefully; give over to destruction; be seized with anger; address angrily, inveigh against; — ة *damdama-t*, anger; invective; murmur, noise, tumult.

(دمر) *damar*, U, INF. *dimâr*, *dumûr*, *damâra-t*, give over to destruction, destroy, annihilate; — INF. *dumûr*, enter without permission, intrude; — II. INF. *tadmîr*, annihilate, destroy; — III. INF. *mudâmara-t*, watch through the night; — V. INF. *tadammur*, be annihilated, perish; murmur against.

(دمرغ) *dumarig*, entirely red.

(دمس) *damas*, I, U, INF. *dumûs*, be dense; — INF. *dams*, be made undiscernible by effacing the traces; bury; conceal; — make peace; — II. INF. *tadmîs*, conceal; bury; — III. INF. *mudâmasa-t*, conceal from; — V. INF. *tadammus*, anoint one's self; — VII. INF. *indimâs*, enter.

دمستق *dumustuq*, pl. *damâsiq*, court official.

(دمش) *damiś*, A, INF. *damaś*, be agitated.

(دمشق) *damśaq*, INF. ة, perform speedily, despatch.

دمشق *dimiśq*, *dimaśq*, Damascus; — *damśaq*, *dimśiq*, nimble, speedy; — ى *dimiśqiyy*, of Damascus; damask blade.

(دمص) *damaṣ*, U, INF. *damṣ*, hasten, speed; drop young or lay eggs before the time; — دمص *damiṣ*, A, INF. *damaṣ*, have the eyebrows thick in the middle and thin towards the end; have thin hair.

(دمع) *dama'*, INF. *dam'*, water, run (eyes); cry; — *dami'*, A, INF. *dama'*, water; — II. INF. *tadmî'* =I.; — IV. INF. *idmâ'*, fill; — V. INF. *tadammu'*, shed tears.

دمع *dam'*, ة, pl. *dumû'*, *admu'*, tear; drop; — *dumu'*, traces of tears.

دمعان *dam'ân*, overflowing.

(دمغ) *damag*, A, U, INF. *damg*, injure the brain or skull; parch the brain, bring on a sun-stroke; annihilate; abolish; — II. INF. *tadmîg*, mark by branding; — IV. INF. *idmâg*, compel; — ة *damga-t*, mark by branding.

(دمق) *damaq*, U, INF. *dumûq*, enter without permission; enter into one's hiding-place; INF. *damq*, break another's teeth; — U, I, insert one thing into or join it to another; steal; — II. INF. *tadmîq*, sprinkle the dough over with flour; — VII. INF. *indimâq*, enter without permission; move from the place (n.).

دمق *damaq*, snow-storm; — ة *damaqa-t*, blacksmith's bellows.

دمقاس *dimqâs*, دمقاص *dimqâṣ*, and— دمقس *dimaqs*, دمقص *dimaqṣ*, raw silk.

(دمك) *damak*, U, INF. *dumûk*, run fast; get smooth; — INF. *damk*, rise; twist, grind, pound; cover (stallion).

دملك *dumuk*, pl. of دموك *damûk*.

(دمل) *damal*, U, INF. *daml*, *damalân*, dung, manure; make peace; heal, cure; — *damil*, A, INF. *damal*, be healed, scarred over; suppurate and heal; — II. INF. *tadmîl*, form a tumour or abscess; — III. INF. *mudâmala-t*, treat with kindness or flattery; — VII. INF. *indimâl*, be healed, scarred over; suppurate.

دمل *dummal*, ة, pl. *damâmil*, *damâmîl*, also *dumal*, pl. *dimlân*, tumour, abscess, boil.

دملان *dimlân*, pl. of دمل *dumal*; — *damalân*, INF. of (دمل).

(دملج) *damlaj*, INF. ة, *dimlâj*, make perfect and appropriate to the purpose.

دملج *dumlaj*, *dumluj*, pl. *damâlij*, دملوج *dumlûj*, pl. *damâlîj*, large bracelet for the upper arm.

(دملح) *damlaḥ*, INF. ة, roll, revolve.

(دملص) *dumaliṣ*, shining, bright.

(دملق) *dumaliq*, round and smooth.

دمم *dimam*, glue; blood; pl. of دمة *dimma-t*; — *dumam*, pl. of دمة *dumma-t*.

(دمن) *daman*, U, I, INF. *damn*, dung, manure; — *damin*, A, INF. *daman*, entertain an inveterate grudge against (على *'ala*); get black and putrefy; — II. INF. *tadmîn*, dung; — IV. INF. *idmân*, make durable; attend to a thing zealously, practise a thing assiduously; — V. INF. *tadammun*, become callous; — X. INF. *istidmân*, practise diligently.

دمن *dimn*, dung, manure; — ة *dimna-t*, pl. *dimn*, *diman*, dunghill; surroundings of a house covered with dung, ashes, &c.; traces of old dwellings; false show; inveterate hatred.

(دمه) *damah*, heat of glowing sand; — XII. *idmaumah*, INF. *idmîmâh*, glow, boil; swoon.

دموك *damûk*, pl. *dumuk*, windlass, pulley.

دموى *damawiyy*, ة, bloody; plethoric, full-blooded, of full habit; sanguine.

(دمى) *damî*, INF. *daman*, bleed; flow; INF. *daman*, *dumiyy*, be blood-stained; — II. INF. *tadmiya-t*, cause blood to flow; wound; stain with blood; — IV. INF. *idmâ'*, id.

دمى *damiyy*, bloody; — *dumayy*, a little blood; — *dumiyy*, pl. of دم *dam*; INF. of (دمى); — ة *dumya-t*, pl. دمى *duman*, *duma*, statue; idol; painted figure, puppet.

دمياط *dimyâṭ*, Damietta; — ى *dimyâṭiyy*, a cotton stuff.

دميث *damîs̱*, gentle, mild.

دميس *damîs*, concealed.

دميغ *damîg*, hare-brained; wounded in the brain.

دميم *damîm*, pl. *dimâm*, f. ة, pl. *damâ'im*, short, ill-shaped and despised; ugly.

(دن) *dann*, hum, buzz; INF. *danîn*, speak in a low voice and unintelligibly; — *danin*, A, INF. *danan*, be short-legged, having the chest close to the ground and a high back; — II. INF. *tadnîn*, hum, buzz; — IV. INF. *idnân*, stay, abide.

دن *dann*, pl. *dinân*, large wine-jar, with its flat bottom buried in the ground.

(دنا) *dana'*, دنو *danu'*, INF. *danâ'a-t*, *dunû'a-t*, be of little worth, of bad quality, be vile; act headstrongly; — *dani'*, A, INF. *dana'*, be hump-backed; — IV. INF. *idnâ'*, commit enormities; — V.

INF. *tadannu'*, instigate to villainy.

دنا *duna'â'*, pl. of دنى *dani'*; — *dannâ'*, f. of ادن *adann*, hump-backed, &c.; — ة *danâ'a-t*, meanness; weakness; pusillanimity.

دنابة *dinnâba-t*, small, dwarfish.

دنار *dinnâr*=دينار *dînâr*.

دناسة *danâsa-t*, impurity; pollution.

دناعة *danâ'a-t*, ravenous hunger.

دنانير *danânîr*, pl. of دينار *dînâr*.

دناوة *danâwa-t*, approach; nearness; relationship, INF. of (دنو).

دناى *dan'a*, f. hump-backed; — ة *dinâya-t*=دناوة *danâwa-t*.

دنايا *danâyâ*, pl. of دنية *daniyya-t*.

دنب *danab*, (m.) for ذنب *zanab*, tail; — *dinnab*, ة *dinnaba-t*, small, dwarfish.

دنبلة *dumbala-t*, pl. *danâbil*, tumour, abscess.

(دنج) *danaj*, U, INF. *dinâj*, fix, consolidate, carry out in a solid manner.

دنج *danj*, black sealing-wax.

(دنح) *danaḥ*, INF. *dunûḥ*, be contemptible.

دنح *dinḥ*, epiphany.

دنحبة *danḥaba-t*, treason, treachery.

(دنحس) *danḥas*, corpulent, fleshy.

دنخ *danaḫ*, INF. *danaḫân*, walk with difficulty under a burden; bend the neck; humble one's self; stop at home.

دندان *dindân*, murmur; — ة *dandâna-t*, plantation of mulberry-trees.

(دندل) *dandal*, INF. ة, suspend.

(دندن) *dandan*, INF. ة, hum, buzz; murmur between the teeth, speak unintelligibly, mumble.

دندن *dindan*, ة *dandana-t*, humming, mumbling (s.).

(دنر), II. *dannar*, INF. *tadnîr*, shine, be bright, resplendent; pass. have abundance of gold coin.

(دنس) *danis*, A, INF. *danas*, *danâsa-t*, be soiled, stained, polluted; soil, pollute one's self; — II. INF. *tadnîs*, stain, pollute; desecrate, profane; — V. INF. *tadannus*, soil, stain, pollute one's self; be soiled, &c.; be desecrated, profaned.

دنس *danas*, pl. *adnâs*, pollution, impurity, foulness; — *danis*, pl. *adnâs*, *madânîs*, soiled, polluted, impure, foul; immoral; (m.) desecrated, profane.

(دنع) *dana'*, INF. *dunû'*, *danâ'a-t*, be vile and contemptible; — *dani'*, A, have a ravenous hunger; crave for, be greedy; be vile and contemptible; humble one's self before (ل *li*).

دنع *dani'*, hungry; mean, vile; — *dana'*, meanness; dregs of the populace, rabble.

(دنغ) *danig*, pl. *danaga-t*, vile person, villain.

(دنف) *danif*, suffer from long or chronic disease; be emaciated; approach, be near; grow yellow and decline to setting; — IV. INF. *idnâf*, be dangerously ill, near death; afflict sorely; visit with a severe illness; decline; weaken.

دنف *danaf*, chronic disease; — also *danif*, ة, afflicted with a chronic disease; emaciated.

(دنفس) *dinfis*, stupid, silly (f.).

(دنق) *danaq*, I, U, INF. *dunûq*, trifle, be minutely accurate; fall down from weakness; swoon; grow torpid from cold and die; —II. INF. *tadnîq*, reckon closely; examine minutely, look at sharply and for a long time, decline towards setting; be disfigured or emaciated by illness or grief; be sunk; freeze to death in the snow.

دنق *danq*, sixth part of a *dirham*.

(دنقر) *danqar*, INF. ة, indulge in trifles, trifle, transact business with a paltry accuracy; have a bad pace.

دنكس *dankas*, stop at home; not stir.

دنكلة *dankala-t*, sea-gull.

(دنم), II. *dannam*, INF. *tadnîm*, resound; be mean, vile, contemptible; — ة *dinnama-t*, دنامة *dinnâma-t*, short (woman); ant; atom.

دنن *danan*, INF. of (دن).

(دنو) *danâ*, U, INF. *dunuww*, *danâwa-t*, be or come near, approach; — for *daniw*, INF. دنى *danan*, *dinâya-t*, *danâwa-t*, grow mean, vile, contemptible; — II. INF. *tadniya-t*, bring near, lead up; contemplate what is small as well as what is great in things; — III. INF. *mudânât*, be close to, in one's reach; approach; stand between and close to either; — IV. INF. *idnâ'*, bring near, lead up; bid to approach; be near confinement; — VI. INF. *tadânî*, be near to one another; approach one another; approach; — X. INF. *istidnâ'*, wish one to approach; try to come near one; call up, send for.

دنو *dunuww*, nearness; approach, INF. of (دنو); — ة *dunu'a-t*, vileness, INF. of (دنا).

دنى *daniyy*, ة, near, neighbouring; pl. *adniyâ*, also دنى *dani'*, pl. *duna'â'*, *adân-in*, *adnâ'*, low, mean, vile; worthless, of a bad quality; weak-minded, cowardly; — ة *daniyya-t*, pl. *danâyâ*, anything worthless; weakness, imperfection; villainy; meanness, vice; — *danniyya-t*, cap of a judge.

دنيا *dunyâ*, pl. *duna-n*, the world; worldly goods; man, mankind, people; f. of ادنى *adna*, nearer, and of ادنا *adna'*, meaner, viler.

دنياوى *dunyâwiyy*, ة, worldly, perishable.

دنيق *danîq*, torpor from cold.

دنين *danîn*, humming, buzzing, INF. of (دن).

دنيوى *dunyawiyy*, ة, worldly, perishable.

ده *dah-in*, see دهى *dahî*.

دها *dahâ'*, ة *dahâ'a-t*, cunning, craft; subtleness; INF. of (دهى); — ة *dahât*, pl. of داهى *dâhî*, sagacious, &c.; and of دهى *dahî*.

دهاق *dihâq*, full.

دهاقنة *dahâqina-t*, دهاقين *dahâqîn*, pl. of دهقان *dihqân*, *duhqân*.

دهامج *duhâmij*, camel with two humps.

دهان *dahhân*, who anoints; dealer in oil and fat; whitewasher, painter; — *.

(دهب) *dahb*, routed army.

(دهبل) *dahbal*, INF. ة, cram into one's mouth.

(دهث) *dahas*, INF. *dahs*, push, push back.

(دهثم) *dahsam*, strong camel.

(دهدا) *dahda'*, see دهده *dahdah*.

(دهدع) *dahda'*, INF. ة, call to the goats.

(دهدق) *dahdaq*, INF. ة, *dihdâq*, break; cut into small pieces, hash; move.

(دهدم) *dahdam*, INF. ة, disperse.

(دهدموز) *dahdamûz*, glutton.

(دهدن) *dahdan*, man, mankind, creatures.

(دهده) *dahdah*, INF. ة, دهدا *dahda'*, INF. *dihdâ'*, *dahdât*, roll; throw things one upon another; — II. INF. *tadahduh*, roll (m.), bound.

(دهر) *dahar*, happen, befall.

دهر *dahr*, *dahar*, pl. *duhûr*, *adhur*, time, age, epoch, century; history, course of events, vicissitude, fortune; eternal duration; world; custom, habit.

دهرج *dahraj*, INF. ة, walk along quickly.

(دهرس) *dahras*, pl. *dahâris*, calamity; vivacity.

دهرى *dahriyy*, temporal, worldly, mundane; impious; atheist; materialist; — *duhriyy*, very old.

(دهس) *dahis*, A, INF. *dahas*, be soft and reddish (ground); — IV. INF. *idhâs*, come upon such ground; — XI. *idihâss*, INF. *idhîsâs*=I.

دهس *dahs*, soft reddish ground without sand or clay; — *duhs*, soft sand; pl. and—

دهسا *dahsâ*, f. of ادهس *adhas*, rust-coloured, &c.

(دهسم) *dahsam*, INF. ة, conceal, hide.

(دهش) *dahiś*, A, INF. *dahaś*, be perplexed, bewildered, astonished; pass. *duhiś*, id.; — II. INF. *tadhîś*, IV. INF. *idhâś*, perplex, bewilder, astonish; — VII. INF. *indihâś*, be speechless with astonishment.

دهش *dahiś*, astonished, bewildered; — ة *dahśa-t*, astonishment, fright.

(دهض), IV. *adhaḍ*, INF. *idhâḍ*, hurry.

(دهع) *daha'*, INF. *dah'*, call to or decoy the goats.

(دهف) *dahaf*, INF. *dahf*, take much of a thing.

(دهق) *dahaq*, fill, and, by opposition, pour out with a jerk; cut or break into many pieces; knock down and press to the ground; give part of; torment, torture.

دهق *dahaq*, torture.

دهقان *dihqân*, *duhqân*, pl. *dahâqina-t*, *dahâqîn*, head of a village; squire (Pers.).

(دهقل) *dahqal*, INF. ة, rub and smooth the skin of an animal.

(دهقن) *dahqan*, INF. ة, appoint as the head of a village or prefect of a district; (m.) keep back, delay; — II. INF. *tadahqun*, pass. of the previous; — ة *dahqana-t*, office of the prefect of a village or district; delay.

دهقوع *duhqû'*, violent hunger.

(دهك) *dahak*, INF. *dahk*, pound; stamp; lie with.

(دهكر), II. *tadahkar*, INF. *tadahkur*, roll (n.), be rolled; rush upon; totter, waver to and fro.

(دهكم) *dahkam*, decrepit old man; — II. INF. *tadahkum*, engage imprudently in difficult business; rush upon and maltreat.

(دهل) *dahl*, hour, moment; a little, trifle.

(دهلق) *dahlaq*, INF. ة= دهقل *dahqal*.

(دهليز) *dihlîz*, pl. *dahâlîz*, vestibule, passage, entrance-hall, corridor, gallery; subterranean basement; catacombs; (m.) trenches; ابنا الدهاليز *abnâ-u 'd-dahâlîz-i*, foundlings, bastards.

(دهم) *daham*, INF. *dahm*, come unexpectedly, surprise; — II. INF. *tadhîm*, blacken; — III. INF. *mudâhama-t*, surprise; — IX. INF. *idhimâm*, XI. INF. *idhîmâm*, be black.

دهم *dahm*, pl. *duhûm*, army, legion; somebody, a person, creature; calamity — *duhm*, pl. of ادهم *adham*, black; — ة *duhmat*, blackness.

دهما *duhmâ'*, f. of ادهم *adham*, black.

(دهماص) *dihmâṣ*, solid.

(دهمج) *dahmaj*, INF. ة, walk swift and with short steps.

(دهمس) *dahmas*, INF. ة, whisper to (acc.); advise, counsel; attack, assail, push.

(دهمق) *dahmaq*, INF. ة, break, cut, reduce; relax the bow-string; cook the food soft and prepare it well, and, by opposition, over-do it; well dispose one's speech.

دهمن *dahman*, pl. *dahâmina-t*, royal title (Pers.).

دهموث *duhmûṯ*, liberal.

(دهن) *dahan*, U, INF. *dahn*, *dahna-t*, anoint, oil, grease, smear with pomatum; varnish; whitewash, paint; blacken; — INF. *dahn*, take in, cheat; flog; wet slightly; — *dahan*, U, also *dahin*, A, *dahun*, INF. *dihân*, *dihâna-t*,

have little milk ; — II. INF. *tadhîn*, oil, grease, anoint ; paint, whitewash ; — III. INF. *dihân*, *mudâhana-t*, cover ; take in, cheat, outwit, treat gently ; IV. INF. *idhân*, outwit, deceive ; proceed slowly and lukewarmly in a matter ; — V. INF. *tadahhun*, VII. INF. *indihân*, VIII. INF. *iddihân*, pass. of II.

دهن *dahn*, oiling, anointing, greasing, varnishing, white-washing, painting (s.) ; — *duhn*, pl. *adhan*, *dihân*, fat, grease, ointment, salve ; oil-colour ; varnish ; shoe-black ; slight rain ; — *dahin*, anointed, oiled, fatty ; — ة *duhna-t*, a little ointment ; odour, perfume.

دهنا *dahnâ*, field ; desert.

دهنج *dahnaj*, precious stone (emerald).

دهنى *duhniyy*, oily, greasy, fatty.

(دهو) *dahâ*, U, INF. *dahw*, happen to, befall ; — I, INF. *dahy*, id. ; accuse of stratagem, blame, rebuke ; bring misfortune upon ; — دهى *dahî*, A, INF. *dahy*, *dahâ'*, *dahâ'a-t*, be cunning, sly, subtle ; — V. INF. *tadahhî*, VI. INF. *tadâhî*, act with cunning.

دهوا *dahwâ'*, great calamity ; — *duhawâ'*, pl. of دهى *dahiyy*.

(دهور) *dahwar*, INF. ة, grasp and throw into the air ; throw down ; drop excrement ; take a large morsel ; deliver (a speech) pompously ; break in, pull down.

دهون *dahûn*, see the following ; — *duhûn*, ointment, salve ; pomatum ; shoe-black ; pl. of داهى *dâhî*, sagacious, &c.

دهى *dahî* (دهٍ *dah-in*), pl. *dahûn*, also *dahiyy*, pl. *adhiya-t*, *duhawâ'*, cunning, sly, subtle ; see (دهو).

دو *daww*, desert ; — *daw-in*, see دوى *dawiyy*.

(دو , دوى) *dâ'*, pret. *di'tu*, A, INF. *dâ'*, *dau'*, be ill ; — IV. INF. *idwâ'*, be ill ; make ill ; INF. *idwâ'* and *idâ'a-t*, suspect.

دوا *dawâ'*, *diwâ'*, *duwâ'*, pl. *adwiya-t*, remedy, medicine ; — *diwâ'*, cure ; — ة *dawât*, pl. دوى *dawa*, *duwiyy*, *diwiyy*, *dawâyât*, ink-bottle, ink-stand ; writing-material ; shell of a fruit ; (m.) pipe, canal.

دواب *dawâbb*, pl. of دابة *dâbba-t*, beast.

دوات *dawât*=دواة ; — ى *dawâtiyy*, secretary of state.

دواج *duwâj*, *duwwâj*, an upper garment ; covering, blanket.

دواجن *dawâjin*, pl. of داجن *dâjin*, covering, dark, &c.

دواخل *dawâḥil*, interiors, &c., pl. of داخلة *dâḥila-t* ; pl. of دوخلة *dauḥala-t*.

دواخن *dawâḥin*, دواخين *dawâḥîn*, smoke, &c., pl. of دخان *duḥân*.

دواد *duwâd*, worms ; ring-worm.

دوادار *dawâdâr*, keeper or holder of the ink-stand, secretary of state (Pers.).

دوار *dawâr*, *duwâr*, giddiness ; whirlpool ; — * ; — *dawwâr*, revolving, rolling, whirling ; nimble, swift ; hawker, pedlar ; vagabond ; temple in Mecca ; — ة *dawwâra-t*, circular field ; hoop ; tire of a wheel ; circle ; halo ; lock of hair.

دوارج *dawâriğ*, pl. feet of a horse.

دوارس *dawâris*, pl. of دارس *dâris*, ag. of (درس).

دوارى *dawâriyy*, circular (adj.) ; revolving ; returning periodically.

دواس *dawwâs*, bold ; lion ; cunning ; — ة *duwâsa-t*, troop of men ; — *dawwâsa-t*, nose.

دواسيس *dawâsîs*, spies, pl. of داسوس *dâsûs*.

دواعى *dawâ'î*, vicissitudes ; pl. of داعية *dâ'iya-t*, cause, &c., and of دعوة *da'wa-t*, invocation, &c.

دواغص *dawâgiṣ*, knee-pans, &c., pl. of داغصة *dâgiṣa-t*.

دوافع *dawâfi'*, hindrances, &c., pl. of دافعة *dâfi'a-t*.

دوالب *dawâlib*, دواليب *dawâlîb*, water-wheels; see دولاب *dûlâb*, *daulâb*.

دواليك *dawâlîk*, pl. alternating, in turns, one after the other.

دوام *dawâm*, duration; endurance; —*duwâm*, giddiness;—*dawâmm*, seas, &c., pl. of داما *da'mâ'*, &c.; — ة *duwwâma-t*, pl. *duwwâm*, spinning-top; toy.

دوامك *dawâmik*, calamities, pl. of دامكة *dâmika-t*.

دوانيق *dawânîq*, pl. of دانق *dânaq*, *dâniq*, fraction of a drachm, &c.

دواهى *dawâhî*, calamities, pl. of داهية *dâhiya-t*.

دواوين *dawâwîn*, pl. of ديوان *dîwân*.

دوائح *dawâ'iḥ*, trees with a far-spreading shadow, pl. of دائحة *dâ'iḥa-t*.

دوائر *dawâ'ir*, circles, &c., pl. of دائرة *dâ'ira-t*.

دوائس *dawâ'is*, oxen employed to tread out corn; threshing-floor.

دوائم *dawâ'im*, pl. of دائم *dâ'im*, lasting, &c.

دواية *dawâya-t* (m.)=دواة *dawât*; —*dawâya-t*, *diwâya-t*, thin skin upon the milk.

دوائى *dawâ'iyy*, medical, medicinal.

(دوب) *dâb*, U, INF. *daub*=(داب).

دوبل *daubal*, pl. *dawâbil*, small wild ass; boar; sucking-pig; fox; wolf.

دوثة *dausa-t*, flight from the battle.

(دوج) *dâj*, U, INF. *dauj*, serve, wait upon, attend to.

(دوح) *dâḥ*, U, INF. *dauḥ*, be big and protruding; be tall; — INF. *tadwîḥ*, disperse one's cattle; dissipate one's fortune; — VII. INF. *indiyâḥ*=I.; — ة *dauḥa-t*, pl. *dauḥ* tall tree; trunk of a tree; orchard; very large house.

دوحاس *dauḥâs*, whitlow.

(دوخ) *dâḫ*, U, INF. *dauḫ*, be low, mean, contemptible; humble one's self; subdue, conquer; (m.) be giddy;—II. INF. *tadwîḫ*, subdue, conquer; make contemptible, humiliate; travel about; (m.) make giddy; — IV. INF. *idâḫa-t*, throw away; — ة *dauḫa-t*, giddiness, seediness; nausea.

دوخلة *dauḫala-t*, *dauḫalla-t*, pl. *dawâliḫ*, basket of palm-leaves.

(دود) *dâd*, A, INF. *daud*, be worm-bitten, worm-eaten, or full of worms; — II. INF. *tadwîd* and V. INF. *tadawwud*, id.

دود *dûd*, ة, pl. *dîdân*, worm.

دوداة *dauda'a-t*, *daudât*, noise of a crowd, &c.; swing, rocking-board.

دودو *du'du'*, pl. *da'âdî*, the last nights of the month.

(دودى) *dauda*, INF. *daudât*, rock one's self.

(دور) *dâr*, U, INF. *daur*, *dawarân*, move in a circle, revolve, walk round; wander over, travel through; be in motion, in working order; lead or carry about, hawk; look for one everywhere; pass. دير به *dîr bi-hi*, د عليه *dîr 'ale-hi*, he was seized with giddiness; — II. INF. *tadyîr*, revolve (a.); lead about; seek everywhere; set going, wind up (a watch); make round; — III. INF. *diwâr*, *mudâwara-t*, take a turn with, lead about; INF. *mudâwara-t*, show regard to; handle a thing to set it going; look furtively at; — IV. INF. *idâra-t*, turn round, revolve (a.); set going; circulate (a.); wind round; make inclined to; fix one's thoughts upon; turn aside from (a.); pass. be seized with giddiness; — V. INF. *tadawwur*, revolve (n.); be round or circular; — VII. INF. *indiyâr*, be docile; turn, turn aside; — VIII. INF. *iddiyâr*, circulate,

revolve (n.); — X. INF. *istidâra-t* = V.

دور *daur*, pl. *adwâr*, rotation; circle, cycle; turn; vicissitude; age, period, epoch; roundabout way; fit of a fever; storey; the world; — *dûr*, houses, &c., pl. of دار *dâr* and دارة *dâra-t*; — ة *daura-t*, rotation, circulation, cycle; roundabout way.

دورات *dûrât*, houses, pl. of دار *dâr*.

دوران *dûran*, id.; — *dawarân*, rotation, circulation; giddiness; INF. of (دور).

دورق *dauraq*, water-jug with handles and a spout.

دورمز *dauramaz*, snake.

دوری *dauriyy*, ة, periodical, intermittent; — *dûriyy*, someone, somebody; — ة *dauriyya-t*, turn, alternation.

(دوس) *dâs*, U, INF. *daus*, *diyâs*, *diyâsa-t*, tread, stamp; tread under foot; humble, lower; lie with; smooth, polish; — INF. *dawâsa-t*, tread out the corn, thresh; — VII. INF. *indiyâs*, be trodden upon, humbled, lowered; be trodden out, threshed.

دوس *daus*, ة *dausa-t*, treading, threshing (s.); — *dûs*, polish, brightness.

(دوش) *dawiś*, A, INF. *dawaś*, be dimmed, weakened or sunk (eye, from illness).

(دوص), II. *dawwaṣ*, INF. *tadwîṣ*, descend.

(دوع) *dâʿ*, U, INF. *dauʿ*, move the feet or hands quickly.

(دوغ) *dâg*, U, INF. *daug*, be seized by an epidemic; destroy, annihilate; be cheap; — ة *dauga-t*, epidemic; cold (s.).

(دوف) *dâf*, U, INF. *dauf*, mix; moisten; dissolve in water.

دوفان *dûfân*, nightmare, incubus.

(دوق) *dâq*, U, INF. *dauq*, *dawaq*, *duwûq*, *duwûqa-t*, *dawâqa-t*, be of a weak intellect, mad; be emaciated; refuse milk or water; taste a dish; — IV. INF. *idâqa-t*, surround.

دوقانية *dauqâniyya-t*, دوقة *dauqa-t*, madness; ruin, destruction.

دوقل *dauqal*, mast; penis.

(دوك) *dâk*, U, INF. *dauk*, *madâk*, grind, pound; dip into water, bury in the sand or ground; get into confusion or discord; be visited by an epidemic; lie with; — ة *dauka-t*, tumult, quarrel, fight; calamity.

(دول) *dâl*, U, INF. *daul*, be in continual rotation; change, alter, undergo vicissitudes; be worn out; hang down flabbily; — INF. *daul*, *dâla-t*, become renowned; — III. INF. *mudâwala-t*, cause to revolve, to follow each other, to alternate; confer with; handle arms, practise in their use; — IV. INF. *idâla-t*, transfer from one to the other; give a turn; — VI. INF. *tadâwul*, do alternately, reach to one another; circulate (a.); snatch from one another; do frequently, from day to day; confer.

دول *daul*, vicissitude; state, destiny; turn; — ة *daula-t*; pl. *dawal*, *diwal*, *duwal*, *duwalât*, *dûlât*, vicissitude, change of time and fortune; period; dynasty; empire, dominion, sovereignty; wealth and power; luck, good fortune; — *duwala-t*, misfortune, calamity.

دولاب *dûlâb*, *daulâb*, pl. *dawâlîb*, water-wheel; mill; labyrinth; intrigue.

دولتلو *daulatlû*, Excellency (Turk.).

دولوك *du'lûk*, pl. *da'âlîk*, important matter or business.

دولول *du'lûl*, pl. *da'âlîl*, confusion; disaster.

(دوم) *dâm*, U, A, INF. *daum*, *dawâm*, *daimûma-t*, last, continue; endure, persist; remain; stagnate; — I, INF. *daim*, rain continuously; — II. INF. *tadwîm*,

intoxicate completely; describe a curve in the sky, circles in the air; play with a spinning-top; rain continuously; — III. INF. *mudâwama-t*, do or practise without interruption; show diligence and perseverance in a matter (على *'ala*), persist; — IV. INF. *idâma-t*, make to last, preserve, prolong; carry on persistently; rain continuously; — V. INF. *tadawwum*, wait, wait for, expect; — X. INF. *istidâma-t*, continue; be everlasting; wish a thing to be everlasting; tarry; persist; describe circles in the air, hover quietly.

دوم *daum*, continual, lasting; everlasting; duration; — ة *dauma-t*, pl. *daum*, wild palm-tree.

(دون) *dân*, U, INF. *daun*, be of a bad quality; be weak, mean, vile, despised; — II. INF. *tadwîn*, gather stray poems into a collection; enter into a list or roll; note down; write out an account; — V. INF. *tadawwun*, be registered, inscribed, noted down.

دون *dûn*, prep. under, and, by opposition, above; lower down; on or towards this side; close by; except; دونك *dûnaka*, it is yours! take it! — *dûn*, adj. low, mean, vile, bad.

(دوه), II. *dawwah*, INF. *tadwîh*, call to or decoy a camel; — V. INF. *tadawwuh*, change, alter; befall suddenly.

دووى *dawawiyy*, secretary of state.

(دوى) *dawî*, A, INF. *dawan*, be ill; hum, buzz; make a noise, be noisy; — II. INF. *tadwiya-t*, hum, buzz; be covered with a thin skin; — III. INF. *mudâwât*, treat an illness or a patient, heal; — IV. INF. *idwâ'*, make ill; give an echo; — VI. INF. *tadâwî*, treat one's self medically, undergo a cure.

دوى *dawa*, pl. of دواة *dawât*; — *dawan*, ill; pl. *adwâ'*, illness; — *dawî* (دو *daw-in*), ة, ill; — دوى *dawiyy*, someone, somebody; hum, buzz, noise; echo; — *duwiyy*, pl. of دواة; — *dawwiyy*, desert; inhabitant of the desert; someone, somebody; — ة *dawiyya-t*, desert; order of the templars; — II. *dawwa*, INF. *tadwiya-t*, go into the desert; — *dawî'*, v. see (دو).

دويبة *duwaibba-t*, little animal.

دويد *duwaid*, little worm.

دويدار *dawîdâr*=دوادار *dawâdâr*.

دويرة *duwaira-t*, little house, cot.

دويك *duwaik*, little jar.

دوين *duwain*, a little farther below.

دويهية *duwaihiyya-t*, calamity, disaster.

ديابيج *dayâbîj*, pl. of ديباج *dîbâj*.

دياجى *dayâjî*, pl. ديجاة *daijât*.

دياجير *dayâjîr*, pl. of ديجور *daijûr*.

ديار *diyâr*, pl. of ديرة *daira-t*; — *dayyâr*, someone, somebody; superior of a convent, prior; monk; — ة *diyâra-t*, and—

ديارات *diyârât*, houses, &c., pl. of دار *dâr*.

دياس *diyâs*, ة *diyâsa-t*, treading, threshing, INF. of (دوس); — *dayyâs*, thresher.

دياميس *dayâmîs*, pl. of ديماس *daimâs*.

دياميم *dayâmîm*, pl. of ديمومة *daimûma-t*.

ديان *dayyân*, requiter, judge; administrator; religious; — ة *diyâna-t*, religiousness; conscientiousness; religious worship.

دياوين *dayâwîn*, pl. of ديوان *dîwân*.

ديباج *dîbâj*, pl. *dayâbîj*, *dabâbîj*, brocade; embroidered gold-stuff; ornamental book-title, preface; — ة *dîbâja-t*, du. *dîbajatân*, the cheeks; countenance; — ى *dîbâjiyy*, seller of brocade.

(ديث), II. *dayyas̱*, INF. *tadyîs̱*, subdue; render contemptible; — V. INF. *tadayyus̱*, carry on the trade of a procurer, pimp.

(دیج) *dâj*, I, INF. *daij*, *dayajân*, walk like a decrepit old man.

دیجاة *daijât*, pl. *dayâjî*, deep darkness.

دیجوج *daijûj*, very dark.

دیجور *daijûr*, pl. *dayâjîr*, dust, earth; darkness; dark.

دیحان *daiḥân*, locust.

(دیح) *dîḥ*, pl. *diyaḥa-t*, bunch of dates; — II. *dayyaḥ*, INF. *tadyîḥ*, subdue, conquer.

(دید) *daid*, game, sport, jest; — II. *dayyad*, INF. *tadyîd*, be worm-bitten.

دیدا *dî'dâ'*, pl. *da'âdî'*, last nights of the month; INF. of دادا *da'da'*.

دیدان *daidân*, custom, habit; sport, jest; — *dîdân*, pl. of دود *dûd*.

دیدب *daidab*, wild ass; also دیدبان *dîdabân*, دیذبان *daizabân*, watcher, guard; vanguard; — *daidab*, INF. ة, mount guard, be a sentinel.

دیدن *daidan*, ة *daidana-t*, custom, habit.

(دیر), V. *tadayyar*, INF. *tadayyur*, reside; make one's domicile.

دیر *dair*, pl. *adyâr*, *duyûr*, *adyira-t*, convent; wine-house;—ة *daira-t*, pl. *diyâr*, circumference.

دیران *dîrân*, houses, &c., pl. of دار *dâr*; — ی *dairâniyy*, superior of a convent.

(دیس) *dais*, nipple, teat; — ة *dîsa-t*, pl. *dîs*, *diyas*, dense forest.

دیسق *daisaq*, slab of silver; silver ornaments for women; large dish.

(دیش) *dîś*, dung-hill cock.

(دیص) *dâṣ*, I, INF. *dayaṣân*, deviate, diverge; be movable; — INF. *daiṣ*, abscond; flee from battle; steal; fall from a respected state into contempt; be nimble, agile; — VII. INF. *indiyâṣ*, drop from the hand.

(دئص) *da'iṣ*, A, INF. *da'aṣ*, be mischievous, petulant; be very fat.

(دیق) *dâq*, I, INF. *daiq*, make rickety, relax.

دیك *dîk*, pl. *duyûk*, *adyâk*, *diyaka-t*, dung-hill cock; cock; د هندی *dîk hindiyy*, turkey; — ة *dîka-t*, hen.

دئل *du'il*, jackal.

دیم *daim*, INF. of (دوم); — ة *dîma-t*, pl. *diyâm*, *duyûm*, *diyamât*, *dîmât*, steady rain; (m.) striped cotton-stuff.

دیماس *daimâs*, *dîmâs*, pl. *dayâmîs*, *damâmîs*, dark prison, dungeon; bath.

دیموم *daimûm*, desert; — ة *daimûma-t*, pl. *dayamîm*, id.; duration, INF. of (دوم).

(دین) *dân*, I, INF. *dain*, be a debtor, owe money; borrow; lend; compel; render contemptible; submit, yield, obey; —INF. *dain*, *dîn*, requite, reward; benefit; — INF. *dîn*, deliver judgment, sentence; judge hard upon; — INF. *diyâna-t*, be religious, be a believer; profess Islâm; — II. INF. *tadyîn*, lend money; leave one undisturbed in his religion; — III. INF. *mudâyana-t*, lend money, give or take credit; requite; judge hard upon others; — IV. INF. *idâna-t*, lend money; borrow; — V. INF. *tadayyun*, borrow money; incur debts; be indebted; be religious; — VI. INF. *tadâyun*, owe to or credit one another; — VIII. INF. *iddiyân*, borrow, take credit, buy or sell on credit; — X. INF. *istidâna-t*, borrow; demand payment of a debt.

دین *dain*, pl. *duyûn*, *adyun*, *dîna-t*, debt, money obligation; علیه د *'ale-hi dîn*, he owes money; له د *la-hu dîn*, money is owed to him; — *dîn*, pl. *adyân*, creed, religious worship or doctrine, belief; custom, habit; judg-

ment, **sentence**; requital; do-minion, power, victory; د و دولة‎ *din wa daula-t*, church and state; — *dayyin*, religious; pious, conscientious; powerful; conqueror; — ة *dina-t*, incessant rain; debt.

دينار‎ *dinâr*, pl. *danânir*, a gold coin *dinar*; weight of 1½ drachm.

ديرونة‎ *dainûna-t*, judgment, sentence.

ديني‎ *diniyy*, religious, referring to religion.

دية‎ *diya-t*, blood-money, fine or mulct for murder or wounding, due; INF. of (ودى‎).

ديوان‎ *diwân*, pl. *dawówin*, also *daiwân*, pl. *dayâwin*, royal court; court of justice, tri-

bunal; council of state; session; assembly-hall, hall; divan, sofa; collection of an author's poems, arranged according to the final letters of the end-rhymes in the order of the alphabet; roll, register, archives; — ى‎ *diwâniyy*, an official style of writing.

ديوث‎ *dayyûs̱*, cuckold; pimp, procurer.

ديور‎ *dayyûr*, someone, somebody.

ديوك‎ *duyûk*, pl. of ديك‎ *dik*.

ديوم‎ *duyûm*, pl. of ديمة‎ *dima-t*; — *dayyûm*, everlasting.

ديون‎ *duyûn*, pl. of دين‎ *dain*.

دئى‎ *da'iyy*, pl. of داى‎ *da'y*, داية‎ *da'ya-t*, place of the camel's hump where it is touched by the saddle; — *dayyi'*, ة‎, ill, unwell.

ذ

ذ‎ *ẕ*, ninth letter of the alphabet; as a numerical sign = 700; abbreviation for the month ذو الحجة‎ *ẕû 'l-ḥijja-t*, as اذ‎ is an abbreviation for ذو القعدة‎ *ẕû 'l-qa'da-t*.

ذا‎ *ẕâ*, this, this one; ايها ذا‎ *ayyahâ ẕâ*, sîrrah!

(ذأب‎) *ẕa'ab*, INF. *ẕa'b*, gather, assemble (a.); resound loudly, make a thundering noise; cry out; urge on; drive away, repel, frighten; blame, make little of, despise; adorn with curls; — ذئب‎ *ẕa'ib*, A, INF. *ẕa'ab*, also ذوب‎ *ẕa'ub*, INF. *ẕa'âba-t*, be like a wolf; be impious; also pass. *ẕu'ib*, fear the wolf; pass. suffer damage by a wolf; — V. INF. *taẕa''ub*, resemble a wolf; — VI. INF. *taẕâ'ub*, imitate a wolf; — X. INF. *istiẕâb*, look like a wolf.

ذأب‎ *ẕâbb*, unable to stand quiet.

ذابر‎ *ẕâbir*, studious; learned.

ذابل‎ *ẕâbil*, pl. *ẕubul*, *ẕubbal*, *ẕawâbil*, flexible; spear; withered.

ذات‎ *ẕât*, f. of ذو‎ *ẕû*, pl. *ẕawât*, *ûlât*, mistress, possessor (f.); endowed with, containing; essence, substance; person, individual; material object (اسم‎ *ism aẕ-ẕât*, noun); identity, self; spontaneousness; ذ البين‎ *ẕât al-bain*, concord; يوم ذات‎ *ẕât-a yaum-in*, one day, once; ذ ليلة‎ *ẕât-a lailat-in*, on a certain night.

(ذأت‎) *ẕa'at*, INF. *ẕa't*, throttle savagely.

ذاتى‎ *ẕâtiyy*, ة‎, essential, natural, material; personal; particular, selfish; zeal.

(ذأج‎) *ẕa'aj*, INF. *ẕa'j*, drink or lap greedily, and, by opposition, drink slowly, sip; tear; kill; be red; — ذئج‎ *ẕa'ij*, A, INF. *ẕa'aj*, drink or lap greedily,

drink slowly, sip ; — VII. INF. *inẓi'âj*, be torn.

ذاج *ẓâjj*, who is just returning from a journey.

ذادة *ẓâda-t*, pl. of ذائد *ẓâ'id*.

(ذاذا) *ẓa'ẓa'*, INF. *ẓa'ẓâ'*, *ẓa'ẓâ'a-t*, II. INF. *taẓa'ẓu'*, totter in walking.

(ذار) *ẓa'ar*, smear the teat of a camel with ordure to wean the young one ; — ذئر *ẓa'ir*, A, INF. *ẓa'ar*, fear and flee from ; despise ; detest, abhor ; be angry ; make bold, revolt against ; be refractory ; be accustomed to, persist in ;—III. INF. *muẓâ'ara-t*, be refractory ; — IV. INF. *iẓ'âr*, provoke to anger ; force to take refuge with (الى *ila*).

ذارع *ẓâri'*, pl. *ẓawâri'*, small wine-bag.

(ذاط) *ẓa'aṭ*, INF. *ẓa'ṭ*=(ذات) slaughter, kill ; throttle, worry to death ; fill ; be full.

ذاعر *ẓâ'ir*, frightened ; timid, timorous.

(ذاف) *ẓa'af*, INF. *ẓa'f*, *ẓa'fân*, die suddenly ; — VII. INF. *inẓi'âf*, lose breath ; choke, suffocate (n.).

ذاف *ẓa'f*, sudden death.

ذاقنة *ẓâqina-t*, pl. *ẓawâqin*, Adam's apple, larynx.

ذاك *ẓâk-a*, that, that one.

ذاكرة *ẓâkira-t*, memory.

ذاكى *ẓâkî*, ة, smelling strongly ; musk.

ذال *ẓâl*, name of the letter ذ *ẓ*.

(ذال) *ẓa'al*, INF. *ẓa'al*, *ẓa'alân*, walk with a light step and proudly.

ذالان *ẓa'lân*, *ẓu'lân*, wolf ; jackal ; pl. *ẓa'âlîl*, their pace ; INF. of the previous.

ذالك *ẓâlik-a*, that one, yonder.

(ذام) *ẓa'am*, INF. *ẓa'm*, make little of, despise, blame ; drive away ; — IV. INF. *iẓ'âm*, frighten.

ذام *ẓa'm*, *ẓâm*, anything blameworthy ; fault ; blame, rebuke.

ذان *ẓân*, id. ;—*ẓân-i*, these two; du. of ذا *ẓâ*.

ذانب *ẓânib*, follower, partisan.

ذانك *ẓânik-a*, *ẓânnik-a*, those two, du. of ذاك *ẓâk-a*.

ذاهبة *ẓâhiba-t*, pl. *ẓawâhib*, camels on a journey.

ذاو *ẓa'w*, INF. of ذاى ; — *ẓâw-in*, see ذاوى *ẓâwî* ; — ة *ẓa'wa-t*, thin, lean (cattle).

ذاوى *ẓâwî* (ذاو *ẓâw-in*), withered, arid.

(ذاى) *ẓa'a*, A, U, INF. *ẓa'w*, drive camels ; marry and lie with ; — A, INF. *ẓa'w*, wither.

ذائب *ẓâ'ib*, melting, &c., ag. of (ذوب) ; ذ المال *ẓâ'ib al-mâl*, live-stock (slaves, cattle, &c.).

ذائد *ẓâ'id*, pl. *ẓuwwad*, *ẓuwwâd*, *ẓâda-t*, who repels, defends his right.

ذائق *ẓâ'iq*, tasting ; who is made to feel (pain, &c.) ; — ة *ẓâ'iqa-t*, (sense or organ of) taste.

ذائك *ẓâ'ik-a*=ذالك *ẓâlik-a*, that, that one.

ذائل *ẓâ'il*, long-tailed.

(ذب) *ẓabb*, U, INF. *ẓabb*, keep off, repel, forbid, turn from by rebuke ; not be able to keep quiet, go hither and thither ; — INF. *ẓabb*, *ẓabab*, *ẓubûb*, be dried up, parched ; be emaciated ; lose colour ; — I, INF. *ẓabb*, wither ; — II. INF. *taẓbîb*, repel with violence, prevent ; dry up (a.), parch.

ذب *ẓabb*, wild bullock ; pl. of the following.

ذباب *ẓubâb*, pl. *aẓibba-t*, *ẓibbân*, *ẓubb*, fly, gnat, midge ; bee ; (ذبان الهند *ẓibbân al-hind*, Spanish flies) ; the image in the eye ; edge of a sword ; measles, purples ; — *dabbâb*, who wards off, defends his harem ; — ة *ẓubâba-t*, a fly, a bee, noun of unity of *ẓubâb* ; — *ẓabbâba-t*, hanging down, flaccid, flabby ; — ى *ẓubâbiyy*, swelling of the cornea of the eye.

ذباح *ẓibâḥ*, sore throat; — also *ẓubâḥ*, angina, croup.
ذبال *ẓubâl*, tumour in the hypochondres; — *ẓubâla-t*, *ẓubbâla-t*, pl. *ẓubâl*, wick.
ذبان *ẓibbân*, pl. of ذباب *ẓubâb*; — ة *ẓubâna-t*, *ẓubbâna-t*, a fly.
(ذبح) *ẓabaḥ*, INF. *ẓabḥ*, *ẓabâḥ*, split, tear, sever; cut the throat, slaughter, kill; sacrifice; consecrate, purify; tap a cask; — II. INF. *taẓbîḥ*, bend the head too low in praying; — VI. INF. *taẓâbuḥ*, kill one another; — VII. INF. *inẓibâḥ*, be slaughtered, sacrificed; be hoarse; — VIII. INF. *iẓẓibâḥ*, take an animal for a sacrifice.
ذبح *ẓabḥ*, slaughtering, sacrificing (s.); victim, sacrifice; — *ẓibḥ*, victim, sacrifice; — *ẓubaḥ*, a kind of mushroom; — ة *ẓibḥa-t*, *ẓibaḥa-t*, *ẓubaḥa-t*, hoarseness; soreness of the throat; suffocation by blood.
(ذبذب) *ẓabẓab*, INF. ة, swing to and fro (n.); move (a.); defend; hurt, torment; — II. INF *taẓabẓub*, swing to and fro, vibrate, oscillate; move (n.), tremble; waver between two things, hesitate.
ذبذب *ẓabẓab*, penis; — ة *ẓabẓaba-t*, pl. *ẓabâẓib*, anything suspended and vibrating; tongue; penis; testicle; fringes, tassels.
(ذبر) *ẓabar*, U, I, INF. *ẓabr*, write, copy; mark a text with the vowel-points; read secretly to one's self; study; know, comprehend; — I, INF. *ẓibâra-t*, look closely at; — *ẓabir*, A, INF. *ẓabar*, be angry.
ذبر *ẓabr*, pl. *ẓibâr*, book, manuscript; leaf of paper; knowledge; language; — *ẓabir*, easy to read.
(ذبل) *ẓabal*, U, INF. *ẓabl*, *ẓubûl*, be withered, flaccid; be thin and weak; — *ẓabul*, be withered; — II. INF. *taẓbîl*, wither (a.), dry up; weaken; emaciate (a.); — V. INF. *taẓabbul*, balance in walking.
ذبل *ẓabl*, shell or back of a tortoise; — *ẓubul*, pl. of ذابل *ẓâbil*; — ة *ẓubla-t*, dryness of the lips.
ذبلا *ẓablâ'*, having dry lips (f.).
ذبلان *ẓablân*, withered, flaccid; thin, lean; weak.
ذبنة *ẓubna-t*, dryness of the lips.
(ذبو) *ẓabâ*, U, be flaccid and emaciated.
ذبيح *ẓabîḥ*, ة, slaughtered, sacrificed; destined to be slaughtered; — ة *ẓabîḥa-t*, pl. *ẓabâ'iḥ*, victim, sacrifice; suffocation by blood.
(ذج) *ẓajj*, INF. *ẓajj*, drink; be just returning from a journey.
(ذجل) *ẓajal*, U, INF. *ẓajl*, be unjust towards (acc.).
(ذح) *ẓaḥḥ*, beat with the palm of the hand; grind, pound, reduce to powder; cut wood; lie with.
(ذحج) *ẓaḥaj*, peel, shell; push from the place, carry off; — IV. INF. *iẓḥâj*, remain, abide.
(ذحذح) *ẓaḥẓaḥ*, INF. ة, walk fast with short steps; carry off.
(ذحل) *ẓaḥl*, pl. *aẓḥâl*, *ẓuḥûl*, revenge, vindictiveness; hatred; spite.
(ذحلط) *ẓaḥlaṭ*, talk confusedly.
(ذحم) *ẓaḥam*=(ذأم).
(ذحمل) *ẓaḥmal*, INF. ة, roll, revolve (a.).
(ذحو) *ẓaḥâ*, U, A, INF. *ẓaḥw*, urge on violently; lie with.
(ذحى) *ẓaḥa*, I, INF. *ẓaḥy*, beat wool; fall upon.
ذحذاخ *ẓaḥẓâḥ*, who examines everything; cautious.
(ذخر) *ẓaḥar*, INF. *ẓuḥr*, *ẓaḥr*, put by for future use; put into the treasury; save, make savings; spare; — II. INF. *taẓḥîr*, heap up riches; (m.) transport stores, ammunition, &c.; provision an army; prime (a gun); — IV. INF. *iẓḥâr*, VIII. INF. *iẓẓiḥâr*=I.

ذعر ẓuḥr, pl. aẓḥâr, savings, provisions.

ذعير ẓaḥîr, adopted son ;—ة ẓaḥîra-t, pl. ẓaḥâ'ir, savings ; treasure ; stores, provisions ; ammunition, provender ; priming-powder ; fusee ; (m.) adoption ; relic of a saint.

ذر ẓar, IMP. of وذر , leave it alone ; — ẓar', something, anything ; INF. of (وذر) ; — ẓarr, ة , pl. ẓarrât, very small ant, atom, mote ; — ة ẓura-t, a coarse kind of millet ; maize.

(ذر) ẓarr, U, INF. ẓarr, pound, grind ; scatter, sprinkle, strew ; raise the dead ; — U, A, turn grey on the fore-part of the head ; — INF. ẓurûr, germinate ; rise ; peep forth ; show the first germs ; INF. ẓarr, ẓurûr, wrinkle (n.), shrink.

(ذرأ) ẓara', INF. ẓar', create ; increase, multiply ; disperse ; sow over ; lose the teeth ; —also ذرى ẓari', A, INF. ẓara', turn grey.

ذرأ ẓurâ, maize ; millet ; — ẓar-an =ذرى ẓaran.

ذراب ẓurâb, poison ; — ة ẓarâba-t, incurability ; a disease of the stomach.

ذراح ẓarâḥ, watery milk ; — ẓurâḥ, ẓurrâḥ, pl. ẓarârîḥ, Spanish fly.

ذرارة ẓarâra-t, flying motes.

ذرارى ẓarâri, ẓarariyy, pl. of ذرية ẓurriyya-t.

ذراريح ẓarârîḥ, pl. of ذراح ẓurâḥ, ẓurrâḥ, and ذرح ẓurrah.

ذراع ẓirâ', pl. aẓru', ẓur'ân, forearm ; fore-foot ; arm ; ell, yard, cubit ; power.

ذراوة ẓurâwa-t, chaff before the wind.

(ذرب) ẓarab, INF. ẓarb, sharpen ; — ẓarib, A, INF. ẓarab, ẓarâba-t, be sharp ; speak sharply, speak ill ; be incurable ; — A, INF. ẓarab, ẓarâba-t, ẓurûba-t, be disordered (stomach, &c.) ;—II. INF. taẓrib, sharpen.

ذرب ẓarab, pl. aẓrâb, obscene talk ; —ẓarib, pl. ẓurb, f. ة , pl. ẓaribât, sharp, having a sharp tongue ; — ة ẓirba-t, treason, treachery ; pl. ẓirab, swelling (s.) ; swollen gland.

(ذرح) ẓaraḥ, INF. ẓarḥ, render poisonous by Spanish flies ; scatter to the winds.

ذرح ẓurrah, ذرحرح ẓurahrah, ẓuruhruh, ẓurrahrah, ẓurruhruh, ذرحوح ẓurḥûḥ, pl. ẓarârîḥ, Spanish fly.

(ذرذر) ẓarẓar, INF. ة , scatter, strew.

(ذرز) ẓariz, A, INF. ẓaraz, live in plenty and enjoyment.

(ذرع) ẓara', INF. ẓar', measure by one's arm or the cubit ; intercede with one (عند 'ind) for another (ل li) ; throttle with one's arms from behind ; — ẓari', A, INF. ẓara', drink from a skin bag ; intercede ; be tired ; desire ; — IV. INF. iẓrâ', take by the arm ; — V. INF. taẓarru', measure by the ell ; go beyond bounds in one's speech ; — VII. INF. inẓirâ', get far in advance ; — VIII. INF. iẓẓirâ', push forth the arm from beneath a cloak, &c. ; — X. INF. istiẓrâ', prepare for one's self a hiding-place ; seek cover or shelter.

ذرع ẓar', range of the stretched-out arm ; power, influence ; bestowal ; — ẓara', desire, hope ; hiding-place of a hunter ; pl. ẓir'ân, calf of the wild cow.

ذرعان ẓir'ân, pl. of the previous ; — ẓu'rân, pl. of ذراع ẓirâ'.

(ذرف) ẓaraf, I, INF. ẓarf, ẓurûf, ẓarîf, ẓarafân, taẓrâf, flow ; shed tears ; INF. ẓarafân, walk like an ill or weak person ; — II. INF. taẓrîf, taẓrifa-t, taẓrâf, shed tears ; exceed one hundred.

(ذرق) ẓaraq, U, I, INF. ẓarq, drop excrement ; spring, gush forth ; fall ; — IV. INF. iẓrâq, drop excrement.

ذرق ẓarq, excrement of a bird.

(ذرم) *ẓaram*, U, INF. *ẓarm*, give birth before time.

(ذرمل) *ẓarmal*, INF. ة, drop excrement; place before the guest bread hurriedly baked in the ashes.

ذرنوح *ẓurnûḥ*, Spanish fly.

(ذرو) *ẓarâ*, U, I, INF. *ẓarw*, also ذرى *ẓara*, INF. *ẓary*, carry off; throw the corn against the wind to clean it, winnow; sow; give over, leave; be carried off, disappear, go away; run fast; break (n.); lose the teeth;—U, INF. *ẓarw*, pass quickly by; II. INF. *taẓriya-t*, carry off; winnow; search the ground for money;—IV. INF. *iẓrâ'*, carry off; throw off; pull down from; winnow; scatter, shed;—V. INF. *taẓarrî*, be winnowed; mount a summit or the hump of a camel;—V. and VI. INF. *taẓârî*, betake one's self under the shadow of a tree or under anybody's protection;—VII. INF. *inẓirâ'*, be carried off, scattered, winnowed;—X. INF. *istiẓrâ'*=VI.; seek shelter;—ة *ẓurwa-t*, *ẓirwa-t*, pl. ذرى *ẓuran*, *ẓura*, summit, peak; hump of a camel; apogee; great wealth.

ذروبة *ẓurûba-t*, stomach-ache.

ذروح *ẓarûḥ*, *ẓurûḥ*, *ẓurrûḥ*, Spanish fly.

ذرور *ẓarûr*, pl. *aẓirra-t*, what is powdered and scattered; collyrium, eye paint;—*.

(ذرى) see (ذرو).

ذرى *ẓaran*, pl. *aẓrâ'*, projecting roof to shelter from the weather; shelter, protection;—*ẓuran*, pl. of ذروة *ẓurwa-t*;—*ẓarî'*, sown over,—*ẓirriyy*, well-tempered (sword);—ة *ẓurriyya-t*, *ẓarriyya-t*, *ẓirriyya-t*, pl. *-ât* and ذرارى *ẓarârî*, *ẓarâriyy*, children, grandchildren, descendants, progeny.

(ذش) *ẓaśś*, travel fast.

ذعار *ẓa''âr*, inspiring with terror.

ذعاع *ẓa'â'*, ة, troop, herd.

ذعاف *ẓu'âf*, pl. *ẓu'uf*, deadly poison.

(ذعب), V. INF. *taẓa''ub*, frighten, terrify; flow steadily.

ذعبان *ẓu'bân*, young wolf.

(ذعت) *ẓa'at*, INF. *ẓa't*, worry savagely; throttle; roll in the dust; urge on or push back violently.

(ذعج) *ẓa'aj*, INF. *ẓa'j*, push or urge on violently; lie with.

(ذعذع) *ẓa'ẓa'*, INF. ة, scatter, waste, dissipate; betray secrets, make public; shake violently.

(ذعر) *ẓa'ar*, INF. *ẓa'r*, frighten, terrify;—V. INF. *taśa''ur*, pass.

ذعر *ẓa'ar*, *ẓu'r*, fright, terror; consternation;—*ẓu'ar*, anything frightful;—ذعرة *ẓu'ra-t*, and—

ذعرا *ẓa'râ'*, fundament.

(ذعط) *ẓa'aṭ*, INF. *ẓa'ṭ*, slaughter.

(ذعف) *ẓa'af*, INF. *ẓa'f*, poison;—also *ẓa'if*, A, INF. *ẓa'af*, *ẓa'afân*, die;—VII. INF. *inẓi'ab*, get out of breath in running.

ذعف *ẓa'f*, deadly poison;—also *ẓa'af* and ذعفان *ẓa'afân*, death;—*ẓu'uf*, pl. of ذعاف *ẓu'âf*.

(ذعق) *ẓa'aq*, INF. *ẓa'q*, cry out at and frighten.

(ذعل) *ẓa'al*, U, INF. *ẓa'l*, confess after having denied first.

(ذعلب), II. INF. *taẓa'lub*, sneak away, abscond;—IV. INF. *iẓli'bâb*, go away hurriedly; lay one's self on the side;—ة *ẓi'liba-t*, swift she-camel; ostrich; pl. *ẓa'âlîb*, strips of cloth; rags, tatters; hem of a garment.

(ذعلف) *ẓa'laf*, INF. ة, lead astray and destroy.

(ذعلوق) *ẓu'lûq*, a kind of leek; hot-headed youth.

(ذعن) *ẓa'in*, A, INF. *ẓa'an*, obey, submit;—IV. INF. *iẓ'ân*, id.

ذعور *ẓa'ûr*, frightened, timid, shy; anxious for one's good fame (woman).

(ذغ) *ẓagg*, U, INF. *ẓagg*, lie with.

ذغمور ẕugmûr, full of hatred.

(ذف) ẕaff, I, INF. ẕaff, spread rapidly and destructively; — U, INF. ẕaff, ẕafaf, ẕifâf, despatch a wounded man; hasten; be easily done; — II. INF. tazfîf, despatch a wounded man; facilitate.

(ذفاف) ẕifâf, ẕufâf, pl. ẕufuf, deadly poison; small quantity of water; INF. of the previous; — ẕufâf, quick, swift.

(ذفذف) ẕafẕaf, INF. ة, despatch a wounded man; step along proudly.

(ذفر) ẕafir, A, INF. ẕafar, also IV. INF. izfâr, smell strongly or badly.

ذفر ẕafar, ة ẕafara-t, strong smell, stench; — ẕafir, ة, smelling strongly or badly.

(ذفط) ẕafaṭ, I, INF. ẕafṭ = (ذقط).

(ذفطس) ẕafṭas, INF. ة = (ذفطس), lose one's cattle or fortune.

ذفف ẕafaf, INF. of (ذف); — ẕufuf, pl. of ذفاف ẕifâf.

ذفل ẕifl, thin pitch; any thin dripping fluid.

ذفيف ẕafîf, ة, quick; deadly.

ذقاحة ẕuqâha-t, accusing falsely.

(ذقذاق) ẕaqzâq, speaking fluently.

(ذقح), V. tazaqqah, INF. tazaqquh, accuse falsely.

(ذقط) ẕaqaṭ, I, INF. ẕaqṭ, ẕuqṭ, cover (male animal); drop excrement.

(ذقن) ẕaqan, ẕiqan, pl. aẕqân, ẕuqûn, chin; beard on the chin, beard; — ẕaqan, U, INF. ẕaqn, strike on the chin; lean the chin against; — ẕuqn, pl. and—

ذقنا ẕaqnâ, f. of اذقن aẕqan, have a long or hanging chin.

ذكا ẕakâ', quick understanding; intelligence, wit, sagacity; live coal; — ẕukâ', sun; ابن ذكا ibn ẕukâ, dawn of morning; — ة ẕakât, animal to be slaughtered or sacrificed; INF. of (ذكى).

ذكارة ẕukkâra-t, male palm-tree.

ذكاوة ẕakâwa-t, sagacity; wit.

(ذكذك) ẕakẕâk, INF. ة, tickle; — ة ẕakẕaka-t, vivacity.

(ذكر) ẕakar, U, INF. ẕakr, hit on the penis; call back to memory, remember; mention, praise; impute; relate; allege by quoting an authority; — U, INF. ẕikr, ẕukr, taẕkur, keep in remembrance, recall to memory; — II. INF. taẕkîr, make of the masculine gender; temper the edge of a cutting tool; recall to one's memory, remind of (2 acc.); insinuate; admonish; — III. INF. muẕâkara-t, remember; confer with; mention or allege in one's presence; — IV. INF. iẕkâr, drop male young ones; remind of (2 acc.); — V. INF. taẕakkur, remember, think of, consider; listen to admonitions; — VI. INF. taẕâkur, recall mutually to memory; confer with one another;—VIII. INF. iẕẕikâr, X. INF. istiẕkâr, remember.

ذكر ẕikr, remembrance; memory; fame, renown, praise, glory; high birth or rank; mention, report, relation, narrative; anything memorable; invocation of the name of God, piety; also ة ẕikra-t, eulogy; — ẕukr, remembrance; edge (of a sword, &c.); — ẕakar, pl. ẕukûr, ẕukûra-t, ẕukrân, ẕukâr, ẕikâra-t, ẕikara-t, male (adj. s.); tempered iron, steel; pl. ẕukûr, maẕâkir, maẕâkîr, ẕukrân, penis; — ẕakir, who remembers, recites, quotes; — ة ẕikra-t, mention; eulogy; renown, celebrity;—ẕukra-t, id.; steel edge of an axe; virility;— ذكرى ẕikra, remembrance; admonition; repentance.

(ذكو) ẕakâ, U, INF. ẕakw, ẕukuww, ẕakan, ẕakâ, blaze; — ذكى ẕaka, be quick and sharp (intellect); smell strongly; — INF. ذكا ẕakan, ẕakât, slaughter, sacrifice; — ẕaki, A, INF. ذكا ẕakan, ẕakâ, also ذكو ẕaku', INF.

ذكاوة *ẓakâwa-t*, be quick and sharp; push (tooth); blaze; — II. INF. *taẓkiya-t*, cause to blaze, blow into a flame; slaughter; be fat, corpulent; grow old, become or be an old man; — IV. INF. *iẓkâ'*, make to blaze, kindle; — X. INF. *istiẓkâ'*, blaze, flare.

ذكورة *ẓukûra-t*, purity from any admixture; pl. of ذكر *ẓakar*.

ذكورية *ẓukûriyya-t*, manhood, virility.

(ذكى), see (ذكو); — *ẓakiyy*, ة, pl. *aẓkiyâ*, of a vivid mind, sharp-witted, intelligent; sharp, strong (smell), smelling strongly; blazing; slaughtered.

ذكير *ẓakîr*, steel; — also *ẓikkîr*, having a good memory; — *ẓikkîr*, who mentions frequently.

(ذل) *ẓall*, I, INF. *ẓull*, *ẓilla-t*, *ẓalâla-t*, *ẓulâla-t*, *maẓalla-t*, be low, vile, contemptible, of obscure descent, poor, despised; humble one's self, submit; resign one's self; be patient, meek; — II. INF. *taẓlîl*, IV. INF. *iẓlâl*, render contemptible, humble, humiliate; despise, deem contemptible; — V. INF. *taẓallul*, submit, humble one's self, yield; — X. INF. *istiẓlâl*, make light of, despise; tame, subdue.

ذل *ẓill*, low rank or condition; humiliation; submission, obedience; meekness, obsequiousness, yielding disposition; pl. *aẓlâl*, low, mean; trodden; — *ẓull*, humiliation, infamy, disgrace; — ة *ẓilla-t*, contemptibleness; submissiveness; slight, offence.

ذلاح *ẓullâḥ*, watered milk.

ذلاقة *ẓalâqa-t*, fluency of speech.

ذلال *ẓilâl*, pl. of ذليل *ẓalîl*; — ة *ẓalâla-t*, *ẓulâla-t*, contemptibleness; INF. of (ذل).

ذلان *ẓullân*, mean, vile, contemptible.

(ذلج) *ẓalaj*, U, INF. *ẓalj*, lap, sip.

(ذلذل) *ẓalẓal*, *ẓilẓil*, *ẓulaẓil*, ة *ẓalẓala-t*, &c., pl. *ẓalâẓil*, lower part of a shirt, skirt; — II. *taẓalẓal*, INF. *taẓalẓul*, hang flabbily and swing to and fro.

(ذلعب), III. *iẓla'abb*, INF. *iẓli'bâb*, scamper away; lie on one's side.

(ذلغ) *ẓalag*, A, INF. *ẓalg*, fatten the food; eat; lie with; — *ẓalig*, A, INF. *ẓalag*, be turned up; — VII. INF. *inẓilâg*, have soft dates; be sore.

(ذلف) *ẓalif*, A, INF. *ẓalaf*, be small with a flat tip (nose); have such a nose.

(ذلق) *ẓalaq*, U, INF. *ẓalq*, sharpen; be fluent and eloquent; weaken; drop excrement; — *ẓaliq*, A, INF. *ẓalaq*, be sharp and pointed; be fluent and eloquent; give light, shine; be nearly fainting or dying; waver to and fro; — *ẓaluq*, INF. *ẓalâqa-t*, be fluent and eloquent; — II. INF. *taẓlîq*, sharpen, point; — IV. INF. *iẓlâq*, id.; move to and fro (a.), agitate; shine; weaken; — VII. INF. *inẓilâq*, terminate in a point, taper.

ذلق *ẓalq*, *ẓaliq*, ة, sharp and pointed, sharp; ready of speech, fluent; — *ẓalq*, tip of the tongue; also *ẓalaq*, fluency; — *ẓulq*, pl. of اذلق *aẓlaq*, sharp; fluent.

ذلك *ẓâlik*, f. *tilk*, that, that one, yonder.

(ذلم) *ẓalam*, shallow mouth of a river.

ذلول *ẓalûl*, pl. *ẓulul*, *aẓilla-t*, also ى *ẓalûla*, *ẓalûliyy*, pl. *-ûn*, obedient, obsequious, meek, patient.

(ذلى) *ẓala*, INF. *ẓaly*, cull; (also V., XII.) be humble, submissive; — IV. INF. *iẓlâ'*, pluck; — V. INF. *taẓallî*, see I.; — XII. *iẓlaula*, INF. *iẓlîlâ'*, see I.; sneak away; be flabby.

(ذليق) *ẓalîq*, ة, sharp; fluent, ready of speech.

ذليل *ẓalîl*, pl. *ẓilâl*, *aẓillâ'*, *aẓilla-t*, humbled, humiliated; contemptible; submissive; obsequious; meek.

(ذم) *ẓamm*, U, INF. *ẓamm*, *maẓamma-t*, blame, disapprove; flow with mucus; I, U, be ugly of face;—II. INF. *taẓmîm*, blame, criticise severely; — IV. INF. *iẓmâm*, find fault with; disdain; do anything blameworthy; take under one's protection, protect; — V. INF. *taẓammum*, keep clear of blame, behave irreproachably; — VI. INF. *taẓâmm*, blame one another; — VII. INF. *inẓimâm*, get blamed; — X. INF. *istiẓmâm*, deserve or draw upon one's self blame.

ذم *ẓamm*, blame, rebuke; pl. *ẓumûm*, anything blameworthy, fault; — also *ẓimm*, blamed, blameworthy;—*ẓimm*, wedding, feast; protection; allies; — ة *ẓamma-t*, pl. *ẓimâm*, well with little water; — *ẓimma-t*, pl. *ẓimam*, *ẓimamât*, protection, shelter; clientship, alliance; responsibility; guarantee, security, bail (براءة ذمة *barât-u ẓimmat-in*, safe-conduct, passport); debt, debit; allies; client; tributaries; conscience, consienciousness; wedding, feast; (m.) moral theology.

(ذما) *ẓama'*, INF. *ẓam'*, be troublesome, molest.

ذما *ẓamâ'*, last convulsions; motion, emotion; INF. of (ذمى).

ذمار *ẓimâr*, right, law; one's people, good fame, anything to be defended; — ة *ẓamâra-t*, standing bravely by one's own (s.).

ذمام *ẓimâm*, pl. *aẓimma-t*, duty of protection, clientship; protection; honour; duty; right; pl. of ذمة *ẓamma-t*;—*ẓammâm*, fault-finder; calumniator, slanderer; — ة *ẓamâma-t*, *ẓimâma-t*, protection, securing (s.); — *ẓumâma-t*, rest, remainder.

(ذمت) *ẓamat*, I, INF. *ẓamt*, look altered, grieved; emaciate (n.).

(ذمحل) *ẓamḥal*, INF. ة, roll, revolve (a.).

(ذمذم) *ẓamẓam*, INF. ة, give only a little.

(ذمر) *ẓamar*, U, INF. *ẓamr*, instigate by blame, rebuke or threats, encourage, incite; threaten, frighten; roar; — II. INF. *taẓmîr*, define, determinate; — V. INF. *taẓammur*, blame, reproach one's self; threaten, inveigh against; — VI. INF. *taẓâmur*, incite each other to combat.

ذمر *ẓimr*, pl. *aẓmâr*, brave; prudent; a sharp fellow; calamity.

(ذمط) *ẓamaṭ*, I, INF. *ẓamṭ*, slaughter.

ذمقر, III. اذمقر *iẓmaqarr*, INF. *iẓmiqrâr*, be cheesy and capable of being cut (milk).

(ذمل) *ẓamal*, U, I, INF. *ẓaml*, *ẓumûl*, *ẓamîl*, *ẓamalân*, walk slowly, and, by opposition, walk fast; — II. INF. *taẓmîl*, cause to walk slowly.

(ذملق) *ẓamlaq*, INF. ة, flatter, cajole.

ذملق *ẓamallaq*, flattering; eloquent; quick; sharp.

ذمم *ẓimam*, ذممات *ẓimamât*, pl. of ذمة *ẓimma-t*.

(ذمه) *ẓamih*, A, INF. *ẓamah*, be violent, intense.

ذموم *ẓamûm*, blamer, fault-finder; — *.

(ذمى) *ẓamâ*, I, INF. *ẓamy*, *ẓamâ'*, quiver or sprawl in the last convulsions; — INF. *ẓamy*, molest; I, INF. *ẓamayân*, walk fast, hasten; — *ẓamî*, A, INF. *ẓamâ'*, move to and fro; quiver or sprawl in the last convulsions; — give a deadly blow or stroke, hit fatally; — X. INF. *istiẓmâ'*, gather another's things and take them away.

ذمی *ẓimmiyy*, client, protégé, tributary.
ذمیر *ẓamîr*, brave in defence; handsome.
ذمیل *ẓamîl*, slow walk.
(ذمیم) *ẓamîm*, ة, blameworthy; blamed; client; mucus; — ة *ẓamîma-t*, palsy.
(ذن) *ẓann*, I, INF. *ẓanan*, *ẓanîn*, flow from the nose; walk with the utmost feebleness; — *ẓanin*, A, INF. *ẓanan*, suffer from thin mucus flowing from the nose.
ذناب *ẓinâb*, ة *ẓinâba-t*, pl. *ẓanâ'ib*, watercourse; mouth of a river; pl. of *ẓunûb*;—*ẓunâba-t*, *ẓinâba-t*, tail; end; appendix; — *ẓunâba-t*, top of a shoe; follower.
ذنابی *ẓunâba*, tail of a bird.
ذنان *ẓunân*, thin mucus.
ذنائب *ẓanâ'ib*, pl. of ذناب *ẓinâb* and ذنوب *ẓanûb*.
(ذنب) *ẓanab*, I; U, follow step by step; — II. INF. *taẓnîb*, put a tail to; provide with an appendix, supplement, &c.; consider guilty; — IV. INF. *iẓnâb*, commit a fault or crime; — V. INF. *taẓannub*, let a lappet of the turban hang down; follow step by step; consider guilty.
ذنب *ẓamb*, pl. *ẓunûb*, pl. pl. *ẓunûbât*, fault, crime, guilt; — *ẓanab*, pl. *aẓnâb*, tail, end (نجم ابو ذنب *najm abû ẓanab*, comet); lappet; length of the hair; long; end of a valley, mouth of a river; — ة *ẓanaba-t*, tail; end; river-mouth; — ات *ẓanabât*, populace, rabble.
ذنوب *ẓanûb*, pl. *aẓniba-t*, *ẓanâ'ib*, *ẓinâb*, long-tailed; share, lot, destiny; du. *ẓanûbân*, the loins; — *ẓunûb*, ذنوبات, pl. and pl. pl. of ذنب *ẓamb*.
ذنین *ẓanîn*, mucus; INF. of (ذن).
ذه *ẓih*, this, this one, f. of ذا *ẓâ*; — *ẓahh*, sharpness of intellect, sagacity.
ذهاب *ẓahâb*, going away, disappearing (s.); — *.

(ذهب) *ẓahab*, A, INF. *ẓahâb*, *ẓuhûb*, *maẓhab* go away, go, pass, disappear; go to; go with (ب *bi*), carry off, rob; think, deem; follow up; — *ẓahib*, A, INF. *ẓahab*, come suddenly upon gold and be dazzled by it; — II. INF. *taẓhîb*, gild, cover with gold; — IV. INF. *iẓhâb*, carry off, abduct; rob; cause to disappear; destroy; gild; — V. INF. *taẓahhub*, be gilt.
ذهب *ẓahab*, pl. *ẓuhûb*, *aẓhâb*, *ẓuhbân*, gold; pl. *ẓihâb*, *aẓhâb*, yolk; — ة *ẓahaba-t*, lump of gold; gold coin; — *ẓihba-t*, pl. *ẓihâb*, shower; — ی *ẓahabiyy*, ة, golden; — يّة *ẓahabiyya-t*, gold piece; Nile boat.
(ذهر) *ẓahir*, A, INF. *ẓahar*, have black teeth.
(ذهل) *ẓahal*, INF. *ẓahl*, *ẓuhûl*, forget, neglect; — IV. INF. *iẓhâl*, occupy so as to make forget other things, cause to forget; astonish, bewilder; — VII. INF. *inẓihâl*, be astonished, bewildered.
ذهلول *ẓuhlûl*, generous horse.
(ذهن) *ẓahan*, surpass in intellect or sagacity; INF. *ẓihn*, cause one to forget a thing; — III. INF. *muẓâhana-t*, vie in sagacity; —IV. INF. *iẓhân*, cause to forget; — X. INF. *istiẓhân*, id.
ذهن *ẓihn*, pl. *aẓhân*, intellect, sagacity, genius, talent; memory; — *ẓahan*, id.; — *ẓihn*, fat.
(ذهو) *ẓahâ*, U, INF. *ẓahw*, be proud.
ذهوب *ẓuhûb*, departure; disappearance; INF. of ذهب; — *.
ذهیب *ẓahîb*, gilt.
ذهین *ẓahîn*, ingenious, witty, talented.
ذو *ẓû* (gen. ذی *ẓî*, acc. ذا *ẓâ*), du. *ẓawân*, pl. *ẓawûn*, master, possessor, endowed with, containing; — who, which = الذی *allaẓî*.
ذواب *ẓawwâb*, easily melting.

ذوابل *ẓawâbil*, pl. of ذابل *ẓâbil*, flexible.

ذوابة *ẓu'âba-t, ẓuwâba-t*, pl. *ẓawâ'ib*, fore-lock ; highest nobility ; dignity.

ذوات *ẓawât*, pl. of ذات *ẓât*, mistress, &c.

ذواد *ẓawwâd*, who defends his right.

ذوارع *ẓawâri'*, wine-bags, pl. of ذارع *ẓâri'*.

ذواف *ẓu'âf*, sudden death; killing speedily.

ذواق *ẓawâq*, taste; what is taken of a thing to taste it; INF. of (ذوق); — *ẓawwâq*, who tastes; grieved, sorrowful.

ذواقن *ẓawâqin*, pl. of ذاقنة *ẓâqina-t*, larynx.

ذوالة *ẓu'âla-t*, pl. *ẓu'lân, ẓi'lân*, wolf, jackal.

ذواة *ẓawât*, fruit-rind.

ذواهب *ẓawâhib*, pl. of ذاهبة *ẓâhiba-t*, journeying camels.

ذوائب *ẓawâ'ib*, pl. of ذوابة *ẓu'âba-t, ẓuwâba-t*.

(ذوب) *ẓâb*, U, INF. *ẓaub, ẓawabân*, dissolve (n.), melt (n.), thaw; grow hotter; be an indispensable duty; eat honey continually; lose one's senses; — II. INF. *taẓwîb*, melt; — IV. INF. *iẓâba-t*, id.; set a-going; put into order; invade; — X. INF. *istiẓâba-t*, ask for honey.

ذوب *ẓaub*, fluid (adj., s.); purest honey; يا ذوب *yâ ẓaub*, with difficulty, hardly, just (m.).

ذوبان *ẓûbân*, hair on the neck (of a camel, horse, &c.); — *ẓu'bân*, pl. of ذئب *ẓi'b*; — ذوبان *ẓawabân*, INF. of (ذوب).

(ذوج) *ẓâj*, U, INF. *ẓauj*, drink.

ذوج *ẓa'uj*, intensely red.

(ذوح) *ẓâḥ*, U, INF. *ẓauḥ*, drive together; walk with a loud or heavy step; — II. INF. *taẓwîḥ*, distribute here and there; dissipate.

(ذود) *ẓâd*, U, INF. *ẓaud, ẓiyâd*, drive; drive back, keep off; — IV. INF. *iẓâda-t*, help another to drive back or to defend his own.

ذود *ẓaud*, f. sing. and pl., pl. also *aẓwâd*, small number of she-camels (2 to 10); — *ẓuwwad*, pl. of ذائد *ẓâ'id*, who repels, defends.

(ذودح) *ẓaudaḥ*, ذودخ *ẓaudaḫ*, impotent.

(ذور) *ẓâr*, U, INF. *ẓaur*, frighten; — A, INF. *ẓaur*, feel aversion, abhor; — IV. INF. *iẓâra-t*, frighten; — ة *ẓûra-t*, earth, dust; pl. ذور *ẓuwar*, crop of a bird.

(ذوط) *ẓâṭ*, U, INF. *ẓauṭ*, throttle.

(ذوع) *ẓâ'*, U, INF. *ẓau'*, require and use up; — IV. INF. *iẓâ'a-t*, exhaust a pond; take away, rob.

(ذوف) *ẓâf*, U, INF. *ẓauf*, walk with short and stumbling steps.

ذوفان *ẓu'fân, ẓûfân*, deadly poison.

(ذوق) *ẓâq*, U, INF. *ẓauq, ẓawâq, maẓâq, maẓâqa-t*, taste; try, probe; suffer, undergo; — II. INF. *taẓwîq*, give to taste, make to suffer; — IV. INF. *iẓâqa-t*, id.; — V. INF. *taẓawwuq*, taste repeatedly.

ذوق *ẓauq*, taste; good taste; sense or organ of taste; enjoyment, pleasure, اهل ذوق *ahl-u ẓauq-in*, voluptuary.

ذولق *ẓaulaq*, top, tip; — ية *ẓaulaqiyya-t*, the lingual letters (ل ن ر).

(ذون), V. *taẓawwun*, be rich; live in affluence.

ذوو *ẓawû* (before cas. constr.), ذوون *ẓuwûn*, pl. of ذو *ẓû*.

ذووب *ẓa'ûb*, fat.

(ذوى) *ẓawa*, I, *ẓawî*, A, INF. *ẓuwiyy*, be withered, dry; — IV. INF. *iẓwâ'*, wither (a.).

ذويل *ẓawîl*, withered, dried up.

ذى *ẓî*, this, this one, f. of ذا *ẓâ*; obl. case of ذو *ẓû*.

(ذيا), II. *ẓayya'*, cook meat quite

soft ; — V. INF. *taẓayyî* ; pass. of the previous.

ذيا *ẓayyâ*, dim. of ذا *ẓâ*, this, this one.

ذئاب *ẓi'âb*, pl. of ذئب *ẓi'b*.

ذياج *ẓiyâj*, boon-companionship ; — *.

ذياك *ẓayyâk-a*, dim. of ذاك *ẓâk-a*, that, that one.

ذيال *ẓayyâl*, long-tailed ; having a large trail, a numerous retinue ; ابو ذ *abû ẓayyâl-in*, ox ;—ة *ẓayyâ-la-t*, needle and thread.

(ذئب), see (ذاب).

ذئب *ẓaib*, vice, fault ; — *ẓi'b*, *ẓîb*, pl. *aẓ'ub*, *ẓi'âb*, *ẓu'bân*, wolf ; wild dog (دا الذئب *dâ'-u 'ẓ-ẓi'b-i*, ravenous hunger) ; hut ; — ة *ẓi'ba-t*, she-wolf ; a throat-disease of the camel.

ذئبان *ẓi'bân*, *ẓîbân*=ذوبان *ẓûbân*.

ذيت و ذيت *ẓait-a wa ẓait-a*, in this manner and in that, one way or the other.

(ذيج) *ẓâj*, I, INF. *ẓaij*, drink ; — III. INF. *ẓiyâj*, keep company in drinking, be one's boon companion.

(ذئج), see (ذاج).

ذيخ *ẓîḥ*, pl. *ẓuyûḥ*, *ẓiyaḥa-t*, *aẓyâḥ*, wolf ; male hairy hyena (f. ة *ẓîḥa-t*) ; fine stallion ; bold, brave ; — II. *ẓayyaḥ*, INF. *taẓyîḥ*, humble, subdue ; — IV. INF. *iẓâ-ḥa-t*, circle or turn around.

(ذير) *ẓâr*, INF. *ẓair*, feel aversion, detest, abhor.

ذئر *ẓa'ir*, bold ; refractory ; raving mad ; — see (ذار) ; — ة *ẓa'ira-t*, anything abominable, abomination.

(ذيع) *ẓâ'*, I, INF. *ẓai'*, *ẓuyû'*, *ẓa-ya'ân*, *ẓai'û'a-t*, become public ; — IV. INF. *iẓâ'a-t*, make public.

ذيعان *ẓaya'ân*, and—

ذيعوعة *ẓai'û'a-t*, publicity, INF. of the previous.

ذئفان *ẓi'fân*, *ẓîfân*, *ẓaifân*, *ẓayafân*, deadly poison.

ذيك *ẓîk-a*, that, that one, f. of ذاك *ẓâk-a*.

(ذيل) *ẓâl*, I, INF. *ẓail*, have a train (garment) ; wear a train ; walk proudly along trailing one's garment ; be low, mean, despised ; be thin, lean ; come down in the world ; — II. INF. *taẓyîl*, provide a garment with a train ; add an appendix ; — IV. INF. *iẓâla-t*, have a train ; make little of, slight, neglect ; — V. INF. *taẓayyul*, step along proudly ;—VI. INF. *taẓâyul*, come down in the world

ذيل *ẓail*, pl. *ẓuyûl*, *aẓyul*, *aẓyâl*, lower part of a thing, touching the ground ; tail ; skirt, hem, train, trail ; fringes ; appendix, supplement, postscript ; lower margin of a book ; shelter, protection ; ذيل ذائل *ẓail ẓâ'il*, lowness ; contempt.

ذئلان *ẓi'lân*, pl. of ذؤالة *ẓu'âla-t*.

(ذيم) *ẓâm*, I, INF. *ẓaim*, *ẓâm*, blame, reproach, rebuke.

ذيم *ẓaim*, *ẓîm*, also ذين *ẓîn*, blame, reproach, rebuke, fault.

ذية ذية *ẓayyat-a ẓayyat-a*=ذيت ذيت *ẓait-a ẓait-a*.

ذيوع *ẓuyû'*, publicity ; INF. of (ذيع).

ر

ر *r*, as a numerical sign=200 ; abbreviation for the moon (as the last letter of قمر *qamar*) and for the month ربيع الاخر *rabî' al-âḥir*.

را *râ'*, name of the letter ر *r* ; palma Christi ; foam of the sea ; a large kind of tick (insect) ; — *ra''â'*, sagacious ; — ة *ra'a-t*, INF. of (رأى).

رأفة *ra'âfa-t*, mercy.
(رأب) *ra'ab*, INF. *ra'b*, mend; reconcile; push forth grass again after being mown; — IV. INF. *ir'âb*, mend; — V. INF. *tara''ub*, move (n.).
راب *ra'b*, pl. رئاب *ri'âb*, herd of 70 camels; great chief; flaw; — *râb*, value, price; — *râb-in*, see رابى *râbî*; — *ra''âb*, tinker; — *râbb*, step-father; ة *râbba-t*, step-mother.
رابح *râbiḥ*, ة, bringing gain; gainer; pl. *ribâḥ*, camel-foal.
رابض *râbiḍ*, crouching; inhabitant; — ة *râbiḍa-t*, angels who were, with Adam, cast on the earth.
رابط *râbiṭ*, ة, who binds, ties up, fastens, ag. of (ربط); union, tie; frontier-soldier; renouncing the world, philosopher; ر الدرب *râbiṭ ad-durb*, highway robber; — ة *râbiṭa-t*, pl. *rawâbiṭ*, bandage; band, tie, chain; catch-word of a page; regularity; system; order; troops in array; conspiracy, plot, intrigue.
رابع *râbi'*, ة, fourth; quartan (ague).
رابغ *râbig*, luxuriant; pleasant.
(رابل) *ra'bal*, INF. ة, walk strongly leaning to the side from pain in the claws or feet.
رابل *ra'âbil*, lions, pl. of رئبل *ri'bal*, *rîbal*; — ة *ra'bala-t*, cunning, slyness.
(رابوق) *râbûq*, snare, net (m.).
رابى *râbî* (راب *râb-in*), ة, ascending, increasing; — ة *râbiya-t*, pl. *rawâbî*, hill.
رات *rât*, pl. *ruwwât*, straw; — *rât-in*, see راتى *râtî*.
راتب *râtib*, pl. *rawâtib*, firm, solid; daily allowance, ration; pay; pension.
راتخ *râtiḥ*, thin.
راتع *râti'*, pl. *ritâ'*, *rutu'*, *rutta'*, *rutû'*, freely pasturing on rich ground, living in affluence (adj.).
راتى *râtî* (رات *rât-in*), scholar; learned doctor.
راتيانج *râtiyânaj*, راتينج *râtînaj*, راتين *râtîn*, resin.
راتينجى *râtinajiyy*, ة, r esinous.
راج *râj-in*, see راجى *râjî*.
راجبة *râjiba-t*, pl. *rawâjib*, uppermost joint of the finger.
راجح *râjiḥ*, pl. *rujuḥ*, preponderating; excelling, paramount.
راجع *râji'*, pl. *ruja'*, returning; referring to something previous (pronoun, &c.); pl. *rawâji'*, yard (of a sail).
راجفة *râjifa-t*, first blast of the trumpet of Judgment.
راجل *râjil*, pl. *rajl*, *rijâl*, *rajjâla-t*, *rujjâl*, رجالى (*rujjâla*, *rajâla*, *rujâla*), *rujlân*; *rajla-t*, *rijla-t*, رجلى *rajla*, *arâjil*, *arâjîl*, pedestrian; good walker; foot-soldier.
راجن *râjin*, accustomed; tame.
راجى *râjî* (راج *râj-in*), ة, who requests, hopes, expects; petitioner.
راح *râḥ*, wine; windy day; gladness, cheerfulness; — ة *râḥa-t*, rest, repose, ease (بيت الر *bait ar-râḥa-t*, privy, water-closet); pl. *râḥ*, *râḥât*, palm of the hand; (m.) baker's peel.
راحل *râḥil*, pl. *ruḥḥal*, *ruḥḥâl*, ag. of (رحل), traveller; leader of a caravan; — ة *râḥila-t*, caravan; pl. *rawâḥil*, saddle-beast, beast of burden for a caravan.
راحول *râḥûl*, camel-saddle.
راخ *râḫ-in*, راخى *râḫî*, living in affluence (adj.).
(راد) *ra'id*, A, INF. *ra'd*, shine in the sun-light, be bright; — V. INF. *tara''ud*, tremble, be tremulous; blow now from the north, now from the south; — VIII. INF. *irti'âd*, be tremulous.
راد *ra'd*, ة *ra'da-t*, handsome girl; pl. *ar'âd*, middle of the fore-

noon, hour when the sun shines in full brightness; lower jaw; — *râdd*, ة, who gives back, replies, refuses, refutes; — ة *râda-t*, pl. of رائد *râ'id*; — *râdda-t*, reply; position, rank; profit advantage.

رادع *râdi'*, perfumed; hindering, preventing (adj.).

رادفة *râdifa-t*, second blast of the trumpet of Judgment; pl. *rawâdif*, palm-shoot.

رادن *râdin*, saffron.

رادوف *râdûf*, pl. *rawâdîf*, fat.

رادى *râdî*, bad, wicked, corrupt; *ar-râdî*, lion.

(رارا) *ra'ra'*, INF. ة, move, turn; wink; look fixedly at; stare round; shine, be bright; wag the tail; look at one's self in a mirror.

راز *râz*, pl. ة *râza-t*, architect.

رازح *râziḥ*, quite tired out, jaded to death.

رازقى *râziqiyy*, ة, poor; — ة *râzaqiyya-t*, a linen-stuff; wine.

رازيانج *râziyânaj*, fennel (Pers.).

(راس) *ra'as*, I, A, INF. *ri'âsa-t*, rule as a chief, lead, govern as a prefect; be a chief, head of a tribe, prefect; injure on the head; — *ra'us*, be a chief; — II. *ra''as*, *rayyas*, INF. *tar'îs*, *taryîs*, make one a chief, leader, prefect; (m.) *rawwas*, INF. *tarwîs*, point, sharpen into a point; — V. INF. *tara''us*, *tarayyus*, become or make one's self a chief, &c.; (m.) INF. *tarawwus*, become pointed; taper; — VIII. INF. *irti'âs*, be appointed as a chief, &c., over (على *'ala*).

راس *ra's*, pl. اروس, اراس *ar'us*, *ru'us*, *ru'ûs*, head, peak, summit; projecting point; promontory; chief, leader, captain; principal part, beginning; end, extremity, conclusion; large tribe, powerful confederacy; head of cattle; capital; solstice; على راس ستين *'ala ra's-i sittîn*, as a sexagenarian; على الراس والعين *'ala 'r-râs wa-'ain*, most willingly.

راسات *râsât*, capital, funds (m.).

راسب *râsib*, firm; mild, meek, gentle; tame; sediment.

راسخ *râsiḥ*, firm, solid, firmly rooted, durable.

راسخت *râsuḥt*, antimony (Pers.).

راسوم *râsûm*, wooden seal.

راسى *râsî* (راس *râs-in*), ة, f. pl. *râsiyât*, *rawâsî*, at anchor, moored; firm, unmovable.

راشح *râśiḥ*, ag. of (رشح); foal able to follow its dam; pl. *rawâśiḥ*, reptile; a mountain moist at its foot.

راشد *râśid*, ag. of (رشد); orthodox, pious; (m.) who can manage his affairs himself, of age; ام راشد *umm-u râśid-in*, mouse.

راشق *râśiq*, ag. of (رشق); darting; (adj.) archer, thrower of the javelin; slender, well-made, alert.

راشوم *râśûm*, seal for corn.

راشى *râśi* (راش *râś-in*), who bribes.

راصد *râṣid*, pl. *ruṣṣad*, *ruṣṣâd*, who observes, spies, pursues; lion.

راض *râḍ-in*, see راضى *râḍî*; — ة *râḍa-t*, pl. of رائض *râ'iḍ*.

راضب *râḍib*, ة, lotus-tree.

راضع *râḍi'*, pl. *ruḍḍa'*, *ruḍḍâ'*, sucking; — also ة *râḍi'a-t*, pl. *rawâḍi'*, milk-tooth.

راضى *râḍî* (راض *râḍ-in*), ة, pl. *ruḍât*, agreeing, consenting, content; agreeable, pleasant.

راطب *râṭib*, moist, fresh.

راع *râ'-in*, see راعى *râ'î*.

راعد *râ'id*, ة *râ'ida-t*, pl. *rawâ'id*, thundering.

راعى *râ'î* (راع *râ'-in*), pl. *ru'ât*, *ru'yân*, *ru'â'*, *ri'â'*, pasturing, grazing, browsing; tending, watching, guarding; herdsman, watchman, protector; governor; — ة *râ'iya-t*, shepherdess; herd, flock.

راغ *râg-in*, راغى *râgî*, foaming; ef-

fervescent; lowing;—ة râgiya-t, she-camel; camels.

(راف) ra'af, U, INF. ra'fa-t, be very compassionate and kind;—ra'if, A, INF. ra'af and ra'uf, INF. ra'âfa-t, id.; — III. INF. murâ-'afa-t, murâwafa-t, id.; — VI. INF. tarâ'uf, show kindness to (على 'ala).

راف ra'f, wine; compassionate; — also ة ra'fa-t, compassion; mildness, gentleness; bounty.

رافح râfiḥ, commodious, comfortable; abundant.

رافد râfid, who supports, gives; — also ة râfida-t, pl. rawâfid, rafters; Euphrates; ar-râfidân, Euphrates and Tigris.

رافض râfiḍ, ة, who throws, flings; who leaves in the lurch, forsakes, rejects; — ة râfiḍa-t; pl. rawâfiḍ, deserter, apostate, renegade, heretic.

رافع râfi', ag. of رفع; bearer, deliverer; who takes away, removes; accuser, plaintiff.

رافغ râfig, pl. rawâfig, luxurious.

راق râq-in, see راقى râqî.

راقب râqib, ag. of (رقب); rival.

راقد râqid, pl. ruqqad, ruqûd, who lies and sleeps.

راقود râqûd, pl. rawâqîd, oblong pitched vessel for wine; a measure; a small fish.

رقوص raqûṣ, dancer.

راقى râqî (راق râq-in), ة, pl. râqûn, ruqât, rawâqî, sorcerer, magician; magic; — râqî, arrack, brandy (Turk.).

راكب râkib, pl. rukkâb, rukbân, rakaba-t, rakb, ag. of (ركب), who rides or drives; mountain-summit.

راكد râkid, ة, pl. rawâkid, quiet, stable (adj.), still, stagnating; in equilibrium.

راكع râki', pl. rukka', who bows, kneels down.

راكوب râkûb, hanging branch of a palm-tree; (m.) short ladder.

(رال) ra'l, f. ة, pl. ri'âl, ri'lân, ارؤل ar'ul, ri'âla-t, the young of an ostrich; pl. ri'yâl, lion; — X. INF. istir'âl, have large teeth and be old; be tall.

رام râm-in, see رامى râmî.

(رام) ra'am, INF. ra'm, twist a rope tight; mend; — رئم ra'im, A, INF. ra'm, like, be addicted to (acc.); INF. ri'mân, be fond of her foal: — INF. ra'm, ri'mân, close and heal (wound); — IV. INF. ir'âm, render a she-camel fond of a strange foal; heal (a.); — V. INF. tara''um, be full of compassion for, of fondness towards (acc.).

رامج râmij, decoy-bird.

رامح râmiḥ, lance-bearer; horned.

رامس râmis, grave-digger.

رامق râmiq, pl. rumuq, who looks at enviously; decoy-bird.

رامك râmik, adulterated musk.

راموز ramûz, lake; root, origin; type, model.

راموس râmûs, tomb.

رامى râmî (رام râm-in), pl. rumât, who throws, flings, hits; archer; Sagittarius; mocker, scoffer.

ران rân, gaiters; (m.) pond; — rânn, ة, sounding, resounding, vibrating; sighing; — rân-in, see رانى rânî.

رانج rânij, nut; cocoa-nut (Pers.)

رانفة rânifa-t, pl. rawânif, lower edge of a tent; hem of a shirt; ball of the thumb.

رانى rânî (ران rân-in), who looks at admiringly.

راه râh-in, see راهى râhî.

راهب râhib, pl. ruhbân, Christian monk; hermit; mystic (s.); lion; — ة râhiba-t, pl. -ât, nun; râhiba-t, anything terrifying.

راهن râhin, firm, solid; lasting; well ordered; who bets, pawns.

راهى râhî (راه râh-in), ة, at ease, comfortable; — ة râhiya-t, wine.

راو râw-in, see راوى râwî.

راوق râwuq, راووق râwûq, filter, strainer; wine-vessel; cup.

راول *ra'ul*, راوول *ra'ûl*, saliva and foam of a horse.

راوند *râwand*, rhubarb ;—ى *râwandiyy*, irritable, prone to anger (m.).

راوى *râwî* (راو *râw-in*), pl. *ruwât*, *râwûn*, hander down of traditions, narrator ; (m.) who perceives, ponders, remembers ; — *râwiyy*, referring to the flag or standard ; — ة *râwiya-t*, pl. *rawâyâ*, water-bag ; animal carrying water ; hander down of traditions.

(راى) *ra'a*, aor. *yara*, IMP. ارا *ir'a*, را *ra'*, INF. *ru'ya-t*, *ra'y*, *ra'a-t*, *ra'ya-t*, *ri'yân*, *ru'yân*, see, perceive, notice ; judge, opine, think, deem true, deem ; pronounce one's opinion ; know ; be willing ; — INF. *ru'ya-t*, see in a dream ; injure in the lungs ; plant the flag ; give fire ; strike fire ; — II. INF. *tar'iya-t*, dissimulate ; (m.) *rawwa*, *warra*, INF. *tarwiya-t*, *tawriya-t*, show a thing to (2 acc.) ; — III. INF. *murâyât*, see one another ; confer ; INF. *murâ'ât*, *ri'yâ'*, *riyâ'*, dissimulate, dissemble ;—IV. INF. *irâ'*, *irâ'a-t*, show (2 acc.) ; INF. *irâ'*, become prudent, intelligent, wise, and, by opposition, look foolish, stupid ; — V. INF. *tara''î*, show one's self, appear ; reflect one's self ; — VI. INF. *tarâ'î*, come in sight of one another, see each other ; reflect one's self ; — VIII. INF. *irti'â'*, perceive, see, recognise, ponder over, consider ; think, believe, be of opinion ; give one's opinion, judge ; — X. INF. *isti'râ'*, see, recognise ; wish to see ; ask for another's opinion.

راى *ra'y*, pl. *ar'â'*, *ârâ'*, *ary*, *rayy*, *riyy*, رئى *ra'iyy*, opinion, view ; sentiment ; advice, vote, decision ; sentence, aphorism ; doctrine ; aspect, form ; اصحاب الر *aṣḥâb-u 'r-ra'y-i*, metaphysicians, idealists ; — ة *râya-t*, pl. *râyât*, *rây*, standard, flag, sign ; — *ra'a-t*, id. ; INF. of (راى).

رائب *râ'ib*, thick, curdled ; complicated ; (m.) muddy.

رائج *râ'ij*, selling well (adj.) ; having currency ; رائج الوقت *râ'ij al-waqt*, opportune, timely ; fashionable, current ; fashion.

رائح *râ'iḥ*, ة, ag. of (روح) ; pl. *rawaḥ*, coming home in the evening ; — ة *ra'iḥa-t*, pl. *rawâ'iḥ*, smell ; odour, fragrance ; stench ; blood ; evening rain.

رائد *râ'id*, pl. *ruwwâd*, *râda-t*, ag. of (رود) ; forager ; herdsman ; guide ; handle of a (hand-) mill ; — also ة *râ'ida-t*, breeze, gentle current of air.

رائس *râ'is*, head, chief.

رائض *râ'iḍ*, horse-breaker ; clever.

رائع *râ'i'*, pl. *ar'â'*, *arwâ'*, what causes fear or astonishment ; terrible, astonishing, pleasant ; generous fleet horse ;—ة *râ'i'a-t*, pl. *rawâ'i'*, event of the above description.

رائف *râ'if*, compassionate.

رائق *râ'iq*, pl. *rûq*, *rûqa-t*, pure, clear, serene, fair, beautiful, lovely ; fasting ; dry bread ; pure water.

رائل *râ'il*, salivating.

رائم *râ'im*, ة *râ'ima-t*, fond.

رائى *râ'î*, who sees, perceives ; — *râ'iyy*, *râyiyy*, referring to the flag or standard.

(رب) *rabb*, U, INF. *rabb*, be lord and master, exercise dominion over (acc.) ; possess ; gather (a.) ; increase (a.) ; abide ; put into good order, arrange, improve, ameliorate ; complete ; give a skin bag a good smell and taste by smearing it with syrup ; INF. *rabb*, feed, nourish, bring up ; — for *rabib*, A, bring up, educate ; — II. INF. *tarbîb*, *taribba-t*, rear, educate ; — IV. INF. *irbâb*, abide in a place ; — V. INF. *tarabbub*,

declare and bear one's self as master of a land, a slave, &c.; rear, educate; — VIII. INF. *irtibâb*, rear, educate.

رب *rabb*, pl. *arbâb*, *rubûb*, *rabb*, lord, master, owner, possessor; ارباب الدولة *arbâb ad-daula-t*, grandees; ارباب المجلس *arbâb al-majlis*, members of the council; ارباب القبور *arbâb al-qubûr*, the dead; — *rubb*, pl. *ribâb*, *rubûb*, jam, syrup; رب السوس *rubb as-sûs*, liquorice-juice; — *rubb-a*, *rabb-a*, frequently; perhaps; many a; ربه رجلا *rubba-hu rajul-an*, oftentimes it happens that a man, &c.; — ة *rabba-t*, mistress; house-mother; — *ribba-t*, carob-tree; — also *rubba-t*, pl. *aribba-t*, *ribâb*, myriad; ten thousand; immense number; — *rubba-t*, plenty, abundance; thick boiled fruit-syrup.

(ربا) *raba'*, INF. *rab'*, mount a watch-tower and observe; keep guard; serve as a scout or spy; lift up; elevate; improve; be high, sublime; cause to disappear; — III. INF. *murâba'a-t*, observe; watch over, guard; — VIII. INF. *irtibâ'*, mount a watch-tower to look out; serve as a scout or spy.

ربا *riban*, *riba*, *ribâ'*, du. *ribawân*, *rîbayân*, gain in selling; usury, usurious interest; — *rabâ*, hills, pl. of ربوة *rabwa-t*, *ribwa-t*, *rubwa-t*.

رباب *rabâb*, ة, white cloud; — also ة *rabâba-t*, a fiddle with one or two strings; — *; — ة *ribâba-t*, supreme authority; divinity, deity; covenant; bundle of arrows for the game.

ربابنة *rabâbina-t*, pl. of ربان *rubbân*.

ربابى *rabâbiyy*, player on the fiddle.

رباجة *rabâja-t*, stupidity.

رباح *rabâḥ*, gain; usury; civet; — *; — *rubbâḥ*, male ape; kid.

رباض *rabbâḍ*, crouching lion.

رباط *ribâṭ*, boundary stone towards an enemy's country; troop of armed horses; tied up horses; pl. *ribâṭât*, firm building, caravanserai; block-house; garrison-town, barracks; hospice of monks; pl. *rubuṭ*, tie, rope, fetter; union; obligation, duty, engagement; corner-stone; suspension of a priest; — ة *ribâṭa-t*, firmness and courage.

رباع *rabâ'*, state, condition; — *ribâ'*, pl. of رباعى *rabâ'î*, ربع *rab'* and ربيع *rabî'*; — *; — *rubâ'*, four, *rubâ'an*, by fours; — ة *rabâ'a-t*, *ribâ'a-t*, condition, state; manner, method; sect; religion.

رباعى *rabâ'î*, ة, pl. *rub'*, *rubu'*, *ruba'*, *arbâ'*, *ribâ'*, *rib'ân*, *ru'bân*, f. *rabâ'iyât*, animal that has lost its teeth *rabâ'iya-t* (sheep 4 years old, horse 5, camel 7); —*rubâ'iyy*, having four radicals; pl. *-ât*, quatrain; — ة *rabâ'iya-t*, one of the teeth between the two middle front teeth and the corner teeth.

ربالة *rabâla-t*, plumpness.

ربان *rubbân*, pl. *rabâbina-t*, captain (of a ship); — ة *rabâna-t*, violin, fiddle; — ى *rabbâniyy*, divine; pl. *-ûn*, theologian, rabbi; — *rubbâniyy*, captain (of a ship).

رباوة *ribâwa-t*, hill.

ربايا *rabâyâ*, pl. of ربيئة *rabî'a-t*.

ربائب *rabâ'ib*, pl. of ربيبة *rabîba-t*.

ربب *rabab*, plenty of good water.

(ربت) *rabat*, I, INF. *rabt*, bring up, educate; —INF. *rabat*, be locked; — II. INF. *tarbît*, educate.

ربت *rubat*, *rabat*, *rubbat-a*, *rabbat-a*, ربتما *rubbatamâ*, *rabbatamâ*, often, frequently, perhaps, may be.

(ربث) *rabas̱*, U, INF. *rabs̱*, prevent, hinder; — II. INF. *tarbîs̱*, id.; — V. INF. *tarabbus̱*, tarry, delay, defer; — VIII. INF. *irtibâs̱*, IX. INF. *irbis̱âs̱*, disperse (n.); — VIII., IX., XI. INF. *irbîs̱âs̱*, take

a bad turn (affairs, &c.); XI. be hindered, prevented.

(ربج) *rabuj*, INF. *rabâja-t*, be stupid, senseless; — IV. INF. *irbâj*, beget small children; — V. INF. *tarabbuj*, show love and care for (على *'ala*) the children.

ربج *rabj*, small coin.

(ربح) *rabiḥ*, A, INF. *ribḥ*, gain in trade, &c.; — II. INF. *tarbîḥ*, cause to gain; — III. INF. *murâbaḥa-t*, sell with profit; cause to gain; — IV. INF. *irbâḥ*, cause to gain; milk in the morning and at noon; — V. INF. *tarabbuḥ*, be thunderstruck, bewildered, perplexed.

ربح *ribḥ*, *rubḥ*, pl. *arbâḥ*, profit; interest; usury; pl. *ribâḥ*, foals of camels; see رابح *râbiḥ*.

(ربحل) *ribaḥl*, ة, well-made, well-shaped; powerful, of a high rank.

(ربخ) *rabaḫ*, I, INF. *rabâḫ*, faint during coition; — *rabiḫ*, A, id.; have a difficult road; (m.) faint, swoon; crouch on one's heels; kneel down; duck; brood.

(ربد) *rabad*, U, INF. *rubûd*, stop, stay, remain; keep back, fetter, tie up; — V. INF. *tarabbud*, change (n.); be covered with clouds; frown; — IX. INF. *irbidâd*, change colour; — IX. and XI. INF. *irbîdâd*, be of a dark ashy grey.

ربد *rabd*, *rabad*, thin mud or dung; — *rubad*, damascening a blade (s.); — ة *rubda-t*, dark ash colour.

ربدا *rabdâ'*, f. (*rubd*, pl.) of اربد *arbad*, ash-coloured, &c.

(ربذ) *rabiẓ*, A, INF. *rabaẓ*, be skilful in handling; — IV. INF. *irbâẓ*, cut off; — ة *ribẓa-t*, *rabaẓa-t*, pl. *ribâẓ*, *ribaẓ*, fleak of wool for ornament or to anoint and wipe with; stopper.

(ربرب) *rabrab*, pl. *rabârib*, herd of wild oxen.

ربرق *rabraq*, nightshade (plant).

(ربز) *rabaz*, slap with the palm of the hand; — *rabuz*, INF. *rabâza-t*, be fleshy, plump; fill a skin bag; — VIII. INF. *irtibâz*, be complete.

(ربس) *rabas*, U, INF. *rabs*, slap; fill a skin bag; be plump, firm of flesh; — VIII. INF. *irtibâs*, be plump and firm; be mixed; — IX. INF. *irbisâs*, depart; come down, take a bad turn (affairs).

ربس *ribs*, ربسا *rabsâ'*, pl. *rubs*, great calamity.

(ربش) *rabaś*, the white of the nails; — IV. INF. *irbâś*, green.

(ربص) *rabaṣ*, U, INF. *rabṣ*, watch an opportunity, wait for; be in store; (m.) water the land in autumn, before sowing; — II. INF. *tarbîṣ*, expect, hope from; (m.) be resolute and persevering; — V. INF. *tarabbuṣ*, watch an opportunity; wait for (ب *bi*); spy out; (m.) hold out in one's post; — ة *rubṣa-t*, expectation, hope; (m.) seed in irrigated ground; variegation, gaudiness.

(ربض) *rabaḍ*, I, INF. *rabḍ*, *rabḍa-t*, *ribḍa-t*, lie with crossed feet; sit or lie in wait; — U, I, alight with, visit; — II. INF. *tarbîḍ*, half fill a skin bag; — IV. INF. *irbâḍ*, allow the sheep to lie down, to rest; provide for the expenditure of one's family; be scorching hot.

ربض *rabḍ*, *rubḍ*, *rabaḍ*, *rubaḍ*, wedded wife; mother; sister; — *rubḍ*, centre, foundation; — *rabaḍ*, pl. *arbâḍ*, anything to fall back upon; home, family, fortune; ramparts; suburb; — ة *ribḍa-t*, battle-field with dead bodies; corpse; body; figure; troop.

(ربط) *rabaṭ*, I, U, tie, tie up, fasten; retain, seize; restrain, rein, rule; bring into order, into a system; take hold of; waylay;

render impotent by a spell; suspend a priest; — INF. *ribâṭa-t,* take courage, strengthen the heart; — III. INF. *ribâṭ, murâbaṭa-t,* persevere in a thing; be on guard in a frontier-station; plot with, conspire; — VI. INF. *tarâṭub,* conspire, take mutual obligations; — VII. INF. *irribâṭ,* get tied up; get suspended; — VIII. INF. *irtibâṭ,* tie, tie up; keep the horse ready for mounting guard.

ربط *rubuṭ,* pl. of رباط *ribâṭ*; — ة *rabṭa-t,* pl. *rabṭ, rabaṭât,* band, rope, string; bundle, parcel, packet.

(ربع) *raba',* come to the water on the fourth day; — A, U, I, INF. *rab',* be the fourth or fortieth, come as the fourth; twist the rope four-fold; take the fourth part of a property, every fourth man, come on every fourth day; pass. suffer from quartan ague; — A, INF. *rab',* stay, remain, abide; stop, wait for; restrain one's self, abstain, desist; lean towards compassionately; be in spring-time; pass. be visited by a spring rain; have a rich pasture, pasture freely; lift up a stone to try one's strength; lift a load with another by a lever to place it on the camel's back; gallop; — II. INF. *tarbî',* give a square or quadrangular form; square; do a thing four times; multiply by four; put the horses on the spring pasture; — III. INF. *murâba'a-t,* help another to load by means of a lever; bear the fourth part of a gain or loss; INF. *ribâ', murâba'a-t,* make a contract for spring-time; — IV. INF. *irbâ',* become four from three; enter on spring-time; beget children in a youthful age; have four camels; visit a sick person on the fourth day; lose the teeth رباعية *rabâ'iya-t*; — V. INF. *tara''ub,* sit down cross-legged squarely; be square or quadrangular; be on the spring pasture; be well fed; — VIII. INF. *irtibâ',* lift a stone to try one's strength; pass the spring-time anywhere; grow fat on the spring pasture; — X. INF. *istirbâ',* be heaped up; rise; be strong for a journey.

ربع *rab',* pl. *ribâ', rubû', arbu', arbâ',* spring sojourn, spring camp; home, dwelling, house; troop; — *rib',* watering of the camel on the fourth day; حمى الربع *ḥumma ar-rib',* quartan ague; — *rub',* pl. *arbâ',* fourth part; fourth part of a *dinar*; — *rabi',* state, condition; — *ruba',* pl. *ribâ', arbâ',* camel-foal dropped in spring; — *ruba'-a,* by fours; — *rab', rubu', ruba',* pl. of رباعي *rabâ'î*; — *rubu',* pl. of ربيع *rabî'*; — ة *rab'a-t,* pl. *rab'ât, raba'ât,* of middle height; thick-set, stubby; box, case; pl. *raba'ât, rabi'â-t,* stations; habitations; — *riba'a-t,* state, condition.

ربعان *rib'ân,* pl. of رباعي *rabâ'î.*

ربعي *rib'iyy,* brought forth in spring; spring-like; — ة *rub'iyya-t,* small gold coin.

(ربغ) *rabag,* U, INF. *rabg,* lead an easy life; — IV. INF. *irbâg,* allow the camel to drink at any time.

ربغ *rabug,* enjoyment of life; novelty and freshness; — *rabig,* impudent, insolent.

(ربق) *rabaq,* U, I, INF. *rabq,* put another's head into a noose; catch a bird by its head in a noose or snare; entrap, entangle; — INF. *rabq, ribq,* bind, tie up, fetter; — II. INF. *tarbîq,* provide a string with nooses; dispose a speech well; water, moisten; — V. INF. *tarabbuq,* hang round the neck; — VIII.

INF. *irtibâq*, be caught in a noose or snare; get entangled in a matter.

ربق *ribq*, string with nooses or snares; noose, snare; — ة *rib-qa-t*, *rabqa-t*, pl. *ribaq*, *ribâq*, *arbâq*, noose, snare; yoke; halter.

(ربك) *rabak*, U, INF. *rabk*, mix, mix up, confuse; throw one into a mire; mend, make good, make up for; prepare the dish ربيكة *rabîka-t*; — *rabik*, A, INF. *rabak*, be entangled in a complicated and difficult matter; — VIII. INF. *irtibâk*, be mixed, mixed up, confused; be difficult and complicated; be in a plight; get into or be pushed into a mire, stick in it; stop short in one's speech and stammer; — XI. INF. *irbîkâk*, abstain, desist; be confused in one's mind.

ربك *rabik*, *rubak*, *ribakk*, entangled in difficulties, in a plight.

(ربل) *rabal*, U, I, INF. *rabl*, be numerous, multiply (n.), have many children and cattle; also IV. INF. *irbâl*, and V. produce many trees, greening afresh in autumn, or fresh autumn-grass; — V. INF. *tarabbul*, see IV.; be plump; go hunting;—VIII. INF. *irtibâl*, be numerous.

ربل *rabl*, pl. *rubûl*, tree greening afresh in autumn; autumn-grass; — *ribl*, *rabil*, ة, plump, fleshy; — ة *rabla-t*, *rabala-t*, fleshy part of the hips, the breasts, &c.

(ربم) *rabam*, dense vegetation.

ربما *rubbamâ*, *rubamâ*, *rabbamâ*, *rabamâ*, often, frequently it happens that, perhaps, may be.

(ربن), IV. اربن *arban*, INF. *irbân*, give a pawn or pledge to (acc.); — V. INF. *tarabbun*, be captain of a ship.

(ربو) *rabâ*, U, INF. *ribâ*, *rubuww*, increase, grow, grow up; rise; mount a hill, be on its top; — INF. *rabw*, *rabuww*, grow up, be brought up; — INF. *rabw*, suffer from asthma; snort; — pret. *rabai-tu*, INF. *raba'*, *rubiyy*, grow up, be brought up; be lord, master, dominate; — II. INF. *tarbiya-t*, feed, bring up, rear, educate; take care of, cultivate; III. INF. *marâbât*, flatter, cajole; lend on interest, carry on usury; — IV. INF. *irbâ'*, make to grow; increase; give in addition; carry on usury; — V. INF. *tarabbî*, bring up, educate; be brought up, educated, reared.

ربو *rabw*, hill; asthma; swollen gland; increase, growth; pl. *arbâ'*, troop; — ة *rabwa-t*, *rib-wa-t*, *rubwa-t*, pl. *rubâ*, ربى *ruban*, *rubiyy*, hill, height; — *ribwa-t*, pl. *rabwât*, ten thousand; myriad.

ربوا *ribwâ'*, usury.

ربوان *ribawân*, du. of ربا *rib-an*.

ربوب *rabûb*, step-son; — *rubûb*, pl. of رب *rabb*; — ى *rabûbiyy*, divine, theological; — ية *rubûbiyya-t*, dominion; deity, divinity; swelling, swollen gland.

ربوض *rabûḍ*, pl. *rubuḍ*, big, large, wide; populated.

ربون *rabûn*, pawn, pledge.

ربى *rabi'*, *rabiyy*, body-guard; — *ruban*, *rubiyy*, pl. of ربوة *rab-wa-t*; — *rabbî*, my lord; — *rubban*, pl. *rubâb*, benefit, bounty; wealth, ease, comfort; —*ribbiyy*, ten thousand; myriad; — *rubbiyy*, seller of syrup or jam; — ة *rabiyya-t*, pl. of ربيئة *rabî'a-t*.

ربيب *rabîb*, pl. *aribbâ'*, brought up; foster-child; adopted son; slave; confederate, ally; king; step-son, step-father; — ة *rabî-ba-t*, pl. *rabâ'ib*, step-daughter

or daughter by adoption; step-mother; nurse.

ربيث *rabîs̱*, hindered; — ة *rabîs̱a-t*, ى *ribbîs̱a*, pl. *rabâ'is̱*, hindrance; what averts evil.

ربيدة *rabîda-t*, book-case; compartment.

ربيز *rabîz*, firm of flesh; witty, elegant.

ربيط *rabîṭ*, ة, bound, tied up; firm, solid; monk, hermit; — ة *rabîṭa-t*, plot, conspiracy, intrigue.

ربيع *rabî'*, pl. *arbi'a-t*, *arbi'â'*, *ribâ'*, spring; sprin grain; spring vegetation, verdure, pasture; the two months *rabî'*; pl. *arbi'â'*, brook, rivulet; pl. *rubu'*, fourth part; (m.) comrade, companion, partner; ابو الر *abû 'r-rabî'*, hoopoo; — ى *rabî'iyy*, brought forth in spring; spring-like.

ام ربيق *umm rubaiq*, calamity; — ة *rabîqa-t*, caught in a noose or snare.

ربيك *rabîk*, entangled in difficulties; — also ة *rabîka-t*, dish of dates with flour, butter, milk, or cheese; — *rabîka-t*, miry pool, puddle.

ربيل *rabîl*, robber; — ة *rabîla-t*, plumpness; easy circumstances.

ربيئة *rabî'a-t*, pl. *rabâyâ*, spy; body-guard.

(رت) *ratt*, for *ratit*, A, INF. *ratat*, have a heavy tongue and stammer; — IV. INF. *irtât*, make one a stammerer.

رت *ratt*, pl. *ruttân*, *rutût*, chieftain, prince; pl. *rutût*, pig; — *rutt*, pl. and رتا *rattâ'*, f. of ارت *aratt*, stammerer; — ة *rutta-t*, stammering (s.).

(رتا) *rata'*, A, INF. *rutû'*, make a knot; throttle; stay, abide; be dismissed, go away, depart; INF. *rat'ân*, gallop with short steps; — IV. INF. *irtâ'*, laugh in a subdued manner.

رتاج *ritâj*, door with smaller doors in it; doorway, entrance; Mecca; — ة *ritâja-t*, pl. *ratâ'ij*, rock.

رتاع *ritâ'*, INF. of رتع *rata'*; pl. of راتع *râti'*, pasturing freely.

رتام *ritâm*, رتائم *ratâ'im*, pl. of رتيمة *ratîma-t*.

رتان *rat'ân*, short gallop; smile; — *ruttân*, pl. of رت *ratt*.

(رتب) *ratab*, U, INF. *rutûb*, be firm, solid; stand unmoved; — *ratib*, A, INF. *ratab*, stand upright, be planted up; — II. INF. *tartîb*, make firm, fix, consolidate; put into good order, arrange well; — IV. INF. *irtâb*, raise, make to stand upright; — V. INF. *tarattub*, be firm, solid, unshakeable; get into shape; result; — ة *rutba-t*, pl. *rutab*, round of a ladder; step; grade, degree; rank, dignity; order; ceremony (كتاب الرتب *kitâb-u 'r-rutab*, ritual).

(رتج) *rataj*, U, INF. *ratj*, lock, shut up; INF. *ratajân*, try to walk alone; — *ratij*, A, INF. *rataj*, have a heavy tongue, an impediment; — IV. INF. *irtâj*, lock the door; pass. (also VIII. and X.) be hindered, impeded; — VIII. INF. *irtitâj*, see IV.; be locked, shut up; — X. INF. *istirtâj*, see IV.

رتج *rataj* = رتاج *ritâj*.

(رتح) *rataḥ*, U, INF. *rutûḥ*, be soft and thin; remain, stay, abide; shrink from, desist; — ة *rataḥa-t*, thin mud.

(رترت) *ratrat*, INF. ة, be unable to pronounce the letter ت *t*; stammer; talk idly.

(رتع) *rata'*, INF. *rat'*, *ritâ'*, *rutû'*, eat and drink freely; live in affluence and enjoyment; — IV. INF. *irtâ'*, allow the camels to pasture freely.

رتع *rutta'*, *ruttu'*, pl. of راتع *râti'*, pasturing freely; — ة *rut'a-t*, affluence, plenty and enjoyment.

(رتق) *rataq*, U, INF. *ratq*, mend, restore, stitch together, solder, cement, &c.; bring into order again; lock, shut; — *ratiq*, A, INF. *rataq*, *rataqa-t*, be unfit for coition (woman); — VIII. INF. *irtitâq*, be mended, &c., pass. of *rataq*.

رتق *rataq*, ة *rataqa-t*, unfitness of a woman for coition; — ة *rataqa-t*, pl. *rataq*, step; tread.

رتقا *ratqâ'*, pl. *rutq*, unfit for coition (f.).

(رتك) *ratak*, U, INF. *ratk*, *ratak*, *ratakân*, walk with short steps; — IV. INF. *irtâk*, laugh in a subdued manner.

(رتل) *ratal*, INF. *ratl*, also *ratil*, A, INF. *ratal*, be beautiful, in good order; be white and fresh (teeth); — II. INF. *tartîl*, arrange in good order; read the Koran deliberately, distinctly and well; sing; — V. INF. *tarattul*, deliver a speech slowly.

رتل *ratil*, having white and fresh teeth; clear and fresh; cold.

(رتم) *ratam*, I, INF. *ratm*, squash, smash; grow up; eat of the plant رتم *ratam* and faint from it; — IV. INF. *irtâm*, twist a thread round one's finger as a reminder.

رتم *ratam*, ة, broom (plant), gorse; — ة *ratma-t*, pl. *rutm*, a thread wound round the finger as a reminder.

(رتن) *ratan*, U, INF. *ratn*, mix, mingle.

(رتو) *ratâ*, U, INF. *ratw*, bring one thing near another; stitch together, mend; tie up; contract, and, by opposition, make loose, relax; strengthen the courage; weaken, lessen; draw or let down the bucket slowly; step, step forward; INF. *ratw*, *rutuww*, nod the head; — II. INF. *tartiya-t*, mend, restore.

رتو *rutû'*, INF. of (رتا); — *rutuww*, INF. of (رتو); — ة *ratwa-t*, step; bow-shot (distance); reach of the eye; mile; a short space of time.

رتوب *rutûb*, INF. of (رتب).

رتوع *rutû'*, INF. of (رتع); pl. of راتع, pasturing freely.

رتى *rutta*, f. stammering.

رتيلا *rutailâ'*, pl. *rutailât*, *rutailawât*, large spider, tarantula.

رتيم *ratîm*, squashed, broken; — ة *ratîma-t*, pl. *ratâ'im*, *ritâm*, thread twisted round a finger to make one remember a thing; a notch for the sake of remembrance.

(رث) *raṣṣ*, I, INF. *raṣâṣa-t*, be worn, threadbare, dirty; be old and dry; — IV. INF. *irṣâṣ* = I.; wear out; dirty; — VIII. INF. *irtiṣâṣ*, gather rags, old carpets, lumber, rubbish, &c.; — X. INF. *istirṣâṣ*, find old and worn out, deem useless.

رث *raṣṣ*, ة, pl. *riṣâṣ*, old, worn, tattered, squalid; rags, old carpets, &c.; — ة *riṣa-t*, inheriting, INF. of (ورث); — *riṣṣa-t*, pl. *riṣaṣ*, tatters, rags, old carpets, rubbish, lumber; shabbiness; rabble.

(رثا) *raṣa'*, milk fresh milk into sour to make it thick; make milk sour; prepare the dish رثية *raṣiyya-t*; mix together; subside, calm down; lament or eulogise the dead.

رثا *riṣâ'*, lamentation; eulogy; elegiac poem; — ة *raṣṣâ'a-t*, female mourner, mourning woman.

رثاث *riṣâṣ*, pl. of رث; — ة *riṣâṣa-t*, *raṣâṣa-t*, threadbareness, raggedness.

رثان *raṣân*, intermittent rain.

(رثن), V. *taraṣṣan*, INF. *taraṣṣun*, anoint the face.

(رثو) *raṣâ*, U, INF. *raṣw*, lament

and eulogise the dead; remember and quote another's words.
رثوثة rasûsa-t, threadbareness.
(رثى) rasa, I, INF. rasy, risâ', risâya-t, marsât, marsiya-t, lament or eulogise the dead, compose an elegy in honour of; lament, bewail; feel compassion, pity; condole with (ل li); — INF. risâya-t, remember and quote another's words; — rasî, A, INF. rasan, have pain in the hands, feet or joints; be thin; — II. INF. tarsiya-t, V. INF. tarassî, lament or eulogise the dead; — ة rasya-t, pain in the joints; stupidity; — ة rasiyya-t, rasî'a-t, fresh milk mixed with sour.
رثيث rasîs, worn out, threadbare; wounded, half dead.
رثيد rasîd, piled up.
(رج) rajj, U, INF. rajj, move (a.), shake (a.), cause to tremble; tremble, shake (n.); waver, be agitated; be troubled; restrain, prevent; make a door; — VIII. INF. irtijâj, be moved, agitated, tremble, shake (n.); — ة rajja-t, trembling, shaking (s.); agitation; noise, tumult.
رجا rajan, rajâ', pl. arjâ', side, wall of a well; flank; quarter; coast; — rajâ', hope, wish, request; fear; — ة rajâ'a-t, rajât, hope, fear.
(رجا), IV. arja', INF. irjâ', delay, defer; not shoot anything.
رجاح rajâḥ, pl. rujuḥ, having full hips (f.); — ة rajâḥa-t, excellence; preference; probability; — rujjâḥa-t, swing, rocking-board.
رجاد rajâd, transfer of the sheaves to the threshing-floor; — rajjâd, who brings in sheaves.
رجازة rijâza-t, tare, balancing weight; litter, sedan-chair.
رجاس rajjâs, thundering, roaring; agitated sea; — ة rajâsa-t, disgraceful action; dirt, impurity.
رجاع rijâ', return; repetition; pl. arji'a-t, ruju', halter of a camel; — *
رجاف rajjâf, who trembles; day of resurrection; sea.
رجال rijâl, rujjâl, ة rajjâla-t, rujjâla-t, pl. of راجل râjil and رجل rajil.
رجالات rijâlât, pl. of رجل rajul.
رجالى rujjâla, rajâla, rujâla, pl. of راجل râjil, رجل rajil, rajul, رجلى rajla and رجيل rajîl.
رجام rijâm, large stone; tomb-stone; — pl of رجمة rujma-t.
رجاوة rajâwa-t, hope, fear.
(رجب) rajab, U, INF. rajb, be ashamed; INF. rajb, rujûb, honour, venerate; — rajib, A, INF. rajab, honour, venerate; fear; be ashamed; — II. INF. tarjîb, IV. INF. irjâb, honour, venerate; prop up.
رجب rajab, pl. arjâb, rujûb, rijâb, rajabât, name of a month; — ة rujba-t, pl. rujab, prop of a tree; snare or trap for a wolf; pl. rawâjib, first joint of a finger.
(رجح) rajaḥ, A, I, U, INF. rujûḥ, rujḥân, sink, weigh over; surpass; be more probable; — II. INF. tarjîḥ, cause the scale to sink; give more than the full weight; make one thing heavier than another; prefer; represent as more probable; — III. INF. murâjaḥa-t, have one's self weighed against another; rock one's self with another on a swing, &c.; — IV. INF. irjâḥ, give more than the full weight; — V. INF. tarajjuḥ, weigh heavier; be preferable, prevail; swing; — VIII. INF. irtijâḥ, rock one's self.
رجح rujaḥ, pl. of راجح râjiḥ and رجاح rajâḥ.
رجحان rujḥân, rajaḥân, the sinking of the scale, preponderating (s.); preference; superiority; — ة rujḥâniyya-t, excellence.
(رجحن), III. irjaḥann, INF. irjiḥnân,

weigh heavier; swing to and fro.

(رجد) *rajad*, U, INF. *rajâd*, bring in corn; pass. *rujid*, tremble; — II. INF. *tarjîd*, pass. tremble; — IV. INF. *irjâd*, cause to tremble.

رجراج *rajrâj*, trembling; mercury, quicksilver; — ة *rajrâja-t*, agitated crowd.

(رجرج) *rajraj*, INF. ة, be agitated, wave to and fro, tremble; be tired; — II. INF. *tarajruj*, tremble.

(رجز) *rajaz*, INF. *rajz*, compose or recite verses in the metre *rajaz*; (m.) thunder; get angry; — V. INF. *târajjuz*, roll; grow angry; — VIII. INF. *irtijâz*, compose verses in the metre *rajaz*.

رجز *rijz*, *rujz*, punishment, chastisement; dirt; plague; idolatry; — *rajaz*, trembling disease of a camel; name of a metre (مستفعلن *mustaf'ilun* six times repeated).

(رجس) *rajas*, U, INF. *rajs*, roar; thunder; measure the depth of the water; I, U, prevent, keep back from; — *rajis*, A, INF. *rajas*, disgrace one's self; be dirty, polluted; — *rajus*, INF. *rajâsa-t* (also pass. *rujis*), id.; — IV. INF. *irjâs*, measure the depth of the water; — VIII. INF. *irtijâs*, be shaken, shake (n.); thunder.

رجس *rijs*, *rajas*, pl. *arjâs*, disgraceful action; pollution, dirt; punishment; — *rajis*, *rijs*, disgraced; dirty.

(رجع) *raja'*, I, INF. *rujû'*, *marji'*, *marji'a-t*, *ruja'*, *ruj'ân*, return, come back; mend (n.), repent; refer grammatically; repeat; desist, renounce; INF. *raj'*, lead or bring back; be useful, profitable; INF. *raj'*, *marja'*, *marji'*, turn away from one thing and towards another; — II. INF. *tarji'*, cause to return, bring or fetch back; repeat; return, restore to; tattoo the face; — III. INF. *murâja'a-t*, revert to a thing, repeat; look repeatedly at or into; take back a divorced wife; — IV. INF. *irjâ'*, cause to return, bring or fetch back; give back anything bought; — VI. INF. *tarâju'*, return together; come back; — VIII. INF. *irtijâ'*, lead or bring back; take back; return; mend (n.), repent, get converted; — X. INF. *istirjâ'*, demand back, reclaim; demand one's return; pronounce the phrase "To God we belong and to Him we return!"; snivel.

رجع *raj'*, return; reply to a letter; (m.) receipt; profit, advantage; tattoo lines in the face; pl. *rijâ'*, *rij'ân*, *ruj'ân*, channel, gutter; place with stagnating water; repeated rain; excrement of wild animals; plague; — *ruja'*, pl. of راجع *râji'*, returning, &c.; — *ruju'*, pl. of رجاع *rijâ'*; — ة *raja'a-t*, *rija'a-t*, return; jubilee; metempsychosis; retrocession of a star; — *rija'a-t*, marrying a divorced wife again; — *rija'a-t*, *ruj'a-t*, *ruja'a-t*, reply to a letter; (m.) receipt.

رجعان *ruj'ân*, return, INF. of (رجع).

رجعى *ruj'a*, return; reply to a letter; — *raj'iyy*, the second fruit of a year.

(رجف) *rajaf*, U, INF. *rajf*, *rajafân*, *rujûf*, *rajîf*, move, shake (a.); be violently moved, shaken; shake (n.), tremble; be agitated; resound, pass. be rumoured; prepare for war; — II. INF. *tarjîf*, cause to shake or tremble; — IV. INF. *irjâf*, shake, tremble; excite the populace, spread false rumours; — V. INF. *tarajjuf*, be agitated; tremble; waver; be easily made to waver or tremble; — ة *rajfa-t*

shaking (s.), shock of an earthquake; convulsion.

رجفان *rajafân*, violent agitation; trembling, shaking (s.); earthquake.

(رجل) *rajal*, U, INF. *rajl*, beat on the foot; (also VIII.) bind and suspend by the feet; — *rajil*, A, INF. *rajal*, have a white spot on the foot; INF. *rajal*, *rujla-t*, be a pedestrian, walk on foot; be half smooth, half curled; — II. INF. *tarjîl*, bring help; encourage; dress the hair so as to be half smooth, half curled; — IV. INF. *irjâl*, bid one to walk on foot; grant a delay or respite; — V. INF. *tarajjul*, walk on foot; dismount (n.); look like a man (woman); become marriageable;—VIII. INF. *irtijâl*, see I.; speak extempore, improvise; act headstrongly; slacken its course to rest (horse).

رجل *rajl*, pedestrian; foot-soldiers; — *rijl*, pl. *arjul*, *rijalât*, *rijilât*, foot; hind-foot; foot of a mountain; extremity; ر الباب . *rijl al-bâb*, hinge of a door; pl. *arjâl*, swarm of locusts; part or half of what a skin bag holds; — *rajil*, pl. *rajl*, *rijâl*, *rajla-t*, *rajla*, *rujjâl*, *rajjâla-t*, *rujjâla*, *rajâla*, *rujâla*, *rujlân*, pl. pl. *arâjil*, *arâjil*, *arjila-t*, pedestrian, traveller on foot; foal which is allowed to suck freely; pl. *rajjâla-t*, retinue, servants, messengers; — *rajul*, pl. *rijâl*, *rijâlât*, *rijla-t*, *rajla-t*, *rijala-t*, *arâjil*, *marjal*, man; powerful man, man of great physical strength; common man (opposed to a leader, &c.); pl. *arjâl*, *rajâla*, hair half smooth, half curled; having such hair (also *rajil*, *rajal*); — ة *rajla-t*, firm step; — *rijla-t*, pl. *rijal*, watercourse from stony parts into the plain; — *rujla-t*, manhood; being a good walker; travelling on foot (s.);—*rajula-t*, virago.

رجلان *rajlân*, pl. *rajla*, pedestrian; — *rujlân*, pl. of رجيل *rajîl*.

رجلى *rajla*, stony road; pl. *rijâl*, *rajâla*, women travelling on foot; pl. of راجل *râjil*, رجلان *rajlân*, and رجل *rajil*; — ة *rujliyya-t*, manhood.

(رجم) *rajam*, U, INF. *rajm*, pelt with stones, stone, kill; calumniate, slander; inveigh against, execrate, curse; mark the tomb by a stone; drive away, expel; break off; interrupt; leave in the lurch, forsake; run hurriedly by; surmise, suppose, try to guess; — III. INF. *murâjama-t*, pelt with stones in combat; try to ward off by throwing stones or shooting; vie in efforts; — VI. INF. *tarâjûm*, pelt each other with stones; — VIII. INF. *irtijâm*, be heaped up.

رجم *rajm*, what is thrown or flung, projectile; stoning; blame; execration, curse; surmise, supposition, guess; tomb; pit; — ة *rujma-t*, pl. *rujam*, *rijâm*, heap of stones; tomb-stone; tomb.

(رجن) *rajan*, U, INF. *rujûn*, stay, abide; accustom one's self to a place; INF. *rajn* (also II.), keep an animal in the stable and feed it badly; — *rajin*, A, INF. *rajan*, stay and accustom one's self to a place; INF. *rujûn*, be kept in the stable; — II. INF. *tarjîn*, see I.; — VIII. INF. *irtijân*, be complicated and difficult.

(رجه) *rajah*, I, INF. *rajh*, hold with the teeth;—IV. INF. *irjâh*, defer, delay.

(رجو) *rajâ*, U, INF. *rajw*, *rajâ'*, *rajât*, *rajâ'a-t*, *rajâwa-t*, *marjât*, hope for, expect; hope, expect or ask for a thing from; fear; — رجى *rajî'*, A, INF. *raj-an*,

cease to speak, be interrupted;— II. INF. *tarjiya-t*, hope, expect; cause to hope; — IV. INF. *irjâ'*, defer, delay; — V. INF. *tarajjî*, hope, expect; implore, entreat; submit (n.); — VIII. INF. *irtijâ'*, hope, fear;—ة *rajwa-t*, ى *rajwa*, hope; fear.

رجود *rajûd*, who brings in corn.

رجوس *rajûs*, roaring, thundering.

رجوع *rujû'*, return; reply, answer; relation, reference; success; advantage, profit; proof, demonstration; — ة *rajû'a-t*, answer.

رجولة *rajûla-t*, رجولية *rajûliyya-t*, *rujûliyya-t*, manhood, manliness.

رجوم *rajûm*, stoned; cursed.

(رجى) see (رجو).

رجيح *rajîḥ*, surpassing, excellent.

رجيدة *rajîda-t*, bringing in of the corn.

رجيع *rajî'*, ة, brought back; pl. *ruju'*, *rajâ'i'*, animal returning tired and at once put to use again; what returns without being sold; cold food.

رجيف *rajîf*, shaking, trembling (s.); — *rijjîf*, who trembles, shaker.

رجيل *rajîl*, pl. *rujâla*, good walker; pedestrian; hard; improvised; — *rujail*, little man, manikin.

رجيم *rajîm*, stoned, cursed (Satan).

رجين *rajîn*, deadly poison; — ة *rajîna-t*, resin, gum; troop.

رحا *raḥan*, mill.

رحاب *riḥâb*, pl. of رحبة *raḥba-t*; — *ruḥâb*, wide, spacious; — ة *raḥâba-t*, spaciousness; commodiousness.

رحاض *ruḥâḍ*, perspiration after a fit of fever.

رحاق *ruḥâq*, pure, generous.

رحال *riḥâl*, pl. of رحل; camp; — *raḥḥâl*, who travels much; good camel-rider; pl. ة, nomads; maker of camel-saddles; — *ruḥḥâl*, travellers, &c., pl. of

راحل *râḥil*; — ة *riḥâla-t*, pl. *raḥâ'il*, leather saddle.

(رحامس) *ruḥâmis*, bold, brave.

رحائب *raḥâ'ib*, pl. vast plains.

(رحب) *raḥub*, INF. *ruḥb*, *raḥâba-t*, also *raḥib*, A, INF. *raḥab*, be expanded, wide, spacious, commodious; — II. INF. *tarḥîb*, widen, make more commodious; welcome; make room for a new-comer; — IV. INF. *irḥâb*, be wide, spacious; widen;—V. INF. *taraḥḥub*, welcome.

رحب *raḥb*, ة, wide, spacious, commodious; — *ruḥb*, spaciousness; comfortable place; *ruḥb-an*, welcome! — ة *raḥba-t*, *raḥaba-t*, pl. *raḥb*, *raḥab*, *riḥâb*, *raḥbât*, *raḥabât*, comfortable place; wide field or plain.

رحح *raḥaḥ*, broad hoof; — *ruḥuḥ*, pl. wide dishes.

رحراح *raḥrâḥ*, رحرح *raḥraḥ*, رحرحان *raḥraḥân*, broad, wide, spacious; commodious and abundant.

(رحرح) *raḥraḥ*, INF. ة, speak obscurely; conceal from.

(رحض) *raḥaḍ*, I, INF. *raḥḍ*, wash, clean; — II. pass. perspire violently after a fit of fever; — IV. INF. *irḥâḍ*, wash; — VIII. INF. *irtiḥâḍ*, be rebuked; be disgraced, dishonoured.

رحضا *ruḥaḍâ'*, perspiration after a fit of fever.

(رحف), IV. *arḥaf*, INF. *irḥâf*, sharpen.

(رحل) *raḥal*, INF. *raḥl*, saddle the camel; INF. *raḥl*, *raḥîl*, depart, emigrate; suffer patiently; strike with the sword; — II. INF. *tarḥîl*, cause one to travel, to remove, to emigrate; cause to start, expedite, despatch; — III. INF. *murâḥala-t*, help in saddling, departing, &c.; — IV. INF. *irḥâl*, make the camel ready for travelling; give one a camel to ride upon; — V. INF. *taraḥḥul*, set out, emigrate; ride a restive camel;—VIII. INF.

irtiḥâl, saddle the camel; depart, emigrate; travel, ride.

رحل *raḥl*, pl. *arḥul*, *riḥâl*, camel-saddle; quarter, dwelling; removed household furniture; (m.) also ة *raḥla-t*, reading-desk, pulpit; — *ruḥḥal*, travellers, &c., pl. of راحل *râḥil*; — ة *riḥla-t*, removal, emigration, departure, journey; saddling of a camel; death; — *ruḥla-t*, being ready for travelling; departure; journey; direction or destination of a journey.

(رحم) *raḥim*, A, INF. *raḥma-t*, *marḥama-t*, *ruḥm*, *ruḥum*, be compassionate, kind, merciful, take pity upon (acc. or على *'ala*); INF. *raḥm*, *raḥam*, also pass. *ruḥim* and — *raḥum*, INF. *raḥâma-t*, have disease in the womb after giving birth; — II. INF. *tarḥîm*, call God's mercy upon; — V. INF. *taraḥḥum*, feel compassion for, have mercy upon (على *'ala*); — VI. INF. *tarâḥum*, feel compassion for one another; — X. INF. *istirḥâm*, implore for compassion or mercy.

رحم *raḥim*, *riḥm*, pl. *arḥâm*, womb; kindred relations, ties of blood; compassion, mercy; — *ruḥm*, *ruḥum*, mercy, commiseration; ام رحم *umm-u ruḥm-in*, Mecca; — ة *raḥma-t*, compassion, commiseration, mercy; pardon.

رحما *raḥmâ'*, suffering from the womb.

رحمان *raḥmân*, merciful, compassionate; God; — ى *raḥmâniyy*, divine.

رحموت *raḥamût*, رحمى *ruḥma*, compassion, commiseration; mercy; pardon.

رحة *raḥḥa-t*, coiled up snake.

(رحو) *raḥâ*, U, INF. *raḥw*, build a mill; turn the mill; grind; also V. INF. *taraḥḥî*, coil itself up.

رحول *raḥûl*, ة *raḥûla-t*, very fit for travelling.

رحوم *raḥûm*, suffering from disease of the womb; compassionate, merciful.

رحوى *raḥawiyy*, revolving (adj.).

رحى, رحا *raḥan*, *raḥa*, f. pl. *arḥ-in*, *arḥî*, *arḥiyy*, *arḥâ'*, *raḥiyy*, *ruḥiyy*, *arḥiya-t*, mill, hand-mill; mill-stone.

رحيب *raḥîb*, spacious, wide, commodious.

رحيض *raḥîḍ*, washed, clean.

رحيق *raḥîq*, pure, generous wine; a perfume; a river of Paradise.

رحيل *raḥîl*, departure, journey; death; saddled; fit for travelling.

رحيم *raḥîm*, compassionate; merciful; related by blood; sincere in friendship.

(رخ) *raḫḫ*, U, INF. *raḫḫ*, tread upon, tread under foot; mix the wine; — IV. INF. *irḫâḫ*, attend zealously to (فى *fî*); — VIII. INF. *irtiḫâḫ*, be soft, relaxed, weak, irresolute; be uncertain; be complicated.

رخ *raḫḫ*, soft, relaxed, irresolute; — *ruḫḫ*, pl. *riḫaḫa-t*, *riḫâḫ*, the fabulous bird Roc; castle in chess.

رخا *raḫan*, softness, relaxedness; INF. of (رخى); — *raḫâ'*, abundance, affluence, ease; — also *ruḫâ'*, softness, relaxedness, weakness; — *ruḫâ'*, breeze; — *raḫḫâ'*, pl. *raḫâḫiyy*, soft yielding ground.

رخاخ *raḫâḫ*, commodious, comfortable, at ease, soft; — *.

رخاصة *raḫâṣa-t*, cheapness; softness, flexibility, pliableness; delicateness of the body.

رخافة *raḫâfa-t*, thinness.

رخام *ruḫâm*, marble; alabaster; — ة *raḫâma-t*, softness, gentleness, tenderness; — *riḫâmat*, heavy stone; — *ruḫâma-t*, sun-dial; — ى *ruḫâma*, gentle breeze; — *ruḫâmiyy*, of marble.

رخاوة *rahâwa-t, ruhâwa-t*, softness, relaxedness; indifference.

رخائص *rahâ'iṣ*, pl. of رخصة *rahṣa-t*.

رخبين *rihbîn*, sour milk (Pers.).

رخت *raht*, pl. *ruhût*, household furniture, carpets, bedding, clothes; housings, saddle-cloth; — II. *rahha-t*, INF. *tarhît*, cover the horse with the saddle-cloth, with housings.

رخخة *rihaha-t*, pl. of رخ *ruhh*.

رخشة *rahśa-t*, movement; — V. INF. *tarahhuś*, move (n.); — VII. INF. *irtihâś*, be moved, agitated.

(رخص) *rahaṣ*, INF. *rahâṣa-t, ruhûṣa-t*, be soft, flexible, pliable, of a delicate frame; INF. *ruhś, ruhû-ṣa-t*, be cheap, get cheaper, fall in price; be kind towards (ل *li*); — II. INF. *tarhîṣ*, lower the price, sell cheap; soften, make pliable; make easier; show kindness, make an allowance, permit, grant leave or furlough; — IV. INF. *irhâṣ*, make cheap; find cheap; buy cheap; — VIII. INF. *irtihâṣ*, reckon cheap; find cheap; buy cheap; — X. INF. *istirhâṣ*, id.; wish to buy cheap.

رخص *rahṣ*, soft, pliable, delicate; — *ruhṣ*, cheapness; indulgence, permission; — ة *rahṣa-t*, pl. *rahâ'iṣ*, soft, delicate; — *ruhṣa-t, ruhu-ṣa-t*, benevolence; kindness; allowance; furlough; leave.

(رخف) *rahaf*, U; — *rahif*, A, INF. *rahaf*; — *rahuf*, INF. *rahâfa-t, ruhûfa-t*, be thin and watery.

رخف *rahf*, ة *rahfa-t*, pl. *rihâf*, cream, thin butter, watery dough, thin mud; — *rahfa-t*, pl. *rihâf*, pumice-stone.

(رخل) *rihl, rahil*, ة *rihla-t*, pl. *rihâl, ruhâl, arhul, rihlân, rihala-t, rahala-t*, lamb.

(رخم) *raham*, U, INF. *rahm*, be soft and pleasant; have a sweet voice; feel compassion; — I, U, A, INF. *rahm, raham, rahama-t*, soothe a child, play with it; — U, INF. *rahm, raham, raha..ıa-t*, sit on the eggs; — *rahim*, A, INF. *raham*, treat kindly; — *rahum*, INF. *rahâma-t*, be soft and pleasant; have a sweet voice; be smooth and level; — II. INF. *tarhîm*, have a soft voice; soften one's tone; slur over the last part of a name; execute in or lay out with marble; cause the hen to brood; — IV. INF. *irhâm*, brood.

رخم *raham*, thick milk; kindness, gentleness; noun of unity ة, a bird of the eagle kind; pelican; — also ة *rahama-t*, caress bestowed upon a child.

(رخو) see (رخى).

رخو *rahw, rihw, ruhw*, ة, soft, relaxed; thin; — *rihw, ruhw*, also ة *rihwa-t, ruhwa-t*, softness, relaxedness.

رخود *rihwadd*, ة, fleshy with delicate bones; — ة *rahwada-t*, delicacy; luxuriousness, luxury, abundance.

رخوصة *ruhûṣa-t*, cheapness; softness, flexibility.

رخوفة *ruhûfa-t*, thinness, wateriness.

(رخى) *rahî*, A, INF. *rahan, ruhâ', rihwa-t*, be soft, relaxed, loose, weak; — *rahû*, INF. *rahâwa-t*, id.; — *rahâ*, U, INF. *rahâ'*, also *rahî, rahû*, and pass. *ruhî*, live in affluence; — II. INF. *tarhîya-t*, soften, loosen, relax, unstring; — III. INF. *murâhât*, be near confinement; — IV. INF. *irhâ'*, soften, loosen; let down the veil or curtain; give the reins to the horse; let the beard grow long; let loose, let go, give up; — VI. INF. *tarâhî*, yield weakly, show one's self cowardly, lazy, negligent; desist, renounce; relax (n.); give up; be interrupted or abolished; — VIII. INF. *irtihâ'*, X. INF. *istirhâ'*, relax (n.); yield, renounce a claim; be thin.

رخى *rahiyy*, soft, relaxed; flexible;

thin ; commodious, spacious ; comfortable ; living in ease.

رخيخ *raḫîḫ*, soft; relaxed, weak, without vigour.

رخيص *raḫîṣ*, ة, cheap ; soft ; tender, delicate ; sudden and easy (death).

رخيفة *raḫîfa-t*, pl. *riḫâf*, lump of soft dough ; soft butter.

رخيم *raḫîm*, ة, soft (ة *raḫîma-t*, having a sweet voice, f.) ; soft and smooth.

(رد) *radd*, U, INF. *radd*, *riddîda*, *maradd*, *mardûd*, turn back, turn off, keep off ; refuse ; avert ; refute ; bring back, return, restore ; reply, answer ; revert ; bring back to a former state, to reason, to virtue ; shut the door or set it ajar ; vomit ; — II. INF. *tardâd*, *tardîd*, refuse or repel violently ; recall to memory ; — III. INF. *murâdda-t*, *ridâd*, return (a.), give back, requite ; oppose, fight ; — V. INF. *taraddud*, frequent (acc. or الى *ila*) ; be frequently refused or repelled ; remember or remind frequently ; waver ; alternate ; — VI. INF. *tarâdd*, reverse ; — VIII. INF. *irtidâd*, be brought back ; return (n.) ; recover (n.) ; be converted to (الى *ila*) ; apostatize (عن *'an*) ; — X. INF. *istirdâd*, demand back, take back, receive back.

رد *rad-in*, see ردى ; — *radd*, refusal ; repulse ; refutation ; hindrance ; restitution, return ; reply ; restoration to a former state ; vomiting ; bad ; worthless ; — *rid'*, helper ; help ; — ة *ridda-t*, return ; refusal, repulse ; repeated watering of the camels ; echo, burden (of a song) ; apostasy ; putting new soles to the shoes ; bran.

(ردا) *rada'*, INF. *rad'*, prop a wall ; give a support to ; assist, help ; pelt ; take good care of the camels ; — *radu'*, INF. *radâ'a-t*, be bad, corrupt ; — IV. INF. *irdâ'*, make bad, corrupt ; act badly or wickedly ; prop, support, assist, help ; consolidate ; calm down (a.) ; increase ; let down the veil.

ردا *rid'*, companion, fellow, helper ; help ; counterpoise ; load ; prop ; — *ridâ'*, pl. *ardiya-t*, wrapper, cloak ; jewelled girdle ; debts ; غمر الردا *gamr ar-ridâ'*, very liberal ; — ة *radât*, pl. *rada-n*, hard stone, rock ; — *ridât*, mantle, cloak ; — *radâ'a-t*, wickedness, INF. of (ردا).

رداح *radâḥ*, pl. *ruduḥ*, heavily laden ; having heavy hips ; having numerous camp-followers (army) ; large dish ; vast plain ; — ة *radâḥa-t*, den of a hyena.

رداد *radâd*, *ridâd*, repulse, aversion ; *ridâd*, opposition, INF. III. of (رد) ; — *raddâd*, who sets broken bones.

رداع *ridâ'*, thin mud ; — *rudâ'*, relapse ; indisposition ; — *raddâ'*, strong, efficacious ; — ة *ridâ'a-t*, trap or pit for wolves.

رداف *ridâf*, ى *rudâfa*, pl. of رديف *radîf* ; — ة *ridâfa-t*, rank next to the king or leader.

رداه *ridâh*, pl. of ردهة *radha-t*.

ردادة *radâwa-t*, badness, wickedness (m.).

(ردب) *radb*, trodden road which ceases suddenly ; — V. *taraddab*, INF. *taraddub*, treat kindly.

(ردج) *radaj*, U, INF. *radajân*, move slowly and step by step.

(ردح) *radaḥ*, INF. *radḥ*, enlarge the tent ; cement, loam ; be in good proportions ; perform one's business well.

ردح *ruduḥ*, pl. of رداح *radâḥ* ; — ة *rudḥa-t*, curtain before a bedroom ; piece put into the cloth of a tent to enlarge it ; opportunity ; — ى *rudḥiyy*, greengrocer.

(ردخ) *radaḥ*, INF. *radḥ*, break anything hollow.

(ردس) *radas*, U, I, INF. *rads*, pelt with large stones; break the walls; stamp or level the ground; — U, I, break one stone with another; go away with a thing; — V. INF. *taraddus*, fall down.

(ردع) *rada'*, INF. *rad'*, repel, keep off, hinder, prevent; dissuade, dehort, warn, make strong remonstrance; dye, stain; paint the nose with saffron, change colour, grow pale; fall on the ground and rebound; lie with; pass. *rudi'*, have a relapse; — VII. INF. *irridâ'*, VIII. INF. *irtidâ'*, be repelled, prevented, hindered; abstain; yield to remonstrance.

ردع *rad'*, hindrance, dissuasion, remonstrance; neck; saffron; stain of blood, saffron, ointment, &c.

(ردعل) *rida'l*, small, little.

(ردغ) *radig*, A, INF. *radag*, be loamy, muddy; — IV. INF. *irdâg*, id.; moisten; be scarce; — VIII. INF. *irtidâg*, fall into the mud.

ردغ *radig*, loamy, muddy; — ة *radga-t*, *radaga-t*, pl. *radg*, *radag*, *ridâg*, moist clay or loam; thick mud.

(ردف) *radaf*, U, INF. *radf*, come behind another, follow; rise in succession; — *radif*, A, INF. *radaf*, come behind, follow; — III. INF. *murâdafa-t*, squat one upon another, cluster; carry another rider behind; ride behind another on the same beast; be a reserve man; be substitute for a prince, &c.; be able to stand substitute for anyone, equal; be synonymous; — IV. INF. *irdâf*, come behind, follow, succeed; bid to mount behind another; take up a second rider; add; tow; — VI. INF. *tarâduf*, succeed one another; second; be synonymous; carry a second rider; — VIII. INF. *irtidâf*, mount or ride behind; attack in the rear; — X. INF. *istirdâf*, ask to be allowed to mount behind.

ردف *ridf*, pl. *ardâf*, hind part, croup; who mounts behind the rider; what follows or succeeds; substitute; viceroy; *ar-ridfân*, day and night.

(ردق) = (ردج).

(ردم) *radam*, I, INF. *radm*, stop a breach or hole, shut up, fill up a well with earth, obstruct; heap up rubbish; mend; — U, continue without interruption; — captivate; cause to resound; flow; green afresh; INF. *rudâm*, break wind; — V. INF. *taraddum*, mend, patch up; be worn and patched up; — VIII. INF. *irtidâm*, wear old patched-up clothes.

ردم *radm*, pl. *rudûm*, wall; boundary-wall; ruins of a wall; worthless, useless; — *rudum*, pl. of رديم *radîm*.

(ردن) *radan*, I, INF. *radn*, pile up and order; coil; spin; cause the fire to smoke; (m.) purr; — *radin*, A, INF. *radan*, be wrinkled, shrivelled; — II. INF. *tardîn*, IV. INF. *irdân*, put cuffs, fringes, &c., to a sleeve; — VIII. INF. *irtidân*, prepare a spindle or distaff for one's self.

ردن *rudn*, pl. *ardân*, cuff with fringes; sleeve; purse; — *radan*, spun silk; thread, in threads.

(رده) *radah*, INF. *radh*, pelt with stones; build a large house or palace; excel; — ة *radha-t*, pl. *radh*, *ridâh*, *ruddah*, pit with stagnating water; large house; palace; pl. *radah*, rocky hill.

(ردو) *radâ*, U, INF. *radw*, pelt with stones.

ردو *radu'*, see (ردا).

(ردى) *rada*, I, INF. *rady*, *radayân*, stamp the ground; go a moderate pace; go away; hop, walk in hops; hop on one foot;

grow, increase; surpass in number (above 50); run against; pelt with stones; break with a stone; fall into a well; — *radî*, A, INF. *radan*, perish, get annihilated, destroyed; — II. INF. *tardiya-t*, clothe with a wrapper or mantle; — IV. INF. *irdâ'*, ruin, destroy; cause to fall; urge the horse to a moderate pace; increase (n.); surpass fifty; — V. INF. *taraddî*, put on a wrapper or mantle, be clad with it; fall into a well from a mountain; — VIII. INF. *irtidâ'*, put on a wrapper or mantle; stamp the ground; go a moderate pace.

ردى *radî*, ة, bad, pernicious; — *radan*, INF. of the previous, destruction; — *radan*, pl. of رداة *radât*; — *radiyy*, ة, *radî'*, pl. *ardâ'*, *radî*, pl. *ardi'â'*, bad, worthless; — *raddî*, reprobate, wicked; — *rudda*, repudiated wife; — ة *ridya-t*, manner of wearing one's mantle.

رديحا *rudaiḥan*, during a long space of time.

رديدى *riddîda*, restitution, &c.; INF. of (رد).

رديف *radîf*, pl. *ridâf*, *rudâfa*, who rides behind another on the same beast; who comes behind another; reserve, reserve troops; addition; burden (of a song); constellation which rises when the opposite one sets; pl. *rudâfa*, who assist one another.

رديم *radîm*, pl. *rudum*, worn out and patched up; buried in rubbish.

رديني *rudainiyy*, ة *rudainiyya-t*, lance.

(رذ) *razz*, INF. *razâz*, also pass. *ruzz*, rain slightly; — IV. INF. *irzâz*, id.; leak.

رذاذ *razâz*, slight rain.

رذال *ruzâl*, *rizâl*, ة *ruzâla-t*, *rizâla-t*, rabble, dregs of the populace; pl. *arzila-t*, a worthless fellow; — ة *razâla-t*, meanness, villany, infamy; — ى *ruzâla*, pl. of رذيل *razîl*.

رذاة *ruzât*, pl. of رذى *raziyy*.

رذاوة *razâwa-t*, abject state.

رذايا *razâyâ*, pl. of رذية *raziyya-t*.

(رذل) *razil*, A, *razul*, U, INF. *razâla-t*, *ruzûla-t*, be mean, bad, reprobate, worthless; — *razal*, INF. *razl*, render worthless, bad, reprobate; lower, abase, degrade; despise; reject, disapprove; — II. INF. *tarzîl*, abase; despise; revile; — IV. INF. *irzâl*, render contemptible, despise, disdain, reject; keep bad company; — VI. INF. *tarâzul*, commit vile actions; be insolent towards (على *'ala*); — X. INF. *istirzâl*, deem vile and wicked; despise.

رذل *razl*, pl. *ruzûl*, *arzâl*, *ruzzal*, vile, abject, mean, impure, indecent, obscene.

رذلا *ruzalâ'*, pl. of رذيل *razîl*.

(رذم) *razam*, I, U, INF. *razm*, *ruzûm*, *razamân*, flow, run; — *razim*, A, INF. *razam*, be full to overflowing.

رذم *razam*, worn-out clothes; — *ruzum*, pl. of رذوم *ruzûm*.

رذولة *ruzûla-t*, meanness, vileness.

رذوم *ruzûm*, pl. *ruzum*, full to overflowing; fluid.

(رذى) *razî*, A, INF. *razâwa-t*, be jaded, emaciated; — IV. INF. *irzâ'*, jade, emaciate.

رذى *raziyy*, pl. *ruzât*, f. ة, pl. *razâyâ*, emaciated and jaded.

رذيل *razîl*, ة, pl. *ruzalâ'*, *ruzâla*, mean, vile, abject, wicked; *ruzâla*, abject rabble; — ة *razîla-t*, pl. *razâ'il*, anything worthless, bad; vile action or quality, vice.

(رز) *razz*, U, I, INF. *razz*, thrust the sting into the ground to lay ova; stick a thing into the earth, or one thing into another; pierce; patter with rain; — II. INF. *tarzîz*, polish, smooth; —

VIII. INF. *irtizâz*, refuse a request; stick in the target.

رز *rizz*, distant sound; rolling of thunder; — *ruzz*, rice; — *ruz'*, pl. *arzâ'*, damage, loss; calamity; — ة *razza-t*, pl. *-ât*, *razaz*, hinge, iron band of a bolt.

(رزا) *raza'*, A, INF. *ruz'*, diminish; (also VIII.) take forfeit from, damage; befall and harm; scoff or mock at; — INF. *ruz'*, *marzi'a-t*, accept a benefit, a present; — رزی *razi'*, diminish another's property; — VIII. INF. *irtizâ'*, see I.

رزادیق *razâdîq*, pl. of رزداق *ruzdâq*.

رزاز *razâz*, lead; — *razzâz*, rice-merchant.

رزاغ *rizâg*, pl. of رزغة *razaga-t*.

رزاق *razzâq*, the giver of the daily bread, God.

رزاقی *razâqîyy*, bunch of grapes (Pers.).

رزام *rizâm*, pl. *ruzzâm*, haughty and harsh; — *razzâm*, roaring.

رزان *razân*, modest woman; — *; — ة *razâna-t*, modesty; firmness of character and gravity of manners; weight.

رزايا *razâyâ*, pl. of رزئة *razi'a-t*.

(رزب) *razab*, U, INF. *razb*, adhere to the place, not stir from it.

(رزح) *razaḥ*, U, INF. *razâḥ*, *ruzâḥ*, break down from tiredness and emaciation; be jaded; be bad; — INF. *razḥ*, pierce with a lance; — II. INF. *tarzîḥ*, jade the camel.

(رزح) *ruzzaḥ*, رزحی *razha*, jaded and half-dead camels.

(رزخ) *razaḫ*, U, INF. *razḫ*, pierce with a lance.

رزداق *ruzdâq*, pl. *-ât*, *razâdîq*, market-town; district with a market.

رزدق *razdaq*, row, range.

(رزرز) *razraz*, INF. ة, move, shake (a.); counterpoise a load.

رزز *razaz*, pl. of رزة *razza-t*.

(رزغ) *razig*, A, INF. *razag*, stick in the mud; be in a plight; — III. INF. *murâzaga-t*, act invidiously towards; — IV. INF. *irzâg*, moisten the ground and produce mud; be very muddy; come in digging upon moist clay; be scarce; = X.; — X. INF. *istirzâg*, try to get hold of the property of one considered to be weak.

رزغ *razig*, sticking in the mud; in a plight; — ة *razaga-t*, pl. *razag*, *rizâg*, moist clay or loam, mud.

(رزف) *razaf*, I, INF. *razîf*, roar; hasten the pace, trot; hurry from fear; approach, come up; — IV. INF. *irzâf*, roar; come up.

رزفات *razafât*, pl. suburbs; surroundings, neighbourhood.

(رزق) *razaq*, U, INF. *razq*, give sustenance, the daily bread; preserve, feed, nourish; grant; pass. receive from God; — VIII. INF. *irtizâq*, receive or take the necessaries of life; — X. INF. *istirzâq*, pray for the necessaries of life.

رزق *rizq*, pl. *arzâq*, sustenance, daily bread, food; property, possessions, immovables; ration, pay, wages, pension; present; rain; — ة *razqa-t*, pl. *razaqât*, ration, pay; possessions; immovables.

(رزم) *razam*, I, U, INF. *razm*, wrap up, embale, make a packet of; — I, U, INF. *ruzâm*, *ruzûm*, be so weak and emaciated as not to be able to rise; die; accept, take; give birth; overthrow an adversary and kneel upon him; — II. INF. *tarzîm*, embale, pack up; make up a bundle; invade a country not to leave it again; — III. INF. *murâzama-t*, join two things; — IV. INF. *irzâm*, sound, roll; — ة *razma-t*, *rizma-t*, violent blow; — *rizma-t* (also *razma-t*, *ruzma-t*), pl. *rizam*, *razam*, *ruzam*, packet, bale;

bundle; sheaf; (m.) ream of paper; — *razama-t*, affectionate sound of a camel to its foal; roar.

(رزن) *razan*, U, INF. *razn*, lift up a thing to estimate its weight; stop, remain; — *razun*, INF. *razâna-t*, be heavy, weighty; show gravity, dignity, and perseverance; — V. INF. *tarazzun*, show one's self grave and persevering; bear one's self gravely; give one's self a dignified air; — VI. INF. *tarâzun*, stand opposite each other.

رزن *razn*, pl. *ruzûn*, *rizân*, elevated plain; — *rizn*, tract of land; side, edge; — ة *rizna-t*, pl. *rizân*, stagnating water; pond.

رزوح *ruzûḥ*, extreme tiredness.

رزوف *razûf*, long-legged; making long strides.

(رزى) *raza*, I, INF. *razy*, accept benefits from (acc.); — IV. INF. *irzâ'*, take refuge with anybody and rely on his protection.

رزى *ruzziyy*, rice-merchant; — ة *razî'a-t*, *raziyya-t*, pl. *razâyâ*, damage, injury; calamity; affliction.

رزيح *razîḥ*, jaded, emaciated.

رزيم *razîm*, roar.

رزين *razîn*, grave, dignified; heavy, weighty; dignity; — *razzîn*, wild maize (m.).

(رس) *rass*, U, INF. *rass*, dig a well; bury the dead; conceal, keep secret; pry into other people's circumstances; pacify, and, by opposition, stir up discord; repeat inwardly; = (رز); — III. INF. *murâssa-t*, begin; — VI. INF. *tarâss*, communicate secrets to one another, whisper to; — VIII. INF. *irtisâs*, become public.

رس *rass*, prelude; beginning; first symptoms of an illness, of love, &c.; well; — ة *rassa-t*, strong tree; mast; — *russa-t*, hat, cap.

رسابة *rasûba-t*, sediment.

رساتيق *rasâtîq*, pl. of رستاق *rustâq*.

رساعة *risâ'a-t*, pl. *rasâ'i'*, plaited strap as an ornament to the scabbard.

رسالة *risâla-t*, *rasâla-t*, pl. *-ât*, *rasâ'il*, mission, missive, message; messenger; letter; treatise; epistle; gift of prophecy; prophet; *rasâla-t*, apostolic mission; missionary work; missionaries; pl. *rasâ'il*, business transactions.

رسام *rassâm*, designer, draughtsman, drawer of maps, painter, writer; — ة *rasâma-t*, ordination of a priest.

رسائع *rasâ'i'*, pl. of رساعة *risâ'a-t*.

رسائل *rasâ'il*, pl. of رسالة *risâla-t*; — ى *rasâ'iliyy*, who reads the Epistle; sub-deacon.

(رسب) *rasab*, U, INF. *rusûb*, sink in water, settle (as sediment); be sunk; — *rasub*, sink in water; — IV. INF. *irsâb*, have the eyes sunk.

رستاق *rustâq*, *rastâq*, pl. *rasâtîq*, *rasâtiq*, market-town; fine country with villages and country-houses; camp; good order; peasant; corporal (Pers.).

(رستق) *rastaq*, INF. ة, order or arrange well, organise; tune an instrument; — II. INF. *tarastuq*, be well ordered, nicely arranged or laid out.

(رسح) *rasaḥ*, thinness of the hips; — IV. INF. *irsâḥ*, cause the hips to grow thin.

(رسخ) *rasaḥ*, U, INF. *rusûḥ*, be founded, established; be firm, solid; cake; dry up (n.); soak into the ground; — II. *tarsîḥ*, IV. INF. *irsâḥ*, establish, consolidate; impress deeply on the memory; — V. INF. *tarassuḥ*, be firmly established, consolidated.

رسداق *rusdâq* = رستاق *rustâq*.

(رسرس) *rasras*, INF. ة, be strong enough to rise under the load.

(رسع) *rasa'*, INF. *ras'*, have the eye-lids sticking together from illness; have the joints relaxed; bind an amulet against the evil eye to a child's hand or foot; — *rasi'*, A, INF. *rasa'*, be sore (eye) or have sore eyes; — II. INF. *tasrî'*, split a strap to plait another with it.

(رسغ) *rusg, rusug*, pl. *arsâg, arsug*, smallest part of a horse's foot; wrist; — *rasag*, weakness of the feet; — II. *rassag*, INF. *tarsîg*, cause the life to pass in affluence and comfort; arrange one's speech well; moisten the ground.

(رسف) *rasaf*, U, INF. *rasf, rasîf, rasafân*, walk as if the feet were tied together.

(رسل) *rasal*, INF. *rasl*, send a message or a messenger; — *rasil*, A, INF. *rasl*, hang down long; — INF. *rasl, risâla-t*, walk leisurely; — II. INF. *tarsîl*, be rich in milk; give abundantly milk to drink; — II. INF. *murâsala-t*, send to, correspond with; — IV. INF. *irsâl*, despatch, dismiss; send; bid to send; carry on negligently; compose a treatise; — V. INF. *tarassul*, act leisurely or negligently; read slowly; — VI. INF. *tarâsul*, send a message to one another; correspond; alternate (in versifying); — X. INF. *istirsâl*, show kindness or benevolence; have familiar intercourse; hang down long.

رسل *rasl*, ة, walking leisurely (adj.); hanging down (adj.); — *risl*, ة *risla-t, rasla-t*, ease, slowness, comfortableness, convenience; steadiness; milk of a pregnant animal; — *rusl, rusul*, pl. of رسول *rasûl*, رسيل *rasîl*; — *rusul*, girl yet unveiled.

رسلا *rusalâ'*, pl. of رسول *rasûl*, رسيل *rasîl*.

(رسم) *rasam*, U, INF. *rasm*, engrave lines or signs; impress traces; draw, sketch, delineate; write; seal, mark; prescribe, impose, fix a pay, &c.; institute a feast; consecrate or ordain a priest; — U, INF. *rasîm*, leave tracks or traces; — U, INF. *rasm*, conceal the traces, leaving them recoverable; be hidden in the ground, be dead; — II. INF. *tarsîm*, register, inscribe; prescribe, order; — IV. INF. *irsâm*, urge the camel to a vigorous pace; — V. INF. *tarassum*, investigate the traces of a dwelling; examine a place to build upon, to dig a well, &c.; — VIII. INF. *irtisâm*, receive a command; allow one's self to be commanded; obey; receive ordination.

رسم *rasm*, well; pl. *rusûm, arsum*, trace, impression, mark, line, stroke; drawing, map, sketch; plan of a building, outlines of the foundation, foundation; inscription; prescription, order, edict; tax, duty, impost; institution of a feast; pl. *rusûm, rusûma-t*, principles; fundamental rules, constitution, customs, ceremonial; taxes, duties, postage; — ى *rasmiyy*, ة, according to rule, normal, official, legitimate; pensioner, servant; *rasmiyyât*, prescriptions, rules, norms; duties, taxes, imposts.

(رسن) *rasan*, U, I, INF. *rasn*, tie with a rope; also IV. INF. *irsân*, halter a horse.

رسن *rasan*, pl. *arsun, arsân*, rope; nose-string; halter.

(رسو) *rasâ*, U, INF. *rasw, rusuww*, stand firm; keep one's stand; lie at anchor; be calm, grave, dignified; quote part of the traditions; INF. *rasw*, pacify; — III. INF. *murâsât*, vie in swimming; — IV. INF. *irsâ'*, consolidate; put at anchor; be firmly at anchor, well moored; — ة *raswa-t*, pl. رسى *risan*, bracelet.

رسوب rasûb, piercing, penetrating; gland of the penis; — rusûb, sediment.

رسوخ rusûḥ, ية rusûḥiyya-t, firmness; perseverance; firm stand; solidity.

رسول rasûl, pl. arsul, rusul, rusl, rusalâ', sent; envoy, ambassador, missionary, apostle, prophet; — ى rasûliyy, apostolic.

رسوم rasûm, imprinting traces or tracks;—rusûm, رسومات rusûmât, pl. of رسم rasm.

رسى rasiyy, firm, persevering, unshakable; solid; middle pole of a tent.

رسيس rasîs, prelude; beginning; first symptoms of an illness, love, &c.; anything firm, solid; prudent, intelligent; rumour.

رسيغ rasîg, abundant, comfortable.

رسيل rasîl, pl. rusalâ', rusul, arsul, sent; messenger; message; who sends or is sent to; partisan, follower, helper.

رسيم rasîm, a pace of the camel.

(رش) raśś, U, INF. raśś, tarśâś, sprinkle, shed, strew, sow; rain slightly; — IV. INF. irśâś, rain slightly; be large and bleed abundantly (wound); cause the horse to perspire, urge it to run; — V. INF. taraśśus, be sprinkled, sprinkled over.

رش raśś, pl. riśâś, sprinkling (s.); light rain; dew; — ة raśśa-t, thin jet of water; thin rain; shower.

(رشا) raśa', INF. raś', drop young ones; lie with.

رشا, رش raś', pl. arśâ', the young of a gazelle; — riśâ', pl. arśiya-t, string, rope; pedicle of a fruit; INF. III. of (رشو).

رشاح raśśâḥ, perspiring; running, flowing, leaking, oozing.

رشاد raśâd, entering on the right road; right direction; right and reasonable way of acting; victory, triumph; cress; — ة raśâda-t, justice; pl. raśâd, stone which fills the hand.

رشاش raśâś, sprinkling, trickling; noun of unity ة raśâśa-t, drop; — riśâś, pl. of رش raśś; — ة raśśâśa-t, sprinkle; watering-pot.

رشاقة raśâqa-t, skill, ability, subtility; beauty and elegance.

رشانة raśâna-t, parasitism.

رشبة ruśba-t, shell of a cocoa-nut used as a spoon.

(رشح) raśaḥ, perspire, drip with perspiration; leak, ooze; trickle; filter, strain; give little; bribe; skip; — II. INF. tarśîḥ, bring up; drill; feed or tend well; lick the newly-born young; bring on a cold; — IV. INF. irśâḥ, deem fit, suitable; — V. INF. taraśśuḥ, be well brought up; be fit, suitable; be able to walk; ooze; perspire; (m.) have a cold; — X. INF. istirśâḥ, rear, bring up, educate; be grown up.

رشح raśḥ, ة raśḥa-t, perspiring (s.); oozing (s.); filtering (s.); secretion; cold; — raśaḥ, sweat, perspiration.

(رشد) raśad, U, INF. ruśd, raśâd, enter on the right path, be well guided; (m.) be of age; — raśid, A, INF. raśad, id.; — IV. INF. irśâd, lead on the right path, guide, preserve from error; — VIII. INF. irtiśâd, X. INF. istirśâd, walk on the right path; be well guided or ask for guidance.

رشد ruśd, entering on the right path (s.); right conduct combined with firmness; — raśad, the right path; — ة raśda-t, riśda-t, lawful wedlock; — ى ruśdiyy, ة, reasonable, right, correct; — ية ruśdiyya-t, right guidance.

(رشرش) raśraś, INF. ة, be soft; be equal to the enemy, have

no need to fear him; (m.) besprinkle.

رهرش *raśraś*, رهراش *raśrâś*, soft bone; stale but soft bread.

(رهف) *raśaf*, U, I, INF. *raśf*; also *raśif*, A, INF. *raśaf*, and II. INF. *tarśîf*, IV., V. INF. *taraśśuf*, VIII. INF. *irtiśâf*, suck, sip; quaff; — IV. INF. *irśâf*, see I.; allow to suck or sip.

(رهق) *raśaq*, U, INF. *raśq*, throw or shoot at, pelt; — *raśuq*, INF. *raśâqa-t*, have an elegant figure; be skilful and subtle; perform quickly and skilfully; — III. INF. *murâśaqa-t*, throw or shoot at, pelt; travel with; — IV. INF. *irśâq*, throw or shoot at a place; fix the look sharply upon; stretch the neck.

رهق *riśq*, shot arrow, projectile, its flight; art of shooting; shot; — *raśaq*, pl. of رهيق *raśîq*; — *raśiq*, of elegant figure; skilful, nimble, agile.

رهك *riśk*, having a long beard.

(رهم) *raśam*, U, INF. *raśm*, write; mark the heaps of corn, mark; (m.) baptise a child in apprehension of death; halter a horse; — *raśim*, A, INF. *raśam*, smell a dish and covet it; — II. INF. *tarśîm*, write; — IV. INF. *irśâm*, mark; push forth leaves.

رهم *raśm*, marking; (m.) baptism of a dying child; — *raśam*, first sprouts of a seed; black spot on the face of a hyena; traces of rain; — ة *raśma-t*, muzzle; halter.

(رهن) *raśan*, U, INF. *raśn*, *ruśûn*, act the parasite, sponge; put the head into the pot (dog); — *raśun*, INF. *raśâna-t*, come uninvited to a meal or banquet, act the parasite.

رهن *raśn*, *raśan*, river-mouth.

(رهو) *raśû*, U, INF. *raśw*, bribe; be kind towards, assist; try to conciliate by a gift; — V. INF. *taraśśî*, confederate for mutual revenge; — VIII. INF. *irtiśâ'*, accept a present; allow one's self to be bribed; — X. INF. *istirśâ'*, ask for a bribe; — ة *raśwa-t*, *riśwa-t*, *ruśwa-t*, pl. رها,

رهى *ruśan*, *riśan*, *riśwât*, *riśawât*, present, bribe; dung.

رهيح *raśîḥ*, sweat, perspiration, exudation.

رهيد *raśîd*, who guides on the right path; well guided; hitting on the right thing, wise; — ة *raśîda-t*, Rosetta.

رهيف *raśîf*, sucking (s.).

رهيق *raśîq*, of an elegant figure; shooting fast.

(رص) *raṣṣ*, U, INF. *raṣṣ*, fit one thing to another and join them, cement; put into good order; press, press upon, beat; — II. INF. *tarṣîṣ*=I.; cover or glaze with lead; — VI. INF. *tarâṣuṣ*, be ranged; — ة *raṣṣa-t*, callosity; — *riṣṣa-t*, veil.

رصا *raṣṣâ'*, f. of ارص *araṣṣ*, having well-set teeth.

رصاد *raṣṣâd*, observer, watcher; astronomer, mathematician; custom-receiver; watch-tower, observatory; — *ruṣṣâd*, pl. of راصد *râṣid*, who observes, &c.; — *.

رصاص *raṣâṣ*, lead; tin; — *raṣṣâṣ*, tinker; — ة *raṣâṣa-t*, leaden ball, bullet; — *raṣṣâṣa-t*, miser; gutter-stones.

رصاع *raṣâ'*, sexual intercourse; — *raṣṣâ'*, who indulges frequently in it.

رصاغ *riṣâg*, tether for a horse.

رصاف *riṣâf*, pl. of رصيف *raṣîf*; — ة *raṣâfa-t*, firmness.

رصانة *raṣâna-t*, firmness, gravity, dignified manners.

(رصح) *raṣaḥ*, U, INF. *ruṣûḥ*, be firm, persevering.

(رصد) *raṣad*, U, INF. *raṣd*, *raṣad*, observe attentively, watch; waylay; — pass. *ruṣid*, get wetted by rain; — IV. INF. *irṣâd*, pre-

pare for, use for; requite; — V. INF. *taraṣṣud*, observe attentively; watch; fix the look sharply upon; expect, hope for; — VIII. INF. *irtiṣâd*, id.

رصد *raṣd*, *raṣad*, observation (بيت الرصد *bait ar-raṣd*, observatory); superintendence; guard; waylaying; *raṣd*, remainder (in a calculation); — *raṣad*, *riṣd*, pl. *arṣâd*, observer, watcher, guardsmen, satellites; — *ruṣṣad*, pl. of راصد *râṣid*, who observes, &c.; — ة *raṣda-t*, pl. *riṣâd*, heavy shower; — *ruṣda-t*, lion's den; ring in which the sword hangs at the belt.

(رصرص) *raṣraṣ*, INF. ة, consolidate; stand firm; load a gun.

(رصع) *raṣa'*, INF. *raṣ'*, beat with the hand, slap; grind between two stones; stab, wound deeply, make to penetrate deeply; INF. *raṣâ'*, lie with; INF. *ruṣû'*, stay, remain, abide; — *raṣi'*, A, INF. *raṣa'*, have thin hips; stick; be smeared with ointments; — II. INF. *tarṣî'*, join one thing to another; inlay with precious stones, gold, &c.; embroider; embellish, adorn; order, decree; — V. INF. *taraṣṣu'*, be inlaid with precious stones, gold, marble, &c.; be adorned.

(رصف) *raṣaf*, U, INF. *raṣf*, put stones side by side, make a pavement; join the feet in the praying posture; fix the head of an arrow; be fit, proper; — *raṣuf*, INF. *raṣâfa-t*, be firmly joined, solid; — VI. INF. *tarâṣuf*, be ranged, arrayed.

رصف *raṣf*, *raṣaf*, ة, stones put side by side, pavement; — ة *raṣfa-t*, pl. *riṣâf*, sinew to fix the head of an arrow.

رصفا *raṣfâ'*, woman with a narrow pelvis.

(رصم) *raṣam*, U, INF. *raṣm*, come to a narrow mountain-pass.

(رصن) *raṣan*, U, INF. *raṣn*, complete, finish; inveigh against; rebuke; — *raṣun*, INF. *raṣâna-t*, be firm, solid; — II. INF. *tarṣîn*, acquire thorough knowledge of a thing, master it; — IV. INF. *irṣân*, make firm, consolidate.

رصن *raṣn*, completion, conclusion.

(رصو) *raṣâ*, U, INF. *raṣw*, make firm, solid, consolidate; — IV. INF. *irṣâ'*, adhere to a place.

رصيد *raṣîd*, lying in ambush (adj.); observer.

رصيص *raṣîṣ*, piled up, ranged; veil which leaves only the eyes uncovered.

رصيعة *raṣî'a-t*, pl. *raṣâ'i'*, ornamental boss in belt, bridle, &c.; sword-ring; pounded wheat boiled with butter.

رصيف *raṣîf*, well and solidly worked or performed; firm, decisive; paved street, causeway; (m.) rocky place; pl. *riṣâf*, sinew of a horse.

رصين *raṣîn*, firm, solid, consolidated; firm of character, steady, dignified; ill, aching; benevolent, kind, favourable.

(رض) *raḍḍ*, U, INF. *raḍḍ*, break or pound coarsely; crush; bruise; — II. INF. *tarḍîd*, pound vehemently, bruise violently; — V. INF. *taraḍḍud*, be broken, pounded, bruised.

رض *raḍd*, dates dissolved in milk; — also ة *raḍḍa-t*, bruise, contusion.

رضا *riḍâ'*, agreeing (s.), consent, permission; being pleased (s.), favour; devotedness; — ة *ruḍât*, pl. of راضى, agreeing (adj.), consenting, &c.

رضاب *ruḍâb*, spittle (not ejected); grain; drop of dew; — *.

رضاض *ruḍâḍ*, large fragment.

رضاع *riḍâ'*, sucking (s.), INF. III. (رضع); — *raḍḍâ'*, suckling (adj., s.); miser; — *ruḍḍâ'*, pl. of راضع, sucking (adj.); — ة *raḍâ'a-t*, avarice, sordidness, filthiness;

south-west wind;—also *riḍâ'a-t*, sucking (s.).

(رضب) *raḍab*, U, INF. *raḍb* (also V.), suck the lips of the beloved one; stream violently;—V. INF. *taraḍḍub*, see I.

(رضح) *raḍah*, INF. *raḍh*, break, break into pieces;—V. INF. *taraḍḍuh*, pass. of the previous;—VIII. INF. *irtiḍâh*, excuse one's self, apologise.

(رضخ) *raḍaḥ*, A, INF. *raḍḥ*, break, smash; throw violently on the ground; pelt with stones; make a small present; dole out; (m.) submit to, obey.

(رضد) *raḍad*, U, INF. *raḍd*, pile upon one another.

رضراض *raḍrâḍ*, رضرض *raḍraḍ*, gravel, pebbles.

(رضرض) *raḍraḍ*, INF. ة, break into large pieces or fragments, pound; (m.) bruise;—II. INF. *taraḍruḍ*, pass. of the previous.

(رضع) *raḍi'*, A, *raḍa'*, I, INF. *raḍ'*, *raḍa'*, *raḍi'*, *raḍâ'*, *riḍâ'*, *raḍâ'a-t*, *riḍâ'a-t*, suck; ask for milk;—*raḍi'*, A, be mean, miserly, ungenerous;—II. INF. *tarḍî'*, IV. INF. *irḍâ'*, suckle, give suck;—VIII. INF. *irtiḍâ'*, suck, be suckled with; quaff; take in with the mother's milk.

رضع *raḍ'*, sucking (s.);—*raḍi'*, what is sucked; pl. *ruḍu'*, suckling, sucking child, &c.;—*ruḍḍa'*, pl. of راضع *râḍi'* and رضيع *raḍî'*, sucking (adj.).

رضعا *ruḍa'â'*, رضعان *ruḍa'ân*, pl. of رضيع *raḍî'*.

(رضف) *raḍaf*, I, INF. *raḍf*, roast, warm or boil by means of heated stones; cauterise; drop excrement; fold up a cushion or pillow.

رضف *raḍf*, ة *raḍfa-t*, heated stone; calamity;—ة *raḍfa-t*, *raḍafa-t*, pl. *raḍf*, *raḍaf*, bones of a horse between the knee-pan and the hollow of the knee.

(رضك), IV. *arḍak*, INF. *irḍâk*, open and close the eyes alternately.

(رضم) *raḍam*, I, INF. *raḍm*, walk slowly and heavily; trip; furrow, till; sit always at home; throw on the ground; throw one's self on the ground; pile up stones, build, pave;—INF. *raḍamân*, make short steps.

رضم *raḍm*, *raḍam*, ة, also رضام *riḍâm*, large stone for building.

(رضو) *raḍâ*, U, INF. *raḍw*, overcome one's displeasure, content, satisfy;—رضى *raḍî*, A, INF. *riḍ-an*, *ruḍ-an*, *riḍwân*, *ruḍwân*, *marḍât*, be content, pleased with; declare one's self satisfied, consent, agree; accept one's favour;—III. INF. *murâḍât*, *riḍâ'*, try to satisfy, conciliate, try to reconcile to an enemy; try to please better than another;—IV. INF. *irḍâ'*, satisfy; gratify; move to consent;—V. INF. *taraḍḍî*, try to satisfy, to please;—VI. INF. *tarâḍî*, be satisfied with one another; get reconciled to one another; agree;—VIII. INF. *irtiḍâ'*, be satisfied with; approve; think fit for one's service or company, consider as the right man;—X. INF. *istirḍâ'* =V.; beg to be satisfied or to consent.

رضوان *riḍwân*, *ruḍwân*, consent, approval, being pleased with, favour; blessing; Paradise, the angel of Paradise; INF. of (رضو);—*riḍawân*, du. of رضى, رضا *riḍan*.

(رضى) see (رضو).

رضى *raḍî*, pl. *raḍûn*, satisfied, content, agreeing (adj.);—also رضا *riḍ-an*, du. *riḍawân*, *riḍayân*, consent, approval, being well pleased (s.); favour;—*raḍiyy*, pl. *arḍiyâ'*, satisfied, content; agreeable; desirable.

رضيح *raḍîh*, broken.

رضيد *raḍîd*, piled up.

رضيض *raḍîḍ*, coarsely pounded.

رضيع *raḍî'*, pl. *ruḍḍâ'*, *riḍâ'*, *raḍâ'i'*, *raḍḍa'*, *ruḍa'â'*, *ruḍa'ân*, suckling, child at the mother's breast; foster-brother.

رضيم *raḍîm*, built solidly in stone.

(رط), IV. *araṭṭ*, INF. *irṭâṭ*, be stupid; scream, be noisy, boisterous; not stir from the place.

(رطا) *raṭa'*, INF. *raṭ'*, lie with; drop excrement; discontent; — IV. INF. *irṭâ'*, become marriageable; — X. INF. *istirṭâ'*, grow stupid, mad.

رطا *raṭa'*, stupidity, folly, madness; — *raṭ'â'*, pl. *raṭ'a'ât*, stupid (woman); — *riṭâ'*, pl. of رطى *raṭiyy*.

رطابة *raṭâba-t*, freshness and delicacy.

رطازات *ruṭâzât*, fables, fairy-tales, wonderful stories.

رطاط *riṭâṭ*, رطائط *raṭâ'iṭ*, pl. of رطيط *raṭîṭ*.

رطانة *raṭâna-t*, foreign and barbarous language.

(رطب) *raṭab*, U, INF. *raṭâba-t*, be ripe, fresh and juicy; — INF. *raṭb*, *ruṭûb*, feed (a.) on fresh dates, feed the cattle on fresh herbs; — *raṭib*, be fresh, juicy, moist and delicate; — *raṭub*, INF. *raṭâba-t*, *ruṭûba-t*, id.; — II. INF. *tarṭîb*, moisten, wet; feed (a.) on fresh dates; — IV. INF. *irṭâb*, have just grown ripe, be fresh and juicy; bear such dates; — V. INF. *taraṭṭub*, get moistened.

رطب *raṭb*, *raṭib*, ة, moist; fresh and tender; pliable of character; لولو رطب *lu'lu' raṭb*, precious pearl; — *ruṭb*, *ruṭub*, ة *ruṭba-t*, *ruṭuba-t*, fresh herbage and foliage; moisture; — *ruṭab*, ة, pl. *arṭâb*, *riṭâb*, ripe date, still fresh and juicy; — ة *raṭba-t*, pl. *riṭâb*, fresh green fodder, especially clover; delicate girl.

(رطز) *raṭaz*, weak; dull; thin; — U, INF. *raṭz*, sprawl, kick about; skip (m.).

رطزات *raṭazât*=رطازات *ruṭâzât*.

(رطس) *raṭas*, I, INF. *raṭs*, beat with the palm of the hand, slap.

(رطع) *raṭa'*, INF. *raṭ'*, lie with.

(رطل) *raṭal*, U, INF. *raṭl*, run; weigh with the hand; — II. INF. *tarṭîl*, make the hair soft by ointments, &c.; weigh by pounds; — V. INF. *taraṭṭul*, walk with difficulty; be weak of limbs, be soft.

رطل *raṭl*, *riṭl*, pl. *arṭâl*, pound of 12 ounces; a wine-measure= ½ من *mann*; — *raṭl*, *raṭil*, weak in the limbs.

(رطم) *raṭam*, U, INF. *raṭm*, throw into the mud; entangle in difficulties or unpleasant things; drop excrement; — VIII. INF. *irtiṭâm*, be thrown into the mud; be hopelessly entangled; — ة *ruṭma-t*, great plight; hopeless entanglement.

(رطن) *raṭan*, U, INF. *raṭâna-t*, *riṭâna-t*, speak to in a foreign language, not Arabic; mumble, mutter to; — III. INF. *murâṭana-t*, id.; — VI. INF. *tarâṭun*, speak in such a way or mutter to one another.

(رطو) *raṭâ*, U, INF. *raṭw*, lie with.

رطوبة *ruṭûba-t*, moisture; freshness; tenderness, delicacy.

رطى *raṭî'*, *raṭiyy*, ة, pl. *riṭâ'*, stupid; dull.

رطيب *raṭîb*, moist, fresh and tender; pliable, supple; pl. *riṭâb*, ripe and juicy.

رطيط *raṭîṭ*, pl. *riṭâṭ*, *raṭâ'iṭ*, clamour, tumult; folly, madness; foolish, mad.

رطينا, رطينى *ruṭaina*, unintelligible or barbarous language, mutter.

(رع) *ra''*, U, INF. *ra''*, subside, calm down, be calm; — ة *ri'a-t*, abstinence from anything unlawful; victim, sacrifice.

رعا *ri'â'*, ة *ru'ât*, pl. of راعى *râ'i*, herdsman.
رعاب *ru'âb*, cry of the ostrich.
رعابيب *ra'âbîb*, pl. of رعبوب *ru'bûb*.
رعابيل *ra'âbîl*, pl. of رعبلة *ri'bala-t* and رعبولة *ru'bûla-t*.
رعاد *ra''âd*, thundering; torpedo-fish.
رعاس *ra''âs*, trembling.
(رعاع) *ra'â'*, wicked young people; rabble;—ة *ra'â'a-t*, female ostrich.
رعاف *ru'âf*, bleeding from the nose (s.); hæmorrhage.
رعافى *ru'âfiyy*, liberal, generous.
رعال *ru'âl*, mucus;—*;—ة *ra'âla-t*, stupidity; folly.
رعام *ra'âm*, sharpness of sight;—*ru'âm*, pl. *ar'ima-t*, mucus of diseased sheep.
رعايا *ra'âyâ*, pl. of رعية *ra'iyya-t*.
رعاية *ri'âya-t*, protection, guard, tending of a flock; regard, observance; kindness, indulgence, favour; (m.) itch, cancer, gangrene.
(رعب) *ra'ab*, INF. *ra'b*, frighten, terrify; threaten; fill a basin; cut off;—INF. *ru'b*, coo loudly; frighten; be afraid, fear;—II. INF. *tar'îb*, IV. INF. *ir'âb*, frighten; threaten;—VIII. INF. *irti'âb*, frighten; be afraid, fear.
رعب *ru'b*, fright, fear; pl. *ri'aba-t*, hole into which the head of a spear or arrow is placed.
(رعبل) *ra'bal*, INF. ة, cut into pieces; tear; break; marry a stupid woman.
رعبل *ra'bal*, wearing tattered clothes; stupid (woman);—ة *ri'bala-t*, pl. *ra'âbil*, id.; torn.
رعبوب *ru'bûb*, pl. *ra'âbîb*, very timorous; weak;—also ة *ru-bûba-t* and رعبيب *ri'bîb*, tall and at the same time delicate girl; piece of a camel's hump.
رعبولة *ru'bûla-t*, pl. *ra'bâ'il*, torn garment.
(رعث) *ra'as̱*, INF. *ra's̱*, bite and take some flesh off; have flesh-lappets with white-points hanging from the neck (goat);—*ra'is̱*, A, INF. *ra'as̱*, id.;—V. INF. *tara''us̱*, VIII. INF. *irti'âs̱*, wear ornaments for the ear.
رعث *ra's̱*, *ra'as̱*, ة *ra's̱a-t*, *ra'as̱a-t*, woollen tassel of a litter; ة, pl. *ri'âs̱*, ear-ring, pendant; pl. *ra'as̱ât*, flesh-lappet of a cock, sheep, &c.
(رعج) *ra'aj*, INF. *ra'j*, move (a.), agitate; enrich; flash continually;—*ra'ij*, A, INF. *ra'aj*, be very numerous;—IV. INF. *ir'âj*, agitate, disquiet; grow rich;—VIII. INF. *irti'âj*, be moved, agitated, disquieted.
(رعد) *ra'ad*, A, U, INF. *ra'd*, thunder; frighten, terrify, threaten, thunder against; show one's self in shining ornaments, sparkle with jewellery;—IV. INF. *ir'âd*, thunder; threaten; be struck by a thunder-bolt; pass. be seized with fear, tremble;—VIII. INF. *irti'âd*, tremble with terror, be violently agitated.
رعد *ra'd*, pl. *ru'ûd*, thunder, thunder-clap; ذات ر *zât-u ra'd-in*, war;—ة *ra'da-t*, *ri'da-t*, trembling, shivering; fear, terror.
رعديد *ri'dîd*, pl. *ra'âdîd*, very timorous; (m.) blockhead.
(رعرع) *ra'ra'*, INF. ة, cause to thrive; train a horse; shine and wave to and fro;—II. thrive and grow; be nimble, agile; be rickety, move loosely.
رعرع *ra'ra'*, *ru'ru'*, also رعراع *ra'râ'*, pl. *ra'âri'*, tall, handsome youth.
(رعز) *ra'az*, U, INF. *ra'z*, lie with;—III. INF. *murâ'aza-t*, be shrunk, contracted.
(رعس) *ra'as*, INF. *ra's*, tremble; walk slowly; INF. *ra'asân*, tremble, shake (n.).
(رعش) *ra'aś*, INF. *ra'ś*, and *ra'iś*, A, INF. *ra'aś*, tremble, shake (n.);—IV. INF. *ir'âś*, cause to

tremble ; — VIII. INF. *irti'âś* =I.

رعش *ra'aś*, trembling, shaking (s.); convulsions ; — *ra'iś*, trembling (adj.); timid, timorous ; — ة *ra'śa-t*, *ri'śa-t*, fit of trembling, convulsion, violent agitation.

رعشن *ra'śan*, رعشيش *ra'śîś*, trembling, timid, timorous ; — *ra'śan*, m., رعشا *ra'śâ'*, f., quick, swift, fleet.

(رعص) *ra'aṣ*, INF. *ra'ṣ*, move (a.), shake (a.), pull, draw, drag ; — IV., INF. *ir'âṣ*, id. ; — V. INF. *tara''uṣ*, VIII. INF. *irti'âṣ*, wind itself, writhe ; be shaken ; VIII. tremble violently ; rise (price).

(رعظ) *ra'aẕ*, INF. *ra'ẕ*, make a hole in a spear or arrow to fix in the head, or break either at that part ; — *ra'iẕ*, A, INF. *ra'aẕ*, break (n.) there.

رعظ *ru'ẕ*, pl. *ar'âẕ*, hole in a spear or arrow to fix the head in.

(رعف) *ra'af*, A, U, INF. *ra'f*, *ru'âf*, bleed from the nose ; bleed ; — U, A, INF. *ra'f*, get the lead in running ; — *ra'if*, A, INF. *ra'af*, flow from the nose, flow ; — *ra'uf* and pass. *ru'if*, id. ; — IV. INF. *ir'âf*, urge to make haste ; fill ; — V. INF. *tara''uf*, bleed from the nose ; — VIII. INF. *irti'âf*, step up, advance ; — X. INF. *istir'âf*, id.

(رعق) *ra'aq*, INF. *ra'q*, *ra'îq*, make a rumbling noise.

(رعل) *ra'al*, INF. *ra'l*, pierce with a spear ; strike with a sword ; — *ra'il*, A, INF. *ra'al*, be stupid, imbecile ; — II. INF. *tar'îl*, make an incision in a camel's or sheep's ear ; — IV. INF. *ir'âl*=I. ; — X. INF. *istir'âl*, walk behind one another ; precede ; — ة *ra'la-t*, pl. *ri'âl*, *ar'âl*, *arâ'il*, herd, troop (20 to 25), the foremost in a troop ; many servants, numerous family ; palm-tree ; ابو رعلة *abû ri'la-t*, wolf.

(رعم) *ra'am*, INF. *ru'âm*, be very thin and suffer from a flow of mucus (sheep) ; — U, INF. *ra'm*, observe, contemplate ; guard, watch over ; — *ra'um*, INF. *ra'â-ma-t*, be thin and suffer from a flow of mucus.

رعم *ri'm*, fat ; ام رعم *umm-u ri'm-in*, hyena.

(رعن) *ra'an*, U, INF. *ra'n*, be relaxed, soft, cowardly ; be stupid ; be big but stupid ; — *ra'in*, A, INF. *ra'an*, also *ra'un*, INF. *ru'ûna-t*, id.

رعن *ra'n*, pl. *ri'ân*, *ru'un*, jutting part of a mountain ; promontory ; mountain-chain ; — *ra'an*, relaxation ; — *ru'un*, pl. girls.

رعنا *ra'nâ'*, soft, delicate ; Balsorah ; f. of ارعن, talkative, stupid, &c.

(رعو) *ra'â*, U, INF. *ra'w*, *ri'w*, *ru'w*, *ra'wa-t*, *ri'wa-t*, *ru'wa-t*, *ru'yâ*, acknowledge and desist from an error or a sin, abstain from what is unlawful ; — VIII. INF. ارعا *irdi'â'*, id. ; — *ir'awa*, INF. *ir'iwâ'*, id. ; — ة *ra'wa-t*, *ri'wa-t*, *ru'wa-t*, رعوى *ra'wan*, *ri'wan*, *ru'wan*, guarding one's self from error or sin, abstinence from what is unlawful ; turning back from evil, conversion.

رعوس *ra'ûs*, trembling.

رعولى *ra'waliyy*, badly roasted.

رعونة *ra'ûna-t*, laxity, relaxedness, softness ; cowardice ; stupidity.

(رعى) *ra'a*, INF. *ra'y*, *mar'an*, *ri'âya-t*, browse, graze, pasture freely ; tend the cattle ; allow the cattle to graze ; be a herdsman ; INF. *ri'âya-t*, govern, guard, take care of, administer, be dutiful ; INF. *ra'y*, observe the setting of the stars ; observe good manners and decency, have regard to ; — III. INF. *murâ'ât*, graze together with another animal ; observe the setting of the stars, the course of events ; have friendly regard for, guard, take care of, manage, administer ;

(m.) cause an itching on the skin; — IV. INF. *ir'â'*, lead to the pasture, pasture (a.); have plenty of green food; spare one's life; lend one's ear to, listen; — V. INF. *tara''i*, VIII. INF. *irti'â'*, pasture (n.), graze, browse; — X. INF. *istir'â'*, beg to take care of or protect; ask permission for pasturing on another's ground.

رعى *ra'y*, pasturing (s.); — *ri'y*, pl. *ar'â'*, green food, pasture; — *ra'iyy*, pastured, tended; guarded, protected; — ة *ri'ya-t*, pasturing, grazing, browsing (s.); — *ra'iyya-t*, pl. *ra'âyâ*, pasturing flock; subjects, subject; parish.

رعيا *ru'yâ*, guard, care and the object of it; INF. of (رعى).

رعيان *ru'yân*, pl. of راعى *râ'i*, herdsman, &c.

رعيب *ra'îb*, frightened; dripping with fat.

رعيدا *ru'aidâ'*, chips, parings.

رعيق *ra'îq*, rumbling noise in the bowels.

رغا *rugâ'*, cry, roar.

رغام *ragâm*, sand and dust; soft ground; — *rugâm*, mucus, snot.

رغاوة *rugâwa-t*, *rigâwa-t*, foam, froth, syllabub.

(رغب) *ragib*, A, INF. *ragb*, *rugb*, *ragba-t*, desire, crave, wish for, incline to (الى *ila*); turn away from, be averse (عن *'an*); — INF. *ragab*, *rugba-t*, *ragba-t*, رغبى *ragba*, *rugba*, *ragbâ'*, *ragabân*, *ragabût*, رغبوتى *ragabûta*, call humbly and fervently on God, pray; entreat humbly and instantly; — *ragub*, INF. *rugb*, *rugub*, be greedy and voracious; be wide and spacious; — II. INF. *targîb*, inspire with a desire, cause to wish for; incite, encourage; fill with aversion, turn from; — III. INF. *murâgaba-t*, show one's self eager; — IV. INF. *irgâb*=II.; — VIII. INF. *irtigâb*, desire, wish for.

رغب *rugb*, craving (s.), greed, greediness; voraciousness; — *ragab*, craving, longing for, love; — ة *ragba-t*, ardent desire, longing for, wish; eagerness, zeal, diligence; courage; anything desired, object of a wish; preference; esteem, sympathy, inclination, affection; pleasure in a thing.

(رغث) *ragas*, A, INF. *rags*, suck; pierce repeatedly; have one's means exhausted by bestowing on beggars, &c.; — IV. INF. *irgâs*, suckle, give suck; — VIII. INF. *irtigâs*, suck.

رغثا *rugasâ'*, du. *rugasâwân*, base of the udder; milk-veins.

(رغد) *ragid*, A, INF. *ragad*, be blessed with everything that is good, live in affluence; — *ragud*, INF. *ragâda-t*, id.; — IV. INF. *irgâd*, rejoice in abundant pastures or crops, live in ease and affluence; — X. INF. *istirgâd*, consider one's life plentiful or blessed.

رغد *ragd*, life in ease and affluence; abundant and pleasant; — *ragad*, id.; people who live in ease and affluence.

(رغرغ) *ragrag*, INF. ة, live in affluence; lead the camels to water whenever they like.

(رغز), X. *istargaz*, INF. *istirgâz*, consider weak, soft.

(رغس) *ragas*, INF. *rags*, grant riches to, enrich; make numerous, multiply; — IV. INF. *irgâs*, id.; — X. INF. *istirgâs*, consider weak and soft.

رغس *rags*, riches, wealth; pl. *argâs*, gift, present, favour, blessing.

(رغش) *ragaś*, INF. *ragś*, excite a tumult, revolt against; stir up mischief; — II. INF. *targîś*, increase (a.).

(رغف) *ragaf*, INF. *ragf*, ball,

knead; — IV. INF. *irgâf*, sharpen one's look upon; walk fast.

رغف *ruguf*, رغفان *rugfân*, pl. of رغيف *ragîf*.

(رغل) *ragal*, INF. *rugl*, suck; — IV. INF. *irgâl*, suckle, give suck; form into grain (corn); lean towards, err.

رغل *ragl*, corn just forming into grain; — ة *rugla-t*, prepuce.

(رغلد), III. *irgaladd*, INF. *irgildâd*, live in affluence.

(رغم) *ragam*, INF. *ragm*, compel; do in spite of; humiliate; feel aversion or disgust for; — *ragim*, A, feel aversion, disgust; be humbled and despised; — II. INF. *targîm*, say to a person رغما رغما *ragm-an ragm-an*, humiliation upon you! — III. INF. *murâgama-t*, feel aversion, disgust, abhorrence; provoke to anger; get angry; shun, avoid; treat with hostility; — IV. INF. *irgâm*, push one's nose into the dust, humble, humiliate; compel, force; provoke to anger; torment, vex, oppress, hinder; blacken one's face, i.e., cause him to be despised; — V. INF. *taraggum*, be angry; cry out, roar (camel).

رغم *ragm*, aversion, abhorrence; anger; compulsion, force, violence; humiliation, contempt, insult; rind, skin; *ragm-an*, against one's will, in spite of.

(رغن) *ragan*, INF. *ragn*, lend a favourable ear; eat and drink with enjoyment; desire, wish for; lean upon; — IV. INF. *irgân*, lend a favourable ear; inspire with longing for; ease, facilitate; despise.

رغن *raganna*, perhaps.

(رغو) *ragâ*, U, INF. *rugâ'*, *ragawân*, cry out, roar; bellow; cry violently (child); — رغى *raga*, رغا *ragâ*, U, INF. *ragw*, be covered with foam or froth, effervesce; — II. INF. *targiya-t*, cause to foam or effervesce; provoke to anger; — IV. INF. *irgâ'*, cause to roar or bellow; roar, bellow, clamour; foam, throw up froth; scum, remove the froth, &c.; — VI. INF. *tarâgî*, roar to one another; — VIII. INF. *irtigâ'*, drink the froth off the milk.

رغو *raguww*, roaring much; — ة *ragwa-t*, *rigwa-t*, *rugwa-t*, pl. رغى *rugan*, foam, froth; effervescence; thin skin upon the milk; — *ragwa-t*, rock.

رغيب *ragîb*, ة, desired, wished for; esteemed, valued; greedy, voracious, avaricious; pl. *rigâb*, yielding much milk; deep and large; spacious; — ة *ragîba-t*, pl. *ragâ'ib*, anything desirable; valuable present; riches, wealth; *ar-ragâ'ib*, supererogations; ليلة الرغائب *lailat-u 'r-ragâ'ib*, night of Mohammed's birth.

رغيد *ragîd*, easy and affluent; living in ease and affluence; pleasant; — ة *ragîda-t*, milk-pap.

رغيغة *ragîga-t*, life in ease and affluence.

رغيف *ragîf*, pl. *argifa-t*, *ruguf*, *rugfân*, *tarâgîf*, flat cake or loaf, roll.

(رف) *raff*, U, I, INF. *raff*, spread the wings for flying; wink; suck; eat much; eat or kiss with the edge of the lips; be eager for, crave; be easily induced; surround from all sides and protect; treat kindly; honour; be serviceable in everything; — I, INF. *raff*, *rafîf*, shine, gleam; — for *rafif*, A, INF. *rafaf*, be thin; — IV. INF. *irfâf*, spread the wings (over the eggs); — VIII. INF. *irtifâf*, shine, be bright, gleam.

رف *raff*, pl. *rufûf*, large sill, cornice, sideboard of shelves; board, deal; arch; herd; fold for cattle; swarm, flock; daily fit of a fever; — *ruff*, straw,

chaff ; — ة *rifa-t*, greening (adj.) ; — *rufa-t*, fig ; also *ruf-fa-t*, straw, chopped straw ; — *raffa-t*, a draught of milk ; برفة عين *bi-raffat-i 'ain-in*, in a trice.

(رفا) *rafa'*, INF. *raf'*, mend anything torn ; re-establish a friendship, make peace ; quiet, free from fear ; bring a ship near the land ; — II. INF. *tarfî'*, *tarfi'a-t*, congratulate a newly-married couple with the words بالرفا و البنين *bi 'r-rifâ'-i wa 'l-banîna*, live in peace and enjoyment of children ; — III. INF. *murâfa'a-t*, show personal regard to, flatter, cajole ; — IV. INF. *irfâ'*, lean to the side ; approach ; bring near ; comb hair and beard ; take refuge with ; = III. ; — VI. INF. *tarâfu'*, agree and work into one another's hands.

رفا *rifâ'*, concord, peace ; — *rufâ'*, rag, tatter ; — *raffâ'*, who mends, patches up.

رفات *rufât*, anything broken into small pieces ; broken bones.

رفادة *rifâda-t*, bandage ; saddle-cushion.

رفاض *rafâḍ*, fragment.

رفاع *rafâ'*, abundant crops on the field ; — also *rifâ'*, bringing in of the sheaves ; (m.) carnival ; — *raffâ'*, who lifts up, raises ; — ة *rafâ'a-t*, *rifâ'a-t*, *rufâ'a-t*, raising of the voice ; — *rifâ'a-t*, elevation ; high rank ; authority ; subtlety, fineness ; — *rifâ'a-t*, *rufâ'a-t*, hip-improvers.

رفاغة *rafâġa-t*, abundance, affluence.

رفاغية *rafâġiyya-t*, pleasant life.

رفاق *rifâq*, companionship on a journey ; assistance, help ; rope to tie up a camel ; pl. of رفقة *rafqa-t* and رفيق *rafîq* ; — ة *rafâqa-t*, sociability ; kindness ; friendly help ; — *rufâqa-t*, travelling-company.

رفال *rafâl*, flowing down (hair).

رفاهة *rafâha-t*, رفاهية *rafâhiyya-t*, ease and affluence ; comfort ; enjoyment of life.

(رفت) *rafat*, U, I, INF. *raft*, break into small pieces ; smash a bone ; be broken into small fragments ; be abrupt, fragmentary, a fragment ; (m.) refuse, reject, push aside ; — II. INF. *tarfît*, (m.) pay transit-duty ; — IX. INF. *irtifât*, be broken, abrupt, fragmentary, a fragment ; be torn.

رفت *rufat*, who breaks everything ; straw, chaff.

رفتية *raftiyya-t*, transit-duty (m.).

رفث *rafa<u>s</u>*, U, INF. *raf<u>s</u>*, *rufû<u>s</u>*, also *rafi<u>s</u>*, A, INF. *rafa<u>s</u>*, and *rafu<u>s</u>*, talk obscenities (to a woman) ; lie with ; — IV. INF. *irfâ<u>s</u>*, talk ribaldry.

(رفح), II. *raffaḥ*, INF. *tarfîḥ*, congratulate a newly-married couple.

(رفخ) *rafaḫ*, also V. INF. *taraffuḫ*, rise ; swell (m.).

(رفد) *rafad*, I, INF. *rafd*, give for a present, give ; help, assist ; (also IV.) put the saddle-cloth on a beast ; lift, lift up ; — II. INF. *tarfîd*, honour, raise to great dignity ; — III. INF. *murâfada-t*, make a present ; help, assist ; — IV. INF. *irfâd*, see I. ; present with ; — VI. INF. *tarâfud*, assist one another ; — VIII. INF. *irtifâd*, acquire ; gain ; — X. INF. *istirfâd*, ask for a present or help.

رفد *rafd*, saddle-cloth ; — also *rifd*, large cup ; — *rifd*, pl. *rufûd*, *arfâd*, present, gift, benefit, favour ; help, assistance.

رفدان *rufadân*, soft boiled egg (m.).

رفراف *rafrâf*, a kind of finch ; ostrich.

(رفرف) *rafraf*, INF. ة, spread the wings ; wish well to, protect

(على *'ala*); circle round the hen; sound, resound.

رفرف *rafraf*, pl. *rafârif*, sill, shelf, sideboard of shelves; a green cloth for bedding; bed, pillow; cushion of the blessed in Paradise; lappet, anything hanging; hanging branches, ornament of a helmet, &c.; arch, window.

(رفز) *rafaz*, I, INF. *rafz*, beat; throb.

(رفس) *rafas*, I, U, INF. *rafs*, *rifâs*, kick; tie up the camel with a rope (رفاس *rifâs*), (m.) have a strong tension.

رفس *rafs*, ة, kicking (s.); *rafs*, key-stone.

(رفش) *rafaś*, U, INF. *rafś*, shovel away; diminish, grind, pound; eat and drink well; INF. *rufûś*, spend much on a thing; — *rafiś*, A, INF. *rafaś*, have large ears; — II. INF. *tarfiś*, let the beard grow long (like a shovel); —IV. INF. *irfâś*, live luxuriously; stop in a place.

رفش *rafś*, *rufś*, shovel; shoulder-blade; الرفش و القفش *ar-rafś wa 'l-qafś*, indulging in food and sexual enjoyment.

(رفص) *rafaṣ*, INF. *rafṣ*, kick; have a strong tension; threaten to fall in; — VI. INF. *tarâfuṣ*, draw water in turns; — VIII. INF. *irtifâṣ*, become dear, expensive; — ة *rufṣa-t*, turn, opportunity.

(رفض) *rafaḍ*, I, U, INF. *rafḍ*, *rufûḍ*, abandon, forsake, leave in the lurch; allow to pasture freely; give up, let go, renounce, reject; throw, fling; be large; begin to cluster; — U, INF. *rufûḍ*, pasture freely; — II. INF. *tarfîḍ*, leave little water in the skin bag; — IV. INF. *irfâḍ*, allow the camels to pasture freely; — V. INF. *taraffuḍ*, disperse and disappear; get broken; leave or renounce one's people, one's religion, desert; — VI. INF. *tarâfuḍ*, break forth, flow; — VII. INF. *irrifâḍ*, be forsaken, rejected, spurned; — IX. INF. *irfiḍâḍ*, disperse and disappear; flow; — X. INF. *istirfâḍ*, be wide, large.

رفض *rafḍ*, repudiation, exclusion; *rafḍ*, *rafaḍ*, pl. *arfâḍ*, freely pasturing camels.

(رفع) *rafa'*, INF. *raf'*, lift, lift up, raise, hoist; raise the voice, name aloud; appeal; put a word in the nominative, pronounce it with *ḍamma-t*; remove; cause to disappear; urge to a quicker pace; INF. *raf'*, *marfû'*, walk apace; INF. *rafa'ân*, come to higher regions; INF. *ruf'ân*, bring a matter before the king or judge; ascribe certain words to an author; — *rafu'*, INF. *rafâ'a-t*, have a loud voice; be loud; INF. *rif'a-t*, be highly placed, of high rank or authority; — II. INF. *tarfî'*, lift up; hoist; urge to a quicker pace; remove from the battle-field, &c.; (m.) make thinner, refine; make carnival; — III. INF. *murâfa'a-t*, bring a matter or summon a person before the judge; appeal; spare one's life; — V. INF. *taraffu'*, raise one's self; grow proud; behave haughtily towards (على *'ala*); live at ease; (m.) be thin, fine; — VI. INF. *tarâfu'*, bring a cause together before the king or judge; carry on a law-suit against one another; wrangle; — VIII. INF. *irtifâ'*, lift up, raise, elevate; get elevated, promoted; grow proud; amount to; get removed, disappear; — X. INF. *istirfâ'*, demand a thing to be lifted up, raised, removed.

رفع *raf'*, raising (s.); removal, causing to disappear; the vowel *u* (*ḍamma-t*), nominative; — ة *raf'a-t*, elevation; — *rif'a-t*, high

rank, authority; fineness, thinness.

رفعان *ruf'ân, rafa'ân*, INF. of (رفع).

(رفغ) *rafag*, INF. *rafâga-t*, be comfortable and enjoyable (life); — V. INF. *taraffug*, lead such a life; lie with.

رفغ *rafg*, plenty, affluence; fertility, and, by opposition, sterile ground; pl. *arfâg*, rabble; pl. *rifâg*, soft and level ground; — *rafg, rufg*, pl. *arfâg, rufûg*, dirt of the nails, &c.; arm-pit, junction of the thighs.

رفغا *rafgâ'*, woman with closely-joining thighs.

رفغنية *rufagniya-t*, plenty, affluence.

رفف *rafaf*, thinness, fineness.

(رفق) *rafaq*, U, INF. *rifq*, help, assist, favour, profit (a.); — U, INF. *rifq, marfiq, marfaq, mirfaq*, be gentle, kind towards (ب *bi* or على *'ala*); — U, INF. *rifq*, be no longer in distress, improve one's circumstances, be able to help one's self; — INF. *rafq*, push against another's elbow; tie the fore-feet of a camel; — *rafiq*, A, INF. *rafaq*, be gentle, kind towards; have a contorted elbow; (m.) have the advantage over (على *'ala*); —*rafuq*, INF. *rafâqa-t*, be gentle, kind towards; be one's companion, accompany; — III. INF. *murâfaqa-t*, be one's companion, accompany; assist; be useful to (acc.); — IV. INF. *irfâq*, be gentle, kind towards; bestow; profit (a.); — V. INF. *taraffuq*, show one's self gentle or kind towards; be one's inseparable companion; show one's self active and easy in a matter; — VI. INF. *tarâfuq*, join company and assist one another; be companions, partners; — VIII. INF. *irtifâq*, show one's self gentle and kind; be assisted, find help; profit (n.), gain advantage; lean on one's elbow; — X. INF. *istirfâq*, ask for a kindness, for a favour, for help.

رفق *rifq*, kindness, gentleness, compassion, favour, grace; what helps, is profitable, sufficiency, ease, comfortable condition; — ة *rafqa-t, rifqa-t, rufqa-t*, pl. *rufaq, rifâq, arfâq*, companionship; the companions; travelling-company; — *rufqa-t*, and—

رفقا *rufaqâ'*, pl. of رفيق *rafîq*.

(رفل) *rafal*, U, INF. *rafl*, be awkward, clumsy; spoil everything, bungle; — U, INF. *rafl, rafalân*, trail the garments, walk along pompously; walk as if proud of one's clothes; saunter; INF. *rafl*, collect water in a well; — *rafil*, A, INF. *rafal*, be awkward, clumsy; — II. INF. *tarfîl*, trail the garments; elevate, praise, and, by opposition, abuse and revile; make one a king, a great lord, &c.; bring into possession of (2 acc.); collect water in a well; (m.) have flabby ears; — IV. INF. *irfâl*, trail the garments; walk pompously.

رفل *rafil*, ة (f. also رفلا *raflâ*), awkward, clumsy; stupid, not of any use; comfortable, affluent; — *rifall*, ة, trailing; long-tailed.

رفن *rafn*, egg; — *rifann*=رفل *rifall*.

(رفه) *rafah*, INF. *rafh, rifh, rufûh*, also *rafih*, A, INF. *rafah*, lead a comfortable and enjoyable life; go freely to the water at any time;—*rafuh*, INF. *rafâha-t*, be comfortable and enjoyable; — II. INF. *tarfîh*, grant a comfortable and enjoyable life; also IV., allow the camels to drink freely; be indulgent with a debtor; — IV. INF. *irfâh*, see II.; also V. INF. *taraffuh*, and X. INF. *istirfâh*, lead a comfortable and enjoyable life.

رفه *rifh*, comfortable enjoyment of life; — *rufah*, straw, chopped straw.

رفهان *rafhân*, living in luxury (adj.).

رفهنية *rufahniya-t*, comfortable enjoyment of life.

(رفو) *rafâ*, U, INF. *rafw*, mend, darn, make whole; quiet, free from fear; — II. INF. *tarfiya-t*, congratulate a newly-married couple; — III. INF. *rifâ'*, *murâfât*, id.; live together in peace.

رفو *rafw*, fine seam.

رفوا *rafwâ'*, f. of ارفى *arfa*, having long and flabby ears.

رفيص *rafîṣ*, table-companion; companion.

رفيض *rafîḍ*, rejected, thrown away as useless; broken.

رفيع *rafî'*, ة, lifting up (adj.); high, elevated, sublime; loud, having a loud voice; thin, fine, subtle; very small; — ة *rafî'a-t*, matter brought before the king or judge.

رفيغ *rafîg*, comfortable, affluent.

رفيف *rafîf*, thin, fine; sky-light; shining with dew; lily; roof.

رفيق *rafîq*, pl. *rufaqâ'*, *rufqa-t*, *rifâq*, kind, gentle, mild; companion, comrade, friend, helper; — ة *rafîqa-t*, trowsers.

رفيه *rafîh*, living in enjoyment (adj.).

(رق) *raqq*, for *raqaq*, I, INF. *riqqa-t*, be or become thin, fine; be seized with compassion or tenderness for (ل *li*); grow ashamed; INF. *riqq*, become a slave; — II. INF. *tarqîq*, make thin or fine, refine; make weak, pliable; flatten; use a word metaphorically; — IV. INF. *irqâq*, make thin, fine, weak; flatten; be thin, fine, weak; be badly off; enslave, make a slave of; — V. INF. *taraqquq*, feel compassion or tenderness; get thin, fine, flat; — X. INF. *istirqâq*, be thin, fine, weak; make a slave of, take as a slave; be almost exhausted.

رق *raqq*, pl. *ruqûq*, thin, fine; thin parchment; sheet of paper; book, roll; a large tortoise; — *riqq*, slavery; slave, servant; dominion, right of possession; thin, compassionate, tender; parchment, paper; — *ruqq*, pl. *riqâq*, soft ground; — ة *riqa-t*, first vegetation; pl. *riqûn*, coin; — *raqqa-t*, thinness, fineness; pl. *riqâq*, banks exposed to inundations; — *riqqa-t*, thinness, fineness; compassion; sympathy; delicacy; softness of the voice; feeling of weakness; shame; poverty and helplessness.

(رقا) *raqa'*, INF. *raq'*, *ruqû'*, cease to flow; be stirred up; — INF. *raq'*, stir up discord, and, by opposition, pacify; mount, ascend; — IV. INF. *irqâ'*, stifle, stanch; produce perspiration.

رقا *raqâ*, ruin, destruction, disaster, calamity; — *raqqâ'*, pl. *-ûn*, sorcerer.

رقاب *riqâb*, INF. III. of (رقب); pl. of رقبة *raqaba-t*; — ة *raqâba-t*, expectation; — *raqqâba-t*, superintendent of the luggage.

رقاحة *raqâḥa-t*, gain; traffic.

رقاحى *raqâḥiyy*, merchant, tradesman, clerk; manager.

رقاد *ruqâd*, night-sleep.

رقارق *ruqâriq*, vast shallow sheet of water; thin vapour; shining, bright.

رقاش *raqâś*, glittering snake.

رقاص *raqqâṣ*, dancer; balance or pendulum of a clock; letter-carrier; messenger.

رقاع *riqâ'*, . of رقعة *ruq'a-t*; — ة *raqâ'a-t*, stupidity; — ى *riqâ'iyy*, epistolary style of handwriting.

رقاق *raqâq*, hot; — *riqâq*, pl. of رق *ruqq*, رقة *raqqa-t*, and رقيق *raqîq*; — *ruqâq*, thin; slow pace of a camel; — *ruqqâq*, thin; —

ة *raqâqa-t*, thinness; — *ruqâqa-t*, pl. *ruqâq*, *riqâq*, thin cake or loaf, cracknel.

رقان *riqân*, saffron; henna.

(رقب) *raqab*, U, INF. *raqûb*, *ruqûb*, *raqaba-t*, *riqba-t*, *riqbân*, *raqâba-t*, observe attentively, be on the watch for, watch, expect; guard; spy out; bind by the neck; — III. INF. *riqâb*, *murâqaba-t*, observe, watch, spy out; fear; show respect; fear God; — IV. INF. *irqâb*, allow the use of a house or land for a life-time (2 acc.); — V. INF. *taraqqub*, observe, spy out; watch; hope for; expect; fear God; — VIII. INF. *irtiqâb*, observe; expect; be or stand high; tower.

رقب *raqab*, thinness of the neck; — *ruqub*, pl. of رقيب *raqîb*; — ة *raqaba-t*, pl. *raqab*, *riqâb*, *arqub*, *raqabât*, root of the neck, neck (خيط الر *ḥaiṭ ar-raqaba-t*, spinal marrow); slave, serf, subject; submissiveness; — *raqba-t*, environs, esplanade (m.); — *riqba-t*, distant relations; space, interval; guard; vigilance, caution, fear.

رقبان *raqabân*, رقبانى *raqabâniyy*, having a thick neck.

رقبى *ruqba*, house which falls back to the previous owner after the death of the present tenant.

(رقح), II. *raqqaḥ*, INF. *tarqîḥ*, administer well one's fortune; manage well one's life; maintain; — IV. INF. *irqâḥ*, perform well; — V. INF. *taraqquḥ*, earn a livelihood for one's family.

(رقد) *raqad*, U, INF. *raqd*, *ruqâd*, *ruqûd*, go to sleep, sleep, rest (at night-time); — II. INF. *tarqîd*, send to sleep, lull into sleep; — IV. INF. *irqâd*, id.; remain, stay; — IX. INF. *irqidâd*, hasten, act quickly.

رقد *raqd*, sleep; — *ruqqad*, pl. of راقد *râqid*, agent of (رقد); — ة *raqda-t*, sleep; time during which one sleeps without awakening; space of time between death and resurrection; — *ruqada-t*, sleeper.

رقدان *raqadân*, rejoicing (s.); leaping, jumping (s.).

رقراق *raqrâq*, moving of a mirage; flashing, shining (adj.).

(رقرق) *raqraq*, INF. ة, sprinkle water here and there in small quantities; shake the water, mix a drink; — II. INF. *taraqruq*, move and glitter, come and go, appear and disappear.

(رقز) *raqaz*, INF. *raqz*, spring, skip, dance; beat, throb.

(رقش) *raqaś*, U, INF. *raqś*, paint with different colours, variegate; write elegantly; leave traces, marks; — II. INF. *tarqîś*, variegate; adorn one's speech, embellish; interlard one's speech with lies; — V. INF. *taraqquś*, be variegated, parti-coloured; be adorned; adorn one's self; — VIII. INF. *irtiqâś*, mix in close fight.

رقش *raqś*, gaudy picture, gaudiness; marks on the face; adorning (s.); — *ruqś*, pl. and—

رقشا *raqśâ'*, f. of ارقش *arqaś*, spotted black and white; a spotted snake.

(رقص) *raqaṣ*, U, INF. *raqṣ*, dance, skip; move to and fro, undulate; ferment and bubble, effervesce; INF. *raqṣ*, *raqaṣ*, *raqaṣân*, gallop; — II. INF. *tarqîṣ*, make dance, dandle; put into gallop; — IV. INF. *irqâṣ*, id.; — V. INF. *taraqquṣ*, dance, skip, gallop.

رقص *raqṣ*, dance; waltz; gallop.

(رقط), II. *raqqaṭ*, INF. *tarqîṭ*, variegate, make parti-coloured, gaudy; V. INF. *taraqquṭ*, be bespattered, soiled; — IX. *irqaṭṭ*, INF. *irqiṭâṭ*, be variegated, be spotted black and white; — XI. *irqâṭṭ*, INF. *irqîṭâṭ*, id.; — ة

ruqṭa-t, white spotted with black or vice versâ.

رقطا *raqṭâ'*, f. of ارقط *arqaṭ*, spotted, &c.

(رقع) *raqa'*, INF. *raq'a-t*, patch up; mend or support a decaying well; pierce, hit; scoff at, lampoon, satirise; — *raqu'*, INF. *raqâ'a-t*, be imbecile, commit follies; — II. INF. *tarqî'*, patch in many places, mend; — V. INF. *taraqqu'*, be patched up; earn a sustenance; — VI. INF. *tarâqu'*, act stupidly or foolishly towards (على *'ala*); — VIII. INF. *irtiqâ'*, care for, take care of; — X. INF. *istirqâ'*, want mending, patching up.

رقع *raq'*, the seventh heaven; husband; — *raqi'*, stupid, foolish; — ة *ruq'a-t*, patch; piece of paper to write upon; scrap; short letter, note; written report of one who is not a minister; an epistolary style of handwriting; cataplasm; territory, precinct; رقعة الشطرنج *ruq'a-t aś-śaṭranj*, chess-board; — *ruqa'a-t*, pl. *ruqa'*, a tree resembling a plane-tree with a fig-like fruit.

(رقف) *raqaf*, U, tremble, shiver; — IV. INF. *irqâf*, be seized with a shiver.

رقق *raqaq*, soft ground with a harder layer beneath; weakness; need of money.

(رقل), IV. *arqal*, INF. *irqâl*, stride fast, hasten; wander through; — ة *raqla-t*, pl. *raql*, *riqâl*, high palm-tree.

(رقم) *raqam*, U, INF. *raqm*, write; point a text; stripe stuff; embroider; — II. INF. *tarqîm*, write; stripe; embroider.

رقم *raqm*, pl. *arqâm*, writing (s.); numbers, numerical signs; stripe; striped stuff; — also *raqam*, *raqim*, much; calamity; — ة *raqma-t*, garden, meadow; shore, bank; mallows; — ى *raqamiyy*, jasper.

(رقن) *raqan*, INF. *raqn* (also II.), dye red with henna; write in beautiful characters; point a text; cross a figure in an account, &c.; write in narrow lines; (m.) plane a board; — II. INF. *tarqîn*, see above; — IV. INF. *irqân*, dye red with henna; saturate a dish with fat; — V. INF. *taraqqun*, dye one's self with henna; — VIII. INF. *irtiqân*, be dyed with henna or saffron.

رقو *raqw*, ة *raqwa-t*, sand-hill; — *raqû'*, remedy for stanching the blood; blood-money; INF. of (رقا); — ة *ruqwa-t*=رقية *ruqya-t*.

رقوب *raqûb*, bereft of children; ام الرقوب *umm ar-raqûb*, calamity; — *.

رقود *ruqûd*, sleep.

رقوط *raqwaṭ*, INF. ة=(رقط) II.

رقون *raqûn*, *ruqûn*, saffron, henna; — *riqûn*, coins, pl. of رقة *riqa-t*.

(رقى) *raqî*, A, INF. *raqy*, *ruqiyy*, ascend a ladder or stairs; mount on the roof, mount, ascend; — *raqa*, I, INF. *raqy*, *ruqiyy*, *ruqya-t*, use magic against, charm, spell; — II. INF. *tarqiya-t*, raise by degrees, elevate, exalt; speak to in a loud voice; — IV. INF. *irqâ'*, promote, cause to advance or rise by degrees; — V. INF. *taraqqî*, rise or advance by degrees; make progress; profit; — VIII. INF. *irtiqâ'*, ascend; rise higher or highest; receive the higher ordinations; — X. INF. *istirqâ'*, ask to use magic, to charm.

رقى *ruqan*, pl. of رقية *ruqya-t*, below; — *raqiyy*, tender melon; — *ruqqa*, thin, fluid; — ة *ruqya-t*, رقوة *ruqwa-t*, pl. *ruqan*, magic; sorcery; spell, charm; amulet; — *riqqiyya-t*, slavery; — *ruqayya-t*, female name.

رقيب *raqîb*, pl. *ruqabâ'*, who guards, preserves (God);

watcher, night-watcher; sentinel; overseer, superintendent; spy, informer; rival; station of the moon or a star in opposition to another; third arrow in the game; pl. *-ât, ruqub*, poisonous snake.

(رقيع) *raqî'*, of weak intellect; pl. *arqi'a-t*, firmament, lowest heaven.

رقيق *raqîq*, ة, pl. *riqâq, ariqqâ'*, thin, fine, subtle; soft, sensitive, sentimental; slim; in narrow circumstances; m. and f., sing. and pl., pl. also *riqâq*, slave;—ة *raqîqa-t*, female slave, slave-girl; pl. *raqâ'iq*, subtleties; anything transcendental.

رقيم *raqîm*, pl. *raqâ'im*, slab or stone with an inscription; scripture, book; inkstand; reasonable, sensible; — ة *raqîma-t*, prudent and chaste (f.); line, handwriting, letter.

رقين *raqîn*, coin; dirham.

(رك) *rakk*, I, INF. *rakk, rakâka-t*, be very thin and fine; be weak; — U, INF. *rakk*, put one upon another; touch, feel; lie with; wind round one's neck; (m.) macadamize;=IV.; — II. INF. *tarkîk*, talk unintelligibly or faultily; — IV. INF. *irkâk*, rain slightly upon the earth; — VII. INF. *irrikâk*, be stamped, macadamized; be filled up; — VIII. INF. *irtikâk*, tremble, waver, be irresolute; be agitated; stop short sometimes in an otherwise eloquent speech; entangle one's self in difficulties; — X. INF. *istirkâk*, deem too thin, weak, insignificant.

رك *rakk, rikk*, pl. *rikâk, arkâk*, thin rain.

ركا *rakâ'*, echo; — also *rakkâ'*, screech of an owl; — *rikâ'*, pl. of ركوة *rakwa-t*.

ركاب *rikâb*, pl. *rukub*, stirrup; pl. *rikâbât, rukub, rakâ'ib*, camel to ride upon or carry loads; — *rakkâb*, pl. of راكب *râkib*, who rides or drives; — ة *rakkâba-t*, hanging branch of a palm-tree; — ى *rikâbiyy*, oil brought on camels from Syria; pl. ة, stirrup-holder.

ركاز *rikâz*, pl. *rakâ'iz*, precious ore; lump of gold or silver; buried treasures; mines.

ركاس *rikâs*, rope to halter a camel with.

ركاك *rikâk*, pl. of رك *rakk*, ركيك *rakîk* and ركيكة *rakîka-t*; — *rukâk*, ة *rukâka-t*, weak and despised man; — ة *rakâka-t*, thinness, fineness, weakness; idiotcy; trembling handwriting.

ركال *rakkâl*, seller of leeks.

ركام *rakâm, rukâm*, heap; sand-heap; heaped up clouds; crowd.

ركانة *rakâna-t*, firmness; earnestness; severity; perseverance.

ركايا *rakâyâ*, pl. of ركية *rakiyya-t*.

ركائب *rakâ'ib*, pl. of ركاب *rikâb*.

ركائز *rakâ'iz*, pl. of ركاز *rikâz* and ركيزة *rakîza-t*.

(ركب) *rakib*, A, INF. *rukûb, markab*, ride, drive, sail, make use of any vehicle; embark, mount; ر البحر *rakib al-baḥr*, travel on the sea; follow (one's head or desires); commit (a crime); — U, hit or strike on the knee or with one's knee; — *rakib*, A, INF. *rakab*, have a large knee; — II. INF. *tarkîb*, mount (a.); give a horse in exchange for half of the booty; be practicable for horsemen (road); be able to carry a rider; put one thing upon another; compose, mix; join, insert, fit (a.); — IV. INF. *irkâb*, mount (a.), give a horse or vehicle; be able to carry a rider;—V. INF. *tarakkub*, be composed, put one upon another, joined to or inserted into one another, fitted to each other; — VI. INF. *tarâkub*, be put on the top of one another,

heaped up, closely joined; — VIII. INF. *irtikâb*, commit a crime; ride, drive; — X. INF. *istirkâb*, bid to mount.

ركب *rakb* (also ة *rakaba-t*), pl. *arkub*, *rukûb*, troop of horsemen, of riders; cavalcade. cortege; pl. of راكب *râkib*, who rides or drives; — *rakab*, pl. *arkâb*, *arâkîb*, exterior pudenda, hair on them; — *rukub*, pl. of راكب *râkib* and ركيب *rakib*; — ة *rakba-t*, good riding-camel; — *rikba-t*, art or manner of riding, horsemanship; — *rukba-t*, pl. *rukab*, *rukbât*, *rukubât*, knee; elbow; — *rikaba-t*, and—

ركبان *rukbân*, pl. of راكب *râkib*, who rides or drives, &c.; — ة *rakbâna-t*, and—

ركباة *rakbât*, saddle-camel.

ركبوت *rakabût*, ركبوتى *rakabûta*, good saddle-camel.

(ركح) *rakaḥ*, INF. *rakḥ*, lean upon (على *'ala*); INF. *rukûḥ*, bend (n.), incline towards (الى *ila*); turn repeatedly towards, return to (الى *ila*); put one thing above the other; — IV. INF. *irkâḥ*, lean upon, lean against; cause one to lean against, to take refuge with; — V. INF. *tarakkuḥ*, live at ease in a house, live freely; abide remain; — VIII. INF. *irtikâḥ*, rely upon.

ركح *rukḥ*, pl. *rukûḥ*, *arkâḥ*, base and angle of projection; foot and slope of a mountain; middle house-floor; yard; pl. *arkâḥ*, foundation; — ة *rukḥa-t*, courtyard.

ركحا *rakḥâ'*, f. rugged.

(ركد) *rakad*, U, INF. *rukûd*, stop, halt, rest; be calm, quiet, at rest; culminate; — be in equilibrium.

ركرك *rakrak*, INF. ة, be weak; — II. INF. *tarakruk*, shake the milk in the skin bag and churn it.

(ركز) *rakaz*, U, I, INF. *rakz*, plant in the ground (a lance, flag, &c.); form veins of gold and silver in the earth; beat, throb; (m.) be quiet, at rest, settle quietly in a place and remain there; — II. INF. *tarkîz*, fix; fasten; quiet (m.); — IV. INF. *irkâz*, find veins of precious metal or buried treasures; — V. INF. *tarakkuz*, be fixed, fastened, quiet (m.); — VIII. INF. *irtikâz*, be planted in the earth; be fixed; beat, throb.

ركز *rakz*, ة *rikza-t*, fastness, firmness, perseverance; (m.) rest, pause; — *rikz*, low sound; sentiment, sensation; pl. *rikâz*, vein of gold or silver; — ة *rikza-t*, lump of gold or silver.

(ركس) *rakas*, U, INF. *raks*, overturn, turn topsy-turvy; tie with the rope ركاس *rikâs*; — IV. INF. *irkâs*, overturn; reject; refute; get breasts; — VIII. INF. *irtikâs*, get overturned; meet with adventures; be pressed, hemmed in.

ركس *raks*, turning topsy-turvy (s.); — *riks*, dirt.

(ركض) *rakaḍ*, U, INF. *rakḍ*, move the feet; step, tread, kick; move anything with the feet; spur, urge to full career; run, gallop; flee; push; — II. INF. *tarkîḍ*, make to run, put into gallop; — III. INF. *murâkaḍa-t*, vie in running, race; — IV. INF. *irkâḍ*, be in that stage of pregnancy when the embryo begins to move; — VI. INF. *tarâkuḍ*, race with one another; — VIII. INF. *irtikâḍ*, move in the womb; bestir one's self in one's affairs.

ركض *rakḍ*, swift run, gallop; — ة *rakḍa-t*, motion, impulse.

(ركع) *raka'*, INF. *rukû'*, bow to the ground, touch the ground with one's face; prostrate one's self; kneel down and adore; be bent with old age; become poor after being rich; — II. INF. *tarkî'*,

IV. INF. *irkâ'*, make one kneel down.

ركع *rukka'*, pl. of راكع *râki'*, ag. of the previous ; — ة *rak'a-t*, a bowing down or prostration in prayer ; — *ruk'a-t*, pl. *ruka'*, hollow ground.

(ركف), VIII. *irtakaf*, INF. *irtikâf*, remain lying on the ground.

(ركل) *rakal*, U, INF. *rakl*, put into gallop ; kick against ; — II. INF. *tarkîl*, paw the ground ; — V. INF. *tarakkul*, push the mattock into the ground with one's foot.

ركل *rakl*, leek ; — ة *rakla-t*, bunch of herbs.

(ركم) *rakam*, U, INF. *rakm*, carry together, heap up ; — VI. INF. *tarâkum*, VIII. INF. *irtikâm*, be heaped one upon another ; gather closely (n.) ; multiply (n.).

ركم *rakam*, heaped-up clouds ; — ة *rukma-t*, hay-stack.

(ركن) *rakan*, U, A, INF. *rukûn*, lean upon, rely upon, trust in (الى *ila*) ; — *rakin*, A, INF. *rakan*, id. ; — *rakun*, INF. *rakâna-t*, *rakâniya-t*, *rukûna-t*, be firm and persevering ; be calm, grow calm ; — II. INF. *tarkîn*, fix, make firm ; quiet, calm (a.) ; make similar ; — V. INF. *tarakkun*, be firm, steady, persevering ; be fixed, consolidated ; be strong, powerful.

ركن *rukn*, pl. *arkân*, *arâkîn*, the firm part of a thing on which it rests ; support, prop, pillar, column ; angle of a building, corner-stone ; the corner of the Kaaba where the black stone is lying ; aid, protection ; power, greatness ; base ; element ; principal part, fundamental condition, essential principle ; foot of a verse ; اركان الحرب *arkân al-harb*, general staff ; اركان الدولة *arkân ad-daula-t*, grandees.

(ركو) *rakâ*, U, INF. *rakw*, dig up the ground ; fasten, fix ; mend, restore ; blame, rebuke ; accuse falsely of a crime ; remain, abide ; delay, defer, put off ; double a camel's load ; — IV. INF. *irkâ'*, reproach with ; delay, defer ; take refuge with ; prepare an army ; — ة *rakwa-t*, pl. *rakwât*, *rikâ'*, small skin bag ; small flask or water-vessel ; (m.) coffee or tea-things ; — *rakwa-t*, *rikwa-t*, *rukwa-t*, pl. *rukiyy*, *rakâyâ*, *rakawât*, small boat.

ركوب *rakûb*, on horseback, mounted ; — also ة *rakûba-t*, pl. *rakâ'ib*, saddle-beast ; carriage ; trodden road ; — *rukûb*, INF. of (ركب) ; bend in a cane or reed ; pl. of راكب *râkib*, who rides or drives, &c., and of ركب *rakb*.

ركود *rukûd*, INF. of (ركد) ; quietude, rest, pause ; calm (of the winds).

ركون *rukûn*, trust, confidence, reliance ; — ة *rakâna-t*, *rukûna-t*, firmness, &c.

ركى *rakiyy*, weak ; — *rukiyy*, pl. of ركوة *rakwa-t* ; — *rukka*, easily-melting fat ; — ة *rakiyya-t*, pl. *rakiyy*, *rakâyâ*, well.

ركيب *rakîb*, placed upon, inserted, set in ; who rides or drives in company with others ; vegetable garden ; pl. *rukub*, planted in a row.

ركيزة *rakîza-t*, pl. *rakâ'iz*, fossils, precious metals ; (m.) pillar, column, post.

ركيك *rakîk*, pl. *rikâk*, thin, fine ; subtle ; weak, despised ; stupid ; — ة *rakîka-t*, pl. *rikâk*, fine rain.

ركين *rakîn*, firm, solid, strong ; persevering calm, steady ; — *rukain*, mouse ; jerboa ; mole.

(رم) *ramm*, U, I, INF. *ramm*, *maramma-t*, mend, restore ; pluck branches with the lips ; browse, eat ; — I, INF. *rimm*, *rimma-t*,

ramîm, be carious, worm-eaten; moulder; — II. INF. *tarmîm*, mend, restore; — IV. INF. *irmâm*, putrefy, become carious; be old and worn; be silent; be inclined to; — VIII. INF. *irtimâm*, browse; begin to have a hump; — X. INF. *istirmâm*, need mending, restoring.

رم *ramm*, something, anything; — *ramm*, *rumm*, flight, escape; — *rimm*, moist ground; marrow; putrefaction of the bones; — ة *rimma-t*, pl. *rimam*, *rimâm*, carious or putrifying bone; mark; ship-worm; — *rumma-t*, pl. *rumam*, *rimâm*, worn rope; halter; — *rumma-t*, *ruma-t*, forehead.

(رما) *rama'*, INF. *ram'*, *rumû'*, stop, remain, abide; surpass in number (a hundred); believe to be true; — IV. INF. *irmâ'*, surpass in number (a hundred); approach, be near.

رما *ramâ'*, usury; increase; — *rimâ'*, shooting, throwing (s.); — *rammâ'*, white; — ة *rumât*, pl. of رامى *râmî*, who shoots, &c.

رماث *rammâs*, maker of rafts; rower.

رماح *rammâḥ*, maker of lances; who throws lances, lancer; ة *rammâḥa-t*, shooting far; — ة *rimâḥa-t*, art of making lances; poverty.

رماحس *rumâḥis*, strong and bold.

رماد *ramâd*, ashes; potash; — ة *ramâda-t*, murrain in consequence of frost or hail; — ى *ramâdiyy*, ash-coloured.

رماز *rammâz*, who speaks mysteriously by signs, &c.; who proposes riddles; mysterious, enigmatical, puzzling; — ة *rammâza-t*, winking (courtesan); large army.

رماع *rumâ'*, pains in the hips or loins, lumbago; — ة *rammâ'a-t*, bones of the crown of the head.

رماق *ramâq*, *rimâq*, small competence, pittance; furtive side-glance.

رمال *rumâl*, *rimâl*, basket-work of palm-leaves; woof of a garment; — *; — *rammâl*, soothsayer, especially from figures in the sand.

رمام *rimâm*, *rumâm*, decayed, putrefied; — ة *rumâma-t*, competence.

رمان *rummân*, ة, pomegranate; pomegranate-tree; ر الخشخاش *rummân al-ḥaśḥâś*, poppy; — ة *rummâna-t*, weight in the balance; sword; pommel; epaulet; tripe, guts; — ى *rummâniyy*, seller of pomegranates; like to or of the colour of a pomegranate; red; ruby.

رمايا *ramâyâ*, pl. of رمى *ramiyy*.

رماية *rimâya-t*, shooting, &c. (s.), INF. of (رمى).

(رمث) *ramas*, U, INF. *rams*, mend, restore, wipe with the hand; — *ramis*, A, INF. *ramas*, be difficult and complicated; be sick from eating the plant رمث *rims*; — IV. INF. *irmâs* (also II. INF. *tarmîs*), leave some milk in the udder; (also X.) put by or save part of one's fortune; surpass; soften; — X. INF. *istirmâs*, see IV.

رمث *rims*, pl. *rimâs*, *armâs*, a bitter plant used as food for camels; — *ramas*, pl. *rimâs*, wooden raft; remainder of milk in the udder; abundance.

(رمج) *ramaj*, U, INF. *ramj*, drop excrement; — II. INF. *tarmîj*, efface the writing.

رمج *rimj*, dung of birds.

(رمح) *ramaḥ*, INF. *ramḥ*, pierce with a lance; kick; flash; run, gallop.

رمح *ramḥ*, (m.) course, gallop; — *rumḥ*, pl. *rimâḥ*, *armâḥ*, lance, spear; ر الجن *rimâḥ al-jinn*,

plague; العقرب ر rimâḥ al-'aqrab, sting of a scorpion); poverty.

(رمح) *rimḥ*, thicket; — ة *rumḥa-t*, *rimaḥa-t*, pl. *rumaḥ*, *rimaḥ*, unripe date; — IV. *armaḥ*, INF. *irmâḥ*, bear unripe dates; become docile and obedient; grow old and fat.

(رمد) *ramad*, U, I, fall upon a tribe to destroy it; — I, INF. *ramd*, *ramâda-t*, perish by frost or hail; — *ramid*, A, INF. *ramad*, become sore and running, suffer from sore eyes; — II. INF. *tarmîd*, put into the ashes; throw ashes at, soil with ashes; turn into ashes; — IV. be afflicted with frost or a murrain, grow poor; make the eyes run; — IX. INF. *irmidâd*, become painful and running; be ash-coloured; turn pale.

رمد *rumd*, fly; pl. of ارمد *armad*, ash-coloured; — *ramad*, ophthalmia; running eyes; — *ramid*, ة, also (m.) رمدان *ramdân*, suffering from ophthalmia; running; — ة *rimda-t*, rest, remainder.

رمدا *ramdâ'*, f. of ارمد *armad*, ash-coloured; ostrich.

(رمرم), II. INF. *taramrum*, move the lips as if speaking.

(رمز) *ramaz*, U, INF. *ramz*, *rumz*, *ramaz*, wink, give a sign by movement of the lips, brows, tongue or hand; allude to; scarcely be able to move from heaviness; fill; — INF. *ramazân*, jump up; spur, urge on; — *ramuz*, INF. *ramâza-t*, be very mobile, agile, nimble; be prudent, wise, intelligent; be powerful, of high birth or rank, honoured; — V. INF. *tarammuz*, be agitated, disquieted; move on the seats as if about to rise; — XI. INF. *irmîzâz*, leave a place, and, by opposition, adhere to a place.

رمز *ramz*, *ramaz*, *rumz*, noun of unity ة *ramza-t*, pl. *rumûz*, wink, sign; allusion; allegory; riddle; abbreviation in writing; mysterious circumstance; — *rumz*, fat camels; — ى *ramziyy*, by way of allusion; symbolic, allegorical.

(رمس) *ramas*, U, INF. *rams*, throw at; shoot, hit; conceal, hide from, make a secret of; cover with earth; bury; dip the head into water; — VIII. INF. *irtimâs*, be plunged into the water.

رمس *rams*, pl. *rumûs*, *armâs*, grave, tomb.

(رمش) *ramaś*, I, U, INF. *ramś*, throw at; wink; touch, take up with the finger-tops; feed the cattle scantily; — IV. INF. *irmâś*, green; look at with eyes winking from weakness; drop tears from weakness of the eyes.

رمش *ramś*, bunch of herbs; — *ramaś*, luxuriant vegetation; inflammation and running of the eyes; — ة *ramśa-t*, wink, blinking of the eye.

رمشا *ramśâ'*, f. of ارمش *armaś*, having inflamed and running eyes, &c.

(رمص) *ramaṣ*, U, INF. *ramṣ*, make up for a calamity, compensate for a loss; make peace; tie together anything broken, mend; drop excrement; gain.

(رمض) *ramaḍ*, I, INF. *ramḍ*, cut open a sheep and roast it in its skin upon heated stones under glowing ashes; pasture a herd on dried-up ground; — I, U, sharpen the head of a spear between stones; — *ramiḍ*, A, INF. *ramaḍ*, heat sand and stones; be hot; — IV. INF. *irmâḍ*, burn (a.); — VIII. INF. *irtimâḍ*, burn with grief or pain.

رمضا *ramḍâ'*, burnt by the sun; heated stone.

رمضان *ramaḍân*, pl. *-ât*, *-ûn*, *armiḍa-t*, the (ninth) month of fasting.

رمضى *ramḍa*, *ramaḍa*, rain towards the end of summer.

(رمط) *ramaṭ*, I, INF. *ramṭ*, blame, rebuke, taunt.

(رمع) *rama'*, INF. *rama'ân*, tremble; beckon; nod the head; give birth; run, drop tears; — INF. *ram'*, *rama'ân*, walk apace; — *rami'*, A, INF. *rama'*, be pale from pain in the womb or the hips; have pain in the loins (from drawing water); — V. INF. *tarammu'*, tremble (with rage).

(رمعل), III. *irma'all*, INF. *irma'lâl*, salivate (n.); drip with fat; flow uninterruptedly; be wet through; walk fast; cry aloud, scream.

(رمعن), III. *irma'ann*, INF. *irmi'nân*, flow.

(رمغ) *ramag*, INF. *ramg*, rub with the hand; — II. INF. *tarmîg*, arrange one's speech in good order.

(رمق) *ramaq*, U, INF. *ramq*, *ramaqân*, glance at furtively, view; — INF. *rumûq*, look stealthily and continuously at; — II. INF. *tarmîq*, look at continuously; slur over a work; arrange one's speech in good order; — V. INF. *tarammuq*, drink slowly, suck.

رمق *ramaq*, pl. *armâq*, last spark of life in one dying; — *ramaq*, pl. *rimâq*, herd; — *ramiq*, just expiring; — *ramiq*, ة *rumqa-t*, pl. *rumaq*, barely sufficient for life; — *rumuq*, pl. of رامق *râmiq*, who looks at with envy, and of رموق *ramûq*.

(رمك) *ramak*, U, INF. *rumûk*, stop, remain, abide; — IV. INF. *irmâk*, cause to abide in a place; — IX. INF. *irmikâk*, be emaciated; be ash-coloured; be of low extraction; — ة *ramaka-t*, pl. *rimâk*, *ramakât*, *ramak*, *armâk*, inferior mare left with the foals to lead them; — *rumka-t*, ash-colour of old camels.

(رمل) *ramal*, U, INF. *raml*, sprinkle or strew with sand; allow sand to get into a dish; soil with blood; weave thinly; embroider with pearls; — U, INF. *ramal*, *ramalân*, *marmal*, walk apace; — II. INF. *tarmîl*, strew with sand; weave thinly; — IV. INF. *irmâl*, weave thinly; become a widow or widower; eat up the provisions; grow poor, be crushed to the dust; falsify a speech; — V. INF. *tarammul*, be stained with blood; become a widow or widower.

رمل *raml*, ة, pl. *rimâl*, *armul*, sand; ضرب ر *ḍarb-u raml-in*, geomancy; ضراب ر *ḍarrâb-u raml-in*, geomancer; — *ramal*, geomancy, soothsaying from figures in the sand; increase, growth; name of a metre (فاعلاتن *fâ'ilâtun* six times repeated); pl. *armâl*, fine rain; — ة *ramla-t*, sand-heap; — *rumla-t*, pl. *rumal*, *armâl*, black lines.

رملا *ramlâ'*, f. white with black feet; dry and sterile.

رملى *ramliyy*, geomancer; — f. ة, sandy; — ة *ramliyya-t*, sandy place, place of execution; ساعة رملية *sâ'a-t ramliyya-t*, hourglass.

رمم *rimam*, *rumam*, pl. of رمة *rimma-t*, *rumma-t*, respectively.

(رمه) *ramih*, A, INF. *ramah*, be glowing hot.

رمو *rumû'*, INF. of (رما).

رموح *ramûḥ*, given to kicking.

رموس *ramûs*, raft.

رموق *ramûq*, pl. *rumuq*, poor, starving; envious.

(رمى) *rama*, I, INF. *ramy*, *rimâya-t*, throw; shoot arrows, shoot, fling; hit and kill; throw down; cut off (the head); throw out (a hint, &c.); help;

blame, inveigh against; surpass in number (50); drop excrement; — III. INF. *rimâ'*, *tarmâ'*, *murâmât*, vie in throwing, shooting, &c.; throw, &c., each from his side; — IV. surpass in number (50); throw out, eject; — VI. INF. *tarâmî*, throw, &c., at one another; throw one's self at another's feet in supplication; be relaxed, hang down flaccidly; arrive at, travel afar (news, &c.); — VIII. INF. *irtimâ'*, be thrown, &c.; be hit, killed; throw, &c., at one another; fall down in a swoon; throw, shoot, hit.

رمى *ramy*, throwing, flinging, shooting (s.); — *rim-an*, the hissing of a projectile; — *ramiyy*, ة, pl. *armâ'*, *armiya-t*, *ramâyâ*, thrown at, hit; *ramiyya-t*, hit prey of a hunter; — ة *ramya-t*, throw, shot.

رميح *rumaiḥ*, small lance, javelin.

رميز *ramîz*, agile, nimble, mobile; prudent, reasonable, intelligent; of noble birth; honoured, dignified; — *rumaiz*, stick, staff.

رميس *ramîs*, secret, concealed; buried.

رميض *ramîḍ*, ة, sharp; sharpened between stones.

رميم *ramîm*, putrid, carious, rotten; old, worn; INF. of (رم).

(رن) *rann*, I, INF. *ranîn*, *ranna-t*, cry out; give a sound, resound, whiz, ring, tingle; sigh, groan; listen to (الى *ila*); — II. INF. *tarnîn*, cause to sound, to resound, &c.; — IV. INF. *irnân*, cry out; complain, lament; resound; listen to; — ة *ranna-t*, sound, voice.

(رنا) *rana'*, INF. *ran'*, look at, view, contemplate; walk heavily.

رنا *ran-an*, *ranâ*, what is worth looking at, captivating (adj.); — *runâ'*, sound, (musical) tone; joy, emotion; dance; — *rannâ'*, admirer of the fair sex, starer at ladies.

رناس *runnâs*, madder.

رنان *rannân*, sounding, resounding; vibrating.

(رنجح) *ranjaḥ*, INF. ة, hum a song.

(رنجس) *ranjis*=نرجس *narjis*, narcissus.

(رنح) *ranḥ*, giddiness; a certain part of the brain said to resemble a sparrow; — II. *rannaḥ*, INF. *tarnîḥ*, make giddy; cause to reel, to swoon; confuse; bend the branches; reel; — V. INF. *tarannuḥ*, drink slowly, sip, suck; also VIII. INF. *irtinâḥ*, reel.

(رنخ) *ranaẖ*, U, INF. *ranẖ*, be very weak and slack; be dark; — II. INF. *tarnîẖ*, make very weak; humble; (m.) wet through; — V. INF. *tarannuẖ*, hold fast; (m.) be wet through.

(رند) *rand*, an aromatic tree of the desert, myrtle.

رندج *randaj*, plane (tool).

رنز *runz*, rice.

(رنع) *rana'*, INF. *runû'*, change colour and waste away, emaciate (n.); drive away the flies by shaking the head; play.

(رنف) *ranf*, *ranaf*, wild willow-tree; — IV. *arnaf*, INF. *irnâf*, hang down the ears from tiredness; walk apace.

(رنق) *ranaq*, U, INF. *ranq*, *runûq*, be troubled, muddy (water, &c.); — *raniq*, A, INF. *ranaq*, id.; — II. INF. *tarnîq*, trouble the water, dim the eyes, and, by opposition, clear, make clear; remain, abide; differ in opinion; soar with spread wings; be weak, dim; — IV. INF. *irnâq*, wave the flag for an attack; — V. INF. *tarannuq*, be troubled, dim.

رنق *ranq*, *ranaq*, *raniq*, troubled.

رنقا *ranqâ'*, brooding; pl. *ranqawât*, sterile.

(رنم) *ranim*, INF. *ranîm*, sing with a soft voice, modulate; — II.

INF. *tarnîm*, id.; resound; — V. INF. *tarannum*, modulate, chant psalms.

رنم *ranam*, sound; song; —*runum*, pl. female singers; — ة *ranama-t*, musical tone; melody, air.

(رنو) *ranâ*, U, INF. *ran-an*, *runuww*, look at steadily and with admiration, gaze; be captivated; rejoice and dance; listen attentively; — II. INF. *tarniya-t*, (also IV.) enchant, captivate; rejoice (a.), cheer; — III. INF. *murânât*, adore, flatter; — IV. INF. *irnâ'*, see II.

رنو *ranuww*, who gazes at admiringly; admirer of the fair sex; — *runuww*, INF. of (رنو).

رنى *runna*, the sixth month; *ar-runna*, man, mankind, all.

رنيم *ranîm*, song, hymn.

رنين *ranîn*, sound, tone; echo; vibration, resonance; sighing, groaning (s.).

(ره) *rahh*, wide and shallow.

رها *rihâ'*, pl. of رهو *rahw*; — الرها *ar-ruhâ'*, Edessa.

رهاب *rihâb*, pl. of رهب *rahb*; — ة *ruhâba-t*, *ruhhâba-t*, *rahhâba-t*, pl. *rahâb*, breast-bone.

رهابنة *rahâbina-t*, رهابين *rahâbîn*, pl. of رهبان *ruhbân*.

رهادة *rahâda-t*, softness, delicacy.

رهاص *rahhâṣ*, who makes or smears with mortar; who builds clay walls.

رهاط *rihâṭ*, furniture; pl. *arhiṭa-t*, skin to cut straps from.

رهافة *rahâfa-t*, thinness, fineness.

رهاق *rihâq*, *ruhâq*, a considerable number.

رهام *rahâm*, lean sheep or goats; — *ruhâm*, numerous; many; tame birds; — *.

رهان *rihân*, bet, wager.

رهاوى *ruhâwiyy*, of or from Edessa.

(رهب) *rahib*, A, INF. *rahb*, *ruhb*, *rahab*, *rahba-t*, *ruhbân*, *rahabân*, fear; — II. INF. *tarhîb*, inspire with fear, frighten; be worn out by a journey; induce to enter on a clerical life, to become a monk; — IV. INF. *irhâb*, frighten into flight; — V. INF. *tarahhub*, devote one's self to God, enter on a clerical life, become a monk; — VIII. INF. *irtihâb*, fear; — X. INF. *istirhâb*, try to frighten, frighten.

رهب *rahab*, *rahb*, *ruhb*, fear, fright, terror; — *rahb*, pl. *rihâb*, sharp head of an arrow or spear; — ة *rahba-t*, fear; monastic life; monachism.

رهبا *rahbâ'*, *ruhbâ'*, fear.

رهبان *ruhbân*, pl. *-ûn*, *rahâbîn*, *rahâbina-t*, monk; Christian priest; pl. of راهب *râhib*, monk, &c.; — ى *rahbâniyy*, *ruhbâniyy*, ة, monachal, ecclesiastical, clerical; — ة *rahbâniyya-t*, *ruhbâniyya-t*, monachism; ascetic life.

(رهبل) *rahbal*, unintelligible speech; — ة *rahbala-t*, tottering or jerking walk; — II. INF. *tarahbul*, walk in such a manner.

رهبنة *rahbana-t*, monachism; monastic life.

رهبوت *rahabût*, رهبوتى *rahabûta*, رهبى *rahba*, *ruhba*, fear.

(رهج) *rahj*, *rahaj*, dust; tumult; waving, glittering (s.); — *rahaj*, INF. *rahj*, waver to and fro; flicker, glitter, scintillate; — IV. INF. *irhâj*, id.; raise dust; rain abundantly; strongly fumigate a house.

(رهد) *rahad*, rub violently; — II. INF. *tarhîd*, show great stupidity.

(رهدل) *rahdal*, weak, stupid; — *rahdal*, also رهدن *rahdan*, INF. ة, chat, chatter (m.); — II. INF. *tarahdul*, chat, chatter with one another; converse; behave arrogantly; — ة *rahdala-t*, arrogance.

(رهدن) *rahdan*, INF. ة, tarry, hesitate; be kept back, retained; walk in a circle; see (رهدل).

رهدن *rahdan, rihdan, ruhdan*, pl. *rahâdin*, cowardly, mean; — also ة *rahdana-t, ruhdunna-t*, and رهدون *ruhdûn*, Mecca sparrow; — ة *rahdana-t*, chat, conversation.

رهراه *rahrâh*, رهره *rahrah*, wide and shallow; — also رهروه *ruhrûh*, white and delicate (body).

(رهره) *rahrah*, INF. ة, keep open house; (also II.) be white and delicate; — II. INF. *tarahruh*, see I.; shine, beam, be brilliant; be in good humour, in high spirits, wantonly merry; — ة *rahraha-t*, brightness, lustre; brilliancy of complexion.

(رهز) *rahaz*, INF. *rahz, rahazân*, move violently (especially in coition).

(رهس) *rahas*, INF. *rahs*, tread violently under foot; — V. INF. *tarahhus*, be moved, agitated, shaken; waver; — VIII. INF. *irtihâs*, knock together and hurt each other; be full of water; throng.

رهش *rahś*, sesame-flour; — ة *ruhśa-t*, unpretending liberality; — VIII. INF. *irtihâś*, be thin and easily made to tremble (bow); destroy, annihilate; tremble.

رهشوش *ruhśûś*, liberal; — ة *ruhśûśa-t*, unpretending liberality.

(رهص) *rahaṣ*, INF. *rahṣ*, press, be hard upon; urge to haste; blame; (also IV.) make the first layer of a wall, build a clay wall; — *rahiṣ*, A, INF. *rahaṣ*, and pass. *ruhiṣ*, have the hoof hurt by stones and limp; — III. INF. *murâhaṣa-t*, take an opportunity to come down upon a debtor; — IV. INF. *irhâṣ*, see I.; impart all that is good to.

رهص *rihṣ*, lowest stone layer of a wall; mortar, cement; — ة *rahṣa-t*, soreness of the hoof.

(رهط) *rahaṭ*, INF. *rahṭ*, take large bits; devour greedily; assemble (n.); — VIII. INF. *irtihâṭ*, assemble (n.).

رهط *rahṭ, rahaṭ*, pl. *arhâṭ, arhuṭ, arâhiṭ, arâhîṭ*, family, race (especially below 10 and without women); company; — *rahṭ*, pl. *rihâṭ*, petticoat of leather for women and children.

(رهف) *rahaf*, INF. *rahf*, make thin, sharpen, whet; — *rahuf*, INF. *rahâfa-t*, be thin, sharp; be pretty and delicate; — IV. INF. *irhâf*, sharpen, whet, grind; — VIII. INF. *irtihâf*, receive kindly.

رهطا *ruhaṭâ'*, رهطة *ruhaṭa-t*, hole of a field-mouse or jerboa.

(رهق) *rahiq*, INF. *rahaq*, overtake, reach from behind, come close up to; cover, veil; be stupid and frivolous, (m.) be quite dumbfounded by an agreeable surprise, be almost spell-bound; tell lies; hasten; be always disposed to wrong and violence; — III. INF. *murâhaqa-t*, be near puberty or full age; — IV. INF. *irhâq*, instigate to wrong and violence; charge one with anything beyond his power (2 acc.), worry; astonish, prepare an agreeable surprise; — VII. INF. *irrihâq*, be stupid; be agreeably surprised.

رهق *rahaq*, stupidity and frivolity; unjust over-burdening.

(رهك) *rahak*, INF. *rahk*, crush between two stones; grind or pound violently; remain, abide; — VIII. INF. *irtihâk*, be weak or relaxed in limbs and joints; step not firmly; — ة *rahka-t*, weakness; — *rahaka-t, ruhaka-t*, weakling; good-for-nothing fellow.

(رهل) *rahil*, A, INF. *rahal*, be soft and tremulous; (also V.) have soft tremulous flesh; be inflated, swollen; — V. INF. *tarahhul*, see I.

رهل *rahl*, water round the embryo; — *rahil*, soft and tremulous.

(رهم), IV. *arham*, INF. *irhâm*, rain steadily; — ة *rihma-t*, pl. *riham*, *rihâm*, fine steady rain.

(رهمج) *rahmaj*, wide, spacious.

(رهمس) *rahmas*, INF. ة, whisper to, talk into one's ears; say or place in one's way unpleasant things.

(رهن) *rahan*, INF. *rahn*, pawn, give as a pledge, on mortgage, as a hostage; restrain; be settled, fixed in a place; last; make to last; — A, INF. *ruhûn*, be emaciated; — III. INF. *rihân*, *murâhana-t*, bet, make a wager; pawn; — IV. INF. *irhân*, pawn to (2 acc.); mortgage; give a pledge; demand a pledge (2 acc.); deliver as a hostage; make to last; give for a length of time; raise the price; pay in advance; weaken; — VI. INF. *tarâhun*, bet with one another, give a pledge mutually; — VIII. INF. *irtihân*, take or receive a pledge; receive as a hostage; be given as a pledge or hostage; be mortgaged; have bound by a pledge; — X. INF. *istirhân*, demand a pledge; receive a pledge or hostage.

رهن *rahn*, pl. *rihân*, *ruhûn*, *rahîn*, *ruhun*, pledge, pawn; mortgage; hostage; — رهن مال *rihn mâl*, manager, administrator.

رهنا *ruhanâ'*, pl. of رهين *rahîn*.

رهنامج *rahnâmaj*, mariner's chart; travelling-guide (Pers.).

(رهو) *rahâ*, U, INF. *rahw*, open the legs wide, sit or walk so; walk slowly and comfortably; be calm; spread the wings; — III. INF. *murâhât*, be near to (acc.); — IV. INF. *irhâ'*, lower the price, under-sell; give food and drink for a permanency; come to a place; — VIII. INF. *irtihâ'*, be mixed and in confusion; prepare the dish رهية *rahiyya-t*.

رهو *rahw*, pl. *rihâ'*, aqueduct, canal; crane (bird); width of the wings of a bird; width of the thighs; calm.

رهواج *rahwâj*, of a light step.

رهوان *rahwân*, id.; ambler.

رهوج *rahûj*, soft, delicate; — ة *rahwaja-t*, light step of a horse.

رهودية *rahwadiyya-t*, kindness, friendliness, favour; help, aid, assistance.

رهوس *rahwas*, glutton.

(رهوط), II. *tarahwuṭ*, walk proudly, give one's self airs.

رهوق *rahûq*, making wide steps; fleet.

(رهوك) *rahwak*, INF. ة, have weak or relaxed limbs and walk unsteadily.

رهوك *rahwak*, plump and delicate.

رهوم *rahûm*, who has no will or opinion of his own.

(رهيا) *rahya'*, INF. ة, be weak, impotent; have no will or opinion of one's own; by opposition, plan and execute deliberately; fix or carry a load not equally balanced; — II. INF. *tarahyu'*, totter; lean to one side in walking; lose self-reliance in a matter and desist from it.

رهيدة *rahîda-t*, delicate girl; — also رهية *rahiyya-t*, wheat cooked in milk.

رهيش *rahîś*, knocking together of the fore-feet of a saddle-beast; thin; weak; fleshless; — also ة *rahîśa-t*, abounding in milk.

رهيص *rahîṣ*, sore through stones (hoof); cruel.

رهيط *ruhaiṭ*, small number of men.

رهيف *rahîf*, thin and sharp.

رهيق *rahîq*, wine.

رهين *rahîn*, ة, given as a pawn, pledge, mortgage, security or hostage; submissive; pl. *ruhanâ'*, hostages; — also ة *rahîna-t*, pl. *rahâ'in*, pledge, mortgage, hostage.

رهية *rahiyya-t*, see رهيدة *rahîda-t*.

(روا), II. *rawwa'*, INF. *tarwî'*, *tarwiya-t*, well consider, weigh the

consequences and not precipitate the answer.

روا *rawâ'*, sweet, wholesome; the well Zemzem; — *riwâ'*, pl. *arwiya-t*, packing-rope; — *ruwâ'*, *ru'â'*, loveliness, grace, comeliness; — ة *ruwât*, pl. of راوى *râwî*, narrator, &c.

روابط *rawâbiṭ*, bandages, &c., pl. of رابطة *râbiṭa-t*.

روابى *rawâbî*, hills, pl. of رابية *râbiya-t*.

روات *ruwwât*, pl. of رات *rât*, straw.

رواتب *rawâtib*, pl. of راتب *râtib*, fix, &c.

رواج *rawâj*, selling well; current; usual, customary; good sale; use; (m.) zeal, hurry.

رواجب *rawâjib*, upper joints of the fingers, pl. of راجبة *râjiba-t*.

رواجع *rawâji'*, pl. of راجع *râji'*, yard (of a sail).

رواح *rawâḥ*, afternoon; evening; rest, repose; also *riwâḥ*, walking (s.), INF. of (روح); — ة *rawâḥa-t*, rest, repose, ease, comfort.

رواحل *rawâḥil*, pl. of راحلة *râḥila-t*, saddle-beast.

رواد *riwâd*, wish, desire, request, INF. III. of (رود); — *ruwwâd*, foragers, scouts, &c., pl. of رائد *râ'id*.

روادف *rawâdif*, pl. of رادفة *râdifa-t*, palm-shoot.

رواذق *rawâẕiq*, pl. of روذق *rauẕaq*.

روازن *rawâzin*, pl. of روزن *rauzan*.

رواس *rawwâs*, رواسى *rawwâsiyy*, cattle-dealer.

رواسى *rawâsî*, pl. f. of راسى *râsî*, firm at anchor, &c.; — *ru'âsiyy*, having a large head.

رواسيم *rawâsîm*, books of the pagan Arabs.

رواش *rawwâś*, selling well.

رواشح *rawâśiḥ*, exudations; reptiles; pl. of راشح *râśiḥ*.

رواض *ruwwâḍ*, horse-breakers, pl. of رائض *râ'iḍ*.

رواضع *rawâḍi'*, milk-teeth, pl. of راضعة *râḍi'a-t*.

رواعد *rawâ'id*, pl. f. of راعد *râ'id*, thundering; ذات رواعد *ẕât rawâ'id*, calamity.

رواعف *rawâ'if*, pl. of راعف *râ'if*, bleeding, &c.; spears.

رواغ *rawâg*, flight, retreat; trot; — *rawwâg*, not straightforward, cunning; fox; — ة *riwâga-t*, arena for wrestlers.

روافد *rawâfid*, pl. of رافد *râfid*, ة *râfida-t*, rafter.

روافض *rawâfiḍ*, deserters, &c., pl. of رافضة *râfiḍa-t*.

رواق *riwâq*, *ruwâq*, pl. *arwiqa-t*, *rûq*, tent, any tent-like building; awning, projecting roof, gallery; peristyle; stoa; balcony, portico; audience-hall; eye-brow; — ى *riwâqiyy*, stoic; — *rawâqî*, sorcerers, pl. of راقى *râqî*.

رواقيد *rawâqîd*, pl. large vessels for wine.

رواكد *rawâkid*, pl. of راكد *râkid*, quiet, stable, &c.

روال *ru'âl*, *ruwâl*, spittle or foam of a horse; supernumerary tooth.

روام *ru'âm*, *ruwâm*, spittle or foam of a camel.

روامس *rawâmis*, pl. of رامس *râmis*, wind which effaces traces; night-birds, night-beasts.

روانف *rawânif*, lower edges of tents, hems of shirts, pl. of رانفة *rânifa-t*.

روانق *rawâniq*, pl. of رونقة *rauniqa-t*.

رواهش *rawâhiś*, veins on the back of the hand, or on the feet of horses.

روائص *rawâ'iṣ*, stones wounding the hoofs.

رواية *riwâya-t*, tradition; tale; anecdote; recitation; information; seeking of instruction; authority of one who hands down traditions; INF. of (روى).

روائح *rawâ'iḥ*, odours, &c., pl. of رائحة *râ'iḥa-t*.

روائم *rawâ'im*, pl. tripods.

(روب) *râb*, U, INF. *raub*, *ru'ub*, curdle, turn sour, coagulate

(m.) get dirty; be bewildered; be lazy, slack, relaxed; be tired; be near death; tell lies; — II. INF. *tarwîb*, IV. INF. *irâba-t*, cause the milk to curdle; — V. INF. *tarawwub*, be curdled.

روب *raub*, ة *rauba-t*, curdled milk; *raub*, fraud in commerce; — ة *rauba-t*, *rûba-t*, what causes the milk to curdle, runnet; who sows discord; sperm of the stallion; anything urgent; — ة *ru'ba-t*, pl. *ri'âb*, solder.

روبان *raubân*, relaxed; bewildered.

روبج *raubaj*, small coin.

روبع *rauba'*, ة *rauba'a-t*, small, little.

(روث) *râs̱*, U, INF. *raus̱*, drop excrement; soil with excrement; — ة *rausa-t*, pl. *raus̱*, *arwâs̱*, dung.

(روج) *râj*, U, INF. *rawâj*, sell well, have course, be current, be obtainable; be changeable, uncertain; — II. INF. *tarwîj*, procure a speedy sale for, give currency; bring or perform speedily, despatch; — V. INF. *tarawwuj*, go round a thing without being able to approach it; — ة *rauja-t*, speed, haste, eagerness.

روجيل *rûjail* = رجيل *rujail*, little man, manikin.

(روح) *râḥ*, U, INF. *rawâḥ*, go, travel or blow at evening-time, go to (الى *ila*); go away, depart; be lost to (على *'ala*); have course, be current; — INF. *rauḥ*, *rawâḥ*, come at evening-time; — A, INF. *râḥ*, *rawâḥ*, *ru'uḥ*, *riyâḥa-t*, be near fulfilment, be at rest, have one's mind set at rest; — A, INF. *râḥa-t*, be willing; be light and skilful (hand); be a stallion; push forth leaves; — A, I, INF. *râḥa-t*, notice by the smell, smell; receive benefits; — A, INF. *rîḥ*, blow violently, be very windy; touch, blow at, fan; — A, INF. *ruwûḥ*, be prone to give, be liberal; — *rawiḥ*, A, INF. *rawaḥ*, be wide, spacious, commodious; — II. INF. *tarwiḥ*, drive into the fold; also (m.) *rayyaḥ*, INF. *taryîḥ*, procure rest, set at rest, pension; smell at; blow at, fan; air; perfume; lose, feel as a loss; (m.) leak, miscarry (woman), destroy; — III. INF. *murâwaḥa-t*, come at evening-time; stand alternately on the right or left foot; — IV. INF. *irâḥa-t*, drive in or milk the camels (especially at evening); allow one to rest, set at rest, give rest; die; come into the wind; smell badly; recognise by the smell, smell; — V. INF. *tarawwuḥ*, travel, come or do anything at evening-time; fan one's self; (m.) *tarayyaḥ*, INF. *tarayyuḥ*, bend, crack (fresh wood); — VIII. INF. *irtiyâḥ*, rest, take breath; be willing and ready to do or perform, be brisk, condescend easily, be gracious; strive for, aspire to; — X. INF. *istirâḥa-t*, *istirwâḥ*, rest, find repose and ease; be at rest; credit a report; rely upon; recognise by the smell, smell, smell at, get wind of.

روح *rauḥ*, rest, repose; redress; quietude of mind; cheerfulness, joy; compassion; divine mercy; refreshing breeze; pleasant; good fortune and ease; — *rûḥ*, m. f., pl. *arwâḥ*, breath of life, spirits, life; soul, mind; word or spirit of God, revelation, prophecy; Christ; the Koran; demon, ghost; روح القدس *rûḥ-u 'l-quds-i*, Gabriel, Mohammed; الروح القدس *ar-rûḥ al-qudus*, the Holy Ghost; روح توتيا *rûḥ tûtiyâ'*, mercury, tin; *arwâḥ*, spirits, intoxicating drinks; — ة *rauḥa-t*, rest, repose; tranquility of mind; pleasure; evening, evening-time; (m.)

coming, going, travelling (s.), especially at even.

روحا *rauḥâ*, f. of اروح *arwaḥ*, wide, spacious.

روحاني *rauḥâniyy*, good, agreeable; — *ruḥâniyy*, pl. *-ûn*, spiritual, holy; angel, ghost, fairy; mercury; — ة *ruḥâniyya-t*, spirituality, holiness.

(روخ), V. *tarawwaḥ*, INF. *tarawwuḥ*, fall into the mud.

(رود) *râd*, U, INF. *raud*, *riyâd*, seek, seek food and water, forage; come and go, go to and fro, roam about; move to and fro, shift; — INF. *rawadân*, frequent the neighbours, be always visiting; — III. INF. *murâdât*, *riwâd*, wish, will; demand, entice, seduce; — IV. INF. *irâda-t*, wish, will, want; demand; INF. *irwâd*, *murwad*, *marwad*, be slow and leisurely (in walking), walk on at leisure; — VIII. INF. *irtiyâd*, wish, will, desire, seek, seek food.

رود *raud*, pleasant, agreeable; — *rûd*, slow but steady walk; — *ru'd*, ة *ru'ada-t*, *ru'uda-t*, handsome girl.

رودس *rûdis*, island of Rhodes.

رودك *raudak*, lovely, blooming; — *raudak*, INF. ة, embellish.

(روذ) *râẓ*, U, INF. *rauẓa-t*, come and go.

روذق *rauẓaq*, pl. *rawâẓiq*, stripped-off skin; kid skinned for being roasted.

روذكة *rauẓaka-t*, pl. *rawâẓik*, small.

(روز) *râz*, U, INF. *rauz*, weigh by the hand; weigh, ponder over, consider; try by experience, test; live on one's estate and manage it well; demand, ask from (عند *'and*).

روزن *rauzan*, ة *rauzana-t*, pl. *rawâzin*, window (Pers.).

(روس) *râs*, U, INF. *raus*, step along haughtily; carry away offal, &c.; eat well or much; — II. INF. *tarwîs*, sharpen, point; also V. INF. *tarawwus*, get pointed, taper.

روس *ru'us*, heads, &c., pl. of راس *ra's*.

روسا *ru'asâ'*, pl. of رئيس *ra'îs*.

روسختج *rûsaḫtaj*, antimony.

روسم *rausam*, mark, trace; large seal for marking corn-heaps, &c.

(روش) *râś*, U, INF. *rauś*, eat much, and, by opposition, eat little; weaken in the hips; — II. INF. *tarawwuś*, have a strong beard.

روش *rawwaś*, hairy, bearded.

روشم *rauśam* = روسم *rausam*.

روشن *rauśan*, window.

(روص) *râṣ*, U, INF. *rauṣ*, grow wise.

(روض) *râḍ*, U, INF. *rauḍ*, *riyâḍ*, *riyâḍa-t*, tame, rein, exercise, dress, train; drill soldiers; change a place into a meadow or garden by growing grass and plants in it; — III. INF. *murâwaḍa-t*, beguile, cajole; — V. INF. *tarawwuḍ*, be well trained, drilled, exercised; grow healthy, be thoroughly healthy; — VIII. INF. *irtiyâḍ*, get drilled, trained, exercised.

روض *rauḍ*, some water; — ة *rauḍa-t*, pl. *rauḍ*, *rauḍât*, *riyâḍ*, *rîḍân*, place with water and consequently abounding in grass and herbs; meadow, plot; kitchen garden, garden with rich vegetation; Paradise; mausoleum.

(روط) *râṭ*, U, I, INF. *rauṭ*, flee into the mountains and sand-hills; deviate.

روط *rauṭ*, pl. *arwâṭ*, spars, short beams.

(روع) *râ'*, U, INF. *rau'*, *ruwû'*, frighten, terrify; surprise; fear; please; be quenched; — U, I, INF. *ruwâ'*, return; — II. INF. *tarwî'*, IV. INF. *irâ'a-t*, frighten; — V. INF. *tarawwu'*, VIII. INF. *irtiwâ'*, be frightened, fear.

روع *rau'*, ة *rau'a-t*, fear, fright; — *rû'*, seat of fear, heart, mind;

— *rawa'*, surprise; surprising beauty.

روعا *rau'â*, f. of اروع *arwa'*, surprising, pleasing, &c.

(روغ) *râg*, U, INF. *raug*, *ragawân*, turn from the straight way, to approach stealthily, steal up to a person to strike him; act slyly; — II. INF. *tarwîg*, butter or grease a dish; — III. INF. *murâwaga-t*, act insidiously towards (acc.); — IV. INF. *irâga-t*, VIII. INF. *irtiyâg*, strive for, desire, seek, steal against.

(روف) *râf*, A, INF. *rauf*, pardon; have compassion.

روف *rauf*, ة *raufa-t*, compassion; — *ra'uf*, kind; God.

(روق) *râq*, U, INF. *rauq*, be pure, clear; become clear, clear (n.), settle; recover; fill with admiration, please, charm, be choice, excel, surpass; — *rawiq*, A, INF. *rawaq*, have long teeth; — II. INF. *tarwîq*, clear (a.), strain; have a portico, an awning; change an old garment for a new one by addition of some money; (m.) recover; (m.) give one a breakfast; — IV. INF. *irâqa-t*, pour out; — V. INF. *tarawwuq*, breakfast.

روق *rauq*, pl. *arwâq*, vestibule, portico; canopy, baldachin; tent; awning, veil, curtain; horn; pure, clear; bloom of youth; — *rûq*, pl. of رواق *riwâq*; *rûq*, ة *rûqa-t*, pl. of رائق *râ'iq*, pure, clear, fair, &c.; — ة *rauqa-t*, surpassing beauty; — *rûqa-t*, a handsome boy or girl, a fair one, anything beautiful.

روك *rûk*, community; — ة *rauka-t*, wave; — *rauka-t*, and—

روكا *raukâ'*, screech of an owl; echo.

روكی *raukiyy*, common.

(رول), II. *rawwal*, INF. *tarwîl*, butter the bread, put fat on it; salivate (n.).

(روم) *râm*, U, INF. *raum*, *marâm*, crave for, desire strongly; — II. INF. *tarwîm*, set one to seek a thing; remain, stay, abide, tarry; — V. INF. *tarawwum*, mock at, deride.

روم *raum*, craving, desire, wish; — *rûm*, Rome; Greece, Roumelia; pl. *arwâm*, Romans, Greeks, Byzantines; بحر الروم *bahr ar-rûm*, Mediterranean; روم و حبش *rûm wa habaś*, north and south, the whole world; — ة *rûma-t*, glue.

رومانی *rûmâniyy*, ruby-coloured.

رومی *rûmiyy*, ة, Roman, Grecian; — ة *rûmiya-t*, *rûmiyya-t*, Rome; Greece; Turkey; رومية صغرى *rûmiya-t ṣugra*, Asia Minor.

رون *raun*, border of a sown field; — *rûn*, pl. *ruwûn*, hardness, violence; adversity; — *ri'un*, lungs, pl. of رئة *ri'a-t*.

روند *riwand*, rhubarb.

رونق *raunaq*, splendour, lustre, brilliancy; beauty, elegance; adornment; — ة *raunaqa-t*, pl. روانق *rawâniq*, troubled (water).

روودة *ra'ûda-t*, handsome girl; — *ru'ûda-t*, slowness.

رووس *ru'ûs*, heads, &c., pl. of راس *ra's*.

رووف *ra'ûf*, compassionate, kind.

(روه) *râh*, U, INF. *rauh*, *ruwâh*, undulate on the ground (water).

(روی) *rawa*, I, INF. *riwâya-t*, quote as the words of another, refer to one as an authority, relate; twist a rope; bring water to, draw water for, give to drink; tie the rider to the camel; consider, ponder over, examine; — *rawî*, A, INF. *rayy riyy*, *riwan*, quench one's thirst; be sufficiently watered; — II. INF. *tarwiya-t*, (also IV.) water, give to drink; bid to quote another's words, to recite his verses; consider, ponder; prepare one's speech; (also IV.) impregnate, saturate; (also IV.) show; — IV. INF. *irwâ'*, see II.; water

sufficiently; quench; — II. INF. *tarawwî*, quench one's thirst; be sufficiently watered; quote another's words, recite his verses; relate; speak after sufficient preparation; — VIII. INF. *irtiyâ'*, quench one's thirst; be sufficiently watered; consider, take thought; — X. INF. *istiryâ'*, consider well.

روى *riwan*, abundant and good drinking-water; plenty; INF. of (روى); — *rawiyy*, letter upon which the rhyme of a poem depends; good and sufficient for quenching the thirst; — *ru'iyy*, beautiful face; — ة *ru'ya-t*, aspect; vision, apparition; consideration, notion, opinion; inspection, perusal, revision; — *rawiyya-t*=روئة *rawi'a-t*.

رويا *ru'yâ*, *rûyâ*, pl. روى *ru'an*, vision, vision in a dream, apparition; aspect.

رويان *ra'yân*, INF. of (رأى).

رويجل *ruwaijil*, little man, manikin.

رويحة *rawîḥa-t*, ease, rest, repose, tranquillity.

رويد *ruwaid*, slow quiet walk; gentle and composed manners; *ruwaid-an*, رويدك *ruwaidaka*, gently! be gentle with (acc.), leave him alone!

رويدا *ruwaidâ'*, رويدية *ruwaidiya-t*, *ruwaidiyya-t*, gentle walk; kindness, help, aid.

رويغة *ruwaiga-t*, cunning, stratagem.

روئة *rawi'a-t*, mature consideration, close examination; balance, remainder.

رى *rayy*, *riyy*, quenching of thirst; full draught; plentiful watering; luxuriant verdure; affluence; — *riyy*, fine aspect, beautiful form; — *ri'*, aspect; — ة *riya-t*, tinder; INF. of (روى), burn, blaze; — *ri'a-t*, *riya-t*, pl. *ri'ât*, *ri'ûn*, lung; ذات الرئة *ẕât ar-ri'a-t*, inflammation of the lungs; — *rayya-t*, watering (s.); plenty, abundance; — also *riyya-t*, abounding in water; — *riyya-t*, perception, cognition, knowledge.

(ريا), را *râ'*, see, perceive; — II. INF. *taryi'a-t*, loosen again the cord for strangling; consider, ponder, think over; — III. INF. *murâya'a-t*, fear, be on one's guard against (acc.).

ريا *riyâ'*, dissembling, hypocrisy; aspect, appearance; in sight of one another; — *rayyâ'*, *rayy-an*, odour, fragrance; fragrant breeze.

رياب *rayyâb*, terrifying, terrific; — *ri'âb*, camel-herds, &c., pl. of راب *ra'b*; pl. of روبة *ru'ba-t*.

رئات *ri'ât*, lungs, pl. of رئة *ri'a-t*.

رباح *rayâḥ*, wine; — also *riyâḥ*, afternoon; — *riyâḥ*, pl. of ريح *rîḥ*.

رياحين *rayâḥîn*, pl. of ريحان *rîḥân*.

ريازة *riyâza-t*, supervision in the building of a house, &c., office of an architect; consideration.

رئاس *ri'âs*, pommel of a sword; — ة *ri'âsa-t*, ruling, governing (s.); dominion, command; presidency; princeliness; ecclesiastical government (opposed to سياسة *siyâsa-t*, political government).

رياش *riyâš*, embroidered ornamental vest; plenty and ease; — *; — *rayyâš*, who feathers arrows.

رياض *riyâḍ*, training, drill, exercise; INF. of (روض); pl. of روضة *rauḍa-t*; — ة *riyâḍa-t*, training; drill, exercise; discipline; self-mortification, ascetic life; (m.) spiritual exercises; (m.) rest, tranquillity; (m.) full health; — ى *riyâḍiyy*, ة, referring to discipline, disciplinary; practical; علوم رياضية *'ulûm riyâḍiyya-t*, practical sciences, mathematics.

رياغ *riyâg*, fertility, plenty; — ة *riyâga-t*, arena for wrestling.

ريافة *riyâfa-t*, finding of wells.

ريال *riyâl*, spittle; — *riyâl*, pl.

riyalât, real, dollar, piece of five piastres ; — *ri'âl*, ة *ri'âla-t*, young ostriches, pl. of رال *ra'l*.

ريان *rayyân*, f. *rayya*, pl. *riwâ'*, whose thirst is quenched ; impregnated, saturated ; sappy, greening, fresh ; beautiful.

ربائى *riyâ'iyy*, hypocritical, dissembling.

(ريب) *râb*, I, INF. *raib*, *rîba-t*, unsettle one's opinions or resolutions, inspire with doubts, scruples, suspicions, fear ; — IV., INF. *irâba-t*, id. ; become doubtful, suspect ; — VIII. INF. *irtiyâb*, X. INF. *istirâba-t*, be uncertain, doubtful, suspicious.

ريب *raib*, uncertainty, doubt, suspicion, ill fame ; what inspires with suspicion or fear ; guilt, crime ; vicissitude ; calamity ; — ة *rîba-t*, pl. *riyab*, doubt, suspicion, bad opinion ; doubtful deed ; pl. *riyab*, adversities, embarrassments.

رئبال *ri'bâl*, *rîbâl*, pl. *ra'âbil*, *ra'âbîl*, lion.

(ريث) *râs̱*, I, INF. *rais̱*, tarry, hesitate ; reach too late ; — II. INF. *taryîs̱*, soften ; be tired ; — IV. INF. *irâs̱a-t*, detain, delay (a.) ; — V. INF. *tarayyus̱*, tarry, hesitate, delay (n.) ; — X. INF. *istirâs̱a-t*, consider slow, lazy, find tardy.

ريث *rais̱*, quantity, measure, space ; *rais̱-a*, ريثما *rais̱a-mâ*, as long as, while, when, till ; —*rayyis̱*, tardy, delaying, slow, lazy ; — ة *rais̱a-t*, delay, postponement, procrastination.

(ريح) see (روح), II. and V.

ريح *rîḥ*, pl. *arwâḥ*, *aryâḥ*, *riyâḥ*, *riyaḥ*, breath of air, breeze, wind ; (also m. ريحية *rîḥiyya-t*) flatulence ; smell ; odour, fragrance ; victory ; power ; good fortune ; rheum ; — *rayyiḥ*, breezy ; fragrant ; — ة *rîḥa-t*, wind ; — *rayyiḥa-t*, a plant.

ريحان *rîḥân*, sustenance, daily bread ; offspring, son ; — also ة *rîḥâna-t*, pl. *rayâḥîn*, basil, myrtle, in general an aromatic plant ; — ى *riḥâniyy*, emerald.

ريحى *rîḥiyy*, causing flatulence.

(ريخ) *râḥ*, I, INF. *raiḥ*, *ruyûḥ*, be tired, relaxed, slack ; — II. INF. *taryîḥ*, relax (a.), unnerve.

ريد *raid*, pl. *ruyûd*, mountain-knoll ; cliff ; — *ra'id*, co-eval, in equal circumstances ; — ة *raida-t*, also—

ريدانة *raidâna-t*, soft breeze.

ريذجان *raiẕajân*, camel loaded with goods.

(رير), pass. *rîr*, have a plentiful year, grow fat from plenty of food ; — II. INF. *taryîr*, id. ; grow too fat ; — IV. INF. *irâra-t*, soften the brain or marrow.

رير *rair*, spittle, saliva ; marrow.

(ريس) *râs*, I, INF. *rais*, *rayasân*, walk pompously with violent movements of the body ; INF. *rais*, take possession of and retain ; for (راس), be at the head of the people or tribe ; — II. INF. *taryîs*, make one chief or leader ; — V. INF. *tarayyus*, become chief ; take the leadership.

رئس *ra'is*, *rayyis*, chief, leader, captain.

(ريش) *râś*, I, INF. *raiś*, (also II. and IV.) feather an arrow, plume, provide a friend with food and clothing ; collect a fortune and household things ; — II. INF. *taryîś*, see I. ; — IV. INF. *irâśa-t*, see I. ; be hairy ; — VIII. INF. *irtiyâś*, be in good circumstances.

ريش *rîś*, ة, pl. *riyâś*, *aryâś*, feather ; hair of the beard ; embroidered garment ; wealth, affluence ; food, nourishment ; — ة *rîśa-t*, a feather ; (m.) lancet ; (m.) small key-stone ; iron bar ; (m.) circle.

ريصار *rîṣâr*, pl. *rawâṣîr*, pickled onions.

ريض *rayyiḍ*, not yet quite trained ;

still rather wild; disciple, novice; — ة *rîḍa-t*, watery place.

ريضان *rîḍân*, pl. of روضة *rauḍa-t*.

ريطة *raiṭa-t*, thin light garment of one piece of linen; kerchief.

(ريع) *râ'*, I, INF. *rai'*, *riyâ'*, *ruyû'*, *raya'ân*, grow, increase; prosper, thrive; be in flourishing circumstances; be good; return; — INF. *rai'*, move to and fro, undulate; fear; — II. INF. *taryî'*, be assembled; — IV. INF. *irâ'a-t*, thrive luxuriantly; increase; — V. INF. *tarayyu'*, undulate; assemble (n.); delay over and over again; also X. INF. *istirâ'a-t*, be astonished, bewildered, perplexed.

ريع *rai'*, *rai'ân*, *raya'ân*, growth and thriving of plants; the best part of; prime, bloom of youth; — *rai'*, *rî'*, ة, pl. *riyâ'*, hill, mountain-path; — ة *rî'a-t*, conscientious abstinence; abstemiousness.

(ريغ), II. INF. *taryîg*, grease or butter a dish.

ريغ *rîg*, dust, earth; perishableness.

(رئف) see (راف).

(ريف) *râf*, I, INF. *raif*, (also II. and IV.) come to fertile regions; graze on such; — II. INF. *taryîf*, IV. INF. *irâfa-t*, see I.; IV. yield abundant produce.

ريف *rîf*, pl. *aryâf*, *ruyûf*, fertile tract, particularly in the neighbourhood of water, well-watered land, oasis; — *ra'if*, kind; — *rayyif*, fertile.

ريفية *rîfiyya-t*, fertile field or plain.

(ريق) *râq*, I, INF. *raiq*, shine and undulate (mirage, &c.); be poured out, spread (n.) on the ground; shine, glitter; INF. *ruyûq*, expire; — II. INF. *taryîq*, moisten with spittle; — IV. INF. *irâqa-t*, pour out, spill; — V. INF. *tarayyuq*, shine and undulate; break one's fast, breakfast.

ريق *raiq*, *rayyiq*, (also *rîq*) the first and best of a thing, prime, bloom of youth; — *rîq*, pl. *aryâk*, spittle (especially of one fasting, therefore على الريق, fasting); breakfast; the last gasp; — *rayyiq*, fasting; — *rîqa-t*, spittle.

ريقان *raiqân*, (m.) = يرقان *yaraqân*, *yarqân*, jaundice.

(ريل) *râl*, I, INF. *rail*, also II. INF. *taryîl*, V. INF. *tarayyul*, salivate (n.).

رئلان *ri'lân*, young ostriches, pl. of رال *ra'l*.

(ريم) *râm*, I, INF. *raim*, abandon, forsake; be far; be separate; leave a place, remove; cease; lean to the side; — INF. *raim*, *ramayân*, close and heal (wound); — II. INF. *taryîm*, stay, abide, remain; be supernumerary, remainder.

ريم *raim*, growth, increase; surplus, rest, remainder; round of a ladder; — *ri'm*, *raim*, pl. *ar'âm*, *ârâm*, milk-white gazelle; — *ru'im*, the buttocks.

رئمان *ri'mân*, INF. of (رام) and *rayaman*, INF. of (ريم), closing and healing of a wound.

(رين) *rân*, I, INF. *rain*, *ruyûn*, possess entirely; oppress; conquer, subdue; pass. fall into difficulties beyond remedy; be corrupted, of mean disposition; — IV. INF. *irâna-t*, lose one's cattle.

رين *rain*, sin, vice; dirt; rust; — ة *raina-t*, wine.

(ريه) *râh*, I, INF. *raih*, come and go; — V. INF. *tarayyuh*, appear and disappear.

ريهقان *raihuqân*, saffron.

ريوال *rîwâl*, spittle.

ريوح *rayûḥ*, breezy.

ريون *ri'ûn*, pl. of رئة *ri'a-t*; — *ruyûn*, INF. of (رين).

رئى *ri'y*, aspect, form, face; — *ra'iyy*, *ri'iyy*, seeing, perceiving (adj.); who or what is seen,

perceived; genius, demon; a large snake; exhibited good; pl. of راى *ra'y*, opinion.

رئيس *ra'îs* (ريس *rayyis*), pl. *ru'asâ*, chief, chieftain, leader, captain; abbot, prior, superior; president; — *ri''îs*, great chieftain; — ة *ra'îsa-t*, abbess, lady superior; الاعضا الرئيسة *al-a'dâ ar-ra'îsa-t*, the nobler parts of the body (brain, heart, liver, testicles).

ز

ز *z*, as a numerical sign=7; abbreviation for Saturday, as the seventh day of the week, and Scorpion, as the seventh sign of the zodiac.

زا *zâ'*, name of the letter ز *z*; pl. *azwâ'*, glutton, voracious eater; — *zâ'*, 3 pret. see (زوا).

(زاب) *za'ab*, INF. *za'b*, take up an easy burden and carry it quickly off; urge on; drink in long draughts.

زابب *za'âbib*, pl. glass bottles.

(زابج) *za'baj*, all, the whole of.

(زابر) *za'bar*, all, the whole of; — *za'bar*, INF. ة, be shaggy; be fringed; fringe a garment; — III. *izba'arr*, INF. *izbi'râr*, bristle (n. and a.).

(زابق) *za'baq*, INF. ة, rub coins, &c., with mercury.

(زابل) *za'bal*, *za'bil*, *zâbal*, *zâbil*, short, small, dwarfish.

زابن *zâbin*, satellite, beadle, bailiff.

زابوقة *zâbûqa-t*, corner.

(زات) *za'at*, INF. *za't*, fill with rage.

زاج *zâj*, vitriol; sulphate of iron; (shoe-) blacking; ز ابيض *zâj abyaḍ*, alum; — *zâj-in*, see زاجى *zâjî*.

(زاج) *za'aj*, INF. *zâj*, create enmity.

زاجر *zâjir*, pl. *zawâjir*, repelling, repulsive; preventing, forbidding; blaming; ابو زاجر *abû zâjir*, crow; — ة *zâjira-t*, pl. *-ât*, *zawâjir*, defense; rebuke, reproof; predictions; the angels of winds and clouds.

زاجل *za'jal*, *zâjal*, a small spear; javelin; — *zâjil*, crying out, singing; حمام الزاجل *ḥamâm az-zâjil*, carrier pigeon; — *zâjil*, *zâjal*, pl. *zawâjil*, wooden stopper of a skin bag; military leader.

زاجى *zâjî* (زاج *zâj-in*), small; contemptible; — *zâjiyy*, containing vitriol; of the colour of vitriol, black.

زاحف *zâḥif*, ة, pl. *zawâḥif*, dragging one's self along wearily.

زاخر *zâḫir*, swelling; over-full; liberal; in joyful emotion; of very high birth or rank; pl. *zawâḫir*, the agitated sea.

زاخف *zâḫif*, boasting, arrogant.

(زاد) *za'ad*, INF. *za'd*, inspire with fear, frighten.

زاد *zâd*, pl. *azwâd*, *azwida-t*, provender, travelling-provisions; pelf.

(زار) *za'ar*, I, A, INF. *za'r*, *za'îr*, also *za'ir*, A, INF. *za'ar*, IV. INF. *iz'âr*, V. INF. *taza''ur*, roar; shriek.

زار *za'r*, roar; *zâr-in*, see زارى *zârî*; — ة *za'ra-t*, reed-bank; — *zâra-t*, herd of camels; crop (of a bird); — *zârra-t*, a camel-fly.

زارع *zâri'*, pl. *zurrâ'*, sower, planter, peasant.

زارى *zârî* (زار *zâr-in*), who scolds, inveighs.

(زازا) *za'za'*, INF. ة, move, shake (a.); inspire with fear, frighten; run fast with raised head and tail (ostrich); — II. INF. *taza'zu'*, be moved, shaken; show one's

self cowardly, fear; desist from fear.

(زاط) *za'aṭ*, INF. *zi'âṭ*, talk much and boisterously.

زاطية *zâṭiya-t*, pl. *zawâṭî*, strumpet.

زاعب *zâ'ib*, guide on a journey; head of a spear.

زاعبى *zâ'ibiyy*, a kind of spear.

زاعر *zâ'ir*, malignant, malicious; gipsy.

زاعط *zâ'iṭ*, sudden and violent (death).

زاعة *zâ'a-t*, satellites; vanguard.

زاغ *zâg*, pl. *zîgân*, small crow, rook; — *zâg-in*, زاغى *zâgî*, pl. *zâga-t*, swerving from truth.

(زاف) *za'af*, INF. *za'f*, urge to speed; — IV. INF. *iz'âf*, rush upon a wounded man and kill him.

زاف *za'f*, sudden death.

زافرة *zâfira-t*, pl. *zawâfir*, assembly; troop; squadron, battalion; support, pillar, buttress.

زاق *zâq-in*, زاقى *zâqî*, pl. *zawâqî*, crying out, shrieking.

(زاك) *za'ak*, INF. *za'akân*, walk proudly with violent movements of the body; — VI. INF. *tazâ'uk*, be ashamed.

زاك *zâk-in*, زاكى *zâkî*, ة, pure, pious.

زال *zâll*, not of full weight (money).

(زام) *za'am*, INF. *za'm*, *zu'âm*, die suddenly; swallow greedily; frighten; impart uncertain news on hearsay; pass. *zu'im*, be seized with great terror; — *za'im*, A, INF. *za'am*=pass. of the previous; cry out; — II. INF. *taz'îm*, frighten; — IV. INF. *iz'âm*, compel, force; — VIII. INF. *izdi'âm*, terrify.

زام *zâm*, fourth part of the day, a watch of the day (du. *zâmân*, half a day); fourth part, quarter; — *za'm*, ة *za'ma-t*, loud cry, shriek; report from hearsay; sufficient provender, necessity; wind, air; — *zâmm*, pl. *zamam*, who binds, ties; proudly silent, proud; — ة *zâma-t*, society, sect.

(زامج) *za'maj*, all, the whole of it.

زامح *zâmiḥ*, abscess.

زامخ *zâmiḫ*, pl. *zummaḫ*, proud; high-minded; over-full.

زامر *zâmir*, f. ة, piper.

زامل *zâmil*, following (adj.); — ة *zâmil-at*, beast of burden; overload.

زان *zân-in*, see below; — ة *zâna-t*, indigestion; — ى *zânî* (زان *zân-in*), pl. *zunât*, fornicator, adulterer; f. ة *zâniya-t*, pl. *zawânî*, adulteress.

زاهد *zâhid*, abstemious, chaste; pious, religious; monk; hermit; ascetic (s.); mystic (s.); bigoted; hypocrite.

زاهر *zâhir*, blooming; shining, resplendent; clear, distinct; — ة *zâhira-t*, flower.

زاهق *zâhiq*, pl. *zuhq*, *zuhuq*, put to flight; disappearing, perishing, perishable, vain; — ة *zâhiqa-t*, soul that leaves the body.

زاهل *zâhil*, tranquil, secure.

زاوق *zâ'uq*, زاووق *zâ'ûq*, mercury, quicksilver.

زاوية *zâwiya-t*, pl. *zawâyâ*, angle, corner, edge; cell, hermitage.

(زاى) *za'a*, INF. *za'y*, be proud; bring the bride to the husband; — IV. INF. *iz'â*, prevent from moving (full belly).

زائد *zâ'id*, increasing, superfluous, too much of; more; not radical (letter); — ة *zâ'ida-t*, pl. *zawâ'id*, anything added, supernumerary, superfluous; زائدة الكبد *zâ'ida-t al-kabd*, lobe of the liver.

زائر *zâ'ir*, roaring; — *zâyir*, pl. *-ûn*, *zuwwâr*, *zuwwar*, visitor, pilgrim.

زائغ *zâ'ig*, erring; heretic.

زائف *zâ'if*, pl. *ziyâf*, *azyâf*, clipped (coin); lion.

زائل *zâ'il*, ceasing, decreasing, disappearing, waning, perishable, fleet; moving, alive; — ة *zâ'ila-t*, pl. *zawâ'il*, living being, perish-

able or transitory things; stars in motion.

زائن *zâ'in*, adorned.

(زب) *zabb*, INF. *zabab*, be near setting; — U, INF. *zabb*, fill; A, I, be long-haired, shaggy, dishevelled; have a full head of hair, thick eye-brows; — II. INF. *tarbîb* (also IV.), dry grapes or figs; (also V.) have foam in the corners of the mouth; — IV. INF. *izbâb*, see II.; be near setting; — V. INF. *tazabbub*, see II.; — VIII. INF. *izdibâb*, be filled.

زب *zubb*, point of the beard; pl. *azubb*, *azbâb*, *zibâb*, *zababa-t*, penis.

زبا *zabbâ'*, f. of ازب *azabb*, hairy, &c.

زباب *zabâb*, ة, mole, field-mouse; blind; ignorant; messenger; — *; — *zabbâb*, seller of raisins.

زباد *zabâd*, civet; — *zubbâd*, worthless.

(زبار), III. *izba'arr*, INF. *izbi'râr*, bristle (n. and a.).

زباريق *zabârîq*, pl. convulsions of the dying.

زبال *zibâl*, what an ant or bee takes into its mouth; — also *zubâl*, ة *zubâla-t*, very little; — *zabbâl*, who deals with dung; — ة *zabâla-t*, dung.

زبان *zabân*, sting of an insect; refractory, rebellious; — also *zubân*, tongue (Pers.); — *zubân*, 16th station of the moon.

زبانی *zabânî*, satellite; guardian of hell; du. *zabâniyân*, the pincers of a scorpion; — ة *zabâniya-t*, pl. of زبنية *zibniya-t*.

زبب *zabab*, hairiness, INF. of (زب); thick hair; down; — ة *zababa-t*, pl. of زب *zubb*.

زبتل *zabtal*, short, small, dwarfish.

(زبد) *zabad*, U, INF. *zabd*, shake the milk-bag to make butter; feed (a.) on cream or fresh butter (acc.); take the cream from the milk; take the best of a thing; — I, INF. *zabd*, give little; — II. INF. *tazbîd*, foam; pluck cotton; — IV. INF. *izbâd*, foam, froth, effervesce; — V. INF. *tazabbud*, foam; hasten; take the best of a thing; swallow.

زبد *zabad*, pl. *azbâd*, foam, froth; (m.) substance, essence of a thing; — *zubd*, ة *zubda-t*, pl. *zubad*, cream, fresh butter; the best part of a thing; quintessence; selection; — ى *zubdiyy*, creamy; — ية *zabdiyya-t*, large deep dish.

(زبر) *zabar*, U, I, INF. *zabr*, copy a book, copy, write; — U, pelt with stones; fill with stones; pile up stones for building; speak; hint at; bear patiently; turn off a supplicant roughly; prevent, hinder; lop a vine-tree; — II. INF. *tazbara-t*, copy.

زبر *zibr*, pl. *zubûr*, anything written, scripture; the Psalms; — *zibbir*, very strong, powerful; — ة *zubra-t*, pl. *zubar*, *zubur*, lump of iron; lump, piece; anvil; the back (between the shoulders); shoulder; hair of a lion's mane; 11th station of the moon.

زبرا *zabrâ'*, back (between the shoulders).

(زبرج) *zibrij*, design or embroidery of a garment; jewellery; gold ornaments.

(زبرجد) *zabarjad*, chrysolite; emerald; topaz.

(زبرق) *zabraq*, INF. ة, dye yellow or red.

زبرقان *zibriqân*, moon; having a thin beard.

(زبزب) *zabzab*, INF. ة, be angry; flee from the battle.

(زبط) *zabaṭ*, I, INF. *zabṭ*, quack.

زبطانة *zabṭâna-t*, blow-pipe.

(زبع), V. INF. *tazabbu'*, burn with anger; be harsh and malignant.

(زبغ) *zabag*, novelty; all, the whole of it.

(زبق) *zabaq*, I, U, INF. *zabq*, pluck the beard; mix one thing with another, blend; prevent, hinder; shut up, confine; = VII.; — VII. INF. *inzibâq*, enter, steal in.

(زبل) *zabal*, I, INF. *zabl*, manure a field; soil with dung; — II. INF. *tazbîl*, IV. INF. *izbâl*, id.

زبل *zibl*, dung, manure; — *zubul*, pl. of زبيل *zabîl*; — ة *zubla-t*, mouthful.

زبلان *ziblân*, *zublân*, pl. of زبيل *zabîl*.

(زبن) *zaban*, I, INF. *zabn* (also III.), sell the fruit of a tree in the lump; deposit as a security or pledge; push, push back, keep off; — III. INF. *muzâbana-t*, see I.; push, push back.

زبنية *zibniya-t*, refractory, rebellious; guardian of hell; — pl. *zabâniya-t*, life-guardsman, satellite.

زبهمة *zabhama-t*, haste; a carriage.

زبور *zabûr*, pl. *zubur*, written; scripture, writing; book; the Psalms; — *zubûr*, pl. of زبر *zibr*.

زبون *zabûn*, malicious, mischievous; kicking; violent; cunning, sly; weak, frail; submissive; simpleton; partner, who deals with another, customer, buyer; (m.) pl. *azbina-t*, vest, bodice; — *zabbûn*, ة *zabbûna-t*, pride; refractoriness; — ة *zabbûna-t*, *zubbûna-t*, flank-protection; neck.

زبى *zaba*, I, INF. *zaby*, take up, carry; urge on; do evil to (acc.); — II. INF. *tazbiya-t*, urge on; dig a den or keep for lions; — IV. INF. *izbâ'*, carry; — V. INF. *tazabbî*, dig a den or keep for lions; — VI. INF. *tazâbî*, walk hesitatingly; show pride; — VIII. INF. *izdibâ'*, carry, urge on; — ة *zubya-t*, pl. زبى *zuban*, high ground that cannot be reached by the water; lion-keep.

زبيب *zabîb*, ة, dried grapes (raisins), figs or dates; foam, froth; poison of a snake; — ة *zabîba-t*, abscess in the hand; — *zubaiba-t*, a female name; — ى *zabîbiyy*, seller of raisins; wine made of raisins.

زبيدة *zubaida-t*, marigold; a female name.

زبير *zabîr*, scripture, writing, book; calamity; ة, written, before-mentioned.

زبيل *zabîl*, dung, manure; — also *zibbîl*, pl. *zubul*, *ziblân*, *zublân*, hollowed pumpkin used as a vessel; basket; leathern bag.

(زت) *zatt*, U, INF. *zatt*, adorn the bride; (m.) throw, shoot; (m.) send away, dismiss, expel; — II. INF. *taztît*, adorn the bride; — V. INF. *tazattut*, be adorned.

(زتخ) *zataḥ*, U, INF. *zutûḥ*, stick firmly in the skin (insect).

(زج) *zajj*, U, INF. *zajj*, pierce with the point of a lance; throw; shoot arrows; run; — for *zajij*, A, INF. *zajaj*, be thin and long; — II. *tazjîj*, make the eye-brows thin and long; — provide the lance with an iron point.

زج *zujj*, pl. *zijaja-t*, *zijâj*, top of the elbow; head of an arrow or spear; pl. and—

زجا *zajjâ'*, f. of *azajj*, having thin long eye-lashes or brows, &c.

زجاج *zajâj*, *zijâj*, *zujâj*, ة, glass, crystal; window-pane; tumbler; eye; corner-tooth; — *; — *zajjâj*, glazier; — ى *zajâjiyy*, ة, of glass, of crystal; glass-maker, glazier.

حمام الزجال *ḥamâm az-zajjâl*, carrier-pigeon.

زججة *zijaja-t*, pl. of زج *zujj*.

(زجح) *zajaḥ*, INF. *zajḥ*, scratch.

(زجر) *zajar*, U, INF. *zajr*, drive back, scare (by shouting, &c., especially birds, to take omen from their flight); urge on; drop excrement; forbid, hinder, prevent; blame, scold; — VII. INF. *inzijâr*, be driven away,

scared, scolded; — VIII. INF. *izdijâr*, drive away by shouting, &c.; be driven away, thrown off, prevented.

زجر *zajr*, *zajar*, pl. *zujûr*, omen or prediction from the flight of birds; defence; blame, scolding, threat; punishment; violence; — *zajr*, pl. *zujûr*, a large fish, sturgeon; — ى *zajriyy*, forbidden; — ية *zajriyya-t*, duty on spirits (m.).

(زجل) *zajal*, throw, throw away; refuse, reject; pierce with the point of a lance; emit the sperm into the womb; send out a carrier-pigeon; — *zajil*, A, INF. *zajal*, sport in a boisterous manner; sing beautifully; raise the voice, shout.

زجل *zajal*, boisterous merriment; shouting (s.); singing (s.); — *zajil*, resounding with thunder; high-pitched; singer; blown through by a hissing wind; — ة *zujla-t*, pl. *zujal*, crowd, troop; part, particle.

زجلا *zajlâ'*, f. swift, fleet.

(زجم) *zajam*, INF. *zajm*, speak in a very low voice; listen to what is spoken thus; — ة *zajma-t*, word uttered in a low voice.

(زجنجل) *zajanjal*, polished mirror.

زجنة *zajna-t*=زجمة *zajma-t*.

(زجو) *zajâ*, U, INF. *zajw*, *zajâ'*, *zujuww*, come to pass easily, bring about successfully; be paid in without difficulty (taxes); stop short laughing; INF. *zajw*, drive, drive away; — II. INF. *tazjiya-t*, drive slowly; pass (the time, &c.);=IV.; — IV. INF. *izjâ'*, drive; push back; prevent; pass the time; — V. INF. *tazajjî*, be content, satisfied.

(زح) *zaḥḥ*, U, INF. *zaḥḥ*, push from its place; drive away; move quickly to and fro (a.).

زحار *zuḥâr*, ة *zuḥâra-t*, dysentery; asthma; — *zaḥḥâr*, who breathes with difficulty and groans.

زحاف *zuḥâf*, ة *ziḥâfa-t*, deviation; suppression of the second letter of a *sabab* if it is quiescent, or rendering it quiescent if it is movable (in poetry); — *zaḥḥâf*, creeping on the ground, crawling.

زحام *ziḥâm*, crowd, throng, INF. of (زحم).

زحاميك *zaḥâmîk*, pl. of *zuḥmûk*.

(زحب) *zaḥab*, INF. *zaḥb*, be near, approach.

(زحر) *zaḥar*, I, A, INF. *zaḥr*, *zaḥîr*, *zuḥâr*, *zuḥâra-t*, utter or produce a sound; breathe heavily and groan; give birth; grumble, growl; act., pass. and II., INF. *tazḥîr*, suffer from dysentery.

زحر *zuḥar*, زحران *zaḥrân*, miser; — زحرة *zaḥra-t*, throe (in childbirth).

(زحزح) *zaḥzaḥ*, INF. ة, remove, turn from; chase away; — II. INF. *tazaḥzuḥ*, pass. of the previous.

(زحف) *zaḥaf*, INF. *zaḥf*, *zuḥûf*, *zaḥafân*, advance, advance towards, be foremost in battle; crawl, creep; rebound; drag one's self along wearily; (m.) remove the snow; — IV. INF. *izḥâf*, assemble (n.) for a review; reach the goal; drag one's self along wearily; — V. INF. *tazaḥḥuf*, advance; — VI. INF. *tazâḥuf*, advance against one another; — VIII. INF. *izdiḥâf*, advance towards.

زحف *zaḥf*, pl. *zuḥûf*, army advancing for battle; combat.

(زحك) *zaḥak*, INF. *zaḥk*, be tired; stop, abide; be near, approach, and, by opposition, be far, remove to a distance (n.); — III. INF. *muzâḥaka-t*, remove (a.); — IV. INF. *izḥâk*, have a tired beast for riding; — VI. INF. *tazâḥuk*, be near each other, and, by opposition, be far from one another.

(زحل) *zaḥal*, INF. *zaḥl*, *zuḥûl*, leave one's place or be removed from it; be tired; remain behind; fall in, slip (land); — II. INF. *tazḥîl*, take or draw from a place; — IV. INF. *izḥâl*, id.; remove (a.); cause to take refuge; — V. INF. *tazaḥḥul*, remove (n.) from a place.

زحل *zaḥl*, change of place; taking (s.) from a place, removal; downfall, crash, landslip;—*zaḥil*, who removes (n.);—*zuḥal*, planet Saturn.

زحلف *zaḥlaf*, INF. ة, roll, revolve (a.); fill; give; speed on; remove, drive away; — II. INF. be rolled, revolved, pushed; — III. INF. *izliḥfâf*, remove (n.) from a place (عن *'an*).

(زحلق) *zaḥlaq*, (زحلك) *zaḥlak*, INF. ة, roll, revolve (a.); — II. INF. *tazaḥluk*, roll or glide down.

زحلوط *zuḥlûṭ*, mean, miserly.

زحلوفة *zuḥlûfa-t*, pl. *zaḥâlif*, *zaḥâlîf*, زحلوقة *zuḥlûqa-t*, pl. *zaḥâliq*, زحلوكة *zuḥlûka-t*, pl. *zaḥâlîk*, smooth slope for children to slide down upon; slide or track of sliding.

زحلول *zuḥlûl*, narrow precipitous place.

زحليل *zaḥlîl*=the previous; what slips, leaves its place.

(زحم) *zaḥam*, INF. *zaḥm*, *ziḥâm*, press, throng; — III. INF. *muzâḥama-t*, press upon; be near, close on; — VI. INF. *tazâḥum*, press one another; — VIII. INF. *izdiḥâm*, id.; be pressed, be in a throng.

زحم *zaḥm*, pressing or thronging crowd; — ة *zaḥma-t*, *zuḥma-t*, throng; molestation, trouble, hardships; evil, illness; throes of childbirth.

زحمر *zaḥmar*, INF. ة, fill.

زحموك *zuḥmûk*, pl. *zaḥâmîk*, flaxen silk.

(زحن) *zaḥan*, INF. *zaḥn*, be slow, tarry; remove (a.) from a place; — V. INF. *tazaḥḥun*=I.; undertake a thing reluctantly.

زحن *zaḥn*, *zuḥan*, ة, small; — ة *zaḥna-t*, violent heat; caravan; —*zuḥna-t*, bend of a valley.

زحوف *zaḥûf*, dragging itself along wearily (camel); — *.

(زحول), II. *tazaḥwal*, INF. *tazaḥwul*, remove (n.).

زحول *zuḥûl*=زحل *zaḥl*.

زحير *zaḥîr*, dysentery, asthma.

(زخ) *zaḫḫ*, U, INF. *zaḫḫ*, push or throw down; jump, leap; lie with; emit urine; cause the camel to stride apace; be angry with (acc.); (m.) stoop; — I, INF. *zaḫḫ*, *zaḫîḫ*, shine, glow; — ة *zaḫḫa-t*, rage, fury; hatred; envy.

زخار *ziḫâr*, boasting (s.); — *zaḫḫâr*, swelling, raging; over-full, overflowing; exceeding, supernumerary;—ى *zuḫâriyy*, luxuriant; — also *zaḫâriyy*, luxuriant verdure, freshness, bloom.

(زخر) *zaḫar*, INF. *zaḫr*, *zuḫûr*, be full and swell; flow over; be agitated, rise in masses; boil violently; rage, be infuriated; grow high; boast; surpass in glory; cheer, rejoice (a.); cause to grow fat; fill; — III. INF. *muzâḫara-t*, boast towards; — V. INF. *tazaḫḫur*, flow over, inundate.

زخر *zaḫr*, overflowing (s.), inundation.

(زخرط) *ziḫriṭ*, mucus (of sheep).

(زخرف) *zuḫruf*, ة *zaḫrafa-t*, pl. *zaḫârif*, false gold, false ornaments or jewellery; tinsel; gilding, gloss; tinsel of a speech; *zuḫruf*, wordly pomp, vanities of the world; pl. water-ditches; ships; mermaids.

زخرف *zaḫraf*, INF. ة, guild; adorn; adorn with false ornaments or

jewellery; tinsel one's speech; — II. INF. *tazaḥruf*, pass.

زخروط *zuḥrûṭ*, decrepit.

زخزب *zuḥzubb*, stout and firm of flesh.

زخزخ *zaḥzaḥ*, INF. ة, lie with.

(زخف) *zaḥaf*, INF. *zaḥf*, *zaḥîf*, be proud, vain-glorious; boast; — II. *tazḥîf*, make many words.

(زخلب) *zaḥlab*, INF. ة, make a fool of, make fun of.

(زخم) *zaḥam*, A, INF. *zaḥm*, push back violently; — *zaḥim*, A, INF. *zaḥam*, be deteriorated, putrid, gamey; — II. INF. *taḥzîm*, push back violently; — IV. INF. *izḥâm*, be putrid; — VIII. INF. *izdiḥâm*, carry a burden.

زخم *zaḥm*, violence, violent temper; — *zaḥim*, putrid; — ة *zaḥama-t*, stench; — ة *zaḥma-t*, stirrup-strap (m.).

زخور *zaḥwar*, ى *zaḥwariyy*, luxuriant; pompous, bombastic; — II. *tazaḥwar*, INF. *tazaḥwur*, boast, glory.

زخيخ *zaḥîḥ*, glow, INF. of (زخ).

زخيم *ziḥḥîm*, violent.

(زدب) *zidb*, pl. *azdâb*, share, portion.

(زدع) *zada'*, INF. *zad'*, sleep with.

(زدغ), V. *tazaddag*, INF. *tazaddug*, lean on a cushion or pillow.

(زدف), IV. *azdaf*, INF. *izdâf*, be dark.

(زدق) *zidq*=صدق *ṣidq*, sincerity.

(زدو) *zadâ*, U, INF. *zadw*, play at holes (with nuts); INF. *zuduww*, stretch the hand for (الى *ila*); — IV. INF. *izdâ'*, confer benefits.

(زر) *zarr*, for *zarar*, U, INF. *zarr*, provide with buttons; bite; chase; pierce with a lance; pluck out hair; compress the eyes; become wiser; — for *zarir*, exercise violence towards an enemy; grow wise; — II. INF. *tazrîr*, provide with buttons; — III. INF. *muzârra-t*, bite; — IV. INF. *izrâr*, provide with buttons; button; — V. INF. *tazarrur*, have buttons; be to be buttoned.

زر *zirr*, pl. *azrâr*, *zurûr*, button; bud; knob, buckle, boss; bird's egg; joint; — ة *zira-t*, INF. of (وزر), burden one's conscience, commit a crime; — *zirra-t*, trace or mark of a bite.

(زرا), IV. *azra'*, INF. *izrâ'*, stand in high estimation with (ب *bi*).

زرابة *zarâba-t*, shutting up (s.) in a fold.

زرابى *zarâbiyy*, pl. of زربى *zirbiyy*, زربية *zirbiyya-t*.

زراد *zarrâd*, maker of coats of mail.

زراريق *zarâriq*, pl. of زرق *zurraq*.

زرازرة *zarâzira-t*, pl. of زرزار *zirzâr*.

زرازير *zarâzîr*, pl. of زرزور *zurzûr*.

زراط *zirâṭ*, street.

زراع *zarrâ'*, sower, husbandman; — *zurrâ'*, pl. of زارع *zâri'*, sowing, &c.; — * ; — ة *zirâ'a-t*, agriculture.

زراف *zarrâf*, also ة *zarâfa-t*, *zurâfa-t*, *zurrâfa-t*, pl. زرافى *zurâfa*, *zarâfiyy*, (m.) *zarâ'if*, giraffe, camelopard; — ة *zarâfa-t*, *zarrâfa-t*, pl. *-ât*, troop of 10 men; — *zurâfa-t*, great liar.

زراق *zarrâq*, hypocrite; rogue, rascal; — ة *zarrâqa-t*, watering-pot.

زراقم *zarâqim*, pl. snakes.

(زرأم), III. *izra'amm*, INF. *izri'mâm*, cease to flow, to run.

زراهمة *zurâhima-t*, spotless girl.

زراية *zirâya-t*, invective, INF. of (زرى).

(زرب) *zarab*, U, INF. *zarb*, make a (sheep-) fold; drive the cattle into the fold; shut up, imprison; — *zarib*, A, flow, run; run out; flow over; — VII. INF. *inzirâb*, be put into a fold, shut up, imprisoned; repair to one's ambush or hiding-place (hunter); — IX. *izrabb*, INF. *izribâb*, begin to wither and grow yellow.

زرب *zarb*, *zirb*, pl. *zurûb*, fold (for

cattle); hunting-hut, ambush, hiding-place; — *zirb*, canal; — ة *zarba-t*, putting (s.) into the fold.

زرباب *zirbâb*, gold; brightness, gloss; yellowness.

زربول *zarbûl*, pl. *zarâbîl*, high-heeled shoes.

زربون *zarbûn*, perch (fish);—*zurbûn*, *zarabûn*, slipper.

زربى *zirbiyy*, *zurbiyy*, ة *zirbiyya-t*, *zurbiyya-t*, pl. *zarâbiyy*, cushion, pillow, bolster, anything to lean upon; — ة *zirbiyya-t*, *zurbiyya-t*, pl. *zarâbiyy*, large precious carpet; spring, fountain.

(زرت) *zarat*, INF. *zart*, throttle, strangle.

(زرج) *zaraj*, U, INF. *zarj*, pierce with a lance.

زرجون *zarajûn*, *zarjûn*, vine; vine-shoot.

زرجينة *zarjîna-t*, id.; wine; golden, yellow as gold.

(زرح) *zaraḥ*, INF. *zarḥ*, break one's head or a limb; — *zariḥ*, A, INF. *zaraḥ*, wander from place to place.

(زرد) *zarad*, U, INF. *zard*, throttle, strangle; make a coat of mail; join rings into a chain; knit; — *zarid*, A, INF. *zard*, swallow; — II. INF. *tazrîd*, link rings into a chain; — VIII. INF. *izdirâd*, swallow.

زرد *zarad*, pl. *azrâd*, *zurûd*, coat of mail; — ة *zarada-t*, ring, link of a chain; zebra.

(زردب) *zardab*, INF. ة, strangle.

(زردم) *zardam*, INF. ة, strangle, throttle; swallow; — ة *zardama-t*, throat.

زردية *zàradiyya-t*, small coat of mail, corselet; helmet.

زرزار *zarzâr*, witty, ingenious; — *zirzâr*, pl. *zarâzîr*, leader of 10,000 men.

(زرزر) *zarzar*, INF. ة, sing, whistle; (m.) button.

زرزر *zurzur*, starling.

(زرزق) *zarzaq*, INF. ة, drink without placing the vessel to the mouth.

زرزور *zurzûr*, pl. *zarâzîr*, starling.

زرزير *zarzîr*, prudent and firm.

(زرط) *zaraṭ*, I, INF. *zarṭ*, swallow.

(زرع) *zara'*, INF. *zar'*, sow, scatter seed; let the seed grow or thrive; give strength for; — III. INF. *muzâra'a-t*, give a field and seed for part of the produce, sow a field together with another; — IV. INF. *izrâ'*, have seed for sowing; shoot up high; — VII. INF. *inzirâ'*, be scattered; be sown over; — VIII. INF. *izdirâ'*=I.

زرع *zar'*, pl. *zurû'*, seed; sown field; child.

زرغب *zargab*, raw skins; — ى *zargabiyy*, tanner.

(زرف) *zaraf*, U, INF. *zarf*, spring upon; spring forth; advance against; (also II.) make many words and tell lies; speed along; INF. *zarîf*, walk slowly; — U, INF. *zarf*,—*zarif*, A, INF. *zaraf*, break out again (wound); II. INF. *tazrîf*, see I.; — VII. INF. *inzirâf*, penetrate, pierce; cease; go after pastures.

زرفن *zarfan*, INF. ة, curl the hair of the temples into ringlets or crotchets.

زرفين *zurfîn*, *zirfîn*, door-ring; ring (Pers.).

(زرق) *zaraq*, U, I, INF. *zarq*, drop excrement; (also IV.) squint so that almost only the white of the eye is visible; — U, thrust at with the lance; throw off saddle and load; — *zariq*, A, INF. *zaraq*, be blue, bluish, greenish; grow blue; grow livid; be blind; — II. INF. *tazrîq*, make blue; — IV. INF. *izrâq*, see I.; — V. INF. *tazarruq* =IX. and XI.;—VII. INF. *inzirâq*, penetrate; throw one's self on the back; — IX. INF. *izriqâq*, XI. INF. *izrîqâq*, be or grow blue, bluish, greenish.

زرق *zaraq*, ة *zurqa-t*, blue, bluish colour, lividity; — *zarq*, hypocrisy (Pers.); — *zurq*, pl. of أزرق *azraq*, blue, &c.; — *zurraq*, pl. *zarârîq*, a white falcon.

(زرك) *zarik*, A, INF. *zarak*, be of a bad disposition; — *zarak*, INF. *zark*, press, throng (m.); — II. INF. *tazrîk*, press to the wall; drive into a corner; vex; — III. INF. *muzâraka-t*, drive into a corner; — VI. INF. *tazâruk*, press one another; — ة *zarka-t*, throng (m.).

(زركش) *zarkaś*, gold brocade; stuff embroidered with gold;—*zarkaś*, INF. ة, embroider with gold; make gold brocade; adorn.

(زرم) *zarim*, A, INF. *zaram*, cease to flow or run, be interrupted; give birth; — II. INF. *tazrîm*, break off, interrupt, cause to cease; render miserly; — VIII. INF. *izdirâm*, swallow.

زرمانقة *zarmânaqa-t*, woollen tunic without sleeves.

زرموج *zurmûj*, shoe.

(زرنق) *zarnaq*, INF. ة, clothe; cover; (also II.) irrigate; provide a well with زرنوقان *zurnûqân* (q.v.); — II. INF. *tazarnuq*, be clad, dress (n.).

زرنوق *zurnûq*, brook, rivulet; du. *zurnûqân*, two pillars joined by a cross-beam and placed over a well, to carry the bucket.

زرنيخ *zarnîḥ*, arsenic.

(زرى) *zara*, I, INF. *zary*, *zuryân*, *zirâya-t*, *mazrât*, *mazriya-t*, scold, blame; blacken, slander; — IV. INF. *izrâ'*=I.; contemn, despise; take a thing easy; render contemptible, shame;—VIII. *izdirâ'*, contemn, despise; insult, offend, inveigh against;—X. INF. *istizrâ'* =VIII.

زرياب *ziryâb*, solution of gold for gilding (Pers.).

زريبة *zarîba-t*, pl. *zarâ'ib*, fold (for cattle); hunting-hut, ambush, hiding-place; lair; entrance.

زرير *zarîr*, witty, ingenious; inflamation of the eyes; INF. of (زر).

زريع *zarî'*, prepared for sowing; — *zirrî'*, what grows by itself from fallen grain; — ة *zarî'a-t*, sown field; seed on the field; cause, reason.

(زز) *zazz*, U, INF. *zazz*, touch slightly on the neck.

(زط) *zaṭṭ*, U, INF. *zaṭṭ*, buzz.

زعار *zu'âr*, pl. of زاعر *zâ'ir*, malicious, &c.;—ة *za'âra-t*, *za''âra-t*, malice, malicious disposition.

زعازع *za'âzi'*, pl. of زعزع *za'za'*; — *zu'âzi'*, hurricane.

زعاف *zu'âf*, sudden death; killing suddenly.

زعافر *za'âfir*, زعافير *za'âfîr*, pl. of زعفران *za'farân*.

زعافق *za'âfiq*, pl. of زعفوق *zu'fûq*.

زعاق *zu'âq*, thick brackish water; — *za''âq*, quick, swift; — ة *za'âqa-t*, INF. of (زعق).

زعاقيق *za'âqîq*, pl. of زعقوقة *zu'qûqa-t*.

زعامة *za'âma-t*, power, authority, command; glory, honour; INF. of (زعم); — also *za''âma-t*, cow; — *zi'âma-t*, share of the booty; large fief granted for services in warfare.

(زعب) *za'ab*, INF. *za'b*, push away, drive away, chase; fill; carry a full skin bag, &c.; walk under a heavy burden; be full of water; press upon one another; load; cut or break off; give part of; (m.) overwhelm with reproaches; — INF. *za'îb*, croak; — V. INF. *taza''ub*, be cheerful, merry; — VIII. INF. *izdi'âb*, cut or break off; take up a burden to carry it.

زعب *zi'b*, a little money; — *zu'b*, pl. of أزعب *az'ab*, small, despised; — ة *za'ba-t*, *zu'ba-t*, small property; — *za'ba-t*, reproach, rebuke (m.).

زعبج *za'baj*, thin white cloud.

(زعبر) *za'bar*, INF. ة, cheat, trick

by sleight of hand, pick, take from slily (على *'ala*); — ة *za'bara-t*, deceit; jugglery, legerdemain, sleight of hand.

(زعبق) *za'baq*, INF. ة, scatter; dissipate.

زعبوبة *zu'bûba-t*, well-made woman of a white complexion.

زعتر *za'tar*, thyme.

(زعج) *za'aj*, INF. *za'j*, drive away, push away; snatch violently from a place, tear or pull out; disquiet, vex, torment, molest; cry out; — *za'ij*, A, INF. *za'aj*, be disquieted, troubled; — IV. INF. *iz'âj*, disquiet; torment; tear or pull out; drive away, repel, rout; — VII. INF. *inzi'âj*, be disquieted, tormented, troubled, molested; be torn from the place, snatched away, chased off.

زعج *za'aj*, ة *za'aja-t*, trouble, molestation; weariness; annoyance.

زعجلة *za'jala-t*, maliciousness of disposition.

(زعر) *za'ar*, INF. *za'r*, lie with; — *za'ir*, A, INF. *za'ar*, be thin (hair, &c.); — IX. INF. *iz'irâr*, XI. INF. *iz'îrâr*, id.

زعر *za'ir*, having thin hair.

زعر *zu'r*, pl. and—

زعرا *za'râ'*, f. of ازعر *az'ar*, having thin hair, &c.

زعرور *zu'rûr*, medlar-tree, medlar; wild plum.

زعزاع *za'zâ'*, hurricane-like.

(زعزع) *za'za'*, INF. ة, shake violently; — II. INF. *taza'zu'*, pass.

زعزع *za'za'*, pl. *za'âzi'*, shaking violently, stormy; storm, tempest; — ة *za'za'a-t*, pl. *za'âzi'*, shaking (s.), shock; pl. storm; adversities.

زعزوع *zu'zû'*, mane of a horse.

(زعط) *za'aṭ*, INF. *za'ṭ*, throttle, strangle; bray.

(زعف) *za'af'*, INF. *za'f*, kill on the spot; strike dead; — IV. INF. *iz'âf*, id.

زعف *za'f*, killing (s.), murder.

زعفر *za'far*, INF. ة, dye or season with saffron.

زعفران *za'farân*, pl. *za'âfir*, *za'âfîr*, saffron; rust; — ى *za'farâniyy*, saffron-coloured; seasoned with saffron.

(زعفوق) *zu'fûq*, of a malicious disposition.

(زعق) *za'aq*, INF. *za'q*, cry out, cry to or call out to, frighten; — pass. be afraid at night-time; urge on; raise dust; sting; — *za'iq*, A, INF. *za'aq*, fear; speed from fear; — *za'uq*, INF. *za'âqa-t*, be thick and brackish.

زعق *za'iq*, timorous; swift, nimble.

زعقوقة *zu'qûqa-t*, pl. *za'âqîq*, young partridge.

زعكة *za'ka-t*, stay, sojourn; pause.

(زعل) *za'il*, A, INF. *za'al*, be cheerful; move cheerfully without being spurred; (m.) be ill-tempered, annoyed, wearied, bored; — II. INF. *taz'îl*, annoy, weary, bore (m.); — III. INF. *muzâ'ala-t*, offend, hurt, vex (m.); — V. INF. *taza''ul*, be cheerful, lively.

زعل *za'il*, cheerful; — (m.) also زعلان *za'lân*, morose, ill-tempered, bored; — ة *za'ala-t*, bad temper, weariness, being bored (s.).

زعلجة *za'laja-t*, maliciousness of disposition.

(زعم) *za'am*, U, INF. *za'm*, *zi'm*, *zu'm*, say, pretend, assert; be of opinion; talk over, give one's opinion on a subject; impart one's opinion to another (2 acc.); — U, INF. *za'm*, *za'âma-t*, stand security for (ب *bi*); — *za'im*, A, INF. *za'am*, desire, demand; — *za'um*, INF. *za'âma-t*, be lord, leader, prince; — II. INF. *taz'îm*, claim; — III. INF. *muzâ'ama-t*, press upon; be near, close to; — IV. INF. *iz'âm*, make eager for, render covetous, cause to desire; obey; — V. INF. *taza''um*, assert falsely, lie.

زعم *za'm*, assertion, opinion, surmise.
زعما *zu'amâ'*, pl. of زعيم *za'îm*.
(زعن) *za'an*, INF. *za'n*, bow, bend.
(زعنف) *za'naf*, INF. ة, dress the hair of and adorn the bride; — ة *zi'nafa-t*, *za'nafa-t*, pl. *za'ânif*, small, dwarfish; vile, mean, contemptible; worthless; mixed troop from different tribes; troop, detachment; rag hanging from a garment; tanned goat-skin with the feet; calamity; pl. *za'ânif*, fins.
(زعو) *za'â*, U, INF. *za'w*, act justly.
زعيق *za'îq*, frightened.
زعيم *za'îm*, pl. *zu'amâ'*, claimant without a right; who stands security, bail; — ة *za'îma-t*, master, lord, leader, prince; owner of a large fief.
زغابة *zugâba-t*, زغابى *zugâba*, down.
زغاد *zaggâd*, swelling, flowing over.
زغار *zugâr*, pl. worms.
زغاريت *zagârît*, jubilations and rejoicings of the women at a wedding, &c.
زغاليل *zagâlîl*, pl. of زغلول *zuglûl*.
(زغب) *zagib*, A, INF. *zagab*, (also XI.) be covered with down; have thin hair; — II. INF. *tazgîb*, id.; — IV. INF. *izgâb*, begin to green; — XI. INF. *izgîbâb*=I.
زغب *zagab*, down; thin hair; hair of the embryo; — *zugab*, ash-coloured.
(زغبج) *zagbaj*, wild olive.
(زغبد) *zagbad*, cream, fresh butter.
زغبر *zagbar*, *zagbur*, ة *zagbara-t*, *zagbura-t*, soft hair of new carpets, &c.; — *zagbar*, INF. ة, be new and have long soft hair.
(زغد) *zagad*, INF. *zagd*, roar; press the skin bag until the butter comes out; throttle; incite against; —IV. INF. *izgâd*, suckle, give suck.
(زغدب) *zagdab*, INF. ة, be angry; be boisterous and obtruding.
(زغر) *zagar*, INF. *zagr*, snatch from (one) with violence; overflow; abound.
زغر *zagr*, abundance, affluence.
(زغرب) *zagrab*, flowing abundantly; deep; — *zagrab*, INF. ة, laugh.
(زغرت) *zagrat*, INF. ة, utter shouts of rejoicing.
(زغزغ) *zagzag*, INF. ة, speak with a weak unintelligible voice; conceal; make fun of, scoff at; endeavour to open a skin bag; (m.) be built with little solidity.
زغزغ *zagzag*, agile, nimble; — ة *zagzaga-t*, unintelligible speech; (m.) unsolidity of a building.
(زغف) *zagaf*, INF. *zagf*, pierce with a lance; be abundant; mingle lies with one's speech; — VIII. INF. *izdigâf*, take much of a thing; — ة *zagfa-t*, *zagafa-t*, pl. *zagf*, *zagaf*, *azgâf*, *zugûf*, fine, closely-wrought coat of mail.
(زغل) *zagal*, U, INF. *zagl*, pour out water repeatedly, expectorate; emit urine; suck; also IV. feed the young ones; also IV. alloy metals, falsify money; —IV. INF. *izgâl*, see I.
زغل *zagal*, false, counterfeit; — ة *zugla-t*, pl. *zugl*, what is expectorated or emitted at one time; what is drunk at one time and therefore poured into a smaller vessel, a little; fundament.
زغلمة *zaglama-t*, *zuglama-t*, doubt, suspicion, surmise; secret hatred, grudge.
(زغلط) *zaglat*, INF. ة=زغرت *zagrat*.
زغلوطة *zuglûta-t*, pl. *zagâlît*=زغاريت *zagârît*.
زغلول *zuglûl*, pl. *zagâlîl*, agile, nimble, quick; child; young of a bird.
(زغم), V. INF. *tazaggum*, prolong the bellowing or roaring, repeat it.
(زغمل) *zugmul*, secret hatred, grudge.
زغموم *zugmûm*, stammering (adj.).

(زغو) *zagâ*, U, INF. *zagw*, cry, scream; exercise justice.

زغوم *zagûm*, stammering, stuttering (adj.).

(زف) *zaff*, U, INF. *zaff*, *zifâf*, lead the bride in procession to the bridegroom's house; flash; — I, INF. *zaff*, *zufûf*, *zafîf*, hurry in running or flying, career; INF. *zaff*, *zafîf*, spread the wings, alight; I, INF. *zaff*, blow; — IV. INF. *izfâf*, lead the bride in procession to (الى *ila*).

زف *ziff*, young feathers, down; — ة *zuffa-t*, troop, crowd; bridal procession; procession.

زفاف *zifâf*, wedding-procession; bridal night.

زفانة *zufâna-t*, tongue.

(زفت) *zafat*, U, INF. *zaft*, fill; burn with anger against (acc.); urge on; drive back, repel, prevent; molest, tire; whisper; — II. INF. *tazfît*, pitch.

زفت *zift*, resin; pitch.

(زفد) *zafad*, U, INF. *zafd*, fill; feed copiously.

(زفر) *zafar*, I, INF. *zafr*, *zafîr*, give vent to previously pent-up breath; sigh; puff; crackle; draw water; INF. *zafr*, carry; — II. INF. *tazfîr*, break the fast; cause to break the fast; talk obscenely; — V. INF. *tazaffur*, break the fast; — VIII. INF. *izdifâr*, carry, lade.

زفر *zifr*, load, burden; travelling-company, troop; — *zafar*, dirt; food forbidden for a fasting-day; also (m.) *zifr*, support, prop, pillar; — *zifir*, dirty, filthy; obscene; rude, impudent, insolent; dirt in a pipe-tube; — *zufar*, one powerful and brave; lord, master, prince; lion; sea, powerful stream; strong camel; troop, battalion, squadron; — ة *zafra-t*, middle of the body, waist; — also *zufra-t*, sighing (s.), deep sigh; puff; breathing (adj.); animal; scum of boiling meat.

(زفزف) *zafzaf*, INF. ة, run fast; rush up; shake the grass and cause it to rustle (wind); spread the wings, alight.

(زفن) *zafan*, I, INF. *zafn*, kick, tread; dance.

زفن *zifn*, roof for protection.

زفوف *zafûf*, swift, precipitate; striding apace; — *

زفون *zafûn*, female dancer.

(زفى) *zafa*, I, INF. *zafy*, *zafayân*, chase the clouds; resound, twang (n.); make an object appear higher; spread the wings and run against; — IV. INF. *izfâ'*, bring from one place to another.

زفير *zafîr*, sighing (s.); braying of an ass; INF. of (زفر); calamity; = زفر *zifir*.

(زق) *zaqq*, U, INF. *zaqq*, feed the young ones; drop excrement; (m.) transport.

زق *ziqq*, pl. *azqâq*, *ziqâq*, *zuqqâq*, *zuqqân*, skin bag for wine; skin bag; — *zuqq*, pl. *zaqaqa-t*, wine; — ة *zuqqa-t*, a small bird.

زقا *zaqâ'*, *zuqâ'*, crowing (s.); crying out (s.); echo.

زقاع *zuqâ'*, crowing (s.), INF. of (زقع).

زقاق *zuqâq*, m. and f., pl. *zuqqân*, *aziqqa-t*, narrow street, alley, lane; passage between two rows of booths or stalls, market-place; بحر الزقاق *bahr az-zuqâq*, Straits of Gibraltar; (m.) transport; — *; — *zaqqâq*, maker of skin bags for wine; — ى *zuqâqiyy*, belonging to the streets, common, vulgar.

زقان *zuqqân*, pl. of زق *ziqq*, and of زقاق *zuqâq*.

(زقب) *zaqab*, U, INF. *zaqb*, drive into the hole, slip into the hole; — II. INF. *tazqîb*, cry out, shriek.

زقب *zaqab*, near; — also *zuqub*, ة

zaqaba-t, pl. zaqab, narrow path, alley, lane.

زقح zaqḥ, gibberish of a monkey.

زقزاق zaqzâq, dandling of a child.

(زقزق) zaqzaq, INF. ة, feed the young ones; drop excrement; walk swiftly and lightly; twitter; giggle; speak with great volubility; INF. ة, and zaqzâq, dandle a child; — ة zaqzaqa-t, twitter; sharp tone; swiftness, fluency, volubility.

(زقع) zaqa', INF. zaq', zuqû', break wind; cry out, crow.

(زقف) zaqaf, U, INF. zaqf, snatch, seize quickly; — V. INF. tazaqquf, VIII. INF. izdiqâf, id.; VIII. steal.

زققة zaqaqa-t, pl. ring-doves; pl. of زق zuqq, wine.

زقل zuql, pl. robbers, thieves; — ة zaqla-t, bludgeon, cudgel (m.).

(زقم) zaqam, U, INF. zaqm, swallow at one gulp; eat of the dish زقوم zaqqûm; — II. INF. tazqîm, cause to swallow; feed the young ones; — IV. INF. izqâm=II.; — VIII. INF. izdiqâm=I.

زقم zaqm, wedge; — ة zâqma-t, plague.

(زقن) zaqan, U, INF. zaqn, take up and carry; — IV. INF. izqân, help to carry.

(زقو) zaqâ, U, INF. zaqw, zuqâ', shriek, screech; crow; answer, respond.

زقوم zaqqûm, zaqûm, tree of hell, the fruit of which are devils' heads; food of hell; a resinous thorn-tree; fresh dates with cream; (m.) oleander, rose-laurel.

(زقى) zaqa, I, INF. zaqy=(زقو); — ة zaqya-t, shriek, screech, crowing (s.); — zuqya-t, small heap or pile (of money, &c.).

زقيلة zaqîla-t, narrow street; lane.

(زك) zakk, I, INF. zakîk, circle round the hen; INF. zakk, run, trip; drop excrement; fill; — I, INF. zakk, zakak, zakîk, walk with short steps (from weakness); — ة zikka-t, arms, armour; — zukka-t, anger, rage; grief, sorrow.

(زكا) zaka', INF. zak', beat; pay promptly (2 acc.); flee, seek refuge with (الى ila); lie with; — VIII. INF. izdikâ', have a debt paid to one's self.

زكا zak-an, even (opposed to odd), equal; — zuka', zukâ', ة zuka'a-t, who pays promptly; a rich man; — zakâ', purity, piety; INF. of (زكو); sagacity (for ذكا ẕakâ'); — ة (also زكوة) zakât, pl. زكا zak-an, purity; sanctification of a property by alms-giving; alms (pl. also zakawât).

زكام zukâm, cold, rheum, catarrh.

زكانة zakâna-t, زكانية zakâniyya-t, right guess; certain knowledge.

زكاوة zakâwa-t, purity, innocence; honesty, uprightness, frankness; sharpness of intellect, sagacity.

(زكب) zakab, U, INF. zakb, zakab, bear the child at one effort; lie with; fill; — ة zukba-t, embryo; sperm.

(زكت) zakat, U, INF. zakt, fill; cause to remember (2 acc.).

(زكر) zakar, U, INF. zakr, fill; — II. INF. tazkîr, id.; be large (of belly) and at the same time healthy; — V. INF. tazakkur, be full, swell with food; — ة zukra-t, pl. zukar, small skin bag; belly, paunch; — ى zakariyy, زكريا zakariyyâ, Zacharias; — zakriyy, zakariyy, entirely red.

زكزك zakzak, INF. ة, make short steps (from weakness); (m.) tickle; — II. INF. tazakzuk, arm one's self.

(زكم) zakam, U, INF. zakm, cause a cold or catarrh; emit (sperm); fill; pass. and zakim, have a cold, suffer from a catarrh; — II. INF. tazkîm, IV. INF. izkâm, bring on a cold; — V. INF. tazak-

kum, have a cold ; — ة *zukma-t*, cold, catarrh; last-born offspring; rude man, ruffian.

(زكن) *zakin*, A, INF. *zakan*, understand, conceive, know ; recognise by exterior signs, infer, surmise, suspect ; — II. INF. *tazkîn*, be undecided in one's judgment, have suspicions ; — III. INF. *muzâkana-t*, be near (1000) in number ; — IV. INF. *izkân*, understand, conceive ; recognise by outward signs ; make one to understand, to recognise by certain signs.

زكن *zakn*, surmise, suspicion ; — *zakin*, good physiognomist ; — *zukan*, good watcher.

زكوات *zakawât*, زكوة *zakât*, see under زكا.

(زكى) *zakî*, A, INF. زكا *zak-an*, grow, increase ; be thirsty.

زكى *zak-an*, in pairs, even ; — *zakiyy*, ة, pl. *azkiyâ'*, pure, innocent, pious ; virtuous ; just, honest, upright ; who gives the lawful alms ; rich ; strongly-grown ; ingenious, sagacious.

زكيبة *zakîba-t*, sack.

زكيك *zakîk*, INF. of (زك).

زكين *zakîn*, hair of a newly-born child.

(زل) *zall* (*zalal*), I, INF. *zall*, *zulûl*, *zalîl*, *zillîla*, *zillîlâ'*, *mazilla-t*, slip, stumble ; fail, sin ; make a slip of the tongue ; pass away ; INF. *zulûl*, *zalîl*, pass by hurriedly ; INF. *zulûl*, slip from the hand ; fall in price or be not of full weight ; — for *zalil*, A, INF. *zalal*, glide, slip ; commit an error of speech ; have thin thighs ; — IV. INF. *izlâl*, cause to slip, to trip, to sin ; turn from one's opinion ; bestow a benefit on (الى *ila*) ; — X. INF. *istizlâl*, cause to slip ; seduce.

زل *zull*, slippery ; — ة *zalla-t*, slip, false step ; fall ; error, fault, sin ; wedding ; remainder of a meal ; present, gift ; — *zulla-t*, slippery place ; difficulty of breathing, asthmatic fit ; — also *zalla-t*, obliging service.

زلابى *zulâbiyy*, ة *zalâbiya-t*, pan-cake.

زلاج *zilâj*, bolt.

زلاغيط *zalâgîṭ*, pl. of زلغوطة *zulgûṭa-t* = زغلوطة *zuglûṭa-t*.

زلاقة *zalâqa-t*, slippery place ; hind parts of an animal ; — *zallâqa-t*, slide.

زلاقيم *zalâqîm*, pl. of زلقوم *zulqûm*.

زلال *zulâl*, who slips easily ; what glides easily down ; pure, clear, and wholesome ; ز خضر *zulâl ḥiḍr*, the water of life ; ز البيض, the white of an egg.

زلالل *zulâlil*, clear, pure.

زلالى *zalâliyy*, pl. of زلية *zilliyya-t*.

(زلام), III. *izla'amm*, INF. *izli'mâm*, ripen, burst open ; be high, sublime ; stand high.

(زلب) *zalib*, A, INF. *zalab*, be always with its mother (child) ; — VIII. INF. *izdilâb*, steal ; — ة *zulba-t*, white ivy ; arrow.

(زلج) *zalaj*, I, INF. *zalj*, *zalîj*, glide along swiftly and lightly ; INF. *zalj*, bolt ; — INF. *zalajân*, precede, get in advance of ; — II. INF. *tazlîj*, make one's words publicly known ; — IV. INF. *izlâj*, bolt or lock the door ; — V. INF. *tazalluj* = I. ; slip.

(زلح) *zalaḥ*, INF. *zalḥ*, taste of a dish.

زلح *zalḥ*, anything vain or idle ; in vain ; — *zuluḥ*, pl. large dishes.

(زلحب) *zalḥab*, slipping (adj.) ; — II. *tazalḥab*, INF. *tazalḥub*, slip.

(زلحف) *zalḥaf*, INF. ة, chase away ; remove ; — ة *zalḥafa-t*, great calamity ; tortoise.

زلحلح *zalaḥlaḥ*, light of body ; ة, thin and large (cake) ; wide and shallow.

(زلحم) *zulḥam*, cloak with hood.

(زلخ) *zalaḫ*, I, INF. *zalḫ*, pierce with a lance ; — U, INF. *zalḫân*, *zalaḫân*, get in advance ; — *zaliḫ*, A, INF. *zalaḫ*, be fat.

زلح *zalḥ*, *zaliḥ*, slippery place; — ة *zullaḥa-t*, slide; pain in the hips.

زلحفة *zalḥafa-t*, calamity.

(زلدب) *zaldab*, INF. ة, swallow.

(زلز) *zaliz*, A, INF. *zalaz*, be restless, move continually to and fro.

زلزال *zalzâl*, trembling (s.).

(زلزل) *zalzal*, INF. *zalzâl*, *zilzâl*, *zulzâl*, *zalzala-t*, shake (a.); — II. INF. *tazalzul*, shake (n.) violently and repeatedly; — ة *zalzala-t*, pl. *zalâzil*, earthquake; pl. calamities.

(زلط) *zalaṭ*, I, INF. *zalṭ*, walk fast; pull off one's clothes; — II. INF. *tazlîṭ*, strip (a.); — V. INF. *tazalluṭ*, strip; be naked.

زلط *zalṭ*, quick walk; (m.) nakedness; — also *zalaṭ*, naked; smooth; smooth pebble.

زلع *zala'*, INF. *zal'*, burn one's foot; take slyly; swallow without chewing; — *zali'*, A, INF. *zala'*, be in a bad condition; — II. INF. *tazlî'*, give to devour, to eat; — IV. INF. *izlâ'*, id.; — VIII. INF. *izdilâ'*, take slyly; wrong.

زلع *zal'*, crack in the skin; — ة *zal'a-t*, bad wound.

(زلعب), III. *izla'abb*, INF. *izli'bâb*, clash violently; be dense, thick.

زلعوم *zul'ûm*, pl. *zalâ'îm*, throat, gullet.

زلغ *zalag*, U, INF. *zulûg*, rise; flare or blaze up.

(زلغب), III. *izlagabb*, INF. *izligbâb*, begin to grow again (hair); grow feathers.

(زلغط) *zalgaṭ*, INF. ة, utter shouts of rejoicing=زغلط *zaglaṭ*, زغرط *zagraṭ*.

زلغوطة *zulgûṭa-t*, pl. *zalâgîṭ*, jubilation, shout of rejoicing.

(زلف) *zalaf*, I, INF. *zalf*, *zalîf*, approach, be near; — II. INF. *tazlîf*, add anything in relating; — IV. INF. *izlâf*, cause to approach, bring near; — V. INF. *tazalluf*, VIII. INF. *izdilâf*, advance, approach, be near one another.

زلف *zalaf*, nearness, neighbourhood; advance, step in advance, step; degree, stairs, ladder; — *zilf*, garden, meadow, lawn; — ة *zulfa-t*, زلفى *zulfa*, nearness, proximity; rank, degree, dignity; resting-place, station; — *zulfa-t*, pl. *zulaf*, *zulfât*, *zulufât*, *zulafât*, part of the night, night-watch; dish; pl. *zulaf*, lock of hair, curl; up-stroke of a letter; —*zalafa-t*, pl. *zalaf*, cistern, well, pond; bottle; dish.

(زلق) *zalaq*, U, INF. *zalq*, slip, glide; leave a place; I, INF. *zalq*, cause to slip; remove (a.) from a place; shave the head; — *zaliq*, A, INF. *zalaq*, slip, leave a place; — II. INF. *tazlîq*, IV. INF. *izlâq*, cause to slip; smooth; — V. INF. *tazalluq*, slide on the ice; become fair, shining, bright; get a white and brilliant complexion.

زلق *zalq*, *zalaq*, slippery place; slipping (s.); ز الامعا *zalaq al-am'â'*, diarrhœa; ز الكلية *zalaq al-kulya-t*, diabetes; — *zaliq*, slippery; hind-parts of an animal; — ة *zalqa-t*, slip, fall; slippery place;—*zalaqa-t*, smooth stone; woman.

زلقوم *zulqûm*, pl. *zalâqîm*, gullet, throat.

زلل *zalal*, slipping (s.), tripping (s.), fall; error, slip of the tongue, faulty expression; under weight; defect; INF. of زل; slippery.

(زلم) *zalam*, U, INF. *zalm*, commit an error; speak thoughtlessly; talk idly; fill; make trifling, cut off, maim; smooth, fashion (an arrow, &c.); — II. INF. *tazlîm*, fill; smooth, make even; turn the mill; — VIII. INF. *izdilâm*, cut off, maim.

زلم *zalam*, *zulam*, pl. *azlâm*, unfeathered arrow (for casting

lots, &c.); cloven hoof; a domestic cat; — ة zalma-t, zulma-t, zalama-t, zulama-t, true, genuine; — ة zalama-t, lappet of flesh on the throat of a goat; — zulma-t, pl. zilâm, in straitened circumstances; pedestrian, foot-soldier.

زلنبع zulambi', confection of almonds baked in sesame-oil.

زلنبور zalambûr, the devil of marriages.

زله zalh, the beauty of blossoms; well-stone; astonishment; — zalah, grief, sorrow.

(زلهب) zalhab, having a thin beard; not fleshy.

زلوج zalûj, quick; steep slope, precipice; easily slipping from the hand.

زلوق zalûq, swift, fleet; long, lengthy, extended.

زلول zulûl, slipping (s.), INF. of (زل).

زليج zalîj, swift, fleet; INF. of (زلج).

زليق zullâiq, nectarine.

زليل zalîl, pure, clear, wholesome; — zalîl, and—

زليلى zillîla, INF. of (زل); — ة zilliya-t, pl. zalâliyy, woollen blanket without hair and stripes.

(زم) zamm, U, INF. zamm, tie together, strap; muzzle the camel; bridle; fasten the shoe with a strap; lift the head; be proud; fill; get in advance; seize a lamb (wolf); — VII. INF. inzimâm, be tied or strapped together; — VIII. INF. izdimâm, be proud, haughty; seize a lamb.

(زمات), III. izma'att, INF. izmi'tât, be variegated, parti-coloured; — ة zamâta-t, gravity, dignity.

زماح zummâh, a large bird which steals children.

زمار zimâr, cry of the ostrich; pl. of زمير zamîr; — zammâr, flute-player, piper; — ة zimâra-t, art of a flute-player or piper; — zammâra-t, flute, pipe, flageolet; strumpet.

زماع zamâ', zimâ', boldness; perseverance; firm resolution, INF. of (زمع); — ة zammâ'a-t, back part, reverse.

زمال zimâl, pl. zumul, azmila-t, cover of a travelling-bag; lameness of a camel; — *; — zummâl, ة zummâla-t, cowardly, timid; — zammâla-t, beast of burden (m.).

زمام zimâm, pl. azimma-t, bridle, line, guiding-rope; cord, string; register, table; — zummâm, high, grown high.

زمان zamân, pl. azmân, azmina-t, azmun, time, epoch, season, moment; tense (in grammar); temporality, world; fortune; weather; — ة zamâna-t, love; pl. -ât, weakness, especially in the foot of an animal; INF. of (زمن); — ى zamâniyy, temporal; worldly.

زمانئذ zamâna'iz-in, at that very time.

زماورد zumâward, dish of flour, almonds and honey.

(زمت) zamut, INF. zamâta-t, possess gravity, dignity, power.

زمت zummat, a parti-coloured bird.

(زمج) zamaj, U, INF. zamj, fill; stir up discord; enter unannounced; — zamij, A, INF. zamaj, be angry.

زمج zamaj, anger; — zamij, angry; — zummaj, a species of eagle; — ة zimijja-t, beak of an ostrich.

(زمجر) zamjar, INF. ة, roar, growl; rage, clamour; — II. INF. tazamjur, id.; — III. izmajarr, INF. izmijrâr, produce or utter a sound.

زمجر zamjar, pl. zamâjir, zamâjîr, long tube, pipe; arrow; — ة zamjara-t, clamour, noise, tumult (also zimajr); flute, pipe; strumpet.

زمجيل zimjîl, leopard.

(زمح), II. *zammaḥ*, INF. *tazmîḥ*, kill the bird زماح *zummâḥ*.

زمح *zummaḥ*, beggarly; small, paltry, contemptible; ugly; black.

(زمخ) *zamaḥ*, INF. *zamḥ*, be proud, haughty.

زمخ *zummaḥ*, pl. of زامخ *zâmiḥ*, proud, &c.

(زمخر) *zamḥar*, INF. ة, roar; be violent; bud.

زمخر *zamḥar*=زمجر *zamjar*; — ة *zamḥara-t*, strumpet.

(زمر) *zamar*, U, INF. *zamr*, *zamîr*, play on the flute; spread about what has been told; incite against; INF. *zamr*, fill; INF. *zamarân*, flee; — I, INF. *zimâr*, cry out; — *zamir*, A, INF. *zamar*, have little of a man, have a thin beard, be cowardly; have little wool; — II. INF. *tazmîr*, play on the flute; sing, chant.

زمر *zumr*, pl. *zumûr*, flute, flageolet, hautboy, pipe; song, hymn; (m.) snout of a pig; — *zamir*, having a thin beard; cowardly; pretty of face; — *zimirr*, strong, violent; — ة *zumra-t*, pl. *zumar*, troop; family; class of men; category; association, party, corporation, corps, (corporative) body.

زمرد *zumurrud*, *zumurud*, *zumrud*, emerald; — ى *zumurrudiyy*, emerald-coloured.

(زمزم) *zamzam*, INF. ة, hum, buzz, resound for a length of time; mumble; roar.

زمزم *zamzam*, *zumazim*, in abundance; the well *zamzam*, the well of Hagar; — ة *zamzama-t*, humming (s.), rustling (s.), echo; song; — *zimzima-t*, pl. *zamâzim*, troop of people; herd.

(زمط) *zamaṭ*, INF. *zamṭ*, escape; get loose, slip off.

(زمع) *zama'*, INF. *zama'ân*, be swift and mobile; run fast, and, by opposition, walk slowly; — *zami'*, A, INF. *zama'*, be seized with wonder or fear; — II. INF. *tazmî'*, set to a thing with energy and perseverance; — III. INF. *zimâ'*, *muzâma'a-t*, be bold; — IV. INF. *izmâ'*=II.

زمع *zama'*, astonishment, perplexity, fright, horror; supernumerary finger; — *zumma'*, drone; stingless wasp; — ة *zama'a-t*, pl. *zama'*, *zimâ'*, horny excrescence behind the hoof of an animal; spur of a cock; vine-shoot; pl. *azmâ'*, small river, valley.

زمعا *zuma'â'*, pl. of زميع *zamî'*.

زمعان *zama'ân*, INF. of (زمع).

(زمق) *zamaq*, I, U, INF. *zamq*, pluck; unlock, open.

(زمك) *zamak*, U, INF. *zamk*, incite to violent anger against (على *'ala*); fill; — II. INF. *tazmîk*, fit tightly (m.); — XI. INF. *izmîkâk*, be violently enraged.

زمك *zamak*, anger; — also *zimikk*, زمكى *zimikka*, rump of a bird; — ة *zamaka-t*, choleric.

(زمل) *zamal*, U, INF. *zaml*, *zimâl*, *zamalân*, run as if limping; — U, I, INF. *zimâl*, run leaning to one side, from unequal weight of the load, run and carry; follow on one's heels; — INF. *zaml*, have one riding behind or on the other side; — U, INF. *zumûl*, follow on one's heels; chisel a stone; — II. INF. *tazmîl*, bid to mount behind or to follow; wrap in one's clothes; — III. INF. *muzâmala-t*, be of equal weight with another, counter-balance; — V. INF. *tazammul*, wrap one's self in one's clothes; — VIII. INF. *izdimâl*, id.; carry off a burden at one time.

زمل *ziml*, who mounts or is mounted behind another; load, burden; half a sackful; — *zimal*, *zumal*, *zummal*, weak, languid, cowardly; — ة *zumla-t*, travelling company, troop; — *zamala-t*, a family, many.

زملا *zumalâ'*, pl. of زميل *zamîl*.

زملق *zumaliq, zummaliq*, who emits his sperm before coition is completed.

زمم *zummam*, pl. of زام *zâmm*, who binds, &c.

(زمن) *zamin*, A, INF. *zaman, zumna-t, zamâna-t*, be seized with a chronic disease or permanent lameness; INF. *zumna-t*, be worn out with old age and fatigue; — III. INF. *muzâmana-t*, make a temporary compact; — IV. INF. *izmân*, last long; be old, ancient.

زمن *zaman*, pl. *azmân, azmina-t, azmun*, time; chronic disease; — *zamin*, pl. *-ûn, zamna*, worn out by old age; suffering from a chronic disease, palsied; — ة *zamana-t*, a certain or appointed time; — ى *zamaniyy*, temporal, perishable; — *zamna*, pl. of زمين *zamîn*.

(زمه) *zamih*, A, INF. *zamah*=ذمه *ẕamih*, be violent; — *zamah*, INF. *zamh*, burn, parch.

(زمهر) *zamhar*, INF. ة, be red with burning anger; — III. *izmaharr*, INF. *izmihrâr*, be violent; be very cold; frown; sparkle.

زمهرير *zamharîr*, violent cold; the forty days after the winter solstice; moon.

(زمهل), III. *izmahall*, INF. *izmihlâl*, fall; dissolve.

زموع *zamû'*, quick, nimble, alert.

زمولة *zammûla-t*, spout of a vessel (m.).

زموم *zamûm*, mercury, quicksilver.

زميت *zamît, zimmît*, staid, grave, dignified; modest and gentle.

زمير *zamîr*, playing (s.) on the flute, INF. of (زمر); pl. *zimâr*, small; handsome fellow; — *zimmîr*, a fish.

زميع *zamî'*, pl. *zuma'â'*, alert, nimble, brisk; enterprising; prudent.

زميل *zamîl*, pl. *zumalâ'*, who mounts behind another; companion, comrade, fellow-traveller, partner, fellow-pupil, colleague; — *zumail, zummail*, ة *zumaila-t, zummaila-t, zimmîl, zimyal*, cowardly; lazy.

زمين *zamîn*, pl. *zumna*, worn out by old age, suffering from a chronic disease, palsied; — *zumain*, a little while; ذات الزمين *ẕât az-zumain*, a little while ago.

(زن) *zann*, U, INF. *zann*, have an opinion of, judge; wither, shrink; — II. INF. *taznîn*, feed always on the vegetable زن *zinn*; — IV. INF. *iznân*=I.

زن *zinn*, a small pea-like vegetable; oats; — ة *zina-t*, weighing (s.), INF. of (وزن); weight; quantity of a syllable; proper measure and proportion; *zinat-an*, opposite, face to face; — *zinna-t*, tasting badly; ابو زنة *abû zinna-t*, monkey.

(زنا) *zanâ*, INF. *zan'*, be quick, alert; hasten; be merry; — INF. *zan', zunû'*, stick to a place, adhere to the ground; ascend a mountain; flee, take refuge with (الى *ila*); approach; throttle, strangle; — II. INF. *tazni'a-t*, drive into a corner.

زنا *zinan, zinâ, zinâ'*, fornication, adultery; ولد زنا *walad zinâ'*, bastard; — *zannâ'*, fornicator; — ة *zunât*, pl. of زانى *zânî*, fornicator, adulterer; — *zannâ'a-t*, female ape.

زنابير *zanâbîr*, pl. of زنبور *zumbûr*.

زناج *zinâj*, requital.

زناد *zinâd*, fire-shafts; — *zannâd*, cock of a gun (m.).

زنادق *zanâdiq*, زناديق *zanâdîq*, pl. of زنديق *zindîq*.

زنار *zunnâr*, ة *zunnâra-t*, pl. *zanânîr*, girdle (especially of Christians, Jews, Magians); stole.

زناط *zinâṭ*, throng.

زناطرة *zanâṭira-t*, restless multitude.

زناق *zinâq*, necklace; — *zunâq*, collar for mules; ring of a bridle

beneath the chin; clamp for the nose of a horse to keep it quiet while being shoed.

زنانير *zanânîr*, gravel, shingle; flies, gnats; pl. of زنار *zunnâr*.

زناوى *zinawiyy*, زنائى *zinâ'iyy*, fornicator; whorish; adulterous.

(زنب) *zanib*, A, INF. *zanab*, be fat.

زنبار *zimbâr*, wasp; plane-tree.

(زنبر) *zambar*, lion; — *zumbur*, small; glib, witty; — ة *zumbura-t*, trigger.

زنبرى *zambariyy*, great; — ة *zambariyya-t*, a ship.

(زنبق) *zambaq*, lily; jessamine-oil; flute, pipe; ام زنبق *umm zambaq*, wine.

زنبور *zumbûr*, ة, pl. *zanâbîr*, wasp, hornet, bee; glib, witty.

زنبوع *zumbû'*, perennial fruit.

زنبيل *zumbîl*, pl. *zanâbîl*, basket of palm-leaves.

(زنتر), II. *tazantar*, INF. *tazantur*, walk proudly; get into a violent rage; be capricious, irritable, peevish; — ة *zantara-t*, proud walk; embarrassment, difficulty; (m.) caprice, peevishness, irritableness.

زنتو *zantû*, زنتور *zantûr*, a stringed instrument.

(زنج) *zanj*, *zinj*, pl. *zunûj*, Ethiopian, negro; drum; — *zanaj*, thirst; — III. *zânaj*, INF. *zinâj*, requite.

زنجار *zinjâr*, verdigris.

زنجب *zunjab*, زنجبان *zunjabân*, girdle, belt; — ة *zanjaba-t*, false hips.

زنجبيل *zanjabîl*, ginger; a river in Paradise; wine.

(زنجر) *zanjar*, INF. ة, snap one's fingers at; — also II. INF. *tazanjur*, be covered with verdigris or rust; — ة *zanjara-t*, snap.

(زنجفر) *zunjufr*, cinnabar.

زنجفيل *zanjafîl*=زنجبيل *zanjabîl*.

زنجى *zanjiyy*, ة, Ethiopian (adj. and s.); Nubian, negro.

زنجير *zinjîr*, *zanjîr*, pl. *zanâjîr*, chain (Pers.).

(زنح) *zaḥah*, INF. *zanḥ*, praise; push, drive; press, oppress; — III. INF. *muzânaḥa-t*, vie in praising; — V. INF. *tazannuḥ*, praise one's self immoderately; exalt one's self above one's station.

(زنخ) *zanaḥ*, U, I, INF. *zunûḥ*, imbed firmly in the skin; — *zaniḥ*, A, INF. *zanaḥ*, become rancid and smell badly; — II. INF. *tazniḥ*, id.

زنخ *zaniḥ*, rancid.

(زنخر) *zanḥar*, INF. ة, blow from the nostrils, snort.

زند *zanad*, U, INF. *zand*, fill; strike fire; — *zanid*, A, INF. *zanad*, be thirsty; — II. INF. *taznîd*, increase (a.), cause to grow, to augment; fill; tell lies; strike fire; punish beyond measure; — IV. INF. *iznâd*, grow, increase (n.); increase (a.); — V. INF. *tazannud*, be angry.

زند *zand*, pl. *zinâd*, *aznâd*, *aznud*, materials to strike fire, fire-shaft; pl. *zunûd*, fore-arm; wrist; knuckle of the hand, of the elbow; maniple of a priest.

(زندق) *zandaq*, زندقى *zandaqiyy*, very avaricious; — II. *tazandaq*, INF. *tazanduq*, profess Manicheism; profess a religion only externally; — ة *zandaqa-t*, Manicheism, Sadducism, heresy; unbelief.

زنديق *zindîq*, pl. *zanâdiqa-t*, *zanâdîq*, Manichean; Sadducee; heretic, unbeliever, hypocrite.

(زنر) *zanar*, U, INF. *zanr*, fill; gird with the زنار *zunnâr*; — II. INF. *taznîr*, gird; — V. INF. *tazannur*, gird one's self; be thin, fine, subtle.

زنزلخت *zanzalaḥa-t*, Persian lilac; acacia.

(زنط) *zinṭ*, throng; — VI. INF. *tazânuṭ*, throng one another.

زنطرة *zanṭara-t*=زنترة *zantara-t*.

(زنف) *zanif*, A, INF. *zanaf*, be angry; — V. INF. *tazannuf*, id.

زنفجة *zanfaja-t*, calamity.

(زنق) *zanaq*, I, INF. *zanq*, put a chin-ring to a bridle; also II. and IV. keep one's family scantily; also II. tie up, strap; — II. INF. *taznîq*, see I.; — IV. INF. *iznâq*, see I.; — ة *zanaqa-t*, small and narrow street, alley, lane; throng; ذو زنقة *zû zanaqa-t*, trapezoid.

زنقلة *zanqala-t*, throat; crop.

زنقير *zinqir*, parings of the nails; skin of a date; a little, trifle.

زنكاوة *zankâwa-t*, stirrup.

زنكة *zanaka-t*, lobe of the liver.

زنكية *zankiyya-t*, stirrup (m.).

زنكين *zengîn*, زنكيل *zengîl*, a rich and odd person (Turk.).

(زنم) *zanam*, excrescence behind the hoof; — ة *zanama-t*, du. *zanamatân*, flesh-lappet on the throat of a goat; point of the notch of an arrow.

زنهار *zinhâr*, beware! take care!

(زنهر) *zanhar*, ة, look at sharply with protruding eyes.

(زنو) *zanâ*, U, INF. *zunuww*, be narrow.

زنوى *zanawiyy*, *zinawiyy*, fornicator; meretricious, adulterous; — *zinawiyy*, referring to measure and weight.

(زنى) *zana*, INF. زنا *zinan*, *zinâ'*, fornicate, commit adultery; — II. INF. *tazniya-t*, call one a fornicator or adulterer; — III. INF. *muzânât*, *zinâ'*, commit fornication or adultery with; call one a fornicator.

زنى *ziniyy*, referring to measure and weight; — *zaniyy*, *zanna*, narrow; — ة, ابن زنية *ibn zanya-t* (*zinya-t*), son of a whore; bastard.

زنير *zunnair*, girdle, belt.

زنيم *zanîm*, bastard; intruder; impostor; additional, superfluous; stick.

زنين *zanîn*, suffering from dysury.

زه *zih*, well done! bravo!

زها *zahâ'*, beautiful flower, blossom; — *zuhâ'*, ة *zuhât*, number, quantity; about.

زهاد *zuhhâd*, pl. of زاهد *zâhid*, abstemious, &c.; — ة *zahâda-t*, religious life; piety, ascetic life; self-denial; — *zahhâda-t*, devotee, ascetic.

زهاليق *zahâlîq*, pl. زهلوق *zuhlûq*.

(زهب) *zihb*, ة *zuhba-t*, provender, provisions, ammunition; part of the property, the cattle; — V. INF. *tazahhub*, provide one's self with provisions and ammunition; — VIII. INF. *izdihâb*, carry off or take part of another's property.

(زهد) *zahad*, INF. *zuhd*, be without desire for a thing, look at it with indifference, abstain from (في); devote one's self to the service of God, lead an ascetic life; — *zahid*, A, INF. *zahad*; — *zahud*, INF. *zahâda-t*, id.; — *zahad*, INF. *zahd*, estimate approximately; — II. INF. *tazhîd*, cause to look at a thing with indifference, to despise it, avert from it; — IV. INF. *izhâd*, estimate; — V. INF. *tazahhud*, show contempt for the world and entire devotedness to God; devote one's self to God or an ascetic life; — VIII. INF. *izdihâd*, count (a.) for little.

زهد *zuhd*, indifference; contempt for the world; abstinence, abstemiousness; temperance; devotedness to God; — *zahad*, pl. *zihâd*, part of one's property devoted to God; alms.

(زهدم) *zahdam*, a hawk; lion.

(زهر) *zahar*, INF. *zuhûr*, shine, sparkle, be brilliant; bloom, expand blossoms; parch; — *zahir*, A, INF. *zahar*, be bright and beautiful; — *zahur*, INF. *zahâra-t*, *zuhûra-t*, id.; — II. INF. *tazhîr*, make to bloom; — IV. INF. *izhâr*, expand blossoms; expand (n.); shine; cause the

fire to blaze; — VIII. INF. *izdihâr*; shine, glitter.

زهر *zuhr*, the shining stars, pl. of أزهر *azhar*, shining, &c.; — *zuhar*, the first three days of the month; new moonlight; — ة *zahra-t*, *zahara-t*, pl. *zahr*, *azhâr*, *zuhûr*, *azhur*, pl. pl. *azâhîr*, blossom, flower; the best or most exquisite part of a thing; ما زهر *mâ' zahr*, essence of orange flowers; — *zuhra-t*, shining whiteness, brightness, beauty; — also *zuhara-t*, planet Venus; blossom, flower.

زهزج *zahzaj*, pl. *zahâzij*, cry or hissing of the demons in the desert.

(زهزق) *zahzaq*, INF. ة, dandle a child; laugh violently.

(زهف) *zahaf*, INF. *zuhûf*, be mean, contemptible; be near death; perish; tell lies; — *zahif*, A, INF. *zahaf*, be light, swift, alert; carry off light things; — IV. INF. *izhâf*, take away, destroy; despatch (a wounded man); be seized with astonishment or joy; hurt, injure; hit; tell lies; — V. INF. *tazahhuf*, recede, retreat; — VII. INF. *inzihâf*, jump; — VIII. INF. *izdihâf*, carry off light things, carry off, carry.

(زهق) *zahaq*, INF. *zuhûq*, abound in marrow; be thick; wane, vanish, perish; be vain, perishable; expire; INF. *zahq*, *zuhûq*, get in advance; precede; INF. *zuhûq*, reach the mark; — *zahiq*, A, INF. *zahaq*, expire; — IV. INF. *izhâq*, abound in marrow; cause vain things to perish; destroy; dissipate; make an arrow reach the mark; — VII. INF. *inzihâq*, get in advance.

زهق *zahiq*, light, agile; — *zuhq*, *zuhuq*, pl. of زاهق *zâhiq*, routed, &c.

زهقى *zahaqa*, pl. horses getting in advance of others.

(زهك) *zahak*, INF. *zahk*, crush between two stones; raise dust.

(زهل) *zahal*, INF. *zahl*, keep aloof from evil; — *zahil*, A, INF. *zahal*, be smooth, bare, bald, white.

(زهلب) *zahlab*, having little beard.

(زهلج) *zahlaj*, INF. ة, flatter, cajole.

(زهلق) *zahlaq*, INF. ة, make to be of a pure white; — II. INF. *tazahluq*, be of a pure white; be clean; be fat.

زهلق *zihliq*, quick, agile; violent wind; lamp.

(زهلوق) *zahlûq*, pl. *zahâlîq*, smooth, even, level.

(زهم) *zaham*, U, INF. *zahm*, abound in marrow; repel, hinder; overwhelm with words; — *zahim*, A, INF. *zaham*, suffer from indigestion; be greasy, dirty; — also *zahum*, INF. *zuhûma-t*, smell badly, be putrid; — III. INF. *muzâhama-t*, be hostile to (acc.); be estranged from, separate from, and, by opposition, be near to, approach; — ة *zuhma-t*, smell of bad fat.

زهمان *zahmân*, suffering from indigestion.

(زهمع) *zahma'*, INF. ة, adorn; — II. INF. *tazahmu'*, pass.; arm one's self, prepare one's self.

(زهو) *zahâ*, U, INF. *zahw*, *zuhuww*, *zahâ'*, shine, bloom and thrive; appear or be beautiful; be grown tall, be high; be or become proud, boast, glory; infatuate; (also II.) begin to redden (ripening date); shine; make the sword flash; INF. *zahw*, tell lies, lie; make little of; — INF. *zahw*, pass. *zuhî*, be proud of, boast of (ب *bi*); — II. INF. *tazhiya-t*, see I.; — IV. INF. *izhâ'*, disdain, despise; be proud, boast; be high; — VIII. INF. *izdihâ'*, make little of, disdain; boast; revive the spirits; lead to pride.

زهو *zahw*, brightness and beauty; fine aspect, fair face, beautiful flower; pride, vain-glory; vanities; lie; — also *zuhuww*, date which begins to redden and ripen.
(زهوط) *zahwaṭ*, INF. ة, make large bits.
زهوق *zahûq*, vain, perishable.
زهومة *zuhûma-t*, stench; INF. of (زهم).
زهى *zahiyy*, bright and beautiful; vain, proud; — *zuhan*, splendour of this world; — *zihî*, splendid! bravo!
زهيد *zahîd*, abstemious; contenting one's self; very frugal; inconsiderable, little; narrow and deficient in water.
زهير *zahîr*, emaciated; brought low; melancholy.
زو *zaww*, a couple, pair; fate, destiny; — *zau'*, pl. *zau'ât*, vicissitude.
(زوا), زا *za'*, U, INF. *zau'*, visit.
زواب *zu'âb*, change, alteration.
زوابع *zawâbi'*, pl. of زوبعة *zauba'a-t*.
زواج *ziwâj*, marriage, wedlock.
زواجر *zawâjir*, defences, rebukes, pl. of زاجرة *zâjira-t*.
زواجل *zawâjil*, pl. of زاجل *zâjil*, stopper of a skin bag; leader.
زواح *zawâḥ*, going away (s.), departure, INF. of (زوح).
زواحف *zawâḥif*, pl. f. of زاحف *zâḥif*, weary.
زواد *zawâd*, provender (m.); — ة *zawwâda-t*, id.; الزوادة الاخيرة *az-zawwâda-t al-aḥîra-t*, extreme unction.
زوار *ziwâr*, pl. *azwira-t*, means of support and protection; — *zu'âr*, roar of a lion; — *zuwâr*, visit; INF. of (زور); — *zawwâr*, visitor, stranger, pilgrim; — *zuwwâr*, pl. of زاير *zâyir*, visitor, pilgrim; — ة *zuwâra-t*, visit; INF. of (زور).
زوارق *zawâriq*, pl. of زورق *zauraq*.
زواف *zu'âf*, hastening (s.), acceleration; sudden death.

زوافر *zawâfir*, assemblies, &c., pl. of زافرة *zâfira-t*.
زواق *zawwâq*, decorator, painter (of rooms, &c.); — ى *zawâqî*, pl. of زاقى *zâqî*, crying out (adj.)
زواقيل *zawâqîl*, pl. robbers.
زوال *zawâl*, going away (s.); departure; cessation, disappearance, end; setting of the sun; descent; decline, change for the worse, injury, harm; — *
زوام *zu'âm*, sudden and violent death; — ى *zu'âma*, combat, slaughter, massacre.
زوان *zawân*, *ziwân*, *zuwân*, *zu'ân*, *zau'ân*, *ziw'ân*, darnel, tare, weed; — ى *zawânî*, adulteresses, pl. of زانية *zâniya-t*.
زواهر *zawâhir*, brilliant ornaments, jewellery, &c., pl. of زاهرة *zâhira-t*.
زوايا *zawâyâ*, angles, &c. pl. of زاوية *zâwiya-t*.
زوائد *zawâ'id*, additions, &c., pl. of زائدة *zâ'ida-t*; — ى *zawâ'idiyy*, who has an additional limb or part of the body.
زوائل *zawâ'il*, women; stars; game, prey of a hunter, pl. of زائلة *zâ'ila-t*.
(زوب) *zâb*, U, INF. *zaub*, flow; save one's self by flight.
(زوبر) *zaubar*, INF. ة, be long-haired, shaggy; have a selvedge.
زوبر *zaubar*, all, totality; selvedge.
زوبعة *zauba'a-t*, a wicked demon; pl. *zawâbi'*, whirlwind, hurricane.
(زوج) *zâj*, U, INF. *zauj*, incite people against one another; — II. INF. *tazwîj*, join two things or persons, pair, couple; marry (a.); — III. INF. *muzâwaja-t*, *ziwâj*, be coupled, paired; — IV. INF. *izâja-t*, join well the different parts of a speech; — V. INF. *tazawwuj*, marry (n.); — VI. INF. *tazâwuj*, be coupled, paired; — VIII. INF. *izdiwâj*, id.

زوج *zauj*, pl. *azwâj*, *ziwaja-t*, what makes a pair or couple with another, husband, wife, couple; du. *zaujân*, husband and wife, male and female; covering of a camel-litter; even number; — ة *zauja-t*, wife; — ى *zaujiyy*, coupled; matrimonial; — ية *zaujiyya-t*, the connection existing between a couple or pair.

(زوح) *zâḥ*, U, INF. *zauḥ*, disperse, and, by opposition, unite; disappear, remove (n.) from the place; INF. *zawâḥ*, go away, depart; — IV. INF. *izâḥa-t*, push a thing from its place, remove it, take it away; — VII. INF. *inziyâḥ*, remove to a distance, depart.

(زود) *zâd*, U, INF. *zaud*, supply one's self for a journey; — II. INF. *tazwîd*, supply, increase; — IV. INF. *izâda-t*=II.; — V. INF. *tazawwud*=I.; — X. INF. *istizâda-t*, demand provender or supply.

زود *zaud*, increase, growth; surplus; — *zu'd*, *zu'ud*, fright, INF. of (زأد).

(زور) *zâr*, U, INF. *zaur*, *zuwâr*, *ziyâra-t*, *mazâr*, visit; tie up the camel with the rope زوار *ziwâr*; — *zawir*, A, INF. *zawar*, be inclined, slope; have the chest or one side of the body crooked; — II. INF. *tazwîr*, cause or allow a place to be visited; honour a visitor; falsify; declare evidence to be false; commit an error in writing; disguise one's self; adorn; — III. INF. *muzâwara-t*, look askance at; — IV. INF. *izâra-t*, cause to visit; — VI. INF. *tazâwur*, visit one another; = IX.; — VIII. INF. *izdiwâr*, visit; — IX. INF. *izwirâr*, deviate, go askant; swerve aside; be confused in colour, tarnished; remove from (عن *'an*); — X. INF. *istizâra-t*, ask for a visit; — XI. INF. *izwîrâr*=IX.

زور *zaur*, middle and highest part of the chest; breast-bone; visitor, visitors; prince, chief, leader; vision in a dream; resolution; — *zûr*, lie, falsity; idolatry; idol; pl. of أزور *azwar* leaning to one side, &c.; (m' for جور *jaur*) violence, wrong; — *zawar*, inequality, crookedness; — *ziwwar*, *ziwarr*, chief; *ziwarr*, hard, firm; — *zuwwar*, pl. of زائر *zâ'ir*, *zâyir*, visitor, pilgrim; — ة *zaura-t*, visit; pilgrimage.

زوراء *zaurâ'*, f. of أزور *azwar*, leaning to one side, &c.

(زورق) *zauraq*, pl. *zawâriq*, boat, skiff, gondola; — II. INF. *tazauruq*, drop excrement.

زورقي *zauraqiyy*, heel-bone.

زوزاة *zauzâ'a-t*, haste.

(زوزق) *zauzaq*, INF. ة, embellish, adorn.

(زوزك) *zauzak*, INF. ة, move the hips in walking.

(زوزى) *zauza*, INF. زوزاة *zauzât*, despise; drive away, drive; go with quick and small steps and raising the back (cattle).

(زوش) *zauś*, *zûś*, bad slave.

(زوط), II. *zawwaṭ*, INF. *tazwîṭ*, make large bits.

(زوع) *zâ'*, U, INF. *zau'*, urge on the camel by shaking the reins; turn aside; cut a slice of melon for another (ل *li*).

زوع *zû'*, *zuwa'*, spider; — ة *zau'a-t*, slice of melon.

(زوغ) *zâg*, U, INF. *zaug*, leave one's place; deviate, swerve; be inclined, lean towards; be sprained; pull the camel by the reins; — INF. *zawagân*, swerve from the truth.

زوغل *zaugal*, INF. ة, falsify money, cheat in gaming.

(زوف) *zâf*, U, INF. *zauf*, step with outspread wings and sweeping the ground with the tail; walk with relaxed limbs.

زوف *zûfâ*, زوفى *zûfa*, hyssop

(زوق), II. *zawwaq*, INF. *tazwîq*, embellish, decorate; gild; rub coins with mercury; adorn one's speech; — V. INF. *tazawwuq*, be adorned, decorated.

زوق *zuwaq*, mercury, quicksilver.

(زوقل) *zauqal*, INF. ة, let the two ends of the turban hang down.

(زوك) *zâk*, U, INF. *zauk*, *zawakân*, strut with swinging shoulders (like a raven).

(زول) *zâl*, U, A, INF. *zawâl*, *zuwûl*, *zawîl*, *zawalân*, cease to be in a place, remove; cease, perish; with negative: continue to; — INF. *zawâl*, *zuwûl*, *ziyâl*, *zawalân*, decline towards setting; separate (n.) from (عن *'an*); — II. INF. *tazwîl*, take from its place, remove (a.); cause to cease, to disappear; destroy; abolish, repeal; — III. INF. *ziwâl*, *muzâwala-t*, intend, endeavour to bring about, to provide; deal with; — IV. INF. *izâla-t*=II.; — VII. INF. *inziyâl*, be separated.

زول *zaul*, pl. *azwâl*, person, individual; witty, ingenuous; liberal, generous, brave; a hawk.

زولات *zu'alât*, witty fellows, wags.

(زوم) *zaum*, a dish of milk; — *zûm*, pl. *azwâm*, juice of a fruit; water wrung out of washed linen.

(زون) *zûn*, *zaun*, dwarf; — *zûn*, idol; — *ziwann*, ة, small, insignificant; — ة *zûna-t*, adornment, ornament.

زوورة *zu'ûra-t*, crop of a bird.

(زوى) *zawa*, I, INF. *zayy*, *zawiyy*, take away, remove (a.); hinder; conceal, keep secret; fold, roll up; frown; pass. *zuwî*, it is decreed by God; — II. INF. *tazwiya-t*, gather into a corner; =V.; — V. *tazawwî*, sit in a corner; retire to a corner; live in retirement; — VII. INF. *inziwâ'*, be removed; be concealed; hide one's self, retire to a corner; shrink.

زويل *zawîl*, INF. of (زول).

زى *zayy*, INF. of (زوى); — *ziyy*, (m.) *zayy*, pl. *azyâ'*, outer aspect, exterior, shape, form, costume, garb, fashion, manner; in the manner of, as, how; زى ما *ziyy mâ*, as.

زيات *zayyât*, seller of oil, oil-merchant.

زياح *ziyyâḥ*, pl. *ziyyâḥât*, procession (of Christians); benediction with the most holy sacrament (m.).

زياد *ziyâd*, ة *ziyâda-t*, increase, surplus, addition; بزيادة *biziyâda-t*, too much, too; حروف الزيادة *ḥurûf az-ziyâda-t*, servile letters.

زيار *ziyâr*, means of protection or aid; resource; vice (of a locksmith); barnacle, torchenes; bow; — ة *ziyâra-t*, visit; pilgrimage; bow.

زيازى *zayâzî*, pl. of زيزاة *zîzâ'a-t*.

زياط *ziyâṭ*, cry, outcry; — *zayyâṭ*, crying out, shouting.

زياف *zayyâf*, lion; — *.

زيان *zayân*, fine, handsome; — *ziyân*, adornment.

زيائد *zayâ'id*, redundances, superfluities; excrescences.

(زيب), V. *tazayyab*, INF. *tazayyub*, be firm, compact.

زئبر *zi'bar*, *zi'bur*, shagginess of newly-made cloth.

زيبق *zi'baq*, *zîbaq*, mercury, quicksilver.

زيبل *zi'bil*, *zîbil*, calamity.

(زيت) *zât*, I, INF. *zait*, put oil to a dish; feed (a.) on oil; — II. INF. *tazyît*, put oil to a dish; provide oil, supply with oil; — IV. INF. *izâta-t*, have abundance of oil; — V. INF. *tazayyut*, be oiled; be provided with oil; — VIII. INF. *izdiyât*=V.

زيت *zait*, pl. *zuyût*, (olive-) oil.

زيتون *zaitûn*, ة, pl. *zawâtîn*, olive-

tree; — ة *zaitûna-t*, an olive; — ى *zaituniyy*, oily.

زيج *zîj*, measuring cord; — pl. زيجات *zîjât*, astronomical tables (Pers.).

(زيح) *zâḥ*, INF. *zaiḥ*, *zayûḥ*, *zuyûḥ*, *zayaḥân*, be far; remove (n.) to a distant place, depart; — II. INF. *tazyîḥ*, carry the image of a saint or the most holy sacrament in procession; walk in procession; give the benediction; draw a line (m.); — IV. INF. *izâḥa-t*, remove (a.) to a distant place; cut short (a pretext, &c.);—V. INF. *tazayyuḥ*, be carried in procession; be led from place to place or for a walk; — VII. INF. *inziyâḥ*=I.

زيح *zîḥ*, pl. *azyâḥ*, line, stroke, tracing (s.).

(زيخ) *zâḫ*, I, INF. *zaiḫ*, *zayaḫân*, act unjustly, commit iniquity; withdraw from a place; — IV. INF. *izâḫa-t*, take from a place, remove (a.); — V. INF. *tazayyuḫ*, be removed.

(زيد) *zâd*, I, INF. *zaid*, *zîd*, *zayad*, *ziyâda-t*, *mazîd*, *zaidân*, increase, augment, multiply (n.); become dearer, more expensive; surmount a number, measure or quantity; surpass; be supernumerary; increase (a.), give more, overwhelm; — II. *zayyad*, *zawwad*, INF. *tazwîd*, increase (a.); cause to grow, augment (a.); raise the price; buy dearly; — III. INF. *muzâyada-t*, buy dearly; — V. INF. *tazayyud*, increase (n.); be raised; add, add lies; exaggerate; — VI. INF. *tazâyud*, surpass one another; become dearer; — VIII. INF. *izdiyâd*, increase, multiply (n.); — X. INF. *istizâda-t*, ask for more.

زيد *zaid*, increase, growth; more, a surplus; male proper name.

زيدان *zaidân*, increase, &c., INF. of (زيد).

زير *zîr*, pl. *azyâr*, *azwâr*, *ziyara-t*, large bucket; pitched wine-jar; noun of unity ة, linen, flax; button or loop of a dress; string of a lute; treble voice; fond of women; — (زئر), see (زار); — *za'ir*, roaring, bellowing (adj.) — II. *zayyar*, INF. *tazyîr*, hold the nose of a horse with the زيار *ziyâr* while shoeing it; — V. INF. *tazayyur*, be pressed; be driven into a corner; — ة *zîra-t*, piece, portion; visit.

زيزا *zaizâ*, rugged ground; nib of a pen; — also زيزاءة *zîzâ'a-t*, *zîzât*, زيزى *zaiza*, pl. *zayâzî*, hillock.

زيزفون *zaizafûn*, fleet she-camel; an aromatic willow.

(زيط) *zâṭ*, I, INF. *zaiṭ*, *ziyâṭ*, cry out.

(زيغ) *zâg*, I, INF. *zaig*, *zayagân*, *zaigûga-t*, be inclined, lean (n.), swerve; leave one's place; go astray; decline towards setting; grow dim; — IV. INF. *izâga-t*, cause to swerve, to go astray; — V. INF. *tazayyug*, adorn one's self.

زيغان *zayagân*, INF. of (زيغ); — *zîgân*, crows, pl. of زاغ *zâg*.

زيغوغة *zaigûga-t*, deviation, &c., INF. of (زيغ).

(زيف) *zâf*, I, INF. *zaif*, *zayafân*, walk proudly; hasten; — INF. *zuyûf*, be not of full weight, be clipped (coin); INF. *zaif*, falsify or clip coins; — II. INF. *tazyîf*, falsify or clip coins.

زيف *zaif*, projecting corner of a wall; noun of unity ة, battlements, stairs; pl. *ziyâf*, *azyâf*, *zuyûf*, base coin.

(زيق) *zîq*, pl. *azyâq*, collar of a shirt; زيق الشيطان *zîq aś-śaiṭân*, gossamer; — V. INF. *tazayyuq*, be adorned and have the eyes painted with collyrium.

(زيك) *zâk*, I, INF. *zayakân*, walk proudly with violent movements of the body.

(زيل) *zâl*, A, I, INF. *zail*, remove

(a.) from the place; A, INF. *zail*, cease; with a negative: continue; — A, INF. *zayal*, have wide thighs; — II. INF. *tazyîl*, separate (a.); — III. INF. *ziyâl*, *muzâyala-t*, separate from (n.), move away from; quit; — IV. INF. *izâla-t*, take away, remove (a.); cause to cease; abolish, repeal, suppress; cause to disappear; — V. INF. *tazayyul*, be separated, dissolved; — VI. INF. *tazâyul*, separate from one another; — VII. INF. *inziyâl*, get separated from one another.

(زيم) *zâm*, I, INF. *zaim*, silence; — V. INF. *tazayyum*, disperse (n.).

زئم *zi'm*, eye; aspect; — *za'im*, see (زأم); — *za'im*, frightened; — ة *zîma-t*, troop of camels (2–15).

(زين) *zân*, I, INF. *zain*, adorn; (m.) weigh (a.); — II. INF. *tazyîn*, adorn, embellish, decorate, deck out; praise up; — IV. INF. *izyân*, *izâna-t*=II.; — V. INF. *tazayyun*, get adorned, adorn one's self; — VIII. INF. *izziyân*, IX. INF. *izyinân* =V.

زين *zain*, pl. *azyân*, adornment, ornament, decoration, distinction; cock's comb; — ة *zîna-t*, adornment; splendour, pomp.

زينب *zainab*, an aromatic tree; female proper name; coward.

زينهار *zînhâr*=زنهار *zinhâr*, beware! &c.

زيوان *zîwân*, oats (m.).

(زي), II. *zayya*, INF. *tazyiya-t*, give the shape, form, costume of; — V. INF. *tazayyî*, have the shape, form, costume of; dress (a.), adorn one's self.

زئير *za'îr*, roaring (adj.); roar; INF. of (زأر).

س

س *s*, twelfth letter of the Arabic alphabet; as a numerical sign= 60; abbreviation for سلام *salâm*, peace, hail.

س *sa*, prefixed to an aorist in order to give it the meaning of immediate future.

سا *sâ'*, see (سوأ).

سآل *sa''âl*, who continually puts questions.

سآمة, see سأمة *sa'âma-t*.

(سأب) *sa'ab*, INF. *sa'b*, throttle, worry to death; make wide; quench one's thirst; — سئب *sa'ib*, A, INF. *sa'ab*, quench one's thirst.

سأب *sa'b*, pl. *su'ûb*, large skin bag; — *sâbb*, who inveighs, reviles, insults.

ساباط *sâbât*, pl. *sâbâtât*, *sabâwît*, covered passage, corridor.

سابح *sâbih*, f. ة, pl. *subbâh*, swimmer; — also ة *sâbiha-t*, pl. *sawâbih*, fleet horse; pl. *sâbihât*, ships; stars; spirits of the believers.

سابرى *sâbiriyy*, finest cloth; finest coats of mail; best dates.

سابع *sâbi'*, ة, seventh.

سابغ *sâbig*, ample; long and rich; abundant; complete, copious, extensive; — ة *sâbiga-t*, pl. *sawâbig*, long and wide coat of mail.

سابق *sâbiq*, pl. *subbâq*, *subbaq*, f. ة, pl. *sawâbiq*, previous, preceding, old; former; John the Baptist as precursor of Christ; *sâbiq-an*, in olden times, of old, formerly, long ago; who gets in advance, conquers; winning race-horse; — ة *sâbiqa-t*, pl. *sawâbiq*, past time; priority, superiority, preeminence; old right or custom; precedent; progress; first dis-

position or symptoms of an illness; antecedent; — ية sâbiqiyya-t, priority.

سابل sâbil, pouring (adj.); — ة sâbila-t, pl. sawâbil, trodden roads; passers-by, travellers; travelling-company.

سبيا sâbiyâ', pl. sawâbî, membrane which surrounds the embryo in the womb; fertile and numerous.

(سات) sa'at, INF. sa't, throttle.

سات sa'at, du. sa'atân, the sides of the throat; — sâtt, sixth.

ساج sâj, ة, iron plate for baking bread, roasting, &c.; fire-screen; table of a money-changer; pl. sâjât, castanets; pl. sâjât, sîjân, frontlet; plane-tree; ebony.

ساجد sâjid, ة, pl. sujjad, sujûd, prostrate; adorer; — ة sâjida-t, bowing (adj.); dim.

ساجع sâji', writer of rhymed prose; — ة sâji'a-t, pl. sawâji', cooing (adj.).

ساجم sâjim, pl. sawâjim, flowing.

ساجور sâjûr, pl. sawâjîr, piece of wood tied to a dog's neck.

ساجی sâjî (ساج sâj-in), ة, pl. sawâjî, calm, quiet; dark.

ساح sâhh, ة, pl. sihâh, suhhâh, very fat; — ة sâha-t, pl. -ât, sâh, sûh, yard; open place between tents, houses, &c.; vestibule; out-house, dwelling; precinct; region; shore, coast.

ساحر sâhir, ة, pl. sahara-t, suharâ', enchanting; sorcerer, magician.

ساحل sâhil, pl. sawâhil, sea-coast, shore; Phœnicia.

ساحية sâhiya-t, rain-flood.

ساخر sâhir, who scoffs; buffoon.

ساخن sâhin, ة, hot; pl. suhhân, feverish, sick, ill.

(ساد) sa'ad, INF. sa'd, sa'ad, throttle; — سئد sa'id, A, INF. sa'ad, drink; break open again; — IV. INF. is'âd, walk apace; travel all night through without resting in the morning.

ساد sâdd, stopping, damming in (adj.); redressing, remedying (adj.); — ة sâda-t, lords, pl. of سائد sâ'id and سيد sayyid; — sâdda-t, open but dim eye.

سادات , سادة sâdât, lords, &c., pl. of سيد sayyid.

سادج sâdij, pl. suddâj, unfermented; unmixed; simple, natural, sincere; — ية sâdijiyya-t, smooth surface without any design; natural simplicity, absence of any ornament.

سادر sâdir, thunderstruck, perplexed, giddy, dazzled, careless, reckless, obdurate.

سادس sâdis, ة, sixth.

سادن sâdin, pl. sadana-t, watcher or servant of a temple.

سادوم sâdûm, Sodom.

سادومی sâdûmiyy, Sodomite; — ة sâdûmiyya-t, sodomy, pederasty.

(سار) sa'ar, INF. sa'r, leave something in the pot or the cup; — سئر sa'ir, A, INF. sa'ar, remain; — IV. INF. is'âr, leave.

سار sârr, ة, giving joy, cheering (adj.); joyful; — sâr-in, see ساری sârî.

سارب sârib, who walks freely, pasturing freely; visible.

سارف sârif, ag. of (سرف); corroding, corrosive.

سارق sâriq, pl. surrâq, thief; سارق اليد sâriq al-yad, weak of hand; — ة sâriqa-t, pl. sawâriq, female thief; large kettle, cauldron; pillory; iron chains.

سارورا sârûrâ', joy.

ساروقة sârûqa-t, a small saw.

ساری sârî (سار sâr-in), pl. سراة surât, travelling at night; piercing, penetrating; reaching; contagious; — ة sâriya-t, pl. sawârî, column; mast.

سا سم sa'sam, sâsam, ebony-tree.

ساسة sâsa-t, pl. of سايس sâyis.

ساسية sâsiya-t, red cap.

ساطح *sâṭiḥ*, God, the spreader of the earth.

ساطر *sâṭir*, butcher; satellite, life-guardsman; bailiff.

ساطع *sâṭi'*, what rises and spreads, far-spread; clear, evident.

ساطل *sâṭil*, rising.

ساطن *sâṭin*, bad, wicked, corrupt.

ساطور *sâṭûr*, pl. *sawâṭîr*, large butcher's knife.

ساطى *sâṭî* (ساط *sâṭ-in*), ة, furious and biting (stallion); rushing on impetuously, attacking furiously; irresistible; long.

ساعاتى *sâ'âtiyy*, watch-maker.

ساعاتئذ *sâ'âta'iẓ-in*, at that very hour.

ساعد *sâ'id*, pl. *sawâ'id*, fore-arm; armlet; neck of a violin; assistance;—ة *sâ'ida-t*, supporting beam; lion.

ساعل *sâ'il*, gargle, throat; coughing (adj.).

ساع *sâ'in*, see ساعى *sâ'î*; — ة *sâ'a-t*, pl. *-ât*, *sâ'*, hour; moment; little while, short time; hour of resurrection; watch, clock.

ساعور *sâ'ûr*, stove; — also ة *sâ'ûra-t*, fire.

ساعى *sâ'î* (ساع *sâ'in*), pl. *su'ât*, who runs, hastens; express; messenger; eager, zealous (ساعى بالفساد *sâ'î bi 'l-fasâd*, mischievous, eager to stir up mischief); prefect; superior, judge; tax-gatherer; defamer.

ساغب *sâgib*, pl. *sigâb*, hungry and weary.

(سأف) *sa'af*, A, INF. *sa'f*, be rent, be pared, peeled, separated into fibres; — سئف *sa'if*, A, INF. *sa'af*, id.; — سوف *sa'uf*, INF. *sa'âfa-t*, be afflicted with murrain.

سأف *sa'af*, wolf's hair; bristles; *sâf-in*, see سافى *sâfî*; — *sâf*, ة *sâfa-t*, stone layer of a wall; — ة *sâfa-t*, pl. *sâf*, layer of ground between sand and stone.

سافر *sâfir*, pl. *suffâr*, *asfâr*, traveller; pl. *safara-t*, clerk, scribe; angel who registers the deeds of men; mediator; pl. *sawâfir*, unveiled, clearly seen; — ة *sâfira-t*, travelling company, wandering tribe.

سافك *sâfik*, shedding, ag. of (سفك); sword.

سافل *sâfil*, lower part, further down; low, mean, vile, bad; أسفل السافلين *asfal as-sâfilîn*, the vilest of the vile, the damned; — ة *sâfila-t*, lower half of the body, lower parts of it.

سافنة *sâfina-t*, pl. *sawâfin*, sweeping the ground, raising dust (wind).

سافى *sâfî* (ساف *sâf-in*), pl. *sawâfî*, wind raising dust; also سافيا *sâfiya*, dust and wind.

ساق *sâq*, pl. *sûq*, *su'ûq*, *sîqân*, *as'uq*, leg; trunk, stalk; column, pillar; side of an angle; perpendicular; scale (of a balance); genus, gender, kind; pain, torment; ساق على ساق *sâq 'ala sâq*, leg across leg, i.e. deep thought, meditation; — *sâq-in*, see ساقى *sâqî*; — ة *sâqa-t*, rear-guard; strap of the stirrup.

ساقط *sâqiṭ*, pl. *suqqâṭ*, falling, thrown down; مرض س *marḍ sâqiṭ*, epilepsy; less valuable furniture; despised, worthless, bad; miscarriage; — ة *sâqiṭa-t*, pl. *sawâqiṭ*, سقطى *sakṭa*, of little value, cheap; fallen leaf; fallen word.

ساقور *sâqûr*, glow, glowing fire; iron for heating, curling-iron.

ساقوطة *sâqûṭa-t*, bolt; latch.

ساقى *sâqî* (ساق *sâq-in*), pl. *suqât*, *suqiyy*, *suqqa*, who waters or gives to drink, cup-bearer; water-carrier; — ة *sâqiya-t*, pl. *sawâqî*, canal for irrigating, channel, river-arm; female cup-bearer.

ساكب *sâkib*, who pours out, &c., ag. of (سكب); Aquarius.

ساكت *sâkit*, silent, ag. of سكت; dumb.

ساكر *sâkir*, still, quiet.
ساكف *sâkif*, threshold.
ساكن *sâkin*, ة, quiet; quiescent letter; calmed; pl. *sukkân*, inhabitant.
ساكوت *sâkût*, one silent; — ة *sâkûta-t*, id.; silence.
(سال) *sa'al*, IMP. *is'al*, *as'al*, *sal*, INF. *su'âl*, *sa'la-t*, *sa'âla-t*, *tas'âl*, *mas'ala-t*, ask, question, ask for, beg; — III. INF. *musâ'ala-t*, *musâyala-t*, ask, ask for, beg; (m.) *sâyal*, injure, damage; — IV. INF. *is'âl*, grant a request; — V. INF. *tasa''ul*, beg (alms); — VI. INF. *tasâ'ul*, *tasâyul*, question one another.
سال *sâll*, drawing, ag. of (سل); pl. *sullân*, *sawâll*, wide valley; — ة *sa'la-t*, INF. of (سال).
سالار *sâlâr*, commander, general, chief-justice (Pers.).
سالب *sâlib*, who steals, &c., ag. of (سلب); negative, privative; pl. *sawâlib*, miscarrying (woman); — ة *sâliba-t*, negative sentence; — ية *sâlabiyya-t*, sage (plant).
سالح *sâliḥ*, armed.
سالخ *sâliḫ*, skinning, skinner, &c., ag. of (سلخ); scab; snake which has thrown off its slough; f. ة, black.
سالغ *sâlig*, m. f. losing the teeth (after the sixth year, cattle).
سالف *sâlif*, pl. *sullâf*, preceding; former, past; who pays in advance; pl. *sawâlif*, predecessor; — ة *sâlifa-t*, pl. *sawâlif*, things past, old stories; olden times; side of a horse's fore-neck, neck; (m.) *sawâlif*, hair falling over the ears and temples.
سالقة *sâliqa-t*, wailing (f.).
سالك *sâlik*, ag. of (سلك); traveller; frequented; usual, customary; devotee, ascetic.
سالم *sâlim*, sound and safe; in perfect condition; secure; free from (من *min*); regular (verb, plural); — ة *sâlima-t*, sage (plant).
(سام) *sa'im*, A, INF. *sa'm*, *sa'am*, *sa'âma-t*, *sa'âm*, be tired, weary, disgusted of, feel aversion, be wearied, annoyed; — IV. INF. *is'âm*, cause weariness, disgust, annoyance, bore.
سام *sa'm*, death; — *sâm*, Shem, son of Noah; — *sâmm*, ة, poisonous, venomous, pestilential; hot with a poisonous wind; poisonous wind; peculiar; — ة *sâma-t*, pl. *sâm*, gold, silver; veins of gold or silver; hole for water; pl. *siyam*, cavity of a well; — *sa'âma-t*, weariness, satiety, disgust; — *sâmma-t*, poisonous animal; intimate friend; patrician; death.
سامح *sâmiḥ*, pl. *sumûḥ*, liberal, beneficent; forgiving, indulgent.
سامد *sâmid*, careless, toying.
سامر *sâmir*, pl. *sâmira-t*, *summar*, *summâr*, conversing (adj.); who gathers and converses by moonlight, night-talker; — ة *sâmira-t*, Samaritans; — ى *sâmariyy*, Samaritan; ة *sâmariyya-t*, Samaria.
سامع *sâmi'*, ة, hearing, hearer; listening, obeying, obedient; — ة *sâmi'a-t*, ear; hearing (s.), sense of hearing.
سامغان *sâmigân*, du. the corners of the mouth.
سامل *sâmil*, peace-maker; earning one's livelihood by industry.
سامم *sâmim*, poisoner, mixer of poison.
سامن *sâmin*, fat; buttery, rich in butter.
سامه *sâmih*, pl. *summah*, perplexed, bewildered.
سامى *sâmî* (سام *sâm-in*), pl. *sumât*, lofty, sublime; emanating from the sultan or the grand-vizier; complete; hunter; pl. *sawâmî*, bearing his head high (stallion).
سانح *sâniḥ*, ة, pl. *sawâniḥ*, turning the right side towards, therefore: auguring well, auspicious,

lucky; happening, befalling; game coming in sight, turning up; — ة *sâniḥa-t*, pl. *-ât*, *sawâniḥ*, fore-token, omen; revelation; edict; event.

سانى *sânî* (سان *sân-in*), ة, pl. *sawânî*, drawing and carrying water; — ة *sâniya-t*, large bucket for drawing water.

ساهج *sâhij*, ة, blowing violently.

ساهر *sâhir*, waking, sleepless; — ة *sâhira-t*, earth, surface of the earth; waterless desert; hell; = سهور *sahûr*.

ساهمة *sâhima-t*, pl. *sawâhim*, emaciated she-camel.

ساهور *sâhûr*, sheath into which the eclipsed moon is said to withdraw; shadow of the earth; halo; moon; moonlight; sleeplessness, waking (s.).

ساهى *sâhî* (ساه *sâh-in*), careless, negligent, absent-minded; bewildered, perplexed.

(ساو) *sa'â*, INF. *sa'w*, intend; — INF. *sa'w*, *sa'y*, stretch (cloth) until it tears; — ساى *sa'a*, run; stir up enmity; — سآا *sa'â*, 1. pret. *sa'autu*, INF. *sa'w*, be in a bad condition, suffer damage; do evil, damage, injure; — IV. INF. *is'â'*, provide the bow with a head.

ساى *sa'a*, see the previous; — ة *sâya-t*, equality, evenness.

سايب *sâyib*, flowing, running; forsaken, abandoned; — ة *sâ'iba-t*, pl. *suyyab*, set free.

سايح *sâyiḥ*, pl. *suwwâḥ*, traveller, wanderer; who fasts in a mosque, who mortifies himself, hermit, wandering dervish; running, flowing; spreading, current.

سائد *sâ'id*, pl. *sâda-t*, *sayâ'id*, master, lord, prince.

ساير *sâyir*, ag. of (سير); wanderer, traveller; current, usual, customary; — *sâ'ir*, ag. of (سار), remaining; the rest, the remainder, all; — ة *sâyira-t*, travelling company.

سايس *sâyis*, pl. *siyâs*, *sâsa-t*, administrator, governor, regent; equerry, groom; corroded, decaying (tooth).

سايط *sâyiṭ*, ة, who scourges; swimming in water, much watered.

سايع *sâyi'*, lost, useless.

سايغ *sâyig* (also سايغ لايغ *sâyig lâyig*), gliding pleasantly down the throat; lawful, beseeming.

سايف *sâyif*, armed with a sword.

سايق *sâyiq*, pl. *suwwâq*, who urges on, driver, coachman; — ة *sâyiqa-t*, urging cause, motive.

سايل *sâyil*, flowing, liquid; — *sâ'il*, who questions, who proposes a question, who requests; beggar; — ة *sâyila-t*, pl. *sawâyil*, fluid (s.).

سائم *sâ'im*, ة, pl. *sawâ'im*, grazing, pasturing; — ة *sâ'ima-t*, pl. *sawâ'im*, grazing cattle, herd.

(سب) *sabb*, U, INF. *sabb*, cut; wound; INF. *sabb*, *sibbîba*, inveigh against, revile (acc. or ل *li*); — II. INF. *tasbîb*, cause, be the motive; procure an opportunity; inveigh violently against; — III. INF. *sibâb*, *musâbba-t*, inveigh, overwhelm with abuse, revile; — V. INF. *tasabbub*, be the cause of; carry on a retail trade; earn one's livelihood by working; — VI. INF. *tasâbub*, revile one another; — VIII. INF. *istibâb*, id.

سب *sabb*, invective, abuse; rebuke; — *sibb*, pl. *subûb*, who reviles much; calumniator, slanderer; turban; net for the hair; — ة *sabba-t*, a time, a while; week; buttocks; — *sibba-t*, fore-finger, index; — *subba-t*, invective, abuse; shame; who is abused by everybody.

(سبا) *saba'*, INF. *sab'*, *sabâ'*, *sibâ'*, *masba'*, buy; neglect; take by the hand; skin, flay; scourge

so as to tear the skin; scorch and cause to shrink; — IV. INF. *isbâ'*, submit humbly to the law of God, submit; — VIII. INF. *istibâ'*, buy wine.

سبا *sabâ'*, drift wood; — *sibâ'*, captivity; imported wine; — *sabbâ'*, wine-merchant; — ة *sub'a-t*, long journey.

سباب *sibâb*, abuse, invective; — *sabbâb*, abuser, reviler; — ة *sabbâba-t*, fore-finger, index.

سبابيط *sabâbîṭ*, pl. of سباط *sabbâṭ*.

سبات *subât*, sleep, rest, repose; lethargy; alert and cunning.

سباتى *subâtiyy*, lethargic; struck with apoplexy.

سباج *sabbâj*, who sells shells.

سباح *sabbâḥ*, swimmer; — *subbâḥ*, pl. of *sâbiḥ*; — ة *sibâḥa-t*, art of swimming; — *sabbâḥa-t*, fore-finger, index.

سبادرة *sabâdira-t*, pl. idlers.

سبار *sibâr*, surgeon's probe.

سباريت *sabârît*, pl. of سبروت *subrût*.

سبارينا *sabârînâ*, sarsaparilla.

سباط *sabâṭ*, fever; — *subâṭ*, February; — *subâṭa-t*, offal, sweepings; plentiousness; — *; — *sabbâṭ*, pl. *sabâbiṭ*, shoe.

سباع *sibâ'*, pl. of سبع *sabu'*; — ى *subâ'iyy*, composed of seven letters; seven years old; bulky; enormous; full in body.

سباق *sibâq*, eagerness to get the lead, INF. III. of (سبق); superiority, pre-eminence; — *sabbâq*, who is in advance, superior, pre-eminent; — *subbâq*, pl. of سابق *sâbiq*.

سباك *sabbâk*, who melts, founds, founder.

سبالة *sibâla-t*, moustache.

سبايا *sabâyâ*, pl. of سبى *sabiyy*.

سبب *sabab*, pl. *asbâb*, cause, reason, motive; argument, subject; means of living; household furniture, thing; small goods, retail goods; materials; kinship; tent-rope; element of a foot of verse, composed of two letters (خفيف *ḥafîf* if a movable letter is followed by a quiescent one, ثقيل *saqîl* if both are movable); — ة *subaba-t*, reviler, abuser, slanderer; — ية *sababiyya-t*, reason, cause; causality.

(سبت) *sabat*, U, I, INF. *sabt*, rest, sleep; keep the Sabbath; make holiday, be idle; cut off, behead; shave; let the hair hang down; be perplexed; — IV. enter on the Sabbath; — VII. INF. *insibât*, be prolonged, protracted, be long.

سبت *sabt*, pl. *asbut*, *subût*, Sabbath; rest; week, time, while; — *sibt*, tanned hide; — *sibitt*, anise; — ة *sabta-t*, Ceuta; a while; herd of goats.

سبتا *sabtâ'*, f. desert.

سبج *sabaj*, ة, small black shell; — ة *subja-t*, a black garment or carpet; sleeveless dress, shirt; — II. *sabbaj*, INF. *tasbîj*, fit (a.), order, arrange (m.); — V. INF. *tasabbuj*, put on the *subja-t*.

(سبح) *sabaḥ*, A, INF. *sabḥ*, *sibâḥa-t*, swim; float; career; praise God with the words سبحان الله *subḥân-a 'l-lâh-i*; make many words; make a long journey; spread; INF. *sabḥ*, work for one's living; dig the ground; sleep, rest; be free of, have done with (عن *'an*); — II. INF. *tasbîḥ*, *tasbiḥa-t*, praise God; pray; cause to swim, to float; set adrift; — III. INF. *musâbaḥa-t*, vie in swimming with (acc.); — IV. INF. *isḥâb*, cause to swim, wash, set afloat.

سبح *sabḥ*, praise of God; swimming (s.); — ة *sabḥa-t*, *subḥa-t*, glory of God; — *sabḥa-t*, garment of skins; — *subḥa-t*, pl. *subaḥ*, *subuḥât*, bead of a rosary; rosary; supererogatory prayers.

سبحا *subaḥâ'*, pl. of سبوح *sabûḥ*.

سبحان *subḥân*, praise, glorification; سبحان من كذا *subḥân-a min kaẕâ*, how exquisite! how wonderful! — ى *subḥâniyy*, divine.

سبحل *sibaḥl*, سبحلل *sibaḥlal*, thick, bulky, massive; — *sabḥal*, and—

سبحن *sabḥan*, INF. ة, repeat the words سبحان الله *subḥân-a 'l-lâh-i*; *sabḥan*, wonder at.

(سبخ) *sabaḥ*, U, INF. *sabḥ*, be at leisure, be idle; sleep deeply; remove to a great distance, be far; — II. INF. *tasbîḥ*, alleviate; moderate; — IV. INF. *isbâḥ*, contain salt; meet with salt in digging; — ة *sabḥa-t*, *sabaḥa-t*, *sabiḥa-t*, pl. *sibâḥ*, salty ground; salt marsh.

(سبد) *sabad*, U, INF. *sabd*, shave off the hair; — II. INF. *tasbîd*, IV. INF. *isbâd*, id.

سبد *sibd*, pl. *asbâd*, wolf; thief; calamity; — *sabad*, cloth of goat's hair; wool; — *subad*, pl. *sibdân*, hair of the pudenda; calamity.

سبذة *sabaẕa-t*, pl. *sabaẕ*, large basket.

(سبر) *sabar*, U, INF. *sabr*, probe or clean a wound; sound; — II. INF. *tasbîr*, place on guard; mount guard, be on guard; — VIII. INF. *istibâr*=I.

سبر *sabr*, probing, sounding (s.); examination and knowledge resulting from it; destiny; lion; — *sabr*, *sibr*, pl. *asbâr*, form, shape, fashion, manner, taste; colour; beauty; root, origin; — *sibr*, abuse, invective; — *sabar*, nail in the axle-tree; — ة *sabra-t*, pl. *sabarât*, cold morning.

سبرات *sibrât*, سبرت *subrut*, poor, wretched, miserable; — ة *sabrata-t*, being (s.) contented.

(سبرج) *sabraj*, INF. ة, cover, hide, conceal.

سبروت *subrût*, سبريت *sibrît*, pl. *sabârît*, poor, wretched, miserable; waste ground, desert.

سبزوات *sabzawât*, greens (Pers.).

(سبسب) *sabsab*, INF. ة, cause to flow; — II. INF. *tasabsub*, flow.

سبسب *sabsab*, pl. *sabâsib*, vast plain; desert; extensive; (m.) lash, hair of the brow.

(سبط) *sabiṭ*, A, INF. *sabṭ*, *sabaṭ*, be smooth; — *sabuṭ*, INF. *sabâṭa-t*, *subûṭa-t*, id.; INF. *sabâṭa-t*, be far-spread and abundant; pass. *subiṭ*, suffer from fever; — IV. INF. *isbâṭ*, be silent; lie on the ground at full length.

سبط *sibṭ*, pl. *asbâṭ*, Hebrew tribe; grandson, descendant; — *sabṭ*, *sabaṭ*, smooth hair; slender; liberal; — *sabiṭ*, smooth; slender.

سبطانة *sabaṭâna-t*, blow-pipe; pike, spear.

(سبطر) *sabṭar*, INF. ة, execute an order obediently; — III. *isbaṭarr*, INF. *isbiṭrâr*, lay one's self on the side and stretch one's self; be extended; walk apace.

سبطر *sibaṭr*, crouching to take a leap.

(سبع) *saba'*, A, I, INF. *sab'*, complete the number of seven; twist sevenfold; take the seventh part of one's property; shoot; frighten; fall upon, bite, tear, devour; rob a sheep from the flock; abuse, revile; — II. INF. *tasbî'*, divide into seven parts, make sevenfold, return sevenfold; frighten; — IV. INF. *isbâ'*, be or become seven.

سبع *sab'*, f., سبعة m., seven; du. *as-sab'ân*, the seven heavens and the seven earths; سبع المثانى *sab'-u 'l-maṯânî*, the first chapter of the Koran; — *sub'*, pl. *asbâ'*, seventh part; — *sabu'*, *sab'*, *saba'*, pl. *asbu'*, *sibâ'*, voracious animal, lion; — ة *sabu'a-t*, *sab'a-t*, lioness.

سبعون *sab'ûn*, seventy; seventieth.

سبعى *sabu'iyy*, ة, wild and cruel, savage like a wild beast; — ة *sabu'iyya-t*, savageness, cruelty.

(سبغ) *sabag*, U, INF. *subûg*, trail on the ground; be abundant, abound; travel to, come to; — IV. INF. *isbâg*, make a garment ample and long; extend over the whole of the body; give in abundance.

سبغ *subug*, clad in a long coat of mail; — ة *sabga-t*, plenty, abundance, affluence.

(سبغل), III. *isbagall*, INF. *isbiglâl*, be wet through; be oiled, anointed.

(سبق) *sabaq*, I, U, INF. *sabq*, get in advance, get the lead of, overtake; come first to the goal; get the better of, have the precedence, anticipate; come before time; precede; — II. INF. *tasbîq*, cause to get in advance; (m.) get in advance, overtake; give and take stakes in a race; — III. INF. *musâbaqa-t*, (also VIII.) try to overtake one another, vie with one another, rival one another; — VII. INF. *insibâq*, be overtaken, surpassed; remain behind; — VIII. INF. *istibâq*= VI.; get in advance, be foremost; rival in running or shooting.

سبق *sabq*, getting in advance (s.), precedence, superiority; — *sabaq*, ة *subqa-t*, pl. *asbâq*, *sibâq*, stake in a race, pledge in contracting a marriage; — *sabaq*, example, model, pattern; lesson; — *subbaq*, pl. of سابق *sâbiq*; — (*sibq*) du. *sibqân*, the two betters; — ة *sabqa-t*, getting in advance; precedence; anything preceding.

(سبك) *sabak*, I, INF. *sabk*, melt metals, found and cast into a form; — VI. INF. *tasâbuk*, pass. of the previous.

سبك *sabk*, founding or casting of metals; formation, disposition, construction of a sentence.

(سبكر), III. *isbakarr*, INF. *isbikrâr*, lay one's self on the side and stretch one's self; be well made.

سبل *sabal*, rain; spear; cataract (of the eye); — also *subl*, noun of unity *sabala-t*, *subla-t*, ear (of corn); — *subul*, pl. of سبيل *sabîl*; — ة *sabla-t*, *sabala-t*, pl. *sibâl*, moustache; garments; — *subla-t*, extended rain; — II. *sabbal*, INF. *tasbîl*, consecrate to a pious use; protract, prolong; trail the garment; set free, dismiss; rain abundantly; shed tears; form ears (corn); abound in travellers, be much travelled over; — IV. INF. *isbâl*, trail the garments, lower the veil.

سبلا *sablâ'*, f. having long eyelashes.

سبلانى *sabalâniyy*, having long moustaches.

(سبن), *asbân*, pl., fine kerchief.

سبنتى *sabanta*, pl. *sabânit*, سبندى *sabanda*, pl. *sabânid*, *sabânida-t*, bold, wild; leopard; an embroidered silk stuff.

(سبه) *subih*, pass. *subbih*, pass. II. (m. *sabah*, U) INF. *sabah*, delirate, dote.

سبه *sabah*, dotage.

سبوح *sabûḥ*, pl. *subaḥâ'*, swimmer; safe (horse); — *subbûḥ*, holy; — ة *sabûḥa-t*, Mecca; the valley of Mina.

سبورة *sabbûra-t*, writing-tablet, slate.

سبوع *subû'*, week; *subû'-an*, seven times.

سبوق *sabûq*, surpassing.

سبولة *sabûla-t*, full ear of corn.

(سبى) *saba*, I, INF. *saby*, *sibâ'*, make prisoner, lead into captivity or slavery; captivate one's attention, one's heart; import wine; INF. *saby*, send into distant foreign lands, into captivity; — VIII. INF. *insibâ'*, make prisoner.

سبى *saby*, captivity; pl. *sibiyy*, led far away or into captivity;

women (as captives or slaves); — *sabiyy*, pl. *sabâyâ*, prisoner of war; who is led far away; drift wood; — also *saby*, thrown off slough of a snake; — ة *sabî'a-t*, wine; — *sabiyya-t*, سبيئة *sabî'a-t*, pl. *sabâyâ*, slough; spoil, booty; imported wine.

سبيب *sabîb*, pl. *sabâ'ib*, reviler, slanderer; — also ة *sabîba-t*, pl. *sabâ'ib*, tuft of hair, hair falling over the forehead, mane, tail; — ة *sabîba-t*, garment of linen, piece of thin linen.

سبيبى *sibbîba*, abuse, INF. of (سب).

سبيجة *sabîja-t*, a black garment or carpet; sleeveless dress, shirt.

سبيخ *sabîḥ*, ة *sabîḥa-t*, pl. *sabâ'iḥ*, fleak of cotton; offal, parings, feathers, &c.; deep sleep.

سبيكة *sabîka-t*, pl. *sabâ'ik*, bar of gold or silver, ingot; *sabâ'ik*, meltings.

سبيل *sabîl*, pl. *subul*, way, path, road; manner, method; means and ways; kinship; necessary connection; distribution of water; public fountain; ابن السبيل *ibn-u 's-sabîl-i*, wanderer; فى سبيل الله *fî sibîl-i 'l-lâh-i*, in the cause of God, in holy warfare; — ة *sabîla-t*, road, path.

ست *sat*, *satt*, indecent talk; vice; stain; — ـ *sitt*, pl. *sittât*, mistress, lady, gentlewoman (ستى *sittî*, madam); grandmother; — *sitt* (for سدس *sids*), f., ة *sitta-t*, m. six.

ستار *sitâr*, pl. *sutur*, veil; — *sattâr*, guardsman of the curtain, chamberlain, who veils carefully; who covers sin, pardons; — *suttâr*, complines, evening prayers (m.); — ة *sitâra-t*, pl. *satâ'ir*, anything that veils or covers, curtain, covering, veil; protection; palisade.

ستالة *sutâla-t*, bad remainder.

ستائر *satâ'ir*, pl. of ستارة *sitâra-t*.

(ستب) *satb*, a quick pace; — *satab*, walking languidly.

(ستر) *satar*, U, INF. *satr*, cover, veil, envelop; protect; — II. INF. *tastîr*, id.; keep a girl veiled; — V. INF. *tasattur*, be covered, veiled; cover, veil one's self; — VIII. INF. *istitâr* = V.

ستر *sitr*, pl. *sutûr*, *astâr*, veil, curtain, cover; protection; modesty, shame, bashfulness; prudence; — *sutur*, pl. of ستار *sitâr*; — ة *sutra-t*, anything that covers or veils.

ستل *satal*, U, INF. *satl*, come forth in succession, succeed one another; — *satil*, A, INF. *satal*, follow.

ستمائة *sittumi'a-t*, six hundred.

(سته) *sath*, buttock; — *satih*, having large buttocks; pederast, sodomite.

(سته) *satah*, INF. *sath*, follow from behind.

ستهم *suthum* = سته *satih*.

(ستو) *satâ*, U, INF. *satw*, hasten.

ستوق *sattûq*, *suttûq*, ة, forged, not of full weight.

ستون *sittûn*, sixty; sixtieth.

ستى *sittî*, madam! miss!

ستيتة *sutaita-t*, damsel.

ستير *satîr*, ة, veiled; bashful, chaste; who covers other people's faults; — *sittîr*, *sattîr*, who veils himself.

ستين *sittîn*, (n.) sixty; sixtieth.

سج *sajj*, U, INF. *sajj*, loam (a wall).

سجاح *sijâḥ*, opposite, in front of; — *sujâḥ*, atmosphere.

سجاد *sajjâd*, prostrate in adoration; — ة *sujjâda-t*, pl. *sajâjîd*, prayer-carpet; oratory, mosque.

سجاع *sajjâ'*, ة *sajjâ'a-t*, composer of rhymed prose.

سجاف *sajâf*, *sijâf*, curtain; fringe.

سجان *sajjân*, jailer.

سجايا *sajâyâ*, pl. of سجية *sajiyya-t*.

(سجب) *sajb*, pl. *sujb*, old leathern flask.

سجج *sujuj*, flat loam roofs.

(سجح) *sajah*, U, INF. *sajh*, coo; (also II.) gloss over, tell in a disguised manner; — *sajih*, A, INF. *sajh*, *sajâha-t*, be smooth and well-shaped (cheek); — II. INF. *tasjîh*, see I.; pass over with indulgence, pardon; — IV. INF. *isjâh*, pardon, treat with indulgence; — VII. INF. *insijâh*, show generosity.

سجح *sujh*, smoothness, evenness; high-road; — also *sujuh*, measure, seize; — *sajah*, symmetry; — *sujuh*, smooth, even; gentle; — ة *sajha-t*, natural disposition, temper.

سجحا *sajhâ'*, f. of اسجح *asjah*, well-proportioned.

(سجد) *sajad*, U, INF. *sujûd*, bow in reverence, prostrate one's self in prayer or adoration; adore; be low or bent down, and, by opposition, stand erect; — *sajid*, A, INF. *sajad*, be swollen; — IV. INF. *isjâd*, bend the head, bow; revere, honour.

سجد *sujjad*, pl. of ساجد *sâjid*; — ة *sajda-t*, bow; prostration.

(سجر) *sajar*, U, INF. *sajr*, heat the stove; light the fire; INF. *sajr*, *sujûr*, protract a tender cry for her foal; feel, cause to swell; INF. *sajr*, tie a piece of wood to a dog's neck; — II. INF. *tasjîr*, cause the water to flow, shed, fill the sea, swell (a.); pass. *sujir*, swell (n.); — III. INF. *musâjara-t*, cultivate one's friendship; — VII. INF. *insijâr*, step along in an unbroken line; — ة *sujra-t*, pl. *sujur*, small cistern for rain-water; — also *sajar*, red spot in the white of the eye.

سجرا *sujarâ'*, pl. of سجير *sajîr*.

سجس *sajis*, A, INF. *sâjas*, be corrupted, be turbid, troubled, muddy; be agitated; — II. INF. *tasjîs*, trouble, agitate; — V. INF. *tasajjus*=I.

سجس *sajas*, turbidness, muddiness; agitation, tumult; — *sajis*, troubled, turbid.

سجسج *sajsaj*, temperate.

(سجع) *saja'*, A, INF. *saj'*, coo; rhyme, speak in rhymed prose; protract the sound of the voice; intend, purpose; — II. INF. *tasjî'*, speak in rhymed prose.

سجع *saj'*, pl. *asjâ'*, *asâji'*, rhymed prose; assonance; cadence; — *sujja'*, pl. of سجوع *sajû'*.

(سجف) *sajif*, A, INF. *sajaf*, have a slim waist and slender body; = II.; — II. INF. *tasjîf*, let down the curtain; — IV. INF. *isjâf*, id.; be dark.

سجف *sajf*, *sijf*, pl. *sujûf*, *asjâf*, curtain, veil; — *sajaf*, slender waist; — ة *sajfa-t*, an hour of the night.

(سجل) *sajal*, U, INF. *sajl*, pour out; (also II.) throw down; — II. INF. *tasjîl*, see I.; sign a public document; seal, put one's seal to; register, enter; recommend a petition by a marginal note; — III. INF. *musâjala-t*, vie in glory with; — IV. INF. *isjâl*, draw up a document, fill; give full buckets or large presents; possess many goods; neglect, forget; — VI. vie in glory with one another; — VII. INF. *insijâl*, be poured out.

سجل *sajl*, pl. *sijâl*, *sujûl*, large bucket full of water; — *sijl*, pl. *sujul*, also *sijill*, pl. *sijillât*, roll of parchment to write upon, volume; public document, deed, diploma; edict; protocol; public writer, notary.

سجلا *sajlâ'*, woman with hanging breasts.

سجلاط *sijillât*, jessamine; particoloured linen; covering for protection.

(سجم) *sajam*, U, INF. *sijâm*, *sujûm*, flow, stream, be shed;

INF. *sajm*, shed tears; cause rain to pour; — U, I, INF. *sajm*, *sujûm*, *sajamân*, shed abundantly or cause to fall in drops; — INF. *sajm*, *sujûm*, delay, defer; — II. INF. *tasjîm*, cause to flow, to stream; — V. INF. *tasajjum*, flow, stream; be shed; — VII. INF. *insijâm*=V.

(سجن) *sajan*, U, INF. *sajn*, confine, imprison; conceal in one's heart; — II. INF. *tasjîn*, split; surround the foot of the palm-tree with watering-ditches.

سجن *sijn*, pl. *sujûn*, prison; imprisonment, confinement.

سجنا *sujanâ'*, سجنى *sajna*, pl. of سجين *sajîn*.

سجنجل *sajanjal*, pl. *sanâjil*, looking-glass; spectacles; gold, silver; saffron; pure, clear.

سجة *sajja-t*, thin milk.

(سجهر), III. *isjaharr*, INF. *isjihrâr*, move to and fro, undulate.

(سجو) *sajâ*, U, INF. *sujuww*, and سجى *saja*, be quiet, settle; be quiet, dark and long; protract a tender call for her foal; — INF. *tasjiya-t*, shroud the dead; — III. INF. *masâjât*, touch; carry on, manage, handle a thing; — IV. INF. *isjâ'*, abound in milk.

سجوا *sajwâ'*, f. quiet.

سجود *sujûd*, prosternation, adoration; — pl. of ساجد *sâjid*, adoring, &c.

سجور *sajûr*, chips for burning.

سجوع *sajû'*, pl. *sujju'*, cooing.

سجول *sajûl*, overflowing; — *.

سجوم *sajûm*, crying, shedding tears; raining; — *.

سجى *saja*, see (سجو); — ة *sajiyya-t*, pl. *sajâyâ*, natural disposition, quality, constitution, temper; custom, habit.

سجيح *sajîḥ*, smooth and soft; high-road; — ة *sajîḥa-t*, natural disposition; measure, symmetry.

سجير *sajîr*, pl. *sujarâ'*, faithful friend.

سجيس *sajîs*, troubled, turbid; سجيس الاوجس *sajîs al-awjus* (*al-awjas*), سجيس حجيس *sajîs-a ḥajîs-in*, never.

سجيل *sajîl*, ة *sajîla-t*, bucket; — *sijjîl*, hard bricks; stones baked in hell-fire, on which the sins are registered.

سجين *sajîn*, pl. *sujanâ'*, *sajna*, f. ة, pl. *sajâ'in*, *sajna*, imprisoned; — *sijjîn*, terrible prison, dungeon; bottom of hell; =*sajîl*; inveterate bachelor.

(سح) *saḥḥ*, U, INF. *saḥḥ*, pour out plenteously; make many words; INF. *saḥḥ*, *suḥûḥ*, be poured out, shed; flow down; beat, cudgel; — INF. *suḥûḥ*, *suḥûḥa-t*, be very fat.

سحا *siḥâ'*, ة, pl. *asḥiya-t*, membrane or strip of papyrus for binding books; cover of a book; a thorny plant; — *saḥḥâ*, who shovels; rainy; hot wind; — ة *saḥât*, pl. ساحا *sâḥan*, region; quadrangular place, square, yard; bat (animal); a thorny tree; =ة *siḥâ'a-t*, above.

سحاب *saḥâb*, mercury, quicksilver; — ة *saḥâba-t*, pl. *saḥâb* (also sing.), *suḥub*, *saḥâ'ib*, cloud; length; سحاب البحر *saḥâb al-baḥr*, sea-sponge; — (m.) *saḥḥâba-t*, drawer (of a chest, &c.).

سحاح *saḥâḥ*, air, atmosphere; — *siḥâḥ*, *suḥâḥ*, fat; herd; — *saḥḥâḥ*, raining, weeping.

سحاحير *saḥâḥîr*, pl. of سحارة *saḥḥâra-t*.

سحادل *suḥâdil*, penis; du. *suḥâdilân*, the testicles.

سحار *saḥḥâr*, f. ة, great sorcerer or magician; early riser; — ة *suḥâra-t*, wind-pipe and lung of a sheep; — *saḥḥâra-t*, pl. *saḥâḥîr*, box for the transport of grapes (m.); — *saḥḥâra-t*, jugglery; toy.

سحاف *siḥâf*, dysentery; — *suḥâf*, consumption.

سحاق *saḥḥâq*, who rubs violently;

— ة *saḥḥâqa-t*, woman who indulges in self-pollution.

سحال *siḥâl*, bridle, bit; muzzle; — *suḥâl*, roaring, bellowing (s.); — ة *suḥâla-t*, filings, parings, husks of corn; bran; rabble.

سحام *suḥâm*, darkness.

سحائب *saḥâ'ib*, pl. of سحابة *saḥâba-t*.

سحاية *siḥâya-t*, pl. *asḥiya-t*=سحاءة *siḥâ'a-t*.

(سحب) *saḥab*, INF. *saḥb*, trail; droop to the ground; eat and drink greedily; — V. INF. *tasaḥḥub*, be pert, insolent towards (على *'ala*); — VII. INF. *insiḥâb*, be trailed.

سحب *suḥub*, pl. of سحابة *saḥâba-t*; — ة *suḥba-t*, covering, veil.

سحبان *saḥbân*, name of a celebrated orator; hence: ى *saḥbâniyy*, eloquent like Saḥbân.

سحبل *saḥbal*, thick and hanging.

(سحت) *saḥat*, INF. *saḥt*, out-root, exterminate, annihilate; take the fat off the meat; draw an unlawful gain; — IV. INF. *isḥât* =I.; be unlawful, dishonest.

سحت *suḥt*, *suḥut*, pl. *asḥât*, anything unlawful.

(سحج) *saḥaj*, INF. *saḥj*, peel, skin; scratch; comb the hair slightly; run moderately;—II. INF. *tasḥîj*, scratch the skin; — VII. INF. *insiḥâj*, be skinned.

سحج *saḥj*, dysentery.

(سحجل) *saḥjal*, INF. ة, rub, polish.

(سحر) *saḥar*, INF. *saḥr*, *siḥr*, practice magic or sorcery; bewitch by spells; captivate, fascinate; deceive, delude; gild; remove (n.) to a great distance;—*saḥir*, A, INF. *saḥar*, be up early, do anything early in the morning; —II. INF. *tasḥîr*, practice magic, bewitch; fascinate; deceive; come early in the morning; (m.) place water in the open air during the night to cool it; —IV. INF. *isḥâr*, practice magic; bewitch; deceive; be or become anything in the morning; arrive, travel, &c., early; — V. INF. *tasaḥḥur*, take a morning meal; — VIII. INF. *istiḥâr*, row in earliest morning; depart early.

سحر *saḥr*, *saḥar*, *suḥr*, pl. *suḥûr*, *asḥâr*, lung; — *siḥr*, magic, sorcery, spell; magic charms; anything charming, captivating, fascinating, deceiving, deluding; — *saḥar*, pl. *asḥâr*, early morning; dawn; — ة *suḥra-t*, first dawn of the morning; — *saḥara-t* and—

سحرا *suḥarâ'*, pl. of ساحر *sâḥir*, sorcerer, &c.

سحرى *saḥariyy*, ة *saḥariyya-t*, before or at daybreak.

سحساح *saḥsâḥ*, pouring rain; ة, overflowing.

سحسح *saḥsaḥ*, pouring rain; — also ة *saḥsaḥa-t*, yard, square; — II. INF. *tasaḥsuḥ*, pour down (n.).

(سحط) *saḥaṭ*, INF. *saḥṭ*, *suḥâṭa-t*, *saḥâṭa-t*, *masḥaṭ*, kill quickly, despatch, slaughter; choke (a.); mix wine with water; — VII. INF. *insiḥâṭ*, slip from the hand; glide down.

(سحف) *saḥaf*, INF. *saḥf*, scrape the hair from a skin; extirpate the hair; shave the head; loosen the fat of the back, the flesh from the bones; chase away the clouds; burn (a.); eat at will;— ة *saḥfa-t*, pl. *suḥuf*, *siḥâf*, fat of the back.

(سحفر), IV. *isḥanfar*, INF. *isḥinfâr*, utter a speech hurriedly and vehemently.

(سحق) *saḥaq*, INF. *saḥq*, pound, crush, grind to powder; hurt; sweep the floor; blow away the traces; wear, use up; soften hard things by rubbing; crack lice; shave the head; exhaust

the tears; trot; — *saḥiq*, A, INF. *suḥq*, be at a great distance; — *saḥuq*, INF. *suḥûqa-t*, id.; be high; be worn; — IV. INF. *isḥâq*, remove far (a.); wear out, use up, spoil; — VII. INF. *insiḥâq*, be crushed, pounded, ground; be contrite; expand (n.), extend (n.).

سحق *saḥq*, rubbing, grinding (s.); worn garment; thin cloud; trot; — *suḥq*, *suḥuq*, far distance, great remoteness; سحقا له *suḥq-an la-hu*, far away with him! — *suḥq*, pl. of سحوق *saḥûq*.

سحك *saḥak*, for سحق *saḥaq*.

سحكوك *suḥkûk*, entirely black; — IV. *isḥankak*, INF. *isḥinkâk*, be pitch dark; offer great difficulties to (على *'ala*).

(سحل) *saḥal*, INF. *saḥl*, peel, skin; sweep, scour; rub, scratch; blame, abuse, revile; pay down in ready money; have one's self paid in ready money; give a hundred strokes; weave or twist with simple threads; twine; — INF. *saḥl*, *suḥûl*, weep; — A, I, INF. *saḥîl*, *suḥâl*, bray, roar; — III. INF. *musâḥala-t*, go to or arrive at the sea-coast; — IV. INF. *isḥâl*, find blamed, abused; — VII. INF. *insiḥâl*, get peeled, skinned; be smooth, slippery; be glib in speech.

سحل *saḥl*, pl. *suḥul*, *suḥûl*, *asḥâl*, texture or rope made from simple threads; a white cotton garment; ready money; — ة *suḥala-t*, young hare.

سحم *saḥam*, ة *suḥma-t*, blackness; *saḥam*, iron; — IV. INF. *isḥâm*, rain.

(سحن) *saḥan*, INF. *saḥn*, break, break into pieces; smooth by rubbing, polish; rub colours; — III. INF. *musâḥana-t*, go to meet; have friendly intercourse with; =V.; — V. INF. *tasaḥḥun*, look well at a thing; — VII. INF. *insiḥân*, be broken, broken into pieces, ground to powder.

سحن *saḥn*, rubbing, grinding (s.); — ة *saḥna-t*, *saḥana-t*, سحنا *saḥnâ*, pl. *saḥanât*, exterior; form, figure; complexion.

(سحو) *saḥâ*, سحى *saḥa*, A, I, U, INF. *saḥy*, shovel or sweep away; shave off the hair; bind books in parchment; — سحى *saḥa*, draw off a membrane; — II. INF. *tasḥiya-t*, bind (books); — VIII. INF. *istiḥâ'*, shave.

سحوح *saḥûḥ*, raining.

سحور *saḥûr*, slight morning meal during the fast of Ramaḍân; — *.

سحوق *saḥûq*, pl. *suḥq*, having a long body, a high trunk; — ة *suḥûqa-t*, INF. of (سحق).

سحول *saḥûl*, bleacher, fuller; name of a town in Yaman; — *.

سحير *saḥîr*, suffering from colic; paunch-bellied; — *suḥair*, early in the morning.

سحيف *saḥîf*, ة *saḥîfa-t*, rattling of a mill; — ة *saḥîfa-t*, rain that washes away everything; layer of fat in the back.

سحيق *saḥîq*, far distant, absent; difficult to understand; medicine in powder form; — ة *saḥîqa-t*, heavy shower, downpour.

سحيل *saḥîl*, simple, simple in thread; roar, bellowing (s.); — ة *suḥaila-t*, lizard.

(سخ) *saḫḫ*, U, INF. *saḫḫ*, penetrate deeply into a country, into the ground; thrust the sting into the ground.

سخا *saḫâ'*, liberality, bounty.

سخاب *siḫâb*, pl. *suḫub*, necklace of aromatic berries, &c.; — *saḫḫâb*, clamorous, noisy.

سخاخين *saḫâḫîn*, pl. of سخين *siḫḫîn*; — *suḫâḫîn*, hot, inflamed; heat, inflamation.

سخاسخ *saḫâsiḫ*, soft ground without sand.

سخافة *saḫâfa-t*, weakness of intellect.

سخالة *suḥâla-t*, offal, rubbish.

سخام *suḥâm*, blackness of the kettle; coal; black (adj., s.); soft; disgracing fault; — ة *suḥâma-t*, podex.

سخّان *suḥḥân*, pl. of ساخن *sâḥin*, hot; — ة *saḥâna-t*, heat.

سخانية *saḥâniyya-t*, joke, jest (m.).

سخاوة *saḥâwa-t*, liberality.

سخاوى *saḥâwa*, pl. of سخوا *saḥwâ*; — ة *saḥâwiyya-t*, pl. *saḥâwiyy*, vast tract of soft ground.

سخايا *saḥâyâ*, pl. of سخية *saḥiyya-t*.

سخب *saḥab*, clamour; — *suḥub*, pl. of سخاب *saḥâb*.

سخت *saḥt*, violent (Pers.).

سختيان *suḥtiyân*, goat-skin; Morocco leather.

سخد *saḥd*, hot; — *suḥd*, water; — II. pass. *suḥḥid*, stick close together; be pale and swollen.

(سخر) *saḥar*, INF. *siḥriyyâ*, compel to labour without wages; have a fair wind; — *saḥir*, A, INF. *saḥr*, *suḥr*, *saḥar*, *suḥur*, *suḥra-t*, *masḥar*, mock at, scoff at, laugh at, make fun of; — II. INF. *tasḥîr*, force to compulsory service; make requisitions in the name of government; subdue, tame, control; — V. INF. *tasaḥḥur*, be forced to compulsory labour; also X. INF. *istisḥâr*, mock at, laugh at; — ة *suḥra-t*, forced to compulsory labour; compulsory labour; requisition; what is done or to be got gratis; object of mockery, butt; — *suḥara-t*, mocker, scoffer.

سخريا *siḥriyyâ*, compulsory labour, INF. of (سخر).

سخرية *suḥriyya-t*, mocking, scoffing (s.); joke, jest.

(سخط) *saḥiṭ*, A, INF. *saḥaṭ*, be provoked to anger, be angry; — IV. INF. *isḥâṭ*, provoke to anger, anger; — V. INF. *tasaḥḥuṭ*=I.; be dissatisfied with a thing or gift.

سخط *suḥṭ*, *suḥuṭ*, *saḥaṭ*, ة *suḥṭa-t*, displeasure, vexation, anger.

(سخف) *saḥuf*, INF. *saḥâfa-t*, be weak, deficient; have a weak intellect; — INF. *suḥf*, be burst; — V. INF. *tasaḥḥuf*, show one's self stupid or behave stupidly towards (acc.).

سخف *saḥf*, ة *saḥfa-t*, poor pittance, insufficiency of sustenance; — also *suḥf*, ة *suḥfa-t*, weakness of intellect; emaciation from hunger.

(سخل) *saḥal*, INF. *saḥl*, drive back, repel, prevent, hinder; clean, sift; take fraudulently; — II. INF. *tasḥîl*, accuse, blame; — IV. INF. *isḥâl*, detain, delay.

سخل *suḥḥal*, mean, vile; bad dates with soft stones; — ة *saḥla-t*, pl. *saḥl*, *siḥâl*, *suḥlân*, *siḥala-t*, newly-dropped lamb or kid.

(سخم) *saḥam*, ة *suḥma-t*, blackness; (m.) disgracing crime; — II. INF. *tasḥîm*, blacken; dishonour, disgrace; commit a disgracing crime; anger; — V. INF. *tasaḥḥum*, hate; — ة *suḥma-t*, hatred.

(سخن) *saḥan*, U, INF. *suḥn*, *suḥna-t*, grow hot, be hot; — INF. *saḥn*, *suḥûn*, *saḥna-t*, get heated and run (eye); — *saḥin*, A, INF. *saḥan*, be or grow hot; — *saḥun*, INF. *saḥâna-t*, *suḥûna-t*, id.; have a fever; be ill; — II. INF. *tasḥîn*, warm, heat; cause a fever, make ill; — IV. INF. *isḥân*, warm, heat; inflame the eye and cause it to run.

سخنان *saḥnân*, *suḥnân*, ة, hot.

(سخو , سخى) *saḥâ*, U, سخى *saḥa*, A, سخى *saḥî*, A, and سخو *saḥû*, INF. *saḥâ'*, *saḥw*, *suḥuwwa-t*, be generous, liberal, bountiful; abstain, refrain from; — *saḥâ*, U, INF. *saḥw*, سخى *saḥa*, INF. *saḥy*, stir up the fire beneath the kettle; cease to move, rest; سخى *saḥî*, A, INF. سخا *saḥan*, be lame; — II. INF. *tasḥiya-t*,

abstain, refrain from ; — V. INF. *tasahhî*, wish to show one's self always liberal and generous.

سخوا *sahwâ'*, pl. *sahâwa*, *sahâwî*, vast tract of soft ground ; — *suhawâ'*, pl. of سخى *sahiyy*.

سخون *sahûn*, warm, hot ; warmed-up broth ; — * ; — ة *suhûna-t*, being heated (s.) ; inflammation (of the eye) ; fever ; illness.

(سخى) see (سخو) ; — *sahiyy*, pl. *ashiyâ'*, *suhâwâ'*, f. ة, *-ât*, *sahâyâ*, liberal, generous, high-minded ; — also *sahî*, lame (in the shoulder).

سخيت *sahît*, violent, strong, rough.

سخيف *sahîf*, thin, weak of texture ; of a weak intellect.

سخيلة *suhaila-t*, lambkin, kid.

سخيمة *sahîma-t*, pl. *sahâ'im*, hatred ; ill-will ; dirt, filth.

سخين *sahîn*, heated, hot ; inflamed ; painful ; — *sihhîn*, pl. *sahâhîn*, mattock ; butcher's knife ; hot ; — ة *sahîna-t*, pap of flour and milk.

(سد) *sadd*, U, INF. *sadd*, stop (a hole, a bottle, &c.) ; bar an entrance or a road, barricade ; dam in, close a dam ; mend a breach or damage ; repair ; fill a gap, grant compensation ; redeem a debt by goods, &c. ; — I, be truthful ; hit on the right thing, be to the point ; — I, A, be well arranged, solidly founded ; INF. *sadâd*, be straightforward, just, sincere, loyal ; — II. INF. *tasdîd*, straighten ; guide rightly ; lead back to the right path ; — IV. INF. *isdâd*, strive for and reach what is right ; hit the point ; — VII. INF. *insidâd*, be stopped, closed, barred ; — VIII. INF. *istidâd*, be straight ; be rightly guided ; = VII. ; accept the payment of a debt in goods, &c., instead of money.

سد *sadd*, mountain ; pl. *asdâd*, any artificial hindrance : barrier ; dam ; rampart ; boundary-post ; pl. *asidda-t*, bodily infirmity or impediment ; — *sidd*, truthful, true ; — *sudd*, mountain ; pl. *sudûd*, natural or artificial impediment : barrier, &c. ; dark cloud ; cloud of locusts ; pl. *sidada-t*, rocks barring a river ; — ة *sadda-t*, stoppage, bar, hindrance, impediment ; strait (of the sea) ; — *sudda-t*, pl. *sudad*, doorway ; vestibule ; door, threshold ; long bench ; seat, sofa, chair ; inveterate cold.

سداب *sadâb*, ة *sadâba-t*, rue (plant).

سداج *saddâj*, liar ; — *suddâj*, pl. of ساذج *sâdij*, unfermented, &c. ; — ة *sadâja-t*, simplicity.

سداد *sadâd*, what is straight, right, true ; the path of truth and salvation ; دار السداد *dâr-u 's-sadâd*, Bagdad ; — *sidâd*, ة, stopper, cork ; border-garrison ; scanty means of subsistence ; — *sudâd*, cold, rheum.

سدار *sidâr*, veil, curtain ; — ة *sadâra-t*, perplexity, bewilderment.

سداس سداس *sudâs sudâs*, by sixes ; — ى *sudâsiyy*, six years old ; consisting of seven letters.

سدافة *sidâfa-t*, curtain, veil.

سدان *sadân*, curtain, veil ; — *saddân*, anvil ; — ة *sadâna-t*, service of the temple ; office of a sacristan ; — *.

سداة *sadât*, pl. *asdiya-t*, du. *sadayân*, woof ; bounty, present.

(سدج) *sadaj*, U, INF. *sadj*, suspect ; — V. INF. *tasadduj*, show one's self to be a liar ; — VII. INF. *insidâj*, fall on one's face.

(سدح) *sadah*, slaughter and stretch on the ground ; kill ; throw on the face or on the back ; make the camel kneel down ; stay, abide ; fill ; enjoy the husband's favour ; bear him many children ; — II. INF. *tasdîh*, kill ; — VII. INF. *insidâh*, be thrown on the back.

(سدخ), VII. *insadaḥ*, INF. *insidâḥ*, be spread, extended.

سدد *sadad*, straightness ; — *sudad*, pl. of سدة *sudda-t* ; blind eyes ; — ة *sidada-t*, pl. of *sudd*, obstructing rocks in a river.

(سدر) *sadar*, U, INF. *sadr*, let the hair hang down ; — *sadir*, A, INF. *sadar*, be perplexed, bewildered, dumbfounded ; be dazzled by the heat ; — VII. INF. *insidâr*, hang down.

سدر *sidr*, ة , pl. *sidar*, *sidrât*, *sidirât*, *sidarât*, *sudûr*, lotus-tree (سدرة المنتهى *sidrat al-muntaha* or س طوبى *sidra-t ṭûba*, lotus of salvation in the seventh heaven) ; — *sadar*, perplexity, bewilderment ; giddiness ; seasickness ; — *sadir*, confused, bewildered ; giddy ; sea ; — *suddar*, a game.

(سدس) *sadas*, U, INF. *sads*, take the sixth part of one's property ; — I, come the sixth, be the sixth ; — II. INF. *tasdîs*, multiply by six ; repeat six times ; make sexagonal ; — IV. INF. *isdâs*, be six of them.

سدس *sids*, watering of the camels on the sixth day ; — *suds*, sixth part ;=دانق , q.v. ; pl. of سديس *sadîs*.

(سدع) *sada'*, INF. *sad'*, beat one thing with another, knock together ; slaughter ; stretch out, spread ; pass. be oppressed by calamities ; — ة *sud'a-t*, calamity.

(سدف) *sadaf*, ة *sadfa-t*, *sudfa-t*, darkness ; first twilight, dawn ; — *sudfa-t*, door, doorway, entrance-curtain ; — IV. INF. *isdâf*, be dark ; shine ; be dimmed ; sleep ; lift or let fall the veil ; open the door to let in light ; light ; turn aside from.

(سدك) *sadik*, A, INF. *sadk*, *sadak*, attend to ; cleave to ; — II. INF. *tasdîk*, pile up dates in a vessel.

سدك *sadik*, zealously devoted ; nimble, alert ; fit, proper, appropriate.

(سدل) *sadal*, U, I, INF. *sadl*, let down, trail (a.) ; — I, tear, split ; depart, travel ; — IV. INF. *isdâl*= I. ; — V. INF. *tasaddul*, be let down, trail (n.) ; — VII. INF. *insidâl*, trail (n.) ; fall down, sink.

سدل *sidl*, *sudl*, pl. *sudûl*, *asdâl*, *asdul*, veil, covering, wrapping ; —*sidl*, trinket of pearls hanging down to the breast.

(سدم) *sadam*, U, INF. *sadm*, shut, lock ; — *sadim*, A, INF. *sadam*, be sad, sorrowful, repenting ; feel anger, abhorrence ; be eager for ; — VII. INF. *insidâm*, be healed.

سدم *sadam*, grief ; repentance ; — also *sadim*, rutting ; — *sudum*, *sudm*, pl. *asdâm*, stopped-up well.

سدمان *sadmân*, sorrowful ; repenting.

(سدن) *sadan*, U, INF. *sadn*, *sidâna-t*, *sadâna-t*, attend to the service of the temple ; serve ; — U, I, loosen a dress, let down a veil or curtain, perform the office of a chamberlain.

سدن *sadn*, service of the temple ; office of a sacristan ; — *sidn*, *sadan*, pl. *asdân*, veil, curtain ; — ة *sadana-t*, pl. of سادن *sâdin*, guard-keeper or servant in a temple.

(سدى , سدو) *sadâ*, U, INF. *sadw*, سدى *sada*, INF. *sady*, reach for ; intend, aim at, proceed to ; walk with long strides ; — *sada*, I, make the woof ; plot treason ; — *sadî*, A, INF. *sadan*, begin to ripen ; be abundantly moistened by the dew ; — II. INF. *tasdiya-t*, make the woof, weave ; hatch treason ; bestow benefits ; — IV. INF. *isdâ'*, make the woof ; overwhelm with bounties ; make peace ; let the camels

walk at large; — V. INF. *tasaddî*, be woven; make the woof; ascend the top and sit upon it; — VIII. INF. *istidâ'*, stretch out the hand, reach for.

سدوم *sudûm*, Sodom.

سدى *sadan*, night-dew; — also *sady*, woof; benefit, bounty, present; — *sudan*, left to one's self; at large; in vain, gratis, to no purpose; lost; — *sadî*, ة, dewy; soft at the pedicle, beginning to ripen.

سديان *sadayân*, du. of سداة *sadât*.

سديد *sadîd*, straight, in the right direction; well arranged; obstructing, damming in.

سديس *sadîs*, m. f., pl. *suds*, sixth part; six (respectively eight) years old; tooth of such an animal.

سديف *sadîf*, fat of the camel's hump.

سديل *sadîl*, pl. *sudûl*, *asdul*, *sadâ'il*, cloth cover of a camel-litter; curtain.

سدين *sadîn*, fat; blood; wool; curtain, veil.

سذب *saẕab*, rue (plant); — ة *suẕba-t*, sheath, case.

سذق *saẕaq*, a falcon; illuminated night of a festival.

سذوم *saẕûm*=سدوم *sadûm*.

(سر) *sarr*, U, INF. *surr*, *surûr*, *surra-n*, *tasirra-t*, *masarra-t*, gladden, cheer, rejoice (a.); satisfy; — INF. *sarr*, cut off the navel-string; hurt the navel; — *sarir*, A, INF. *sarr*, complain of pain in the navel; — II. INF. *tasrîr*, cheer, gladden, rejoice (a.); — III. INF. *musârra-t*, whisper to, impart a secret; — IV. INF. *isrâr*, keep secret, keep to one's self; impart a secret, whisper to; hold secretly, or, by opposition, prepare openly (a banquet, &c.); — V. INF. *tasarrur*, keep a concubine; — VI. INF. *tasârur*, impart secrets to one another; — VII. INF. *insirâr*, be gladdened, satisfied, rejoice (n.); — X. INF. *istisrâr*, conceal one's self from (عن *'an*); be covered by clouds (moon).

سر *sarr*, who gladdens, bestows benefits (in secret); — *sirr*, pl. *asrâr*, secret, hidden thought, mystery; sacrament; wedlock; heart, core, innermost and best part; root, origin; tomb; secret sign; pudenda; coition, fornication; (m.) toast, pledging (s.) in wine; pl. *asirra-t*, *asrâr*, pl. pl. *asârîr*, lines of the palm; — *surr*, pl. *assira-t*, navel-string; — *suru'*, *surra'*, pl. of سرو *sarû'*; — ة *surra-t*, pl. *-ât*, *surar*, navel; middle; heart; what rejoices the heart.

(سرا) *sara'*, INF. *sar'*, lay ova; be very prolific; — II. INF. *tasri'a-t*, id.

سرا *sirr-an*, secretly; — *sarâ'*, a tree of which bows are made; — *sarrâ* (f. of اسر *asarr*), joy, pleasure; — ة *sar'a-t*, *sir'a-t*, *sirâ'a-t*, ovum of the locust; spawn; — *sarât*, summit; best part; middle; pl. *sawarât*, back, croup; — *sarât*, pl. of سرى *sariyy*; — *surât*, night-travellers, &c., pl. of سارى *sârî*.

سراب *sarâb*, mirage.

سرابيل *sarâbîl*, pl. of سربال *sirbâl*.

سراج *sirâj*, pl. *suruj*, burning wick; lighted lantern; lamp, candlestick, chandelier; torch; sun; — *sarrâj*, saddler; groom; — ة *sirâja-t*, profession of a saddler; — ى *sirâjiyy*, shining.

سراح *sarâḥ*, setting free, setting at large; dismissal; divorce; — *sarâḥ*, *sirâḥ*, and—

سراحين *sarâḥîn*, pl. of سرحان *sarḥân*.

سرادق *surâdiq*, pl. *surâdiqât*, entrance-curtain; drapery, hangings; baldachin; protection; dense dust or smoke.

سرار *sarâr*, last night of the month; navel-string; also ة *sarâra-t*, best and most beautiful part;

sarâra-t, excellent condition; — *sirâr*, pl. *asirra-t*, lines in the hand or on the forehead.

سراری *sarâriyy*, pl. of سرية *surriyya-t*.

سراط *sirâṭ*, street, road; — *surâṭ*, ى *surâṭiyy*, sharp.

سراع *sirâ'*, pl. of سريع *sarî'*; — ة *surâ'a-t*, haste, hurry; hastening, hurried.

سرافين *sarâfîn*, Seraphim.

سراق *sarrâq*, great thief, arch-thief; — *surrâq*, thieves, pl. of سارق *sâriq*.

سراويل *sarâwîl*, pl. *sarâwîlât*, trowsers; more usually considered as pl. of سروال *sirwâl* (see de Sacy's Harîri, p. 288).

سراى *sarây*, palace, castle (Pers.); —ة *sarâya-t*, id. (m.);—*sirâya-t*, night-journey; spreading, propagating, circulating (s.); contagion, infection, INF. of (سرى).

سرايا *sarâyâ*, pl. of سرية *sariyya-t*; palace, castle.

(سرب) *sarab*, U, INF. *surûb*, pasture freely (n.); travel through; flow, run; derive; — *sarib*, A, INF. *sarab*, leak, ooze; — pass. *surib*, be prevented from breathing; — II. INF. *tasrîb*, let the camels walk in troops; drive the cattle from the pasture into the stable; cause to advance, to march on; dismiss; (m.) go home from work; — V. INF. *tasarrub*, creep into the burrow, burrow; — VII. INF. *insirâb*=V.; be protracted; be derived from.

سرب *sarb*, stitch; — *sirb*, *sarb*, pl. *asrâb*, troop, herd, flock; road, way, manner; heart, mind; — *sarab*, lair of an animal; burrow; dropping water; aqueduct, canal; — *sarib*, ة, leaking; — ة *sarba-t*, stitch; short day's journey; — *surba-t*, pl. *surûb*, *asrâb*, herd, flock, troop (20–30 horsemen); many, large number; sect; institution.

سرباخ *sirbâḫ*, vast desert.

سربال *sirbâl*, pl. *sarâbîl*, shirt; dress; wide trowsers; cuirass, armour, coat of mail.

سربخ *sarbaḫ*, vast plain; — ة *sarbaḫa-t*, alertness, nimbleness, briskness.

(سربط) *surbiṭ*, be long and thin.

سربل *sarbal*, INF. ة, put on the سربال *sirbâl*; dress, arm (a.); — II. INF. *tasarbul*, dress, arm (n.).

سرتاح *sirtâḥ*, generous.

(سرج) *saraj*, U, INF. *sarj*, saddle; adorn, deck out, decorate; plait the hair; — *sarij*, A, INF. *saraj*, have a handsome face, shine, be brilliant; tell lies; — II. INF. *tasrîj*, saddle; adorn; plait the hair; (m.) sew in long stitches; — IV. INF. *isrâj*, saddle; light the lamp.

سرج *sarj*, pl. *surûj*, saddle; — *suruj*, pl. of سراج *sirâj*.

سرجم *sarjam*, rape (vegetable).

سرجين *sirjîn*, dung.

(سرح) *saraḥ*, INF. *sarḥ*, *surûḥ*, pasture freely; allow to pasture freely, set at large, set free, dismiss; let the hair flow down; disclose one's thoughts; be in thoughts, absent-minded; break forth, advance; — *sariḥ*, A, INF. *saraḥ*, proceed gently in one's actions; — II. INF. *tasrîḥ*, allow to pasture freely; make to stray; dismiss, repudiate, repel; loose the hair and let it flow down; — VII. INF. *insirâḥ*, undress, strip (n.); flow without hindrance and enter into (water).

سرح *sarḥ*, freely pasturing herd; setting free, setting at large (s.); courtyard; — *suruḥ*, walking apace, swift; — ة *sarḥa-t*, pl. *sarḥ*, high tree; س العساكر *sarḥa-t al-'asâkir*, campaign.

سرحان *sirḥân* (also سرحال *sirḥâl*), pl. *sarâḥ*, *sirâḥ*, *sarâḥîn*, wolf, lion;

middle of a fountain; ذنب السرحان *zanab as-sirḥân*, first dawn of morning.

سرحوب *surḥûb*, long and swift; tall; jackal; a sea-demon.

(سرد) *sarad*, I, U, INF. *sard, sirâd*, pierce, bore through; sew together; make a coat of mail; dispose a speech well and in good order; word, rehearse, read fluently; keep the fast without interruption; (m.) sift; nibble or gnaw at; — II. INF. *tasrîd*, pierce, bore through.

سرد *sard*, meshwork; coat of mail; unbroken series, coherence, connection; *as-sard*, the months *Ẓulqa'da, Ẓulḥijja* and *Muḥarram*.

سرداب *sirdâb*, pl. *sarâdîb*, ice-cellar (Pers.).

سردق *sardaq*, ة, cover with a baldachin.

سردولة *sardûla-t*, walnut.

سر *sarar* middle; — also *sirar*, pl. *asrâr, asârîr*, navel-string; lines in the hand or on the forehead; last night of the month; — *surar*, pl. of سرة *surra-t*; — *surur, surar*, pl. of سرير *sarîr*.

(سرس) *saris*, A, INF. *saras*, be impotent; be weak; grow wise, cautious and firm after imprudence; be of a malicious or wicked disposition.

سرس *saris*, pl. *sirâs*, impotent; weak; prudent, cautious.

سرسا *surasâ'*, pl. of سريس *sarîs*.

سرسام *sirsâm*, fever with headache and inflammation of the throat.

(سرسب) *sarsab*, INF. ة, make one doubtful, raise one's scruples, render irresolute; — II. INF. *tasarsub*, pass.

(سرسر) *sarsar*, INF. ة, sharpen, whet, grind; — II. INF. *tasarsur*, be thinly woven.

سرسور *sursûr*, prudent, cautious and economical.

(سرط) *saraṭ*, U, INF. *saraṭân*, swallow; — *sariṭ*, A, INF. *saraṭ*, id.; — V. INF. *tasarruṭ*, id.; — VII. INF. *insirâṭ*, glide easily down the throat; — VIII. INF. *istirâṭ* = I.

سرطان *saraṭân*, craw-fish, crab; Cancer of the zodiac; cancerous disease, gangrene; — INF. of (سرط).

سرطع *sarṭa'*, INF. ة, run with all one's might (from fear); (m.) stamp.

سرطل *sarṭal*, too long and high, and therefore tottering; — ة *sarṭala-t*, tottering (s.).

(سرع) *saru'*, INF. *sira', sur'a-t*, be quick, swift; hasten, hurry; — III. INF. *musâra'a-t*, vie in speed; hasten towards; — IV. INF. *isrâ'*, walk apace, hasten; despatch; have a fleet animal; — V. INF. *tasarru'*, hasten to accomplish; speed; hasten towards (الى *ila*); — VI. INF. *tasâru'*, vie with one another in speed.

سرع *sar', sir'*, tender branch; vine-shoot; youth; — *sara', sira'*, ة *sur'a-t*, haste, hurry.

سرعان *sar'ân, sara'ân*, the most noble, the best; the swiftest horses; — *sir'ân, sur'ân*, pl. of سريع *sarî'*.

سرعسكر *sari'askar*, general (Pers.).

(سرعف) *sar'af*, INF. ة, feed (a.) well.

سرعوب *sur'ûb*, weasel.

سرعوف *sur'ûf*, tender; slender, slim.

(سرغ) *sarg*, pl. *surûg*, vine-shoot; — *sarig*, A, INF. *sarag*, eat grapes with the stalks.

(سرف) *saraf*, U, INF. *sarf, sirâf*, eat a tree bare; spoil the child by too much milk; — *sarif*, A, INF. *saraf*, neglect; exceed the bounds; accustom one's self to drink wine; — IV. INF. *isrâf*, make an excessive expenditure,

dissipate, squander; exceed, commit excesses.

سرف *saraf*, neglect, negligence; dissipation; excess; custom, habit; corrosion; — *sarif*, negligent, lazy; stupid; — ة *surfa-t*, white ant; teredo; caterpillar; — *sarifa-t*, abounding in ants.

(سرق) *saraq*, INF. *sarq*, *saraq*, *sariq*, *saraqa-t*, *sariqa-t*, take away clandestinely, steal; — *sariq*, A, INF. *saraq*, be hidden, concealed; be weak; — II. INF. *tasrîq*, accuse, of theft; call a thief; — III. INF. *musâraqa-t*, do behind another's back; look stealthily at; — V. INF. steal or carry off one thing after the other; — VII. INF. *insirâq*, be stolen; steal out of one's sight; be weak; — VIII. INF. *istirâq*, carry off clandestinely; steal.

سرق *sarq*, *saraq*, *sariq*, ة *sarqa-t*, *sariqa-t*, theft, plunder; — *saraq*, ة, strip of white silk; silk.

سرقع *surqu'*, sour date-wine.

(سرقن) *sarqan*, INF. ة, dung, manure.

سرقين *sirqîn*, *sarqîn*, dung.

(سرك) *sarik*, A, INF. *sarak*, grow weak and thin.

سركار *sarkâr*, overseer, superintendent; royal court, government (Pers.).

(سركل) *sarkal*, INF. ة, exile, banish; — II. INF. *tasarkul*, pass. of the previous.

سرم *surm*, pl. *asrâm*, rectum; — *saram*, pain in the rectum or anus; — II. *sarram*, INF. *tasrîm*, cut into pieces.

سرمان *surmân*, a hornet.

(سرمد) *sarmad*, lasting, everlasting, eternal.

سرمدى *sarmadiyy*, eternal; — ة *sarmadiyya-t*, eternity.

(سرمط) *sarmaṭ*, long; — II. INF. *tasarmuṭ*, be thin (hair).

سرموجة *sarmûja-t*, slipper (m.).

سرناف *sirnâf*, long, tall.

سرنج *saranj*, red lead; red; a wound-salve.

سرندى *saranda*, f. سرنداة *sarandât*, quick, resolute and active, energetic; — IV. *isranda*, INF. *isrindâ'*, overcome, get the better of, surpass.

سرنديب *sarandîb*, Ceylon.

سرنوف *sarnûf*, sparrow-hawk.

(سرهب) *sarhab*, never satiated glutton; drunkard.

(سرهد) *sarhad*, INF. ة, feed well (a.).

(سرو) *sarâ*, U, INF. *sarw*, lay eggs, spawn; put off one's clothes; put off; have a manly and generous character, be high-souled; — سرى *sarî*, A, id.; — سرو *sarû*, INF. سرا *saran*, *sarâ'*, *sarâwa-t*, id.; — II. INF. *tasriya-t*, throw off one's clothes; — IV. INF. *isrâ'*, id.; — V. INF. *tasarrî*, show one's self generous, liberal; — VIII. INF. *istirâ'*, select; take the best for one's self.

سرو *sarw*, ة, cypress; rising of the ground; greatness, glory, nobility; generosity, liberality; liberal man; — *sarû'*, pl. سر *suru'*, *surra'*, locust depositing ova; — ة *sirwa-t*, *surwa-t*, pl. سرى *siran*, small arrow; *sirwa-t*, locust just come out of the egg.

سروا *surawâ'*, pl. of سرى *sariyy*.

سروات *sarawât*, pl. of سراة *sarât*; — pl. pl. of سرى *sariyy*.

سروال *sirwâl*, pl. *sirwâlât*, *sarâwîl*, (also سراوين *sarâwîn*), wide trowsers, drawers.

سروجى *sarûjiyy*, of Sarûj; — *surûjiyy*, saddler.

سروح *surûḥ*, absence of mind; — *.

سرور *surûr*, joy, pleasure, satisfaction, INF. of (سر).

سروعة *sarwa'a-t*, sand-hill.

سروف *sarûf*, powerful, great.

سرول *sarwal*, INF. ة, put trowsers on to; — II. INF. *tasarwul*, put on trowsers.

سرومط *saraumaṭ*, long.

سرويل *sirwîl*, pl. *sarâwîl*, trowsers; drawers.

سرى *sara*, I, INF. *sura-n*, *sarya-t*, *surya-t*, *sirâya-t*, *masra-n*, travel at night; appear at night; travel, march; cause to travel; work, operate (as poison, &c.); spread; I, U, undress (a. and n.); — II. INF. *tasriya-t*, send out a squadron, a detachment; — III. INF. *musârât*, travel in company with; — IV. INF. *isrâ'*, travel at night; travel, march, come; cause to travel at night; — V. INF. *tasarrî* (also VII.), be taken away, removed, dispersed; disappear, vanish, subside; keep a concubine, live in concubinage.

سرى *suran*, night-journey; march; generosity, liberality; — *surran*, INF. of (سر);—*sariyy*, pl. *asriya-t*, *suryân*, ditch for the irrigation of a palm-tree plantation; pl. *asriyâ'*, *surawâ'*, *suran*, *sarât* (pl. pl. *sarawât*), f. ة, pl. *-ât*, *sarâyâ*, liberal, generous, noble; prince; the most exquisite, the best; — *sirriyy*, mysterious; sacramental; allegorical; — ة *sarya-t*, *surya-t*, pl. *sura-n*, night journey; — *sirya-t*, locust just crept out of the egg; — *sariyya-t*, pl. *sarâyâ*, troop, division, brigade (400–500); expedition, raid; — *surriya-t*, pl. *sarâriyy*, concubine; slave-girl taken in marriage.

سريان *sarayân*, night-journey; spreading (s.), infection, contagion; — *suryân*, pl. of سرى *sariyy*; — ى *suryâniyy*, Syriac.

سريج *suraij*, small saddle; handsome nose.

سريح *sarîḥ*, bare, without saddle; fluent, light; — ة *sarîha-t*, pl. *sarâ'iḥ*, strips of leather for sewing; long strip of anything.

سريد *sarîd*, awl; — ة *sarîda-t*, pl. *sarâ'id*, strip of leather.

سرير *sarîr*, pl. *asirra-t*, *surur*, *surar*, throne, sofa, couch; cradle; bier; estrade; residence, capital; — ة *sarîra-t*, pl. *sarâ'ir*, secret, mystery; hidden thought.

سريس *sarîs*, pl. *surasâ'*, impotent (for coition).

سريط *surait*, dish of flour, honey and water.

سريطا *suraiṭâ*, سريطى *suraiṭa*, what glides easily through the throat; easy to perform.

سريع *sarî'*, pl. *sur'ân*, f. ة, pl. *sirâ'*, hastening, hasty, hurried, quick.

سريف *sarîf*, row of vine-plants.

(سسا), III. *sâsâ*, INF. *musâsât*, chide and threaten.

(سطا) *saṭa'*, INF. *saṭ'*, lie with.

سطاع *siṭâ'*, pillar; long pole.

سطام *siṭâm*, stopper, cork; bolt; poker; edge of a sword, &c.

(سطح) *saṭaḥ*, INF. *saṭḥ*, spread; roll thin and flat; level, flatten, give a flat roof to a house; throw one on his back, lay him on his side; — II. INF. *tasṭîḥ*, spread, make smooth and level; — VII. INF. *insiṭâḥ*, pass. of II.; lie extended on the back.

سطح *saṭḥ*, pl. *suṭûḥ*, level, plain surface; flat roof, terrace, platform, ceiling; — ى *saṭḥiyy*, ة, flat; superficial; referring to a surface.

(سطر) *saṭar*, U, INF. *saṭr*, write, form letters, draw lines; compose or tell stories; cut with the sword; — II. INF. *tasṭîr*=I.; — IV. INF. *isṭâr*, skip a line or what is written on it; — V. INF. *tasaṭṭur*, be written, drawn, traced; talk or profess idle or false things; — VIII. INF. *istiṭâr*, write.

سطر *saṭr*, *saṭar*, pl. *suṭûr*, *asṭur*, *asṭâr*, *asâṭîr*, stroke, line, row, writing; — ة *suṭra-t*, wish.

سطرلاب *suṭurlâb*, astrolabe.

سطط *suṭuṭ*, pl. transgressors, oppressors, tyrants.

(سطع) *saṭa'*, I, INF. *suṭû'*, *saṭî'*, rise and spread; mount into one's nose; be light, bright;

INF. *saṭ'*, clap the hands; touch with the hand; — *saṭi'*, A, INF. *saṭa'*, have a long neck.

(سطل) *saṭl*, pl. *suṭûl*, vessel with an ear; bucket; — VII. *insaṭal*, INF. *insiṭâl*, be perplexed, stunned (m.).

(سطم) *saṭam*, U, INF. *saṭm*, shut the door; bar; stop.

سطم *saṭm*, edge of a sword; — *suṭum*, pl. roots, origins.

(سطن) *saṭan*, prop, support, strengthen, consolidate; — II. INF. *tasṭîn*, id.

سطة *siṭa-t*, middle, being (s.) in the middle, INF. of (وسط).

(سطو) *saṭâ*, U, INF. *saṭw*, *saṭwa-t*, assail, leap upon, attack, overcome; be restive, headstrong; rise and swell; taste of a dish; — III. INF. *musâṭât*, be hard and unjust towards (acc.); — V. INF. *tasaṭṭî*, wrong, attack unjustly, pick a quarrel with (على *'ala*); — ة *saṭwa-t*, surprise, attack; offensive power, power, despotism.

سطيح *saṭîḥ*, flat, spread out; lying on the back; fallen so as not to be able to rise again; killed; — also ة *saṭîḥa-t*, large water-bag made of three skins; — *saṭîḥa-t*, plane surface.

سع *su''*, vetch; wild wheat; — ة *sa'a-t*, *si'a-t*, spaciousness, ease, opportunity, power, extent.

سعا *sa''â'*, planning, plotting, intriguing (adj.); — ة *sa'â-t*, ability, skill; possession, power; — *su'ât*, pl. of ساعي *sâ'î*, q.v.

سعابر *sa'âbir*, vetch, darnel, tare.

سعابيب *sa'âbîb*, phlegm; spittle; honey in clammy threads.

سعادة *sa'âda-t*, happiness; highness, majesty (a title); دار الس *dâr as-sa'âda-t*, Constantinople.

سعادين *sa'âdîn*, pl. of سعدان *sa'dân*.

سعار *su'âr*, pl. *si'rân*, *su'ur*, glow, fire; voracious hunger; calamity.

سعاط *su'âṭ*, sharp (sense of) smell.

سعال *su'âl*, cough; س ساعل *su'âl sâ'il*, violent hunger.

سعالى *sa'âlî*, pl. of سعلا *si'lâ'*.

سعانين *sa'ânîn*, Palm Sunday.

سعاية *si'âya-t*, calumny; spying and informing against custom-officers, &c.

سعب *sa'b*, anything clammy, thick fluid; — *sa'ab*, INF. *sa'b*, be clammy, gluey, thick and fluid; — V. INF. *tasa''ub*, thicken (n.); — VII. INF. *insi'âb*, flow, run.

(سعبر) *sa'bar*, ة *sa'bara-t*, overflowing well; abundant; cheap.

سعتر *sa'tar*, thyme.

(سعد) *sa'ad*, A, INF. *sa'd*, *su'ûd*, be fortunate; be propitious; — سعد *sa'id*, A, INF. *sa'âda-t*, be happy, lucky, successful; — pass. *su'id*, id.; — III. INF. *musâ'ada-t*, help, assist, prosper (a.); — IV. INF. *is'âd*, make happy, fortunate, help, assist; — V. INF. *tasa''ud*, seek the plant سعدان *sa'dân* for a pasture; — X. INF. *istis'âd*, seek fortune; find one's happiness in (ب *bi*); find one happy, fortunate; deem propitious or auspicious.

سعد *sa'd*, pl. *su'ûd*, good fortune, luck, success, happiness; propitious augury; du. *as-sa'dân*, Venus and Jupiter.

سعدا *su'adâ'*, pl. of سعيد *sa'îd*.

سعدان *sa'dân*, a plant making excellent food for camels; (m.) pl. *sa'âdîn*, ape, monkey; — *su'dan*, prosperity, salvation, blessing; — ة *sa'dâna-t*, nipple of the (female) breast; wart, callosity, knob; pigeon; a thorny plant.

سعدى *sa'da*, f. of اسعد *as'ad*, more or most fortunate.

سعر *sa'ar*, INF. *sa'r*, light or stir the fire; kindle war; pass. *su'ir*, be met by the poisonous wind سموم *samûm*; get enraged, mad; — II. INF. *tas'îr*, light, kindle, stir; fix the price,

estimate, tax; — IV. INF. *is'âr* = II.; — V. INF. *tasa''ur*, be stirred and burn brightly; be fixed; — VIII. INF. *isti'âr*, be stirred and burn brightly; kindle (n.).

سعر *si'r*, pl. *as'âr*, set price, price; — *su'r*, voracious hunger; infection; — also *su'ur*, heat, fury, pain; — *su'ur*, pl. of سعار *sa'âr* and سعير *sa'îr*; — *sa'ir*, pl. سعرى *sa'ra*, enraged, furious.

سعران *si'rân*, pl. of سعار *sa'âr*.

سعرى *sa'ra*, pl. of سعر *sa'ir*.

(سعسع) *sa'sa'*, INF. ة, call the goats; be decrepit; anoint the hair with oil; — II. INF. *tasa'su'*, be decrepit; tremble with old age; totter; be nearly finished.

(سعط) *sa'aṭ*, A, U, INF. *sa'ṭ*, make one snuff a medicine; — IV. INF. *is'âṭ*, id.; — VIII. INF. *istis'âṭ*, snuff a medicine.

سعف *sa'af*, INF. *sa'f*, carry to an end, complete; manage another's affairs; — *sa'if*, A, INF. *sa'af*, be chapped round the nails; — II. INF. *tas'îf*, mix (musk) with other perfumes; — III. INF. *musâ'afa-t*, help, assist; — IV. INF. *is'âf*, carry to an end, complete; help, help to, assist; alight.

سعف *sa'af*, ة, branch or leaf of a palm-tree; a disease of the camel; pl. *su'ûf*, household things as dowry of a bride; valuable property; — also *sa'f*, mountain-summit; — ة *sa'fa-t*, *sa'afa-t*, ulcers or scurf on the head of a child.

(سعل) *sa'al*, U, INF. *su'âl*, *su'la-t*, cough; — U, INF. *sa'l*, be brisk; — X. INF. *istis'âl*, be like a fury; — ة *sa'la-t*, cough.

سعلا *si'lâ'*, ة *si'lât*, pl. *sa'âlî*, a female demon; hag, fury, megaera; cunning, sly (f.).

(سعم) *sa'am*, INF. *sa'm*, walk very fast.

(سعن) *sa'n*, fat; wine; — *su'n*, pl. *si'ana-t*, large leathern flask; — ة *sa'na-t*, fortunate, and, by opposition, unfortunate; — *su'na-t*, roof for shade, baldachin; — IV. INF. *is'ân*, make a roof for shade; — V. INF. *tasa''un*, be full of fat.

سعوا *si'wâ'*, *su'wâ'*, an hour of the night.

سعود *su'ûd*, ة *su'ûda-t*, luck, good fortune, happiness; happy augury.

سعوط *sa'ûṭ*, *su'ûṭ*, medicine to be snuffed; snuff (tobacco).

سعوة *sa'wa-t*, pl. *sa'w*, lighted wax-candle; — *si'wa-t*, shameless woman; = سوا.

(سعى) *sa'a*, INF. *sa'y*, hasten, run, hurry to a place; perform; work together with (مع *ma'*); take pains and care in (فى *fî* or ل *li*); earn for one's family; carry on the trade of a prostitute; INF. *si'âya-t*, inform against, denounce, calumniate, blacken one's character; preside over the public charity or the collection of tithes; — III. INF. *musâ'ât*, vie with in efforts; — IV. INF. *is'â'*, cause one to work and earn; promote one's affairs; — X. INF. *istis'â*, demand work from (acc.); live by working as.

سعى *sa'y*, endeavour, effort, exertion, zeal; co-operation; career, course.

سعيد *sa'îd*, ة, pl. *su'adâ'*, fortunate.

سعير *sa'îr*, pl. *su'ur*, flame, blaze; a division of hell appropriated to unbelievers; — *su'air*, an idol.

سعيط *sa'îṭ*, tartar (of wine); flavour of wine; strong smell; myrobalan.

سعيع *sa'î'*, vetch, darnel, tare.

سغاب *sagâb*, pl. of سغب *sagib*; — *sigâb*, pl. of ساغب *sâgib*, hungry and weary; — ة *sagâba-t*, hunger and weariness, exhaustion.

(سغب) *sagab*, U, INF. *sagb*, *suqûb*, *sagâba-t*, *masgaba-t*, suffer pain from hunger and exhaustion; — *sagib*, A, INF. *sagab*, id.; — — IV. INF. *isgâb*, fall into such condition.

سغب *sagb*, *sagab*, hunger; — *sagib*, pl. *sigâb*, and—

سغبان *sagbân*, f. سغبى *sagba*, hungry.

سغبل *sagbal*, INF. ة, take butter or any by-dish with bread; grease or butter a dish; anoint the head; — II. INF. *tasagbul*, put on (a coat of mail, &c.).

سغبى *sagba*, f. of سغبان *sagbân*.

(سغد) *sugid*, (pass.) be swollen.

سغد سغد *sagd sagd*, thin rain.

(سغر) *sagar*, INF. *sagr*, repel, drive away.

سغسغ *sagsag*, INF. ة, remove (a.); tread into or roll in the dust; butter or grease a dish very abundantly; grease the hair; — II. INF. *tasagsug*, be loose, rickety; enter into the ground.

(سغل) *sagil*, A, INF. *sagal*, be short and ugly with thin legs.

(سغم) *sagam*, A, INF. *sagm*, lie with without completing coition.

سغما *sagman*, against one's will.

سف *saf*, abbreviated for سوف *sauf*.

سف *saff*, U, INF. *safîf*, skim the ground (in flying); INF. *saff*, entwine palm-leaves together (to make baskets, &c.); — *safîf*, I, A, *saff*, U, INF. *saff* (also IV. and VIII.), take medicine in pills or powder; — IV. INF. *isfâf*, see I.; skim the ground; stoop; twine palm-leaves together; sharpen one's look, look sharply at; engage in trifles or subtleties; instil balm into a wound; — VIII. INF. *istifâf*, see I.

سف *saff*, male palm-blossom; — *siff*, *suff*, a flying serpent; — ة *suffa-t*, dry medicine (pills, powder); corn; basket of palm-leaves.

سفا *safan*, dust, earth; thorn-tree, thorn; — *sifâ'*, medicine.

سفاح *sifâḥ*, fornication, INF. 3 of (سفح); — *saffâḥ*, blood-shedder; fornicator; liberal; eloquent.

سفاد *sifâd*, copulation (of animals).

سفار *sifâr*, travelling in company, travelling (s.); projecting roof; pl. *asfira-t*, *sufur*, *safâ'ir*, bridle for the camel's nose; — *saffâr*, bookseller; — *suffâr*, travellers, &c., pl. of سافر *sâfir*; — ة *sifâra-t*, mediation; embassy; — *sufâra-t*, sweepings.

سفارج *safârij*, pl. of سفرجل *safarjal*.

سفاسرة *safâsira-t*, سفاسير *safâsîr*, pl. of سفسير *sifsîr*.

سفاطة *safâṭa-t*, kindness, bounty, liberality;—ة *sufâṭa-t*, household things, furniture.

سفافيد *safâfîd*, pl. of سفود *saffûd*.

سفاقة *safâqa-t*, denseness, density.

سفاك *saffâk*, blood-shedder; cruel, blood-thirsty; very eloquent, eminent orator.

سفال *safâl*, ة *safâla-t*, lowliness; misery; — ة *sufâla-t*, id.; lowest part, ground.

سفان *saffân*, ship-builder; captain; — ة *sifâna-t*, profession of a ship-builder; — *saffâna-t*, pearl.

سفاناج *sifânâj*, spinach (Pers.).

سفاه *safâh*, *sifâh*, foolishness; — *sifâh*, pl. of سفيه *safîh*; — ة *safâha-t*, foolishness; impudence; thoughtlessness.

سفائر *safâ'ir*, pl. of سفار *sifâr*.

(سفت) *safit*, A, INF. *saft*, drink much without quenching one's thirst.

(سفتج) *saftaj*, INF. ة, have a draft given instead of ready money.

سفتجة *saftaja-t*, pl. *safâtij*, bill of exchange, letter of credit.

سفج *safj*, violent blast of wind.

سفجر *safjar*, small.

(سفح) *safaḥ*, INF. *safḥ*, shed; INF. *safḥ*, *sufûḥ*, shed tears; INF. *safḥ*, *sufûḥ*, *safaḥân*, flow, be shed; — III. INF. *sifâḥ*, *musâfaḥa-t*, fornicate; neglect, be

careless about a thing; — VI. INF. *tasâfuḥ*, fornicate.

سفح *safḥ*, pl. *sufûḥ*, lower part of a mountain-slope; foot of a mountain.

(سفد) *safad*, I, *safid*, A, INF. *sifâd*, cover (male animal); — II. INF. *tasfîd*, put flesh on the spit; — IV. INF. *isfâd*, cause to cover.

(سفر) *safar*, I, INF. *safr*, sweep the house; remove, disperse, chase away; take off the turban, the veil; unveil (n.), discover; shine; write, copy; bridle a camel's nose; INF. *safr*, *sifâra-t*, act as a mediator, try to make peace; begin to subside; — INF. *sufûr*, set out on a journey, depart, travel; — *safir*, A, INF. *safar*, depart; — II. INF. *tasfîr*, bridle the camel's nose; send on a journey; send away, despatch; — III. INF. *sifâr*, *musâfara-t*, depart, travel; — IV. INF. *isfâr*, shine, beam; enter on the time of dawn; disperse; write, copy; — V. INF. *tasaffur*, set out on a journey; — VII. INF. *insifâr*, hang or flow down (hair).

سفر *safr*, pl. *sufûr*, trace; — *sifr*, pl. *asfâr*, written book; book, volume, holy scripture; — *safar*, pl. *asfâr*, departure, journey, travel; campaign, military expedition; — *sufur*, pl. of سفار *sifâr*; — ة *safra-t*, a journey; a campaign; — *sufra-t*, pl. *sufar*, large table-cloth; table-board, table; — *safara-t*, pl. of سافر, mediator, envoy, &c.

سفرا *sufarâ'*, pl. of سفير *safîr*.

سفرجل *safarjal*, pl. *-ât*, *safârij*, *safârîj*, quince.

سفرنية *safarniyya-t*, projecting roof (m.).

سفرى *safariyy*, referring to a journey, travelling.

سفساف *safsâf*, bad, worthless.

سفسطة *safasṭa-t*, sophism.

سفسطى *safasṭiyy*, sophistical.

سفسف *safsaf*, INF. ة, sift flour; bungle.

سفسقة *safsaqa-t*, *sifsiqa-t*, bright undulating lines on a sword-blade; flash of the blade.

سفسير *sifsîr*, pl. *safâsîr*, *safâsira-t*, manager, administrator; courier, messenger; sent.

سفسيقة *sifsîqa-t*=سفسقة *safsaqa-t*.

(سفط) *safuṭ*, INF. *safâṭa-t*, be kind and liberal; — II. INF. *tasfîṭ*, loam; mend; make a wall with a single row of stones; — VIII. INF. *istifâṭ*, drink up the whole.

سفط *safaṭ*, pl. *asfâṭ*, basket; box; sack.

(سفع) *safa'*, INF. *saf'*, beat with the wings; box the ears; beat; mark; scorch the face; attract, pull towards one's self; — III. INF. *musâfa'a-t*, endeavour to drive away; — V. INF. *tasaffu'*, get scorched; — ة *suf'a-t*, pl. *suf'*, blackness mingled with red.

(سفق) *safaq*, U, INF. *safq* (also IV.), open the door wide, and, by opposition, close it; box on the ears; — *safuq*, INF. *safâqa-t*, be coarse and stiff (cloth, &c.); — IV. INF. *isfâq*, see I.; — ة *safqa-t*, striking (s.) a bargain.

(سفك) *safak*, I, INF. *safk*, shed; pour out a flow of words.

سفك *safk*, shedding; — ة *sufka-t*, wink, twinkle, glance.

(سفل) *safal*, U, INF. *safâl*, *sufûl*, be deep down; be low, mean, contemptible; INF. *sufûl*, descend, come down; INF. *safl*, *sufl*, *sifâl*, occupy a low position or rank, be of a low standard; — *safil*, I, INF. *safal*, be below, at the bottom, be low; — *saful*, INF. *safâla-t*, id.; be mean, despised; — II. INF. *tasfîl*, take down, lower; — V. INF. *tasafful*, occupy a low rank or degree; lower one's self,

سفل *safl, sufl,* lowness, lowliness; — *sufl, sifl,* the lower part, bottom; — *safil,* ة, low, mean; — ة *sifla-t,* lowness; meanness; — also *safila-t,* rabble, dregs of the populace.

سفلى *sufla,* f. of اسفل *asfal,* low, &c.; — *sufliyy,* ة, at the bottom, low; mean; worthless; earthly; pl. *suffliyyât,* worldly things; matters of secondary importance, incidents.

(سفن) *safan,* I, INF. *safn,* scrape off the rind, peel; — U, also *safin,* A, INF. *safan,* blow away.

سفن *safan,* anything serving to smooth or polish (stone, file, &c.); — *sufun,* pl. of سفينة *safîna-t.*

سفنج *safanj,* sponge; — ة *safannaja-t,* female ostrich.

(سفه) *safah,* U, INF. *safh,* render stupid, call stupid; get the better in reviling; be occupied; — *safih,* A, INF. *safah,* be unwise, stupid, foolish; be impudent; drink to excess; — *safuh,* INF. *safâh, safâha-t,* be stupid, foolish; — II. INF. *tasfîh,* deem, declare or treat as stupid, foolish or impudent; — III. INF. *musâfaha-t,* treat as foolish; show one's self foolish; revile; drink to excess; — IV. INF. *isfâh,* cause to get very thirsty; — V. deprive one of his property by cunning; — VI. INF. *tasâfuh,* show one's self or pretend to be stupid; revile one another.

سفه *safah,* stupidity, foolishness; (m.) impudence; shamlessness; — *suffah,* and—

سفها *sufahâ',* pl. of سفيه *safîh.*

(سفو) *safâ,* U, INF. *sufuww,* be alert, nimble, brisk; — سفى *safa,* I, INF. *safy* (also IV.), carry off; INF. سفا *safan,* have little hair falling over the forehead (horse); — سفى *safî,* A, INF. سفا *safan, safâ',* be chapped; be stupid, foolish; — III. INF. *sifâ', musâfât,* treat as stupid or foolish; cure, restore to health; — IV. INF. *isfâ',* see I.; — VIII. INF. *istifâ',* turn (the face) towards.

سفوا *safwâ',* f. of اسفى *asfa,* good ambler, &c.

سفود *saffûd,* pl. *safâfîd,* roasting or toasting-fork; poker.

سفور *saffûr,* a fish armed with spikes; — ة *saffûra-t,* writing-tablet.

سفوف *safûf,* pl. *safûfât,* medicine in powder form.

سفوك *safûk,* who sheds blood; cruel; soul, self; liar.

سفون *safûn,* pl. *sawâfîn,* sweeping (adj.); — *sufûn,* pl. of سفينة *safîna-t.*

سفى, see (سفو), *safiyy,* violent.

سفيا *safyâ'* = سفوا *safwâ'.*

سفيح *safîḥ,* coarse garment; large sack; eighth (losing) arrow in the game.

سفير *safîr,* pl. *sufarâ',* ambassador, envoy; mediator; broker; — ة *safîra-t,* chain round the neck, necklace.

سفيك *safîk,* shed.

سفيل *safîl,* low; mean; miserable.

سفين *safîn,* wedge; — ة *safîna-t,* pl. *safâ'in, sufun, safîn, sufûn,* ship; oblong entry-book.

سفيه *safîh,* pl. *sufahâ', sifâh,* f. ة, pl. *-ât, safâ'ih, suffah, sifâh,* stupid, foolish; impudent, insolent, pert.

(سق) *saqq,* U, INF. *saqq,* drop excrements.

سقا *siqâ',* pl. *asqiya-t, asqiyât, asâqî,* skin bag; — *saqqâ',* water-carrier; seller of water; who waters the field; cup-bearer; pelican; — ة *suqât,* cup-bearers, &c., pl. of ساقى *sâqî.*

سقار *saqqâr,* wretch, scamp, rascal; liar.

سقاط *saqâṭ, saqqâṭ,* sharp sword; — *siqâṭ,* falling, stumbling, tripping (s.); error, faulty speech; quick speech and repartee; — *suqâṭ,* anything fallen off; (also ة *su-*

qâṭa-t) rabble ;— *saqqâṭ*, broker ; retail dealer ; — *suqqâṭ*, pl. of ساقط *sâqiṭ*, falling (adj.), &c. ; — ة *saqqâṭa-t*, latch of a door (m.).

سقاع *siqâ'*, nose-ring of the camel ; garment of a mendicant or dervish ; veil.

سقال *saqqâl*, polisher ; — ة *saqâla-t*, scaffolding ; scaffold.

سقالبة *saqâliba-t*, pl. of سقلبى *saqlabiyy*.

سقام *saqâm*, ة *saqâma-t*, illness, ailing, infirmity, damage ; — *siqâm*, pl. of سقيم *saqîm*.

سقاوة *saqâwa-t*, catarrhal flux (of horses, &c.).

سقاية *siqâya-t*, *suqâya-t*, drinking-vessel ; watering-place ; a measure for fluids ; wine ;—*siqâya-t*, watering (s.) ; tempering of the iron ; — *saqqâya-t*, female water-carrier.

(سقب) *saqab*, U, INF. *suqûb*, also *saqib*, A, INF. *saqab*, be or stand near.

سقب *saqb*, f. ة, pl. *siqâb*, *suqûb*, *suqbân*, *asqub*, newly-born foal ; pl. *siqbân*, middle pole of a tent ; long.

(سقت) *saqit*, A, INF. *saqt*, *saqat*, be unfortunate, lack the blessing of God.

سقت *saqit*, unfortunate.

سقح *saqaḥ*, ة *saqaḥa-t*, baldness of the forehead.

(سقد), II. *saqqad*, INF. *tasqîd*, make a horse slender ; — ة *suqda-t*, pl. *suqad*, a red finch.

(سقر) *saqar*, U, INF. *saqr*, singe, scorch ; pimp ; — IV. INF. *isqâr*, bear sweet dates.

سقر *saqr*, hawk, falcon ; — *saqar*, hell-fire ; — ة *saqara-t*, glowing of the sun.

سقراط *suqrâṭ*, Socrates.

سقرقع *suqurqa'*, beer of millet.

(سقسق) *saqsaq*, INF. ة, drop excrement.

(سقط) *saqaṭ*, U, INF. *suqûṭ*, *masqaṭ*, fall, fall down, drop, decay ; trip, err ; commit an error of speech ; set ; be dropped or born ; drop in, come, alight, pass the night ; cease ; — II. INF. *tasqîṭ*, cause to fall ; spoil, corrupt ; (m.) lay out, incrust ; damask a blade ; — III. INF. *siqâṭ*, *musâqaṭa-t*, cause to fall, throw down ; drop one thing after another ; drop (a.) ; — IV. INF. *isqâṭ*, let fall, drop ; throw down ; give up, renounce ; make a miscarriage ; abolish, repeal ; subtract ; make a fault, commit an error ; — V. INF. *tasaqquṭ*, bring to fall, cause to commit a fault or error ; (m.) be or become defective, be spoiled ; — VI. INF. *tasâquṭ*, *issâquṭ*, drop one after another (n.), tumble in by degrees ; rush into (على *'ala*).

سقط *saqṭ*, subtraction ; dew, hoar-frost, snow ; also *siqṭ*, lower edge ; *saqṭ*, *siqṭ*, *suqṭ*, miscarriage ; spark from a fire-stick ;— *saqaṭ*, pl. *asqâṭ*, defective goods, refuse ; offal, sweepings ; defect ; essential fault or damage ; shame ; impotence ; error in calculation, in writing, &c. ; rude speech, rudeness ; — ة *saqṭa-t*, pl. *siqâṭ*, fall ; fault, error.

سقطى *saqṭa*, pl. of ساقطة *sâqiṭa-t*, of little value, cheap, &c. ; — *saqaṭiyy*, fripperer, second-hand dealer ; pedlar.

سقطيم *siqṭîm*, a kind of mouse.

(سقع) *saqa'*, INF. *saq'*, crow ; hit, beat ; go away with anything.

سقع *suq'*, bank, shore, edge of a well.

(سقف) *saqaf*, U, INF. *saqf*, roof ; — INF. سقيفى *siqqîfa*, become a bishop ; — II. INF. *tasqîf*, provide with a roof or ceiling ; make bishop ;—V. INF. *tasaqquf*, be provided with a roof or ceiling ; become a bishop.

سقف *saqf*, pl. *suqûf*, *suquf*, *suqfân*,

roof; ceiling; sky; — *suqf*, *suquff*, bishop; — *suquf*, pl. of سقيف *saqîf*; — ى *saqfiyy*, rafter (m.).

سقق *suquq*, pl. calumniators, slanderers.

(سقل) *saqal*, U, INF. *saql*, smooth, polish.

سقل *suql*, the hypochondres; — *saqil*, slender, slim of waist.

(سقلب) *saqlab*, INF. ة, throw down, overthrow, cut down; (m.) turn, turn round (a.); — ى *saqlabiyy*, pl. *saqâliba-t*, slave, Slavonian.

(سقم) *saqim*, U, INF. *saqam*, be weak and ailing; — *saqum*, id.; — IV. INF. *isqâm*, make ill.

سقم *suqm*, *saqam*, pl. *asqâm*, illness; languor.

سقما *suqamâ'*, سقمى *saqma*, pl. of سقيم *saqîm*.

(سقن), IV. *asqan*, INF. *isqân*, polish a sword completely.

سقنقور *saqanqûr*, a piece of muslin to envelop letters.

سقوط *saqûṭ*, falling (adj.), fallen off, dropped; — *suqûṭ*, falling, stumbling, erring (s.); downfall, decay, ruin.

سقوفية *suqûfiyya-t*, roof.

سقوة *saqwa-t*, poisoned drink.

(سقى) *saqa*, I, INF. *saqy*, give to drink, water; pledge in wine, &c.; put into the bag; be dropsical; temper; poison; blacken the character of the absent; wish rain (happiness) to a person; see II.; — II. INF. *tasqiya-t*, give to drink or water abundantly; fill the glass for, pledge in drink; (also I., III. and IV.) show water to (acc.); — III. INF. *musâqât*, see II.; — IV. INF. *isqâ'*, see II.; water the field; — V. INF. *tasaqqî*, be watered; be impregnated, imbibe, absorb; get tempered; — VI. INF. *tasâqî*, give to drink to one another, pledge each other in drink; — VIII. INF. *istiqâ'*, ask for water; pray for rain; draw water; drink; — X. INF. *istisqâ'*, ask for drink; draw water; be dropsical.

سقى *saqy*, giving to drink, watering (سقيا له *saqyan la-hu*, may God give him rain!); tempering of iron; — *siqy*, pl. *asqiya-t*, water for drinking or irrigating; irrigated, watered; — *siqy*, *saqy*, water in the belly, &c., dropsy; — *suqqa*, pl. of ساقى, who waters, &c.; — *saqiyy*, pl. *asqiya-t*, abundantly raining cloud; palm-tree; — *suqiyy*, pl. of ساقى *sâqî*.

سقيا *suqyâ*, shower.

سقيط *saqîṭ*, pl. سقطى *saqṭa*, snow, ice, hoar-frost, hail, dew; — *saqîṭ*, ة, weak of intellect.

سقيف *saqîf*, pl. *suquf*, roof; — ة *saqîfa-t*, pl. *saqâ'if*, large shingle or flat stone for roofing; deck of a ship; long bench in front of a house.

سقيفى *siqqîfa*, office of a bishop; INF. of (سقف).

سقيم *saqîm*, pl. *siqâm*, سقمى *saqma*, *suqamâ'*, ill, ailing, weak; not sufficiently attested, apocryphal.

(سك) *sakk*, U, INF. *sakk*, stop, bar, obstruct; fortify a door with iron plates or nails; coin; cut off; drop excrement; (m.) stumble and fall; — *sakik*, A, INF. *sakak*, have small ears, too narrow a cavity of the ear, be deaf; — V. INF. *tasakkuk*, humble, humiliate; — VIII. INF. *istikâk*, be too narrow or deaf (ear); be densely grown.

سك *sakk*, trip and fall; pl. *sikâk*, *sukûk*, nail; iron band; closely wrought coat of mail; — *sukk*, juice of the myrobalan; — ة *sikka-t*, pl. *sikak*, ploughshare; mattock, hoe; high road (سكة حديد *sikka-t ḥadîd*, railroad); die for coining; coin; right of coining; دار السكة *dâr as-sikka-t*, mint.

سكا *sikâ'*, importunate begging.
سكابج *sakâbij*, pl. of سكباج *sikbâj*.
سكات *sukât*, silence;—also *sukâta-t*, by what one is silenced; end, conclusion.
سكار *sakkâr*, seller of date-wine;—ى *sakâra*, *sukâra*, pl. of سكران *sakrân*.
سكاف *sakkâf*, shoe-maker; — ة *sikâfa-t*, profession of a shoe-maker.
سكاك *sikâk*, row of tents or houses; pl. of سك *sakk* and سكى *sakka*; —*sukâk*, ة *sukâka-t*, atmosphere; — *sakkâk*,—
سكاكينى *sakâkîniyy*, and—
سكان *sakkân*, cutler; — *sukkân*, helm, rudder; anchor; pl. of ساكن *sâkin*, inhabitant; — ة *sa-kâna-t*, poverty.
(سكب) *sakab*, U, INF. *sakb*, *taskâb*, pour out; melt and cast metals; INF. *sukûb*, be poured out, flow; — VII. INF. *insikâb*, be poured out, molten, cast into a mould.
سكب *sakb*, pouring out, melting, casting (s.); cast; brass, lead; flowing; lasting rain; generous, wide stepping (horse).
سكباج *sikbâj*, pl. *sakâbij*, dish of hashed meat boiled in vinegar.
(سكت) *sakat*, U, INF. *sakt*, *sukât*, *sukût*, be silent; subside; die; — II. INF. *taskît*, silence, impose silence; — III. INF. *musâkata-t*, be silent towards, not talk to; — IV. INF. *iskât*, silence; keep silent.
سكت *sakt*, ة *sakta-t*, silence; pause in singing; — *sakta-t*, apoplectic stroke, apoplexy.
(سكج), II. *sakkaj*, INF. *taskîj*, do anything as well or badly as the circumstances or tools will allow; make the best of a thing.
(سكر) *sakar*, U, INF. *sakr*, fill; dam in a river; — U, INF. *sukûr*, *sakarân*, calm down, subside; — *sakir*, A, INF. *sakr*, *sukr*, *sakar*, *sukur*, *sakarân*, be drunk, get one's self drunk; INF. *sakar*, be full; burn with anger; — II. INF. *taskîr*, intoxicate; cover to suffocation, suffocate, smother; (m.) lock the door; pass. get dimmed; — IV. INF. *iskâr*, intoxicate; — VI. INF. *tasâkur*, feign drunkenness; — X. INF. *istiskâr*, rain abundantly.
سكر *sakr*, ة, intoxicated, drunk; drunkenness, intoxication; — also *sakar*, filling, replenishing (s.), repletion; — *sikr*, pl. *sukûr*, river-dam; damming in (s.); (m.) aqueduct, brook; — *sukr*, intoxication; intoxicating drink, wine; — *sakar*, id.; rage; grudge; — *sakir*, ة, given to drunkenness; — *sukkar*, sugar; ة *sukkara-t*, piece of sugar; — ة *sakra-t*, pl. *sakarât*, intoxication; pl. agony; deep grief;—*sakra-t*, *sukkara-t*, pl. *sakâkir*, wooden lock.
سكران *sakrân*, f. ة and سكرى *sakra*, pl. سكارى *sakâra*, *sukâra*, *sakra*, intoxicated, drunk; — *sakarân*, drunkenness; — ية *sakrâniyya-t*, intoxication.
سكرجة *sukurruja-t*, *sukurja-t*, pl. *sakârîj*, saucer.
سكرى *sakra*, f. of سكران *sakrân*; — *sukriyy*, given to drunkenness; — *sukkariyy*, of sugar.
سكسكة *saksaka-t*, weakness; bravery.
(سكع) *saka'*, INF. *sak'*, also *saki'*, A, INF. *saka'*, deviate; wander at random, seek adventures, stroll; depart, go away; *saka'*, (m.) sleep, fall asleep; — V. INF. *tasakku'*, engage in idle and frivolous pursuits; seek adventures; depart.
سكع *sak'*, (m.) sleep, sleepiness; — *saki'*, strange, foreign; — *suka'*, confused, perplexed.
(سكف) *sakif*, A, INF. *sakaf*, provide the door with a threshold; — II. INF. *taskîf*=IV.; — IV. INF. *iskâf*, carry on the profession of a shoe-maker, become a shoe-

maker; mend shoes; — V. INF. *tasakkuf*=I.; — ة *sakfa-t*, mending of shoes, cobbling.

سكك *sakak*, deafness, INF. of (سك); *sikak*, pl. of سكّة *sikka-t*.

(سكم) *sakam*, U, INF. *sakm*, walk wearily and with short steps.

(سكن) *sakan*, U, INF. *sukûn*, be or get quiet, rest; dwell, live, inhabit; retire to rest; subside, calm down, vanish; rely upon; be uttered without a vowel; have possession of (demon); grow poor and despised; — *sakun*, INF. *sakâna-t*, be poor, in misery; — II. INF. *taskîn*, calm (a.), pacify; allow or cause one to dwell in a place, settle (a.); utter a consonant without a vowel; — IV. INF. *iskân*, allow another to live in one's house, give it to him for a dwelling (2 acc.); calm, quiet (a.); impoverish, reduce to misery, be poor, in misery; — V. INF. *tasakkun*, be poor and in misery; — VII. INF. *insikân*, be inhabited, be inhabitable; — VIII. INF. *istikân*, humble one's self before, submit to; (m.) wait for.

سكن *sakn*, pl. *askân*, inhabitant; — *sakan*, habitation, dwelling, abode; domestic tranquillity; household; — ة *sukna-t*, what quiets a child; remainder in the pot; — *sakana-t*, pl. of ساكن *sâkin*, inhabitant; — *sakina-t*, dwelling.

سكنجبين *sikanjabîn*, oxymel.

سكنى *sukna*, dwelling, abode, place of sojourn.

سكوب *sakûb*, flowing; — *.

سكوت *sakût*, silent; — *.

سكور *sakûr*, given to drunkenness; — *.

سكوك *sakûk*, narrow well; — *.

سكون *sukûn*, quiet, rest; dwelling, &c.; INF. of (سكن); quiescence of a consonant and its sign ـْ; poverty, misery; — ة *sukûna-t*, dwelling, inhabiting (s.).

(سكى), III. *sâka*, INF. *musâkât*, importune by begging or soliciting.

سكى *sakka*, pl. *sikâk*, iron band; nail; — *sakkiyy*, nail; die for coining; — *sikkiyy*, stamped, coined; dinâr.

سكيب *sakîb*, flowing, fluid.

سكيت *sikkît*, always silent, taciturn; — *sukait*, *sukkait*, silent; tenth horse in a race.

سكير *sikkîr*, always drunk, habitual drunkard; dead drunk.

سكيران *sukairân*, slightly drunk; tipsy.

سكين *sikkîn*, (m., f.) ة, pl. *sakâkîn*, knife; — ة *sakîna-t*, pl. *sakâ'in*, calmness, quiet; presence of God among men; divine law; — *sikkîna-t*, id.

(سل) *sall*, U, INF. *sall*, draw out slowly; draw the sword; I, lose the teeth; pass. *sull*, suffer from consumption; — IV. INF. *islâl*, draw or pull out slowly; afflict with consumption; — V. INF. *tasallul*, slip away (n.); — VII. INF. *insilâl*, id.; slip in; (m.) suffer from consumption; — VIII. INF. *istilâl*, draw the sword; — X. INF. *istislâl*, draw away.

سل *sal*, IMP. of (سال), to ask; — *sall*, ة *salla-t*, pl. *silâl*, *sallât*, basket with a leathern covering for victuals; — *sill*, *sull*, consumption; hectic fever; — ة *salla-t*, unnoticed theft.

(سلا) *sala'*, INF. *sal'*, purify the butter; press sesame-oil; clean the palm-tree from thorns; beat; pay promptly.

سلا *salan*, pl. *aslâ'*, membrane which surrounds the embryo; — *salâ'*, pl. *as'ila-t*, molten butter.

سلاب *silâb*, pl. *sulub*, black mourning dress; — ة *sallâba-t*, robber; female thief.

سلاجقة *salâjiqa-t*, the Seljukian dynasty.

سلاح *silâḥ*, pl. *asliḥa-t*, ة *silâḥa-t*, pl. *asliḥât*, arms ; — *sulâḥ*, ة *sulâḥa-t*, excrement.

سلاحدار *silâḥdâr*, pl. *silâḥdâriyya-t*, sword-bearer, arms-bearer.

سلاحف *salâḥif*, pl. سلحفا *sulaḥfâ*, &c.

سلاخ *sallâḥ*, skinner ; — ة *sulâḥa-t*, offal in skinning.

سلاس *sulâs*, weakness of mind or intellect ; — ة *salâsa-t*, docility, sociability, easy manners ; obedience.

سلاسل *salâsil*, sweet soft water ; — *.

سلاطة *salâṭa-t*, dominion ; glibness of tongue.

سلاطين *salâṭîn*, pl. of سلطان *sulṭân*.

سلاف *sulâf*, anything oozing, exuding ; — also ة *sulâfa-t*, must ; best wine ; vanguard ; — *sullâf*, pl. of سالف *sâlif*, preceding, &c., and of سلف *salaf*.

سلاق *sulâq*, eruption of the skin ; tubercle ; looseness of the teeth ; — also *sullâq*, ascension (to heaven) ; — *sallâq*, loud-voiced ; great orator ; — ى *sulâqiyy*, f. ة, greyhound.

سلال *silâl*, pl. of سل *sall* and سلة *salla-t*, *silla-t* ; — *sulâl*, consumption ; hectic fever ; — *sallâl*, maker of baskets ; stealer of cattle ; — ة *sulâla-t*, anything drawn out of another ; sperm ; gonorrhœa ; embryo ; purest vital parts ; pl. *salâ'il*, son ; progeny.

سلام *salâm*, peace, quiet and security, well-being, welfare, prosperity, salvation ; salutation ; name of God ; — *silâm*, pl. of سلم *salm*, *silm*, and of سلمة *salima-t* ; — *sulâm*, bones of the fingers, hands ; — ة *salâma-t*, perfect condition, health, wholesomeness, well-being ; security, weal, salvation ; — *sallâma-t*, a female proper name ; — ى *salâma*, south wind ; — *sulâma*, pl. *sulâmiyât*, finger-bones ; — *salâmiyy*, of or from Bagdad (مدينة السلام *madîna-t as-salâm*, دار السلام *dâr as-salâm*).

سلان *sullân*, wide valleys, pl. of سال *sâll*.

سلائب *salâ'ib*, pl. of سلوب *salûb*, سليب *salîb*.

سلائل *salâ'il*, pl. of سلالة *salâla-t*.

(سلب) *salab*, U, INF. *salb*, *salab*, take from with violence ; rob, plunder, steal ; (m.) spin raw silk ; — *salib*, A, INF. *salab*, wear black mourning apparel ; — V. INF. *tasallub*, mourn for the husband ; — VII. INF. *insilâb*, be robbed, plundered, stolen ; run very fast ; — VIII. INF. *istilâb*, rob, plunder, steal.

سلب *salb*, robbery, plunder, theft ; depriving ; absence, lack of anything ; negation, restriction ; (m.) spun silk ; — *silb*, handle of the plough, plough-tail ; — *salab*, pl. *aslâb*, stolen goods, theft, plunder, booty ; the bark of a tree ; — *salib*, long-stretched and light ; swift, quick ; — *sulub*, pl. of سلاب *salâb* and سليب *salîb* ; — ة *sulba-t*, nakedness.

(سلبط), II. *tasalbaṭ*, INF. *tasalbuṭ*, play the parasite, sponge.

سلبى *salba*, pl. of سليب *salîb* ; — *salbiyy*, denying (adj.), negative.

(سلت) *salat*, U, I, INF. *salt*, draw one thing out of another ; wipe, wipe away ; shave ; cut, cut off the nose, the head ; beat ; drop excrement ; steal away (n.).

سلت *sult*, husk of barley ; — ة *saltat-an*, insensibly, suddenly.

سلتا *saltâ'*, a woman who has not dyed her finger-tops, f. of اسلت *aslat*.

(سلتم) *siltim*, calamity, disaster ; year of famine ; a demon ; — also *saltam*, something, anything.

سلتين *siltîn*, palm-tree with ditches for watering.

(سلج) *salaj*, U, INF. *salj*, have the diarrhœa (from eating the plant *sullaj*); — *salij*, A, INF. *salj*, *salajân*, swallow a morsel; suck (foal); — V. INF. *tasalluj*, swallow; also VIII. INF. *istilâj*, drink much.

سلج *salj*, present, gift; — *sulaj*, oyster; — *sullaj*, a herb.

سلجان *salajân*, INF. of (سلج); — *sillijân*, gullet, throat; — *sullajân*=*sullaj*.

سلجم *saljam*, pl. *salâjim*, long, large; dense; turnip.

(سلح) *saliḥ*, A, INF. *salḥ*, drop excrement; — II. INF. *tasliḥ*, arm; equip; give a nice taste to a butter-bag by the juice سلح *sulḥ*; — IV. INF. *islâḥ*, make drop excrement, drop excrement; — V. INF. *tasalluḥ*, arm, equip one's self; — VII. INF. *insilâḥ*, draw towards the end.

سلح *sulḥ*, see II. (سلح); — *sulaḥ*, pl. *silḥân*, young partridge; — *silaḥ*, and—

سلحان *salḥân*, arms.

(سلحب), III. *islaḥabb*, INF. *isliḥbâb*, be straight and distinct.

سلحفا *sulaḥfâ*, *sulaḥfâ'*, ة *sulaḥfât*, *silaḥfât*, سلحفى *sulaḥfa*, ة *sulaḥfiya-t*, pl. *salâḥif*, tortoise, turtle.

(سلخ) *salaḥ*, U, A, INF. *salḥ*, skin, flay; throw off the slough; undress; produce the day out of the night; cheat, overcharge; — VII. INF. *insilâḥ*, get skinned, flayed; get cheated; draw towards the end; proceed out of the night; — IX. INF. *isliḥâḥ*, lie with the breast on the ground.

سلخ *salḥ*, end of the month; skinning, flaying, cheating (s.); skin, slough; — *silḥ*, slough; — *salaḥ*, thread on the spindle.

سلخد *sillaḥd*, pl. *salâḥid*, strong.

(سلس) *salis*, A, INF. *salas*, be docile, manageable; easy-going, tractable, be tame, familiar; obey; run continually; (also IV.) be deprived of the lower branches; be old, half rotten; pass. *sulis*, be of a weak intellect; — II. *taslîs*, adorn a trinket with jewels, pearls, &c.; render docile; refine spirits by repeated distillation; — IV. INF. *islâs*, see I.; make a miscarriage.

سلس *salas*, docility; diabetes; — *salis*, docile, sociable, easy-going; tame, familiar; (m.) phlegmatic; suffering from diabetes; — ة *salisa-t*, a thistle.

سلسال *salsâl*, sweet, soft, cold water or drink.

سلسبيل *salsabîl*, sweet milk; mild wine; a spring in Paradise; spring, source.

(سلسل) *salsal*, INF. ة, chain together, concatinate; eat; pour; (m.) draw up a pedigree; — II. INF. *tasalsul*, flow down; form a chain (n.), be concatinated; come in an unbroken succession.

سلسل *salsal*=سلسال *salsâl*; — *silsil*, ة *silsila-t*, pl. *salâsil*, chain; rope; unbroken succession, tradition; (m.) genealogy, pedigree; long flash of lightning.

(سلط) *saliṭ*, A, INF. *salâṭa-t*, be absolute, be despotic, hard, violent; be sarcastic, glib of tongue; — *saluṭ*, INF. *salâṭa-t*, *sulûṭa-t*, id.; — II. INF. *tasliṭ*, make one an absolute master, give him power over others, make him a proxy; (m.) make a roof &c. to slant; — V. INF. *tasalluṭ*, exercise or usurp absolute power; treat harshly; master; exceed in height, dominate; slant.

سلط *sulṭ*, ة *sulṭa-t*, conferred power, authority; influence; — ة *salṭa-t*, jacket (m.); — *silṭa-t*, pl. *silaṭ*, *silâṭ*, long arrow.

سلطان *sulṭân*, *suluṭân*, absolute power, dominion; violence; f. ة,

pl. *salâṭîn*, absolute ruler, sultan, emperor; سلطان الثانى *sulṭân as-sânî*, governor, lieutenant; — pl. of سليط *salîṭ*; — ى *sulṭâniyy*, imperial.

(سلطح) *sultuḥ*, slanting, rising gradually;—IV. *islanṭaḥ*, INF. *islinṭâḥ*, fall on the face; be long and wide.

(سلطع), IV. *islanṭa'*, INF. *islinṭâ'*, lie down on one's back.

سلطعون *salṭa'ûn*, crab, crayfish.

(سلطن) *salṭan*, INF. II. make one an absolute ruler, sultan, emperor; — II. INF. *tasalṭun*, become sultan; play the sultan; grow angry; — ة *salṭana-t*, absolute power, dominion.

(سلع) *sala'*, INF. *sal'*, split, cleave; —*sali'*, A, INF. *sala'*, be chapped; be leprous;—V. INF. *tasallu'*, be split, cleft; split (n.), burst; be wounded; break; — VII. INF. *insilâ'*=V.

سلع *sal'*, pl. *sulû'*, split, cleft; chap; mountain-cleft; — *sil'*, pl. *aslâ'*, *sulû'*, similarity; similar; mountain-cleft; — *sala'*, leprosy; poison; a bitter tree, aloes; rent, breach; — ة *sal'a-t*, *sala'a-t*, pl. *-ât*, *silâ'*, rent, breach; wound, bruise; — *sil'a-t*, pl. *sila'*, wares, merchandise, goods; household things; anything for sale; (m.) anything worthless, bad.

سلعام *sil'âm*, having a large snout and a wide gullet; wolf (also ابو سلعامة *abû sil'âma-t*).

(سلغ) *salag*, INF. *sulûg*, get the eye-teeth or dog-teeth; INF. *salg*, smash the head.

(سلغف) *salgaf*, INF. ة, swallow, devour; — *salgaf*, strong, stout.

(سلف) *salaf*, U, INF. *salf*, harrow; level, plane; INF. *salf*, *sulûf*, precede in time; come sooner to (الى *ila*); — U, INF. *salaf*, have happened, be passed; — II. INF. *taslîf*, let one thing precede another; send in advance; take anything before dinner; =IV.; — III. INF. *musâlafa-t*, travel together with; precede; — IV. INF. *islâf*, advance money without interest; pay in advance; — V. INF. *tasalluf*, lend money to be redeemed in goods; have goods paid in advance; take anything before dinner;—VI. INF. *tasâluf*, become related by marriage; — X. INF. *istislâf*, demand payment in advance; borrow money.

سلف *salf*, pl. *asluf*, *sulûf*, large travelling-bag, portmanteau; — *silf*, *salif*, pl. *aslâf*, husband of a wife's sister, brother-in-law; skin; — *sulf*, woman above 40; pl. of سلوف *sulûf*; — *salaf*, payment in advance; loan without interest; good deed; pl. *sullâf*, *aslâf*, predecessor, ancestor, men of old; — *sulaf*, pl. *silfân*, *sulfân*, young partridge; — ة *silfa-t*, relationship of sisters married to brothers; sister-in-law; — *sulfa-t*, pl. *sulaf*, meal before dinner, breakfast; *sulfat-an*, one after another, in succession.

(سلفع) *salfa'*, bold; broad-chested.

(سلق) *salaq*, U, INF. *salq*, boil; throw on the back; loosen the flesh from the bones; pierce with a lance; singe, scorch; hurt by words; run; — II. INF. *taslîq*, gather herbs, greens, &c.; —V. INF. *tasalluq*, scale the wall, climb, stand on the top of; — VII. INF. *insilâq*, get boiled, cooked; be seized by the disease سلاف *sulâq*, q.v.

سلق *silq*, greens, kitchen-herbs; beet-root; pl. *sulqân*, place where water flows; channel; pl. *sulqân*, *silqân*, wolf; — *salaq*, ة *salaqa-t*, pl. *aslâq*, *sulqân*, *silqân*, good low ground, plain; — ة *silqa-t*, pl. *silq*, *silaq*, she-wolf; pl. *sulqân*, *silqân*, impudent and boisterous woman.

(سلقد) *silqid*, thin-flanked horse; — *salqad*, INF. ة, make the horse lean.

(سلقع) *salqa'*, INF. ة, be poor; — IV. INF. *islinqâ'*, flash through the clouds; glow.

سلقع *salqa'*, male ostrich; pl. *salâqi'*, rugged ground; desert.

(سلقم) *salqam*, INF. ة, gnash the teeth; have a bad opinion of (acc.).

سلقم *salqam*, lion.

سلقى *salqa*, pierce with a lance; throw on the back; — II. INF. *tasalqî*, and IV. INF. *islinqâ'*, lie on the back; fall backwards, throw one's self back.

(سلك) *salak*, U, INF. *salk*, cause to enter, to enter on; put into; — INF. *salk*, *sulûk*, enter a place; walk; behave, conduct one's self; have course; be usual; pass a thread; = IV.; — II. reel off thread or silk; put money into currency; introduce a custom; — IV. INF. *islâk*, cause to enter a place or on a road, lead; put into; — VII. INF. *insilâk*, be practicable (road); begin to understand the usages of society; walk.

سلك *silk*, pl. *sulûk*, vine-prop; — *sulak*, f. ة, pl. *silkân*, young partridge or *qaṭa*; — ة *silka-t*, pl. *silk*, *aslâk*, *sulûk*, thread, string; wire, telegraph-wire; row, line, furrow; path; career, way of living, conduct; manner; assembly, party of friends.

سلكى *salka*, direct stroke or thrust; straightforward bargain.

(سلم) *salim*, A, INF. *salâm*, *salâma-t*, be or remain healthy, in sound condition; be well; be without a blemish; escape safely; — *salam*, I, INF. *salm*, make (a bucket) of the bark of the tree *salam*; bite; — II. INF. *taslîm*, preserve in good health or condition; save, preserve from evil; give over, hand, transmit, assign; surrender, submit; admit; wish a blessing, salute; be proclaimed as caliph; — III. INF. *musâlama-t*, make or keep the peace with, make a truce; live in peace with (acc.); — IV. INF. *islâm*, keep sound and safe; attain to safety, tranquillity and prosperity; give over to; deliver up, betray; submit, resign one's self to the will of God; profess Islâm, become a Muslim; pay in advance; — V. INF. *tasallum*, accept anything handed over, accept the surrender; take possession or be put into possession of; take upon one's self the supervision or direction of a thing; become a Muslim; — VI. INF. *tasâlum*, make peace, become reconciled; — VIII. INF. *istilâm*, touch anything given over, take or receive it; touch the holy stone of the Ka'ba with hand and mouth; — X. INF. *istislâm*, yield, surrender, obey, be submissive.

سلم *salm*, peace; pl. *silâm*, *aslum*, bucket; — *silm*, peace, truce, concord, salvation; Islâm; pl. *silâm*, *aslâm*, who keeps peace; — *salam*, payment in advance; transmission, surrender, captivity; salutation; *salam*, noun of unity ة, name of a thorn-tree; — *sullam*, pl. *salâlim*, *salâlîm*, ladder, stairs; stirrup; — ة *salima-t*, pl. *silâm*, stone.

سلما *sulamâ'*, pl. of سليم *salîm*.

(سلمج) *salmaj*, pl. *salâmij*, long head of an arrow.

(سلهب) *salhab*, ة *salhaba-t*, pl. *salâhib*, *salâhiba-t*, having a long body, thin flanks; — III. *islahabb*, INF. *islihbâb*, have a long body, thin flanks.

(سلو) *salâ*, U, INF. *salw*, *suluww*, *salwân*, console one's self about a thing and forget it, put out of one's mind, disregard; — سلى *salî*, A, INF. *suliyy*, id.; —

II. INF. *tasliya-t*, console for the loss of, divert, cheer, amuse; — IV. INF. *islâ'*, id.; be safe; — V. INF. *tasallî*=I.; divert or amuse one's self; — VII. INF. *insilâ'*, depart from; — VIII. INF. *istilâ*, be fat.

سلوان *salwân*, consolation for a loss; — *sulwân*, anything that consoles, cheers, diverts; a love-spell; an elixir; — ة *sulwâna-t*, *salwâna-t*, a shell, &c., as an amulet; *sulwâna-t*, honey.

سلواة *salwât*, noun of unity of سلوى *salwa*, quail.

سلوب *salûb*, pl. *salâ'ib*, *sulub*, subject to having miscarriages.

سلوطة *sulûṭa-t*, dominion, INF. of (سلط).

سلوف *salûf*, pl. *sulf*, running to the water in advance of others; swift, fleet; — *.

سلوق *salûq*, natural disposition, character; name of a town, whence: ى *salûqiyy*, f. ة, greyhound (bred in *Salûq*); — ية *salûqiyya-t*, cabin of the captain.

سلوك *sulûk*, march, journey, travel; way of living, conduct, behaviour; proceeding; good manners; usage, custom, habit; commerce; — *.

سلوة *salwa-t*, *sulwa-t*, remedy against grief or love-sickness; consolation, tranquillity, happiness; diversion, amusement, pleasure; — *salwa-t*, pl. *-ât*, and—

سلوى *salwa*, noun of unity سلواة *salwât*, pl. *salâwî*, quail; — *salwa*, honey; consolation.

(سلى) see (سلو); — *salî*, A, INF. سلا *salan*, have the membrane سلا *salan* torn; — II. INF. *tasliya-t*, draw this membrane out.

سلى *sala-n*=سلا *sal-an*; — *saliyy*, consoled, contented.

سليب *salîb*, pl. سلبى *salba*, deprived of leaves and fruit; deprived of one's senses, mad, distracted; bark, bast; pl. *sulub*, having had a miscarriage.

سليج *salîj*, savoury, relishing, dainty.

سليح *salîḥ*, apostle.

سليخ *salîḫ*, fallow field; — ة *salîḫa-t*, oil of the myrobalan; cassia; child, descendant.

سليس *salîs*, well-speaking.

سليط *salîṭ*, violent; sharp, ground; sarcastic; eloquent; pl. *sulṭân*, sesame-oil, olive-oil; — ة *salîṭa-t*, boisterous shrew.

سليف *salîf*, past; ancestor.

سليق *salîq*, pl. *sulk*, what falls from a tree, leaves, branches; kitchen-herbs; beet-root; pearl-barley and dish of it; — *salîqa-t*, what is boiled, cooked; kitchen-herbs; natural disposition, genius, character; custom, usage.

سليل *salîl*, new-born child; boy, lad, son; pl. *sullân*, wide valley; middle of a valley; spinal marrow; — ة *salîla-t*, girl, daughter; long strip, shred; muscle of the loins; long slice of bread.

سليم *salîm*, sound, safe, healthy, whole; without blemish; good-natured, inoffensive, peaceable, tame; wounded by a snake or scorpion.

سليمان *sulaimân*, Solomon; — ى *sulaimâniyy*, Solomonic; arsenic; sublimate.

(سم) *samm*, U, INF. *samm*, poison; grant a particular favour; be granted particularly; purpose, resolve upon; stop; mend; make peace; examine closely; meet with the poisonous wind سموم *samûm*; — II. INF. *tasmîm*, poison; — IV. INF. *ismâm*, id.; — VII. INF. *insimâm*, get poisoned; grow irritated, embittered.

سم *samm*, pl. *simâm*, *sumûm*, hole; eye of a needle; poison; mother-of-pearl; intention, purpose, aim; — ة *sima-t*, pl. *simât*, sign, mark; stigma; distinction:

INF. of (وسم); — *summa-t*, pl. *sumam*, mat of palm-leaves; — also *simma-t*, podex.

سما *samâ'*, pl. *asmiya-t*, *samawât*, *samâ'î*, heaven; firmament; roof; pl. *samiyy*, سمى, سما *suman*, *asmiya-t*, id.; rain, heavy downpour; باب السما *bâb as-samâ'*, galaxy; — ة *samât*, *simât*, sign.

سماح *samâḥ*, ة *samâḥa-t*, kindness, liberality, generosity, bounty; mercy, grace; leave, permission; — *.

سماخ *simâḫ*, ear; cavity of the ear.

سماد *samâd*, dung with ashes.

سمادير *samâdîr*, pl. of سمدور *sumdûr*.

سمار *samâr*, much-watered milk; — *summâr*, night-talkers, &c., pl. of سامر *sâmir*.

سماسرة *samâsira-t*, سماسير *samâsîr*, pl. of سمسار *simsâr*.

سماط *simâṭ*, pl. *sumuṭ*, row, series, order; — also *sumâṭ*, pl. *asmiṭa-t*, *sumuṭ*, tablecloth on which the meal is served; dressed table; banquet, entertainment.

سماع *samâ'*, hearing, listening (s.); reputation, good name, character; grammatical parlance; dance and music of the dervishes; — *sammâ'*, hearer, listener, auditor; — ة *samâ'a-t*, listening (s.); audience; — *sammâ'a-t*, hearing (adj.); — ى *samâ'iyy*, founded on the usage of a language; usual, common, vulgar; handed down by tradition, traditional; arbitrary, irregular.

سماق *sumâq*, pure; sheer; — *summâq*, sumach-tree and its fruit; — ى *summâqiyy*, seller of sumach; — *sammâqiyy*, a species of marble.

سماك *simâk*, pl. *sumuk*, anything supporting; upper part of the chest; name of two stars; (m.) roof; — *sammâk*, fisherman; — *summâk*, sumach.

(سمال), III. *isma'all*, INF. *ismi'lâl*, have a slim waist; shorten (n.).

سمام *samâm*, a species of swallow; f. ة, swift, nimble, alert; — *; — ة *samâma-t*, body, figure, person, face; banner, flag.

سمان *simân*, pl. of سمين *samîn*; — *sammân*, seller of butter; grocer; — ة *samâna-t*, fatness; — *sumâna-t*, ى *sumâna*, quail.

سمانجونى *samânjûniyy*, sky-blue, azure (Pers.).

سماوات *samâwât*, pl. سما *samâ'*.

سماوة *samâwa-t*, roof; form, figure, mould.

سماوى *samâwiyy*, heavenly; sky-blue; north-east wind; light breeze; zephyr.

سمائم *samâ'im*, pl. of سموم *samûm*.

سمائى *samâ'î*, pl. of سما *samâ'*; — *samâ'iyy*, heavenly.

(سمت) *samat*, U, I, INF. *samt*, proceed towards an aim, try to reach, intend; do or say the right thing; — II. INF. *tasmît*, invoke the name of God over (على *'ala*); — III. INF. *musâmata-t*, go in the direction of (acc.).

سمت *samt*, tendency or direction towards an aim; road; right proceeding; conduct, deportment; manner; direction, point of the compass; سمت الراس *samt ar-râs*, zenith, نظير السمت *naẓîr as-samt*, nadir; — ى *samtiyy*, who disposes well his thoughts and speech.

(سمج) *samuj*, INF. *samâja-t*, be ugly, horrid to look at; — II. INF. *tasmîj*, make ugly; — X. INF. *istismâj*, find ugly.

سمج *samj*, *samij*, pl. *simâj*, ugly, horrid; indecent.

(سمجر) *samjar*, INF. ة, water the milk much.

(سمح) *samuḥ*, INF. *samḥ*, *simâḥ*, *sumûḥ*, *samâḥa-t*, *sumûḥa-t*, be

kind, liberal, generous; grant generously, bestow liberally, supply abundantly; grace, pardon; — II. INF. *tasmîḥ*, act kindly; walk with a light and noiseless step; straighten; — III. INF. *musâmaḥa-t*, act with kindness or indulgence towards, pardon, excuse; remit, present with; — IV. INF. *ismâḥ*, be kind, liberal, generous; — V. INF. *tasammuḥ*, show kindness; — VI. INF. *tasâmuḥ*, act kindly towards one another; pardon or excuse mutually; become reconciled.

سمح *samḥ*, pl. *sumaḥâ'*, *masâmîḥ*, f. ة, pl. *simâḥ*, kind, liberal, generous; indulgent, forgiving, placable; smooth; without knots.

سمحاق *simḥâq*, scalp or wound in it.

(سمخ) *samaḫ*, injure the ear-hole; begin to sprout; — ة *simḫa-t*, hearing (s.).

(سمد) *samad*, U, INF. *sumûd*, stand as if thunderstruck; be grieved; bear one's head high from pride; toy; be careless; sing a song; exert one's self in a matter; walk apace; — II. INF. *tasmîd*, manure with dung and ashes; — IX. INF. *ismidâd*, XI. INF. *ismîdâd*, swell with anger.

سمد *samd*, eternal.

(سمدر), III. *ismadarr*, INF. *ismidrâr*. be dimmed.

سمدور *sumdûr*, pl. *samâdîr*, dimmed eyesight; gloomy pictures before the eye; monarch.

(سمر) *samar*, U, INF. *samr*, *sumûr*, pass the night awake and in conversation; — U, INF. *samr*, burn or tear out the eye; water milk much; shoot the arrow; graze off herbs; drink; — I, U, fix with nails; drive nails into; — *samir*, *samur*, INF. *sumra-t*, (also IX. and XI.) be brown, dark yellow; — II. INF. *tasmîr*, fasten with nails — III. INF. *musâmara-t*, converse with at night-time; — V. INF. *tasammur*, be fastened with nails; — IX. INF. *ismirâr*, XI. INF. *ismîrâr*, see I.

سمر *samar*, nightly conversation, night-talk; night, darkness, shade of night, shadow of the moon; fairy-tale; — *sumr*, the lances, pl. of اسمر *asmar*, brown, &c.; — *summar*, night-talkers, &c., pl. of سامر *sâmir*; — ة *sumra-t*, brown or dark yellow (s.); — *samara-t*, pl. Samaritans; — *samura-t*, pl. *-ât*, *samur*, *asmur*, Egyptian thorn.

سمرج له *samrij la-hu*, give him!

سمروت *sumrût*, سمرود *sumrûd*, long, tall.

سمرى *samariyy*, who talks, converses, tells stories at night-time.

سمسار *simsâr*, pl. *samâsir*, *samâsira-t*, *samâsîr*, broker, factor; mediator, peace-maker; — ة *simsâra-t*, tale-bearing woman.

سمسر *samsar*, INF. ة, carry on the profession of a broker; — ة *samsara-t*, fee of a broker, brokerage.

سمسق *samsaq*, *simsiq*, *sumsuq*, *sumsaq*, jessamine; sweet marjoram.

(سمسم) *samsam*, INF. ة, run.

سمسم *samsam*, fox, cat; — *simsim*, sesame; coriander-seed; — *sumsum*, ة *simsima-t*, pl. *samâsim*, red ant; — *sumsum*, and—

سمسمان *sumsumân*, ى *sumsumâniyy*, nimble, alert.

(سمط) *samaṭ*, U, I, INF. *samṭ*, scald; hang, suspend; sharpen, whet, grind; — U, INF. *sumûṭ*, begin to turn sour; be silent; — II. INF. *tasmîṭ*, be silent; strap to the saddle; land and moor a ship; — IV. INF. *ismâṭ*, be silent; — V. INF. *tasammuṭ*, be tied up, suspended.

سمط *simṭ*, pl. *sumûṭ*, *asmuṭ*, thread,

string, string of pearls; long saddle-strap to tie up the luggage; nimble, alert; — *sumṭ*, a woollen garment; — *sumuṭ*, pl. of سماط *simâṭ*; — ى *simṭiyy*, quatrain with rhyme of the third and fourth line.

(سمع) *sami'*, A, INF. *sam'*, *sim'*, *samâ'*, *samâ'a-t*, *samâ'iya-t*, hear; listen; listen to and accept advice; obey; hear any work explained; — II. INF. *tasmî'*, publish or spread news, make public; disgrace; cause to hear, rehearse to; — IV. INF. *ismâ'*, cause to hear, bring to one's hearing; — V. INF. *tasammu'*, lend an ear, listen to, try to understand one; obey one's word; — VIII. INF. *istimâ'*, pay attention, listen, lend an ear, understand; steal a hearing, listen secretly; obey.

سمع *sam'*, pl. *asmâ'*, *asmu'*, *asâmi'*, hearing (s., *sam'-an*, in reach of hearing); sense of hearing; anything heard, hear-say; good repute; — *sim'*, hearing (s.); good repute; — *sumu'*, pl. of سموع *samû'*; — ة *sim'a-t*, cross between a hyena and she-wolf; — *sam'a-t*, a hearing; — *sim'a-t*, way of hearing; — *sum'a-t*, sound; good repute, fame; hypocrisy; — *sami'a-t*, hearing (adj.).

سمعا *suma'â*, pl. of سميع *samî'*.

سمعان *sim'ân*, Simeon.

(سمعج) *sam'aj*, thick sweet milk.

سمعى *sam'iyy*, on hear-say; by way of mouth.

(سمغد) *simagd*, tall and strong.

(سمق) *samaq*, U, INF. *sumûq*, be high-grown.

(سمقر), III. *ismaqarr*, INF. *ismiqrâr*, be very hot.

(سمك) *samak*, U, INF. *samk*, raise to great height; INF. *sumûk*, be very high.

سمك *samk*, height, depth, thickness; stature; roof; ceiling; — *samak*, pl. *simâk*, *sumûk*, *asmâk*, noun of unity ة, pl. *-ât*, fish; (m.) saddle; pillow; — *sumuk*, pl. of سماك *simâk*.

(سمل) *samal*, U, INF. *saml*, tear out the eye; make peace; clean a well or pond from mud; (also II.) bring up little water; INF. *sumûl*, be old and worn; — II. INF. *tasmîl*, see I.; — IV. INF. *ismâl*, make peace; be old and worn; — V. INF. *tasammul*, be given to drink; — VIII. INF. *istimâl*, tear out an eye.

سمل *samal*, *samil*, old, worn, threadbare; worn garment, rag; — ة *samala-t*, pl. *samal*, *simâl*, small remainder of water in a well; mud.

سملاخ *simlâḫ*=صملاخ *ṣimlâḫ*, interior of the ear, &c.

(سملج) *samlaj*, INF. ة, sip slowly.

سملق *samlaq*, pl. *samâliq*, soft level ground.

سمم *sumam*, pl. of سمة *summa-t*.

(سمن) *saman*, U, INF. *samn*, butter a dish; feed on butter or grease (a.); — *samin*, A, INF. *saman*, *samâna-t*, be or grow fat, be corpulent; — II. INF. *tasmîn*, fatten; batten; butter; — IV. INF. *ismân*, be naturally fat; have or give anything fat; batten; — X. INF. *istismân*, take for fat; ask for fat.

سمن *samn*, pl. *sumûn*, *sumnân*, *asmun*, molten butter, grease; cream; — *siman*, fatness; — ة *samna-t*, a little grease; — *sumna-t*, a plant the seed of which fattens; — *summana-t*, pl. *summan*, *samâmin*, thrush, fieldfare.

سمندر *samandar*, salamander.

(سمه) *samah*, INF. *sumûh*, run unwearyingly; be as if thunderstruck, dumbfounded; — II. INF. *tasmîh*, allow the camels to pasture at large.

سمه *summah*, pl. of *sâmih*, thunderstruck, bewildered.

(سمهر) *samhar*, INF. ة, be hard; bear only one ear (stalk of corn); — III. *ismaharr*, INF. *ismihrâr*, be hard and dry; be straight and symmetrical; be very dense; — ى *samhariyy*, strong and hard; Indian lance.

(سمو) *samâ*, U, (pret. *samautu*, *samai-tu*) INF. *sumuww*, be high, elevated, sublime; rise high and be visible far and wide; raise, elevate; ascend, mount; go for a hunting expedition; intend, purpose; INF. *samw*, call one by his name (2 acc.); — *samû*, INF. *samâwa-t*, cover (stallion); — II. INF. *tasmiya-t*, give a name to, name; mention; — III. INF. *musâmât*, vie with in height, greatness, boast against, surpass in greatness; — IV. INF. *ismâ'*, raise, elevate; profess; name; — V. INF. *tasammî*, be called, named; give one's self a name, call one's self; be called after, referred to; — VI. INF. *tasâmî*, vie in height or greatness with one another, boast, be proud; be high; — X. INF. *istismâ'*, ask for one's name.

سمو *sumuww*, height; greatness.

سموات *samawât*, pl. of سما *samâ'*.

سموح *samûḥ*, kind, indulgent, affable, liberal; — *sumûḥ*, ة *sumûḥa-t*, kindness, indulgence, affability, liberality.

سمود *sumûd*, pride; — *.

سمور *samûr*, swift, fleet; — *sammûr*, Siberian weasel, Norway rat, sable, sable-fur.

سموع *samû'*, pl. *sumu'*, hearing; who hears everything (God.).

سمول *samûl*, old and worn;—*sumûl*, threadbareness; — *.

سموم *samûm*, pl. *samâ'im*, hot poisonous wind; — *.

سموه *sumûh*, astonishment, INF. of (سمه).

سموى *samawiyy*, *simawiyy*, ة, by name, nominal, referring to the name.

سمى *siman*, name; — *suman*, good repute, fame; — *samiyy*, pl. *asmiyâ'*, high, sublime; homogenious, of the same name, namesake; similar; — *sumiyy*, pl. of سما *samâ'*; — ة *sammiyya-t*, being poisonous (s.), virulence.

سميج *samîj*, pl. *simâj*, ugly; indecent.

سميد *samîd*, سميذ *samîẕ*, white bread; finest flour (Pers.).

سميدع *samaida'*, a brave one, hero; prince.

سمير *samîr*, time, age, epoch; nightly conversation, night-talk or place of such; — *simmîr*, given to such conversation, talk-fellow, companion.

سميط *samîṭ*, ة; scalded (and thereby made hairless); pl. *asmâṭ*, simple, not lined, not double-soled; nimble, alert; — also *sumaiṭ*, regular brick building.

سميع *samî'*, ة, hearing, obeying; — *samî'*, hearer; who hears everything, God.

سميك *samîk*, high, deep, thick.

سميكا *sumaikâ'*, a small dried fish.

سميل *samîl*, old, threadbare.

سمين *samîn*, ة, pl. *simân*, fat; buttered, greased; corpulent; —ة *samîna-t*, fat clayey ground.

سميها *sumaihâ'*, *summaihâ'*, سميهى *sumaiha*, *summaiha*, lie; vanity, nothingness; atmosphere; mote.

(سن) *sann*, U, INF. *sann*, sharpen, grind; provide a lance with the iron point سنان *sanân*; thrust with a lance; bite; sharpen the appetite; clean the teeth; form, shape; make vessels of clay; pour water slowly over; sprinkle water in one's face; (also VIII.) introduce a law or usage, observe such and instigate others to observe it, ordain; explain; enter on; urge to haste; throw over one

a coat of mail; pass. *sunn*, be grazed bare; — II. INF. *tasnîn*, sharpen, grind; excite or sharpen the appetite; dispose well and deliver skilfully one's speech; point the lance against (الى *ila*); — IV. INF. *isnân*, be advanced in years; have large teeth; make teeth; pour water over; — VIII. INF. *istinân*, see I.; rub one's teeth; enter on a road; jump briskly to and fro, skip, gallop, course away; undulate; accustom or exercise one's self; — X. INF. *istisnân*, have large teeth; be advanced in years; be commodious; enter on a road.

سن *sann*, sharpening, grinding (s.); forming, shaping (s.) — *sinn*, pl. *asnân*, *asinna-t*, *asunn*, tooth; pl. *isnân*, bits (wards) of a key; nib of a pen; f. pl. *asnân*, age of life, age (طاعن فى السن *ṭâ'an fî 's-sinn*, advanced in years); — *sunn*, pl. *sunûn*, swallow; — ة *sana-t*, pl. *sanûn* (*sinûn*, *sunûn*), year; pl. *sinûn*, sterile ground; famine; — *sina-t*, carelessness, negligence, sluggishness; sleepiness, sleep; — *sanna-t*, she-bear; — *sinna-t*, double-edged axe; ploughshare; coin, money; — *sunna-t*, pl. *sunan*, roundness of the face, face; forehead, temple; form, figure, shape; nature; way of acting, rule of life; custom, usage; divine law; tradition; circumcision; punishment, torment, pain.

سنا *sanan*, *sanâ*, brightness, clearness; senna; — *sanâ'*, height, elevation, sublimeness; senna, senna-leaves.

سناب *sanâb*, great corruption; — *sinâb*, ة *sinâba-t*, lengthy.

سناج *sinâj*, stain of soot; lamp.

سناجل *sanâjil*, pl. of سجنجل *sajanjal*.

سناخة *sanâḫa-t*, shavings, scrapings; dirt.

سناد *sinâd*, assistance; large animal; rhinoceros.

سنادين *sanâdîn*, pl. of سندان *sandân*.

سنار *sunnâr*, pl. *sanânîr*, cat; — ة *sinnâra-t*, pl. *sanânîr*, fishing-hook; knitting-needle.

سناط *sinâṭ*, *sunâṭ*, pl. *sunuṭ*, *asnâṭ*, beardless; — ة *sanâṭa-t*, beardlessness.

سناعة *sanâ'a-t*, symmetry, fine proportions.

سناف *sinâf*, pl. *sunuf*, breast-harness of the camel.

سناكرة *sanâkira-t*, pl. of سنكرى *sankariyy*.

سنام *sanâm*, pl. *asnima-t*, hump of a camel; elevation, hill, projection, promontory; support, prop, principal part.

سناموره *sanâmûra-t*, anchovy.

سنان *sinân*, pl. *asinna-t*, head of a spear; spear; head of an arrow; point of a needle; grinding-stone; — *; — *sannân*, grinder.

سنانير *sanânîr*, pl. of سنور *sinnaur*, سنار *sunnâr* and سنارة *sinnâra-t*.

سنايا *sanâyâ*, eminent, distinguished personages.

سناية *sinâya-t*, the whole of.

(سنب) *sanib*, pl. *sunûb*, running well; — ة *samba-t*, *simba-t*, maliciousness; — *samba-t*, time, while.

سنبا *sambâ'*, سنبات *sambât*, podex; — *sambât*, *simbât*, maliciousness.

سنبادج *sumbâdaj*, emery; grindstone.

(سنبر) *sambar*, wise, knowing.

(سنبس) *sambas*, INF. ة, hasten.

سنبك *sumbuk*, pl. *sanâbik*, front side of a horse's hoof; a running pace; crest of a helmet; formerly; time; awl, punch; small boat, skiff.

سنبل *sumbul*, hyacinth; spikenard; — ة *sumbula-t*, pl. *sumbul*, *sanâ-*

bil, ear (of corn); Virgo; — *sambal*, INF. ة, form ears.

سنبتة *sambata-t*, time, while.

سنبوسق *sambûsaq*, سنبوسك *sambûsak*, pie; small meat pies (Pers.).

سنبوق *sumbûq*, small boat, skiff.

سنبول *sumbûl*, ear (of corn).

سنت *sanat*, year, year of famine; — *sanit*, ة, worthless, useless; sterile; — II. *sannat*, INF. *tasnît*, put caraway-seeds into the pot; — III. INF. *musânata-t*, search the ground for plants; — IV. INF. *isnât*, suffer a year of famine.

(سنتب) *suntub*, malicious, mischievous; — ة *santaba-t*, inveterate vice.

(سنج) *sanaj*, U, INF. *sanj*, blacken with smoke, &c.; — II. INF. *tasnîj*, id.; cause stiffness or a rheumatism of the neck.

سنج *sanj*, equilibrium; — ة *sanja-t*, scale; weight; — *sunja-t*, pl. *sunj*, white with spots of black; — *sunuja-t*, red jujube.

سنجاب *sinjâb*, grey squirrel; its fur; ermine; — ى *sinjâbiyy*, grey.

سنجرف *sinjarf*, cinnabar.

سنجق *sinjaq*, *sanjaq*, pl. *-ât*, *sanâjiq*, standard, flag (Pers.); a province with a banner of its own.

(سنح) *sanaḥ*, INF. *sanḥ*, *sunḥ*, *sunûḥ*, occur, present itself, offer itself; happen; befall; hint at a thing with hidden words; turn from one's opinion; — INF. *sunûḥ*, come from the left and offering the right side to the hunter; come within shot; be favourable, promoting, conducive to a purpose; be easy, succeed well; — II. INF. *tasnîḥ*, facilitate, render possible; stick out (to receive a blow); — III. INF. *musânaḥa-t*=I.; ـّـ V. INF. *tasannuḥ*, ask for an explanation; — X. INF. *istisnâḥ*, id.

سنح *sunḥ*, good omen; good fortune after misfortune; middle of the road.

(سنحنح) *sanaḥnaḥ*, sleepless.

(سنخ) *sanaẖ*, INF. *sunûẖ*, be firm, be solid; — *saniẖ*, A, INF. *sanaẖ*, be rancid and smell badly; be intemperate; — II. INF. *tasnîẖ*, ask, demand.

سنخ *sinẖ*, pl. *sunûẖ*, *asnâẖ*, root; origin, cause, reason; paroxysm of a fever; — *sanaẖ*, rankness; — *saniẖ*, visited by an epidemic; — ة *sanẖa-t*, *sanaẖa-t*, bad smell.

(سند) *sanad*, U, INF. *sunûd*, lean upon; rely upon, confide in; support; belong to; ascend; be near, close to; — II. INF. *tasnîd*, support firmly; pile up; — III. INF. *musânada-t*, *sinâd*, help, assist; compensate for, requite; — IV. INF. *isnâd*, cause to lean upon or against; support an assertion by an authority; trace back to; approach; ascend; cause to ascend; have dealings with; — VI. INF. *tasânud*, VIII. INF. *istinâd*, rely upon, confide in.

سند *sanad*, pl. *asnâd*, support, anything to fall back upon, refuge; prop, supporting beam; mountain slope; affinity, kinship, relation; written acknowledgment of any kind, deed, patent, mandate, diploma; a striped stuff; — *sind*, India; Sind, people of Sind.

سنداب *sinda'b*, strong.

سندان *sandân*, pl. *sanâdîn*, anvil; — *sindân*, big, strong.

(سندر) *sandar*, INF. ة, step apace; hurry, hasten.

سندر *sandar*, birch-tree; a kind of gum.

سندروس *sandarûs*, *sindarûs*, Sandarach; red arsenic; varnish, lac; juniper-tree.

سندس *sundus*, brocade; silk interwoven with gold or silver; fine silk; — ى *sundusiyy*, of brocade.

سندوق **sundûq**, trunk, chest, portmanteau.
سندى **sindiyy**, of or from Sind.
سنديان **sindiyân**, holm-oak.
(سنر) *sanir*, A, INF. *sanar*, be obstinate, headstrong, peevish; — II. INF. *tasnîr*, id.
(سنسن) *sinsin*, thirst; pl. *sanâsin*, projecting part of a rib or vetebra; paddle.
(سنط) *sanuṭ*, INF. *sanâṭa-t*, be beardless.
سنط *sinṭ*, wrist; — *sanaṭ*, a thorny acacia; — *sunuṭ*, pl. of سناط *sinâṭ*, سنوط *sanûṭ*, and سنوطى *sanûṭa*.
سنطاب *sinṭâb*, sledge-hammer.
سنطلة *sanṭala-t*, length.
سنطير *sanṭîr*, harp; (m.) piano.
(سنع) *sanaʻ*, U, A, INF. *sunûʻ*, be finely and symmetrically made; be tall, slender; — *sanuʻ*, INF. *sanâʻa-t*, id.; — IV. INF. *isnâʻ*, beget handsome children; suffer pain in the wrist or ankle.
سنع *sinʻ*, pl. *sinaʻa-t*, *asnâʻ*, wrist, ankle; — *sanaʻ*, symmetry, fine proportion.
سنعا *sanaʻâʼ*, f. uncircumcised.
سنعبة *sunʻuba-t*, weasel; gland of the lip.
(سنف) *sanaf*, I, U, INF. *sanf*, gird the camel with the breast-harness; — IV. INF. *isnâf*, id.
سنف *sinf*, vetch, darnel; — *sunuf*, pl. of سناف *sinâf*; — ة *sinfa-t*, branch stripped of its leaves; leaf; pl. *sinf*, *sinafa-t*, skin or shell of a fruit, husk.
(سنق) *saniq*, A, INF. *sanaq*, have indigestion from milk; — IV. INF. *isnâq*, effeminate.
سنك *sunuk*, open highroads.
سنكر *sankar*, INF. ة, carry on the trade of a tinker; —ى *sankariyy*, pl. *sanâkira-t*, tinker; gipsy.
(سنم) *sanim*, A, INF. *sanam*, be tall and have a high hump, be high; — II. INF. *tasnîm*, make the camel to grow tall and high-humped; make a thing convex; fill; complete a sum; — V. INF. *tasannum*, mount the camel's back, ride upon it; ascend a height or summit, be on it; — VIII. INF. *istinâm*, id.
سنم *sanim*, high-humped; high; blossoming, blooming; — *sunnam*, cow; — ة *sanama-t*, top, summit; blossom.
سنمار *sinimmâr*, who does not sleep at night; moon; robber; name of a celebrated architect.
سنن *sanan*, camels which lift the front feet at the same time in running; road, path; career; custom, usage, rule of conduct; — also *sinan*, *sunan*, *sunun*, surface of the road; — *sunan*, pl. of سنة *sunna-t*.
(سنه) *sanih*, A, INF. *sanah*, have existed for many years, be advanced in age; — III. INF. *sinâh*, *musânaha-t*, bear fruit every second year; make a contract for a year with (acc.); — V. INF. *tasannuh*, be very old, antiquated, old-fashioned; be old, stale, deteriorated.
سنه *sanah*, pl. *sanahât*, *sanawât*, year.
(سنو) *sanâ*, U, INF. *sanw*, *sanâwa-t*, irrigate by means of the water-wheel or with the help of a camel; draw water; rain upon; flare and blaze; flash; open the door; — سنى *sanî*, A, INF. *sanâʼ*, be high, elevated, sublime; be celebrated, eminent, bright, beautiful; — II. INF. *tasniya-t*, raise, elevate; remove difficulties, make easy, facilitate; alleviate; — III. INF. *sinâʼ*, *musânât*, make a contract for a year with; hire for a year; — IV. INF. *isnâʼ*, raise, elevate; last or remain through the whole year, stay; — V. INF. *tasannî*, be easy to be done, come easily; change (n.), deteriorate; — VIII. INF. *istinâʼ*,

be afflicted with a year of famine; — x. INF. *istisnâ'*, find high, sublime, bright, beautiful, set high.

سنوا *sanwâ'*, f. sterile.

سنوات *sanawât*, pl. of سنة *sanah*.

سنوت *sanût*, irritable; liar; — *sannût*, *sinnaut*, cummin, caraway-seeds, fennel, anise; cream, cheese; honey.

سنوح *sunûḥ*, appearance, occurrence, happening (s.); sudden idea, occurring thought; manifestation, explanation; success.

سنور *sinnaur*, pl. *sanânîr*, cat; prince, head of the family; vertebra of the neck; base of the tail; — *sanawwar*, armour; coat of leather.

سنوط *sanûṭ*, سنوطى *sanûṭa*, pl. *sunuṭ*, *asnâṭ*, beardless.

سنون *sanûn*, wooden pencil for rubbing the teeth, tooth-pick; — also *sinûn*, *sunûn*, pl. of سنة *sana-t*.

سنونو *sunûnû*, swallow.

سنوى *sanawiyy*, ة, yearly.

سنى *sanî*, see (سنو); — *saniyy*, ة, high, sublime, noble; magnificent, splendid, precious; beautiful; — *sunniyy*, lawful; traditional; Sunnite.

سنيت *sanît*, barren, sterile.

سنيج *sanîj*, lamp.

سنيح *sanîḥ*, coming from the left and turning the right side towards the hunter; female ornaments.

سنيد *sanîd*, not genuine; adulterated; bastard.

سنيع *sanî'*, ة, of beautiful symmetry, finely proportioned; — ة *sanî'a-t*, pl. *sanâ'i'*, mountain-path.

سنين *sanîn*, ة, sharp, polished; lance; co-eval, of the same age; bare pasture-ground; obl. case of the pl. of سنة *sana-t*; — ة *sanîna-t*, pl. *sanâ'in*, wind; high sand-hill; — *sunaina-t*, little tooth.

(سه) *sah*, *sih*, the buttocks; their roundness.

سها *sihâ'*, pl. of سهو *sahw* and سهوة *sahwa-t*.

سهاد *suhâd*, sleeplessness.

سهار *suhâr*, waking at night (s.); — *sahhâr*, who remains awake; watchman.

سهاف *suhâf*, unquenchable thirst.

سهاك *sahhâk*, exceedingly eloquent, choice orator.

سهالة *sahâla-t*, facility, ease, INF. of (سهل).

سهام *sahâm*, summer-heat; gossamer; — *; — *suhâm*, emaciation; — *sahhâm*, archer.

سهاوة *sahâwa-t*, light step.

(سهب) *sahab*, INF. *sahb*, take; be lengthy in one's speech; — IV. INF. *ishâb*, lengthen; make many words, be lengthy; exceed the bounds; be exceedingly greedy; meet with sand instead of water in digging; pass. *suhib*, change colour from love-sickness or fear, go mad from the bite of a snake; — VIII. INF. *istihâb*, make many words; bestow many presents.

سهب *sahb*, vast desert; — also *sahib*, wide-stepping; — *suhb*, pl. *suhûb*, level ground; desert; — ة *sahba-t*, deep (adj.).

(سهج) *sahaj*, INF. *sahj*, pound, grind; blow violently, sweep the ground; travel all night.

سهج *suhhaj*, pl. of ساهج *sâhij*, ag. of the previous.

سهجر *sahjar*, INF. ة, run like one in fear.

(سهد) *sahid*, A, INF. *sahad*, be sleepless, awake through the night; — II. INF. *tashîd*, make sleepless.

سهد *suhud*, who sleeps little; very vigilant and prudent, circumspect; — ة *suhda-t*, sleeplessness.

(سهر) *sahir*, A, INF. *sahar*, wake the night through, be awake, wake with another at night;

watch over; — II. INF. *tashîr*, cause to wake; — III. INF. *musâhara-t*, wake with another, vie in remaining awake; — IV. INF. *ishâr*, cause to wake.

سهر *sahar*, waking, being awake (s.); — ة *sahra-t*, evening party; — *suhara-t*, sleepless.

سهران *sahrân*, awake.

(سهف) *sahaf*, INF. *sahf*, writhe in convulsions of agony; — *sahif*, A, INF. *sahaf*, suffer exceedingly of intense thirst; die; — VIII. INF. *istishâf*, make light of, value little.

(سهك) *sahak*, U, INF. *sahk*, blow violently and raise dust; grind; INF. *suhûk*, run swiftly and lightly; — *sahik*, A, INF. *sahak*, smell badly.

سهك *sahik*, ة, smelling from perspiration.

(سهل) *sahal*, come into or travel through the plain; — *sahul*, INF. *suhûla-t*, be level, smooth; INF. *sahâla-t*, be easy, facile, commodious, comfortable; — II. INF. *tashîl*, level, smooth; facilitate, render easy or possible; — III. INF. *musâhala-t*, be obliging, accommodating, complaisant towards; — IV. INF. *ishâl*, purge, ease the bowels, have stool; come into the plain; — V. INF. *tasahhul*, be level; be easy; make easy, ease, facilitate; — VI. INF. *tasâhul*, be facile, accommodating, friendly towards one another.

سهل *sahl*, pl. *suhûl*, plain (s.); f. ة, level (adj.); — also *sahil*, ة, easy; soft, smooth; ة *sahila-t*, having soft ground; — ة *sahla-t*, soft level ground; — *sihla-t*, gravel; stones in the bladder.

(سهم) *saham*, INF. *suhûm*, be thin, discoloured, pale; look austere, frown; win in the game of arrows; pass. *suhim*, fall in with the poisonous wind *samûm*, be exposed to the heat of the sun; — *sahum*, INF. *suhûma-t*, be thin and pale; pass. *suhim*, id.; — III. INF. *musâhama-t*, cast lots with; gamble with (acc.); have a share in, be a shareholder, a partner in a commercial company; agree with; assist; — IV. INF. *ishâm*, cast lots between; make many words; — VI. INF. *tasahum*, VIII. INF. *istihâm*, X. INF. *istishâm*, cast lots, divide between each other.

سهم *sahm*, pl. *sihâm*, arrow; lot, share, portion; lottery-ticket; cosine; principal beam of support in house or tent; mast; pl. *suhmân*, *suhma-t*, share, portion; — ة *suhma-t*, share, portion; kinship, relationship.

(سهن), pl. اسهان *ashân*, soft sand.

(سهو) *sahâ*, U, INF. *sahw*, *suhuww*, forget one thing over another, overlook, neglect; INF. *sahwa-t*, id.; — *sahû*, INF. *sahâwa-t*, get accustomed to be ridden, walk quietly; — III. INF. *musâhât*, neglect those present.

سهو *sahw*, forgetfulness, neglect, oversight, absence of mind; pl. *sihâ'*, tranquillity, mildness, modesty; play; f. ة, quiet, gentle; — ة *sahwa-t*, pl. *sihâ'*, rock; bench in front of the house; niche; small storeroom; tent; curtain.

سهوا *sahwâ'*, first watch of the night.

سهوان *sahwân*, forgetful, negligent, heedless, thoughtless.

سهوج *sahûj*, *sahwaj*, blowing violently.

سهود *sahûd*, *sahwad*, fresh, tender; big and strong.

(سهوق) *sahwaq*, liar; juicy, full of sap; long-legged; storm.

سهوك *sahwak*, INF. ة, hit deadly; — II. INF. *tasahwuk*, perish, die; walk slowly; — *sahûk*, storm; a species of the eagle; — ة *sahûka-t*, smell from perspiration.

سهول *sahûl*, purging, purgative; —

*; — ة *suhûla-t*, ease, facility, comfortableness; mildness, gentleness, softness.

سهوم *sahûm*, severe, austere, grim, frowning; an eagle; — *.

سهى *suhan*, small star in Ursa Major.

سهيل *suhail*, Canopus.

(سو) *sâ'*, U, INF. *sau'*, *sawâ'*, *sawâ'a-t*, *sawâya-t*, *sawâ'iya-t*, *masâ'*, *masâ'a-t*, *masâya-t*, *masâ'iya-t*, *masâ'iyya-t*, act badly, maltreat, injure; grieve (a.); be bad; displease; — IV. INF. *isâ'a-t*, treat badly, offend, grieve; make worse, spoil; — VIII. INF. *istiyâ'*, suffer evil.

سو *sau*, abbreviation for سوف *sauf*; — *sau'*, evil (s.); bad, evil (adj.); — *sû'*, pl. *aswâ'*, evil, calamity, malice, treachery; hell; — ة *su'a-t*, horn of the bow; — *sau'a-t*, bad action; pl. *sau'ât*, *sawwât*, pudenda.

سوا *sawâ*, pl. *aswâ'*, *sawâsiya-t*, سواس *sawâs-in*, *sawâsî*, *sawâsiwa-t*, equal, in pairs, coupled, together, the same; equality; mediocrity, middle; summit, top; another; except; — *siwâ*, equal; INF. of (سو); — ة *sau'a-t*, abomination, ugliness, ignominy; fornication; pudenda.

سوابى *sawâbî*, pl. of سابيا *sâbiyâ'*, membrane which surrounds the embryo in the womb, &c.

سوابيط *sawâbîṭ*, corridors, pl. of ساباط *sâbâṭ*.

سوات *sawwât*, pl. of سوة *sau'a-t*.

سواح *sawwâḥ*, traveller; — *suwwâḥ*, travellers, &c., pl. of سايح *sâyiḥ*.

سواخ *suwâḫ*, pl. سواخى *suwwâḫa*, soft yielding ground.

سواد *sawâd*, blackness; pl. *aswida-t*, *asâwid*, black point or dark figure in the distance; black mourning apparel; melancholy; populace, rabble; large crowd; distant tents, villages, towns; س العين *sawâd al-'ain*, the black of the eye; the beloved one; س القلب *sawâd al-qalb*, bottom of the heart, innermost thought, original sin; س البطن *sawâd al-baṭn*, liver; — *suwâd*, a disease.

سوادى *sawâdiyy*, inhabitant of a town, townsman.

سوار *siwâr*, *suwâr*, pl. *aswira-t*, *asâwir*, *asâwira-t*, *sûr*, *su'ûr*, bracelet, arm-ring; — *; — *suwâr*, sharpness, tartness, strength.

سواسوة *sawâsiwa-t*, سواسى *sawâsî*, pl. of سوا *sawâ'*.

سواط *sawwâṭ*, public scourger, executioner.

سواع *suwâ'*, first night-watch; a short time; rest, quiet; name of an idol.

سواغ *suwâg*, lawfulness, decency.

سواف *sawâf*, a cucumber; — *; — also *suwâf*, *su'âf*, fatal epidemic.

سوافك *sawâfik*, swords, pl. f. of سافكة *sâfika-t*, ag. of (سفك).

سوافل *sawâfil*, lower parts of the body, pl. f. of سافلة *sâfila-t*.

سوافين *sawâfîn*, pl. of سفون *safûn*, sweeping, &c.

سواق *sawwâq*, cattle-driver; who urges to haste; — *suwwâq*, pl. of سايق *sâyiq*, driver, &c.

سواك *siwâk*, the rubbing of the teeth; pl. *suwuk*, tooth-pick.

سوال *su'âl*, *suwâl*, pl. *as'ila-t*, *aswila-t*, question, request; — *su''âl*, beggars, pl. of سائل *sâ'il*; — *sawâll*, large valleys, pl. of سال *sâll*.

سوام *sawâm*, going to the pasture; — *; — ة *sawwâma-t*, cattle (m.).

سوامد الليل *sawâmid-u 'l-lail-i*, uninterrupted night-journeys.

سواى *sû'a*, f. ugly, horrid, abominable; hell-fire; evil, pain.

سوايا *sawâyâ*, pl. of سوى *sawiyy*, ة.

سواية *sawâya-t*, سوائية *sawâ'iya-t*, INF. of (سو).

سوب *su'ub*, skin bags, pl. of ساب *sa'b*; — ة *sûba-t*, long journey.

سوبان *su'bân*, manager, overseer, superintendent; — *sûbân*, name of a valley.

سوبيا *sûbiyâ'*, سوبيئة *sûbî'a-t*, سوبية *sûbiyya-t*, a cooling drink made of melon-kernels.

(سوج) *sâj*, U, INF. *sauj*, *suwâj*, *sawajân*, walk along slowly; INF. *sawajân*, come and go.

(سوجر) *saujar*, INF. ة, put the ساجور *sâjûr* (q.v.) to a dog's neck; — *saujar*, willow.

سوح *sûḥ*, court-yards, &c., pl. of ساحة *sâḥa-t*.

سوحل *sauḥal*, INF. ة, arrive at the sea-shore; land.

(سوخ) *sâḥ*, U, INF. *sauḥ*, *suwûḥ*, *sawaḥân*, sink in the mud; settle in the water as sediment; — INF. *suyûḥ*, *suwûḥ*, *sawaḥân*, swallow up.

(سود) *sâd*, U, INF. *sûd*, *sûdad*, *su'dud*, *siyâda-t*, *saidûda-t*, be head or leader of (acc.) a tribe, rule, command; — *sawid*, be black; — II. INF. *taswîd*, choose or invest as a chief, leader, prince; place in power; paint black, blacken, slander; make a first draft, a rough copy; be bold, courageous; (m.) manure a field; — III. INF. *musâwada-t*, vie with for the leadership or in blackness; — IV. INF. *isâda-t*, bear a son who becomes a chief or prince; — V. INF. *tasawwud*, be made a chief or prince; get blackened; marry; (m.) get manured; — VIII. INF. *istiyâd*, deprive a tribe of their chief or prince; — IX. INF. *iswidâd*, XI. INF. *iswîdâd*, be or get black.

سود *sûd*, dominion, leadership; pl. of اسود *aswad*, black.

سوداء *saudâ'*, black gall; melancholy, f. of اسود *aswad*.

سودان *sûdân*, negroes, pl. of اسود *aswad*; — ى *sûdâniyy*, negro-like, black; — ة *sudâniyya-t*, black sparrow.

سوداوى *saudâwiyy*, melancholic; hypochondriac (adj. s.).

سودد *sûdad*, *su'dud*, leadership, princeship, dominion, INF. of (سود).

سودل *saudal*, moustache; — *saudal*, INF. ة, have a long moustache.

سودن *saudan*, INF. ة, grieve (a.), sadden, make ill-tempered; — II. INF. *tasaudun*, be or become so.

سوذانق *sûẕâniq*, *sauẕâniq*, *sûẕânaq*, سوذانيق *sauẕânîq*, *suẕâniq*, سوذانوق *sauẕânuq* (also spelled with د), sparrow-hawk.

سوذق *sauẕaq*, bracelet; heart; — also *sûẕaq*, a species of falcon; link of a chain; — ى *sauẕaqiyy*, lively, sprightly, ardent, prudent, cunning.

(سور) *sâr*, U, INF. *saur*, scale the wall; leap against, attack; INF. *saur*, *suwûr*, get into one's head; — II. INF. *taswîr*, surround a place with walls, ramparts, &c.; adorn with bracelets; — III. INF. *siwâr*, *musâwara-t*, leap against, attack; — V. INF. scale the wall; be surrounded by walls, fortified; put on bracelets.

سور *sûr*, pl. *aswâr*, *sîrân*, wall, ramparts; — pl. of سوار *siwâr*; — *su'r*, pl. *as'âr*, anything left, rest, remainder; — ة *saura-t*, assault, attack; power of dominion; strength, severity, violence; also *sûra-t*, trace, mark, sign; — *sûra-t*, pl. *sûr*, *suwar*, rank, degree, dignity; high building; a layer of stones in a wall; pl. *suwar*, *sûrât*, chapter or verse of the Korân.

سورية *sûriya-t*, Syria.

(سوس) *sâs*, U, INF. *siyâsa-t*, rule a people, lead, command; direct; break in, lead, dress a horse, be groom; — A, INF. *saus*, and *sawis*, A, INF. *sawas* (II., IV., V., and pass. *sîs*), be eaten by or troubled with moths, worms,

lice, &c.; be carious; — II. INF. *taswîs*, see I.; make one a regent or governor; — IV. INF. *isâsa-t*, V. INF. *tasawwus*, see I.

سوس *sûs*, nature, natural disposition; root, origin; pl. *sîsân*, liquorice; noun of unity ة, moth, mite, worm; — ة *sûsa-t*, worm-holes; germ of discord; Susa.

سوسن *sausan*, *sûsan*, سوسان *sûsân*, lily.

(سوط) *sâṭ*, U, INF. *sauṭ*, whip, scourge; mix together; stir (a.); INF. *sawaṭân*, be oppressed, grieved; — II. INF. *taswîṭ*, mix together or stir about; — VIII. INF. *istiwâṭ*, be confused.

سوط *sauṭ*, pl. *siyâṭ*, *aswâṭ*, whip, scourge; punishment; pain; violence; severity; share, portion.

(سوطر) *sauṭar*, INF. ة, superintend, have the supervision.

(سوع) *sâ'*, U, INF. *sau'*, be allowed to pasture at large; — III. INF. *musâwa'a-t*, hire out one's services to another for an hour; — IV. INF. *isâ'a-t*, allow to pasture at large; neglect; lose; be delayed or put off from one hour to another.

سوع *sau'*, side; a part of the night.

سوعا *sau'â'*, disastrous hour; calamity; — *suwa'â'*, effusion of sperm.

(سوغ) *sâg*, U, INF. *saug*, *sawâg*, *suwâg*, *sawagân*, pass the throat easily, do good, be of easy digestion; be permitted, lawful, suitable, decent; — II. INF. *taswîg*, allow, permit, make convenient, decent; — IV. INF. *isâga-t*, make digestible; pass the throat easily; receive; — ة *sauga-t*, the next-born.

سوغان *sawagân*, lawfulness; decency.

(سوف) *sâf*, U, INF. *sauf*, smell at, sniff at, smell; exercise patience; — U, A, die of an epidemic; — II. INF. *taswîf*, smell or sniff at; say to one سوف *saufa*, i.e. it will be, the thing is feasible, delay, put off; — IV. INF. *isâfa-t*, lose the cattle by an epidemic; — VIII. INF. *istiyâf*, smell at, smell.

سوف *saufa* (abbreviated سو *sau*, س), placed before an aorist, changes it into future; — *sauf*, wish, desire, hope, patience; philosopher; — *sa'uf*, see (سأف); — ة *sûfa-t*, pl. *sûf*, *suwaf*, soft ground between a layer of stone and sand; ground, earth.

(سوق) *sâq*, U, INF. *sauq*, *siyâqa-t*, *siyâq*, *masâq*, drive, urge on, stir; send the dowry into the bride's house; — INF. *sauq*, *siyâq*, lie in the last gasps; hurt the leg; — V. INF. *tasawwuq*, carry on retail trade, trade in small goods; make purchases; — VII. INF. *insiyâq*, be driven; — VIII. INF. *istiyâq*, drive.

سوق *sauq*, driving (s.), impulse, carrying on (s.); — *sûq*, (m. f.), pl. *aswâq*, market, market-place, bazaar, public place; combat, boxing match, broil, dint of battle; pl. of ساق *sâq*, leg, &c.; — ة *sûqa-t*, pl. *suwaq*, common people, rabble of the market-place; subjects.

سوقا *sauqâ'*, f. of أسوق *aswaq*, long-legged.

سوقعة *sauqa'a-t*, hole at the top of a pudding with the sauce in it; edge, border, angle, corner.

سوقى *sûqiyy*, referring to the market, market-trader; plebeian; common.

(سوك) *sâk*, U, INF. *sauk*, rub, clean the teeth; — II. INF. *taswîk*, id.; — VIII. INF. *istiyâk*, clean one's teeth.

سوك *suwuk*, pl. of سواك *siwâk*.

(سوكر) *saukar*, INF. ة, assure a

house, goods, &c.; make a cigarette, smoke cigarettes (m.); — ة saukira-t, assurance of a house, &c.

(سول) *sâl*, A, INF. *siwâl*, *suwâl*, ask, demand; — *sawil*, A, INF. *sawal*, have a flabby hanging belly; — II. INF. *taswîl*, make covet, tempt.

سول *su'l*, *sûl*, thing in question, point of question; desire, wish, what seems desirable; — ة *saula-t*, flabbiness of the belly; dove-cot; — *su'la-t*, *sûla-t*, point in question, matter of debate; — *su'ala-t*, *suwala-t*, who asks many questions.

سولع *saula'*, bitter aloes.

(سوم) *sâm*, U, INF. *saum*, pasture at large; act to one's liking; pass by; fly around, hover around; impose anything difficult, force, impel; injure, do violence; — INF. *saum*, *suwâm*, ask or offer a price for, offer a higher price; — II. INF. *taswîm*, impose anything hard; allow the cattle to pasture at large; give to another the free management of one's cattle or fortune; allow one to act according to his own will; mark a horse by branding; — III. INF. *siwâm*, *musâwama-t*, quote a price, ask for the price, make an offer on it, offer more; — IV. INF. *isâma-t*, lead the cattle to the pasture, let graze; — VIII. INF. *istiyâm*, quote, make an offer on it, offer a higher one.

سوم *saum*, price; — ة *sûma-t*, id.; estimation, valuation; mark by branding.

(سومك) *saumak*, INF. ة, tie the vine to a stick (m.).

سوملة *saumala-t*, small cup.

(سون) *saun*, flabbiness of the belly; — V. *tasawwan*, INF. *tasawwun*, be flabby.

سوهق *sauhaq*, juicy, full of sap; liar; — ة *sauhaqa-t*, water-pipe; canal.

سوور *su'ûr*, ة *su'ûra-t*, pl. of سوار *siwâr*.

سووق *su'ûq*, legs, &c., pl. of ساق *sâq*.

سووم *sa'ûm*, languid, peevish, pettish.

(سوى) *sawa*, INF. *siwan*, intend, purpose; be worth, have the value of, cost; — II. INF. *taswiya-t*, make one thing equal to another, consider as equal, put on the same line, treat equally; level; create, shape, form; do, make; — III. INF. *musâwât*, equalise; bring about an agreement or reconciliation between two persons, settle between them what is right and satisfactory to both; — IV. INF. *iswâ'*, equalise; level; — V. INF. *tasawwî*, be made equal, be levelled; — VI. INF. *tasâwî*, be equal; be levelled; come to an agreement; — VIII. INF. *istiyâ'*, be equal; be in equilibrium; be moderate, just, equitable; be straightened; be in the prime; be patient; be ripe, well cooked; rise (to heaven); pass from one thing finished to something else; take hold of, get into possession of.

سوى *sawan*, *sawa*, intention, purpose, aim, end; — *siwa*, *suwa*, equal, same; middling; equality; justice; mediocrity; another; except; — *suwa*, straight and level; — *sau'a*, evil; badness, wickedness; — *sû'a*, bad action, evil deed; — *sawiyy*, ة, pl. *aswiyâ*, *sawâyâ*, equal, symmetrical, proportional, parallel; smooth and even; straight; whole, in good condition; — ة *sawiyya-t*, equality; levelness, straightness; pl. *sawâyâ*, pack-saddle.

سويد *suwaid*, blackish.

سويدا *suwaidâ'*, f. blackish, dark

black spot; coriander; grief; melancholy; سويداء القلب *suwaidâ' al-qalb*, bottom of the heart, original sin.

سويس *suwîs, suwais*, Suez.

سويطا *suwaiṭâ'*, broth with onions.

سويعاتى *suwai'âtiyy*, changing at every moment, fickle.

سويعة *suwai'a-t*, a little while.

سويق *sawîq*, pl. *aswiqa-t*, pounded wheat, oats, &c., in balls or in broth; wine.

سى *sai*=سو *sau*, abbreviated for سوف *sauf-a*; — *sai', sî'*, milk in the udder or flowing out by itself; — *sayy*, desert; — *sîyy*, id.; equal, du. *siyyân*, two equal things; pleasantness of life; — *sayyi'*, evil, bad; — ة *siya-t, si'a-t*, horn or notch of the bow; — *siyya-t*, equality, equal.

سياب *sayâb, sayyâb, suyyâb*, ة, unripe date; — ة *sayâba-t*, wine.

سياج *siyâj*, pl. *siyâjât, aswija-t, asyâj*, thorn-hedge; hedge, garden wall.

سياح *sayyâḥ*, traveller, pilgrim; — ة *siyâḥa-t*, long journey; pilgrimage.

سيادة *siyâda-t*, dominion; descent from Mohammed by Fatima.

سيار *sayyâr*, ة, who walks, wanders, travels much; traveller; — also ة *sayyâra-t*, travelling-company; planet;—*sayyâr*, door-post (m.).

سياس *siyâs*, administrators, grooms, &c., pl. of سايس *sâyis*; — *sayyâs*, who governs or administers well; —ة *siyâsa-t*, government; policy, politics; administration of justice, administration; courtliness; punishment, chastisement; — ى *sayâsiyy*, pl. سيسا *sîsâ'*; — *siyâsiyy*, ة, referring to government or administration; political.

سياط *siyâṭ*, pl. stalks of leek; — pl. of سوط *sauṭ*.

سياع *sayâ'*, juniper-tree; — *sayâ'*, *siyâ'*, clay mixed with straw for building purposes.

سياف *sayyâf*, pl. *sayyâfa-t*, sword-bearer; executioner; furbisher; — ى *sayâfî*, pl. of سيف *sîf*.

سياق *siyâq*, driving, urging on, INF. of (سوق); consequence; logical connection; state of things, case; course; reason; — ة *siyâqa-t*, counting by the letters as numerical signs.

سيال *sayyâl*, flowing rapidly; fluid; raining heavily; of a pure water (precious stone); a fish; — ة *sayâla-t*, pl. *siyâl*, a milky thorn-plant; — *sayyâla-t*, mountain-current.

سيان *siyyân*, du. of سى *sîyy*.

سيائد *sayâ'id*, lords, princes, pl. of سائد *sâ'id*.

سيائق *sayâ'iq*, pl. of سيقة *sayyiqa-t*.

(سيب) *sâb*, I, INF. *saib*, flow, run; run away, escape; walk briskly, glide; go at large, be left behind, abandoned; — II. INF. *tasyîb*, allow to pasture at large; leave behind, abandon, leave in the lurch; allow to escape; set free; — VII. INF. *insiyâb*, flow; walk apace, glide swiftly, go onward, go abroad; escape; be left behind or in the lurch; intrude.

سيب *saib*, flowing, streaming (s.), stream; pl. *suyûb*, favour, bounty, present; oar;—*sîb*, water-course; — *sa'ib* (v.), quench one's thirst, see (ساب); — *suyyab*, pl. of سائبة *sâ'iba-t*, set free.

(سيج), II. *sayyaj*, INF. *tasyîj*, hedge in; — V. INF. *tasayyuj*, pass.

سيجان *sîjân*, fillets, pl. of ساج *sâj*.

(سيح) *sâḥ*, I, INF. *saiḥ*, *sayaḥân*, flow on the surface of the ground, spread; melt; — INF. *saiḥ, suyûḥ, siyâḥa-t, sayaḥân*, travel, make long journeys or a pilgrimage, make off; — II. INF. *tasyîḥ*, make to flow, melt; — IV. INF. *isâḥa-t*, cause to stream; — VII. INF. *insiyâḥ*, enlarge (n.).

سيح *saiḥ*, pl. *suyûḥ*, *asyâḥ*, running water.

سيحان *sayaḥân*, travelling, flowing (s.); fusibility.

(سيخ) *sâḥ*, I, INF. *saiḥ*, *sayaḥân*, sink in anything soft; be firm, solid.

سيخ *sîḥ*, pl. *asyâḥ*, spit (for roasting); fork; table-knife.

سيد *sîd*, pl. *sîdân*, wolf, lion; — *sa'id*, (v.) drink, &c., see (ساد); — *sayyid* (m. *sîd*), pl. *sâda-t*, *sâdât*, *sayâ'id*, (m.) *asyâd*, master, lord, prince; title of a descendant from Mohammed through Fatima; liberal, mild; wise; — also *siyyad*, old goat; — ة *sayyida-t*, mistress, princess, particularly applied to Fatima, as the masc. *sayyid* to Mohammed.

سيدارة *sîdâra-t*, cloth worn by women between the hair and headgear.

سيدودة *saidûda-t*, dominion, INF. of (سود); descent from Mohammed through Fatima.

سيدى *sayyidî* (m. *sîdî*), sir! monsieur! — *sayyidiyy*, referring to a lord or master.

سيذاق *saiẕâq*, سيذقان *saiẕaqân*, سيذنوق *saiẕanûq*, سيذنيق *saiẕanîq*=سوذانق *sauẕâniq*.

(سير) *sâr*, I, INF. *sair*, *sairûra-t*, *tasyâr*, *masîr*, *masîra-t*, step along, pace, go, depart, travel; conduct one's self; cause to depart, to travel; — II. INF. *tasyîr*, cause to travel, send away; expel, drive off; bring into circulation, spread (a.), tell abroad; — III. INF. *masâyara-t*, vie in walking swiftly; travel with, converse with familiarity; — IV. INF. *isâra-t*, cause one to set out, to travel; — V. INF. *tasayyur*, travel or voyage afar; — VI. INF. *tasâyur*, travel in company; — VIII. INF. *istiyâr*, supply one's self for a journey.

سير *sair*, pl. *suyûr*, walk, march, travel, voyage; road; way, manner; spectacle, sight; pl. *suyûr*, strip of leather, strap, thong; — ة *sîra-t*, walk, pleasure-walk; pl. *siyar*, conduct, way of living; biography, chronic, romance; conversation; travelling-provisions; ways and means; measures; — *suyara-t*, who walks much.

سيران *sairân*, walk, pleasure-walk, country-trip; — *sîrân*, pl. of سور *sûr*.

سيرورة *sairûra-t*, walk, INF. of (سير).

سيس *sayis*, A, = سيس *sîs*, pass. of (سوس).

سيسا *sîsâ'*, pl. *sayâsiyy*, joining of the vertebræ; boundary, limit.

سيسان *sîsân*, pl. of سوس *sûs*.

سيطر *saiṭar*, INF. ة, be manager, overseer, superintendent, master; — II. INF. *tasaiṭur*, id.; govern.

سيطل *saiṭal*, bucket.

(سيع) *sâ'*, I, INF. *sai'*, *suyû'*, flow, dissolve, move (n.), undulate; pasture at large.

(سيغ) *sâg*, I, INF. *saig*, flow or glide easily down the throat.

(سيف) *sâf*, I, INF. *saif*, strike with the sword; be chapped; — III. INF. *musâyafa-t*, fight with; — IV. INF. *isâfa-t*, pierce; — VI. INF. *tasâyuf*, fight one another; — VIII. INF. *istiyâf*, strike with the sword.

سيف *saif*, pl. *suyûf*, *asyuf*, *asyâf*, *masîfa-t*, sword, sabre; — also *sîf*, sword-fish; — *sîf*, pl. *sayâfî*, *asyâf*, river-bank, sea-coast, shore; — *sa'if*, A, (v.) be chapped, &c., see (ساف); — *sa'if*, chapped.

سيفان *saifân*, ة, long and thin.

سيقان *sîqân*, legs, &c., pl. of ساق *sâq*.

سيقل *saiqal*, pl. *sayâqila-t*, polisher.

سيقية *saiqiyya-t*, booty taken from the enemy; pl. *sayâ'iq*, hiding-place of a hunter.

سيكارة *sîkâra-t*, cigarette (m.).

سيكف *saikaf*, shoe-maker.

سيكورتا *sîkûrtâ*, assurance (It. securita).

سيكون *saikûn*, small wood.

(سيل) *sâl*, I, INF. *sail*, *sayalân*, flow, run; stretch over the horse's forehead and nose (white spot); — II. INF. *tasyîl*, cause to flow, to stream; — IV. INF. *isâla-t*, id.

سيل *sail*, pl. *suyûl*, river, stream, torrent after a water-spout; running in streams (adj.); — ة *saila-t*, *sîla-t*, stream; heavy shower; water-spout; — *saila-t*, waistcoat-pocket (m.).

سيلان *sailân*, Ceylon;—*sîlân*, handle of a knife, hilt of a sword; — *sayalân*, flow, flux, INF. of (سيل).

سيم *sa'im*, (v.) be tired, weary, &c., see (سام); — *sa'im*, weary, annoyed; — *siyam*, pl. of سامة *sâma-t*, cavity of a well; — ة *sîma-t*, sign, mark; price; set rate.

سيما *sîman*, *sîma*, *sîmâ'*, sign, token, mark, stigma; — *sîmâ*, *siyya-mâ* (for سي ما *siyya mâ*), above all, especially, likewise.

سيمسنجرف *sîmasanjarf*, cinnabar; red ink.

سيمى *sîma*=سيما *sîmâ*.

سيميا *sîmiyâ*, natural magic; charm or spell of beauty; — *sîmiyâ'*, sign, mark.

سين *sîn*, name of the letter س; lock of hair, curl.

سيهج *saihaj*, سيهك *saihak*, سيهوج *saihûj*, سيهوك *saihûk*, violent.

سيورى *suyûriyy*, strap-maker, belt-maker.

سيى *sayyi'*, bad, evil, wicked; — ة *sayyi'a-t*, *sai'a-t*, malice, viciousness, crime; evil, pain; dearth and famine; panic.

سئيم *sa'îm*, weary, tired of.

ش

ش *ś*, as a numerical sign=300; abbreviation for شمال *śamâl*, north, and the month شعبان *śa'bân*.

شا *śâ'*, see (شو); — ة, شاة *śât*, pl. *śâ'*, *śiyâh*, *śiwâh*, *aśâwih*, شوى *śawa*, *śaih*, *śîh*, *śayyih*, شواهى *śawâha*, sheep; gelded ram; goat; deer; doe; ostrich; woman.

شاب *śâbb*, pl. *śabâb*, *śubbân*, *aśbâb*, *śababa-t*, young man, youth; f. ة, pl. *śawâbb*, young woman, girl; young.

شابر الميزان *śâbir-u 'l-mîzân-i*, thief.

شابك *śâbik*, intricate, complicated.

شابيب *śa'âbîb*, rain-storms, &c., pl. of شوبوب *śu'bûb*.

شات *śât-in*, شاتى *śâtî*, winterly, cold.

(شاج) *śa'aj*, INF. *sa'j*, grieve (a.).

شاجر *śâjir*, pl. شواجر *śawâjir*, ag. of (شجر); adversity.

شاجن *śâjin*, grieved; — ة *śâjina-t*, pl. *śawâjin*, way through a valley abounding in trees.

شاحح *śâḥiḥ*, miserly, avaricious, a niggard; not of full weight, too little.

شاحم *śâḥim*, seller of fat.

شاحن *śâḥin*, full; laden, freighted; full of hatred.

شاحية *śâḥiya-t*, pl. *śawâḥiyy*, yawning, opening the mouth wide, f.

شاخص *śâḫiṣ*, ag. of (شخص), traveller.

شاد *śâd-in*, see شادى *śâdî*; — *śâdd*, ag. of (شد); overseer, superintendent, governor.

شادح *śâdiḥ*, plentiful, abundant.

شادخ *śâdiḫ*, young and tender; — ة *śâdiḫa-t*, whiteness of a horse's forehead reaching to the nose.

شادروان *śâdrawân*, water-spout, fountain (Pers.).
شادن *śâdin*, young gazelle; pretty; — ة *śâdina-t*, also—
شادنج *śâdanaj*, blood-stone (Pers.).
شادى *śâdî* (شاد *śâd-in*), who sings well, singer, reciter, declaimer; driver.
شاذ *śâẕẕ*, ة, pl. *śuẕẕûẕ*, *śawâẕẕ*, solitary, secluded, alone; unusual, irregular, rare, wonderful; pl. exceptions; — ة *śâẕẕa-t*, rare reading.
شاذنج *śâẕanaj*, hemp-seed.
شار *śâr-in*, see شارى *śârî*; — ة *śâra-t*, figure, form; clothing; furniture; adornments; fatness.
شارب *śârib*, pl. *śarb*, *śurub*, *śurûb*, drinker, drunkard; weariness, languidness, weakness; pl. *śawârib*, moustache; — ة *śâriba-t*, inhabitants of the shore.
شارح *śâriḥ*, pl. *śurrâḥ*, commentator, glosser, annotator; rural policeman.
شارخ *śâriḫ*, pl. *śarḫ*, young man, youth.
شارد *śârid*, pl. *śarad*, f. ة, pl. *śawârid*, *śurrad*, fleeing, fugitive; deviating; slanting from; false, insidious; range.
شارز *śâriz*, pl. *śurrâz*, punisher, chastiser.
شارع *śâri'*, ة, pl. *śurra'*, *śurû'*, engaging in, beginning (adj.); going into the water; situated by the high-road; also ة *śâri'a-t*, high-road, large street; giver of a new law, prophet; — ة *śâri'a-t*, pl. *śawâri'*, pointed (lance); setting (star).
شارف *śârif*, pl. *śurraf*, of high rank, noble; wine-jar; pl. *śuruf*, temptation; — also ة *śârifa-t*, pl. *śawârif*, *śuruf*, *śurraf*, *śurûf*, decrepit.
شاروق *śârûq*, mortar, cement; ashes.
شارى *śârî* (شار *śâr-in*), buyer, purchaser; pl. شراة *śurât*, quarrelsome; schismatic (s.), heretic.

شارز *śa'âriz*, pl. of شعراز *śi'râz*, curdled whey, &c.
(شاز) *śa'az*, INF. *śa'z*, lie with; — شئز *śa'iz*, A, INF. *śa'z*, *śu'za-t*, be hard and rugged; be disquieted, agitated, frightened; pass. *śu'iz*, id.
شاز *śa'z*, rough, rugged, hard; ة, fat.
(شاس), شئس *śa'is*, A, INF. *śa'as*, be hard and firm; be hard and rugged.
شاس *śa's*, pl. شئيس *sa'îs*, *śu's*, rugged and stony; hard; — *śâss*, thin, lean; — ى *śâsi'*, rough, rugged, hard; cruel; — ية *śâsiya-t*, pl. *śawâsî*, cap worn under the turban.
شاش *śâś*, turban-cloth.
(شاشا) *śa'śa'*, call the ass to the water; fail to conceive or be fructified; — II. INF. *taśaśu'*, be dispersed; be low in the world, have deteriorated.
شاشية *śâśiya-t*, pl. *śawâśî*, small turban.
شاصب *śâṣib*, full of hardship, miserable; lean, thin.
شاصر *śâṣir*, pl. *aśṣâr*, young deer whose horns begin to sprout; — ة *śâṣira-t*, net, trap, snare, noose.
شاط *śâṭṭ*, ة, tall and straight; far; acting wrongly.
شاطر *śâṭir*, pl. *śuṭṭâr*, who torments or forsakes his family, his people; cunning, sly, impudent; bold, energetic, able, devil of a fellow; runner; chess-player.
شاطف *śâṭif*, missing (shot, &c.).
شاطل *śâṭil*, purge, purgative (s.).
شاطن *śâṭin*, wicked, bad, malicious, mischievous.
شاطى *śâṭi'*, pl. *śawâṭi'*, *śuṭ'ân*, river-bank, sea-shore.
شاع *śâ'-in*, see شاعى *śâ'î*; — ة *śâ'a-t*, published; woman.
شاعبان *śâ'ibân*, du. the shoulders.
شاعر *śâ'ir*, pl. *śu'arâ'*, poet; ة *śâ'ira-t*, poetess.

شاعل *śâ'il*, lighting, kindling (adj.); shining (adj.); — ة *śâ'ila-t*, pl. *śawâ'il*, flame, light.

شاعى *śâ'î* (شاع *śâ'-in*), ة, pl. *śawâ'i'*, far distant.

شاغر *śâgir*, pl. *śawâgir*, given up, undefended; camel-saddle.

شاغل *śâgil*, who occupies others; what requires attention.

(شاف), شئف *śa'if*, A, INF. *śa'af*, and pass. *śu'if*, suffer from an abscess on the sole; — INF. *śa'f*, *śa'fa-t*, hate.

شاف *śâf-in*, see شافى *śâfî*; — ة abscess on the sole of the foot from cauterisation; — *śa'afa-t*, pl. of شائف *śâ'if*.

شافع *śâfi'*, intercessor, defender; ة, seeing double.

شافعى *śâfi'iyy*, name of the founder of one of the four Mahommedan law schools; his follower; — ة *śâfi'iyya-t*, their sect.

شافه *śâfih*, thirsty.

شافى *śâfî* (شاف *śâf-in*), salutary, healing, curing; efficacious; satisfactory to the mind; sincere, truthful, clear, definite.

شاق *śâqq*, ة, troublesome, difficult, hard, enforced (labour); splitting, cleaving (adj.).

شاقل *śâqul*, شاقول *śâqûl*, stick with an iron point; pendulum; plummet.

شاقى *śâqî*, pl. *śawâqî*, high; mountain-knoll; miserable; criminal.

شاك *śâk*, fully armed; — *śâk-in*, see شاكى *śâkî*; —*śâkk*, pl. *śukkâk*, fully armed; prickly, thorny.

شاكر *śâkir*, who thanks, praises; thankful; valet de place; — ة *śâkira-t*, bag, pouch, pocket; — ى *śâkiriyy*, pl. ة, servant; follower, partisan, disciple.

شاكل *śâkil*, similarity; road; — ة *śâkila-t*, figure, form; pl. *śawâkil*, membrane of the hypochondres of a horse; side, parts, direction; intention, purpose; road, rule, way, manner; way of thinking, belief, creed.

شاكى *śâkî* (شاك *śâk-in*), fully armed.

شالج *śâlij*, *śâlaj*, half a قفيز *qafîz*, q.v.

شالم *śâlam*, vetch, darnel.

شالوق *śâlûq*, landslip; waterfall (m.).

(شام) *śa'am*, be of bad omen or augury, unauspicious, unpropitious; — شوم *śa'um*, and pass. شئم *śu'im*, id.; pass. be hated by (على *'ala*); — IV. INF. *iś'âm*, travel to Syria; — V. INF. *taśa''um*, pass one's self for a Syrian; — VI. INF. *taśâ'um*, come to Syria; consider as a bad omen, augur evil from (ب *bi*).

شام *śâm*, *śa'am*, Syria; Damascus; *śâm*, ة, smelling (adj.); — ة *śâma-t*, pl. *śâm*, *śâmât*, *śiyâm*, *śiyâmât*, black spot or mole, spot; stain, blemish; speck in the moon; sign, mark; black she-camel; — *śa'ma-t*, left side; Syria; Damascus; bad omen, calamity, ignominy; — *śa'âma-t*, misfortune, calamity; — *śâmma-t*, nose.

شامت *śâmit*, rejoicing in another's misfortune; malignant.

شامخ *śâmiḥ*, pl. *śummaḥ*, f. ة, pl. *śawâmiḥ*, high, sublime; pl. *śawâmiḥ*, heights.

شامظ *śâmiẓ*, pl. *śummaẓ*, *śawâmiẓ*, pregnant; fructified; scorpion.

شامس *śâmis*, pl. *śums*, *śawâmis*, given to throwing off the rider, restive.

شامط *śâmiṭ*, large pot holding a whole sheep.

شامل *śa'mal*, north; — *śâmil*, extended and comprehensive; general; implicated, concerned in; allied.

شامى *śa'miyy*, *śa'âmiyy*, *śâmiyy*, ة, Syriac (adj.), Syrian (s.); native of Damascus; — ة *śa'miyya-t*, &c., the Syrians.

(شان) *śa'an*, INF. *śa'n*, notice, remark, take into regard; purpose, aim at; perform well and intel-

ligently; announce, report, make known; destroy, spoil; — VIII. INF. *iśti'ân*, intend, purpose.

شان *śa'n*, pl. *śu'ûn*, *śi'ân*, thing, matter, affair; intention, purpose; regard; quality, nature, habit, disposition; estimation, honour, dignity, rank; will, pleasure; pl. *śu'ûn*, joining of the seams of the skull; pl. *aś'un*, *śu'n*, strips of fertile ground on mountains.

شانب *śânib*, having fresh teeth and a sweet breath.

شانف *śânif*, hater; traitor.

شانئ *śâni'*, pl. *śunnâ'*, *śunât*, hater, enemy; — *śa'niyy*, referring to one's rank, authority, &c.

شاه *śâh*, *śah-in* = شاهى *śâhî*; — *śâh*, king, king in chess (Pers.).

شاهانى *śâhâniyy*, kingly, royal.

شاهب *śâhib*, ash-coloured.

شاهد *śâhid*, pl. *śuhûd*, *śuhhad*, *śahd*, *aśhâd*, *śawâhid*, eye-witness, anyone present, evidence; martyr; notary; — ة *śâhida-t*, pl. *śawâhid*, female witness; text quoted as evidence; earth.

شاهدانج *śâhdânaj*, شاهدانق *śâhdânaq*, hemp-seed.

شاهق *śâhiq*, ة, high; braying; artery; — ة *śâhiqa-t*, pl. *śawâhiq*, high mountain-range, mountain-summits.

شاهنشاه *śâhinśâh*, king of kings (Pers.).

شاهى *śâhî* (شاه *śâh*, *śâh-in*), penetrating, sagacious; — *śâhiyy*, referring to sheep; — ة *śâhiya-t*, a falcon, hawk.

شاهين *śâhîn*, pl. *śawâhîn*, *śawâhîn*, white falcon, royal hawk; beam or tongue of a balance.

(شاو), شاى *śa'a* (pret. *śa'au-tu*), INF. *śa'w*, precede, go in advance, get the lead; remove mud and earth out of a well; — V. INF. *taśa''uw*, be separated; — VIII. INF. *iśti'â*, hear, listen; get the lead.

شاو *śa'w*, basket; extreme limit; ultimate aim; — *śâw-in*, شاوى *śâwî*, who roasts meat; — *śâwiyy*, referring to sheep; abounding in sheep; — ة *śâwiyya-t*, dried up, withered; refuse.

شاى *śa'a*, see (شاو).

شائب *śâ'ib*, hoary, grey-haired; who mixes, brings into confusion; — ة *śâ'iba-t*, pl. *śawâ'ib*, dirt, mud, impurity, pollution; blemish, flaw; mixed hue; suspicion; abomination; calamity.

شائع *śâ'i'*, spread about, become public; celebrated; belonging to several in common.

شائف *śâ'if*, pl. *śa'afa-t*, who hates, enemy; (m.) who sees, perceives.

شائق *śâ'iq*, exciting desire; loved; desirable, charming.

شائك *śâ'ik*, thorny, pricking (adj.); fully armed.

شائل *śâ'il*, pl. *śuwwal*, who lifts up, takes away, carries off; pl. *śuwwal*, *śuyyal*, *śiyyal*, *śiwâl*, milkless.

شائم *śâ'im*, left; portending calamity; who watches.

شائه *śâ'ih*, sagacious, penetrating; lynx.

(شب) *śabb*, I, INF. *śabâb*, *śabîba-t*, grow up, become a young man; — U, INF. *śabb*, *śubûb*, light a fire, kindle; stir up, excite; act. and pass. *śubb*, be kindled and burn; be high; — U, I, INF. *śibâb*, *śubûb*, *śabîb*, leap briskly, lifting the front feet at the same time, leap, overleap one's self with (ب *bi*); — II. INF. *taśbîb*, praise the beauty of the beloved; — IV. INF. *iśbâb*, have young men for sons; be old; — V. INF. *taśabbub*, compose love-poetry, make gallant verses in praise of a woman.

شب *śabb*, vitriol; alum; height; — *śibb*, young wild bullock; — ة *śabba-t*, pl. *śabâ'ib*, young girl, damsel.

شبا *śaban*, water-moss ; — ة *śabât*, pl. شبا *śaban*, شبى *śaba*, *śabawât*, top or end of anything, edge ; sting of a scorpion ; a species of scorpion ; — *śab'a-t*, bolt of a lock.

شباب *śabâb*, growing up (s.), youth, prime ; — * ; — *śibâb*, skipping ; — ة *śibâba-t*, *śabbâba-t*, reed-pipe, flute.

شبابيك *śabâbîk*, pl. of شباك *śabbâk*, ة.

شبارق *śabâriq*, torn ; — *śubâriq*, id. ; drawers, pants ; — *.

شباط *śubâṭ*, February.

شباع *śibâ'*, pl. of شبعان *śab'ân* ; — ة *śaba'a-t*, *śabâ'a-t*, satiation ; — *śubâ'a-t*, what remains after the eaters are satisfied.

شباك *śibâk*, trellis-work ; lattice windows ; pl. of شبكة *śabaka-t*.

شباك *śubbâk*, ة *śubbâka-t*, pl. *śabâbîk*, net, net- or trellis-work ; lattice-work of a window, window.

شبام *śibâm*, gag ; muzzle ; string for fastening the veil.

شبان *śubbân*, pl. of شاب *śâbb*.

شباه *śibâh*, pl. of شبيه *śabîh* ; — ة *śabâha-t*, similarity, resemblance.

شبائب *śabâ'ib*, pl. of شبة *śabba-t*.

شبائح *śabâ'iḥ*, wooden framework of a camel-saddle.

شبب *śabab*, young of cattle or sheep ; — ة *śababa-t*, pl. of شاب *śâbb*.

(شبت) *śabit*, anise.

(شبث) *śabis̱*, A, INF. *śabas̱*, adhere, stick to, hold fast with the hands, claws, &c., clutch ; — V. INF. *taśabbus̱*, id. ; take a firm grip of, bring every means to bear upon ; be attached.

شبث *śabas̱*, scolopendra, milliped ; sea-spider ; — *śabis̱*, adhering firmly, holding in a firm grip ; also ة *śubas̱a-t*, faithfully attached ; — *śibiss*, anise.

شبج *śabaj*, high door or doors ; — IV. *aśbaj*, INF. *iśbâj*, repel, refuse, turn off.

شبح *śabaḥ*, INF. *śabḥ*, split, cleave asunder ; extend a skin between pegs ; stretch out the hand, the arms ; stand ready for service before (ل *li*) ; — *śabuḥ*, INF. *śabâḥa-t*, be broad in the arms ; stretch one's self ; — II. INF. *taśbîḥ*, spread ; extend and stretch (a.) ; enlarge, widen ; have weak sight, see double or confusedly.

شبح *śabḥ*, *śabaḥ*, extension, width ; — *śabaḥ*, pl. *aśbâḥ*, *śubûḥ*, indistinct object in the distance ; figure, form ; phantom ; high door ; — ة *śabḥa-t*, ring lined with felt to tie up a horse by.

شبحان *śabḥân*, long.

شبخ *śabḫ*, sound produced by milking.

(شبدع) *śibdi'*, *śibda'*, ة, pl. *śabâdi'*, scorpion ; tongue ; çalamity.

(شبذر) *śabẕar*, a species of clover.

(شبر) *śabar*, I, U, INF. *śabr*, measure by the span ; give, bestow ; — *śabir*, A, INF. *śabar*, be boisterously merry ; — II. INF. *taśbîr*, measure by the span ; make gestures, gesticulate ; — IV. INF. *iśbâr*, give.

شبر *śabr*, wedlock ; matrimonial right ; morning-gift, dowry ; fee of a courtesan ; also *śibr*, life, age ; — *śibr*, pl. *aśbâr*, span between index and thumb (قصير الشبر *qaṣîr aś-śibr*, small, dwarfish) ; — *śabar*, gift ; sacrifice ; mass (church-service) ; wealth, power ; gospel.

شبرذة *śabraẕa-t*, swiftness, quickness (m.).

(شبرق) *śabraq*, INF. ة, *śibrâq*, tear (a.) ; cut into pieces ; tear the prey ; — II. INF. *taśabruq*, dress one's self up ; get one's self ready.

شبرق *śabraq*, pl. *śabâriq*, *śabârîq*, torn ; rags, tatters.

شبرم *śubrum*, a plant with a milky

root and lentil-like seed; also *śabram*, short.

شبريات *śabriyât*, riding-basket on the camel.

(شبزق) *śabzaq*, possessed and thrown down by the devil.

(شبشب) *śabśab*, INF. ة, complete.

(شبص) *śabaṣ*, roughness; — V. INF. *taśabbuṣ*, be closely entwined.

شبص *śabṣ*, being (s.) closely entwined.

(شبط) *śabaṭ*, INF. *śabṭ*, draw magic lines in the sand; sweep away; make incisions, cup; (m.) efface, blot out.

شبع *śabi'*, A, INF. *śab'*, *śiba'*, *śaba'*, eat one's fill; be satiated, satisfied; be tired of a thing, disgusted with it; — *śabu'*, INF. *śabâ'a-t*, be vigorous; — II. INF. *taśbî'*, satiate, satisfy; colour richly; — IV. INF. *iśbâ'*=II.; — V. INF. *taśabbu'*, surfeit, cram into one's self; feign to be satisfied; boast of riches.

شبع *śab'*, *śiba'*, satiety; — *śib'*, *śaba'*, ة *śub'a-t*, what satiates.

شبعان *śab'ân*, f. ة, and شبعى *śab'a*, pl. *śibâ'*, satiated, full.

(شبق) *śabiq*, INF. *śabaq*, be voluptuous, lecherous, libidinous; loathe.

شبق *śabaq*, lewdness, voluptuousness, lust; — *śabiq*, lecherous, libidinous; — *śubuq*, pipe-tube; switch, rod (m.).

شبك *śabak*, I, INF. *śabk*, put one thing into another, entwine, entangle, involve; — INF. *śubûk*, be intricate, entangled; — II. INF. *taśbîk*, entangle, entwine, knit together; — V. INF. *taśabbuk*, pass. of the previous; — VI. INF. *taśâbuk*, get mutually entangled, entwined, knit together; — VIII. INF. *iśtibâk*=V.; be in many ways related; — ة *śabaka-t*, pl. *śabak*, *śibâk*, fishing-net; knit veil; network; trellis, trelliswork; noose; complication, intricacy, confusion; — *śabka-t*, family connection, relationship.

(شبل) *śibl*, pl. *aśbâl*, *śubûl*, *śibâl*, *asbul*, cub, whelp; — *śabal*, INF. *śubûl*, grow, grow tall; grow up under favourable circumstances; — II. INF. *taśbîl*, sew with large stitches, stitch together; — IV. INF. *iśbâl*, favour, assist (على *'ala*).

(شبم) *śabam*, U, INF. *śabm* (also II.), gag the kid to prevent it from sucking; gag; — *śabim*, A, INF. *śabam*, be cold; be chilly, frozen; — II. INF. *tasbîm*, see I.

شبم *śabim*, cold, fresh; ة, fat; — *śibamm*, gag.

(شبن) *śaban*, be tender, delicate; be near, approach.

(شبه) *śabih*, A, INF. *śabah*, be similar, resemble; — II. INF. *taśbîh*, compare; assimilate; make or represent two things so much alike as to be distinguished with difficulty; cause uncertainty and doubt; — III. INF. *muśâbaha-t*, be similar, resemble; — IV. INF. *iśbâh*, id.; — V. INF. *taśabbuh*, resemble, allow of comparison; imitate; — VI. *taśâbuh*, resemble one another; be obscure, doubtful; — VII. INF. *inśibâh*, get doubtful or uneasy about a matter, grow suspicious with regard to (فى *fî*); — VIII. INF. *iśtibâh*, resemble; be obscure, doubtful.

شبه *śibh*, *śabah*, pl. *aśbâh*, *maśâbih*, similarity; anything similar, alike, like to; likeness, figure; anything uncertain, doubtful; brass; — *śabah*, pl. *aśbâh*, a large tree; of brass; — ة *śubha-t*, pl. -*ât*, *śubah*, similarity; uncertainty, doubt, objection, suspicion; anything obscure, ambiguous, allowing of different interpretations; — ى *śibhiyy*, of brass.

(شبو) *sabâ*, U, INF. *śabw*, be high,

elevated, sublime; stand upright on the hind legs; be bright again; light a fire; — شبى *śaba*, A, INF. *śab-an*, cover the mare (m.); — IV. INF. *iśbâ'*, give, bestow, present with; favour, honour.

شبوات *śabawât*, pl. of شباة *śabât*.

شبوب *śabûb*, youthful and vigorous; — *.

شبوبية *śabûbiyya-t*, youth, youthfulness.

شبور *śabbûr*, a kind of trumpet.

شبوط *śabûṭ*, *śabbûṭ*, *śubbûṭ*, pl. *śabâbîṭ*, perch (fish).

شبوق *śabbûq*, young tree; young oak-tree.

شبى *śaba*, v. see (شبو).

شبيبة *śabîba-t*, شبيبية *śabîbiyya-t*, youth, youthfulness.

شبيط *śabîṭ*, perch (fish).

شبيع *śabî'*, satiated, full, well provided; richly dyed; robust, blunt.

شبيكة *śabîka-t*, net or trelliswork; net.

شبين *śabîn*, god-father, sponsor.

شبيه *śabîh*, pl. *śibâh*, *asbâh*, similar; uncertain, doubtful, ambiguous; likeness, image, portrait; شبيه معين *śabîh ma'în*, rhomboid.

(شت) *śatt*, I, INF. *śatt*, *śatât*, *śatît*, separate, scatter, disperse; INF. *śatt*, *śatât* (also V.), be separated, scattered, dispersed; be absent-minded; — II. INF. *taśtît*=I.; divert or distract the mind; — V. INF. *taśattut*, see I.; — VII. INF. *inśitât*, VIII. INF. *iśtitât*, be separated, dispersed.

شت *śatt*, pl. *aśtât*, *śutût*, separate, scattered, dispersed; separation, dispersion; *aśtât-an*, in divisions; شتوت من الناس *śutût min an-nâs*, different classes of men.

شتا *śatan*, entrance of a valley; — *śitâ'*, pl. *śutiyy*, *aśtiya-t*, winter, rainy season; cold; rain; pl. of شتوة *śatwa-t*.

شتات *śatât*, dispersion, INF. of (شت); scattered means; *śatât-a śatât-a*, in scattered groups.

شتام *śattâm*, impudent reviler; — ة *śatâma-t*, ugliness, repulsiveness, INF. of (شتم).

شتان ما بين *śattân mâ bain*, what a difference between— !

(شتر) *śatar*, I, INF. *śatr*, cut or tear into irregular pieces; mangle, wound, hurt, abuse; — *śatir*, A, INF. *śatar*, be cut, torn, ragged, tattered; be wrinkled, shrivelled; (also VII.) be chapped, have chapped eye-lids or lips; — II. INF. *taśtîr*, revile, slander; — VII. INF. *inśitâr*, see I.; be cut, torn, mangled.

شتر *śatar*, being chapped or inversed (of the eye-lids); — ة *śutra-t*, space between two fingers.

(شتع) *śati'*, A, INF. *śata'*, be depressed, dejected, fretful.

(شتغ) *śatag*, I, INF. *śatg*, tread under foot, give over to contempt; subdue; — IV. INF. *iśtâg*, spoil.

(شتل) *śatal*, INF. *śatl*, plant cabbage, greens, &c.

شتل *śatl*, ة, plant; stalk; ش قرنفل *śatla-t qaramful*, carnation-plant.

(شتم) *śatam*, U, I, INF. *śatm*, *maśtama-t*, *maśtuma-t*, abuse, revile, inveigh against; — *śatum*, INF. *śatâma-t*, be ugly, repulsive; — II. INF. *taśtîm*, revile, abuse; — III. INF. *muśâtama-t*, inveigh against; — VI. INF. *taśâtum*, revile one another.

شتم *śatm*, pl. *śutûm*, invective, abuse.

(شتن) *śatan*, U, INF. *śatn*, weave.

(شتو) *śatâ*, U, INF. *śatw*, pass the winter, winter, hibernate; suffer from want in winter; — II. INF. *taśtiya-t*, hibernate; suffice for the winter; rain; — IV. set in (winter); suffer from want in winter-time; — V. INF. *taśattî*, hibernate.

هتوة *śatwa-t*, pl. *śitâ'*, winter.

هتوى *śatwiyy, śatawiyy*, ة, winterly; — ة *śatawiyya-t*, winter.

هتى *śatta* (sing. pl. and ad.), dispersed, scattered, manifold, diverse, mixed; مكتب صنائع ش *maktab ṣanâ'i' śatta*, polytechnic school; — *śatiyy*, winter-rain; — *śutiyy*, pl. of هتا *śitâ'*; — ة *śatiyya-t*, winter.

هتيت *śatît*, pl. *śatta*, separate, dispersed, scattered; separation, INF. of (هت).

هتيم *śatîm*, abused, reviled; despised, worthless; ugly, repulsive, horrid; — ة *śatîma-t*, pl. *śatâ'im*, abuse, invective, revilement.

هث *śass*, an aromatic herb used for tanning; wild nut; bee; pl. *śisâs*, broken column of a rock.

هثا *śasan*, entrance of a valley.

(هثر) *śasir*, A, INF. *śasar*, be disfigured by a tubercle on the eye-lids.

هثر *śisr*, pl. *śusûr*, mountain-knoll; summit; — *śasir*, broken.

(هثل) *śasil*, A, INF. *śasal*, be thick; — *śasul*, INF. *śasâla-t*, id.

(هثن) *śasin*, A, INF. *śasan*; — *śasun*, INF. *śasan, śusûna-t*, be hard and rough, be callous; have hard lips from eating thorns.

هثير *śasîr*, what a stream carries away.

(هج) *śajj*, U, I, INF. *śajj*, cleave or break the head; be wounded or scarred; plough the sea; traverse the desert; mix the wine with water; — II. INF. *taśjîj*, cleave the head; — III. INF. *muśâjja-t*, cleave or try to cleave one's head.

هج *śajj-in*, see هجى *śajî*; — ة *śujja-t*, pl. *śijâj*, broken skull, wound in the head.

هجا *śajan*, what sticks in the throat and causes anguish; anguish, chimera; — ة *śajâ'a-t*, anguish, anxiety.

هجاب *śijâb*, wooden tripod or trestle for washed linen, &c., towel-horse; stopper.

هجاذ *śajâẕ*, fine rain.

هجار *śijâr*, wooden bolt; deal boards of a floor; wooden gag; also *śajâr*, pl. *śujur*, framework of a camel-litter; open litter; — *.

هجاع *śajâ', śijâ', śujâ'*, ة, pl. *śaj'a-t, śij'a-t, śuj'a-t, śaja'a-t, śij'ân, śuj'ân*, bold, courageous, brave; — ش نجاع *śujâ' nujâ'*, courageous, brave; — *śujâ', śijâ'*, pl. *śij'ân, śuj'ân*, a species of snake; — *śijâ'*; pl. of هجيع *śajî'*.

هجاعة *śajâ'a-t*, bravery, courage, boldness.

(هجب) *śajab*, U, INF. *śujûb*, perish; — U, INF. *śajb*, doom to destruction, ruin; (m.) sentence to death; grieve; occupy; stretch, lengthen, pull out; stop; (m.) carry off, take along with one's self; — *śajib*, A, INF. *śajab*, perish; be grieved, sorrowful.

هجب *śajab*, ruin, perdition, destruction; misfortune; sentence of death; grief, sorrow; column; dry skin bag; long; — *śajib*, perishing, doomed; grieved.

هجذة *śajẕa-t*, gentle rain.

هجر *śajar*, U, INF. *śajr*, turn aside from (a.), avert, estrange; refuse, keep off, hinder; be disputed between; tie up, chain to (الى *ila*); prop up; support; open; force the beast to open the mouth by pulling the reins; pierce; — *śajir*, A, INF. *śajar*, be many, numerous; paint over with foliage and flowers; get filled with new-grown trees; — III. INF. *muśâjara-t*, quarrel with; gnaw a tree; graze off all the herbs; — IV. INF. *iśjâr*, abound in trees or stalk plants; — VI. INF. *taśâjur*, differ in opinion, dispute, quarrel; pierce one another

with lances; — VIII. INF. iśtijâr, place the hand to the chin.

شجر śajr, object of dispute, disputed matter or question; pl. aśjâr, śujûr, śijâr, chin; corner of the mouth, opening of the mouth; — śajar, palate; — śajar, śijar, ة, pl. aśjâr, plant with a woody stalk, tree; — śajir, woody, abounding in trees; — ى śajariyy, ة, referring to trees; tree-like, of a tree; referring to the palate, palatal; — ية śajariyya-t, plantation of trees; pleasure-grove, nursery, shrubbery, orchard.

(شجع) śaja', INF. śaj', surpass in courage and bravery; — śaju', INF. śajâ'a-t, be courageous, brave; — II. INF. taśjî', encourage; deem brave; — V. INF. taśajju', show one's self brave; play the part of the brave; take courage.

شجع śuji', ة, courageous, brave; brisk, alert, nimble; — śuju', pl. of اشجع aśja' and شجيع śajî', brave, courageous; — ة śaj'a-t, &c., pl. of شجاع śajâ'.

شجعا śaj'â, f. of اشجع aśja', — śuja'â', pl. of شجيع śajî', see above.

شجعان śij'ân, śuj'ân, pl. of شجاع śajâ', شجيع śajî'.

شجعم śaj'am, lion; long; neck.

(شجغ) śajag, INF. śajg, move the feet quickly.

(شجم) śajam, ruin, perdition, death.

(شجن) śajan, U, INF. śajn, prevent, hinder from; INF. śajn, śujûn, grieve (a.), cause anxiety; be intertwined; — śajin, A, INF. śajan; — śajun, INF. śujûn, be grieved, sorrowful; — II. INF. taśjîn, grieve (a.), render sorrowful, sadden; — IV. INF. iśjân, id.; — V. INF. taśajjun, be intertwined.

شجن śajan, pl. śujûn, aśjân, grief, pain, sorrow; urgent business; branch, branching (s.), ramification; pl. śujûn, by-paths; ways, ways and means, intentions; ذو شجون zû śujûn, intricate, complicated, mixed; — ة śajna-t, śijna-t, śujna-t, ramification, branch.

(شجو) śajâ, U, INF. śajw, grieve deeply, cause anguish, and, by opposition, excite intensely by anything joyful; overcome, conquer, subdue; be disputed, stir up discord; — شجى śajî, A, INF. شجا śajan, be grieved, in anxiety; have a fit of suffocation, of asthma; choke; — IV. INF. iśjâ', excite intensely by anything sad or joyful; rebuke, torment.

شجوا śajwâ', desert difficult to traverse.

شجوب śajûb, f. oppressed of heart.

شجى śajî, v., see (شجو); — śajî (شج śajjin), śajiyy, ة, grieved, anxious, in anxiety; pre-occupied, engrossed; صوت شجى ṣaut śajî, harmonious voice.

شجيج śajîj, split, broken, wounded in the head.

شجير śajîr, ة, abounding in trees or plants with a stalk; strange; — ة śujaira-t, little tree, shrub.

شجيع śajî', pl. śuju', śijâ', śij'ân, śuj'ân, śuja'â', f. ة, pl. śajâyi', courageous, brave.

(شح) śaḥḥ (pret. śaḥaḥ-tu), U, I, — (pret. śaḥiḥ-tu), A, INF. śaḥḥ, be greedy, avaricious, a niggard; subside and yield but little more water; — III. INF. muśaḥḥa-t, show one's self miserly towards (على 'ala); — VI. INF. taśâḥuḥ, grudge one another a thing.

شح śuḥḥ, śaḥḥ, śiḥḥ, avarice; decrease, lessening (s.); — ة śiḥḥa-t, what is niggardly guarded.

شحا śaḥan, wide, spacious.

شحاج śaḥḥâj, braying (adj.); بنات ش banât-u śaḥḥâj-in, mules.

شحاح śaḥâḥ, miserly, avaricious; a little; shallow; sterile; — śiḥâḥ, pl. of شحيح śaḥîḥ; — *

شحاذ *śaḥḥâẓ*, obtrusive beggar; intruder; grinder; — ة *śiḥâza-t*, beggary; obtrusiveness.

شحار *śaḥḥâr*, soot; blackish ground.

شحارير *śaḥârîr*, pl. of شحرور *śuḥrûr*.

شحاطة *śaḥḥâṭa-t*, line, stroke, trace; (m.) phosphoric match.

شحام *śaḥḥâm*, seller of fat, &c.; — ة *śaḥâma-t*, fatness, INF. of (شحم).

شحاف *śiḥâf*, milk.

(شحب) *śaḥab*, scrape off the ground with a shovel; *śaḥab*, *śaḥub*, INF. *śuḥûb*, *śuḥûba-t*, also pass. *śuḥib*, be changed, disfigured by exertion, hunger, illness.

شحتار *śaḥtâr*, soot (m.).

شحتر *śaḥtar*, INF. ة, blacken with soot (m.).

شحتلة *śaḥtala-t*, pinch of snuff.

شحج *śaḥaj*, A, I, INF. *śaḥâj*, *śaḥîj*, *śaḥajân*, bray, cry out; have a rough voice.

شحدد *śuḥdud*, شحدود *śuḥdûd*, malicious.

(شحذ) *śaḥaẓ*, INF. *śaḥẓ*, sharpen, whet, grind; burn the stomach; sharpen the appetite; importune with solicitations; ask for alms, beg; throw a glance at; urge on violently; chase away; peel; burn with anger; — IV. INF. *iśḥâẓ*, sharpen, grind.

شحرور *śuḥrûr*, pl. *śaḥârîr*, blackbird.

(شحط) *śaḥṭaṭ*, INF. ة, delight.

(شحف) *śaḥaf*, skin, flay.

(شحك) *śaḥak*, gag a kid to prevent it from sucking.

(شحم) *śaḥam*, INF. *śaḥm*, (a.) give fat to eat, feed (a.) on fat; grease, smear with fat;—*śaḥim*, A, INF. *śaḥam*, be greedy for fat; — *śaḥum*, INF. *śaḥâma-t*, abound in fat;—II. INF. *taśḥîm*, grease, smear with fat; — IV. INF. *iśḥâm*, be fat.

شحم *śaḥm*, pl. *śuḥûm*, fat, lard, grease; pulp; — *śaḥam*, greedy for fat; fat; more pulpy than juicy; — ة *śaḥma-t*, a slice of lard, some fat; pulp; ش الاذن *śaḥma-t al-uzn*, lobe of the ear; ش العين *śaḥma-t al-'ain*, the white of the eye.

(شحن) *śaḥan*, INF. *śaḥn*, fill, load; garrison; drive away; I, U, — *śaḥin*, A, chase, pursue far without reaching; — *śaḥin*, A, INF. *śaḥan*, bear a grudge, hate; — III. INF. *muśâḥana-t*, hate; — IV. INF. *iśḥân*, fill, load; garrison; — ة *śiḥna-t*, deep grudge; daily allowance of food, ration; troop, garrison; pl. *śiḥân*, شحانى *śiḥâna*, guardsman; commander of a town, prefect of police, superintendent.

شحنا *śaḥnâ'*, deep grudge, bitter hatred.

(شحو) *śaḥâ*, U, INF. *śaḥw*, open the mouth, be open; — IV. INF. *iśḥâ'*, open the mouth; — V. INF. *taśaḥḥî*, speak freely about a person (على *'ala*); — ة *śaḥwa-t*, step, pace.

شحوا *śaḥwâ'*, wide open.

(شحى) *śaḥî*, A, INF. *śaḥan*, stand wide open.

شحيح *śaḥîḥ*, pl. *śiḥâḥ*, *aśiḥḥa-t*, *aśiḥḥâ'*, f. ة, pl. *śaḥâ'iḥ*, miserly, avaricious; poor in milk; poor in water.

شحيج *śaḥîḥ*, croaking (s.), INF. of (شحج).

شحيم *śaḥîm*, fat; fond of eating fat; — also ة *śaḥîma-t*, breviary (m.).

(شخ) *śaḫḫ*, I, INF. *śaḫḫ*, *śaḫîḫ*, make water; snore; make a gurgling noise.

شخاخ *śaḫḫâḫ*, who makes much water; — ة *śaḫḫâḫa-t*, urine.

شخارة *śaḫḫâra-t*, wind-pipe.

(شخب) *śaḫab*, A, U, INF. *śaḫb*, *maśḫab*, flow in rays, make the milk flow in rays.

شخب *śaḫb*, *śuḫb*, milk flowing in rays;—ة *śuḫba-t*, pl. *śiḫâb*, ray of milk.

(شخت) *śaḫut*, INF. *śaḫt*, be slender, slim; cut or tear into narrow

strips; — II. INF. *taśḫîṭ*, bring, transmit.

شخت *śaḫt*, slender, slim.

شختور *śaḫtûr*, ة, pl. *śaḫâtîr*, boat.

(شخدب) *śuḫdub*, pl. *śaḫâdib*, reptile.

(شخذ), IV. *aśḫaẓ*, INF. *iśḫâẓ*, irritate, incite.

(شخر) *śaḫar*, I, INF. *śaḫr*, *śaḫîr*, snore; snuffle; neigh; bray.

(شخز) *śaḫaz*, A, INF. *śaḫz*, shake (n.), waver; agitate, confuse; set against one another (بين *bain*); molest, vex, grieve; pierce; tear out an eye.

(شخس) *śaḫas*, INF. *śaḫs*, be violently agitated; waver; (also VI.) yawn; — IV. INF. *iśḫâs*, slander, calumniate; — VI. INF. *taśâḫus*, see I.

(شخشب) *śaḫśab*, INF. ة, call forth doubts or scruples in another (acc.).

شخشخ *śaḫśaḫ*, INF. ة, clash, clatter.

شخشور *śaḫśûr*, trowsers.

(شخص)* *śaḫaṣ*, INF. *śuḫûṣ*, be high, lofty, sublime; rise high, tower above other things, show itself distinctly; appear; strike against the palate; over-reach the mark; swell; fix the eyes upon, stare at; pass. *śuḫiṣ*, be astonished or terrified; depart, travel; go to; — *śaḫuṣ*, be tall and corpulent; — II. INF. *taśḫîṣ*, cause a thing to appear, to show itself distinctly; make the diagnosis of an illness; imagine, represent to one's mind; — IV. INF. *iśḫâṣ*, frighten, agitate, disquiet; be at hand; slander; over-reach the mark; bring about; — V. INF. *taśaḫḫuṣ*, appear, show itself; present itself to the eye or mind.

شخص *śaḫṣ*, pl. *aśḫuṣ*, *śuḫûṣ*, *aśḫâṣ*, object, dark figure in the distance; person, individual; — ى *śaḫṣiyy*, ة, personal; — ية *śaḫṣiyya-t*, personality, rank, nobility.

(شخل) *śaḫal*, INF. *śaḫl*, clear, strain (wine); milk.

(شخم) *śaḫam*, be deteriorated, putrid; — *śaḫim*, id.; — II. INF. *taśḫîm*, spoil, deteriorate (a.).

شخوتة *śuḫûta-t*, slenderness, slimness.

شخوص *śuḫûṣ*, becoming visible (s.), appearance, INF. of (شخص).

شخيت *śaḫît*, slender, slim.

شخيخ *śaḫîḫ*, snoring (s.).

شخير *śaḫîr*, snoring, snuffling, snorting, neighing (s.); — *śiḫḫîr*, who snores, &c., loudly.

شخيص *śaḫîṣ*, ة, tall and corpulent; considerable, important, a somebody; lord, prince.

شخيف *śiḫḫîf*, stout, corpulent.

(شد) *śadd*, U, I, INF. *śadd*, strap, fasten tight; compress, press; bind a book; strengthen, fortify, brace; fix; act with vigour, exert one's self, make efforts; gain strength, increase in violence or intensity; urge on, spur, demand categorically, insist; saddle; be already advanced (day); — U, I, INF. *śadd*, run; rush upon, attack; U, INF. *śadda-t*, attack, make an assault; — II. INF. *taśdîd*, fortify, strengthen, brace; double a consonant, mark it with *taśdîd* ـّ; condense, thicken; — III. INF. *muśâdda-t*, press one hard, persecute and maltreat; — IV. INF. *iśdâd*, have a strong beast for riding; — V. INF. *taśaddud*, get or show one's self hard, violent, severe; get fortified, strengthened; devote all one's strength to a matter; get thick, condensed; — VIII. INF. *iśtidâd*, be strong, intense, violent; be troublesome, burdensome, press upon; grow stronger, increase in strength; get condensed, grow thick; double one's zeal and efforts; run.

شد *śadd*, violence, strength; severity; pl. *śudûd*, a covering

for the head; — ة *śadda-t*, onslaught, attack; parcel, bale of merchandise; pack (of cards); — *śidda-t*, violence, severity, intensity; hardness; strength; misfortune, calamity, misery, need; a war-ship.

هداد *śaddâd*, oppressor, tyrant; — *śidâd*, harshness; severity; pl. of هديد *śadîd*.

هداه *śudâh*, astonishment, bewilderment, confusion; occupation.

(هدح) *śadaḥ*, INF. *śadḥ*, be fat; be free and unrestrained; — VII. INF. *inśidâḥ*, lie down and stretch the legs asunder; — ة *śudḥa-t*, liberty, opportunity; room, spaciousness, width.

(هدخ) *śadaḫ*, INF. *śadḫ*, break anything hollow; break the head; squash; hit with a lance; hit in the part of the neck where the head is cut off in decapitating; reach as far as the nose (whiteness on a horse's forehead); bend, lean towards; — II. INF. *taśdîḫ*, break or wound heads.

هدخ *śadaḫ*, miscarriage; — ة *śadḫa-t*, slice (of an apple, &c.); soft, juicy.

(هدف) *śadaf*, I, INF. *śadf*, cut into several pieces; — IV. INF. *idśâf*, be dark.

هدف *śadaf*, dark object in the distance, body, person, individual; darkness; height, greatness, nobility; joy; — *śadif*, great; quick to attack; — *śuduf*, pl. of اهدف *aśdaf*, left-handed, &c.; — ة *śadfa-t*, *śudfa-t*, darkness; — *śudfa-t*, part; *śudfat-an*, piecemeal.

(هدق) *śadiq*, A, INF. *śadaq*, have broad corners of the mouth; — *śadaq*, INF. *śadq*, open wide; — II. INF. *taśdîq*, V. INF. *taśadduq*, bend strongly the corners of the mouth so as to talk more quickly, talk very fluently.

هدق *śidq*, *śadq*, pl. *aśdâq*, corner of the mouth; edge of a valley; — *śudq*, pl. and—

هدقا *śadqâ'*, f. of اهدق *aśdaq*, having broad corners of the mouth, fluent, eloquent.

هدقم *śadqam*, having a large mouth; lion.

هدن *śadan*, U, INF. *śudûn*, grow strong, be able to walk, to do without its dam (young of an animal).

(هده) *śadah*, A, INF. *śadh*, shatter; (also IV.) astonish, confuse, bewilder; — IV. INF. *iśdâh*, see I.; — VII. INF. *inśidâh*, VIII. INF. *iśtidâh*, pass. of the previous.

هده *śadah*, confusion, bewilderment, embarrassment; — *śadh*, *śudh*, occupation.

(هدو) *śadâ*, U, INF. *śadw*, urge on; sing, recite verses; acquire some literary or musical accomplishment; — IV. INF. *iśdâ'*, sing beautifully.

هدى *śudda*, misfortune, calamity; distress.

هديد *śadîd*, ة, pl. *aśiddâ'*, *śidâd*, violent, strong, intense, severe, hard, difficult; vigorous, powerful; persevering, firm; avaricious; thick, tight; oppressive; — ة *śadîda-t*, pl. *śadâ'id*, adversity, calamity; necessity, need.

(هذ) *śaẕẕ*, U, I, INF. *śaẕẕ*, *suẕûẕ*, be separate, isolated; separate (n.), isolate one's self; be odd, irregular, make an exception; U, INF. *śaẕẕ*, separate (a.), sunder, set apart; — II. INF. *taśẕîẕ*, separate (a.), sunder, isolate; lay aside; except from a rule; — IV. INF. *iśẕâẕ*=II.

هذا *śaẕan*, strength of an odour; salt; hunger; damage, evil; scab; — ة *śaẕât*, dog-fly.

هذاذ *śuẕẕâẕ*, people who live dispersed amongst foreign tribes; few.

هذام *śaẕâm*, salt; sting.

هذان *śiẕẕân*, lotus-tree.

(هذب) *śaẓab*, U, I, INF. *śaẓb*, draw off, peel; cut off, lop; prune, lop off the branches; refuse, repel, defend; — II. INF. *taśẓîb*, skin, peel; prune.

هذب *śaẓab*, pl. *aśẓâb*, household things, furniture, carpets, &c.; rind, crust, bark; dam; — ة *śaẓaba-t*, pl. *śaẓab*, cut off dry branches.

(هذر) *śaẓr*, ة, pl. *śuẓûr*, small particles of gold, small glass beads; هذر بذر *śaẓr-a baẓr-a*, *śiẓr-a biẓr-a*, هذر مذر *śiẓr-a miẓr-a*, scattered in all directions, pell-mell, helter-skelter;—V. INF. *taśaẓẓur*, be ready or prepared for combat; be quickly at hand, be alert, nimble; frighten, threaten; vent one's anger.

(هذف) *śaẓaf*, INF. *śaẓf*, get, obtain.

(هذو) *śaẓâ*, U, INF. *śaẓw*, damage, injure, hurt, torment; perfume one's self with musk, smell of musk; break; — IV. INF. *iśẓâ'*, injure, damage; remove, keep off, repel.

هذوذ *śuẓûẓ*, separation, isolation; peculiarity; irregularity, INF. of (هذ).

(هذى), II. *sazza*, INF. *taśẓiya-t*, hear of a thing and inform others about it.

هذى *śaẓan*, n. u. هذاة *śaẓât*, dog-fly.

(هر) *śarr* (pret. *śarar-tu*), U, I, INF. *śarr*, be bad, evil, wicked, impious, or act badly, &c.; INF. *śurr*, blame, rebuke; (also II. and IV.) expose to the sun or air; — for *śarir*, A, INF. *śarr*, be bad, act badly; — for *śarur*, INF. *śarâra-t*, id.; — II. INF. *taśrîr*, see I.; bring one into bad repute; — III. INF. *muśârra-t*, act boldly against, show enmity towards; — IV. INF. *iśrâr*, see I.; call bad, accuse of malice, bring into bad repute; make public, spread abroad; — VIII. INF. *iśtirâr*, chew the cud; — X. INF. *istiśrâr*, possess a large herd of camels.

هر *śarr*, *śurr*, pl. *śurûr*, evil, anything bad, badness, wickedness, malice; damage, injury; (m.) war, battle; — *śarr*, ة; pl. *aśrâr*, *śirâr*, bad, evil, wicked, malicious; — ة *śirra-t*, ardour of youth; anger; desire, craving, eagerness; malice.

هرا *śarâ'*, side, direction; — *śirâ'*, purchase, bargain, sale; purchase-money; — *śarrâ'*, buyer, purchaser; — ة *śarât*, best part, and, by opposition, worst part of a flock; — *śurât*, pl. of هارى *śârî*, quarrelsome, &c.

(هراب), III. *iśra'abb*, INF. *iśri'bâb*, stretch one's neck to see, be a-stretch.

هراب *śarâb*, pl. *aśriba-t*, drink, beverage; wine; pl. *śarâbât*, drinks, syrups, sherbets; — *śarrâb*, drunkard; — *śurrâb*, pl. of هارب *śârib*, who drinks, &c.; — ة *śarrâba-t*, pl. *śarrârîb*, tassel.

هراباتى *śarâbâtiyy*, seller of sherbets.

هرابى *śarâbiyy*, drinker of wine; wine-merchant.

هرابيبة *śurâbîba-t*, stretching of the neck for the purpose of seeing.

هراج *śirâj*, sesame-oil.

هراح *śarrâḥ*, commentator, explainer; — *śurrâḥ*, commentators, &c., pl. of هارح *śâriḥ*.

هراحيب *śarâḥîb*, pl. of هرحوب *śurḥûb*.

هرار *śarâr*, *śirâr*, ة, spark; — ة *śarâra-t*, malice, INF. of (هر).

هراريب *śarârîb*, pl. of هرابة *śarrâba-t*.

هراريز *śarârîz*, pl. of هثراز *śi'râz*, curdled whey.

هراريف *śarârîf*, pl. of هراف *śurrâf*.

هراز *śirâz*, obstinacy; malice; dispute; — *śurrâz*, tormentors, pl.

of شارز *śâriz* ; — ة *śarâza-t*, hardness, obdurateness, malice.

شراس *śarrâs*, شراسى *śarâsî*, hard ; — ة *śarâsa-t*, maliciousness ; quarrelsomeness.

شراسيف *śarâsîf*, pl. of شرسوف *śursûf*.

شراشر *śarâśir*, the whole of the body ; soul, mind ; love ; pl. of شرشرة *śarśara-t*.

شراع *śirâ'*, pl. *aśrâ'*, *aśri'a-t*, *śuru'*, sail ; tent ; protecting roof ; bow-string ; spear ; neck of a camel ; — *śarrâ'*, linen-draper ; — ة *śarâ'a-t*, boldness, bravery ; —ى *śurâ'iyy*, long, long-necked.

شراف *śurrâf*, ة *śurrâfa-t*, pl. *śarârif*, pinnacle, battlement ; — ة *śarâfa-t*, nobility, high rank.

شراك *śirâk*, pl. *śuruk*, *aśruk*, shoe-string ; allowance of food ; — * ; — ة *śirâka-t*, companionship, partnership, company.

شران *śarrân*, evil ; a fly.

شرانق *śarâniq*, *śurâniq*, slough ; tattered clothes ; — *.

شرانى *śarrâniyy*, who bears malice ; quarreller, maker of mischief.

شراهة *śarâha-t*, greediness, appetite.

شرايين *śarâyîn*, pl. of شريان *śaryân*.

(شرب) *śarib*, A, INF. *śarb*, *śirb*, *śurb*, *taśrab*, *maśrab*, drink ; imbibe, suck, absorb ; be taken with, penetrated with ; smoke tobacco ; be thirsty ; — *śaraba*, U, INF. *śarb*, apprehend, understand, see into ; belie ; — II. INF. *taśrîb*, give to drink ; impregnate, saturate ; cause one to understand, render intelligible ; — III. INF. *muśâraba-t*, drink in company with (acc.) ; — IV. INF. *iśrâb*=II. pass. *uśrib*, be imbued, mingled with ; — V. INF. *taśarrub*, be saturated, impregnated, imbued ; imbibe, absorb ; saturate, impregnate.

شرب *śarb* (*śirb*, *śurb*), drinking (s.) ; — *śarb*, drinkers, pl. of شارب *śârib* ; — *śirb*, *śurb*, drink, beverage, water, draught ; — ة *śarba-t*, drink, draught (also *śurba-t*) ; water-jug with a long narrow neck ; purge ; — *śaraba-t*, sherbet, liquor, lemonade ; well for watering palm-trees ; — *śuraba-t*, great drinker ; — *śarabba-t*, place abounding in grass but treeless ; way, manner.

(شربك) *śarbak*, INF. ة, entangle, confuse ; — ة *śarbaka-t*, and—

شربوكة *śurbûka-t*, confusion, entanglement, embarrassment.

شربين *śarbîn*, cedar ; a species of cypress ; larch-tree.

(شرث) *śaris*, A, INF. *śaras*, be thick and chapped ; pass. *śuris* and II. pass. *śurris*, be not equally smooth and straight.

شرث *śaris*, sharp ; — ة *śarsa-t*, *śursa-t*, old shoe ; shoe.

(شرج) *śaraj*, U, INF. *śarj*, pile up bricks ; mix ; (also II. and IV.) draw the strings of a purse ; gather ; tell lies ; make common cause with ; — II. INF. *taśrîj*, sew with long stitches ; see I. ; — III. INF. *muśâraja-t*, remind by similarity ; — IV. INF. *iśrâj*, see I. ; — V. INF. *taśarruj*, be intermixed, mingled.

شرج *śarj*, pl. *śirâj*, *śurûj*, *aśruj*, rocky water-course towards the plain ; purse or its string ; troop, company, fellowship, sect ; colour ; manner, way ; similarity ; kind, sort ; pl. *śurûj*, *aśrâj*, rent, split ; — also *śaraj*, nature, disposition ; habit, kind, manner.

(شرجب) *śarjab*, long-stretched.

(شرجع) *śarja'*, INF. ة, cut smooth a quadrangular piece of wood ; cut oblong.

شرجع *śarja'*, bier ; long.

شرجم *śarjam*, rape (vegetable).

(شرح) *śarah*, open, unlock the door ; widen, enlarge, spread ; expound, explain, comment on ; understand, apprehend, conceive ; cut into pieces ; saw asunder ; lie with, deflower ; — II. INF. *taśrîh*,

carve meat; dissect; enlarge, widen; cut open and spread in the sun (figs to be dried); — VII. INF. *inśirâḥ*, be enlarged, widened, spread; be explained, commented upon; be in good humour.

شرح *śarḥ*, pl. *śurûḥ*, explanation, commentary; tale, relation, narrative; — *śariḥ*, ة, wide, open, affording a fine view; — ة *śarḥa-t*, piece or slice of meat.

(شرخ) *śaraḫ*, U, INF. *śurûḫ*, grow up; INF. *śarḫ*, *śurûḫ*, break through, pierce.

شرخ *śarḫ*, pl. *śurûḫ*, root, origin, beginning; prime of youth; start; point, top; wedge; progeny; an equal; du. the two equal parts; *śarḫ*, youths, pl. of شارخ *śâriḫ*.

شرخوب *śurḫûb*, pl. *śarâḫîb*, vertebra.

(شرد) *śarad*, U, INF. *śirâd*, *śurâd*, *śurûd*, flee, escape, roam as a fugitive; disperse; (m.) deviate from the straight line; — II. INF. *taśrîd*, scare and disperse, put to flight, drive into the desert; separate, scatter; cause to deviate from the straight line; cut into long slices; — IV. INF. *iśrâd*=II.

شرد *śard*, rain driven aslant by the wind; — *śarad*, pl. of شارد *śârid*, fugitive, &c.; — *śurud*, pl. of شرود *śarûd*; — *śurrad*, poems passing on from mouth to mouth.

(شردق), II. *taśardaq*, INF. *taśarduq*, get anything into one's throat and cough.

شرذمة *śirẓima-t*, pl. *śarâẓim*, small number of men; piece, slice; pl. rags, tatters.

شرر *śarar*, malice; *śarar*, ة, spark.

(شرز) *śaraz*, U, INF. *śarz*, cut; — II. INF. *taśrîz*, punish, chastise; revile, abuse; — III. INF. *muśâraza-t*, quarrel with; behave maliciously towards; — IV. INF. *iśrâz*, throw helplessly into adversity.

شرز *śarz*, rough to the touch; difficult; violent; difficulty, violence; — also ة *śarza-t*, annihilation; — *śaraz*, pure, unmixed.

(شرس) *śaras*, U, INF. *śars*, pull by the reins; hurt by hard words; soften a skin in water; U, devour; — *śaris*, A, INF. *śaras*, *śarîs*, *śarâsa-t*, be unsociable, quarrelsome, malicious; please, be liked; — III. INF. *śirâs*, *muśârasa-t*, treat with harshness and severity; — VI. INF. *taśârus*, live continually in dispute or quarrel.

شرس *śaras*, malice, maliciousness; also *śirs*, a thorny plant; — *śaris*, unsociable, difficult to deal with, quarrelsome, malicious.

شرسفة *śarsafa-t*, malignant disposition.

شرسوف *śursûf*, pl. *śarâsîf*, cartilage of the ribs.

شرش *śirś*, pl. *śurûś*, root; blood-vessel, vein (m.).

شرشاوة *śarśâwa-t*, window, trellis of a window (m.).

(شرشر) *śarśar*, INF. ة, cut into pieces; bite; graze off and chew; sharpen, whet; trail; — ة *śarśara-t*, pl. *śarâśir*, furniture, household things.

شرشف *śarśaf*, pl. *śarâśif*, bed-cloth, sheet (m.).

(شرص) *śaraṣ*, U, INF. *śarṣ*, just begin to walk; pull, draw; take the lead in conversation.

شرص *śaraṣ*, incision in a camel's nose for the ring of the bridle; ruggedness of the ground; — *śirṣ*, pl. *śiraṣa-t*, *śirâṣ*, baldness about the temples; — ة *śirṣa-t*, du. *śirṣatân*, the temples.

(شرط) *śaraṭ*, U, I, INF. *śarṭ*, make a condition, stipulate; make incisions in the skin, scarify, cup; fasten with a string of palm-bast; (m.) tear into pieces; — *śariṭ*, A, INF. *śaraṭ*, get into a

difficult position, into a plight; — II. INF. *taśrîṭ*, scarify, cup; (m.) make small chains or rosaries; — III. INF. *muśâraṭa-t*, stipulate with, bet with (acc.); — IV. INF. *iśrâṭ*, make preparations, get one's self ready; — V. INF. *taśarruṭ*, fix one's thoughts upon a matter; — VI. INF. *taśâruṭ*, enter mutually on conditions, stipulate, make many reservations or provisos; grant under conditions; — X. INF. *istiśrâṭ*, get into a bad condition.

شرط *śarṭ*, pl. *śurûṭ*, condition, reservation, proviso, stipulation, article of a compact, contract; prescription; obligation; incision, scarification; pl. *aśrâṭ*, low, mean; — *śaraṭ*, pl. *aśrâṭ*, notch, sign, token; cutting of the ground, channel; du. *śaraṭân*, two stars in the horns of the ram; — *śuruṭ*, pl. of شريط *śarîṭ*; — ة *śurṭa-t*, pl. *śuraṭ*, anything stipulated, condition; bodyguard; vanguard; policeman, bailiff; allies, helpers; kind, species; — ى *śarṭiyy*, ة, according to condition, stipulated; conditional; — *śurṭiyy*, *śuraṭiyy*, pl. *śuraṭ*, body-guardsman, satellite; bailiff; — ية *śarṭiyya-t*, conditionality; conditional sentence; compact, contract, stipulation.

(شرع) *śara'*, INF. *śar'*, prescribe a road to walk upon or a law to follow, lead, give laws; have an outlet or passage into the street; publish; be open and distinct; strip the skin; lift very high; INF. *śar'*, *śurû'*, go into the water; engage in a business, begin; make ready for; be straight; stretch the neck; — II. INF. *taśrî'*, mark or show the way distinctly; open a path; lead the cattle to the most convenient watering-place; make clear; lift up; — III. INF. *muśâra'a-t*, summon before the judge, open a law-suit against; — IV. INF. *iśrâ'*, open the door towards the street; point the lance against; mark or show the way; cause to enter on a road; lead the animal to the water; make clear; lift up; — V. INF. *taśarru'*, study law; observe the law; — VI. INF. *taśâru'*, be engaged in a law-suit against one another.

شرع *śar'*, divine law; prescripts of Mohammed; religion; justice; — also *śara'*, manner, way; equal; *śara'*, common property; — *śir'*, string of a lute; shoe-lace; — ة *śir'a-t*, pl. *śir'*, *śirâ'*, *aśrâ'*, the straight road; the divine law, religion; pl. *śir'*, *śar'*, what is equal to another; string of a lute.

شرعاف *śir'âf*, sheath of the male blossom of the palm-tree.

(شرعب) *śar'ab*, INF. ة, cut into long strips; — *śar'ab*, long.

شرعى *śar'iyy*, ة, legitimate, according to law, just; — *śir'iyy*, bow-string; equal.

شرغ *śarg*, *śirg*, *śarag*, a small frog.

(شرف) *śaraf*, U, INF. *śaraf*, be high; tower over; surpass, conquer; provide a wall with battlements; INF. *śurûf*, be old; — *śarif*, A, INF. *śaraf*, be high; dominate the surrounding parts; — *śaruf*, INF. *śarâfa-t*, be eminent in glory, rank, dignity; be old; INF. *śaraf*, occupy a high rank; — II. INF. *taśrîf*, make celebrated, ennoble; distinguish, honour; provide a wall with battlements; — III. INF. *muśârafa-t*, vie in glory, &c. with; tower over, be eminent, dominate; be distinguished; ascend, mount; — IV. INF. *iśrâf*, threaten, impend, be near, close at hand; be high, tower, dominate, over-

hang; look down from on high; ascend, be on the top; — v. INF. *taśarruf*, be distinguished, ennobled, honoured; — VIII. INF. *iśtirâf*, raise one's self high, lift one's self up; — x. INF. *istiśrâf*, id.; look at with lifted up head and screening the eyes with the hand; disregard one's right.

شرف *śaraf*, height, greatness, distinction, honour, glory, nobility, descent from Mohammed, dignity; high spot, top; (horse-) race; pl. of شريف *śarîf*; — *śurf*, pl. of اشرف *aśraf*, high, noble, &c.; — *śuruf*, *śurraf*, pl. of شارف *śârif*, ag. of (شرف); — ة *śurfa-t*, pl. *śuraf*, height, greatness, honour, dignity; good fortune; pl. *śuraf*, *śurafât*, battlements; gallery of a minaret.

شرفا *śarfâ'*, f. of اشرف, high, noble, &c.; — *śurafâ'*, pl. of شريف *śarîf*.

شرفية *śarafiyya-t*, nobility, high rank; honourability.

(شرق) *śaraq*, U, INF. *śarq*, split, cut in two; (m.) swallow in a moment, sip, imbibe; — U, INF. *śarq*, *śurûq*, rise; shine; cull; — *śariq*, A, INF. *śaraq*, have the ears split; redden; have a fit of suffocation, choke; be near setting, shine dimly; — II. expose strips of meat in the sun to dry; go east; turn towards the east; almost choke an animal; — IV. INF. *iśrâq*, rise, shine, beam; light up; cause the sun to rise; — v. INF. *taśarruq*, sit down in a sunny place; — VII. INF. *inśirâq*, be split, broken; — XIII. *iśrauraq*, INF. *iśrîrâq*, choke with tears.

شرق *śarq*, sun-rise; east, orient; sun-light; sun; split, cleft; — also *śariq*, lean; — *śarq*, *śirq*, light shining through a chink; — *śurq*, pl. of شارق *śâriq*, rising, shining; — *śaraq*, ة *śurqa-t*, choking fit; — *śuruq*, pl. of شريق *śarîq*; — ة *śarqa-t*, sunny place; also *śariqa-t*, rising sun.

شرقراق *śaraqrâq*, *śiriqrâq*, green magpie.

(شرقط) *śarqaṭ*, INF. ة, emit sparks, scintillate (m.).

شرقوطة *śurqûṭa-t*, pl. *śarâqîṭ*, spark (m.).

شرقی *śarqiyy*, ة, eastern, oriental.

(شرك) *śarik*, A, INF. *śirka-t*, be a partner, fellow, companion; have the laces torn; — II. INF. *taśrîk*, provide a shoe with laces; confuse, entangle; be shareholder in a commercial concern or company, &c.; — III. INF. *śirâk*, *muśâraka-t*, be in partnership with, take into partnership; — IV. INF. *iśrâk*, take into partnership, allow to share in a thing, admit into a society; give an associate to God, be a polytheist; provide a shoe with laces; — VI. INF. *taśâruk*, enter into partnership with; — VIII. INF. *iśtirâk*, id.; be admitted into a society.

شرك *śirk*, pl. *aśrâk*, fellowship, company, association, partnership; share, lot; partner, companion, shareholder; polytheism, polytheist; Christian; hypocrisy; — *śarak*, ة, pl. *śuruk*, *aśrâk*, *śirâk*, net of a fowler, noose, snare; pl. open roads; — *śuruk*, pl. of شراك *śirâk*; (m.) agio, discount; — ة *śirka-t*, *śurka-t*, fellowship, association, company (commercial), congregation, brotherhood; community, commonalty.

شركا *śurakâ'*, pl. of شريك *śarîk*.

(شركل) *śarkal*, INF. ة, entangle, confuse, embarrass; — II. INF. *taśarkul*, be entangled, &c.

شركی *śurakiyy*, quickly and frequently repeated, quick.

(شرم) *śaram*, I, INF. *śarm*, graze (in passing), wound slightly; split, tear; blunt; cut off the

tip of the nose; give little; — *śarim*, A, INF. *śaram*, have the tip cut off (nose); — II. INF. *taśrîm*, split, tear violently; — III. INF. *taśarrum*, be split, torn, blunted; — VII. INF. *inśirâm*, id.

شرم *śarm*, pl. *śurûm*, split, rent; notch, gap; precipice, abyss, whirlpool; gulf, bay.

شرما *śarmâ'*, f. deflowered.

(شرمح) *śarmaḥ*, pl. *śarâmiḥ*, *śarâmiḥa-t*, strong; — also *śarammaḥ*, long.

(شرمط) *śarmaṭ*, INF. ة, tear into tatters.

شرموطة *śarmûṭa-t*, pl. *śarâmiṭ*, rag, tatter; strumpet.

(شرن) *śarin*, A, INF. *śarn*, be split.

شرنبث *śarambaṣ*, شرنبذ *śarambaẓ*, stout, big.

(شرنق) *śarnaq*, INF. ة, cut; change into a chrysalis; — ة *śarnaqa-t*, pl. *śarâniq*, chrysalis, cocoon.

شرنوق *śurnûq*, small frog.

(شره) *śarih*, A, INF. *śarah*, be greedy for food or drink; eat or drink greedily; — VI. INF. *taśâruh*, id.; be intemperate.

شره *śarah*, greed, gluttony; —*śarih*, and—

شرهان *śarhân*, greedy, intemperate; glutton.

(شرهف) *śarhaf*, INF. ة, feed well (a.).

شرو *śarw*, *śirw*, honey; — ة *śarwa-t*, purchase, anything purchased.

شرواض *śirwâḍ*, pl. *śarâwiḍ*, fat, soft.

شروال *śirwâl*, pl. *śarâwîl*, trowsers.

شرود *sarûd*, pl. *śurud*, fleeing in terror; fugitive.

شروع *śurû'*, beginning, commencement; undertaking (s.), INF. of (شرع).

شروق *śurûq*, sunrise.

(شرول) *śarwal*, INF. ة, put trowsers on to (m.).

شروم *śarûm*, f. deflowered.

شروى *śarwa*, equal (adj., s.).

(شرى) *śara*, I, INF. *śirâ'*, *śiran*, buy; rescue, redeem, save; sell; expose to the sun for drying; scoff at, make contemptible; — *śarî*, A, INF. *śaran*, spread rapidly; shine brilliantly, flash; INF. *śary*, feel an itching on the skin, get an eruption; — III. INF. *śirâ'*, *muśârât*, conclude a bargain with (acc.); dispute, quarrel; — IV. INF. *iśrâ'*, shine, flash; fill; — V. INF. *taśarrî*, be dispersed, scattered, separated; — VIII. INF. *iśtirâ'*, buy; sell; exchange for; acquire, earn; shine; — X. INF. *istiśrâ'*, walk apace; dispatch one's business; quicken; be important; — XII. *iśraura*, INF. *iśrîrâ'*, be moved, agitated, waver, oscillate.

شرى *śary*, purchase; sale; *śary*, ة, coloquintida; — *śarî*, selected; having an eruption (on the skin); — *śaran*, pustules, eruption; road; mountain; woody and mountainous tract; pl. *aśrâ'*, tract, district; — *śiran*, pl. *aśriya-t*, bargain; — *śurra*, very bad; angry, malicious, f. of اشر *aśarr*, worse; — *śariyy*, swift and wide-stepping; — ة *śariyya-t*, manner, fashion, method; nature, natural disposition.

شريان *śaryân*, *śiryân*, pl. *śarâyîn*, artery; name of a tree.

شريب *śarîb*, drinkable; drinking companion; — *śirrîb*, given to drink, drunkard.

شريج *śarîj*, wood split in two; similar, equal; equality; du. *śarîjân*, two different colours.

شريح *śarîḥ*, ة *śarîḥa-t*, long shreds of meat.

شريد *śarîd*, fugitive, exile; wanderer.

شرير *śarîr*, ة, pl. *aśrâr*, *aśirrâ'*, bad, evil, wicked, malicious; sea-shore; — *śirrîr*, scoundrel, scamp; — ة *śarîra-t*, packing-needle.

شریس *śarîs*, maliciousness; malicious, malignant; lion.

شریصة *śarîṣa-t*, pl. *śarâ'iṣ*, cheek.

شریط *śarîṭ*, pl. *śuruṭ*, rope or string of palm-bast; chest, trunk; (m.) iron wire; lace-work, fringe, galloon; — ة *śarîṭa-t*, pl. *śarâ'iṭ*, condition, stipulation, reservation, proviso; (pl. also *śuruṭ*) ruler, lever, plumb-line; brass wire.

شریع *śarî'*, bold; finest linen; — ة *śarî'a-t*, pl. *śarâ'i'*, prescript of religion, law; law-book; justice; level road; threshold.

شریف *śarîf*, ة, pl. *śaraf*, *śurafâ'*, *aśrâf*, noble, of noble lineage (particularly descending from Mohammed), honoured, celebrated; excellent, eminent; du. *aś-śarîfân*, eye and ear.

شریق *śarîq*, rising sun; east; pl. *śuruq*, youthful, handsome.

شریك *śarîk*, pl. *aśrâk*, *śurakâ'*, f. ة, pl. *śarâ'ik*, partner, companion; fellow, schoolfellow.

شریم *śarîm*, deflowered; pudenda; plane (tool).

(شز) *śazz* (pret. *śaziz-tu*), A, INF. *śazâza-t*, be dry and hard.

شز *śazz*, dry and hard.

(شزب) *śazab*, U, INF. *śazb*, *śuzûb*, be hard and rugged; be slender and muscular; — *śazib*, A, INF. *śazab*, id.

شزب *śazb*, hardness and ruggedness; — *śuzzab*, pl. of شازب *śâzib*, ag. of (شزب); — ة *śazba-t*, emaciated she-camel; — *śuzba-t*, opportunity.

(شزر) *śazar*, I, INF. *śazr*, look askance at; hit on the eye; pierce; — I, U, (also X.) twist from the left or outside; plait; — V. INF. *taśazzur*, be angry; be ready for combat; — VI. INF. *taśâzur*, look askance at one another; — X. INF. *istiśzâr*, see I.; pass. of the same.

شزر *śazr*, violence; difficulty; unequal; — ة *śuzra-t*, redness of the eyes; looking askance (s.).

شزرا *śazrâ'*, f. of اشزر *aśzar*, red; looking askance (adj.).

(شزن) *śazin*, A, (also *śazan*) INF. *śazan*, be very tired; INF. *śazan*, *śuzûna-t*, be hard and rough; INF. *śazan*, be brisk, alert; — V. INF. *taśazzun*, be hard; rise to quarrel with.

شزن *śazn*, *śuzun*, die; — *śazan*, pl. *śuzûn*, hard rugged place; tiredness, weariness; poverty; — also *śuzn*, *śuzun*, side, direction, region.

(شزو) *śazâ*, U, INF. *śazw*, be high.

شزوب *śuzûb*, pl. of شزیب *śazîb*; — *.

شزونة *śuzûna-t*, hardness and ruggedness, INF. of (شزن).

شزیب *śazîb*, pl. *śuzûb*, hard dry branch.

شزیز *śazîz*, dry and hard.

(شس) *śass*, U, INF. *śusûs*, be dry, withered.

شس *śass*, pl. *śisâs*, *śusûs*, *śasîs*, hard ground; name of a plant.

(شسب) *śasib*, A, INF. *śasab*; — *śasub*, INF. *śasâba-t*, be withered, shrunk.

شسب *śisb*, bow; — *śusb*, pl. of شاسب *śâsib*, lean.

شستجة *śustuja-t*, towel.

(شسع) *śasa'*, INF. *śas'*, *śusû'*, be very far distant; provide the sandals with straps; — *śasi'*, A, INF. *śasa'*, have the straps broken; have a gap between the teeth.

شسع *śis'*, pl. *śusû'*, *aśsâ'*, strap of a sandal; border, edge, seam; side, direction, region; — *śus'*, pl. of شاسع *śâsi'* and شسوع *śasû'*, very far distant, &c.

(شسف) *śasaf*, U, I, INF. *śusûf*, be dry and emaciated; wither, dry up (a.); — *śasuf*, INF. *śasâfa-t*, *śisâfa-t*, wither, dry up (n.).

(شسل) *śasl*, plump, fat.

شسوع *śasû'*, pl. *śus'*, very far distant; — *śusû'*, far distance; — *.

شسیف *śasîf*, withering, drying up (a.); withered, dry.

(ششقل) *śaśqal*, INF. ة, counterfeit or falsify coins.

ششم *śiśm*, a grain employed against ophthalmia;—ة *śiśma-t*, commonplaces, phrases (m.).

ششنة *śiśna-t*, model, pattern, sample (m.).

(شص) *śaṣṣ*, I, INF. *śiṣâṣ*, *śuṣûṣ*, have little milk; prevent, hinder; be hard, difficult, toilsome; stifle one's pain and submit in patience; go, depart; —IV. INF. *iśṣâṣ*, prevent, hinder, remove.

شص *śiṣṣ*, *śaṣṣ*, pl. *śuṣûṣ*, fishing-hook, hook; clever thief.

شصاب *śaṣṣâb*, butcher.

شصار *śiṣâr*, torchenes of a camel.

شصاصا *śaṣâṣâ'*, year of famine, need, distress; hurry; pressing business.

شصائص *śaṣa'iṣ*, pl. of شصوص *śaṣûṣ*.

(شصب) *śaṣab*, U, INF. *śaṣb*, scald off the hair; skin; INF. *śaṣb*, *śaṣab*, be dry and hard;—U, INF. *śuṣûb*, be hard, toilsome; —*śaṣib*, A, INF. *śaṣab*, be difficult.

شصب *śiṣb*, pl. *aśṣâb*, distress, misery; destiny, lot.

(شصر) *śaṣar*, U, INF. *śaṣr*, prick with a thorn; stitch together; gore; pierce; leap; put the شصار *śiṣâr* (see above) to a camel's nose.

شصر *śaṣar*, *śaṣr*, ة, pl. *aśṣâr*, young gazelle growing strong and beginning to make use of the horns.

(شصو) *śaṣâ*, U, INF. *śaṣw*, *śuṣuww*, be rigidly fixed upon; be carried high into the air; be quite full;—U, I, INF. *śuṣiyy*, swell (dead body);—شصى *śaṣî*, id.; —IV. INF. *iśṣâ'*, fix one's look upon.

شصوص *śaṣûṣ*, pl. *śuṣûṣ*, *śaṣâ'iṣ*, poor in milk; sterile;—*śuṣûṣ*, sterility;—*.

شصيبة *śaṣîba-t*, pl. *śaṣâ'ib*, calamity; toilsome life, hardship.

شصير *śaṣîr*, prick of a thorn.

(شط) *śaṭṭ*, U, I, INF. *śaṭṭ*, *śuṭûṭ*, be far distant; be extreme in, overrun, treat with injustice, press upon; I, INF. *śaṭîṭ*, judge unjustly;—II. INF. *taśṭîṭ*, go or travel along the bank of a river, land;—IV. INF. *iśṭâṭ*, exceed the boundaries of justice, &c., wrong, treat with injustice, judge unjustly; demand too high a price;—VIII. INF. *iśtiṭâṭ*, be far distant; go beyond measure; judge unjustly.

شط *śaṭṭ*, pl. *śuṭûṭ*, *śuṭṭân*, river-bank, shore; Tigris;—ة *śaṭṭa-t*, well made, of beautiful form (girl);—*śiṭṭa-t*, distance.

(شطا) *śaṭa'*, INF. *śaṭ'*, *śuṭû'*, shoot or sprout forth; go along the bank, follow the bank of a river or the ridge of a valley; saddle the camel; conquer, subdue; overburden; lie with; be equal to a burden;—V. INF. *taśaṭṭu'*, follow the river-bank.

شطا *śaṭ'*, pl. *śuṭû'*, palm-shoot; river-bank, edge; end;—*śaṭan*, small splinters.

شطاح *śaṭṭâḥ*, shameless; obscene.

شطار *śuṭṭâr*, pl. of شاطر *śâṭir*, q.v.; —ة *śaṭâra-t*, skill, cleverness, fineness, subtility; cunning; boldness, INF. of (شطر).

شطاط *śaṭâṭ*, *śiṭâṭ*, high and elegant stature;—also ة *śaṭâṭa-t*, distance.

شطان *śuṭ'ân*, pl. of شاطى *śâṭî'*, *śuṭṭân*, pl. of شط *śaṭṭ*, banks, shores.

شطائط *śaṭâ'iṭ*, pl. of شطوط *śaṭûṭ*.

(شطب) *śaṭab*, U, INF. *śaṭb*, cut into strips, split; lean to the side; deviate, decline; be far distant; —II. INF. *taśṭîb*, damask a blade; scarify, cup;—V. INF. *taśaṭṭub*, get one's self cupped;—VIII. INF. *iśtiṭâb*, flow.

شطب *śaṭb*, fresh and green; *śaṭb*, ة *śaṭba-t*, *śiṭba-t*, slender;—ة *śaṭba-t*, fresh branch; sword;

— *śuṭba-t*, *śuṭaba-t*, pl. *śuṭab*, *śuṭub*, *śuṭûb*, undulating lines on a blade; long strip.

(شطح) *śaṭaḥ*, fill one's self with drink.

(شطر) *śaṭar*, U, INF. *śaṭr*, divide into two equal parts, halve; milk only two teats; milk only half of the milk; — U, INF. *śuṭûr*, squint; be malignant; separate in anger from one's people, forsake them; — *śaṭur*, INF. *śaṭâra-t*, have one udder longer than the other; INF. *śaṭâra-t*, *śuṭûra-t*, be malignant and cunning, treat one's people in such a manner; (m.) be very skilful, clever; — II. divide into two equal parts; make one malignant and cunning; (m.) make one skilful; — III. INF. *muśâṭara-t*, share with another by halves; — V. INF. *taśaṭṭur*, show one's self cunning.

شطر *śaṭr*, pl. *aśṭur*, *suṭûr*, half, part; hemistich, cæsura; side, direction, region; the two front or the two hind teats of a camel; — *śuṭr*, *śuṭur*, very distant; — ة *śiṭra-t*, half of them boys, half girls (number of children).

شطران *śaṭrân*, f. شطرى *śaṭra*, half full.

شطرنج *śiṭranj*, *śaṭranj*, chess.

(شطس) *śaṭas*, depart, set out on a journey.

شطس *śaṭs*, cunning, slyness; —*śuṭs*, refractoriness; lie.

شطط *śaṭaṭ*, excess, what is beyond bounds; what is superfluous; injustice, fraud, abuse; great lie.

شطع *śaṭi'*, A, INF. *śaṭa'*, be weakened by illness.

(شطف) *śaṭaf*, U, INF. *śaṭf*, remove (n.), depart, set out, desist; be far away; roam about; wash, rinse; — II. INF. *taśṭîf*, wash, rinse; — V. INF. *taśaṭṭuf*, wash one's hands.

(شطم) *śaṭam*, U, INF. *śaṭm*, lie with.

(شطن) *śaṭan*, U, INF. *śaṭn*, oppose another to turn him from his purpose; bind; travel to; INF. *śuṭûn*, be far distant.

شطن *śaṭan*, pl. *aśṭân*, long rope.

شطو *śaṭw*, side, region; — *śuṭû'*, INF. of (شطا), pl. of شطا *śaṭ'*.

شطوط *śaṭûṭ*, شطوطى *śaṭauṭa*, pl. *śaṭâ'iṭ*, camel with a large hump; — *.

شطوف *śaṭûf*, distant.

شطون *śaṭûn*, distant, remote; deep.

(شطى) *śaṭî*, A, INF. *śuṭiyy*, swell; — II. INF. *taśṭiya-t*, skin and dissect the slaughtered camel; — V. INF. *taśaṭṭî*, be broken into small pieces or break into splinters; — VII. INF. *inśiṭâ'*, be derived, propagated.

شطى *śaṭiyy*, pl. *śiṭyân*, circumference, bulk; piece of ground; — ة *śaṭiyya-t*, small splinter.

(شطيا) *śaṭya'*, INF. ة, be badly advised and irresolute.

شطيبة *śaṭîba-t*, pl. *śaṭâ'ib*, long strip of leather or meat; pl. different sects; adversities.

شطير *śaṭîr*, *śiṭṭîr*, distant, remote; strange, foreign; half.

شطيط *śaṭîṭ*, injustice.

(شظ) *śazz*, U, INF. *śazz*, be hard, painful to, vex, torment, press upon; have an erection; stretch the tail; (also IV.) join two sacks or bales by a crooked piece of wood placed on the back of the beast of burden; (also II. and IV.) disperse (a.), drive away; disperse (n.); — II. INF. *taśẓîẓ*, IV. INF. *iśẓâẓ*, see I.

شظا *śazan*, small splinters, shreds; the small bones in a horse's knee; INF. of (شظى).

شظاظ *śaẓâẓ*, dispersion; — *śiẓâẓ*, pl. *aśiẓẓa-t*, yoke-like piece of wood to carry the burden (see (شظ)).

شظاف *śaẓâf*, distress, misery; — *śiẓâf*, distance; — *.

شظايا *śaẕâyâ*, pl. of *śaẕiyya-t*.
(شظف) *śaẕaf*, U, INF. *śaẕf*, hinder, prevent; geld a ram; — *śaẕif*, A, INF. *śaẕaf*, be hard, rough; be toilsome and full of privations; lead a hard life; penetrate between skin and flesh; — *śaẕuf*, INF. *śaẕâfa-t*, grow hard.
شظف *śiẕf*, pl. *śiẕafa-t*, chip, billet, log; — *śaẕaf*, pl. *śiẕâf*, distress, misery, privation, hard life; — *śaẕif*, hard, toilsome, full of privations; — also *śuẕuf*, malignant, quarrelsome; — ة *śaẕifa-t*, hard ground.
شظيف *śaẕîf*, hard.
شظو *śaẕw*, side, direction, region.
شظوظ *śaẕûẕ*, hard, harsh, rough.
(شظى) *śaẕî*, A, INF. شظا *śaẕan*, be broken into splinters, burst, break (n.); tremble; swell; — V. INF. *taśaẕẕî*, get shivered; — ة *śaẕiyya-t*, pl. *śaẕâya*, *śaẕiyy*, *śiẕẕiyy*, piece of wood; small splinter, shin-bone; — also *śiẕya-t*, projecting rock.
شظيظ *śaẕîẕ*, shivered, broken into splinters; fastened to the شظاظ *śiẕâẕ* (see above).
(شع) *śa''*, U, INF. *śa''*, *śu'â'*, spurt out; I, disperse and spread in all directions; attack in scattered troops from several sides; INF. *śu''*, *śa'î'*, hasten, hurry; — IV. INF. *iś'â'*, emit rays, beam; — VII. INF. *inśi'â'*, break into the flock (wolf).
شع *śu''*, شعاع *śu'â'*, ة, pl. *śu'u'*, *śi'â'*, *aśi''a-t*, sunbeam, ray; — ة *śa'a-t*, INF. of وشع *waśa'*, mix, &c.
شعاب *śi'âb*, INF. III. of (شعب); pl. of شعب *śi'b*; — *śa''âb*, tinker.
شعار *śa'âr*, trees, plants, vegetation; thicket; — also *śi'âr*, pl. *śu'ur*, *aś'ira-t*, under-garment, shirt, vest; sign, badge, insignia; watchword; ceremonies, custom, usage; — *; — ة *śi'âra-t*, pl. *śa'â'ir*, customs, observances (particularly of the pilgrimage).
شعارير *śa'ârîr*, pl. of شعرور *śu'rûr*.
شعاع *śa'â'*, *śi'â'*, *śu'â'*, beard of a corn-ear; — *śu'â'*, ة, pl. *śi'â'*, *aśi''a-t*, *śu'u'*, sunbeam; (m.) monstrance, pyx; — ى *śu'â'iyy*, ray-like, radiated.
شعاف *śu'âf*, madness; — *.
شعانينة *śu'ânîna-t*, pl. *śa'ânîn*, twigs, branches; عيد الشعانين *'îd aś-śa'ânîn*, Palm Sunday.
شعائر *śa'â'ir*, pl. of شعارة *śi'âra-t* and شعيرة *śa'îra-t*.
(شعب) *śa'ab*, INF. *śa'b*, gather, unite; mend; disperse; split, cut; spoil, injure; get separated; leave one's people; appear; — *śa'ib*, A, INF. *śa'ab*, be broad in the shoulders; have a large space between the horns; — II. INF. *taś'îb*, split, divide, ramify; beat with the tail to the right and left; — III. INF. *śi'âb*, *muśâ'aba-t*, separate from (n.); — V. INF. *taśabbu'*, split (n.), ramify (n.); be dispersed, scattered; be far from; desist; — VII. *inśi'âb*, split, ramify (n.); get separated, dispersed.
شعب *śa'b*, pl. *śu'ûb*, troop, band, tribe, people, nation; distance; split, cleft; — *śi'b*, pl. *śi'âb*, mountain-path, path; cleft, narrow pass, valley, water-course; — *śu'b*, pl. of اشعب *aś'ab*, broad in the shoulders, having the horns distant from one another; — *śu'ub*, pl. of شعيب *śa'îb*; — ة *śu'ba-t*, pl. *śu'ab*, *śi'âb*, ramification, twig, branch; finger; part, piece; distance between two objects; mountain-cleft; water-course, channel.
شعبان *śa'bân*, pl. *śa'bânât*, *śa'âbîn*, name of the eighth Arabian month.
(شعبذ) *śa'baẕ*, INF. ة, juggle.
(شعبط) *śa'bat*, INF. ة, climb, scale.
(شعث) *śa'iṯ*, A, INF. *śa'aṯ*, be dis-

persed; get into disorder; be separated into fibres or threads; — INF. *śa'as̱*, *śu'ûs̱a-t*, have the hair dishevelled and untidy; — II. INF. *taś'îs̱*, disperse, scatter; separate into fibres; bring into disorder;—V. INF. *taśa''us̱*, pass. of the previous.

شعث *śa'as̱*, disorder; — *śa'is̱*, dispersed, disorderly; also—

شعثان *śa's̱ân*, dishevelled.

(شعر) *śa'ar*, U, INF. *śi'r*, *śa'r*, *śa'ra-t*, *śi'ra-t*, *śu'ra-t*, *śu'ûr*, *śi'ra*, *śu'ra*, *śu'ûra-t*, *maś'ûr*, *maś'ûra-t*, *maś'ûrâ'*, know, notice, observe, feel; — U, INF. *śi'r*, *śa'ar*, compose poetry, make verses; surpass as a poet; — *śa'ir*, A, INF. *śa'ar*, be hairy, shaggy; have slaves; — *śa'ur*, be a poet; know, notice; — II. INF. *taś'îr*, line the inside with fur, &c.; grow hairy, shaggy; — III. INF. *muśâ'ara-t*, vie as a poet with; sleep with another in the same under-garment; touch one skin to skin; — IV. INF. *iś'âr*, cause to notice, inform, make known to (acc.); mark the animal for sacrifice; grow hair (embryo); clothe with the شعار *śi'âr*; provide the handle of a knife or the hilt of a sword with a knob or pommel; — V. INF. *taśa''ur*, grow hair; — VI. INF. *taśâ'ur*, deal in poetry, pass one's self for a poet; — X. INF. *istiś'âr*, grow hair; put on the شعار *śi'âr*; feel anxiety, fear; apprehend.

شعر *śa'r*, *śâ'ar*, ة, pl. *śi'âr*, *śu'ûr*, *aś'âr*, hair; شعر مستعار *śa'r musta'âr*, periwig; — *śi'r*, pl. *aś'âr*, knowing (s.), knowledge; noticing (s.), perception, sensation; poetry, poem, verses; — *śu'r*, plants, trees, vegetation; pl. of اشعر *aś'ar*, hairy, &c.; — *śa'ir*, ة, hairy; — *śu'ur*, pl. of شعار *śi'âr*; — ة *śi'ra-t*, hair of the pubes; pudenda.

شعرا *śa'râ'*, f. of اشعر *aś'ar*, hairy, &c.; — *śu'arâ'*, pl. of شاعر *śâ'ir*, poet.

شعرانى *śa'râniyy*, very hairy.

شعرور *śu'rûr*, pl. *śa'ârîr*, versifier; — also ة *śa'rûra-t*, a small cucumber; a fly.

شعرى *śi'ra*, dog-star, Syrius; — *śi'riyy*, poetical; — ة *śa'riyya-t*, transparent veil; wire-work, trellis-work; vermicelli.

(شعشع) *śa'śa'*, INF. ة, mix; water the wine; shine, sparkle; — II. INF. *taśa'śu'*, draw towards the end.

(شعصب) *śa'ṣab*, INF. ة, be decrepit.

شعصور *śu'ṣûr*, wild nut.

(شعط) *śa'aṭ*, INF. *śa'ṭ*, get angry, fly into a passion.

شعع *śu'u'*, pl. of شعاع *śu'â'*

(شعف) *śa'af*, INF. *śa'af*, enflame, take entirely hold of, madden (love, &c.); — *śa'if*, A, INF. *śa'af*, be madly in love; lose the hair of the eye-lids.

شعف *śa'af*, passionate love; infatuation; a disease of the camel which makes it lose the hair of the eye-lids; highest point, top; — ة *śa'afa-t*, pl. *-ât*, *śa'af*, *śu'ûf*, *śi'âf*, mountain-summit; topmost part of the heart; lock of hair; — also *śa'fa-t*, pl. *śa'afât*, gentle rain.

(شعل) *śa'al*, INF. *śa'l*, light a fire, kindle; kindle war; enflame the heart; give one's self entirely over to a thing, be extreme in it; burn with love; — *śa'il*, A, INF. *śa'al*, have a white forehead, mane and tail; — II. INF. *taś'îl*, kindle; excite war, passion, &c.; — IV. INF. *iś'âl*=II.; — V. INF. *taśa''ul*, be kindled, burn; burn with love; — VIII. INF. *išti'âl*, ignite, burn; enflame; get covered with white hair.

شعل *śa'al*, white hair of the forehead and tail; — ة *śu'la-t*, pl. *śu'ul*, *śu'ûl*, burning piece of

wood; tinder; flame; brightness, light.
شعلان *śa'lân*, kindled, inflamed, burning.
شعلع *śa'alla'*, great, high.
(شعلق), II. *taśa'laq*, INF. *taśa'luq*, climb, scale.
(شعم) *śa'am*, U, INF. *śa'm*, pacify.
(شعن) *śa'an*, scattered dry leaves or parts of plants; — *śa'an* and IV. dishevel; — IV. INF. *iś'ân*, see I.; seize in combat the hair of the adversary's forehead; — XI. *iśa'ânn*, INF. *iś'înân*, be dishevelled.
(شعنب) *śa'nab*, INF. ة, have the horns bent backwards.
(شعنلع) *śa'anla'*, great, high.
(شعو) *śa'â*, U, INF. *śa'w*, bristle, stand on end; — IV. INF. *iś'â'*, scatter troops in all directions for plunder; exert one's self zealously in (ب *bi*).
شعوب *śa'ûb*, death; — *.
(شعوذ) *śa'waẓ*, INF. ة, juggle.
شعوذة *śa'waẓa-t*, jugglery; legerdemain, sleight of hand.
شعوذى *śa'waẓiyy*, juggler; courier, express.
شعور *śu'ûr*, INF. of (شعر); consciousness, intellect; knowledge; ارباب شعور *arbâb śû'ûr*, the learned.
شعيب *śa'îb*, pl. *śu'ub*, travelling-bag with partitions; — *śu'aib*, name of Moses's father-in-law, Jethro.
شعير *śa'îr*, barley; comrade; — ة *śa'îra-t*, grain of barley; knob at the handle of a knife or the hilt of a sword; pl. *śa'â'ir*, victim, animal to be sacrificed; ceremonies of the pilgrimage; — *śu'aira-t*, little hair.
شعيع *śa'î'*, cart, carriage.
شعيفات *śu'aifât*, little curls on the forehead.
شعيل *śa'îl*, having a white tail; — ة *śa'îla-t*, pl. *śa'â'il*, *śa'îl*, *śu'ul*, burning wick; burning match.
(شغ) *śagg*, U, INF. *śagg*, scatter about; go different ways, separate (n.).
شغا *śagâ*, *śagan*, splayness of tooth.
شغاب *śaggâb*, stirrer up of discord, of a tumult.
شغارة *śaggâra-t*, flint-stone.
شغاف *śagâf*, the innermost heart, core; pericardium; original sin; — also *śugâf*, pain in the pericardium or about the liver.
(شغب) *śagab*, U, INF. *śagb*, deviate; A, INF. *śagab*, stir up discord, revolt, tumult; — II. INF. *taśgîb*, foment discord; — III. INF. *muśâgaba-t*, try to injure one, make a quarrel with.
شغب *śagab*, *śagb*, discord, tumult, revolt; — *śagib*, *śigabb*, trouble-maker, factionist.
شغبر *śagbar*, شغبز *śagbaz*, jackal; — II. *taśagbar*, INF. *taśagbur*, get entangled, mixed up.
(شغر) *śagar*, INF. *śagr*, lift the leg to make water (dog); be far from; be given up and left defenceless; drive away, expel; be separated, dispersed; — III. INF. *muśâgara-t*, intermarry without mutually giving a dowry; — IV. INF. *iśgâr*, march separate from others; — V. INF. *taśaggur*, career; — VIII. INF. *iśtigâr*, be numerous, be complicated; be far distant.
شغر بغر *śigar-a bigar-a*, in all directions.
(شغز) *śagaz*, INF. *śagz*, behave impudently against; stir up discord, excite a tumult.
(شغزب) *śagzab*, powerful wrestler; — also شغرب *śagrab*, INF. ة, trip in wrestling; — II. INF. *taśagrub*, blow sideways.
شغزبى *śagzaba*, ة *śagzabiyya-t*, شغربية *śagrabiyya-t*, tripping in wrestling.
شغشغ *śagśag*, INF. ة, turn the lance inside the body of the wounded, pierce with the lance; move the bit in the mouth of a horse that

is to be broken in; roar; coo; hasten, hurry (n.).

(شغف) *śagaf*, INF. *śagf*, hurt in the pericardium or about the liver; inspire with violent love; — *śagif*, A, INF. *śagaf*, be passionately in love; — VII. INF. *inśigâf*, id.

شغف *śagf* = شغاف *śagâf*; — *śagaf*, passionate love.

شغفر *śagfar*, handsome woman.

(شغل) *śagal*, INF. *śagl*, *śugl*, occupy (a.), give work; engross; divert from one occupation by means of another; be occupied, engrossed; — II. INF. *taśgîl*, occupy (a.); give work; — IV. INF. *iśgâl*, id.; — VI. INF. *taśâgal*, occupy one's self with, busy one's self, pretend to be busy or occupied; be detained from a place by an occupation; — VIII. INF. *iśtigâl*, be occupied, engrossed with; work.

شغل *śagl*, *śugl*, *śagal*, *śugul*, pl. *aśgâl*, *śugûl*, n. u. ة *śugla-t*, pl. *śuglât*, occupation, work, business; — *śagil*, occupied, busy; — ة *śagla-t*, pl. *śugal*, corn-stack.

(شغم) *śagim*, greedy.

(شغنب) *śagnab*, شغنوب *śugnûb*, tender branch; — *śagnab*, INF. ة, be bifurcated.

شغنة *śugna-t*, pl. *śugan*, tender branch; burden; bundle.

(شغو) *śagâ*, U, INF. *śagw*, be of unequal length; — شغى *śagî*, A, INF. شغا *śagan*, id.; — II. INF. *taśgiya-t*, emit urine in drops; — IV. INF. *iśgâ'*, hinder, obstruct.

شغوا *śagwâ'*, شغيا *śagyâ'*, f. of اغشى *agśa*, having teeth of unequal length, splay-toothed.

شغير *śiggîr*, who stirs up discord.

شغيزة *śagîza-t*, packing-needle.

شغيل *śagîl*, occupied, busy.

(شف) *śaff*, I, INF. *śafaf*, *śufûf*, *śafîf*, increase, multiply, and, by opposition, lessen, diminish; be very fine, thin, clear, transparent; — I, INF. *śufûf*, be emaciated; — U, emaciate; get moved, excited, agitated; — I, INF. *śiff*, multiply (n.), increase (n.), exceed, and, by opposition, diminish, remain short of; — IV. INF. *iśfâf*, prefer; — VI. INF. *taśâfuf*, drink out; — VIII. INF. *iśtifâf*, id.; — X. INF. *istiśfâf*, try to see through anything transparent, discern; fill with longing for (الى *ila*); exhaust.

شف *śaff*, *śiff*, gain, surplus, increase; loss, decrease, abatement; wind; pl. *śufûf*, transparent material or dress; — ة *śafa-t*, *śifa-t*, pl. *śafawât*, *śifâh*, lip (بنت الش *bint aś-śafa-t*, word, speech); praise; edge, border; — ة *śaffa-t*, pl. *śifâf*, *śufuf*, lip; — *śiffa-t*, *śaffa-t*, gain, increase; decrease.

شفا *śafa*, *śaf-an*, pl. *aśfâ'*, *śufiyy*, *śiffiyy*, edge, border, seam, corner, angle, end; last remains of life, light, &c.; — *śifâ'*, healing, curing (s.), INF. of (شفو); pl. *aśfiya-t*, *aśâfî*, medicine, remedy; cure, recovery.

شفارج *'śufârij*, tray or plate with sweets, flowers, &c.

شفاشف *śufâśif*, pitch of thirst.

شفاعة *śafâ'a-t*, *śifâ'a-t*, intercession, recommendation.

شفاف *śaffâf*, thin and transparent; — *śifâf*, pl. of شفيف *śafîf* and شفة *śaffa-t*; — ة *śafâfa-t*, transparency; — *śufâfa-t*, remains of water in a vessel.

شفان *śaffân*, cold wind with rain.

شفاه *śifâh*, conversation, INF. III. of (شفه); pl. of شفة *śafa-t* and شفهة *śafaha-t*.

شفاهى *śifâhiyy*, by way of mouth; labial; — *śufâhiyy*, having thick lips.

(شفتر) *śaftar*, INF. ة, be dispersed; (m.) have the nether lip thicker and protruding; — III. *iśfatarr*, INF. *iśfitrâr*, be dispersed; get broken.

شفتن *śaftan*, INF. ة, lie with.
شفتورة *śaftûra-t*, thick nether lip (m.).
(شفر) *śafir*, A, INF. *śafâra-t*, be inclined to sexual pleasure and easily satisfied (woman); diminish, lessen (n.); — II. INF. *taśfîr*, come to the edge or end; be near setting; diminish, waste away (n.).
شفر *śufr*, *śafr*, pl. *âśfâr*, edge, border, seam; extreme limit, end; somebody, anybody; — ة *śafra-t*, pl. *śifâr*, border, seam; edge of a sword, &c.; broad blade; knife; knife of a shoemaker or gardener; servant; somebody; also *śufra-t*, sufficient store or provisions; — *śufra-t*, pl. *aśfâr*, edge of the eye-lids; knife of a shoemaker.
(شفز) *śafaz*, I, INF. *śafz*, kick with the fore part of the foot.
شفشاف *śafśâf*, cold.
(شفشف) *śafśaf*, INF. ة, emaciate; dry up and bend; burn, scorch; emit; sprinkle; tremble; be mixed.
شفشق *śafśaq*, pl. *śafâśiq*, paddle of a water-wheel (m.).
شفشليق *śafśalîq*, withered old woman.
(شفع) *śafa'*, INF. *śaf'*, make equal what was unequal before, pair, couple; adjust, round up; INF. *śafâ'a-t*, intercede, speak in favour of (ل *li* or فى *fî*); assist in damaging another; — INF. *śaf'*, *śif'*, have a foal and be big with young again; — II. INF. *taśfî'*, accept one's intercession; — V. INF. *taśaffu'*, intercede with (الى *ila*); — X. INF. *istiśfâ'*, ask for one's intercession.
شفع *śaf'*, things equal, making a couple or pair with another; even number; created beings as couples or pairs; a festival in Mecca; — ة *śuf'a-t*, pairing, coupling (s.); right of pre-emption on neighbouring grounds; rescue; madness.
شفعا *śufa'â'*, pl. of شفيع *śafî'*.
شفف *śafaf*, little of a thing; INF. of (شف); — *śufuf*, pl. of شفة *śaffa-t*.
(شفق) *śafaq*, U, I, INF. *śafaq*, *śafaqa-t*, feel compassion with, have mercy upon, pardon (على *'ala*); love tenderly; — I, be on one's guard; be afraid; — *śafiq*, A, INF. *śafaq*, be anxiously concerned in one's welfare; — IV. INF. *iśfâq*, be on one's guard against; fear and shun; have compassion with; diminish (a.); — V. INF. *taśaffuq*, have compassion.
شفق *śafaq*, pl. *aśfâq*, evening twilight; ruddy light; compassion, tender sympathy; shore, tract of the coast; — ة *śafaqa-t*, compassion, solicitude, fond attachment.
شفقان *śafqân*, compassionate, kind.
شفلقة *śafallaqa-t*, a game in which one tries to hit the other's buttocks.
(شفن) *śafan*, I, INF. *śufûn*; — *śafin*, A, look askance at (with wonder and contempt).
شفن *śafin*, *śafn*, *śufan*, sagacious.
شفنين *śifnîn*, *śafnîn*, pl. *śafânîn*, turtle-dove.
(شفه) *śafah*, INF. *śafh*, strike on the lip; divert from a thing by other occupation; exhaust another's property by obtrusive begging; — III. INF. *śifâh*, *muśâfaha-t*, bring one's lips close to another's, approach, be near; tell to one's face, communicate by word of mouth; — ة *śafaha-t*, pl. *śifâh*, lip; — ى *śafahiyy*, ة, referring to the lips, labial.
(شفو) *śafâ*, U, INF. *śafw*, be near setting; appear; — شفى *śafa*, I, INF. *śifâ'*, cure, heal, pass. *śufî*, recover; — *śafî*, A, INF.

شفا *safan*, set; — IV. INF. *iśfâ'*, be quite close to (على *'ala*); give as a remedy; cure, restore to health; — V. INF. *taśaffî*, recover; calm down, get pacified; satisfy one's revengefulness; — VIII. INF. *iśtifâ'*, recover; rejoice in an enemy's calamity; — X. ask to be cured or for a remedy; consider as a remedy; try to get satisfaction, to vent one's revengefulness.

شفوات *śafawât*, pl. of شفة *śafa-t*.

شفوف *śufûf*, transparency, INF. of (شف); — *.

شفوق *śafûq*, compassionate, merciful.

شفوى *śafawiyy*, referring to the lips, labial.

شفى *śafî*, (v.) see (شفو); — *śafiyy*, labial; — *śufiyy*, pl. of شفا *śafan*.

شفير *śafîr*, edge, border, seam, end.

شفيع *śafî'*, pl. *śufa'â'*, intercessor, advocate, mediator, protector; ش حايط, possessor of neighbouring ground having a right of pre-emption.

شفيف *śafîf*, thin, transparent; pl. *śifâf*, scorching effect of heat or cold; little of, few.

شفيق *śafîq*, compassionate, solicitous, well-wisher.

شفيهة *śufaiha-t*, small lip.

(شق) *śaqq*, U, INF. *śaqq*, split, cleave, tear asunder; pierce through; separate (a.); make one's way through a crowd; renounce one's people, stir up discord; INF. *śaqq*, *maśaqqa-t*, be troublesome, difficult to deal with, unbearable; bear up with; throw into difficulties, molest; (m.) visit; — II. INF. *taśqîq*, split into many fragments, shatter; pronounce distinctly; — III. INF. *śiqâq*, *muśâqqa-t*, separate from, renounce, become hostile to, act with hostility towards (acc.); — V. INF. *taśaqquq*, split (n.), separate (n.) into fibres; — VI. INF. *taśâquq*, separate from one another, become enemies; — VII. INF. *inśiqâq*, get split, separated; separate (n.); turn a schismatic; — VIII. INF. *iśtiqâq*, take half of; derive a word; swerve from the matter in dispute.

شق *śaqq*, pl. *śuqûq*, split, rent; half (s.); side; dawn (of morning); molestation; — *śiqq*, half (s.); one side of a thing; uterine brother; the beloved (f.);—*śuqq*, pl. of شقا *śuqqâ'*; — ة *śaqqa-t*, visit (m.); — *śiqqa-t*, *śuqqa-t*, pl. *śiqaq*, *śuqaq*, half (s.); rag; chip; long piece of cloth; garment open in front; door-wing; distance; long and difficult journey; great hardship; — *śûqqa-t*, folded piece of paper or cloth, note, scrap, letter; diploma, mandate (m.).

(شقا) *śaqa'*, INF. *śaq'*, *śuqû'*, pierce through; cleave or hurt the head; part the hair.

شقا *śaqan*, *śaqa*, also *śaqâ'*, *śiqâ'*, misery, distress; impudence; — *śaqqâ*, pl. *śuqq*, wide in the womb.

شقاحط *śaqâḥiṭ*, pl. of شقحطب *śaqaḥṭab*.

شقاحة *śaqâḥa-t*, ugliness, horridness, abomination, infamy.

شقاذى *śaqâẓa*, pl. of شقذ *śaqẓ*.

شقار *śuqqâr*, pl. of شقر *śaqir*; name of a fish.

شقارى *śuqâra*, lie; pl. of شقر *śaqir*.

شقاطب *śaqâṭib*, pl. شقحطب *śaqaḥṭab*.

شقافة *śuqâfa-t*, potsherds.

شقاق *śiqâq*, separation, renunciation, discord, dissension, hostility, rebellion; — *śuqâq*, pl. chaps of the skin.

شقاوة *śaqâwa-t*, *śiqâwa-t*, distress, misery; impudence; malice, rebellion, murder and robbery.

شقاوى *śiqâwiyy*, miserable, in distress.

شقب *śaqb*, *śiqb*, pl. *śiqâb*, *śiqaba-t*, *śaqaba-t*, *śuqûb*, mountain-cleft; cavity in a rock where birds build their nests; narrow mountain-pass; low-ground with stagnating water;—*śiqb*, *śaqab*, a tree with lotus-like fruit.

(شقح) *śaqah*, INF. *śaqh*, break (a.); lift the leg to make water; soil, pollute;—*śaquh*, INF. *śaqâha-t*, be ugly, horrid, abominable; be mean, vile, infamous; make fun of, scoff at, scold;—IV. INF. *iśqâh*, remove (a.) to a great distance; have dates beginning to ripen;—ة *śuqha-t*, red intermingled with white.

(شقحطب) *śaqahtab*, pl. *śaqâhit*, *śaqâtib*, ram with strong horns.

شقحى *śuqahiyy*, red.

شقدة *śiqda-t*, good grass for food.

(شقذ) *śaqaz*, I, INF. *śaqz*, depart, emigrate;—*śaqiz*, A, INF. *śaqaz*, have a malignant look, injure by it;—III. INF. *muśâqaza-t*, oppose with hostility;—IV. INF. *iśqâz*, expel, drive away.

شقذ *śaqz*, *śiqz*, fault, blemish, blame; also *śuqaz* and شقذان *śiqzân*, pl. *śaqâza*, young of the chameleon; young of the *qata* or of the sparrow-hawk; also *śiqzân*, *śaqazân*, wolf;—*śaqiz*, id.; also *śaqazân*, having a malignant look; sleepless.

شقذا *śaqzâ'*, شقذى *śaqaza*, hungry eagle.

(شقر) *śaqir*, A, INF. *śaqar*, *śuqra-t*, be of a light red, bay; have red hair;—*śaqur*, id.;—IX. *iśqarr*, INF. *iśqirâr*, id.

شقر *śaqr*, pl. *śuqûr*, pressing and necessary business;—*śaqir*, ة, pl. *śaqirât*, *śuqqâr*, *siqrân*, *śuqâra*, *śuqqâra*, anemony; red tulip;—*śuqar*, cock; lie;—ة *śuqra-t*, light red, bay-colour.

شقراق *śaqrâq*, *śiqrâq*, *śaqarrâq*, *śiqarrâq*, green magpie; green woodpecker.

شقران *śiqrân*, anemony; pl. of شقر *śaqir*.

(شقشق) *śaqśaq*, INF. ة, pronounce distinctly; twitter, peep; talk very glibly; roar, cry out;—ة *śiqśiqa-t*, pl. *śaqâśiq*, part of a camel's throat which is protruded in roaring, sound produced by it; glibness of tongue, great eloquence; Persian belt;—ى *śiqśiqiyy*, loud.

(شقص) *śiqs*, portion, share, lot; piece of ground; partnership; a good horse;—II. *śaqqas*, INF. *taśqîs*, divide and distribute in equal parts.

شقطية *śaqatiyya-t*, tuft of hair in the middle of the head (m.).

(شقع) *śaqa'*, put the mouth to the vessel and drink; injure by the evil eye; heap up, pile up;—II. INF. *taśqî'*, offend by reviling what another honours; revile on account of one's religion.

(شقف) *śaqaf*, pl. *śiqâf*, earthen pot; potsherd;—*śaqaf*, and II. *śaqqaf*, INF. *taśqîf*, cut into pieces, split;—ة *śaqfa-t*, pl. *śaqaf*, *śiqaf*, potsherd; chip; piece; small coin.

شقق *śaqaq*, length of a horse's body;—*śiqaq*, pl. of شقة *śiqqa-t*.

(شقل) *śaqal*, U, INF. *śaql*, weigh a coin or money; lie with; (m.) lift up, pull up, hoist.

(شقلب) *śaqlab*, INF. ة, turn topsy-turvy; overthrow; tumble over; stir (n.), bestir one's self;—II. INF. *taśaqlub*, be overthrown, tumble; roll about, turn restlessly from one side to the other (in bed).

شقم *śaqam*, ة, a species of date; a species of the palm-tree.

(شقن) *śaqan*, INF. *śaqn*, do little, give scantily, diminish (a.);—*śaqun*, INF. *śuqûna-t*, be little, paltry;—IV. INF. *iśqân*, have

but a small fortune; give little.

شقن *śaqn, śaqin*, little of, paltry.

(شقح), II. *śaqqah*, INF. *taśqih*, have dates which begin to ripen.

(شقو) *śaqâ*, U, make miserable, throw into calamities; surpass in bearing up with distress; — شقى *śaqî*, A, INF. *śaq-an, śaqâ', śaqwa-t, śiqwa-t, śaqâwa-t, śiqâwa-t*, be miserable, unfortunate, unhappy; — شقى *śaqa*, split, tear asunder; I, INF. *śaqq*, pierce through; — III. INF. *muśâqât*, vie in bearing up with distress; assist in need of war; — IV. INF. *iśqâ'*, throw into misery, render unhappy; comb the hair or beard; — ة *śaqwa-t, śiqwa-t*, misery, distress, misfortune; malice; INF. of (شقى).

شقور *śaqûr, śuqûr*, urgent business; — *

شقول *śaqûl*, plummet.

شقى *śaqî, śaqa* (v.), see (شقو); — *śaqiyy*, ة, pl. *aśqiyâ'*, miserable, distressed, unhappy, wretched; impudent; villain, criminal, robber and murderer, rebel; — ة *śaqiyya-t*, malice; doings of a robber and murderer (m.).

شقيح *śaqîḥ*, disfigured, ugly; weakened.

شقيذ *śaqîẕ*, sleepless; having a malignant look.

شقيص *śaqîṣ*, partner, shareholder; partnership, share.

شقيط *śaqîṭ*, شقيظ *śaqîẕ*, earthenware.

شقيق *śaqîq*, pl. *aśiqqâ'*, split, torn; one half or side; uterine brother; — ة *śaqîqa-t*, pl. *śaqâ'iq*, split, rent (s.); one half or side; one-sided headache; mountain-pass; uterine sister; also *śaqîq*, pl. *śaqâ'iq*, anemony; peony; ش الما *śaqîq al-mâ'*, wood-violet.

شقين *śaqîn*, little of, little, small, paltry.

(شك) *śakk*, U, INF. *śakk*, doubt, be doubtful, suspect; be scandalised; cause doubts or scruples; scandalise; pierce with a lance to the bones, pierce through; lean upon or against; lean towards, adhere, cohere; halt, limp; arm one's self from head to foot; build the houses in one row; — II. INF. *taśkîk*, cause doubts or scruples, scandalise; — V. INF. *taśakkuk*, have doubts, suspicions; scruples; be scandalised; — VII. INF. *inśikâk*, be thrust into.

شك *śakk*, pl. *śukûk*, doubt, uncertainty, suspicion, scruple, scandal, hesitation; small rent or split; arsenic; — *śikk*, upper garment; case, sheath; — *śukk*, split, schism, tumult, commotions; — ة *śakka-t*, thrust of a lance; wound in the side; (m.) frontlet of gold-pieces; — *śikka-t*, pl. *śikak*, arms, equipment for war; wedge driven in for the purpose of fastening; — *śukka-t*, difficulty; split; schism.

(شكا) *śaka'*, INF. *śak*, penetrate, pierce through; grow; — شكى *śakî*, A, INF. *śaka'*, be chapped; — IV. INF. *iśkâ'*, push forth branches.

شكا *śakâ'*, illness; complaint; — ة *śakât*, id.; accusation, reproach; fault.

شكارة *śakâra-t*, piece, portion; small piece of cultivated ground (m.).

شكاز *śakkâz*, ة *śakkâza-t*, who prematurely emits the sperm in coition.

شكاسة *śakâsa-t*, a malignant repulsive being.

شكاعى *śukâ'a, śakâ'a*, a thin thorn.

شكاك *śakâk*, region, side; — *śikâk*, houses built in a single row; — *śukkâk*, pl. of شاك *śâkk*, completely armed; — ة *śakâka-t*, tract of land.

شكال *śikâl*, similarity, likeness, accordance; INF. III. of (شكل); pl. *śukul*, tether; girth; — ة

śikâla-t, mingled hue of red and white.

شكاه *śikâh*, similarity; neighbourhood; — *.

شكاوة *śakâwa-t*, complaint.

شكائر *śakâ'ir*, pl. front locks.

شكاية *śikâya-t*, *śakâya-t*, complaint; accusation.

شكب *śukb*, gift, present; requital, reward.

(شكد) *śakad*, U, INF. *śakd*, give; — II. INF. *taśkîd*, present with; — IV. INF. *iśkâd*, id.; acquire anything valueless.

شكد *śakd*, present; thank.

(شكر) *śakar*, U, INF. *śukr*, *śukûr*, *śukrân*, thank; praise; reward; (also IV.) sprout; *śakir*, A, INF. *śakar*, abound in milk, in water; be rich, liberal; be fat; — III. INF. *muśâkara-t*, prove thankful to (acc.); — IV. abound in milk; have cattle abounding in milk; see I.; — V. INF. *taśakkur*, thank one (ل *li*) for (acc.); speak but well of (من *min*); — VIII. INF. *iśtikâr*, abound in milk; rain plenteously.

شكر *śakr*, coition; also *śikr*, pudenda of a woman; — *śukr*, pl. *śukûr*, thanks, protestation of thankfulness; praise; reward from God; — *śukur*, pl. of شكير *śakîr*; — *śukkar*, pl. of شاكر *śâkir*, thankful, &c.; —ة *śakara-t*, abundance of milk in the udder; —*śakira-t*, pl. *-ât*, *śakâra*, *śakra*, abounding in milk.

شكران *śukrân*, thanks, thankfulness; praise, glorification.

شكرانية *śukrâniyya-t*, thankfulness, gratitude.

شكرية *śakariyya-t*, return of the camels from the spring pastures.

(شكز) *śakaz*, U, INF. *śakz*, tip with the finger; sting with words, slander, backbite; pierce with a lance; lie with.

(شكس) *śakus*, INF. *śakâsa-t*, be malignant, difficult to deal with, unsociable; — III. INF. *muśâkasa-t*, show one's self thus towards (acc.); — VI. INF. *taśâkus*, be so towards one another.

شكس *śaks*, *śakis*, *śakus*, ة, pl. *śuks*, bearing ill-will, malignant, difficult to deal with, unsociable.

شكشكة *śakśaka-t*, sharp arms; armour.

شكص *śakiṣ*=شكس *śakis*.

(شكع) *śaka'*, INF. *śak'*, pull up the head of a camel by the bridle; — *śaki'*, A, INF. *śaka'*, groan much, feel pain; be angry; be full of pain; — IV. INF. *iśkâ'*, provoke to anger, molest.

شكع *śaki'*, sleepless; ill-tempered, out of humour, peevish.

شكك *śikak*, pl. of شكة *śikka-t*; — *śukuk*, pl. of شكيكة *śakîka-t*.

(شكل) *śakal*, U, INF. *śakl*, tie three feet of a beast together; mark a text with the vowel-points; (also II. and IV.) place two shades of colour, &c. side by side; just begin to get red and ripen; — *śakil*, A, INF. *śakal*, be ambiguous, obscure, complicated, difficult; be of mixed hue, as black and white, red and white, &c.; be coquettish; — II. INF. *taśkîl*, tether, tie up; vocalise; form, shape; see I.; tuck up the clothes or sleeves; plait the hair on both sides of the forehead; — III. INF. *muśâkala-t*, resemble another, remind (one) of another by features or qualities; agree, accord, suit, fit; — IV. INF. *iśkâl*, be ambiguous, obscure, confused, difficult; vocalise; see I.; be of a mixed hue; — V. INF. *taśakkul*, get into shape, take such or such a form; be vocalised; get shaded with different hues; — VI. INF. *taśâkul*, resemble one another, agree, fit together.

شكل *śakl*, pl. *aśkâl*, *śukûl*, resemblance; exterior, personal de-

scription; shape, form, figure; manner, way, fashion, taste; garb; kind, species, variety; religion, creed, belief; coquettishness; vocalisation of a text; suppression of the second and seventh letter of a foot when both are quiescent; pl. *aśkâl*, difficult and complicated matter; object of dispute; — *śikl*, resemblance; phantom, bugbear; coquettishness; — *śukl*, pl. of اشكل *aśkal*, of mixed hue; — *śukul*, pl. of شكال *śikâl*; — ة *śukla-t*, red mixed with white; reddish whiteness; shading of two hues.

شكلا *śaklâ'*, f. of اشكل *aśkal*, of mixed hue.

(شكم) *śakam*, U, INF. *śakm*, *śakîm*, bite; INF. *śakm*, requite, give a present in return, reward; bribe; bridle; = *śakim*, A, INF. *śakam*, be hungry; — IV. reward, reciprocate a present.

شكم *śukm*, reward, reciprocation of a present; present; pl. of شكيمة *śakîma-t*; — *śakim*, lion.

شكمى *śukma*, mutual present.

(شكه), III. *śâkah*, INF. *śikâh*, *muśâkaha-t*, resemble, be related; — IV. INF. *iśkâh*, be complicated, difficult; — VI. INF. *taśâkuh*, resemble one another.

(شكو) *śakâ*, U, (also شكى *śaka*, I) INF. *śakwân*, *śakwa*, *śakût*, *śakâwa-t*, *śikâya-t*, *śakiyya-t*, complain; accuse; feel pain or complain of such; — INF. *śakw*, *śakwa*, *śakât*, befall, visit sorely (illness, &c.); — II. INF. *taśkiya-t*, allow one to complain, listen to his complaints; prepare the skin bag for making butter; — IV. INF. *iśkâ'*, cause to complain, listen to one's complaints, and, by opposition, cut short one's complaints; injure and pain still more; — V. INF. *taśakkî*, complain, complain to, bring forth a complaint or accusation; — VI. INF. *taśâkî*, complain of one another; accuse or reproach each other; — VIII. INF. *iśtikâ'*, complain; ache; complain to, accuse; use the following: — ة *śakwa-t*, pl. *śakawât*, *śikâ'*, bag of kid-skin for milk or water; complaint.

شكوا *śakwâ*, complaint.

شكوثا *śakûsa'*, شكوثى *śakûsa*, flax-silk.

شكور *śakûr*, very thankful; thanking (adj.); paying, worth the trouble; satisfied with a little; — *.

شكورية *śukûriyya-t*, chicory.

شكوى *śakwa*, complaint; accusation; pain, ache, suffering, illness.

شكى *śaka*, (v.) see (شكو); — *śakî'*, (v.) see (شكا); — *śukka*, sharp bit; — *śakkiy*, ة, who always complains or ails; who is complained of; — *śakiyy*, doubtful; uncertain; irresolute, hesitating; — ة *śakiyya-t*, complaint; rest.

شكير *śakîr*, pl. *śukur*, bark of a tree; shoots of a root; small leaves, branches, feathers, &c., between larger ones; hair in the face and neck.

شكيكة *śakîka-t*, pl. *śakâ'ik*, *śukuk*, troop, people; sect; custom, usage; gullet; fruit-basket.

شكيل *śakîl*, well formed, handsome, pretty.

شكيم *śakîm*, INF. of (شكم); — ة *śakîma-t*, pl. *śakâ'im*, *śukm*, *śakîm*, handle of a vessel or pot; bit of a bridle (شديد الش *śadîd aś-śakîma-t*, hard of mouth, restive); maliciousness; haughtiness; poison; rust, dirt; hunting panther.

(شل) *śall*, U, INF. *śall*, *śalal*, drive away the camels, drive away; INF. *śall*, sew with wide stitches, stitch together; shed tears; — A, INF. *śall*, *śalal*, be dried up, withered, maimed; — IV. INF. *iślâl*, cause the hand to wither;

— VII. INF. *inśilâl*, be driven away.

هلا *śalan*, limb, &c.=هلو *śilw*; — *śallâ'*, dried up or withered hand.

هلافة *śallâfa-t*, courtesan; concubine.

هلاق *śalâq*, stick; scourge; scourging (s.); refractory; — *śallâq*, wallet of a beggar.

هلال *śalâl*, withering of an arm or hand; — *śallâl*, who urges on violently.

هلايا *śalâyâ*, pl. of هلية *śaliyya-t*.

(هلبن) *śalban*, INF. ة, render pretty, elegant; — II. INF. *taśalbun*, be or become pretty; — ة *śalbana-t*, beauty, elegance (m.).

هلبى *śalabiyy*, pretty, handsome, elegant; barber.

هلجم *śaljam*, turnip (Pers.).

(هلح) *śalaḥ*, A, INF. *śalḥ*, strip (n.); (m.) put off the frock, renounce the ecclesiastical state; reject, leave aside; — undress, strip (a.); unfrock, secularise a monk or priest; plunder; carry on highway robbery; — V. INF. *taśalluḥ*, be robbed.

هلحا *śalḥan*, *śalḥâ'*, pl. *śulḥ*, sharp sword.

هلحف *śillaḥf*, of a weak frame, of a vacillating gait.

(هلع) *śalaḥ*, cut to pieces with a sword.

هلع *śalḥ*, volley; root, origin, race; sperm.

(هلخب) *śalḥab*, stammering.

(هلدق), II. *taśaldaq*, INF. *taśalduq*, rob with violence, plunder; — ة *śaldaqa-t*, theft, robbery.

هلش *śilś*, pl. *śulûś*, root; — *śaliś*, awkward, clumsy; — II. *śalaś*, INF. *taślîś*, take root, push the roots deeply into the ground.

(هلشل) *śalśal*, INF. ة, emit in drops; fall in drops, trickle; — II. INF. *taśalśul*, id.; shed.

هلشل *śalśal*, ة *śalśala-t*, dropping, trickling (s.); — *śulśul*, lean, thin; nimble, alert; also *śalśal*, willing to serve, to render services.

(هلط) *śalṭ*, knife; — ة *śilṭa-t*, pl. *śilaṭ*, long thin arrow.

هلطا *śalṭâ'*, knife.

(هلغ) *śalag*, INF. *śalg*, break one's skull.

هلغم *śalgam*, turnip; pl. *śalâgim*, moustache.

(هلق) *śalaq*, I, INF. *śalq*, whip, flog, scourge; split lengthwise; go off, fire off, give a volley; lie with; tumble in, slip (earth); — VIII. INF. *iśtilâq*, get wind of, suspect, surmise; find out (a secret).

هلق *śilq*, *śaliq*, a small fish; eel; — *śilqa-t*, ova of the Lybian lizard; — *śalaqa-t*, wooden hammer; horse-breakers, equerries.

هلل *śalal*, withering of the hand; stain which cannot be taken out; driving away (s.) — *śulal*, *śulul*=هلول *śulûl*.

هلو *śilw*, pl. *aślâ'*, limb; body; stump; rest, ruins; — ة *śilwa-t*, limb, piece, portion.

هلوش *śalûś*, awkward, clumsy.

هلوك *śalûk*, *śilûk*, هلوق *śalûq*, *śilûq*, sirocco.

هلول *śalûl*, nimble, alert; willing to serve, to render services, friendly, obliging; old.

هليح *śalîḥ*, small carpet, mat; sound.

هليك *śalîk*, volley.

هليل *śalîl*, pl. *aśilla-t*, *śilla-t*, under garment beneath a coat of mail; horse-cloth; swelling muscles of the neck and back; mucus; innermost part.

هلية *śaliyya-t*, pl. *śalâyâ*, remains of cattle; piece; part, portion.

(هم) *śamm* (*śamamtu*), U, INF. *śamm*, *śamîm*, *śimmîma*, smell (a.); take air, go into the open air; deviate; be proud; — *śamimtu*, A, smell; — pass. *summ*, be tested, probed; — II.

(also IV.) INF. *taśmîm*, smell (a.), make smell; — III. INF. *muśâmma-t*, smell at; — IV. INF. *iśmâm*, see II.; walk along with uplifted head; deviate; — V. INF. *taśammum*, VIII. INF. *iś-timâm*, smell; — X. INF. *istiś-mâm*, want to smell; inhale the smell.

شم *śamm*, smelling (s.), sense of smell, smell; — ة *śamma-t*, smell; a little of, a spark; pinch (of snuff); — *śumm*, pl. and—

شمّا *śammâ'*, f. of اشم *aśamm*, having a straight nose, &c.

شمات *śamât*, ة *śamâta-t*, rejoicing at another's misfortune; *śa-mâta-t*, tumult; — *śimât*, and—

شماتى *śamâta*, pl. who have been disappointed, deceived in their hopes.

شماج *śamâj*, skin of a grape, &c., that is thrown away in eating; a little of.

شمار *śamâr*, fennel.

شمارق *śamâriq*, شماريق *śamârîq*, torn.

شماريج *śamârîj*, pl. of شمراج *śimrâj*.

شماريخ *śamârîḥ*, pl. of شمراخ *śimrâḥ* and شمروخ *śumrûḥ*.

(شماز), III. *iśma'azz*, INF. *iśmi'zâz*, contract (n.), shrink, shudder; feel horror, shrink from.

شماس *śammâs*, pl. *śamâmisa-t*, priest, deacon; priest's attendant at mass.

شماص *śumâṣ*, haste, hurry.

شماط *śimâṭ*, greens; aromatic herbs for seasoning.

شماطيط *śamâṭîṭ*, pl. of شمطاط *śimṭâṭ*.

شماع *śammâ'*, seller of wax; chandler.

شمال *śamâl*, *śam'al*, *śam'all*, pl. *śamâ'il*, north; left hand or side; — *śimâl*, pl. *-ât*, north-wind; pl. *aśmul*, *śamâ'il*, *śumul*, left hand or side (ذو شمالين *ẕû śimâlain*, amphidexter); bad omen or augury; handful of ears; pl. *śamâ'il*, natural disposition, character, virtues; case, sheath; — *

شمالى *śamâliyy*, ة, northern (النور الشمالى *an-nûr aś-śamâliyy*, aurora borealis); cold day.

شماليل *śamâlîl*, pl. of شملول *śumlûl*.

شمام *śimâm*, smelling at (s.); — *śammâm*, ة *śammâma-t*, a fragrant striped melon; pl. *-ât*, perfumes; — ة *śamâma-t*, nosegay; — *śammâma-t*, wick-holder.

شمامسة *śamâmisa-t*, pl. of شماس *śammâs*.

شماميط *śamâmîṭ*, pl. of شموط *śam-mûṭ*.

شماميل *śamâmîl*, pl. of شمول *śam-mûl*.

شمائل *samâ'il*, pl. of شمال *śamâl*, *śimâl* and شميلة *śamîla-t*.

شمبا *śambâ'*, having clean teeth and a sweet breath.

(شمت) *śamit*, A, INF. *śamat*, *śa-mâta-t*, rejoice at another's misfortune; — II. INF. *taśmît*, (also IV.) blast one's hopes, disappoint; (also IV.) cause to rejoice at another's misfortune; wish a blessing to one who sneezes; — IV. INF. *iśmât*, see II.; — V. INF. *taśammut*, get disappointed; return without booty; — VIII. INF. *iśtimât*, begin to grow fat.

(شمج) *śamaj*, U, INF. *śamj*, sew with long stitches; urge to haste.

(شمجر) *śamjar*, INF. ة, flee in terror, run away from fear.

(شمحط) *śamḥaṭ*, شمحاط *śimḥâṭ*, شمحوط *śumḥûṭ*, disproportionately long.

(شمخ) *śamaḥ*, INF. *śamḥ*, *śumûḥ*, be high, lofty; bear one's head high, be proud; — II. heighten, raise, elevate; turn up; — VI. INF. *taśâmuḥ*, be very high; turn proud.

شمخ *śamaḥ*, high and distant aim; — *śummaḥ*, pl. of شامخ *śâmiḥ*, high.

(شمخر) *śamḥar*, INF. ة, be proud,

haughty; — III. *iśmaḥarr*, INF. *iśmiḥrâr*, be tall, high.

شمخر *śummaḥr*, *śimmaḥr*, haughty, proud.

شمخز *śummaḥz*, *śimmaḥz*, sagacious; great, bulky, gigantic; — ة *śummaḥza-t*, and—

شمخزيزة *śummaḥzîza-t*, great old age.

(شمظ) *śamaẓ*, I, INF. *śamẓ*, *śimâẓ*, *śumûẓ*, have conceived, be fructified; tuck up.

شمظ *śummaẓ*, pl. of شامظ *śâmiẓ*, pregnant, fructified; — ة *śamaẓa-t*, fructification of the palm-tree.

شمظار *śimẓâr*, شمظر *śamẓar*, *śimẓar*, quick pace or walk; — ة *śimẓâra-t*, id.; nimble, alert, agile.

(شمر) *śamar*, U, I, INF. *śamr*, walk with drawn sinews, walk with a light step and elegantly, walk proudly; hasten, hurry; draw together, contract; tuck up; cut the dates from the tree; — II. INF. *taśmîr*=I.; — IV. INF. *iśmâr*, urge to haste; — V. INF. *taśammur*, tuck up one's garments; make ready for; walk fast; walk leisurely; — VIII. INF. *iśtimâr*, walk apace.

شمر *śimr*, liberal; nimble, alert; looking sharply at, examining carefully; — *śamar*, part of Arabia, in the north of Najd; — *śimirr*, great, portentous.

شمراج *śimrâj*, pl. *śamârîj*, lie.

شمراخ *śimrâḫ*, pl. *śamârîḫ*, branch of a palm-tree with a bunch of dates; vine-shoot; bunch of grapes; mountain-summit; whiteness of a horse's forehead.

(شمرج) *śumruj*, thin tissue; — *śamraj*, INF. ة, sew badly and with long stitches; interlard one's speech with lies; nurse and nourish well.

(شمرخ) *śamraḫ*, INF ة, cut off the dates.

(شمردل) *śamardal*, شمرذل *śamarẓal*, long; swift; fine, handsome.

شمرة *śamra-t*, fennel.

شمروج *śumrûj*=شمرج *śumruj*.

شمروخ *śumrûḫ*=شمراخ *śimrâḫ*.

شمرى *śamariyy*, *śimiriyy*, *śumariyy*, *śimmariyy*, ة, nimble, alert, agile.

شمرير *śamrîr*, cap.

(شمز) *śamaz*, U, INF. *śamz*, feel aversion, abhor, shrink from, run away; — V. INF. *taśammuz*, contract (n.), shrink, frown.

(شمس) *śamas*, I, U, INF. *śams*, be bright and sunny; show hatred and enmity; — INF. *śimâs*, *śumûs*, be restive; — *śamis*, A, INF. *śamas*, be sunny; — II. INF. *taśmîs*, expose to the sun; serve at mass; — IV. INF. *iśmâs*, be sunny; — V. INF. *taśammus*, be exposed in the sun; lie down in the sun; bask.

شمس *śams*, f. pl. *śumûs*, sun; gold; source, spring; middle and head-piece (of an ornament); — *śums*, pl. of شموس *śamûs*; — ة *śamsa-t*, pl. *śamasât*, image of the sun; idol, statue, image; plate of a door-lock.

شمسل *śimsil*, elephant.

شمسى *śimsiyy*, ة, referring to the sun, solar; sunny; — ة *śamsiyya-t*, sun-shade; (m.) umbrella.

شمشقة *śimśiqa-t*=شقشقة *śiqśiqa-t*.

شمشم *śamśam*, INF. ة, do repeatedly or with interruptions.

(شمص) *śamaṣ*, INF. *śamṣ*, urge on violently; beat;—*śamiṣ*, A, INF. *śamaṣ*, talk quickly; — II. INF. *taśmîṣ*, urge on violently, goad an animal into restiveness; — VII. INF. *inśimâṣ*, be seized with terror.

(شمصر) *śamṣar*, INF. ة, press hard, drive into a corner.

(شمط) *śamaṭ*, mix; fill; lose its dates or leaves; (m.) grasp, take away everything; pull

(the ear); — *śamiṭ*, A, INF. *śamaṭ*, turn grey; (m.) grow suddenly.

شمط *śumṭ*, pl. شمطا *śumṭâ'*, f. شمطان *śumṭân*, pl. of اشمط *aśmaṭ*, turning grey.

شمطاط *śimṭâṭ*, pl. *śamâṭîṭ*, troop; rag, tatter.

شمطوط *śumṭûṭ*, great, tall, long;= the previous.

شمطيط *śimṭîṭ*, pl. *śamâṭîṭ*=شمطاط *śimṭâṭ*.

(شمظ) *śamaẓ*, U, INF. *śamẓ*, prevent, hinder; mix; take away gradually and in small quantities; try to instigate, to move.

(شمع) *śam'*, *śama'*, ة, pl. *śumû'* wax; wax-candle, candle, torch, lantern; ش عسلی *śam' 'asaliyy*, yellow wax; ش كافوری *śam' kâfûriyy*, white wax; — ة *śam'a-t*, pl. *śam'*, *śumû'*, wax-candle; piece of wax or of a candle.

(شمع) *śama'*, INF. *śam'*, *śumû'*, *maśma'a-t*, play, sport; INF. *śumû'*, be dispersed; — II. INF. *taśmî'*, cover or smear with wax, wax; cause to play; — IV. INF. *iśmâ'*, shine.

شمعدان *śam'dân*, pl. *śamâ'idîn*, candlestick (Pers.).

(شمعط), III. *isma'aṭṭ*, INF. *iśmi'ṭâṭ*, be full of anger.

(شمعل) *śam'al*, ة *śam'ala-t*, brisk, nimble, alert; — *śam'al*, INF. ة, get dispersed; — II. INF. *taśam'ul*, get dispersed; — III. *iśma'all*, INF. *iśmi'lâl*, impend, be close at hand; disperse and seek eagerly; walk fast; — ة *śam'ala-t*, Jewish way of reading holy scripture.

(شمعون) *śam'ûn*, Simeon.

شمعی *śam'iyy*, of wax, waxen; seller of wax.

(شمق) *śamiq*, A, INF. *śamaq*, be boisterously merry, almost mad with merriment; — V. INF. *taśammuq*, id.; sink (in mud, &c.).

شمق *śimiqq*, ة, great, tall, long.

(شمل) *śamal*, U, INF. *śaml*, *śumûl*, hold, contain, encompass; extend to all, have effect upon all; surround from all sides admit the stallion and conceive; INF. *śaml*, attack from the left; expose to the north wind; — *śamil*, A, INF. *śamal*, *śumûl*, wrap up in a cloak; comprise all, apply or extend to all; meet with a north wind; — II. INF. *taśmîl*, (also IV.) make to comprise or contain; expose to the north wind; — IV. INF. *iśmâl*, see II.; have north wind; blow from the north; wrap one up in a cloak; — V. INF. *taśammul*, wrap one's self up in one's clothes or a cloak; — VIII. INF. *iśtimâl*, id.; comprise, contain, consist of (على *'ala*); surround from all sides, encompass; extend to all, be general.

شمل *śaml*, collection, union; reunion, seeing again (s.); covering, veiling (s.); comprehension, conception; north wind; also *śamal*, great number, troop; — *śiml*, *śimill*, bunch of dates; — *śamal*, shoulder; pl. *aśmâl*, small quantity; a handfull of ears; north wind; — *śumul*, pl. of شمال *śimâl*; — ة *śamla-t*, pl. *śimâl*, cloak; kerchief, small turban; — *śimla-t*, way of wrapping one's self up in a cloak; — *śumla-t*, generality: ام الشملة *umm aś-śumla-t*, the world, wine; — *śamala-t*, small quantity; — *śimilla-t*, and—

شملال *śimlâl*, pl. *śamâlîl*, swift, fleet; the left hand.

شملل *śamlal*, INF. ة, be alert, agile, nimble; walk apace.

شملول *śumlûl*, pl. *śamâlîl*, small quantity; shoulder.

شمم *śamam*, height, sublimity; summit; length and straightness of the nose; nearness; distance; INF. of (شم).

(شمهذ) *śamhaẕ*, sharp; iron; swift

and having sharp teeth; — *śamhaẓ*, INF. ة, make thin; sharpen.

(همو) *śamâ*, U, INF. *śumuww*, be high, lofty, sublime; be highly honoured; — II. INF. *taśmiya-t*, smell (a.).

هموح *śamûḥ*, wide, stretching far; — *śumûḥ*, height; pride, INF. of (همح).

همور *śammûr*, diamond.

هموس *śamûs*, pl. *śums*, *śumus*, restive, headstrong, impatient of a rider; wine; — *śumûs*, restiveness; headstrongness; — *.

هموص *śamûṣ*, nimble, brisk.

هموط *śammûṭ*, pl. *śamâmîṭ*, skein; yarn on the spindle.

هموع *śamû'*, disposed to play and sport; — *.

همول *śamûl*, cooled; pure wine; north wind; — *śumûl*, encompassing, &c.; contents, collection of the mind, INF. of (همل); — *śammûl*, pl. *śamâmîl*, mulberry; raspberry (m.).

هموم *śamûm*, fragrant.

هميت *śamît*, rebuke, scolding; quarrel, tumult, clamour, screaming.

همير *śimmîr*, brisk, nimble, alert.

هميس *śamîs*, exposed to the sun, sunny; — ة *śumaisa-t*, little sun.

هميط *śamîṭ*, mixed; of two colours.

هميل *śamîl*, north wind; — ة *śamîla-t*, pl. *śamâ'il*, natural disposition, character, quality, virtue, talents.

هميم *śamîm*, INF. of (هم); odour, perfume; fragrant; smelling (adj.); high, lofty, sublime; — ة *śamîma-t*, odour, stench.

هميمى *śimmîma*, odour, smell, INF. of (هم).

(هن) *śann*, U, INF. *śann*, pour out slowly, water the wine; (also IV.) disperse (a.) the troops for plunder; — II. INF. *taśnîn*, sprinkle with sand; — IV. INF. *iśnân*, see I.; — V. INF. *taśannun*, be old and worn out; — VI. INF. *taśânun*, id.; be wrinkled; be mixed; — X. INF. *istiśnân*, grow lean, thin.

هن *śann*, ة, pl. *śinân*, old withered skin-bag.

(هنا) *śana'*, هنى *śani'*, A, INF. *śan'*, *śin'*, *śun'*, *śanâ'a-t*, *śan'ân*, *śana'ân*, *śana'âna-t*, *maśna'*, *maśna'a-t*, *masnu'a-t*, hate, detest (ب *bi*); admit one's claim on a debt and pay him.

هنا *śunnâ'*, pl. of هانى *śânî*, hater, enemy; — ة *śunât*, id.; — *śanâ'at*, hatred, detestation, abhorrence.

هنابث *śunâbiṯ*, lion; thick, stout.

هناتين *śanâtîn*, pl. of هنتان *śintân* and هنتيان *śintiyân*.

هناح *śanâḥ*, young camel; also: ى *śanâḥiyy*, ة, big and clumsy; — *śinâḥ*, pl. *śunuḥ*, drunkard.

هناخ *śinâḫ*, mountain-knob.

هناخيب *śanâḫîb*, pl. of هنخاب *śinḫâb* and هنخوب *sunḫûb*.

هنار *śanâr*, disgrace, dishonour.

هنارى *śunara*, cat.

هناص *śanâṣ*, هناصى *śanâṣiyy*, *śunâṣiyy*, tall, strong and swift.

هناط *śinâṭ*, pl. *śinâṭât*, *śanâ'iṭ*, woman with a rosy complexion.

هناظ *śinâẓ*, mountain-summit; fleshiness.

هناظى *śanâẓî*, pl. of هنظات *śanẓât* and هنظوة *śunẓuwa-t*.

هناع *śanâ'*, ة *śanâ'a-t*, ugliness, abomination, ignominy.

هناعيف *śanâ'îf*, pl. of هنعاف *śin'âf*.

هناق *śanâq*, *śinâq*, tall, long; — *śinâq*, string to tie up a skin-bag; bow-string; acceptance of the blood-money.

هنان *śanân*, *śan'ân*, f. ة and هناى *śan'a*, hating, detesting (adj.); hateful, hated; — *śinân*, pl. of هن *śann*; — *śunân*, cold water; dripping; ة *śunâna-t*, anything dripping, drops.

هنائط *śanâ'iṭ*, pl. of هناط *śinâṭ*.

هنائية *śanâ'iya-t*, f. hated, hostile.

(هنب) *śanib*, A, INF. *śanab*, have

fresh and beautiful teeth, fresh lips; be cold.

هنب *śanab*, beauty, purity, freshness and sharpness of the teeth; cold; pl. *śanabât, aśnâb*, moustache; — ة *śumba-t*, coldness.

هنبا *śambâ'*=همبا.

(هنبث) *śambas̱*, INF. ة, adhere, put one's hand to; take hold of the heart.

هنبث *śambas̱*, lion; — *śumbas̱*, hard, rough; — ة *śambas̱a-t*, affection, inclination.

(هنبل) *śambal*, INF. ة, kiss.

هنبل *śumbul*, pl. *śanâbil*, measure of 6 مد *madd*.

هنتان *śintân*=هنتيان *śintiyân*.

(هنتر) *śantar*, INF. ة, tear (a.); — ة *śantara-t*, pl. *śanâtir*, space between the fingers; finger; earring.

هنتيان *śintiyân*, pl. *śanâtîn*, very wide trowsers.

(هنث) *śanis̱*, A, INF. be thick.

هنج *śanij*, A, INF. *śanaj*, be wrinkled; — II. INF. *taśnîj*, cause a rheumatism of the neck, a stiff neck; — V. INF. *taśannuj*, be wrinkled; have a stiff neck.

هنج *śanaj*, being wrinkled (s.); he-camel; — *śanij*, having a stiff neck.

هنجار *śinjâr*, bugloss.

هنح *śanuḥ*, pl. of هناح *śinâḥ*.

(هنح), II. *śannaḥ*, INF. *taśnîḥ*, clean the palm-tree from thorns.

هنخاب *śinḫâb*=هنخوب *śunḫûb*.

هنخف *śinnaḫf*, stout, corpulent; tall, long; — ة *śanḫafa-t*, pride, vanity.

هنخوب *śunḫûb*, ة *śunḫûba-t*, pl. *śanâḫîb*, mountain-summit; shoulder-blade; vertebra.

هنذاخ *śinẕâḫ*, *śunẕâḫ*, هنذاخى *śunẕâḫiyy*, and—

هنذخ *śunẕaḫ*, هندخ *śundaḫ*, ة *śunẕuḫa-t*, entertainment after the completion of a building, after a happy return from a journey, &c.; — *śanẕaḫ*, INF. ة, prepare such an entertainment; — *śunẕuḫ*, big, stout, fleshy, strong; lion.

(هنر), II. *śannar*, INF. *taśnîr*, blame, reproach with anything shameful or dishonourable.

(هنزر) *śanzar*, INF. ة, be rough, rude.

هنشنة *śinśina-t*, nature, disposition, temper; custom, habit, usage; sample, model, pattern.

(هنص) *śanaṣ*, U, INF. *śunûṣ*, adhere, stick to; attend to carefully; — *śaniṣ*, id.

هنصرة *śanṣara-t*, roughness, violence; adversity, calamity.

هنصير *śinṣîr*=the previous; refuge.

(هنط) *śunuṭ*, steaks.

(هنطط) *śanṭaṭ*, INF. ة, disperse (a.); — II. INF. *taśanṭuṭ*, disperse (n.).

هنطوف *śunṭûf*, summit; gable.

هنظاة *śanẕât*, pl. *śanâẕî*, mountain-summit.

(هنظر) *śanẕar*, INF. ة, abuse, revile.

هنظورة *śunẕûra-t*, rolling fragment of a rock.

هنظوف *śunẕûf*, twig, branch.

هنظوة *śunẕuwa-t*, pl. *śanâẕî*=هنظاة *śanẕât*.

هنظيان *śinẕiyân*, disagreeable, boisterous (woman); shrew.

هنظير *śinẕîr*, rolling fragment of a rock; large flat stone; also ة *śinẕîra-t*, perverse, corrupt, obscene; — ة *śinẕîra-t*, promontory; mountain-peak.

(هنع) *śana'*, INF. *śan'*, find ugly, horrid, abominable; dishonour, revile; despise; accuse; separate a rag entirely into fibres; — *śani'*, A, INF. *śun'*, find ugly, detestable, horrid; — *śanu'*, INF. *śana'a-t*, be ugly, &c.; — II. INF. *taśnî'*, make ugly, &c.; say abominations of (على *'ala*), dishonour, disgrace; — IV. INF. *iśnâ'*, be quick, hasten; — V. INF. *taśannu'*, walk apace; mount on horseback, ride; prepare for combat; — X. INF.

istiśnâ', find ugly, horrid, abominable.

هنع *śan'*, abomination ; — *śani'*, ugly, infamous, abominable ; — ة *śun'a-t*, ugliness, baseness, infamy, abomination.

هنعا *śan'â'*, f. of اهنع *aśna'*, ugly, &c.

(هنعاب) *śin'âb*, tall, long.

(هنعاف) *śin'âf*, pl. *śanâ'if*, mountain-summit; high mountain; mountain-yoke; also—

هنعف *śinna'f*, big but weak; — *śan'af*, INF. ة, be tall, long; — ة *śan'afa-t*, tallness, length.

هنعم *śinna'm*, big, corpulent.

هنعوف *śun'ûf* = هنعاف *śin'âf*.

هنغاب *śingâb*, long flexible branch; long rope; tall.

(هنغب) *śungub*, long, thin.

هنغرة *śangara-t*, perversity, corruption.

هنغف *śinnagf*, of bad proportions; loosely built or constructed.

هنغم *śinnagm*, long, tall; *śinnagm-an*, against will, unwillingly.

هنغوب *śungûb*, long thin rope, twig, or mineral vein.

هنغير *śingîr*, unchaste, depraved; — ة *śingîra-t*, depravity.

(هنف) *śanaf*, U, INF. *śanf*, look askance at; — *śanif*, A, INF. *śanaf*, hate; be intelligent, considerate; have the upper lip turned up; — II. INF. *taśnîf*, adorn with ear-rings; — V. INF. *taśannuf*, adorn one's self with ear-rings.

هنف *śanf*, pl. *śunûf*, ear-ring, pendant; — *śanif*, hating (adj.).

هنفار *śanfâr*, light, nimble; — ة *śinfâra-t*, and—

هنفيرة *śinfira-t*, nimbleness, alertness, agility.

هنفرى *śanfara*, name of a poet and celebrated runner.

(هنق) *śanaq*, I, U, INF. *śanq* (also IV.), pull up the head of a camel by the reins; tie up an animal by the head; tie up; worry, throttle; hang (a.); — *śaniq*, A, INF. *śanaq*, be devoted, attached; — II. place the هنيق *śanîq* into the bee-hive; — III. INF. *śinâq*, *muśânaqa-t*, mix one's cattle with another's; — IV. INF. *iśnâq*, see I.

هنق *śanq*, throttling, hanging (s.); — *śanaq*, pl. *aśnâq*, number (of sheep, &c.) between two given ones for which a rise in taxation takes place; payment of a remainder (as of blood-money, &c.); rest, remainder; rope; — *śaniq*, greatly given to, eager for, infatuated with.

هنقا *śanqâ'*, f. feeding the young ones.

(هنك), II. *śannak*, INF. *taśnîk*, lift up the head.

(هنم) *śanam*, U, INF. *śanm*, scratch with the nails.

هنوع *śunû'*, infamy, abomination.

هنوة *śanû'a-t*, *śunû'a-t*, *śanuwwa-t*, hatred of anything impure.

هنى *śaniyy*, hated, hateful.

هنيب *śanib*, having beautiful fresh teeth.

هنير *śinnîr*, ة *śinnîra-t*, depraved, infamous, rascal.

هنيز *śinnîz*, fennel-seed.

هنيع *śanî'*, ة, ugly, repulsive, abominable, infamous; — ة *śanî'a-t*, pl. *śanâ'i'*, anything infamous, abomination.

هنيق *śanîq*, piece of wood placed across a bee-hive; bastard; ة *śanîqa-t*, coquette (s.); — *śinnîq*, self-complacent, vain.

هنين *śanîn*, watered milk; drops.

ههاب *śahâb*, ة *śuhâba-t*, watered milk; — *śihâb*, pl. *śuhub*, *śuhb*, *śuhbân*, *śihbân*, *aśhub*, brilliant star; shooting star; flame (ش الحرب *śihâb al-ḥarb*, hero); nimble, alert.

ههاد *śahâd*, pl. testimonies; — *; — ة *śahâda-t*, testimony, evidence; profession of faith; martyrdom; passage of a text, quotation; testimonial, certificate; being

present and witnessing (s.); visible world; — *śihâda-t*, roast lamb.

شهار *śihâr*, contract for a month, monthly rent.

شهاق *śuhâq*, sighing, groaning (s.).

شهام *śahâm*, sorceress, hag; — *; — ة *śahâma-t*, sagacity, wit, alertness, energy, boldness, bravery.

شهاوى *śahâwa*, pl. of شهوان *śahwân*, شهوى *śahwa*.

(شهب) *śahab*, A, INF. *śahb*, scorch the skin, spoil the complexion; destroy a tribe or their cattle; beget grey foals; — *śahib*, A, INF. *śahab*, be ash-coloured; shine, flare; — *śahub*, id.; — II. INF. *taśhîb*, scorch, spoil the complexion; — IX. *iśhabb*, INF. *iśhibâb*, be ash-coloured.

شهب *śahab*, ash-colour; — *śuhub*, *śuhb*, pl. of شهاب *śihâb*; — ة *śuhba-t*, ash-colour; mixture of white and black.

شهبا *śahbâ'*, ash-coloured; clear and cold; with flashing arms; sterile, f. of اشهب *aśhab*.

شهبان *śuhbân*, *śihbân*, pl. of شهاب *śihâb*; — *śahabân*, name of a tree.

(شهبر) *śahbar*, INF. ة, be ash-coloured; be whitish; be near crying.

شهبر *śahbar*, long, broad and thick.

شهجبة *śahjaba-t*, confusion.

(شهد) *śahid*, A, INF. *śuhûd*, witness, be present; give witness, testimony, evidence; profess; affirm by oath; — *śahud*, INF. *śahâda-t*, give testimony, evidence; — II. INF. *taśhîd*, call to witness, take as a witness; emit sperm (without coition); — III. INF. *muśâhada-t*, be an eye-witness; convince one's self by sight; be present; — IV. INF. *iśhâd*, wish for one's presence; bring up; call to witness; pass. *uśhid*, die as a martyr; — V. INF. *taśahhud*, pronounce the profession of faith; — VI. INF. *taśâhud*, see one another; — X. INF. *istiśhâd*, call to witness; pass. *ustuśhid*, suffer martyrdom.

شهد *śahd*, *śuhd*, pl. *śihâd*, yellow honey; honeycomb; — *śahd*, *śuhhad*, eye-witnesses, &c., pl. of شاهد *śâhid*; — ة *śahda-t*, best honey.

شهدا *śahdan*, in one's presence; — *śuhadâ*, pl. of شهيد *śahîd*.

شهدانج *śahdânij*, شهدانق *śahdâniq*, شهدانة *śahdâna-t*, hemp-seed (Pers.).

(شهدر) *śahdar*, ة, between three and four years old; well to do, rich.

(شهر) *śahar*, U, INF. *śahr*, make generally publish, spread abroad; make one to be talked of; draw and brandish the sword; brandish a knife against (على *'ala*); — II. INF. *taśhîr*, make known, publish, spread; — III. INF. *śihâr*, *muśâhara-t*, make a contract or hire out for a month; — IV. INF. *iśhâr*=II.; enter on a month; pass the month; have been in a place for a month; — VIII. INF. *iśtihâr*, become generally known; get celebrated, win a name; publish; celebrate as famous.

شهر *śahr*, pl. *śuhûr*, *aśhur*, month; moon, new moon; — ة *śuhra-t*, becoming (s.) public, celebrity, fame, repute, ill-fame; rumour.

(شهرب) *śahrab*, ة, old.

شهرق *śahraq*, weaver's spindle.

شهرى *śahriyy*, ة, monthly; — ة *śahriyya-t*, monthly pay or salary; — *śihriyya-t*, beast of burden.

(شهق) *śahaq*, A, I, *śahiq*, A, INF. *śuhâq*, *śahîq*, *taśhâq*, sob, groan; hiccough; roar, bray; injure by the evil eye; be high; — ة *śahqa-t*, hiccough; death-rattle.

(شهل) *śahil*, A, INF. *śahal*, be dark blue with a reddish lustre; have such eyes; — II. *taśhîl*, hasten

one's work, despatch (m.); — III. INF. *muśâhala-t*, wrong, disgrace; — V. INF. *taśahhul*, lose one's good looks; — IX. *iśhall*, INF. *iśhilâl*=I.; — ة *śahla-t*, old man, old woman; — *śuhla-t*, dark blue (s.) with a reddish lustre.

شهلا *śahlâ'*, of a dark blue; pressing business.

(شهم) *saham*, INF. *śahm*, *śuhûm*, frighten; INF. *śahm*, call out to a horse; — *śahum*, INF. *śahâma-t*, be sharp, sagacious; possess great vitality, be quick, vigorous, energetic, bold; be strong and swift.

شهم *śahm*, pl. *śihâm*, sharp of intellect, sagacious; energetic, bold; pl. *śuhûm*, strong and swift; very powerful.

شهنشين *śahniśîn*, balcony (Pers.).

(شهنق) *śahnaq*, INF. ة, cry out, bray.

(شهو) *śahâ*, U, شهى *śahî*, A, INF. *śahwa-t*, crave for, desire, have appetite; be desirable, relishing; — II. INF. *taśhiya-t*, call forth a longing, desire, appetite; desire; — III. INF. *muśâhât*, resemble; — IV. INF. *iśhâ'*, fulfil one's desire, give him what he is wishing for; look at malignantly; — V. INF. *taśahhî*, desire passionately; wish for everything; — VIII. covet, have an appetite, a wish or desire for; — ة *śahwa-t*, pl. *śahwât*, *śahawât*, desire, craving, covetousness, appetite; passion.

شهوان *śahwân*, f. شهوى *śahwa*, pl. *śahâwa*, and ى *śahwâniyy*, ة, desiring passionately, covetous, greedy, sensual, voluptuous.

شهوى *śahwa*, f. of شهوان *śahwân*; — *śahwiyy*, covetous, greedy, sensual.

شهى *śahî*, (v.) see (شهو); *śahiyy*, full of desire, sensual; relishing, desirable, precious.

شهيد *śahîd*, *śihîd*, pl. *aśhâd*, *śuhûd*, *śuhadâ'*, witness; martyr.

شهير *śahîr*, generally known, celebrated, notorious, ill-reputed.

شهيق *śahîq*, hiccough, sobbing, death-rattle.

شهيم *śahîm*, sharp-witted, sagacious.

(شو) *śâ'*, U, I, INF. *śau'*, precede, get in advance of; grieve (a.); astonish.

شوا *śiwâ'*, *śuwâ'*, anything roasted, roast meat, joint; — *śawwâ'*, who roasts; — ة *śawât*, scalp; — *śiwât*, *śiwâ'a-t*, a slice of roast meat.

شواب *śawwâb*, young women, girls, pl. of شابة *śâbba-t*.

شوابك *śawâbik*, pl. of *śaubak*.

شوابصة *śawâbiṣa-t*, pl. of شوباصى *śaubâṣiyy*.

شواحى *śawâḥî*, pl. of شوحية *śûḥiyya-t*.

شواذ *śawâẕẕ*, pl. of شاذ *śâẕẕ*, solitary, &c.

شوار *śawâr*, INF. of (شور); shape, form, figure; beauty; clothing; fatness; also *śiwâr*, *śuwâr*, utensils, things; pudenda; — *śuwâr*, edge of an amphitheatrically rising field; parapet (m.).

شوارز *śawârîz*, pl. of شيراز *śîrâz*.

شواش *śawâś*, disturbance, turbidness, trouble, discord.

شواشى *śawâśî*, pl. of شوشة *śûśa-t*.

شواطى *śawâṭî'*, river-banks, pl. of شاطى *śâṭi'*.

شواظ *śiwâẕ*, *śawâẕ*, flame without smoke; great smoke; great thirst or heat; clamour.

شواق *śawâqq*, difficult matters, difficulties, adversities.

شوال *śiwâl*, raising, elevating (s.), INF. of (شول); pl. of شائل *śâ'il*, milkless; — *śawwâl*, pl. *śawwâlât*, *śawâwîl*, the tenth Arabian month; — ة *śawwâla-t*, scorpion; slandering woman.

شوامت *śawâmit*, feet (of animals).

شوانى *śawânî*, pl. of شونة *śauna-t*.

شواه *śiwâh*, sheep, pl. of شاة *śât*.

هواهن *śawâhin*, هواهين *śawâhîn*, royal hawks, &c., pl. of شاهين *śâhîn*.

هواهى *śawâha*, sheep, pl. of شاة *śât*.

هوائع *śawâ'i'*, anything scattered, dispersed.

هواية *śiwâya-t*, *śawâya-t*, *śuwâya-t*, worst remainder; crust of bread; — *śuwâya-t*, a piece of roast meat; light matter; — *śuwwâya-t*, frying-pan.

(هوب) *śâb*, U, INF. *śaub*, *śiyâb*, mix, confuse, trouble; water the milk; (also II.) defend, ward off; — II. INF. *taświb*, see I.; be very hot; — VII. INF. *inśiyâb*, VIII. INF. *iśtiyâb*, be mixed.

هوب *śaub*, mixture; anything mixed; (m.) heat; — ة *śauba-t*, fraud, deceit.

هوباصى *śaubâṣiyy*, pl. *śawâbiṣa-t*, field-watchman (m.).

(هوبص) *śaubaṣ*, INF. ة, appoint as a field-watchman; — II. *taśaubuṣ*, discharge the duty of a field-watchman (m.).

هوبصة *śaubaṣa-t*, duty of a field-watchman.

هوبج *śûbaj*, هوبق *śûbaq*, (m.) هوبك *śaubak*, pl. *śawâbik*, roller for dough.

هوبوب *śu'bûb*, pl. *śa'âbîb*, heavy shower, rain-storm; violence, intensity.

(هوح), II. *śawwaḥ*, INF. *taświḥ*, refuse, reject, disapprove.

هوح *śûḥ*, fir-tree; — ة *śûḥa-t*, hawk, kite.

هوحية *śûḥiyya-t*, pl. *śawâḥî*, beam.

هوخط *śauḥaṭ*, corn-ear; bunch of fruit.

(هود , هوذ), II. *śawwad*, INF. *taświd*, *śawwaẓ*, INF. *taświẓ*, stand high; — V. INF. *taśawwud*, *taśawwuẓ*, id.

هودانيق *śûdânîq*, a species of woodpecker.

هودكان *śaudakân*, hunting-net; arms.

(هوذ), II. *śawwaẓ*, INF. *taświẓ*, put on the turban; cover the sun; decline towards setting; rise above the horizon; see (هود); — V. INF. *taśawwuẓ*, VIII. INF. *iśtiyâẓ*, don the turban.

هوذانق *śauẓânaq*, a species of the falcon.

هوذب *śauẓab*, tall and handsome.

هوذر *śauẓar*, long veil for going out; a shirt.

(هوذق) *śauẓaq*, seize with the fingers or claws; — *śauẓaq*, bracelet.

(هور) *śâr*, U, INF. *śaur*, *śiyâr*, *śiyâra-t*, *maśâr*, *maśûra-t*, take out the honey; advise to; INF. *śaur*, *śawâr*, exhibit (a horse, slave, &c.); be well kept and fed, keep and feed well; — II. INF. *taświr*, exhibit, wink or beckon, point out, show; cause to blush with shame, uncover one's nakedness, confuse; (m.) be at death's door; — III. INF. *muśâwara-t*, ask for advice, consult; — IV. INF. *iśâra-t*, give a hint, wink or point at; command; advise; ride a horse for exhibition; make the fire to flame high; — V. INF. *taśawwur*, get ashamed, confused; — VI. INF. *taśâwur*, consult one another, hold a consultation; — VIII. INF. *iśtiyâr*, take out the honey; — X. INF. *istiśâra-t*, id.; ask for advice, consult.

هور *śaur*, taken-out honey; (m.) advice, hint; also ة *śûra-t*, intrinsic quality; form, shape, figure, beauty; clothing; fatness; — ة *śaura-t*, shame, confusion; also *śûra-t*, scene, theatre; — *śûra-t*, bee-hive.

هورا *śuwarâ'*, pl. of هير *śayyir*.

هوران *śaurân*, *śûrân*, saffron in blossom.

هورباج *śûrabâj*, broth, soup.

هورج *śauraj*, salt-steppe.

هورى *śûra*, consultation; advice;

commission, order; — *śaura*, a sea-plant.
(هوز), pass. هير *śîz*, INF. *śauz*, be violently in love with.
هوز *śu'uz*, ة *śu'uza-t*, INF. of (هاز).
هوزب *śauzab*, token, sign, trace.
(هوس) *śâs*, U, INF. *śaus*, rub the teeth; — *śâs*, *śawis*, A, INF. *śawas*, compress the eye-lids to see better; look askance at; — VI. INF. *taśâwus*, look with one eye; = *śawis*.
هوس *śûs*, pl. of اهوس *aśwas*, blinking, squinting; — *śu'us*, pl. of هاس *śa's*, rough and stony, hard.
(هوش), II. *śawwaś*, INF. *taświś*, disturb, trouble, grieve (a.), annoy; confuse; — V. INF. *taśawwuś*, pass.; — VI. INF. *taśâwûś*, be mixed up; — ة *śûśa-t*, pl. *śawâśî*, tuft of hair on the crown of the head; crest of a bird.
هوها *śauśâ'*, ة *śauśâ't*, swift camel.
هوهب *śauśab*, scorpion; louse; ant.
(هوص) *śâṣ*, U, INF. *śauṣ*, rub the teeth; chew the toothpick; rub, clean, wash; take a thing from its place; — U, A, have toothache, belly-ache; move in the womb (embryo).
هوص *śauṣ*, tooth-ache.
هوصا *śauṣâ'*, f. squinting.
(هوصر) *śauṣar* = (هصر).
(هوط) *śauṭ*, pl. *aśwâṭ*, *śiwâṭ*, course of a horse up to the goal, career; going (s.) round the Caaba; — II. *śawwaṭ*, INF. *taświṭ*, make a long journey; make the horse run until it is getting tired; cook the meat well; make the kettle boil; scorch.
(هوظ), VI. INF. *taśâwuẓ*, abuse one another.
(هوع) *śawi'*, A, INF. *śawa'*, having bristling hair; have one cheek white.
هوع *śau'*, born immediately after another; — *śû'*, tamarisk.
هوغر *śaugar*, strongly built; — ة *śaugara-t*, basket of palm-leaves.
(هوف) *śâf*, U, INF. *śauf*, smooth, polish; pass. get adorned; smear with pitch; perceive, see; — II. INF. *taświf*, let see, show; — IV. INF. *iśâfa-t*, tower over; dominate; fear; — V. INF. *taśawwuf*, adorn one's self, dress up; set to work, undertake; look from above, gaze; — VIII. INF. *iśtiyâf*, look at, gaze at; observe; thicken (n.); — ة *śaufa-t*, look, aspect, sight; skill in measuring with the eye, correct estimation.
هوفان *śûfân*, oats.
(هوق) *śâq*, U, INF. *śauq*, fill with longing and desire, charm, fill with affection, with passionate love; tie the rope to a pole; — II. INF. *taświq*, fill with longing or passionate love; — V. INF. *taśawwuq*, pass.; fall in love; — VIII. INF. *iśtiyâq*, long for, crave, desire passionately.
هوق *śauq*, pl. *aśwâq*, violent desire, ardent longing or craving, passionate love; zeal; briskness, cheerfulness; — *śûq*, pl. of اهوق *aśwaq*, longing, desirous; long; — ى *śauqiyy*, ة, longing for, desirous, in love; — ية *śauqiyya-t*, beginning of a letter expressing the writer's longing.
(هوك) *śâk*, U, INF. *śauk*, prick, wound; pull out a thorn; — A, INF. *śâka-t*, *śîka-t*, fall into or meet with thorns, walk on thorns; — A, INF. *śauk*, show one's self brave in war; be armed from head to foot; — II. INF. *taświk*, have thorns; provide with thorns; prickle; show again stumps of hair; — IV. INF. *iśâka-t*, have thorns; prick with thorns; — V. INF. *taśawwuk*, prick one's self in thorns.
هوك *śauk*, pl. *aśwâk*, thorn, prickle; point; thistle; — *śawik*, thorny,

prickly; fully armed; — ة *śau-ka-t*, thorn, sting, prickle; tongue of a buckle; spur; fork; arms and their points; clash of combatants; slaughter, massacre; thrust, wound; bravery; military power; power, greatness, pomp, majesty.

شوكحة *śaukaḥa-t*, pl. *śaukaḥ*, large door with smaller outlets.

شوكران *śaukarân*, wormwood; fennel; hellebore.

(شول) *śâl*, U, INF. *śaul*, *śawalân*, lift up, take from the place; carry a burden; ascend; be raised, lifted up; remove, emigrate; vanish; fall short; (m.) distil; rear, breed; — II. *śayyal*, INF. *taświl*, despatch, carry out; advance (a.), cause to make rapid progress; comfort, encourage; — IV. INF. *iśâla-t*, lift up; take from the place; carry a burden; — VII. INF. *inśiyâl*, pass. of the previous.

شول *śaul*, pl. *aświl*, remainder of water; small property; nimble, alert; — *śûl*, vegetables; — *śuwwal*, pl. of شائل *śâ'il*, q.v.; — ة *śaula-t*, sting of a scorpion; name of a woman who always gave bad advice; — *śawila-t*, scorpion.

شولم *śaulam*, vetch, darnel.

شوم *śu'm*, evil omen, ill luck, misfortune, calamity; also *śûm*, unpropitious, portentous; hopeless, miserable, unhappy; black camels; — ة *śûma-t*, haughtiness, pride; avarice.

شومار *śûmâr*, fennel (m.).

(شومل) *śaumal*, north.

شومى *śu'ma*, left hand or side; — ة *śûmiyya-t*, avarice, niggardliness.

(شون) *śân*, U, INF. *śaun*, open; — be light-minded.

شون *śu'un*, things, affairs, &c., pl. of شان *śa'n*; — ة *śauna-t*, pl. *śawânî*, corn magazine; barn; little castle or fort; ship of a pirate; stupid woman.

شوندر *śawandar*, carrot (Pers.).

شونوز *śu'nûz*, شونيز *śûnîz*, coriander-seed.

(شوه) *śâh*, U, INF. *śauh*, *śauha-t*, be ugly; rise, rise higher; desire, wish for; injure by the evil eye; frighten; envy; — *śawih*, A, INF. *śawah*, be ugly; be long, and, by opposition, be short; — II. INF. *taświya-t*, render ugly, disfigure; throw an evil eye upon; — V. INF. *taśawwuh*, render one's self unrecognizable; — ة *śûha-t*, distance.

شوها *śauhâ'*, f. of اشوه *aśwah*, ugly, &c.

شوهب *śauhab*, male hedgehog.

شوون *śu'ûn* = شون *śu'un*, above.

(شوى) *śawa*, I, INF. *śayy*, roast; heat water; cut off a slice of roast meat; — II. INF. *taświya-t*, roast; have roasted; feed (a.) on roast meat; wound in a not dangerous place; — IV. INF. *iświâ'*, have meat roasted; feed (a.) on roast meat; — VII. INF. *inśiwâ'*, be roasted; — VIII. INF. *iśtiwâ'*, id.; roast meat for one's self.

شوى *śawan*, *śawa*, anything paltry, worthless, valueless; hands, feet, any place where a wound is not fatal; skull, scalp; pl. of شاة *śât*, sheep, and of شواة *śawât*, scalp; — *śawiyy*, ة, roasted; — *śuwayy*, a little thing, a trifle; *śuwayy śuwayy*, little by little, piece-meal; — ة *śawiyya-t*, pl. *śawâya*, remainder of a flock, or people; — *śuwayya-t*, *śuwai'a-t*, a small thing, trifle; *śuway-yatan śuwayyatan*, little by little.

شويخ *śuwaiḥ*, little old man.

شويعر *śuwai'r*, poetaster.

شويكة *śuwaika-t*, small thorn.

شويهة *śuwaiha-t*, lambkin.

شى *śai*, (m.) *śe*, *śî*, pl. *aśyâ'*,

aśyâwât, aśâwât, aśâwa, aśâyâ, aśyâyâ, aśâwih, thing, object, some, something (لا هى *lâ śai*, nothing, بلا هى *bi-lâ śai*, m. *bilâś*, for nothing, gratis); unknown quantity, square-root; هى الله *śai'u 'l-lâhi*, the will of God; is in vulgar Arabic placed after other words to express a question, or together with *mâ*, a negation; — *śayy, śiyy*, stammering; *śayy*, INF. of (هوى); — ة *śiya-t*, pl. *śiyât*, a different or glaring colour; colour; sign, mark, fault; sheep; — *śi'a-t*, will, wish, INF. of (هيى).

(هيا) هيى *śayî*, ها *śâ'* (pret. *śi-'tu*), A, INF. هى *śai', maśi'a-t, maśâ'a-t, maśâ'iya-t*, will, wish; ان ها الله *in śâ' 'l-lâh*, if it please God, let us hope; — II. INF. *taśyî'*, urge to, incite, move; disfigure; — V. INF. *taśayyu'*, calm down; — ة *śi'at*, will, wish.

هياب *śiyâb*, mixture.

هيات *śiyât*, pl. of هية *śiya-t*.

هياح *śiyâḥ*, defect; zeal, effort, care; fear, precaution; — *.

هيار *śiyâr*=هوار *śawâr*; pl. *aśyur, śuyur, śîr*, Saturday; pl. of هير *śayyir*; also ة *śiyârâ-t*, INF. of (هور).

هياص *śiyâṣ*, maliciousness.

هياط *śiyâṭ*, smell of burnt food; pl. of هوط *śauṭ*; — ة *śiyâṭa-t*, INF. of (هيط).

هياطين *śayâṭîn*, pl. of هيطان *śaiṭân*.

هياظمة *śayâẓima-t*, pl. of هيظم *śaiẓam*.

هياع *śiyâ'*, shepherd's pipe; also *śayâ'*, chips; — *.

هياف *śiyâf*, a collyrium; any remedy for the eyes.

هيال *śayyâl*, porter.

هيام *śayâm, śiyâm*, soft ground; — *.

هئان *śi'ân*, things, affairs, pl. of هان *śa'n*.

هياه *śiyâh*, sheep, pl. of هاة *śât*.

(هيب) *śâb*, I, INF. *śaib, śaiba-t, maśyab*, turn grey by age, get old; — II. INF. *taśyîb*, make grey; cause to appear old; — IV. INF. *iśâba-t*, id.

هيب *śaib*, grey hair; old age; — *śîb, śuyub*, pl. of اهيب *aśyab*, grey-haired, hoary, &c.; — ة *śaiba-t*, grey hair; ش العجوز *śaiba-t al'ajûz*, white moss.

هيبا *śaibâ'*, f. of اهيب *aśyab*, hoary.

هيبان *śaibân*, clouded cold and rainless; also *śîbân*, a winter month.

هيت *śît*, parti-coloured linen, cotton.

هيتعور *śaita'ûr*, هيتغور *śaitagûr*, oats.

هيث *śîs*, Seth.

(هيح) *śâḥ*, I, INF. *śaiḥ*, perform with zeal, diligence and care; fear, be on one's guard, and, by opposition, be bold, brave; — II. INF. *taśyîḥ*, warn to be on one's guard, caution, make cautious; (m.) provide the silkworms with fragrant plants; — III. INF. *śiyâḥ, muśâyaḥa-t*, set to a thing with zeal and cautiously; — IV. INF. *iśâḥa-t*, id.; produce in abundance the grass هيح *śîḥ*.

هيح *śîḥ*, pl. *aśyâḥ*, absinthum, wormwood; fragrant plants for silkworms; (also هيحان *śaiḥân*) zealous and cautious; a striped stuff of Yemen.

(هيخ) *śâḫ*, I, INF. *śayaḫ, śaiḫûḫa-t, śuyûḫa-t, śuyûḫiyya-t, śaiḫûḫiyya-t*, age, be or grow old, become an old man; — II. INF. *taśyîḫ*, be old, an old man; call or make one a *śaiḫ*; rebuke, blame; disgrace; — V. INF. *taśayyuḫ*, grow old; have one's self called a *śaiḫ*.

هيخ *śaiḫ*, pl. *śuyûḫ, śiyûḫ, aśyâḫ, śiyaḫa-t, śîḫa-t, śîḫân, maśyaḫa-t, maśîḫa-t, maśâyiḫ, maśyûḫâ', maśyuḫâ'*, old man (above 50); head of a family or tribe; doctor, teacher, preacher, spiritual guide; prefect of the dervishes; abbot; ش الاسلام

śaiḥ al-islâm, religious chief of the Moslim; ش البلد *śaiḥ al-balad*, mayor; ش النار *śaiḥ an-nâr*, Satan; — ة *śaiḥa-t*, elderly woman; coloquintida; — *śîḥa-t*, *śiyaḥa-t*, INF. of (شيخ).

شيخوخة *śaiḥûḥa-t*, شيخوخية *śaiḥûḥiyya-t*, old age, INF. of (شيخ).

شيخون *śaiḥûn*, old man.

(شيد) *śâd*, I, cover a wall with mortar; (also II.) give a great height to a wall or building, build up; perish; — INF. *śiyâd*, call the camels; (also II.) rub with perfumes; — II. INF. *taśyîd*, see I.; — IV. INF. *iśâda-t*, give a great height to a building; raise the voice, speak or pronounce loudly; make known, publish; ruin.

شيد *śîd*, mortar, cement.

شيذارة *śîẕâra-t*, jealous (man).

شيذاق *śaiẕâq*, شيذق *śaiẕaq*, شيذقان *śaiẕaqân*, a variety of the falcon.

شيذمان *śaiẕumân*, wolf; — ة *śaiẕumâna-t*, young she-camel.

شيذة *śaiẕa-t*, a way of rolling the turban.

شير *śîr*, lion (Pers.); — *śîr*, pl. *śiyâr*, rock (m.); — *śiyar*, plant with a stalk; tree; — *śuyur*, *śîr*, pl. of شيار *śiyâr*; — *śayyir*, pl. *śiyâr*, well nourished, fat; excellent; pl. *śuwarâ'*, counsellor, minister.

شيراز *śîrâz*, *śi'râz*, pl. *śawârîz*, *śarârîz*, *śa'ârîz*, curdled whey; a kind of cheese; conserves.

شيرج *śîraj*, sesame-oil.

شيز *śîz*, شيزى *śîza*, Indian ebony; combs, plates, bows made of it; nut-tree; — pass. of (شوز); — *śa'iz*, (v.) see (شاز); rough, rugged.

شئس *śa'is*, (v.) see (شاس); rough, rugged.

شيش *śîś*, a bad variety of dates; (m.) pl. *aśyâś*, ram-rod; — ة *śîśa-t*, glass; bottle; glass pipe for smoking.

شيص *śîṣ*, شيصا *śîṣâ'*, a bad kind of dates with a soft stone; toothache; belly-ache; a fish; — ة *śîṣa-t*, prey.

شيصبان *śaiṣabân*, male ant; a demon; devil.

(شيط) *śâṭ*, I, INF. *śaiṭ*, *śiyâṭa-t*, *śaiṭûṭa-t*, be slightly burnt; taste as if burnt; have particles of burnt food adhering to it (pot); be boiled too thick or over-boiled; take fire, grow passionate, get angry; perish; — II. INF. *taśyîṭ*, burn (a.) slightly; — IV. INF. *iśâṭa-t*, id.; ruin, destroy; — V. INF. *taśayyuṭ*, be burnt; be emaciated, exhausted; — X. INF. *istiśâṭa-t*, take fire; get angry, burn with rage; fly swiftly; despatch (a business).

شيطان *śaiṭân*, pl. *śayâṭîn*, Satan, devil; tempter, seducer; impious and proud; malignant; restless, intent on mischief; sly, cunning; possessed by demons; a snake; — ى *śaiṭâniyy*, ة, Satanic, devilish; — ية *śaiṭâniyya-t*, Satanic malice; Satanic pride; devilishness.

(شيطن) *śaiṭan*, INF. ة, II. INF. *taśaiṭun*, be Satanical, rebellious, possessed of Satanic pride; — ة *śaiṭana-t*, Satanic maliciousness or pride, devilishness.

شيطى *śaiṭiyy*, dust in the air.

(شيظ) *śâẓ*, I, INF. *śaiẓ*, penetrate into the skin, the flesh; — VI. INF. *taśâyuẓ*, abuse one another.

شيظان *śaiẓân*, hard, cruel.

شيظم *śaiẓam*, شيظامى *śaiẓâmiyy*, pl. *sayâẓima-t*, big and strong; lion.

(شيع) *śâ'*, I, INF. *śai'*, *śuyû'*, *śai'û'a-t*, *śaya'ân*, *maśâ'*, spread (n.), become publicly known; fill; — II. INF. *taśyî'*, spread (a.), make public, publish; escort; burn; replenish the

fire; encourage; — III. INF. *muśâya'a-t*, escort; follow, be one's partisan or disciple; help, assist; — IV. INF. *iśâ'a-t*, spread news, publish a secret; — V. INF. *taśayyu'*, profess the faith of the Shiites; — VI. INF. *taśâyu'*, form a sect or party.

شيع *śai'*, pl. *aśyâ'*, amount, quantity, measure; space; born immediately after another; whelp of a lion; also *śî'*, follower, partisan, disciple; — *śayyi'*, pl. *śuya'â'*, partisan, follower, helper; f. ة *śayyi'a-t*, common; — ة *śî'a-t*, pl. *śiya'*, *aśyâ'*, troop of followers, partisans or helpers; party; sect; *aś-śî'a-t*, the Shiites, followers of Ali; — *śayyi'a-t*, common property.

شيعوعة *śai'û'a-t*, becoming (s.) publicly known, publication, spreading of news, &c., INF. of (شيع).

شيعى *śiya'iyy*, Shiite; — ة *śiya'iyya-t*, connexion with the Shiites.

شيف *śîf*, thorns on the back of a palm-leaf; — II. *śayyaf*, INF. *taśyîf*, prepare a remedy for the eyes; — *śa'if*, (v.) see (شاف); — ة *śayyifa-t*, and—

شيفان *śayyifân*, van-guard. outpost; scout, spy.

(شيق) *śâq*, I, tie up.

شيق *śîq*, mountain-chain; high inaccessible part of a mountain; mountain-cleft; also ة *śîqa-t*, a small white duck; n. u. ة, hair in a horse's tail; — *śayyiq*, ardently longing; covetous, lascivious; dainty, lickerish.

شيكة *śîka-t*, INF. of (شوك).

شيل *śail*, the lifting and carrying away of a burden; — *śayyal*, (v.) see (شول) II.; — *śuyyal*, pl. of شائل *śâ'il*, milkless; — ة *śaila-t*, burden.

شيلم *śailam*, darnel.

(شيم) *śâm*, I, INF. *śaim*, put one thing into another; thrust into; enter; draw the sword; observe the flashes of lightning and the clouds to forecast rain; watch, wait for; be marked with a black spot of beauty or mole; — INF. *śaim*, *śuyûm*, attack in proper order; — IV. INF. *iśâma-t*, enter, penetrate; — V. INF. *taśayyum*, penetrate; take after one's father; — VII. INF. *inśiyâm*, VIII. INF. *iśtiyâm*, penetrate.

شيم *śîm*, pl. of اشيم *aśyam*, having a black mole; —*śu'im*, (v.) pass. see (شام);—*śayam*, hard ground; — ة *śîma-t*, *śi'ma-t*, pl. *śiyam*, natural disposition, inborn qualities, character, habits; *śiyam-an*, according to his nature.

شيما *śaimâ'*, f. of اشيم *aśyam*, having a black mole.

شيمذان *śaimuẕân*, wolf.

(شين) *śân*, I, INF. *śain*, disfigure and damage, spoil, disgrace, dishonour; — II. INF. *taśyîn*, write the letter ش.

شين *śain*, ugliness, defect, fault, vice, disgrace; — *śîn*, name of the letter ش; — *śayyin*, ugly, defective; disgraceful, infamous, abominable.

شينيز *śînîz*, coriander-seed.

(شيه) *śâh*, I, injure by the evil eye; accuse; revile.

شيه *śaih*, *śîh*, *śayyih*, sheep, pl. of شاة *śât*.

شيهم *śaiham*, male hedgehog; — ة *śaihama-t*, old slut, hag.

شيوخ *śuyûḫ*, pl. of شيخ *śaiḫ*; — ة *śuyûḫa-t*, and—

شيوخية *śuyûḫiyya-t*, old age.

شيوع *śayû'*, fire-wood, fuel; — *śuyû'*, ة *śuyû'a-t*, INF. of (شيع).

شيوه *śayûh*, disgraceful, infamous.

شيى *śayi*, (v.) see (شيا); — *śuyai'*, small thing, trifle, a little; — *śayiyy*, stammerer.

هثيت *śa'ît*, given to stumbling.
هييخ *śuyaiḥ*, little old man.
هثيس *śa'îs*, pl. of هاس *śa's*, rough and stony.

هيئة *śi'a-t*, will, wish.
هيى *śuyaiy'*, small thing, trifle, a little.

ص

ص *ṣ*, as a numerical sign=90; abbreviation for صفر *ṣafar*, name of the second Arabian month; in the Koran, sign for the pause, as abbreviation for مرخص *muraḥḥaṣ*.
صا *ṣâ'*, صاءة *ṣa'ât*, صاة *ṣâ'a-t*, fluid which surrounds the embryo in the womb; placenta of a sheep.
صاب *ṣâb*, ة, coloquintida; — *ṣa'ab*, INF. of (صئب); — *ṣâbb*, pouring out (adj.); — ة *ṣaba-t*, calamity; punishment; madness.
صابح *ṣâbiḥ*, clear, evident.
صابر *ṣâbir*, suffering, patient, &c., ag. of (صبر); ابو صابر *abû ṣâbir*, salt.
صابغ *ṣâbig*, ag. of (صبغ); (m.) who baptizes; — ة *ṣâbiga-t*, having the udders swelling with milk.
صابورة *ṣâbûra-t*, ballast.
صابورية *ṣâbûriyya-t*, pl. -*ât*, *ṣawâbîr*, basket of rushes to carry earth with.
صابون *ṣâbûn*, soap; — ى *ṣâbûniyy*, soap-boiler.
صابية *ṣâbiya-t*, north-east wind.
صات *ṣât*, loud-voiced.
صاح *ṣâḥ-i*, see صاحب *ṣâḥib*; — *ṣâḥ-in*, see صاحى *ṣâḥî*; — ة *ṣâḥa-t*, sterile ground.
صاحب *ṣâḥib*, ة, pl. *ṣaḥb*, *ṣiḥâb*, *ṣaḥâba-t*, *ṣiḥâba-t*, *ṣuḥbân*, *aṣḥâb*, pl. pl. *aṣâḥîb*, companion, fellow, friend; master, lord, prefect, possessor; inhabitant; frequent in composition, as: صاحب الحوت, companion or inhabitant of the fish, i.e. Jonah; اصحاب النار *aṣḥâb an-nâr*, the inhabitants of the fire, i.e. the damned, &c.; — ة *ṣâḥiba-t*, f. wife.
يا صاحبى *yâ ṣâḥibî*, O my friend, abbreviated يا صاح *yâ ṣâḥi*.
صاحى *ṣâḥî* (صاح *ṣâḥ-in*), clear; (m.) conscious, recovered from a fit or drunkenness, sober; nimble, brisk, alert.
صاخ *ṣâḫḫ*, deafening, stunning, stupefying (adj.); — ة *ṣâḫa-t*, pl. *ṣâḫ*, *ṣâḫât*, swelling of a bone and scar (from a blow); calamity; — *ṣâḫḫa-t*, deafening noise; last judgment; disaster, calamity.
صاخد *ṣâḫid*, lonely, having no son or brother.
صاخر *ṣâḫir*, clatter; — ة *ṣâḫira-t*, a pebble; erratic stone; earthen vessel.
صاد *ṣâd*, copper, brass; brass vessel; catarrhal flux; name of the letter ص *ṣ*; — *ṣâd-in*, see صادى *ṣâdî*; — ة *ṣâda-t*, suffering from a catarrhal flux (camel).
صادر *ṣâdir*, pl. *ṣadar*, returning from the watering-place, opposed to وارد *wârid*, going there (ما له صادر ولا وارد, he possesses nothing at all); springing forth, issuing, derived.
صادع *ṣâdi'*, ag. of (صدع), splitting; walking apace; stretching far; morning dawn.
صادق *ṣâdiq*, truthful, sincere; perfect; effective.
صادى *ṣâdî* (صاد *ṣâd-in*), ة, pl. *ṣawâd-in*, thirsty.
صار *ṣâr-in*, see صارى *ṣârî*; — *ṣârr*, who draws together, pulls the strings of a purse; always af-

fording coolness or shade ; — ة *ṣûra-t*, mountain-ridge ; musk-rat ; — *ṣârra-t*, pl. *ṣarâyir*, *ṣawârr*, what needs must happen, necessity ; thirst.

صارخ *ṣâriḥ*, crying out ; *aṣ-ṣâriḥ*, calling for help ; coming to help ; — ة *ṣâriḥa-t*, cry for help ; help.

صارد *ṣârid*, pl. *ṣawârid*, piercing through ; cold.

صارف *ṣârif*, hot (bitch) ; who spends or changes money ; extravagant, dissipating ; forger ; — ة *ṣârifa-t*, pl. *ṣawârif*, vicissitude, change of fortune.

صارم *ṣârim*, pl. *ṣawârim*, cutting, sharp ; energetic, bold ; severe, harsh ; lion.

صاروج *ṣârûj*, chalk mixed with sand ; gypsum.

صارور *ṣârûr*, صاروراء *ṣârûrâ'*, صارورة *ṣârûra-t*, who has not performed the pilgrimage to Mecca ; unmarried.

صارى *ṣârî* (صار *ṣâr-in*), pl. *ṣurrâ'*, *ṣarâriyy*, sailor ; — ة *ṣâriya-t*, mast ; cross-beam of a ship ; column ; trunk of a palm-tree ; well with foul water ; sailor.

(صاصا) *ṣa'ṣa'*, INF. *ṣa'ṣa'a-t*, try to open the eyes, be scarcely able to open them (puppy) ; be cowardly, wanting in courage ; submit from fear ; produce a sound ; fail to be fructified.

صاع *ṣâ'*, ة, pl. *aṣwu'*, *aṣ'u'*, *aṣwâ'*, *ṣû'*, *ṣi'ân*, a measure for fruit ; 1,040 dirhams ; level place ; playground.

صاعب *ṣâ'ib*, offering hindrances.

صاعد *ṣâ'id*, ascending, climbing ; — *ṣâ'id-an*, above (speaking of a number), henceforth.

صاعقة *ṣâ'iqa-t*, pl. *ṣawâ'iq*, thunder and lightning ; clap, crash ; cry of despair or agony ; execution, death ; scourge of the angel of the winds.

صاغ *ṣâg*, pure, unmixed, genuine ; honest, upright ; healthy ; — *ṣâg-in*, see صاغى *ṣâgî*.

صاغر *ṣâgir*, pl. *ṣagara-t*, who humbles himself of his own will.

صاغى *ṣâgî* (صاغ *ṣâg-in*), ة, inclining towards ; listening, attentive ; — ة *ṣâgiya-t*, who ask for advice, protection or help, clients, friends.

صاف *ṣâf*, summer-rain ;=صايف *ṣâyif*, hot ; also *ṣâf-in*=صايف *ṣâyif*, woolly ; — *ṣâf-in*, see صافى *ṣâfî* ; — *ṣâff*, who places in lines, arrays, ranges ; in lines, in battle order ; — ة *ṣâffa-t*, pl. *ṣawâff*, stepping with the two front feet at the same time and in an equal line ; *ṣawâff-a*, in file and line ; الصافات صفا *aṣ-ṣâffât-u ṣaff-an*, the ranks of glorifying angels.

صافر *ṣâfir*, ag. of (صفر) ; bird ; person.

صافقة *ṣâfiqa-t*, troop of guests ; pl. *ṣawâfiq*, blows of misfortune ; calamities.

صافور *ṣâfûr*, ة *ṣâfûra-t*, pipe, flageolet.

صافى *ṣâfî* (صاف *ṣâf-in*), ة, pure, clear, unmixed ; serene, bright ; serenity, purity ; cold ; shining, flashing.

صاق *ṣâq*=ساق *sâq*, leg, &c.

صاقر *ṣâqir*, stone-breaker ; having sharp eyesight ; — ة *ṣâqira-t*, calamity.

صاقور *ṣâqûr*, hammer for breaking stones ; heavy axe ; — ة *ṣâqûra-t*, space between the dura mater and skull ; third heaven ; tongue.

صاقعة *ṣâqi'a-t*, for صاعقة *ṣâ'iqa-t*.

صاك *ṣa'k*, INF. of (صئك) ; — ة *ṣa'aka-t*, smell of damp wood.

صال *ṣâl-in*, see صالى *ṣâlî* ; — *ṣâll*, falling down and furrowing the ground (rain) ; — ة *ṣa'âla-t*, INF. of (صول) ; — *ṣâlla-t*, blow of destiny.

صالب *ṣâlib*, loins ; shivering.

صالح *ṣâliḥ*, ة, pl. *ṣâliḥun*, *ṣullâḥ*, in good condition, sound, whole ;

honest, upright, good ; (m.) good (s.), interest, advantage ; pl. *ṣâliḥât*, good actions.
صالح *ṣâliḥ*, scab.
صالدة *ṣâlida-t*, pl. *ṣawâlid*, gnashing (adj. f.).
صالغ *ṣâlig*, pl. *ṣullag*, *ṣawâlig*, five or six years old (sheep, cattle).
صالى *ṣâlî* (صال *ṣâl-in*), pl. *ṣuliyy*, heated, burnt.
(صام) *ṣa'am*, lead ; — *ṣa'im*, drink much water.
صامت *ṣâmit*, silent ; irrational, brute ; inanimate ; gold, silver, furniture, and such like property, opposed to slaves and cattle (ناطق *nâṭiq*) ; thick ; herd of 20 camels.
صامد *ṣâmid*, hard, massive ; (m.) put by money, savings.
صامغان *ṣâmigân*, du. the corners of the mouth.
صامق *ṣâmiq*, hungry or thirsty.
صامل *ṣâmil*, dried up, withered.
صامورة *ṣâmûra-t*, very sour milk.
صانع *ṣâni'*, ة, pl. *ṣunnâ'*, ag. of (صنع) ; artisan, artist ; workman, apprentice ; servant ; industrious, skilful.
صانق *ṣâniq*, strong, firm ; pl. *ṣanaqa-t*, clever in rearing camels.
صانى *ṣânî*, always serving.
صاهروج *ṣâharûj*, chalk mixed with sand ; gypsum (Pers.).
صاهل *ṣâhil*, neighing ; given to kicking and biting ; ذو صاهل *ẕû ṣâhil*, f. ذات ص *ẕât ṣâhil*, irascible and malignant ;—ة *ṣâlita-t*, pl. *ṣawâhil*, neighing (s.) ; humming, buzzing ; clatter.
صاهور *ṣâhûr*=ساهور *sâhûr*.
صاو *ṣâw-in*, صاوى *ṣâwî*, ة, dried up, withered.
(صاى) *ṣa'a*, INF. صئى *ṣa'iyy*, *ṣi'iyy*, *ṣu'iyy*, peep ; whistle, neigh, grunt, bark ; — IV. INF. *iṣ'â'*, cause to peep, &c.
صاى *ṣa'î*, barking, yapping (s.) ; — ة *ṣâya-t*, overcoat ; cassock.
صايب *ṣâyib*, pl. *ṣibân*, going straight to the aim ; hitting, to the point, right, true.
صايت *ṣâyit*, crying out, sounding.
صايح *ṣâyiḥ*, crying out ; public crier ; — ة *ṣâyiḥa-t*, outcry, clamour, lamentation.
صايد *ṣâyid*, hunter ; ابن ص *ibn ṣâyid*, Anti-Christ.
صاير *ṣâyir*, what becomes or has become, happening, happened, what is to happen, destiny ; — ة *ṣâyira-t*, hay.
صايغ *ṣâyig*, pl. *ṣuyyâg*, fashioner ; goldsmith ; artist ; creator.
صايف *ṣâyif*, woolly, see (صوف) ; very hot ; summer-rain ; who begets children in his old age, see (صيف) ; — ة *ṣâyifa-t*, pl. *ṣawâyif*, summer provisions ; summer campaign.
صايق *ṣâyiq*, adhering, sticking to.
صائكة *ṣa'ika-t*, smell of damp wood.
صائل *ṣâ'il*, arrogant, overbearing ; furious.
صايم *ṣâyim*, fasting (adj.) ; fast-day ; — *ṣâ'im*, thirsty.
صائى *ṣâ'î*, renegade, apostate.
(صب) *ṣabb*, U, INF. *ṣabb*, pour out, shed ; be poured out ; descend ; — for *ṣabib*, A, INF. *ṣabâba-t*, long for, love tenderly ; pass. be destroyed or squandered ; — IV. INF. *iṣbâb*, descend ; — V. INF. *taṣabbub*, VII. INF. *inṣibâb*, VIII. INF. *iṣtibâb*, be poured out ; — VI. INF. *taṣâbub*, drink out what remains in a cup ; — VII. see V. ; go eagerly to.
صب *ṣabb*, poured out ; f. ة, full of longing or love ; lover ; — *ṣubb*, anything poured out.
(صبا) *ṣaba'*, INF. *ṣab'*, *ṣubû'*, change from one religion to another ; also صبو *ṣabu'*, INF. *ṣubû'a-t*, become a Sabean ; lead against (على *'ala*) ; appear ; (also IV.) rise ; (also IV.) touch ; — IV. INF. *iṣbâ'*, meet unexpectedly with the enemy ; see I.
صبا *ṣab-an*, *ṣabâ*, pl. *ṣabawât*, *aṣbâ'*,

east wind, zephyr, vernal breeze; — *ṣibâ*, pleasure.
صبابة *ṣabâba-t*, love; —*ṣubâba-t*, rest of a fluid; drop.
صباح *ṣabâḥ*, early morning; —*ṣibâḥ*, pl. of صبيح *ṣabîḥ*; — *ṣubâḥ*, brightness, clearness; — *ṣubâḥ*, *ṣubbâḥ*, beautiful, fair, friendly; — ة *ṣabâḥa-t*, beauty, fairness, friendliness.
صبار *ṣibâr*, patience; stopper, cork; pl. of صبرة *ṣubra-t*; — *ṣubâr*, *ṣubbâr*, fruit of the tamarind; — *ṣabbâr*, very patient; — ة *ṣibâra-t*, *ṣubâra-t*, *ṣabâra-t*, stones; splinters; — *ṣabbâra-t*, hard, stony ground; severe cold; aloes.
صباصب *ṣubâṣib*, big.
صباغ *ṣibâg*, dye; — *; — *ṣabbâg*, dyer; liar.
صباوة *ṣabâwa-t*, childhood.
صبايا *ṣabâyâ*, pl. of صبية *ṣabiyya-t*.
صبب *ṣabab*, flowing off, ebbing (s.); pl. *aṣbâb*, descending (s.); declivity, slope.
(صبث) *ṣabaṡ*, INF. *ṣabṡ*, mend, darn.
(صبح) *ṣabaḥ*, come early in the morning to (acc.); — *ṣabiḥ*, INF. *ṣabaḥ*, *ṣubḥa-t*, have black hair with a red lustre; shine, flash; — *ṣabuḥ*, INF. *ṣabâḥa-t*, be fair, beautiful, lovely; — II. INF. *taṣbîḥ*, cause it to be morning; wish good-morning; come in the morning to (acc.); give a morning draught; bring to the water after a night's journey; — IV. INF. *iṣbâḥ*, grow morning; enter on the morning of a day; become in the morning, become; awake (n.), attend; use as lighting material; — V. INF. *taṣabbuḥ*, make a morning sleep; take breakfast; — VIII. INF. *iṣṭibâḥ*, light a lamp; take a morning draught; — X. INF. *istiṣbâḥ*, make a lamp ready, procure a light.
صبح *ṣubḥ*, *ṣibḥ*, pl. *aṣbâḥ*, day-break, dawn, light of the morning; ام ص *umm-u ṣubḥ-in*, Mecca; —*ṣabaḥ*, glimmer, gleam; reddish black; — ة *ṣubḥa-t*, *ṣabḥa-t*, morning sleep; — *ṣubḥa-t*, early meal, breakfast; reddish blackness.
صبحان *ṣabḥân*, f. صبحى *ṣabḥa*, who takes a morning draught; fair, beautiful.
صبحى *ṣabḥiyy*, early, of the morning.
صبخة *ṣabḥa-t*, salty ground.
(صبر) *ṣabar*, I, INF. *ṣabr*, tie up; prevent from; bind one in order to kill him; force, compel; restrain one's desire, have patience, wait for; — INF. *ṣabr*, *ṣabara-t*, stand security, offer bail; — II. INF. *taṣbîr*, give or command patience; heap up without measuring; embalm; — III. INF. *muṣâbara-t*, *ṣibâr*, have patience with (acc.); — IV. INF. *iṣbâr*, give or recommend patience; fall into a calamity; sit on a stony hill; eat of the cake صبيرة *ṣabîra-t*; cork or stop a vessel; turn bitter; — V. INF. *taṣabbur*, VIII. INF. *iṣṭibâr*, exercise patience; VIII. revenge one's self upon (من *min*); — INF. *istiṣbâr*, be dense or compact.
صبر *ṣabr*, patience; abstemiousness; * myrrh; يمين الصبر *yamîn aṣ-ṣabr*, enforced oath; — *ṣibr*, *ṣubr*, pl. *aṣbâr*, side, edge, border; white cloud; — *ṣubr*, *ṣubur*, gravelly ground; — *ṣabar*, ice; — *ṣabir*, juice of bitter plants; myrrh; — *ṣubur*, pl. of صبير *ṣabîr*; — ة *ṣabra-t*, severe cold; mud at the border of a well; — *ṣubra-t*, pl. *ṣubar*, heap of corn; ballast; pl. *ṣibâr*, big stones in heaps.
صبرا *ṣubarâ'*, pl. of صبير *ṣabîr*.
صبصاب *ṣabṣâb*, big; = بصباص *baṣbâṣ*, fast, swift; alert; small quantity of water, bread, &c.
(صبصب) *ṣabṣab*, INF. ة, separate,

divide; disperse (a.), dissipate; efface, blot out; — II. INF. *taṣabṣub*, disperse (n.); get effaced, blotted out; have passed for the greater part; be hostile or froward towards (على *'ala*); be intense.

صبصب *ṣabṣab*, big.

(صبع) *ṣaba'*, INF. *ṣab'*, point at (contemptuously); point out; put the finger on the orifice of a vessel in decanting.

صبع *ṣab'*, pride, haughtiness.

(صبغ) *ṣabag*, U, I, A, INF. *ṣabg*, *ṣibag*, dye; immerse, dip into; be lengthy; wink; — INF. *ṣubûg*, be of a full colour; — II. INF. *taṣbîg*, dye; colour, ripen; — IV. INF. *iṣbâg*, begin to have ripe fruit; complete; — V. INF. *taṣabbug*, embrace a religion; — VIII. INF. *iṣṭibâg*, make a ragout.

صبغ *ṣibg*, *ṣibag*, pl. *aṣbâg*, dipping of a stuff into a dye; baptism; dye, colour; — *ṣibg*, pl. *ṣibâg*, ragout, stew, sauce; — ة *ṣibga-t*, dye, colour; religion; baptism; — *ṣubga-t*, date beginning to colour; — ى *ṣibgiyy*, seller of dyes or colours.

(صبن) *ṣaban*, I, INF. *ṣabn*, turn a thing from its destination; prepare to cast the dice; — II. INF. *taṣbîn*, lather; — VII. INF. *inṣibân*, VIII. INF. *iṣṭibân*, turn or go away from (عن *'an*).

(صبو) *ṣabâ*, U, INF. *ṣabw*, صبى *ṣaba-n*, *ṣabâ'*, *ṣubwa-t*, *ṣubuww*, be childish; — INF. *ṣabwa-t*, *ṣubwa-t*, *ṣubuww*, be in love; incline towards; desire for; lay the head on the grass; blow; — صبى *ṣabî*, INF. *ṣabâ'*, act childishly; be in love; pass. *ṣubî*, have east wind; — III. INF. *muṣâbât*, couch the lance; recite a verse faultily; pronounce wrongly; build awry; turn the sword and put it into the scabbard; — IV. INF. *iṣbâ'*, have a little boy; inspire with love; meet with an east wind; — V. INF. *taṣabbî*, inspire with love; (also VI.) seduce a woman; — VI. INF. *taṣâbî*, see V.; fall in love; (also X.) behave childishly; — X. INF. *istiṣbâ'*, see VI.; deem childish.

صبو *ṣabu'*, v. see (صبا); — *ṣubû'*, rise (of a star, &c.), INF. of (صبا); — ة *ṣabwa-t*, boyishness; — *ṣibwa-t*, and—

صبوان *ṣibwân*, *ṣubwân*, pl. of صبى *ṣabiyy*.

صبوب *ṣabûb*, poured out.

صبوح *ṣabûḥ*, morning draught; morning milk; milked early in the morning.

صبور *ṣabûr*, patient; enduring; gentle; ام صبور *umm ṣabûr*, hard ground, calamity, war.

صبى *ṣabî*, *ṣubî*, v. see (صبو); — *ṣiba-n*, ardour of youthful love; — *ṣabiyy*, pl. *ṣibwa-t*, *ṣabya-t*, *ṣibya-t*, *ṣibwân*, *ṣabwân*, *ṣibyân*, *ṣabyân*, *aṣb-in*, *aṣbiya-t*, boy, lad, youth; servant-boy, servant; pupil of the eye; projecting or jutting part; — ة *ṣabiyya-t*, pl. *ṣabâyâ*, young girl; — *ṣubayya-t*, little boys.

صبيان *ṣibyân*, *ṣubyân*, pl. of صبى *ṣabiyy*.

صبيب *ṣabîb*, poured out, shed; sweat, perspiration; juice of the leaves of henna; fluid honey; hoar frost; blood; edge of a sword, &c.

صبيح *ṣabîḥ*, ة, pl. *ṣibâḥ*, fair, beautiful, friendly; — ة *ṣabîḥa-t*, early morning.

صبير *ṣabîr*, pl. *ṣubarâ'*, patient, enduring; bail, security; administrator; having no son or brother; pl. *ṣubur*, stony hill; heaped up clouds; corn-heap; also ة *ṣabîra-t*, thin bread-cake.

(صت) *ṣatt*, INF. *ṣatt*, push back, stop; cry out loudly; overwhelm (with calamity, abuse, &c.); —

III. INF. *muṣâtta-t, ṣitât*, dispute, quarrel with (acc.); — VI. INF. *taṣâtut*, dispute, quarrel with one another.

صت *ṣatt*, push, slap; — *ṣatt, ṣitt*, ة *ṣatta-t*, crowd of people; — *ṣitt*, ة *ṣitta-t*, contrary (s.).

(صتا) *ṣata'*, take an important matter in hand.

صتام *ṣatâm*, big and strongly developed.

صتت *ṣatat*, vis-a-vis (s.).

(صتع) *ṣata'*, INF. *ṣat'*, throw down; — V. INF. *taṣattu'*, come repeatedly; come and go; come with empty hands.

صتع *ṣata'*, strength and flexibility of an ostrich's neck; wild ass.

(صتم), II. *ṣattam*, INF. *taṣtîm*, complete a number, round off; — V. INF. *taṣattum*, run fast.

صتم *ṣatm, ṣatam*, pl. *ṣutm*, stout and strong; in full vigour of manhood; full, complete; — ة *ṣatma-t*, hard rock, stone.

صتيت *ṣatît*, shout, clamour; crowd of people.

صتيمة *ṣatîma-t*, hard rock, stone.

(صته) *ṣatah*, render contemptible, abase, humble; — II. INF. *taṣtîh*, id.

(صتو) *ṣatâ*, U, skip in walking.

(صج) *ṣajj*, INF. *ṣajj*, clash iron against iron.

صجج *ṣujuj*, clatter.

(صح) *ṣaḥḥ*, recover, be healthy; be without fault or blemish; be authentic, valid; prosper, thrive; succeed; — II. INF. *taṣḥîḥ*, make to recover, heal, cure; correct, mend; level, smooth; legalise; liquidate; — IV. INF. *iṣḥâḥ*, make healthy; have one's people and cattle healthy.

صح *ṣaḥ*, abbreviation for صحيح *ṣaḥîḥ*, right; — *ṣaḥḥ*, postscript; — ة *ṣiḥḥa-t*, health; soundness, wholeness, correctness; completeness; good condition; validity.

صحابة *ṣaḥâba-t, ṣiḥâba-t*, companionship; *aṣ-ṣaḥâba-t*, the companions of Mohammed.

صحابى *ṣaḥâbiyy*, companion of Mohammed.

صحاح *ṣaḥâḥ*, pl. *aṣiḥḥa-t*, whole, complete; sound, healthy; faultless; — *ṣiḥâḥ*, pl. of صحيح *ṣaḥîḥ*.

صحار *ṣuḥâr*, sweat, perspiration; fever.

صحارا *ṣaḥâr-an, ṣiḥâr-an*, publicly.

صحارى *ṣaḥâra, ṣaḥârî*, pl. of صحرا *ṣaḥrâ*.

صحاف *ṣiḥâf*, pl. *ṣuḥuf*, water-vessel; — *ṣaḥḥâf*, book-binder; bookseller; — *.

(صحب) *ṣaḥab*, skin; — *ṣaḥib*, A, INF. *ṣuḥba-t, ṣaḥâba-t, ṣiḥâba-t*, be one's companion, accompany, carry with one's self; — III. INF. *muṣâḥaba-t*, offer one's self as a companion to, take for a companion; become sociable; — IV. INF. *iṣḥâb*, associate (a.), give for a companion, endow with; get a companion; grow tame or docile; guard, watch over; prevent; — V. INF. *taṣaḥḥub*, be ashamed; — VI. INF. *taṣâḥub*, make friends with one another; — VIII. INF. *iṣtiḥâb*, guard, watch over, watch; keep company with one another; contract a friendship; — X. INF. *istiṣḥab*, wish or take for a companion; be attached to, adhere, belong to.

صحب *ṣaḥb*, pl. of صاحب *ṣâḥib*; — ة *ṣuḥba-t*, companionship, friendship; company; commerce; in company of, by means or by the care of; (m.) chandelier; nosegay.

صحبان *ṣuḥbân*, pl. of صاحب *ṣâḥib*.

(صحر) *ṣaḥar*, boil milk; inflict a sunstroke; extend (n.) far; — IV. INF. *iṣḥâr*, travel into the plain or desert; be far extended; be one-eyed; — XI. *iṣḥârr*, INF. *iṣḥîrâr*, become withered or red (by withering).

صحر *ṣaḥar*, grey on a red ground;

—*ṣuḥar*, pl. of صحرا *ṣaḥrâ'*; — *ṣuḥr*, name of Lokman's sister; — ة *ṣuḥra-t*, pl. *ṣuḥar*, cleft of a rock; mixture of white and red; — *ṣaḥrat-an*, *ṣuḥrat-an*, quite distinctly; ص نحرة *ṣaḥrat-an naḥrat-an*, before the eyes of all.

صحرا *ṣaḥrâ'*, f. white mixed with red; brown; pl. *ṣaḥara*, *ṣaḥârî*, *ṣaḥrâwât*, *ṣuḥar*, waste plain, desert (Sahara); plain with loose ground.

(صحصح) *ṣaḥṣaḥ*, INF. ة, be clear, doubtless.

صحصح *ṣaḥṣaḥ*, صحصاح *ṣaḥṣâḥ*, صحصحان *ṣaḥṣaḥân*, pl. *ṣaḥâṣiḥ*, flat plain; ترهات صحاصح *turrahât ṣaḥâṣiḥ*, vain things, vanities; — صحصح *ṣuḥṣuḥ*, صحصوح *ṣuḥṣûḥ*, trifler, giving one's mind to trifles.

(صحف) *ṣaḥaf*, dig the ground; — II. INF. *taṣḥîf*, read or write faultily; — IV. INF. *iṣḥâf*, join leaves or pamphlets into a volume; — V. INF. *taṣaḥḥuf*, pass. of II.

صحف *ṣuḥuf*, pl. of صحاف *ṣiḥâf* and صحيفة *ṣaḥîfa-t*; — ة *ṣaḥfa-t*, pl. *ṣaḥafât*, *ṣiḥâf*, large dish; ص السارى *ṣaḥfa-t as-ṣârî*, bower.

(صحل) *ṣaḥil*, A, INF. *ṣaḥal*, be hoarse, harsh and broken (voice).

صحل *ṣaḥil*, hoarse.

(صحم), VIII. *iṣtaḥam*, INF. *iṣtiḥâm*, stand up; — XI. *iṣḥâmm*, INF. *iṣḥîmâm*, be very green; grow partly yellow; wither; show a withered vegetation; — ة *ṣuḥma-t*, yellowish black (s.); dirty black (s.); mixture of red and white.

(صحن) *ṣaḥan*, INF. *ṣaḥn*, beat; make peace; offer on a plate; ask for, beg.

صحن *ṣaḥn*, pl. *ṣuḥûn*, inner hollow part of a hoof; large cup; plate; cavity of the ear; interior; courtyard; du. *ṣaḥnân*, castanets; — ة *ṣaḥna-t*, pl. *ṣaḥanât*, blow; plate; — *ṣuḥna-t*, soft ground in the midst of stony.

صحنا *ṣaḥnâ'*, *ṣiḥnâ'*, ة *ṣaḥnât*, a small salt fish; *ṣaḥnâ'*, cavity (of the ear).

(صحو) *ṣaḥâ*, U, INF. *ṣaḥw*, be clear, serene; sleep one's self sober; become reasonable; — صحى *ṣaḥî*, be clear, serene; recover (from intoxication, love, &c.); attend, be on one's guard; — IV. INF. *iṣḥâ'*, be clear, be sober; clear up.

صحو *ṣaḥw*, clear, serene; sober serenity, clearness of thought.

صحور *ṣaḥûr*, white intermixed with red; kicking (adj.).

صحون *ṣaḥûn*, kicking (adj.); —*.

صحى *ṣaḥî* (v.), see (صحو).

صحيح *ṣaḥîḥ*, pl. *ṣiḥâḥ*, *ṣaḥâyiḥ*, *aṣiḥḥâ'*, complete, perfect, whole; sound, healthy; correct; true; authentic; valid; regular; pl. *ṣaḥâyiḥ*, the thummim of the Jewish priest; *ṣaḥîḥ-an*, yes, it is true.

صحير *ṣaḥîr*, bray; — ة *ṣaḥîra-t*, milk boiled by heated stones; hence dim. صحيرا *ṣuḥairâ'*, id.

صحيف *ṣaḥîf*, surface of the ground; — ة *ṣaḥîfa-t*, pl. *ṣaḥâyif*, *ṣuḥuf*, leaf (of a book); list; letter; book; newspaper; small dish.

(صخ) *ṣaḫḫ*, U, INF. *ṣaḫḫ*, beat one hard thing against another; INF. *ṣaḫḫ*, *ṣaḫîḫ*, clash, clatter; peck open tumours on the back of a camel (raven); — I, INF. *ṣaḫḫ*, deafen by a blow or by cries.

صخ *ṣaḫ-in*, see صخى *ṣaḫî*; — ة *ṣaḫḫa-t*, clash.

صخاب *ṣaḫḫâb*, f. ة, screamer, shouter.

صخاة *ṣaḫâ'a-t*, dirt, stain.

(صخب) *ṣaḫib*, A, INF. *ṣaḫab*, cry out, scream, shout; — VI. INF. *taṣâḫub*, brawl; — VIII. INF. *iṣtiḫâb*, clamour, mingle their cries (birds, &c.).

صخب *ṣaḫab*, clamour, noise, tu-

mult ; — *ṣaḥib*, clamouring, deafening with noise, roaring (waves) ; — ة *ṣaḥba-t*, *ṣuḥubba-t*, f. screaming, clamouring ; bubbling (source) ; *ṣaḥba-t*, amulet.

صخبان *ṣaḥbân*, pl. *ṣuḥbân*, screamer, brawler.

(صخت), XI. *iṣḥâtt*, INF. *iṣḥîtât*, subside ; recover.

(صخد) *ṣaḥad*, INF. *ṣaḥd*, singe, scorch ; shriek ; — INF. *ṣuḥûd*, listen to (الى *ila*) ; — *ṣaḥid*, A, INF. *ṣaḥad*, be very hot ; — IV. INF. *iṣḥâd*, expose one's self to the heat of the sun, bask.

صخدان *ṣaḥdân*, *ṣaḥadân*, hot.

(صخر) *ṣaḥr*, *ṣaḥar*, pl. *ṣuḥûr*, noun of unity ة *ṣaḥra-t*, *ṣaḥara-t*, pl. *ṣaḥarât*, large rock ; hard stone ; crag, cliff ; — *ṣaḥir*, rocky, stony ; —IV. INF. *iṣḥâr*, come into rocky parts ; be rocky.

(صخف) *ṣaḥaf*, INF. *ṣaḥf*, dig the ground.

(صخم) *ṣaḥam*, INF. *ṣaḥm*, scorch.

صخما *ṣaḥmâ'*, stony hill with soft ground alternately.

(صخو) *ṣaḥâ*, U, INF. *ṣaḥw*, stir the fire ; — صخى *ṣaḥî*, INF. *ṣaḥa-n*, be soiled.

صخوب *ṣaḥûb*, f. ة, screamer, brawler.

صخود *ṣaḥûd*, very hot.

صخى *ṣaḥî* (v.), see (صخو) ; — *ṣaḥî* (صخ *ṣaḥ-in*), dirty.

صخيخ *ṣaḥîḥ*, INF. of (صخ).

صخير *ṣaḥîr*, large rock.

(صد) *ṣadd*, INF. *ṣudûd*, turn (n.) from ; turn to (acc.) ; — INF. *ṣadd* (also IV.), hinder ; turn (a.) from ; — I, U, INF. *ṣadîd*, cry out, shout ; — II. INF. *taṣdîd*, clap the hands ; — IV. INF. *iṣdâd*, see I. ; suppurate ; — V. INF. *taṣaddud*, *taṣaddî*, come to meet, meet, hit upon ; — VII. INF. *inṣidâd*, be prevented ; — VIII. INF. *iṣtidâd*, veil one's self.

صد *ṣadd*, turning away (s.) ; preventing (s.) ; denial, refusal ; aversion ;—*ṣadd*, *ṣudd*, mountain-chain ; tract of a valley ; river-bed ; side ; — *ṣada'*, slender ; rust ; — *ṣad-in*, see صدى *ṣadî*.

(صدا) *ṣada'*, scratch the rust from a mirror to use it as collyrium ; — صدى *ṣadi'*, INF. *ṣada'*, *ṣadâ'a-t*, be of a reddish black ; rust ; rise and look ; — II. INF. *taṣdi'a-t* =صدا *ṣada'* ; — V. INF. *taṣaddu'*, step forth to meet ; undertake, begin.

صدا *ṣad-an*, صدى *ṣada-n*, pl. *aṣdâ'*, thirst ; voice, echo ; owl which is said to fly out of a dead man's head ; corpse ; a cricket ; a black fish ; expectation ; good breeder of cattle ; — *ṣadâ'*, rust ; — *ṣidâ'*, INF. of (صدو) ; — *ṣaddâ'*, name of a fountain ; — ة *ṣudât*, rust colour.

صداح *ṣaddâḥ*, screamer, shouter ; — *.

صداد *ṣidâd*, veil ; — *ṣuddâd*, pl. *ṣadâ'id*, road to the watering-place ; snake, lizard.

صدار *ṣidâr*, short skirt ; bodice ; mark by branding on the chest of an animal ; — * ; — ة *ṣadâra-t*, صديرة *ṣadîra-t*, pl. *ṣadâ'ir*, part of a valley rising above others ; — *ṣadâra-t*, superior rank, pre-eminence, rank of a prime minister.

صداع *ṣudâ'*, headache, megrim.

صداغ *ṣidâg*, marks on the temples ; — ة *ṣadâga-t*, weakness, INF. of (صدغ).

صداق *ṣadâq*, *ṣidâq*, pl. *ṣudq*, *ṣuduq*, presents to the parents of a bride ; — * ; — ة *ṣadâqa-t*, faithfulness ; friendship.

صدام *ṣidâm*, a head-disease of mules and horses.

صدائد *ṣadâ'id*, pl. of صداد *ṣuddâd*.

صدائر *ṣadâ'ir*, pl. of صدارة *ṣadâra-t* and صديرة *ṣadîra-t*.

(صدح) *ṣadaḥ*, INF. *ṣadḥ*, *ṣudâḥ*, cry out, crow, shout, sing, chant.

صدح *ṣadaḥ*, stony hill; heap of stones as a road-mark; flag; pl. *ṣidḥân*, black; negro; — ة *ṣadḥa-t*, shell or pearl as an amulet.

صدد *ṣadad*, neighbourhood, proximity; vis-a-vis; business in hand, intention.

(صدر) *ṣadar*, I, U, INF. *ṣadr, maṣdar*, return, especially from the watering-place; issue (n.), proceed, result; lead back; bit or strike on the chest; — II. INF. *taṣdîr*, lead back; be in advance by the length of the chest; provide a book with a title and preface; begin a letter; place in the seat of honour; turn towards; fasten the saddle on the camel's chest; — III. INF. *ṣidâr, muṣâdara-t*, demand with importunity; — IV. INF. *iṣdâr*, lead back; issue an order; invent; — V. INF. *taṣaddur*, sit in the place of honour, preside; protrude the chest in sitting; advance, take the lead.

صدر *ṣadr*, m. f. pl. *ṣudûr*, the foremost or upper part of anything, beginning; chest, breast, heart (بنات الصدر *banât aṣ-ṣadr*, cares, ذات الصدر *ẕât aṣ-ṣadr*, inflammation of the chest); the foremost seat, place of honour; leader, president, chairman (الصدر الاعظم *aṣ-ṣadr al-'aẓam*, prime minister); صدر عدالة *ṣadr 'adâla-t*, high court of justice; — *ṣadar*, return from the watering-place; — ة *ṣudra-t*, pl. *ṣudar*, chest, breast; cuirass; bodice, waistcoat; — ى *ṣadriyy*, referring to the chest or breast, pectoral; highest, supreme; foremost; — ية *ṣadriyya-t*, bodice, waistcoat, vest; breast-plate; corselet; breast, chest.

(صدع) *ṣada'*, INF. *ṣad'*, split, rend; divide; break forth; traverse; distinguish, disclose accurately, hit the point; carry out, accomplish; appeal to one's generosity; lean to, turn from (a.); — II. INF. *taṣdî'*, split, break; molest, weary, annoy, make one's head ache; pass. suffer from a headache; — V. INF. *taṣaddu'*, be split, disperse (n.), open (n.); — VII. INF. *inṣidâ'*, split, break (n.).

صدع *ṣad'*, cleft, rent; piece; troop, procession; shaft of an arrow; shoot of a plant; split (adj.); — *ṣid'*, piece, part, fragment; troop; — *ṣada'*, young and strong; troop; rust; — *ṣudu'*, pl. of صديع *ṣadî'*; — ة *ṣid'a-t*, herd, flock; piece, half of; pl. *ṣada'â-t*, differences of opinion, sects.

(صدغ) *ṣadag*, A, INF. *ṣadg*, walk side by side (temple by temple); kill (an ant); turn (a.) from, prevent, deny; — *ṣadug*, INF. *ṣadâga-t*, be seven days old, be weak; — also II. INF. *taṣdîg*, mark the camel on the temples by branding; — III. INF. *muṣâdaga-t*, walk side by side with.

(صدف) *ṣadaf*, I, INF. *ṣadf*, turn from (n. and a.); — INF. *ṣadf*, *ṣudûf*, turn round and lean to; — III. INF. *muṣâdafa-t*, meet with; — IV. INF. *iṣdâf*, turn from (a.), prevent; — V. INF. *taṣadduf*, turn from (n.).

صدف *ṣadaf*, ة, pl. *aṣdâf*, shell; pearl-oyster; shell-like cavity; cavity of the ear; highest part, top; mountain-cutting; — ة *ṣadfa-t*, meeting, casual meeting; *ṣadfat-an, bi-ṣadfat-in*, by chance, accidentally.

صدق *ṣadaq*, U, INF. *ṣadq*, be truthful and sincere; tell the truth; prove true; become aware of; — II. INF. *taṣdîq*, be very truthful or sincere; consider truthful, believe; affirm; make true; flee straight on; — III. INF. *ṣidâq*, *muṣâdaqa-t*, be a true friend to (acc.); acknowledge a contract

as valid; — IV. INF. *iṣdâq*, give the morning gift; — V. INF. *taṣadduq*, give alms to (على *'ala*); receive alms; — VI. INF. *taṣâduq*, confide in one another; be true friends.

صدق *ṣadq*, truth, sincerity; pl. *ṣudq*, *ṣuduq*, true, truthful, sincere; complete; f. ة, unerring, but hard or cruel; — *ṣidq*, truth, sincerity, frankness; strength, vigour, excellence; praise, good repute; — *ṣudq*, *ṣuduq*, pl. of صداق *ṣadâq*, *ṣidâq* and صدوق *ṣadûq*; — ة *ṣadaqa-t*, alms prescribed by law; — *ṣadaqa-t*, *ṣadqa-t* (also *ṣudqa-t*, *ṣaduqa-t*, *ṣudaqa-t*), morning gift; dowry.

صدقا *ṣadaqâ'*, صدقان *ṣudqân*, pl. of صديق *ṣadîq*.

(صدم) *ṣadam*, I, INF. *ṣadm*, strike (hard bodies) against one another; befall; guard off, drive away; — III. *muṣâdama-t*, fight; — VI. INF. *taṣâdum* (also VIII.), beat or fight one another; throng; clash together; — VIII. INF. *iṣṭidâm*, see VI.; clash together; — ة *ṣadma-t*, clash, stroke; calamity; baldness of the temples; du. *ṣadmatân*, *ṣidmatân*, the sides of the forehead, the temples.

(صدو) *ṣadâ*, U, INF. *ṣadw*, clap the hands; — صدى *ṣadî*, A, INF. *ṣada-n*, be thirsty; rust, be rusty; — II. INF. *taṣdiya-t*, clap the hands; — III. INF. *muṣâdât*, flatter, cajole; cover; go to meet; hinder, oppose; imitate; — IV. INF. *iṣdâ'*, re-echo; die; — V. *taṣaddî*, go to meet; oppose; bring one's self to, essay, try.

صدوح *ṣadûḥ*, screamer, shouter, clamourer.

صدود *ṣadûd*, a girl's dress; a kind of collyrium; deceiving (adj.); impostor; — *ṣudûd*, aversion, &c., INF. of (صد).

صدوف *ṣadûf*, coquette (s.); having a foul breath.

صدوق *ṣadûq*, pl. *ṣudq*, *ṣuduq*, truthful, sincere.

صدى *ṣada-n* = صدا *ṣad-an*; — *ṣadî'* (v.), see (صدأ); (adj.) rusty, dirty; — *ṣadî* (v.), see (صدو); (adj.) also صد *ṣad-in*, and—

صديان *ṣadyân*, f. *ṣadyâ'*, thirsty.

صديد *ṣadîd*, cry, shout; pl. *ṣudud*, water flowing from a wound; blood and pus; sweat.

صدير *ṣudair*, ة *ṣudaira-t*, bodice, waistcoat; — ة *ṣadîra-t* = صدارة *ṣadâra-t*.

صديع *ṣadî'*, pl. *ṣudu'*, cleft, split; morning-dawn; half (s.); split (adj.); new patch upon an old cloth; young; herd, flock.

صديغ *ṣadîg*, child up to the seventh day; weak.

صديق *ṣadîq*, pl. *ṣudaqâ'*, *aṣdiqâ'*, *ṣudqân*, *aṣâdiq*, f. ة, true friend; — *ṣiddîq*, ة, most truthful; who keeps his word; Joseph, Abu Bekr; — *ṣudayyiq*, little friend.

(صر) *ṣarr*, U, INF. *ṣarr*, tie up a purse; pack, embale; tie up the udders of a she-camel; (also IV.) lay the ears close against the head; — I, INF. *ṣarr*, *ṣarîr*, produce a sound; INF. *ṣarîr*, tingle (ears); pass. suffer from the cold (plant); — II. INF. *taṣrîr*, advance, go ahead; — III. INF. *muṣârra-t*, force, compel; — IV. INF. *iṣrâr*, see I.; purpose, persist in, try to accomplish; get leaves; — VII. INF. *inṣirâr*, be bundled up, embaled; — VIII. INF. *iṣṭirâr*, be narrow.

صر *ṣarr*, ة, tied up, bundled up; be quiet! silence! — *ṣirr*, severe cold; cold wind; hoar-frost; mildew, blight; a yellow finch; — ة *ṣarra-t*, violence, intensity; heat; crowd; austere looks; tumult; grief; — *ṣirra-t*, severe cold; deafening noise; dust; — *ṣurra-t*, pl. *ṣurar*, purse.

(صرا) *ṣara'*=(صرح), scream, cry out, shout.

صرا *ṣirâ'*, pl. of صراية *ṣarâya-t*; — *ṣarrâ'*, f. of اصر *aṣarr*, hard; — *ṣurrâ'*, pl. of صارى *ṣârî*, sailor; deadly, poisonous; — ة *ṣarât*, stagnating water; not milked for a long time (sheep).

صراب *ṣirâb*, seed.

صراح *ṣarâḥ*, *ṣurâḥ*, pure, unmixed; *ṣurâḥ*, publicity; open speech; *ṣurâḥ*, ى *ṣurâḥiyy*, wine-bottle; — *; — *ṣurrâḥ*, eatable locust; —ة *ṣarâḥa-t*, purity; *ṣarâḥat-an*, openly, publicly;—ية *ṣurâḥiya-t*, pure wine; —*ṣurrâḥiyya-t*, wine-bottle.

صراخ *ṣurâḥ*, cry, shout; — *ṣarrâḥ*, f. ة, screamer; peacock.

صراد *ṣurrâd*, bright rainless cloud.

صرار *ṣirâr*, pl. *aṣirra-t*, string to tie up the udder of a camel; *ṣirâr*, heights not reached by the water;—*ṣarrâr*, screamer; what makes a screeching noise; — *; — ة *ṣarâra-t*, pl. of صرور *ṣarûr*; — ى *ṣarâriyy*, pl. -*ûn*, sailor.

صراط *ṣirâṭ*, pl. *ṣuruṭ*, road; the bridge of hell; — *ṣurâṭ*, long sword.

صراعة *ṣurrâ'a-t*, good wrestler.

صراف *ṣirâf*, pl. of صريفة *ṣarîfa-t*; — *ṣarrâf*, pl. *ṣayârifa-t*, money-changer, banker; grammarian; — ة *ṣarâfa-t*, an exchange; agio; banking-house.

صرام *ṣarâm*, *ṣirâm*, harvest-time (particularly for dates); war; — *ṣurâm*, war; calamity; sword; last milk in the udder;—*ṣarrâm*, seller of hides; — ة *ṣarâma-t*, harshness; bravery; — ى *ṣarâmiyy*, pl. of صرمة *ṣarma-t*.

صران *ṣurrân*, mastic-tree.

صرائر *ṣarâ'ir*, pl. of صارة *ṣârra-t* and صريرة *ṣarîra-t*.

صراية *ṣarâya-t*, pl. *ṣirâ'*, ripening coloquintida.

(صرب) *ṣarab*, INF. *ṣarb*, cut off; make sour milk; restrain the urine; bring on constipation; produce fresh plants; — *ṣarib*, INF. *ṣarab*, gather, collect (n.); — II. INF. *taṣrîb*, eat sour milk or the gum *ṣarb*; — IV. INF. *iṣrâb*, give; — VIII. INF. *iṣṭirâb*, make sour milk; — XI. INF. *isrîbâb*, be smooth.

صرب *ṣarb*, *ṣarab*, ة, sour milk; gum of the tree طلح *ṭalḥ*; a red dye; — *ṣirb*, small huts; — *ṣurb*, pl. of صريب *ṣarîb*; — ة *ṣarba-t*, *ṣaraba-t*, plants pushing forth fresh shoots.

(صرحة) *ṣarbaḥa-t*, agility, nimbleness.

صربى *ṣarba*, cattle only to be milked for guests.

(صرج), II. *ṣarraj*, INF. *taṣrîj*, give a coat of chalk.

(صرح) *ṣaraḥ*, expound clearly, explain, publish; — *ṣaruḥ*, INF. *ṣarâḥa-t*, *ṣurûḥa-t*, be pure; — II. INF. *taṣrîḥ*, speak distinctly; say one's opinion openly; publish; be clear, evident; be pure, clear; miss; — III. INF. *muṣâraḥa-t*, *ṣirâḥ*, *ṣurâḥ*, act openly; speak out; — IV. INF. *iṣrâḥ*, publish, make known; be clear and known.

صرح *ṣarḥ*, pl. *ṣurûḥ*, high building; castle; — *ṣaraḥ*, pure, unmixed; — ة *ṣarḥa-t*, hard ground; floor, vestibule; publicity; *ṣarḥat-an*, publicly, openly, boldly.

صرحا *ṣuraḥâ'*, pl. of صريح *ṣarîḥ*.

(صرخ) *ṣaraḥ*, INF. *ṣurâḥ*, cry out, call loudly; — IV. INF. *iṣrâḥ*, help, bring assistance; — V. INF. *taṣarruḥ*, try to cry out; — VI. INF. *taṣâruḥ*, VIII. INF. *iṣṭirâḥ*, cry or call to one another; — X. INF. *istiṣrâḥ*, call to one for help; — ة *ṣarḥa-t*, cry; call to prayer.

صرخبة *ṣarḥaba-t*, alertness, nimbleness.

صرخد *ṣarḥad*, صرخدية *ṣarḥadiyya-t*, wine.

(صرد) *ṣarid*, A, INF. *ṣarad*, freeze easily; be sore under the saddle; let out the froth of the milk; be free, turn away from, miss; pierce through the aim; — II. INF. *taṣrîd*, lessen, give in small quantity; water insufficiently; — IV. INF. *iṣrâd*, send the arrow through the aim.

صرد *ṣard*, pure, unmixed; sincere; notorious; cold (adj., s.); nail which fixes the head to the spear; high point; also *ṣarad*, numerous; — *ṣarid*, sensible to the cold, chilly; sore on the back; piercing; — *ṣurad*, pl. *ṣirdân*, a bird of prey; white spot from a scar.

صرر *ṣarar*, ة, ear (yet without corn); — *ṣurar*, pl. of صرة *ṣurra-t*.

(صرصر) *ṣarṣar*, INF. ة, cry; whistle.

صرصر *ṣarṣar*, *ṣurṣur*, cricket; cock; clamour, noise; cold and whistling; cold (s.); — ة *ṣarṣara-t*, whistling of the wind; pl. *ṣarâṣir*, cry of the hawk; cooing of the dove; pl. big and strong camels.

(صرع) *ṣara'*, INF. *ṣar'*, *ṣir'*, *maṣra'*, throw on the ground; pass. *ṣuri'*, have an epileptic fit, a violent headache; (also II.) make a folding door, a verse of two hemistichs; — II. INF. *taṣrî'*, see I.; (also VIII.) throw violently on the ground; — III. INF. *muṣâra'a-t*, wrestle; fight a duel; — V. INF. *taṣarru'*, consist of two hemistichs; — VIII. INF. *iṣṭirâ'*, see II.

صرع *ṣar'*, pl. *ṣurû'*, *aṣru'*, kind, species; condition, state, form; epilepsy; violent headache with spasms; staggers; also *ṣir'*, pl. *ṣurû'*, similar, alike; the other half; *ṣuru'*, pl. of صروع *ṣarû'* and صريع *ṣarî'*; — ة *ṣar'a-t*, kind, condition; time, turn; also *ṣir'a-t*, throwing to the ground, flooring (s.); precipitation; — *ṣura'a-t*, skilful wrestler.

صرعى *ṣar'a*, pl. of صريع *ṣarî'*.

(صرف) *ṣaraf*, I, INF. *ṣarf*, turn, turn round; turn off, refuse, prevent; send away, dismiss, despatch; send to (2 acc.); spend; leave the wine unmixed; drink wine; — INF. *ṣarâfa-t*, change money; — INF. *ṣurûf*, *ṣirâf*, be hot (bitch, &c.); — INF., *ṣarîf*, creak; — II. INF. *taṣrîf*, overturn; despatch; free one's self from anything; inflect (grammar); explain verses; turn, lead (a horse); change direction; drink pure wine; spend; change money; give authority or jurisdiction, confide the management of a fortune; circulate (as the blood); — III. INF. *muṣârafa-t*, finish a business with despatch; take advantage of; — IV. INF. *iṣrâf*, grant leave or furlough; — V. INF. *taṣarruf*, have authority, jurisdiction, full power, the management; use one's self freely; — VII. INF. *inṣirâf*, *munṣaraf*, depart, remove, go away; resign a post, retire; get finished; be inflected; — VIII. INF. *iṣṭirâf*, work for one's living or gain; — X. INF. *istiṣrâf*, pray to God to avert an evil.

صرف *ṣarf*, change; du. *aṣ-ṣarfân*, day and night; repentance; religious duty; cleverness and activity; ransom; full weight or measure; gain; an exchange; agio; vicissitude; pl. *ṣurûf*, calamity; averting of an evil; inflection, that part of grammar which treats of it; — *ṣirf*, pure, unmixed; a red colour; *ṣirf-an*, by all means, in every respect; — *ṣuruf*, pl. of صريفة *ṣarîfa-t*.

صرفان *ṣarafân*, death; cupper, lead; an inferior kind of date.

صرفى *ṣarfiyy*, grammarian; grammatical.

(صرق) *ṣaraq*, thin, fine; — *ṣuruq*, pl. of صريقة *ṣarîqa-t*.
(صرقع) *ṣarqa'*, INF. ة, snap the fingers.
(صرم) *ṣaram*, I, INF. *ṣarm*, *ṣurm*, cut off; cull, pluck; stay, abide; break, tear (n.); — *ṣarum*, INF. *ṣarâma-t*, be brave, hard, severe; be sharp, cutting; — II. INF. *taṣrîm*, cut the udders of a camel; cut or tear into pieces; — IV. INF. *iṣrâm*, get ripe for the harvest; be poor with a large family; — V. INF. *taṣarrum*, be cut into pieces; be at an end; be brave, sharp, alert; — VII. INF. *inṣirâm*, be cut into pieces, tear (n.); be finished; separate (n.); — VIII. INF. *iṣṭirâm*, cut, reap.
صرم *ṣarm*, *ṣurm*, *ṣuram*, separation; breach, rupture; *ṣarm*, leather; — *ṣirm*, pl. *aṣrâm*, *aṣârim*, *aṣârîm*, *ṣurmân*, crowd; village; shoeing of a horse; horse-shoe; manner, kind, species; — *ṣurm*, pl. of صرما *ṣarmâ'*; — ة *ṣarma-t*, pl. *ṣaram*, *ṣarâmiyy*, shoe; — *ṣirma-t*, pl. *ṣiram*, herd of camels (10 to 50).
صرما *ṣarmâ'*, pl. *ṣurm*, waterless desert; milkless camel; cooking-vessel, pot.
صرماية *ṣarmâya-t*, shoe (m.).
(صرنفح) *ṣaranfaḥ*, screaming much.
(صرنقح) *ṣaranqaḥ*, hard; who gives nothing away; subtle and prudent.
(صرو) *ṣarâ*, U, INF. *ṣarw*, look at, gaze at.
صروحة *ṣurûḥa-t*, purity.
صرود *ṣurûd*, arctic zone.
صرور *ṣarûr*, ة *ṣarûra-t*, صرورا *ṣarûrâ'* صروری *ṣarûrîyy*, who does not join in the pilgrimage to Mecca; unmarried.
صروع *ṣarû'*, pl. *ṣuru'*, wrestler.
صروف *ṣarûf*, gnashing the teeth; — *.
صروم *ṣarûm*, sharp, cutting; active, energetic.

(صرى) *ṣara*, I, INF. *ṣary*, cut, cut off, lop; refuse, repel; prevent; guard, protect; grant a refuge, save; be as a captive or hostage with; settle a dispute; be an adequate substitute for; keep back the water or sperm, refrain from coition; advance at the head of; lag behind; be high, and, by opposition, be low; fold, bend together; — صرى *ṣarî*, be kept back; stagnate, get foul; — II. INF. *taṣriya-t*, leave unmilked for several days; — IV. INF. *iṣrâ'*, sell a sheep which has been left unmilked for several days as abounding in milk.
صرى *ṣaran*, *ṣuran*, *ṣiran*, *ṣarâ*, &c., stagnating water; *ṣaran*, spoiled milk; rest, remainder; — *ṣirra*, *ṣurra*, firm resolution; trouble and toil; — *ṣurra*, sheep not milked for several days; — *ṣarriyy*, *ṣirriy*, paid in cash, ready (money).
صريا *ṣaryâ* = صرى *ṣurra*.
صريب *ṣarîb*, pl. *ṣurb*, sour milk, or dish made of it.
صريح *ṣarîḥ*, pl. *ṣuraḥâ'*, *ṣarâ'iḥ*, pure, unmixed; of pure origin, thoroughbred; clear, evident, open; doubtless.
صريخ *ṣarîḫ*, cry for help; who cries for help; helper.
صريد *ṣarîd*, injured by the frost, blasted; — *ṣurraid*, bright rainless cloud; — ة *ṣarîda-t*, pl. *ṣarâ'id*, head of cattle uninjured by the cold.
صرير *ṣarîr*, scream, shout, noise; creaking; ة, shouting, screaming, sounding; — ة *ṣarîra-t*, pl. *ṣarâ'ir*, scream, cry, sound.
صريع *ṣarî'*, pl. *ṣar'a*, thrown to the ground; epileptic; hostage; pl. *ṣuru'*, broken branch; roughly-made bow; — *ṣirrî'*, skilful wrestler.
صريف *ṣarîf*, creaking, gnashing of the teeth; pure silver; milk fresh

from the cow; withered tree; — *ṣirrîf*, gnashing the teeth violently; — ة *ṣarîfa-t*, pl. *ṣuruf*, *ṣirâf*, coll. *ṣarîf*, withered palm-branch.

صريقة *ṣarîqa-t*, pl. *ṣarîq*, *ṣuruq*, *ṣarâ'iq*, a thin cake.

صريم *ṣarîm*, cut off; isolated small sandhill; heap of sheaves; morning dawn, and, by opposition, dark night; bare ground; — ة *ṣarîma-t*, resolution; firm; ness; perseverance; pl. *ṣarâ'im*, isolated sandhill.

صطر *ṣaṭr*, pl. *asṭur*, *ṣuṭûr*, line, handwriting; — *ṣaṭar*, kid.

صطل *ṣaṭal*, bucket.

صعا *ṣi'â'*, pl. of صعو *ṣa'w*.

امور صعاتر *umûr ṣa'âtir*, difficulties; unpleasantnesses.

صعار *ṣa''âr*, haughty; — *.

صعارير *ṣa'ârîr*, pl. of صعرر *ṣu'urrur*.

صعالك *ṣa'âlik*, صعاليك *ṣa'âlîk*, pl. of صعلوك *ṣu'lûk*.

صعائد *ṣa'â'id*, pl. of صعود *ṣa'ûd*.

(صعب) *ṣa'ub*, INF. *ṣu'ûba-t*, be hard, difficult; be troublesome, disobedient, refractory; — II. INF. *taṣ'îb*, make difficult; — III. INF. *muṣâ'aba-t*, make difficulties to; — IV. INF. *iṣ'âb*, be hard, difficult; find difficult; leave a refractory camel; — V. INF. *taṣa''ub*, be or make difficult; — X. INF. *istiṣ'âb*, be or find difficult; be refractory.

صعب *ṣa'b*, pl. *ṣi'âb*, ة, pl. *ṣab'ât*, hard, difficult; refractory; *aṣ-ṣa'b*, lion.

صعبوب *ṣu'bûb*, pl. *ṣa'âbîb*, hard, difficult.

(صعت) *ṣa't*, thick-set; صعت الربة *ṣa't ar-ruba-t*, of a handsome figure.

(صعتر) *ṣa'tar*, thyme.

صعتر *ṣa'tar*, INF. ة, feed on thyme; adorn.

(صعد) *ṣa'id*, A, INF. *ṣu'ûd*, *ṣa'ad*, *ṣu'ud*, mount, ascend; — II. INF. *taṣ'îd*, ascend; descend; melt fat; sublimate; cause to evaporate; draw (breath); — IV. INF. *iṣ'âd*, mount, ascend, go uphill; travel by land; descend; come to Mecca; — V. INF. *taṣa''ud*, VI. INF. *taṣâ'ud*, be difficult, troublesome; also VIII. INF. *iṣṭi'âd*, ascend.

صعد *ṣa'd*, high; — *ṣu'd*, top, the top part; — *ṣa'ad*, terrible punishment, pain, torture; — *ṣu'ud*, pl. of صعود *ṣa'ûd* and صعيد *ṣa'îd*; — ة *ṣa'da-t*, pl. *ṣa'adât*, *ṣi'âd*, straight shaft of a lance, straightly-made woman; she-ass; utensil, tool.

صعدا *ṣa'dâ'*, molestation; — *ṣu'adâ'*, pl. صعداوى *ṣu'adâwâ*, deep sigh.

صعدات *ṣu'udât*, pl. of صعيد *ṣa'îd*.

صعدد *ṣu'dud*, pain, torment, torture.

(صعر) *ṣa'ir*, A, INF. *ṣa'ar*, be distorted, wry; have the neck distorted (camel); be small; — II. INF. *taṣ'îr*, III. INF. *muṣâ'ara-t*, IV. INF. *iṣ'âr*, distort the face (from contempt) or have it distorted by nature; — V. INF. *taṣa''ur*, have the face distorted.

صعر *ṣa'ar*, wry or distorted face; turning proudly away (s.); distorted neck of a camel; — صعر *ṣu'r*, pl. of اصعر *aṣ'ar*, declining (star).

(صعرر) *ṣa'rar*, INF. ة, form into a ball; — II. have the form of a ball, be globular; — IV. *iṣ'anrar*, INF. *iṣ'inrâr*, ball, coil one's self up.

صعرر *ṣu'urrur*, صعرور *ṣu'rûr*, pl. *ṣa'ârîr*, a resin, gum.

(صعصع) *ṣa'ṣa'*, INF. ة, separate, disperse; fear; move (a.); anoint; — II. INF. *taṣa'ṣu'*, be moved; be dispersed, dishevelled; yield; be timid; humble one's self, abase one's self; dishevel; destroy.

صعصع *ṣa'ṣa'*, *ṣu'ṣu'*, pl. *ṣa'âṣi'*, dispersed; a bird; — ة *ṣa'ṣa'a-t*, a purging plant.

(معف) *ṣu'if*, pass. tremble.

معف *ṣa'f*, pl. *ṣi'âf*, a small bird; honey-wine, mead; — ة *ṣa'fa-t*, trembling.

معفان *ṣa'fân*, fond of mead.

(معفر) *ṣa'far*, INF. ة, scare and disperse; also II. INF. *taṣa'fur*, be distorted.

معفق *ṣa'faq*, معفقى *ṣa'faqiyy*, معفوق *ṣa'fûq*, pl. *ṣa'âfiq*, *ṣa'âfiqa-t*, market-thief; contemptible fellow.

(معق) *ṣa'aq*, INF. *ṣâ'iqa-t*, strike with lightning; — *ṣa'iq*, INF. *ṣa'q*, *ṣa'aq*, *ṣa'qa-t*, *taṣ'âq*, swoon, faint; die; — IV. INF. *iṣ'âq*, cause to swoon.

معق *ṣa'aq*, loud cry; — *ṣa'iq*, screaming, crying out (adj.); stunned.

معقر *ṣu'qur*, spawn.

معل *ṣa'il*, and XI. *iṣ'âll*, INF. *iṣ'îlâl*, have a small head and thin neck.

معل *ṣa'l*, having a small head and thin neck; bald; — *ṣa'al*, the above quality; — ة *ṣa'la-t*, palm-tree which is not straight and has thin branches.

معلا *ṣa'lâ*, f. of اصعل *aṣ'al*, bald.

(معلك) *ṣa'lak*, INF. ة, impoverish; make convex at the top; fatten; —II. INF. *taṣa'luk*, become poor; become a robber, a scamp; — ة *ṣa'laka-t*, poverty.

معلوك *ṣu'lûk*, pl. *ṣa'âlîk*, *ṣa'âlik*, poor; beggar; robber.

معمور *ṣu'mûr*, water-wheel; bucket.

(معن), IV. *aṣ'an*, have a small head and little intellect; — IX. *iṣ'ann*, INF. *iṣ'inân*, be thin and pretty.

معنب *ṣa'nab*, having a small head.

(معو) *ṣa'â*, INF. *ṣa'w*, be thin and small.

معو *ṣa'w*, ة, pl. *ṣi'â'*, *ṣa'wât*, red-headed finch;—ة *ṣa'wa-t*, having a small head.

معوب *ṣa'ûb*, difficult; restive, refractory; — ة *ṣu'ûba-t*, difficulty; restiveness.

معود *ṣa'ûd*, pl. *ṣu'ud*, *ṣa'â'id*, steep; steep summit, height; the mountains of hell; great difficulty; heavy punishment; — *ṣu'ûd*, mounting, ascending (s.); ascension (feast of).

معودا *ṣa'ûdâ'*, steepest summit.

معوط *ṣa'ûṭ*, snuff.

معون *ṣi'wann*, f. ة, ostrich.

معيد *ṣa'îd*, plur. *ṣu'ud*, *ṣu'udât*, earth, ground, road; mounting, ascending (s.); tomb; upper, the upper part; *ṣu'ud-an*, upward; on high;—ة *ṣa'îda-t*, pl. *ṣawâ'id*, burnt offering.

(صغ) *ṣagg*, U, INF. *ṣagg*, eat much.

صغا *ṣag-an*, *ṣagâ*, inclination.

صغاب *ṣugâb*, ova of ants.

صغار *ṣigâr*, smallness; minority; pl. of صغير *ṣagîr*; — *ṣugâr*, small, little; — ة *ṣagâra-t*, paltriness; weakness; contemptibleness; subjection.

صغانة *ṣagâna-t*, castanets.

صغبل *ṣagbal*=سغبل *sagbal*.

(صغر) *ṣagir*, *ṣagur*, INF. *ṣagar*, *ṣigar*, *ṣagâra-t*, *ṣugrân*, be small, paltry, insignificant; — INF. *ṣigr*, *ṣigâr*, grow small; humble one's self; be young, under age; be younger; — *ṣagir*, A, INF. *ṣagar*, be despised, made little of; — *ṣagur*, INF. *ṣugr*, *ṣigar*, *ṣigâr*, *ṣagâr*, *ṣagâra-t*, *ṣugrân*, submit cowardly; turn towards setting; — II. INF. *taṣgîr*, make small, lessen, diminish;—IV. INF. *iṣgâr*, id.; cause to be despised; produce young ones; — VI. INF. *taṣâgir*, appear contemptible in one's own eyes; humble one's self; show one's self contemptible; —X. INF. *istiṣgâr*, consider small, make little of, slight, abuse; choose the smallest.

صغر *ṣugr*, contempt, disdain; — *ṣigar*, smallness; light weight; minority;—ة *ṣigra-t*, the younger, the inferior ones; — *ṣagara-t*, pl.

of *ṣâgir*, who humbles himself of his own accord.

صغرا *ṣugrâ*=صغرى *ṣugrâ*; — *ṣugarâ'*, pl. of صغير *ṣagîr*.

صغران *ṣugrân*, small, little, paltry; INF. of (صغر).

صغرى *ṣugrâ*, smaller, less; the minor proposition.

صغصغ *ṣagṣag*, INF. ة, comb the hair up so as to be neither curly nor smooth; put fat or butter to.

صغل *ṣagil*, small; ill-shaped.

(صغو) *ṣagâ*, U, I, INF. *ṣagw*, *ṣuguww*, incline towards (الى *ila*); turn towards setting; — صغى *ṣagî*, A, INF. *ṣagan*, *ṣugiyy*, incline (n.); incline and listen; — IV. INF. *iṣgâ'*, incline one's ear towards, listen to; be attentive; make a vessel to incline; diminish; turn the head towards the saddle as if to listen.

صغو *ṣagw*, *ṣigw*, *ṣuguww*, inclination; love; — *ṣigw*, hollow of a spoon; inside of a well, bucket, &c.

صغوا *ṣagwâ'*, setting (adj., f.).

صغى *ṣagî*, (v.) see (صغو); — *ṣagan*, *ṣagy*, *ṣugiyy*, inclination.

صغير *ṣagîr*, pl. *ṣigâr*, *ṣugarâ'*, small, insignificant, paltry; under age; — *ṣugayyir*, dim. exceedingly small, &c.; — ة *ṣagîra-t*, venial sin, peccadillo.

(صف) *ṣaff*, U, INF. *ṣaff*, range in a line; array in battle-order; set in print (m.); milk into two or three buckets standing in a line; spread the wings; place the feet in a line; provide the saddle with a seat; — II. INF. *taṣfîf*, place in a line, range; — III. INF. *muṣâffa-t*, array one's self opposite another (for combat); sit on the opposite bench; — IV. INF. *iṣfâf*, provide the saddle with a seat; — VI. INF. *taṣâff*, stand arrayed in lines; — VIII. INF. *iṣṭifâf*, stand in a line.

صف *ṣaff*, pl. *ṣufûf*, row, line; battle-order; setting in type; — ة *ṣifa-t*, quality; adjective, epithet, attribute, INF. of (وصف); —*ṣuffa-t*, pl. *ṣufaf*, bench; stone bench; sofa; sill, shelf, console; a small part, a little of; a short while, a trice; seat of a saddle; اهل الص *ahlu 'ṣ-ṣuffa-t*, the companions of Mohammed.

صفا *ṣafâ'*, clearness, purity; cheerfulness, gladness, joy; amusement, recreation; true friendship; affection; — *ṣifâ*, INF. III. of (صفو); — ة *ṣafât*, pl. *ṣafawât*, *aṣfâ'*, *ṣufiyy*, *ṣifiyy*, *ṣafan*, *ṣafâ'*, large bare rock, rock.

صفاح *ṣuffâḥ*, broad stone; blade; pl. *ṣuffâḥât*, *ṣafâfîḥ*, having a big hump (camel); — *.

صفاد *ṣifâd*, pl. *aṣfâd*, chain.

صفار *ṣufâr*, whistling (s.); yellow colour; yellow water in the belly; sheep-louse; — *; — *ṣaffâr*, copper-smith; — ة *ṣufâra-t*, *ṣafâra-t*, pl. *ṣifâr*, withered plants; — ى *ṣufâriyya-t*, yellow-hammer; canary-bird; golden thrush.

صفافيح *ṣafâfîḥ*, pl. of صفاح *ṣuffâḥ*.

صفاق *ṣaffâq*, travelling wholesale merchant; — ة *ṣafâqa-t*, impudence.

صفايا *ṣafâyâ*, pl. of صفى *ṣafiyy*.

صفائق *ṣafâ'iq*, pl. of صفوق *ṣafûq*.

صفائى *ṣafâ'î*, purity (m.).

(صفت) *ṣafat*, INF. *ṣaft*, pardon an offence; — V. INF. *taṣaffut*, *taṣafṣut*, show one's self strong, superior in power, hard.

صفت *ṣifitt*, صفتان *ṣifittân*, *ṣiffitân*, صفتيت *ṣiftît*, strong, eminently powerful, tyrannical; conqueror; firm of flesh; — ة *ṣafta-t*, superior power; victory.

(صفح) *ṣafaḥ*, INF. *ṣafḥ*, turn aside (n.); pardon; refuse; admit the camels to the watering-place one after another; let pass in

review one by one; turn leaf by leaf; blink (eye-lids); attend to (فى *fî*); give to drink; strike with the blade; flatten; clap the hands; — INF. *ṣufûḥ*, lose the milk; — II. INF. *taṣfîḥ*, flatten, beat flat or into leaves; cover with metal plates; clap the hands; — III. INF. *ṣifâḥ*, show the broad side; INF. *muṣâfaḥa-t*, (also VI.) take by the hand; (m.) pardon; — IV. INF. *iṣfâḥ*, turn off, refuse; overturn; flatten; — V. INF. *taṣaffuḥ*, look at a thing from the broad side; attend to; be beaten flat or into leaves; — VI. INF. *taṣâfuḥ*, take each other by the hand; get reconciled.

(صفح) *ṣafḥ*, pl. *ṣifâḥ*, side, broadside; cheek; lower mountain-slope; pardon; — *ṣufḥ*, the flat or broad side; — *ṣafaḥ*, excessive width of the forehead; — ة *ṣafḥa-t*, pl. *ṣafaḥât*, side; side of a leaf.

(صفد) *ṣafad*, I, INF. *ṣafd*, also II. INF. *taṣfîd* and IV. INF. *iṣfâd*, tie up, fasten; — IV. present with.

صفد *ṣafad*, present; pl. *aṣfâd*, tie, bond, fetter.

(صفر) *ṣafar*, I, INF. *ṣafîr*, whistle, pipe; call by whistling (the ass to the watering-place); — *ṣafir*, A, INF. *ṣafar*, *ṣufûr*, be empty; — pass. *ṣufir*, suffer from bilious phlegm; — II. INF. *taṣfîr*, dye yellow; empty, void; whistle; — IV. INF. *iṣfâr*, be poor; empty; be empty; — IX. INF. *iṣfirâr*, XI. INF. *iṣfîrâr*, be yellow; be black; turn pale, blanch (n.).

صفر *ṣafr*, *ṣifr*, *ṣafir*, *ṣufr*, *ṣufur*, pl. *aṣfâr*, empty; — *ṣifr*, pl. *ṣifrât*, zero; also *ṣufr*, copper; brass; gold; — *ṣafar*, chlorosis, jaundice; emptiness; hunger, fright; heart; understanding, intellect; alliance, league, covenant; pl. *aṣfâr*, month Safar; transferring Safar into Muharram (du. *aṣ-ṣafrân*, Safar and Muharram); — ة *ṣafra-t*, hunger; — *ṣufra-t*, yellow or black (s.); paleness, pallor; yolk of an egg; copper, brass; دا الص *dâ' aṣ-ṣufra-t*, syphilis.

صفرا *ṣafrâ'*, gold; gall; bee; locust without ova.

صفرات *ṣifrât*, pl. of صفر *ṣifr*.

صفراية *ṣafrâya-t*=صفارية *ṣufâriyya-t*.

صفرد *ṣifrid*, *ṣifrud*, pl. *ṣafârida-t*, lark; nightingale.

(صفرن) *ṣafran*, INF. ة, be giddy.

صفرى *ṣafariyy*, ة *ṣafariyya-t*, autumn; autumn rain; an autumn plant; — ة *ṣufriyya-t*, dried unripe dates of Yemen (for making conserves).

صفريت *ṣifrît*, pl. *ṣafârît*, poor, needy.

صفصاف *ṣafṣâf*, ة, willow.

(صفصف) *ṣafṣaf*, plain; — *ṣafṣaf*, INF. ة, travel by one's self in the plain; range (m.); — *ṣufṣuf*, sparrow; — ة *ṣafṣafa-t*, chirping of a sparrow.

(صفع) *ṣafa'*, INF. *ṣaf'*, cuff, box the ear; — III. INF. *muṣâfa'a-t*, treat one to boxes on the ear.

صفعان *ṣaf'ân*, pl. *ṣafâ'ina-t*, who meekly receives boxes on the ear.

(صفغ) *ṣafag*, INF. *ṣafg*, strew in a medicine in form of powder.

صفف *ṣufaf*, pl. of صفة *ṣuffa-t*.

صفق *ṣafaq*, I, INF. *ṣafq*, clap; refuse, repel, turn off; — INF. *ṣafq*, *ṣafqa-t*, clap the hands (especially in sign of a bargain concluded); strike with the sword; flap the wings; close or lock the door, and, by opposition, open; close the eyes; play on the lute, play on an instrument; move the trees; depart; fill; alight, put up in an inn; decant wine, &c.; cover, smear with (ب *bi*); — *ṣafuq*,

INF. *ṣafâqa-t*, be thick and strong (stuff); be impudent;— II. INF. *taṣfîq*, clap the hands; strike a bargain; flap the wings; decant wine; make the camels change pasture; depart; go round; — III. INF. *muṣâfaqa-t*, turn to the other side (in lying down); have throes of child-birth; wear two garments one above the other; — IV. INF. *iṣfâq*, turn off, refuse; close or lock; fill; decant wine; agree upon; receive sufficient food; milk the small cattle only once a day; — V. INF. *taṣaffuq*, be refused, sent from one to the other; set to work; roll about (n.); be moved by the wind; — VI. INF. *taṣâfuq*, clasp hands with one another, strike a bargain; — VII. INF. *inṣifâq*, be turned off, refused; be moved; be touched, played upon (lute).

صفق *ṣafq*, pl. *ṣufûq*, side; cheek; the nether jaw of a horse; face; mountain-slope; clapping or clasping of the hands; also *ṣafaq*, impure water from a new skin bag; — *ṣifq*, wing of a door; window-shutter; — *ṣufq*, *ṣafaq*, side; — *ṣufuq*, pl. of صفوق *ṣafûq*; — ة *ṣafqa-t*, clapping or clasping of the hands; bargain; contract.

صفقى *ṣifiqqā*=صفقة *ṣafqa-t*.

(صفن) *ṣafan*, I, INF. *ṣufûn*, stand on three legs, the hoof of the fourth slightly touching the ground; place the feet in one line; throw on the ground; (m.) wonder, look at with astonishment; — II. INF. *taṣfîn*, build a nest; — VI. INF. *taṣâfun*, divide the water between each other.

صفن *ṣafn*, ة, pl. *aṣfân*, *ṣufn*, *ṣufun*, *ṣufnân*, scrotum; a table-cloth of leather, serving also as a bag to carry food and eating-utensils; faucial bag of the camel; (m.) wonder, astonishment; — *ṣafan*, pl. *aṣfân*, scrotum; wasp-nest; corn-ear; — *ṣufn*, *ṣufun*, leathern vessel for washing; leathern bag, skin bag.

(صفو) *ṣafâ*, U, INF. *ṣafw*, *ṣafâ'*, *ṣufuww*, be pure, clear, serene; be pure of heart; take the best part; remain as a clear gain; — INF. *ṣafw*, also *ṣafû*, INF. *ṣafâwa-t*, have plenty of milk; — II. INF. *taṣfiya-t*, clear, strain, filter, decant; — III. INF. *muṣâfât*, *ṣifâ'*, act with sincerity towards; — IV. INF. *iṣfâ'*, id.; clear, strain; be void of a thing; have no sperm left; cease to lay eggs; cease to compose poetry; prefer; — VI. INF. *taṣâfî*, act with sincerity towards one another; — VIII. INF. *iṣṭifâ'*, choose, select, arrange to one's liking; — X. INF. *istiṣfâ'*, id.; deem very pure, good, sincere; take the better part, the cream; take all.

صفو *ṣafw*, *ṣufuww*, purity, clearness; *ṣafw*, pure water; purity of the heart; the best part of a thing; — ة *ṣafwa-t*, *ṣifwa-t*, *ṣufwa-t*, the best part; Mohammed; sincere friend; purity; (m.) selection; homogeneousness.

صفوا *ṣafwâ'*, bare rock; — ة *ṣafwât*, pl. *ṣafwân*, *ṣafawân*, id.

صفوات *ṣafawât*, pl. of صفاة *ṣafât*.

صفوان *ṣafwân*, bright cold day; — ة *ṣafwâna-t*, bare rock.

صفوح *ṣafûḥ*, liberal; forgiving; woman who shows only the side, not the face.

صفوف *ṣafûf*, placing the feet in a line (adj.); filling many vessels one after the other (milch camel); — *.

صفوق *ṣafûq*, steep; soft; pl. *ṣufuq*, *ṣafâ'iq*, smooth and steep rock; pl. *ṣufuq*, *ṣifâq*, thin under-skin; membrane of the bowels.

صفون *ṣafûn*, standing on three legs; — *ṣufûn*, pl. of صافن *ṣâfin*, ag. of (صفن); — *.

صفى *ṣafiyy*, ة, pl. *aṣfiyâ'*, pure; the best part; sincerely attached; friend; *ṣafiyy*, ة *ṣafiyya-t*, pl. *ṣafâyâ*, part of the booty which the leader takes first; camel abounding in milk; very fertile palm-tree; — *ṣufiyy*, pl. of صفاة *ṣafât*; — ة *ṣufayya-t*, first cold day.

صفيح *ṣafîḥ*, sky, heaven; the broad side; broad blade; sheet metal, tin plate; skull; — ة *ṣafîḥa-t*, pl. *ṣafâ'iḥ*, broad side; blade; plate; thin flag-stone; slate; pallet; skin of the face.

صفير *ṣafîr*, whistling, piping (s.); sapphire; — *ṣufair*, cassia sophera; — ة *ṣafîra-t*, isolated sand-hill.

صفيف *ṣafîf*, placed in a row.

صفيق *ṣafîq*, coarse and thick; impudent.

(صق) *ṣaqq*, I, INF. *ṣaqq*, produce a whistling or hissing sound.

صق *ṣaqq*, sound of a nail which is being driven in.

صقار *ṣaqqâr*, who rears hawks; seller of date-honey; liar, swearer, slanderer; infidel; — *

صقارى *ṣuqâra*, evident slander.

صقاع *ṣiqâ'*, cloth placed between the head and veil to protect the latter from grease; veil; muzzle for the mouth or nose of a camel; mark on the back part of a camel's head; — *.

صقال *ṣiqâl*, smoothing (s.); polish, brightness; side; belly; — *ṣaqqâl*, polisher; — ة *ṣaqâla-t*, scaffolding (s.), scaffold; stand.

صقالبة *ṣaqâliba-t*, Sclavonians, pl. of صقلاب *ṣiqlâb*.

(صقب) *ṣaqab*, U, INF. *ṣaqb*, beat with the fist; erect, raise; gather; chirp, twitter; — *ṣaqib*, A, INF. *ṣaqab*, be near, opposite, and, by opposition, be far; — III. INF. *muṣâqaba-t*, *ṣiqâb*, place one's self face to face with (acc.); follow one's lead; accommodate, equalize, make to agree; — IV. INF. *iṣqâb*, bring near; be near, close at hand.

صقب *ṣaqb*, pl. *ṣiqâb*, *ṣuqbân*, long and vigorous, thin and strong; embryo of a camel; pl. *ṣuqûb*, tent-pole; — *ṣaqab*, affinity, relationship, and, by opposition, remoteness, contrast; related.

(صقح) *ṣaqiḥ*, A, INF. *ṣaqḥ*, be bald; — *ṣuqḥ*, pl. of اصقح *aṣqaḥ*, bald; — ة *ṣaqḥa-t*, baldness.

صقحا *ṣaqḥâ'*, f. of اصقح *aṣqaḥ*, bald.

(صقر) *ṣaqar*, U, INF. *ṣaqr*, *ṣaqra-t*, singe, scorch; — INF. *ṣaqr*, beat; break stones; be very sour; light a fire; throw on the ground; — II. INF. *taṣqîr*, light a fire; — IV. INF. *iṣqâr*, be very hot; — V. INF. *taṣaqqur*, hunt with a hawk; burn (n.); stay, abide; — VIII. INF. *iṣṭiqâr*, burn (n.); — IX. *iṣqarr*, INF. *iṣqirâr*, be very sour.

صقر *ṣaqr*, pl. *aṣqur*, *ṣuqûr*, *ṣiqâr*, *ṣuqûra-t*, *ṣiqâra-t*, *ṣuqr*, bird of prey; hawk; sour milk (some sour milk, ة *ṣaqra-t*); intense heat of the sun (also ة *ṣaqra-t*); propensity for anything unlawful; membrane round the lobes of the liver; pl. *ṣuqûr*, *ṣiqâr*, undeserved curse; liberal man; also *ṣaqar*, sugar of dates or grapes, or syrup therefrom; — *ṣaqar*, very sacchariferous dates; hell; — *ṣaqir*, sacchariferous; — *ṣuqar*, notorious lie; — ة *ṣaqara-t*, muddy remains of water; — *ṣaqira-t*, sharp, sagacious (woman).

(صقع) *ṣaqa'*, A, INF. *ṣaq'*, depart, deviate; beat; mark, brand; throw on the ground; fall on the ground as an adorer; utter a lie; — INF. *ṣaq'*, *ṣaqî'*, *ṣuqâ'*, crow; — INF. *ṣaq'*, strike (light-

ning); — *ṣaqiʻ*, A, INF. *ṣaqaʻ*, be struck by lightning; be white in the middle of the head; pass. be covered with hoar-frost; tumble in; — II. INF. *taṣqîʻ*, affirm by oath; chill through; freeze to death in snow or ice; — IV. cover (the earth, as hoar-frost); meet with hoar-frost.

صقع *ṣuqʻ*, region, tract; — *ṣaqaʻ*, melancholy in consequence of hot weather; — *ṣaqiʻ*, melancholic; — ة *ṣuqa-t*, white spot on the forehead; hoar-frost, cold, frost.

صقعا *ṣaqʻâʼ*, sun.

صقعب *ṣaqʻab*, long; creaking, gnashing (adj.).

(صقعر) *ṣaqʻar*, INF. ة, shout into one's ear; — III. INF. *iṣqʻirâr*, flee from the heat of the sun.

صقعر *ṣuqʻur*, water; foul water.

صقعل *ṣaqʻal*, dry dates in milk; — ة *ṣaqʻala-t*, cold.

صقعى *ṣaqaʻiyy*, *ṣaqaʻâ*, firstling.

صقغ *ṣuqg*= صقع *ṣuqʻ*.

(صقل) *ṣaqal*, U, INF. *ṣaql*, *ṣiqâl*, smooth, polish; emaciate; throw on the ground; beat.

صقل *ṣuql*, side, hypochondrium; agile, swift, fleet; — *ṣaqil*, thin, lean; — *ṣaqal*, length of the side, flank; — ة *ṣuqla-t*, *ṣaqla-t*, hypochondrium; — *ṣaqala-t*, polishers, pl. of صاقل *ṣâqil*.

صقلاب *ṣiqlâb*, voracious; red; Lard; pl. *ṣaqâliba-t*, Sclavonians, Russians, &c.

صقور *ṣaqqûr*, cuckold.

صقوف *ṣuqûf*, roof, shelter.

صقيع *ṣaqîʻ*, hoar-frost; a species of wasp.

صقيل *ṣaqîl*, smooth, polished.

(صك) *ṣakk*, U, INF. *ṣakk*, beat violently; lock; — for *ṣakik*, A, INF. *ṣakak*, tremble, knock (knees); trip (n.), make a false step; — VIII. INF. *iṣtikâk*, knock the knees together.

صك *ṣakk*, pl. *ṣukûk*, *ṣikâk*, *aṣukk*, judicial act, signed sentence; deed, document; slip, false step; — *ṣakka-t*, intense heat of mid-day; knock.

صكاك *ṣakâk*, air, atmosphere; — *ṣakkâk*, clerk of the court (of justice); — *.

(صكو) *ṣakâ*, U, INF. *ṣakw*, stick to a thing, attend to it zealously.

صكيك *ṣakîk*, weak and stupid.

(صل) *ṣall*, I, INF. *ṣalîl*, sound, clink, clatter, clash, rumble, grumble; — INF. *ṣulûl*, rot, be putrid, be foul; — INF. *ṣall*, purify, strain, clear, clean; be cleaned, cleared, strained; — U, befall; — I, line with leather; — II. INF. *taṣlîl*, be putrid; — IV. INF. *iṣlâl*, id.; befoul the water.

صل *ṣall*, *ṣill*, pl. *aṣlâl*, rain; — *ṣill*, ة, pl. *aṣlâl*, *ṣilâl*, serpent with a human face; basilisk; vicious, malignant; calamity; sharp sword; similar, alike, equal; a tree; — *ṣull*, foul, putrid, rancid; — ة *ṣila-t*, gift; conjunctive sentence; INF. of (وصل).

صلا *ṣalan*, du. *ṣalawân*, pl. *ṣalawât*, *aṣlâʼ*, middle of the back; buttocks of a horse; space between the vulva and anus of a mare; — *ṣalan*, *ṣalâʼ*, conflagration, fire; anything burnt or roasted; — ة *ṣalât*, prayer; *ṣalâʼa-t*, forehead; pl. *ṣiliyy*, *ṣaliyy*, stone on which perfumes are ground.

صلابة *ṣalâba-t*, hardness; obduracy.

صلاتة *ṣalâta-t*, INF. of (صلت); (m.) salad.

صلاح *ṣalâḥ*, soundness, good or healthy condition; beautiful order; peace; (m.) good actions, justice; also *ṣalâḥi*, Mecca; — *; — *ṣullâḥ*, pl. of صالح *ṣâliḥ*, sound, &c.

صلاد *ṣallâd*, not taking fire (wood).

صلاصل *ṣulâṣil*, braying (adj.).

صلاطح *ṣulâṭiḥ*, spacious, roomy, wide.

صلاطة *ṣalâṭa-t*, salad.

صلاع *ṣilâ'*, heat of the sun; — *ṣullâ'*, ة, broad hard stone; deficient in vegetation.

صلافى *ṣalâfâ*, pl. of صلف *ṣalif*; — *ṣalâfî*, pl. of اصلف *aṣlaf*, hard and sterile.

صلاقة *ṣulâqa-t*, stagnating and befouled water.

صلاقيم *ṣalâqîm*, pl. heads; teeth; dog-teeth.

صلال *ṣilâl*, a herb; also ة *ṣilâla-t*, pl. *aṣilla-t*, inner side or upper part of a shoe; — * ; — *ṣallâl*, foul, deteriorated; sounding, creaking.

صلام *ṣallâm*, *ṣullâm*, marrow of the lotus-fruit; — ة *ṣalâma-t*, *ṣilâma-t*, *ṣulâma-t*, isolated troop of men.

(صلب) *ṣalab*, I, INF. *ṣalb*, crucify; torment violently and unceasingly; roast; draw the marrow out of the bones; — I, U, burn (n.); — *ṣalib*, INF. *ṣalâba-t*, be hard and firm; — II. INF. *taṣlîb*, id.; harden, make hard; crucify; make the sign of the cross; print a stuff with cross-patterns; grow hard; — V. INF. *taṣallub*, grow hard; lie down crosswise; — VIII. INF. *iṣtilâb*, draw the marrow out of the bones.

صلب *ṣalb*, crucifixion; — *ṣulb*, ة, hard; hardened; pl. *aṣlub*, *aṣlâb*, *ṣilaba-t*, spine; loins; strength, vigour; nobility; middle; pl. *ṣilaba-t*, far-stretching stony tract of land; — *ṣalab*, marrow, spine, loins; — *ṣalib*, hard, hardened; — *ṣulab*, a bird; — *ṣulub*, pl. of صليب *ṣalîb*; — *ṣullab*, hard; grind-stone.

صلبان *ṣulbân*, pl. of صليب *ṣalîb*.

صلبوب *ṣulbûb*, flute.

صلبى *ṣulbiyy*, referring to the loins; — *ṣullabiyy*, ة *ṣullabiyya-t*, grind-stone; polishing-stone; sharpened, sharp.

(صلت) *ṣalat*, pierce with the sword; pour out; — U, INF. *ṣalt*, make the horse to prance; — I, have little fat and much water; — *ṣalut*, INF. *ṣalâta-t*, have a large and bright forehead; — IV. INF. *iṣlât*, draw the sword; unsheathe; — VII. INF. *inṣilât*, lag behind in walking; slip away.

صلت *ṣalt*, large and bright forehead; sharp and bright sword; a large knife; hairless; able in business transactions; — *ṣilt*, thief; — *ṣult*, drawn from the scabbard; pl. *aṣlât*, large knife.

صلتان *ṣalatân*, pl. *ṣiltan*, swift; strong; hairless.

(صلج) *ṣalaj*, U, INF. *ṣalj*, melt (a.), knead, rub; beat; — III. pass. *ṣûlij*, be crooked, hooked; be of genuine silver; — VI. INF. *taṣâluj*, feign deafness.

صلج *ṣalaj*, deafness; — *ṣuluj*, genuine coins; — *ṣullaj*, ة, silkworm; cocoon.

(صلح) *ṣalaḥ*, INF. *ṣalâḥ*, *ṣulûḥ*; — *ṣaluḥ*, INF. *ṣalâḥa-t*, be in good or perfect condition; be honest, upright; suit, respond, answer the purpose, be adequate; — II. INF. *taṣlîḥ*, mend, improve (a.); tune; — III. INF. *muṣâlaḥa-t*, *ṣilâḥ*, get reconciled with (acc.); make peace; — IV. INF. *iṣlâḥ*, mend, improve, put in order; tune; bestow benefits on (الى *ila*); — V. INF. *taṣalluḥ*, be mended; — VI. INF. *taṣâluḥ*, make peace, get reconciled; — VIII. INF. *iṣṭilâḥ*, id.; agree upon (على *'ala*); mend, improve (n.); — X. INF. *istiṣlâḥ*, wish or find a thing good; happen by good chance; ask for peace, for reconciliation.

صلح *ṣilḥ*, in good condition, perfect; — *ṣulḥ*, peace, reconciliation; — *ṣaliḥ*, proper name.

صلحا *ṣulaḥâ'*, pl. of صليح *ṣalîḥ*.

(صلخ) *ṣalaḫ*, deafness; — VI. INF. *taṣâluḫ*, feign deafness; — IX.

iṣlaḥḥ, INF. *iṣliḥâḥ*, lie down on one side.

صلحا *ṣalḥâ'*, f. صلحى, pl. of اصلح *aṣlaḥ*, scabious.

صلحام *ṣilḥâm*, long, strong.

(صلخد) *ṣalḥad*, *ṣilḥad*, *ṣillaḥd*, صلخاد *ṣilḥâd*, صلاخد *ṣulâḥid*, صلخدى *ṣalaḥdâ*, f. *ṣalaḥdât*, pl. *ṣulâḥid*, strong; strenuous in running; — III. *iṣlaḥadd*, INF. *iṣliḥdâd*, stand upright.

صلخف *ṣillaḥf*, utensils; قصعة صلخفة *qaṣ'a-t ṣillaḥfa-t*, large drinking-vessel.

(صلخم) *ṣalḥam*, *ṣilḥamm*, violent, intense, piercing; steep; — III. *iṣlaḥamm*, INF. *iṣliḥmâm*, stand upright; be angry.

(صلد) *ṣalad*, I, INF. *ṣald*, beat the ground with the fore-feet in running; ascend; gnash; be or grow hard or dry; be shining (bald head); — INF. *ṣulûd*, give a sound without fire (fire-stick); — *ṣalud*, INF. *ṣalâda-t*, be avaricious, miserly; — II. INF. *taṣlîd*, id.; — IV. INF. *iṣlâd*, be hard; give a sound without fire.

صلد *ṣald*, avaricious, miserly; (m.) smooth; ة, strong; — *ṣald*, *ṣild*, pl. *aṣlâd*, hard, bare, sterile; not given to perspiring.

صلداء *ṣildâ'*, ة *ṣildâ'a-t*, rugged ground.

صلدام *ṣildâm*, strong; lion.

(صلدح) *ṣaldaḥ*, ة, broad.

(صلدم) *ṣildim*, ة, pl. *ṣalâdim*, big, strong and hard of hoof; lion.

صلصال *ṣalṣâl*, loam, clay; sound.

(صلصل) *ṣalṣal*, INF. ة, sound, resound, creak, tinkle; re-echo; frighten, intimidate, threaten; kill the leader of an army; pronounce in an affected and swaggering manner; — II. INF. *taṣalṣul*, sound repeatedly, resound.

صلصل *ṣalṣal*, front hair of a horse; white hair in the mane; — *ṣulṣul*, pl. *ṣalâṣil*, id.; *ṣulṣul*, braying; wild pigeon (also ة *ṣulṣula-t*); small cup; skilful herdsman; sediment of water or oil (also ة *ṣalṣala-t*, *ṣulṣula-t*); bald spot; — ة *ṣulṣula-t*, baldness.

(صلط), II. *ṣallaṭ*, INF. *taṣlîṭ*, make an absolute master of, invest with dominion, confer full power on (acc.).

صلطح *ṣalṭaḥ*, ة, thick, broad; — IV. *iṣlanṭaḥ*, INF. *iṣlinṭâḥ*, be broad, wide.

(صلع) *ṣali'*, A, INF. *ṣala'*, be bald; — II. INF. *taṣlî'*, excuse one's self, apologise; — V. INF. *taṣallu'*, VII. INF. *inṣilâ'*, rise, come forth from behind the clouds, reach the middle of the sky; — VIII. INF. *iṣṭilâ'*, have bald spots; be soiled.

صلع *ṣul'*, صلعان *ṣul'ân*, pl. صلعا *ṣal'â'*, f. of اصلع *aṣla'*, bald; — *ṣala'*, baldness; — *ṣulla'*, broad stone; bare spot of ground; — ة *ṣul'a-t*, bald or bare spot; forehead; — *ṣula'a-t*, smooth stone.

صلعم, abbreviation for صلى الله عليه و سلم *ṣalla 'l-lâhu 'alaihi wa sallama*, after the name of Mohammed.

(صلغ) *ṣalag*, INF. *ṣulûg*, get the eye-teeth; — *ṣalag*, red mountain; — *ṣullag*, pl. of صالغ *ṣâlig*; — ة *ṣalga-t*, large ship; — *ṣalaga-t*, four (or six) years old and fat.

(صلف) *ṣalif*, A, INF. *ṣalaf*, afford little nourishment; be loathsome to (عند *'ind*); say unpleasant things to (ل *li*); be fastidious, morose; boast (of things which one has not got); —IV. INF. *iṣlâf*, breathe heavily; have little good in one's self; hate; make hateful; — V. INF. *taṣalluf*, flatter; affect ingenuity and delicacy; boast; seek bitter herbs (from being satiated with sweet ones); come to a stony tract; be of a hard disposition.

صلف *ṣalf*, ة *ṣalfa-t*, empty space in

the heart of a palm-tree; — *ṣalif*, pl. *-ûn*, *ṣulafâ'*, *ṣalâfâ*, boasting, pretending, fastidious; without authority or estimation; insipid; heavy vessel with little water in it; thundering cloud with little rain; — ة *ṣalifa-t*, pl. *-ât*, *ṣalâ'if*, loathsome to the husband.

صلفا *ṣalfâ'*, hard ground or stone, f. of اصلف *aṣlaf*; — *ṣulafâ'*, pl. of صلف *ṣalif*; — ة *ṣalfâ'a-t*, stony ground; rock.

(صلفع) *ṣalfa'*, INF. ة, cut off; shave; grow poor.

(صلق) *ṣalaq*, I, INF. *ṣalq*, cry aloud, scream; beat; lie with; bring a great calamity or defeat upon; scorch; — IV. INF. *iṣlâq*, cry aloud; — V. INF. *taṣalluq*, cry out in the throes of child-birth; roll about (n. from pain); — X. INF. *istiṣlâq*, gnash the teeth.

صلق *ṣalq*, *ṣaliq*, loud sound or cry; — *ṣalaq*, pl. *aṣlâq*, *aṣâliq*, level field; pl. *ṣalaqât*, the gnashing teeth of a stallion.

صلقاب *ṣilqâb*, whose teeth grow sharp by continual gnashing.

(صلقع) *ṣalqa'*, INF. ة=صلفع *ṣalfa'*; raise the voice.

(صلقم) *ṣalqam*, INF. ة, gnash the teeth; — *ṣalqam*, gnashing (adj.); lion; stout; — *ṣilqim*, old woman; thick, stout.

(صلك) *ṣilak*, what flows from a sheep's udder before the first milk; — II. *ṣallak*, INF. *taṣlîk*, tie up the camel's udder to prevent the foal from sucking.

(صلم) *ṣalam*, U, I, INF. *ṣalm*, cut off the nose and ears; — II. INF. *taṣlîm*, id.; — VIII. INF. *iṣṭilâm*, eradicate, destroy, annihilate.

صلم *ṣalm*, suppression of a *watad mafrûq* at the end of a foot; — *ṣalam*, brave or bold man; — ة *ṣalma-t*, helmet.

(صلمح) *ṣalmaḥ*, INF. ة, shave.

(صلمع) *ṣalma'*, INF. ة, tear or pull out; shave; smooth; grow poor; — ة *ṣalma'a-t*, poverty.

صلندحة *ṣalandaḥa-t*, *ṣulandaḥa-t*, strong.

(صلنفح) *ṣalanfaḥ*, given to screaming, clamorous, boisterous.

صلنقا *ṣalanqâ'*, صلنقى *ṣalanqâ*, talkative, garrulous.

صلنقح *ṣalanqaḥ*=صرنقح *ṣaranqaḥ*.

صلهام *ṣilhâm*, lion.

(صلهب) *ṣalhab*, long, tall; large; also صلهباة *ṣalhabât*, صلهبى *ṣalhaba*, strong and enduring; — III. *iṣlahabb*, INF. *iṣlihbâb*, be stretched out at full length.

(صلهج) *ṣalhaj*, large rock; strong camel.

(صلو) *ṣalâ*, U, INF. *ṣalw*, beat on the middle of the back; — صلى *ṣalî*, A, INF. *ṣalâ*, have the middle of the back lowered (mare before giving birth); — II. INF. *ṣalaut*, pray, INF. *taṣliya-t*, bless, send a blessing upon (على *'ala*); follow close on the first horse (in a race); urge on; — IV. INF. *iṣlâ'*=صلى *ṣalî*, above; — V. INF. *taṣallî*, be blessed; (m.) receive the blessing of the church (couple to be married); — ة *ṣalaut*, *ṣalât* (also صلاة *ṣalât*), pl. *ṣalawât*, invocation of God; adoration; mercy; *aṣ-ṣalawât*, Jewish temples.

صلوات *ṣalawât*, (compare the previous) and—

صلوان *ṣalawân*, see صلا *ṣalan*.

صلوح *ṣalûḥ*, good condition.

صلوخ *ṣalûḫ*, ruin, destruction.

صلود *ṣalûd*, not perspiring (defect of a horse); hard, dry, withered; not giving any fire; milkless; isolated; — *ṣulûd*, hardness of the ground; avarice.

صلودد *ṣalaudad*, hard; smooth.

صلودح *ṣalûdaḥ*, hard; strong.

صلور *ṣillaur*, a fish.

(صلا , صلى) *ṣalâ* (1 pret. *ṣalai-tu*), I, INF. *ṣaly*, roast meat; throw

into the fire; warm, heat; hold in the fire a long time; beguile; lay snares or traps for (ل *li*); (m.) cock a gun; — *ṣalî*, INF. *ṣaly*, *ṣiliyy*, *ṣalâ'*, *ṣilâ'*, support the heat; burn; — II. INF. *taṣliya-t*, throw into the fire; roast (a.); warm; — IV. INF. *iṣlâ'*, throw or hold a long time in the fire; — V. INF. *taṣallî*, support the heat; warm one's self at the fire; burn; make a stick pliable by the fire; — VIII. INF. *iṣṭilâ'*, warm or burn one's self at the fire; feel or support the fire.

صلى *ṣaliyy*, roasted; — *ṣilliy*, *ṣaliyy*, pl. of صلاءة *ṣalâ'a-t*; — *ṣuliyy*, pl. of صال *ṣâl-in*, صالى *ṣâlî*, heated, burnt.

صليب *ṣalîb*, hard; pl. *ṣulub*, *ṣulbân*, cross (s.); stigma, mark by branding; flag; troop of 10,000; pl. *ṣulub*, marrow; the crucified.

صليجة *ṣalîja-t*, the pure part of silver.

صليح *ṣalîḥ*, pl. *ṣulaḥâ'*, good, upright.

صليد *ṣalîd*, single, solitary, isolated; shining, resplendent.

صليع *ṣalî'*, without vegetation.

صليعا *ṣulai'â*, great calamity.

صليف *ṣalîf*, broader side of a hill; two pieces of wood placed across a camel's saddle to fix the litter upon.

صليق *ṣalîq*, ة, smooth; — ة *ṣalîqa-t*, pl. *ṣalâ'iq*, soft roasted meat; thin bread.

(صم) *ṣamm*, INF. *ṣamm*, close, shut up, stop up; beat; — *ṣamm*, *ṣamim*, A, INF. *ṣamm*, *ṣamam*, be stopped, be deaf; — II. INF. *taṣmîm*, proceed in a matter; take a firm resolution; bite and hold with the teeth; pierce the bone; give sufficient food to a horse; trust a thing to another's memory; silence; — IV. INF. *iṣmâm*, deafen; stop up a bottle; meet with a deaf person, find one deaf; talk to deaf ears; — VI. INF. *taṣâmm*, pretend to be deaf.

صم *ṣimm*, fit, able, clever; lion; calamity; — *ṣumm*, pl. of اصم *aṣamm*, deaf; — ة *ṣimma-t*, pl. *ṣimam*, stopper, cork; calamity; male snake; female hedgehog; able man; lion.

(صما) *ṣamâ*, INF. *ṣam'*, rise and ascend; incite, anger; — VII. INF. *inṣimâ'*, allow one's self to get excited.

صما *ṣammâ'*, f. of اصم *aṣamm*, deaf.

صمات *ṣumât*, what silences; mouthful, morsel; sudden thirst; performance, execution of a work.

صماح *ṣumâḥ*, sweat; caustic (s., also صماحى *ṣumâḥiyy*); small quadruped; ointment for sore feet.

صماخ *ṣimâḫ*, pl. *aṣmiḫa-t*, cavity of the ear; ear; a little water.

صماد *ṣimâd*, stopper; head-band.

صمادح *ṣumâdiḥ*, ى *ṣumâdiḥiyy*, strong; lion; pure, select; distinct.

صمارى *ṣamârā*, *ṣumârā*, *ṣumâriyy*, the buttocks.

صماريد *ṣamârîd*, tracts of hard ground; fat sheep, and, by opposition, lean ones.

صماصم *ṣumâṣim*, ة, fit, able; fiery; lion.

صمالح *ṣumâliḥ*, thick milk.

صماليخ *ṣamâlîḫ*, pl. of صملاخ *ṣimlâḫ*.

صمام *ṣamâm-i*, great calamity; — *ṣimâm*, ة *ṣimâma-t*, stopper; cork.

صمان *ṣummân*, pl. of اصم *aṣamm*, deaf.

(صمت) *ṣamat*, U, INF. *ṣamt*, *ṣumât*, *ṣumût*, cease to speak, be silent; — II. INF. *taṣmît*, be silent; silence; — IV. INF. *iṣmât*, id.; make massive, without a hollow space; be hard.

صمت *ṣamt*, being silent (s.), silence; — ة *ṣimta-t*, *ṣumta-t*, a morsel (to silence children).

صمج *ṣamaj*, ة, lantern.

صمح *ṣamaḥ*, I, A, INF. *ṣamḥ*, scorch the brain; beat, scourge; make difficulties.

صمحا *ṣimḥâ'*, ة *ṣimḥâ'a-t*, stony ground.

صمحمح *ṣamaḥmaḥ*, ة *ṣamaḥmaḥa-t*, ى *ṣamaḥmaḥiyy*, thick-set and strong; smoothly shaven.

(صمخ) *ṣamaḫ*, injure the cavity of the ear; strike with the whole hand on the eye; burn, parch.

صمخ *ṣimḫ*, ear-wax (m.).

صمخاة *ṣamḫât*, stony ground.

(صمد)* *ṣamad*, go to visit; beat; set up, raise, plant; (m.) exhibit; parch; stop up;—*ṣumud*, INF. *ṣamûd*, be massive; be free of debt; — II. INF. *taṣmîd*, go to see, visit; put by, place aside as net gain; liquidate; — III. INF. *ṣimâd*, fight with.

صمد *ṣamd*, stony rising ground; mark of burning from the sun; — *ṣamad*, head of the family; independent lord and master; everlasting, God; massive; enduring; people without subsistence or resources; — ة *ṣamda-t*, rock in soft ground; sterile.

(صمدح) *ṣamdaḥ*, INF. ة, be hot.

(صمر) *ṣamar*, U, INF. *ṣamr*, *ṣumûr*, be avaricious; stop (n.); — I, and *ṣamir*, A, INF. *ṣamar*, be wanting in sweetness; — II. INF. *taṣmîr*, refuse from avarice; enter on the time of sun-set; — IV. INF. *iṣmâr*, refuse from avarice; enter on the time of sunset; be wanting in sweetness.

صمر *ṣamr*, smell of fresh musk; stench; — *ṣimr*, place where the water stops in a plain; — *ṣumr*, pl. *aṣmâr*, edge of the cup; — *ṣamir*, ة, smelling badly; — ة *ṣamra-t*, milk that is not sweet.

صمصام *ṣamṣâm*, ة *ṣamṣâma-t*, sharp and unyielding sword; *ṣamṣâm*, mettled (horse).

صمصم *ṣamṣam*, very avaricious, miserly; — *ṣimṣim*, short, thick-set; able, bold; — *ṣumaṣim*, id.; lion; — ة *ṣamṣama-t*, growling of a hedgehog; — also *ṣimṣima-t*, the best part of the people; pl. *ṣimṣim*, troop, crowd.

(صمع) *ṣama'*, INF. *ṣam'*, beat, go to and dissuade; — *ṣami'*, A, INF. *ṣama'*, be headstrong; commit errors in speaking; — II. INF. *taṣmî'*, take a firm resolution; pile up; give a conic form, point at the top; — VII. INF. *inṣimâ'*, persist in; — hence صومع *ṣauma'*, INF. ة, make conic or point at the top; gather, collect.

صمع *ṣum'*, صمعان *ṣum'ân*, pl., and صمعا *ṣam'â'*, f. of اصمع *aṣma'*, ascending, &c., q.v.; *ṣama'â'*, side of the neck from the ear to the collar-bone.

(صمعد), III. *iṣma'add*, INF. *iṣmi'dâd*, go quickly away.

(صمعر) *ṣam'ar*, hard; strong; — ة *ṣam'ara-t*, fur cap; anything thick; — ى *ṣam'ariyy*, hard, strong; common; entirely red; — ية *ṣam'ariyya-t*, a poisonous snake.

صمعور *ṣum'ûr*, thick-set and strong.

صمعيوت *ṣam'ayût*, headstrong.

(صمغ) *ṣamg*, *ṣamag*, gum, India-rubber; resin; صمغ بطم *ṣamag buṭm*, colophony; — II. *ṣammag*, INF. *taṣmîg*, put gum into the ink, gum; — IV. INF. *iṣmâg*, produce gum; secrete spittle in the corners of the mouth; yield fresh milk; — X. INF. *istiṣmâg*, make incisions in a tree to cause gum to flow; have an abscess; — ة *ṣamga-t*, a drop of gum; abscess.

صمغان *ṣamgân*, whose eyes, ears or mouth secrete matter.

صمغى *ṣamgiyy*, gum-like.

(صمق), IV. *aṣmaq*, INF. *iṣmâq*, put the door ajar, lock, tie up; have a deteriorated taste; — ة *ṣamaqa-t*, deteriorated milk or water.

(صمقر) *ṣamqar*, INF. ة, also III.

iṣmaqarr, INF. *iṣmiqrâr*, be sour; III. be hot, burn violently.

(صمك), XI. *iṣmâkk*, INF. *iṣmîkâk*, be angry; turn thick (milk); — ة *ṣamaka-t*, strong.

صمكمك *ṣamakmak*, of an offensive smell; strong, brave.

صمكوك *ṣamakûk*, صمكيك *ṣamakîk*, strong, enduring; thick, sticky; stupid, clumsy, malicious.

(صمل) *ṣamal*, U, INF. *ṣaml*, cudgel; INF. *ṣaml*, *ṣumûl*, be hard and firm; abstain from food; — XI. *iṣma'all*, INF. *iṣmîlâl*, grow entwined; — hence: صومل *ṣaumal*, INF. ة, suffer from dryness of the skin.

صمل *ṣumul*, strongly built or made.

صملاخ *ṣimlâḥ*, صملوخ *ṣumlûḥ*, pl. *ṣamâlîḥ*, the interior of the ear together with the ear-wax; pl. tendrils of a plant.

صموت *ṣamût*, silent; heavy; deeply penetrating; full; *ṣumût*, silence.

صموح *ṣamûḥ*, hard; hot.

(صمى) *ṣama*, I, INF. *ṣamayân*, leap upon, rush against; hurry, hasten; — INF. *ṣamy*, remain dead on the spot; succeed well, prosper; — IV. INF. *iṣmâ'*, kill on the spot; bite the bridle in advancing; — VII. INF. *inṣimâ'*, be poured down; pounce; be swift.

صميان *ṣamayân*, pl. *ṣimyân*, brave in attack; quick, swift; INF. of (صمى).

صميت *ṣimmît*, very silent; taciturn.

صميدح *ṣamaidaḥ*, hot day; hard, strong.

صمير *ṣamîr*, having dry muscles; smelling from perspiration; — *ṣumair*, time of sun-set.

صميل *ṣamîl*, dried up, withered.

صميم *ṣamîm*, root; principal part; kernel; bottom of the heart; of pure origin, pure, noble; intense; hard, firm; bone; skeleton; egg-shell.

(صن) *ṣinn*, basket with a cover; smelling badly; — IV. *aṣann*, INF. *iṣnân*, smell from the armpits; turn up the nose from pride; be angry; refuse the stallion; be deteriorated; persist in; — ة *ṣinna-t*, smell of the arm-pits.

صنا *ṣanan*, *ṣanâ'*, ashes.

صناب *ṣinâb*, mustard; also ة *ṣinâba-t*, having a lengthy belly and back; — ى *ṣinâbiyy*, of the colour of mustard.

صناتيت *ṣanâtît*, pl. of صنوت *ṣannût*.

صناج *ṣannâj*, ة *ṣannâja-t*, who plays the castanets; ليلة صناجة *laila-t ṣannâja-t*, moon-lit night.

صناحية *ṣunâḥiyya-t*, big.

صنادل *ṣunâdil*, having a big head; strong; — *ṣanâdila-t*, pl. of صندلانى *ṣandalâniyy*.

صناديق *ṣanâdîq*, pl. of صندوق *ṣandûq*.

صنار *ṣinâr*, *ṣinnâr*, plane-tree; — *ṣannâr*, angler; (ص الحوت *ṣannâr al-ḥaut*, eel); — ة *ṣinnâra-t*, pl. *ṣanânîr*, head-piece of the spindle; leathern handle; ear; uneducated man; fishing-line; hammer; knitting-needle.

صناطير *ṣanâṭîr*, pl. of صنطور *ṣanṭûr*.

صناع *ṣanâ'*, pl. *ṣunu'*, skilled in art, skilful; weir; — *ṣunnâ'*, artisans, &c., pl. of صانع *ṣâni'*; — ة *ṣinâ'a-t*, pl. *ṣanâ'i'*, art, handicraft; — *ṣannâ'a-t*, weir; — ى *ṣinâ'iyy*, artificial, artful.

(صنافر) *ṣunâfir*, essence of anything; — ة *ṣunâfira-t*, limit of the horizon; ولد ص *walad ṣunâfira-t*, child of a father unknown.

صناق *ṣinâq*, crying aloud.

صنان *ṣunân*, pl. *aṣinna-t*, smell of the arm-pits; — *ṣannân*, able, clever; excelling.

صنانير *ṣanânîr*, pl. of صنارة *ṣinnâra-t*.

صنائع *ṣanâ'i'*, pl. of صناعة *ṣanâ'a-t* and صنيعة *ṣanî'a-t*.

صناية *ṣinâya-t*, the whole of a thing.

(صنبر) *ṣambar*, INF. ة, stand isolated, having a weak stem and few dates.
صنبر *ṣambar*, thin, weak; — *ṣinnabir*, intense cold of winter; the second of the seven days called ايام العجوز *ayyâm al-'ajûz*.
صنبرص *ṣambariṣ*, rat.
(صنبع) *ṣamba'*, INF. ة, shrink, shrink back.
صنبعر *ṣimba'r*, of a bad kind, degenerate.
صنبل *ṣumbal*, *ṣumbul*, very cunning.
صنبور *ṣumbûr*, canal; drinking-tube; crane; isolated palm with a weak stem and little fruit; isolated man; weak and unprotected; small boy; calamity; cold wind.
(صنت) *ṣant*, mimosa nilotica; — IV. *aṣnat*, INF. *iṣnât*, fix, fasten, consolidate.
(صنتع) *ṣunta'*, hard-headed; bony.
صنتوت *ṣantût*, صنتيت *ṣintît*=صنت *ṣant*.
صنتور *ṣantûr*=صنطور *ṣanṭûr*.
(صنج) *ṣanaj*, U, INF. *ṣunûj*, send away, drive home; cudgel; — II. INF. *taṣnîj*, throw on the ground.
صنج *ṣanj*, pl. *ṣunûj*, castanets, cymbals; Persian harp; — *ṣunuj*, castanets of ebony; — ة *ṣanja-t*, weight, balance.
صنخ *ṣinḥ*, pl. *aṣnâḥ*, root, origin, cause; root of a tooth; — *ṣaniḥ*, teething (adj.); — ة *ṣanaḥa-t*, dirt.
(صنخاب) *ṣinḥâb*, stout camel.
(صنخر) *ṣinḥir*, *ṣunaḥir*, stout; tall and strong; *ṣinḥir*, full-grown unripe date; — *ṣinḥarr*, stupid.
(صندد) *ṣindid*, excellent prince; high mountain-peak; of high birth or rank.
(صندح) *ṣandaḥ*, broad rock.
صندعة *ṣinda'a-t*, pointed peak.
(صندل) *ṣandal*, INF. ة, grow stout and big-headed (camel); — II. INF. *taṣandul*, court women.
صندلانى *ṣandalâniyy*, pl. *ṣanâdila-t*, and—
صندنانى *ṣandanâniyy*, apothecary.
صندوق *ṣandûq*, pl. *ṣanâdîq*, chest, box, trunk.
صنديد *ṣindîd*, pl. *ṣanâdîd*, excellent prince; strong; powerful; صناديد القدر *ṣanâdîd al-qadr*, blows of misfortune.
صنطور *ṣanṭûr*, pl. *ṣanâṭîr*, tympanum; a kind of piano.
(صنع) *ṣana'*, INF. *ṣan'*, *ṣun'*, do, make; INF. *ṣun'*, show one's self obliging; create; INF. *ṣan'*, *ṣan'a-t*, take good care of a horse; pass. *ṣuni'*, be well fed; — II. INF. *taṣnî'*, care well for, feed well, make handsome and plump (a girl); perform or arrange skilfully; — III. INF. *muṣâna'a-t*, bribe; flatter, court; not show all its swiftness (horse); — IV. INF. *iṣnâ'*, take care of, fatten; assist, instruct; — V. INF. *taṣannu'*, adorn one's self, deck one's self out, dress up, dress the hair; be affected in speech or manners; — VI. INF. *taṣânu'*, think of and exert one's self for gain; — VIII. INF. *iṣṭinâ'*, confer benefits, educate, bring out; receive benefits; give an entertainment; choose one to perform a business; order, have made for one's self; make, invent.
صنع *ṣin'*, pl. *aṣnâ'*, clever, skilful; (roasting-) spit; roast meat, joint; table-cloth (of leather); turban; garment; tailor; water-reservoir; — *ṣun'*, *ṣan'*, deed, action; kindness; — *ṣana'*, *ṣani'*, clever, skilful; — *ṣunu'*, pl. of صناع *ṣanâ'* and صنيع *ṣanî'*; — ة *ṣan'a-t*, deed; work.
صنعا *ṣan'â'*, town in Arabia.
صنعانى *ṣan'âniyy*, of Ṣan'â'.
صنعبة *ṣana'ba-t*, strong she-camel.
صنعى *ṣun'a*, *ṣana'a*, *ṣin'a*, *ṣunu'a*, skilful man.
(صنف) *ṣanf*, *ṣinf*, pl. *aṣnâf*, *ṣunûf*, kind, species; article of trade; guild, corporation; — *ṣinf*,

quality; also ة ṣinfa-t, ṣanifa-t, seam, border of a garment; — II. ṣannaf, INF. taṣnîf, separate, classify; compose a book; push forth leaves; sprout, bud; get chapped; — ى ṣanfiyy, an Indian wood for fumigating.

(صنق) ṣaniq, A, INF. ṣanaq, smell offensively; — IV. INF. iṣnâq, pay continual care to (على 'ala); manage well one's fortune.

صنق ṣaniq, ة ṣaniqa-t, strong and firm; big.

(صنم) ṣanim, A, INF. ṣanam, be very offensive, loathsome; be vigorous; — II. INF. taṣnîm, make idols for one's self; form, make an image of, picture; make camels to abound in milk.

صنم ṣanam, pl. aṣnâm, idol; the beloved; — ṣanim, strong, vigorous; pl. f. ṣanimât, camels which yield milk in thick rays; — ة ṣanama-t, calamity; tube; quill.

صنهاج ṣinhâj, ة ṣinhâja-t, born from a slave by a slave.

صنو ṣanw, pl. ṣunuww, thicket; water or stones between two mountains; — ṣinw, ṣunw, an equal; not isolated, forming a group; pl. ṣinwân, aṣnâ', id.; uterine brother; son; cousin; deserted well; a little water; — ة ṣinwa-t, sister; daughter; lady-cousin.

صنوبر ṣanaubar, pine-tree; fir; resin of a fir-tree.

صنوت ṣannût, pl. ṣanânît, small basket; case for a flask.

صنور ṣinnaur, avaricious; mean.

(صنى), IV. aṣna, INF. iṣnâ', V. taṣanna, INF. taṣannî, soil one's self with ashes.

صنى ṣunayy, a little water in a ravine.

صنيع ṣanî', made more pliable by use, inured; well kept and fed; skilful; prepared food; — ṣanî', ة ṣanî'a-t, pl. ṣanâ'i', work, deed, good action; kindness, benefit; benefited, educated by, protégé; — ة ṣanî'a-t, new invention; aṣ-ṣanî'a-t, minister, ambassador; pl. aṣ-ṣanâ'i', retinue; body-guard.

صه ṣah, صه صه ṣah-in ṣah, be quiet! silence!

صها ṣihâ', pl. of صهوة ṣahwa-t.

صهاب ṣuhâb, name of a celebrated camel stallion; — ى ṣuhâbiyy, descending from Ṣuhâb; light red, bay-coloured, fair; estate from which the tithes have not been paid; who keeps no books; cruel; full.

صهارج ṣuhârij, صهريج ṣihrîj, pl. ṣahârîj, cistern.

صهارة ṣuhâra-t, grease, fat, marrow.

صهال ṣuhâl, neighing (s.); — ṣahhâl, neighing frequently.

(صهب) ṣahib, A, INF. ṣahab, ṣuhba-t, ṣuhûba-t, be light red, bay, fair; — IV. INF. iṣhâb, beget young one's of such a colour.

صهب ṣahab, ة ṣuhba-t, bay colour; — ṣuhb, pl. and—

صهبا ṣahbâ', f. of أصهب aṣhab, light red, bay, fair; wine.

(صهد) ṣahad, scorch, parch.

صهدان ṣahdân, intense heat.

(صهر) ṣahar, INF. ṣahr, scorch or parch intensely; anoint; melt (a.); — III. INF. muṣâhara-t, IV. INF. iṣhâr, become related by intermarriage, ally one's self by marriage; IV. approach one another; melt (a.); — VII. INF. inṣihâr, get melted, melt (n.); — VIII. INF. iṣṭihâr, melt (a.); eat grease or fat; also X. INF. istiṣhâr, shine like fat.

صهر ṣahr, melting (s.); hot; — ṣihr, relationship by intermarriage; kindred; pl. aṣhâr, ṣuharâ', related; father-in-law; son-in-law; brother-in-law (husband of a sister); tomb; — ة ṣihra-t, sister-in-law.

صهرا ṣuharâ', pl. of صهر ṣihr.

صهرى *ṣihriyy*, صهريج *ṣihrîj*, cistern.

(صهصلق) *ṣahṣaliq*, صهصليق *ṣahṣalîq*, strong, loud; boisterous or screaming woman.

(صهصه) *ṣahṣah*, INF. ة, bid to keep silence.

صهطلة *ṣahṭala-t*, softness.

(صهل) *ṣahal*, I, A, INF. *ṣahîl*, neigh; — VI. INF. *taṣâhul*, neigh alternately.

صهل *ṣahal*, rough or hoarse voice.

صهميم *ṣihmîm*, noble leader; mischievous, restive, headstrong; fee of a soothsayer; pure, sheer; — II. INF. *taṣahmum*, behave like a noble leader.

صهوة *ṣahwa-t*, pl. *ṣihâ'*, hole with water in a plain; source, spring; mountain-yoke; pl. *ṣihâ'*, *ṣahawât*, hind-part of a camel's hump, of the croup of a horse; pl. *ṣuha-n*, watch-tower on a mountain-top.

(صهى) *ṣahâ*, INF. *ṣahy*, be very rich; also *ṣahî*, INF. *ṣahan*, have a wound from which the blood runs;—III. INF. *muṣâhât*, mount on the croup of a camel or horse; — IV. INF. *iṣhâ'*, smear an ill child with fat or butter and place it in the sun; feel pain in the croup.

صهى *ṣahan*, INF. of the previous; — *ṣuhan*, pl. of صهوة *ṣahwa-t*.

صهيل *ṣahîl*, neighing (s.).

صو *ṣaww*, empty; — ة *ṣuwwa-t*, pl. *ṣuwan*, pl. pl. *aṣwâ'*, hill; grave-mound; place where the winds separate; echo; a troop of game; pl. *ṣawwân*, stone as a road-mark.

صواب *ṣawâb*, what is right, true, proper, to the point; sound judgment; success; — *ṣu'âb*, ة, pl. *ṣi'bân*, nit; — ة *ṣuwwâba-t*, the best of the people; — ى *ṣawâbiyy*, right, just, reasonable.

صواح *ṣuwâḥ*, perspiration of a horse; watery milk; gypsum; elevation of the ground; palm-branch; — ة *ṣuwwâha-t*, dishevelled hair.

صواخ *ṣuwwâḫ*, muddy ground.

صواد *ṣawâd-in*, صوادى *ṣawâdî*, pl. of صادى *ṣâdî*, thirsty.

صوادف *ṣawâdif*, pl. camels waiting for their turn to drink.

صوادى *ṣawâdî*, high palm-trees; see صواد *ṣawâdin*, above.

صوار *ṣiwâr*, *ṣuwâr*, *ṣuwwâr*, صيار *ṣiyyâr*, pl. *ṣirân*, yoke of oxen; pl. *aṣwira-t*, grain of musk; perfume; du. *ṣiwârân*, the two sides of the mouth; — *ṣawwâr*, peeping (adj.); — *ṣawârr*, pl. of صارة *ṣârra-t*, what needs must happen, necessity, &c.; — ى *ṣawârî*, masts, &c., pl. of صارية *ṣâriya-t*.

صواع *ṣuwâ'*, cup; — *ṣuwâ'*, *ṣiwâ'* = صاع, a fruit-measure.

صواعد *ṣawâ'id*, burnt-offerings, pl. of صعيدة *ṣa'îda-t*.

صواف *ṣawwâf*, wool-merchant; — *ṣawâff*, pl. of صافة *ṣâffa-t*, q.v.

صواقع *ṣawâqi'*, pl. of صاقعة *ṣâqi'a-t*, lightning, and of صوقعة *ṣauqa'a-t*.

صواكيم *ṣawâkîm*, pl. blows of misfortune.

صوالجة *ṣawâlija-t*, pl. of صولجان *ṣaulajân*.

صوام *ṣawâm*, waterless; — *ṣuwwâm*, pl. of صايم *ṣâyim*, fasting.

صوامع *ṣawâmi'*, pl. of صومع *ṣauma'*.

صوان *ṣawân*, *ṣiwân*, *ṣuwân*, صيان *ṣayân*, *ṣiyân*, *ṣuyân*, pl. *aṣwina-t*, clothes-press, wardrobe; festival tent; — *ṣawwân*, ة, quartz, pebble; flint-stone; anus; *ṣawwân*, pl. of صوة *ṣuwwa-t*; — ى *ṣawwâniyy*, Chinese.

(صوب) *ṣâb*, U, INF. *ṣaub*, pour out; water; be poured out; INF. *ṣaub*, *muṣâb*, come from above; INF. *ṣaub*, *ṣaib*, *ṣaibûba-t*, hit the aim; come to, reach, attain; — II. INF. *taṣyîb*, say to one اصبت *aṣabta*, you have hit the point; justify; bend the head; let the horse run; — III. INF. *muṣâwaba-t*, attack; — IV.

INF. *iṣâba-t*, let down from above; hit the mark, hit on the right thing, speak or act to the point; wish to do so, wish, intend; find, obtain; destroy, afflict; — V. INF. *taṣawwub*, let one's self down; fall; — VI. INF. *taṣâwub*, go the right way; — VII. INF. *inṣiyâb*, be poured out; be visited with a calamity; — X. INF. *istiṣâba-t*, *istiṣwâb*, find good, approve of.

صوب *ṣaub*, heavy shower; side; the right direction; the right thing; happy issue; — ة *ṣûba-t*, a bitter plant; — *ṣu'ba-t*, place where corn, dates, &c., are stored up, barn; heap; indefinite number.

صوبج *ṣaubaj*, rolling-pin, wooden roller for flattening the dough.

(صوت) *ṣât*, U, A, INF. *ṣaut*, produce a sound; call; — II. INF. *taṣwît*, id.; call to (على *'ala*); — IV. INF. *iṣâba-t*=I; — VII. INF. *inṣiyât*, hear the call and answer; resound, re-echo; follow a call; come at a call; go back; get straight again.

صوت *ṣaut*, pl. *aṣwât*, sound, call, voice; good name, fame; *al-aṣwât*, the interjections.

صوج *ṣûj*, fault, defect (m.).

صوجان *ṣaujân*, hard and dry.

(صوح) *ṣâḥ*, U, INF. *ṣauḥ*, split, cleave (a.); — II. INF. *taṣwîḥ*, dry up, wither (a.), parch up; — V. INF. *taṣawwuḥ*, get split, split (n.); be dishevelled; dry up; — VII. INF. *inṣiyâḥ*, get split, dishevelled, torn; shine.

صوح *ṣauḥ*, *ṣûḥ*, steep bank; mountain-side.

صوحان *ṣûḥân*, dried up, withered.

(صوخ) *ṣâḫ*, U, sink in the mud; — IV. INF. *iṣâḫa-t*, listen; be silent.

(صود), II. *ṣawwad*, INF. *taṣwîd*, write the letter ص *ṣ*.

(صور) *ṣâr*, U, I, INF. *ṣaur*, bend (a.), incline to one side; turn the face towards; cut into pieces, dissect, split; decide; — U, produce a sound, call; collect, and, by opposition, separate, disperse; — *ṣawir*, A, INF. *ṣawar*, bend, incline (n.); break (n.); — II. INF. *taṣwîr*, represent by an image; form, paint, draw, picture; imagine; — IV. INF. *iṣâra-t*, bend sideways (a.); cause to waver; break; dispose, make willing; — V. INF. *taṣawwur*, be represented by an image; be conceived, imagined; imagine; be made to waver, fall; — VII. INF. *inṣiyâr*, be bent or inclined; be made to waver; be broken; become inclined, disposed.

صور *ṣaur*, pl. *ṣîrân*, small palm-tree; palm-root; river-bank; hunting-horn; *aṣ-ṣûr*, Tyre; — ة *ṣûra-t*, pl. *ṣûr*, *ṣuwar*, *ṣiwar*, form, shape, figure, image, picture; appearance; species; manner; character; — ى *ṣûriyy*, formal; express, explicit.

(صوص) *ṣûṣ*, avaricious, miserly; (m.) pl. *ṣîṣân*, chick.

(صوصى) *ṣauṣa*, peep.

صوط *ṣauṭ*, pattering of drops; = سوط *sauṭ*, whip, &c.

(صوع) *ṣâ'*, U, INF. *ṣau'*, measure corn by the measure صاع *ṣâ'*; separate, scatter; terrify; come one after the other; — II. INF. *taṣwî'*, dry up (a.); prepare a place (for picking wool); make a thing pointed at the top and round at the sides; — V. INF. *taṣawwu'*, dry up (n.); split (n.), bend (n.), fall out; disperse entirely and far (n.); — VII. INF. *inṣiyâ'*, hasten back; cease; disperse (n.).

(صوغ) *ṣâg*, U, INF. *ṣaug*, form, shape, fashion, create; invent; carry on the craft of a goldsmith; penetrate, impregnate, soak; = (سوغ) go well down the

throat; — V. INF. *taṣawwug*, VII. INF. *inṣiyâg*, be formed, shaped.

صوغ *ṣaug*, form, shape; kind; born immediately after; ة, made after the same model; du. *ṣûgân*, a pair, couple; pl. f. *ṣûgât*, productions.

(صوف) *ṣâf*, U, INF. *ṣauf*, *ṣu'ûf*, bear wool; — U, I, miss the aim; — *ṣawif*, A, INF. *ṣawaf*, have plenty of wool; be turned away; — II. INF. *taṣwîf*, make one's speech obscure after the manner of a philosopher or Ṣûfî; — IV. INF. *iṣâfa-t*, turn off, avert; — V. INF. *taṣawwuf*, behave like a Ṣûfî; become a Ṣûfî.

صوف *ṣûf*, pl. *aṣwâf*, wool; بصوف رقبته *bi-ṣûf-i raqabati-hi*, gratis, for nothing, in vain;—*ṣawif*, woolly, covered with thick wool; — ة *ṣûfa-t*, fleak of wool.

صوفان *ṣûfân*, tinder (m.); — ة *ṣûfâna-t*, a kitchen-herb; — ى *ṣûfâniyy*, ة, covered with thick wool.

صوفى *ṣûfî*, Ṣûfî, a mystic, philosopher.

(صوق) *ṣâq*, urge on; — V. INF. *taṣawwuq*, pollute one's self with excrement, &c.

صوق *ṣûq* = سوق *sûq*, market, &c.

صوقر *ṣauqar*, large hammer or axe.

(صوقر) *ṣauqar*, INF. ة, produce the sound—

صوقرير *ṣauqarîr*, repeated cooing.

(صوقع) *ṣauqa'*, INF. ة, strike on the middle of the head;—ة *ṣauqa'a-t*, pl. *ṣawâqi'*, middle of the head; white spot on a horse's skin; hole in the middle of the dish ثريدة *ṯarîda-t* to place the butter in; brunt of the battle.

(صوك) *ṣâk*, U, INF. *ṣauk*, adhere, stick to; — V. INF. *taṣawwuk*, pollute one's self with excrement, sperm, &c.

صوك *ṣauk*, sperm; صوك و بوك *ṣauk wa bauk*, life, vitality; اول صوك و بوك *awwal-a ṣauk-in wa bauk-in*, first of all.

(صول) *ṣâl*, U, INF. *ṣâl*, *ṣaul*, *ṣuwûl*, *ṣiyâl*, *ṣawalân*, *maṣâla-t*, attack furiously, assault boldly; overpower; — INF. *ṣaul*, also *ṣa'ul*, INF. *ṣa'âla-t*, try to kill from fury; be furious, enraged; — — INF. *ṣaul*, *ṣavla-t*, leap upon; pass. *ṣîl*, be decreed by fate to (ل *li*); — II. INF. *taṣwîl*, wash out impurities, extract the essence; sweep; stir locusts in roasting them; — III. INF. *muṣâwala-t*, *ṣiyâl*, *ṣiyâla-t*, leap upon; rush against; — VI. INF. *taṣâwul*, rush against one another in the attack.

صول *ṣa'ul*, furious, enraged; — ة *ṣaula-t*, violence, fury; strength, power; sudden attack; — *ṣûla-t*, wheat from which impurities have been washed out.

صولب *ṣaulab*, صوليب *ṣaulîb*, seed after ploughing.

صولج *ṣaulaj*, silver; ة, unmixed.

صولجان *ṣaulajân*, pl. *ṣawâlija-t*, the Persian mace in the game at balls.

صولع *ṣaula'*, shining.

صولق *ṣaulaq*, girdle, belt.

(صوم) *ṣâm*, U, INF. *ṣaum*, *ṣiyâm*, abstain from food, drink, speech, sexual intercourse, travelling, working; fast; taste (death from excess of hunger); stand without food; be silent; subside; be noon-time; drop excrement; seek shade under the tree صوم *ṣaum*;—II. INF. *taṣwîm*, cause to fast; — VIII. INF. *iṣtiyâm*, abstain from food, &c.; fast.

صوم *ṣaum*, abstinence; fasting (s.); fasting-month *Ramaḍân*; abstaining, fasting (adj.); Christian church; excrement of an ostrich; an ugly tree; — *ṣuwwam*, pl. of صايم *ṣâyim*, fasting (adj.).

صومان *ṣaumân*, pl. *ṣiyâm*, *ṣuyâmâ*, fasting (adj.).

صومر *ṣaumar*, ة *ṣaumara-t*, basil (plant).

صومع *ṣauma'*, ة *ṣauma'a-t*, pl. *ṣawâmi'*, monk's cell; tower; pointed cap; eagle; — *ṣauma'*, (v.) see (صمع).

صومل *ṣaumal*, name of a tree; — *ṣaumal*, (v.) see (صمل).

(صون) *ṣân*, U, INF. *ṣaun*, *ṣiyân*, *ṣiyâna-t*, protect, preserve, respect; stand on the edge of the hoof; — II. INF. *taṣwîn*, protect; wall in; — VIII. INF. *iṣtiyân*, protect.

صون *ṣaun*, protection, guard; reserve, moderation; — ة *ṣauna-t*, box for perfumes.

(صوى) *ṣawâ*, I, INF. *ṣuwiyy*, dry up, wither (n.); — *ṣawî*, A, INF. *ṣawa-n*, *ṣaw-an*, id.; be strong; — II. INF. *taṣwiya-t*, IV. INF. *iṣwâ'*, dry up, wither (n.); II. spare an animal (as by not milking or overworking it).

صوى *ṣuwan*, pl. of صوة *ṣuwwa-t*; — *ṣawiyy*, dried up, withered; — *ṣuwiyy*, INF. of (صوى).

صويب *ṣawîb*, well guided.

(صيا), II. *ṣayya'*, INF. *taṣyî'*, wash the head not quite clean; have dates on the point of ripening; — ة *ṣai'a-t*, *ṣiyâ'a-t*, placenta.

صياب *ṣayyâb*, who hits the point or the aim; — *ṣuyyâb*, *ṣuyâb*, ة *ṣuyyâba-t*, *ṣuyâba-t*, root; principal part; the best part, the best of; — ة *ṣuyyâba-t*, lord, master.

صياجة *ṣayyâja-t*, clear (night).

صياح *ṣiyâḥ*, cry, crowing of the cock; — *ṣayyâḥ*, a perfume for washing; screamer.

صياخيد *ṣayâḫîd*, pl. of صيخود *ṣaiḫûd*.

صياد *ṣayyâd*, hunter; fisherman; lion; ابن صياد *ibn ṣayyâd*, Anti-Christ; — ة *ṣiyâda-t*, hunting, fishing (s.).

صيادلة *ṣayâdila-t*, pl. of صيدلانى *saidalâniyy*.

صيار *ṣiyâr*, rattle; — *ṣiyyâr*=صوار *ṣiwâr*, &c.; — ة *ṣiyâra-t*, sheep-fold.

صياص *ṣayâṣ-in*, صياصى *ṣayâṣi*, pl. of صيصة *ṣaiṣa-t*.

صياط *ṣiyâṭ*, clamour, noise.

صياغ *ṣayyâg*, gold-smith; — *ṣuyyâg*, pl. of صايغ *ṣâyig*, fashioner, &c.; — ة *ṣiyâga-t*, goldsmith's art.

صيال *ṣiyâl*, ة *ṣiyâla-t*, INF. of (صول).

صيام *ṣiyâm*, INF. of (صوم); — *ṣiyâm*, صيامى *ṣuyâmâ*, pl. of صومان *ṣaumân*, fasting (adj.); — *ṣuyyâm*, pl. of صايم *ṣâyim*, fasting (adj.).

صيان *ṣayân*, *ṣiyân*, *ṣuyân*, see صوان *ṣawân*; — *ṣiyân*, ة *ṣiyâna-t*, INF of (صون); — ة *ṣiyâna-t*, prudence, caution; chastity; modesty.

(صيب) *ṣâb*, I, INF. *ṣaib*, hit the aim; — *ṣa'ib*, INF. *ṣa'ab*, be satiated, have one's fill; — also IV. INF. *iṣ'âb*, have the head full of nits.

صيب *ṣaib*, INF. of (صوب); — *ṣuyub*, pl. of صيوب *ṣayûb*; — *ṣayyib*, pouring out rain; heavy rain.

صئبان *ṣi'bân*, *ṣîbân*, pl. of صواب *ṣu'ab*, nit; — *ṣîbân*, pl. of صايب *ṣâyib*, hitting (adj.).

(صئبل) *ṣi'bil*, calamity.

صيبوبة *ṣaibûba-t*, INF. of (صوب).

(صيت) *ṣît*, renown, honour, glory; hammer; worker in metal; — II. *ṣayyat*, INF. *taṣyît*, make renowned, celebrated; — V. INF. *taṣayyut*, become so; — *ṣayyit*, loud-voiced; — ة *ṣîta-t*, honour, renown.

(صيح) *ṣâḥ*, I, INF. *ṣaiḥ*, *ṣaiḥa-t*, *ṣiyâḥ*, *ṣayâḥ*, *ṣayaḥân*, cry very loud; call to; crow; grow high; grow long; pass. صيح بهم *ṣîḥ bi-him*, they were terrified; صيح فيهم *ṣîḥ fi-him*, they died, perished; — II. INF. *taṣyîḥ*, cry out; =*taṣwîḥ*, dry up (a.), parch; — III. INF. *muṣâyaḥa-t*, call to; — V. INF. *taṣayyuḥ*, dry up (n.); split, break (n.); be dishevelled; — VI. INF. *taṣâyuḥ*, call to one another; burst, break (n.).

صيح *ṣaiḥ*, crying out (s.), crowing of the cock; cleft, coming forth from a cleft; sun-rise; — ة *ṣaiḥa-t*, cry; divine punishment; remonstrance.

صيحان *ṣayaḥân*, INF. of (صيح).

صيحاد *ṣaiḥâd*, hard.

صيحدون *ṣaiḥadûn*, hardness.

صيخود *ṣaiḫûd*, very hot; pl. *ṣayâḫîd*, hard.

(صيد) *ṣâd*, I, A, INF. *ṣaid*, hunt; cause one to bend the neck; — *ṣa'id*, A, INF. *ṣayad*, have the neck bent or inclined; bear the head high (from pride); — IV. INF. *iṣâda-t*, bring on a catarrhal flux, or, by opposition, heal from it; — V. INF. *taṣayyud*, live by hunting, capture by hunting or fishing; — VIII. INF. *iṣṭiyâd*, hunt; capture by hunting or fishing; make a prey.

صيد *ṣaid*, hunt, fishing (s.); prey of a hunter, game; prey, booty; *ṣîd*, pl. *aṣyâd*, *aṣâ'id*, catarrhal flux of camels; — *ṣayad*, id.; — *ṣuyud*, *ṣîd*, pl. of صيود *ṣayûd*.

صيدا *ṣaidâ'*, f. of اصيد *aṣyad* hard uneven ground, &c.; Sidon.

صيداح *ṣaidâḥ*, screaming much.

صيدان *ṣaidân*, stoneware; copper; gold; fox; — ة *ṣaidâna-t*, female demon, goblin of the desert; shrew.

صيدح *ṣaidaḥ*, neighing violently; — ى *ṣaidaḥiyy*, crying aloud.

صيدق *ṣaidaq*, faithful; king; Pleiades.

صيدلانى *ṣaidalâniyy*, pl. *ṣayâdila-t*, apothecary.

صيدلة *ṣaidala-t*, perfume; pharmacy.

صيدن *ṣaidan*, hyena; fox; king; a coarse garment.

صيدنانى *ṣaidanânî*, fox; apothecary.

صيدى *ṣaidiyy*, of copper.

(صير) *ṣâr*, I, INF. *ṣair*, *maṣîr*, *ṣairûra-t*, become, get, grow, turn, turn out; happen; go to the water, go, return; cut; bend, incline (a.); — II. INF. *taṣyîr*, IV. INF. *iṣâra-t*, cause to become, make, turn into; shut up the water, — V. INF. *taṣayyur*, remind of one by resemblance.

صير *ṣair*, *ṣîr*, event, issue; — *ṣîr*, water resorted to; chink; small salt fish or dish of it; Jewish high priest; for the French Sire! — *ṣayyir*, troop; tomb; well-shaped; — ة *ṣîra-t*, pl. *ṣîr*, *ṣiyar*, sheep-fold; establishment for breeding sheep.

صيران *ṣîrân*, pl. of صوار *ṣiwâr*, &c., and صور *ṣaur*.

صيرف *ṣairaf*, صيرفى *ṣairafiyy*, pl. *ṣayârifa-t*, *ṣayârîf*, experienced and able in business transactions; versatile; money-changer.

صيرم *ṣairam*, persevering and faithful; calamity; a meal taken once in 24 hours.

صيرورة *ṣairûra-t*, INF. of (صير).

(صيص) *ṣâṣ*, I, INF. *ṣaiṣ*, also II. INF. *taṣyîṣ*, IV. INF. *iṣâṣa-t*, produce inferior fruit.

صيص *ṣîṣ*, صيصا *ṣîṣâ'*, *ṣi'ṣâ'*, inferior dates with a soft stone and wanting in sweetness (from imperfect fructification); — ة *ṣîṣa-t*, صيصية *ṣîṣiyya-t*, pl. *ṣayâṣin*, *ṣayâṣî*, spur of a cock; horn; loom; castle; stick for beating down the dates; good shepherd.

صئصى *ṣi'ṣi'*, *ṣîṣi*, root.

(صيع) *ṣâ'*, I, INF. *ṣai'*, separate, disperse, scatter; attack; — V. INF. *taṣayyu'*, overflow the banks; stay, abide; — VII. INF. *inṣiyâ'*, see (صوع).

صيعان *ṣî'ân*, pl. of صاع *ṣâ'*, a fruit-measure (=4 مد *mudd*).

صيعرى *ṣai'ariyy*, big; احمر ص *aḥmar ṣai'ariyy*, crimson; — ة *ṣai'ariyya-t*, oblique pace; mark by branding on a camel's neck.

(صيغ) II. *ṣayyag*, INF. *taṣyîg*, soak bread, &c., in fat or sauce.

صيغ *ṣayyig*, forger of lies; — ة *ṣîga-t*, form; grammatical form;

law-formula; origin; trinkets, articles of jewellery; — *ṣayyiga-t* = ثريدة *s̲arîda-t*, broth, bread-soup.
(صيف) *ṣâf*, I, INF. *ṣaif*, pass the summer; pass. *ṣîf*, be fructified by the summer rain; — INF. *ṣaif*, *ṣayûfa-t*, miss the aim; — II. INF. *taṣyîf*, suffice for the summer; — III. INF. *muṣâyafa-t*, hire one's services for the summer; — IV. INF. *iṣâfa-t*, enter on summer; beget children in one's old age; avert; — V. INF. *taṣayyuf*, pass the summer.
صيف *ṣaif*, pl. *aṣyâf*, ة *ṣaifa-t*, pl. *ṣiyaf*, summer; — *ṣayyif*, summer rain; — ى *ṣaifiyy*, of the summer, referring to the summer; summer rain; born in summer or in the father's old age.
(صيق) *ṣîq*, wind; cloud of dust (also ة *ṣîqa-t*, pl. *ṣiyaq*); sound, tone; perspiration; offensive smell of animals; red sap-wood of a palm-tree; pl. *ṣîqân*, sparrow.
صيقل *ṣaiqal*, pl. *ṣayâqil*, *ṣayâqila-t*, furbisher, polisher.
صيقم *ṣaiqam*, offensive to the smell.
(صيك) *ṣâk*, I, INF. *ṣaik*, adhere; — *ṣa'ik*, perspire and smell of it; curdle; adhere; — III. INF. *muṣa'aka-t*, treat harshly.
صئك *ṣa'ik*, violent, rough, harsh.
(صيل) *ṣâl*, I = (صول).
صئل *ṣa'il*, furious, enraged.
صيلخود *ṣailaḥûd*, strong.
صيلم *ṣailam*, difficult, dangerous; calamity; sword; = صيرم *ṣairam*, meal taken once in 24 hours; — ة *ṣailama-t*, sanguinary battle.
صئم *ṣa'im*, (v.) see (صام); — *ṣiyyam*, thick-set; — *ṣiyyam*, *ṣuyyam*, pl. of صايم, fasting (adj.).
صين *ṣîn*, China.
صينى *ṣîniyy*, Chinese; — ة *ṣîniyya-t*, pl. *ṣawânî*, Chinese porcelain, china-ware; plate; dish; tray.
صيهج *ṣaihaj* = صلهج *ṣalhaj*.
صيهوج *ṣaihûj*, smooth.
صيوان *ṣîwân*, pl. *ṣawâwîn*, palace; festival-tent; tent.
صيوب *ṣayûb*, pl. *ṣuyub* = صويب *ṣawîb* and صيب *ṣayyib*.
صيود *ṣayûd*, pl. *ṣuyud*, *ṣîd*, hunter; — *ṣayyûd*, hitting the aim (adj.).
صيور *ṣayyûr*, ة *ṣayyûra-t*, end, issue, event; *ṣayyûr*, understanding, intelligence, prudence (ام صيور *umm ṣayyûr*, difficult matter); hay.
صئى *ṣa'iyy*, *ṣu'iyy*, peeping (s.).
صئل *ṣa'il*, neighing (s.).

ض

ض *ḍ*, as a numerical sign = 800.
ضابث *ḍâbis̲*, adhering (adj.).
ضابح *ḍâbiḥ*, snorting horse.
ضابط *ḍâbiṭ*, holding fast; strong; horse; lion; prudent, cautious; who keeps order; lord, master; governor; policeman; officer; ضابط الكل *ḍâbiṭ al-kull*, the Almighty; — also ة *ḍâbita-t*, list; law, rule.
ضابى *ḍâbî*, hot ashes.
ضاج *ḍâjj*, screamer.
ضاجع *ḍâji'*, lazy; sluggard; stupid; pl. *ḍawâji'*, winding of a river; bending (adj. n.); pl. stars; — ة *ḍâji'a-t*, river-mouth; full; numerous.
ضاحة *ḍâḥa-t*, eye; face.
ضاحك *ḍâḥik*, laughing; flashing, coruscating, lightening (adj.); — ة *ḍâḥika-t*, pl. *ḍawâḥik*, tooth-like, projecting (white rocks).
ضاحى *ḍâḥi*, projecting; exposed to the sun; — ة *ḍâḥiya-t*, pl. *ḍawâḥî*,

such a place; region, tract, province, district, quarter; ض برانية ḍâḥiya-t barrâniyya-t, suburb.

ضاحة ḍâḥa-t, ضاحية ḍâḥiyya-t, calamity.

ضاد ḍâd, name of the letter ض ḍ; — ḍa'd, pudenda of a woman.

(ضاد) ḍa'ad, INF. ḍa'd, quarrel, dispute; pass. ḍu'id, INF. ḍu'âd, suffer from a cold or catarrh; — IV. INF. iḍ'âd, cause to have a cold.

ضادى ḍâdî, pl. ḍudât, angry; pl. ḍawâdî, word which provokes anger.

ضار ḍâr-in, see ضارى ḍârî; — ḍârr, hurtful, injurious.

ضارب ḍârib, ag. of (ضرب), beating, throbbing; who mints; pestle; pedestrian, traveller; swimmer; pl. ḍawârib, situated towards; tract; valley with trees; partly-clouded night; president in the game of arrows.

ضارع ḍâri', weak; humble; submissive; small.

ضارور ḍârûr, ة ḍârûra-t, necessity; exigency of a metre; narrow.

ضاروراء ḍârûrâ', necessity; need, scarcity, famine; calamity; loss, damage.

ضارى ḍârî (ضار ḍâr-in), sporting-dog; pl. ḍawârî, beasts of prey.

(ضاز) ḍa'az, INF. ḍa'z, ḍa'az, wrong, act unjustly towards one.

ضازى ḍa'za, ضوزى ḍu'za, ضئزى ḍi'za, incomplete, defective (share, portion).

ضاضا ḍa'ḍa', ة ḍa'ḍa'a-t, ضوضى ḍauḍan, ضوضا ḍauḍâ', battle-cry; tumult, turmoil.

ضاط ḍa'iṭ, see (ضئط).

ضائل ḍâ'il, strong male camel.

ضاغط ḍâgiṭ, overseer; tax-gatherer.

ضاغن ḍâgin, restive, lazy.

ضافط ḍâfiṭ, merchant travelling with goods; loaded camel; — ة ḍâfiṭa-t, id.; dregs of the populace.

ضافى ḍâfî, long, trailing.

(ضال) ḍa'al, make one's self small; — ḍa'ul, INF. ḍa'âla-t, ḍu'ûla-t, ḍa'îla-t, be small, thin, weak, contemptible; — VI. INF. taḍâ'ul, id.; make one's self small; — VIII. INF. iḍṭi'âl = ḍa'ul.

ضال ḍâl, wild lotus; — ḍâll, ة, pl. ḍawâll, erring, wandering, roaming about (adj.); wanderer; forgetting; f. stray animal; — ة ḍâla-t, arms, bows.

ضالع ḍâli', gone astray; lamed, palsied.

ضام ḍâmm, contracting (adj.).

ضامر ḍâmir, pl. ḍummar, slender; pliable.

ضامن ḍâmin, bail, who stands security; pl. ḍawâmin, camel big with young; — ة ḍâmina-t, palm-trees within the precincts of a city; — ى ḍâminiyy, who stands security; — ية ḍâminiyya-t, security, warranty.

(ضان) ḍa'n, pl. aḍ'ân, aḍ'un, ḍa'în, sheep; pl. of ضائن ḍâ'in; — IV. INF. iḍ'ân, have plenty of sheep; separate one's sheep from the goats; — ة ḍa'na-t, ring for a camel's nose made of a sinew.

ضانى ḍâni', fertile, prolific; — ḍa'niyy, referring to a sheep, sheepish; — ة ḍâni'a-t, pl. ḍawânî, fertile, prolific; wealth, riches.

ضاهر ḍâhir, mountain-summit; valley.

ضاهلة ḍâhila-t, yielding little water.

ضاوى ḍâwî, night-farer, night-wanderer; — ḍâwi', morning-star; — ḍâwiyy, ة, delicate, weak.

(ضاى) ḍa'a, INF. ḍa'y, have a thin delicate body.

ضائع ḍâ'i', pl. ḍiyâ', ḍuyya', lost; vain, fruitless; empty; hungry; loss.

ضائق ḍâ'iq, narrow, strait.

ضائن ḍâ'in, pl. ḍa'n, ḍa'an, ḍa'în, gelded ram; having a flabby belly; eating little; well-made; large white sand-hills; — ة ḍâ'ina-t, pl. ḍawâ'in, sheep; — ى

dâ'iniyy, of a gelded ram; mutton.

(ضب) *dabb*, I, INF. *dabb*, flow, run, drip; suffer from the disease ضب *dabb* (see below); milk; be silent; gather in one's hand, take the whole of a thing; keep together; be hostile, hate; adhere to the ground; — for *dabib*, A, INF. *dabab*, have a swelling of the chest, knee or hoof; be full of lizards; — *dabab*, INF. *dabâba-t*, id.; — II. INF. *tadbîb*, gather, collect; give syrup to a child; put the iron bolt or bar to a door; — IV. INF. *idbâb*, abound in lizards; be silent; collect; scream, cry out; talk; make a hostile invasion; come in scattered troops; be thick, rich (head of hair); be densely grown over; stick to; seize and hold; be on the point of obtaining one's end; leak; be foggy; conceal; set all to work, be many at a work; talk much at the same time (many people); cause to flow, to run; give syrup to a child; — V. INF. *tadabbub*, have a plump neck; — VII. *indibâb*, be gathered in the hand; be kept in order; be kept together.

ضب *dabb*, *dibb*, hatred; anger; *dabb*, bold; insolent, pert; strong; pl. *dibâb*, unopened blossom of a palm-tree; f. *dabba-t*, pl. *adubb*, *dibâb*, *dubbân*, *madabba-t*, an eatable lizard; *dabb*, tumour on the lip with bleeding; swelling of a camel's bones; — ة *dabba-t*, skin of a lizard; pl. *dibâb*, unopened palm-blossom; iron bolt or bar of a door.

(ضبا) *daba'*, INF. *dab'*, *dubû'*, adhere to the ground; throw on the ground; hide (n.); try to surprise, threaten; seek refuge; be ashamed.

ضباب *dabâb*, ة, fog, mist, vapour; — *

ضباث *dabâs*, *dabbâs*, ضباثم *dubâsim*, lion; — *dubâs*, soft parts of a lion's paw; — ية *dubâsiya-t*, fleshy arm.

ضباح *dabâh*, screech of an owl; bark of a fox; — *

ضبار *dibâr*, *dubâr*, pl. books; — *dabbâr*, name of a dog; — *dubbâr*, a tree; — ة *dabâra-t*, denseness; — *dibâra-t*, *dubâra-t*, small bundle, parcel; pl. *dabâ'ir*, troop, company.

(ضبارز) *dubâriz*, thick, stout; firm; strong.

ضبارك *dabârik*, pl. of ضبراك *dibrâk*.

ضبارم *dubârim*, ة *dubârima-t*, strong lion; bold against the enemy.

ضباضب *dubâdib*, short and clumsy; bold, active, energetic; insolent, impudent; farcical.

ضباعى *dabâ'a*, pl. of ضبعة *dabi'a-t*.

ضباعين *dabâ'în*, pl. of ضبعان *dib'ân*.

ضباغط *dabâgit*, pl. of ضبغطى *d abgata*.

ضبائر *dabâ'ir*, pl. of ضبارة *dibâra-t*.

ضبب *dabab*, swelling in a camel's foot; INF. of (ضب); — *dabib*, full of lizards.

(ضبث) *dabas*, I, INF. *dabs*, seize; beat; feel; — VIII. INF. *idtibâs*, seize with the hand.

(ضبث) *dabis*, ضبثم *dabsam*, lion; — ة *dabsa-t*, mark by branding.

(ضبج) *dabaj*, INF. *dabj*, throw one's self on the ground.

(ضبح) *dabah*, INF. *dabh*, *dubâh*, snort in running; run; singe, scorch; — III. INF. *mudâbaha-t*, inveigh against; — VI. INF. *tadâbuh*, snort; — VII. INF. *indibâh*, be singed, scorched.

ضبح *dibh*, ashes.

(ضبد) *dabad*, INF. *dabd*, mingle ripe and unripe dates; — II. INF. *tadbîd*, remind of things which provoke to anger.

ضبد *dabad*, anger.

(ضبر) *dabar*, I, INF. *dabr*, *dabarân*,

leap with contracted feet; range stones; — U, range the leaves of a book;— II. INF. *taḍbîr*, gather; I. and II. be firmly made; strong of bones.

ضبر *ḍabr*, nutmeg; wild pomegranate; troop of assailers; pl. *ḍubûr*, siege-engines covered with hides; — *ḍabr*, *ḍabir*, walnut-tree; — *ḍibr*, arm-pit; — *ḍibbîr*, leaping into the air (adj.).

ضبراك *ḍibrâk*, pl. *ḍabârik*, big and strong.

ضبران *ḍabarân*, INF. of (ضبر).

ضبرك *ḍibrik*, having thick hips.

(ضبز) *ḍabaz*, INF. *ḍabz*, look passionately or savagely at (adj.).

ضبز *ḍabiz*, looking savagely (wolf).

(ضبس) *ḍabas*, INF. *ḍabs*, press for payment; — *ḍabis*, A, INF. *ḍabas*, be malignant.

ضبس شر *ḍibs śarr-in*, malicious; — *ḍabis*, id.; calamity.

(ضبضب) *ḍibḍib*, fat; insolent, pert.

(ضبضب) *ḍabḍab*, INF. ة, be misty, foggy, covered with fog (m.).

(ضبط) *ḍabaṭ*, I, INF. *ḍabṭ*, *ḍabâṭa-t*, hold fast; keep one's self possessed of; keep in order, manage, administer, govern; enter (in a book, &c.), note down; (m.) take possession of, confiscate, sequester; settle (an account); level (a gun); know accurately; — *ḍabiṭ*, A, INF. *ḍabaṭ*, do with both hands; pass. *ḍubiṭ*, be entirely rained over; — IV. INF. *iḍbâṭ*, mark the words with the signs of inflection; — V. INF. *taḍabbuṭ*, take possession of a thing by violence; snatch some food or eat rapidly; — VII. INF. *inḍibâṭ*, be fastened, consolidated; (m.) be confiscated; be done with accuracy or punctuality.

ضبط *ḍabṭ*, keeping in order (s.); government; regulation; control; entry; orthography; confiscation, sequestration; taking possession of (s.); consolidation; accuracy; punctuality; — *ḍabaṭ*, being equally skilful with both hands.

(ضبطر) *ḍibaṭr*, lion; strongly-built.

ضبطى *ḍabṭiyy*, confiscator; confiscated.

(ضبع) *ḍaba'*, INF. *ḍab'*, stretch out the arm against, beat; exercise violence; raise the hands to God against, curse; make the way free, make room; — INF. *ḍab'*, *ḍubû'*, *ḍaba'ân*, stretch the fore-feet in pacing; run; incline to peace; portion; — *ḍabi'*, A, INF. *ḍaba'*, *ḍabâ'a-t*, be hot (camel); — II. INF. *taḍbî'*, stretch the fore feet; be cowardly, timid; prevent from obtaining the prey by stepping between; — IV. INF. *iḍbâ'*, be hot (she-camel); — VIII. INF. *iḍṭibâ'*, take the cloak under the right arm and throw it over the left shoulder.

ضبع *ḍab'*, pl. *aḍbâ'*, arm; arm-pit; long hill; a quiet pace; hyena; ضبعا لبعا *ḍab'an lab'an*, in vain; — *ḍab'*, *ḍib'*, *ḍub'*, land, territory, dominion; protection; — *ḍab'*, *ḍabu'*, pl. *aḍbu'*, *ḍibâ'*, *ḍub'*, *ḍubu'*, *maḍba'a-t*, female hyena (pl. *ḍibâ'*, small star in Arcturus); hunger; year of dearth; — *ḍaba'*, rut; — ة *ḍabu'a-t*, female hyena; rut; — *ḍabi'a-t*, pl. *ḍibâ'*, *ḍabâ'a*, hot, rutting.

ضبغطرى *ḍabagṭara*, big, strong; mad; hyena; also—

ضبغطى *ḍabagṭa*, pl. *ḍabâgiṭ*, bugbear, scare-crow.

(ضبن) *ḍaban*, avert; — IV. INF. *iḍbân*, weaken; take under one's arm; press in sitting; — II. INF. *taḍbîn*, VIII. INF. *iḍṭibân*, take under one's arm.

ضبن *ḍabn*, averting (s.), prevention; — *ḍabn*, *ḍibn*, place between the arm-pit and short ribs; *ḍibn*, hard; — *ḍaban*, loss, defect; — *ḍabin*, narrow space; little and

useless; lamed; — ة ḍabna-t, ḍibna-t, ḍubna-t, ḍabina-t, domestics; dependents; poor people.

ضبنط ḍabannaṭ, ضبنطى ḍabanṭā, strong, powerful.

(ضبو) ḍabâ, U, INF. ḍabw, ḍubiyy, singe, roast; take refuge; — IV. INF. iḍbâ', seize; hold back; be on the point of obtaining one's end; disappoint; throw back; lift up; have a thin, delicate body.

ضبوب ḍabûb, making water in running (beast of burden); having narrow teats; — *.

ضبوث ḍabûṡ, doubtfully fat; lion.

ضبور ḍabûr, lion; — *.

ضبوك ḍubûk, pl. furrows, grooves.

ضبى ḍabî', adhering to the ground; man; — ḍubiyy, INF. of ضبو.

ضبيب ḍabîb, edge of a sword; — ة ḍabîba-t, syrup; crocodile.

ضبير ḍabîr, strong; bold; penis.

ضبيز ḍabîz, looking savagely (wolf).

ضبيس ḍabîs, malignant.

ضبيطر ḍubaiṭir, strong lion.

ضتيرب ḍutairib, slight shock.

(ضج) ḍajj, I, INF. ḍajj, ḍajîj, cry out; clamour; quack, croak; groan from exhaustion and succumb; — II. INF. taḍjîj, depart; lean to the side; strew poison (for birds, &c.); — III. INF. ḍijâj, muḍâjja-t, wrong, do injustice to (acc.); cause disorder, tumult; — IV. INF. iḍjâj, cry out, clamour; — ة ḍajja-t, clamour, noise, tumult.

ضجاج ḍajâj, clamour, tumult; violence; a kind of pearls; concha veneris; ivory; — ḍijâj, an eatable gum; any tree with poisonous fruit.

(ضجهر) ḍajhar, INF. ة, fill; — III. INF. iḍjihrâr, pass.

(ضجر) ḍajir, A, INF. ḍajar, be grieved, put to anxiety; roar; — II. INF. taḍjîr, IV. INF. iḍjâr, grieve (acc.), render sorrowful; — V. INF. taḍajjur, grieve (n.); be in anxiety; be angry.

ضجر ḍajar, ة ḍujra-t, anxiety; grief; ill-humour; — ḍajr, ḍajir, narrow, strait; — ḍajir, grieved, sorrowful; noisy.

(ضجع) ḍaja', INF. ḍaj', ḍujû', lie on the side; deviate; decline towards setting; — II. INF. taḍjî', do less than duty requires; be near setting; — III. INF. muḍâja'a-t, lie side by side with; — IV. INF. iḍjâ', lay or bid to lie on the side; press down, let down; empty; — V. INF. taḍajju', be lazy, remiss; remain stationary; — VII. INF. inḍijâ', lie on the side; — VIII. INF. iḍṭijâ', id.; bend or press the chest to the ground for prayer.

ضجع ḍaj', ة, washing-material (potash, &c.); a kind of cucumber; — ḍij', inclination, affection; — ة ḍaj'a-t, ḍaja'a-t, ḍij'a-t, lying on the side (s.); — ḍaj'a-t, ḍij'a-t, ḍuj'a-t, weakness of intellect, sleepiness, indolence, laziness; ḍuj'a-t, ḍuja'a-t, and—

ضجعى ḍij'iyy, ḍuj'iyy, ة ḍij'iyya-t, ḍuj'iyya-t, who sleeps much, lie-a-bed; lazy, idle.

(ضجم) ḍajim, INF. ḍajam, be wry, distorted, crooked; — VI. INF. taḍâjum, be under dispute; — IX. INF. iḍjimâm, XI. INF. iḍjîmâm, have the mouth distorted.

ضجم ḍajam, wryness, distortedness, crookedness.

ضجوج ḍajûj, roaring, crying out, clamouring (adj.).

ضجور ḍajûr, ill-humoured, morose; roaring.

ضجوع ḍajû', weak of intellect; disobedient; large bucket; bent towards the earth; slow rain-cloud; — *.

ضجيج ḍajîj, noise, clamour, tumult.

ضجيع ḍajî', bed-fellow; hunger.

ضح ḍiḥḥ, sun; sun-light; exposed to the sun; vast plain; — ة

ḍaḥa-t, ḍiḥa-t, INF. of (وضح), be evident.

ضحا *ḍaḥa'*, breakfast, meat; INF. of (ضحى).

ضحاك *ḍaḥḥâk*, laugher; long way; mid-way; name of a king.

ضحايا *ḍaḥâyâ*, pl. of ضحية *ḍaḥiyya-t*.

ضحضاح *ḍaḥḍâḥ*, ضحضح *ḍaḥḍaḥ*, shallow.

(ضحضح) *ḍaḥḍaḥ*, INF. *ḍaḥḍaḥ*, ة *ḍaḥḍaḥa-t*, undulate; — II. INF. *taḍaḥḍuḥ*, id.

(ضحك) *ḍaḥik*, A, INF. *ḍaḥk, ḍiḥk, ḍaḥik, ḍiḥik*, laugh aloud, laugh, laugh at; lighten; — INF. *ḍaḥak*, wonder, be startled; burst out laughing; lighten; have the menses; exude gum; — III. INF. *muḍâḥaka-t*, laugh to, vie in laughing; — II. INF. *taḍḥîk*, IV. INF. *iḍḥâk*, make laugh; — V. INF. *taḍaḥḥuk*, laugh, laugh at; — VI. INF. *taḍâḥuk*, laugh to one another, tell each other laughable things; laugh at one another; — X. INF. *istiḍḥâk*, laugh; want to laugh; take a laughable aspect of things.

ضحك *ḍaḥk, ḍaḥik, ḍiḥk, ḍiḥik*, laughter, &c.; — *ḍaḥk*, fresh butter; froth of milk; white honey; snow; blossoms; white front teeth; middle of the way; — *ḍuḥk*, pl. of ضحوك *ḍaḥûk*; — ة *ḍaḥka-t*, laughter; — *ḍuḥka-t*, object of laughter; — *ḍuḥaka-t, ḍuḥukka-t*, laugher, scoffer, satirist.

(ضحل) *ḍaḥal*, INF. *ḍaḥl*, be scarce; be shallow.

ضحل *ḍaḥl*, pl. *ḍiḥâl, ḍuḥûl, aḍḥâl*, scarce and shallow water.

(ضحو) *ḍaḥâ*, U, INF. *ḍaḥw*, be clear, visible in the sun-light; — U, INF. *ḍaḥw, duḥuww, ḍuḥiyy*, go into the sunshine; also ضحى *ḍaḥa*, INF. *ḍaḥw, ḍuḥiyy*, be exposed to the sun; — INF. *ḍuḥuww*, show itself; be distinctly visible; — ضحى *ḍaḥi*, A, INF. *ḍaḥâ'*, go into the sunshine perspire; — II. INF. *taḍḥiya-t*, feed (a.) in the morning, slaughter or sacrifice a sheep in the morning; act slowly, deliberately, considerately; — III. INF. *muḍâḥât*, come in the morning to (acc.); — IV. INF. *iḍḥâ'*, be or do in the morning; make visible, show; expose to the sun; bring to light; (m.) prove or become such and such a one (m.); be in arrear, remain behind; — V. INF. *taḍaḥḥî*, take a meal or do anything in the morning; be exposed to or stand in the sun; be in arrear, remain behind.

ضحو *ḍaḥw*, ة *ḍaḥwa-t* = ضحى *ḍuḥan*; — *ḍuḥuww*, INF. of (ضحو).

ضحوك *ḍaḥûk*, pl. *ḍuḥk*, very much given to laughing; laughing (adj.); broad, distinctly-visible road

ضحى *ḍaḥa, ḍaḥî*, (v.) see (ضحو); — *ḍuḥan*, ضحا *ḍuḥâ*, middle of the time between sun-rise and mid-day, fore-noon; breakfast-time; fore-noon prayer; sunshine, sun; clearness (of speech, &c.); — *ḍuḥayy*, small part of the fore-noon; — ة *ḍaḥiyya-t* = *ḍuḥan*, above; pl. *ḍaḥâyâ*, sheep sacrificed in the fore-noon; sacrifice, victim.

ضحيا *ḍaḥyâ'*, hairless in the body (woman); clear, bright; white, grey; — *ḍuḥayyâ* = ضحى *ḍuḥayy*.

ضحيان *ḍaḥyân*, ة, basking in the sun; sunny; bright, shining brilliantly; breakfasting (adj.).

(ضخ) *ḍaḫḫ*, weep, run (with tears); spout water.

(ضخز) *ḍaḫaz*, tear out the eye together with the fat.

(ضخم) *ḍaḫum*, INF. *ḍaḫm, ḍaḫâma-t*, be big, stout, corpulent.

ضخم *ḍaḫm*, ة, big and heavy; stout; broad, wide; — *ḍaḫam*, pl. *ḍiḫâm*, big; corpulent; — ة *ḍiḫamma-t*, plump and delicate (woman).

(ضد) *ḍadd*, U, INF. *ḍadd*, get the

better in a dispute or lawsuit; oppose; prevent by friendly remonstrance; fill; — III. INF. *muḍâdda-t*, oppose; form a contrast; — IV. INF. *iḍdâd*, be angry; — VI. INF. *taḍâdd*, oppose, hinder one another; form a contrast to each other; (m.) meet with opposition.

ضد *ḍidd*, pl. *aḍdâd*, opposition, contradiction, counterpart, contrast; opponent, adversary, enemy; assistant, helper; similar; *al-aḍdâd*, words with opposite meanings.

(ضدن) *ḍadan*, I, INF. *ḍadn*, mend, repair, make more convenient.

(ضدى) *ḍadi*, A, INF. *ḍadan*, also *ḍadi'*, be angry; — III. INF. *muḍâdât*, be opposed, be in contradiction, form a contrast; — IV. INF. *iḍdâ'*, fill a vessel entirely; — ة *ḍiddîyya-t*, opposition, contrast.

ضديد *ḍadîd*, opposed, contrasting, contradictory; similar.

(ضر) *ḍarr*, U, INF. *ḍarr*, damage, injure, prevail against; — III. INF. *muḍârra-t*, *ḍirâr*, injure, damage; press one another (in a crowd); — IV. INF. *iḍrâr*, damage, injure; come near, close to; hasten; urge one against his will; take a second wife in addition to a first one; bite the bit; — V. INF. *taḍarrur*, be injured, damaged, hurt; — VII. INF. *inḍirâr*, suffer an injury, damage, wrong; — VIII. INF. *iḍṭirâr*, want, need; force, compel; (m.) be forced; be urged to a thing by need.

ضر *ḍirr*, *ḍurr*, marriage, taking (s.) another wife; — *ḍurr*, calamity, damage, loss; leanness; — ة *ḍarra-t*, pl. *ḍarâ'ir*, the fleshy parts of the fingers and toes; udder; breasts; property; herds of cattle; distress, poverty, sorrow, loss; wife with another wife besides her; pl. *ḍarratân*, the two mill-stones; two fellow-wives; — *ḍurra-t*, necessity, compulsion; loss, damage.

(ضرأ, ضر) *ḍara'*, INF. *ḍar'*, be concealed; — VII. INF. *inḍirâ'*, perish by drought; wither (n.).

ضرا *ḍarâ*, *ḍirâ*, INF. of ضرى *ḍarî*, see (ضرو); — *ḍarrâ'*, pl. *ḍarrâwat*, *aḍurr*, calamity, loss; disease, illness; cattle-plague; — ة *ḍarât*, ضراوة *ḍarâwa-t*, accustoming (s.); training for the hunt, for combat, &c.

ضراب *ḍarrâb*, who beats, beater; mintman; — *

ضرابخانة *ḍarrâbḫâna-t*, mint.

ضراح *ḍirâḥ*, *ḍarâḥ-i*, be gone! away with you; — *ḍurâḥ*, the heavenly palace.

ضرار *ḍirâr*, INF. III. of (ضر); — ة *ḍarâra-t*, loss, damage; cattle-plague; blindness.

ضراس *ḍurâs*, tooth-ache.

ضراسى *ḍurâsā*, pl. of ضريس *ḍarîs*.

ضراط *ḍurâṭ*, fart; — *ḍarrâṭ*, one who breaks wind.

ضراع *ḍirâ'*, ة *ḍarâ'a-t*, INF. of (ضرع); — ة *ḍarâ'a-t*, humility, submissiveness.

ضرافط *ḍurâfiṭ*, corpulent, paunch-bellied.

ضراك *ḍurâk*, strong, vigorous; lion.

ضرام *ḍirâm*, fire-wood; conflagration; — ة *ḍirâma-t*, resinous tree, fir-tree, &c.

ضراوة *ḍarâwa-t*, see ضراة *ḍarât*.

ضرائر *ḍarâ'ir*, pl. of ضرة *ḍarra-t*.

ضراية *ḍarâya-t*, INF. of ضرى *ḍarî*, see (ضرو).

(ضرب) *ḍarab*, I, INF. *ḍarb*, beat, hit; cut off; pitch (a tent); coin; quote, make use of (a proverb, simile); play (an instrument); impose (tribute, &c.); move (n.), pass away; be long (night); lay hold upon; inflict; — INF. *ḍarb*, *ḍarabân*, depart, set out, bestir one's self; attack (على *'ala*); mix one thing with (ب *bi*) another; multiply with (فى *fi*); — INF.

ḍirâb, cover (stallion); — U, get the better in beating; pass. *ḍurib*, be covered with hoar-frost; — *ḍarib*, A, INF. *ḍarab*, suffer from the cold; — *ḍarub*, INF. *ḍarâba-t*, give a violent hit, a sound blow; — II. INF. *taḍrîb*, beat violently or repeatedly; mix, mix up; multiply (فى *fi*); stir up discord; sew on a lining or padding; drink of the milk ضريب *ḍarîb*; get overtaken by the snow; be deep-set (eye); — III. INF. *ḍirâb*, fight with; cover (stallion); INF. *muḍâraba-t*, enter into a sleeping partnership; get the better in beating; — IV. INF. *iḍrâb*, make the stallion to cover; stay at home; suffer from hoar-frost; cause all moisture to be absorbed by the ground (hot wind); be well baked; turn away from, renounce, pass to something else; — V. INF. *taḍarrub*, move (n.), be agitated, undulate, fluctuate; beat one's self; — VI. INF. *taḍârub*, beat each other, fight; clash together; — VII. INF. *inḍirâb*, be beaten, hit, afflicted with, befallen; — VIII. INF. *iḍṭirâb*, be moved, excited, agitated; undulate, fluctuate; waver, be precarious, unsolid; beat one another, fight; have anything beaten, forged, coined for one's self; carry on business, bestir one's self for gain; be long but weak; — X. INF. *istiḍrâb*, be white and thick (honey); want the stallion (mare).

ضرب *ḍarb*, blow, push; throw; violence, power; haste, hurry; the playing of musical instruments; minting (s.); multiplication; pl. *ḍurûb*, *aḍrub*, manner, method, form; report of a gun; similarity; similar; pl. *aḍrâb*, contemporaries; who beats much; brave, bold; active and clever; of a slender make and not fleshy; slight, light; coined; sour milk; last foot of the second hemistich; — *ḍarab*, *ḍarb*, white honey; — *ḍarib*, who beats; who multiplies; — ة *ḍarba-t*, pl. *ḍarbât*, *ḍarabât*, a blow, stroke, hit; report of a gun, shot; punishment, torment.

ضربا *ḍurabâ'*, pl. of ضريب *ḍarîb*.

ضربان *ḍarabân*, throbbing of a wound; INF. of (ضرب).

ضربجي *ḍarbajiyy*, spurious (coin).

ضربخانة *ḍarbḥâna-t*, mint.

(ضرج) *ḍaraj*, U, INF. *ḍarj*, split, cleave (a.); soil, stain; impregnate, dye; throw on the ground, fling away; loosen, open wider; urge on the camel with the feet; dispose well and adorn one's speech; dye red; stain with blood; beat the nose so as to bleed; — V. INF. *taḍarruj*, be soiled, stained; split (n.); open (n.); be red, dyed red; show one's self adorned; — VII. INF. *inḍirâj*, be split, split (n.); widen (n.); pounce upon.

(ضرجع) *ḍarja'*, leopard.

(ضرح) *ḍaraḥ*, INF. *ḍarḥ*, refuse, repel, keep off; kick; make a grave for the dead in the middle of a tomb; — INF. *ḍirâḥ*, kick; — INF. *ḍurûḥ*, be dull, slack (market); — III. INF. *muḍâraḥa-t*, revile, abuse; throw at; be near; — IV. INF. *iḍrâḥ*, spoil; spoil the market; remove (a.); — VIII. INF. *inḍirâḥ*=*inḍirâj*.

ضرح *ḍarḥ*, skin, hide, leather; — *ḍaraḥ*, bad, wicked; far.

ضرداخ *ḍirdâḥ*, noble.

(ضردخ) *ḍirdiḥ*, great.

ضرر *ḍarar*, damage, loss, injury; difficulty; distress, need, poverty; straitness; strait; border of a cave; لا ضرر *lâ ḍarar*, it does not matter! there is no harm in it! never mind!

ضرز *ḍarz*, ruggedness and pathlessness of the ground; — *ḍirizz*,

hard; avaricious, miserly; lion; ة ḍirizza-t, short and mean (woman).
(ضرزل) ḍirzil, avaricious, covetous.
(ضرزم) ḍirzim, mordacious viper; — also ḍarzam, she-camel growing old; — ة ḍarzama-t, violent bite.
(ضرس) ḍaras, I, INF. ḍars, bite violently with the molar teeth; rage against; break in a camel (by wounding its nose and passing a strap over the wound); line a well with stones; be silent all day; — ḍaris, be blunt from biting bitter plants (teeth); II. INF. taḍris, bite violently with the molar teeth; inure to warfare; — III. INF. muḍârasa-t, fight against one another; — IV. INF. iḍrâs, blunt the teeth; agitate; silence; — VI. INF. taḍârus, be unequal or disconnected in its parts (building); fight each other.
ضرس ḍars, country with scattered vegetation; — ḍirs, pl. aḍrâs, ḍurûs, tooth, molar tooth; rugged hill; long absorption in prayer; pl. ḍurûs, fine raindrops; stones to cover a well; cover for the eyes (in a woman's veil); — ḍaras, bluntness of the teeth; — ḍaris, irritable.
ضرسامة ḍirsâma-t, unfeeling, mean, vile.
ضرسان ḍarsân, blunt.
ضرضم ḍarḍam, lion; beast of prey.
(ضرط) ḍaraṭ, I, INF. ḍarṭ, ḍariṭ, ḍurâṭ, ḍarîṭ, break wind; — ḍariṭ, A, ḍaraṭ, have a thin beard and thin eyebrows; — II. INF. taḍrîṭ, IV. INF. iḍrâṭ, cause to break wind; produce a farting sound with the mouth, to mock at a person; — ة ḍarṭa-t, wind from behind.
(ضرطم) ḍirṭim, paunch-bellied.
(ضرع) ḍara', — ḍari', A, INF. ḍara', — ḍaru', INF. ḍarâ'a-t, submit, yield, obey, be humble or weak, solicit humbly; — ḍara', INF. ḍurû', approach; set or be near setting; — II. INF. taḍrî', id.; approach stealthily; need repair; — III. INF. muḍâra'a-t, resemble; — IV. INF. iḍrâ', render submissive, humble; put in need of; be on the point of giving birth; present with a fortune; — V. INF. taḍarru', humble one's self; supplicate; approach stealthily; diminish, shorten (n.).
ضرع ḍar', pl. ḍurû', udder; — ḍir', pl. ḍurû', aḍru', similarity, resemblance; similar; thread in a rope; — ḍara', ḍari', humble, submissive, weak; small; — ة ḍara'a-t, humble, low, mean.
ضرعا ḍar'â', having large breasts or udders.
ضرعمط ḍara'miṭ, greedy, covetous, libidinous; thick milk.
ضرغام ḍirgâm, ة ḍirgâma-t, pl. ḍarâgim, lion; ḍirgâma-t, vigorous, powerful; stiff.
(ضرغط), III. iḍragaṭṭ, INF. iḍrigṭâṭ, swell with anger; be very fleshy.
ضرغطة ḍirgaṭa-t, stiff clay.
(ضرغم) ḍargam, INF. ة, II. INF. taḍargum, be bold as a lion; — ḍargam, lion; — ة ḍargama-t, a lion's boldness.
(ضرف) ḍarif, ة ḍarifa-t, wild fig; — ة ḍurfa-t, abundance, affluence.
ضرفاطة ḍirfâṭa-t, ضرفطى ḍirfaṭiyy, corpulent; paunch-bellied.
(ضرفط) ḍarfaṭ, INF. ة, fasten; — II. INF. taḍarfuṭ, sit astride on another's back.
(ضرك) ḍaruk, INF. ḍarâka-t, be struck by misfortune; be poor, blind, stupid; be strong, stout.
ضركا ḍurakâ', pl. of ضريك ḍarîk.
(ضرم) ḍarim, A, INF. ḍaram, burn, be hot; suffer from heat or hunger; burn with anger; eat all; — II. INF. taḍrîm, IV. INF. iḍrâm, X. INF. istiḍrâm, kindle, light or stir up the fire; — V.

INF. *taḍarrum*, burn, blaze; burn with anger; — VIII. INF. *iḍṭirâm*, burn, be consumed by fire; shine (white hair); — X. see II.

ضرم *ḍurm*, *ḍirm*, lavender;—*ḍaram*, heat, fire, fuel; — *ḍarim*, swift; hungry; eaglet; — ة *ḍarama-t*, fire-brand, glow, blaze, fire.

(ضرو) *ḍarâ*, U, INF. *ḍuruww*, bleed; — ضرى *ḍara*, I, INF. *ḍary*, flow; — *ḍarî*, A, INF. *ḍaran*, *ḍary*, *ḍurâwa-t*, *ḍarâ'a-t*, be intent upon, addicted to, entirely devoted to (ب *bi*); INF. *ḍaran*, *ḍirâ'*, *ḍarâ'*, (m.) *ḍarâwa-t*, be trained for hunting, be accustomed to blood, be blood-thirsty; blaze, be hot (as a combat); — II. INF. *taḍriya-t*, accustom or inure to; kindle war; — IV. INF. *iḍrâ'*, accustom to, inure, train for; hound against; drink date-wine; — X. INF. *istiḍrâ'*, fall upon from an ambush; beguile, deceive.

ضرو *ḍarw*, *ḍirw*, juniper berries; — *ḍirw*, a gum-tree; impurity of leprosy; *ḍirw*, f. ة, pl. *aḍr-in*, *aḍrî*, *ḍirâ'*, sporting-dog.

ضروب *ḍarûb*, who beats; — *.

ضروح *ḍarûḥ*, given to kicking; darting the arrow powerfully (bow).

ضرور *ḍarûr*, ضرورى *ḍarûriyy*, ة, necessary, indispensable; essential; compelled; pl. *ḍarûriyyât*, necessaries, wants; — ة *ḍarûra-t*, compulsion, necessity, want, need, exigency.

ضروس *ḍarûs*, given to biting, mordacious.

ضروط *ḍarûṭ*, *ḍirrauṭ*, one who breaks wind; — *ḍarrûṭ*, stout, corpulent.

ضروع *ḍarû'*, humble, meek, submissive; — *.

ضرى *ḍara*, *ḍarî*, (v.) see (ضرو); — *ḍaran*, pl. *aḍr-in*, *aḍrî*, sporting-dog; — *ḍarî*, id.; — *ḍariyy*, bleeding violently; date-wine.

ضريب *ḍarîb*, portion, share, lot, destiny; third arrow in the game; small section of a tribe; beaten; who beats; milk of several camels in the same bucket; snow, hoar-frost, ice; belly; kind, species, quality; similar; pl. *ḍurabâ'*, who casts the arrows in the game; who beats or hits; beaten, hit; — ة *ḍarîba-t*, pl. *ḍarâ'ib*, natural disposition, talent, endowment; tribute; reward; struck by the sword; sword; fleak of cotton.

ضريج *ḍarîj*, swift, rapid; — ى *ḍarîjiyy*, clipped money.

ضريح *ḍarîḥ*, far distant; pl. *ḍarâ'iḥ*, grave in the middle of a tomb.

ضرير *ḍarîr*, ة, pl. *aḍirrâ'*, *aḍrâr*, grown blind; ill and weakened; damaged, injured; loss; patience, endurance; river-bank; soul; jealousy; polygamist.

ضريس *ḍarîs*, pl. *ḍarâsā*, well lined with stones; vertebra; very hungry.

ضريط *ḍarîṭ*, INF. of (ضرط); — ة *ḍurraiṭa-t*, big sheep.

ضريع *ḍarî'*, ة, having large udders or breasts; thorns of a palm-tree, thorn; bitterness of hell; withered tree; weak wine; clear drink.

ضريك *ḍarîk*, pl. *ḍarâ'ik*, *ḍurakâ'*, poor; miserable; blind; lame; stupid; a species of the eagle.

ضريم *ḍarîm*, burnt, burning; — *ḍiryam*, a kind of gum.

(ضز) *ḍazz*, INF. *ḍazaz*, be unable to speak distinctly from narrowness of the mouth or gullet; — IV. INF. *iḍzâz*, be miserly; bite the bit or reins.

ضزاز *ḍazâz*, pl. of اضز *aḍazz*, narrow, strait, &c.

(ضطط) *ḍaṭaṭ*, ضطيط *ḍaṭîṭ*, much; deep; — *ḍuṭuṭ*, calamity, evil.

(ضع) *ḍa'*, train; tame.

ضع *ḍa'*, put down! IMP. of (وضع); = موضوع *mauḍû'*, put down, deposed, lying; — ة *ḍa'a-t*, *ḍi'a-t*,

INF. of (وضع); site; humiliation.

ضعاف *ḍiʻâf*, ضعافى *ḍaʻâfā*, pl. of ضعيف *ḍaʻif*; — ة *ḍaʻâfa-t*, weakness.

(ضعز) *ḍaʻaz*, INF. *ḍaʻz*, tread under foot.

ضعضاع *ḍaʻḍâʻ*, ضعضع *ḍaʻḍaʻ*, weak; imbecile.

(ضعضع) *ḍàʻḍaʻ*, INF. ة, make level with the ground, raze; humble, humiliate; (m.) scatter, disperse;—II. INF. *taḍaʻḍuʻ*, humble one's self before (ل *li*); grow poor; (m.) be dispersed, scattered; be spoiled; be despised;—ة *daʻḍaʻa-t*, humiliation; downfall, ruin.

(ضعط) *ḍaʻaṭ*, INF. *ḍaʻṭ*, slaughter.

(ضعف) *ḍaʻaf*, U, INF. *ḍaʻf*, *ḍuʻf*, be weak, be not equal to; grow weak and thin; — A, INF. *daʻf*, be superior in number and power; double; — *ḍaʻuf*, INF. *ḍaʻâfa-t*, *ḍaʻâfiya-t*, be weak; — II. INF. *taḍʻîf*, weaken; emaciate; double; double up; deem weak; — III. INF. *muḍâʻafa-t*, double; give twice as much; — IV. INF. *iḍʻâf*, weaken, emaciate; double; have a weak animal; pass. receive twice as much; — V. INF. *taḍaʻʻuf* (also X.), deem weak; — VI. INF. *taḍâʻuf*, be doubled; — X. INF. *istiḍʻâf*, see V.

ضعف *ḍaʻf*, weakness; leanness; human sperm; — *diʻf*, pl. *aḍʻâf*, similar, equal; capital punishment; du. *ḍiʻfân*, anything doubled, a couple; اضعاف الكتب *aḍʻâf al-kutub*, space between the lines; — *ḍuʻf*, weakness; fault, defect; — *ḍaʻaf*, weakness; doubled or lined clothes; — ة *ḍaʻfa-t*, weak people, invalids.

ضعفا *ḍuʻafâʼ*, pl. of ضعيف *ḍaʻîf*.

ضعفان *ḍaʻfân*, pl. *ḍaʻâfā*, weak; — *ḍiʻfan* (du. of ضعف *ḍiʻf*), a couple.

ضعفى *ḍaʻfā*, pl. of ضعيف *ḍaʻîf*.

(ضعل) *ḍaʻil*, A, INF. *ḍaʻal*, be weakly (child, from too close relationship of the parents).

(ضعو) *ḍaʻâ*, U, INF. *ḍaʻw*, conceal one's self, hide (n.).

ضعوف *ḍaʻûf*, weak.

ضعيف *ḍaʻif*, ة, pl. *diʻâf*, *duʻafâʼ*, *ḍaʻafa-t*, *ḍaʻfā*, *ḍaʻâfā*, weak; timid; sick, thin; stupid; blind; not supported by authority, untrustworthy; du. *ḍaʻîfân*, wife and slave.

ضغا *ḍugâʼ*, INF. of (ضغو).

ضغاب *ḍugâb*, cry.

ضغابيس *ḍagâbîs*, pl. of ضغبوس *ḍugbûs*.

ضغامة *ḍugâma-t*, anything chewed, spit out.

(ضغب) *ḍagab*, INF. *ḍagb*, cry; frighten; lie with.

ضغبوس *ḍugbûs*, pl. *ḍagâbîs*, a small cucumber; a prickly herb; young fox; not old and not fat; weak.

(ضغث) *ḍagas̱*, give a confused report; mix up; examine the fatness of a camel's hump; rustle, whistle; wash insufficiently; — II. INF. *taḍgîs̱*, VIII. INF. *iḍṭigâs̱*, seize a handful of herbs or roots.

ضغث *ḍigs̱*, *ḍags̱*, pl. *aḍgâs̱*, handful of herbs or roots; handful; intricacy, confusion.

(ضغد) *ḍagad*, INF. *ḍagd*, throttle, choke (a.).

ضغدرة *ḍaqdara-t*, pl. *ḍagâdir*, hen.

(ضغرس) *ḍagras*, voracious, greedy.

(ضغز) *ḍigz*, lion; savage animal.

(ضغضغ) *ḍagḍag*, INF. ة, chew with difficulty or not sufficiently; swallow down; pronounce indistinctly; stammer; make many words.

ضغضغة *ḍagḍaga-t*, chewing (s.); idle talk.

(ضغط) *ḍagaṭ*, INF. *ḍagṭ*, press, press against (الى *ila*), push; — III. INF. *muḍâgaṭa-t*, VI. INF. *taḍâguṭ*, press one another; — VII. INF. *inḍigâṭ*, press one's self against

the wall ;— ة *ḍagṭa-t*, pressing against (s.) ; narrowness ; — *ḍugṭa-t*, difficulty ; narrowness, pressure ; anxiety ; remissness of a debtor ; *ḍugṭat-an*, by force.

ضغطى *ḍagṭā*, pl. of ضغيط *ḍagîṭ*.

(ضغم) *ḍagam*, INF. *ḍagm*, bite, fill the mouth with a thing one likes.

(ضغن) *ḍagan*, INF. *ḍagan*, hate ; lean towards ;—VI. INF. *taḍâgun*, hate one another ; be prone to hatred ;—VIII. INF. *iḍṭigân*, hate one another ; take under the arm.

ضغن *ḍign*, pl. *aḍgân*, hatred, ill-will ; inclination, attachment ; region ; shoulder of the camel ; — *ḍagin*, ة, bent, crooked.

(ضغو) *ḍagâ*, U, INF. *ḍagw*, show one's self submissive ; cheat in a game ; — INF. *ḍagw*, *ḍugâ'*, cry out (as a cat, &c.) ; — IV. INF. *iḍgâ'*, cause to cry out ; — VI. INF. *taḍâgî*, cry out to one another.

ضغوث *ḍagûs*, camel felt (for its fatness).

ضغيب *ḍagîb*, cry.

ضغيط *ḍagîṭ*, well overflowed by another ; pl. *ḍagṭā*, weak of intellect ; — ة *ḍagîṭa-t*, weak plant.

(ضغيغ) *ḍagîg*, abundance of corn ; the whole of ; — ة *ḍagîga-t*, abundance, affluence ; magnificent garden ; multitude ; thin dough or paste ; cake.

ضغيفة *ḍagîfa-t*, greening, blooming ; fresh verdure.

ضغينة *ḍagîna-t*, pl. *ḍagâ'in*, hatred ; inclination, affection.

ضغينى *ḍaginiyy*, lion.

(ضف) *ḍaff*, U, INF. *ḍaff*, *ḍafaf*, press one another in eating or at the water ; — INF. *ḍaff*, milk with the whole hand ; gather ; bend one's fingers and warm them at the fire ; — VI. INF. *taḍâff*, press one another ; be in straitened circumstances.

ضف *ḍaff*, narrow, strait, straitened ; — *ḍuff*, pl. *ḍiffa-t*, *ḍifafa-t*, tick ; — ة *ḍaffa-t*, troop of people hastening to the water ; crowd, press, throng ; stream ; bank ; — *ḍiffa-t*, bank ; wall of a well.

ضفا *ḍafan*, du. *ḍafwân*, side.

ضفادع *ḍafâdi'*, ضفادى *ḍafâdî*, pl. of ضفدع *ḍafda'*.

ضفاريط *ḍafârîṭ*, pl. of ضفروط *ḍufrûṭ*.

ضفاز *ḍaffâz*, slanderer.

ضفاط *ḍaffâṭ*, hirer out of camels ; camel-driver ; travelling slave- or cattle-dealer ; fat and clumsy ; lazy ; peevish, morose ; clamorous ; having diarrhœa ;—*ḍuffâṭ*, dregs of the populace ; — ة *ḍafâṭa-t*, drum ; drummer ; INF. of (ضفط) ; — *ḍaffâṭa-t*, travelling-company ; loaded camel or other beast of burden.

ضفافة *ḍafâfa-t*, weak of intellect, imbecile.

(ضفد) *ḍafad*, I, INF. *ḍafd*, beat with the palm of the hand, slap ; — XI. INF. *iḍfidâd*, swell with anger.

(ضفدع) *ḍafda'*, *ḍifdi'*, *ḍufda'*, ة, pl. *ḍafâdi'*, *ḍafâdi*, frog (the frogs of his belly are croaking = he is hungry) ; swelling beneath the tongue.

ضفدع *ḍafda'*, INF. ة, have frogs in it (water).

(ضفر) *ḍafar*, I, INF. *ḍafr*, plait ; tie the hair together ; twist a rope ; hasten, hurry (a.) ; build a house without cementing the stones ; throw food into the mouth of a beast of burden ; — II. INF. *taḍfîr*, plait ; — III. INF. *muḍâfara-t*, help ; — VI. INF. *taḍâfur*, help one another ; — VII. INF. *indifâr*, be twisted together.

ضفر *ḍafr*, ة *ḍafra-t*, pl. *ḍufûr*, *ḍufur*, rope for fastening a load ; plait or lock of hair ; pl. *ḍufûr*, sand-hill ; structure of stone without mortar ; — ة *ḍafira-t*, pl. *ḍafir*, sand-hill ; quiver with arrows ; an insect.

(ضفرط) *ḍafraṭ*, INF. ة, be big and strong;—*ḍifriṭ*, big and strong; — ة *ḍafraṭa-t*, bigness and strength.

ضفروط *ḍufrûṭ*, pl. *ḍafâriṭ*, wrinkle between the nose and cheek or round the corner of the eye, crow-feet.

(ضفز) *ḍafaz*, U, INF. *ḍafz*, force a morsel into one's mouth; push back, repel; lie with; run, jump; push, kick; put the bit into the horse's mouth; — VIII. INF. *iḍṭifâz*, put a morsel into one's mouth against his will.

ضفز *ḍafz*, morsel forced into one's mouth; coition; shock, impetus, impulse; push, blow; — *ḍafaz*, ground barley.

(ضفس) *ḍafas*, I, INF. *ḍafs*, gather thistles and give them to the camel.

ضفضفة *ḍafḍafa-t*, troop of men, number of people.

(ضفط) *ḍafaṭ*, U, INF. *ḍaft*, tie together; ride continually upon (على *'ala*);—*ḍafuṭ*, INF. *ḍafâṭa-t*, be stupid, imbecile; have a paunch; — VI. INF. *taḍâfuṭ*, be firm and thick.

ضفط *ḍifiṭṭ*, clumsy, heavy; peevish, morose; fleshy and full of sap; —ة *ḍafṭa-t*, pl. *ḍafaṭâṭ*, stupidity, silliness, idiotcy; weakness.

ضفطى *ḍafṭa*, pl. of ضفيط *ḍafiṭ*.

(ضفع) *ḍafa'*, INF. *ḍaf'*, drop excrement; break wind.

ضفع *ḍaf'*, excrement of an elephant.

ضفف *ḍafaf*, insufficient measure; more eaters and drinkers than food or water; numerous attendants; household; throng of people; need, anxiety; haste; weakness; — ة *ḍifafa-t*, pl. of ضف *ḍuff*.

(ضفق) *ḍafaq*, I, INF. *ḍafq*, ease the bowels once.

(ضفن) *ḍafan*, I, INF. *ḍafn*, come and sit by; ease the bowels; perform an urgent business; lie with; knock the foot against, stumble; load; kick on the buttocks; throw on the ground; — VI. INF. *taḍâfun*, help one another; — VIII. INF. *iḍṭifân*, kick a man who is behind one.

ضفن *ḍifann*, ة *ḍifanna-t*, *ḍifinn*, ضفندد *ḍafandad*, big and stupid; short and thick.

(ضفند) *ḍafannad*, soft and gorbellied.

(ضفنس) *ḍafannas*, soft, flabby; numerous.

(ضفنط) *ḍafanṭ*, soft and fat.

(ضفو) *ḍafâ*, U, INF. *ḍafw*, be complete, cover the whole body; abound; overflow.

ضفو *ḍafw*, abundance; side; — ة *ḍafwa-t*, abundance, affluence.

ضفوان *ḍafwân*, du. of ضفا *ḍafan*.

ضفور *ḍufûr*, pl. of ضفر *ḍafr*, ة *ḍafra-t*.

ضفوف *ḍafûf*, having plenty of milk.

ضفير *ḍafîr*, sea-shore; belt, girth; plait of hair; (m.) nail; — ة *ḍafîra-t*, pl. *ḍafâ'ir*, braid of hair, plait; pig-tail; sand-hill.

ضفيز *ḍafîz*, thick; coarsely ground; — ة *ḍafîza-t*, pl. *ḍafâ'iz*, large morsel, mouthful.

ضفيط *ḍafîṭ*, pl. *ḍafṭa*, stupid; defective; fat, soft; liberal, generous.

ضفيف *ḍafîf*, traitor; Judas; — ة *ḍafîfa-t*, greening, blooming.

(ضق) *ḍaqq*, I, INF. *ḍaqq*, sound, resound, re-echo.

(ضك) *ḍakk*, U, INF. *ḍakk*, press, press upon.

ضكاضك *ḍukâḍik*, ضكضاك *ḍakḍâk*, ة, firm of flesh; short, thick-set.

(ضكز) *ḍakaz*, U, INF. *ḍakz*, press violently with the hand; calumniate, slander.

(ضكضك) *ḍakḍak*, INF. ة, press; walk apace; — II. INF. *taḍakḍuk*, rejoice; — ة *ḍakḍaka-t*, quick walk; throng, crowd, press.

(ضكل) *ḍakl*, small quantity of water.

(ضل) *ḍall*, I, INF. *ḍalâl*, *ḍalâla-t*, go astray, wander; err, commit an error or fault; be unknown;

be lost; lose; die and moulder; be concealed or contained in; forget; — for *ḍalil*, A, miss (a road, &c.); — II. INF. *taḍlîl*, cause to wander or err, lead astray; seduce; corrupt; accuse of error; lose; — IV. INF. *iḍlâl*, cause to err; lead into or keep in error; lose; bury in the ground, conceal; — V. INF. *taḍallul*, err, commit an error; — X. INF. *istiḍlâl*, allow one to fall into error or destruction.

ضل *ḍall*, error; — ضل بن ضل *ḍillu bnu ḍill-in*, *ḍullu bnu ḍull-in*, who persists in error, utterly reprobate, unknown by his own or his father's merits; ضل الاضلال *ḍullu 'l-aḍlâl*, utterly reprobate, quite abject, worthless; — *ḍull*, loss; going astray (s.), error, aberration; — ة *ḍalla-t*, aberration of the mind; error; going astray (s.); talk of the absent; worthless; — *ḍilla-t*, error; fault; *ḍillat-an*, with impunity; لضلة *li-ḍilla-t*, illegitimate; — *ḍulla-t*, skill as a guide.

ضلاضل *ḍalâḍil*, remainder of water; — *ḍulâḍil*, clever guide.

ضلاعة *ḍalâ'a-t*, strength; strongly built.

ضلال *ḍalâl*, ة *ḍalâla-t*, INF. of (ضل); error; destruction; — *ḍullâl*, pl. wanderers.

(ضلضل) *ḍalḍal*, *ḍulaḍil*, *ḍulḍul*, stony; — ة *ḍalḍala-t*, error; — *ḍalḍala-t*, *ḍulḍula-t*, *ḍulaḍila-t*, stones which a man can lift up; stony, rugged (ground which easily makes one lose one's way).

(ضلع) *ḍala'*, bend, incline (n.); wrong, do violence to (على *'ala*); be crooked; fill one's self with food or drink (up to the ribs); beat on the ribs; — *ḍali'*, A, INF. *ḍala'*, be crooked; be lame, limp (from nature; if by accident, they say *ḍala'*, INF. *ḍal'*); — *ḍalu'*, INF. *ḍalâ'a-t*, have strong ribs; (m.) be equal to a burden; — II. INF. *taḍlî'*, bend, incline (a.); make crooked; make a work difficult or awkward, undo; — IV. INF. *iḍlâ'*, bend (a.), cause to lean; — V. INF. *taḍallu'*, fill one's self to the ribs; — VIII. INF. *iḍḍilâ'*, be able to bear.

ضلع *ḍal'*, leaning towards, inclination; — *ḍil'*, *ḍila'* (f.); pl. *ḍulû'*, *aḍlâ'*, *aḍlu'*, *aḍâli'*, rib; side of a triangle, base; square number; *ḍulû'*, hilly tracts, roads in such; — *ḍul'*, pl. of اضلع *aḍla'* and ضليع *ḍalî'*; — *ḍala'*, strength; endurance, perseverance; pressing debt; crookedness, lameness; — *ḍila'*, isolated low mountain; tract of land; line; anything resembling a rib; lute; mark by branding behind the ribs; — *ḍali'*, crooked and lame; — ة *ḍil'a-t*, side; — *ḍila'a-t*, a small fish.

ضلعا *ḍula'â*, pl. of ضليع *ḍalî'*.

ضلفع *ḍalfa'*, INF. ة, shave the head.

ضلفة *ḍalfa-t*, pl. *ḍalf*, window-shutter.

ضلل *ḍalal*, error; running water.

ضلوعة *ḍalû'a-t*, slightly bent bow.

ضلول *ḍalûl*, loitering about; wanderer.

(ضلى) *ḍalâ*, I, INF. *ḍaly*, perish; — V. INF. *taḍallî*, join the erring and heretics.

ضليع *ḍalî'*, pl. *ḍul'*, *aḍlâ'*, having strong ribs; strongly-made; enduring; have a large mouth and closely-set teeth.

ضليل *ḍalîl*, *ḍallîl*, who greatly errs.

(ضم) *ḍamm*, U, INF. *ḍamm*, gather, hoard, join, bring near; concentrate, centralise; gird; mark or pronounce with ضمة *ḍamma-t*; — III. INF. *muḍâmma-t*, join (a.), adjoin to one's self; — VI. INF. *taḍâmm*, join, assemble (n.); be joined, associated; — VII. INF. *inḍimâm*, get joined,

added, annexed; associate with (الى *ila*); — VIII. INF. *iḍṭimâm*, associate to one's self, take to one's self; contain, comprehend; — X. INF. *istiḍmâm*, receive.

ضم *ḍamm*, hoarding (s.), INF. of (ضم); — *ḍamm*, ة *ḍamma-t*, the vowel *u*; — *ḍimm*, great calamity; — ة *ḍamma-t*, pl. race-horses.

ضماد *ḍamâd*, poultice; — *ḍimâd*, ة *ḍimâda-t*, bandage; plaster; — *ḍimâd*, having (s.) two lovers.

ضمار *ḍimâr*, anything uncertain; an idol.

ضمارز *ḍumâriz*, big; old and milkless.

ضماريط *ḍamârîṭ*, pl. of ضمروط *ḍumrûṭ*.

ضمازر *ḍumâzir*, strong.

ضماضم *ḍumâḍim*, lion; angry.

ضمام *ḍimâm*, *ḍumâm*, cement; — *ḍumâm*, great calamity: — ة *ḍimâma-t*, burden, bundle; du. the edges of a book; — *ḍamâma-t*, book-cover.

ضمان *ḍamân*, security, bail; farming (s. of taxes); — also ة *ḍamâna-t*, bodily infirmity; palsy; — *ḍimân*, reward; compensation, damages.

ضمائن *ḍamâ'in*, natural gifts.

(ضمج) *ḍamij*, U, INF. *ḍamj*, rub the body with perfume until it almost drops off; — *ḍamij*, A, INF. *ḍamaj*, rut; adhere to the ground; — II. INF. *taḍmîj*, rub in, smear with; — IV. INF. *iḍmâj*, adhere to the ground.

(ضمحل) *ḍamḥal*, INF. ة, disperse, dissipate; — III. *iḍmaḥall*, INF. *iḍmiḥlâl*, depart, disappear; be driven away; be loosened.

(ضمحن), III. *iḍmaḥann*, INF. *iḍmiḥnân*=the previous.

(ضمخ) *ḍamaḥ*, U, INF. *ḍamḥ*, rub or smear a thing with perfume until it almost drops; — II. INF. *taḍmîḥ*, id.; — V. INF. *taḍammuḥ*, VII. INF. *inḍimâḥ*, VIII. INF. *iḍṭimâḥ*, be rubbed, anointed; — ة *ḍimḥa-t*, fat, plump; dropping juice (date).

(ضمخر) *ḍummaḥr*, proud; big and fat.

(ضمخز) *ḍimaḥz*, *ḍumaḥz*, big, stout.

(ضمد) *ḍamad*, U, I, INF. *ḍamd*, dress a wound; twist a bandage or fillet round the head; strike on the head; have two lovers; flatter, cajole; — *ḍamid*, A, INF. *ḍamad*, be dry, wither; hate; — II. INF. *taḍmîd*, dress a wound; gather, assemble (a.); begin to form leaves; — V. INF. *taḍammud*, be dressed with a bandage.

ضمد *ḍamd*, wet, moist, damp; dry; fat; lean; best or worst head of a flock; woman with two lovers; — *ḍimd*, friend; — *ḍamad*, dryness; hatred; arrear of a debt, INF. of (ضمد).

(ضمر) *ḍamar*, U, INF. *ḍumûr*, *ḍamur*, be slender, have thin flanks; be weak, small, frail; — II. INF. *taḍmîr*, reduce a horse from fat to lean food, emaciate it by exercise in the race-course; — IV. INF. *iḍmâr*, id.; conceal one's thoughts; make disappear; meditate, contemplate a thing, imagine; use one's best endeavours; — V. INF. *taḍammur*, grow thin, get wrinkled (face); — VIII. INF. *iḍṭimâr*, have thin flanks.

ضمر *ḍamr*, ة, thin, slender; narrow; have thin eye-brows or eye-bones; concealment; — *ḍumr*, *ḍumur*, leanness, slenderness; — *ḍummar*, pl. of ضامر, slender, flexible.

ضمران *ḍamrân*, sweet basil; — *ḍumrân*, a dog.

(ضمرز) *ḍamraz*, INF. ة, be disagreeable, difficult, rough.

ضمرز *ḍamraz*, lion; — *ḍamruz*, hard ground; — *ḍimriz*, old and milkless; strong; — ة *ḍamruza-t*, rugged ground; corpulent, disagreeable (woman).

(ضمروط) *ḍumrûṭ*, secret or narrow place; pl. *ḍamârîṭ*, wrinkle between the nose and cheek.
(ضمز) *ḍamaz*, U, I, INF. *ḍamz*, be silent; pause in chewing the cud; watch carefully over another's property; be stingy with (على *'ala*); swallow the morsel.
ضمز *ḍamz*, rugged place; isolated hill with red stones.
(ضمزر) *ḍamzar*, INF. ة, be disagreeable, difficult, rough.
ضمزر *ḍamzar*, hard; corpulent, big; lion; — *ḍimzir*, strong.
(ضمس) *ḍamas*, I, INF. *ḍams*, chew secretly.
ضمضام *ḍamḍâm*, who takes everything.
(ضمضم) *ḍamḍam*, INF. ة, summon one's courage, raise one's self to heroism; take everything; roar.
ضمضم *ḍamḍam*, corpulent; — also *ḍumaḍim*, lion; angry, bold.
(ضمعج) *ḍam'aj*, pl. *ḍamâ'ij*, stout and well-made.
(ضمك), XI. *iḍma'akk*, INF. *iḍmîkâk*, be full of sap; sprout forth (a.); swell.
(ضمن) *ḍamin*, A, INF. *ḍamn*, *ḍamân*, stand security; take in farm (taxes, &c.); ail, have a bodily infirmity; — II. INF. *taḍmîn*, impose a duty upon (acc.); make one responsible for; leave or lend for use; rent or farm out; put into a case; bury; insert; give to understand, imply; — V. INF. *taḍammun*, stand security, give a pledge; be warranted, assured; be farmed out; take under one's protection; buy or hire from; contain.
ضمن *ḍimn*, inside, interior, contents; enclosure (of a letter); (*ḍimn-an*, enclosed, herewith); envelope; endorsement; meaning, idea; security, assurance; help; — *ḍaman*, indisposition, ailment; — *ḍamin*, pl. *ḍamna*, unwell, ailing, lingering; invalid; love-sick, in love; implicit; warranted; — ة *ḍumna-t*, bodily infirmity, ailment.
ضمنى *ḍamna*, pl. of ضمن *ḍamin*; — *ḍimniyy*, enclosed, annexed.
ضموز *ḍamûz*, silent; lion; isolated hill with red stones.
ضموم *ḍamûm*, river between two mountains.
(ضمى) *ḍama*, I, INF. *ḍamy*, wrong.
ضمير *ḍamîr*, pl. *ḍamâ'ir*, mind, heart, soul, consciousness; thought, idea; secret; pronoun; dried grapes, raisins; — *ḍimmîr*, secret.
(ضميل) *ḍamîl*, dry; — ة *ḍamîla-t*, limping, decrepit (f.).
ضميم *ḍamîm*, joined, added, annexed; — ة *ḍamîma-t*, pl. *ḍamâ'im*, addition, increase; supplement.
ضمين *ḍamîn*, who stands bail or security; who undertakes, contractor.
(ضن) *ḍann* (1 pret. *ḍanin-tu*), I, A, INF. *ḍanâna-t*, *ḍinn*, adhere to, cling to; be miserly; — VIII. INF. *iḍṭinân*, id.
ضن *ḍan'*, *ḍin'*, see ضنا; — *ḍan-in*, see ضنى *ḍanî*; — *ḍinn*, avaricious, miserly; peculiar by nature; — ة *ḍanna-t*, economy, parsimony.
(ضنا) *ḍana'*, ضنى *ḍanî'*, A, INF. *ḍan'*, *ḍunû'*, have many children; abound; disappear, depart; hide (n.); — IV. INF. *iḍnâ'*, have many children; have plenty of cattle; — VIII. INF. *iḍṭinâ'*, be ashamed and withdraw.
ضنا, ضن, *ḍan'*, *ḍin'*, pl. *ḍunû'*, children, numerous progeny; root; origin; — *ḍin'*, a mineral; — ة *ḍun'a-t*, *ḍunâ'a-t*, need, distress; grief, sorrow.
ضناط *ḍinâṭ*, people thronging to a well.
ضناك *ḍanâk*, *ḍinâk*, firm of flesh; have swelling hips; — *ḍunâk*,

cold, rheum; — *ḍun'ak*, ة, big, tall; firm of flesh; — ة *ḍanâka-t* weakness of character; narrowness, straitness; extreme need.
ضنانة *ḍanâna-t*, INF. of (ضن).
ضنائن *ḍanâ'in*, pl. divine gifts; surpassing qualities.
(ضنب) *ḍanab*, I, INF. *ḍamb*, throw on the ground; seize.
(ضنبس) *ḍimbis*, enervated.
(ضندل) *ḍandal*, big-headed.
(ضنط) *ḍanaṭ*, U, INF. *ḍanṭ*, take two lovers; — *ḍaniṭ*, A, INF. *ḍanaṭ*, have firm flesh; — VII. INF. *indinâṭ*, press one another, throng.
ضنط *ḍanṭ*, narrowness, straitness; woman with two lovers; — *ḍanaṭ*, liveliness, briskness, nimbleness; scarcity of corn; fat.
(ضنك) *ḍanuk*, INF. *ḍank*, *ḍanâka-t*, *ḍunûka-t*, be narrow; — INF. *ḍanâka-t*, be weak in body and mind; (m.) be in extreme distress; be hard, severe; — *ḍanik*, A, pass in poverty (life); — pass. *ḍunik*, have a cold.
ضنك *ḍank*, *ḍanik*, weak of intellect; narrow, strait; distressed, poverty-stricken; hard, severe; — *ḍank*, distress; — ة *ḍunka-t*, cold, rheum.
ضنن *ḍanan*, able, clever, skilful; brave.
ضنو *ḍanw*, *ḍinw*, children, progeny; — *ḍunû'*, pl. of ضنا *ḍan'*; INF. of (ضنا).
ضنوط *ḍanûṭ*, woman with two lovers.
ضنوكة *ḍunûka-t*, narrowness, straitness.
ضنى *ḍana*, *ḍanî*, I, A, INF. *ḍanâ'*, *ḍana-n*, have many children; grow larger and be abundant; — *ḍanî*, A, INF. *ḍana-n*, linger with disease; be thin and small; — III. INF. *muḍânât*, torment, vex; — IV. INF. *iḍnâ'*, torment, molest, weaken, consume slowly; — VII. INF. *inḍinâ'*, linger; grow thin, emaciate (n.); get worn out; — VIII. INF. *iḍṭinâ'*, be ill, linger, be emaciated.
ضنى *ḍanî* (ضن *ḍan-in*), ة, thin, emaciated; ill, lingering; — *ḍanan*, id.; sickness, lingering illness (as from love); — *ḍani'*, (v.) see (ضنا).
ضنيك *ḍanîk*, weak; weak of intellect; servant; poverty; cut off.
ضنين *ḍanîn*, avaricious, who clings to, miser.
(ضه) *ḍahh*, U, INF. *ḍahh*, resemble (with acc.).
(ضها), III. INF. *muḍâhât*=the previous; treat kindly.
(ضهب) *ḍahab*, A, INF. *ḍahb*, bring on a change by fire; — INF. *ḍuhûb*, be weak, unlike a man; — II. INF. *tadhîb*, roast on a hot stone or imperfectly; hold the bow to the fire to straighten it; — III. INF. *muḍâhaba-t*, treat one meanly.
ضهب *ḍahb*, mixed, medley.
ضهبا *ḍahbâ'*, straightened by the fire.
(ضهت) *ḍahat*, INF. *ḍaht*, stamp any thing into the ground.
(ضهج), IV. INF. *iḍhâj*, miscarry (she-camel).
(ضهد) *ḍahad*, INF. *ḍahd*, do violence to, treat unjustly and tyrannically; persecute, press hard; — VIII. INF. *iḍṭihâd*, do violence to (acc.), persecute; — ة *ḍuhda-t*, who submits to everybody.
(ضهر) *ḍahr*, pl. *ḍuhûr*, mountain-peak; tortoise.
(ضهز) *ḍahaz*, INF. *ḍahz*, tread violently under foot; lie with; chew in the front part of the mouth.
(ضهزم) *ḍihzim*, low, mean, vile.
(ضهس) *ḍahas*, chew in the front part of the mouth.
(ضهضب) *ḍahḍab*, INF. ة, gather (fire-wood).
(ضهل) *ḍahal*, INF. *ḍuhûl*, gather (n.) in the vessel; — INF. *ḍahl*, *ḍuhûl*, gather (n.) in small

quantities, by degrees; have little milk; be scarce; yield little water; give too little; return; come to (الى *ila*); — IV. INF. *iḍhâl*, have dates on the point of ripening; be on the point of ripening; — X. INF. *istiḍhâl*, question as much as possible.

ضهل *ḍahl*, milk in a vessel; little water; anything collected; — *ḍuhul*, pl. of ضهول *ḍahûl*; — ة *ḍahla-t*, a little, a trifle.

ضهوا *ḍahwâ'*, without vegetation; woman without bosom.

ضهول *ḍahûl*, pl. *ḍuhal*, yielding but little milk or water; laying many eggs; — *.

ضهوة *ḍahwa-t*, pl. *aḍhâ'*, pond.

(ضهى) *ḍahî*, A, INF. *ḍaha-n*, have no menses, no bosom and no milk; produce nothing; — III. INF. *muḍâhât*, resemble (with acc.); — IV. INF. *iḍhâ'*, let the camels graze on thistles; marry a woman without menses, bosom or milk.

ضهى *ḍahiyy*, similar, corresponding; — *ḍuhy*, pl. of ضهيا *ḍahyâ'*.

(ضهيا) *ḍahya'*, INF. ة, make one's affairs worse instead of better, make evil worse.

ضهيا *ḍahyâ'*, ة *ḍahya'a-t*, woman without menses, bosom, or milk; desert; a kind of thistle.

ضهيد *ḍahyad*, hard; firm; strong.

(ضو) *ḍâ'*, U, INF. *ḍau'*, *ḍuwâ'*, shine, glitter, gleam; — II. INF. *taḍwî'a-t*, light up; light, make light; turn from (n.); — III. INF. *muḍâwât*, enlighten, speak clearly to a person; — IV. INF. *iḍâ'a-t*, shine, beam; light up; show in the light; illuminate; — V. INF. *taḍa''u*, stand in the dark and look into a lit-up place; be lighted, lit up, illuminated; — X. *istiḍâ'a-t*, ask for light, enlightenment, advice.

ضو *ḍaw-in*, see ضوى *ḍawî*; — *ḍau'*, *ḍû'*, pl. *aḍwâ'*, light; الضو الازرق *aḍ-ḍau' al-azraq*, twilight; الضو الاسود *aḍ-ḍau' al-aswad*, crepuscule; — ة *ḍuwwa-t*, noise, turmoil, tumult.

ضوا *ḍiwâ'*, light, brightness; — *; — ة *ḍawât*, tumour, swelling; noise, tumult.

ضواجع *ḍawâji'*, crowd of people; pl. of ضاجع *ḍâji'*, bend in a river, &c.

ضواد *ḍu'âd*, INF. of (ضئد).

ضوادى *ḍawâdî*, angering words; lies; flatteries.

ضوارب *ḍawârib*, migrating birds in search of food; pl. of ضارب, situated towards, tract of land, &c.

ضواريب *ḍawârîb*, mutual blows.

ضوازة *ḍuwâza-t*, stick used as a tooth-brush.

ضواضى *ḍuwâḍî*, thick, stout; — ة *ḍuwâḍiya-t*, calamity.

ضواطر *ḍawâṭir*, pl. of ضوطر *ḍauṭar*.

ضواع *ḍuwâ'*, screech of an owl; — *ḍawwâ'*, fox.

ضواكة *ḍawâka-t*, troop, number of people.

ضوال *ḍawâll*, pl. of ضال *ḍâll*, erring, wandering, &c.

ضوائع *ḍawâ'i'*, lean camels.

(ضوب) *ḍâb*, U, INF. *ḍaub*, lay an ambush for an enemy.

ضوبان *ḍaubân*, *ḍûbân*, *ḍu'bân*, big and strong camels; — *ḍûbân*, withers of a camel.

ضوتع *ḍauta'*, blockhead.

(ضوج) *ḍâj*, U, INF. *ḍauj*, bend (n.), deviate; swerve from (عن *'an*); be broad; be wearied, not knowing what to do; — V. INF. *taḍawwuj*, have many windings, meander; — VII. INF. *inḍiyâj*, be broad.

ضوج *ḍauj*, pl. *aḍwâj*, bend of a river.

ضوجان *ḍaujân*, ة *ḍaujâna-t*, hard, dry.

(ضوح), II. *ḍawwaḥ*, INF. *taḍwîḥ*, mix milk with water.

ضود *ḍu'd*, ة *ḍu'da-t*, cold, rheum.

(ضور) *ḍâr*, U, INF. *ḍaur*, suffer from

violent hunger; hurt, injure, damage; — V. INF. *taḍawwur*, writhe; roar from hunger; — X. INF. *istiḍâra-t*, desire the bull.

ضور *ḍaur*, violent hunger; injury; — *ḍûr*, black cloud; — ة *ḍûra-t*, poor; despised.

(ضوز) *ḍâz*, U, INF. *ḍauz*, chew; wrong.

ضوز *ḍauz*, ة *duwaza-t*, toothpick.

ضوزى *ḍu'za*, defective, incomplete.

(ضوس) *ḍâs*, U, INF. *ḍaus*, eat.

ضوضا *ḍauḍâ'*, ة *ḍauḍât*, battle-cry; tumult, clamour, noise.

ضوضو *ḍu'ḍu'*, a bird; also *ḍu'ḍû'*, root, origin; mine; numerous progeny.

(ضوضى) *ḍauḍa*, INF. ة, clamour, be noisy, tumultuous.

(ضوط) *ḍawaṭ*, sprained jaw; — II. *ḍawwaṭ*, INF. *taḍwîṭ*, gather (a.).

ضوطار *ḍauṭâr*, who goes to the market without money in order to earn something.

(ضوطر) *ḍauṭar*, ضيطر *ḍaiṭar*, pl. *-ûn*, *ḍayâṭir*, *ḍayâṭira-t*, big and strong, but good for nothing; ى *ḍauṭarā*, id.; ابو ضوطرى *abû ḍauṭarā*, hunger.

(ضوع) *ḍâ'*, U, INF. *ḍau'*, move, shake, swing (a.); frighten, terrify; molest, bring to grief, agitate; emaciate (a.); feed; be brought in motion and spread an odour (good or bad); writhe while crying; — V. *taḍawwu'*, be moved and spread an odour; also VII. INF. *inḍiyâ'*, writhe; spread the wings to be fed (young birds).

ضوع *ḍiwa'*, *ḍuwa'*, pl. *aḍwâ'*, *ḍi'ân*, owl; screech-owl; crow.

ضوقى *ḍûqā*, f. of اضيق *aḍyaq*, narrower.

(ضوك) *ḍâk*, U, INF. *ḍauk*, cover (stallion); — V. INF. *taḍawwuk*, pollute one's self with one's excrement; — VIII. INF. *iḍṭiwâk*, inveigh against, scold violently.

(ضوكع) *ḍauka'*, INF. ة, get tired with walking; — II. INF. *taḍauku'*, be tired, lazy; — ة *ḍauka'a-t*, heavy and stupid; f. walking with difficulty.

ضولا *ḍu'alâ'*, pl. of ضئيل *ḍa'îl*.

ضولج *ḍaulaj*, fine silver.

ضولة *ḍu'ala-t*, thin, weak.

(ضوم) *ḍâm*, U, INF. *ḍaum*=(ضيم).

ضومران *ḍaumarân*, sweet basil.

(ضون) *ḍân*, INF. *ḍauna-t*, also V. INF. *taḍawwun*, have many children (man).

ضون *ḍaun*, gastric acid of the camel, runnet; — ة *ḍauna-t*, young deer; many children.

(ضوى) *ḍawa*, I, INF. *ḍayy*, *ḍuwiyy*, retire to, take refuge with (الى *ila*); come at night-time; inquire for (الى *ila*); — *ḍawî*, A, INF. *ḍawa-n*, have thin bones, be thin, lean; be weak; wither (n.); — IV. INF. *iḍwâ'*, be weak, thin; wither; weaken; give birth to a weak child; wrong; manage a thing not well; — VII. INF. *inḍiyâ'*, resort to, join, take refuge with (الى *ila*).

ضوى *ḍawî*, thin, lean; having delicate bones; — *ḍawiyy*, shining, bright; (m.) clear space, interval.

ضويضية *ḍuwaiḍiya-t*, calamity; furious stallion; hot she-camel.

ضويطة *ḍawîṭa-t*, mud in water; melted butter; soft dough or paste, bread.

ضويكة *ḍawîka-t*, troop, number of people.

ضى *ḍayy*, INF. of (ضوى).

(ضيا), II. *ḍayya'*, INF. *taḍyi'a-t*, have many children.

ضيا *ḍiyâ'*, light, brightness, gleam.

ضياح *ḍayâḥ*, watery.

ضياريب *ḍayârîb*, pl. of ضيراب *ḍairâb*.

ضياط *ḍayyâṭ*, fat and shuffling in walking.

ضياطر *ḍayâṭir*, ة *ḍayâṭira-t*, pl. of ضوطر *ḍauṭar*.

ضياع *ḍayâ'*, people of the household; attendants; an aroma; INF. of (ضيع); ruin, destruction,

loss; — *ḍiyâ'*, pl. of ضائع *ḍâ'i'*, lost, &c., and of ضيعة *ḍai'a-t*.

ضيافة *ḍiyâfa-t*, being a guest; hospitality; invitation; entertainment, banquet; دار الض *dâr aḍ-ḍiyâfa-t*, hospitable convent; inn.

ضياق *ḍiyâq*, INF. of (ضيق).

ضئال *ḍi'âl*, pl. of ضئيل *ḍa'îl*.

ضيان *ḍayân*, lasting, enduring, strong.

ضياون *ḍayâwin*, pl. of ضيون *ḍaiwan*.

ضيائي *ḍiyâ'iyy*, shining, bright, brilliant.

ضئب *ḍi'b*, *ḍaib*, pearl; an animal of the sea.

(ضئبل) *ḍi'bil*, *ḍi'bul*, calamity.

ضيثم *ḍaisam*, lion.

(ضيج) *ḍâj*, I, INF. *ḍuyûj*, *ḍayajân*, lean to one side, incline (n.).

(ضيح) *ḍâḥ*, I, INF. *ḍaiḥ*, water the milk; be deserted; — II. INF. *taḍyîḥ*, give watered milk to drink; — V. *taḍayyuḥ*, be watered; drink watered milk.

ضيح *ḍaiḥ*, watered milk; honey; wild dates; — *ḍîḥ*, sun.

(ضير) *ḍâr*, I, INF. *ḍair*, injure, hurt, harm.

ضيراب *ḍîrâb*, pl. *ḍayârîb*, *ḍawârîb*, mutual blows.

ضيرم *ḍairam*, burnt.

(ضيز) *ḍâz*, I, INF. *ḍaiz*, wrong; oppress, tyrannize over (acc.).

ضيزان *ḍaizân*, stallion who has never covered.

ضيزن *ḍaizan*, who loves or marries his father's wife; who wants to draw water first; forestaller; punctual, reliable; family.

ضيزى *ḍîza*, *ḍi'za*, defective, incomplete.

(ضيس) *ḍâs*, I, INF. *ḍais*, begin to wither.

ضيس *ḍais*, *ḍayyis*, beginning to wither.

ضئضئ *ḍi'ḍi'*, *ḍi'ḍiyy*=ضوضو *ḍu'ḍu'*.

(ضيط) *ḍâṭ*, I, INF. *ḍaiṭ*, *ḍayaṭân*,— *ḍa'iṭ*, A, INF. *ḍa'aṭ*, walk with a shake of the shoulders and fleshy parts.

ضئط *ḍa'iṭ*, who walks in the above manner.

ضيطار *ḍaiṭâr*, see ضوطار *ḍauṭâr*.

ضيطان *ḍayaṭân*, INF. of (ضيط, ضيطن *ḍaiṭan*); — *ḍaiṭân*, whose shoulders shake from fat.

ضيطر *ḍaiṭar*, see ضوطر *ḍauṭar*.

ضيطن *ḍaiṭan*, INF. ة, *ḍayaṭân*=(ضيط).

(ضيع) *ḍâ'*, I, INF. *ḍai'*, *ḍi'*, *ḍaya'*, *ḍai'a-t*, perish; lose one's way, go astray; spread an odour; — II. INF. *taḍyî'*, destroy by negligence; lose, waste, squander; — IV. INF. *iḍâ'a-t*, id.; have great landed property, many estates; — V. INF. *taḍayyu'*, spread an odour; — X. INF. *istiḍâ'a-t*, deem lost (m.).

ضيع *ḍai'*, loss; — *ḍuyya'*, pl. of ضائع *ḍâ'i'*, lost, &c.; — ة *ḍai'a-t*, pl. *ḍiya'*, *ḍiyâ'*, *ḍai'ât*, landed estate; immovable goods; field; land and sea; occupation, trade, handicraft; lack, INF. of (ضيع).

ضيعان *ḍî'ân*, pl. of ضوع *ḍiwa'*, *ḍuwa'*; — *ḍaya'ân*, loss; يا ضيعانه *yâ ḍaya'âna-ku*, what a pity for him! (m.)

ضيغم *ḍaigam*, ى *ḍaigamiyy*, biter; lion.

(ضيف) *ḍâf*, I, INF. *ḍaif*, *ḍiyâfa-t*, alight as a guest; befall; INF. *ḍaif*, lean towards; decline towards setting; miss the aim, swerve; have the menses; — II. INF. *taḍyîf*, lean or incline towards; bend (a.); cause to alight as a guest; receive hospitably; — IV. INF. *iḍâfa-t*, bend, incline (a.); cause to alight as a guest or seek refuge with (الى *ila*); receive hospitably; join, add, put two nouns in the state of construction; lean against (a.); be in fear or anxiety; flee; run fast; be near, on the point of; — V. INF. *taḍayyuf*, alight as a guest; decline; — VI. INF. *taḍâyuf*, be close to one's side; be in relation to

one another; — VII. INF. *indiyâf*, be or come near to, touch, join; be added or joined; — X. INF. *istidâfa-t*, seek help, refuge or hospitality.

ضيف *daif*, pl. *adyâf*, *duyûf*, *dîfân*, *adâyif*, guest, stranger (also f.); — *dîf*, arm; du. *dîfân*, the two banks of a river; — ة *daifa-t*, female guest, strange woman; woman who has the menses.

ضيفن *daifan*, companion of a guest; unbidden comer, intruder, parasite, sponger.

(ضيق) *dâq*, I, INF. *daiq*, *dîq*, be narrow, strait, straitened; shrink; be beyond one's power (عنه *'an-hu*); press (as time); be oppressed, impatient (heart); be narrow-minded, close, miserly; — II. INF. *tadyîq*, straiten, make narrow or too narrow; bring into distress; restrain; be hard, severe towards; keep in close confinement; — III. INF. *mudâyaqa-t*, oppress, treat with harshness or severity; — IV. INF. *idâqa-t*, make narrow, straiten; fall into distress; — V. INF. *tadayyuq* (also VI.), be narrow; find one's self hemmed in; — VI. INF. *tadâyuq*, see V.; make a hostile onset upon (على *'ala*); — VII. INF. *indiyâq*, find one's self in a strait, in distress (m.).

ضيق *daiq*, *dîq*, strait, distress, poverty; anxiety; doubt; — *daiq*, *dayyiq*, narrow, strait; restrained; avaricious, miserly; — ة *daiqa-t*, one of the stations of the moon; — *daiqa-t*, *dîqa-t*, pl. *dîq*, distress, poverty, straitness of circumstances; anguish.

ضيقى *dîqā*, f. of اضيق *adyaq*, narrower.

(ضيك) *dâk*, I, INF. *daik*, *daikân*, burn with rage against (على *'ala*).

ضيكل *daikal*, pl. *dayâkil*, *dayâkila-t*, thick, fleshy; naked, poor.

ضئل *da'il*, pl. *di'âl*, thin, lean, weak.

(ضيم) *dâm*, I, INF. *daim*, injure, wrong; deceive; oppress; — IV. INF. *idâma-t*, id.; cause pain (illness); — VII. INF. *indiyâm*, be injured; suffer, be afflicted with a fatal disease (m.); — X. INF. *istidâma-t*, hurt, injure, oppress, assail.

ضيم *daim*, pl. *duyûm*, injustice; oppression; injury; assault; — *dîm*, mountain-slope.

ضيمران *daimurân*, an aromatic plant.

(ضين), III. INF. *mudâyana-t*, serve a long time, last long.

ضئنى *di'niyy*, lambskin bag for making butter.

ضيهب *daihab*, roasting-spit; place for roasting.

ضيور *dayûr*, want, need, distress.

ضئولة *du'ûla-t*, slimness, slenderness.

ضيون *daiwan*, pl. *dayâwin*, wild cat; tom-cat.

ضييعة *duyai'a-t*, little estate.

ضئيل *da'îl*, pl. *du'alâ'*, *di'âl*, thin, lean; weak; poor; — ة *da'îla-t*, a snake; uvula, glottis.

ضئين *da'în*, pl. of ضان *da'n* and ضائن *dâ'in*, sheep; — *duyain*, *duyayyin*, also—

ضييون *duyaiwin*, small wild cat, tom-cat.

ط

ط *ṭ*, as a numerical sign=9; symbol for capricorn as the ninth sign in the zodiac; in the Koran abbreviation for مطلق *muṭlaq*, generally acknowledged pause.

طا *ṭâ*, name of the letter ط *ṭ*; — ة *ṭâ'a-t*, clay, mud; — *ta'a-t*, INF. of (وطی), tread, &c.

طاب *ṭâb*, perfume, fragrance; — ة *ṭâba-t*, wine; Medina; (m.) ball, game at balls.

طاباق *ṭâbâq*, large brick.

طابان *ṭâbân*, damasked blade.

طابخ *ṭâbiḫ*, pl. *ṭubbaḫ*, cook; angel of hell; fever; — ة *ṭâbiḫa-t*, mid-day heat.

طابع *ṭâba'*, *ṭâbi'*, pl. *ṭawâbi'*, seal-ring; die for branding; stamp; impression; — *ṭâbi'*, printer; who seals; stamps, marks; firm gait.

طابق *ṭâbaq*, *ṭâbiq*, pl. *ṭawâbiq*, *ṭawâbîq*, large brick; frying-pan; cellar, cave; trap-door; storey, floor; limb; hand; half of a sheep; what is sufficient for two or three persons.

طابن *ṭâbiň*, very intelligent, clever.

طابور *ṭâbûr*, legion.

طابون *ṭâbûn*, fire-hole.

طاجن *ṭâjin*, *ṭâjin*, pl. *ṭawâjin*, frying-pan.

طاح *ṭâḥ-in*, see طاحی *ṭâḥî*.

طاحل *ṭâḥil*, troubled, turbid; ill-coloured.

طاحن *ṭâḥin*, who grinds; miller; ox in a tread-mill; — also ة *ṭâḥina-t*, pl. *ṭawâḥin*, molar tooth.

طاحون *ṭâḥûn*, ة *ṭâḥûna-t*, water-mill, mill.

طاحی *ṭâḥî* (طاح *ṭâḥ-in*), extended; wide and high; filling everything; crowd of people.

طاخر *ṭâḫir*, darkening cloud.

طاخی *ṭâḫî* (طاخ *ṭâḫ-in*), thick, dense.

طاد *ṭâd*, hot, rutting (she-camel); heavy, clumsy; — *ṭâd-in*=

طادی *ṭâdî*, ة, ancient, of old.

طار *ṭâr*, circle, disc; tambourine; a circle of people; — *ṭârr*, whose moustache is beginning to grow.

طارد *ṭârid*, pursuer, persecutor; expeller.

طارف *ṭârif*, newly-acquired or dis-covered; new, interesting, rare; — ة *ṭârifa-t*, plenty of money; new acquisitions; pl. *ṭawârif*, eye; dormer-window in a tent; beasts of prey.

طارق *ṭâriq*, ة, pl. *ṭurrâq*, who beats; night-traveller; soothsayer; morning-star; — ة *ṭârîqa-t*, pl. *ṭawâriq*, family, tribe, race; small seat; event; calamity befalling in the night; female soothsayer.

طارقية *ṭârîqiyya-t*, collar; neck-tie.

طارمة *ṭârima-t*, wooden house with a high roof.

طارونی *ṭârûniyy*, raw silk.

طاری *ṭârî*, pl. *ṭurrâ'*, *ṭur'â'*, coming up suddenly; — ة *ṭârî'a-t*, cala-mity.

طازج *ṭâzaj*, fresh; healthy, sound, pure; — ة *ṭâzija-t*, pl. *ṭawâzij*, genuine coin.

طاس *ṭâs*, pl. *ṭâsât*, cup, saucer; plate, tray; brocade; طاس افلاك *ṭâs aflâk*, sky; — ة *ṭâssa-t*, pene-trating deeply; (m.) pl. *ṭusûs*, saucer, cup.

طاط *ṭâṭ*, long; slender; strong; quarrelsome; hot, rutting; cotton; — ة *ṭâṭa-t*, pl. of طائط *ṭâ'iṭ*.

(طاطا) *ṭa'ṭa'*, INF. ة, hang the head; throw down; let in; relax the reins to make the horse run faster; urge on with the thighs; squander rapidly one's own; — II. INF. *taṭa'ṭu'*,

hang down; hang the head before (الى *ila*); be bent, inclined; be low.

طاطا *ṭa'ṭa'*, camel with a short and thick neck; deepening of the ground.

طاع *ṭâ'*, obedient; — ة *ṭâ'a-t*, obedience; submissiveness; worship of God.

طاعن *ṭâ'in*, piercing, thrusting; penetrating deeply (ط فى السن *ṭâ'in fi 's-sinn*, deep in years, aged); blaming (adj.); slanderer.

طاعون *ṭâ'ûn*, pl. *ṭawâ'in*, the plague; rampant disease, epidemic.

طاغوت *ṭâgût*, pl. *ṭawâgît*, *ṭawâgî*, name of an idol; Satan; sorcerer, soothsayer; rebel; impostor; seducer, tempter; sectarian, heretic.

طاغى *ṭâgî* (طاغ *ṭâg-in*), disobedient; rebel; tyrant; Byzantine emperor; (m.) seducer; liar, impostor; — ة *ṭâgiya-t*, pl. *ṭawâgî*, chief of rebels; tyrant; Byzantine emperor; proud and insolent; an idol; lightning and thunder-clap; cry of pain; sins.

طاف *ṭâf*, who walks about much; wool in the neck; — *ṭâf-in*, see طافى *ṭâfî*; — ة *ṭâfa-t*, wave of ground; enclosure of a garden.

طافح *ṭâfiḥ*, full to overflowing.

طافلة *ṭâfila-t*, good, benefit, advantage.

طافى *ṭâfî* (طاف *ṭâf-in*), extinguished, gone out; swimming on the top, floating.

طاق *ṭâq*, pl. *ṭâqât*, *ṭîqân*, arch; vault; cupola, dome; a tree; a garment; open; mountain-knoll; projecting part; balcony; window; throne; opening, hole; unique, odd, strange; one of two pieces; fold, layer, stratum; — pl. *ṭûq*, thread in a rope; — ة *ṭâqa-t*, might, power, capacity, faculty; patience; rest; arch of a vault; window; opening; hole in a wall; layer, stratum, row; thread; bundle; handful.

طاقم *ṭâqim*, pl. *ṭuqûm*, handsome new garment; armour (m.).

طاقية *ṭâqiya-t*, *ṭâqiyya-t*, pl. *ṭawâqî*, fillet; white under-cap; balcony; projecting roof; cornice.

طال *ṭâl-in*, see طالى *ṭâlî*; — ة *ṭâla-t*, she-ass.

طالب *ṭâlib*, pl. *ṭullâb*, *ṭullab*, *ṭalaba-t*, *ṭalab*, ag. of (طلب), who demands, seeks, &c.; beggar; examining judge; investigator, searcher; — ة *ṭâliba-t*, hot (bitch).

طالح *ṭâliḥ*, pl. *-ûn*, *ṭullaḥ*, *ṭullâḥ*, bad, corrupt; tired, sullen.

طالع *ṭâli'*, pl. *ṭawâli'*, ag. of (طلع), ascending, rising, appearing, &c.; twilight; new moon; star; lucky star; fate, destiny.

طالق *ṭâliq*, pl. *ṭullaq*, divorced; left at large; — ة *ṭâliqa-t*, pl. *ṭawâliq*, id.; mild.

طالم *ṭâlim*, pl. *ṭalama-t*, baker.

طالما *ṭâla-mâ*, *ṭâl-mâ*, it is a long time since . . . . ; frequently.

طالوت *ṭâlût*, طالوط *ṭâlûṭ*, King Saul.

طالى *ṭâlî* (طال *ṭâl-in*), covered with green mud; dark.

طاليان *ṭâliyân*, ى *ṭâliyâniyy*, Italian (adj., s.).

طام *ṭâmm*, victorious; — ة *ṭâmma-t*, calamity; resurrection.

طامث *ṭâmiṣ*, having the menses.

طامح *ṭâmiḥ*, high; high-minded; violent.

طامر *ṭâmir*, flea; ط بن طامر *ṭâmir bnu ṭâmir*, perfect stranger.

طامس *ṭâmis*, pl. *ṭawâmis*, far distant, invisible; effaced; heartless; who conceals.

طامع *ṭâmi'*, pl. *ṭuma'â'*, *ṭamâ'a*, *aṭmâ'*, desirous, greedy; ambitious; — ة *ṭâmi'a-t*, appetite.

طامل *ṭâmil*, corrupt, shameless.

طامور *ṭâmûr*, pl. *ṭawâmîr*, book, volume, roll.

طامى *ṭâmî*, swelling, overflowing.

طان *ṭân*, loamy, clayey; body.

طانز *ṭâniz*, satirical, sarcastic.
طانی *ṭânî*, pl. *ṭunât*, fornicator.
طاهر *ṭâhir*, ة, pl. *aṭhâr*, *ṭahârā*, *-ûn*, pure; chaste; not having the menses.
طاهل *ṭâhil*, foul (water).
طاهی *ṭâhî*, pl. *ṭuhât*, *ṭuha-n*, cook; baker; cooking, &c.
طاوس *ṭâ'us*, *ṭâwus*, طاووس *ṭâwûs*, pl. *aṭwâs*, *ṭawâwîs*, peacock; dandy, fop; green fields; silver.
طاوی *ṭâwî*, ة, hungry; who folds; — *ṭâwiyy*, somebody, anybody.
طائب *ṭâ'ib*, good, handsome, right.
طائح *ṭa'iḥ*, lost, gone astray; (m.) who throws himself down from on high.
طائر *ṭâ'ir*, flying; pl. *ṭair*, *aṭyâr*, *ṭuyûr*, bird; angel; deed, work, task; fore-token (evil); anger, passion; brain; dignity, honour, good fortune; daily bread.
طائش *ṭâ'iś*, light-minded, flighty, fickle; absent-minded, thoughtless.
طائط *ṭâ'iṭ*, pl. *ṭâṭa-t*, *aṭwâṭ*, angry, quarrelsome, pugnacious; long, tall.
طائع *ṭâ'i'*, pl. *ṭuwwa'*, obedient, willing.
طائف *ṭâ'if*, pl. *ṭuwwâf*, circulating, going round; ox who turns the mill; watchmen, guard, patrol; rampart; projecting rock; good slave; middle of the bow; spectre, phantom, vision, apparition; temptation; — ة *ṭâ'ifa-t*, pl. *ṭawâ'if*, people, tribe, family; guild, band, gang; company; retinue; person, individual; part, portion; du. *ṭâ'ifatân*, Jews and Christians.
طائق *ṭâ'iq*, who can, is able.
طائل *ṭâ'il*, long; might, power; wealth; advantage, profit; excellence; — ة *ṭâ'ila-t*, pl. *ṭawâ'il*, power, wealth, riches; excellence; enmity, hostility, hatred.
طاية *ṭâya-t*, flat roof; plain surface; place for drying; broad stone.

طائی *ṭâ'iyy*, belonging to the tribe of طی *ṭayy*.
(طب) *ṭabb*, I, INF. *ṭabb*, *ṭibb*, *ṭubb*, heal, cure; — INF. *ṭabâba-t*, be a physician; treat gently and kindly; excel in knowledge and art; double the seam of a bag with a strip of leather; (m.) lay one's head upon; make a vessel stand on its mouth; — II. INF. *taṭbîb*, double well the seams of a bag; shake the milk in a suspended bag to make butter; put a piece into a garment to make it wider; (m.) heal, cure; — III. INF. *muṭâbba-t*, heal, cure; — V. INF. *taṭabbub*, be a physician; pretend to be a good physician without being such; (m.) undergo a treatment; — X. INF. *istiṭbâb*, ask for a treatment or remedy, have one's self medically treated.
طب *ṭabb*, ة, able, skilful, practised in (ب *bi*); physician; — *ṭibb*, *ṭubb*, remedy, physic (علم طب *'ilm-u ṭibb-in*, medical science or art); sorcery, magic; art, skill; benevolence, courtesy, politeness; assistance; — *ṭibb*, wish, inclination: natural disposition, habit, state, condition; illness; — ة *ṭibba-t*, pl. *ṭibab*, long strip; goat-skin; long garment open in front; sunbeam; house; — *ṭubba-t*, pl. *ṭibâb*, strip of leather; (m.) plug.
طباب *ṭabâb*, ة *ṭibâba-t*, long cloud; — ة *ṭabâba-t*, medical science; — *ṭibâba-t*, strip of cloth or leather; girth-leather.
طباخ *ṭabâḥ*, *ṭubâḥ*, vigour, strength, firmness; fatness; — *ṭabbâḥ*, cook; — ة *ṭibâḥa-t*, art of cooking; — *ṭubâḥa-t*, what foams over.
طباخية *ṭabâḥiyya-t*, *ṭubâḥiyya-t*, handsome woman.
بنات طبار *banât ṭabâr-a*, great calamities; — *ṭubbâr*, a tree similar to the fig-tree.

طباشير *ṭabâśîr*, chalk; الصبح ط *ṭabâśîr aṣ-ṣubḥ*, morning-dawn.

طباع *ṭibâ'*, natural disposition, nature; temper; intellectual gifts, genius, judgment; — *; — *ṭabbâ'*, furbisher; potter; who seals; printer, typographer; — ة *ṭibâ'a-t*, profession of a *ṭabbâ'*; دار الط *dâr aṭ-ṭibâ'a-t*, printing-house.

طباق *ṭibâq*, ة *ṭibâqa-t*, what fits something else; lid, cover, upper part; antithesis, contrast; — *; — *ṭabbâq*, bookbinder; — *ṭubbâq*, a medicinal tree.

طباقا *ṭabâqâ'*, weak; impotent; fat; stammerer.

طبال *ṭabbâl*, ة *ṭabbâla-t*, drummer; — ة *ṭibâla-t*, beating the drum (s.).

طباة *ṭab'a-t*, nature, disposition.

طباهج *ṭabâhaj*, ة *ṭabâhija-t*, dish of hashed meat, eggs and onions.

طبائب *ṭabâ'ib*, medical sciences.

طبائح *ṭabâ'iḥ*, hot poisonous winds.

طبائعى *ṭabâ'i'iyy*, natural.

طبب *ṭibab*, pl. of طبة *ṭibba-t*.

(طبج) *ṭabaj*, INF. *ṭabj*, beat on the head or anything hollow; — *ṭabij*, A, INF. *ṭabaj*, be stupid, silly, imbecile; — V. INF. *taṭabbuj*, vary in one's speech, make new distinctions.

طبجى *ṭubjiyy*, pl. ة, artilleryman, gunner.

(طبخ) *ṭabaḫ*, U, A, INF. *ṭabḫ*, cook; burn bricks, &c.; bake; make boil; ripen (a.); — II. INF. *taṭbîḫ*, grow up, grow big; cook, ripen (a.); — VII. INF. *inṭibâḫ*, be cooked, baked; — VIII. INF. *iṭṭibâḫ*, id.; make a decoction for one's self.

طبخ *ṭabḫ*, cooking, baking (s.); art of cooking; جيد الط *jayyid aṭ-ṭabḫ*, well-baked, well-done; — *ṭubbaḫ*, pl. of طابخ *ṭâbiḫ*; — ة *ṭabḫa-t*, quite stupid; portion of meat; (m.) almanac, calendar.

(طبر) *ṭabar*, U, INF. *ṭabr*, leap; cover (stallion); conceal one's self, hide (n.).

طبر *ṭibr*, projecting angle; side-curtain; supporting pillar; pure gold (تبر *tibr*); — *ṭabar*, axe, hatchet.

طبرانى *ṭabarâniyy*, of or from Tiberias.

طبردارية *ṭabar-dâriyya-t*, axe-bearers, sappers.

طبرزد *ṭabarzad*, طبرزذ *ṭabarzaẓ*, طبرزل *ṭabarzal*, طبرزن *ṭabarzan*, hard white sugar; sugar-candy; conserves of roses.

طبرزين *ṭabarzîn*, battle-axe (Pers.).

طبرس *ṭabras*, *ṭibris*, liar.

طبرى *ṭabariyy*, of or from Tiberias or Tabaristan; third part of a *dirham*; — ة *ṭabariyya-t*, Tiberias.

(طبز) *ṭabaz*, lie with; fill.

طبز *ṭibz*, mountain-knoll; corner-stone; camel with two humps.

(طبس) *ṭabs*, black; — *ṭibs*, wolf; — *ṭabas*, U, INF. *ṭabs*, sink in mud; — II. *ṭabbas*, INF. *taṭbîs*, smear with mud; roll in the mud (n.); smear or coat with loam; tap on the hand.

طبش *ṭabś*, men, people.

طبطاب *ṭabṭâb*, ة *ṭabṭâba-t*, racket, battledore in the game at balls.

(طبطب) *ṭabṭab*, INF. ة, sound, produce a sound; murmur, ripple, purl; growl, grumble; — II. INF. *taṭabṭub*, id.

طبطبية *ṭabṭabiyya-t*, some braided work with which dancers beat one another.

(طبع) *ṭaba'*, INF. *ṭab'*, seal, stamp, mark, impress; print; coin; stud; rust (a.); forge a sword; form, make; shut up (the heart, على *'ala*); knock on the back part of the head; fill; pass. *ṭubi'*, have the stamp, form, nature of (على *'ala*) a thing; — *ṭabi'*, A, INF. *ṭaba'*, be dirty, filthy, mean; be rusty; be disgraced; pass. id.; — II. INF.

taṭbî‘, impress the seal, &c., strongly, make a strong impression; dirty, soil; fill; burden; (m.) break in a horse, train it for racing; — V. INF. *taṭabbu‘*, have or show such or such a stamp, nature, character; be full; be accustomed; — VII. INF. *inṭibâ‘*, be stamped, impressed; be sealed, printed, printed upon; be tamed, docile.

طبع *ṭab‘*, pl. *ṭibâ‘*, impression of a seal or stamp; coining, printing (s.); nature, character, temper, habit; genius, mind, intellect; model, form, shape; resemblance; — *ṭib‘*, pl. *aṭbâ‘*, river, canal; watering-place; full measure; bag for making butter; rust, dirt; — *ṭaba‘*, rust, dirt; disgrace, ignominy; — *ṭabi‘*, rusty, dirty; miserly; shameless; — ة *ṭabi‘a-t*, proof-sheet.

طبعان *ṭub‘ân*, sealing-wax.

طبعي *ṭab‘iyy*, natural.

(طبق) *ṭabaq*, I, INF. *ṭabq*, cover, veil; close; fold up; fall in upon; — *ṭabiq*, A, INF. *ṭabq*, *ṭabaq*, be shortened, curtailed; cling to the side; be closed; be passed; begin, attempt; — II. INF. *taṭbîq*, cover entirely, provide with a lid or cover; rain over the whole country; be general; fold up; close the hands; pile up in layers; make one thing fit another; place the hands between the thighs (in praying); cut the joint without injuring the bone; hit on the right thing or on the point; lift the two front feet or the two hind feet at the same time in running; — III. INF. *muṭâbaqa-t*, *ṭibâq*, fit (a.), conform (a.), make suitable; fit (n.), agree, be in harmony or accordance; yield; put on one cloth over another; place the hind feet in the tracks of the front feet; make short steps; be accustomed; — IV. INF. *iṭbâq*, cover; provide with a lid or cover; surround from all sides; adhere to; agree; conclude a bargain; appear numerous; be excellent; — V. INF. *taṭabbuq*, be covered; — VI. INF. *taṭâbuq*, come to an agreement; agree; conspire, plot; — VII. INF. *inṭibâq*, be covered; be closed.

طبق *ṭabaq*, pl. *aṭbâq*, *aṭbiqa-t*, cover, covering, lid; flat dish, plate, slab, table; layer; story, bee-hive; leaf, leaf of metal, foil; what suits, belongs to, fits another thing (*ṭabq-an ‘an ṭabq-in*, one above another, layer by layer); surface of the earth; general, far-spreading; what the earth offers; firmament; troop, swarm; the greater part of day or night; generation (20 years); age, century; condition, state; a fabulous tortoise (بنات ط *banât ṭabq-in*, ام ط *umm ṭabq-in*, calamity); — *ṭibq*, ة, exactly fitting, belonging to; accurate; troop, swarm, crowd; hour; space of time; bird-lime; a fruit; *ṭibq-an*, during a long time; — *ṭubq*, pl. of طبيق *ṭabîq*; — *ṭabaq-an*, one after the other; layer by layer; — ة *ṭibqa-t*, an hour of the day; pl. *ṭibaq*, *ṭibq*, noose, springe; — *ṭabaqa-t*, what follows or resembles another thing; layer, row, degree, storey; generation; class, category; race; troop; — *ṭabiqa-t*, shortened, curtailed; contorted.

(طبل) *ṭabal*, U, INF. *ṭabl*, II. INF. *taṭbîl*, drum, beat the drum.

طبل *ṭabl*, pl. *aṭbâl*, *ṭubûl*, drum; tambourine; stake (in a game); saving-box; people, men; tribute; — ة *ṭabla-t*, a drum-shaped pail.

طبليط *ṭablîṭ*, pl. *ṭabâlîṭ*, altar-stone; altar.
طبلية *ṭabliyya-t*, tribute; (m.) a low table for taking meals.
(طبن) *ṭaban*, I, INF. *ṭabn*, *ṭabâna-t*, *ṭubûna-t*, *ṭabâniya-t*,—*ṭabin*, A, INF. *ṭaban*, have knowledge of (ل *li*), understand a thing; — III. INF. *muṭâbana-t*, deepen; agree with (acc.); — XI. INF. *iṭbînân*, be low, deepened.
طبن *ṭabn*, *ṭibn*, *ṭubn*, *ṭaban*, troop of people; number of men; (اى طبن *ayyu ṭabn-in*, what countryman?); — *ṭubn*, lute, guitar; — *ṭabin*, knowing, understanding; — *ṭuban*, a kind of backgammon; bait; — ة *ṭibna-t*, pl. *ṭiban*, comprehension, knowledge; — *ṭubna-t*, tone of a lute; pl. *ṭuban*, backgammon.
طبنجة *ṭabanja-t*, pistol (m.).
(طبندر) *ṭabandar*, dispute, quarrel; calamity.
(طبو) *ṭabâ*, U, INF. *ṭabw*, call, invite; — VIII. INF. *iṭṭibâ'*, id.; make friends with and kill afterwards.
طبوا *ṭabwâ'*, she-camel with long udders; important matter.
طبور *ṭabûr*, Tiberias; Tabor.
طبوع *ṭabbû'*, tick (insect); — *.
طبونة *ṭubûna-t*, knowledge, comprehension; INF. of (طبن).
(طبى) *ṭabâ*, I, INF. *ṭaby*, turn, turn from, avert; call, invite; — *ṭabî*, A, INF. *ṭaban*, have hanging udders; — IV. INF. *iṭbâ'*, call, invite.
طبى *ṭiby*, *ṭuby*, pl. *aṭbâ'*, udder; — *ṭabiyy*, agreeing, consenting; easy to be milked; — *ṭibbiy*, *ṭubiyy*, medical, medicinal; — ة *ṭabiyya-t*=طبوا *ṭabwâ'*.
طبيب *ṭabîb*, pl. *aṭibbâ'*, *aṭibba-t*, physician, doctor; master; learned, skilful; — ة *ṭabîba-t*, stripe; — ى *ṭabîbiyy*, medical, medicinal.
طبيجة *ṭibbîja-t*, the buttocks.
طبيخ *ṭabîḫ*, cooked; decoction, broth; liquor; brick; pavement; mortar, cement; fever-heat; — *ṭibbiḫ*, melon.
طبيس *ṭabîs*, overflowing.
طبيعة *ṭabî'a-t*, pl. *-ât*, *ṭabâ'i'*, nature, quality, essence; disposition, character, temper, genius; instinct; rough nature (opposed to gracefulness); علم الطبيعات *'ilm aṭ-ṭabî'ât*, natural science.
طبيعى *ṭabî'iyy*, natural; inborn.
طبيق *ṭabîq*, pl. *ṭubq*, hour of the night; space of time; what fits another thing; *ṭabîq-an*, for a long time; — ة *ṭabîqa-t*, anything fitting, suitable, pleasant; (m.) conspiracy, plot.
(طتو) *ṭatâ*, U, INF. *ṭatw*, go, depart.
طتيليق *ṭutailîq*, moderate extent (dim. of اطلاق *iṭṭilâq*).
(طث) *ṭaṯṯ*, game with a spinning-top.
(طثا) *ṭaṯa'*, INF. *ṭaṯ'*, play with a spinning-top; ease the bowels; vomit.
(طثر) *ṭaṯar*, U, INF. *ṭaṯr*, *ṭuṯûr*, be thick and creamy; — II. INF. *taṭṯîr*, id.; — IV. INF. *iṭṯâr*, increase, multiply; — ة *ṭaṯra-t*, thick milk with cream; water with a thick sediment, mud or moss; wool; fat of the shoulders; abundance, affluence.
(طثرج) *ṭaṯraj*, small yellow ant.
(طثن) *ṭaṯn*, *ṭiṯn*, *ṭuṯn*, merriment, song, harmony; good fortune.
طثى *ṭaṯan*, small pieces of wood, chips.
طثيار *ṭaṯyâr*, lion; a brave one, hero; fly.
(طجن) *ṭajan*, U, INF. *ṭajn*, fry in a pan, roast.
(طح) *ṭaḥḥ*, U, INF. *ṭaḥḥ*, spread, tread flat with the heel; — IV. INF. *iṭḥâḥ*, let fall, drop; throw down; — VII. INF. *inṭiḥâḥ*, be spread.

طحا *ṭaḥan*, vast plain.
طحار *ṭuḥâr*, sigh; pain.
طحاف *ṭaḥâf*, hovering on high.
طحال *ṭiḥâl*, pl. *ṭuḥul*, milt; pl. (m.) coal-dust, sediment, dregs; — *ṭuḥâl*, disease of the milt.
طحامر *ṭuḥâmir*, thick, bellied.
طحان *ṭaḥḥân*, f. ة, miller; — ة *ṭiḥâna-t*, profession of a miller.
طحاوى *ṭaḥawî*, kites flying round corpses.
(طحث) *ṭaḥas*, INF. *ṭaḥs*, push back with the hand.
طحح *ṭuḥuḥ*, shavings (from the plane).
(طحر) *ṭaḥar*, INF. *ṭaḥr*, throw out; urge on; lie with; cut out the prepuce; — I, fetch a deep breath; sigh, groan; (m.) be afflicted with dysentery; — IV. INF. *iṭḥâr*, cut out the prepuce.
طحر *ṭaḥr*, small cloud; — ة *ṭaḥara-t*, fleak of a cloud.
(طحرب) *ṭaḥrab*, INF. ة, fill; break wind.
طحرب *ṭiḥrab*, chips, shavings; woodwork; — ة *ṭaḥraba-t*, *ṭiḥriba-t*, *ṭuḥruba-t*, dress; rag, tatter; little cloud.
طحرف *ṭiḥrif*, ة *ṭiḥrifa-t*, thin.
(طحرم) *ṭaḥram*, INF. ة, fill; put a string to the bow; — ة *ṭiḥrima-t*, tatter, rag.
طحرور *ṭuḥrûr*, ة *ṭuḥrûra-t*, طحريرة *ṭiḥrîra-t*=طحرة *ṭaḥara-t*.
(طحز) *ṭaḥaz*, INF. *ṭaḥz*, tell lies.
طحز *ṭaḥz*, coition; — *ṭiḥz*, lie.
(طحس) *ṭaḥas*, INF. *ṭaḥs*, lie with.
طحطاح *ṭaḥṭâḥ*, lion.
(طحطح) *ṭaḥṭaḥ*, INF. ة, *ṭaḥṭâḥ*, break; tear and scatter; disperse and destroy; smile submissively, smirk; — ة *ṭiḥṭiḥa-t*, rag, tatter; hair.
(طحك) *ṭuḥḥak*, pl. (camels) not yet having their side-teeth.
(طحل) *ṭaḥal*, INF. *ṭaḥl*, wound in the milt; pass. complain of pain in the milt; fill; — *ṭaḥil*, A, INF. *ṭaḥal*, have the milt large; be foul and smell offensively; be grey with a shade of white.
طحل *ṭaḥil*, irritable; splenetic; full; black; turbid, muddy; light grey; — *ṭuḥul*, pl. of طحال *ṭiḥâl*; — ة *ṭuḥla-t*, grey with a shade of white; dirty white or greenish.
طحلا *ṭaḥlâ'*, f. of اطحل *aṭḥal*, muddy, turbid, &c.
(طحلب) *ṭaḥlab*, INF. ة, be covered with green moss; be covered with green; shear camels; kill.
طحلب *ṭaḥlab*, *ṭiḥlab*, *ṭuḥlab*, pl. *ṭaḥâlib*, water-moss; — ة *ṭiḥliba-t*, rag, tatter; hair.
طحلمة *ṭiḥlima-t*, small cloud.
(طحم) *ṭaḥam*, INF. *ṭaḥm*, rush along impetuously; rush upon; — ة *ṭaḥma-t*, mass; the greater part; turmoil, tumult; *ṭaḥma-t*, *ṭiḥma-t*, *ṭuḥma-t*, impulse; departure; crowd; bustle, turmoil; — *ṭuḥama-t*, fearless in combat; plenty of camels.
(طحمر) *ṭaḥmar*, INF. ة, jump, leap; fill; put a string to the bow; — ة *ṭiḥmira-t*, little cloud; hair; something, anything.
طحمير *ṭiḥmîr*, little cloud.
(طحن) *ṭaḥan*, INF. *ṭaḥn*, turn round (mill); roll in a circle; grind; crush to powder; — II. INF. *taṭḥîn*, grind, pound, crush; — V. *taṭaḥḥun*, VII. INF. *inṭiḥân*, pass. of II.
طحن *ṭiḥn*, flour; anything ground or pounded; — *ṭuḥan*, dwarf; a small animal; a kind of scorpion.
(طحو , طحى) *ṭaḥâ*, INF. *ṭaḥw*, spread (a.); be spread; lie on one's side; depart, disappear, speed on; carry away; — *ṭaḥâ*, U, INF. *ṭaḥw*, depart; perish; throw down on the face.
طحور *ṭaḥûr*, quick, swift; flowing rapidly;—also ة *ṭaḥûra-t*, throwing out.

طحوم *ṭaḥûm*, carrying away; impetuous.

طحون *ṭaḥûn*, who grinds or crushes; crowd overthrowing everything; hot battle; many camels (about 300).

(طحى) see (طحو); — ة *ṭaḥya-t*, little cloud.

طحير *ṭaḥîr*, sigh; pain which takes away the breath; colic, dysentery.

طحين *ṭaḥîn*, flour; an oil-cake.

(طخ) *ṭaḥḥ*, U, INF. *ṭaḥḥ*, fling far away, remove; lie with; address hard words to (ل *li*).

طخ طخ *ṭiḥ ṭiḥ*, interjection of one who laughs.

طخا *ṭaḥâ'*, high cloud; sorrow, care.

طخارم *ṭuḥârim*, angry, enraged.

طخارير *ṭaḥârîr*, pl. of طخرور *ṭuḥrûr*.

طخارية *ṭaḥâriya-t*, brisk she-ass.

طخاطخ *ṭuḥâṭiḥ*, obscurities.

طخاف *ṭaḥâf*, high cloud; — *.

طخامة *ṭaḥâma-t*, pride, INF. of (طخم).

طخر *ṭaḥr*, very thin cloud.

طخربة *ṭaḥraba-t*, طخربية *ṭuḥrubiyya-t* = طحربة *ṭaḥraba-t*.

طخرور *ṭuḥrûr*, pl. *ṭaḥârîr*, thin cloud; lean and weak; stranger; pl. dispersed crowd.

طخز *ṭiḥz*, lie.

طخس *ṭiḥs*, root, origin.

طخش *ṭaḥiś*, A, INF. *ṭaḥś*, *ṭaḥaś*, be dark.

طخطاخ *ṭaḥṭâḥ*, bearing ill-will, malignant; dense clouds; tinkling of a necklace; anything rubbed off.

طخطخ *ṭaḥṭaḥ*, INF. ة, make equal and join one thing or part to another; — ة *ṭaḥṭaḥa-t*, giggling, laughing (s.).

(طخف) *ṭaḥf*, grief, sorrow; high cloud; sour milk; — ة *ṭaḥfa-t*, pl. *ṭiḥâf*, thin cloud.

طخفا *ṭaḥfâ*, having a black mouth (she-ass).

(طخم) *ṭaḥam*, INF. *ṭaḥm*,—*ṭaḥum*, INF. *ṭaḥâma-t*, be proud; — IX. INF. *iṭḥimâm*, burn blackish; — ة *ṭaḥma-t*, herd of goats; — *ṭuḥma-t*, blackness of the tip of the nose.

طخميل *ṭiḥmîl*, rock.

(طخو) *ṭaḥâ*, INF. *ṭaḥw*, *ṭuḥuww*, be dark; — ة *ṭaḥwa-t*, thin cloud.

طخوخ *ṭuḥûḥ*, malice; hardness; quarrelsomeness.

طخوم *ṭuḥûm*, boundaries.

طخى *ṭuḥayy*, cock; — ة *ṭaḥya-t*, *ṭuḥya-t*, fleak of a cloud; pl. *ṭaḥyûn*, stupid; — *ṭaḥya-t*, *ṭiḥya-t*, *ṭuḥya-t*, darkness. obscurity.

طخيا *ṭaḥyâ*, dark, obscure (f.).

طخيفة *ṭaḥîfa-t*, broth with meat.

طخيم *ṭaḥîm*, dry; black; meat.

طدة *ṭida-t*, INF. of (وطد), make firm, consolidate, &c.

(طر) *ṭarr*, U, INF. *ṭarr*, urge on violently; drive together in one place; INF. *ṭarr*, *ṭurûr*, sharpen; restore; coat a well with loam; — U, I, sprout, push forth (n.); cut, cut to pieces, cleave; cut off (the purse); take away; box one's ears; fall off; mount along the banks of a river; go along a river; — IV. INF. *iṭrâr*, throw down; cut off, lop off; irritate against; show one's self amorous.

طر *ṭarr*, hair growing again; — *ṭurr*, totality (*ṭurr-an*, altogether); hair hanging in front; — ة *ṭarra-t*, waist; impregnation, making pregnant; — *ṭurra-t*, pl. *ṭurar*, *ṭirâr*, *aṭrâr*, river-bank, edge of a valley; coast, shore; boundary tract, tract; selvedge; border, hem; front locks; hair of the forehead, toupet; travelling-pack, wallet; long narrow cloud; — (for طغرة *ṭugra-t*) royal sign-manual, signature.

(طرا) *ṭara'*, INF. *ṭar'*, *ṭurû'*, fall upon unexpectedly, appear suddenly, rise; — طرو *ṭaru'*, INF.

ṭarâ'a-t, ṭarâ', be fresh, juicy, full of sap; — IV. INF. *iṭrâ'*, eulogise, raise to the clouds.

طرا *ṭaran*, not earth-like; the numberless beings of creation; — *ṭarâ'*, ة *ṭarâ'a-t*, INF. of طرو *ṭaru'*, under (طرا); — *ṭurrâ'*, *ṭura'â'*, pl. of طارى *ṭârî*, who comes suddenly, falls unexpectedly upon; — ة *ṭur'a-t*, power of the stream.

طرابيش *ṭarâbîś*, pl. of طربوش *ṭarbûś*.

طرابيل *ṭarâbîl*, pl. of طربال *ṭarbâl* and طربيل *ṭarbîl*.

طراح *ṭarâḥ*, distant place; — *ṭarrâḥ*, architect; — ة *ṭarrâḥa-t*, covering, coverlet; small mattress; cushion, pillow; — ى *ṭurâḥiyy*, far.

طراخنة *ṭarâḫina-t*, pl. of طرخان *ṭarḫân*.

طراد *ṭirâd*, hunting-spear; a hunter's stratagem; — *ṭarrâd*, who drives away; fleet boat; flat roof; roomy place; long day; tiring out one's patience.

طرار *ṭarrâr*, cut-purse, pick-pocket; — *.

طراز *ṭirâz*, *ṭarâz*, embroidery; border, hem; manner, habit, custom; — *ṭarrâz*, embroiderer.

طرازدان *ṭirâzdân*, case for a balance (Pers.).

طراف *ṭirâf*, pl. *ṭurf*, *ṭarâ'if*, leathern tent; what has been mown on the borders; nobility, gentility (*ṭirâf-an*, by inheritance); dispute, quarrel.

طرافش *ṭurâfiś*, malignant.

طراق *ṭirâq*, pl. *ṭurq*, sole of leather; double leather; double piece; leather of a helmet; crest of a helmet; mark on the ear of a sheep; — *ṭirrâq*, theriac; counterpoison; — *ṭurrâq*, pl. of طارق *ṭâriq*.

طرامة *ṭurâma-t*, impurity upon the teeth.

طران *ṭur'ân*, bad; ى *ṭur'âniyy*, coming suddenly.

طراوة *ṭarâwa-t*, freshness and tenderness.

طرائز *ṭarâ'iz*, embroidered fringes.

(طرب) *ṭarib*, A, INF. *ṭarab*, be agitated in emotion; be delighted; be in festive mood, celebrate a feast; sing or make music; wander (from the road); — II. INF. *taṭrîb*, excite, agitate, cheer or sadden; sing or make music; — IV. INF. *iṭrâb*, V. INF. *taṭarrub*, agitate; cheer or sadden; try to do so; — X. INF. *istiṭrâb*, wish for emotion; wish to be cheered up; urge the camels by singing.

طرب *ṭirb*, pl. *ṭirâb*, agitated, in emotion; — *ṭarab*, agitation, emotion; joy, rejoicing; sorrow, grief; music; — *ṭarib*, agitated; joyful, delighted; home-sick.

طربال *ṭirbâl*, pl. *ṭarâbîl*, watch-tower; church-tower, steeple; tower; castle; high mountain-knoll; projection of a wall; road-mark.

طربوش *ṭarbûś*, pl. *ṭarâbîś*, red cap, fez.

طربون *ṭarbûn*, vine-tendrils.

طربيل *ṭirbîl*, pl. *ṭarâbîl*, threshing-roller; flail.

طربين *ṭarbîn* = طربون *ṭarbûn*.

طرث *ṭarṯ*, new building; — *ṭirṯ*, tip of the clitoris.

طرثخة *ṭarṯaḫa-t*, lightness; light-mindedness, levity.

(طرثم) *ṭarṯam*, INF. ة, silently fix the eyes on the ground from anger or pride.

طرثوث *ṭurṯûṯ*, pl. *ṭarâṯîṯ*, a kind of truffle; gland of the penis; pl. a medicinal wood.

طرجهارة *ṭarjahâra-t*, *ṭirjihâra-t*, طرجهالة *ṭarjahâla-t*, *ṭirjahâla-t*, drinking-vessel, cup; bottle.

(طرح) *ṭaraḥ*, INF. *ṭarḥ*, throw far away; remove; turn from (a.), avert; impose; play at chess; make a miscarriage; bear fruit; raise (a cry of alarm); — *ṭariḥ*, A, INF. *ṭaraḥ*, be of a mischie-

vous disposition; enjoy good fortune and ease; — II. INF. *taṭrîḥ*, throw far away, remove to a great distance (a.); make a miscarriage; breed fowls; extend or elevate a building; — III. INF. *muṭâraḥa-t*, converse, propose questions to one another, ask to sing; — IV. INF. *iṭrâḥ*, throw far away; remove (a.); throw one's self down; — VII. INF. *inṭirâḥ*, be thrown away; throw one's self down; — VIII. INF. *iṭṭirâḥ*, throw far away, reject; remove (a.).

طرح *ṭarḥ*, throw; mud in the water; — *ṭirḥ*, *ṭurraḥ*, thrown away; removed; *ṭirḥ*, miscarriage; — *ṭaraḥ*, distant; ط الصوت *ṭaraḥ aṣ-ṣaut*, cry of alarm; signal; — ة *ṭarḥa-t*, a coarse wrapper or over-all; veil reaching to the feet.

طرحان *ṭarḥân*, thrown, cast; weakened.

(طرحوم) *ṭurḥûm*, large, great; foul. corrupted.

طرحى *ṭarḥa*, pl. of طريح *ṭarîḥ*.

طرخ *ṭarẖ*, ة *ṭarẖa-t*, reservoir at the mouth of a canal.

طرخان *ṭarẖân*, pl. *ṭarâẖina-t*, prince in Khorasan; a plant.

طرخشة *ṭarẖaṣa-t*=طرخشة *ṭarṣaẖa-t*.

(طرخف) *ṭirẖif*, ة *ṭirẖifa-t*, fluid butter.

(طرخم), III. *iṭraẖamm*, INF. *iṭriẖmâm*, be purblind, have dim eyes; be very dark; see مطرخم *muṭraẖimm*.

طرخون *ṭarẖûn*, tarragon.

(طرد) *ṭarad*, INF. *ṭard*, *ṭarad*, push away, drive away, repel; expel, repudiate, banish; pursue, chase; drive together; meet and pass by; — II. INF. *taṭrîd*, drive away; pursue, chase; clack a whip; — III. INF. *ṭirâd*, *muṭârada-t*, attack one another, charge; — IV. INF. *iṭrâd*, order one's expulsion or banishment; agree upon a prize for running a race; overtake and get the lead of; — VII. INF. *inṭirâd*, be expelled, banished; — VIII. INF. *iṭṭirâd*, id.; succeed one another, come immediately after one another; be well connected (arguments, &c.); prosper; flow, run; chase; be extended, lengthened; — X. INF. *istiṭrâd*, drive away, chase; deceive an enemy by a feigned flight and fall upon them; swerve from one's subject; adduce arguments without order or conclusiveness.

طرد *ṭard*, expulsion, repudiation, banishment; chase, hunt; bale of merchandise, colli; — *ṭarid*, befouled water; — ة *ṭirda-t*, cavalry-charge.

(طردس) *ṭardas*, INF. ة, fasten, consolidate.

طرر *ṭurar*, pl. of طرة *ṭurra-t*.

(طرز) *ṭariz*, A, INF. *ṭaraz*, become handsome and slender; mend, improve (n.); dress finely; — II. INF. *taṭrîz*, embroider a garment with figures; — V. INF. *taṭarruz*, be embroidered with figures.

طرز *ṭarz*, form, shape, figure; manner; rule.

(طرس) *ṭaras*, U, INF. *ṭars*, efface, blot out, extinguish; — II. INF. *taṭrîs*, paint black; refresh effaced writing; — V. INF. *taṭarrus*, eat and drink always daintily; shun from pride or fastidiousness; abstain, turn from (n.).

طرس *ṭirs*, pl. *aṭrâs*, *ṭurûs*, leaf, sheet of paper, page; writing, letter, book.

(طرسع) *ṭarsaʻ*, INF. ة, run fast from fear.

(طرسم) *ṭarsam*, INF. ة, fix the look silently upon the ground; yield, desist.

(طرش) *ṭariś*, A, INF. *ṭaraś*, be slightly deaf; — *ṭaraś*, U, INF. *ṭarś*, whitewash a wall; scratch

(as a pen); — II. INF. *taṭrîś*, deafen; scatter; — V. INF. *taṭarruś*, recover and be again able to walk; stand out, be conspicuous; — VI. INF. *taṭâruś*, feign deafness.

طرش *ṭarś*, a white earth to white-wash walls (m.); pl. *ṭurûś*, small cattle;—*ṭurś*, deaf people, pl. of اطرش *aṭraś*; — *ṭaraś*, deafness; — ة *ṭurśa-t*, slight deafness.

طرشا *ṭarśâ'*, f. of اطرش *aṭraś*, deaf.

(طرشح) *ṭarśaḥ*, INF. ة, enervate; — ة *ṭarḥaśa-t*, enervation.

(طرشم) *ṭarśam*, INF. ة, be very dark.

(طرط) *ṭariṭ*, A, INF. *ṭaraṭ*, be stupid; have thin lashes and eye-brows.

طرط *ṭaraṭ*, stupidity;—*ṭariṭ*, stupid; having thin eye-brows.

(طرطب) *ṭarṭab*, INF. ة, call the goats by whistling to be milked; call or drive away small cattle; make a rumbling noise (water).

طرطب *ṭurṭubb*, large and flabby female breast; — ة *ṭurṭubba-t*, ى *ṭurṭubba*, طرطبانية *ṭurṭubâniy-ya-t*, having long hanging breasts or udders.

طرطبيس *ṭarṭabîs*, abundance of water; she-camel abounding in milk; old woman.

(طرطر) *ṭarṭar*, INF. ة, chatter and boast; call the sheep; sound cracked.

طرطر *ṭurṭur*, IMP., frequently abide in the house of God!

طرطش *ṭarṭaś*, INF. ة, scratch (pen).

(طرطق) *ṭarṭaq*, INF. ة, crack one's fingers or joints (m.).

طرطور *ṭurṭûr*, long and thin; weak; thin high cap; — *ṭaraṭûr*, sauce, broth (m.).

طرطير *ṭarṭîr*, tartar (salt).

(طرعب) *ṭar'ab*, immoderately long or tall.

(طرغش) *ṭargaś*, INF. ة, recover and be able to walk again; — III. *iṭragaśś*, INF. *iṭrigśâś*, id.; have rain and good pastures after drought; stir (n.).

(طرغم), III. *'iṭragamm*, INF. *iṭrigmâm*, be proud.

(طرف) *ṭaraf*, I, INF. *ṭaraf*, turn off, repel; slap, box the ears; press the eye-lids together, blink, wink; look at, glance; hurt the eye so that it runs; (m.) press olives; — *ṭarif*, A, INF. *ṭaraf*, graze on the borders of a pasture-ground (separate from the others); — *ṭaruf*, INF. *ṭarâfa-t*, be new, recently acquired; descend in a long and direct line from the first ancestor, be of old nobility; — II. INF. *taṭrîf*, drive back straggling camels; attack the extremities of an army or throw them back on the main body; throw back the foremost horsemen; drive towards the sides; skirt, walk along or towards the edge; lose the teeth; dye the finger-tops with henna; — IV. INF. *iṭrâf*, present with anything novel, rare, curious; make a present; close the eyes; produce in abundance the plant طريفة *ṭarîfa-t*; be of old nobility, &c. (see طريف *ṭarîf*); pass. be on both sides printed upon with figures or lines (staff); — V. INF. *taṭarruf*, skirt, go along the edge; graze on the borders of the pasture-ground; — VIII. INF. *iṭṭirâf*, acquire or purchase anything novel, beautiful, rare; — X. INF. *istiṭrâf*, find novel and beautiful; deem of old nobility.

طرف *ṭarf*, pl. *aṭrâf*, extremity, border, edge, top; du. *aṭ-ṭarfan*, the feet; cue; end, issue; enemy; wife; eye, glance, look, blinking (s.); blow, push, clap; nobleman — *ṭirf*, nobleman, high-born; pl. *ṭurûf*, generous (of animals)

generous horse, good steed; fresh; newly-acquired; graceful; pleasant; fickle, soon wearied; who wishes for everything; — *ṭurf*, pl. of طراف *ṭirâf* and طريف *ṭarîf*; — *ṭaraf*, pl. *aṭrâf*, part, side; anything confining another; tract, region, district, coast; edge, border; end, top; extremities of the body; du. *ṭarafân*, tongue and penis, mouth and anus, the two sides of a question, death or recovery, father's and mother's side; pl. who are at the sides or hindmost lateral parts, additional circumstances, incidents, the lowest or most eminent; *ṭaraf*, near relative, father, brother, uncle; nobleman; — *ṭarif*, not adhering or attached to one; fickle; restless; of old nobility; — ة *ṭarfa-t*, look, glance, blink; blow, clap; scar; tamarisk; — *ṭurfa-t*, pl. *ṭuraf*, soreness of the eye; beauty, novelty; rarity, curiosity; new acquisition; dessert; — *ṭarifa-t*, restless, unsteady.

طرفا *ṭarfâ'*, ة, tamarisk.

طرفاس *ṭirfâs*, heap of sand round a tree.

طرفانى *ṭarafâniyy*, extreme; what is the border, the edge, the end.

(طرفس) *ṭarfas*, INF. ة, sharpen one's look; put on many clothes; be dark; be frequented; be muddy.

طرفسا *ṭirfisâ'*, f. dark; darkness.

طرفسان *ṭirfisân*, darkness; heap of sand round a tree.

(طرفش) *ṭarfaś*, INF. ة, recover; be weak and dim; look with half-closed eyes.

(طرق) *ṭaraq*, I, INF. *ṭarq*, beat, knock; box the ears; beat wool; ring (a bell); hammer; throw pebbles (for vaticination); befoul the water; pass. be weak of intellect; — U, INF. *ṭarq*, *ṭurûq*, come at night-time; cover the mare; fall upon, surprise; — *ṭariq*, A, INF. *ṭaraq*, drink impure water; have crooked legs or weak knees; be piled close together; — II. INF. *taṭrîq*, open the way, make room; be on the point of laying eggs; drop excrement; give birth with difficulty; acknowledge a debt previously denied; tie the camels up to prevent them from grazing; cover a shield, double a sole, &c.; — III. INF. *muṭâraqa-t*, put on one garment over another; double a sole; — IV. INF. *iṭrâq*, be silent and fix the eyes on the ground; lend one's stallion to another for the purpose of covering; allow to perform sexual intercourse; be given to sport; come darker and darker upon (night); come one after the other; cover with leather, double; — V. INF. *taṭarruq*, find means for a thing; obtain; — VI. INF. *taṭâruq*, follow one in the track of the other; — VIII. INF. *iṭṭirâq*, id.; disperse (n.); break down from weakness of the knees; be densely feathered; — X. INF. *istiṭrâq*, borrow another's stallion; have one's fortune told; accustom one's self to a thing.

طرق *ṭarq*, turn, time, once; blow, strike; weakness of intellect; befouled water; palm-tree; covering stallion; sperm; — *ṭirq*, fat; fattiness; strength, courage; trade, calling, profession; — *ṭurq*, pl. of طراق *ṭirâq* and طريق *ṭarîq*; — *ṭaraq*, pl. *aṭrâq*, place where water collects; fold; — *ṭuruq*, pl. of طريق *ṭarîq*; — ة *ṭarqa-t*, handicraft, trade, calling, profession; net or noose of a bird-catcher; once; one blow; — *ṭirqa-t*, net, noose, snare; one thing on the

top of another; — *ṭurqa-t*, pl. *ṭuraq*, handiwork; line of sight on a bow; way, road; habit, custom; one thing on the top of another, fold upon fold; heap of stones; darkness; stupid; desire, greed, greediness; — *ṭaraqa-t*, pl. *ṭaraq*, train of camels; track of camels; noose, snare; — *ṭuraqa-t*, who travels at night after his friends.

(طرم) *ṭarim*, A, INF. *ṭaram*, be full of honey; — IV. INF. *iṭrâm*, be green or unclean; have foul breath (from unclean teeth); — V. INF. *taṭarrum*, get confused in one's speech; — VIII. INF. *iṭṭirâm*=IV.

طرم *ṭarm*, *ṭirm*, butter; honey; honey-comb; — *ṭurm*, coal-pan; a tree; — ة *ṭarma-t*, *ṭirma-t*, *ṭurma-t*, excrescence on the upper lip; — *ṭarma-t*, liver; — *ṭurma-t*, coal-pan.

طرماح *ṭirimmâḥ*, of noble birth and celebrated; penetrating and prudent; also *ṭirmâḥ*, long.

طرماد *ṭirmâd*, boaster.

(طرمح) *ṭarmaḥ*, INF. ة, raise high; heighten, lengthen.

طرمح *ṭarmaḥ*, making long strides.

طرمحانية *ṭarmaḥâniyya-t*, haughtiness.

(طرمذ) *ṭarmaẓ*, INF. ة, boast, swagger.

طرمذار *ṭarmaẓâr*, طرمذان *ṭirmiẓân*, طرمذة *ṭirmiẓa-t*, boaster.

(طرمس) *ṭarmas*, INF. ة, shrink; desist from fighting and flee; efface; frown; — III. *iṭramass*, INF. *iṭrimsâs*, be dark.

طرمسا *ṭirmisâ'*, dense darkness; thin cloud; dust.

(طرمش) *ṭarmaś*, INF. ة, be dark.

(طرموث) *ṭurmûṯ*, weak; cake baked in the ashes.

طرموح *ṭurmûḥ*, long, tall.

طرموس *ṭurmûs*, cake baked in the ashes.

(طرموق) *ṭurmûq*, bat (animal).

(طرن) *ṭurn*, raw silk.

طرنجبين *ṭaranjbîn*, manna.

(طرهم), III. *iṭrahamm*, INF. *iṭrihmâm*, be well-made (youth).

(طرو) *ṭarâ*, U, INF. *ṭuruww*, come from afar; — طرى *ṭarî*, طرو *ṭarû*, INF. *ṭarâwa-t*, *ṭarâ'a-t*, *ṭarâ'*, *ṭarât*, be fresh and tender, be freshly plucked; — II. INF. *taṭriya-t*, freshen; refresh perfumes by admixture; season; refresh, sprinkle over, soften; — IV. INF. *iṭrâ'*, season; eulogise; — V. INF. *taṭarrî*, refresh one's self; — XII. *iṭraura*, INF. *iṭrîrâ'*, have a swollen belly.

طروب *ṭarûb*, excited, agitated.

طروح *ṭarûḥ*, far distant; shooting far; having long branches; begetting a child; — ة *ṭurûḥa-t*, tax, duty, tribute.

طروقة *ṭarûqa-t*, marriageable, mature.

(طرى) *ṭarî*, A, INF. *ṭaran*, step up to, pass by; INF. *ṭarayân*, happen, come to pass.

طرى *ṭariyy*, *ṭarî'*, fresh and tender; — *ṭurra*, chased she-ass.

طرياق *ṭiryâq*, theriac; opium; — ى *ṭiryâqiyy*, opium-chewer.

طريان *ṭarayân*, event, anything unpleasant; — *ṭirriyân*, tray with food.

طريح *ṭarîḥ*, cast away; despised; — *ṭirrîḥ*, small salt fish; anchovy.

طريد *ṭarîd*, expelled, exiled; trunk of a tree; bunch of dates; long; born immediately after his brother; du. day and night; — ة *ṭarîda-t*, pl. *ṭarâ'id*, chased game, game; camels driven away or stolen; pl. yachts; strip of silk; tract of land.

طرير *ṭarîr*, sharp, sagacious penetrating; having a moustache beginning to grow.

طريف *ṭarîf*, pl. *ṭurf*, newly acquired; of old nobility; strange,

odd ; — ة *ṭarîfa-t*, pl. *ṭarâ'if*, beautiful and rare furniture.

طريق *ṭarîq*, pl. *ṭurq*, *ṭuruq*, *aṭruq*, *aṭriqâ'*, *aṭriqa-t*, *ṭuruqât*, way, road, path ; manner, means ; — *ṭirîq*, blow ; — *ṭuraiq*, palm-tree ; ام طريق *umm ṭuraiq*, hyena ; — *ṭirrîq*, silent and fixing the eyes on the ground ; — ة *ṭarîqa-t*, pl. *ṭarâ'iq*, road, path ; stroke, furrow, strip, strip of cloth ; way, manner, habit, custom ; means, expedient, device ; condition, state ; stick of an umbrella ; high palm-tree (pl. *ṭarîq*) ; leader, pl. chiefs ; order of monks or dervishes ; melody ; — *ṭirrîqa-t*, softness, gentleness ; weakness ; soft level ground.

(طريم) *ṭaryam*, INF. ة, be deteriorated ; be piled up ; — II. INF. *taṭaryum*, stick in the mud.

طريم *ṭiryam*, thick heap of clouds ; honey.

(طرين) *ṭaryan*, lie about drunk.

طرين *ṭiryan*, thin clay or loam.

(طزر) *ṭazar*, U, INF. *ṭazr*, push back with the fist.

طزر *ṭazar*, summer-house.

(طزع) *ṭaza'*, INF. *ṭaz'*, lie with ; be unwilling to fight ; — *ṭazi'*, A, INF. *ṭaza'*, be without food and money.

طزع *ṭazi'*, طزيع *ṭazî'*, without means ; having neither bread nor money ; greedy.

(طس) *ṭass*, U, INF. *ṭass*, quarrel with (acc.), scold ; silence ; dip into the water (a.) ; depart, go ; — II. INF. *taṭsîs*, go away, depart.

طس *ṭass*, ة *ṭassa-t*, *ṭissa-t*, pl. *ṭusûs*, *ṭisâs*, *ṭasîs*, *ṭassât*, cup.

(طسا) *ṭasa'*, INF. *ṭas'*, طسى *ṭasi'*, A, INF. *ṭasa'*, have the stomach-ache ; feel satiety and disgust ; — طسا *ṭasa'*, be ashamed ; — IV. INF. *iṭsâ'*, cause stomach-ache or disgust.

طساس *ṭassâs*, maker of cups ; — * ; — ة *ṭisâsa-t*, making of cups.

طساسيج *ṭasâsîj*, pl. of طسوج *ṭassûj*.

طسام *ṭasâm*, *ṭusâm*, *ṭassâm*, طسان *ṭassân*, whirled up dust.

طست *ṭast*, pl. *ṭisâs*, cup.

طستخان *ṭastiḥân*, tray.

(طسع) *ṭasa'*, INF. *ṭas'*, lie with ; travel ; — *ṭasi'*, A, INF. *ṭasa'*, be without means, resourceless.

طسع *ṭasi'*, without means, resourceless.

طسق *ṭasq*, *ṭisq*, طسك *ṭask*, tax, duty ; a measure.

(طسل) *ṭasal*, U, INF. *ṭasl*, move and shine (mirage).

طسل *ṭasl*, running water.

(طسم) *ṭasam*, I, INF. *ṭusûm*, be effaced, blotted out ; — INF. *ṭasm*, efface, blot out ; — *ṭasim*, A, INF. *ṭasam*, have the stomach-ache ; — IV. INF. *iṭsâm*, cause stomach-ache ; — VII. INF. *inṭisâm*, be effaced, blotted out.

طسم *ṭasam*, darkness ; dust.

طسوج *ṭassûj*, pl. *ṭasâsîj*, 24th part of a drachm, 4th part of the دانق *dânaq* ; coast ; tract.

(طسى) *ṭasî*, A, INF. *ṭasan*, have the stomach-ache.

طسيت *ṭusait*, طسيس *ṭusais*, little cup ; — *.

طسيع *ṭasî'*, without means, resourceless.

مياه طسيم *miyâh-u ṭusaim-in*, water of deceit, deception.

(طش) *ṭass*, U, I, INF. *ṭaśś*, rain slightly ; pass. *ṭuśś*, be seized with a cold ; (m.) get decomposed, boil, crackle, shudder ; — IV. INF. *iṭśâś*, rain slightly.

طش *ṭaśś*, slight rain ; — ة *ṭaśśa-t*, طشطشة *ṭaśṭaśa-t*, decomposition crackling, boiling, hissing ; noise ; shudder (m.) ; — *ṭiśśa-t*, infant ; — *ṭuśśa-t*, cold.

(طشا) *ṭaśa'*, INF. *ṭaś'*, lie with — IV. INF. *iṭśâ'*, have a cold ; — ة *ṭuśś'a-t*, *ṭuśśa'a-t*, cold.

طشاش *ṭaśâś*, *ṭuśâś*, cold.

طشت *ṭaśt*, طشط *ṭaśṭ*, pl. *ṭuśûṭ*, cup, basin.
طشطشة *ṭaśṭaśa-t*, see طشة *ṭaśśa-t* under طش *ṭaśś*.
طشيش *ṭaśîś*, slight rain.
(طص) *ṭaṣṣ*, U, see.
(طع) *ṭa‘‘*, U, INF. *ṭa‘‘*, lick.
طعام *ṭa‘âm*, pl. *aṭ‘ima-t*, *aṭ‘imât*, food, meal; wheat, corn; water of the well Zamzam.
طعامية *ṭa‘âmiyya-t*, expenditure for food.
طعان *ṭa‘‘ân*, combatant with the lance; slanderer; — *.
(طعب) *ṭa‘b*, pleasure.
(طعشنة) *ṭa‘sana-t*, shrew; غنم ط *ganam ṭa‘sana-t*, small cattle.
(طعر) *ṭa‘ar*, INF. *ṭa‘r*, lie with; compel to submit to judgment.
(طعز) *ṭa‘az*, INF. *ṭa‘z*, push back; lie with.
طعزبة *ṭa‘zaba-t*, mockery, derision, banter, scorn.
(طعس) *ṭa‘as*, INF. *ṭa‘s*, lie with.
(طعسب) *ṭa‘sab*, INF. ة, run astray.
(طعسف) *ṭa‘saf*, tread the ground violently (in walking).
طعطع *ṭa‘ṭa‘*, level ground; — ة *ṭa‘ṭa‘a-t*, sound produced by licking, sucking, &c.; smacking (s.).
(طعل) *ṭa‘al*, INF. *ṭa‘l*, blame, revile.
(طعم) *ṭa‘im*, A, INF. *ṭa‘m*, *ṭa‘âm*, eat, consume food; be satiated; — INF. *ṭa‘am*, take to the graft; (m.) be vaccinated; (m.) be provided with a bait; — INF. *ṭu‘m*, taste (a.); savour, relish; be able to perform; — II. INF. *taṭ‘îm*, graft; vaccinate; provide with a bait; be full of marrow; — III. INF. *muṭâ‘ama-t*, (also VI.) bill; — IV. INF. *iṭ‘âm*, feed, give to eat; bear ripe fruit; graft; (m.) put the match to a gun; (m.) poison; — V. INF. *taṭa‘‘um*, taste of (a.); (m.) be grafted, be vaccinated; — VI. INF. *taṭâ‘um*, see III.; — VIII. INF. *iṭṭi‘am*, grow savoury; take to education; — X. INF. *istiṭ‘âm*, ask for food; relish, find savoury.
طعم *ṭa‘m*, pl. *ṭu‘ûm*, taste, savour; dainty food; — *ṭu‘m*, food, dish; (m.) bait; (m.) fish; taste; intelligence; power; — *ṭa‘im*, dainty in one's food; — ة *ṭi‘ma-t*, manner of eating, of tasting; — *ṭu‘ma-t*, pl. *ṭu‘am*, food, dish, meal; invitation; bait; match of a gun; dining-place; prey; gain, earnings income; woof.
(طعن) *ṭa‘an*, U, A, INF. *ṭan‘*, thrust or pierce with a lance; — INF. *ṭa‘n*, *ṭa‘nân*, abuse, revile, tarnish (one's honour); penetrate; advance (in years), be aged; travel the night through; go with loosened reins; pass. be seized with the plague; receive a lance-thrust; — III. INF. *ṭi‘ân*, (also VI., VIII.) fight one another with lances; — VI. INF. *taṭâ‘un*, *ṭi‘innân*, see III.; — VII. INF. *inṭi‘ân*, receive a lance-thrust; be seized with the plague; — VIII. INF. *iṭṭi‘ân*, see III.
طعن *ṭu‘n*, pl. of طعين *ṭa‘în*; — ة *ṭa‘na-t*, lance-thrust; calumny, abuse, taunt; plague-blister.
طعنان *ṭa‘nân*, *ṭi‘innân*, INF. of (طعن), I. and VI.
طعوم *ṭa‘ûm*, طعيم *ṭa‘îm*, well fed; — *; — ة *ṭa‘ûma-t*, sheep to be slaughtered.
طعين *ṭa‘în*, pl. طعن *ṭu‘n*, pierced by a lance; afflicted with the plague.
طغ *ṭagg*, bull.
طغا *ṭagan*, sound, tone; — ة *ṭugât*, pl. of طاغى *ṭâgî*, disobedient, &c.
طغام *ṭagâm*, ة, common class, the vulgar; stupid and vulgar.
(طغر) *ṭagar*=(دغر).
طغرا *ṭugrâ*, طغرة *ṭugra-t*, royal sign-manual, imperial signature (Pers.).
(طغم) *ṭagam*, sea; mass of water; — ة *ṭugma-t*, choir of angels.

طغمشة *ṭagmaśa-t*, weakness of the eyes.
طغموش *ṭugmûś*, devil; devilish.
(طغو) *ṭagâ*, U, INF. *ṭugwa*, *ṭugwân* =(طغى).
طغو *ṭagw*, ة *ṭagwa-t*, pl. *ṭagawât*, high place; mountain-summit; a little of, a trifle.
طغوا *ṭagwâ*=طغوى *ṭagwā*=طغيان *ṭigyân*.
طغوان *ṭugwân*, INF. of (طغو).
طغومة *ṭugûma-t*, طغومية *ṭugûmiyya-t*, vileness, vulgarity, stupidity.
طغوى *ṭagwâ*=طغيان *ṭigyân*, *ṭugyân*; —*ṭugwa*, INF. of (طغو).
(طغى) *ṭaga*, *ṭagî*, INF. *ṭagy*, *ṭigyân*, *ṭugyân*, exceed the bounds; become excessive in refractoriness, rebellion, injustice, cruelty, unbelief; be seduced; swell, be agitated, boil; rise; low; — II. INF. *taṭgiya-t*, make one a tyrant, an emperor; — IV. INF. *iṭgâ'*, allow one to exceed the bounds; make rebellious, tyrannical, cruel; seduce; — ة *ṭagya-t*, highest summit; smooth stone; a little, trifle, particle.
طغيا *ṭagyâ*, *ṭugyâ*, wild cow.
طغيان *ṭigyân*, *ṭugyân*,. rebellion; impiety; seduction; INF. of (طغى).
(طف) *ṭaff*, U, INF. *ṭaff*, *ṭufûf*, be near to (من *min*); offer the outer side; present one's self; reach and lift up; be near setting; (m.) INF. *ṭufûf*, fill to the brim; clap the wings; rush upon, throng; — II. INF. *taṭfîf*, not quite fill the measure, measure badly; clap the wings; jump with; bring near; sting one's people; — IV. INF. *iṭfâf*, be near; offer the side; threaten, impend; bring near; fill the measure to the brim; give birth prematurely; conceal insidiously; deceive, lay traps, waylay; have knowledge of, understand; throw a stone at; contain; — X. INF. *istiṭfâf*, be near; offer or present one's self; be high.
طف *ṭaff*, tract of land, shore; outside; swift;—*ṭaff*, طفف *ṭafaf*, what makes the measure brimful or full to overflowing.
طفاح *ṭifâḥ*, abundance; swelling over (s.); — ة *ṭufâḥa-t*, what swells or boils over; foam, froth, scum.
طفاسة *ṭafâsa-t*, dirt; INF. of (طفس).
طفاف *ṭafâf*, *ṭifâf*, darkness of the night; — *ṭafâf*, *ṭifâf*, *ṭufâf*, ة *ṭufâfa-t*, what makes full or over-full; brim, edge; — *ṭaffâf*, swift, fleet.
طفال *ṭafâl*, *ṭufâl*, dry loam or clay; — طفال *ṭifâl*, pl. of طفل *ṭafl*; — ة *ṭafâla-t*, tender age, childhood.
طفان *ṭaffân*, brimful.
طفانين *ṭafânîn*, lies; idle talk; holding back (s.); remaining behind (s.).
طفانية *ṭafâniya-t*, nickname.
طفاوة *ṭufâwa-t*, halo; what swells, boils or foams over; springtime.
(طفح) *ṭafaḥ*, INF. *ṭafḥ*, *ṭufûḥ*, be brimful; boil or flow over; fill to the brim; be full of wine; give mature birth; raise; go away; happen; — II. INF. *taṭfîḥ*, IV. INF. *iṭfâḥ*, fill to the brim; — VIII. INF. *iṭṭifâḥ*, scum off, skim.
طفحان *ṭafḥân*, f. *ṭafḥâ'*, brimful, overflowing.
(طفظ) *ṭafaẓ*, I, INF. *ṭafẓ*, bury.
طفظ *ṭafẓ*, *ṭafaẓ*, pl. *aṭfâẓ*, tomb.
(طفر) *ṭafar*, I, INF. *ṭafr*, *ṭafra-t*, *ṭufûr*, jump up (against a wall to reach what is behind); jump down; — II. INF. *taṭfîr*, make the horse jump up; put to flight, drive away; secrete cream; — IV. INF. *iṭfâr*, knock the heels against the groins of a horse (fault in riding); — VI. INF. *taṭâfur*, dispute about words; — ة *ṭafra-t*, leap or

jump of a horse; foam, froth; budding of trees; eruption of pustules.
(طفس) *ṭafas*, I, INF. *ṭafs*, lie with; — U, INF. *ṭufûs*, die; — *ṭafis*, A, INF. *ṭafas*, *ṭafâsa-t*, be dirty, untidy, neglect one's self.
طفس *ṭafas*, dirt; — *ṭafis*, dirty.
(طفش) *ṭafaś*, I, INF. *ṭafś*, lie with; soil, dirty; flee into an unknown country, be a fugitive; — V. INF. *taṭaffuś*, lie with; stain, soil.
طفشيقون *ṭafśîqûn*, poison for arrows.
طفشيل *ṭafśîl*, porridge; porridge of lentils.
طفطاف *ṭafṭâf*, coast; outside, exterior.
(طفطف) *ṭafṭaf*, INF. ة, grow weak, disheartened; (m.) flap the wings; (m.) be on the point of going out (burning wick); — ة *ṭafṭafa-t*, *ṭifṭifa-t*, pl. *ṭafâṭif*, soft parts of the belly, hypochondres.
طفف *ṭafaf*, ة *ṭafafa-t* = طف *ṭaff*.
(طفق) *ṭafiq*, A, INF. *ṭafaq*,—*ṭafaq*, I, INF. *ṭafq*, *ṭufûq*, begin; — *ṭafiq*, A, INF. *ṭafaq*, adhere to a place; — *ṭafaq*, INF. *ṭufûq*, obtain one's wish; — IV. INF. *iṭfâq*, allow one to obtain one's wish.
(طفل) *ṭafal*, U, INF. *ṭufûl*, decline towards setting; enter on the evening time; be red in setting; rise; — U, INF. *ṭafl*, feed well the foal (she-camel); — *ṭafil*, A, INF. *ṭafal*, perish in the dust (plant); — *ṭaful*, INF. *ṭafâla-t*, be soft and tender; (m.) INF. *ṭufûla-t*, be still young, be still a child; — II. INF. *taṭfîl*, dispose one's speech well; break upon; decline towards setting; feed the foal well; drive the she-camel slowly, so that the foals may be able to follow her; sponge, intrude, molest by intruding; pass. perish in the dust; IV. INF. *iṭfâl*, be near setting and turn red; enter on the evening time; have a child or young not yet able to follow; be near confinement; — V. INF. *taṭafful*, sponge, play *ṭufail*, come uninvited as a guest.
طفل *ṭafl*, pl. *ṭifâl*, *ṭufûl*, young and tender; — *ṭifl*, pl. *aṭfâl*, child, young of an animal; originating from, part of; need; sunset; night; — *ṭafal*, tender age, childhood; time between afternoon and sunset; last part of the forenoon; evening twilight, crepuscule, evening; darkness; rain; — ة *ṭafla-t*, delicate girl.
طفليل *ṭiflîl*, uninvited guest, intruder.
طفلية *ṭifliya-t*, childhood.
(طفن) *ṭafan*, U, INF. *ṭafn*, die; imprison, confine; — XI. *iṭfa'ann*, INF. *iṭfi'nân*, dwell peaceably; be well mannered.
طفنش *ṭafannaś*, broad in the forefeet.
طفنشا *ṭafanśa'*, *ṭafanśâ'*, purblind timid, timorous, weak.
طفنشل *ṭafanśal*, weak.
(طفو) *ṭafâ*, U, INF. *ṭafw*, *ṭufuww*, appear on the top of; run very fast; die; engage in a thing.
طفو *ṭufû'*, going out, getting extinguished (s.), INF. of (طفى); — ة *ṭafwa-t*, a thin plant.
طفولة *ṭufûla-t*, طفولية *ṭufûliyya-t*, tender childhood.
(طفى) *ṭafi'*, A, INF. *ṭufû'*, get extinguished, go out; be dim, darkened; — II. INF. *taṭfi'a-t*, IV. INF. *iṭfâ'*, extinguish; — VII. INF. *inṭifâ'*, get or be extinguished.
طفى *ṭufy*, ة, leaf of the dwarf-palm; stripe, stroke; a poisonous snake.
طفيشل *ṭafaiśal*, porridge.
طفيف *ṭafîf*, a little, trifle; paltry; (m.) what flows over in measuring.
طفيل *ṭafîl*, muddy water; — *ṭifyal*, child, young of an animal; —

ṭufail, little child, infant; — *ṭufail*, طفيلى *ṭufailiyy*, parasite, intruder.

(طق) *ṭaq*, *ṭiq*, imitative sound, as of a stone falling, &c.; — *ṭaqq*, U, INF. *ṭaqq*, produce a sound; crack, burst; — *ṭaqq*, sound, tone, crack.

طقش *ṭaqś*, pl. *ṭuqûś*, order; church-constitution, liturgy (τάξις); (m.) tax; weather; — ى *ṭaqśiyy*, liturgical.

(طقطق) *ṭaqṭaq*, INF. ة, make the ground resound with the hoof; crack the fingers or joints; — ة *ṭaqṭaqa-t*, cracking, resounding (s.).

(طقم), II. *ṭaqqam*, INF. *taṭqîm*, clothe afresh; bridle a horse; — IV. INF. *iṭqâm*, id.; — V. INF. *taṭaqqum*, dress in holiday-clothes; be richly caparisoned.

طقم *ṭaqm*, pl. *ṭuqûm*, garment; caparison.

(طقو) *ṭaqâ*, U, INF. *ṭaqw*, walk fast.

(طل) *ṭall*, U, INF. *ṭall*, moisten slightly the ground; grant a delay of payment; hurt, injure; — INF. *ṭull*, get moistened; urge on the camels; — INF. *ṭall*, *ṭulûl*, shed blood with impunity; shed blood, kill; be shed; — INF. *ṭalâla-t*, astonish, please; (m.) be convenient; show one's self, offer a view; smear, cover with; — IV. INF. *iṭlâl*, shed blood; tower, hang over, dominate the neighbourhood, look from above; offer a view; be moistened; — VI. INF. *taṭâll*, lift up or stretch one's self to look; — X. INF. *istiṭlâl*, tower over, dominate, offer a view; please.

طل *ṭall*, pl. *ṭilâl*, *ṭilal*, slight rain, shower; dew; milk; beautiful, charming, lovely; very old man; — *ṭall*, *ṭill*, snake; — *ṭull*, milk (draught of); blood; fat; — ة *ṭalla-t*, handsome woman; wife; delicious wine or perfumes; dewy garden; fine view; abundance and splendour; immodest old (woman); — *ṭilla-t*, pl. of طليل *ṭalîl*; — *ṭulla-t*, pl. *ṭulal*, neck; draught of milk.

طلا *ṭalan*, *ṭalâ*, pl. *aṭlâ'*, du. *ṭalayân*, child, young of an animal; person, form, figure; dangerously ill; wish, pleasure; thirst; smeared with pitch, smeared; — also *ṭalw*, pl. *aṭlâ'*, *ṭilâ'*, *ṭilyân*, *ṭulyân*, new-born gazelle; the young of a cloven-footed animal; small; spittle dried up in the mouth; — *ṭilan*, *ṭilâ*, pleasure; *ṭilâ*, gold (Pers.); — *ṭilâ'*, pitch, salve, ointment; syrup; juice of grapes; delicious wine; abuse; tether; — *ṭulâ'*, thin skin on blood; — *ṭallâ'*, seller of syrup, &c.; unavenged blood; — *ṭullâ'*, blood; thin skin on blood; — ة *ṭulât*, pl. *ṭula-n*, neck; scabious she-camel; cloth to rub camels with.

طلاب *ṭilâb*, INF. III. of (طلب); — *ṭallâb*, who seeks, investigates, demands; — *ṭullâb*, pl. of طالب *ṭâlib*, who asks, &c.

طلاح *ṭalâḥ*, bad condition (opposed to صلاح *ṣalâḥ*); — *ṭilâḥ*, acacia; pl. of طليح *ṭalîḥ*; — *ṭullâḥ*, pl. of طالح *ṭâliḥ*, bad, corrupt, &c.; — ة *ṭalâḥa-t*, INF. of (طلح); — ى *ṭulâḥiyy*, *ṭilâḥiyy*, ة, grazing on the acacia.

طلاسة *ṭallâsa-t*, cloth for wiping, duster.

طلاطل *ṭulâṭil*, ة, *ṭulâṭila-t*, death.

طلاع *ṭilâ'*, pl. *ṭul'*, what serves to fill up (earth, ground, &c.); what is smeared upon, salve, ointment, &c.

طلافح *ṭulâfiḥ*, fluid marrow; — *.

طلاق *ṭalâq*, divorce; — ة *ṭalâqa-t*, frank merriment; eloquence; freedom and openness of manner.

طلال *ṭilâl*, pl. of طل *ṭall*; — ة *ṭa-*

lâla-t, cheerfulness, merriment; beauty; what shows itself in the distance, form, trace, ruins of a dwelling-place; INF. of (طل).

طلام *ṭullâm*, hemp-seed;—ى *ṭalâmî*, cakes, loaves of bread, pl. of طلمة *ṭulma-t*.

طلاوة *ṭalâwa-t*, expectation; delay; — *ṭalâwa-t*, *ṭilâwa-t*, *ṭulâwa-t*, fairness, beauty, elegance, charm, gracefulness; thin skin on blood or milk; remains of food in the mouth; spittle drying up in the mouth; sorcery, magic; — *ṭalâwa-t*, neck.

طلاية *ṭilâya-t*, *ṭalâya-t*, outpost; guard; patrol.

(طلب) *ṭalab*, U, INF. *ṭalab*, wish, demand, ask, seek; long for; — *ṭalib*, A, INF. *ṭalab*, be far distant; — II. INF. *taṭlîb*, demand repeatedly, beg instantly; — III. INF. *muṭâlaba-t*, *ṭilâb*, demand one's right or payment from (acc.) another; call to account; claim, reclaim; punish; — IV. INF. *iṭlâb*, compel to demand or beg; cause one to need a thing (2 acc.); give what is asked; be far distant; — V. INF. *taṭallub*, demand or beg repeatedly and instantly; — VII. INF. *inṭilâb*, be sought or wished for (m.); — VIII. INF. *iṭṭilâb*= V.

طلب *ṭalb*, scholar; priest; — *ṭilb*, pl. *aṭlâb*, *ṭilaba-t*, *ṭilâb*, lover, mistress; anything sought or wished for; — *ṭalab*, what is sought; request, desire, demand; investigation; reclamation; requisition; money-claim; salary; — *ṭalab*, *ṭallab*, pl. of طالب *ṭâlib*, who asks, demands, &c.; — *ṭulub*, pl. of طلوب *ṭalûb*; — ة *ṭilba-i*, *ṭalba-t*, anything sought for, beloved, mistress; demand, request, claim, reclamation; prayer, litany; — *ṭulba-t*, long journey; angels who register the deeds of men; — *ṭalaba-t*, pl. of طالب *ṭâlib*, who asks, demands, &c.; — *ṭaliba-t*, anything sought for.

طلبا *ṭulabâ'*, pl. of طليب *ṭalîb*.

طلبي *ṭalabiyy*, sought.

طلتوفة *ṭaltûfa-t*, uvula; its swelling.

(طلث) *ṭalas*, U, INF. *ṭulûs*, flow, run; — II. INF. *taṭlîs*, surpass in number or quantity; — ة *ṭulsa-t*, weak in body and mind.

(طلح) *ṭalaḥ*, INF. *ṭalḥ*, *ṭalâḥa-t*, be jaded; jade; — *ṭaliḥ*, A, INF. *ṭalaḥ*, have the colic from feeding on the acacia; have an empty stomach;—II. INF. *taṭlîḥ*, jade; insist upon; fill to the brim;— IV. INF. *iṭlâḥ*, be jaded; jade.

طلح *ṭalḥ*, palm-blossom; banana; thorny acacia; muddy water; emaciated, jaded; having empty entrails; — *ṭilḥ*, pl. *aṭlâḥ*, jaded; herdsman; friend of women; tick, louse; — *ṭalaḥ*, favour of fortune; wealth; — *ṭaliḥ*, ة, having the colic from feeding on the acacia; ة *ṭaliḥa-t*, producing acacias; du. *ṭaliḥân*, camel and its rider; — *ṭullaḥ*, pl. of طليح *ṭalîḥ*; — ة *ṭalḥa-t*, acacia.

(طلحث) *ṭalḥas*, INF. ة, embarrass, disgrace; stain, soil.

(طلحف) *ṭilaḥf*, *ṭilḥaff*, violent hunger; — also طلحاف *ṭilḥâf*, طلحيف *ṭilḥîf*, violent.

طلحوم *ṭulḥûm*, foul water.

طلحية *ṭalḥiyya-t*, sheet of paper.

(طلخ) *ṭalaḫ*, INF. *ṭalḫ*, stain, dirty, pollute; bespatter with muddy water; blacken; efface; — IX. *iṭlaḫḫ*, INF. *iṭliḫâḫ*, be bathed in tears flow.

طلخ *ṭalḫ*, foul water; dirt, mud.

طلخا *ṭalḫâ'*, f. stupid.

طلخام *ṭilḫâm*, female elephant.

(طلخث) *ṭalḫas*, INF. ة, stain, sully; disgrace.

طلخف *ṭilḫaf*, طلخيف *ṭilḫîf*, violent.

طلخوم *ṭulḥûm*=طلحوم *ṭulḥûm*.

(طلس) *ṭalas*, I, INF. *ṭals*, efface; bring before; waste away, grow blind; pass. be imprisoned; — II. INF. *taṭlîs*, efface; (m.) grow blind; — V. INF. *taṭallus*, be effaced; be used as a head-gear (طيلسان *ṭailasân*, q.v.); — VII. INF. *inṭilâs*, be veiled in mysterious darkness.

طلس *ṭals*=طيلسان *ṭailasân*; — *ṭils*, pl. *aṭlâs*, smooth, hairless; effaced, erased; leaf, sheet of paper, page; dirty; old; — ة *ṭulsa-t*, grey satin.

(طلسم) *ṭalsam*, INF. ة, fix the eyes on the ground; look sullen; recede from the combat; use talismans; surround with spells.

طلسم *ṭilsam*, pl. *ṭilsamât*, *ṭalâsim*, talisman, amulet; صاحب طلسمات *ṣâḥib ṭalismât*, maker of talismans; —ى *ṭilsamiyy*, having the power of a talisman.

طلش *ṭalś*, knife.

(طلطل) *ṭalṭal*, INF. ة, move (a.).

طلطل *ṭalṭal*, ة *ṭalṭala-t*, calamity; — *ṭulṭul*, chronic disease.

طلطين *ṭulṭain*, calamity.

(طلع) *ṭala'*, U, INF. *ṭulû'*, *maṭla'*, *maṭli'*, rise; — U, INF. *ṭulû'*,— *ṭali'*, A, ascend a mountain, mount; break forth; put forth blossoms; — U, A, INF. *ṭulû'*, come upon, befall; surprise; observe; go, depart; visit, reach; (m.) go out, leave the house, leave the service; originate; become; occur; know, understand; — *ṭali'*, A, ascend; — II. INF. *taṭlî'*, (m.) *ṭaila'*, cause to ascend, to come forth, to go out; put forth blossoms; fill up the measure; (m.) complete, earn, see, perceive; — III. INF. *ṭilâ'*, *muṭâla'a-t*, look at attentively; see, revise, peruse, study; show, propound, allow an insight or perusal; — IV. INF. *iṭlâ'*, cause to ascend, to appear, to come forth; put forth blossoms; draw one's attention to; disclose, make known, impart a secret; render services; vomit; shoot beyond the aim; urge to haste; appear, rise; come; — V. INF. *taṭallu'*, look out for; expect, endeavour; look at attentively; survey, enjoy a view from above; know; be entirely full; totter in walking; — VIII. INF. *iṭṭilâ'*, appear, rise; put forth blossoms; examine, study, know; see, perceive; come upon unexpectedly; reach; ascend; be fit for (ل *li*); vomit; — X. INF. *istiṭlâ'*, investigate, inquire for, try to find out one's intentions; make search for; ask to show; go away with.

طلع *ṭal'*, leaf of a blossom; spathe of the palm-tree; palm-shoot; number, quantity, measure; — *ṭil'*, lowland; tract, region; a long snake; sight; perception; care; insight into a secret; — *ṭul'*, pl. of طلاع *ṭilâ'*; — ة *ṭal'a-t*, aspect, sight; face; ascending (s.), rising ground, sloping terrace; (m.) death, burial; prepuce; — *ṭul'a-t*, considerate; peeping forth (woman, opposed to خباة *ḥuba'a-t*, hiding, withdrawing).

طلعا *ṭula'â'*, vomiting (s.).

(طلغ) *ṭalag*, INF. *ṭalg*, *ṭalagân*, be weak, languid, faint.

طلغان *ṭalagân*, tired, weak; tiredness, weakness, languidness.

(طلف), II. *ṭallaf*, INF. *taṭlîf*, be more, surpass; — IV. INF. *iṭlâf*, give, present; leave unpunished, unavenged; remain so.

طلف *ṭalf-an*, *ṭalaf-an*, (adv.) with impunity, without revenge; — *ṭalaf*, present; liberty, leave; easy; pleasant; brimful.

(طلفح) *ṭalfaḥ*, INF. ة, make thin, fine.

طلفح *ṭalfaḥ*, pl. *ṭalâfiḥ*, large and broad.

(طلق) *ṭalaq*, U, *ṭaluq*, INF. *ṭalâq*,

get divorced; be left at large; — INF. *ṭalq*, *ṭulûq*, hurry to water which is a day's journey distant; — INF. *ṭalq*, open one's hand for a bounty; give; leave to one's disposal; (m.) fire off a gun; — *ṭaliq*, A, be far distant; — *ṭaluq*, be divorced; INF. *ṭulûqa-t*, *ṭalâqa-t*, be open and cheerful; be temperate, not too hot; — INF. *ṭalq*, lie in the throes of child-birth; — II. INF. *taṭlîq*, dismiss a wife, divorce (a.); leave, abandon; fructify (the palm-tree); recover (from a violent pain); — IV. INF. *iṭlâq*, divorce (a.); leave at large, set free; open one's hand for a bounty; present with; poison; fructify; generalize; let go, drop, fire off; — V. INF. *taṭalluq*, get dismissed, divorced; hasten by; be open and cheerful; — VII. INF. *inṭilâq*, be set free, dismissed; set out; go away with, carry off; be open and cheerful; — VIII. INF. *iṭṭilâq*, cheer up (n.); — X. INF. *istiṭlâq*, get eased (bowels); get loosened; allow the she-camel to pasture at large.

(طلق) *ṭalq*, *ṭalaq*, course, running (s.), race; shot, volley; — *ṭalq*, *ṭaliq*, طليق *ṭalîq*, ة, set free; free, unrestrained; open; — *ṭalq*, ة, temperate, moderate; simple; unfettered; liberal; cheerful; glib; pl. *aṭlâq*, deer, gazelle; sporting-dog; untethered camel; wine; — *ṭalq*, *ṭilq*, talc; — *ṭilq*, permitted, lawful; free; frank, open; eloquent; the best; — *ṭulq*, unfettered, untethered; — *ṭalaq*, night-journey to the water; tether; part, portion; pl. *aṭlâq*, entrails; — *ṭaliq*, free, frank, open; eloquent; — *ṭulaq*, eloquent; unfettered; — *ṭuluq*, pl. *aṭlâq*, untethered; eloquent; liberal; — *ṭuluq*, pl. freedmen; — *ṭullaq*, pl. of طالق *ṭâliq*, divorced, &c.; — ة *ṭulaqa-t*, man who divorces frequently.

طلقا *ṭulaqâ'*, pl. of طليق *ṭalîq*.

طلل *ṭalal*, pl. *aṭlâl*, *ṭulûl*, object, form, person; anything elevated; house-top; ruins of a dwelling, ruins of a camp; sail; sitting-room; surface of water; fresh, juicy, green, verdant; — *ṭilal*, pl. of طل *ṭall*; — *ṭulal*, pl. of طلة *ṭulla-t*; — *ṭulul*, pl. of طليل *ṭalîl*.

(طلم) *ṭalam*, U, INF. *ṭalm*, form the cake; — II. INF. *taṭlîm*, knead the dough.

طلم *ṭulm*, kneading-trough; — *ṭalam*, impurity of the mouth; — ة *ṭulma-t*, pl. *ṭulam*, *ṭalâmî*, bread baked in the ashes; cake; — *ṭalama-t*, pl. of طالم *ṭâlim*, baker.

(طلنس), IV. *iṭlansa*, INF. *iṭlinsâ'*, perspire all over.

(طلنش), IV. *iṭlanśa*, INF. *iṭlinśâ'*, wander from place to place.

(طلنفا) *ṭalanfa'*, *ṭalanfâ'*, طلنفى *ṭalanfa*, f. talkative; — IV. *iṭlanfa'*, INF. *iṭlinfâ'*, adhere to the ground.

طلنفح *ṭalanfaḥ*, having empty bowels, hungry; jaded, tired.

(طله) *ṭalah*, U, INF. *ṭalh*, wander about wearily and sulkily.

طله *ṭulh*, pastures with little grass left, pl. of اطله *aṭlah*; — *ṭulah*, thin cloud; — ة *ṭulha-t*, rests, remains (of a property).

(طلهيس) *ṭalahyas*, *ṭilhîs*, large army; *ṭalahyas*, darkness of the night.

(طلو) *ṭalâ*, U, tie up; INF. *ṭalâwa-t*, hesitate, tarry.

طلو *ṭalw*=طلا *ṭal-an*; — *ṭilw*, small and slender; wolf; — ة *ṭalwa-t*, string, rope; — *ṭilwa-t*, young (of an animal); — *ṭalwa-t*, brightness of dawn; neck.

طلوا *ṭulawâ'*, delay; expectation.

طلوان *ṭulwân*, *ṭalawân*=the pre-

vious; spittle drying up in the mouth.

طلوب *ṭalûb*, pl. *ṭulub*, seeking eagerly.

طلوع *ṭulû'*, ascent, rise; sprouting (s.), INF. of (طلع); (m.) pustule, abscess.

طلوقة *ṭulûqa-t*=طلاقة *ṭulâqa-t*.

(طلى) *ṭala*, I, INF. *ṭaly*, rub in, smear, cover with (as with gold, &c.); tie up a lamb to keep it away from its dam; — *ṭalî*, A, INF. *ṭal-an*, have yellow teeth; — II. INF. *taṭliya-t*, rub in, smear; abuse, revile; visit and nurse the sick; sing and make music; — IV. INF. *iṭlâ'*, incline to; follow one's inclination; bow the head and die; — V. INF. *taṭallî*, be rubbed, smeared; follow one's inclinations and pleasures; — VIII. INF. *iṭṭilâ'*, be rubbed, smeared.

طلى *ṭala-n*=طلا *ṭal-an*; — *ṭilan*, pleasure; — *ṭulan*, *ṭullan*, draught of milk; — *ṭaliyy*, having yellow teeth; yellowness of the teeth; tied up; smeared, anointed; pl. *ṭulyân*, lamb; — ة *ṭulya-t*, pl. *ṭula-n*, neck.

طليا *ṭalyâ*, smeared; scabious; scab.

طليان *ṭilyân*, yellowness of the teeth; pl. of طلى *ṭaliyy*; — *ṭalayân*, pl. of طلا *ṭal-an*.

طليب *ṭalîb*, pl. *ṭulabâ'*, seeking, investigating (adj.); student; freeman; *ṭalîb*, f. ة, betrothed.

طليح *ṭalîḥ*, ة, pl. *ṭilâḥ*, *ṭullaḥ*, *ṭalâ'iḥ*, tired, jaded; sheep-louse.

طليس *ṭillîs*, blind.

طليعة *ṭalî'a-t*, pl. *ṭalâ'i'*, vanguard, outpost; scout, spy.

طليف *ṭalîf*, received; gratis, for nothing, worthless.

طليق *ṭalîq*, pl. *ṭulaqâ'*, set free, emancipated; frank and open, cheerful; eloquent; — *ṭillîq*, who divorces frequently.

طليل *ṭalîl*, sweet; unavenged; pl. *aṭilla-t*, *ṭilla-t*, *ṭulul*, mat of palm-bast.

(طم) *ṭamm*, U, INF. *ṭamm*, *ṭumûm*, abound and overflow; drown, surpass; (m.) bury; fill to overflowing; shave the head; cut, plait or dress the hair; sit or nestle in the summit of a tree; — I, U, INF. *ṭamm*, *ṭamîm*, be swift; — II. INF. *taṭmîm*, fall upon a branch; — IV. INF. *iṭmâm*, be long and fit to be cut (hair); — VII. INF. *inṭimâm*, be quite full, entirely covered; be swallowed, buried; — X. INF. *istiṭmâm*=IV.

طم *ṭamm*, sea; mass of water; — *ṭimm*, water; sea; what the water carries off; male ostrich; large penis; noble mare; large number; abundance, wealth; anything wonderful; admiration; prudent, cunning, sly; — ة *ṭumma-t*, piece of mud.

طماح *ṭimâḥ*, obstinacy, headstrongness; avarice, covetousness; longing for; ambition; — *ṭammâḥ*, greedy, covetous, avaricious; ambitious; — ة *ṭammâḥa-t*, f. coquettish and obstinate; — *ṭummâḥa-t*, mattress.

طماحر *ṭumâḥir*, insatiable.

طماخر *ṭumâḥir*, male camel.

طمار *ṭamâr-a*, *ṭamâr-i*, height, hill; بنات ط *banât ṭamâr-i*, calamity.

طماسة *ṭamâsa-t*, surmise, INF. of (طمس).

طماع *ṭamâ'*, desire, eagerness, greed, INF. of (طمع); — *ṭammâ'*, greedy, covetous; — ة *ṭamâ'a-t*, greed, desire, covetousness.

طماعى *ṭamâ'ā*, pl. of طامع *ṭâmi'*, greedy, desirous, &c., and of طمع *ṭami'*; — ة *ṭamâ'iya-t*, greed, desire.

طماليح *ṭamâlîḥ*, small white clouds.

(طامن , طمان) *ṭam'an*, *ṭa'man*, INF. ة, lean one's back against; rest; — II. *taṭa'mun*, descend into a hole or cavity; — III.

iṭma'ann, INF. *iṭmi'nân*, *ṭuma'nîna-t*, dwell or sit peaceably; enjoy security; trust in; be low, level; show one's self submissive, yield.

طمانينة *ṭuma'nîna-t*, *ṭumânîna-t*, rest, quiet, tranquillity of mind; levelness; INF. of the previous.

(طمث) *ṭamas̱*, I, U, INF. *ṭams̱*, deflower, lie with for the first time; touch for the first time (a pasture); — U, INF. *ṭams̱*, have the menses; be impure.

طمث *ṭams̱*, *ṭims̱*, menses; dirt, impurity, pollution; vice.

(طمح) *ṭamaḥ*, INF. *ṭamḥ*, *ṭimâḥ*, *ṭamâḥ*, have higher things in view; look at attentively or longingly, gaze; strive to rise, to obtain higher rank or dignity; be disobedient; make the highest efforts to obtain a thing; go or run away with; fall to the ground; — INF. *ṭimâḥ*, be disobedient, refractory, restive; — II. INF. *taṭmîḥ*, raise the fore-feet; — IV. INF. *iṭmâḥ*, have higher things in view.

طمحات *ṭamaḥât*, pl. calamity.

(طمحر), III. *iṭmaḥarr*, INF. *iṭmiḥrâr*, drink one's fill.

طمحرير *ṭamḥarîr*=طماحر *ṭumâḥir*.

(طمخ) *ṭamaẖ*, U, INF. *ṭamẖ*, be proud, haughty.

(طمخر), III. *iṭmaẖarr*, INF. *iṭmiẖrâr* =اطمحر *iṭmaḥarr*.

طمخرير *ṭamẖarîr*=طمحرير *ṭamḥarîr*.

(طمر) *ṭamar*, U, INF. *ṭamr*, dig under, bury; conceal; fill (a.); swell (n.); — I, INF. *ṭamr*, *ṭumûr*, *ṭimâr*, leap, leap up; skip, hop; — INF. *ṭumûr*, travel, set out on a journey; pass. have a violent tooth-ache; — *ṭamir*, A, INF. *ṭamar*, swell; — II. INF. *taṭmîr*, fold up; let down the curtains; — VIII. INF. *iṭṭimâr*, jump from behind upon the horse.

طمر *ṭimr*, pl. *aṭmâr*, tattered garment, ragged coat; poor; penniless; a green magpie; noble, generous, mettled; — *ṭummar*, root, origin, cause; youthful inexperience; — *ṭimirr*, ة, *ṭimirra-t*, mettled horse; — ة *ṭummara-t*, early youth.

(طمرس) *ṭamras*, INF. ة, shrink, contract (n.); desist.

طمرس *ṭimris*, liar; villain.

طمرسا *ṭimrisâ'*, dust.

طمرر *ṭimrir*, mettled horse.

طمرور *ṭumrûr*=طمر *ṭimr*.

طمروس *ṭumrûs*, bread baked in the ashes; lamb; foal six months old; liar, villain.

طمرير *ṭimrîr*, mettled horse.

(طمس) *ṭamas*, U, I, INF. *ṭumûs*, be effaced, extinguished; — INF. *ṭams*, efface, extinguish; destroy, annihilate; see far; be far distant; (m.) be blind; dip deep into the water; — I, INF. *ṭamâsa-t*, surmise, suppose, estimate approximately; — II. INF. *taṭmîs*, efface the traces; (m.) blind; — IV. INF. *iṭmâs*, destroy, annihilate; — V. INF. *taṭammus*, be effaced, extinguished, have disappeared.

طمس *ṭams*, obliteration of traces.

(طمسل) *ṭamsal*, INF. ة, be unfit for coition.

طمسل *ṭumsul*, pl. *ṭamâsila-t*, thief.

طمسلى *ṭamsala*, damage, calamity; *'ala 't-ṭamsala*, stealthily, like a thief.

(طمش) *ṭamś*, pl. *ṭumûś*, man; people, men.

طمطام *ṭamṭâm*, middle of the sea.

(طمطم) *ṭamṭam*, INF. ة, swim in the middle of the sea; pronounce Arabic badly; stammer; twitter, chirp.

طمطم *ṭimṭim* (طمطمى *ṭimṭimiyy*, طمطمانى *ṭimṭimâniyy*), pl. *ṭamâṭim*, speaking barbarously; stammering; a species of short-eared sheep; — طمطمانية *ṭimṭimâniyya-t*, objectionable provincialism.

(طمع) *ṭami'*, A, INF. *ṭama'*, *ṭamâ'*, *ṭamâ'iya-t*, long for, desire, covet what belongs to others; satisfy one's greed, steal; (m.) allow one's self everything towards; — *ṭamu'*, INF. *ṭamâ'a-t*, be very greedy or covetous; — II. INF. *taṭmî'*, and IV. INF. *iṭmâ'*, embolden one against another; IV. make covet.

طمع *ṭama'*, greed, covetousness; ambition; pl. *aṭmâ'*, pay, wages; day of payment; anything coveted, desired, craved for; — *ṭami'*, *ṭamu'*, pl. *ṭami'ûn*, *ṭuma'â'*, *ṭamâ'a*, *aṭmâ'*, greedy, covetous; ambitious.

(طمخ) *ṭamig*, A, INF. *ṭamag*, be full of impure matter (eye).

طمغا *ṭamgâ'*, mark by branding; stamp; edict; diploma.

(طمل) *ṭamal*, U, INF. *ṭaml*, urge on violently; roll out the dough; dye deeply; stain; — *ṭamil*, A, INF. *ṭamal*, be stained; — II. INF. *taṭmîl*, roll out the dough; (m.) give a round shape; — IV. INF. *iṭmâl*, efface, blot out; — V. INF. *taṭammul*, be stained; — VII. INF. *inṭimâl*, be the companion of robbers; — VIII. INF. *iṭṭimâl*, exhaust, drink out.

طمل *ṭaml*, creation; created things, creatures; — *ṭiml*, deeply coloured garment; black, dark green; common, worthless; muddy water, pl. *ṭumûl*, stupid; ludicrous, farcical; obstinate, sullen, sulky, peevish; dirty; poor; worn-out, ragged, torn; bare, bald; necklace; — *ṭimill*, bald wolf; — ة *ṭamla-t*, *ṭumla-t*, *ṭamala-t*, mud, muddy water; — *ṭimla-t*, id.; weak woman; *ṭumla-t*, dirty bargain.

طملال *ṭimlâl*, poor, pitiable; naked, bare, bald; wicked, bad; thief..

(طملس) *ṭamlas*, INF. ة, show great zeal; flatter cunningly; hate.

طملس *ṭamallas*, dry; thin; — ة *ṭamlasa-t*, hatred.

طملول *ṭumlûl*, طمليل *ṭimlîl*=طملال *ṭimlâl*.

(طمن) *ṭamn*, pl. *ṭumûn*, quiet, tranquil; — II. *ṭamman*, INF. *taṭmîn*, quiet, tranquillise (m.); — VI. INF. *taṭâmun*, stoop to enter (m.).

(طمو) *ṭamâ*, U, INF. *ṭumuww*=(طمى).

طمور *ṭimmaur*, root, origin.

طمول *ṭamûl*, pl. *ṭumûl*, corrupt, shameless; — * ; — *ṭammûl*, ة *ṭammûla-t*, ball of dough; snowball; badly-risen dough.; — ة *ṭumûla-t*, corruption, corruptness, shamelessness.

(طمى) *ṭami'*, be unclean, impure; — II. INF. *taṭmi'a-t*, consider unclean; impure; — *ṭama*, I, INF. *ṭamy*, *ṭumiyy*, rise high, swell, overflow; grow high; be thin; run quickly by.

طميس *ṭamîs*, blind, blinded, dazzled.

طميع *ṭimmî'*, very greedy.

طميل *ṭamîl*, blood-stained; broad thorn of a palm-tree; concealed; muddy water; rolled out; mat; necklace; — also ة *ṭamîla-t*, kid.

طميم *ṭamîm*, noble fleet horse.

طميئن *ṭumai'in*, quite at rest; — ة *ṭumai'ina-t*, a little rest.

(طن) *ṭann*, U, INF. *ṭanîn*, produce a metallic sound, tinkle, hum, buzz; quack; tingle (ear); die; — II. INF. *taṭnîn*, tinkle, hum; — IV. INF. *iṭnân*, make tinkle, cause to sound, cause the ears to tingle; cut off, amputate.

طن *ṭin'*, last gasp of breath; remains of water in a well; dead ashes; illness, disease; lust, lustfulness, fornication; lion's den; high ground without water; bare ground; garden; purpose, intention, plan; dwelling, resting-place, station; bed,

pillow; stone inclosure for cattle; — *ṭinn*, sweet fresh date; — *ṭunn*, pl. *aṭnân*, *ṭinân*, the human body; load carried on the camel's back between the loads carried on both sides; bundle of reeds; — ة *ṭanna-t*, tinkling, sounding (s.); — *ṭunna-t*, stalk of reed out of a bundle.

(طنا) *ṭana'*, A, INF. *ṭan'*, be ashamed; — طنى *ṭani'*, A, INF. *ṭana'*, have the milt grown fast to the side; be ashamed to speak out; — IV. INF. *iṭnâ'*, be inclined to alight at an inn, &c., to go to bed, to drink; let alive; — ة *ṭana'a-t*, pl. fornicators; — *ṭunât*, pl. of طانى *ṭânî*, id.

طناب *ṭanâb*, *ṭinâb*, tent-rope; rope-ladder, scaling ladder; springe.

طنابر *ṭanâbir*, pl. of طنبور *ṭumbûr*..

طناز *ṭannâz*, jocose, facetious; satirical.

طنافة *ṭanâfa-t*, abstemiousness, continence.

طنان *ṭannân*, tinkling, resounding (adj.); — *.

(طنب) *ṭanib*, A, INF. *ṭanab*, be bent, crooked; be strung (bow); have long and weak legs, have a long back; — II. INF. *taṭnîb*, fix a tent by stretching the ropes; tie the milk-bag to the pole for making butter by shaking it; abide in a dwelling; howl; have long flanks; be exceedingly zealous; (m.) be proud; — IV. INF. *iṭnâb*, exceed the bounds; raise much dust; walk one behind the other; have a long course; amplify (in praise or blame).

طنب *ṭanab*, a tree; INF. of the previous; — *ṭunub*, pl. *aṭnâb*, *ṭinaba-t*, tent-rope; strap which fixes the string to the bow; string; root of a tree; ط الاطناب *ṭunub al-iṭnâb*, bombastic style.

طنبا *ṭambâ'*, f. of اطنب, having a long back, weak legs.

طنبار *ṭimbâr*, lute.

(طنبازيز) *ṭambâzîz*, pudenda of a woman.

(طنبل) *ṭambal*, INF. ة, prove stupid (after pretending to be wise).

طنبور *ṭumbûr*, pl. *ṭanâbîr*, also ة *ṭumbûra-t*, lute; — ى *ṭumbûriyy*, انى *ṭumbûrâniyy*, player on the lute.

(طنشر) *ṭanṣar*, INF. ة, eat so much fat that indigestion follows; — II. INF. *taṭanṣur*, have indigestion from eating fat.

(طنج) *ṭanj*, pl. *ṭunûj*, saddle-strap; pl. kinds; leaves of a book, sheets of paper stitched together.

طنجرة *ṭanjara-t*, pl. *ṭanâjir*, طنجير *ṭinjîr*, pl. *ṭanâjîr*, frying-pan; kettle, pot.

(طنح) *ṭaniḥ*, A, INF. *ṭanaḥ*, suffer from indigestion; be fat.

(طنخ) *ṭaniḫ*, A, INF. *ṭanaḫ*, suffer from indigestion; be too fat; — II. INF. *taṭnîḫ*, IV. INF. *iṭnâḫ*, bring on indigestion.

طنخ *ṭinḫ*, part of the night; — ة *ṭanaḫa-t*, stupid.

(طنز) *ṭanaz*, U, INF. *ṭanz*, mock at, ridicule, taunt, scoff.

طنز *ṭanz*, joke, mockery; a fish.

(طنس) *ṭanas*, dense darkness.

(طنش), II. *ṭannaś*, INF. *taṭnîś*, be silent, quiet.

ذو طنطان *zû ṭanṭân*, noisy, clamorous, tumultuous.

(طنطن) *ṭanṭan*, INF. ة, tinkle, sound, hum, resound, re-echo; — ة *ṭanṭana-t*, metallic sound, tinkling (s.); echo; hum, murmur; pomp.

طنطور *ṭanṭûr*, head-ornament of metal for women (m.).

(طنف) *ṭanif*, A, INF. *ṭanaf*, be suspected; — INF. *ṭanaf*, *ṭanâfa-t*, *ṭunûfa-t*, have a bad heart; — INF. *ṭanâfa-t*, scorn, abstain from; — II. INF. *taṭnîf*, suspect; protect a wall by putting thorns, &c., on it; make desirous

for; — v. INF. *taṭannuf*, feel a desire, long for; come upon unexpectedly.

طنف *ṭanf*, *ṭunf*, *ṭanaf*, *ṭunuf*, pl. *aṭnâf*, *ṭunûf*, mountain-knoll; projecting part of a wall; anything projecting; — *ṭanaf*, red straps; suspicion, — *ṭanif*, suspected; malignant; poor eater.

(طنفس) *ṭanfas*, INF. ة, deteriorate, degenerate; put on many clothes.

طنفس *ṭinfis*, corrupt, degenerated, disfigured; — ة *ṭanfasa-t*, *ṭanfisa-t*, *ṭanfusa-t*, *ṭinfasa-t*, *ṭinfisa-t*, *ṭunfusa-t*, pl. *ṭanâfis*, coarse shaggy cloth or carpet; mat of palm-leaves; garment.

(طنفش) *ṭanfaś*, INF. ة, look close at; press the eyelids together, make the eyes small.

طنفش *ṭanfaś*, ى *ṭanfaśiyy*, طنفشا *ṭanfaśâ'*, weak, cowardly.

طنو *ṭanw*, bed, couch; — *ṭunw* = طنى *ṭiny*.

(طنى) *ṭanî*, A, INF. *ṭanan*, buy palm-trees, buy dates by the weight; persist in fornication; have the milt and liver adhering to the left side; — INF. *ṭinan*, get cured (from the bite of a scorpion); — II. INF. *taṭniya-t*, cure one who has the above disease; cauterise the camel in the side; — IV. INF. *iṭnâ'*, persist in fornication; have the milt as above described; buy trees, sell dates; strike a blow not fatal; let live; incline to being suspicious; turn lazily to the couch.

طنى *ṭany*, suspicion; extinguished; illness, disease; water-moss; — *ṭiny*, fornication; — *ṭanan*, *ṭanî*, having the milt adhering to the side; — *ṭani'*, see (طنا); — *ṭunniyy*, strong and corpulent.

طنين *ṭanîn*, tinkling, humming (s.); tingling of the ears, &c.; INF. of (طن).

(طه) *ṭah*, silence! be quiet! O man!

طها *ṭahâ'*, ة *ṭahâṭ*, high cloud; — ة *ṭuhât*, pl. of طاهى *ṭâhiyy*, cook, &c.

طهار *ṭahhâr*, who purifies; — ة *ṭahâra-t*, purity, sanctity; — ى *ṭahârâ*, pl. of طاهر *ṭâhir*, pure, chaste.

طهاطه *ṭahâṭih*, neighing (s.).

طهاف *ṭahâf*, high cloud; — ة *ṭuhâfa-t*, also طهاوة *ṭuhâwa-t*, thin skin upon milk or blood.

طهاية *ṭahâya-t*, preparation, dressing.

(طهبل) *ṭahbal*, INF. ة, travel, set out on a journey.

طهثة *ṭuhsa-t*, big and stupid.

(طهر) *ṭahar*, INF. *ṭahr*, remove (a.); — INF. *ṭuhr*, *ṭahûr*, — *ṭahur*, INF. *ṭahâra-t*, be pure; be clean again after the menses, &c.; — II. INF. *taṭhîr*, purify, cleanse, wash; — III. INF. *muṭâhara-t*, cleanse; circumcise; — v. INF. *taṭahhur*, *iṭṭahur*, be pure, clean; cleanse one's self, wash (n.); abstain from sin.

طهر *ṭuhr*, purity, chastity; — *ṭahir*, pl. *-ûn*, *aṭhâr*, pure; — ة *ṭuhra-t*, purity, cleanness.

طهران *ṭuhrân*, pure, clean.

(طهس) *ṭahas*, INF. *ṭahs*, enter a country, come to.

(طهش) *ṭahaś*, INF. *ṭahś*, spoil, get confused and spoil a work in consequence.

(طهطا) *ṭahṭâ'*, young handsome horse.

(طهف) *ṭahf*, *ṭahaf*, a grass with eatable seed; *ṭahf*, millet or bread of it; — *aṭhaf*, INF. *iṭhâf*, grow luxuriantly; give part of one's own to another; utter one's words rapidly; be flabby; — ة *ṭahfa-t*, the upper part of fresh chives; زبدة ط *zubda-t ṭahfa-t*, fresh cream or butter; — *ṭihfa-t*, part, portion, piece; — *ṭahaffa-t*, cloth placed beneath the saddle.

(طهفل) *ṭahfal*, INF. ة, eat continually bread of millet.
(طهق) *ṭahaq*, INF. *ṭahq*, walk fast.
طهق *ṭahaq*, quick walk.
(طهل) *ṭahal*, *ṭahil*, A, INF. *ṭahal*, be spoiled, be putrid.
طهل *ṭahl*, foul, putrid; — ة *ṭuhla-t*, a delicate vegetable; a small quantity of food.
(طهلب) *ṭahlab*, INF. ة, travel into a country.
طهلئة *ṭihli'a-t*, small cloud; darkness.
(طهم) *ṭahm*, *ṭuhm*, kind or race of men; — II. *ṭahham*, INF. *taṭhîm*, abhor, loathe, detest; be thick, plump; be handsome of form; — V. INF. *taṭahhum*, abhor; get estranged from (عن *'an*); — ة *ṭuhma-t*, black with a shade of yellow, whitish red; — *ṭahima-t*, having thin, fleshless face (f.).
طهملى *ṭahmaliyy*, black and dwarfish.
(طهنبى) *ṭahamba*, strong camel.
(طهو) *ṭahâ*, U, A, INF. *ṭahw*, *ṭuhuww*, *ṭuhiyy*, *ṭahâya-t*, prepare meat by boiling or roasting; — INF. *ṭahw*, travel into a country; — IV. INF. *iṭhâ'*, be a master in one's art.
طهو *ṭahw*, work, labour.
طهور *ṭahûr*, cleansing, washing (s.).
طهى *ṭahan*, particles of straw; — *ṭuhan*, anything cooked, decoction; wolf; pl. of طاهى *ṭâhî*, cook, &c.; — *ṭuhiyy*, INF. of (طهو).
طهيا *ṭahyâ'*, somebody, a person.
طهيان *ṭahayân*, summit; offal, shavings.
طهياية *ṭahyâya-t*, preparation of meat.
طهير *ṭahîr*, pl. *ṭahâra*, pure, clean.
(طهيل) *ṭahyal*, INF. ة, eat of the vegetable طهلة *ṭuhla-t*; — ة *ṭahîla-t*, *ṭih'ila-t*, *ṭihli'a-t*, fresh mortar falling from the sides of a well; stupid and useless.
(طو) *ṭâ'*, U, INF. *ṭau'*, come and go; — A, depart, go far away; — INF. *ṭâ'a-t*, go far to a pasture-ground; — VI. INF. *taṭâyu'*, rise high.
طو *ṭaw-in*, see طوى *ṭawî*.
طواب *ṭawwâb*, brick-maker, tiler.
طواحين *ṭawâḥîn*, water-mills, pl. of طاحونة *ṭâḥûna-t*.
طواخ *ṭawwâḫ*, offensive.
طوار *ṭawâr*, opposite and of equal extent; similar, corresponding; — *ṭawâr*, *ṭiwâr*, extent of the area of a house.
(طواز) *ṭawwâz*, soft to the touch.
طواس *ṭawâs*, one of the three last nights of a month.
طواشى *ṭawâšiyy*, pl. ة, eunuch; gelding.
طواط *ṭuwâṭ*, apt, able; foaming with rut.
طواعن *ṭawâ'in*, pl. of طاعون *ṭâ'ûn*, plague.
طواعية *ṭawâ'iya-t*, obedience.
طواغى *ṭawâġî*, طواغيت *ṭawâġît*, rebels, &c., pl. of طاغوت.
طواف *ṭawâf*, walk or procession round; part, portion; — *ṭawwâf*, who partakes in the procession; going around (adj.); vagabond, vagrant; surrounding with careful attention; inundation; — *ṭuwwâf*, pl. of طائف *ṭâ'if*, circulating, &c.
طوال *ṭawâl*, duration, while, length; ط الدهر *ṭawâl ad-dahr*, never; — *ṭiwâl*, pl. of طويل *ṭawîl*; — *ṭuwâl*, long and big, tall; — *ṭuwwâl*, very long and big, gigantic.
طوامير *ṭawâmîr*, books, rolls, leaves, &c., pl. of طامور *ṭâmûr* and طومار *ṭûmâr*.
طواويس *ṭawâwîs*, peacocks, pl. of طاوس *ṭâ'us*.
طوائح *ṭawâ'iḥ*, pl. calamities from all sides, shocks.
طوائق *ṭawâ'iq*, pl. necklaces, chains.
(طوب) *ṭûb*, brick; — for Turk. طوپ *ṭûp*, cannon; cannon-ball; ball.
طوبا *ṭûbâ*=طوبى *ṭûba*.
طوباز *ṭûbâz*, topaz.
طوبالة *ṭûbâla-t*, sheep.
طوبانى *ṭûbâniyy*, and—

طوباوى *ṭûbâwiyy*, happy, blissful; beatified; — ة *ṭûbâwiyya-t*, bliss; beatification (m.).

طوبجى *ṭûbjiyy* (for Turk. طوپچى *ṭopchiyy*), cannonier.

طوبخانة *ṭûb-ḥâna-t*, arsenal.

طوبى *ṭûba*, f. of اطيب *aṭyab*, better, &c.; a tree of paradise; blessing; hail! well done! pl. of طيبة *ṭayyiba-t*.

طوتماج *ṭûtmâj*=طودماج *ṭûdamâj*.

(طوح) *ṭâḥ*, U, I, INF. *ṭauḥ*, perish, waste away, be close on ruin; fall, drop; go away, depart; go astray, wander; lead amiss; throw one's self down from on high; — II. INF. *taṭwîḥ*, cause to stray; lead amiss; drive hither and thither; cast; send one whence he will not come back, into a dangerous desert, &c.; fill one with longing or passion for (ب *bi*); beat; render shy, timid; — III. INF. *muṭâwaḥa-t*, throw one upon another; — IV. INF. *iṭâḥa-t*, cause the hair to fall out; cause a thing to perish or be lost; — V. INF. *taṭawwuḥ*, wander about; — VI. INF. *taṭâwuḥ*, pelt one another (ب *bi*) with anything (acc.).

طوح *ṭawaḥ*, ة, distant aim, intention.

(طوخ) *ṭâḫ*, U, INF. *ṭauḫ*, disgrace by word or deed.

(طود) *ṭâd*, U, INF. *ṭaud*, stand firm; — II. INF. *taṭwîd*, (also V.) roam about in the country, in the mountains; — IV. INF. *iṭâda-t*, fix, consolidate; — V. INF. *taṭawwud*, see II.; — VII. INF. *inṭiyâd*, rise into the air (as a building, &c.).

طود *ṭaud*, pl. *ṭiwada-t*, *aṭwâd*, high mountain with a broad base; sandhill.

طودماج *ṭûdamâj*, vermicelli in broth.

(طور) *ṭâr*, U, step up to, approach; INF. *ṭaur*, *ṭawarân*, go around anything.

طور *ṭaur*, *ṭûr*, opposite and of equal extent; similar, corresponding; pl. *aṭwâr*, measure, bound, quantity; manner, way, method; behaviour; kind, category; anything separating, boundary; turn, time; — *ṭûr*, pl. *aṭwâr*, mountain; Mount Sinai; — *ṭûr*, courtyard; — ة *ṭiwara-t*, bad sign; unpropitious augury.

طوران *ṭawarân*, INF. of (طور); — ى *ṭûrâniyy*, somebody, anybody; a wild pigeon.

طورى *ṭûriyy*, wild; = the previous.

(طوس) *ṭâs*, U, INF. *ṭaus*, tread under; be blooming again after illness; — II. INF. *taṭwîs*, go away with; adorn, deck out; — V. INF. *taṭawwus*, adorn one's self; boast.

طوس *ṭûs*, duration; a medicine to strengthen the memory; the city of Ṭûs; — ى *ṭûsiyy*, of or from Ṭûs; a kind of purple.

(طوش), II. *ṭawwaś*, INF. *taṭwîś*, put off a creditor; geld, castrate; (m.) stun, dumbfound.

طوش *ṭauś*, levity; absence of mind; — ة *ṭauśa-t*, id.; thoughtlessness, inconsiderate action; (m.) noise, tumult, revolution.

(طوط) *ṭâṭ*, U, INF. *ṭuwûṭ*, rut; — A, INF. *ṭuyûṭ*, id.; roar with rut.

طوط *ṭûṭ*, long, tall; small; strong and courageous; quarrelsome; cotton; a kind of rush; sparrow-hawk; bat (animal); a snake; hot water pipe in a bath; rutting.

(طوطر) *ṭauṭar*, INF. ة, throw repeatedly.

(طوع) *ṭâ'*, U, A, INF. *ṭau'*, be obedient, willing, docile; give to dispose of; second a speaker; — II. INF. *taṭwî'*, render docile, tame; admit, give permission or power; — III. INF. *muṭâwa'a-t*, consent, agree, condescend; fit with; follow; — IV. INF. *iṭâ'a-t*, obey; place at one's disposal; present ripe fruit

(tree); — V. *taṭawwu'*, obey; supererogate; — VI. INF. *taṭâwu'*, obey, yield, allow one's self to be guided; use one's efforts for;. try to carry out; — X. INF. *istiṭâ'a-t*, obey; have the power to, be able.

طوع *ṭau'*, obedience; accord; obedient, docile, yielding; *ṭau-an*, of free will; (m.) pl. *aṭwâ'* (also طوغ *ṭaug*, pl. *aṭwâg*), horse's tail carried before a pacha; —*ṭuwwa'*, pl. of طائع *ṭâ'i'*, obedient; — ة *ṭuwa'a-t*, who obeys everybody.

طوغری *ṭûgriyy*, straight on, right ahead (Turk.).

(طوف) *ṭâf*, U, INF. *ṭauf*, *ṭawâf*, *ṭawafân*, go around, circulate, describe a circle round; — INF. *ṭauf*, go out to ease the bowels; — II. INF. *taṭwîf*, *taṭwâf*, go repeatedly around; lead round; — IV. INF. *iṭâfa-t*, go around; go in company; — V. INF. *taṭawwuf*, X. INF. *istiṭâfa-t*, go around.

طوف *ṭauf*, going around (s.), round, patrol; inflated bladders or bags to carry rafts; raft; human excrement; storm; inundation, deluge; — *ṭûf*, hair or wool in the neck; — ة *ṭaufa-t*, storm; heavy shower.

طوفان *ṭûfân*, ة, continuous rain; far-reaching storm or calamity; deluge; general mortality; dark night; storm; irritable person, given to anger; great quantity; — *ṭawafân*, INF. of (طوف); — ى *ṭûfâniyy*, hurricane-like; quarrelsome.

(طوق) *ṭâq*, U, INF. *ṭauq*, *ṭâqa-t*, be able to, have the power of; be able to support; — II. INF. *taṭwîq*, enable, empower, make possible, facilitate; trouble with, commission; put a chain round one's neck; promote one's interests; permit; —IV. INF. *iṭâqa-t*, be able to; — V. INF. *taṭṭawuq*, *iṭṭawuq*, put a chain round one's neck; halter one's self; — VII. INF. *inṭiyâq*, be bearable, supportable.

طوق *ṭauq*, power, ability, capability; range of the mind; power of endurance; pl. *aṭwâq*, neck-chain; collar; ruff, frill; what surrounds other things, circle, ring, halo; opening, hole, window; climbing-rope; pillory; —ة *ṭauqa-t*, plain surrounded by mountains or rocky ground.

(طول) *ṭâl*, U, INF. *ṭûl*, be long, stretch to a great extent, last long; be or last too long; be tall; surpass in length or tallness; overcome finally; benefit; (m.) be able to reach with one's hand; — *ṭawil*, A, INF. *ṭawal*, have a long upper lip; — II. INF. *taṭwîl*, lengthen; relax the tether; grant a respite or delay; (m.) be long at a thing; tarry, be backward; — III. INF. *muṭâwala-t*, vie with in length, tallness, riches, power; put off for a length of time; — IV. INF. *iṭâla-t*, *iṭwâl*, lengthen, protract, prolong; give birth to a big child or children; — V. INF. *taṭawwul*, stretch one's self; grow longer; oblige by benefits; — VI. INF. *taṭâwul*, lengthen (n.); stretch one's self to see far; raise one's self above another, be proud towards; be powerful; overreach, take unlawful possession of; be long or too long; — X. INF. *istiṭâla-t*, be long; lengthen (n.); surpass; have the upper hand; exalt one's self, be proud towards (على *'ala*); kill the greater number of enemies in a battle.

طول *ṭaul*, merit; wealth; power; bounty; — *ṭaul*, *ṭûl*, *ṭuwal*, *ṭiwal*, duration of life, duration, while; absence; — *ṭûl*, pl. *aṭwâl*, length; longitude; long

duration; long-suffering (s.); — *ṭawal*, immoderate length of the upper lip (camel); — *ṭiwal*, *ṭiwall*, long tether; — *ṭuwal*, pl. of طولى *ṭûla*; — *ṭuwwal*, a long-legged water-bird; — ة *ṭûla-t*, length, duration.

طولاب *ṭûlâb*, for دولاب, chest, chest of drawers.

طولانى *ṭûlâniyy*, long; high; loud.

طولع *ṭaulaʻ*, vomiting (s.).

طولمبة *ṭûlumba-t*, a hydraulic musical instrument; trumpet; pump; fire-engine.

طولى *ṭûla*, pl. *ṭuwal*, longer, taller, f. of اطول *aṭwal*; high rank; pl. the (seven) long chapters of the Koran.

طومار *ṭûmâr*, pl. *ṭawâmîr*, book, roll, scroll, leaf, sheet of paper; account, invoice; writing in large letters.

طومة *ṭûma-t*, calamity; death; female tortoise.

طووى *ṭu'iyy*, *ṭuwawiyy*, somebody, anybody.

(طوى) *ṭawa*, I, INF. *ṭayy*, fold, fold up; roll up, close (a book); conceal; draw in the sails; turn from; go to, stay with, pass by; travel; shorten; fast of one's own accord; praise God twice in prayer; wall the inside of a well; enter (on a road); — *ṭawî*, A, INF. *ṭawan*, be folded up; hunger; — IV. INF. *iṭwâ'*, hunger violently; — V. INF. *taṭawwî*, coil one's self up; be folded up; — VI. INF. *taṭâwî*, entwine one another; — VII. INF. *inṭiwâ'*, VIII. INF. *iṭṭiwâ'*, be folded or rolled up.

طوى *ṭawan*, hunger; — *ṭiwan*, *ṭuwan*, what may be folded or rolled, or is so; pliable; walk, promenading (s.); — *ṭawî*, thin, empty; — *ṭoy*, feast (Turk.); — *ṭawiyy*, folded, rolled; bale of linen; bundle; walled, pl. *aṭwâ*, well; an hour of the night; — *ṭu'iyy*, somebody, anybody; — ة *ṭawiyya-t*, fold; anything folded or rolled; fixed habit, character; folds of the heart, secret thoughts; intention; well walled inside.

طوير *ṭuwair*, small bird, insect.

طويس *ṭuwais*, little peacock.

طويل *ṭawîl*, ة, pl. *ṭiwâl*, *ṭiyâl*, long, tall; great; lasting long; vast; lengthy, prolix; name of a metre (*faʻûlun mafâʻîlun* four times repeated); — ة *ṭawîla-t*, long string, tether; string of pearls; large stable, royal or public stable.

طوئى *ṭu'iyy*, somebody, anybody.

طويئر *ṭuwai'ir*, little bird, insect.

طى *ṭayy*, INF. of (طوى), folding (s.); fold, crease; envelope; interior, inclosure; walled inside of a well; hunger; suppression of the fourth letter of a foot when it is quiescent; name of a tribe; — ة *ṭi'a-t*, INF. of (وطى), tread, &c.; — *ṭayya-t*, secret thought; intention; — *ṭiyya-t*, *ṭiya-t*, id.; fold; way of folding; distant goal of a journey; nature, quality.

طيا *ṭayyâ'*, f. of طيان *ṭayyân*.

طياب *ṭiyâb*, good things; a kind of dates; — *ṭuyyâb*, most excellent, sweet, pure; fragrance.

طيار *ṭiyâr*, INF. III. of (طير); — *ṭayyâr*, ة, flying, winged; swift; mercury; ريح ط *rîḥ ṭayyâr*, flying gout, rheumatism; — ة *ṭayyâra-t*, fast sailing ship; kite (toy); levity; ray (fish).

طياش *ṭayyâś*, light-minded, full of levity, fickle.

طيال *ṭiyâl*, duration of life; while, time; absence; pl. of طويل *ṭawîl*.

طيالس *ṭayâlis*, ة *ṭayâlisa-t*, pl. of طيلسان *ṭailasân*; — ى *ṭayâlisiyy*, maker of *ṭailasâns*.

طيان *ṭayyân*, f. طيا *ṭayyâ'*, famished, starved; who has to deal with loam or mortar (طين *ṭain*);

paver; — ة *ṭiyâna-t*, profession of a paver.

طياهيج *ṭayâhîj*, pl. of طيهوج *ṭaihûj*.

(طيب) *ṭâb*, I, INF. *ṭâb*, *ṭîb*, *ṭîba-t*, *taṭyâb*, be good, pleasant, sweet, fragrant, pure; be in good condition; fare well with; improve (n.); recover; be pleased, be of good cheer; be able to do without (عن *'an*); produce herbs and plants; make pleasant, sweeten; — II. INF. *taṭyîb*, make or find pleasant; improve (a.), better; perfume; embalm; — III. INF. *muṭâyaba-t*, play or sport (with); (m.) feign friendliness; — IV. INF. *iṭâba-t*, make pleasant, sweeten, purify; clean one's self by shaving and washing; find good and pleasant; present good and clean food; speak friendly; have good children; contract a lawful marriage; — V. INF. *taṭayyub*, be of a good and pure disposition; be perfumed, smell sweetly; be embalmed; — X. INF. *istiṭâba-t*, find good, sweet, pleasant; please (n.); find better, prefer; clean one's self; have the hair of the pubes shaved; ask for sweet water.

طيب *ṭîb*, ة *ṭîba-t*, INF. of (طيب); *ṭîb*, pl. *aṭyâb*, anything good, pleasant; perfume, aromatic essence, balm; the best of anything; anything lawful; good will, pleasure; perfumed; — *ṭayyib*, ة, good, excellent, pleasant, sweet; fragrant; lawful; ة *ṭayyiba-t*, Medina; pl. *-ât*, *ṭûba*, pleasant things, dainty viands; good deeds; — ة *ṭîba-t*, anything lawful; best wine; well Zamzam; — *ṭiyaba-t*, captivity on honest grounds.

طيبى *ṭîba*, Paradise; a tree in Paradise.

طيثار *ṭaiṡâr*, fearless; lion; fly.

طيجن *ṭaijan*, frying-pan.

(طيح) *ṭâḥ*, I, INF. *ṭaiḥ*=(طوح); — II. INF. *taṭyîḥ*, throw away to perish; spoil; confuse and lead astray; — IV. INF. *iṭâḥa-t*, spoil, squander; — V. INF. *taṭayyuḥ*, be thrown away, dispersed.

طيح *ṭaiḥ*, wooden middle part of a plough; — ة *ṭaiḥa-t*, cause for discord.

(طيخ) *ṭâḫ*, I, INF. *ṭaiḫ*, be polluted by anything abominable; pollute; be haughty; follow vain pursuits; — II. INF. *taṭyîḫ*, pollute; fill with fat and flesh; ruin; — V. INF. *taṭayyuḫ*, be polluted by anything abominable.

طيخ *ṭîḫ*, pride; *ṭîḫ ṭîḫ*, imitative sound of laughter; — ة *ṭaiḫa-t*, stupid; useless; tumult, insurrection, revolt, disturbance.

(طير) *ṭâr*, INF. *ṭayarân*, *ṭair*, *ṭairûra-t*, fly, fly or run away; fly into a passion; hurry up; bring quickly; be long (hair); — II. INF. *taṭyîr*, (also IV.) let fly, cause to fly; distribute one's property; II. cover all the she-camels; throw off the first hair; supplant; blow up, blast; — III. INF. *muṭâyara-t*, let fly, cause to fly; — IV. INF. *iṭâra-t*, see II.; drive away, dispel; — V. INF. *tatayyur*, *iṭṭayyur*, take a bad omen from (ب *bi*, من *min*); (m.) be launched (balloon); — VI. INF. *taṭâyur*, disperse (n.), scatter (n.), fly about; be long; cover the sky entirely; — VII. INF. *inṭiyâr*, split (n.); — X. INF. *istiṭâra-t*, disperse, scatter (n.); spread (n.), be widened; burst entirely; get chapped, rent; draw the sword quickly; fly away, be carried off; want coition; get suddenly frightened, shy; fly, run.

طير *ṭair*, pl. *ṭuyûr*, *aṭyâr*, bird; evil augury; levity; pl. of طائر, bird; — ة *ṭîra-t*, *ṭiyara-t*, evil augury; — *ṭaira-t*, levity.

طيران *ṭayarân*, INF. of (طير).
طيرورة *ṭairûra-t*, INF. of (طير); levity.
طيز *ṭîz*, pl. *aṭyâz*, buttocks (m.).
(طيس) *ṭâs*, I, INF. *ṭais*, be numerous.
طيس *ṭais*, great number, quantity or bulk; dust; animals with a numerous breed; myriads of.
طيسر *ṭaisar*, plenty, fulness, abundance.
طيسع *ṭaisa'*, roomy place; greedy.
طيسل *ṭaisal*, great number, quantity or bulk; dust; violent wind; dark; mirage; basin, dish; — *ṭaisal*, INF. ة, make large gains in small journeys.
(طيش) *ṭâś*, I, INF. *ṭaiś*, be thoughtless and fickle; have lost one's mind; be absent-minded; miss the aim; — IV. INF. *iṭâśa-t*, make to miss the aim.
طيش *ṭaiś*, levity, thoughtlessness, fickleness, caprice; distraction.
طيشان *ṭaiśân*=the previous; slight motion.
(طيط) *ṭîṭ*, stupid; tall, slender.
طيطان *ṭîṭân*, wild chives or leek.
طيطوى *ṭaiṭawa*, a water-bird.
(طيع) *ṭâ'*, I, INF. *ṭai'*, obey; — II. INF. *taṭyî'*, vex, be troublesome, annoy (m.).
طيع *ṭayyi'*, pl. *ṭuwwa'*, obedient; *ṭayyi'-an*, willingly, with pleasure.
(طيف) *ṭâf*, I, INF. *ṭaif*, *maṭâf*, appear (phantom, &c.); — II. INF. *taṭyîf*, walk frequently around.
طيف *ṭaif*, vision in a dream, apparition, phantom, spectre, rage; fury, furious madness; suggestion or inspiration of the devil; — *ṭayyif*, id.
طيفور *ṭaifûr*, little bird, insect.
طيقان *ṭîqân*, arches, &c., pl. of طاق *ṭâq*.
طيل *ṭîl*, *ṭiyal*, ة *ṭîla-t*, duration of life; while; absence; — *ṭiyal*, *ṭiyall*, long rope, tether; — ة *ṭayyila-t*, contrary wind.
طيلس *ṭailas*, *ṭailis*, *ṭailus*, طيلسان *ṭailasân*, pl. *ṭayâlis*, *ṭayâlisa-t*, the ends or lappets of a turban hanging down behind; headgear, hat; wrapper; head-band of a judge; — hence *ṭailas*, INF. ة, put on the *ṭailas* or *ṭailasân*.
طئلهة *ṭi'liha-t*=طهلئة *ṭihli'a-t*.
(طيم) *ṭâm*, I, INF. *ṭaim*, form, shape; act correctly and well.
(طين) *ṭân*, I, INF. *ṭain*, smear or coat with loam; seal with sealing-earth; work well in loam, &c.; form, shape; — II. INF. *taṭyîn*, cover with loam; — V. INF. *taṭayyun*, be soiled with loam; be covered with loam.
طين *ṭîn*, loam, clay; sealing-earth, red chalk; mud, puddle; سليل الطين *salîl aṭ-ṭîn*, Adam; human form or shape; — ة *ṭîna-t*, lump of clay, &c.; nature, natural disposition, constitution, temper; — ى *ṭîniyy*, earthy; inborn.
طيور *ṭuyûr*, pl. of طير *ṭair*; — ط فيور *ṭayyûr fayyûr*, quick, active, penetrating.
طيورى *ṭuyûriyy*, seller of birds.
طيوط *ṭuyûṭ*, impetuosity; rut; calamity.
طيهوج *ṭaihûj*, pl. *ṭayâhîj*, small kind of partridge.

ظ

ظ ẕ, as a numerical sign=900.
(ظاب) ẕa'ab, INF. ẕa'b, cry out; bleat; marry;— III. INF. muẕâ'aba-t, become brothers-in-law by marrying two sisters.
ظاب ẕa'b, ẕâb, clamour, noise, tumult; wrong, oppression; pl. aẕ'ub, ẕu'ûb, marriage; husband of a wife's sister.
(ظات) ẕa'at, INF. ẕa't, throttle, strangle.
(ظار) ẕa'ar, INF. ẕa'r, ẕi'âr, make a mother or she-camel fond of another's child or foal, so as to give it suck; be and do so; dispose towards; tie up the nose of a she-camel for the above purpose so as to make her forget the smell of her foal; move one to a thing under difficulties;— III. INF. muẕâ'ara-t, ẕi'âr, take a child to give it suck; take a wet nurse; also IV. INF. iẕ'âr, dispose towards another's child or foal; — VIII. INF. iẕẕi'âr, be fond of another's foal; procure a nurse for a child;— X. INF. istiẕ'âr, be hot (bitch).
ظارى ẕâri, given to biting, mordacious.
(ظاظا) ẕa'ẕa', INF. ة, ẕa'ẕâ', bleat with rut; speak with a lisp and indistinctly.
ظاعن ẕâ'in, traveller.
ظاغية ẕâgiya-t, wet nurse, nurse.
ظاف ẕâf, fur, coat (of an animal); hair in the neck.
ظاف ẕa'af, INF. ẕa'f, push away, drive off, repel.
ظافر ẕâfir, victorious, conquering.
ظالع ẕâli', pl. ẕulla', one-sided; limping; suspected; rutting, hot.
ظالم ẕâlim, pl. ẕalama-t, tyrannic, oppressive, cruel; tyrant, oppressor; a plant.
(ظام) ẕa'am, INF. ẕa'm, marry another's sister; lie with;— III. INF. muẕâ'ama-t, marry sisters, become brothers-in-law.
ظام ẕa'm, ẕâm=ظاب ẕa'b, ẕâb.
ظان ẕânn, who indulges his thoughts; who renders others suspected.
ظاهر ẕâhir, ة, externally appearing; distinct, clear, evident; external; exoteric; superficial; exterior, surface; ẕâhir-an, by heart; عين ظاهرة 'ain ẕâhira-t, protruding eye; God;— ة ẕâhira-t, pl. ẕawâhir, race, family; midday; mid-day watering; pl. projecting parts of the ground; —herbs;—ى ẕâhiriyy, external; apparent, seeming (adj.);— ية ẕâhiriyya-t, external appearance.
(ظب) ẕubb, ة, mimosa;— ة ẕuba-t, pl. aẕb-in, aẕbî, ẕubât, ẕubûn, ẕibûn, ẕuba-n, crooked point of a sword or arrow.
ظبا ẕibâ', pl. of ظبى ẕaby, ة;— ة ẕab'a-t, lame hyena.
ظبظاب ẕabẕâb, pl. ẕabâẕib, pain, illness; pustules in the face or on the eye-lids; fault, blemish; clamour, threat; pl. bleating of sheep.
(ظبظب) ẕubẕib, INF. ة, have a fever; —II. INF. taẕabẕub, make a slight fall.
ظبى ẕaby, f. ة, pl. aẕb-in, aẕbî, ẕibâ, ẕubiyy, ẕabayât, gazelle, mountain-goat; mark by branding; name of a star;— ẕuba-n, pl. of ظبة ẕuba-t;— ة ẕabya-t, cow; pl. ẕibâ', vulva; pocket; purse; bend of a valley;— ى ẕabyiyy, of a gazelle.
ظج ẕajj, U, INF. ẕajj, call for assistance in a battle.
(ظر) ẕarr, INF. maẕarra-t, loosen a sharp stone; kill a camel with

a sharp stone; — IV. INF. *izrâr*, walk upon sharp stones; sharpen a pebble to strike fire with; sting by words, offend, irritate.

ظر *zirr*, ة *zirra-t*, ظرر *zurar*, ة *zurara-t*, pl. *zirâr*, *zirrân*, stone with sharp knife-like edge.

ظرا *zar'*, ice; frozen mud.

ظرابی *zarâbiyy*, ظرابین *zarâbîn*, pl. of ظربا *zirbâ'*, ظربان *zaribân*.

ظراف *zirâf*, pl. of ظریف *zarîf*; — *zurâf*, pl. *zurafâ'*, also *zurrâf*, pl. *-ûn*, ingenious, witty; elegant; — ة *zarâfa-t*, wit, humour, grace of speech; elegance, fineness, skill.

ظران *zirrân*, pl. of ظر *zirr*; —*zurrân*, pl. of ظریر *zarîr*.

(ظرب) *zarib*, A, INF. *zarab*, adhere, stick to; — II. pass. *zurrib*, be firm, solid.

ظرب *zarib*, pl. *zirâb*, sharp projection of a rock; mountain, hill; — *zurubb*, short and thick-set.

ظربا *zirbâ'*, ظربان *zaribân*, pl. *zirba*, *zarâbîn*, *zarâbiyy*, pole-cat.

ظرر *zurar*, ة *zurara-t*, see ظر *zirr*.

ظرظار *zurzâr*=ظر *zirr*.

(ظرف) *zaruf*, INF. *zarf*, *zarâfa-t*, be ingenious, witty, sharp of intellect; be eloquent, skilful, graceful, elegant; — II. INF. *tazrîf*, embellish, adorn; — IV. INF. *izrâf*, have children as described under I.; put into a vessel or upon a saucer; — V. INF. *tazarruf*, show one's self ingenious, &c., want to be considered so; play the elegant; embellish one's self; be adorned; —X. INF. *istizrâf*, deem ingenious, &c.

ظرف *zarf*, pl. *zurûf*, vessel, saucer of metal; box, paste-board box, purse, bag; egg-çup; adverb, adverbial expression denoting place or time; wit, sagacity; gracefulness, elegance, culture; — *zuruf*, and—

ظرفا *zurafâ'*, ظرفان *zurfân*, pl. of ظریف *zarîf*.

ظرفی *zarfiyy*, adverbial, expressive of place or time; — *zarafiyy*, witty, elegant; — ة *zarfiyya-t*, local inclusion.

ظروری *zaraura*, prudent, cunning, sly.

ظروف *zurûf*, pl. of ظرف *zarf* and ظریف *zarîf*.

(ظری) *zara*, I, INF. *zary*, flow; have the diarrhœa; — *zarî*, A, INF. *zaran*, be sagacious, sharp, cunning; — XII. INF. *izrîrâ'*, have a swollen belly, be paunch-bellied, suffer from fatness.

ظریاط *ziryât*, ة *ziryata-t*, loam, clay.

ظریر *zarîr*, full of sharp stones; pl. *zurrân*, *azirra-t*, stone to mark the road.

ظریف *zarîf*, ة, pl. *zurafâ'*, *zuruf*, *zirâf*, *zurûf*, *zurfân*, sagacious, sharp-witted, witty, graceful, elegant, polite, skilful; — ة *zarîfa-t*, pl. *zarâ'if*, anything graceful, elegant; witty saying, wit; elegance, tidiness.

ظش *zašš*, rugged, stony place.

ظعام *zi'âm*, ظعان *zi'ân*, rope of a litter; litter.

(ظعن) *za'an*, INF. *za'n*, *za'an*, travel; set forth; — IV. INF. *iz'ân*, cause to travel; allow to travel in a litter; —VIII. INF. *izzi'ân*, travel in a litter.

ظعن *za'n*, *za'an*, wandering, travelling (s.); — *zu'un*, pl. of ظعون *za'ûn*; — *zu'n*, *zu'un*, pl. of ظعینة *za'îna-t*.

ظعون *za'ûn*, pl. *zu'un*, camel of burden (gentle animal).

ظعینة *za'îna-t*, pl. *zu'n*, *zu'un*, *za'â'in*, *az'ân*, litter to carry women; woman in it; married woman.

(ظف) *zaff*, U, INF. *zaff*, tie together the fore-feet of a camel; — X. INF. *istizfâf*, follow the track unremittingly.

ظف *zaff*, miserable life, long dearth.

ظفار *ẕafâr*, an aromatic spice; clove.

(ظفر) *ẕafar*, I, INF. *ẕafr*, scratch in the face; sit; — *ẕafir*, A, INF. *ẕafar*, obtain one's wish, get the better, be victorious; take possession of; be covered with a pellicle (eye); — II. INF. *taẕfîr*, wound with the nails or claws; bear plants which may be scratched out with the nails; have nail-like excrescences; rub the finger-nails on leather to smooth them; pray for one to gain the victory; render victorious; perfume one's clothes with cloves; — III. INF. *muẕâfara-t*, help one to gain the victory or to be successful; — IV. INF. *iẕfâr*, scratch the face; help one to obtain, to be successful or victorious; make to prevail, grant victory; wish victory; — VIII. INF. *iẕẕifâr*, press the nails into (على *'ala*); clutch, seize with the claws; have success, obtain one's wish, be victorious.

ظفر *ẕufr*, *ẕufur*, pl. *aẕfâr*, finger-nail; claw; ذو ظ *ẕû ẕufur-in*, camels and sheep; ما ظ *mâ ẕufr*, nobody; — *ẕufr*, pellicle upon the eye; top of the bow; — *ẕafar*, obtainment, success, victory; level ground; — *ẕafir*, who obtains, overcomes, gets the better; victorious, conqueror; ة, covered with a pellicle (eye); — ة *ẕufra-t*, corrosive plant used to destroy warts; — *ẕafara-t*, pellicle upon the eye.

ظفف *ẕafaf*, insufficiency, &c.=ضفف *ḍafaf*.

ظفير *ẕafîr*, obtaining or conquering everything; — ة *ẕafîra-t*, wild mint.

(ظل) *ẕall* (1 pret. *ẕal-tu*, *ẕil-tu*), INF. *ẕall*, *ẕulûl*, do a thing all day long (in poetry also at night-time); become; last; stay continually; — II. INF. *taẕlîl*, overshadow; bring into the shade or shadow; threaten with the whip; — IV. INF. *iẕlâl*, be shady; cover, overshadow; be so near as to be reached by the shadow; be near, impend; — V. INF. *taẕallul*, be in the shade; — X. INF. *istiẕlâl*, seek the shade and sit down in it; be shaded by (ب *bi*, من *min*); have the tendrils entwined; be deep-set (eyes); come from the inside.

ظل *ẕill*, pl. *ẕilâl*, *ẕulûl*, *aẕlâl*, shadow, shade; shady garden; paradise; protection, help, assistance; dark cloud; darkness; night; phantom, spectre; cover, lid, scabbard; shape, figure, person; the Sultan (as shadow of God on earth); greatness, sublimity, distinction, eminence, rareness; power, night; colours of the day, shades of colour, bloom of youth; heat of summer; fringe, hairy side of a cloth; tangent; ظ الذهب *ẕill aẕ-ẕahab*, quicksilver; — ة *ẕalla-t*, remaining, staying, abiding (s.); health; — *ẕulla-t*, pl. *ẕulal*, anything shady (also *ẕilla-t*); shade, cover, cloud; pl. *ẕulal*, *ẕilâl*, shaded bench, &c.

ظلوم *ẕalûm*, disorderly; very cruel; tyrannical; — *.

(ظلى), V. *taẕalla*, INF. *taẕallî*=V. of (ظل); — ة *ẕilliyya-t*, shading (s.); quality of being the shadow of God; tangent.

ظليف *ẕalîf*, pl. *ẕulf*, *ẕuluf*, perverse, abject, reprobate; in a bad condition; rough, rugged; toilsome; difficulty; hardness; base of the neck; =ظلف *ẕalif*, abstemious, chaste; *ẕalîf-an*, in vain; — also ة *ẕalîfa-t*, the whole of.

ظليل *ẕalîl*, shady, cool; lasting (hence ظل ظ *ẕill ẕalîl*, paradise); — ة *ẕalîla-t*, whirlpool in deep

water; pl. *zalâ'il*, garden with a thicket of trees.

ظليم *zalîm*, wronged, injured, damaged; also ة *zalîma-t*, milk not quite sour; virgin land, earth out of a freshly-dug well; pl. *zilmân*, *zulmân*, male ostrich; a constellation; — *zillîm*, most tyrannical; — ة *zalîma-t*, wrongfully taken; injustice; complaint of such.

ظم *zam-in*, see ظمى *zamî*;—*zim'*, pl. *azmâ'*, thirst; desire, craving; time between two waterings; duration (of life); ظ الحمار *zim' al-himâr*, a very short time, a little.

(ظما), ظمى *zami'*, A, INF. *zam'*, *zama'*, *zamâ'*, *zamâ'a-t*, thirst, be very thirsty; long for ardently, crave for; — II. INF. *tazmiya-t*, IV. INF. *izmâ'*, let one thirst; let a horse grow thin.

ظما *zaman*, reddish brown;—*zimâ'*, pl. of ظمان *zam'ân* and ظمى *zamî*; — ة *zamâ'a-t*, perverse nature; INF. of (ظما).

ظمان *zam'ân*, pl. *zimâ'*, *zumâ'*, f. ة, and ظماى *zam'a*, thirsty; hot; f. *zam'a*, a hot scorching wind.

(ظمخ) *zamih*, *zimh*, a kind of plane-tree; fig-tree.

ظمى *zami'*, see (ظما); — *zamî* (ظم *zam-in*), ة, pl. *zimâ'*, *zumâ'*, thirsty; lean, fleshless.

ظميا *zamyâ*, f. of اظمى *azma*, brown, &c.

(ظن) *zann*, U, INF. *zann*, *zunûn*, think, opine, suppose; doubt; consider true; deem; — IV. INF. *iznân*, suspect; cause to be suspected; have an opinion about (ب *bi*); — V. INF. *tazannî*, opine, think; — VIII. INF. *izzinân*, suspect.

ظن *zann*, pl. *zunûn*, *azânîn*, opinion, supposition, surmise; knowledge, persuasion;—ة *zinna-t*, pl. *zinan*, *zanâ'in*, opinion, surmise.

ظنابيب *zanâbîb*, pl. of ظنبوب *zumbûb*.

ظنانة *zannâna-t*, speaking ignorantly.

(ظنب) *zimb*, foot of a tree; — ة *zumba-t*, sinew of a camel's neck to fix the feathers of an arrow.

ظنبوب *zumbûb*, pl. *zanâbîb*, hip-bone.

ظنمة *zanama-t*, a draught of milk before the cream has been taken off.

ظنون *zanûn*, full of suppositions, suspicious; weak of intellect; doubtful; well with but little water; high-born lady (as a wife); — *.

(ظنى), V. INF. *tazannî*, see V. of (ظن); — *zanniyy*, supposed, surmised.

ظنين *zanîn*, pl. *azinna-t*, supposed, presumed, presumptive, putative.

ظهار *zahâr*, stony surface; — *; — *zuhâr*, pl. *zuhrân*, crowd, multitude; shorter side of the feathers of an arrow;—ة *zahâra-t*, INF. of (ظهر); (m.) pad placed under a burden to be carried on the back; — *zihâra-t*, outer side (of a garment, &c.); — ى *zahâriyy*, pl. of ظهرى *zihriyy*; — ية *zuhâriyya-t*, way of throwing one's adversary on the back.

(ظهر) *zahar*, INF. *zuhûr*, appear, become distinctly visible; sprout, bud; bring out, make known; elevate; — INF. *zahr*, *zuhûr*, help, assist; find one's opportunity against and get the better of; ascend (a roof); take hold (of a secret); throw behind, forget, neglect; — A, INF. *zahr*, boast of a thing; beat on the back; keep an animal ready to mount; — *zahir*, A, INF. *zahar*, have a pain in the back; — *zahur*, INF. *zahâra-t*, have a strong back; — II. INF. *tazhîr*, forget, neg-

lect; dismiss a wife, set out for a journey at noon-time; — III. INF. *muzâhara-t*, *zihâr*, cover one's back, protect; put on a garment over another one; fit two things; separate from a wife; — IV. INF. *izhâr*, bring to light, make publicly known, proclaim; make evident; attest; show, make show of, pretend; render successful, help to conquer an enemy; neglect; enter on mid-day or travel in it; say by heart; — V. INF. *tazahhur*, dismiss a wife; — VI. INF. *tazâhur*, show one's self, appear; make a show of, pretend; boast; cover each other's back, help one another; turn the back to one another, desert each other; publish; separate (n.); — VIII. INF. *izzihâr*, neglect; keep an animal ready to be mounted; — X. INF. *istizhâr*, id.; ask for help; seek shelter; conquer; help; place a thing behind one's self to be able to protect it; be able to recite, recite by heart; wish to get at the bottom of a thing.

ظهر *zahr*, pl. *azhur*, *zuhûr*, *zuhrân*, back; the opposite side or outer side; surface; road in the desert; road; saddle-beast, camel ready to be mounted; deck of a ship; summit; exoteric sense of the Koran; wealth, power, strength; cover, protection, help; anything neglected, absent, hidden; tradition, intelligence, news; old kettle; — *zuhr*, (m. f.) pl. *azhâr*, time immediately after noon; time of the first mid-day prayer; — *zahir*, suffering from a pain in the back; — ة *zihra-t*, helper; help, assistance; — *zihra-t*, *zahara-t*, *zuhra-t*, family, relations, allies; household furniture; — *zuhra-t*, helper; tortoise.

ظهران *zuhrân*, pl. of ظهر *zahr* and ظهار *zuhâr*.

ظهرى *zihriyy*, thrown behind, forgotten; pl. *zahâriyy*, always ready to be mounted.

ظهور *zahûr*, prominent, high; — *zuhûr*, INF. of (ظهر); birth; event; reign, dominion; glory; (m.) stool (easing of the bowels); — *

ظهير *zahîr*, afflicted with a pain in the back; strong of back; helper, assistant, patron; — ة *zahîra-t*, pl. *zahâ'ir*, middle of the day; time of the first noon-day prayer; strong-backed she-camel.

ظؤار *zu'âr*, ظور *zu'r*, ة *zu'ra-t*, pl. of ظئر *zi'r*.

ظورى *zu'ra*, cow desiring the bull.

(ظوف) *zâf*, U, A, INF. *zauf*, *za'f*, push away, drive off.

ظوف *zûf*, hair on the neck.

ظوة *zau'a-t*, stupid, foolish, mad.

ظووب *zu'ûb*, pl. of ظاب *za'b*.

ظوور *za'ûr*, ة *za'ûra-t*, she-camel who gives suck to another's foal; — *zu'ûr*, ة *zu'ûra-t*, pl. of ظئر *zi'r*.

(ظوى), IV. *azwa*, INF. *izwâ'*, be stupid, foolish.

ظى *zayy*, honey; — ة *zayya-t*, corpse on the point of bursting.

(ظيا), II. INF. *tazyî'*, grieve, annoy, molest; — ة *zaia-t*, stupid; blockhead.

ظئار *zi'âr*, INF. III. of (ظار).

ظيان *zayyân*, wild jasmine; honey; a plant containing tannin.

ظئر *zi'r*, pl. *az'ur*, *az'âr*, *zu'ûr*, *zu'ûra-t*, *zu'âr*, *zu'r*, *zu'ra-t*, (wet-) nurse; foster-mother; benevolent; buttress.

ع

ع ', as a numerical sign = 70.
عابث *'âbis*, player, toyer, jester.
عابد *'âbid*, pl. *-ûn*, *'abada-t*, *'ubbâd*, adorer, servant of God; pious; angry; scorning (adj.), denying; — ة *'âbida-t*, nun.
عابر *'âbir*, crossing a river; passer by, traveller; past, bygone; perishable, of short duration, fleet; expounder, commentator, interpreter; — ة *'âbira-t*, existent; admissible.
عابس *'âbis*, pl. *'awâbis*, frowning (adj.); — *al-'âbis*, lion.
عابية *'âbiya-t*, f. handsome.
عات *'ât-in*, see عاتى *'âtî*.
عاتر *'âtir*, pl. *'utur*, lustful.
عاتق *'âtiq*, pl. *'utq*, set free; fledged; old, ancient; old wine, an old bow (also ة *'âtiqa-t*); pl. *'awâtiq*, who frees, sets free; girl in her father's house; wine-bag; middle of the back, shoulder; needle of a balance.
عاتك *'âtik*, noble; excellent, pure, bright; fickle, quarrelsome; also ة *'âtika-t*, old bow; — ة *'âtika-t*, unfecundated palm-tree.
عاتم *'âtim*, late; f. pl. *'âtimât*, clouded stars.
عاتن *'âtin*, pl. *'utun*, strong, violent.
عاتة *'âtih*, pl. *'utahâ'*, who spreads abroad other people's talk, tale-bearer.
عاتى *'âtî*, pl. *'utiyy*, *'utât*, haughty, insolent; exaggerating (adj.); old man.
عاثور *'âsûr*, pitfall; dangerous place; calamity, evil.
عاثى *'âsî*, pl. *'usât*, *'usiyy*, insolent, impudent; disastrous.
عاج *'âj*, ivory; tortoise-shell; gentle (camel); — *'âjj*, frequented, full; — ة *'âja-t*, piece of ivory.
عاجب *'âjib*, wonderful.
عاجز *'âjiz*, pl. *'awâjiz*, *'ujjaz*, *'ajaza-t*, weak, exhausted; impotent; imbecile; down in the world and hopeless.
عاجل *'âjil*, in a hurry, hastening, mobile; quickly passing, perishable, fleeting; present, not delayed.
عاجمة *'âjima-t*, biting (adj.); tooth.
عاجن *'âjin*, who kneads the dough; ة *'âjina-t*, middle of a place.
عاجى *'âjiyy*, of ivory.
عاد *'âd*, name of an ancient Arabic tribe; — *'âdd*, common divisor of two commensurable numbers; pl. *-ûn*, who counts; — ة *'âda-t*, pl. *-ât*, *'awâ'id*, *'âd*, *'îd*, custom, habit, manner; customary gift or present; menses.
عادتى *'âdatiyy*, usual, customary; habitual sinner.
عادل *'âdil*, pl. *'udâl*, *'uddal*, *'adl*, just, upright, equitable; honest witness; giving judgment; pl. *'udûl*, notary, judge; deviating, deflecting, varying; similar, equal; polytheist.
عادم *'âdim*, annihilated, lost.
عاد *'âd-in*, عادى *'âdî*, pl. *'ida*, *'uda*, who hastens by, runner; اى عادى *ayyu 'âdî*, what kind of a man? pl. *'udât*, transgressor, oppressor; lion; — *'âdiyy*, referring to the tribe of *'Âd*; hence old, ancient; f. ة, usual, habitual, customary, of every day; — ة *'âdiya-t*, injustice; transgression; hostility; front troops; racing (s.); what draws off attention; interval, distance; pl. *'âdiyât*, swift horses or camels; pl. *'awâdî*, camels grazing on vine-tendrils.
عاذ *'âz-in*, see عاذى *'âzî*.

عاذب *'âẓib*, unwilling to eat from excessive thirst; in the open air.

عاذر *'âẓir*, who excuses, accepts excuses; who circumcises; scab of a wound; also ة *'âẓira-t*, excrement, dung.

عاذل *'âẓil*, pl. *'aẓala-t*, *'uẓẓâl*, *'uẓẓal*, blamer, fault-finder, censurer; pl. *'awâẓil*, vein bleeding during the menses; month *śa'bân* or *śawwâl*.

عاذور *'âẓûr*, pl. *'awâẓîr*, calamity; also—

عاذوراء *'aẓûrâ'*, pain in the throat when swallowing; inflammation of the larynx.

عاذى *'âẓî* (عاذ *'âẓ-in*), ة, far from the water; healthy, wholesome.

عار *'âr*, reproach, shame, disgrace, infamy; blush, bashfulness, modesty; — *'ârr*, scabious, mangy; — ة *'âra-t*, anything borrowed; loan.

عارب *'ârib*, ة, deep; abounding in water; of pure blood.

عارض *'âriḍ*, what happens, accidental; accident; calamity; comer; holding a review; general; crisis of an illness; cheek; molar tooth; what intercepts the vision (mountain, cloud, &c.); present, gift; old and lame; — ة *'âriḍa-t*, pl. *'awâriḍ*, accident, event; pressing business; note, memorandum, notice; side of the face, cheek; eruption on the cheek; eloquence; skill, courage and agility; camel to be slaughtered; cross-beam, lintel of a door; pl. incidents, accidental circumstances; — ى *'âriḍiyy*, accidental.

عارف *'ârif*, ة (pl. *'awârif*), knowing, intelligent, sagacious; expert; patient; well-known; a saint; captain; — ة *'ârifa-t*, pl. *'awârif*, gift, present, bounty, favour.

عارك *'ârik*, pl. *'awârik*, having the menses; who rubs, kneads, brushes.

عارم *'ârim*, violent, hard, insolent; piebald; cold; suckling.

عارن *'ârin*, far, distant; *al-'ârin*, lion.

عارورة *'ârûra-t*, spiteful; avaricious, miserly; unhappy, unfortunate; without a hump (camel).

عارى *'ârî*, ة, pl. *'urât*, naked; hairless, bald; free (of cares, &c.); simple; ignorant; surprising; — ة *'âriya-t*, pl. *'awârî*, also *'âriyya-t*, pl. *'awâriyy*, anything borrowed, loan.

عاريتى *'âriyyatiyy*, borrowed, spurious, false; of every day, common; fleeting, passing quickly, ephemeral.

عازب *'âzib*, single, unmarried; bachelor; distant pasture, grazing on a distant pasture; — ة *'âziba-t*, f. of the previous, spinster; she-camel.

عازر *'âzar*, Lazarus; — *'âzir*, censurer.

عازف *'âzif*, singer, musician; ag. of (عزف).

عازم *'âzim*, pl. *'uzzâm*, who purposes anything, contemplates a journey, a visit, &c.; resolute; contractor, undertaker.

عاس *'âs-in*, see عاسى *'âsî*; — *'âss*, pl. *'asas*, *'asîs*, night-watchman; patrol.

عاسل *'âsil*, who seeks for honey; trembling, vibrating; pl. *'usul*, a just man, of good fame; pl. *'ussal*, *'awâsil*, wolf; — ة *'âsila-t*, bee-hive with honey; wolf.

عاسم *'âsim*, who works for his bread; greedy.

عاسى *'âsî*, palm-tree; bunch of dates; (عاس *'âs-in*) hard, dry.

عاش *'âś-in*, see عاشى *'âśî*.

عاشب *'âśib*, ة, full of herbs.

عاشر *'âśir*, ة, tenth; tithe; tax-gatherer; — ة *'âśira-t*, pl. *-ât*, female hyena; pl. *'awâśir*, every tenth verse of the Koran; pl.

a'śâr, gain in a play; portion of a camel's meat.

عاشق *'âśiq*, in love, lover, f. ة, mistress; — ة *'âśiqa-t*, ivy; — ية *'âśiqiyya-t*, amorousness.

عاشورا *'âśûrâ'*, عاشورى *'âśûra*, pl. *'awâśîr*, the 10th of *Muḥarram*; a sweetmeat.

عاشى *'âśî* (عاش *'âś-in*), who eats in the evening; who prepares for a journey.

عاص *'âṣ-in*, see عاصى *'âṣî*.

عاصف *'âṣif*, ة, violent, stormy; deviating, swerving, missing; bent; — ة *'âṣifa-t*, pl. *'awâṣif*, storm.

عاصم *'âṣim*, defended, protected; chaste, virtuous; ابو عاصم *abû 'âṣim*, beer;—ة *'âṣima-t*, Medina; pl. *'awâṣim*, capital.

عاصى *'âṣî* (عاص *'âṣ-in*), pl. *'uṣât*, refractory, rebellious; sinful; Orontes; ة *'âṣiya-t*, unaccessible.

عاض *'âḍḍ*, biting (adj.); also ة *'aḍḍa-t*, camel grazing on the plant عض *'iḍḍ*.

عاضه *'âḍih*, pl. *'awâḍih*, sorcerer, magician; deadly snake; also *'âḍiha-t*, camel grazing on the plant عضاه *'iḍâh*.

عاطر *'âṭir*, pl. *'uṭur*, fragrant, perfumed; benevolent, noble, generous; who is fond of perfumes.

عاطس *'âṭis*, ة, sneezing (adj.).

عاطش *'âṭiś*, thirsty.

عاطف *'âṭif*, pl. *'uṭf*, inclined; benevolent; sheet, shroud, wrapper; the sixth horse in a race; also ة *'âṭifa-t*, particle of conjunction; — ة *'âṭifa-t*, pl. *'awâṭif*, benevolence; sympathy; affection of kinship.

عاطل *'âṭil*, empty, vain, useless; free, unoccupied; pl. *'awâṭil*, *'uṭṭal*, unadorned; without any good quality; verses made up of words without any pointed letter; (m.) damaged, bad; good for nothing fellow; ill beyond recovery.

عاطم *'âṭim*, pl. *'uṭum*, fallen, extinct (nations).

عاطن *'âṭin*, ة *'âṭina-t*, pl. *'awâṭin*, *'uṭun*, camel lying down by the well after drinking.

عاطوس *'âṭûs*, what causes to sneeze; snuff.

عاطوف *'âṭûf*, springe, noose.

عاطى *'âṭî*, who gives or takes.

عاظل *'âẕil*, pl. *'aẕla*, clustering close together.

عاف *'âf*, plain with soft ground.

عافطة *'âfiṭa-t*, sheep; shepherdess.

عافور *'âfûr*, calamity.

عافى *'âfî*, ة (عاف *'âf-in*), pl. *'ufât*, abundant, numerous, luxuriant; forgiving; who asks for bread or a favour, suppliant; newcomer, guest; meat left in a borrowed kettle as a compensation; long-haired; pl. *'ufiyy*, effaced; who effaces or destroys; —ة *'âfiya-t*, what makes to recover or comforts; health, welfare; pl. *'awâfî*, seeking food, water or a favour, guest.

عاق *'âq*, croaking of a raven; — *'âqq*, pl. *'aqaqa-t*, أعقة *a'iqqa-t*, disobedient, refractory, rebellious.

عاقب *'âqib*, last-comer, Mohammed (as the last of the prophets); successor, lieutenant, substitute; — ة *'âqiba-t*, pl. *'awâqib*, end, final result, issue; final; short; reward; son, child, offspring, descendant.

عاقر *'âqir*, pl. *'uqqar*, *'awâqir*, barren (woman); unable to beget children; sterile; vast sand-plain; sand-hill; peerless (woman).

عاقف *'âqif*, having crooked legs.

عاقل *'âqil*, ة, pl. *'uqalâ'*, *'uqqâl*, reasonable, endowed with reason, prudent; mountain-goat; hind; who are entitled to an inheritance; (m.) priest of the Druses

— ة *'âqila-t*, attire-woman; magistrate, authorities; relations on father's side who pay the blood-money.

عاقور *'âqûr*, producing soreness.

عاقول *'âqûl*, pl. *'awâqîl*, bend in a river; whirlpool; wave, billow; river; complicated affair; pathless tract; sand-heap; astringents.

عاقولى *'âqûla*, city of Kufa.

عاكب *'âkib*, pl. *'ukûb*, standing; pressed, thronged; great crowd.

عاكف *'âkif*, pl. *'ukuf*, zealously attending; devotee staying in a sacred place.

عاكل *'âkil*, pl. *'ukâl*, dwarf; miser; of evil augury.

عاكوب *'âkûb*, dust.

عال *'âl-in*, see عالى *'âlî*; — ة *'âla-t*, umbrella; protecting roof made of branches; female ostrich; poverty; pl. of عائل *'â'il*, poor and of عيل *'ayyil* family; — *'âlla-t*, camels watered twice.

عالج *'âlij*, pl. *'awâlij*, heaped in layers; grazing on the plant علجان *'alajân*.

عالط *'âliṭ*, poet; slanderer.

عالك *'âlik*, what is to be chewed, hard; tough.

عالم *'âlam*, pl. *-ûn*, *'awâlim*, universe, world, kingdom (as animal, &c.); time, age, epoch; elements; creatures, men, people; — *'âlim*, pl. *'ullâm*, knowing, learned; theoretical; — ى *'âlamiyy*, worldly, secular, layman.

عالة *'âlih*, vain, fickle; female ostrich.

عالى *'âlî* (عال *'âl-in*), on high, high; عالى الكعب *'âlî al-ka'b*, of high rank; — *'âliyy*=على *'aliyy*, high, &c.; of *Hijáz*;— ة *'âliya-t*, pl. *'awâlî*, the upper part; point of a lance, lance; climax; high, sublime; sublimeness; upper Arabia, Hijâz; *al-'awâlî*, the regions outside Medina.

عام *'âm*, pl. اعوام *a'wâm*, year, day; *al-'âm*, this year; ع الاول *'âm-al-awwal*, last year; ع الاول *'âm 'âm al-awwal*, or عامين الاولين *'âmen al-awwalen*, the year before last; — *'âmm*, ة, perfect, accomplished, complete; year; — *'âmm* and *'âm*, ة, general, concerning all, common, public; community, commonwealth; *al-'âmm*, and pl. *al-'awâmm*, the common people; — ة *'âma-t*, pl. *'âm*, handful; turban; head of a horseman towering above others; inflated bags as support of rafts; — *'âmma-t*, pl. *'amam*, community, commonwealth; association; the common people, all, everybody, the public; resurrection; raft.

عامر *'âmir*, ة, pl. *'ummâr*, inhabited, cultivated, flourishing, wealthy; well preserved and in use; inhabitant; visitor; peasant, rustic; family; royal; snake; young of a hyena (ام عامر *umm 'âmir*, hyena); — ة *'âmira-t*, cultivated ground; long-lived; full treasury; royal exchequer; pl. *'awâmir*, snake.

عامص *'âmiṣ*, name of a dish.

عامل *'âmil*, who does, makes, performs; pl. *'amala-t*, *'ummâl*, *'umalâ'*, workman; official; tax-gatherer; agent; governor; practical; ع الطبع *'âmil aṭ-ṭab'*, power of nature, organic or animal life; — also ة *'âmila-t*, pl. *'awâmil*, governing, any grammatical word or relation governing a case.

عامه *'âmih*, pl. *'ummah*, confused.

عامود *'âmûd*, pl. *'awâmîd*, column, pillar; pedigree.

عامى *'âmmiyy*, *'âmiyy*, concerning all, public; general; common, vulgar; plebeian; ignorant, ignoramus; a year old.

عان *'ân-in*, see عانى *'ânî*; — *'ânn*, long rope; — ة *'âna-t*, pl. *'ûn*, hair of the pubes; herd of wild

asses; she-ass; a constellation; — *'ânna-t*, a cloud.

عانب *'ânib*, who possesses grapes.

عانت *'ânit*, for عانس *'ânis*.

عاند *'ânid*, pl. *'unnad*, *'awânid*, deviating, swerving from the path; obstinate, refractory; undutiful; vagrant, vagabond; flowing, not to be stanched.

عانذة *'âniza-t*, base of the chin or ear.

عانس *'ânis*, pl. *'awânis*, *'uns*, *'unnas*, *'unûs*, marriageable girl in her father's house; old spinster or bachelor; ة, full-grown; handsome, fat and full-grown.

عانقا *'âniqâ'*, hole of the field-mouse.

عانك *'ânik*, pathless sand-hills; partisan, follower; necessary; fat woman; red; having the menses.

عانى *'ânî* (عان *'ân-in*), pl. *'unât*, captured, made captive; flowing; grieving (a.); careful, full of solicitude.

عاهر *'âhir*, dissolute; fornicator, fornicatress; — ة *'âhira-t*, strumpet, hag, sorceress; female thief.

عاهل *'âhil*, emperor; without a husband.

عاهن *'âhin*, pl. *'awâhin*, palm-branch; member, limb; a vein; inherited; home-bred (camel); permanently settled; present; poor; weakened, relaxed.

عاهة *'âha-t*, damage, injury; bodily infirmity; pest; cattle-plague; mildew.

عاوز *'âwiz*, poor, needy; in want of.

عائب *'â'ib*, thick milk.

عائث *'â'is*, lion.

عائد *'â'id*, returning; what recurs in regular turns; what results from, proceeds; referring to; pl. *'aud*, *'uwwad*, *'uwwâd*, who visits the sick; who pays, restores; — ة *'â'ida-t*, pl. *'awâ'id*, habit, custom; revenue, gain, profit, proceeds; toll, taxes; reward; present, favour; benevolence; compassion.

عائذ *'â'iz*, pl. *'ûz*, *'ûzân*, mare on the 10th to 15th day after parturition.

عائر *'â'ir*, mote, &c., in the eye; عائرة عينين *'â'ira-t 'ainen*, what fills both eyes, abundance, affluence.

عائز *'â'iz*, in want of; needy, poor.

عائش *'â'iś*, living in ease.

عائض *'â'iḍ*, given in exchange or compensation; عائضين *'â'iḍîn*, عوض العا *'auḍa al-'â'iḍîn*, always, ever; never.

عائط *'â'iṭ*, pl. *'ûṭ*, *'îṭ*, *'uyya-t*, *'ûṭaṭ*, *'auṭaṭ*, *'auṭuṭ*, not conceiving for several years (woman, camel, &c.).

عائف *'â'if*, feeling disgust, loathing; ashamed; f. ة, soothsayer.

عائق *'â'iq*, pl. *'uwwaq*, what hinders.

عائل *'â'il*, inclining towards one side; preponderant, victorious; pl. *'âla-t*, *'uyyal*, *'aila*, poor, needy.

عائم *'â'im*, swimming.

عائن *'â'in*, spectator, looker on; casting the evil eye upon; somebody; — ة *'â'ina-t*, what comes into sight; herd, flock.

عائهة *'â'iha-t*, clamour.

(عب) *'abb*, U, INF. *'abb*, drink with the mouth close to the water or without breathing between, drink; produce a sound by falling into the water (bucket); be long; — INF. *'ubâb*, throw up large billows; — V. INF. *ta'abbub*, be addicted to wine.

عب *'ab*, *'abb*, sun-light; — *'ubb*, lower part of the sleeve; pl. *'ibâb*, armpit; bosom of a garment; — *'ab'*, sunlight; — also *'ib'*, equal, similar; bale of merchandise; — *'ib'*, pl. اعبا *a'bâ'*, id.; load, luggage; — ة

'ubba-t, pl. *'ubab*, berry of the nightshade; currant.

(عبا) *'aba'*, INF. *'ab'*, prepare, make ready, put into order; gather, equip and array an army; mix perfumes; make, do; heed; — II. INF. *ta'bi'a-t*, *tabyî'*, prepare, order, arrange; array an army; — VIII. INF. *i'tibâ'*, intercept the blood of the menses with a cloth.

عبا *'abâ'*, ة, pl. *a'biya-t*, (m.) *'ubiyy*, coarse cloth; wrapper, cloak; pl. *a'biya-t*, stupid and lazy; — ة *'abât*, *'abâ'a-t*, pl. *'ibâ'*, *'abâ'ât*, *'abâwât*, cloth or wrapper of goat's-hair.

عباب *'abâb*, drinking (s.), draught; — *'ubâb*, mass of water; billow; inundation; the first, uppermost; palm-leaf; — *'abbâb*, who makes himself drunk.

عبابيد *'abâbîd*, what separates (n.), diverges (men, animals, roads, chains of mountains, &c.).

عباد *'ubbâd*, pl. of عابد *'âbid*, adorer, &c.; — *; — ة *'ibâda-t*, adoration of God; pious work; obedience.

عبادلة *'abâdila-t*, the 220 companions of Mohammed.

عباديد *'abâdîd*=عباديب *'abâdîb*.

عبار *'abbâr*, strong; fit for travelling; — ة *'ibâra-t*, explanation, interpretation, commentary; figure of speech, metaphor; meaning, expression, synonym; word, phrase, speech, sermon, dialect; style; (m.) compound; — ى *'abâra*, pl. of عبران *'abrân* and عبرى *'abra*.

عباس *'abbâs*, frowning; *al-'abbâs*, lion; — ى *'abbâsiyy*, Abbasides.

عباط *'ibâṭ*, pl. of عبيط *'abîṭ*.

عباقية *'abâqiya-t*, cunning rogue, robber; a thorny tree; scar in the face.

عباقيس *'abâqîs*, عباقيل *'abâqîl*, rest, remainders, traces.

عبال *'abâl*, wild rose-tree; — ة *'abâlla-t*, *'abâla-t*, burden, load.

عبام *'abâm*, stammering; babbler, idle talker; — *'ubâm*, great quantity (of water); — ة *'abâma-t*, stupidity.

عباما *'abâmâ'*, stupid.

عبائر *'abâ'ir*, pl. of عبور *'abûr*.

عباية *'abâya-t*=عباة *'abât*; troublesome, burdensome; cruel, unjust, iniquitous.

عبائى *'abâ'iyy*, saddle-cloth.

عبب *'ubab*, pl. of عبة *'ubba-t*; — *'ubub*, swelling waters.

(عبث) *'abis*, A, INF. *'abas*, play, toy; hurt, injure; make free with; — I, INF. *abs*, mix; prepare for one's self the dish *'abîsa-t*.

عبث *'abas*, ة, toying (s.); idle doings, futilities; absurdity.

عبجة *'abaja-t*, stupid, useless and disagreeable.

(عبد) *'abad*, U, INF. *'ubûda-t*, *'ubudiyya-t*, *'ibâda-t*, adore, worship, serve God; — *'abid*, A, INF. *'abad*, be angry; have the mange very badly; regret, repent of; blame, rebuke; be greedy; deny; — *'abud*, INF. *'abâda-t*, be a slave; (m.) be pious; — II. INF. *ta'bîd*, enslave, take a slave; run away; tarry, hesitate; smear the camel with pitch; cause to enter on a road; — IV. INF. *ib'âd*, give as a slave or servant; take as a slave; assault and beat; assemble (n.); pass. get tired out and refuse service; — V. INF. *ta'abbud*, serve God; devote one's self to (ل *li*); be a pious Muslim; be refractory, restive; jade a camel; take or treat as a slave or servant; impose a task on a slave; be angry; — X. INF. *isti'bâd*, make or take as a slave, subjugate.

(عبد) *'abd*, pl. *-ûn*, *'abîd*, *'ibâd*, *a'bud*, *a'âbid*, *'ibdân*, *'ubdân*, *'ibiddân*, *'ibiddâ'*, *'ibidda*, *'abud*, *'ubud*, *ma'bada-t*, *ma'âbid*, *ma'bûdâ'*,

slave, negro, servant; man; pl. *'ibâd*, servants of God; men, people, attendants, retinue; a fragrant herb; short broad head of a spear; mercury; — *'abad*, INF. of (عبد); — *'abid*, ashamed; refusing (adj.); — ة *'abda-t*, female slave, negress; — *'abada-t*, abhorrence; endurance; durability; strength; corpulence; life; stone for pounding perfumes; pl. of عابد *'âbid*, adorer, &c.

عبدا *'ibiddâ'*, عبدان *'ibdân*, &c., pl. of عبد *'abd*.

عبدل *'abdal*, slave, servant.

عبدلى *'abdaliyy*, عبدلاوى *'ubdalâwiyy*, mallow.

عبدى *'abdiyy*, slavish; devoted to the service, to worship;—*'ibidda*, pl. of عبد *'abd*.

(عبر) *'abar*, U, INF. *'abr*, *'ubûr*, cross a valley, a river, a road; bring over; go away, depart; pass away; die; — INF. *'abr*, read in a low voice to one's self; open a book; make out the weight or value; leave a ram unshorn for a year; cry, weep; — I, U, INF. *'abr*, scare away birds; — U, INF. *'abr*, *'ibâra-t*, interpret, explain, expound; communicate news, notify; — *'abir*, A, INF. *'abar*, take for an example or warning; cry, weep; — II. INF. *ta'bîr*, bring over the water; pass (a.); interpret (a dream), explain, expound; denote by a metaphor; weigh gold pieces one by one or superficially; show one's inflamed eyes to another; overpower, oppress, subdue; destroy, ruin, annihilate; — IV. INF. *i'bâr*, leave the sheep unshorn; — VIII. INF. *i'tibâr*, wonder at; take warning; consider well; notice and take into account; — X. INF. *isti'bâr*, have one's dream interpreted by (acc.); take an example or warning; take into account; examine coins by the weight, estimate goods; be sorrowful and cry, be moved to tears.

عبر *'abr*, *'ibr*, *'ubr*, river-bank, shore; — *'abr*, *'ibr*, numerous; بنات عبر *banât 'ibr-in*, lie; absurdity; — *'ubr*, *'abar*, heat in the eyes, inflammation of the eyes; what calls forth tears; — *'ubr*, bereft of a son (woman); eagle; swift clouds; — *'abar*, preterite of the verb; ابو العبر *abû 'l-'abar*, impudent jester; — *'abir*, ة, crying, weeping; — *'ubur*, pl. of عبور *'abûr*; — ة *'abra-t*, pl. *'abarât*, *'ibar*, tear; suppressed grief; explanation; river-bank, shore; — *'ibra-t*, example, warning; anything wonderful; notice; esteem, consideration; bank, shore; — *'ubra-t*, inflammation of or heat in the eyes; numerous troop; a shell; — *'abara-t*, inflammation of the eyes; tears.

عبرود *'ubrûd*, tender and supple; relaxed.

عبرى *'abra*, pl. *'abâra*, crying, weeping, tearful; — *'ibriyy*, Hebraic; — *'ubriyy*, river-lotus; — ة *'ibriyya-t*, Hebrew (language).

(عبس) *'abas*, I, INF. *'abs*, *'ubûs*, frown, contract the brows, look severe; — *'abis*, A, INF. *'abas*, get dry and adhere (dirt); — II. INF. *ta'bîs*, frown, look severe; — V. INF. show austerity, look severe, sulkiness.

عبس *'abs*, thyme; — *'ibs*, vile, mean; — *'abas*, adhering dry dung.

(عبسر) *'absar*, عبسور *'ubsûr*, swift.

(عبش) *'abś*, anything fit, appropriate, becoming; — *'abś*, *'abaś*, negligence; — II. *'abbaś*, INF. *ta'bîś*, have the hair in disorder; be untidy in one's appearance; — ة *'abśa-t*, *'abaśa-t*, negligence.

(عبط) *'abaṭ*, I, INF. *'abṭ*, slaughter a young, fat and entirely sound animal; tear anything new, get torn; spoil anything new and whole; dig on untouched ground; injure the udder so as to bleed; befall undeservedly; forge lies against; blame, censure; raise dust; sweep the ground; rush into the combat; urge the horse to run until it perspires; (m.) embrace; — IV. INF. *i'bâṭ*, carry off in the prime of youth; — VI. INF. *ta'âbuṭ*, seize one another in wrestling; — VIII. INF. *i'tibâṭ*, slaughter a sound animal; blame; sweep the ground; dig in untouched ground; forge a lie against; =IV.

عبط *'abṭ*, mere lie; — *'ubuṭ*, pl. of عبيط *'abîṭ*; — ة *'ubṭa-t*, freshness, novelty; prime.

عبعاب *'ab'âb*, tall, strong and handsome.

(عبعب) *'ab'ab*, INF. ة, flee, take to flight; (m.) place under one's arm; — II. INF. *ta'ab'ub*, take and eat the whole of; (m.) carry under the arm, in one's bosom.

عبعب *'ab'ab*, strength and gracefulness of youth; = عبعاب *'ab'âb*; a wide garment; soft carpet.

(عبق) *'abiq*, A, INF. *'abaq*, *'abâqa-t*, *'abâqiya-t*, adhere; (m.) evaporate; be permanently settled; be passionately addicted or attached to (ب *bi*); — II. INF. *ta'bîq*, smell of perfume; perfume; penetrate; — V. INF. *ta'abbuq*, be impregnated; — VII. INF. *in'ibâq*, gather and adhere; be full of sorrow; be occupied, taken up (time, &c.); — XV. *i'banqa*, INF. *i'binqâ'*, be mischievous, malicious.

عبق *'abaq*, exhalation, evaporation, smell; — *'abiq*, ة, smelling of perfume; — ة *'abqa-t*, oppression (of the heart); — *'abaqa-t*, adhering butter.

(عبقر) *'abqar*, INF. ة, shine (mirage).

عبقر *'abqar*, a powerful demon; his dwelling-place; — *'abqarr*, *'abqurr*, hail; — ة *'abqara-t*, id.; delicate and handsome (f.); — ى *'abqariyy*, unsurpassed; tall and handsome; extraordinary; violent, severe; leader, prince, chief; mere lie; cloth or carpet made in 'Abqar; — ة *'abqariyya-t*, highest perfection; generosity, liberality.

(عبك) *'abak*, U, INF. *'abk*, mix; — ة *'abaka-t*, crumb of bread; small piece, trifle, a little; adhering bits of butter; malignant and hateful.

(عبل) *'abal*, U, INF. *'abl*, twist a rope; bind, tie up; — I, INF. *'abl*, strip the tree of its leaves; put a broad head to an arrow; refuse, reject, repel; lay hold on, arrest; cut; go away with, carry off; — INF. *'ubûl*, also *'abil*, A, INF. *'abal*, and *'abul*, INF. *'abâla-t*, be thick; — II. INF. *ta'bîl*, strip a tree of its leaves; — IV. INF. *i'bâl*, be thick and white; be stripped of the leaves; have the first leaves.

عبل *'abl*, *'abil*, ة, pl. *'ibâl*, thick, stout; — *'abl*, pl. اعبال *a'bâl*, falling leaf; first leaves; — ة *'abla-t*, pl. -*ât*, *'ibâl*, formed in perfect beauty (f.).

عبلا *'ablâ'*, f. of اعبل *a'bal*, thick, &c.; white, far-visible rock.

(عبم) *'abum*, INF. *'abâma-t*, be stupid, foolish, a fool.

عبم *'ibamm*, big and long.

(عبن) *'aban*, U, INF. *'abn*, be thick, coarse and rough; — IV. INF. *i'bân*, take a stout and strong camel.

عبن *'ubun*, strong fine men; — *'abann*, ة, tall and strong; — ة *'abna-t*, strength.

عبناة *'abannât*, pl. *'abannâyât*, tall and fat she-camel.

عبنبل *'abambal*, tall and strong.

(عبنجر) *'abanjar*, tall and stout.

عبنقا *'abanqâ*, ة *'abanqât*, having sharp claws.

عبنقس *'abanqas*, bad and relaxed; originating from strangers.

عبنقسا *'abanqasâ'*, lively, brisk; cheerful.

عبنك *'abannak*, firm, strong.

عبنى *'abanna*, f. *'abannât*, tall and strong.

عبهال *'ibhâl*, blame, censure, reproach.

(عبهر) *'abhar*, narcissus, jasmine; ة, fleshy, delicate and tall; delicate and well-made; storax-tree.

(عبهل) *'abhal*, INF. ة, allow the camel to pasture at large; — INF. ة, *'ibhâl*, blame, censure.

(عبو) *'abâ*, U, INF. *'abw*, shine, be bright; order, array, arrange; — II. INF. *ta'biya-t*, array, marshal an army; (m.) fill; pass a thread through a needle; — IV. INF. *i'bâ'*, (m.) fill entirely, cram into; set plants close together; — V. INF. *ta'abbî*, be arrayed, put into order; (m.) be full; — VI. INF. *ta'âbî*, help to feed each one his neighbour.

عبودة *'ubûda-t*, slavery, state of a slave or servant, service.

عبودية *'ubûdiyya-t*=the previous; servility, submissiveness.

عبور *'abûr*, pl. *'abâ'ir*, lambkin; pl. *'ubur*, uncircumcised; — *

عبوس *'abwas*, large number; — *'abûs*, frowning, looking severe, austere, grim; disastrous; lion; — *; — ة *'ubûsa-t*, and—

عبوسية *'abûsiyya-t*, austerity, sullenness.

عبول *'abûl*, fate, death.

عبى *'abiyy*, ordered, arrayed; crammed, closely pressed, packed; dense; — *'ubba*, woman whose children are dead; — ة *'ibiyya-t*, *'ubiyya-t*, haughtiness, vain-glory, idle boast.

عبيث *'abîs̱*, a plant; — *'ibbîs̱*, great gambler; — ة *'abîs̱a-t*, mixture (food, &c.); of a mixed race; cream-cheese (اقط *aqaṭ*).

عبيثران *'abais̱arân*, a thorny plant; difficulty, calamity.

عبيد *'abîd*, pl. of عبد *'abd*; — *'ubaid*, little slave; — ة *'ubaida-t*, belly, paunch; gut.

عبير *'abîr*, ambergris; perfume; saffron; pl. *'ubr*, fully-feathered (arrow); numerous.

عبيط *'abîṭ*, pure; fresh; pl. *'ubuṭ*, *'ibâṭ*, slaughtered sound animal; its flesh; torn.

عبيلة *'abîla-t*, f. strong, rough, coarse.

(عت) *'att*, U, INF. *'att*, rehearse repeatedly to (acc.); molest, importune; blame, rebuke, make a scene; — III. INF. *mu'âtta-t*, *'itât*, scold, dispute with (acc.); — IV. INF. *i'tât*, persuade to undergo anything burdensome; — V. INF. *ta'attut*, blunder in speech and repeat one's self frequently.

عتاب *'itâb*, reproach, blame, rebuke.

عتاد *'atâd*, pl. *a'tud*, preparation, making ready, equipment; large cup; also ة *'atâda-t*, INF. of (عتد).

عتار *'atâr*, penis; — *'attâr*, strong horse; bold man; wild rugged tract.

عتاق *'atâq*, setting free, emancipation; freedom; nobility; — *'itâq*, pl. of عتيق *'atîq*; — *'utâq*, good old wine; — ة *'atâqa-t*, emancipation, freedom, INF. of (عتق).

عتال *'attâl*, turf-cutter.

عتان *'itân*, dung and salt for tanning.

عتاة *'utât*, pl. of عاتى *'âtî*.

عتاهة *'atâha-t*, stupidity, folly, madness; also—

عتاهية *'atâhiyya-t*, wanderers, travellers; stupid, foolish, mad.

(عتب) *'atab*, U, I, INF. *'atb*, *'atabân*, *ma'tab*, *ma'taba-t*, *ma'tiba-t*, be angry; — INF. *'atb*, *'itâb*, *'ittîba*, *ta'tâb*, *ma'tib*, blame, rebuke, chide; — INF. *'atb*, *'atabân*, *ta'tâb*, limp, hop; cross the threshold; — II. INF. *ta'tîb*, tighten the belt, the string of the trowsers; provide the door with a threshold; relinquish the destination of a journey and remain staying elsewhere; — III. INF. *'itâb*, *mu'âtaba-t*, blame, rebuke, scold; INF. *mu'âtaba-t*, (also V. and VI.) quarrel as lovers do; — IV. INF. *i'tâb*, content, please (a.), render a service; receive again into favour; deviate, turn aside; — V. INF. *ta'attub*, VI. INF. *ta'âtub*, see III.; — VIII. INF. *i'titâb*, turn aside; leave a thing and pass to another; turn from an easy road to a more difficult one; ascend a mountain instead of turning it; go straight towards the aim; — X. INF. *isti'tâb*, content, satisfy; beg one to be satisfied, to receive you again into his favour; intend to scold; turn aside.

عتب *'itb*, who scolds or blames much; — *'atab*, space between the index and middle finger, or middle and ring finger; step, degree; bridge of a musical instrument; evil, unpleasantness; ruin; ruggedness; — ة *'ataba-t*, pl. *'atab*, *'atabât*, *a'tâb*, degree, step; threshold; flooring; · foot-stool; unpleasantness, difficulty; wife.

عتبان *'itbân*, عتبى *'utba*, favour, good-will, benevolence.

عتت *'atat*, hardness, roughness, bluntness (of speech).

(عتد) *'atud*, INF. *'atâda-t*, *'atâd*, be ready; — II. INF. *ta'tîd*, IV. INF. *i'tâd*, make ready, prepare; — V. INF. *ta'attud*, devote great diligence to (فى *fî*).

عتد *'atid*, *'atad*, perfect, faultless; — ة *'utda-t*, travelling things; = عتاد *'atâd*.

عتدان *'itdân*, pl. of عتود *'atûd*.

(عتر) *'atar*, I, INF. *'atr*, *'atarân*, be hard, strong; tremble, vibrate; — INF. *'atr*, *'utûr*, be hard and erected (penis); — INF. *'atr*, kill (the sheep of sacrifice).

عتر *'atr*, *'itr*, penis; — *'atr*, kid; gazelle; — *'itr*, origin; descent; marjoram; capers; an idol; animal to be sacrificed; delirium; — *'atar*, strength, power; — *'utur*, pl. of عاتر *'âtir*, عتور *'atûr*; — ة *'itra-t*, grains of musk; family, kindred; sweet marjoram; capers; sweet spittle; beauty and sharpness of the teeth; ع العينين *'itrat al-'ainen*, abundance, affluence.

(عترب) *'utrub*, sumach.

(عترس) *'atras*, INF. ة, take in a rough and violent manner.

عترس *'atras*, *'atarras*, short and strongly built; broad-chested; also—

عترسان *'utrasân*, lion; cock.

(عترف) *'atraf*, INF. ة, be hard, violent; — II. INF. *ta'atruf*, feign blindness.

عترفان *'utrufan*, house-cock.

عتروف *'utrûf*, عتريف *'itrîf*, ة, froward and impious; strong.

عتريس *'itrîs*, powerful tyrant; wood-demon; calamity.

(عتس) *'atas*, I, INF. *'ats*, bend (a.).

(عتعت) *'at'at*, INF. ة, call the goats.

عتعت *'ut'ut*, *'at'at*, kid; tall and strong; — ة *'at'ata-t*, madness.

(عتف) *'ataf*, I, INF. *'atf*, pull out hair.

عتف *'itf*, part of the night.

(عتق) *'ataq*, U, also عتق *'atuq*, INF. *'atâqa-t*, be old, ancient; *'atuq*, INF. *'atâqa-t*, be old and good (wine); — U, I, be generous and swift, get the lead of

the others (horse); — I, INF. *'atq*, *'ataq*, also *'atuq*, INF. *'atâqa-t*, be set free, be free; — I, INF. *'atq*, *'itq*, also *'atuq*, *'atâqa-t*, have again a delicate skin after illness; be sacred and binding (oath); — U, INF. *'ataq*, also *'atuq*, INF. *'atâqa-t*, be in good condition; be marriageable; be an old maiden; — U, INF. *'atq*, bite; keep one's property or cattle in good condition; — II. INF. *ta'tîq*, let grow old, keep long; bite; set free; — IV. INF. *i'tâq*, set free; urge on the horse; dig out afresh an old well; keep one's property in good condition; appropriate a place by fencing it in.

عتق *'atq*, setting free (s.), emancipation; old wine; — *'itq*, old age (of wine, &c.); excellence; beauty; honour; power; good condition; freedom; a tree; — *'utq*, old age; pl. of عاتق *'âtiq*; — *'utuq*, a tree.

عتقا *'utaqâ'*, pl. of عتيق *'atîq*.

(عتك) *'atak*, I, INF. *'atk*, attack repeatedly in a battle; intend to bite; grow red (old bow); place the hands on the breast; go straight towards the aim; do without hindrance; — INF. *'utûk*, go or travel alone; venture to perjure one's self; do or bring to one anything good or bad; be haughty and refractory towards the husband; be very sour; adhere, stick to; wander through a country; turn towards a place.

عتك *'atk*, *'atak*, space of time, age, old age.

(عتل) *'atal*, U, I, INF. *'atl*, drag along with violence; drag before the prince; lead the camel by the bridle; (m.) carry a burden, help to carry the burden of grief, share in one's sorrow; — *'atil*, A, INF. *'atal*, be prone to do evil or injury; — III. INF. *mu'âtala-t*, trouble one's self with, toil for a thing; — V. INF. *ta'attul*, stir from the place; — VII. INF. *in'itâl*, be dragged along.

عتل *'atil*, *'itill*, *'utull*, prone to evil; hard, rude, rough; — *'utull*, thick; — ة *'atala-t*, large clod of earth; spade; borer of a carpenter; crowbar; wooden lever; cudgel, bludgeon; Persian bow.

عتلا *'utalâ'*, pl. of عتيل *'atîl*.

(عتم) *'atam*, I, INF. *'atm*, desist from (عن *'an*); tarry, be too late, do a thing too late; be in the first stage; grow dark; pull out hair; — U, I, be milked in the evening; — II. INF. *ta'tîm*, desist; tarry; come or do too late; travel or drive the cattle home or to the watering-place in the first third of the night; hover above one's head; — IV. INF. *i'tâm*, tarry; be too late; be but in the first stage; grow dark or night; be dark; travel, &c., at night (see II.); also VIII. INF. *i'titâm*, and X. INF. *isti'tâm*, milk in the evening.

عتم *'atm*, ة *'atma-t*, darkness; — *'utm*, *'utum*, wild olive-tree; — ة *'atama-t*, first third of the night; coming home of the cattle; darkness.

(عتن) *'atan*, I, U, INF. *'atn*, throw into prison; — IV. INF. *i'tân*, be hard upon one's debtors.

عتن *'utun*, pl. of عتون *'atûn*.

(عته), pass. *'utih*, INF. *'ath*, *'uth*, *'utâh*, lose one's mind; be senseless, out of mind, confused; be addicted to science; spread abroad and distort one's words to injure him; — V. INF. *ta'attuh*, be out of mind, confused, or show one's self so; feign to be stupid or negligent; be extravagant in food or clothing.

عته *'atah*, dotage.

عتها *'utahâ'*, pl. of عاته *'âtih* and عتيه *'atîh*.
(عتو) *'atâ*, U, INF. *'utuww*, *'utiyy*, *'itiyy*, (m.) *'atw*, be haughty, exceed the bounds ; — INF. *'atiyy*, *'utiyy*, become decrepit ; — V. INF. *ta'attî*, affect haughty manners.
عتو *'atw*, *'utuww*, haughtiness.
عتوارة *'itwâra-t*, grain of musk ; dwarf ; *'itwâra-t*, *'utwâra-t*, name of a tribe.
عتوب *'atûb*, who allows himself to be scolded.
عتود *'atûd*, pl. *a'tida-t*, *'iddân*, *'itdân*, one year old kid ; lotus-tree ; acacia.
عتور *'atûr*, pl. *'utur*, hot and open (vulva) ; — *
عتول *'itwal*, *'itawwal*, impotent.
عتون *'atûn*, pl. *'utun*, strong, powerful, violent.
عتوه *'atûh*, mad.
(عتى) *'ata*=(عتو).
عتى *'atiyy*, pl. *'utiyy*, overbearing, haughty ;—*'utiyy*, *'itiyy*, haughtiness ;—*'atta*, for حتى *hatta*, until.
عتيبة *'atîba-t*, of evil repute.
عتيبى *'ittîba*, scolding (s.), rebuke.
عتيد *'atîd*, ة, prepared, ready, stored ; — ة *'atîda-t*, table with perfumes for a bride or bridegroom.
عتيرة *'atîra-t*, victim, sacrifice.
عتيق *'atîq*, ة, pl. *'utaqâ'*, f. *'atâ'iq*, set free, emancipated, free ; old and good (wine) ; ancient, old-fashioned ; chronic ; having a delicate and clear complexion ; pl. *'itâq*, noble, generous, excellent ; the best of a thing ; wine or juice thickened by boiling ; wine ; water ; milk ; fat ; salve, ointment ; fomentation ; vulture.
عتيك *'atîk*, sultry, close.
عتيل *'atîl*, pl. *'utalâ'*, mercenary (s., adj.) ; hireling, servant ; heavy (disease).
(عث) *'a<u>ss</u>*, U, INF. *'a<u>ss</u>*, eat up or destroy the wool (moth) ; importune ; bite ; — II. INF. *ta'<u>s</u>î<u>s</u>*, III. INF. *'i<u>s</u>â<u>s</u>*, *mu'â<u>ss</u>a-t*, quaver in singing, modulate ; — VI. INF. *ta'â<u>ss</u>*, give as a reason, take for a pretext ; — VIII. INF. *i'ti<u>s</u>â<u>s</u>*, keep back from doing good.
عث *'a<u>ss</u>*, importunity ; bite of a snake ; — ة *'u<u>ss</u>a-t*, pl. *'u<u>ss</u>*, *'u<u>s</u>a<u>s</u>*, *'u<u>s</u>û<u>s</u>*, moth, book-worm ; impudent jade or old woman.
عثا *'a<u>ss</u>â'*, snake ; — ة *'u<u>s</u>ât*, pl. of عاثى *'â<u>s</u>î*, impudent, disastrous.
عثاث *'i<u>s</u>â<u>s</u>*, trill, quaver ; pl. snakes.
عثاجل *'u<u>s</u>âjil*, big-bellied.
عثار *'a<u>s</u>âr*, calamity ; — *'i<u>s</u>âr*, tripping, stumbling (s.).
عثاكيل *'a<u>s</u>âkîl*, pl. of عثكال *'i<u>s</u>kâl*, عثكول *'u<u>s</u>kûl*.
عثالط *'u<u>s</u>âli<u>t</u>*, thick, consistent.
عثان *'u<u>s</u>ân*, pl. *awâ<u>s</u>in*, smoke ; dust ; — *.
عثانين *'a<u>s</u>ânîn*, pl. of عثنون *'u<u>s</u>nûn*.
عثث *'u<u>s</u>a<u>s</u>*, pl. of عثة *'u<u>ss</u>a-t*.
(عثج) *'a<u>s</u>aj*, I, INF. *'a<u>s</u>j*, drink in small quantities but long and much.
عثج *'a<u>s</u>j*, *'a<u>s</u>aj*, part of the night ; — also ة *'u<u>s</u>ja-t*, troop of travellers.
عثجج *'a<u>s</u>jaj*, numerous crowd.
(عثجل) *'a<u>s</u>jal*, INF. ة, be able to rise but with difficulty (from old age or illness).
عثجل *'a<u>s</u>jal*, bulging out, wide.
(عثر) *'a<u>s</u>ar*, I, U,— *'a<u>s</u>ir*, A,— *'a<u>s</u>ur*, INF. *'a<u>s</u>r*, *'i<u>s</u>âr*, *'a<u>s</u>îr*, stumble, trip and fall ; — *'a<u>s</u>ar*, I, U, throb, beat ; tell lies ; — U, INF. *'a<u>s</u>r*, *'u<u>s</u>ûr*, get a casual insight into a matter (على *'ala*), hit on ; — II. INF. *ta'<u>s</u>îr*, cause to stumble, to trip ; (m.) bring to fall, abase, ruin ; — IV. INF. *i'<u>s</u>âr*, id. ; let one get insight into (على *'ala*) ; inform ; accuse, denounce ; — V. INF. *ta'a<u>ss</u>ur*, stumble, trip ; get confused ; (m.) come to fall, fall into misery.
عثر *'a<u>s</u>r*, *'a<u>s</u>ar*, moistened only by

rain ; — 'asr, fate, death ; — 'usr, eagle ; — 'usr, 'asar, lie ; — ة 'asra-t, pl. 'asarât, stumbling, tripping (s.) ; trip, false step ; offence ; sin ; fate, death.

(عثرب) 'usrub, ة 'usruba-t, a kind of pomegranate.

عثرى 'asariyy=عثر 'asr, 'asar ; not caring for God or the world.

(عثعث) 'as'as, INF. ة, move, shake (a.) ; stay, abide ; lean upon or against.

عثعث 'as'as, perdition, destruction ; — also ة 'as'asa-t, barren sand-hill ; soft ground ; soft part of the thigh ; pl. 'asâ'is, calamities.

(عثق) 'asaq, high-road ; a tree ; — IV. INF. i'sâq, produce a rich harvest ; — ة 'asaqa-t, very rich, fertile.

(عثك) 'asak, 'usak, 'usuk, palm-roots ; — ة 'asaka-t, watery mud.

عثكال 'iskâl, عثكول 'uskûl, ة 'uskûla-t, pl. 'asâkîl, palm-branch with many bunches of dates.

(عثكل) 'askal, INF. ة, adorn with fringes ; run heavily ; — II. INF. ta'askul, bare many bunches of dates.

عثكول 'uskûl, ة, see 'iskâl ; — ة 'uskûla-t, hangings in shape of fringes.

(عثل) 'asil, A, INF. 'asal, abound ; be coarse and thick ; — 'asal, U, INF. 'asl, be healed so as to be distorted.

عثل 'isl, manager, administrator ; — 'asal, 'asil, much ; big and fleshy ; — 'usul, pl. of عثول 'asûl.

(عثلب) 'aslab, INF. ة, take wood for a fire-stick from a tree without knowing whether it is fit ; roast quickly in the ashes ; pound but coarsely from haste ; swallow the water greedily ; separate, disperse (a.) ; grow decrepit ; — II. INF. ta'aslub, waste away and emaciate (n.).

(عثلط) 'usalit, thick, consistent.

عثلول 'uslûl, nerve of a horse's mane.

(عثم) 'asam, U, INF. 'asm, be healed so as to be crooked ; heal so (a.) ; sew with large stitches ; get a scab without healing ; — IV. INF. i'sâm, sew but slightly, stitch ; — VIII. INF. i'tisâm, id. ; perform in an illusory manner ; ask for and receive help ; stretch out the hand (for giving).

عثم 'asam, crookedly-healed bone.

عثما 'asmâ', hand healed so as to become distorted.

عثمان 'usmân, a young (of an animal) ; Osmân ; — ى 'usmâniyy, Ottoman.

عثمثم 'asamsam, ة, violent ; big and strong, lion.

عثمرة 'usmura-t, skin of grapes, husk.

(عثن) 'asan, U, INF. 'asn, 'usân, 'usûn, smoke ; ascend ; — 'asin, A, INF. 'asan, smell of perfumes ; — II. INF. ta'sîn, smoke ; perfume ; cause discord and revolt ; — IV. INF. i'sân, smoke.

عثن 'isn, wool ; a herb ; manager, administrator ; — 'asan, smoke ; pl. a'sân, small idol ; — 'asin, spoiled by smoke.

عثنون 'usnûn, pl. 'asânîn, point of a beard ; long beard ; rain beginning to fall ; pl. beginning ; the first of ; hanging drops or cones.

(عثو) 'asâ, U, INF. 'asw, — عثى 'asa, I, A, — 'asî, A, INF. 'usy, 'isiyy, 'asayân, do harm, corrupt, cause mischief ; — ة 'aswa-t, pl. 'ussa, long hair.

عثوا 'aswâ', f. of اعثى a'sa, blackish, &c. ; female hyena ; decrepit old woman.

عثوث 'usûs, pl. of عثة 'ussa-t.

عثور 'asûr, stumbling, tripping (adj.) ; vain, futile ; — *.

عثول 'asûl, pl. 'usul, stupid ; thick and rough ; — 'iswall (also عثولى 'aswaliyy), having thick hair ;

matted (hair, beard); — *'iswall* (also عشوثل *'asausal*), stupid and weak.

عشى *'asa*, etc., see (عشو); — *'usa*, pl. plants; — *'ussa*, pl. of عشوة *'aswa-t*; — *'ussî*, pl. of عاشى *'âsî*, impudent; disastrous, mischievous.

عثيان *'isyân'* male hyena.

عثيثة *'usaisa-t*, little moth.

عثير *'isyar*, dust; earth; mud; trace, impression.

عثيل *'isyal*, male hyena.

(عج) *'ajj*, I, A, INF. *'ajj*, *'ajîj*, cry aloud, roar, bellow, bleat; call the camel; ride or travel in many different ways; blow violently and raise the dust; — II. INF. *ta'jîj*, fill with smoke; — IV. INF. *i'jâj*, blow violently; ride or travel in various ways; — V. INF. *ta'ajjuj*, be full of smoke.

عج *'ajj*, clamour; roaring, bellowing (s.); — ة *'ujja-t*, omelet, pancake.

عجاب *'ujâb*, wonderful; wonder; — *ujjâb*, very wonderful.

عجاج *'ajâj*, dust; smoke; stupid; — *'ajjâj*, dusty; windy; screamer, clamourer; roaring (adj.); — ة *'ajâja-t*, whirling of dust or smoke; clamour, noise; large flock.

عجاجيل *'ajâjîl*, pl. of عجول *'ijjaul*.

عجارف *'ajârif*, عجاريف *'ajârîf*, calamities; violence of the rain.

عجارير *'ajârîr*, pl. of عجرور *'ujrûr*.

عجاريز *'ajârîz*, pl. of عجروز *'ujrûz*.

عجاف *'ijâf*, calamity, fate; time; coloquintida; pl. of اعجف *a'jaf*, lean, thin.

عجال *'ijâl*, pl. of عجلة *'ajala-t*, عجلان *'ajlân* and عجيل *'ajîl*; — *'ujjâl*, a few dates eaten in haste; handful of dates; — ة *'ijâla-t*, *'ujâla-t*, what is ready and at hand, hasty meal; early corn; hastily done; *'ijâlat-an*, at once, immediately; *'ijâla-t*, a plant.

عجالد *'ujâlid*, عجالز *'ujâliz*, عجالط *'ujâliṭ*, thick cheese-like milk.

عجالى *'ajâla*, *'ujâla*, pl. of عجلان *'ajlân*.

عجام *'ujâm*, stone of a fruit; — *'ajjâm*, bat (animal); mountain-swallow.

عجان *'ijân*, pl. *a'jina-t*, *'ujun*, perineum; neck below the chin; foundation; — *'ajjân*, blockhead.

عجانس *'ajânis*, beetles.

عجاوة *'ajâwa-t*, pulpy date; — *'ujawa-t*, *'ijawa-t*, milk; — *'ujâwa-t*, pl. *'uja*, *'ujiyy*, *'ajâyâ*, sinew from the knee to the hoof.

(عجاهن) *'ujâhin*, pl. *'ajâhina-t*, servant; cook; best man (of a bridegroom); porcupine; — ة *'ujâhina-t*, bridesmaid.

عجايا *'ajâyâ*, pl. of عجاوة *'ujâwa-t* and عجى *'ajiyy*.

عجائبى *'ajâ'ibiyy*, wonder-working.

عجائز *'ajâ'iz*, pl. of عجوز *'ajûz*.

عجائل *'ajâ'il*, pl. of عجول *'ajûl*.

(عجب) *'ajib*, A, INF. *'ajab*, wonder, be astonished at (من *min*); — II. INF. *ta'jîb*, astonish, surprise, cause to wonder; — IV. INF. *i'jâb*, astonish agreeably; please (n.), fascinate; wonder, rejoice at (acc.); pass. *'ujib*, (ب *bi*) id.; admire; — V. INF. *ta'ajjub*, wonder, be astonished; inspire with love; — VIII. INF. *i'tijâb*, X. INF. *isti'jâb*, wonder.

عجب *'ajb*, pl. *'ujûb*, tail-bone; hind part; end of sandy tracts; — *'ajb*, *'ijb*, *'ujb*, fond of women; — *'ujb*, self-complacency, pride, vanity; — *'ajab*, wonder, astonishment (*'ajab-an*, oh wonder!); being pleasing to God; ابو العجب *abû 'l-'ajab*, fate, destiny.

عجبا *'ajbâ'*, f. of اعجب *a'jab*, more wonderful, &c., q.v.; marvel of beauty.

(عجد) *'ajd*, *'ujd*, pressed grapes; raisin; — *'ajad*, ة, raven.

(عجر) *'ajar*, I, INF. *'ajr*, bend the

neck; — INF. *'ajr, 'ajarân*, run quickly past; raise the two fore-feet at the same time in running; run away with (the rider); attack, charge; hinder, prevent; importune, set upon; — *'ajir*, A, INF. *'ajar*, be stout, big, paunch-bellied; be knotty; be still unripe or green; be hard and strong; — III. INF. *mu'âjara-t*, run quickly past; — V. INF. *ta'ajjur*, be folded upon itself, cover itself; — VIII. INF. *i'tijâr*; put on the turban with a few twists; cover the head with the under-cap معجر *ma'jar*; give birth against hope.

عجر *'ajar*, excrescence, knot, knob; — *'ajir, 'ajur*, knotty, knobby; thick above the joint; still unripe or green; — ة *'ijra-t*, way of twisting the turban; — *'ujra-t*, pl. *'ujar*, knob, knot, button; anything complicated; fault; (m.) unripeness of fruit; عجره و بجره *'ujaru-hu wa bujaru-hu*, what one does openly and secretly, one's wrongs and cares.

عجرا *'ajrâ'*, knotty stick.

(عجرد) *'ajrad*, nimble, alert; corpulent; — *'ajarrad*, ة, clamorous, given to screaming; bold; bare, naked; bald, hairless.

(عجرف), II. *ta'ajraf*, INF. *ta'ajruf*, show haughtiness; inconsiderately impose anything distasteful; treat harshly; *ta'ajruf*= عجرفية *'ajrafiyya-t*.

عجرفة *'ajrafa-t*, haughtiness; harsh words; also—

عجرفية *'ajrafiyya-t*, haste, precipitation; rashness, boldness, fearlessness.

(عجرقب) *'ajarqab*, vile and abject; suspected.

(عجرم) *'ajram*, INF. ة, hasten, hurry.

عجرم *'ajram*, base of the tail; a thorny shrub; also *'ujrum*, hard; brave; also *'ijrim*, thickset and strong; — *'ujrum*, ة, strong; — ة *'ajrama-t, 'ijrima-t, 'ujruma-t*, herd of camels (50 to 100, also 200).

عجرور *'ujrûr*, pl. *'ajârîr*, عجروز *'ajrûz*, pl. *'ajârîz*, furrow in the sand.

عجروف *'ujrûf*, a long-legged insect; alert, agile; — also ة *'ujrûfa-t*, old woman.

عجرى *'ujriyy*, lie; calamity.

(عجز) *'ajaz*, I, INF. *'ajz, 'ajazân, 'ujûz, ma'jaz, ma'jaza-t, ma'jiz, ma'jiza-t*, be weak, be too weak, be not equal to (ل *li*); — INF. *'ujûz*, grow old, age; anticipate, overtake, get the lead of; — *'ajiz*, A, INF. *'ajaz*, be weak; — INF. *'ajaz, 'ujz*, have large buttocks; — *'ajuz*, grow old; — II. INF. *ta'jîz*, grow old; pass. have large hips; deem or declare weak, too weak, impotent; prevent; (m.) weary, make desperate; — III. INF. *mu'âjaza-t*, depart so as not to be overtaken again; try to come in advance of (acc.); incline (n.) towards (الى *'ila*); — IV. INF. *i'jâz*, make or find one weak, impotent; do wonders, puzzle, baffle; escape; pass one over as too weak; surpass one's power; — V. INF. *ta'ajjuz*, ride on the hind-parts of the camel.

عجز *'ajz*, weakness; impotence; incapacity; poverty; hilt of a sword; a bird; بنات العج *banât al-'ajz*, arrows; pl. *a'jâz*, trunk of a tree; — *'ijz*, handle of a bow; — *'ujz*, pl. of اعجز *a'jaz*, having large buttocks or hips; — *'ujz, 'ajz, 'ijz*, buttock, hip, rump, croup; — *'ajuz, 'ajaz, 'ajiz*, id.; penultimate letter; — *'ujuz*, pl. of عجوز *'ajûz*; — ة *'ijza-t, 'ujza-t*, the last-born child, nestling; — *'ajaza-t*, the poor, pl. of عاجز *'âjiz*.

عجزا *'ajzâ'*, f. of اعجز *a'jaz*, having large hips.

عجران *'ajzân*, too weak; impotent; — *'ajazân*, weakness; INF. of (عجر).

(عجس) *'ajas*, I, INF. *'ajs*, keep back, prevent; seize, hold; lose the way from playfulness (camel); — INF. *'ujûs*, come along with a noisy rush (large train of camels); — V. INF. *ta'ajjus*, keep in sight and pursue; rain upon in shower after shower; go out towards the end of the night; keep back, retain, prevent; cause a delay to (ب *bi*); remain behind; blame, put to shame.

عجس *'ajs*, *'ijs*, *'ujs*, middle or hand-piece of the bow; — also ة *'ujsa-t*, last part of the night, morning-dawn; —*'ajus*, pl. *a'jâs*, buttocks, rump, croup.

عجسمة *'ajsama-t*, nimbleness, alertness, haste.

(عجعج) *'aj'aj*, INF. ة, cry out loud and repeatedly; call the camel; roar, groan; bleat.

(عجف) *'ajaf*, I, INF. *'ajf*, *'ujûf*, abstain from food in spite of one's appetite so that a hungry one may eat; devote one's self entirely to nursing a sick person; forbear with; — I, U, INF. *'ajf*, allow to grow thin, emaciate (a.); get mollified; be distant from; — *'ajif*, A, INF. *'ajaf*,— *'ajuf*, emaciate (n.); — II. INF. *ta'jîf*, abstain from food, &c. (as I.); eat without getting satisfied; — IV. INF. *i'jâf*, devote one's self entirely to nursing the sick; emaciate (a.); have lean cattle.

عجف *'ajaf*, leanness, thinness; — ة *'ajifa-t*, thin (f.).

عجفى *'ajfa*, pl. of عجيف *'ajîf*.

(عجل) *'ajil*, A, INF. *'ajal*, *'ajala-t*, hasten, hurry (n.); — II. INF. *ta'jil*, id.; urge to haste, hurry (a.); bid to bring quickly; do a thing quickly or hastily; accelerate; overtake, get the lead of; send in advance; give or pay in advance; form the cheese اقط *aqt* into long pieces; — III. INF. *mu'âjala-t*, do a thing in haste; vie in haste; urge to haste; do suddenly; — IV. INF. *i'jâl*, urge to haste; anticipate, get in advance of; give birth prematurely; — V. INF. *ta'ajjul*, hasten (n.); bid to make haste; have anything given to one's self in advance; form the cheese into long pieces; — X. INF. *isti'jâl*, urge to haste; hurry one's self; be over-hasty; get in advance; keep a calf.

عجل *'ijl*, pl. *'ujûl*, *'ijâl*, calf; — *'ujl*, what is soon ready or at hand; — *'ajal*, haste; mud; — *'ajil*, *'ajul*, hasty, in a hurry; alert, nimble; — ة *'ajala-t*, haste, hurry; pl. *'ajal*, *a'jâl*, *'ijâl*, carriage, cart; water-wheel; mud, loam, clay; — عجلة *'ijla-t*, pl. *'ijal*, *'ijâl*, *'ajâl*, she-calf; skin-bag; water-wheel; —*'ujla-t*, soon ready or at hand; milk fresh from the cow, &c.

عجلان *'ajlân*, pl. *'ajâla*, *'ujâla*, *'ijâl*, f. *'ajla*, pl. *'ajâlî*, hasty, in a hurry.

(عجلد) *'ujalid*, عجلط *'ujalit*, thick sour milk.

عجلى *'ajla*, f. of عجلان *'ajlân*.

(عجم) *'ajam*, U, INF. *'ajm*, *'ujûm*, bite, chew (to examine the hardness of a thing, &c.); test; brandish a sword to try it); cut; hit upon, gaze at; — INF. *'ajm*, mark a text with the vowel-points; — II. INF. *ta'jîm*=the previous; —III. INF. *mu'âjama-t*, bite (to examine the hardness); — IV. INF. *i'jâm*, speak or write barbarously or unintelligibly; point letters or a text; shut or lock the door; boil strongly; — VI. INF. *ta'âjum*, be unintelligible, obscure; — VII. INF. *'ini'jâm*, id.; — X. INF. *isti'jâm*, be silent, be unable to answer;

be unintelligible, obscure; be no longer able to read (from sleepiness); find obscure.

عجم *'ajm*, pl. *'ujûm*, young camels; base of the tail; back-bone; intelligent; — *'ajam*, pl. *a'jâm*, not an Arab, barbarian, especially Persian; *al-'ajam*, Persia; stone of a fruit; young camels; — ة *'ajama-t*, stone of a fruit; — *'ujma-t*, sand-hill; difficulty in speaking Arabic; — ى *'ajamiyy*, pl. *'ajam*, not an Arab, barbarian, Persian; Persian earthenware; — ية *'ajamiyya-t*, quality of not being an Arab, &c.

(عجن) *'ajan*, U, I, INF. *'ajn*, knead or work upon with the whole hand; slap on the buttocks; stamp the ground; go with the help of the hands (old man); — *'ajin*, A, INF. *'ajan*, have a tumour in the pudenda or the buttocks; be very fat; — II. INF. *ta'jîm*, knead; be dough-like; — IV. INF. *i'jân*, have the buttocks swollen; ride a fat camel; go on board a ship; — VII. INF. *ini'jân*, be kneaded; — VIII. *i'tijân*, knead.

عجن *'ajin*, ة, strong and fat; having a tumour in the genital parts; — *'ujun*, pl. of عجان *'ajân* and عجين *'ajîn*.

(عجه), II. *'ajjah*, sow discord by slandering; — V. INF. *ta'ajjuh*, feign stupidity or ignorance; be complicated.

عجهرة *'ajhara-t*, excess of thickness.

عجهن, II. *ta'ajhan*, woo and win a woman; be عجاهن *'ujâhin*, q.v.

(عجو) *'ajâ*, U, INF. *'ajw*, delay the suckling of a child, suckle it too late; give suck; open; show a cross face; be mischievous; oppress; — II. INF. *ta'jiya-t*, show a cross face, frown; — III. INF. *mu'âjât*, suckle too late; bring up on another woman's milk or on food; — ة *'ajwa-t*, firm pulpy date; fine date of Medina; conserve of dates; (m.) stone.

عجوبة *'ujûba-t*, pl. *a'âjîb*, anything wonderful; wonder.

عجوز *'ajûz*, ة, pl. *'ajâ'iz*, *'ujuz*, old woman; old man; decrepit; impotent; — *'ujûz*, weakness; INF. of (عجز).

عجول *'ajûl*, hasty, in a hurry; death; breakfast; pl. *'ujul*, *'ajâ'il*, deprived of her foals, bereft of her children; disconsolate; — *'ujul*, pl. of عجل *'ijl*; — *'ijjaul*, pl. *'ajâjîl*, male calf; handful of dates.

عجى *'uja*, pl. of عجاوة *'ujâwa-t*; — *'ajiyy*, ة, pl. *'ajâyâ*, motherless and suckled by another.

عجيب *'ajîb*, ة, pl. *'ajâ'ib*, wonderful, marvellous; — ة *'ajîba-t*, pl. *'ajâ'ib*, anything extraordinary, astonishing; wonder, marvel.

عجيج *'ajîj*, screaming (s.), clamour INF. of (عج).

عجير *'ajîr*, impotent.

عجيز *'ajîz*, impotent; the buttocks; — *'ujayyiz*, little old woman; — ة *'ajîza-t*, hips of a woman.

عجيسا *'ajîsâ'*, impotent (stallion); — also *'ijjîsâ'*, slow pace.

عجيف *'ajîf*, pl. *'ajfa*, lean, thin.

عجيل *'ajîl*, *'ijjîl*, hurrying; pl. *'ijâl*, *'ajâla*, *'ujâla*, swift, nimble, agile.

عجين *'ajîn*, pl. *'ujun*, kneaded; dough; electuary; jam, decoction; — ة *'ajîna-t*, multitude, crowd, troop; effeminate; stupid; ام ع *umm 'ajîna-t*, pelican; — ى *'ajîniyy*, dough-like, doughy.

(عد) *'add*, U, I, INF. *'add*, count, count up; count for, consider; — II. INF. *ta'dâd*, count; recount, enumerate (the merits of the dead); make numerous,

multiply; INF. *ta'did*, put by for the time of need; — III. INF. *'idâd*, *mu'âdda-t*, count for or amongst (فى *fî*); cast lots, obtain by lot; — IV. INF. *i'dâd*, prepare, make ready, equip; put by; gather riches; count among (مع *ma'*); — V. INF. *ta'addud*, be prepared, ready; multiply; (n.) be reckoned, counted; be equipped, fitted out; — also VI. INF. *ta'âdd*, surpass a number (على *'ala*); — VIII. INF. *i'tidâd*, be counted, reckoned; count, reckon among (ب *bi*); be ready, prepared; be inaccessible; boast; (m.) be proud; — X. INF. *isti'dâd*, prepare for, be ready; equip, make ready.

عد *'add*, telling over, counting, calculation; number; — *'idd*, pl. *a'dâd*, the hitting number; number, multitude; equal; fellow, companion; permanently flowing; — *'udd*, pustule, small blister; — ة *'ida-t*, promise; threat; term; INF. of (وعد); — *'idda-t*, number; multitude; time during which a woman is inaccessible (on account of the menses, of divorce, of mourning); — *'udda-t*, pl. *'udad*, preparation, equipment, outfit; store; means; (m.) totality of tools, instruments, &c.; (m.) saddle; pustule, small blister.

عدا *'adâ*, ما عدا *mâ 'adâ*, except that, except; — *'adâ'*, transgression; removal; — also *'idâ'*, course, race; equally long and broad, fitting, corresponding; — *'idâ'*, pl. of عدو *'idw* and عدوة *'idwa-t*; — *'addâ'*, good runner; — ة *'udât*, pl. of عادى, transgressor, &c.

عداد *'idâd*, number, counting (s.), telling up (s.); being counted (s.); equal; fellow, companion; making ready (s.), preparing (s.).

عدادين *'adâdîn*, pl. of عدان *'adân*, *'addân*.

عدار *'addâr*, sailor; (m.) pioneer, sapper.

عداف *'udâf*, something, some (eatable).

عدالة *'adâla-t*, equity, justice; right; court of justice.

عدامة *'adâma-t*, stupidity.

عدان *'adân*, coast, shore; also *'addan*, pl. *'adâdîn*, fixed time of a public distribution (of water, &c.); — ة *'adâna-t*, troop; = عدينة *'adîna-t*.

عداوة *'adâwa-t*, enmity, hostility, hatred.

عدبى *'udabiyy*, excellent, high-minded, generous; blameless, stainless.

(عدث) *'ads*, gentleness of disposition.

عدد *'adad*, pl. *a'dâd*, number; years of life; multitude, crowd; family; — *'udad*, pl. of عدة *'udda-t*; — ى *'adadiyy*, numerical.

(عدر) *'adar*, be bold against (على *'ala*); (m.) dig, entrench; — *'adir*, A, INF. *'adar*, abound in rain-water.

عدر *'adr*, *'udr*, heavy rain.

(عدس) *'adas*, I, INF. *'ads*, serve; tend the cattle; tread violently, stamp; work zealously, endeavour to earn; call the mule by عدس *'adas!* surmise; INF. *'ads*, *'idâs*, *'udûs*, *'adasân*, depart, set out on a journey; pass. *'udis*, have a lentil-shaped eruption on the skin; — III. INF. *mu'âdasa-t*, travel continually.

عدس *'adas*, ة, lentil; pustule, lens; — ة *'adasa-t*, lens of glass; (m.) macadam; — ية *'adasiyya-t*, dish of lentils.

(عدف) *'adaf*, I, INF. *'adf*, eat; — V. INF. *ta'adduf*, taste but little food.

عدف *'adf*, some food; small present; — *'idf*, origin; also *'idaf*,

troop (of 10 to 50); —*'udf*, pl. of عدوف *'adûf*; —*'adaf*, bit of straw, mote (&c. in the eye); — ة *'adfa-t*, origin; —*'idfa-t*, pl. *'idaf*, portion, part; the upper chest; troop of 10 to 50; hem of a garment; short under-garment; —*'idfa-t*, *'adafa-t*, pl. *'idaf*, *'adaf*, root of a tree in the ground.

(عدق) *'adaq*, I, INF. *'adq*, gather, collect; surmise without being certain; dip the hand into water for a thing; —*'adiq*, A, INF. *'adaq*, id.; — II. INF. *ta'dîq*, surmise, suppose; — IV. INF. *i'dâq*, dip the hand into water.

عدق *'adaq*, ة, pl. *'uduq*, harpoon; hook to draw the bucket out of the well.

(عدك) *'adak*, beat wool.

(عدل) *'adal*, I, INF. *'adl*, *'adâla-t*, *'udûla-t*, *ma'dila-t*, *ma'dala-t*, exercise justice, give righteous judgment; — INF. *'adl*, weigh (a.), weigh equally; ride on the same beast with another; counterbalance, be equal in weight, be equal; make equal; mediate; hesitate or waver between two things; requite, make up for; straighten; make a bend; leave covering (stallion); drive away the stallion; — INF. *'adl*, *'udûl*, deviate; abstain, desist; — INF. *'udûl*, return; —*'adul*, INF. *'adâla-t*, *'adal*, be just; — II. INF. *ta'dîl*, give judgment according to the right; make equal in size or weight, declare to be equal; set into the right proportion; straighten; lead straight; weigh rightly (a.); place the balance in equilibrium; admit as lawful (a witness); drink to excess; (m.) grow thick or stout; — III. INF. *mu'âdala-t*, be or make equal in size or weight; understand two things, have two strings to one bow; compare one's self to, place one's self on a level with (ب *bi*); bring about an agreement or settlement between; ride on the same beast; INF. also *'idâl*, hesitate in a difficult matter; be crooked; — IV. INF. *i'dâl*, make just, right, straight, fit, corresponding; —V. INF. *ta'addul*, be equal or in equilibrium; — VII. INF. *in'idâl*, deviate, swerve from (عن *'an*); — VIII. INF. *i'tidâl*, be right, just; keep the middle or equilibrium between two things with regard to quality or quantity; be proportionate, symmetrical; grow equal; (m.) grow stout, corpulent; — X. INF. *isti'dâl*, find right or just; grow corpulent.

عدل *'adl*, justice, equity; righteousness, uprightness, honesty; right measure; ة, just, upright, honest; lawful, admissible; of equal value; compensation; reward; ransom; deviation from what is right, anomaly; also *'udal*, pl. of عادل *'âdil*, just, &c.; —*'idl*, pl. *a'dâl*, *'idâl*, *'udûl*, equal, of equal weight; bale of merchandise; of equal value; similar, corresponding; —*'adal*, equilibration of the two side-loads; — *'adil*, just; proportionate; (m.) healthy and but little corpulent;—ة *'udala-t*, *'adala-t*, admissible witness.

عدلا *'udalâ'*, pl. of عديل *'adîl*.

عدلية *'adliyya-t*, justice.

(عدم) *'adim*, A, INF. *'udm*, *'adam*, miss, lack; escape, be wanting, fail; —*'adum*, INF. *'adâma-t*, be stupid, lack sense; be spoiled, destroyed, annihilated; — IV. INF. *i'dâm*, deprive or rob of (2 acc.), impoverish, destroy, ruin, annihilate; be wanting, missing; prevent, hinder; INF. *'udm*, *'idâm*, grow poor; — VII. INF. *in'idâm*, get destroyed, disappear; be spoiled; — X.

INF. *isti'dâm*, consider as spoiled, lost, worthless.

عدم *'adam*, *'udm*, *'udum*, non-existence, nonentity; destruction, annihilation; want; poverty; corresponds to the prefix un-, in- before English nouns; — *'adim*, pl. *'udamâ'*, poor, needy.

عدمل *'udmul*, ى *'udmuliyy*, pl. *'adâmil*, old and thick.

عدمول *'udmûl*, pl. *'adâmîl*, old; frog.

عدمى *'adamiyy*, not existing; — ة *'adamiyya-t*, non-existence; nonentity, nothing, nothingness.

(عدن) *'adan*, I, U, INF. *'adn*, *'udûn*, stay or dwell permanently; keep to the same pasture-ground; I, INF. *'adn*, dung, manure; cut; take out of the ground; grow high; — II. INF. *ta'dîn*, manure; break the ground with a pick-axe, search for minerals, exploit a mine; fix the time of public distribution; fill one's self with drink; — V. INF. be fixed (time of distribution).

عدن *'adn*, permanent abode; Paradise, Eden; — *'adan*, Aden.

(عدو) *'adâ*, U, INF. *'adw*, *'adawân*, *ta'dâ'*, *'ad-an*, run, run fast; escape; — INF. *'adw*, *'uduww*, *'adâ'*, *'udwân*, *'idwân*, *'udwa*, do violence, commit injustice; — INF. *'adâ'*, *'udwân*, *'adawân*, steal, rob; — INF. *'adw*, *'udwân*, turn (a.) from one thing and occupy with another; prevent, hinder; leap at; pass by, leave undone; hesitate; transgress; — عدى *'adî*, A, INF. *'adan*, hate, be hostile to (ل *li*); — (m.) عدا *'adâ*, INF. *'udwân*, be hostile; — II. INF. *ta'diya-t*, cause to cross, to overstep, to transgress; cause to pass by, to leave off, to go elsewhere, to do something else; make a verb active or transitive; turn from (n.), leave off; pass through; (m.) enter a house; — III. INF. *mu'âdât*, *'idâ'*, turn quickly from one thing to another; shoot one after the other (game); run after, pursue; treat with hostility; resist, oppose; — IV. INF. *i'dâ'*, overstep the bounds; transgress; exercise violence against, tyrannize over (على *'ala*); urge to jump or run; transfer; infect; help the oppressed, lend assistance; summon before the judge; judge in favour of; — V. INF. *ta'addî*, wrong; usurp; pass from one to the other; be transitive; overstep the bounds; leave off, be able to leave off; take the wife's dowry; — VI. INF. *ta'âdî*, vie in running; be unlevel and not fit to settle upon; be far; remove, separate (n.); be infected by or infect one another; — VII. INF. *in'idâ'*, be infected by; — VIII. INF. *i'tidâ'*, wrong, be hostile to (على *'ala*); — X. INF. *isti'dâ'*, call to help or for protection against; ask the judge to summon the adversary; declare one's self an enemy of, become hostile to; urge to run.

عدو *'adw*, run, course; — *'idw*, pl. *'idâ'*, extent, extension; boundary; flat stone for covering; — *'aduww*, f. ة, pl. *a'dâ'*, *a'âdî*, *'udât*, *'uda-n*, *'ida-n*, enemy; — *'aduww*, *'uduww*, run, course; transgression; — ة *'adwa-t*, *'idwa-t*, *'udwa-t*, pl. *'idâ'*, river-side, bank; — *'adwa-t*, crossing, passing over (s.), transition; attack; career; — *'idwa-t*, *'udwa-t*=*'idw*; pl. *'idâ'*, *'udyât*, high place.

عدوان *'udwân*, enmity, hostility; wrong, violence, injustice, transgression; INF. of (عدو).

عدوب *'adûb*, plenty of sand.

عدوس *'adûs*, bold; hyena; — *

عدوف *'adûf*, ة *'adûfa-t*, pl. *'adf*, anything eatable.
عدوقة *'adwaqa-t*, pl. *'uduq*=عدق *'adaq*.
عدول *'udûl*, deviation; desistence; defection; pl. of عادل *'âdil*, just, &c.; — * ; — ة *'udûla-t*, justice.
عدوم *'adûm*, poor, needy, indigent.
عدوى *'adwa*, help; counsel (in a law-suit); infection; — *'udwa*, wrong, hostility, enmity; INF. of (عدو); — *'adawiyy*, hostile; — *'idawiyy*, by way of promise, promissory.
عدى *'adî*, see (عدو); — *'adan*, river-bank; — *'idan*, pl. *a'dâ'*, region, tract; flat stones for covering; intermediate beams; strangers, enemies; — *'idan*, *'udan*, pl. of عدو *'aduww*; — *'adiyy*, pl. of عادى *'âdî*, runner; — *'idiyy*, promissory; — *'udayy*, dim. of عدو *'aduww*, enemy.
عديات *'udyât*, pl. of عدوة *'udwa-t*.
عديد *'adîd*, numerous; counted; number; equal; companion, fellow; one of; — ة *'adîda-t*, lot, share.
عديل *'adîl*, pl. *'udalâ'*, equal to the counterpoise, to the load or weight on the other side; rider on one side of the camel; equal; just; rival.
عديم *'adîm*, lacking, missing (adj.); deprived, without (corresponding to the prefix un-, in- of English adjectives); not in existence; poor; stupid.
عدينة *'adîna-t*, pl. *'adâ'in*, patch of leather.
عذاب *'azâb*, pl. *a'ziba-t*, punishment; pain, torment; martyrdom; — ة *'azâba-t*, womb, pudenda of a woman.
عذار *'izâr*, pl. *'uzr*, cheek; side; chaw; down on the cheeks; face; bridle-strap over the chaws; bridle for the (camel's) nose; shame; extensive sand-hill.
عذارى *'azâra*, pl. of عذرا *'azrâ'*.

(عذافر) *'uzâfir*, pl. *'azâfira-t*, big and strong; *al-'uzâfir*, lion.
عذال *'azzâl*, severe critic; censurer, blasphemer; — *'uzzâl*, pl. of عاذل *'âzil*, censurer; — ة *'azzâla-t*, buttocks.
عذام *'azzâm*, pl. *'uzum*, fly; — *'azzâm*, *'uzzâm*, ة *'azzâma-t*, *'uzzâma-t*, an aromatic herb, camelopodium.
عذانة *'azâna-t*, buttocks.
عذاة *'azât*, pl. *'azawât*, healthy and fertile ground; — *'azâ'a-t*, good climate.
(عذب) *'azab*, I, INF. *'azb*, hinder, prevent; leave, leave undone; be unable to eat from violent thirst; — *'azib*, A, INF. *'azab*, be covered with moss, sea-weed, &c.; — *'azub*, I[illegible] *'uzûba-t*, be sweet, of pleasan[illegible]ste; — II. INF. *ta'zîb*, prevent, [illegible]p off; punish, vex, torment; [illegible]rovide the whip with a thong; — IV. INF. *i'zâb*, prevent, hinder; clear the water of moss, &c.; have sweet water; — V. INF. *ta'azzub*, be punished, tormented; suffer pain; — VIII. INF. *i'tizâb*, let the lappets of the turban hang down behind; — X. INF. *isti'zâb*, leave, leave undone; draw sweet water; find the water sweet; find delightful.
عذب *'azb*, sweet, of pleasant taste; eloquent; — *'azab*, ة, pl. *'azabât*, stalk, blade, straw; twig, branch; end, top, lappet, fringe; thread, strap; tip of the tongue; thong; top-leather of a shoe; — *'azib*, covered with dirt, with impurities; — ة *'azba-t*, *'azaba-t*, *'aziba-t*, water-lentil; — *'aziba-t*, chaff; foam, froth; noose; — ى *'azabiyy*, magnanimous.
(عذج) *'azaj*, U, INF. *'azj*, drink.
(عذر) *'azar*, I, INF. *'uzr*, *'uzur*, *'uzra*, *'ma'zira-t*, *ma'zura-t*, excuse, accept one's excuse; — I, INF. *'azr*, *'uzr*, be guilty and

disgraced; circumcise; — U, I, INF. *'azr*, *'uzr*, tighten the bridle round the jaws; pass. *'uzir*, be seized with an inflammation of the uvula; be a virgin, be maiden-like; — II. INF. *ta'zîr*, proffer lying excuses; get a downy beard; pollute with excrement; efface the traces of a house; celebrate by an entertainment (the circumcision, &c.); invite to such; circumcise; mark a camel; do less than is required; — III. INF. *mu'âzara-t*, proffer lying excuses; — IV. INF. *i'zâr*, excuse; proffer excuses; have a good excuse; be excused with, have one's self excused with; do less than is required, remain short of; carry out with diligence; be covered with guilt and disgrace; bridle or saddle the horse; circumcise, give an entertainment; act justly and fairly; beat so as to leave scars; ease the bowels; contain much dirt and filth; pass. incur deadly danger; — V. INF. *ta'azzur*, excuse one's self, apologise; deny one's self; be polluted; do less than is required; be difficult, be too hard for (على *'ala*); be poor; be effaced; flee; — VIII. INF. *i'tizâr*, excuse one's self, apologise; be effaced; complain; let the lappets of the turban hang down behind; fail, be exhausted (water); deflower; — X. INF. *isti'zâr*, apologise.

عذر *'uzr*, pl. *a'zâr*, excuse; success; victory; virginity (ابو عذرها *abû 'uzri-hâ*, the master of her virginity, first husband); menses; — ة *'izra-t*, pl. *'izar*, excuse, pretext; — *'uzra-t*, pl. *'uzar*, mane, tuft of hair; prepuce, clitoris; circumcision; uvula and its inflammation; sign; flag; — *'azira-t*, dung; human excrement; chaff; company.

عذرا *'azrâ'*, pl. *'azâra*, *'azârî*, *'azrawât*, virgin.

(عذف) *'azaf*, I, INF. *'azf*,—V. INF. *ta'azzuf*, eat.

عذف *'azf*, anything eatable.

(عذفر), II. INF. *ta'azfur*, get angry, fly into a passion.

(عذق) *'azaq*, I, INF. *'azq*, mark (a sheep); bring into evil repute; ascribe, impute; have the diarrhœa; drive other horses away and possess himself of the mare; push forth ears; take the clusters of dates from the palm-tree; let the lappets of the turban hang down behind; — II. INF. *ta'zîq*, take the clusters of dates from the tree; — IV. INF. *i'zâq*, mark a sheep; push forth ears; make over a business or the dominion; — VIII. INF. *i'tizâq*, let the two ends of the turban hang down behind; allot or ascribe (ب *bi*) as peculiar to (acc.); mark a camel.

عذق *'azq*, pl. *a'zuq*, *'izâq*, palm-tree loaded with fruit; — *'izq*, pl. *a'zâq*, *'uzûq*, bunch or cluster of dates; branch; glory; — *'aziq*, clever, skilful, prudent; fragrant;—ة *'azqa-t*, *'izqa-t*, mark for sheep (a flock of wool of different colour used as such).

(عذل) *'azal*, U, INF. *'azl*, blame, censure, reproach with; — II. INF. *ta'zîl*, id.; — V. INF. *ta'azzul*, allow one's self to be censured, expose one's self to blame; — VIII. INF. *i'tizâl*, id.; be censured; blame one's self; persist in, persevere; throw or shoot a second time.

عذل *'azl*, *'azal*, blame, censure; — *'uzul*, sultry days; — *'uzzal*, ة *'azala-t*, censurers, pl. of عاذل *'âzil*; — ة *'uzala-t*, censurer.

عذلاج *'izlâj*, pleasant, agreeable.

(عذلج) *'azlaj*, INF. ة, fill; feed well.

عذلط *'uzaliṭ*=عثلط *'uṣaliṭ*, thick.

(عذلق), II. INF. *ta'azluq*, swing in walking.

عذلوج *'uzlûj*, ة, well fed.

عذلوق *'uzlûq*, alert fellow.

(عذم) *'azam*, I, INF. *'azm*, *'izâm*, seize with the teeth, bite, chew violently; blame, rebuke; refuse, reject, repel; — INF. *'azam*, scold.

عذم *'azam*, a plant; — *'uzum*, pl. of عذام *'azzâm*.

عذمذم *'azamzam*, measuring by estimation; great mortality.

(عذو) *'azâ*, U, INF. *'azw*, have good air or a healthy climate; — *'azu'*, INF. *'azâwa-t*, also عذى *'azî*, A, INF. *'azan*, id.; be fertile; — X. INF. *isti'zâ'*, find a place healthy and feel well there.

عذوف *'azûf*, anything eatable; tasting (s.).

عذى *'azî*, see (عذو); — *'aziyy*, ة, healthy, salubrious; — ة *'aziya-t* = عذاة *'azât*; straw.

عذير *'azîr*, pl. *'uzur*, who excuses; defender; festival, entertainment.

عذيمة *'azîma-t*, pl. *'azâ'im*, blame, censure, rebuke; palm-tree with stoneless dates.

(عر) *'arr*, U, I, INF. *'arr*, be scabious, mangy; also pass. *'urr*, suffer from the falling out of the hair; do evil to (acc.); vex; reproach with anything base; meet with a poor one who dares not beg; — U, manure; — U, INF. *'urra-t*, drop excrement; — I, INF. *'arâr*, cry out (male ostrich); (m.) roar, bellow; — for *'arir*, A, INF. *'arr*, be small; — II. INF. *ta'rîr*, manure; entrust with a business; vex, grieve; — III. INF. *mu'ârra-t*, *'irâr*, cry out; — VI. INF. *ta'ârr*, be restless in bed and talk; start out of a dream talking; — VIII. INF. *i'tirâr*, beg without speaking, beg; pass. be solicited; — X. INF. *isti'râr*, be visited by the itch (tribe).

عر *'arr*, itch, scab, mange; evil; disgrace; f. ة, an early-weaned child; — *'urr*, itch, scab; a boil in the neck; falling out of a camel's hair; dung (of birds); servant lad, slave; — ة *'arra-t*, courage, bravery; — *'urra-t*, dung; scab; sin; shame, disgrace.

عرا *'arâ'*, pl. *a'riya-t*, *a'râ'*, open place, yard, court-yard; surface of the ground; — also *'irâ'*, desert; INF. III. of (عرى); — *'arrâ'*, girl; f. of اعر *a'arr*, scabby, mangy, &c.; — ة *'arât*, courtyard; vestibule; shore, coast; tract, field; frost; — *'urât*, pl. of عارى *'ârî*, naked, &c.

عراب *'irâb*, handsome Arabian horses or camels; — ة *'irâba-t*, *'arâba-t*, obscene language, indecent talk.

عراج *'urâj*, pl. hyenas.

عرادة *'arâda-t*, state, condition; female locust; — *'arrâda-t*, balister, catapult.

عراديس *'arâdîs*, pl. joints of the fingers, knuckles.

عرار *'arâr*, a fragrant herb; requital; equal in strength or quantity; f. ة, early weaned; — ة *'arâra-t*, root; the first and best of anything; strength, power; pomp, splendour, magnificence; badness, wickedness.

عراز *'urrâz*, pl. slanderers.

عراس *'irâs*, rope or tether for camels; — *'arrâs*, seller of young camels.

عراص *'irâṣ*, pl. of عرصة *'arṣa-t*; — *'arrâṣ*, continually lightning or flashing; lightning (s.).

عراصيف *'arâṣîf*, pl. of عرصاف *'irṣâf*.

عراض *'irâḍ*, pl. *'urḍ*, half (s.); the greater part; side, tract, part; iron for marking a camel's hoof; pl. of عرض *'urḍ*, عريض *'arîḍ*; INF. of (عرض); — *'urâḍ*, ة, broad; — ة *'arâḍa-t*, INF. of عرض *'aruḍ*;

— *'urâḍa-t*, gift in victuals; provender.
عراعر *'urâ'ir*, fat; pl. *'arâ'ir*, chief, nobleman; —*.
عراف *'arrâf*, soothsayer; physician; — ة *'arâfa-t*, second rank; —*.
عرافج *'arâfij*, pl. pathless deserts.
عرافيص *'arâfîṣ*, pl. of عرفاص *'irfâṣ*.
عراق *'irâq*, pl. *'uruq*, *a'riqa-t*, leather lining; pl. *'uruq*, sea-shore; chain of mountains; flesh about the hoof; border of the ear; court-yard; rectum; Irâq; du. *al-'irâqân*, Kufa and Balsorah;— *'urâq*, picked bone; scanty meal; shower of rain; water; —*; — ى *'irâqiyy*, of or from Irâq.
عراقيب *'arâqîb*, pl. عرقوب *'urqûb*.
عراقيل *'arâqîl*, pl. difficulties.
عرام *'urâm*, nibbled, barkless; —*.
عران *'irân*, turning point of the winds; piece of wood across a camel's nose; nail, tack; horn; den of the hyena; combat; far distant.
عرانية *'urâniyya-t*, open sea; flood.
عراهين *'arâhîn*, pl. of عرهون *'urhûn*.
عراوة *'arâwa-t*, buphthalmus silvester.
عرايا *'arâyâ*, pl. of عرية *'ariyya-t*.
عرائس *'arâ'is*, pl. of عروس *'arûs*.
(عرب) *'arab*, I, INF. *'arb*, eat; — *'arib*, A, INF. *'arab*, suffer from indigestion; swell and suppurate; leave scars or marks; be deep, abound in water; separate, put by, put aside; — *'arub*, INF. *'urûba-t*, be pure Arabic (speech); — II. INF. *ta'rîb*, speak obscenely, talk ribaldry; use vulgar language to (على *'ala*); denounce one's language or actions as vulgar; utter one's speech in pure Arabic; introduce a foreign word into the Arabic language; speak for, explain another's intentions; make for one's self an Arabian bow; separate, put-aside; cut off the branches of a palm-tree; drink much of pure water; render the cow hot (bull); give earnest-money; — IV. INF. *i'râb*, speak out frankly and openly, explain distinctly; make a horse jump, urge it to run; recognise a horse as Arabian by its neighing; show itself so; get a son of Arabian complexion; speak distinctly and pure Arabic; pronounce with Arabic vocalisation; speak ribaldry; prevent one from using vulgar language; lie with or invite a woman to do so by hints; marry an amorous woman; irrigate but every third or fourth day; give a pledge or earnest-money; — V. INF. *ta'arrub*, be translated into Arabic; become a Bedouin, inhabit the desert; talk ribaldry, use vulgar language; be separated, put aside; — X. INF. *isti'râb*, become clients of the Arabs, take to Arabian ways; talk obscenely or vulgarly; be hot (cow).
عرب *'arb*, *'arab*, briskness; — *'urb*, Arabs living in towns; generous horses; — *'arab*, great quantity of pure water; — *'arib*, id.; ailing (stomach); — *'urub*, pl. of عروب *'arûb*; — ة *'araba-t*, pl. *'arab*, rapid stream; soul, self; wheel; pl. *'arabât*, carriage; pl. pontoon-bridge;—*'ariba-t*, Arabs of pure blood.
عربان *'urbân*, pl. *'arâbîn*, pledge, earnest-money; — ة *'arabâna-t*, carriage, cart.
عربب *'urbub*, plenty of pure water; scar, mark from a wound.
(عربج) *'urbuj*, *'irbuj*, fat dog; sporting-dog.
عربجى *'arabajiyy*, pl. ة, coachman (m.).
(عربد) *'arbad*, INF. ة, show ill-will, offend a friend or boon companion, be a troublesome guest.
عربد *'irbadd*, *'irbidd*, strong; habit, custom; a snake; — ة *'arbada-t*,

quarrelsomeness, drunken humour; quarrel, dispute, fight; revolt, sedition.

عربرب *'arabrab*, eatable sumach.

(عربس) *'irbis*, plain land fit for culture; resting-place, station; — *'arbas*, INF. ة, bring into confusion, disturb; — II. INF. *ta'arbus*, get confused.

(عربش) *'arbaś*, INF. ة, II. INF. *ta'arbuś*, climb.

(عربض) *'irbaḍ*, thick, stout.

(عربن) *'arban*, INF. ة, give a pledge, deposit, earnest-money.

عربون *'urbûn*, pledge, earnest-money.

عربى *'arabiyy*, ة, Arab, Arabic, Arabian; Arabic language; pl. *'arabiyyât*, Arabic literature, Arabic idioms; white barley.

عربيد *'irbîd*, quarreller, troublesome guest.

عرت *'arat*, A, I, INF. *'art*, be hard; be shaken; lighten, flash, shine; rub with the hand.

عرتبة *'artaba-t*, عرتمة *'artama-t*, tip or soft parts of the nose; dimple in the upper lip; على عرتمته *'ala 'artamat-hu*, under his nose, in spite of him.

(عرتن) *'artan*, *'artun*, *'aratan*, عرتون *'aratûn*, a tree containing tannin; — hence *'artan*, INF. ة, tan with this plant.

(عرث) *'aras̱*, I, U, INF. *'ars̱*, remove; lift up; lay aside; rub with the hand.

عرثمة *'ars̱ama-t*=عرتبة *'artaba-t*.

(عرج) *'araj*, U, INF. *'urûj*, *ma'raj*, mount (pass. *'urij*, be borne aloft); limp (from an accident); — *'arij*, A, INF. *'araj*, limp naturally; turn to the west, set; — *'aruj*, id.; — II. INF. *ta'rîj*, build in a sloping line, in steps; abide; linger; enter on the time of sunset; turn a little aside from the road to halt or alight; — IV. INF. *i'râj*, make to limp; have a certain number of camels or give it (see عرج *'arj* below); enter on the time of sunset; — V. INF. *ta'arruj*, be built in a slope or steps; abide; limp; turn from the road; — VI. INF. *ta'âruj*, feign a limp; — VII. INF. *in'irâj*, bend (n.); be inclined, sloping; set; — XIV. INF. *i'rinjâj*, attend diligently to (فى *fi*).

عرج *'arj*, *'irj*, pl. *a'râj*, *'urûj*, train of camels (80–90; 150; 500–1000); — *'urj*, pl. of اعرج *a'raj*, limping; — *'araj*, limp; — ة *'arja-t*, bend; deviation; round-about way; slope, inclination.

عرجا *'arjâ'*, f. of اعرج *a'raj*, limping; hyena.

عرجان *'arajân*, limp, lameness.

(عرجد) *'urjad*, *'urjudd*, pedicle of a date.

عرجلة *'arjala-t*, troop; herd, flock.

عرجن *'arjan*, INF. ة, print a stuff with the figures of عرجون *'urjûn*; beat with *'urjûn*; smear with blood, saffron or any dye.

عرجود *'urjûd*, pedicle of a date.

عرجون *'urjûn*, pl. *'arâjîn*, bunch of dates; branch of a palm-tree; a mushroom.

(عرد) *'arad*, U, INF. *'ard*, shoot up, grow; throw or fling far; — *'arid*, A, INF. *'arad*, flee, take to flight; — II. INF. *ta'rîd*, flee; penetrate; lose the way, remain behind; stand high and decline towards setting; — V. INF. *ta'arrud*, be put to flight.

عرد *'ard*, hard, firm, stiff; ass; base of the neck; — *'arid*, *'urudd*, hard.

عردس *'ardas*, INF. ة, throw to the ground.

عردل *'ardal*, hard, firm, stiff.

عردم *'ardam*, id.; rough, rude; neck.

عردمان *'urdumân*, obdurate, headstrong.

عرر *'arar*, itch, scab, mange; INF. of (عر).

(عرز) *'araz*, I, INF. *'arz*, tear out

violently; blame, rebuke; be thick and strong; be contracted; show a thing grasped in one's hand; — *'ariz*, A, INF. *'araz*, be strong and hard; — II. INF. *ta'rîz*, conceal, hide (a.); hint at; be contracted; spoil, corrupt; — III. INF. *mu'âraza-t*, hinder, oppose from hatred or obstinacy; be contracted; — IV. INF. *i'râz*, spoil; — V. INF. *ta'arruz*, be difficult; — VI. INF. *ta'âruz*, be contracted; be difficult, violent, hard.

عرزال *'irzâl*, pl. *'arâzîl*, hut in a tree for a watchman; hut, tent; lair.

عرزب *'arzab*, *'irzabb*, hard, firm.

عرزم *'arzam*, firm; also *'irzamm*, lion; — IV. *a'ranzam*, INF. *i'rinzâm*, be contracted.

(عرس) *'aras*, U, INF. *'ars*, tie the fore-foot of the camel to its neck; turn from; be always cheerful; — *'aris*, A, INF. *'aras*, be confused, perplexed; be too merry or boisterous; be attached to, diligent in (ب *bi*); be stingy with one's own; — II. INF. *ta'rîs*, allow one's self a short rest towards the end of the night; abide in a place (ل *li*); indulge in profligacy; — IV. INF. *i'râs*, snatch a short rest towards the end of the night; be attached to, diligent in (ب *bi*); prepare a wedding entertainment; bring the bride home; visit one's wives; — V. INF. *ta'arrus*, show love to one's wife; — VIII. INF. *i'tirâs*, separate (n.).

عرس *'ars*, partition-wall; middle pillar or pole of a tent; rope; — *'ars*, *'urs*, pl. *a'râs*, weaned camel-foal; — *'irs*, pl. *a'râs*, betrothed, bride, wife, husband (du. *'arsân*, husband and wife); lioness; ابن عرس *abn-u 'irs-in*, pl. بنات ع *banât-u 'irs-in*, weasel; — *'urs*, *'urus*, pl. *'urusât*, *a'râs*, wedding; — *'aris*, astonished, perplexed, dumbfounded; lion; — *'urus*, pl. of عروس *'arûs*; — ى *'irsiyy*, of the colour of a weasel.

(عرش) *'araś*, I, U. INF. *'arś*, build, build a hut or arbour in (ل *li*) the vineyard; stand still (dog); lose one's senses from joy or merriment; — INF. *'arś*, *'urûś*, bind the vine-branches to poles; (m.) entwine (n.); wall up a well with stone and roof it with wood; beat on the neck; stay, abide; pass. be kindled and kept burning; — *'ariś*, A, INF. *'araś*, lose one's senses from joy; press a debtor, dun; turn from, leave, quit; be stingy with one's own; — II. INF. *ta'rîś*, build a hut or arbour; roof a house; tie the vine-branches to poles; rush upon the she-ass; delay; pass. be kindled and kept burning; — IV. INF. *i'râś*, build a hut or arbour; — V. INF. *ta'arruś*, stay permanently in a place; stick to a thing; (m.) roost, nest; — VIII. INF. *i'tirâś*, build for one's self a hut or arbour; overgrow the roof of such; mount a horse, ride; — XIII. INF. *i'riwwâś*, id.; — hence (عروش), II. INF. *ta'arwuś*, id.

عرش *'arś*, pl. *'urûś*, *'uruś*, *a'râś*, *'iraśa-t*, throne, seat of honour; palace, castle; roof, vault, alcove; hut, tent; nest; tribe; pillar, support; letter; instep; leader; Mecca; ذو العرش *ẓû 'l-'arś*, God; ع و فرس *'arś wa fars*, heaven and earth; — *'arś*, *'urś*, pl. *'iraśa-t*, *a'râś*, part of the foot between instep and toes; — *'urś*, base of the neck; ear; stout; — *'uruś*, pl. of عريش *'arîś*.

(عرص) *'araṣ*, I, INF. *'arṣ*, lighten continually; be always moving; (m.) pander; — *'ariṣ*, A, INF. *'araṣ*, flash violently; be brisk; be deteriorated by dampness;

—II. INF. *ta'rîṣ*, expose flesh for drying it; (m.) pander;—IV. INF. *i'râṣ*, be always moving; totter, be rickety;—V. INF. *ta'arruṣ*, stay, abide;—VIII. INF. *i'tirâṣ*, play and jump about; tremble, quiver.

عرص *'ariṣ*, *'arṣ*, flashing frequently;—ة *'arṣa-t*, pl. *'araṣât*, *'irâṣ*, *a'râṣ*, open place, square, yard, courtyard; plain; surface: arena; battle-field; chess-board, عرصة العرصات *'arṣa-t al-'araṣât*, place of the last Judgment.

(عرض) *'araḍ*, I, INF. *'arḍ*, offer, present, show itself; happen, occur; U, come to meet (ل *li*), turn from (عن *'an*); befall; show, bring to mind, place before the eyes; exhibit; give over to; lead; turn aside; touch or hit in, or attack from, the side; hold a review; turn over the leaves of a book; give or take in exchange; cheat in selling;—U, I, buckle on the sword sideways; leap against the enemy with the head bent sideways, be jaded, diseased; die without an illness; die from surfeit; fill; graze off the highest branches; come into the neighbourhood of Mecca and Medina; pass. *'uriḍ*, be seized with madness;—*'ariḍ*, A, INF. *'araḍ*, appear;—I, A, meet and frighten; be jaded or diseased; die from surfeit;—*'aruḍ*, INF. *'irâḍ*, *'arâḍa-t*, be broad, wide, large; lie widthways;—II. INF. *ta'rîḍ*, place one thing opposite the other; make broad, wide, large; offer, bring presents; expose, explain; exchange; hint at; write indistinctly, illegibly; defame, slander, abuse; under-do the meat; mark the camel at the hoof; circumcise children; be eloquent;—III. INF. *mu'âraḍa-t*, oppose, hinder, disturb, thwart, cross, contradict; receive and treat one as he did you; keep up with; walk by the side of the road; have an oblique position; go aside, turn from, shun; meet on one's road; try to cheat in selling; compare, collate; INF. *'irâḍ*, *mu'âraḍa-t*, give birth to an illegitimate child;—IV. INF. *i'râḍ*, appear, show itself; present, lay before; offer, offer the side, offer itself; set out on a distant and long journey; go far in a thing; be excessive; turn away; prevent; give birth to an illegitimate child; geld, castrate; make broad, wide, large;—V. INF. *ta'arruḍ*, seize on a thing that offers itself; undertake, venture, essay; happen, befall; oppose; be exhibited; tarnish (one's fame); walk now to the right, now to the left; be wry, crooked; be broadened, widened; be broad, wide, large; perish;—VI. INF. *ta'âruḍ*, oppose; thwart, contradict one another; do as one is done to;—VIII. INF. *i'tirâḍ*, happen, occur, befall; present one's self to; oppose, cross, contradict, interrupt; go to; meet with one and abuse him; hit deadly with an arrow; undertake rashly and impetuously; lie across; come forth instead of another; prevent; be disobedient to the bridle; ride on a restive camel; ride to a review; hold a review, pass in review; find the ground overgrown and graze it off; be brisk; begin the month with a later day than the first; be unable to perform the sexual act;—X. INF. *isti'râḍ*, beg to present, to put before, to exhibit, to offer, to expose, &c.; beg a girl to show her face; make the game offer its side;

ask from, question; look on, take sight of, compare; kill indiscriminately; give indiscriminately to all; find the ground overgrown and graze it off; (m.) broaden (n.); be steep, precipitous, inclined.

عرض *'arḍ*, happening (s.), event; presentation, representation; exhibition; review; review of souls, last Judgment; memoir, petition; offer, proposition, motion; side; (pl. *'urûḍ*) breadth; latitude; (pl. *'urûḍ*) goods, merchandise, movables; mountain-slope; valley; large army, multitude; darkening cloud; hour, hour of night; madness; briskness; —

'irḍ, pl. *a'râḍ*, good fame, honour, family honour; sense of honour; good quality; soul, mental part; the human body and any perspiring part of it; limb; pore; sweat; perspiration; odour of the body; mountain-slope; valley with water, trees and villages; side of the neck; skin, hide, leather; army; multitude of locusts; large cloud; who flies madly.

'urḍ, pl. *'irâḍ*, side, flank; mountain-slope, foot of a mountain; middle of a river, of the sea; broad side of a sword; the bulk of men; a pace; the principal part; *'urḍ-an*, as may be, at hap-hazard; ع السفر *'urḍ as-safar*, fit for travelling; pl. of عارض *'âriḍ*, molar tooth.

'araḍ, pl. *a'râḍ*, event, accident, calamity, illness; *'araḍ-an*, accidentally, unintentionally; (chance) gain or booty; accidental quality; not lasting, perishable, good things of the world; goods, merchandise; desire, craving; army; —.

'uruḍ, side; boundary, limit, end; corner of the eye; casual present; ع عن *'an 'uruḍ-in*, from the side, as may be, indiscriminately.

ة *'arḍa-t*, representation, exposition, exhibition; review; offer, tender; — *'urḍa-t*, intention, aim; inclination, favour; what is exposed to loss; pretext, subterfuge; impediment, obstruction, hindrance; place for the foundation; suiting, fitting, appropriate; an equal, companion, fellow; subject to criticism or blame.

ى *'arḍa*, a kind of cloth; — *'urḍî*, camp (Turk.); — *'iridda*, briskness; — *'arḍiyy*, memoir, petition; ة, not firm in the saddle; restive, difficult to ride; — *'araḍiyy*, accidental, casual, unessential; venial; — ية *'urḍiyya-t*, restiveness, refractoriness.

(عرط) *'araṭ*, U, INF. *'arṭ*, graze on shrubs and lose the teeth in consequence; (m.) gnaw at; — also VIII. INF. *i'tirâṭ*, slander the absent.

(عرطب) *'arṭab*, ة *'arṭaba-t*, *'urṭaba-t*, harp, lute; Abyssinian cymbal.

(عرعر) *'ar'ar*, INF. ة, uncork; pull out an eye; (m.) roar, bellow; — II. *ta'ar'ur*, have the itch, the mange.

عرعر *'ar'ar*, mountain-cypress; — ة *'ar'ara-t*, cork, stopper; — *'ur'ura-t*, pl. *'arâ'ir*, id.; mountain-top; the uppermost and best part; partition of the nose; nose; abdomen, pudenda.

(عرف) *'araf*, I, INF. *ma'rifa-t*, *'irfân*, *'iriffân*, *'irfa-t*, know, know well and accurately, become acquainted with; be able to distinguish from (من *min*); acknowledge, avow, confess; lie with (ل *li*); requite, reward; be patient; become known, become a chief (aor. U); — U, INF. *'arf*, shear off the horse's mane; — I, INF. *'irâfa-t*, soothsay, be a soothsayer; — pass. INF. *'arf*,

have boils on the hand; — *'arif*, A, INF. *'araf*, have a strong odour, a pleasant smell, be fragrant; — *'aruf*, INF. *'arâfa-t*, become an acquaintance, a chief, a prince; (m.) be a soothsayer; — II. INF. *ta'rîf*, make known to, inform of, teach; own, confess; define; make definite (a noun by the article); (m.) hear one's confession; make fragrant or pleasant; visit Mount 'Arafat; — IV. INF. *i'râf*, communicate to, inform of (2 acc.); have a long mane; have a fine comb or crest (cock, &c.); — V. INF. *ta'arruf*, try to recognise, inquire for, question and learn; make one's acquaintance; become known, make one's self known; be defined; do a thing competently, with intelligence; — VI. INF. *ta'âruf*, recognise one another; — VII. INF. *in'irâf*, be or become known; be discovered, made known; — VIII. INF. *i'tirâf*, recognise; acknowledge; know; own, avow, confess; profess the faith; (m.) say confession, try to find one out, question, inquire; make one's self known, state one's name and quality; hint at; be patient; be obedient, docile, submissive; — X. INF. *isti'râf*, ask for information; try to learn, or get information; make one's self known; (m.) wish to say confession, go to confession; — XII. INF. *i'rîrâf*, be ready for evil; have a long mane; throw up high waves; foam; lift one's self above the horse's mane; mount the heights.

عرف *'arf*, odour, scent; a plant; — *'irf*, knowledge, distinction, discernment; patience; slowness; — *'urf*, what is generally known, truism; known form; avowal, confession; (*'urf-an*, as is known, avowedly, certainly); comb of a cock, crest, mane (*'urf-an*, in rows, numerously as the hairs of a mane); pl. *'uraf*, *a'râf*, high place, height, sand-hill; what comes from on high (winds, &c.); bounty, benefit, present, favour, liberality; what is just, good, agreeable; righteousness; corresponding, fitting, equal; wall between heaven and hell; name by which a person goes, alias; dialect; political administration; oppression, tyranny; pl. *a'râf*, a kind of palm-tree; pl. of اعرف *a'raf*, maned, crested, and of عروف *'arûf*, patient, persevering; — *'uruf*, comb, crest, mane; height; sand-hill; — ة *'arfa-t*, odour, scent; wind; boil on the hand; investigation; — *'irfa-t*, investigation, scrutiny, disquisition; knowledge; acquaintance; — *'urfa-t*, company, association, guild, college; master of a guild; fertile tract; pl. *'uraf*, *a'râf*, sand-hill with high grass; pl. *'uraf*, boundary, partition-wall; high place, height; — *'arafa-t*, watch, guard (body of men); mountain near Mecca (يوم ع *yaum 'arafa-t*, the day of pilgrimage to it).

عرفا *'urf-an*, see the previous; — *'arfâ'*, f. of *a'raf*, crested; hyena; — *'urafâ'*, pl. of عريف *'arîf*.

عرفات *'arafât*, mountain near Mecca.

(عرفاس) *'irfâs*, pl. *'arâfîs*, strong camel; lion.

(عرفاص) *'irfâṣ*, pl. *'arâfiṣ*, scourge; rope.

عرفان *'irfân* (*'iriffân*), knowledge, instruction, mental culture; recognition; avowal, confession; — *'iriffân*, *'uruffân*, a large kind of locust.

(عرفج) *'arfaj*, ة, a thorny plant.

(عرفط) *'urfuṭ*, a kind of Mimosa.

عرفى *urfiyy*, ة, sacred by custom; referring to the political ad-

ministration; oppressive, tyrannical; accumulated; accessory; aphoristic; evident, generally admitted; — ة *'urfiyya-t*, an evident proposition, general truth, truism; aphorism.

(عرق) *'araq*, U, INF. *'arq*, *ma'raq*, gnaw at, pick a bone; depart, set out; double the leather of a bag; pass. *'uriq*, INF. *'arq*, be emaciated, bare; — *'ariq*, A, INF. *'araq*, sweat, perspire; be lazy; — *'aruq*, root (n.), be rooted, originate; be of noble birth; — II. INF. *ta'rîq*, make perspire; (m.) parboil; (also IV.) mix but little water to the wine; not quite fill the bucket; — IV. INF. *i'râq*, see II.; give pure wine to drink; put forth numerous and strong roots; exceed in vileness or generosity; be in or come to 'Irâq; — V. INF. *ta'arruq*, pick; get another's head under one's arm and throw him on the ground; — X. INF. *isti'râq*, make or try to make one's self perspire.

عرق *'arq*, *'araq*, trodden path; basket of palm-leaves: pl. *'irâq*, *'urâq*, bone; milk in the udder; foundation of a wall; — *'irq*, pl. *'urûq*, *a'râq*, *'irâq*, root; origin; vein; sap (especially of plants used for dyeing); metallic vein; sinew; a little, a drop, a shade; natural propensity; blade, stalk, leaf, &c.; milk; the body; numerous progeny; mountain-knoll, mountain; alkaline ground; pl. *'urûq*, sand-hill; ع النسا *'irq an-nasâ*, hip-gout, sciatica; ع ظالم *'irq ẓâlim*, expropriation; *'araq*, pl. *a'râq*, sweat, perspiration, exudation; moisture; distilled liquor, brandy; milk; juice, sap; date-honey; dried currants; reward; present; profit, gain; run of a horse; pl. *a'râq*, *'urûq*, layer of bricks, mud-wall; row of beasts or birds; mountain-paths; oppression, molestation; — *'ariq*, smelling or tasting of sweat; — *'uraq*, much perspiring; — *'uruq*, pl. of عراق *'irâq*; — ة *'arqa-t*, mountain-path; — *'irqa-t*, root; capital, stock of trade; — *'araqa-t*, row, layer, train; series; transversal piece of wood; strap; — *'uraqa-t*, who perspires much.

عرقان *'arqân*, perspiring.

عرقاة *'arqât*, clear water; INF. of (عرقى); — *'araqât*, *'irqât*, root; capital, stock of trade.

(عرقب) *'arqab*, INF. ة, hough a beast for riding; lift the hind-legs of a beast and make it stop; use stratagem; desist; — II. *ta'arqub*, be houghed; travel through winding valleys; mount a horse from behind; (m.) be complicated, difficult.

عرقچين *'araqchîn*, cloth to wipe the perspiration (m.), handkerchief.

(عرقد) *'arqad*, INF. ة, twist a rope very tight.

عرقسوسى *'irqsûsiyy*, seller of liquorice-juice (ع السوس *'irq as-sûs*).

(عرقص) *'arqaṣ*, INF. ة, skip, dance; creep.

(عرقل) *'arqal*, INF. ة, renounce a purpose; distort the meaning of one's words; put a bad construction on one's words or actions; (m.) embarrass, complicate; — II. INF. *ta'arqul*, (m.) be embarrassed, complicated; be lame, palsied; have a spasm.

عرقوب *'urqûb*, pl. *'arâqîb*, hollow of the knee; narrow winding path; narrow bend of a valley; عراقيب الامور *'arâqîb al-amûr*, difficult affairs; wile, deceit; impostor.

عرقوة *'arquwa-t*, pl. *'arâqî*, transversal piece of wood.

(عرقى) *'arqa*, INF. *'arqât*, place

pieces of wood across the bucket.

عرقيل *'irqîl*, yolk of an egg.

عرقية *'araqiyya-t*, pl. *'arâqî*, under-cap; towel.

(عرك) *'arak*, U, INF. *'ark*, rub, smooth; rub sore; (m.) knead; (m.) stir up; (m.) brew; use up by wearing; make wise; bring evil upon; pull one's ears; wrestle with; feel, touch; allow to pasture at large; eat herbs; — U, INF. *'ark*, *'arâk*, *'urûk*, have the menses; — *'arik*, A, INF. *'arak*, be brave; — III. INF. *'irâk*, *mu'âraka-t*, wrestle, fight with; — IV. INF. *i'râk*, have the menses; — VI. INF. *ta'âruk*, wrestle, fight; — VIII. INF. *i'tirâk*, press one another in wrestling or at the water; wipe one's self with a cloth; be used up, worn out; (m.) be kneaded, stirred up.

عرك *'ark*, rubbing (s.); (m.) kneading, stirring up (s.); experience, practice; excrement of wild beasts; — *'arak*, sound, tone; fishermen, sailors, pl. of عركى *'arakiyy*; — *'arik*, tone, sound; experienced, proved; powerful combatant, wrestler; clashing; — ة *'arka-t*, rubbing, kneading (s.); throng, press, crowd; one turn, once; experience, practice.

(عركس) *'arkas*, INF. ة, gather, collect, heap up, hoard; — IV. INF. *i'rinkâs*, be accumulated, heaped up; be of a deep black.

عركل *'arkal*, drum; — ة *'arkala-t*, troop of lions.

عركى *'arakiyy*, pl. *'arak*, *'araka-t*, fisherman, sailor.

(عرم) *'aram*, U, I, INF. *'arm*, gnaw, pick, nibble; suck; bring calamity upon (acc.); — INF. *'urâm*, be violent, hard-hearted; be overbearing and mischievous; (m.) bind books; — *'arim*, A, INF. *'aram*, be soft; — *'arum*, INF. *'arâma-t*, be violent, hard-hearted, malignant; — II. INF. *ta'rîm*, mix; (m.) heap up, fill up the measure; — IV. INF. *i'râm*, accuse falsely; — V. INF. *ta'arrum*, pick a bone; be heaped up; (m.) be measured full; (m.) swell; (m.) be full of pride, vanity; — VII. INF. *in'irâm*, be bound (book); — VIII. INF. *i'tirâm*, be violent, hard-hearted, malignant; be restive.

عرم *'arm*, (m.) binding of a book; water-spout, inundation; fat; well; — *'urm*, eggs of the *Kaṭa*; pl. of أعرم *a'ram*, spotted white and black, &c.; — *'aram*, black with white stripes or spots; — *'arim*, dam; torrent; breaking of a dam; hard-hearted; — ة *'arma-t*, *'arama-t*, heap; — *'urma-t*, black striped or spotted with white; — *'arima-t*, vineyard; field-mouse; water-spout; dam.

عرما *'armâ'*, f. of أعرم *a'ram*, see the previous.

عرماض *'irmâḍ*, green surface of water.

عرمان *'urmân*, pl. of *a'ram*, uncircumcised, and of عريم *'arîm*.

عرمرم *'aramram*, numerous; violent; general.

(عرمس) *'irmis*, pl. *'arâmis*, rock; hardened, inured to work; — *'arammas*, very prudent, successful.

(عرمض) *'armaḍ*, *'irmaḍ*, a tree; sea-weed; water-lentil; — *'armaḍ*, INF. ة, *'irmâḍ*, be covered with sea-weed.

(عرن) *'aran*, I, U, INF. *'arn*, put the عران *'irân* (piece of wood) into the camel's nose; pass. *'urin*, suffer pain from it; — U, practise persistently; twist a sinew round the arrow; — INF. *'irân*, be far distant; — *'urin*, A, INF. *'aran*, have the withers chapped, or ulcers on the

throat; — II. INF. *ta'rîn*, fix the head of a spear with a nail; — IV. INF. *i'rân*, always eat meat; have mangy camels or foals with broken legs.

عرن *'irn, 'aran*, smell of anything cooked; — *'aran*, anything cooked; smoke; the deep of the sea; deep; ulcer on the throat; chaps on the withers of a camel; — *'urun*, pl. of عرين *'arîn*.

(عرناس) *'irnâs*, mountain-knoll; nose; a bird; spindle; vine-branches.

عرند *'urund*, عرندد *'arandad*, thick, hard.

عرندس *'arandas*, strong; torrent.

عرنوس *'arnûs*, pl. *'arânîs*, maize-stalk.

عرنين *'irnîn*, pl. *'arânîn*, the first, the best of a thing; base of the nose; cartilage of the nose; prince; army.

عرهون *'urhûn*, pl. *'arâhîn*, a mushroom.

(عرو) *'arâ*, U, INF. *'arw*, ask for a service; come up to, approach, visit; occur, happen; pass. *'urî*, be seized with a shiver of fever; — II. INF. *ta'riya-t*, provide with a handle, &c. (see عروة *'urwa-t* below); — VIII. INF. *i'tirâ'*, ask for a service; visit, befall; occur to the mind.

عرو *'arw*, sudden approach (of a calamity, &c.); — *'irw*, pl. *a'râ'*, side; negligent; — ة *'urwa-t*, pl. *'ura-n*, also *'irwa-t*, pl. *'ira-n*. handle, haft; loop, button-hole; ع الوثقى *'urwa-t al-wusqa*, the safe handle, Islâm.

عروا *'urawâ'*, ague-fit, paroxysm; roar of a lion.

عروب *'arûb*, also ة *'arûba-t*, pl. *'urub*, loving; — ة *'arûba-t*, Friday; also ية *'arûbiyya-t*, pure Arabic, Arabism.

عرور *'urûr*, mange; — *.

عروس *'arûs*, pl. *'urus*, bridegroom; also ة *'arûsa-t*, pl. *'arâ'is*, fiancée, bride, wife; ابيات عرائس *abyât 'arâ'is*, verses consisting of words of which all the letters are pointed; — ى *'arûsiyy*, bridal.

(عروش), II. INF. *ta'arwuś*, devote one's self to a thing; ride.

عروض *'arûḍ*, pl. *a'ârîḍ*, tent-pole; poetry, poem; verse; metre; prosody; anything necessary, want, need; impediment; path; boundary; much; restive; — *; — ى *'arûḍiyy*, metrical, prosodical.

عروف *'arûf*, ة *'arûfa-t*, intelligent; pl. *'urf*, patient, persevering.

عروك *'urûk*, sailors;—INF. of (عرك).

عرون *'arûn*, hard of withers (horse).

(عرى) *'ara*, I, visit, befall, fall upon; — *'arî*, A, INF. *'ury*, *'urya-t*, be naked, stripped; be free, vacant; — II. INF. *ta'riya-t*, bare, strip; — III. INF. *mu'ârât*, ride unsaddled horses; — IV. INF. *i'râ'*, bare, strip; forsake a friend; present one with the date-crops of the year; travel to or settle in an open country; be exposed to the wind; refresh one's self in the evening breeze; — V. INF. *ta'arrî*, be naked, stripped; strip one's self; — X. INF. *isti'râ*, eat the dates off the tree; — XII. INF. *i'rîrâ'*, travel alone through a country; do anything disgraceful; ride on (acc.) an unsaddled horse.

عرى *'uran, 'ury*, nakedness; — *'uran, 'iran*, pl. of عروة *'urwa-t*, *'irwa-t*; — *'ury*, pl. *a'râ'*, unsaddled; — *'urra*, bad woman; — *'ariyy*, ة *'ariyya-t*, cold wind; — ة *'irya-t, 'urya-t*, nakedness; uncovered parts of the body; — *'urya-t*, INF. of (عرى); — *'ariyya-t*, pl. *'arâyâ*, anything left to usufruct.

عريان *'uryân*, ة; quite naked; long-legged.

عريج *'arîj*, lame; flat, dull

عريد *'arîd*, far; habit, custom.
عرير *'arîr*, stranger, foreigner, traveller.
عريس *'arîs*, bridegroom; (m.) child; ة *'arîsa-t*, ferret;—*'irrîs*, ة *'irrîsa-t*, lion's den.
عريش *'arîś*; pl. *'uruś*, hut, roof for shade; throne; camel-litter;—also ة *'arîśa-t*, pl. *'arâ'iś*, arbour, vine-arbour; tap-room.
عريض *'arîḍ*, ة, pl. *'irâḍ*, broad; wide, vast, extended; in abundance, plentiful; pl. *'irḍân*, *'urḍân*, one-year-old kid;—*'irrîḍ*, who hinders others, is in the way;— ة *'arîḍa-t*, petition.
عريط *'iryaṭ*, ع ام *umm 'iryaṭ*, scorpion.
عريف *'arîf*, pl. *'urafâ'*, well informed; acquaintance; lieutenant of a leader; leader.
عريك *'arîk*, stout and strongly built;— ة *'arîka-t*, pl. *'arâ'ik*, nature, natural disposition; soul, self; hump of a camel.
عريم *'arîm*, pl. *'urmân*, calamity; water-pit, cistern.
عرين *'arîn*, ة *'arîna-t*, pl. *'urun*, lair; lion's den, hole of a snake, &c.; thicket, wood; area of a house; town; game, prey of a hunter; meat; power, glory; (m.) imbecile.
(عز) *'azz*, I, INF. *'izz*, *'izza-t*, *'azâza-t*, be loved, dear, honoured, powerful; become rich and powerful after poverty; INF. *'izz*, *'azâza-t*, be rare, difficult to get, scarce; flow, run;—I, A, be hard to bear;—I, INF. *'izz*, be honoured;—U, INF. *'izz*, surpass in honour and power; surpass or try to surpass in eloquence;—U, INF. *'uzûz*, *'izâz*, also *'azuz*, INF. *'azâza-t*, have narrow papillæ of the udder;—II. INF. *ta'zîz*, make honoured and powerful; strengthen; honour; cause the earth to be sticky (rain);—III. INF. *mu'âzza-t*, vie with in honour and authority; try to surpass or surpass in eloquence;—IV. INF. *i'zâz*, make honoured and powerful; strengthen, fortify; honour; love dearly; deem rare or precious; prefer; deny to another, keep for one's self; have narrow papillæ of the udder; show signs of pregnancy by swelling of the udder; give birth with difficulty; meet with hard ground; pass. be sorely visited; be pained by another's misfortune;—V. INF. *ta'azzuz*, become honoured and powerful; become scarce and dear; be firm of flesh; have narrow papillæ;—VII. INF. *in'izâz*, be refused as too precious;—VIII. INF. *i'tizâz*, become honoured and powerful, consider one's self to be so or behave as such; boast of another's favour; be proud of; become important; surpass in authority;—X. INF. *isti'zâz*, befall in a violent degree, overwhelm; visit with illness and death (God); outdo, get under; stick close together.
عز *'izz*, power, authority, honour, glory; overbearingness; pleasure; violent; rare, scarce;—ة *'iza-t*, pl. *'izûn*, *'iza-n*, troop; sect;—*'azza-t*, young doe;—*'izza-t*, power, majesty, glory; rareness, scarcity, dearth.
عزا *'azâ'*, patience; receiving of visits of condolence; funeral; INF. of (عزو, عزى).
عزاب *'uzzâb*, pl. of عزب *'azab*.
عزار *'izâr*, blame, rebuke;—*'azzâr*, who rebukes violently.
عزاز *'izâz*, ة *'azâza-t*, INF. of (عز);—*'izâz*, ة *'izâza-t*, pl. of عزيز *'azîz*.
عزاف *'azzâf*, thunder-cloud; thundering, blustering; calling on the demons.
عزاقة *'azzâqa-t*, buttocks; anus.
عزال *'izâl*, weak;—ى *'azâlî*, *'azâla*, pl. of عزلا *'azlâ'*.

عرام *'azzâm*, snake-charmer; lion; — *'uzzâm*, pl. of عازم *'âzim*, resolved, resolute.

عزاه *'izâh*, pl. of عزه *'izh*, &c.

(عزب) *'azab*, U, I, INF. *'uzûb*, be absent, far; be hidden, concealed; leave in retirement; go, depart; roam about; be uninhabited; — U, INF. *'uzûba-t*, be single, a bachelor, a spinster; — II. INF. *ta'zîb*, leave anything begun for a long time unfinished; — IV. INF. *i'zâb*, be far away; remove, send away; have far-roaming camels; — V. INF. *ta'azzub*, be unmarried.

عزب *'azab* (m. f.), pl. *a'zâb*, *'uzzâb* (f. also *'azbâ'*, *'azaba-t*), unmarried person, bachelor, spinster; — ة *'uzba-t*, single life, celibacy.

(عزج) *'azaj*, U, INF. *'azj*, push back, repel; lie with; turn up the ground.

(عزد) *'azad*, I, INF. *'azd*, lie with.

(عزر) *'azar*, I, INF. *'azr*, blame; help, assist (acc.); prevent, hinder; lie with; compel; instruct in religious duties; — II. INF. *ta'zîr*, rebuke violently; beat hard, punish by beating; help; strengthen; praise, honour; load; (m.) get worse (wound).

عزر *'azr*, blame, rebuke, remonstrance.

عزرائل *'izrâ'îl*, the angel of death.

(عزط) *'azaṭ*, U, INF. *'azṭ*, lie with.

(عزف) *'azaf*, U, I, INF. *'uzûf*, abstain, get weary and give up or leave; INF. *'azf*, *'azîf*, hiss, cry out (demons in the desert); utter a hissing or rattling sound (dying child); sing to the cittern or guitar; — I, INF. *'azf*, be addicted to eating and drinking; — II. INF. *ta'zîf*, call on the demons of the desert.

عزف *'azf*, whistling of the wind, of moving sand; voices of the demons; pl. *ma'âzif*, a stringed instrument; — *'uzf*, ring-dove.

(عزق) *'azaq*, I, INF. *'azq*, dig up the ground; — U, run fast; keep back; beat in a dangerous place; — *'aziq*, A, INF. *'azaq*, adhere to, be permanently attached.

عزق *'aziq*, pl. *'uzuq*, malignant.

(عزل) *'azal*, I, INF. *'azl*, remove, set aside; depose; separate from the crowd; break up the camp; (m.) relieve the guard; pass. have the menses; — II. INF. *ta'zîl*, remove (a.), set aside; depose; (m.) empty, clean, purge; (m.) change domicile, remove (n.); — IV. INF. *i'zâl*, remove (a.), set aside; — V. INF. *ta'azzul*, be removed, set aside, deposed; remove (n.); resign; (m.) take a purge; — VI. INF. *ta'âzul*, remove from one another; — VII. INF. *in'izâl*, VIII. INF. *i'tizâl*=V.; VIII. desert; separate (n.) from the community.

عزل *'azl*, dismissal, deposition; leisure; — *'uzl*, weak; pl. of اعزل *a'zal*, who separates himself, &c.; — *'uzl*, *'azal*, being (s.) without arms, without office; leisure; — ة *'azla-t*, dismissal; resignation, retirement; — *'azala-t*, hip-bone.

عزلا *'azlâ'*, pl. *'azâlî*, *'azâla*, mouth of a skin bag; anus.

عزلان *'uzlân*, pl. of اعزل *a'zal*, who separates himself, &c.

(عزلب) *'azlab*, INF. ة, lie with.

(عزم) *'azam*, I, INF. *'azm*, *'uzm*, *ma'zam*, *ma'zim*, *'uzmân*, *'azîm*, *'azîma-t*, be resolved and carry out one's resolution; be firmly resolved upon; go, resort to (الى *ila*); conjure, charm, read spells; summon, invite; — V. INF. *ta'azzum* carry firmly in one's mind; — VII. INF. *in'izâm*, be invited to an entertainment; — VIII. INF. *i'tizâm*=V.; carry out one's resolution by every means; career along.

عزم *'azm*, pl. *'uzûm*, firm resolution, resolve; pl. *'uzum*, husks of grapes; — ة *'azma-t*, resolve; determination; divine decree; unavoidable; right; duty; — *'uzma-t*, pl. *'uzam*, relations on father's side; race; — *'azama-t*, true friends; — ى *'azmiyy*, persevering; who keeps his word, faithful to one's promise.

(عزن), IV. *a'zan*, INF. *i'zân*, divide with, share with.

(عزه) *'izh*, *'azih*, also عزهى *'izha*, *'izhiyy*, عزهاة *'izhât*, *'izhâ'a-t*, pl. *'izhûn*, *'uzhûn*, *'izâh*, who abstains from women and pleasure; timid, bashful; who spoils the game.

عزهول *'uzhûl*, pl. *'azâhîl*, pasturing at large; nimble, light.

(عزو) *'azâ*, U, INF. *'azw*, father upon; father one's self upon; ascribe; — V. INF. *ta'azzî*, VIII. INF. *i'tizâ*, id.; — ة *'izwa-t*, fathering, tracing back to an ancestor (s.); kinship; relation, reference.

عزوبة *'azûba-t*, celibacy.

عزوف *'azûf*, loathing (adj.), weary of; impatient of baseness.

عزوق *'azwaq*, unripe, acid.

عزوم *'azûm*, resolved, resolute; — ة *'azûma-t*, *'uzûma-t*, pic-nic, country trip.

عزون *'izûn*, pl. of عزة *'iza-t*.

(عزى) *'azâ*, I, INF. *'azy*=(عزو); — *'azî*, A, INF. *'azan*, *'azâ'*, be patient, suffer patiently; console one's self; allow one's self to be consoled; receive visits of condolence; — II. INF. *ta'ziya-t*, recommend patience, console, condole with; make visits of condolence; — V. INF. *ta'azzî*, allow one's self to be consoled, console one's self, be patient; — VI. INF. *ta'âzî*, console one another; — VIII. INF. *i'tizâ'*, boast in combat of a filiation, make one's self kin to.

عزى *'azî*, *'aziyy*, patient; — *'iza*, *'izan*, pl. of عزة *'iza-t*; — *'uzza*, f. of أعز *a'azz*, dearer; an idol.

عزيب *'azîb*, bachelor; pl. of عازب *'âzib*, distant pasture, or pasturing on such.

عزيز *'azîz*, pl. *'izâz*, *'izâza-t*, *a'izza-t*, *a'izzâ'*, powerful, mighty, honoured, glorious; rare, precious, dear, beloved.

عزيزا *'uzaizâ'*, عزيزى *'uzaiza*, croup (of a horse).

عزيف *'azîf*, voice of the demons in the desert; sound.

عزيم *'azîm*, resolved; bitter, embittered (enemy); — *; — ة *'azîma-t*, pl. *'azâ'im*, *'azîm*, resolution, purpose; perseverance; conjuration, spell, charm; law prescribed by the Koran; enterprise, undertaking (ماضى العـ *mâḍî al-'azîma-t*, successful); departure, setting sail; invitation to an entertainment.

عزية *'izya-t*=عزوة *'izwa-t*.

(عس) *'ass*, U, INF. *'ass*, *'asas*, keep night-watch, patrol; spy; arrive late; give but little to eat; pasture alone; — II. INF. *ta'sîs*, press out; — VIII. INF. *i'tisâs*, patrol; spy; walk about; gain, earn.

عس *'ass*, night-watch, patrol; watchfulness; spying (s.); — *'uss*, pl. *'isâs*, *'isasa-t*, large cup; penis.

عسارة *'asâra-t*, difficulty.

عساس *'isâs*, pl. of عس *'ass*; — *'assâs*, night-watchman; spy; wolf; probe; sounding-lead, plummet.

عساف *'usâf*, agony.

عسال *'assâl*, sweet as honey; honey-gatherer; trembling; wolf; — ة *'assâla-t*, bee; bee-hive.

عساليج *'asâlîj*, pl. of عسلوج *'uslûj*.

(عسب) *'asab*, I, INF. *'asb*, cover (stallion); hire a stallion; — II. INF. *ta'sîb*, weed (m.); — IV. INF. *i'sâb*, run away; — X. INF. *isti'sâb*, want the stallion (mare); loathe, abhor.

عسب *'asb*, covering (s.), copulation; — *'asib*, uncombed.
عسبر *'usbur*, ة *'usbura-t*, leopard.
(عسبل) *'asbal*, INF. ة, come and go in turns and repeatedly.
(عسج) *'asaj*, U, INF. *'asj*, stretch out the neck in walking; — *'asij*, A, INF. *'asaj*, get ill from eating the plant عسوجة *'asûja-t*; — IX. INF. *i'sijâj*, bend in walking from old age.
(عسجد) *'asjad*, gold; jewel; — ى *'asjadiyy*, golden.
(عسجر) *'asjar*, INF. ة, look sharply at; be enduring on the march; salt.
عسجر *'asjar*, salt.
(عسد) *'asad*, I, INF. *'asd*, depart, set out, travel; twist a rope tight; lie with.
(عسر) *'asar*, U, I, INF. *'asr*, *'usr*, press hard upon a debtor; be difficult, be hard to bear; oppose, be hostile to; give birth with difficulty; cause molestation; come from the left; — I, INF. *'asr*, *'asarân*, lift the tail in walking; pass. *'usir*= the following; — *'asir*, A, INF. *'asar*, *'usur*, *ma'sûr*, be hard, difficult; be miserly; use the left as well as the right, be left-handed; — *'asur*, INF. *'usr*, *'usur*, *'asâra-t*, be difficult; be hard, oppressive, hostile; — II. INF. *ta'sîr*, render difficult, put difficulties in one's way; be hostile, oppose; come from the left; — III. INF. *mu'âsara-t*, raise difficulties and hindrances; — IV. INF. *i'sâr*, press hard upon a debtor; find difficulties in (فى *fî*); give birth with difficulty; be barren; grow poor; — V. INF. *ta'assur*, be difficult and complicated; be hard to bear; be obscure, difficult to understand; — VI. INF. *ta'âsur*, be difficult and complicated; place difficulties in one another's way, thwart one another; enter in turns on difficult matters; — VIII. INF. *i'tisâr*, take an untamed camel to ride upon; take from a son's property against his will; compel; — X. INF. *isti'sâr*, demand anything difficult from (acc.); be difficult and complicated; find difficult.
عسر *'usr* (*'asar*, *'usur*), difficulty (as in making water, breathing, &c.), hardship, need, distress, plight; — *'asar*, ill-temper; — *'asir*, difficult, complicated; hard, oppressive; ill-humoured; — ة *'usra-t*, difficulty; adversity.
عسرا *'asrâ'*, f. of اعسر *a'sar*, left-handed, &c.
عسراوى *'asrâwiyy*, who uses the left hand equally as well as the right, left-handed.
عسرى *'usra*, difficulty; adversity.
عسس *'asas*, INF. of (عس); pl. of عاس *'âss*, night-watchman, patrol.
عسعاس *'as'âs*, mirage; wolf.
(عسعس) *'as'as*, INF. ة, rove about at night (wolf); come near the earth (cloud); darkness begins to come or go; make a matter difficult and complicated; move (a.); — II. INF. *ta'as'us*, set out for prey; smell.
عسعس *'as'as*, pl. *'asâ'is*, wolf; hedgehog.
(عسف) *'asaf*, I, INF. *'asf*, deviate, swerve from the road, walk on at random; wander in the desert; be cruel and oppressive; demand one's service; heed, take good care of; work for; utter a death-rattle; walk about at night and seek; — II. INF. *ta'sîf*, tire out; (m.) take away the spider-webs, weed; — IV. INF. *i'sâf*, force a slave to hard work; treat harshly; walk on at random by night; always drink from a large cup; have a dying child; — V. INF. *ta-*

'*assuf*, lose one's way; act without a plan; treat harshly and unjustly; — VII. INF. *in'isâf*, be bent; — VIII. INF. *i'tisâf*, lose one's way; act unjustly; force with violence; take one as a slave.

عسف '*asf*, injustice, violence, wrong; large cup; — (ة '*asfa-t*) pl. '*asafât*, last gasp, agony.

عسفا '*usafâ'*, pl. of عسيف '*asîf*.

(عسق) '*asiq*, A, INF. '*asaq*, adhere, be attached to (ب *bi*); long for; demand persistently.

عسق '*asaq*, malice; anxiety, anguish; darkness; — '*asiq*, malignant, mischievous; — '*usuq*, pl. hard creditors.

(عسقب) '*asqab*, (عسقف) '*asqaf*, INF. ة, be unable to shed tears; — ة '*isqiba-t*, pl. '*isqib*, '*asâqib*, small side-clusters of dates.

(عسقل) '*asqal*, INF. ة, move to and fro, undulate (mirage); — pl. '*asâqil*, and—

عسقول '*usqûl*, pl. '*asâqîl*, mirage; a large white bulbous plant.

(عسك) '*asik*, A, INF. '*asak*, adhere to (ب *bi*).

(عسكر) '*askar*, INF. ة, gather, assemble (n.); fall into calamities; be very dark; collect an army; pitch a camp;—II. INF. *ta'askur*, assemble (n.), form an army or corps.

عسكر '*askar*, pl. '*asâkir*, soldier; army; large number, troop, crowd; — ة '*askara-t*, recruiting (s.), levy; — ى '*askariyy*, pl. ة, soldier; foot-soldier; — ية '*askariyya-t*, military service.

(عسل) '*asal*, I, U, INF. '*asl*, season a dish with honey; take out honey; feed (a.) on honey, give one honey to take with him; say sweet things in praise of (acc.); render one dear to men; — I, lie with, marry; — I, INF. '*asl*, '*usûl*, '*aslân*, shake much (n. long lance); — I, INF. '*asl*, '*aslân*, lift up the head and shake it in running (horse, &c.); walk fast; — A, INF. '*asal*, taste of a dish; — INF. '*asal*, '*asalân*, be moved by the wind; — II. INF. *ta'sîl*, season with honey, gather honey; give honey; — X. INF. *isti'sâl*, ask for honey.

عسل '*isl*, overseer of the herds; — '*asal*, pl. *a'sâl*, '*usul*, '*usl*, '*usûl*, '*uslân*, honey (*a'sâl*, honeycombs); water-bubble, glory; ruin ('*asal-an*, perdition on you! عليك العل '*alai-ka al-'asal*, look sharp!); — '*asil*, swift of fingers; — '*usul*, pl. of عاسل '*âsil*, honey-gatherer, &c., عسول '*asûl* and عسيل '*asîl*; —'*ussal*, pl. of عاسل '*âsil*, wolf; — ة '*asala-t*, a little honey; — ابو عسلة *abû 'isla-t*, wolf.

(عسلج) '*aslaj*, INF. ة, put forth fresh tender branches.

عسلج '*usluj*, pl. '*asâlij*, tender shoot, tender, delicate; — '*asallaj*, dainty.

(عسلط) '*aslaṭ*, INF. ة, talk confusedly.

(عسلق) '*aslaq*, '*isliq*, '*asallaq*, ة, pl. '*asâliq*, ugly; malignant; beast of prey; male ostrich; long-necked; nimble, alert, mobile; vapour, mirage.

عسلوج '*uslûj*, pl. '*asâlîj*, tender shoot; — ة '*uslûja-t*, id.; tender (f.).

عسلى '*asaliyy*, sweet as honey.

(عسم) '*asam*, I, INF. '*asm*, wish for, desire; — INF. '*asm*, '*usûm*, try to gain, to earn; — I, take pains or trouble in; rush into the middle of the turmoil; be unclean, have the lids sticking together; — '*asim*, A, INF. '*asam*, have a withered or distorted hand or foot; — IV. INF. *i'sâm*, be unclean; cause the hand or foot to wither; — VIII. INF. *i'tisâm*, give what is wished for; put on torn shoes.

عسم '*asam*, withering of hand or foot; — '*usm*, pl. of اعسم *a'sam*,

having a withered limb;—*'usum*, pl. of عاسم *'âsim*, عسوم *'asûm*, working for a livelihood; — ة *'asma-t*, morsel of dry bread.
(عسمط) *'asmaṭ*, INF. ة, mix.
(عسن) *'asin*, A, INF. *'asan*, agree well with so as to make fat; — II. *ta'sîn*, cause to lose flesh; — IV. INF. *i'sân*, (also V.) produce but few plants; — V. INF. *ta'assun*, see IV.; resemble one's father; seek the traces, investigate; — X. INF. *isti'sân*, eat but little.
عسن *'asn*, tall of stature with fair complexion and rich hair; —*'asn*, *'isn*, *'usn*, fat; —*'isn*, equal, alike. resembling; — *'asin*, fat, in good condition; — *'usun*, fat; good food.
(عسنج) *'asannaj*, male ostrich.
(عسو) *'asâ*, U, INF. *'asâ'*, *'usuww*, also عسى *'asa*, INF. *'asan*, grow hard or dry; grow callous; be very dark; — INF. *'asw*, *'asâ'*, *'usuww*, *'usiyy*, also عسى *'asî*, A, INF. *'asan*, grow very old: — II. INF. *ta'siya-t*, make the hands callous; wither plants.
عسو *'asw*, wax; wax candle; — *'usuww*, hardness, callosity.
عسوب *'asûb*, queen bee; chieftain, prince.
عسوس *'asûs*, looking out for a prey or booty; good-for-nothing fellow, impudent; *al-'asûs*, wolf.
عسوف *'asûf*, oppressor; cruel, unjust.
عسول *'asûl*, pl. *'usul*, good man; trembling; — *
عسوم *'asûm*, pl. *'usum*, who earns his bread by working; — *'usûm*, poverty; bread-crusts; — *.
(عسى) *'asa*, may be that (followed by ان *an* and the aor., also by an affixed personal pronoun and the aor.; or by a participle); — IV. INF. *i'sâ'*, be fit, appropriate; — see (عسو).
عسى *'asî*, *'asiyy*, fit, appropriate, suitable.
عسيب *'asîb*, instep; longest feather in the wing; pl. *'usbân*, *'usub*, bare palm-branch; also ة *'asîba-t*, pl. *'us* , tail-bone.
عسير *'asîr*, difficult; oppressive, hard; unfavourable; يوم ع *yaum 'asîr*, day of the last Judgment.
عسيس *'asîs*, pl. of عاس *'âss*, night-watchman, patrol.
عسيف *'asîf*, pl. *'usafâ*, day-labourer; servant; decrepit old man.
عسيل *'asîl*, pl. *'usul*, penis.
(عش) *'aśś*, U, INF. *'aśś*, seek, look for; gather, collect (a.); earn, gain; beat; mend, darn; dole; remain in the nest; expel a tribe from their dwellings; — for *'aśuś*, *'aśiś*, INF. *'aśaś*, *'aśâśa-t*, *'uśûśa-t*, have a thin stem and but few branches; — for *'aśiś*, INF. *'aśâśa-t*, *'uśûśa-t*, *'aśaś*, be thin, lean; — II. INF. *ta'śîś*, build a nest in a tree; dry up (n.); get mouldy; have but few branches; — IV. INF. *i'śâś*, cause to grow thin; expel from their dwellings; scare up game; turn from (a.), avert; meet with rugged ground; — VII. INF. *in'iśâś*, be darned; — VIII. INF. *i'tiśâś*, build a nest; bring but few provisions.
عش *'aśś*, small; lean, thin; nest; rugged; ة, pl. *'iśâś*, having thin branches; — *'uśś*, pl. *'iśâś*, *'iśaśa-t*, *a'śâś*, bird's-nest in a tree.
عشا *'aśâ'*, pl. *a'śiya-t*, supper (العشا السرى *al-'aśâ' as-sirriyy*, the Holy Supper); night-blindness; — *'iśâ'*, evening; first part oı watch of the night; night-prayer.
عشاب *'aśśâb*, herbalist, seller of herbs; — ة *'aśśâba-t*, abundance of grass; luxuriant vegetation.
عشار *'iśâr*, familiar intercourse; pl. of عشرا *'uśarâ'*; — *; — *'uśâr*, by tens;—*'aśśâr*, collector of tithes, tax-gatherer.

عشارى *'uśâriyy*, consisting of ten parts; ten yards long; a Nile-boat.

عشاش *'aśâś*, ة *'aśâśa-t*, INF. of (عش); — *'iśâś*, pl. of عش *'aśś*.

عشاق *'uśâq*, favourite, darling; — *'aśśâq*, madly in love; — *'uśśâq*, pl. of عاشق *'âśiq*, lover, &c.

عشان *'uśśân*, base of a palm-branch; — ة *'uśâna-t*, id.; trunk of a tree.

عشاوة *'aśâwa-t*, night-blindness.

عشايا *'aśâyâ*, pl. of عشية *'aśiyya-t*.

(عشب) *'aśib*, A, INF. *'aśab*, dry up, get stale; (m.) eat green-meat, grow fat on it; — II. INF. *ta'śîb*, cover itself with grass, with green food; (m.) gather or weed such; — IV. INF. *i'śâb*, cover itself with grass; find green food; grow fat on it; give one a decrepit camel; — V. INF. *ta'aśśub*, get fat on green-meat; — X. INF. *isti'śâb*, seek green food or herbs; — XII. INF. *i'śîśâb*, produce plenty of green food.

عشب *'uśb*, grass, green food, green-meat; — *'aśab*, grown-up people; — *'aśib*, ة, abounding in grass; — ة *'uśba-t*, sarsaparilla; — *'aśaba-t*, old, decrepit; dwarf; poor person, beggar.

(عشجب) *'aśjab*, lame in the hips.

(عشجذ) *'aśjaẓ*, INF. ة, rain gently.

(عشد) *'aśad*, I, INF. *'aśd*, gather (a.).

(عشر) *'aśar*, I, U, INF. *'aśr*, *'uśr*, *'uśûr*, take the tenth from, tithe; — I, come as the tenth; make ten out of nine; make twenty; be pregnant in the tenth month; — II. INF. *ta'śîr*, id.; be big with young, abstain from the male; take ten or the tenth; tithe; decimate; take every ten verses of the Koran together; — III. INF. *mu'âśara-t*, *'iśâr*, have familiar intercourse with (acc.); visit frequently; converse with; — IV. INF. *i'śâr*, be pregnant in the tenth month; become ten; have camels which drink but every tenth day; — VI. INF. *ta'âśur*, have familiar intercourse; entertain each other; be sociable.

عشر *'iśr*, watering of the camels on the tenth day; — *'uśr*, pl. *'uśûr*, *a'śâr*, tenth part; the tenth, tithe; piece, fragment; — *'aśar*, ten (f.); — *'uśar*, a tree; the 10th, 11th and 12th days of the month; — *'iśra-t*, company; social intercourse; pleasure; banquet, drinking-bout; — *'aśara-t*, ten (m.); a ten, denary.

عشرا *'uśarâ'*, pl. *'uśarâwât*, *'iśâr*, pregnant (in the tenth month); summit; pl. of عشير *'aśîr*.

(عشرب) *'aśrab*, *'aśarrab*, darting arrow; running; lion; bold.

(عشرق) *'aśraq*, INF. ة, grow green, be green, verdant.

عشرق *'iśriq*, *'uśriq*, a medicinal plant.

(عشرم) *'aśram*, rough, hard, strong; — *'aśarram*, id.; bold; = عشرب *'aśrab*, *'aśarrab*.

عشرون *'iśrûn*, (m.) *'iśrîn*, twenty, a score.

عشرى *'uśriyy*, to be tithed; decimal.

(عشز) *'aśaz*, I, INF. *'aśazân*, walk like one who has only one leg; lean on a staff.

(عشزب) *'aśzab*, strong, brave; lion.

(عشزن) *'aśzan*, INF. ة, cope with, oppose.

عشزن *'aśazzan*, hard, strong.

عششة *'iśaśa-t*, pl. of عش *'uśś*.

(عشط) *'aśaṭ*, I, INF. *'aśṭ*, pull out.

(عشف), IV. INF. *i'śâf*, fail to thrive on the food eaten; refuse, loathe; be approved of, praised.

(عشق) *'aśiq*, A, INF. *'iśq*, *ma'śaq*, *'aśaq*, love passionately; be blind with love; be attached to, well disposed towards; — II. INF. *ta'śîq*, put one thing

into another (m.); — V. INF. *ta'aśśuq*, fall in love, show one's self to be in love; — VI. INF. *ta'âśuq*, be in love with one another.

عشق *'iśq*, love; passion of love; amorousness; — *'aśaq*, ة, ivy.

(عشم) *'aśim*, A, INF. *'aśm*, *'uśûm*, be dried up, withered; be greedy; hope for advantages; — *'aśam*, U, INF. *'aśm*, begin to grow fat; — V. INF. *ta'aśśum*, be withered; be greedy, hope for advantages.

عشم *'aśam*, greediness; selfish expectation; dry bread; — *'aśim*, a tree; — *'uśum*, pl. of عاشم *'âśim*, ag. of (عشم); — ة *'aśama-t*, wish, desire, greed; piece of dry bread; decrepit; decrepitude.

عشما *'aśmâ'*, f. of اعشم *'âśam*, of a mixed colour, &c.

(عشن) *'aśan*, U, INF. *'aśn*, speak according to one's opinion or surmise; — II. INF. *ta'śîn*, id.; — V. INF. *ta'aśsun*, cull dates beginning from the lowest branches; — VIII. INF. *i'tiśân*= I. and V.; fall upon in an aggressive manner without a just cause.

عشنج *'aśannaj*, wrinkled; morose.

(عشو) *'aśâ*, U, INF. *'aśw*, *'aśâwa-t*, also عشى *'aśî*, A, INF. *'aśan*, see badly, be night-blind; — INF. *'aśw*, *'uśuww*, perceive a fire at night and go towards it; assemble at one's place in the evening; go to at night, go to; go away; — INF. *'aśw*, be evening-time; come in the evening; take supper; pasture the camels at night; — also عشى *'aśa*, INF. *'aśw*, *'aśy*, give supper to (acc.); — *'aśî*, A, INF. *'aśan*, be night-blind; pasture (n.) at night; act unjustly; — II. INF. *ta'śiya-t*, give supper to (acc.); let the camels pasture at night; blind; dazzle birds at night with a fire in order to catch them; be night-blind; pretend to be so; treat gently; — IV. INF. *i'śâ'*, make night-blind, blind, dim the sight; feign to be night-blind; give supper to (acc.); bestow a present on (acc.); — V. INF. *ta'aśśî*, take supper; — VI. INF. *ta'âśî*, feign to be night-blind, blind, ignorant; — VIII. set out in the evening; go towards a fire at night; — X. INF. *isti'śâ'*, follow the guidance of a fire; find one perplexed, confused; — ة *'aśwa-t*, dense darkness; anything dark, dangerous; — *'iśwa-t*, love-game; coquettishness; — also *'uśwa-t*, night-fire.

عشوا *'aśwâ*, f. of اعشى *a'śa*, night-blind; blind she-camel.

عشور *'aśûr*, sociable (m.); — *'uśûr*, pl. of عشر *'uśr* and عشير *'aśîr*.

عشورا *'aśûrâ'*, the tenth (or ninth) of Muḥarram.

عشوف *'uśûf*, withered tree.

عشوى *'aśawiyy*, belonging or referring to the evening, evening-; — ة *'aśawiyya-t*, dark place.

(عشى) see (عشو).

عشى *'aśy*, supper; — *'aśan*, *'aśa*, night-blindness; — *'iśa*, pl. *a'śiya-t*, supper; evening-food; — *'aśî*, night-blind; — *'aśśiyy*, pl. *'aśiyya-t*, cook (m.); — *'aśiyy*, evening; first night-watch; — *'uśiyy*, pl. of اعشى *a'śa*, night-blind; — ة *'aśiyya-t*, pl. *-ât*, *'aśâyâ*, evening; cloud.

عشيان *'aśyân*, who takes supper.

عشيب *'aśib*, abounding in grass.

عشير *'aśîr*, pl. *a'śirâ'*, *'uśûr*, *a'śâr*, tenth part; cry of the hyena; pl. *'uśarâ'*, comrade, fellow, mate, friend; husband; wife; — ة *'aśîra-t*, pl. *'aśâ'ir*, relations by blood, kindred; family, race; association, company.

عشيق *'aśîq*, f. ة, lover, in love; — *'iśśîq*, mad with love.

(عص) *'aṣṣ* (pret. *'aṣiṣ-tu*), A, INF.

'aṣṣ, 'aṣaṣ, be hard, firm, strong; U, INF. *'aṣṣ*, press on a spring, &c.; compress air (m.); — II. INF. *ta'ṣîṣ*, press hard upon a debtor, dun; — VII. INF. *in'iṣâṣ*, VIII. INF. *i'tiṣâṣ*, be pressed, dunned; be compressed.

عص *'aṣṣ*, root, origin; (m.) pressure, compression.

عصا *'aṣan, 'aṣâ*, du. *'aṣawân*, pl. *'uṣiyy, 'iṣiyy, a'ṣ-in, a'ṣî, a'ṣâ'*, staff, stick; punishment, chastisement; wooden handle; sceptre; crosier; dominion; penis; lingual bone, tongue; Muslim fraternity or community; شق الع *śaqq al-'aṣâ*, stir up discord; — ة *'aṣâ-t*, staff.

عصاب *'iṣâb*, ribbon, bandage; kerchief, fillet; turban; handle; handful; — *'aṣṣâb*, seller of yarn; — ة *'iṣâba-t*, ribbon, band, bandage; head-band, kerchief, fillet, turban; troop of horsemen, troop, company, herd; flag; (m.) delicacy, tact, sense of honour.

عصار *'aṣâr, 'uṣâr*, ة *'aṣâra-t, 'uṣâra-t*, pressed-out juice; must; extract; — *'iṣâr*, mass of dust; fart; time; — *'aṣṣâr*, who presses olives or grapes.

عصافة *'uṣâfa-t*, chaff.

عصافير *'aṣâfîr*, pl. of عصفور *'uṣfûr*.

عصاقيا *'aṣâqiyâ'*, عصاقية *'aṣâqiya-t*, tumult.

عصاقيل *'aṣâqîl*, pl. whirlwinds, tornadoes.

عصال *'iṣâl*, crooked; pl. of اعصل *a'ṣal*, distorted; — *.

عصام *'aṣâm*, pl. *a'ṣâm*, collar for a dog; — *'iṣâm*, pl. *a'ṣima-t*, top of the tail; pl. *'iṣâm, a'ṣima-t, 'uṣum*, rope for the bucket; string; handle; a collyrium; — ة *'aṣâma-t*, head-band; — ى *'iṣâmiyy*, like 'Iṣâm's (model among the Arabs of a man who is great by his own merits), noble, generous.

عصامير *'aṣâmîr*, pl. of عصمور *'uṣmûr*.

عصاوة *'aṣâwa-t, 'iṣâwa-t, 'uṣâwa-t*, refractoriness, rebellion.

عصائب *'aṣâ'ib*, pl. of عصابة *'iṣâba-t*.

(عصب) *'aṣab*, I, INF. *'aṣb*, fold, bend, bind, strap; tie together; remove by tying (the testicles of a he-goat); tie round the hips of a she-camel to make her yield more milk; tie round; surround; assemble (n.); be zealous and persevering; dry up; — INF. *'aṣb, 'iṣâb*, grasp; — INF. *'aṣb, 'uṣûb*, be dirty, unclean; — INF. *'uṣûb*, be dry (year); — *'aṣib*, A, INF. *'aṣab*, be rich in nerves, sinews, muscles; surround; assemble (n.); be in a red glow; — II. wrap round, bind round with the turban, hence make one a chief or lord; starve (a.); spoil, destroy; (m.) form a party, a league; — IV. INF. *i'ṣâb*, tie fast or have tied fast; make every effort; — V. INF. *ta'aṣṣub*, wrap the turban tight round one's head; show a strong public spirit, embrace a cause passionately, be a fanatic, sectarian, a zealot; be obstinate, stubborn; confederate, conspire, unite into a party; content one's self; — VII. INF. *in'iṣâb*, be violent, intense, hard, firm, strong; — VIII. INF. *i'tiṣâb*, be wrapped round with the turban; wrap the turban round; put on a diadem; form a troop; tie round the hips of a she-camel (see I.); content one's self; — XII. INF. *i'ṣîṣâb*, make the utmost exertions; assemble (n.); be hot, dangerous; grow worse.

عصب *'aṣb*, cotton-thread; — *'aṣb, 'uṣb, 'aṣab*, ivy; — *'aṣab*, ة, pl. *a'ṣâb*, nerve; sinew, tendon; muscle; band, ribbon, long strip of cloth, scarf; chieftain; grandees; also ات *'aṣabât*, somewhat distant relations; — ة *'iṣba-t*, way of twisting the

turban; — *'uṣba-t*, pl. *'uṣab*, troop (10 to 40); a kind of resin; (m.) party, league, plot, conspiracy, cabal; — *'aṣaba-t*, hereditary portion, inheritance.

عصبصب *'aṣabṣab*, hard, disastrous (day).

عصبى *'aṣabiyy*, sinewy; nervous; muscular; — ة *'aṣabiyya-t*, family-spirit; patriotism; party- or corporation-spirit; zealous partisanship; fanaticisms; sense of honour, ambition.

(عصد) *'aṣad*, I, INF. *'aṣd*, bend, fold, fold up; stir up (anything boiling); lie with; compel; — INF. *'uṣûd*, die; — *'aṣid*, A, INF. *'aṣad*, id.; — II. INF. *ta'ṣîd*, starch (m.); — IV. INF. *i'ṣâd*, fold up; lend a stallion; — V. INF. *ta'aṣṣud*, get starched (m.).

عصد *'aṣd*, sperm.

(عصر) *'aṣar*, I, INF. *'aṣr*, press out, wring out; keep back, retain, prevent; present with; — INF. *'uṣr*, take refuge with; — *'aṣur*, be watered by the rain; — II. INF. *ta'ṣîr*, grow marriageable; put forth ears; have completed three quarters of his course (sun); — III. INF. *mu'âṣara-t*, be coeval with; — IV. INF. *i'ṣâr*, enter on the afternoon time; grow marriageable, have the menses and stop indoors, give birth; be on the point of pouring forth rain (cloud); pass. be rained upon; — V. INF. *ta'aṣṣur*, be pressed out; take refuge with; — VII. INF. *in'iṣâr*, be pressed out; be pressed upon; be dirtied by dust; — VIII. INF. *i'tiṣâr*, be pressed or wrung out; press out for one's self; extort a gift or the return of a gift; extort payment; spill down the food by slowly drinking; be miserly; prevent, hinder; take refuge with (ب *bi*).

عصر *'aṣr*, day or night (du. *al-'aṣrân*, day and night); evening; morning; also *'aṣar*, afternoon; — *'aṣr*, *'iṣr*, *'uṣr*, *'uṣur*, pl. *a'ṣâr*, *'uṣûr*, *a'ṣur*, *'uṣur*, time; season; age, century, era, reign; — *'uṣr*, dust; also *'aṣar*, refuge; — ة *'uṣra-t*, refuge, asylum; time; — *'aṣara-t*, whirlwind, tornado; cloud of dust.

عصرن, II. *ta'aṣran*, INF. *ta'aṣrun*, take an afternoon meal (m.).

عصرونية *'aṣrûniyya-t*, afternoon meal.

عصرى *'aṣriyy*, ة, opportune, seasonable.

عصص *'aṣaṣ*, *'uṣuṣ*, base of the tail; rump-bone.

(عصعص) *'aṣ'aṣ*, *'uṣ'uṣ*, *'uṣa'iṣ*, rump-bone; ة *'aṣ'aṣa-t*, &c., pain in the rump-bone; — *'uṣ'uṣ*, good-for-nothing fellow, scamp.

(عصف) *'aṣaf*, I, INF. *'aṣf*, *'uṣûf*, blow violently; try to earn for one's family; take away from, destroy; incline (n.); walk apace, hurry; — INF. *'aṣf*, cut off the crops while unripe; — IV. INF. *i'ṣâf*, blow violently; snatch away; destroy; perish; hurry past; turn round the well thirstily and beating the ground (camel); put forth leaves and blades; — VIII. INF. *i'tiṣâf*, endeavour to gain.

عصف *'aṣf*, ة, pl. *'uṣûf*, young blade and leaf; straw; blowing of the wind, storm.

(عصفر) *'uṣfur*, saffron in bloom; — hence *'aṣfar*, INF. ة, dye with saffron, dye red or yellow; — II. INF. *ta'aṣfur*, pass.; be distorted.

عصفور *'uṣfûr*, ة, pl. *'aṣâfîr*, sparrow, finch; any small bird; male locust; protuberance of the os frontis; white spot of a horse; book; prince; عصافير المنذر *'aṣâfîr al-munẓir*, a superior race of camels; — ة *'uṣfûra-t*, pack-thread, string; — ى *'uṣfûriyy*, two-humped camel.

عصقول *'uṣqûl*, male locust.

(عصل) *'aṣal*, U, INF. *'aṣl*, bend (a.), make crooked; make water; — *'aṣil*, A, INF. *'aṣal*, be bent, crooked.

عصل *'aṣal*, crookedness, bend; pl. *a'ṣâl*, gut; a tree; rose-laurel; — *'aṣil*, pl. *'iṣâl*, crooked and hardened; — *'uṣl*, pl. and—

عصلا *'aṣlâ'*, f. of اعصل *a'ṣal*, crooked, distorted.

(عصلب) *'aṣlab*, INF. ة, be strong of muscle and nerves.

عصلب *'aṣlub*, عصلبى *'aṣlubiyy*, big and strong.

(عصلد) *'aṣlad*, عصلود *'uṣlûd*, strong, hard.

(عصم) *'aṣam*, I, INF. *'aṣm*, gain; prevent; guard, keep, preserve; grant a letter of safe-conduct; protect, defend; take refuge with; put a string or strap to the skin bag; — *'aṣim*, A, INF. *'aṣam*, have a white spot on the fore-foot; — IV. INF. *i'ṣâm*, guard, protect, &c.; put a string to the skin bag; prepare a place of refuge for (acc.); defend one's self; keep to; seize the horse's mane; ride indifferently; — VII. INF. *in'iṣâm*, be defended; protect one's self; — VIII. INF. *i'tiṣâm*, take hold of (ب *bi*); take refuge with (ب *bi*); protect, defend one's self; be innocent, guiltless; — X. INF. *isti'ṣâm*, seek refuge; try to protect one's self.

عصم *'uṣm*, ة *'uṣma-t*, pl. *a'ṣâm*, whiteness on the fore-feet; — *'uṣm*, mountain-goats, pl. of عصما *'aṣmâ'* (f. of اعصم *a'ṣâm*); — *'uṣum*, traces, remainders; pl. of عصام *'iṣâm*; — ة *'iṣma-t*, protection, guard; abstemiousness, chastity, innocence; incorruptibility, integrity; immunity; good name; — also *'uṣma-t*, pl. *'iṣam*, *a'ṣum*, *'aṣama-t*, *a'ṣâm*, chain round the neck, necklace; collar for a dog.

عصمور *'uṣmûr*, pl. *'aṣâmîr*, water-wheel with a bucket.

(عصن), IV. *a'ṣan*, INF. *i'ṣân*, be crooked and difficult.

(عصو) *'aṣâ*, U, INF. *'aṣa-n*, *'aṣw*, beat with a stick or strike with a sword; use or handle as a stick; give a stick to (acc.); dress a wound; unite people (for a good or bad purpose); — عصى *'aṣî*, A, INF. *'aṣan*, seize a stick; seize a sword, strike with it; — II. INF. *ta'ṣiya-t*, give a stick to (acc.); — III. INF. *mu'âṣât*, beat with a stick; — IV. INF. *i'ṣâ'*, put forth branches without bearing fruit; — VIII. INF. *i'tiṣâ'*, lean on a staff; use the sword as a stick; cut a stick for one's self.

عصود *'aṣwad*, INF. ة, II. INF. *ta'aṣwud*, fight one another with clamour, brawl.

عصوص *'uṣûṣ*=عصص *'aṣaṣ*.

عصوف *'aṣûf*, pl. *'uṣf*, violent; storm; rapid as a storm; — *'uṣûf*, wine.

عصوم *'aṣûm*, voracious; glutton.

(عصى) *'aṣa*, I, INF. *'iṣyân*, *'aṣy*, *ma'ṣiya-t*, *'aṣâwa-t*, be refractory, rebellious, resist; — II. INF. *ta'ṣiya-t*, stir up rebellion; render difficult, impossible; — III. INF. *ma'âṣât*, revolt against; — V. INF. *ta'aṣṣi*, be difficult and complicated; — VIII. INF. *i'tiṣâ'*, be hard; — X. INF. *isti'ṣâ'*, revolt, rebel; find difficult; resist remedy; — *'aṣî*, see (عصو).

عصى *'aṣiyy*, refractory, rebellious; apostate, renegade; river Orontes; — *'iṣiyy*, *'uṣiyy*, pl. of عصا *'aṣâ*; — ة *'uṣayya-t*, little staff.

عصيان *'iṣyân*, disobedience; rebellion; sin; INF. of (عصى).

عصيب *'aṣîb*, violent; hot; disastrous day; pl. *a'ṣiba-t*, *'uṣub*, the intestines as food; sausage.

عصيدة *'aṣîda-t*, a thick broth, flour made consistent by boiling, starch; pudding; syrup.

عصير *'aṣîr*, pressed out; — also ة *'aṣîra-t*, juice; must.

عصيف *'aṣîf*, violent.

عصيفر *'uṣaifir*, **عصيفير** *'uṣaifîr*, little sparrow; — ة *'uṣaifira-t*, yellow violet.

عصيم *'aṣîm*, traces, remainders; dirt, filth.

(عض) *'aḍḍ*, A, INF. *'aḍḍ*, *'aḍîḍ*, seize with the teeth or tongue and bite; bite (one's fingers as a sign of repentance or grief); treat badly; taunt; bear patiently; — INF. *'aḍîḍ*, stick to one's companion; — for *'aḍiḍ*, A, bite; be sly, cunning; — II. INF. *ta'ḍîḍ*, bite; draw from a deep well; feed the camel; sport with a female slave; — III. INF. *'iḍâḍ*, *mu'âḍḍa-t*, bite one another; — IV. INF. *i'ḍâḍ*, make one to bite; give to taste (the sword); be deep and full of water; abound with the plant عض *'iḍḍ*; have camels feeding on it; — VI. INF. *ta'âḍḍ*, bite one another; — VII. INF. *in'iḍâḍ*, be bitten.

عض *'aḍḍ*, biting (s.), bite; — *'iḍḍ*, pl. *'uḍûḍ*, malignant; calamity; apt, clever; also *'uḍḍ*, pl. *a'ḍâḍ*, a thorny plant; — *'uḍḍ*, food for a camel; branches, trunks of trees; — ة *'iḍa-t*, pl. *'iḍûn*, *'iḍawât*, section, part, portion; — *'aḍḍa-t*, bite.

عضاب *'aḍḍâb*, reviler, slanderer, blasphemer; — *.

عضاد *'aḍâd*, *'uḍâd*, **عضادى** *'aḍâdiyy*, *'uḍâdiyy*, ة, big and strongly built; thick of arm; — *'iḍâd*, bracelet; — *; — ة *'iḍâda-t*, pl. *'aḍâ'id*, side-part; buttress; pillar, column, post.

عضارس *'uḍâris*, hail.

عضارط *'uḍâriṭ*, day-labourer.

عضاض *'aḍâḍ*, thick, big; anything eatable; — *'iḍâḍ*, biting (s.), mordacity; INF. III. of (عض); pl. of **عضوض** *'aḍûḍ*; — *'uḍâḍ*, *'uḍḍâḍ*, base of the nose; — ى *'uḍâḍiyy*, fat; delicate, tender.

عضال *'uḍâl*, *'aḍḍâl*, important; difficult; grave, mortal (disease).

عضام *'iḍâm*, os lumbale; — *.

عضاه *'iḍâh*, ة, pl. *'iḍûn*, *'iḍawât* a thorny shrub.

عضائية *'aḍâ'iyya-t*, membership, see **عضو** *'uḍw*.

(عضب) *'aḍab*, I, INF. *'aḍb*, cut off, lop; prevent; scold, taunt; beat; stab, pierce; return, desist; deprive of motion; make a sheep or camel **عضبا** *'aḍbâ'*; — *'aḍib*, INF. *'aḍab*, have a horn broken; — *'aḍub*, INF. *'uḍûb*, *'uḍûba-t*, have a malicious tongue; — III. INF. *'iḍâb*, *mu'âḍaba-t*, prevent, hinder; — IV. INF. *i'ḍâb*, make a camel or sheep **عضبا** *'aḍbâ'*.

عضب *'aḍb*, sharp of tongue, glib; sharp; sword; thoughtless, light-minded, full of levity.

عضبا *'aḍbâ'*, f. of **اعضب** *a'ḍab*, having a horn broken or an ear split.

(عضد) *'aḍad*, U, INF. *'aḍd*, hit on the arm or upper arm; help; help one (acc.) to (ب *bi*); make sore; tie two beasts of burden together by their thighs; — I, cut; lop, prune; — pass. *'uḍid*, have pain in the arm; — *'aḍid*, A, INF. *'aḍad*, have pain in the upper thigh; — II. INF. *ta'ḍîd*, swerve to the right and left; — III. INF. *mu'âḍada-t*, *'iḍâd*, help, assist; — IV. INF. *i'ḍâd*=II.; — VI. INF. *ta'âḍud*, help one another; find help; — VIII. INF. *i'tiḍâd*, take upon one's arm or shoulders; ask help from (ب *bi*); take as a helper; — X. INF. *isti'ḍâd*, prune; gather fruit.

عضد *'aḍd*, *'uḍd*, *'iḍd*, *'aḍid*, *'aḍud*, *'uḍud*, pl. *a'ḍâd*, upper arm, upper part of an animal's leg; help, assistance; helper; pedes-

tal, base; side; — *'aḍad*, pain in the arm; — ة *'aḍida-t*, arm; hand.

عضدان *'iḍdân*, pl. of عضيد *'aḍîd*.

(عضر) *'aḍar*, INF. *'aḍr*, speak publicly.

(عضرس) *'aḍras*, pl. *'aḍâris*, hail, snow, cold; cold water; — *'iḍris*, a plant.

(عضرط) *'aḍraṭ*, *'iḍriṭ*, buttocks; — *'iḍriṭ*, os lumbale; perineum; — *'uḍruṭ*, day-labourer; pl. *'aḍâriṭ*, also—

عضروط *'uḍrûṭ*, pl. *'aḍârîṭ*, hireling; vile person.

(عضز) *'aḍaz*, I, INF. *'aḍz*, keep off, guard off, prevent; chew.

عضض *'uḍaḍ*, pl. of عضوض *'aḍûḍ*.

عضعض *'aḍ'aḍ*, INF. ة, bite.

(عضل) *'aḍal*, U, INF. *'aḍl*, oppress, vex; be difficult, molest, importune; — A, U, I, INF. *'aḍl*, *'iḍl*, *'iḍlân*, prevent a woman by force from marrying; — *'aḍil*, A, INF. *'aḍal*, be very muscular; — II. INF. *ta'ḍîl*, make troublesome, difficult, unbearable; (m.) vex, torment; prevent from marrying; be narrow, strait; be too small for the inhabitants; be troublesome, importune; give birth or lay eggs with difficulty; — IV. INF. *i'ḍâl*, id.; be difficult, toilsome, insurmountable; depress, tire out; (also V.) baffle; — V. INF. *ta'aḍḍul*, see IV.; become incurable; — XI. INF. *i'ḍîlâl*, be closely entwined and grown together.

عضل *'iḍl*, malignant; — *'aḍal*, pl. -*ât*, *'iḍlân*, *'uḍlân*, field-mouse; — *'aḍil*, muscular; — ة *'uḍla-t*, pl. *'uḍl*, *'uḍal*, calamity; tight knot; — *'aḍala-t*, pl. *'aḍal*, muscle; piece of flesh.

(عضم) *'aḍm*, mountain-goats; pl. *'uḍm*, *a'ḍima-t*, handle of the plough, plough-tail; winnowing-fan, cribble; tail-bone, extremity of the back-bone; pl. *'iḍâm*, hand-piece of the bow.

عضمز *'aḍammaz*, ة, hard; miserly, avaricious; lion; — ة *'aḍammaza-t*, ugly old woman.

عضمور *'uḍmûr*, water-wheel; bucket.

(عضه) *'aḍah*, A, INF. *'aḍh*, *'aḍah*, *'aḍîha-t*, *'iḍha-t*, lie, tell lies; slander, calumniate; practise sorcery; INF. *'aḍh*, eat of the thorn-bush عضاه *'iḍâh*; — *'aḍih*, A, INF. *'aḍah*, be sick from doing so; lie, slander; — I. and II. INF. *ta'ḍîh*, prune the عضاه *'iḍâh*; — IV. INF. *i'ḍâh*, lie, slander; produce the *'iḍâh*; prune it; have camels feeding on it.

عضه *'iḍah*, pl. *'iḍûn*, lie; calumny; sorcery, magic; — also ة *'iḍa-t*, a thorny shrub.

(عضهل) *'aḍhal*, INF. ة, stop up, cork.

(عضو) *'aḍâ*, U, INF. *'aḍw*, dissect; separate, sever, seclude; — II. INF. *ta'ḍiya-t*=I.

عضو *'uḍw*, *'iḍw*, pl. *a'ḍâ'*, limb; member; — *'uḍuww*, welfare, well-being, ease.

عضوض *'aḍûḍ*, pl. *'uḍaḍ*, *'iḍâḍ*, what can be bitten; mordacious, given to biting; deep; — *.

عضون *'iḍûn*, pl. of عضاه *'iḍâh*, عضه *'iḍah* and عضة *'iḍa-t*.

عضوى *'iḍwiyy*, *'aḍawiyy*, having limbs or joints; referring to limbs or members.

عضيد *aḍîd*, pl. *'iddân*, low palm-tree; row of palms.

عضيض *'aḍîḍ*, of the same age, coeval; contemporaneous; calamity; — *.

عضيلة *'aḍîla-t*, muscle.

عضيهة *'aḍîha-t*, *'uḍaiha-t*, lie, slander, calumny.

(عط) *'aṭṭ*, U, INF. *'aṭṭ*, rend (without severing); throw to the ground; conquer, overcome; — II. INF. *ta'ṭîṭ*, rend; — V. INF. *ta'aṭṭuṭ*, VII. INF. *in'iṭâṭ*, be rent, torn, bent; — VIII. INF. *i'tiṭâṭ*, split, rend.

عطا *'aṭan, 'aṭâ'*, pl. *a'ṭiya-t*, gift, present.

عطار *'aṭṭâr*, f. ة, perfumer; druggist; — ة *'iṭâra-t*, profession of a perfumer or druggist; — *'aṭṭâra-t*, excellent.

عطارد *'uṭârid*, planet Mercury; quicksilver.

عطاس *'uṭâs*, sneezing (s.); morning dawn; — *'aṭṭâs*, who sneezes.

عطاش *'aṭâś*, pl. *'aṭśan, 'aṭśa*, thirsty; — *'uṭâś*, pain from thirst.

عطاف *'iṭâf*, pl. *'uṭf*, upper garment; sword; — *'aṭṭâf*, strongly bent.

عطالة *'aṭâla-t*, inactivity; unconcern, carelessness; vacancies, holidays.

عطايا *'aṭâyâ*, pl. of عطية *'aṭiyya-t*.

(عطب) *'aṭab*, U, INF. *'aṭb, 'uṭûb*, be soft, tender; ruin; hurt, injure; — *'aṭib*, A, INF. *'aṭab*, perish miserably; be jaded, broken down; be violently enraged; — II. INF. *ta'ṭîb*, handle the wine so as to make it fragrant; begin to bud; also IV. INF. *i'ṭâb*, harm, injure, destroy; despise; — VII. INF. *in'iṭâb*, perish; be injured, harmed; — VIII. INF. *i'tiṭâb*, take embers with the cloth عطبة *'uṭba-t*.

عطب *'aṭb, 'aṭab*, calamity; ruin, perishing (s.); loss; (m.) injury; — *'uṭb, 'uṭub*, cotton; — ة *'uṭba-t*, fleak of cotton; cloth to take and carry embers with.

(عطر) *'aṭir*, A, INF. *'aṭar*, smell of perfumes; — II. INF. *ta'ṭîr*, perfume; be a perfumer or druggist; — V. INF. *ta'aṭṭur*, be fragrant; perfume one's self; live yet unmarried in the paternal house; = *ta'allul*, be unadorned; find fragrant or perfumed.

عطر *'iṭr*, pl. *'uṭûr*, perfume; essence; — *'aṭar*, scent, fragrance, aroma; — *'aṭir*, ة, scented, fragrant, aromatic, perfumed; — *'uṭur*, pl. of عاطر *'âṭir*, fragrant; — ى *'iṭriyy*, عطر=ة *'aṭir*; — pl. f. *'iṭriyyât*, perfumes.

(عطس) *'aṭas*, I, U, INF. *'aṭs, 'uṭâs*, sneeze; peep forth, appear (dawn); die; run straight against you (game); — II. INF. *ta'ṭîs*, make to sneeze; sneeze violently; — ة *'aṭsa-t*, sneeze; similar.

(عطش) *'aṭiś*, A, INF. *'aṭaś*, be thirsty, thirst for, desire violently; — II. INF. *ta'ṭiś*, make to thirst, cause thirst; — IV. INF. *i'ṭâś*, make or allow to thirst; have thirsty cattle; keep the camels long from the water; — V. INF. *ta'aṭṭuś*, suffer thirst; force one's self to endure thirst; desire violently.

عطش *'aṭaś*, thirst; — *'aṭiś*, ة, thirsty; — ة *'aṭśa-t*, violent thirst.

عطشان *'aṭśân*, f. ة, and عطشى *'aṭśa*, pl. *'aṭśa, 'aṭâśa*, and f. *'iṭâś*, thirsty; desirous, craving; dried up, parched.

(عطعط) *'aṭ'aṭ*, cry out, clamour (combatants).

(عطف) *'aṭaf*, I, INF. *'aṭf*, incline, bend (n.), lean to; be benevolent, favourable to (على *'ala*); turn; rush upon; turn from, depart; double up a pillow; join two words or sentences by a copulative particle; — *'aṭif*, A, INF. *'aṭaf*, have long eyelashes; — II. INF. *ta'ṭîf*, fold up, bend; make to lean or incline; dispose well towards, make favourable to (على *'ala*); inspire with sympathy; make an upper garment; — V. INF. *ta'aṭṭuf*, be inclined, well-disposed, favourable; yield; put on an upper garment; — VI. INF. *ta'âṭuf*, have good will, sympathy towards one another; walk with a bent head; walk along proudly; — VII. INF.

in'iṭâf, be inclined, folded, bent; be moved by (فى *fi*); change one's direction; turn back; be inclined towards (الى *ila*); — VIII. INF. *i'tiṭâf*, put on an upper garment; — X. INF. *isti'ṭâf*, make inclined, win for; try to gain sympathy; solicit.

عطف *'aṭf*, inclination; bend; turning; sympathy, affection, favour, kindness; conjunction (حرف العطف *ḥarf al-'aṭf*, copulative particle); point of a bow; present; — *'iṭf*, pl. *a'ṭâf*, side of the neck; anything bent, curved, lineaments of the body, outlines; armpit; — *'uṭf*, pl. of عاطف *'âṭif*, inclined, &c., of عطاف *'iṭâf* and عطوف *'aṭûf*; — ة *'aṭfa-t*, turn, bend; round-about way; lane, alley; necklace as amulet; — *'iṭfa-t*, ivy; — *'aṭafa-t*, bent or curved piece of wood.

(عطل) *'aṭil*, A, INF. *'aṭal*, *'uṭûl*, be unadorned; lack property, education, &c.; INF. *'aṭal*, be tall, of high stature; (m.) be spoiled, no longer of use; — II. INF. *ta'ṭîl*, deprive one's wife of adornments; deprive of one's property; leave without work, unemployed; empty; free; destroy, devastate, ruin; (m.) injure, cause loss to (على *'ala*); (m.) lend at interest; — V. INF. *ta'aṭṭul*, be unadorned; be unemployed; (m.) suffer loss, damage, injury; (m.) be spoiled; (m.) be lent at interest; — X. INF. *isti'ṭâl*, find damaged, spoiled, believe to be lost; give up (a patient).

عطل *'aṭl*, *'aṭal*, absence of adornment, simplicity; inactivity; inefficiency; — *'uṭl*, (m.) damage, loss; (m.) palsy; عطل المال *'uṭl al-mâl*, interest; — *'uṭl*, *'uṭul*, poor, needy; uncultivated, uneducated; — *uṭul*, pl. *a'ṭâl*, *'uṭṭal*, unadorned; unarmed; without a thread (needle); — *'aṭil*, ة, handsome, clean; without vowel-points; = عاطل *'âṭil*, vacant, empty, vain, &c.; — *'uṭṭal*, pl. of عاطل *'âṭil*; — ة *'uṭla-t*, leisure; inactivity; absence of adornment.

عطلان *'aṭlân*, inactive, unemployed; spoiled, useless.

(عطلس) *'aṭallas*, long.

(عطم) *'uṭm*, carded wool; — VIII. INF. *i'tiṭâm*, perish.

(عطن) *'aṭan*, I, U, INF. *'aṭn*, apply salt, &c., to hides, so as to remove the hair; — INF. *'uṭûn*, rest by the water (camels); — *'aṭin*, A, INF. *'aṭan*, deteriorate and putrefy (hides); moulder, decay; — II. INF. *ta'ṭîn*, treat hides as under I.; putrefy, deteriorate, get decomposed; prepare a place for the camels to rest by the water; rest by the water; — IV. INF. *i'ṭân*, have camels resting by the water, or drive them there; — VII. INF. *in'iṭân*, be treated as under I.

عطن *'aṭan*, pl. *a'ṭân*, *'uṭûn*, *'aṭana-t*, *'uṭṭan*, place where camels are resting by the water; fold; — *'atàn*, ة *'aṭana-t*, decomposition; putrefaction, decay, stench; — *'aṭin*, putrefying, offensive to the smell.

(عطو) *'aṭâ*, U, INF. *'aṭw*, receive, take with the hand; lift up the head or the hand; overcome; (m.) give, grant; — II. INF. *ta'ṭiya-t*, serve, work for (acc.); urge to haste; — III. INF. *mu'âṭât*, give, present with; receive; serve; — IV. INF. *i'ṭâ'*, give, present with, bestow on (2 acc.); give pay; let one's self be guided by (acc.); — V. INF. *ta'aṭṭî*, ask for a gift from (2 acc.); set zealously to a work; hasten (n.); — VI. INF. *ta'âṭî*, give or reach to one another; receive; take, take without a right; stand on tip-toe and

stretch out the hand for a thing; try to anticipate one another in taking; take reciprocally; set zealously to a work; take to poetry; undertake; attempt; (m.) interfere, meddle; (m.) have relations to one another; — VII. INF. *in'itâ'*, be given, granted; — X. INF. *isti'tâ'*, ask for a gift.

عطود *'atawwad*, quick pace; open; noble; sharp; long; whole; difficult.

عطوس *'utûs*, snuff; اللجم الع *al-lujam al-'utûs*, death.

عطوف *'atûf*, pl. *'utf*, well-inclined, benevolent; noose, springe; wrapper, cloak, mantle; — ة *'atûfa-t*, inclination, affection, benevolence.

عطون *'atûn*, resting by the water.

عطوى *'atwa*, good bow.

(عطى) *'ata*, I, give; — *'utayy*, small gift, dole; — ة *'atiyya-t*, pl. *-ât*, *'atâyâ*, gift, present; pay.

عطيد *'atayyad*=عطود *'atawwad*.

عطيف *'atîf*, gentle, yielding, docile (woman).

عطيل *'atîl*, long palm-branch; lamed, palsied, impotent.

عطيم *'atîm*, pl. *'utum*, perished, lost.

عطين *'atîn*, ة *'atîna-t*, putrefying, decaying, offensive to the smell.

(عظ) *'azz*, U, INF. *'azz*, press hard upon, bite; throw on the ground; — III. INF. *mu'âzza-t*, bite; INF. *mu'âzza-t*, *'izâz*, fight furiously, be pressed hard in combat; — IV. INF. *i'zâz*, make one a brave combatant or warrior; — ة *'iza-t*, sermon, exhortation, INF. of (وعظ); — *'azza-t*, impetuosity.

عظا *'izâ'*, pl. of — ة *'azâ'a-t*, a species of lizard.

عظارة *'izâra-t*, drunkenness.

عظام *'izâm*, pl. عظم *'azm* and عظيم *'azîm*; — *'uzâm*, *'uzzâm*, great; — ة *'azâma-t*, greatness; pomp; pride, — also *'izâma-t*, false hips, hip-improver; — ى *'azâmiyy*, proud of one's ancestors.

(عظب) *'azab*, I, INF. *'azb*, *'uzûb*, persevere patiently; attend well to one's cattle and fortune; dry up (n.); become callous; — INF. move the rump quickly to and fro; — *'azib*, A, INF. *'azab*, endure or persevere patiently; be fat; — II. INF. *ta'zîb*, thwart.

(عظر) *'azir*, A, INF. *'azar*, abhor, loathe, be disgusted with (فى *fî*); — IV. INF. *i'zâr*, cause stomach-ache, bring on indigestion.

(عظعظ) *'az'az*, INF. ة, *'iz'âz*, tremble and whirl round (arrow).

(عظل) *'azal*, U, INF. *'azl*, also *'azil*, A, INF. *'azal*, stick fast together (dogs); — II. INF. *ta'zîl*, agree upon; — III. INF. *'izâl*, *mu'âzala-t* = I.; INF. *'izâl*, insert another's verses into one's own; — V. INF. *ta'azzul*, come together; — VI. INF. *ta'âzul*, VIII. INF. *i'tizâl*=I.

عظل *'uzul*, pl. paederasts.

عظلام *'izlâm*, dark dust.

عظلم *'izlim*, indigo; — also ة *'azlama-t*, darkness, night.

(عظم) *'azam*, INF. *'azm*, throw a bone to the dog; — INF. *'azma-t*, beat or hit on the bones; — *'azum*, INF. *'izâm*, *'azama-t*, be great; be important; be terrible; make a deep impression upon (على *'ala*); — II. INF. *ta'zîm*, deem great, make much of; make great, elevate, honour, praise; exaggerate; cut up a sheep; — IV. INF. *i'zâm*, honour, praise; deem great, important; give a bone to eat; — V. INF. *ta'azzum*, be honoured, praised; appear great; exalt one's self, be overbearing, proud, haughty; become great, considerable, important; — X. INF. *isti'zâm*, deem great, admire; find astonishing; be proud; take the largest part.

عظم *'azm*, pl. *a'zum*, *'izâm*, *'izâma-t*, bone; — *'izm*, greatness; — *'uzm*, greatness; bulk, extent, thickness; pride; crowd, multitude; also *'azm*, principal part; — *'azam*, high-road; — *'izam*, greatness, pomp; — ة *'uzma-t*, bulk, extent, circumference, thickness; false hip; — *'azama-t*, greatness; majesty; power; pomp; pride, vanity; thick part of the arm; pl. *'azamât*, grandees, princes.

عظماء *'uzamâ'*, pl. of عظيم *'azîm*.

عظمى *'uzma*, f. of اعظم *a'zam*, greater, &c.

(عظو) *'azâ*, U, INF. *'azw*, hurt, injure, wrong; slander; administer poison clandestinely; turn from what is good (a.); — عظى *'aza*, A, INF. *'azan*, have the belly swollen from feeding on عنظوان *'unzuwân*.

عظور *'azûr*, pl. *'uzur*, full of wine (bag).

عظى *'aza*, see (عظو).

عظيم *'azîm*, ة, pl. *'izâm*, *'uzamâ*, great; much, many; glorious, magnificent, majestic; important; terrible; (m.) bravo! well-done! — *'uzaim*, small bone; — ة *'azîma-t*, pl. *'azâ'im*, great event, crime, calamity; mighty trouble.

(عف) *'aff*, U, I, INF. *'aff*, *'afâf*, *'afâfa-t*, *'iffa-t*, abstain from what is unlawful; be chaste; — INF. *'aff*, collect or remain in the udder; (m.) except, spare (عن *'an*); — II. INF. *ta'fîf*, make abstemious, chaste; — IV. INF. *i'fâf*, id.; pass. be milked so that some milk remains in the udder; — V. *ta'affuf*, live or try to live abstemiously, chastely; — VI. INF. *ta'âff*, milk a second time; use medicine; — VIII. INF. *i'tifâf*, pick up dry herbs from the ground with the tongue (camel); — X. INF. *isti'fâf*, id.; abstain.

عف *'aff*, ة, abstemious, chaste; — ة *'affa-t*, chaste woman; — *'iffa-t*, chastity, abstemiousness, continence; incorruptibility, integrity.

عفاء *'afâ'*, effacing (s.), passing away (s.), decay; dust; foal of an ass; rain; — *'ifâ*, long hair, long feathers; pl. of عفو *'afw*, &c.; — ة *'ufât*, pl. of عافى *'âfî*, abundant, suppliant, &c.

عفار *'afâr*, flour; dry or stale bread; a tree; — *'affâr*, gleaner; — ة *'afâra-t*, red willow; malice, malignity; also ية *'afâriyya-t*, gleaning (s.); gleanings; — ى *'afâra*, pl. of عفرية *'ifriya-t*; — ية, عفارية نفارية *'ufâriya-t nufâriya-t*, anything unheard-of, awful, terrible.

عفاز *'afâz*, walnut; — ة *'afâza-t*, hill; — ة *'ufâza-t*, *'uffâza-t*, fruit of the cotton-tree.

عفاش *'ufâś*, having a thick beard; — ة *'ufâśa-t*, rabble, populace.

عفاص *'ifâs*, purse; stopper, cork.

عفاط *'affât*, stammerer; — ة *'affâta-t*, shepherdess.

عفاف *'afâf*, ة *'afâfa-t*, abstemiousness, continence, chastity; — *'ifâf*, medicine, remedy.

عفاقة *'affâqa-t*, buttocks; rabble, populace.

عفاك *'afâk*, may God pardon thee! bravo! well done!

عفان *'iffân*, right time, nick of time.

(عفاهن) *'ufâhin*, strong, enduring.

عفاوة *'afâwa-t*, *'ifâwa-t*, *'ufâwa-t*, scum of the pot; gravy; (m.) thickness.

(عفت) *'afat*, I, INF. *'aft*, break by twisting, break without severing; speak Arabic with difficulty.

عفتان *'ifittân*, ى *'ifittâniyy*, big; fleshy.

(عفج) *'afaj*, I, INF. *'afj*, beat; lie with; — V. INF. *ta'affuj*, go askance.

عفج *'afj*, *'ifj*, *'afaj*, *'afij*, pl. *a'fâj*, gut; — ة *'afja-t*, &c., id.; pond.

(عفد) *'afad*, I, INF. *'afd*, *'afadân*, jump without running; — VIII. INF. *i'tifâd*, shut one's self up and die from hunger to avoid begging; believe firmly.

عفد *'afd*, pigeons and such-like birds.

(عفر) *'afar*, I, INF. *'afr*, roll in the dust (a.); tread into the dust; dust over (a.), cover with dust; throw on the ground; water for the first time; fructify the palm-tree; (m.) scold; — *'afir*, A, INF. *'afar*, be dust-coloured; — II. INF. *ta'fîr*, roll in the dust (a.); humble, abase; (m.) pick from the dust or ground, glean; wean; dry meat in the sun or in hot sand; (m.) scold; — III. INF. *mu'âfara-t*, attend well to one's cattle or business; — V. INF. *ta'affur*, fall into the dust, become dusty; be gleaned; be fat; become powerful, able, self-possessed, &c. (see عفريت *'ifrît*); — VII. INF. *in'ifâr*, become dusty; — VIII. INF. *i'tifâr*, id.; throw into the dust; be powerful, &c.; attack; tear to pieces; — X. INF. *isti'fâr*, skim over the dusty ground.

عفر *'afr*, *'afar*, pl. *a'fâr*, dust, earth; — *'ifr*, pig; villain; devil; — *'ufr*, pl. *a'fâr*, *'ifâr*, id.; strong, brave; 7th to 9th of the month; عن عفر *'an 'ufr-in*, after a month; pl. of اعفر *a'far*, reddish-white, &c.; — *'ufar*, time; month; — ة *'ifra-t*, *'ufra-t*, mane; feathers of the neck; — *'ufra-t*, dust-colour; reddish-white (s.); — *'ufra-t*, *'ufurra-t*, beginning of the cold; highest heat.

عفرا *'afrâ*, feathers of the neck; — *'afrâ'*, f. of اعفر *a'far*, reddish-white, &c.; 13th night of the month.

عفراس *'ifrâs*, devouring lion.

(عفرت), II. INF. *ta'afrut*, grow wicked as a devil; be exceedingly troublesome and importune.

(عفرس) *'afras*, INF. ة, throw to the ground and conquer.

عفرس *'ifris*, عفريس *'ifrîs*, عفروس *'ufrûs*, عفرنس *'afarnas*, عفرنى *'afarna*, devouring lion.

عفرناة *'afarnât*, strong, robust (camel).

عفرى *'afra*, ة *'ifriya-t*, pl. *'afâra*, feathers of the neck; mane; front hair of a horse; — *'ifriyy*, ة *'ifriya-t*, malicious, mischievous; ill-looking.

عفريت *'ifrît*, pl. *'afârît*, gigantic and powerful demon; devil; — also *'ifirrît*, عفرين *'ifrîn*, *'ifirrîn*, powerful, self-possessed, able, capable, skilful, cunning; terrible; *'ifirrîn*, a kind of scorpion.

(عفز) *'afaz*, U, INF. *'afz*, sport with one's wife; make the camels kneel down; — III. INF. *mu'âfaza-t*, sport with one's wife.

(عفزر) *'afzar*, quick, hastening in advance.

(عفس) *'afas*, I, INF. *'afs*, prevent; use daily; urge on violently; knead, rub; kick on the buttocks; draw to the ground; — III. INF. *'ifâs*, *mu'âfasa-t*, try to draw down, to get under in wrestling; — VI. INF. *ta'âfus*, wrestle; — VII. INF. *in'ifâs*, be rolled in the dust and dirtied; — VIII. INF. *i'tifâs*, be violently shaken; wrestle.

(عفش) *'afaś*, I, INF. *'afś*, gather, collect, especially worthless things; — II. INF. *ta'fîś*, be dishevelled (m.); be densely grown.

عفش *'afś*, ة *'afśa-t*, useless stuff, rubbish; refuse; lumber; baggage; — *'afś*, (m.) soldier or boy of the baggage-train.

(عفشج) *'afśaj*, long, thick.

(عفشل) *'afśal*, عفشليل *'afśalîl*, stolid, lazy, indolent.

(عفص) *'afaṣ*, I, INF. *'afṣ*, pull out;

throw down in wrestling; bend, fold; lie with; distort; tie up the mouth of a bottle; — II. INF. *ta'fîṣ*, dye with gall-nut; — IV. INF. *i'fâṣ*, tie up a bottle; — VIII. INF. *i'tifâṣ*, receive payment of a debt.

عفص *'afṣ*, gall-nut, gall-nut tree; — *'afaṣ*, wryness of the nose; — *'afiṣ*, astringent, styptic, acid.

(عفضج) *'ufḍij*, INF. ة, be fat.

(عفط) *'afaṭ*, I, INF. *'afṭ*, *'afiṭ*, *'afaṭân*, break wind; INF. *'afṭ*, *'afîṭ*, sneeze; INF. *'afṭ*, stammer; call the sheep by smacking the lips; (m.) scold.

عفط *'afṭ*, fart; sneeze; — *'afiṭ*, farting (adj.).

(عفطل) *'afṭal*, INF. ة, mix.

(عفعف) *'af'af*, fruit of the *ṭalaḥ*-tree; — *'af'af*, INF. ة, eat of this fruit.

عففة *'afafa-t*, pl. of عف *'aff*.

(عفق) *'afaq*, I, INF. *'afq*, be absent, out of sight, invisible; break wind; whip, lash; cover the she-ass frequently; awake after a short sleep; work in an illusory manner; return frequently; go frequently to and from the water; be allowed to pasture at large; gather, collect (a.); hold off, prevent, detain; — INF. *'afq*, *'afâq*, milk frequently; walk fast; — II. INF. *ta'fîq*, drive back; — III. INF. *mu'âfaqa-t*, flatter and deceive, beguile; break in repeatedly (wolf); — IV. come and go repeatedly and to no purpose; — V. INF. *ta-'affuq*, take refuge with (ب *bi*); — VII. INF. *'in'ifâq*, get on; — VIII. INF. *i'tifâq*, rush upon a prey; — ة *'afqa-t*, absence; a game.

عفقس *'afqas*, INF. ة, deprave the good; — III. INF. *i'finqâs*, be difficult to manage.

(عفقل) *'afqal*, having a big face.

(عفك) *'afak*, I, INF. *'afk*, speak confusedly; — *'afik*, A, INF. *'afk*, *'afak*, be very stupid.

عفك *'afik*, very stupid.

عفكا *'afkâ'*, f. of اعفك *a'fak*, very stupid, &c.; restive she-camel.

(عفل) *'afal*, examine the fatness of a sheep by feeling; — *'afil*, A, INF. *'afal*, have a rupture in the pudenda; — II. INF. *ta'fîl*, pretend that a woman has such a rupture; cure it.

عفل *'afal*, fat of the scrotum; — ة *'afala-t*, rupture in the pudenda of a woman.

عفلا *'aflâ'*, f. afflicted with a rupture in the pudenda.

(عفلط) *'aflaṭ*, INF. ة, mix.

عفلط *'ifliṭ*, *'afallaṭ*, عفليط *'iflîṭ*, stupid.

(عفن) *'afan*, U, INF. *'afn*, ascend a mountain; putrefy (a.) the flesh or meat; — *'afin*, A, INF. *'afan*, *'ufûna-t*, putrefy (n.), decay; get putrid, offensive to the smell; — II. INF. *ta'fîn*, putrefy (a.); (m.) get putrid; — IV. INF. *i'fân*, have the skin worn out and perforated; — V. INF. *ta'affun*, putrefy and decay, moulder.

عفن *'afan*, putrefaction; stench; miasma; (m.) impurity in the stomach; — *'afin*, also ى *'afaniyy*, putrescent.

(عفنش) *'afnaś*, INF. ة, be dense, thick; — *'afannaś*, dense; thick.

عفنشل *'afanśal* = عفشل *'afśal*.

(عفه) *'afah*, A, INF. *'ufûh*, be closely pressed together, crammed.

(عفو) *'afâ*, U, INF. *'afw*, efface, blot out the traces, wear out; be effaced, razed; — INF. *'afâ'*, *'ufuww*, id.; pardon; exempt, spare; be long and dense; be thick; be densely grown over; be numerous; shear; be pure, not troubled by passengers (water); surpass; leave; leave undone; — II. INF. *ta'fiya-t*, efface (على *'ala*); let the hair (of the camel) grow; make a thread thick; arrange well, mend (على *'ala*); — III. INF.

mu'âfât, preserve in health and wealth; restore to health; — IV. INF. *i'fâ'*, preserve in good health; cure, heal, protect; dispense from (a.), excuse from (عن *'an*, من *min*); let the hair (of the camel) grow thick; let the beard grow; give the best part of one's property, give everything; pay entirely, make up; — V. INF. *ta'affi*, be effaced; (m.) be thick, dense, get thick; — VI. INF. *ta'âfi*, recover; abandon; — VIII. INF. *i'tifâ'* (m.) and X. INF. *isti'fâ'*, beg to be dispensed, excused from, spared (من *min*); resign; ask for a gift or favour; pick out with the lips the drier herbs (camel).

عفو *'afw*, effacing (s.); pardon, amnesty, forgiveness; dispensation, exemption, sparing (s.); excuse; bounty, favour, present; good pasture-ground; the greatest and best part; balance (of an account); easy; — *'afw*, *'ifw*, *'ufw*, pl. *'afwa-t*, *'ifâ'*, foal of an ass; — *'affuww*, who pardons much, forgiving, forbearing; — *'ufuww*, effacing (s.), INF. of (عفو); — ة *'afwa-t*, forgiveness, pardon; blood-money; — *'afwa-t*, *'ifwa-t*, *'ufwa-t*, scum of the pot; — *'ifwa-t*, *'ufwa-t*, female foal of an ass.

عفوصة *'ufûṣa-t*, astringent acidity.

عفونة *'afûna-t*, putrefaction; stench.

عفير *'afîr*, meat dried in sand; dry bread; avaricious, miserly.

عفيط *'afîṭ*, sneezing (s.); breaking wind (s.).

عفيف *'afîf*, f. *a'iffâ'*, abstemious, chaste; — ة *'afîfa-t*, pl. *-ât*, *'afâ'if*, chaste woman.

عفيك *'afîk*, very stupid.

(عق) *'aqq*, U, INF. *'aqq*, split, cleave; make the cloud to rain (wind); sacrifice a sheep when the hair of the child is cut for the first time; shoot the arrow into the air; — U, INF. *'uqûq*, *ma'aqqa-t*, be disobedient, refractory, resist; — I, INF. *'aqâq*, *'aqaq*, *'uqûq*, be big with young; INF. *'aqaq*, be split; be rent, break (n.); — IV. INF. *i'qâq*, make bitter; push forth shoots on the ground; be big with young; — VII. INF. *in'iqâq*, be split, split (n.), burst, break (n.); rise; be tightly knit; — VIII. INF. *i'tiqâq*, burst (n.); draw the sword.

عق *'aqq*, disobedient; — also *'iqq*, deep furrow, rent; — *'uqq*, bitter; — ة *'iqqa-t*, pl. *'iqaq*, furrow, split, cleft; — *'uqqa-t*, a-toy.

عقا *'iqâ'*, pl. of عقوة *'aqwa-t*; — ة *'aqât*, pl. *'iqâ'*, house, court.

عقاب *'iqâb*, end; punishment; — *; — *'uqâb*, pl. *a'qub*, *'uqbân*, *'iqbân*, black eagle; sea-eagle; constellation of the eagle; name of a celebrated horse; projecting stone; channel, gutter.

عقابيس *'aqâbîs*, pl. calamities.

عقاد *'aqqâd*, lace-maker; — ة *'iqâda-t*, knitting (s.), lace-making.

عقار *'aqâr*, pl. *-ât*, landed property; immovables; *'aqâra-t*, land, estate; — *'uqâr*, wine; — *; — *'aqqâr*, pl. *'aqâqîr*, simple; root; an aromatic plant, drug; — ة *'uqâra-t*, *'aqâra-t*, sterility, barrenness; — ى *'aqâra*, houghed.

عقاص *'iqâṣ*, plaiting-band; — *

عقافة *'uqâfa-t*, cramp-iron, clasp.

عقاق *'aqâq*, disobedience; INF. of (عق); also *'iqâq*, being big with young (s.); — *'iqâq*, pl. of عقق *'uquq*, pregnant, عقوق *'aqûq*, bitter.

عقاقير *'aqâqîr*, pl. of عقار *'aqqâr*; — ى *'aqâqîriyy*, druggist.

عقاقيل *'aqâqîl*, pl. of عقنقل *'aqanqal*.

عقال *'iqâl*, annual tax; pl. *'uqul*, foot-rope, tether; (m.) head-band; — *'uqqâl*, lameness of a horse; pl. of عاقل *'âqil*, reasonable, &c.

عقام *'aqâm*, pl. *'uqamâ'*, barren,

sterile; unaffected; — *'iqâm*, pl. of عقيم *'aqîm*; — *'uqâm*, disastrous, calamitous.

(عقب) *'aqab*, U, INF. *'aqb*, beat on the heel; follow at one's heels, follow, succeed; pursue, persecute, spy after; wrap a sinew round the arrow; — II. INF. *ta'qîb*, follow at one's heels; kick with the heel; wait, tarry; let one thing succeed another, repeat in quick succession; try repeatedly to obtain; wait after prayer quietly for the next prayer-time; stay and wait; turn or look round; grow yellow; — III. INF. *mu'âqaba-t*, follow at one's heels; do a thing alternately with; come or use alternately, relieve (as a guard); be alternately used or employed; INF. *'iqâb*, punish for a transgression; carry off booty or gain; — IV. INF. *i'qâb*, follow, succeed; ride alternately with (acc.); let one thing succeed another, bring on; use alternately for one another; befall at intervals; die and leave children; reward, requite; return a borrowed pot with some broth, &c., left in it as a compensation; — V. INF. *ta'aqqub*, fall upon from behind; follow at one's heels; punish; requite with evil; doubt and inquire repeatedly, inquire minutely; learn the issue or result; try to entrap or to make stumble; — VI. INF. *ta'âqub*, succeed one another, alternate; be punished; — VIII. INF. *i'tiqâb*, succeed, come after; do alternately; retain, retain goods until full payment; obtain or find ultimately; — X. INF. *isti'qâb*, expect or wish for as a final result; follow one's track; try to entrap or to make stumble.

عقب *'aqb*, pl. *'iqâb*, run of a horse immediately after a first run; *'aqb*, son, grandson, offspring, progeny; heel; what follows immediately; — *'uqb*, pl. *a'qâb*, *'uqub*, end, issue; consequence, result; — *'aqab*, iron at the lower end of a lance; — *'aqib*, pl. *a'qâb*, heel; end; children, progeny; — ة *'iqba-t*, track, trace; traces of beauty; rest, remainder; sediment, dregs; — *'uqba-t*, progeny; rotation, revolution (of time); turn, alternative (*'uqbat-an*, once); — *'uqba-t*, *'iqba-t*, external, extraneous; — *'aqaba-t*, pl. *'iqâb*, hill, mountain, high place; steep road; pl. *'aqab*, sinew, tendon.

عقبا *'uqbâ*, for عقبى *'uqba*.

عقبان *'uqbân*, end of the month; — *'uqbân*, *'iqbân*, pl. of عقاب *'uqâb*.

عقبر *'aqbar*, dwelling-place of the genii; — ى *'aqbariyy*, sprite, fairy, goblin.

(عقبل), II. INF. *ta'aqbul*, come immediately after another; — ة *'uqbila-t*, immediate successor.

عقبول *'uqbûl*, ة *'uqbûla-t*, pl. *'aqâbil*, traces; remains, remainders; calamity.

عقبى *'uqba*, end, issue; reward, recompense, requital, punishment; life eternal.

(عقد) *'aqad*, I, INF. *'aqd*, tie, knit, make a knot; conclude a bargain or contract; build across (bridge); place (the crown upon one's head); make one (ل *li*) a leader; warrant; set (one's heart) upon; form seed-pods; make an arch or vault; count; pass. be gathered; — *'aqid*, A, INF. *'aqad*, speak with an impediment; be on the point of forming (seed-pod); thicken (n.), get consistent; hang together (dogs); — II. INF. *ta'qîd*, tie together with a knot, connect; arch, vault; thicken (a.), make consistent (by boiling, &c.); — III. INF. *mu'âqada-t*,

conclude a contract or compact with; — IV. INF. *i'qâd*, thicken, (a.) make consistent; — V. INF. *ta'aqqud*, be tied together; be entangled, complicated; be arched, like an arch; thicken (n.), grow consistent; be heaped up; — VI. INF. *ta'âqud*, make a compact, a covenant between one another; hang together; — VII. INF. *in'iqâd*, be tied together, connected; be established, concluded; be arched; cease to flow (milk in the breast); be transferred to; — VIII. INF. *i'tiqâd*, be tied together, connected; be hard and knotty; believe firmly; acquire; — X. INF. *isti'qâd*, believe; be credulous, superstitious; rut, be hot.

عقد *'aqd*, tying together (s.), binding (صاحب العقد والحل *ṣâḥib al-'aqd wa 'l-ḥall*, lord of binding and loosening, possessor of supreme power); making of magic knots; tie, bond; connection, cohesion; alloy; pl. *'uqûd*, denary number; compact, contract, covenant; seed-pod; pl. *'uqûd*, *'uqûdât*, vault, arch; opinion, belief; — *'iqd*, pl. *'uqûd*, knot; neck-lace; *al-'uqûd*, doubloons; *'uqûd*, thick shrubs; عقود الحساب *'uqûd al-ḥiṣâb*, total of an account; — *'aqid*, knotty; short but strong; thick, impervious; difficult; ع اللسان, speaking with an impediment; — ة *'uqda-t*, pl. *'uqad*, knot; difficulty; plot of a drama; magic knot; thong of a whip; joint; bundle; compact, covenant; fief, feudal estate; vault; — *'aqada-t*, base of the tongue; — also *'aqida-t*, sand-hill.

(عقر) *'aqar*, I, INF. *'aqr*, wound, make sore; hough; jade; destroy; cut out the top together with the pith (of a palm-tree to make it wither); eat green-food; keep fettered a long time; meet with game; — I, INF. *'aqr*, *'uqr*, *'aqâr*, be sterile, barren; — *'aqir*, A, INF. *'aqar*, be almost petrified with terror; — *'aqur*, INF. *'uqr*, *'aqâra-t*, *'uqâra-t*, be sterile, barren; be unsuccessful, resultless; — II. INF. *ta'qîr*, make very sore; hough; — III. INF. *mu'âqara-t*, vie with the enemy in houghing; taunt, defame, insult; persist, persevere in (acc.); be addicted to; — IV. INF. *i'qâr*, terrify, startle, dumbfound; possess many estates; afflict a woman with a uterine disease or with barrenness; leave a field fallow; — V. INF. *ta'aqqur*, last; be thick everywhere (fat of a camel); be high; be back-sore; — VI. INF. *ta'âqur*, vie in houghing; — VII. INF. *in'iqâr*, be wounded, hurt, sore, back-sore; be maimed; be kept in chains a long time; (m.) be in love; — VIII. INF. *i'tiqâr*, be hurt, back-sore; observe the flight of birds without being able to interpret it; let the wine out of the skin bag; — X. INF. *isti'qâr*, howl.

عقر *'aqr*, soreness of the back; palace, castle; — *'uqr*, pl. *a'qâr*, middle and principal part of the house; most intense heat of the fire; the best verses; dowry; damages for defloration; barrenness, sterility; food, green-meat; بيضة الع *baiḍa-t al-'aqr*, cock's egg, anything impossible; — *'aqar*, calamity; — *'uqar*, making sore (adj.); — *'uqur*, pl. of عقور *'aqûr*; — *'uqqar*, pl. of عاقر *'âqir*, barren, &c.; — ة *'aqra-t*, *'uqra-t*, barrenness, sterility; — *'uqara-t*, suffering from a womb-disease; making the back sore; an amulet worn by women.

عقرا *'aqrâ'*, high, heaped up.

(عقرب) *'aqrab*, n. u. and f. ة, scorpion; pl. *'aqârib*, needle; (m.)

hand of a watch; sting; tack; bolt (for shooting); latchet; hook, cramp-iron, clasp; — *'aqraba-t*, alert maid-servant; — *aqrab*, INF. ة, bend, curve, make crooked; — II. INF. *ta'aqrub*, be curved, crooked.

عقربا *'aqrabâ'*, female, and—

عقربان *'aqrabân*, male scorpion.

عقرطل *'aqarṭal*, *'iqarṭal*, female elephant.

عقرق *'uqurruq*, frog.

عقرى *'aqra*, having the menses; pl. of عقير *'aqîr*; — *'uqra*, immovables; landed estate.

(عقز) *'aqaz*, INF. *'aqz*, swarm (ants).

(عقش) *'aqaś*, bend; gather, collect.

(عقص) *'aqaṣ*, I, INF. *'aqṣ*, twist and plait; sting, bite; — *'aqiṣ*, A, INF. *'aqaṣ*, be miserly and malicious; be curved round the ears (horn of a wether); — II. INF. *ta'qîṣ*, sting, bite; feel a sting (m.); — V. INF. *ta'aqquṣ*, VII. INF. *in'iqâṣ*, be stung or bitten.

عقص *'aqṣ*, sting, bite; — *'aqiṣ*, miserly; malicious; — ة *'aqṣa-t*, sting; stinging (s.); — *'iqṣa-t*, pl. *'iqaṣ*, *'iqâṣ*, plait of hair adorned with jewels, pearls, &c.; — *'uqṣa-t*, knot, knob.

عقصا *'aqṣâ'*, f. of اعقص *a'qaṣ*, having the horns bent backwards, &c.

(عقط) *'aqaṭ*, I, INF. *'aqṭ*, wrap round, enfold, bind up.

(عقعق) *'aq'aq*, pl. *'aqâ'iq*, magpie; — hence *'aq'aq*, INF. ة, chatter, be garrulous.

(عقف) *'aqaf*, I, INF. *'aqf*, bend, curve, make crooked; wind, twist, plait; — II. INF. *ta'qîf*, id.; — V. INF. *ta'aqquf*, VII. INF. *in'iqâf*, be bent, curved.

عقف *'aqf*, fox; — ة *'uqfa-t*, bend, curve.

عقفا *'aqfâ'*, f. iron hook like a stick, cramp-iron; f. of اعقف *a'qaf*, bent, crooked, &c.

(عقفر) *'aqfar*, INF. ة, IV. *i'qranfar*, INF. *i'qrinfâr*, ruin; — II. INF. *ta'aqfur*, perish.

عقق *'aqaq*, INF. of (عق); — *'iqaq*, pl. of عقة *'iqqa-t*; — *'uqaq*, disobedient; — *'uquq*, pl. *'iqâq*, big with young; pl. of عقوق *'aqûq*; — ة *'aqaqa-t*, pl. of عاق *'âqq*, disobedient, &c.

(عقل) *'aqal*, I, INF. *'aql*, tie up; — I, U, INF. *'aql*, constipate, astringe; — I, INF. *'aql*, *ma'qûl*, possess one's full intellect, be endowed with reason, be reasonable; I, INF. *'aql*, understand, comprehend; atone for murder by money, pay blood-money; renounce revenge for blood-money; consecrate to a pious purpose; — I, INF. *'aql*, *'uqûl*, ascend a mountain; take refuge with (الى *'ila*); trip up; feed on the plant عاقول *'âqûl*; — *'aqil*, A, INF. *'aqal*, be knock-kneed; — II. INF. *ta'qîl*, make reasonable; be very reasonable; tie up the legs of a camel; bear sour grapes; — III. *mu'âqala-t*, vie in understanding, intellect; be equal with reference to the blood-money; — IV. INF. *i'qâl*, deem or find reasonable, intelligent; pay an annual tax; have a very short shadow (at mid-day); — V. INF. *ta'aqqul*, show one's self reasonable or intelligent; join the hands so as to help another to mount; cross the legs; — VI. INF. *ta'âqul*, vie in reasonableness; feign prudence; be willing to revenge or to make atonement by money for blood-shed among themselves; — VIII. INF. *i'tiqâl*, tie up the legs of a camel; cross the legs; take between one's legs; put the lance between the leg and stirrup; trip up; tremble, shake; accept blood-money for the murdered; pass. be bound, imprisoned.

عقل *'aql*, pl. *'uqûl*, understanding, reason, intellect; sound judgment; wisdom; Holy Ghost; heart, mind; memory; asylum; fortress; blood-money; — *'uqul*, pl. of عقال *'iqâl*; — ة *'uqla-t*, pl. *'uqal*, tripping up (s.); a spell; impediment of the tongue.

عقلا *'aqlâ'*, f. of اعقل *a'qal*, more reasonable, &c.; — *'uqalâ'*, pl. of عاقل *'âqil*, reasonable, &c.

عقلى *'aqliyy*, ة, mental, spiritual, intellectual; philosophical; prudent; — pl. f. *'aqliyyât*, objects of meditation.

(عقم) *'aqam*, U, INF. *'aqm*, *'uqm*,— *'aqim*, A, INF. *'aqam*,—*'aqum* and pass. *'uqim*, be barren; — *'aqam*, I, INF. *'aqm*, make barren; pass. dry up, wither; — *'aqim*, A, INF. *'aqam*, be silent; — II. INF. *ta'qîm*, make barren; silence; — III. INF. *mu'âqama-t*, dispute with, quarrel with (acc.); — IV. INF. *i'qâm*, make barren; — VI. INF. *ta'âqum*, be punished; — VIII. INF. *i'tiqâm*, try the first water in digging a well to see whether it is worth while to dig on.

عقم *'aqm*, *'iqm*, ة *'aqma-t*, *'iqma-t*, red, variegated; — *'uqm*, barrenness; — ة *'aqama-t*, phase of the moon;—ى *'aqma*, pl. of عقيم *'aqîm*; — *'uqmiyy*, antiquated; noble, of high rank or birth, liberal.

(عقنقل) *'aqanqal*, pl. *'aqâqil*, broad valley; sand-hill; cup; sword.

(عقو) *'aqâ*, U, INF. *'aqw*, prevent, detain, delay; be hoisted, raised high; (also VIII.) meet with a lateral source in digging a well; — U, I, abhor; — VIII. INF. *i'tiqâ'*, see I.; be prevented; — ة *'aqwa-t*, pl. *'iqâ'*, house, manor; yard, open place in front of the house; surroundings of a house; precinct.

عقوب *'aqûb*, successor; — *; — ة *'uqûba-t*, punishment.

عقود *'uqûd*, عقودات *'uqûdât*, pl. of عقد *'aqd*.

عقور *'aqûr*, pl. *'uqur*, given to biting; mordacious; oppressive, making the back sore (saddle); wounded, sore.

عقوص *'uqûṣ*=عقيصة *'aqîṣa-t*;—*'aqqûṣ*, sting, prickle.

عقوق *'aqûq*, pl. *'uquq*, *'iqâq*, big with young; — *'uqûq*, disobedience, revolt; resistance; INF. of (عق).

عقول *'aqûl*, reasonable, intelligent, prudent, wise; astringent (s.); — *

(عقى) *'aqa*, I, INF. *'aqy*, give to drink, water; abhor, detest; drop the first excrement; — II. INF. *ta'qiya-t*, give to drink, water; shoot an arrow into the air; soar high; pass. come; — IV. INF. *i'qâ'*, be very bitter; find bitter and spit out; — VIII. pass. *u'tuqî*, come.

عقى *'iqy*, pl. *a'qâ'*, first excrement of a new-born.

عقيان *'iqyân*, pure gold.

عقيب *'aqîb*, succeeding immediately.

عقيد *'aqîd*, ة, connected, tied together; thickened, consistent; allied; bound by contract, by one's word, &c.; (m.) commander of an army; — ة *'aqîda-t*, pl. *'aqâ'id*, article of creed; creed, belief; religious conviction; conserves of roses; sweets.

عقير *'aqîr*, ة, pl. *'aqra*, wounded; back-sore; houghed; lamed; perplexed, dumbfounded; childless; —*'iqqîr*, pl. *'aqâqîr*, a tree; — ة *'aqîra-t*, wounded animal; (m.) game; (m.) carcass, carrion; voice of one weeping, singing, reading, shrill note.

عقيص *'iqqîṣ*, miser; tripe, guts, bowels; — ة *'aqîṣa-t*, tress of hair with its adornments.

عقيق *'aqîq*, ة, pl. *'aqâ'iq*, agate; cornelian; coral; any adorn-

ment of red stones for the neck; pl. *a'iqqa-t*, bed of a torrent; ravine; — ة *'aqîqa-t*, flash of lightning; hair of the new-born; feast of the first hair-cut; patron's day; sacrifice of atonement, alms.

عقيلة *'aqîla-t*, the most noble and precious part of anything; what is kept jealously (woman, &c.).

عقيلى *'uqqaila*, unripe fruit.

عقيم *'aqîm*, ة, pl. *'aqâ'im*, *'uqum*, *'uqm*, sterile, barren; pl. *'uqamâ'*, *'iqâm*, *'aqma*, childless; in vain, useless; to no purpose; this world; disastrous, calamitous; day of the last Judgment.

(عك) *'akk*, U, INF. *'akk*, be very sultry and without wind; importune or vex repeatedly, tire, weary, disturb, worry; be continuous; ask to be told the same thing over again; attack; conquer, convict; beat, whip, flog; delay payment; explain; prevent; open a road; change the colour of one's hair; — III. INF. *mu'âkka-t*, attack; — IV. INF. *i'kâk*, change the colour of her hair after having conceived (she-camel).

عك *'akk*, perseverance, endurance; sultry, close; brave; also ة *'akka-t*, violent attack of fever; — ة *'akka-t*, *'ukka-t*, pl. *'ikâk*, oppressive heat; Ascalon or Acre; — *'ukka-t*, pl. *'ukak*, *'ikâk*, bag for making butter.

عكا *'akkâ'*, Acre; — *'ikâ'*, pl. of عكوة *'akwa-t*.

عكاب *'ukâb*, smoke, dust.

عكابس *'ukâbis*, large number of camels (1000).

عكار *'akâr*, sediment, dregs; — *'akkâr*, who attacks repeatedly.

عكاز *'akkâz*, ة *'akkâza-t*, pl. *'akâkiz*, *'akâkîz*, stick mounted with iron; crutch; shepherd's staff; crosier of a bishop.

عكاس *'ikâs*, rope for a camel.

عكاش *'ukkâś*, ة *'ukkâśa-t*, spider; spider-web; *'ukkâś*, flag; — ة *'akâśa-t*, awkwardness, clumsiness; embarrassment (m.).

عكاظ *'ukâẕ*, the old market or fair of Mecca; — ى *'ukâẕiyy*, goods from there (leather).

عكاك *'ikâk*, sultriness; pl. of عكة *'akka-t*, *'ukka-t*.

عكاكز *'akâkiz*, عكاكيز *'akâkîz*, pl. of عكازة *'akkâza-t*.

عكال *'ikâl*, rope for a camel, string; chains, fetters.

عكالد *'ukâlid*, thick milk.

عكام *'ikâm*, pl. *'ukum*, pack-cloth or string for bales of merchandise; — *'akkâm*, packer, loader, camel-driver, &c.; pitcher of a tent.

عكامس *'ukâmis*, very dark; = عكابس *'ukâbis*.

(عكان) *'ikăn*, neck.

(عكب) *'akab*, U, INF. *'ukûb*, stop, stand; boil; — *'akib*, A, INF. *'akab*, have a heavy chin and thick lips; have the fingers or toes set close together; — II. INF. *ta'kîb*, smoke; — V. INF. *ta'akkub*, occupy entirely, engross, dominate; — VIII. INF. *i'tikâb*, raise dust; be raised.

عكب *'akb*, dust; nimble, alert, brisk; — *'akab*, thickness; — *'ukub*, pl. of عنكب *'ankab*; — *'ikkab*, thick-set dwarf.

عكبا *'akbâ'*, f. thick and ugly.

(عكبز) *'ukbuz*, gland of the penis.

(عكبس) *'ukabis*, large number of camels (about 1000); — II. INF. *ta'akbus*, be heaped or piled upon one another.

(عكبش) *'akbaś*, INF. ة, fasten with a string; — II. INF. *ta'akbuś*, adhere firmly.

عكث *'akṯ*, concord, union.

(عكد) *'akad*, I, INF. *'akd*, be possible, become possible for (acc.); flee, seek refuge; — *'akid*, A, INF. *'akad*, be fat; persist in (ب *bi*); — IV. INF. *i'kâd*, flee; — VIII. INF. *i'tikâd*, persist, be

zealous in (acc.); — X. INF. *isti'kâd*, be fat; cling to for refuge.

عكد *'ukd*, middle; — *'akad*, ة *'akada-t*, base of the tongue; — *'akid*, ة, fat; — ة *'akda-t*, extremity of the back-bone; power, might, strength.

(عكر) *'akar*, I, INF. *'akr*, *'ukûr*, return to the attack; run away with the rider and return to its own people (camel); (m.) trouble, make turbid; — *'akir*, A, INF. *'akar*, be turbid, muddy; — II. INF. *ta'kîr*, trouble, make turbid, dirty; grieve (a.); — IV. INF. *i'kâr*, have a troop of camels; be fat; be grieved, moved; — VI. INF. *ta'âkur*, mix together, mingle; — VIII. INF. *i'tikâr*, be very dark; bring dense clouds of dust; attack repeatedly and mix in combat; be lasting and vigorous.

عكر *'ikr*, root, origin; — *'akar*, sediment, dregs, impurity; rust; — *'akir*, turbid, troubled, muddy, impure; — ة *'akra-t*, renewed attack; — *'akara-t*, pl. *'akar*, troop of camels (about 100).

(عكرد) *'akrad*, INF. ة, be fat and strong; run away with the rider and return to its people.

(عِكرش) *'ikriś*, a plant; — ة *'ikriśa-t*, female hare.

(عكرم) *'ikrim*, darkness; — ة *'ikrima-t*, pl. *'akârim*, dove.

(عكز) *'akaz*, INF. *'akz*, lean on a staff; walk on crutches; thrust the lance into the ground; be guided by (ب *bi*); — *'akiz*, A, INF. *'akaz*, be shrunk, wrinkled; — II. INF. *ta'kîz*, mount a lance with iron; lean on a staff; — V. INF. *ta'akkuz*, id.

عكز *'ikz*, malignant; miserly, avaricious.

(عكس) *'akas*, I, INF. *'aks*, turn topsy-turvy; reverse the order; go against the grain; do the contrary; distort the meaning; reflect light, reverberate; (m.) hinder, thwart; bring to fall, ruin morally, corrupt; tie up a camel to break it in; pour sour milk over a dish; — II. INF. *ta'kîs*, IV. INF. *i'kâs*, bring to fall, overthrow, make miserable; spoil, corrupt; — III. INF. *'ikâs*, *mu'âkasa-t*, engage in a hand to hand fight with, combat; (m.) thwart, bring to fall; — V. INF. *ta'akkus*, wind one's self like a snake in walking; — VII. INF. *in'ikâs*, be turned topsy-turvy; be reflected, mirror one's self; — VIII. INF. *i'tikâs*, be turned upside-down, be reversed; take a bad turn or issue.

عكس *'aks*, turning upside-down (s.), overthrow; rebound, reflection; echo; rumour; contrary (بالعكس *bi-'l-'aks*, on the contrary, vice versa, reciprocally, one another); — ى *'aksiyy*, contrary (adj.), contrariwise.

(عكش) *'akaś*, I, INF. *'akś*, gather, assemble, collect (a.); make a web; return to the attack; surround, hem in; bind fast; — *'akiś*, A, INF. *'akaś*, be dense, curly; — II. INF. *ta'kîś*, grow mouldy; — V. INF. *ta'akkuś*, be dense, curly; shrink; contract the feet for making a web.

عكش *'akiś*, collector; collection; curled; good-for-nothing, useless; (m.) awkward, clumsy.

(عكص) *'akaṣ*, I, INF. *'akṣ*, repel, drive back, turn off, refuse; — *'akiṣ*, A, INF. *'akaṣ*, be malignant; be restive, refractory; — V. INF. *ta'akkuṣ*, give scantily.

عكص *'akaṣ*, being thick-set (s.), compactness; malice; — *'akiṣ*, ة, malignant, mischievous; difficult (to pass through, to walk over).

(عكظ) *'akaẕ*, I, INF. *'akẕ*, keep back, prevent; rub; tame; — II. *ta'kîẕ*, keep back, prevent, hinder; render difficult, disturb; com-

mand more emphatically, give a stricter order; — III. INF. *mu'âkaẓa-t*, delay payment; — V. INF. *ta'akkuẓ*, be complicated and difficult; undertake a long and toilsome journey; — VI. INF. *ta'âkuẓ*, quarrel with one another; surpass one another in pride.

(عكف) *'akaf*, I, U, INF. *'akf*, bend, curve, fold; keep, retain; prevent; re-arrange anything brought out of order, restore, mend; — I, INF. *'ukûf*, stay, remain; attend to zealously; attach one's self to; surround, fly round, hover round; — also II. INF. *ta'kîf*, plait, dress the hair; — III. INF. *mu'âkafa-t*, cling to, be tied to one's apron-strings; — V. INF. *ta'akkuf*, abide permanently; — VII. INF. *in'ikâf*, id.; be folded, bent, curved; — VIII. INF. *i'tikâf*, attend to with zeal; attend assiduously to the mosque.

عكف *'akf*, bend, fold; hair-dress; — *'akif*, curled, frizzled; — also عاكف *'âkif*, pl. *'ukûf*, attending zealously or assiduously (adj.); — ة *'akfa-t*, curved knife.

عكك *'akak*, oppressive heat, sultriness, closeness; — *ukak*, pl. of عكّة *'ukka-t*.

(عكل) *'akal*, I, U, INF. *'akl*, collect (a.), drive together; put one thing upon another, pile up; keep in prison, keep captive; throw down; bind, tie up; carry on assiduously; suppose, surmise, think; say one's opinion in a matter; — *'akil*, A, INF. *'akal*, get dirty, greasy; be doubtful, unintelligible; — IV. INF. *i'kâl*, id.; — VIII. INF. *i'tikâl*, id.; retire, resign; attack one another with the horns.

عكل *'ikl*, *'akl*, pl. *a'kâl*, mean, vile, miserly; — *'ukul*, dwarfs, misers, &c., pl. of عاكل *'âkil*.

عكلد *'ukalid*, عكلط *'ukaliṭ*, thick milk.

(عكم) *'akam*, I, INF. *'akm*, wrap up in a cloth, make up a bale, embale; load an animal; fasten with a string, cord; wait for (الى *ila*), expect; attack; desist; be fat; keep close, preserve; pass. be prevented from visiting a person; — II. INF. *ta'kîm*, be very fat; — IV. INF. *i'kâm*, help one in embaling or loading; — VIII. INF. *i'tikâm*, equalise the two side-loads; be closely heaped up.

عكم *'ikm*, pl. *a'kâm*, pack-cloth; half of the load, load of one side; pulley of the well; pl. *'ukûm*, bundle of clothes; — *'ukum*, pl. of عكام *'ikâm*.

عكمس *'akmas*, INF. ة, be dark.

(عكن), ة *'ukna-t*, pl. *'ukan*, *a'kân*, fold of fat of the belly; — V. INF. *ta'akkun*, have folds of fat.

عكنكع *'akanka'*, male demon of the desert.

(عكو) *'akâ*, U, INF. *'akw*, tie the horse's tail into a knot; comb and tie up the hair; use the *izâr* as a large belt; rise; impregnate (the she-camel); put into chains; be big and fat; be kind towards one's own; keep the excrement partly back; — II. INF. *ta'kiya-t*, wrap a fresh sinew round the hand-piece of a lance, &c.; — ة *'akwa-t*, *'ukwa-t*, pl. *'uka-n*, *'ikâ'*, hairless base of a horse's tail; middle; time, turn; twisted sinews; trowser-band, belt.

عكوب *'akûb*, dust; eatable thistle; — *'ukûb*, crowd, throng; INF. of (عكب).

عكوز *'akwaz*=عكاز *'akkâz*.

عكوف *'ukûf*, pl. of عاكف *'âkif*, zealously attending, assiduous; — *.

(عكى) *'aka*, I, INF. *'aky*, also II. and IV. use the *izâr* as a large belt; die; — II. INF. *ta'kiya-t*,

IV. INF. *i'kâ'*, see I.; IV. put into chains.

عكى *'akiyy*, pure milk.

عكيس *'akîs*, vine-shoot; sour milk; mess of flour and sour milk; — ة *'akîsa-t*, dark night.

عكيك *'akîk*, pl. *'ikâk*, oppressive heat; paroxysm.

(عل) *'all*, I, U, INF. *'all*, water a second time or immediately after the first time, give plenty of water; beat unceasingly; — I, U, INF. *'all*, *'alal*, water, &c., as above; repeat, do over again; engross the mind; (m.) purify, refine; pass. be eaten of; — I, be ill, have an infirmity or defect; be protracted; — II. INF. *ta'lîl*, water repeatedly, do anything repeatedly; quiet by offering one thing instead of another one wished for, draw off the attention, divert, beguile; cause, be cause or pretext, discuss the reasons of anything, allege reasons or pretexts; purify, refine; — IV. INF. *i'lâl*, water repeatedly; drive the camels from the watering-place before they are satisfied, stint; afflict with an illness; — V. INF. *ta'allul*, occupy, divert, amuse one's self with anything; solace one's self, beguile one's self; sport with one's wife; get up after confinement; allege reasons or pretexts, excuse one's self; (m.) be purified, refined, of best quality; — VI. INF. *ta'âll*, exhaust the last strength; get up after confinement; — VII. INF. *in'ilâl*, be ill, have an infirmity; have one of the weak letters ا, و or ى; — VIII. INF. *i'tilâl*=VII.; allege reasons or pretexts; occupy, divert, beguile one's self; turn one from his occupation or purpose.

عل *'al*, what is above, at the top, uppermost; من عل *min 'al-in*, from on high; — *'al-in*, see على *'alî*; — *'all*, who frequents women; emaciated; *'ull*, id.; a large louse; — *'all-a*, perhaps, may be that, followed by the pronominal affixes and the aorist; — ة *'alla-t*, concubine, fellow-wife; — *'illa-t*, pl. *-ât*, *'ilal*, pl. pl. *a'lâl*, illness, suffering infirmity; wicked inclination; imperfection, defect; cause, reason; pretext, subterfuge; distraction, diversion; dirt; حروف العلة *ḥurûf al-'illa-t*, the weak letters ا, و and ى.

علا *'alâ*, high; — *'alâ'*, height, greatness, dignity; — ة *'alât*, pl. *'al-an*, *'alâ*, anvil.

علاب *'ilâb*, pl. of علبة *'ilba-t*; — *'ullâb*, *'alâb*, and — ى *'ullâbiyy*, *'alâbiyy*, lead, tin; — *'alâbiyy*, pl. of علبا *'ilbâ'*.

بنو علات *banû 'allât*, sons of the same father and different mothers.

علاثة *'ulâsa-t*, mixture; a mess of cheese.

علاج *'ilâj*, medical treatment, cure; management; medicine; — *

علاجيم *'alâjîm*, pl. of علجوم *'uljûm*.

علاد *'alâd-in*, ى *'alâdî*, pl. of علندى *'alanda*.

علاس *'ulâs*, anything to eat, eatable, food.

(علاص) *'ilâṣ*, money advanced against a share in the gain; — *.

علاط *'ilâṭ*, pl. *'uluṭ*, *a'liṭa-t*, rope round the neck of a camel; mark across a camel's neck; ring of a pigeon's neck; thread; gossamer; quarrel; calamity.

علاف *'allâf*, who provides food for animals; — *

علافيات *'ilâfiyât*, pl. strong pack-saddles.

علاق *'alâq*, ة *'alâqa-t*, pl. *'alâ'iq*, sufficient food; livelihood, profession, trade; relations; desire, longing; attachment, friendship; hatred, enmity; connection, reference; interest;

pulley of a well; bucket; morning-gift to the wife; — ة *'ilâqa-t*, pl. *'alâ'iq*, straps, ropes, &c., for suspending (also *'allâqa-t*); bond; true love; — ية *'alâqiya-t*, attached, devoted; pl. *'ulâqa*, title, nickname.

علاك *'alâk*, *'ulâk*, anything eatable, what can be chewed; — *'allâk*, seller of mastic for chewing; quack, mountebank; silly talker.

علالم *'alâlim*, worlds, pl. of عالم *'âlam*.

علالة *'ulâla-t*, distraction, diversion; remains, remainders, a drop.

علالى *'alâliyy*, pl. of *'illiyya-t*.

علام *'alâm*, sign; aim; — *'ilâm*, pl. of علم *'alam*; — *'ulâm*, *'ullâm*, sparrow-hawk; — *'allâm*, omniscient; very learned; — *'ullâm*, very learned; pl. of عالم *'âlim*, knowing, &c.; — ة *'alâma-t*, pl. *'alâm*, *'alâ'im*, sign, token, mark; signature; symbol; symptom, diagnosis; flag, standard; pedigree; stone as a road-mark; boundary-stone; phenomenon, prodigy (pl. *'alâ'im*, rain-bow); noise; — *'allâma-t*, very learned man, great scholar; — *'ullâma-t*, indication, proof, demonstration; — ى *'allâmiyy*, very wise, prudent.

علاميد *'alâmîd*, pl. of علماد *'ilmâd*.

علان *'ilân*, acting openly (s.), INF. III. of (علن); — *'allân*, ة, ignorant, stupid.

علاند *'alânid*, pl. of علندى *'alanda*.

علانى *'alâniyy*, ة, pl. *-ûn*, public, notorious, generally known; — ة *'alâniyya-t*, publicity, notoriety, general spread.

علاه *'ilâh*, ى *'alâha*, pl. of علهان *'alhân*.

علاوة *'alâwa-t*, superabundance, excess; height; also *'ulâwa-t*, the topmost and best part of; — *ilâwa-t*, pl. *'alâwa*, *'alâwiyy*, what is at the top of something else; addition, supplement, appendix; increase.

علائق *'alâ'iq*, pl. of علاقة *'alâqa-t* and عليقة *'alîqa-t*.

علائم *'alâ'im*, pl. of علامة *'alâma-t*.

علاية *'alâya-t*, height; high place.

(علب) *'alab*, U, INF. *'alb*, (also II.) mark by an incision or impression; cut off; I, U, (also II.) twist a fresh sinew round the hilt of a sword; be hard, rough; grow hard and offensive to the smell (meat); — *'alib*, A, INF. *'alab*, be hard, rough, tough; grow thick and woody; be offensive to the smell; be blunted; have a sore throat on both sides; — II. INF. *ta'lîb*, see I.; — X. INF. *isti'lâb*, be offensive to the smell; find (the food) too coarse and loathsome.

علب *'alb*, pl. *'ulûb*, impression, trace, mark; stony place (also *'ilb*, pl. *'ulûb*); — *'ilb*, *'ulb*, *'alib*, old and tough; — ة *'ilba-t*, a hard wood; also *'ulba-t*, pl. *'ulab*, *'ilâb*, box, band-box, chest, trunk; ع نشوق *'ilba-t naśûq*, snuff-box; bucket; high palm-tree.

علبا *'ilbâ'*, *'albâ*, pl. *'alâb-in*, *'alâbî*, muscle or nerve of the neck.

علبوبة *'ulbûba-t*, better sort of people, educated classes.

علبى *'alba*, pierce the neck-muscle of a slave; have a strongly-marked neck-nerve.

(علث) *'alas*, I, INF. *'als*, mix; gather, collect (a.); knead, rub, dress (leather); give no fire; — *'alis*, A, INF. *'alas*, fight unceasingly and violently; lay traps for, try to impute a crime to (ل *li*); be attached, devoted; make in an imperfect manner; — VIII. INF. *i'tilâs*, take without choosing; make a chance match.

علث *'alis*, supposed bastard; — ة *'ulsa-t*, food for the day.

(علج) *'alaj*, INF. *'alj*, surpass in management, attendance, care, &c.; — III. INF. *'ilâj*, *mu'âlaja-t*,

take in hand, handle, manipulate, manage, vie with another in anything; nurse, treat medically, cure; try to help one; wrestle, fight; (m.) quarrel, dispute; (m.) barter for the price; — VI. INF. *ta'âluj*, carry on in common; treat one's self or have one's self treated medically; brawl, quarrel, barter with one another; — VIII. INF. *i'tilâj*, wrestle; clash together; be luxuriantly grown over; — X. INF. *isti'lâj*, grow thick.

علج *'ilj*, pl. *'ulûj*, *a'lâj*, *ma'lûjâ'*, *ma'lûja*, *'ilaja-t*, infidel and barbarian; renegade; strong wild ass; rough, wild, savage; — *'alij*, *'ulaj*, *'ullaj*, grave and able.

علجان *'alajân*, a plant; rocking walk of a she-camel.

علجم *'aljam*, long, tall.

علجوم *'uljûm*, pl. *'alâjîm*, strong, powerful, fit for work (camel); male frog; duck; wave, billow; wild he-goat; dragon; louse; palm-garden; deep water.

(علد) *'alid*, A, INF. *'alad*, be hard; — XIII. INF. *i'liwwâd*, be heavy; — XV. INF. *i'lindâ'*, be big and fat.

(علز) *'aliz*, A, INF. *'alaz*, be restless; — IV. INF. *i'lâz*, weaken.

علز *'aliz*, restless; miserly.

(علس) *'alas*, I, INF. *'als*, enjoy; eat, drink; — II. INF. *ta'lîs*, give to eat or drink; increase (n.); cry out.

علس *'als*, food and drink; — *'alas*, big louse; a kind of ant; lentil; a kind of wheat.

علش *'alś*, greed.

(علص), II. *'allaṣ*, INF. *ta'lîṣ*, cause stomach-ache or indigestion; — III. INF. *'ilâṣ*, fight with, try to beat; — VIII. INF. *i'tilâṣ*, receive little; — ة *'ulṣa-t*, a little, a trifle.

(علض) *'alaḍ*, I, INF. *'alḍ*, shake a thing to pull it out.

(علط) *'alaṭ*, I, U, INF. *'alṭ*, (also II.) mark a camel across the neck; slander, revile; shoot at; — II. INF. *ta'lîṭ*, see I.; take the rope from the neck; — VIII. INF. *i'tilâṭ*, begin to quarrel with (acc. and ب *bi*); — XIII. INF. *i'liwwâṭ*, take hold of the camel's neck and mount it; ride a camel without bridle and saddle; cling to; cover (male camel); engage thoughtlessly in a matter; captivate and bind.

علط *'alṭ*, patch or spot of beauty; — *'uluṭ*, pl. of اعليط *i'lîṭ*, mark across a camel's neck, &c., and علاط *'ilâṭ*; — ة *'ulṭa-t*, chain for the neck, necklace; = *'alṭ*.

(علطس) *'alṭas*, INF. ة, wander without a guide.

(علعل) *'al'al*, extremity of the chest-bone; — also علعال *'âl'âl*, lark; — II. INF. *ta'al'ul*, be loose and rickety.

علعول *'al'ûl*, waving to and fro, undulating; combat; lasting.

(علف) *'alaf*, I, INF. *'alf*, feed (a.); drink much; — II. INF. *ta'lîf*, feed well, batten (also IV.); form seed-pods; bear pods (also IV.); — IV. INF. *i'lâf*, see II.; — V. INF. *ta'alluf*, be well fed, grow fat; — VIII. INF. *i'tilâf* = V.; pluck the food with the lips; — X. INF. *isti'lâf*, ask for food by neighing; grow fat.

علف *'ilf*, drunkard; glutton; also *'ulf*, a tree; — *'ulf*, *'uluf*, pl. of علوفة *'alûfa-t*; — *'alaf*, pl. *'ilâf*, *a'lâf*, *'ulûf*, grass, hay, green-meat; food; — *'ullaf*, fruit of the acacia; — ة *'alfa-t*, feeding (s.); meal.

(علفص) *'alfaṣ*, INF. ة, order, command, advise imperiously; compel; try in vain to trip up.

(علفط) *'alfaṭ*, INF. ة, mix (a.).

(علفق) *'alfaq*, moss, sea-weed, &c., on the top of the water.

(علق) *'alaq*, U, INF. *'alq*, also *'aliq*. A, INF. *'alaq*, browse leaves from high trees;—U, INF. *'alq*, revile; —*'aliq*, A, INF. *'alaq*, hang on, be suspended, tied to, hooked in (ب *bi*, فى *fi* or acc.); cleave to; be caught in a snare, trap or net; begin (followed by an aor.);— INF. *'ilq*, *'alaq*, *'ulûq*, *'alâqa-t*, be attached to, love; cling to; know, learn; conceive by (من), get big with (ب); pass. adhere;— II. INF. *ta'lîq*, append, suspend, tie to, hook in or to; make marginal notes, extract superficially; hang the food-bag round an animals neck; set leeches; give one a camel with provisions to take with him; (m.) mount afresh (an iron tool); (m.) ignite, catch fire; (m.) break out; (m.) kindle; (m.) lock up; pass. be in love;— III. INF *mu'âlaqa-t*, lay a wager with (acc.), bet one;— IV. INF. *i'lâq*, append, attach, tie together, fasten; set leeches; captivate, gain one's affection; set the claws in; have the prey in a snare, trap or net; provide a thing with a noose, thong or handle to suspend it by; find anything precious; bring on a great calamity;— V. INF. *ta'alluq*, be suspended from, attached to; adhere firmly; be devoted to; fall in love with, devote one's self to (all followed by ب *bi*); tie (an amulet, &c.) round one's neck; do a thing superficially, slur over; put forth roots;— VIII. INF. *i'tilâq*, adhere to, hold on to (ب *bi*); love (acc.);— X. INF. *isti'lâq*, try to get a hold on, to make one's self a hanger-on.

علق *'ilq*, ة, pl. *'uluq*, *a'lâq*, anything precious; livelihood, earnings; shield; sword; leather bag; addicted to;—*'alaq*, what sticks to, holds on to (also *'aliq*, pl. *'ulûq*); leech; curdled blood; gallows-bird;—ة *'ulqa-t*, attachment, affection, love; pl. *'ulaq*, sufficient food or earnings, sufficiency; something; pl. *-ât*, property; riches, wealth; precious possession;— *'alaqa-t*, pl. *-ât*, leech; drop of blood.

(علقم) *'alqam*, ة, pl. *'alâqim*, coloquintida; anything bitter;— *'alqam*, INF. ة, be bitter; make bitter;—ة *'alqama-t*, bitterness.

(علك) *'alak*, I, U, INF. *'alk*, chew and turn about in the mouth; chew the bit; gnash the teeth; (m.) talk silly things;— II. INF. *ta'lîk*=I.; knead, rub or work a thing well; administer well a fortune;— XIV. INF. *i'linkâk*, be dense, thick.

علك *'ilk*, pl. *'ulûk*, gum fit to be chewed, mastic;— *'alak*, paste; —*'alik*, fit to be chewed; elastic; pliable; tough like gum; pl. *'alikât*, molar teeth;—ة *'ilka-t* =*'ilk*; what is chewed and turned about in the mouth; trifle, nothingness, a thing of no value.

علكد *'alkad*, *'ilkid*, *'ulkud*, thick, big.

(علكس), IV. INF. *i'linkâs*, be dark.

(علكم) *'alkam*, thick;—ة *'alkama-t*, thickness.

علل *'alal*, INF. of (عل);— *'ilal*, pl. of علة *'illa-t*.

(علم) *'alam*, I, U, INF. *'alm*, mark, denote, put a sign to;— I, INF. *'alm*, split the upper lip;— U, INF. *'alm*, surpass in knowledge; — *'alim*, A, INF. *'ilm*, know, learn; notice; be aware of; excel by knowledge; distinguish from (من *min*); establish well and solidly; INF. *'ilm*, have the upper lip split;— II. INF. *ta'lîm*, *'illâm*, teach, make known to (2 acc.); be a teacher; sign (a document, &c.); make one's self recognisable by a

sign or token; — III. INF. *mu'âlama-t*, vie in knowledge; — IV. INF. *i'lâm*, let know, make known to, inform; mark one's merchandise with a sign; make one's horse or one's self recognisable by a sign; — V. INF. *ta'allum*, learn; instruct one's self, study; know, understand; establish well and solidly; — VI. INF. *ta'âlum*, know, understand; — X. INF. *isti'lâm*, want to know, inquire, question one about a thing (2 acc.).

علم *'alm*, beings, creatures; world; — *'ilm*, pl. *'ulûm*, knowledge, science; scholarship, learnedness; communication; theory; art; known; — *'alam*, sign, token, mark; pattern; boundary or road-mark; flag, standard, colours; strip of cloth, lacing (s.), hem; epaulet, shoulder-piece; split in the upper lip; proper noun, name; chieftain, principal person; glory (of a land or people); pl. *'ilâm*, *a'lâm*, mountain, hill.

علما *'almâ'*, f. of اعلم *a'lam*, more learned, &c.; — *'ulamâ'*, pl. of عليم *'alîm*.

علماد *'ilmâd*, ة *'ilmâda-t*, pl. *'alâmida-t*, *'alâmîd*, anything to be coiled up; clue, hank, skein, thread.

علمانى *'ilmâniyy*, worldly; layman.

علمدار *'alamdâr*, pl. *'alamdâriyya-t*, standard-bearer, colour-bearer, ensign (m.).

علمى *'ilmiyy*, ة, scientific, referring to science or knowledge.

(علن) *'alan*, I, U, INF. *'aln*, *'ulûn*, *'alâniya-t*, become manifest, public; make known, publish, reveal; — *'alin*, A, INF. *'alan*, — also *'alun*, become publicly known, transpire; — III. INF. *'ilân*, *mu'âlana-t*, act openly towards; reveal, communicate to (2 acc.); — IV. INF. *i'lân*, reveal, publish, make known, notify, advertise; act openly; — VIII. INF. *i'tilân*, become publicly known; — X. INF. *isti'lân*, id.; be revealed.

علن *'alan*, publicity; *'alan-an*, publicly, notoriously; — ة *'ulana-t*, blabber.

علنداة *'alandât*, a thorny plant.

(علندس) *'alandas*, ة, strong; lion.

(علندى) *'alanda*, *'ulanda*, pl. *'alânid*, *'alâd-in*, *'alâdî*, big and strong; — also —

علنى *'alaniyy*, ة, public, manifest, notorious; — ة *'alaniyya-t*, publicity, notoriety.

(عله) *'alih*, A, INF. *'alah*, be intoxicated; be stunned, thunderstruck, dumbfounded; run to and fro from terror; become subject to reproach; be vile, malignant; be hungry; be brisk, shake the bridle from playfulness.

علهان *'alhân*, f. *'alha*, pl. *'ilâh*, *'alâha*, hungry; fiery, mettled; ostrich.

(علهج) *'alhaj*, INF. ة, soften a hide by the fire (to eat it in time of famine); a tree.

(علهد) *'alhad*, INF. ة, feed well (a.).

(علهس) *'alhas*, INF. ة, handle roughly.

(علهص) *'alhaṣ*, علهض *'alhaḍ*, try to uncork a bottle; try to pull out an eye; treat roughly; obtain from (من *min*).

علهى *'alha*, f. of علهان *'alhân*.

(علو) *'alâ*, U, INF. *'uluww*, be high, highly situated; excel, be eminent, sublime; be proud, haughty; tower above; be at the summit of; rise; be advanced; set on high, raise, exalt, make great; mount; ride upon (acc.); overpower, conquer; press down; pierce from above; — على *'ala*, I, INF. *'aly*, *'iliyy*, ascend, mount; — *'alî*, A, INF. *'alâ'*, be high, elevated, sublime; stand high in au-

thority or rank; — II. INF. *ta'liya-t*, raise, elevate, exalt; lift up; mount; take down the luggage; put a preface to a book; — III. INF. *mu'âlât*, mount; make to mount; impose a thing (ب *bi*) upon (على *'ala*); make two things equally high; exalt; come to Upper Arabia; make known, publish, announce; call to one عال عنى *'âl-i 'annî*, away from me! begone! — IV. INF. *i'lâ'*, set on high, raise, rear; mount; descend; get out of bed; make one's beast jump; come to Upper Arabia; — V. INF. *ta'allî*, be high; rise gradually; stand high, be powerful; become proud; get up again, be recovered; — VI. INF. *ta'âlî*, be high; rise; be powerful (الله تعالى *allah-u ta'âla*, God who is powerful or exalted, God Almighty); attain to greatness or glory; ascend, be advanced; IMP. تعال *ta'âl-a*, *ta'âl*, come here! — X. INF. *isti'lâ'*, ascend, mount, rise; find high or too high; surpass, overcome; be advanced; — XII. INF. *i'lîlâ'*, mount, ascend.

علو *'alw*, *'ulw*, *'ilw*, the topmost and best part; height; greatness, sublimeness; upper story; *'alw-an*, by force; — *'aluww*, height, greatness; — *'uluww*, INF. of (علو).

علوان *'ulwân*, preface, title, address.

علوج *'alûj*, embassy, ambassador; — *'ulûj*, pl. of علج *'ilj*.

(علود) *'alwad*, INF. ة, adhere to a place; — *'ilwadd*, long, tall; grandee.

علوز *'illauz*, colic; madness.

علوس *'alûs*, eatable; — *'illaus*, colic.

علوش *'illauś*, علوض *'illauḍ*, jackal; greedy.

علوص *'illauṣ*, colic.

علوفة *'alûfa-t*, pl. *'uluf*, *'ulf*, food, green-meat; pay, hire; — *'ulûfa-t*, pl. *'alâ'if*, fed in the stable, cattle for fattening; pay, wages, salary.

علوق *'alûq*, fœtus.

علومة *'ullûma-t*, sign, wink, hint (m.).

(علون) *'alwan*, INF. ة, *'ulwân*, put a title to a book, an address to a letter.

علوى *'ulwiyy*, high, sublime; from higher regions, heavenly; angel; outer planet; of Upper Arabia; — *'alawiyy*, sublime; descendent of Ali; — ة *'ulwiyya-t*, sublimity; pl. *-ât*, high qualities.

(على) *'ala*, see (علو).

على *'ala*, upon, on the top of, above; at, by; to; in; against; towards; according to; with regard to; concerning; on account of; during; along; in spite of; to one's charge (عليه ل *'alai-hu lî*, he owes to); على به *'alayya bi-hi*, up to me with him! bring him before me! على ان, providing, in so far as, although, notwithstanding that; على روس الاقران *'ala rûs al-aqrân*, over the head of his equals; — *'alî* (عل *'al-in*), high place; (m.) of best quality, first-rate; من ع *min 'alî*, from on high; — *'ily*, pl. grandees, noblemen; — *'ula-n*, *'ula*, height, sublimeness, nobility; pl. of اعلى *a'la*, higher, &c.; — *'aliyy*, ة, pl. *'ilya-t*, high, sublime; powerful, of high rank or birth; — *'iliyy*, height; — *'illiyy*, pl. *-ûn*, *'illiyya-t*, high, sublime; *'illiyûn*, the seventh heaven, the blest, angels; — ة *'aliyya-t*, descendants of Ali; — *'illiyya-t*, *'alliyya-t*, upper room; parlour; garret; balcony.

عليا *'alyâ'*, summit; Heaven; anything sublime; noble deed; important matter; — *'ulyâ*, f. of اعلى *a'la*, higher, &c.

علیان *'ilyân, 'illiyân*, tall and stout, big; loud; male hyena;—*'ulyân*, title, superscription.

عليث *'alis*, wheat mixed with oats.

عليف *'alîf*, ة, fed; fat.

عليق *'aliq*, suspended; pl. *'alâ'iq*, a portion of food, ration; parchment; — *'ullaiq*, عليقى *'ullaiqa*, ة, thorn-bush; flax-silk; توت العـ *tût al-'ullaiq*, wild mulberry, blackberry, bramble; — ة *'aliqa-t*, pl. *'alâ'iq*, attachment, affection, inclination; relation; commerce, traffic; hanging lamp; morning-gift.

عليل *'alîl*, ة, pl. *a'illâ'*, weak, ill, infirm, invalid.

عليم *'alîm*, pl. *'ulamâ'*, learned, wise; doctor of law and divinity.

(عم) *'amm*, U, INF. *'umûm*, be common to all, concern all, comprise all, give an equal share to all, &c.; cover entirely, involve; — INF. *'umûma-t*, become a (paternal) uncle; — INF. *'amm*, be covered with a turban, head-band, diadem, &c.; — II. INF. *ta'mîm*, crown with a turban; hence pass. be made an Imam, judge, leader; be frothy; make common, generalise; comprise all, extend to all; (m.) fill the measure to the brim; call one an uncle; — VIII. INF. *i'timâm*, put on the turban, helmet, &c.; be frothy; be full grown; — X. INF. *isti'mâm*, put on the turban, helmet, &c.; acknowledge as an uncle.

عم *'am*, abbreviation for عليه السلام *'alai-hi as-salâm*, peace be upon him! — *'am*, pl. *'amû*, shortened IMP. of (نعم), health to you! — *'amm*, pl. *a'mâm*, *'umûma-t*, *a'imma-t*, *a'umm*, pl. pl. *a'mumûn*, father's brother, paternal uncle; father-in-law; large number of men; generality; f. ة *'amma-t*, father's sister, paternal aunt; — *'amm-a* =عما *'ammâ*, for عن ما *'an mâ*, wherefrom; — ة *'imma-t*, way of putting on the turban.

عما *'amâ*, truly, certainly, indeed; — *'ammâ*, for عن ما *'an mâ*, wherefrom; — *'amâ'*, deviation, aberration; blindness; cloud.

عماد *'imâd*, ة, high building; column, support, pillar, tent-pole, pilaster; house, tent (اهل العـ *ahl al-'imâd*, inhabitants of tents); trustworthiness; trustworthy guide, messenger, &c.; the pron. of the 3rd person used as copula;—also ة *'imâda-t*, baptism.

عمار *'amâr*, salutation, greeting; gift; myrtle; — *'imâr*, cultivation; inhabited country; — *'ammâr*, cultivator, settler, colonist; architect, mason; firm in duty and belief; mild, agreeable, benevolent; — *'ummâr*, pl. inhabitants, visitors; — ة *'amâra-t*, pl. *'amâ'ir*, small tribe, division of a tribe; salutation; gift; — *'imâra-t*, pl. *'amâ'ir*, sign of cultivation; cultivation, culture, colonisation; building, dwelling-place; pious foundation; building for protection; (m.) fleet; adoration of God; 4th degree of relationship; — *.

عمارطة *'amâriṭa-t*, عماريط *'amârîṭ*, pl. of عمروط *'umrûṭ*.

عماريس *'amârîs*, pl. of عمروس *'umrûs*.

عماس *'amâs*, calamity; furious battle; pl. *'ums*, *'umus*, dark; difficult.

عماص *'imâṣ* having running eyes, bleáredness (m.).

عماق *'imâq*, pl. of عميق *'amîq*; — ة *'amâqa-t*, depth.

عمال *'ammâl*, ة, occupied, employed; able workman; just now; — *'ummâl*, pl. of عامل *'âmil*, who makes, performs, agent, &c.;—ة *'amâla-t*, activity, performance; district; — also *'imâla-t*, *'umâla-t*, wages; tools.

عمام *'imâm*, ة, pl. *'amâ'im*, head-

band, turban; raft; hooka-tube with mouth-piece.

عمان *'umân*, Omân; — *'ummân*, ocean.

عماوة *'amâwa-t*=عماية *'amâya-t*.

عمائر *'amâ'ir*, pl. of عمارة *'amâra-t*, *'imâra-t*.

عمائم *'amâ'im*, pl. of عمامة *'imâma-t*.

عماية *'amâya-t*, blindness; infatuation; aberration, error; twilight.

(عمت) *'amat*, I, INF. *'amt*, form a clew of wool to have it spun; subdue, conquer; prevent, hinder; beat at random with a stick.

عمت *'umut*, pl. of عميت *'amît*.

(عمج) *'amaj*, U, INF. *'amj*, walk fast; swim; swerve to the right and left in walking (also V.); — V. INF. *ta'ammuj*, wind in creeping (n.).

عمج *'amaj*, *'umaj*, snake.

(عمد) *'amad*, I, INF. *'amd*, support by a pillar, column, &c.; prop up an invalid, place a pillow beneath him; oppress heavily; molest, vex, render gloomy; cause to fall; cudgel; pierce, empale; purpose, resolve upon; attend to, undertake; go to; retire, withdraw; baptise; wonder; — *'amid*, A, INF. *'amad*, be angry; be seized with astonishment or pain; cling to, adhere; swell; be sore at the inner side of the hump; be moistened and made sticky by the rain; — II. INF. *ta'mîd*, dam in a water-course; support by a pillar, &c.; baptise; cause to make a firm resolution; — IV. INF. *i'mâd*, support by a pillar, &c.; — V. INF. *ta'ammud*, resolve firmly upon; do purposely; go to (acc.); be baptised; — VII. INF. *in'imâd*, be supported by a pillar; be baptised; — VIII. INF. *i'timâd*, lean upon; rely upon, trust in; dare to do, venture; obey (the bridle); travel on (all night through); resolve firmly upon; get baptised.

عمد *'amd*, firm resolution, purpose, intention; wilfulness; predestination; — *'imd*, pl. *a'mâd*, branch, twig; — *'amid*, backsore; — *'umudd*, ة, in the full prime of youth; — ة *'amda-t*, confidence, reliance; — *'umda-t*, support, pillar; distinguished person, minister; influential; trustworthy messenger or guide, scout, reconnoiterer, herald, &c.

عمدان *'umdân*, trustworthy messenger, scout, &c.; — *'ummadân*, long, tall; — ى *'ummudâniyy*, ة, in the full prime of youth.

(عمر) *'amar*, U, INF. *'amr*, cultivate and inhabit a land; worship God; visit frequently, frequent; — INF. *'imâra-t*, make or keep a house or land well inhabited and flourishing; preserve alive; give for life; be in good condition, flourish; — INF. *'umûra-t*, *'imâra-t*, cling to; — I, U, INF. *'amr*, *'amâra-t*, live long; — *'amir*, A, INF. *'amar*, *'amr*, *'umr*, live long; be in good condition and inhabited, flourish; — *'amur*, id.; be frequented, well visited (market); — II. INF. *ta'mîr*, cultivate the ground; populate a land well and preserve it in flourishing condition; colonise; build, raise buildings; provide well (as a lamp with oil, &c.); preserve alive for a long time; pray to God (acc.) to let one live long; give for life; weave or sew well; — IV. INF. *i'mâr*, cause one to cultivate and inhabit a land; make and keep a house inhabited; make rich; find or describe a a land as cultivated and inhabited; visit, alight; enable one to make the pilgrimage; give for life; make the wedding at the bride's home; — V. INF.

ta'ammur, be well cultivated, populated and flourishing; be built, raised;—VIII. INF. *i'timâr*, visit or alight frequently at (acc.); stay, abide; stay as a pilgrim in Mecca; — X. INF. *isti'mâr*, make an inhabitant, naturalize; intend to cultivate a place, to make it inhabited.

عمر *'amr*, belief, creed, religion; ear-ring, nose-ring; — *'amr*, *'umr*, pl. *'umûr*, the gums; sugar-date tree; — *'umr*, *'amr*, pl. *a'mâr*, life-time, life; age; enjoyment of life; a long time; mosque; ذو عمرين *ẕû 'amrain*, amphibious animal; — *'amar*, kerchief used as a veil; — *'amîr*, long-lived; — *'umar*, Omar, du. Abu Bekr and Omar; — *'umur*, life; age; — ة *'amra-t*, head-cover; turban; ابو ع *abû 'amra-t*, hunger and distress; — *'umra-t*, pl. *'umar*, pilgrimage to Mecca;—du. *'amaratân*, the two bones of the base of the tongue.

عمرا *'umr-an*, never (in his life).

عمران *'imrân*, Imrân, father of Moses; — *'umrân*, cultivated, inhabited; sociable, humane; human society; culture; cultivated land.

عمرد *'amarrud*, long, stretched; bad, wicked.

عمرو *'amr*, pl. *a'mur*, *'umûr*, Amr, Amru (proper name); ام عمرو *umm 'amr*, hyena.

عمرود *'umrûd*, very long; stretched, stretching (n.).

عمروس *'umrûs*, pl. *'amârîs*, sucking lamb or foal.

عمروط *'umrûṭ*, pl. *'amâriṭa-t*, *'amârîṭ*, robber; scamp.

عمرى *'umra*, living, livelihood, pension; — *umriyy*, old; river-lotus.

عمريط *'amrîṭ*=عمروط *'umrûṭ*.

عمس *'amas*, U, INF. *'ams*, be worn by use, no longer readable (book); conceal, secrete; feign ignorance; — *'amis*, A, INF. *'ams*, *'amas*, *'umûs*, be oppressive and dark; — *'amus*, INF. *'amâsa-t*, id.; — III. INF. *mu'âmasa-t*, work against in an underhand manner; whisper in one's ear; — IV. INF. *i'mâs*, conceal, secrete; — V. INF. *ta'ammus*, be uncertain in a matter (acc.); — VI. INF. *ta'âmus*, feign unconcern; feign blindness, ignorance; leave one in uncertainty or doubt.

عمس *'ams*, difficult; terrible war; — *'ums*, *'umus*, dark nights; pl. of عماس *'amâs*.

(عمش) *'amaś*, U, INF. *'amś*, hit or beat unintentionally; — *'amiś*, A, INF. *'amaś*, suffer from weakness of the eyes or bleáredness; fit; recover; — II. INF. *ta'mîś*, cause the body to recover; — IV. INF. *i'mâś*, restore to health, mend; — VI. INF. *ta'âmuś*, neglect; — X. INF. *isti'mâś*, deem stupid.

عمش *'amaś*, blearedness, soreness of the eyes.

عمشا *'amśâ*, f. of اعمش, bleared-eyed.

عمشوش *'umśûś*, grape-stalk without berries.

(عمص) *'umṣ*, a dish; — *'amiṣ*, fond of acidities; — *'amiṣ*, A, INF. *'amaṣ*, be blear-eyed.

(عمط) *'amiṭ*, A, INF. *'amaṭ*, vilify, fail to acknowledge; —VIII. INF. *i'timâṭ*, vilify.

(عمعم) *'am'am*, INF. ة, have a large army round one's self; enlarge; — II. INF. *ta'am'um*, become great, numerous, assume great proportions.

(عمق) *'amuq*, INF. *'amâqa-t*, be deep; — *'amuq*, *'amiq*, INF. *'amq*, *'amâqa-t*, be long, stretch (n.) long; — II. INF. *ta'mîq*, make deep, deepen; — IV. INF. *i'mâq*, id.; make to penetrate deeply; — V. INF. *ta'ammuq*, be deep; immerse one's self entirely, try to get at the bottom

of a thing; make deep studies; — X. INF. *isti'mâq*, find deep.

عمق *'amq*, *'umq*, pl. *a'mâq*, depth; extended desert; dates drying in the sun; — *'amaq*, right, claim; — *'umuq*, depth; also *'imaq*, pl. of عميق *'amîq*.

عمقية *'amqiyya-t*, depth (m.).

عمكوس *'umkûs*, ass.

(عمل) *'amil*, A, INF. *'amal*, work, perform; do; practise, profess; produce an effect; be brisk; walk fast; exercise an influence; govern a case; take pains with (على *'ala*); work to an end; take care of; last without interruption; — II. INF. *ta'mîl*, pay one his fee or wages; make one an administrator or governor; suppurate, grow cancerous; — III. INF. *mu'âmala-t*, transact business with; act in common with; treat in such or such a way; — IV. INF. *i'mâl*, cause to work, make work, ply one's hands; set a-working; set one's mind on a work; urge; jade; — V. INF. *ta'ammul*, work at; be tired; — VI. INF. *ta'âmul*, have dealings with one another; treat one another in such or such a way; — VII. INF. *in'imâl*, be being done, carried out, accomplished; — VIII. INF. *i'timâl*, do the work one's self; — X. INF. *isti'mâl*, bid work; employ in a work; use, make use of; hire workmen; make one an administrator, governor, &c.

عمل *'aml*, business, office; province, district, sphere; — *'amal*, pl. *a'mâl*, deed, action; way of acting; occupation, practice; toil, work, labour; execution, performance; administration; effect, efficacy, influence; grammatical governance; (m.) fabrication; (m.) pus; — *'amil*, ة, acting, working, effecting; fit for work; — ة *'amla-t*, theft; deceit; treachery; — *'imla-t*, action; way of acting; event, affair; disposition; currency; — also *'umla-t*, fee, wages; — *'amala-t*, work-people; *'amila-t*, work, action, deed.

عملا *'umalâ'*, pl. of عامل *'âmil*, agent, &c., and عميل *'amîl*.

عملان *'amalân*, action.

(عملس) *'amlas*, INF. ة, walk fast, hasten (n.).

عملس *'amallas*, indefatigable; wolf.

(عملق) *'amlaq*, INF. ة, drop the excrement easily; engage more deeply in.

عملوش *'umlûś*=عمشوش *'umśûś*.

عملى *'amaliyy*, ة, practical; artificial, counterfeited; — ة *'amaliyya-t*, practice.

عمم *'amam*, perfect, complete; general, comprising all; generality; multitude; extent, bulk, thickness; pl. of عامة, community, &c.; — *'umum*, perfect bodily condition; pl. of عميم *'amîm*.

(عمن) *'aman*, I, INF. *'amn*, stay, remain, abide; — *'amin*, A, INF. *'aman*, id.; — II. INF. *ta'mîn*, travel to 'Umân; — IV. INF. *i'mân*, id.; stay permanently.

عمن *'umun*, pl. permanent settlers; — *'amman*=عن من *'an man*, from whom, &c.

(عمه) *'amah*, INF. *'amh*, *'umûh*, *'amahân*, *'umûha-t*, wander astray; be perplexed, confused, baffled as to which way to go; be embarrassed for an excuse; — *'amih*, A, INF. *'amah*, id.; be without road-marks; — II. INF. *ta'mîh*, act blindly; treat hard without proof of guilt; — VI. INF. *ta'âmuh*=I.

عمه *'amih*, perplexed, thunderstruck, dumbfounded; — *'ummah*, pl. عامه *'âmih*, confused.

عمها *'amhâ*, f. without a road-mark.

(عمو) *'amw*, pl. *a'mâ'*, error; submissiveness.

عمو *'ammû*, عموجة *'amûja-t*, uncle.

عمود *'amûd*, pl. *a'mida-t*, *'amad*, *'umud*, column, pillar; support, prop; base; vertical line; pedigree; cudgel, bludgeon, mace; chief, chieftain; trustworthy messenger; large vein; scale-beam; first ray of dawn; — ى *'amûdiyy*, perpendicular.

عموق *'umûq*, depth.

عمول *'amûl*, industrious; — ة *'umûla-t*, order (for a work), commission; pay for such; interest, provision, percentage.

عموم *'amûm*, generality; — ة *'umûma-t*, pl. of عم; being a paternal uncle; kinship on father's side; — ى *'umûmiyy*, ة, general; — ية *'umûmiyya-t*, generality.

عمون *'amûn*, pl. of عمى *'amî*, blind.

عموه *'umûh*, ة *'umûha-t*, INF. of (عمه).

عموى *'amawiyy*, according to the manner of the blind, the stupid.

(عمى) *'ama*, I, INF. *'amy*, flow, run; throw out foam, impurities, &c.; roar and foam (camel); come at noon; — *'amî*, A, INF. *'aman*, be or grow blind; fail to see a thing, be stupid; be dark, obscure; — II. INF. *ta'miya-t*, make blind, blind, dazzle; darken (a.), render obscure; involve in riddles; pass. عميت عليه *'ummiya-t 'alai-hi*, it grows dark around him, he dies; — IV. INF. *i'mâ'*=II.; find blind; be stupid; come at noon; — V. INF. *ta'ammî*, be blind, feign blindness; be dark, enigmatical; — VI. INF. *ta'âmî*, feign blindness.

عمى *'amy*, blindness; — *'umy*, pl. of اعمى *a'ma*, blind; — *'aman*, *'ama*, blindness; dust; size, form, figure; — *'amî*, ة, pl. *'amûn*, blind; ignorant; — *'ammî*, my uncle; — *'umma*, at the edge of the grave, on the point of death; — *'ammiyy*, father's brother, paternal uncle; — *ummiyy*, man of the people; plebeian; — ة *'amya-t*, choice; who is chosen, elected; — *'amiyya-t*, f. blind; also *'umiyya-t*, error, going astray, aberration; dispute, quarrel; — *'ummiyya-t*, *'immiyya-t*, ignorance; blind pride or obstinacy; bigotry.

عميا *'amyâ*, f. of اعمى *a'ma*, blind; على العميا *'ala 'l-immiyyâ'*, blindly.

عميان *'amyân*, blind; — *'umyân*, pl. of اعمى *a'ma*, blind.

على العمياني *'ala 'l-'amyâniyy*, blindly.

عميت *'amît*, ة, pl. *a'mita-t*, *'umut*, clew of wool.

عميد *'amîd*, support, prop; leader, chief; governor, lieutenant; love-sick.

عمير *amîr*, cultivated and inhabited; coarse; — ابو ع *abû 'umair*, penis; — ة *'amîra-t*, bee-hive; — جلد ع *jald 'umaira-t*, onanism.

عميس *'amîs*, dark, obscure; ة, على الع *'ala 'l-'amîsa-t*, false (oath).

عميق *'amîq*, ة, pl. *'umuq*, *'imaq*, *'amâ'iq*, *'imâq*, deep; far, far-stretching or extending.

عميل *'amîl*, pl. *'umalâ'*, workman; tax-gatherer; business friend, correspondent.

عميم *'amîm*, perfect, full, complete; upper class; pl. *'umum*, general, common to all, concerning or comprising all; assembled; abundant, plenteous; ة, pl. *'umum*, full-grown.

عمينة *'amîna-t*, level ground.

(عن) *'ann*, I, U, INF. *'ann*, *'anân*, *'unûn*, present itself to view, appear, happen; refrain (also IV.); provide the bit with a bridle (also II.); put a title to a book, an address to a letter (also II. and IV.); abuse, revile; pass. *'unn*, II. *'unnin*, and IV. *u'inn*, be declared by the judge

to be impotent, become impotent by a spell; INF. *'anîn*, sigh; complain; — II. INF. *ta'nîn*, see I.; — III. INF. *'inân*, *mu'ânna-t*, show one's self to, step forth against, oppose, resist; — IV. INF *i'nân*, see I.; turn to (a.); — VIII. INF. *i'tinân*, appear; pass. be informed, apprized of.

عن *'an*, prep. from, away from; instead of, for; with regard to; in accordance with; on account of, after; upon; in; about; — *'ann-a*, perhaps, may be, by chance; — ة *'unna-t*, pl. *'unan*, *'inân*, impotence; fireplace; rope.

عنا *'anan*, pl. *a'nâ'*, side; — *'anâ'*, trouble, pain, weariness; molestation; sorrow, grief; adversity; — *'inâ'*, INF. III. of (عنى); — *'annâ*=عن نا *'an nâ*, from (&c.) us; — ة *'unât*, pl. of عانى *'ânî*, captive, &c.; — *'anâ'a-t* =عناية *'anâya-t*, *'inâya-t*.

عناب *'annâb*, seller of grapes; — *'unnâb*, jujube-tree; fruit of the *arâk*; — ى *'unnâbiyy*, nut-brown.

عناثى *'anâsî*, pl. of عنثوة *'ansuwa-t*, *'unsuwa-t*.

عناج *'inâj*, pl. *a'nija-t*, rope of the bucket; connection, causality; foundation, base.

عناد *'inâd*, obstinacy, stubbornness; contention.

عنادل *'anâdil*, pl. of عندليب *'andalîb*; du. *'anâdilan*, the testicles.

عنادى *'inâdiyy*, refractory.

عناس *'inâs*, mirror, looking-glass; — *.

عناش *'inâś*, who fights, combatant; — *.

عناصى *'anâṣî*, pl. of عنصاة *'inṣât*, &c.

عنافة *'anâfa-t*, troublesomeness; — *.

عناق *'anâq*, pl. *a'nuq*, *'unûq*, young goat; misfortune, calamity; ع الارض *'anâq al-arḍ*, badger; — *'inâq*, embrace, INF. III. of (عنق); — ة *'anâqa-t*, deception, delusion.

عناقيد *'anâqîd*, pl. of عنقود *'unqûd*.

عناك *'anâk*, sand-hill.

عنان *'anân*, ة, cloud; — *'inân*, apparition; pl. *a'inna-t*, *'unun*, rein, bridle, curb; vein; du. *'inânân*, the two halves, the whole; resistance, INF. III. of (عن); pl. of عنة *'unna-t*; — *'annân*, slow, hesitating; (m.) who sighs frequently; — ة *'anâna-t*, aversion to women.

عناية *'anâya-t*, *'inâya-t*, succour; favour, grace; patronage; present, bounty; solicitude; providence; meaning; half silk; INF. of (عنى).

(عنب) *'inab*, pl. *a'nâb*, bunch of grapes; — ة *'inaba-t*, berry of grapes; ع الثعلب *'inaba-t as-sa'lab*, nightshade; currant; — II. *'annab*, INF. *ta'nîb*, produce grapes; (m.) leave the grapes to the last on the vine-tree.

عنبب *'umbab*, body of water.

عنبج *'umbuj*, عنبوج *'umbûj*, stupid; lazy; paunch-bellied.

(عنبر) *'ambar*, m. f. ambergris; a sea-fish; shield made of its skin; saffron; night; magazine, store-house, barn; also ة *'ambara-t*, cold of winter; — ى *'ambariyy*, of ambergris; perfumed with it; (m.) a liquor.

عنبس *'ambas*, pl. *'anâbis*, lion.

عنبى *'inabiyy*, made of grapes.

(عنت) *'anit*, A, INF. *'anat*, be corrupted, deteriorated; perish; commit a crime; commit adultery, fornication; succumb to an accusation; undertake anything burdensome; be visited with troubles, get into great embarrassments; break again (healed bone); — II. INF. *ta'nît* (also IV.), urge to anything burdensome; vex; bring into trouble; — IV. INF. *i'nât*, see

II.; break again a scarcely-healed bone; ruin; — V. INF. *ta'annut*, observe and point out other people's weaknesses; act violently towards; make difficulties, show reluctance.

عنت *'anat*, great embarrassment; perdition, ruin, corruption; sin; fornication; — *'anit*, broken afresh.

عنتت *'antat*, INF. ة, deviate; be high.

(عنتر) *'antar*, INF. ة, rush boldly into danger, display bravery; pierce with a lance; hum, buzz; — II. INF. *ta'antur*, boast of one's courage.

عنتر *'antar*, ة *'antara-t*, name of a poet and hero of romance; blue fly; — ة *'antara-t*, fearless bravery; — ى *'antariyy*, a short under-garment.

(عنتل) *'antal*, INF. ة, tear to pieces.

عنثل *'ansal*, ام ع *umm 'ansal*, hyena.

عنثة *'ansa-t*, *'insa-t*, *'unsa-t*, عنثوة *'ansuwa-t*, *'unsawa-t*, pl. *'anâsî*, the plant حلى *haliyy* (white thistle) in a dry state; hay.

(عنج) *'anaj*, U, INF. *'anj*, prevent the camel by the bridle from kneeling down; put a rope to the bucket; — IV. INF. *i'nâj*, see I.; establish well and solidly; complain of a pain in the hips.

(عنجد) *'anjad*, *'unjad*, *'unjud*, smallest stoneless sort of grapes; raisin; — *'anjad*, INF. ة, turn into raisins.

(عنجر) *'anjar*, INF. ة, smack the lips; put the lips out and curl them.

عنجوج *'anjûj*, pl. *'anâjîj*, excellent horse or camel; stretching (n.).

عنجورة *'unjûra-t*, case for a bottle.

(عند) *'anad*, U,—also *'anud*, INF. *'unûd*, deviate, swerve from; bleed so as not to be staunched; — I, INF. *'unûd*, oppose and reject what is right; separate (n.), seclude one's self; be restive, refractory, disobedient; — III. INF. *'inâd*, *mu'ânada-t*, remove from, desist; oppose; attend zealously to; — IV. INF. *i'nâd*, go away, depart; bleed; vomit; oppose; equal in friendship, &c.; — VI. INF. *ta'ânud*, oppose one another; — X. INF. *isti'nâd*, persist obstinately, be headstrong; overpower; take hold of the bit, run away; beat with a stick among the people; turn to the mouth of the skin-bag and drink; step towards, repair to.

عند *'and*, *'ind*, *'und*, *'anad*, side; *'and-a*, *'ind-a*, *'und-a*, (m.) *'and*, at the side, by, with, in presence of; — *'ind*, heart, mind; — *'unud*, pl. of عنود *'anûd*, عنيد *'anîd*.

عنداو *'inda'dw*; brave, bold, courageous; — ة *'inda'wa-t*, id.; calamity; wile, stratagem, deceit.

(عندر) *'andar*, INF. ة, be violent.

عندقة *'unduqa-t*, abdomen.

(عندل) *'andal*, INF. ة, have strong sinews; sing, warble (as a nightingale).

عندليب *'andalîb*, pl. *'anâdil*, nightingale.

عندم *'andam*, dragon's blood; Brazil-wood; any light-red dye.

عندى *'indiyy*, ة, founded only on individual opinion; pl. ات *'indiyyât*, individual notions or opinions.

عنذى *'anza*, INF. ة, instigate, incite.

(عنز) *'anaz*, U, INF. *'anz*, deviate, depart from (عن), swerve; pierce with a spear; — II. be goatlike, do as goats do; play on the bag-pipes; (m.) have a swollen belly; — IV. INF. *i'nâz*, cause one to depart from; — VIII. INF. *i'tinâz*, X. INF. *isti'nâz*, deviate, turn aside, swerve or depart from.

عنز *'anz*, ة, pl. *'inâz*, *'unûz*, *a'nuz*, goat; — ة *'anaza-t*, short spear; edge of an axe; a weasel.

(عنزب) *'unzub*, eatable sumach.

عنزروت *'anzarût*, sarcocol; Persian ointment for the eyes.

عنزهوة *'inzahwa-t*, عنزهانى *'unzahâniyy*, who abstains from women and pleasure; timid, shy; who spoils a game.

(عنس) *'anas*, I, U, INF. *'ans*, bend (a.); INF. *'inâs*, *'unûs*, stay a long time unmarried at home; change, alter (a.); — *'anis*, A, INF. *'anas*, remain a long time unmarried; look frequently into the mirror; — II. INF. *ta'nîs*, (also IV.) leave a girl for a long time unmarried; pass. remain so; — IV. INF. *i'nâs*, see II.; change, alter (a.); — XII. *i'naunas*, INF. *i'nînâs*, be strong and have long hair (camel's tail).

عنس *'ans*, strong she-camel; eagle; bend, winding, crookedness; — *'uns*, pl. of عانس *'ânis*, marriageable girl staying at home, &c.

(عنش) *'anaś*, U, INF. *'anś*, bend (a.), curve; drive away; urge on; — III. INF. *mu'ânaśa-t*, seize round the neck and fight against (also VIII.); — VI. INF. *ta'ânuś*, seize one another round the neck; — VIII. INF. *i'tinâś*, see III.; wrong, injure.

(عنشط) *'anśaṭ*, INF. ة, be angry.

عنشط *'anśaṭ*, *'anaśśaṭ*, pl. *'anâśiṭ*, malignant.

(عنص), IV. *a'naṣ*, INF. *i'nâṣ*, have but little hair left on the head.

عنصاة *'inṣât*, pl. *'anâṣ-in*, *'anâṣî*, scattered remainders.

(عنصر) *'unṣar*, care, zeal; intention; want, need; sorrow, grief; calamity; — *'unṣur*, *'unṣar*, pl. *'anâṣir*, *'anâṣîr*, origin; descent; essence, substance; chemical element, base; temper; estimation; — ة *'anṣara-t*, feast of Tabernacles; Whitsuntide.

عنصرى *'unṣuriyy*, ة, elementary; — ة *'unṣuriyya-t*, element.

(عنصل) *'unṣul*, *'unṣal*, عنصلا *'unṣulâ'*, *'unṣalâ'*, pl. *'anâṣil*, wild onion; leek.

عنصوة *'anṣuwa-t*, *'inṣuwa-t*, *'unṣuwa-t*, عنصية *'inṣiya-t*=عنصاة *'inṣât*.

(عنط) *'anaṭ*, length, particularly of the neck.

(عنظب) *'unẓub*, *'unẓab*, عنظاب *'inẓâb*, *'unẓâb*, ة *'unẓâba-t*, عنظبا *'unẓubâ*, عنظبان *'unẓubân*, big locust.

عنظر *'anẓar*, INF. ة, skip like a goat; get proud.

(عنظل) *'anẓal*, INF. ة, run.

عنظل *'anẓal*, spider-web.

عنظوان *'unẓuwân*, a saline plant; liberal; boaster; obscene talker; mixer of poison.

(عنظى) *'anẓa*, INF. ة, talk obscenely to (ب *bi*).

(عنعن) *'an'an*, INF. ة, pronounce the ء like ع; trace one's origin to, trace back to the source; (m.) sigh.

(عنف) *'anaf*, INF. *'anf*, *'inf*, *'unf*, treat harshly and violently; — *'anuf*, INF. عنافة *'anâfa-t*, id.; — II. INF. *ta'nîf*, id.; find fault with, rebuke; — IV. INF. *i'nâf*, treat harshly and violently; undertake, begin; — V. INF *ta'annuf*, manage roughly or awkwardly; — VIII. INF. *i'tinâf*, take by force; undertake without knowledge; undertake, do for the first time; have an aversion to, loathe; be not fit or suitable; emigrate, remove; graze off the first grass.

عنف *'anf*, *'unf*, harshness; violence; roughness, rough treatment; beginning commencement; — *'unf*, ة *'unfa-t*, aversion, loathing (s.).

(عنفش) *'anfaś*, INF. ة, be thick and handsome (beard).

(عنفص) *'infiṣ*, ة *'infiṣa-t*, impudent jade; — *'anfaṣ*, INF. ة, show

one's self haughty, bad-tempered, arrogant.

(عنفط) *'unfuṭ*, ة, pl. *'anâfiṭ*, vile, malicious; badger.

(عنفق) *'anfaq*, ة *'anfaqa-t*, lightness; — ة *'anfaqa-t*, hair of the beard between the nether lip and chin.

(عنفك) *'anfak*, stupid; burdensome, importunate.

عنفو *'unfuww*, ة *'unfuwwa-t*, عنفوان *'unfuwân*, beginning; freshness, prime, bloom of youth.

عنفى *'unfiyy*, ة, violent, oppressive.

(عنق) *'anaq*, hide (n.) in the hole or burrow, burrow; — *'aniq*, A, INF. *'anaq*, have a long neck; — II. INF. *ta'nîq*, seize by the neck; tower, project; be long; swell; deceive, delude; bear one's head high; disperse the dust; — III. INF. *mu'ânaqa-t*, *'inâq*, take by the neck and draw towards one's self, embrace (also an occupation); — IV. INF. *i'nâq*, put a collar on a dog; run with a stretched-out neck; have a long stalk or pedicle; stand high in ears; dispel the dust; set; — V. INF. *ta'annuq*, creep into the hole, burrow; — VI. INF. *ta-'ânuq*, embrace one another; — VIII. INF. *i'tinâk*, seize one another by the neck; embrace one another.

عنق *'unq*, *'unuq*, *'unaq*, pl. *a'nâq*, *a'nuq*, (m. f.) neck; pedicle; — *'unq*, grandees; — *'anaq*, length of the neck; a pace of the camel; — *'unuq*, inclined towards, solicitous for (الى *ila*).

عنقا *'anqâ'*, f. of اعنق *a'naq*, long-necked; griffin; phœnix; rare in its kind.

عنقاد *'inqâd*, cluster, bunch; bunch of grapes.

(عنقد) *'anqad*, INF. ة, begin to form berries.

(عنقر) *'anqar*, *'anqur*, ة, first shoot; offspring, progeny; pith of the palm-tree.

عنقريب *'an-qarîb*, soon, shortly, presently.

(عنقز) *'anqaz*, sweet marjoram; penis of the ass; — ة *'anqaza-t*, flag; poison; calamity.

(عنقس) *'anqas*, cunning and malicious.

(عنقش) *'anqaś*, INF. ة, adhere, stick to; — II. INF. *ta'anquś*, be tightly twisted round (ب *bi*).

(عنقفير) *'anqafîr*, calamity; scorpion.

عنقود *'unqûd*, pl. *'anâqîd*, cluster, bunch of fruit; bunch of grapes.

(عنك) *'anak*, U, INF. *'ank*, *'unûk*, be pathless and heaped up high (sand of the desert); wade through the sand with difficulty (also VIII.); be thick; be very red; be refractory; depart, set out on a journey; leap at repeatedly and recede again; lock the door; — IV. INF. *i'nâk*, lock; deal in clothes; get into deep sand; — V. INF. *ta'annuk*, be heaped up high and difficult to wade through; — VIII. INF. *i'tinâk*, see I.

عنك *'ank*, *'ink*, *'unk*, the larger part of anything; — *'ink*, door; — *'ink*, *'anak*, root, origin; — *'unk*, pl. of عنيك *'anîk*; — *'an-ka*, from (&c.) thee.

(عنكب) *'ankab*, ة *'ankaba-t*, pl. *'anâkib*, *'ikâb*, *'ukub*, *'anâkib*, spider.

عنكباة *'ankabât*, عنكبوت *'ankabût*, pl. *'ankabûtât*, *'anâkîb*, spider.

(عنكش) *'ankaś*, INF. ة, dry up, wither (n.); curl; — II. INF. *ta'ankuś*, dry up, wither; keep curly (n.).

عنكليس *'ankilîs*, eel.

(عنم) *'anam*, tree with a red fruit; vine-branches; — II. *'annam*, INF. *ta'nîm*, dye red; — IV. *a'nam*, INF. *i'nâm*, browse

off the *'anam* tree; — ى *'anamiyy*, red, rose-coloured.

عنن *'anan*, pl. *a'nân*, appearing object, apparition; region; side; evil; — *'unan*, pl. of عنة *'unna-t*; — *unun*, pl. of عنان *'inân*.

(عنو) *'anâ*, U, fill with anxiety, with sorrow; — INF. *'unuww*, be bent (face of the sorrowful); humble one's self before, bow down to (ل *li*); obey; — INF. *'anâ'*, *'unuww*, live as a captive; abase one's self; suffer; be wearied, exhausted; happen, befall; be hard, difficult, burdensome; — A, I, take out, lead out; produce; publish; snuffle at; let the water leak out; — عنى *'anî*, A, live as a captive; — II. INF. *ta'niya-t*, keep captive; make one suffer, afflict, tire, exhaust; — III. INF. *mu'ânât*, suffer, bear, support; — IV. (1 pret. *a'nai-tu*) INF. *i'nâ'*, make one a supplicant; publish, make public, reveal; lead out; produce; — VI. INF. *ta'ânî*, humble one's self; — ة *'anwa-t*, anything brought to light, made public; violence, compulsion (*'anwat-an*, by force, violently); love.

عنوان *'unwân*, *'inwân*, title of a book; superscription, address; index; title; royal signature; front; beginning; pretext; manner, method, quality.

عنوت *'anût*, steep.

عنود *'anûd*, pl. *'unud*, obstinate, headstrong, refractory; raincloud; — *.

عنوس *'anûs*, pl. of عانس *'ânis*, marriageable girl staying at home.

عنوق *'unûq*, pl. of عناق *'anâq*.

عنون *'anûn*, enduring and swift.

(عنون) *'anwan*, INF. ة, provide a book with a title, address a letter.

(عنى) *'ana*, I, INF. *'any*, *'inâya-t*, mean, signify; concern, refer to; — I, INF *'anâya-t*, *'inâya-t*, *'iniyy*, fill with anxiety, engross, trouble; — I, INF. *'any*, happen, occur, befall; produce; do good, agree with; — INF. *'anâ'*, be a captive; agree with, do good; — *'anî*, A, INF. *'anan*, be in anxiety about; pass. *'unî*, id.; INF. *'anâ'*, be tired, exhausted, unwell; — II. INF. *ta'niya-t*, tire; grieve (a.); put a title to a book; — III. INF. *mu'ânât*, manage, take care of, attend to; bear up with; — IV. INF. *i'nâ'*, express, mean, signify, allude to; keep captive; produce; tire out; — V. INF. *ta'annî*, tire out; grow tired; take pains with (acc.); trouble one's self about; — VI. INF. *ta'ânî*, vie in taking pains with; — VIII. INF. *i'tinâ'*, attend to, do carefully; observe attentively; be troubled about (ب *bi*); — X. INF. *isti'nâ*, give all one's attention and care to; carry on an art, a trade.

عنى *'anî* (عن *'an-in*), anxious, solicitous; — *'inan*, a little; — *'unan*, care, solicitude; — ة *'anya-t*, pain, care; — *'aniyya-t*, dry camel-dung.

عنيان *'inyân*, title, address.

عنيد *'anîd*, ~~pl. *'unud*~~, obstinate, refractory.

عنيز *'anîz*, unfortunate, unhappy; — ة *'unaiza-t*, little goat; a female proper name.

عنيف *'anîf*, ة, pl. *'unuf*, violent, oppressive, cruel.

عنيق *'anîq*, neck; embracing, embraced; a pace of the camel (= عنق *'anaq*).

عنيقيد *'unaiqîd*, little bunch of grapes, &c.

عنيك *'anîk*, pl. *'unk*, sand-heap.

عنيكب *'unaikib*, little spider.

عنين *'innîn*, impotent; — ة *'innîna-t*, impotence; having an aversion to men.

(عه) *'ahh*, impudent, shameless, insolent.

عهاد *'ihâd*, spring shower; —*.
عهارة *'ahâra-t*, fornication; sin; —*.
(عهب) *'ahib*, A, INF. *'ahab*, be ignorant of (ب *bi* or acc.); — hence عوهب *'aukab*, INF. ة, lead into error.
عهبا *'ihibbâ'*, عهبى *'ihibba*, early youth; reign.
(عهد) *'ahid*, A, INF. *'ahad*, prescribe, enjoin, charge with; stipulate, covenant, make a contract or compact; give by will; confer an appanage, a province, a fief upon (الى *ila*); appoint as a successor; precede; stand security for (ل *li*); meet, have an appointment, visit; observe; fulfil one's promise; see; know; suppose; treat with reverence; pass. be visited by the first spring-rain; — III. INF. *mu'âhada-t*, see, see again, visit; oblige, by contract; promise the same on one's own part; covenant; stand security; — IV. INF. *i'hâd*, offer security; — V. INF. *ta'ahhud*, bind one's self to, promise, warrant; inquire again and again after; attend always carefully to; visit, frequent; do repeatedly, be in the habit of; remind of the past; warrant; — VI. INF. *ta'âhud*, make a compact with one another; bind one by contract to an obligation; visit; = VIII.; — VIII. INF. *i'tihâd*, attend carefully to; — X. INF. *isti'hâd*, bind one by contract; exact a written agreement.
عهد *'ahd*, pl. *'uhûd*, contract, compact, covenant; obligation; vow; oath; will, testament (also in a Biblical sense); promise of protection, clientship, security, guarantee; commission, prescription; diploma of investiture; government; reign, epoch, time; knowledge of a thing; faithfulness, fidelity; place where a thing operates, where a thing is found; preeminence; honour, reverence; pl. *'ihâd*, *'uhûd*, spring shower; — *'ahid*, vicegerent, regent; — ة *'ahda-t*, *'ihda-t*, spring shower; — *'uhda-t*, obligation, stipulation; security; compact, covenant; affair; fine, mulct; fief, tenure; appanage; province, department; office, occupation, employment; undersigned witnesses; proof of the truth.
(عهر) *'ahar*, INF. *'ahr*, *'ihr*, *'uhr*, *'ahûr*, *'ahâra-t*, *'uhûra-t*, visit a woman to commit fornication with her (also III.); live in sin; steal; — III. INF. *'ihâr*, see I.
عهر *'ihr*, fornication, sin; — ة *'ahira-t*, fornicatress, whore.
(عهن) *'ahan*, U, INF. *'ahn*, dry up, wither (n.); stay, remain, abide; depart; take pains with, attend carefully to (فى *fî*); do readily; also = (عهد); — I, INF. *'ahn*, be bent and broken (without being severed).
عهن *'ihn*, good manager and overseer of the cattle; also ة *'ihna-t*, pl. *'uhûn*, dyed wool; — ة *'ihna-t*, hatred, rage; — *'uhna-t*, bend, breach, rupture.
(عهو) *'ihw*, foal of an ass; perfect camel.
عهيد *'ahîd*, ة, bound by contract; allied; tributary; contemporaneous; very old; — ى *'uhhaida*, security, bail.
عوا *'awwâ'*, dog, snarling dog; buttocks; 13th station of the moon.
عواثن *'awâsin*, pl. of عثان *'usân*, smoke, dust.
عواج *'awwâj*, dealer or artist in ebony or tortoise-shell.
عواد *'iwâd*, INF. III. of (عود); doing repeatedly (s.), custom, habit; — *'awwâd*, player on the lute; who visits the sick; — *'uwwâd*, pl. of عائد *'â'id*, who visits the sick, who pays back, restores; — ة *'uwâda-t*, visiting the sick

(s.); anything warmed up; return;—'awwâda-t, female player on the lute.

عواظ 'awâẓ, disapproval; 'awâẓ-an, against one's will.

عواذير 'awâẕîr, pl. of عاذور 'âẕûr, calamity.

عوار 'awâr, 'iwâr, 'uwâr, mote, &c., in the eye; defect, fault; rent; — 'uwwâr, pl. 'awâwir, 'awâwîr, mote in the eye; imposture; who does not see the way; timid, weak; swallow.

عوارق 'awâriq, pl. molar teeth.

عواس 'awwâs, night-watch, patrol.

عواشير 'awâśîr, pl. of عاشورا, the 10th (or 9th) of *Muharram*, &c.

عواصر 'awâṣir, pl. stones for pressing grapes.

عواصم 'awâṣim, a district of Antioch.

عواض 'awâḍḍ, pl. of عاضة 'âḍḍa-t, camel feeding on عض 'iḍḍ; — 'iwâḍ, exchange, INF. III. of (عوض).

عواف 'uwâf, ة 'uwâfa-t, prey.

عواقيل 'awâqîl, pl. of عاقول 'âqûl, bend of a river, &c.

عوام 'awwâm, swimmer; swimming (adj.); raft; — 'awâmm, pl. of عام 'âmm, general, common, &c.

عواميد 'awâmîd, pl. of عامود 'âmûd, column, pedigree, &c.

عوان 'awân, pl. 'ûn, of middle age; married woman; no longer virginal (m. and f.); long, sanguinary (war); —*

عواور 'awâwir, عواوير 'awâwîr, pl. of عوار 'uwwâr.

عوائد 'awâ'id, pl. of عائدة 'â'ida-t and عادة 'âda-t, custom, habit, &c.

(عوث) 'âs, U, INF. 'aus, perplex and thereby prevent; — II. INF. ta'wîs, id.; — V. INF. ta'awwus, be perplexed.

عوثية 'ûsiyya-t, locusts baked in flour.

(عوج) 'âj, U, INF. 'auj, ma'âj, stay, remain; alight in passing by; cause to stay; cede, desist; turn aside (a.); turn the head; be anxious about (ب bi); — for 'awij, A, INF. 'awaj, be crooked; be difficult, complicated; — II. INF. ta'wîj, make crooked, bend (a.), curve; make of ivory; — V. INF. ta'awwuj, grow crooked, bend (n.); = IX.; — VII. INF. in'iwâj = IX.; lean towards; — IX. INF. i'wijâj, be crooked, distorted, reversed; go crookedly, be perverse, insincere.

عوج 'awaj, 'iwaj, crookedness; perversity; — 'ûj, pl. and—

عوجا 'aujâ', f. of اعوج a'waj, crooked, &c.; bow.

(عود) 'âd, U, INF. 'aud, 'auda-t, ma'âd, turn back, return; do again, repeatedly (followed by an aor.); with negative: do no longer; — INF. 'aud, examine repeatedly; fall as a share or profit to (ل li); turn to disadvantage; benefit by; favour repeatedly; INF. 'aud, 'iyâd, repeat; INF. 'aud, 'iyâd, 'iyâda-t, 'uwâda-t, visit, frequent; do a thing so often that it becomes a habit; practise; turn off, refuse (a petitioner); change, alter (a.); — II. INF. ta'wîd, accustom to (2 acc.); exercise in, teach; eat warmed-up food; grow old; — III. INF. 'iwâd, mu'âwada-t, do repeatedly, habitually, by habit and assiduously; return to, befall repeatedly; importune by repeated questions; return from a journey; call to memory;—IV. INF. i'âda-t, repeat; do repeatedly; lead back; restore; have for a habit; imitate; — V. INF. ta'awwud, accustom one's self; be accustomed; be practised and experienced; visit; — VI. INF. ta'âwud, join a leader in crowds; — VIII. INF. i'tiyâd, return, lead back; accustom one's self to (على 'ala); make it a habit; be accustomed, visit; — X. INF.

isti'âda-t, ask to return or repeat; call back; accustom one's self to.

عود *'aud*, ة *'auda-t*, return; repetition; habit, custom; *'aud*, ة, pl. *'iyada-t*, *'iwada-t*, old; also *'uwwad*, pl. of عائد *'â'id*, who visits the sick; — *'ûd*, pl. *'îdân*, *a'wâd*, wood, trunk, branches; tree; aloes; lute, cithern; rail, splint; mare, horse (Magrebian); — ة *'auda-t*, inclosure (of mulberry-trees).

عودق *'audaq*, ة *'audaqa-t*, hook for the bucket at a well.

(عوذ) *'âẓ*, U, adhere close to the bone (flesh); — INF. *'auẓ*, *'iyâẓ*, *ma'âẓ*, *ma'âẓa-t* (also V. and X.), take refuge with God, commend one's self to God; — INF. *'iyâẓ* (also IV.), have borne recently; — II. INF. *ta'wîẓ*, cause or force one to seek refuge; grant refuge, protect (also IV.); consecrate; — IV. INF. *i'âẓa-t*, *i'wâẓ*, see I.; — V. INF. *ta'awwuẓ*, see I.; — VI. INF. *ta'âwuẓ*, take refuge with one another; — X. INF. *isti'âẓa-t*, see I.

عوذ *'auẓ*, abhorrence; عوذ بالله *'auẓ bi 'l-lâh*, God forbid; — *'awaẓ*, refuge to God; abhorrence; *'awaẓ-an*, unwillingly, by a narrow escape; — *'uwwaẓ*, flesh on the bone; — ة *'ûẓa-t*, pl. *'ûẓ*, talisman, amulet, charm; refuge.

عوذان *'ûẓân* (also عوذ *'ûẓ*), pl. of عائذ *'â'iẓ*, mare on the 10th to 15th day after dropping young.

(عور) *'âr*, U, INF. *'aur*, make one-eyed, deprive of an eye; U, I, take away, spoil, destroy; efface, blot out; — aor. *ya'âr*, — also *'awir*, A, INF. *'awar*, be one-eyed, be blind (one eye); be full of rents, ambushes, dangers (a place); be spoiled; — II. INF. *ta'wîr*, deprive of one eye; ruin, give over to destruction; obstruct a well; (m.) damage, maim; hinder, prevent; refuse a request; = III.; — III. INF. *mu'âwara-t*, fix accurately the measure and weight of a thing; — IV. INF. *i'wâr*, make one-eyed; be full of rents, ambushes, dangers, &c.; INF. *i'âra-t*, lend (2 acc.); borrow; exchange; show or present one's self; offer the side, lay one's self open to an enemy; — V. INF. *ta'awwur*, borrow; (m.) be damaged, maimed; — VI. INF. *ta'âwur*, lend to one another; blot out the traces of a dwelling; — VIII. INF. *i'tiwâr*, lend mutually; — IX. INF. *i'wirâr*, be one-eyed; — X. INF. *isti'âra-t*, borrow; use in a metaphorical sense; be by one's self; be transferred to others; — XI. INF. *i'wîrâr*, be one-eyed.

عور *'ûr*, عوران *'ûrân*, pl. of اعور *a'war*, one-eyed, &c.; — *'awir*, full of rents, &c.; — ة *'aura-t*, *'awra-t*, pl. *'aurât*, *'awarât*, rent, cleft; parts between the navel and knee, pudenda; disgrace, ignominy; vice, fault; weakness, weak point; blindness of one eye; — *'awira-t*, place full of rents, ambushes, dangers, &c.

عورا *'aurâ'*, f. of اعور *a'war*, one-eyed, &c.; obscene language or action, ribaldry; solecism, barbarism; waterless desert.

(عوز) *'âz*, U, INF. *'auz*, flee, escape; — *'awiz*, A, INF. *'awaz*, escape, be lacking, be not in existence; be poor, needy; want; — IV. INF. *i'wâz*, be poor, needy; impoverish; be necessary but out of reach; escape, fail; be difficult; — VIII. INF. *i'tiyâz*, want, need.

عوز *'auz*, ة, grape-stone; — *'awaz*, pl. *ma'âwiz*, need, want; — *'awiz*, needy; عوز لوز *'awiz lawiz*, extremely poor.

(عوس) *'âs*, U, INF. *'aus*, *'awasân*, roam about at night-time; seek

for a prey; INF. *'aus, 'iyâsa-t,* manage or administer well; support one's family, toil for it; — *'awis,* A, INF. *'awas,* have the corners of the mouth deeply drawn in.

عوس *'aus,* pen-knife, knife.

عوسا *'ausâ,* f. of اعوس *a'was,* who draws in the corners of the mouth, &c.

عوسج *'ausaj,* ة *'ausaja-t,* a thorny shrub.

(عوص) *'âṣ,* INF. *'awaṣ, 'iyâṣ,* be obscure, difficult to understand; be difficult; — *'awiṣ,* A, INF. *'awaṣ,* id.; — II. INF. *ta'wîṣ,* produce or recite obscure verses; — III. INF. *mu'âwaṣa-t,* try to throw down; — IV. *a'waṣ,* INF. *'awaṣ, 'iyâṣ,* press the adversary into a corner; speak in a strange, unintelligible manner; — VIII. INF. *i'tiyâṣ,* be obscure, difficult and complicated; be hard in understanding; fail to conceive (camel).

عوصا *'auṣâ',* f. of اعوص *a'waṣ,* difficult to understand, &c.; difficult matter; يركب العوصا *yarkab al-'auṣâ',* he runs risks.

(عوض) *'âḍ,* U, INF. *'auḍ, 'iwaḍ, 'iyâḍ,* do or give one thing instead of another, compensate; — II. INF. *ta'wîḍ,* id.; substitute; — III. INF. *mu'âwaḍa-t,* IV. INF. *i'âḍa-t,* id.; — V. INF. *ta'awwuḍ,* receive or take in compensation for (عن *'an*); — VIII. INF. *i'tiyâḍ,* id.; put one thing in place of another; exchange; — X. INF. *isti'âḍa-t,* claim compensation or damages; wish for an exchange.

عوض *'iwaḍ,* pl. *a'wâḍ,* compensation; requital, reward; stead.

(عوط) *'âṭ,* U, I, INF. *'auṭ, 'aiṭ,* fail to conceive for several years (also V., VIII.); be long (also V.); — V. INF. *ta'awwuṭ*=I.; — VIII. INF. *i'tiyâṭ,* see I.; be difficult, complicated.

عوط *'ûṭ,* عوطط *'ûṭaṭ,* &c., pl. of عائط *'â'iṭ,* not conceiving for several years.

عوطب *'auṭab,* calamity; precipice, abyss.

عوعا *'au'â',* clamour, noise, tumult.

عوعو *'au'au,* ة *'au'aua-t,* howling, barking (s.).

(عوف) *'âf,* U, INF. *'auf,* adhere to; be attached to; fly round, circle round; — II. INF. *ta'wîf,* pass over in silence; (m.) spare, exempt; — V. INF. *ta'awwuf,* seek for prey at night-time.

عوف *'auf,* state, condition; affair, concern, matter; luck, good fortune; — ى *'aufiyy,* devoted; attached.

(عوق) *'âq,* U, INF. *'auq,* hinder, prevent, check, avert; detain, delay; be in the way; — II. INF. *ta'wîq,* hinder, prevent; — IV. INF. *i'âqa-t,* id.; INF. *i'wâq,* refuse further service (beast); run short (provisions); — V. INF. *ta'awwuq,* be hindered, prevented; tarry, hesitate, delay; — VII. INF. *in'iyâq,* be hindered, prevented; — VIII. INF. *i'tiyâq,* id.; find hindrances; prevent, hinder; be detained, be a captive.

عوق *'auq,* hindrance, delay; time; — *'auq, 'ûq, 'awiq,* ة *'auqa-t,* &c., casual impediment or obstruction; — *'auq, 'ûq,* pl. *a'wâq,* good for nothing; — *'awaq,* hunger; — *'awiq,* hungry; — *'uwaq, 'uwwaq,* ة *'uwaqa-t,* who is always in the way; coward; *'uwwaq,* pl. of عائق *'â'iq,* what hinders.

(عوك) *'âk,* A, INF. *'auk,* face about and attack again, assault; turn to, approach; return home; take refuge; hope; INF. *'auk, ma'âk,* gain, earn; — III. INF. *mu'âwaka-t,* fight one another; — VIII. INF. *i'tiwâk,* press one another.

عوك *'auk,* movement, motion; thing.

عوكر *'aukar,* INF. ة, trouble, make turbid; — II. INF. *ta'aukur,* be turbid.

عوكشة *'aukaśa-t,* winnowing-van, cribble.

(عول) *'âl,* U, I, INF. *'aul,* deviate from what is right, be unjust; fall short; — U, I, incline to one side (balance); exact more than what is right, be exacted unduly; be very difficult; press down, oppress, break (a.); also pass. *'îl,* be exhausted; — INF. *'aul, 'uwûl, 'iyâla-t,* support one's family, sustain; (m.) nurse, take care of; — INF. *'aul, 'iyâla-t,* have many to keep; — II. INF. *ta'wîl,* rely upon, believe one; resolve upon (على *'ala*); invoke one's help; lament; make a roof of branches as protection against the rain; behave provokingly; — IV. INF. *i'âla-t, i'wâl,* sustain one's family; have many to keep; be poor; exact more than is due; crave for, be greedy; *a'wal,* lament, wail; resound; behave provokingly; — VIII. INF. *i'tiyâl,* wail, lament.

عول *'aul,* aberration; sustenance of one's family; also ة *'aula-t,* lamentation; — *'iwal,* reliance; call for help; — ة *'aula-t,* travelling-provisions.

(عوم) *'âm,* U, INF. *'aum,* swim; float; walk along; — II. INF. *ta'wîm,* make swim; launch; place the corn in sheaves; bear fruit but every second year (also III.); heap up the measure; — III. INF. *mu'âwama-t,* see II.; hire or rent for a year; make a contract for a year.

عوم *'aum,* ة *'auma-t,* swimming (s.); navigation; abundance; — *'uwwam,* pl. of عائم *'â'im,* swimming (adj.); — ة *'ûma-t,* pl. *'uwam,* a small aquatic animal.

(عون) *'ân,* U, INF. *'uwûn,* enter on middle age; be no longer a virgin; become a wife, a matron; — II. INF. *ta'wîm,* id.; cover frequently (ass); receive another's share; help; — III. INF. *'iwâm, mu'âwana-t,* help, assist; — IV. INF. *i'âna-t,* id.; deliver, free; — VI. INF. *ta'âwun,* help one another; — VIII. INF. *i'tiyân,* id.; — X. INF. *isti'âna-t,* ask for help or assistance; shave the hair of the pudenda.

عون *'aun,* ة *'auna-t,* help, assistance; pl. *a'wân,* helper, ally; servant, satellite, lifeguardsman; (m.) giant; — *'ûn,* pl. of عانة *'âna-t,* hair of the pudenda, &c., and of عوان *'awân.*

عونجى *'aunjiyy,* detective; confidant; informer (m.).

عونى *'auniyy,* helping (adj.), serviceable.

(عوه) *'âh,* I, INF. *'uwûh,* suffer misfortune, loss; have an infirmity; pass. *'îh,* id.; (m.) hurt one's self; — II. INF. *ta'wîh,* cause a damage, an illness; (m.) maim; suffer a loss of cattle or fruit (also IV.); make a halt towards morning, be detained, stay, abide; — IV. INF. *i'âha-t, i'wâh,* see II.; — V. INF. *ta'awwuh,* have an infirmity.

عوة *'awwa-t,* clamour, turmoil; also *'uwwa-t,* the buttocks.

عوهب *'auhab,* INF. ة, lead into error.

(عوى) *'awa,* I, INF. *'ayy, 'uwâ', 'awwa-t, 'awiyy, 'awiyya-t,* howl, growl; condole with; turn aside; direct; plait, twist, bend; be thirty years old and strong of hand; convict of a lie or false pretences; incite to rebellion; — II. INF. *ta'wiya-t,* turn, bend (a.); howl, bark; — III. *mu'âwât,* lament, wail, howl with; — VI. INF. *ta'âwî,*

howl to one another (wolves, &c.); — X. INF. *isti'wâ'*, cause a dog to howl; ask for legal assistance, for help; call the people to revolt.

عوى *'awiyy*, ة *'awiyya-t*, howl.

عويسية *'awaisiyya-t*, pen-knife, knife.

عويص *'awîṣ*, puzzle.

عويل *'awîl*, ة *'awîla-t*, howling (s.); wailing, lamentation for the dead; — *'awîl*, travelling-provisions (m.).

عويم *'uwaim*, dim. of عام *'âm*, year; ذات عويم *ẑât-a 'uwaim*, last year.

(عوين) *'uwain*, little eye; pl. *'uwainât*, spectacles.

(عى) *'ayya*, INF. *'ayy*, *'ayâ'*, stop short in anything, slacken, be not equal to it; stammer; — عيى *'ayî*, A, INF. *'iyy*, id.; be ignorant; be weak, tired, slack; — II. INF. *ta'yiya-t*, speak indistinctly; be or get tired; tire (a.); be too difficult for; weaken, prostrate beyond recovery; — V. INF. *ta'ayyî*, VI. INF. *ta'âyî*, be not equal to (ب *bi* or على *'ala*); — X. INF. *isti'yâ'*, id.

عى *'ayy*, INF. of (عوى); pl. *a'yâ'*, incapable, relaxing; impotent; stammering (adj.); *'ayy*, *'iyy*, INF. of (عى).

عيا *'ayâ'*, pl. *a'yâ'*, difficult; incurable; impotent.

عياب *'iyâb*, pl. of عيبة *'aiba-t*; — *'ayyâb*, ة *'ayyâba-t*, reviler, slanderer.

عياث *'ayyâs̱*, lion.

عياد *'iyâd*, ة *'iyâda-t*, frequent return; repeated visit of the sick; habit, practice.

عياذ *'iyâẑ*, seeking refuge (s.); عياذاً بالله *'iyâẑ-an bi 'l-lâh*, God forbid.

عيار *'iyâr*, standard measure or weight; touchstone; criterion; regulation of a watch, &c.; — *; — *'ayyâr*, ة, who turns and twists about; impostor, quack; who stirs up disturbances; impudent fraud; lion; — ة *'iyâra-t*, publicity; anything borrowed; anything false, spurious, counterfeit; INF. of (عير).

عياسة *'iyâsa-t*, good management.

عياش *'ayyâś*, who knows how to live; gormandizer.

عياص *'iyâṣ*, difficulty, obscurity (عوص).

عياض *'iyâḍ*, requital, compensation; exchange (عوض).

عياط *'iyâṭ*, clamour, tumult, outcry; — *'ayyâṭ*, screamer; — *.

عياف *'iyâf*, aversion; — ة *'iyâfa-t*, augury; elegance, distinction.

عياقة *'iyâqa-t*, skill, cleverness; (m.) elegance.

عيال *'iyâl*, family, household, dependents; pl. of عيل *'ayyil*; — ة *'iyâla-t*, food; sustenance.

عيان *'ayân*, distinct; public, notorious; — *'iyân*, seeing (s.) with one's own eyes; distinctness; evidence; publicity; pl. *a'yina-t*, *'uyun*, plough-share; — *'ayyân*, tired, weak, unwell; incapable; — ة *'iyâna-t*, rainflood; being (s.) an eye-witness; personal observation; spying (s.); spy; — ى *'iyâniyy*, eye-witness; spy.

عيايا *'ayâyâ'* = عى *'ayy*, incapable, &c.

عيائل *'ayâ'il*, pl. of عيل *'ayyil*.

(عيب) *'âb*, I, INF. *'aib*, be defective, faulty, deteriorated, spoiled; be bad; have faults, vices; make defective, deteriorate, spoil, corrupt; blame, rebuke, find fault with; revile, abuse; accuse; — II. INF. *ta'yîb*, make defective, deteriorate, spoil; accuse; revile; put down as a fault or vice, impute such; surpass in faults, vices; shame another by one's own excellences; — V. INF. *ta'ayyub*, be defective, faulty, spoiled; — VII. INF. *in'iyâb*, id.; — X. INF. *isti'âba-t*, find defective, bad, blameworthy.

عيب *'aib*, pl. *'uyûb*, fault, defect; blame; disgrace; vice, ignominy; — ة *'aiba-t*, pl. *'iyab*, *'iyâb*, *'aibât*, id.; travelling-bag, trunk, wardrobe; *al-'iyâb*, heart, mind; — ة *'uyaba-t*, reviler, slanderer.

(عيث) *'âs̱*, I, INF. *'ais̱*, damage, injure, spoil, destroy; rage; — II. INF. *ta'yîs̱*, begin (with aor.); feel for, grope; — V. INF. *ta'ayyus̱*, drink not its fill (camel).

عيثام *'ais̱âm*, plane-tree.

عيثر *'ais̱ar*, trace; essence; thing.

(عيج) *'âj*, I, INF. *'aij*, find pleasant, agreeable; be concerned at, heed; quench one's thirst; find relief by a remedy.

(عيد) *'âd*, I, INF. *'aid*, come repeatedly; visit the sick; — II. INF. *ta'yîd*, celebrate a feast, keep festival; wish joy to a feast (also III.); make a festival for; — III. INF. *mu'âyada-t*, see II.; — V. INF. *ta'ayyud*, try to injure by the evil eye; abuse her fellow wives and raise the hand against them.

عيد *'îd*, pl. *a'yâd*, feast, feast day; access (of regret, &c.); — ة *'iyada-t*, pl. of عود.

عيدان *'aidân*, ة, high palm-tree; — *'îdân*, pl. of عود *'ûd*.

عيدى *'îdiyy*, ة, festive; — ة *'îdiyya-t*, festive-gift.

(عير) *'âr*, I, INF. *'air*, *'ayâra-t*, *'iyâra-t*, roam about, rove, wander, run away; travel; rage; go and come frequently; take away; spoil; become known; — II. INF. *ta'yîr*, reproach with (ب *bi* or 2 acc.); revile, dishonour; verify a weight or coin; gauge; be covered with green mud; — III. INF. *'iyâr*, *mu'âyara-t*, determine the difference between (بين *bain*); roam about; — IV. INF. *i'âra-t*, allow to rove; — V. INF. *ta'ayyur*, be weighed; be gauged, legalised; disgrace one's self; — VI. INF. *ta'âyur*, revile one another.

عير *'air*, f. ة, pl. *'iyâr*, *'uyûr*, *'uyûra-t*, *'iyârât*, *a'yâr*, *ma'yûrâ'*, wild ass; ass (كجوف عير *ka-jauf-i 'air-in*, useless); lord, master, prince; middle and thicker part; back; pupil of the eye, look; — *'îr*, pl. *'irât*, *'iyarât*, caravan, train of beasts of burden.

عيران *'îrân*, pl. of اعور *a'war*, one-eyed; — ة *'airâna-t*, fleet she-camel.

عيزار *'aizâr*, vigorous, brisk.

(عيس) *'âs*, I, INF. *'ais*, cover and get with young; — IV. INF. *i'yâs*, lack verdure; — V. INF. *ta'ayyus*, be of a greyish or yellowish whiteness.

عيس *'ais*, sperm of the stallion; — *'îs*, pl. and—

عيسا *'aisâ'*, f. of اعيس *a'yâs*, yellowish-white; white she-camel; female locust.

عيسوى *'îsawiyy*, ة, referring to Jesus; Christian (adj. s.).

عيسى *'îsa*, Jesus; — *'îsiyy*, Christian (adj.).

(عيش) *'âś*, I, INF. *'aiś*, *'îśa-t*, *'aiśûśa-t*, *ma'âś*, *ma'îś*, *ma'îśa-t*, live, gain one's living; enjoy life; pass. *'îś*, be kept alive, live; — II. INF. *ta'yîś*, make one to live, let live; enliven; keep, feed, sustain; — IV. INF. *i'âśa-t*, keep alive, let live; — V. INF. *ta'ayyuś*, try to gain a living; — VIII. INF. *i'tiyâś*, live upon.

عيش *'aiś*, life; living, livelihood; enjoyment of life; bread; — ة *'îśa-t*, way of life; ease, enjoyable life.

عيشا *'îśâ'*, maternal womb.

عيشم *'aiśam*, mouldy, stale.

عيشوشة *'aiśûśa-t*, INF. of (عيش); ease, enjoyable life.

عيص *'aiṣ* (also عيصو *'îṣû*), Esau; — *'îṣ*, ة *'îṣa-t*, pl. *'iṣân*, *a'yâṣ*, thicket; root.

(عيط) *'âṭ*, I, INF. *'aiṭ*, *'iyâṭ*, fail to get with child for several years (also V. and VIII.); — *'ayiṭ*, A, INF. *'ayaṭ* (also V.), have a long neck; — II. INF. *ta'yîṭ*, cry out, scream; clamour; call to; scold; — V. INF. *ta'ayyuṭ*, see I.; ooze; flow; scream, clamour, make a tumult; — VI. INF. *ta'âyuṭ*, cry out at one another, scold one another; — VIII. INF. *i'tiyâṭ*, see I.

عيط *'îṭ*, pl. of عايط *'âyiṭ*, failing to conceive for several years, and of اعيط *a'yâṭ*, f. عيطا *'aiṭâ'*, long-necked, &c.; — ة *'aiṭa-t*, out-cry, scream, shout.

(عيع), II. *'ayya'*, INF. *ta'yî'*, desist from one's purpose.

(عيف) *'âf*, A, I, INF. *'aif*, *'ayafân*, *'iyâf*, *'iyâfa-t*, loathe, refuse, dislike, be unwilling; leave, forsake; — I, INF. *'iyâfa-t*, take augury from the flight of birds; INF. *'aif*, hover above, circle around; — VII. INF. *in'iyâf*, leave undone; be abandoned; be excepted; — VIII. INF. *i'tiyâf*, make provision for a journey.

(عيق) *'âq*, I, INF. *'aiq*=(عوق); — II. INF. *ta'yîq*, cry out, shout, scream.

عيق *'aiq*, hindrance, impediment; — also *'ayyiq*, who is only in the way, useless; — also ة *'aiqa-t*, sea-shore.

(عيك) *'âk*, I, INF. *'ayakân*, move the shoulders in walking; — ة *'aika-t*, forest-thicket.

(عيل) *'âl*, I, (also V.) balance one's self proudly in walking; — INF. *'ail*, *'aila-t*, *'uyûl*, *ma'îl*, grow poor; be unable to sustain one's family any longer; — INF. *'ail*, *ma'îl*, impoverish, forsake, desert, escape; — INF. *'ail*, *'uyûl*, travel about; — II. INF. *ta'yîl*, sustain one's family; sustain them in a poor or neglectful way; receive into one's family; allow the horse to graze at large; — IV. INF. *i'âla-t*, have a large family to keep; be poor; crave for; seek for people; — V. INF. *ta'ayyul*, see I.

عيل *'ayyil*, pl. *a'yila-t*, *a'wila-t*, *'âla-t*, *'iyâl*, *'ayâyil*, wife; family; who belongs to the household; — *'uyyal*, pl. of عائل *'â'il*, poor; — ة *'aila-t*, family; poverty, penury; — ى *'aila*, pl. of عائل *'â'il*, poor.

(عيم) *'âm*, A, I, INF. *'aim*, *'aima-t*, have a violent thirst for milk; lack milk; — IV. INF. *i'âma-t*, id.; leave without milk; — VIII. INF. *i'tiyâm*, take away the best part; — ة *'aima-t*, thirst; — *'îma-t*, best part of a property.

عيمان *'aimân*, f. *'aima*, thirsty for milk.

(عين) *'ân*, I, INF. *'ain*, *'ayanân*, flow, gush, well; meet with a spring in digging; hurt the eye; — INF. *'ain*, fix one's look upon, try to injure by the evil eye; — INF. *'iyâna-t*, make inquiries and bring information; — *'ayin*, A, INF. *'ayan*, have large eyes, have the black of the eyes large; — II. INF. *ta'yîn*, make evident, clear, recognisable; define, determine, specify; mark, characterize; distinguish; except; pierce, make holes in; form eyes; bud, bloom; buy on credit up to a fixed term; fix prices for a certain time; enlist (a.); stir up war; form the letter ع; — III. INF. *'iyân*, *mu'âyana-t*, fix the eyes upon, see with one's own eyes, spy; behold, perceive; feel, be sensible of; — IV. *a'yan*, meet with a well in digging; INF. *i'âna-t*, look sharp at, try to injure by the evil eye; — V. INF. *ta'ayyun*, be evident; be marked, characterized, defined, determined, specified; be peculiar to, inseparable from, incumbent on; be particularly

attached to; try to injure by the evil eye; have many eyes or holes; take money in advance; enlist (n.); — VIII. INF. *i'tiyân*, look out from a watch-tower and observe; spy out; bring information; fix one's look upon, try to injure by the evil eye; take the whole or the best part; buy on credit.

عين *'ain*, pl. *'uyûn*, *a'yun*, spring, source; lasting rain; pl. *'uyûn*, *a'yun*, *a'yân*, pl. pl. *a'yûnât*, eye (على عينى *'ala 'ainî*, upon my eye, willingly); *'uyûn*, *'uyûnât*, spectacles; look; aspect; bud; hole, opening; mesh; link of a chain or coat of mail; mien, physiognomy; influence of the evil eye; substance, essence, the best of a thing; choice point; original model; self, the same, identically equal, copy; sun, sun-beams; appearance; what is in existence, ready at hand (money); gold piece, coin; uterine brother; belonging to the family, member of the family, citizen; somebody; troop, number of people; young wild bullock; letter ع, second radical of a root; *al-a'yân*, the great ones of the realm, grandees; pl. *'uyûn*, *a'yun*, scout, watchman; ع الحياة *'ain al-hayât*, mercury; ع الشمس *'ain aś-śams*, disc of the sun, opal; ع القطر *'ain al-qaṭr*, brimstone; — *'în*, wild cattle; pl. of اعين, large-eyed, and of عيون *'ayûn*; *'ayan*, people of the house-hold; citizens; — *'uyun*, pl. of عيان *'iyân* and عيون *'ayûn*; — *'ayyin*, full of eyes or holes; — ة *'aina-t*, lasting rain; — *'îna-t*, advance of money; the best part of a property.

عينا *'ain-an*, exactly so, indeed; — *'ainâ'*, f. of اعين *a'yan*, large-eyed, &c.; distinct, well-ordered speech.

عينى *'ainiyy*, ة, essential, natural; genuine; equal, identical; original; authentic; ready; — ة *'ainiyya-t*, sample, pattern, model.

(عيه) *'âh*, I, INF. *'aih*, meet with a loss or injury, be damaged.

عيوب *'ayûb*, blameworthy; — *

عيوف *'ayûf*, loathing; baseness.

عيوق *'ayyûq*, capella (constellation); (m.) pretty, handsome.

عيون *'ayûn*, pl. *'în*, *'uyun*, who looks at fixedly and frequently, who looks at with an evil eye; — *.

عيى *'ayiyy*, pl. *a'yiyâ'*, *a'yiya-t* = عى *'ayy*, stammering, &c.

عيير *'uyair*, little ass.

عيينة *'uyaina-t*, little eye.

غ

غ *g*, as a numerical sign = 1000; denotes quadrature in the aspects of the stars.

غابر *gâbir*, ة, pl. *gubbar*, *gawâbir*, remaining, left; gone, passed, fleeting, ceasing; future, future tense.

غابط *gâbiṭ*, pl. *gubuṭ*, who finds enviable, envier, rival.

غابن *gâbin*, impostor; relaxed.

غاب *gâb-in*, غابى *gâbî*, weak-minded, forgetful; — ة *gâba-t*, pl. *gâb*, lowland; thicket; lair of a wild beast.

غابية *gâbiya-t*, top-sail.

غاد *gâd-in*, see غادى *gâdî*; — ة *gâda-t*, f. fresh, tender; tender branch.

غادوف *gâdûf*, oar.

غادى *gâdî* (غاد *gâd-in*), ة, who rises early, does anything early in the morning ; — ة *gâdiya-t*, early rain.

غاذ *gâẕ-in*, غاذى *gâẕiyy*, ة, digestive ; nutritious ; ة *gâẕiy-ya-t*, digestion ; foster-mother ; — *gâẕẕ*, fistula of the lachrymal gland.

غار *gâr*, pl. *agwâr*, *gîrân*, cave ; lair ; socket of the eye ; interior of the mouth (du. mouth and pudenda, anus and pudenda) ; a measurement ; army, squadron, troop of plundering enemies ; jealousy, envy ; dust ; — *gârr*, pl. *gurûr*, anything vain, frivolous ; seducing ; negligent ; slack ; — ة *gâra-t*, invasion, raid ; plunder ; gallop ; squadron ; a kind of laurel ; navel.

غارب *gârib*, who comes from afar ; setting (adj.) ; crest of a wave ; pl. *gawârib*, part between hump and neck of a camel, hump, neck.

غارز *gâriz*, pl. *gurraz*, yielding but little milk ; thrusting in anything pointed, a sword, sting, &c.

غارض *gâriḍ*, who does anything early in the morning ; long.

غارق *gâriq*, immersed ; sunk ; shipwrecked.

غارم *gârim*, debtor.

غازل *gâzil*, spider ; — ة *gâzila-t*, pl. *guzzal*, *gawâzil*, spinster (female spinner).

غازى *gâzî* (*gâz-in*), pl. *guzza*, *guzziyy*, *guzzâ'*, *guzât*, who wages war against the infidel ; commander ; conqueror ; — ة *gâziya-t*, conquering expedition, hostile invasion, war against the infidel.

غاسق *gâsiq*, first part of the night.

غاسل *gâsil*, ة, washer ; — ة *gâsila-t*, woman who washes the dead.

غاسول *gâsûl*, what cleanses well ; soap.

غاش *gâś-in*, see غاشى *gâśî* ; — *gâśś*, deceptive.

غاشم *gâśim*, unjust, tyrannous.

غاشى *gâśî* (غاش *gâś-in*), who covers, presents himself, comes, &c. ; — ة *gâśiya-t*, pl. *gawâśî*, covering ; saddle-cloth ; pericardium ; colic ; resurrection ; hell ; pl. sorrows ; friends, servants, attendants.

غاص *gâṣṣ*, choking (adj.).

غاصب *gâṣib*, who uses violence ; tyrant ; robber.

غاطس *gâṭis*, pl. *gawâṭis*, immersed ; clad in armour ; (m.) delirious.

غاطى *gâṭî* (غاط *gâṭ-in*), ة, covering (adj.) ; — ة *gâṭiya-t*, vine-tree.

غافصة *gâfiṣa-t*, pl. *gawâfiṣ*, mishap, accident, disaster.

غافى *gâfî*, sleepy.

غاق *gâq*, ة *gâqa-t*, crow.

غال *gâl*, pl. *gâlât*, lock of a door ; — *gâl-in*, see غالى *gâlî* ; — *gâll*, pl. *gallân*, thirsty ; flat land ; fertile.

غالب *gâlib*, ag. of (غلب), overcoming, &c. ; majority ; frequent ; victor, conqueror.

غالبية *gâlibiyya-t*, victory ; superior or supreme power.

غالى *gâlî* (غال *gâl-in*), ة, pl. *galât*, dear, expensive, costly, precious ; seething, boiling (adj.) ; zealot ; — ة *gâliya-t*, pl. *gawâlî*, perfume of musk and ambergris.

غام *gâmm*, covering (adj.) ; sultry, close, oppressive ; sorrowful.

غامد *gâmiḍ*, under cargo, loaded.

غامر *gâmir*, non-inhabited, uncultivated, opposed to عامر *'âmir* ; swamping everything ; (m.) embracing (adj.) ; pl. *-ât*, deserts.

غامض *gâmiḍ*. pl. *gawâmiḍ*, deep, deep-set ; difficult to understand, obscure, enigmatical, mysterious ; vile, mean, common ; slack, weak ; — ة *gâmiḍa-t*, pl. *gawâmiḍ*, anything obscure, mystery.

غاميا *gamiyâ'*, mouse-holes.

(غانظ) *gâniẓ*, throat.

غانم *gânim*, loaded with booty; successful.

غانى *gânî* (غان *gân-in*), ة, rich, able to do without a thing; singing (adj.); — ة *gâniya-t*, pl. *gawânî*, beautiful even without adornment, modest and chaste; female singer.

غاووش *gâwûś*, seed-cucumber.

غاوى *gâwî*, pl. *gâwûn*, *guwât*, erring; seduced; seducer; Satan; — ة *gâwiya-t*, knapsack, satchel, skin bag.

غائب *gâ'ib*, *gâyib*, ة, pl. *guyyab*, *gayab*, *guyyâb*, *gawâyib*, absent, hidden, concealed; mysterious; disappearing; invisible; transcendental; third person.

غائر *gâ'ir*, *gâyir*, disappearing in the ground; galloping; jealous, envious; على الغ *'ala 'l-gâyir*, by heart; — ة *gâ'ira-t*, *gâyira-t*, noon; mid-day slumber, siesta.

غائص *gâ'iṣ*, *gâyiṣ*, who plunges, diver; sunken, depraved.

غائض *gâ'iḍ*, *gâyiḍ*, falling, sinking, decreasing.

غائط *gâ'iṭ*, *gâyiṭ*, pl. *gûṭ*, *agwâṭ*, *giyâṭ*, *giṭân*, flat plain; ambush; human excrement; dung-pit.

غائل *gâ'il*, *gâyil*, breaking upon suddenly; death; demon; — ة *gâ'ila-t*, *gâyila-t*, pl. *gawâyil*, misfortune, calamity; torment, vexation; enforced service; pain; rent, breach; pregnant woman who gives suck.

غاية *gâya-t*, pl. *-ât* and *gây*, end, limit, goal, extremity, extreme; standard; boundary-pole; last resource; *bi 'l-gâya-t*, in the extreme, very much.

(غب) *gabb*, I, INF. *gabb*, *gibb*, *gubûb*, be watered every second day; come every second day; do a thing every second or third day; pass the night; putrefy; be brought to an end, be successful; recover; sip; — II. INF. *tagbîb*, seize the sheep by the throat; slacken, relax; keep off; — IV. INF. *igbâb*, befall or visit every third day; study with interruptions; water the camels every second day; pass the night; putrefy.

غب *gibb*, watering (s.) on every second day; recurrence on every third day (of a fever); rare visit; end, issue; *gibb-a*, after; *gibb-an*, rarely; — *gubb*, who travels to the interior of a country; pl. *agbâb*, *gubûb*, watery lowland; swelling of the waves; — ة *gubba-t*, sip, draught.

(غبا) *gaba'*, INF. *gab'*, repair to.

غبار *gubâr*, dust; grief, sadness, affliction; torment, vexation.

غباشة *gabâśa-t*, weak eye-sight (m.).

غباشير *gabâśîr*, morning twilight.

غبانة *gabâna-t*, silliness.

غباوة *gabâwa-t*, INF. of (غبى); stupidity, folly; secret hatred, grudge.

غبب *gabab*, loose flesh beneath the chin; dewlap.

غبث *gabaṯ*, U, INF. *gabṯ*, mix cream-cheese with butter; — IX. INF. *igbiṯâṯ*, be ash-coloured.

(غبج) *gabij*, A, INF. *gabaj*, sip, lap; — ة *gabja-t*, sip, draught.

(غبر) *gabar*, U, INF. *gubûr*, tarry, abide; remain, be left; pass; be passed, be gone; be to come, impend; be dust-coloured, dusty; — *gabir*, A, INF. *gabar*, get corrupted, putrefy; — II. INF. *tagbîr*, dirty with dust; throw dust into one's face; milk the remainder of the milk; — IV. INF. *igbâr*, raise dust; exert one's self to the utmost in (فى *fî*); rain heavily; be dust-coloured; — V. INF. *tagabbur*, milk the remainder of the milk; be dust-covered; — IX. INF. *igbirâr*, be or become dust-coloured.

غبر *gibr*, secret hatred; — *gubr*, pl.

agbâr, anything left, remainder of milk in the udder; pl. of اغبر *agbar*, dust-coloured; — *gabar*, unheard of calamity; dust;—*gabir*, putrescent; bursting again (vein);—*gubbar*, *gubar* =*gubr*; pl. of غابر *gâbir*, remaining, left, &c.; — ة *gabra-t*, *gabara-t*, dust; — *gubra-t*, dust-colour; —*gubbara-t*, remainder.

غبرا *gabrâ'*, pl. *gubr*, f. of اغبر *agbar*, dust-coloured, &c.; earth, dust.

غبران *gubrân*, pl. *gabârîn*, two dates on one pedicle.

(غبس) *gabas*, A, INF. *gabs*, be dark; — IX. INF. *igbisâs*, XI. INF. *igbîsâs*, id.

غبس *gabas*, darkness; dirt-colour; — *gubs*, pl. and—

غبسا *gabsâ'*, f. of اغبس *agbas*, greyish-brown.

(غبش) *gabiś*, A, INF. *gabaś*, be on the point of turning into dawn (night); be dark; — II. INF. *tagbîś*, see things as in a twilight (m.); — IV. INF. *igbâs*= I.; — V. INF. *tagabbuś*, wrong, injure.

غبش *gabaś*, ة *gubśa-t*, pl. *agbâś*, twilight of the morning; — *gabiś*, dark.

(غبص) *gabiṣ*, A, INF. *gabaṣ*, be unclean, running (eye).

(غبط) *gabaṭ*, I, feel the buttocks and back to examine the fatness of an animal; — I, INF. *gabṭ*, *gibṭa-t*, also *gabiṭ*, A, find one's position enviable, envy, be jealous; — II. INF. *tagbîṭ*, place one in an enviable position; — IV. INF. *igbâṭ*, leave the saddle on the beast's back; visit continually; rain unceasingly; cover the ground densely; — V. INF. *tagabbuṭ*, rejoice in; be angry with; — VII. INF. *ingibâṭ*, be angry (m.); — VIII. INF. *igtibâṭ*, be in an enviable position; rejoice in (ب *bi*).

غبط *gabṭ*, ة *gibṭa-t*, enviable state, good fortune, luck; envy; — *gubuṭ*, pl. of غابط *gâbiṭ* and غبيط *gabîṭ*.

غبغب *gabgab*=غبب *gabab*.

(غبق) *gabaq*, U, INF. *gabq*, offer or take an evening draught; — V. INF. *tagabbuq*, milk in the evening; — VIII. INF. *igtibâq*, take an evening draught.

(غبن) *gaban*, U, INF. *gabn*, *gaban*, deceive, defraud; pass. *gubin*, be foolish; — U, A, have no knowledge of, ignore; INF. *gabn*, fold up, turn in; — *gabin*, A, INF. *gabn*, *gaban*, forget, neglect from thoughtlessness; INF. *gaban*, *gabâna-t*, be imbecile, thoughtless, easy to be deceived; ignore; — III. INF. *mugâbana-t*, deceive; — VI. INF. *tagâbun*, deceive one another; — VIII. *igtibân*, take under one's arm.

غبن *gabn*, deceit, fraud; — *gaban*, imbecility; forgetfulness; — ة *gabna-t*, turned-in part of a garment.

غبو *gabw*, fainting-fit; (m.) light fog, mist; — ة *gabwa-t*, *gubuwwa-t*, forgetfulness.

(غبى) *gabî*, A, INF. *gaban*, *gabâwa-t*, fail to understand, to conceive; be concealed, obscure, unintelligible; escape; swoon, faint; — II. INF. *tagbiya-t*, clip and pull out the hair; cover, conceal; — IV. INF. *igbâ'*, send down a heavy rain; — V. INF. *tagabbî*, be hidden, concealed, obscure; — VI. INF. *tagâbî*, neglect, be thoughtless about; feign carelessness; — VIII. INF. *igtibâ'*=V.; wish to make a fool of.

غبى *gabiyy*, imbecile, foolish, forgetful; selfish; — *gubiyy*, forgetfulness; — ة *gabya-t*, heavy shower; whirling cloud of dust; sunset.

غبيرا *gubairâ'*, an intoxicating drink made of millet.
غبيس *gubais*, wolf.
غبيط *gabîṭ*, pl. *gubuṭ*, camel-saddle for women; abyss in a river; deep place.
غبين *gabîn*, imbecile, fool; — ة *gabîna-t*, imbecility; deceit.
(غت) *gatt*, U, INF. *gatt*, plunge into the water; vex, grieve; hold one's mouth and nose shut, choke (a.); suppress one's laughter; silence; take one sip or draught after another; let one thing follow another.
غتل *gatil*, A, INF. *gatal*, be densely grown over with trees, bear a luxuriant growth of trees.
(غتم) *gatm*, oppressive heat; — *gutm*, pl. of اغتم *agtam*, speaking unintelligibly or barbarously; — ة *gutma-t*, barbarism, solecism; — IV. *agtam*, INF. *igtâm*, importune by visiting too frequently; — VIII. INF. *igtitâm*, id.; suffer from nausea.
غتمى *gutmiyy*, who speaks unintelligibly.
(غث) *gaṯṯ*, A, I, INF. *gaṯâṯa-t*, *guṯûṯa-t* (also IV.), be lean, thin; be false, spurious; — I, INF. *gaṯṯ*, cause pain; — I, INF. *gaṯṯ*, *gaṯîṯ* (also IV.), flow with pus; — II. INF. *tagṯîṯ*, grow fat by degrees; — IV. INF. *igṯâṯ*, see I.; — X. INF. *istigṯâṯ*, press the pus out of a wound.
غث *gaṯṯ*, ة, pl. *giṯâṯ*, lean, thin; false, spurious; bad, wicked, abominable; غث وثمين *gaṯṯ wa ṯamîn*, little and much, poor and rich, weak and strong, good and bad.
غثا *guṯâ'*, *guṯṯâ'*, pl. *agṯâ'*, foam, impurities, &c., upon a stream.
غثار *guṯâr*, hyena.
غثر *gaṯar*, U, INF. *gaṯr*, be covered with luxuriant vegetation; — ooze out honey; — XI. INF. *igṯîrâr*, be shaggy.
غثر *gaṯr*, ة *gaṯara-t*, rabble, dregs of the populace; — *gaṯar*, shaggy, coarse-haired cloth; — ة *gaṯra-t*, abundance, plenty, cheapness; — *guṯra-t*, black mingled with red, dirty green.
غثعث *gaṯ'aṯ*, INF. ة, stay, abide; fight without a weapon.
(غثم) *gaṯam*, U, INF. *gaṯm*, give the best part of one's property.
غثم *guṯm*, ة *gaṯima-t*, tripe, guts; — ة *guṯma-t*, blackish grey.
(غثمر) *gaṯmar*, INF. ة, allow one's goods and cattle to perish.
(غثو) *gaṯâ*, U, INF. *gaṯw*, carry many leaves, impurities, &c. along with its foam.
غثوثة *guṯûṯa-t*, INF. of (غث).
غثى *gaṯa*, I, INF. *gaṯy*=(غثو); wash away and spoil the hay (torrent); I, A, confuse; beat and kick; — INF. *gaṯy*, *gaṯayân*, be moved, agitated; be covered with clouds; be luxuriantly grown over; — IV. wash away and spoil hay, &c.
غثيث *gaṯîṯ*, pus, discharged matter; — *; — ة *gaṯîṯa-t*, corruption, putrescent flesh of a wound.
غد *gad*, next morning, morrow; بعد غد *ba'd-a gad-in*, the day after to-morrow.
(غد) *gadd*, U, INF. *gadd*, also pass. *gudd*, be covered with plague-blisters; — II. INF. *tagdîd*, id.; receive one's share; — IV. INF. *igdâd*=I.; (m.) have a goiter or a very fleshy chin; — ة *gudda-t*, pl. *gudad*, *gidâd*, *gadâ'id*, knob in the flesh, gland, scrofula; plague-blister; (m.) goiter, double-chin; portion, share.
غدا *gadâ'*, pl. *agdiya-t*, breakfast, morning meal, luncheon, dinner; — *gidâ'*, food, victuals; coming (s.) early in the morning; — ة *gadât*, pl. *gadawât*, early morning; *al-gadât*, this morning; غداة غد *gadât-a gadd-in*, to-morrow morning; غداتئذ *gadâta'iz-in*, on that morning.

غداد *gidâd*, pl. of غدة *gudda-t*.
غدار *gaddâr*, ة, very perfidious, treacherous; arch-traitor; —*; — ة *gaddâra-t*, a small pistol, hidden weapon.
غداف *gudâf*, pl. *gidfân*, black raven, vulture; black hair; — ى *gudâfiyy*, black-haired, raven-locked.
غدايا *gadâyá*, pl. of غدية *gadya-t*.
غدائد *gadâ'id*, pl. of غدة *gudda-t*.
(غدب) *gudubb*, thick and fleshy.
غدد *gadad*, camel-plague; — *gudad*, gut,; pl. of غدة *gudda-t*.
(غدر) *gadar*, I, U, INF. *gadr*, lag behind the flock; — INF. *gada-rân*, *gadr*, leave in the lurch, betray, deceive; compel, force; — I, drink out of a pond; — *gadir*, A, INF. *gadar*, lag behind the flock; leave in the lurch; become a traitor; — II. INF. *tadgîr*, form a pond; — III. INF. *gidâr*, *mugâdara-t*, leave in such or such a state, forsake (also IV.); leave in the lurch, betray; — IV. INF. *igdâr*, see III.; — VI. INF. *tagâdur*, betray one another; — VII. INF. *ingidâr*, be betrayed, deceived; — VIII. INF. *igtidâr*, make or take a milk-soup; — X. INF. *istigdâr*, get covered with ponds and pools.
غدر *gadr*, treason, treachery, perfidy; ingratitude; — *gadar*, anything abandoned or left behind; stony, rugged ground; — *gudar*, *gadar*, ة, pool, water-ditch; — *gudur*, pl. of غدير *gadîr*; pl. traitors; — ة *gudra-t*, anything left behind; — *gadira-t*, f. also—
غدرا *gadrâ'*, f. dark.
غدران *gudrân*, pl. of غدير *gadîr*.
(غدغد) *gadgad*, INF. ة, have a goiter or a double-chin.
(غدف) *gadaf*, U, INF. *gadf*, be very liberal towards (ل *li*), bestow many presents on him; — II. INF. *tagdîf*, wish one to go to the devil (m.); — IV. INF. *idgâf*, lower the veil or curtain; spread darkness; bestow liberal presents on (على *'ala*, ب *bi*); — VIII. INF. *igtidâf*, receive much from (من *min*).
غدف *gadaf*, abundance and ease; — *gidaff*, lion.
غدفان *gidfân*, pl. of غداف *gudâf*.
(غدفل) *gadfal*, INF. ة, live in luxury.
غدفل *gidafl*, pl. *gadâfil*, worn garment; at ease, abundant.
(غدق) *gadiq*, A, INF. *gadaq*, be spacious and abounding in water; — IV. INF. *igdâq*, be abundant, plenteous.
غدق *gadaq*, abundant and good water.
غدن *gadan*, softness, juiciness (ة *gudna-t*, *gudunna-t*, id.); faintness, languidness, drowsiness; — V. INF. *tagaddun*, bend, incline (n.); — X. INF. *istigdân*, be long and thick; be luxuriant.
(غدو) *gadâ*, U, INF. *gadw*, *guduww*, *gudwa-t*, go or come in the early morning, before sunrise; feed, nourish; — غدى *gadî*, A, INF. *gadan*, take breakfast; — II. INF. *tagdiya-t*, bid breakfast, give a breakfast or meal; — III. INF. *mugâdât*, come in the early morning to (acc.); be early; — V. INF. *tagaddî*, breakfast, take a meal; — VIII. INF. *igtidâ'* = III.
غدو *gadw*, *guduww*, morning, morrow; — ة *gudwa-t*, pl. *-ât*, *gudan*, early morning, earliness.
غدور *gadûr*, treacherous.
غدوى *gadawiyy*, happening on the following morning; future; — ة *gadwiyya-t*, early morning, earliness.
غدى *gadî*, *gadan*, see (غدو); — *gudan*, pl. of غدوة *gudwa-t*; — *gadiyy* = غدوى *gadawiyy*; (m.) to-morrow, soon, later on; — ة

gadya-t, pl. *gadâyâ*, *gadayât*, early morning, earliness.

غديان *gadyân*, f. *gadyâ'*, breakfasting.

غدير *gadîr*, pl. *gudur*, *gudrân*, *agdira-t*, pond, pool, water; treacherous; — *giddîr*, exceedingly treacherous; — ة *gadîra-t*, pl. *gadâ'ir*, lock of hair; tress of hair; pit; abandoned sheep, camel, &c.; milk-pottage.

(غذ) *gazz*, I, U, INF. *gazz*, suppurate; — II. INF. *tagzîz*, diminish, lessen (a.); — IV. INF. *igzâz*, suppurate; accelerate one's walk, hasten.

غذا *gizâ'*, pl. *agziya-t*, food, nourishment, meal.

(غذر), VIII. INF. *igtizâr*, make a milk-pottage and eat of it.

(غذرم) *gazram*, INF. ة, sell in a lump without weighing or measuring; speak confusedly.

(غذغذ) *gazgaz*, INF. ة, diminish (a.).

(غذم) *gazam*, U, INF. *gazm*, give one (ل *li*) the best of (من *min*); — U, also *gazim*, A, INF. *gazam*, eat greedily; — V. INF. *tagazzum*, taste of a dish; chew anything soft; — VIII. INF. *igtizâm*, eat greedily.

(غذمر) *gazmar*, INF. ة, sell in a lump; speak confusedly; mix up; act capriciously; — II. INF. *tagazmur*, cry out, scream.

(غذو) *gazâ*, U, INF. *gazw*, feed, nourish; be nutritious, invigorate, strengthen; INF. *gazawân*, flow; — II. INF. *tagziya-t*, nourish, feed; bring up, rear, educate; — V. INF. *tagazzî*, VIII. INF. *igtizâ'*, take food, feed on, eat one's fill.

غذوى *gazawiyy*, غذى *gaziyy*, pl. *gizâ'*, new-born.

غذيذة *gazîza-t*, pus, discharged matter.

غذيرة *gazîra-t*, milk-pottage warmed by a heated stone.

(غر) *garr*, U, INF. *garr*, *girra-t*, *gurûr*, deceive with empty hopes, delude; — U, INF. *garr*, *girâr*, feed the young ones; tend the flocks, pasture (a.); sink in the ground (water); — *garir*, I, INF. *garâra-t*, be inexperienced and easily deceived; — A, INF. *garar*, *gurra-t*, *garâra-t*, have a white spot on the forehead, be white; — II. INF. *tagrîr*, *tagirra-t*, delude, rush blindly into danger; — III. INF. *mugârra-t*, yield but little milk; be impotent; INF. *girâr*, be dull (market); — IV. INF. *igrâr*, be abundant; — VII. INF. *ingirâr*, allow one's self to be deceived by false hopes, deluded, seduced; — VIII. INF. *igtirâr*=VII.; be careless, thoughtless.

غر *garr*, pl. *gurûr*, fold, wrinkle; rent; — *girr*, ة, pl. *agrâr*, inexperienced, easily deceived; — *gurr*, food of young birds; fold, split, groove, channel, canal; (m.) pl. *girâr*, little bell, handbell; pl. of اغر *agarr*, having a white spot on the forehead, bright, &c.; — ة *girra-t*, pl. *girar*, inexperience, simplicity; thoughtlessness; infatuation; — *gurra-t*, pl. *gurar*, white spot on the forehead; brow; dawn of the morning; new moon; anything white, bright, bright look, bright brow; the best, most exquisite of a thing; beginning of the month, first day of it.

غرا *gar-an*, *garâ*, glue; — *girâ'*, id.; violent desire, ardent longing, craving; INF. III. of (غرو); — *garrâ*, f. of اغر *agarr*, white, bright, shining, resplendent, brilliant.

غراب *gurâb*, pl. *agriba-t*, bend of the scabbard; edge, point; pl. *agrub*, *agriba-t*, *girbân*, *gurb*, *garâbîn*, raven, crow; a ship, corvet, sloop; ة *gurâba-t*, beginning; edge (of a sword, &c.); — ة *garâba-t*, oddness of

expression; anything strange, extraordinary.

غرابيل *garâbîl*, pl. of غربال *girbâl*; — ى *garâbîliyy*, maker of sieves.

غراث *girâs*, غراثى *garâsa*, pl. of غرثان *garsân*.

غراد *garâd*, ة *garâda-t*, pl. *girâd*, a kind of mushroom.

غرار *girâr*, INF. III. of (غر); a little; haste, hurry; manner, model, form, fashion; pl. *agirra-t*, point of a lance, head of an arrow or spear, edge of a sword, &c.; — *garrâr*, deceiver, deceiving; — ة *garâra-t*, inexperience; على غ *'ala garârat-in*, suddenly, unexpectedly; — *girâra-t*, pl. *garâ'ir*, a large sack; a measurement (12 pecks); a coarse carpet-cloth.

غراس *girâs*, time for planting; shoot; pl. of غرس *gars*; — *garrâs*, planter; learned.

غراضيف *garâḍîf*, pl. of غرضوف *gurḍûf*.

غراف *girâf*, a measurement; — *garrâf*, spacious; over-full; — ة *gurâfa-t*, drinking (s.) out of the hand.

غرام *garâm*, desire, longing, craving, passion, greediness; also *gurm* and ة *garâma-t*, mulct, fine-money; debt which must be paid; due, obligation; transgression; punishment; pain, torment, torture; loss; calamity.

غران *gurrân*, pl. of اغر *agarr*, having a white spot on the forehead, bright, &c., and of غرير *garîr*.

غرانق *garâniq*, غرانيق *garânîq*, pl. of غرنوق *girnauq*, *gurnûq*; — *gurâniq*, m. and f., f. also ة, pl. *garâniq*, *garâniqa-t*, *garânîq*, youthfully delicate and handsome.

غرائر *garâ'ir*, pl. of غرارة *girâra-t* and غرير *garîr*.

(غرب) *garab*, U, INF. *garb*, *gurûb*, pass away, depart, disappear, hide (n.); INF. *gurûb*, set (sun); be far, concealed, darkened, eclipsed; persist; — U, INF. *gurb*, *gurba-t*, leave house and home; — *garib*, A, INF. *garab*, be black; — *garub*, INF. *gurba-t*, be strange, odd, obscure, difficult to understand; leave house and home; live in foreign parts; — II. INF. *tagrîb*, go far away, go west; expel from one's home, exile; — IV. INF. *igrâb*, go far away or to the west; do, utter or bring anything strange, odd, extraordinary; — V. INF. *tagarrub*, go far away; become estranged from one's home; travel or live in foreign parts; be made to look strange or changed; — VIII. INF. *igtirâb*, travel abroad; take a foreigner for a wife; — X. INF. *istigrâb*, find strange, odd, extraordinary; wonder and burst out laughing; be excessive in merriment; be bewildered.

غرب *garb*, sunset; west; the north-west of Africa; travelling abroad, emigration; flow of tears, pl. *gurûb*, tears, lachrymal ducts; most projecting part; head of an arrow, edge; tip of the tongue, sharpness of tongue; violence; quickness, briskness; leathern bag; — *gurb*, absence in foreign parts; pl. of غراب *gurâb*; — *garab*, pl. *gurûb*, silver, silver cup; cup, bucket; willow, poplar; — *gurub*, stranger, foreigner; — ة *garba-t*, removal, departure; — *gurba-t*, long journey and absence; foreign country; exile; emigration; misery.

غربا *gurabâ'*, pl. of غريب *garîb*.

غربال *girbâl*, pl. *garâbîl*, large sieve, fan; drum.

غربان *girbân*, pl. of غراب *gurâb*.

(غربل) *garbal*, INF. ة, sift; cut off; destroy, kill; (m.) examine, try, test.

غربى *garbiyy*, ة, westerly, western;

west wind; (m.) of the Latin rite.

(غرث) *gari<u>s</u>*, A, INF. *gara<u>s</u>*, be starved, famished.

غرثان *gar<u>s</u>ân*, f. *gar<u>s</u>a*, pl. *gar<u>s</u>a*, *garâ<u>s</u>a*, *girâ<u>s</u>*, hungry, famished.

(غرد) *garid*, A, INF. *garad*, sing, warble, twitter; — II. INF. *tagrîd*, IV. INF. *igrâd*, V. INF. *tagarrud*, id.; — X. INF. *istigrâd*, cause or invite to sing; — XV. *igranda*, INF. *igrindâ'*, assault and get the better of.

غرد *gard*, pl. *girada-t*, a kind of mushroom.

(غردق) *gardaq*, INF. ة, cover entirely; let down the veil or curtain.

غرر *garar*, INF. of (غر); — *girar*, pl. of غرة *girra-t*; — *gurar*, pl. of غرة *gurra-t*; the first three nights of the month.

(غرز) *garaz*, I, INF. *garz*, prick; thrust into; deposit ova; — INF. *garz*, *girâz*, yield but little milk; — II. INF. *tagrîz*, thrust deeply into; deposit ova; penetrate deeply; pass. be not milked; — V. INF. *tagarruz*, VII. INF. *ingirâz*, penetrate deeply; — VIII. INF. *igtirâz*, put the foot into the stirrup.

غرز *garz*, stirrup of leather; pl. *gurûz*, graft, scion, shoot; seam; — ة *gurza-t*, pl. *guraz*, prick, prick of a needle, stitch; seam; dimple; shoot, scion; — *gurraz*, pl. of غارز, ag. of (غرز).

(غرس) *garas*, I, INF. *gars*, plant, set; sink (a.); fasten, fix; — IV. INF. *igrâs*=I.; — VII. INF. *ingirâs*, be planted, set.

غرس *gars*, planting, setting (s.); *gars*, (m.) *girs*, ة, pl. *girâs*, *agrâs*, (m.) *gurûs*, shoot; proselyte; client, protégé.

غرش *girś*, pl. *gurûś*, piaster (m.).

(غرض) *garaḍ*, I, INF. *garḍ*, strap the girth-leather across the camel's chest; fill, fill but partly; wean before the proper time; cull fresh fruit; carry out before time; prevent, hinder; — *gariḍ*, A, INF. *garaḍ*, long ardently for, desire violently; abhor, be tired of, be passionately averse; fear; — *garuḍ*, INF. *giraḍ*, be fresh; — II. INF. *tagrîḍ*, fill; exhaust; gather fruit when fresh; eat while fresh; — IV. INF. *igrâḍ*, fill; passionately take the part of (مع *ma'*); — V. INF. *tagarruḍ*, id.; — X. INF. *istigrâḍ*, accuse of partisanship with, of partiality for.

غرض *garaḍ*, pl. *agrâḍ*, target, aim, end; wish; private interest; inclination, taste; partisanship, party-spirit, (m.) party; hatred, grudge, malice; (m.) affair, business; the principal thing; pl. *gurûḍ*, *agrâḍ*,—also ة *gurḍa-t*, *girḍa-t*, pl. *gurḍ*, *guruḍ*, girth of a camel.

غرضوف *gurḍûf*, pl. *garâḍîf*, cartilage.

غرضية *garaḍiyya-t*, private advantage, exclusive interest; partiality; party-intrigue.

(غرغر) *gargar*, INF. ة, produce a gurgling sound, gurgle; seethe, boil; — II. INF. *tagargur*, id.; gush forth; imitate one gurgling.

غرغر *girgir*, ة, guinea-hen; — ة *gargara-t*, gurgling (s.); death-rattle; seething, boiling (s.).

غرف *garaf*, I, U, INF. *garf*, take water with the hand or a spoon; — U, lop; shear; tan; — *garif*, A, INF. *garaf*, have colic from feeding on the plant غرف *garf*; — VII. INF. *ingirâf*, be taken with the hand or spoon; be lopped; — VIII. INF. *igtirâf*, take water with the hand or a spoon.

غرف *garf*, *garaf*, a plant used for tanning; *garf*, leaves and branches used as fuel; — ة *garfa-t*, a handful or spoonful;

— *girfa-t*, drinking out of one's hand; pl. *giraf*, sandal; — *gurfa-t*, pl. *gurfât*, *gurafât*, *gurufât*, *guraf*, upper dining-room; garret, gallery, balcony; the seventh heaven; pl. *girâf*, handful or spoonful.

(غرق) *gariq*, A, INF. *garaq* (*garq*), plunge or dip into water (a. and n.); drown (n.); suffer shipwreck; rush into; take a draught; — II. INF. *tagrîq*, plunge or throw into the water; drown (a.); strangle; destroy; — IV. INF. *igrâq*, plunge or throw into the water, drown; rush precipitately into; exceed all bounds, exaggerate; — V. INF. *tagarruq*, plunge, drown, sink (n.); immerse one's self (in study, &c.); — X. INF. *istigrâq*, plunge (n.); take the whole; exceed; generalize; — XII. *igrauraq*, INF. *igrîrâq*, be bathed in tears, be drowned.

غرق *garq*, *garaq*, ة *garqa-t*, *garaqa-t*, sinking, drowning (s.); shipwreck; — *gariq*, immersed, sinking (adj.); ة *gariqa-t*, excessively irrigated ground; — *gurqa-t*, pl. *guraq*, draught.

غرقا *garqa'*, INF. ة, lay eggs without shells.

غرقان *garqân*, sunk, immersed, drowned, shipwrecked.

غرقد *garqad*, a thorn-tree.

غرقل *garqal*, INF. ة, deteriorate, putrefy; pour water over one's head.

(غرقى) *garqa*, pl. of غريق *garîq*; — *girqi'*, the white of an egg, the thin skin around it.

غرل *garil*, long; — ة *gurla-t*, prepuce.

(غرم) *garim*, A, INF. *garam*, *garâma-t*, be obliged, bound by duty; be a debtor, owe; pass. be in love with; — II. INF. *tagrîm*, impose a debt or payment upon, fine, tax; enforce the fulfilment of an obligation; divide a payment between several debtors; — IV. INF. *igrâm*, cause one to get into debt; enforce payment; make one fall in love, infatuate; — V. INF. *tagarrum*, take an obligation, payment, fine, &c., upon one's self; (m.) be divided, assessed; — VII. INF. *ingirâm*, be in love, infatuated; — VIII. INF. *igtirâm*, acknowledge or contract a debt; pay a debt.

غرم *gurm* = غرامة *garâma-t*.

غرما *guramâ'*, pl. of غريم *garîm*.

(غرمول) *gurmûl*, big penis (of a horse).

(غرن) *garin*, A, INF. *garan*, dry up.

غرن *garan*, pl. *agrân*, eagle; crawfish; — *garin*, weak; — ة *gurna-t*, kneading-trough, trough.

(غرنشم), IV. *igranśam*, INF. *igrinśâm*, have shrivelled flesh, a flaccid belly.

غرنوق *girnauq*, *gurnûq*, pl. *garânîq*, *garâniq*, *garâniqa-t*, delicate, slender youth or plant; crane (bird).

(غرو) *garâ*, A, INF. *garw*, *girâ'*, smear with glue or paste; glue, paste; bedaub, be grown to, adhere; be seized with admiration, wonder at; — غرى *garî*, A, INF. *gar-an*, *girâ'*, be intent upon (ب *bi*); have cold water; — II. INF. *tagriya-t*, glue, paste; bedaub, besmear; make to adhere; pass. be intent upon (ب *bi*); — IV. INF. *igrâ'*, cause to desire; instigate, urge, incite against; stir up enmity; pass. be given to; — V. INF. *tagarrî*, be glued.

غرو *garw*, astonishment, wonder.

غروب *gurûb*, sunset, west; — *.

غرور *garûr*, deceptive, deceitful; impostor, cheat, seducer; Satan; worldly things; — *gurûr*, infatuation; confidence or pride in vain things; vain or delusive things, pl. of غار *gârr*; — *.

غروف *garûf*, accessible, attainable; bucket.

غروى *garwa*=غرو *garw*; violent desire, craving.

غرى *garan*, beauty; — *garî*, v. see (غرو); — *gurra*, princess; — *gariyy*, beautiful.

غريب *garîb*, ة, pl. *gurabâ'*, strange, foreign; foreigner, stranger, traveller; odd, extraordinary, unheard-of, rare; forsaken, poor, miserable; raven-black; — ة *garîba-t*, pl. *garâ'ib*, strange, extraordinary, wonderful occurrence.

غرير *garîr*, ة, pl. *agirra-t*, *agirrâ'*, *garâ'ir*, inexperienced and easily deceived; pl. *gurrân*, agreeable disposition, easy-going temper, graciousness, grace; security, warning; bail (person), warner; bright, brilliant.

غريزة *garîza-t*, pl. *garâ'iz*, nature; natural disposition or gift; endowment, talent, character; natural impulse, instinct.

غريزى *garîziyy*, ة, natural, inborn; instinctive; physical, animal (adj.).

غريسة *garîsa-t*, pl. *garâ'is*, shoot, young tree.

غريض *garîḍ*, ة, fresh.

غريف *garîf*, ة *garîfa-t*, thicket; reed-bank; — *giryaf*, papyrus.

غريق *garîq*, pl. *garqa*, sunk, drowned; shipwrecked; immersed, engrossed.

غريم *garîm*, pl. *guramâ'*, debtor; creditor; who gives cause for offence, offender; (m.) with whom one has to deal, competitor, rival; share in a bankruptcy stock; bankruptcy.

غرين *garîn*, *giryan*, thin loam or clay; butter; folly.

(غز) *gazz* (for *gaziz*), A, INF. *gazaz*, elect, select (for a companion); protect by some amulet from the evil eye; — U, INF. *gazz*, put into, immerse; prick; penetrate; rush into; — III. INF. *gizâz*, be beforehand with; — IV. INF. *igzâz*, be provided with densely-set thorns; have a difficult parturition; — VI. INF. *tagâzz*, dispute about a thing; — VII. INF. *ingizâz*, be put into; rush into, penetrate; — VIII. INF. *igtizâz*, select.

غز *guzz*, inner corners of the mouth; a Turkish tribe; — ة *gazza-t*, Gaza.

غزا *guzzâ'*, pl. of غازى, who wars against infidels, &c.

غزار *gizâr*, pl. of غزير *gazîr*; — *gazzâr*, ة, rush; — ة *gazâra-t*, plenty, abundance.

غزاز *guzzâz*, pl. kind people; — *.

غزال *gazâl*, f. and n. u. ة, pl. *gizla-t*, *gizlân*, young gazelle or deer; delicate person; bridge of a violin; ة *gazâla-t*, rising sun; غ الضحى *gazâla-t aḍ-ḍuḥa*, first fifth of the day, breakfast; — *gazzâl*, spinner; seller or maker of yarn; — ة *gazzâla-t*, spin-house; spider; spindle full of yarn or flax.

غزاة *gazât*, غزاوة *gazâwa-t*, pl. *gazawât*, raid, especially against infidels; — *guzât*, pl. of غازى *gâzî*, who wars against infidels.

غزتة *gazeta-t*, غازتة *gâzeta-t*, newspaper (m.).

(غزر) *gazur*, INF. *gazr*, *guzr*, *gazâra-t*, abound; yield in abundance; — IV. INF. *igzâr*, make still more abundant, increase; benefit abundantly; (m.) cover itself with rushes; — X. INF. *istigzâr*, find abundant, deem plenteous; give in order to get still more.

غزر *gazr*, abundance, plenty.

(غزل) *gazal*, I, INF. *gazl*, draw into threads, spin; — *gazil*, A, INF. *gazal*, court a woman, make love to; compose love-poetry; desist from worrying a plaintive gazelle; — II. *tagzîl*, make spin or draw into threads; — III. INF. *mugâzala-t*, court a woman, make love to; — IV. INF. *igzâl*,

have young; — V. INF. *tagazzul* = III.; — VI. INF. *tagâzul*, make love to one another; — VII. INF. *ingizâl*, be spun; — VIII. INF. *igtizâl*, spin.

غزل *gazl*, spinning (s.); thread; — *gazal*, love-talk, love-verses, ode, sonnet; — *gazil*, erotic poet; — *guzzal*, pl. of غازلة *gâzila-t*, spinster; — ة *gizla-t*, and—

غزلان *gizlân*, pl. of غزال *gazâl*.

غزليات *gazliyyât*, verses, love talk.

(غزو) *gazâ*, U, INF. *gazw*, strive for, intend, purpose, wish; — INF. *gazw*, *gazâwa-t*, *gazawân*, make a raid upon, invade, especially infidels; turn against; — II. INF. *tagziya-t*, cause to make an incursion or raid; place troops in the field and equip them; attack the enemy; — IV. INF. *igzâ'*, id.; —VI. INF. *tagâzî*, make incursions into each other's country.

غزو *gazw*, purpose, intention; incursion, raid (n. u. ة *gazwa-t*), campaign; attack.

غزوات *gazawât*, pl. of غزاة *gazât*.

غزوان *gazawân*, INF. of (غزو).

غزوى *gazawiyy*, warlike, military; hero.

غزى *guzza*, pl. of غازى *gâzî*, who wars against infidels.

غزير *gazîr*, ة, pl. *gizâr*, abundant, plentiful; yielding plenty of milk; numerous, frequent.

(غس) *gass*, U, INF. *gass*, enter and travel through a country; plunge or throw into the water; find fault with, blame; — VII. INF. *ingisâs*, be thrown into the water, immersed; be under water.

غس *guss*, contemptible.

غساق *gassâq*, putrid matter flowing from the damned.

غسال *gassâl*, f. ة, washer; washer of the dead; — ة *gusâla-t*, dirty water; washed; — ى *gasâla*, pl. of غسيلة *gasîla-t*.

غساة *gasât*, pl. *gasa*, *gasayât*, unripe dates.

(غسر) *gasar*, U, INF. *gasr*, cover a mare not hot; press hard upon a debtor; — V. INF. *tagassur*, be entangled; be difficult, complicated; be turbid.

غسر *gasir*, complicated, difficult.

(غسف) *gasaf*, darkness; — IV. *agsaf*, INF. *igsâf*, step in the dark.

(غسق) *gasaq*, I, INF. *gasq*, *gasaq*, *gusûq*, *gasaqân*, be very dark; drop, trickle; — INF. *gasaqân*, *gusûq*, be troubled, dimmed; be bathed in tears, flow; — *gasiq*, A, INF. *gasaq*, id.; — IV. INF. *igsâq*, be very dark; enter on the first darkness of night.

غسق *gasaq*, first darkness of night; gloom.

(غسل) *gasal*, I, INF. *gasl*, *gusl*, wash, cleanse; beat, flog; — II. INF. *tagsîl*, wash clean; — V. INF. *tagassul*, wash (n.), bathe; perform the religious ablutions; — VII. INF. *ingisâl*, be washed, cleansed; — VIII. INF. *igtisâl* = V.

غسل *gasl*, *gusl*, *gusul*, pl. *agsâl*, washing (s.); ablution; — *gisl*, water for washing; perfumes, &c.; — ة *gisla-t*, *gasla-t*, water for washing; ابو غ *abû gisla-t*, wolf.

غسلا *gusalâ'*, pl. of غسيل *gasîl*.

(غسلب) *gaslab*, INF. ة, snatch out of one's hand, take from (من *min*).

غسلى *gasla*, pl. of غسيل *gasîl*.

غسلين *gislîn*, what comes back from the laundress after being washed; washed; putrid matter flowing from the damned; hell-fire.

(غسم) *gasam*, U, INF. *gusûm*, be dark.

(غسن) *gasan*, U, INF. *gasn*, chew.

غسن *gusn*, weak; — ة *gusna-t*, also غسناة *gusnât*, pl. *gusan*, lock of hair.

(غسو) *gasâ*, U, INF. *gusuww*, be dark; — غسى *gasî*, A, INF. *gasan*, id.; — IV. INF. *igsâ'*, id.

غسوس *gasûs*, food, nourishment.

غسول *gasûl*, anything used for washing: soap, potash, &c.

غسى *gasa*, pl. of غساة *gasât*; — *gasî*, *gasan*, see (غسو).

غسيل *gasîl*, pl. *gasla*, *gusalâ'*, f. ة, pl. *gasâla*, washed.

(غش) *gaśś*, U, INF. *giśś*, delude, deceive; falsify, counterfeit; — II. INF. *tagśîś*, id.; — VII. INF. *ingiśâś*, allow one's self to be deluded or deceived; — VIII. INF. *igtiśâś*, allow one's self to be entrapped by delusions or false advice; — X. INF. *istigśâś*, deem false or an impostor.

غش *giśś*, deceit, fraud; insidiousness; forgery, spuriousness, bad quality; hatred; — *guśś*, false, impostor; forger.

غشا *giśâ'*, cover, covering; saddle-cloth; membrane (of the eye, brain, &c.); lid, scabbard, sheath; shell of a fruit; pericardium.

غشاش *giśâś*, twilight; *giśâś-an*, in the dusk, suddenly; — *gaśśâś*, great impostor.

غشاوة *gaśâwa-t*, *giśâwa-t*, *guśâwa-t* = غشا; veil; dimmed look.

غشاية *giśâya-t*, *guśâya-t*, veil.

غشب *gaśb*, injustice.

(غشق) *ġaśaq*, INF. *gaśq*, pound, beat.

(غشم) *gaśam*, U, INF. *gaśm*, treat unjustly, wrong; — I, INF. *gaśam*, do a thing in a wrong or thoughtless manner; gather wood in the dark; (m.) be stupid, ignorant; — V. INF. *tagaśśum*, wrong, treat unjustly; deem or find one stupid or ignorant.

غشم *gaśm*, wrong, arbitrariness; — *guśm*, ignorance, stupidity; — *gaśam*, darkness of night.

غشما *guśamâ'*, pl. of غشيم *gaśîm*.

(غشمر) *gaśmar*, INF. ة, come suddenly up; undertake unhesitatingly or inconsiderately; act headstrongly; — II. INF. *tagaśmur*, take hold of by violence; be angry.

غشمرة *gaśmara-t*, pl. *gaśâmir*, *gaśmariyya-t*, violence; arbitrariness; clamour.

غشمشم *gaśamśam*, energetic, bold, irresistible.

(غشن) *gaśan*, I, INF. *gaśn*, beat, hit; — V. INF. *tagaśśun*, be covered with floating dung.

(غشو) *gaśâ*, U, INF. *gaśw*, approach, draw near to; pass. غشى على *guśî 'ala*, INF. *gaśy*, *gaśayân*, swoon, faint; — غشى *gaśî*, A, INF. *gaśâwa-t*, cover, envelop, veil; come to, surprise, fall upon, visit; surround an army; lie with; — II. INF. *tagśiya-t*, cover, veil; conceal; make swoon or faint; — IV. INF. *igśâ'*, id.; come to, surprise and surround (also V.); cause one to come to, &c. (2 acc.); — V. INF. *tagaśśî*, see IV.; cover; lie with; cover or veil one's self; — X. استغشى ثيابه *istagśa siyâba-hu*, bury one's head in one's garments.

غشو *gaśw*, fruit of the lotus-tree; — ة *gaśwa-t*, *giśwa-t*, *guśwa-t*, veil; — *gaśwa-t*, fainting-fit.

غشوا *gaśwâ'*, f. of اغشى *agśa*, having the head entirely white.

غشوش *gaśûś*, great impostor.

غشوم *gaśûm*, unjust; arbitrary; — ية *guśûmiyya-t*, stupidity; inexperience.

غشى *gaśy*, ة *gaśya-t*, swoon, fainting-fit; stupor; — ة *guśya-t*, veil.

غشيان *gaśayân*, INF. of (غشو); fainting-fit.

غشيم *gaśîm*, pl. *guśamâ'*, stupid, inexperienced; (m.) quarry-stone.

(غص) *gaṣṣ* (for *gaṣaṣ* and *gaṣiṣ*), A, INF. *gaṣaṣ*, have a choking-fit, choke; be oppressed, full of anxiety be full to choking

(house); — II. INF. *tagṣîṣ*, choke (a.), smother; oppress, fill with anxiety; — VIII. INF. *igtiṣâṣ*, have a choking-fit; be full of anguish; — ة *guṣṣa-t*, pl. *guṣaṣ*, what sticks in the throat; choking-fit; anxiety, anguish.

غصاب *gaṣṣâb*, bird of prey.

غصان *gaṣṣân*, on the point of choking; full of anxiety or anguish.

(غصب) *gaṣab*, I, INF. *gaṣb*, take from by violence or unlawfully; compel, force; — III. INF. *mugâṣaba-t*, take from by violence, do violence to, force, compel; — VI. INF. *tagâṣub*, compel one another; — VII. INF. *ingiṣâb*, be compelled; — VIII. INF. *igtiṣâb* =III.

غصب *gaṣb*, taking by violence; violence, force, compulsion; robbery, plunder; غصبا عنه *gaṣb-an 'an-hu*, against one's will.

غصبانية *gaṣbâniyya-t*, violence, force, compulsion.

غصص *gaṣaṣ*, INF. of (غص); — *guṣaṣ*, pl. of غصة *guṣṣa-t*.

(غصلج) *gaṣlaj*, cook, salt or season a dish not sufficiently.

(غصن) *gaṣan*, I, INF. *gaṣn*, hold out a branch to; snatch, take; cut off; prevent, turn from; — II. INF. *tagṣîn*, have many branches and twigs; — also IV. INF. *igṣân*, have large stones (grapes).

(غض) *gaḍḍ*, U, INF. *gaḍḍ*, *gaḍâḍ*, *giḍâḍ*, *gaḍâḍa-t*, lower the eyes to the ground, look down; turn the eyes from; be indulgent with, forbear; suppress, soften (the voice); hinder; diminish, lessen (a.); break off; — A, INF. *gaḍâḍa-t*, *guḍûḍa-t*, be full of sap, vigorous, pliable; — IV. INF. *igḍâḍ*, have many branches and a rich foliage.

غض *gaḍḍ*, ة, fresh, tender, blooming and full of sap; downcast glance; pl. *giḍâḍ*, newly-born; — ة *guḍḍa-t*, loss; poverty.

غضاب *giḍâb*, غضابى *gaḍâba*, pl. of غضبان *gaḍbân*; — *giḍâb*, small-pox.

غضابى *guḍâbiyy*, unsociable, quarrelsome, unaccomodating.

غضارب *guḍârib*, well watered and abounding in vegetation.

غضارة *gaḍâra-t*, plenty, abundance, ease; — also *giḍâra-t*, pl. *gaḍâ'ir*, earthen dish.

غضاريف *gaḍârîf*, pl. of غضروف *guḍrûf*.

غضاض *gaḍâḍ*, *guḍâḍ*, base of the nose; — *; — ة *gaḍâḍa-t*, luxuriance of vegetation; defectiveness, damage.

غضاة *gaḍât*, pl. *gaḍ-an*, a tree of the tamarisk kind.

(غضب) *gaḍib*, A, INF. *gaḍab*, *magḍaba-t*, get angry, be angry; grow passionate for, defend; protect; also pass. *guḍib*, suffer from small-pox; — III. INF. *mugâḍaba-t*, be angry with, speak roughly and angrily to; — IV. INF. *igḍâb*, provoke to anger, anger, incite against (على *'ala*); — V. INF. *tagaḍḍub*, get angry.

غضب *gaḍab*, anger, rage; — *gaḍib*, angry, enraged; — *guḍubb*, irascible, easily provoked, fierce, grim; — ة *gaḍba-t*, fit of anger; pock-mark; (m.) disgrace, calamity; — ة *guḍubba-t*, very irascible.

غضبان *gaḍbân*, f. ة, and *gaḍba*, pl. *giḍâb*, *gaḍba*, *gaḍâba*, angry, wrathful; catapult.

(غضر) *gaḍar*, U, INF. *gaḍr*, bless with abundance; — I, go away from, leave (عن *'an*); lean to; (على *'ala*); prevent, hinder; cut off; give part of one's own to another; — *gaḍir*, A, INF. *gaḍar*, attain to abundance; — V. INF. *tagaḍḍur*, leave, abandon.

غضر *gaḍir*, ة, at ease, comfortable, abundant.

غضرا *gaḍrâ'*, plenty, abundance of

(من *min*); ease; good consistent clay.

(غضرب) *gaḍrab*, well watered and abounding in vegetation.

(غضرم) *gaḍram*, *giḍrim*, with a soft clayey ground; red clay.

غضروف *guḍrûf*, pl. *gaḍârîf*, cartilage.

(غضغض) *gaḍgaḍ*, INF. ة, diminish (a. and n.); sink (n.);—II. INF. *tagaḍguḍ*, diminish (n.).

(غضف) *gaḍaf*, I, INF. *gaḍf*, break to pieces; drop the ears; start running;—*gaḍif*, A, INF. *gaḍaf*, have drooping ears;—II. INF. *tagḍîf*, let hang down, droop;—IV. INF. *igḍâf*, be dark, be black; be on the point of raining;—V. INF. *tagaḍḍuf*, swing to and fro in walking; incline to (على *'ala*);—VII. INF. *ingiḍâb*, meet with dust; fall in ruins.

غضف *guḍf*, pl. of *agḍaf*, having drooping ears, &c.;—also ة *gaḍafa-t*, black *qaṭa* bird.

(غضفر) *gaḍfar*, INF. ة, be heavy.

غضفر *gaḍfar*, rude, rough, unjust.

(غضل), *igḍa'all*, INF. *igḍîlâl*, have many branches and dense foliage.

(غضن) *gaḍan*, U, I, INF. *gaḍn*, prevent, hinder; miscarry (camel);—II. INF. *tagḍîn*, id.;—III. INF. *mugâḍana-t*, look at with compressed eye-lids, compress the eye-lids;—IV. INF. *igḍân*, rain continuously;—V. INF. *tagaḍḍun*, be wrinkled; have wrinkles or creases.

غضن *gaḍn*, *gaḍan*, ة, pl. *guḍûn*, wrinkle, crease; فى غضون ذالك *fî guḍûn ẕâlik*, meanwhile.

غضنفر *gaḍanfar*, lion; hero, champion; violent, cruel.

(غضو) *gaḍâ*, U, INF. *gaḍw*, be dark and cover everything;—INF. *guḍuww*, be in good condition and abundant;—غضى *gaḍî*, A, INF. *gaḍ-an*, have the colic from feeding on the tree غضاة *gaḍât*;—IV. INF. *igḍâ'*, compress the eye-lids, close the eyes and turn them aside, wink at, indulge; be very dark;—V. INF. *tagaḍḍî*, overlook, neglect;—VI. INF. *tagâḍî*, pretend not to see a thing; disregard, neglect.

غضوب *gaḍûb*, irascible, irritable, prone to anger.

غضى *gaḍa*, wood;—*gaḍî*, v. see (غضو).

غضيض *gaḍîḍ*, pl. *agiḍḍa-t*, weak, decreasing; downcast; poor; fresh and juicy;—ة *gaḍîḍa-t*, loss; poverty.

(غط) *gaṭṭ*, I, U, INF. *gaṭṭ*, dip (a.) into the water;—INF. *gaṭîṭ*, roar, snort; snore, produce a rattling noise; roost, alight;—III. INF. *giṭâṭ*, *mugâṭṭa-t*, try to immerse;—VII. INF. *ingiṭâṭ*, get immersed; dive;—VIII. INF. *igtiṭâṭ*, press down the mare to cover her.

غط *gaṭṭ*, ة, immersion.

غطا *giṭâ'*, pl. *agṭiya-t*, covering, veil.

غطارفة *gaṭârifa-t*, pl. of غطريف *giṭrîf*.

غطاس *giṭâs*, immersion, baptism;—*gaṭṭâs*, who immerses; diver.

غطاط *gaṭâṭ*, ة, bird *qaṭa*; also *guṭâṭ*, first dawn of the morning;—*

(غطر) *gaṭar*, I, INF. *gaṭr*, swing the arms proudly in walking.

(غطرس) *gaṭras*, INF. ة, be full of self-admiration; step along proudly; exalt one's self above others; provoke to anger;—II. INF. *tagaṭrus*, give one's self airs, step along proudly, be overbearing; be provoked to anger.

غطرس *giṭris*, غطريس *giṭrîs*, pl. *gaṭâris*, *gaṭârîs*, overbearing and unjust;—ة *gaṭrasa-t*, haughtiness.

(غطرف) *gaṭraf*, INF. ة, be proud and overbearing;—II. INF. *tagaṭruf*, id.; step along proudly.

غطريس *giṭrîs*, pl. *gaṭârîs*, see غطرس *giṭris*.

غطريف *giṭrîf*, pl. *gaṭârifa-t*, noble generous lord; lord; young sparrow-hawk.
(غطس) *gaṭas*, I, INF. *gaṭs*, immerse; be immersed, plunge (n.), dive; — II. INF. *tagṭîs*, immerse, baptize; — V. INF. *tagaṭṭus*, plunge (n.), dive; bathe.
غطش *gaṭaś*, I, INF. *gaṭś*, be dark; — INF. *gaṭś*, *gaṭaśân*, walk along slowly from illness or old age; — *gaṭiś*, A, INF. *gaṭaś*, be weak, dim; — IV. INF. *igṭâś*, be dark; make dark.
غطشا *gaṭśâ'*, f. of اغطش *agṭaś*, dim-sighted, &c.
(غطغط) *gaṭgaṭ*, INF. ة, be violently agitated (sea); boil briskly; — II. INF. *tagaṭguṭ*, id.
غطف *gaṭaf*, pleasantness of life.
غطفان *gaṭafân*, name of an Arabian tribe.
(غطل) *gaṭal*, U, INF. *gaṭl*, be covered with clouds; — *gaṭil*, A, INF. *gaṭal*, be very dark.
(غطم) *giṭamm*, the high sea; numerous assembly; exceedingly liberal; abundant.
(غطمش) *gaṭmaś*, INF. ة, take by violence.
(غطمط) *gaṭmaṭ*, INF. ة, billow, be high, agitated (sea); boil briskly; rush along with a roaring noise.
غطمطم *gaṭamṭam*, high sea.
غطمطيط *gaṭmaṭîṭ*, uproar of the sea.
(غطو) *gaṭâ*, U, INF. *gaṭw*, *guṭuww*, be dark; cover, veil, envelop in darkness; inundate; — غطى *gaṭî*, A, INF. *gaṭy*, *guṭy*, be in the prime and vigour of youth; walk along at a good pace; be dark; — II. INF. *tagṭiya-t*, cover, veil; — V. INF. *tagaṭṭî*, VIII. INF. *igtiṭâ'*, cover or veil one's self; be veiled.
غطوس *gaṭûs*, who is fond of diving, who engages boldly; foolhardy.
غطيط *gaṭîṭ*, roar, snorting, snore, rattle; — ة *guṭaiṭa-t*, fog.

(غطيل) *gaṭyal*, INF. ة, have plenty of cattle and slaves; deal in cattle.
(غف) *gaff*, dry leaves; — *guff*, ة *guffa-t*, daily ration, sufficient food; — VIII. *igtaff*, INF. *igtifâf*, have sufficient food; produce fat; I. *gaff*, and VIII. throng around (m.).
غفا *gafan*, chaff.
غفار *gifâr*, helmet; — *gufâr*, hair on the neck, the jaws, &c.; — *gaffâr*, who is very forgiving; — ة *gifâra-t*, *gafâra-t*, pl. *gafâ'ir*, cloth worn beneath the veil to keep it clean; (m.) surplice of a priest; helmet; sheet over a couch.
(غفر) *gafar*, I, INF. *gafr*, cover, veil, put into; dye (grey hair); — INF. *gafr*, *gifra-t*, *gufûr*, *gafîr*, *gafîra-t*, *gufrân*, *magfira-t*, pardon, forgive; perform well; — also *gafir*, A, INF. *gafar*, break out again (wound), become worse again (patient); — *gafir*, be coarse-haired, shaggy; — II. INF. *tagfîr*, provide with an indulgence; wear a surplice (m.); — VI. INF. *tagâfur*, pardon one another; — VII. INF. *ingifâr*, be pardoned; — X. INF. *istigfâr*, ask pardon; — XI. INF. *igfîrâr*, be rough-haired, shaggy.
غفر *gafr*, 15th station of the moon; — *gufr*, pl. *agfâr*, *gifara-t*, *gufûr*, young of the chamois; — *gafar*, hair on the throat, the jaws, in the neck; (m.) escort; — *gafir*, ة, hairy on the throat, the jaws, and in the neck; — *gufur*, pl. of غفور *gafûr*; — ة *gifra-t*, pardon, forgiveness; — *gufra-t*, covering, cover, lid.
غفران *gufrân*, pardon; absolution; سنة الغ *sanat al-gufrân*, year of the Jubilee.
غفرجى *gafarjiyy*, pl. ة, man belonging to an escort.
(غفش) *gafaś*, impurity of the eye.
(غفص), III. *gâfaṣ*, INF. *mugâfaṣa-t*,

fall upon unexpectedly and overpower.

(غفق) *gafaq*, I, INF. *gafq*, break wind; come to the water at any hour; frequent the she-ass; beat or whip frequently; INF. *gafqa-t*, slumber lightly; — II. INF. *tagfîq*, slumber lightly; — V. INF. *tagaffuq*, drink all day long; — VIII. INF. *igtifâq*, surround, encompass.

(غفلَ) *gafal*, U, INF. *gufûl*, neglect, disregard from carelessness; be neglectful, careless; — II. INF. *tagfîl*, render negligent, careless, indolent, obtuse; cover, veil; — III. INF. *mugâfala-t*, profit by one's negligence or carelessness; — IV. INF. *igfâl*, neglect, leave undone, forget; render negligent; leave unmarked, without a sign; — V. INF. *tagafful*, VI. INF. *tagâful*, neglect, disregard, leave undone.

غفل *gufl*, pl. *agfâl*, without a mark or sign (road in the desert, arrow, &c.); unknown, nameless, anonymous; blank (in a lottery); — *gafal*, forgetfulness, negligence; — *guffal*, pl. of غافل *gâfil*, ag. of (غفل); — ة *gafla-t*, negligence; forgetfulness; suddenness, unexpectedness.

غفلان *gaflân*, forgetful, negligent; — *guflân*, negligence.

(غفو) *gafâ*, U, INF. *gafw*, *gufuww*, be on the point of falling asleep, fall aslumber, sleep; float on the water; — غفى *gafa*, I, INF. *gafy*, clean the wheat from chaff, winnow; — *gafî*, A, INF. *gafya-t*, fall aslumber, sleep; float; — IV. INF. *igfâ'*, id.; clean from chaff; have much chaff.

غفو *gafw*, ة *gafwa-t*, falling asleep.

غفور *gafûr*, pl. *gufur*, very forgiving; — *gufûr*, pardon, forgiveness.

غفول *gufûl*, negligence.

غفى *gafa*, *gafî*, v. see (غفو); — *gafan*, *gafa*, chaff; — ة *gafya-t*, falling asleep.

غفير *gafîr*, covering everything; enveloping and veiling; numerous; = غفر *gafar*; (m.) man belonging to an escort; — *gafîr*, ة *gafîra-t*, INF. of (غفر).

(غق) *gaqq*, I, INF. *gaqq*, *gaqîq*, boil or bubble audibly; croak; make a gargling noise.

غقغق *gaqgaq*, INF. ة, croak, screech.

(غل) *gall*, U, INF. *gall*, put one thing into another, insert, join together; be put or placed into; be admitted, enter; penetrate; put on the under-garment غلالة *gilâla-t*; yield crops or a revenue (estate); take part of the booty, embezzle; turn from what is right; bind, fetter, chain; — pass. *gull*, INF. *gull*, *gulla-t*, thirst, suffer from violent thirst; — INF. *gill*, *galîl*, *gulûl*, thirst for revenge, be full of hatred; — INF. *gulûl*, use treachery, deceit; — for *galil*, A, INF. *galal*, be thirsty; — II. INF. *taglîl*, fetter, chain; perfume; — IV. INF. *iglâl*, embezzle, deceive, defraud; consider as an impostor or traitor; yield crops or a revenue; furnish corn, convey provisions; let thirst; — V. INF. *tagallul*, be loaded with chains; enter, penetrate; — VII. INF. *ingilâl*, be admitted, enter; — VIII. INF. *igtilâl*, be thirsty; perfume one's self; put on an under-garment; — X. INF. *istiglâl*, gather in, draw revenues, gain, advantage, rent.

غل *gill*, secret hatred, deep grudge; — *gull*, violent thirst; heat in the bowels; torment; pl. *aglâl*, iron chain for the neck, iron collar; handcuffs; pillory; yoke; — ة *galla-t*, pl. *-ât*, *gilâl*, produce of the harvest; crops; revenue, gain; house-rent; wages,

earnings ; —*gulla-t*, pl. *gulal*, burning thirst ; an under-garment.

غلا *galâ'*, dearness, dearth ; —*gilâ'*, pl. of *galwa-t* ; — ة *gulât*, pl. of غالى *gâlî*, dear, &c.

غلاب *gallâb*, who conquers frequently.

غلاظ *gilâẕ*, pl. of غليظ *galîẕ* ; — *gulâẕ*, thick, coarse, rough ;—ة *gilâẕa-t*, thickness ; roughness, rudeness ; density strength.

غلاف *gilâf*, pl. *gulf*, *guluf*, *gullaf*, sheath, scabbard, case ; letter-envelope ; box, capsule ; fruit-shell ; cover ; prepuce ; pericardium ;—ى *gilâfiyy*, sheathed, provided with a shell, testaceous animal.

غلاقة *galâqa-t*, lock ; conclusion, end.

غلال *gulâl*, pl. of غليل *galîl* ; — ة *gilâla-t*, pl. *galâ'il*, short under-garment ; false hip, &c.

غلام *gulâm*, pl. *gilma-t*, *gilmân*, *aglima-t*, boy, lad, youth ; slave, servant, page, satellite, courier ; — ة *gulâma-t*, girl, slave-girl ; — ى *gulâmiyy*, youthful ; —ية *gulâmiyya-t*, prime of youth.

غلان *gallân*, thirsty.

غلائل *galâ'il*, pl. of غلالة *gilâla-t* and غليل *galîl*.

(غلب) *galab*, I, INF. *galb*, *galab*, *galaba-t*, *gulubba*, *gilibba*, *gulubba-t*, *gulabba-t*, *galâbiya-t*, *maglab*, *maglaba-t*, surpass, overcome, vanquish, conquer ; snatch from ; be beforehand with ; overreach ; (m.) use every effort to persuade ; — *galib*, A, INF. *galab*, have a thick neck ; — II. INF. *taglîb*, render victorious, let overcome, let one get the upper hand ; — III. INF. *mugâlaba-t*, try to overcome, to conquer, to get the better of ; conquer ; possess one's self of ; make one's self lord and master of ; — VII. INF. *ingilâb*, be overcome, vanquished, overreached ; — X. INF. *istiglâb*, deem one to be easily conquered, deem weak.

غلب *galb*, victory ; upper hand, superior power ; — *gulb*, pl. of اغلب *aglab*, having a thick neck, &c. ; — ة *galaba-t*, victory, superiority, supremacy ; dominion ; more frequent occurrence ; crowd, multitude ; (m.) idle talk ; — *gulabba-t*, *gulubba-t*, victory.

غلبى *gulubba*, *gilibba*, victory.

(غلت) *galat*, U, INF. *galt*, annul a mercantile transaction ; — *galit*, A, INF. *galat*, make a mistake ; — V. INF. *tagallut*, and VIII. INF. *igtilât*, take by surprise or catch one who is careless.

غلت *galat*, ة *galta-t*, error in calculation.

(غلث) *galas̱*, I, INF. *gals̱*=(غلت) ; fail to give light, to go off ; — *galis̱*, A, INF. *galas̱*, fight furiously ; worry ; — II. INF. *taglîs̱*, deceive one's hope or expectation ; (m.) grieve (a.) ; — III. INF. *mugâlas̱a-t*, fail to give light, to go off ; come to close quarters with (ب *bi*) ; worry ; — VIII. INF. *igtilâs̱*, fail to give light.

غلث *galas̱*, furious combat ;—*galis̱*, fighting furiously (adj.).

(غلج) *galaj*, I, INF. *galj*, run with an equal pace ;—V. INF. *tagalluj*, treat with violence ; lap.

(غلس) *galas*, pl. *aglâs*, last darkness of the night ; *galas-an*, before dawn ; — II. *gallas*, INF. *taglîs*, travel or do anything at that time ; — IV. INF. *iglâs*, id.

(غلص) *galaṣ*, U, INF. *galṣ*, seize one's throat or cut it.

(غلصم) *galṣam*, INF. ة *galṣama-t*= the previous ; — ة *galṣama-t*, pl. *galâṣim*, throat, larynx ; base of the tongue.

(غلط) *galiṭ*, A, INF. *galaṭ*, err, be mistaken, commit an error ; make a mistake in speaking or in calculation ; — II. INF. *taglîṭ*,

accuse of an error or fault; cause one to err or commit a fault; deceive; — III. INF. *gilâṭ*, *mugâlaṭa-t*, try to involve one in error, mislead by sophistical reasoning; venture, risk; fail to give light, to go off; — IV. INF. *iglâṭ*, involve in error, &c.; — V. INF. *tagalluṭ*, err, commit a fault; contain erroneous statements; — VI. INF. *tagâluṭ*, try to deceive one another.

غلط *galaṭ*, ة *galṭa-t*, error, mistake, fault, oversight, slip of the tongue or pen.

غلطان *galṭân*, who errs, commits faults.

(غلظ) *galaẕ*, I, also *galuẕ*, INF. *gilaẕ*, *galẕa-t*, *gilẕa-t*, *gulẕa-t*, *gilâẕa-t*, be or grow big, stout; be coarse; thicken (n.), be or become consistent; be rough, rugged; be rude, rough in manner, impolite; be harsh, cruel, inhumane; be obtuse, dull, stupid; — *galuẕ*, grow into grains; — II. INF. *taglîẕ*, make thick, consistent, coarse, rough, hard; treat roughly or harshly; — IV. INF. *iglâẕ*, treat or receive roughly, be rough with, utter a word aloud, particularly emphasizing the consonants; — X. INF. *istiglâẕ*, turn or find thick, rough, hard, &c.

غلظ *galẕ*, rugged ground; — *gilaẕ*, *gilẕ*, thickness; roughness of manner, rudeness; — ة *gilẕa-t*, *galẕa-t*, *gulẕa-t*, thickness, hardness, roughness, rudeness.

(غلغل) *galgal*, INF. ة, walk apace, hasten (n.); reach (news); put into, insert, let in; be admitted, penetrate, engage deeply in (فى *fî*); (m.) mix up, confuse; — II. INF. *tagalgul*, be admitted, introduced, inserted, joined; penetrate; get mixed up, confused.

غلغلة *galgala-t*, insertion, introduction; quick walk; (m.) confusion, hurly-burly.

(غلف) *galaf*, U, INF. *galf*, sheathe, put into a scabbard, case, etui, box, envelope, &c.; (m.) coat a wall with a mixture of loam (clay) and straw; — *galif*, A, INF. *galaf*, be uncircumcised; — II. INF. *taglîf*, put into a case; put a letter into an envelope; perfume; — IV. INF. *iglâf*, id.; make a case, &c. for a thing; — V. INF. *tagalluf*, be put into a case, into an envelope; perfume one's self; — VIII. INF. *igtilâf*, be provided with a case, &c.

غلف *galf*, putting into a case, envelope, &c.; (m.) coat of mud, mud wall; — *gulf*, pl. of اغلف *aglaf*, sheathing (adj.), uncircumcised, and غلاف *gilâf*; — ة *gulfa-t*, prepuce.

غلفا *galfâ'*, f. of اغلف *aglaf*, see the previous.

(غلفق) *galfaq*, INF. ة, be or grow poor; غ الكلام *galfaq al-kalâm*, be a bad speaker, speak badly.

غلفق *galfaq*, a sea-weed, water-moss; comfortable life, ease.

(غلق) *galaq*, I, U, INF. *galq*, shut, shut up; travel far; — *galiq*, A, INF. *galaq*, give a pledge or pawn; — II. INF. *taglîq*, shut well, shut all doors; — III. INF. *mugâlaqa-t*, lay a wager; — IV. INF. *iglâq*, shut the door; make the camel's back sore beyond remedy; compel to (على *'ala*); — VI. INF. *tagâluq*, lay a wager between one another; — VII. INF. *ingilâq*, be shut; — X. INF. *istiglâq*, shut; conclude, finish; bind the buyer to a bargain; be obscure, hard of understanding.

غلق *galq*, shutting (s.); — *galaq*, pl. *aglâq*, *agâlîq*, bolt, keyless wooden lock; key-stone; — *galiq*, shut; obscure, hard of understanding; — ة *galqa-t*, *gil-*

qa-t, غلقى *galqa*, a bitter or poisonous shrub.

غلل *galal*, pl. *aglâl*, violent thirst; heat in the bowels; water beneath shrubs; — *gulal*, pl. of غلة *gulla-t*.

(غلم) *galim*, A, INF. *galam*, *gulma-t*, be overcome by carnal desire; be rutting and enraged; — IV. INF. *iglâm*, excite to rut; — VIII. INF. *igtilâm*=I.

غلم *galim*, ة, rutting, hot; — ة *gulma-t*, rut; — *gilma-t*, and—

غلمان *gilmân*, pl. of غلام *gulâm*.

(غلن) *galan*, U, INF. *galn*, attain early to maturity of understanding; (m.) calm down (n. wind, sea); — II. INF. *taglîn*, id. (m.).

(غلو) *galâ*, U, INF. *galâ'*, be dear, expensive; sell dearly; get dearer, rise in price; — INF. *guluww*, exceed the bounds, be excessive; — INF. *galw*, *guluww*, shoot high at a distant aim; — INF. *guluww*, overreach the aim; grow dense, high and luxuriant; overgrow; attain soon to maturity; — II. INF. *tagliya-t*, raise the price, overcharge; — III. INF. *mugâlât*, exceed the bounds, go too far; INF. *gilâ'*, *mugâlât*, shoot at a distant aim; sell too dear, heighten the price; — IV. INF. *iglâ'*=II.; grow high and luxuriant; strip off the leaves; — V. INF. *tagallî*, perfume one's self; — VI. INF. *tagâlî*, grow high and luxuriant; — VIII. INF. *igtilâ'*, run fast, hurry along; — X. INF. *istiglâ'*, find too dear; buy or sell dearly; try to buy the most expensive and best; — XII. *iglaula*, INF. *iglîlâ'*=VI.

غلو *galw*, *guluww*, excess, exaggeration; hyperbole; — *guluww*, heat of youth; attack, charge; — ة *galwa-t*, pl. *gilâ'*, *galawât*, bow-shot; a hundred steps or paces.

غلوا *gulwâ'*, *gulawâ'*, overshooting the mark (s.); petulance.

غلوان *gulwân*, heat of youth; excess, exaggeration.

غلول *galûl*, easily-digested food; impostor; — *gulûl*, thirst; embezzlement; INF. of (غل).

غلوط *galûṭ*, ة *galûṭa-t*, what is liable to be misunderstood.

غلومة *gulûma-t*, غلومية *gulûmiyya-t*, youthfulness.

غلوى *galwa*, a perfume.

(غلى) *gala*, I, INF. *galy*, *galayân*, seethe, boil; — *galî*, A, id.; — II. INF. *tagliya-t*, boil (a.), make boil; beckon and greet from afar; — IV. INF. *iglâ'*, id.; — V. INF. *tagallî*, perfume one's self; — VII. INF. *ingilâ'*, be boiled, decocted.

غلى *galy*, ة, boiling, seething (s.); — *galiyy*, dear, expensive.

غليان *galayân*, boiling, seething (s.); — *gilyân*, *galyân*, hydraulic pipe.

غليظ *galîẓ*, ة, pl. *gilâẓ*, thick, coarse, hard, rough, rude; obtuse; dull of intellect; miserly, niggardly; opaque; — ة *galîẓa-t*, rugged ground; thick bottle.

غليل *galîl*, pl. *galâ'il*, violent thirst; thirst for revenge, vindictiveness; passionateness of hatred or love; thirsty; — ة *galîla-t*, pl. *galâ'il*, coat of mail; an under-garment.

غليم *gillîm*, ة, rutting, hot; — *gulayyim*, lad.

غلينة *galîna-t*, calm of the sea (m., γαλήνη).

غليون *galyûn*, hydraulic pipe; galleon, high-boarded ship.

(غم) *gamm*, U, INF. *gamm*, cover entirely; fill with sorrow, grieve (a.); oppress with heat; muzzle; pass. be covered by clouds, invisible; be unknown or unintelligible; — II. INF. *tagmîm*, cover entirely and en-

velop; — IV. INF. *igmâm*, fill with sorrow, grieve (a.); fill with the greatest anxiety; oppress with heat; be covered with clouds; — VI. INF. *tagâmm*, feign grief; — VII. INF. *ingimâm*, be covered, enveloped; (also VIII. INF. *igtimâm*) be sorrowful; grieve (n.).

غم *gamm*, pl. *gumûm*, sorrow, grief, anxiety; — ة *gamma-t*, cloudy or excessively hot (night); (m.) head and feet of a sacrificed sheep; — *gumma-t*, anxiety; darkness; pain.

غما *gamâ'*, grief, sorrowfulness; — *gimâ'*, roof; visor; — *gammâ'* f. of اغم *agamm*, covering all, more grievous, &c.; covered sky; sadness; calamity.

غمار *gamâr*, *gimâr*, *gumâr*, crowd of people, throng; — *; — ة *gamâra-t*, inexperience, ignorance.

غماز *gammâz*, slanderer; informer; — ة *gammâza-t*, f. winking; coquette; dimple in the cheek.

غماسة *gammâsa-t*, pl. *gammâs*, plungeon, sea-diver (bird).

غماض *gamâḍ*, *gimâḍ*, wink of the eyes; a little sleep; — *gammâḍ*, who winks and makes signs; — ة *gamâḍa-t*, *gumûḍa-t*, INF. of (غمض).

غمام *gumâm*, cold, rheum; — ة *gamâma-t*, pl. *gamâm*, *gamâ'im*, cloud; — *gimâma-t*, pl. *gamâ'im*, muzzle; veil for the eyes; bridle; — also *gumâma-t*, prepuce.

غمان *gammân*, grieved, sorrowful.

(غمت) *gamat*, I, INF. *gamt*, burden the stomach and cause giddiness; dip (a.) into the water; — *gamit*, A, INF. *gamat*, suffer from indigestion and headache.

(غمج) *gamaj*, I, INF. *gamj*, — also *gamij*, A, INF. *gamaj*, sip.

غمجار *gimjâr*, varnish.

غمجر *gamjar*, INF. ة, varnish; rain upon plenteously, water thoroughly; sip.

(غمد) *gamad*, I, U, sheathe; — INF. *gumûd*, cover the thorns with the leaves; — *gamid*, A, INF. *gamad*, have abundance or scarcity of water; — II. INF. *tagmîd*, cover, conceal; close the eyes; — IV. INF. *igmâd*, sheathe; put one thing into another; — V. INF. *tagammud*, sheathe; veil, conceal, cover with one's mercy; — VIII. INF. *igtimâd*, enter on the night.

غمد *gimd*, pl. *agmâd*, *gumûd*, sheath, scabbard, etui, case; shell, husk, pod; tunic, wrapper.

(غمذر) *gamẓar*, INF. ة, fill the measure to overflowing.

(غمر) *gamar*, U, INF. *gamr*, cover entirely; embrace; — U, INF. *gamâra-t*, *gumûra-t*, be abundant, stand high (water); — *gamir*, A, INF. *gamar*, be soiled with grease; be angry with, have a grudge against; — *gamur*, INF. *gamâra-t*, be stupid; — II. INF. *tagmîr*, (m.) put into heaps or sheaves; paint the face; — III. INF. *mugâmara-t*, attack furiously; — V. INF. *tagammur*, rush blindly into; (m.) be put into heaps or sheaves; — VI. INF. *tagâmur*, embrace one another; — VII. INF. *ingimâr*, be immersed, covered with water; — VIII. INF. *igtimâr*, cover; immerse; be immersed.

غمر *gamr*, ة, pl. *gimâr*, *gumûr*, body of water which covers everything; very liberal; ample; great multitude; — *gimr*, *gamar*, pl. *gumûr*, ill-will; — *gimr*, *gumr*, pl. *agmâr*, inexperienced, uncultured, simpleton; — *gumr*, pl. *agmâr*, (m.) armful, sheaf; (m.) embrace; saffron; — *gamar*, smell of meat, fish, &c.; — *gamir*, ة, smelling offensively; — *gumar*, little bowl, cup; — ة *gamra-t*, pl.

gamarât, *gimâr*, large body of water, depth (غمرات الموت *gamarât al-maut*, abyss of death, agony); also pl. *gumar*, multitude; adversity, calamity; — ة *gumra-t*, a paint for the face; saffron.

(غمز) *gamaz*, I, INF. *gamz*, make a sign, beckon, wink; slander, denounce, inform against (ب *bi*); feel an animal to examine its fatness; — III. INF. *mugâmaza-t*, make a sign to, beckon, wink; accuse, charge with; — IV. INF. *igmâz*, calumniate, slander; — VI. INF. *tagâmuz*, make signs to one another; have a secret understanding with one another; — VIII. INF. *igtimâz*, talk with ill-will of; slander.

غمز *gamz*, ة *gamza-t*, wink; blinking of the eye; love-sign, love-token.

(غمس) *gamas*, I, INF. *gams*, dip into water, immerse, wet; dye; set; cement; — II. INF. *tagmîs*, immerse, wet; drink little; — III. INF. *mugâmasa-t*, try to immerse; rush to the combat; — VII. INF. *ingimâs*, VIII. INF. *igtimâs*, get immersed, wetted; plunge into; be cemented.

(غمش) *gamiś*, I, INF. *gamaś*, become dim-sighted (from hunger or thirst); (m.) scratch; — IV. INF. *igmâś*=I.

(غمص) *gamaṣ*, I, INF. *gamṣ*, disdain, despise; slander, accuse falsely; be ungrateful; —*gamiṣ*, A, INF. *gamaṣ*, run with impure matter; disdain, despise; —VIII. INF. *igtimâṣ*, disdain, despise.

غمص *gamaṣ*, impurity of the eye; — *gumṣ*, pl. and—

غمصا *gamṣâ*, f. of اغمص, having running eyes, blear-eyed.

(غمض) *gamaḍ*, U, INF. *gumûḍ*, be low and flat; be obscure (speech); — I, show one's self yielding, accommodating; travel to; penetrate; — *gamuḍ*, INF. *gamâḍa-t*, *gumûḍa-t*, be low and flat; INF. *gumûḍa-t*, be obscure; — II. INF. *tagmîḍ*, compress the eye-lids strongly; close the eyes; render obscure; give at a low price, cheaply; — IV. INF. *igmâḍ*, close the eyes at (على *'ala*); show one's self yielding, accommodating; — V. INF. *tagammuḍ*, close (n.); — VII. INF. *ingimâḍ*, VIII. INF. *igtimâḍ*, close and open again alternately (n.); be obscure; VIII. be closed.

غمض *gamḍ*, pl. *gumûḍ*, flat lowland; indulgence; — *gumḍ*, closing of the eyes.

(غمط) *gamaṭ*, I, INF. *gamṭ*, — *gamiṭ*, A, INF. *gamaṭ*, disdain, slight, despise; be ungrateful; live inconsiderately, disorderly; sip greedily; — IV. INF. *igmâṭ*, last for ever; — V. INF. *tagammuṭ*, cover with earth; — VIII. INF. *igtimâṭ*, get beforehand with; get the better of with words; disappear without leaving a trace.

غمط *gamṭ*, low and flat.

(غمغم) *gamgam*, INF. ة, roar, bellow, cry out; be obscure; — II. INF. *tagamgum*, speak unintelligibly.

(غمق) *gamiq*, *gamaq*, A, *gamuq*, INF. *gamaq*, be very moist, wet; (m.) be deep; — II. INF. *tagmîq*, deepen (a.), hollow; fathom by deep thought.

غمق *gumq*, depth (m.); — *gamiq*, spoiled by too much moisture.

(غمل) *gamal*, U, INF. *gaml*, put hides into the ground until they soften and lose their hair; make to perspire by covering up; put fruit into straw; pile up grapes; — *gamil*, A, INF. *gamal*, deteriorate, grow bad.

(غملج) *gamlaj*, *gamallaj*, غملاج *gimlâj*, غمالج *gumâlij*, غملوج *gumlûj*, ة, غمليج *gimlîj*, ة, fickle, inconsistent, changeable.

(غملس) *gamallas*, malicious and insolent; wolf.
(غملط) *gamallaṭ*, long-necked.
غملول *gumlûl*, valley with luxuriant vegetation.
(غمن) *gaman*, U, INF. *gamn*, put into the ground; make perspire by covering up.
(غمو) *gamâ*, U, INF. *gamw*, cover.
غموس *gamûs*, deep; dark, obscure, difficult; premeditated; false (oath).
غموص *gamûṣ* (ال *al-*), little dog, dog-star; false (oath).
غموم *gumûm*, pl. of غم *gamm*.
(غمى), pass. *gumî*, faint and recover (على *'ala*);—II. INF. *tagmiya-t*, cover a roof; pass. faint (على *'ala*).
غمى *gamy*, *gaman*, fainting-fit; clouding over (s.); — *gaman*, pl. *agmâ'*, swooning, fainting (adj.); pl. *agmâ'*, *agmiya-t*, roof, covering of a house; visor; — *gamma*, clouded over or very sultry; — also *gumma*, difficulty, calamity.
غميان *gamyân*, swooning, fainting (m.).
غمير *gamîr*, pl. *agmirâ'*, body of water.
غميزة *gamîza-t*, anything desirable; exposed to slander.
غميس *gamîs*, dark; unknown; darkness.
غميصا *gumaiṣâ* (ال *al-*), the little dog-star.
(غن) *gann*, A, INF. *gunna-t*, sound, resound; speak through the nose; grow full (also IV.); abound in trees (also IV.); — IV. INF. *ignân*, hum, buzz; resound (with the hum of flies, &c.); see I.
غن *gann-a*, perhaps, may be; — ة *gunna-t*, sound; hum; growl; speaking through the nose.
غنا *ganâ'*, INF. of (غنى); sufficing (s.), sufficiency; riches, wealth; power; profit, advantage, gain; usefulness; — *ginâ'*, song, air, melody; — *gannâ'*, f. of اغن *agann*, speaking through the nose, &c.
غنائم *ganâ'im*, pl. of غنم *ganam* and غنيمة *ganîma-t*.
غنام *gannâm*, pl. *gannâma-t*, sheep-dealer.
غنانى *ganâniyy*, pl. of غنية *ganniyya-t*.
(غنب) *gamb*, plenty of booty.
(غنث) *ganiṯ*, A, INF. *ganaṯ*, drink and fetch a deep sigh after; be malignant.
(غنثر) *ganṯar*, INF. ة, have thick hair; — II. INF. *tаganṯur*, drink without thirst.
غنثر *ganṯar*, *gunṯur*, fool; — ة *ganṯara-t*, a blue fly.
(غنج) *ganij*, A, INF. *ganaj*, also pass. *gunij*, be coquettish, take coquettish airs; be in love, (m.) pull faces; — II. INF. *tagnîj*=I.; (m.) spoil a child by over-indulgence; — V. INF. *tagannuj* =I.
غنج *gunj*, *gunuj*, غناج *gunâj*, coquetry; (m.) wry faces, grimaces; — *ganij*, ة, coquettish.
(غنجل) *gunjul*, pl. *ganâjil*, badger.
غندبة *gunduba-t*, غندوب *gundûb*, pl. *ganâdib*, swollen glands of the throat, mumps.
(غندر) *gundar*, *gundur*, غندور *gundûr*, big and fat (young man); fop, coxcomb; effeminate dandy; — *gandar*, INF. ة, effeminate, pamper, over-indulge; — II. INF. *tagandur*, be effeminate; play the coxcomb;—ة *gandara-t*, effeminating, pampering (s.); effeminacy; foppishness.
غندوب *gundûb*, see غندبة *gunduba-t*.
غندور *gundûr*, see غندر *gandar*.
(غنص) *ganiṣ*, A, INF. *ganaṣ*, have the chest oppressed.
(غنظ) *ganaẓ*, I, INF. *ganẓ*, oppress heavily, depress deeply; be on the point of death from grief.
غنظ *ganẓ*, *ganaẓ*, grief which brings near to death.

(غنظى) *ganza*, INF. *ganzâ'a-t*, revile; talk obscenely.

غنظيان *ginziyân*, shameless; ribald.

(غنم) *ganim*, A, INF. *ganm*, *gunm*, *ganam*, *gunmân*, *ganîma-t*, carry off as booty; — INF. *gunm*, win easily; — II. INF. *tagnîm*, cede part of the booty, present, enrich; — V. INF. *tagannum*, deem or get a prize; — VIII. INF. *igtinâm*=V.; — VIII. and X. INF. *istignâm*, profit quickly by an opportunity.

غنم *ganam* (f.), pl. *gunûm*, *ganâ'im*, *agnâm*, sheep; small cattle; — *gunm*, gain, booty, prize.

(غنى) *ganî*, A, INF. *ginan*, *ganâ'*, be rich, find one's self rich enough, content one's self, be satisfied; be content with one thing instead of another; be able to dispense with; be contented with her husband and her own unadorned beauty, be chaste and modest; have enough to live upon, live; INF. *ganan*, stay, remain; meet with; marry; be at a place; — II. INF. *tagniya-t*, make rich, content, give enough; sing an air to; address one's wife with words of love; praise, blame satirically; — IV. INF. *ignâ'*, make rich, content; suffice; be able to dispense with (عن *'an*).

غنى *gina*, *gana*, riches, wealth; being able to do without (s.); — *ganiyy*, ة, pl. *agniyâ'*, rich; able to dispense with (عن *'an*); — ة *gunya-t*, *ginya-t*, sufficiency; wealth; — *ganiyya-t*, pl. *ganâniyy*, song, melody.

غنيان *gunyân*, sufficiency, wealth.

غنيم *ganîm*, booty, prey, gain; — ة *ganîma-t*, pl. *ganâ'im*, id.; plenty, abundance; — *gunaima-t*, little sheep.

(غهب) *gahib*, A, INF. *gahab*, neglect, forget; — VIII. INF. *igtihâb*, travel in the darkness of night.

غهب *gahab*, carelessness, negligence; *gahab-an*, unawares.

غهق *gahiq*, having a long body.

غواث *guwâs*, *gawâs*, cry for help; help.

غوار *gawwâr*, whirlpool, eddy.

غواش *gawâś*, noise, tumult.

غواص *gawwâṣ*, diver; pearl-fisher; penetrating deeply.

غواة *guwât*, pl. of غاو *gâw-in*, غاوى *gâwî*, erring, &c.

غواية *gawâya-t*, error, misconduct, INF. of (غوى).

(غوث) *gâs*, U, INF. *gaus*, help, come to help; — II. INF. *tagwîs*, call for help; (m.) appeal; — IV. INF. *igâsa-t*, *magûsa-t*, come to help, succour; — VII. INF. *ingiyâs*, get help; — X. INF. *istigâsa-t*, call to help; (m.) appeal.

غوث *gaus*, call or cry for help; help; appeal.

(غوج) *gâj*, U, INF. *gauj*, be bent, inclined, bend (n.); — V. INF. *tagawwuj*, id.

(غور) *gâr*, U, INF. *gaur*, *gu'ûr*, descend into a valley; disappear in the ground, sink; — U, A, INF. *gaur*, *gu'ûr*, sink back into its socket (eye), lie deep in its socket, be deep-set; — U, INF. *gaur*, *gu'ûr*, *giyâr*, enter, penetrate; — INF. *giyâr*, *gu'ûr*, set; be very hot; — INF. *giyâr*, bless with rain and fertility; come to help with; — INF. *gâra-t*, make a foray, a raid; gallop; — II. INF. *tagwîr*, descend into lowlands; sink; rest on a journey at noontide; — III. INF. *mugâwara-t*, make a foray on a tribe; plunder one's territory; — IV. INF. *igâra-t*, descend into lowlands; make a foray; gallop against (ب *bi*); — V. INF. *tagawwur*, come to low ground; — VI. INF. *tagâwur*, devastate and plunder one another's country; — VIII. INF. *igtiyâr*, have advantage from,

profit by ; — x. INF. *istigâra-t*, wish to come to soft low ground; send one's horsemen against a hostile tribe; make a foray; gallop; grow fat.

غور *gaur*, bottom, the lowest part; depth; cavity, socket, cave; low ground; enclosed valley, valley; depth of mind; deep thought, meditation; — *gûr*, a measure;—*giwar*, blood-money; — ة *gaura-t*, sun; mid-day.

(غوز) *gâz*, U, INF. *gauz*, intend, purpose.

(غوش) (m.) *gâś*, — II. *gawwaś*, INF. *tagwiś*, make a noise, a tumult; — ة *gauśa-t*, noise, tumult.

(غوص) *gâṣ*, U, INF. *gauṣ*, *giyâṣ*, *giyâṣa-t*, *magâṣ*, plunge, dive (n.); try to get at the bottom of a thing; make water.

غوص *gauṣ*, diving (s.), immersion.

(غوط) *gâṭ*, U, INF. *gauṭ*, enter; hide (n.) anywhere; sink; dig, excavate; — II. INF. *tagwîṭ*, deepen (a.); swallow large pieces; — IV. INF. *igâṭa-t*, immerse; — V. INF. *tagawwuṭ*, have stool; — VII. INF. *ingiyâṭ*, be bent, crooked.

غوط *gûṭ*, pl. of غائط *gâ'iṭ*, flat plain, &c.; — ة *gûṭa-t*, well-watered fertile valley, especially round Damascus; — ة *gauṭa-t*, dipping, diving, sinking (s.).

(غوغا) *gaugâ'*, noisy crowd; tumult, uproar, skirmish.

(غول) *gâl*, U, INF. *gaul*, seize and carry off unexpectedly, abduct, rob; spoil, destroy; be vast; — II. INF. *tagwîl*, devour like a demon (m.); — III. INF. *mugâwala-t*, set to a thing quickly; — V. INF. *tagawwul*, take different shapes, change one's form (as a demon); — VI. INF. *tagâwul*, try to capture, to destroy one another; — VIII. INF. *igtiyâl*, seize suddenly, assail, destroy.

غول *gaul*, sudden calamity, destruction; drunkenness; headache; — *gûl*, id.; pl. *gîlân*, *agwâl*, wicked demon, goblin (also female); pl. *agwâl*, snake; death and destruction;—*guwwal*, comfortable.

غومنة *gômana-t*, cable (m. from the It.).

(غون), V. *tagawwan*, INF. *tagawwun*, persist in revolt; advance bravely in combat.

غوهق *gauhaq*=غيهق *gaihaq*.

غوور *gu'ûr*, INF. of (غور).

(غوى) *gawa*, I, INF. *gayy*, err; induce into error, lead astray, seduce;—*gawî*, A, INF. *gawâya-t*, err, go astray, be seduced; — *gawa*, I, *gawî*, A, INF. *gawan*, refuse to suck and get emaciated (foal, lamb); — *gawî*, A, INF. *gawan*, long for, hanker after, lust for (m.); — II. INF. *tagwiya-t*, lead astray, seduce; — IV. INF. *igwâ'*=II.; — VII. INF. *ingiwâ'*, be led astray, seduced; (m.) long for, have a propensity for or hankering after; — X. INF. *istigwâ'*, try to lead astray, into error, or to seduce; seduce.

غوى *gawiyy*, ة, pl. *guwât*, erring; seduced; transgressor.

غوير *guwair*, little cave.

غويص *gawîṣ*, deep; obscure.

(غى) *gayy* (1 pret. *gayai-tu*), I, INF. *gayy*, plant a flag, a standard.

غى *gayy*, error, sin; despair; leading into error (s.); seduction; — ة *gayya-t*, precipitation; ولد غ *walad gayya-t*, bastard; — *giyya-t*, error; (m.) anything desirable; (m.) fashion.

غياب *gayâb*, absence; also *giyâb*, ة *giyâba-t*, concealment, invisibility, supersensuousness; sunset; — *; — *gayyâb*, who slanders the absent, backbiter; — *guyyâb*, pl. of غائب *gâ'ib*, *gâyib*, absent, &c.; — ة *giyâba-t*, depth, bottom.

غياث *giyâs̱*, ة *giyâs̱a-t*, help; call or cry for help.

غياذير *gayâẕîr*, pl. of غيذار *gaiẕâr*.

غيار *giyâr*, jealousy; exchange of goods; change; distinguishing sign for Jews, Christians, &c.; (m.) alteration of the features, maceration; (m.) putting on afresh an old horse-shoe.

غيارى *gayâra*, pl. of غيران *gairân*, غيرى *gaira*.

غياص *giyâṣ*, ة *giyâṣa-t*, diving; deep study or thought.

غياط *giyâṭ*, pl. of غائط *gâ'iṭ*, *gâyiṭ*, flat plain, &c.

غياظ *giyâẓ*, anger; offence, insult.

غيان *gayân*, mercury; — *gayyân*, erring; seduced.

(غيب) *gâb*, I, INF. *gaib*, *gaiba-t*, *giyâb*, *gaibûba-t*, *guyûb*, *guyûba-t*, *magâb*, *magîb*, be absent; remove, depart; lose one's mind; — INF. *giyâb*, *giyâba-t*, *gayâb*, *guyûba-t*, *gîba-t*, be hidden, concealed; disappear, set; penetrate deeply; be dark, obscure, doubtful; backbite; — II. INF. *tagyîb*, conceal, make disappear, render invisible; (m.) learn by heart; — III. INF. *mugâyaba-t*, be hidden or concealed from, hide from (n.); profit from one's absence; address an absent person; — IV. INF. *igâba-t*, have an absent husband; — V. INF. *tagayyub*, remove, depart, disappear; (m.) be learnt by heart; — VIII. INF. *igtiyâb*, backbite, slander; — X. INF. *istigâba-t*, try to hide from (n.), to profit from one's absence.

غيب *gaib*, pl. *giyâb*, *guyûb*, absence, concealment; doubt; what is hidden or obscure, secret, mystery; invisible; *gaib-an*, by heart; — *gayab*, *guyyab*, pl. of غائب *gâ'ib*, *gâyib*, absent, &c.; — ة *gaiba-t*, absence, concealment; exile; being absorbed by the contemplation of transcendental things, mysticism; pl. *gaibât*, mysteries, secrets; — *gîba-t*, backbiting (s.).

غيبوبة *gaibûba-t*, absence.

غيبى *gaibiyy*, ة, absent, concealed; mysterious; belonging to the invisible world; heavenly.

(غيث) *gâs̱*, I. INF. *gais̱*, water with rain, rain upon, water; shine.

غيث *gais̱*, abundant and far-spread rain; ذات الغ *ẕât al-gais̱*, perennial (source), in full gallop (horse); — *gayyis̱*, raining abundantly.

(غيد) *gayid*, A, INF. *gayad*, be slender and delicate; be soft and tender.

غيد *gîd*, pl., غيداء *gaidâ'*, غيدى *gaida*, f. of اغيد *agyad*, young, tender and supple, &c.; — *gayad*, delicacy, tenderness, suppleness.

غيدان *gaidân*, delicate and slender.

غيذار *gaiẕâr*, pl. *gayâẕîr*, ass.

(غير) *gâr*, A, (m.) I, INF. *gâr*, *gair*, *gaira-t*, (m.) *gîra-t*, *giyâr*, be jealous; feel jealousy, envy; — I, INF. *giyâr*, provide, furnish provisions; bestow benefits, rain, &c., upon (acc.); profit (a.), be useful to (acc.); — II. INF. *tagyîr*, change, alter, transform; (m.) alter (n.), emaciate (n.); — III. INF. *mugâyara-t*, feel jealous with; INF. *giyâr*, *mugâyara-t*, carry on exchange with (acc.); — IV. INF. *igâra-t*, render jealous; twist a rope; — V. INF. *tagayyur*, be changed, alter (n.), transform one's self; (m.) emaciate (n.); — VI. INF. *tagâyur*, be jealous of one another; be different from one another; — VII. INF. *ingiyâr*, be tormented by jealousy, envy; — VIII. INF. *igtiyâr*, id.; procure provisions (n.); — X. INF. *istigâra-t*, excite jealousy, emulation.

غير *gair*, diminution; difference; INF. of (غير); pl. *agyâr*, another

(followed by pron. aff.); serves as a privative before adjectives, as: غير خالص *gair ḥâliṣ*, impure, &c.; بغير *bi-gair*, except, without; بنات غير *banât-u gair-in*, lies; — *gîr*, jealousy; pl. *agyâr*, blood-money; — *giyar*, pl. vicissitudes of fortune; — *guyur*, pl. of غيور *gayûr*; — ة *gaira-t*, *gîra-t*, pl. *giyar*, jealousy; emulation, ambition, higher aspirations, patriotism, &c.; — *gîra-t*, pl. *giyar*, provisions, supply; rain; blood-money.

غيران *gairân*, pl. *gayâra*, *guyâra*, f. *gaira*, pl. *gayâra*, jealous; — *gîrân*, pl. of غار *gâr*, cave, den, &c.

غيرية *gairiyya-t*, change, alteration; non-existence.

(غيس) *gais*, mud, dung; — لمم غيس *limam gîs*, rich locks of hair behind the ear.

غيسان *gaisân*, youth; — ة *gaisâna-t* (also غيسبات *gaisât*), bloom of youth; — ى *gaisâniyy*, youthful.

(غيض) *gâḍ*, I, INF. *gaiḍ*, *magâḍ*, diminish, decrease, sink away; be failing, be rare; lessen (a.); — II. INF. *tagyîd*, diminish (a.), lessen (a.), let subside, make to sink away; enter the thicket (lion); — VII. INF. *ingiyâḍ*, sink away, decrease, grow scarce.

غيض *gaiḍ*, decrease, diminution, sinking away; scarcity; غ من فيض *gaiḍ min faiḍ*, little after plenty; — ة *gaiḍa-t*, pl. *giyâḍ*, *agyâḍ*, thicket with some water, reedy bank, wood; grove.

(غيط) *gâṭ*, I, INF. *gaiṭ*, enter anywhere and conceal one's self.

غيط *gîṭ*, pl. *gîṭân*, field (m.).

(غيظ) *gâẓ*, I, INF. *gaiẓ*, provoke to anger, irritate, offend; enter; dive; conceal one's self; — II. INF. *tagyîẓ*, provoke to anger, irritate, offend; — III. INF. *mugâyaẓa-t*, id.; — IV. INF. *igâẓa-t*, id.; — V. INF. *tagayyuẓ*, be enraged; — VI. INF. *tagâyuẓ*, irritate, provoke, offend one another; — VII. INF. *ingiyâẓ*, be provoked, offended; — VIII. INF. *igtiyâẓ*, be angry, burst out in anger.

غيظ *gaiẓ*, anger, burst of anger, rage.

(غيف) *gâf*, I, INF. *gayafân*, bend to the right and left with its branches.

غيف *gaif*, flock of birds; — ة *gaifa-t*, lair or den of a lion.

(غيق), II. *gayyaq*, INF. *tagyîq*, ruin one's fortune; think and act confusedly or inconsistently; perplex; — V. INF. *tagayyuq*, grow dim.

(غيل) *gâl*, I, INF. *gail* (also IV.), give suck to a child in spite of being pregnant or indulging in coition; — INF. *giyâl*, get into a morass or thicket; — IV. INF. *igâla-t*, *igyâl*=I.; — V. INF. *tagayyul*, be densely grown; — VIII. INF. *igtiyâl*, grow fat; — X. INF. *istigyâl*, grow dense in foliage.

غيل *gail*, the giving suck of a pregnant woman; حليب غ *ḥalîb gail-in*, the milk of a pregnant woman; — *gîl*, pl. *guyûl*, *agyâl*, morass; reedy bank, thicket; — ة *gîla-t*, pl. *giyal*, sudden destruction; treacherous attack; stratagem, treachery; — *gaila-t*, f. fat.

ام غيلان *umm gailân*, Egyptian thorn, acacia; — *gîlân*, pl. of غول *gûl*.

غيلم *gailam*, tortoise; frog; — also غيلمى *gailamiyy*, boy with a large head and plentiful hair.

(غيم) *gâm*, I, INF. *gaim*, be thirsty; be consumed by inner heat; be covered with clouds; — II. INF. *tagyîm*, be covered with clouds; be foggy; — IV. INF. *igâma-t*, *igyâm*, be thirsty; be covered with clouds; be foggy; INF. *igyâm*, have the sky covered

with clouds; —v. INF. *tagayyum*, be cloudy, foggy.

غيم *gaim*, pl. *guyûm*, cloud; thirst, heat in the bowels; anger, vexation, grief; — ة *gaima-t*, cloud.

غيمان *gaimân*, f. *gaimâ'*, *gaima*, thirsty; with heated bowels.

(غين) *gân*, I, INF. *gain*, be thirsty; be troubled, vexed; be oppressed with debts; pass. be covered with clouds; — IV. INF. *igâna-t*, engross and oppress.

غين *gain*, thirst; thin cloud; letter غ.

غيناء *gainâ'*, f. of أغين *agyan*, dark green; having dense foliage; long; mountain-peak.

غيهب *gaihab*, pl. *gayâhib*, darkness; pitch-dark, coal-black.

غيهق *gaihaq*, briskness; folly; = غهق *gahiq*.

غيهم *gaiham*, darkness.

غيوب *guyûb*, pl. of غيب *gaib*; also ة *guyûba-t*, INF. of (غيب).

غيور *gayûr*, pl. *guyur*, jealous (m. f.); resting from work.

غيول *guyûl*, pl. of غيل *gîl*.

غيوم *guyûm*, pl. of غيم *gaim*.

ف

ف *f*, as a numerical sign = 80; denotes in the almanac the altitude of the moon; — *fa*, and, and then, and thereupon, so then, joined in writing to the following word.

فا *fâ*, acc. of فوه *fûh*, mouth; — *fâ'*, name of the letter ف; denotes in grammar the first radical of any root.

فاا *fa'a*, see (فاو).

(فات), VIII. *ifta'a-t*, INF. *ifti'ât*, tell lies against (على *'ala*); have one's peculiar opinion and follow it; pass. die suddenly.

فاتح *fâtiḥ*, pl. *fataḥa-t*, who opens, conquers; victor, conqueror; semi-dark or light colour; — ة *fâtiḥa-t*, pl. *fawâtiḥ*, opening, beginning (adj., s.), overture, introduction, exordium; *al-fâtiḥa-t*, the opening Sura of the Koran.

فاتر *fâtir*, dull; peevish; languid; lukewarm; dim.

فاتك *fâtik*, pl. *futtâk*, bold, daring; spurner of the law; lost to honour; robber.

فاتن *fâtin*, pl. *futtân*, charming, enchanting; seducing; tempter, Satan; trouble-maker, factionist; seduced.

فاتور *fâtûr*, lukewarm.

فاثور *fâs̱ûr*, large dish or cup; ornamental table; boundary-post; dignity; place of honour.

فاج *fâj-in*, see فاجى *fâjî*.

فاجر *fâjir*, ة, pl. *fujjâr*, *fajara-t*, *fawâjir*, licentious, profligate; sinner, fornicator, liar; sorcerer; rebellious, insolent; false (oath).

فاجع *fâji'*, grievous, painful; — ة *fâji'a-t*, calamity.

فاجل *fâjil*, gambler; gainer, winner.

فاجور *fâjûr*, licentious, profligate; fornicator.

فاجى *fâjî* (فاج *fâj-in*), who opens.

فاحش *fâḥiś*, ة, shameless, obscene; excessive, unproportional; — ة *fâḥiśa-t*, fornicatress, whore; pl. *fawâḥiś*, sin, fornication.

فاحص *fâḥiṣ*, who examines, investigates.

فاحم *fâḥim*, coal-black.

فاختة *fâḫita-t*, pl. *fawâḫit*, ring-dove; a female proper name.

فاختى *fâḫitiyy*, dove-coloured; passing from one colour into another.

فاخر *fâḫir*, f. ة, boaster; excellent; delightful, delicious; precious, costly, magnificent.

فاخورة *fâḫûra-t*, earthenware.

فاخورى *fâḫûriyy*, potter.

(فاد) *fa'ad*, A, INF. *fa'd*, injure in the heart; oppress the heart; suffer from oppression of the heart, be afflicted with heart-disease (pass. *fu'id*, id.); bake bread in the hot ashes; — *fa'id*, have heart-disease; — V. INF. *tafa''ud*, be kindled, burn; — VIII. INF. *ifti'âd*, kindle, light; roast (a.).

فادح *fâdiḥ*, ة, difficult; oppressive; — ة *fâdiḥa-t*, pl. *fawâdiḥ*, calamity.

فادر *fâdir*, pl. *fudr*, weak, tired out, exhausted; — ة *fâdira-t*, summit of a rock.

فادن *fâdin*, plummet, plumb-line (m.).

فادى *fâdî* (فاد *fâd-in*), who redeems, ransoms; Saviour.

فاذا *fa-iẕâ*, then, therefore, consequently.

(فار) *fa'ar*, INF. *fa'r*, dig out; bury in the ground.

فار *fa'r*, *fâr*, ة, pl. *fu'ûr*, *fi'ara-t*, *fi'rân*, *fîrân*, mouse; rat; musk; —*fârr*, pl. *farr*, fleeing, fugitive, deserter; — ة *fa'ra-t*, *fâra-t*, a little bag with musk; strong smell; (m.) plane (tool).

فارد *fârid*, ة, single; unique, exquisite.

فارز *fâriz*, separating, &c., ag. of (فرز); distinct, clear; queen ant.

فارس *fâris*, riding on horse-back; tearing to pieces (beast of prey); pl. *fawâris*, *fursân*, horseman; knight; lion; Persian; physiognomist; — ى *fârisiyy*, *fârsiyy*, ة, Persian (adj., s.); — ية *al-fârisiyya-t*, the Persian language.

فارض *fâriḍ*, pl. *furraḍ*, corpulent; thick; bulky; old, aged; old cow.

فارط *fâriṭ*, pl. *furrâṭ*, guide; who beats down fruit; (m.) lost; (m.) escaped.

فارع *fâri'*, high, towering; pl. *fara'a-t*, ally, confederate; — ة *fâri'a-t*, pl. *fawâri'*, towering mountain-peak.

فارغ *fârig*, ة, pl. *furrag*, *furrâg*, empty, emptied; having finished one's work, free of work, at leisure; free of cares.

فارق *fâriq*, ة, separating, &c., ag. of (فرق); f. pl. *fâriqât*, angels who distinguish the lie from the truth.

فارك *fârik*, woman who hates her husband.

فارن *fârin*, ة, who bakes.

فاره *fârih*, ة, pl. *furrah*, *furraha-t*, *furha-t*, *furuh*, *furh*, skilful, active, brisk; running well.

فاروق *fârûq*, ة, extremely timid; distinguishing between lie and truth.

فازر *fâzir*, ة, broad, wide.

(فاس) *fa's*, INF. *fa's*, cut or hew with the axe; beat on the back of the head.

فاس *fâs*, fez; — *fa's* (f.), pl. *fu'us*, *fu'ûs*, *af'us*, axe; iron part of the bridle; projecting part of the occiput.

فاسد *fâsid*, pl. *fasda*, destructive; spoiled, corrupted, good-for-nothing; ف المزاج *fâsid al-mizâj*, indisposed, unwell.

فاسق *fâsiq*, ة, pl. *fasaqa-t*, *fussâq*, shameless, dissolute, licentious; fornicator, rake; sodomite; not admissible as a witness.

فاسيا *fâsiyâ'*, فاسية *fâsiya-t*, a beetle.

فاش *fâś-in*, see فاشى; — ة *fâśśa-t*, refractory (wife).

فاشوش *fâśûś*, spoiled, deteriorated; empty (m.).

فاشى *fâśî* (فاش *fâś-in*), ة, published, made known; spreading far; propagated, multiplied; — ة *fâśiya-t*, pl. *fawâśî*, cattle, property.

فاصل *fâṣil*, ة, separating; decid-

ing; decisive, peremptory, final; — ة *fâṣila-t*, intervening space, interstice, interval; distinction, difference; pl. *fawâṣil*, jewel or large pearl between smaller ones.

فاض *fâḍ-in*, see فاضى *fâḍî*; — ة *fâḍa-t*, large cuirass; — *fâḍḍa-t*, pl. *fawâḍḍ*, calamity.

فاضح *fâḍiḥ*, offending, disgracing, &c., ag. of (فضح); gross (fault, mistake); clear, bright (day).

فاضل *fâḍil*, ة, overflowing, &c.; abundant; virtuous; cultivated; —ة *fâḍila-t*, pl. *fawâḍil*, anything superfluous; increase, gain; distinction, privilege; present, bounty; advance (of money).

فاضى *fâḍî* (فاض *fâḍ-in*), free of work, at leisure; void, emptied (m.).

فاطر *fâṭir*, creator; who breakfasts.

فاطم *fâṭim*, young of an animal on the point of being weaned; — ة *fâṭima-t*, pl. *fawâṭim*, mother weaning her child; female proper name.

فاطمية *fâṭimiyya-t*, the descendants of Fâṭima.

فاع *fâ-'in*, see فاعى *fâ'î*.

فاعل *fâ'il*, making, doing, &c.; author, perpetrator, agent; governing, participle present or active, noun in the nominative; what produces an effect, effective; paederast (a.); pl. *fa'ala-t*, working man, artisan; — ى *fâ'iliyy*, ة, operating, effective; — ية *fâ'iliyya-t*, efficacy, influence; governing of a word.

فاعى *fâ'î* (فاع *fâ'-in*), angry; foaming.

فاغر *fâgir*, wide open; — ة *fâgira-t*, cubeb.

(فاق) *fa'aq*, INF. *fu'âq*, belch, hiccough.

فاقد *fâqid*, widowed, orphaned.

فاقرة *fâqira-t*, pl. *fawâqir*, calamity; bridle.

فاقع *fâqi'*, bursting; crimson, bright yellow; pure, bright; — ة *fâqi'a-t*, pl. *fawâqi'*, calamity.

فاقيا *fâqi'â'*, membrane surrounding an embryo.

فاك *fâkk*, pl. *fakaka-t*, *fikâk*, weak and imbecile; decrepit; who separates, loosens.

فاكه *fâkih*, who possesses fruit; ة, tenderly reared; merry, cheerful; — ة *fâkiha-t*, pl. *fawâkih*, fruit.

فاكهانى *fâkihâniyy*, fruit-seller, fruiterer.

فاكورة *fâkûra-t*, window-sash fastening (m.).

(فال) *fa'l*, *fâl*, pl. *fu'ul*, *af'ul*, fore-token, omen, augury; (m.) superstition; لا فال عليك *lâ fa'l 'alai-ka*, it portends no evil to you! — *fa'al*, II. *fa''al*, INF. *taf'îl*, (m.) *fawwal*, INF. *tafwîl*, augur well by (على *'ala*, ب *bi*), take as a good omen; II. cause one to take as an omen; — V. INF. *tafa''ul*, VI. INF. *tafâ'ul*, VIII. INF. *ifti'âl*, X. INF. *istif'âl*, (m.) *istifwâl*, take as an omen, augur by (ب *bi*); — (m.) VI. and X. be superstitious; — *fâl*, pl. *afyâl*, imbecile, weak of intellect.

فالت *fâlit*, escaped, free, without a bridle; indecent (speech); — ى *fâlitiyy*, good-for-nothing fellow, scamp (m.)

فالج *fâlij*, hemiplegia; splitting in two, halving (adj.).

فالع *fâli'*, burst, having rents or splits; — ة *fâli'a-t*, pl. *fawâli'*, calamity, evil.

فالق *fâliq*, who splits, halves; creator; — ة *fâliqa-t*, valley, low ground.

فالوذ *fâlûẕ* (فالود *fâlûd*, فالودج *falûdaj*, فالودق *fâlûdaq*), sweetmeat of flour, water and honey.

فالى *fa'liyy*, *fâliyy*, interpreter of signs, augur, soothsayer.

فاليز *fâlîz*, pl. *fawâlîz*, kitchen garden; — ى *fâlîziyy*, kitchen gardener.

(فام) *fa'am*, INF. *fa'm*, quench one's thirst with water; take the mouth full of herbs; be full; — *fa'im*, A, INF. *ta'am*, be fat.

فاما *fa-ammâ*, furthermore.

فامی *fâmiyy*, seller of corn, corn-chandler.

فان *fân-in*, see فانی *fânî*;—*fa'inna*, and then behold.

فانوس *fânûs*, pl. *fawânîs*, light-house; lantern (ف خيال *fânûs ḥayâl*, magic lantern); tell-tale, slanderer.

فانی *fânî* (فان *fân-in*), ة, perishable, fleeting, changeable, frail.

فانيذ *fânîẕ*, pure sugar-candy.

فاه *fâh*, pl. *afhâh*, mouth.

(فاو), فاا *fa'a* (1 pret. *fa au-tu*, *fa'ai-tu*), INF. *fa'w*, *fa'y*, split, cleave (a.); cut open, prick open; — III. INF. *mufa'awa-t*, return; — IV. INF. *if'â'*, come to a mountain-cleft; inflict an open wound upon.

فاو *fa'w*, mountain-cleft, mountain-pass.

فای *fa'y*, INF. of (فاو).

فائت *fâ'it*, passing, passing by, escaping (adj.); lost; (m.) entering.

فائح *fâ'iḥ*, spreading an odour; fragrant;—ة *fâ'iḥa-t*, pl. *fawâ'iḥ*, odour, fragrance, scent.

فائدة *fâ'ida-t*, pl. *fawâ'id*, usefulness, profit, advantage; gain; interest; profitable saying, moral, useful remark, note, annotation; sign.

فائر *fâ'ir*, boiling; rage, fury, hatred; pl. *fûr*, hind.

فائز *fâ'iz*, who gains his end, prevails, succeeds, gainer, conqueror; who escapes; who turns from; lintel.

فائش *fâ'iś*, afloat; boasting (adj.); proud.

فائض *fâ'iḍ*, overflowing; spreading; superfluous; excellent, distinguished; usurious interest.

فائغة *fa'iga-t*, pungent stupefying odour.

فائق *fâ'iq*, surpassing, pre-eminent, superior, the best; genius; transcendental; uppermost vertebra; (m.) remembering, awaking (n.), recovering.

فائن *fâ'in*, miserly, niggardly.

فبها *fa-bi-hâ*, well done!

(فت) *fatt*, U, INF. *fatt*, break with the fingers, break into crumbs, crumble; maim, — II. INF. *taftît*=I.; — V. INF. *tafattut*, be broken into crumbs, crumble (n.); — VII. INF. *infitât*, id.

فت *fatt*, breaking into crumbs, crumbling (s.); cleft in a stone; — ة *fita-t*, pl. *fitûn*, water-pot; —*fatta-t*, anything broken into crumbs; ragout.

(فتا) *fata'*, INF. *fat'*, break (a.); — also فتى *fati'*, فتو *fatu'*, cease; — IV. INF. *iftâ'*, id.

فتا *fatâ'*, youthful age, youth; nobility, chivalry, chivalrous conduct; — *fitâ'*, pl. of فتى *fatiyy*; — ة *fatât*, pl. *fatayât*, young girl.

فتات *futât*, fragment, small piece; crumb of bread; —*fattât*, who breaks into crumbs.

فتاح *fattâḥ*, who opens, unlocks; conqueror, victor; judge; God; pl. *fatâtîḥ*, a bird; — ة *fatâḥa-t*, help, assistance, succour; victory, conquest; —*futâḥa-t*, *fitâḥa-t*, sentence of a judge, decision.

فتار *fitâr*, weakness, dulness; lukewarmness; — *futâr*, incipient drunkenness.

فتاش *fattâś*, who investigates minutely; scout, spy.

فتافت *fatâfit*, whispering (s.).

فتاق *fitâq*, *fatâq*, leaven; —*fitâq*, rupture, hernia.

فتاك *fattâk*, bold robber; devastator; — *futtâk*, pl. of فاتك *fâtik*.

فتال *fattâl*, rope-maker; nightingale.

فتان *fitân*, saddle-cloth (of leather); —*fattân*, mint-warden; essayer; f. ة, seducer; tempter; Satan; trouble-maker, factionist; seductive; du. the two angels of death.

فتاوى *fatâwa*, pl. of فتوى *fatwa*.

(فتح) *fataḥ*, INF. *fatḥ*, open (a. n.); conquer, occupy, take possession of; disclose to (على *'ala*); explain, expound; prompt; assist; begin; decide; mark a consonant with the vowel *fatḥa-t*; offer (a price); broach (a subject, &c.); فتح الفال *fataḥ al-fa'l*, take as an omen; — II. INF. *taftîḥ*, open (a.); cause to open (n.), to disclose itself; hatch; open the mind, cultivate; open (n.), expand; be threadbare; — III. INF. *mufâtaḥa-t*, begin together with (acc.); broach; — V. INF. *tafattuḥ*, be open; open (n.); open one's heart, disclose; expand, develop (n.); — VI. INF. *tafâtuḥ*, disclose to one another, make intimate communications; — VII. INF. *infitâḥ*, be opened; — VIII. INF. *iftitâḥ*, open (a.); disclose; begin; conquer, take possession of; — X. INF. *istiftâḥ*, open, bid open, have the first use or enjoyment of a thing; make the first purchase at; take in the first money; begin to speak; call for one's help; ask one for the explanation of (2 acc.).

فتح *fatḥ*, opening, beginning (s.); pl. *futûḥ*, *futûḥât*, disclosure, overture, beginning; occupation of a fortified place, conquest, victory; help; also ة *fatḥa-t*, the vowel sign َ; —*futuḥ*, wide, open.

(فتخ) *fataḥ*, INF. *fatḥ*, bend, make supple; —*fatiḥ*, A, INF. *fataḥ*, have soft, long, relaxed limbs; — IV. INF. *iftâḥ*, groan from fatigue; — ة *fatḥa-t*, *fataḥa-t*, pl. *fataḥ*, *futûḥ*, *fataḥât*, ring (round hand or foot); finger-ring without a stone.

فتخا *fatḥâ'*, f. of افتخ *aftaḥ*, having soft limbs, &c.; having large udders or breasts.

(فتر) *fatar*, U, I, INF. *fitâr*, *futûr*, grow tired, weary, slack; relax and rest; lose strength and courage; desist, cease, slacken; be or get lukewarm; measure by the span; — INF. *futûr*, be weak and relaxed of joint; — II. INF. *taftîr*, weaken, relax (a.), tire out; make to cease; make lukewarm; remit part of a punishment; — IV. INF. *iftâr*, weaken (a.); relax (a.); — V. INF. *tafattur*, grow lukewarm; — VI. INF. *tafâtur*, act in a lukewarm, lax, cowardly manner.

فتر *fitr*, span between thumb and index-finger; — *fatar*, weariness, relaxedness, languidness, weakness; —*fittar*, torpedo-fish; — ة *fatrat*=*fatar*; interval (between two prophets, between wars, &c.); interregnum.

(فترص) *fatraṣ*, INF. ة, cut off.

(فتش) *fataś*, U, I, INF. *fatś*, seek carefully; investigate, try to find out, inquire; — II. INF. *taftîś*, id.;—III. INF. *mufâtâśa-t*, search one; seek carefully, investigate.

فتش *fatś*, search, investigation.

فتفت *fatfat*, INF. ة, drink short of its fill (camel); (m.) crumble; pound, grind to powder; scatter, disperse; — II. INF. *tafatfut*, crumble (n.); be pounded, ground to powder.

(فتغ) *fatag*, INF. *fatg*, tread to pieces, crush under foot; — V. INF. *tafattug*, get crushed, ground (by the molar teeth).

(فتق) *fataq*, U, I, INF. *fatq*, split, break off, break loose (a.); rip open; put much leaven to the dough; strengthen musk by another perfume; — *fatiq*, A, INF. *fataq*, yield abundant

crops; be afflicted with a rupture, hernia; have large pudenda (woman); — II. INF. *taftîq*, split or rip open entirely; (m.) invent; — IV. INF. *iftâq*, pierce, break through, penetrate; have the sky clearing up (traveller); — V. INF. *tafattuq*, be split, ripped open, &c.; split (n.); burst; — VII. INF. *infitâq* =V.

فتق *fatq*, bursting (s.); rupture, hernia; split; separation; loosing (فتق ورتق *fatq wa ratq*, loosing and binding, supreme power); open place; — *fataq*, abundant harvest; plenty; dawn, dusk; — *futuq*, talkative, garrulous.

فتقا *fatqâ'*, f. of افتق *aftaq*, afflicted with a rupture; having large pudenda.

(فتك) *fatak*, U, I, INF. *fatk*, *fitk*, *futk*, *futûk*, undertake anything that crosses one's mind; be foolhardy, venturesome; persist in; talk at random; fall upon unexpectedly and treacherously; break upon from an ambush and wound or kill, slay; overpower; ravish a girl; — II. INF. *taftîk*, ravish a woman; card cotton; — IV. INF. *iftâq*, ravish a girl; break from an ambush and kill.

فتك *fatk*, foolhardiness; want of moral principles; violence; ravishment.

(فتل) *fatal*, I, INF. *fatl*, twist, plait; rub into threads; turn one's head; turn the face aside; — II. INF. *taflîl*, twist the rope tight or double; — V. (and VII.) INF. *tafattul*, be twisted; apostatize, change party; — VII. INF. *infitâl*, see V.; turn from (عن *'an*), cease.

فتل *fatl*, twisting of a rope; — *futl*, pl. and—

فتلا *fatlâ'*, f. of افتل *aftal*, having the legs wide apart, &c.

(فتن) *fatan*, I, INF. *fatn*, *futûn*, *fitna-t*, *maftûn*, try, probe, test, tempt; be visited or tempted by calamity (also pass.); incite to rebellion; stir up revolt or discord; charm by beauty, captivate; madden; fill with admiration; melt metals; burn; — *fatun*, be enchanted, seduced by (ب *bi*, m.); — IV. INF. *iftân*, tempt; enchant, captivate, fill with admiration, seduce; incite to revolt or discord, stir up disturbances; — VII. INF. *infitân*, be enchanted, seduced; be entangled in a revolt; — VIII. INF. *iftitân*, incite to revolt, &c.; be enchanted, seduced (pass. be madly in love with ب *bi*); tempt; fall out with.

فتن *fatn*, internal commotions, revolt, insurrection; — *futun*, pl. of فتين *fatîn*; — ة *fitna-t*, pl. *fitan*=*fatn*; civil war; tumult, war; mischief, disorder, scandal; discord; visitation, temptation, seduction; trouble of mind; calamity; malice; sin; punishment; calumny.

(فتو) *fatâ*, U, surpass in generosity or liberality; — فتى *fatî*, A, INF. *fatâ'*, be of a youthful age, be a youth; — II. INF. *taftiya-t* pass. *futtiyat*, be kept from conversing and playing with boys (girl); — III. INF. *mufâtât*, vie in generosity and liberality with; — IV. INF. *iftâ'*, advise in a matter; give a decision in question of law; give one (acc.) a definition of (ب *bi*); authorise; — V. INF. *tafattî*, be kept from boys; be high-minded and liberal; — VI. INF. *tafâtî*, id.; have recourse to the Mufti; — X. INF. *istiftâ'*, ask for an opinion on a point of law; consult a lawyer.

فتو *futuww*, ة *fitwa-t*, pl., فتوان *fatawân*, du. of فتى *fat-an*, *fata*; — ة *futuwwa-t*, youth; noble

manliness, chivalry; generosity, liberality.

فتوا *fatwâ'* = فتوى *fatwa.*

فتوت *fatût*, broken into crumbs, crumbled.

فتوح *fatûḥ*, beginning of the spring rains; —*futûḥ*, ات *futûḥât*, pl. of فتح *fatḥ*; —ى *futûḥiyy*, jacket or vest without sleeves.

فتور *futûr*, lukewarmness; languidness, relaxation, faintness, exhaustion.

فتون *fitûn*, pl. of فتة *fita-t*.

فتوى *fatwa*, *futwa*, فتيا *fatyâ'*, *futyâ'*, pl. *fatâwa*, *fatâwî*, legal decision, answer of a Muftî to a question of law, fetwa; —*fatawiyy*, crumbled, fragmentary.

فتى *fatan*, *fata*, du. *fatawân*, *fatayân*, pl. *futuww*, *futiyy*, *fitwa-t*, *fitya-t*, *fityân*, youth, young nobleman, knight; generous, liberal; slave; page; eunuch; —*fatiyy*, ة, pl. *fitâ'*, young, new; (m.) strong and courageous.

فتيا *fatyâ'*, *futyâ'* = فتوى *fatwa.*

فتيات *fatayât*, pl. of فتاة *fatât.*

فتيان *fatayân*, du. of فتى *fatan.*

فتيت *fatît*, crumbled, broken into crumbs.

فتيق *fatîq*, shining, resplendent; east, dawn of morning; split, burst.

فتيل *fatîl*, ة, twisted; also ة *fatîla-t*, pl. *fatâ'il*, rope, string, packing-thread; fibre; wick; match of a gun, &c.; lint; dirt rubbed off from the skin; (m.) small glass bottle, phial; حجر الف *ḥajar al-fatîla-t*, asbestos.

فتين *fatîn*, burnt; pl. *futun*, burnt stony ground.

(فث) *fass*, U, INF. *fass*, empty.

(فثا) *fasa'*, INF. *fas'*, *fusû'*, cool down (a.); INF. *fas'*, calm down one's anger (a.); keep from, turn from (عن *'an*); foam (boiling milk); — IV. INF. *ifsâ'*, be tired, weary; stay, abide; — VII. INF. *infisâ'*, cool or calm down (n.).

فثاثيد *fasâsîd*, فثافيد *fasâfîd*, white cumulous clouds.

(فثج) *fasaj*, U, INF. *fasj*, diminish (a.); cool down; be weighed down, burdened; — II. INF. *tafsîj*, be weighed down, bear heavily; — IV. INF. *ifsâj*, leave, abandon; be tired and weary.

(فثح) *fasiḥ*, pl. *afsâḥ*, belly, paunch; a thick snake.

(فثد), II. *fassad*, INF. *tafsîd*, line armour with cloth.

(فثغ) *fasag*, INF. *fasg*, shatter.

فثو *fusû'*, INF. of (فثا).

فثى, IV. *afsa*, INF. *ifsâ'*, be tired, weary.

(فج) *fajj*, U, INF. *fajj*, open the legs; be splay-footed; widen a bow; (m.) cut asunder, in two; — II. INF. *tafjâj*, prevent the fruit from ripening; split into several pieces; — IV. INF. *ifjâj*, open the legs wide; — V. INF. *tafajjuj*, be cut or split into many pieces; — VI. INF. *tafâjj*, keep the legs opened wide (camel in being milked); make wide steps; — VII. INF. *infijâj*, be split.

فج *fajj*, pl. *fijâj*, broad valley-path; saddle of mountain, defile, pass; dung in the guts or the rennet; —*fijj*, (m.) *fajj*, unripe; water-melon (of Syria); — ة *fujja-t*, pl. *fujaj*, interval; split, cut.

(فجا) *faja'*, INF. *faj'a-t*, *fujâ'a-t*, fall upon unexpectedly; fall upon and take hold of; come inopportunely to; INF. *faj'*, lie with; — فجى *fajî*, A, INF. *faja'*, fall upon unexpectedly, come inopportunely; — III. INF. *mufâjât*, id.; surprise; — VIII. INF. *iftijâ'*, fall upon unexpectedly, seize and carry off.

فجا *fajan*, *faja* = فجوة *fajwa-t*; — *fajjâ*, f. of أفج *afajj*, splay-footed; having the hand-piece

too far distant from the string; — ة *faj'a-t*, INF. of (فجا); — *fujâ'a-t*, id.; what falls upon suddenly (death, calamity); surprise.

فجاج *fijâj*, pl. of فج *fajj*; — *fujâj*, broad valley-path, saddle of mountain, defile, pass; — ة *fajâja-t*, unripeness, unripe fruit.

فجار *fijâr*, fornication, adultery; corruption (يا فجار *yâ fijâr-i*, strumpet! whore!); roads, paths; pl. *afjira-t*, perfidy, treacherous war; — *; — *fujjâr*, pl. of فاجر *fâjir*.

فجج *fajaj*, wide distance between the legs or feet; — *fujaj*, pl. of فجة *fujja-t*.

(فجر) *fajar*, U, INF. *fajr*, drain, drain off; — INF. *fajr*, *fujûr*, go wrong, sin, live dissolutely, forni te; swerve from the truth, lie; slip from the saddle; revolt against (acc.); (m.) talk ribaldry; (m.) make a hole or incision for draining; — II. INF. *tafjîr*, drain, water, make to gush forth; — III. INF. *fijâr*, commit fornication with (acc.); — IV. INF. *ifjâr*, drain; be anywhere at the time of daybreak; find one to be impious, a fornicator; go wrong, live dissolutely, fornicate, swerve from the truth; be an infidel; — V. INF. *tafajjur*, VII. INF. *infijâr*, flow off; break forth, appear; V. flow over (eyes); VII. break upon suddenly; — VIII. INF. *iftijâr*, invent lies.

فجر *fajr*, first light of the morning, daybreak; split, opening, hole; — *fujr*, pl. of فجور *fajûr*; — ة *fajra-t*, lie; profligacy; — also *fujra-t*, water-course in a valley, canal; — *fajara-t*, pl. of فاجر *fâjir*.

(فجس) *fajas*, U, INF. *fajs*, be proud, haughty, give one's self airs, treat with violence; be the first in doing a disgraceful thing; — IV. INF. *ifjâs*, boast falsely.

(فجش) *fajaś*, U, INF. *fajś*, smash, shatter; widen (a.).

(فجع) *faja'*, INF. *faj'*, grieve (a.), pain; befall, bring loss upon; pass. *fuji'*, suffer a heavy loss; — II. INF. *tafjî'*, grieve (a.), pain; — V. INF. *tafajju'*, suffer calamity and loss; be sorely visited; feel compassion for (ل *li*); — ة *faja'a-t*, calamity, loss.

فجفاج *fajfâj*, فجفج *fajfaj*, *fujfuj*, talkative, garrulous.

(فجل) *fajal*, U, INF. *fajl*, — *fajil*, A, INF. *fajal*, be thick and soft; — II. INF. *tafjîl*, make broad, broaden (a.).

فجل *fujl*, *fujul*, ة, pl. *fujûl*, radish.

(فجم) *fajam*, U, INF. *fajm*, blunt, jag, make full of notches (m.); — II. INF. *tafjîm*, id.; — V. INF. *tafajjum*, VII. INF. *infijâm*, be blunt, jagged, full of notches.

فجم *fajm*, jagging, making full of notches; — also ة *fajma-t*, jag, notch in a sword.

فجن *fajn*, rue (plant).

(فجو) *fajâ*, U, INF. *fajw*, open (the door, the legs); — فجى *fajî*, A, INF. *faj-an*, widen a bow; having the legs or knees wide apart; be big-bellied; — II. INF. *tafjiya-t*, lay open, uncover; do away, remove; — VII. INF. *infijâ'*, be opened, open (n.), be ajar, gape; — ة *fajwa-t*, pl. *fajawât*, *fijâ'*, *fajâ'*, interval, distance; gap, opening between mountains; open tract.

فجوا *fajwâ'*, f. of افجا *afjâ*, splay-footed, big-bellied; spacious ground.

فجور *fajûr*, pl. *fujur*, dissolute, profligate, rake; — *fujûr*, impiety, fornication, profligacy; (m.) ribaldry, obscene talk; ف القرابة *fujûr al-qarâba-t*, incest.

فجيع *fajî'*, ة, grievous, distressing; causing loss; — ة *fajî'a-t*, pl. *fajâ'i'*, calamity, loss, grief.

(فح) *faḥḥ*, U, I, INF. *faḥḥ*, *faḥîḥ*, *tafḥâḥ*, hiss; INF. *faḥḥ*, *faḥîḥ*, snore; — ة *fuḥḥa-t*, hotness (of pepper, &c.).

فحا *faḥan*, *faḥa*, *fiḥa*, pl. *afḥâ'*, spices, onion, greens.

فحاحيل *faḥâḥîl*, pl. of فحال *fuḥḥâl*.

فحام *faḥḥâm*, charcoal-burner; coalman; — *.

فحاوى *faḥâwî*, pl. of فحوى *faḥwan*.

(فحت) *faḥat*, dig.

(فحث) *faḥas̱*, INF. *faḥs̱*, examine, investigate; — VIII. INF. *iftiḥâs̱*, be examined, investigated.

فحث *faḥis̱*, paunch; excrement in it.

(فحج) *faḥaj*, A, INF. *faḥj* (also II. and V.), turn the toes in and the heels out in walking; be proud, haughty; — II. INF. *tafḥîj*, see I.; — IV. INF. *ifḥâj*, abstain; deviate, swerve; place the legs of an animal apart in milking; — V. INF. *tafaḥḥuj*, see I.

(فحر), VIII. *iftaḥar*, INF. *iftiḥâr*, give one's opinion without anybody following it.

(فحس) *faḥas*, INF. *faḥs*, take out of the hand with the tongue or lips.

(فحش) *faḥuś*, U, INF. *faḥś*, be utterly impious and lost to shame; talk ribaldry; — II. INF. *tafḥîś*, IV. INF. *ifḥâś*, talk ribaldry or act obscenely towards (على *'ala*); — V. INF. *tafaḥḥuś*, VI. INF. *tafâḥuś*, be obscene in speech and action; — X. INF. *istifḥâś*, find obscene, shameless.

فحش *faḥś*, shamelessness, baseness; ribaldry.

فحشا *faḥśâ'*, shameful action; niggardliness in alms, &c.

فحشى *faḥśiyy*, ة, shameless; unchaste, lewd; — ة *faḥśiyya-t*, shameful action, lewdness.

(فحص) *faḥaṣ*, examine minutely, investigate; explore, inquire; — V. INF. *tafaḥḥuṣ*, examine minutely, investigate, inquire after; — VII. INF. *infiḥâṣ*, pass. of the previous; — VIII. INF. *iftiḥâṣ*=V.; — X. INF. *istifḥâṣ*, investigate, make inquiries.

فحص *faḥṣ*, examination, investigation.

(فحض) *faḥaḍ*, INF. *faḥḍ*, break (anything soft).

فحطل *fiḥaṭl*, time before creation; deluge.

(فحفح) *faḥfaḥ*, INF. ة, be sincere in love and friendship; be hoarse; snore.

(فحل) *faḥal*, INF. *faḥl*, admit the stallion to the she-camels; select a good stallion for the herd; — IV. INF. *ifḥâl*, lend one's stallion to a neighbour (2 acc.); — V. INF. *tafaḥḥul*, have but manly qualities, nothing effeminate; — VIII. INF. *iftiḥâl*, select a good stallion; — X. INF. *istifḥâl*, deem thoroughly manful, energetic, brave.

فحل *faḥl*, pl. *fiḥâl*, *fuḥûl*, *fiḥâla-t*, *fuḥûla-t*, *afḥul*, stallion; having manly qualities, manful; energetic and brave; eminent man, the first amongst his equals, chief; male palm-tree; mat made of its leaves; pl. *fuḥûl*, good narrators, poets, satirists; — ة *fiḥla-t*, aptness; capability of a stallion; manliness, energy.

(فحم) *faḥam*, U, INF. *fuḥûm*, be dried up (well); A, INF. *faḥm*, *fuḥûm*, *fuḥâm*, have the voice stifled by tears; pass. *fuḥim*, id.; — *faḥim*, A, INF. *faḥam*, id.; — *faḥum*, INF. *fuḥûm*, *fuḥûma-t*, be (coal-) black; — II. INF. *tafḥîm*, make black, blacken (a.); blacken with coal; (m.) have the voice stifled with tears; (m.) get carbonised, reduced to coal; — IV. INF. *ifḥâm*, stifle; silence.

فحم *faḥm, faḥam*, ة, pl. *fiḥâm, fuḥûm*, coal; — ة *faḥma-t*, twilight, dusk, darkness; — ى *faḥmiyy*, ة, referring to coal, carbonic; اصل ف *aṣl faḥmiyy*, carbon.

فحولة *fuḥûla-t*=فحلة *fiḥla-t*, pl. of فحل *faḥl*.

فحوة *faḥwa-t*, finest honey.

فحوى *faḥwan, faḥwa*, pl. *faḥâwî*, sense, meaning; purport; argument.

(فحى), II. *faḥḥa*, INF. *tafḥiya-t*, spice or season strongly; allude to, speak in allusions.

فحيح *faḥîḥ*, hissing (s.).

فحيل *faḥîl*, fit for covering; distinguished, excellent.

فحيم *faḥîm*, coal-black.

(فخ) *faḫḫ*, I, INF. *faḫḫ, faḫîḫ*, snore; spread (n.), emanate; — INF. *faḫîḫ*, hiss;—INF. *faḫḫ, faḫḫa-t, faḫaḫ*, be relaxed.

فخ *faḫḫ*, pl. *fiḫâḫ, fuḫûḫ*, springe, noose, snare; net; weakness of the feet.

فخار *faḫâr*, glory; — *; —*faḫḫâr*, potter; potter's clay; — ة *faḫâra-t*, boasting (s.);—*faḫḫâra-t*, pottery, earthenware, chinaware; — ى *faḫḫâriyy*, potter.

فخام *fiḫâm*, pl. of فخم *faḫm* and فخيم *faḫîm*; — ة *faḫâma-t*, corpulence; bulkiness; importance; high rank.

(فخت) *faḫat*, INF. *faḫt*, cut off; uncover; beat or strike on the head; pierce, break through; dig, dig out; coo;=II. INF. *tafḫît*=I.; speak evil of (فى *fî*), slander; — V. INF. *tafaḫḫut*, wonder; — VII. INF. *infiḫât*, be broken through.

فخت *faḫt*, ة *faḫta-t*, hole, breach; *faḫt*, springe, noose.

(فخج) *faḫaj*, INF. *faḫj*, be proud; —*faḫij*, A, INF. *faḫaj*, turn the toes in and the heels out in walking.

(فخذ) *faḫaẕ*, INF. *faḫẕ*, hurt in the thigh; — II. INF. *tafḫîẕ*, cross the legs.

فخذ *faḫiẕ, faḫẕ, fiḫẕ*, pl. *afḫâẕ*, thigh, leg; *faḫiẕ*, division of a tribe, near relations.

(فخر) *faḫar*, INF. *faḫr, faḫâr, faḫâra-t, fiḫḫîra, fiḫḫîrâ'*, glory, boast; declare one to be more celebrated than another; — U, surpass in glory and nobility; —*faḫir*, A, INF. *faḫar*, boast; disdain, refuse with disgust, loathe; — II. INF. *tafḫîr*, esteem one higher than another as to merit, glory, nobility; — III. INF. *fiḫâr, mufâḫara-t*, boast against, try to surpass in glory; — V. INF. *tafaḫḫur*, glory, boast; — VI. INF. *tafâḫur*, vie in glory; boast of (ب *bi*); — VIII. INF. *iftiḫâr*, glory, boast; — X. INF. *istifḫâr*, find excellent, magnificent; try to acquire or obtain anything excellent as affording honour.

فخر *faḫr, faḫar*, glory, celebrity; glorying, boasting (s.); — ة *faḫra-t*, what brings glory.

فخرانية *faḫrâniyya-t*, glory, good fortune, felicity.

فخرى *faḫriyy*, ة, glorious; — ة *faḫriyya-t*, eulogy, encomium.

(فخز) *faḫaz*, INF. *faḫz*,—*faḫiz*, A, INF. *faḫaz*, glory, boast falsely; out-boast another; — III. INF. *mufâḫaza-t*, try to out-do in boasting falsely.

(فخش) *faḫaś*, INF. *faḫś*, lose, squander, neglect.

(فخفخ) *faḫfaḫ*, INF. ة, glory, boast.

(فخل), II. *tafaḫḫal*, INF. *tafaḫḫul*, show great calmness and mildness.

(فخم) *faḫum*, INF. *faḫâma-t*, be thick, corpulent, bulky; enjoy general esteem; — II. INF. *tafḫîm*, honour, show great regard for; emphasise, read or speak with emphasis; — V.

INF. *tafaḥḥum*, be honoured, esteemed.

فخم *faḥm*, pl. *fiḥâm*, highly esteemed, honoured; great, big; spoken with emphasis.

فخور *faḥûr*, boaster;—*fuḥûr*, boasting (s.).

فخيخ *faḥîḥ*, hissing (s.), snoring (s.).

فخير *faḥîr*, celebrated; boasting (adj.);—*fiḥḥîr*, boasting in the highest degree;—ى *fiḥḥîra*, also—

فخيرا *fiḥḥîrâ'*, glory; boasting (s.).

فخيم *faḥîm*, pl. *fiḥâm*, f. ة, pl. *faḥîmât*, highly esteemed, honoured; illustrious; great.

(**فد**) *fadd*, I, **INF.** *fadîd*, call, cry out; trample; run; threaten.

فدا *fadan*, *fidan*=*fidâ'*;—*fadâ'*, corn-stack;—*fidâ'*, ransom; sacrifice, self-sacrifice; فدا عن *fidâ'-an 'an*, instead of.

فداد *faddâd*, crying out loud; loud-voiced; proud;—ة *faddâda-t*, frog.

فدادين *fadâdîn*, pl. of فدان *faddân*.

فدار *fadâr*, anything kept ready to replace another (m.).

فدام *fidâm*, *fadâm*, veil for the mouth or face of a Parsee; turban; muzzle for oxen; stopper; strainer, colander;—*;—ة *fadâma-t*, **INF.** of (**فدم**).

فدان *fadân*, pl. *afdina-t*, فدان *faddân*, pl. *fadâdîn*, a yoke of oxen; a field-measure, acre; plough.

فداوى *fadâwiyy*, who sacrifices himself; volunteer.

فدائى *fidâ'iyy*=the previous.

(**فدح**) *fadaḥ*, **INF.** *fadḥ*, press heavily upon (acc.).

(**فدخ**) *fadaḥ*, **INF.** *fadḥ*, shatter.

(**فدر**) *fadar*, I, **INF.** *fadr*, *fudûr*, be weak, cover no longer (stallion); get cold.

فدر *fadar*, pl. *fudûr*, *mafdara-t*, *mafdura-t*, full-grown mountain-goat;—*fadir*, stupid; brittle;—*fudr*, pl. of فادر *fâdir*;—*fudur*, pl. of فدور *fadûr*;—*fudurr*, silver;—ة *fidra-t*, pl. *fidar*, slice of meat; part, portion.

(**فدس**) *fuds*, pl. *fidasa-t*, spider;—**IV.** *afdas*, **INF.** *ifdâs*, have spider-webs in one's vessels.

(**فدش**) *fadaś*, U, **INF.** *fadś*, shatter.

(**فدع**) *fadi'*, A, **INF.** *fada'*, have the hand or foot turned in;—**II.** **INF.** *tafdî'*, bring on this condition.

فدع *fada'*, ة, distortion of a joint; defect in the hoof.

فدعا *fad'â'*, f. of افدع *afda'*, having a distorted joint, ostrich.

(**فدغ**) *fadag*, **INF.** *fadg*, break, smash; (m.) wound in the head;—**VII.** **INF.** *infidâg*, be smashed, shattered; (m.) be wounded in the head.

فدغ *fadag*, wound in the head (m.).

(**فدغم**) *fadgam*, tall and handsome; fleshy; full of sap, juicy;—pass. *fudgim*, have a full and handsome face.

(**فدفد**) *fadfad*, **INF.** ة, cry out violently; run away in flight.

فدفد *fadfad*, pl. *fadâfid*, plain of hard ground; desert;—*fudafid*, thick milk;—also *fudfud*, loud-voiced.

(**فدك**), **II.** *faddak*, **INF.** *tafdîk*, clean cotton.

(**فدم**) *fadam*, I, **INF.** *fadm*, cover the face, the mouth;—*fadum*, **INF.** *fadâma-t*, have a heavy tongue, an impediment; stammer; be stupid, imbecile; be rude;—**II.** **INF.** *tafdîm*, cover with the فدام *fidâm*, q.v.; stop up.

فدم *fadm*, ة, pl. *fidâm*, *afdâm*, having an impediment, stammering (adj.); stupid, imbecile, rude.

(**فدن**) *fadan*, a red dye; pl. *afdân*, castle, palace;—**II.** *faddan*, **INF.** *tafdîn*, fatten camels; build high, like a castle.

فدور *fadûr*, pl. *fudur*, full-grown mountain-goat; — *

فدوم *faddûm*, veil for the mouth (of a Parsee); strainer, colander; — ة *fudûma-t*, stammering (s.).

فدوية *fidawiyya-t*, self-sacrificing devotedness.

(فدى , فدا) *fada*, I, INF. *fadan*, *fidan*, *fidâ'*, ransom; rescue; save by sacrificing one's self; — II. INF. *tafdiya-t*, say جعلت فداك *ju'il-tu fidâka*, may I be made your ransom! show unbounded devotedness; — III. INF. *mufâdât*, ransom; — VI. INF. *tafâdî*, ransom one another; — VII. INF. *infidâ'*, be ransomed, rescued, saved; — VIII. INF. *iftidâ'*, ransom, redeem; defend one's self against (من *min*).

فدى *fidan*, *fadan*=فدا *fidâ'*.

فديد *fadîd*, clamour, tumult, noise; course; great number of camels; —*.

(فذ) *fazz*, INF. *fazz*, be alone, isolated; push violently away, chase; — IV. INF. *ifzâz*, give birth to but one young one;—V. INF. *tafazzuz*, be alone, isolated; take for one's self alone, or only one for one's self.

فذ *fazz*, pl. *fuzûz*, *afzâz*, alone, single, isolated; the first arrow in the game; فذ بذ *fazz bazz*, odd, queer, strange.

فذاذا *fuzâzan*, *fuzzâzan*, فذاذى *fazâza*, *fuzâza*, single, each by itself.

فذاك *fazâka*, well.

فذالك *fa-zâlika*, and thus; *fazâlik*, pl. of فذلكة *fazlaka-t*.

(فذح), V. *tafazzah*, INF. *tafazzuh*, VII. *infazah*, INF. *infizâh*, put the legs apart to make water.

(فذفذ) *fazfaz*, INF. ة, crouch in order to leap forth.

فذلك *fazlak*, INF. ة, sum up, pronounce the result; — ة *fazlaka-t*, pl. *fazâlik*, summing up, sum; synopsis, index, register; appendix.

(فر) *farr*, I, INF. *farr*, *firâr*, *mafarr*, *mafirr*, flee, run away, desert, escape; — U, INF. *farr*, *farâr*, *firâr*, *furâr*, determine the age of an animal by examining its teeth; examine, test; — IV. INF. *ifrâr*, put to flight; — VIII. INF. *iftirâr*, show the teeth in laughing; smile; flash; — X. INF. *istifrâr*, flee, try to escape.

فر *farr* (m. f., sing. du. pl.), fugitive; flight, escape; كر وفر *karr wa farr*, attack and retreat; pl. of فار *fârr*, fugitive, deserter; — *furr*, ة *furra-t*, belonging to the better, more respectable (of a people); — ة *fira-t*, abundance, affluence, INF. of (وفر); — *farra-t*, flight; — *firra-t*, quail (m.); — *furra-t*, severity, harshness; intense heat; mixture.

فرا *fara'*, *farâ'*, pl. *firâ'*, *afrâ'*, *afru'*, wild ass or its grown foal; — *farrâ'*, furrier; f. of افر *afarr*, bright, shining; fair; showing beautiful teeth in smiling.

فرات *furât*, pl. *fartân*, Euphrates; very sweet water (also ما ف *mâ' furât*); sea; du. *furâtân*, Euphrates and Tigris.

فراج *farrâj*, who dispels grief, who cheers up; — ة *farâja-t*, upper garment; fur.

فراح *farâh*, joy, merriment; — ى *farâhî*, pl. of فارح *fârih*, ag. of (فرح).

فراخى *farâhî*, spaciousness, width; abundance, affluence (m.).

فراد *furâd-a*, *farâd-a*, فرادا *furâdan*, *firâdan*, فرادى *furâda*, one after the other, singly; —*; —*farrâd*, maker of gold beads, &c.; — ة *farâda-t*, bale of merchandise; load of the camel on one side; (m.) shoe.

فرادى *furâda*, see the previous; pl. of فرد *fard*.

فراديس *farâdîs*, pl. of فردوس *firdaus*.

فرار *firâr, farâr* (ة *farâra-t*), *furâr*, flight, escape; mercury, quicksilver; — *furâr*, examining; young deer; wild goat (also pl.);—*farrâr*, fugitive, deserter; mercury; — ى *farâriyy*, pl. ة, commander.

فراريج *farârîj*, pl. of فروج *farrûj*.

فرازد *farâzid*, فرازق *farâziq*, pl. of فرزدق *farazdaq*.

فرازين *farâzîn*, pl. of فرزان *firzân*.

فراس *farrâs*, lion; — ة *farâsa-t*, equestrian art, horsemanship; chivalrousness;—*firâsa-t*, physiognomy; discernment, sagacity.

فراسن *farâsin*, pl. of فرسن *firsin*; — *furâsin*, lion.

فراسيون *farâsiyûn*, wild leek.

فراش *farâś*, ة, moth, butterfly; fickle person; (m.) mill-wheel; (m.) river-bed;—*firâś*, pl. *furuś*, *furûś*, bed, couch, matress, cushion, pillow; wife; bird's nest; — *; —*farrâś*, chamberlain; who takes charge of the spreading of carpets, making of beds, pitching of tents, &c.; hangman, executioner; — ة *farâśa-t*, pl. *farâś*, *farâ'iś*, catch or bolt of a lock; — ة *firâśa-t*, فراشية *farrâśiyya-t*, office of a *farrâś*.

فراض *firâḍ*, river-mouth; roads, streets; a garment; — *.

فراط *firâṭ*, INF. III. of (فرط); — *furrâṭ*, pl. of فارط, guide, &c.; — ة *farâṭa-t*, small coin (m.); — *firâṭa-t*, INF. of (فرط); — *furâṭa-t*, water which the first-comer gets.

فراعنة *farâ'ina-t*, pl. of فرعون *fir'aun*, &c.

فراعة *farâ'a-t*, pen-wiper; — *furrâ'a-t*, axe, hatchet.

فراغ *farâg*, pl. *-ât*, tare, weight of the cases, &c., in which goods are packed; — *; — *firâg*, pl. *afriga-t*, finishing (s.), termination; vacancy, leisure, rest; large leathern bucket; *li 'l-firâg*, in vain; —*furrâg*, at leisure, unemployed; — ة *farâga-t*, leisure, rest; hollow, cavity; INF. of (فرغ).

فرافر *furâfir*, lion.

فرافص *furâfiṣ*, ة *furâfiṣa-t*, tall, strong lion; strong man.

فرافير *farâfîr*, pl. of فرفور *furfûr*.

فراق *firâq, farâq*, separation, grief on account of separation; — ى *firâqiyy*, referring to separation, particularly applied to a poem.

فرام *firâm*, ة *firâma-t*, cloth used by women during the menses; — *farrâm*, who cuts up tobacco.

فرامين *farâmîn*, pl. of فرمان *firmân*.

فران *farrân*, baker.

(فرانس) *furânis*, lion; thick-necked; — ة *farânisa-t*, pl. of فرناس *firnâs*;—*farânsa-t*, France; frank (coin).

فرانسوى *farânsawiyy*, ة, French.

فرانسيز *farânsîz*, Frenchmen (coll.).

فرانق *furâniq*, leader of an army; courier; lion.

فراهة *farâha-t*, فراهية *farâhiyya-t*, liveliness and ingenuity, sprightliness; INF. of (فره).

فراهيد *farâhîd*, pl. of فرهود *furhûd*.

فرائضى *farâ'iḍiyy*, well versed in the Mohammedan law of inheritance.

(فرب), II. *farrab*, INF. *tafrîb*, constringe the pudenda of a woman by medicaments.

(فرت) *farat*, U, INF. *fart*, be impious; —*farit*, A, INF. *farat*, turn imbecile, grow stupid; — *farut*, INF. *furûta-t*, be very sweet.

فرتان *fartân*, pl. of فرات *furât*.

(فرتح) *fartaḥ*, INF. ة, grow gentle; stop and stand quiet.

(فرتك) *fartak*, INF. ة, cut very small; spoil a work.

(فرتن) *fartan*, INF. ة, speak indistinctly and incoherently; walk with short steps.

فرتونة *furtûna-t*, storm, tempest (m.).

فرتيكة *furtaika-t*, fork (m.).

(فرث) *faras̱*, I, U, INF. *fars̱*, empty; — I, INF. *fars̱* (also II.), cut up the liver, split; — U, INF. *fars̱* (also V. and VII.), be troubled in mind; — *faris̱*, A, INF. *faras̱*, get satiated; get dispersed; — II. INF. *tafrîs̱*, see I.; — V. INF. *tafarrus̱*, VII. INF. *infirâs̱*, see I.

فرث *fars̱*, pl. *furûs̱*, dung in the paunch.

(فرثد) *fars̱ad*, INF. ة, be fleshy and full.

(فرج) *faraj*, I, INF. *farj*, put asunder, separate, split; open the door or put it ajar; dispel (the clouds, sorrows, &c.); console, alleviate; —*farij*, A, INF. *faraj*, be free of care, cheerful; have the legs open so as to show the pudenda;—II. INF. *tafrîj*, separate, split, put asunder; remove, dispel; comfort; cheer by the sight of a thing, show; — IV. INF. *ifrâj*, be separate; — V. INF. *tafarruj*, be separate, gape, stand apart, stand open; be freed from care, comforted; rejoice in a sight, look at with pleasure; take a pleasure-walk, a trip, loiter about, travel and see everything; — VII. INF. *infirâj*, be separate, stand apart or asunder; be comforted.

فرج *farj*, comfort, recreation of the mind; gap, opening, split; open boundaries; pl. *furûj*, pudenda, particularly of a woman; — *faraj*, joy after sorrow, comfort, relief; —*farij*, cheerful;—*furuj*, gaping (adj.);—ة *farja-t*, *firja-t*, *furja-t*, cheer after sorrow; freeness of care, contentment; comforting sight, pleasant spectacle or scenery; — *furja-t*, pl. *furaj*, gap, interstice; rent in a wall; breach; access, opportunity; (m.) brush.

فرجار *firjâr*, فرجارز *farjâriz*, pair of compasses; — ى *firjâriyy*, made by the compass.

(فرجل) *farjal*, INF. ة, walk fast and with long steps.

(فرجن) *farjan*, INF. ة, curry a horse.

فرجون *firjaun*, فرجول *firjaul*, curry-comb, comb.

فرجى *farajiyy*, ة *farajiyya-t*, upper garment, fur coat.

(فرح) *fariḥ*, A, INF. *faraḥ*, rejoice (n.), be cheerful, merry, content; — II. INF. *tafrîḥ*, rejoice (a.), cheer, content.

فرح *faraḥ*, ة *farḥa-t*, *furḥa-t*, joy, cheerfulness, merriment, contentment, wantonness; — *fariḥ*, ة, rejoicing, cheerful, content, wanton, boisterously merry.

فرحان *farḥân*, f. ة, and *farḥa*, pl. *farḥa*, *farâḥa*, glad, cheerful, merry, content; — ة *farḥâna-t*, a mushroom.

(فرحج) *farḥaj*, ة, set the legs wide apart in walking.

فرحى *farḥa*, f. and pl. of فرحان *farḥân*.

(فرخ) *fariḫ*, A, INF. *faraḫ*, be calm and fearless; duck to the ground; — II. INF. *tafrîḫ*, get young ones; allow a chick to creep out (egg); germinate, put forth shoots; — IV. INF. *ifrâḫ* =II.; — X. INF. *istifrâḫ*, keep poultry, &c., for the sake of the young.

فرخ *farḫ*, f. ة, pl. *afruḫ*, *afrâḫ*, *firâḫ*, *furûḫ*, *firḫân*, *afriḫa-t*, young of a bird, chick; young of any animal; young plant, germ, shoot; pl. *firâḫ*, plant beginning to branch; — ة *farḫa-t*, hen; a germ or shoot.

(فرد) *farad*, U, — *farid*, A, — *farud*, INF. *furûd*, be single, by itself, isolated; be alone; be unique; be simple, not compound; act by one's self; — II. INF. *tafrîd*, seclude and devote one's self to a meditative life, to studies; II. and IV.: separate, single

out, isolate; make unequal to another, make odd; reduce to the simplest expression; — IV. INF. *ifrâd*, be alone; act by one's self; bring forth only one young one; see II.; — V. INF. *tafarrud*, seclude one's self; be alone, isolated; act by one's self; distinguish one's self, be without an equal; — VII. INF. *infirâd*, seclude one's self; retire into solitude; be alone, isolated, unique; act by one's self; be simple, not compound; — X. INF. *istifrâd*, wish to be alone, wish for seclusion or solitude; select for one's own use; wait for the moment when anyone is alone; be alone, isolated; act by one's self.

فرد *fard*, pl. *firâd*, one of a pair or two equal things; the half; anything single, odd; pl. *furâda, afrâd, furûd*, unique, without an equal; singular; individual, one; with a negative: nobody; فرد الفرد *fard al-fard*, indivisible; جوهر ف *jauhar fard*, atom, monad; pl. *afrâd*, private persons, individuals; ف حقيقة *fard ḥaqîqa-t*, memoir; ف سوال *fard suwâl*, petition; — (m.) *fard*, pl. *furûda-t*, pistol; — *farad, farid, farud, furud*, alone, by one's self; unique, incomparable, excellent; — ة *farda-t*, pl. *fardât, farad*, bale of merchandise; load on one side of a beast of burden; (m.) shoe; — *farda-t, firda-t*, capitation-tax; custom-tax (by piece).

فردان *fardân*, isolated; alone.

فردانية *fardâniyya-t*; being unique (s.); isolation, singleness; oneness, unity.

فردد *fardad*, excellent.

(فردس) *fardas*, INF. ة, throw on the ground, throw down; fill the basket entirely.

فردوس *firdaus*, pl. *farâdîs*, Paradise.

فردى *farda*, singly; — *fardiyy*, tax-roll; catalogue; — ة *fardiyya-t*, being unique; oneness; pl. *fardiyyât*, specific remedies.

فررة *farara-t*, fugitive; deserter.

(فرز) *faraz*, I, INF. *farz*, separate (a.), set apart, secrete; select; distinguish, discern; — II. INF. *tafriza-t*, prescribe measure and aim; decide at one's pleasure upon another; — III. INF. *mufâraza-t*, break off, interrupt; dissolve the community or partnership with; settle a business with; — IV. INF. *ifrâz*, separate, set apart, distinguish; — VIII. INF. *iftirâz*, settle a matter by one's self without asking anybody.

فرز *farz*, separation, distinction.

فرزان *firzân*, pl. *farâzîn, farâzina-t*, queen in chess.

(فرزدق) *farazdaq*, ة, pl. *farâzid, farâziq*, lump of dough; crumbs of bread.

(فرزع) *furzu'*, cotton-seed; — ة *furzu'a-t*, pl. *farâzi'*, handful of food, ration of food; — II. *tafarza'*, INF. *tafarzu'*, be divided into rations.

(فرزل) *farzal*, INF. ة, fetter, chain up.

فرزل *firzil*, fetters; — *furzul*, thick.

فرزن *farzan*, INF. ة, become queen (pawn in chess); (m.) see, perceive, look at, observe.

(فرس) *faras*, I, INF. *fars*, break the neck, crush; tear the prey into pieces, kill; — *farus*, INF. *farâsa-t, furûsiyya-t, furûsa-t*, excel in horsemanship, in breaking in horses, be a connoisseur of horses; — III. INF. *mufârasa-t*, make one a horseman or knight; encourage; — V. INF. *tafarrus*, fix the eyes firmly upon, look sharply at; read in the physiognomy of a person; show one's self as a horseman; — VIII. INF. *iftirâs*, tear the prey.

فرس *faras* (m. f.), pl. *furûs*, *afrâs*, horse, mare; knight in chess; — *firs*, a plant; — *furs*, Persia; pl. of فارس *fâris*, Persian; — ة *farasa-t*, mare.

فرساح *firsâḥ*, wide tract of land.

فرسان *fursân*, pl. of فارس, horseman, knight.

فرسخ *farsaḥ*, pl. *farâsiḥ*, parasang, league (about 18,000 feet); — *farsaḥ*, INF. ة, subside, diminish (cold, &c.); — II. INF. *tafarsuḥ*, IV. INF. *ifrinsâḥ*, id.

(فرسق) *firsiq*, فرسك *firsik*, smooth peach.

(فرسن) *firsin*, pl. *farâsin*, hoof.

فرسى *farsa*, pl. of فريس *farîs*; — *fursiyy*, ة, Persian (adj., s.); pl. *fursiyyât*, Persian things, Persian locutions.

(فرش) *faraś*, U, INF. *farś*, *firâś*, spread on the floor, spread out; render easy, convenient, commodious; furnish a house; make the bed; disperse; — II. INF. *tafrîś*, spread a carpet or mat for (2 acc.); floor the house with flat stones; spread and move the wings; hover above; keep off the sun by its branches; have dense and extended branches; creep out (silk-moth); — IV. INF. *ifrâś*, spread a carpet for (2 acc.); — V. INF. *tafarruś*, be spread like a carpet; hover above with outspread wings; have dense and extended branches; — VII. INF. *infirâś*, be spread out; — VIII. INF. *iftirâś*, spread out; be spread; use anything to lie upon; tread under foot; throw to the ground; conquer, vanquish.

فرش *farś*, pl. *furûś*, anything spread on the floor: carpet, mat, mattress, bed, board; camel not used for carrying burdens; wide field, open space, yard; — *furuś*, pl. of فراش *firâś*; — ة *farśa-t*, carpet; mat; mattress; bed; — *firśa-t*, way of spreading a carpet, of arranging the bed; face; — (m.) *furśa-t*, brush.

(فرشح) *farśaḥ*, INF. ة, *farśaḥa*, open the legs; put asunder, widen (a.); — ة *farśaḥa-t*, width, spaciousness.

(فرص) *faraṣ*, U, INF. *farṣ*, cut, split, tear; injure the horse at the فريصة *farîṣa-t*; — IV. INF. *ifrâṣ*, offer itself to (acc.), be favourable (opportunity); — VIII. INF. *iftirâṣ*, X. INF. *istifrâṣ*, avail one's self of an opportunity.

فرص *farṣ*, ـة, stone of the wild date; — ة *furṣa-t*, pl. *furaṣ*, turn; opportunity, favourable moment; superiority, supremacy.

فرصاد *firṣâd*, stone of a grape; mulberry-tree; mulberry; a red colour.

(فرصع) *farṣa'*, pl. *farâṣi'*, separation of the hoof.

(فرصم) *farṣam*, INF. ة, break off, cut off.

(فرض) *faraḍ*, I, INF. *farḍ*, make incisions, notches; impose as a duty; predict, announce; assign; fix an inheritance, revenue, pension; make a supposition, suppose, surmise; — also *fariḍ*, A, INF. *faraḍ* and *faruḍ*, INF. *farâḍa-t*, be old; know well the commandments of God; — II. INF. *tafrîḍ*, make incisions, notches; make law; explain a chapter of the Koran or the Divine Commandments; — IV. INF. *ifrâḍ*, impose as a duty; appoint or give a salary; give, bestow; — V. INF. *tafarruḍ*, have incisions, notches; — VII. INF. *infirâḍ*, be prescribed, imposed as a duty; — VIII. INF. *iftirâḍ*, prescribe, impose as a duty; receive pay; (m.) suppose, surmise.

فرض *farḍ*, pl. *firâḍ*, *furûḍ*, incision, notch; commandment of God, religious duty; legal prescrip-

tion; supposition, surmise, hypothesis (*farḍ-an*, by way of supposition, example, &c., distinctly, certainly); pl. *furûḍ*, legal share; salary, pay, pension; present; — ة *farḍa-t*, ground-rent; patent-duty; prescribed prayer; — *furḍa-t*, pl. *furaḍ*, *furûḍ*, incision, notch; anchorage, sea-port; river-mouth; mouth of an ink-stand; hole in the threshold in which the door turns.

(فرضخ) *firḍiḥ*, scorpion.

(فرضم) *firḍim*, old sheep; toothless.

فرضول *farḍûl*, cock of a gun.

فرضى *faraḍiyy*, *farḍiyy*, ة, referring to divine commandments; well versed in the divine law; hypothetical; — ة *faraḍiyya-t*, religious duty.

(فرط) *faraṭ*, U, INF. *furûṭ*, hasten in advance of others, overtake, reach; — INF. *farṭ*, *farâṭa-t*, hasten a night before to the watering-place, to make all necessary preparations; come unexpectedly, befall, happen, occur; exceed the bounds, be reckless, grow imprudent; send; conquer; INF. *farṭ*, be negligent; disregard, lose or miss by negligence; escape, be forgotten; beat off fruit; — II. INF. *tafrîṭ*, transgress, exceed, commit excesses; praise excessively; run fast; overtake, get in advance of (على *'ala*); send a messenger or ambassador; be remiss, neglect; — III. INF. *firâṭ*, *mufâraṭa-t*, try to get in advance of; meet; — IV. INF. *ifrâṭ*, exceed the bounds; exaggerate; fill to overflowing; burden beyond one's strength; hasten (n.); leave undone, forget; — V. INF. *tafarruṭ*, come in advance of others; — VII. INF. *infirâṭ*, be dissolved; (m.) be dispersed, disperse (n.); (m.) be beaten down (fruit); — X. INF. *istifrâṭ*, find something wished for to be bought cheaply.

فرط *farṭ*, pl. *afruṭ*, *afrâṭ*, what is excessive, excess, exaggeration; negligence, missing (s.); superiority; short time passed (3 to 15 days); — *faraṭ*, who hastens to the watering-place before others; — *fariṭ*, low price; cheap (m.); — *furuṭ*, what is excessive; iniquity; (m.) small coin, change; pl. *afrâṭ*, high hill; — ة *farṭa-t*, coming ahead of the adversary in running; excess; sin.

(فرطح) *farṭaḥ*, INF. ة, widen (a.), enlarge, make broad (a.).

(فرطس) *farṭas*, protrude the snout.

فرطونة *firṭûna-t*, storm, tempest (m.).

فرطيسة *firṭîsa-t*, snout of a pig.

(فرع) *fara'*, INF. *far'*, mount; descend; brandish a cudgel above one's head; INF. *far'*, *furû'*, surpass; pacify; (m.) prune a tree; — *fari'*, A, INF. *fara'*, have long hair; — II. INF. *tafrî'*, mount; descend; derive; put forth new branches; divide, distribute; tear (a.); — IV. INF. *ifrâ'*, mount; descend; put forth new branches; sacrifice the first foal of a camel; — V. INF. *tafarru'*, spread in all directions; be derived from a principle; — VIII. INF. *iftirâ'*, deflower.

فرع *far'*, pl. *furû'*, top of a branch; top; branch, twig, shoot; long hair; ramification; branching out (s.); derivation; corrolary — *fara'*, pl. *furû'*, the first foal of a camel or young of a sheep (as a sacrifice); — ة *far'a-t*, pl. *firâ'*, mountain-summit; pl. *far'*, also *fara'a-t*, pl. *fara'*, louse; (m.) top-leather; *fara'a-t*, pl. of فارع *fâri'*, ally, confederate.

(فرعن), II. *tafar'an*, INF. *tafar'un*,

be like Pharaoh; play the tyrant.

فرعون *fir'aun*, *fur'ûn*, *far'ûn*, pl. *farâ'ina-t*, Pharaoh; tyrant; crocodile.

فرعى *far'iyy*, ة, first-born, first; derived, indirect, secondary.

(فرغ) *farag*, U, A, empty; INF. *farâg*, *furûg*, bring to an end, complete, finish, have done with; be idle, at leisure, have time for (ل *li*); undertake; be empty; — INF. *furûg*, be dead; — *farig*, A, INF. *farag*, bring to an end, finish, have done with; — *farug*, INF. *farâga-t*, be large; be disquieted, agitated, excited; — II. INF. *tafrîg*, empty a vessel; pour out; free one from a work to employ him at another; fire off a gun, make a shot; — IV. INF. *ifrâg*, empty; pour out; exhaust; give abundantly; shed blood; cast; have a place emptied; exert one's strength, make every effort; — V. INF. *tafarrug*, have done with; have time for, be at leisure; attend carefully to (ل *li*); — VIII. INF. *iftirâg*, pour out water for one's self; — X. INF. *istifrâg*, exert one's self to the utmost; empty; throw out; vomit; pull out, pull.

فرغ *farig*, empty, void; having done (adj.), at leisure, idle; sluggard; — *firg*, unavenged blood (*firg-an*, with impunity); — *furrag*, pl. of فارغ *fârig*, empty, &c.

فرغا *fargâ'*, f. of افرغ *afrag*, free of care, &c.

فرفار *farfâr*, ة, full of levity, flighty; talkative, garrulous.

(فرفح) *farfaḥ*, soft and level ground; — *farfaḥ*, INF. ة, open (n.); cheer up (n.).

(فرفخ) *farfaḫ* (m.), فرفخين *farfaḫîn*, a kitchen herb.

(فرفر) *farfar*, INF. ة, cry out at; break, cut; move, shake; tear to pieces; calumniate, slander; walk with short steps; be full of levity; creep out (silk-moth).

فرفر *farfar*, ة *farfara-t*, haste, precipitation; levity; spinning-top; — *furfur*, young of an animal.

فرفور *furfûr*, pl. *farâfîr*, butterfly; (m.) also فرفورى *farfûriyy*, porcelain.

(فرق) *faraq*, U, INF. *farq*, *farqân*, split, separate (a.); part the hair; distinguish; expound, explain; determine, order, ordain; INF. *furûq*, separate (n.); — *fariq*, A, INF. *faraq*, fear; be afraid, be timorous; — II. INF. *tafriqa-t*, *tafrîq*, separate; distinguish; disperse; divide a work between (على *'ala*); INF. *tafrîq*, terrify; — III. INF. *firâq*, *mufâraqa-t*, separate with grief (n.), leave; die; — IV. INF. *ifrâq*, recover; be better (in health); — V. INF. *tafarruq*, *tafrâq*, be dispersed, separate; disperse, separate (n.); — VI. INF. *tafâruq*, separate from one another (n.); — VII. INF. *infirâq*, be separate, separate (n.); — VIII. INF. *iftirâq*, separate (n.); fall out.

فرق *farq*, separation; difference; discord; parting of the hair; — *firq*, pl. *furûq*, separate part; small flock; — *faraq*, pl. *afrâq*, interval, interstice; fear; pl. *farqân*, a medical measure; — *fariq*, timorous; — *furuq*, pl. of فريق *farîq*; — ة *firqa-t*, pl. *firaq*, *afâriqa-t*, *afrâq*, *afârîq*, troop of people, number of men; division, detachment; party, sect; — *furqa-t*, separation; grief for separation; distinction; interval, interstice.

فرقان *furqân*, what teaches to distinguish between good and evil; any sacred book, religious text, the Koran; salvation; bifurcation of the Red Sea; pl. of فرق

faraq ; — ى *furqâniyy*, referring or belonging to the Koran.

فرقد *farqad*, pl. *farâqid*, calf ; β of ursa major ; du. *farqadân*, β and γ in ursa minor.

(فرقع) *farqa'*, INF. ة, run very fast ; wring one's neck ; snap the fingers ; break wind ; produce a noise ; — II. INF. *tafarqu'*, snap (the fingers) ; — ة *farqa'a-t*, snapping of the fingers ; — *furqu'a-t*, the buttocks.

(فرقم) *farqam*, gland of the penis.

(فرك) *farak*, U, INF. *fark*, rub between the fingers or hands ; pick the grains out of ears ; rub the dirt out of a cloth ; (m.) rub with ointment ; (m.) make rods ; also *farik*, A, INF. *fark*, *firk*, *furûk*, *furukkân*, hate ; *farik*, A, INF. *farak*, be loose at the root ; — II. INF. *tafrîk*, rub violently between the fingers or hands ; — III. INF. *mufâraka-t*, dismiss, leave ; abandon ; — IV. INF. *ifrâk*, be friable, easy to be picked out ; begin to ripen ; — V. INF. *tafarruk*, slip or stumble in walking or talking ; — VII. INF. *infirâk*, be rubbed between the fingers, picked out ; — VIII. INF. *iftirâk*, (m.) rub between the fingers ; pick out the grains ; move about restlessly.

فرك *firk*, فركان *furukkân*, hatred between married people ; — *furk*, rubbing between the fingers (s.) ; — *farik*, rubbed off ; ة, loose ; — *furuk*, pl. of فروك *farûk*.

(فركح) *farkaḥ*, INF. ة, have the buttocks wide apart ; separate the legs immoderately in walking.

(فركش) *farkaś*, INF. ة, bring one to fall, trip up ; embarrass, disconcert ; — II. INF. *tafarkuś*, come to fall ; lose one's composure, get embarrassed, disconcerted.

(فرم) *faram*, U, INF. *farm*, cut small, hash ; lose the milk-teeth ; — II. INF. *tafrîm*, cut or hash very small, mince ; — IV. INF. *ifrâm*, fall out to make room for new teeth ; fill ; — V. INF. *tafarrum*, be hashed, minced ; — VII. INF. *infirâm*, id. ; (m.) fall out ; (m.) be jagged, full of notches ; (m.) break (n.) into splinters ; — VIII. INF. *iftirâm*, wear a menstrual cloth ; — X. INF. *istifrâm*, constringe the womb by medicaments.

فرم *farm*, hashing, mincing (s.) ; — also ة *farma-t*, an astringent for the womb ; — ة *farma-t*, what is cut off at a time in mincing meat, &c. ; small fragment ; chop, steak ; splinter of wood.

فرمان *firmân*, pl. *farâmîn*, Imperial edict, decree, passport, &c.

(فرن) *furn*, pl. *afrân*, oven, furnace.

(فرنا) *farnâ*, INF. ة, cut or tear into pieces ; break the neck (a.), kill.

فرناس *firnâs*, thick-necked lion ; strong ; pl. *farânisa-t*, *farânîs*, village chief.

فرنب *firnib*, mouse ; small jerboa.

(فرنج) *faranj*, the Franks, Europeans ; — ى *faranjiyy*, ة, Frank, European (adj., s.).

(فرند) *firind*, pl. *farânid*, sword ; damascening and polish ; quality of a blade ; — *firnid*, pl. *farânid*, herbs for seasoning.

فرنسا *faransâ*, *firansâ*, France.

فرنساوى *faransâwiyy*, *firansâwiyy*, ة, French.

فرنع *firni'*, *furnu'*, louse.

(فرنق) *furnuq*, bad, spoiled, corrupt ; — II. *tafarnaq*, INF. *tafarnuq*, grow bad, deteriorate, get corrupted ; be erect, pricked up (ears).

فرنى *furniyy*, ة, baked in the oven ;

-— ة *furniyya-t*, pl. *farâniyy*, loaf (fresh from the oven).

(فرة) *farih*, A, INF. *farah*, be brisk, agile and playful;—*faruh*, INF. *farâha-t*, *farâhiya-t*, be clever, sharp, inventive; — II. INF. *tafrîh*, IV. INF. *ifrâh*, drop a brisk foal; — X. INF. *istifrâh*, try to train one's horses well.

فرة *farih*, brisk, playful, active, clever; —*firruh*, iron; —*furrah*, brisk and playful foals; —*farrah*, *furh*, *furuh*, ة *furraha-t*, pl. of فارة *fârih*=*farih*.

(فرهد) *furhud* (*farhad*, فرهذ *furhuẓ*, *farhaẓ*), pl. *farâhîd*, thick-set; vigorous and full of sap; young of the mountain-goat; pl. lambs.

(فرو) *farw*, pl. *firâ'*, fur; lined with fur; fur coat, furred robe; — II. *farrâ*, INF. *tafriya-t*, line with fur, fur;—VIII. *iftara*, INF. *iftirâ'*, wear or put on a fur coat; — ة *farwa-t*, pl. *firâ'*, fur coat (ابو ف *abû farwa-t*, chestnut); scalp; diadem; head-gear; box of a beggar (ذو ف *ẓû farwa-t*, beggar); wealth, abundance.

فروت *furût*, corruption, INF. of (فرت); — ة *furûta-t*, sweetness of the water.

فروج *furûj*, comfort; contentment; — *; —*farrûj*, a child's shirt; also *furrûj*, pl. *farârîj*, f. ة, chicken.

فروح *farûḥ*, glad, joyful.

فروخ *farrûḫ*, brothers of Isaac and Ishmael; — *.

فرود *farwad*, incomparable, matchless, peerless.

فرور *farûr*, ة *farûra-t*, fugitive; — also *furrûr*, kid, lamb, young deer.

فروز *farwaz*, INF. ة, die, perish.

فروس *farûs*, lion; — *; —ة *furûsa-t*, فروسية *furûsiyya-t*, horsemanship, equestrian art; skill; sharpness of intellect, sagacity.

فروطى *furûṭiyy*, spendthrift (m.).

فروغ *farûg*, constellation of the Twins; — *furûg*, termination of one's work, ceasing (s.), rest.

فروق *farûq*, *farrûq*, ة *farûqa-t*, *farrûqa-t*, timid, timorous;—*furûq*, pl. of فريق *farîq*; — *; — ة *farûqa-t*, armful; fat of the kidneys.

فروك *farûk*, pl. *furuk*, woman who hates her husband.

فروهة *furûha-t*, briskness, INF. of (فرة).

(فرى) *fara*, I, INF. *fary*, cut, cleave, sever; fashion; wander about a country; forge lies; —*farî*, A, INF. *faran*, *fara*, be astonished, perplexed, confused; admire one's self; — II. INF. *tafriya-t*, cut out a cloth or dress, fashion; — IV. INF. *ifrâ'*, id.; spoil by cutting; teach to cut out a dress, &c.; — V. INF. *tafarrî*, be cut out, fashioned; be cut, torn, spoiled; disclose; — VII. INF. *infirâ'*, id.; — VIII. INF. *iftirâ'*, forge lies against (على *'ala*); lie; (m.) wrong, offend, seek a quarrel with, attack.

فرى *fary*, *faran*, *farî*, see the previous; — *furra*, fugitives, army on the flight; — *fariyy*, ة, great, extraordinary; important; new, unheard-of; fresh; made, made up, artificial; invented, mendaceous; — ة *farya-t*, heat; a milking; —*firya-t*, pl. *firan*, *fira*, lie, invention, fiction.

فريح *farîḥ*, merry, glad, cheerful.

فريخ *furaiḫ*, little bird, chick.

فريد *farîd*, pl. *farâ'id*, jewel, pearl (large one), gold-foil between smaller pearls; ة, single, separate; one, one thing; unique, incomparable, peerless (ف الدهر *farîd ad-dahr*, phœnix of the age); vertebral column, spine; — ة *farîda-t*, large precious pearl, gem.

فرير *farîr*, pl. *furâr*, young deer, kid, lamb; mouth of the horse.

فريس *farîs*, pl. *farsa*, torn to pieces, devoured; killed, slain; wooden ring, ring at the end of a noose;

furais, little horse; — ة *farîsa-t*, prey of a lion, crushing of it, torn prey; prey.

فريسى *farîsiyy*, *firrîsiyy*, Pharisee.

فريش *farîś*, pl. *farâ'iś*, hoofed animal having just borne; concubine.

فريصة *farîṣa-t*, pl. *farîṣ*, *farâ'iṣ*, jugular vein of a horse; shoulder, loin.

فريض *farîḍ*, notched, indented; according to divine law; old; — ة *farîḍa-t*, pl. *farâ'iḍ*, divine commandment, indispensable law or duty; tithe from cattle; portion, share, inheritance; knowledge of the law of inheritance; decrepit old woman.

فريط *firrîṭ*, spendthrift (m.).

فريع *furai'*, tyrant in a small way; — ة *furai'a-t*, small louse.

فريغ *farîg*, wide; wide-stepping; — ة *farîga-t*, large wound; large bottle.

فريق *farîq*, pl. *afriqâ'*, *afriqa-t*, *furuq*, *furûq*, division, class; detachment of troops, squadron; large number of people; (m.) lieutenant-general, general of a division; party;—ة *farîqa-t*, separate division; a single person or thing; du. *al-farîqatân*, both kind of creatures, men and genii.

فريك *farîk*, ripe, dry, friable; toasted cheese, Welsh rare-bit.

(فز) *fazz*, I, INF. *fazîz*, flow, run, bleed; — INF. *fazz*, start up, jump up, jump; desert, retire, withdraw, desist; separate one's self, act by one's self; — INF. *fazâza-t*, *fuzûza-t*, be excited with joy, burn, be enflamed (with passion, &c.); — II. INF. *tafzîz*, cause one to start up, to run away, desist, &c., scare off, frighten away; — IV. INF. *ifzâz*, id.;—V. INF. *tafazzuz*, be grieved; — X. INF. *istifzâz*, disquiet, agitate, excite.

فز *fazz*, pl. *afzâz*, easily excited and fickle; young deer; — ة *fazza-t*, jump.

فزارة *fazâra-t*, female leopard.

فزازة *fazâza-t*, emotion, excitement.

فزاعة *fazzâ'a-t*, who frightens; scarecrow.

(فزد) *fuzd*, blood of a camel.

(فزر) *fazar*, U, INF. *fazr*, tear (a.); (m.) open the belly and take out the intestines, disembowel; flog one's back; have a large protuberance on the chest or back; — II. INF. *tafzîr*, tear (a.) in many places, (m.) disembowel; — IV. INF. *ifzâr*, tear, break (a.); — V. INF. *tafazzur*, be torn; (m.) burst (n.); (m.) be disembowelled; — VII. INF. *infizâr*, id.

فزر *fizr*, rent, split; small flock of sheep; kid; root, origin; swelling in the hypochondres;—*fizar*, pl. rents, clefts; — ة *fuzra-t*, large protuberance on the chest or back.

فزرا *fazrâ'*, f. plump, full and fleshy.

(فزع) *faza'*, INF. *fiz'*, also *fazi'*, A, INF. *faza'*, be frightened, fear, be afraid of (من *min*); flee for help to (الى *ila*, من *min*), cal for help; help; awake (n.); — II. INF. *tafzî'*, frighten; free from fear; — IV. INF. *ifzâ'*, id.; help, assist; — V. INF. *tafazzu'*, be seized with fear, be afraid.

فزع *faza'*, pl. *afzâ'*, fear, fright, terror; cry for help, out-cry; help; — *fazi'*, terrified, frightened; timorous; — ة *fuza'a-t*, easy to be frightened.

فزعان *faz'ân*, frightened, terror-stricken.

فزفز *fazfaz*, INF. ة, dispel, drive away.

فزوزة *fazûza-t*, emotion, excitement.

فزيع *fizzî'*, very timorous.

(فسا) *fasa'*, INF. *fas'*, tear (a.); flog one's back; prevent, hinder; — فسى *fasi'*, have a protruding chest and drawn-in back; hav

pain in the back and hips so as to be unable to get up; — II. INF. *tafsî'*, *tafsi'a-t*, tear (a.) lengthways.

فسا *fusâ'*, noiseless fart; — *fassâ'*, farter.

فساح *fasâḥ*, spacious; — *; — ة *fasâḥa-t*, spaciousness, width, commodiousness; بالفساحة *bi 'l-fasâḥa-t*, abundantly.

فساد *fasâd*, pl. *-ât*, corruption, corruptness; infamy, nefariousness; act of violence; mischief, revolt, rebellion; discord; drought; want; unhealthy condition; — *fussâd*, pl. of فاسد *fâsid*, pernicious, corrupt, &c.

فساط *fussâṭ*, *fissâṭ*=فسطاط *fusṭâṭ*.

فساطين *fasâṭîn*, pl. of فسطان *fusṭân*.

فساق *fussâq*, pl. of فاسق *fâsiq*, reprobate, &c.

فسالة *fusâla-t*, dross of iron.

فستات *fustât*, *fistât*, فستاط *fustâṭ*=فسطاط *fusṭâṭ*.

(فستق) *fustaq*, *fustuq*, pistachio-nut and tree; pine-tree.

فستقية *fustiqiyya-t*, basin with jet-d'eau.

(فسج), II. *fassaj*, INF. *tafsîj*, open the legs.

(فسح) *fasaḥ*, INF. *fasḥ*, be wide, spacious; make room for; procure a passport for; — *fasaḥ*, INF. *fasâḥa-t*, be wide, spacious; — II. INF. *tafsîḥ*, make wide, widen; make room for, procure an opportunity to, make one more comfortable; procure an exemption, dispensation, &c.; — V. INF. *tafassuḥ*, make room for; be widened, made more spacious; sit comfortably; (m.) receive as dispensation or exceptional permission, &c.; — VII. INF. *infisâḥ*, be wide, spacious; widen (n.); breathe again freely, feel comfortable, be elated with joy.

فسح *fasḥ*, widening (s.), enlargement; dispensation, permission; passport; Easter; — *fusḥ*, broad-chested; — *fusuḥ*, spacious; — ة *fusḥa-t*, width, spaciousness; vast space; liberty of action, permission; holidays, vacation; truce.

(فسخ) *fasaḫ*, INF. *fasḫ*, separate; suppress, abolish, repeal; recant, cancel a business transaction, dissolve a marriage; sprain a limb; corrupt one's mind; grow disabled, weak, old, worn; ignore; — *fasiḫ*, A, INF. *fasaḫ*, be separated, abolished, cancelled, put out of course, &c.; be spoiled, deteriorated; — II. INF. *tafsîḫ*, separate, dissolve, disperse; (m.) cut, cleave, split; (m.) be split, chapped; (m.) be entirely spoiled or corrupt; (m.) commit sodomy; — V. INF. *tafassuḫ*, be severed, dissolved, sprained; be cut into pieces or slices; split (n.), burst (n.); — VII. INF. *infisâḫ*, get severed, fall to pieces; be abolished, annulled, cancelled.

فسخ *fasḫ*, separation of the parts, dissolution; also ة *fasḫa-t*, abolition; annulment, cancellation; — ة *fasḫa-t*, (m.) split, schism; (m.) portion, piece, fragment; (m.) unfit to transact business; weak.

(فسد) *fasad*, U, I, INF. *fasâd*, *fusûd*, be corrupted; — *fasud*, id.; — II. INF. *tafsîd*, spoil, corrupt; — IV. INF. *ifsâd*, corrupt, ruin; stir up mischief, discord, revolt; blacken one's character, incite against; — V. INF. *tafassud*, be spoiled; be badly educated; — VII. INF. *infisâd*, be spoiled, corrupted; — X. INF. *istifsâd*, endeavour to spoil, to stir up mischief.

فسد *fasad*, discord; false report; — ة *fasada-t*, pl. of فاسد *fâsid*, pernicious, corrupted, &c.; — ى *fasadiyy*, who spoils, stirs up mischief, discord, &c.; informer, eavesdropper.

(فسر) *fasar*, I, U, INF. *fasr*, dis-

close, expound, explain; examine the urine; — II. INF. *tafsîr*, *tafsira-t*, disclose; explain, interpret, comment upon; — *tafsira-t*, diagnosis by the urine; — V. INF. *tafassur*, be expounded, interpreted, commented upon; — X. INF. *istifsâr*, ask for an explanation, interpretation, &c., inquire, question.

فسر *fasr*, disclosure; explanation.

فسس *fusus*, pl. of فسيس *fasîs*.

فسطاط *fusṭâṭ*, pl. *fasâṭîṭ*, large tent of a coarse cotton stuff or goats'-hair; ancient name of Cairo; large town.

فسطان *fusṭân*, pl. *fasâṭîn*, jacket, vest, upper garment (m.).

فسفاس *fasfâs*, فسفس *fasfas*, very stupid; blunt (sword); *fisfâs*, *fisfas*, pl. *fasâfis*, bug.

(فسق) *fasaq*, I, U, also *fasuq*, INF. *fisq*, *fusûq*, swerve from the commandments of God; give one's self over to immorality and a dissolute life, commit fornication, adultery; come out of the shell (ripe date); — II. INF. *tafsîq*, corrupt one's morals; deem guilty or accuse of fornication, adultery, &c.; declare one to be vicious.

فسق *fisq*, profligacy, dissolute life; fornication, adultery; viciousness; revolt, rebellion; — *fasiq*, profligate, dissolute, vicious; — *fusaq*, exceedingly vicious; — ة *fasaqa-t*, pl. of فاسق *fâsiq*, shameless, profligate, &c.

فسقية *fasaqiyya-t*, pl. *-ât*, *fasâqiyy*, basin with jet-d'eau; cistern; pl. burial-place.

(فسكل) *faskal*, INF. ة, lag behind, come last; cause one to lag behind.

فسكل *fiskîl*, *fuskul*, فسكول *fuskûl*, *fiskaul*, lazy, coming last; bad.

(فسل) *fasal*, U, INF. *fasl*, wean a child; — pass. *fusil*, also *fasil*, A, INF. *fasal*, and *fasul*, INF. *fasâla-t*, *fusûla-t*, be bad, vile, mean, miserly, of inferior quality, spoiled, deteriorated; — IV. INF. *ifsâl*, declare to be bad, of inferior quality, throw amongst the refuse; cut off a palm-shoot and plant it for one's self.

فسل *fasl*, pl. *fusalâ'*, *fusl*, *fusûl*, *fisâl*, *fusûla-t*, *afsul*, mean, low, miserly, bad, of inferior quality; vine-shoot; — ة *fasla-t*, palm-shoot.

فسلان *fuslân*, pl. of فسيلة *fasîla-t*.

(فسو) *fasâ*, U, INF. *fasw*, *fusâ'*, fart inaudibly; — VI. INF. *tafâsî*, stretch the hind parts to emit wind (beetle); — ة *faswa-t*, inaudible fart, emission of wind.

فسولة *fusûla-t*, INF. of (فسل) and pl. of فسل *fasl*.

فسيح *fasîḥ*, wide, spacious.

فسيخ *fasîḫ*, weak, unfit, incapable.

فسيد *fasîd*, pl. *fasda*, corrupt.

فسيس *fasîs*, pl. *fusus*, weak in mind and body.

(فسيط) *fasîṭ*, parings of the finger-nails; pedicle of a date.

فسيفسا *fusaifisâ'*, mosaic work.

فسيق *fissîq*, thoroughly vicious.

فسيلة *fasîla-t*, pl. *fasîl*, *fuslân* *fasâ'il*, palm-shoot.

(فش) *faśś*, U, INF. *faśś*, press the air out of; let the air out (a. and n.); belch, eructate; — II. INF. *tafśîś*, press the air out of; calm down (a.), quiet, pacify; — VII. INF. *infiśâś*, stream out; let out the air (n.), collapse.

فش *faśś*, emission of air, collapse, subsiding of a tumour; a coarse material.

فشا *faśâ'*, growing generation of cattle.

فشار *fuśâr*, idle talk; swagger, lies; — *faśśâr*, great talker; swaggerer, liar (m.).

فشاط *faśśâṭ*=فشار *faśśâr* (m.).

فشاقة *faśśâqa-t*, فشاكة *faśśâka-t*, rocket.

(فشج) *faśaj*, I, INF. *faśj*, open the

legs, put the legs apart; — II.
INF. tafśîj, V. INF. tafaśśuj, id.

(فشح) faśaḥ, INF. faśḥ, open the
legs; deviate from the right
way; turn aside, desert a cause,
apostatize, resign; (m.) unrobe
(n.), renounce the clerical state;
— II. INF. tafśîḥ, cause one to
deviate, &c.

(فشخ) faśaḫ, INF. faśḫ, slap on the
head or neck, box one's ears;
maltreat; tell lies; (m.) make
a step;—II. INF. tafśîḫ, pull one's
joints; make large steps; — VII.
INF. infiśâḫ, get between another's legs (m.).

فشخ faśḫ, step; — ة faśḫa-t, one
step, width of a step.

(فشر) faśur, be excessive in talk,
swagger, lie.

(فشط) faśaṭ, U, talk at random,
exaggerate, lie (m.); — II. INF.
tafśîṭ, id.; — VII. INF. infiśâṭ,
be broken.

فشط faśṭ, idle talk, exaggeration,
lie (m.).

(فشع) faśa', INF. faś', be dry at
the top (ear of corn).

(فشغ) faśag, INF. faśg, tower above,
cover; cudgel from above; — ة
faśga-t, ivy.

فشفش faśfaś, INF. ة, be a great
liar, be very mendacious; be
weak of intellect; squirt about
the urine.

(فشق) faśaq, U, INF. faśq, break
(a.); eat rapidly and vora-
ciously; — I, give one's self
over to pleasure and a luxu-
rious·life; — faśiq, A, INF. faśaq,
be brisk and merry, run away
(slave).·

(فشك) faśak, U, INF. faśk, mix up,
confuse (m.).

فشك fiśk, ة fiśka-t, dry dung (m.);
— ة faśaka-t, pl. faśak, car-
touch, cartridge (m.); بيت
الفشك bait al-faśak, cartridge-
box.

(فشل)·faśil, A, INF. faśal, be imbecile, lazy, weak, relaxed,

cowardly; (m.) be deceived in
one's hopes, be unsuccessful;
— faśal (m.) and IV. INF. ifśâl,
deceive one's hopes, cause one
to be unsuccessful; refuse,
turn off, render discontented;
disconcert, turn one's head; —
VII. INF. infiśâl = I. faśil.

فشل faśl, disappointment, unsuc-
cessfulness; pl. afśâl, also faśil,
pl. fuśl, imbecile, lazy, cowardly;
— faśal, imbecility, laziness,
cowardice.

فشلا faślâ', f. of افشل afśal, left-
handed; left hand.

(فشو) faśâ', U, INF. faśw, fuśuww,
fuśiyy, spread (n.), become
public; — II. INF. tafśiya-t, id.;
— IV. INF. ifśâ', spread (a.),
make public, communicate, show
forth; — V. INF. tafaśśî = I.; be
rampant; — VII. INF. infiśâ',
be spread, make known.

فشيش faśiś, hollow, empty,
spoiled.

(فص) faṣṣ, U, INF. faṣṣ, separate,
detach, pull out from; whine,
whimper; — I, INF. faṣiṣ, be
moist and purulent (wound)
— II. INF. tafṣîṣ, detach, separate, take out, husk; enclose,
frame, set (as a jewel), incrust;
— VII. INF. infiṣâṣ, be detached;
separated.

فص faṣṣ, eloquence; also fuṣṣ, fiṣṣ,
pl. fuṣûṣ, separation, detaching
(s.), loosening (s.); distinction;
kernel; stone or setting of a
ring; pupil of the eye; joint;
— ة faṣṣa-t, a kind of clover.

فصا faṣâ, ة, stone of a grape.

فصاح faṣâḥ, pl. of فصح faṣḥ and فصيح
faṣîḥ; — ة faṣâḥa-t, eloquence
and clearness of speech.

فصاد fiṣâd, ة fiṣâda-t, faṣâda-t, pl.
faṣâ'id, bleeding; — faṣṣâd, who
bleeds, surgeon.

فصاص faṣṣâṣ, who sets precious
stones, &c.

فصال fiṣâl, weaning (s.); cancelling
of a contract, &c., separation of

friends; pl. of فصيل *faṣîl*; — *faṣṣâl*, fault-finder, censurer; flatterer.

(فصح) *faṣaḥ*, INF. *faṣḥ*, break forth and shine in full splendour; be scummed (also II. and IV.); — *faṣuḥ*, INF. *faṣâḥa-t*, speak clearly, distinctly, fluently and with an elegant utterance; — II. INF. *tafṣîḥ*, make clear; speak distinctly and elegantly; see I.; — IV. INF. *ifṣâḥ*, explain distinctly and in elegant language; be eloquent; declare; break forth (morning); be clear, distinct, evident; celebrate Easter; see I.; — V. INF. *tafaṣṣuḥ*, speak or endeavour to speak clearly and elegantly; — VI. INF. *tafâṣuḥ*, take pains to speak clearly and eloquently; — X. INF. *istifṣâḥ*, find eloquent.

فصح *faṣḥ*, pl. *fuṣaḥâ'*, *fiṣâḥ*, *fuṣuḥ*, speaking distinctly and elegantly, eloquent; — *fiṣḥ*, *faṣḥ*, Easter.

فصحا *fuṣaḥâ'*, pl. of the previous and of فصيح *faṣîḥ*.

فصحى *faṣḥa*, f. of افصح, more or most eloquent, &c.; — *faṣḥiyy*, referring to Easter, pascal.

(فصخ) *faṣaḫ*, INF. *faṣḫ*, neglect, feign ignorance; sprain the hand; pass. *fuṣiḫ*, be overreached, cheated.

(فصد) *faṣad*, I, INF. *faṣd*, *fiṣâd*, bleed (a.); destine as a present to (ل *li*); — II. INF. *tafṣîd*, bleed (a.) repeatedly; — V. INF. *tafaṣṣud*, VII. INF. *infiṣâd*, be bled; — VIII. INF. *iftiṣâd*, bleed (a.).

فصد *faṣd*, bleeding (s.); blood made into a sausage; —ة *faṣda-t*, dates with blood.

(فصع) *faṣa'*, INF. *faṣ'*, press the fresh date to make it come out of the shell; knead and soften with the fingers; take or scrape off the shell of an almond; pull the prepuce over the gland; put off the turban; — also II. INF. *tafṣî'*, give to, bestow upon (ل *li*); — VIII. INF. *iftiṣâ'*, press and open; right one's self by force; —ة *fuṣ'a-t*, prepuce drawn over the gland.

فصعا *faṣ'a'*, female mouse.

فصعان *faṣ'ân*, always bare-headed.

(فصعل) *fiṣ'il*, *fuṣ'ul*, scorpion or its young; wicked person.

(فصفص) *faṣfaṣ*, INF. ة, give reliable information; be precipitate in speech; separate, disperse (a.); — II. INF. *tafaṣfuṣ*, separate (n.) from; disperse (n.) in all directions; — ة *fiṣfaṣa-t*, clover, trefoil.

(فصل) *faṣal*, I, INF. *faṣl*, cut off or separate one thing from another, separate, detach; distinguish between; break the continuity of anything; fix or barter for (a price); decide; — U, INF. *fuṣûl*, depart, remove from (من *min*, عن *'an*); — I, INF. *fiṣâl*, *faṣl*, wean; — II. INF. *tafṣîl*, cut or separate into several parts; cut out the material for a dress; set off by intervening parts; divide; detail; make a distinct plan; — III. INF. *mufâṣala-t*, separate (n.) from, rid one's self of; settle finally with; dissolve a partnership, cancel a contract; agree finally upon a price; — IV. INF. *ifṣâl*, die; — V. INF. *tafaṣṣul*, be cut out; — VI. INF. *tafâṣul*, agree upon a price; — VII. INF. *infiṣâl*, be separated; be decided, terminated; depart, remove from (عن *'an*); — VIII. INF. *iftiṣâl*, wean.

فصل *faṣl*, pl. *fuṣûl*, separation, distinction; incision; division, chapter, paragraph; season; joints; interstice; copula (pron. of the 3rd person); point; difference; decision; hitting or telling speech; sagacity; يوم

يوم الف yaum al-faṣl, day of the last judgment; ف الخطاب faṣl al-ḫiṭâb, the words اما بعد ammâ ba'd, which separate an introduction from the text, exposition; — ة faṣla-t, division, chapter, section.

فصلان faṣlân, fiṣlân, pl. of فصيل faṣîl.

فصلى faṣliyy, season; the official year beginning July 1st (m.).

(فصم) faṣam, I, INF. faṣm, break, cut (a.); pass. fuṣim, fall in (house); — V. INF. tafaṣṣum, be broken, break (n.); — VII. INF. infiṣâm, be broken, torn off; burst (n.).

(فصى) faṣa, I, INF. faṣy, separate, loosen; dismiss, give leave to depart, set free; — II. INF. tafṣiya-t, free; — IV. INF. ifṣâ', be freed, get rid of; be at an end, terminate, finish (n.); — V. INF. tafaṣṣî, VII. INF. infiṣâ', be rescued, liberated, freed.

فصى faṣan, grape-stone.

فصيح faṣîḥ, pl. fuṣaḥâ', fiṣâḥ, fuṣuḥ, f. ة, pl. fiṣâḥ, faṣâ'iḥ, eloquent; clear and distinct.

فصيخ faṣîḫ, ة faṣîḫa-t, unfortunate, unhappy, miserable.

فصيد faṣîd, bled.

فصيل faṣîl, pl. fuṣlân, fiṣlân, fiṣâl, weaned child or foal, &c.; smaller wall outside a circumvallation; parapet; — ة faṣîla-t, female colt of a camel; nearest relations in a tribe, family, small tribe; — ات fuṣailât, pl. commas.

(فض) faḍḍ, INF. faḍḍ, break off, detach; open, unseal; divide, disperse; decide, solve; harm; deflower; — II. INF. tafḍîḍ, silver over, plate with silver; — V. INF. tafaḍḍuḍ, be separated, dispersed; be silvered over; — VII. INF. infiḍâḍ, be broken, break (n.); get loose, dispersed; separate and disperse (n.); — VIII. INF. iftiḍâḍ, deflower; — ة faḍḍa-t, fiḍḍa-t, pl. fiḍaḍ, rocky high-land; — fiḍḍa-t, (m.) faḍḍa-t, silver; a small coin, para.

فضا faḍâ', open tract, field, plain; open place between houses or tents; passage, vestibule; inner part of a mosque; (m.) empty space, vacuum, chaos; — fiḍâ', purling or rippling water.

فضاح fiḍâḥ, ة fiḍâḥa-t, faḍâḥa-t, infamy; — faḍḍâḥ, who exposes infamy, dishonours, disgraces (المدام ف al-mudâm faḍḍâḥ, in vino veritas).

فضاض fiḍâḍ, pieces of rock; — fuḍâḍ, fiḍâḍ, fragment, potsherd, splinter.

فضال fiḍâl, every-day dress; wine; — *; — faḍḍâl, excellent, well-deserving man; — ة fuḍâla-t, remainder, rest; what is superfluous; — ى fuḍâlā, pl. people with high aspirations.

فضاوة faḍâwa-t, leisure time (m.).

(فضج), V. tafaḍḍaj, INF. tafaḍḍuj, perspire; — VII. INF. infiḍâj, id.

(فضح) faḍaḥ, INF. faḍḥ, disclose one's infamy or crime, expose, shame, disgrace; break forth (dawn); — faḍiḥ, be white, whitish; — IV. INF. ifḍâḥ, break forth; — VII. INF. infiḍâḥ, be covered with disgrace, be exposed, expose one's self; — VIII. INF. iftiḍâḥ, id.; — ة fuḍḥa-t, dead white.

(فضخ) faḍaḫ, INF. faḍḫ, beat in pieces, dash, shatter, pull out an eye; pour out water; — VII. INF. infiḍâḫ, open, break (n.); — VIII. INF. iftiḍâḫ, beat in pieces, dash, shatter.

فضض faḍaḍ, fuḍaḍ, what spurts or splinters off; — fiḍaḍ, pl. of فضة fiḍḍa-t.

(فضع) faḍa', INF. faḍ', break wind; drop excrement.

(فضخ) *faḍag*, INF. *faḍg*, break (a.).
فضفاض *faḍfâḍ*, wide, comfortable; trailing, training; abundant; — ة *faḍfâḍa-t*, f. full.
فضفض *faḍfaḍ*, INF. ة, be wide, large, comfortable; be abundant, easy.
(فضل) *faḍal*, U, INF. *faḍl*, be superfluous, superabundant, and therefore left; U, I, leave a remnant, a surplus; remain, keep alive, survive; surpass; — *faḍil*, A, INF. *faḍal*, be superabundant, remain; — II. INF. *tafḍîl*, make to surpass, render superior, deem to be so, prefer to (على *'ala*); exalt, praise; leave a remainder, a surplus; — III. INF. *fiḍâl*, *mufâḍala-t*, vie in excellence; — IV. INF. *ifḍâl*, consider one's self superior to (على *'ala*); surpass, be pre-eminent; treat with kindness and generosity; bestow benefits upon, deserve well of (على *'ala*); leave a remainder; — V. INF. *tafaḍḍul*, bestow a favour, a service, honour upon; be pleased to, have the kindness of; arrogate preference over (على *'ala*); wear an every-day dress, but one dress; — VI. INF. *tafâḍul*, vie in excellence with one another; show the difference between one another; — X. INF. *istifḍâl*, leave a remnant; have anything superfluous, have to spare, be able to do without.
فضل *faḍl*, pl. *fuḍûl*, *afḍâl*, anything superfluous, surplus, superabundance; completeness; rest, remainder; pre-eminence, surpassing excellence, superiority; learning, knowledge, scholarship; present, bounty, benefit; favour, service, obligingness; بفضل الله *bi-faḍl-i 'l-lâh-i*, for God's sake; *faḍl-an*, furthermore, how much the more so, not to mention that, moreover; — ة *faḍla-t*, pl. *faḍalât*, *fiḍâl*, remainder, surplus; overweight, addition; every-day dress, night-dress; excrement.
فضلا *faḍl-an*, see the previous; — *fuḍalâ'*, pl. of فضيل *faḍîl*.
(فضو) *faḍâ*, U, INF. *faḍâ'*, *fuḍuww*, be wide, vast, spacious; — IV. INF. *ifḍâ'*, go into the open fields; come to; lie with, tear the pudenda of a woman; push things so far that; jade.
فضو *fuḍuww*, spaciousness; INF. of the previous; — ة *faḍwa-t*, free time, leisure.
فضوح *faḍûḥ*, covered with disgrace; — *fuḍûḥ*, ة *fuḍûḥa-t*, disgrace, ignominy.
فضول *faḍûl*, what exceeds bounds, a surplus; exaggerated; arrogant; — *fuḍûl*, encroachment, excess; — ى *fuḍûliyy*, *faḍûliyy*, intermeddler; intrusive; idle talker; swaggering, boasting (adj.).
(فضى) *faḍî*, A, INF. *faḍâwa-t*, (m.) be empty; be unoccupied, have leisure; — II. INF. *tafḍiya-t*, empty, clear away; — IV. INF. *ifḍâ'*, bring matters to the point that, push a thing so far that; tend to; lead; come to, obtain; — V. INF. *tafaḍḍî*, get rid of; have leisure for; — X. INF. *istifḍâ'*, have nothing more to do, be at leisure.
فضى *faḍan*, *faḍa*, empty space; chaos; — *fiḍḍiyy*, ة, of silver.
فضيج *faḍîj*, sweat, perspiration.
فضيح *faḍîḥ*, bad householder; ة, dishonoured, disgraced; disgraceful, infamous; — ة *faḍîḥa-t*, pl. *faḍâ'iḥ*, disgraceful action, disgrace; ignominy.
فضيخ *faḍîḥ*, pressed-out juice of grapes; date-wine.
فضيض *faḍîḍ*, what spurts or splinters off; pure running water.
فضيل *faḍîl*, ة, pl. *fuḍalâ'*, excellent; virtuous; deserving; — ة *faḍîla-t*, pl. *faḍâ'il*, surplus, superabundance, plenteousness; superabundant merit; virtue; pre-

ference; eminence; Eminency; favour, benefit, service; learning, scholarship.

(فطا) *faṭa'*, INF. *faṭ'*, *faṭ'a-t*, beat on the back; throw on the ground; lie with; break wind, drop excrement; foam; shatter; burden with anything unpleasant, overburden; — فطى *faṭi'*, A, INF. *faṭa'*, *fuṭa't*, have a protruding chest and hollow back; be flat-nosed.

فطار *fuṭâr*, blunt, jagged; — ى *fuṭâriyy*, who is neither good nor bad.

فطاطيرى *faṭâṭîriyy*, pastrycook.

فطام *fiṭâm*, weaning (s.); (m.) muzzle.

فطانة *faṭâna-t*, فطانية *faṭâniya-t*, intelligence, quick understanding, sagacity.

(فطح) *faṭaḥ*, INF. *faṭḥ*, widen, make broad (a.); plane; cudgel; fructify the palm-tree; give birth; — *faṭiḥ*, A, INF. *faṭaḥ*, be broad, large; be fructified; — II. INF. *tafṭîḥ*, make broad (a.).

فطحل *fiṭaḥl*, time of the chaos; time before the Deluge; inundation.

(فطذ) *faṭaẓ*, I, INF. *faṭẓ*, drive away, prevent, hinder.

(فطر) *fatar*, U, I, INF. *faṭr*, split, cleave; begin, do first or for the first time, open a road; create out of nothing; fail to leaven the dough, bake unleavened bread from haste; — INF. *faṭr*, *fuṭûr*, pierce through (tooth); — INF. *faṭr*, *fiṭr*, break the fast, breakfast; — II. INF. *tafṭîr*, cause to break the fast; make one breakfast; (m.) be unleavened, fail to rise (also V.); — IV. INF. *ifṭâr*, break the fast; cause to break the fast, make one breakfast; — V. INF. *tafaṭṭur*, be split, broken; see II.; — VII. INF. *infiṭâr*, be split, split (n.), get chapped; bud forth.

فطر *faṭr*, pl. *fuṭûr*, split, rent; sperm; — *fiṭr*, breaking of the fast; feast following the month of *Ramaḍân*; breaking the fast, breakfasting (adj.); — *fuṭr*, *fuṭur*, unleavened; a poisonous mushroom; champignon; — ة *fiṭra-t*, creation; natural disposition, quality, make; creative power; alms, sacrifice; mass, host; prudence, cunning; pl. *fiṭar*, the created beings.

فطرى *faṭra*, unleavened; — *faṭriyy*, *fiṭriyy*, ة, inborn, natural.

(فطز) *faṭaz*, I, INF. *faṭz*, die.

(فطس) *faṭas*,* I, INF. *fuṭûs*, die, expire; (m.) choke (n.); — INF. *faṭs*, tell to one's face; beat broad; — *faṭis*, A, INF. *faṭas*, be flat-nosed; — II. INF. *tafṭîs*, choke, throttle; — ة *faṭsa-t*, glass bead, &c. as a spell or amulet; — *faṭasa-t*, flatness of the nose; (m.) suffocation, choke.

فطسان *faṭsân*, choked, suffocated (m.).

(فطش), VII. *infaṭaś*, INF. *infiṭâś*, be broken.

(فطفط) *faṭfaṭ*, INF. ة, drop excrement; speak unintelligibly.

(فطم) *faṭam*, I, INF. *faṭm*, *fiṭâm*, wean; turn from; cut off; (m.) put on the muzzle; — II. INF. *tafṭîm*, cease to bear fruit; — IV. INF. *ifṭâm*, be old enough to be weaned; — VII. INF. *infiṭâm*, be weaned; be muzzled.

فطم *fuṭum*, pl. فطيم *faṭîm*.

(فطن) *faṭan*, U, INF. *faṭn*, *fiṭn*, *fuṭn*, *fuṭun*, apprehend, conceive, understand, be aware of; remember; — *faṭin*, A, INF. *faṭan*, — also *faṭun*, INF. *faṭâna-t*, *faṭâniya-t*, *fuṭûna-t*, be intelligent, sharp, sagacious; — II. INF. *tafṭîn*, make to comprehend; call to one's memory; — V. INF. *tafaṭṭun*, ponder, think over; remember.

فطن *faṭn*, *fiṭn*, *fuṭn*, *fuṭun*, intel-

ligence; comprehension; sagacity; — *faṭin*, *faṭun*, ة, pl. *fuṭn*, intelligent, sagacious; — ة *fiṭna-t*, pl. *fiṭan*, intelligence, sagacity; an intelligent person.

(فطه) *faṭah*, breadth of the back.

(فطو) *faṭâ*, U, INF. *faṭw*, urge on violently.

فطور *faṭûr*, breakfast; — * ; — ة *faṭûra-t*, sheep sacrificed on the feast *al-fiṭr*.

فطوس *fuṭûs*, death.

فطون *faṭûn*, intelligent, sagacious, sharp of intellect; — ة *faṭûna-t*, intelligence.

فطير *faṭîr*, unleavened dough, bread which has not risen; anything precipitate; — ة *faṭîra-t*, pl. *faṭâ'ir*, pastry, tart; = فطورة *faṭûra-t*.

فطيس *faṭîs*, choked, suffocated; — *fiṭṭîs*, pl. *faṭâṭîs*, blacksmith's large hammer, sledge.

فطيم *faṭîm*, ة, pl. *fuṭum*, weaned, weanling.

فطين *faṭîn*, intelligent, sharp, sagacious, penetrating.

(فظ) *fazz*, U, INF. *fazz*, press out the water from a camel's stomach (for drinking); — for *faẓiẓ*, A, INF. *fiẓâẓ*, *faẓâẓa-t*, be cruel, inhumane, harsh, rough.

فظ *faẓẓ*, water in a camel's stomach; inhumane, harsh, rough; فظ بظ *faẓẓ baẓẓ*, big and fat.

(فظا) *faẓan*, *faẓa*, womb.

فظاظ *fiẓâẓ*, ة *faẓâẓa-t*, harshness, roughness, bluntness.

فظاعة *faẓâ'a-t*, horridness, ugliness; abomination; great difficulty; INF. of (فظع).

فظظ *faẓaẓ*, water in a camel's stomach.

(فظع) *faẓi'*, A, INF. *faẓa'*, deem to be great and beyond one's power; be not equal to; be full; — *faẓu'*, INF. *faẓâ'a-t*, be horrid and ugly; — II. INF. *tafẓî'*, describe as too great and difficult; picture emphatically, describe graphically; — IV. INF. *ifẓâ'*, be horrid, ugly, abominable; fill with aversion; become exceedingly burdensome; — V. INF. *tafaẓẓu'*, X. INF. *istifẓâ'*, find horrid, ugly, abominable.

(فظى) *faẓan*, *faẓa*, womb; — IV. *afẓa*, INF. *ifẓâ'*, have a wicked disposition.

فظيظ *faẓîẓ*, harsh, rough, blunt; animal sperm.

فظيع *faẓî'*, horrid, ugly, abominable; very difficult.

فعارير *fa'ârîr*, a plant used for food.

فعال *fa'âl*, deed; benefit, bounty; noble activity; misdeed; pl. *fu'ul*, handle of an axe; — *fi'âl*, pl. *fu'ûl*, id.; pl. of فعل *fi'l*; — *fa''âl*, perpetrator; who acts, does a thing; very effective; *al-fa''âl*, God.

(فعر) *fa'ar*, A, INF. *fa'r*, feed on the herb *fa'ârîr*; (m.) chide, scold.

(فعفع) *fa'fa'*, kid; active fellow, nimble lad; — INF. ة, call the herd with *fa'fa'*; — II. INF. *tafa'fu'*, hasten.

(فعل) *fa'al*, INF. *fa l*, bestir one's self, act, do, perform; exercise influence upon (ب *bi*); — VII. INF. *infi'âl*, be done, made, performed; be influenced by hatred, grief, &c.; — VIII. INF. *ifti'âl*, perpetrate, perform, act; form by art, invent; forge lies.

فعل *fi'l*, pl. *fi'âl*, *af'âl*, pl. pl. *afâ'îl*, deed, action, performance; efficacy; verb; *fi'l-an*, *bi 'l-fi'l*, indeed, really; — *fu'ul*, pl. of فعال *fa'âl*; — ة *fi'la-t*, *fa'ala-t*, a deed, an action; — *fa'ila-t*, custom, habit; — ى *fi'liyy*, ة, real; effective, efficacious; active, transitive; derived from a verb; — ية *fi'liyya-t*, reality, actuality.

(فعم) *fa'am*, INF. *fa'm*, fill, fill up; — *fa'um*, INF. *fa'âma-t*, *fu'ûma-t*, be full; be muscular, fleshy; be

well-made and have full hips; — IV. INF. *if'âm*, fill with; — XII. *if'an'am*, INF. *if'i'âm*, be full to overflowing.

فعم *fa'm*, a kind of roses; ة, fleshy.

فعول *fa'ûl*, effective, efficacious; perpetrator.

(فعى), V. INF. *tafa''î*, be mischievous like a snake (m.).

فعيل *fi''îl*, very active.

(فغ) *fagg*, INF. *fagga-t*, spread (n.); — ة *fagga-t*, diffusion of an odour.

فغافرة *fagâfira-t*, pl. of فغفور *fagfûr*.

(فغر) *fagar*, A, U, INF. *fagr*, open the mouth; open (n.); expand, blossom; — IV. INF. *ifgâr*, open the mouth; — VII. INF. *infigâr*, be open; bloom; — ة *fagra-t*, rising of the Pleiades; — *fugra-t*, pl. *fugar*, mouth of a river.

فغفور *fagfûr*, pl. *fagâfira-t*, title of the Emperors of China; Chinese porcelain; — ى *fagfûriyy*, chinaware.

(فغم) *fagam*, INF. *fagm*, *fugûm*, fill the nose so as almost to prevent breathing (odour); free the respiration; kiss one's wife; suck its dam; — INF. *fugûm*, open (n.), expand; — *fagim*, A, INF. *fagam*, crave for, be set upon a thing, infatuated with it; — III. INF. *mufâgama-t*, kiss one's wife; — V. INF. *tafaggum*, open (n.).

فغم *fugm*, *fugum*, mouth; chin with beard; — *fagim*, greedy, craving for; — ة *fagma-t*, scent, odour, fragrance.

(فغو) *fagâ*, U, INF. *fagw*, spread (n.); become known; fade, wither; — bear the blossom فاغية *fâgiya-t*.

فغو *fagw*, فاغية *fâgiya-t*, blossom of the cypress-tree.

(فق) *faqq*, U, INF. *faqq*, open (a.), separate, set apart; — VII. INF. *infiqâq*, be separated.

(فقا) *faqa'*, INF. *faq'*, prick open, open (a.), pull out; deprive of sight; — II. *tafqi'a-t*, pull out; (m.) husk, peel, take off the crust; — V. INF. *tafaqqu'*, be pulled out; be torn, split, rent; pierce the ground; (m.) be peeled, husked, &c.; — VII. INF. *infiqâ'*=V.; — ة *fuqa'a-t*, membrane round the head of the embryo.

فقاح *fiqâḥ*, pl. of فقحة *faqḥa-t*; — *fuqqâḥ*, flowers with hair or fibres; Schoenanthus (plant); beautiful woman; — ة *faqâḥa-t*, palm; open mind; (m.) impudence.

فقارة *faqâra-t*, pl. *faqâr*, vertebra; ذو الفقار *ẕû 'l-faqâr*, a celebrated sword; — ى *faqâriyy*, vertebral.

فقاس *fuqâs*, aching of the limbs, rheumatism.

فقاع *fuqâ'*, *fiqâ'*, reddish; crimson; deep yellow; — *faqqâ'*, very white; (m.) green, unripe; dirty, corrupt; — *fuqqâ'*, a kind of beer; a sherbet; boaster, braggart; — ة *faqqâ'a-t*, pl. *faqâqî'*, bubble; — ى *fuqâ'iyy*, crimson; deep yellow; — *fuqqâ'iyy*, beer-room keeper, beer-seller.

فقاقيع *faqâqî'*, pl. of فقاعة *faqqâ'a-t*.

فقامة *faqâma-t*, importance.

فقاه *fiqâh*, legal dispute; — ة *faqâha-t*, jurisprudence, knowledge of the law; mental culture.

(فقح) *faqaḥ*, INF. *faqḥ*, open the eyes for the first time (also II.); bloom, blossom; take a medicine in solid form; injure at the anus; (m.) be insolent; — II. INF. *tafqîḥ*, see I.; — V. INF. *tafaqquḥ*, open (n.); expand, develop (n.); — VI. INF. *tafâquḥ*, place their backs against one another.

فقح *faqḥ*, anus; — ة *faqḥa-t*, pl. *fiqâḥ*, id.; palm (of the hand); blossom; a cloth used as a girdle for a pilgrim's cloak.

(فقحل) *faqḥal*, INF. ة, to be easily provoked, prone to anger;—*fuqḥul*, irascible, prone to anger.

(فقح) *faqaḥ*, INF. *faqḥ*, *fiqâḥ*, beat on the head or anything hollow.

(فقد) *faqd*, INF. *faqd*, *fiqdân*, *fuqdân*, seek for anything lost; also INF. *fuqûd*, lose a person by death, miss sorely;—IV. INF. *ifqâd*, cause one to lose or miss (2 acc.);—V. INF. *tafaqqud*, VIII. INF. *iftiqâd*, seek for anything lost; miss one and seek for him; visit a sick person or one's wife; visit with a calamity, &c., try, examine; review;—X. INF. *istifqâd*, become aware of a loss, miss sorely; visit; visit with a calamity, &c.

فقد *faqd*, loss of a thing or person (also فقدان *fiqdân*, *fuqdân*); a plant; a kind of mead made of raisins, honey, &c. (also فقدد *fuqdud*).

(فقر) *faqar*, I, U, INF. *faqr*, dig; pierce, bore through; perforate the young camel's nose to put a training-cord through; break one's neck or spine; (m.) press grapes;—*faqir*, A, INF. *faqar*, have pain in the vertebræ from injury or illness;—*faqur*, INF. *faqâra-t*, be poor;—II. INF. *tafqîr*, dig; pierce, perforate;—IV. INF. *ifqâr*, impoverish, render poor; (verbal noun, *fuqra*), lend one's camel (ب *bi*) to another (acc.); expose the side to the hunter's shot;—V. INF. *tafaqqur*, be pressed (fruit);—VIII. INF. *iftiqâr*, be perforated; be or become poor, a beggar;—X. INF. *istifqâr*, deem one poor.

فقر *faqr*, pl. *mafâqir*, *fuqûr*, poverty; ascetic life; care, sorrow;—*fuqr*, poverty; pl. *fuqar*, side;—*faqir*, having a vertebra broken;—*fuqur*, pl. of *faqîr*;—ة *faqra-t*, *faqr*, a plant;—also *fiqra-t*, *fuqra-t*, pl. *fiqarât*, *faqarât*, *fiqrân*, *fiqirân*, *fiqar*, vertebra; the finest couplet in a poem, choice saying in rhymed prose; rhyme; line, paragraph;—*fiqra-t*, mark, sign;—*fuqra-t*, kinship; ditch; opening in a shirt for the head.

فقرا *fuqarâ'*, pl. of فقير *faqîr*, ة.

فقرى *fuqra*, loan of one's camel to another to carry a load or ride upon, see IV. (فقر).

(فقز) *faqaz*, I, *faqz*, die.

(فقس) *faqas*, I, INF. *fuqûs*, die; INF. *faqs*, break the egg and make come out or spoil its contents (bird), hatch; kill; creep out of the egg; expand, blossom; prevent by force; pull one down by his hair; (m.) shoot, fire off a gun; (m.) lose patience, grow ill-tempered, get vexed;—II. INF. *tafqîs*, make ill-tempered, irritate; melt and clear butter;—III. INF. *mufâqasa-t*, tap eggs together (in play);—V. INF. *tafaqqus*, be cleared, purified;—VI. INF. *tafâqus*, tap eggs together;—VII. INF. *infiqâs*, be turned over; be broken, break (n.); run out (spring);—ة *faqsa-t*, running out of a spring; sudden fit of ill temper (m.).

فقسان *faqsân*, ill-tempered; peevish.

(فقش) *faqaś*, U, INF. *faqś*, break with the hand; break, splinter (n.);—II. INF. *tafqîś*, break (a.); peel, take off the shell, &c.;—V. INF. *tafaqquś*, break, splinter (n.).

خمر فقش *ḥamr faqś*, fermented wine.

(فقص) *faqaṣ*, I, INF. *faqṣ*, break (a.); obtain, reach.

فقط *faqaṭ*, only, and that's all (postponed);—II. *faqqaṭ*, INF. *tafqîṭ*, write the words *fa-qaṭ* at the end of an account to prevent any spurious addition.

(فقع) *faqa'*, A, U, INF. *fuqû'*, be of

a deep yellow or crimson, of a pure colour in general; shine, be bright; break down (a.), crush; burst, burst with anger; die with laughter, die from heat; snap the fingers; thrive; — A, INF. *faq'*, steal; break wind; — *faqi'*, A, INF. *faqa'*, be of a deep red; — II. INF. *tafqî'*, cause to break or burst; crack rose-leaves, &c.; speak fluently; dye red; — IV. INF. *ifqâ'*, grow poor.

فقع *faq'*, *fiq'*, ة *faq'a-t*, *fiq'a-t*, snapping of the fingers; (m.) blame, rebuke; vexation; — *faq'*, *fiq'*, pl. *fiqa'a-t*, white soft mushroom (despised); — *fuq'*, pl. of افقع *afqa'*, very white; — *faqa'*, being (s.) of a deep red.

فقعسة *faq'asa-t*, stupidity.

فقفاق *faqfâq*, silly talk; silly, stupid; — also ة *faqfâqa-t*, silly talker.

(فقفق) *faqfaq*, INF. ة, bark from fear; grow very poor; (m.) indulge in silly talk; sing (boiling kettle); — ة *faqfaqa-t*, empty talk.

فقفوق *fuqfûq*, intellect, sagacity.

(فقل) *faqal*, U, INF. *faql*, winnow the corn, ventilate the threshing-floor; — IV. INF. *ifqâl*, be exceedingly fertile.

فقل *faql*, great fertility, luxuriance; — *fuql*, a poisonous fish.

(فقم) *faqam*, U, INF. *faqm*, *fuqûm*, be of great importance; — INF. *faqm*, seize by the jaw or nose; lie with; — *faqim*, A, INF. *faqam*, be full; be surfeited; INF. *faqm*, *faqam*, be boisterously merry, wanton; have the upper front teeth projecting; be abundant; be exhausted, scarce; — *faqum*, INF. *faqâma-t*, be difficult; be important; — III. INF. *mufâqama-t*, lie with; — VI. INF. *tafâqum*, be of great importance.

فقم *faqm*, *fuqm*, jaw; — *faqim*, intelligent, ingenious; superior, getting the better of his adversary; — *fuqm*, *fuqum*, mouth; *fuqm*, pl. and—

فقما *faqmâ'*, f. of افقم *afqam*, having the upper front teeth projecting.

(فقه) *faqah*, surpass in the knowledge of law or divinity; — *faqih*, A, INF. *fiqh*, be well versed in law and divinity, be learned, wise, sagacious; understand; — *faquh*, INF. *faqâha-t*, id.; be a doctor of law and divinity; — II. INF. *tafqîh*, make one learned in law and divinity; make wise and intelligent; teach; — III. INF. *mufâqaha-t*, discuss legal and theological questions with, vie with in legal or theological learning; — IV. INF. *ifqâh*=II.; make understand; — V. INF. *tafaqquh*, study law and theology; grow learned, wise, intelligent; understand.

فقه *fiqh*, knowledge, learning (especially in law and divinity); intelligence, understanding; — *faqih*, *faquh*, ة, learned in law and divinity; wise and intelligent.

فقها *fuqahâ'*, pl. of فقيه *faqîh*.

فقهى *fiqhiyy*, legal and theological; school-master.

(فقو) *faqâ*, U, INF. *faqw*, follow one's track; — ة *fuqwa-t*, pl. *fuqa*, notch of a bow.

فقود *fuqûd*, missing (s.), loss.

فقوس *faqqûs*, فقوص *faqqûṣ*, melon not yet ripe, small melon.

فقوم *fuqûm*, importance.

فقى *faqi'*, constipation in a camel; camel afflicted with it; — *fuqa*, pl. of فقوة *fuqwa-t*.

فقيد *faqîd*, missing, bereaved of, deprived; lost.

فقير *faqîr*, pl. *fuqarâ'*, poor, needy; beggar, mendicant, dervish; in need of; having the nose pierced (camel); having the spine broken; — ة *faqîra-t*, pl.

fuqâ'ir and *fuqarâ'*, beggar-woman.

فقيشة *fuqaiśa-t*, fold in the skirt of a garment to make it wider if wished ; — pl. *fuqaiśât*, castanets.

فقيص *faqîṣ*, broken.

فقيع *faqî'*, reddish, red ; dirty ; corrupt ; —*fiqqi'*, entirely white ; (m.) green, unripe.

فقيم *fuqaim*, quiver (for arrows) ; porcupine.

فقيه *faqîh*, pl. *fuqahâ'*, f. ة, pl. also *fuqahâ'* and *faqâ'ih*, well versed in jurisprudence and theology, doctor of law and divinity ; scholar ; teacher ; wise, intelligent.

فك *fakk*, U, INF. *fakk*, separate ; loose, untie ; disentangle, remove difficulties ; open the hand and drop what was in it ; sprain a limb ; be infirm and decrepit ; — INF. *fakk*, *fakâk*, *fikâk*, rescue, ransom, set at liberty, free, deliver ; — INF. *fakk*, *fukûk*, redeem a pledge or pawn ; — for *fakik*, A, INF. *fakak*, be sprained ; be broken ; INF. *fakk*, *fakka-t*,— also *fakuk*, grow stupid ; — II. INF. *tafkîk*, loosen, detach, separate ; free ; disentangle ; — V. INF. *tafakkuk*, be sprained ; be loosened, broken ; be disentangled ; — VII. INF. *infikâk*, be detached, separated ; separate (n.) ; get loose ; be sprained ; cease ; with negative, do a thing continually ; rid one's self of ; — VIII. INF. *iftikâk*, redeem a pledge or pawn ; — X. INF. *istifkâk*, try to detach, to loose, to separate ; detach, separate.

فك *fakk*, loosing, separating, detaching (s.) ; opening (s.) ; redeeming (s.) ; liberation, ransom ; dislocation, fracture ; pl. *afkâk*, *fukûk*, jaw ; articulation of the jaws ; bridle, bit ; — ة *fakka-t*, loosing, detaching (s.) ; dislocation ; lassitude ; stupidity ; (m.) disentanglement.

فكاك *fakâk*, *fikâk*, loosing (s.), ransom, liberation, rescue ; — *fikâk*, pledge and price to redeem it ; pl. of فاك *fâkk*, imbecile, &c. ; — *fakkâk*, who looses, separates, frees.

فكاهة *fukâha-t*, *fakâha-t*, merriment, pleasantry.

(فكر) *fakar*, U, INF. *fakr*, think, ponder over (فى *fî*) ; — II. INF. *tafkîr*, make one think of, remind ; think ; — III. INF. *mufâkara-t*, (m.) contradict ; oppose, thwart ; — IV. INF. *ifkâr* =II. ; — V. INF. *tafakkur*, think, meditate, be thoughtful ; — VI. INF. *tafâkur*, contradict and thwart one another ; — VIII. INF. *iftikâr*, think of (فى *fî*).

فكر *fikr*, *fakr*, pl. *afkâr*, thought ; thoughtful attention ; idea ; — *fikr*, need ; — ة *fikra-t*, pl. *fikar*, id. ; care, grief, sorrowfulness.

فكش *fakaś*, U, INF. *fakś*, sprain ; be sprained ; — VII. INF. *infikâś*, be sprained (m.).

فكش *fikś*, ة *fakśa-t*, dislocation, distortion.

(فكع) *faki'*, A, INF. *fak'*, *fukû'*, cast the eyes down from grief or emotion.

فكك *fakak*, dislocation ; fracture ; — ة *fakaka-t*, pl. of فاك *fâkk*, imbecile, &c.

(فكل), VIII. INF. *iftikâl*, give care and attention to (فى *fî*).

(فكن) *fakan*, U, INF. *fakn*, persist in (فى *fî*) ; — V. INF. *tafakkun*, be seized with grief ; repent ; wonder ; be thoughtful, ponder ; — ة *fukna-t*, repentance, regret, grief.

(فكه) *fakih*, A, INF. *fakah*, *fakahân*, be very joyful and merry ; INF. *fakh*, *fakâha-t*, jest, cheer up by jesting ; be seized with admiration ; — II. INF. *tafkîh*, bring or give fruit to (acc.) ; cheer up by jesting ; — III. *mufâ-*

kaha-t, jest with ; — v. INF. *tafakkuh*, be cheerful and jest; rejoice in, be pleased with (ب *bi*) ; be seized with admiration; — VI. INF. *tafâkuh*, jest with one another.

فكه *fakih*, who eats fruit; who is merry and jests; witty person, wit.

فكور *fakûr*, who thinks much.

(فكون), II. INF. *tafakwun*, eat fruit, satisfy one's appetite with fruit.

فكير *fikkîr*, very thoughtful, meditative.

فكيهة *fakîha-t*, mirth, cheerfulness, pleasantry.

فل *ful*=فلان *fulân*.

(فل) *fall*, U, INF. *fall*, blunt or jag the blade of a sword, break (a.) ; rout, put to flight; flee, run away; be blunt, jagged; — II. INF. *taflîl*, break, blunt, jag; rout; cause one to run away; — IV. INF. *iflâl*, be deprived of all resources; — V. INF. *tafallul*, get broken, blunt, jagged; be routed; — VII. INF. *infilâl*=v. ; be broken out (tooth).

فل *fall*, pl. *fulûl*, *aflâl*, *filâl*, breach, rent, jag; a part or a single fugitive of a routed army; defeat and flight; —*fall*, *fill*, pl. *aflâl*, rainless desert ; — *full*, pl. *fulûl*, Arabian jasmine.

فلا *falâ*, INF. *fal'*, corrupt ; — ة *falât*, pl. *fal-an*, *falawât*, *fuluww*, *fuliyy*, *filiyy*, *aflâ'*, vast waterless desert ; (m.) open space; (m.) atmosphere; فى الف *fî 'l-falât*, in the open air.

فلات *fulât*, pl. ladies ; — * ; — ى *falâtiyy*, good-for-nothing fellow, scamp.

فلاح *falâḥ*, good fortune, happiness, welfare, blessing, success; rescue, salvation, liberation ; asylum; security; —*fallâḥ*, pl. *-ûn*, *falâliḥ*, peasant, husbandman, plougher ; sailor ; — ة *falâḥa-t*, agriculture, husbandry.

فلاز *fallâz*, kitchen-gardener.

فلاسفة *falâsifa-t*, pl. of فيلسوف *failasûf*, *fîlasûf*.

فلاس *fallâs*, money-changer ; — ة *falâsa-t*, bankruptcy.

فلاطن *falâṭun*, فلاطون *falâṭûn*, Plato.

فلاق *filâq*, curdling of the milk; — also *fulâq*, anything separate; — ة *falâqa-t*, stocks or block for a criminal; —*fulâqa-t*, pl. *filâq*, fragments of bricks.

فلاكة *falâka-t*, evil, calamity.

فلال *fullâl*, defeated part of an army.

فلاليج *falâlîj*, pl. of فلوجة *fallûja-t*.

فلان *fulân*, f. ة, a certain person, so and so, such a one; — ى *fulâniyy*, referring to so and so; a certain.

فلاورة *falâwira-t*, pl. apothecaries.

فلاوى *falâwa*, pl. of فلو *fuluww*.

فلائق *falâ'iq* (فلائك *fulâ'ik*), pl. of فلوقة *fulûqa-t*, فلوكة *falûka-t*.

فلاية *filâya-t*, lousing (s.).

(فلت) *falat*, I, INF. *falt*, rescue, liberate, free; **escape**; loose one's self, get **rid of**; — II. INF. *taflît*, loose, **detach**; free, rescue, make one to **escape**; — III. INF. *filât*, come **suddenly** or unexpectedly upon, **surprise**; — IV. INF. *iflât*, make one **to** escape, rescue ; escape ; — **v.** INF. *tafallut*, escape, **get rid** of; — VII. INF. *infilât*, id.; — VIII. INF. *iftilât*, make a speech ex tempore; pass. *uftulit*, die suddenly.

فلت *falat*, escape; —*fulat*, *fult*, swift, fleet;— ة *falta-t*, pl. *falatât*, sudden attack, surprise (*faltatan*, suddenly); last night of the month; pl. slips of the tongue, escaped errors, &c.

فلتان *filtân*, *falatân*, swift, fleet; — *falatân*, free, rid of, unrestrained; hard, strong, bold; a hunting-bird.

(فلج) *falaj*, U, I, INF. *falj*, split in two; furrow the ground; divide, distribute ; vanquish

one's adversary; be successful, prosper; escape; impose taxes; pass. *fulij*, be seized with hemiplegy; — *falij*, A, INF. *falaj*, stand apart, have the toes, teeth, &c. standing apart; — II. INF. *taflîj*, split (a.); divide, distribute; — IV. INF. *iflâj*, get the better of one's adversary in a debate or disputation, triumph; afflict with hemiplegy; — V. INF. *tafalluj*, be split into several parts; get chapped.

فلج *falj*, victory, triumph; pl. *fulûj*, half; piece, portion; division; water-course; flow of tears; — *fulj*, ة *fulja-t*, victory; success; escape, rescue; — *falaj*, also—

فلجان *falajân*, separation of the toes, fingers, teeth, &c.; regularity.

(فلح) *falaḥ*, INF. *falḥ*, split, furrow the ground, plough; till the ground, carry on agriculture; be successful, make progress; deceive insidiously; — *faliḥ*, A, INF. *falaḥ*, also *faluḥ*, be split; — II. INF. *taflîḥ*, make one till a field; make one a peasant or husbandman: — IV. INF. *iflâḥ*, be successful, prosper, thrive; live upon; — VII. INF. *infilâḥ*, be tilled, cultivated; — X. INF. *istiflâḥ*, force one to do field-work; — ة *falaḥa-t*, sown field.

(فلحس) *falḥas*, greedy; dog; old bear; who watches the time of people's meals to intrude upon them; name of a chief of the Banû S'aibân, who, after receiving his share of the booty, exacted one for his wife and another for his camel,—hence: II. *tafalḥas*, INF. *tafalḥus*, make impudent demands; be a parasite, sponge; — ة *falḥasa-t*, woman with thin hips.

(فلخ) *falaḫ*, I, INF. *falḫ*, split in two, break (a.); make distinctly known; — II. INF. *taflîḫ*, hit, strike.

(فلذ) *falaẕ*, I, INF. *falẕ*, cut into slices, cut a slice for (ل *li*); give on the spur of the moment and abundantly; — II. INF. *taflîẕ*, cut into slices or pieces; — VIII. INF. *iftilâẕ*, take from another part of his property (2 acc.).

فلذ *filẕ*, pl. *aflâẕ*, liver of a camel; piece, slice; — ة *filẕa-t*, pl. *filaẕ*, piece, slice; part, portion.

فلسطون *filasṭûn*, *falisṭûn*, فلسطين *filasṭîn*, *falasṭîn*, Palestine.

(فلسف), II. *tafalsaf*, INF. *tafalsuf*, philosophize, reason; — ة *falsafa-t*, *filsafa-t*, philosophy; — ى *falsafiyy*, philosophical.

(فلص) *falaṣ*, U, escape, get one's self out of; — II. INF. *taflîṣ*, rescue, free; — IV. INF. *iflâṣ*, V. INF. *tafalluṣ*, VII. INF. *infilâṣ*, escape; — VIII. INF. *iftilâṣ*, take out of one's hand.

(فلط) *falaṭ*, U, INF. *falṭ*, be terrified by, shrink from (عن *'an*); (m.) flatten (a.), make broader; — IV. INF. *iflâṭ*, fall upon suddenly, surprise; — VII. INF. *infilâṭ*, be flattened; — VIII. INF. *iftilâṭ*, pass. of IV.

فلط *falaṭ*, anything sudden, unexpected.

(فلطح) *falṭaḥ*, INF. ة, extend, spread, make broad (a.), flatten (a.); — II. INF. *tafalṭuḥ*, pass.

(فلطس), II. INF. *tafalṭus*, be flat, broad (nose).

فلطاس *filṭâs*, فلطوس *filṭûs*, *falṭûs*, فلطيس *filṭîs*, thick gland of the penis; — ة *filṭîsa-t*, snout of a pig.

(فلع) *fala'*, INF. *fal'*, split, cleave (a. & n.), cut; burst (n.); get chapped; — II. INF. *taflî'*, split, cleave (a.), cut; — V. INF. *tafallu'*, VII. INF. *infilâ'*, split (n.), burst (n.), get chapped.

فلع *fil'*, ة *fil'a-t*, *fal'*, pl. *fulû'*, split, chap; — *ful'*, pl. of فلوع *falû'*;

— ة *fil'a-t*, slice of a camel's hump.

(فلغ) *falag*, A, INF. *falg*, break in one's head.

فلفل *filfil*, *falfal*, pepper; —*falfal*, INF. ة, pepper; (m.) burn (like pepper); walk proudly and with short steps; rub one's teeth with the *miswâk*; — II. INF. *tafalful*, be peppered.

(فلق) *falaq*, I, INF. *falq*, split (a.), tear (a.), cut; cause the dawn to break forth; shear; — II. INF. *taflîq*, split (a.), cut; — IV. INF. *iflâq*, produce anything wonderful, a masterpiece; — V. INF. *tafalluq*, be split, torn, chapped; — VII. INF. *infilâq*= V.; open (n.); — VIII. INF. *iftilâq*, produce anything extraordinary.

فلق *falq*, pl. *fulûq*, split, cleft, orifice (من فلق فيه *min falq-i fî-hi*, from his own mouth); — *filq*, ة *filqa-t*, pl. *filaq*, half, part, portion; —*falaq*, pl. *aflâq*, mountain-cleft; first dawn of the morning; stocks for a prisoner or one to be bastinadoed; remainder of milk; — ة *filqa-t*, anything wonderful, calamity.

(فلقح) *falqaḥ*, INF. ة, eat or drink all that there is in a dish or vessel; — II. INF. *tafalquḥ*, meet people cheerfully; (m.) learn good manners, be sociable and polite; — ة *falqaḥa-t*, polite manners; — ى *falqaḥiyy*, who laughs in people's faces.

(فلقس) *falqas*, miserly, filthy.

(فلقط) *falqaṭ*, INF. ة, be hasty or precipitate in walk or speech.

(فلك) *falk*, U, INF. *falk*, be round; be spherical; —*falik*, A, INF. *falak*, have round breasts; — II. INF. *taflîk*, be round or spherical; have round breasts; (m.) persist in; (m.) apply one's self to astronomy or astrology, predict from the stars; — IV. INF. *iflâk*, be round.

فلك *falak*, pl. *aflâk*, *fuluk*, *fulk*, anything round or spherical, ball, globe; sphere of the sky; rotation of the sky; astronomy, astrology; influence of the stars; (m.) weather; —*fulk* (f. and m.), sing. and pl., pl. also *fuluk*, large ship; — ة *falka-t*, pl. *filâk*, noun of unity of *falak*; —*falka-t*, *filka-t*, ring of a spindle; buttock; — ى *falakiyy*, ة, heavenly, referring to the sky, astronomical; pl. ة, astronomer.

(فلم), VIII. *iftalam*, INF. *iftilâm*, maim one's nose.

(فلندح) *falandaḥ*, thick.

فلنقس *falanqas*, son of a slave and a free woman.

فلهد *falhad*, *fulhud*, فلهود *fulhûd*, corpulent boy approaching puberty.

فلهم *falham*, shuttle; pudenda of a woman; large well.

(فلو) *falâ*, U, INF. *falw*, *falâ'*, wean; bring up, educate; strike; set out on a journey; — IV. INF. *iflâ'*, wean; have a foal fit to be weaned, or generally a sucking foal.

فلو *filw*, f. ة, pl. *aflâ'*, foal; — *fuluww*, *faluww*, f. ة, pl. *falâwa*, id.; —*fuluww*, and—

فلوات *falawât*, pl. of فلاة *falât*.

فلوج *fallûj*, scribe, clerk; — ة *fallûja-t*, pl. *falâlîj*, sown field.

فلوس *fulûs*, money, pl. of فلس *fals*.

فلوع *falû'*, pl. *ful'*, sharp.

فلوكة *fulûka-t* (فلوقة *fulûqa-t*), pl. *falâ'ik* (*falâ'iq*), ship, barque, felucca.

(فلى) *fala*, I, INF. *faly*, strike with a sword; louse; study a poem, try to understand it; (m.) examine, search; — فلى *falî*, A, INF. *fal-an*, be cut off; — II. INF. *tafliya-t*, louse; — V. INF. *tafallî*, catch lice or fleas; do nothing, be idle; — VI. INF.

tafâlî, X. INF. *istiflâ'*, have one's self loused, ask to be loused.

فلى *fulla*, beaten, put to flight; — *fuliyy*, pl. of فلاة *falât*.

فليج *falîj*, having the teeth separated; — ة *falîja-t*, part of a tent; wainscoting.

فليق *falîq*, ة *falîqa-t*, wonder, calamity; —*fallaiq*, peach, plum, &c. which can be loosed from its stone; — ة *falîqa-t*, thin hair.

فليل *falîl*, jagged, broken, decayed (tooth); — also *falîla-t*, large knot of hair.

(فم) *fam*, *fim*, *fum*, *famm*, pl. *afmâm*, *afwâh*, mouth, orifice.

فموى *famawiyy*, فمى *famiyy*, *fimiyy*, *fumiyy*, referring to the mouth or orifice; oral.

(فن) *fann*, U, INF. *fann*, drive along; deceive, cheat; delay payment (of a debt); put variety into; adorn, deck out; (m.) throw away, reject; — II. INF. *tafnîn*, bring, show, demand various things; mix up different things; put variety into; embellish, adorn; divide into classes, categories, departments, &c., make rich in resources, clever, industrious; — V. INF. *tafannun*, branch out in different classes, catagories, &c.; show one's self rich in resources, clever, industrious, active in various ways; follow up various pursuits; — VIII. INF. *iftinân*, produce a variety of things, show one's self rich in resources and clever, be versatile.

فن *fan'*, troop, number of people; —*fann*, pl. *funûn*, *afnân*, *afânîn*, species, kind, category, branch of science or art; manner, way; adornment, embellishment; resource; device, trick, artifice; — ة *fanna-t*, hour, short while; —*funna-t*, plenty of food.

فنا *fanan*, *fana*, Solanum hortense; —*fanâ'*, perishableness, nothingness, non-existence; INF. of (فنى); perishable, fleeting; — *finâ'*, pl. *afniya-t*, *funiyy*, inclosure in front of a house, courtyard; —*fannâ'*, copiously ramified; — ة *fanât*, pl. *fanawât*, doe; pl. *fan-an*, Solanum hortense.

فناجين *fanâjîn*, pl. of فنجان *finjân*.

فناخر *funâḫir*, ة, having a bulky body, inflated nostrils.

فناديد *fanâdîd*, pl. of فنداوة *finda'wa-t*.

فنار *fanâr*, lighthouse; lantern (m.).

فنتق *funtuq*, caravanserai.

فنجان *finjân*, pl. *fanâjîn*, china cup, coffee-cup.

فنجر *fanjar*, INF. ة, open the eyes wide and in an insolent manner; — ة *fanjara-t*, insolence, impudence; —ى *fanjariyy*, impudent, insolent.

(فنجل) *fanjal*, who has the toes turned in and the heels turned out; — *funjul*, badger; — ة *fanjala-t*, unsteady walk (from weakness); large distance of the legs and feet from one another.

(فنح) *fanaḥ*, A, INF. *fanḥ*, drink without fully quenching its thirst (horse, &c.).

(فنخ) *fanaḫ*, U, INF. *fanḫ*, bruise a bone without breaking it; subdue, overcome; humiliate; — II. INF. *tanfîḫ*, overcome, subdue.

فنخر *fanḫar*, INF. ة, inflate the nostrils, give one's self haughty airs.

(فند) *fanid*, A, INF. *fanad*, be delirious, dote; err, commit a fault; lie; — II. INF. *tafnîd*, consider as a dotard or liar; accuse of a lie, belie; refute; rebuke; (m.) divide into classes or categories; (m.) distinguish or expound clearly; (m.) sow discord; — IV. INF. *ifnâd*, dote;

err ; — v. INF. *tafannud*, (m.) pass. of II. (m.).

فند *fand*, trick, stratagem, wile ; — *find*, *fand*, pl. *afnâd*, branch ; class, category ; mountain, mountain-tract ; name of a man proverbial for his slowness ; — *find*, pl. *funûd*, small wax candle ; — *fanad*, lie ; ingratitude.

فنداق *fundâq*, book of receipts and expenditure.

فنداوة *finda'wa-t*, فنداية *finda'ya-t*, pl. *fanâdîd*, sharp axe or hatchet.

(فندس) *fandas*, INF. ة , run.

(فندش) *fandaś*, INF. ة , vanquish, conquer.

فندق *funduq*, hazel-nut ; — also *finduq*, pl. *fanâdiq*, hotel, inn.

فندقانى *funduqâniyy*, hotel-keeper.

فندير *findîr*, ة *findîra-t*, pl. *fanâdîr*, large mountain-crag.

(فنش), II. *fannaś*, INF. *tafnîś*, slacken, relax.

(فنشع) *fanśaḥ*, INF. ة , be tired, weary ; desist, lag behind ; be very old ; also II. INF. *tafanśuḥ*, keep the legs wide apart.

فنطاس *finṭâs*, hold of a ship with water in it ; reservoir.

فنطيس *finṭîs*, pl. *fanâṭîs*, mean, vile ; flat-nosed ; — ة *finṭîsa-t*, snout of a pig.

(فنع) *fani'*, A, INF. *fana'*, have plenty ; prosper, increase.

فنع *fana'*, wealth ; honour ; liberality ; scent, fragrance ;—*fani'*, rich.

فنق *funuq*, young and fat (camel) ; delicate and tenderly reared ; — II. *fannaq*, INF. *tafnîq*, rear tenderly ; make one's life easy ; — III. INF. *mufânaqa-t*, benefit, favour ; make one's life easy ; — IV. INF. *ifnâq*, lead an easy life after hardship ; — v. INF. *tafannuq*, lead a comfortable life.

(فنك) *fanak*, INF. *funûk*, stay, remain, abide ; be diligent in, attend to (فى *fî*) ; press with importunity ; lie ; — *fanik*, A, INF. *fanak*, be unjust, hostile ; vanquish, overcome (على *'ala*) ; — III. INF. *mufânaka-t*, undertake ; — IV. INF. *ifnâk*, attend to with diligence.

فنك *fank*, combat ; victory, conquest ; also *fanak*, anything wonderful ; — *fank*, *fink*, door ; — *fanak*, pl. *afnâk*, weasel ; beaver.

فنن *fanan*, pl. *afnân*, *afânîn*, branch, twig ; manner, way.

فنوا *fanwâ'*, branchy, shady, f.

فنوات *fanawât*, pl. of فناة *fanât*.

(فنى) *fana*, *fanî*, A, INF. *fanan*, *fanâ'*, dwindle away, vanish, disappear; be perishable, mortal ; be infirm, decrepit ; run short, be used up ; perish, die ; — III. INF. *mufânât*, court, flatter, curry favour with (acc.) ; — IV. INF. *ifnâ'*, make disappear, destroy ; — VI. INF. *tafânî*, destroy one another ; be perished.

فنى *fanan*, perishableness ;—*funiyy*, pl. of فنا *finâ'*.

فنيق *fanîq*, pl. *funuq*, *afnâq*, noble stallion ;— ة *fanîqa-t*, pl. *fanâ'iq*, large sack for putting earth in.

فه *fahh*, ة , weak ; stammerer ; — ة *fahha-t*, stammering ; slip ; forgetfulness.

فهاد *fahhâd*, who trains panthers, &c. for hunting.

فهام *fahhâm*, very intelligent and learned ;— ة *fahâma-t*, *fihâma-t*, and—

فهامية *fahâmiyya-t*, intelligence, understanding, discernment.

فهاهة *fahâha-t*, stammering.

(فهد) *fahad*, INF. *fahd*, manage an absent person's business well ; — *fahid*, A, INF. *fahad*, be similar to or sleep like a hunting-panther ; neglect everything from sleepiness ; — v. INF. *tafahhud*, be like a hunting-panther, i.e. proud or drowsy.

فهد *fahd*, pl. *fuhûd*, *afhud*, hunting-

panther, ounce; — *fahid, fihid*, sleepy, drowsy like a hunting-panther.

(فهر) *fahar*, INF. *fahr, fahar*, excite one's self with a woman and afterwards lie with another.

فهر *fihr*, pl. *afhâr, fuhûr*, stone of the size of a hand; — *fuhr*, Jewish feast of Purim.

فهرس *fihris*, ة *fihrisa-t*, فهرست *fihrist*, pl. *fahâris*, index, summary; rule, canon; preface; — *fahras*, INF. ة, provide a book with an index.

(فهض) *fahaḍ*, INF. *fahḍ*, break (a.).

فهفه *fahfah*, weak; stammering (adj.).

(فهق) *fahaq*, INF. *fahq, fahaq*, injure the first vertebra; — *fahiq*, A, INF. *fahq, fahaq*, be full; — IV. INF. *ifhâq*, fill; — also V. INF. *tafahhuq*, and VII. INF. *infihâq*, extend far; — ة *fahqa-t*, pl. *fihâq*, first vertebra.

فهم *fahim*, A, INF. *fahm, faham, fahâma-t, fihâma-t, fahâmiya-t*, understand, comprehend; — II. INF. *tafhîm*, IV. INF. *ifhâm*, make understand, teach; — V. INF. *tafahhum*, understand by degrees; — VII. INF. *infihâm*, be understood; — VIII. INF. *iftihâm*, understand, comprehend, conceive; — X. INF. *istifhâm*, wish to understand; ask for explanation.

فهم *fahm, faham*, pl. *fuhûm*, understanding, comprehension, intellect; — *fahim*, of a quick understanding.

(فهه) *fahih*, A, INF. *fahah*, be weak; stammer; forget; — IV. INF. *ifhâh*, weaken; cause to forget.

(فهو) *fahâ*, U, INF. *fahw*, neglect.

فهيرة *fahîra-t*, milk and flour cooked by a heated stone.

فهيم *fahîm*, quick of understanding.

فو *fû*, pl. *afwâh*, mouth; valerian (plant); — ة *fuwwa-t*, madder, rubia tinctorum.

فوات *fawât*, INF. of (فوت).

فواد *fu'âd*, (m.) *fawâd*, pl. *af'ida-t*, the nobler intestines: heart, lung, liver; heart, mind.

فوار *fuwâr*, foam, froth; INF. of (فور); — *fawwâr*, boiling and throwing up large bubbles; very irascible.

فوارة *fu'âra-t*, fennel and dates as food for a confined woman; — *fuwâra-t*, heat of a boiling kettle; — *fawwâra-t*, gush of water; jet-d'eau, spring, fount.

فواشق *fawâśiq*, فواشك *fawâśik*, see فوشق *fauśaq*.

فواض *fawâḍḍ*, pl. of فاضة *fâḍḍa-t*, calamity.

فواق *fuwâq*, pl. *afwiqa-t, âfiqa-t*, lank and awkwardly built; last gasps of a dying person; interval between two milkings (*fawâq-an fawâq-an*, from time to time); — *fu'âq*, hiccough.

فوال *fawwâl*, seller of beans.

فوائه *fawâ'ih*, pl. of فوهة *fuwwaha-t*.

(فوت) *fât*, U, INF. *faut, fawât*, pass by sideways, escape; pass, pass by; be no longer the fashion; miss, fail to reach; get beforehand with; leave behind, abandon; عاد فات *'âd fât*, go to and fro; (m.) enter (فى *fî*); — II. INF. *tafwît*, cause to pass, to escape, to leave; (m.) to enter; — IV. INF. *ifâta-t*, make to lose; — V. INF. *tafawwut*, escape; overcome; see VIII.; — VI. INF. *tafâwut*, be at a great distance from one another, be distinguished from one another, be different; (m.) exceed bounds; — VII. INF. *infiyât*, be overtaken, passed over by; — VIII. INF. *iftiyât*, escape; act wilfully disregarding another's authority, be excessively insolent (also V.); decide against (also V.); — X. INF. *istifâta-t*,

avail one's self of an opportunity.

فوت *faut*, pl. *afwât*, distance; excelling (s.); *faut-a*, in reach of and yet not attainable; death, destruction, annihilation; — ة *fauta-t*, passing over (s.); payment.

فوتنج *fûtanaj*, mint (plant).

(فوج) *fâj*, U, INF. *fauj*, diffuse odour, perfume; be cold; — IV. INF. *ifâja-t*, run.

فوج *fauj*, pl. *fuwûj*, *afwâj*, pl. pl. *afâwij*, *afâwîj*, troop, number of men, legion, regiment, battalion; division, class, category.

(فوح) *fâḥ*, I, INF. *faiḥ*, be wide, spacious; — U, I, INF. *fauḥ*, *faiḥ*, *fuwûḥ*, *fayaḥân*, *fawaḥân*, diffuse odour, perfume; bleed abundantly (n.); boil; — IV. INF. *ifâḥa-t*, spread odour; bleed; shed blood; boil; (m.) uncover, make appear, show.

فوح *fauḥ*, pl. *afwâḥ*, odour; — ة *fauḥa-t*, a waft of odour.

فوحان *fawaḥân*, INF. of (فوح).

(فوخ) *fâḫ*, U, I, INF. *fauḫ*, *fawaḫân*, spread odour, emit scent;—INF. *fawaḫân*, blow (wind); break wind.

(فود) *fâd*, U, INF. *faud*, mingle one thing with another; die; run short, waste or dwindle away; last; — IV. INF. *ifâda-t*, kill; enrich lastingly.

فود *faud*, pl. *afwâd*, temple, where the hair is richest; rich lock of hair; the two halves of a load.

فودج *faudaj*, camel-litter.

(فور) *fâr*, U, I, INF. *faur*, *fu'ûr*, *fawarân*, boil, bubble; throw out foam or froth; rise, spout; fly into a passion; throb violently; cause to boil, to bubble; INF. *fawarân*, shed blood; INF. *fuwâr*, *fawarân*, spread odour; INF. *fawar*, provide a balance with فيارات *fiyârân*, q.v.; — II. INF. *tafwîr*, cause to boil, to bubble; (m.) hunt for rats and mice; prepare food for a confined woman; — IV. INF. *ifâra-t*, cause to boil, to bubble.

فور *faur*, ebullition; excitement, heat; hatred; precipitation; *faur-an*, من فوره *min fauri-hi*, at once, on the spur of the moment; — *fûr*, pl. of فائر *fâ'ir*, hind; — *fu'ar*, male mouse; — ة *faura-t*, violent outburst of anger; intense heat; mountain-ridge, table-land of a mountain; — *fûra-t*, young deer.

فوران *fawarân*, INF. of (فور).

(فوز) *fâz*, U, INF. *fauz*, take possession of, attain one's end, gain, win; take along with; escape; perish, die; — II. INF. *tafwîz*, die; — IV. INF. *ifâza-t*, cause one to obtain, to carry off; render successful, victorious.

فوز *fauz*, gain, success, victory; good fortune; escape, rescue; — ة *fauza-t*, victory and success.

(فوسق) *fausaq*, INF. ة, be consumed by an obnoxious worm (فاسوق *fâsûq*).

(فوش) *fâś*, U, INF. *fauś*, be haughty, vain-glorious, boast; float, drift; evaporate; subside; — II. INF. *tafwîś*, make drift, bring afloat again, help up; — ة *fauśa-t*, ebullition of anger; emptying (s.), decrease (m.).

فوشش *fauśaś*, INF. ة, be empty, spoiled (nut, &c.).

فوشق *fauśaq*, (m.) فوشك *fauśak*, pl. *fawâśîq*, *fawâśîk*, cartouche, charge of a gun or cannon.

(فوص) *fawaṣ*, III. INF. *mufâwaṣa-t*, explain a saying or tradition; — IV. INF. *ifâṣa-t*, id.

(فوض), II. *fawwaḍ*, INF. *tafwîḍ*, give full power, authority, jurisdiction to (الى *ila*); commit one's case to; bestow honours or favours upon; marry a woman without a dowry; — III. INF. *mufâwaḍa-t*, have equal rights with (acc.), enter into partnership on equal terms;

converse; compensate for; — v. INF. *tafawwuḍ*, be charged with, commissioned, authorised; — VI. INF. *tafâwuḍ*, have equal rights with one another, keep partnership, converse.

فوضوضى *fauḍûḍa*, partnership; community of property.

فوضى *fauḍa*=the previous; communism, anarchy; equally divided amongst all (cattle); mixed.

فوطة *fûṭa-t*, pl. *fuwaṭ*, *fûṭ*, apron, napkin; handkerchief; purse; treasury.

(فوغ) *fâg*, U, INF. *faug*, spread, emit scent; — ة *fauga-t*, scent, odour, fragrance.

(فوف) *fâf*, U, INF. *fauf*, make a sign with the nails of the thumb and fore-finger to declare "you shall not have as much as that"; — II. INF. *tafwîf*, stripe with white.

فوف *fûf*, ة, pl. *afwâf*, white spots on the finger-nails; pith of the papyrus.

فوفل *faufal*, *fûfal*, Indian betel-tree and its nut.

(فوق) *fâq*, U, INF. *fauq*, *fawâq*, *fawaqân*, be superior to, surpass; — INF. *fawâq*, *fuwâq*, hiccough, belch; — INF. *fuwâq*, *fuwûq*, expire; break an arrow at the notch; awake (n.), recover one's senses; (m.) remember; — *fawiq*, A, INF. *fâq*, *fauq*, *fawaq*, be broken at the notch; — II. INF. *tafwîq*, provide the arrow with a notch; (m.) awake (a.), make one recover his senses; (m.) remind (also *fayyaq*); — IV. INF. *ifâqa-t*, 1 pret. *afaqt-u*, *afwaqt-u*, place the arrow with its notch on the bow-string; recover (from illness, a swoon, &c.); — V. INF. *tafawwuq*, rise or exalt one's self above others; (m.) remember or try to remember; drink from time to time, one time after another; — X. INF. *istifâqa-t*, recover.

فوق *fauq*, upon, above, beyond, over; — *fûq*, ة *fûqa-t*, pl. *fuwaq*, *fûqa-n*, *afwâq*, lank and awkwardly built; notch of an arrow (du. *al-fûqân*, its ends); arrow; — ة *fawaqa-t*, highly educated men, orators.

فوقا *fauqâ'*, f. double-notched; gland of the penis.

فوقانى *fauqâniyy*, ة, upper; pointed at the top (letter).

فوقى *fauqiyy*, ة=the previous; — ة *fauqiyya-t*, superiority, superior rank.

(فول) *fûl*, ة, bean; vetch; — *fu'ul*, pl. of فال *fa'l*, omen, &c.

فولاذ *fûlâẓ* (also فولاد *fûlâd*), best steel.

(فوم) *fûm*, garlic; grey peas; wheat or other corn for bread; bread; — *fu'um*, pl. فئام *fi'âm*; — ة *fûma-t*, ear (of corn).

فونس *faunas*, INF. ة, fish at night by a lantern.

(فوه) *fâh*, U, INF. *fauh*, utter, speak; address (acc.); — *fawih*, A, INF. *fawah*, have a large mouth; — III. *fâwah*, *fâha*, INF. *mufâwaha-t*, *mufâhât*, converse; vie in glory with; — V. INF. *tafawwuh*, utter, deliver (a speech); — VI. INF. *tafâwuh*, converse with one another.

فوه *fûh*, pl. *afwâh*, *afhâh*, mouth; pl. *afwâh*, *afâwîh*, mouth, orifice; perfumes; fragrant flowers; =فوة *fuwwa-t*; — ة *fauha-t*, mouth, word; — *fûha-t*, *fuwwaha-t*, pl. *fûhât*, *fawâ'ih*, mouth, orifice, opening, entrance, crater; — ى *fûhiyy*, by word of mouth, oral.

فوها *fauhâ'*, f. of افوه *afwah*, having a large mouth, &c.

فويت *fuwait*, m. f. who acts wilfully.

فويق *fuwaiq*, a little above.

فويطة *fuwaiṭa-t*, strip of cloth.

فويه *fuwaih*, little mouth.

(فى) *fâ'*, I, INF. *fai'*, return;

change place and alter; gain booty; take back a divorced woman after paying a fine; — II. INF. *tafyi'a-t*, give shade; — IV. INF. *ifâ'a-t*, return; let return, lead back; give as booty; — V. INF. *tafayyu'*, be in the shadow, shade one's self; change place (shadow); — X. INF. *istifâ'a-t*, obtain as booty.

فى *fî*, in, among, with regard to, upon, on account of, in the midst of; oblique case of فو *fû*, mouth, &c.; — *fai'*, return; pl. *afyâ'*, *fuyû'*, shadow; booty, plunder; taxes, tribute; (m.) price, fee, tariff of post; pl. *fi'ât*, currencies, money-standards; — *fiyya*, concerning me, what regards myself, prep. فى with suffixed pronoun of the 1 person; my mouth, for فو *fû* with the same; — ة *fi'a-t*, pl. *fi'un*, *fi'ât*, army, troop; one's people.

فياح *fayâḥ*, f. *fayâḥ-i*, give way! cry of invaders; — *fayyâḥ*, ة, wide, vast; — ة *fayyâḥa-t*, f. with full udders.

فياد *fayyâd*, ة *fayyâda-t*, swaggering; male owl; devouring everything.

فياران *fiyârân*, du. the two prongs between which the tongue of a balance moves.

فياش *fiyâś*, boasting (s.); — *fayyâś*, boaster.

فياشل *fayâśil*, pl. of فيشلة *faiśala-t* = فيش *faiś*, ة.

فياض *fayyâḍ*, overflowing; most liberal and beneficent.

فياف *fiyâf*, pl. of فيف *faif*; — ى *fayâfî*, pl. of فيفا *faifâ'*.

فياق *fuyâq*, awakening (s.); remembrance, recollection (m.).

فيال *fiyâl*, *fayâl*, *fi'âl*, a game of children (hiding anything in the sand and guessing for it); — *fayyâl*, elephant-leader, karnak; — ة *fiyâla-t*, weakness of intellect, imbecility.

فئام *fi'âm*, pl. *fu'um*, padding of a camel-litter; crowd, troop.

فياة *fai'a-t*, return; time, season.

فيج *faij*, pl. *fuyûj*, runner, courier, satellite.

(فيح) *fâḥ*, I, INF. *faiḥ*, *fayaḥân*, spread; boil; bleed (n.); INF. *faiḥ*, *fuyûḥ*, spread fertility; — *fayiḥ*, A, INF. *fayaḥ*, make wide steps; be wide, spacious; — IV. INF. *ifâḥa-t*, cool, afford coolness.

فيح *fayaḥ*, spaciousness; — ة *faiḥa-t*, dish.

فيحا *faiḥâ'*, f. of افيح *afyaḥ*, roomy, spacious; spiced soup; name of Basra.

(فيحن) *faiḥan*, rue; — *faiḥan*, INF. ة, put rue into.

(فيخ) *fâḫ*, I, INF. *faiḫ* = (فوخ).

(فيد) *fâd*, I, INF. *faid*, moisten, wet; die; avoid, guard one's self against (عن *'an*); last; waste away, dwindle; be haughty (also V.); accrue, fall to one's share; (m.) profit, serve for; — II. INF. *tafyîd*, lend money on interest; — IV. INF. *ifâda-t*, profit (a.), bring advantage; serve for a lesson, afford instruction; allow to profit by (2 acc.); render services; bestow upon; profit (n.); give a complete sense or meaning; — V. INF. *tafayyud*, be lent on interest; see I.; — VI. INF. *tafâyud*, profit one another; — X. INF. *istifâda-t*, profit from or by; gain lasting wealth; seek or strive for profit.

فئد *fa'id*, v. see (فاد).

فيدم *faidam*, فيدن *faidan*, plummet, plumb-line (m.).

فيدوس *faidûs*, recreation, holidays (m.)

(فئر) *fa'ir*, ة, abounding in mice; — ة *fi'ara-t*, and—

فئران *fi'rân*, (m.) *fîrân*, pl. of فار *fa'r*, *fâr*, mouse, rat.

فيرورج *fîrûraj*, turquoise (Pers.).

(فيز) *fiyazz*, muscular; — VII. INF. *infiyâz*, separate (n.).

(فيش) *fâś*, I, INF. *faiś*, cover (he-ass); — also III. INF. *fiyâś*, *mufâyaśa-t*, be vain-glorious, boast falsely; — IV. INF. *ifâśa-t*, arrogate falsely.

فيش *faiś*, ة *faiśa-t*, gland of the penis.

(فيص) *fâṣ*, I, INF. *faiṣ*, depart, wander; cease; — IV. INF. *ifâṣa-t*, flee, run away.

فيصل *faiṣal*, decision; decree; separation; arbitrator, judge; — ة *faiṣala-t*, decision; — ى *faiṣaliyy*, arbitrator.

(فيض) *fâḍ*, I, INF. *faiḍ*, *fuyûḍ*, *fiyûḍ*, *faiḍûḍa-t*, *fayaḍân*, abound, flow freely; be unable to conceal, communicate; spread; become known; be superfluous; exceed; INF. *faiḍ*, *fuyûḍ*, die; — II. INF. *tafyîḍ*, cause to overflow; — IV. INF. *ifâḍa-t*, pour water over one's self; pour out; spread; give abundantly; give one's self to; flow in a discourse, be profuse or prolix, expatiate; return; — X. INF. *istifâḍa-t*, be brimful, on the point of overflowing; want one to pour out, to make overflow; spread (n.).

فيض *faiḍ*, pl. *fuyûḍ*, overflowing (s.), abundance, affluence; pl. *fuyûḍât*, inundations; unbounded liberality, generosity, clemency; death; the river Nile; river by Basra; excellent race-horse; — ة *faiḍa-t*, pouring out, overflowing (s.).

فيضان *fayaḍân*, فيضوضة *faiḍûḍa-t*, abundance, affluence, INF. of (فيض).

(فيظ) *fâẓ*, I, INF. *faiẓ*, *fuyûẓ*, *fayaẓân*, *faiẓûẓa-t*, die.

فيظ *faiẓ*, death.

فيع *fai'*, ة *fai'a-t*, beginning, undertaking (s.).

(فيف) *faif*, pl. *afyâf*, *fiyâf*, *fuyûf*, waste plain.

فيفا *faifâ'*, *faifan*, ة *faifât*, pl. *fayâfi*, dangerous desert, plain.

(فيق) *fâq*, I, INF. *faiq*, expire, die; — II. فيق *fayyaq*, see (فوق); — IV. INF. *ifyâq*, excel; — ة *faiqa-t*, pl. *faiq*, *afwâq*, pl. pl. *afâwîq*, awakening (s. n.); remembrance, recollection; flow of milk; gathering of the milk in the udder between two milkings; — *fîqa-t*, interval between two showers.

(فيل) *fâl*, I, INF. *fail*, *failûla-t*, be weak; — II. INF. *tafwîl*, weaken, render imbecile; deem to be so; — V. INF. *tafayyul*, grow big and strong like an elephant; grow big and fat; be weak; — X. INF. *istifyâl*, be like an elephant.

فيل *fîl*, pl. *afyâl*, *fuyûl*, *fiyala-t*, male elephant; bishop in chess; clumsy, heavy; imbecile, weak of intellect (also *fail*, *fayyil*); ذات الفيل *ẓât al-fîl*, elephantiasis; سن الفيل *sinn al-fîl*, ivory; — ة *fîla-t*, female elephant.

فيلق *failaq*, pl. *fayâliq*, army, legion; calamity; silkworm.

فيلسوف *failasûf*, *fîlasûf*, pl. *falâsifa-t*, philosopher, particularly applied to Aristotle.

فيلكون *failakûn*, roller for flattening the dough (m.).

فيلولة *failûla-t*, weakness of intellect, imbecility.

(فيم) *fayyim*, pl. *fuyûm*, strong man.

فيم *fîma*, فيما *fîmâ*=فى ما, while.

(فين) *fân*, I, INF. *fain*, come; (m.) also VI. INF. *tafâyun*, be miserly, niggardly; — ة *faina-t*, time, hour, moment; (m.) avarice, niggardliness.

فيه *fîh*, mouth; — *fî-hi*, in it, in him; — *fayyih*, ة, eloquent; voracious.

فيهج *faihaj*, cup; wine.

فيهك *faihak*, stupid woman.

فيو *fuyû'*, pl. of فى *fai'*.

فيوضات *fuyûḍât*, pl. of فيض *faid*.

فئون *fi'ûn*, pl. of فئة *fi'a-t*.

فيئة *fî'a-t*, return; = فياة *fai'a-t*, فئة *fi'a-t*.

ق

ق *q*, as a numerical sign=100; — *qi*, IMP. of (وقى), guard, protect, &c.

قا *qâ'*, see (قيا).

(قاب) *qa'ab*, INF. *qa'b*, eat; drink; —*qa'ib*, A, INF. *qa'b*, *qa'ab*, drink much, fill one's self with wine.

قاب *qâb*, distance, interval; length of the half of a bow; quantity; — ة *qâba-t*, egg.

قابض *qâbiḍ*, who seizes with the hand and holds; who takes possession of, sequestrates; tax-gatherer, collector; ق الارواح *qâbiḍ al-arwâḥ*, the angel of death, Israfil; pl. *-ât*, astringent (s.).

قابل *qâbil*, ة, who receives, accepts; who consents; who approaches, comes up; coming, future, next year; receptive, admitting, capable, worthy, susceptible, subject to; Cain; — ة *qâbila-t*, midwife; next night; — ية *qâbiliyya-t*, capacity, susceptibility, disposition, talent; possibility, feasibility; desire, appetite.

قاتر *qâtir*, well-proportioned, symmetrical; economical, thrifty, miserly.

قاتل *qâtil*, killing, fatal; pl. *qatala-t*, *quttâl*, murderer; ق الذئب *qâtil az-zi'b*, wolf's milk.

قاتم *qâtim*, قاتن *qâtin*, brown; blackish; dark.

قاتول *qâtûl*, murderer; shedding blood; — ى *qâtûliyy*, killing, fatal.

قاثم *qâsim*, very liberal.

قاحب *qâḥib*, violent, intense.

قاحد *qâḥid*, single, solitary.

قاحزات *qâḥizât*, pl. calamities.

قاحط *qâḥiṭ*, pl. *qawâḥiṭ*, hard, difficult.

قاحف *qâḥif*, pl. *quḥf*, carrying off everything.

قاحل *qâḥil*, dried up, withered.

قاحم قاحم *qâḥim qâḥim*, black.

قاحة *qâḥa-t*, inner courtyard.

قاحوف *qâḥûf*, ة *qâḥûfa-t*, shovel (m.).

قادح *qâdiḥ*, who strikes fire; slanderer; violent, intense; — ة *qâdiḥa-t*, worm (in a tooth or tree).

قادر *qâdir*, ة, powerful; absolute, despotic; equal to a thing, fit, capable.

قادم *qâdim*, pl. *qudum*, *quddâm*, who arrives, returns; in front, foremost; next, coming; pl. *qawâdim*, head; — ة *qâdima-t*, pl. *qawâdim*, front part; front piece of a saddle; vanguard; pl. the foremost feathers.

قادة *qâda-t*, pl. of قائد *qâ'id*.

قادوس *qâdûs*, pl. *qawâdîs*, bucket to draw water; vessel.

قادور *qâdûr*, misanthropist; — ة *qâdûra-t*, dirt, filth, sin.

قار *qâr*, pitch, tar; — *qârr*, ة, cold; comforting the heart; who dwells permanently; who avows, confesses; — ة *qâra-t*, pl. *-ât*, *qâr*, *qûr*, *qîrân*, isolated hill; large black stone.

قاراة *qârât*, fixed domicile, town, city.

قارب *qârib*, pl. *qawârib*, boat of a ship; who hastens to the water at night-time.

قارت *qârit*, bruised, crushed; discoloured; who takes everything for himself; best dry musk.

قارح *qâriḥ*, who has all his teeth; who has experienced much; lion; ة, pl. *qirâḥ*, *qawâriḥ*, *qurraḥ*, *maqâriḥ*, full-grown; five years old (cattle).

قارس *qâris*, very cold; icy; intense frost; old.

قارشة *qâriśa-t*, bleeding wound on the head.

قارص *qâriṣ*, who or what pricks; boy; sour; (m.) wooden lever, crowbar; — ة *qâriṣa-t*, pl. *qawâriṣ*, stinging taunt.

قارض *qâriḍ*, corrosive; gnawing, nibbling (adj.); money-lender.

قارظ *qâriẓ*, gathering the fruit of the acacia-tree or the leaves of the سلم *salam*, q.v.; رجع رجوع القارظين *raja'-a rujû'-a 'l-qâriẓain-i*, he never returns.

قارع *qâri'*, who knocks at the door; who casts lots; — ة *qâri'a-t*, pl. *qawâri'*, adversity, offence; evil; curse, bane; *al-qâri'a-t*, day of the last judgment; public road.

قارن *qârin*, companion, helper; who unites in couples; yokes together.

قرورة *qarûra-t*, pl. *qawârîr*, glass bottle, phial; alabaster vase; pupil of the eye.

قارون *qârûn*, Korah, according to the Mohammedans, a cousin of Moses, proverbial for his wealth and avarice.

قارى *qâri'*, pl. *-ûn*, *qurrâ'*, *qara'a-t*, reader, reader of the Koran; pious, devotee; dervish, monk; — *qârî*, inhabitant of a village; — ة *qâriya-t*, (m.) *qârriya-t*, pl. *qawârî*, a bird prognosticating rain; witness who spies upon others; testimony, evidence; point, edge.

قاز *qâzz*, Satan.

قازوزة *qâzûza-t*, pl. *qâzûz*, small goblet, cup.

قاس *qâs*, quantity, measure, length; — *qâs-in*, see قاسى *qâsî*.

قاسط *qâsiṭ*, unjust, tyrannical.

قاسى *qâsî* (قاس *qâs-in*), ة, pl. *qusât*, hard, unfeeling.

قاش *qâś*, cable; — قاش ماش *qâś mâś*, utensils, things, stuffs, materials.

قاشب *qâśib*, tailor; imbecile, weak of intellect.

قاشح *qâśiḥ*, thick, coarse (cloth).

قاشر *qâśir*, ة, peeling, &c., ag. of (قشر); the last horse in a race; all but skirting the ground.

قاشور *qâśûr*, ة, excoriating or skinning everything (adj.); year of famine; disastrous, calamitous; last horse in a race.

قاص *qâṣ-in*, see قاصى *qâṣî*; — *qâṣṣ*, narrator.

قاصب *qâṣib*, piper; butcher.

قاصد *qâṣid*, ة, pl. *quṣṣâd*, who intends, &c., ag. of (قصد); near; traveller; visitor; express (messenger), courier; (m.) delegate of the Pope.

قاصر *qâṣir*, ة, pl. *quṣṣar*, short, small, insufficient, defective; minor, under-aged; cold.

قاصعا *qâṣi'â'*, pl. *qawâṣi'*, hole of the field-mouse.

قاصل *qâṣil*, sharp.

قاصى *qâṣî* (قاص *qâṣ-in*), ة, pl. *aqṣâ'*, far distant; — ة *qâṣiya-t*, tract, region, district; pl. *qawâṣî*, small river.

قاض *qâḍ-in*, see قاضى *qâḍî*.

قاضب *qâḍib*, pl. *qawâḍib*, *quḍb*, sharp.

قاضوى *qâḍawiyy*, ة, judicial.

قاضى *qâḍî* (قاض *qâḍ-in*), pl. *quḍât*, who decides definitely; judge, cadi (ق القضاة *qâḍî al-quḍât*, chief justice); who makes an end of it, executes, performs a duty; — *qâḍiyy*, ة, judicial; — ة *qâḍiya-t*, fate, destiny, death; settled matter; alms.

قاطب *qâṭib*, frowning, &c., ag. of (قطب); who surrounds, invests; lion; (m.) cross-beam; — ة *qâṭiba-t*, everybody; *qâṭibat-an*, altogether; with or without negative: by no means, not at all.

قاطر *qâṭir*, dropping, &c., ag. of (قطر); resin, gum; (m.) mule.

قاطرجى *qâṭirjiyy*, muleteer (Turk.).

قاطع *qâṭi'*, pl. *quṭṭâ'*, cutting, &c., ag. of (قطع); (ق الطريق *qâṭi' aṭ-ṭarîq*, pl. *quṭṭâ'*, *quṭ'*, highwayman, robber; ق الرحم *qâṭi' ar-raḥim*, who abandons his people); sharp; penetrating; categorical; sour and thick; secant; (m.) lean; (m.) emaciating (adj.); (m.) river-bank (ق النهر *qâṭi' an-nahr*, on the other side of the river).

قاطن *qâṭin*, ة, pl. *quṭṭân*, *qaṭîn*, *qâṭina-t*, settled inhabitant, resident; servant.

قاطوع *qâṭû'*, worm in a fruit (m.).

قاع *qâ'*, pl. *qî'*, *qî'a-t*, *qî'ân*, *aqwu'*, *aqwâ'*, plain, flat tract of land; — ة *qâ'a-t*, paved courtyard, floor; upper state room; saloon; vast plain.

قاعد *qâ'id*, pl. *qu'ûd*, who sits, &c., ag. of (قعد); settled, resident; full so as to stand upright (sack); idle; pl. *qawâ'id*, who keeps indoors, matron; discharged soldier; dwarf palm; pl. *qa'ad*, sectarian, heretic; — ة *qâ'ida-t*, pl. *qawâ'id*, foundation, base, pedestal, foot of a column, &c.; fundamental rule, system, principle, canon; model, pattern; manner, way, method; usage; capital (town).

قاعف *qâ'if*, heavy shower; torrent.

قاعلة *qâ'ila-t*, pl. *qawâ'il*, high and extensive mountain-range.

قاف *qâf*, a fabulous mountain-chain; Caucasus; — *qâf-in*, see قافى *qâfî*; — ة *qâfa-t*, pl. of قائف *qâ'if*.

قافز *qâfiz*, pl. *qawâfiz*, rearing (horse).

قافل *qâfil*, dry; having a withered skin or hand; pl. *quffâl*, returning from a journey; — ة *qâfila-t*, pl. *qawâfil*, caravan.

قافور *qâfûr*, spathe of the palm-blossom.

قافوزة *qâfûza-t*, cup, wine-glass.

قافى *qâfî* (قاف *qâf-in*), follower, attendant, servant; — ة *qâfiya-t*, pl. *qawâfî*, rhyme, metre, poem; back of the neck.

(قاقا) *qa'qa'*, INF. ة, croak.

قاقا *qa'qâ'*, croaking (s.).

قاقلة *qâqulla-t*, قاقولة *qâqûla-t*, cardamum.

قاقم *qâqum*, ermine (Turk.).

قال *qâl-in*, see قالى *qâlî*; — قال و قيل *qâl wa qîl*, talk; — ة *qâla-t*, speech; rumour, report (evil); flow of talk.

(قالب) *qâlib*, turning, &c., ag. of (قلب); pl. *qawâlib*, form, mould, model; cast; last (of a shoemaker); material form, exterior; framework, scaffolding; variety; ق سكر *qâlib sukkar*, sugar-loaf.

قالبجى *qâlibjiyy*, founder.

قالبى *qâlibiyy*, cast in a mould.

قالم *qâlim*, pl. *qalama-t*, bachelor.

قالى *qâlî* (قال *qâl-in*), who roasts; who hates; — *qâliyy*, carpet, curtain.

قاليون *qâliyûn*, hydraulic pipe (Pers.).

قامة *qâma-t*, stature, figure; cubit (measurement); shirt; pl. *qiyam*, pulley of a well.

قاموس *qâmûs*, pl. *qawâmîs*, ocean, high sea, abyss of the sea; dictionary.

قاموع *qâmû'*, pl. *qawâmî'*, chimney; cone, anything conical (m.).

قان *qân*, a tree; — *qân-in*, see قانى *qânî*.

قانت *qânit*, ة, pious; assiduous in prayer.

قانص *qâniṣ*, hunter; — ة *qâniṣa-t*, pl. *qawâniṣ*, stomach and intestines of a bird, crop.

قانون *qânûn*, pl. *qawânîn*, fundamental rule, canon; law, norm, precept; law-code; duty, task; penance; a kind of cithern; — ى *qânûniyy*, canonical, according to law or rule, legal.

قانى *qânî* (قان *qân-in*), who owns, possessor; — *qâni'*, *qânî*, crimson.

قاه *qâh*, obedience; power, dignity.

قاهر *qâhir*, f. ة, victor, conqueror; victorious; — ة *qâhira-t*, victrix (Cairo); breast, bosom.

قاوق *qâwuq*, pl. *qawâwîq*, doctor's cap; hat of a Maronite priest (m.).

(قاى) *qa'a*, INF. *qa'y*, acknowledge a debt or obligation.

قائبة *qâ'iba-t*, egg (the breaking one).

قائت *qâ'it*, sufficient sustenance, competence.

قائد *qâ'id*, pl. *quwwâd*, *quwwad*, *qâda-t*, guide; leader, commander; police officer.

قائف *qâ'if*, pl. *qâfa-t*, who easily draws inferences from external signs, physiognomist; seeker for tracks.

قائل *qâ'il*, who says, speaks, &c., ag. of (قول); pl. *quwwal*, *quyyal*, *quwûl*, speaker; who firmly maintains a thing; author; pl. *qail*, *quyyal*, *quyyâl*, who makes a siesta; — ة *qâ'ila-t*, mid-day slumber, siesta.

قائم *qâ'im*, ة, pl. *quwwam*, *quyyam*, *quwwâm*, *quyyâm*, rising, standing, &c., ag. of (قوم); upright, vertical; unshakable; resisting; revolting against; lasting, enduring; steady; vigilant; hilt of a sword; pl. *qawama-t*, prefect, superintendant, guardian; — ة *qâ'ima-t*, pl. *qawâ'im*, foot of a quadruped; perpendicular (s.); right angle; leaf of a book, register, list, memorandum-book; invoice; ticket; bank-note; bulletin; hilt of a sword; trunk of a vine-tree; hour.

قائن *qâ'in*, Cain; — ى *qâ'iniyy*, قاينى *qâyîniyy*, referring to Cain, of Cain; (m.) bad, insupportable.

(قب) *qabb*, I, INF. *qabb*, cut off; (m.) lift a little; (m.) depart, flee; — I, INF. *qubûb*, brawl; relax, wither; — U, INF. *qabb*, *qabîb*, gnash the teeth; — I, U, INF. *qabb*, wither; — *qabb*, INF. *qabb*, also *qabib*, A, INF. *qabab*, be thin, slender; — II. INF. *taqbîb*, be dry, withered; provide a building with a cupola; make convex, vault; — V. INF. *taqabbub*, be provided with a cupola; be convex, vaulted; — V. INF. *inqibâb*, be lifted; — VIII. INF. *iqtibâb*, cut off the hand.

قب *qabb*, chief, prince, king (also *qibb*); good stallion; axle-tree; scale-beam; — *qibb*, extremity of the back-bone; — *qubb*, pl. of اقب *aqabb*, slender of waist; — ة *qibba-t*, *qiba-t*, tripe of a sheep; hedge-hog; — *qubba-t*, pl. *qibâb*, *qubab*, cupola, vault; alcove; tower; cathedral, dome; tent, tabernacle; sunshade; palanquin; litter, sedan-chair; mountain-summit; (m.) thick vine-pole; (m.) collar; scale-beam.

(قبا) *qaba'*, INF. *qab'*, eat; fill one's self with drink.

قبا *qabâ'*, pl. *aqbiya-t*, an upper garment, kaftan (Pers.); — ق قوسين *qibâ' qausain*, two lengths of a bow, two yards; — *qabbâ'*, f. of اقب *aqabb*, slender of waist.

قباب *qibâb*, a fish; pl. of قبة *qubba-t*; — *qubâb*, sharp; broad, flat; — *qabbâb*, lion.

قبابر *qabâbir*, pl. of *qubbara-t*.

قبابيع *qabâbî'*, pl. of قبوع *qabbû'*.

قباتر *qubâtir*, short, dwarfish.

قباح *qabâḥ*, upper joint of the knee; — *qibâḥ*, قباحى *qabâḥa*, pl. of قبيح *qabîḥ*; — *qubbâḥ*, bear; — ة *qabâḥa-t*, ugliness; vileness, ignominy, infamous action; INF. of (قبح).

قباض *qabbâḍ*, who seizes and holds, who grasps; also ة *qabbâḍa-t*, a good driver (of cattle, &c.); — ة *qabâḍa-t*, swiftness, quickness.

قباقيب *qabâqîb*, pl. of قبقاب *qabqâb*.

قبال *qibâl*, latchet of a sandal (m.)=*qubâlat-a* ; — ة *qabâla-t*, bail, security ; obligation by contract, stipulation ; rent-money ; — *qibâla-t*, id. ; office of a midwife ; — *qubâlat-a*, in front of, over against.

قبان *qabbân*, steelyard (sort of balance) ; who weighs for the market people ; حمار ق *ḥimâr-u qabbân-in*, cricket (insect).

قبائر *qabâ'ir*, pl. of قبرا *qubrâ'*.

قبب *qabab*, slenderness of the waist ; — *qubab*, pl. of قبة *qubba-t*.

قبتر *qubtur*, short, dwarfish.

(قبث) *qabas̱*, I, INF. *qabs̱*, seize and hold, grasp.

قبج *qabj*, ة *qabja-t*, pl. *qibâj*, partridge (Pers.).

(قبح) *qabuḥ*, INF. *qabḥ*, *qubḥ*, *qabâḥ*, *qubûḥ*, *qabâḥa-t*, *qubûḥa-t*, be ugly, vile, infamous, abominable ; — II. INF. *taqbîḥ*, make ugly, &c. ; treat as worthless or abject ; reproach with ; — III. INF. *muqâbaḥa-t*, treat with ignominy, revile, insult ; — IV. INF. *iqbâḥ*, utter vile, infamous, abominable things ; act meanly, shamefully ; — VI. INF. *taqâbuḥ*, revile one another ; — X. INF. *istiqbâḥ*, find or consider vile, abominable, &c. ; detest, abhor.

قبح *qabḥ*, *qubḥ*, ugliness, foulness, vice ; قبحا له *qubḥ-an la-hu*, abomination on him ! — ى *qabḥa*, pl. of قبيح *qabîḥ*.

(قبر) *qabar*, U, I, INF. *qabr*, *maqbar*, bury, inter ; plant afresh ; — II. INF. *taqbîr*, bury several dead ; cause to bury, have buried ; — IV. INF. *iqbâr*, make a tomb for ; have buried ; allow or order one's burial ; — VII. INF. *inqibâr*, be buried.

قبر *qabr*, pl. *qubûr*, tomb, sepulchre, sepulchral monument ; — *qubbar*, ة, pl. *qabâbir*, and—

قبرا *qubrâ'*, pl. *qabâ'ir*, sky-lark.

قبرس *qubrus*, Cyprus ; — ى *qubrusiyy*, of Cyprus.

(قبز) *qibz*, vile, mean, miserly ; short ; small.

(قبس) *qabas*, I, INF. *qabs*, fetch fire from (من *min*) ; learn from ; give fire ; teach ; borrow passages from an author ; — *qabis*, A, INF. *qabas*, fecundate quickly (stallion) ; — *qabus*, INF. *qabâsa-t*, id. ; — IV. INF. *iqbâs*, give fire ; teach ; — VIII. INF. *iqtibâs*, fetch fire from, kindle at ; learn from ; borrow passages from ; draw advantage from (من *min*) ; catch ; — X. INF. *istiqbâs*, ask for fire.

قبس *qabas*, fire kindled at a larger one, brand ; — *qibs*, root, origin ; — ة *qabsa-t*, fetching fire (s.) ; borrowing passages ; loan.

(قبص) *qabaṣ*, I, INF. *qabṣ*, take with the finger-tips, take a pinch ; stop an animal from drinking before it has quenched its thirst ; cover (stallion) ; be brisk, playful ; — ة *qabṣa-t*, *qubṣa-t*, pinch.

(قبض) *qabaḍ*, I, INF. *qabḍ*, close the hand, make a fist ; seize and hold, grasp ; arrest ; take away ; contract, astringe ; draw in the wings and pounce down ; receive money, cash a cheque, get payment ; keep back from ; — II. INF. *taqbîḍ*, give into one's hand to hold it ; collect ; make a payment to ; — V. INF. *taqabbuḍ*, contract (n.), shrink ; get constipated ; restrain one's self ; be paid, received ; — VI. INF. *taqâbuḍ*, receive mutually one's due (buyer and seller) ; — VII. INF. *inqibâḍ*, contract (n.), shrink ; shorten (n.) ; withdraw from the world ; get constipated ; be oppressed, grieved ; be received, paid.

قبض *qabḍ*, grasping (s.) ; taking possession (s.), possession ; confiscation ; constipation ; receipt

of a sum; suppression of the fifth letter of a foot when it is quiescent ; — *qabaḍ*, tribute, tax, impost; taking possession of another's property, usurpation ; — ﺓ *qabḍa-t*, closing of the hand; handle, haft, hilt (hence: sword, knife, &c.); — *qubḍa-t*, whát can be seized by the hand, handful.

(قبط) *qabaṭ*, U, INF. *qabṭ*, seize and hold, grasp; (m.) tremble with fear; — II. INF. *taqbîṭ*, make to tremble (m.) ; — V. INF. *taqab-buṭ*, tremble with fear (m.).

قبط *qibṭ*, Egypt; Copts;—ﺓ *qabṭa-t*, trembling from fear (s.) ; — ى *qibṭiyy*, *qubṭiyy*, ﺓ, pl. *qabâ-ṭiyy*, *qabâṭî*, Copt ;—ﺔ *qibṭiyya-t*, Egyptian linen.

(قبع) *qabaʿ*, INF. *qubûʿ*, draw in the head (hedgehog) ; cover the head with one's garment, &c.; lag behind; depart, travel; (m.) be slightly lifted up; (m.) pull out a tooth;=VIII.; — INF. *qabʿ*, bend the head in praying ; fetch a deep sigh ; grunt ; cry out, roar ; — II. INF. *taqbîʿ*, hide the head in one's clothes, under a hood, &c.; (m.) take away, lift up, gather ; (m.) cause one to flee, to run away ; —VII. INF. *inqibâʿ*, withdraw to its nest; — VIII. INF. *iqtibâʿ*, drink from the mouth of the water-bag.

قبع *qubʿ*, hood, cowl; trumpet ; — *qubaʿ*, hedgehog; — ﺓ *qubbaʿa-t*, hood, cowl.

(قبعثر) *qabaʿṯar*, having a huge body.

قباقب *qabqâb*, pl. *qabâqîb*, wooden shoes.

قبقب *qabqab*, INF. ﺓ, produce a sound: neigh, roar, growl, rumble, &c. ; be stupid, crazy ; (m.) lift slightly ; — II. INF. *taqabqub*, be slightly lifted ; wear wooden shoes (m.) ; — ﺓ *qabqaba-t*, voice; neighing (s.).

قبل *qabil*, A, INF. *qabûl*, *qubûl*, receive, accept, admit ; take from ; consent, agree; obey, yield to ; — *qabal*, U, INF. *qabl*, squint ; — U, INF. *qabl*, *qabûl*, *qubûl*, blow from the south ; — U, INF. *qabl*, set to a thing and persevere in it ; — A, INF. *qabl*, provide the sandal with a string or strap; approach, be near ; — *qabal*, U, also *qabil*, A, INF. *qibâla-t*, act as a midwife ; — A, I, U, INF. *qabâla-t*, stand security for (ب *bi*) ; — *qabil*, A, INF. *qabal*, squint ; — II. INF. *taqbîl*, kiss (respectfully) ; — INF. *taqabbul*, undertake a work by contract ; — III. INF. *muqâ-bala-t*, be in front of, stand opposite to (acc.) ; come to meet and receive friendly ; give an audience ; have an audience ; confront, compare, collate ; correspond to; compensate; punish; put a string to the sandal ; — IV. INF. *iqbâl*, approach ; come to meet and receive friendly ; turn towards (على *ʿala*) ; set zealously to (على *ʿala*) ; put a string to the sandal ; grow wise ; yield much (estate, &c.) ; thrive, be abundant ; — V. INF. *taqabbul*, receive ; accept; consent ; be granted, complied with ; be kissed ; travel to the south ; — INF. *taqbîl*, undertake by contract ; — VI. INF. *taqâbul*, meet face to face ; be confronted ; be compared, collated ; — VII. INF. *inqibâl*, be received, admitted ; — VIII. INF. *iqtibâl*, receive, accept; speak ex tempore ; begin, undertake ; — IX. INF. *iqbilâl* (also XI.), squint ; — X. INF. *istiqbâl*, go to meet and receive ; receive in a vessel, &c. ; place one's self in front of, opposite to (acc.) ; turn towards; impend ; — XI. INF. *iqbilâl*=IX.

قبل *qabl*, antecedency ; *qabl-un*,

qabl-u, من ق *min qabl-u*, *qabl-an*, previously, formerly; *qabl-a*, prep. before; — *qubl*, aim, intention, end; also *qubul*, pudenda; front part; beginning; — *qabal*, mountain-slope in front; mountain-summit; sand-hill; *qabal-an*, ex tempore; also *qubal-an*, *qubul-an*, for the first time; — *qibal*, side, direction; presence; power, authority; — ة *qibla-t*, side towards which one turns, especially in prayer, direction of Mecca (du. *qiblatân*, Mecca and Jerusalem); south; tomb of Mohammed; temple, altar; worship; manner, method; — *qubla-t*, kiss; bail, security; — *qabala-t*, spindle; shell or pearl used as an amulet; — ى *qibliyy*, southern, meridional; — ية *qibliyya-t*, compass showing the direction of Mecca.

(قبن) *qaban*, I, INF. *qubûn*, set out on a journey, go abroad; — II. INF. *taqbîn*, weigh by the steelyard; — IV. INF. *iqbân*, flee, run fast; — V. INF. *taqabbun*, be weighed by the steelyard.

(قبو) *qabâ*, U, INF. *qabw*, pick up; gather, cull; raise a building high; injure (على *ala*); — II. INF. *taqbiya-t*, prepare, range; cut out the material for a *qabâ'*; (m.) make a hole; (m.) make convex; — IV. INF. *iqbâ'*, provide a building with a cupola, vault; — V. INF. *taqabbî*, put on a *qabâ'*; (m.) be slightly vaulted, convex; (m.) grow proud.

قبو *qabw*, pl. *aqbiya-t*, vault, cellar, cave, cavity; (m.) stone building.

قبوع *qabbû'*, pl. *qabâbî'*, woollen cap.

قبول *qabûl* (*qubûl*), consent, acceptance; south wind, east wind; beauty; — ية *qabûliyya-t*, receipt, acknowledgment of a payment, &c.

قبيح *qabîḥ*, ة, pl. *qibâḥ*, *qabâḥa*, *qabḥa*, ugly, vile, infamous abominable; — ة *qabîḥa-t*, pl. *qabâ'iḥ*, infamy, vile action, abomination.

قبيصة *qabîṣa-t*, what is picked up; earth, gravel; — *qubaiṣa-t*, little screech-owl.

قبيض *qabîḍ*, constipated.

قبيل *qabîl*, bail, security; obedience, fellow-wife; kind, species, category; side; pl. *qubul*, mixed multitude, medley crowd; *qabîl-an*, before (me), in (my) presence; — *qubail-an*, a little before; — ة *qabîla-t*, pl. *qabâ'il*, nomadic tribe; generation, kinship.

قبين *qabîn*, quick in business.

(قت) *qatt*, U, INF. *qatt*, *qittîtâ*, interpret one's words falsely; calumniate, slander; spy after (الى *ila*); cut into strips; diminish (a.); prepare, make ready; gather by degrees; follow the track; — II. INF. *taqtît*, interpret falsely; — VIII. INF. *iqtitât*, uproot, eradicate, destroy.

قتا *qittâ'*, *quttâ'* (m.) = قثا *qiṯṯâ'*, *quṯṯâ'*.

قتات *qattât*, tale-bearer, spy.

قتاد *qatâd*, pl. *aqtâd*, *aqtud*, *qutûd*, a thorn-tree.

قتار *qutâr*, smell of roast meat, burnt food, &c.; perfume.

قتال *qatâl*, soul; remains of life; body; — *qitâl*, skirmish, battle, slaughter, massacre, INF. III. of (قتل); — *qattâl*, murderer; murderous; fatal; — *quttâl*, pl. of قاتل *qâtil*, killing, &c.

قتام *qatâm*, dust; dark reddish brown.

قتاية *qitâya-t*, cucumber (m.).

(قتب) *qatab*, INF. *qatb*, place roast tripe before one (acc.); — IV. INF. *iqtâb*, put a pack-saddle on the camel.

قتب *qitb*, ة, pl. *aqtâb*, intestine, tripe; small pack-saddle of a camel; vessels for a camel to

bear water; — *qatab*, pl. *aqtâb*, small pack-saddle; — *qatib*, close, miserly; easily provoked, irascible; — ى *qutabiyy*, belonging to the tribe قتيبة *Qutaiba-t*.

(قتد) *qatid*, A, INF. *qatad*, feed (n.) on the tree *qatâd*; have the stomach-ache from doing so; — II. INF. *taqtîd*, prepare food for the camel from this tree.

قتد *qatad*, pl. *qutûd*, *aqtud*, *aqtâd*, wooden framework of a camel-saddle, saddle; — ة *qatida-t*, f. having the stomach-ache from feeding on the tree *qatâd*.

(قتر) *qatar*, U, I, INF. *qatr*, *qutûr*, live economically, spend but little; be niggardly to one's people; spread a smell (roast meat, &c.); — *qatir*, A, INF. *qatar*, spread a smell; — II. INF. *taqtîr*, be niggardly to one's people (على *'ala*); — IV. INF. *iqtâr*=II.; be poor; — V. INF. *taqattur*, prepare for the combat.

قتر *qitr*, roundish head of an arrow; — *qutr*, *qutur*, tract, zone, region, side; — ة *qatra-t*, pl. *qatar*, dust upon anything; — *qitra-t*, devil; — *qutra-t*, pl. *qutar*, ambush of a hunter, hunting-hut.

(قتع) *qata'*, INF. *qutû'*, be vile, abject; — III. INF. *muqâta'a-t*, fight with, contend against (acc.).

(قتل) *qatal*, U, INF. *qatl*, *taqtâl*, kill, execute; beat; curse; mix water with wine; — II. INF. *taqtîl*, kill with one stroke; — III. INF. *qitâl*, *qîtâl*, *muqâtala-t*, fight one, wage war against; (m.) quarrel with; curse; — IV. give over to death, have one killed or executed; — V. INF. *taqattul*, make the utmost efforts, work one's self to death, stake one's life on a thing; be killed; — VI. INF. *taqâtul*, combat with one another, fight; — VI. INF. *inqitâl*, be killed; succumb; — VIII. *iqtatal* and *qittal*, aor. *yaqtatil*, *yaqattil*, combat with one another, fight; — X. INF. *istiqtâl*, seek death; stake one's life.

قتل *qatl*, ة, murder, execution; slaughter; — *qitl*, pl. *aqtâl*, enemy, adversary in a combat; equal, comrade, cousin; — *qutl*, *qutul*, pl. of قتول; — ة *qatla-t*, (m.) a sound thrashing; — *qitla-t*, way of killing, of executing a criminal; — *qatala-t*, pl. of قاتل *qâtil*, murderer; — ى *qatla*, pl. of قتيل *qatîl*; — *qatliyy*, murderer.

(قتم) *qatam*, U, INF. *qatûm*, rise; be dark-coloured, of a dark reddish brown; be dense; — *qatim*, A, INF. *qatam*, *qatâm*, rise; — IX. INF. *iqtimâm*, be dark-coloured, of a dark reddish brown; be dense; — ة *qatma-t*, a dark reddish brown; — *qatama-t*, bad smell.

(قتن) *qatan*, U, INF. *qutûn*, get dried; — *qatun*, INF. *qatâna-t*, eat but little; — IV. INF. *iqtân*, id.; emaciate (n.), grow thin; kill lice.

(قتو) *qatâ*, U, INF. *qatw*, *qat-an*, *qita-n*, *quta-n*, *maqta-n*, serve well (one's king, &c.); — VIII. INF. *iqtitâ'*, take into one's service.

قتود *qutûd*, pl. of قتاد *qatâd* and قتد *qatad*.

قتور *qatûr*, niggardly, miserly; — *qutûr*, niggardliness, avarice.

قتول *qatûl*, pl. *qutl*, *qutul*, bloodthirsty, sanguinary; — *qitwall*, stammerer; enervated.

قتيبة *qutaiba-t*, small piece of tripe; name of a tribe.

قتيتى *qittîtâ*, tale-bearing, INF. of (قت).

قتيل *qatîl*, ة, pl. *qatla*, killed, murdered; executed; who has succumbed.

(قث) *qas̱s̱*, U, INF. *qas̱s̱*, pull towards one's self; drive; cut down, pull out; — VIII. INF. *iqtis̱âs̱*, cut down, pull out.

قثا *qis̱s̱â'*, *qus̱s̱â'*, ة, cucumber; ق الحمار *qis̱s̱â' al-ḥimâr*, wild cucumber; — IV. INF. *iqs̱â'*, produce plenty of cucumbers.

قثام *qas̱âm*, female hyena; wench.

(قثد) *qas̱ad*, ة, a plant similar to the cucumber; — *qas̱ad*, I, INF. *qas̱d*, eat of this plant.

(قثر), V. INF. *taqas̱s̱ur*, be seized with fear, shrink back; — ة *qas̱ra-t*, and—

(قثرد) *qas̱rad*, *qis̱rid*, *qus̱rud*, household things, furniture.

(قثقث) *qas̱qas̱*, INF. ة, fill the measure to the brim; shake a pole to pull it out.

(قثم) *qas̱am*, U, INF. *qas̱m*, give the best part of one's own to another; — I, INF. hoard up; pollute with excrement; — *qas̱im*, A, INF. *qas̱am*, also *qas̱um*, INF. *qus̱ma-t*, be polluted with excrement; — *qas̱um*, INF. *qas̱m*, *qas̱âma-t*, be dusty; — VIII. INF. *iqtis̱âm*, hoard; take to one's self; carry along with; take all or great part; uproot, destroy; — ة *qus̱ma-t*, ash-colour; dust; pollution.

(قثو) *qas̱â*, U, INF. *qas̱w*, hoard; chew; — VIII. INF. *iqtis̱â'*, hoard.

قثول *qis̱wall*, stammerer, enervated; flaccid, withered.

قثى *qas̱a*=(قثو).

قثيثة *qas̱îs̱a-t*, herd; troop.

قثيرة *qus̱aira-t*, small furniture.

(قح) *qaḥḥ*, INF. *qaḥîḥ*, drink in large gulps; (m.) cough; — U, INF. *qaḥâḥa-t*, *quḥûḥa-t*, be pure, unmixed; be the pure truth; INF. *quḥûḥa-t*, be unripe, indigestible.

قح *quḥḥ*, pl. *aqḥâḥ*, pure, unmixed; genuine, truthful, unsophisticated; unripe, indigestible; — ة *qaḥa-t*, *qiḥa-t*, INF. of (وقح), be hard, be impudent, &c.; — *qaḥḥa-t*, cough (m.).

قحاب *qiḥâb*, pl. of قحبة *qaḥba-t*; — *quḥâb*, cough.

قحاح *quḥâḥ*, the best and purest; — ة *qaḥâḥa-t*, INF. of (قح).

قحاد *qiḥâd*, pl. of قحدة *qaḥada-t*; — *qaḥḥâd*, lonely, without a son or brother.

قحاف *qiḥâf*, wine; — *; — *quḥâf*, rapid; — ة *qaḥâfa-t*, taking everything (s.), making a clean dish of it.

قحامة *qaḥâma-t*, decrepit old age.

(قحب) *qaḥab*, U, INF. *qaḥb*, *quḥâb*, cough; (m.) lead a dissolute life; — II. INF. *taqḥîb*=I.; — ة *qaḥba-t*, cough; pl. *qiḥâb*, whore, prostitute.

(قحث) *qaḥas̱*, INF. *qaḥs̱*, seize from behind.

(قحثر) *qaḥs̱ar*, INF. ة, scatter from the hand.

(قحد) *qaḥad*, INF. *qaḥd*, have a large base of the hump; — ة *qaḥada-t*, pl. *qiḥâd*, base of a camel's hump; — *qaḥda-t*, having (adj.) a large base of the hump.

(قحر) *qaḥr*, pl. *quḥûr*, decrepitude from old age.

(قحز) *qaḥaz*, INF. *qaḥz*, jump about; be restless, agitated; cudgel; — INF. *qaḥz*, *quḥûz*, drop down like one dead; — II. INF. *taqḥîz*, cudgel; speak roughly to (ل *li*); incite, instigate; — V. INF. *taqaḥḥuz*, use rough language.

(قحزل) *qaḥzal*, INF. ة, throw down and cudgel.

(قحزن) *qaḥzan*, INF. ة, cudgel one so as to make him drop down; — II. INF. *taqaḥzun*, drop down under blows.

(قحش), III. *qâḥaś*, INF. *muqâḥaśa-t*, lead a toilsome life; — VIII. INF. *iqtiḥâś*, search or rummage in every direction.

(قحص) *qaḥaṣ*, INF. *qaḥṣ*, pass by rapidly, go away rapidly; sweep

the house; skip, jump; run; kick, push back; — II. INF. *taqḥîṣ*, push back with repeated kicks; keep one at a distance, turn off, refuse.

قحص *qaḥṣ*, jump, leap: rapid course; kick.

(قحط) *qaḥaṭ*, INF. *qaḥṭ*, beat violently; INF. *qaḥṭ*, *quḥûṭ*, also pass. *quḥiṭ*, be rainless and unfertile, fail, stop away; (m.) cleanse, rub or scrape off the dirt, polish, furbish; — *qaḥiṭ*, A, INF. *qaḥaṭ*, be rainless and unfertile; fail (rain); suffer from want of rain.

قحط *qaḥṭ*, scarcity of rain, drought and famine; want, need.

قحطان *qaḥṭân*, Qaḥṭân or Yoktân, ancestor of the South Arabians.

(قحطب) *qaḥṭab*, INF. ة, throw down; attack with the raised sword.

قحطى *qaḥṭiyy*, glutton, gormandizer.

(قحف) *qaḥaf*, INF. *qaḥf*, beat on the skull, break one's skull, wound at the head; — also VIII. INF. *iqtiḥâf*, drink out the vessel, make a clean dish of it, take everything.

قحف *qiḥf*, pl. *quḥûf*, *aqḥâf*, *qiḥafa-t*, skull; a round wooden cup; cap; — *quḥf*, pl. of قاحف *qâḥif*.

(قحقح) *qaḥqaḥ*, INF. ة, laugh aloud.

(قحل) *qaḥal*, INF. *qaḥl*, *quḥûl*, dry up (n.), wither, be dry; be nothing but skin and bones; pass. *quḥil*, and — *qaḥil*, A, INF. *qaḥal*, id.; — III. INF. *muqâḥala-t*, attend zealously to; — IV. INF. *iqḥâl*, dry (a.); cause one to be nothing but skin and bones.

قحل *qaḥl*, *qaḥil*, being nothing but skin and bones; dry, withered.

(قحم) *qaḥam*, U, INF. *quḥûm*, rush heedlessly into (فى *fî*); wander; come up, approach; — II. INF. *taqḥîm*, cause one to rush heedlessly into; spur one's horse into the river, &c.; throw off; — IV. INF. *iqḥâm*, id.; rush to ruin; — V. INF. *taqaḥḥum*, rush heedlessly into; — VIII. INF. *iqtiḥâm*, id.; let one's self down; plunge into (acc.).

قحم *qaḥm*, reckless, foolhardy undertaking; ة, old, decrepit; — ة *quḥma-t*=*qaḥm* (s.); pl. *quḥam*, dangers, difficulties; distress of a year of famine.

(قحو) *qaḥâ*, U, INF. *qaḥw*, take all of.

قحوان *quḥwân*, pl. *aqâḥ-in*, *aqâḥiyy*, camomile.

قحوحة *quḥûḥa-t*, INF. of (قح).

قحوط *quḥûṭ*, drought, year of famine.

قحوم *qaḥûm*, decrepit; — ة *quḥûma-t*, decrepitude.

قحيط *qaḥîṭ*, dry, hard.

(قخر) *qaḥar*, INF. *qaḥr*, strike anything dry or hard against another.

(قخز) *qaḥaz*, INF. *qaḥza-t*=the previous.

(قد) *qadd*, U, INF. *qadd*, cut, tear (a.), cut or tear into strips, shred; cut off at the root; break off a speech; wander all through the desert; — II. INF. *taqdîd*, cut or tear entirely; shred, cut into long strips (meat to dry it); — V. INF. *taqaddud*, be cut into strips; — VII. INF. *inqidâd*, id.; be split; — VIII. INF. *iqtidâd*=VII.; cut, tear; arrange affairs; — X. INF. *istiqdâd*, proceed steadily in the same way.

قد *qad*, really, certainly; already; just now; sometimes; enough, sufficient for (acc. or gen. in construction, as: قد زيدا درهم *qad zaid-an dirham-un*, or قد زيد د *qad-u zaid-in dirham-un*, a dirham is sufficient for Zaid); — *qadd*, pl. *qidâd*, *qudûd*, *aqudd*, *aqidda-t*, stature, size, figure; length; definite measure or quantity

(قد اى شى qadd-u ayy-i śa'y-in, (m.) قد ايش qadd eś, قداش qaddâś, how much? بقدايش bi-qadd-eś, for how much? at what price?); equal of a person or thing; lamb's-skin; strip, shred; split; cæsura;—qidd, pl. qudûd, aqudd, strip of untanned leather; strap, scourge; a leathern vessel; — ة qidda-t, pl. qidad, aqidda-t, strip of untanned leather; troop, sect.

قداح qaddâḥ, who strikes fire; flint-stone, tinder-box, matches (also ة qaddâḥa-t); glass and crockery-ware maker; — *; — ة qidâḥa-t, fabrication of crockery and glass-ware.

(قداحس) qudâḥis, brave one, hero; lion.

قداد qadâd, hedgehog; — *

قداديس qadâdîs, pl. of قداس quddâs.

قداديم qadâdîm, pl. of قدوم quddûm.

قدار qidâr, qudâr, power, influence; valuation, estimation; — qudâr, cook; — ة qadâra-t, power.

قداس qudâs, rosary; — quddâs, pl. qadâdîs, host, holy wafer, mass, liturgy; — ة qadâsa-t, holiness.

قداش qaddâś, how much? see قد qadd.

قداف qudâf, plate, dish.

قدام qudâm, old; — qaddâm, qud-dâm, leader, prince; — quddâm, butcher; front part; quddâm-a, in front of, before, towards, in the direction of; ق البعض qud-dâm-a 'l-ba'ḍ, a short time ago; pl. of قادم qâdim; — ى qudâma, pl. of قديم qadîm; — qudâmā, vanguard of an army.

قدائم qadâ'im, pl. of قدوم qadûm and قديمة qadîma-t.

(قدح) qadaḥ, INF. qadḥ, strike fire; bore; revile, curse, attack one's pedigree; take out with a ladle; (also II.) sink into its socket (eye); — II. INF. taqdîḥ, make many holes in, pierce in many places; see I.; — V. INF. taqad-duḥ, VII. INF. inqidâḥ, be perforated, pierced; — VIII. INF. iqtidâḥ, strike fire; take out with a ladle.

قدح qadḥ, fire produced by rubbing the fire-sticks; rebuke, abuse, curse, imprecation, satire; — qidḥ, pl. qidâḥ, aqduḥ, aqdâḥ, aqâdîḥ, arrow (without head and feathers to be used in casting lots), lot, portion; satire, epigram; hole, perforation; — qadaḥ, pl. aqdâḥ, drinking-cup, tumbler; — ة qad-ḥa-t, qidḥa-t, a striking of the fire-sticks; — qudḥa-t, broth.

قدد qidad, pl. of قدة qidda-t.

(قدر) qadar, I, U, INF. qudra-t, maqdara-t, maqdira-t, muqdura-t, qadâra-t, qudûra-t, qudûr, qidrân, qudrân, qadâr, qidâr, be able; — INF. qadr, prize highly, value, honour; estimate, appreciate; — U, I, INF. qadr, measure, take one's measurement; make one thing proportionate to another, fit (a.); suppose, take for granted; — I, INF. qadâra-t, prepare, make ready; fix a time for (acc.); — U, I, INF. qadr, qadar, decree for, destine to (على 'ala), fix one's fate; oppress; distribute; — INF. qadr, cook in a pot or kettle; — qadir, A, INF. qadar, be able; have a short neck; — II. INF. taqdîr, preordain for (على 'ala); dispose; consider a thing well; render possible, facilitate; make powerful; fix in measure and quantity and distribute; value, estimate; (m.) take one's measurement; make proportionate, fit (a.); suppose, take for granted; — IV. INF. iqdâr, make powerful; give authority over; — V. INF. taqaddur, be pre-ordained; be well considered and managed; have the power or meaning of, be equal in sense with; (m.) be supposed, taken for granted;

— VIII. INF. *iqtidâr*, be powerful, have great influence; become rich and powerful.

قدر *qadr*, pl. *aqdâr*, pre-ordained destiny, predestination, fate; will of God, divine decree, providence; might, power, position, influence, wealth; measure, dimension, quantity; worth, value; ليلة القدر *lailat al-qadr*, the night when the Koran was sent down; — *qidr*, ة, pl. *qudûr*, *qidarât*, *qidirât*, *aqdur*, pot, kettle; — *qudr*, measure and quantity; price, value, worth; — *qadar*, pl. *aqdâr*, fate, destiny; power; definite measure or quantity; amount; — ة *qadra-t*, measurement of a cloth, shoe, &c.; — *qudra-t*, might, power, authority, wealth; omnipotence; courage; — *qadara-t*, narrow bottle.

قدران *qidrân*, power, INF. of (قدر).

قدرتى *qudratiyy*, done by the omnipotence of God.

قدرى *qadriyy*, predestined by fate; an order of dervishes; — *qadariyy*, who believes in the freedom of will (opposed to جبرى *jabariyy*, fatalist); — ة *qadariyya-t*, sect of such believers.

(قدس) *qadus*, U, INF. *quds*, be pure, immaculate, holy; — II. INF. *taqdîs*, purify; sanctify; consecrate to God; say or hear the mass; — V. INF. *taqaddus*, be purified, sanctified, consecrated; — VI. INF. *taqâdus*, play the saint; — X. INF. *istiqdâs*, deem holy.

قدس *quds*, purity, holiness; Paradise; *al-quds*, Jerusalem; — *qadas*, small cup or plate; — *qudus*, purity, sanctity; saint, holy; — ى *qudsiyy*, holy; paradisiac; of Jerusalem; Gabriel.

(قدع) *qada'*, INF. *qad'*, keep back, restrain; prevent, hinder; dispatch, execute; drink intermittingly; — *qadi'*, A, INF. *qada'*, be weak; be near, impend; — IV. INF. *iqdâ'*, restrain; prevent.

قدع *qadi'*, ة, timid; modest; not drinkable; blear-eyed; — ة *qid'a-t*, a short overcoat.

(قدف) *qadaf*, U, INF. *qadf*, scoop water with the hand; exhaust; pour out; (m.) keep off, prevent.

(قدم) *qadam*, U, INF. *qudm*, *qudûm*, precede, step in front of, approach, come up; arrive; return, come back; attack; be bold; — *qadim*, A, INF. *qudûm*, *qidmân*, *maqdam*, return from a journey; come to, arrive at (acc.); approach, step up to (على *'ala*); — *qadim*, A, INF. *qadam*, be bold; — *qadum*, INF. *qidam*, *qadâma-t*, precede in time, be old or ancient; be eternal; — II. INF. *taqdîm*, *taqdima-t*, bid to advance, to attack boldly, to lead; make one a leader, chief, judge; step in front, lead; send in advance; do a thing before another; prefer; place before, offer; order, command; — IV. INF. *iqdâm*, bid to advance, to attack boldly; advance boldly to the attack; undertake courageously, be bold; — V. INF. *taqaddum*, pass. of the active meanings of II.; = II. in its neuter meanings; — VI. INF. *taqâdum* = *qadum*; — VII. INF. *inqidâm*, be measured by feet (m.); — X. INF. *istiqdâm*, want to take the lead, lead; show one's self eager to advance or attack boldly; send in advance; deem old or ancient.

قدم *qadm*, INF. of the previous; a red cloth; — *qidm*, *qidam*, olden times, former centuries; *qidman*, of old, once on a time, formerly; — *qadam*, pl. *aqdâm*, *aqdum*, foot, front part of the

foot; step; foot or step as a measurement; precedence; place of honour; pre-eminence; m. f. sing. and pl. (f. also ة), pre-eminent; — also *qadim*, ة, bold; — *qidam*, precedence, preference; antiquity; — *qudum*, advance; valiant; pl. of قادم *qâdim* and قدوم *qadûm*; — ة *qudma-t*, pompous way of walking; advance to the attack, boldness; step, track; precedence; preliminary steps; — *qadama-t*, step; degree, grade.

قدما *qudamâ'*, pl. of قديم *qadîm*.

قدمان *qidmân*, return, — ى *qudmâniyy*, front part, front.

قدموس *qudmûs*, pl. *qadâmîs*, old, ancient.

قدومية *qudûmiyya-t*, pre-eminence; pomposity.

(قدن) *qadn*, sufficiency.

(قدو) *qadâ*, U, INF. *qadw*, *qadâwa-t*, taste nice; arrive, return; be near; — قدى *qadî*, A, INF. *qadan*, *qadâwa-t*, taste nice; — V. INF. *taqaddî*, keep on the right way; — VIII. INF. *iqtidâ'*, imitate, emulate, copy; — ة *qadwa-t*, *qidwa-t*, *qudwa-t*, model for imitation, good example; pattern; trodden path.

قدورة *qadûra-t*, power, influence.

قدوس *qadûs*, bold; — *qaddûs*, *quddûs*, pure, holy; most holy; — ية *qudûsiyya-t*, holiness, sanctity.

قدوم *qadûm*, advancing boldly; pl. *qadâ'im*, *qudum*, also *quddûm*, pl. *qadâdîm*, hatchet, axe; — *qudûm*, arrival, return (especially from the pilgrimage); first appearance; accession to the throne; — ية *qudûmiyya-t*, present of welcome, welcome.

(قدى) *qada*, I, INF. *qady*, taste nice; come out of the desert through famine; INF. *qadayân*, run fast; — III. INF. *muqâdât*, act in an opposite manner to (acc.).

قدى *qadiyy*, tasting or smelling nice; — ة *qidya-t*, condition, state; manner, custom; — *qadiyya-t*, present.

قديد *qadîd*, shreds of meat dried in the sun.

قديديون *qadîdiyyûn*, followers of an army, especially artizans, &c.

قدير *qadîr*, powerful; all-powerful, omnipotent; able to; cooked in a pot or kettle; — *qudair*, ة *qudaira-t*, small pot.

قديم *qadîm*, ة, pl. *qudamâ'*, *qudâma*, *qadâ'im*, old, ancient; eternal; — *qiddîm*, leader, prince; — ى *qadîmiyy*, old, ancient, antiquated, old-fashioned.

(قذ) *qaẕẕ*, INF. *qaẕẕ*, clip accurately; — also IV. INF. *iqẕâẕ*, feather an arrow; — ة *quẕẕa-t*, pl. *quẕaẕ*, feather, feathering of an arrow; ear; lip of the pudenda; pl. *qiẕẕân*, flea.

قذا *qaẕ-an*, ة *qaẕât* = قذى *qaẕa-n*.

قذاذة *quẕâẕa-t*, filing of metal; pl. *quẕâẕât*, filings.

قذاريف *qaẕârîf*, pl. of قذروف *quẕrûf*.

قذاف *qiẕâf*, swift gallop; — * ; — *qaẕẕâf*, who flings with all his might; rower, galley-slave; also ة *qaẕẕâfa-t*, scales of a balance; ballista, catapult.

قذال *qaẕâl*, pl. *quẕul*, *aqẕila-t*, hind-part of a horse's head.

قذان *qiẕẕân*, and—

قذذ *quẕaẕ*, pl. of قذة *quẕẕa-t*, hind-part of the head; flea.

(قذر) *qaẕar*, U, INF. *qaẕr*, be unclean, soiled; soil; — *qaẕir*, A, INF. *qaẕar*, be unclean, soiled; have anything dirty; — *qaẕur*, INF. *qaẕâra-t*, be unclean, soiled; — II. INF. *taqẕîr*, soil; — IV. INF. *iqẕâr*, make many words; — V. INF. *taqaẕẕur*, find unclean, dirty, and turn from with disgust; keep clean, guard against (عن *'an*).

قذر *qaẕar*, pl. *aqẕâr*, dirt, uncleanliness; — *qaẕir*, *qaẕr*, *qaẕar*, *qaẕur*,

ة, dirty; — ة quẓara-t, who is anxious to keep clean.

قذروف quẓrûf, pl. qaẓârîf, vice, opprobrium, reproach.

قذع qaẓa‘, cudgel; abuse; — II. INF. taqẓî‘, soil; — III. INF. muqâẓa‘a-t, surpass in abuse; — IV. INF. iqẓâ‘, abuse.

قذع qaẓa‘, filthy talk, filth.

(قذف) qaẓaf, I, INF. qaẓf, throw, cast, fling; drive away by throwing stones at; abuse, accuse of fornication or adultery; vomit, expectorate; row; — II. INF. taqẓîf, abuse, imprecate; vomit; row; — VI. INF. taqâẓuf, throw stones at one another, abuse one another, repel; — X. INF. istiqẓâf, throw stones at, abuse.

قذف qaẓf, abuse; accusation; rowing (s.); also qaẓaf, pl. quẓâf, quẓufât, side of a valley, river-bank; — qaẓaf, quẓuf, far distant; — ة quẓfa-t, pl. quẓaf, quẓuf, qiẓâf, quẓufât, battlement; mountain-peak.

(قذقذ), II. INF. taqaẓquẓ, ascend a mountain; fall into a well and perish.

(قذل) qaẓal, U, INF. qaẓl, beat on the hind-part of the head; swerve from what is right, act unjustly; accuse; be zealous, eager.

قذل qaẓl, wrong (s.) — qaẓal, vice; reproach; — quẓul, pl. of قذال qaẓâl.

(قذم) qaẓam = قثم qasam; — qaẓim, A, INF. quẓma-t, sip; — VII. INF. inqiẓâm, hasten (n.).

قذم qaẓim, quẓam, violent and quick; very liberal; — quẓum, pl. perennial wells in the rock.

(قذن), IV. aqẓan, display many vices.

قذوف qaẓûf, far distant.

(قذى) qaẓa, I, INF. qaẓy, qaẓan, quẓiyy, qaẓayân, exude a white matter (eye); step up to; — qaẓî, A, INF. qaẓan, qaẓayân, catch a mote, ache from a mote; — II. INF. taqẓiya-t, set a mote in the eye; pluck out a mote; — III. INF. muqâẓât, impart, requite; — IV. INF. iqẓâ’, set a mote into the eye.

قذى, قذا, ة qaẓan, ة qaẓât, mote in the eye; — qaẓî, qaẓiyy, suffering pain from a mote in the eye, aching; — qiẓa, pl. aqẓâ’, quẓiyy, earth reduced to powder.

(قر) qarr, I, INF. qarr, qarâr, qurûr, taqirra-t, stay permanently in a place, dwell quietly; persist; — I, drink its fill at a time; be satisfied at a time; INF. qarr, qarîr, cease to cluck; — U, INF. qarîr, hiss; — A, I, U, be cold, fresh (pass. qurr, suffer from cold, freeze); pour cold water into the boiling kettle or over one's head; whisper secrets; — I, INF. qarra-t, qurra-t, qurûr, be refreshed or consoled by a pleasant sight (eye), (pass. قر به عينا qurr-a bi-hi ain-an, be quieted and consoled by); (m.) confess, avow; — II. INF. taqrîr, cause one to stay, to reside permanently; aver, state the proofs of a fact; decide upon, determine; draw up a document; force to confess; — III. INF. qirâr, muqârra-t, be quiet; share with another (acc.) an easy mind about a thing; persist together with another; dwell permanently together with another; — IV. INF. iqrâr, cause to stay permanently, settle (a.); leave one quiet at his work; visit with cold; cool one's eye, i.e. quiet and console him; confess the truth; — V. INF. taqarrur, be stated, proved, averred, ratified; be determined, decided upon; be confessed; — VIII. INF. iqtirâr, adhere to; refresh one's self with, treat one's self to; — X.

INF. *istiqrâr*, settle (n.), dwell permanently, inhabit; rest, refresh one's self; force to confess.

قر *qar'*, *qur'*, pl. *qurû'*, *aqrâ'*, *aqru'*, menses; being clear of them; pl. *aqrâ'*, rhyme; — *qarr*, fixed residence, settlement; rest; fowl; comfort of the eye; ة, cold, fresh; — *qirr*, green frog; — *qurr*, freshness, cold; cold of winter; resting-place; — ة *qira-t*, INF. of (وقر); modest, steady deportment; flock with herdsman; family; — *qarra-t*, *qirra-t*, *qurra-t*, frog; — *qirra-t*, freshness, cold; — also *qurra-t*, cooling, i.e. comfort of the eye, darling; cress.

(قرا) *qara'*, A, U, INF. *qar'*, *qara'*, *qirâ'a-t*, *qur'ân*, read; read to or with; receive instruction from (على *'ala*); recite; quote from the Koran; present in the name of another; — INF. *qara'*, *qarâ'*, pick up, gather; — INF. *qarâ'*, *qurû'*, conceive, get big with young, give birth; — II. INF. *taqri'a-t*, make or teach one to read; — III. INF. *qirâ'*, *muqâra'a-t*, read with (acc.); — IV. INF. *iqrâ'*=II.; send in writing (greetings, &c.); have the menses; be clear of them; — V. INF. *taqarru'*, devote one's self to sacred studies and piety; — VII. INF. *inqirâ'*, be read, recited; — VIII. INF. *iqtirâ'*, read, recite; transmit a greeting; — X. INF. *istiqrâ'*, ask one to read; desist from the she-camel (stallion).

قرا *qaran*, back; — *qarâ'*, *qirâ'*, INF. of (قرا) and (قرى); — *qarrâ'*, pl. *qarrâ'ûn*, who reads well; — *qurrâ'*, pl. *qurrâ'ûn*, *qarâri'*, monk, holy man; pl. of قارى *qâri'*; — ة *qir'a-t*, plague, epidemic (s.); — *qara'a-t*, pl. of قارى *qâri'*, reader; — *qirâ'a-t*, reading (s.), reading of the Koran.

قراب *qarâb*, near; — *qirâb*, pl. *qarub*, sheath, scabbard, case, etui; quiver; pl. of قربان *qarbân* and قريب *qarîb*; — *; — *qurâb*, sagacity; — *qarrâb*, pedestrian, foot-soldier; — ة *qarâba-t*, pl. *-ât*, *qarâ'ib*, kinship, relations; — *qirâba-t*, night-march to get to the water; — *qarrâba-t*, bottle, decanter.

قرابيس *qarâbîs*, pl. of قربوس *qarabûs*, *qurbûs*.

قرابين *qarâbîn*, pl. of قربان *qurbân*.

قراح *qarâḥ*, pl. *aqriḥa-t*, sown field without trees upon; ground free of salt; pure (water); — *qirâḥ*, pl. of قارح *qâriḥ*, full-grown, &c.

قراد *qurâd*, pl. *qirdân*, tick (insect), louse; nipple; — *qarrâd*, monkey leader; — ى *qarrâdiyy*, little ass of a monkey leader.

قرار *qarâr*, ة *qarâra-t*, fixed residence, domicile; secure dwelling; stability; steadiness; perseverance; rest, quietude; patience; assurance, promise, agreement; security; truth; consent; deepest spot, bottom, low plain; pool; — ة *qurâra-t*, what remains in the pot and is washed out of it; — ى *qarâriyy*, permanently settled; artizan, working man, firmly agreed upon; (m.) truthful; — *qarâri'*, pl. of قرا *qurrâ'*.

قراريط *qarârîṭ*, tamarind-seed; pl. of قراط *qirrâṭ* and قيراط *qîrâṭ*, carat.

قراسة *qarrâsa-t*, refrigerator.

قراسيا *qarâsiyâ*, قراسية *qarâsiya-t*, see قراصيا *qarâṣiyâ*.

قراسم *qarâsim*, ة *qarâsima-t*, tick (insect), louse.

قراص *qurrâṣ*, camomile; احمر ق *aḥmar qurrâṣ*, crimson; — ة *qarrâṣa-t*, reviler, censurer, fault-finder.

قراصيا *qarâṣiyâ*, قراصية *qarâṣiya-t*, cherry; a kind of plum.

قراض *qirâḍ*, sleeping partnership; loan raised by a governor on interest; debt; — ة *qurâḍa-t*, what falls off in nibbling; dross, filings.

قراضبة *qarâḍiba-t*, pl. of قرضاب *qirḍâb*, قرضوب *qurḍûb*.

قراط *qirâṭ*, candle, lamp; wick; candle-snuff; pl. *aqriṭa-t*, ring for a (camel's) nose; — *qirrâṭ*, pl. *qarârîṭ*, carat.

قراطيس *qarâṭîs*, pl. of قرطاس *qarṭâs*.

قرافة *qarâfa-t*, cemetery; — *qurâfa-t*, a kind of bark (of a tree).

قراقر *qarâqar*, rumbling (s.), rumbling noise, noise; — *qurâqir*, ى *qurâqiriyy*, melodious.

قراقير *qarâqîr*, pl. of قرقور *qurqûr*.

قرام *qirâm*, pl. *qurum*, embroidered curtain, coverlet, veil.

قراميد *qarâmîd*, pl. of قرمود *qurmûd*.

قراميل *qarâmîl*, pl. of قرمول *qurmûl*.

قران *qirân*, close union, association; pilgrimage in common; conjuncture of the planets; — * ; — *qur'ân*, *qurân*, reading (s.); piece for reading, book; the Koran; — *qarrân*, bottle; — ى *qurâna*, pl. closely united; — *qur'âniyy*, referring or belonging to the Koran.

قراية *qirâya-t*, reading (s.).

(قرب) *qarab*, U, INF. *qirâba-t* (also *qarib*, A, INF. *qarab*), travel the night through in order to get to the water; — U, INF. *qarb*, sheathe the sword; — *qarib*, A, INF. *qirbân*, be near to (acc.); feel pain in the hypochondrium; — *qarub*, INF. *qurb*, *qirbân*, *qurbân*, be near to (من *min*, الى *ila*, or acc.); approach; impend; be closely related; — II. INF. *taqrîb*, bring near, lead up, approach (a.); present, offer, offer up a sacrifice; (m.) give the holy communion; lift up the two front feet at the same time; — III. INF. *qirâb*, *muqâraba-t*, be near to (acc.); live close by; approach; be on the point of; be nearly full; be closely related; — IV. INF. *iqrâb*, nearly fill up; sheathe the sword; be on the point of parturition; — V. INF. *taqarrub*, *tiqirrâb*, approach, come nearer; seek greater intimacy or relationship with (الى *ila*); curry favour with; (m.) communicate (n.); — VI. INF. *taqârub*, be near one another; approach one another; come nearer; — VIII. INF. *iqtirâb*, approach; — X. INF. *istiqrâb*, find near; prefer and take the thing nearest at hand.

قرب *qurb*, (m.) *qirb*, nearness of place, time or relationship; also *qurub*, pl. *aqrâb*, *qurûb*, hypochondres; — *qarab*, night-march to the watering-place; relationship; pain in the hypochondres; — *qurub*, pl. of قراب *qirâb*; — ة *qirba-t*, pl. *qirbât*, *qirabât*, *qiribât*, *qirab*, skin bag for milk or water; — *qurba-t*, pl. *qurab*, *qurubât*, kinship, relations; pious offering to conciliate the favour of God; service.

قربوس *qarabûs*, *qurbûs*, pl. *qarâbîs*, pommel of a saddle, front saddle-bow; ق الذقن *qurbûs az-zaqn*, chin.

قربى *qarba*, f. of قربان *qarbân*; — *qurbâ*, kinship; — ة *qurbiyya-t*, nearness, proximity.

(قرت) *qarat*, U, INF. *qurût*, dry up and gather beneath the skin (discoloured blood); bruise; — *qarit*, A, INF. *qarat*, be discoloured, have disfigured features.

قرت *qarat*, ice, snow; jelly; — du. *qarratân*, morning and evening; — ة *qarta-t*, bruise; cataract (of the eye).

(قرث) *qaraṡ*, U, INF. *qarṡ*, grieve (a.); — *qariṡ*, A, INF. *qaraṡ*, toil for gain.

(قرثع) *qarsa'*, stupid and impudent (woman).

(قرح) *qaraḥ*, INF. *qarḥ*, wound; hurt with words; cover with ulcers; bring on an ulcer or abscess; convict of wrong; dig a well in a waterless place; (m.) cough; — A, INF. *qurûḥ*, have all its teeth, be five years old; be visibly big with young; —*qariḥ*, A, INF. *qaraḥ*, be covered with ulcers; ulcerate; have all its teeth; — II. INF. *taqrîḥ*, accustom to, prepare for (a.); — V. INF. *taqarruḥ*, be covered with ulcers; ulcerate; (m.) prepare for (n.); — VIII. INF. *iqtirâḥ*, urge, desire one to; speak ex tempore, improvise verses; do a thing as the first, open a path, invent; select.

قرح *qarḥ*, pl. *qurûḥ*, wound; ulcer; hurt; — *qurḥ*, pain from a wound; very painful wound; beginning; the first three nights of a month; — *qariḥ*, covered with ulcers; suppurating, sore; — *qurraḥ*, pl. of قارح *qâriḥ*, having all its teeth, &c.; — ة *qarḥa-t*, wound; ulcer; (m.) cough; — ى *qarḥa*, pl. of قريح *qarîḥ*.

(قرد) *qarad*, I, INF. *qard*, collect, gather, hoard up; — *qarid*, A, INF. *qarad*, be spoiled, get matted, become curly; be attacked by worms; be yellow; be speechless (also II. and IV.); — II. INF. *taqrîd*, see I.; louse a camel; (m.) wish one to blazes; — IV. INF. *iqrâd*, see I.; rest; submit to (الى *ila*).

قرد *qird*, pl. *qurûd*, *qirada-t*, *qarida-t*, *qirad*, *aqrâd*, ape, monkey; (m.) wicked demon, devil; — *qurd*, pl. *qirdân*, louse; tick (insect); — *qarid*, heaped up; full of lice; — ة *qirda-t*, pl. *qirad*, female ape.

قرداحى *qardâḥiyy*, armourer (m.).

قردان *qirdân*, pl. of قراد *qurâd*.

(قردح) *qardaḥ*, INF. ة, confess on being questioned; submit; (m.) be an armourer.

قردح *qardaḥ*, *qurduḥ*, a striped garment; — ة *qardaḥa-t*, trade of an armourer.

قردحجى *qardaḥjiyy*, armourer.

قردد *qardad*, hard ground.

(قردس) *qardas*, INF. ة, fasten, tie up; call to a puppy.

قردع *qirda'*, louse of a camel or a fowl; hen.

قردم *qardam*, stammerer.

قردمانى *qurdamâniyy*, ة *qurdamâniyya-t*, lined armour; cap of a helmet.

(قرز) *qaraz*, U, INF. *qarz*, take with the finger-tips; pinch; sting; — VII. INF. *inqirâz*, be hurt by words; — ة *qarza-t*, a pinch (of snuff, &c.).

قرزام *qirzâm*, poetaster.

(قرزل) *qarzal*, INF. ة, coil the hair up on the top of the head; (m.) truss up the garments.

قرزل *qurzul*, bad, vile; knot of hair on the top of the head.

(قرزم) *qarzam*, INF. ة, make bad verses.

قرزوم *qurzûm*, table of a shoe-maker to cut the leather upon; wooden part of an anvil.

(قرس) *qaras*, I, INF. *qars*, also *qaris*, A, INF. *qaras*, be intense (cold); freeze, curdle; — II. INF. *taqrîs*, freeze (a.); hurt, injure.

قرس *qars*, intense cold; cold, icy.

(قرش) *qaraś*, I, U, INF. *qarś*, cut off; gnaw at; gather from all sides; earn, gain; have much money; — II. INF. *taqrîś*, earn, gain; turn into money; (m.) curdle; incite; — III. INF. *muqâraśa-t*, (m.) intermeddle; have dealings with; — IV. INF. *iqrâś*, hoard up money, grow rich; injure a bone without fracture; slander; — VIII. INF. *iqtirâś*, earn, gain; — X. INF. *istiqrâś*, deem rich.

قرش *qarś*, a fish of prey; — *qirś*, pl. *qurûś*, piaster.

قرشام *qirśâm*, pl. *qarâśim*, large louse; — ة *qirśâma-t*, kite, sparrow-hawk.

(قرشب) *qirśabb*, pl. *qarâśib*, paunch-bellied; old; ill-tempered, peevish.

(قرشح) *qarśaḥ*, INF. ة, hop in short leaps.

قرشع *qirśiʻ*, heat in the chest and throat.

قرشوم *qurśûm*=قرشام *qirśâm*.

قرشي *quraśiyy*, of the tribe of Koreish.

(قرص) *qaraṣ*, U, INF. *qarṣ*, pinch, pull with two fingers; sting, prick; taunt with epigrams, &c.; clutch; cut off; cleanse dirty clothes; flatten the dough; make flat loaves of it; — *qariṣ*, A, INF. *qaraṣ*, be of a slanderous disposition; — II. INF. *taqrîṣ*, hurt deeply by epigrams, &c.; form the dough into flat round loaves; — V. INF. *taqarruṣ*, be formed into flat loaves; — VII. INF. *inqirâṣ*, be pinched, pricked, stung.

قرص *qurṣ*, pl. *aqrâṣ*, *qiraṣa-t*, flat disc; round loaf; cake, tart; honeycomb; pastils, lozenges; golden disc as ornament for a lady's head, brooch, frontlet, diadem; disc of the sun; — ة *qurṣa-t*, pl. *quraṣ*, disc; loaf of bread; round slice of bread; holy wafer; disc of the sun.

(قرصب) *qarṣab*, INF. ة, cut off.

(قرصم) *qarṣam*, INF. ة, cut, break.

قرصن *qarṣan*, pl. *qarâṣin*, corsair, pirate (m.); — *qarṣan*, INF. ة, cruise as a pirate.

(قرصوف) *qurṣûf*, sharp.

(قرض) *qaraḍ*, INF. *qarḍ*, cut; gnaw, nibble; impart, reward; lend money; recite; swerve to the right and left in walking; depart from (acc.); die or be on the point of death; — *qariḍ* (also *qaruḍ*), A, INF. *qaraḍ*, die; pass from one thing to another; — II. INF. *taqrîḍ*, cut; gnaw; exalt with praise; blame; — III. INF. *qirâḍ*, *muqâraḍa-t*, lend one money to carry on a business for a share in the gain, lend one money (on interest or without); — IV. INF. *iqrâḍ*, lend money (2 acc.); — VI. INF. *taqâruḍ*, requite one another; return (a visit, &c.); lend money to one another; recite verses to one another; — VII. INF. *inqirâḍ*, die out, become extinguished, perish; terminate, expire (time); — VIII. INF. *iqtirâḍ*, take a loan; — X. INF. *istiqrâḍ*, try to make a loan, borrow money.

قرض *qarḍ*, gnawing, nibbling (s.); also *qirḍ*, pl. *qurûḍ*, loan, debt; =قراض *qirâḍ*; — ة *qarḍa-t*, loan.

قرضاب *qirḍâb*, pl. *qarâḍiba-t*, who devours everything; one famished; lion; robber; sharp sword.

(قرضب) *qarḍab*, INF. ة, cut off; gather meat in a pot; eat all; eat anything dry.

(قرضم) *qarḍam*, INF. ة, cut off; take all.

قرضوب *qurḍûb*, pl. *qarâḍiba-t*=قرضاب *qirḍâb*.

قرضي *qarḍiyy*, ة, borrowed; — ة *qarḍiyya-t*, loan.

(قرط) *qaraṭ*, U, INF. *qarṭ*, cut into small pieces (also II.); (m.) cut off or withhold from one part of what is due to him; — *qariṭ*, A, INF. *qaraṭ*, have flabby ears; — II. INF. *taqrîṭ*, see I.; adorn the ear with ear-rings; (m.) gnaw at, clip (coins), make incisions, indent, pinch; give too little to eat, be niggardly with, withhold part from one's due; keep the bridle of an excited horse short; put the reins behind a horse's ears; — V. INF. *taqarruṭ*, be cut into small pieces (also VII.); be

withheld (also VII.); be adorned with ear-rings; (m.) be gnawed or nibbled at; be clipped; — VII. INF. *inqirâṭ*, see V.

قرط *qirṭ*, leek; — *qurṭ*, pl. *aqriṭa-t*, *aqrâṭ*, *qirâṭ*, *qurûṭ*, *qiraṭa-t*, ear-ring, pendant; diadem; a cluster of bananas; — ة *qurṭa-t*, piece, splinter.

قرطاس *qarṭâs*, *qirṭâs*, *qurṭâs*, pl. *qarâṭîs*, sheet of paper; paper; papers, writings, pamphlets, books; — *qirṭâs*, aim; — ى *qarṭâsiyy*, of paper; seller of paper, stationer.

قرطال *qirṭâl*, ة *qirṭâla-t*, see قرطل *qirṭall*.

قرطام *qirṭâm*, a disease by which the extremities rot off (m.).

(قرطب) *qarṭab*, INF. ة, throw one down on his back; cut the bones of a slaughtered animal; render one powerless, bind one's hands; — II. INF. *taqarṭub*, be cut off, amputated; be powerless, unable to do anything.

قرطب *qurṭub*, thorns (m.); — ة *qurṭuba-t*, Cordova; — ى *qurṭuba*, sword; — *qirṭibba*, a game; a way of throwing a person down.

قرطس *qarṭas*, *qirṭas*=قرطاس *qarṭâs*, &c.; — *qarṭas*, INF. ة, hit the mark; — II. INF. *taqarṭus*, perish.

قرطف *qarṭaf*, velvet; satin.

قرطق *qarṭaq*, pl. *qarâṭiq*, an upper garment; — *qarṭaq*, INF. ة, clothe one with it; — II. INF. *taqarṭuq*, be clad with it.

(قرطل) *qirṭall*, ة *qirṭalla-t*, قرطالة *qirṭâla-t*, pl. *qirṭâl*, *qarâṭil*, basket, fruit-basket.

(قرطم) *qarṭam*, INF. ة, cut, cut off; — *qirṭim*, *qurṭum*, saffron-seed.

(قرظ) *qaraẓ*, gather the leaves of the *salam*-tree; tan therewith; cut off; laud, eulogize; — *qariẓ*, A, INF. *qaraẓ*, grow wealthy (after lowliness); — II. INF. *taqrîẓ*, eulogize; — VI. INF. *taqâruẓ*, praise one another.

قرظ *qaraẓ*, leaves of the *salam*-tree, fruit of the acacia *sanaṭ*.

(قرع) *qara'*, A, INF. *qar'*, knock, rap, strike; cudgel; beat the drum; INF. *qar'*, *qirâ'*, cover (stallion); — U, INF. *qar'*, cast lots, be winner in casting lots; — *qari'*, A, INF. *qara'*, accept advice; conquer in throwing the javelin or spear; be bald; have the itch; also *qara'*, INF. *qar'*, be empty, deserted, bare; — II. INF. *taqrî'*, cover; inveigh against, scold, rebuke; molest people so as to cause them to leave a place; (m.) cut off the crown of a tree; — III. INF. *muqâra'a-t*, come to close quarters with; cast lots with; gamble with (acc.); — IV. INF. *iqrâ'*, cast lots, decide by lot; lend one's stallion to another; — V. INF. *taqarru'*, (m.) be deprived of its crown (tree); have the head shaved; — VI. INF. *taqâru'*, cast lots or play at dice with one another; quarrel; — VII. INF. *inqirâ'*, have the itch; — VIII. INF. *iqtirâ'*, cast lots; have one's own lot drawn; elect, choose; (m.) come to blows with; — X. INF. *istiqrâ'*, ask for one's stallion.

قرع *qar'*, knocking, rapping (s.); ة, pumpkin, gourd; a tumid pustule; bottom, ground, depth; — *qur'*, pl. of اقرع *aqra'*, bald, bare, &c.; — ة *qur'a-t*, pl. *qura'*, lot; casting lots (s.); choice by lots, ballot; — *qara'a-t*, baldness; bald head, head; (m.) itch; — ى *qar'a*, pl. of قريع *qarî'*.

قرعا *qar'â*, f., قرعان *qur'ân*, pl. of اقرع *aqra'*, bald, bare, &c.

(قرعب), III. *iqra'abb*, INF. *iqri'bâb*, shrink (from cold).

(قرعث), II. *taqar'as̱*, INF. *taqar'us̱*, assemble (n.).

(قرعف), II. *taqar'af*, INF. *taqar'uf*, III. *iqra'aff*, INF. *iqri'fâf*, shrink.

(قرف) *qaraf*, I, INF. *qarf*, rind, bark, peel; skin, lay bare; act harshly or violently towards, maltreat; suspect of, accuse of (ب *bi*); try to earn sustenance for one's family; tell lies; mix; —*qarif*, A, INF. *qaraf*, be on the point of falling ill; (m.) loathe; — II. INF. *taqrîf*, maltreat; accuse; cause disgust, make to loathe; — III. INF. *qirâf*, *muqârafa-t*, engage in sin, pollute one's self with sin; approach; lie with; — IV. INF. *iqrâf*, revile, abuse; draw suspicion upon, accuse; mix with (n.); (m.) cause disgust, make to loathe; — VIII. INF. *iqtirâf*, try to earn; commit (a crime); — X. INF. *istiqrâf*, feel disgust, loathe.

قرف *qarf*, *qarif*, pl. *qirâf*, worthy, apt; — *qirf*, rind, bark, crust, shell; — *qurf*, pl. of قروف *qurûf*; — *qâraf*, disgust, loathing; — ة *qirfa-t*, pl. *qiraf*, rind, bark; shell of a pomegranate; cinnamon; gain; suspicion.

(قرفص) *qarfaṣ*, INF. ة, sit on the ground with the knees drawn closely to the body and the hands joined in front of them; bind one's hands beneath his feet.

قرفصا *qurfuṣâ*, قرفصى *qarfaṣā*, *qirfiṣā*, *qurfuṣā*, pl. *qarâfiṣ*, way of sitting described under قرفص *qarfaṣ*.

(قرفط) *qarfaṭ*, INF. ة, walk with short steps; — IV. *iqranfaṭ*, INF. *iqrinfâṭ*, be shrunk.

(قرفع), II. *taqarfa'*, INF. *taqarfu'*, be shrunk; — IV. pass: *uqrunfa'* (عليه *'alai-hi*), recover from a swoon.

(قرق) *qaraq*, suppose; deceive; cluck; — *qariq*, A, INF. *qaraq*, travel in a plain or desert; (m.) be afflicted with a rupture of the testicles or groins; — II. INF. *taqrîq*, cluck; (m.) cause a hen to brood; (m.) remain quiet, motionless; — VII. INF. *inqirâq*, be afflicted with a rupture of the testicles or groins.

قرق *qarq*, clucking of a hen; rumbling in the bowels; — *qurq*, confiscation, embargo; rupture of the testicles or groins; — *qariq*, level, flat; — ة *qurqa-t*, brood-hen.

قرقارية *qurqariyya-t*, hollow in a tree (m.).

(قرقب) *qarqab*, *qurqub*, *qurqubb*, belly.

قرقدون *qarqadûn*, squirrel.

(قرقر) *qarqar*, INF. ة, coo; roar; crow; laugh to choking; rumble, grumble; (m.) complain; (m.) be hollow; — II. INF. *taqarqur*, rumble, grumble, growl; complain.

قرقر *qarqar*, soft level ground (also ة *qarqara-t*); suburbs; — ة *qarqara-t*, pl. *qarâqir*, cooing of a dove; rumbling, grumbling, growling; complaining, querulousness.

(قرقس) *qarqas*, قرقص *qarqaṣ*, INF. ة decoy or call a dog.

قرقس *qirqis*, a desert-fly.

(قرقش) *qarqaś*, INF. ة, gnaw at (m.).

(قرقض) *qarqaḍ*, INF. ة = the previous (m.).

قرقضون *qarqaḍûn*, pl. *qarâqiḍîn*, squirrel; ق ممتن *qarqaḍûn mumtin*, pole-cat, skunk.

(قرقط) *qarqaṭ*, INF. ة, gnaw the bit; nibble at.

(قرقع) *qarqa'*, INF. ة, make a rumbling noise, clatter, creak; publish, make publicly known; — II. INF. *taqarqu'*, be published, made public; — ة *qara'a-t*, creaking or rumbling of a cart; noise, tumult; becoming public (s.), public noise.

(قرقف) *qarqaf*, INF. ة, frighten so as to make tremble; tremble; be violent, boisterous; pass. and — II. INF. *taqarquf*, chatter from cold.

(قرقل) *qarqal, qarqall*, pl. *qarâqil*, a woman's shift.
(قرقم) *qarqam*, INF. ة, feed a child badly.
قرقور *qurqûr*, pl. *qarâqîr*, large long ship; (m.) lamb.
قرقوش *qurqûś*, cartilage.
قرقوص *qurqûṣ*, young dog, puppy.
قرقوف *qurqûf*, very strong wine.
قرقى *qurqiyy*, confiscated.
(قرم) *qaram*, U, INF. *qarm*, cut a piece of the skin of a camel's nose as a mark; retain, hold; rind, peel, bark; revile, abuse; eat; — I, INF. *qarm, qurûm, qaramân, maqram*, gnaw at, nibble at; (m.) cut off the top of a thing; — *qarim*, A, INF. *qaram*, have a strong appetite for meat; long for; — II. INF. *taqrîm*, mark a camel by cutting the skin of the nose; — IV. INF. *iqrâm*, free from work and keep only for copulation; — V. INF. *taqarrum*, eat like a child or an animal which has just been weaned.
قرم *qarm*, pl. *qurûm*, excellent stallion, breeder; camel kept only for copulation or to be slaughtered; chief of a tribe, master, lord, prince; — *qirm, qirim*, Crimea; — *qaram*, strong appetite for meat; greediness; — *qarim*, carnivorous; — ة *qarma-t*, notch; also *qurma-t*, incision in a camel's nose with a piece of skin hanging down as a mark; — *qurma-t* (m.) = قرمية *qirmiyya-t*.
قرما *qarmâ'*, camel with an incision as described above.
قرماص *qirmâṣ*, see قرمص *qirmiṣ*.
(قرمد) *qarmad*, INF. ة, cover with gypsum; pave or build with bricks; write closely.
قرمد *qarmad*, anything smeared on; brick; lime-stone; — ة *qarmada-t*, tile-kiln.
(قرمز) *qirmiz*, Kermes; crimson; — ى *qirmiziyy*, scarlet, red, crimson.
(قرمش) *qarmaś*, INF. ة, spoil, ruin; gather, collect (a.).
(قرمص) *qarmaṣ*, INF. ة, retire to a hole in the ground (from cold).
قرمص *qirmiṣ*, قرماص *qirmâṣ*, قرموص *qurmûṣ*, pl. *qarâmîṣ*, hole in the ground to shelter a herdsman, &c. from the cold; ambush of a hunter, hunting-hut.
(قرمط) *qarmaṭ*, INF. ة, write very closely; make small steps; — IV. *iqramma-ṭ*, INF. *iqrimmâṭ*, be shrunk, wrinkled; — ة *qarmaṭa-t*, close writing; *al-qarmaṭa-t*, a sect; *qarâmiṭa-t*, its followers.
(قرمل) *qirmil*, pl. *qarâmil*, double-humped camel.
قرمود *qurmûd*, pl. *qarâmîd*, mountain-goat; fruit of the قضاة *qaḍât*-tree.
قرموص *qurmûṣ* = قرمص *qirmiṣ*.
قرموط *qarmûṭ*, little imp, urchin, pigmy, manikin (m.).
قرمول *qurmûl*, pl. *qarâmil, qarâmîl*, curling-paper.
قرميد *qirmîd*, pl. *qarâmîd*, brick; canal of earthen pipes.
قرمية *qirmiyya-t*, pl. *qarâmî*, trunk of a tree.
(قرن) *qaran*, I, U, INF. *qarn*, join one thing to another, yoke together; identify one thing with another; — U, INF. *qirân*, perform two things at the same time; — *qarin*, A, INF. *qaran*, have the eye-brows joined; — II. INF. *taqrîn*, join several things, bind several animals or prisoners to the same string; make conical; — III. INF. *qirân, muqârana-t*, enter into partnership with; be of the same age with, be one's comrade; — IV. INF. *iqrân*, join one thing to another; perform two things at the same time; be equal to; help, assist; — V. INF. *taqarrun*, form a projecting angle; — VIII.

INF. *iqtirân*, join with (n.); be joined, yoked together, married; join immediately (n.).

قرن *qarn*, pl. *qurûn*, horn; point, edge; feeler; side-lock; fleak of wool; side of the forehead where the horns grow; entrance; border of the rising sun, first rays of the sun; trumpet of the last judgment; pl. *aqrân*, string of bast; pl. *qurûn*, *qirân*, projecting hill or mountain; shower; start of a horse; nobleman, prince, lord; time of forty years, generation; decade, century, age; coevals; comrade; troop; — *qirn*, pl. *aqrân*, one's equal in bravery, &c.; adversary; coeval; contemporaneous; shell of a fruit; — *qaran*, pl. *aqrân*, string to tie two camels, &c. together; quiver of leather; — ة *qurna-t*, pl. *qarâni*, projecting angle or corner; edge of a sword; head of a spear.

قرنا *qarnâ*, f. of اقرن *aqran*, tied together; a horned snake.

قرناس *qirnâs*, *qurnâs*, mountain-summit; back of an axe.

قرنبيس *qirambîs*, قرنبيط *qarnabîṭ*, cauliflower.

(قرنس) *qarnas*, INF. ة, moult, run away bristling the feathers of the throat (cock).

(قرنص) *qarnaṣ*, INF. ة, run away with bristled feathers; get a hawk for hunting; hunt, chase.

(قرنفل) *qaramful*, قرنفول *qaramfûl*, cloves.

قرنوص *qurnûṣ*, pl. *qarânîṣ*, seam of a boot.

(قره) *qarih*, A, *qarah*, have bad and yellow teeth: have the skin blackened or spotted; have the jaundice.

(قرهب) *qarhab*, pl. *qarâhib*, old big ox; chief.

(قرو) *qarâ*, U, INF. *qarw*, tend to, go to; travel from one country to another; follow up a thing with perseverance; pierce with a lance; swell; — IV. INF. *iqrâ'*, have pain in the back; — VIII. INF. *iqtirâ'*, strive after with perseverance; — X. INF. *istiqrâ'*, id.; follow.

قرو *qarw*, pl. *quruww*, water vessel for the camel foals; far-stretching tract; hydrocele, rupture of the testicles; manner, way; pl. *aqrâ'*, *aqr-in*, *aqrî*, *aqriwa-t*, *quriyy*, trough to feed dogs; outlet of a wine-press; — *qurû'*, pl. of قر *qar'*; — ة *qarwa-t*, rupture of the groins or testicles.

قرواح *qirwâḥ*, vast field.

قروانى *qarwâniyy*, afflicted with a rupture of the testicles or groins.

قرور *qarûr*, cold; — *

قروف *qurûf*, pl. *qurf*, very intrusive and quarrelsome.

قرون *qarûn*, ة *qarûna-t*, soul, self; — *

قروى *qarawiyy*, *qurawiyy*, inhabitant of a village or town; rural, rustic.

(قرى) *qara*, I, INF. *qiran*, *qarâ'*, receive hospitably; shelter, entertain, feed, refresh; — I, INF. *qaran*, *qary*, collect water in a reservoir; chew the cud; travel from land to land; — IV. INF. *iqrâ'*, ask for a hospitable reception; come as a guest to; — V. INF. *taqarrî*, go after the water; — VIII. INF. *iqtirâ'*, ask for a hospitable reception; (m.) suffice and refresh (food); travel, wend one's way, visit.

قرى *qaran*, pl. *aqrâ'*, back; — *qiran*, meal placed before a guest, food, entertainment, feasting; hospitality; — ة *qarya-t*, *qirya-t*, pl. *qur-an*, *qura*, village, hamlet, town.

قريب *qarîb* (sing. and pl.), ة, pl. *qirâb*, near, close at hand (in space and time); pl. *aqribâ'*, related; probable; one's neighbour, fellow man.

قريت *qarît*, jelly; ice.
قريح *qarîḥ*, pl. *qarḥa*, wounded; sore; ulcerating, covered with ulcers; clear, pure; — *qirrîḥ*, suppurating very much; — ة *qarîḥa-t*, natural disposition, character, talent, genius, flow of wit, inclination and gift for.
قريد *quraid*, little monkey.
قرير *qarîr*, ة, cool, fresh; refreshed, consoled; ق العين *qarîr al-'ain*, happy.
قريس *qarîs*, icy cold; jelly, especially of fish.
قريش *qarîś*, ة *qarîśa-t*, soft sourish cheese; — *quraiś*, name of the tribe Koreish.
قريص *qarîṣ*, *qurraiṣ*, nettle.
قريض *qarîḍ*, poetry, verse.
قريظ *qarîẓ*, laudation, eulogy, panegyric on a living person.
قريع *qarî'*, exquisite, excellent; ق الدهر *qarî' ad-dahr*, hero of the age; despised, contemptible; good stallion; adversary in a game; also *qirrî'*, leader, chief; — ة *qarî'a-t*, best part of one's property; little bell.
قرين *qarîn*, pl. *quranâ'*, *aqrân*, joined, yoked together, married; jointly liable; companion, partner, comrade, one's equal; ally; husband; coeval; immediately joining; related; demon attached to a person; soul, self; ق القبول *qarîn al-qabûl*, acceptable; — ة *qarîna-t*, pl. *qarâ'in*, female companion, friend, wife, mate, spouse; company, union, association; incident; cause; consequence, corollary; surmise, supposition; context; soul; (m.) ugly wench; دور قرائن *dûr qarâ'in*, opposite houses.
قريى *qarayiyy*, inhabitant of a village or town.
(قز) *qazz*, I, U, INF. *qazz*, feel aversion; INF. *quzz*, loathe anything impure; U, I, INF. *qazz*, leap, leap upon, crouch in order to leap; — V. INF. *taqazzuz*, feel aversion, loathe; flee from (من *min*) with loathing.
قز *qazz*, pl. *quzûz*, raw silk, floss-silk; silk; silk-worm; also *qizz*, *quzz*, ة, pl. *aqizzâ'*, who loathes anything impure; — ة *quza-t*, a snake; a game.
قزاح *qazzâḥ*, greengrocer.
قزاز *qazâz*, *qizâz*, glass, glass-ware; also ة *qazâza-t*, *qizâza-t*, bottle; —*qazzâz*, silk-manufacturer, silk-spinner; lace-maker.
قزاق *qazzâq*, light-armed soldier; Cossack; robber.
(قزب) *qazab*, U, INF. *qazb*, have frequent sexual intercourse with (acc.); — *qazib*, A, INF. *qazab*, be hard and strong.
(قزبر) *qazbar*, INF. ة, lie with.
(قزح) *qazaḥ*, INF. *qazḥ*, season a dish; (also *qaziḥ*) INF. *qazḥ*, *quzûḥ*, make water; (m.) cut off a tree at the root; (m.) extirpate a corn; — INF. *qazḥ*, *qazaḥân*, run out in drops; — II. INF. *taqzîḥ*, season.
قزح *qizḥ*, *qazḥ*, pl. *aqzâḥ*, onion-seed; greens for seasoning; — *quzaḥ*, Satan; the angel of clouds; قوس قزح *qaus-u quzaḥ-a* or *quzaḥ-in*, rainbow; — ى *quzaḥiyy*, of the colours of the rainbow.
قزدير *qazdîr*, tin.
(قزع) *qaza'*, INF. *quzû'*, be swift of motion, fleet; be quick, expeditious; be slow; — II. INF. *taqzî'*, urge to run; make one apt for business, instruct; despatch, send; shave the head so as to leave only stray tufts of hair.
قزع *qaza'*, ة, separate parts of a cloud; stray tufts of hair; stray rag.
(قزل) *qazal*, I, INF. *qazalân*, *qazl*, leap, leap upon; walk as one one who limps; — *qazil*, U, INF. *qazal*, limp much.
(قزم) *qazam*, U, I, INF. *qazm*, accuse

of a vice;—*qazim*, A, INF. *qazam*, be mean and contemptible, be small, mean-looking and poor.

قزم *qazam*, *qazim*, *quzum* (sing., pl. m. f.), f. also ة, pl. *quzum*, *qazâma*, *aqzâm*, mean and contemptible; small, mean-looking and poor;—*qazam*, insignificant look.

(قزن), IV. *aqzan*, INF. *iqzân*, break a leg.

(قزو) *qazâ*, U, INF. *qazw*, play at the game *quza-t*; tap the ground with the point of a stick; loathe anything impure; — IV. INF. *iqzâ'*, incur blame or abuse.

(قزى) *qazî*, A, INF. *qazy*, move, be rickety; — II. INF. *taqziya-t*, throw to the ground, strike down and kill.

قزى *qizy*, nickname; — *qazziyy*, silken.

قزيح *qazîḥ*, handsome, pretty.

قزيز *qazîz*, sprinkling bottle.

(قس) *qass*, U, I, INF. *qass*, slander, injure by calumnies; — U, INF. *qass*, *qiss*, *quss*, wish for, seek, aim at; — U, INF. *qass*, pick a bone entirely and suck it out; go to the pasture by itself; tend the camel well; drive; — INF. *qussûsa-t*, *qissîsa-t*, become a priest; — II. INF. *taqsîs*, tend the camels well; — V. INF. *taqassus*, wish, strive for; hear.

قس *qass*, *qiss*, pl. *qusûs*, *qasâwisa-t*, (Christian) priest, ecclesiastic; —ة *qassa-t*, little village or town.

قساح *qusâḥ*, hard and dry; — ة *qasâḥa-t*, hardness.

قساطرة *qasâṭira-t*, pl. of قسطرى *qasṭariyy*.

قسافسة *qasâfisa-t*, pl. of قسيس *qasîs*.

قسام *qasâm*, beauty; heat of midday; — *qassâm*, distributor; who divides by testament; — ة *qasâma-t*, beauty; oath; keeping of an oath; truce or peace between Muslims and Infidels; — *qusâma-t*, alms.

قسان *qussân*, pl. of قسيس *qasîs*.

قساة *qusât*, pl. of قاسى *qâsî*, hard, unfeeling.

قساوسة *qasâwisa-t*, pl. of قس *qass* and قسيس *qasîs*.

قساوة *qasâwa-t*, hardheartedness; sorrow, grief; misfortune, calamity; INF. of (قسو).

(قسب) *qasab*, I, INF. *qasb*, flow, run; turn towards setting; — *qasub*, INF. *qusûb*, *qusûba-t*, be hard.

(قسبر) *qasbar*, INF. ة, lie with.

(قسح) *qasaḥ*, INF. *qasâḥa-t*, *qusûḥa-t*, be hard; be always sexually excited, suffer from priapism; twist.

(قسر) *qasar*, U, INF. *qasr*, force, compel; do to one anything against his will; — III. INF. *muqâsara-t*, do violence to; — VIII. INF. *iqtisâr*=I.

قسر *qasr*, violence, compulsion; — ى *qasariyy*, by force.

قسس *qusus*, pl. intelligent, clever.

(قسط) *qasaṭ*, I, INF. *qasṭ*, *qusûṭ*, swerve from what is right, act unjustly; separate (a.), disperse (a.); — I, U, INF. *qisṭ*, exercise justice, distribute justly; — *qasiṭ*, A, INF. *qasaṭ*, have a thin neck; have hard sinews of the foot; INF. *qusûṭ*, be hard and dry;—II. INF. *taqsîṭ*, divide, distribute; pay by instalments; be niggardly; (m.) talk much, relate; — IV. INF. *iqsâṭ*, exercise justice; give right weight and measure.

قسط *qisṭ*, justice; right weight and measure; a measurement, bushel; part, portion, share; also ة *qisṭa-t*, dividend, pay, rent, pension; rate, tax; balance;—*qusṭ*, a medicinal herb; also ة *qusṭa-t*, leg; —*qasaṭ*, inflexibility of a horse's hind legs.

قسطار *qisṭâr*, *qusṭâr*, money-changer, banker; balance; the oldest in a village.

قسطاس *qisṭâs, qusṭâs*, large balance; — *qusṭâs*, large curtain.
قسطان *qusṭân*, dust; also قسطانى *qusṭâniyy*, ة *qusṭâniyya-t*, rainbow.
(قسطر) *qasṭar*, money-changer, banker; — *qasṭar*, INF. ة, separate the bad coin from the good; — ى *qasṭariyy*, cunning and subtle like a money-changer.
(قسطل) *qasṭal*, dust; ام ق *umm-u qasṭal-in*, calamity; — *qusṭul*, chestnut; — ة *qasṭala-t*, roaring of the camel; murmuring of a stream; Castile.
قسطلان *qasṭalân*, dust.
قسطلانية *qasṭalâniyya-t*, ruddiness of the dawn; rainbow; a red stuff.
قسطنطينية *qusṭanṭiniyya-t*, Constantinople.
(قسقس) *qasqas*, INF. ة, brandish a stick, &c.; hasten on a journey; pick and suck out a bone; — II. INF. *taqasqus*, listen, hear.
(قسم) *qasam*, I, INF. *qasm*, divide, distribute; determine according to weight and measure; transact a business with justice and fairness; disperse (a.); — *qasum*, INF. *qasâma-t*, be handsome of face; — II. INF. *taqsîm*, divide, distribute; — III. INF. *muqâsama-t*, divide a thing with another (2 acc.); — IV. INF. *iqsâm*, swear by the name of God; — V. INF. *taqassum*, disperse (a.); — VI. INF. *taqâsum*, divide between one another; take mutual oaths; — VII. INF. *inqisâm*, be divided, distributed; — VIII. INF. *iqtisâm*, divide between each other; — X. INF. *istiqsâm*, ask for distribution, especially by lot; demand one's share; demand an oath from (acc.).
قسم *qasm*, division, distribution; also *qism*, natural disposition or quality, custom, habit; — *qism*, pl. *aqsâm, aqsimâ', qasîm, aqâsîm*, part, portion, share; kind, species; — *qusm*, pl. of قسيم *qasîm*; — *qasam*, pl. *aqsâm*, oath; beauty; — ة *qisma-t*, division, distribution; share, portion, lot; destiny, fate; — *qasima-t, qasama-t*, face; beauty; box for perfumes; phial.
قسما *qusamâ'*, pl. of قسيم.
(قسن), IV. *aqsan*, have the hands hard from work; — XI. *iqsa'ann*, INF. *iqsînân, qasânîna-t*, grow dry and hard; be very old; be very dark.
قسنى *qasniyy*, galbanum.
(قسو) *qasâ*, U, INF. *qasw, qasâ', qaswa-t, qasâwa-t*, harden (n.), be hard; be of bad silver (coin); — III. INF. *muqâsât*, harden one's self against, endure, suffer; forbear with; be hard towards (acc.).
(قسور) *qaswar*, INF. ة, grow luxuriantly; be old.
قسور *qaswar*, lion; ة, powerful, strong.
قسوس *qusûs*, ivy; pl. of قس *qass*; — ة *qussûsa-t*, priesthood; — ى *qussûsiyy*, priestly, sacerdotal; — ية *qussûsiyya-t*, office of a priest, priesthood.
قسوى *qusawiyy*, referring to a bow.
قسى *qasî*, pl. *qisyân*, f. ة, pl. *-ât*, hard, rough, severe; spurious, of bad silver; — *qisiyy, qusiyy*, pl. of قوس *qaus*, bow.
قسيس *qasîs*, pl. *qussân, aqissa-t*, also *qissîs*, pl. *-ûn, qasâwisa-t*, vulg. *qasâfisa-t*, (Christian) priest, ecclesiastic, clergyman; — ة *qissîsa-t*, office of a priest.
قسيسية *qissîsiyya-t*, dignity of a presbyter.
قسيم *qasîm*, pl. *qusm*, pretty, handsome of face; pl. *qusamâ'*, share, portion; pl. *aqsimâ', qusamâ'*, who shares with, co-heir; bound to one by oath; — *; — ة *qasîma-t*, oath; pl. *qasâ'im*, perfume-box.

(قش) *qaśś*, U, I, INF. *quśûś*, be well, improve again (after illness, &c.); walk like one emaciated; eat of this and that; gather (a.).

قش *qaśś*, a bad kind of palm-tree; — ة *qiśśa-t*, little girl; female monkey.

قشا *qaśan*, spittle; — *qiśâ'*, pl. of قشوة *qaśwa-t*.

قشارة *quśâra-t*, peelings, parings.

قشافة *qaśâfa-t*, misery.

قشام *quśâm*, ة *quśâma-t*, pl. *qusuma-t*, bread-crumbs; remains of food.

(قشب) *qaśab*, admix; poison a drink; pollute; spoil, corrupt; vex; revile, abuse; = VIII.; — *qaśub*, INF. *qaśâba-t*, be bright and pure; — II. INF. *taqśîb*, pollute; — VIII. INF. *iqtiśâb* merit praise or blame.

قشب *qaśb*, *qiśb*, *qaśab*, pl. *aqśâb*, poison; — *qiśb*, soul; a plant; rust; — *quśb*, pl. of قشيب *qaśîb*.

قشبار *qiśbâr*, rough.

قشبر *qiśbarr*, thick.

(قشد) *qaśad*, INF. *qaśd*, uncover, bare, strip; — ة *qiśda-t*, cream; fresh butter; sediment of butter.

(قشر) *qaśar*, I, U, INF. *qaśr*, rind, peel, skin, shell, bark; bring calamity upon, be disastrous to (acc.); — II. INF. *taqśîr*, rind, bark, skin, peel; — V. INF. *taqaśśur*, VII. INF. *inqiśâr*, pass. of II.

قشر *qiśr*, ة *qiśra-t*, pl. *quśûr*, rind, bark, skin, shell, crust; — ى *qiśriyy*, of rind, &c.

قشرا *qaśrâ'*, f. of اقشر *aqśar*, peeled, &c.

(قشط) *qaśaṭ*, U, INF. *qaśṭ*, take off, uncover, bare, strip; skin, flay; cudgel, give the bastinado; — V. INF. *taqaśśuṭ*, VII. INF. *inqiśâṭ*, be clear, serene.

(قشع) *qaśa'*, INF. *qaś*, disperse, dispel; uncover, bare, take off; milk; — *qaśi'*, A, INF. *qaśa'*, be frivolous, fickle, full of levity; — IV. INF. *iqśâ'*, disperse, dispel; — V. INF. *taqaśśu'*, VII. INF. *inqiśâ'*, pass. of the previous.

قشع *qaś'* (also ة *qaśa-t*), part of a cloud; (also *qiś'*, *quś'*) sweepings of a bath; thin crust of ice; crust; table-cloth; (also ة *qaś'a-t*, *qiś'a-t*) pl. *qiśa'*, dry skin; pl. *quśû'*, tent of hides; — *qaśi'*, frivolous, full of levity.

(قشعر), III. *iqśa'arr*, INF. *iqśi'râr*, shudder, shiver, be bristling; be rigid with cold; be sterile, barren.

قشعريرة *quśa'rîra-t*, shudder; feverish shivering, ague-fit.

(قشعم) *qaś'am*, pl. *qaśâ'im*, very old; thick, stout; lion; ام ق *umm-u qaś'am-in*, death, calamity, war.

(قشف) *qaśif*, A, INF. *qaśaf*, have the skin scarified and discoloured, be dirty-looking, live in squalor and misery; — *qaśuf*, INF. *qaśâfa-t*, id.; — V. INF. *taqaśśuf*, live in squalor and misery; (m.) lead an ascetic life.

قشف *qaśf*, *qaśaf*, who lives in squalor and misery; — *qaśaf*, squalor; life in squalor and misery; (m.) ascetic life; — *qaśif*, dirty, filthy, miserable; hard and oppressive; ascetic.

قشق *qaśaq*, curry-comb (Turk.).

(قشقش) *qaśqaś*, INF. ة, recover; heal (a.), cure; (m.) gather wood; — II. INF. *taqaśquś*, get cured.

(قشم) *qaśam*, U, INF. *qaśm*, eat the best and leave the rest; select; sift, winnow; eat much; split palm-leaves in order to sew them together; die.

قشم *qiśm*, nature; also *qaśm*, pl. *quśûm*, canal; ready food; bodily constitution; — *quśm*, pl. of قشيم *qaśîm*.

قشمش *qiśmiś*, raisin (Pers.).

(قشو) *qaśâ*, U, INF. *qaśm*, rind,

peel, strip, skin; scrape; turn on a lathe; rub the face; (m.) skim; — II. INF. *taqśiya-t*=I.; — IV. INF. *iqśâ'*, grow poor after being rich; — ة *qaśwa-t* (also m. قشوية *qaświyya-t*), pl. *qaśawât*, *qiśâ'*, straw basket; *qaśwa-t*, what is skimmed off; froth, cream, &c.

(قشور) *qaśwar*, INF. ة, cudgel, beat.

قشومة *qaśûma-t*, pl. of قشام *qaśâm*.

قشى *qaśiyy*, bad (money).

قشيب *qaśîb*, pl. *quśb*, *quśub*, bright and clean, new, fresh; old; polished; rusty.

قشيش *qaśîś*, rustling of the slough of a snake.

قشيم *qaśîm*, pl. *quśm*, dry fruit of the dwarf-palm.

(قص) *qaṣṣ*, U, INF. *qaṣṣ*, cut off, clip (with scissors); INF. *qaṣaṣ*, impart, communicate, tell; make a speech, lecture; — U, INF. *qaṣṣ*, *qaṣaṣ*, follow one's tracks; INF. *qaṣṣ*, be near, impend; bring near to death; — II. INF. *taqṣîṣ*, cover with gypsum; — III. INF. *qiṣâṣ*, *muqâṣṣa-t*, requite, revenge one's self upon; chastise; impart an equal share to, settle with; — IV. INF. *iqṣâ'*, bring near to death; charge one with taking revenge upon another (من *min*); — V. INF. *taqaṣṣuṣ*, be cut off, clipped; remember one's words; follow one's tracks; — VI. INF. *taqâṣṣ*, impart equal shares to one another; requite, give tit for tat, take mutual revenge; be chastised, punished; — VII. INF. *inqiṣâṣ*, be clipped; — VIII. INF. *iqtiṣâṣ*, follow one's tracks, retrace; report accurately another's words; relate, tell; use reprisals with (من *min*); — X. INF. *istiqṣâṣ*, ask one to tell; ask one to requite, to revenge.

قص *qaṣṣ*, cutting off, clipping (s.); قص الشعر *qaṣṣ aś-śa'r*, hair-cutting, tonsure; clipped wool; pl. *qiṣâṣ*, top or middle of the chest; gypsum; — *quṣṣ*, womb, vulva; — ة *qaṣṣa-t*, *qiṣṣa-t*, pl. *qiṣâṣ*, gypsum; —*qiṣṣa-t*, pl. *qiṣaṣ*, event; affair; law-case; (pl. also *aqâṣîṣ*) tale, story, relation, petition; pudenda; *al-qiṣṣat-a*, in short; — *quṣṣa-t*, pl. *quṣaṣ*, *qiṣâṣ*, front-lock, toupee; pl. *quṣaṣ*, string of pearls on a veil; shell, husk.

قصا *qaṣan*, *qaṣâ'*, distance, direction; yard in front of a house.

قصاب *qiṣâb*, pl. of قصبة *qaṣaba-t*; — *qaṣṣâb*, pl. *-ân*, butcher; flute-player, piper; — ة *qaṣâba-t*, head-cloth of women; — *qiṣâba-t*, trade of a butcher; art of playing the flute; — *quṣṣâba-t*, pl. *quṣṣâb*, pipe, tube; flute; — ية *qaṣṣâbiyya-t*, taxes imposed on a butcher.

قصاد *quṣṣâd*, pl. of قاصد *qâṣid*, who intends, &c.; (m.) straight towards; just in front; — ة *qaṣâda-t*, apostolical delegation; INF. of (قصد).

قصار *qaṣâr*, negligence, laziness, shortcoming;— *;—*quṣâr*, *qaṣâr*, end, conclusion, termination; last end; — *qaṣṣâr*, abstemious; fuller, washer, bleacher; — ة *qaṣâra-t*, shortness, smallness; — *qiṣâra-t*, trade of a fuller, &c.; pl. of قصيرة *qaṣîra-t*; — *quṣâra-t*, straw with ears; — ى *quṣârā*, end, termination, extreme; last end.

قصاص *qiṣâṣ* (also قصاصا *qiṣâṣâ'*), requital, tit for tat, retaliation; revenge, revenge for bloodshed; chastisement, punishment; capital punishment; — *; — *quṣâṣ*, place where hair is growing; — ة *quṣâṣa-t*, cuttings (of hair), parings; scrap.

قصاع *qiṣâ'*, pl. of قصعة *qaṣ'a-t*; — ة *quṣâ'a-t*, hole of the field-mouse.

(قصال), III. *iqṣa'all*, INF. *iqṣîlâl*, take, seize, grasp; stay, remain.
قصال *qaṣṣâl*, sharp; lion; — ة *quṣâla-t*, refuse in winnowing, chaff; mote.
قصايا *qaṣâyâ*, pl. of قصية *qaṣiyya-t*.
(قصب) *qaṣab*, I, INF. *qaṣb*, cut, cut off; dissect; cut stones; (m.) interweave, fringe or lace a garment; accuse, revile, disgrace; INF. *qaṣb*, *quṣûb*, lift up the head unwilling to drink (camel); prevent from drinking its fill; — II. INF. *taqṣîb*, cut off, cut into pieces, dissect; carve; lace; revile; push forth leaves; curl the hair; — IV. INF. *iqṣâb*, have camels unwilling to drink; — V. INF. *taqaṣṣub*, pass. of II.; — VIII. INF. *iqtiṣâb*, cut off.
قصب *quṣb*, pl. *aqṣâb*, back; gut; string of a musical instrument; side, hypochondres; — *qaṣab*, reed, any reed-like plant; tube, pipe; aqueduct; lachrymal ducts; flute, reed-pipe; wind-pipe; reed-pen, pen; thread of gold or silver; finger-bone; pearl or precious stone set about with rubies; Egyptian linen; citadel; — ة *qaṣaba-t*, pl. *qiṣâb*, reed-plant; hollow piece of reed between two knots; tube; pipe-tube; wind-pipe; artery; marrowy bone; nasal bone; a measurement; capital, town, large village; principal part of a city, citadel; curl of hair; — *quṣba-t*, gut; — ى *qaṣabiyy*, made of reed; tubular; fine Egyptian cambric.
قصبا *qaṣbâ'*, reed-plants.
(قصبل) *qaṣbal*, INF. ة, eat all.
قصبور *qaṣbûr*, coriander.
(قصد) *qaṣad*, I, INF. *qaṣd*, intend, purpose; move towards; aim at; try to injure or kill; fall upon; rely upon; dedicate; break (a.) in the middle; be just; keep the golden mean; economise; make poems; — *qaṣud*, INF. *qaṣâda-t*, be fat; — IV. INF. *iqṣâd*, hit the mark, pierce and kill; — V. INF. *taqaṣṣud*, be broken in the middle; purpose; move towards, repair to; — VIII. INF. *iqtiṣâd*, keep the golden mean; be economical; keep books; make poems.
قصد *qaṣd*, intention, purpose, resolution, end, aim; purport; way, road; — *qaṣad*, a kind of thorn; — *qaṣid*, broken; — ة *qiṣda-t*, fragment, piece.
قصدان *quṣdân*, pl. of قصيد *qaṣîd*.
(قصدر) *qaṣdar*, INF. ة, tin.
(قصدن) *qaṣdan*, INF. ة, compose a laudatory poem on; sing songs.
قصدير *qaṣdîr*, tin.
(قصر) *qaṣar*, U, INF. *qaṣr*, *qiṣr*, *qiṣar*, be short, be too short; — U, INF. *quṣûr*, be not equal to a thing and desist from (عن *'an*); get the worst of it; fall short of; subside, calm down (n.); grow dear; grow cheap; — U, INF. *qaṣr*, cut short the prayer; — I, INF. *qaṣr*, shorten (a.); shut up; keep back; grow dense; decline towards evening; INF. *qaṣr*, clean, full, wash; bleach; — *qaṣir*, A, INF. *qaṣar*, *qiṣar*, suffer from a stiff neck; — *qaṣur*, INF. *qaṣâra-t*, be short; — II. INF. *taqṣîr*, shorten (a.), abbreviate; clip the hair; be not equal to one's task, fall short of; lag behind, be slothful; fail in strength; subside; wash, full; — III. INF. *muqâṣara-t*, punish, chastise; — IV. INF. *iqṣâr*, desist from; be powerless; be old and weak; bear small children; — V. INF. *taqaṣṣur*, shrink, shorten (n.); — VI. INF. *taqâṣur*, feign to be short; crouch, shrink; be not equal to and desist; (m.) be punished, chastised; — VII. INF. *inqiṣâr*, be cleaned, fulled, washed, bleached; get white;

— VIII. INF. *iqtiṣâr*, limit one's self to, be content with; — X. INF. *istiqṣâr*, find short or too short.

قصر *qaṣr*, shortness, smallness; shortening (s.); shrinking, contraction; restriction; suppression of the second letter of a *sabab ḥafîf* at the end of a foot and making the first quiescent; end, last end, aim; evening, twilight; also *qaṣar*, doing too little, falling short, shortcoming; sluggishness, weakness, impotence; fulling, bleaching; pl. *quṣûr*, large stone building, castle, palace, fortress; — *qaṣar*, having a stiff neck; — *qiṣar*, shortness; — *quṣṣar*, pl. of قاصر *qâṣir*, short, &c.; — ة *qaṣra-t*, *quṣra-t*, shortness; nearest degree of relationship; — *qaṣara-t*, nuptial chamber; pl. *-ât*, husk of a grain of wheat; pl. *aqṣâr*, base of the neck, neck.

قصرا *qaṣrâ'*, f. of اقصر *aqṣar*, shorter, &c.; — *quṣarâ'*, pl. of قصير *qaṣîr*.

قصرى *quṣra*, short rib; a snake; — *qaṣriyy*, noble, of high birth.

قصرين *qaṣrîn*, coarse straw.

قصص *qaṣaṣ*, tale, INF. of (قص); chest; — *qiṣaṣ*, *quṣaṣ*, pl. of قصة *qiṣṣa-t*, *quṣṣa-t*.

قصطل *qaṣṭal*, dust.

(قصع) *qaṣa'*, INF. *qaṣ'*, swallow water; chew; quench the thirst; prevent the growth of a child; keep indoors; kill a louse between the nails; despise; fill (n.) with blood (wound); — *qaṣi'*, A, INF. *qaṣ'*, *qaṣa'*,— also *qaṣu'*, INF. *qaṣâ'a-t*, fail to thrive; — II. INF. *taqṣî'*, quench the thirst; keep always indoors; (m.) cover the flat roof with turf and then with earth.

قصع *qaṣi'*, backward in growth; — ة *qaṣa'a-t*, pl. *qiṣa'*, *qiṣâ'*, *qaṣa'ât*, dish for two persons; trough; scale of a balance; قصعة الصارى *qaṣa'at aṣ-ṣârî*, tops (of the masts); (m.) roof covered with turf; — *quṣ'a-t*, pl. *quṣa'*, prepuce drawn over the gland; also *quṣa'a-t*, hole of the field-mouse.

قصعا *quṣâ'a'* (قصاعة *quṣâ'a-t*, قاصعا *qâṣi'â'*, قصيعا *quṣai'â'*), pl. *qawâṣi'*, hole of the field-mouse.

(قصعل) *quṣ'ul*, *qiṣ'il*, contemptible; scorpion; — III. *iqṣa'all*, INF. *iqṣi'lâl*, culminate.

(قصف) *qaṣaf*, I, INF. *qaṣf*, break, cut off, shatter; press and push; INF. *quṣûf*, indulge in eating and drinking; amuse one's self; — INF. *qaṣîf*, roar and resound (thunder); sound; — *qaṣif*, A, INF. *qaṣaf*, be weak, brittle, not strong enough; break (n.) in the middle; bend (n.); — IV. INF. *iqṣâf*, be thin, weak; — V. INF. *taqaṣṣuf*, break (n.), get broken; — VI. INF. *taqâṣuf*, assemble and throng; — VII. INF. *inqiṣâf*=V.; be pushed back; leave and pass on.

قصف *qaṣf*, indulgence in eating and drinking; amusement, sport, frolic; — *qaṣif*, broken; brittle; —ة *qaṣfa-t*, pushing (s.), throng; violent roaring of a camel; pl. *qaṣf*, *quṣfân*, part of a sand-hill, torn off by the storm; — *qiṣfa-t*, pl. *qiṣaf*, fragment, piece.

(قصقص) *qaṣqaṣ*, INF. ة, call or decoy young dogs; (m.) cut off the tops of the hair; — *qaṣqaṣ*, hairy part of the chest; — *quṣquṣ*, ة *quṣquṣa-t*, short, thick-set and strong; lion.

(قصل) *qaṣal*, I, INF. *qaṣl*, cut off; mow green food; give green food to the horse; — V. INF. *taqaṣṣul*, VII. INF. *inqiṣâl*, be cut off, mown; — VIII. INF. *iqtiṣâl*, cut off; be cut off.

قصل *qaṣl*, cutting off, mowing (s.); also *qiṣl*, *qaṣal*, chaff, stubble; — *qiṣl*, ة *qiṣla-t*, troop of camels

(30 to 40); — ة qaṣla-t, chaff; stubble; sheaf.

(قصم) qaṣam, I, INF. qaṣm, break entirely; return from whence one came; — V. INF. taqaṣṣum, VII. INF. inqiṣâm, be broken.

قصم qaṣm, qiṣm, quṣm, ة qaṣma-t, &c., fragment, piece;—qaṣm, suppression of the mu and making quiescent the l of mufâ'alatun, changing it into fâ'altun = maf'ûlun;—qaṣam, breach, fracture;— qaṣim, brittle; — quṣam, who breaks everything;—quṣum, pl. of قصيمة qaṣîma-t.

(قصمل) qaṣmal, INF. ة, break, cut off; walk with short steps; throw down.

(قصنصع) qaṣanṣa', short, dwarfish.

(قصو) qaṣâ, U, INF. qaṣw, quṣuww, qaṣa-n, qaṣâ', be very far distant; remove (n.) to a great distance; — U, INF. qaṣw, maim at the tops of the ears; — قصي qaṣî, A, INF. qaṣan, qaṣâ', be far distant; — III. INF. muqâṣât, dispute about who is more distant or lives farther away; — IV. INF. iqṣâ', remove (a.) to a great distance; — V. INF. taqaṣṣî, be far distant; be sent away to a great distance; flee, escape; penetrate deeply into a matter; — X. INF. istiqṣâ', send or wish far away; try to fathom, to penetrate deeply into a matter.

قصوا qaṣwâ', f. of اقصى aqṣa, having the ears clipped, &c.; a she-camel of Mohammed's.

قصود qaṣûd, marrow.

قصور quṣûr, falling short, shortcoming (s.); insufficiency, weakness, impotence; sluggishness, negligence, forgetfulness; defect, fault; transgression, sin; — *; — ة qaṣûra-t, nuptial chamber, cabinet.

قصوف quṣûf, over-indulgence in eating and drinking.

قصوى quṣwa, f. of اقصى aqṣa, farther, farthest.

قصى qaṣan, qaṣa, distance, direction; see (قصو); — qaṣṣiy, ة, pl. aqṣâ', far distant; — quṣṣayy, a proper name; — ة qaṣiyya-t, pl. qaṣâyâ, very valuable and kept free from work (camel).

قصيا quṣyâ = قصوى quṣwa.

(قصيب) qaṣîb, ة, accurately cut; — ة qaṣîba-t, pl. qaṣâ'ib, twisted curl; reed, reed-pipe.

قصيد qaṣîd, pl. quṣdân, qaṣâ'id, poem of some length, laudatory poem; — ة qaṣîda-t, pl. qaṣîd, qaṣâ'id, id.; romance.

قصير qaṣîr, pl. qiṣâr, quṣarâ', f. ة, pl. qiṣâr, qiṣâra-t, short; too short, defective; small; imp; — quṣair, town on the Red Sea.

قصيرا quṣairâ', قصيرى quṣaira, last rib.

قصيعا quṣai'â', see قصعا quṣa'â'.

قصيعة quṣai'a-t, small dish.

قصيف qaṣîf, broken; — *

قصيل qaṣîl, green food.

(قض) qaḍḍ, U, INF. qaḍḍ, pierce, perforate, bore (pearls, &c.); deflower; put anything dry, as sugar, &c. into a fluid dish; rub, grind, pound; send horsemen against the enemy; pull out; INF. qaḍîḍ, crack, gnash; — qaḍiḍ, be mixed with anything dry; eat of such food; be hard; — IV. INF. iqḍâḍ, add anything dry to a dish; be too hard, be stone-strewed; — V. INF. taqaḍḍuḍ, taqaḍḍî, pounce down;—VII. INF. inqiḍâḍ, spread in all directions and rush against the enemy; swoop down; fall; threaten ruin; — VIII. INF. iqtiḍâḍ, deflower; — X. INF. istiqḍâḍ, find a place or bed hard to lie upon.

قض qaḍḍ, full of pebbles and gravel and therefore hard; small gravel; — ة qiḍa-t, pl. qiḍûn, qiḍât,

qiḍa-n, a herb; — *quḍa-t*, fault, vice;—*qaḍḍa-t*, *qiḍḍa-t*, pl. *qiḍâḍ*, pounded pebbles, shingle; remains; *qiḍḍa-t*, virginal blood, virginity.

قضا *qaḍ'* (also قض *qaḍ'*), INF. of (قضى); — *qaḍan*, *qaḍa*, *qaḍâ'*, pl. *aqḍiya-t*, fate, destiny; death; decision; decree; judgment, sentence; jurisdiction; dominion; execution; payment of a debt; event, accident; (m.) use, service;—ة *quḍât*, membrane round the head of an embryo; pl. of قاضى *qâḍî*, judge, &c.

قضاب *qaḍḍâb*, ة *qaḍḍâba-t*, sharp; apt; — ة *quḍâba-t*, clippings of trees.

قضاض *qiḍâḍ*, pl. of قضة *qiḍḍa-t*.

قضاع *quḍâ'*, colic, gripes; also ة *quḍâ'a-t*, fine dust; —ة *qaḍâ'a-t*, beaver; hunting-panther.

قضاف *qiḍâf*, pl. of قضفة *qaḍafa-t* and قضيف *qaḍîf*.

قضايا *qaḍâyâ* pl. of قضية *qâḍiyya-t*.

(قضب) *qaḍab*, I, INF. *qaḍb*, cut off, lop off; beat with a rod; ride an untrained beast; (m.) make an extract, condense; — II. INF. *taqḍîb*, cut off, prune; (m.) sew, make a seam;—V. INF. *taqaḍḍub*, be cut off, pruned; — VII. INF. *inqiḍâb*, id.; — VIII. INF. *iqtiḍâb*, cut off, prune; ride an untrained beast; speak ex tempore, improvise; make an extract.

قضب *qaḍb*, lopped off branches; also ة *qaḍba-t*, freshly mown clover;—*quḍb*, young branches; pl. of قاضب *qâḍib*, sharp; — *quḍub*, pl. of قضيب *qaḍîb*; — ة *qaḍba-t*, pl. *qaḍabât*, tender branch.

قضبان *quḍbân*, pl. of قضيب *qaḍîb*.

قضض *qaḍaḍ*, gravel and sand; sandy food; INF. of (قض).

(قضع) *qaḍa'*, I, INF. *qaḍ'*, subdue, tame; — II. INF. *taqḍî'*, colic; — V. INF. *taqaḍḍu'*, be cut, separated, dispersed; —VII. INF. *inqiḍâ'*, be far away from one's people.

قضع *qaḍ'*, colic, gripes; — ة *quḍ'a-t*, perdition, vice, pollution.

(قضعم) *qaḍ'am*, greatly advanced in years; decrepit.

(قضف) *qaḍif*, A, *qaḍuf*, INF. *qaḍaf*, *qiḍaf*, *qaḍâfa-t*, be thin and slender.

قضف *qaḍaf*, thinness, leanness; — ة *qaḍafa-t*, *qaṭa* bird; pl. *qaḍaf*, *qiḍâf*, *qiḍfân*, *quḍfân*, rocky hill; — *qiḍâfa-t*, shifting sand-hill.

(قضقض) *qaḍqaḍ*, INF. ة, tear to pieces and crush; — II. INF. *taqaḍquḍ*, be dispersed.

(قضم) *qaḍim*, A, INF. *qaḍm*, nibble at; break, cut; do anything leisurely; — *qaḍim*, A, INF. *qaḍam*, have decayed and black teeth, be decayed and black; — IV. INF. *iqḍâm*, feed the horse on oats.

قضم *qaḍam*, sword; pl. of *qaḍîm*;— *qaḍim*, old and jagged; — ة *qiḍma-t*, anything dry and cracking under the teeth; roasted grey peas.

(قضى) *qaḍa*, I, INF. *qaḍy*, *qaḍâ'*, *qaḍiyya-t*, decide, decide upon, resolve, pre-ordain, order, prescribe; judge, deliver sentence; condemn; impose; INF. *qaḍâ'*, execute, perform, complete; make, create; pay entirely; be extreme in; fulfil one's destiny, die; kill, exterminate; pass (the time); inform; — II. INF. *taqḍiya-t*, *qiḍḍâ'*, execute, carry out, complete; INF. *taqḍiya-t*, make one a judge; (m.) suffice for; — III. INF. *muqâḍât*, summon before the judge; — V. INF. *taqaḍḍî*, be carried out, completed; be at an end, cease; be past; — VI. INF. *taqâḍî*, have a law-suit against; demand payment from; receive payment (2 acc.); — VII. INF. *inqiḍâ'*, be carried out, com-

pleted; cease, be past; die; demand payment, exact; admit; decide, decide upon; be required, necessary, beseeming; — X. INF. *istiqḍâ'*, ask one to decide as a judge (2 acc.); pass. *ustuqḍî*, be appointed as a judge; demand for one's own use.

(قضى) *qaḍi'*, A, INF. *qaḍa'*, rot, fall to pieces, break (n.); be red and have the corners sore (eye); — *qaḍi'*, A, INF. *qaḍ'*, eat up, consume; — V. INF. *taqaḍḍu'*, give to eat, feed.

قضى *qaḍi'*, ة, rotten; — ة *qaḍiyya-t*, pl. *qaḍâyâ*, judgment, sentence, decision; order, command; dominion; fate, death; statement, assertion, question, proposition; article of faith; fact, thing, matter, affair; law-suit; story; requisite (s.).

قضيب *qaḍîb*, pl. *quḍub*, sharp; pl. *quḍbân*, *qiḍbân*, slender branch, switch, rod; iron bar, rail; penis.

قضيض *qaḍîḍ*, cracking; INF. of (قض); coarse gravel; بقضيضهم *bi-qaḍîḍ-hum*, all of them.

قضيف *qaḍîf*, pl. *qiḍâf*, *quḍfân*, thin, slender.

قضيم *qaḍîm*, pl. *qaḍam*, what cracks under the teeth; white parchment; table-cloth of leather; old and jagged.

(قط) *qaṭṭ*, U, INF. *qaṭṭ*, cut; mend a pen; (m.) desist; — I, INF. *qaṭṭ*, *quṭûṭ*, also pass. *quṭṭ*, grow dear, rise in price; — A, INF. *qaṭâṭa-t*, — also *qaṭiṭ*, A, INF. *qaṭaṭ*, be short and curly; — VII. INF. *inqiṭâṭ*, be cut, mended (pen), pruned.

قط *qaṭ*, *qaṭṭ*, only (placed after); *qaṭ*, *qaṭṭ-u*, sufficiency; — *qaṭṭ-u*, *quṭṭ-i*, *quṭṭ-u*, *qaṭ-u*, *quṭ-u*, vulg. *qaṭṭ*, ever; with negative: never, not at all; — *qaṭṭ*, short and curly; — *qiṭṭ*, pl. *qiṭâṭ*, *aqṭâṭ*, *qiṭaṭa-t*, tom-cat; pl. *quṭûṭ*, account-book; decision of a judge; money-order, cheque; diploma; — ة *qaṭṭa-t*, nib of a pen; — *qiṭṭa-t*, pl. *qiṭaṭ*, cat.

قطا *qaṭan*, *qaṭâ'*, ة, pl. *qaṭawât*, *qaṭayât*, bird *qaṭa* (ardea stellaris).

قطاب *qiṭâb*, mixture; — *qaṭṭâb*, cross-beam; (m.) always; — ة *qaṭâba-t*, subterranean aqueduct; sluice, flood-gate.

قطاج *qaṭâj*, *qiṭâj*, cable, rope.

قطار *qiṭâr*, pl. *quṭur*, *quṭurât*, row of camels; row; — *; — ة *quṭâra-t*, droppings; — *qaṭṭâra-t*, pl. *qaṭâṭîr*, place where pitch is boiled; — ى *quṭâriyy*, a poisonous snake.

قطاط *qiṭâṭ*, curly-haired; pl. *aqiṭṭa-t*, model, pattern; — *; — *qaṭṭâṭ*, turner.

قطاطير *qaṭâṭîr*, pl. of قطارة *qaṭṭâra-t*.

قطاطين *qaṭâṭîn*, pl. of قطين *qiṭṭîn*.

قطاع *qiṭâ'*, pl. of قطع *qiṭ'* and قطيع *qaṭî'*; INF. of (قطع); — *quṭâ'*, sweets; — *qaṭṭâ'*, sharp, cutting; who cuts much; secant; — *quṭṭâ'*, pl. of قاطع *qâṭi'*, cutting, &c.; — ة *quṭâ'a-t*, pl. *qaṭâ'i'*, cuttings; fasting (s.); — *qaṭṭâ'a-t*, mason's hammer.

قطاف *qaṭâf*, *qiṭâf*, grape-gathering, vintage; slow pace of a horse; — *qaṭṭâf*, grape-gatherer, vintager; — ة *quṭâfa-t*, gleanings in grape-gathering; (m.) best food, delicacies.

قطام *qaṭâm*, greedy for meat; hawk; — ى *qaṭâmiyy*, *quṭâmiyy*, id.; sagacious.

قطان *qaṭṭân*, pl. *quṭun*, cotton-spinner or seller; — *quṭṭân*, pl. of قاطن *qâṭin*, resident, &c.

قطايات *qaṭâyât*, pl. of قطاة *qaṭât*.

قطائط *qaṭâ'iṭ*, pl. detachments.

قطائع *qaṭâ'i'*, pl. of قطاعة *qaṭâ'a-t* and قطيعة *qaṭî'a-t*.

(قطب) *qaṭab*, I, INF. *qaṭb*, *quṭûb*, frown; concentrate; assemble (n.); cut; anger; mix wine; fill; bind the ends of a sack together; (m.) mend anything

torn; (m.) reach from one wall to the other (cross-beam); — II. INF. *taqṭîb*, frown; mix wine; sew together again, sew a wound; — V. INF. *taqaṭṭub*, be wrinkled, frowning; be sewn together; — VI. INF. *taqâṭub*, concentrate (n.) from all sides to surround one; — VII. INF. *inqiṭâb*, be contracted, wrinkled, frowning; be sewn together again.

قطب *qaṭb, qiṭb, quṭb, quṭub*, axle-tree; — *quṭb*, pl. *aqṭâb, quṭûb, qiṭaba-t*, pole, polar star; axis, pivot; leader, prince, chief, the first of; — ة *quṭba-t*, pl. *quṭab*, axis; head of a spear used as a mark; (m.) stitch *qiṭibba*; — ى *quṭbiyy*, ة, polar; — *qiṭibba*, a plant of which strong ropes are made.

(قطج) *qaṭaj*, U, INF. *qaṭj*, twist a rope tight; draw up the bucket with the rope *qiṭâj*.

(قطر) *qaṭar*, U, INF. *qaṭr, quṭûr, qaṭarân*, fall or flow in drops, drop, trickle; make to drop, drop (a.) into; smear the camel with pitch; INF. *qaṭr*, tie camels, mules, &c. one behind the other so as to form a row; tow a ship; — INF. *quṭûr*, travel fast; — II. INF. *taqṭîr*, IV. INF. *iqṭâr*, drop (a.), drop into, distil; throw one on his side; make the beasts march in a row; — V. INF. *taqaṭṭur*, fall on the side; throw one (ب *bi*) on his side; drop (n.), fall in drops; — VI. INF. *taqâṭur*, walk in a row or chain; drop together; come from all sides at the same time; — X. INF. *istiqṭâr*, cause to drop, distil.

قطر *qaṭr*, pl. *qiṭâr*, what drops; rain; drop; dropping, distilling (s.); — *qiṭr*, brass; — *quṭr*, pl. *aqṭâr*, side; climate, region; diameter; also *quṭur*, wood for fumigation, aloes; — *quṭur*, pl. of قطار *qiṭâr*; — ة *qaṭra-t*, pl. *qaṭr*, drop; a little, a bit.

قطرات *quṭurât*, pl. of قطار *qiṭâr*.

قطران *qaṭrân, qiṭrân, qaṭirân*, fluid pitch, tar; — *qaṭarân*, INF. of (قطر).

(قطرب) *qaṭrab*, INF. ة, hasten (n.), make haste; throw to the ground; — II. INF. *taqaṭrub*, move one's head like the animal *quṭrub*.

قطرب *quṭrub*, pl. *qaṭârib*, a wicked demon; were-wolf; melancholy, demoniacal possession; a small ever-moving animal.

قطرميز *qaṭarmîz*, large bottle (Turk.).

(قطرن) *qaṭran*, INF. ة, smear with pitch, pitch, tar.

قطروب *quṭrûb*=قطرب *quṭrub*.

قطرى *qiṭriyy*, ة *qiṭriyya-t*, a striped stuff.

قطريب *qaṭrîb*, peg by which the oxen are tied to a plough.

قطط *qaṭaṭ*, pl. *qiṭâṭ*, curly head of hair or a person having such; INF. of (قط); — *qiṭaṭ*, pl. of قطة *qiṭṭa-t*; — ة *qiṭaṭa-t*, pl. of قط *qiṭṭ*.

(قطع) *qaṭa'*, INF. *qaṭ', tiqiṭṭâ', maqṭa'*, cut, cut off, lop, amputate; break off, tear off, sever; separate from a friend, cut an acquaintance, spurn; separate by a wall, &c.; estrange; decide between; ق الطريق *qaṭa' aṭ-ṭarîq*, infest the high road, carry on highway robbery; turn aside from; enter (one's head); pass (the time); order peremptorily; fix (a ransom, &c.); destroy; cause to cease; stanch; (m.) suspend a priest; give up hope; renounce a title, claim, &c.; dry up; lose its power (medicine); thicken (n.); digest; (m.) fast; be sufficient for a dress; have the stuff for a dress cut off; fit; beat, cudgel; — INF. *qaṭ', quṭû'*, swim over or cross a river, cross a mountain; wander through; — INF. *qaṭâ', qiṭâ', quṭû'*, mi-

grate from colder parts to warmer ones; — pass. *quṭi'*, suffer from asthma; be forced to renounce; — *qaṭi'*, A, INF. *qaṭa'*,— *qaṭu'*, INF. *qaṭâ'a-t*, be no longer able to speak, become paralysed (tongue); — II. INF. *taqṭî'*, cut off entirely or into many pieces; scan; bring across a river; pass (the time); get ahead of, overtake; suffice for a dress; (m.) use up a dress; mix the wine; — III. INF. *muqâṭa'a-t*, separate from (n.), renounce, cut one's acquaintance; interrupt; (m.) give work at a fixed price; — IV. INF. *iqṭâ'*, make one cut or cut off; bring across a river; convince; give a fief to (2 acc.); cease to lay eggs; pass. be separated from one's people; — V. INF. *taqaṭṭu'*, be cut, cut off, broken off, severed; be cut in pieces; fall in rags; decay; be cancelled; cancel; be mixed with water; — VI. INF. *taqâṭu'*, get separated, estranged; separate (n.); VII. INF. *inqiṭâ'*, be cut off; break, tear (n.); get detached; separate (n.); be interrupted, be forced to interrupt or renounce; be at an end, cease; be unable to march on; run short, dry up; give one's self entirely up to; — VIII. INF. *iqtiṭâ'*, cut off for one's self, take out; — X. INF. *istiqṭâ'*, demand an estate as a fief.

قطع *qaṭ'*, cutting off (s.), cut, amputation; section; intersection; conic section: ق زائد *qaṭ' zâ'id*, hyperbola, ق ناقص *qaṭ'' nâqiṣ*, ellipsis, ق مكافى *qaṭ' mukâfî*, parabola; breach of friendship; interruption, termination, end; suppression of the last letter of a *watad majmû'* at the end of a foot and making the preceding one quiescent; partition-wall; suspension from office; interdict; *qaṭ'an*, by all means, with and without negative: not at all, by no means; — *qiṭ'*, pl. *aqṭâ'*, place of a cut or breach; cut off branch; darkest part of the night; night-watch; pl. *qiṭâ'*, *aqṭu'*, *aqṭâ'*, small broad head of an arrow; *qiṭ'*, highway robber; wicked, bad; also *quṭ'*, asthma, shortness of breath; ceasing (s.); — *quṭ'*, highway robber; pl. of اقطع *aqṭa'*, cut off, &c., and قاطع *qâṭi'*, cutting, &c.; also *quṭu'*, pl. of قطيع *qaṭî*; — ة *qiṭ'a-t*, pl. *qiṭa'*, cut off piece; piece, slice; segment; part, a little, mite; rags, tatters, strophe; last part of the night; clipped hair; size of a book; — *quṭ'a-t*, pl. *quṭa'*, ceasing (s.), subsiding, sinking (of the water in a well); piece of land, field, acre; pl. *qaṭa'*, place of a cut, stump of an amputated limb; pl. *quṭa'*, cut, form, design.

قطعا *qaṭ'â*, f. of اقطع *aqṭa'*, cut off, &c.; — *qiṭ'â'*, *quṭ'â'*, قطعان *quṭ'ân*, pl. of قطيع *qaṭî'*.

(قطعر), III. *iqṭa'arr*, INF. *iqṭi'râr*, be short of breath.

(قطعن), III. *iqṭa'ann*, INF. *iqṭi'nân* = the previous.

قطعى *qaṭ'iyy*, ة, separating, disjunctive; categorical, determined; (m.) wicked, bad; highway robber.

(قطف) *qaṭaf*, I, INF. *qaṭf*, cull, pluck; gather; scratch; bolt, sift; treat to delicate food; — IV. INF. *iqṭâf*, be ripe for the harvest; — V. INF. *taqaṭṭuf*, be finely sifted; — VII. INF. *inqiṭâf*, be culled, gathered; — VII. INF. *iqtiṭâf*, cull, gather, select.

قطف *qaṭf*, gathering of fruit or grapes; suppressing a *sabab ḥafîf* at the end of a foot and rendering the previous consonant quiescent; pl. *quṭûf*, scratch, chap, rent; — *qiṭf*, pl.

quṭûf, bunch of grapes, cluster; culled fruit; — *qaṭaf*, ة *qaṭafa-t*, trace, track; — *quṭuf*, pl. of قطوف *qaṭûf* and قطيفة *qaṭîfa-t*; — ة *qaṭfa-t*, harvest.

(قطقط) *qaṭqaṭ*, INF. ة, rain; cry out (as the *qaṭa* bird); — II. INF. *taqaṭquṭ*, walk fast and with short steps; be headstrong.

قطقط *qiṭqiṭ*, slight rain, hail.

(قطل) *qaṭal*, U, I, INF. *qaṭl*, cut off, amputate, behead; — II. INF. *taqṭîl*, id.

(قطلب) *qaṭlab*, wild currant; strawberry-tree.

(قطم) *qaṭam*, I, INF. *qaṭm*, bite, seize with the teeth and taste; cut off; — *qaṭim*, A, INF. *qaṭam*, have an eager desire for; — VII. INF. *inqiṭâm*, be cut off; — ة *qaṭma-t*, fragment, piece.

قطمير *qiṭmîr*, split in a date-stone and membrane in it; membrane round a fruit-stone; also قطمور *quṭmûr*, name of the dog of the Seven Sleepers.

(قطن) *qaṭan*, U, INF. *quṭûn*, inhabit; serve; — *qaṭin*, A, INF. *qaṭan*, bend (n.); — II. INF. *taqṭîn*, grow woolly, mouldy.

قطن *quṭn*, *quṭun*, *quṭunn*, pl. *aqṭân*, cotton; — *qaṭan*, trunk (of the body); — *quṭun*, pl. of قطين *qaṭîn*; — ة *quṭna-t*, flake of cotton; — *qaṭina-t*, tripe; — ى *qaṭniyy*, ة, of cotton; — ية *quṭniyya-t*, *qiṭniyya-t*, pl. *qaṭâniyy*, shell-fruit; peas, lentils, beans, millet; fruit in general (except wheat, oats, grapes, and dates).

(قطو) *qaṭâ*, U, INF. *qaṭw*, walk slowly; cry.

قطوات *qaṭawât*, pl. of قطا *qaṭan*.

قطوب *qaṭûb*, frowning, austere; lion; — *.

قطوع *qaṭû'*, interrupting suddenly (adj.); danger; — *qaṭṭû'*, large log of wood (m.); — *

قطوف *qaṭûf*, pl. *quṭuf*, short-stepping; — *

قطونا *qaṭûnâ*, *qiṭûnâ*, flea-bane.

قطيب *qaṭîb*, mixed; — ة *qaṭîba-t*, troop, crowd.

قطيرة *quṭaira-t*, small drop; a little, mite.

قطيع *qaṭî'*, pl. *quṭ'*, *quṭu'*, *qiṭâ'*, *quṭ'ân*, *aqṭu'*, *aqâṭi'*, *aqṭi'a-t*, cut off branch; pl. *qiṭâ'*, *quṭ'ân*, *aqṭâ'*, *aqâṭi'*, part of a herd, herd, flock; pl. *quṭa'â'*, whip; equal, similar; — *qiṭṭî'*, digesting well; — ة *qaṭî'a-t*, pl. *qaṭâ'i'*, estrangement, separation, breaking off the connection; piece of land, fief; tax, custom.

قطيل *qaṭîl*, cut off.

قطيمة *qaṭîma-t*, fragment, piece.

قطين *qaṭîn*, sing. and pl., pl. also *quṭun*, inhabitant of a house; people of a house, household, servants; — *qiṭṭîn*, pl. *qaṭâṭîn*, large cave; — ة *qaṭîna-t*, people of the house, household; shell-fruit.

(قع) *qa''*, U, INF. *qa''*, irritate by bold speech; meet with bitter water in digging.

قعاد *qu'âd*, lameness of the hips; — ة *qu'âda-t*, woman.

قعارة *qa'âra-t*, depth.

قعاص *qu'âṣ*, fatal disease of sheep from surfeit; — *qa''âṣ*, who kills at once; lion.

قعاع *qu'â'*, bitter water.

قعال *qu''âl*, ة, vine-blossom.

قعائد *qa'â'id*, pl. of قعدة *qa'da-t*, قعود *qa'ûd* and قعيدة *qa'îda-t*.

(قعب) *qa'b*, pl. *qi'âb*, *qi'aba-t*, *aq'ub*, cup (for one person); — *qu'b*, deep ravine, cave; water-hole; — II. *qa''ab*, INF. *taq'îb*, be cup-like; impart depth to one's speech; — ة *qa'ba-t*, small box.

قعبرى *qa'bariyy*, hard, miserly.

(قعبل) *qa'bal*, *qi'bil*, white mushroom.

(قعث) *qa'aṯ*, INF. *qa'ṯa-t*, give but little, give niggardly; — II. INF.

taq'îṣ, destroy entirely; — IV. INF. *iq'âṣ*, be lavish of one's own; make a liberal gift.

(قعشب) *qa'ṣab*, قعشبان *qa'ṣbân*, much, many, plentiful.

(قعشر) *qa'ṣar*, INF. ة, uproot, extirpate, destroy entirely.

(قعد) *qa'ad*, U, INF. *qu'ûd*, *maq'ad*, sit down, sit; remain sitting, abide, dwell; be pensioned; roost; invite to sit, seat; stand; be stiff; be idle; desist from (عن *an*), cease, bear no fruit every second year; make a stand against (ب *bi*); neglect; keep from; prepare (n.) for war; — II. INF. *taq'îd*, invite to sit, seat; make stiff; keep as a guest, take as a servant into one's house; — III. INF. *muqâ'ada-t*, sit down by, sit at the side of (acc.); — IV. INF. *iq'âd*, invite to sit; prevent from, force to renounce; limp; pass. be tied to the place, be lame; — V. INF. *taqa''ud*, VI. INF. *taqâ'ud*, delay, put off, have no mind for, neglect; — VIII. INF. *iqti'âd*, sit down, take as a seat, take a camel, &c. to ride upon; — XIV. *iq'andad*, INF. *iq'indâd*, settle, stay, remain.

قعد *qi'd*, companion; — *qa'ad*, deserted soldiers; heretic; — *qu'ud*, قعدان *qi'dân*, pl. of قعود *qa'ûd*; — ة *qa'da-t*, sitting (s.), session; seat, buttocks; — *qi'da-t*, way of sitting; youngest child, nestling; ذو القعدة *ẕû 'l-qi'da-t*, eleventh month of the Arabs; — *qu'da-t*, pl. *qu'dân*, ass; the camel for daily riding; saddle; — *qu'ada-t*, stable, stationary; sluggard, slothful; — ى *qi'diyy*, *qu'diyy*, weak; sedentary, stationary; — *qa'adiyy*, heretic.

(قعر) *qa'ar*, A, INF. *qa'r*, dig deep, deepen (a.); fathom; empty the cup to the bottom; eat up; excavate; extirpate; — *qa'ur*, be deep; — II. INF. *taq'îr*, dig deep, make deep, deepen (a.); (also V.) draw out the corners of the mouth in speaking; — IV. INF. *iq'âr*, make a solid bottom to a well; — V. INF. *taqa''ur*, be excavated, deepened; be hollow and empty; let one's self down into a depth; see II.; — VII. INF. *inqi'âr*, be excavated, deepened, hollow, empty; be extirpated, cut off by the root.

قعر *qa'r*, pl. *qu'ûr*, bottom, ground, depth; excavation, pit; hold of a ship, keel; also قعران *qa'rân*, deep dish; — ة *qa'ra-t*, pit.

(قعرط) *qa'raṭ*, INF. ة, demolish.

(قعز) *qa'az*, INF. *qa'z*, fill; drink out quickly.

(قعس) *qa'is*, A, INF. *qa'as*, have the chest protruding and the back drawn in; recede; — VI. INF. *taqâ'us*, affect the above quality; strain against; fall short of one's duty; — XIV. *iq'ansas*, INF. *iq'insâs*, have the above quality (I.) in a high degree.

قعس *qa'is*, having a protruding chest and hollow back.

(قعسر) *qa'sar*, INF. ة, take hold of; be hard, firm, solid; — ى *qa'sariyy*, beam by which an ass turns the wheel of a mill.

(قعش) *qa'aś*, INF. *qa'ś*, gather (a.); destroy, demolish; bend (a.), bend towards one's self; — VII. INF. *inqi'âś*, emigrate; be destroyed.

قعش *qa'ś*, pl. *qu'ûś*, camel-litter for women.

(قعص) *qa'aṣ*, INF. *qa'ṣ*, kill on the spot; remain dead on the spot; pass. *qu'iṣ*, be seized with the disease قعاص *qu'âṣ*; — *qa'iṣ*, A, keep the milk back.

(قعط) *qa'aṭ*, INF. *qa'ṭ*, press hard upon a debtor; fasten the turban on the head; be a coward, fear; throw to the ground; be angry; cry out

violently; urge on violently; uncover, bare; — *qa'iṭ*, A, INF. *qa'aṭ*, be contemptible and despised; — II. INF. *taq'iṭ*, be shameless in speech; — IV. INF. *iq'âṭ*, render contemptible; cry out violently.

(قعظ), IV. *aq'aẓ*, INF. *iq'âẓ*, molest, press hard.

(قعف) *qa'af*, INF. *qa'f*, pull out by the root, exterminate; consume entirely; carry off stones; — *qa'if*, A, INF. *qa'af*, fall, tumble in; — V. INF. *taqa''uf*, be moved from its place; — VII. INF. *inqi'âf*, id.; be no longer in its place.

قعق *qa'q*, pl. *qu'qân*, raven (m.).

قعقاع *qa'qâ'*, clatter, clash, rattle (s.); feverish shivering.

(قعقر) *qa'qar*, INF. ة, heap up stones (m.).

(قعقع) *qa'qa'*, INF. ة, *qi'qâ'*, clatter, clash, rattle; thunder; (m.) croak; shake the arrows (in the game); — II. INF. *taqa'qu'*, move (n.) or be shaken with a noise; have creaking boots; (m.) croak.

قعقع *qa'qa'*, raven; — ة *qa'qa'a-t*, clatter, clash, rattle; — *qu'qu'*, stork.

قعقور *qa'qûr*, heap of stones; boundary-stone.

(قعل) *qa'l*, poles to prop vine-trees or to dry dates upon; — IV. INF. *iq'âl*, open (n.), expand; — XI. *iqa'all*, INF. *iq'i'lâl*, id.

(قعم) *qa'am*, INF. *qa'm*, cry out, mew; — *qa'im*, A, INF. *qa'am*, be seized with a fatal disease; — IV. INF. *iq'âm*, rise in the sky; bite and kill; pass. *uq'im* = *qa'im*.

قعموط *qu'mûṭ*, swaddling-cloth.

(قعن) *qa'in*, A, INF. *qa'an*, be very short.

قعنا *qa'nâ'*, f. of اقعن *aq'an*, having a short up-turned nose; pug-nosed.

(قعو) *qa'â*, U, INF. *qa'w*, *qu'uww* (also VIII.), cover the mare, tread the hen; — قعى *qa'î*, A, INF. *qa'an*, have the top of the nose large and up-turned; — IV. INF. *iq'â'*, id.; sit on the buttocks; lean the back against anything in sitting.

قعو *qa'w*, pl. *qu'iyy*, pulley.

قعواش *qa'wâš*, pl. *qa'âwîš*, hole in the earth, cave.

قعود *qa'ûd*, ة *qa'ûda-t*, pl. *qu'ud*, *qa'â'id*, *qi'dân*, *aqdi'a-t*, young camel fit to be ridden; — *qu'ûd*, INF. of (قعد); sojourn; inactivity; state of a pensioner.

قعور *qa'ûr*, deep; — *qu'ûr*, pl. of قعر *qa'r*.

قعوش *qa'waš*, INF. ة, throw down; (m.) dig a hole in the ground; — II. INF. *taqa'wuš*, be destroyed.

قعى *qa'î*, V. see (قعو); — *qu'iyy*, pl. of قعو *qa'w*.

قعيد *qa'îd*, who sits at the side of, keeps him company, companion (du. *qa'îdân*, the two guardian angels); contemporary; ally; who lags behind, sluggard, lazy; hunting-prey; — ة *qa'îda-t*, wife, concubine.

قعير *qa'îr*, ة, deep.

(قف) *qaff*, U, INF. *qufûf*, purloin the coin (money-changer); (m.) crouch, squat down; — INF. *qufûf*, *qafîf*, wither, dry up, dry; — INF. *qufûf*, stand on end from fear (hair); — IV. INF. *iqfâf*, cease to lay eggs.

قف *qif*, IMP. of وقف, *waqif*, stand, &c.; — *quff*, pl. *qifâf*, *aqfâf*, stony hill; stone-heap; hole of the axe; — ة *qaffa-t*, weak man; also *qiffa-t*, *qaffa-t*, feverish shivering, ague-fit, chill; — *quffa-t*, pl. *qufaf*, large basket; boat.

قفا *qafan*, *qafa*, *qafâ'*, pl. *qifiyy*, *qufiyy*, *qifîn*, *aqf-in*, *aqfî*, *aqfâ'*, *aqfiya-t*, hind part of the head, occiput, neck; head, skull; back side, reverse; pursuit.

قفاحتة *qafâtaḥta-t*, cornice (m.).
(قفاخر) *qufâḥir*, ة, thick, full.
قفار *qafâr*, dry bread ; — * .
قفاز *quffâz*, glove ; muff.
قفاص *qaffâṣ*, maker of cages.
قفاع *qifâ'*, pl. of قفعة *qaf'a-t* ; — *qaffâ'*, niggardly ; — ة *quffâ'a-t*, nest ; — ى *qufâ'iyy*, crimson.
قفاق *qaffâq*, who purloins money ; — *.
قفافير *qafâfîr*, pl. of قفورة *qaffûra-t*.
قفال *qaffâl*, lock-smith ; — *quffâl*, pl. of قافل *qâfil*, returning from a journey.
قفان *qaffân*, occiput, neck ; end.
قفاند *qafânid*, pl. of قفندد *qafandad*.
قفاوة *qafâwa-t*, honour shown to a guest, favour ; joy ; قفاوة عنه *qafâwat-an 'an-hu*, behind one's back, without one's knowing.
قفتان *qaftân*, overcoat (Turk.).
(قفح) *qafaḥ*, INF. *qafḥ*, abhor, turn aside from, loathe ; abstain from (عن *'an*).
(قفخ) *qafaḫ*, INF. *qafḫ*, *qifâḫ*, beat, strike, especially on the head or anything hollow ; — IV. INF. *iqfâḫ*, be hot (cow).
(قفد) *qafad*, I, INF. *qafd*, slap slightly on the neck ; wind the turban entirely round the head, so that nothing hangs down ; complete.
قفدا *qafdâ'*, way of winding the turban as prescribed in the previous.
قفدان *qafadân*, ة *qafadâna-t*, small box for drugs.
قفدر *qafdar*, ugly.
(قفر) *qafar*, U, INF. *qafr*, follow one's tracks, place one's foot in another's track ; (m.) acknowledge, verify, try, test ; — *qafir*, A, INF. *qafar*, be but little ; be without a side-dish ; be not fleshy ; — IV. INF. *iqfâr*, be waste, depopulated, deserted ; come to the desert ; find a town laid waste and deserted ; — V. INF. *taqaffur*, follow one's tracks ; — VII. INF. *inqifâr*, (m.) be acknowledged, verified, averred ; (m.) be tried, tested ; — VIII. INF. *iqtifâr*=V.
قفر *qafr*, ة, pl. *qifâr*, *qufûr*, desert without water and vegetation ; desert, empty, waste ; *qafr-a*, in the open air ; ق اليهود *qafr al-yahûd*, asphalte ; — ى *qafra*, desert (s.).
(قفز) *qafaz*, I, INF. *qafz*, *qafazân*, *qufâz*, *qufûz*, jump, leap ; die ; — II. INF. *taqfîz*, make jump ; have the mare covered ; — ة *qafza-t*, ى *qafaza*, jump, leap.
قفزان *qufzân*, pl. of قفيز *qafîz* ; — *qafazân*, INF. of (قفز).
(قفس) *qafas*, U, INF. *qafs*, *qufûs*, die ; seize by the hair ; tear away violently and angrily ; tie up the feet.
قفس *qafs*, cage ; — *qufs*, a tribe of robbers.
قفسا *qafsâ'*, f. of *aqfas*, born of a free woman by a slave, &c. ; stomach, intestines.
(قفش) *qafaś*, U, INF. *qafś*, take and collect ; beat ; eat greedily ; indulge in sexual intercourse ; milk hastily.
(قفص) *qafaṣ*, U, INF. *qafṣ*, tie the feet together ; put a bird into a cage ; reduce to a smaller place or size, bring the parts nearer to one another ; cause pain to (acc.) ; — *qafiṣ*, A, INF. *qafaṣ*, be nimble and brisk ; shrink with cold ; suffer from heart-burn ; — II. INF. *taqfîṣ*, encage a bird ; — IV. INF. *iqfâṣ*, have a cage.
قفص *qafaṣ*, pl. *aqfâṣ*, bird's cage ; basket ; trellis-work.
قفصل *qufṣul*, lion.
(قفط) *qafaṭ*, U, I, INF. *qafṭ*, cover, fecundate ; requite ; look austere, frown ; — VI. INF. *taqâfuṭ*, copulate (n.).
قفطان *qafṭân*=قفتان *qafṭân*.
(قفطل) *qafṭal*, INF. ة, take out of one's hand, from under one's nose.

(قفع) *qafa'*, INF. *qaf'*, beat on the fingers with a rod; prevent, hinder; — *qafi'*, A, INF. *qafa'*, have the ears shrivelled up, be shrivelled; have the toes crooked; — II. *taqfî'*, preserve in a vessel; — V. INF. *taqaffu'*, be shrivelled; — VII. INF. *inqifâ'*, be prevented.

قفع *qafa'*, anxiety, trouble, hardship; — ة *qaf'a-t*, pl. *qifâ'*, basket made of palm-leaves without a handle.

قفف *qufaf*, pl. of قفة *quffa-t*.

(قفقف) *qafqaf*, INF. ة, tremble with cold; shiver; chatter (teeth); — II. INF. *taqafquf*, id.

قفقف *qafqaf*, chin and beard of a camel; wing of an ostrich.

(قفل) *qafal*, I, U, INF. *qufûl*, return from a journey, &c.; carry on a usurious corn-trade; lock, lock up; — U, also *qafil*, A, INF. *qafl*, dry up, wither; — I, INF. *qafl*, *qufûl*, estimate; store victuals for a time of need; — I, INF. *qufûl*, rut furiously; — II. INF. *taqfîl*, dry up, wither; lock the door; — IV. INF. *iqfâl*, id.; push the bolt; cause to return, lead back; — V. INF. *taqafful*, VII. INF. *inqifâl*, VIII. INF. *iqtifâl*, get locked; — X. INF. *istiqfâl*, be miserly, niggardly.

قفل *qafl*, ة, dry, withered; — *qufl*, pl. *aqfâl*, *aqful*, *qufûl*, lock, bolt (ق رومى *qufl rûmiyy*, padlock); flag, banner; skein; (m.) caravan; — *qafal*, people returning from a journey, ة *qafala-t*, caravan; — ة *qafla-t*, occiput.

(قفن) *qafan*, U, INF. *qafn*, beat, cudgel, flog, whip; strike in the neck; kill, slaughter; fight; lick out a vessel; — I, INF. *qufûn*, die; — VIII. INF. *iqtifân*, kill, slaughter.

قفن *qafan*, occiput.

(قفند) *qafannad*, big- and hard-headed.

قفندد *qafandad*, pl. *-ûn*, *qafânid*, broad-shouldered.

(قفو) *qafâ*, U, INF. *qafw*, *qufuww*, walk behind one (acc.), follow the track of, persecute; imitate; (m.) disappear behind anything; impart, bestow; efface one's traces; accuse publicly of a crime, of adultery; — *qafû*, قفى *qafa*, I, INF. *qafy*, beat on the back part of the head; — II. INF. *taqfiya-t*, cause or bid to follow, send after; follow one's track; make verses to rhyme; — III. INF. *muqâfât*, profit from one's absence, to do a thing behind his back; — IV. INF. *iqfâ'*, cause to follow; impart, bestow; honour a guest; eat of a dish made in one's honour; — V. INF. *taqaffî*, follow one's track; (m.) disappear behind; receive with distinction; rhyme; — VIII. INF. *iqtifâ'*, follow, imitate; impart; claim; prefer, select; — X. INF. *istiqfâ'*, beat in the neck; (m.) = III.

قفو *qafw*, imitation; — ة *qafwa-t*, *qifwa-t*, back-part, hind-part; (m.) cloth embroidered with gold leaves, worn by women on their backs.

قفورة *qaffûra-t*, pl. *qafâfîr*, large basket covered with clay to preserve corn in.

قفول *qufûl*, return; — *.

(قفى) *qafi'*, A, INF. *qafa'*, have the plants spoiled by too much rain or dust; — VIII. INF. *iqtifâ'*, tear, burst (n.).

قفى *qafa*, *qafy*, V. see (قفو); — *qafiyy*, who comes behind another, successor; honoured guest; dish made in honour of a guest; benevolent; — *qiffiyy*, pl. of قفا *qafan*.

قفير *qafîr*, dry bread; basket; beehive.

قفيز *qafîz*, pl. *qufzân*, *aqfiza-t*, a measure = 12 صاع *ṣâ'*; a mea-

surement of surface=144 square miles.

قفيص *qafîṣ*, plough-share.

قفين *qafîn*, killed by a blow in the neck; — *qifîn*, pl. of قفا *qafan*.

قفة *qaqqa-t*, excrement of a child.

(قل) *qall*, I, INF. *qill*, *qull*, *qilla-t*, *qulâl*, be but little, be of small number or quantity; be scarce, happen rarely; diminish (n.), decrease; declare to be little; INF. *qulâl*, lift up and carry; — II. INF. *taqlîl*, diminish (a.); — IV. INF. *iqlâl*=II.; be rare, happen rarely; grow poor; find but little; bring but little; lift up and carry; lift, raise, support; bear with; — V. INF. *taqallul*, be lessened, diminish (n.); — VI. INF. *taqâll*, find too little; — X. *istaqall*, INF. *istiqlâl*, find small in number, too little, too paltry; despise, contemn; depart, remove (n.); lift up and carry; rise, soar; seize; have absolute power.

قل *qill*, *qull*, small number or quantity, little; scarceness, rareness; — *qill*, trembling (s.); — *qull*, solitary, lonely, isolated; — ة *qilla-t*, pl. *qilal*, littleness, small quantity, scarceness; few things; want, poverty; fit of trembling; — *qulla-t*, pl. *qulal*, highest point, top, summit; tower; head; knob; earthen water-jug.

قلا *qalâ'*, hatred, detestation; — *qallâ*, who roasts; maker of frying-pans; burner of potash.

قلاب *qilâb*, wolf; — *qulâb*, a disease of the heart; — *qallâb*, forger, falsifier of money; — *qullâb*, hook, grapnel.

قلادة *qilâda-t*, pl. *qalâ'id*, necklace; chaplet; investiture; piece, head (of elephants); pl. exquisite old poems.

قلار *qillâr*, ى *qillâriyy*, white fig.

قلاس *qallâs*, foaming; maker of caps; — ى *qalâsî*, *qalâsiyy*, pl. of قلنسوة *qalansuwa-t*, &c.

قلاص *qallâṣ*, rising.

قلاع *qilâ'*, pl. of قلع *qal'* and قلعة *qal'a-t*; — *qulâ'*, ulcers in the mouth; a disease of the tongue; St. Andrew's fire (a consuming illness); — *qulâ'* ة (also *qullâ'a-t*), dry clay, glebe, clod of earth; stone of a catapult; — *qallâ'*, beadle; slanderer, informer; — ة *qilâ'a-t*, sail.

قلافة *qilâfa-t*, calking of a ship; — *qulâfa-t*, rind, crust, shell.

قلامة *qulâma-t*, parings, offal in cutting the nails or mending pens.

قلانس *qalânis*, قلانيس *qalânîs*, pl. of قلنسوة *qalansuwa-t*.

قلايا *qalâyâ*, pl. of قلية *qaliyya-t*.

قلائد *qalâ'id*, pl. of قلادة *qilâda-t*.

قلائص *qalâ'iṣ*, pl. of قلوص *qalûṣ*.

قلاية *qillâya-t*, pl. *-ât*, *qalâliyy*, cell, room; patriarchate.

(قلب) *qalab*, I, INF. *qalb*, turn, overturn, turn topsy-turvy, rummage, search; overthrow; transform; exchange (pass. change one's opinions, change colour, turn into); take the marrow out of a palm; turn from; turn towards or against; take to one's self; — U, I, INF. *qalb*, hit or injure in the heart; pass. be seized with the heart-disease قلاب *qulâb*; — *qalib*, A, INF. *qalab*, be turned up, have the lips turned up; — II. INF. *taqlîb*, turn, overturn, &c.; manipulate; prove, probe; transact business; — IV. INF. *iqlâb*, take one to one's self (God); turn; — V. INF. *taqallub*, be turned, turned over, &c.; veer, shift, be restless; change; be fickle, changeable, inconsistent; adventure; — VII. INF. *inqilâb*, *munqalab*, be turned upside down, topsy-turvy; be changed, transformed, metamorphosed; be converted to

(الى *ila*); veer, turn round, return; be turned from.

قلب *qalb*, (m.) *qulb*, turn, change, tacking about (s.); vicissitude; exchange, interchange; reverse; pl. *qulûb*, heart; mind, soul, secret thought; centre, core, kernel, marrow; best and purest part, essence; ة, pure of origin; perverted; counterfeit, spurious, adulterated; *qalb, qilb, qulb*, pl. *qilaba-t, aqlâb, qalûb*, marrow of a palm-tree; — *qulb*, pure of origin; bracelet; pl. of اقلب *aqlîb*, turned upside down, &c., and قليب *qalîb*; — *qalab*, being turned up of the lip; — *qullab*, who changes at every moment, fickle; — ة *qalba-t*, turn; change; tack; change of opinion; fickleness; — *qulba-t*, pure origin; — *qalaba-t*, heart-ache; — ى *qalabiyy*, ة, hearty, intimate; internals; — *qulabiyy*, versatile; changeable.

(قلت) *qalit*, A, INF. *qalat*, perish; — IV. INF. *iqlât*, give over to destruction.

قلت *qalt*, pl. *qilât*, mountain-cave with water; cavity, hole; — *qult*, saxifrage (plant).

(قلح) *qaliḥ*, A, INF. *qalaḥ*, be of a dirty yellow (tooth) or have such teeth; — II. INF. *taqlîḥ*, remove this evil.

قلح *qaliḥ*, dirty; — *qulḥ*, pl. and—

قلحا *qalḥâ'*, f. of أقلح *aqlaḥ*, having yellow teeth.

(قلخ) *qalaḫ*, INF. *qalḫ*, *qalîḫ*, roar; beat dry things about so as to rustle; up-root; tear off; — II. INF. *taqlîḫ*, whip violently, flog; grow strong, hard.

(قلد) *qalad*, I, INF. *qald*, collect in a reservoir or vessel; befall every day; twist; irrigate; put around; beat metal thin and plate with it; — II. INF. *taqlîd*, wind round; adorn with a necklace, put on a neck-tie, gird with a sword, invest, make one a prince, give him full power; hand down old poems, sayings, truths, traditions, &c.; (m.) imitate, ape, represent on the stage; — V. INF. *taqallud*, put round one's neck; adorn one's self or be adorned with a necklace; buckle on the sword; get invested; be handed down; (m.) imitate, ape; — X. INF. *istiqlâd*, ape.

قلد *qild*, periodical access of fever; pl. *qulûd*, hole in a rock with water; — ة *qilda-t*, sediment of butter.

(قلذ) *qalaẓ*, tick (insect), sheep-louse; — ة *qaliẓa-t*, lousy.

(قلز) *qalaz*, U, I, INF. *qalz*, drink from the ground, sip, lap; let drink; thrust a stick into the ground; beat; shoot, hit; leap, jump; — II. INF. *taqlîz*, thrust the sting into the ground (locust for depositing its ova).

قلز *quluzz*, *qilizz*, hard and strong; very hard copper.

(قلزم) *qalzam*, INF. ة, swallow; blame, rebuke; — II. INF. *taqalzum*, swallow; die of avarice.

قلزم *qulzum*, ancient town near Mount Sinai; بحر القلزم *baḥr al-qulzum*, Red Sea.

(قلس) *qalas*, I, INF. *qals*, vomit; let wine or water flow over; drink much wine; — II. INF. *taqlîs*, play on the cymbals; sing and dance to them; prepare a solemn reception; place the cap قلنسوة *qalansuwa-t* upon one.

قلساة *qalsât*, INF. of قلسى *qalsa*, q.v. under (قلنس).

قلسوة *qalaswa-t*, see قلنسوة *qalansuwa-t*.

(قلش) *qalaś*, U, INF. *qalś*, remove the crust from a wound; stick to the feet, &c. (wet ground); — II. INF. *taqlîś*, fall off; stick to.

قلشين *qalśîn*, pl. *qalâśîn*, stocking sock; galoches (m.).

(قلص) *qalaṣ*, I, INF. *qulûṣ*, jump; vomit; rise; be contracted, wrinkled (also II.); shrink; — also *qaliṣ*, A, INF. *qalaṣ*, be disturbed (mind); — II. INF. *taqlîṣ*, see I.; — V. INF. *taqalluṣ*, be contracted, wrinkled, shrunk; shorten (n.).

قلص *qalaṣ*, disturbance of mind; — *quluṣ*, pl. of قلوص *qalûṣ*.

(قلط) *qalṭ*, ugliness of face; — (m.) *qalaṭ*, U, INF. *qalṭ*, empty a reservoir; clean; polish, scrape off; — VII. INF. *inqilâṭ*, be emptied, cleaned; be expelled; depart; —*qalaṭ*, without proviso, unconditionally (m.).

(قلع) *qala'*, INF. *qal'*, tear from its place, pull out, uproot, extract; pull off one's clothes, undress; dig out stones; overthrow, destroy, extirpate; depose; pass. be covered with small ulcers; — *qali'*, A, INF. *qala'*, sit not firmly on a chair or in the saddle; stand not firmly in wrestling; be rickety, fall easily; be dull of understanding; — II. INF. *taqlî'*, take away; depose; expel; — IV. INF. *iqlâ'*, *muqla'*, set sail; be turned from, desist, withdraw from; leave; fail; enter on the seventh year; — V. INF. *taqallu'*, be taken away, pulled out, digged out, deposed; — VII. INF. *inqilâ'*=V.; depart; — VIII. INF. *iqtilâ'*=I.; and pass. of it; rob.

قلع *qal'*, taking away, pulling out, up-rooting, extirpation, deposition; (also ة *qal'a-t*) pl. *qulû'*, *aqlu'*, *qilâ'*, *qila'a-t*, pouch of a herdsman, satchel, knapsack; *qal'*, *qil'*, *qala'*, intermission of a fever; — *qil'*, pl. *qulû'*, *qilâ'*, sail; — *qala'*, thickened blood; scurf, itch; — *qali'*, unsteady; tripping, slipping (adj.); — ة *qal'a-t*, *qil'a-t*, pl. *qilâ'*, *qulû'*, fortress, fortification, castle; — *qil'a-t*, pl. *qila'*, half of anything split asunder; — *qul'a-t*, *qula'a-t*, unsettled dwelling, restless sitting; — *qala'a-t*, pl. *qilâ'*, *qila'*, mass of rock difficult to pass round or cross; large stone; — ى *qala'iyy*, Indian tin.

(قلف) *qalaf*, I, INF. *qalf*, bark, rind, peel, take off the bast; cut off the prepuce, circumcise; INF. *qalf*, *qalfa-t*, tap a cask; foam, froth; calk and tar a ship; — *qalif*, A, INF. *qalaf*, have the prepuce left; — II. INF. *taqlîf*, calk a ship.

قلف *qilf*, rind, crust; — *qulf*, pl., قلفا *qalfâ'*, f. of اقلف *aqlaf*, circumcised, &c.; — *quluf*, pl. of قليفة *qalîfa-t*; — ة *qulfa-t*, prepuce.

(قلفط) *qalfaṭ*, INF. ة, calk a ship.

(قلق) *qaliq*, A, INF. *qalaq*, be agitated, disquieted, shaken; quake, waver; — IV. INF. *iqlâq*, agitate, disquiet, disturb, cause to quake; — V. INF. *taqalluq*, be agitated, disquieted, convulsed.

قلق *qalaq*, agitation, disquietude, trouble, anxiety; — *qaliq*, agitated, disquieted.

قلقاس *qulqâs*, colocassia; ق افرنجى *qulqâs afranjiyy*, potato.

قلقال *qalqâl*, agitation.

قلقان *qalqân*, agitated (m.).

(قلقس) *qalqas*, INF. ة, burn the tongue like the plant قلقاس *qulqâs*.

(قلقل) *qalqal*, INF. ة, *qalqâl*, *qilqâl*, move (a.), shake, agitate; sound, resound; (m.) stammer; — II. INF. *taqalqul*, be moved, shaken, agitated; be lifted up from the ground; —ة *qalqala-t*, agitation; (m.) stammering.

قلل *qilal*, *qulal*, pl. of قلة *qilla-t*, *qulla-t*, respectively; — *qulul*, pl. of قليل *qalîl*.

(قلم) *qalam*, I, INF. *qalam*, cut, pare, (m.) make stripes, stripe;

— II. INF. *taqlîm*, cut much or frequently; stripe.

قلم *qalam*, pl. *aqlâm*, *qilâm*, reed, reed-pen, pen (ق رصاص *qalam raṣâṣ*, pencil); graving tool; written character, handwriting, writing (القلم القديم *al-qalam al-qadîm*, hieroglyphics); manner of writing, style; stroke, line, alinea; (m.) stripe in variegated stuffs; (m.) arithmetical rule; arrow in the game; scion, graft; tubular bone; — ة *qalama-t*, bachelors, pl. of قالم *qâlim*.

قلما *qalla-mâ*, it rarely happens that.

قلمتراش *qalamtirâś*, *qalamtrâś*, pen-knife (Pers.).

قلمس *qalammas*, overflowing; waves of the sea; large army.

ابو قلمون *abû qalamûn*, chameleon.

قلمى *qalamiyy*, cystalline, crystallised; — ة *qalamiyya-t*, fee of a copyist; office of finances.

قلندر *qalandar*, beardless mendicant; — ية *qalandariyya-t*, order of beardless mendicants.

(قلنس) *qalnas*, INF. ة, also قلسى *qalsa*, INF. قلساة *qalsât*, put the cap قلنسوة *qalansuwa-t* on one.

قلنسوة *qalansuwa-t*, قلنسية *qalansiya-t*, *qalaswa-t*, pl. *qalânis*, *qalânîs*, *qalâs-in*, *qalâsî*, *qalâsiyy*, cap; hat of a Greek priest.

قلهب *qalhab*, old, thick.

(قلو) *qalâ*, U, INF. *qalw*, drive violently; run away with the rider; fry in a pan, roast; INF. *qil-an*, *qilâ'*, hate.

قلو *qilw*, nimble, alert; potash; young ass; — ة *qilwa-t*, runaway horse or camel.

قلوب *qalûb*, very dexterous, versatile; also *qallûb*, *qillaub*, wolf; — *.

قلوسة *qallûsa-t*, cap (m.).

قلوص *qalûṣ*, pl. *qalû'iṣ*, *qulaṣ*, *qilâṣ*, young she-camel just fit to be ridden; female ostrich with her young; young bustard; — *

قلولى *qalaula*, goose.

قلوم *qulûm*, hunting-hut.

(قلى) *qala*, I, INF. *qaly*, fry in the pan, roast, stew; beat on the head; — I, INF. *qila-n*, *qilâ'*, *maqliya-t*, hate passionately, detest and leave; — V. INF. *taqallî*, burn with anger; also VII. INF. *inqilâ'*, be roasted, fried.

قلى *qaly*, roasting, frying (s.); — *qila*, *qily*, ash of alkaline plants, potash, soda, &c.; sesame-oil; — *qilan*, hatred; — *qulan*, pl. crowns of heads, summits of mountains; — *qaliyy*, hostile, inimical; — ة *qaliyya-t*, pl. *qalâyâ*, fried, roasted; — *qilliyya-t*, pl. *qalâlî*, monk's cell, convent.

قليب *qalîb* (m. f.), pl. *aqliba-t*, *qulb*, *qulub*, old well or one not walled up inside; — ب *qulaib*, little heart; — *qillîb*, wolf.

قليسية *qalaisiyya-t*, little cap.

قليط *qalîṭ*, who is afflicted with— *qillîṭ*, ة *qillîṭa-t*, hydrocele, rupture of the scrotum or testicles.

قليفة *qalîfa-t*, pl. *qalîf*, *quluf*, basket for dates.

قليل *qalîl*, pl. *-ûn*, *qulul*, *qululûn*, *qilâl*, *qalâ'il*, *aqillâ'*, few, little, of small number or quantity; a little, trifle; scarce; short, thin, paltry, insignificant-looking; *qalîl-an*, rarely; *qalîl-an qalîl-an*, little by little, by degrees.

قليميا *qilîmiyâ*, dross, filings; daughter of Adam.

قلينسة *qulainisa-t*, little cap.

قليون *qalyûn*, hydraulic pipe.

(قم) *qamm*, U, INF. *qamm*, sweep the house; fecundate the mare; eat up from the ground; eat all; be dry, withered; — V. INF. *taqammum*, ascend the summit of a mountain; — VIII. INF. *iqtimâm*, eat all.

قم *qumm*, pl. *qimâm*, sleeve; — ة *qimma-t*, pl. *qimam*, crown,

highest point, vertex, apex; body, bodily make, form; troop, people.

(قما) *qama'*, INF. *qam'*, *qamâ'*, *qumû'*, also *qamu'*, INF. *qamâ'a-t*, *qumû'a-t*, be fat; — A, INF. *qam'a-t*, *qum'a-t*, *qim'a-t*, also *qamu'*, INF. *qamâ'a-t*, be small and insignificant-looking, be mean and contemptible; — IV. INF. *iqmâ'*, be fat; have fat camels; cause to be despised; — V. INF. *taqammu'*, gather by degrees; take the best for one's self; suit as a dwelling; — ة *qam'a-t*, place where the sun does not shine; plenty of food.

قماحة *qummâḥa-t*, saffron; barm, yeast.

قمار *qimâr*, game of chance, particularly at dice; — ى *qamâriyy*, pl. of قمرية *qamriyya-t*; — *qumâriyy*, of Cape Komorin; finest aloes.

(قمارص) *qumâriṣ*, sour.

قماس *qammâs*, diver; — *.

قماش *qumâś*, pl. *aqmiśa-t*, material for clothes, stuff; linen; household things, lumber, rubbish; rabble.

قماط *qimâṭ*, pl. *qumuṭ*, *aqmiṭa-t*, swaddling-cloth; rope; tricks.

قماعيل *qamâ'îl*, pl. of قمعولة *qum'ûla-t*.

قماقم *qamâqim*, small lice, ticks; pl. of قمقم *qumqum*, ة *qumquma-t*.

قمامسة *qamâmisa-t*, pl. of قمس *qummas*.

قمامة *qumâma-t*, pl. *-ât*, *qumâm*, sweepings; mixed crowd; كنيسة الق *kanîsa-t al-qumâma-t*, church of the Holy Sepulchre in Jerusalem.

قماميس *qamâmîs*, pl. of قميس *qimmîs*.

(قمح) *qamaḥ*, INF. *qumûḥ*, lift up the head and refuse to drink; — *qamiḥ*, A, INF. *qamḥ*, take medicine in a solid form; — II. INF. *taqmîḥ*, abound in grain; shoot into ears; bud; — IV. INF. *iqmâḥ*=II.; make to lift up the head; lift up the head and lower the eyes; — V. INF. *taqammuḥ*, VII. INF. *inqimâḥ* =I.

قمح *qamḥ*, wheat, corn, grain; — *qummaḥ*, pl. of قامح *qâmiḥ*, ag. of (قمح); — ة *qamḥa-t*, grain of wheat; grain (weight); bud.

قمحدوة *qamaḥduwa-t*, pl. *qamâdiḥ*, occiput; protuberance behind the ear.

(قمخ), IV. *aqmaḥ*, carry high (the nose, ب *bi*); sit like one who feels honoured.

(قمد) *qamad*, I, INF. *qamd*, refuse, scorn; persist in; — *qamid*, A, INF. *qamad*, have a long and thick neck; — IV. INF. *iqmâd*, stretch the neck after, look at (الى *ila*).

قمد *qumudd*, ة, long-necked; hard, strong, stiff.

(قمر) *qamar*, U, I, INF. *qamr*, play at dice or any game of chance; win in doing so, win at (acc.); gain, earn; — *qamir*, A, INF. *qamar*, shine with a yellowish or greenish-white hue; be not able to sleep in the moonlight; be a lunatic, a night-walker; be moon- or snow-blind; abound; drink its fill; — III. INF. *qimâr*, *muqâmara-t*, play at dice or any game of chance with; contradict, dispute with, get the better of in a dispute; — IV. INF. *iqmâr*, have moonlight (traveller); be moonlit; wait for the moon's rising; — V. INF. *taqammur*, play at dice; win in doing so; — VI. INF. *taqâmur*, play at dice with one another; contradict one another; dispute.

قمر *qamar*, pl. *aqmâr*, moon; luminary; du. *qamarân*, sun and moon; handsome face; — *qumr*, Cape Komorin; pl. of اقمر *aqmar*, shining, &c., and of

قمرية *qumriyya-t*; — *qamir*, abundant; ة, moonlit; — ة *qumra-t*, glitter or colour of yellowish or greenish-white.

قمرا *qamrâ'*, f. of اقمر *aqmar*, shining, &c.; moonlit night; moonlight; a bird.

قمرى *qamariyy*, ة, lunar; moonlike; lunatic; piece of five piasters; — ة *qumriyya-t*, pl. *qamâriyy*, *qumr*, turtle-dove.

(قمز) *qamaz*, U, INF. *qamz*, scrape together and pick up with the finger-tips; gather; (m.) jump; — II. INF. *taqmîz*, make jump; — IV. INF. *iqmâz*, acquire anything worthless.

قمز *qamaz*, worst part, anything worthless; — ة *qamza-t*, jump, leap (m.); — *qumza-t*, handful.

(قمس) *qamas*, I, U, INF. *qams*, dive, dip or plunge into the water (a.); surpass in diving; move in the maternal body (embryo); — III. INF. *muqâmasa-t*, *qimâs*, vie in diving; — IV. INF. *iqmâs*, immerse, plunge into (a.); dive; turn towards setting, set.

قمس *qummas*, pl. *qamâmisa-t*, patrician; count; leader of 10,000.

(قمش) *qamaś*, U, INF. *qamś*, gather from the ground; — II. INF. *taqmîś*, id.; — V. INF. *taqammuś*, eat what one can get, the bad included; — ة *qamśa-t*, whip (m.).

(قمص) *qamaṣ*, I, U, INF. *qamṣ*, *qimâṣ*, *qumâṣ*, walk lifting up and lowering the two front feet at the same time, gallop; beat and drive the ship; — INF. *qimâṣ*, *qumâṣ*, *qimiṣṣa*, jump; — V. INF. *taqammuṣ*, put on the shirt قميص *qamîṣ*; robe one's self; migrate from body to body.

قمص *qumuṣ*, قمصان *qumṣân*, pl. of قميص *qamîṣ*.

(قمط) *qamaṭ*, U, I, INF. *qamṭ*, bind a sheep by its fore-feet, bind a captive hand and foot; tie the camels in a row behind one another; swaddle; bandage the head; taste; take; be tart; — II. INF. *taqmîṭ*, bind one hand and foot; — III. INF. *muqâmaṭa-t*, seize one body to body to throw him down; — V. INF. *taqammuṭ*, be swaddled, wrapped up, bandaged; bandage one's own head.

قمط *qimṭ*, rope; — *qumuṭ*, pl. of قماط *qimâṭ*; — ة *qamṭa-t*, fillet, bandage; small turban; (m.) tartness of wine.

(قمطر) *qamṭar*, INF. ة, tie up the mouth of a skin bag; lie with; pass. assume a cheesy taste; pass. shrink, contract (n.); — III. *iqmaṭarr*, INF. *iqmiṭrâr*, writhe and bend its tail (scorpion); be disastrous.

قمطر *qimaṭr*, case of a book; bookcase (also ة *qimaṭra-t*); log of wood tied to the foot of a prisoner.

قمطرير *qamṭarîr*, disastrous; violent.

قمطلص *qamṭalaṣ*, chilblain.

(قمع) *qama'*, INF. *qam'*, subdue, tame; beat on the head; prevent by force; break, destroy, exterminate; put the funnel to a skin bag; drink out greedily; enter upon, engage in; — *qami'*, A, INF. *qama'*, suffer from a fistula of the lachrymal ducts or from inflammation of the corners of the eye; — II. INF. *taqmî'*, put on the funnel; make in the shape of a funnel; — IV. INF. *iqmâ'*, subdue, tame; — V. INF. *taqammu'*, be formed in the shape of a funnel; (m.) put on a black veil; — VII. INF. *inqimâ'*, be subdued, tamed; restrain one's self; steal in; return; — VIII. INF. *iqtimâ'*, drink out greedily.

قمع *qam'*, subjugating, taming (s.); submission; — *qim'*, *qima'*, pl. *qumû'*, funnel; cavity in

which the pedicule of a fruit is placed; fruit-shell; — *qama'*, inflammation of the eyes; — ة *qum'a-t*, *qam'a-t*, *qama'a-t*, pl. *qum'*, best part of one's property; — *qama'a-t*, pl. *qama'*, *maqâmi'*, camel-fly.

قمعا *qam'â'*, f. (قمع *qum'*, pl.) of اقمع *aqma'*, having a thick knee, having inflamed eye-lids.

(قمعل) *qam'al*, INF. ة, be chief of the family or tribe, first of the herdsmen; bloom, blossom.

قمعل *qum'ul*, clitoris; large cup.

(قمعوث) *qum'ûs*, cuckold; pimp, procurer.

قمعول *qum'ûl*, large cup; — ة *qum'ûla-t*, pl. *qamâ'il*, bud; chalice; knot in a vein.

قمقام *qamqâm*, *qumqâm*, deep sea; great crowd; prince; — ة *qamqâma-t*, smallest kind of lice.

(قمقم) *qamqam*, INF. ة, gather; surround; seize; afflict with small lice; — II. INF. *taqamqum*, be immersed; murmur.

قمقم *qumqum*, great crowd of people; also ة *qumquma-t*, pl. *qamâqim*, cup; basin; perfume in a bottle to be sprinkled over the guests.

(قمل) *qaml*, ة, louse, vermin; — *qamil*, lousy; — *qummal*, ة, a small camel-louse; — ة *qummala-t*, louse of a plant; worm in the corn; ear-wig.

قمل *qamil*, A, INF. *qamal*, be covered with lice; — II. INF. *taqmîl*, id. (m.); — IV. INF. *iqmâl*, show the first leaves.

قمم *qimam*, pl. of قمة *qimma-t*.

(قمن) *qamn*, manner, way, method; near; neighbour; — *qaman*, *qamin*, fit, suited, worthy; — V. INF. *taqammun*, endeavour, strive for, wish for.

قمنا *qumanâ'*, pl. of قمين *qamîn*.

(قمه) *qamah*, slight touch of appetite; — *qummah*, pl. of قامه *qâmih*, travelling camel, or a camel lifting up its head; — V. INF. *taqammuh*, depart without knowing whither.

(قمهد) *qamhad*, mean and ugly; — *qumhad*, who remains, sedentary; — III. *iqmahadd*, INF. *iqmihdâd*, lift up the head; stay, abide.

قمو *qumû'*, ة *qumû'a-t*, INF. of (قما).

قموس *qamûs*, deep and full.

قموط *qammûṭ*, rod (m.).

قموع *qamû'*, afflicted with a fistula of the lachrymal ducts.

(قمى), III. *qâma*, INF. *muqâmât*, fit, suit.

قمى *qamî'*, small, contemptible.

قميحة *qamîḥa-t*, a digestive powder.

قمير *qamîr*, pl. *aqmâr*, adversary in a game of chance; — *qumair*, little moon.

قميس *qimmîs*, pl. *qamâmîs*, sea.

قميص *qamîṣ*, jumping (adj.); pl. *qumuṣ*, *aqmiṣa-t*, *qumṣân*, shirt; under-vest; linen overcoat, blouse, tunic; surplice.

قميعة *qamî'a-t*, pl. *qamâ'i'*, protuberance behind a horse's ear.

قمين *qamîn*, pl. *qumanâ'*, fit, worthy; oven to heat baths; (m.) baker's oven.

(قن) *qann*, U, INF. *qann*, question, inquire for news; seek with the eyes; flog, cudgel; — VIII. INF. *iqtinân*, stand upright, be planted up; take as a slave; be silent; — X. INF. *istiqnân*, stay with the cattle and drink of their milk.

قن *qinn* (m. f., sing. pl.), pl. also *aqnân*, *aqinna-t*, slave, son of slaves born in the house; — *qunn*, pl. *qinân*, shirt-sleeve; (m.) poultry-stall; — ة *qinna-t*, pl. *qinan*, fibre of a palm-rope; — *qunna-t*, pl. *qunan*, *qinân*, *qunûn*, mountain-peak.

(قنا) *qana'*, INF. *qunû'*, be very red, dyed red; INF. *qan'*, dye the beard black; — A, INF. *qan'*, water the milk; cause one's death (acc.), kill; — قنى *qani'*,

A, INF. *qana'*, die, perish, rot;—II. INF. *taqni'a-t*, dye red; dye the beard black;—IV. INF. *iqnâ'*, kill, cause one's death.

قنا *qanan, qana*, hook of an eagle's beak or an aquiline nose;—*qana'*, canal;—*qannâ'*, spear-maker; spearman; skilful in finding water; ق الارض *qannâ' al-arḍ*, hoopoe;—ة *qanât*, pl. *qanawât, qana-n, qinâ', qaniyy, qanayât*, reed; reed-lance, lance; spine; pl. *quniyy, qanawât, aqniya-t*, subterranean canal.

قناب *qinâb*, bow-string; claw of a lion;—*qinnâb*, rope, string, pack-thread;—ة *qunnâba-t*, husk of grain.

قناتة *qanâta-t*, abstemiousness.

قناحة *qunnâḥa-t*, long key.

قناد *qannâd*, maker of sugar-candy; confectioner.

قنارة *qinnâra-t, qannâra-t*, butcher's stall; butcher's hook; shambles.

قناص *qannâṣ*, hunter.

قناطة *qanâṭa-t*, despair.

قناطير *qanâṭîr*, pl. of قنطار *qinṭâr* and قنطرة *qanṭara-t*

قناع *qinâ'*, pl. *qunu'*, wide veil for the head; pericardium; armour;—ة *qanâ'a-t*, contentedness, contentment, satisfaction; moderation; sobriety, frugality, temperance; conviction.

قناق *qinâq*, pl. *qinâqât*, resting-place, station, staple, relay; quarters.

قناقن *qunâqin*, pl. *qanâqin*, skilful in finding water.

قنان *qanân*, name of a mountain;—*qunân*, shirt-sleeve;—*;—ى *qanânî*, pl. of قنينة *qinnîna-t*.

(قنب) *qanab*, INF. *qanûb*, set;—U, INF. *qamb*, break forth (blossom); enter; prune the vine-tree;—II. INF. *taqnîb*, stretch, extend (a rope);—IV. INF. *iqnâb*, form a troop (of 30 to 40);—V. INF. *taqannub*, id.

قنب *qumb*, sheath of a horse's penis; large sail;—*qinnab, qunnab*, hemp; rope of hemp; pack-thread, string.

(قنبر) *qambar*, INF. ة, make proud by praise (m.);—II. INF. *taqambur*, grow proud, display self-sufficiency.

قنبر *qambar*, ة *qambara-t*, pl. *qanâbir*, bomb, shell;—ة *qumbura-t*, قنبرا *qumburâ'*, pl. *qanâbir*, lark; *qumbura-t*, crest of a bird;—ى *qumburiyy*, crested, cock.

قنبرانية *qumburâniyya-t*, crested (f.), hen.

(قنبض) *qumbuḍ*, snake.

(قنبل) *qambal*, INF. ة, become possessor or leader of a troop of horsemen;—ة *qambala-t*, pl. *qanâbil*, troop of horse, squadron.

قنبى *qunnabiyy, qinnabiyy*, hempen.

قنبيط *qimbîṭ, qunnabîṭ*, cauliflower.

(قنت) *qanat*, U, INF. *qunût*, obey God and adore Him in purity of heart;—*qanut*, INF. *qanâta-t*, take but little food;—IV. INF. *iqnât*, submit to God and call on Him; pray much; curse one's enemy; fight long and frequently against the infidel.

قند *qand*, sugar-candy;—II. INF. *taqnîd*, candy.

قنداق *qindâq*, ritual, missal (m.);—*qandâq*, pl. *qandâqât*=

قندق *qandaq*, pl. *qanâdiq*, gun-stock (m.).

(قندل) *qandal*, INF. ة, be big-headed; be indolent in walking; light candles round a dying person.

قندلة *qandala-t*, pl. *qanâdil*, pannier.

قندول *qandûl*, a shrub whose blossoms yield a fine oil.

قندى *qandiyy*, of sugar-candy.

قنديد *qindîd*, sugar-candy; wine; ambergris; musk; saffron.

قنديل *qindîl, qandîl*, pl. *qanâdîl*, candlestick, lamp, chandelier.

(قنز) *qinz*, a small cup;—IV. *aqnaz*, INF. *iqnâz*, drink out of it.

(قنزع) *qanza'*, INF. ة, raise the crest; flee from the adversary (cock); — ة *qunzu'a-t*, *qinzi'a-t*, pl. *qanâzi'*, cock's-comb.

(قنس) *qans*, *qins*, root, origin; — *qins*, pl. *qunûs*, crown of the head; — IV. *aqnas*, INF. *iqnâs*, claim a noble origin while being of low extraction.

(قنسر) *qansar*, *qinsarr*, *qinnasr*, old, decrepit; — *qansar*, INF. ة, cause to shrivel and render decrepit; — II. INF. *taqansur*, grow old and decrepit; — ى *qansariyy*, old, decrepit; — *qinnasriyy*, of Kinnasrîn.

(قنش), II. pass. *qunniś*, be given or spent scantily.

قنشورة *qunśûra-t*, woman who has not any menses.

(قنص) *qanaṣ*, I, INF. *qanṣ*, hunt, catch or kill in hunting; — V. INF. *taqannuṣ*, VIII. INF. *iqtinâṣ*, id.

قنص *qanṣ*, hunt; — *qanaṣ*, hunting-prey.

(قنصل) *qunṣul*, short; pl. *qanâṣil*, vulg. قنصو *qunṣû*, pl. *qunṣuwât*, consul.

قنصلية *qunṣûliyya-t*, consulate.

(قنط) *qanaṭ*, INF. *qanṭ*, prevent, hinder; — U, I, INF. *qunûṭ*, — *qaniṭ*, A, INF. *qanaṭ*, — *qanuṭ*, INF. *qanâṭa-t*, despair, lose courage; — II. INF. *taqnîṭ*, throw into despair, discourage; — IV. INF. *iqnâṭ*, id.

قنط *qanaṭ*, despair; — *qaniṭ*, desperate.

قنطار *qinṭâr*, pl. *qanâṭîr*, hundredweight; talent (1000 and more *dînars*); (m.) steelyard (balance).

(قنطر) *qanṭar*, INF. ة, leave the desert and settle in a village or town; own money by talents; (m.) produce a hundredweight of fruit; lie with; stay a long time with; vault; fall beneath the rider; — II. INF. *taqanṭur*, rear, fall down; — ة *qanṭara-t*, pl. *qanâṭir*, *qanâṭîr*, bridge; vault, arch; lofty building, arcade; aqueduct; causeway.

(قنع) *qana'*, INF. *qunû'*, solicit, pray humbly, beg; submit; ascend a mountain, mount; be contented with (ب *bi*)'; — INF. *qan'*, put the orifice of the bag to one's mouth in order to drink; — *qani'*, A, INF. *qana'*, *qun'ân*, *qanâ'a-t*, be contented with; be able to do without (عن *'an*); allow one's self to be convinced, be convinced; — II. INF. *taqnî'*, content; bid to be satisfied; convince, persuade; put on the veil قناع *qinâ'*; veil; — IV. INF. *iqnâ'*, content; convince; raise (the head); — V. INF. *taqannu'*, be contented; be convinced; put on the veil *qinâ'*, veil one's self; — VIII. INF. *iqtinâ'*, content one's self.

قنع *qin'*, root, origin; pl. *aqna'*, arms, weapons; — *qun'*, trumpet; — *qana'*, contentment, contentedness; — *qani'*, content; — *qunu'*, pl. of قناع *qinâ'*; — ة *qin'a-t*, pl. *qin'*, *qin'ân*, low ground.

قنعان *qun'ân*, sufficient.

(قنف) *qanif*, A, INF. *qanaf*, be covered with cracked clay; (m.) feel aversion; — II. INF. *taqnîf*, cut with the sword; — IV. INF. *iqnâf*, have a large army; = X.; — V. INF. *taqannuf*, feel aversion (m.); — X. INF. *istiqnâf*, have a collected mind and one's affairs in good order.

قنف *qinnaf*, deposited clay which has cracked.

قنفد *qunfud*, *qunfad*, قنفذ *qunfuẓ*, *qunfaẓ*, ة *qunfuda-t*, &c., pl. *qanâfid*, *qanâfiẓ*, porcupine; hedgehog; mouse, rat (ق بحرى *qunfud*, &c. *baḥriyy*, beaver); projecting bone behind a camel's ear; high sand-hill; —

II. INF. *taqanfuẓ*, give a sound thrashing.

(قنفش) *qanfaś*, INF. ة, shrink, contract (n.); be shrivelled, wrinkled; snatch; (m.) be untidy and unkempt; gather quickly.

(قنق), II. *qannaq*, INF. *taqnîq*, make a halt, alight (Turk.).

قنقريص *qanqariṣ*, a kind of vermicelli.

قنقن *qinqin*, *qanqan*, skilful guide, particularly to the water.

(قنم) *qanim*, A, INF. *qanam*, smell offensively, smell of oil; be rank; — II. INF. *taqnîm*, personify; — V. INF. *taqannum*, be personified; — ة *qanama-t*, offensive smell; — *qanima-t*, offensively-smelling (hand).

قنه *qinah*, *qinnah*, galbanum.

(قنو) *qanâ*, U, INF. *qanw*, *qunuww*, *qunwân*, *qunwa-t*, *qinwa-t*, *qunya-t*, *qinya-t*, acquire; procure for one's own use; possess; create; — I, INF. *qanw*, preserve shame, remain virginal; pass. be kept indoors; — قنى *qanî*, A, INF. *qanan*, acquire; be rich in cattle; preserve shame; — II. INF. *taqniya-t*, place in possession of, make one a rich proprietor, enrich; dig a canal for the water; — IV. INF. *iqnâ'*, enrich, make rich; preserve shame; — V. INF. *taqannî*, spend not all, but save for the future; — VIII. INF. *iqtinâ'*, acquire, procure (n.); possess; — X. INF. *istiqnâ'* (m.) = VIII.

قنو *qinw*, *qunw*, ة, pl. *aqnâ'*, *qunwân*, *qanwân*, *qinwân*, *qunyân*, *qanyân*, *qinyân*, bunch of dates; tender shoot; — *qanû'*, INF. of (قنا); ruddiness; — ة *qinwa-t*, *qunwa-t*, acquisition; property; possession of cattle.

قنوا *qanwâ'*, f. of اقنى *aqna*, having an aquiline nose; — ت *qanawât*, pl. of قناة *qanât*.

قنوان *qunwân*, INF. of (قنو); — *qunwân*, &c., pl. of قنو *qinw*, *qunw*.

قنوت *qunût*, piety, submission to the will of God.

(قنور) *qanawwar*, big-headed.

قنوط *qanûṭ*, desperate; — *qunûṭ*, despair.

قنوع *qanû'*, content; — *qunû'*, humble prayer, supplication; contentedness.

قنون *qunûn*, pl. of قنة *qunna-t*.

(قنى) *qana*, I, INF. *qany*, *qinyân*, *qunyân*, acquire; content; — *qanî*, A, INF. *qinan*, be content; — II. INF. *taqniya-t*, content; — III. INF. *muqânât*, mix; fit (n.) suit; — IV. INF. *iqnâ'*, content; place in possession of; — see (قنو).

قنى *qani'*, V. see (قنا); — *qinan*, *qina*, contented mind, contentedness; — *qanan*, *qaniyy*, *quniyy*, pl. of قناة *qanât*; — ة *qinya-t*, *qunya-t*, pl. *qinan*, acquisition; property; store; INF. of (قنو).

قنيان *qinyân*, *qunyân*, acquisition, property; INF. of (قنى); *qunyân*, &c., pl. of قنو *qinw*, *qunw*.

قنيص *qanîṣ*, hunter, chaser; — ة *qanîṣa-t*, pl. *qanîṣ*, hunt, hunting-prey.

قنيط *qanîṭ*, desperate, despairing.

قنيع *qanî'*, content, satisfied; convinced.

قنين *qinnîn*, Greek bow; — ة *qinnîna-t*, pl. *qanânî*, glass bottle; phial; little can.

قه *qih*, forbid! — *qahh*, loud laughter; — ة *qiha-t*, pure milk.

قهاب *quhâb*, ى *quhâbiyy*, white.

قهار *qahhâr*, vanquisher, conqueror, oppressor; avenger; irresistible, powerful; almighty.

قهارمة *qahârima-t*, pl. of قهرمان *qahramân*.

قهاوى *qahâwî*, pl. of قهوة *qahwa-t*.

(قهب) *qahib*, A, INF. *qahab*, be grey; — *qahb*, grey; — ة *quhba-t*, greyness.

(قهبل) *qahbal*, face; — INF. ة, say to one حيا الله قهبلك *ḥayyâ al-lâh-u qahbalak*, bless your face!

(قهد) *qahad*, A, INF. *qahd*, walk with short steps.

قهد *qahd*, pl. *qihâd*, a reddish kind of sheep with small ears; bright-coloured; dark-coloured; stag.

(قهر) *qahar*, INF. *qahr*, subdue, tame by force, overcome, conquer, oppress; compel; maltreat; harm; irritate; pass. be boiled soft; — III. INF. *muqâhara-t*, treat with violence and harshness; — IV. INF. *iqhâr*, find subdued; — VII. INF. *inqihâr*, be compelled by violence; be driven to extremities, be irritated, dissatisfied.

قهر *qahr*, ة *qahra-t*, exercise of superior power; submission, compulsion, violent treatment; overwhelming grief or anger; — ة *quhra-t*, id.; (m.) miserable condition.

قهربان *qahrabân*, amber (Pers.).

قهرمان *qahramân*, pl. *qahârima-t*, major-domo, steward, manager, administrator; holder of power, judge; — ة *qahramâna-t*, housekeeper.

قهرمة *qahrama-t*, administration, management.

قهرى *qahriyy*, having power of punishment, penal jurisdiction.

(قهز) *qahiz*, A, INF. *qahaz*, leap, leap upon.

قهز *qahz*, a red woollen stuff mixed with silk.

قهزب *qahzab*, short, dwarfish.

(قهقر) *qahqar*, INF. ة, go backwards, come back; (m.) abase, despise, embitter one's life; — II. INF. *taqahqur*, pass. of the previous: lead a miserable life.

قهقرى *qahqara*, retrograde movement; retreat; miserable life.

قهقز *qahqaz*, ة, black.

(قهقع) *qahqa'*, INF. *qihqâ'*, show the teeth and grin (wolf, bear, &c.).

(قهقه) *qahqah*, INF. ة, II. INF. *taqahquh*, laugh immoderately; — ة *qahqaha-t*, immoderate laughter.

(قهل) *qahal*, INF. *qahl*, *quhûl*, be dry, shrivelled; INF. *qahl*, be ungrateful; blacken one's character; — *qahil*, A, INF. *qahal*, be dry, shrunk, shrivelled; be dirty, keep one's self untidy, wash rarely; — IV. INF. *iqhâl*, undertake anything unexpected; — V. INF. *taqahhul*, be shrivelled; keep one's self untidy; — VII. INF. *inqihâl*, be weak and sink (from old age).

(قهم) *qahim*, A, INF. *qaham*, have no appetite; — IV. INF. *iqhâm*, id.; loathe; desire for.

(قهمز) *qahmaz*, INF. ة, leap, jump.

قهمزى *qahmaza*, running (s.) with uplifted body; swiftness.

قهوة *qahwa-t*, wine; coffee; pl. *qahâwî*, coffee-house, coffee- or guest-room.

قهوهجى *qahwahjiyy* (قهوجى *qahwajiyy*), pl. ة, coffee-house keeper.

(قهى) *qahî*, A, INF. *qahan*, have no appetite; — IV. INF. *iqhâ'*, id.; turn (a.) from (عن *'an*).

قهيز *qahîz*, coarse silk.

قوا *qawan*, *qawâ'*, *qiwâ'*, desolate place; desert; open air.

قوابى *qawâbiyy*, pl. of قوبا *qûbâ'*.

قوات *quwât*, provender.

قواد *qawwâd*, f. ة, pimp, procurer, broker; guide, conductor, guard; nose; — *quwwâd*, pl. of قائد *qâ'id*, guide, leader, &c.

قوارة *quwâra-t*, *quwwâra-t*, circular cut in the middle of anything, round hole.

قوارى *qawârî*, pl. of قارية *qâriya-t*, q.v.; — *qawâriyy*, tailor.

قوارير *qawârîr*, pl. of قارورة *qârûra-t*, glass bottle, &c.

قواس *quwâs*, report of a gun; — *qawwâs*, pl. *qawwâsa-t*, bow-

maker; archer; Kawwâs, policeman.

قواصر *qawâṣir*, pl. of قوصرة *qauṣara-t*.

قواصع *qawâṣi'*, pl. of قاصعا *qâṣi'â'*.

قواطع *qawâṭi'*, pl. birds of passage.

قواقى *qawâqî*, pl. of قيقاة *qîqâ'a-t*.

قوال *qawwâl*, ة *qawwâla-t*, very talkative, garrulous; eloquent; حمام ق *ḥamâm qawwâl*, cuckoo.

قوام *qawâm*, upright gait, stature; justice, equity; right measure; truth, reality; normal state; (m.) quick (*qawâm-an*, at once, directly, without ceremony); also *qiwâm*, essence, subsistence, consistency, substance; foundation; sustenance, means, money; support of the family; direction; — *qiwâm*, pl. of قويم *qawîm*; — *qawwâm*, standing upright, straight; well-ordered; firm, solid; superior;—*quwwâm*, pl. of قائم *qâ'im*, rising, standing, &c.

قوامع *qawâmi'*, pl. of قاموع *qâmû'*, chimney, &c.

قوانين *qawânîn*, pl. of قانون *qânûn*, fundamental rule, &c.

قواويق *qawâwîq*, pl. of قاوق *qâwuq*, doctor's cap, &c.

(قوب) *qâb*, U, INF. *qaub*, dig; break (a.); flee; approach, be near; — II. INF. *taqwîb*, dig out; — V. INF. *taqawwub*, be torn out by the root; be broken; open (n.); — VII. INF. *inqiyâb*, be dug out; be broken, open (n.); — VIII. INF. *iqtiyâb*, elect.

قوب *qûb*, pl. *aqwâb*, young of a bird, chick; (m.) lever; — *quwab*, egg-shell.

قوبا *qûbâ'*, *quwabâ'*, قوبة *quwaba-t*, pl. *quwwab*, *qawâbiyy*, tetter, dry scab.

(قوت) *qât*, U, INF. *qaut*, *qût*, *qiyâta-t*, nourish, feed, keep, sustain; strengthen, invigorate; — II. INF. *taqwît*, id.; — IV. INF. *iqâta-t*, id.; be equal to; — V. INF. *taqawwut*, pass. of I.; nourish, strengthen one's self; — X. INF. *istiqâta-t*, try to nourish one's self; ask for food or sustenance.

قوت *qût*, pl. *aqwât*, food, victuals, sustenance;— ة *qûta-t*, provisions for one day, ration.

(قوح) *qâḥ*, U, INF. *qauḥ*, be purulent, suppurate; sweep the house; — II. INF. *taqwîḥ*, sweep; — IV. INF. *iqâḥa-t*, refuse a gift to the supplicant.

قوح *qûḥ*, pl. of قاحة *qâḥa-t*, middle yard.

(قوخ) *qâḫ*, U, INF. *qauḫ*, be diseased.

(قود) *qâd*, U, INF. *qaud*, *qiyâda-t*, *maqâda-t*, *qaidûda-t*, *taqwâd*, lead, guide, rule; — INF. *qiyâda-t*, pander; — *qawid*, A, INF. *qawad*, have a long back or neck; — II. INF. *taqwîd*, *taqwâd*, lead, drag along; — IV. INF. *iqâda-t*, lead, guide; make obedient, obsequious; give one horses to lead; charge one to revenge another; — VII. INF. *inqiyâd*, allow one's self to be guided, yield, obey; — VIII. INF. *iqtiyâd*, lead; be led; gain; — X. INF. *istiqâda-t*, lead; yield to; have for a guide; demand from the judge the execution of a murderer, exact vengeance.

قود *qaud*, leading, guiding (s.); — *qawad*, requital, vengeance, revenge for bloodshed; — *quwwad*, pl. of قائد *qâ'id*, leader, &c.

(قور) *qâr*, U, INF. *qaur*, walk on tip-toe; surround the prey; make a circular cut or a round hole in anything (also II.); circumcise (a girl); — *qawir*, A, INF. *qawar*, be deprived of an eye; — II. INF. *taqwîr*, see I.; — V. INF. *taqawwur*, have a circular cut or round hole; writhe; — VII. INF. *inqiyâr*, fall, incline, bend (n.); — VIII. INF. *iqtiyâr*,

iqtiwâr, make a circular cut; be needy, want; examine.

قور *qaur*, cutting out (s.), circumcision; — *qûr*, pl. of قارة *qâra-t*, isolated hill, &c.; — *qawar*, being one-eyed (s.); being bleareyed (s.).

قورا *qaurâ'*, f. of اقور *aqwar*, spacious.

(قورم) *qauram*, INF. ة, salt fat or butter; — ة *qaurama-t*, salt butter or fat.

قوز *qauz*, pl. *aqwâz*, *qîzân*, *aqâwiz*, *aqâwîz*, high round sand-hill; — *qawwaz*, INF. *taqwîz*, be luxuriant; — V. INF. *taqawwuz*, run; be demolished, fall in; — VIII. INF. *iqtiyâz*, eat up.

قوزع *qauza'*, INF. ة, be conquered and flee.

(قوس) *qâs*, U, INF. *qaus*, *qiyâs*, determine the measure of a thing, measure it by; — INF. *qaus*, go in advance, get the lead of, overtake; — *qawis*, A, INF. *qawas*, have a crooked back; — II. INF. *taqwîs*, be crooked, bent; shoot off a bow or gun; — V. INF. *taqawwus*, be crooked, bent; be hit by a shot; — VIII. INF. *iqtiyâs*, measure; be in everything like one's father; — X. INF. *istiqwâs*, be bent with old age.

قوس *qaus* (f. m.), pl. *qusiyy*, *qisiyy*, *qiyâs*, *aqwâs*, bow (ق البندق *qaus al-bunduq*, cross-bow; ق الجلاهق *qaus al-julâhiq*, catapult, ballista; ق قزح *qaus quzah*, rainbow); segment; fore-arm; ell, yard; fiddlestick; card (for carding wool); — *qûs*, convent, cell; — *qawas*, bend of the back; — ى *qausiyy*, ة, of the shape of a bow; of the colours of the rainbow; — *qûsiyy*, hard, difficult (times).

(قوش) *qûś*, small man; (m.) pl. *aqwâś*, crupper; — II. *qawwaś*, INF. *taqwîś*, put the crupper on a horse.

قوصرة *qauṣara-t*, pl. *qawâṣir*, a kind of basket; cornice.

قوصف *qauṣaf*, coarse carpet.

(قوض) *qâḍ*, U, INF. *qauḍ*, demolish, sever the connection between parts; strike (a tent); — II. INF. *taqwîḍ*=I.; — V. INF. *taqawwuḍ*, VII. INF. *inqiyâḍ*, be destroyed, demolished, be broken up, disarranged.

(قوط) *qauṭ*, pl. *aqwâṭ*, herd of sheep (100); — ة *qauṭa-t*, large basket for dates; (m.) pressed dates.

(قوطب) *qauṭab*, INF. ة, surround from all sides, infest; overtake and cut off one's way.

قوطع *qauṭa'*, INF. ة, be worm-eaten.

(قوظ) *qauẓ*, heat of midsummer.

(قوع) *qâ'*, U, INF. *qau'*, *qiyâ'*, cover (stallion); withdraw, desist, remain behind; — INF. *qawa'ân*, limp; — VIII. INF. *iqtiyâ'*, be hot, rutting.

(قوف) *qâf*, U, INF. *qauf*, *qiyâfa-t*, follow one's track; draw inferences from external signs as to the interior state; suck the udder; — V. INF. *taqawwuf*, direct in speaking, prompt; — VIII. INF. *iqtiyâf*, follow one's track.

قوف *qûf*, the upper edge of the ear; edge, border.

(قوق) *qâq*, U, INF. *qauq*, cluck.

(قوقا) *qauqa'*, INF. ة=the previous.

قوقل *qauqal*, male partridge.

(قوقى) *qauqa*, INF. *qauqât*, cluck.

(قول) *qâl*, U, INF. *qâl*, *qaul*, *qîl*, *qaula-t*, *maqâl*, *maqâla-t*, speak, say, propose an opinion or doctrine; think; possess one's self of, conquer; beat, hit; kill; cause one to say, to speak about, to recite; pretend that one has said; — III. INF. *muqâwala-t*, speak with (acc.), converse; agree; object; — IV. INF. *iqwâl*, *iqâla-t*, cause one to say; pretend that one has said; INF.

iqâla-t, cancel a commercial transaction; excuse, pardon; — V. INF. *taqawwul*, invent as said by another, fable; — VI. INF. *taqâwul*, converse; — VII. INF. *inqiyâl*, be said, pretended, stated; — VIII. INF. *iqtiyâl*, dispose of, have in one's power; elect; — X. INF. *istiqâla-t*, wish to cancel a contract of purchase or sale; ask for pardon.

قول *qaul*, pl. *aqwâl*, *aqâwîl*, saying, word, speech, sentence; agreement, promise, contract;—*qu'ul*, pl. of قوول *qa'ûl*; — *quwwal*, pl. of قائل *qâ'il*, who says; — ة *qaula-t*, speech; INF. of (قول); — *quwala-t*, eloquent; talkative, garrulous.

(قولج) *qaulaj*, INF. ة, have the colic (m.).

قولنج *qaulanj*, *qûlanj*, colic.

قولى *qauliyy*, literal.

(قوم) *qâm*, U, INF. *qaum*, *qâma-t*, *qauma-t*, *qiyâm*, rise and stand upright; be erected; stand, stand motionless, remain standing; be unable to proceed (tired beast); remain, abide; break up the camp, depart; revive, recover; repair to (الى *ila*); rise against, revolt; rise to honour one; set at, put hand to, perform, complete; be animated (market); be dull; cost; — II. INF. *taqwîm*, make to stand upright, erect, straighten; bid to rise; put into order, set going again; mend, correct; fix the price of (acc.), estimate; pass. *quwwim*, be drawn (game); — III. INF. *qiwâm*, *muqâwama-t*, stand by; oppose, dispute with; make a stand against, defy; — IV. INF. *qâma-t*, *iqâma-t*, bid to stand, cause to rise; set up, erect; install, invest, appoint to; set in front, make leader of (على *'ala*); awake (a.); raise the dead; straighten; abide, stay; break up the camp, depart; cause to do so; persist in (فى *fî*, على *'ala*); persevere, endure; arrange well; execute, perform; call for prayer; devote one's self to (على *'ala*); besiege; carry (on a law-suit); — V. INF. *taqawwum*, be straightened, put into order, mended, corrected; — VI. INF. *taqâwum*, rise to combat against; be ready to oppose one another; defy or make a stand against one another; — VIII. INF. *iqtiyâm*, maim one's nose; — X. INF. *istiqâma-t*, rise and keep upright; be upright, straight, in good order; fix the price, estimate; cost; stay, abide; be in the family-way.

قوم *qaum*, standing up, rising, placing upright, remaining, abiding, &c., INF. of the previous; pl. *aqwâm*, pl. pl. *aqâwim*, *aqâ'im*, *aqâwîm*, people, nation, tribe; some people, someone, a certain; family; sect; *al-qaum*, the enemy; — *qawwam*, pl. of قائم *qâ'im*, rising, standing, &c.; — ة *qauma-t*, standing upright (s.); time during which one is standing (in prayer, &c.); stature, figure; (m.) insurrection, revolution.

قومس *qaumas*, prince, leader; open sea.

قومية *qaumiyya-t*, bond or connection between the members of a tribe; livelihood, sustenance; stature, figure.

(قون), V. *taqawwan*, INF. *taqawwun*, taunt; praise highly;—ة *qûna-t*, piece of tin-plate for making repairs; pl. *quwan*, medal.

قونس *qaunas*, pl. *qawânis*, crest of a helmet; crown of the head; — *qaunas*, INF. ة, beat an animal between the ears.

قونية *qûniyya-t*, Iconium.

(قوه), II. *qawwah*, INF. *taqwîh*, cry out, call; drive the prey into

the net ; — VI. INF. *taqâwuh*, cry out or call to one another.

قوة *quwwa-t*, pl. *quwa-n*, *qiwa-n*, *quwwât*, strength, power, faculty, sense, sensitive power.

قؤود *qa'ûd*, obedient, trained.

قؤول *qu'ûl*, pl. *qu'ul*, talkative; eloquent; — *quwûl*, pl. of قائل *qâ'il*, who says, &c.

(قوى) *qawa*, surpass in strength or power; — *qawî*, A, INF. *qawa-n*, be or grow strong, vigorous, powerful; be or grow rich; cope with (ب *bi*); be superior to (على *'ala*); be empty, deserted; be famished; be withheld;—II. INF. *taqwiya-t*, strengthen, make vigorous, encourage; — III. INF. *muqâwât*, vie in strength, wrestle with; impart strength to; — IV. INF. *iqwâ'*, grow strong; be rich; be poor, have no victuals left, live in misery; have a strong beast for riding; be empty, deserted; live in a deserted country; use different rhyme vowels in a poem; — V. INF. *taqawwî*, be or grow strong, vigorous; secure one's self against (على *'ala*); — VI. INF. *taqâwî*, out-bid one another; — VIII. INF. *iqtiwâ'*, be strong, vigorous; claim for one's self and defend.

قوى *quwan*, *qiwan*, pl. of قوة *quwwa-t*; — *qawiyy*, ة, pl. *aqwiyâ'*, strong, vigorous, powerful; — *quwayy*, young of an animal.

قويس *quwais*, ة *quwaisa-t*, little bow; — ة *quwaisa-t*, sage (plant).

قويم *qawîm*, pl. *qiwâm*, *qiyâm*, straight and upright; true (religion); well-made, of handsome form; firm, solid; established; rectitude; — *quwaim*, ة *quwaima-t*, small people or tribe; — ة *quwaima-t*, a little while.

قى *qai'*, vomiting (s.); — ة *qiyya-t*, ounce (weight).

(قيا) *qâ'*, I, INF. *qai'*, vomit; be saturated with colour; — II. INF. *taqyi'a-t*, make to vomit, give an emetic; — IV. INF. *iqâ'a-t*=II.; — V. INF. *taqayyu'*, VI. INF. *taqâyu'*, X. INF. *istiqâ'a-t*, vomit.

قيا *quyâ'*, vomiting (s.), emetic.

قياتة *qiyâta-t*, nourishing, feeding (s.).

قياد *qiyâd*, rein, halter; — ة *qiyâda-t*, leading, reining (s.); pandering.

قيار *qayyâr*, seller of pitch or tar.

قياس *qiyâs*, measure, measuring (s.), comparison; rule, analogy, paradigm, example; logical conclusion, syllogism; surmise, supposition, hypothesis; (m.) pl. *-ât*, chilblain; pl. of قوس *qaus*; — ى *qiyâsiyy*, ة, regular, according to rule; by way of surmise.

قياظ *qiyâẕ*, heat of summer.

قيافة *qiyâfa-t*, appearance, resemblance, imitation; gait, manner, costume; inference from external signs, physiognomics.

قياقى *qayâqî*, pl. of قيقاة *qîqâ'a-t*.

قيال *quyyâl*, pl. of قائل *qâ'il*, who says, &c.; — ة *qiyâla-t*, mid-day, mid-day slumber, siesta.

قيام *qiyâm*, rising, standing upright; resurrection; departure; performance; persistence; support, subsistence, sustenance; base; pl. of قويم *qawîm*; — *qayyâm*, what subsists by itself; eternal; God; — *quyyâm*, pl. of قائم *qâ'im*, rising, standing, &c.; — ة *qiyâma-t*, resurrection, day of the Last Judgment; tumult, revolt; calamity.

قيان *qiyân*, pl. of قين *qain*, ة.

قئب *qa'ib*, see (قاب).

قيت *qît*, ة *qîta-t*, provisions for one day, ration.

(قيث), V. *taqayyaṡ*, INF. *taqayyuṡ*, gather, collect (a.); prevent, hinder.

(قيح) *qâḥ*, I, INF. *qaiḥ*, suppurate; —*qaiḥ*, II. INF. *taqyîḥ*, V. INF. *taqayyuḥ*, id.

قيح *qaiḥ*, pl. *quyûḥ*, pus, suppuration.

(قيد), pass. *qîd*, get bound; — II. *qayyad*, INF. *taqyîd*, bind, fetter, chain; enter in a book, inscribe, register; provide with vowels; limit, restrict the sense of a word; consider as important, regard carefully, keep one's eye upon; defend, forbid; — V. INF. *taqayyud*, be bound, fettered; be registered, enrolled, inscribed; enlist or enrol (n.); devote zeal and care to; be devoted to.

قيد *qaid*, pl. *quyûd*, *aqyâd*, fetter, chain, bond; strap; registration; contract; deed, document; diligence, effort; restriction; rule, norm; ق الاسنان *qaid al-asnân*, gums; *qaid*, also *qayyid*, obedient, obsequious; — *qîd*, quantity; value; length (of a lance).

قيدود *qaidûd*, pl. *qayâdîd*, long, extended;—ة *qaidûda-t*, leading (s.), guidance.

قيدى *qaidiyy*, prisoner (m.).

قيذار *qaiẕâr*, Kedar, son of Ismael.

(قير) *qîr*, pitch, tar; — II. *qayyar*, INF. *taqyîr*, pitch, tar; — VIII. INF. *iqtiyâr*, examine, test.

قيراط *qîrâṭ*, pl. *qarârîṭ*, carat=4 قمحة *qamḥa-t* or grains=$\frac{1}{24}$ مثقال *misqâl*.

قيران *qîrân*, pl. of قارة *qâra-t*, isolated hill.

قيروان *qairawân*, *qairuwân*, caravan (Pers.); Cyrene.

قيروطى *qairûṭiyy*, oil-cloth.

قيزان *qîzân*, pl. of قوز *qauz*.

(قيس) *qâs*, I, INF. *qais*, *qiyâs*, measure one thing by another; compare; infer from analogy, draw a conclusion; — III. INF. *qiyâs*, *muqâyasa-t*, measure; investigate, examine; compare; requite, give measure for measure; draw a conclusion; (m.) insert rafters, &c. according to measurement;—V. INF. *taqayyus*, keep to the tribe Kais Gailân;— VI. INF. *taqâyus*, be measured by, compared with; be collated, confronted; — VII. INF. *inqiyâs*, be measured, compared, collated; — VIII. INF. *iqtiyâs*, measure, compare; be like one's father, take after him.

قيس *qais*, measuring, comparing (s.); a proper name; — *qîs*, quantity, measure.

قيسرية *qîsariyya-t*, Cesarea; (m.) large houses with arcades, shops, &c.; barracks.

(قيص) *qâṣ*, I, INF. *qaiṣ*, fall out (tooth); stir, move about; — V. INF. *taqayyuṣ*, roar; fall in; — VIII. INF. *iqtiyâṣ*, fall out; fall in ruins.

قيصارية *qaiṣâriyya-t*, Cesarea.

قيصر *qaiṣar*, pl. *qayâṣir*, *qayâṣira-t*, Cæsar, emperor.

قيصرى *qaiṣariyy*, ة, imperial; — ة *qaiṣariyya-t*, imperial dignity; Cesarea.

قيصوم *qaiṣûm*, a plant.

(قيض) *qâḍ*, I, INF. *qaiḍ*, exchange, give in exchange; make one thing similar to another; break through the shell; be broken; — II. INF. *taqyîḍ*, send to, give for a companion; — III. INF. *muqâyaḍa-t*, *qiyâḍ*, offer in exchange, make an exchange with (acc.), give one thing for another; — V. INF. *taqayyuḍ*, be in ruins; — VI. INF. *taqâyuḍ*, make an exchange between one another; — VII. INF. *inqiyâḍ*, be in ruins; — VIII. INF. *iqtiyâḍ*, tear out by the root, exterminate.

قيض *qaiḍ*, egg-shell; —*qayyiḍ*, who offers an exchange; du. seller and purchaser.

قيطان *qîṭân*, lacing, trimming (m.).

(قيطن) *qaiṭan*, INF. ة, lace, trim.
قيطون *qaiṭûn*, bed-room, dormitory; pantry; cave, cellar.
(قيظ) *qâẕ*, I, INF. *qaiẕ*, be hot as in high summer; yield no rain; pass the summer; — II. INF. *taqyîẕ*, be very hot; yield no rain; — III. INF. *qiyâẕ*, *muqâyaẕa-t*, arrange with one for the summer-time; — V. INF. *taqayyuẕ*, pass the summer; pass the summer in the desert.
قيظ *qaiẕ*, pl. *aqyâẕ*, *quyûẕ*, high summer; midsummer; want of rain, drought, heat; — ى *qaiẕiyy*, of the high summer, midsummerly.
(قيع) *qâ'*, I, INF. *qai'*, grunt.
قيع *qî'*, قيعان *qî'ân*, pl. of قاع *qâ'*, plain.
(قيف), II. *qayyaf*, INF. *taqyîf*, examine and follow one's tracks; examine, test, criticise; (m.) mock at; — V. INF. *taqayyuf*, follow, pursue; examine.
قيف *qaif*, examination; criticism; (m.) fault-finding, lampoon; — *qîf*, funnel; — ة *qîfa-t*, trace, remainder.
قيفال *qîfâl*, قيفل *qîfal*, vena cephalica.
(قيق) *qâq*, I, INF. *qaiq*, cluck.
قيق *qîq*, chain of mountains surrounding the world; very long; stupid; — ة *qîqa-t*, inner membrane of an egg; white of an egg.
قيقاءة *qîqâ'a-t*, pl. *qawâqî*, *qayâqî*, *qiyaq*, rough ground; also *qîqât*, a drinking-vessel.
قيقب *qaiqab*, saddle; wood of which a saddle is made.
قئقئ *qi'qi'*, *qîqi'* = قيقة *qîqa-t*.
(قيل) *qâl*, I, INF. *qail*, *qâ'ila-t*, *qailûla-t*, *maqâl*, *maqîl*, slumber in the middle of the day, make siesta; be idle; milk, water or drink at mid-day; — INF. *qail*, cancel a transaction, recall a promise; — II. INF. *taqyîl*, give one milk to drink at mid-day; — III. INF. *muqâyala-t*, do one thing in compensation or requital for another; exchange; — IV. INF. *iqâla-t*, see I.; free from, rid from; pardon; water the camels at noon; — V. INF. *taqayyul*, resemble one's father, remind of him, take after him; slumber, milk, drink at noon; collect (n.); — VI. INF. *taqâyul*, cancel a transaction between one another, release one another of a promise; — VII. INF. *inqiyâl*, get free, rid of; — VIII. INF. *iqtiyâl*, exchange; = X.; — X. INF. *istiqâla-t*, ask to have a transaction cancelled, to be released of a promise, to be rid of.
قيل *qail*, pl. *aqyâl*, *aqwâl*, king of the Himyarites; also *quyyal*, pl. of قائل *qâ'il*, who keeps siesta; also *qîl*, rupture; swelling of the testicles; — *qîl*, word, speech, particularly repartee.
قيلولة *qailûla-t*, mid-day slumber, siesta.
قيم *qiyam*, pl. of قامة *qâma-t*, pulley of a well; — *qayyim*, ة, true; manager, prefect, superintendent; guardian; prince; — *quyyam*, pl. of قائم *qâ'im*, rising, standing, &c.; — ة *qîma-t*, pl. *qiyam*, price, value, worth; estimation; stature, figure; perseverance; resurrection.
قيمومة *qaimûma-t*, self-relying existence; unchangeableness.
(قين) *qân*, I, INF. *qain*, forge the iron, hammer; gather what is dispersed; mend; deck out, adorn; form, create; — II. INF. *taqyîn*, comb, dress the hair, adorn; — V. INF. *taqayyun*, be adorned; — XI. *iqta'ann*, *iqtânn*, INF. *iqtînân*, bloom magnificently.
قين *qain*, trade of a blacksmith; pl. *quyûn*, *aqyân*, blacksmith; pl. *qiyân*, prisoner, slave, ser-

vant; — ة qaina-t, pl. -ât, qiyân, maid-servant; lady's-maid; female singer; the buttocks.

قيهل qaihal, ة qaihala-t, face; sight.

قيو qayû', qayyuww, who vomits; emetic.

قيور qayyûr, of low extraction.

قيوم qayyûm, durable; everlasting, unchangeable; God.

ك

ك k, as a numeral sign=20; — ka, as, like, governs the oblique case, and is in writing joined to the following word; — ka, f. ki, pronominal suffix of the 2nd pers. sing.

كا kâ', ة kâ'a-t, weak, cowardly.

(كاب) ka'ib, A, INF. ka'b, ka'ba-t, ka'âba-t, be very much depressed, sad; — IV. INF. ik'âb, depress, grieve, sadden; — VIII. INF. ikti'âb=I.

كاب kâb-in=كابى kâbî; — ka'b, كابا ka'bâ', ة ka'ba-t, ka'âba-t, grief, sorrow, depression.

كابح kâbiḥ, pl. kawâbiḥ, bad augury.

كابد kâbid, evil to be endured.

كابر kâbir, great.

كابس kâbis, projecting; alone, solitary; who surprises, falls upon; who presses, oppresses.

كابوس kâbûs, pl. kawâbîs, nightmare; (m.) plough.

كابى kâbî (كاب kâb-in), who drops his head from sleepiness; who trips, falls; faint, feeble; high (ك الرماد kâbî ar-ramâd, very hospitable).

كاتب kâtib, pl. kuttâb, kataba-t, katâbît, writer, scribe, clerk, secretary.

كاتم kâtim, who conceals, keeps secret; secret, concealed; ك الاسرار kâtim al-asrâr, confidential secretary; cryptographer; (m.) constipated.

كاتوليكى kâtûlîkiyy, Catholic (m.).

كاثر kâsir, numerous, much, many.

(كاج) ka'aj, A, INF. ka'j, be very stupid.

كاح kâḥ, pl. akyâḥ, kuyûḥ, mountain-slope, mountain-ridge.

كاحط kâḥiṭ, dry, rainless.

كاحل kâḥil, pl. kawâḥil, ankle.

كاخ kâḫ, hut without a window; pl. kiwaḫa-t, upper apartment.

(كاد) ka'ad, A, INF. ka'd, be sad; be earnestly devoted to and concerned in; — V. INF. taka''ud, grieve, fill with anxiety; — VI. INF. takâ'ud, id.

كاد kâdd, who takes pains, toils.

كادا ka'dâ', sorrow, grief; fear; prudence, foresight; severity, cruelty.

كادح kâdiḥ, who toils, troubles himself, makes efforts; (m.) limping (adj.).

كاذب kâẕib, pl. kuẕẕab, kaẕaba-t, kawâẕib, liar; false, deceitful; — ة kâẕiba-t, lie.

كارث kâris, ة, pl. kawâris, grievous, depressing; grief; calamity.

كارح kâriḥ, ة kâriḥa-t, human wind-pipe.

كارز kâriz, كاروز kârûz, preacher.

كارع kâri', who drinks in sips.

كاركاه kârkâh, machine, engine, weaver's loom; alembic.

كاروبيم kârûbîm, pl. kârûbiyûn, cherubim.

كاروز karûz, see كارز kâriz.

كاز kâz, shears to cut leather or tin-plate, &c. (m.).

كاس kâs-in, see كاسى kâsî; — kâs, pl. ku'us, ki'âs, ka'sât, akwus,

cup, goblet, tumbler; cup of wine, wine; — ة *kâsa-t*, cup (m.).

كاسب *kâsib*, who earns, gains; working-man, artisan; executor; ابو كاسب *abû kâsib*, wolf.

كاسد *kâsid*, worthless; selling badly; dull (market); little credible; brute (animal).

كاسر *kâsir*, pl. *kussar*, f. ة, pl. *kawâsir*, who breaks, conquers; rapacious animal, bird of prey.

كاسف *kâsif*, pressed; disastrous; darkened, eclipsed; looking gloomy.

كاسل *kâsil*, lazy, slow.

كاسى *kâsî* (كاس *kâs-in*), dressing, clothing (part.); dressed, clad.

(كاش) *ka'aś*, A, INF. *ka'ś*, eat.

كاش *kâśś*, looking gloomy, austere.

كاشح *kâśiḥ*, secret enemy; enemy.

كاشد *kâśid*, who toils for his family.

كاشف *kâśif*, who uncovers, &c., ag. of (كشف); overseer; (m.) probe; — ة *kâśifa-t*, revelation, communication; apocalypse.

كاشم *kâśim*, assafœtida.

(كاص) *ka'aṣ*, INF. *ka'ṣ*, overcome, tame, subdue, humble; eat; eat and drink much; eat and drink but little.

كاظم *kâẕim*, suppressing (one's anger); keeping back one's breath; pl. *kuẕẕam*, not chewing the cud; silent.

كاع *kâ'*, wrist; — *kâ'-in*, see كاعى *ka'î*.

كاعب *kâ'ib*, pl. *kawâ'ib*, swelling breast; girl having such, high-bosomed.

كاعى *kâ'î* (كاع *kâ'-in*), cowardly; deserter, run-away.

كاغذ *kâgiẕ* (كاغد *kâgid*), paper; letter; document (Pers.).

كاف *kâf*, name of the letter ك *k*; — *kâf-in*, see كافى *kâfî*; — *kâff*, pl. *kafafa-t*, who prevents, hinders; hindrance; who seams or borders garments; — ة *kâffa-t*, totality; all.

كافر *kâfir*, pl. *kuffâr*, *kafara-t*, *kifâr*, f. ة, pl. *kawâfir*, infidel; renegade, apostate; ungratuful; peasant, rustic, husbandman.

كافل *kâfil*, pl. *kuffal*, manager, agent, administrator; who stands bail, security; who fasts much and observes silence.

كافور *kâfûr*, pl. *kawâfîr*, *kawâfir*, blossom or spathe of the palm-tree; camphor; — ى *kâfûriyy*, prepared with camphor.

كافى *kâfî* (كاف *kâf-in*), ة, pl. *kufât*, sufficient, enough; what completely compensates for anything else; effective; able, apt, skilful.

(كاكا) *ka'ka'*, INF. ة, be a coward, run away; assemble (n.); — II. INF. *taka'ku'*=I.

كاكنج *kâkanj*, nightshade (plant).

(كال) *ka'al*, INF. *ka'l*, *ka'la-t*, *ku'ûla-t*, transfer a debt, sell or buy it.

كال *kâll*, thick and blunt.

كالب *kâlib*, breeder of dogs.

كالح *kâliḥ*, severe-looking, austere; unfavourable; cold.

كام *kâm*, for كم *kam*, how much? — *kâm-in*, see كامى *kâmî*.

كامح *kâmiḥ*, who holds high the horse's bridle.

كامد *kâmid*, sad, depressed; faint, feeble.

كامل *kâmil*, pl. *kamala-t*, perfect, complete, in full number, total; learned; folio (size); name of a metre, *mutafâ'ilun* six times repeated.

كامن *kâmin*, ة, concealed, hidden; in ambush.

كامى *kâmî* (كام *kâm-in*), completely armed.

(كان) *ka'an*, INF. *ka'n*, be hard, violent.

كان *kân-in*, see كانى *kânî*; — *ka'an*, *ka'anna*, as if, as though; — *kânn*, quiet, pacified.

كانا *ka'ana*, like me.

كانز *kâniz*, firm and hard, compact.

كانس *kânis*, pl. *kunnas*, hiding in its den or lair.

كانع *kâni'*, ة *kâni'a-t*, pl. *kawâni'*, flat (nose).

كانفة *kânifa-t*, bulwark, entrenchment.

كانون *kânûn*, pl. *kawânîn*, warming-pan; hearth, stove; كانون الاول *kânûn al-awwal*, December; كانون الثاني *kânûn as-sâni*, January.

كانى *kânî* (كان *kân-in*), who speaks symbolically or by allusion; — *ka'annî*, as I.

كاهب *kâhib*, reddish brown.

كاهل *kâhil*, slow, lazy, indolent; middle-aged, steady; ill; Pacific (ocean); pl. *kawâhil*, space between the shoulders; back; withers; shoulder.

كاهن *kâhin*, pl. *kahana-t*, *kuhhân*, soothsayer; magician; priest.

كاو *kâw-in*, كاوى *kâwî*, caustic.

كاويا *kâwiyâ*, instrument for cauterization, brand-iron.

كاى (كاى) *ka'a*, INF. *ka'y*, hurt by words; — IV. INF. *ik'â'*, have aversion against (عن *'an*).

كاى *ka'ayy*, how much, how many?

كائد *kâ'id*, deceitful.

كائش *kâ'iš*, very active, zealous.

كائع *kâ'i'*, pl. *kâ'a-t*, timid.

كائن *kâ'in*, ة, being, existing (adj.); being (s.), creature; الكائن المطلق *al-kâ'in al-mutlaq*, the absolute being, God; — *ka'ayyin, ka'a'in*, how much? how many? — ة *kâ'ina-t*, being, creature (pl. *al-kâ'inât*, everything created); accident, event.

كب (كب) *kabb*, U, INF. *kabb*, throw one with the face to the ground, overthrow; roll up thread; prepare in the shape of small balls, make balls; (m.) pour out; — II. INF. *takbîb*, prepare the dish كباب *kabâb*; roll up thread; prepare in the shape of small balls; — IV. INF. *ikbâb*, throw with the face on the ground; be thrown down, fall; drop the head; bend over (n.), lean

against; keep intent upon (على *'ala*); (m.) pour out; — V. INF. *takabbub*, be rolled up; — VII. INF. *inkibâb*, fall on one's face; be overthrown; be intent upon; go over and adhere to; (m.) be poured out.

كب *kubb*, a bitter salt plant; — ة *kuba-t*, pl. *kubûn*, sweepings; — *kabba-t*, blow, push, attack; — *kubba-t*, pl. *kubab, kubâb*, troop of horses or men; skein; meat ball; fat hen.

كبا *kib-an*=كبى *kiba-n*; — *kabâ'*, spring of water; moon-beams; frankincense; —*kibâ'*, pl. *kuba-n, kuba*, aloes-wood.

كباب *kabâb*, hashed meat roasted with onions and eggs; roast meat; joint; — *kubâb*, shifting sand-hill; herd of camels; pl. of كبة *kubba-t*; — ة *kabâba-t*, cubeb.

كباث *kabâs̱*, fruit of the *arak*-tree in the first stage of ripeness.

كباخ *kubâḵ*, greatness, pomp.

كباد *kibâd*, endurance; — *kubâd*, a disease of the liver; — *kubbâd*, candied lemon peel; — ة *kabâda-t*, small bow for beginners.

كبار *kibâr*, pl. of كبر *kabar* and كبير *kabîr*; — *kubâr, kubbâr*, very great; — *kibbâr*, INF. II. of (كبر).

كباس *kubâs*, big-headed; — ة *kibâsa-t*, pl. -ât, *kabâ'is*, bunch of dates.

كبان *kubân*, millet.

كباس *kabâ'is*, pl. of كباسة *kibâsa-t*.

كباية *kubbâya-t*, tumbler.

كبب *kubab*, pl. of كبة *kubba-t*.

كبت (كبت) *kabat*, I, INF. *kabt*, throw down; subdue, tame; destroy; put to shame; break; repel an insult by force.

كبتل (كبتل) *kabtal*, INF. ة, form into balls; pour forth invectives against (ل *li*).

كبتولة *kabtûla-t*, ball, globe (m.).

كبث (كبث) *kabas̱*, U, INF. *kabs̱*, cover meat and spoil it thereby; — *kabis̱*, A, INF. *kabas̱*, be putrid

and smell offensively; — II. INF. *takbîṣ*, place the ship on her side to unload her.

(كبح) *kabaḥ*, INF. *kabḥ*, pull up a horse; restrain, prevent, hinder; — IV. INF. *ikbâḥ*=I.; — VII. INF. *inkibâḥ*, be prevented, hindered.

كبح *kabḥ*, refraining, restraining (s.); — *kubḥ*, sour milk for curdling.

(كبد) *kabad*, I, U, INF. *kabd*, injure in the liver; purpose; press hard upon; pass. *kubid*, suffer from the liver; — *kabid*, A, INF. *kabad*, suffer from the liver; be big; — II. INF. *takbîd*, culminate; — III. INF. *kibâd*, *mukâbada-t*, harden one's self against suffering, endure; — IV. INF. *ikbâd*, bring into the zenith; — V. INF. *takabbud*, culminate; be in the zenith; place one's self in the middle; suffer, endure; purpose.

كبد *kabd*, *kibd*, *kabid* (m. f.), pl. *akbâd*, *kubûd*, liver; heart; intestines; middle, depth; principal part; zenith; *kabid*, belly, stomach, interior; place where the bow is seized; — *kabad*, liver-complaint; adversity; severe cold.

كبدا *kabdâ'*, f. of اكبد *akbad*, big, paunch-bellied, &c.; zenith; hand-mill; bow with a thick hand-piece.

(كبر) *kabar*, U, INF. *kabr*, surpass in age; — *kabir*, A, INF. *kibar*, *makbir*, be of an advanced age; — *kabur*, INF. *kubr*, *kibar*, *kabâra-t*, be tall and corpulent; grow tall; grow, increase; — II. INF. *kibbâr*, *takbîr*, make great, cause to grow, enlarge; call great and sublime, praise; say الله اكبر *allâh akbar*, God is great! — III. INF. *mukâbara-t*, treat with haughtiness; harden one's self against; (m.) suffer, bear, endure; — IV. INF. *ikbâr*, deem great; make much of; — V. INF. *takabbur*, grow proud and haughty; — VI. INF. *takâbur*, assume haughty airs; — X. INF. *istikbâr*, consider one's self to be great; grow proud; deem great and important; wish for or select the greatest.

كبر *kibr*, greatness, glory, pride, pomp, power; great sin; — *kubr*, greatness, glory, consideration; principal part; *kubr*, *kuburr*, ة *kubra-t*, *kuburra-t*, head of a family; — *kabar*, ة, pl. *kibâr*, *akbâr*, capers (spice); drum; — *kibar*, greatness; old age; — *kubar*, pl. of كبرى *kubra*; — ة *kabra-t*, *kabura-t*, old age; — *kibra-t*, greatness; pride; last-born son or daughter; great sin.

كبرا *kubarâ'*, pl. of كبير *kabîr*.

(كبرت) *kabrat*, INF. ة, cover with brimstone.

كبرى *kubra*, f. of اكبر *akbar*, greater; pl. *kubar*, *kubrayât*, major proposition; — ة *kabariyya-t*, dish seasoned with capers.

كبريا *kibriyâ'*, greatness; power; pride, haughtiness.

كبريت *kibrît*, brimstone; match, lunt; ذهب ك *ẓahab kibrît*, pure gold.

(كبس) *kabas*, I, INF. *kabs*, fill up, stop up; invest, besiege; fall upon and take by surprise; hide the head in one's garments; insert an intercalary day in the fourth year; (m.) press upon (a spring, &c.), exercise pressure; (m.) conserve in vinegar; — II. INF. *takbîs*, train young oxen for work; — V. INF. *takabbus*, be filled or stopped up; (m.) be trained for work; — VII. INF. *inkibâs*, be attacked from all sides and infested; be pressed; be heaped or stopped up.

كبس *kabs*, surprise, assault; pressure; conserving fruit in vinegar (s.); — *kibs*, earth with which a

well is filled up; big head; clay-hut; — *kubbas*, hard, granitic; — ة *kabsa-t*, surprise, sudden attack.

(كبش) *kabś*, pl. *kibâś*, *akbuś*, *akbâś*, ram; battering-ram; buttress; leader; — ة *kabśa-t*, kindred; party; — III. INF. *mukâbaśa-t*, join hands; come to close quarters.

(كبع) *kaba'*, INF. *kab'*, cut, cut off; prevent; separate the bad coin from the good; INF. *kubû'*, submit to (n.).

(كبكب) *kabkab*, INF. ة, overturn, overthrow; throw from above; (m.) round, form round; (m.) pour out, spill, scatter; — II. INF. *takabkub*, wrap one's self up in one's garment; (m. be rounded; (m.) be poured out, spilt, scattered.

(كبل) *kabal*, I, INF. *kabl*, fetter a prisoner; keep prisoner; delay a creditor; — II. INF. *takbîl*, fetter a prisoner; — V. INF. *takabbul*, pass. of the previous.

كبل *kabl*, *kibl*, pl. *kubûl*, heavy fetter.

(كبن) *kaban*, U, I, INF. *kabn*, double the seam of a cloth or dress; transfer a benefit from (عن *'an*) one person to (الى *ila*) another; — I, INF. *kabn*, *kubûn*, trot gently, run with short steps; — INF. *kubûn*, be quiet; — XI. *ikba'ann*, INF. *ikbi'nân*, be shrunk, contracted.

كبن *kubunn*, ة *kubunna-t*, miser, niggard.

(كبو) *kabâ*, U, INF. *kabw*, *kubuww*, fall on one's face; trip, tumble, fall; drop the head forward, fall asleep; fail to give light; rise; wither (n.); fade; — II. INF. *takbiya-t*, perfume or fumigate one's clothes; cover the fire up with ashes; — IV. INF. *ikbâ'*, fail to give fire; cause the material to do so; disfigure one's face; — V. INF. *takabbî*, throw down; — VII. INF. *inkibâ'*, throw one's self with the face on the ground; trip, slip; — VIII. INF. *iktibâ'*=VII.; bend over the censer so as to perfume one's clothes; — ة *kabwa-t*, falling upon one's face (s.); tripping, stumbling (s.); failing of the igniting material to give fire; dust, dust colour; — *kubwa-t*, censer.

كبوع *kubû'*, submission, submissiveness.

كبوك *kabbûk*, lark.

كبون *kibûn*, pl. of كبى *kiban*; — *kubûn*, INF. of (كبن); pl. of كبة *kuba-t*.

كبى , كبا *kibân*, *kiba*, pl. *kibûn*, *akbâ'*, sweepings; anything worthless; — *kuban*, pl. of كبا *kibâ'*.

كبيث *kabîs̱*, putrid.

كبيدا *kubaidâ'*, ة *kubaida-t*, zenith.

كبير *kabîr*, ة, pl. *kibâr*, *kubarâ'*, *makbûrâ'*, great, tall; important; powerful, honoured; aged; older; — ة *kabîra-t*, pl. *kabâ'ir*, great crime; abomination.

كبيس *kabîs*, preserved in vinegar; also ة *kabîsa-t*, leap-year.

(كت) *katt*, I, INF. *katît*, walk slowly or hasten with short steps; I, INF. *katt*, *katît*, low gently; boil; grieve or anger by misdeeds; humble; — U, INF. *katt*, *katît*, whisper into one's ear; (m.) pour out, spill; — IV. INF. *iktât*, whisper into the ear; — VII. INF. *inkitât*, be poured out, spilled (m.); — ة *katta-t*, verdure, vegetation.

كتاب *kitâb*, pl. *kutub*, *kutb*, writing (s.), book, volume; letter; commission; sentence; prescription, law; document; contract of marriage; destiny, fate; inkstand; writing-school; *al-kitâb*, the Koran, Bible; اهل الكتاب *ahl al-kitâb*, people who have sacred scriptures, scholars; — *kuttâb*, pl. *katâlîb*, small arrow

for practice; writing-school; pl. of كاتب *kâtib*, writer, &c.; — ة *kitâba-t*, art of writing, calligraphy; writing, inscription, epitaph; title; deed, document; contract of emancipation; letter; tax; — ى *kitâbiyy*, referring to writing or to a book; Jew.

كتاتيب *katâtîb*, pl. of كاتب *kâtib* and كتاب *kuttâb*.

كتاف *kitâf*, pl. *kutf*, rope, fetter, chain; — *kutâf*, pain in the shoulder.

كتام *kitâm*, constipation, costiveness.

كتان *kattân*, flax, linen; water-moss, sea-weed.

(كتب) *katab*, U, INF. *katb*, *kitâb*, *kitâba-t*, write; be a writer, compose writings; impose by writing, prescribe; pre-ordain; leave by a written will; — U, I, INF. *katb*, fasten, sew doubly; — II. INF. *taktîb*, write; make write; teach to write, teach calligraphy; — III. INF. *mukâtaba-t*, write to, correspond with; fix a ransom for one's self (slave); engage to emancipate a slave for a certain sum; — IV. INF. *iktâb*, make write; give to write; dictate; teach writing or calligraphy; — V. INF. *taqattub*, assemble in squadrons or regiments; — VI. INF. *takâtub*, write to one another, be in correspondence; — VIII. INF. *iktitâb*, write; write after dictation; note down; be inscribed, registered; ask one to dictate; compose; fasten tightly or sew doubly; — X. INF. *istiktâb*, ask to write or dictate; dictate to (2 acc.); make one one's secretary.

كتب *kutub*, pl. of كتاب *kitâb*; — ة *kitba-t*, writing, scripture, inscription; — *kutba-t*, stitch, seam; — *kataba-t*, pl. of كاتب *kâtib*; — ى *kutubiyy*, according to scripture; book-seller; — ة *kutubiyya-t*, library; book-shop.

(كتح) *kataḥ*, INF. *katḥ*, eat to satiety; eat the ground bare; cover with dust; tear off the clothes (wind); scratch the skin.

(كتد) *katad*, *katid*, pl. *kutûd*, *aktâd*, place where the shoulder-blades come nearest one another.

(كتر) *katr*, quantity; quality; dignity; small camel-litter; *katr*, *kitr*, *katar*, ة *katra-t*, &c., large camel-hump; — *kitr*, vault, arch, cupola; — IV. *aktar*, INF. *iktâr*, have a large hump.

(كتع) *kata'*, INF. *kat'*, go away with, escape with, rob; be always active and ready for work; INF. *kutû'*, travel far into a country; flee; swear, take an oath; m. also *kati'*, A, INF. *kata'*, shrink, contract (n.); be contracted, crippled; — II. INF. *taktî'*, cut small; — VI. INF. *takâtu'*, follow one another.

كتع *kat'*, crippled state; — *kuta'*, pl. *kit'ân*, contemptible; whelp of a fox, wolf; — ة *kit'a-t*, pl. *kita'*, small piece; — *kut'a-t*, *kata'a-t*, pl. *kuta'*, *kitâ'*, small bucket.

كتعا *kat'â'*, female slave, maid-servant; جمعا كتعا *jam'â'a kat'â'a*, altogether entirely.

(كتف) *kataf*, I, INF. *katf*, beat on the shoulder; hurt on the shoulder; tie one's hands to the back, gag; cross the arms or legs; walk slowly or move the shoulders in walking; mend a vessel; detest; have high shoulder-blades; — INF. *kitf*, *kitfân* (*katf*, *katafân*), to fly striking the wings against the tail; — INF. *katafân*, step along quickly; — *katif*, A, INF. *kataf*, walk slowly; INF. *katf*, *kataf*, have large shoulder-blades; — II. INF. *taktîf*, gag; cross the

arms or legs; mend a vessel; have high shoulder-blades; — V. INF. *takattuf*, protrude the shoulder-blades in walking; be gagged, have one's hands tied to the back; have the arms or legs crossed; — VII. INF. *inkitâf*, be crossed over the other leg.

كتف *kitf*, *kataf*, *katif*, pl. *aktâf*, *kitafa-t*, shoulder-blade, shoulder; mountain-slope; — *kutf*, pl. (كتفا *katfâ'*, f.) of اكتف *aktaf*, having large shoulder-blades or being lame in the shoulder; — *kataf*, broadness of the shoulders.

كتفان *kutfân*, *kitfân*, ة, locust just beginning to fly.

(كتكت) *katkat*, INF. ة, walk slowly; hasten with small steps; laugh low.

كتكت *katkat*, floss-silk; wadding.

كتكوت *kutkût*, pl. *katâkît*, chicken.

كتل *katal*, U, INF. *katl*, bind, fetter, imprison; heap up; — *katil*, A, INF. *katal*, cohere, be glued together; — II. INF. *taktîl*, heap up; — V. INF. *takattul*, be heaped up; walk like a dwarf; — VII. INF. *inkitâl*, depart, pass on, pass by; — ة *kutla-t*, pl. *kutal*, heap; piece of meat.

(كتلك) *katlak*, INF. ة, become a Catholic.

(كتم) *katam*, U, INF. *katm*, *kitmân*, conceal, hide (a.); master one's anger; (m.) be constipated; — II. INF. *taktîm*, conceal carefully; master well one's anger; — III. INF. *mukâtama-t*, conceal; keep one's secret; — VI. INF. *takâtum*, conceal from one another; — VII. INF. *inkitâm*, be concealed, hidden; hide one's self; — VIII. INF. *iktitâm*, conceal; — X. INF. *istiktâm*, ask one to be silent about a thing (2 acc.).

كتم *katm*, concealing, hiding (s.); — *kutm*, leaf of indigo; pl. (كتما *katmâ'*, f.) of اكتم *aktam*, paunch-bellied; — *katam*, a herb for dying the hair; — ة *kitma-t*, anything concealed, secret; — *kutama-t*, who conceals everything.

(كتن) *katin*, A, INF. *katan*, be dirty, soiled; make dirty, soil; be glued together, cohere; — II. INF. *taktîn*, make to cohere, glue together; — IV. INF. *iktân*, id.

كتن *katan*, dirt; *katin*, dirty; — *kattan*, linen.

(كتو) *katâ*, U, INF. *katw*, walk with short steps; — IV. INF. *iktâ'*, conquer one's enemy; — XII. *iktauta*, INF. *iktîtâ'*, be full of anger; stammer; praise one's self immoderately.

كتوال *kutwâl*, porter of a palace; commissary of police.

كتوم *katûm*, pl. *kutum*, very reticent, very reserved; solid.

كتونة *kattûna-t*, surplice, alb.

كتيب *katîb*, firmly sewn; — ة *katîba-t*, pl. *katâ'ib*, division of an army, regiment; battalion, squadron; document, diploma, edict.

كتيت *katît*, low cry; boiling (s.); lint; tow-yarn, oakum.

كتيف *katîf*, pl. *kutf*, broad; hoop (of a cask); — ة *katîfa-t*, pl. *katâ'if*, iron-plate to coat a door; troop; malignity, hatred.

كتيلة *kutaila-t*, wen.

(كث) *kass* (*kasis*), A, INF. *kasâsa-t*, *kasas*, *kusûsa-t*, be thick, condensed; be thick, short and curly; — U, INF. *kass*, drop (excrement, ب *bi*); — IV. INF. *iksâs*, have a thick beard.

كث *kass*, pl. *kisâs*, *kass*, f. ة, thick, dense; having thick hair, a thick beard; densely crowded; — ة *kassa-t*, thick beard.

(كثا) *kasa'*, INF. *kas'*, rise to the top and leave pure water beneath (milk); froth (n.); skim; grow, be high and densely-grown; — II. INF. *taksi'a-t*,

sprout, grow luxuriantly, be densely-grown; INF. *taskî'*, id.; eat off the froth or cream.

كثا *kassâ'*, f. thick, dense; — ة *kas'a-t*, froth, cream of the milk; also *kasât*, pl. كثى *kasa-n*, a kind of cress, bank-cresses.

كثار *kasâr*, *kisâr*, pl. troops; — *kusâr*, great quantity.

كثافة *kasâfa-t*, thickness, denseness; luxuriance; plenty, abundance; rudeness.

(كثب) *kasab*, U, I, INF. *kasb*, gather (a.), heap up; gather (n.), assemble; pour out; enter; — II. INF. *taksîb*, be but little; — III. INF. *mukâsaba-t*, approach; put itself within shot; — VII. INF. *inkisâb*, be heaped up.

كثب *kasab*, nearness, proximity; — *kusub*, *kusbân*, pl. of كثيب *kasîb*; — ة *kusba-t*, pl. *kusab*, milk yielded at one milking.

كثبا *kasbâ'*, earth.

كثج *kasaj*, I, INF. *kasj*, eat what is sufficient; gather stores for one's family.

(كثح) *kasah*, U, INF. *kash*, bare, uncover (عن *'an*); make dusty; gather, collect (a.); disperse (a.); take as much as one likes; — VI. INF. *takâsuh*, strike at one another with the sword.

(كثر) *kasar*, U, surpass in number or quantity; — *kasur*, INF. *kasra-t*, *kasâra-t*, be much, many, numerous; increase (n.), multiply (n.), be exuberant; appear or happen frequently; — II. INF. *taksîr*, increase (a.), multiply (a.); do a thing frequently; do too much, exceed the bounds, be excessive; — III. INF. *mukâsara-t*, vie or dispute with regard to quantity; frequent; — IV. INF. *iksâr*, increase (a.); procure in abundance; be rich; make many words; — V. INF. *takassur*, increase, multiply (n.), grow numerous, be exuberant; grow rich; — VI. INF. *takâsur*, be numerous, come in large numbers; multiply (n.); vie or dispute with regard to quantity; — X. INF. *istiksâr*, demand much of (2 acc. or acc. and من *min*); take much; find much, too much, too frequent; استكثره بخير *istiksar-hu bi-hair-in*, wish one increase of happiness, give thanks to.

كثر *kasr*, much, many; — *kisr*, *kusr*, great number, plenty, abundance; much, too much; — ة *kasra-t*, *kisra-t*, plenty, abundance; plurality, majority; frequency; too much; — ى *kusrā*, doing too much; excess.

(كثع) *kasa'*, INF. *kas'* (also II.), have cream; — INF. *kusû'* (also II.), have diarrhœa; — INF. *kas'*, *kusû'*, be full of blood, be very red (lips); — II. INF. *taksî'*, see I.; be healed externally; — ة *kas'a-t*, *kus'a-t*, froth, cream; — *kus'a-t*, dimple in the lip; — *kasa'a-t*, clay, mud.

كثعم *kas'am*, panther, jaguar.

(كثف) *kasuf*, INF. *kasâfa-t*, be thick, thicken (n.), condense (m.); be densely-grown; be rough and rude; — II. INF. *taksîf*, thicken, condense (a.); make numerous; — IV. INF. *iksâf*, be near, within shot; — VI. INF. *takâsuf*, behave roughly, rudely; be dense, compact.

كثف *kasf*, dense crowd, throng, great quantity.

(كثكث) *kaskas*, INF. ة, have a thick beard.

كثكث *kaskas*, *kiskis*, dust mingled with pebbles.

(كثل) *kasal*, U, INF. *kasl*, gather, heap up.

كثل *kasl*, great quantity; cornstack.

(كثم) *kasam*, U, INF. *kasm*, eat anything soft; carry together, heap up; fill; follow a track; turn from (a.); — *kasim*, A, INF. *kasam*, approach; be slow, tarry;

— IV. INF. *ikṣâm*, fill; — V. INF. *takassum*, stand perplexed and hesitate; — VII. INF. *inkiṣâm*, be sad.

كثم *kaṣim*, ة, thick.

كثنة *kuṣna-t*, plate of basket-work for flowers; small mat of palm-leaves.

(كثو) *kuṣw*, heaped up earth; a little milk; *qaṭa*-bird.

كثوثة *kuṣûṣa-t*, thickness, density.

كثى *kaṣan*, pl. of كثاة *kaṣât*.

كثيب *kaṣîb*, pl. *akṣiba-t*, *kuṣub*, *kuṣbân*, sand-hill heaped up by the wind; — ى *kaṣîbiyy*, round like a hill.

كثيث *kaṣîṣ*, thick, dense.

كثير *kaṣîr*, ة, pl. *kiṣâr*, much, many, numerous; abundant; frequently recurring; too much; long (time); *kaṣîr-an*, abundantly, often, very; *kaṣîrat-an*, frequently.

كثيرا *kaṣîrâ'*, resin of the tragacanth.

كثيف *kaṣîf*, ة, thick, dense, compact; rough, coarse, rude; shady; numerous, in abundance, plentiful.

(كج) *kajj*, INF. *kajj*, play at balls; — ة *kujja-t*, game at balls.

(كح) *kuḥḥ*, ة, pure, unmixed, of pure blood.

كحال *kiḥâl*, antimony, collyrium; — *kuḥâl*, pl. of كحيل *kuḥail*; — *kaḥḥâl*, who applies collyrium to the eye; oculist; —ة *kiḥâla-t*, art of an oculist or of preparing paints for the eye; — ى *kaḥḥâliyy*, referring to this art.

كحائل *kaḥâ'il*, pl. of كحل *kaḥil* and كحيل *kaḥîl*, *kuḥail*.

(كحب) *kaḥab*, INF. *kaḥb*, beat on the buttocks; — bear unripe or sour grapes.

كحب *kaḥb*, the buttocks; ة, unripe or sour grapes.

(كحت) *kaḥat*, INF. *kaḥt*, clean; drive away (m.).

(كحث) *kaḥaṣ*, INF. *kaḥṣ*, give with both hands.

(كحص) *kaḥaṣ*, INF. *kaḥṣ*, efface; be wiped away; be effaced; stir up the ground with the foot and search; — INF. *kuḥûṣ*, be old and in ruins; be effaced; escape, come out of sight; — II. INF. *takḥîṣ*, ruin; efface, blot out.

(كحط) *kaḥuṭ*, fail to come (rain); — — *kaḥṭ*, drought, distress.

(كحف) *kaḥaf*, INF. *kaḥf*, tread out one's shoes; — VII. INF. *inkiḥâf*, be trodden out.

كحف *kaḥf*, pl. *kuḥûf*, limb.

(كحل) *kaḥal*, A, U, INF. *kaḥl*, apply collyrium to one's eyes; — A, be unfertile and harm the people; — *kaḥil*, A, INF. *kaḥal*, have naturally black eye-lashes or eyes; = IV.; — II. INF. *takḥîl*, apply collyrium to one's eyes; (m.) prevent from seeing, blind, throw dust into one's eyes; (m.) cement the stones of a wall; — IV. INF. *ikḥâl* (also I., V., VIII., XI.), be covered with plants just beginning to green; — V. INF. *takaḥḥul*, apply collyrium to one's eyes; have the eyes painted with collyrium; see IV.; — VIII. INF. *iktiḥâl*, apply collyrium; see IV.; — XI. INF. *ikḥîlâl*, see IV.

كحل *kaḥl*, unfertile year; distress; sky; — *kuḥl*, pl. *akḥâl*, antimony in powder form to paint the eye-lids black, collyrium; pl. *akâḥil*, herbs for seasoning; — *kaḥal*, blackness of the eyes; — *kaḥil*, pl. *kaḥla*, *kaḥâ'il*, painted black with antimony, &c.

كحلا *kaḥlâ'*, f. of اكحل *akḥal*, having the eyes black by nature or art, &c.

كحلى *kuḥliyy*, dark-blue, azure-blue.

كحمة *kaḥma-t*, eye.

(كحى) *kaḥa*, INF. *kaḥy*, be spoiled, corrupted.

كحيل *kaḥîl*, pl. *kaḥâ'il*, *kaḥla*,

painted black with antimony; — *kuḥail*, asphalt; (m.) also *kuḥailân*, pl. *kuḥâl*, *kaḥâ'il*, horse of the best breed.

كحيلا *kaḥailâ'*, ox-tongue (plant).

(كح) *kiḥ*, *kiḥḥ*, *kaḥḥ*, fie! for shame!

كح *kaḥḥ*, I, INF. *kaḥḥ*, *kaḥîḥ*, snore; hiss (as a snake); — ة *kaḥḥa-t*, snoring, hissing (s.); chameleon.

(كخم) *kaḥam*, INF. *kaḥm*, push away; drive off.

كخيخ *kaḥîḥ*, snoring (s.).

(كد) *kadd*, U, INF. *kadd*, undergo troubles, take pains, toil hard; cause troubles to, molest, weary; bid or urge to work; goad; beckon; comb the head; — II. INF. *takdîd*, chase; — IV. INF. *ikdâd*, be miserly, tenacious; — VIII. INF. *iktidâd*, ask one to undergo a trouble or undertake a work; bid to be diligent; borrow a mortar from (2 acc.); — X. INF. *istikdâd*, bid to be diligent.

كد *kadd*, pain, trouble, toil, hardship, labour; effort, exertion, diligence (بالكد *bi 'l-kadd*, with difficulty, hardly); mortar; examination, investigation; — ة *kidda-t*, rough, rugged.

(كدا) *kada'*, INF. *kad'*, *kudû'*, suffer from the cold and be kept back in the ground; be behind in growth from lack of water; (also II.) injure a plant and keep it back (cold); — كدى *kadi'*, A, INF. *kada'*, be small and weak; — II. INF. *takdi'a-t*, see I.

كدادة *kudâda-t*, remains of food; sediment in a kettle.

كداديس *kadâdîs*, pl. of كداس *kuddâs*.

كدارة *kadâra-t*, turbidness, impurity; — *kudâra-t*=كدادة *kudâda-t*.

كداس *kidâs*, sneezing (s.);—*kuddâs*, pl. *kadâdîs*, heap of unthreshed corn; heap of sheaves; — ة *kudâsa-t*, anything snatched together.

كدام *kudâm*, old man; a plant; — ة *kudâma-t*, remains of food.

كدان *kaddân*, pumice-stone (m.); — ة *kadâna-t*, meanness, vileness.

كداية *kudâya-t*, heap; plenty of food and drink.

(كدب) *kadb*, *kadab*, *kadib*, *kudb*, white spot on a nail; — *kadib*, watery, thin.

(كدج) *kadaj*, drink to satiety.

(كدح) *kadaḥ*, INF. *kadḥ*, exert one's self, make every effort to carry a thing out or to reach a person; earn a sustenance for one's family; scratch, disfigure; part the hair; (m.) walk with difficulty, limp; — II. INF. *takdîḥ*, scratch, wound by biting;— V. INF. *takadduḥ*, be lacerated, chapped; — VIII. INF. *iktidâḥ*, earn a living for one's family.

كدح *kadḥ*, effort, exertion, painstaking, (m.) impediment in walking, limp; pl. *kudûḥ*, hurt by scratching.

كددة *kadada-t*, *kudada-t*, remains of broth.

(كدر) *kadar*, U, INF. *kudra-t*, *kudûr*, be troubled, muddy, turbid; — *kadir*, A, INF. *kadar*, id.; be unfortunate, have ill luck; be troubled by misfortune; — *kadur*, INF. *kadâra-t*, *kudûra-t* =*kadir*; — II. INF. *takdîr*, trouble, make turbid, dirty; molest, weary, tire out; — V. INF. *takaddur*, be troubled, muddy, turbid; have evil fortune; be molested, wearied; grow weary, tired of; be troubled by misfortune; — VII. INF. *inkidâr*, rush upon; pounce, swoop down; fall; be quick, hasty.

كدر *kadr*, *kadir*, troubled, turbid; faint; troublesome, importunate;—*kudr*, pl. (كدرا *kadrâ'*, f.)

of اكدر *akdar*, troubled; turbid; — *kadar*, pl. *akdâr*, turbidness, impurities; darkness, gloom; gloomy disposition, weariness, ennui; — ة *kudra-t*, turbidness, impurity; — *kadara-t*, pl. *kadar*, handful of cut-off fruit; large lump; mud of a cistern; — ى *kudriyy*, thin cloud; a species of the *qaṭa*-bird.

(كدس) *kadas*, I, INF. *kads*, *kidâs*, *kadasân*, sneeze; urge on a laden beast; throw down; heap up; — II. INF. *takdîs*, heap up; — V. INF. *takaddus*, walk as if oppressed by the load; be heaped up.

كدس *kuds*, pl. *akdâs*, heap of cut corn.

(كدش) *kadaś*, I, INF. *kadś*, scratch; wound by a sword or lance; cut; urge on; drive violently back; try to gain a living for one's family; receive a present; receive; (m.) bite; (m.) degenerate; — II. INF. *takdîś*, bite.

كدش *kudś*, pl. of *kadîś*; — ة *kadśa-t*, bite.

كدع *kada'*, INF. *kad'*, drive, drive back, repel.

(كدف) *kadaf*, clatter of the hoof; noise; — IV. INF. *ikdâf*, make the ground resound with the clatter of hoofs.

(كدكد) *kadkad*, INF. ة, *kidkâd*, laugh immoderately; polish a blade; — II. INF. *takadkud*, urge on violently.

(كدم) *kadam*, U, I, INF. *kadm*, seize with the lips or teeth; bite; stamp with an iron instrument, brand, mark; chase the game; — III. INF. *mukâdama-t*, be able to reach by the lips only; — ة *kadama-t*, mark, impression.

كدن *kadan*, U, INF. *kadn*, gird one's self; yoke oxen to the plough; — *kadin*, A, INF. *kadan*, be black; be grazed off to the root; — VII. INF. *inkidân*, be yoked to the plough.

(كده) *kadah*, INF. *kadh*, scratch the face, disfigure; beat so as to leave marks; break (a.); part the hair with a comb; overcome; — II. INF. *takdîh*=I.; — V. INF. *takadduh*, be broken, break (n.).

(كدو) *kadâ*, U, INF. *kadw*, *kuduww*, be hard, have but scarce vegetation; grow badly; — INF. *kidâ'*, deny a gift; — I, INF. *kady*, give but little, be miserly; — كدى *kadî*, A, INF. *kadan*, vomit when coughing; choke (n.); have colic from drinking milk; — IV. INF. *ikdâ'*, be miserly, avaricious; be exhausted; delay; be baffled.

كدو *kudû'*, INF. of (كدا).

كدود *kadûd*, laborious.

كدورة *kadûra-t*, turbidness; pl. *-ât*, impurity in a fluid; grief, anxiety.

كدى *kadî*, *kadan*, see (كدو); — *kadiyy*, having no smell, inodorous (musk); — ة *kudya-t*, pl. *kud-an*, hard ground or clod; calamity.

كديد *kadîd*, rugged tract; ground trodden by hoofs.

كدير *kadîr*, troubled, turbid.

كديرا *kudairâ'*, milk and pounded dates as a dish.

كديس *kadîs*, heap of sheaves.

كديش *kadîś*, pl. *kudś*, horse of a low breed; cart-horse.

كدين *kadîn*, girdle, belt.

(كذ) *kazz*, INF. *kazz*, be rough.

كذا *kazâ*, like this, thus; ك و ك *kazâ wa kazâ*, so and so, such an one, and so on, etcætera.

كذاب *kizâb*, *kuzâb*, lie; — *kazzâb*, liar, impostor.

كذان *kazzân*, soft clay-stone; pumice-stone.

(كذب) *kazab*, I, INF. *kizb*, *kazib*, *kizâb*, *kizzâb*, *kazba-t*, *kizba-t*, lie, tell lies, be a liar, deceive, cheat; be an indispensable duty; *kazib*, A, lie, tell lies to; — II. INF. *kizzâb*, *takzîb*, accuse

of lying, declare one to be a liar, a thing to be a lie; give the lie to; كذب ذاته *kazzab zâta-hu*, belie one's self, contradict one's self, fail; — III. INF. *kizâb*, *mukâzaba-t*, tell lies to; — IV. INF. *ikzâb*, make one a liar, bid one to tell lies; find one to be a liar, accuse of lying; — V. INF. *takazzub*, be given to lying; be accused of lying, given the lie; — X. INF. *istikzâb*, deem one to be a liar, accuse of lying.

كذب *kizb*, *kazib*, lie, untruth, fraud, deceit; — *kuzb*, white spot on the nail; — *kuzub*, pl. of كذوب *kazûb*; — *kuzzab*, pl. of كاذب *kâzib*; — ة *kazba-t*, *kizba-t*, lie; — *kazaba-t*, pl. of كاذب *kâzib*; — *kuzaba-t*, liar; — ى *kuzba*, lie; — *kizbiyy*, ة, mendacious.

كذبان *kazbân*, liar; — *kuzbân*, lie.

(كذح) *kazah*, INF. *kazh*, throw dust and stones at.

كذلك *kazalik*, like that, thus; likewise, none the less.

كذوب *kazûb*, pl. *kuzub*, liar; — ة *kazûba-t*, lie; soul.

كذى *kaza*=كذا *kazâ*.

كذينق *kuzînaq*, fulling-bat.

(كر) *karr*, INF. *karr*, *kurûr*, return to, flee and attack afresh with a sudden turn; repel; desist; lean to; (m.) fall, tumble, roll down; (m.) unroll itself; — INF. *kurûr*, pass away (time); — I, A, INF. *karîr*, produce a rattle in the throat; — II. INF. *takrâr*, *takrîr*, *takirra-t*, repeat; do anything repeatedly; purify, refine, extract the quintessence; — V. INF. *takarrur*, be repeated; be purified, refined.

كر *karr*, pl. *kirâr*, *kurûr*, rope of bast or fibres of palm-leaves; pl. *kurûr*, cable; pl. *akrâr*, *kirâr*, a measure (=6 ass-loads or 12 وسق *wasq*); (m.) pl. *kirâr*, foal of an ass, colt; pl. *akrâr*, an upper garment; — ة *kura-t* (m. also *kurra-t*), pl. *-ât*, *kurûn*, *kirîn*, *kariyy*, *kura-n*, globe, ball; — *karra-t*, pl. *-ât*, *kirâr*, repetition, recurrence; taking to flight and returning to the attack; attack, charge; turn, time (*karrat-an*, once, sometimes, at once); (m.) one hundred thousand.

كرا *karan*, male swan; — *kirâ'*, ة *kirât*, hire, rent; wages, salary; anything hired; load of a mule; INF. III. of (كرو).

كرابيج *karâbîj*, pl. of كرباج *kirbâj*.

كرابيس *karâbîs*, pl. of كرباس *kirbâs*; — ى *karâbîsiyy*, of fine white muslin.

كراث *karrâs*, *kurrâs*, leek.

كراحين *karâhîn*, pl. of كرحانة *karhâna-t*.

كرادس *karâdis*, كراديس *karâdîs*, pl. of كردوسة *kurdûsa-t*.

كرار *karâr*, pearl or shell used as an amulet; pantry; — *; — *karrâr*, strenuous in attacking; impetuous.

كرارجى *karârjiyy*, major-domo, steward.

كرارزة *karâriza-t*, pl. of كرز *kurraz*.

كراز *kurâz*, *kurrâz*, pl. *kirzân*, earthen jar with a narrow orifice; — *karrâz*, pl. *karârîz*, ram carrying on his horn the herdsman's satchel; big he-goat; — ة *karâza-t*, sermon.

كراسة *kurrâsa-t*, pl. *kurrâs*, *karârîs* paper stitched together, copybook; pamphlet; number of a periodical; book; Koran.

كراسى *karâsiyy*, pl. of كرسى *kursiyy*; — ة *kurâsiya-t*, small copy-book.

كراع *kurâ'*, pl. *akru'*, *akâri'*, smaller part of the shin-bone of sheep or oxen; sheep-foot; pl. *kir'ân*, extremity, limb; projecting rock; — ى *kurâ'iyy*, seller of sheep's feet.

كرام *kirâm*, pl. of كريم *karîm*; — *kurâm*, *kurrâm*, very noble and generous; — *karrâm*, vine-dresser; — ة *karâma-t*, gene-

rosity, liberality; honour, dignity; pl. *karâm*, cover of a pot or jar; pl. *-ât*, miracle.

كرامية *karâmiyya-t*, favour, present, bounty.

كران *kirân*, lute; cymbal.

كرانيف *karânîf*, pl. of كرناف *kirnâf*.

كراهة *karâha-t*, كراهية *karâhiyya-t*, abhorrence, aversion.

كراوين *karâwîn*, pl. of كروان *karawân*.

كراية *kirâya-t*=كرا *kirâ'*, hire, &c.

كراييس *karâyîs*, pl. of كرياس *kiryâs*.

(كرب) *karab*, U, INF. *karb*, tighten one's bonds; twist a rope; grieve (a.); overburden with work; load an animal; (m.) inflate the belly; be near doing anything; be near setting; — INF. *karb*, *kirâb*, plough; furrow the field; — *karib*, A, INF. *karab*, break (n.); — II. INF. *takrîb*, molest; overburden with work; — IV. INF. *ikrâb*, grieve; put a rope to the bucket; — VII. INF. *inkirâb*, VIII. INF. *iktirâb*, grieve (n.); (m.) have the stomach surfeited.

كرب *karb*, pl. *kurûb*, grief, sorrow; — *kurb*, near, on the point of; — *karab* (sing. and pl.), rope of a bucket; base of a palm-leaf; — ة *kurba-t*, pl. *kurab*, grief; sorrow; (m.) indigestion.

كرباج *kirbâj*, pl. *karâbîj*, horse-whip, scourge.

كرباس *kirbâs*, pl. *karâbîs*, fine white linen (cotton, muslin); — ى *kirbâsiyy*, made of it; seller of it.

كربال *kirbâl*, pl. *karâbîl*, instrument for cleaning cotton; sieve.

(كربج) *karbaj*, INF. ة, shrink, contract (n.), grow torpid.

كربج *kurbaj*, shop; tavern, taproom.

كربش *karbaś*, INF. ة, take prisoner and bind; also كربس *karbas*, walk like one fettered; — II. INF. *takarbuś*, be shrunk, shrivelled, wrinkled.

(كربل) *karbal*, INF. ة, walk through mud; wade in or plunge into water; mix one thing with (ب *bi*) another; winnow the wheat; (m.) gag, bind.

كربلا *karbalâ'*, Kerbela.

(كرتع) *karta'*, INF. ة, intermeddle; (m.) molest, disquiet; (m.) benumb; — II. INF. *takartu'*, (m.) be mixed up with, entangled in; (m.) be benumbed.

(كرتن) *kartan*, (m.) INF. ة, impose a quarantine, quarantine (a.); — INF. *takartun*, keep quarantine.

(كرث) *karas̱*, U, I, INF. *kars̱*, oppress, be heavy upon; molest; decant; — IV. INF. *ikrâs̱*=I.; — VII. INF. *inkirâs̱*, break (n.); — VIII. INF. *iktirâs̱*, be grieved, be concerned in, need.

(كرثأ) *kars̱a'*, INF. ة, be thick, dense; — II. INF. *takars̱u'*, id.

(كرج) *karij*, A, INF. *karaj* (also V.), be spoiled, mouldy;—(m.) *karaj*, U, INF. *karj*, collect and stream towards one point (water); (m.) run, run with short steps; (m.) read fluently;—V. INF. *takarruj*, see I.

كرج *karj*, fluent reading; — *kurj*, Georgia; — *kurraj*, colt, foal; — ى *kurjiyy*, Georgian; — *kurrajiyy*, Sodomite.

(كرح) *kirḥ*, pl. *akrâḥ*, monk's cell; hermitage.

كرخانة *karḥâna-t*, *kirḥâna-t*, pl. *karâḥîn*, manufactory, workshop.

(كرد) *karad*, U, INF. *kard*, urge on; pursue; cut off, shear; — III. INF. *mukârada-t*, pursue.

كرد *kurd*, pl. *akrâd*, Kurd; also ة *kurda-t*, a field-measure.

كردان *kurdân*, neck-chain of precious metal.

(كردس) *kardas*, INF. ة, divide the horsemen into squadrons; (m. also كردش *kardaś*) gather sheaves

and place them together; — II. INF. *takardus*, be gathered, placed together; be short and thick-set.

كردوس *kurdûs*, ة *kurdûsa-t*, pl. *karâdîs*, *karadis*, squadron of horsemen, squadron; *kurdûs* (m. also كردوش *kurdûś*), heap; piece of meat.

كردى *kurdiyy*, ة, Kurdish.

(كرز) *karaz*, I, INF. *kurûz*, enter; hide (n.); take refuge with (الى *ila*); lean towards; — I, INF. *karz*, *karâza-t*, preach the Gospel; — *kariz*, A, INF. *karaz*, eat much cheese; — II. INF. *takrîz*, celebrate the carnival; moult; — III. INF. *mukâraza-t*, take refuge in a place and hide there.

كرز *karz*, preaching of the Gospel; — *kurz*, pl. *kiraza-t*, a herdsman's satchel; portmanteau; — *karaz*, cherry, cherry-tree; big ram or he-goat; — *kurraz*, pl. *karâriza-t*, hawk, falcon; clever, masterly; also ى *kurraziyy*, good-for nothing fellow, worthless person, miser.

كرزان *kirzân*, pl. of كراز *kurâz*, *kurrâz*.

(كرزل) *karzal*, INF. ة, tie up the hair on the crown of the head; tuck up one's garments.

(كرزن) *karzan*, *kirzin*, كرزين *kirzîn*, pl. *karâzin*, large hatchet, axe.

(كرس) *karas*, I, INF. *kars*, (m.) clean the stable; — II. INF. *takrîs*, lay the foundation of a house; consecrate, dedicate; — IV. INF. *ikrâs*, put lambs, goats, &c. into the stable; — V. INF. *takarrus*, be consecrated or devoted to God; — VII. INF. *inkirâs*, be cleaned; fall over, fall into.

كرس *kirs*, pl. *akrâs*, *akâris*, *akârîs*, adjoining house; pl. connected buildings; stable for lambs, goats, pigeons, &c.; excrement sticking to the tails of animals, the walls of stables, &c.; string of pearls.

كرستة m. *karasta-t*, timber, wood; material of any workman (Turk.).

(كرسح) m. *karsaḥ*, INF. ة, cripple, lame;—II. *takarsuḥ*, be crippled, lamed.

(كرسع) *karsa'*, INF. ة, run; hit one on the outer bone of the wrist.

(كرسف) *karsaf*, INF. ة, hough the camel; tie a camel's feet close together; place the cotton stopper into the ink-bottle.

كرسف *kursuf*, pl. *karâsif*, old cotton; also ة *kursufa-t*, cotton stopper.

(كرسم) *karsam*, INF. ة, fix the eyes silently on the ground.

كرسنة *karsana-t*, (m.) *kursanna-t*, black vetch; a medicinal plant.

كرسوع *kursû'*, pl. *karâsî'*, outer bone of the wrist;—ة *kursû'a-t*, troop.

كرسى *kursiyy*, pl. *karâsiyy*, throne, arm-chair, chair, bench of the judges; throne of God, highest heaven; base of a column; setting of a ring; residence, seat, see.

(كرش) *kariś*, A, INF. *karaś*, be wrinkled; be at the head of many after isolation; — II. INF. *takrîś*, frown; disembowel an animal; (also IV.) grow paunch-bellied; — IV. INF. *ikrâś*, see II.; — V. INF. *takarruś*, be wrinkled, contracted; assemble (n.).

كرش *kirś*, *kariś*, pl. *kurûś*, belly or stomach of man or ruminants; tripe; womb; crowd of people; children and household.

كرشا *karśâ'*, f. of اكرش *akraś*, paunch-bellied.

(كرص) *karaṣ*, I, INF. *karṣ*, scrape cheese; mix dates with cheese; — II. INF. *takrîṣ*, eat of this dish; — VIII. INF. *iktirâṣ*, gather (a.).

(كرض) *karaḍ*, U, INF. *karḍ*, take the sperm out of the covered she-

camel's womb ; — INF. *kirâḍ*, prepare the dish كريض *karîḍ*.

(كرظ) *karaẓ*, U, INF. *karẓ*, injure one's honour.

(كرع) *kara'*, INF. *kar'*, *kurû'*, sip water ; injure at the shin-bone ; — *kari'*, A, INF. *kara'*, sip water ; have thin shin-bones, feel pain in the shin-bone ; desire a man ; — II. INF. *takrî'*, drink much in sipping ;—V. INF. *takarru'*, make one's ablutions before prayer.

كرعان *kir'ân*, pl. of كراع *kurâ'*.

(كرف) *karaf*, U, I, INF. *karf*, smell the water of the she-ass ; (m.) urge on, goad ; (m.) remove the sweepings ; — VII. INF. *inkirâf*, be goaded ; be removed.

(كرفا) *karfa'*, INF. ة, froth ; be mixed up ;—II. INF. *takarfu'*, be thick, dense.

(كرفت) m. *karfat*, INF. ة, drop, let roll down ; — II. INF. *takarfut*, fall, roll down.

كرفس *karafs*, parsley, celery ; — *kurfus*, cotton.

كرك *karik*, red ; — ة *karaka-t*, alembic.

(كركب) *kurkub*, an aromatic plant ; — *karkab*, INF. ة, disarrange, confuse ; be noisy ; — II. INF. *takarkub*, be entirely out of order ; get confused, entangled ; — ة *karkaba-t*, disorder, confusion ; noise, tumult.

كركدن *karkaddan*, m. *karkadann*, كركدان *karkadân*, rhinoceros.

(كركر) *karkar*, INF. ة, repeat ; cut corn ; turn a mill ; gather and heap up ; drive the clouds together ; laugh loud and repeatedly ; take to flight ; keep back ; (m.) murmur, rumble ; — II. INF. *takarkur*, spin in the air, turn about, be versatile ; — ة *karkara-t*, immoderate laughter ; confusion, hurly-burly ; rumbling noise in the belly ; — *kirkira-t*, callosity on the chest of a camel.

كركم *kurkum*, *karkum*, saffron.

كركند *karkand*, a red precious stone.

كركى *kurkiyy*, pl. *karâkiyy*, crane (bird).

(كرم) *karam*, U, INF. *karm*, surpass in generosity or liberality ; — *karum*, INF. *karam*, *karama-t*, *karâma-t*, be generous, high-minded, liberal, beneficent ; — II. INF. *takrîm*, *takrima-t*, pronounce one to be generous, &c., exalt, honour above others, honour ;—III. INF. *mukârama-t*, vie in generosity ; do anything in honour of ; — IV. INF. *ikrâm*, pronounce one to be generous, &c. ; honour, receive with marks of honour ; show one's self generous and beneficent ; give as a present, bestow alms upon ; —V. INF. *takarrum*, be honoured, overwhelmed with marks of honour ; be liberal towards ; present with ; — also VI. INF. *takârum*, be stainless, irreproachable ; abstain from anything mean ; — X. INF. *istikrâm*, find generous, liberal, venerable.

كرم *karm*, pl. *kurûm*, vine-tree ; — *karam*, *kurm* (also كرمان *kurmân*), generosity, liberality, grace ; *karam*, noble, kind ; also *kuram*, good, fertile ; — ة *karma-t*, vine-tree ; vine-branch ; — *kurma-t*, *karama-t*, generosity ; kindness (كرمة عينك *kurmat-a 'ainak*, in honour of you) ; — ى *kurma*, generosity, kindness.

كرما *kuramâ'*, pl. of كريم *karîm*.

(كرمد) *karmad*, INF. ة, run after.

كرمل *kirmil*, Mount Carmel.

كرناف *kirnâf*, pl. *karânîf*, trunk of a palm-tree without branches.

(كرنب) *karnab*, INF. ة, place the dish كرنيب *karnîb*, before the guest ; eat of this dish.

كرنب *karamb*, *kuramb*, cauliflower ; — ية *karambiyya-t*, dish of cauliflower.

(كرنش) m. *karnaś*, INF. ة, also II. INF. *takarnuś*, be wrinkled.

(كرنف) *karnaf*, INF. ة, strike off with the sword; strike, beat; take the branches off a palm-tree.

كرنيب *karnîb*, *kirnîb*, dish of milk and dates; pl. *kurânîb*, shell of a pumpkin used for drawing water; — ة *kirnîba-t*, very thin person, skeleton.

كرنيفة *karnîfa-t*, (m.) gun-stock; — *kirnîfa-t*, thick nose.

(كره) *karih*, INF. *karh*, *kurh*, *karâha-t*, *karâhiyya-t*, *makraha-t*, *makruha-t*, feel aversion or abhorrence at (acc.), loathe; — *karuh*, INF. *karâha-t*, inspire with aversion or abhorrence; be loathsome, ugly, detestable, abominable; — II. INF. *takrîh*, render loathsome or hateful; make one feel abhorrence or aversion, disgust; — IV. INF. *ikrâh*, force one against his inclination; — V. INF. *takarruh*, feel aversion or abhorrence, (m.) murmur; — VII. INF. *inkirâh*, be detested, hated; — X. INF. *istikrâh*, find loathsome, horrid, abominable; feel aversion, abhorrence.

(كرو) *karâ*, U, INF. *karw*, also كرى *kara*, I, INF. *kary*, dig out earth; dig a canal; consolidate the inside of a well with beams; do repeatedly; play at balls; make in form of a ball; walk apace; run fast; — m. *kara*, let, rent (a.), hire out; — *karî*, A, INF. *kara-n*, slumber, sleep; — III. INF. *kirâ'*, *mukârât*, let, rent, hire out (2 acc.); be a muleteer or ass-driver; — IV. INF. *ikrâ'*, rent (a.), hire out; increase; decrease; delay; — V. INF. *takarrî*, sleep; — VII. INF. *inkirâ'*, be hired out; — VIII. INF. *iktirâ'*, hire, take into one's service; — X. INF. *istikrâ'*, id.

كرو *karw*, *kirw*, hire, wages, pay; — ة *kirwa-t*, *kurwa-t*, id.; load of a mule.

كروان *karawân*, pl. *kirwân*, *karâwîn*, red-legged partridge; crane (bird); bustard; swan.

كروبى *karûbiyy*, pl. *-ûn*, *karûbîn*, cherubim.

كرور *kurûr*, passing space of time.

كروس *karawwas*, *karawwus*, big-headed; — ة · *karrûsa-t*, كروصة *karrûṣa-t*, state coach, landau.

كروى *kurawiyy*, ة, globular, spherical; pl. *kurawiyyât*, spherical trigonometry.

كرويا *karawiyâ'*, caraway.

كرى *kara*, *karî*, v. see (كرو); — *karan*, *kara*, sleepiness, drowsiness; = كروان *karawân*; — *karî* (كر *kar-in*), *kariyy*, sleepy; hirer-out, muleteer; — *kariyy*, *kuran*, pl. of كرة *kura-t*; — *kuriyy*, spherical; — *kurra*, once; a single attack.

كرياس *kiryâs*, pl. *karâyîs*, privy on the roof of a house.

كريان *karyân*, sleepy, drowsy.

كريب *karîb*, grieved, sorrowful; surfeited; — ة *karîba-t*, pl. *karâ'ib*, calamity.

كريت *karît*, entire, full.

كريث *karîs̱*, vexatious; wearied of, disgusted with.

كرير *karîr*, sound produced by one choking; death-rattle; — *.

كريزة *karîza-t*, carnival.

كريص *karîṣ*, كريض *karîḍ*, dish of dates mixed with the cheese اقط *aqṭ*.

كريع *karî'*, who drinks by sipping.

كريم *karîm*, pl. *akrimâ'*, *kuramâ'*, *kirâm*, generous, noble-minded, liberal, beneficent; kind, gracious; venerable, honoured; God; (m.) a kind of turtle-dove; — ة *karîma-t*, pl. *karâ'im*, noble, honoured person; high-born lady, princess; the daughter of the house; precious object or limb (*al-karîmatân*, the two eyes); fertile ground; — ية *karâmiyya-t*, kindness, beneficence, graciousness.

كرين *kirîn*, pl. of كرة *kura-t*; — ة *karîna-t*, pl. *kirân*, female musician or singer.

كريه *karîh*, ة, loathsome, detestable, hateful, abominable; ugly; *al-karîh*, lion; — ة *karîha-t*, pl. *karâ'ih*, adversity, misery of war, war.

(كز) *kazz*, U, INF. *kazâza-t*, *kuzûza-t*, be dried up and shrivelled; shrink; — INF. *kazz*, shorten, make narrower; be shortened; shiver with cold; feel aversion; gnash (the teeth, على *'ala*); — INF. *kazâza-t*, be miserly; — IV. INF. *ikzâz*, visit with the disease كزاز *kuzâz*; — VIII. INF. *iktizâz*, be shrivelled, shrunk.

كز *kazz*, ة, dry, withered, shrivelled, shrunk; hard and inflexible, stiff; miserly, niggardly.

كزاز *kuzâz*, shivering from cold, cold shiver; rheumatism.

كزبرة *kuzbura-t*, coriander.

(كزم) *kazam*, U, INF. *kazm*, break with the front-teeth; open and eat the contents; — *kazim*, A, INF. *kazam*, have short fingers, a short nose; be miserly; — II. INF. *takzîm*, have the toes bent downwards; — IV. INF. *ikzâm*, shrink, contract (n.); be shrivelled; eat one's fill.

كزم *kazam*, avarice; shortness of the fingers or nose; — *kuzam*, a kind of finch; nightingale.

كزمازج *kizmâzaj*, tamarisk.

كزوزة *kuzûza-t*, INF. of (كز).

(كزى) *kaza*, I, INF. *kazy*, show one's self kind.

(كس) *kass*, U, INF. *kass*, grind or pound to powder; — *kasis*, A, have small short teeth.

كس *kuss*, pl. *aksâs*, pudenda of a woman; — *kas'*, pl. *kusû'*, part of the night; — *kus'*, pl. *aksâ'*, back-part, hind-parts.

(كسا) *kasa'*, INF. *kas'*, follow, pursue; drive an animal in the tracks of the preceding one; get the better in a dispute or lawsuit; strike with the sword.

كسا *kasâ'*, honour, glory; — *kisâ'*, pl. *aksiya-t*, upper garment, dress; pl. of كسوة *kiswa-t*..

كساب *kassâb*, who earns or gains much.

كساحة *kusâḥa-t*, paralysis, palsy.

كساد *kasâd*, dulness of the market, lack of purchasers, slackness.

كسار *kusâr*, ة, fragments; — *kassâr*, who breaks much; — ة *kusâra-t*, recently-plouged field (m.); — ى *kasâra*, pl. of كسير *kasîr*.

كساسرة *kasâsira-t*, pl. of كسرى *kasra*.

كسافة *kasâfa-t*, eclipse; turbid sediment.

كسالة *kasâla-t*, laziness, slowness, negligence; difficulty; embarrassment; affliction.

كسالى *kasâla*, pl. of كسلان *kaslân*.

كساوى *kasâwî*, pl. of كسوة *kiswa-t*.

(كسب) *kasab*, I, INF. *kisb*, try to earn a living, earn, gain; gather riches, knowledge; — II. INF. *taksîb*, cause one to earn, to gain; leave one a share in the gain; — IV. INF. *iksâb*, make to earn or gain; — V. INF. *takassub*, try to earn, to gain; acquire knowledge; make progress; — VIII. INF. *iktisâb*, try to earn; earn, gain; — X. INF. *istiksâb*, id.; make to work for gain, to be industrious.

كسب *kasb*, *kisb*, earnings, gain; — *kusb*, husk, sediment produced in pressing oil; — ة *kisba-t*, earnings; trade.

كسبان *kasbân*, who earns, gains.

(كسبر) *kusbar*, pl. *kasâbir*, bracelet of ivory; — ة *kusbura-t*, *kusbara-t*, coriander.

(كست) *kust*, Costus (shrub); — ة *kasta-t*, and—

كستانة *kastâna-t*, chestnut.

(كسح) *kasaḥ*, INF. *kasḥ*, sweep; prune; take all, grasp, snatch away; (m.) beat, flog, punish; — *kasiḥ*, A, INF. *kasaḥ*, be weakened or lamed in hand or foot,

be crippled; limp; — VIII. INF. *iktisâḥ*, take all.

كسحان *kasḥân*, lame of hand or foot; — *kusḥân*, pl. of اكسح *aksaḥ*, lame.

(كسد) *kasad*, U, *kasud*, INF. *kasâd*, *kusûd*, find no purchaser; sell badly; be dull; — IV. INF. *iksâd*, have a dull market; be dull; — VII. INF. *inkisâd*, return to.

كسد *kusd*=كست *kust*.

(كسر) *kasar*, I, INF. *kasr*, break (a.); wreck; break the battle-line and rout; overthrow, ruin; quench; pay the price for the crops in advance; INF. *kasr*, *kusûr*, draw in the wings to alight; cast down one's looks; point with the vowel *kasra-t*; — II. INF. *taksîr*, break into many pieces; (m.) reprimand, refine, civilize; slur over in speaking, pronounce badly; — III. INF. *mukâsara-t*, join immediately; share the same room with; barter with (acc.); — V. INF. *takassur*, be broken into many pieces; be reprimanded, refined, civilized; — VII. INF. *inkisâr*, be broken; be routed; fail, become a bankrupt; — VIII. INF. *iktisâr*, break (n.).

كسر *kasr*, pl. *kusûr*, *kusûrât*, breach, fracture; fraction (in arithmetic); contrition, affliction; vowel *i* ـِ; also *kisr*, pl. *kusûr*, *aksâr*, side; side-wall of a house; lowest flap of a tent with entrance-opening; habitation; limb, leg; — *kussar*, pl. of كاسر *kâsir*, who breaks, &c.; — ة *kasra-t*, vowel *i* ـِ; fracture; defeat; contrition; — *kisra-t*, pl. *kisar*, fragment; slice of bread.

كسروى *kisrawiyy*, royal, imperial.

كسرى *kasra*, pl. of كسير *kasîr*; also *kisra*, pl. *kusûr*, *akâsir*, *akâsira-t*, *kasâsira-t*, title of the Persian kings.

(كسطل) *kasṭal*, كسطال *kasṭâl*, كسطان *kasṭân*, dust.

(كسع) *kasaʻ*, INF. *kasʻ*, beat and kick one on the back; whip a spinning-top; — VIII. INF. *iktisâʻ*, press the tail (ب *bi*) between the legs; — ة *kusʻa-t*, pl. *kusaʻ*, white spot on the forehead; beast of burden; slave.

(كسف) *kasaf*, I, INF. *kasf*, cut up; hough; darken, eclipse; — INF. *kusûf*, also VII. INF. *inkisâf*, be eclipsed.

كسف *kasf*, eclipse; (more usually كشف *kaśf*), suppression of the last letter of a *watad mafrûk* at the end of a foot (*mafʻûlâtu* becoming *mafʻûlun*); — ة *kisfa-t*, pl. *kisaf*, *kisf*, *aksâf*, *kusûf*, part of a cloud; fragment, part.

(كسكس) *kaskas*, INF. ة, pound minutely.

كسكس *kuskus*, flour boiled in milk; pap.

(كسل) *kasil*, A, INF. *kasal*, be lazy, idle, negligent; neglect (عن *ʻan*); — IV. INF. *iksâl*, render lazy, negligent; — VI. INF. *takâsul*, be or feign to be lazy, negligent; live in idleness.

كسل *kasal*, laziness; — *kasil*, ة, lazy, negligent; idle.

كسلان *kaslân*, ة, pl. *kasâla*, *kisâla*, *kusâla*, *kasâlî*, *kaslā*, lazy, negligent; cowardly.

(كسم) *kasam*, I, INF. *kasm*, fritter; toil to support one's family; stir up.

كسم m. *kasm*, way, manner, method; shape, fashion; costume, livery.

(كسمل) *kasmal*, INF. ة, walk with short steps.

(كسو) *kasâ*, U, INF. *kasw*, put a dress upon (2 acc.), clothe; — كسى *kasî*, A, INF. *kasan*, dress (n.), be dressed; — II. INF. *taksiya-t*, dress (a.), clothe; — III. INF. *mukâsât*, vie in glory with (acc.); — V. INF. *takassî*,

dress (n.); — VIII. INF. *iktisâ'*, id.; be dressed.

كسو *kusû'*, pl. of كس *kas'*; — ة *kiswa-t*, *kuswa-t*, pl. *kusa-n*, *kisâ'*, *kasâwî*, dress, garment; clothing.

كسى *kusy*, pl. *aksâ*, back-part, hind-parts; — *kusan*, pl. of كسوة *kiswa-t*, *kuswa-t*.

كسيح *kasîḥ*, *kusaiḥ*, paralyzed, crippled; weak, powerless.

كسيد *kasîd*, very slack of sale; contemptible, low, mean.

كسير *kasîr*, pl. *kasra*, *kasâra*, broken; routed.

كسيس *kasîs*, dried and pounded meat for provisions; date-wine.

كسيف *kasîf*, ة, thick, muddy, turbid; — ة *kasîfa-t*, sediment, dregs.

(كش) *kaśś*, I, INF. *kaśîś*, rustle in the dry leaves; roar, bellow, low; chase away the flies; frown, look austere; — ة *kaśśa-t*, austere face (m.); — *kuśśa-t*, fore-lock; ك العجوز *kuśśat al-'ajûz*, moss.

(كشا) *kaśa'*, INF. *kaś'*, eat cucumbers; roast meat until it is entirely dried up; strike off with a sword; lie with; — كشى *kaśi'*, A, INF. *kaś'*, *kaśa'*, be full of food.

كشاحة *kaśśâḥa-t*, secret hatred, deep grudge.

كشاف *kaśśâf*, who unveils, reveals, investigates, explains, reports; — *kiśâf*, getting big with young in two consecutive years.

كشامرة *kaśâmira-t*, pl. of كشميرى *kiśmîriyy*.

(كشب) *kaśab*, I, INF. *kaśb*, also II. INF. *takśîb*, swallow greedily.

كشتبان *kiśtibân*, pl. *kaśâtibîn*, thimble; a little, trifle.

(كشح) *kaśaḥ*, U, INF. *kaśḥ*, bear a grudge against (ل *li*); pass. *kuśiḥ*, suffer from the disease كشح *kaśaḥ*; — II. INF. *takśîḥ*, mark by branding at the place كشح *kaśḥ*; peel; (m.) disperse (n.), clear up; — III. INF. *mukâśaḥa-t*, bear a grudge against; — V. INF. *takaśśuḥ*, lie with; — VII. INF. *inkiśâḥ*, disperse (n.).

كشح *kaśḥ*, pl. *kuśûḥ*, place between the hypochondres and false ribs; side, waist; — *kaśaḥ*, pleurisy.

(كشخ), II. *kaśśaḥ*, INF. *takśîḥ*, and— كشخن *kaśḥan*, INF. ة, call one:

كشخان *kaśḥân*, *kiśḥân*, cuckold.

(كشد) *kaśad*, I, INF. *kaśd*, bite at or off; milk with three fingers.

كشد *kaśad*, who toils for his family; — *kuśud*, pl. of كاشد *kâśid* and كشود *kaśûd*, both=*kaśad*.

(كشر) *kaśar*, I, INF. *kaśr*, uncover, bare, show the teeth (عن *'an*); smile, laugh; — *kaśir*, A, INF. *kaśar*, flee, take to flight; — II. INF. *takśîr*=I.; ك على نابه *kaśśar 'ala nâbi-hi*, pull faces; — III. INF. *mukâśara-t*, show the teeth; smile or laugh at; — ة *kiśra-t*, showing of the teeth.

(كشط) *kaśaṭ*, I, INF. *kaśṭ*, take off (the cover or veil); skin, flay; skim; — VII. INF. *inkiśâṭ*, be taken off, uncovered; disperse (n.), pass away, subside; — VIII. INF. *iktiśâṭ*, take off the covering.

كشع *kaśa'*, INF. *kaś'*, go, depart; — *kaśi'*, A, INF. *kaśa'*, be in anxiety, in sorrow.

(كشف) *kaśaf*, I, INF. *kaśf*, *kâśifa-t*, uncover, bare, unveil, reveal; publish, communicate; expose; investigate into the facts of a case; reconnoitre; visit (a sick person, على *'ala*); — *kaśif*, A, INF. *kaśaf*, be put to flight; have an open forehead and temples by pushing back the hair; — II. INF. *takśîf*, uncover, reveal; cause one to do so; compel one to disclose or communicate; — III. INF. *mukâśafa-t*, disclose to (acc.); show openly (a.); try to discover, to find out; — V. INF. *takaśśuf*, be disclosed, show one's self openly (n.), be known; — VII. INF.

inkiśâf, be uncovered, disclosed, unveiled; be reconnoitred; show one's self openly; be removed; — X. INF. *istikśâf*, ask one to disclose, to communicate; try to discover, to find out.

كشف *kaśf*, uncovering, baring, unveiling, revealing; disclosure, exposure; making public; discovery; investigation; official report; gauze; see كسف *kasf*; — ة *kaśafa-t*, place on the forehead free of hair.

كشفانية m. *kaśfâniyya-t*, present at a visit paid to a sick person.

كشك *kaśk*, *kiśk*, (oatmeal) porridge; oats.

(كشكش) *kaśkaś*, INF. ة, rustle in the grass (snake); flee, take to flight.

كشكش m. *kaśkaś*, doubled up; hem; fold, drapery.

كشكية *kaśkiyya-t*, oatmeal porridge.

(كشم) *kaśam*, U, INF. *kaśm*, cut off the nose;—*kaśim*, A, INF. *kaśam*, have a bodily defect; have a spoiled reputation.

كشم *kaśm*, hunting-panther.

(كشمر) *kaśmar*, INF. ة, break (a.) the nose; be on the point of crying.

كشمش *kiśmiś*, raisin; Armenian apricot with a bitter kernel.

كشمير *kaśmîr*, Cashmere; Cashmere shawl; — ى *kiśmîriyy*, pl. *kaśâmira-t*, of Cashmere.

كشنى *kuśnā*, vetch.

(كشو) *kaśâ*, U, INF. *kaśw*=(كشا).

كشوت *kuśût*, كشوث *kaśûs̱*, *kuśûs̱*, كشوثى *kaśûs̱a*, كشوثا *kaśûs̱â'*, floss-silk.

كشود *kaśûd*, pl. *kuśud*=كشد *kaśad*.

كشى *kaśi'*, roasted meat, roast beef; — ة *kuśya-t*, pl. *kuśa-n*, fat parts of the crocodile or Lybian lizard.

كشيش *kaśîś*, rustling of a snake, INF. of (كش).

(كص) *kaṣṣ*, I, INF. *kaṣṣ*, *kaṣîṣ*, have a thin shrill voice; chirp; — I, INF. *kaṣṣ*, be gathered, assembled; — IV. INF. *ikṣâṣ*, take to flight; — VI. INF. *takâṣṣ*, VIII. INF. *iktiṣâṣ*, assemble (n.) and throng one another.

(كصم) *kaṣam*, INF. *kaṣm*, push back violently; INF. *kuṣûm*, retreat, flee, return without having obtained one's object.

(كصى) *kaṣa*, I, INF. *kaṣy*, fall into contempt.

كصيص *kaṣîṣ*, shrill voice; chirping; emotion; trembling.

(كضكض) *kaḍkaḍ*, INF. ة, walk fast.

(كضل) *kaḍal*, I, INF. *kaḍl*, repel, drive back, turn off.

(كظ) *kaẕẕ*, U, INF. *kaẕẕ*, molest and take the breath from; be full, surfeited; m. loathe, feel aversion at; — U, INF. *kaẕâẕ*, *kaẕâẕa-t*, oppress, put to great anxiety; — VIII. INF. *iktiẕâẕ*, be molested by the food; be full of water.

كظ *kaẕẕ*, oppressed, depressed; كظ لظ *kaẕẕ laẕẕ*, ill-tempered; — ة *kiẕẕa-t*, surfeit, indigestion, nausea.

كظام *kiẕâm*, what serves to stop up; firmness; — *; — ة *kiẕâma-t*, place for the feathering of an arrow; sinew to be twisted round an arrow; rope for the camel's nose; well from which a canal proceeds.

(كظب) *kaẕab*, U, INF. *kuẕûb*, be as if bolstered up with fat.

(كظر) *kaẕar*, notch a bow for the arrow.

كظر *kuẕr*, notch of a bow.

(كظكظ) *kaẕkaẕ*, INF. ة, be equally extended.

(كظم) *kaẕam*, I, INF. *kuẕûm*, abstain from chewing the cud; keep back one's breath; — I, INF. *kaẕm*, suppress one's anger; silence, make speechless; shut the door; dam off a water-course; pass. *kuẕim*, INF. *kuẕûm*, be silent with anger or grief.

كظم *kaẕm*, breath; — *kaẕam*, pl.

kizâm, mouth; gullet; bronchial canal, wind-pipe; — *kuzzam*, pl. of كاظم *kâzim*, suppressing, &c.
(كظو) *kazâ*, U, INF. *kazw*, be hard, firm, solid; — V. INF. *takazzî*, rise and grow round.
كظيظ *kazîz*, oppressed, depressed.
كظيم *kazîm*, who suppresses his anger; sorrowful; lock, bolt; — ة *kazîma-t*, large water-bottle of leather.
(كع) *ka'*, I, U, INF. *ku'û'*, be weak and timid; — IV. INF. *ik'â'*, render timid, frighten off, prevent.
كعاب *ka'âb*, having swelling breasts.
كعاسيم *ka'âsîm*, pl. of كعسوم *ku'sûm*.
كعام *ka'âm*, muzzle of the camel.
(كعب) *ka'ab*, U, I, INF. *ku'ûb*, *ki'âb*, *ku'ûba-t*, have swelling breasts, swell; — A, INF. *ka'b*, fill; — II. INF. *tak'îb*, make square or cubic; raise a number to its cube; furnish with trellis-work in squares; swell; follow on one's heels; — IV. INF. *ik'âb*, hasten; be cubic or square.
كعب *ka'b*, pl. *ki'âb*, *ku'ûb*, *ak'ub*, knuckle, joint, ankle; heel; pl. *ki'âb*, *ku'b*, die; cube; pl. *kû'ûb*, knob in a reed or lance; glory, honouring; proper name of a man proverbial for his generosity; — *ku'b*, breast, bosom; — ة *ka'ba-t*, die; square building; temple in Mecca; *al-ka'batân*, the temples of Mecca and Jerusalem.
(كعبر) *ka'bar*, INF. ة, strike off the knuckle, the head-part of a bone; — ة *ku'bura-t*, *ku'burra-t*, pl. *ka'âbir*, knob in a stalk or reed; knuckle of the thumb; *ka'âbîr*, pl. husks, shells.
(كعبش) *ka'baś*, INF. ة, seize and bind, strap up.
كعبى *ka'biyy*, cubic, square.
(كعت) *ka't*, ة, short, small; — IV. INF. *ik'ât*, depart hurriedly; sit down.
كعتان *ki'tân*, pl. of كعيت *ku'ait*.
(كعتر) *ka'tar*, INF. ة, reel in walking like one intoxicated; run fast, hasten, hurry.
(كعثب) *ka'sab*, thick; — II. INF. *taka'sub*, be full and rounded.
(كعد) *ka'd*, sack; — ة *ka'da-t*, stopper.
(كعدب) *ka'dab*, ة *ka'daba-t*, lazy, cowardly; — ة *ku'duba-t*, water-bubble.
(كعدل) *ka'dal*, pl. *ka'âdil*, basket of willow in which oil is pressed.
(كعر) *ka'ir*, A, INF. *ka'ar*, be big-bellied and fat; also II. INF. *tak'îr* and IV. INF. *ik'âr*, grow fat in the back; — m. *ka'ar*, INF. *ka'r*, drive away ignominiously; scold; chase up game.
كعر *ka'ir*, big-bellied and fat; — ة *ka'ra-t*. tumour like a swollen tonsil, &c.
(كعز) *ka'az*, INF. *ka'z*, scrape together with the fingers; (m.) fall on one's head; cut a somersault.
(كعس) *ka's*, pl. *ki'âs*, bone of the hand or foot.
(كعسم) *ka'sam*, INF. ة, turn the back and flee.
كعسم *ka'sam*, pl. *ka'âsim*, wild ass.
كعسوم *ku'sûm*, pl. *ka'âsîm*, domesticated ass.
(كعص) *ka'aṣ*, INF. *ka'ṣ*, eat; eat or drink much.
(كعك) *ka'k*, ة, biscuit, tart, bun, twist.
(كعكع) *ka'ka'*, INF. ة, render timorous, frighten off, prevent; — II. INF. *taka'ku'*, allow one's self to be frightened, to be scared off.
(كعل) *ka'l*, fresh dung; — V. INF. *taka''ul*, adhere toughly to.
(كعم) *ka'am*, INF. *ka'm*, muzzle a

camel; stop up a bottle; INF. *ka'm, ka'am*, kiss; (m.) place obstacles in one's way, oppose, thwart; (m.) conquer, overcome; — III. INF. *mukâ'ama-t*, lie with; hinder, prevent.

كعم *ki'm*, pl. *ki'âm*, case, sheath; — ة, m. *ka'ma-t*, opposition, hindrance.

(كعن), IV. *ak'an*, INF. *ik'ân*, lose one's spirits, relax.

(كعنب) *ka'nab*, short; lion.

(كعنش), II. *taka'nuś*, engage deeply in; be caught in the net.

(كعو) *ka'â*, U, INF. *ka'w*, be remiss, lazy, cowardly; — II. INF. *tak'iya-t*, discourage, fatigue.

كعيت *ku'ait*, pl. *ki'tân*, nightingale.

كعيم *ka'îm*, muzzled; m. hindered, thwarted, vanquished.

(كف) *kaff*, U, INF. *kaff*, double up and sew a hem, hem, seam; sew in tight; avert, turn off, stay (a.); desist, refrain; be dazzled (eye, also pass. *kuff*); draw the strings of a purse; wrap up in bandages; fill to overflowing; — VII. INF. *inkifâf*, be seamed or hemmed; be hindered; desist, refrain; depart; — X. INF. *istikfâf*, stretch out the hand to give or to beg for alms; shade one's eyes with the hand to see better; stand round and look at.

كف *kaff*, desisting, refraining, abstaining, self-restraint; defence; suppression of the seventh letter of a foot if it is quiescent; pl. *akuff, kufûf, kuff*, palm of the hand, hand; foot, sole; handful; plenty, abundance; (m. pl. *kufûf*) glove; كف مريم *kaff maryam*, peony (Jericho rose); — *kif'*, river-bed; — *kuf'* = كفو *kafw*; — ة *kif-fa-t, kaffa-t*, pl. *kifaf, kifâf*, scale (of a balance); hollow of the hand, the palate, anything round and hollow; — *kuffa-t*, pl. *kufaf, kifâf*, edge, border, seam, hem; pl. *kifâf*, sandy tract; *kuffa-t, kiffa-t*, net (for catching), ring in it.

(كفا) *kafa'*, INF. *kaf'*, turn upside down; turn (a.) from one thing to another; follow; flee; chase away; despatch; — also *kafu'*, INF. *kafâ'a-t*, be equal to, fit, suitable, able; be sufficiently instructed; — III. INF. *kifâ'*, *mukâfa'a-t*, turn from (a.), prevent; be equal to, be a match for, resemble; recede, flee; reward, requite; observe; — IV. INF. *ikfâ'*, be turned upside down; be inclined; turn upside down, incline (a.); — VI. INF. *takâfu'*, be equal to, a match for one another; respond to one another; — VII. INF. *inkifâ'*, be turned upside down; retreat, take to flight; turn homeward.

كفا *kafâ'*, *kifâ'*, equality, parity; resemblance, similarity; reward, requital; pl. *akfâ'*, equal, a match for, similar; — *kifâ'* = كفاية *kifâya-t*; pl. of كفي *kafî'*; — ة *kufât*, pl. of كافي *kâfî*, sufficient, &c.; — *kaf'a-t, kuf'a-t*, produce of the year; — *kafâ'a-t*, *kifâ'a-t*, equality, similarity.

كفات *kifât*, place where anything is gathered; *kifât-an*, suddenly (die); — *kaffât*, lion.

كفاح *kifâḥ*, fight, combat, battle, war, contention.

كفار *kifâr, kuffâr*, pl. of كافر *kâfir*, infidel, &c.; — *kaffâr*, very ungrateful; very impious; farmer, husbandman; — ة *kaffâra-t*, penance, atonement, expiation.

كفاف *kafâf*, sufficient sustenance, sufficiency, daily bread; equal, unharmed; — *kifâf*, edge, border; edge of a sword; better part of a thing; — *; — ة *kafâfa-t*, seaming or hemming of a garment.

كفالة *kafâla-t*, bail, security, pledge.

كفاية *kifâya-t*, sufficing (s.), sufficient quantity; skill.

(كفت) *kafat*, I, INF. *kaft*, take up,

draw to one's self; tuck up one's garments; gather, add piece to piece; turn off (a.), prevent, hinder; (m.) cross the legs; — INF. *kaft*, *kifât*, *kafît*, *kafatân*, fly or run fast; — II. INF. *takfît*, draw to one's self; — VII. INF. *inkifât*, be tucked up; be prevented, hindered; — ة *kafta-t*, burial-ground in Medina.

(كفح) *kafaḥ*, INF. *kafḥ*, uncover, unveil, reveal, disclose; look straight into one's face or speak to one while doing so; attack boldly and come to close quarters; beat; pull up the reins; — *kafiḥ*, A, INF. *kafaḥ*, be timorous, cowardly; be ashamed; — III. INF. *kifâḥ*, *mukâfaḥa-t*, look straight into one's face; come to close quarters with (acc.); intercede with one (فى *fî*) for another (ل *li*).

كفح *kafaḥ*, hand-to-hand fight.

(كفخ) *kafaḫ*, INF. *kafḫ*, beat, beat on the head; — ة *kafḫa-t*, white cream or butter.

(كفر) *kafar*, I, INF. *kafr*, cover, conceal; — U, INF. *kafr*, *kufr*, *kufûr*, *kufrân*, be unbelieving in God, be impious, an infidel; renounce the faith; renounce, deny, be ungrateful; (m.) blaspheme, curse, swear; — II. INF. *takfîr*, cover; make up for, atone; redeem (an oath, عن *'an*); pardon; make one impious or an infidel; cause one to blaspheme, to curse, to swear; make one king and throw one's self in the dust before him; bow to, placing the hand on one's heart (also I.); — III. INF. *mukâfara-t*, deny a debt to (2 acc.); — IV. INF. *ikfâr*, call or deem impious; — — VIII. INF. *inkifâr*, live permanently in the village.

كفر *kafr*, unbelief; throwing (s.) one's self down before a king, bow, obeisance; pl. *kufûr*, village, hamlet; also *kifr*, darkness of night; — *kufr*, impiety, unbelief; apostacy; ingratitude; denial (كفر نفسه *kufr-u nafsi-hi*, self-denial); pitch; — *kafar*, spathe of the palm-blossom; a kind of eagle; — *kufur*, pl. of كفور *kafûr*; — ة *kafra-t*, darkness; — *kafara-t*, pl. of كافر *kâfir*, infidel, &c.; — ى *kufurra*, spathe of the palm-blossom.

كفران *kufrân*=كفر *kufr*.

(كفس) *kafis*, A, INF. *kafas*, have crooked toes.

كفف *kafaf*, sufficient living, sufficiency; — *kifaf*, *kufaf*, pl. of كفة *kiffa-t*, *kuffa-t*, respectively; — ة *kafafa-t*, pl. of كاف *kâff*, who prevents, &c.

(كفكف) *kafkâf*, INF. ة, repel repeatedly, prevent, hinder, restrain; (m.) wrap up; — II. INF. *takafkuf*, be prevented, abstain; (m.) wrap one's self up in one's clothes.

(كفل) *kafal*, U, INF. *kafl*, feed, take charge of; U, I, INF. *kafl*, *kufûl*, stand security for (ب *bi* or عن *'an*); — *kafil*, A, INF. *kafal*, — also *kaful*, INF. *kafâla-t*, stand security; — II. INF. *takfîl*, make one bail or security, warrant; — IV. INF. *ikfâl*, secure payment by bail; assure goods, &c.; — V. INF. *takafful*, stand security; — VII. INF. *inkifâl*, be secured by bail; — VIII. INF. *iktifâl*, cover the camel with the saddle-cloth.

كفل *kifl*, anything double; equal, corresponding; part, portion; pl. *akfâl*, saddle-cloth for a camel; — *kafal*, pl. *akfâl*, hind-parts; croup; — *kuffal*, pl. of كافل *kâfil*, who stands security, &c.

كفلا *kufalâ'*, pl. of كفيل *kafîl*.

(كفن) *kafan*, I, INF. *kafn*, spin wool; put the bread on the

ashes to bake it; (also II.) shroud or bury the dead; — II. INF. *takfîn*, see I.; — V. INF. *takaffun*, be buried.

كفن *kafan*, pl. *akfân*, winding-sheet, shroud.

(كفهر), III. *ikfaharr*, INF. *ikfihrâr*, shine in a dark night; be very dark, gloomy; look severe and austere.

كفو *kafw*, pl. *kifâ'*, *kafû'*, pl. *akfâ'*, equal, corresponding, a match for; sufficiently instructed; — *kafu'*, v. see (كفا).

كفور *kafûr*, pl. *kufur*, very ungrateful; very impious; — *kufûr*, unbelief, impiety; — *.

(كفى) *kafa*, I, INF. *kifâya-t*, suffice; give sufficiently, content; exempt, free, spare; do anything requisite instead of another; — II. INF. *takfiya-t*, give enough, content; suffice; finish, complete; — III. INF. *kifâ'*, *mukâfât*, requite, retaliate; suffice; — VIII. INF. *iktifâ'*, have enough and be contented; — X. INF. *istikfâ'*, id.; find sufficient; ask one to give enough, to act satisfactorily.

كفى *kafy*, *kify*, *kufy*, *kafiyy*, sufficient; — ة *kufya-t*, pl. *kufa-n*, sufficiency; food, sustenance.

كفيت *kafît*, swift; — *.

كفيح *kafîḥ*, equal, similar; bedfellow, husband; unexpected guest.

كفيف *kafîf*, blind.

كفيل *kafîl*, pl. *kufalâ'*, security, bail; who stands bail or security; equal, similar.

كفيى *kafî'*, ة, pl. *kifâ'*, equal, similar.

كك *kak*=كذالك *kazâlik*, likewise.

(كل) *kall*, I, INF. *kalla-t*, *killa-t*, *kalâl*, *kulûl*, *kalâla-t*, *kulûla-t*, be exhausted and tired; be weary; be dim, blunt, dull; be heavy; be entirely orphaned or childless; INF. *kalâla-t*, subside; — II. INF. *taklîl*, crown; place a wreath on the head; join in wedlock (a.), marry (a.); be dim, dull, blunt; apply one's self zealously to; forsake one's people; smile; — IV. INF. *iklâl*, fatigue, exhaust, jade; blunt; have a jaded beast; — V. INF. *takallul*, be crowned, wear a crown or diadem; crown; (also VII. and VIII.) lighten slightly; — VII. INF. *inkilâl*, see V.; be blunt; laugh; — VIII. INF. *iktilâl*, see V.

كل *kall*, pl. *kulûl*, tiredness, weariness, fatigue, exhaustion; heavy burden; oppression, wrong; calamity; dim, dull, blunt; entirely orphaned or childless; family; — *kull*, totality; the whole of, all of; — ة *kalla-t*, blunt knife; — *killa-t*, bluntness, dulness, dimness; pl. *kilâl*, *kilal*, state, condition; veil, curtain to protect against flies; (m.) pl. *kilal*, ball, globe; — *kulla-t*, every one, each, f.; delay.

(كلا) *kala'*, INF. *kal'*, *kilâ'*, *kilâ'a-t*, guard, keep, preserve; beat, whip; fix repeatedly one's look at; have a delay granted; be finished, completed; abound in food; — كلى *kali'*, A, INF. *kala'*, abound in food; feed (n.); — II. INF. *taklî'*, move the ship to the shore; keep back, retain; hope for (فى *fî*); — IV. INF. *iklâ'*, abound in food; look repeatedly at; — VIII. INF. *iktilâ'*, be on one's guard, heed; accept partial payment and grant the debtor a delay; abound in food.

كلا *kilâ*, du. f. *kiltâ*, both of; — *kallâ*, no! by no means, on the contrary; by all means, at any rate, truly; — *kallâ'*, safe anchorage; docks; — ة *kul'a-t*, debt for payment of which a delay has been granted; pledge; anything bought on credit; — *kilâ'a-t*, guard, protection.

كلاب **kalâb**, hydrophobia; madness; — *; — **kallâb**, breeder of dogs; —**kullâb**, pl. **kalâlîb**, hook, harpoon; spur; saw; **kalâlîb**, claws of a hawk; — ة **kallâba-t**, tongs, pincers.

كلابزى **kalâbiziyy**, pl. **kalâbiza-t**, dog-keeper.

كلاثب *kalâsib*, miserly, avaricious.

كلاح **kilâḥ**, **kalâḥ**, **kulâḥ**, day, year; —**kulâḥ**, ة **kulâḥa-t**, austere face, sour looks.

كلاس **kallâs**, very sharp; chalk-burner, maker of gypsum.

كلاع **kulâ'**, endurance in the combat; — ى **kulâ'iyy**, brave.

كلاكل *kulâkil*, short, thick and strong.

كلال *kalâl*, ة *kalâla-t*, weariness, exhaustion; dimness, dulness, bluntness; — *; — ة *kalâla-t*, one who has no parents or children left.

كلاليب *kalâlîb*, pl. of كلاب *kullâb* and كلوب *kallûb*.

كلام *kalâm*, speech, word; conversation, controversy; sentence, phrase, proposition; علم الك *'ilm al-kalâm*, rhetoric, dogmatics, scholastic theology, metaphysics; — *.

كلاوى *kalâwiyy*, pl. of كلية *kulya-t*.

كلاية *kilâya-t*, guard, keeping.

(كلب) *kalab*, U, INF. *kalb*, border with a strip of leather; spur; — INF. *kalb*, bark like a dog; — *kalib*, A, INF. *kalab*, be seized with hydrophobia, be mad; be enraged with anger; be seized with an unquenchable thirst; bark; be very cold, be hard; be very greedy; —II. INF. *taklîb*, keep firmly together (m.); —III. INF. *kilâb*, *mukâlaba-t*, be malicious towards; —IV. INF. *iklâb*, have enraged camels; — VI. INF. *takâlub*, *taklâb*, rush simultaneously at one another; rush upon like greedy dogs; — X. INF. *istiklâb*, be seized with hydrophobia, turn mad; bark like a dog.

كلب **kalb**, pl. **kilâb**, **kilâbât**, **kalîb**, **aklub**, **akâlib**, dog; rapacious animal; lion (ك البحر **kalb al-baḥr**, shark; ك الما **kalb** [ة **kalba-t**] **al-mâ'**, beaver); strip of leather, strap; handle of a mill, mill-clog; — **kalab**, hydrophobia; raving madness; malice; violence, hardship; ravenous hunger, greed; — **kalib**, ة, pl. **kalba**, seized with hydrophobia, enraged, mad; hard; — ة **kalba-t**, bitch (ام ك **umm kalba-t**, fever); a thorny shrub; du. **kalbatân**, blacksmith's tongs; — **kulba-t**, cell; cellar, cave, cavern; severity; a thorn; — ى **kalbiyy**, dog-like, canine, ravenous (hunger).

كلبان **kalbân**, seized with hydrophobia; enraged, mad; belonging to the tribe **kalb**.

(كلت) *kalat*, I, INF. *kalt*, gather, assemble (a.); pour over, decant, pour in; spur; throw; — VII. INF. *inkilât*, be decanted, poured in; — VIII. INF. *iktilât*, drink; — ة *kulta-t*, portion of food or corn; bundle of hay or wood; quantum, ration.

(كلتب) *kaltab*, INF. ة, dissimulate cunningly.

(كلث), VII. *inkalas*, INF. *inkilâs*, advance, come up.

(كلثب) *kalsab*, miserly, avaricious.

(كلثم) *kalsam*, INF. ة, have a very full but still handsome face.

كلثوم *kulsûm*, fulness of the face; elephant; streamer.

(كلج) *kalaj*, generous and brave; — *kuluj*, pl. brave ones.

(كلح) *kalaḥ*, INF. *kulâḥ*, *kulûḥ*, look austere, be frowning; — II. INF. *taklîḥ*, frown; — III. INF. *mukâlaḥa-t*, receive with a frowning face, treat harshly; — IV. INF. *iklâḥ*, V. INF. *takalluḥ*=I.; — ة *kalaḥa-t*, mouth, parts about the mouth.

(كلحب) *kalḥab*, INF. ة, strike with the sword; flicker and crackle.

(كلحم) ***kilḥim***, earth; dust.

كلد ***kalad***, hard, rough, rugged; weasel; leopard; — ة *kalda-t*, rugged tract; ابو ك *abû kalda-t*, hyena.

(كلدح) *kaldaḥ*, strong, hard; old woman.

(كلز) *kalaz*, I, INF. *kalz*, gather, assemble (a.); — II. INF. *taklîz*, id.; — XI. *ikla'azz*, INF. *ikli'zâz*, crouch, bend (as a bad horseman).

كلس *kils*, chalk; — II. INF. *taklîs*, plaster with chalk or lime; calcine (a.); fall upon; see V.; — IV. INF. *iklâs*, plaster with lime; — V. INF. *takallus*, receive a coating of lime; (also II.) be impregnated with water; — ة *kalsa-t*, dark ash-colour.

(كلسم) *kalsam*, INF. ة, perform one's duty negligently; depart hurriedly; advance towards.

(كلصم) *kalṣam*, INF. ة, take to flight.

(كلط) *kuluṭ*, pl. wantonly or boisterously merry people.

(كلع) *kala'*, INF. *kal'*, be dirty; dry upon the head (dirt); INF. *kal'*, *kulâ'*, have the hoofs chapped; — *kali'*, A, INF. *kala'*, be dirty and chapped; be very scabby; — IV. INF. *iklâ'*, disfigure, stain.

كلع *kil'*, pl. *kila'a-t*, hard and rough, dirty, ugly; mean, vile; —*kala'*, dirt; heat of battle; — *kali'*, dirty; — ة *kala'a-t*, part of a herd.

(كلغب) *kulgub*, an alkaline plant used in washing.

(كلف) *kalif*, A, INF. *kalaf*, spend zeal, pains and costs on a thing; be eager; be or fall in love with (ب *bi*); — (m.) *kalaf*, INF. *kalf*, take good care of, feed or keep or keep well; — II. INF. *taklîf*, impose a difficult matter upon; molest, make difficulties, ceremonies, trouble; (m.) cost; — IV. INF. *iklâf*, cause one to take pains; — V. INF. *takalluf*, undertake anything difficult or troublesome, take pains; feign; spend money upon; cost; — XI. INF. *iklîfâf*, assume a dark yellow colour.

كلف *kilf*, lover; — *kulf*, pl. of اكلف *aklaf*, dark yellow, brown; — *kalaf*, pains and care taken; amorousness; pl. *aklâf*, brown spots, freckles; costs; also ة *kulfa-t*, blackish yellow; — ة *kulfa-t*, freckles; pl. *kulaf*, pain, trouble, labour, hardship; costs, expenses.

(كلكل) *kalkal*, *kalkall*, also كلكال *kalkâl*, pl. *kalâkil*, upper part of the chest; callous part of a camel's chest; place where the horse is girt; pl. troops.

كلكل m. *kalkal*, INF. ة, grow callous; — II. INF. *takalkul*, id.; — ة *kalkala-t*, callosity.

كلكلان *kulkullân*, steward, major-domo, factotum.

كلل *kalal*, state, condition; — *kilal*, pl. of كلة *killa-t*.

(كلم) *kalam* I, INF. *kalm*, wound; — II. INF. *taklîm*, *killâm*, wound; utter, speak; speak to, talk to, converse with (acc.); — III. INF. *mukâlama-t*, speak to, converse with; — V. INF. *takallum*, *tikillâm*, talk, converse, speak a language (acc. or ب *bi*); — VIII. INF. *takâlum*, speak, confer, converse with one another.

كلم *kalm*, pl. *kilâm*, *kulûm*, wound; — *kalim*, incomplete sentence, word without meaning; — *kalima-t*, *kilma-t*, pl. *kalimât*, *kalim*, word, speech, sentence; — *kilama-t*, pl. *kilam*, id.; — ى *kalmā*, pl. of كليم *kalîm*.

كلما *kulla-mâ*, as often as, each time when; — *kullu-mâ*, whatsoever.

كلمانى *kalmâniyy*, *kalamâniyy*, *killimâniyy*, *kilimmâniyy*, eloquent.

كلمس *kalmas*, INF. ة, depart, go away.

(كلهس) *kalhas*, INF. ة, fear; attend carefully to (على *'ala*); attack boldly.

كلواذ *kilwâẕ*, ark of the covenant; ام ك *ummu kilwâẕ*, calamity.

كلوب *kallûb*, pl. *kalâlîb*=كلاب *kullâb*.

كلوف *kalûf*, difficult, toilsome.

كلوة *kulwa-t*, pl. *kula-n*, kidney.

كلوى *kilwiyy*, referring to both.

(كلى) *kala*, I, INF. *kaly*, injure in the kidneys; — *kalî*, A, INF. *kalan*, suffer from the kidneys; — VIII. INF. *iktilâ'*, id.

كلى *kilai*, obl. case of كلا *kilâ*, both; — *kulan*, pl. of كلوة *kulwa-t*; — *kulliyy*, ة, entire, total, universal; comprehensive, full of meaning; — *kali'*, ة, abounding in food; — ة *kulya-t*, pl. *kula-n*, *kulyât*, (m.) *kalâwiyy*, kidney; part of a bow between the handpiece and the ends; — *kulliyya-t*, totality; pl. *kulliyyât*, all created things, collected works, everything necessary, generalities; — *kali'a-t*, ground abounding in food.

كليب *kalîb*, pack of hounds.

كليسا *kilîsâ*, كليسة *kilîsa-t*, church (m.).

كليل *kalîl*, blunt; dim-sighted, blear-eyed; stammering.

كليم *kalîm*, pl. *kalma*, wounded; who speaks or is spoken to; ك الله *kalîmu 'l-lâh-i*, Moses.

كلين *killîn*, double (wall).

(كم) *kamm*, U, INF. *kamm*, *kumûm*, cover, conceal, protect, stop, shut up; provide with an envelope; put a sleeve to; muzzle the bullock; assemble; pass. be budding; — II. INF. *takmîm*, bud; — IV. INF. *ikmâm*, id.; provide with sleeves.

كم *kam*, how much? how many? — *kamm*, quantity, multitude; — *kimm*, pl. *akmâm*, *kimâm*, *akimma-t*, *akâmîm*, spathe of the palm-blossom, spathe; shell; rose-bud; — *kumm*, pl. *akmâm*, *kimama-t*, sleeve; — *kam'*, pl. *akmu'*, *kam'a-t*, mushroom; truffle; — ة *kumma-t*, pl. *kimâm*, a kind of cap or hat.

(كما) *kama'*, INF. *kam'* (also IV.), feed (a.) on mushrooms or truffles; — كمى *kamî*, A, INF. *kamâ'*, be foot-sore; be chapped; — IV. produce plenty of mushrooms; see I.; — V. INF. *takammu'*, detest, abhor.

كما *ka-mâ*, as, even as, just as; — *kammâ'*, seller of mushrooms or truffles; — ة *kumât*, pl. of كمى *kamiyy*; — *kam'a-t*, mushroom; truffle.

كماتة *kamâta-t*, reddish brown; كماتى *kamâtiyy*, horses of such colour.

كماجة *kamâja-t*, finest flour.

كماحة *kumâḥa-t*, niggardliness, avarice.

كماد *kimâd*, ة *kimâda-t*, fomentation; colic, gripes.

كماشة *kamâśa-t*, agility; sufficiency; — *kammâśa-t*, pincers.

كمال *kamâl*, completeness; pl. *-ât*, perfection; conclusion; rest; — *kummâl*, pl. of كامل *kâmil*, complete, &c.

كمالية *kamâliyya-t*, perfection.

كمام *kimâm*, pl. *akimma-t*, muzzle; — *; — ة *kimâma-t*, pl. *kimâm*, id.; spathe.

كمان (m.) *kamân*, also, likewise; again, once more.

(كمت) *kamat*, U, INF. *kamt*, suppress one's anger; — *kamut*, INF. *kamt*, *kamta-t*, *kamâta-t*, be reddish brown; — II. INF. *takmît*, dye reddish brown; — IX. INF. *ikmitât*, XI. INF. *ikmîtât*, XII. *ikmaumat*, INF. *ikmîmât*, be reddish brown; — ة *kumta-t*, reddish brown colour.

(كمتر) *kamtar*, INF. ة, walk or run with short steps; fill; tie up at the top.

كمتر *kumtur*, كماتر *kumâtir*, short and thick; hard and strong.

(كمثر) *kamsar*, INF. ة, be compact.

كمثرى *kumasrâ*, *kummasrâ*, n.u. كمثراة *kumasrât*, pear.

كمج *kamaj*, groin.

(كمح) *kamah*, INF. *kamh*, pull up the reins (also IV.); be niggardly, miserly; — IV. INF. *ikmâh*, see I.; begin to put forth leaves.

كمح *kamih*, pulling up the reins (adj.).

(كمخ) *kamah*, INF. *kamh*, pull up the reins; كمخ بانفه *kamah bi-anfi-hi*, be proud; drop excrement; — *kamih*, A, INF. *kamah*, also II. INF. *takmîh*, be covered with tartar; be covered (tongue); — ة *kamha-t*, tartar.

(كمد) *kamad*, U, INF. *kamd*, unstiffen, full; — *kamid*, A, INF. *kamad*, be ill and sad; be unstiffened by wear; be somewhat faded; — II. INF. *takmîd*, warm the bed, foment; — IV. INF. *ikmâd*, make sad and ill; cause to fade; — VII. INF. *inkimâd*, be grieved; — IX. INF. *ikmidâd*, be somewhat faded; be pale.

كمد *kamd*, *kamad*, fading (s.); paleness; sad look; sadness; — *kamid*, sad and pale; — ة *kumda-t*, paleness; — *kumudda-t*, penis.

(كمر) *kamar*, U, INF. *kamr*, exceed in size of the gland of the penis; (m.) cover, veil, conceal; — VII. INF. *inkimâr*, (m.) be covered, concealed.

كمر *kimr*, soft date fallen off the tree; — *kamar*, pl. *akmâr*, leathern belt for carrying money (Pers.); — *kumurr*, having a large penis; also ة *kumurra-t*, penis; — ة *kamara-t*, pl. *-ât*, *kamar*, *kimâr*, gland of the penis; penis.

كمرك *kumruk*, toll, custom (m.).

(كمز) *kamaz*, I, INF. *kamz*, roll into a ball with the hands; — ة *kumza-t*, pl. *kumaz*, bunch of dates; heap of earth or sand.

(كمس) *kamas*, U, INF. *kumûs*, be austere, morose.

(كمش) *kamaś*, U, INF. *kamś*, tie up the udder of a camel; maim in the limbs; grasp; run short; — *kamiś*, A, INF. *kamaś*, make folds, get wrinkled; contract (n.), shorten (n.); — II. INF. *takmîś*, grasp as much as possible; — V. INF. *takammuś*, fit closely, stick to; walk fast; — VI. INF. *takâmuś*, come to close quarters; — VII. INF. *inkimâś*, hasten; be seized with the hand, grasped; — ة *kamśa-t*, handful.

(كمع) *kama'*, INF. *kam'*, cut off; drink all; — III. INF. *mukâma'a-t*, sleep with one under the same cover skin to skin; — VIII. INF. *iktimâ'*, drink out of the orifice of the water-bag.

كمع *kim'*, a garment; edge of a river; bed-fellow; house; — *kami'*, weak; bowing to everybody's will.

كمكام *kamkâm*, a kind of gum.

(كمكم), II. INF. *takamkum*, cover one's self with the cap كمة *kumma-t*; put on one's clothes (في *fî*).

(كمل) *kamal*, U, *kamil*, A, *kamul*, INF. *kamâl*, *kumûl*, be entire, whole, complete, perfect; be finished; be sovereign; — II. INF. *takmîl*, finish, complete, perfect; — IV. INF. *ikmâl*=II.; — V. INF. *takammul*, be finished, completed, perfect; — VI. INF. *takâmul*=V.; — VIII. INF. *iktimâl*=V.; — X. INF. *istikmâl*, complete, perfect; find or wish finished or perfect; collect the remainder of a debt.

كمل *kamal*, the whole, entirety; — *kummal*, ة *kamala-t*, pl. of كامل *kâmil*, complete, perfect, &c.

كملول *kumlûl*, a vegetable; desert.

كممة *kimama-t*, pl. of كم *kumm*.

(كمن) *kaman*, U, INF. *kumûn*, hide (n.); lay one's self in ambush,

watch for; — *kamin*, A, id.; also pass. *kumin*, be seized with weakness of the eyes; — IV. INF. *ikmân*, conceal, hide (a.); — V. INF. *takammun*, keep one's self hidden in an ambush; — VIII. INF. *iktimân*, hide (n.); — ة *kamna-t*, pl. *kimân*, people in ambush; — *kumna-t*, weakness of the eye.

كمن *ka-man*, like him who.

كمنتير *kamantîr*, burial-place of the dervishes; dirty place (m.).

كمنجة *kamanja-t*, a kind of violin (m.).

كمنون *kimnûn*=كمون *kammûn*.

(كمه) *kamih*, A, INF. *kamah*, be blind; be night-blind; be misty; grow pale; — also V. INF. *takammuh*, wander at random.

كمه *kamih*, born blind.

(كمهل) *kamhal*, INF. ة, tuck up one's garments; gather (a.); refuse one his right; — II. INF. *takamhul*, be gathered; — III. INF. *ikmihlâl*, shrink from cold.

(كمو) *kamû*, be armed from head to foot; be brave.

كمودة *kumûda-t*, paleness, pallor.

كمون *kammûn*, cumin, caraway; — ى *kammûnîyy*, seasoned with cumin or caraway-seed.

كموى *kamwā*, moonlit night.

(كمى) *kama*, I, INF. *kamy*, withhold one's evidence (also IV.); arm one's self; — *kamî*, A, INF. *kaman*, be armed from head to foot; be brave; — IV. INF. *ikmâ'*, see I.; kill armed or brave men; — V. INF. *takammî*, be wholly armed; cover, veil; pass. lose all its brave ones (army).

كمى *kamiyy*, pl. *kumât*, *akmâ'*, armed from head to foot; brave; warrior; — *kammiyy*, how much? how many? — ة *kammiyya-t*, quantity.

كميت *kumait*, pl. *kumt*, *kamâtiyy*, reddish brown (horse); ruddy wine; ك احم *kumait aḥamm*, chestnut-coloured; ك مدمى *kumait mudamma*, light chestnut; — ة *kamîtat-an*, *bi-kamîta-t*, entirely.

كميثرة *kumaisira-t*, little pear.

كميد *kamîd*, grieved, sad.

كميش *kamîś*, quick, sagacious; girded up.

كميع *kamî'*, bed-fellow.

كميل *kamîl*, finished, complete, perfect.

كميم *kamîm*, wrapped up, enveloped.

كميمثرة *kamaimisra-t*, little pear.

كمين *kamîn*, concealed, hidden; lying in ambush; ambush.

(كن) *kann*, U, INF. *kann*, *kunûn*, cover, veil; keep concealed, secret; guard, watch over; shade; (m.) subside; — II. INF. *taknîn*, cover, veil, conceal; — IV. INF. *iknân*, id.; suppress one's anger; quiet, calm (a.), pacify; — VIII. INF. *iktinân*, cover, be covered; — X. INF. *istiknân*, keep concealed; retire to one's dwelling, to one's home; be covered, protected.

كن *kinn*, pl. *aknân*, veil, envelope, cover; court-yard, interior of the house, home; asylum, refuge; sun-shade; cocoon; — ة *kanna-t*, pl. *kanâ'in*, son's or brother's wife; (m.) quiet, tranquillity of mind; — *kinna-t*, veil, cover, envelope, anything shading; — *kunna-t*, pl. *-ât*, *kinân*, roof for protection against rain or sun, particularly over a door.

كنابد *kanâbid*, كنابظ *kanâbiẓ*, ugly of face.

كناد *kannâd*, very ungrateful; impious; rebel.

كنار *kinâr*, hem, border, edge (Pers.); (m.) archives; (m.) canary-bird; — *kunâr*, fruit of the lotus-tree; — *kinnâr*, ة *kinnâra-t*, *kannâra-t*, pl. *-ât*, *kanânîr*, lute, harp; tambourine.

كناز *kanâz*, *kinâz*, store of dates; — *kinâz*, pl. *kunuz*, firm of flesh.
كناس *kinâs*, pl. *kunus*, *kunnas*, lair, covert; — *kannâs*, sweeper; miser; — ة *kunâsa-t*, sweepings.
كناهات *kunnâśât*, principles, rudiments (in book-titles).
كناص *kunâṣ*, strong, vigorous.
كناف *kinâf*, help; — ة *kanâfa-t*, a kind of pie.
كنان *kinân*, pl. *akinna-t*, cover, veil, envelope, shelter; — *; — ة *kinâna-t*, pl. *kanâ'in*, quiver (for arrows.).
كنانير *kanânîr*, pl. of كنارة *kinnâra-t*.
كناة *kunât*, pl. of كانى *kânî*, who speaks metaphorically.
كنائس *kanâ'is*, pl. of كنيسة *kanîsa-t*; — ى *kanâ'isiyy*, ecclesiastical.
كنائن *kanâ'in*, pl. of كنانة *kinâna-t* and كنة *kanna-t*.
كناية *kinâya-t*, metaphor, metonomy; nickname; allusion to (عن *'an*).
(كنب) *kanab*, I, INF. *kamb*, gather up, collect; — U, INF. *kunûb*, be thick and rough; grow rich; — *kanib*, A, INF. *kanab*, be callous; — IV. INF. *iknâb*, be thick and rough; be callous; restrain (one's tongue).
كنب *kanib*, hemp.
كنبار *kimbâr*, rope of the fibres of the cocoa.
(كنبث) *kambas*, INF. ة, also II. INF. *takambus*, be shrunk, shrivelled; be niggardly.
(كنبش), II. *takambaś*, INF. *takambuś*, be mixed.
كنبوش *kumbûś*, cloth beneath the saddle.
(كنت) *kanat*, U, INF. *kant*, be of vigorous make; — *kanit*, A, INF. *kanat*, be rough, hard stiff.
(كنتب) *kuntub*, كناتب *kunâtib*, dwarf.
(كنتع) *kuntu'*, short; dwarf.
كنتى *kuntiyy*, big, strong; old, decrepit; egotistical, selfish.

(كنثا) *kanṣa'*, INF. ة, be dense and long (beard).
(كنثح) *kanṣaḥ* (كنتح *kantaḥ*), crazy.
كنثة *kunṣa-t*, small basket for aromatics.
(كند) *kanad*, INF. *kand*, cut; — I, INF. *kunûd*, be ungrateful for a benefit (acc.); be rebellious.
كند *kunud*, ungrateful.
كندر *kundur*, frankincense; — ة *kandara-t*, hawk's nest; (m.) shoe.
كندرجى *kandarjiyy*, shoe-maker (m.).
كندش *kunduś*, magpie.
كندل *kundul*, copper vessel for carrying water.
(كنز) *kanaz*, I, INF. *kanz*, bury in the ground, dig in; put into the purse, pocket, &c.; push into the ground (lance); hoard up treasures; store dates; — *kaniz*, A, INF. *kanaz*; — also VIII. INF. *iktinâz*, be firm of flesh, compact; VIII. be hoarded up.
كنز *kanz*, pl. *kunûz*, treasure; — *kunuz*, pl. of كناز *kinâz*.
(كنس) *kanas*, I, INF. *kunûs* (also V.), retire to its lair (game); — I, INF. *kans*, sweep the house; — II. INF. *taknîs*, sweep; — V. INF. *takannus*, see I.; be swept (also VII.); go into the tent; — VII. INF. *inkinâs*, see V.
كنس *kans*, sweeping (s.); — *kunus*, *kunnas*, pl. of كناس *kinâs*; — *kunnas*, pl. of كانس *kânis*, hiding in its covert or lair.
(كنش) *kanaś*, U, INF. *kanś*, twist, plait; — IV. INF. *iknâś*, bid to make haste and finish.
(كنص), II. INF. *taknîṣ*, turn up the nose in mockery.
(كنظ) *kanaẓ*, I, U, INF. *kanẓ*, put to anxiety, grieve; — V. INF. *takannuẓ*, id.; — ة *kanẓa-t*, anxiety.
(كنع) *kana'*, INF. *kunû'*, be shrunk, shrivelled; be near, impend; shun, shrink from; decline to-

wards setting; crave for (في *fî*); humble one's self; stick to, adhere; — *kani'*, A, INF. *kana'*, be withered and shrivelled; be thrown on one's chin; — II. INF. *taknî'*, contract; cut off the arms; make the hand to wither; — IV. INF. *iknâ'*, draw in the wings to alight; — VIII. INF. *iktinâ'*, assemble (n.).

كنع *kin'*, last third of the night; root, origin; — *kani'*, shrivelled and weak from old age.

كنعان *kan'ân*, Canaan.

(كنعد) *kan'ad*, pl. *kanâ'id*, sturgeon, sword-fish.

(كنف) *kanaf*, U, INF. *kanf*, watch over, guard, shelter; — U, I, surround with a hedge or fold, keep enclosed in it; help, come to assistance; turn from (n.), desist; — II. INF. *taknîf*, surround from all sides, encompass; — III. INF. *mukânafa-t*, help one, come to his assistance; — IV. INF. *iknâf*, guard; help; — V. INF. *takannuf*, surround from all sides; — VI. INF. *takânuf*, form a circle; — VIII. INF. *iktinâf*, surround, invest; make a fold for the camels; take under one's protection.

كنف *kinf*, pl. *aknâf*, bag for utensils; needle-box of a shoemaker; — *kunf*, pl. of كنيف *kanîf*; — *kanaf*, pl. *aknâf*, side; slope, bank; enclosure before a house; shelter, protection, place of refuge, asylum; wing of a bird; shade; — ة *kanafa-t*, side.

كنفرة *kinfira-t*, tip of the nose.

(كنفش) *kanfaś*, INF. ة, be untidy in appearance.

(كنكن) *kankan*, INF. ة, take to flight; be lazy; sit always at home; (m.) gossip; (m.) contradict continually.

كنمة *kanma-t*, wound.

(كنه) *kunh*, substance, essence; real truth; quantity; limit, pitch, sum; aspect, shape, manner; point of time, epoch; — IV. *aknah*, INF. *iknâh*, reach the end, the highest point, the acme; — VIII. INF. *iktinâh*, id.

(كنهف) *kanhaf*, INF. ة, leave hurriedly.

(كنو) *kanâ*, U, كنى *kana*, I, INF. *kinâya-t*, hint at, indicate by metaphor or symbol, intimate, allude to; — INF. *kinya-t*, *kunya-t*, designate by a nickname; (m.) be one's substitute, supply; — II. INF. *takniya-t*, designate by a nickname; — IV. INF. *iknâ'* = II.; — V. INF. *takannî*, VIII. INF. *iktinâ'*, go by or assume a nickname.

كنود *kanûd*, ungrateful; impious; faithless; rebellious; — *kunûd*, ingratitude.

كنى *kana*, v. see (كنو); — *kaniyy*, referring to the nickname; pl. *akniyâ'*, having the same nickname; — ة *kinya-t*, *kunya-t*, pl. *kuna-n*, nickname.

كنيت *kanît*, holding water well, water-tight (bag, &c.).

كنيز *kanîz*, dates stored up for the winter.

كنيس *kanîs*, synagogue; temple of an idol; — ة *kanîsa-t*, pl. *kanâ'is*, church; synagogue; beautiful woman; — *kunayyisa-t*, little church.

(كنيف) *kanîf*, pl. *kunf*, covered side-place; privy, water-closet; sewer; wash-house; fold; veil; shield.

كنين *kanîn*, concealed; well-guarded, carefully preserved.

(كه) *kahh*, I, INF. *kuhûh*, be old and decrepit; INF. *kahh*, breathe into one's face; — ة *kahha-t*, old she-camel; old woman.

كها *kihâ'*, glorying (s.), self-praise, INF. of (كهى); — ة *kahât*, big, fat.

كهام *kahâm*, blunt; heavy; old and decrepit.

كهان *kuhhân*, pl. of كاهن *kâhin*, soothsayer, &c.; — ة *kihâna-t*,

soothsaying (s.), divination; priesthood.

(كهب) *kahib*, A, INF. *kahab*,—*kahub*, INF. *kuhûb*; — also IX. INF. *ik-hibâb*, and XI. INF. *ikhîbâb*, be of the colour — ة *kuhba-t*, blackish or bluish-grey.

كهب *kahb*, old.

(كهد) *kahad*, INF. *kahd*, *kahadân*, run fast, hurry; be very tired; be obtrusive; — IV. INF. *ikhâd*, be tired; tire, weary, molest; bid to hasten.

(كهر) *kahar*, INF. *kahr*, be advanced; be intense; scold; look severe and indignant; receive one thus; play, sport, joke; laugh; tame, subdue, oppress.

كهرب *kahrub*, yellow amber; — *kahrab*, INF. ة, electrify; — II. INF. *takahrub*, be electrified.

كهربا *kahrubâ*, yellow amber; — ي *kahrubâ'iyy*, ة, electric; — ية *kahrubâ'iyya-t*, electricity.

(كهف) *kahf*, pl. *kuhûf*, spacious cave (اصحاب الكهف *aṣḥâb al-kahf*, the seven sleepers); refuge, asylum;—V. INF. *takahhuf*, have caves; enter a cave.

(كهكه) *kahkah*, INF. ة, blow into one's hands to warm them; roar; cry out with fear.

(كهل) *kahal*, INF. *kuhûl*, enter on the age of maturity; — III. INF. *mukâhala-t*, id.; be of advanced age; be married; — VIII. INF. *iktihâl*=I.; begin to turn grey.

كهل *kahl*, pl. *kuhhal*, *kihâl*, *kuhûl*, *kuhlân*, *kahlûn*, f. ة, pl. *kahlât*, *kahalât*, *kuhalâ'*, of a mature age, elderly; getting the first grey hair.

(كهم) *kaham*, U, INF. *kahm*, depress, render low-spirited; — *kahim*, A, INF. *kaham*, be obtuse, blunt; — IV. INF. *ikhâm*, be dim, weak (sight).

(كهن) *kahan*, A, U, INF. *kahâna-t*, foretell the future, soothsay; be priest or soothsayer; — *kahun*, INF. *kahâna-t*, id.; — II. INF. *takhîn*, exercise the office of a priest or soothsayer; — V. INF. *takahhun*, soothsay; — ة *kahana-t*, pl. of كاهن *kâhin*, soothsayer, &c.

كهنوت *kahnût*, priesthood.

كهول *kahwal*, *kahûl*, spider; — *; — ة *kuhûla-t*, ية *kuhûliyya-t*, mature age; steadiness; laziness.

كهوه *kuhûh*, decrepitude.

(كهى) *kahi'*, A, INF. *kahan*, have foul breath, an impure complexion; be weak, cowardly; — III. INF. *kihâ'*, *mukâhât*, glory, try to surpass in glory; — IV. INF. *ikhâ'*, warm one's finger-tips by breathing upon them.

كهيل *kuhyal*, a middle-aged man, nearer to youth.

كو *kuww*, *kaww*, ة *kuwwa-t*, *kawwa-t*, pl. *kiwâ'*, *kuwiyy*, *kiwa-n*, window, dormer-window.

(كوا) *kâ'* (1 pret. *ku'tu*), U, INF. *kâ'*, *kau'*, *ka'w*, also *ki'*, I, INF. *kai'*, *kai'a-t*, desist from fear; — IV. INF. *ikâ'*, *ikâ'a-t*, deter from.

كوا *kiwâ'*, invective; pl. of كو *kuww*, ة;—*kawwâ'*, who inveighs against.

كواثر *kawâṡir*, pl. of كوثر *kauṡar*.

كواحص *kawâḥiṣ*, pl. effaced traces.

كوارة *kiwâra-t*, *kuwâra-t*, *kuwwâra-t*, pl. -*ât*, *kawâ'ir*, bee-hive; receptacle for corn in the shape of a bee-hive made of small twigs and earth.

كواسب *kawâsib*, pl. wild beasts; limbs, extremities.

كوافر *kawâfir*, pl. of كافرة *kâfara-t*, infidels, f. &c., and كافور *kâfûr*, spathe, &c.

كواكب *kawâkib*, pl. of كوكب *kaukab*.

كوانين *kawânîn*, pl. of كانون *kânûn*, stove, &c.

كوائر *kawâ'ir*, pl. of كوارة *kiwâra-t*.

كوائف *kawâ'if*, pl. details, contents.

(كوب) *kâb*, U, INF. *kaub*, drink out of—

كوب *kûb*, pl. *akwâb*, a large cup without handle or spout; — ة

kûba-t, chess; a kind of drum; a kind of lute.

كوتى *kauta*, *kûtiyy*, short, dwarf.

(كوث) *kauṣ*, pl. *akwâṣ*, shoe; short boot.

كوثر *kauṣar*, pl. *kawâṣir*, principal river of Paradise; plenty, abundance, much; liberal.

كوثل *kauṣal*, stern of a ship; helmet.

كوثة *kauṣa-t*, fertility; cheapness of corn.

(كوح) *kâḥ*, U, INF. *kauḥ*, get the better in a combat; dip into the water; bury in the ground; — II. INF. *takwîḥ*, conquer, vanquish; subdue, humble; repel; — III. INF. *mukâwaḥa-t*, id.; combat against; provoke by invectives; — VI. INF. *takâwuḥ*, try to injure one another as much as possible.

كوخ *kûḥ*, pl. *akwâḥ*, *kûḥân*, *kîḥân*, *kiwaḥa-t*, hut of reed or cane without windows.

كوهن m. *kauhan*, INF. ة, appoint as one's minister.

(كود) *kâd*, A, INF. *kaud*, *makâd*, *makâda-t*, be on the point of (followed by the aor.): كاد يفعل *kâd yaf'al*, he was on the point of doing, he almost did; و لا كودا *wa lâ kaud-an*, by no means.

كود *kaud*, pl. *ahwâd*, troop, squadron, legion; — ة *kauda-t*, pl. *akwâd*, heap of earth.

(كودا) *kaudâ'*, INF. ة, run.

كودن *kaudan*, ى *kaudaniyy*, pack-horse, sumpter; mule; elephant.

(كور) *kâr*, U, INF. *kaur*, wind in a spiral form; roll along; hasten; dig up the ground; fall down, tumble; — II. INF. *takwîr*=I.; carry together, heap up, fasten; cause to follow; throw down; pass. be eclipsed; — IV. INF. *ikâra-t*, deem weak, despise; — V. INF. *takawwur*, be thrown down, fall; — VIII. INF. *iktiyâr*, id.; be turbaned; walk fast; lift the tail in running; — X. INF. *istikâra-t*, hasten; take the burden on one's back.

كور *kaur*, plenty; — *kûr*, pl. *akwâr*, *akwur*, *kîrân*, camel-saddle; hearth, stove; furnace, hearth of a forge; bellows; crucible; funnel of a mill; wasp-nest; — ة *kûra-t*, pl. *kuwar*, *kûr*, small town; tract, district; land.

(كوز) *kâz*, U, INF. *kauz*, gather, unite; be gathered in one point, concentrated (also V.); drink out of.

كوز *kûz*, pl. كيزان *kîzân*, *kizawa-t*, *akwâz*, a water-vessel with handles and a narrow neck without a spout.

(كوس) *kâs*, U, INF. *kaus*, be thrown head over heels; throw a somersault; throw down; walk on three feet; walk slowly; coil one's self up; abate the price.

كوس *kûs*, heaped-up sand-hill; pl. *-ât*, drum; a triangle of equal sides for measuring.

كوسج *kausaj*, *kûsaj* (m. كوسة *kûsa-t*), having a thin beard; toothless; sword-fish; — *kausaj*, INF. ة, grow a thin beard, get toothless.

كوسى *kûsa*, pumpkin; ingenious, witty, clever (woman); — *kûsiyy*, having short fore-feet.

(كوش) *kâś*, U, INF. *kauś*, be afraid and call for help; lie with; (m.) exert one's self; — II. INF. *takwîś*, grasp, heap up, concentrate troops; — V. INF. *takawwuś*, be concentrated; — ة *kûśa-t*, pl. *kuwaś*, heap; troop, detachment; great zeal and exertion (m.).

كوشان *kauśân*, rice with fish.

كوصة *ku'ṣa-t*, inured to bear hunger and thirst.

(كوع) *kâ'*, U, INF. *kau'*, walk on one side of the foot; — pret. *ku'tu*, aor. *yakâ'*, *yakî'*, yield from fear, desist; — *kawi'*, A, INF. *kawa'*, have large wrists

or ankles; — II. INF. *takwî'*, dip a wounded limb into warm oil to stanch the blood; — V. INF. *takawwu'*, be distorted; (m.) pass. of II.

كوع *kû'*, pl. *akwâ'*, inner knuckle of the wrist or ankle; elbow.

(كوف) *kâf*, U, INF. *kauf*, double in the sides of a skin bag; — II. INF. *takwîf*, cut leather; reel off; — V. INF. *takawwuf*, pretend or appear to be a native of Kufa; INF. also *kaufân*, be circular; — ة *kûfa-t*, round hill of red sand; Kufa; blame, blemish, fault.

كوفان *kaufân*, *kûfân*, *kuwwafân*, *kawwafân*, Kufa; round sand-hill; anything round, circle; honour, dignity.

كوفى *kûfiyy*, ة, of Kufa; *al-kûfiyyûn*, the Kufic grammarians; — ة *kûfiyya-t*, pl. *kawâfiyy*, reel, windle; a woman's gear.

كوكب *kaukab*, ة, pl. *kawâkib*, star, planet; chief, prince; pupil (of the eye); — ة *kaukaba-t*, troop of people; — *kaukab*, INF. ة, shine, glitter, sparkle.

(كوكى) *kauka*, INF. *kaukawa-t*, walk jerkily.

(كول), V. INF. *takawwul*, be gathered, assembled; approach with invectives and threatening blows; — VI. INF. *takâwul*, be not equal to a thing; — VII. INF. *inkiyâl*=V.; — ة *ku'ula-t*, transfer of a debt, INF. of (كال).

كولان *kaulân*, *kûlân*, papyrus plant; a kind of rush for mats.

كولح *kaulaḥ*, ugly.

كولك *kaulak*, wooden bucket (Pers.).

(كوم) *kâm*, U, cover (stallion); lie with; — *kawim*, A, INF. *kawam*, have a big hump; — II. INF. *takwîm*, make a heap, heap up; — V. INF. *takawwum*, be heaped up.

كوم *kûm*, pl. *kîmân*, heap; dung-hill, dung-pit; — ة *kûma-t*, pl. *akwâm*, heap of earth; (m.) stock in trade, capital, funds.

(كون) *kân*, U, INF. *kaun*, *kainûna-t*, happen, take place; INF. *kaun*, *kiyân*, be, exist, be in a state or place; think, imagine; stand security for (على *'ala*); — II. INF. *takwîn*, call into existence, create, form; — V. INF. *takawwun*, be created, formed, receive life, exist; — VIII. INF. *iktiyân*, be, exist; stand security for (على *'ala*); — X. INF. *istikâna-t*, submit.(n.); be humble.

كون *kaun*, pl. *akwân*, being, existence, essence, substance; condition, circumstance (*li-kaun-i*, *kaun-a*, because); what exists, all, universe; du. *al-kaunân*, both worlds, things material and spiritual, men and angels; rest; event; news; (m.) war, combat; — ى *kaumiyy*, being, existing (adj.); — *kûniyy*, very old.

(كوه) *kâh*, U, INF. *kauh*, make one breathe to see whether he has drunk wine; — *kawih*, A, INF. *kawah*, be perplexed, dumb-founded; — V. INF. *takawwuh*, extend and claim all one's activity (business, &c.).

كوهد *kauhad*, trembling with old age.

كوود *ka'ûd*, difficult to mount or ascend.

(كوى) *kawa*, I, INF. *kayy*, cauterise; burn; (m.) iron; — II. INF. *takwiya-t*, cauterise repeatedly or in several places; iron; — III. INF. *mukâwât*, abuse, insult; — V. INF. *takawwî*, be cauterised; be ironed; — VII. INF. *inkiwâ'*, be cauterised; feel a burning pain; — VIII. INF. *iktiwâ'*, have one's self cauterised.

كوى *kiwan*, pl. of كو *kuww*, ة *kuwwa-t*, — *kauy*, ironing (s.); —*kuwwiyy*, referring or belonging to the window.

كويس *kuwayyis*, ة, handsome, pretty, dim. of كيس *kayyis*.

(كى) *kâ'*, I, INF. *kai'*, see (كو).

كى *kai*, in order that, so that; — *kayy*, ة, cauterisation; cautery; ironing (s.); — *kai'*, fear; timorous; — ة *kayya-t*, cauterised place on the skin.

كياج *ki'âj*, malicious stupidity.

كئاس *ki'âs*, pl. of كاس *ka's*, cup; — ة *kayâsa-t*, *kiyâsa-t*, sagacity, penetration; fineness, delicacy; beauty, grace, elegance.

كيال *kayyâl*, who measures, weighs; — ة *kiyâla-t*, measuring, weighing (s.); fee for measuring.

كيان *kiyân*, being (s.), existence; essence of man, inborn nature; also ة *kiyâna-t*, bail, security; — ية pl. *kiyâniyyât*, natural science.

كئاة *kai'a-t*, fear.

كئب *ka'ib*, V. see (كاب); — *ka'ib*, grieved, sorrowful.

كيت *kaita*, thus; *kaita wa kaita*, *kaita wa kaiti*, so and so; — II. *kayya-t*, INF. *takyît*, stop up, fill; alleviate, lighten (a.).

(كيح) *kâḥ*, I, INF. *kaiḥ*, penetrate, pierce.

كيح *kaiḥ*, thick and rough; — *kîḥ*, pl. *akyâḥ*, *kuyûḥ*, mountain-slope, side; — *kayaḥ*, thickness and roughness.

كيخان *kîḥân*, pl. of كوخ *kûḥ*.

كيخم *kaiḥam*, great king (title).

(كيد) *kâd*, I, INF. *kaid*, *makîda-t*, deceive cunningly, conquer by stratagem, outwit; lay snares or traps to; — II. INF. *takyîd*, be obstinate; be revengeful (m.); — III. INF. *mukâyada-t*, lay snares, try to deceive; — IV. INF. *ikâda-t*, be obstinate (m.); — VII. INF. *inkiyâd*, VIII. INF. *iktiyâd*, allow one's self to be deceived, ensnared.

كيد *kaid*, pl. *kiyâd*, stratagem, cunning, deceit; snare, ambush; obstinacy; vindictiveness; malice; ك الله, divine punishment for perfidy and insidiousness.

كيذبان *kaiẕabân*, *kaiẕubân*, liar.

(كير) *kâr*, I, INF. *kiyâr*, raise the tail in running.

كير *kîr*, pl. *akyâr*, *kiyara-t*, *kîrân*, blacksmith's bellows; — m. *kîr*, master, lord, *kîr wa kîr*, your Reverence, title of the Greek Patriarch.

كيران *kîrân*, pl. of the previous and of كور *kûr*.

(كيس) *kâs*, I, INF. *kais*, *kiyâsa-t*, be cunning, subtle, sly, wide-awake, wise; be handsome, pretty; — INF. *kais*, surpass in cunning; — II. INF. *takyîs*, render cunning, &c.; make handsome, &c.; (m.) put into a bag or purse; — III. INF. *mukâyasa-t*, vie with in cunning, try to surpass in intelligence; — V. INF. *takayyus*, show one's self cunning and subtle; grow handsome, pretty; be put into a purse or bag.

كيس *kais*, cunning, intelligence, finesse; beauty, elegance; — *kîs*, pl. *akyâs*, *kiyasa-t*, bag, purse; scrotum; — *kayyis*, ة, pl. *kîsā*, *akyâs*, cunning, fine, subtle; intelligent; handsome, pretty.

كيسان *kaisân*, fraud, treachery.

كيسبة *kaisaba-t*, wolf.

كيسوم *kaisûm*, pl. *akâsim*, luxuriant; great quantities of food.

كيسى *kîsā*, pl. of كيس *kayyis*.

(كيص) *kâṣ*, I, INF. *kaiṣ*, *kayaṣân*, *kuyûṣ*, lose courage and desist; take care of one's self only; eat much; carry on; hasten, walk fast.

كيص *kaiṣ*, avarice; — *kîṣ*, *kayyiṣ*, narrow-minded; miserly, avaricious; — *kiyaṣ*, *kiyaṣṣ*, muscular.

(كيع) *kâ'*, I, A, INF. *kai'*, *kai'û'a-t*, desist from fear.

(كيف) *kâf*, I, INF. *kaif*, cut, cut off, lop; — II. INF. *takyîf*, cut off entirely; (m.) bring one into good humour, amuse well; (m.) make one tipsy, intoxicate; (m.) qualify; — V. INF. *takayyuf*, diminish (a.); (m.) be in good humour, enjoy one's self, carouse; (m.) be qualified, show or assume such or such qualities; — VII. INF. *inkiyâf*, be cut off.

كيف *kaif*, how? (ك بك *kaifa bak*, ك كيفك *kaif kaifak*, how do you do?); as; vulg. *kef*, well-being, good humour, enjoyment, carouse, excitement from opium, &c.; — ة *kaifa-t*, section, segment; wedge-like piece in clothes, &c.

كيفما *kaifa-mâ*, howsoever.

كيفى *kaifiyy*, intoxicating; drunk; — ة *kaifiyya-t*, quality; way, manner; particulars; amusement, pleasure-party; raised spirits, excitement.

كيكا *kaikâ'*, worthless.

كيكة *kaika-t*, كيكية *kaikiyya-t*, pl. *kaiyâkî*, egg.

(كيل) *kâl*, I, INF. *kail*, *makâl*, *makîl*, measure, weigh; measure out to, impart, give (2 acc.); measure one thing by another; fail to give fire; — II. INF. *takyîl*, measure, weigh; — III. INF. *mukâyala-t*, measure out corn to; retaliate; dispute with, vie; — V. INF. *takayyul*, be measured; — VIII. INF. *iktiyâl*, measure, measure out to, impart, give.

كيل *kail*, measure, especially for corn, =6 مد *mudd*; capacity of a measure; — *kayyil*, offal, rubbish, refuse; the most exquisite; — ة *kaila-t*, small measure for corn, =2 مد *mudd*.

كيلا *kai-lâ*, in order that not, lest.

كيلجة *kailaja-t*, pl. *kayâlija-t*, a corn-measure ($\frac{15}{16}$ منا *manâ*).

كيلوس *kailûs*, *kîlûs*, chyle.

كيما *kai-mâ*, in order that; why?

كيمان *kîmân*, pl. of كوم *kûm*, ة.

كيميا *kîmiyâ'*, chemistry, alchemy; elixir; philosopher's stone; اهل ك *ahl kîmiyâ'*, alchemist; quack.

كيمياوى *kîmiyâwiyy*, ة, chemical.

كيمخت *kaimuḫt*, raw hides (Pers.).

(كين) *kân*, I, INF. *kain*, humble one's self, be submissive; — IV. INF. *ikâna-t*, humble; — VIII. INF. *iktiyân*, be sad; — X. INF. *istikâna-t*=I.

كين *kain*, pl. *kuyûn*, caruncle in the womb; — ة *kaina-t*, bail, security; lotus-tree; — *kîna-t*, plight, bad state of things.

كينونة *kainûna-t*, being (s.), existence, INF. of (كون).

(كيه) *kâh*, I, INF. *kaih*, make one breathe to see whether he has been drinking wine.

كيه *kayyih*, shunned as an impostor.

كيوان *kaiwân*, planet Saturn (Pers.).

كيوح *kuyûḥ*, mountain-slopes, &c., pl. of كاح and كيح *kîḥ*.

كيول *kayyûl*, rear-guard of an army; timid; filings; offal, rubbish; the most exquisite.

كيى *kai'*, timorous, timid; — ة *kai'a-t*, fear; timorous.

كئيب *ka'îb*, grieved, sorrowful.

كييكة *kuyaika-t*, كييكية *kuyaikiya-t*, little egg.

كئين *ka'în*, how many?

ل

ل *l*, as a numerical sign=30; abbreviation for ليل *lail*, night, مقابلة *muqâbala-t*, opposite aspect, زحل *zuḥal*, the planet Saturn, and the month of شوال *śawwâl*;—

la (joined in writing with the following word), truly, indeed, certainly; particle introducing an oath, as: لعمرك *la-'amru-ka*, by thy life!—or in exclamations of wonder or for help;—

li, prep. to, before pronominal affixes *la*, expressing our dative or possessive; for the sake of, on account of, for the purpose of; according to; لان *li'anna*, conj. governing the subjunctive (*naṣb*) of a verb, in order that; if expressing a command, the jussive with suppression of the final vowel follows, as: لينفق *layanfuq*, let him spend alms.

لا *lâ*, not; no (followed by the accusative, as: لا ابا له *lâ abâ la-hu*, he has no father); لا جرم *lâ jaram*, by all means, necessarily;—*lâ'-i*, which, f. pl. of التى *allatî*;—*la''â'*, and—

لاال *la''âl*, seller of pearls.

لاامة *la'âma-t*, blameworthy disposition or conduct.

لااة *la'ât* (also لاة *la'ât*), doe; shield.

لاب لك *lâb-a lak-a*, you must by all means.

لابث *lâbis*, who tarries, delays; staying longer.

لابد *lâbid*, riches, wealth; *al-lâbid*, lion;—*lâbud*, musical key;—*lâ-budd*, there is no help, no doubt, no escape.

لابس *lâbis*, clad; dressing, covering (adj.).

لابق *lâbiq*, fitting (dress).

لابن *lâbin*, abounding in milk, yielding plenty of milk;—ة *lâbina-t*, pl. *lawâbin*, udder, breast.

لات *lât*, name of a goddess.

لاتح *lâtiḥ*, intelligent, clever.

لاتى *lâtî*, f. pl. which.

لاث *lâs*, ة, densely grown.

لاثم *lâsim*, pl. *lusm*, who breaks.

لاجل *li-ajl-i*, on account of.

لاح *lâḥḥ*, narrow, strait.

لاحب *lâḥib*, open (high road).

لاحد *lâḥid*, niched tomb.

لاحس *lâḥis*, ة, pl. *lawâḥis*, licking; hard.

لاحظة *lâḥiza-t*, pl. *lawâḥiz*, glancing; look, glance.

لاحق *lâḥiq*, reaching; adjoining; appendix.

لاحم *lâḥim*, pl. *lawâḥim*, eating meat, carnivorous.

لاحن *lâḥin*, pronouncing faultily.

لاحوس *lâḥûs*, unfortunate, unhappy.

لاخ *lâḫḫ*, narrow.

لاد *lâdd*, adversary.

لاذة *lâza-t*, pl. *lâz*, dress of raw Chinese silk.

لازم *lâzim*, ة, necessary, urgent, unavoidable; closely adhering to, inseparable (لازم ملزوم *lâzim malzûm*, closest friendship); entirely addicted or devoted to; worthy, fit; intransitive, neuter; ل البنا *lâzim al-binâ'*, indeclinable;—ة *lâzima-t*, pl. *lawâzim*, what is necessary, indispensable duty; obligation, debt.

لازورد *lâzward*, lapis lazuli;—ى *lazwardiyy*, azure blue.

لازوق *lâzûq*, sticking-plaster.

لاسيما *lâ-siyyamâ*, particularly, especially.

لاصف *lâṣif*, stone containing antimony.

لاصق *lâṣiq*, adhering, sticking; low (building).

(لاط) *la'aṭ*, INF. *la'ṭ*, demand or ask urgently; press for payment; be harsh, severe; hit, wound.

لاط *lâṭṭ*, miserly, niggardly; — ة *lâṭa-t*, sodomites, pl. of لائط *lâ'iṭ*.

لاطى *lâṭi'*, who seeks refuge; — ة *lâṭi'a-t*, severe wound in the head.

(لاظ) *la'aẓ*, INF. *la'ẓ*, turn off; grieve (a.); press, dun.

لاع *lâ'*, pl. *lâ'ûn*, *lâ'a-t*, *alwâ'*, timid, timorous; ill-humoured, peevish; impatient; malicious; — *lâ'-in*, see لاعى *lâ'î*; — ة *lâ'a-t*, discreet woman.

لاعج *lâ'ij*, violent, ardent.

لاعطا *lâ'iṭ-an*, sideways.

لاعى *lâ'î* (لاع *lâ'-in*), licking; — *lâ'iya-t*, a plant of great purgative and vomitive power.

لاغية *lâgiya-t*, faulty speech; foolish and ribald talk.

(لاف) *la'af*, INF. *la'f*, eat nicely.

لافح *lâfiḥ*, pl. *lawâfiḥ*, scorching.

لافظة *lâfiẓa-t*, sea; mill; world; feeding bird; cock.

لاقح *lâqiḥ*, pl. *lawâqiḥ*, big with young.

(لاك), IV. INF. *il'âk*, send as a messenger.

لاكن *lâkin*, but.

لاكى *lâkî*, censurer, fault-finder; malicious.

لال *la'âl*, pearls; — *la''âl*, ة *li'âla-t*, and—

لالا *la'la'*, *lâla''â'*, seller of pearls; — *la'lâ'*, gladness.

(لالا) *la'la'*, INF. ة, shine, glitter, light, sparkle; ogle; wag the tail; shed tears; — II. INF. *tala'lu'*, shine, flash.

لالى *la'âlî*, pearls, pl. of لولو *lu'lu'*.

(لام) *la'am*, INF. *la'm*, accuse of a vile disposition; dress a wound; mend; pacify; unite two things, reconcile (بين *ben*, *bain*); — لوم *la'um*, INF. *lu'm*, *la'âma-t*, *mal'ama-t*, be of a vile disposition, miserly, niggardly; — II. *tal'îm*, mend; pacify; — III. INF. *mulâ'ama-t*, id.; agree with, accord with; be fitted to; — IV. INF. *il'âm*, represent one as vile, miserly; have such children; mend broken things; — VIII. *ilti'âm*, be considered vile; agree and fit well; assemble (n.); — X. INF. *istil'âm*, put on a coat of mail.

لام *la'm*, mended; — ة *lâma-t*, anything blameworthy; also *la'ma-t*, pl. *la'm*, closely-wrought coat of mail; — *lâmma-t*, malignant; threatening.

لامان *lâmân*, ignoble, vile, miserly.

لامس *lâmis*, ة, touching, feeling; — ة *lâmisa-t*, sense of touch or feeling.

لامع *lâmi'*, ة, shining, flashing, resplendent; — ة *lâmi'a-t*, soft skull of the new-born; pl. *lawâmi'*, trembling light, glitter.

لامى *lâmiyy*, rhyming on the letter ل; in the shape of the letter ل; — ة *lâmiyya-t*, poem rhyming on the letter ل.

لان *lân*, for الان *alân*, now, just now; — *la'anna*, perhaps; — *li-anna*, for the reason that, because, for; with pronominal affix لاننى *li-anna-nî*, لانى *li'annî*, for I, لانك *li-anna-ka*, for thou, &c.

لاه *lâh*, God; — *lâh-in*, see لاهى *lâhî*; — ة *lâha-t*, snake, serpent.

لاهز *lâhiz*, narrowly surrounding chain of mountains.

لاهوت *lâhût*, Godhead, divinity.

لاهى *lâhî* (لاه *lâh-in*), dallying away the time; erring from levity; careless.

لاوا *lâwâ'*, distress, misfortune.

(لاى) *la'a*, INF. *la'y*, be slow, irresolute; be poor, unfortunate; — IV. INF. *il'â'*, get into distress and misfortune.

لاى *la'y*, slowness, irresoluteness; while; misfortune, distress,

hardship ; *la'y-an mâ*, with great difficulty ; — *la-an*, pl. *al'â'*, wild bullock, wild cow ; misfortune, hardship.

لائب *lâ'ib*, pl. *lu'ûb*, *lawâ'ib*, thirsty.

لائث *lâ'is̱*, densely grown ; lion.

لائح *lâ'iḥ*, appearing ; distinct, clear ; bright, shining ; — ة *lâ'iḥa-t*, pl. *lawâ'iḥ*, anything evident ; clearness ; proof, demonstration.

لائس *lâ'is*, voluptuary.

لائط *lâ'iṭ*, pl. *lâṭa-t*, sodomite.

لائق *lâ'iq*, ة, fit, appropriate.

لائك *lâ'ik*, cynical fault-finder.

لائم *lâ'im*, pl. *luwwam*, *luwwâm*, *luyyâm*, censurer, blamer, accuser ; — ة *lâ'ima-t*, blame, reproach, accusation.

لائى *lâ'iyy*, referring to لا *lâ*, not ; negative, refusing, declining, denying.

لب *labb*, U, INF. *labb*, stay, remain, abide ; stand opposite ; — for *labib*, A, be sound in head and heart ; — *labub*, INF. *labâba-t*, id. ; — II. INF. *talbîb*, seize by the throat ; — IV. INF. *ilbâb*, stay, remain, fix in a place ; be pulpy, full of marrow ; adorn the horse with a breast-piece ; — V. INF. *talabbub*, gird one's self.

لب *lab*, ة *laba-t*, lioness ; — *lubb*, pl. *lubûb*, principal part and middle ; the purest and best ; essence ; marrow, kernel ; crumb of bread ; pl. *albâb*, *alubb*, *albub*, heart, mind, intellect ; — ة *labba-t*, throat of an animal ; place where it is killed ; excellent (wife) ; — *lubba-t*, breast ; heart.

(لبا) *laba'*, INF. *lab'*, milk a sheep after parturition ; place such milk before the guest.

لبا *liba'*, milk obtained after parturition ; — ة *labât*, *lab'a-t*, lioness.

لباب *libâb*, pl. of لبيب *labîb* ; — *lubâb*, pure, stainless ; choice (adj.) ; pure essence ; pulp or marrow of fruit ; — ة *labâba-t*, *lubâba-t*, mind, intellect.

لباث *labâs̱*, ة *labâs̱a-t*, delay.

لباد *labbâd*, maker of felt ;—*lubbâd*, ة *lubbâda-t*, felt ; mattress of felt, wrapper of felt, cap of felt ; ل السرج *lubbâda-t as-sarj*, saddle-cloth.

لباس *libâs*, pl. *albisa-t*, garment, dress, robe, costume ; trowsers, drawers ; confusion, hurly-burly ; decency, bashfulness ; ل الرجل *libâs ar-rajul*, wife ; ل المرأة *libâs al-mar'a-t*, husband ; ل الباس *libâs al-ba's*, great calamity ; — *labbâs*, who has many clothes ; who causes confusion ; who dissimulates.

لباط *labbâṭ*, who kicks.

لباقة *labâqa-t*, wit and cleverness ; gracefulness, elegance ; the fitting of clothes.

لباكة *lubâka-t*, multitude, plenty.

لبالب *labâlib*, bellowing ; لباليب *labâlîb*, pl. of لبلوب *lublûb*.

لبان *labân*, chest, breast, bosom ; breast-piece ; — *libân*, sucking of milk ; fostering ; — * ; — *lubân*, resin of the alder-tree, &c. as incense ; benzoin ; — *labbân*, brick-maker ; seller of sour milk ; — ة *lubâna-t*, pl. -*ât*, *lubân*, voluntary good work, undertaking ; urgent business or want.

لبائن *labâ'in*, pl. of لبون *labûn*.

لبب *labab*, pl. *albâb*, throat, place on the neck for an ornament ; breast-piece, breast-plate for a horse.

(لبت) *labat*, U, INF. *labt*, distort the hand ; beat with a rope on the chest or belly.

(لبث) *labis̱*, A, INF. *labs̱*, *lubs̱*, *labas̱*, *lubâs̱*, *libâs̱*, *lubâs̱a-t*, *labîs̱a-t*, tarry, stay longer, remain ; — II. INF. *talbîs̱*, cause delay, detain ; — IV. INF. *ilbâs̱*, id. ; — V. INF. *talabbus̱*, delay,

tarry; — x. INF. *istilbâs̲*, deem
tarrying, delaying.

لبـــث *labs̲*, halt; — *lubs̲*, ة *lubs̲a-t*,
delay, longer stay; — *labis̲*,
who tarries, delays; staying
longer.

(لبج) *labaj*, U, INF. *labj*, throw on
the ground; beat, cudgel; — ة
lubja-t, *labaja-t*, *lubuja-t*, pl.
labaj, *lubaj*, trap for wolves.

(لبح) *labaḥ*, INF. *labḥ*, grow old;
— II. INF. *talbîḥ*, IV. INF. *ilbâḥ*,
id.

لبح *labaḥ*, old man; bravery.

(لبخ) *labaḫ*, INF. *labḫ*, beat, cudgel;
abuse; take from; try to obtain
by stratagem; set traps or
snares; kill; (m.) lay on a
plaster; — ة *labḫa-t*, pl. *labaḫ*,
plaster, cataplasm.

(لبد) *labad*, U, INF. *lubûd*, stay,
remain; abide, adhere, stick
to; stand firm in the ground;
duck; cram into a sack; press
hair or wool so as to form felt;
card wool; — *labid*, A, INF. *labad*,
stay, abide; adhere firmly; —
II. INF. *talbîd*, cover the ground
and cause its particles to stick
together; fix upon (n.), adhere;
beat firm; (m.) kick about and
be noisy; — IV. INF. *ilbâd*, stay,
abide; adhere; join, cause to
stick together; — V. INF. *ta-
labbud*, stick together; — VII.
INF. *inlibâd*, be crammed, well
stuffed; — VIII. INF. *iltibâd*, id.;
stick closely together.

لبد *libd*, *labd*, pl. *lubûd*, *albâd*,
moist hair or wool sticking
together or compressed; felt;
saddle-cloth; affairs; — *labad*,
wool, felt; mat; — *labid*, *lubad*,
pl. *lubûd*, who stays always at
home, does not go after gain;
— *lubad*, *lubbad*, great wealth,
plenty, abundance; *lubad*, the
seventh vulture of Loqmân the
'Adite; — ة *libda-t*, *lubda-t*, hair
or wool sticking closely together;

cloth of felt; dense crowd; pl.
libad, *lubad*, lion's mane; ابو لبد
abû libad, ذو لبد *z̲û libad*, lion; —
ى *lubbadā*, densely crowded.

(لبز) *labaz*, I, INF. *labz*, eat hurriedly and greedily; swallow
quickly; beat violently; INF.
libz, dress a wound.

(لبس) *labas*, I, INF. *labs*, cover; obscure, render dark or indistinct,
confuse; mingle; — *labis*, A,
INF. *lubs*, put on a dress, dress
(n.); associate with (acc.); —
II. INF. *talbîs*, cover; obscure;
try to conceal; deceive, dissemble; clothe, invest; — III.
INF. *mulâbasa-t*, intermeddle
with, take a matter into one's
hand, carry on; accustom one's
self to; — IV. INF. *ilbâs*, cover,
clothe (2 acc.); — V. INF. *ta-
labbus*, cover one's self, dress
(n.); disguise one's self, wear
a mask; intermeddle with (ب
bi); — VIII. INF. *iltibâs*, be
dark, obscure, confused, enigmatical.

لبس *labs*, confusion, lack of clearness, secrecy; hurly-burly, chaos;
— *libs*, pl. *lubûs*, clothing, dress,
garment; cover; scalp; — *lubs*,
putting on and wearing of
clothes; long commerce, association; — ة *libsa-t*, way of
dressing; — *lubsa-t*, confusion,
want of clearness, doubt, anything doubtful.

(لبش) m. *labaś*, luggage, things,
chattels; — II. INF. *talbîś*, pack
one's things, make ready for a
journey, set out.

(لبط) *labaṭ*, U, INF. *labṭ*, throw on
the ground; kick, kick at; pass.
lubiṭ, INF. *labṭ*, *labaṭ*, catch a
cold; — II. INF. *talbîṭ*, throw on
the ground; kick; — V. INF.
talabbuṭ, lie down, throw one's
self down, roll (n.) on the
ground; — VIII. INF. *iltibâṭ*, lie
down; — ة *labṭa-t*, kick, kicking;
cold, rheum.

لبعا *lab'an*, (adv.) unrevenged (blood shed).

(لبق) *labaq*, U, INF. *labq*, soften; — *labiq*, A, INF. *labaq*, be intelligent and skilful; fit; beseem; be elegant; — *labuq*, INF. *labâqa-t*, id.; — II. INF. *talbîq*, employ stratagem and artifices; soften, steep in broth; (m.) embellish.

لبق *labq*, ة, intelligence and skill; — *labiq*, ة, intelligent and skilful; experienced; whose dress fits well; adorned, elegant; fitting.

(لبك) *labak*, U, INF. *labk*, mix; confuse; prejudice, bias against; — II. INF. *talbîk*, mix; confuse; hinder; — V. INF. *talabbuk*, be confused, hindered, thwarted; — VIII. INF. *iltibâk*, id.; be prejudiced, prepossessed, biassed.

لبك *labk*, ة *labka-t*, mixture, confusion;—*labik*, mixed, confused; — ة *labaka-t*, mouthful.

لبلاب *lablâb*, ivy; wall-wort.

(لبلب) *lablab*, INF. ة, lick the new-born tenderly; fondle the child; be dispersed; (m.) chat, chatter.

لبلوب *lublûb*, pl. *labâlîb*, end of a branch, shoot, bud; pulp of a fruit.

(لبم) *labim*, A, INF. *labam*, be unequal.

(لبن) *laban*, I, INF. *labn*, eat much; beat violently; beat or bruise the breast; — I, U, give milk to drink; — *labin*, A, INF. *laban*, have plenty of milk in the udder; — II. INF. *talbîn*, suckle; make bricks; — IV. INF. *ilbân*, have plenty of milk in the udder; be rich in milk; — V. INF. *talabbun*, tarry, delay; — VIII. INF. *iltibân*, suck milk; — X. INF. *istilbân*, ask for milk.

لبن *libn*, *labin*, *libin*, ة, brick, tile (dried in the sun); (m.) quarry-stone; — *libn*, *lubn*, pl. of لبون *labûn*; — *laban*, pl. *albân*, *libân*, milk, sour milk; resin, gum; quicksilver; — ة *labina-t*, pl. *-ât*, *labin*, wedge-like piece of a shirt beneath the arm-pit.

لبنان *lubnân*, Libanon; — ى *lubnâniyy*, of or from the Libanon.

لبنى *lubnā*, a resinous tree; female proper name; — ة *labaniyya-t*, dish of milk; milk diet.

لبوخ *lubûẖ*, fleshiness.

لبود *labûd*, sheep-louse; — ى *lubûdiyy*, felt-maker.

لبوس *labûs*, clothing; coat of mail.

لبون *labûn*, ة *labûna-t*, pl. *libân*, *libn*, *lubn*, *labâ'in*, having the udder full of milk; ابن لبون *ibn labûn*, entering on the third year (camel).

لبوة *labwa-t*, *libwa-t*, *labuwa-t*, *lubawa-t*, *labu'a-t*, *luba'a-t*, *lab'a-t*, pl. *lab'ât*, *labuwât*, *lubu'*, *lubû'*, lioness.

(لبى) *labî*, A, INF. *laby*, eat much; — II. INF. *talbiya-t*, perform readily the prescriptions for the pilgrimage; pronounce the words لبيك *labbai-ka*, here I am for your service; obey, respond, accede to.

لبيب *labîb*, pl. *alibbâ'*, gifted with intelligence and skill; man of head and heart; active, persevering; — ة *labîba-t*, a coat without sleeves; upper and front part of anything.

لبيث *labîs*, malicious.

لبيخ *labîẖ*, fleshy;—ة *labîẖa-t*, little bag for musk.

لبيد *labîd*, bag for provender suspended at a horse's neck; male proper name.

لبيس *labîs*, worn-out; dressed; similar, alike.

لبيق *labîq*, ة, intelligent, clever and active; adorned, elegant; — ة *labîqa-t*, coquette.

لبيك *labbai-ka*, see (لبى); — ة *labîka-t*, dish of flour and sour milk or of dates and butter.

لبين *labîn*, fed on milk; — بو لبين

abû lubain, penis; — ة *labîna-t*, having milk in the udder; shirt-front; — ى *lubainā*, daughter of the devil.

(لت) *latt*, U, INF. *latt*, bind tightly together, strap; mix two things by stirring them up; break, pound; scrape; (m.) chatter; pass. be united in friendship; — VII. INF. *inlitât*, be mingled and stirred up; be scraped.

لت *latt*, blow; (m.) idle talk; pl. *lutût*, a drinking-glass with a long neck; — ة *latta-t*, anything paltry, trifle.

(لتا) *lata'*, INF. *lat'*, push on the chest, push back; throw or beat at with a stone; fix the eyes upon; break wind; drop excrement.

لتات *lutât*, anything pounded; — *lattât*, great talker.

لتاح *lutâh*, intelligent, clever.

(لتب) *latab*, U, INF. *latb*, *lutûb*, adhere, stick; stand firm; fasten, strap, lace; put on a dress; pierce; — II. INF. *taltîb*, fasten, strap, lace.

(لتح) *latah*, INF. *lath*, throw pebbles into one's face, blind one's eyes; beat; injure by the evil eye; — *latih*, A, INF. *latah*, be hungry.

لتح *lath*, *latih*, ة *lutaha-t*, لتحان *lathân*, intelligent and skilful; *lathân*, f. *latha*, hungry; —*latah*, hunger.

(لتخ) *latah*, INF. *lath*, throw dirt at, soil; flog so as to tear the skin; wound; flay; — ة *latha-t*, soiling, dirtying (s.); blow.

(لتد) *latad*, I, INF. *latd*, beat with the fist.

(لتز) *lataz*, U, I, INF. *latz*, beat with the fist, box; push aside, drive away.

(لتغ) *latag*, INF. *latg*, beat with the fist; sting, bite; (m.) lisp, speak thickly.

(لتلت) *latlat*, INF. ة, stammer, talk silly things; — *latlata-t*, perjury.

(لتم) *latam*, U, INF. *latm*, pierce a camel's throat with a lance; throw, shoot, dart; beat; wound.

(لتن) *latin*, sweet; — ة *latna-t*, anything indispensable; — *lutunna-t*, hedgehog.

(لث) *lass*, I, INF. *lass*, molest; last several days; stay, remain, abide; mix, mingle; (m.) chat, chatter; — IV. INF. *ilsâs*, molest; stay, abide; — ة *lisa-t*, pl. *-ât*, *lisa-n*, gums; a tree.

(لثا) *lasa'*, INF. *las'*, lap up the contents of a vessel; — ة *lasât*, uvula.

لثام *lisâm*, veil for the mouth and cheeks, comforter.

(لثد) *lasad*, I, INF. *lasd*, pile up side by side.

(لثط) *lasat*, I, INF. *last*, throw; beat slightly; blame slightly.

لثعة *las'a-t*, part of the lip connected with the gums.

(لثغ) *lasig*, A, INF. *lasag*, have an impediment of the tongue and pronounce thickly, as: غ, ل or ى for ر, ث for س.

لثغ *lasag*, ة *lusga-t*, the above fault of pronunciation.

(لثق) *lasiq*, A, INF. *lasaq*, be bedewed, moist; be calm and dewy; — II. INF. *talsîq*, corrupt, spoil; — IV. INF. *ilsâq*, moisten, bedew.

لثق *lasaq*, moisture; — *lasiq*, wet, moist.

لثلاث *laslâs*, ة *laslâsa-t*, sluggish, irresolute; inactive; talker.

لثلث *laslas*, cleave to and molest, obtrude; be weak; retain; be sluggish, irresolute, inactive; chatter, indulge in idle talk; speak unintelligibly; roll (a.) in the dust; — II. INF. *talaslus*, roll (n.) in the dust; dirty one's self; — ة *laslasa-t*, soiling (s.); idle talk.

(لثم) *lasam*, I, INF. *lasm*, stamp the gravel with the hoof; wound the hoof; beat on the nose with

the fist; cover the lower part of the face with the لثام *lisâm*; — *lasîm*, A, INF. *lasm*, kiss; give one a لثام *lisâm*; — II. INF. *talsîm*, cover the lower part of one's face with the لثام *lisâm*; — V. INF. *talassum* (also VIII.), cover one's self with the لثام *lisâm*; wear a comforter; — VI. INF. *talâsum*, kiss one another; — VIII. INF. *iltisâm*, see V.; kiss.

لثم *lasm*, ة, kiss; — ة *lisma-t*, way of wearing the لثام *lisâm*.

(لثو) *lasâ*, U, لثى *lasa*, I, INF. *lasy*, drink slowly; lick out greedily; — *lasî*, A, INF. *lasan*, be wet, moist; flow with gum or resin; — IV. INF. *ilsâ'*, emit gum or resin; — V. INF. *talassî*, gather such.

لثوى *liswiyy*, referring to the gums.

لثى *lasa*, *lasî*, v. see (لثو); — *lasan*, *lasa*, thin resin or gum; dew; moisture; — *lasî*, moist, wet; — *lisan*, pl. of لثة *lisa-t*.

(لج) *lajj* (*lajajtu*, *lajijtu*), I, A, INF. *lajâj*, *lajâja-t*, be unyielding, obstinate; insist upon, carry through with perseverance; molest; — II. INF. *taljîj*, come on the high sea; plunge into the deep; founder, suffer shipwreck; — III. INF. *mulâjja-t*, dispute obstinately with (acc.); — IV. INF. *iljâj*, molest, press; — VIII. INF. *iltijâj*, be deep, deeply furrowed; sound confusedly (voices); — X. INF. *istiljâj*, claim persistently; adhere to one's oath.

لج *lujj*, ة *lujja-t*, pl. *lujâj*, *lijâj*, enormous quantity; immense mass of water; high sea; the deep; abyss of the sea; — ة *lija-t*, INF. of ولج *walaj*, enter, &c.; — *lajja-t*, clamour, tumult, noise; — *lujja-t*, silver; looking-glass, mirror; pupil of the eye.

(لجا) *laja'*, INF. *laj'*, *malja'*, take refuge with (الى *ila*); — لجى *laji'*, id.; — II. INF. *talji'a-t*, force, compel; force to seek refuge; — IV. INF. *iljâ'*=II.; — VIII. INF. *iltijâ'*=I.; ask for one's protection.

لجا *laja'*, refuge, asylum; — ة *laja'a-t*, female frog.

لجاج *lajâj*, ة *lajâja-t*, quarrel, quarrelsomeness, contentiousness; molestation, obtrusiveness; — *lijâj*, quarrel, dispute; hard riding; — *; — *lajjâj*, quarrelsome; obtrusive.

لجاذ *lijâz*, fish-glue; quarrel, dispute.

لجاف *lijâf*, threshold.

لجام *lijâm*, pl. *lujum*, *aljima-t*, bridle, curb; cloth to intercept the menses.

لجان *lijân*, restiveness.

لجاون *lajâwun*, legion (m.).

(لجب) *lajib*, A, INF. *lajab*, cry out, clamour; be agitated (sea); — *lajub*, INF. *lujûba-t*, be exhausted of or abound in milk.

لجب *lajib*, ذو ل *zû lajab*, thundering; numerous and boisterous (army); — ة *lajba-t*, *lijba-t*, *lujba-t*, *lajaba-t*, *lajiba-t*, *lijaba-t*, pl. *lijâb*, ewe without milk.

لجج *lujaj*, pl. of لج *lujj*; — ة *lujaja-t*, quarrelsome; obtrusive.

(لجح) *lujh*, hole in the bottom of a well or in a canal; — *lajah*, running eyes.

(لجذ) *lajaz*, U, INF. *lajz*, eat, consume; graze off the first green food; take but little; lick out a vessel.

(لجز) *lajiz*, ductile, sticky like resin, &c.

(لجف) *lajaf*, I, INF. *lajf*, beat violently; dig a hole for one's self; — II. INF. *taljîf*, dig into the side of a well.

لجف *lajaf*, pl. *aljâf*, well; ditch, pit; dam, weir.

(لجلج) *lajlaj*, INF. ة, chew and turn about in the mouth; repeat

words frequently in the speech;
— II. INF. *talajluj*, id.

(لجم) *lajam*, U, INF. *lajm*, sow;
m.=IV.; — II. INF. *taljim*, rise
to the mouth; — IV. INF. *iljâm*,
bridle a horse; restrain, refrain; — V. INF. *talajjum*, intercept the menses with a cloth;
— VII. INF. *inlijâm*, be bridled;
be restrained, refrained; — VIII.
INF. *iltijâm*, id.

لجم *lujm*, air, atmosphere; also
lajam, *lujam*, frog; — *lajam*,
part of the horse's cheek covered
by the bridle; — *lujum*, pl. of
لجام *lijâm*.

(لجن) *lajan*, U, INF. *lajn*, lick;
(also II.) beat down leaves and
mingle them with oats or flour
for the food of a camel; — *lajin*,
A, INF. *lajan*, stick to, adhere;
lean to.

لجن *lajin*, dirt; — ة *lajna-t*, as-
senting majority.

لجوج *lajûj*, ة *lujûja-t*, quarrelsome;
obtrusive.

لجون *lajûn*, restive; — *.

(لجى), VIII. INF. *iltijâ'*, claim
falsely descent from (الى *ila*).

لجى *lujjiyy*, *lijjiyy*, fathomless
(sea).

لجيفة *lajîfa-t*, door-post.

لجين *lajin*, beaten off leaves for
food; foam in the corners of a
camel's mouth; — *lujain*, silver.

(لح) *laḥḥ*, I, INF. *laḥḥ*, be next
of kin; approach, be near; —
laḥiḥ, A, INF. *laḥaḥ*, have the
eye-lids sticking together; —
IV. INF. *ilḥâḥ*, importune and
ask boisterously; persist in;
be restive; rain continuously;
press the back of an animal;
bring near, approach (a.).

لح *laḥḥ*, nearest degree of relationship.

لحا *liḥâ'*, inner bark, bast; rind,
crust; INF. III. of (لحى); —
liḥan, pl. of لحية *liḥya-t*.

لحادة *luḥâda-t*, grammatical fault.

لحاس *laḥḥâs*, licker, lickerish per-

son, sweet-tooth; — ة *laḥḥâsa-t*,
lioness.

لحاظ *laḥâẓ*, outer corner of the
eye; — ة *liḥâẓa-t*, look, glance;
observation.

لحاف *liḥâf*, pl. *luḥuf*, wrapper;
cover, blanket; woman; armour,
coat of mail.

لحام *liḥâm*, *luḥâm*, solder; *liḥâm*,
soldering; — *laḥḥâm*, butcher,
seller of meat.

لحان *laḥḥân*, ة *laḥḥâna-t*, who pronounces badly, commits frequent errors of language; — ة
laḥâna-t, fault of pronunciation;
— ية *laḥâniyya-t*, faulty pronunciation.

(لحب) *laḥab*, INF. *laḥb*, strike with
the sword; make an impression,
leave a trace; cut lengthwise;
mark out or clear the road;
tread out a path; go straight
on, quickly along; INF. *luḥûb*,
be broad and open (high road);
— *laḥib*, A, INF. *laḥab*, be thin
with old age; —VIII. INF. *iltiḥâb*,
march on the high road.

لحب *laḥb*, open high road; — *laḥib*,
broad and trodden (path).

(لحت) *laḥat*, INF. *laḥt*, beat,
cudgel; peel.

(لحج) *laḥaj*, INF. *laḥj*, beat; hit
in the eye; injure by the evil
eye; take refuge with; — *laḥij*,
A, INF. *laḥaj*, stick in the scabbard; — II. INF. *talḥîj*, represent
falsely, inform falsely; — IV.
INF. *ilḥâj*, VIII. INF. *iltiḥâj*, force
to take refuge, compel.

لحج *luḥj*, corner in the house;
corner of the eye; also *laḥj*,
pl. *alḥâj*, socket of the eye,
cavity, cave; — *laḥij*, narrow,
strait.

(لحد) *laḥad*, INF. *laḥd*, dig a niche
in an older tomb and bury the
dead in it, bury; lean towards;
— II. INF. *talḥîd* id.; — IV.
INF. *ilḥâd*, id.; swerve from the
right way, from faith, become a

heretic; — VIII. INF. *iltiḥâd*, lean to.

لحد *laḥd*, *luḥd*, pl. *luḥûd*, *alḥâd*, lateral grave or niche in a tomb, tomb.

(لحز) *laḥaz*, INF. *laḥz*, set upon, press hard; — *laḥiz*, A, INF. *laḥaz*, be narrow-minded, morose, miserly; — V. *talaḥḥuz*, id.; — VI. INF. *talâḥuz*, say hard things to one another; recite obscure verses to one another.

لحز *laḥiz*, *laḥz*, narrow-minded, miserly.

(لحس) *laḥas*, INF. *laḥs*, eat up the wool; — *laḥis*, A, INF. *laḥs*, *laḥsa-t*, *luḥsa-t*, *malḥas*, lick, lap; — II. INF. *talḥîs*, allow to lick out; — VIII. INF. *iltiḥâs*, receive payment of a debt.

(لحص) *laḥaṣ*, INF. *laḥṣ*, engage in a business; (also II.) know a case well and represent it clearly; — II. INF. *talḥîṣ*, see I.; drive into a corner, press hard; — VIII. INF. *iltiḥâṣ*, force, compel.

لحصان *laḥaṣân*, quick run, swiftness.

(لحط) *laḥaṭ*, sprinkle, moisten; push violently, drive away.

(لحظ) *laḥaẓ*, INF. *laḥẓ*, *laḥaẓân*, look askance at, glance sideways; regard, notice; understand, comprehend; — III. INF. *liḥâẓ*, *mulâḥaẓa-t*, look at attentively, observe, have regard to; be attentive; guard, take care of; — VI. INF. *talâḥuẓ*, look askance at one another, observe, notice, have regard to; be an object of attention and care.

لحظ *laḥẓ*, pl. *alḥâẓ*, outer corner of the eye; eye; look; glance; — ة *laḥẓa-t*, glance, sideward glance; twinkling of an eye, moment.

(لحف) *laḥaf*, INF. *laḥf*, wrap up; lick; — IV. INF. *ilḥâf*, wrap up; put a dress on to, robe; molest, press; — V. INF. *talaḥḥuf*, wrap one's self up; dress (n.); (m.) stay in bed; — VIII. INF. *iltiḥâf* = V.; be dressed.'

لحف *laḥf*, foot of a mountain of moderate height; — *luḥuf*, pl. of لحاف *liḥâf*; — ة *liḥfa-t*, way of wrapping one's self up or dressing.

(لحق) *laḥiq*, A, INF. *laḥq*, *laḥâq*, reach, overtake; catch; pursue; cling to; — INF. *luḥûq*, be thin, slender; — II. INF. *talḥîq*, give or grant according to circumstances; — III. INF. *mulâḥaqa-t*, reach, overtake, catch; — IV. INF. *ilḥâq*, id.; cause to reach; annex, make an addition to; — VI. INF. *talâḥuq*, reach, overtake, catch one another; arrive one after another, succeed one another without interruption; — VIII. INF. *iltiḥâq*, reach, overtake; join with; be added, annexed, affiliated; — X. INF. *istilḥâq*, try to reach, pursue; try to gain, or to annex; appropriate.

لحق *laḥaq*, what follows, joins; pl. *alḥâq*, land sown over after an inundation.

(لحك) *laḥak*, INF. *laḥk*, make to stick fast together, solder; administer medicine to (acc.); — *laḥik*, A, INF. *laḥak*, lick; — III. INF. *mulâḥaka-t*, VI. INF. *talâḥuk*, make to adhere firmly.

لحكا *laḥakâ'*, لحكة *laḥaka-t*, lizard.

(لحلح) *laḥlaḥ*, INF. ة, stop in a place; (m.) remove, change place; — II. INF. *talaḥluḥ* = I.; (m.) relish, find pleasure in.

(لحم) *laḥam*, U, INF. *laḥm*, make firm, work solidly; solder; gnaw a bone; — A, INF. *laḥm*, feed (a.) on meat; — *laḥim*, A, INF. *laḥam*, stick to a place; have an appetite for meat; INF. *laḥm*, be fleshy; — *laḥum*, INF. *laḥâma-t*, be fleshy; have an appetite for meat; eat flesh; — pass. *luḥîm*, be killed; — II. INF. *talḥîm*, make

firm, work solidly; solder; weave; — III. INF. *mulâḥama-t*, join (a.); solder; unite with a family by marriage; — IV. INF. *ilḥâm*, join (a.); solder; have plenty of meat in the house; be fleshy, fat; fight furiously, slaughter; weave the woof; versify; finish; — V. INF. *talaḥḥum*, grow embittered; kill one another, slaughter; be soldered; — VIII. INF. *iltiḥâm*, join, unite, close (n.); form flesh and heal (wound); grow embittered.

لحم *laḥm*, *laḥam*, pl. *liḥâm*, *luḥûm*, *liḥmân*, *luḥmân*, *alḥum*, flesh, meat; pulp; — *laḥim*, pl. *lawâḥim*, carnivorous; greedy after flesh or meat; — ة *laḥma-t*, piece of flesh or meat; — *luḥma-t*, pl. *luḥam*, woof; relationship; skin of the flesh.

(لحن) *laḥan*, INF. *laḥn*, lean to, be well disposed to; talk to one so as to be only understood by him; understand, comprehend; INF. *laḥn*, *laḥan*, *luḥûn*, *laḥâna-t*, *laḥâniya-t*, make faults in reading, pronounce or write false vowels, commit barbarisms; — *laḥin*, A, INF. *laḥan*, understand what has been said; modulate in singing; — II. INF. *talḥîn*, pronounce faultily; notice errors of language, find one to speak ungrammatically; modulate in reading; — IV. INF. *ilḥân*, make one to understand (2 acc.).

لحن *laḥn*, pl. *luḥûn*, *alḥân*, tone, sound, note, accord, melody; modulation; chant; air; singing of a bird; way of speaking; dialect; error of language; meaning of a word; — ة *luḥna-t*, *laḥana-t*, who commits errors in speaking; — *luḥana-t*, who criticises others on this account.

(لحو) *laḥâ*, U, INF. *laḥw*, take off the bast of a tree; insult, vilify; — VIII. INF. *iltiḥâ'*, take off the bast.

(لحوج) *laḥwaj*, INF. ة, represent falsely; inform falsely.

لحوح *luḥûḥ*, a kind of cake.

لحود *laḥûd*, deep; — *.

لحوس *laḥwas*, greedy; — *laḥûs*, lickerish after sweets.

لحوق *luḥûq*, reaching, overtaking (s.); arrival; union.

لحون *luḥûn*, error in speech.

لحوى *liḥawiyy*, referring to the beard or chin.

(لحى) *laḥa*, INF. *laḥy*, take off the bast; blame, rebuke, chide; curse, abase, ruin; — III. INF. *liḥâ'*, *mulâḥât*, dispute with, contend; — IV. INF. *ilḥâ'*, blame; — V. INF. *talaḥḥî*, tie together the ends of the turban beneath the chin and throw them back over the shoulder; — VI. INF. *talâḥî*, dispute with one another; rebuke; — VIII. INF. *iltiḥâ'*, begin to grow (beard); grow a beard, have a beard.

لحى *laḥy*, pl. *alḥî*, *luḥiyy*, chin; rind, bast; — *laḥan*, pl. *alḥî*, *luḥiyy*, places where the beard grows, cheeks and chin; — ة *liḥya-t*, pl. *liḥa-n*, *luḥa-n*, beard.

لحيانى *liḥyâniyy*, long-bearded.

لحيب *laḥîb*, thin in the back.

لحيج *laḥîj*, mendacity and fraud.

لحيجا *luḥaijâ'*, recantation.

لحيزا *luḥaizâ'*, treasure.

لحيظ *laḥîẓ*, equal, similar.

لحيف *laḥîf*, an upper garment.

لحيم *laḥîm*, fleshy, fat; killed; similar; fit.

(لخ) *laḫḫ*, U, INF. *laḫḫ*, run (with tears); speak unintelligibly or barbarously; investigate; — VIII. INF. *iltijâj*, be densely grown; be entangled, complicated, mixed up.

لخاقيق *laḫâqîq*, pl. of لخقوق *luḫqûq*.

لخام *laḫâm*, bones; — ة *laḫâma-t*, fleshiness.

(لخب) *laḥab*, A, U, lie with; box on the ear, beat.
(لخبط) *laḥbaṭ*, INF. ة, mix up, confuse; — ة *laḥbaṭa-t*, confusion, hurly-burly.
لخت *laḥt*, big, corpulent.
(لخج) *laḥij*, A, INF. *laḥaj*, exude impure matter and stick together (eye-lids); — ة *laḥija-t*, sticky.
(لخجم) *laḥjam*, big-bellied; open road.
لخز *laḥz*, sharp knife.
(لخص) *laḥiṣ*, A, INF. *laḥaṣ*, have the upper eye-lid fleshy; be swollen all round (eye); — II. INF. *talḥîṣ*, purify; extract the purest part, the quintessence; sum up, recapitulate; make a report; deliver one's speech distinctly.
لخص *laḥiṣ*, too fleshy.
لخصا *laḥṣâ'*, f. swollen.
(لخع) *laḥi'*, A, INF. *laḥa'*, be relaxed.
(لخف) *laḥaf*, INF. *laḥf*, beat violently; enlarge the mark of an animal (by branding).
لخقوق *luḥqûq*, pl. *laḥâqîq*, hole or rent in the earth.
لخلخانى *laḥlaḥâniyy*, speaking badly.
لخلخة *laḥlaḥa-t*, aromatic ball.
(لخم) *laḥam*, INF. *laḥm*, cut; strike on the face.
لخم *luḥm*, a sea-fish; — ة *laḥma-t*, weariness, heaviness; languidness.
(لخن) *laḥin*, A, INF. *laḥan*, smell offensively; be rank, foul, rotten.
(لخو) *laḥâ*, U, INF. *laḥw*, administer a medicine through the nose.
لخوا *laḥwâ'*, f. of الخى *alḥa*, talkative; a species of eagle.
لخوخ *laḥûḥ*, stained, impure.
(لخى) *laḥa*, I, INF. *laḥy*, administer a medicine through the nose, cause to sneeze; present, bestow upon (acc.);—*laḥî*, A, INF. *laḥan*, be talkative; — III. INF. *ilḥâ'*, *mulâḥât*, befriend.
لخى , لخا *laḥan*, instrument for administering a medicine through the nose.
لخيفة *laḥîfa-t*, murmuring of the water or wind, rustling of a bird, &c.
(لد) *ladd*, U, INF. *ladd*, quarrel, dispute; be quarrelsome; — INF. *ladd*, *ludûd*, prepare or administer the medicine لدود *ladûd*; — II. INF. *taldîd*, disgrace, dishonour; — III. INF. *mulâdda-t*, repel from; — INF. *lidâd*, *mulâdda-t*, dispute or quarrel with;—V. INF. *taladdud*, swerve to the right and left.
لد *lad-u*, *lad*, *lud*, at, by, to, with; — لد *ludd*, pl. of الد *aladd*, quarrelsome, contentious; — ة *lida-t*, INF. of ولد *walad*, birth; birthday; pl. *lidât*, *lidûn*, born at the same time, coeval, contemporary.
لدا *ladâ*=لدى *lada*.
لداد *lidâd*, pl. quarrelsome people.
لداغ *luddâg*, sting, prickle, thorn; —ة *laddâga-t*, biting speech or person.
لدام *lidâm*, patching, mending; patch.
لدانة *ladâna-t*, softness.
(لدح) *ladaḥ*, INF. *ladḥ*, beat slightly with the hand, slap.
لدد *ladad*, quarrel, dispute, contention; disputatiousness.
(لدس) *ladas*, U, INF. *lads*, throw stones at; lick; slap; provide the camel with leathern soles; — IV. INF. *ildâs*, grow green, be verdant.
(لدغ) *ladag*, INF. *ladg*, *taldâg*, bite, sting; hurt by words; — ة *ladga-t*, sting, poisonous bite.
لدغا *ludagâ'*, لدغى *ladga*, pl. of لديغ *ladîg*.
(لدك) *ladik*, A, INF. *ladak*, *ladk*, adhere firmly.
(لدم) *ladam*, I, INF. *ladm*, slap the face; beat her face (woman);

beat flat; patch, patch up; — II. INF. *taldîm*, patch, patch up; solder; — IV. INF. *ildâm*, visit continually (fever); — V. INF. *taladdum*, be torn, worn out; — VIII. INF. *itlidâm*, be disquieted, agitated.

لدم *ladam*, acknowledgment of kinship, family honour; — ة *ladma-t*, piece, part, portion.

(لدن) *ladun*, INF. *ludûna-t*, *ladâna-t*, be soft to the touch; be supple, pliable; — II. INF. *taldîn*, make soft and tender; — V. INF. *taladdun*, abide, stay; make excuses and tarry or delay.

لدن *ladn*, ة, pl. *ludn*, *lidân*, soft, smooth, delicate, tender; supple, pliable; — *ladan*, *ladin*, *ladun*, *ludun*, *ludn-u*, *ladn-i*, at, by, to, with; — ة *ludunna-t*, what is necessary to be done, indispensable.

لدود *ladûd*, adversary; pl. *alidda-t*, medicine to be administered by a tube into the mouth; sore throat; — *.

لدون *lidûn*, pl. of لدة *lida-t*; — ة *ludûna-t*, softness, smoothness, pliancy.

لدى *lada*, at, by, to, with.

لديد *ladîd*, pl. *alidda-t*=لدود *ladûd*; du. *ladîdân*, banks of a river, sides of a valley; the sides of the neck beneath the ears; — ة *ladîda-t*, blooming garden.

لديس *ladîs*, pl. *aldâs*, fleshy.

لديغ *ladîg*, pl. *ludagâ'*, *ladga*, stung by a scorpion, bitten by a snake, hurt by words.

لديم *ladîm*, torn, patched up.

(لذ) *lazz* (for *laziz*), A, INF. *lazâz*, *lazâza-t*, find sweet, agreeable, delightful; enjoy; eat and drink well; be sweet, agreeable, delightful; — II. INF. *talzîz*, make sweet, &c.; delight; give pleasure, enjoyment; — V. INF. *talazzuz*, feel pleasure; enjoy, delight in (ب *bi*, or acc.); — VIII. INF. *iltizâz*=V.; be agreeable, give enjoyment; — X. INF. *istilzâz*, feel pleasure, satisfaction, enjoyment; find pleasant, delightful.

لذ *lazz*, sweet, agreeable, pleasant, delightful; *al-lazz*, sleep; — *luzz*, pl. of لذيذ *lazîz*; — ة *lazza-t*, pleasure, enjoyment, delight, voluptuousness; taste; *al-lazza-t*, wine.

لذاذ *lazâz*, ة *lazâza-t*, enjoyment, pleasure, delight; — *lizâz*, pl. of لذيذ *lazîz*.

لذاع *lazzâ'*, hurting with words, biting, stinging; pungent; liar.

(لذب) *lazab*, U, INF. *luzûb*, stay, abide.

(لذج) *lazaj*, U, INF. *lazj*, drink in sips; importune by asking or begging.

(لذع) *laza'*, INF. *laz'*, burn; hurt by words; brand, cauterise; — V. INF. *talazzu'*, look about to the right and left; — VII. INF. *inlizâ'*, VIII. INF. *iltizâ'*, be injured by fire, burned; feel a burning pain; be hurt by words.

لذع *laza'*, ة *laza'a-t*, cauterisation, mark by branding, stigma; hurt by words; لذعة شمس *laza'a-t šams*, sun-stroke.

لذلاذ *lazlâz*, nimble; *al-lazlâz*, wolf.

(لذلذ) *lazlaz*, INF. ة, be nimble.

لذلك *li-zâlik*, on account of this, therefore.

(لذم) *lazim*, A, INF. *lazm*, please (n.); stick to a place, stay, abide; cause to remain with.

(لذى) *lazî*, A, INF. *lazan*, attend zealously to; remain in a place (ب *bi*).

لذيذ *lazîz*, pl. *luzz*, *lizâz*, sweet, pleasant, delightful; *al-lazîz*, wine.

(لز) *lazz*, U, INF. *lazz*, *lazaz*, *lazâz*, join two things closely together, unite, make to cling together; write in narrow lines; be connected, adhere, stick to; pierce;

m. press hard, molest, jade; — III. INF. *lizâz*, be joined to, united with, adhere to; — IV. INF. *ilzâz*, unite closely; write narrowly; — ة *lazza-t*, extreme tiredness of an overburdened beast.

(لزا) *laza'*, INF. *laz'*, give; fill up; feed well; give birth;— II. INF. *talzi'a-t*, give; feed well; — IV. INF. *ilzâ'*, fill.

لزاب *lazzâb*, ة, alder-tree, a kind of wild cedar.

لزاز *lizâz*, bolt of a door, turn-pike, bar; filled with hatred; energetic, clinging to one's purpose; — *.

لزاق *lizâq*, glue; connection.

لزام *lazâm*, ة *lazâma-t*, necessity; steady perseverance; — *lizâm*, death; upright judge; who has continual commerce with; — *lazzâm*, farmer, tenant.

لزان *lazzân*, broom (plant).

(لزب) *lazab*, U, INF. *luzûb*, adhere firmly; cling to; cohere, be thick and tough; stand firm; be firm, solid; be hard, sterile (year); — *lazib*, A, INF. *lazab*, stick to (ب *bi*); — *lazub*, INF. *lazb*, cohere closely by having their parts interjoined.

لزب *lizb*, narrow path; — *lazib*, pl. *lizâb*, little, few; — ة *lazba-t*, pl. *lazb*, *lazabât*, distress, calamity, famine.

(لزج) *lazij*, U, INF. *lazaj*, *luzûj*, m. *lazaj*, U, be ductile; stretch, extend (n.); be elastic; stick to, adhere.

لزج *lazij*, ductile, elastic; resin-like, sticky; — ة *lazija-t*, who sticks always at home.

لزز *lazaz*, bolt, bar; (m.) molestation, importunity.

(لزق) *laziq*, A, INF. *luzûq*, stick to, adhere; — II. INF. *talzîq*, unite, join (a.), glue together; — IV. INF. *ilzâq*, id.;—VIII. INF. *iltizâq* =I.; cohere.

لزق *lazq*, side; — *lizq*, joining immediately; next neighbour, inseparable companion; — ة *lazqa-t*, poultice, cataplasm.

لزك *lazk*, closing of the edges of a wound.

(لزلز), II. INF. *talazluz*, be moved, agitated, shaken.

(لزم) *lazim*, A, INF. *lazm*, *lazâm*, *luzma-t*, *luzûm*, *luzmân*, *lazâma-t*, be addicted to, persist in, attend to perseveringly; adhere to a place; be inseparable from; be necessary, incumbent, indispensable; follow of necessity; — III. INF. *lizâm*, *mulâzama-t*, attend to steadily and zealously, be inseparable from, cling to, beset; — IV. INF. *ilzâm*, adjoin (a.), associate (a.), impose as a duty; compel; be incumbent upon (acc.); — VIII. INF. *iltizâm*, take upon one's self as a duty; be bound by contract or oath; be responsible; farm; be forced, compelled; embrace; — X. INF. *istilzâm*, demand as a duty or necessary consequence; find necessary or incumbent; — ة *luzama-t*, who constantly clings to a place or person.

(لزن) *lazan*, U, INF. *lazn*, throng together in a narrow space; — *lazin*, A, INF. *lazan*, id.; — VI. INF. *talâzun*, id.

لزوب *luzûb*, dearth, famine.

لزوجة *lazûja-t*, ductility, elasticity, stickiness; sticky substance.

لزوق *lazûq*, poultice, cataplasm, plaster; — * .

لزوم *luzûm*, necessity; necessary connection or consequence; obligation, debt.

لزيز *lazîz*, pl. *lazâ'iz*, breast-bone; لزيز شر *lazîz-u śarr-in*, entirely given to evil.

لزيق *lazîq*, inseparable companion; next neighbour.

(لس) *lass*, U, INF. *lass*, eat; lick out; pluck the grass with the lips.

لساس *lusâs*, first grass-tops.

لساع *lassâ'*, stinging, biting (adj.).

لسان *lisân*, m. f., pl. *lusn, alsun, alsina-t*, tongue; speech, style; ل الحال *lisân al-ḥâl*, what speaks for itself, what the circumstances of the case show; ذو لسانين *ẕû lisânain*, double-dealing, false; ل المزمار *lisân al-mizmâr*, larynx; ل القلزم *lisân al-qalzum*, Red Sea; — *lisân-an*, by word of mouth; — *lassân*, eloquent; — *lussân*, a plant; — ى *lisâniyy*, referring to the tongue, lingual; — ية *lassâniyya-t*, eloquence.

(لسب) *lasab*, A, I, INF. *lasb*, bite; whip;—*lasib*, A, INF. *lasab*, lick; adhere, stick to;—ة *lasba-t*, bite, sting.

(لسد) *lasad*, I, INF. *lasd*,—*lasid*, A, INF. *lasad*, suck, suck out the udder; lick out.

لسس *lusus*, who attend well to camels (pl.).

(لسع) *lasa'*, INF. *las'*, *las'a-t*, sting, bite; hurt by words; depart, set out on a journey;—ة *las'a-t*, sting, bite; stinging speech; — *lusa'a-t*, wicked tongue.

(لسق) *lasiq*, A, INF. *lusûq*, adhere, stick to; INF. *lasaq*, have the lung adhering to the ribs; — IV. INF. *ilsâq*, glue, make stick together; compel to stick to; — VIII. INF. *iltisâq*, stick to; glue.

(لسم) *lasam*, INF. *lisâm*, taste; — *lasim*, A, INF. *lusûm*, adhere, be addicted or devoted to; — INF. *lasam*, grow silent (from weariness); — IV. INF. *ilsâm*, make to taste; silence; make to understand; compel; demand; — X. INF. *istilsâm*, demand, ask for.

(لسن) *lasan*, U, INF. *lasn*, seize or hold one's tongue; get the better of in speaking; abuse violently; sting, bite; — *lasin*, A, INF. *lasan*, be eloquent; — II. INF. *talsîn*, make in the shape of a tongue, linguiform, pointed; allude to; — III. INF. *mulâsana-t*, fight one with words, let one's tongue loose against; — IV. INF. *ilsân*, make linguiform, pointed; be another's mouth-piece.

لسن *lisn*, language, tongue, dialect; — *lusn*, pl. of لسان *lisân* and السن *alsan*, eloquent; — *lasan*, eloquence; *lasin*, pl. *lusn*, eloquent; linguiform, pointed.

(لسو) *lasâ*, U, INF. *lasw*, eat greedily.

لسوب *lasûb*, *lassûb*, to be licked; something, a bit.

لسيع *lasî'*, stung, bitten.

لسيق *lasîq*, inseparable companion.

(لش) *laśś*, U, INF. *laśś*, drive away.

لش *laśś*, sumach; a kind of peas.

(لشلش) *laślaś*, INF. ة, be seized with fear so as to drop excrement; run to and fro from fear.

لشن *laśn*, *laśan*, *laśin*, delicate, smooth, pretty;—*laśan*, support, prop.

(لشو) *laśâ*, U, INF. *laśw*, be abased after elevation;—III. INF. *mulâśât*, suppress, destroy, annihilate; — VI. INF. *talâśî*, id.; (m.) be annihilated, vanish.

(لص) *laṣṣ*, U, INF. *laṣṣ*, do secretly; shut the door; — A, INF. *laṣaṣ*, *laṣâṣ*, *luṣûṣa-t*, *laṣûṣiya-t*, *luṣûṣiya-t*, be a robber; — V. INF. *talaṣṣuṣ*, become a robber, take to robbery; spy out secretly.

لص *laṣṣ*, *liṣṣ*, *luṣṣ*, pl. *luṣûṣ*, *alṣâṣ*, f. ة, pl. *laṣṣât*, *laṣâ'iṣ*, thief, robber.

لصاص *laṣâṣ*, robbery.

لصائص *laṣâ'iṣ*, pl. of لصة *laṣṣa-t*.

(لصب) *laṣib*, A, INF. *laṣb*, stick fast in the scabbard; adhere firmly to the bone; be tight upon the finger.

لصب *liṣb*, pl. *liṣâb*, *luṣûb*, mountain-cleft, pass, valley; — *laṣib*, miserly; a kind of oats.

لصت *laṣt*, *liṣt*, *luṣt*, pl. *luṣût*, robber.

لصص *laṣaṣ*, narrowness of the shoulders, teeth, &c.

(لصغ) *laṣag*, U, INF. *luṣûg*, be dry and stick to the bones (skin of a thin person).

(لصف) *laṣaf*, U, INF. *laṣf*, place in order side by side or pile up; — U, INF. *laṣîf*, shine, flash; — *laṣif*, A, INF. *laṣaf*=(لصغ).

لصف *laṣaf*, caper-tree.

(لصق) *laṣiq*, A, INF. *luṣûq*, adhere, stick to, be closely joined; be devoted to, cling to; — *laṣiq*, A, INF. *laṣaq*, have the lungs adhering to the sides; — II. INF. *talṣîq*, fasten, glue together, join (a.); — III. INF. *mulâṣaqa-t*, cling to; — IV. INF. *ilṣâq*=II.; cause to adhere; — VIII. INF. *iltiṣâq*, adhere, stick to, cohere.

لصق *liṣq*, side; inseparable companion.

لصلص *laṣlaṣ*, INF. ة, move (a.), set in motion.

(لصو) *laṣâ*, U, INF. *laṣw*,—لصى *laṣa*, I, INF. *laṣy*, *laṣî*, A, accuse.

لصوص *luṣûṣ*, ة *luṣûṣa-t*, ية *luṣûṣiya-t*, robbery; — *.

لصيف *laṣîf*, shining, flashing (adj.); glitter, flash.

لصيق *laṣîq*, inseparable companion.

لضلض *laḍlaḍ*, look out to the right and left.

(لضم) *laḍam*, I, INF. *laḍm*, use violence against, press hard; (m.) join two things.

(لضو) *laḍâ*, U, INF. *laḍw*, be experienced, skilful, proficient.

(لضى) *laḍa*, I, INF. *laḍy*, be always at one's heels.

(لط) *laṭṭ*, I, INF. *laṭṭ*, attend zealously to; join, fasten; put the tail between the legs; be unable to get one's money; veil, conceal; shut; — IV. INF. *ilṭâṭ*, deny a debt; repudiate; veil, conceal.

لط *laṭṭ*, pl. *liṭâṭ*, necklace; — ة *laṭṭa-t*, vermicelli.

(لطا) *laṭa'*, INF. *laṭ'*, *luṭû'*,—لطى *laṭi'*, A, INF. *laṭa'*, stick in the ground, be near the ground; be short, dwarfish; cudgel; — ة *laṭât*, place; forehead; weight, burden, load.

لطاط *laṭâṭ*, year of scarcity; — *liṭâṭ*, mountain-summit, mountain-crag; — *.

لطاع *laṭṭâ'*, who licks his fingers.

لطافة *laṭâfa-t*, kindness, benevolence; delicate conduct; loveliness, gracefulness, beauty; subtility; thinness, fineness; pleasantry, wit.

لطام *liṭâm*, boxing (s.).

(لطب) *laṭab*, be dry and stick to the bones.

(لطث) *laṭas̱*, U, INF. *laṭs̱*, slap, beat with anything flat; beat violently; gather (a.); throw at; grieve, put to anxiety.

(لطح) *laṭaḥ*, INF. *laṭḥ*, slap lightly on the back; throw on the ground.

(لطخ) *laṭaẖ*, INF. *laṭẖ*, soil, bespatter; accuse, disgrace; beat; — II. INF. *talṭîẖ*, soil, stain; — V. INF. *talaṭṭuẖ*, be soiled, stained, dishonoured; pollute one's self; — VIII. INF. *iltiṭâẖ*, soil or pollute one's self.

لطخ *laṭiẖ*, uncleanly, dirty, soiled; — ة *laṭẖa-t*, stain; — *luṭaẖa-t*, pl. *luṭaẖât*, idiot, fool.

(لطس) *laṭas*, U, INF. *laṭs*, beat; box on the ear; throw at; beat to pieces.

(لطش) *laṭaś*, U, INF. *laṭś*, give a blow or push, beat; — II. INF. *talṭiś*, have knowledge of (ب *bi*); — ة *laṭśa-t*, blow, push; caprice, humour; mania; stag-gers.

(لطع) *laṭa'*, INF. *laṭ'*, — *laṭi'*, A, lick; kick on the buttocks, beat, cudgel, push; hit; efface; enter (in writing); (m.) set fire to, light and burn; — II. (m.) INF. *talṭî'*, burn in several places; — V. INF. *talaṭṭu'*, VII.

INF. *inliṭâ'*, be burned, receive marks of burning; — VIII. INF. *iltiṭâ'*, lick off.

لطع *laṭ'*, pl. *alṭâ'*, gums; — ة *laṭ'a-t*, wound from burning (m.).

(لطف) *laṭaf*, U, INF. *luṭf*, be near, approach; be kind and friendly towards (ب *bi*, ل *li*); — *laṭuf*, INF. *laṭf*, *laṭâfa-t*, be small, fine, thin, subtle, delicate; behave with delicacy towards, be gracious to (ب *bi*); — II. INF. *talṭîf*, render graceful, delicate, tender; soften, allay, moderate; — III. INF. *mulâṭafa-t*, treat with kindness and benevolence; flatter, cajole, caress; — IV. INF. *ilṭâf*, bestow benefits upon (acc.), deserve well of (ب *bi*); — V. INF. *talaṭṭuf*, show friendliness and kindness; be polite, courteous; flatter, caress; favour; be well up in, contrive; — VI. INF. *talâṭuf*, show one's self benevolent, conciliatory, delicate; be favourable to; — X. INF. *istilṭâf*, find pretty, delicate.

لطف *luṭf*, pl. *alṭâf*, kindness, benevolence, friendliness; help and protection of God; subtlety; also *laṭaf*, bounty, favour; (m.) slight indisposition; بيت اللطف *bait al-luṭf*, wine-house; — ة *laṭafa-t*, present, favour; — ى *luṭfiyy*, brought up with one's own children, adopted.

لطفان *laṭfân*, kind, friendly.

(لطلط) *liṭliṭ*, having strong teeth; old and toothless; decrepit.

(لطم) *laṭam*, I, INF. *laṭm*, beat with the hand, box on the ear; glue, attach, fasten on; — II. INF. *talṭîm*, box the ears violently; — III. INF. *liṭâm*, *mulâṭama-t*, box the ears; — VI. INF. *talâṭum*, box each other's ears; also VIII. INF. *iltiṭâm*, clash (waves); — ة *laṭma-t*, box on the ear; blow; — ى *laṭamiyy*, aromatic.

(لطو) *laṭâ*, U, take refuge on a rock or in a cave.

لطو *luṭû'*, INF. of (لطا); — ة *laṭwa-t*, protected place.

لطوخ *laṭûḫ*, dirt, pollution.

(لطى) *laṭa*, INF. *laṭy*, stick to a place, remain, abide; — *laṭî*, A, INF. *laṭan*, molest, importune; suppose, suspect of.

لطى *laṭî'*, V. see (لطا); — *laṭi'*, dwarfish.

لطيف *laṭîf*, ة, pl. *liṭâf*, graceful, pretty, handsome, elegant; kind, benevolent, friendly; thin, delicate, subtle; — ة *laṭîfa-t*, pl. *laṭâ'if*, anything pretty, exquisite, choice; elegant expression, witty saying, pleasantry; *laṭâ'if*, funny tales, jokes.

لطيم *laṭîm*, pl. *luṭum*, boxed on the ears; beaten; weaned camel-foal; orphan; the last but one (ninth) horse in a race; musk; wave; horse white on one knee; — ة *laṭîma-t*, pl. *laṭâ'im*, musk; perfume-vial; market for perfumes; train of camels laden with perfumes.

(لظ) *laẕẕ*, U, INF. *laẕẕ*, *laẕîẕ*, follow continually, cling to, molest, importune, press hard; drive away; — IV. INF. *ilẕâẕ*, cling to; stay, abide; continue, last.

لظ *laẕẕ*, لظ كظ *laẕẕ kaẕẕ*, لظلاظ *laẕlâẕ*, hard, malignant.

(لظلظ) *laẕlaẕ*, INF. ة, writhe; shake the head angrily; — II. INF. *talaẕluẕ*, id.

لظه *laẕah*, I, INF. *laẕh*, beat with the palm of the hand, slap.

(لظى) *laẕî*, A, INF. *laẕan*, blaze, flare; — II. INF. *talẕiya-t*, stir up the fire so as to blaze; — V. INF. *talaẕẕî*, VIII. INF. *iltiẕâ'*, burn brightly, be flaming, blaze.

لظى *laẕan*, fire, flame; *al-laẕan*, hell-fire.

لظيظ *laẕîẕ*, perseverance.

(لع) *la''*, INF. *la''*, shine; — IV. INF. *il'â'*, produce the plant لعاعة *lu'â'a-t*; — ة *la''a-t*, handsome and chaste.

لعاب *lu'âb*, spittle, saliva, sliver of

children; phlegm, mucus; dew; ل عنكبوت lu'âb 'ankabût, spider-web; ل الشمس lu'âb aś-śams, gossamer; ل النحل lu'âb an-naḥl, honey; — la''âb, who plays much; gambler; — ى lu'âbiyy, mucous, slimy, sticky.

لعاع lu'â', young grass; — ة lu'â'a-t, id.; chicory, endive.

لعان li'ân, ية la'âniyya-t, imprecation, curse excommunication; — *; — ة li'âna-t, reprobateness, depravity.

لعاة la'ât, bitch.

(لعب) la'ab, INF. la'b, salivate, slaver; — la'ib, A, INF. la'b, li'b, la'ib, tal'âb, play, sport, gamble; make sport of, take in; — II. INF. tal'ib, cause or allow one to play; — III. INF. mulâ'aba-t, play, sport, converse with (acc.); make game of, cheat; — IV. INF. il'âb, slaver, salivate; make or allow to play; — V. INF. tala''ub, play repeatedly; — VI. INF. talâ'ub, make sport of.

لعب la'b, li'b, la'ib, play, game, sport, conversation; — li'b, la'ib, given to playing or gambling; — ة la'ba-t, lu'ba-t, pl. lu'ab, game, sport; toy, puppet, plaything; everybody's butt; image in the pupil of the eye; — li'ba-t, way of playing; — lu'aba-t, given to playing or gambling.

(لعث) la'is̱, A, INF. la'as̱, be slow and clumsy.

(لعثم) la's̱am, INF. ة, tarry, hesitate, delay; stop short (in speaking), hinder; — II. INF. tala's̱um, id.

(لعج) la'aj, A, INF. la'j, stir the heart; pain; burn.

(لعذم) la'ẓam, INF. ة = (لعثم); — II. INF. tala'ẓum, eat, devour, swallow.

(لعز) la'az, INF. la'z, lick the young one; beat on the chest; lie with.

(لعس) la'as, INF. la's, — m. لعوس la'was, INF. ة, bite; (m.) chew; — la'is, A, INF. la'as, have dark red, blackish lips; — V. INF. tala''us, tala''wus, be chewed; — ة la'sa-t, chewing (s.).

(لعص) la'iṣ, A, INF. la'aṣ, be difficult; be greedy, voracious.

(لعض) la'aḍ, INF. la'ḍ, take up with the tongue.

(لعط) la'aṭ, INF. la'ṭ, brand or cauterise on the throat; hit; wound; injure by the evil eye; hasten; go to the pasture; lick; (m.) withdraw one's favour from (acc.).

لعط la'ṭ, pl. al'âṭ, tattoo; — ة lu'ṭa-t, evil eye, injury by it; tattooed lines; (m.) being forsaken by God; lack of rain.

(لعف) la'if, A, INF. la'af, detest, hate; — IV. INF. il'âf, V. INF. tala''uf, drink blood; look angrily around and be ready to attack.

(لعق) la'iq, A, INF. la'qa-t, lu'qa-t, lick (ل اصبعه la'iq aṣba'a-hu, die); scrape off the dish; — II. INF. tal'iq, make to lick up.

لعق la'iq, lickerish; — ة la'qa-t, lu'qa-t, what can be licked up at a time.

لعل la'l, ruby (Pers.); — la'al, la'alla, perhaps, may be (followed by the pronominal affixes).

لعلاع la'lâ', coward.

(لعلع) la'lâ', INF. ة, break (a.); = II.; — II. INF. tala'lu', shine; let the tongue hang out; be famished, exhausted and sad; pass. of I.

لعلع la'la', pl. la'âli', mirage; wolf; — ة la'la'a-t, utter exhaustion from hunger; sadness, depression.

لعن la'an, INF. la'n, curse, imprecate evil upon; expel, excommunicate; — II. INF. tal'în, punish, torment, torture; — III. INF. li'ân, mulâ'ana-t, break

forth in imprecations against, curse; — VI. INF. *talâ'un*, curse one another; — VIII. INF. *ilti'ân*, be cursed.

لعن *la'n*, curse, imprecation, expulsion, excommunication; blame, rebuke; — *la'anna*, perhaps; — ة *la'na-t*, pl. *la'anât*, *li'ân*, imprecation, curse; — *lu'ana-t*, pl. *lu'an*, who curses much.

(لعو), IV. *al'a*, INF. *il'â'*, produce the grass لعاع *la'â'*; — V. INF. *tala''î*, become thick, consistent (honey); go to fetch the grass لعاع *la'â'*.

لعو *la'w*, pl. *li'â'*, malicious and mean; glutton; ة, greedy; — ة *la'wa-t*, bitch; — also *lu'wa-t*, extreme hunger.

لعوب *la'ûb*, who plays much; great gambler; frivolous, flighty (woman); — ة *la''ûba-t*, game, play, sport, conversation or its object.

لعوس *la'was*, greedy; wolf; — *la'was*, INF. ة, bite.

لعوض *la'waḍ*, jackal.

(لعوق) *la'waq*, INF. ة, make haste.

لعوق *la'ûq*, licked; electuary; — *la'waq*, ignorant.

لعيب *li''îb*, who plays much; great gambler.

لعيعة *la'î'a-t*, bread of millet.

لعين *la'în*, cursed, accursed, execrable, expulsed, excommunicated; transformed into a monster; scarecrow; wolf; cursing (adj.).

لغا *lagan*, tone, sound, voice, noise.

لغاز *laggâz*, who speaks in riddles; calumniator, slanderer.

لغاف *laggâf*, boaster, braggart.

(لغام) *lugâm*, foam (from the mouth of a camel).

لغاوس *lagâwis*, pl. of لغوس *lagwas*.

(لغب) *lagab*, U, A, INF. *lagb*, *lagûb*, *lugûb*, be extremely tired; — A, INF. *lagb*, spoil, injure; tell an untruth; lick out, lap up; — *lagib*, A, INF. *lagab*, — *lagub*, be extremely tired; — II. INF. *talgîb*, IV. INF. *ilgâb*, V. INF. *talaggub*, tire exceedingly, jade.

لغب *lagab*, hair in the neck.

لغثون *lugsûn*, pl. *lagâsîn*, inner walls of the nose.

(لغد) *lagad*, INF. *lagd*, lead the camels on the right way and keep them in order; prick the ears; prevent, hinder; — VIII. INF. *iltigâd*, prevent from taking.

لغد *lagd*, لغدود *lugdûd*, لغديد *ligdîd*, flesh on the throat and beneath the chin and ears.

(لغز) *lagaz*, U, INF. *lagz*, alter, change the shape of a thing, distort, pervert; — IV. INF. *ilgâz*, obscure the meaning of a speech; speak in riddles; make or propose riddles; allude obscurely to (عن *'an*).

لغز *lugz*, *lagaz*, *lugaz*, *luguz*, pl. *algâz*, riddle; mystery; *lugz*, *lagz*, *lagaz*, pl. *algâz*, labyrinth; hole of a lizard, mouse, &c., burrow.

(لغط) *lagaṭ*, INF. *lagṭ*, *ligâṭ* (also II.), be clamorous, noisy; INF. *lagṭ*, *lagîṭ*, coo; — II. INF. *talgîṭ*, see I.

لغط *lagṭ*, *lagaṭ*, pl. *algâṭ*, clamour, noise, turmoil.

(لغف) *lagif*, A, INF. *lagaf*, form into balls and eat; — III. INF. *mulâgafa-t*, meet, encounter; kiss; — IV. INF. *ilgâf*, associate with thieves; — ة *lugfa-t*, mouthful, morsel.

لغفا *lugafâ'*, pl. of لغيف *lagîf*.

(لغلغ) *laglag*, INF. ة, stammer; steep the bread in broth and eat it.

(لغم) *lagam*, INF. *lagm*, foam; tell uncertain things abroad; — V. INF. *talaggum*, anoint the lips.

لغم m. *lugm*, pl. *lugûm*, *lugûma-t*, mine; springing of mines and instrument for it.

لغمجى *lugumjî*, *lagimjî*, miner.

(لغن) *lagn*, youthful ardour; — *lugn* (also لغنون *lugnûn*, pl. *la-*

gânîn), flesh of the palate and throat; nerve of the ear; cartilage of the ear; ear; — *laganna*, perhaps.

لغة *luga-t*, pl. *lugât*, *lugûn*, *luga-n*, language, dialect; word, phrase; dictionary.

(لغو) *lagâ*, U, INF. *lagw*, speak; speak vainly, indulge in idle talk; bark; coo; be deceived in one's hopes, disappointed; — لغى *lagî*, A, INF. *lagan*, *lâgiya-t*, *malgât*, make mistakes, commit errors (in speaking); talk rubbish; INF. *lagan*, be addicted to (ب *bi*); — IV. INF. *ilgâ'*, exclude, eliminate, put away, eschew; abolish; pass by or over, forget, disregard, neglect; deceive one's hopes; — VI. INF. *talâgî*, talk to one another; — X. INF. *istilgâ'*, listen attentively.

لغو *lagw*, idle talk; anything worthless; talk, conversation; topic of conversation; — ة *lagwa-t*, topic; idiom, brogue.

لغوس *lagwas*, pl. *lagâwis*, wolf; glutton; thief, robber; tender grass.

لغون *lugûn*, pl. of لغة *luga-t*.

لغوى *lagwa*, silly talk; — *lugawiyy*, *lagawiyy*, referring or belonging to a language, an idiom; etymological; lexicographic; lexicographer; literal meaning.

لغى *lagan*, idle talk; error of speech; anything worthless; — *lugan*, pl. of لغة *luga-t*; — ة *lugayya-t*, slight mistake in speaking; trivial word, triviality.

لغيث *lagîs*, mixed; mixture.

لغيزا *lugaizâ*, لغيزى *lugaizā*, riddle, enigma.

لغيف *lagîf*, pl. *lugafâ'*, friend, comrade; associate of thieves, concealer of stolen goods; — ة *lagîfa-t*, thick stiff pap or broth.

(لف) *laff*, U, INF. *laff*, be densely grown; wrap up, envelop, roll or fold up; join (a.); belong to; come to close quarters; assemble (n.); bend, double up (n.); — II. INF. *talfîf*, wrap up carefully or entirely; — IV. INF. *ilfâf*, cover with, envelop in one's own clothes; put the head under the wings; — V. INF. *talaffuf*, wrap one's self up; — VIII. INF. *iltifâf*=V.; be luxuriant and densely entwined.

لف *laff*, folding, enveloping, wrapping up (s.); fold, envelope; round-about way; ceremonies; — *liff*, pl. *lufûf*, mixed crowd, band; assemblage; *liff*, *laff*, pl. *alfâf*, densely-grown trees and gardens; — *luff*, pl. (لفا *laffâ'*, f.) of الف *alaff*, engaged in complicated business, &c.; — ة *laffa-t*, *liffa-t*, dense orchard; *laffa-t*, filled pie.

(لفا) *lafa'*, INF. *laf'*, *lafâ'*, peel, bark, shell, skin, disperse the clouds; beat; repel, turn off, refuse; prevent, avert; slander; pay a debt entirely or partially; — لفى *lafî*, A, INF. *lafa'*, survive, remain; — IV. INF. *ilfâ'*, preserve alive; — VIII. INF. *iltifâ'*, peel, bark, skin.

لفا *lafâ'*, trifle, small part.

لفاح *luffâḥ*, mandrake.

لفاظ *lifâz*, *lufâz*, herbs for seasoning; — *laffâz*, eloquent; — ة *lufâza-t*, pl. *-ât*, *lafâz*, what is expectorated; utterance, word; remainders, scraps.

لفاع *lifâ'*, wrapper, covering; veil; a garment for women.

لفافة *lifâfa-t*, pl. *lafâ'if*, swaddling-band; bandage; socks; envelope, covering.

لفام *lifâm*, cloth covering the mouth and nose.

لفائف *lafâ'if*, pl. of لفافة *lifâfa-t*.

لفاية *lafâya-t*, m. foreigners, the fluctuating population of a city; colony; INF. of (لفى).

(لفت) *lafat*, I, INF. *laft*, turn, roll

about in the mouth; fold; turn from (a. and n.); INF. *laft, lift*, bark a tree; — V. INF. *talaffut*, turn repeatedly (n.), turn to gaze at; — VIII. INF. *iltifât*, turn round after; turn friendly towards, have care and regard for (الى *ila*).

لفت *lift*, rape, turnip, cole-rape; half; side, edge; inclination towards; — ة *lafta-t*, turning aside; side-glance (حسن اللفتة *ḥusn al-lafta-t*, benevolence); fold; tour, trip; round-about way; — ية *liftiyya-t*, a dish of rapes or turnips.

(لفث), X. *istalfas̱*, INF. *istilfâs̱*, entice out of a hiding-place.

(لفج) *lafj*, misery, lowliness; — IV. INF. *ilfâj*, be poor, miserable (also X.); force one to take refuge with strangers; — X. INF. *istilfâj*, see I.

(لفح) *lafaḥ*, INF. *lafḥ*, *lafaḥân*, burn, scorch; — INF. *lafḥ*, inflict a slight stroke with the sword; (m.) eat and swallow greedily; — ة *lafḥa-t*, what is greedily swallowed at one gulp.

(لفخ) *lafaḫ*, INF. *lafḫ*, beat on the head, box on the ear.

(لفط) *lufṭ*, rape, turnip.

(لفظ) *lafaẓ*, I, INF. *lafẓ*, cast out, expectorate, utter; — V. INF. *talaffuẓ*, utter, pronounce, speak; — VII. INF. *inlifâẓ*, be pronounced, uttered.

لفظ *lafẓ*, ة, pl. *alfâẓ*, word, utterance, pronunciation; — ى *lafẓiyy*, pronounced, uttered, by word of mouth.

(لفع) *lafa'*, INF. *laf'*, cover the head; veil; — II. INF. *talfî'*, id.; — V. INF. *talaffu'*, be covered; wrap one's self up; ignite, blaze; — VIII. INF. *iltifâ'*, be covered with a garment (ب *bi*).

(لفق) *lafaq*, I, INF. *lafq*, sew the two ends of a cloth together; hem, seam; be not able to obtain one's wish; let the hawk fly in vain; — *lafiq*, A, INF. *lafaq*, begin, commence; — II. INF. *talfîq*, sew two pieces together; join, unite (a.), dispose one's speech well; interpolate, falsify by interpolation, hatch lies; (m.) perform in an illusory manner, bungle, daub; — V. INF. *talaffuq*, reach, catch; — VI. INF. *talâfuq*, be gathered again and in good circumstances (dispersed tribe); — VII. INF. *inlifâq*, be sewn together; be hemmed, seamed.

لفق *lifq*, ة *lafqa-t*, hem of a garment, border of a cloth.

(لفلف) *laflaf*, INF. ة, swallow greedily; wrap up, envelop; gather together from all sides; — II. INF. *talafluf*, be enveloped, wrap one's self up.

لفلف *laflaf*, لفلاف *laflâf*, weak.

(لفم) *lafim*, A, INF. *lafam*, wrap one's self up in the لفام *lifâm* (also V.); — I, pierce the partition of the nose to insert a ring; — V. INF. *talaffum*, see I.

(لفو) *lafâ*, U, INF. *lafw*, wrong; — لفى *lafa*, I, INF. *lifâya-t*, return; visit frequently, frequent; — II. INF. *talfiya-t*, invite frequently; — IV. INF. *ilfâ'*, find; — VI. INF. *talâfî*, mend; make up for a loss.

لفى *lafi'*, see (لفا).

لفيظ *lafîẓ*, uttered, pronounced.

لفيف *lafîf*, wrapped up, under an envelope, enclosed; mixed; mixed crowd; intimate friend; verb with two weak letters.

(لق) *laqq*, U, INF. *laqq*, beat with the hand, slap; (m.) lick, lap; (m.) be loose, rickety; (m.) rumble.

لقا *liqâ'*, meeting (s.), encounter; being opposite, in front of (s.); combat; meeting (adj.); pl. of لقوة *laqwa-t*; — ة *laqât*, meeting (s.); middle of the road.

لقاح *laqâḥ*, fecundation; male

blossom of the palm-tree; — *liqâḥ*, sperm of the stallion; milch-camel; pl. of لقحة *liqḥa-t* and لقوح *laqûḥ*; — *laqqâḥ*, who fecundates.

لقاط *liqâṭ*, opposite, in front of; — *luqâṭ*, gleanings; — ة *luqâṭa-t*, id.; offal, anything worthless.

لقالق *laqâliq*, pl. of لقلاق *laqlâq*, لقلق *laqlaq*.

لقانة *laqâna-t*, لقانية *laqâniyya-t*, quick comprehension.

لقاية *liqâya-t*, meeting, finding (s.).

(لقب) *laqab*, pl. *alqâb*, nickname, title of honour; word; — II. INF. *talqîb*, give a nickname, a title; — V. INF. *talaqqub*, have or assume a nickname.

(لقث) *laqis̠*, A, INF. *laqs̠*, take off everything quickly; — *laqus̠*, INF. *laqs̠*, mix; — II. INF. *talqîs̠*, mix.

(لقح) *laqiḥ*, A, INF. *laqḥ*, *laqaḥ*, *laqâḥ*, conceive, grow big with young; throw, throw down; — II. INF. *talqîḥ*, fecundate the female palm-blossom; make big with young; (m.) vaccinate; throw, throw down; — IV. INF. *ilqâḥ*, fecundate, make big with young; — V. INF. *talaqquḥ*, appear big with young without being so; (also VIII.) be thrown down, stretch one's self down at full length; — VIII. INF. *iltiqâḥ*, see V.; be made fruitful; — X. INF. *istilqâḥ*, want fecundation.

لقح *luqqaḥ*, pl. of لقوح *laqûḥ*; — ة *liqḥa-t*, pl. *liqaḥ*, *liqâḥ*, big with young; milch camel (also *laqḥa-t*); suckling woman; a kind of eagle; a kind of crow; pl. *liqâḥ*, soul.

(لقز) *laqaz*, U, INF. *laqz*, beat one with the hand on his chest.

(لقس) *laqas*, U, I, INF. *laqs*, overwhelm with reproaches, blame, scold; dispose for; catch with the mouth; — *laqis*, A, INF. *laqas*, incline passionately towards; have aversion, disgust, loathe; — II. INF. *talqîs*, keep back, delay (a.); — V. INF. *talaqqus*, be kept back, delayed (m.); delay (n.); ripen slowly and late.

لقس *laqs*, itch, scab; — *laqis*, who reviles, ridicules.

(لقش) *laqaś*, U, INF. *laqś*, talk with; — III. INF. *malâqaśa-t*, converse with.

لقش *laqś*, conversation; — *luqś*, core of a fir-tree.

(لقص) *laqaṣ*, INF. *laqṣ*, burn the skin; — *laqiṣ*, A, INF. *laqaṣ*, be narrow, strait; loathe; — VIII. INF. *iltiqâṣ*, take.

لقص *laqiṣ*, narrow, strait; talkative; sinful.

(لقط) *laqaṭ*, U, INF. *laqṭ*, gather up, pick from the ground, glean; patch; (m.) overtake in running, seize, take hold of; — INF. *liqṭ*, escape the sickle (ear); — II. INF. *talqîṭ*, gather from all sides (a.); glean; (m.) catch, seize; — III. INF. *liqâṭ*, *mulâqaṭa-t*, stand opposite, in front of; (m.) reach, overtake, catch, seize; butt with the horns; — V. INF. *talaqquṭ*, pick up from all sides; be picked up, gathered; (m.) be seized; — VI. INF. *talâquṭ*, reach, catch; butt at one another with the horns; — VIII. INF. *iltiqâṭ*, pick up from the ground, gather.

لقط *laqaṭ*, pl. *alqâṭ*, what is picked up, gleaned; gold-dust in a mine; a little, trifle; — ة *luqṭa-t*, *luqaṭa-t*, pl. *laqaṭ*, what is picked up, found, masterless; stray animal; foundling; (m.) pl. *laqâ'iṭ*, string, small cord.

لقطا *luqaṭâ'*, pl. of لقيط *laqîṭ*.

(لقع) *laqa'*, INF. *laqa'ân*, hurry by, pass; — INF. *laq'*, suck; throw away; hit; injure by the evil eye; bite; get the better of (in words); — III. INF. *mulâqa'a-t*, try to get the better of;

— v. INF. *talaqqu'*, utter inconsiderate words; — VIII. INF. *iltiqâ'*, change, fade.

(لقف) *laqif*, A, INF. *laqf*, *laqafân* (also v., VIII.), catch, catch and swallow; (also VIII.) comprehend quickly; — INF. *laqaf*, fall in, decay; — II. INF. *talqîf*, swallow; — v. INF. *taqalluf*, see I.; swallow eagerly one's words; — VIII. INF. *iltiqâf*, see I.

لقف *laqf*, quickness in seizing or comprehending; لقف ثقف *laqf saqf*, *laqif*, quick of comprehension; — *laqaf*, pl. *alqâf*, wall of a well; — *laqif*, tumbled in, sunk.

لقلاق *laqlâq*, pl. *laqâlîq*, stork; sound, noise, tumult; chatter; لقلاق بقلاق *laqlâq baqlâq*, talkative, garrulous.

(لقلق) *laqlaq*, INF. ة, keep up a rattling noise (as a stork); produce a tremulous sound; move the jaws tremulously and put out the tongue (snake); smack with the tongue; (m.) bespatter; — II. INF. *talaqluq*, move (n.); (m.) bespatter one's self.

لقلق *laqlaq*, tongue; pl. *laqâliq*, stork; — ة *laqlaqa-t*, clapping of wings; rattle of a stork; smacking with the tongue.

(لقم) *laqam*, U, INF. *laqm*, bar the way; — *laqim*, A, INF. *laqm*, swallow, devour, eat hastily; (m.) cut bread; cut into slices or pieces; — II. INF. *talqîm*, make to swallow; (m.) feed birds; (m.) pour the ground coffee into the boiling water; — IV. INF. *ilqâm*, make to swallow; — v. INF. *talaqqum*, be cut into small pieces; — VIII. INF. *iltiqâm*, swallow quickly.

لقم *laqam*, middle of the road; — ة *luqma-t*, *laqma-t*, pl. *luqam*, morsel, mouthful.

لقمان *luqmân*, name of a sage and composer of fables.

(لقن) *laqin*, A, INF. *laqn*, *laqna-t*, *laqâna-t*, *laqâniya-t*, excel by quick comprehension, comprehend quickly; — II. INF. *talqîn*, make to understand, instruct; teach; insinuate, inspire; dictate; — IV. INF. *ilqân*, learn quickly by heart; — v. INF. *talaqqun*, comprehend quickly; learn; (m.) allow one's self to be advised or inspired by.

لقن *laqn*, ة *laqna-t*, quick comprehension; — *liqn*, what one leans upon, support, pillar, protection; side, edge, border, coast, shore; — *laqan*, pl. *alqân*, wash-basin; — *laqin*, *liqn*, quick of comprehension.

(لقو) *laqâ*, A, INF. *laqw*, afflict with the disease لقوة *laqwa-t*; — ة *laqwa-t*, distortion of the corner of the mouth by apoplexy; convulsions of the face; ذو اللقوة *zû al-laqwa-t*, a species of eagle; *laqwa-t*, *liqwa-t*, pl. *liqâ'*, *alqâ'*, female eagle; nimble, active woman.

لقوح *laqûḥ*, pl. *luqqaḥ*, *liqâḥ*, big with young; female of an animal with young ones.

لقونة m. *laqûna-t*, لاقونة *lâqûna-t*, cement made of resin and ground brick.

(لقى) *laqî*, A, INF. *luqan*, *liqy*, *luqy*, *liqâ'*, *liqâ'a-t*, *laqâ'a-t*, *liqâya-t*, *liqyân*, *liqyâna-t*, *luqyân*, *luqyâna-t*, *luqya-t*, *liqiyy*, *luqiyy*, *laqât*, *tilqâ'*, meet, encounter, perceive, find; (m.) be made solidly, stand wear and tear, last; (m.) lean upon; — II. INF. *talqiya-t*, hold out to, show, explain; — III. INF. *liqâ'*, *mulâqât*, go to meet one, meet, encounter; — IV. INF. *ilqâ'*, throw on the ground, throw away, fling; propose, offer; impute, ascribe; lean one thing against another; put upon one's

back, burden with; — v. INF. *talaqqî*, meet, encounter; go to meet with, receive with; receive or learn from; — VI. INF. *talâqî*, meet face to face; — VIII. INF. *iltiqâ'*, go to meet, meet; meet one another; be found, be to be found; — X. INF. *istiqlâ'*, catch what is thrown down; lie or throw one's self on one's back; fall back.

لقى ***laqan***, pl. *alqâ'*, what is thrown **away as** worthless, refuse; — ***luqan***, meeting, encounter; — ***laqiyy***, one met with; what is found or met with; du. *laqiyyân*, two people who meet; abject, bad; — ة *luqya-t*, meeting (s.).

لقيان *liqyân*, *luqyân*, ة *liqyâna-t*, *luqyâna-t*, meeting, encounter.

لقيس (m.) *liqqîs*, who or what makes itself to be waited for; ripening late.

لقيط *laqîṭ*, pl. *luqaṭâ'*, picked from the ground, found; foundling; — ة *laqîṭa-t*, m. f. utterly abject, despised.

لقيف *laqîf*=لقف *laqif*.

لقيم *laqîm*, what is swallowed at one gulp; mouthful.

(لك) *lakk*, U, INF. *lakk*, give one a blow with the fist, push back; loosen the flesh from the bone; — VIII. INF. *iltikâk*, be pressed together, crammed, straitened; throng (n.), concentrate (n.); make mistakes in speaking; (m.) be involved in unpleasant affairs, be unsafe, waver.

لك *lakk*, mixture; flesh; a plant for dyeing goat-skins (*lukk*, its juice); lac, sealing-wax; pl. *lukûk*, a hundred thousand; — ة *lakka-t*, blow with the fist.

(لكا) *laka'*, INF. *lak'*, beat with a scourge; throw on the ground; pay one the whole of a debt; — لكى *laki'*, A, INF. *laka'*, stay, abide; addict one's self entirely to; — V. INF. *talakku'*, make excuses, prevaricate; desist; tarry, hesitate.

لكا *lakkâ*, leather dyed with لك *lukk*.

لكاع *lakâ'i*, stupid, vile (woman); wretch; — ة *lakâ'a-t*, dirt, vileness.

لكاف *likâf*, saddle-cloth; pack-saddle.

لكاك *likâk*, pl. *lukak*, pression, pressure; firm of flesh.

لكام *lakkâm*, very hard.

لكانة *lukâna-t*, sausage.

(لكث) *lakas̱*, U, INF. *laks̱*, beat; over-burden; — *lakis̱*, A, INF. *lakas̱*, have ulcers in the mouth; adhere, stick to.

(لكح) *lakaḥ*, INF. *lakḥ*, beat with the fist; (m.) lick; — II. INF. *talkîḥ*=I.; — V. INF. *talakkuḥ*, be licked.

(لكد) *lakad*, U, INF. *lakd*, beat with the hand; kick; — *lakid*, A, INF. *lakad*, adhere visibly; — V. INF. *talakkud*, cohere; be firm of flesh.

لكد *lakad*, sesame-seed.

(لكز) *lakaz*, U, INF. *lakz*, beat with the fist on the chest or chin, box; push back, repel; — V. INF. *talakkuz*, criticise, censure, satirize.

لكش *lakuś*, U, INF. *lakś*, fix the price, defend its transgression; beat the beast of burden; — VII. INF. *inlikâś*, be fixed; be beaten; — ة *lakśa-t*, blow.

(لكض) *lakaḍ*, U, INF. *lakḍ*, beat with the fist.

(لكع) *laka'*, INF. *lak'*, sting; — *laki'*, A, INF. *laka'*, adhere, stick to; INF. *laka'*, *lakâ'a-t*, be dirty and vile.

لكع *lik'*, dwarf; — *luka'*, vile, dirty, miserly; servile; stupid; slave, villain, rogue; child; young of an animal, foal; dirt; — ة *luka'a-t*, mare.

لكك *lukak*, pl. of لكاك *likâk*.

(لكف) m. *lakaf*, U, make every

effort to move one to consent; — II. INF. *talkîf*, id.

(لكلك) *l ukluk*, thick, short.

لكلك *laklak*, give repeated blows with the fist.

(لكم) *lakam*, U, INF. *lakm*, beat with the fist on the chest and push back; — III. INF. *mulâkama-t*, beat with the fist; — VI. INF. *talâkum*, beat one another, box; — ة *lakma-t*, blow with the fist.

(لكن) *lakin*, A, INF. *lakan*, *lukna-t*, *lukûna-t*, *luknûna-t*, speak with an impediment, speak Arabic indifferently, express one's self with difficulty.

لكن (for لاكن) *lâkin*, *lâkinn-a*, but, yet, however (followed by the pronominal affixes); — *lakan*, pl. *alkân*, basin; — ة *lukna-t*, لكونة *lukûna-t*, difficulty of pronunciation.

(لكى) *lakî*, A, INF. *lakan*, be entirely devoted or addicted to; be greedy.

لكى *li-kai*, لكى ان *li-kaian*, لكى ما *li-kai mâ*, in order that, so that; لكيلا *li-kai-lâ*, lest; — *lakiyy*, entirely devoted to, addicted.

لكيع *lakî'*, dirty, filthy, vile.

لكيك *lakîk*, pl. *likâk*, closely joined, compact.

(لم) *lamm*, U, INF. *lamm*, gather (a.), amass; concentrate; mend, put into good condition; alight, dwell; — IV. INF. *ilmâm*, alight, dwell; come, arrive, befall; — VII. INF. *inlimâm*, be gathered; — VIII. INF. *iltimâm*, gather, assemble, unite (n.); alight, dwell; visit.

لم *lam*, not; — *li-ma*=لما *li-mâ*, why? what for? — ة *lamma-t*, fate; calamity; violence; slight madness; — *limma-t*, pl. *limâm*, locks of hair, curls; also *luma-t*, equal, comrade, coeval; company; leader, chief.

(لما) *lama'*, INF. *lam'*, set hand to; take all, steal; cast one's look upon; — IV. INF. *ilmâ'*, steal secretly; deny one's right; — V. INF. *talammu'*, cover; — VIII. INF. *iltimâ'*, chose or take for one's self; pass. change (n.).

لما *la-mâ*, certainly not; — *li-mâ*, why? for what reason? — *lammâ*, when, after; not yet, never.

لماج *lamâj*, very little.

لماذا *li-mâ-zâ*, why then?

لماز *lammâz*, لمزة *lumaza-t*, reviler, slanderer.

لماظ *lamâz*, light food, a little food; — ة *lamâza-t*, remains of food in the mouth.

لماع *lammâ'*, shining brightly, flashing; — *; — ة *lammâ'a-t*, tract where a mirage is seen.

لمام *limâm*, pl. of لمة *limma-t*; *limâm-an*, rarely; — *lammâm*, gatherer, collector.

(لمج) *lamaj*, U, INF. *lamj*, eat with the sides of the mouth; — V. INF. *talammuj*, taste but little food, take a luncheon; — ة *lumja-t*, luncheon; breakfast.

(لمح) *lamaḥ*, INF. *lamḥ*, look stealthily at, catch a glance; spy at; — INF. *lamḥ*, *lamaḥân*, *talmâḥ*, shine, glitter, sparkle; — II. INF. *talmîḥ*, speak obscurely, hint at; — VIII. INF. *iltimâḥ*, cast a stealthy glance at.

لمح *lamḥ*, glance; moment; truth, evidence; — ة *laḥma-t*, glance, wink; glitter; *lamḥat-an lamḥat-an*, at every moment; pl. *malâmiḥ*, resemblance; features which remind of the father; — *luḥma-t*, pl. *lumaḥ*, shining spot or place.

(لمخ), III. *lâmaḥ*, INF. *limâḥ*, *mulâmaḥa-t*, box one's ears.

(لمد) *lamad*, I, INF. *lamd*, submit to, be obsequious.

لمدان *lamdân*, submissive, obsequious.

(لمذ) *lamaẕ*, U, INF. *lamẕ*=(لمج).

(لمز) *lamaz*, U, I, INF. *lamz*, wink at, revile, abuse, slander; beat, push.
لمز *lamz*, calumny; — ة *lamza-t*, wink, hint; — *lumaza-t* = لماز *lammâz*.
(لمس) *lamas*, U, I, INF. *lams*, touch, feel; seek, inquire after; — III. INF. *mulâmasa-t*, touch, feel; lie with; — V. INF. *talammus*, seek and inquire for repeatedly;— VIII. INF. *iltimâs*, beg instantly, entreat.
لمس *lams*, feeling, touch; sense of touch or feeling.
(لمش) *lamś*, toying; futility.
(لمص) *lamaṣ*, U, INF. *lamṣ*, dip the fingers into honey, &c. and lick it off; pinch; — II. INF. *talmîṣ*, stick to; glue (m.).
(لمط) *lamaṭ*, U, INF. *lamṭ*, be moved, restless, agitated; totter; pierce; — VIII. INF. *iltimâṭ*, take away, fail to pay a debt.
(لمظ) *lamaẓ*, U, INF. *lamẓ*, roll the tongue over (also V.); taste food; pay one's debt to (acc.); — V. INF. *talammuẓ*, see I.; dart forth the tongue (snake); — VIII. INF. *iltimâẓ*, throw quickly into one's mouth.
(لمع) *lama'*, INF. *lam'*, *lama'ân*, shine, flash; glitter, sparkle; — II. INF. *talmî'*, shine very brightly, flash; make to shine, to flash; — IV. INF. *ilmâ'*, snap the fingers, beckon; steal; — VIII. INF. *iltimâ'*, rob; flash, gleam.
لمع *lam'*, ة, flash, brightness; — *lum'a-t*, pl. *limâ'*, *luma'*, withering parts of a plant; part of the body not wetted in washing; isolated quotations from an author.
لمعان *lam'ân*, shining, flashing (adj.); — *lama'ân*, shining, flashing (s.).
(لمق) *lamaq*, I, INF. *lamq*, beat with the palm of the hand, slap; look at; efface, blot out; — II. INF. *talmîq*, (m.) do a work superficially, slur over; — V. INF. *talammuq*, taste some food.
(لمك) *lamak*, U, INF. *lamk*, knead dough.
(لملم) *lamlam*, INF. ة, gather, get together; round; wish, desire, crave for; — II. INF. *talamlum*, be gathered.
لملم *lamlam*, numerous.
لملوم *lamlûm*, troop.
لمم *lamam*, pardonable sins; slight madness, craziness; — *.
لمن *li-man*, for whom? to whom? for whose sake? on whose account?
(لمو) *lamâ*, U, INF. *lamw*, take all.
(لمى) *lama*, I, INF. *lamy*, have dark lips; — *lamî*, A, INF. *laman*, id.
لميا *lamyâ'*, f. of المى *alma*, having dark lips, dark brown, &c.
لن *lan*, by no means, not at all.
(لهّ) *lahh*, U, INF. *lahh*, smooth the hair and make it glossy.
له *leh*, Poland; — *la-hu*, to him.
لها *la-hâ*, to her; — *luhâ'*, number, quantity, multitude; — ة *lahât*, pl. *lahawât*, *lahayât*, *luhiyy*, *lihiyy*, *lah-an*, *lihâ'*, uvula.
لهاب *lihâb*, ة *lihâba-t*, pl. of لهب *lihb*; *lihâb*, pl. of لهبان *lahbân*; — *luhâb*, ة *luhâba-t*, flame; thirst.
لهاث *lahâṡ*, *luhâṡ*, burning thirst; *luhâṡ*, agony.
لهاد *luhâd*, hiccough; sigh.
لهاف *lihâf*, لهافى *lahâfâ*, pl. of لهفى *lahfâ*.
لهام *luhâm*, immense army.
(لهب) *lahib*, A, INF. *lahb*, *lahab*, *luhâb*, *lahîb*, *lahabân*, flame, blaze; INF. *lahab*, suffer from intense thirst; — IV. INF. *ilhâb*, make the fire to blaze; — V. INF. *talahhub*, flare up; — VIII. INF. *iltihâb*, id.; get inflamed (parts of the body).
لهب *lahb*, *lahab*, flaming, blazing (s.); *lahab*, flame without smoke;

redness; — *lihb*, pl. *lihâb*, *lihâba-t*, *luhûb*, *alhâb*, mountain-rent, ravine; pass; steep precipice; — ة *luhba-t*, thirst; shining of the flame; bright whiteness.

لهبان *lahbân*, f. لهبى *lahbā*, pl. *lihâb*, burning, blazing (adj.); violently thirsty; — *lahabân*, blazing (s.); heat; thirst.

(لهث) *lahas̱*, INF. *lahs̱*, *luhâs̱*, let the tongue hang out from thirst or tiredness; be out of breath; (m.) fetch breath, breathe; — *lahis̱*, A, INF. *lahas̱*, be thirsty; — VIII. INF. *iltihâs*, let the tongue hang out.

لهث *lahas̱*, thirst; — ة *luhs̱a-t*, thirst, weariness.

لهثان *lahs̱ân*, thirst; f. لهثى *lahs̱ā*, thirsty.

(لهج) *lahij*, A, INF. *lahaj*, be addicted to; set one's mind upon, long for; love passionately; speak of the object of one's love; — II. INF. *talhîj*, place a luncheon before (acc.); — IV. INF. *ilhâj*, addict one's self to; pass. *ulhij*, be given to.

لهج *lahij*, addicted to, infatuated with, in love; — ـة *lahja-t*, *lahaja-t*, tip of the tongue; tongue; voice, tone; speech; — *luhja-t*, luncheon.

(لهجم) *lahjam*, broad cup; broad road; — II. *talahjum*, be distinct and broad; be passionately addicted to.

(لهد) *lahad*, INF. *lahd*, oppress; jade; beat, push.

(لهذم) *lahẓam*, INF. ة, cut; — II. INF. *talahẓum*, id.; eat.

لهذم *lahẓam*, pl. لهاذم *lahâẓim*, sharp.

(لهز) *lahaz*, INF. *lahz*, mix with people, have intercourse with; also II. INF. *talhîz*, strike one with the fist on the chest or chin.

لهزمة *lihzima-t*, pl. *lahâzim*, projecting part of the nether jaw below the ear; — *lahzam*, INF. ة, cut this part off.

(لهس) *lahas*, INF. *lahs*, lick; throw one's self greedily upon the food; — III. INF. *mulâhasa-t*, throw one's self greedily upon and push others aside.

لهسم *luhsum*, pl. *lahâsim*, narrowness of a stream.

(لهط) *lahaṭ*, INF. *lahṭ*, beat with the palm of the hand; aim; shoot an arrow; (m.) swallow greedily.

(لهع) *lahiʻ*, A, INF. *lahaʻ*, be obliging and accommodating; draw out the corners of the mouth in speaking.

لهع *lahiʻ*, obliging, accommodating.

(لهف) *lahif*, A, INF. *lahaf*, regret deeply, bemoan; be grieved and agitated; be out of breath; — II. INF. *tahlîf*, sigh, call out يا لهف *yâ lahf-a*; — IV. INF. *ilhâf*, be greedy after (ل *li*); — V. INF. *talahhuf*, bewail a loss, bemoan; long and sigh for (الى *ila*); — VIII. INF. *iltihâf*, blaze; grow excited (horse).

لهف *lahf*, regret, pity; يا لهف *yâ lahf-a*, *yâ lahf-i*, oh! alas! يا لهفه *yâ lahfa-hu*, how unfortunate he is! يا لهفى عليك *yâ lahfî ʻale-ka*, how I pity you!

لهفان *lahfân*, f. لهفى *lahfā*, pl. *lahâfā*, *lihâf*, sighing (adj.); unfortunate, unhappy, worthy of pity, deplorable.

(لهق) *lahaq*, INF. *lahq*, be very white, shine brightly; — *lahiq*, A, INF. *lahaq*, id.

لهق *lahaq*, *lahiq*, ة, entirely white; *lahiq*, pl. *lihâq*, white bullock; brownish camel.

(لهله) *lahlah*, INF. ة, weave the cloth thin; — II. INF. *talahluh*, seek for a little food.

لهله *lahlah*, cloth thin of thread and loosely woven; — *luhluh*, ة *luhluha-t*, pl. *lahâlih*, plain with a mirage.

(لهم) *lahim*, A, INF. *lahm*, *laham* (also V. and VIII.), swallow at

one gulp ; — IV. INF. *ilhâm*, make one swallow; inspire; — V. INF. *talahhum*, VIII. INF. *iltihâm*=I.; — X. INF. *istilhâm*, ask or pray for inspiration, advice, patience.

لهم *lihm*, pl. *luhûm*, old; — *lahim*, *luham*, greedy, voracious; — *lihamm*, getting the lead in a race; liberal; wise; ocean.

(لهن), II. *lahhan*, INF. *talhîn*, bring a present from a journey (also IV.); place a luncheon before; — IV. INF. *ilhân*, see I.; — ة *luhna-t*, present brought from a journey; luncheon.

(لهو) *lahâ*, U, INF. *lahw*, *luhuww*, be pleased with, pass away the time, toy, be wanton; — INF. *luhiyy*, *lahyân*, get over the loss of a thing, forget; — لهى *lahî*, A, INF. *lahan*, like, love, enjoy a thing (ب *bi*); console one's self for a loss, forget it (عن *'an*); — II. INF. *talhiya-t*, make one forget a loss; be careless about (عن *'an*); amuse, divert; — III. INF. *mulâhât*, id.; — IV. INF. *ilhâ'*, occupy, engross; delight; call to diversion; turn from, avert; fill the funnel of a mill; — V. INF. *talahhî*, get over a loss; mind a thing no longer; occupy one's self with (ب *bi*); — VI. INF. *talâhî*, amuse one's self, enjoy one's self; — VIII. INF. *iltihâ'*, be engrossed with a thing so as to forget another; amuse one's self with; toy.

لهو *lahw*, pastime; jest; diversion; wantonness; toy, plaything; (m.) dialect; — ة *lahwa-t*, *luhwa-t*, pl. *luhan*, what the miller throws into the funnel of a mill, grist; two hands full of gold or silver, 1,000 pieces; costly present.

لهوات *lahawât*, pl. of لهاة *lahât*.

(لهوج) *lahwaj*, INF. ة, boil the meat imperfectly; perform precipitately, slur over a work; — II. INF. *talahwuj*=I.; be underdone.

(لهوق) *lahwaq*, INF. ة, boast, be vainglorious.

لهوى *lahwiyy*, uttered by the uvula.

لهى *lahî*, v. see (لهو); — *luhan*, pl. of لهوة *lahwa-t*; — *lehiyy*, Pole; — ة *luhya-t*, costly present.

(لهيب) *lahîb*, blaze, flaring of the fire; glow, heat; passion, ardour of love; inflammation.

لهيد *lahîd*, tired; — ة *lahîda-t*, soup, broth.

لهيف *lahîf*, ة, pl. *lihâf*, grieved, sorrowful, sad, sighing; who has been wronged; out of breath.

لهيم *lahîm*, *luhaim*, fate, death; — *luhaim*, kettle; ام ل *umm luhaim*, calamity; — *lihhîm*, swift race-horse.

لو *lau*, if; لوان *lau-anna*, perhaps, may be that; — ة *lawwa-t*, ugliness of face; — *luwwa-t*, a fragrant wood.

لوا *liwâ'*, winding (s.), bend; pl. *alwiya-t*, flag, standard, banner; small province; — *lawwâ'*, a bird; — ة *lau'a-t*, pudenda; anything shameful, shame, disgrace.

لواب *lu'âb*, thirst; — *luwâb*, id.; spittle.

لواح *luwâḥ*, thirst; — *lawwâḥ*, scorching, blackening.

لواذ *liwâẕ*, refuge.

لواز *lawwâz*, seller of almonds.

لوازم *lawâzim*, ات *lawâzimât*, requisites, wants; perquisites, pl. of لازمة *lâzima-t*.

لواص *lawâṣ*, honey; honey-cake.

لواصب *lawâṣib*, deep narrow valleys.

لواط *liwâṭ*, ة *liwâṭa-t*, sodomy, pæderasty; — *lawwâṭ*, sodomite.

لواطف *lawâṭif*, the short ribs.

لواف *lawwâf*, carpet-maker; spinner.

لواق *lawâq*, a little, a small quantity.

لواقن *lawâqin*, abdomen.

لوالك *lawâk*=لواق *lawâq*.

لوالب *lawâlib*, pl. of لولب *laulab*.

لوام *lu'âm*, feathering of an arrow; necessity, need, count; — *law-wâm*, who blames much; — *luwwâm*, pl. of لائم, censurer.

لواى *liwây*, standard, banner; — ة *liwâya-t*, flag-staff.

لوايا *lawâyâ*, pl. of لوية *lawiyya-t*.

(لوب) *lâb*, U, INF. *luwâb*, *lawa-bân*, be thirsty, stand thirsting around the water without being able to get properly to it; — II. mix or anoint with the perfume ملاب *malâb*.

لوب *lu'ub*, *lûb*, *laub*, thirst; — ة *lûba-t*, Libya; Ethiopia; Ethiopian, negro; tract with black stone; — ى *lûbiyy*, لابى *lâbiyy*, Libyan, Ethiopian, negro.

لوبا *lûbâ*, لوبيا *lûbîyâ*, لوبية *lûbiya-t*, bean.

(لوت) *lât*, U, INF. *laut*, answer what one has not been asked for, conceal; لات حين, it is no time now for (oblique case).

(لوث) *lâs*, U, INF. *laus*, wrap the turban round one's head; go around; roll about in the mouth; turn in the fat; take refuge with; stick always at home; — II. *talwîs*, prevent, hinder; soil; — V. INF. *talaw-wus*, be soiled, polluted, befouled; befoul one's self; — VIII. INF. *iltiwâs*, be entangled, complicated.

لوث *laus*, ة *lausa-t*, dirt, mud; — *lûsa-t*, excitement, agitation, impetuosity; laziness, languidness; stupidity; fleshiness.

(لوج) *lâj*, U, INF. *lauj*, turn about in the mouth; — II. INF. *talwîj*, deviate, turn aside from the road, swerve.

(لوح) *lah*, U, INF. *lauh*, appear, lower, shine, lighten, flash; seem; — INF. *lauh*, *lûh*, *luwâh*, *luwûh*, *lawahân*, be thirsty; INF. *lauh* (also II.), change one's colour, disfigure; scorch, embrown; — II. see I.; make to flash; hold out bread to a dog; scorch, make swarthy; begin to ripen; — IV. INF. *ilâha-t*, appear; shine; shrink from; — VIII. INF. *iltiyâh*, suffer from thirst.

لوح *lauh*, ة, pl. *alwâh*, board, slab, slate to write upon; plank; wing of a door; shoulder-blade; also لوح *lûh*, air, atmosphere; — *lûh*, *lu'ûh*, thirst.

لوحش الله *lauhaś al-lâh*, God forbid! well done! bravo!

(لوخ) *lâh*, U, INF. *lauh*, mix; — VIII. INF. *iltiyâh*, get mixed.

(لود) *lawid*, A, INF. *lawad*, be perverse, corrupt, defiant, refractory.

(لوذ) *lâz*, U, INF. *lauz*, *lawâz*, *liwâz*, *luwâz*, *liyâz*, take for shelter or cover; take refuge with; be under one's protection; surround; — III. INF. *liyâz*, *mu-lâwaza-t*, take for shelter and refuge, flee to (ب *bi*); — IV. INF. *ilâza-t*, surround.

لوذ *lauz*, pl. *alwâz*, asylum; bend of a valley; mountain-chain.

لوذع *lauza'*, لوذعى *lauza'iyy*, ingenious, witty; clever.

(لوز) *lâz*, U, INF. *lauz*, take refuge with (الى *ila*, ب *bi*); be under one's protection, depend on, belong to; become free, escape; eat; — II. INF. *talwîz*, fill with almonds.

لوز *lauz*, ة, almond; almond-tree; tonsil, parotid gland; confectionery of almonds; ل الهند *lauz al-hind*, quince.

لوزينج *lauzînaj*, لوزية *lauziyya-t*, confectionery of almonds.

(لوس) *lâs*, U, INF. *laus*, be fond of dainties, sweetmeats, &c.; turn about in the mouth; taste food.

(لوش) m. *lâś*, U, INF. *lauś*, be excessively tired and out of breath; be unable to move on; — II. INF. *talwîś*, id.; tire to the utmost, put out of breath.

(لوص) *lâṣ*, U, INF. *lauṣ*, peep through chinks, &c.; deviate, turn aside from the road, swerve; (m.) grow weary, become impatient.

لوص *lauṣ*, tooth-ache; pain in the ears; sore throat; — ة *lauṣa-t*, pain in the hips; sciatica; (m.) weariness, ennui, impatience.

(لوط) *lâṭ*, U, I, INF. *lauṭ*, *laiṭ*, be in one's mind; bring together; smear, coat with loam, &c.; be a sodomite, pæderast; prevent, hinder, turn from (a.); — III. INF. *mulâwaṭa-t*, commit pæderasty with;—VIII. INF. *iltiyâṭ*, shoot at;—also X. INF. *istilâṭa-t*, claim unjustly as one's son.

لوط *lûṭ*, Lot; — ى *lûṭiyy*, sodomite; bandit.

(لوظ) *lâẓ*, U, INF. *lauẓ*=(لاظ).

(لوع) *lâ'*, U, INF. *lau'*, take hold of and cause to fall sick (love); change one's colour, scorch; INF. *lau'a-t*, feel sick from fright, grief, &c.; be ill; INF. *lau'*, *lu'û'*, be cowardly, perverse, avaricious; — II. INF. *talwî'*, cause one to suffer, weaken;—V. INF. *talawwu'*, feel unwell, suffer pain; — VIII. INF. *iltiyâ'*, burn with love; be depressed, saddened; — ة *lau'a-t*, love-pain; heart-sickness; passion; sorrow; illness.

(لوغ) *lâg*, U, INF. *laug*, roll about in the mouth and throw out.

(لوف) *lâf*, U, INF. *lauf*, eat, chew.

لوف *lûf*, a plant, dragon's-wort.

(لوق) *lâq*, U, INF. *lauq*, soften; slap; put wool into the ink-flask; — II. INF. *talwîq*, butter a dish; (m.) distort, curve.

لوق *lauq*, stupidity; — ة *lauqa-t*, incurvation, distortion.

(لوك) *lâk*, U, INF. *lauk*, turn about in the mouth and chew; chew slightly; attack one's honour.

لولا *lau-lâ*, if not, unless; may be followed by the pronominal suffixes, as: لولاهُ *lau-lâ-hu*, unless he, &c.; — *laulâ'*, calamity, misfortune, loss; — ة *laulât*, INF. of (لولى).

لولب *laulab*, pl. *lawâlib*, tube of an alembic; tube, canal; spire, screw; (m.) spiral staircase; — لولبى *laulabî-y*, spiral, screw-formed.

(لولق) m.;—II. INF. *talauluq*, make sport of.

لولو *lu'lu'*, ة, pl. *la'âli'*, *la'âlî*, pearl, jewel; — ة *lu'lu'a-t*, doe; — ى *lu'lu'iyy*, pearl-coloured; dealer in pearls.

لولوان *lu'lu'ân*, pearl-coloured.

لولى *laula*, INF. ة, make one a governor.

(لوم) *lâm*, U, INF. *laum*, *lauma-t*, *malâm*, *malâma-t*, blame, rebuke, reproach, scold; — II. INF. *talwîm*, blame violently; — III. INF. *liwâm*, *mulâwama-t* = I.; — IV. INF. *ilâma-t* = II.; do anything blameworthy, deserve blame;—V. INF. *talawwum*, wait, tarry, delay (n.); — VI. INF. *talâwum*, reproach one another; — VIII. INF. *iltiyâm*, be blamed, rebuked; — X. INF. *istilâma-t*, show one's self blameworthy.

لوم *laum*, blame, rebuke, reproach; fault, transgression; — *lu'm*, avarice, meanness, vice; — *luwwam*, pl. of لائم *lâ'im*, censurer, &c.; — ة *lauma-t*, blame, reproach; best honey; — *lûma-t*, who is accused, defendant; expectation, delay; — *luwama-t*, who finds fault with others, censurer; reproach.

لوما *laumâ'*, blame, reproach; — *lu'amâ'*, pl. of لئيم *la'îm*.

لومان *lu'mân*, who deserves blame; pl. of لئيم *la'îm*.

لومى *laumā*, blame, rebuke, re proach.

لون *laun*, pl. *alwân*, colour; exterior, form, shape; kind, sort,

species ; — II. *lawwan*, INF. *talwîn*, colour ; — V. INF. *talawwun*, be coloured ; be of many kinds, vary, change, be fickle ;— X. *ilwann*, INF. *ilwinân*, be coloured.

(لوه) *lâh*, U, INF. *lauh*, *lawahân*, shine and undulate (mirage) ; create.

(لوى) *lawa*, I, INF. *layy*, *luwiyy*, bend, turn to the right or left, incline ; twist ; heed, mind ; desist ; grow twenty years old ; INF. *layy*, *liyy*, *liyân*, delay the payment of a debt, deny a debt ; — INF. *layy*, *layân*, conceal from (عن *'an*) ; — *lawî*, A, INF. *lawan*, turn (n.), bend (n.), incline (n.), be bent or crooked, make a bend ; be partial to ; waver ; suffer from colic ; — II. INF. *talwiya-t*, bend &c. much (a.) ; turn the head ; — III. INF. *liwâ'*, join with, make common cause with (مع *ma'*) ; — IV. INF. *ilwâ'*, bend, turn, twist (a.) ; bend or turn the head ; turn the conversation to another topic ; delay a creditor ; give a sign with ; — V. INF. *talawwî*, be twisted ; turn, bend (n.) ; writhe (n.), move, stir (n.) ; — VII. INF. *illiwâ'*, id. ; incline more to one side ; be or grow perverse ; — VIII. INF. *iltiyâ'*=VII. ; be bent ; grow too difficult for (على *'ala*) ; desist from (عن *'an*).

لوى *liwan*, *liwa*, pl. *alwiya-t*, *alwâ'*, bend, curve ; pl. of لية *layya-t* ; — *luwan*, anything vain, futile ; — *lawiyy*, withered ; — *lawwiyy*, referring to the particle لو *lau*, conditional ; — ة *lawiyya-t*, pl. *lawâyâ*, food kept for anybody.

لى *lî*, to me ; — *layy*, winding, bending, twisting (s.) ; folds ; — *luyy*, pl. of الوى *alwa*, bent backwards, &c. ; — ة *layya-t*, pl. *liwa-n*, bend, fold, twist (ل قلب *layya-t qalb*, palpitation) ; woman ; relationship ; — *al-liyya-t*, aloes-wood.

(ليا), IV. *alya'*, INF. *ilyâ'*, be slow.

ليا *liyâ'*, a kind of vetch ; — *layyâ'*, f. of الوى *alwa*, bent backwards, &c.

لياح *layâḥ*, *liyâḥ*, of a pure white ; morning.

لياذ *liyâẓ*, ة *liyâẓa-t*, refuge.

لياط *liyâṭ*, advantage, profit, usury ; loam, cement ; dung ; pl. of ليطة *lîṭa-t* ; — *layyâṭ*, active man.

لياق *layâq*, perseverance ; vast grass-plot ; — *liyâq*, flame, heat ; — ة *liyâqa-t*, appropriateness, fitness ; what is befitting, beseeming ; decency ; elegance ; worthiness, merit ; aptitude, capability ; prudence.

ليالى *layâlî*, pl. of ليل *lail* and ليلى *laila*.

ليام *li'âm*, pl. of لئيم *la'îm* ; — ة *liyâma-t*=لوم *lu'm*.

ليان *layân*, softness ; pleasantness ; — *liyân*, gentleness ; INF. of (لين) and (لوى) ; — * .

ليايل *layâyil*, pl. of ليل *lail*.

(ليت) *lât*, I, INF. *lait*, prevent, hinder, avert ; (also IV.) diminish ; deceive, wrong ; — IV. INF. *ilâta-t*, see I.

ليت *laita*, يا ليت *yâ laita*, if only ! would that ! (may be followed by an accusative or the pronominal suffixes) ; ليت شعرى , if I but knew or had known ; ليت و لعل *laita wa la'alla*, if and but, excuses, subterfuges.

(ليث) *laiṡ*, pl. *luyûṡ*, lion ; strong capable man ; a kind of spider ; — *lîṡ*, a plant ; (also *layyiṡ*) dense grass ; pl. of اليث *alyaṡ*, strong, courageous ; — II. *layyaṡ*, and pass. *luyyiṡ*, be like a lion ; perform great deeds ; — V. INF. *talayyuṡ*, id.

(ليز) *lâz*, I, INF. *laiz*, flee, seek refuge.

(ليس) *laisa*, not to be, not to have been, governing the acc. of the predicate; followed by a pronoun in the acc.=except, as: ليسك *laisa-ka*, ليس اياك *laisa iyyâ-ka*, except thee.

ليس *lîs*, pl. of اليس *alyas*, courageous, &c.; — *layas*, boldness, courage; carelessness, negligence; — II. m. *layyas*, INF. *talyîs*, coat or cement a wall; white-wash; fasten on, glue to; — VI. INF. *talâyus*, be of a good disposition.

(ليص) *lâṣ*, I, INF. *laiṣ*, go aside, deviate; (also IV.) shake in order to pull out; — IV. INF. *ilâṣa-t*, see I.; ask for a thing (عن *'an*) from (acc.).

(ليط) *lâṭ*, I, INF. *laiṭ*, accurse; wound, harm, injure; befit, beseem.

ليط *laiṭ*, *lîṭ*, colour; — *lîṭ*, skin, rind, crust; temper, bodily constitution; — ة *lîṭa-t*, pl. *lîṭ*, *liyâṭ*, *alyâṭ*, reed; lance; bow; temper.

ليطان *laiṭân*, Satan.

(ليع) *lâ'*, I, INF. *laya'ân*, be weary and sullen; INF. *lai'*, be cowardly, timorous, perverse.

(ليغ) *lâg*, I, INF. *laig*, beg, request, demand (2 acc.).

(ليف) *lâf*, I, INF. *laif*, eat; — II. INF. *talyîf*, have many and strong fibres.

ليف *lîf*, fibres, especially of the palm-tree, &c.

ليفس *liyafs*, bold, courageous.

(ليق) *lâq*, I, INF. *laiq*, befit, beseem; fit well; care for; preserve carefully; cling to, keep by; take refuge with (ب *bi*); I, INF. *laiq*, *lîqa-t*=IV.; — IV. INF. *ilâqa-t*, provide the ink-flask with fresh cotton impregnated with ink; — VIII. INF. *iltiyâq*, be entirely devoted and cling faithfully to; — X. INF. *istilâqa-t*, find fit, appropriate, beseeming; — ة *lîqa-t*, cotton or raw silk impregnated with ink; loam, cement.

ليل *lail*, ة, pl. *layâl-in*, *layâlî*, *layâyil*, night; *al-laila-t*, last night; ليلتئذ *lailata'iẕ-in*, in that very night; ذات ليلة *ẕât-a lailat-in*, one night; — *lail*, female bustard and her young; — III. *lâyal*, INF. *mulâyala-t*, implore one's protection for a night, make a compact for a night.

ليلا *li'allâ*=لان لا *li-ann lâ*, lest; — *lailâ'*, f. of اليل *alyal*, long and dark; — ة *lailât*, night.

ليلى *laila*, pl. *layâl-in*, *layâlî*, fragrance of wine; a female proper name; ام ليلى *umm laila*, red wine; — *lailiyy*, nightly, nocturnal.

لئم *li'm*, *lîm*, concord, peace; — *luyyam*, pl. censurers, accusers.

ليمون *laimûn*, *lîmûn*, lemon, citron.

(لين) *lân*, I, INF. *lain*, *liyân*, be or grow soft, tender, delicate; be of a gentle disposition; — II. INF. *talyîn*, soften (a.); pacify; purge; — III. INF. *liyân*, *mulâyana-t*, treat gently and kindly; — IV. INF. *ilâna-t*, *ilyân*=II.; — V. INF. *talayyun*, soften (n.); calm down (n.); — X. INF. *istilâna-t*, find or deem soft and delicate.

لين *lain*, softness, delicacy, gentleness; soft, delicate, tender, gentle, kind, supple, pliable; — *lîn*, softness, tenderness, delicacy; (حرف اللين *ḥarf al-lîn*, soft consonant); ة, pl. *liyân*, best kind of palms; — *layyin*, ة, pl. *-ûn*, *alyinâ'*, soft, tender, delicate; tanned; gentle, sociable; — ة *laina-t*, leathern cushion; — ة *lîna-t*, softness; effeminacy; — ى *lainiyy*, ة, soft consonant.

(ليه) *lâh*, I, INF. *laih*, be covered, veiled; be high, sublime.

ليوان *lîwân*, pl. *lawâwîn*, vestibule with columns, portico, anteroom.

لين ة *luyûna-t*, softness, tenderness, delicacy.

لييل *luyail*, ية *luyailiya-t*, short night.

لئيم *la'îm*, pl. *li'âm*, *lu'amâ'*, *lu'mân*, abject, vile, cowardly, niggardly; pl. *al'âm*, *li'âm*, equal, similar.

م

م *m*, as a numerical sign=40; abbreviation for Sunday and the month of *Muḥarram*; — *ma*, in composition for ما *mâ*.

ما *mâ*, which, what, whatever, all that which; how, how much! as long as; what? not; — *mâ'* (for ماء), pl. *miyâh*, *amwâh*, water; fluid, juice, sap; sperm; gloss, brightness (ما الوجه *mâh al-wajh*, serenity of the face, honour, perspiration).

مآبر *ma'âbir*, pl. of مئبر *mi'bar*, ة, large needle, &c.

مآذن *ma'âẕin*, pl. of مئذنة *mi'ẕana-t*, minaret, tower.

مآرين *ma'ârîn*, pl. of مئران *mi'rân*, hiding-place of the game.

مآزر *ma'âzir*, pl. of مئزر *mi'zar*, veil, &c.

مآزيب *ma'âzib*, pl. of مئزاب *mi'zâb*, aqueduct, &c.

مآل *ma'âl*, return, INF. of (اول).

مآلى *ma'âlî*, pl. of مئلاة *mi'lât*, cloth round the waist of mourning women.

مآويد *ma'âwîd*, calamities.

مآب *ma'âb*, pl. *ma'âwib*, place which contains, to which one returns continually; reference; resort; hearth, focus; resting-place, station; return.

مآباة *ma'bât*, refusal, denial; f. of مأبى *ma'bā*.

مأبد *ma'bid*, place, habitation, dwelling.

مأبض *ma'biḍ*, pl. *ma'âbiḍ*, hollow of the knee, inner side of the elbow.

مأبلة *ma'bala-t*, place full of camels.

مأبور *ma'bûr*, ة, stung; suspected; (f.) fecundated.

مأبى *ma'bā*, f. *ma'bât*, abominable; — *ma'âbiyy*, ة, pestilential.

مابين *mâ-bain*, between, among; interval.

ماتع *mâti'*, long; preponderating, sinking (scale of a balance); tightly twisted; excellent.

مأتم *ma'tam*, pl. *ma'âtim*, calamity; mourning, mourning assembly, gathering of the mourning-women.

ماتن *mâtin*, real author.

ماتة *mâtta-t*, pl. *mawâtt*, honour, authority, consideration; reason, cause, occasion; means to obtain favour.

مأتونا *ma'tûnâ'*, pl. of اتان *itân*, *atân*, she-ass.

مأتى *ma'tā*, appearance, aspect; opposite side, place which one comes from; place of meeting, appointment; what is accessible or attainable; — *ma'tiyy*, patient of اتى *ata*, coming to pass, arriving, happening.

مأثاة *ma'sât*, calumny, slander.

مأثد *ma'sid*, scout, spy.

مأثرة *ma'sara-t*, *ma'sura-t*, what leaves a trace, glorious deed, exploit, feat; eminent performance; memorial; tower; greatness, glory, honour.

ماثل *mâsil*, effaced; — ة *mâsila-t*, shining, giving light; lampstand, chandelier.

ماثم *ma'sam*, ة *ma'sama-t*, pl. *ma'âsim*, sin, wrong; also *ma'sim*, punishment.

ماثور *ma'sûr*, patient of (اثر), chosen, &c.; recorded; remarkable; far-famed; noble; tradition; excellent sword.

ماثية *ma'siya-t*, calumny, slander.

ماج *ma'j*, bitter, salt, briny; stupid; excited, agitated; excitement, agitation; battle; — *mâjj*, salivating; weak and imbecile, especially from old age.

ماجد *mâjid*, glorious, praiseworthy.

ماجريات *mâjarayât*, events, adventures.

ماجعة *mâji'a-t*, strumpet.

ماجل *ma'jal*, *mâjil*, pl. *ma'âjil*, watering-place, pond; — *mâjil*, ة, covered with blisters.

ماجن *mâjin*, pl. *mujjân*, who talks at random or acts recklessly, impudent.

ماجوج *ma'jûj*, Magog, son of Japhet; the Scythians; Eastern Tartary.

ماجور *ma'jûr*, rewarded, paid; a vessel; flower-pot.

ماح *mâḥ*, yoke; the white of an egg; — ة *mâḥa-t*, square courtyard, vestibule.

ماحش *mâḥiś*, glutton; burning.

ماحصل *mâ-ḥaṣal*, result, produce; gain; revenue.

ماحط *mâḥiṭ*, dry.

ماحق *mâḥiq*, pl. *mawâḥiq*, patient of (محق), effacing, &c.; hot; intense; sharp; heat.

ماحل *mâḥil*, dry, arid; niggard.

ماحوز *mâḥûz*, a fragrant plant.

ماح *mâḥ-in*, ماحى *mâḥî*, effacing, blotting out.

ماخذ *mâ'ḫaẕ*, bait; place where anything is to be found, taken or derived from; origin, source; mine; receptacle; *ma'âḫiẕ*, pl. nets, snares, nooses, &c.

ماخرة *mâḫira-t*, pl. *mawâḫir*, furrowing the sea (ship).

ماخض *mâḫiḍ*, pl. *mawâḫiḍ*, in the throes of child-birth; on the point of confinement.

ماخل *mâḫil*, fugitive.

ماخور *mâḫûr*, pl. *mawâḫir*, *mawâḫîr*, wine-house; gambling-hell; brothel; company therein.

ماخير *ma'âḫîr*, hind parts.

(ماد) *ma'ad*, INF. *ma'd*, become juicy and begin to grow; be tender.

ماد *ma'd*, ة, juicy, tender; — *mâdd*, extending, stretching; wire-maker; — ة *mâdda-t*, pl. *mawadd*, matter, material; humour of the body; article, stipulation; object; steady increase.

مادبة *ma'daba-t*, *ma'duba-t*, pl. *ma'âdib*, entertainment, festival, banquet.

مادخ *mâdiḫ*, great; magnificent, excellent.

مادة *mâdih*, pl. *muddah*, who praises.

مادور *ma'dûr*, pl. *ma'âdîr*, broken.

مادوم *ma'dûm*, bread to be eaten with meat or fish.

مادى *mâddiyy*, ة, material, referring to matter.

ماذ *mâẕ*, good-natured; cheerful.

ماذل *mâẕil*, weak; languishing.

ماذن *mu'aẕẕin*, who calls to prayer; — ة *ma'ẕana-t*, pl. *ma'âẕin*, tower, minaret.

ماذونية *ma'ẕûniyya-t*, permission, leave, furlough (m.).

ماذى *mâẕiyy*, fresh and purest honey; also ة *mâẕiyya-t*, smooth armour; — ة *mâẕiyya-t*, gentle, mild (f.).

ماذيانات *mâẕiyânât*, water-courses.

(مار) *ma'ar*, INF. *ma'r*, fill a skin bag; stir up enmity; — مئر *ma'ir*, A, INF. *ma'ar*, conceive hatred, enmity against; break open again (wound); — III. INF. *mi'âr*, *mumâ'ara-t*, stir up enmity; — VIII. INF. *imti'âr*, be full of hatred against (على *'ala*).

مار *mâr*, ى *mârî*, master, lord, saint; — *mârr*, passing, passing by, past; pl. *mârra-t*, the passers-by.

مارب *ma'rab*, time or place where anything is to happen;—*ma'rab*, *ma'rib*, ة *ma'raba-t*, *ma'riba-t*, *ma'ruba-t*, pl. *ma'ârib*, what needs must happen, unavoidable, indispensable; need, want, necessity; aim, intention, purpose; — *ma'rib*, celebrated place in Yemen.

مارج *mârij*, flame without smoke.

مارخ *mâriḫ*, flowing.

مارد *mârid*, pl. *marada-t*, haughty, arrogant, defiant; rebel; devil, demon; pestle.

مارز *ma'riz*, place of refuge, ambush.

مارس *mâris*, sown field, crop.

مارستان *mâristân*, hospital; asylum.

مارض *mâriḍ*, ill.

مارع *mâri'*, place abounding with grass.

مارق *mâriq*, pl. *mâriqa-t*, apostate, schismatic, heretic; (m.) passer-by; thin as broth.

مارن *mârin*, supple but strong; tip of the nose, nose; pestle.

ماروت *mârût*, a fallen angel, companion to هاروت *hârût*.

مارورة *mârûra-t*, plump but delicate girl.

ماروش *ma'rûś*, created, formed.

ماروض *ma'rûḍ*, worm-eaten; afflicted with a cold; possessed by a demon, epileptic.

ماروط *ma'rûṭ*, tanned with the bark of the tree ارطى *arṭa*.

ماروق *ma'rûq*, blighted.

ماروك *ma'rûk*, origin, root.

مارومة *ma'rûma-t*, of handsome form (girl); deserted, empty.

مارى *mârî*, ة, of a bright whiteness; a garment; *mârî*=مار *mâr*; also ة *mâriyya-t*, *qaṭa*-bird; — ة *mâriya-t*, a female proper name (Mary).

مازفة *mâzifa-t*, pl. *ma'âzif*, human excrement.

مازق *ma'ziq*, narrow battle-field; war, battle.

مازم *ma'zim*, pl. *ma'âzim*, narrow place; mountain-pass; narrow battle-field; straitened circumstances.

مازن *mâzin*, ova of ants.

مازو *ma'zuww*, worn-out.

مازى *mâzî*, separate, apart.

(ماس) *ma'as*, INF. *ma's*, be angry with; stir up enmity; — مئس *ma'is*, A, INF. *ma'as*, gape, be large (wound).

ماس *mâs*, fickle, full of levity, frivolous; diamond; — *mâss*, ة, touching, adjacent, adjoining; closely related; urgent and important.

ماسدة *ma'sada-t*, tract abounding with lions; thicket full of lions.

ماسط *mâsiṭ*, salt (adj.); purgative.

ماسو *ma'suww*, healed.

ماسوا *mâ-sawâ*, except, besides; external; worldly things.

ماسور *ma'sûr*, taken prisoner, bound; afflicted with disury; — ة *ma'sûra-t*, tube of a pipe; water-pipe; barrel of a gun.

ماسى *mâsî'*=ماجن *mâjin*.

(ماش) *ma'aś*, INF. *ma'ś*, repel, keep off; wash the ground.

ماش *mâś*, bad furniture; a kind of vetch or pea; — *mâś-in*, see ماشى *mâśî*.

ماشط *mâśiṭ*, ة, ag. of (مشط), comb, &c.; — ة *mâśiṭa-t*, woman who dresses the hair of a bride.

ماشور *mâśûr*, sawn.

ماشى *mâśî* (ماش *mâś-in*), pl. *muśât*, pedestrian, foot-soldier; rich in cattle; narrator; *mâśiy-an*, on foot; — ة *mâśiya-t*, pl. *mawâśî*, cattle.

ماشير *ma'âśîr*, pl. of مئشار *mi'śâr*, saw.

(ماص) *ma'aṣ*, noble white camels; — *mâṣṣ*, sucking.

ماصر *ma'ṣar*, *ma'ṣir*, pl. *ma'âṣir*, prison.

ماصل *mâṣil*, leaking; sour; a little, paltry.

ماض *mâḍ-in*, see ماضى *mâḍî*.

ماضغ *mâḍig*, agent of (مضغ), chew; du. *mâḍigân*, two veins in the jaws, jaws; — ة *mâḍiga-t*, jaw.

ماضوى *mâḍawiyy*, referring to the past.

ماضى *mâḍî* (ماض *mâḍ-in*), ة, passed; past (s.); dead; quick, nimble; penetrating, sharp; effective, successful; lion; who signs, puts his seal to; past tense, preterite.

ماطر *mâṭir*, pl. *mawâṭir*, rainy.

ماطور *ma'ṭûr*, well with a side gallery; — ة *ma'ṭûra-t*, pail.

ماطوم *ma'ṭûm*, constipated.

ماعدا *mâ-'adâ*, without regard to, not considering, besides, moreover, excepting.

ماعز *ma'iz*, m. f., f. also ة, pl. *mawâ'iz*, goat; goat-skin; sinewy, strong; cunning, versatile.

ماعوط m. *ma'ûṭ*, heavy shower.

ماعون *mâ'ûn*, pl. *mawâ'în*, household utensils; bark, boat; (m.) ream of paper; taxes upon the believers.

ماعى *mâ'î*, juicy, tender.

مافوق *ma'fûq*, imbecile; credulous; deceived in one's hopes, disappointed; unfortunate.

مافون *ma'fûn*, rotten, foul; stupid; lazy and good-for-nothing.

(ماق), مئق *ma'iq*, A, INF. *ma'aq* (also VIII.), sob; — IV. INF. *im'âq*, fall a-sobbing; — VIII. INF. *imti'âq*=I.; — ة *ma'qa-t*, sobbing, sighing.

ماق *ma'q*, *mâq*, ة *ma'qa-t*, *mâqa-t*, inner corner of the eye.

ماقط *mâqiṭ*, quite exhausted; pl. *muquṭ*, bridle, halter, rope of the bucket; soothsayer; also *ma'qiṭ*, narrowest part of a battle-field; thick of the battle.

ماقى *ma'qan*, pl. *ma'âq-in*, *ma'âqî*, also *mâqi'*, *mâq-in*, *mâqî*, pl. *mawâqi'*, *mawâqî*, inner corner of the eye.

ماكت *mâkit*, ماكث *mâkis*, staying, dwelling; lasting, durable.

ماكد *mâkid*, ة, lasting, yielding milk or water all the year round; perennial.

ماكر *mâkir*, pl. *makara-t*, cunning impostor.

ماكس *mâkis*, tax-gatherer.

ماكل *ma'kal*, INF. of (اكل), eat, &c.; — ة *ma'kala-t*, *ma'kula-t*, food, victuals; feasting; pantry.

ماكم *ma'kam*, *ma'kim*, ة *ma'kama-t*, pl. *ma'âkim*, protruding hip.

ماكول *ma'kûl*, pat. of (اكل), eaten, eatable; article of food; pl. *ma'kûlât*, victuals; — *mâkûl*, pl. *mawâkîl*, id.

ماكوم *ma'kûm*, pale with grief, grieved.

(مال) *ma'al*, مئل *ma'il*, A, INF. *ma'âla-t*, *mu'ûla-t*, grow thick and fat; INF. *ma'l*,—also *ma'ul*, INF. *ma'âla-t*, be not prepared for.

مال *mâl*, pl. *amwâl*, property, possession (كتاب مالى *kitâb mâlî*, my book); fortune, money, revenue, rent; wealth, riches; finances; cube of a number; مال ضامن *mâl ḍâmin*, bail; ة, pl. *mâla-t*, *mâlûn*, rich, wealthy; — *ma'âl*, return; end of man, death; place where one returns to, refuge, resort; centre; essence, substance; real meaning, tendency, pith; aim, issue, consequences; — *mâll*, tired, weary, sulky; — ة *mâla-t*, see above; pl. of مائل *mâ'il*; — *ma'la-t*, pl. *mi'âl*, meadow; mill; wheel of a mill.

مالج *mâlaj*=مالق *mâlaq*.

مالح *mâliḥ*, salt (adj.), briny.

مالطة *mâlṭa-t*, Malta.

مالطى *mâlṭiyy*, Maltese.

مالغ *mâlig*, pl. *mullâg*, impure, abject, reprobate; fornicator.

مالف *ma'laf*, familiar place; abode; company.

مالق *mâlaq*, *mâliq*, roller (to level the ground); trowel (Pers.); — *mâliq*, flatterer.

مالك *mâlik*, pl. *umlûk*, possessor, owner, master; the angel of hell; م الحزين *mâlik al-ḥazîn*, heron; pl. *mullâk*, *mullak*, f. ة, king; — *ma'lak*, angel; — ة *ma'luka-t*, pl. *ma'âlik*, message, missive; — ى *mâlikiyy*, ة, kingly, royal; — ية *mâlikiyya-t*, possession, right of possession.

مالو *ma'luww*, tanned with the bark of the tree الا *al-an*.

مالوس *ma'lûs*, mad, possessed by a demon.

مالوش m. *mâlûś*, pl. *mawâlîś*, wall-cricket.

مالوق *ma'lûq*, mad.

مالوك *ma'lûk*, ambassador, envoy.

مالولة *ma'lûla-t*, languid, sullen.

مالون *mâlûn*, pl. of مال *mâl*.

مالوه *ma'lûh*, adored.

مالى *ma'âlî*, pl. of مئلاة *mi'lât*; — *ma'âliyy*, ة, referring to the future life; central; having a tendency; — *mâli'*, filling (adj.), full; — *mâliyy*, rich; referring to fortune and revenue, financial; — ة *mâliyya-t*, finances; wealth.

ماليخوليا *mâlîḥolîyâ*, melancholy.

(ماما) *ma'ma'*, INF. ة, bleat.

مامل *ma'mal*, place hoped for, object of hope.

مامن *ma'man*, place of safety; person in whom one confides.

ماموت *ma'mût*, determinate, fixed.

مامود *ma'mûd*, term, end, aim.

مامور *ma'mûr*, pat. of (امر), ordered, &c.; order, command, precept; delegate, plenipotentiary, official; — ة *ma'mûra-t*, numerous; order, command.

مامورية *ma'mûriyya-t*, order, command, commission; office; obedience.

مامول *ma'mûl*, hoped-for, desired, expected; hope, expectation.

ماموم *ma'mûm*, injured in the dura mater or the brain.

مامون *ma'mûn*, secured, &c.; exempt; spared; person in whom one confides, trustworthy; persevering and reliable; uncle on mother's side.

ماموه *ma'mûh*, afflicted with an eruption of the skin; mad.

ماميثا *mâmîṯâ*, sap of a kind of poppy.

(مان) *ma'an*, INF. *ma'n*, hit in the hypochondres; provision; — II. INF. *tam'ina-t*, prepare, make ready; = III.; — III. INF. *mumâ'ana-t*, consider carefully; — ة *ma'na-t*, pl. *-ât*, *mu'ûn*, *mu'un*, hypochondres; abdomen; fat of the peritoneum.

مانع *mâni'*, pl. *mana'a-t*, pat. of (منع), hindering, &c.; pl. also *mawâni'*, hindrance, obstacle; prevention; inaccessible, inconquerable, opposing a strong defence; miserly.

مانوس *ma'nûs*, familiar; familiar friend or companion, house-companion; — ة *ma'nûsa-t*, fire.

مانوى *mânawiyy*, Manichean.

ماه *mâh*, water; town, city; ة, stupid, cowardly; — ة *mâha-t*, full well; measles.

ماهج *mâhij*, thin (fluid).

ماهد *mâhid*, who speaks; God.

ماهر *mâhir*, pl. *mahara-t*, prudent and experienced, well-versed, master of one's art.

ماهن *mâhin*, domestic-servant.

ماهول *ma'hûl*, ة, populated, inhabited; — ة *ma'hûla-t*, inhabitable house.

ماهى *mâhî*, who makes water to spring; — *mâhiyy*, ة, watery, stupid, cowardly; Median; — ة *mâhiyya-t*, quality, nature, essence of a thing (what a thing is); state, condition; appointment, salary.

(ماو) *ma'â*, U, INF. *ma'w*, widen, stretch, lengthen out; — INF. *mu'â'*, mew; — V. INF. *tama''î*, be widened, stretched, lengthened.

ماو *ma'w*, violence, vehemence, severity; — ة *ma'wa-t*, low ground; — *ma'âwa-t*, hospitality.

ماوا *ma'wâ* = ماوى *ma'wan*; — ة *ma'wât*, habitation.

ماوب *ma'âwib*, pl. of ماب.

ماود *ma'âwid*, pl. evils, calamities.

ما ورا *mâ warâ'*, what is behind; ما ورا النهر *mâ warâ 'n-nahar*, Transoxiana.

ماوز *ma'waz*, place abounding with geese.

ماوف *ma'ûf*, injured, hurt.

ماولع *mu'aula'*, ماولق *mu'aulaq*, mad.

ماوى *mâwî*, blue (m.); — *ma'wan*, *ma'wa*, *ma'wî*, n. u. ماواة *ma'wât*, habitation, dwelling; quarter; place of refuge, asylum; paradise; — *ma'wiyy*, ة, watery; terminating or rhyming in ما;— ة *mâwiyya-t*, watery substance, juice, sap (m.); — *ma'wiya-t*, compassion; — *ma'wiyya-t*, pl. *ma'wiyy*, mirror, looking-glass.

(ماى) *ma'a*, INF. *ma'y*, widen, stretch; stir up discord; set to a work with utmost zeal; put forth leaves; — IV. INF. *im'â*, be one hundred, make full a hundred; — V. INF. *tama''î*, be widened.

ماى *mâ'iyy*=مائى; — ة *mi'a-t*, pl. *mi'ûn*, *mi'ât*, *mi'a*, *miyy*, hundred.

مائت *mâ'it*, dying; موت م *maut mâ'it*, slow hard death.

مائدة *mâ'ida-t*, pl. *mawâ'id*, table (particularly covered with food); circle, circumference.

مائر *mâ'ir*, pl. *muyyâr*, *mayyâra-t*, who travels about; importer; corn-merchant; purveyor, contractor; — ة *mâ'ira-t*, flowing (blood).

مائس *ma'is*, walking proudly along.

مائع *mâ'i'*, pl. *mawâ'i'*, fluid; melting; also ة *mâ'i'a-t*, pl. *mâ'i'ât*, fluid (s.); oil of myrrh and other fluid perfumes; flowing hair on the forehead of a horse.

مائق *mâ'iq*, pl. *mauqa*, stupid.

مايوس *ma'yûs*, despairing; — ية *ma'yûsiyya-t*, despair.

مائى , مامى *mâ'iyy*, watery, referring to water, aquatic; referring to the particle ما *mâ*; — ة *mâ'iya-t*, mewing animal, cat;—*mâ'iyya-t*, quality, nature, essence of a thing; watery substance, juice, sap.

مباح *mubâḥ*, allowed, left to one's free will, indifferent; common or open to all; pl. f. *mubâḥât*, indifferent actions, permitted pleasures; — ية *mubâhiyya-t*, allowableness.

مباد *mubâd*, annihilated, destroyed.

. مبا *mubâ . .*, ة . . مبا *mubâ . . t*, to be looked for under (. . ب III.), for instance—

مبادر *mubâdir*, ag. of (بدر III.), hastening to the front, &c.; mature youth; — ة *mubâdara-t*, INF. of the same; haste, zeal; undertaking; beginning, attack.

مبادهة *mubâdaha-t*, surprise.

مبادى *mubâdî*, pl. of مبدا *mabdâ'*, مبدو *mabdu'*.

مباذاة *mubâẕa'a-t*, obscenity.

مباذرة *mubâẕara-t*, dissipation.

مبار *mabârr*, pl. of مبر *mubirr*; — ة *mubârra-t*, benevolence; fulfilment of one's duty.

مباراة *mubârât*, contention, competition;—*mubâra'a-t*, dismissal of a wife in an amicable way; separation from a partner.

مبارى *mabârî*, pl. of مبراة *mibrât*; —*mubârî* (*mubâr-in*), adversary, competitor, rival.

مبازمة *mubâzama-t*, resolution; undertaking.

مباشر *mubâśir*, ag. III. of (بشر), who carries out by himself, &c.; agent, factor, plenipotentiary, proxy; inspector; — ة *mubâśara-t*, personal management, superintendence, inspection; beginning; good tidings.

مباصرة *mubâṣara-t*, out-look, watch.
مباطنة *mubâṭana-t*, secret consultation.
مباع *mubâ'*, for sale.
مباغضة *mubâgaḍa-t*, mutual hatred.
مباك *mibâk*, little stick to stir about the ink.
مباكات *mubâkât*, crying in common.
مبال *mabâl*, urinary canal; — ة *mubâla-t*, solicitude.
مبالغة *mubâlaga-t*, INF. III. of (بلغ); exaggeration; hyperbola; industry; emphasis; superiority.
مبالى *mubâlî* (مبال *mubâl-in*), solicitous, attentive, intent upon.
مبان *mubân*, separated; — *mabân-in*, and—
مبانى *mabânî*, pl. of مبنى *mabna*.
مباة *mabâ'a-t*, habitation; lair; resting-place for camels; nest of bees; womb, matrice.
مباهاة *mubâhât*, vainglory, boasting, arrogance; glory, honour.
مباهت *mubâhit*, liar;—ة *mubâhata-t*, telling lies.
مباوك *mubâwik*, intermeddler.
مبت *mubitt*, who divorces irrevocably his wife.
مبتاع *mubtâ'*, seller; sold, bought.
مبتدا *mubtada'*, anything begun; beginning, commencement; substantive, subject.
. مبت *mubt* . ., to be looked for under (. . ب VIII.), as—
مبتدع *mubtada'*, patient, *mubtadi'*, agent of (بدع VIII.); *mubtadi'*, innovator, sectarian.
مبتدى *mubtadî*, beginner, disciple, novice.
مبتر *mubattar*, clipped, maimed; incomplete.
مبترى *mubtara*, cut smooth with a hatchet.
مبتغى *mubtaga*, pl. *mubtagayât*, much desired, sought for; requisite, due; — *mubtagî*, craving for; lion.
مبتل *mubattal*, formed in perfect beauty; — *mubtill*, moistened, wetted through; recovering (adj.).
مبتلى *mubtala*, visited by calamity; addicted to; — *mubtalî*, who exacts an oath.
مبتهر *mubtahar*, spoken of publicly.
مبتوت *mabtût*, decisive; — ة *mabtûta-t*, divorced (woman).
مبتئش *mubta'iś*, who accuses destiny.
مبثور *mabsûr*, envied; very rich.
مبحبح *mubaḥbaḥ*, considerable.
مبحث *mabḥas*, pl. *mabâḥis*, place or time of examination; examination, investigation or anything which deserves such; — ة *mabḥisa-t*, pl. *mabâḥis*, investigation, disquisition, debate, disputation; pl. points under debate.
مبحر *mubḥar*, briny.
مبحزج *mubaḥzaj*, boiling.
مبحوح *mabḥûḥ*, hoarse.
مبخرة *mabḫara-t*, what brings on a a foul breath; pl. *mabâḫir*, censer.
مبخضة *mibḫaḍa-t*, churn.
مبخلة *mabḫala-t*, object of avarice or of solicitude.
مبخوت *mabḫût*, fortunate.
مبخور *mabḫûr*, perfumed; intoxicated.
مبدا *mabdan*, wilderness, desert; — *mabda'*, *mubda'*, ة *mabda'a-t*, pl. *mabâdi'*, beginning, commencement; origin, source; principle, fundamental proposition.
مبدد *mubaddad*, dispersed; squandered.
مبدع *mabda'*, new invention; place or time of invention; fiction; pl. f. *mubda'ât*, innovations, heresies; — *mubdi'*, inventor, innovator, heretic; forger of lies.
مبدن *mubaddan*, corpulent.
مبده *mibdah*, improvisator; — *mubdah*, ex tempore; improvised.

مبدو *mabdau*, desert ; — *mabdu'*, *mabdû'*, pl. *mabâdi'*, *mabâdî*, anything begun ; beginning, commencement ; — *mabdû'*, afflicted with small-pox.
مبدوح *mabdûḥ*, far-stretched.
مبدى *mubdî*, beginner ; inventor ; who makes known ; experienced.
مبذل *mibẕal*, ة, pl. *mubâẕil*, worn-out or every-day garment.
مبذم *mibẕam*, strong.
مبذول *mabẕûl*, spent, squandered ; costly present.
مبر *mubirr*, pl. *mabârr*, strong, more powerful ; prudent ; excelling ; — ة *mabarra-t*, pl. *-ât*, good work ; pious foundation ; love for parents or children ; bounty.
مبرا *mabran*, *mabra*, place where a pen is mended ; — *mibra*, pen-knife ; razor ; knife ; hatchet ; — ة *mibrât*, pl. *mabârî*, pen-knife ; carving-knife ; file ; — *mubrât*, she-camel with a nose-ring.
مبربر *mubarbir*, lion.
مبرد *mabrad*, ة *mabrada-t*, refreshment ; — *mibrad*, pl. *mabârid*, file ; — *mubrid*, cooling ; post-master ; — *mubarrad*, cooled ; handsome of face ; also *mubrad*, struck by hail ; — *mubarrid*, cooling ; pl. *-ât*, refreshments.
مبردانة *mibridâna-t*, cold food.
مبرز *mabraz*, pl. *mabâriz*, battle-field ; amphitheatre ; privy.
مبرشة *mibraśa-t*, rasp for scraping cheese (m.).
مبرغث *mubargas̱*, full of fleas.
مبرق *mabraq*, morning-dawn.
مبرقع *mubarqa'*, veiled ; ة, having a white head ; — ة *mubarqi'a-t*, white spot on a horse's fore-head.
مبرك *mabrak*, pl. *mabârik*, place where the camel kneels down ; — ة *mubrika-t*, fire.
مبرم *mibram*, pl. *mabârim*, spindle of a spinning-wheel ; — *mubram*, doubly-twisted or spun, strong ; irresistible (fate) ; — *mubrim*, strengthening ; obtrusive ; morose ; urgent.
مبرور *mabrûr*, justified, acquitted ; received into the mercy of God ; pious, dutiful ; equitable, just.
مبروز *mabrûz*, published, edited (book) ; — *mubarwaz*, framed (picture, m.).
مبروض *mabrûḍ*, leprous ; grown poor by liberality.
مبروة *mabruwwa-t*, she-camel with a nose-ring.
مبرى *mubra*, healed, cured ; — *mubarra*, freed, free ; — *mabriyy*, cut, carved, mended (pen).
مبزر *mibzar*, beetle (of a washer).
مبزغ *mibzag*, pl. *mabâzig*, lancet of a veterinary surgeon.
مبزقة *mibzaqa-t*, spittoon.
مبزل *mibzal*, ة *mibzala-t*, strainer for wine.
مبزم *mibzam*, tooth.
مبزور *mabzûr*, having a large progeny.
مبسط *mabsaṭ*, open space ; — *mibsaṭ*, place where the carpets, &c. are spread.
مبسم *mabsam*, pl. *mabâsim*, smiling (s.) ; — *mabsim*, pl. *mabâsim*, smiling lips, smiling teeth, beauty.
مبسور *mabsûr*, afflicted with piles.
مبشر *mubaśśir*, ag. of (بشر II.), who brings glad tidings, &c. ; preacher, evangelist, paraclete ; pl. f. *mubaśśirât*, clouds announcing rain.
مبصر *mabṣar*, ة *mabṣara-t*, convincing proof, evident fact ; — * ; — ة *mubṣira-t*, evident sign.
مبضع *mibḍa'*, pl. *mabâḍi'*, lancet ; pen-knife, carving-knife or tool.
مبطان *mibṭân*, paunch-bellied, glutton.
مبطاة *mabṭa'a-t*, delay.
مبطخة *mabṭaḫa-t*, melon-field.
مبطن *mubaṭṭan*, having the belly flat from hunger ; lined ; — ة *mabaṭṭana-t*, having an elegant

waist (woman); small boat, felucca.
مبطة *mibaṭṭa-t*, lancet.
مبطول *mabṭûl*, lamed, paralysed.
مبطون *mabṭûn*, extended; suffering from colic.
مبظرة *mubazzira-t*, woman who circumcises girls.
مبعث *mab'as*, message.
مبعد *mib'ad*, who travels far; — *.
مبعر *mab'ar*, gut; also *mib'ar*, dunghill; stable; — ة *mab'ara-t*, anus (of animals).
مبعوض *mab'ûḍ*, tormented by flies.
مبعوق *mab'ûq*, burst; embossed.
مبغاة *mabgât*, place where or manner in which anything is sought for.
مبغولا *mabgûlâ'*, pl. of بغل *bagl*, mule.
مبغى *mabgî*, honoured, sought for; — *mabgiyy*, wronged.
مبق *mibaqq*, talkative, garrulous.
مبقرة *mabqara-t*, path, road.
مبقل *mubqil*, pushing forth leaves; — ة *mabqala-t*, *mabqula-t*, pl. *mabâqil* kitchen-garden.
مبقم *mubaqqam*, dyed red with basil-wood.
مبقوث *mabqûs*, hated; confused.
مبقور *mabqûr*, burst.
مبكار *mibkâr*, premature, early; fertile.
مبكر *mubkir*, early rain; — also *mubakkir*, who sets out or does anything early in the morning, early riser.
مبكل *mubakkal*, provided with buckles or buttons.
مبكم *mubakkim*, silent, dumb.
مبكونة *mabkûna-t*, abject, depraved (f.).
مبل *miball*, resolute; — *mubill*, companion, helper.
مبلبل *mubalbil*, who brings on confusion, revolutionist.
مبلة *muballa-t*, well arranged, in good order.
مبلد *mublid*, old well.
مبلس *mublis*, despairing, desperate; silent; gloomy, morose.
مبلط *mubliṭ*, what leads to beggary; also *mublaṭ*, beggar; — *mubliṭ*, *muballiṭ*, pavior.
مبلع *mabla'*, gullet; sink-hole, drain; — *mibla'*, glutton.
مبلغ *mablag*, pl. *mabâlig*, sum, amount; result, product, quotient; place of arrival; goal, aim; acme; a multitude, many; — *.
مبلق *mablaq*, grater; — *.
مبلم *mublim*, swelling, swollen.
مبلندى *mublandî*, fleshy, strong.
مبلود *mablûd*, stupid, imbecile, timid.
مبناة *mabnât*, *mibnât*, tanned skin as a seat; portmanteau.
مبندق *mubandiq*, fusileer.
مبنى *mabnan*, *mabnî*, pl. *mabân-in*, *mabânî*, building (s.); foundation; — *mubnî*, instigator; — *mabniyy*, ة, built, founded; indeclinable; terminating or rhyming in (ب *bi*).
مبهرر *mubahrir*, dazzlingly beautiful.
مبهم *mubham*, unknown; indistinct, dark, obscure; general, indefinite; dumb; locked, closed; strictly forbidden; demonstrative pronoun; — *mubhim*, who conceals, speaks obscurely.
مبهول *mabhûl*, stupid, imbecile, timid.
مبهيات *mubahiyyât*, aphrodisiacs.
مبوأ *mubawwa'*, *mabwâ'*, dwelling, lodging, quarter; night-lodging.
مبوس *mubawwis*, kissing (adj.).
مبول *mibwal*, ة *mibwala-t*, urinal, pot; bladder; — *mubwil*, *mubawwil*, diuretic.
مبيت *mabît*, place where the night is passed; night-lodging; bedroom; house; INF. of (بيت); — ة *mubayyata-t*, married woman.
مبيح *mubîḥ*, ag. of (بوح IV.), who makes known, &c.; lion.
مبيد *mubîd*, destroyer; God.
مبيض *mubîḍ*, place where eggs are

laid or ova deposited; — *mubîḍ*, bleacher, fuller; — * .

مبيطر *mubaiṭir*, veterinary surgeon; smith; — *mubaiṭar*, shoed (m.).

مبيع *mabî'*, sale; sold; — *mubî'*, seller; — *mubî'iyy*, for sale (m.).

مبين *mubîn*, distinct, clear, manifest, evident; true; — * .

مبيوع *mabyû'*, sold, what can be bought, for sale.

مبيى *mubî'*, ة, hard, difficult.

(مت) *matt*, U, INF. *matt*, stretch; pull the rope out of the well, draw water.

(متا) *mata'*, INF. *mat'*, beat, cudgel; stretch.

متاب *matâb*, turning back (s.), repentance, penance; place where one returns to; — ة *mutâba-t*, penitential vow.

. متا *muta'* . ., to be looked for under (. . ا v.); — *mutâ* . ., ة *mutâ* . . *t*, to be looked for under (. . ت III.), for instance—

متابت *muta'abbit*, ag. of (ابت v.), glowing.

متابع *mutâbi'*, ag. of (تبع III.), following; successor, partisan; obedient; — *mutâba'*, pat. of the same; strong, firm; — ة *mutâba'a-t*, INF. of the same; following (s.), obedience.

متابى *muta'abbî*, refractory.

متاثث *muta'assis*, ag. of (اث v.), having handsome furniture; well-to-do.

متاثر *muta'assir*, receiving an impression; confounded, grieved.

متاجر *matâjir*, pl. merchandise, goods; — ة *mutâjara-t*, commerce, traffic.

متاجل *muta'ajjil*, coming in time; hitting the aim.

متاح *mutâḥ*, fixed, appointed, ordained; (day) of death; — *mattâḥ*, long; astride.

متاحد *muta'aḥḥid*, united.

متاخر *muta'aḥḥir*, ag. of (اخر v.), lagging behind, &c.; modern.

متاخى *muta'aḥḥî*, acting like a brother; — *muta'âḥî*, united in brotherhood.

متادب *muta'addib*, *muta'addab*, well educated, literary, refined, polite; chastised.

متاذى *muta'azzî*, hurt, injured, grieved.

متاريس *matârîs*, pl. of متراس *mitrâs*.

متاركة *mutâraka-t*, INF. of (ترك III.); truce, amnesty.

متاسر *muta'assir*, apologizing, making excuses (adj.); who seeks a delay or respite.

متاسى *muta'âsî*, comforting and assisting one another; — *muta'assî*, who consoles himself or allows himself to be consoled, who suffers patiently.

متاع *matâ'*, pl. *amti'at*, usufruct; property, possessions; goods, merchandise; furniture, utensils, household things, clothes, &c.; penis; metals; profit, gain: f. ة, pl. *mutû'*, expressing possession, as: كتاب متاعك *kitâb matâ'ak*, thy book; بغلة متاعة الرجل *bagla-t muta'a-t ar-rajul*, the man's mule, &c.

متاعيس *matâ'is*, pl. of متعوس *mat'ûs*.

متاق *mit'aq*, strong and swift.

متالاة *mutâlât*, succession; musical accompaniment.

متالم *muta'allim*, ag. of (الم v.), suffering pain, &c.; compassionate.

متالى *mutâlî*, succeeding, following; who accompanies (in music); f. pl. *mutâliyât*, things following in succession.

متام *matâ-ma*, how long? until when? — *mit'âm*, woman who bears twins; also *mit'am*, *mutâ'am*, pl. *mata'îm*, woven with a double woof; — ة *muta'ama-t*, such a texture.

متامل *muta'ammil*, ag. of (امل v.), looking at long and attentively, &c., thoughtful, contemplative.

متامة *mutâmama-t*, INF. of (تم

III.); endeavour to complete a thing.

متانث *muta'anniṡ*, female, effeminate; lady's man.

متانة *matâna-t*, firmness, solidity, strength, power of resistance; strength of will; obstinacy, obduracy; fortification, castle; — *mutânna-t*, comparison.

متاهه *muta'ahhih*, sighing.

متايم *muta'ayyim*, ag. of (ايم v.), widowed; single, unmarried.

متائيم *matâ'îm*, pl. of متام *mit'âm*.

متب *mutibb*, weakening (adj.).

. . . . مت *muta* . . . ., to be looked for under (. . . . II.), (. . . v.) or (. . . VI.), throwing out a letter of prolongation or a doubled letter, as: متبختر *muta-baḥtir*, ag. of (بختر *baḥtar* II.), pompous; — متباد *muta-bâdd* (for *muta-bâdid*), ag. of (بدد *badad*, بد VI.), who comes to close quarters; — متبدّد *muta-baddid*, ag. of (بد v.), dispersed.

متبادل *mutabâdil*, ag. of (بدل VI.), exchanging; alternate, stepping in alternately for one another; mutual, reciprocal.

متبادى *mutabâdî*, taking after the inhabitants of the desert, rude, barbarous, grown wild, savage.

متبارى *mutabâri'*, *mutabârî*, contending with, opposing, competing with one another; du. day and night.

متباطى *mutabâṭi'*, who delays, tarries, lags behind; lazy.

متبجل *mutabajjil*, feeling honoured.

متبختر *mutabaḥtir*, pompous.

متبدع *mutabaddi'*, innovator, sectarian, heretic.

متبدى *mutabaddî*, beginner; inhabitant of the desert.

متبرر *mutabarrir*, pious, godly; true, just; — *mutabarrar*, justified, acquitted.

متبرى *mutabarra*, acquitted; — *mutabarrî*, guiltless, free.

متبس *muttabiṣ*, ag. of (يبس VIII.), dry, withered.

متبصبص *mutabaṣbiṣ*, ag. of (بصبص II.), wagging the tail; flattering.

متبصل *mutabaṣṣil*, enfolded in one another.

متبع *mutbi'*, who follows; — *muttabi'*, ag. of (تبع VIII.), id.; who pursues or seeks eagerly; client, protégé.

متبل *mutbal*, *mutabbal*, seasoned with greens; — *mutbil*, seasoning; what harms, weakens.

متبن *matban*, ة *matbana-t*, loft for straw or hay; — *muttabin*, wearing the short trowsers تبان *tubbân*; — *mutabban*, straw-coloured; — *mutabbin*, sagacious, prudent.

متبنى *mutabanna*, adopted; — *mutabannî*, who adopts.

متبوع *matbû'*, pat. of (تبع), followed, &c.; leader, prince, chief, sovereign; high-priest; prefect; — *mutabawwi'*, ag. of (بوع v.), long, &c.

متبول *matbûl*, pat. of (تبل), sick; weakened, unnerved, maddened; mad; — *mutabawwil*, ag. of (بول v.), making water.

متبيت *mutabayyit*, married.

متتابع *mutatâbi'*, ag. of (تبع VI.), happening or doing in succession, &c.; finely and symmetrically made (horse).

متتالى *mutatâlî*, following one another in unbroken succession.

متتهته *mutatahtih*, stammering.

متثاقل *mutaṡâqil*, heavy, clumsy; sullen, lazy; cowardly.

متثاوب *mutaṡâwib*, متثائب *mutaṡâ'ib*, yawning (m.).

متثبب *mutaṡabbib*, consolidated, ordered; who carries through with perseverance.

متجاثى *mutajâṡî*, sitting on one's knees.

متجازى *mutajâzî*, pressing creditor.

متجاعل *mutajâ'il*, who fixes the price or wages.

متجافى *mutajâfî*, inclined sideways, sliding off.

متجانب *mutajânib*, shunning, on one's guard; cautious.
متجانس *mutajânis*, of the same kind, homogeneous.
متجانن *mutajânin*, half mad.
متجاور *mutajâwir*, neighbouring.
متجبر *mutajabbir*, ag. of (جبر v.), set (bone), &c.; *al-mutajabbir*, lion.
متجر *matjar*, commerce, traffic; pl. *matâjir*, article of trade, merchandise; — *mutjir*, *muttajir*, trader, merchant; — *muttajar*, ة *matjara-t*, commercial place; land with markets; — ى *matjariyy*, commercial.
متجزى *mutajazzi'*, divided into parts; contented.
متجسس *mutajassis*, who spies out; scout, spy.
متجلد *mutajallid*, ag. of (جلد v.), hardy, &c.; covered with leather; covered with a skin.
متجلى *mutajallî*, lit up, shining, resplendent, transfigured, refulgent; revealing one's self in all splendour.
متجنن *mutajannin*, possessed by a demon, mad; entirely grown over.
متجه *muttajih*, ag. of (وجه viii.), occurring thought.
متجوز *mutajawwiz*, performing one's duty negligently; taking great liberties.
متجوع *mutajawwi'*, starving one's self.
متجيش *mutajayyiś*, passing review (army); excited, agitated.
(متح) *mataḥ*, INF. *matḥ*, draw water from the well; drop excrement; cut off; pull out; beat; be long; — also II. INF. *tamtîḥ*, and IV. INF. *imtâḥ*, deposit ova; — VIII. INF. *imtitâḥ*, draw out, pull out.
متحاب *mutaḥâbb*, loving one another, mutual friend.
متحات *mutaḥâtt*, falling off (as leaves).
متحاث *mutaḥâss*, inciting, encouraging one another.
متحاشي *mutaḥâśî*, keeping aloof from one another, avoiding one another.
متحامل *mutaḥâmil*, patient.
متحتم *mutaḥattam*, indispensable.
متحجر *mutaḥajjir*, petrified; hardened; suppurating.
متحد *muttaḥid*, ag. of (وحد VIII.), united, &c. (م المركز *muttaḥid al-markaz*, concentric); isolated; — ية *muttaḥidiyya-t*, concord; isolation.
متحرس *mutaḥarris*, cautious.
متحرف *mutaḥarrif*, altered, transformed; — ة *mutaḥarrifa-t*, taxes on trade and industry.
متحرم *mutaḥarrim*, forbidden, inaccessible, sacred; outcast, fugitive.
متحزب *mutaḥazzib*, partisans, confederates, allies.
متحصل *mutaḥaṣṣil*, who procures, produces, earns; pl. f. *mutaḥaṣṣilât*, productions.
متحف *mutḥaf*, given as a present; — *mutḥif*, who makes a present.
متحقق *mutaḥaqqaq*, verified; ascertained, true; probable; — *mutaḥaqqiq*, who verifies.
متحل *muttaḥil*, ag. of (وحل VIII.), making a proviso.
متحلحل *mutaḥalḥil*, dissolving (adj. n.), scattering.
متحم *mutaḥḥam*, dark brown; — ة *mutaḥḥama-t*, *mutḥama-t*, striped stuff of Yemen.
متحمد *mutaḥammid*, who deserves praise or thanks.
متحنى *mutaḥannî*, bent, curved.
متحول *mutaḥawwil*, changing place and form; versatile, cunning; (m.) executory soldier to exact the taxes.
متحير *mutaḥayyar*, perplexed, dumbfounded, thunder-struck; — ة *muḥayyara-t*, planet.
متحيز *mutaḥayyiz*, received with others, associated; member of a society; containing, filling a place, referring to space; coiled up; deserter.
(متخ) *mataḥ*, U, A, INF. *matḥ*, pull out; drop excrement, &c.=

(متع); — VIII. INF. *imtitâḥ*, pull out, take away.
متخارج *mutaḥârij*, sharing in the expenses.
متخالف *mutaḥâlif* (خلف VI.), different; standing opposite.
متخبر *mutaḥabbir*, newsmonger.
متخت *mutaḥḥat*, covered with boards; estrade, platform.
متختح *mutaḥtaḥ*, rotten, worm-eaten.
متخذ *muttaḥiz* (اخذ VIII.), who takes, accepts or prepares for himself; beginner.
متخشن *mutaḥaśśin*, rude, rough.
متخطى *mutaḥaṭṭî*, overstepping, transgressing; overstepped.
متخلص *mutaḥalliṣ*, who saves himself, &c.; successful.
متخلف *mutaḥallif*, who lags behind, &c.; who breaks his word; adversary.
متخلق *mutaḥalliq*, who takes after others, &c.; who teaches the fine arts; liar.
متخلى *mutaḥallî* (خلو V.), who keeps himself free, free, unencumbered, vacant.
متخم *matḥim*, indigestible; — *muttaḥim* (تخم VIII.), suffering from indigestion;— ة *matḥama-t*, indigestible food or dish.
متخوم *matḥûm*, suffering from indigestion.
متخيل *mutaḥayyil*, indulging in fancies or illusions, fantastic; — ة *mutaḥayyila-t*, قوة م *quwwa-t mutaḥayyila-t*, imagination, phantasy.
(متد) *matad*, U, INF. *mutûd*, stay, abide.
متداخل *mutadâḥil*, involved.
متدارك *mutadârik*, reaching, &c.; name of a metre (*fâ'ilun* — ◡ — eight times repeated).
متداكس *mutadâkis*, very numerous; difficult, hard; difficult to approach, inaccessible.
متدانى *mutadânî* (دنو VI.), near to one another.
متداول *mutadâwil*, alternating, &c.; current (money); of everyday life, vulgar (language).
متداوم *mutadâwim*, turning about continually, spinning, warbling; — ة *mutadâwama-t*, continual rotation.
متدثر *mutadaṡṡir*, wrapping one's self up in one's clothes; prostituted, infamous (m. f.).
متدعى *mutada''î* (دعو V.), claimant, pretender.
متدلى *mutadallî* (دلو V.), hanging down and swinging; merry.
متدين *mutadayyin*, religious, orthodox; greatly in debt.
متذايل *mutaẓâyil*, mean, low, lowly.
متذكرة *mutaẓakkira-t*, virago.
(متر) *matar*, INF. *matr*, cut off; stretch; — VIII. INF. *immitâr*, be stretched.
متراجع *mutarâji'*, returning, coming back; brought back.
مترادف *mutarâdif*, succeeding one another, &c.; successive, continual; simultaneous; synonymous.
مترامس *mitrâs*, pl. *matârîs*, rampart, entrenchment; (m.) barricade.
متراضى *mutarâḍî* (رضو VI.), satisfied with one another; agreeing with one another.
متراكب *mutarâkib*, piled upon one another, &c.; firm, strong, solid.
مترب *matrab*, INF., *mutrib*, ag. of (ترب IV.);— ة *matraba-t*, poverty, beggary, misery.
متربض *mutarabbiḍ*, unable to stir (from weakness); struck down, slain.
متربى *mutarabbî* (ربو V.), who brings up, &c.; who makes preserves of fruit; preserved.
مترتب *mutarattib*, solid and well-arranged, &c.; ordained; happening, befalling; springing forth, originating; consisting of; forming a class.
مترتل *mutarattil*, singing, chanting.
مترج *mutarraj*, red, orange-coloured.
مترجرج *mutarajraj*, quivering, vibrating.

مترجم *mutarjim*, translator, interpreter.

مترجى *mutarajjî* (رجو v.), hoping, begging; petitioner, supplicant.

مترحل *mutaraḥḥil*, mounted and ready to start; traveller.

مترخص *mutaraḫḫiṣ*, who takes leave, leave of absence.

متردد *mutaraddid*, who comes and goes frequently, &c.; irresolute; offering resistance, adversary; pl. the passers by.

متردى *mutaraddî*, wrapped in the cloak ردا *ridâ'*; dressed, clad.

مترس *mitras*, ة *mitrasa-t*, pl. *matâris*, cover, rampart, parapet, entrenchment; *mitrasa-t*, shield, armour; — *mutarris*, arming or covering one's self with a shield.

مترسمل *mutarasmil*, capitalist (m.).

مترص *mutraṣ*, *mutarraṣ*, firm, strong; well poised, in equilibrium.

مترف *mutraf*, living in continual ease and affluence; effeminate; — *mutrif*, *mutarrif*, effeminating; sumptuous.

متركم *mutarakkim*, heaped or piled up.

مترنم *mutarannim*, singing, chanting psalms; trilling, cooing.

مترنن *mutarannin*, resounding sonorously.

مترهب *mutarahhib*, (God-) fearing, monk, &c.; who threatens, frightens.

مترهل *mutarahhil*, loose, relaxed.

متروبص m. *mutaraubiṣ*, thoroughly purified, refined, fine, pure (gold, &c.).

متروك *matrûk*, abandoned, &c.; pl. f. *matrûkât*, property left behind, inheritance; superfluous luggage.

متريض *mutarayyiḍ*, pensioned; in good health.

متزايد *mutazâyid*, gradually increasing; growing too much or many.

متزايل *mutazâyil*, separate, distant; ceasing, fleeting, transitory; injured, damaged, spoiled, corrupted.

متزر *mutazzir*, guilty.

متزعزع *mutaza'za'*, shaken, rickety.

متزفر *mutazaffir*, who is dispensed from fasting.

متزلع *mutazalli'*, chapped (skin).

متزن *muttazin* (وزن VIII.), well measured, metrically correct.

متزيى *mutazayyî*, fashionable.

(متس) *matas*, U, INF. *mats*, throw dung or excrement at; — I, INF. *mats*, try to pull out.

متسابق *mutasâbiq*, trying to overtake one another; betting with one another (at a race).

متسارع *mutasâri'*, pretending to be in a hurry.

متسالم *mutasâlim*, living in peace with one another.

متسربل *mutasarbil*, wearing large trowsers; wearing a shirt, a cuirass.

متسع *muttasi'* (وسع VIII.), far extended.

متسلح *mutasalliḥ*, armed from head to foot.

متسلم *mutasallim*, who takes possession of, &c.; vice-governor, commander of a town.

متسم *muttasim* (وسم VIII.), sealed; characterised.

متسمى *mutasammî* (سمو v.), named.

متسوق *mutasawwiq*, visiting the market.

(متش) *mataś*, I, INF. *matś*, separate by the fingers; milk easily.

متشابه *mutaśâbih*, similar, equal; allegorical, metaphorical; difficult, complicated, equivocal, obscure; — ة *mutaśâbiha-t*, simile, allegory; consonance, homophony, play on words, pun.

متشاخص *mutaśâḫiṣ*, different.

متشاعر *mutaśâ'ir*, who passes himself as a poet, poetaster.

متشخص *mutaśaḫḫiṣ*, appearing, &c.; different.

متشرب *mutaśarrib*, imbibing, &c.; spreading, rampant, infecting, contageous.

متشرع *mutaśarri'*, learned in law, jurist, lawyer.

متشرف *mutaśarrif*, feeling honoured; honoured, respected.

متشكل *mutaśakkil*, taking this or that shape, &c.; similar.

متشكى *mutaśakkî* (شكو v.), complaining, discontented.

متشمم *mutaśammim*, inhaling an odour, snuffling.

متشى *muttaśî* (اهى viii.), healed.

متصادف *mutaṣâdif*, meeting one another.

متصاعب *mutaṣâ'ib*, difficult, refractory.

متصاعد *mutaṣâ'ad*, ascended gradually, difficult to ascend;—*mutaṣâ'id*, ascending gradually and with difficulty.

متصام *mutaṣâmm*, feigning deafness.

متصدى *mutaṣaddî* (صدو v.), coming to meet, presenting one's self; offering resistance; enterprising, undertaking; scribe, clerk.

متصرف *mutaṣarrif*, freely disposing of anything, &c.; owner, master; absolute commander, governor of a province, exercising jurisdiction; extravagant, lavish; — ات *mutaṣarrafât*, declension and conjugation, inflections.

متصف *muttaṣif* (وصف viii.), possessing or claiming a quality; described; describer; praiseworthy.

متصل *muttaṣil* (وصل viii.), bordering upon, adjacent, cohering, closely connected; sharing in; uninterrupted; — ة *muttaṣila-t*, pronominal suffix.

متصلب *mutaṣallib*, hard, severe.

متصوت *mutaṣawwit*, sounding, resounding.

متصوف *mutaṣawwif*, behaving like a Sufî, mystic.

متضام *mutaḍâmm*, united, &c.; pressed together, compact, heaped up.

متضايق *mutaḍâyiq*, straitened, in utmost distress; dying.

متضح *muttaḍiḥ* (وضح viii.), open, clear, evident.

متضع *muttaḍi'* (وضع viii.), humiliating or abusing one's self.

متطارق *mutaṭâriq*, walking or coming behind one another.

متطامن *mutaṭâmin*, bent, inclined; submissive.

متطاهر *mutaṭâhir*, purified.

متطاول *mutaṭâwil*, stretching, &c.; rising on tip-toe; reaching for; long, oblong.

متطرق *mutaṭarriq*, making way for one's self; happening, befalling; guide.

متطوع *mutaṭawwi'*, obedient, volunteer.

متع *mata'*, enjoy, have the usufruct, derive advantage from; INF. *mutû'*, be advanced and near evening; be strong, firm; be of a deep red; be generous, liberal; — also *matu'*, INF. *matâ'a-t*, be long; be ingenious, witty; — II. INF. *tamtî'*, preserve alive and allow to enter on adolescence (also IV.); allow one the enjoyment or usufruct of (2 acc. or acc. and ب *bi*); give a dowry to a divorced wife; — IV. INF. *imtâ'*, see II.; enjoy, have the usufruct; be rich in furniture, utensils, &c.; be useful; be no longer in need of (عن *'an*); — V. INF. *tamattu'*, enjoy, have the usufruct; amuse one's self, find pleasure in (ب *bi*, من *min*); — X. INF. *istimtâ'* =V.

متعادل *muta'âdil*, parallel to one another.

متعادى *muta'âdî* (عدو VI.), hostile to one another; ة, rugged and stony.

متعارف *mata'âraf*, renowned, celebrated; —*muta'ârif*, well known to one another; usual, customary.

متعاشى *muta'âśî* (عشو VI.), who pretends not to see anything.

متعاطى *muta'âṭî* (عطو VI.), giving

to one another, &c.; who carries on commerce or a trade.

متعاكس *muta'âkis*, reversed, perverted.

متعال *muta'âl-in*, ى *muta'âlî*, sublime; the Most High.

متعاون *muta'âwin*, bound to help one another; — ة *muta'âwana-t*, woman of mature age, matron.

متعب *mat'ab*, pl. *matâ'ib*, trouble, hardship; — *; — ة *mat'aba-t*, difficult place; — ات *mut'ibât*, difficulties.

متعبد *muta'abbad*, consecrated to worship; — *mata'abbid*, devoted to God, religious, devout; devoted, submissive; — ات *muta'abbadât*, ceremonies of the pilgrimage.

متعتب *muta'attib*, complaining of a person (على *'ala*).

متعدد *muta'addid*, very numerous; varied; prepared, ready.

متعدى *muta'addî* (عدو v.), transgressing, wronging, encroaching; unjust; tyrant; transitive.

متعذر *muta'azzir*, apologising; deserving of excuse; difficult, impossible.

متعرب *muta'arrib*, taking after the Arabs, passing one's self for an Arab, be a half-bred Arab.

متعرق *muta'arriq*, wishing to learn, &c.; intruding by questions; confessing.

متعزب *muta'azzib*, bachelor.

متعشم *muta'aśśim*, desirous, hopeful.

متعشى *muta'aśśî* (عشو v.), who takes supper.

متعطف *mata'aṭṭif*, inclined, &c.; bend of a valley, winding (s.).

متعظ *mutta'iẕ* (وعظ VIII.), who listens to a sermon, accepts admonition; admonished.

متعفن *muta'affin*, corrupted, foul, putrid; full of miasma; worn out.

متعقل *muta'aqqil*, thinking; intelligent; grave, steady.

متعلق *muta'allaq*, place where anything is suspended; point where the interest lies; — ة *muta'alliqa-t*, dependency, appurtenance; belongings, family.

متعلم *muta'allim*, instructing one's self, &c.; disciple, pupil, student; instructed.

متعة *mut'a-t*, *mit'a-t*, pl. *muta'*, *mita'*, what is necessary to life, what one may enjoy; use, usufruct (نكاح متعة *nikâḥ mut'a-t*, marriage for a time, for some days; م الطلاق *mut'a-t aṭ-ṭalâq*, dowry of a divorced wife); — *mut'a-t*, visit to the holy places.

متعوج *muta'awwaj*, crooked; wrong, false.

متعوس *mat'ûs*, pl. *matâ'is*, fallen, lost, ruined.

متعوق *muta'awwiq*, hindered, delayed; embarrassed.

متعوه *muta'awwih*, weakened, disfigured; lamed; maimed.

متعيش *muta'ayyiś*, who has enough to live upon, who earns his living.

متعيف *muta'ayyif*, soothsayer, augur.

متعين *muta'ayyin*, evident, &c.; distinguishing one's self, renowned; — ة *muta'ayyana-t*, post, command, office.

متغاضى *mutagâḍî* (غضو VI.), caring little for, neglecting or overlooking a thing.

متغافل *mutagâfil*, feigning indifference; neglectful, inattentive.

متغرق *mutagarriq*, plunged into the the water, wetted through, drenched.

متغطى *mutagaṭṭî* (غطو v.), covered, veiled.

متغلب *mutagallib*, victorious, having the upper hand, tyrant.

متغمس *mutagammas*, dipped into; dyed.

متغير *mutagayyir*, changed; changing colour; disfigured,

perturbed; spoiled; changeable, fickle.

متفاقد *mutafâqid*, missing one another.

متفاقم *mutafâqim*, of greatest importance; monstrous.

متفال *mitfâl*, having foul breath; — *mutafa''al*, of good augury; — *mutafa''il*, auguring well from.

متفائل *mutafâ'il*, soothsayer.

متفتش *mutafattiś*, seeking, examining.

متفحل *mutafaḥḥil*, like a stallion, very manful.

متفحة *matfaḥa-t*, apple-garden.

متفر *mutfir*, budding; — *muttafir* (وفر viii.), numerous, multiplied.

متفرد *mutafarrid*, separating (n.), &c.; rebel.

متفرز *mutafarriz*, separate, secluded, isolated.

متفرع *mutafarri'*, branching out, &c.; appertaining to; — ة *mutafarri'a-t*, ramifications, dependencies, appurtenances.

متفرق *mutafarriq*, separating, dissipating, &c. (adj. n.); — ة *mutafarriqa-t*, escort-man, messenger on horseback.

متفضض *mutafaḍḍiḍ*, broken (seal); dispersed.

متفق *mutaffiq* (وفق viii.), agreeing, confederated, allied.

متفقح *mutafaqqaḥ*, wide awake; petulant, mischievous.

متفقد *mutafaqqid*, missing, longing for.

متفلك *mutafallik*, spherical.

متفهم *mutafahhim*, who tries to understand, who comprehends.

متفوق *mutafawwiq*, surpassing, superior; excessive.

متقادم *mutaqâdim*, having precedence; old, ancient, antiquated.

متقارب *mutaqârib*, approaching one another; name of a metre (*fa'ûlun* ⏑ — — eight times repeated).

متقارن *mutaqârin*, united with one another, yoked together.

متقاعد *mutaqâ'id*, settled, stationary; pensioned, dismissed; delaying payment; inactive, lazy.

متقامر *mataqâmir*, gambler, better.

متقرب *mutaqarrib*, approaching one another; having access, favourite or kinsman (of the king); devotee; near, close at hand.

متقرى *mutaqarri'* (قرا v.), devoted to the study of sacred writings.

متقن *mutqan*, perfect, solidly made; — *mutqin*, who makes solidly; — *mutaqqin* (يقن viii.), knowing for certain, understanding well.

متقون *matqûn* = متقن *mutqan*.

متقى *mutaqqî*, who is on his guard, cautious; God-fearing.

متقيى *mutaqayyi'* (قيا v.), vomiting.

(متك) *matak*, INF. *matk*, cut, cut in pieces.

متك *matk*, anything cut off, piece; also *mutk*, *mutuk*, proboscis of a fly; urinary canal; clitoris; lily, narcissus; — *mutukk*, a vein of the penis.

متكا *matkâ'*, clitoris; uncircumcised, f.; — *muttaka'*, couch, sofa, cushion to lean upon.

متكارى *mutakârî*, who hires.

متكاشف *mutakâśif*, making disclosures to one another.

متكافى *mutakâfî*, responding to one another.

متكاهل *mutakâhil*, negligent, neglectful.

متكبد *mutakabbid*, ready; standing in the meridian.

متكبر *mutakabbir*, proud, &c.; sublime; God.

متكسى *mutakassî* (كسو v.), dressing (adj. n.), dressed.

متكلف *mutakallaf*, performed with pains or produced with cost, sought for, valued, precious; forced, compelled; — *mutakallif*, taking pains with, &c.; purveyor; intermeddler; who feigns, who pretends to.

متكلم *mutakallim*, who speaks, &c.; first person (in grammar); eloquent.
متكمم *mutakammim*, armed from head to foot.
متكنى *mutakannî*, allegorical.
متكى *muttaki'* (وكا VIII.), leaning upon or against; supported, propped up.
(متل) *matal*, U, INF. *matl*, shake, move (a.).
متل *mitall*, firm, strong; — *mutill*, who leads, ties up, distils.
متلاحق *mutalâḥiq*, following each other in unbroken succession; supervening, added.
متلاحك *mutalâḥiq*, inserted into one another, involved.
متلاحمة *mutalâḥima-t*, flesh-wound on the head.
متلاشى *mutalâśî*, wasting away, fleeting, subject to annihilation, vain.
متلاف *mitlâf*, extravagant, squandering, spendthrift.
متلالى *mutala'li'* (لالا II.), glittering, shining, flashing.
متلبك *mutalabbik*, complicated.
متلجم *mutalajjim*, bridled.
متلحف *mutalaḥḥif*, wrapped up.
متلد *mutlad*, inherited property; — *mutlid*, owner of such; — *mutallad*, old; — *mutallid*, who hoards up avariciously.
متلزج *mutalazzij*, ductile, resinous.
متلطى *mutalaṭṭî*, who seeks a refuge, finds protection.
متلف *matlaf*, dangerous place, desert; — *mitlaf*, dissipating, squandering; — *mutlif*, who spoils, destroys, wastes, dissipates; consuming.
متلفق *mutalaffiq*, joining well together, firmly connected.
متلقس *mutalaqqis*, delayed, late.
متلقى *mutalaqqî*, meeting, arriving, &c.; conceiving (woman); collector, tax-gatherer.
متلهث *mutalahhis*, panting with thirst; greedy.

متلهوج *mutalahwij*, over-hasty, precipitate.
متلوط *mutalawwiṭ*, sodomite.
متلوع *mutalawwi'*, disquieted, grieved.
متلوه *matlûh*, mad.
متلوى *mutalawwî*, distorted.
متلى *mutlî*, ة *mutliya-t*, pl. *matâlî*, *mutallayât*, she-camel with her foal.
متلين *mutalayyin*, softened, &c.; mild, kind, gentle.
متم *mutamm*, perfect, completed; superadded; — *mutimm*, completing; full moon.
متماجد *mutamâjid*, vying in glory.
متماحل *mutamâḥil*, long; extended, vast; distant; lengthy and difficult.
متماسى *mutamâsî* (مسو VI.), cancerous, mortified (wound); worm-eaten.
متمائن *mutamâ'in*, hypocritical.
متمت *matmat*, INF. ة, try to become related with (الى *ila*).
متمدح *mutamaddiḥ*, eager for praise.
متمدن *mutamaddin*, settled in a town; civilized, cultivated, refined, polite; well-to-do.
متمرن *mutamarrin*, accustomed to overcome difficulties, inured, exercised.
متمزق *mutamazziq*, torn.
متمسخ *mutamassaḥ*, transformed.
متمكن *mutamakkin*, powerful, stable, consolidated, &c.; noun with three cases, triptote.
متمم *mutmam*, completed, perfect; — *mutammim*, completing, &c.; supplementary; supplementary angle.
متمنى *mutamannî*, who desires, hopes, &c.; optative (mood).
متن *matan*, U, INF. *matn*, beat violently; lie with; swear, take an oath; set out on a journey; — U, INF. *mutûn*, stay, abide; — *matun*, INF. *matâna-t*, be firm, strong, enduring, hardy; — III. INF. *mumâtana-t*, grant a delay

of payment, prolong; — IV. INF. *imtân*, beat one on the back.

متن *matn*, pl. *mitân*, hard rising of the ground, knoll; mountain-summit; pl. *mutûn*, (m. f.) lower part of the back, croup; principal part or thing; middle of the road; bulwark, fortress; text; — *mutinn*, far distant.

متناسب *mutanâsib*, fitting, proportional, &c.; اربع متناسبة *arba' mutanâsiba-t*, the four terms of proportion, rule of three.

متناكح *mutanâkiḥ*, marrying one another, lying with one another; related by intermarriage.

متناوب *mutanâwib*, waiting each for his turn; alternately, by turns.

متناولات *mutanâwalât*, victuals.

متنبج *mutanabbij*, swollen.

متنبه *mutanabbih*, awake, vigilant, on one's guard; prudent, wise by experience.

متنحى *mutanaḥḥa*, place of retirement; — *mutanaḥḥî*, retiring, living in retirement or seclusion; separate.

متنزه *mutanazzah*, spot pleasant for a walk, &c.

متنصح *mutanaṣṣiḥ*, who accepts advice, wise by experience.

متنظف *mutanaẓẓif*, cleanly, tidy, neat.

متنفر *mutanaffir*, detesting, abhorring.

متنفس *mutanaffis*, breathing; living being; taking breath, resting.

متنقد *mutanaqqid*, paying in ready money.

متنيح *mutanayyiḥ*, resting in peace.

(متح) *matah*, INF. *math*, draw or pull up (the bucket out of the well); — *matih*, A, INF. *matah*, err, persist in error; — V. INF. *tamattuh*, arrogate praise; — VI. INF. *tamâtuh*, be far from one another.

متهادن *mutahâdin*, quiet, peaceful.

متهافت *mutahâfit*, rushing precipitately into, &c.; old, worn out.

متهالك *mutahâlik*, rushing to perdition; passionately taken with.

متهاود *mutahâwid*, cheap.

متهاون *mutahâwin*, who despises, neglects.

متهدم *mutahaddim*, in ruins; decrepit.

متهذب *mutahaẓẓib*, pruned; well educated.

متهلهل *mutahalhil*, trembling with joyful excitement.

متهم *muttaham* (وهم VIII.), suspected, accused; guilty; — *muttahim*, *muthim* (تهم IV.), who suspects, causes one to be suspected; — *muttahim*, violent, intense (heat, &c.).

متهنى *mutahanni'* (هنا V.), refreshed by food, &c.

متهور *mutahawwir*, furious, enraged; foolhardy, thoughtless; falling in ruins; tumbling from above.

متهيب *mutahayyab*, terrible; *al-mutahayyib*, lion.

متهيى *mutahayyi'*, preparing one's self, making ready.

(متو) *matâ*, U, INF. *matw*, stride apace; stretch.

متواتر *mutawâtir*, following one another, &c.; well authenticated by continuous evidence, doubtless.

متوارد *mutawârid*, coming one after another, following.

متواسط *mutawâsiṭ*, being in the middle; middling; mediator.

متواضع *mutawâḍi'*, humble, submissive, &c.; condescending.

متواطى *mutawâṭi'*, coming to an agreement with another; humbling one's self.

متوافق *mutawâfiq*, agreeing, &c.; commensurable.

متوالى *mutawâlî*, following one another without interruption, successive; f. pl. *mutawâliyât*, consequences; pl. *matâwila-t*, sect of the *Mutawâlîs* (Shiites).

متوائم *mutawâ'im*, harmonious.

متوبل *mutaubal*, seasoned with herbs.

متوج *matûj*, long; well.
متوجب *mutawajjib*, what is duty, beseeming.
متوح *matûḥ*, draw-well; who draws water; stretching far.
متوحد *mutawaḥḥid*, isolated, &c.; unique; *al-mutawaḥḥid*, God.
متوخم *mutawaḥḥim*, indigestible.
متودع *mutawaddi'*, kind, gentle.
متورع *mutawarri'*, master of one's self; abstemious, pious.
متوسط *mutawassiṭ*, being in the middle, mediating, &c.; middling, indifferent, neither good nor bad; متوسطو الحال *mutawassaṭû 'l-ḥâl*, those concerned in the case.
متوصف *mutawaṣṣif*, described; praised, celebrated.
متوصل *mutawaṣṣil*, who desires to be united with, to come to; united, joined; dependent; arrived.
متوصم *mutawaṣṣim*, weakened by fever; languishing.
متوضا *mutawaḍḍa'*, lavatory; privy.
متوضح *mutawaḍḍiḥ*, distinct, clear, evident; hypochondres.
متوفر *mutawaffir*, numerous, plentiful.
متوفى *mutawaffan*, *mutawaffa*, received in the mercy of God, dead; — *mutawaffî*, who receives (God); who pays his debt in full.
متوق *mutawwaq*, craved for, desired; *mutawwiq*, desirous.
متوقد *mutawaqqid*, burning, glowing; sharp (of intellect).
متوم *mutawwam*, adorned with a necklace.
متون *mutûn*, INF. of (متن); pl. of متن *matn*.
متى *mata*, when? at what time? when; — *mutta*, id.; Matthew.
متياح *mityâḥ*, متيح *mityaḥ*, intermeddler; — *mityâḥ*, *mutyaḥ*, ordained, decreed (fate).
متيح *mittîḥ*, long and flexible; — ة *mittîḥa-t*, stalk; staff; — *mittîḥa-t*, *matyaḥa-t*, *mityaḥa-t*, palm-branch.
متئس *mutta'is*, despairing, desperate.
متيسر *mutayassir*, facilitated, easy; easy to be got; ready; who has good luck and success.
متئم *mut'im*, bearing twins; — *mutayyam*, enslaved; — *mutayyim*, enslaving.
متيما *mataimâ*, whenever.
متين *matîn*, strong; enduring, persevering; text.
متيه *matyah*, ة *matyaha-t*, *matîha-t*, *mutîha-t*, desert where one loses one's self.
متيوسا *matyûsâ*, he-goats, pl. of تيس *tais*.
متئى *mutta'î*, quiet, gentle.
(مث) *maṡṡ*, U, INF. *maṡṡ*, wipe, clean; anoint; perspire, ooze.
مثاب *maṡâb*, ة, middle of the well, place on its edge where the drawer stands; cistern, pond; place where one always returns to, place of assembling, of meeting; caravanserai; — *maṡâb*, reward; — *muṡâb*, rewarded, requited; — ة *maṡâba-t*, degree, rank; place, point; value; class, category.
مثار *muṡâr*, ploughed.
مثافيد *maṡâfîd*, pl. lining.
مثاقيل *maṡâqîl*, pl. of مثقال *miṡqâl*.
مثال *miṡâl*, pl. *amṡila-t*, *muṡl*, *muṡul*, resemblance, anything equal or similar; image, type, model, example; form, formula, formulary; simile, allegory, parable, fable, tale; vision in a dream; manner, method; definite quantity; order, command, written order; retaliation; assimilated verb (beginning with و or ى); bed, carpet; — ى *miṡâliyy*, equal, similar.
مثانة *maṡâna-t*, bladder; womb.
مثانى *maṡânî*, pl. of مثناة *maṡnât* and مثنى *maṡna*.
مثاهاة *maṡâhât*, conference, colloquy.

مثاوى *masâwî*, pl. of مثوى *maswa*.
مثبج *musabbaj*, confused ; — ة *musabbaja-t*, owl.
مثبر *masbir*, place of assembly.
مثبنة *masbana-t*, pocket or bag for toilet-utensils.
مثبور *masbûr*, annihilated.
مثج *masaj*, U, INF. *masj*, mix ; give one to eat.
مثجر *musajjar*, knotty.
مثخبج *musahbij*, with soft loose flesh.
مثخن *mushan*, seriously wounded ; — *mushin*, serious.
(مثد) *masad*, U, INF. *masd*, spy out the enemy hidden between rocks.
مثراد *misrâd*, instrument for killing cattle ; bread broken into the broth.
مثراة *masrât*, what increases wealth.
مثرد *misrad*, dish for the mess ثريد *sarîd*.
مثرطل *musartil*, trailing the robes.
(مثط) *masat*, I, INF. *mast*, press with the hand to the ground.
مثطوع *mastû'*, afflicted with a cold.
(مثع) *masa'*, A, U, INF. *mas'* ; — *masi'*, A, INF. *masa'*, walk in vulgar fashion (woman).
مثعا *mas'â'*, woman walking in vulgar fashion ; hyena.
مثعب *mas'ab*, aqueduct, canal.
مثعل *mas'al*, ة *mas'ala-t*, مثعلب *mus'alib*, ة *mus'aliba-t*, region abounding with foxes.
مثعنجر *mus'anjar*, high sea.
مثغر *masgar*, pl. *masâgir*, open boundary place.
مثغور *masgûr*, gap-toothed ; made breaches into.
مثفاة *misfât*, branding-iron.
مثفى *misfa*, *musaffa*, f. *musaffiya-t*, *musaffât*, *misfât*, thrice married.
مثقال *misqâl*, pl. *masâqîl*, weight (especially for jewels, &c.) ; weight of $1\frac{3}{7}$ ($1\frac{1}{7}$) drachms ; gold piece of this weight ; a silver coin ; coin.
مثقب *misqab*, pl. *masâqib*, a large borer, gimlet ; sharp of intellect, sagacious ; also *masqab*, broad road ; — ة *musaqqaba-t*, pierced pearl.
مثكال *miskâl*, مثكل *muskil*, pl. *masâkîl*, bereft of children ; — ة *maskala-t*, spear (bereaving of children) ; — *muskila-t*, elegy on the death of children.
(مثل) *masal*, U, INF. *masl*, make one similar to the other, compare ; resemble ; — U, INF. *masl*, *musla-t*, make an example of ; INF. *musûl*, stand upright ; — *masul*, INF. *masâla-t*, stand upright ; be eminent, superior, excellent ; — II. INF. *tamsîl*, *tamsâl*, represent in images, show in an image or model, describe, give a simile or example ; make equal or similar, assimilate ; compare ; quote an example ; represent by image, portrait, or statue ; take a simile from ; mutilate ; — III. INF. *mumâsala-t*, be one and the same with ; resemble, remind of by resemblance ; compare, show the similarity between two things ; imitate ; — IV. INF. *imsâl*, make an example of by punishment ; kill the murderer in retaliation ; — V. INF. *tamassul*, make one's self similar to another, become similar to him, assimilate one's self ; imitate ; quote an example or give a simile ; imagine ; stand erect and ready for service ; — VI. INF. *tamâsul*, grow similar to one another ; imitate each other ; — VIII. INF. *imtisâl*, place one's self upright before (ل *li*) ; obey an order ; imagine ; take a thing as a simile, make a proverb of it ; adduce a tradition, a proof ; retaliate.
مثل *misl*, pl. *amsâl*, similarity, resemblance, what is equal in quality, size or number ; like (مثل ماثل *misl-u mâsil*, equal in every respect) ;—*musl*, *musul*, pl.

of مثال *misâl*;—*masal*, pl. *amsâl*, anything similar, equal, similarity; (pl. also *masalât*) image, simile, parable, proverb, fable, tale; sentence, maxim; example, model; similar case, precedent; quality, state; ضرب م *darab masal-an*, use as a simile, set up or quote a proverb; *masal-an*, for instance; — ة *musla-t*, *musula-t*, exemplary punishment; example, model.

مثلبة *maslaba-t*, *masluba-t*, pl. *masâlib*, injury, defect, want; blame, evil report.

مثلث *maslas*, ة *maslisa-t*, third string of the lute; by threes; — *muslas*, reduced to three; — *musallas*, ة, tripled, divided by three; trilateral, triangular, triangle; marked with three dots (letter); pronounceable with the three vowels; a kind of mulled wine; *al-musallasât*, trigonometry.

مثلج *muslij*, snowing, snowy; — ة *maslaja-t*, pl. *masâlij*, ice-cellar.

مثلما *misla-mâ*, like, as.

مثلوث *maslûs*, triple; triangular.

مثلوج *maslûj*, covered with snow; cold (used also of the mind).

مثلى *musla*, f. of امثل *amsal*, coming nearest to the model, &c.; — ة *masliya-t*, similarity, resemblance.

مثماث *masmâs*, complicated matter; shake, concussion.

(مثمث) *masmas*, INF. ة, *mismâs*, leak; move, shake (a.); confuse.

مثمج *musmij*, f. ة, embroiderer of garments.

مثمر *musmar*, ripe to be culled; — *musmir*, fruit-bearing, &c.; — bearing interest.

مثمل *masmil*, asylum; — *musammal*, deadly (poison); — ة *masmala-t*, large well; — *mismala-t*, basket of palm-leaves; shepherd's pouch or satchel.

مثمن *musamman*, octagon; — *; — ة *mismana-t*, travelling-bag.

مثمور *masmûr*, abundant; numerous.

(مثن) *masan*, U, I, INF. *masn*, hit on the bladder;—*masin*, A, INF. *masan*, suffer from the bladder, be unable to retain the water.

مثن *masin*, f. مثنا *masnâ'*, suffering from the bladder; — *musinn*, old and decrepit.

مثناة *masnât*, pl. *masâniya-t*, bent, curve; consisting of two equal parts, distich; subtraction; power; also *misnât*, pl. *masânî*, fold; tetrastich; rope; song; vocal music; the Mishnah; double-twisted string.

مثنوى *masnawiyy*, rhyming in its half verses (poem); a moral poem of this description.

مثنى *masna*, • two by two; n.u. *masnât*, pl. *masânî*, bend, curve; divided, separate; distich rhyming in its half verses; second chord of the lute; double twisted string; *al-masânî*, sections of the Koran, especially the 1st Sûra: the twice-read chapter; the Koran; — *masniyy*, doubled, folded; of a double thread; twice ploughed; — *musanna*, f. *musannât*, doubled, repeated; in the dual case; marked with two dots; the second, the younger of two people with the same name; copy.

مثوب *mas'ub*, lazy, slow; — ة *masûba-t*, *maswaba-t*, reward; pl. *-ât*, good deeds meeting with reward.

مثورة *maswara-t*, country abounding with oxen.

مثول *musûl*, standing (s.) upright before one's master to receive his orders; waiting (s.), attendance.

مثوول *maswûl*, giddy; crazed.

مثوى *maswa*, pl. مثاو *masâw-in*, مثاوى *masâwî*, dwelling, abode,

sojourn; inn, hotel (ابو المثوى *abû'l-maṡwa*, innkeeper).

مثيب *muṡayyab*, no longer a virgin, deflowered.

مثيرة *muṡîra-t*, cow at the plough.

مثيل *maṡîl*, equal, similar; eminent, excellent; great; ة *maṡîla-t*, example, verses quoted as an example; lesson;—*muṡail*, dim. slightly similar.

(مج) *majj*, U, INF. *majj*, spit out; (m.) inhale, imbibe.

مج *majj*, a kind of lentils.

مجا . *mujâ* ., to be looked for under (جو . , جب . IV.), pass. as—

مجاب *mujâb*, pat. of (جوب IV.), answered, having received an answer, accepted, heard by God (prayers).

مجاج *mujâj*, cut-off branch; mushroom; — *mujâj*, saliva (م العنب *mujâj al-'inab*, wine, م النحل *mujâj an-naḥl*, honey); millet; — *majjâj*, pompous.

مجاد *mijâd*, emulation, vying (s.) for glory; — *mujâdd*, having a law-suit against; — ة *majâda-t*, glory, distinction; — *mujâdda-t*, law-suit, legal contest.

مجا . *mujâ* . ., *mujâ* . . ة, to be looked for under (. . ج III.), as—

مجادل *mujâdil*, ag. of (جدل III.), disputing with, &c.; — ة *mujâdala-t*, INF. of the same; dispute, quarrel, contest, combat.

مجاديف *majâdîf*, pl. of مجداف *mijdâf*.

مجار *mijâr*, profiting (s.); tether of a camel; — *mujâr* (جور IV.), protected, fugitive; — *mujârr*, who torments, tortures.

مجاراة *mujârât*, running a race with (s.), emulation, competing (s.), contest.

مجاريح *majârîḥ*, pl. of مجروح *majrûḥ*.

مجاز *majâz*, passing, passing by (s.); passage, road (م الزقاق *majâz az-zuqâq*, Strait of Gibraltar); figurative speech, allegory, metaphor; insincere; superficial, worldly, profane; also ة *majâza-t*, plantation of nut-trees; — *mujâz*, allowed, permitted.

مجازاة *mujâzât*, requital; chastisement.

مجازى *majâziyy*, figurative; allegorical; insincere; superficial, worldly; — *.

مجاس *majâss*, pl. of مجسة *majassa-t*.

مجاع *majâ'*, hunger; — *mujjâ'*, gruel; — ة *majâ'a-t*, hungering (s.); impudence; pl. *majâ'i'*, year of famine, distress; — *mujjâ'a-t*, *majjâ'a-t*, impudent.

مجاعيل *majâ'îl*, pl. of مجعول *maj'ûl*.

مجال *majâl*, place of exercise, of combat, battlefield; skirmish; circle; sphere (of action), elbowroom; power, capacity, possibility, opportunity; road, passage; career; — *maj'al*, pl. *majâ'il*, assembly; — *mijâl*, pl. of مجلة *majla-t*; — *majâll*, pl. of مجلة *majalla-t*.

مجالدة *mujâlada-t*, combat with swords; combat of gladiators.

مجامد *mujâmid*, next neighbour.

مجان *majjân*, what is in abundance, to be got for nothing; *majjân-an*, gratis; — *mujjân*, pl. of ماجن *mâjin*, talking at random, &c.;—*majânn*, pl. of مجن *mijann*; — ة *majâna-t*, thoughtlessness; pertness;—*mujânna-t*, blackness of the face.

مجانق *majâniq*, مجانيق *majânîq*, pl. of منجنيق *manjanîq*.

مجانى *majânî*, profit, advantage, gain.

مجانين *majânîn*, pl. of مجنون *majnûn*, mad, and of منجنون *manjanûn*, water-wheel, &c.

مجاهرة *mujâhara-t*, open enmity; reproach.

مجاهز *mujâhiz*, rich, wealthy.

مجاهيل *majâhîl*, pl. of مجهول *majhûl*.

مجاور *mujâwir*, ة, neighbouring, &c.; servant of a mosque, sweeper; — ة *mujâwara-t*, neighbouring (s.), being neighbourly (s.); protection.

مجاوز *mujâwiz*, passing, &c.; transitive (verb).

مجاولة *mujâwala-t*, combat.

مجائع *majâ'i'*, pl. of مجاعة *majâ'a-t*.

مجائل *majâ'il*, pl. of مجال *maj'al*.

. . مجـ *muja . .*, to be looked for under (. . ج II.), as—

مجبب *mujabbab*, pat. of (جب II.), having the legs white from the knees downward; — *mujabbib*, ag. of the same, fleeing.

. . مجـ *muj . .*, to be looked for under (. . ج IV.), as—

مجبن *mujbin*, ag. of (جبن IV.), curdling, cheesy, &c.; — ة *majbana-t*, what makes a man cowardly; what causes the milk to turn into cheese, rennet.

مجبة *majabba-t*, high-road.

. و . مجـ *maj . û .*, to be looked for under (. . ج), as—

مجبوب *majbûb*, pat. of (جب), gelded, castrated; — ة *majbûba-t*, a leather bag.

مجبور *majbûr*, compelled; set (bone); restored to better circumstances; — ة *majbûra-t*, Medina; — ية *majbûriyya-t*, compulsion.

مجتاز *mujtâz*, passing, travelling.

مجتبا *mujtaba*, elected, pat. of (جبو VIII.); — مجتبى *mujtabî*, electing, selecting; collector.

مجتر *mujtarr*, pulled, dragged along; — *mujtarir*, chewing the cud, ruminating.

مجترى *mujtari'* (جرا VIII.), bold; *al-mujtari'*, lion.

مجتمع *mujtama'*, place of assembly.

مجتهد *mujtahid*, who exerts himself, &c.; lawyer entitled to give decisions.

مجثاث *mijṡâṡ*, مجثة *mijaṡṡa-t*, borer.

مجثم *majṡim*, seat; roost; lair.

(مجح) *majaḥ*, INF. *majḥ*, be proud; — *majiḥ*, A, INF. *majaḥ*, rejoice; — V. INF. *tamajjuḥ*, be proud.

مجحر *majḥar*, pl. *majâḥir*, place of refuge, asylum.

(مجد) *majad*, U, INF. *majd*, surpass others in glory, be eminent; — U, INF. *majd*, *mujûd*, come to rich pasture grounds; have its fill, or nearly so, of green food; — *majud*, INF. *majâda-t*, excel by glory; — II. INF. *tamjîd*, praise, glorify, exalt; deem celebrated; feed the camels to satiety on green food; — III. INF. *mijâd*, vie in glory; — IV. INF. *imjâd*, glorify, overwhelm with praise; — V. INF. *tamajjud*, be glorified, praised; glory; — VI. INF. *tamâjud*, glorify one another; — X. INF. *istimjâd*, claim or excel in glory, honour, privileges, &c.

مجد *majd*, pl. *amjâd*, glory, praise, distinction.

مجداب *mijdâb*, land of famine.

مجداح *mijdâḥ*, sea-coast.

مجداف *mijdâf*, pl. *majâdîf*, wing; oar.

مجدال *mijdâl*, quarrelsome.

مجدح *mijdaḥ*, paddle or spoon for stirring up.

مجدر *majdar*, ة *majdara-t*, place where small-pox is rampant; — *mujaddar*, suffering from small-pox, pock-marked; ة *mujaddara-t*, pillaw with lentils; — ة *majdara-t*, worthy, fit.

مجدف *mijdaf*, pl. *majâdif*, wing; oar; — *mujaddaf* (عليه *'alai-hi*), in bad circumstances; — *mujaddif*, ungrateful; blaspheming.

مجدل *majdal*, troop; — *mijdal*, pl. *majâdil*, stronghold, fortress; quarrelsome.

مجدوب *majdûb*, hard, sterile; (m.) crazy, mad.

مجدور *majdûr*, marked by small-pox; worthy, fit.

مجدول *majdûl*, twisted, plaited; — *mujadwal*, bordered by lines and divided into columns.

مجذاف *mijẓâf*, ة *mijẓâfa-t*, oar.

مجذم *mijẓam*, leprous;—*mujaẓẓam*, id.; cut off, maimed.

مجذوب *majẓûb*, attracted, &c.; fanatic, enthusiast; half mad, frantic.

مجذور *majẓûr*, reduced to the square root.

(مجر) *majar*, U, INF. *majr*, be thirsty; — *majir*, A, INF. *majar*, have the stomach full of water without being satiated; — III. INF. *mijâr*, *mumâjara-t*, sell with profit; — IV. INF. *imjâr*, id.

مجر *majr*, much, many, numerous; numerous army; profit in selling; interest; thirst; — *majar*, m. the Hungarians; Hungarian ducat; — *majarr*, water-course; supporting beam (head-beam); — *mijarr*, harrow;— ة *majarra-t*, galaxy.

مجرا *majrâ*=مجرى *majra*;—*mijrâ'*, runner.

مجرد *mijrad*, pl. *majârid*, surgical instrument for cleaning the teeth; — *mujarrad*, stripped, &c.; exercised, experienced, probed; unmarried, single, lonely; only, but for; first form of a verb; pl. f. *mujarradât*, bodiless beings, spirits, angels; abstractions; — ى *mujarradiyy*, lonely, solitary (m.); — ية *mujarradiyya-t*, solitude.

مجرف *mujarraf*, robbed of all, denuded; — *mujarrif*, carrying off everything; — ة *mijrafa-t*, shovel, spade, hoe.

مجرم *mujrim*, criminal, sinner; — *mujarram*, whole, entire.

مجروح *majrûḥ*, pl. *majârîḥ*, wounded, hurt, refused; refuted.

مجروم *majrûm*, corpulent.

مجرى *majra*, مجرا *majrâ*, pl. *majârî*, water-course, channel, river-bed; canal, aqueduct; course of a ship; — *mujra*, made to flow; made current, carried out, executed; also *majriyy*, inflected; — *mujrî*, making to flow; making current, carrying out; executor;—*majariyy*, Hungarian;—ة *mujriya-t*, wild beast or bitch with young ones.

مجز *mijazz*, sickle; scissors, shears; — *mujizz*, ripe for the harvest.

مجزا *majza'*, *mujza'*, ة *majza'a-t*, *mujza'a-t*, satisfying (s.), satisfaction, INF. of (جزا);—*mujazza'*, divided into parts or portions.

مجزب *mijzab*, outwardly moral.

مجزر *majzir*, ة *majzira-t*, pl. *majâzir*, slaughter-house; —*mujzir*, to be slaughtered.

مجزفة *mijzafa-t*, fishing-net.

مجزم *mijzam*, full.

مجزى *mujzî*, sufficient; appropriate.

(مجس), II. *majjas*, INF. *tamjîs*, make one a worshipper of fire; — V. INF. *tamajjus*, become such.

مجس *majass*, ة *majassa-t*, pl. *majâss*, place to be felt, pulse.

(مجسد) *mijsad*, part of a garment which touches the body; — *mujsad*, pl. *majâsid*, red; dyed with saffron; — *mujassad*, id.; full, sonorous (voice).

مجسم *mujassam*, corporeal, &c.; massy, massive; solid body; م كثير القواعد *mujassam kaṡîr al-qawâ'id*, polyhedron.

مجش *mijaśś*, ة *mijaśśa-t*, hand-mill.

(مجع) *maja'*, INF. *maj'*, *maj'a-t*, be shameless, impudent and obtrusive;—*maji'*, A,—*maju'*, INF. *majâ'a-t*, id.

مجع *mij'*, stupid, foolish; — ة *maj'a-t*, *muj'a-t*, *muja'a-t*, id.; — *maji'a-t*, f. talking ribaldry.

مجعب *mij'ab*, strong wrestler.

مجعد *muja''ad*, thick, consistent; curled.

مجعر *maj'ar*, fundament of a bird.

مجعول *maj'ûl*, put down, &c.; pl. *majâ'il*, salary, wages, pension.

مجفر *majfar*, anti-venereal food; — *mujaffar*, entirely white.

مجفو *majfuww*, مجفى *majfiyy*, who has been wronged.

(مجل) *majal*, U, INF. *majl*, *mujûl*, cover (n.) with blisters (hand from working); heal (n.); — ة *majla-t*, pl. *majl*, *mijâl*, blister on the hand from working; — *majila-t*, hand covered with blisters; — *mujalla-t*, pl. *majâll*, roll, book, scientific work of high standard.

مجلو *majluww*, ة, polished, shining, bright; ة, unveiled (bride).

مجلوه *majlûh*, without door or curtain.

مجلى *majlan*, *majla*, pl. *majâlî*, front part of the head which first grows bald; — *mijla*, baldness of the forehead; — *mujallan*, مجلا *mujallâ*, (جلو II.) polished, &c.; transfigured (Christ); — *mujallî*, polishing, &c.; f. pl. ات *mujalliyât*, purging medicines.

مجم *majamm*, breast; also *majimm*, part of a well that contains water; — *mujimm*, filling up the measure; heaping up.

(مجمج) *majmaj*, INF. ة, trace the letters indisctinctly in writing; utter or express one's self indistinctly, stammer; — II. INF. *tamajmuj*, be closed.

مجمر *mijmar*, ة *mijmara-t*, pl. *majâmir*, censer, coal-basin; also *mujmar*, incense, perfumes; — ة *majmara-t*, blacksmith's furnace.

مجمع *majma'*, *majmi'*, pl. *majâmi'*, place of assembly, hall; assembly, council; crowd, multitude, quantity; miscellany; (m.) card-box; meeting of rivers or seas; — *; — ة *majma'a-t*, place of assembly; sand-hill; desert; memorandum-book, miscellanies.

مجمم *mujammam*, brimful, heaped; having the hair tied up into a knot; (m.) shorn.

مجموع *majmû'*, pl. *majâmî'*, collected, gathered, &c.; the whole of; crowd; sum, total; — ة *majmû'a-t*, book of extracts, scrap-book, album, miscellanies, memorandum-book.

مجمول *majmûl*, predicate.

(مجن) *majan*, U, INF. *mujûn*, be thick, rough and hard; — U, INF. *mujn*, *mujûn*, *majâna-t*, talk or act inconsiderately.

مجن *mijann*, pl. *majânn*, shield; — *mujann*, mad, possessed of a demon; — ة *majanna-t*, madness; place inhabited by demons; — *mijanna-t*, shield.

مجنا *mujna'*, convex shield without any iron part; — ة *mujna-t*, tomb.

مجنب *majnab*, INF. of (جنب); also *mijnab*, much, many, numerous; — *mijnab*, shield; curtain, veil; — *mujnab*, shield; — *mujnib*, foreign, strange; — ة *mujannaba-t*, van-guard; — du. f. تان *mujannibatân*, the two wings of an army.

مجنف *mijnaf*, inclined; — *mujnif*, deviating from the right way, from what is right.

(مجنق) *majnaq*, INF. ة, fling stones by the ballista.

مجنوب *majnûb*, leading horse; suffering from pleurisy; brought by the south wind.

مجنون *majnûn*, pl. *majânîn*, possessed by a demon, raving; mad with love; — ية *majnûniyya-t*, madness.

مجنه *mujannah*, tray of reed or rushes.

مجنى *majnan*, pl. *majânî*, anything gathered, plucked, reaped; — *majniyy*, plucked, culled; — *.

مجهار *mijhâr*, مجهر *mijhar*, outspoken.

مجهز *mujhiz*, sudden.

مجهل *majhal*, pathless desert; — ة *majhala-t*, sign of ignorance; what propagates ignorance.

مجهود *majhûd*, jaded, &c.; hardship, labour; zeal, exertion, utmost effort.

مجهول *majhûl*, pl. *majâhîl*, unknown, ignored; passive mood; anonymous.

مجهى *mujhî*, open, distinct; clear, serene (sky); without a curtain.

مجواد *mijwâd*, who produces beautiful things (poet).

مجوب *mijwab*, scissors; shield; — ة *majûba-t*, answer.

مجود *mujawwad*, well done or performed; seized with love-passion; — *mujawwid*, who does a thing well, writes beautifully; scholar, linguist; singer.

مجوسى *majûsiyy*, pl. *majûs*, Magian, worshipper of fire; — ة *majûsiyya-t*, their sect.

مجوعة *majwa'a-t*, hunger, distress.

مجوف *majûf*, stout, corpulent; — *maj'uf*, timorous; — * .

مجول *mijwal*, shield; girl's chemise; rings for ornament, amulet, &c.; silver; wild ass; — * .

مجون *mujûn*, impudence; gay talk.

مجوهر *majauhar*, studded with jewels; — ات, pl. f. *mujauharât*, jewellery.

مجووف *maj'ûf*, frightened; hungry.

مجى *maji*, *majiyy* = مجيى *maji'*.

مجيد *majîd*, glorified, celebrated; *al-majîd*, God; — *mujîd*, who produces beautiful things; near, impending (death); — ى *majîdiyy*, dollar coined under Sultan *Abdul-majîd*; — ية *majîdiyya-t*, his decoration.

مجيع *majî'*, dish of milk and dates.

مجيى *majî'*, coming (s.), arrival; origin.

(مح) *maḥḥ*, I, A, INF. *maḥḥ*, *maḥaḥ*, *muḥûḥ*, be worn out; — ة *muḥḥa-t*, yolk.

محابا *muḥâbâ'*, ة *muḥâbât*, honouring (s.); friendly regard; partizanship, taking one's part; respect of person.

محابة *muḥâbba-t*, love.

محابى *muḥâbî* (محاب *muḥâb-in*), partial to.

محابيب *maḥâbîb*, pl. of محبوب *maḥbûb*.

محابيس *maḥâbîs*, pl. of محبوس *maḥbûs*.

محاج *miḥâj*, granted delays of payment; — *maḥâjj*, pl. of محجة *maḥajja-t*; — ة *muḥâjja-t*, defence of a legal cause, pleading (s.).

محاح *maḥâḥ*, salty ground; — *muḥâḥ*, hunger; — *maḥḥâḥ*, liar, impostor; who assails others with unfounded accusations.

محاد *muḥâdd*, adjacent, bordering on; who hinders, adversary, opponent; — ة *muḥâdda-t*, contiguity; limitation; hindrance.

محاذاة *muḥâẕât*, opposition, being opposite or parallel; answering (s.).

محاذى *muḥâẕi* (حذو III.), opposite, in front of, parallel.

محاذير *maḥâẕîr*, pl. of محذور *maḥẕûr*.

محار *maḥâr*, place where one returns to; shell; oyster; also ة *maḥâra-t*, return; — ة *maḥâra-t*, shell; oyster; cavity of the ear; palate; joint of the shoulders; strip; tract, region.

محاريب *maḥârîb*, pl. of محراب *miḥrâb*.

محاريم *maḥârîm*, pl. of محرم *muḥarram*.

محارين *maḥârîn*, pl. of محران *miḥrân*.

محاسب *muḥâsib*, accountant, auditor, examiner of accounts; — ة *muḥâsaba-t*, office of such; settling of accounts; arithmetic.

محاسن *maḥâsin*, pl. of حسن *ḥusn*, fine qualities or actions, beauties, excellencies, advantages.

محاش *maḥâś*, valuables, goods, pieces of furniture; — *muḥâś*, roasted; — *maḥâśś*, pl. of محشة *maḥaśśa-t*.

محاشاة *muḥâśât*, exception.

محاشى *maḥâśi'*, coarse clothes; — *maḥâśî*, pl. of محشى *miḥśan*.

محاص *maḥâṣ*, flight, INF. of (حيص); — *maḥâṣṣ*, shining, resplendent, lighting up; — *muḥâṣṣ*, who takes his portion, shareholder; — ة *muḥâṣṣa-t*, dividing or sharing with others.

محاصيل *maḥâṣîl*, pl. of محصول *maḥṣûl*.

محاض *maḥâḍ*, menses; — *; — ة *muḥâḍḍa-t*, stimulating, inciting, encouraging (s.).

محاضر *muḥâḍir*, present, ready; — ة *muḥâḍara-t*, being present, appearing, presenting one's self (s.); pleading in a court of justice; disputation; conversation.

محاضرية *muḥâḍariyyat-an*, on the spot, at once.

محاط *maḥâṭ*, inclosure, fold; — *

محافاة *muḥâfât*, quarrel, dispute.

محافظ *muḥâfiẓ*, guarding, defending, &c.; soldier of a garrison; commander of a fortress; — ة *muḥâfaẓa-t*, guard, protection, &c.; regard, attendance; sense of shame and decency.

محافل *muḥâfil*, who maintains his honour.

محافة *muḥâfa-t*, litter for women.

محاق *maḥâq*, *miḥâq*, *muḥâq*, waning of the moon; annihilation; — *muḥâqq*, opponent in a lawsuit; — ة *muḥâqqa-t*, law-suit, legal contest.

محاقين *maḥâqîn*, pl. of محقان *miḥqân*.

محاكاة *muḥâkât*, tale, report, narration; similarity, imitation.

محاكمة *muḥâkama-t*, summoning before the judge, &c.; lawsuit; wrangling.

محاكة *maḥâka-t*, workshop of a weaver; — *maḥâkka-t*, rubbing against one another (s.), resistance; electricity.

محاكى *muḥâkî* (حكو III.), imitating; talking.

محال *maḥâl*, stratagem, artifice, deceit; power; spine; — *miḥâl*, versatility, cunning, stratagem; Michael; — *muḥâl*, impossible, absurd, nonsensical; pl. *muḥâlât*, impossibilities; contradiction; perverseness; — *maḥḥâl*, cunning, sly; cunning fellow; devil; — *maḥâll*, pl. of محل *maḥall*; — ة *maḥâla-t*, pl. *maḥâl*, artifice, deceit; vertebra of a camel; (pl. also *maḥâwil*) pulley of a well; power, possibility (لا محالة *lâ maḥâlat-a*, there is no help, it is necessary, no doubt, in full earnest); — *maḥâlla-t*, pl. *maḥâll*, place, square, street, quarter.

محالف *muḥâlif*, conspirator; — ة *muḥâlafa-t*, conspiracy; alliance.

محام *muḥâmm*, persevering, firm.

محاماة *muḥâmât*, protection, defence, pleading for.

محامى *muḥâmî* (محام *muḥâm-in*), defender, advocate.

محانث *maḥâniṣ*, abominations.

محانة *maḥâna-t*, bend of a river.

محاور *maḥâwir*, pl. of محور *miḥwar*; — ة *muḥâwara-t*, conversation, &c.; dialogue, usage of a language, idiomatic expression, idiom.

محاوى *maḥâwî*, miscellanies.

محايا *maḥâyâ*, pl. of محيا *maḥyâ*; — ة *muḥâyât*, making to blush, putting to shame, abashing (s.); blushing (s.), shame; bringing up of a child.

محبر *miḥbar*, ة *maḥbara-t*, *maḥbira-t*, *maḥbura-t*, *maḥburra-t*, pl. *maḥâbir*, ink-flask, ink-stand.

محبس *maḥbas*, imprisoning, keeping captive, imprisonment; — *maḥbis*, pl. *muḥâbis*, prison,

dungeon; dam; ring without a stone; — *miḥbas*, embroidered coverlet, bedding; — *; — *muḥabbis*, who prevents; — ة *maḥbasa-t*, pl. *maḥâbis*, hermitage.

محبل *maḥbal*, time of conception and gestation; also *maḥbil*, womb, matrice;—*;—*muḥabbal*, bushy; rope.

محبة *maḥabba-t*, love, friendship; benevolence.

محبوب *maḥbûb*, pl. *maḥâbîb*, beloved; lover; — ة *maḥbûba-t*, mistress, lady-love.

محبور *maḥbûr*, happy, joyous.

محبوك *maḥbûk*, solidly woven; strong in the legs.

محبول *maḥbûl*, caught in a net; involved in difficulties.

محبون *maḥbûn*, dropsical.

(محت) *maḥut*, INF. *maḥâta-t*, be intensely hot; — IV. INF. *imḥât*, fill with anger, provoke.

محت *maḥt*, hard; difficult, violent; close, sultry; pl. *muḥût*, *muḥatâ'*, intelligent; sagacious; pure (of blood).

محتا . *muḥtâ* ., to be looked for under (حو . , حى . VIII.), as—

محتاج *muḥtâj*, ag. or pat. of حوج VIII., in want of (الى *ila*); wanted, necessary.

محتال *muḥtâl*, ة, cunning, deceitful; knave; — ة *muḥtâla-t*, procuress.

محت . . *muḥta* . ., to be looked for under (. . ح VIII.), as—

محتبس *muḥtabis*, ag. of (حبس VIII.), who keeps back, restrains, restricts; suffering from dysury;—*muḥtabbas*, pat. of id., kept back, imprisoned.

محتج *muḥtajj*, *muḥtajij*, who quarrels, disputes, pleads.

محتد *maḥtid*, root, origin; race; mature;—*muḥtadd*, violent, impetuous; flight, escape.

محترف *muḥtarif*, artizan; — *muḥtaraf*, workshop;—ة *muḥtarifa-t*, taxes on trade and industry.

محترم *muḥtarim*, who defends his honour; — *.

محتزم *muḥtazim*, girded; clad in armour, armed.

محتسب *muḥtasib*, who takes in account, &c.; accountant; overseer of the market; excise-collector; prefect of police.

محتشى *muḥtaśî* (حشو VIII.), filled, crammed; ة, having false breasts, hips, &c.

محتضر *muḥtaḍar*, near death, in the last gasps; — *.

محتضن *muḥtaḍan*, upper part of the chest; — *.

محتظى *muḥtaẕî* (حظو VIII.), fortunate, successful; favourite.

محتفل *muḥtafal*, place of assembly; assembly.

محتكر *muḥtakir*, who buys up the corn, speculator, usurer, monopolist.

محتملات *muḥtamilât*, suppositions, possibilities; — *.

محتوم *maḥtûm*, settled, decided upon, fixed by decree.

محتى *muḥtā*, strongly built.

محث *muḥiṡṡ*, محثث *muḥaṡṡiṡ*, who spurs, urges on, stimulates; — ة *maḥaṡṡa-t*, stimulation.

محثو *maḥṡuww*, dispersed, scattered.

محج *maḥaj*, INF. *maḥj*, skin, bark; make flexible by rubbing; wipe; sweep the ground; — III. INF. *miḥâj*, *mumâḥaja-t*, grant a delay of payment; — ة *maḥajja-t*, pl. *maḥâjj*, highroad, causeway; thesis, assertion; anything proved.

محجا *maḥja'*, refuge, asylum; — ة *miḥjât* (m. and f., sing. and pl.), worthy, fit.

محجاج *miḥjâj*, quarrelsome; probe; a kind of harrow.

محجام *miḥjâm*, coward.

محجر *maḥjar*, anything forbidden; — *maḥjir*, *miḥjar*, pl. *maḥâjir*, socket of the eye; surroundings of a town; orchard; quarry; —

muḥajjar, petrified; surrounded with clouds.

محجز *miḥjaz*, bar, screen.

محجم *miḥjam*, ة *miḥjama-t*, pl. *maḥâjim*, cupping-glass;—*muḥjim*, cowardly;—ة *maḥjama-t*, pl. *maḥâjim*, place where the cupping-glass is put.

محجن *miḥjan*, ة *miḥjana-t*, pl. *maḥâjin*, stick crooked at the top, crosier.

محجوب *maḥjûb*, veiled, &c.; ashamed; embarrassed; blind from birth.

محجوج *maḥjûj*, what is resorted to, where a pilgrimage is made to; house of pilgrimage, temple at Mecca; aim, end, purpose.

محجوز *maḥjûz*, hindered, &c.; tied up; girded.

محجول *maḥjûl*, white-footed (horse).

محجى *maḥjiyy*, enigmatic;—*muḥjî*, miserly, avaricious, greedy.

محد *maḥadd*, flight, escape.

محدب *muḥaddab*, hump-backed; convex.

محدث *muḥdas*, created; new, modern; also ة *muḥdasa-t*, anything new, strange, unwished-for;— * ;— ات *muḥaddisât*, events, stories.

محدس *maḥdis*, question, request; wish, intention.

محدلة *miḥdala-t*, pl. *maḥâdil*, cylinder, roller.

محدود *maḥdûd*, limited, sharpened, &c.; expelled;— ات *maḥdûdât*, legal punishments.

محذا *miḥẕâ'*, who reviles, abuses; —ة *miḥẕât*, shoe-maker's nippers.

محذم *miḥẕam*, sharp.

محذور *maḥẕûr*, pl. *maḥâẕîr*, what is to be guarded against; accident, calamity; fear, anxiety, apprehension;— ة *maḥẕûra-t*, id.; war; scarecrow.

محر *muḥirr*, hot.

محراب *miḥrâb*, pl. *maḥârîb*, prayer-niche of a mosque; garret, parlour, hall; battle-field; warrior, warlike.

محراث *miḥrâs*, pl. *maḥârîs*, plough.

محراف *miḥrâf*, probe.

محراك *miḥrâk*, poker; little stick to stir up; intriguer, agitator, revolutionist.

محران *miḥrân*, pl. *maḥârîn*, honeycomb, honey; cotton-seed.

محرب *miḥrab*, ة *miḥraba-t*, warlike, bellicose;— *.

محرث *miḥras*, pl. *maḥâris*, plough.

محرد *maḥrid*, pl. *maḥârid*, moustaches, beard of a camel, &c.; — *muḥarrad*, curved, arched.

محرز *muḥriz*, cautious (ابو م *abû muḥriz*, sparrow);— *muḥarraz*, carefully preserved, guarded;— ة *muḥriza-t*, chaste woman.

محرض *miḥraḍ*, ة *miḥraḍa-t*, vessel for ashes and alkalis;— *.

محرف *maḥrif*, place where one stays or moves, workshop, &c.; — *muḥarrif*, who transposes, &c.; diagonal; cut in a sharp angle; anagram.

محرق *miḥraq*, file;— *;— ة *muḥraqa-t*, burnt-offering.

محرم *maḥram*, pl. *maḥârim*, forbidden, anything unlawful; ذو م *ẕû maḥram*, who has access to the harem: near relation, slave-girl, person of trust, confidant;— *;— *muḥarram*, pl. *muḥarramât*, anything forbidden; pl. also *muḥârim*, *muḥârîm*, the month *Muḥarram*; ة *muḥarrama-t*, not yet quite trained (camel);— *maḥrama-t*, *maḥruma-t*, pl. *-ât*, *maḥârim*, anything inviolable, sacred, forbidden; wife; failure, disappointment, denial;— ية *maḥramiyya-t*, close relationship, intimate friendship, access to the closest circle.

محرن *miḥran*, instrument for cleaning cotton.

محروب *maḥrûb*, robbed; poor.

محرور *maḥrûr*, set free; hot, hot-

tempered, choleric (also ى *maḥrûriyy*); written.

محروسة *maḥrûsa-t*, fortified and garrisoned town, large town, large ship.

محروقة *maḥrûqa-t*, fuel.

محروم *maḥrûm*, forbidden, &c.; disappointed; unfortunate, indigent;—ية *maḥrûmiyya-t*, being excluded, outcast; disappointment, failure.

محرى *miḥran*, pudenda of a woman; — *maḥriyy*, worthy, fit; — *maḥariyy*, a species of dromedary.

(محز) *maḥaz*, INF. *maḥz*, *miḥâz*, lie with; strike the chest with the fist.

محز *maḥazz*, incision, indentation, articulation; — *miḥazz*, sharp, bitter (in words).

محزان *miḥzân*, sad, sorrowful.

محزرة *maḥzara-t*, estimation, evaluation.

محزز *muḥazzaz*, indented.

محزم *maḥzim*, pl. *maḥâzim*, place where the girth is put on; — *miḥzam*, ة *miḥzama-t*, pl. *maḥâzim*, girth, girdle, belt; — *.

محزون *maḥzûn*, grieved, &c.; wearing mourning-apparel.

(محس) *maḥas*, INF. *maḥs*, knead; scrape and tan.

محس *miḥass*, ة *miḥassa-t*, currycomb; — *.

محسا *maḥsâ*, mouth.

محساب *miḥsâb*, counting-board.

محسبة *maḥsaba-t*, thinking, conceiving (s.), INF. of (حسب); — *miḥsaba-t*, small cushion or pillow.

محسر *maḥsar*, *maḥsir*, face; nature, natural disposition; interior, heart; — ة *miḥsara-t*, broom, brush.

محسمة *maḥsama-t*, efficacious remedy.

محسن *muḥassan*, handsome, beautiful; praiseworthy; — ة *muḥassana-t*, praiseworthy quality, fine performance or action; — *;

— ة *maḥsina-t*, anything beautiful, good; — ات *muḥsanât*, *muḥsinât*, beautiful and chaste women.

محسوب *maḥsûb*, counted, reckoned, &c.; — *maḥsûb-an*, with regard to, on account of.

محسوس *maḥsûs*, felt, perceived, perceptible.

(محش) *maḥaś*, INF. *maḥś*, peel off the skin; carry off; burn the skin, scorch; — VIII. INF. *imtiḥâś*, burn; efface, blot out, erase.

محش *maḥś*, blotting out, erasing (s.); — *maḥaśś*, *miḥaśś*, sickle, scythe; grass-plot; hay-loft; — ة *maḥaśśa-t*, country yielding plenty of hay; pl. *maḥâśś*, buttocks; — *miḥaśśa-t*, hay-stack; hay-loft; poker.

محشا *miḥśa'*, *miḥśâ'*, pl. *maḥâśî*, coarse garment, plaid; trowsers; — ة *maḥśât*=محشى *maḥśan*.

محشر *maḥśar*, *maḥśir*, pl. *maḥâśir*, place of assembly; last judgment; cattle-plague.

محشو *maḥśuww*, filled, stuffed.

محشود *maḥśûd*, supported, defended; surrounded with servants, well attended to.

محشوم *maḥśûm*, modest, steady, sedate.

محشى *maḥśan*, stomach and bowels; — *miḥśan*, pl. *maḥâśî*, false hips, breasts, &c.; — *maḥśiyy*, filled, stuffed, crammed; — *muḥaśśa*, provided with marginal notes.

(محص) *maḥaṣ*, INF. *maḥṣ*, run fast; flee; stamp the ground; kick, sprawl; shine, flash; refine gold in the fire;—II. INF. *tamḥîṣ*, take away, remove; pardon; visit by calamities, try;—IV. INF. *imḥâṣ*, shine with fresh brightness; — VII. INF. *inmiḥâṣ*, id.

محص *maḥṣ*, strong, vigorous; — *muḥiṣṣ*, who gives away his share; who deposes, dethrones.

محصال *miḥṣâl*, scraper, scraping-tool.

محصاة *maḥṣât*, محصبة *maḥṣaba-t*, gravelly ground.

محصد *miḥṣad*, pl. *maḥâṣid*, sickle; — * ; — *muḥaṣṣad*, enduring, firm.

محصل *muḥaṣṣil*, who procures, earns, &c.; tax-gatherer or farmer; — *.

محصمة *miḥṣama-t*, iron club.

محصن *miḥṣan*, lock, bolt;—*muḥṣan*, well guarded; — ة *muḥṣana-t*, *muḥṣina-t*, chaste lady; — *muḥaṣṣana-t*, carefully-guarded woman.

محصوب *maḥṣûb*, afflicted with small-pox or typhus.

محصود *maḥṣûd*, reaped; harvest, crops.

محصول *maḥṣûl*, what results, &c.; result, produce; gain; harvest; tax, excise; pl. *maḥṣûlât*, productions, fruits of the field.

محصى *maḥṣiyy*, suffering from calculus; — *.

(محض) *maḥaḍ*, INF. *maḥḍ*, give one pure milk to drink; bestow sincere advice or love upon (2 acc.); — *maḥiḍ*, A, INF. *maḥaḍ*, drink pure milk; — *maḥuḍ*, INF. *muḥûḍa-t*, be of pure descent; be pure, unmixed; — III. INF. *mumâḥaḍa-t* (also IV.), treat with sincerity; — IV. INF. *imḥâḍ*, see III.; give pure milk to drink; — VIII. INF. *imtiḥâḍ*, drink pure milk.

محض *maḥḍ*, m. and f., sing. and pl. f. also ة, of pure blood (Arab); pure, unmixed; sheer, mere; only; purity; pure truth; pl. *miḥâḍ*, pure milk; — *maḥiḍ*, who has an appetite for pure milk.

محضار *maḥḍâr*, ready, fresh of vigour.

محضر *maḥḍar*, pl. *maḥâḍir*, presence, confrontation; aspect; inhabited place, fixed domicile, residence; place of assembly; circle; royal court; those present, audience; judicial document; petition, round robin; legal deed; act of drama; race (run); natural disposition, character; — *muḥḍir*, who summons to a court of justice, usher.

محضن *maḥḍan*, *maḥḍin*, pl. *maḥâḍin*, nest of a brooding hen.

(محط) = (مخط); — VIII. INF. *imtiḥâṭ*, draw the sword; draw out.

محط *maḥaṭṭ*, ة *maḥaṭṭa-t*, place for alighting and unloading; station, staple, relay; anchorage; abode; end of a sentence, period, full stop, cæsura;—*miḥaṭṭ*, ة *miḥaṭṭa-t*, steel pencil to draw figures on leather, arms, &c.

محطب *miḥṭab*, sickle, hedging-bill.

(محظ), III. *mâḥaẓ*, INF. *mumâḥaẓa-t*, force the she-camel to lie down (stallion).

محظور *maḥẓûr*, enclosed, inaccessible, &c.; forbidden; pl. *maḥẓûrât*, forbidden things.

محظوظ *maḥẓûẓ*, favoured by fortune, lucky, happy, content;—ية *maḥẓûẓiyya-t*, joy and contentment, pleasure.

محظى *muḥẓan*, favoured; — ة *maḥẓiyya-t* concubine.

محفار *miḥfâr*, spade; — ة *miḥfâra-t*, sand-pit (m.).

محفد *maḥfid*, pl. *maḥâfid*, origin, descent, race; also *miḥfad*, manger.

محفر *miḥfar*, ة *miḥfara-t*, pl. *maḥâfir*, tool for digging, spade; — ة *maḥfara-t*, pl. *maḥâfir*, place where they dig; sand-pit.

محفظة *maḥfaẓa-t*, place for keeping, magazine; case; م الادراك *maḥfaẓat al-idrâk*, memory.

محفل *maḥfil*, place or time of assembly, assembly, company, congress, council, tribunal, court of justice; gallery; — *.

محفة *miḥaffa-t*, open camel-litter for women.

محفور *maḥfûr*, dug, hollowed; notch, mark; also ى *maḥfûriyy*, large carpet.

محفوف *maḥfûf*, surrounded, enveloped, &c.; pressed by poverty, needy.

(محق) *maḥaq*, INF. *maḥq*, efface, blot out, destroy, annihilate, ruin; burn, scorch; (also II.) withdraw one's blessing from, render unfortunate; — II. INF. *tamḥîq*, destroy or blot out entirely; see I.; — V. INF. *tamaḥḥuq*, be destroyed, blotted out; perish; — VII. INF. *inmiḥâq*, VIII. INF. *imtiḥâq*, id.

محق *maḥq*, destruction, annihilation; — *muḥiqq*, who confirms, attests, speaks the truth.

محقان *miḥqân*, pl. *maḥâqîn*, pond, reservoir; fish-pond.

محقد *maḥqid*, root, origin.

محقرة *maḥqara-t*, vileness, meanness.

محقق *muḥaqqiq*, who confirms, &c.; who seeks and teaches the truth, sage, philosopher; — *.

محقلة *maḥqala-t*, pl. *maḥâqil*, arable land, sown field.

محقن *miḥqan*, ة *miḥqana-t*, syringe.

محقو *maḥquww*, *maḥqiyy*, suffering from colic.

محقوق *maḥqûq*, worthy, fit.

محقوقف *muḥqauqif*, crouching (حقف XII.).

(محك) *maḥak*, INF. *maḥk*, quarrel, begin a quarrel; — III. INF. *mumâḥaka-t*, id.; — IV. INF. *imḥâk*, be quarrelsome; — VI. INF. *tamâḥuk*, quarrel with one another.

محك *maḥik*, محكان *maḥkân*, quarrelsome, churlish; — *miḥakk*, touchstone.

محكد *maḥkid*, root, origin; refuge, asylum.

محكم *muḥkam*, firm, strong, solid; fixed, certain; clear, distinct; — *muḥakkam*, appointed as a judge; wise, unshakable; — *; — ة *maḥkama-t*, pl. *maḥâkim*, court of justice, tribunal, town hall.

محكوم *maḥkûm*, decreed, ordained, &c.; under command, subject, servant; invested with power and authority; م به *maḥkûm bi-hi*, predicate.

محكى *maḥkiyy*, narrated, handed down by tradition.

(محل) *maḥal*, INF. *maḥl*, be sterile; — I, INF. *maḥl*, *miḥâl*, injure one by malignant insinuation or information with the prince (الى *ila*); — *maḥil*, A, — *maḥul*, id.; INF. *muḥûl*, be sterile; — III. INF. *miḥâl*, *mumâḥala-t*, vie with in cunning; intrigue against, be hostile to (acc.); — IV. INF. *imḥâl*, be sterile, dry; suffer from want of food; make sterile; — V. INF. *tamaḥḥul*, intrigue.

محل *maḥl*, ة *maḥla-t*, sterility, want of rain, dearth; dry, withered (*maḥla-t*, dry land); useless; cunning, stratagem, deceit; — *maḥall*, pl. *maḥâll*, station, place, spot, position; abode, quarter; time and opportunity; delay, respite; fitting, appropriate; (m.) assembly in the house of a dead person; — *maḥill*, term of payment; place of sacrifice; — *muḥill*, mourning for a dead husband; — ة *maḥalla-t*, quarter of a town, street, station, inn; community; review; — *miḥalla-t*, reel, windle, hasp; — du. *muḥillatân*, pot and handmill.

محلا *miḥlâ'*, ة *miḥlâ'a-t*, scraper.

محلاب *miḥlâb*, milk-pail.

محلاج *miḥlâj*, instrument for cleaning cotton; baker's roller.

محلال *miḥlâl*, place of assembly.

محلب *maḥlab*, an aromatic grain; honey; also *miḥlab*, milk-pail.

محلج *miḥlaj*, axis of a pulley; also

ة *miḥlaja-t*, board on which cotton is cleaned; cotton-reel.

محلحل *muḥalḥal*, prince, powerful man.

محلف *muḥlif*, who exacts an oath; doubtful; غير م *gair muḥlif*, doubtless, distinct, bright and pure (colour).

محلق *miḥlaq*, ة *miḥlaqa-t*, pl. *maḥâliq*, scraping-tool; razor; —*.

محلل *muḥallil*, who allows, solves, &c.; who marries a divorced woman in order to dismiss her, so that the first husband may marry her again; — ات *muḥallilât*, solvents.

محلم *muḥlim*, dreaming.

محلنكك *muḥlankik*, coal-black, pitch-dark.

محلوب *maḥlûb*, milked; (m.) milk-pail.

محلوفا *maḥlûfâ'*, oath.

محلول *maḥlûl*, solved, &c.; acquitted, broken (spell); allowed, permitted, vacant; solution (medicine); weakened, relaxed.

محلى *muḥla*, sweets; — *muḥlî*, who anoints the eyes with collyrium; —*muḥallâ*, adorned, gilt, sweetened; — *muḥallî*, who adorns, gilds, sweetens.

محم *miḥamm*, kettle for heating water; — *muḥimm*, ة, feverish; — ة *maḥamma-t*, district where fevers are frequent; aim, end, intention.

محماصة *miḥmâṣa-t*, cunning female thief.

(محمح) *maḥmaḥ*, INF. ة, love sincerely; — II. INF. *tamaḥmuḥ*, be merry.

محمد *maḥmid*, *maḥmad*, praising (s.); — *muḥmid*, who deserves praise; — *muḥammad*, highly praised; proper name; —*; — ة *maḥmida-t*, *maḥmada-t*, pl. *maḥâmid*, praise, glory; praiseworthy deed or quality; — ى *muḥammadiyy*, ة, Mohammedan (adj., s.); *muḥammadiyya-t*, Islâm.

محمر *miḥmar*, pl. *maḥâmir*, pack-horse; —*; — *muḥmarr*, red.

محمصة *maḥmaṣa-t*, (m.) stove; (m.) stew of meat and roasted onions.

محمل *maḥmil*, that which carries; double camel-litter; stand on which every year the new silk drapery for the Kaba is carried to Mecca; this drapery; silk, velvet; bier; portable basket, hamper; — *miḥmal*, sword-belt; —*.

محمود *maḥmûd*, praised, &c.; proper name; — ة *maḥmûda-t*, ية *maḥmûdiyya-t*, scammony; — ى *maḥmûdiyy*, small silver coin (8½ pence).

محمور *maḥmûr*, suffering from indigestion (horse, &c.).

محمورا *maḥmûrâ'*, pl. of حمار *ḥimâr*, ass.

محموز *maḥmûz*, sour, tart; lively, fiery, ardent; strong, powerful.

محموق *maḥmûq*, afflicted with small-pox.

محمول *maḥmûl*, carried, loaded, &c.; imputed; permitted; bearable; founded upon; attribute; fœtus; — ة *maḥmûla-t*, load, freight, cargo; a kind of wheat.

محموم *maḥmûm*, heated; afflicted with fever; decreed, ordained.

محمى *maḥmiyy*, ة, protected; client; (*maḥmiyya-t*, protected town); feverish; also *maḥmî*, lion; *maḥmiyy*, *muḥma*, heated, glowing; — *muḥmî*, heating; — ة *maḥmiya-t*, protection.

(محن) *maḥan*, INF. *maḥn*, beat; put to the test (also III., VIII.); make trials, experiments; wear out a garment; = II.; — II. INF. *tamḥîn*, soften, shave, scrape off the hair (leather); — III. INF. *mumâḥana-t*, put to the test; — VIII. INF. *imtiḥân*, id.; examine.

محن *maḥan*, tiredness from work; soft; — ة *miḥna-t*, pl. *miḥan*, trouble, pain, hardship, vexation, sorrow, calamity; hard work or service.

محنث *muḥnis*, miserable wretch, abject rascal.

محنجة *miḥnaja-t*, tool, instrument.

محنك *muḥnak*, *muḥannak*, tried, put to the test; wise by experience.

محنون *maḥnûn*, mad, epileptic.

محنى *muḥanna* (حنو II.), bent, curved;—ة *maḥniya-t*, bend of a river; unlevel ground.

(محو) *maḥâ*, U, A, INF. *maḥw*, efface entirely, destroy; wipe off; be entirely effaced, destroyed, blotted out; vanish, perish; — II. INF. *taḥmiya-t*, efface, destroy; — VII. INF. *immiḥâ'*, VIII. INF. *imtiḥâ'*, be effaced, destroyed; vanish, disappear.

محو *maḥw*, effacing, blotting out, erasing; abolishing, repealing, annulling (s.); — ة *maḥwa-t*, id.; shower of rain; disgrace; hour.

محوج *muḥwij*, in want of, needing.

محور *miḥwar*, ة *miḥwara-t*, pl. *maḥâwir*, axis, pivot; dough-roller; — *muḥawwar*, rounded (bread); quite white (flour); — *muḥawwir*, bleacher; — ة *maḥwara-t*, *maḥwura-t*, answer.

محوصل *muḥauṣal*, having a crop; bellied.

محوط *muḥawwaṭ*, enclosed, hedged in; ة *muḥawwaṭa-t*, enclosure;— *muḥawwiṭ*, surrounding, encompassing; watchman, guard-keeper; ة *muḥawwiṭa-t*, fence, hedge, wall.

محوق *maḥûq*, swept, rubbed; — *; — ة *miḥwaqa-t*, broom to sweep a threshing-floor.

محوكة *maḥwaka-t*, combat, battle.

محول *maḥûl*, cunning; intriguer; — *.

محوى *maḥwiyy*, collected, gathered, contained.

(محى) *maḥa*, A, I, INF. *maḥy*, efface, blot out, destroy.

محى *muḥy-in*, see محيى.

محيا *muḥyâ'*, pl. *maḥyâyâ*, place where and time when one lives, life; lively, brisk, merry; — *muḥayyâ*, face, cheek; — ة *maḥyât*, place abounding with snakes.

محيان *miḥyân*, time, period.

محيد *maḥîd*, bend, curve; point of deviation where one leaves a road; turning (s.) aside; refuge, escape.

محيص *maḥîṣ*, flight, escape; polished, shining, glossy.

محيض *maḥîḍ*, the menses.

محيط *muḥîṭ*, ag. of (حوط IV.), surrounding, &c.; periphery, circumference; البحر الم *al-baḥr al-muḥîṭ*, ocean, title of comprehensive works.

محيل *muḥîl*, deceitful, impostor; who assigns the payment of a debt to another, draws upon (على *'ala*).

محيم *miḥyam*, intelligent, spirited, ingenious.

محيوس *maḥyûs*, whose parents are both children of slaves.

محيى *muḥyî* (محى *muḥy-in*), ة, vivifying, bringing to life again, reanimating; making to bloom; — *muḥayyî*, vivifying (God).

(مخ) *muḫḫ*, pl. *miḫâḫ*, *miḫaḫa-t*, marrow, brain; kernel; pulp; purest and best part, quintessence; م البيض *muḫḫ al-baiḍ*, yolk; — II. *maḫḫaḫ*, INF. *tamḫîḫ*, take the marrow out of a bone; — IV. INF. *imḫâḫ*, have plenty of marrow; — V. INF. *tamaḫḫuḫ*, VIII. INF. *imtiḫâḫ* = II.; — ة *muḫḫa-t*, marrow.

مخا *muḫâ*, town of Moka.

مخابرة *muḫâbara-t*, mutual information, correspondence.

مخابيط *maḫâbîṭ*, pl. of مخباط *miḫbâṭ*.

مخاتيم *maḥâtîm*, pl. of مختوم *maḥtûm*.

مخاخ *miḥâḥ*, pl. of مخ *muḥḥ*; — ة *muḥâḥa-t*, marrow.

مخاد *maḥâdd*, pl. of مخدة *miḥad-da-t*.

مخادم *maḥâdim*, pl. servants, slaves, eunuchs; family.

مخاديم *maḥâdîm*, pl. of مخدوم *maḥdûm*.

مخاذيل *maḥâẕîl*, pl. of مخذول *maḥẕûl*.

مخاريق *maḥâriq*, pl. of مخراق *miḥrâq*.

مخازى *maḥâzî*, pl. of مخزاة *maḥzât*.

مخاض *maḥâḍ*, *miḥâḍ*, throes of child-birth; she-camels big with young; — ة *maḥâḍa-t*, pl. *maḥâḍ*, *maḥâwiḍ*, ford, shallow (s.); — *muḥâḍḍa-t*, INF. of (خض III.).

مخاط *muḥâṭ*, mucus; م الشيطان, gossamer; — ى *muḥâṭiyy*, mucous.

مخاطب *muḥâṭab*, second person; — *.

مخاطرة *muḥâṭara-t*, risk, hazard, danger; — *.

مخافة *maḥâfa-t*, pl. *maḥâwif*, fear; fright, terror, danger.

مخالط *muḥâliṭ*, who intermeddles, engages in, partner; — *.

مخالفة *muḥâlafa-t*, antithesis, contradiction, contrast; opposition, resistance, refractoriness, rebellion, disobedience, transgression; discord, enmity.

مخالة *maḥâla-t*, imagination, idea, fancy, vanity; INF. of (خيل).

مخالى *maḥâlî*, pl. of مخلاة *miḥlât*.

مخاليق *maḥâlîq*, pl. of مخلوقة *maḥ-lûqa-t*.

مخاوذ ملاوذ *muḥâwiẕ mulâwiẕ*, complicated, intricate.

مخاوض *maḥâwiḍ*, pl. of مخاضة *maḥâḍa-t*; — ة *muḥâwaḍa-t*, passing of a ford on horseback.

مخبا *maḥbâ'*, pl. *maḥâbi'*, hiding-place; privy; — ة *muḥba'a-t*, *muḥabba'a-t*, kept hidden, secret.

مخباية *maḥbâya-t*, anything hidden, secret treasure (m.).

مخبث *muḥbiṯ*, مخبثان *maḥbaṯân*, vile, perverse; — ة *maḥbaṯa-t*, vileness, perverseness.

مخبر *maḥbar*, real inner state, reality; also ة *maḥbara-t*, knowledge from information, experience, proving (s.); — *.

مخبز *maḥbaz*, ة *maḥbaza-t*, pl. *ma-ḥâbiz*, bakehouse, oven.

مخبصة *miḥbaṣa-t*, pl. *maḥâbiṣ*, spoon for stirring.

مخبط *miḥbaṭ*, pl. *maḥâbiṭ*, stick for beating down leaves; — *muḥab-baṭ*, troubled in one's senses; — *muḥabbiṭ*, troubling the senses.

مخبو *maḥbû'*, hidden, concealed.

مخبى *muḥabba*, f. *muḥabbât*, hidden, concealed.

مختا *muḥtâ* ., to be looked for under (. خو , . خى VIII.), as—

مختار *muḥtâr*, pat. of (خير VIII.), elected, selected; the best, the most exquisite; ag. of the same: who selects, who acts with a free will, who has the choice; invested with authority and power.

مختبا *muḥtaba'*, anything hidden; hiding-place.

مخت *muḥta* . ., to be looked for under (. . خ VIII.), as—

مختبط *muḥtabiṭ*, ag. of (خبط VIII.), sprawling; excited, agitated, confused.

مختبى *muḥtabi'*, hidden; hiding.

مختتم *muḥtatam*, completed; end, conclusion.

مختر *muḥattir*, intoxicating.

مخترعات *muḥtara'ât*, inventions, new performances; — *.

مختص *muḥtaṣṣ*, peculiar, particular to, &c.; exceeding; familiar friend.

مختصر *muḥtaṣar*, extract, compendium; — *muḥtaṣir*, epitomist.

مختطب *muḥtaṭib*, wooer for another, suitor, matchmaker;

seeking a suitor for one's daughter.

مختفى• *muḥtafî*, hiding one's self; hidden, concealed; despoiler of dead bodies.

مختل• *muḥtall*, weakened; spoiled, disordered; disturbed, ruined; poor, needy; sour.

مختلط• *muḥtaliṭ*, mixed, &c.; holding intercourse with, dealing with, associating with.

مختلعة• *muḥtali'a-t*, woman who demands a divorce on condition of returning her dowry; — *.

مختلق• *muḥtalaq*, well made; invented, feigned, fictitious; lie, fable.

مختوم• *maḥtûm*, sealed (م الابصار *maḥtûm al-abṣâr*, blind, blinded); finished; closed (wound); pl. *maḥâtîm*, a measure.

(مخج) *maḥaj*, INF. *maḥj*, draw the bucket after shaking it until it is full; lie with.

مخخة• *miḥaḥa-t*, pl. of مخ *muḥḥ*.

مخدرة• *muḥaddara-t*, woman or girl kept in the harem; — ات *muḥaddirât*, narcotics; — *.

مخدش• *miḥdaś*, withers of a camel; — *muḥaddaś*, id.; — *.

مخدع• *miḥda'*, *muḥda'*, pl. *maḥâdi'*, magazine; treasury; apartment, room, chamber, cell.

مخدة• *maḥada-t*, help, protection, favour;—*miḥadda-t*, pl. *maḥâdd*, pillow, cushion, bolster; ploughshare.

مخدوم• *maḥdûm*, pl. *maḥâdîm*, served by others (particularly the son of the house); lord, master; — ية *maḥdûmiyya-t*, state of being served, dominion, mastership.

مخذأة• *miḥza'a-t*, knife.

مخذفة• *miḥzafa-t*, stick for flinging a stone, sling.

مخذم• *miḥzam*, *muḥazzam*, sharp.

مخذول• *maḥzûl*, pl. *maḥâzîl*, left in the lurch, abandoned, forsaken; destitute, helpless, miserable.

(مخر) *maḥar*, INF. *maḥr*, *muḥûr*, rush through the sea; part the waves; water the ground, irrigate; — V. INF. *tamaḥḥur*, observe the direction of the wind;=X.; —VIII. INF. *imtiḥâr*, select the best;=X.; — X. INF. *istimḥâr*, turn the nose towards the wind (horse).

مخر• بنات مخر *banât-u maḥr-in*, white summer clouds; — مخر الما *maḥarr al-mâ'*, waterfall, cataract.

مخرا• *maḥra'*, ة *maḥra'a-t*, *maḥrât*, privy.

مخراق• *miḥrâq*, experienced, skilled; wooden sword; pl. *maḥârîq*, incredible lie.

مخرت• *maḥrat*, straight road.

مخرج• *maḥraj*, pl. *maḥârij*, place of issue, issue, outlet, drain-pipe; organ of secretion, anus; privy; expedient; organ of voice; formation of a sound, utterance, final sound, desinence; pl. expenses, costs;—*muḥraj*, brought out, &c.; exiled, banished; result; — *;—*muḥrij*, who brings out, &c.; who pays tribute or a capitation-tax.

مخرز• *miḥraz*, pl. *maḥâriz*, awl, puncheon.

مخرف• *miḥraf*, pl. *maḥârif*, wallet, basket;—ة *maḥrafa-t*, silly talk; fables, fairy-tales; orchard; avenue of trees.

مخرق• *maḥraq*, INF. ة, tell portentous lies, tell stories, swagger.

مخروط• *maḥrûṭ*, turned on the lathe; oval; also *maḥrûṭa-t*, cone; — *muḥrawwiṭ*, swift, fleet; — ى *maḥrûṭiyy*, conic; — يات *maḥrûṭiyyât*, conic sections.

مخزاة• *maḥzât*, pl. *maḥâzî*, putting to shame (s.), abashing; offence, insult.

مخزق• *miḥzâq*, pl. *maḥâziq*, stick with an iron point.

مخزن• *maḥzan*, pl. *maḥâzin*, storeroom, magazine, warehouse, cellar, barn, treasury.

مخزى• *muḥza*, abashed; (m.) de-

mon ;—*muḫzî*, abashing, putting to shame.

مخسوم *maḫsûm*, m. removed; finished.

مخش *miḫaśś*, fearless; penis.

مخشاة *maḫśât*, fear.

مخشنة *maḫśana-t*, roughness.

مخشى *muḫaśśi*, terrible; — ة *maḫśiya-t*, pl. *maḫâśî*, fear.

مخصاب *miḫṣâb*, fertile.

مخصال *miḫṣâl*, sickle.

مخصب *muḫṣib*, fertile.

مخصر *muḫaṣṣar*, slender of waist; — ة *miḫṣara-t*, pl. *maḫâṣir*, support; stick, staff, sceptre; rod, scourge.

مخصف *miḫṣaf*, awl.

مخصل *miḫṣal*, sharp.

مخصوص *maḫṣûṣ*, assigned, ascribed as peculiar to, &c.; personally devoted, familiar, attached in close friendship; *maḫṣûṣ-an*, especially; — ية *maḫṣûṣiyya-t*, particularity, peculiarity; exclusive ownership; personal attachment, familiarity.

مخصى *maḫṣa*, place where a man or animal is gelded; — *maḫṣiyy*, castrated; eunuch; gelding.

(مخض) *maḫaḍ*, A, I, U, shake the milk in a skin bag to turn it into butter; shake violently; — *maḫiḍ*, A, INF. *maḫâḍ*, *miḫâḍ*, lie in the throes of child-birth; — pass. *muḫiḍ*, id.; — V. INF. *tamaḫḫuḍ*, id.; (also VII., VIII.) be shaken for buttering; — VII. INF. *inmiḫâḍ*, be skimmed; see V.; — VIII. INF. *imtiḫâḍ*, see V.

مخض *muḫḫaḍ*, pl. of ماخض, in the throes of child-birth.

مخضب *miḫḍab*, dyer's tub; colour-pot; — *.

مخضد *miḫḍad*, glutton, voracious eater.

مخضر *muḫḍarr*, green;— *muḫaḍḍar*, dyed green.

مخضرم *muḫaḍram*, of an unknown father; mongrel, mulatto; — ة *muḫaḍrama-t*, circumcised, f.

مخضرة *maḫḍara-t*, verdant place, grass-plot, meadow.

مخضل *muḫḍal*, commodious, comfortable; — *muḫḍil*. *muḫaḍḍil*, tender, delicate.

مخضونة *maḫḍûna-t*, pregnant.

(مخط) *maḫaṭ*, A, U, INF. *maḫṭ*, *muḫûṭ*, pierce through and come out on the opposite side; draw the sword; secrete mucus; blow the nose;—II. INF. *tamḫîṭ*, wipe off the mucus; wipe a child's nose; blow the nose; — IV. INF. *imḫâṭ*, cause the arrow to pierce through; — V. INF. *tamaḫḫuṭ*, blow the nose; — VIII. INF. *imtiḫâṭ*, draw the sword.

مخط *maḫiṭ*, pl. *amḫâṭ*, highminded prince; — *miḫaṭṭ*, pencil; ruler (for drawing lines).

مخطاط *miḫṭâṭ*, ruler.

مخطر, II. *tamaḫṭar*, INF. *tamaḫṭur*, balance one's body in walking.

مخطط *muḫaṭṭaṭ*, striped; beginning to grow a beard; handsome pretty; — *.

مخطم *maḫṭam*, woman; — *maḫṭim*, *miḫṭam*, nose, proboscis, snout, beak; — *.

مخطوب *maḫṭûb*, demanded in marriage, betrothed; — ة *maḫṭûba-t*, bride.

مخطور *maḫṭûr*, conceived in the mind, idea, occurrent thought; forbidden.

مخطوف *maḫṭûf*, robbed, carried off, enraptured.

مخطى *muḫṭiyy*, who is mistaken, who errs, sins, misses the aim.

مخف *muḫiff*, light, nimble.

مخفف *muḫaffaf*, eased, &c.; pronounced without the *taśdîd*.

مخفقة *miḫfaqa-t*, ox-tail, scourge.

مخفوق *maḫfûq*, suffering from palpitations of the heart; mad.

مخفى *maḫfiyy*, concealed, hidden, secret.

(مخل) *muḫl*, pl. *amḫâl*, lever, crowbar; — *muḫill*, who disturbs, damages, causes confusion, deserts, betrays.

مخلا *muḫallâ*, ة = مخلى *muḫalla*; — ة *miḫlât*, ة *miḫlâya-t*, pl. *maḫâlî*, fodder-bag.

مخلاب *miḫlâb* = مخلب *miḫlab*.

مخلاط *miḫlâṭ*, intermeddler.

مخلاف *miḫlâf*, who never keeps his word; pl. *maḫâlîf*, ward (of a city).

مخلب *miḫlab*, مخلاب *miḫlâb*, pl. *maḫâlib*, *maḫâlîb*, claw, talon; sickle; surgical instrument; — *muḫlib*, covered with leaves.

مخلخل *muḫalḫal*, place where the anklets are put.

مخلد *muḫallad*, lasting, eternal; vigorous in high old age; durable; abiding always in the same place.

مخلص *maḫlaṣ*, place of refuge, asylum; name which a poet gives himself in the last couplet of a *gazel*; — *muḫalliṣ*, saviour; — *.

مخلط *miḫlaṭ*, intermeddler; — *.

مخلع *muḫalla'*, pulled out, &c.; relaxed, unnerved, weak, powerless; lamed, paralytic, palsied; sprained; without bones (roast meat).

مخلف *muḫallif*, who leaves behind, &c.; successor, substitute, lieutenant; testator; — ات *muḫallafât*, property left behind.

مخلقة *maḫlaqa-t*, well fitting, as if made or created for the purpose.

مخلوط *maḫlûṭ*, mixed, &c.; heterogeneous; confused; — ة *maḫlûṭa-t*, dish of lentils, peas and groats; pl. *maḫlûṭât*, medley of all sorts of things.

مخلوع *maḫlû'*, pulled out, &c.; relaxed, unnerved; deserted.

مخلوقة *maḫlûqa-t*, pl. *-ât*, *maḫâlîq*, creature.

مخلوقية *maḫlûqiyya-t*, state of being created.

مخلول *maḫlûl*, pierced, perforated.

مخلى *miḫla*, sickle; — *muḫalla*, dismissed, set free; left alone; repudiated; — *muḫallî*, who sets free, &c.; first in a race.

مخم *muḫimm*, deteriorated, putrid.

(مخمخ) *maḫmaḫ*, INF. ة, take the marrow out of the bones; delight (a.).

مخمد *muḫmid*, extinguishing a fire; calming, pacifying.

مخمر *muḫammar*, fermented, fermenting; half drunk; — *muḫammir*, what brings on fermentation, &c.; baker.

مخمس *muḫammas*, multiplied by five, pentagonal; also ة *muḫammasa-t*, poem in strophes of five rhymed lines.

مخمصة *maḫmaṣa-t*, hunger, emptiness.

(مخمض) *maḫmaḍ*, INF. ة, rinse a glass; rinse one's mouth.

مخمل *maḫmal*, velvet, plush.

مخمة *miḫamma-t*, broom.

مخمور *maḫmûr*, intoxicated, not yet sober.

مخموم *maḫmûm*, swept, clean.

(مخن) *maḫan*, U, INF. *maḫn*, draw water; lie with; bark, peel; cry, weep.

مخناف *miḫnâf*, impotent stallion.

مخنث *muḫannaṣ*, bent; weak, impotent; sodomite; worthless, good-for-nothing; coward; effeminate, badly educated.

مخنق *maḫnaq*, place of the throat where one is strangled; pl. *maḫâniq*, chain for the neck, necklace; — *muḫannaq*, choked, strangled; = *maḫnaq*; م الخصر *muḫannaq al-ḫuṣr*, very slender of waist; — *muḫanniq*, who strangles, hangman.

مخنة *maḫanna-t*, nose, tip of the nose; nasal sound; entrance, orifice; rights, privileges.

مخوف *maḫûf*, terrible, dangerous; — ة *maḫûfa-t*, danger; — *.

مخيالة *miḫyâla-t*, rain-cloud.

مخيخ *maḫîḫ*, having plenty of marrow.

مخير *muḫayyar*, who has a free choice, left to one's free will;

indifferent ; — *muḥayyir*, who leaves to one's choice; kind, benevolent.

مخيس *muḥayyas*, tamed, humbled; prison.

مخيض *maḥîḍ*, skimmed ; made into butter; butter-milk.

مخيط *maḥîṭ*, *muḥayyaṭ*, sewn ; — *miḥyaṭ*, needle.

مخيف *maḥîf*, threatening ruin (building) ; — *muḥîf*, *muḥayyif*, causing fear.

مخيل *maḥîl*, worthy, fit ; — *muḥîl*, id. ; conceited, vain ; — * ; — ة *maḥîla-t*, *muḥayyala-t*, imagination, power of conception ; conceit, vanity, pride ; pl. *maḥâyil*, anything from which inferences may be drawn, token, sign, indication.

مخيم *muḥîm*, *muḥayyim*, who pitches a tent ; — *muḥayyam*, a camp of tents ; living in tents.

(مد) *madd*, U, INF. *madd*, stretch, extend ; fix the look a long time upon ; spread out ; rise, grow ; flow ; stand high, be advanced (day) ; prolong the life ; grant a delay of payment ; come to one's aid ; take ink from the inkstand ; — II. INF. *tamdîd*, stretch or extend greatly ; — III. INF. *midâd*, *mumâdda-t*, stretch, lengthen ; fight body to body ; — IV. INF. *imdâd*, grant a delay of payment ; help, assist, aid with troops or provisions ; allow one (acc.) profit from (ب *bi*) ; prolong one's life ; provide the inkstand with ink ; suppurate ; — V. INF. *tamaddud*, stretch, extend, lengthen (n.) ; — VI. INF. *tamâdud*, wrestle ; — VIII. INF. *imtidâd*, be stretched, extended ; stretch, extend, lengthen (n.), be long ; — X. INF. *istimdâd*, ask for help, aid, intercession ; take ink out of the inkstand.

مد *madd*, pl. *mudûd*, rising of the water, flood ; stretch, extent, range, reach ; sign of the lengthening of ا ; حروف المد *ḥurûf-u'l-madd-i*, letters of prolongation ; — *mudd*, pl. *amdâd*, *midada-t*, *midâd*, a measure ($1\frac{1}{2}$ to 2 pounds) ; — ة *madda-t*, stretching, extending (s.) ; prolongation of a letter and its sign ; threads of the woof ; — *midda-t*, pl. *midad*, pus ; — *mudda-t*, pl. *mudad*, space of time, while ; end, termination, limit.

مداجاة *mudâjât*, simulation, shamming, hypocrisy.

مداح *maddâḥ*, who praises much ; eulogist.

مداخيل *madâḥîl*, pl. of مدخول *madḥûl*.

مداد *midâd*, ink ; food ; dung, manure ; path, road, sect ; stretching, extending (s.) ; pl. of مد *mudd* and مديد *madîd* ; — *maddâd*, wide-stepping ; ivy.

مدار *madâr*, orb, orbit, circumference, rotation, time of rotation ; centre ; axis, pivot, turning-point ; tropic ; starting-point ; goal ; stand-point, seat ; tread-mill ; motive, reason.

مداراة *mudâra'a-t*, *mudârât*, insinuating manners, winning friendliness, courtesy ; simulated friendship.

مدارسة *mudârasa-t*, study, higher instruction.

مداركة *mudâraka-t*, uninterrupted pursuit ; careful solicitude or attendance.

مداس *madâs*, a kind of coarse shoes ; also ة *madâsa-t*, threshing-floor ; — ة *maddâsa-t*, nose.

مداص *madâṣ*, place of diving ; pearl-fishing.

مداعق *madâ'iq*, water-courses.

مداعى *madâ'î*, pl. of مدعاة *mad'ât* ; —*mudâ'î*, who challenges ; quarrelsome.

مدافى *madâfi'*, pl. of مدفاة *madfa'a-t*.

مداق *madâq*, place of combat ; —

madâqq, pl. of مدق *midaqq*, ة; — ة *mudâqqa-t*, accuracy.
مداك *madâk*, stone on which colours are pounded.
مداكاة *mudâka'a-t*, throng.
مدالث *madâlis*, battle-field.
. مدا *mudâ* ., to be looked for under (. دو , . دي IV.), as—
مدام *mudâm*, pat. of (دوم IV.); lasting, continual; also ة *mudâma-t*, wine.
مدان *madân*, basil (plant); also *mudân*, *maddân*, *muddân*, deep in debt; — *mudân*, judged, sentenced.
مداناة *mudânât*, approach.
مدانس *madânis*, pl. impurities.
مداني *mudânî*, approaching, near.
مداهنة *mudâhana-t*, flattery, hypocrisy, lie, treachery.
مداواة *mudâwât* (also مداوا *mudâwâ*), nursing of the sick, cure, recovery.
مداولة *mudâwala-t*, conference.
مدائين *madâ'în*, pl. of مديان *midyân*.
مدب *madabb*, *madibb*, pl. *madâbb*, place where anything is creeping.
مدبر *mudbir*, who goes backwards, returns; down in the world; — *mudabbir*, who ordains, &c.; governor, manager, director; — ات *mudabbirât*, authorities, powers; angels.
مدبغة *madbaga-t*, pl. *madâbig*, hide in the tanning-pit; also *madbuga-t*, pl. *madâbig*, tanning-pit; tannery.
مدبور *madbûr*, galled, back-sore.
مدبى *madba*, *mudbî*, *madbiyy*, ة *mudbiya-t*, full of locusts.
مدبى *mudabbî*, who hides, conceals.
مدجج *mudajjaj*, armed from head to foot; hedge-hog; — *mudajjij*, cloudy.
(مدح) *madaḥ*, INF. *madḥ*, *midḥa-t*, mention with praise, praise; — II. INF. *tamdîḥ*, praise highly; — V. INF. *tamadduḥ*, praise; praise one's self, boast; — VIII. INF. *imtidâḥ*, praise.
مدح *madḥ*, praise, eulogy; — ة *midḥa-t*, *madḥa-t*, pl. *madaḥât*, *midaḥ*, anything praiseworthy, praise.
مدحاة *midḥât*, children's carriage.
مدحرة *madḥara-t*, driving forth.
مدحوس *madḥûs*, suffering from whitlow.
مدحى *madḥa*, place in the sand where the ostrich deposits its eggs.
(مدخ) *madaḫ*, INF. *madḫ*, be great, large; help, assist completely.
مدخا *mudaḫâ'*, pl. of مديخ *madîḫ*.
مدخر *mudḫar*, humbled; — *mudaḫḫar*, stored up, hoarded, saved.
مدخل *madḫal*, pl. *madâḫil*, entrance, access; vestibule, anteroom; door; time of entrance; interference; influence; complicity, taking part in; pl. revenues, income; — *midḫal*, key; — *mudḫal*, introduced, admitted; ungenuine; adulterated, counterfeited; introduction, preface; — *mudḫil*, who introduces; introduction.
مدخن *madḫan*, pl. *madâḫin*, chimney, flue; hearth; heated room for silk-worms; — *; — ة *midḫana-t*, pl. *madâḫin*, censer; flue.
مدخول *madḫûl*, entered into, &c.; introduced; having a secret fault; weak of intellect; pl. *madâḫil*, revenues, income, gain; ة *madḫûla-t*, deflowered.
مدد *madad*, help, aid, assistance; auxiliaries, subsidies; — *midad*, *mudad*, pl. of مدة *midda-t*, *mudda-t* respectively; — *mudud*, pl. of مديد *madîd*; — ة *midada-t*, pl. of مد *mudd*.
(مدر) *madar*, U, INF. *madr*, coat with mud; — *madir*, A, INF. *madar*, have a big protruding belly; — II. INF. *tamdîr*, coat

with mud ; — VIII. INF. imtidâr, take a piece of clay, a clod.

مدر madar, ة, clod ; centre ; city, village (اهل المدر ahl al-madar, inhabitants of towns, &c., opposed to اهل الوبر ahl al-wabar, inhabitants of tents, nomads) ; — mudirr, promoting the secretion of milk, sweat, urine, &c. ;— ات mudirrât, such remedies.

مدرار midrâr, yielding plenty of milk ; raining abundantly (sky).

مدراس midrâs, school, academy.

مدراة midrât, see مدرى midra.

مدرج madraj, ة madraja-t, pl. madârij, road, path ; conduct ; scroll ; pl. steps, degrees ;— mudraj, put into, inserted, contained ; contents ;— mudrij, who puts into ; — *.

مدرس madras, ة madrasa-t, pl. madâris, higher educational establishment, university, academy ; — midras, book ; — *.

مدرع midra', ة midra'a-t, coarse vest or shirt ; alb of a priest ; — mudarra', wearing armour, cuirassier.

مدره midrah, pl. madârih, chief, prince ; leader.

مدرهم mudarham, rich ; — mudrahimm, old, tottering.

مدروج madrûj, usual, customary.

مدروز mudarwiz, artizan.

مدرى midra, مدراة midrât (and مدرية midriya-t), pl. madârî, horn ; comb ; hair-pin ; pitchfork ; — muddarî, deceitful ; — madarîyy, inhabitant of a town, citizen ; — (m.) midrî, I do not know (for ما ادرى mâ adrî).

(مدس) madas, U, INF. mads, rub.

مدسع madsa', narrow spot ; gullet ; — midsa', guide, leader.

(مدش) madaś, U, INF. madś, eat but little ; give but little ; — madiś, A, INF. madaś, grow dim ; — II. INF. tamdîś, give ; — VIII. INF. imtidâś, take, rob.

مدعا mudda'â, see مدعى mudda'an.

مدعاس mid'âs, pl. مداعس madâ'is, lance ; trodden path.

مدعاة mad'ât, invitation.

مدعر muda''ar, dirt-colour.

مدعس mad'as, anything desirable ; sexual intercourse ; — mid'as, pl. madâ'is, = مدعاس mid'âs.

مدعك mid'ak, instrument for rubbing, polishing ; quarrelsome.

مدعة mad'a-t, cocoanut-shell as a vessel.

مدعو mad'uww, called, invited ; prayed for (له).

مدعى mad'î, who adopts ; — mudda'a (مدعا mudda'â), claimed ; object of a claim or law-suit ; asserted, assertion ; law-suit, process ; advocate ; — mudda'î, claimant, pretender, adversary.

مدغر mudaggar, dirt-coloured ; — ة madgara-t, heated combat.

مدغل mudgil, secret, concealed ; perverse, wily.

مدغم mudgam, hidden ; enclosed, comprised ; also mudaggam, inserted, contracted with and assimilated to the following (letter).

مدف mudiff, uninterrupted.

مدفاة madfa'a-t, warm country.

مدفحة madfaha-t, mouse-trap.

مدفع madfa', water-course ; — midfâ', pl. madâfi', cannon, piece of artillery ; — mudaffa', refused ; denied by everybody ; stranger ; — ة madfa'a-t, means of keeping off, repelling.

مدفن madfan, pl. madâfin, burial-place, tomb.

(مدق) madaq, U, INF. madq, break to pieces.

مدق midaqq, muduqq, ة midaqqa-t, madaqqa-t, pl. madâqq, instrument for breaking, pounding, &c., mallet, sledge-hammer, ram, pestle ; — *.

مدقس midqas, pl. madâqîs, strong ; — midaqs, silk.

مدك midakk, ة, strong and fit for hard work ; — midakk, ramrod.

مدكوبة *madkûba-t,* hot combat.
مدكوك *madkûk,* pounded, flattened, &c.; loaded (gun); hectic.
(مدل) *madl,* contemptible, worthless; thick milk; — V. INF. *tamaddul,* wipe one's self with a towel; cover the face with a veil; — *.
مدلبة *madlaba-t,* place planted with plane trees.
مدلك *midlak,* instrument for grating.
مدلهم *mudlahimm,* pitch dark; old.
مدلول *madlûl,* led up to, &c.; sense, meaning.
مدماجة *midmâja-t,* turban.
مدماك *midmâk,* mason's plummet; layer of stones in a wall.
(مدمد) *madmad,* INF. ة, flee.
مدمد *madmad,* river; rope.
مدمع *madma',* pl. *madâmi',* inner corner of the eye; tear-fount.
مدمغ *mudammag,* hare-brained; marked by branding.
مدمقس *mudamqas,* made of the silk دمقس *dimaqs.*
مدمك *midmak,* dough-roller.
مدمة *midamma-t,* . rake (tool); harrow.
مدموج *madmûj,* adorned.
مدموغ *madmûg,* hare-brained.
مدموم *madmûm,* red as blood.
مدمى *mudma, mudamma,* stained with blood; red as blood.
(مدن) *madan,* U, INF. *mudûn,* stay, dwell; come to town; — II. INF. *tamdîn,* found cities, civilize; — V. INF. *tamaddun,* join in civil society; get civilized, refined.
مدن *mudun,* pl. of مدينة *madîna-t.*
مدنف *mudnif,* suffering from a chronic disease; near death.
مدنى *madaniyy,* ة, living in towns, civilized (موت م *maut madaniyy,* quiet death); made or revealed in Medina; worldly; — *; — ة *mudniya-t,* near confinement.
مده *madh,* praise; — *muddah,* pl. of ماده *mâdih,* who praises.

مدهامة *mudhâmma-t,* luxuriant garden.
مدهن *mudhun,* pl. *madâhin,* oil-jar; phial for ointments.
مدهور *madhûr,* visited with calamities.
مدواس *midwâs,* threshing-instrument; a tool for polishing.
مدوحس *madauhas*=مدحوس *madhûs.*
مدود *midwad,* pl. مداود *madâwid,* manger; — *mudûd,* pl. of مد *madd*; — *mudawwad,* worm-eaten; full of worms.
مدوس *midwas*=مدواس *midwâs.*
مدوف *madûf,* dissolved, macerated.
مدوك *midwak,* stone pestle.
مدوم *midwam,* continual, everlasting.
مدون *madawwin,* who collects into a diwân, who registers, &c.; — ات *mudawwanât,* collective works.
(مدى) *mada,* I, INF. *madan,* stretch, extend; — III. INF. *mumâdât,* grant one a delay or respite; — IV. INF. *imdâ',* id.; be advanced in years; — VI. INF. *tamâdî,* last, continue; be long; persist; go far in; hesitate, tarry; reach the goal.
مدى *madan,* duration, period, term, goal; reach, range; — *mudy,* pl. *amdâ',* a measure; — *mudî',* ة, ill, sick; — *madiyy,* pl. *amdiya-t,* place enclosed with stones, watering-place; channel in front of a reservoir; — ة *madya-t, midya-t, mudya-t,* pl. *madan, midan, mudan,* large knife; handle of a bow; — *mudya-t,* goal, limit.
مديان *midyân,* pl. *madâ'in, madâ'în, madâyîn,* deep in debt; who lends much.
مديح *madîḥ,* ة *madîḥa-t,* anything praiseworthy; praiseworthy deed; praise.
مديخ *madîḫ,* pl. *mudaḫâ',* excellent, magnificent, great; — *middîḫ,* id.
مديد *madîd,* pl. *mudud, midâd,*

stretched, extended, long, great; grass, hay, straw; name of a metre (*fâ'ilâtun fâ'ilun* — ⏑ — — | — ⏑ — four times repeated).

مدير *mudîr*, who turns round, &c.; prefect of a district, governor, director; — ـة *mudîriyya-t*, district, jurisdiction.

مدين *madyan*, Midian; — *madîn*, debtor; rewarded, requited; — *mudayyin*, tolerant in religious matters; who lends, gives credit, creditor; — ة *madîna-t*, pl. *mudn*, *mudun*, *madâ'in*, town; Medina; م السلام *madînat as-salâm*, Bagdad; — ى *midyaniyy*, Midianite; — *madîniyy*, inhabitant of a town; municipal.

مديون *madyûn*, in debt.

مدئى *mud'î*, ill; making ill.

مذ *muẕ*, *miẕ*, since.

مذا *maẕẕa'*, onanist; — ء *miẕâ'*, pl. of مذية *maẕiyya-t*, *maẕya-t*.

مذاب *muẕâb*, molten; — *muẕa''ab*, having forelocks; fringed; — ة *maẕ'aba-t*, tract abounding with wolves.

مذارع *maẕâri'*, مذاريع *maẕârî'*, pl. of مذراع *miẕrâ'*.

مذارف *maẕârif*, pl. lachrymal ducts.

مذاق *maẕâq*, ة *maẕâqa-t*, tasting (s.), taste, palate (صاحب م *ṣâḥib maẕâq*, gormandizer, epicurean); discrimination; — *maẕẕâq*, who dissimulates; insincere.

مذاكير *maẕâkîr*, pl. of ذكر *ẕakar*, penis.

مذام *maẕâmm*, pl. of مذمة *maẕamma-t*.

مذب *maẕabb*, who well defends his people, his wives; — ة *maẕabba-t*, place abounding with flies; — *miẕabba-t*, pl. *maẕẕâb*, fly-flap.

مذبح *maẕbaḥ*, spot of the throat where an animal is killed; slaughter-place, altar of sacrifice; high altar; amphitheatre for gladiators; — *miẕbaḥ*, slaughtering-knife; — *.

مذبذب *muẕabẕib*, suspended and swinging in the air; irresolute.

مذبر *muẕabbar*, written; embroidered; — *muẕabbir*, writing.

مذبوب *maẕbûb*, troubled by flies; raving, furious.

مذبوح *maẕbûḥ*, slaughtered, &c.; hoarse; watered (wine).

(مذح) *maẕiḥ*, A, INF. *maẕaḥ*, have the inner side of the thighs sore; — V. INF. *tamaẕẕuḥ*, suck.

مذح *maẕaḥ*, مذخ *maẕaḥ*, juice of the wild pomegranate; — V. INF. *tamaẕẕuḥ*, suck this juice.

مذخاة *maẕḥât*, treeless tract.

مذخر *maẕḥar*, pl. *maẕâḥir*, storehouse, loft, magazine; pl. bowels.

مذخور *maẕḥûr*, stored, &c.; adopted.

(مذر) *maẕir*, A, INF. *maẕar*, be corrupted, foul; be sick, disordered (stomach); be troubled, disturbed (mind); — II. INF. *tamẕîr*, disperse, separate; — V. INF. *tamaẕẕur*=I.; be dispersed.

مذر *maẕir*, ة, deteriorated, foul; — ة *miẕarra-t*, flail.

مذراع *miẕrâ'*, pl. *maẕâri'*, *maẕârî'*, border district between cultivated land and desert.

مذراة *miẕrât*, see مذرى *miẕran*.

مذرب *miẕrab*, tongue; — *.

مذرق *maẕraq*, INF. ة, throw.

مذروان *miẕrawân*, the two ends of a bow.

مذرى *miẕran*, مذراة *miẕrât*, pl. *maẕârî*, fan (for winnowing), hay-fork; — *muẕrî* (ذرو IV.), winnowing, scattering, &c.

(مذع) *maẕa'*, INF. *maẕ'*, *maẕ'a-t*, inform only partially; take (an oath); flow.

مذعان *miẕ'ân*, tame, obsequious; very obedient.

مذفوف *maẕfûf*, ready, prepared.

(مذق) *maẕaq*, U, INF. *maẕq*, mix with water; (m.) be insipid, disgusting; simulate friendship or love; — III. INF. *mumâẕaqa-t*

=I.; deceive by simulated love; —VIII. INF. *imtiẓâq*, be watered.

مذق• *maẓiq*, insipid, disgusting, loathsome; — *miẓq*, ة *maẓqa-t*, watered milk, mess.

(مذقر), II. *tamaẓqar*, INF. *tamaẓqur*, be corrupt, foul (water).

مذكر *muẓkir*, مذكار• *miẓkâr*, bearing only boys; trying, hard, dangerous; — *muẓakkar*, manly; of tempered steel; — ة, hard, dangerous; —*muẓakkir*, reminding, &c.; warner; calling on the name of God; — ة *maẓkara-t*, anything worthy of mention, mention; — *muẓkara-t*, *muẓakkara-t*, virago; — *muẓakkira-t*, verbal message.

مذكوبة• *maẓkûba-t*, virtuous woman.

مذكى *muẓakkî* (مذك• *muẓakk-in*), six-year-old horse; — *muẓki'*, (m.) wine (in the Eucharist).

(مذل) *maẓal*, U, INF. *maẓl*, *maẓâl*, make known a secret; — *maẓil*, A,—*maẓul*, be unable to keep a secret; —IV. INF. *imẓâl*, IX. INF. *imẓilâl*, get benumbed.

مذل• *maẓl*, torpidity, numbness; — *; — ة *maẓalla-t*, state of abasement, disgrace.

مذلق• *muẓlaq*, pronounced with the tip of the tongue; — *muẓallaq*, sharp; watered.

مذلل• *muẓallal*, humbled; tamed, broken in; — *.

مذلى• *miẓlan*, restless person.

مذم• *muẓimm*, blameworthy, contemptible; damaged; — ة *maẓamma-t*, blame, reproach, abuse; pl. *maẓâmm*, anything blameworthy; clientship, duty of protection; ذو م *ẓû maẓamma-t*, troublesome, molesting; also *maẓimma-t*, shame on account of blame.

(مذمذ) *maẓmaẓ*, INF. ة, tell lies.

مذمر• *muẓammar*, part between the shoulders.

مذموم• *maẓmûm*, blamed; blameworthy.

مذميذ• *miẓmîẓ*, great liar.

مذنب• *miẓnab*, spoon; — *muẓnib*, guilty; sinner, criminal; — *muẓannab*, having a tail; كوكب م *kaukab muẓannab*, comet.

مذهب• *maẓhab*, pl. *maẓâhib*, path which one follows, sect, school; religious belief; opinion; law, rule, custom; root, origin; privy, sewer; INF. of (ذهب); —*muẓhab*, gilt; bay (horse); — *muẓahhab*, gilt, embroidered with gold; — *muẓahhib*, gilder, embroiderer with gold.

مذوب• *miẓwab*, crucible; — ة *miẓwaba-t*, spoon.

مذود• *miẓwad*, fodder-bag; manger; horn of a bull; tongue; — *muẓawwid*, driver.

مذؤوب• *maẓ'ûb*, having a sore throat.

مذؤوف• *maẓ'ûf*, poisoned.

(مذى) *maẓa*, I, INF. *maẓy*, send to the pasture (also II.); lose sperm (without sexual intercourse); — II. INF. *tamẓiya-t*, see I.; — ة *maẓiyya-t*, *maẓya-t*, pl. *maẓiyyât*, *miẓâ'*, woman.

مذياغ• *miẓyâg*, pl. *maẓâyîg*, having many rents; who blabs out.

مذيب• *muẓîb*, causing to melt; — *muẓ'ib*, frightened.

مذيحة• *maẓyaḥa-t*, pl. wolves.

مذيذ• *maẓîẓ*, liar.

مذئر• *muẓ'ir*, who urges on, goads.

مذيع• *muẓî'*, who publishes, makes known; robber.

مذيق• *maẓîq*, watered.

مذيل• *muẓîl*, weak; soft; — *.

مذيم• *maẓîm*, مذيوم• *maẓyûm*, blamed, reproached.

(مر) *marr*, U, INF. *marr*, *murûr*, pass, pass by (acc., ب *bi*, على *'ala*); pass away; happen to, befall (ب *bi*); depart, go away; — *marar*, *marir*, U, A, INF. *marâra-t*, be bitter; — II. INF. *tamrîr*, make bitter, embitter; — III. INF. *mumârra-t*, pass by with; wrestle with; INF. *mumârra-t*, *mirâr*, be dragged up;

—IV. INF. *imrâr*, let one cross a river, let one pass; pass the knife through one's throat; be bitter; make bitter; twist a rope firmly;—VIII. INF. *imtirâr*, pass by, pass over;—X. INF. *istimrâr*, id.; be firm, persevere; last, endure, continue; stay, remain; find bitter.

مر *marr*, passing, passing by, passing away (s.); unbroken duration; time, turn (مرا او مرين *marr-an au marrain*, once or twice); iron shovel;—*murr*, ة, pl. *amrâr*, bitter; ˉ bitterness; myrrh;—ء *mar'*, *mir'*, *mur'*, pl. *mar'ûn*, man; wolf;—ة *marra-t*, pl. *marr*, *marrât*, *mirar*, *mirâr*, *murûr*, a time, a turn: *marrat-an*, ذات م *ẕât-a marrat-in*, once, once upon a time; *mirâr-an*, repeatedly, also ذات المرار *ẕât-a'l-mirâr-i*, sometimes; بالمرة *bi'l-marrat-i*, at once, suddenly;—*mirra-t*, pl. *mirar*, gall; pl. *mirar*, *amrâr*, *marîr*, bodily strength; power; intellect, sound judgment; ذو م *ẕû mirrat-in*, archangel Gabriel;—*murra-t*, pl. *murr*, *amrâr*, a bitter plant (ابو م *abû murrat-in*, devil); du. *al-murratân*, hardness and bitterness.

(مرا) *mara'*, be easily digested, do good;—INF. *mar'*, eat; taste; lie with;—مرى *mari'*, be wholesome, salutary, beneficial; be like a woman (in gait, &c.);—*maru'*, INF. *marâ'a-t*, be good, be beneficial, conducive to health (food, &c.); have a healthy air; INF. *muru'a-t*, be manly, manful, brave; be humane;—IV. INF. *imrâ'*, be beneficial, do one (acc.) good;—V. INF. *tamarru'*, show manliness, humanity;—X. INF. *istimrâ'*, find the food digestible and wholesome; eat sweetly.

مراء *mirâ'*, quarrel; dispute; doubt, INF. of (مرى III.);—ة *murâ'ât*, simulation, hypocrisy;—ة *marâ'at*, digestibleness.

مراب *mir'ab*, who patches up, mends;—ة *murâba-t*, polite insinuating manners; lending money for interest, usury;—*murâba'a-t*, observation, guard, INF. (ربا III.).

مرابط *murâbiṭ*, placed as an outpost at a hostile boundary; garrison-soldier; defender of Islâm; patient, quiet;—ة *murâbaṭa-t*, plotting (s.), conspiracy.

مرابى *murâbî* (مراب *murâb-in*), usurer.

مرابيع *marâbî'*, pl. of مرباع *mirbâ'*.

مراث *marâs̱*, buttocks of a horse.

مراح *mirâḥ*, joy, cheerfulness, merriment;—*murâḥ*, pl. *murḥ*, place of rest or recreation; stable, fold; abode.

مراحلة *murâḥala-t*, lending help in saddling or unloading; departure, starting; travelling-expenses.

مراحى *marâḥa*, pl. of مرح *mariḥ*.

مراحيض *marâḥîḍ*, pl. of مرحاض *mirḥâḍ*.

مراد *marâd* (also *marrâd*, pl. *marârid*), neck;—*murâd*, willed; what one wishes, wants, intends; pl. *-ât*, wish, intention, mind;—ة *marâda-t*, refractoriness, rebelliousness;—*murâdda-t*, repulsion, refusal;—ى *marâdi*, trowsers; feet; pl. of مردى *mirda*;—*murâdî*, according to wish, favourable;—*murâdiyy*, voluntary.

مرار *marâr*, rope;—*mirâr*, INF. of (مر III.); pl. of مرة *marra-t*;—*murâr*, a bitter plant;—ة *marâra-t*, bitterness; pl. *marâ'ir*, gall-bladder.

مرارى *marârî*, pl. of مروراة *maraurât*;—ة *mirâriyya-t*, biliousness.

مراريد *marârîd*, pl. of مراد *marrâd*.

مراز *marâz*, ة *marâza-t*, weight; du. *marâzân*, both breasts.

مرازب *marâzib*, pl. of مرزاب *mirzâb*

—ة *marâziba-t*, pl. of مرزبان *marzubân*.

مرازن *murâzin*, inhabitant of the same house, fellow-lodger; —ة *murâzana-t*, cohabitation.

مراس *marâs*, strength, power; —*mirâs*, id.; active and skilful management of affairs (مرس III.); —*marrâs*, strong, powerful; —ة *marâsa-t*, violence, harshness, severity.

مراسلة *murâsala-t*, correspondence; summons.

مراسم *marâsim*, pl. traces, signs; customs, manners, rules of behaviour, ceremonies, prescriptions.

مراسى *marâsî*, pl. of مرساة *mirsât* and مرسى *marsa*.

مراسيل *marâsîl*, pl. of مرسال *mirsâl*.

مراسيم *marâsîm*, pl. of مرسوم *marsûm*.

مراش *mirâś*, vomiting (s.).

مراض *marâḍ*, pl. *marâ'iḍ*, hard low ground with water; —*mirâḍ*, pl. of مريض *marîḍ*; —*murâḍ*, mildew.

مراضاة *murâḍât*, endeavour to satisfy one; mutual consent.

مراضعة *murâḍa'a-t*, giving suck (s.); handing over of the child to a wet nurse.

مراضى *marâḍa*, pl. of مريض *marîḍ*.

مراضيع *marâḍî'*, pl. of مرضع *murḍi'*.

مراط *mirâṭ*, pl. of مريط *marîṭ*.

مراع *mirâ'*, fat.

مراعاة *murâ'ât*, observation, observance, regard.

مراعف *marâ'if*, nose and surrounding parts.

مراغ *marâg*, ة *marâga-t*, place where an animal rolls about; —ة *marrâga-t*, rolling about frequently.

مراغب *marâgib*, wants, needs, inducements;—*;—ة *murâgaba-t*, desire, craving for, wish, inclination, propensity.

مرافض *marâfiḍ*, open bottoms of valleys.

مراق *marâq-in*, see مراقى *marâqî*; —*marâqq*, pl. of مرق *maraqq*.

مراقاة *murâqât*, circumspection, prudence, cautiousness.

مراقبة *murâqaba-t*, guard, watch, observation, surveillance; contemplation, deep thought.

مراقى *marâqî* (مراق *marâq-in*), مراقيا *marâqiyâ*, hypochondres; *marâqî*, pl. of مرقاة *marqât*.

مراكبى *marâkibiyy*, captain of a ship; charioteer.

مراكى *murâkî*, persevering, enduring; —ة *murâkiya-t*, pl. *marâkî*, a bitter, salt plant.

مراكيب *marâkîb*, pl. of مركوب *markûb*.

مرام *marâm*, pl. -*ât*, desire, striving for, intention, aim, will, wish; ascending (s.).

مراماة *murâmât*, emulation in shooting; shooting at one another.

مرامر *murâmir*, vain, perishable, fleeting, delicate; soft and trembling.

مرانة *marâna-t*, practice; —*murrâna-t*, pl. *murrân*, hard but supple spear.

مرآة *mar'ât*, aspect; face; worthy; —*mir'ât*, pl. *mirâ'in*, *mirâ'î*, *marâyâ*, mirror, looking-glass; —*mar'a-t*, woman, wife; she-wolf; fit, appropriate; easily digested, wholesome.

مراهص *marâhiṣ*, pl. of مرهصة *marhaṣa-t*.

مراهى *marâhî*, pl. of مرهاة *mirhât*.

مراوزة *marâwiza-t*, people of Merv.

مراوفة *murâwafa-t*, kindness, benignity.

مراوق *murâwiq*, next-door neighbour.

مراوون *murâ'ûn*, pl. of مرائى *murâ'î*.

مراوى *marâwî*, pl. of مروى *mirwa*.

مرأى *mar'a*, aspect, features, physiognomy.

مرايا *marâyâ*, lacteal veins; —ة

murâyât, hypocrisy ; — *murâya'a-t*, vigilance.

مرايحة *murâyaḥa-t*, tranquillization.

مرائر *marâ'ir*, pl. of مرارة *marâra-t* and مرير *marîr*.

مرائض *marâ'iḍ*, pl. of مراض *marâḍ*.

مراية *mirâya-t*, mirror, looking-glass.

مرائى *marâ'î* (مرا *marâ'-in*), pl. of مراة *mir'ât* ; — *murâ'î*, pl. *murâ'ûn*, hypocrite.

مرب *marabb*, house, dwelling ; — ة *marabba-t*, dominion ; — *murabba-t*, jam, confitures.

مربا *marba'*, ة *marba't*, hill, high place ; — ء *marbâ'*, ladder, stairs.

مرباع *mirbâ'*, pl. *marâbî'*, place with early grass ; spring rain ; fourth part of the booty ; square-built, short and thick-set.

مربب *murabbab*, boiled in syrup or juice, confitures (pl. *-ât*) ; brought up, educated ; — *murabbib*, who makes confitures.

مربد *mirbad*, stable for camels ; — *murbadd*, ash-coloured.

مربض *marbiḍ*, *marbaḍ*, pl. *marâbiḍ*, sheep-fold ; lair ; lion's den.

مربط *marbaṭ*, *marbiṭ*, stable ; relay of horses ; — *mirbaṭ*, ة *mirbaṭa-t*, chain, rope, strap ; bridle ; packet ; bale of merchandise ; nosegay, batch of flowers.

مربع *marba'*, pl. *marâbi'*, spring tents, spring pasture ; summer habitation ; dwelling ; — *mirba'*, ة *mirba'a-t*, lever, crowbar ; — *murba'*, afflicted with quartan ague ; — *murbi'*, quartan ague ; — *murabba'*, ة, square (adj.), *murabba'*, ة *murabba-t*, square (s.) ; quatrain ; square pillow or cushion.

مربقة *murabbaqa-t*, bread and butter.

مربوب *marbûb*, fed, brought up ; subject (adj. s.), slave.

مربوط *marbûṭ*, tied up, &c. ; suspended, dependent ; grammatically correct ; ascetic, Marabout.

مربوع *marbû'*, quadruple, square ; thick-set ; afflicted with quartan ague.

مربى *marba*, place where one has been brought up ; education ; — *marbiyy*, educated ; increased ; — *murabba*, brought up, protected ; confitures (pl. *murabbayât*) ; — *murabbî*, who brings up and protects ; who makes confitures.

(مرت) *marat*, I, INF. *mart*, smooth ; drive away.

مرت *mart*, pl. *amrât*, *murût*, desert without vegetation ; entirely hairless.

مرتا *murtâ*, pat. of (راى VIII.), wish, view.

مرتا *murtâ* ., to be looked for under (. رو ; . رئ VIII.), as—

مرتاب *murtâb*, ag. of (ريب VIII.), suspecting, doubtful, irresolute ; dependent.

مرتاج *mirtâj*, pl. *marâtij*, bolt ; avenue of trees.

مرتاح *murtâḥ*, rested, comforted, &c. ; the fifth horse in a race.

مرتب *murattab*, arranged, consolidated, &c. ; regular ; ready ; salary, wages ; pl. *-ât*, regular supplies ; — *murattib*, who arranges, &c. ; type-setter, compositor ; — ة *martaba-t*, pl. *marâtib*, step of a ladder or stairs ; degree, rank, dignity, order ; class, category ; hierarchy ; carpet-seat, mattress ; storey ; height ; watch-tower ; full tone (in music).

مرتبا *martaba'*, watch-tower.

مرتبان *martabân*, ى *martabâniyy*, finest porcelain vessel ; a fine texture.

مرتبع *murtaba'*, spring habitation.

. مرة *murta* . . , to be looked for under (. ر VIII.), as—

مرتبق *murtabiq* ag. of (ربق VIII.), complicated, entangled.

مرتج *murtaj*, galena, lead-glance.

مرتجح *murtajiḥ*, swinging up and down; rickety; inclined.
مرتد *murtadd*, refused, expelled; apostate, renegade.
مرتدع *murtadi'*, who allows himself to be prevented, hindered; hindered, turned off, refused; dyed with saffron; perfumed.
مرتزق *murtazaq*, food, sustenance; — *murtaziq*, pensioner, stipendiary, who enjoys free board.
مرتسم *murtasam*, embroidered, painted;—*murtasim*, who obeys, who professes Islâm; devoted to God.
مرتضى *murtaḍa* (رضو VIII.), acceptable, agreeable; *al-murtaḍa*, Ali; — *,
مرتع *marta'*, pl. *marâti'*, place where everything is in abundance; pasture, meadow; food; — *murti'*, fertile.
مرتفع *murtafi'*, high, sublime, &c.; in the nominative case.
مرتفق *murtafaq*, couch; inn; — *murtafiq*, leaning against, supporting one's self; firm, solid.
مرتقى *murtaqa*, ascent; summit; — *.
مرتك *martak*, *murtak*, galena, lead-glance; — *murtakk*, in great embarrassment; not able to help one's self.
مرتكى *murtaka*, who can be relied upon; place of support; — *murtakî*, who leans against, supports himself.
مرتمى *murtamî*, thrown away, &c.; outpost, vanguard.
مرتنة *mirtana-t*, bread and butter.
مرتهن *murtahan*, pledged; pledge, mortgage; — *murtahin*, who takes a pledge, asks for a security or mortgage.
(مرث) *maras̱*, U, INF. *mars̱*, wet, moisten; soften; macerate; crush with the fingers; chew; bite the fingers; suck; beat; — *maris̱*, A, INF. *maras̱*, show patience and gentleness in a dispute; —II. INF. *tamrîs̱*, crush violently; — VII. INF. *inmirâs̱*, be crushed, chewed.
مرث *mars̱*, crushing (s.); — *maris̱*, patient, gentle; — *muriss̱*, old, stale.
مرثاة *mars̱ât*, pl. *marâs̱î*, funeral speech, elegy on a dead person, solemnity in honour of or lamentation for the dead.
مرثد *mars̱ad*, lion; magnanimous.
مرثم *mars̱im*, *mirs̱am*, nose.
مرثية *mars̱iya-t*=مرثاة *mars̱ât*.
(مرج) *maraj*, U, INF. *marj*, send an animal to the pasture; allow to flow freely and to mingle; range freely; mix; — *marij*, A, INF. *maraj*, fit loosely (ring on the finger); be in disorder, in confusion; — IV. INF. *imrâj*= *maraj*.
مرج *marj*, pl. *murûj*, meadow, marsh-land, common; — *maraj*, pasturing freely; — *marij*, in disorder, confused; — *murijj*, near parturition (mare).
مرجا *murja'*, pl. *murja'ûn*, delayed, put off; — ة *marjât*, hope, expectation.
مرجاس *mirjâs*, sounding-lead to measure the depth of a well.
مرجام *mirjâm*, ballista, catapult.
مرجان *marjân*, a seasoning herb; also *murjân*, ة, coral; pearl; sole (fish); — ة *murjâna-t*, a female proper name.
مرجب *murajjib*, preponderant, pre-eminent, more probable.
مرجز *murajjaz*, rhythmical prose without rhyme.
مرجع *marja'*, ة *marji'a-t*, return; — *marji'*, *marja'*, place where one returns to or from, refuge, asylum; ultimate object; repetition; pl. *marâji'*, lower part of the shoulder; —*murji'*, *murajji'*, inviting to return or repetition, advantageous; restorative, restoring (adj.).
مرجف *murjif*, alarmist, agitator; du. *al-murjifân*, water-jug and basin, circulating after meals.

مرجل *marjal*, pl. of رجل *rajul*; man; — *mirjal*, pl. *marâjil*, a large kettle or pot; comb; also *marjal*, a striped garment; — *murjil*, bearing male children; —*murajjal*, painted with human figures; — *.

مرجم *mirjam*, strong; — *murajjam*, equivocal, doubtful.

مرجوح *marjûḥ*, inferior in weight or value, surpassed; — ة *marjûḥa-t*, swing, hammock; — ية *marjûḥiyya-t*, preponderance.

مرجوسة *marjûsa-t*, confusion, hurly-burly.

مرجوع *marjû'*, sent or brought back; also ة *marjû'a-t*, reply, answer.

مرجوم *marjûm*, stoned, worthy to be stoned, devil.

مرجونة *marjûna-t*, pumpkin used as a flask, gourd.

مرجى *murjî*, who delays, puts off; also ة *murjiya-t*, near parturition; — *marjiyy*, shaken, agitated.

(مرح) *mariḥ*, A, INF. *maraḥ*, be merry and boisterous; be nimble and brisk; be proud; walk with head erect; — (m.) *maraḥ*, oil, anoint, rub with ointments; coat slightly with mud; — VII. INF. *inmirâḥ*, pass. of I.

مرح *maraḥ*, liveliness, briskness, wantonness; delight; pride; — *mariḥ*, pl. *marḥa*, *marâḥa*, brisk, wanton, boisterously merry; — ة *mirḥa-t*, warehouse, magazine.

مرحاض *mirḥâḍ*, pl. *marâḥîḍ*, dung-hill; sewer, privy; lavatory.

مرحان *maraḥân*, boisterous merriment, wantonness.

مرحب *marḥab*, width, spaciousness, extended space مرحبا و سهلا *marḥab-an wa sahl-an*, spaciousness and ease; welcome! make yourself at home! willingly; — *marḥab*, INF. ة, welcome one in the above manner.

مرحضة *mirḥaḍa-t*, washing-basin, washing-tub; lavatory, laundry.

مرحل *mirḥal*, fit for travelling; — *muraḥḥal*, saddled, ready to start; embroidered (with a pattern of camel-saddles); — ة *marḥala-t*, pl. *marâḥil*, day's journey; station, inn.

مرحمة *marḥama-t*, pl. *marâḥim*, compassion, mercy; favour, benefit, bounty; good work.

مرحوم *marḥûm*, ة, received in the mercy of God; — ة *marḥûma-t*, Medina.

مرحى *marḥa*, pl. of مرح *mariḥ*; — *marḥan*, battle-field; — *muraḥḥî*, builder of mills.

(مرخ) *maraḫ*, A, INF. *marḫ*, jest, sport; — also II. INF. *tamrîḫ*, anoint, oil and soften; — IV. INF. *imrâḫ*, make soft and thin (dough); — V. INF. *tamarruḫ*, pass. of II.

مرخ *marḫ*, a tree whose wood easily ignites; —*mariḫ*, soft; —*murrâḫ*, wolf; — ة *murḫa-t*, pl. *murḫ*, unripe date.

مرخاء *marḫâ'*, f. pl. *marâḫî*, brisk and swift.

مرخم *muraḫḫim*, polisher of marble; — *.

مرخى *murḫî*, مرخ *murḫ-in*, who suspends or drops, &c.; — *murḫan*, *murḫa*, *marḫiyy*, loose, lax, hanging to the ground; *murḫa*, impotent.

(مرد) *marad*, U, INF. *mard*, cut; blacken one's character; suck at the breast; moisten and soften; INF. *mard* and *marûd*, attend to, practise, inure one's self to (على *'ala*): — U, INF. *murûd*, *murûda-t*, — *marud*, INF. *marâda-t*, persist boldly in opposition or rebellion, excel in boldness amongst rebels; — *marid*, A, INF. *marad*, *murûda-t*, begin to grow a moustache (one otherwise beardless); be beardless; — II. INF. *tamrîd*, *tamrâd*, make a dove-cote; raise high and symmetrically; — V. INF.

tamarrud, show one's self insolent and refractory, rebel.

مرد *mard*, fresh fruit of the tree اراك *arâk*; — *murd*, pl. of امرد *amrad*, beardless, &c.; — *maradd*, return; sending back (s.), refusal, reply; — *muridd*, pl. *marâdd*, with swollen udders; for a long time a bachelor or without sexual intercourse; lascivious, lewd, lecherous; rolling (sea); — ة *marada-t*, pl. of مارد, refractory, &c.; — *maradda-t*, return; gain.

مردا *mardâ'*, f. of امرد *amrad*, bare, &c.; — *muradâ'*, pl. of مريد *marîd*; — ة *mirdât*=مردى *mirda*; latch; upper mill-stone; overcoat.

مردارسنج *murdârsanj*, مرداسنج *murdâsanj*, galena, lead-glance (Pers.).

مردام *mirdâm*, good-for-nothing, worthless.

مردغة *mardaga-t*, pl. *marâdig*, muscles between the shoulder and collar-bone.

مردقوش *mardaqûś*, marjoram (Pers.).

مردن *mirdan*, spindle.

مردود *mardûd*, INF. and pat. of (رد); refused, &c.; abject, despised, repugnant; — ة *mardûda-t*, divorced woman returning to her father's house; — ية *mardûdiyya-t*, repulsion, repudiation.

مردوس *mardûs*, locust.

مردوع *mardû'*, stained; dyed.

مردى *mirda*, pl. *marâdî*, stone or missile thrown by a ballista; م الحرب *mirda al-ḥarb*, hero in warfare; — *mardiyy*, hit by a missile; — *murdiyy*, pl. *marâdiyy*, oar, rowing-pole.

مرذ *maraẓẓ*, مرذوذ *marẓûẓ*, bedewed, wetted by rain.

مرذى *murẓa*, jaded; exposed (child).

مرر *mirar*, pl. of مرة *marra-t*, *mirra-t*.

(مرز) *maraz*, U, INF. *marz*, press slightly with the finger-tips; slap; cut; — III. INF. *mumâraza-t*, accustom, inure, exercise; — VIII. INF. *imtirâz*, take part of; blacken one's character; — ة *mirza-t*, lump of dough; du. *marzatân*, cartilage above the lobe of the ear; — *murza-t*, a kind of vulture; — *marazza-t*, rice-field.

مرزا *murazza'*, very liberal; — *mirzâ'*, slanderer, calumniator.

مرزاب *mirzâb*, pl. *marâzîb*, aqueduct, canal; man-of-war (Pers.).

مرزبان *marzubân*, pl. *marâziba-t*, margrave, count of the marches, marquess, governor of a boundary-district; landed proprietor (Pers.).

مرزبة *marzaba-t*, road; regulation of life; office of a *marzubân*; — *mirzaba-t*, *mirzabba-t*, pl. *marâzib*, iron club, mallet, sledge-hammer, forge-hammer.

مرزز *murazzaz*, polished, smooth; prepared with rice.

مرزنجوش *marzanjûś*, marjoram (Pers.).

مرزوق *marzûq*, provided with food, &c.; well-to-do; pl. *marzûqât*, possessions, property, fortune.

مرزئة *marzi'a-t*, hurt, injury, damage, calamity.

(مرس) *maras*, U, INF. *mars*, macerate and crush with the hand; suck one's finger (child); wipe; slip from the pulley; (m.) make all tricks in a game of cards; — *maris*, A, INF. *maras*, stop because the rope has slipped off (pulley); — III. INF. *mirâs*, *mumârasa-t*, attend carefully to, get practised in (acc.); fight; — V. INF. *tamarrus*, rub one's self against; — VI. INF. *tamârus*, fight with one another; — VIII. INF. *imtirâs*=V.

مرس *mars*, *maris*, kind, form, shape; (m.) *mars*, all tricks in a game; — *maris*, brave; well-

practised ; — ة marasa-t, pl. *amrâs, maras*, string, cord ; gallows ; halter.

مرسا *marsâ*=مرسى *marsan, marsa* ; — ة *marsât*, pl. *marâsî*, anchor.

مرسال *mirsâl*, pl. *marasîl*, walking apace, swift messenger, express.

مرسب *marsab*, pl. *marâsib*, column ; intelligent, considerate, patient ; — *mirsab*, Mohammed's sword.

مرسل *mursal*, sent ; envoy, prophet, apostle (سيد المرسلين *sayyid al-mursalîn*, Mohammed) ; missionary ; — * ; — ة *marsala-t*, apostolic mission ; — *mursala-t*, missive, letter ; chain hanging over the bosom ; *al-mursalât*, letters, angels, winds, horses.

مرسم *murassam*, striped ; م عليه *murassam 'alai-hi*, confined to one's house or to the interior part of a country.

مرسن *marsin, marsan*, pl. *marâsin*, middle of a camel's nose ; nose ; على رغم مرسنه *'ala ragm-i marsani-hi*, against his will.

مرسوم *marsûm*, marked, &c. ; usual, customary ; consecrated ; *marâsîm*, royal letter, mandate, ordinance, passport ; destiny, fate ; salary, pay ; pl. *marâsim*, precepts, customs, usages, ceremonial.

مرسى *marsa, mursa*, pl. *marâsî*, anchorage, harbour ; — *mursa*, fixed ; moored, firmly at anchor.

مرسين *marsîn*, myrtle.

(مرش) *maraś*, I, INF. *marś*, scratch with the nails ; grind with the finger-tips ; eat, swallow greedily ; — VIII. INF. *imtirâś*, snatch out of one's hand, take away from ; earn, gain.

مرش *maraśś*, ة *miraśśa-t*, pl. *marâśś*, sprinkle ; watering-pot ; — *.

مرشا *marśâ'*, f. of امرش *amraś*, mordacious, given to biting ; *al-marśâ'*, ground with luxuriant vegetation.

مرشح *mirśaḥ*, ة *mirśaḥa-t*, cloth placed beneath the saddle.

مرشد *marśad*, pl. *marâśid*, right path ; firm resolution ;—*murśid*, who leads on the right path ; spiritual guide, leader, educator.

مرشف *marśaf*, pl. *marâśif*, place where one sucks ; — *mirśaf*, pl. *marâśif*, means by which one sucks, lips, trunk of an insect, &c.

(مرص) *maraṣ*, U, INF. *marṣ*, press with the hand ; — *mariṣ*, A, INF. *maraṣ*, be beforehand with, go in advance.

مرصاد *mirṣâd*, open road ; look-out for the enemy.

مرصاع *mirṣâ'*, spinning-top.

مرصافة *mirṣâfa-t*, hammer.

مرصد *marṣad*, pl. *marâṣid*, hiding-place ; out-look ; watch ; observatory ; ambush ; road.

مرصص *muraṣṣaṣ*, covered with lead or tin, glazed ; firmly joined, compact.

مرصع *murṣi'*, pl. *marâṣi'*, palm-tree with shoots ; — *muraṣṣa'*, inlaid with gold, studded with jewels.

مرصن *mirṣan*, iron for branding.

مرصوص *marṣûṣ*, solidly joined ; soldered.

مرصون *marṣûn*, cauterised ; tattooed.

(مرض) *mariḍ*, A, INF. *marḍ, maraḍ*, be or fall ill ; — II. INF. *tamrîḍ*, nurse a sick person ; make ill ; weaken ; — IV. INF. *imrâḍ*, cause to fall ill ; find ill ;— VI. INF. *tamâruḍ*, feign to be ill ; — X. INF. *istimrâḍ*, feel ill.

مرض *maraḍ*, pl. *amrâḍ*, illness ; bodily and mental weakness ; م ساقط *maraḍ sâqiṭ*, epilepsy ; also *marḍ*, obscurity, doubt, unbelief ; hypocrisy ; deceit ; loss ; weakness ; languidness ; —*mariḍ*, ill, sick ;— ة *muriḍḍa-t*, thick milk.

مرضا *marḍâ*=مرضى *marḍâ*, pl. of مريض *marîḍ* ; — ة *marḍât*, satis-

faction, pleasure, benevolence, consent.

مرضاح *mirḍâḥ*, مرضاخ *mirḍâḫ*=مرضخة *mirḍaḫa-t*.

مرضافة *mirḍâfa-t*, hot stone for boiling milk.

مرضخة *mirḍaḫa-t*, stone for breaking date-stones, &c.

مرضع *marḍa'*, pl. *marâḍi'*, place where one sucks, teat;—*murḍi'*, pl. *marâḍi'*, *marâḍî'*, also ة *murḍi'a-t*, suckling woman, wet-nurse.

مرضو *marḍuww*, agreeable, pleasant.

مرضى *marḍa*, pl. of مريض *marîḍ*; —*murḍî* (مرض *murḍ-in*), contenting, satisfactory;—*marḍiyy*, agreeable, pleasing, applauded, praiseworthy; consent, approval.

(مرط) *maraṭ*, U, pull out; hasten; gather; secrete; (m.) eat, chew; (m.) tear;—*mariṭ*, A, INF. *maraṭ*, be hairless on the cheek or body; suffer from the falling out of the hair;—II. INF. *tamrîṭ*, pull out hair; —IV. INF. *imrâṭ*, be large enough to be pulled out;—VIII. INF. *imtirâṭ*, grasp, rob; gather; fall out; allow of being pulled out; steal.

مرط *marṭ*, pulling out of hair; rent;—*mirṭ*, pl. *murûṭ*, a woollen or silk stuff and a short shirt, coat, trowsers thereof;—*murṭ*, ة *miraṭa-t*, pl. of امرط *amraṭ*, hairless, &c.;—*muruṭ*, pl. *mirâṭ*, *amrâṭ*, unfeathered arrow.

مرطب *marṭab*, *murṭib*, green (field).

مرطبان *marṭabân*, glazed vessel.

(مرطل) *marṭal*, INF. ة, dirty, pollute; calumniate, slander, revile, abuse; wet; persist in.

مرطوب *marṭûb*, wetted, moist; م المزاج *marṭûb al-mizâj*, phlegmatic.

مرطيزة *murṭaiza-t*, plover.

مرظ *maraẓ*, violent hunger.

(مرع) *mara'*, INF. *mar'*, abound with grass and food; anoint abundantly; comb;—*mari'*, A, INF. *mara'*, abound with food; —*maru'*, INF. *marâ'a-t*, id.;—IV. INF. *imrâ'*, id.;—VII. INF. *inmirâ'*; depart, set out on a journey, travel.

مرع *mari'*, who looks out for food; —ة *mur'a-t*, fat; also *mura'a-t*, pl. *mur'*, *mur'ân*, Asiatic wood-snipe.

مرعا *mar'â*, ة *mar'ât*=مرعى *mar'an*.

مرعبب *mura'bib*, dripping with fat.

مرعبة *mar'aba-t*, what inspires with fear; terrible wilderness.

مرعز *mar'izz*, *mir'izz*, مرعزا *mar'izâ'*, مرعزى *mar'izza*, *mir'izza*, fine goat-hair beneath the coarser one.

مرعل *mir'al*, sharp sword;—*mura''al*, best property, best cattle.

مرعوب *mar'ûb*, frightened; terrible.

مرعوف *mar'ûf*, bleeding from the nose.

مرعون *mar'ûn*, unwell, weak; having a head-ache from the heat.

مرعى *mar'an*, pl. *marâ'î*, pasture, meadow, food; INF. of (رعى); —*mar'iyy*, ة, tended, pastured, ruled, governed; attended to, worthy of attention, important.

(مرغ) *marag*, A, INF. *marg*, graze, feed on grass; stand in the grass; anoint with oil; roll (a.) in the mud, make dirty; throw out foam, mucus, &c.; —*marig*, A, INF. *marag*, be stained, polluted;—II. INF. *tamrâg*, *tamrîg*, allow the horse to roll on the ground;—IV. INF. *imrâg*, salivate;—V. INF. *tamarrug*, roll (n.) on the ground; anoint one's self with oil; make one's self dirty.

مرغ *marg*, anointing with oil, oiling (s.); soiling, dirtying; also

ة *marga-t*, luxuriant garden ;— *marig*, needing to be oiled.

مرغامة *mirgâma-t*, shrew.

مرغاة *mirgât*, instrument for skimming, skimming-spoon, skimmer.

مرغب *murgib*, rich ; — * .

مرغم *margam*, *margim*, nose.

مرغوب *margûb*, desired, &c. ; desirable, beautiful, amiable.

مرفا *marfa'*, *murfa'*, anchorage.

مرفد *mirfad*, pl. *marâfid*, large cup or dish for guests ; false hips ; — *murfid*, rope-dancer.

مرفش *mirfaś*, fan ; ventilator ; winnowing-fan ;— * ;—*mirfaśa-t*, shovel, spade, broom.

مرفض *marfiḍ*, widening of a valley.

مرفع *marfa'*, pl. *marâfi'*, carnival.

مرفق *marfaq*, *marfiq*, *mirfaq*, pl. *marâfiq*, elbow ; advantage, profit ; comforts ; — *marfiq*, pl. *marâfiq*, place to lean the elbows upon ; eaves ; gutter, sewer, privy ; pl. *marâfiq*, wants, needs ; — ة *mirfaqa-t*, pillow, cushion to lean upon.

مرفو *marfuww*, patched, mended, darned.

مرفوع *marfû'*, ة, lifted up, raised, &c. ; honoured ; taken away, put aside ; marked with ـُ, placed in the nominative ; quickened pace.

مرفه *muraffah*, tranquil, content, happy.

(مرق) *maraq*, U, INF. *marq*, fill the pot with rich gravy (also II. and IV.) ; scrape off the wool ; pierce with a lance ; — U, INF. *murûq*, pierce through and come out on the opposite side ; miss the aim ; deviate from true religion or orthodoxy, become a heretic ; (m.) pass, pass by ; — *mariq*, A, INF. *maraq*, lose its dates (palm-tree) ; deteriorate and become watery (egg) ; — II. INF. *tamrîq*, see I. ; allow to pierce, to pass ; — IV. INF. *imrâq*, see I. ; — VII. INF. *inmirâq*, pierce the mark or overshoot it ; shoot many ; — VIII. INF. *imtirâq*, step out quickly, come forth.

مرق *marq*, putrid skin with remains of flesh ; pl. *murûq*, beard of an ear ; فى مرقك *fî marqi-ka*, by your fault ;—*murq*, pl. bald, hairless (wolves) ; — *maraq*, rich gravy ; ة *maraqa-t*, plate or portion of it ; — *mariq*, (m.) shameless, impudent ;—*maraqq*, pl. *marâqq*, hypochondres ; lobe of the ear ; — *muriqq*, elegant (writer) ; having thin hoofs.

مرقاق *mirqâq*, dough-roller.

مرقال *mirqâl*, swift ; rearing.

مرقاة *marqât*, *mirqât* (*marqa'a-t*, *mirqa'a-t*), pl. *marâqî*, stairs, ladder, step.

مرقب *marqab*, ة *marqaba-t*, watch-tower.

مرقد *marqad*, pl. *marâqid*, bedroom, dormitory, resting-place ; bed ; grave ;—*murqid*, *muraqqid*, causing to sleep, narcotic.

مرقشيشا *marqaśîśâ*, marcasite, bismuth.

مرقع *muraqqa'*, patched up, &c. ; well managed ; — *muraqqi'*, who patches up ; manager ; administrator ; economical.

مرقعان *marqa'ân*, ة, foolish, crazy.

مرقق *muraqqaq*, made thin ; fine, &c. ; sharpened, ground.

مرقم *mirqam*, pl. *marâqim*, pencil, style, pen ; pin, crotchet.

مرقوم *marqûm*, written, &c. ; prescribed ; described ; afore-mentioned ; sealed.

مرقى *marqa*, harbour ; — *marqiyy*, bewitched, spell-bound.

مرك *marik*, old sinner, paederast ;— *murakk*, slightly wetted by rain.

مركاح *mirkâḥ*, slipping back (saddle).

مركب *markab*, pl. *marâkib*, vehicle, ship (مركب نار *markab nâr*, steamboat), carriage, beast for riding, camel, ass, horse ; ة *markaba-t*, vehicle, carriage, beast for riding ; — *murakkab*, mounted, &c. ; compound, mixed ; mixture (*murakkabât*, mixtures, com-

pound words); ink; origin, descent; double; — *.

مركز *markaz, markiz*, pl. *marâkiz*, place where the flag is planted in the ground; head-quarters; camp, bivouac; chief town of a province, capital; centre, midst; seat, residence; railway-station.

مركض *mirkaḍ*, poker; chips, fuel; — ة, du. *mirkaḍatân*, the two horns of the bow.

مركع *marka'*, prayer-desk, pew.

مركل *markal*, pl. *marâkil*, road; flanks of a horse; — *mirkal*, foot; — ة *murakkala-t*, trodden path.

مركن *markan*, confidence, trust, credit; — *mirkan*, pl. *marâkin*, washing-bowl; — *.

مركو *markuww*, cistern.

مركوب *markûb*, pl. *marâkîb*, mounted, ridden, &c.; vehicle, beast for riding, steed, carriage; shoe; spade.

مركوز *markûz*, planted in the ground, &c.; implanted, inborn; buried; desire, wish.

مرمات *murimmât*, calamities.

مرماحوز *marmâḥûz*, an aromatic plant, basil.

مرمار *marmâr*, ة, delicate and trembling, soft; very juicy pomegranate.

مرماة *mirmât*, small kind of arrow; also *marmât*, cloven hoof.

مرمتون *marmatûn*, scullion (m.).

مرمد *murammad*, baked in the ashes; — *.

(مرمر) *marmar*, INF. ة, cause bitterness, provoke to anger, anger; be angry; cause to grumble; — II. INF. *tamarmur*, be sore in heart, be angry; be agitated, tremble; grumble.

مرمر *marmar*, marble, alabaster; = مرمار *marmâr*; — ى *marmariyy*, of marble.

مرمريت *marmarît*, مرمريس *marmarîs*, calamity; *marmarîs*, smooth; hard; land without vegetation.

(مرمس) *marmas*, (m.) INF. ة, torment; — II. INF. *tamarmus*, be tormented, tired; — *marmas*, tomb.

مرمش *murammaś*, blear-eyed.

مرمعات *muramma'ât*, false reports.

مرمق *murammaq, murmaqq*, who has scarcely enough to live upon.

مرملة *mirmala-t*, blotting-sand box.

مرمنة *marmana-t*, garden of pomegranates.

مرمة *maramma-t*; reparation, restoration, emendation; loom.

مرموثا *marmûsâ*, confusion.

مرموز *marmûz*, pointed at, alluded to, &c.; symbolical, metaphorical.

مرمى *marma*, pl. *marâmî*, place where one throws to, shoots at, aim, target, game; — *mirma*, مرماة *mirmât*, pl. *marâmî*, missile, projectile, arrow, dart; ballista, catapult, piece of artillery, cannon, battery; hurling (s.); flying splinter; dangerous deserts, far lands; — *marmiyy*, hurled, flung, shot; thrown away; lying on the ground.

مرميس *mirmîs*, rhinoceros.

(مرن) *maran*, U, INF. *murûn*, *marâna-t*, *murûna-t*, be soft with a slight degree of hardness, or vice versa, be elastic; — INF. *murûn*, *marâna-t*, accustom one's self, be inured, practised; — II. INF. *tamrîn*, make soft or hard as above; harden, inure; accustom to (على *'ala*); — V. INF. *tamarrun*, harden or inure one's self, practise.

مرن *marin*, custom, habit; tumult; combat; — *murinn*, sounding, chirping.

مرنان *mirnân*, strong bow.

مرنب *marnab*, abounding with hares; interwoven with hare-hair; a large mouse; — انى *marnabâniyy*, hare-coloured.

مرنحة *marnaḥa-t*, prow.
مرنعة *marna'a-t*, pl. *marâni'*, noise of voices; shouting in a game; comfortable life; fertile season, garden.
(مره) *marih*, A, INF. *marah*, be diseased (eye, from want of collyrium).
مره *marih*, diseased, weak;— ة *murha-t*, pure white, brightness.
مرها *marhâ'*, pl. *murh*, f. of امره *amrah*, dry and white (eye, from want of collyrium); — ة *mirhât*, pl. *marâhî*, swift, fleet (horse).
مرهصة *marhaṣa-t*, pl. *marâhiṣ*, dignity, high rank.
مرهف *murhaf*, thin, slim, sharp.
مرهم *marham*, pl. *marâhim*, poultice, cataplasm; salve, pomatum; — *marham*, INF. ة, apply a poultice, a cataplasm, foment; salve, grease with pomatum.
مرو *marw*, ة, white pebbles as flintstones; an aromatic plant; — *maru'*, see (مرا); — ة *marwa-t*, mountain near Mecca; — *muruwwa-t*, *muru'a-t*, *murû'a-t*, manliness, bravery; humanity, humanisation, refined manners.
مروأة *murû'a-t* = مروة *muruwwa-t*, &c.
مروب *murawwab*, curdled by rennet; also *mirwab*, vessel for making butter.
مروبص *muraubaṣ*, refined (gold); — *muraubiṣ*, refiner.
مروج *murawwaj*, current, &c.; usual, customary; — *murawwij*, seller, dealer; — *.
مروح *marûḥ*, moved or blown by the wind; mettled;—*murawwaḥ*, perfumed; — *murawwiḥ*, perfumer, seller of perfumes; — ة *marwaḥa-t*, pl. *marâwiḥ*, desert; place passed through by the wind; — *mirwaḥa-t*, pl. *mirwaḥ*, *marâwiḥ*, fan, ventilator.
مروخ *marûḫ*, oil, salve, ointment.
مرود *mirwad*, pencil for applying collyrium; axis of a pulley; — *murûd*, refractoriness, rebelliousness; — ة *murûda-t*, beardlessness.
مرور *murûr*, passing, passing by (s.); passage, transit; unbroken succession; lapse of time, superannuation, prescription.
مروراة *marauràt*, pl. *maraura*, *maraurayât*, *marârî*, complete desert.
مروزى *marwaziyy*, pl. *marâwiza-t*, of Merv.
مروص *marûṣ*, swift, fleet.
مروقة (m.) *murawwaqa-t*, bread and butter; — *.
مرون *marûn*, conquered, vanquished; — *murûn*, ة *murûna-t*, softness, elasticity; — *mar'ûn*, pl. of مر *mar'*, man.
مرووس *mar'ûs*, big-headed; wounded in the head; ruled, subject, subaltern.
مروى *mirwa*, pl. *marâwî*, rope to fasten a load; —*murwî*, quenching the thirst (adj.);—*marwiyy*, reported, related, handed down by tradition, asserted; abundantly watered; having one's thirst quenched; also *marawiyy*, of Merv.
(مرى) *mara*, I, INF. *mary*, stroke the udder of the camel for milking; take out, pull out; doubt; deny one's claims; whip; spur; — III. INF. *mirâ'*, *mumârât*, doubt, question, dispute, debate; — IV. INF. *imrâ'*, yield the milk in sprays; — VI. INF. *tamârî*, dispute with one another; doubt; — VIII. INF. *imtirâ'*, doubt; gain, grow rich; draw forth.
مرى *mari'*, v. see (مرا); — *marî'*, easily digested, digestible, wholesome; *al-marî'*, pl. *amri'a-t*, alimentary canal;—*murra*, f. of امر *amarr*, more bitter; — *murriyy*, *muriyy*, a bitter water for sharpening the appetite; — *mariyy*, pl. *marâyâ*, very rich in milk;

— *mar'iyy*, seen, perceived; — ة *mirya-t, murya-t*, full jet of milk from a camel's udder; gallop; doubt; quarrel, dispute; — *murriyya-t*, bitterness.

مريا *maryâ'*, outlook, watch-tower.

مريب *murîb*, raising doubt, doubtful, suspicious, apocryphical; criminal; having doubt or suspicion.

مريج *marîj*, complicated.

مريح *mirrîḥ*, pl. *-ûn, marḥā, marâḥa*, very lively and cheerful.

مريخ *mirrîḫ*, planet Mars; firebrand; iron, steel; long arrow with four rows of feathers; also *murayyaḫ*, dross of silver.

مريد *marîd*, pl. *muradâ'*, refractory, rebellious; — *murîd*, willing, wishing, &c.; disciple, pupil, novice; entirely devoted to God; saint, santon; ة, giving herself over to her lover; — *mirrîd*, very rebellious.

مرير *marîr*, pl. *marâ'ir*, strong; persevering; intention, aim; arid ground; — *murayyar*, obese; — ة *marîra-t*, long and strong rope; strength; perseverance; magnanimity, resoluteness; — also *mirrîra-t*, intention, end.

مريش *marîś, marayyaś*, feathered (arrow).

مريض *marîḍ*, ة, pl. *marḍā, marâḍa, mirâḍ*, ill, sick, unwell; weak; — *murayyaḍ*, dispensed from active service (priest); in good health; — *murayyiḍ*, leader of spiritual exercises.

مريط *marîṭ*, pl. *amrâṭ, mirâṭ*, unfeathered.

مريع *marî'*, terrible, frightful; pl. *amru', amrâ'*, abounding with water and grass.

مرئلة *mur'ila-t*, female ostrich with young ones.

مريم *maryam*, St. Mary, the holy virgin; كف م *kaff-u maryam-a*, Jericho-rose; أبو م *abû maryam-a*, police-officer.

مرينة *murîna-t*, lamprey, murena.

مريء *marî'*, digestible and wholesome; pl. *amri'a-t, muru'*, alimentary canal, œsophagus; — *murai'*, male, ة, *murai'a-t*, female (of an animal); — *mar'iyy*, human; seen, perceived.

(مز) *mazz*, U, INF. *mazz*, suck, imbibe; be sourish, turn sour; (m.) be tasteless, insipid; — *maziz*, A, INF. *mazâza-t*, surpass, excel; — V. INF. *tamazzuz*, imbibe gradually.

مز *mazz*, hard, difficult; — *mizz*, excellence, eminence; measure, quantity; *muzz*, ة, acidulous; tasteless, insipid; — ة *mazza-t*, sweet wine; — *muzza-t* and —

مزا *muzzâ'*, tart wine; — ة *mizât* tyrants; giants.

مزابر *muza'bar, muza'bir*, long-haired, shaggy.

مزابق *muza'baq*, coated with mercury.

مزابنة *muzâbana-t*, selling the fruit while yet on the tree or in the field.

مزاج *mizâj*, pl. *amzija-t*, mixture; water mixed with wine; temper, disposition, constitution, health; الم الشريف *al-mizâj aś-śarîf*, how do you do?

مزاح *mizâḥ*, jesting, joking; *mizâḥ-an*, by way of joke; — *muzâḥ*, ة *muzâḥa-t*, jest, joke, pleasantry; — *mazzâḥ*, very jocular, jester, wag.

مزاحم *muzâḥim*, pressing others, &c.; hindering, hindrance (pl. *mazâḥim*, obstacles); — ة *muzâḥama-t*, pressure, hindrance, difficulty; throng, crowd.

مزاد *mazâd*, selling to the highest bidder, auction; — *; — ة *mazâda-t*, pl. *mazâd, mazâwid, mazâ'id*, large doubled water-bag; bag, sack; bucket.

مزار *mazâr*, visit; place visited, tomb; — ة *mazâra-t*, visit (زور); strength (مزر).

مزارع *mazâri'*, pl. of مزرعة *mazra'a-t*,

and مزدرع *muzdara'*; — *muzâri'*, who tills and sows a field for part of the crops; — ة *muzâ-ra'a-t*, INF. of (زرع III.).
مزاريع *mazârî'*, pl. of مزروع *mazrû'*.
مزاريق *mazârîq*, pl. of مزراق *mizrâq*.
مزازة *mazâza-t*, acidulousness, sourish-sweet taste; (m.) insipidity; abundance, affluence.
مزامير *mazâmîr*, pl. of مزمار *mizmâr* and مزمور *mazmûr*.
مزان *muzzân*, pl. *mazâyin*, *mazâyîn*, adorned.
مزاناة *muzânât*, fornication.
مزاود *mazâwid*, pl. of مزواد *mizwâd*, مزود *mizwad*, and مزادة *mazâda-t*.
مزاولة *muzâwala-t*, diligence and painstaking, effort; wish; care.
مزايا *mazâyâ*, pl. of مزية *maziyya-t*.
مزائد *mazâ'id*, pl. of مزادة *mazâda-t*; —*muzâyada-t*, over-bidding one another, auction.
مزاين *mazâyin*, مزايين *mazâyîn*, pl. of مزان *muzzân*.
مزبر *mizbar*, pencil, style, pen.
مزبرج *muzabraj*, adorned, decked out.
مزبق *muzabbaq*, rubbed with mercury.
مزبلة *mazbala-t*, *mazbula-t*, pl. *mazâ-bil*, dung-hill, dung; hamper.
مزبور *mazbûr*, written, registered, noted down; afore-mentioned.
(مزج) *mazaj*, A, INF. *mazj*, mix (a.); incite against; — III. INF. *mu-mâzaja-t*, mix with (n.), blend; deal with, have commerce with; vie for glory with; — VI. INF. *tamâzuj*, get mixed with one another; — VII. INF. *inmizâj*, VIII. INF. *imtizâj*, get mixed.
مزج *mazaj*, *mizj*, honey; bitter almond; — *mizajj*, short spear.
مزجل *mizjal*, short lance; head of a spear.
مزجى *muzja*, f. مزجاة *muzjât*, little, few, small, paltry, of little value; unfit; — *muzajjî*, who joins a strange tribe.
(مزح) *mazaḥ*, INF. *mazḥ*, jest, joke; — III. INF. *mizâḥ*, *mumâzaḥa-t*, jest with, sport with; — VI. INF. *tamâzuḥ*, jest or sport with one another.
مزح *mazḥ*, jest, joke, sport; ear (of corn); spikenard.
مزحاف *mizḥâf*, dragging one's self along wearily.
مزحف *mazhaf*, place where snakes are crawling; — *.
مزحل *mazḥal*, spot where one departs from, parts with another.
مزحور *mazḥûr*, afflicted with dysentery.
مزخرفات *muzaḥrafât*, false ornaments, tinsel, shams, lies; — *.
مزخة *mazaḫḫa-t*, pudenda of a woman.
(مزد) *mazd*, cold (s.).
مزدا *muzdâ* ., to be looked for under (.زو , .زه VIII.), as—
مزداد *muzdâd*, ag. of (زيد VIII.), increased, grown.
مزداة *mizdât*, little hole in the sand or ground (in a children's game).
. . مزد *muzda* . . , to be looked for under (. . ز VIII.), as—
مزدحم *muzdaḥam* (عليه *'alai-hi*), pat. of (زحم VIII.), place where there is a throng; — * .
مزدرع *muzdara'*, ة *muzdara'a-t*, pl. *mazâri'*, field sown or fit to be sown; — *muzdari'*, sower.
مزدرى *muzdarî* (ال *al-*), lion; — *.
مزدغ *mizdag*, ة *mizdaga-t*, pillow, cushion, bolster.
مزدلف *muzdalif*, approaching, &c.; — ة *muzdalifa-t*, place near Mecca.
مزدهى *muzdahî*, ag. of (زهو VIII.) vain, proud.
مزدوج *muzdawij*, married.
(مزر) *mazar*, U, INF. *mazr*, sip in order to taste; fill entirely; — *mazur*, INF. *mazâra-t*, carry out resolutely and with ability.
مزر *mizr*, *mizar*, a kind of beer made of millet; *mizr*, origin; fool.
مزرا *mizrâ'*, slanderer, reviler; — ة *mazrât*, calumny, abuse.

مزراب *mizrâb*, pl. *mazârîb*, *mazârîba-t*, aqueduct, canal; sewer; gutter, eaves.

مزراق *mizrâq* (مزراغ *mizrâg*), pl. مزاريق *mazârîq*, javelin, pike, short lance.

مزرج *muzarraj*, drunk, intoxicated.

مزرح *mazraḥ*, level ground.

مزرد *mazrad*, gullet; — ة *mizrada-t*, (m.) ية *mizradiyya-t*, pincers, tongs.

مزرعة *mazra'a-t*, *mazru'a-t*, *mazri'a-t*, pl. *mazâri'*, sown field, arable ground; village, hamlet.

مزروعات *mazrû'ât*, sown fields.

مزرية *mazriya-t*, blame, rebuke, abuse, slander.

مزز *mazaz*, distinction.

(مزع) *maza'*, INF. *maz'*, *maz'a-t*, hasten along, begin to run; pick with the fingers (cotton, &c.);— v. burst (n.).

مزع *maz'*, ة *maz'a-t*, light swift walk; — ة *miz'a-t*, fleak of wool, handful of grass or feathers; also *muz'a-t*, pl. *miza'*, morsel.

مزعاج *miz'âj*, restless woman.

مزعافة *miz'âfa-t*, مزعامة *miz'âma-t*, a kind of snake.

مزعبر *muz'abir*, impostor; juggler.

مزعف *muz'af*, salt (adj.); — * *muz'if*, sudden (death); fatal, killing.

مزعفر *muza'far*, dyed or seasoned with saffron; reddish-yellow; a kind of sherbet.

مزعم *maz'am*, pl. *mazâ'im*, bold assertion; uncertain, doubtful.

مزغل *mazgal*, opening in a wall for the water to flow off; — ة *mazgala-t*, small cup.

مزفر *muzfir*, smelling offensively (adj.); filthy, obscene, ribald; — *muzaffar*, deeply - fetched breath; — *muzaffir*, breathing deeply; breaking the fast; dispensed from fasting.

مزفة *mizaffa-t*, litter of a bride in the wedding procession.

مزفور *mazfûr*, strongly built (horse).

مزفي *mazfiyy*, frightened; timorous.

(مزق) *mazaq*, I, INF. *mazq*, *mazqa-t*, tear, tear to pieces; slander, abuse; — U, I, drop excrement; — II. INF. *tamzîq*, tear, rend, destroy; — III. INF. *mumâzaqa-t*, try to overtake in running; — ة *mizqa-t*, torn-off piece, rag; — *muzqa-t*, a small bird.

مزقق *muzaqqaq*, shorn.

مزكن *muzakkin*, physiognomist.

مزكى *muzakkâ*, purified, justified; — *muzakkî*, justifying one's self (by alms and pious works).

مزلاج *mizlâj*, مزلاق *mizlâq*, bolt, latch.

مزلج *muzallaj*, intruder; little, few; mean, low, wicked.

مزلع *muzalla'*, chapped.

مزلعب *muzla'ibb*, swelling.

مزلفة *mazlafa-t*, pl. *mazâlif*, road between desert and cultivated land.

مزلق *mazlaq*, ة *mazlaqa-t*, slippery place; — *mizlaqa-t*, horse's buttock.

مزلم *muzallam*, ة, well-shaped, proportional, symmetrical; nimble, skilful.

مزلة *mazalla-t*, *mazilla-t*, slippery place; *mazilla-t*, slipping (s.), slip.

مزلهم *muzlahimm*, nimble, quick, swift.

مزمار *mizmâr*, ة *mizmâra-t*, pl. *mazâmîr*, flute, pipe.

(مزمز) *mazmaz*, INF. ة, shake or push to and fro; turn sourish; lose its taste, grow insipid; — II. INF. *tamazmuz*, be shaken; be hunted up and dispersed.

مزمع *muzmi'*, resolute and persevering; future.

مزملة *muzammala-t*, earthen vessel for cooling water.

مزمن *muzman*, devastated; — *muzmin*, lasting long; old, ancient; chronic; hesitating; lamed.

مزمور *mazmûr*, pl. *mazâmîr*, psalm, hymn; flute.

(مزن) *mazan*, U, INF. *mazn*, *muzûn*, depart straightway; have a bright face; fill; praise;—II. INF.

tamzîn, fill; praise; — V. INF. *tamazzun*, depart straightway; be accustomed to and practised (in (على *'ala*).

مزن *mazn*, sudden departure, flight; — *muzn*, cloud (حب المزن *ḥabb al-muzn*, hail); — *mazan*, manner, custom, usage; state, condition; — ة *muzna-t*, part of a cloud, rain-cloud, rain (ابن م *ibn muzna-t*, new moon).

مزنجة *maznaja-t*, pl. Abyssinians.

مزند *muzannad*, narrow, strait; narrow-minded; close, miserly; bastard; — *muzannid*, liar; — *.

(مزه) *mazah*, INF. *mazh*, jest with (acc.); — III. INF. *mumâzaha-t*, id.

مزهد *muzhid*, ة, poor, needy.

مزهر *mizhar*, ة *mizhara-t*, pl. *mazâhir*, a kind of lute or violin; — *.

مزهف *mizhaf*, spoon for stirring; — *.

(مزهل) — III. *imzahall*, INF. *imzihlâl*, be dispersed, vanish.

مزهو *mazhuww*, vain, proud.

مزواد *mizwâd*, مزود *mizwad*, pl. *mazâwid*, provision-bag, travelling-bag.

مزور *mazûr*, visited; — *muzawwar*, falsified, &c.; oblique, awry, bent, crooked; — *.

(مزى) *maza*, I, INF. *mazy*, be proud; II. INF. *tamziya-t*, praise, exalt.

مزى *maziyy*, excelling in rare qualities; beautiful; clever, skilful; — ة *maziyya-t*, pl. *mazâyâ*, surplus; excellence; grace; preference, privilege, prerogative.

مزيال *mizyâl*, witty; intermeddler.

مزيج *mazîj*, bitter almond.

مزيح *mazîḥ*, jest, pleasantry, merriment.

مزيد *mazîd*, increase, growth; great quantity; high degree.

مزير *mazîr*, pl. *amâzir*, bold, fearless; strong and skilful; successful; refined, polite; —*muzi'r*, bellowing, lowing (adj.); — *.

مزيز *mazîz*, excellent, distinguished; difficult; little, few.

مزيل *mizyal*, witty, ingenious; — *.

مزين *muzayyin*, decorator; barber; ة *muzayyina-t*, milliner.

(مس) *mass*, U, A, INF. *mass*, *masîs*, *missîsa*, touch slightly; befall; pass. *muss*, be seized with madness, possessed with a demon;— III. INF. *misâs*, *mumâssa-t*, touch, feel; lie with; be in contact with; — VI. INF. *tamâss*, touch or feel one another; be in mutual contact.

مس *mass*, touch, contact; misfortune, calamity; access (of a fever, &c.).

(مسا) *masa'*, INF. *mas'*, *musû'*, talk or act inconsiderately; keep in the middle of the road; tarry, hesitate, delay; cheat; (also IV.) stir up mischief; — IV. INF. *imsâ'*, see I.).

مسا *masâ'*, evening; م امس *masâ'-a ams*, last night, yesternight; — ة ء *masâ'a-t*, pl. *masâwî*, wicked action, crime, baseness; hurt, injury; slander, abuse.

مساب *misa'b*, skin bag; leather flask.

مسابعة *musâba'a-t*, sexual vigour; boasting of such; obscene talk, ribaldry.

مسابقة *musâbaqa-t*, trying to overtake in running, &c.; race; emulation, ambition.

مساتلة *musâtala-t*, unbroken succession.

مساح *masâḥ*, ة *masâḥa-t*, pl. *masâyiḥ*, travelling; stretch, tract; — *massâḥ*, who wipes; land-surveyor, geometrician; — ة *misâḥa-t*, measuring (s.); art of surveying, geometry.

مساحى *masâḥî*, pl. of مسحاة *misḥât*.

مساحيق *masâḥîq*, pl. of مسحاق *misḥâq*, q.v., and منسحق *munsaḥiq*, flowing, running.

مساد *mis'ad*, skin bag for honey or butter; — *.

مسارى *musârî*, lion.

مسارع *masârî'*, pl. of مسراع *misrâ'*.

مساعاة *musâ'ât*, zeal, diligence.

مساعى *masâ'î*, pl. of مسعاة *mas'ât*.

مساعير *masâ'îr*, pl. of مسعار *mis'âr*.

مساغ *masâg*, permission, leave; passage, thoroughfare, road.

مساف *masâf*, distance, stretch of land, tract; nose; — *musâf*, dead; — ة *masâfa-t*, distance, interval; day's journey, station.

مسافر *masâfir*, pl. uncovered parts of the face; — *musâfir*, traveller, stranger, guest; — ة *musâfara-t*, travelling (s.), journey; hospitality.

مساق *masâq*, driving (s.), instigation, motive, direction, INF. of (سوق).

مساك *masâk*, *misâk*, firm hold; avarice; — also *musâk*, pl. *ât*, place which holds water; — ة *masâka-t*, *misâka-t*, avarice.

مساكتة *musâkata-t*, silence; silencing (s.).

مساكن *musâkin*, inhabitant; — *; — ة *musâkana-t*, cohabitation.

مسال *musâl*, side; — *masâll*, pl. of مسلة *misalla-t*; — ة *masâla-t*, beauty of an oval face; — *mas'ala-t*, pl. *masâ'il*, question; point in question, thesis; request, begging (s.).

مساليط *masâlîṭ*, pl. of مسلاط *mislâṭ*.

مسام *masâmm*, ات *masâmmât*, orifices, openings in the body (mouth, nose, &c.); pores.

مسامح *musâmiḥ*, indulgent, &c.; negligent, indifferent, lax, remiss; — ة *musâmaḥa-t*, indulgence, &c.; negligence, remissness, want of energy.

مساميح *masâmîḥ*, pl. of سمح *samḥ*, kind, liberal, &c., and of مسماح *mismâḥ*.

مسامير *masâmîr*, pl. of مسمار *mismâr*.

مساميك *masâmîk*, pl. of مسماك *mismâk* and مسموك *masmûk*.

مسان *masânn*, pl. old; — ات *musânât*, contract for a year.

مسانهة *musânaha-t*, year's salary or pay; contract for a year.

مساهاة *musâhât*, heedlessness, inattention.

مساهل *musâhil*, negligent, indifferent; obliging, social, easy to deal with, easy-going; — ة *musâhala-t*, negligence, indifference; willingness, obligingness, sociability.

مساواة *musâwât*, equalizing | (s.); equality, symmetry; parallelism; evenness; neutrality; fitness.

مساوى *masâwî*, pl. of مساءة *masâ'a-t*; — *.

مساويك *masâwîk*, pl. of مسواك *miswâk*.

مسائح *masâ'iḥ*, pl. of مساحة *masâḥa-t*, مسيحة *masîḥa-t*.

مسائف *masâ'if*, pl. years; famine; — ة *musâyafa-t*, combat with swords, duel.

مسائل *masâ'il*, pl. of مسالة *ma'sala-t* and مسيل *masîl*.

مسابيح *masâyîḥ*, pl. of مسياح *misyâḥ*.

مساية *masâya-t*, مسايئة *masâyi'a-t*, vexation, injury, harm.

مسب *misabb*, ة *masabba-t*, who reviles much.

مسبا *masba'*, road, way; INF. of (سبا).

مسبار *misbâr*, probe; brush (of a painter).

مسبب *musabbab*, caused, &c.; select, excellent; — *musabbib*, causing, &c.; *al-musabbib*, the primary cause, God.

مسبت *musbit*, *musabbit*, narcotic; — ات *musabbitât*, narcotics, opiates.

مسبج *musabbaj*, wide, comfortable, commodious (dress).

مسبح *masbaḥ*, swimming (s.); — *musabbaḥ*, strong (material); — *; — ة *musabbiḥa-t*, fore-finger, index.

مسبرة *masbara-t*, shape, form, figure, manner, method.

مسبعة *masba'a-t*, pl. *masâbi'*, tract with many beasts of prey.

مسبل *musbil*, sixth arrow in the game.

مسبور *masbûr*, well-shaped, of beautiful form.

. . . مست *musta* . . ., to be looked for under (. . . x.), as—

مستاجر *musta'jar*, pat. of (اجر x.), hired, subscribed; — *musta'jir*, ag. of the same, who hires, takes into his service, pays in advance; subscriber.

مستاخر *musta'ḥir*, who lags behind, sluggish.

مستاسر *musta'sir*, who surrenders as a captive.

مستاف *mustâf*, nose.

مستاكل *musta'kil*, extortioner.

مستانف *musta'naf*, still fresh, recently past; impending, to come; — *musta'nif*, beginner; who takes in advance.

مستاهل *musta'hil*, fit, proper, worthy.

مست . ا . *musta . â .*, مست . ﻯ . *musta . î .*, to be looked for under (. و ., . ﻯ . x.), as—

مستبان *mustabân*, pat. of (بين x.), evident, clear.

مستبرز *mustabriz*, challenging, provoking.

مستبصر *mustabṣir*, looking attentively at, &c.; sagacious, penetrating, cautious.

مستبضع *mustabḍi'*, exhibiting goods for sale; merchant.

مستبعد *mustab'ad*, distant, far; unattainable, beyond reach.

. . مست *musta* . ., to be looked for under (. . س VIII.), as—

مستبق *mustàbiq*, ag. of (سبق VIII.), who tries to get in advance of, who overtakes; pressing on.

مستبين *mustabîn*, showing itself distinctly; evident, clear, open.

مستتبع *mustatba'*, followed or attended by others.

مستتر *mustatar*, hiding-place; — *mustatir*, who hides or covers himself; cautious; concealed; understood without being expressed.

مستجلب *mustajlib*, importing, attracting, drawing forth; causing.

مستجمع *mustajmi'*, assembling; containing.

مستحب *mustaḥabb*, loved, &c.; — supererogatory good work; — *.

مستحدث *mustaḥdas̱*, newly invented, anything new, innovation; — *mustaḥdis̱*, who introduces or invents new things.

مستحرب *mustaḥrib*, ready for combat.

مستحضر *mustaḥḍar*, represented, &c.; understood, comprehended; ready.

مستحفظ *mustaḥfiẓ*, who trusts to another's keeping; also *mustaḥfaẓ*, garrison; soldier of a garrison; governor; impressing on one's mind, recollecting.

مستحق *mustaḥaqq*, merit, reward; — *mustaḥiqq*, creditor; — *.

مستحكمات *mustaḥkamât*, fortifications.

مستحلك *mustaḥlik*, coal-black.

مستحيل *mustaḥîl*, impossible, absurd; transformed; — ات *mustaḥîlât*, impossibilities.

مستخلص *mustaḫlaṣ*, exclusively claimed, &c.; entirely liberated, wholly cleaned; — *mustaḫliṣ*, who claims entirely for himself, &c.; tax-gatherer.

مستد *mustadd*, stopped up, diked, embanked.

مستدار *mustadâr*, circle, periphery.

مستدخل *mustadḫil*, who wants to interfere, to intermeddle.

مستدعيات *mustad'àyât*, desire, wish, postulate.

مستدفى *mustadfi'*, warmly dressed.

مستدل *mustadall*, deduced, demonstrated; — *mustadill*, making an induction, drawing an inference.

مستديم *mustadîm*, lasting, &c.; settled, having a fixed residence; old.

مستدين *mustadîn*, who asks for

credit; who seeks his right; judge.

مستذاق *mustazâq*, tasted.

مستذنب *mustaznib*, follower, disciple; lagging behind all others; finished.

مستر *mistar*, veil, covering; — *musattar*, ة, veiled, kept at home, modest, chaste; masked; — *.

مستراح *mustarâḥ*, resting-place; privy.

مسترجى *mustarja*, hoped for, desired, requested, begged for; expected.

مسترخى *mustarḥî*, purgative (s.); — *.

مسترد *mustaradd*, restored, given back.

مسترشى *mustarśî*, who allows himself to be bribed.

مسترضع *mustarḍi'*, suckled, brought up.

مسترق *mustariq*, mobile; weak; listener; — ة *mustariqa-t*, the five intercalary days of the 12th Persian month.

مسترى *mustarî*, lion.

مستريح *mustarîḥ*, m. *mustarayyiḥ*, resting; quiet, comfortable; handy.

مستريض *mustarîḍ*, well watered; abounding with gardens.

مستزاد *mustazâd*, increased, increasing, grown.

مستشار *mustaśâr*, who is consulted; counsellor; under-secretary of State.

مستشفى *mustaśfa*, hospital; — *.

مستصفى *mustaṣfa*, purified, refined.

مستطاب *mustaṭâb*, approved of, good, beautiful, lovely; illustrious, august.

مستطرف *mustaṭraf*, considered as new and interesting, curiosity.

مستطير *mustaṭîr*, flying about in all directions, &c.; furious (camel).

مستطيل *mustaṭîl*, long, lengthy, oblong; parallelogram; finding too long.

مستظير *mustaẓîr*, hot (bitch).

مستع *mista'*, zealous, arduous, quick.

مستعار *musta'âr*, borrowed; metaphorical; false (hair, &c.).

مستعان *musta'ân*, who is called upon for help; God.

مستعجلة *musta'jala-t*, the nearest way.

مستعد *musta'idd*, who makes ready, &c.; ready; worthy, capable.

مستعدل *musta'dil*, in equilibrium; well, in good health.

مستعرب *musta'rib*, who settles in Arabia, makes himself an Arab; — ة *musta'riba-t*, people not of pure Arab blood.

مستعمر *musta'mir*, colonist.

مستعملة *musta'mala-t*, chamber-utensil.

مستعير *musta'îr*, who borrows, uses a metaphor; who lends; alone.

مستغاث *mustagâs*, who is called to help, appealed to; المستغاث عليه *al-mustagâs 'alai-hi*, defendant; المستغاث له — *la-hu*, matter in which an appeal is made; who is helped.

مستغرق *mustagraq*, *mustagriq*, who dives into or engages deeply in; sinking.

مستغزر *mustagzir*, who gives in order to take back with interest.

مستغلات *mustagallât*, produce of the harvest, income.

مستغمد *mustagmid*, in a sheath or case, veiled.

مستغنى *mustagnî*, having plenty of, not wanting any more of, able to do without, &c.; rich, independent, contented; proud, fastidious.

مستفاد *mustafâd*, gained as profit, &c.; learned; contents, meaning, sense.

مستفتى *mustaftî*, who calls for a *fatwa* or decision of the *mufti*; who consults a lawyer.

مستفرغ *mustafrig*, vomitive; — *.

مستفسر *mustafsir*, what requires an explanation; — *.

مستفقد *mustafqid*, missing sadly, &c.; home-sick.
مستفيض *mustafîḍ*, spread abroad (rumour); usual, customary.
مستفيق *mustafîq*, recovering; remembering.
مستقبل *mustaqbil*, ى *mustaqbiliyy*, front side; — *; — يات *mustaqbiliyyât*, things to come.
مستقر *mustaqarr*, fixed domicile, residence, lodging; — *mustaqirr*, confessing; firm, quiet; — *.
مستقصى *mustaqṣî*, eager to learn, investigating assiduously; going far in anything.
مستقطر *mustaqṭir*, distiller.
مستقل *mustaqill*, independent, absolute; firm; persevering; high; — *.
مستقنى *mustaqnî*, who earns, procures for himself.
مستقة *mustaqa-t*, pl. *masâtiq*, fur coat with long sleeves; fiddlestick.
مستقوس *mustaqwis*, formed like a bow.
مستقى *mustaqa*, place where water is drawn; — *.
مستقيد *mustaqîd*, obedient, obsequious.
مستقيم *mustaqîm*, upright, sincere, honest; persevering, firm; — *.
مستكثر *mustakṡir*, finding too much, &c.; increasing.
مستكرى *mustakrî*, who hires, tenant, lessee.
مستكن *mustakinn*, tranquillised, quiet; — *; — ة *mustakinna-t*, hatred, grudge.
مستل *mastal*, narrow path.
مستلزم *mustalzim*, cause, originator, author; — *.
مستمطر *mustamṭir*, in want of rain; praying for rain.
مستميت *mustamît*, seeking death, fearless of death.
مستند *mustanad*, support, assistance; — *.
مستنطق *mustanṭiq*, conferring, inquiring; examining judge, inquisitor.
مستنقع *mustanqa'*, place with stagnant water; pool; — *.
مستهام *mustahâm*, madly in love, love-crazed.
مستهجن *mustahjan*, considered vile, degenerate, ugly.
مستهزل *mustahzil*, jesting; making little of.
مستهزى *mustahzi'*, mocker, scoffer.
مستهلك *mustahlik*, threatening ruin; seeking death, despairing; spendthrift.
مستوبل *mustaubil*, unhealthy.
مستوجب *mustaujib*, cause, originator, author; — *.
مستوحش *mustauḥiś*, grown wild, devastated; sad, grieved.
مستوخم *mustauḫim*, indigestible; unhealthy.
مستودع *mustauda'*, deposit; place where anything is deposited; womb.
مستور *mastûr*, veiled, modest, chaste; abstemious; honest; unknown.
مستوطن *mustauṭan*, permanent residence, settlement; — *mustauṭin*, settler; settled, naturalized.
مستوعب *mustau'ib*, taking the whole of, comprising all, containing.
مستوفى *mustaufî*, accountant; minister of finance; abundant, plentiful; perfect, complete; — *.
مستوقد *mustauqad*, kindling-place.
مستوى *mustawî*, equal; parallel; moderate; of common (grammatical) gender; ripe; well-cooked; — *.
مستيئس *mustai'is*, despairing.
مسجد *masjid*, *masjad*, pl. *masâjid*, place where the forehead of a praying person touches the ground, place of prayer, oratory, (small) mosque; du. *al-masjidân*, the temples of Mecca and Medina; المسجد الاقصى *al-masjid al-'aqṣa*, temple of Jerusalem.

مسجر *misjar*, chips; — *musajjar*, loosened, flowing down (hair).

مسجع *masja'*, intention, aim; middle of the road; — *musajja'*, rhymed prose; — *musajji'*, composer of such.

مسجل *musjal*, free or open to everybody; — *musajjal*, authentic; — *.

مسجنة *masjana-t*, imprisoning (s.).

مسجة *misajja-t*, mason's trowel.

مسجوح *masjûḥ*, side, surface;—also ة *masjûḥa-t*, nature.

مسجور *masjûr*, swelling (sea).

(مسح) *masaḥ*, INF. *masḥ*, pass the hand over anything; wipe; rub in, salve, anoint; feel, touch, stroke; cajole; delude; comb; beat; lie with; survey a field, &c.; travel through; walk apace; INF. *tamsâḥ*, tell lies; — *masiḥ*, A, INF. *masaḥ*, have the hollow of the knees or the inner side of the thighs sore from the roughness of a garment; — II. INF. *tamsîḥ*, wipe vigorously; rub in, salve, anoint; — III. INF. *mumâsaḥa-t*, try to delude one another by flattery; — V. INF. *tamassuḥ*, wipe; wipe one's self; be salved; — VII. INF. *inmisâḥ*, be wiped, salved, anointed; be surveyed; — VIII. INF. *imtisâḥ*, draw the sword.

مسح *masḥ*, wiping, rubbing in, salving (s.); stroking (s.); surveying (s.); — *misḥ*, pl. *musûḥ*, *amsâḥ*, coarse hair- or woollen-stuff; saddle-cloth; sack-cloth; hair-cloth of an ascetic; middle of the road, high-road;—*masaḥ*, soreness of the skin; — *misaḥḥ*, in full gallop; — *musiḥḥ*, hard and dry; — ة *masḥa-t*, *musḥa-t*, wiping (s.), unction; (م المرضى *masḥa-t al-marḍa*, الم الاخيرة *al-masḥa-t al-aḥîra-t*, holy unction); a touch or shade of, a little, trifle; road; plane (tool).

مسحا *masḥâ'*, f. of امسح *amsaḥ*, having a sore skin, &c.; woman with flat breasts, thin thighs; strumpet; — *al-masḥâ*, ground with small pebbles.

مسحاق *misḥâq*, pl. *masâḥîq*, membranes of the skull, of the bowels; thin clouds.

مسحاة *misḥât*, pl. *masâḥî*, shovel, spade.

مسحب *masḥab*, pl. *masâḥib*, place where anything has been dragged along; track; (m.) current of air.

مسحج *misḥaj*, file; rasp.

مسحر *musaḥḥar*, bewitched, spellbound; having lungs.

مسحط *masḥaṭ*, throat.

مسحف *masḥaf*, track of a snake; — ة *misḥafa-t*, tool for scraping bones.

مسحل *misḥal*, pl. *masâḥil*, file; carving-knife or tool; glib tongue; eloquent speaker; bridle, curb; sieve; great liberality; bold, enterprising.

مسحنة *misḥana-t*, pl. *masâḥin*, pestle; grind-stone; pl. gold and silver ore.

مسحور *masḥûr*, bewitched, &c.; unhealthy.

مسحوقونيا *masḥûqûniyâ*, slag of glass.

(مسخ) *masaḫ*, INF. *masḫ*, transform (into a lower shape), disfigure, render ugly; spoil; cause to evaporate, to lose the smell or taste; jade, emaciate (a.); distort one's words or thoughts; — *masiḫ*, *masuḫ*, lose its smell or taste; — II. INF. *tasmîḫ*, render ugly, disfigure; mock at; abash by abuse or scoffing; — IV. INF. *imsâḫ*, open (n.), break up (tumour); — VII. INF. *inmisâḫ*, be rendered ugly, disfigured; be reviled, insulted; — VIII. INF. *imtisâḫ*, draw the sword.

مسخ *masḫ*, pl. *musûḫ*, transformation; transformed person; monster; — *masiḫ*, tasteless, insipid.

مسخاة *misḫât*, poker; chips.

(مسخر) *masḫar*, INF. ة, laugh at, mock at, scoff, revile; — II. INF. *tamasḫur*, id.; be mocked at; — ة *masḫara-t*, pl. *masâḫir*, jest, joke, mockery; disgrace; mummery, masquerade; mask, masked person; buffoon; ridiculous person, butt.

مسخط *masḫaṭ*, indignation.

مسخم *musaḫḫam*, full of hatred.

مسخن *musḫin*, jocose, sportive, facetious; — *; — ة *misḫana-t*, pl. *masâḫin*, kettle for heating water.

مسخوت *masḫût*, smooth, bare, bald.

مسخوط *masḫûṭ*, transformed; having provoked the wrath of God; hateful; inflamed, ignited.

مسخية *misḫiyya-t*, a kind of carpet.

(مسد) *masad*, U, INF. *masd*, twist (a rope); hasten; — II. rub and knead the limbs; fix; strengthen.

مسد *masad*, pl. *misâd*, *amsâd*, rope of palm-fibres; strong rope; iron axe; — *masadd*, hole, gap; barricaded place, barrier.

مسداة *misdât*, a weaver's tool for stretching the woof; bobbin.

مسدد *musaddad*, rightly guided; stopped up, barricaded, shut; — *.

مسدس *masdas*, by sixes; — *musaddas*, six-fold; sexangular; sexangle; cube; cubic; consisting of six lines.

مسدع *misda'*, guide.

مسدى *musda*, *musadda*, warped.

(مسر) *masar*, U, INF. *masr*, pull out; accuse secretly, incite against.

مسر *musirr*, who conceals, keeps secret; who imparts secrets; — ة *masarra-t*, pl. *masârr*, joy, gladness; contentment; pleasure; — *misarra-t*, speaking-trumpet or tube.

مسراع *misrâ'*, quick, prone (to good or evil).

مسراة *masra'a-t*, country abounding with locusts.

مسرب *misrab*, pl. *masârib*, road along which one is going; — ة *masraba-t*, pl. *masârib*, meadow, pasture; also *masruba-t*, orifice of the anus; portico.

مسرج *musraj*, saddled; lit; — ة *masraja-t*, lamp.

مسرح *masraḥ*, pl. *masâriḥ*, extended pasture-ground; field; range; wandering (s.); — *misraḥ*, comb.

مسرد *misrad*, saddler's awl or punch; pl. *masârid*, hair-sieve for sand, &c.; — *musarrad*, firmly sewn (leather); strongly wrought (coat of mail).

مسردبية *musardabiyya-t*, ice-cellar.

مسرط *masraṭ*, *misraṭ*, gullet.

مسرطع *musarṭa'*, stamped; — *musarṭi'*, frivolous, full of levity.

مسروح *masrûḥ*, mirage, Fata Morgana.

مسرود *masrûd*, incantation, spell; — *.

مسروف *masrûf*, worm-eaten.

مسرول *musarwal*, wearing trowsers; white-footed (horse); having the feet feathered (pigeon).

مسرى *masra*, pl. *masârî*, night-journey; road; INF. of (سرى).

(مسط) *masaṭ*, U, INF. *masṭ*, press (a skin bag, &c.) with the fingers in order to empty it; take the sperm out of the camel's uterus; wring out; purge; flog, whip.

مسطار *misṭâr*, new intoxicating wine, must.

مسطبة *musṭaba-t*, pl. *masâṭib* = مصطبة *maṣṭaba-t*, stone bench, &c.

مسطح *misṭaḥ*, pl. *masâṭiḥ*, drying-floor for figs, &c.; pile-work, stockade; dough-roller; mat; — *musaṭṭaḥ*, flat, superficial; plain (s.); — *.

مسطر *misṭar*, ة *misṭara-t*, pl. *masâṭir*, ruler (to draw lines); black lines; line; — *musaṭṭar*, writing (s.); — *; — *musaṭṭir*, writer, clerk; — *.

مسطع *misṭa'*, very eloquent.
مسطور *masṭûr*, described, specified ; — *.
مسع *mis'*, north wind.
مسعار *mis'âr*, poker ; disturber of the peace, stirring up discord.
مسعام *mis'âm*, *mus'âmm*, rapid.
مسعاة *mas'ât*, n.u. of مسعى *mas'an*.
مسعر *mas'ar*, *mus'ur*, thinnest part of a camel's tail ; — *mis'ar*, pl. *masâ'ir*=مسعار *mis'âr* ; — *.
مسعط *mis'aṭ*, *mus'uṭ*, instrument for provoking inhalation by the nose ; snuff-box.
مسعل *mas'al*, throat, wind-pipe.
مسعود *mas'ûd*, happy, prosperous ; gracious, favourable, august.
مسعور *mas'ûr*, scorched by a poisonous wind ; furious ; thirsty.
مسعى *mas'an*, n.u. مسعاة *mas'ât*, pl. *masâ'î*, care, zeal, endeavour ; scheme ; course ; generosity ; highest distinction ; — *mas'iyy*, walking untiringly.
(مسغ), VII. INF. *immisâg*, VIII. INF. *imtisâg*, desist, shrink from.
مسغب *musgabb*, *musaggab*, permitted, lawful ; — * ; — ة *masgaba-t*, ravenous hunger.
مسف *musaff*, changed ; — *musiff*, trifler, punctilious.
مسفر *misfar*, who travels much ; — *musaffir*, cutting off grapes ; — * ; — ة *misfara-t*, broom ; brush ; — *musfira-t*, red ; — *musaffara-t*, clew of thread.
مسفك *misfak*, talkative, garrulous.
مسفن *misfan*, axe ; spade ; wedge.
مسفور *masfûr*, written ; above-mentioned.
مسقام *misqâm*, sickly, weak.
مسقاة *misqât*, *masqât*, watering-place, trough, cistern.
مسقط *masqaṭ*, ة *masqaṭa-t*, falling (s.) ; also *masqiṭ*, pl. *masâqiṭ*, place of falling (م الراس *masqaṭ ar-râs*, birth-place) ; place, spot ; — *musqiṭ*, bringing on abortion ; — * ; — ة *masqaṭa-t*, protector, protection, refuge ; disgraceful action ; place where a sand-hill breaks off.
مسقوم *masqûm*, ill, sick.
مسقوى *masqawiyy*, مسقى *masqiyy*, watered ; impregnated, soaked.
(مسك) *masak*, U, I, INF. *mask*, seize and hold, hold ; be miserly ; be tough ; — *masik*, restrain one's self, contain one's self ; — II. INF. *tamsîk*, set to, seize and hold ; make one to hold, give into one's hands ; give a pledge ; perfume with musk ; — IV. INF. *imsâk*, seize and hold ; contain (acc. or ب *bi*) ; retain, prevent from going ; abstain from (عن *'an*) ; stop short ; — V. INF. *tamassuk*, seize and hold ; take possession of ; cling and hold to ; be perfumed with musk ; — VI. INF. *tamâsuk*, seize and hold ; abstain from ; — VII. INF. *inmisâk*, be seized, retained ; — VIII. INF. *imtisâk*, X. INF. *istimsâk*, seize and hold.
مسك *mask*, seizing and holding (s.), prey, prize ; pl. *musûk*, skin, hide, leather ; — *misk*, musk ; — *musuk*, miserly, avaricious ; — ة *miska-t*, piece of musk ; muscadel ; — *muska-t*, pl. *musak*, handle, heft ; food and drink ; what affords success and security ; sharp intellect ; prey, booty, prize ; also *musuka-t*, miserliness, avarice ; — *masaka-t*, pl. *masak*, bracelet ; fetter ; scalp of the new-born ; — *musaka-t*, pl. *musak*, who keeps a firm hold upon ; miser.
مسكون *maskûn*, inhabited, &c. ; inhabitable ; — ة *maskûna-t* (*al-*), the inhabited part of the world ; — ى *maskûniyy*, general, œcumenical (council).
مسكى *miskiyy*, fragrant with musk ; musk-coloured, dark brown.
مسكين *miskîn*, ة, pl. *ûn*, *masâkîn*, poor, miserable ; beggar ; humble, submissive ; simple of heart ; — ة *miskîna-t*, Medina ; — ية *mis-*

kîniyya-t, poverty, misery, beggary.

(مسل) *masal*, U, INF. *masl*, flow; — VIII. INF. *imtisâl*, draw the sword.

مسل *masal*, pl. *amsila-t*, *musul*, *muslân*, water-course, channel, gutter; — *musul*, pl. of مسيل *masîl*; — ة *masala-t*, question, object; — *misalla-t*, pl. *masâll*, large packing-needle; obelisk.

مسلا *maslâ'*, melted butter; — ة *maslât*, consolation.

مسلاح *mislâḥ*, raw hide; slough.

مسلاط *mislâṭ*, pl. *masâlîṭ*, ward of a key; bolt.

مسلاق *mislâq*, glib of tongue.

مسلان *muslân*, pl. of مسل *masal*, مسيل *masîl*.

مسلحة *maslaḥa-t*, pl. *masâliḥ*, fortified place on the boundary; armed men, warriors, garrison; guardian of heaven.

مسلخ *maslaḥ*, pl. *masâliḥ*, slaughtering-place, skinnery.

مسلسل *musalsal*, enchained, connected; in unbroken succession; striped.

مسلط *musallaṭ*, *musalliṭ*, regent, ruler, governor; — *.

مسلع *misla'*, guide; — *musalla'*, chapped.

مسلفة *mislafa-t*, harrow; trowel.

مسلق *mislaq*, scaling-ladder; rope-ladder; = مسلاق *mislâq*.

مسلك *maslak*, *maslik*, pl. *masâlik*, road, path; institution; rule of conduct, prescript; manner, ways, method; row, line, furrow; — *muslik*, ladder; guide; — *musallak*, thin as a thread; — *musallik*, reeling silk; — ة *maslaka-t*, threadbare seam of a garment; — *mislaka-t*, reel.

مسلم *muslim*, ة, who submits entirely to the will of God, believer, Mohammedan; — *; — II. INF. *tamaslum*, become a Mohammedan.

مسلنقى *muslanqî*, lying on one's back.

مسلوب *maslûb*, robbed, &c.; deprived of one's senses, &c.; refused, denied; also ة *maslûba-t*, raw silk; — ات *maslûbât*, stolen goods or compensation for such.

مسلوع *maslû'*, split, chapped, broken (heart); — ة *maslû'a-t*, high-road.

مسلوقة *maslûqa-t*, pl. *masâlîq*, broth.

مسمات *musammât*, pl. names, denominations.

مسماة *musammât*, f. of مسمى *musamma*.

مسماح *mismâḥ*, kind.

مسمار *mismâr*, pl. *masâmîr*, forked pole of a tent; vine-pole; nail; pin; peg, wedge; — ى *mismâriyy*, nail-like.

مسماك *mismâk*, pl. *masâmîk*, forked tent-pole; vine pole.

مسمح *masmaḥ*, width, breadth.

مسمع *masma'*, place within hearing (*masma'-an*, within hearing-distance); auditory; cavity of the ear; — *misma'*, pl. *masâmi'*, ear, organ of hearing; ear, handle.

مسمكات *masmakât* = مسموكات *masmûkât*.

اهل المسمة *ahl-u 'l-masammat-i* (*musimmat-i*), relations, friends.

مسموع *masmû'*, heard; audible; who is obeyed.

مسموك *masmûk*, high, lofty; pl. *masâmîk* = مسماك *mismâk*; — ات *masmûkât*, sky, firmament.

مسموم *masmûm*, poisoned, &c.; day with a Samûm wind.

مسمى *musamma*, f. مسماة *musammât*, named, denominated, titled.

(مسن) *masan*, draw or pull one thing out of another; INF. *masn*, whip; — *masin*, A, INF. *masan*, be hard and thick; be careless.

مسن *misann*, whetstone, grindstone; — *musinn*, ة, of great old age, old.

مسناة *musannât*, pl. *musannayât*, mound, dam.

مسند *masnad*, *misnad*, ة *misnada-t*,

pl. *masânid*, cushion, pillow; support, back (of a chair, &c.); arm-chair, throne, seat of honour; post of honour, office; — *musnad*, pl. *masânid*, *masânîd*, supported, &c.; الم به *al-musnad bi-hi*, predicate, attribute; الم عليه *al-musnad 'ale-hi*, subject; adulterated, not genuine, bastard; Himyarite character; time, fate, destiny; — *.

مسنف *musnif*, pl. *masânif*, leading horse.

مسنون *masnûn*, sharpened, &c.; bright (complexion); sanctioned by tradition from the Prophet, prescribed, customary; circumcised.

مسهب *mushib*, *mushab*, lengthy in talk, &c.; wide-stepping; who refuses nothing to himself.

مسهك *mashak*, violent current of air; — *mishak*, very eloquent; swift, fleet.

مسهم *musahham*, imprinted with figures of an arrow, striped.

(مسو) *masâ*, U, INF. *masw*, introduce one's hand into the camel's womb to take out the sperm; be restive; come or happen at evening; be evening; — II. INF. *tasmiya-t*, wish good evening; — III. INF. *mumâsât*, visit in the evening; — IV. INF. *imsâ'*, *mumsa*, enter on the evening; become or do in the evening; pass the evening with; — V. INF. *tamassî*, repair to or come home in the evening; — VI. INF. *tamâsî*, turn cancerous (wound); be rotten, worm-eaten.

مسو *musû'*, INF. of (مسا).

مسواط *miswât*, harrow; spatula for stirring.

مسواق *miswâq*, bargain, purchase.

مسواك *miswâk*, pl. *masâwîk*, small piece of wood for rubbing the teeth, tooth-pick.

مسود *musawwad*, ة, blackened, &c.; black-pudding made of camel's blood; *musawwada-t*, rough copy, first draught or sketch; black bottle; — *muswadd*, ة, black.

مسور *masûr*, trodden; — *miswar*, ة *miswara-t*, leather cushion; — *musawwar*, walled in; adorned with bracelets.

مسوس *masûs*, brackish water; pure water; bezoar; — *musawwis*, worm-eaten.

مسوط *miswaṭ*, spatula for stirring.

مسوغات *musawwagât*, lawful things.

مسوق *masûq*, urged on violently; — *miswaq*, ة *miswaqa-t*, stick, whip.

مسول *masûl*, *mas'ûl*=مسئول *mas'ûl*.

مسوون *muswûn*, pl. whole and safe, safe and sound.

(مسى) *masa*, I, INF. *masy*, clear the uterus of a camel from sperm; emaciate (a.); wipe with the hand; travel commodiously; draw the sword; — V. INF. *tamassî*, be cut up; — VI. INF. *tamâsî*, id.; — VIII. INF. *imtisâ'*, be thirsty.

مسى *misy*, *musy*, evening; مسى امسى *musy-a ams-in*, yesternight; — *musi'*=مسيى *musî'*; — *musayy*, dim. of مسا *masâ'*, evening: *musayy-an*, just when it grew evening.

مسياح *misyâḥ*, pl. *masâyîḥ*, telltale; disturber of the peace, who stirs up discord.

مسيانات *musayyânât-a*, in the even ing hours.

مسيب *musayyab*, set free; given as a present, given away; — *musayyib*, squandering, neglectful.

مسيجة *masîja-t*, thorn-hedge.

مسيح *masîḥ*, pl. *musaḥâ'*, wiped, smooth; oiled, anointed (*al-masîḥ*, Messias); — *missîḥ*, who travels much; Antichrist; — *musayyaḥ*, striped; — ة *masîḥa-t*, pl. *masâyiḥ*, bow; curl; — ى *masîḥiyy*, ة, referring to Messias, Christian; *al-masîḥiyya-t*, the religion of Christ.

مسيخ *musîḥ*, transformed; monster;

ugly; deteriorated, spoiled; tasteless, insipid.

مسيد *masîd*, school.

مسير *masîr*, ة *masîra-t*, walk, ride, travel, journey; setting forth (s.); departure; — *musayyar*, sent abroad, &c.; frequently-visited place; striped.

مسيس *masîs*, ى *missîsa*, touch, &c.; INF. of (مس).

مسيط *masîṭ*, ة *masîṭa-t*, muddy water; also ة *musayyiṭa-t*, rivulet, streamlet.

مسيطر *musaiṭir*, guardian, watchman; governor; inspector; minister.

مسيعة *misya'a-t*, trowel.

مسيف *musîf*, girt with a sword; deprived of children; — *musayyaf*, without an impression or stamp (coin); — ة *masîfa-t*, pl. of سيف *saif*, sword.

مسيك *masîk*, holding fast; miserly; nutriment; intellect; f. ة, retaining water (skin bag, ground, &c.); — *missîk*, very avaricious, great miser; — ة *masîka-t*, concubine.

مسيل *masîl*, pl. *masâyil*, *musul*, *amsila-t*, *muslân*, river-bed, water-course, channel, canal, stream.

مسئلة *mas'ala-t*, pl. *masâ'il*, question; request.

مسئول *mas'ûl*, asked, requested; request; — ات *mas'ulât*, questions; — ية *mas'ûliyya-t*, inquiring after (s.), inquiry.

مسيى *masî'*, harming, hurtful; sinner, rebel.

(مش) *maśś*, U, INF. *maśś*, milk but partly, leave milk in the udder; take away by degrees; wipe the hand; be hostile to (acc.); dissolve in water; (also V.) suck the marrow out of a bone; — *maśiś*, A, INF. *maśaś*, have a hard protuberance on the thinner part of the leg (horse); — IV. INF. *imśâś*, abound with marrow; — V. INF. *tamaśśuś*, see I.

مش *maśś*, law-suit, dispute.

مشا *maśan*, a kind of carrot; — *maśâ'*, purgative; — *maśśâ'*, good walker; peripatetic (s.); teacher; slanderer; — ة *muśât*, pl. of ماشى pedestrian, &c.; — *maśâ'a-t*, will.

مشابه *maśâbih*, pl. of شبه *śabah*, resemblance, similar things, similar, &c.; — ة *muśâbaha-t*, similarity; comparison; probability.

مشاتغ *maśâtig*, pl. dangerous places; dangers.

مشاجرة *muśâjara-t*, antagonism, opposition, combat.

مشاحة *muśâḥḥa-t*, dispute; *.

مشاده *maśâdih*, pl. confusing affairs, embarrassments, difficulties.

مشادة *muśâdda-t*, violent opposition; — *.

مشار *maśâr*, bee-hive; — *; — ة *maśâra-t*, pl. *maśâwir*, part of a field or its produce; ox employed for threshing.

مشاراة *muśârât*, contract of purchase; dispute.

مشاربة *muśâraba-t*, drinking-bout, carouse, bacchanal.

مشاركة *muśâraka-t*, forming of a partnership, partnership, association; reciprocity.

مشاريط *maśârîṭ*, pl. of مشراط *miśrâṭ*.

مشاش *muśâś*, soft ground; root, origin; natural disposition, temper, mind; quick and fit for service.

مشاط *maśśâṭ*, ة, who combs, hair-dresser; f. lady's maid; — ة *miśâṭa-t*, combing; art of hair-dressing; — *muśâṭa-t*, hair coming out in combing; — *muśâṭṭa-t*, encroachment, violation of the law.

مشاطر *muśâṭir*, next neighbour; — *.

مشاع *muśâ'*, spread abroad (rumour); common to all, in common possession; yet undivided (inheritance); — ة *maśâ'a-t*, INF. of (شيع).

مشاعر *muśâ'ir*, would-be poet, poetaster ; — * .

مشاعلى *maśâ'iliyy*, hangman, executioner.

مشاغب *muśâgib*, ذو م *zû-maśâgib*, wrangler, caviller, mischievous ; — ة *muśâgaba-t*, quarrelsomeness, raising of a tumult.

مشاق *maśâq*, pruning (s.) ; — *maśâqq*, pl. of مشقة *maśaqqa-t*, *miśaqqa-t* ; —*muśâqq*, separated ; schismatic ; — ة *muśâqa-t*, what falls off in combing or cleaning wool ; floss-silk ; — *muśâqqa-t*, quarrel, dispute.

مشاكى *maśâkiyy*, pl. of مشكاة *miśkât*.

مشالحة *muśâlaha-t*, salutation with a slight bend of the head, drooping arms and open palms.

مشام *maśâmm*, organ or sense of smell, nose ; smelling ; palate ; — ة *maśâmma-t*, smelling at ; — *maś'ama-t*, left hand or side.

مشان *miśân*, rapacious wolf ; impudent and boisterous woman ; also *muśân*, a sweet kind of date.

مشاهدة *muśâhada-t*, evidence of an eye-witness ; aspect, apparition, vision.

مشاهرة *muśâhara-t*, contract for a month ; monthly payment.

مشاهير *maśâhîr*, pl. of مشهور *maśhûr*.

مشاور *maśâwir*, pl. of مشارة *maśâra-t* and مشور *miśwar*.

مشاويذ *maśâwîẕ*, pl. of مشواذ *miśwâẕ*.

مشاوير *maśâwîr*, pl. of مشوار *miśwâr*.

مشايخ *maśâyiḫ*, pl. of شيخ *śaiḫ*, old man, &c.

مشائر *maśâ'ir*, pl. of مشارة *maśâra-t*.

مشائم *maśâ'im*, pl. of مشيمة *maśîma-t*.

مشائن *maśâ'in*, pl. of مشينة *maśîna-t*.

مشائيم *maśâ'îm*, pl. of مشؤم *maś'ûm*.

مشائية *maśâ'iya-t*, volition, will.

مشبح *muśabbaḥ*, dried (fish) ; skinned, peeled ; rough.

مشبر *maśbar*, ة *maśbara-t*, pl. *maśâbir*, the notches or marks on a yard, &c. measure ; — * — * .

مشبك *masbak*, *miśbak*, hinges of a lid, &c.

مشبك *muśabbak*, net-work, trellis-work, lattices ; complicated ; lamed (through a cold).

مشبل *muśbil*, lioness with whelps.

مشبم *muśabbam*, muzzled.

مشبه *muśabbah*, assimilated, &c. ; obscure, equivocal ; — *muśabbih*, assimilating ; who conceives God to be similar to man, anthropomorphist.

مشبوح *maśbûḥ*, split ; broad ; stretched out, extended.

مشبوه *maśbûh*, suspected, ill-reputed.

مشت *muśitt*, dispersing, separating.

مشتا *muśtan*, ة *muśtât*, winter quarters ; winter-cellar ; green-house.

مشتبك *muśtabik*, net-like, complicated ; trellised.

مشتر *muśattar*, cut up, torn ; shrunk, shrivelled, wrinkled.

مشترع *muśtari'*, law-giver, legislator.

مشترك *muśtarak*, ة , possessed in common ; حس م *ḥass muśtarak*, public spirit ; لغة مشتركة *luga-t muśtaraka-t*, word with several meanings ; — *muśtarik*, partner, shareholder, subscriber ; common ; synonymous.

مشترى *maśtara*, purchase, bargain ; — *muśtara*, bought ; ransomed, rescued ;—*muśtarî*, buyer ; planet Jupiter ; a bird.

مشتق *muśtaqq*, derived ; participle.

مشتل *maśtal*, pl. *maśâtil*, seed-bed ; nursery-garden.

مشتم *muśattam*, reviled ; contemptible ; ominous ; abominable, repulsive ; *al-muśattam*, lion ;— ة *maśtama-t*, abuse, invective.

مشتهيات *muśtahayât*, desirable

things; — *muśtahiyât*, desires, appetites, cravings.

مشتور *maśtûr*, badly cut or fitting.

مشتى *maśtan*, winter quarters.

(مشج) *maśaj*, U, INF. *maśj*, mix; trouble, disturb.

مشج *maśaj*, *maśij*, pl. *amśâj*, mixture.

مشجاد *miśjâd*, sling.

مشجب *miśjab*, pl. *maśâjib*, clothes-stand (to perfume them upon).

مشجر *maśjar*, ة *maśjara-t*, pl. *maśâjir*, plantation of trees, nursery; — *miśjar*, clothes-stand; also *maśjar*, frame-work of a camel's litter; small open carriage, dog-cart; — *muśjir*, abounding with trees; — *.

مشجع *maśji'*, utterly mad.

مشجو *maśjuww*, sad.

(مشح) *maśiḥ*, A, INF. *maśaḥ*, be sore in the hollows of the knees or the inner sides of the thighs from wearing rough clothes; — *maśaḥ*, oil, anoint; give the holy unction to a sick person; — IV. INF. *imśâḥ*, be hard; be cleared from clouds; — ة *maśḥa-t*, holy unction.

مشحج *miśḥaj*, wild ass.

مشحذ *miśḥaẕ*, grind-stone.

مشحرة *maśhara-t*, charcoal-kiln; coal-stove.

مشحط *maśḥaṭ*, INF. of (شحط), be far distant, &c.; — *miśḥaṭ*, vine-pole.

مشخل *miśḥal*, ة *miśḥala-t*, filtering-funnel.

مشدح *miśdaḥ*, instrument for shattering; — *muśaddaḥ*, shattered, cut off (head); place of execution.

مشدود *maśdûd*, fastened, &c.; bundle, packet.

مشذب *miśẕab*, pruning-sickle.

(مشر) *maśar*, U, INF. *maśr*, show; put forth tender shoots round the root (also IV. and V.); — *maśir*, A, INF. *maśar*, id.; be merry, brisk, wanton; — IV. INF. *imśâr*, V. INF. *tamaśśur*, see I.; — ة. *maśra-t*, shoot, tender branch; garment, clothing.

مشراط *miśrâṭ*, pl. *maśârîṭ*, lancet, scalpel; structure, shape.

مشراق *miśrâq*, sunny place.

مشرب *maśrab*, pl. *maśârib*, watering-place, pond, reservoir; (also *muśrab*) drink; natural disposition, temper; taste, inclination, propensity; motive, principle of action, sect; — ة *maśraba-t*, *maśruba-t*, pl. *maśârib*, verandah, gallery, saloon; bow window; drinking-bout; soft ground; — *miśraba-t*, pl. *maśârib*, drinking-vessel, earthen jug; — يّة *maśrabiyya-t*, bow window.

مشرح *muśarriḥ*, anatomist.

مشرط *miśraṭ*, ة *miśraṭa-t*, lancet, scalpel; — *muśarriṭ*, belt-maker.

مشرعة *maśra'a-t*, *maśru'a-t*, pl. *maśâri'*, cross-road, road, watering-place, place in a river where water is fetched from.

مشرف *maśraf*, *muśraf*, pl. *maśârif*, height, eminence; high banks with villages; gable, ridge; tower on a height, watch-tower; — *muśrif*, towering above, &c.; overseer, inspector, controller, accountant; — *muśarraf*, exalted, &c.; border, edge.

مشرق *maśraq*, *maśriq*, *maśruq*, pl. *masâriq*, place where the sun rises, sun-rise; east, Orient; du. *al-maśraqân*, east and west; also ة *maśraqa-t*, *maśriqa-t*, *maśruqa-t*, sunny place; — *; — *muśarraq*, temple, oratory; — ى *maśriqiyy*, eastern, Oriental.

مشرك *muśrik*, polytheist; — *; — *muśarrak*, word with numerous meanings; — ى *muśrikiyy*, polytheist.

مشروب *maśrûb*, drunk; drinkable; soaked; — ات *maśrûbât*, drinks, beverages.

مشروح *maśrûḥ*, commented upon, explained; above-mentioned; cheered, refreshed; wine; mirage.

مشروط *maśrûṭ*, stipulated, &c.; conditional.
مشرول *muśarwal*=مسرول *musarwal.*
مشريق *miśrîq*, sunny place.
مشش *maśaś*, hard protuberance on the thin part of a horse's leg; see (مش).
(مشط) *maśaṭ*, U, INF. *maśṭ*, comb; mix; — II. INF. *tamśîṭ*, comb; — V. INF. *tamaśśuṭ*, comb one's self, be combed; — VIII. INF. *imtiśâṭ*, id.
مشط *maśṭ, miśṭ, muśṭ, maśiṭ, muśuṭ, muśuṭṭ*, pl. *amśâṭ, miśâṭ*, comb; rake (gardening tool); middle part (of hand or foot); bridge (of a violin); — *muśṭ*, slave; shoulder-blade; — ة *maśṭa-t*, comb; — *miśṭa-t*, way of combing.
مشطور *maśṭûr*, divided in two equal parts; clipped.
(مشظ) *maśaz̤*, U, INF. *maśz̤*, choose a country for one's residence; — *maśiz̤*, A, INF. *maśaz̤*, have the hand hurt by a thorn or splinter; show the sinews through the flesh (horse); — ة *miśz̤a-t*, splinter.
(مشع) *maśa'*, A, I, INF. *maś'*, take away, carry off; gather, heap up, gain; travel slowly and commodiously; milk sheep; card; chew; beat; — II. INF. *tamśî'*, eat the whole out of a dish; — VIII. INF. *imtiśâ'*, milk all the milk from the udder; — ة *miś'a-t*, fleak of wool.
مشعال *miś'âl*, pl. *maśâ'îl*, skin bag for date-wine.
مشعان *muś'ânn*, having the hair dishevelled.
مشعب *maś'ab*, pl. *maśâ'ib*, broad road between mountains; side path; — *miś'ab*, awl or puncheon for mending pots; — *muśa''ab*, ramified, split; mended.
مشعبذ *muś'abiz̤*=مشعوذ *muś'awiz̤.*
مشعر *maś'ur*, pl. *maśâ'ir*, place consecrated to religious ceremonies, place of sacrifice; holy rites in the temple of Mecca; external sense: sight, hearing, &c.; — *muś'ir*, informing, making known, &c.; also مشعرانى *muś'arâniyy*, hairy, shaggy.
مشعشع *muśa'śa'*, watered; weak, thin; transparent; shining, brilliant; brilliancy.
مشعل *maś'al, miś'al*, ة *maś'ala-t, miś'ala-t*, light, lamp, lantern, torch; — *miś'al*, pl. *maśâ'il*, filter; skin bag for date-wine; — * ; — جى *maś'aljiyy*, torch-bearer.
مشعوذ *muśa'waz̤*, bewitched; — *muśa'wiz̤*, juggler, sorcerer.
مشعور *maś'ûr*, ة *maś'ûra-t*, مشعورا *maś'ûrâ'*, noticing, knowing (s.).
(مشغ) *maśag*, INF. *maśg*, eat or chew anything soft; beat; blame, rebuke; — II. INF. *tamśîg*, dye red; blacken one's character.
مشغ *miśg*, red chalk.
مشغب *miśgab*, who causes a disturbance, trouble-maker, factionist.
مشغلة *maśgala-t*, pl. *maśâgil*, occupation, employment; workhouse, school.
مشفار *miśfâr*, camel's lip.
مشفتر *muśaftir*, having a thick nether-lip; — *muśfatirr*, tucked up, nimble, agile.
مشفح *muśaffaḥ*, always disappointed and unsuccessful.
مشفر *miśfar*, pl. *maśâfir*, camel's lip; violence.
مشفلة *miśfala-t*, pl. *maśâfil*, tripe.
مشفوف *maśfûf*, transparent.
(مشق) *maśaq*, U, INF. *maśq*, stretch, draw out; do anything quickly, accelerate; write in fine large characters; comb; tear (a.); (m.) take the branches or leaves off a mulberry tree; — *maśiq*, A, INF. *maśaq*, be sore on the inner side of the thighs; also pass. *muśiq*, INF. *maśq*, have a slender waist, be of a high stature; — III. INF. *mumâśaqa-t*, provoke by

insults ; — v. INF. *tamaśśuq*, VII. INF. *inmiśâq*, be torn, in rags ; (m.) have the branches cut off (mulberry - tree), be cut off (branches) ; — VIII. INF. *imtiśâq*, take away, snatch from ; cut off a piece ; stretch, draw out, write in bold characters ; milk the whole of the milk ; take the branches or leaves off a mulberry-tree.

مشق *maśq*, slimness of the waist ; copy-slip ; model for exercise ; exercise, practice, use ; also *miśq*, red chalk ;—*miśq*, having a slender waist ; — *muśq*, pl. of امشق *amśaq*, having sore thighs ; *maśaqq*, split, slit, hole, notch ;— ة *miśqa-t*, pl. *miśaq*, fleak of wool ; waste wool in carding, hair coming out in combing ; ragged garment ;—*muśqa-t*, sore spot on the inner side of the thighs ; — *maśaqqa-t*, *miśaqqa-t*, pl. *maśâqq*, hardship, hard work, toil ; distress, calamity.

مشقا *maśqa'*, parting of the hair ; —*miśqa*, *miśqan*, *miśqâ'*, ة *miśqa'a-t*, comb ; — *maśqâ'*, f. of امشق *amśaq*, see *muśq*, above.

مشقر *muśaqqar*, leather flask ; cup.

مشقص *miśqaṣ*, pl. *maśâqiṣ*, broad head of an arrow or spear ; — *muśaqqiṣ*, butcher.

مشقشق *muśaqśiq*, ballad singer ; — * .

مشقى *miśqan*, comb ; — *maśqiyy*, earned by hard work.

مشك *maśakk*, joint, link (in a coat of mail).

مشكاة *miśkât*, pl. *maśâkiyy*, niche in a wall for placing a lamp.

مشكر *muśkir*, ة, yielding plenty of milk ; — ة *maśkara-t*, *muśkira-t*, food productive of milk.

مشكلة *muśkila-t*, pl. *-ât*, (m.) *muśâkil*, difficulty, difficult problem ; — * .

مشكو *maśkuww*, lamented ; complained of, accused ; suspected.

مشكور *maśkûr*, thanked, &c. ; thankworthy, praiseworthy ; acknowledged ; acceptable.

مشكى *maśkiyy*=مشكو *maśkuww*.

(مشل) *maśal*, U, INF. *muśûl*, have but little flesh ; INF. *maśl*, milk but little milk ; also VIII. INF. *imtiśâl*, draw the sword.

مشل *miśall*, alert and ready for service, sociable, friendly.

مشلح *muśallaḥ*, also *maślaḥ*, pl. *maśâliḥ*, ante-room in a bath for undressing ;—*maślaḥ*, cloak ; —*muśalliḥ*, highway robber, robber who commits murder ; — * .

مشلى *miślan*, large spoon ; — *muśalla*, slender, thin.

مشليق *miślîq*, laughing with open mouth.

مشم *muśimm*, nose ; averse.

مشمال *miśmâl*, wrapper, plaid.

مشمخر *muśmaḥirr*, high.

مشمذ *miśmaẕ*, head-band, turban.

(مشمش) *maśmaś*, INF. ة, dissolve in water, macerate ; be alert, quick.

مشمش *maśmaś*, *miśmiś*, ة, apricot ; apricot-tree ; م لوزى *maśmaś lauziyy*, apricot with a sweet kernel, م كليبى *maśmaś kulaibiyy*, ditto with a bitter kernel.

مشمع *muśamma'*, wax-cloth ; — * ; —ة *maśma'a-t*, jest ;—*miśma'a-t*, pl. *maśâmi'*, candle-stick.

مشمعل *muśma'ill*, swift, fleet ; active ; tall.

مشمل *miśmal*, short sword or dagger to be worn beneath the clothes ; also ة *miśmala-t*, wrapper, plaid ; — ة *miśmila-t*, *muśmula-t*, medlar.

مشموم *maśmûm*, smelled, &c. ; perceivable by the smell ; fragrant, perfumed ; musk.

مشمئز *muśma'izz*, feeling fear and aversion.

(مشن) *maśan*, I, INF. *maśn*, beat, flog, whip ; scratch ; give a stroke with the sword which only takes off the skin ; wipe one's hand ; lie with ; — VIII. INF. *imtiśân*, cut off ; snatch

from, drag away by force, rob; draw the sword.

مشن• *miśann*, old shrivelled up skin bag; — ة *maśna-t*, skin-wound, scratch.

مشنا• *maśna'* (also ة *maśna'a-t*), hatred; m. f., sing. pl. ugly; misanthrope;—*miśnâ'*, hated by everybody.

مشنج• *muśannaj*, having a stiff neck from cold; wide, spacious.

مشنق• *muśannaq*, cut into pieces or slices; — *muśanniq*, self-complacent, conceited, vain; — ة *maśnaqa-t*, pl. *maśâniq*, place for hanging, gallows.

مشنو• *maśnu'*, *maśnuww* (مشنى *maśniyy*), hated; — وءة *maśnû'a-t*, hatred.

مشهد• *maśhad*, ة *maśhada-t*, *maśhuda-t*, pl. *maśâhid*, place of meeting or assembly, place where a martyr met with his death, tomb of a martyr or saint, place of pilgrimage; — *.

مشهود• *maśhûd*, witnessed, &c.; place where many people meet; resurrection; Friday; — ة *maśhûda-t*, prayer; — ات *maśhûdât*, personal experiences.

مشهور• *maśhûr*, pl. *maśâhîr*, generally known, celebrated, notorious.

مشهى• *muśahhî*, what sharpens the appetite, relishing.

مشو• *maśw*, *maśuww*, purgative; — ة *maśwa-t*, *miśwa-t* = مشية• *miśya-t*.

مشواذ• *miśwâẓ*, pl. *maśâwîẓ*, turban.

مشوار• *miśwâr* (also مشور *miśwar*, pl. *maśâwir*), instrument for taking out honey; interior, frame of mind; exterior, shape, form; horse- and cattle-market; ة *miśwâra-t*, bee-hive;—*muśwâr*, pl. *maśâwîr*, journey, march; great distance (m.).

مشواة• *miśwât*, (m.) مشواية *miśwâya-t*, frying-pan.

مشوب• *maśûb*, mixed, troubled; — *muśawwib*, who is very hot.

مشوذ• *miśwaẓ*, pl. *maśâwiẓ*, turban; prince, lord.

(مشور) *maśwar*, INF. ة, march, walk, travel (m.).

مشور• *miśwar*, see مشوار• *miśwâr*, council-hall;— ة *maśwara-t*, consultation; advice, lesson; also *maśûra-t*, order, command.

مشوش• *maśûś*, table-cloth and napkin; — *muśawwaś*, troubled, &c.; complicated, entangled.

مشوف• *maśûf*, bright, polished, new; dressed up; furious (stallion).

مشوق• *maśûq*, longingly desired, beloved; desirous, craving for; — *.

مشوك• *muświk*, *muśawwik*, thorny, pricking.

مشوم• *maśûm*, مشووم• *maś'ûm* = مشئوم• *maś'ûm*.

مشوى• *maświyy*, roasted; — *miśwan* = مشواة• *miśwât*.

(مشى) *maśa*, I, INF. *maśy*, *timśâ'*, walk, travel on foot, march; INF. *maśâ'*, have many children; be rich in cattle; — II. INF. *tamśiya-t*, walk; make or bid to walk; set going; purge; slander; — III. INF. *mumâśât*, walk at one's side, keep up with him; — IV. INF. *imśâ'*, make or bid to walk; purge; (also VIII.) have numerous progeny; — V. INF. *tamaśśî*, walk, travel on foot; start; take a pleasure-walk; — VI. INF. *tamâśî*, walk together; — VIII. INF. *imtiśâ'*, see IV.; — X. INF. *istimśâ'*, ask for a purgative.

مشى• *maśy*, walking, travelling on foot (s.), walk, gait; diarrhœa; —*maśiyy*, purgative;—ة *miśya-t*, way of walking, gait, pace; conduct; direction; — *maśî'a-t*, *maśiyya-t* = مشيئة• *maśî'a-t*.

مشياع• *miśyâ'*, who blabs out everything.

مشيب• *maśyab*, grey hair, hoariness, INF. of (شيب); — *maśîb*

grey, hoary ; — *muśayyab*, awry, oblique.

مشيج *maśîj*, pl. *amśâj*, mixed ; mixture.

مشيح *muśîḥ*, zealous, diligent, industrious ; — ى *maśîḥa*, zeal ; mixture ; confusion, hurly-burly.

مشيخة *maśîḫa-t*, assembly of elders ; senate ; dignity of a *śaiḫ* or *śaiḫu 'l-Islâm*.

مشيد *maśîd*, coated with mortar, cemented ; — *muśayyad*, id. ; high ; raised high ; fortified, consolidated, firm, solid ; — *muśayyid*, architect, builder.

مشير *muśîr*, giving a sign, hint, advice ; counsellor ; minister ; brigadier ; — ة *muśîra-t*, fore-finger, index.

مشيط *maśîṭ*, combed.

مشيع *muśi'*, *muśayyi'*, who spreads about news ;— ة *miśya'a-t*, lady's work-basket.

مشيم *maśîm*, having a black mole or beauty-spot ; — ة *maśîma-t*, pl. *maśîm*, *maśâ'im*, membrane which surrounds the fœtus ; pl. *maśâ'im*, disasters, calamities.

مشين *maśîn*, infamous, disgraceful ; f. pl. *maśâ'in*, abominations, vices ;—*muśayyan*, stately, portly, worthy.

مشيوحا *maśyûḥâ'*, zeal ; difficult matter or business.

مشيوخا *maśyûḫâ'*, pl. of شيخ *śaiḫ*, old man, &c.

مشيوم *maśyûm*=مشيم *maśîm*.

مشؤوم *maś'ûm* (مشووم , مشوم), pl. *maśâ'im*, disastrous, ominous, portending evil.

مشيئة *maśî'a-t*, مشئة *maśi'a-t*, مشية *maśiyya-t*, volition, will ; will of God ; fate.

(مص) *maṣṣ* (*maṣaṣ-tu*, *maṣiṣ-tu*), U, A, INF. *maṣṣ*, suck, drink by sucking, sip up ; (m.) have no juice left (fruit) ; — II. INF. *tamṣîṣ*, make suck, give suck, suckle ; — IV. INF. *imṣâṣ*, id. ; — V. INF. *tamaṣṣuṣ*, suck, sip up ; — VII. be sucked up ; have no juice left ; — VIII. INF. *imtiṣâṣ*=V.

مص *maṣṣ*, sucking, sucking up, sipping up (s.) ; قصب مص *qaṣab-u maṣṣ-in*, sugar-cane ; — ة *maṣṣa-t*, suck ; — *muṣṣa-t*, best part of one's property.

مصا *muṣâ* ., مصى . *muṣî* ., to be looked for under (. صو , . صى IV.), as—

مصاب *muṣâb*, pat. of (صوب IV.), hit, &c. ; wounded ; hurt at the hoof ; weak-headed ; sugar-cane ; also ة *muṣâba-t*, calamity.

مصابح *muṣâbiḥ*, f. ة, companion, confidant, favourite ; adjutant ; — ة *muṣâbaḥa-t*, social intercourse, familiarity, conversation ; company, society.

مصابيح *maṣâbîḥ*, pl. of مصباح *miṣbâḥ*.

مصابية *muṣâbiya-t*, calamity.

مصاد *maṣâd*, pl. *amṣida-t*, *muṣdân*, highest peak ; high mountain.

مصادرة *muṣâdara-t*, confiscation ; fine ; contribution ; dispute, opposition.

مصادمة *muṣâdama-t*, shock, concussion, collision.

مصاديق *maṣâdîq*, pl. of مصداق *miṣdâq*.

مصار *miṣâr*, pl. of مصور *maṣûr* ; — *maṣârr*, bowels, intestines.

مصاريع *maṣâri'*, pl. of مصراع *miṣrâ'*.

مصاريف *maṣârîf*, pl. of مصروف *maṣrûf*.

مصارين *maṣârîn*, pl. of مصير *maṣîr*.

مصاص *muṣâṣ*, most exquisite part, cream of ; ة *muṣâṣa-t*, anything to be sucked up, a little, trifle ; spout ; pipe of a syringe ; — *maṣṣâṣ*, who sucks up, sucker, extortioner ; ة *maṣṣâṣa-t*, night-hawk, vampire.

مصاعب *maṣâ'ib*, difficulties, difficult matters.

مصاغ *maṣâg*, pl. *maṣâgât*, ornaments of gold or silver, trinkets, jewelelry.

مصاف *muṣâf-in*, see مصافى *muṣâfî* ;

— *maṣâff*, pl. of مصف *maṣaff*; — ة *muṣâffa-t*, battle-array, battle.

مصافاة *muṣâfât*, sincere friendship, affection, purity of heart, candour.

مصافحة *muṣâfaḥa-t*, shaking of hands; cordiality; pardon, reconciliation.

مصافى *maṣâfî*, pl. of مصفى *miṣfa*, مصفاة *miṣfât*; — *muṣâfî* (مصاف *muṣâf-in*), sincere friend, candid.

مصاقب *muṣâqib*, fitting one another, corresponding, uniform; — ة *muṣâqaba-t*, fitting together (s.), conformity, uniformity.

مصالبة *muṣâlaba-t*, cruciform; vault with cross springers.

مصالة *muṣâla-t*, *maṣâla-t*, what drops off; serum; whey; *maṣâla-t*, INF. of (صول), assault boldly, &c.

مصالى *maṣâlî*, pl. of مصلاة *miṣlât*.

مصاليب *maṣâlîb*, pl. of مصلوب *maṣlûb*.

مصام *maṣâm*, ة *maṣâma-t*, horse-stand.

مصان *maṣân*, den, lair; — * — *maṣṣan*, f. ة, miser.

مصانعة *muṣâna'a-t*, endeavours to win, to bribe, &c.; intrigues; wages.

مصائص *maṣâ'iṣ*, pl. of مصوص *maṣûṣ*.

مصب *maṣabb*, mouth of a river.

مصباح *miṣbâḥ*, pl. *maṣâbîḥ*, light, lamp, lantern; broad arrow-head; also pl. *maṣâbiḥ*, cup (for a morning draught).

مصبح *maṣbaḥ*, *muṣbaḥ*, sun-rise, dawn, morning; place where one passes the morning; — *miṣbaḥ*, pl. *maṣâbiḥ*, cup.

مصبع *maṣba'*, ة *maṣba'a-t*, haughtiness; — *muṣabba'*, frying-pan.

مصبغة *maṣbaga-t*, trade or work-place of a dyer.

مصبنة *maṣbana-t*, soap-manufactory.

مصبور *maṣbûr*, sentenced and expecting execution; — ة *maṣbûra-t*, solemn oath.

مصبوع *maṣbû'*, haughty.

مصبية *maṣbiya-t*, mother of young children, matron; captivating hearts.

(مصت) *maṣat*, U, INF. *maṣt*, lie with; take the sperm out of the camel's uterus; milk the whole of the milk; press the pus out of a wound.

(مصح) *maṣaḥ*, INF. *muṣûḥ*, depart and stay away; be used up; be effaced; waste away, disappear; decrease, diminish; take away.

مصحاب *miṣḥâb*, obsequious, yielding.

مصحاة *miṣḥât*, silver cup.

مصحب *muṣḥib*, submissive.

مصحف *muṣḥaf*, *maṣḥaf*, *miṣḥaf*, pl. *maṣâḥif*, bound book, volume; page, leaf; *al-muṣḥaf*, Koran; — *muṣaḥḥaf*, incorrectly written or read, erroneous reading; — ة *miṣḥafa-t*, pl. *maṣâḥif*, shovel, spade.

مصحنة *miṣḥana-t*, large dish.

مصحة *maṣaḥḥa-t*, *maṣiḥḥa-t*, what is conducive to health.

مصحية *muṣḥiya-t*, serene sky.

(مصخ) *maṣaḫ*, INF. *maṣḫ*, pull out, take out; take off; transform; IV. INF. *imṣâḫ*, put forth leaves; — V. INF. *tamaṣṣuḫ*, VIII. INF. *imtiṣâḫ*, take away.

مصخدة *maṣḫada-t*, pl. *maṣâḫid*, heat of mid-day.

مصخر *muṣḫir*, rocky.

مصخفة *miṣḫafa-t*, shovel, spade.

(مصد) *maṣad*, U, INF. *maṣd*, suck the mother's breast; suck, chew; thunder; lie with; grow intense; humble, humiliate.

مصد *maṣd*, thunder; heat; (also *maṣad*) violent cold; high mountain; — ة *maṣda-t*, coolness, rain.

مصداق *miṣdâq*, pl. *maṣâdîq*, who or what verifies, confirms; criterion, proof, test; argument, demonstration; general truth, truism.

مصدام **miṣdâm,** brave, valiant.
مصدان **muṣdân,** pl. of مصاد *maṣâd*.
مصدر **maṣdar,** pl. **maṣâdir,** issuing, issue, origin, source; place where one returns from; result, outcome, consequence; infinitive; — **muṣaddar,** seated in the place of honour; beginning with; having a large chest; lion; wolf; — * ; — ى *maṣdariyy*, ة, referring to the origin, to the infinitive, &c.; ة *maṣdariyya-t*, import duty.
مصدع *maṣda'*, pl. *maṣâdi'*, level path through a rugged tract; — *miṣda'*, eloquent, intelligent; — *.
مصدغة *miṣdaga-t*, pillow.
مصدق *maṣdaq*, *miṣdaq*, boldness, fearlessness (in construction with ذو *zû*); — * ; — *muṣraddiq*, for متصدق *mutaṣaddiq*, who gives alms.
مصدور *maṣdûr*, suffering in the chest; derived, sent out.
مصدوقة *maṣdûqa-t*, truth.
(مصر) *maṣar*, U, INF. *maṣr* (also VIII.), milk with three finger-tops; — II. INF. *tamṣîr*, yield but little milk; found (cities); make (a city) the capital; — V. INF. *tamaṣṣur*, diminish (n.), be but little, few; milk the last milk of a camel; be made a capital.
مصر *miṣr*, pl. *amṣâr*, *muṣûr*, large town, city, capital; tract, territory; Egypt; Cairo; du. *al-miṣrân*, Kufa and Basra; surroundings; boundary; partition wall, curtain, &c.; sheath, case; sword; red earth; — *muṣirr*, persisting, insisting, pressing; — ة *maṣarra-t*, the urinary and excremental ducts.
مصراع *miṣrâ'*, pl. *maṣârî'*, door-wing; half-verse, hemistitch.
مصران *miṣrân*, du. of مصر *miṣr*, see above; — *muṣrân*, pl. of مصير *maṣîr*; — ة *muṣrâna-t*, gut.
مصرع *maṣra'*, pl. *maṣari'*, wrestling-place, arena; battle-field; INF. of (صرع); — *miṣra'* = مصراع *miṣrâ'*; — *.
مصرف *maṣraf*, pl. *maṣârif*, *maṣârifât*, expenses, costs, expenditure; passage, outlet; quick and easy sale; — *muṣrif*, spendthrift; — *muṣarrif*, money-changer.
مصرم *miṣram*, curved knife for carving in wood, &c.
مصرور *maṣrûr*, tied up, packed; put into the purse.
مصروف *maṣrûf*, turned aside, altered, inflected (gram.); changed, spent (money); pl. *maṣârîf*, expenses, costs;—also ة *maṣrûfa-t*, wine.
مصرى *miṣriyy*, ة, pl. *-ûn*, *maṣârî*, *maṣâriyy*, *maṣârawî*, Egyptian (adj. s.); Cairo; Egyptian sugar; inhabitant of a town, citizen; — ة *miṣriyya-t*, (m.) *maṣriya-t*, pl. *ât*, *maṣârî*, para (coin), penny (pl. money, riches, wealth); cabin.
(مصط) *maṣaṭ*, INF. *maṣṭ*, wring out washed linen.
مصطا . *muṣṭâ* ., to be looked for under (. صو , . صي VIII.), as—
مصطاد *muṣṭâd*, ag. or pat. of (صيد VIII.), hunting, hunted, &c.; hunter; lion; hunting circuit.
مصطار *muṣṭâr*, ة *muṣṭâra-t*, must.
مصطاف *muṣṭâf*, passing the summer; summer habitation.
. . مصط *muṣṭa* . ., to be looked for under (. . ص VIII.), as—
مصطبر *muṣṭabir*, ag. of (صبر VIII.), patient; patience.
مصطبة *maṣṭaba-t*, *miṣṭaba-t*, pl. *maṣâṭib*, large stone bench, platform in front of a house or in a garden; inn for beggars.
مصطح *miṣṭaḥ*, desert; threshing-floor.
مصطدم *muṣṭadam*, place of combat, battle-field.
مصطرع *maṣṭara'*, wrestling-place; — *.
مصطفى *muṣṭafa*, selected, chosen; proper name; *muṣṭafiyy*, مصطفوى *muṣṭafawiyy*, belonging or re-

ferring to Mustafa, Mohammedan.

مصطكا *musṭakâ*, *mastakâ'*, مصطكى *musṭakî*, mastic (for chewing).

مصطلح *muṣṭalaḥ*, agreed upon, &c.; conventional, technical; metaphorical; passable.

مصطلى *muṣṭala*, warming-room.

(مصع) *maṣa'*, INF. *maṣ'*, flash; wag the tail and beat with it; strike with the sword or a whip; beat slightly, hit; hurry by, run fast; drop excrement, &c.; lose courage; INF. *muṣû'*, waste away, fail, become exhausted (milk); pass away, subside; depart;—III. INF. *mumâṣa'a-t*, fight, quarrel; — IV. INF. *imṣâ'*, drop (a fœtus, excrement, &c.); — VIII. INF. *imtiṣâ'*, depart.

مصع *maṣi'*, *maṣ'*, eager for combat, bellicose, reckless fighter; — ة *muṣ'a-t*, *muṣa'a-t*, pl. *muṣ'*, *muṣa'*, a green bird; a fruit.

مصعاد *miṣ'âd*, scaling-ladder; rope-ladder.

مصعب *muṣ'ab*, made difficult; restive; stallion; pl. *maṣâ'ib*, difficulties.

مصعد *miṣ'ad*, pl. *maṣâ'id*, ascent; step, stairs, ladder; — *muṣ'ad*, raised, elevated; — *muṣa''ad*, sublimated, rectified, refined.

مصعوف *maṣ'ûf*, trembling, shuddering.

مصغبة *maṣgaba-t*, hunger, famine.

مصغورا *maṣgûrâ'*, pl. of صغير *ṣagîr*.

مصغى *muṣga*, inclined, well-disposed towards; — *muṣgî*, lending one's ear, listening.

مصف *maṣaff*, pl. *maṣâff*, place where anything is ranged, set up, &c.; battle-array; battle-field; battle.

مصفا *miṣfâ*, مصفاة *miṣfât*, مصفاية *miṣfâya-t*, pl. *maṣâfî*, filter, strainer, colander.

مصفح *muṣfaḥ*, broad (*muṣfaḥ-an*), with the blade); smooth and handsome (face); — *; — ة *muṣaffaḥa-t*, sword.

مصفر *muṣfir*, empty-handed; — *muṣfarr*, yellow, pale.

مصفور *maṣfûr*, famished; bilious.

مصفى *miṣfa*, pl. *muṣâfî*, strainer, colander; — *muṣaffa*, filtered, strained, refined.

مصقع *miṣqa'*, pl. *maṣâqi'*, loud-voiced; eloquent; — *.

مصقل *miṣqal*, ة *miṣqala-t*, pl. *maṣâqil*, shell or any other implement for polishing.

مصك *miṣakk*, ة, strongly made or built; lock, bolt.

(مصل) *maṣal*, U, INF. *maṣl*, drip; be placed on some basket-work to be dried; INF. *muṣûl*, curdle; — IV. INF. *imṣâl*, ruin one's cattle or property; — X. INF. *istimṣâl*, purge.

مصل *maṣl*, whey;—ة *miṣalla-t*, filter, colander.

مصلا *muṣallâ* = مصلى *muṣalla*; — ة *miṣlât*, pl. *maṣâlî*, snare, noose.

مصلات *miṣlât*, pl. *maṣâlît*, alert, active, capable.

مصلت *miṣlat*, id.; — *muṣlat*, lifted up (sword).

مصلح *muṣliḥ*, mending, &c.; peace-maker, reconciler; good, pious; — ة *maṣlaḥa-t*, pl. *maṣâliḥ*, anything promoting, salutary, advantageous; advantage; business, undertaking, enterprise; benevolence; good advice; pl. weal, welfare (of a country, &c.).

مصلطح *muṣaltaḥ*, broad, wide, spacious.

مصلوب *maṣlûb*, pl. *maṣâlîb*, crucified; hung; crucifix; م عليه *maṣlûb 'alai-hi*, afflicted with a fever.

مصلى *muṣlan*, *muṣla*, warming-room; — *maṣliyy*, ة, burnt, roasted; set (snare); ة *maṣliya-t*, soup of whey; — *muṣalla*, blessed, consecrated; place for prayer, oratory; prayer carpet or cushion, praying-desk; — *muṣallî* (مصل *muṣall-in*), praying,

blessing (adj.); preacher; second horse in a race.
مصم *muṣimm*, deaf.
مصماد *miṣmâd*, pl. *maṣâmid*, *maṣâmîd*, she-camel who always yields milk.
مصمت *muṣmat*, massive (not hollow), firm; shut; of one colour; — *muṣammat*, full (a thousand, &c.).
مصمد *muṣmad*, *muṣammad*, massive, firm, solid, hard.
(مصمص) *maṣmaṣ*, INF. ة, sip in with the tip of the tongue and move about in the mouth, rinse the mouth; suck; rinse a vessel.
مصمقر *muṣmaqirr*, very hot.
مصمم *muṣammam*, *muṣammim*, firmly resolved or resolved upon; tending to.
مصمئلة *muṣma'illa-t*, calamity.
مصمية *muṣmiya-t*, projectile killing on the spot, deadly arrow.
مصن *muṣinn*, furious; smelling offensively.
مصنع *maṣna'*, ة *maṣna'a-t*, *maṣnu'a-t*, pl. *maṣâni'*, open cistern; strong building; castle, fortification, stronghold; — * ; — ة *maṣna'a-t*, banquet, drinking-bout.
مصنف *muṣannif*, author, editor; — ات *muṣannafât*, works, writings.
مصنوعات *maṣnû'ât*, all things created, creatures, productions of art, manufactures, works.
مصهر *muṣhir*, allied by marriage.
مصواء *maṣwâ'*, buttocks.
مصوات *miṣwât*, sounding, resounding; screamer, brawler; somebody, anybody.
مصوب *miṣwab*, spoon; — ة *maṣûba-t*, pl. *maṣâwib*, blow, calamity.
مصور *maṣûr*, pl. *miṣâr*, *maṣâ'ir*, yielding but little milk; — * ; — *muṣawwir*, painter, sculptor; — *.
مصوص *maṣûṣ*, pl. *maṣâ'iṣ*, pigeon or fish boiled in vinegar; greatly longing for a husband or lover.
مصول *miṣwal*, pl. *maṣâwil*, reservoir or tub for washing; tub for slaking lime; — ة *miṣwala-t*, broom, brush.
مصومع *muṣauma'* = مصمع *muṣamma'*.
مصون *maṣûn*, مصوون *maṣwûn*, guarded, heeded, protected; healthy; concealed, locked up.
مصيب *muṣîb*, hitting the aim, hitting the point; — ة *muṣîba-t*, calamity; agony.
مصيد *maṣîd*, caught or killed in hunting; — *miṣyad*, ة *miṣyada-t*, *maṣîda-t*, pl. *maṣâyid*, hunting- or fishing-net, noose, trap.
مصير *maṣîr*, place where one finally arrives; sojourn, stay, residence; issue, result; gains (s.), INF. of (صير); pl. *amṣira-t*, *muṣrân*, *maṣârîn*, gut; chylifactory vessel; flank; — ة *muṣaira-t*, little town.
مصيص *maṣîṣ*, wet, moist; — *miṣṣîṣ*, cord, pack-thread; — ة *maṣîṣa-t*, plate, disk.
مصيطر *muṣaiṭir* = مسيطر *musaiṭir*.
مصيف *maṣîf*, summer habitation, country seat, villa; summer; – *muṣayyif*, sufficient for the summer.
مصيقل *muṣaiqal*, polished.
مصيون *maṣyûn*, protected, healthy.
(مض) *maḍḍ*, U, INF. *maḍḍ*, *maḍîḍ*, pain, grief; burn, scorch, bite; INF. *maḍîḍ*, suck strongly; — *maḍiḍ*, A, INF. *maḍaḍ*, feel pain, suffer, be grieved; INF. *maḍîḍ*, *maḍâḍa-t*, id.; INF. *maḍîḍ*, burn, bite; — IV. INF. *imḍâḍ*, cause pain or suffering to (acc.); — VII. (m.) INF. *inmiḍâḍ*, suffer.
مض *maḍḍ*, pain, sorrow, grief; painful, burning; — *miḍḍ-i*, I won't! no! — ة *maḍḍa-t*, sour milk; acrimonious (woman).
مضا *maḍâ'*, INF. of (مضى).
مضار *maḍârr*, pl. of مضرة *maḍarra-t*; — ة *muḍâra-t*, whey; — *muḍârra-t*, injury, INF. of (ضر III.); jealousy between fellow wives (ضرة *ḍarra-t*); polygamy.
مضارب *muḍârab* (به *bi-hi*), multiplicator; — ة *muḍâraba-t*, brawl, fight; sexual intercourse, copulation; sleeping partnership.

مضارع *muḍâri'*, similar, equal, &c.; aorist; — ة *muḍâra'a-t*, similarity; contract between landlord and tenant.

مضاض *muḍâḍ*, pure; brackish; — ة *maḍâḍa-t*, grief, pain.

مضاعف *muḍâ'af*, doubled, &c.; verb whose second and third radical are the same, or which consists of two equal syllables; also those forms of the regular verb in which the last radical is doubled; — ة *muḍâ'afa-t*, doubling.

مضاغ *maḍâg*, chewing (s.); what may be chewed; something, anything; — ة *muḍâga-t*, anything chewed; — *muḍâgga-t*, mad, fool.

مضاف *muḍâf*, added, joined, appended, annexed; accessory; adopted; spurious; appendix, supplement (pl. *muḍâfât*, additions); *al-muḍâf*, word which governs another word (المضاف اليه *al-muḍâf ilai-hi*) in the genitive.

مضامير *muḍâmîr*, pl. of مضمور *maḍmûr*.

مضاهاة *muḍâhât*, similarity, conformity.

مضاواة *muḍâwât*, openness.

مضائف *muḍâ'if*, pl. sides (of a valley, river, &c.).

مضايقة *muḍâyaqa-t*, straitening, obstruction, limitation; straitness; difficulty, need, distress.

مضبا *maḍba'*, hiding-place, loophole; — ة *maḍbât*, hole in the earth for baking; — *muḍbât*, bread baked in the ashes.

مضبث *miḍbas*, lion; pl. *maḍâbis*, lion's claws; fists.

مضبطة *maḍbaṭa-t*, pl. *maḍâbi-t*, roll on which anything is registered; protocol.

مضبعة *maḍba'a-t*, fleshy part of the upper arm; pl. of ضبع *ḍab'*, *ḍubu'*, hyena.

مضبة *maḍabba-t*, pl. *maḍâbb*, place abounding with lizards.

مضبوب *maḍbûb*, gathered and held in the hand; contained, included, enclosed.

مضبوط *maḍbûṭ*, held fast, &c.; solid; regulated; precise, accurate, correct; blameless; vocalised; confiscated.

مضجر *muḍjir*, pl. *maḍâjir*, *maḍâjîr*, morose, peevish, a bore.

مضجع *maḍja'*, pl. *maḍâji'*, resting-place, bed-room, couch, bed, grave; place of combat.

(مضح) *maḍaḥ*, INF. *maḍḥ*, blacken one's character (also IV.); repel, keep off; — IV. INF. *imḍâḥ*, see I.

مضحاك *miḍḥâk*, buxom (woman).

مضحاة *maḍḥât*, sunny place.

مضحك *muḍḥik*, comical; jester; — ة *muḍḥika-t*, *muḍḥaka-t*, funny story, joke, jest.

(مضخ) *maḍaḫ*, INF. *maḍḫ*, rub with perfumes, perfume; — ة *miḍaḫḫa-t*, syringe.

(مضد) *maḍad*, INF. *maḍd*, wrap up the head; — *maḍid*, A, INF. *maḍad*, hate.

(مضر) *maḍur*, U, INF. *maḍr*, *muḍûr*, — *maḍir*, A, INF. *maḍar*, — *maḍur*, turn sour; — II. INF. *tamḍîr*, ruin, destroy; belong to the *Muḍarites*.

مضر *miḍr*, unavenged bloodshed; — *maḍir*, turned sour; very white; — *muḍar*, Mudar, son of Nizâr, first ancestor of an Arab tribe; ية *al-muḍariyya-t*, his descendants, *Muḍarites*; — *muḍirr*, hurtful, pernicious; ة *muḍirra-t*, wife who has a fellow wife; — ة *maḍarra-t*, pl. *-ât*, *maḍârr*, damage, injury, loss; hurtfulness; obligation.

مضراب *miḍrâb*, mallet; knocker; drum-stick; plectrum; fiddlestick.

مضرج *miḍraj*, pl. *maḍârij*, worn out everyday dress; — *muḍarraj*, blood-stained; — *muḍarrij*, lion.

مضرح *maḍraḥ*, ى *maḍraḥiyy*, long-winged; white vulture; hawk.

مضرس *muḍarras*, indented; having rugged prominences.

مضروب *maḍrûb*, ة, beaten, scourged, &c.; proverbial; م فيه *maḍrûb fî-hi*, multiplicator; م عليه *maḍrûb ʻalai-hi*, multiplicand; coining (s.); stamp, sort, kind; injured by hoar-frost; — ة *maḍrûba-t*, scourging; mark from beating, scar.

مضرور *maḍrûr*, hurt, &c.; weak, sickly.

مضض *maḍaḍ*, pain, grief.

مضط *muḍṭ*, comb.

. . مضط *muḍṭa* . . , to be looked for under (. . ض VIII.), as—

مضطجع *muḍṭajaʻ*, pat. of (ضجع VIII.), that which one lies upon, bed, &c.; — *muḍṭajiʻ*, ag. of the same, lying on one's side or back.

مضطر *muḍṭarr* (ضر VIII.), forced, &c.; distressed, needy.

مضطرب *muḍṭarib*, agitated, disquieted, anxious, wavering.

مضعف *muḍʻaf*, مضعوف *maḍʻûf*, blind; — *.

(مضغ) *maḍag*, A, U, INF. *maḍg*, chew, eat; — III. INF. *mumâḍaga-t*, fight furiously with; — IV. INF. *imḍâg*, be good to eat; — VII. INF. *inmiḍâg*, be chewed.

مضغ *maḍg*, chewing (s.); ة *muḍga-t*, pl. *muḍag*, morsel, mouthful; lump of flesh (fœtus); — *muḍdag*, trifles, minutiæ.

مضلة *maḍalla-t*, *maḍilla-t*, *miḍalla-t*, tract where one easily loses one's way.

مضمار *miḍmâr*, pl. *maḍâmîr*, place of exercise; training-ground; race-course; battle-field, puzzle.

مضماض *maḍmâḍ*, *miḍmâḍ*, rinsing of the mouth.

مضمر *muḍmar*, conceived in the mind, &c.; understood without being expressed, inclusive; personal pronoun; — *.

(مضمض) *maḍmaḍ*, INF. ة, *miḍmâḍ*, roll water about in the mouth, rinse the mouth; rinse a vessel; wash a dress; be sleepy; — II. INF. *tamaḍmuḍ*, rinse; follow the track barking; taste.

مضموم *maḍmûm*, added, included, embodied; marked with *ḍamma-t*; — ات *maḍmûmât*, annexations, additions.

مضنون *maḍnûn*, carefully guarded; musk; — ة *maḍnûna-t*, the well Zamzam.

مضنئة *muḍni'a-t*, prolific (woman).

مضوا *muḍawwa'*, lit (lamp).

مضوف *maḍûf*, to be feared; — ة *maḍûfa-t*, need, distress.

(مضى) *maḍa*, I, INF. *muḍiyy*, *muḍuww*, pass, be past; go, go away with, take (ب); — INF. *maḍâ'*, *muḍuww*, go farther in a matter, penetrate more deeply; INF. *maḍâ'*, penetrate deeply, cut (sword); dispose of (merchandise); — II. INF. *tamḍiya-t*, let pass; pass the time; cause to forget; — IV. INF. *imḍâ'*, carry out, execute, complete; let pass; cause to penetrate; sign or seal a document; promise; — V. INF. *tamaḍḍî*, be carried out, executed, brought to a good issue; pass; — VIII. INF. *imtiḍâ'*, draw the sword.

مضى *muḍiyy*, INF. of the previous; — *muḍi'*, lighting up, illuminating, shining (adj.).

مضياع *miḍyâʻ*, spendthrift.

مضياف *miḍyâf*, very hospitable, receiving everybody.

مضير *maḍîr*, sour; very white; — ة *maḍîra-t*, soup of sour milk.

مضيض *maḍîḍ*, grief, INF. of (مض).

مضيعة *maḍîʻa-t*, ruin, destruction, perdition; — *maḍyaʻa-t*, dangerous place.

مضيغة *maḍîga-t*, pl. *maḍîg*, *maḍâ'ig*, projection of the jaw beneath the ear; muscle there.

مضيف *muḍîf*, entertainer; — *; — ة *maḍîfa-t*, *muḍîfa-t*, *maḍyufa-t*, what is to be feared; sorrow, grief.

مضيم *maḍîm*, injured, wronged.

مضيى *muḍî'* = مضى *muḍi'*.

(مط) *maṭṭ*, U, INF. *maṭṭ*, stretch by

pulling, stretch; raise the brows (in pride); pull up the bucket; point with the fingers; lenghthen (n.), stretch one's self;—II. INF. *tamṭîṭ*, revile, abuse, scold; — V. INF. *tamaṭṭuṭ*, stretch one's self; stretch, lengthen (a.); amplify or adorn one's speech.

(مطا) *maṭa'*, INF. *maṭ'*, lie with.

مطا *maṭan*, *mata*, pl. *amṭâ'*, back; protection; yawning (s.); rope of palm-fibre or bast.

مطابقة *muṭâbaqa-t*, conformity, homogeneousness, congruity; direct antithesis.

مطابة *muṭâbba-t*, medical treatment, cure.

مطاحين *maṭâḥîn*, pl. of مطحان *miṭḥân*, mill.

مطاخ *maṭṭâḥ*, stupid, proud, inflated.

مطادة *maṭâda-t*, pl. *maṭâwid*, extended desert.

مطار *maṭâr*, *maṭṭâr*, swift, fleet; also ة *maṭâra-t*, having a wide mouth (well); — ة *maṭâra-t*, tract abounding with birds; — *muṭâra-t*, carrier-pigeon.

مطارنة *maṭârina-t*, مطارين *maṭârîn*, pl. of مطران *miṭrân*.

مطاريق *maṭâriq*, pl. of مطراق *miṭrâq*.

مطاط *maṭâṭ*, thick sour camel's milk; — *miṭâṭ*, *muṭâṭ*, lengthy, far-stretching.

مطاعين *maṭâ'în*, pl. of مطعان *miṭ'ân*.

مطاعيم *matâ'îm*, pl. of مطعوم *maṭ'ûm*.

مطاف *maṭâf*, procession; circuit; haunting of a ghost; also *muṭâf*, sacred place, tomb, &c. round which a procession is made.

مطافيل *muṭâfîl*, pl. of مطفل *mutfil*.

مطاق *muṭâq*, rendered possible.

مطال *miṭâl*, prolongation, delay; — *maṭṭâl*, who defers, delays; helmet-maker; — ة *miṭâla-t*, the profession of such.

مطالبى *maṭâlibiyy*, impostor.

مطالعة *muṭâla'a-t*, observation, consideration, examination; attentive reading; letter.

مطالق *maṭâliq*, pl. of منطلق *munṭaliq*, ag. of (طلق VII.).

مطالى *maṭâlî*, pl. of مطلا *miṭlâ*.

مطامير *maṭâmîr*, pl. of مطمورة *maṭmûra-t*.

مطانب *muṭânib*, tent-neighbour.

مطاوح *muṭâwiḥ*, dangerous parts to which one comes.

مطاود *maṭâwid*, pl. of مطادة *maṭâda-t*.

مطايا *maṭâyâ*, pl. of مطية *maṭiyya-t*.

مطبخ *maṭbaḥ*, pl. *maṭâbiḥ*, kitchen, cooking place; — *miṭbaḥ*, cooking utensils, spoons, &c.; — *muṭabbiḥ*, still growing boy; young of the lizard; — *; — ى *maṭbaḥiyy*, referring to the kitchen, culinary; cook.

مطبع *maṭba'*, ة *maṭba'a-t*, pl. *maṭâbi'*, printing-place, printing-house; — *miṭba'a-t*, pl. *maṭâbi'*; printing-press; — *muṭabba'*, trained (horse); dried (fig); — *.

مطبق *muṭbaq*, covered; folded up; fit; — *muṭbiq*, covering, comprising, encompassing; complete, perfect, entire, general, integral; lasting; — *muṭabbaq*, doubled; closed; fallen in and covering the ground (roof, &c.); — *.

مطبوب *maṭbûb*, placed on its orifice (vessel); bewitched.

مطبوخ *maṭbûḥ*, cooked, &c.; decoction; ripe, mature, experienced; (m.) calendar, almanac.

مطبوع *maṭbû'*, impressed, printed, &c.; sealed; inborn; natural, genuine, simple, pleasant, handsome, excellent..

مطثة *miṭassa-t*, mallet, bat, racket.

مطجن *muṭajjan*, baked in a pan;— *muṭajjana-t*, broth, gravy, stew, ragout.

(مطح) *maṭaḥ*, INF. *maṭḥ*, beat with the hand, slap; lie with.

مطحان *miṭḥân*, ة *miṭḥâna-t*, pl. *maṭâḥîn*, mill; — ة *miṭḥâna-t*, small dish.

مطحر *miṭḥar*, ة, flying far (arrow);

embittered (warfare); — *miṭḥara-t*, spear.

مطحنة *maṭḥana-t*, bakehouse; also *miṭḥana-t*, pl. *maṭâḥin*, mill; — *miṭḥana-t*, small dish.

مطحوم *maṭḥûm*, full.

(مطخ) *maṭaḥ*, INF. *maṭḥ*, eat much; lick; draw water; slap; blacken one's character; — ة *miṭaḥḥa-t*= مطثة *miṭassa-t*.

(مطر) *maṭar*, U, INF. *maṭr*, *maṭar*, rain, rain upon; overwhelm with benefits; fill; take away (ب *bi*); — INF. *muṭûr*, wander through, travel over, travel; INF. *maṭr*, *muṭûr*, step apace; — IV. INF. *imṭâr*, cause to rain; rain; send down;—V. INF. *tamaṭṭur*, expose one's self to the rain.

مطر *maṭr*, pl. *amṭâr*, skin bag for oil; — *muṭr*, custom, usage; — *maṭar*, pl. *amṭâr*, rain; — *maṭir*, rainy; — *muṭirr*, breaking forth (anger); — ة *maṭra-t*, shower of rain, downpour; also *maṭira-t*, *muṭirra-t*, custom, usage; — *maṭara-t*, large water-bag, field-flask.

مطرا *muṭarr-an*, *muṭarra*, ة ,=مطرى *muṭarra-n*; — ة *muṭarrât*, perfumed water.

مطراق *miṭrâq*, pl. *maṭârîq*, following one another in regular order.

مطران *miṭrân*, *maṭrân*, pl. *maṭârina-t*, *maṭârîn*, metropolitan (s.), archbishop.

مطرب *matrab*, ة *maṭraba-t*, pl. *maṭârib*, narrow road, path; — *muṭrib*, cheering, delighting; musician; singer, dancer.

مطرح *maṭraḥ*, place where anything is thrown; mattress;—*miṭraḥ*, far-sighted; — *muṭraḥ*, abject;— *.

مطرد *miṭrad*, pl. *maṭârid*, short hunting spear;—*muṭrad*, banishment; — *muṭarrid*, *muṭarrad*, flowing along freely, repeating itself always in the same manner; steady, firm, constantly observed; periodical; —ة *maṭrada-t*, *miṭrada-t*, high road.

مطرف *muṭraf*, *miṭraf*, pl. *maṭârif*, square garment of silk, bordered and embroidered with figures; — *muṭarraf*, new, fresh, recently past; beginning; rhymed (prose); — *.

مطرق *miṭraq*, ة *miṭraqa-t*, pl. *maṭâriq*, stick for beating wool, tanner's beater, mallet, bat, racket; fighting-club; rapier; sledge-hammer; — *muṭraq*, *muṭraqa-t*, leathern shield; — *muṭarriq*, in the throes of childbirth; — *.

مطرنية *maṭraniyya-t*, episcopal dignity; دار الم *dâr al-maṭraniyya-t*, bishopric.

مطروح *maṭrûḥ*, thrown about, abject, abandoned, abolished; laid (foundations); remainder in subtraction.

مطرور *maṭrûr*, sharpened, polished; — *.

مطروف *maṭrûf*, repelled, &c.; (m.) oil-press.

مطرى *muṭarran*, *muṭarra*, f. مطراة *muṭarrât*, perfumed; made up for show.

مطرير *miṭrîr*, impudent and boisterous woman.

(مطز) *maṭaz*, U, INF. *maṭz*, lie with.

(مطس) *maṭas*, I, INF. *maṭs*, box the ear; drop excrement.

(مطع) *maṭa*, INF. *maṭ'*, *muṭû'*, depart and disappear; chew with the fore-part of the mouth.

مطعام *maṭ'âm*, food, eatable; *miṭ'âm*, very hospitable.

مطعان *maṭ'ân*, pl. *maṭâ'in*, *maṭâ'în*, who is skilled in the use of a lance, pierces with it.

مطعم *maṭ'am*, food, nourishment; taste; — *; — ة *muṭ'ima-t*, hunting-bow; gullet, alimentary canal; du. the two strongest claws of a bird of prey.

مطعن *maṭ'an*, exposed to blame; — *miṭ'an*=مطعان *maṭ'ân*.

مطعوم *maṭ'ûm*, anything eatable, pl. *maṭâ'îm*, grafting (s.), inoculation, vaccination.

مطعون *maṭ'ûn*, pierced; rebuked;

cursed; afflicted with the plague.

مطغمش• *muṭagmiś*, shortsighted, purblind; weak; hidden.

مطف• *muṭiff*, possible; versed in; — *.

مطفاة• *miṭfât*, مطفاية• *miṭfâya-t*, extinguisher.

مطفحة• *miṭfaḥa-t*, skimmer.

مطفل• *muṭfil*, pl. *maṭâfil*, *maṭâfîl*, mother with child, dam with her young.

مطفى• *muṭfa'*, *maṭfiyy*, extinguished; — مطفى الرضف• *muṭfî arraḍf*, extinguishing the fire, calamity.

مطق• *maṭaq*, a disease of the palm-tree; — ة *maṭqa-t*, sweetness; — V. INF. *tamaṭṭuq*, taste; smack the lips.

(مطل•) *maṭal*, U, INF. *maṭl*, melt and forge iron into a helmet; prolong, stretch, lengthen; delay, defer; — III. INF. *miṭâl*, *mumâṭala-t*, delay, put off, keep waiting; — VIII. INF. *imtiṭâl*, id.; be densely grown.

مطل• *muṭl*, delay, respite; — ة *maṭla-t*, *maṭala-t*, muddy remains of water.

مطلا• *miṭlâ*, *miṭlâ'*, pl. *maṭâlî*, rich low ground; lair; narrow canal; — *muṭalla*, gilt.

مطلب• *maṭlab*, ة *maṭlaba-t*, pl. *maṭâlib*, demand, request, question; purpose, intention, aim; what is sought for; buried treasure; — *.

مطلسون• *maṭlasûn*, rafter.

مطلع• *maṭla'*, pl. *maṭâli'*, place of rising, sun-rise; beginning, first hemistich of a verse; — *muṭli'*, allowing an insight into; towering over; — *muṭalla'*, skilful, apt; towering height; resurrection; — *; — ة *muṭla'a-t*, high point; watch-tower.

مطلق• *muṭlaq*, set free, &c.; absolute, general, uncontrolled; supreme; open (air); — *muṭliq*, setting free; purging; — *muṭallaq*, ة, separated, divorced.

مطلوب• *maṭlûb*, desired, &c.; desire, demand, wish; aim, end; — ة *maṭlûba-t*, asked in marriage; what is desired.

مطلوس• *maṭlûs*, rafter.

مطلى• *maṭliyy*, besmeared; gilt; bound; — *muṭalla*, gilt.

مطليق• *miṭlîq*, who divorces frequently.

مطمار• *miṭmâr*, mason's plumb-line; shape, form, figure.

مطمان• *muṭma'an*, reliable; resting-place.

مطمح• *muṭmaḥ*, lifted up, raised (look); pl. *maṭâmiḥ*, place to which the eye is lifted up, sight, spectacle.

مطمر• *miṭmar*, plumb-line; — ة *muṭmira-t*, *muṭammira-t*, dangerous matter.

مطمس• *muṭmas*, blinded, blind.

(مطمط•) *maṭmaṭ*, INF. ة, be very slow; — II. INF. *tamaṭmuṭ*, be thick.

مطمع• *maṭma'*, ة *maṭma'a-t*, pl. *maṭâmi'*, anything desired or desirable, desire; — *.

مطملة• *miṭmala-t*, dough-roller.

مطمه• *muṭammah*, long, tall.

مطمورة• *maṭmûra-t*, pl. *maṭâmîr*, hole in the earth for corn, &c.; casemate.

مطموس• *maṭmûs*, blinded, blind; effaced, blotted out.

مطمئن• *muṭma'inn*, tranquillised, set at rest, comforted; flat, even, level, equal.

مطنب• *maṭnab*, space between shoulder and neck; — *muṭannab*, pitched (tent).

مطنجنة• *muṭanjana-t*, gravy, stew, ragout.

مطهر• *maṭhar*, place of purification, purgatory; — *miṭhar*, instrument; — ة *maṭhara-t*, what serves to clean; also *miṭhara-t*, pl. *maṭâhir*, washing-basin or jug; toothpick; place for ablutions; field-flask; provision-

bag ; — ية *maṭhariyya-t*, purity ; cleanliness.

مطهم *muṭahham*, accomplished, perfect ; of great beauty ; clumsy and fat.

(مطو) *maṭâ*, U, INF. *maṭw*, walk apace, hasten ; travel far ; stretch, extend ; urge to haste ; keep faithfully to ; lie with ; yawn ; open (the eyes) ; — IV. INF. *imṭâ'*, take a beast for riding, mount, burden ; — V. INF. *tamaṭṭî*, lengthen (n.), draw long ; stretch one's self and yawn ; walk along proudly ; — VI. INF. *tamâṭî*, yawn ; — VIII. INF. *imtiṭâ'* = IV.

مطو *maṭw*, *miṭw*, pl. *miṭâ'*, *maṭiyy*, *amṭâ'*, anything long, stretched ; split palm-branch used as a string ; — *miṭw*, equal, companion, comrade ; pl. *miṭâ'*, stalk of a bunch of dates ; ear of millet ;— ة *maṭwa-t*, hour.

مطوا *muṭawâ'*, stretching (s.) ; yawning (s.).

مطواح *miṭwâḥ*, stick, cudgel.

مطواع *miṭwâ'*, submissive, docile, obedient.

مطوع *muṭawwi'*, voluntary ; — ة *muṭawwi'a-t*, volunteers for the holy war.

مطوقة *muṭawwaqa-t*, ring-dove.

مطول *maṭûl*, who delays payment, &c. ; — *miṭwal*, pl. *maṭâwil*, tether.

مطوى *maṭwa*, pl. *maṭâwî*, fold, wrinkle ; roll, page of a book ; — *maṭwiyy*, folded, rolled up ; contained inside ; intended, resolved upon ; occupied ; walled up.

مطى *maṭan*, *maṭu*, pl. *amṭâ'*, stretching (s.), extension ; back ; — ة *maṭiyya-t*, pl. *maṭâyâ*, *amṭâ'*, beast for riding, beast of burden.

مطيبة *maṭyaba-t*, pl. *maṭâyib*, sweetness, delicacy ; pl. choice (dates) ;—*muṭayyaba-t*, Medina.

مطير *maṭyar*, flight (كل مطير *kull-a maṭyar-in*, in all directions) ; — *maṭîr*, rained upon ; — *muṭair*, rain-drop ; — *muṭayyar*, fresh, verdant ; painted with birds ; عود م *'aud muṭayyar*, wood of aloes.

مطيق *muṭîq*, able to, powerful ; enabling, making possible.

مطين *maṭîn*, *muṭayyan*, coated or smeared with mud.

(مظ) *maẕẕ*, U, INF. *maẕẕ*, make little of, blame ; — III. INF. *miẕâẕ*, *mumâẕẕa-t*, be hostile to, dispute with, cling to one's adversary.

مظ *maẕẕ*, pomegranate ; sap of the root of the tree ارطى *arṭa*.

مظارير *maẕârîr*, pl. of مظرور *muẕrûr*.

مظاظ *miẕâẕ*, dispute, ill-will ; — ة *maẕâẕa-t*, strength ; violence, roughness, hardness.

مظال *maẕâll*, pl. of *miẕalla-t*.

مظالمة *muẕâlama-t*, tyranny, oppression.

مظان *maẕânn*, pl. of مظنة *maẕinna-t*.

مظرة *miẕarra-t*, sharp flint stone ; — *maẕarra-t*, place abounding with flint stones.

مظرور *maẕrûr*, pl. *maẕârîr*, sharp stone.

مظروف *maẕrûf*, contained in a vessel ; enveloped.

(مظع) *maẕa'*, INF. *maẕ'*, soften a sinew and make it pliable ; — II. INF. *tamẕî'*, butter or grease much ; — V. INF. *tamaẕẕu'*, lick or lap up all ; lag behind.

مظفار *miẕfâr*, successful and victorious ; hair-pincers.

مظفر *muẕaffar*, favoured with success and victory, victor, conqueror ; having obtained a thing.

مظلام *miẕlâm*, dark, mysterious.

مظلف *muẕallaf*, with a cloven hoof ; increased.

مظلم *muẕlim*, dark, &c. ; dark green ; jet-black ; mysterious ; unknown, obscure ; disastrous, ominous ; — *muẕallam*, pelican ; crow ; — * ; — ة *maẕlama-t*, pl. *maẕâlim*, oppression, cruelty, tyranny ; civil wrong ; complaint and demand to be righted.

مظلّة *mizalla-t, mazalla-t,* pl. *mazâll,* sunshade; shading roof, baldachin, pavilion, tent, bower, tabernacle.

مظلوم *mazlûm,* wronged, oppressed, &c.; innocent, gentle, modest.

(مظمظ) *mazmaz,* INF. ة, swing to and fro (a.).

مظنّة *mazinna-t,* pl. *mazânn,* opinion, surmise, suspicion, object of suspicion; suspicious; place where a thing is supposed to be.

(مظح) *mazah,* U, INF. *mazh,* set out on a journey, travel through.

مظهر *mazhar,* place where anything appears, happens or is to be seen; stage, scene; person or object in which anything manifests itself; ascent, stairs; — *muzahhar,* having a strong back; — *.

مع *ma',* *ma'a,* with, together with, at the same time with, along with, along; مع ذلك *ma' zâlik,* in spite of this, nevertheless; مع ان *ma' an,* although.

(مع) *ma'',* U, INF. *ma'',* melt (n.).

معا *ma'an,* at the same time, together.

معاب *ma'âb,* ة *ma'âba-t,* pl. *ma'â'ib,* blameworthy action or quality, fault, vice.

معابد *ma'âbid,* pl. of عبد *'abd,* slave, &c., and of معبد *ma'bad.*

معاتيق *ma'âtîq,* pl. of معتوق *ma'tûq,* ag. of (عتق).

معاث *ma'âs,* road, wide passage; law; rule; — ة *ma'âssa-t,* quiver, trill.

معاج *ma'âj,* place of resort.

معاجين *ma'âjîn,* pl. of معجون *ma'jûn.*

معاد *ma'âd,* return; place where one returns to; resurrection, the other world, Paradise; Mecca.

معاداة *mu'âdât,* enmity.

معادل *mu'âdil,* restoring the equilibrium, &c.; symmetrical; proportional; just; — ة *mu'âdala-t,* equilibrium, equality, symmetry, proportionality; equation (in mathematics); justice.

معاد *mu'âd-in,* معادى *mu'âdî,* enemy.

معاذ *ma'âz,* ة *ma'âza-t,* refuge, asylum; — ة *ma'âza-t,* amulet.

معاذير *ma'âzîr,* pl. of معذار *mi'zâr.*

معار *mi'âr,* running away with its rider; — *mu'âr,* borrowed; — ة *ma'âra-t,* perverseness, maliciousness; — ى *ma'ârî,* uncovered parts of the body.

معاريج *ma'ârîj,* pl. of معراج *mi'râj.*

معاريض *ma'ârîd,* pl. of معراض *mi'râd.*

معاز *mi'âz,* goat; — *ma''âz,* owner of goats, goat's-herd.

معازيل *mu'âzîl,* pl. of اعزل *a'zal,* who secludes himself, &c., and of معزل *ma'zal.*

معاس *ma''âs,* bold, brave.

معاش *ma'âś,* life, living, livelihood; board, pay, wages, salary; place where one lives.

معاشقة *mu'âśaqa-t,* amorousness, being in love (s.).

معاشيب *ma'âśîb,* pl. of معشاب *mi'-śâb.*

معاصاة *mu'âṣât,* rebellion; — *.

معاصير *ma'âṣîr,* pl. of معصار *mi'ṣâr.*

معاطف *ma'âṭif,* pl. bends, curves, inflections; — ة *mu'âṭafa-t,* friendly inclination, sympathy.

معاطى *ma'âṭî, ma'âṭiyy,* pl. of معطاء *mi'ṭâ'.*

معاف *mu'âf,* see معافى *mu'âfa.*

معافاة *mu'âfât,* health, welfare; pardon; protection.

معافى *mu'âfa* (معاف *mu'âf*), pardoned, excused, acquitted; exempt, dispensed, privileged; free from harm; — *mu'âfî,* ة *mu'afiyya-t,* exemption, privilege, immunity.

معاقة *ma'âqa-t,* depth.

معاك *ma'âk,* refuge; custom, usage, rule; sect; possibility, probability; gaining one's subsistence, INF. of (عوك); — ة *ma'âka-t,* quarrelsomeness, stupidity; — *mu'âkka-t,* bend, turn.

معاكسة *mu'âkasa-t,* reversal of a proposition, contradiction.

معاكيس *ma'âkîs*, pl. of معكوس *ma'kûs*.

معال *mu'âl*, *mu'âl-in*, see معالى *mu'âlî*; — ة *ma'âla-t*, food, fodder; calamity.

معالج *mu'âlij*, who manages, &c.; physician; cook; — ة *mu'âlaja-t*, cure, medical treatment; dispute; haggling; — *.

معالى *ma'âlî*, pl. of معلاة *ma'lât*; — *mu'âlî* (معال *mu'âl-in*, *mu'âl*), higher part; high, tall, great.

معاليق *ma'âlîq*, pl. of معلاق *mi'lâq* and معلوق *ma'lûq*.

معامل *mu'âmil*, who acts with, who promotes, &c.; — ة *mu'âmala-t*, transaction, management, treatment, behaviour; affair, business, traffic, commerce; currency; dissimulation, appearance, false show; province, district, pl. *mu'âmalât*, political relations, transactions, or intercourse.

معامى *ma'âmî*, pl. of معماة *mi'mât*.

معان *ma'ân*, station, resting-place, seat; a town in Syria; — ة *mu'âna-t*, careful management; suffering, bearing (s.); resistance.

معاند *mu'ânid*, obstinate, headstrong, stubborn; adversary, rebel; — ة *mu'ânada-t*, obstinacy, refractoriness.

معانة *ma'âna-t* (*mu'âna-t*), pl. معاون *ma'âwin*, help, assistance; — *mu'ânna-t*, resistance.

معانيق *ma'ânîq*, pl. of معناق *mi'nâq*.

معاهر *mu'âhir*, ة *mu'âhira-t*, fornicatress; — *mu'âhara-t*, fornication.

معاود *mu'âwid*, accustomed, &c.; always zealous; brave one; — ة *mu'âwada-t*, return; backsliding, relapse; repetition; continuous zeal.

معاوز *ma'âwiz*, pl. of عوز *'awaz*, need, want, and of معوز *mi'waz*.

معاوضة *mu'âwaḍa-t*, requital, retaliation; compensation, damages, restitution; exchange, substitution.

معاومة *mu'âwama-t*, contract for a year; allowing an increase of the debt to obtain a delay of payment.

معاون *ma'âwin*, pl. of معانة *ma'âna-t*; — *mu'âwin*, helper, assistant, adjutant, substitute, coadjutor; — ة *mu'âwana-t*, help, assistance, mutual succour; subvention, subsidy, favour.

معاوية *mu'âwiya-t*, whelp of a fox; hot bitch (ابو م *abû mu'âwiya-t*, hunting-panther); a male proper name.

معايى *ma'âyî*, معايا *ma'âyâ*, pl. of معيى *mu'yî*.

معايب *ma'âyib*, *ma'â'ib*, pl. of معاب *ma'âb*, ة.

معاير *ma'âyir*, *ma'â'ir*, pl. of معيار *mi'yâr* and معيرة *ma'îra-t*; — ة *mu'âyara-t*, gauging of a measure or weight.

معاينة *mu'âyana-t*, seeing with one's own eyes, &c.; evidence of an eye-witness; autopsy, inquest; supervision.

معبا *ma'ba'*, path; rule; sect.

معبد *ma'bad*, pl. *ma'âbid*, place of worship, temple, church; — *mi'bad*, shovel, spade, mattock; — *mu'abbad*, subdued, enslaved, tamed; of high rank; — ة *ma'bada-t*, pl. of عبد *'abd*, slave, &c.; — *mu'abbada-t*, tarred (ship).

معبر *ma'bar*, pl. *ma'âbir*, *ma'âbîr*, place of passing or crossing, crossing, ferry, ford, pass; — *mi'bar*, pl. *ma'âbir*, boat, ferry-boat, bridge, pontoon; — *mu'bar*, ة, almost full grown and not yet circumcised; — *mu'abbir*, interpreter of dreams; — *.

معبق *mu'abbaq*, filled, satiated, surfeited; heavy (head), oppressed (heart).

معبلة *mi'bala-t*, pl. *ma'âbil*, long and broad arrow-head.

معبود *ma'bûd*, adored, &c.; idol; — اء *ma'bûdâ'*, pl. of عبد *'abd*, slave, &c.; — ية *ma'bûdiyya-t*, being adored (s.), divinity.

معبور *ma'bûr*, crossed, &c.; ford, crossing, pass.
معبوق *ma'bûq*=معبق *mu'abbaq*.
معبى *mu'abba*, full; stopped (pipe).
(معث) *ma'as*, INF. *ma's*, rub, knead.
معتاد *mu'tâd*, accustomed, customary, usual, of every day; custom, habit, usage.
معتاق *mi'tâq*, who gallops.
معتب *ma'tab*, abuse, fault-finding, INF. of (عتب); — *mu'tib*, burdensome, importunate; — ة *mu'taba-t*, invective, obloquy, blame.
معتبر *mu'tabar*, honoured, respected, honourable, honest; worthy of credit; accredited; authenticated; valid; considerable; well considered.
معتد *mu'tad*, made ready; — *mu'tadd*, counted, reckoned in, included.
معتدل *mu'tadil*, keeping in equilibrium, &c.; moderate; of medium height: proportional, symmetrical; equal; mild, pleasant; (m.) corpulent.
معتدى *mu'tadî*, encroaching, hostile.
معتر *mu'tarr*, poor, needy; begging boldly.
معترض *mu'tariḍ*, who opposes, &c.; by way of parenthesis.
معترف *mu'taraf* (له *la-hu*), father confessor.
معترك *mu'tarak*, battle-field.
معترى *mu'tara*, suddenly overtaken by calamity; seized by an ague or rigor; — *mu'tarî*, surprising, befalling suddenly.
معتزل *mu'tazil*, who secedes, separatist, nonconformist, sectarian.
معتصر *mu'taṣir*, pressed out, &c. (كريم الم *karîm al-mu'taṣar*, who gives willingly when requested); refuge; long life, duration, age.
معتصم *mu'taṣam*, refuge.
معتضد *mu'taḍid*, who claims his right, seeks redress, asks for help.
معتق *mu'attaq*, old, ancient; old and exquisite; — ة *mu'attaqa-t*, old wine, perfume.
معتقدات *mu'taqadât*, articles of a creed.
معتكف *mu'takaf*, place of silent devotion.
معتكل *mu'takil*, complicated, entangled.
معتل *mu'tall*, ill, weak, faint; م العين *mu'tall al-'ain*, verb whose second radical is و or ى.
معتلب *mu'atlab*, lax, loose.
معتم *mu'tim*, *mu'attam*, dark, obscure; faint, dull, not clear (colour).
معتمد *mu'tamad*, man of trust; foreman; book-keeper; — *.
معتوب *ma'tûb*, scolded, blamed, &c.; blameworthy; cursed.
معتوه *ma'tûh*, weak of intellect, childish, doting.
معثب *mu'assab*, eaten by moths.
معثر *mu'assar*, overthrown, humbled, miserable; — ة *ma'sara-t*, pl. *ma'âsir*, stumbling-block.
(معج) *ma'aj*, INF. *ma'j*, walk hurriedly, hasten; blow gently; stir up the collyrium; lie with; — V. INF. *tama''uj*, bend (n.), fold itself up.
معج *ma'j*, combat, excitement; — *mu'ijj*, windy and dusty; — ة *ma'ja-t*, beginning; first bloom.
معجاز *mi'jâz*, who always lags behind, sluggard, weakling; difficult road.
معجب *ma'jab*, ة *ma'jaba-t*, place, object or cause of wonder; — *.
معجر *mi'jar*, under-bonnet of women.
معجز *ma'jaz*, *ma'jiz*, ة *ma'jaza-t*, *ma'jiza-t*, weakness, powerlessness, impotence; — *mu'jiz*, *mu'ajjiz*, weakening, humiliating, making the adversary feel his weakness; molesting, importuning; *mu'jiz*, ة *mu'jiza-t*, wonder, miracle; — *.
معجس *ma'jis*, pl. *ma'âjis*, hand-piece of the bow; bridge of the nose.

معجم *ma'jam*, venerable ;—*mu'jam*, pointed (letter) ; alphabet ; shut, locked ; dark, obscure, unintelligible ; INF. of (عجم) ; — ة *ma'jama-t*, fatness, strength.

معجن *mi'jan*, kneading-trough.

معجوق *ma'jûq*, (m.) in distress, embarrassed ; pressed.

معجون *ma'jûn*, kneaded, &c. ; pl. *ma'âjîn*, dough, paste, jam, electuary ; putty, cement.

معجونجى (m.) *ma'jûnjî*, apothecary, quack.

(معد) *ma'ad*, INF. *ma'd*, travel over ; snatch, take away ; INF. *ma'd*, *mu'ûd*, carry off, rob (ب *bi*) ; hurt in the stomach ; pass. have stomach-ache or gastric fever.

معد *ma'd*, fresh and ripe ; big, thick, compact ; thickness, compactness ; — *ma'add*, side of the back, side, flank, belly ; name of the first ancestor of an Arabian tribe, *Ma'add* son of *'Adnân* ; — * ; — ة *ma'ida-t*, *mi'da-t*, pl. *ma'id*, *mi'ad*, human stomach, belly.

معدان *ma'dân*, having a large stomach.

معدكة *mi'daka-t*, fuller's beater.

معدم *mu'dim*, destroying, annihilating ; depriving, robbing ; poor, needy.

معدن *ma'din*, *ma'dan*, pl. *ma'âdin*, mine ; mineral, metal (علم المعادن *'ilm al-ma'âdin*, mineralogy, metallurgy) ; origin, first principle ; —*mi'dan*, pick-axe for minerals ; — *mu'addin*, miner ; — ى *ma'diniyy*, mineral (adj.), metallurgic ;—يات *ma'daniyya-t*, minerals, metals.

معدو *ma'duww*, treated with hostility.

معدود *ma'dûd*, ة, numbered, reckoned, numerable, small in number ; الايام المعدودات *al-ayâm al-ma'dûdât*, the three days of *taśrîq* after the feast of Bairam.

معدور *ma'dûr*, hacked up ; mattock, hoe, pick-axe.

معدوس *ma'dûs*, having moles.

معدول *ma'dûl*, distorted ; derived (word) ; quiescent (letter).

معدوم *ma'dûm*, missed, lost, not in existence, not real ; — ات *ma'dûmât*, things not real.

معدى *mu'da*, passage, thoroughfare ; — *mu'dî*, passing over ; contagious, catching ; —*mu'addî*, transitive ; —*ma'diyy*=معدو *ma'duww* ; — *ma'adiyy*, ة, coarse, rough ; — ة *ma'diyya-t*, *mu'addiya-t*, ferry-boat, raft.

معذار *mi'zâr*, veil ; excuse.

معذر *mu'azzar*, feast on account of the circumcision ; cheek of a horse ; — * ; — ة *ma'zara-t*, *ma'zira-t*, *ma'zara-t*, pl. *ma'âzir*, excuse.

معذور *ma'zûr*, excused ; excusable ; deceived.

(معر) *ma'ir*, A, INF. *ma'ar*, be spare (hair, &c.) ; lose all the hair ; fall off ; — II. INF. *ta'mîr*, distort the face (in anger) ; (also IV.) grow poor, have nothing to live upon ; — IV. INF. *im'âr*, be spare ; have but little vegetation ; see II. ; — V. INF. *tama''ur*, fall out ; be distorted, disfigured (with anger).

معر *ma'ir*, ة, with spare hair, feathers, or vegetation ; having the hair or nails dropped ; miserable (s.) ; — ة *mu'ra-t*, reddish colour ; — *ma'arra-t*, crime ; disgrace ; injury ; blood-money, debt.

معرا *ma'râ'*, f. of امعر *am'ar*=معر *ma'ir*.

معراج *mi'râj*, pl. *ma'ârîj*, ascent, stairs, ladder ; ascension (ليلة الم *laila-t al-mi'râj*, night of Mohammed's journey).

معراض *mi'râḍ*, pl. *ma'ârîḍ*, argument of a speech, &c. (pl. parables, aphorisms, apophthegms) ; unfeathered arrow.

معراة *ma'rât*=معرى *ma'ra*.

معرب *mu'rab*, declined, declinable; — *mu'rib*, *ma'rib*, horse of pure Arab descent; — *mu'arrab*, made Arabic, expressed in good Arabic; put aside, separated.

معربد *mu'arbid*, drunk; quarrelsome, brawler.

معرج *ma'raj*, ascending; also *mi'raj*, pl. *ma'ârij* = معراج *mi'râj*; — *mu'arraj*, crooked, with crooked lines; striped; — *.

معرس *mi'ras*, good cattle-driver; — *mu'ras*, *mu'arras*, resting-place, station; night-camp; — *mu'arris*, traveller.

معرش *mu'arraś*, shaded by foliage or a roof, &c.; (m.) covered with vine (wall).

معرض *ma'raḍ*, pl. *ma'âriḍ*, place where anything is met with; meeting; event, occurrence; opportunity; cause, motive; slave-market; — *miraḍ*, bride's robe of state; garb, wrapper; — *mu'riḍ*, who makes clear, shows; presenting one's self; turning away; *mu'riḍ-an*, from all sides, in all directions; —*mu'arraḍ*, marked on the sole; — *.

معرف *ma'raf*, pl. *ma'ârif*, uncovered parts of a woman: face, hands, &c.; feature; — *mu'arraf*, place of pilgrimage on Mount 'Arafat; — *; — ة *ma'rafa-t*, place where the mane is growing; cock's comb; — *ma'rifa-t*, pl. *ma'ârif*, knowledge, science, intelligence, prudence; skill, art; acquaintance; the article; *ma'rifat-an*, explicitly, definitely.

معرقل *mu'arqal*, complicated, confused; lamed by gout; beset with (a sin).

معرك *ma'rak*, ة *ma'raka-t*, *ma'ruka-t*, pl. *ma'ârik*, battle-field, place of combat, arena; combat, tumult, turmoil; — *.

معروش *mu'arwaś*, sitting in the shade; — ات *ma'rûśât*, vines grown on trelliswork or on arbours.

معروضاة *ma'rûḍât*, petition, report, memoir.

معروف *ma'rûf*, known, &c.; celebrated; acknowledged to be good, fit, decent, becoming; good conduct; obligingness, kindness, favour, bounty; obedience towards God; gratitude; active voice.

معروك *ma'rûk*, rubbed, &c.; (m.) well mixed, stirred up.

معروم *ma'rûm*, bound (book); — *.

معرى *ma'ra*, معراة *ma'rât*, pl. *ma'ârî*, uncovered parts of the body; spot without vegetation; — *mu'arra*, naked, bare, bald; free, exempt; consisting only of radical sounds; put in the nominative case; — *.

(معز) *ma'az*, INF. *ma'z*, separate the goats from the sheep; — *ma'iz*, A, INF. *ma'az*, be hard; possess many goats; — IV. INF. *im'âz*, id.; — V. INF. *tama''uz*, be contracted, wrinkled; — X. INF. *istim'âz*, bestow care and zeal upon.

معز *ma'z*, *ma'az*, ة, pl. *ma'îz*, goat; — معز *mu'z*, pl. of امعز *am'az*, hard, pebbled; — *mu'izz*, who honours, glorifies, makes celebrated.

معزا *ma'zâ'*, f. of امعز *am'az*, hard, pebbly; — *mi'za*, goats (coll.).

معزابة *mi'zâba-t*, old bachelor.

معزال *mi'zâl*, pl. *ma'âzil*, who keeps apart; without a lance, unarmed, weak; stupid.

معزبة *mi'zaba-t*, maid-servant; also *mu'azziba-t*, woman.

معزف *mi'zaf*, ة *mi'zafa-t*, pl. *ma'âzif*, a stringed instrument; a kind of cymbal.

معزق *mi'zaq*, ة *mi'zaqa-t*, pl. *ma'âziq*, shovel, spade.

معزل *ma'zal*, *ma'zil*, pl. *ma'âzil*, place of seclusion or retreat.

معزم *ma'zam*, undertaking, enter-

prise ; — *mu'azzim*, conjurer, sorcerer.

معزول *ma'zûl*, removed, deposed, &c.; pensioned; *ma'zûl-an*, without an office.

معزوم *ma'zûm*, (m.) invited, guest; — *.

معزى *mi'za*, goats; — *ma'ziyy*, that which allusion is made to; — *mi'ziyy*, miserly, avaricious; — *.

(معس) *ma'as*, INF. *ma's*, rub vigorously; lie with; pierce; despise; (m.) crush; — II. INF. *tam'îs*, crush entirely; — V. INF. *tama''us*, be crushed; — VII. INF. *inmi'âs*, id.; — VIII. INF. *imti'âs*, rub the hind parts on the floor.

معس *ma's*, rubbing, crushing (s.); (m.) على المعس *'ala 'l-ma's*, secretly, groping one's way in the dark; — *ma'ass*, place where one seeks a thing; anything sought for.

معسا *mi'sâ'*, marriageable; — ة *mas'ât*, fit, worthy.

معسر *mu'sir*, in a difficult position; (ة *mu'sira-t*, woman in child-birth); poor, needy; — *; — ة *ma'sara-t*, *ma'sura-t*, difficulty, hardship; poverty.

معسكر *mu'askar*, encamped; camp, head-quarters.

معسل *mu'assal*, prepared with honey; — ة *ma'sala-t*, bee-hive with honey.

معسون *ma'sûn*, intoxicating beverage of hashish.

(معش) *ma'aś*, INF. *ma'ś*, rub slightly.

معش *ma'aśś*, request, desire, wish; — ة *ma'aśśa-t*, rugged ground.

معشاب *mi'śâb*, pl. *ma'âśîb*, place abounding with grass.

معشار *mi'śâr*, the tenth, tithe.

معشب *mu'śib*, abounding with grass.

معشر *ma'śar*, pl. *ma'âśir*, companionship, association, troop; family, kindred; *ma'śar-a ma'śar-a*, by tens; — *mu'aśśar*, tenfold; decagon; — ة *mu'aśśara-t*, big with young (in the tenth month).

معشش *mu'aśśaś*, nest; — *.

معشق *ma'śaq*, love.

معشوقية *ma'śûqiyya-t*, loveliness.

(معص) *ma'iṣ*, INF. *ma'aṣ*, limp; be crooked, distorted; — V. INF. *tama''uṣ*, suffer from colic.

معصار *mi'ṣâr*, pl. *ma'âṣîr*, press (for wine, &c.).

معصب *mu'aṣṣib*, chief of a party, party-leader, partizan; — *.

معصر *mi'ṣar*, ة *mi'ṣara-t*, pl. *ma'âṣir*, press (for wine, &c.); — *mu'ṣir*, pl. *ma'âṣir*, *ma'âṣîr*, marriageable (girl); ات *mu'ṣirât*, rain-clouds; — *mu'aṣṣar*, asylum; — *; — *mu'aṣṣir*, oil-presser; — *; — *ma'aṣara-t*, place where anything is pressed.

معصم *mi'ṣam*, pl. *ma'âṣim*, wrist or place on the upper arm where a bracelet is put; name by which a goat is called to be milked.

معصوم *ma'ṣûm*, defended, &c.; innocent; new born, child; exempt; — ية *ma'ṣûmiyya-t*, innocence, childhood.

معصية *ma'ṣiya-t*, pl. *ma'âṣî*, refractoriness, rebellion; sin.

(معض) *ma'iḍ*, INF. *ma'aḍ*, *ma'ḍ*, be angry and grieved; be complicated, difficult; — II. INF. *tam'îḍ*, anger and grieve; — IV. INF. *im'âḍ*, id.; — VIII. INF. *imti'âḍ*, get angry and grieved.

معض *ma'iḍ*, angry and grieved; — *ma'aḍḍ*, place where the first bite is to be made, where anything may be got at.

معضاد *mi'ḍâd*, معضد *mi'ḍad*, pl. *ma'âḍid*, ring for the upper arm; knife to cut fascines with, butcher's knife; — ة *miḍâda-t*, side-pocket (to be suspended round the neck).

معضل *mu'ḍal*, difficult, hard to understand; — *mu'ḍil*, muscular,

strong; ة, difficult; — ات *mu'-ḍilât*, calamities.

(معط) *ma'aṭ*, INF. *ma'ṭ*, stretch, stretch by pulling; draw (the sword); lie with; miscarry; pull out; break wind; (m.) dip into the water; — *ma'iṭ*, A, INF. *ma'aṭ*, have lost the hair, be bald and ugly; — VII. INF. *in-mi'âṭ*, fall out (hair); — VIII. INF. *imti'âṭ*, id.; draw the sword.

معط *mu'ṭ*, pl. of امعط *am'aṭ*, bald, &c.; — *ma'iṭ*, bald; — ة *mu'ṭa-t*, baldness (ابو م *abû mu'ṭa-t*, wolf).

معطا *ma'ṭâ*, f. of امعط *am'aṭ* (see the previous); — *mi'ṭâ'*, pl. *ma'âṭî*, *ma'âṭiyy*, one very liberal.

معطار *mi'ṭâr*, ة, strongly perfumed.

معطال *mi'ṭâl*, unadorned (woman).

معطب *ma'ṭab*, pl. *ma'âṭib*, dangerous place; danger; fatality; — *mu'ṭib*, economical, thrifty.

معطس *ma'ṭas*, *ma'ṭis*, pl. *ma'âṭis*, nose; — *.

معطش *ma'ṭaś*, pl. *ma'âṭiś*, time when a camel becomes thirsty; — *mu'aṭṭaś*, kept thirsty for a long time; dried up; imprisoned; — ة *ma'ṭaśa-t*, pl. *ma'âṭiś*, dry ground.

معطف *ma'ṭaf*, neck; — *mi'ṭaf*, loose under-garment; sword; bridle; — *.

معطل *mu'aṭṭal*, neglected, disregarded, abolished, antiquated, superannuated, invalid; ineffectual, vain, in vain; escaping; abandoned, uninhabited, uncultivated; injured; unoccupied; lent on interest; — *.

معطن *ma'ṭin*, pl. *ma'âṭin*, resting-place for the cattle round the water; pearl-fishery; — *mu'aṭṭan*, foul, putrid.

معطوف *ma'ṭûf*, bent, &c.; joined by و *wa*, and, or ف *fa*, and then, &c.; — ة *ma'ṭûfa-t*, strongly-bent bow; — ية *ma'ṭûfiyya-t*, connection by و *wa* or ف *fa*.

معطير *mi'ṭîr*, strongly perfumed; using perfumes freely.

معظم *mu'ẓam*, the greater part, majority; best quality or sort; principal, most important; — *; — ة *mu'ẓama-t*, heavy calamity.

معفاج *mi'fâj*, معفجة *mi'faja-t*, stick, cudgel, bludgeon; fuller's beater.

معفرت *mu'afrat*, possessed by the demon عفريت *'ifrît*.

معفس *ma'fis*, joint.

معفش *mu'affaś*, dishevelled, badly combed; hairy and dirty.

معفو *ma'fuww*, *ma'fû*, forgotten, pardoned; included in an amnesty.

(معق) *ma'aq*, INF. *ma'q*, drink greedily; get drunk; swamp, carry away; pass. have the stomach deranged, suffer from indigestion; — *ma'uq*, INF. *ma-'âqa-t*, be deep; — IV. INF. *im'âq*, make deep.

معق *ma'q*, strong wine; malice; indigestion; pl. *am'âq*, vast desert; what a stream carries off; also *mu'q*, removal, remoteness; — ة *ma'aqqa-t*, disobedience, refractoriness.

معقاد *mi'qâd*, amulet worn round the neck.

معقار *mi'qâr*, making sore (saddle).

معقب *mi'qab*, veil; ear-ring; appointed successor; — *; — ات *mu'aqqibât*, the angels of day and night relieving one another.

معقد *ma'qad*, *ma'qid*, pl. *ma'âqid*, place where a knot is made, a business concluded, &c.; knot, tie; — *mu'aqqad*, strongly tied, complicated, intricate, hard to understand; — *; — *mu'aqqid*, who makes knots, sorcerer; who complicates matters; — *.

معقر *mi'qar*=معقار *mi'qâr*; — *mu'qir*, id.; possessing many fields; —

ة *ma'qara-t* = معقرب *mu'aqrib*, see below.

معقرب *mu'aqrab*, strongly bent; twisted, plaited; strongly built, vigorous;—*mu'aqrib*, abounding with scorpions.

معقل *ma'qil*, pl. *ma'âqil*, place which stops or detains one; steep mountain; castle, fortress, stronghold; refuge, asylum; bond, fetter;— ة *ma'qula-t*, pl. *ma'âqil*, blood-money, atonement for murder; — *mu'qala-t*, atoned for (shed blood); — *mi'qala-t*, (m.) & ية *mi'qaliyya-t*, hooked stick.

معقم *ma'qim*, pl. *ma'âqim*, joint of the foot; vertebra; knot, knob (in a reed, &c.).

معقود *ma'qûd*, tied in a knot, &c.; made impotent by sorcery; firm judgment.

معقول *ma'qûl*, seized by the intellect, comprehended, conceived; comprehensible, intelligible; reasonable, wise, considerate; comprehension, understanding; bound, held, restricted; — ات *ma'qûlât*, what is to be seized by the intellect, opposed to محسوسات what is perceived by the senses; metaphysics; — ية *ma'qûliyya-t*, reasonableness, rationality.

معقوم *ma'qûm*, barren; withered.

(معك) *ma'ak*, INF. *ma'k*, rub; roll on the ground; defer, delay, put off; give the sign for combat; vanquish entirely;—*ma'uk*, INF. *ma'âka-t*, be stupid, imbecile; — II. INF. *tam'îk*, roll on the ground (a.); let roll on the ground (a horse); — III. INF. *mumâ'akat*, beat one another, scuffle; — V. INF. *tama''uk*, roll on the ground (n.); — VII. INF. *inmi'âk*, be rubbed.

معك *ma'k*, rubbing (s.); — *ma'ik*, stupid, imbecile; who delays, puts off; also *mi'akk*, quarrelsome.

معكد *ma'kid*, pl. *ma'âkid*, refuge, asylum.

معكل *ma'kal*, prevention, hindrance, obstacle; *mi'kal*, needle; hooked staff, crosier.

معكوس *ma'kûs*, pl. *ma'âkîs*, reversed, topsy-turvy, &c.; contrary; poor; fatal, ominous; miserable; sector; (m.) unhealthy (climate).

معكوف *ma'kûf*, bent, folded, &c.; confiscated.

معكوكا *ma'kûkâ'*, *mu'kûkâ'*, care, grief, sorrow; evil; noise, turmoil, tumult; flying dust.

معكوكة *ma'kûka-t*, plenty, abundance, affluence.

(معل) *ma'al*, INF. *ma'l*, snatch away, rob; hasten (n.); (also IV.) urge to haste, over-hurry (a.); precipitate (a.); walk fast; — IV. INF. *im'âl*, see I.

معل *ma'il*, quick, fast, swift; — *mu'all*, ill, weak.

معلا *mu'alla*, exalted, high, sublime; — ة *ma'lât*, pl. *ma'âlî*, height, greatness, sublimity, dignity, nobility, high virtue, great exploit, merit.

معلاق *mi'lâq*, pl. *ma'âlîq*, what is suspended; ear-ring, pendant; handle, ear; stirrup; peg (to hang upon); door-lock; tongue pl. heart, lungs, liver and spleen.

معلب *mu'allib*, maker of cardboard boxes.

معلف *ma'laf*, pl. *ma'âlif*, feeding-place, stable, manger; — *mi'laf*, fodder-bag; — *.

معلق *ma'laq*, pl. *ma'âliq*, small crocodile; — *mi'laq*, small milk-pail;—*mu'allaq*, suspended, &c.; that on which anything is suspended; attached; attachment; lit (fusee, &c.); pulley of a well; rope of the bucket; bucket; ات *mu'allaqât*, seven old Arabic poems supposed to be suspended in the Kaba; — ة *ma'luqa-t*, blood-money; ذو م *ẕû ma'luqa-t*,

who is everybody's hanger-on; — *mi'laqa-t*, pl. *ma'âliq*, spoon.

معلل *mu'allal*, well founded; in good circumstances; excellent; *mu'allil*, allege pretexts or subterfuges; — *.

معلم *ma'lam*, pl. *ma'âlim*, sign, token, mark, characteristic, signal, road-signs, mile-stones, tracks, trodden paths; desert with road-marks; flag, banner; school, seminary; law, rule, prescript, dogma; surmise; — *mu'lam*, marked, engraved; hemmed (garment); — *mu'allam*, pupil, disciple, apprentice; ة *mu'allama-t*, trained sporting dog; — *mu'allim*, teacher, master, guardian; ة *mu'allima-t*, school, school-mistress; — ية *mu'allamiyya-t*, teaching (s.), instruction.

معلندات *mu'landât*, معلندد *mu'landad*, *mu'landid*, expedients, means of escape.

معلوجا *ma'lûjâ'*, معلوجى *ma'lûja*, pl. of علج *'ilj*, infidel, barbarian, &c.

معلوق *ma'lûq*, suspended, &c.; pl. *ma'âlîq*, grapes suspended for drying; — *mu'lûq*, that to which anything is suspended.

معلول *ma'lûl*, caused, &c.; effect; weak, sickly; pacified; watered (wine).

معلوم *ma'lûm*, known, &c.; clear, evident, certain; of course, yes (in answering); noteworthy, celebrated, distinguished; given (mathematical quantity); coined; date, theme, problem; active voice; income, salary, pension; ات *ma'lûmât*, known things, knowledge, sciences, dates, statements.

معلون *mu'alwan*, provided with an ornamental title.

معلى *mu'lî* (معل *mu'l-in*), who exalts, praises; — *mu'alla*, exalted, most high, praised; — *.

معم *mi'amm*, comprising all, comprehensive, general, universal.

معما *mu'amma*=معمى *mu'amma*; — ة *mi'mât*, *ma'mât*, pl. *ma'âmî*, place where there is nothing to be seen; desolate place; pathless desert.

معمار *mi'mâr*, ى *mi'mâriyy*, pl. *mi'mâriyya-t*, architect, builder; supervisor of a building; — جى *mi'mârjiyy*, mason.

معمد *mu'mad*, high lofty, great; — *mu'ammad*, supported by columns, &c.; love-sick; — *mu'ammid*, supporting, &c.; baptizer.

معمدان *mu'midân*, ى *mu'midâniyy*, baptist (St. John).

معمر *ma'mar*, large well-provided premises or building; — *.

(معمع) *ma'ma'*, INF. ة, travel in hot weather; despatch one's work quickly; — ة *ma'ma'a-t*, crackling or crepitating of the fire; clatter of arms; pl. *ma'âmi'*, noise, tumult, turmoil, combat, battle, war; pl. important matters; alliances; — ى *ma'ma'iyy*, who sides with the successful; coin with the impression مع مع.

معمعان *ma'ma'ân*, great heat; also ى *ma'ma'ânîyy*, very hot.

معمعم *mu'am'am*, swollen, big, numerous.

معمل *ma'mal*, pl. *ma'âmil*, workshop, manufactory; — *mu'mal*, used, employed; trodden (path); — *.

معمم *mu'ammam*, turbaned, &c.; leader, prince; brimful.

معمودانى *ma'mûdâniyy*, baptist, baptizer.

معمودية *ma'mûdiyya-t*, baptism.

معمور *ma'mûr*, cultivated, &c.; البيت الم *al-bait al-ma'mûr*, the house in heaven above the Kaaba; م الجوانب *ma'mûr al-jawânib*, affable, easy of approach, courteous; — ية *ma'mûriyya-t*, state of good cultivation, cosiness, ease, prosperity.

معمول *ma'mûl*, done, made, &c.; artificial; customary; valid;

effect, work; make, performance, execution.

معمى *mu'amma*, riddle, acrostic; enigmatical.

(معن) *ma'an*, INF. *ma'n*, advance quickly and far, get the lead (race-horse); (also IV.) confess; acknowledge a debt; deny one's right; be ungrateful; make water to flow; — IV. INF. *im'ân*, advance quickly and far; (also V.) go far in a matter, work zealously in it, exceed; (also V.) think earnestly of (فى *fî*); fix the look or thoughts intently upon; see I.; — V. INF. *tama''un*, see IV.

معن *ma'n*, water; goat's leather; also ة *ma'na-t*, something, a little; — *mu'un*, pl. of معين *ma'în*.

معناة *ma'nât*, see معنى *ma'nan*.

معناق *mi'nâq*, pl. *ma'ânîq*, having a handsome neck (horse).

معناوى *ma'nâwiyy*=معنوى *ma'nawiyy*.

معنبر *mu'ambar*, perfumed with ambergris; changed, altered.

معنت *mu'nat*, set again (bone); — *mu'nit*, exceedingly importunate; pernicious.

معنتر *mu'antar*, brave like 'Antar.

معنز *mu'annaz*, having a goat's-beard; (m.) swollen; — *.

معنق *ma'niq*, high; — *mu'annaq*, long- or broad-necked; — ة *ma'naqa-t*, uninhabitable, tract; rugged mountain-crag; — *mi'naqa-t*, pl. *ma'ânîq*, necklace; — ات *mu'anniqât*, far-stretching mountains.

معنك *mi'nak*, large bolt; lock.

معنون *ma'nûn*, lunatic; impotent through sorcery; — *mu'anwan*, titled, with an inscription or address.

معنوى *ma'nawiyy*, ة, signifying, included in the meaning, according to the meaning (opposed to لفظى *lafziyy*, according to the sound); intrinsic; true, essential, real; absolute; mental, spiritual, philosophical; speculative; mystical; equivocal, having a double meaning.

معنى *ma'nan*, *ma'na*, معناة *ma'nât*, *ma'niyy*, *man'iya-t*, pl. *ma'âniyy*, sense, meaning, signification; intrinsic nature and value; spirit of a thing, reality; intention, purport; opinion, thought, idea; affair, object, circumstance, fact, state of the case; subject; عالم الم *'âlam al-ma'na*, spiritual world; علم المعنى او المعانى *'ilm al-ma'na, au al-ma'âniyy*, rhetoric; — *ma'niyy*, carefully attending to, concerned about (ب *bi*); — *mu'anna*, tired, exhausted; deeply grieved, afflicted.

معهد *ma'had*, pl. *ma'âhid*, place of appointment, rendezvous; monument; hall.

(معو) *ma'â*, INF. *mu'â'*, mew.

معو *ma'w*, ة, date ripe or on the point of ripening.

معوان *mi'wân*, strong helper, always ready to help.

معوج *mu'awwaj*, bent, crooked; false, unloyal; made of ivory; — *mu'wajj*, crooked.

معود *ma'ûd*, visited and nursed; — *mu'ûd*, INF. of (معد); — *.

معوذتان *mu'awwizatân*, the two last sûras of the Koran.

معور *mu'wir*, base.

معوز *mi'waz*, ة *mi'waza-t*, pl. *ma'âwiz*, every-day dress; swaddling clothes; failure; — *mu'wiz*, needy.

معوشة *ma'ûśa-t*, livelihood.

معوضة *ma'ûḍa-t*, given in compensation, equivalent.

معوق *mu'awwaq*, hindered, delayed; confused, embarrassed; — *mu'awwiq*, hindering, confusing.

معوكر *mu'aukar*, turbid, troubled, with a sediment (m.).

معوكة *ma'waka-t*, combat, battle.

معول *mi'wal*, pl. *ma'âwil*, pickaxe, large hatchet; — *mu'awwal*, confidence; — *.

معونة *ma'ûna-t*, *ma'wana-t*, pl. *ma'ûn*, *mu'âwin*, help, aid, assistance, protection; صاحب المعونة *ṣâḥib al-ma'ûna-t*, minister of police.
معوه *mu'awwah*, weak; ugly, disfigured; (m.) lamed, maimed.
معوود *ma'wûd*=معود *ma'ûd*.
معوى *mi'awiyy*, referring to the intestines, intestinal; — * .
معى *ma'y*, *mi'an*, *mi'a*, pl. *am'â'*, gut, intestines; — *mi'a*, irrigation canal; — ة *ma'iyya-t*, being together, side by side; juxtaposition; company, attendance, retinue; partisanship, partiality; shrewdness.
معيار *mi'yâr*, pl. *ma'âyir*, proof or trade-mark; standard measure or weight, &c., of due weight and alloy; touchstone; shame, disgrace.
معياص *mi'yâṣ*, who raises difficulties.
معيب *ma'îb*, *mu'ayyab*, abused, rebuked; blameworthy; knave; pl. ات fault, vice; — ة *ma'yaba-t*, object of or reason for blame; disgrace.
معيد *mu'îd*, repeating, &c.; able, tried, experienced; well-trained; who brings back all things, God; — * .
معير *mi'yar*, calamity;—*mu'îr*, who lends; — ة *ma'îra-t*, pl. *ma'âyir*, shame, stain of infamy, vice.
معيش *ma'îś*, life; place where one lives; — ة *ma'îśa-t*, pl. *ma'âyiś*, life, living, livelihood; wants; means of enjoyment, المعيشة الضنك *al-ma'îśa-t aḍ-ḍank*, grave, being buried.
معيص *ma'îṣ*, *ma'yaṣ*, dense grove.
معيق *ma'îq*, small; deep; — *mu'îq*, hindering, confusing.
معيكة *ma'îka-t*, buttered toast (m.).
معيل *ma'îl*, need, distress, INF. of (عيل); — *mu'yil*, *mu'îl*, having a numerous family and poor, who has a household; *mu'îl*, lion; leopard; wolf.

معين *ma'în*, pl. *mu'un*, *mu'nân*, water flowing over a surface; source, spring, rill; rhomb (شبيه المعين *śabîh al-ma'în*, rhomboid); = معيون *ma'yûn*; — *mu'în*, helper;—*mu'ayyan*, determined, defined, &c.; assigned, designated; rhomb; with rhombic figures; rue (plant).
معيوراء *ma'yûrâ*, pl. of عير *'air*, wild ass.
معيون *ma'yûn*, معين *ma'în*, looked at with the evil eye; bewitched; gushing forth from a pure well.
معيى *mu'yî*, pl. *ma'âyî*, *ma'âyâ*, weary, tired, exhausted; — *ma'yiyy*=معوى *mi'awiyy*.
مغا *mugâ'*, mewing (s.).
مغا *magâ* ., *migâ* ., *mugâ* ., to be looked for under (. غو , . غي), as—
مغاب *magâb*, INF. of (غيب); absence; accusing or slandering the absent; concealment; — ة *magâbba-t*, final issue, result, success.
مغاث *migâs̱*, dispute, hostility; INF. of (غيث III.); — *mugâs̱*, purgative and vomitive; ة, rained upon.
مغاثير *magâs̱îr*, pl. of مغثور *mugs̱ûr*.
مغاداة *mugâdât*, morning visit.
مغاظ *mugâẓẓ*, hydrophobic (camel).
مغار *magâr*, pl. *magâ'ir*, cave, grotto, loop-hole; — *mugâr*, id.; raid; — *mugârr*, pl. *magârr*, miserly, avaricious; — ة *magâra-t*, *mugâra-t*, cave, grotto, loophole; cleft in the ground, pit; — *mugârra-t*, INF. of (غر III.), scantiness of milk, impotence.
مغاريد *magârîd*, pl. of مغرود *mugrûd*.
مغازلى *magâziliyy*, maker of spindles.
مغاص *magâṣ*, diving; place of diving.
مغافر *magâfir*, pl. of مغفر *migfar*, also *magâfîr*, pl. of مغفار *migfâr*, مغفور *mugfûr*, مغفير *migfîr*.
مغالظة *mugâlaẓa-t*, thickness, compactness; roughness, rudeness.
مغالة *magâla-t*, calumny; treachery, INF. of (مغل).

مغامر *mugâmir*, rushing recklessly into combat, into danger.
مغانى *magânî*, songs, airs; female singers, songstresses; pl. of مغنى *magna*.
مغاوث *magâwis̱*, pl. waters.
مغاوى *magâwî*, pl. of مغواة *magwât*.
مغايبة *mugâyaba-t*, absence from one another; pretending not to see one; talk about the absent;— *.
مغائر *magâ'ir*, pl. of مغارة *magâra-t*; — ة *mugâyara-t*, jealousy, emulation, interchange, contradiction.
مغايير *magâyir*, pl. of مغيار *migyâr*.
مغب *migabb*, ة *magabba-t*, end, issue, result; — *.
مغبر *mugbir*, raising dust; — *mugbarr* (غبر IX.), dust-laden, dirty, dust-coloured; —*mugabbar*, id.; offended.
مغبط *mugabbaṭ*, having deep places (river); irritated.
مغبن *magbin*, pl. *magâbin*, groins; arm-pit.
مغبوطة *magbûṭa-t*, ease, prosperity, good fortune.
مغبون *magbûn*, cheated; stupid, weak.
مغبى *mugabba*, concealed, unintelligible.
مغتا *mugtâ* ., to be looked for under (. غو , . غي VIII.), as—
مغتاب *mugtâb*, ag. of (غيب VIII.), slandering.
مغتال *mugtâl*, assassin.
مغتذى *mugtaẕî*, nourished, fed.
مغتسل *mugtasal*, washing-place, laundry; water for washing; — *.
مغتنم *mugtanam*, considered as a prize, made use of; — *mugtanim*, considering as a prize, taking advantage of, making use of, enjoying.
(مغث) *magas̱*, U, INF. *mags̱*, submerge; dissolve in water, macerate; beat lightly; blacken one's character, dishonour; = III.; mix; — III. INF. *migâs̱*, *mumâgasa-t*, **dispute, fight, wrestle with.**

مغث *mags̱*, combat; vanity, folly; — *magis̱*, good wrestler.
مغثر *migs̱ar*, مغثور *mugs̱ûr*, pl. *magâs̱îr*, juice of plants fit to be consumed.
(مغج) *magaj*, INF. *magj*, run, hasten.
(مغد) *magad*, INF. *magd*, live in luxury, effeminately; grow long and luxuriant; INF. *magd*, *magad*, grow fat, fat; feed luxuriously and effeminately; suck; suck up; — IV. INF. *imgâd*, drink much; give suck.
مغد *magd*, tender, delicate, luxurious, luxuriant, pulpy and juicy; mandrake; a kind of cucumber; *mugidd*, furious; also مغدغد *mugadgid*, being afflicted with a cyst; fat.
مغدر *magdar*, *magdir*, traitor.
مغدف *migdaf*, pl. *magâdif*, oar.
مغدور *magdûr*, betrayed, &c.; (m.) compelled.
مغدى *magda*, morning walk;— *mugaddî*, who gives a breakfast, a dinner.
مغذمر *mugaẕmir*, fantastical person, &c.; leader; who brooks no contradiction.
مغذى *mugẕî*, who gives to eat, feeds; nourishing, strengthening; — *mugaẕẕí*=مغدى *mugaddî*.
(مغر) *magar*, travel fast, travel through; — II. INF. *tamgîr*, mark with red chalk; — ة *magra-t*, *magara-t*, red earth or chalk; (m.) خيط م *ḥaiṭ magra-t*, straight line; — *mugra-t*, *magara-t*, dark reddish colour.
مغراة *migrât*, glue-pot.
مغرب *magrab*, *magrib*, pl. *magârib*, place and time of sun-set; west; North Africa, Barbary; evening; du. west and east; — *mugrib*, who says or does wonderful things, &c.; ingenious; عنقا م *'anqâ' mugrib*, phœnix; — *; — ى *magribiyy*, pl. *magâriba-t*, western, occidental, North African, of Barbary, Magrebian.
مغرد *mugarrad*, *mugarrid*, far dis-

tant ;—*mugarrid*, singing, chirping; modulator.

مغرز *magraz, magriz*, pl. *magâriz*, root, base, seat; place where the wards of a key are put.

مغرس *magris*, pl. *magâris*, place of plantation, plantation, nursery, seed-plot.

مغرض *mugrid*, who keeps to, partisan, partial; intriguer.

مغرف *migraf*, pl. *magârif*, swift, fleet; — ة *migrafa-t*, pl. *magârif*, instrument for scooping, skimmer, large spoon, ladle.

مغرم *magram, mugram*, pl. *magârim*, debt which must needs be paid; — *mugram*, in debt, prisoner for debt; fine; — *.

مغرو *magruww*, glued, pasted over; arrow; spear.

مغرود *mugrûd*, pl. *magârîd*, a kind of mushroom.

مغرور *magrûr*, deceived, &c.; proud, infatuated.

مغروز *magrûz*, put into, &c.; inborn, natural.

مغروسة *magrûsa-t*, confusion, hurly-burly.

مغرى *mugra*, incited, driven to; given to; — *mugrî*, inciting; — *mugarra, magriyy*, glued.

مغزرة *magzara-t*, place of abundance.

مغزال *migzâl*, and—

مغزل *migzal, magzal, mugzal*, pl. *magâzil*, spindle; — *magzal*, love-talk; — ى *migzaliyy*, maker of spindles.

مغزى *magza*, pl. *magâzî*, military expedition, campaign (especially against infidels); war; scene of war; aim, purpose, purport; pl. warlike virtues and deeds.

(مغس) *magas*, INF. *mags*, pierce; feel, touch, grope; — *magis*, also pass. *mugis*=(مغص).

مغس *mags, magas*, colic, gripes.

مغسل *magsal, magsil*, pl. *magâsil*, washing- or bathing-place; washing-tub or bowl; — *migsal*, what is used for washing; — *magsila-t*, laundry.

مغشم *migśam*, bold; self-willed.

مغشوش *magśûś*, falsified, cheated, &c.; deceitful, insincere.

مغشى *mugśa, mugaśśa*, covered, veiled; embroidered;—*magśiyy*, surprised, taken by surprise; م عليه *magśiyy 'alai-hi*, fainting, in a swoon.

(مغص), pass. *mugiṣ*, suffer from colic.

مغص *magṣ*, colic, gripes.

مغضبة *magḍaba-t*, anger, fury, rage.

مغض *mugḍ-in*, مغضى *mugḍî*, dark; dropping or turning aside one's eyes.

(مغط) *magaṭ*, INF. *magṭ*, stretch by pulling; be malleable; make an effort to draw the bow; — V. INF. *tamagguṭ*, stretch (n.); be malleable; stretch one's self out at length; stretch the fore-feet, run very fast, career; — VII. INF. *inmigâṭ* = VIII. INF. *imtigâṭ*, be stretched, extended; be ductile, malleable.

مغط *magṭ*, stretching, extending.

مغطس *migṭas*, pl. *magâṭis*, bathing-tub, bath in it; — *magṭas*, INF. ة, magnetise;—II. INF. *tamagṭus*, pass. of the previous.

مغطى *mugaṭṭa*, covered, veiled.

مغفار *migfâr*, and—

مغفر *migfar, mugfur*, pl. *magâfîr*, *magâfir*=مغثر *migsar*; — *migfar*, ة *migfara-t*, pl. *magâfir*, steel cap, helmet; visor; —*magfara-t*, pardon, indulgence.

مغفل *mugaffal*, careless, neglectful, apathetic, indolent.

مغفور *magfûr*, pardoned; — *mugfûr*, also مغفير *migfîr*, pl. *magâfîr*, *magafir*=مغثر *migsar*.

(مغل) *magal*, INF. *magl*, *magâla-t*, accuse, slander; — U, A, INF. *magl* (also VII.), have colic from swallowing earth (horse); — *magil*, A, INF. *magal* (also IV.), give suck while big with child; — IV. INF. *imgâl*, id.; — VIII. INF. *inmigâl*, see I.

مغل *magl, magal*, milk of a preg-

nant woman ; — *mugall*, ة *mugalla-t*, produce of the harvest ; — *mugill*, traitor ; fruitful in corn ; — ة *magla-t*, colic from swallowing earth.

مغلاط *miglâṭ*, who commits many errors.

مغلاق *miglâq*, pl. *magâlîq*, lock, bolt.

مغلال *miglâl*, yielding abundant crops.

مغلب *maglab*, ة *maglaba-t*, victory, dominion ; — ة *maglaba-t*, place of victory.

مغلط *mugallaṭ*, full of mistakes, abounding with errors ; — ة *maglaṭa-t*, what leads into error, wherein one easily commits an error ; labyrinth ; confused notions ; misleading speech, sophism.

مغلظ *mugallaẕ*, rude, rough ; hard, compact, firm ; rendered difficult.

مغلغل *mugalgal*, inserted ; involved.

مغلف *mugallaf*, in case or envelope, &c. ; envelope ; parcel.

مغلق *miglaq*, pl. *magâliq*, lock, bolt ; what yields a regular income ; — *muglaq*, locked, &c. ; obscure, difficult to understand ; prejudiced.

مغلم *muglim*, hot, rutting ; paederast.

مغلوب *maglûb*, overcome, &c. ; who spends more than he receives ; — ية *maglûbiyya-t*, defeat, submission, servitude.

مغلوط *maglûṭ*, full of mistakes.

مغلوق *muglûq*=مغلاق *miglâq* ; — * .

مغلول *maglûl*, inserted, fettered, &c. ; put in the pillory ; very thirsty.

مغلى *magliyy*, cooked, boiled.

مغليم *miglîm*, ة, hot, rutting.

مغم *mugimm*, distressing, &c. ; covered with clouds ; ة, covered with a dense vegetation.

مغمد *magmad*, pl. *magâmid*, scabbard ; — *

مغمر *mugammar*, rude, uncultivated, inexperienced.

مغمز *magmaz*, object of misinterpretation or blame ; object of desire.

مغمض *magmaḍ*, pl. *magâmiḍ*, low ground ; — * ; — ات *mugammiḍât*, wilfully committed sins.

(مغمغ) *magmag*, INF. ة, chew, masticate (imperfectly) ; mix up, confuse, bring on confusion ; be confused in one's speech ; bungle ; — ة *magmaga-t*, confusion, hurly-burly ; bad case ; mastication ; unintelligible talk.

مغمور *magmûr*, covered ; unknown, obscure ; embraced.

مغمى *magmiyy*, fainting, in a swoon.

مغن *mugn-in*, *mugann-in*, see مغنى *mugni*, *muganni*.

مغناطيس *magnâṭîs*, مغنطيس *magnaṭîs*, magnet, loadstone.

مغناة *magnât*, *mugnât*, compensation, anything substituted for another, sufficiency.

مغنم *magnam*, pl. *magânim*, booty, spoil.

مغنوجة *magnûja-t*, coquette.

مغنى *magna*, pl. *magânî*, pleasant habitation, dwelling, house ; abiding (s.) ; being able to do without (s.) ; expedient ; escape ; the right man in the right place ; — *mugnî* (مغن *mugn-in*), enriching ; compensating for ; rendering possible, making independent of (adj.) ; — *muganni* (مغن *mugann-in*), ة, singer, songster.

مغنيطيس *magnîṭîs*, loadstone.

(مغو) *magâ*, U, INF. *magw*, mew.

مغو *mugw-in*, *mugaww-in*, see مغوى *mugwî*, *mugawwî*.

مغوار *migwâr*, pl. *magâwîr*, *magâwir*, who makes many raids ; warlike ; putting the horse in gallop.

مغواة *magwât*, pl. *magâwî*, tract in which one easily goes astray ; —

mugawwât, pl. *mugawwayât*, id.; pit-fall for game.
مغوثة *magûsa-t*, help, assistance.
مغول *migwal*, long sword; a piece of iron in a whip; ذات م *zât migwal*, very swift (horse); — *.
مغوى *mugwî*, *mugawwî* (مغو *mugw-in*, *mugaww-in*), leading astray, deceiving, deluding; — *; — *magwiyy*, free.
(مغى) *maga*, I, INF. *magy*, speak (vividly and distinctly); (also v.) be soft; — v. INF. *tamaggî*, see I.
مغيب *magîb*, absence, disappearance, sunset; INF. of (غيب); —*magyab*, INF. ة, depart, absent one's self, disappear (m.); — *mugîb*, *mugyib*, ة *mugîba-t*, woman whose husband is absent; — ة *mugayyaba-t*, secret, mystery.
مغيربان *mugairibân*, sunset.
مغيص *magîṣ*, colic, gripes.
مغيل . *mugîl*, *mugyil*, ة *mugîla-t*, *mugyila-t*, woman who has sexual intercourse and gives suck in spite of pregnancy.
مغيلان *mugailân*, a thorn-tree of the desert.
مفا *mufâ'*, slave, servant.
مفاتحة *mufâtaḥa-t*, opening, overture, &c.; beginning; sexual intercourse; argument.
مفاجا *mufâjjan*, walking with the toes turned outwards (adj.); — ة *mufâja'a-t*, *mufâjât*, surprise, sudden attack; unexpected advent (of death, &c.).
مفاجة *mafâja-t*, blockhead.
مفاجى *mufâji'*, attacking suddenly, coming unexpectedly, surprising; *al-mufaji'*, lion.
مفاد *mufâd*, clearly expressed, intelligible; explanation, date; statement, contents; — *mif'ad*, *mif'âd*, ة *mif'ada-t*, pl. *mafâ'id*, poker, spit.
مفارم *mafârim*, pl. astringent washes for women.
مفارة *maf'ara-t*, place abounding with mice.
مفازة *mafâza-t*, flight, escape; pl. *-ât*, *mafâwiz*, place of victory, of flight, of destruction; waterless desert.
مفاص *mafâṣ*, flight, escape.
مفاصلة *mufâṣala-t*, separation, dissolution, &c.; interval.
مفاض *mufâḍ*, ة, wide, spacious, extended, vast; abundantly shed, overflowing; مفاض فيه *mufâḍ fî-hi*, already too much spoken of, over-much discussed; on the same line, level with.
مفاطير *mafâṭîr*, pl. of مفطر *mufṭir*.
مفاعلة *mufâ'ala-t*, day-wages.
مفاعيل *mafâ'îl*, pl. of مفعول *maf'ûl*.
مفاقهة *mufâqaha-t*, discussion on a question of divinity or law.
مفاليج *mafâlîj*, pl. of مفلوج.
مفاليس *mafâlîs*, pl. of مفلس *muflis*.
مفاهاة *mufâhât*, colloquy.
مفاهر *mafâhir*, pl. flesh of the chest.
مفاوز *mafâwiz*, pl. of مفازة.
مفاوصة *mufâwaṣa-t*, clear explanation; clearness, distinctness.
مفاوضة *mafâwaḍa-t*, converse, consultation; letter to an inferior; consent; partnership on equal terms; reciprocity; reply, repartee; requital.
مفائد *mafâ'id*, pl. of مفاد *maf'ad*.
مفتاح *miftâḥ*, pl. مفاتيح *mafâtîḥ*, key.
مفتتات *mufattitât*, instrument for crushing stones in the bladder.
مفتح *maftaḥ*, store-room, magazine; treasure; — *miftaḥ*, pl. *mafâtiḥ*, key; — *mufattaḥ*, having the eyes open, not blind; — *; — ات *mufattiḥât*, purgatives.
مفتخر *muftaḥar*, excellent, magnificent; — *muftaḥir*, boasting; squandering; glorious, celebrated.
مفتدى *muftadî*, redeemer, saviour; — *.
مفترز *muftariz*, cutting off, separating, distinguishing, deciding, decisive.

مفتش *mufattiś*, seeking, &c.; examining judge; censor, syndic.
مفتضح *muftaḍiḥ*, disgraced; clear, evident.
مفتق *maftaq*, opening of a shirt; — *.
مفتل *miftal*, tool for twisting ropes, &c.; — *; — *maftala-t*, body of a spindle.
مفتوح *maftûḥ*, opened, &c.; dilated; light colour; marked with *fatḥa-t*.
مفتول *maftûl*, twisted, &c.; distorted; spoiled.
مفتون *maftûn*, seduced, &c.; temptation, seduction.
مفتى *muftî* (مفت *muft-in*), who is authorised to give valid legal decisions or *fatwas*, superior judge; م الانام *muftî al-anâm*, great *muftî*.
مفثة *mafaṯṯa-t*, abundance, affluence; كثير الم *kaṯîr al-mafaṯṯa-t*, very hospitable.
(مفج) *mafaj*, U, INF. *mafj*, be stupid.
مفج *mufijj*, rounded.
مفجر *mafjar*, place where water runs out; — ة *mafjara-t*, pl. *mafâjir*, broad valley or river-bed.
مفجى *mafjiyy*, opened, open.
مفحص *mafḥaṣ*, pl. *mafâḥiṣ*, nest of the *Qaṭa*-bird.
مفخر *mufaḫḫar*, praised, praiseworthy; — ة *mafḫara-t*, *mafḫura-t*, pl. *mafâḫir*, praiseworthy quality or deed; honour; pl. celebrated persons, celebrities, brilliant points.
مفدر *mufdir*, ة *mafdara-t*, aphrodisiac.
مفدغ *mifdag*, instrument for breaking into pieces.
مفدم *mafdam*, thickly laid (colour); dyed crimson; — *mufaddam*, stopped up, corked; muzzled.
مفر *mafarr*, *mafirr*, flight; — *mafirr*, refuge, asylum; — *mifarr*, swift (helping to escape, horse).
مفراح *mifrâḥ*, joyful, glad.
مفراش *mufrâś*, mattress.
مفراص *mifrâṣ*, مفراض *mifrâḍ* = مفرص *mifraṣ*.
مفرط *mufraṭ*, neglected; — *mufriṭ*, excessive, &c.; transcendental.
مفرصع *mufarṣa'*, with a cloven hoof.
مفرع *mifra'*, pl. *mafâri'*, arbitrator, peace-maker.
مفرغ *mufrag*, ة *mufraga-t*, massive (ring); — *mufarrig*, pouring out, &c.; metal-founder; الالة المفرغة *al-âla-t al-mufarriga-t*, pneumatic machine.
مفرفر *mufarfir*, clapping the wings; fickle, changeable.
مفرق *mafraq*, *mafriq*, pl. *mafâriq*, place where the hair parts; crown of the head; also ة *mafriqa-t*, crossing of roads, cross-way; bifurcation; pl. divergencies; different things.
مفرك *mifrak*, pl. *mafârik*, turnscrew, screw-driver.
مفروز *mafrûz*, separated, &c.; excommunicated.
مفروش *mafrûś*, spread, &c.; carpet.
مفروضات *mafrûḍât*, religious duties, regulations of an order.
مفروع *mafrû'*, ramified; cut off.
مفروغ *mafrûg*, given up; dropped; — *.
مفروك *mafrûk*, rubbed, &c.; deeply dyed.
مفرى *mufarra*, f. مفراة *mufarrât*, wearing a fur coat; furred.
مفزع *mafza'*, ة *mafza'a-t*, refuge, asylum; — ة *mafza'a-t*, reason for fear; scare; — *.
مفسا *mafsa*, anus.
مفسد *mufsid*, corrupting, destroying, &c.; criminal; mutineer, rioter; police spy; ات *mufsidât*, disastrous things; — ة *mafsada-t*, pl. *mafâsid*, source of calamity, dangerous intrigues, mutiny.
مفسوخ *mafsûḫ*, broken, split; chapped; spoiled; abolished; invalidated; — ية *mafsûḫiyya-t*, invalidity.
مفشوش *mafśûś*, emptied of air, emptied by blowing; empty, void, vain, perishable.

مفشى **mufśî** (مفش **mufś-in**), who blabs out secrets.
مفصد *mifṣad*, lancet.
مفصل *mafṣil*, pl. *mafâṣil*, *mafâṣilât*, joint, articulation; دا المفاصل *dâ' al-mufâṣil*, rheumatics, gout; — *miṣfal*, tongue; — *mufaṣṣal*, articulated, &c.; last section of the Koran with the short *sûras*; — *; — ة *mufassala-t*, turning-joint of a lid, &c.
مفضاض *mifḍâḍ*, club for breaking clods, &c.
مفضال *mifḍâl*, very liberal; highly distinguished, eminent.
مفضحة *mafḍaḥa-t*, pl. *mafâḍiḥ*, dishonour, shame, disgrace.
مفضخة *mifḍaḥa-t*, pl. *mafâḍiḥ*, stone for crushing dates, &c.; large, holding much; jug for new wine.
مفضضات *mufaḍḍaḍât*, plated goods, silver plate.
مفضل *mifḍal*, ة *mifḍala-t*, pl. *mafâḍil*, every-day dress of women; — *.
مفضة *mifaḍḍa-t*=مفضاض *mifḍâḍ*.
مفضول *mafḍûl*, surpassed, &c.; conquered.
مفطر *mufṭir*, pl. *mafâṭir*, who breaks a long fast; — *mufaṭṭar*, unleavened.
مفطس *mufaṭṭas*, flat (nose); choked.
مفطمة *mafṭama-t*, (m.) مفطمية *mafṭamiyya-t*, muzzle.
مفطور *mafṭûr*, created, &c.; inborn, natural.
مفعاة *maf'ât*, place abounding with snakes.
مفعول *maf'ûl*, done, effected, &c.; passive, grammatically governed; pl. مفاعيل *mafâ'îl*, effect, result, consequence; — ية *maf'ûliyya-t*, passive state or voice; being in the accusative (s.).
مفقد *mufaqqid*, home-sick.
مفقر *mufaqqar*, pressed (fruit); — *; — ة *mafqara-t*, pl. *mafâqir*, poverty, need.
مفقى *mafqi'*, opened (tumour); burst; peeled, shelled.
مفكك *mufakkak*, مفكوك *mafkûk*, loosed, freed, &c.; weighed (anchor); strained (joint).
مفلح الاسنان *mufallaḥ al-asnân*, having the nether lip split; — *.
مفلس *muflis*, pl. *mafâlîs*, impoverished, a bankrupt, insolvent.
مفلفل *mufalfal*, peppered, &c.; curly.
مفلق *mufliq*, who produces masterpieces; marvellous; — *muflaq*, dried; — *mufallaq*, split, forked; dried (apples); broken (eggs); — *; — ة *maflaqa-t*, *muflaqa-t*, anything unheard of, calamity.
مفلقح *mufalqiḥ*, polite, refined.
مفلوج *maflûj*, pl. *mafâlîj*, lamed on on side, paralytic; afflicted with palsy.
مفلوز *maflûẓ*, of the best steel.
مفلوك *maflûk*, unhappy, miserable, poor; having swelling breasts.
مفلى *muflî* (مفل *mufl-in*), ة *mufliya-t*, mare with a weaned foal; — *.
مفن *mifann*, مفنن *mufannin*, rich in expedients, versed in a hundred arts; — *mufn-in*, see مفنى *mufnî*.
مفنون *mafnûn*, thrown away, abject; — *.
مفنى *mufnî* (مفن *mufn-in*), destroying; dissipating, squandering.
مفهوم *mafhûm*, understood, comprehended; contents, purport, meaning.
مفواد *mifwâd*=مفياد *mifyâd*.
مفواة *mufawwât*, f. of مفوى *mufawwa*.
مفوت *mufawwat*, antiquated, out of fashion; — *mufawwit*, who allows or causes to enter, who introduces.
مفوخر *mufauḥar*, spoiled.
مفود *maf'ud*=مفوود *maf'ûd*.
مفوشش *mufauśaś*, empty, hollow; spoiled (m.).
مفوه *mufawwah*, very eloquent;

talkative ; aromatic, fragrant (wine) ;=the following—

مفؤود *maf'ûd*, wounded in the heart, heart-sick; lifeless, dead; bread baked in the ashes.

مفوى *mufawwa*, f. مفوّاة *mufawwât*, dyed with madder; f. place where madder is growing.

مفى *mufi'*, patron, protector.

مفياد *mifyâd*, who wishes to be useful to everybody, busy-body.

مفياة *mafya'a-t*, shady place or building.

مفيص *mafîṣ*, flight, escape; place of refuge.

مفيق *mufîq*, recovering one's senses or health; excellent, marvellous; —*.

مفيولا *mafyûlâ'*, young elephants.

مفيوءة *mafyû'a-t*, shady place; arbour.

(مق) *maqq*, U, INF. *maqq*, open the female palm-blossom and fecundate it with the pollen; suck the udder; be soft, relaxed; have bad juice;—II. INF. *tamqîq*, feed the young ones (bird); feed one's family but scantily; — V. INF. *tamaqquq*, drink by sips; — VIII. INF. *imtiqâq*, drink all the milk in the udder, suck; — ة *miqa-t*, love, INF. of (ومق).

مقا *maqqâ'*, f. of امق *amaqq*, long, lengthy, lank.

مقاب *miq'âb*, great drinker.

مقابلة *muqâbala-t*, being or standing opposite, &c.; meeting; corresponding; equivalent; requital, retaliation; confrontation; antithesis; opposition; duplicate; check-account, control, control-book, controller; — *muqâbalatan*, in one's presence, to one's face.

مقابيح *maqâbîh*, pl. of مقبوحة *maqbûḥa-t*.

مقاتية *maqâtiya-t*, pl. of مقتوى *maqtawî*.

مقاحم *maqâḥim*, pl. dangerous places, dangers;—ة *muqâḥama-t*, furious attack.

مقاحيم *maqâḥîm*, pl. of مقحام *miqḥâm*.

مقادسة *maqâdisa-t*, pl. of مقدسى *maqdisiyy*.

مقادم *maqâdim*, pl. front parts.

مقادة *maqâda-t*, leading, guidance, INF. of (قود).

مقاديح *maqâdîḥ*, pl. of مقداح *miqdâḥ*.

مقادير *maqâdîr*, pl. of مقدار *miqdâr*, مقدور *maqdûr*.

مقاديم *maqâdîm*, pl. of مقدم *muqdim* and مقدام *miqdâm*.

مقاذيف *maqâẕîf*, pl. of مقذاف *miqẕâf*.

مقار *maqâr-in*, see مقارى *maqârî* ; — *maqârr*, pl. depths, abysses.

مقارضة *muqâraḍa-t*, carrying on business with the capital of a sleeping partner;—*.

مقارع *muqâri'*, adversary; conqueror; prince; leader; — *; — ة *muqâra'a-t*, encounter, skirmish, combat, battle; casting of lots; winning lot; pl. ات blows, strokes.

مقارن *muqârin*, uniting, associating with, &c.; relating, allied; accessory; simultaneous, following immediately after; — ة *muqârana-t*, association, companionship, relationship; coincidence, influence of circumstances, conjunction of the stars.

مقارى *maqârî* (مقار *maqâr-in*), pl. of مقرا *miqrâ'*, مقراة *miqrât*.

مقاريب *maqârîb*, pl. of مقرب *muqrib*.

مقاريض *maqârîḍ*, pl. of مقراض *miqrâḍ*.

مقاص *maqâṣ*, crossbeam in which others are inserted; supports of a mast; scissors, snuffers.

مقاصير *maqâṣîr*, pl. of مقصرة *maqṣara-t* and مقصورة *maqṣûrat*.

مقاصيد *maqâṣîd*, pl. of مقصود *maqṣûd*.

مقاضاة *muqâḍât*, going before a judge (s.).

مقاط *miqâṭ*, short strong rope; swaddling-clothes; — *maqâṭṭ*, pl. of مقط *miqaṭṭ*.

مقاطعة *maqâṭi'a-t*, taxes, custom-duties; toll-places; — *muqâṭa'a-t*, separation, breaking off one's intercourse, &c.; competing; tenure for a time; farming of taxes; state income; wages by the piece; pl. *-ât*, province, district.

مقاطعجى *maqâṭa'ajî*, farmer of taxes, governor.

مقاطيع *maqâṭî'*, pl. of مقطوع *maqṭû'*.

مقاظ *maqâẕ*, summer sojourn.

مقال *maqâl*, speech, word, saying, opinion; — ة *maqâla-t*, passage of a book, book (especially the books of Euclid).

مقاليت *maqâlît*, pl. of *miqlât*.

مقاليد *maqâlîd*, pl. of مقلاد *miqlâd*.

مقاليع *maqâlî'*, pl. of مقلاع *miqlâ'*.

مقام *maqâm*, place, spot; domicile; staying, halting, sojourn, dwelling; station; office, rank, dignity; esteem, consideration; court (of a sovereign); musical tone, tune, song; قائم م *qâ'im maqâm*, lieutenant, vice-governor; — *muqâm*, stopping, making a halt; place and time of halting; — ة *maqâma-t*, sitting, session, assembly, conversation, address; degree, step, rank; musical tone; act, scene.

مقامر *muqâmir*, adversary in a game of chance; — ة *muqâmara-t*, gambling with dice, game of chance.

مقامع *maqâmi'*, pl. of قمعة *qama'a-t*, camel-fly, and of مقمعة *miqmâ'a-t*.

مقامى *maqâmiyy*, local.

مقاوضة *muqâwaḍa-t* = مقايضة *muqâyada-t*.

مقاوة *muqâwa-t*, watch, guard.

مقايسة *muqâyasa-t*, measuring, &c.; comparison, estimation by analogy, parallel (s.); agreement.

مقائم *maqâ'im*, pl. of مقوم *miqwam*.

مقاييد *maqâyîd*, pl. of مقيد *muqayyad*.

مقباس *miqbâs*, pl. *maqâbîs*, fire taken from a larger one to kindle another.

مقبحة *maqbaḥa-t*, what deserves blame, meanness.

مقبر *maqbar*, burying (s.), burial; also ة *maqbara-t*, *maqbira-t*, *maqbara-t*, *miqbara-t*, pl. *maqâbir*, burial-place, cemetery, churchyard, tomb; — ى *maqbariyy*, ة, belonging to a burial-place or tomb, sepulchral; who lives between tombs.

مقبس *miqbas*, pl. *maqâbis* = مقباس *miqbâs*.

مقبص *miqbaṣ*, barricade, hindrance, obstacle; rope extended in front of the race-horses.

مقبض *maqbaḍ*, *maqbiḍ*, *miqbaḍ*, ة *maqbaḍa-t*, &c., pl. *maqâbiḍ*, hand-piece, hilt, handle, occasion, opportunity; — *muqabbaḍ*, contracted, shortened; paid.

مقبط *muqabbaṭ*, trembling with fear.

مقبل *muqbal*, placed in front; — *muqbil*, coming next; fortunate, lucky, favourable; ة *muqbila-t*, next night; — *muqabbal*, kissed; place which is kissed.

مقبو *maqbuww*, contracted.

مقبوح *maqbûḥ*, abject, vile, abominable; — ة *maqbûḥa-t*, pl. *maqâbîḥ*, abomination.

مقبور *maqbûr*, buried; shrouded.

مقبول *maqbûl*, accepted, &c.; agreeable, pleasant, pleasing, welcome, favourite; orthodox; lady-love; — ية *maqbûliyya-t*, agreeableness, pleasantness; state of being beloved or liked, popularity; consent; orthodoxy.

مقبى *maqbiyy*, fat; vaulted, arched, convex.

(مقت) *maqat*, U, INF. *maqt*, *maqâta-t*, hate, detest, abhor; — IV. INF. *imqât*, cause to be hated, inspire with hatred; — VII. INF. *inmiqqât*, be hated.

مقت *maqt*, hatred, aversion; نكاح المقت *nikâḥ al-maqt*, marriage with the step-mother.

مقتا• *muqtâ* ., to be looked for under (. قو , . قي VIII.), as—
مقتاد• *muqtâd*, pat. of (قود VIII.), docile, guidable, submissive.
مقتتل• *muqtatal*, place of execution.
مقتحم• *muqtaḥam*, place of attack, battle-field.
مقتدر• *muqtadar*, rounded, compact.
مقتدى• *muqtada*, who is imitated, followed; worthy of imitation; model, pattern, guide, teacher, public prayer, priest; —*muqtadî* (مقتد• *muqtad-in*), imitating, following, praying after.
مقتر• *muqattar*, fragrant, scented, redolent; — * ; — ة *muqtira-t*, f. redolent of aloes.
مقتصر• *muqtaṣar*, compendium ; — * .
مقتضب• *muqtaḍib*, name of a metre (*maf'ûlâtu mustaf'ilun mustaf'ilun*, — — — ⏑ | — — ⏑ — | — — ⏑ — twice repeated).
مقتضى• *muqtaḍa*, required, &c.; due, need, want, necessity ; aim, end; —*muqtaḍî* (مقتض• *muqtaḍ-in*), requiring, &c.; — ات *muqtaḍiyât*, requisites, necessaries, determining causes, necessary consequences.
مقتفى• *muqtafa*, preferred, honoured; metrical and rhymed ; — *muqtafî* (مقتف• *muqtaf-in*), who imitates.
مقتل• *maqtal*, pl. *maqâtil*, place of killing, battle-field; fatal place in the body; — *muqattil*, *muqittil*, *muquttil*, fighting, combatting; — ة *maqtala-t*, place of execution.
مقتنى• *muqtana*, possession ; — * .
مقتوى• *maqtawî*, pl. *maqtawûn*, *maqâtiwa-t*, *maqâtiya-t*, servant, slave; — *muqtawî*, getting strong.
مقتى• *maqta*, servant; INF. of (قتو); — *maqtiyy*, married with one's step-mother; son from such marriage; — *muqtiyy*, cucumber (m.).
مقثاة• *maqsa'a-t*, cucumber-field.
مقثة• *maqassa-t*, abundance, affluence.
مقثوة• *maqsu'a-t*, cucumber-field.
مقثى• *muqsiyy*, cucumber.
مقحام• *miqḥâm*, pl. *maqâḥîm*, who rushes boldly into danger.
مقحاة• *miqḥât*, wooden shovel.
مقحفة• *miqḥafa-t*, (winnowing-) fan; duster.
مقحو• *maqḥuww*, مقحى• *maqḥiyy*, prepared with camomile.
مقد• *maqadd*, road; level tract; — *miqadd*, nippers of a shoe-maker or saddler; — ة *maqadda-t*, wad.
مقداح• *miqdâḥ*, pl. *maqâdîḥ*, steel for striking fire; gimlet, borer; (m.) intriguer.
مقدار• *miqdâr*, pl. *maqâdîr*, amount, quantity, measure, extent of space or time; value; consideration, authority, influence, power.
مقدام• *miqdâm*, ة *miqdâma-t*, who advances boldly, attacks fiercely.
مقدح• *miqdaḥ*, ة *miqdaḥa-t*, steel for striking fire; large spoon, ladle; — (m.) *maqdaḥ*, INF. ة, intrigue.
مقدر• *muqaddar*, pl. *-ât*, fate, destiny;—*muqaddir*, pre-ordaining, &c.; drawer of maps, architect; — ة *maqdara-t*, fate, destiny; divine providence; also *maqdira-t*, power, capacity, faculty.
مقدس• *maqdis*, holy place, بيت المقدس *bait al-maqdis*, *bait al-muqaddas*, Jerusalem; — *muqaddis*, consecrating, &c.; priest; Jew; — ى *maqdisiyy*, pl. *maqâdisa-t*, of Jerusalem.
مقدم• *maqdam*, arrival, coming (s.); place where one comes from; — *muqdam*, time and occasion of advance; boldness, spirit of enterprise; — *muqdim*, who advances boldly, commands to attack, &c.; leader, colonel; also *muqdam*, ة *muqdima-t*, front part of a camel's saddle, of a ship, &c.; pl. *maqâdîm*, inner corner of the eye, forehead; — *muqaddam*, advanced, &c.; vanguard; subject (in grammar); major (proposition); leader; front part; forehead; inner

corner of the eye; vestibule; former time;—*muqaddam-an*, in olden times, previously, before all things; — *; — ة *muqaddama-t*, front part, front; vanguard; preface, introduction; premise, major; pl. *-ât*, anything previous, preparations, introduction; sacrifice, offering, gift; — *muqaddima-t*, preface; beginning; vanguard; forehead; forelock.

مقدوح *maqdûḥ*, pierced, &c.; (m.) well disposed towards, prepossessed for.

مقدود *maqdûd*, cut into strips, shred, &c.; well made.

مقدور *maqdûr*, pl. *maqâdîr*, preordained, fate; possibility; حسب الم *ḥasba 'l-maqdûr*, according to one's power.

مقدى *maqadiyy*, *maqaddiyy*, mead; — ة *maqadiyya-t*, *maqaddiyya-t*, a stuff.

مقذ *maqaẓẓ*, place of the occiput where the hair is cut; instrument for cutting feathers for an arrow.

مقذاف *miqẓâf*, pl. *maqâẓif*, oar.

مقذذ *muqaẓẓaẓ*, of middle height and well-proportioned.

مقذر *maqẓar*, shunned, object of horror, monster.

مقذف *miqẓaf*, pl. *maqâẓif*, oar.

(مقر) *maqar*, U, INF. *maqr*, break the neck with a club;—*maqir*, A, INF. *maqar*, be sour, bitter; — IV. INF. *imqâr*, soak in vinegar; turn bitter; become tasteless, insipid.

مقر *maqr*, juice of aloes; anything sour or bitter; poison; — *maqir*, bitter, sour; — *maqarr*, abode, dwelling, sojourn; firm stand or seat; chair; buttocks; — *; — ة *maqarra-t*, water-jug or tub.

مقرا *maqra'*, place where the prayers are read, pulpit, praying-desk; — *miqrâ'*, ة very hospitable; — *miqrâ'*, ة *miqrât*, pl. *maqârî*, dish or cup for a guest; basin; reservoir.

مقراص *miqrâṣ*, crooked knife, bill, nippers.

مقراض *miqrâḍ*, pl. *maqârîḍ*, scissors.

مقراع *miqrâ'*, hammer for breaking stones.

مقرب *maqrab*, ة *maqraba-t*, shortest way, short cut; — *muqrib*, pl. *maqârîb*, near confinement or parturition; — *muqarrab*, admitted to closest proximity; favourite, courtier; archangel, cherubim; related; — *; — ة *maqraba-t*, *maqriba-t*, *maqruba-t*, relationship, kinship.

مقرح *muqarraḥ*, be covered with ulcers; — *muqarriḥ*, drawing blisters.

مقرر *muqarrar*, tax, duty; — *.

مقرش *muqriś*, rich.

مقرض *miqraḍ*, scissors; — *muqriḍ*, who lends money on interest; usurer; — ابن م *ibn miqraḍ*, marten.

مقرط *miqraṭ*, scissors (m.); *muqarraṭ*, ة, adorned with ear-rings; place where an ear-ring is put; — *.

مقرطب *muqarṭab*, prevented, unable.

مقرع *miqra'*, vessel for dates; — ة *miqra'a-t*, pl. *maqâri'*, whip, scourge; drum-stick.

مقرف *maqrif*, place where the bark is taken off to get resin or gum; *muqrif*, pl. *maqârif*, born of a free mother from a slave, of a full-bred mare by a bad stallion; who accuses; causing disgust; — *.

مقرفل *muqarfal*, spiced with cloves.

مقرم *miqram*, pl. *maqârim*, gaudily embroidered curtain, coverlet, carpet; — مقرم *muqram*, noble stallion exempt from work; noble, lordly, princely; — *; — ة *miqrama-t*, embroidered veil; bed-clothes; sleeping-room.

مقرمط *muqarmaṭ*, shortened, short,

small ; nibbled at ; close (writing).

مقرن *maqran*, yoke ; — *miqran*, what joins two things ; — *muqrin*, joining, helping, &c. ; (m.) horned ;—* ; — ات , مقرنات الصلوة *muqarranât aṣ-ṣalât*, usages in praying.

مقرنس *muqarnas*, terraced, in form of a terrace.

مقرنى *muqarna*, horned, crested.

مقرو *maqrû'*, *maqruww*, read, readable.

مقرور *maqrûr*, frozen ; refreshed, cooled, cool.

مقروض *maqrûḍ*, cut off ; borrowed ; in debt.

مقروع *maqrû'*, beaten, hit, &c. ; nobleman, prince.

مقروف *maqrûf*, suspected, blamed, accused, &c. ; thin, slender.

مقرونية *maqrûniyya-t*, being joined (s.), union.

مقروى *maqrawiyy*, long-necked.

مقرى *maqra*, place where water collects ; — *miqra*, very hospitable ; n. u. مقراة *miqrât*, pl. *maqârî*, dish or cup for a guest ; — *muqri'*, public reader or prayer.

(مقس) *maqas*, U, INF. *maqs*, immerge ; fill ; break (a.) ; flow ; recite fluently ; — *maqis*, A, INF. *maqas*, faint, swoon, become unwell.

مقساة *maqsât*, what hardens the heart.

مقسم *maqsam*, *miqsam*, part, portion ; — *maqsim*, place of division, place where waters separate, water-shed ; — *muqsam*, oath ; place where an oath is taken ; pl. *-ât*, conjuring entreaties, conjurations ; — *muqassam*, divided, well proportioned, well made ; — * .

مقسوم *maqsûm*, divided, &c. ; dividend ; م عليه *maqsûm 'alai-hi*, divisor.

مقشر *miqšar*, who torments, molests ; — * .

مقشم *maqšam*, pasture ; death.

مقشو *maqšuww*, مقشور *maqšûr*, مقشى *maqšiyy*, shelled, peeled, skinned, barked ; — *maqšiyy*, skimmed.

مقص *miqaṣṣ*, pl. *maqâṣṣ*, scissors, du. *miqaṣṣân*, blades of a pair of scissors ; — *muqiṣṣ*, who claims retaliation, revenge.

مقصال *miqṣâl*, sharp, cutting.

مقصب *muqaṣṣab*, cut in pieces, &c. ; curly, frizzled ; embroidered with gold or silver thread ; — ة *maqṣaba-t*, reed-bank.

مقصد *maqṣad*, *maqṣid*, pl. *maqâṣid*, intention, purpose, aim, end ; wish, desire ; destination ; object aimed at, object of a speech ; chapter, section ; — ة *maqṣada-t*, woman who has many suitors.

مقصر *maqṣar*, *maqṣir*, ة *maqṣara-t*, pl. *maqâṣir*, *maqâṣîr*, dusk, later part of the evening ; — *maqṣir*, wanting, falling short ; — * ; — ة *miqṣara-t*, fuller's beetle.

مقصف *maqṣaf*, pl. *maqâṣif*, country house, summer habitation, summer-house.

مقصل *maqṣal*, pl. *maqâṣil*, field with green food for horses ; onion- or tobacco- field ; — *miṣqal*, sharp, cutting.

مقصود *maqṣûd*, intended, &c. ; pl. *maqâṣîd*, intention, aim, end ; assertion, thesis.

مقصور *maqṣûr*, shortened, &c. ; very white linen ; — ة *maqṣûra-t*, pl. *maqâṣîr*, sanctuary ; most private room ; dressing-room of a bride ; chaste woman (always kept at home) ; edge, border ; near, close ; *maqṣûrat-an*, in the nearest degree of relationship.

مقصوص *maqṣûṣ*, cut, &c. ; castrated ; م له *maqṣûṣ la-hu*, who has been retaliated upon.

مقصى *muqṣa*, very far ; also *maqṣiyy*, with clipped ears.

مقضاب *miqḍâb*, مقضب *miqḍab*, hedging-bill, lopping-knife, pruning-shears ; — *miqḍab*, sharp ; — *miqḍâb*, ة *maqḍaba-t*, good clover-fields.

مقضم *maqḍam*, scanty provisions.

مقضى *maqḍiyy*, decided, decided upon, executed, carried out; obtained; settled, arranged.

(مقط) *maqaṭ*, U, I, INF. *maqṭ*, break (a.); enrage; throw on the ground; throw and catch the ball when it rebounds; tread the hen; twist firmly; — U, INF. *muqûṭ*, be emaciated; — II. INF. *tamqîṭ*, throw on the ground; — VIII. INF. *imtiqâṭ*, pull out, take out.

مقط *maqṭ*, harshness, violence; — *muqṭ*, pl. *amqâṭ*, rope, noose for catching birds; — *muqûṭ*, pl. of ماقط *mâqiṭ*, bridle, halter, &c.; — *maqaṭṭ*, place where the false ribs of a horse terminate; — *miqaṭṭ*, ة *miqaṭṭa-t*, pl. *maqâṭṭ*, piece of bone on which pens are mended or nibbed.

مقطار *miqṭâr*, dropping.

مقطاع *miqṭâ'*, cutting tool; who easily dissolves friendship again.

مقطر *miqṭar*, ة *miqṭara-t*, censer, coal-basin; *miqṭara-t*, stocks (for prisoners).

مقطع *maqṭa'*, cutting, INF. of (قطع); pl. *maqâṭi'*, cut; place of a cut, of separation; interruption; pause, cæsura; piece of linen; quarry, place where anything is broken out from, where it breaks off; ford; pl. public revenues; — *miqṭa'*, cutting-tool, shears for cloth or metal; — *muqṭa'*, torn away from; who is not fond of women; ford; — *muqaṭṭa'*, cut in many pieces, &c.; cut out, cut up; well-made; short, small; — ة *muqaṭṭa'a-t*, watered wine; pl. *muqaṭṭa'ât*, short poems, poetical fragments; short and tight-fitting clothes; printed stuffs, hardware.

مقطف *miqṭaf*, pl. *maqâṭif*, sifter, bolter; — *muqaṭṭaf*, sifted, bolted; plucked, culled; — ة *muqaṭṭafa-t*, dwarf.

مقطم *miqṭam*, claw, crooked nail; — *muqaṭṭam*, a mountain in Egypt.

مقطنة *maqṭana-t*, cotton-plantation.

مقطوطعات *muqṭauṭi'ât*, pl. f. galloping separately.

مقطوع *maqṭû'*, cut, cut off, &c.; captured; decided; fixed; pl. *maqâṭi'*, settled matter, resolution; precipitous, steep; hindered, oppressed (breath), lamed.

مقطوم *maqṭûm*, cut off.

(مقع) *maqa'*, INF. *maq'*, drink quickly and greedily; pass. be reviled or made to be suspected; — VIII. INF. *imtiqâ'*, pass. change colour, grow pale.

مقعد *maq'ad*, pl. *maqâ'id*, place of sitting, seat, chair, cushion, mattress; base; buttocks; sitting-room, saloon; abode, residence; — *muq'ad*, lamed, crippled; also *muqa''ad*, pensioned; veteran (s.); — *; — ة *maq'ada-t*, place of sitting, seat; base; buttocks.

مقعر *muqa''ar*, excavated, hollow, concave; deep.

مقعطة *miq'aṭa-t*, turban-band.

مقعى *muqq'î*, sitting with one's buttocks on the heels.

مقفا *muqaffa*, rhymed; rhythmical.

مقفار *miqfâr*, complete desert.

مقفاص *miqfâṣ*, knob of an iron mace.

مقفر *muqfir*, waste (adj.).

مقفز *muqaffaz*, having the fore-legs white up to the knees.

مقفع *muqaffa'*, shrunk, wrinkled; — ة *miqfa'a-t*, rod.

مقفى *muqfa*, preferred; — *muqaffa*, rhymed, rhythmical.

مقق *maqaq*, length of a horse; — ة *maqaqa-t*, pl. sucking kids or lambs.

(مقل) *maqal*, U, INF. *maql*, look at, contemplate; immerge entirely (a. and n.).

مقل *maql*, bottom of a well; descending into the water; making water; — *muql*, fruit of the wild dwarf-palm, wild date; frankincense; bdellium; resin

of the *mugailân*; — *muqill*, poor, needy; — ة *muqla-t*, the black (also the white) of the eye; eye; middle, centre; سواد الم *sawâd al-muqla-t*, pupil of the eye, what is dearest and most precious.

مقلا• *miqla'*, racket; — ة *miqlât*, مقلاية• *miqlâya-t*, n. u. of مقلى• *miqla*.

مقلات• *miqlât*, pl. *maqâlît*, bearing only once (she-camel); childless.

مقلاد• *miqlâd*, pl. *maqâlîd*, key, lock.

مقلاع• *miqlâ'*, pl. *maqâli'*, pickaxe.

مقلاق• *miqlâq*, restless person.

مقلب• *miqlab*, pl. *miqâlib*, spade; lid of the touch-pan (of a gun).

مقلتة• *maqlata-t*, dangerous place, danger.

مقلد• *miqlad*, pl. *maqâlid*, key; hooked staff, crosier; fodder-bag; a measure; — *muqallad*, imitated, &c.; place of the shoulder where a sword is suspended; — *muqallid*, who imitates, &c.; actor, merry-andrew; — ات *muqalladât*, grand poems handed down from century to century.

مقلع• *maqla'*, pl. *maqâli'*, quarry; — *muqli'*, ة *muqli'a-t*, under sail; — *.

مقلم• *miqlam*, camel's womb; — *muqallam*, stripped; clipped (م الظفر *muqallam az-zufr*, weak, contemptible); long and pointed; also ة *muqallama-t*, unmarried, living single (woman); — ة *miqlama-t*, pen-case.

مقلو• *maqluww*=مقلى• *maqliyy*.

مقلوب• *maqlûb*, overturned, turned upside down, &c.; anagram; م مستوى *maqlûb mustawa*, palindromia.

مقلوفة• *maqlûfa-t*, basket of dates.

مقلى• *miqla*, n. u. مقلاة• *miqlât*, (m.) مقلاية• *miqlâya-t*, pl. *maqâlî*, frying pan; racket (in playing at balls); — *maqliyy*, fried in a pan; — *muqalla*, id.; — ة *maqliya-t*, hatred, INF. of (قلى).

مقماة• *maqma'a-t*, place not shone upon by the sun.

مقمر• *muqmir*, ة *muqmi'ra-t*, moon-lit; — *muqqammar*, be printed with figures of the moon.

مقمط• *muqammat*, swaddled; wrapped up with a bandage.

مقمع• *miqma'*, ة *miqma'a-t*, pl. *maqâmi'*, iron rod or club to lead an elephant; hooked staff, crosier; an instrument of torture in hell.

مقمق• *maqmaq*, INF. ة, be soft, mild, light; soften, tame; suck strongly; speak from the depth of the throat.

مقمل• *muqmil*, *muqammal*, swarming with lice.

مقمن• *maqman*, ة *maqmana-t*, appropriate, fit, worthy.

مقمة• *miqamma-t*, broom, brush; also *maqamma-t*, mouth of cloven-footed animals.

مقموط• *maqmûṭ*, fettered hand and foot; swaddled up.

مقموة• *maqmu'a-t* = مقماة• *maqma'a-t*.

مقناب• *miqnâb*, lion's claw.

مقناطيس• *miqnâṭîs* = مغناطيس• *magnâṭîs*, loadstone.

مقناة• *maqnât*, place always exposed to the sun.

مقنب• *miqnab*, pl. *maqânib*, lion's claw; game-bag; troop of horsemen (thirty to three hundred).

مقند• *muqannad*, مقندى• *muqanda*, prepared with sugar-candy, sugared.

مقنطر• *muqanṭar*, arched, &c.; resting on arches; sun-dial; perfect; ات *muqanṭarât*, bridges, arches, parallels of latitude; — ة *muqanṭara-t*, hundredweight.

مقنطيس• *miqnaṭîs*, magnet, loadstone.

مقنع• *maqna'*, pl. *maqâni'*, sufficient; affording proof, demonstrative; — *miqna'*, ة *miqna'a-t*, pl. *maqâni'*, long fine linen head-cloth of women; — *muqanna'*, covered with an iron helmet; — *; — ة *maqna'a-t*, sufficiency, contentment; wealth; — *muqna'a-t*, shepherd's pipe.

مقنن *muqannan*, arranged, made law ; — *muqannin*, who arranges, law-giver.

مقنود *maqnûd*=مقند *muqannad*.

مقنوة *maqnuwa-t*=مقناة *maqnât*.

مقنى *maqnî*, acquired, possessed ;— *muqnî*, lance-bearer ;— *muqannî*, skilled in finding water ; م الارض *muqannî al-arḍ*, hoopoe.

مقه *maqah*, white mingled with blue; bluish grey ; — *muqh*, pl. and—

مقهاء *maqhâ*, f. of امقه *amqah*, light blue, &c.

مقهقر *muqahqar*, doomed to a miserable life.

مقهور *maqhûr*, subdued, &c. ; to be conquered ; irritated, driven to extremities ; forced, compelled.

(مقو) *maqâ*, U, INF. *maqw*, suck strongly; also مقى *maqa*, I, INF. *maqy*, guard, watch over ; polish (a sword), clean (the teeth).

مقو *maqw*, ة *maqwa-t*, guard.

مقوا = مقوى *muqawwa*.

مقوال *miqwâl*, pl. *maqâwil*, very talkative, garrulous, eloquent.

مقود *maqûd*, *muqawwad*, led with the hand ; — *miqwad*, pl. *maqâwid*, leading-string ; nose-bridle of a camel ; thread.

مقور *muqawwar*, having a round hole cut into (pumpkin) ; tarred; — *maqwarr*, having thin flanks.

مقوس *miqwas*, pl. *maqâwis*, case for a bow ; quiver ; rope in front of the race-horses ; race-course ; — *muqawwar*, in form of a bow ; hit by a shot.

مقوط *muqûṭ*, excessive leanness.

مقوقس *muqauqis*, a pigeon-like bird ; king.

مقول *maqûl*, said ; anything said, word, speech ; also ة *maqûla-t*, topic, matter, object ; mentioned above or below ; kind, category, attribute ;—*miqwal*, pl. *maqâwil*, *maqâwila-t*, tongue ; king, prince ; = مقوال *miqwâl* ; — *muqawwal*, repeatedly said.

مقوم *miqwam*, pl. *maqâ'im*, plough-tail ; — * .

مقونن *muqaunan*, on whom a duty or penance has been imposed.

مقوود *maqwûd*=مقود *maqûd*.

مقوول *maqwûl*=مقول *maqûl*.

مقوى *muqawwa*, strengthened, &c. ; card-board ; card-board box.

مقى *maqa*, v. see (مقو) ;—*muqayyi'*, see مقيى *muqayyî'*.

مقياس *miqyâs*, instrument for measuring, measure ; scale ; hand of a watch or clock ; Nilometer ; quantity.

مقيت *maqît*, hated ;—*muqît*, powerful, able to (على *'ala*) ; who feeds and guards ; overseer ; witness.

مقيد *muqayyad*, pl. *maqâyîd*, fetterred, &c. ; devoted, addicted ; restricted, grammatically determined ; the place where a fetter is put ; verse whose rhyme terminates in a vowelless consonant.

مقيس *maqîs*, measured, compared ; comparison ; — *muqayyas*, responding, analogous, regular ; embroidered, adorned.

مقيسرة *muqaisara-t*, pl. old camels.

مقيض *maqîḍ*, place where eggs are laid.

مقيظ *maqîẓ*, *maqyaẓ*, summer abode ; — * .

مقيل *maqîl*, mid-day slumber, resting place (also *muqayyal*) ; tomb, grave.

مقيم *muqîm*, abiding, residing, &c. ; persevering, enduring.

مقين *muqayyin*, decorator ; — ة *muqayyina-t*, woman who dresses a bride's hair and adorns her, lady's maid.

مقيى *muqayyi'*, *muqî'*, pl. *muqî'ât*, vomitives.

(مك) *makk*, U, INF. suck out ; diminish ; destroy ; drop excrement ; — V. INF. *tamakkuk*, VIII. INF. *imtikâk*, suck out.

مكا *makan*, *maka*, hole of a fox, &c., burrow ; — *mukâ'*, sound produced by blowing into one's hands ; — *mukkâ'*, pl. *makâkî*, small singing-bird.

مكابين *makâbîn*, pl. of مكبونة *makbûna-t*.

مكاتيب *makâtîb*, pl. of مكتوب *maktûb*.

مكاثرة *mukâsara-t*, ostentation; — *.

مكاد *makâd*, ة *makâda-t*, being on the point of doing anything.

مكار *makkâr*, f. ة, cunning impostor, great rogue, rascal; — ات *mukârât*, hiring out, letting (s.).

مكارى *mukârî* (مكار *mukâr-in*), pl. *mukârûn*, *akriyâ'*, *mukâriyya-t*, who hires out camels, horses, mules; camel-driver, muleteer.

مكاس *makkâs*, exciseman, gatherer of taxes or tithes.

مكاسير *makâsîr*, pl. of مكسور *maksûr*.

مكاهرة *mukâśara-t*, false smile, smirk.

مكافاة *mukâfa'a-t*, *mukâfât*, requital, reward; making up for (s.), satisfaction; corresponding, resembling (s.).

مكافل *mukâfil*, neighbour; confederate.

مكافى *mukâfî* (مكاف *mukâf-in*), *mukâfi'*, corresponding, equal; قطع م *qaṭ' mukâfî*, parabola.

مكافيف *makâfîf*, pl. of مكفوف *makfûf*.

مكاك *mukâk*, ة *mukâka-t*, what is sucked at;—ة *mukâka-t*, marrow; — *makkâka-t*, maid-servant.

مكاكى *makâkî*, pl. of مكا *mukkâ'*, also—

مكاكيك *makâkîk*, pl. of مكوك *makkûk*.

مكال *makâl*, measuring, INF. of (كيل); — *mukâl*, fat, tallow, suet.

مكالبة *mukâlaba-t*, scuffle, brawl.

مكامة *mukâma-t*, married woman.

مكان *makân*, pl. *amkina-t*, *amâkin*, place, spot; abode, habitation, house; office, dignity, post; happening, existing (s.); *makân-a*, instead of, in the place of; — ة *makâna-t*, spot; high dignity, power, good circumstances; pl. *-ât*, post, office, dignity; considerateness, steadiness, sedateness; intention, purpose; — ى *makâniyy*, local.

مكاوى *makâwiyy*, pl. of مكواة *mikwât*; — *makkâwiyy*, of Mecca= مكى *makkiyy*.

مكائيل *makâ'îl*, *makâyîl*, pl. of مكيال *mikyâl*.

مكب *mikabb*, pl. *mikabbât*, clew, hank, skein; — *mukibb*, hanging over, inclined; intent, industrious; depressing; — ة *mikabba-t*, cover, covering, lid; provision-bag;—*mukabba-t*, reel.

مكباس *mikbâs*=مكبس *mikbas*.

مكبر *makbir*, ة *makbara-t*, *makbura-t*, great old age.

مكبس *mikbas*, ة *mikbasa-t*, press, hand-press;— *mukabbas*, trained for work; double (flower); — *mukabbis*, dim-sighted, purblind; mean, vile.

مكبن *mukban*, strong in the backbone.

مكبون *makbûn*, having thin bones; short-legged and big-bellied; — ة *makbûna-t*, pl. *makâbîn*, id.

(مكت) *makat*, U, INF. *makt*, stay, abide, remain.

مكتا *muktâ*., to be looked for under (كو ,. كي VIII.), as—

مكتال *muktâl*, pat. of (كيل VIII.), measured.

مكتب *maktab*, pl. *makâtib*, writing-school, preparatory school; office, place of business; — *mukattib*, writing-master; — *; — ة *maktaba-t*, pl. *makâtib*, library.

مكترى *muktarî*, who hires, rents; tenant.

مكتسى *muktasî*, clad, dressed.

مكتفى *muktafi'*, *muktafî* (مكتف *muktaf-in*), content, satisfied.

مكتل *miktal*, pl. *makâtil*, vessel holding 15 صاع *ṣâ'*; — *mukattal*, short, thick-set; corpulent; round; heaped up, in shape of a heap.

مكتمن *muktamin*, concealed.
مكتن *muktann*, hidden; hiding-place of the game.
مكتني *muktanî*, metonymic.
مكتهل *muktahil*, of mature age; grey; blooming.
مكتوب *maktûb*, written; pl. *makâtîb*, writing, letter; sack, bag.
مكتوع *maktû'*, sprained, distorted, disfigured.
مكتوى *muktawa*, cauterised.
مكتئب *mukta'ib*, grieved, saddened, disconsolate; dark, blackish.
(مكث) *makas̱*, *makus̱*, INF. *maks̱*, *miks̱*, *muks̱*, *makas̱*, *mikkîs̱a*, *mikkîs̱â'*, *mukûs̱*, *muks̱ân*, stay, remain, abide, sojourn, wait; — V. INF. *tamakkus̱*, id.
مكث *maks̱*, *miks̱*, *muks̱*, *makas̱*, staying, remaining, waiting; sojourn; delay; على م *'ala muks̱-in*, with delays, at intervals.
مكثار *miks̱âr*, great talker, very garrulous.
مكثان *muks̱ân*, INF. of (مكث).
مكثر *muks̱ir*, rich; also *mukas̱s̱ir*, increasing, &c.; *mukas̱s̱ir*, plural; — ة *maks̱ara-t*, anything increasing.
مكثور *maks̱ûr*, frequented; pressed by creditors.
مكثير *miks̱îr*=مكثار *miks̱âr*.
مكحال *mikḥâl*, مكحل *mikḥal*, pencil for applying collyrium to the eye; — *; — ة *mukḥula-t*, pl. *makâḥil*, box of collyrium; arquebuse; — II. INF. *tamakḥul*, take the collyrium-box to make use of it.
(مكد) *makad*, U, INF. *makd*, *mukûd*, stop (n.), stay, abide; yield less milk.
مكد *mikd*, *mikadd*, comb; — *mukd*, pl. of مكود *makûd*; — *mukidd*, exerting one's self, toiling.
مكدا *makdâ'*, always yielding plenty of milk.
مكدس *makdas*, heap.
مكدم *makdam*, place fit for searching; — *mukaddam*, bitten, seized by the teeth.
مكذبان *makẕabân*, ة *makẕabâna-t*, liar.
مكذبة *makẕaba-t*, *mukẕuba-t*, pl. *makâẕib*, lie.
مكذوب *makẕûb*, proclaimed a liar; م عليه *makẕûb 'alai-hi*, at whose cost lies have been told, falsely accused; also ة *makẕûba-t*, lie.
(مكر) *makar*, U, INF. *makr*, practice artifice, try to deceive by stratagem; whistle; dye red; irrigate; — *makir*, A, INF. *makar*, be red; — II. INF. *tamkîr*, buy up corn for usurious purposes; — III. INF. *mumâkara-t*, try to ensnare, to deceive by artifice; — VIII. INF. *imtikâr*, redden (n.), get dyed red.
مكر *makr*, ة, stratagem, artifice; deceit, fraud, falseness; malice; red chalk; n.u. ة, pl. *mukûr*, a tree; فراخ الم *firâḥ al-makr*, its fruit; — *makarr*, place of combat; — *mikarr*, skilful in evolutions and repeated attack (horsemen); — ة *makra-t*, a kind of clover; — *makara-t*, pl. of ماكر *mâkir*, cunning impostor.
مكرام *mikrâm*, ready to honour others.
مكرب *mikrab*, pl. *makârib*, plough; — *mukrab*, sinewy; firm; grieved; — *.
مكرس *mukras*, *mukarras*, string of pearls.
مكرش *mukriś*, paunch-bellied; — ة *mukarraśa-t*, paunch of a camel dressed with sausages, &c.
مكرص *mikraṣ*, leathern milk-pail.
مكرع *mukra'*, strong in the legs (horse).
مكركب *mukarkab*, excited, agitated, moving about in all directions; confused.
مكرم *makram*, ة *makrama-t*, pl. *makârim*, noble quality or deed; honour, glory, nobility; generosity, liberality, bounty, kindness; good ground; — *; —

mukram, homage ; — *mukarram*, honoured, &c. ; venerable, holy ; ة *mukarrama-t*, Mecca ; الحجر الم *al-ḥajar al-mukarram*, philosopher's-stone ; — *.
مكرنف• *mukarnif*, thick.
مكره• *mukrah*, compelled, against one's will ;— ة *makraha-t*, hatred, aversion, abhorrence ; pl. *makârih*, what excites aversion, adversity, evil, calamity.
مكروش• *makrûś*, paunch-bellied.
مكروم• *makrûm*, honoured with presents.
مكروهة• *makrûha-t*, abominable deed, sin ; harshness, violence, cruelty.
مكرى• *mukrî* (مكر• *mukr-in*), who hires out, lets ;—*mukran*, *mukra*, hired out, let.
مكز• *mukizz*, causing pain.
مكزوبة• *makzûba-t*, black hair mingled with white.
(مكس) *makas*, I, INF. *maks*, deceive in a bargain ; injure, diminish (a.) ; lower the price ; hoard up money ; gather taxes ; oppress tyrannically ; — II. INF. *tamkîs*, gather taxes, &c., be a tax-gatherer ; — III. INF. *mikâs*, *mumâkasa-t*, make an offer against another, outbid ; barter, haggle, quarrel over a bargain ; — VI. INF. *tamâkus*, quarrel over a bargain.
مكس• *maks*, pl. *mukûs*, taxes, duties, tithes ; diminution, damage, fraud in a bargain or contract ; oppression, tyranny.
مكساب• *miksâb*, who gains, earns.
مكسال• *miksâl*, very lazy, slow, great idler.
مكسب• *maksab*, *maksib*, place where a gain is to be made ; also ة *maksiba-t*, pl. *makâsib*, gain.
مكسحة• *miksaḥa-t*, broom, shovel.
مكسر• *maksar*, charcoal ; — *maksir*, place of a breach or rupture, breach, rupture ; opening in a canal to let off the water ; root, origin ; — *mukassar*, broken, &c. ; broken plural ; tamed, calmed down, brought to reason ; — *.
مكسع• *miksa'*, string by which a top is made to spin ; — *mukassa'*, unmarried ; leading a chaste life.
مكسو• *maksuww*, clad, dressed.
مكسور• *maksûr*, broken, &c. ; fraction ; bankrupt ; marked with *kasra-t*.
مكشاح• *mikśâḥ*, مكشح• *mikśaḥ*, axe, hatchet ; edge of a sword.
مكشوف• *makśûf*, disclosed, &c. ; commented upon, explained, revealed.
مكعب• *mak'ab*, pl. *makâ'ib*, low shoe, a kind of slipper ; — *muka''ab*, cubic, &c. ; cube, die ; imprinted with squares ; trellissed in squares ; also *muka''ib*, swelling (bosom) ; — ة *muka'-'aba-t*, palm-basket.
مكفال• *mikfâl*, having large buttocks.
مكفاة• *makfât*, sufficiency.
مكفح• *mikfaḥ*, strong, firm.
مكفر• *mukaffar*, paid with ingratitude ; armed ; atoned for ; made an infidel.
مكفهر• *mukfahirr*, dark ; gloomy, grave ; thick and black (cloud).
مكفول• *makfûl*, trembling with fright ; bailed out.
مكفى• *makfiyy*, sufficiently provided, sufficient ; — *mukaffa*, who himself pays for his board (workman).
(مكل) *makil*, A, INF. *mukûl*, have black mud.
مكل• *makil*, *mukul*, waterless and muddy ; — *mukul*, pl. of مكول• *makûl* ; — ة *makla-t*, *mukla-t*, black mud of a well.
مكلا• *mukalla'*, place protected against the wind ; anchorage, harbour ; river-bank ; — ة *makla'a-t*, place abounding in food.
مكلب• *mukallab*, fettered ; firmly cohering ; — *mukallib*, dog-breeder ; — ة *maklaba-t*, bawding (s.).

مكلس *mukallis*, lime-burner, cement-maker; — *.

مكلف *mukallaf*, expensive, fine, excellent; magnificently adorned; bombastic, overdone; responsible; freckled, full of pimples.

مكلل *mukallal*, crowned, &c.; adorned with jewellery; embroidered with figures of roses (Pers. گل); bordered (especially with flowers).

مكلوب *maklûb*, bitten by a mad dog, afflicted with hydrophobia.

مكلوف *maklûf*, well cared for.

مكلى *mukli'*, abounding with food; — *makliyy*, suffering from the kidneys.

مكماة *makma'a-t*, place abounding with mushrooms or truffles.

مكمح *mukmaḥ*, high; proud.

مكمد *mukammad*, grieved, sorrowful; faded, dull (colour).

مكمك *makmak*, INF. ة, suck out entirely; totter in walking.

مكمل *mikmal*, thorough, perfect; — *.

مكمم *mukammam*, muzzled.

مكمن *makman*, pl. *makâmin*, ambush; hiding-place; — *mukmin*, lying in ambush ,—ة *makmana-t*, hidden treasure.

مكمه *mukammah*, blind from birth.

مكمة *mikamma-t*, muzzle (for asses); harrow.

مكمهل *mukamhal*, cotton-pod with seed.

مكمور *makmûr*, covered, veiled, &c.; pl. *makmûrâ'*, have a big gland of the penis; — ة *makmûra-t*, woman who has had sexual intercourse.

مكموة *makmu'a-t*=مكماة *makma'a-t*.

مكن *makin*, A, INF. *makan*, be full of ova, deposit ova; — *makun*, INF. *makâna-t*, be influential (with the king), powerful; be firm, solidly established; — II. INF. *tamkîn* (also IV.), give power, strength, capacity for (من *min*); let one take root in a land and become powerful; make firm, consolidate; — IV. INF. *imkân*, see II., enable (mostly used impersonally, يمكن it is possible for, &c.); — V. INF. *tamakkun*, have authority and influence; be able to, have the power of, take possession of; be firm, consolidated; take up an abode; — X. INF. *istimkân*, have power of, make one's self master of (من *min*); consolidate one's self.

مكن *makn*, *makin*, ova of locusts or lizards;—*mukann*, hidden; concealed, kept in one's mind; — ة *mikna-t*, *mukna-t*, firmness, solidity; power, might, strength, capacity; possibility; anything possible, not exceeding one's power; credit; — *makina-t*, pl. *makin*, *makinât*, ovum of a locust or lizard; place where ova are deposited; على مكناتهم *'ala makinâti-him*, in full possession of their power.

مكنوز *maknûz*, hoarded up, &c.; ات *maknûzât*, hidden things, thoughts, &c.

مكنون *maknûn*, concealed, &c.; ذو م *ẓû maknûn*, well guarded, precious pearl; — ة *maknûna-t*, well kept at home (girl); well Zamzam.

مكنى *makniyy*, *mukanna*, metonymic; nicknamed; *mukanna*, pronoun.

مكة *makka-t*, Mecca.

مكهرب *mukahrab*, electrified.

(مكو) *makâ*, U, INF. *makw*, *mukâ'*, whistle, chirp; INF. *mukâ'*, break wind; — مكى *makî*, A, INF. *makan*, swell.

مكو *makw*, pl. *amkâ'*, hole of a fox, &c.; burrow; — ة *makwa-t*, anus.

مكوارة *mikwâra-t*, turban.

مكواة *mikwât*, pl. *makâwî*, hot iron for cauterising, cautery; flat-iron.

مكوتعا *mukauti'-an*, quickly, fast.

مكوث *mukûṡ*, staying, abiding, sojourn; delay.
مكود *makûd*, pl. *mukd*, always abounding with milk; — * .
مكوز *mukawwiz*, girt round the loins.
مكور *makwar* (also *makwarr, mikwarr, mukwarr*), camel-saddle; —*mikwar*, ة *mikwara-t*, turban;—*makûr*, cunning impostor; — *; — *mukwarr, mikwarr, makwarr*, مكورى *makwarra, makwariyy*, impudent, shameless, vile; talkative, garrulous; short, broad, and dwarfish.
مكوز *mukawwaz*, long, oblong.
مكوك *makkûk*, pl. *makâkîk, makâkî*, drinking-cup in shape of a ship; a measure=1½ صاع *ṣâ'*; shuttle.
مكول *makûl*, pl. *mukul*, well with mud and but little water; — *; — ى *makûliyy*, muddy; miserly, filthy.
مكون *makûn*, full of ova; depositing ova; — *mukawwin*, creator.
مكوى *mikwa*=مكواة *mikwât*; — *makwiyy*, cauterised; ironed.
مكى *makkiyy*, ة, of or from Mecca; revealed in Mecca.
مكيال *mikyâl*, pl. *makâ'il, makâyil*, a measure for corn, &c.
مكيان *mikyân*, bail, security, guarantee.
مكيث *makîṡ*, steady, sedate, slow.
مكيد *makîd*, using stratagem (s.), INF. of (كيد); — ة *makîda-t*, pl. *makâyid*, artifice, stratagem, ruse; (m.) obstinacy.
مكيس *mukayyis*, attendant in a bath; — *.
مكيفات *mukayyifât*, intoxicating beverages, opiates, &c.
مكيل *makîl*, measuring (s.), INF. of (كيل); also *mikyal*, ة *makîla-t*, *mikyala-t*, pl. *makâyil* = مكيال *mikyâl*; — *.
مكين *makîn*, pl. *mukanâ'*, permanently settled and solidly established; in a firm position; well considered by the king, influential, powerful; consolidated; firm, compact; master of the house; inhabitant;—ة *makîna-t*, authority with the king, influence; sedateness; intention.
مكيول *makyûl*, measured; contents of a measure.
(مل) *mall* (for *malal*), U, INF. *mall*, sew with large stitches; bake bread or roast meat in the ashes or on coals; make the bow or arrow pliable at the fire; hasten, walk fast; (m.) creep, crawl; — for *malil*, A, INF. *malal*, *malla-t, malâl, malâla-t*, be sulky, weary, fretting, peevish; suffer from fever or pain in the back; turn restlessly from side to side (in bed); last too long for, weary (a.), tire out; — IV. INF. *imlâl*, make weary, languid, peevish; bore; dictate to (على *'ala*); — V. INF. *tamallul*, be bored, wearied, &c.; walk apace; join a religion and follow its practices; — VII. INF. *inmilâl*, be sewn with large and loose stitches; — VIII. INF. *imtilâl*, walk apace; roast in the ashes or upon coals;—X. INF. *istimlâl*, find tiresome, wearisome, a bore.
مل *mall*, weary, bored, peevish, languid; live coal; (m.) creeping (s.); — ة *malla-t*, languidness, tiredness, peevishness (ذو م *ẕû malla-t*, languid, &c.); hot ashes, live coals; fever-perspiration;—*milla-t*, pl. *milal*, religion, creed, religious community; people, nation; حقوق الملل *ḥuqûq al-milal*, international law.
(ملا) *mala'*, INF. *mal', mal'a-t, mil'a-t*, fill (2 acc.); satisfy (the heart); help, assist one (acc.) in (على *'ala*); — ملى *mali'*, A, INF. *mala'*, be full, get full; — ملو *malu'*, INF. *malâ', malâ'a-t*, be rich and powerful; have a cold; — III. INF. *mumâla'a-t*, help, assist, aid; — IV. INF. *imlâ*, fill; make very rich; — V. INF. *tamallu'*, get or be full, be filled;

— VI. INF. *tamâlu'*, assist one another; — VIII. INF. *imtilâ'*, get full; — X. INF. *istimlâ'*, ask to fill; try to get rich; fill.

ملا *mal'*, filling, being full (s.); flood (opposed to ebb); — *mil'*, pl. *amlâ'*, quantity which fills up, fulness; — *mala'*, pl. *amlâ'*, number of people filling a place; public, audience; what fills space, a body; full space; consultation for mutual help; nobility, high rank, power, noblemen; host of angels; custom, usage; opinion, view; wish, desire; — *malan, mala*, time, du. *malawân*, day and night; — *malâ'*, ة *malâ'a-t*, wealth, riches; — *milâ'*, pl. of ملان *mal'ân* and مليى *malî'*; — *mulâ'*, surfeit; cold, rheum; — *mullâ* (m.), scholar, schoolmaster, doctor; decoy-bird; — ة *malât*, pl. *malan, mala*, desert; smooth stuff without a border; — *mal'at*, veil of a coarse material; — *mal'a-t, mil'a-t*, filling (s.); *mil'a-t*, way of filling; also *mul'a-t*, surfeit, suffering from it; — *mul'a-t*, cold, rheum; — *malâ'a-t*, wealth, riches; cold, rheum; — *mulâ'a-t*, pl. *mulâ'*, tent, veil, wrapper, dressing-gown of one piece of cloth; surfeit and suffering from it; cold.

ملاا *mula'â'*, pl. of مليى *malî'*.

ملاب *malâb*, a perfume; saffron.

ملابس *mulâbis*, who has commerce with, associates with; — *; — ة *mulâbasa-t*, commerce, intercourse; reference to, relation, connection with.

ملابيس *malâbîs*, pl. of ملبوس *malbûs*.

ملاث *malâs̱*, pl. *malâwis̱*, *malâwis̱a-t*, *malâwîs̱*, of high nobility.

ملاجى *malaji'*, pl. of ملجا *malja'*.

ملاح *milâḥ*, wind driving a ship; veil; protecting roof, shield; pl. of ملح *milḥ* and مليح *malîḥ*; — *mulâḥ, mullâḥ*, handsome, elegant, good; — *mallâḥ*, sailor, pilot; maker or seller of salt; (m.) hoar-frost; — *mullâḥ*, a salty sea-plant; — ة *malâḥa-t*, beauty, elegance; kindness; — *milâḥa-t*, navigation; — *mallâḥa-t*, salt-works, saline.

ملاحد *mulâḥid*, false, hypocritical; intriguer; — ة *mulâḥada-t*, falseness, hypocrisy; intrigues; — *.

ملاحز *malâḥiz*, pl. distress, difficulties.

ملاحم *malâḥim*, fleshy parts; pl. of ملحمة *malḥama-t*; — *.

ملاحى *mulâḥiyy*, a kind of grapes with oval berries; a kind of figs; — ة *mallâḥiyya-t*, navigation.

ملاخ *mallâḫ*, fugitive.

ملاذ *malâẕ*, pl. *malâwiẕ*, refuge, asylum; stronghold, citadel; protection; protector; — *mallâẕ*, ملاذانى *malâẕâniyy*, liar, false friend; — *malâẕẕ*, pl. of ملذة *malaẕẕa-t*; — ة *malâẕa-t*, pl. *malâwiẕ*, raw Chinese silk; trowsers; apron.

ملاز *malâz*, pl. *malâwiz*, refuge, asylum; — *mallâz*, wolf; — ة *malâza-t*, place abounding with almond trees; almond grove; — *mulâzza-t*, union.

ملازم *mulâzim*, clinging to (adj.), &c.; inseparable companion, helper, assistant, servant; adjutant, lieutenant; courtier; grammatically unchangeable; — ة *mulâzama-t*, clinging to (s.), &c.; attachment; dependence; surveillance of a debtor.

ملازيب *malâzîb*, pl. of ملزاب *milzâb*.

ملاس *mallâs*, flatterer; — ة *malâsa-t*, smoothness; — *mallâsa-t*, roller for smoothing and levelling.

ملاشاة *mulâśât*, destructiveness, vandalism.

ملاص *milâṣ*, smooth white stone.

ملاصق *mulâṣiq*, adhering to, &c.; companion, comrade, neighbour; partisan; — ة *mulâṣaqa-t*, adhesion, &c.; contiguity, neighbourhood.

ملاط *milâṭ*, loam, mortar, cement; side of the camel's hump; ابن م *ibn milâṭ*, new moon.

ملاطفة *mulâṭâfa-t*, politeness, friendliness, &c.; jocosity, pleasantry; letter.

ملاع *malâ'*, desert without vegetation.

ملاعيب *malâ'îb*, pl. of ملعوب *mal'ûb*.

ملاعين *malâ'în*, pl. of ملعون *mal'ûn*.

ملاغ *mullâg*, pl. of مالغ *mâlig*, impure, abject, &c.

ملاغم *malâgim*, outer parts of a camel's mouth covered with foam.

ملاق *malâq*, harrow or roller for levelling; — *mallâq*, flatterer.

ملاقاة *mulâqât*, meeting, going to meet, reception; interview, converse.

ملاقى *malâqî*, pl. of ملقى *malqa*, ملقاة *malqât*; — *.

ملاقيح *malâqîḥ*, pl. of ملقوحة *malqûḥa-t*.

ملاقيط *malâqîṭ*, pl. of ملقوط *malqûṭ*.

ملاك *malâk*, self-possession; also *milâk*, principal part which connects the whole, base, foundation (م الجسد *milâk al-jasad*, heart); contract of marriage; — *milâk*, loam, mud; pl. *mulk*, *muluk*, foot of a horse; — *mullâk*, pl. of مالك *mâlik*, possessor, master, &c.; — *mal'ak*, ملك *malak*, pl. *malâ'ik*, *malâ'ika-t*, angel; envoy, messenger; also ة *mal'aka-t*, pl. *malâ'ik*, embassy; missive, letter; — ة *malâka-t*, possession.

ملال *malâl*, ة *malâla-t*, weariness, peevishness, sulkiness, languidness, ennui, impatience, sadness; — *mulâl*, hot ashes, live coals; fever-heat; pains in the back; handle of a sword, bow, &c.; — ة *malâla-t*, sowing (s.) with loose stitches.

ملام *malâm*, ة *malâma-t*, pl. *malâwim*, *malâ'im*, blame, rebuke, abuse, disgrace; — *mal'am*, blameworthy; also *mil'am*, who keeps to mean people, defends them; — *mula''am*, wearing a coat of mail; — ة *mal'ama-t*, meanness.

ملامان *mal'amân*, blameworthy.

ملامتى *malâmatiyy*, pl. ة, who deserves blame, &c.; monks or Sûfis who despise external decorum.

ملامح *malâmiḥ*, features reminding of the father.

ملامسة *mulâmasa-t*, touch, feeling; sexual intercourse.

ملامل *mulâmil*, swift.

ملان *mal'ân*, f. ة, and ملى *mal'a*, pl. *milâ'*, full; — *mil'ân*, for من الان *min alân*, henceforth.

ملاوث *malâwis*, pl. of ملاث *malâs* and ملوث *milwas*.

ملاوذ *malâwiz*, pl. of ملاذ *malâz*, ة.

ملاوز *malâwiz*, pl. of ملاز *malâz*.

ملاوطة *mulâwaṭa-t*, sodomy.

ملاوم *malâwim*, pl. of ملامة *malâma-t*; — ة *mulâwama-t*, mutual reproach.

ملاوة *malâwa-t*, *milâwa-t*, *mulâwa-t*, long space of time.

ملاويث *malâwîs*, pl. of ملاث *malâs* and ملوث *milwas*.

ملى *mal'a*, f. of ملان *mal'ân*.

ملايثة *mulâyasa-t*, boldness like a lion's.

ملايس *mulâyis*, lazy, delaying.

ملائك *malâ'ik*, ة *malâ'ika-t*, pl. of ملاك *mal'ak*, ملك *malak*.

ملائم *malâ'im*, blameworthy actions, reproaches; — *mulâyim*, agreeing, wholesome; mild, gentle, friendly; pliable, docile; soft, tender, smooth, level; corresponding; just; — ة *mulâ'ama-t*, *mulâyama-t*, agreeing (s.); wholesomeness; gentleness, mildness, friendliness, docility; pacification, reconciliation.

ملاينة *mulâyana-t*, conciliation, friendly persuasion or admonition; softness.

ملاية mulâya-t, veil of a coarse material.
ملبد mulbad, covered with a saddle-cloth.
ملبس malbas, anything pleasant, agreeable; also *milbas*, pl. *malâbis*, clothing, costume; — *mulbis*, complicated, obscure; — *mulabbas*, clad, &c.; candied, sugared; — *.
ملبن malban, ة malbana-t, increasing the milk (food); — *milban*, pl. *malâbin*, milk-pail; mould or trough for bricks and tiles; (m.) door- or window-frame; — *mulbin*, ة *mulbina-t*, yielding milk; — *; — ة *milbana-t*, skimmer; spoon.
ملبوب malbûb, man of head and heart, intelligent; covered with a breast-plate (horse).
ملبوس malbûs, pl. *malâbîs*, clad, dressed; worn; — ات *malbûsât*, clothes.
ملبون malbûn, brought up on milk.
ملبى mulabbî, who says Yes to everything, is easily to be got to anything.
(ملت) malat, I, INF. *malt*, move, shake (a.).
ملتا . multâ ., to be looked for under (. لو , . لي VIII.), as—
ملتاث multâs, ag. of (لوث VIII.), complicated, entangled.
ملتاع multâ', deeply grieved.
ملت . . multa . ., to be looked for under (. . ل VIII.), as—
ملتبس multabis, ag. of (لبس VIII.), obscure, equivocal, doubtful; who has frequent intercourse with.
ملتبك multabik, complicated; much occupied; prepossessed.
ملتبية multabiya-t, partnership.
ملتثم multasam, kissed, place which is kissed; — *multasim*, covered with a لثام *lisâm*.
ملتج multajj, deeply furrowed; — ة *multajja-t*, of a deep black (eye).
ملتجا multaja', refuge, asylum; protector.
ملتحد multaḥad, refuge, asylum.
ملتخ multaḫḫ, without self-control (intoxicated person); confused.
ملتد multadd, flight, escape.
ملتزم multazim, taking as a duty upon one's self, &c.; undertaker, farmer, tax-gatherer; resulting necessarily; convinced, convicted.
ملتقى multaqa, place of meeting, tryst; conflux of rivers or seas (Bosphorus).
ملتمسات multamasât, requests, demands.
ملتهى multahî, playing, sporting, jesting.
ملتوت maltût, mixed; anointed or rubbed with; moistened.
ملتوح multawiḥ, appearing, shining.
ملتوخ maltûḫ, dirtied.
ملتوط multawiṭ, who adopts.
ملتئم multa'im, closed (wound); mended, darned, joined.
(ملث) malas, U, INF. *mals*, pacify or quiet by words, coax, cajole; make empty promises; beat lightly; — III. INF. *mumâlasa-t*, treat with dissimulation and falsehood; sport, play, jest with.
ملث mals, malas, ة *mulsa-t*, beginning of night, twilight.
ملثلث mulaslas, talkative; dirty.
(ملج) malaj, U, INF. *malj*, suck but with the edges of the lips; — *malij*, id.; — IV. INF. *imlâj*, give suck; — VIII. INF. *imtilâj*, suck.
ملجا malja', malja, pl. *malâji'*, refuge, asylum; safety, security; resting-place.
ملجوج maljûj (عليه *'alai-hi*), molested.
(ملح) malaḥ, A, I, INF. *malḥ*, salt (a.); give salt to the cattle; — INF. *milḥ*, give suck; — A, slander the absent; — *maluḥ*, INF. *malâḥa-t*, be salty; be handsome, pretty, elegant; — II. INF. *tamlîḥ*, salt strongly; proffer beauti-

ful things (poet); — III. INF. *mumâlaḥa-t*, *milâḥ*, share one's salt, eat at one's table or at the same table with him; behave handsomely towards; — IV. INF. *imlâḥ*, salt much; turn salty; — V. INF. *tamalluḥ*, get salted; (m.) threaten; — X. INF. *istimlâḥ*, find handsome, pretty, elegant; admire; find salty.

ملح *milḥ*, pl. *milaḥ*, *milâḥ*, *milḥa-t*, *amlâḥ*, salt; salt water; salt (adj.), salty; wit, intellect; knowledge; scholar; beauty, loveliness, grace; oath; م البارود *milḥ al-bârûd*, saltpetre; — *mu-liḥḥ*, importunate; — ة *malḥa-t*, abyss of the sea; — *milḥa-t*, oath; clientship, duty of protection; — *mulḥa-t*, pl. *mulaḥ*, witty tale, choice saying, anecdote; elegance; dignified gravity, authority; reverence, awe, fear; blessing, bliss, pleasure.

ملحا *malḥâ'*, f. of املح *amlaḥ*, spotted black and white, &c.; leafless tree; flesh of the back; best part of a camel's hump.

ملحاح *milḥâḥ*, importunate, obtrusive.

ملحان *malḥân*, *milḥân*, month of snow and hoar-frost: 2nd *jumâẓa* or *kânûn*.

ملحج *malḥaj*, pl. *malâḥij*, refuge, asylum; pl. straits, difficulties, distress.

ملحد *mulḥad*, tomb in whose side another is cut; grave-niche; — *mulḥid*, pl. *malâḥid*, *malâḥi-da-t*, infidel, heretic, heathen, theist; impious.

ملحس *malḥas*, licking (s.), INF. of (لحس); — *milḥas*, miser; bold, fearless.

ملحص *malḥaṣ*, refuge, asylum.

ملحف *milḥaf*, ة *milḥafa-t*, pl. *malâ-ḥif*, wrapper, cloak, plaid; blanket.

ملحق *mulḥaq*, added, &c.; written by the reader on the margin; pl. *-ât*, addition, appendix, supplement, postscript; *mulḥaqât*, annexed provinces, dependencies; suffixes; — *.

ملحم *mulḥam*, half silk; — *mulḥim*, weaver; also *mulaḥḥam*, fleshy; — ة *malḥama-t*, pl. *malâḥim*, sanguinary combat, slaughter, massacre; slaughter-house.

ملحن *mulaḥḥin*, who sings psalms; leader of a choir.

ملحود *malḥûd*=ملحد *mulḥad*.

ملحوس *malḥûs*, licked; emaciated; clean.

ملحوظ *malḥûẓ*, looked at, &c.; taken in regard or consideration; surmised, supposed, considered as probable; — ات *malḥûẓât*, thoughts, considerations.

ملحوق *malḥûq*, reached, overtaken.

ملحوم *malḥûm*, joined, soldered; warped; killed.

ملحون *malḥûn*, faulty (speech); full of faults of speech.

ملحي *milḥiyy*, seller of salt.

(ملخ) *malaḥ*, INF. *malḥ*, step apace, travel far; engage in futilities; seize with the hands or teeth; snatch from; — INF. *malḥ*, *malûḥ*, *malâḥa-t*, be exhausted and no longer able to cover (stallion); — *maluḥ*, be tasteless, insipid; — III. INF. *mumâlaḥa-t*, play with; flatter; — VIII. INF. *imti-lâḥ*, pull out; draw the sword.

ملخى *milḥa*, gallipot for drugs; snuff-box.

(ملد) *malad*, U, INF. *mald*, stretch, extend (a.); — *malid*, INF. *malad*, be merry and cheerful, leap with joy; — II. INF. *tamlîd*, soften (a.).

ملد *mald*, soft and delicate; demon of the desert (غول *gûl*); — *malad*, softness, delicacy; youthfulness; freshness of the face.

ملدا *maldâ'*, f. of املد *amlad*, delicate, soft, supple.

ملدام *mildâm*, stone for crushing dates.

ملدان *maladân*, cheerfulness; youthfulness; freshness of the face;

— ة muldâniyya-t, delicate (girl).

ملدس mildas, pl. malâdis = ملطس milṭas; — muladdas, mended, darned; — *.

ملدغ mildag, slanderer.

ملدم mildam = ملدام mildâm; ام م umm mildam, fever; — *.

(ملذ) malaẓ, I, INF. malẓ, tell lies, act differently from what one says; pierce with the lance; rub on the hand; stretch the legs to the utmost in running; — maliẓ, A, INF. malaẓ, be mixed; — VIII. INF. imtilâẓ, receive as a present.

ملذ malẓ, swiftness; — malaẓ, mixture of light and darkness, evening dusk; — malaẓẓ, ة malaẓẓa-t, pl. malâẓẓ, pleasure, enjoyment; voluptuousness.

ملذان malẓân, ى malaẓâniyy, false friend.

ملذذ mulaẓẓaẓ, delightful, delicious.

ملذوع malẓû', stung, bitten; offended; burnt.

(ملز) malaz, U, INF. malz, go away with, carry off; remain behind; — II. INF. tamlîz, free, rescue; — IV. INF. imlâz, carry off; — V. INF. tamalluz, id.; — also VII. INF. inmilâz, free one's self, escape; — VIII. INF. imtilâz, pull out, snatch from.

ملز maliz, muscular; — milazz, very able and zealous.

ملزاب milzâb, pl. malâzîb, great miser.

ملزام milzâm =

ملزم milzam, ة milzama-t, pl. malâzim, pincers; book-binder's press; compress; — mulzam, compelled, forced upon, &c.; convicted, sentenced; — *.

(ملس) malas, U, INF. mals, geld a ram by twisting off his testicles; drive violently; smooth; be mixed with light (darkness); pacify, flatter, coax by stroking; (m.) touch; — malus, INF. malâsa-t, mulûsa-t, be smooth and glossy, satin-like; — II. INF. tamlîs, render smooth and glossy, make satin-like, hot-press; flatter, coax, cajole; caress; — V. INF. tamallus, get smooth; caress; = VII.; — VII. inmilâs, escape, free one's self, slip away from; — VIII. INF. imtilâs, pass. be taken away; — XI. INF. imlisâs, be smooth; = VII.

ملس mals, mixture of light and darkness, twilight; (m.) also malas, mixed, of two ingredients: half silk, &c.; mulatto, mongrel, bastard; — malis, smooth, shaven, shorn.

ملسا malsâ', f. of املس amlas, smooth, &c.; sour milk mixed with sweet; afternoon; month of Safar.

ملسن mulassan, gifted with great eloquence; — *.

ملسون malsûn, liar; having the tongue cut out; — *.

ملسى malasa, smooth, bald; swift.

(ملش) malaś, U, INF. malś, feel, examine with the hand; (m.) pluck out (feathers, hair); — VIII. INF. inmilâś, have the feathers, &c. plucked out.

(ملص) malaṣ, U, INF. malṣ, drop excrement; — maliṣ, A, INF. malaṣ, slip out of the hand; — IV. INF. imlâṣ, let fall, drop; miscarry; — V. INF. tamalluṣ, escape, save one's self; — VII. INF. inmilâṣ, id.

ملص maliṣ, slippery; — ة maliṣa-t, tortoise; — malaṣṣa-t, muliṣṣa-t, tract rendered unsafe by robbers.

ملصق mulṣaq, glued, &c.; associated; allied; contiguous; — also mulaṣṣaq, adopted; — *.

ملصوق malṣûq = ملصق mulṣaq.

(ملط) malaṭ, U, INF. malṭ, coat with mud or mortar; shave off; cement; (m.) scald a bird or animal to pluck its feathers or hair; (m.) pluck; — U, INF. mulûṭ, — also maluṭ, be of mixed

breed, impure blood; — **malit**, A, INF. **malaṭ**, **multa-t**, be hairless on the body; have a thin beard; — II. INF. **tamlîṭ**, cover with mortar, plaster; cement a broken vessel; — VII. INF. *inmilâṭ*, be scalded, plucked (m.).

ملط *malṭ*, coating with mortar, plastering (s.); scalding, plucking (s.); — *milṭ*, pl. *amlâṭ*, *mulûṭ*, thief; ملط م خلط *milṭ ḫilṭ*, of mixed or obscure descent; — ة *malṭa-t*, loam, mortar, cement; compound of ground bricks and resin, mastic; Maltha; — *mulṭa-t*, hairlessness.

ملطا *milṭâ'*, ة *milṭât*, lower membrane of the skull; brain-wound.

ملطاس *milṭâs*=ملطس *milṭas*.

ملطاط *milṭâṭ*, oil-press, sesame-mill; handle of a hand-mill; trowel; profile of a mountain, head, &c.

ملطس *milṭas*, pl. *malâṭis*, stone for crushing dates; broad hammer for breaking stones.

ملطم *mulṭam*, cheek; — *.

ملطوش *malṭûś*, beaten, pushed, touched; capricious; possessed by a demon.

ملطية *malaṭiya-t*, Malatia; — *mulṭiya-t*, scalp-wound.

ملظ *mulizz*, ملظاظ *milẓâẓ*, very importunate, obtrusive; — ة *mulizza-t*, embassy, missive.

(ملع) *mala'*, INF. *mal'* (also II.) skin a sheep from the neck downwards; (m.) also II. tear one's clothes; step apace; — II. INF. *tamlî'*, see I.; — IV. INF. *imlâ'*, step apace, pass by; — V. INF. *tamallu'*, get torn; — VII. INF. *inmilâ'*, step apace.

ملع *mal'*, rent; confederation; — *mulu'*, pl. of مليع *malî'*.

ملعا *mal'â'*, an alkaline plant with a combustible sap.

ملعب *mal'ab*, pl. *malâ'ib*, play, game, sport, jest; play-ground, scene, theatre; ملاعب الريح *malâ'ib ar-rîḥ*, currents of the wind; — ة *mal'aba-t*, plaything, toy, doll; playing-costume.

ملعط *mal'aṭ*, grass and green food, especially round the tents.

ملعقة *mil'aqa-t*, pl. *malâ'iq*, spoon; skimmer.

ملعوب *mal'ûb*, pl. *malâ'ib*, malicious trick, intrigue; salivating (adj.).

ملعوس *mul'awis*, biting, masticating (m.).

ملعوط *mal'ûṭ*, cursed (family).

ملعون *mal'ûn*, pl. *malâ'în*, cursed, damned, excommunicated; (m.) colic of horses.

(ملغ) *milg*, pl. *amlâg*, who talks stupidly and obscenely; — III. *mâlag*, INF. *mumâlaga-t*, talk ribaldry to.

ملغاة *malgât*, fault in speaking.

ملغفة *malgafa-t*, bold gang of robbers.

ملغم *malgam*, softening ointment.

ملغى *mulga*, suppressed, eliminated, passed over, abolished.

ملف *milaff*, ملفاف *milfâf*, bed-cloth.

ملفان *malfân*, pl. *malâfina-t*, doctor, physician (m.).

ملفج *mulfaj*, impoverished, bankrupt.

ملفق *mulaffaq*, lie; — *.

ملفوظات *malfûẓât*, words, sayings.

ملفوف *malfûf*, enveloped, &c. (*malfûf-an*, enclosed); envelope; what forms heads, cabbage.

ملفى *malfa*, place of meeting, rendezvous.

(ملق) *malaq*, U, INF. *malq*, efface, blot out; wash a dress; beat; lie with; suck; — *maliq*, A, INF. *malaq*, flatter falsely; fawn; slip from the finger; — II. INF. *tamlîq*, flatter, caress; — IV. INF. *imlâq*, be or grow poor; — V. INF. *tamalluq*, flatter, cajole; get flattered, caressed; — VII. INF. *inmilâq*, be soft and smooth; escape, free one's self; slip out of the fingers; — VIII. INF. *imtilâq*, be soft and smooth.

ملق *malaq*, flattery; caress; gallop; — *maliq*, ة, flattering,

caressing, pleasant; swift, fleet; — ة *malaqa-t*, smooth stone.

ملقاط *milqâṭ*, pen; tweezers; spider; spider-web.

ملقاة *malqât*, pl. *malâqî*, ramification at the base of the womb; —*mulqât*, anything thrown away.

ملقح *mulqiḥ*, pl. *malâqiḥ*, camel-stallion; fecundating the blossoms of the palm-tree; — *mulaqqaḥ*, fecundated; experienced; thrown to the ground; — ة *mulqaḥa-t*, pl. *malâqiḥ*, fecundated, pregnant; — *malâqiḥ*, winds driving clouds or shaking and fecundating palm-trees.

ملقط *milqaṭ*, pl. *malâqiṭ*, nippers, pincers, tweezers; fork.

ملقن *mulaqqin*, who eulogises or addresses the dead; — *.

ملقو *malquww*, having a distorted face.

ملقوحة *malqûḥa-t*, pl. *malâqîḥ*, mother; fœtus; sperm of a stallion.

ملقوط *malqûṭ*, pl. *malâqîṭ*, picked up; gleaned; foundling; captured (thief).

ملقى *malqa*, place; experienced man (also *malqiyy*, *mulqa*, *mulaqqa*); pl. *malâqî*=ملقاة *malqât*; — *mulqa*, place where anything is thrown to; place of meeting, rendezvous; conflux of waters; ramification of roads; brought low (by fever, &c.); supported; — *mulaqqa*, *malqiyy*, thrown at.

(ملك) *malak*, I, INF. *malk*, *milk*, *mulk*, *malaka-t*, *mamlaka-t*, *mamluka-t*, possess, be master of, rule over; be king, ruler; possess one's self of; vanquish, conquer; occupy, hold (a road, &c.); — INF. *malk*, *milk*, *mulk*, take a wife, marry; — I, INF. *malk*, knead the dough well; — II. INF. *tamlîk* (also IV.), make one possessor of (2 acc.); make the dough to rise; — IV. INF. *imlâk*, see II.; knead the dough well; take possession of; give in marriage; — V. INF. *tamalluk*, make one's self master of, take possession of; become rampant; — VI. INF. *tamâluk*, master one's self; restrain one's self; refrain from; — VIII. INF. *imtilâk*, possess; — X. INF. *istimlâk*, possess one's self of; become possessor.

ملك *malk*, possession (م الولى *malk al-waliyy*, wife); pl. *amlâk*, *mulûk*, possessor; king; slavery, bondage; middle of the road; — *milk*, *mulk*, pl. *amlâk*, possession, property; fortune, estates; right of property; dominion, kingdom; slavery, bondage; middle of the road; — *mulk*, kingdom, empire (دار الم *dâr al-mulk*, capital); royal dignity, power, authority; pea; الم *al-mulk*, م الملكوت *mulk al-malakût*, the visible world, and, by opposition, the invisible world; *mulk* and *muluk*, pl. of ملاك *malâk*; *muluk*, possessions; — *malak*, possession, property; food and water; foundation of a thing's existence; effective cause; for *mal'ak*, pl. *malâ'ika-t*, *malâ'ik*, *amlâk*, messenger (of God), angel; — *malik*, pl. *mulûk*, possessor, king; pirate; حب الملوك *ḥabb al-mulûk*, cherry; — *mullak*, pl. of مليك *malîk* and مالك *mâlik*, king; — ة *malka-t*, royal dignity; also *mulka-t*, possession, property; — *malaka-t*, possession; acquisition; attainment, acquired skill or quality, talent, virtue; habit, custom; slavery; — *malika-t*, mistress, princess, queen; sharp and quick intellect; — *muluka-t*, horse's feet.

ملكا *mulakâ'*, pl. of مليك *malîk*.

ملكد *milkad*, pestle; mallet, hammer.

ملكوت *malakût*, ملكوة *malkuwa-t*, dominion, kingdom, empire; power and majesty; الم *al-malakût*, عالم م *'âlam malakût*,

the kingdom of heaven, the invisible world.
ملكوش *malkûś*, lowest price quoted at a fall in the stocks.
ملكى *milkiyy*, ة, royal, referring to the state and government; farmer; — *mulkiyy*, own, in one's own possession; hereditary; referring to administration, administrative, civil; — *malakiyy*, royal; orthodox; angelical; customary, habitual; ة *al-malakiyya-t*, sect of the Malekites; — ة *milkiyya-t*, right of possession; sovereignty; property.
ملل *malal*, languidness, weariness, sulkiness, impatience; — *milal*, pl. of ملة *milla-t*.
ملمذ *milmaẓ*, liar, false friend.
ملمس *malmas*, touch; place touched; skin, body.
ملمع *milma'*, wing of a bird; — *mulamma'*, shining, flashing, &c.; many-coloured, variegated, piebald; having white stripes in black (ebony); mingled with Arabic and Persian (Turkish); inlaid or sprinkled with gold or silver; dressed up; false, lying; — *mulmi'*, big with young.
(ململ) *malmal*, INF. ة, disquiet, trouble; hasten (n.); — II. INF. *tamalmul*, be restless; — ة *malmala-t*, swiftness.
ململم *mulamlam*, ة, gathered in a heap, very strong; — ة *mulamlama-t*, trunk of an elephant.
ملمة *mulimma-t*, blow of misfortune, calamity.
ملموس *malmûs*, touched; dependent; smoothed; — ات *malmûsât*, tangible things.
ململ *mulmûl*, pencil for applying collyrium; writing-pencil; genital of a fox, camel, &c.
ملموة *malmu'a-t*, receptacle; net, snare, noose.
ملنخوليا *malanḫoliyâ*, melancholy.
ملهم *malham*, voracious; — *mulham*, inspired, revealed; — *.
ملهو *malhuww*, amused, diverted.
ملهوت *malhût*, name of the fish which carries the world.
ملهى *malha*, pl. *malâhî*, place of amusement; music-hall, &c.; pleasure; — *milha*, pl. *malâhî*, toy; musical instrument; pl. carouses, orgies, revels; — *mulhî* (ملة *mulh-in*), diverting, amusing; jester, merry-andrew.
(ملو) *malâ*, U, INF. *malw*, step apace, run; — II. INF. *tamliya-t*, grant for a long time, let enjoy (2 acc.); — III. INF. *mumâlât*, help; — IV. INF. *imlâ'*, be for a long time indulgent and patient with (ل *li*); be long-suffering; let enjoy; dictate to (على *'ala*); write, compose a book; — V. INF. *tamallî*, enjoy; — X. INF. *istimlâ'*, ask for patience and indulgence; write after dictation; — ة *malwa-t*, *milwa-t*, *mulwa-t*, a long time.
ملواح *milwâḥ*, owl as a decoy-bird.
ملوان *malawân*, day and night, du. of ملا *mala*, time.
ملوث *milwas*=ملاث *malâs*.
ملوحة *mulûḥa-t*, salty taste; salt fish; beauty, INF. of (ملح).
ملوخيا *malûḫiyâ*, ملوخية *malûḫiya-t*, mallow.
ملوذ *milwaẓ* = ميلذ *milmaẓ*; — ة *milwaẓa-t*, refuge, asylum.
ملوز *mulawwaz*, filled with almonds; almond-shaped.
ملوسة *mulûsa-t*, smoothness.
ملوظ *milwaẓ*, stick; whip.
ملوع *mulawwa'*, disquieted, troubled, grieved.
ملوف *malûf*, rained upon.
ملوكة *mulûka-t*, possession; bondage.
ملوكى *mulûkiyy*, royal, kingly.
ملول *malûl*, ة, tired, weary, languid, sulky; grieved, sad, melancholy; tragical.
ملولب *mulaulab*=ململ *mulmûl*.
ملووق *malwûq*, bent, folded; distorted.
ملوى *malwa*, pl. *malâwî*, key of a stringed instrument; winch; —

malwiyy, twisted, plaited; — also *mulawwa*, distorted.

ملى• *maliyy*, space of time; length of time; — ملى• *mali'*, v. see (ملا); — *mali'*, full; rich.

مليح• *malîḥ*, pl. *milâḥ*, *amlâḥ*, beautiful, fair, pretty, graceful, lovely, elegant; well done! bravo! salt (adj.); holding salt water; ابو الم *abû al-malîḥ*, lark.

مليخ• *malîḫ*, insipid, dull, flat, weak.

مليز• *malîz*, refuge, asylum.

مليسا• *mulaisâ'*, sour milk mixed with sweet; mid-day; month of *Safar*.

مليع• *malî'*, pl. *mulu'*, vast and bare tract, desert.

مليق• *malîq*, miscarriage; also ة *malîqa-t*, provided with cotton (ink-flask).

مليك• *malîk*, pl. *mulakâ'*, *mullak*, king; م النحل *malîk an-naḥl*, queen-bee.

مليل• *malîl*, baked or cooked in the ashes; — *mulayyal*, long and dark; — ة *malîla-t*, fever-heat.

مليم• *malîm*, blamed, rebuked; — *mulîm*, who blames, rebukes, fault-finder; blame-worthy; evil.

ملينة• *malyana-t*, soft substratum; ذو م *zû malyana-t*, mild, gentle, captivating.

مليه• *malîh*, good, handsome.

مليون• *malyûn*, *milyûn*, pl. *-at*, *malâyîn*, *malâwîn*, million (m.).

مليى• *malî'*, pl. *milâ'*, *amliyâ'*, *mula'â'*, full, rich.

مم abbreviation for ممنوع• *mamnû'*, forbidden, or for مسلم• *musallam*, granted; — *mima* = مما• *mim mâ*, for من ما• *min mâ*, from what? for what reason?

ممات• *mamât*, time or place of death; death; — *mumât*, mortal; antiquated, obsolete; worried to death.

مماثل• *mumâṣil*, comparable, similar, equal, identical; imitating, following an example; — ة *mumâṣala-t*, comparison; similarity; equality; allusion.

مماجرة• *mumâjara-t*, usury.

مماحك• *mumâḥik*, quarrelsome; — ة *mumâḥaka-t*, quarrelsomeness, quarrel.

ممادة• *mumâdda-t*, extension; delay; — *.

مماذق• *mumâẓiq*, false friend; — ة *mumâẓaqa-t*, insincerity.

ممار• *mumâr-in*, مماری• *mumârî*, who doubts, contradicts, disputes.

ممازجة• *mumâzaja-t*, mixture.

ممامس• *mim'as*, swift; slanderer; — *mumâss*, touching, in contact with, bordering upon; خط م *haṭṭ mumâss*, tangent; — ة *mumâssa-t*, touch, contiguity.

مماصاة• *mumâṣât*, swimming with the stream.

مماطل• *mumâṭil*, who delays the fulfilment of a duty, puts off a creditor; — ة *mumâṭala-t*, putting off, delaying (s.).

ممال• *mamâl*, inclination, INF. of (ميل); — *mumâl*, inclined.

مماليك• *mamâlîk*, pl. of مملوك• *mamlûk*.

ممتا• *mumtâ* ., to be looked for under (. مو , . مي VIII.) as—

ممتاز• *mumtâz*, ag. or pat. of (ميز VIII.); distinguished, selected, excellent; privileged.

. . ممت• *mumta* . . , to be looked for under (. . م VIII.), as—

ممتثل• *mumtaṣil*, ag. of (مثل VIII.), standing upright (ready for service), &c.; observing customs, laws, &c.; imitating.

ممتزج• *mumtazij*, mixed; agreeing with one's constitution, constitutional, compatible.

ممتش• *mimtaś*, thief, robber.

ممتلى• *mumtali'*, filled, full.

ممتنع• *mumtani'*, hindered, &c.; forbidden; impossible, inaccessible; who refuses; who refrains; — ات *mumtani'ât*, impossibilities.

ممحال• *mimḥâl*, sterile.

ممحاة• *mimḥât*, duster.

ممحش *mumḥaś*, burnt; — *mumḥiś*, burning; — ة *mumḥiśa-t*, dry year.

ممحوش *mamḥûś*, effaced, erased.

ممحى *mamḥiyy*, blotted out, effaced.

ممخ *mumiḫḫ*, lasting long, troublesome; rich in marrow; ة fat.

ممخض *mimḫaḍ*, *mimḫaḍa-t*, skin bag for making butter.

ممد *mumidd*, stretching, extending; helper, assistant, aid.

ممدد *mumaddad*, long, lengthy, extended, high; tightened with ropes (tent).

ممدر *mumaddar*, plastered, covered with loam;— ة *mimdara-t*, *mamdara-t*, clay-pit;— *mumaddara-t*, pl. fat camels.

ممدود *mamdûd*, stretched, lengthened, &c.; marked with *madda-t*.

ممذقر *mumẕaqirr*, curdled.

ممر *mamarr*, passage, pass, ford; canal; exit, departure; lapse of time; time passed, interval; م الناس *mamarr an-nâs*, the passing away of men, death.

ممراح *mimrâḥ*, mettled, fiery.

ممراض *mimrâḍ*, always sickly.

ممرث *mimras̱*, pl. *mamâris̱*, patient, mild (towards enemies); — *mumarras̱*, ground into powder.

ممرح *mimraḥ*=ممراح *mimrâḥ*.

ممرض *mumriḍ*, waiter on a sick person.

ممرغ *mumarrag*, soiled; — ة *mimraga-t*, cœcum.

ممرق *mamraq*, window.

ممرمر *mumarmar*, embittered, bitter.

ممروث *mamrûs̱*, pounded, made into powder.

ممرور *mamrûr*, bilious.

ممروض *mamrûḍ* = ممراض *mimrâḍ*; ill, sick.

ممروط *mamrûṭ*, made hairless; bitten, bitten at; torn.

ممروغ *mamrûg*, anointed with oil; soiled.

ممرئ *mumri'*, digestible, wholesome.

ممزق *mumazzaq*, torn; tearing (s.).

ممسح *mimsaḥ*, liar; — ة *mimsaḥa-t*, instrument with which a weaver sprinkles the woof; napkin, towel.

ممسك *mamsak*, handle, point of attack, weak point laid open; — *mumsik*, who seizes and holds, &c.; saving, miserly;— *mumassak*, perfumed with musk.

ممسوح *mamsûḥ*, wiped, &c.; polished, smooth.

ممسى *mumsa*, growing evening; INF. of (مسو IV.); monk's cell; — *mumassî*, who bids a good evening.

ممشاة *mamśât*, road, high-road, causeway.

ممشط *mimśaṭ*, comb; — *.

ممشوق *mamśûq*, ة slender; having thin soft flesh; made leafless.

ممشول *mamśûl*, having thin hips.

ممشى *mamśa*, walking; pl. *mamâśî*, walk, pavement, corridor, gallery; also *mamśî*, privy; — *mumśi*, who executes or observes (the law);—*; — *mumaśśî*, who sets a-going, orders to march; who has oxen at the plough.

ممص *mimaṣṣ*, sucking-pipe, siphon.

ممصر *mumaṣṣar*, gay-coloured;—*.

ممصل *mimṣal*, dyer's press or sieve.

ممصوص *mamṣûṣ*, sucked up, &c.; emaciated, thin.

ممض *mumiḍḍ*, biting, pungent.

ممضغة *mamḍaga-t*, mastication; joint of the jaws.

ممضو *mamḍuww*, well managed.

ممضى *mumḍî* (ممض *mumḍ-in*) who signs, the undersigned; — *mumḍa*, signed, sealed; authentic, authenticated.

ممطر *mamṭar*, *mimṭar*, ة *mamṭara-t*, *mimṭara-t*, pl. *mamâṭir*, rain-cloak; — *mumṭir*, rainy.

ممعود *mam'ûd*, suffering from the stomach; — *.

ممغمغ *mumagmig*, who slurs over the words, pronounces badly.

ممكل *mimkal*, pond or well with but little water ;— ة *mamkula-t*, exhausted.

ممكن *mumkan*, *mumakkan*, consolidated, fixed, fortified ; — *mumkin*, possible ; — ات *al-mumkinât*, the possible (created) things.

ممكولة *mamkûla-t*, exhausted (well).

ممل *mumall*, trodden (path) ; — * .

مملاق *mimlâq*, very poor.

مملح *mumallah*, salted ; — ة *mamlaha-t*, salt-works, salt-mine, saline ; — *mimlaha-t*, pl. *mamâlih*, salt-cellar.

مملسة *mimlasa-t*, pl. *mamâlis*, harrow or roller for levelling.

مملق *mimlaq*, trowel ; — *mumliq*, poor ; — * .

مملك *mumallak*, placed in possession, &c. ; king ; — * ; — ة *mamlaka-t*, *mamluka-t*, pl. *mamâlik*, kingdom, empire, state ; land, province ; landed property ; royalty, power ; place of government ; — *mamluka-t*, *mamlaka-t*, *mamlika-t*, possession, INF. of (ملك) ; عبد م *'abd-un mamlukat-un*, &c., bought slave, opposed to عبد قن *'abd-u qinn-in*, slave born in the house.

مملو *mamlû'*, *mamluww*, filled, full.

مملوحات *mamlûhât*, salt pickles.

مملوس *mamlûs*, castrated ; — * .

مملوك *mamlûk*, possessed, &c. ; well kneaded ; pl. *mamâlîk*, slave (bought or captive), Mameluke ; servant ; (m.) apron ; — ة *mamlûka-t*, dominion, empire ; — ية *mamlûkiyya-t*, slavery.

مملول *mamlûl*, baked in the ashes ; tiresome, a bore.

مملى *mumla*, dictated ; orthographically correct.

ممن *mimman*=من من *min man*, by or from whom ; — ان *al-mumminnân*, du. day and night.

ممناة *mamna'a-t*, *mamnât*, black earth.

ممنو *mamnuww*=ممنى *mamniyy*.

ممنوع *mamnû'*, hindered, prevented, &c. ; without nunation or inflection ; — ات *mamnû'ât*, forbidden things.

ممنون *mamnûn*, obliged, owing thanks ; diminished, broken off (غير م *gair mamnûn*, eternal) ; content, satisfied ; — ية *mamnûniyya-t*, obligation.

ممنى *mamniyy*, put to the test, tried, visited ; wishing for (ب *bi*).

ممهر *mumhir*, having a foal ; — * .

ممهو *mamhuww*, watery.

ممهور *mamhûr*, sealed ; — ة *mamhûra-t*, provided with a dowry, bought by a dowry.

ممولا *mamûlâ*, plover.

ممــوم *mamûm*, suffering from pleurisy ; afflicted with smallpox.

ممون *mamûn*, *mumawwan*, kept, fed ; provisioned.

مموه *mumawwah*, gilt, glazed ; counterfeited.

مميت *mumît*, ة , fatal, deadly (sin).

مميل *mamîl*, inclination ; — * .

ممية *mumya-t*, mummy.

ممئى *mam'iyy*, made one hundred.

(من) *mann*, U, INF. *mann*, tire out, jade ; cut off, tear off ; diminish ; —INF. *mann*, *minnîna*, be benevolent, merciful, gracious to (على *'ala*) ;—INF. *minna-t* (also II. and VIII.), reproach one for benefits received ; — II. INF *tamnîn*, see I. ; — III. INF. *mumânna-t*, help one to carry out a thing by repeated assistance ; — IV. INF. *imnân*, weaken ; — VIII. INF. *imtinân*, see I. ; upbraid ; show favour to, bestow benefits on (على *'ala*).

من *man*, he who, she who, those who ; *man* (m. also *mîn*), sometimes declined : du. *manân*, f. *manatân*, pl. *manûn*, f. ة *mana-t*, pl. *manât*, who ? — *min*, from, among, from among, by reason of, with regard to, by, through, since, on (من يومه *min yaumi-hi*,

on the same day); at (من وقته *min waqti-hi*, at the same time, at once); of (من حرير *min ḥarîr-in*, of silk); than; — *mann*, gift, present, bounty, benefit; manna, honey-dew; very fine dust; pl. *amnân*, weight of two pounds (رطلان *ruṭlân*); a measure; pair of scales; weakness; reproach; *minn*, benevolence, favour, mercy; — ة *minna-t*, pl. *minan*, favour; benefit, bounty, kindness; obligation; thanks, praise; reproach for benefits received; — *munna-t*, power, might; weakness.

(منا) *mana'*, U, INF. *man'*, soak a skin to be tanned.

منا *manan*, *mana*, death; du. *manawân*, *manayân*, pl. *amnâ'*, *amn-in*, *amnî*, *maniyy*, *muniyy*, weight of two pounds; a measure; pair of scales; divine decree, fate, destiny; intention; opposite and corresponding; — ة *manât*, weight of two pounds; an idol of Mecca.

مناب *manâb*, substitution, vicariate, representation; post or office supplied.

منات *manât*, pl. f. of من *man*.

مناجاة *munâjât*, familiar conversation, conference; prayer.

مناجذ *manâjiẕ*, moles (serves as pl. to جلذ *julẕ*, جلد *juld*).

مناجى *manâjî*, pl. of منجا *manjâ*.

مناجيب *manâjîb*, pl. of منجاب *minjâb*.

مناجيح *manâjîḥ*, pl. منجح *munjiḥ*.

مناجين *manâjîn*, pl. of منجنون *manjanûn*.

مناح *manâḥ*, mourning for a husband; ة *manâḥa-t*, house of mourning; mourning assembly; — *mannâḥ*, who gives, bestows, makes a present.

مناحس *manâḥis*, calamities, disasters.

مناخ *munâḫ*, pl. *munâḫât*, place where the camel kneels down; lodging, station, resting-place; (m.) climate.

مناخلى *manâḫiliyy*, sieve-maker.

مناخير *manâḫîr*, pl. of منخار *minḫâr* and منخور *munḫûr*.

مناداة *munâdât*, proclamation, public cry, banns of marriage.

منادم *munâdim*, comrade, boon-companion; — ة *munâdama-t*, boon-companionship.

منادة *munâdda-t*, resistance.

منادى *manâdî*, pl. proclamations, public notifications; — *munâdî* (مناد *munâd-in*), who proclaims, public crier, herald, harbinger.

مناديح *manâdîḥ*, pl. deserts.

منار *manâr*, place where a light is seen, where a fire burns; lighthouse; road-stone in the desert; distinct road; minaret; (m.) flag, standard; — *munâr*, illuminated; — ة *manâra-t*, pl. *manâwir*, *manâ'ir*, place of a light or fire; lighthouse; lantern, chandelier, lustre; minaret of a mosque.

منازعة *munâza'a-t*, quarrel, &c.; last gasps, agony.

منازقة *munâzaqa-t*, anger, angry scolding.

منازلة *munâzala-t*, combat, skirmish.

مناسب *munâsib*, fitting, corresponding, conformable, analogous; fit, worthy; referring to, belonging to; — ة *munâsaba-t*, fitness, correspondence, analogy, proportionality; worthiness; relation, connection.

مناسمة *munâsama-t*, intimacy; — *.

مناسيب *manâsîb*, pl. of منسوب *mansûb*.

مناشير *manâśîr*, pl. of منشار *minśâr*, منشور *manśûr*.

مناص *manâṣ*, place of refuge, refuge, flight, escape.

مناصرة *munâṣara-t*, assistance, help.

مناصفة *munâṣafa-t*, division into two equal parts; *munâṣafa-t-an*, in halves.

مناصة *manâṣṣa-t*, dunning a debtor (s.).

مناصيب *manâṣîb*, pl. of منصوب *manṣûb*.

مناط *manâṭ*, great distance, distance between, interval; — *munâṭ*, place where anything is suspended, that on which anything depends.

مناطحة *munâṭaḥa-t*, butting with the horns (s.), combat.

مناطل *manâṭil*, pl. wine- or oil-presses; pressed-out juices.

مناظر *manâẓar*, telescope; — *munâẓir*, resembling, &c.; adversary; overseer, inspector, superintendent, director; — ة *munâẓara-t*, dispute, discussion, controversy; superintendence, care, inspection.

مناظم *manâẓim*, pl. of منظم *manẓim* and نظم *naẓm*.

مناع *mannâ'*, who hinders, prevents, refuses; — ة *manâ'a-t*, inaccessibility; inaccessible, impregnable place.

مناعف *manâ'if*, pl. mountain-summits.

مناغاة *munâgât*, chirping of birds.

مناف *manâf*, an idol; عبد م *'abd manâf*, an Arab tribe; — *min'af*, zealous, exerting one's self; happy, fortunate.

منافاة *munâfât*, incompatability.

منافث *munâfiṡ*, intimate; — *.

منافج *manâfij*, pads used as false hips; false rumour.

منافخ *manâfiḥ*, pl. of منفاخ *minfâḥ* and منفخ *minfaḥ*.

منافرة *munâfara-t*, mutual aversion; jealousy, emulation.

منافسة *munâfasa-t*, competition, envy, enmity; — *.

منافعة *munâfa'a-t*, drawing advantage from, profiting by (s.).

منافق *munâfiq*, hypocrite, double-dealer, liar, impostor; impious, atheist, sacrilegist; — ة *munâfaqa-t*, hypocrisy, &c.; impiety.

منافى *manâfiyy*, belonging to the tribe, عبد مناف *'abd manâf*; — *.

مناقد *manâqid*, pl. of منقاد *minqâd*.

مناقشة *munâqaśa-t*, dispute.

مناقف *manâqif*, pl. of منقاف *minqâf*.

مناقلة *munâqala-t*, mutual information, conversation; circulation of the cup, drinking bout; good trotting.

مناقيب *manâqîb*, pl. of منقاب *minqâb*.

مناقيد *manâqîd*, pl. of منقاد *minqâd*.

مناقير *manâqîr*, pl. of منقار *minqâr*.

مناكح *manâkiḥ*, pl. marriages; wives; — ة *munâkaḥa-t*, marrying (s.).

مناكيد *manâkîd*, pl. of منكود *mankûd*.

مناكير *manâkîr*, pl. of منكر *munkar*.

مناكيش *manâkîś*, pl. of منكوش *mankûś*.

منال *manâl*, manner, means and ways, method; obtaining (s.); present; possession.

منام *manâm*, sleeping-place, bedroom, dormitory, bed; sleep, dream; — ة *manâma-t*, bed; bed-gown; velvet, satin; magazine, shop, warehouse.

منان *manân*, which two? du. of من *man*; — *mannân*, ة, kind; gracious, merciful, liberal; benefactor; who reproaches with benefits received.

مناه *manâh-in*, for مناهى *manâhî*, pl. of منهى *manhiyy*.

مناهيج *manâhîj*, pl. of منهاج *minhâj*

مناهيم *manâhîm*, pl. of منهام *minhâm*.

مناوبة *munâwaba-t*, doing anything in turns; alternation, relief, substitution.

مناور *manâwir*, pl. of منارة *manâra-t*.

مناولة *munâwala-t*, offering, giving, receiving (s.); holy communion.

مناوة *manâwa-t*, *minâwa-t*, reward, requital.

منايا *manâyâ*, pl. of منية *maniyya-t*.

منائر *manâ'ir*, pl. of منارة *manâra-t*.

منبت *mambit*, *mambat*, pl. *manâbit*, place where plants are growing;

— *mumbit*, producing plants; sprouting.
. . . منـ *mun* . . ., before *b* pronounced *mum* . . ., to be looked for under (. . . VII.), as—
منبت *mumbatt*, ag. of (بت VII.), cut off, settled, finally decided.
منبتر *mumbatir*, without progeny.
منبثق *mumbasiq*, breaking forth, issuing, proceeding (adj.).
منبج *mimbaj*, who talks at random, makes empty promises; — *mambaj*, *mambij*, town in Syria; منبجانى *mambajâniyy*, of or from *Mambaj*.
منبذة *mimbaza-t*, cushion.
منبر *mimbar*, pl. *manâbir*, pulpit, chair (of a teacher); reckoning-board, counter; estrade, platform.
منبض *mambid*, place where the beating of the heart is to be felt; pulse; — *mimbad*, instrument for beating cotton.
منبطح *mumbatih*, stretched out; flattened, flat; widened, enlarged.
منبع *mamba'*, pl. *manâbi'*, source, fountain-head, fountain; origin; stream of water.
منبعث *mumba'as*, place where anything springs from, emanates, &c.; — * .
منبعج *mumba'ij*, heretic; — * .
منبعق *mumba'iq*, raining plenteously; liberal; making many words; embossed; — * .
منبه *mumbah*, *mumbih*, forgotten; ة *mumbaha-t*, important business which has been forgotten; — *munabbih*, who awakes, gives good advice, &c.; alarm-bell, alarum; — ة *mambaha-t*, that in which there lies good advice; what makes a man celebrated.
. و . منـ *man . û* ., to be looked for under (. . ذ), as—
منبوذ *mambûz*, pat. of (نبذ), cast away, &c.; exposed in the street, foundling; bastard; spurious, adulterated, not genuine; — * .
منبوش *mambûś*, pulled out by the root; disclosed by searching; — * .
منتاب *muntâb*, visited from time to time, visiting.
منتاخ *mintâh*, tweezers.
منتاش *mintâś*=the previous; — *muntâś*, violently seized and snatched away.
منتاف *mintâf*=منتاخ *mintâh*.
منتان *manatân*, which two women? du. f. of من.
منتاى *munta'a*, distant place; ditch round tents to collect the rain.
منتـ *munta* . ., to be looked for under (. . ذ VIII.), as—
منتبج *muntabij*, ag. of (نبج VIII.) swollen.
منتبه *muntabih*, awaked, warned, instructed; attentive, on one's guard, cautious, prudent.
منتج *mantij*, time of parturition; — *muntaj*, born; brought to light; inferred; — *muntij*, near parturition; — * .
منتجع *muntaja'*, foraging-ground; — * .
منتجل *muntajil*, evident, clear.
منتجة *mintaja-t*, anus.
منتحل *muntahil*, plagiary.
منتحة *mintaha-t*, anus.
منتخى *muntahî*, arrogant and threatening; overbearing.
منتدب *muntadib*, following the call, called (apostle).
منتدح *muntadah*, free; liberty, freedom; — *muntadih*, exempt, free of (عن *'an*).
منتدى *muntada*, place of assembly, council-hall; conference; — * .
منتزه *muntazah*, place for amusement, pleasant spot, pleasure-walk; — *muntazih*, taking a pleasure-walk, &c., enjoying one's self in the open air.
منتسا *muntasa'*, great distance.
منتسج *muntasaj*, woven.
منتسخ *muntasih*, copyist; — * .
منتصر *muntasir*, conqueror; — * .
منتصف *muntasaf*, the golden mean; middle, mid-day; — * .

منتظم *muntazam*, in good order, &c.; regular (troops); — *.

منتعل *munta'il*, wearing shoes; shoed; pedestrian.

منتغ *mintag*, slanderer.

منتفذ *muntafaz*, width, spaciousness, possibility, easy opportunity.

منتفش *muntafiś*, swelling, bursting; bristling; ة, dishevelled, picked (cotton).

منتفى *muntafî* (منتف *muntaf-in*), expelled, &c.; destroyed, annihilated.

منتق *mantaq*, place of a horse's belly which touches the ground in lying down; — *munattiq*, vomitive.

منتقل *muntaqil*, changing place, &c., dead; copied; — ات *muntaqilât*, movables, movable property, furniture.

منتقم *muntaqim*, revenger, God; — *.

منتكر *muntakir*, disguised, incognito.

منتمى *muntamî*, related, belonging to, referring to.

منتها *muntahan*, *muntaha* = منتهى *muntaha*.

منتهر *muntahir*, scolding, &c.; refusing with harshness; bleeding, not to be stanched.

منتهز *muntahiz*, profiting by an opportunity; unrestrained, rude (in laughing).

منتهى *muntaha*, end, extreme, extremity, limit; منتهى الجموع *muntaha al-jumû'*, pl. with *fatha* in the first syllable, *alif* in the second, and ـِ (ي) in the third.

منتين *mintîn*, pl. *manâtîn*, smelling offensively, putrid, foul.

منثا *munsâ* ., to be looked for under (. ثو , . ثي VII.), as—

منثال *munsâl*, ag. of (ثول VII.), swarming, &c.

منثجا *minsaj-an*, in order to ease the bowels; — منثجة *minsaja-t*, anus.

منثر *minsar*, talkative, garrulous; — *munassar*, dispersed, &c.; covered with embroidery, flowers, &c.; weak, unfit.

. . . منث *mun . . .*, to be looked for under (. . . VII.), as—

منثقب *munsaqib*, ag. of (ثقب VII.), pierced, perforated.

منثة *minassa-t*, piece of cloth for rubbing in or anointing.

منثور *mansûr*, dispersed, scattered; كلام م *kalâm mansûr*, prose; white and yellow violet, gilly-flower; wild pepper.

منج *manj*, two or more dates hanging together; — *munj*, a small green shell-fruit.

منجا *manjan*, *manja*, pl. *manâjî*, place, especially on high, where one can escape; rising of the ground; — ة *manjât*, pl. *manâjî*, escape, rescue; place of escape.

منجاب *minjâb*, pl. *manâjîb*, bearing brave and excellent sons; poker.

منجار *minjâr*, a kind of flute or pipe.

منجاش *minjâś*, game-driver.

منجب *munjib*, ة, begetting or bearing heroic sons.

منجبر *munjabir*, cured (broken bone).

منجح *munjiḥ*, pl. *manâjiḥ*, *manâjîḥ*, successful, prosperous; procuring success; of sound judgment.

منجد *minjad*, pl. *manâjid*, broad golden necklace set with jewels; rope; — ة *minjada-t*, whip, rod; — *.

منجذ *munajjaz*, grown wise by sad experience.

منجذر *munjazir*, ebbing.

منجر *munjarr*, pulled, dragged; — ة *manjara-t*, timber-yard, wharf; —*minjara-t*, hot stone for warming water.

منجرد *munjarid*, with short and smooth hair.

منجز *munjiz*, expeditive, &c.; purgative.

منجع *manja'*, pl. *manâji'*, pasture-ground; — *munji'*, nourishing, wholesome (food); pathetic.

منجف *minjaf*, basket.
منجق *manjaq*, INF. ة, throw stones by a ballista.
منجل *minjal*, pl. *manâjil*, sickle; pruning-bill; sponge, wiper, &c.
منجلى *munjalî*, appearing, revealing himself (God).
منجليق *manjalîq* = منجنيق *manjanîq*.
منجم *manjam*, mine; also *minjam*, ankle; — *minjam*, handle of a balance; — *.
منجنون *manjanûn*, منجنين *manjanîn*, pl. *manâjîn*, water-wheel, engine for irrigating; time; destiny.
منجنيق *manjanîq*, *minjanîq* (منجنيك *manjanîk*), pl. *-ât*, *majâniq*, *majânîq*, *manâjîq*, war-engine, catapult, ballista; crane (for lifting); —ى *manjanîqiyy*, maker of such, mechanic, machinist.
منجو *manjuww*, set at liberty; escaped, rescued.
منجور *manjûr*, cut by the carpenter; timber-work; framework, wainscoting; — ة *manjûra-t*, water-wheel.
منجوق *manjûq*, knob, pommel, head; flag on a tower.
منجى *munajjî*, liberating, &c.; redeemer, saviour.
منجيرة *minjîra-t*=منجار *minjâr*.
(منح) *manaḥ*, A, I, INF. *manḥ*, give, bestow, grant (2 acc.); — IV. INF. *imnâḥ*, be near parturition; — V. INF. *tamannuḥ*, give for a present; — VIII. INF. *imtinâḥ*, receive a present; — X. INF. *istimnâḥ*, ask for a present or loan.
منح *manḥ*, giving, granting (s.); — ة *minḥa-t*, pl. *minaḥ*, gift, present; favour, benefit, bounty, blessing.
منحار *minḥâr*, who slaughters and entertains much, liberal.
منحاز *minḥâz*, pestle.
منحاة *manḥât*, long winding canal; اهل المنحاة *ahl al-manḥât*, no relations, strangers.
منحت *minḥat*, pl. *manâḥit*, carpenter's axe; plane; chisel; — *munaḥḥat*, planed; cut.
منحدر *munḥadir*, *munḥadar*, *munḥadur*, *munḥudur*, steep, precipitous; — *.
منحر *manḥar*, place where animals are slaughtered (for sacrifice).
منحرف *munḥaraf*, trapezium; شبيه بالمنحرف *śabîh bi'l-munḥaraf*, trapezoid;— *munḥarif*, deviating, &c.; indirect; sneaking, deceitful.
منحس *munḥis*, disastrous, ill-omened.
منحصر *munḥaṣir*, invested, &c.; restricted; comprised, included.
منحط *munḥatt*, put down, sinking, &c.; depressed; weakened.
منحف *munḥaf*, emaciated.
منحل *manḥal*, heated room for silk-worms; — *munḥall*, solved, loosed.
منحنى *munḥana*, bend of a valley or river; — *munḥanî*, bent, arched, vaulted; pliable; emaciated.
منحوت *manḥût*, cut, planed, &c., statue.
منحور *manḥûr*, gullet, throat.
منحوس *manḥûs*, ill-omened.
منحوف *manḥûf*, emaciated.
منحوى *munḥawî*, rolled or coiled up.
منحى *munaḥḥî*, who observes the rules of grammar; who takes away.
منخار *minḫâr*, pl. *manâḫîr*, nostril.
منخاس *minḫâs*, spur, goad, sting.
منخبة *manḫaba-t*, anus.
منخر *manḫar*, *minḫir*, *munḫur*, *manḫir*, *minḫar*, pl. *manâḫir*, nostril.
منخرب *munaḫrab*, *munaḫrib*, worm-eaten.
منخرق *munḫaraq*, place blown through by the wind; gust of wind; — *.
منخز *minḫaz*, منخس *minḫas*, sting, goad, spur, awl, puncheon.

منخسف *munḥasif*, blinded, blind; eclipsed.
منخع *manḥa'*, joint of the uppermost vertebræ; neck.
منخفض *munḥafiḍ*, suppressed, &c.; marked with *kasra-t*, put in the oblique case.
منخل *munḥal*, *munḥul*, pl. *manâḥil*, sieve, colander, strainer, filter.
منخنق *munḥaniq*, hung (by one's own hands).
منخوت *manḥût*, removed, put out of place, shifted; م الفواد *manḥût al-fuwâd*, timorous.
منخور *munḥûr*, pl. *manâḥîr*, nostril.
منخى *munḥî*, haughtiness, pride, vanity; — *manḥiyy*, haughty, vain.
منداص *mindâṣ*, shameless, frivolous (woman); impudent fellow.
مندب *mandib*, pl. *manâdib*, tears, lamentations; باب الم *bâb al-mandib*, Babelmandeb.
مندح *mandaḥ*, spacious place.
مندرج *mundarij*, included, contained; entered, registered, inserted; rolled up; — ة *mundarija-t*, contents.
مندرس *mundaris*, effaced; worn out.
مندعى *munda'î*, called up; answering, responding, respondent.
منذع *mindag*, satirical; — ة *mindaga-t*, white spots on the nails; =منسغة *minsaga-t*.
مندف *mindaf*, ة *mindafa-t*, instrument for cleaning cotton.
مندق *mundaqq*, pounded, &c.; shot into ruins (wall).
مندل *mandal*, aloes-wood (of Mandal in India); pl. *manâdil*, enchanted circle of a conjurer; — *mindal*, towel, napkin, table-cloth; cloth to gird one's self with; — *mundall*, led, guided.
مندلص *mundaliṣ*, slippery; — *.
مندلى *mandaliyy*, of Mandal, aloes-wood.
مندم *mandam*, repentance; — ة *mandama-t*, cause for repentance.

مندوب *mandûb*, bewailed, &c.; loved.
مندوحة *mandûḥa-t*, vast open country; width; easiness, ease, comfortableness.
مندى *munadda*, moistened, bedewed; watering-place; — ة *mundiya-t*, rebuke addressed to a coward; abuse, offence.
منديل *mandîl*, *mindîl*, pl. *manâdîl*, towel, napkin; table-napkin, table-cloth; *mindîl*, head-band, cloth for girding one's self; handkerchief; cloak, mantle.
منذ *munẓ*, *minẓ*, *munẓ-u* (for من اذ *min iẓ*), since (with nom. or oblique case).
منذر *munẓir*, who warns, &c.; apostle, preacher; name of kings of Hira, or of people belonging to this tribe (pl. مناذرة *manâẓira-t*); ابو الم *abû 'l-munẓir*, cock.
منربة *manraba-t*, calumny, slander.
منز *minazz*, moving to and fro, restless; cradle.
منزحة *minzaḥa-t*, pail, bucket.
منزع *manza'*, pl. *manâzi'*, place from which anything is pulled out, from which one withdraws; — *minza'*, arrow; — *; — ة *manza'a-t*, pl. *manâzi'*, intention, aim, end; after-taste; also *minza'a-t*, pl. *manâzi'*, care, solicitude.
منزغ *minzag*, ة *minzaga-t*, slanderer; *minzaga-t*=منسغة *minsaga-t*.
منزف *minzaf*, ة *minzafa-t*, small bucket.
منزل *manzil*, pl. *manâzil*, place where one alights, hotel, abode; station, day's journey; post-house for relays; position, rank, dignity; station of the moon; also *manzal*, alighting, halting (s.), INF. of (نزل); — *munzil*, who causes to alight, &c.; who offers hospitality, host; — *; — ة *manzila-t*, pl. *manâzil*, house, inn, hotel; alighting, putting up (s.); step; position, rank, degree, dignity; instead of.

منزلق *munzaliq*, slipping; slippery.
منزم *minzam*, tooth; — *.
منزه *munazzah*, kept free from, &c.; pure, holy; — ة *manzaha-t*, pl. *manâzih*, pleasant spot, place of amusement, pleasantness.
منزوء , منزوو *manzû'*, addicted to, infatuated with, greedy for.
منزوع *manzû'*, pulled out; spoiled; (m.) dwarf.
منزوف *manzûf*, exhausted, &c.; silenced by proofs, &c.; drunk; stupid.
منزول *manzûl*, suffering from a cold; — *munzawil*, ceasing, passing away.
منزوى *munzawî*, shrunk, shrivelled, &c.; solitary, hermit.
منس *manas*, cheerfulness, mirth; ة *mansa-t*, f. old; — *minassa-t*, rod, staff.
منساب *mansâb*, place of escape.
منساح *minsâḥ*, brush, broom, sprinkling-brush.
منساق *munsâq*, driven along, &c.; near; relative, relation, successor.
منساة *mansa'a-t*, crediting (s.); also *minsa'a-t*, *mansât*, *minsât*, shepherd's staff; staff of the weak.
منسبت *munsabit*, oblong; ripe; — *.
منسبك *munsabik*, molten.
منسبة *mansaba-t*, love-song, praise of the beloved.
منسج *mansij*, *mansaj*, workshop, or weaver's shop; — *minsaj*, loom; instrument for stretching the woof; — *.
منسجر *munsajir*, loose, flowing (hair); in unbroken succession.
منسجل *munsajil*, poured out; sealed, signed.
منسحق *munsaḥiq*, ground, pounded, &c.; pl. *masâḥîq*, flowing (tears).
منسر *mansir*, troop of horsemen (30 to 200); vanguard; — *mansir*, *minsar*, beak of a bird of prey; — *.
منسرح *munsariḥ*, stretching the legs, pacing along swiftly and lightly; stripped naked; name of a metre: *mustaf'ilun maf'ûlatu mustaf'ilun* — — ◡ — | — — — ◡ | — — ◡ — twice repeated.
منسع *minsa'*, north wind; — ة *minsa'a-t*, ground speedily producing plants.
منسغة *minsaga-t*, bird's wing or tuft of feathers with which a baker dusts the bread.
منسف *minsaf*, pl. *manâsif*, winnowing - fan; also *mansif*, mouth; (m.) hoof; ة *minsafa-t*, mining-tool; tanner's scraping-knife; —*munassaf*, cut with it.
منسفك *munsafik*, shed.
منسك *mansak*, religious submission, devotion; also *mansik*, pl. *manâsik*, place and ceremonies of sacrifice in the valley of Mina, near Mecca; hermitage; solitude.
منسل *mansil*, begetting (s.), generation, progeny; — *munsal*, begotten; — *munsil*, moulting; also (m.) *munassal*, falling in rags (adj.); — *munsall*, stealing away; — stealing in or upon; drawn (sword).
منسلخ *munsalaḥ*, end of the month.
منسلك *munsalik*, entering on a road, on a line of conduct.
منسلى *munsalî*, consoled, comforted.
منسم *mansim*, pl. *manâsim*, sign, mark; road, path; manner, way, method; opinion; sect; aspect, front; sole or hoof of a camel; — *.
منسو *mansû'*, delayed, deferred; credited.
منسوب *mansûb*, ascribed, attributed, &c.; pl. *manâsîb*, love-verses; اسم م *ism mansûb*, relative noun, adjective derived from a noun; — ية *mansûbiyya-t*, relation, appurtenance, relationship,
منسوجات *mansûjât*, textures, tissues; brocades.
منسوف *mansûf* = منسف *munassaf*.

منسى *mansiyy*, forgotten, neglected; — *munsî*, *munassî*, what causes to forget.

منشا *manśa'*, place where one grows up, where anything originates; birth-place, one's country; origin, beginning, source; principle, motive, argument; — *munśa'*, grown up, tall; hoisted; f. ة high-sailed, sailing (ship); — ة *munśât*=منشئاة *munśa'a-t*.

منشار *minśâr*, pl. *manâśîr*, saw; saw-fish; winnowing-fan; — ى *minśariyy*, in form of a saw, saw-like.

منشال *minśâl*, large fork to take meat out of the pot.

منشب *minśab*, net, noose; — *manśab*, what adheres to one; — *munaśśab*, imprinted with figures of arrows.

منشد *manśid*, who recites verses, improvisator.

منشع *manśa'*, INF. of (نشع); — *minśa'*, snuff-box.

منشغة *minśaga-t*, medicine-chest.

منشف *minśaf*, ة *minśafa-t*, pl. *manâśif*, towel; wiper, duster; — *.

منشق *manśaq*, pl. *manâśiq*, nostril; nose; — *.

منشل *minśal*=منشال *minśâl*.

منشم *manśim*, a perfume; — name of a woman who sold perfumes in Mecca.

منشور *manśûr*, spread, &c.; exposed to the sun; sawn; pl. *manâśîr*, royal patent, diploma; prism.

منشى *munśi'*, who produces, calls into life; author, secretary, editor; language-teacher; — ات *munśa'ât*, literary compositions, writings.

منصال *minṣâl*, troop of horsemen under 30.

منصب *manṣib*, *manṣab*, pl. *manâṣib*, place where anything is planted, position, office, dignity; root, origin; — *minṣab*, pl. *manâṣib*, tripod; — *munṣabb*, poured out; love-stricken; — *munaṣṣab*, planted up; straight, erect; — ة *mansabat*, discharge of an office or duty, pain, trouble, care.

منصبغ *munṣabig*, dyed; baptised.

منصح *minṣaḥ*, ة *minṣaḥa-t*, needle.

منصرف *munṣaraf*, success; departure; — *munṣarif*, turned, overturned; dismissed; dispatched; desisting; rebellious; declinable.

منصرم *munṣarim*, cut off.

منصف *manṣaf*, pl. *manâṣif*, middle, half; also *minṣaf*, f. ة, pl. *manâṣif*, servant; — *munṣif*, equitable, just; arbiter, arbitrator.

منصل *munṣul*, *munṣal*, pl. *manâṣil*, sword.

منصة *manaṣṣa-t*, bride-chamber, bridal-couch; stage, scene, theatre; — *minaṣṣa-t*, high chair on which a bride is exhibited to view.

منصور *manṣûr*, who is helped; victor, conqueror.

منصوص *manṣûṣ*, indicated, &c.; confirmed by a passage from the Koran; sanctioned.

منضاج *minḍâj*, spit.

منضام *munḍâm*, severely ill.

منضجات *munḍijât*, what promotes maturity, digestion, suppuration; purgatives.

منضحة *minḍaḥa-t*, منضخة *minḍaḥa-t*, engine for irrigating.

منضم *munḍamm*, added, inserted, annexed; contracted; heaped up.

منضور *manḍûr*, blooming, beautiful, fair.

منطاد *munṭâd*, high.

منطب *minṭab*, ة *minṭaba-t*, strainer, filter.

منطاف *minṭâf*, pl. *manâṭîf*, snuffers.

منطبخ *munṭabiḥ*, cooked; ripe, mature.

منطبع *munṭabi'*, imprinted, &c.; inborn.

منطرة *manṭara-t*, pl. *manâṭir*, place wherefrom a guard-keeper overlooks his district; district or circuit of a guard-keeper (ناطور *nâṭûr*).

منطف *munattaf*, accused of a disgraceful crime; adorned with ear-rings.

منطق *manṭiq*, logical speech; eloquence; logic; — II. INF. *tamanṭuq*, study logic; — *minṭaq*, ة *minṭaqa-t*, girdle; zone (م البروج *mintaqa-t al-burûj*, zodiac); — *manṭaq*, INF. ة, gird; — II. INF. *tamanṭuq*, gird one's self; — ى *mantaqiyy*, logical; — يات *mantaqiyyât*, dialectics.

منطلق *munṭaliq*, set free, &c.; loosened; separated; open and cheerful.

منطوح *manṭûḥ*, gored or killed by a horn.

منطوق *manṭûq*, uttered, expressed; proper (meaning).

منطوى *munṭawî*, folded; put in an envelope, enclosed.

منطيق *minṭîq*, very eloquent.

منظار *minẓâr*, looking-glass.

منظر *manẓar*, looking at (s.); pl. *manâẓir*, aspect, prospect, view; object in sight or looked at; spectacle, scenery; stage, theatre; face, visage, physiognomy, features; belvedere, tower, high building; — ة *manẓara-t*, pl. *manâẓir*, place with a fine view, belvedere; height, high tower, watch-tower, observatory; object looked at; face, physiognomy; spectators; — *minẓara-t*, opera-glass, telescope; — ى *manẓariyy* and—

منظرانى *manẓarâniyy*, of handsome aspect.

منظم *manẓim*, pl. *manâẓim*, place where things are well arranged, in good order; — *.

منظور *manẓûr*, looked at, &c.; visible; approved, acceptable, agreeable; examined, tested; object, intention, view;—ة *manẓûra-t*, calamity; — ية *manẓûriyya-t*, visibility.

منظوم *manẓûm*, well arranged, &c.; metrical, poetical, verse; Pleiades (and other constellations); — ة *manẓûma-t*, verse, anything ranged, string; succession, hierarchy; system.

(منع) *mana'*, A, INF. *man'*, refuse; hinder, prevent, repel; defend, forbid; pass. be indeclinable; — *manu'*, INF. *manâ'a-t*, be inaccessible, difficult of approach, impregnable; — II. INF. *tamnî'*, prevent forcibly or repeatedly, prevent from drinking or sucking, interrupt; refuse; — III. INF. *mumâna'a-t*, refuse; disobey; — V. INF. *tamannu'*, be refused, prevented, repelled; refrain, abstain from; be inaccessible, impregnable, strong (fortress); defend one's self against, parry; — VIII. INF. *imtinâ'*, prevent, forbid; abstain from, keep aloof, refuse to have anything to do with (عن *'an*, من *min*), deny to (على *'ala*); be forbidden, prevented, impossible; — ة *man'a-t*, *mana'a-t*, difficulty of approach, inaccessibility; — *mana'a-t*, dignity; pl. of مانع *mâni'*, who prevents, &c.

منعاف *mun'âf*, set aside, left in the cold, excepted.

منعام *min'âm*, very beneficent, liberal.

منعاة *man'ât*, message of death.

منعرج *mun'araj*, منعطف *mun'aṭaf*, bend; — *.

منعقد *mun'aqid*, tied in a knot, &c.; concluded, settled, decided upon.

منعقر *mun'aqir*, back-sore; (m.) in love.

منعل *man'al*, ة *man'ala-t*, hard ground; — *.

منعم *mun'um*, broom, brush; — *; —ة *muna''ama-t*, benefit, bounty; pleasant life.

منعى *man'a*, pl. *manâ'î*, message of death; prevention, hindrance; abstention; imprisonment; — *man'iyy*, he whose death has been announced; (له *la-hu*), who receives a death-message.

منغم **mungamm, shut, stopped up; muzzled; sorrowful.**
منفاخ *minfâḥ*, bellows.
منفاق *minfâq*, who spends much.
منفتق *munfatiq*, burst; ة *munfatiqa-t*, deflowered; م الكلام *munfatiq al-kalâm*, talkative.
منفجر *munfajir*, dawn of morning; — *.
منفح *minfaḥ*, restless and intermeddling person, busy-body; — ة *minfaḥa-t*, rennet of a lamb.
منفخ *minfaḥ*, pl. *manâfiḥ*, bellows.
منفد *munfid*, who exhausts his provisions; poor; dry, exhausted; — ى *munfadî*, ransomed, rescued.
منفذ *manfaẕ*, *manfiẕ*, pl. *manâfiẕ*, passage, outlet, hole, gap; window.
منفرج *munfarij*, gaping; burst; careless, quiet and cheerful; obtuse (angle).
منفس *manfas*, pl. *manâfis*, opening for breathing, mouth; air-hole, vent-hole; *munfis*, desired, precious; precious things, riches; numerous; abundant; — *.
منفسح *munfasaḥ*, open extensive place; — *.
منفسخ *munfasiḥ*, broken, dissolved; spoiled, put out of order; excluded, excommunicated.
منفش *munfaśś*, letting out air; sunk, fallen (tumour); calmed down.
منفصل *munfaṣal*, place of separation;—*munfaṣil*, separated, &c.; cut off at the joint; disjunctive; weaned.
منفض *minfaḍ*, fan; ventilator; duster; — *; — ة *manfaḍa-t*, pl. *manâfiḍ*, ash-pit.
منفعل *munfa'il*, vexed, offended, discontented.
منفعة *manfa'a-t*, *manfi'a-t*, pl. *manâfi'*, use, employment, profitable use; profit; gain; success; منافع الدارين *manâfi' ad-dâraîn*, the enjoyment of this world and the world to come.

منفل *munfil*, liberal beyond measure; — *munfall*, blunt (sword).
منفوس *manfûs*, greatly desired, precious; new-born.
منفوش *manfûś*, picked (wool); dishevelled; swollen (fruit in water).
منفوض *manfûḍ*, shaken; dusted.
منفى *manfa*, pl. *manâfi*, banishment, place of banishment, exile; — *manfiyy*, rejected; banished; denied, negative.
منقاب *minqâb*, pl. *manâqib*, tube, pipe.
منقاد *minqâd*, pl. *manâqid*, beak; instrument for examining gold and silver coins; — *munqâd*, docile, obedient; soft (ground).
منقار *minqâr*, pl. *manâqir*, beak; point, top; chisel and other pointed instruments.
منقاش *minqâś*=منقش *minqaś*.
منقاف *minqâf*, pl. *manâqîf*, beak; shell used for polishing.
منقال *minqâl*, trotting fast; coal-pan, censer.
منقب *manqab*, mountain-path, pass; passage, street; parts about the navel; — *minqab*, instrument for tapping a dropsical person or for opening an abscess; — *; — ة *manqaba-t*, pl. *manâqib*=*manqab*; bridge; rampart; enclosure; quality which leads to glory and preferment; virtue, talent, glory.
منقبض *munqabiḍ*, shrunk; constipated; ill-tempered.
منقد *munqadd*, cut or split lengthwise.
منقذ *munqiẕ*, saviour, liberator.
منقر *minqar*, ة *minqara-t*, pl. *manâqir*, instrument for hollowing out pumpkins, &c.; pickaxe or hammer; — *munqur*, pl. *manâqir*, well in very hard ground.
منقش *minqaś*, ة *minqaśa-t*, pencil, painting-brush; chisel, engraving-needle; pincers, nippers; — *munaqqiś*, painter; embroiderer; engraver; — *.

منقص *munaqqaṣ*, diminished, &c. incomplete, defective ; — ة *manqaṣa-t*, pl. *manâqiṣ*, decrease, diminution, loss ; defective condition.

منقطع *munqaṭa'*, place where anything is cut off, ceases, breaks off ; — *munqaṭi'*, cut off, &c. ; left in the lurch ; destroyed ; rendered powerless ; م القرين *munqaṭi' al-qarîn*, without an equal.

منقع *manqa'*, ة *manqa'a-t*, pl. *manâqi'*, place where stagnant water collects ; *al-manqa'*, sea, ocean ; — *minqa'*, ة *minqa'a-t*, pl. *manâqi'*, place where an infusion is made, where medicines are macerated ; م الدم *minqa' ad-dam*, guillotine ; — *munqa'*, laid in, preserved (fruit) ; concentrated ; cooling, refreshing ; a wine-measure (18 gallons) ; small cistern of stone ; — ة *minqa'a-t*, *munqa'a-t*, stone kettle.

منقف *manqaf*, unevenness, knot (in smooth wood).

منقل *manqal*, ة *manqala-t*, mountain-path ; day's march, station, halting-place ; a game (kind of back-gammon) ; — *minqal*, *manqal*, coal-pan, censer, portable stove ; — *minqal*, trotting fast ;— ة *minqala-t*, any means of transport ; hamper ; pack-saddle ; sector.

منقلب *munqalab*, reversal ; withdrawing ; place where anything is reversed, turned over, changed ; turn (منقلبنا *munqalabnâ*, it is our turn) ; the future life.

منقود *manqûd*, paid in cash ; cash, ready money ; carefully examined.

منقوع *manqû'*, macerated, &c. ; infusion.

منقوف *manqûf*, pale.

منقول *manqûl*, transported, &c. ; movable goods, furniture.

منقى *manqiyy*, road ; — *munaqqa*, cleaned, &c. ; raisin out of which the stones have been taken.

منكب *mankib*, pl. *manâkib*, shoulder, shoulder-parts ; side ; trace, track ; guide, leader.

منكدر *munkadir*, precipitate, &c. ; طريق الم *ṭarîq al-munkadir*, road from Yemâma to Mecca.

منكر *munkar*, pl. *manâkîr*, belied, &c. ; abominable, abject, forbidden ; م الموت *munkar al-maut*, agony, death-struggle ; *munkar* and نكير *nakîr*, the two angels who examine the souls of the dead ; — *munakkar*, indefinite ; unknown, incognito ; — * ; — ة *munkara-t*, anything unheard of ; pl. *-ât*, abomination, forbidden things.

منكسر *munkasir*, broken, routed, &c. ; fragile, brittle ; broken-hearted, discouraged.

منكش *minkaś*, who examines, investigates.

منكظة *munkaẕa-t*, exertion, haste.

منكع *munka'*, *munakka'*, flat-nosed.

منكف *munakkif*, having protruding jaws.

منكل *mankal*, rock ; also *mankil*, what brings on punishment ; — *minkal*, instrument of torture, torture.

منكمى *munkamî*, hidden.

منكنة *minkana-t*, press (for grapes, &c.).

منكوحة *mankûḥa-t*, married woman.

منكود *mankûd*, pl. *manâkîd*, little, scanty ; miserly ; hard-hearted ; م الحظ *mankûd al-ḥaẕẕ*, unfortunate, cursed.

منكوز *mankûz*, kicked, pricked, goaded.

منكوش *mankûś*, pl. *manâkîś*, hoe, mattock (m.) ; — *.

منكى *munkî*, hurting, infuriating ; —*mankiyy*, wounded, killed.

منلا *manlâ*, judge ; law-scholar.

منم *minamm*, slanderer.

منماص *minmâṣ*, tweezers.

منمحى *munmaḥî*, effaced, blotted out.

منمر *munammar*, spotted as a tiger.
منمص *minmaṣ*=منماص *minmâṣ*.
منمل *minmal*, *munmil*, slanderer; — *munammal*, mended, darned; benumbed; close (writing); ة *munammala-t*, industrious woman (like an ant); — *munmall*, fallen out; stealing away; — ة *manmala-t*, ant-hill, ant-nest.
منمهل *munmahill*, straight and stiff.
منمول *manmûl*, injured by ants.
منن *minan*, pl. of منة *minna-t*.
منها *minhâ*, away from her; subtraction.
منهاج *minhâj*, pl. *manâhij*, high-road.
منهال *minhâl*, see منهل *manhal*.
منهام *minhâm*, pl. *manâhîm*, very obedient.
منهت *munhit*, *minhat*, roaring; lion.
منهتك *munhatik*, torn, rent; injured, hurt.
منهج *manhaj*, pl. *manâhij*, high-road; behaviour, conduct, manners.
منهدم *munhadam*, formed symmetrically; — *.
منهر *manhar*, conduit, aqueduct, canal.
منهس *minhas*, lion.
منهكة *manhaka-t*, cause of weakness.
منهل *manhal*, pl. *manâhil*, watering (s.), watering-place, horse-pond; spring, well; also منهال *minhâl*, very liberal; grave-mound, tomb; — *munhall*, gushing forth in abundance.
منهمر *munhamir*, poured out, &c.; falling in ruins.
منهمة *manhama-t*, carpenter's workshop, timber-yard.
منهوس *manhûs*, منهوش *manhûś*, thin, lean.
منهوك *manhûk*, weakened by illness; — *munhawik*, surprised, perplexed, dumbfounded.
منهوم *manhûm*, insatiable, greedy; passionately addicted.

منهى *munhî* (منه *munh-in*), who brings to an end, decides; decisive, definitive; who brings news; — *munahhî* (منه *munahh-in*), forbidding; — *manhiyy*, forbidden, unlawful; pl. *manâhî*, also f. ة *manhiyya-t*, pl. *-ât*, anything forbidden, sin.
(منو) *manâ*, U, INF. *manw*, put to the test, try; visit, afflict; mete out to.
منو *manû*, obl. c. منى *manî*, acc. منا *manâ*, pl. منون *manûn*, who? — ة *munuwwa-t*, desire; anything desired, longed for.
منواع *minwâ'*, weaver's beam, warping-loom.
منوال *minwâl*, loom, weaver's beam; art of weaving; woof, warp; texture, shape, form, fashion, manner; what is beseeming, duty.
ذات منور *ẕât-u manwar-in*, visible to all.
منوط *manûṭ*, suspended at, tied to, dependent on (ب *bi*); admitted, accepted; entrusted to one's care; obliged; place where anything is suspended.
منوع *manû'*, who hinders, refuses; — *munawwa'*, manifold, specified.
منول *minwal*, loom.
منوم *munawwim*, narcotic; laying (the dust).
منومس *munaumas*, honoured, respected.
منون *manûn*, time; destiny, fate; death; pl. of من *man*, who; f. ة, who bestows favours upon others, obliging; — *munawwan*, pronounced with the *tanwîn*; — ة *manûna-t*, spider.
منوى *manwa*, pl. *manâwî*, intention, purpose, aim; — *munawwî*, mewing.
(منى) *mana*, I, INF. *many*, put to the test, try, visit; mete out to, ordain for; pass. be visited from God; be tempted by, wish for; suffer from seminal loss; — II.

INF. *tamniya-t*, cause one to wish, to long for (2 acc.); — III. INF. *mumânât*, grant the debtor a delay; put one off a long time; — IV. INF. *imnâ'*, suffer from seminal loss; come to the valley of Mina; — V. INF. *tamannî*, desire, long for; read; invent, devise; — VIII. INF. *imtinâ'*, come to the valley of Mina; — X. INF. *istimnâ'*, indulge in onanism.

منى *mana*, destiny, fate, death; measure, quantity; intention; — *mina*, valley of Mina near Mecca; human sperm; — *manî*, obl. case of منو *manû*, who? — *maniyy*, pl. *muny*, seminal loss; human sperm; — ة *manya-t*, pl. *muny*, spermatorrhœa; — *munya-t*, *minya-t*, pl. *muna*, desire, wish; — *munya-t*, name of a town in Egypt; — *maniyya-t*, pl. *manâyâ*, destiny, fate, death.

منيح *manîḥ*, who makes a present; ninth arrow in the game; — ة *manîḥa-t*, pl. *manâ'iḥ*, gift.

منيع *manî'*, inaccessible; impregnable; impossible.

منين *manîn*, weak, and, by opposition, strong; dust.

منيوكة *manyûka-t*, covered (woman).

منيئة *manî'a-t*, hide; tanning-pit.

(مه) *mahh*, U, INF. *mahh*, treat friendly, spare; — *mahih*, A, INF. *mahah*, be kind, friendly; be soft.

مه *mah*=ما *mâ*, what? *mah*, *mahin*, *mah mah*, leave off! gently!

مها *mahâ'*, bend, curve; — ة *mahât*, pl. *mahâ*, *mahawât*, *mahayât*, wild cow; antelope; piece of crystal or white glass; sun.

مهاب *mahâb*, dangerous place; — *mahâbb*, pl. of مهب *mahabb*; — *; — ة *mahâba-t*, fear, awe, respect, reverence; dignified gravity, majesty.

مهابيج *mahâbîj*, pl. of مهباج *mihbâj*.

مهاجر *muhâjir*, fugitive, emigrant; — ة *muhâjara-t*, flight, emigration.

مهاد *mihâd*, pl. *amhida-t*, *muhud*, *muhd*, bed; couch, sofa; chair, arm-chair, throne; cradle; floor; flat country, desert; support; — *mahhâd*, maker of cradles.

مهاداة *muhâdât*, making presents to one another.

مهار *mahâr*, ة *mahâra-t*, skill, proficiency; genius; — *mihâr*, nose-ring of a camel; bridle; also ة *mihâra-t*, pl. of *muhr*.

مهاريس *mahârîs*, pl. of مهراس *mihrâs*.

مهازل *mahâzil*, pl. years of famine.

مهازيل *mahâzîl*, pl. of مهزول *mahzûl*.

مهاصرى *muhâṣiriyy*, striped stuff of Yemen.

مهال *mahâl*, dangerous place; delay, respite, pause, recreation; — *muhâl*, poured out.

مهام *muhâmm*, pl. of مهم *muhimm*; — ة *mahâma-t*, desert.

مهامير *mahâmîz*, pl. of مهماز *mihmâz*.

مهان *muhân*, despised; contemptible; offended; — ة *mahâna-t*, contemptibleness.

مهاه *mahâh*, beauty, freshness; handsome, fair; also ة *mahâha-t*, anything easy, light, paltry.

مهاوش *mahâwiś*, pl. unlawful property.

مهاوى *mahâwî*, pl. of مهوا *mahwâ'*, مهواة *mahwât*, and مهوى *mahwa*.

مهاياة *muhâya'a-t*, community of the usufruct, or of a gain.

مهايجة *muhâyaja-t*, exciting, agitating, infuriating (s.); furious combat.

مهب *mahabb*, pl. *mahâbb*, place where the wind blows through; air-hole; quarter; blowing of the wind.

مهباج *mihbâj*, pl. *mahâbîj*, pestle for pounding coffee.

مهبط *mahbiṭ*, pl. *mahâbiṭ*, place where one descends, alights; — *.

مهبل *mahbil*, *mahbal*, pl. *mahâbil*, womb, matrix; base of the womb; rectum; passage; — *mihbal*, alert, agile, nimble; —

muhabbal, corpulent, clumsy; lost by death.
مهت mihatt, glib.
مهتار mihtâr, prince (Pers.).
مهتبل muhtabil, liar.
مهتجى muhtajî, pl. muhtajûn, satirist.
مهتدى muhtadî, pl. muhtadûn, guided on the right path; proselyte, convert.
مهتر muhtar, doting, delirious; — II. INF. tamahtur, behave proudly, arrogantly towards (على 'ala).
مهتشم muhtaśim, submissive.
مهتلك muhtalik, who rushes into danger; who loses his way.
(مهج) mahaj, A, INF. mahj, suck; lie with; grow handsome again after an illness; — ة muhja-t, pl. muhaj, muhajât, heart-blood, heart; mind, soul, life.
مهجع mihja', thoughtless.
مهجل mahjil, womb, uterus; water-course.
مهجنى mahjanā, مهجنا mahjanâ', مهجنة mahjana-t, pl. contemptible people, disgracing others.
مهجى muhajjî, spelling.
(مهد) mahad, INF. mahd, spread out; attend to a business and draw profit from it; — II. INF. tamhîd, spread; level, plane; carry out, despatch; facilitate; allege or allow an excuse; — V. INF. tamahhud, be spread, levelled, facilitated; be in good condition, flourish; have authority and power; — VIII. INF. imtihâd, spread out.
مهد mahd, bed; cradle; plain, level piece of land; — muhd, ة muhda-t, pl. amhâd, mihada-t, id.; uneven ground, which is to be levelled; muhd, pl. of مهاد mihâd; — mihadd, talkative, garrulous.
مهدا mahda', third part of the night; — mihdâ', who likes to make presents; — ة mahda'a-t, quiet state.
مهدب muhaddab, fringed.
مهدنة mahdana-t, quiet, tranquillity, rest.
مهدى mihda, who likes to make presents; tray, salver; — مهدى mahdiyy, rightly guided; guide; paraclete; — muhaddi', quieting, calming, moderating; — *; — ة mahdiyya-t, gift, present; bride, conducted to her husband's house.
مهذار mihẓâr, ة mihẓâra-t, doting, delirious; talker (m. f.).
مهذب muhaẓẓab, pruned; stainless, just; well-educated, cultivated, refined.
مهذر mihẓar=مهذار mihẓâr.
مهذم mihẓam, sharp.
(مهر) mahar, A, U, INF. mahâra-t, settle a dowry for one's wife; — INF. mahr, mahâr, muhûr, mahâra-t, be clever, excel, distinguish one's self; have practice and experience; — II. INF. tamhîr, demand or take a dowry; — III. INF. mumâhara-t, show one's skill; — IV. INF. imhâr, settle or give a dowry, make a nuptial present; — V. INF. tamahhur, be skilful, excel; be sagacious, penetrating.
مهر mahr, pl. muhûr, dowry, nuptial present; — muhr, f. ة, pl. amhâr, mihâr, mihâra-t, foal of a horse; firstling of an animal; pl. mihara-t, fruit of the colocynth; — ة muhra-t, pl. muhar, muharât, muhurât, young mare; shell worn as an amulet; pl. muhar, cartilage of the ribs; — mahara-t, pl. of ماهر mâhir, clever, experienced, &c.
مهراس mihrâs, pl. mahârîs, mortar (for pounding); stone kettle.
مهراق muhrâq, mahrâq, ة, poured out.
مهرب mahrab, pl. mahârib, flight, escape.
مهرجان mihrajân, autumn (Pers.).
مهرع muhra', trembling; — muhri', lion.
مهرق muhraq, pl. mahâriq, sheet,

page; book; shell for smoothing paper; smooth paper, parchment; sheet of papyrus; piece in a game of draughts; plain, desert.

مهرقان *mahraqân, muhraqân, muhruqân,* sea, ocean.

مهرم *mahram,* ة *mahrama-t,* decrepitude, weakness from old age.

مهری *muhra'*, deteriorated, putrid; — *mahriyy,* ة, pl. *mahârî, mahâriyy,* a breed of camels (of the tribe Mahra); ة *mahriyya-t,* red wheat; — *muharra,* well-cooked.

مهريق *muhrîq,* who pours out, sheds.

(مهز) *mahaz,* INF. *mahz,* repel, prevent; give a push on the breast.

مهزاق *mihzâq,* given to laughing (woman).

مهزام *mihzâm,* poker, stick.

مهزأة *mahza'a-t,* scornful laugh.

مهزر *mahzar,* always deceived.

مهزع *mihza'*, pestle; one who crushes or bruises.

مهزوز *mahzûz,* shaken, &c.; deranged (brains).

مهزول *mahzûl,* pl. *mahâzîl,* emaciated.

(مهش) *mahaś,* INF. *mahś,* burn (a. and n.); scratch with the nails; — VIII. INF. *imtihâś,* burn (n.); shave (n.).

مهشوم *mahśûm,* broken; put to flight, routed.

(مهص) — II. *mahhaṣ,* INF. *tamhîṣ,* clean; — V. INF. *tamahhuṣ,* dive.

مهصا *mahṣâ',* f. without vegetation.

مهصار *mihṣâr,* مهصر *mihṣar,* مهصير *mihṣîr,* lion (who crushes).

مهصم *mihṣam,* lion.

مهضوم *mahḍûm,* well-digested, &c.; sunk; ة, made of reed; — ة *mahḍûma-t,* an aroma.

(مهع) *maha',* blenching (with fear, s.).

مهفهف *muhafhaf,* ة, of a slender waist and brisk.

مهفوت *mahfût,* perplexed; — *.

مهفى *muhaffi,* what leads to poverty, to starvation.

(مهق) *mahiq,* A, INF. *mahaq,* be of a faint white or black; run; — II. INF. *tamhîq,* suck abundantly; — V. INF. *tamahhuq,* drink the whole day.

(مهك) *mahak,* INF. *mahk,* pound minutely; make soft and smooth; enervate (by sexual intercourse); step apace, hasten; lie with; — *mahik,* A, INF. *mahak,* also pass. *muhik,* have no sperm left, be impotent (stallion); — V. INF. *tamahhuk,* perform one's work well; — VII. INF. *inmihâk,* be pounded minutely; — ة *mahka-t,* prime of youth.

مهكر *mahkar,* ة *mahkara-t,* cause for astonishment.

(مهل) *mahal,* INF. *mahl, muhla-t,* proceed slowly and leisurely; be too slow, lag behind; smear the camel with pitch; — II. INF. *tamhîl,* grant a delay or respite; — III. INF. *mumâhala-t,* take one's time with; appoint for a later time; — IV. INF. *imhâl*= II.; put one off with excuses; — V. INF. *tamahhul,* VI. INF. *tamâhul,* proceed slowly and quietly; — X. INF. *istimhâl,* ask for a delay or respite.

مهل *mahl, mahal,* slow and leisurely proceedings; leisure, ease, rest; delay, respite; — *muhl,* metal (especially molten copper or iron); fluid pitch; pus, purulent matter; poison; — ة *mahla-t, mihla-t, muhla-t, mahala-t,* purulent matter from dead bodies; — *muhla-t,* delay, respite; truce; slowness, leisure, preparation; preference, superiority; fluid pitch.

مهلك *mahlik,* ة *mahlaka-t, mahlika-t, mahluka-t,* dangerous place; abyss, desert; — *; ة *mahlika-t,* perdition, ruin, destruction; — *muhlika-t,* anything pernicious, destructive.

مهلل *muhallal,* in the shape of a half-moon, crescent-like; — *muhallil,* praising God.

مهلوس *mahlûs*, stupid; thin, lean; refined (sugar, &c.); made into powder.

مهم *muhimm*, pl. *mahâmm*, important, grave; — * ; — ات *muhimmât*, important matters; cares, efforts, enterprises; necessaries, urgent wants; war-requisites; — ة *mahamma-t*, anxiety, anguish.

مهما *mahmâ*, whatever; all that which; however often; each time when; wherever; however so much; how often? when?

مهمار *mihmâr*, مهمر *mihmar*, talkative, garrulous.

مهماز *mihmâz*, pl. *mahâmîz*, spur.

مهمز *mihmaz*, pl. *mahâmiz*, spur; — * ; — ة *mihmaza-t*, goad.

مهمل *muhmal*, neglected, &c.; obsolete, antiquated; meaningless; unpointed (letter).

مهملج *muhamlij*, pacing at ease; easy.

(مهمه) *mahmah*, INF. ة, say مه مه *mah mah*, give over! leave off! hinder, prevent; — II. INF. *tamahmuh*, desist, abstain from (عن *'an*).

مهمه *mahmah*, ة *mahmaha-t*, pl. *mahâmih*, vast desert.

مهموز *mahmûz*, spurred, &c.; provided with *hamza-t*; (m.) spur.

مهمول *mahmûl* (m.) = مهمل *muhmal*.

(مهن) *mahan*, A, U, INF. *mahn*, *mahna-t*, *mihna-t*, serve, attend to; beat; treat offensively, despise; lie with; — *mahun*, INF. *mahâna-t*, be mean, despised; — VIII. INF. *imtihân*, take into one's service; accept service, become a servant; destine for daily use; abase, despise; — ة *mihna-t*, *mahna-t*, *mahana-t*, *mihana-t*, pl. *mihan*, service, condition of a servant; (m.) handicraft, profession, trade; skill in service; daily use of a thing.

مهنا *mahna'*, what is easy to be got, to be procured; light, digestible, wholesome (food); — *muhanna'*, congratulated; — *muhanâ'*, pl. of مهين *mahîn*.

مهنب *mihnab*, very stupid.

مهند *muhannad*, made of Indian steel, excellent.

مهندس *muhandis*, geometrician, surveyor, engineer, architect; experienced; clever; — *muhandas*, ى *muhandasiyy*, constructed with geometrical accuracy.

مهنى *muhanna'*, congratulated; — *muhanni'*, wishing joy, congratulating.

مهه *mahah*, smoothness; freshness and brightness; smooth; easy, bearable; hope; intention; anything vain; languidness, weariness.

(مهو) *mahâ*, U, INF. beat violently; INF. *mah-an*, *maha*, be sleek (doe); — A, I, INF. *mahy*, gild; *mahû*, INF. *mahûwa-t*, be thin, watery; — IV. INF. *imhâ'*, dilute with water, water; temper; — VIII. INF. *imtihâ'*, sharpen.

مهو *mahw*, watery milk; sharp bright sword; pearls; violent blow; ripe date; cold (s.).

مهوا *mahwâ'*, ة *mahwât*, atmosphere = مهوى *mahwa*.

مهوات *mahawât*, pl. of مهاة *mahât*.

مهواع *mihwâ'*, battle-cry.

مهوب *mahûb* = مهيب *mahîb*.

مهور *muhûr*, skill; — *.

مهوس *muhawwas*, diverted, amused; mad; — *muhawwis*, ى *muhawisiyy*, alchymist.

مهوع *mihwa'* = مهواع *mihwâ'*.

مهول *mahûl*, frightful, terrible; — *.

مهوى *mahwa*, مهواء *mahwâ'*, مهواة *mahwât*, pl. *mahâwî*, *mahâwiyy*, interval between mountains, chasm, ravine, precipice; — *mahwiyy*, loved, desired.

(مهى) *maha*, I, A, INF. *mahy*, dilute with water, water; — I, make thin (a blade); sharpen; gild.

مهى *mahy*, greatest speed of a horse, full career.

مهيب *mahîb*, terrible, frightful; feared; respected, held in awe;

severe, grave; lion; — *muhîb*, calling to, inviting; — ة *mahyaba-t*, cause for fear.

مهيج *muhayyij*, exciting, agitating, pathetic.

مهيدئة *muhaidi'a-t*, modest and tranquil circumstances.

مهيرة *mahîra-t*, pl. *mahâ'ir*, of a noble house and provided with a dowry (woman).

مهيش *muhayyiś*, dense, curly.

مهيص *mahyaṣ*, place where birds drop their excrement.

مهيض *muhîḍ*, broken again after being healed.

مهيع *mahya'*, pl. *mahâ'i'*, broad well-known road.

مهيق *mahîq*, distant country.

مهيك *mahîk*, impotent.

مهيل *mahîl*, terrible; dangerous.

مهيم *mahyam*, well? what is the matter?

مهيمن *muhaimin*, *muhaiman*, protector, guardian (God); who says Amen, confirms; who keeps his promise (God); — *.

مهين *mahîn*, pl. *muhanâ'*, despised, contemptible, bad; servant; little, few; — *muhîn*, offending, insulting, despising; disgraceful.

مهيى *muhayyi'*, who prepares, makes ready, arranges.

(موء) *mâ'*, U, INF. *mû'*, *mu'â'*, mew; — IV. INF. *imwâ'*, imitate the cry of a cat.

موابذة *mawâbiza-t*, pl. of موبذ *maubaẓ*.

موات *mawât*, lifeless, dead; dead bodies, corpses; waste and masterless land; — *mawwât*, near death, about to die.

مواتى *mu'âtî*, favourable.

موائر *mawâsir*, pl. of ميثرة *mîsara-t*; — ة *mu'âsara-t*, preference, choice.

مواثق *mawâsiq*, pl. of موثق *mausiq*; — *.

مواثيق *mawâsîq*, pl. of ميثاق *mîsâq*.

مواج *mawwâj*, agitated (sea).

مواجب *mawâjib*, salary, appointment; — *.

مواجرة *mu'âjara-t*, hiring for wages; payment of wages.

مواجن *mawâjin*, pl. of ميجنة *mîjana-t*.

مواجهة *muwâjaha-t*, meeting face to face, &c.; presence; بالمواجهة *bi-'l-muwâjaha-t*, in front of, in an audible voice.

مواجير *mawâjîr*, pl. of ميجار *mîjâr*.

مواحيد *mawâḥîd*, pl. of ميحاد *mîḥâd*.

مواخاة *mu'aḥât*, brotherly conduct.

مواخذ *mu'âḥaẓ*, not excused, blamed, punished; — *mu'âḥiẓ*, taking amiss, not excusing; — ة *mu'âḥaẓa-t*, taking amiss, blame.

مواخر *mawâḥir*, pl. of ماخرة *mâḥira-t*, furrowing the sea; also:

مواخير *mawâḥîr*, pl. of ماخور *mâḥûr* wine-house, &c.

مواد *mawâdd*, pl. of مادة *mâdda-t*; — ة *muwâdda-t*, mutual affection.

موادع *mawâdi'*, pl. of ميدع *mîda'*; — ة *muwâda'a-t*, reconciliation.

موار *mawwâr*, ة stepping lightly; swift; — ة *muwâra-t*, wool which falls off.

موارات *muwârât*, hiding, burying (s.).

موارب *mu'ârib*, *muwârib*, insincere; cunning impostor; — ة *mu'âraba-t*, imposture, deceit.

موارد *mawârid*, pl. of مورد *maurid*.

موارف *mu'ârif*, contiguous, neighbouring.

موارق *muwâriq*, near; — ة *muwâraqa-t*, nearness, proximity.

مواريث *mawârîs*, pl. of ميراث *mîrâs*.

مواز *mawwâz*, seller of bananas.

موازاة *muwâzât*, parallelism, equal distance; equality of value.

موازب *mawâzib*, pl. of ميزاب *mîzâb*.

موازج *mawâzij*, pl. of موزج *mauzaj*.

موازرة *muwâzara-t*, help, assistance; office of a vezir, a minister.

موازنة *muwâzana-t*, compensation, equilibrium; comparison; consideration, contemplation, pondering (s.).

موازى *muwâzî* (مواز *muwâz-in*), parallel, corresponding exactly, equivalent, equal; about; parallel ruler.

موازيب **mawâzîb**, pl. of ميزاب **mîzâb**.
موازين **mawâzîn**, pl. of ميزان **mîzân**.
مواساة **mu'âsât**, consolation, comfort, encouragement; cure; kindness, benefit, bounty; — *muwâsât*, consolation, assistance.
مواسق *mawâsiq*, مواسيق *mawâsîq*, pl. of واسق, big with young.
مواسم *mawâsim*, pl. of موسم *mausim*, and ميسم *mîsam*.
مواسير *mawâsîr*, pl. of ماسورة *mâsûra-t*.
مواشير *mawâšîr*, pl. of ميشار *mîšâr*.
مواصر *mu'âṣir*, near, neighbouring; neighbours, friends; — ة *mu'âṣara-t*, neighbourhood.
مواصفة *muwâṣafa-t*, purchase from description.
مواصل *mawâṣil*, pl. of موصل *mauṣil*; ة *mawâṣila-t*, pl. Mesopotamians; — *muwâṣala-t*, union; amorous enjoyment; personal meeting, intercourse; doing a thing without interruption; continuance.
مواصة *muwâṣa-t*, dirty water.
مواضع *mawâḍi'*, pl. of موضع *mauḍa'*.
مواضين *mawâḍîn*, pl. of ميضنة *mîḍana-t*.
مواطاة *muwâṭa'a-t*, agreement.
مواطن *mawâṭin*, pl. of موطن *mauṭin*.
مواعد *mawâ'id*, pl. of موعدة *mau'ida-t*; — ة *muwâ'ada-t*, promising, giving one's word (s.).
مواعظ *mawâ'iẓ*, pl. of موعظة *mau'iẓa-t*; — ة *muwâ'aẓa-t*, preaching, admonishing, teaching (s.).
مواعيد *mawâ'îd*, pl. of موعودة *mau'ûda-t*.
مواعين *mawâ'în*, pl. of ماعون *mâ'ûn*, household utensils, &c.
مواغ *muwâg*, mewing.
موافاة *muwâfât*, arrival.
موافقة *muwâfaqa-t*, fitness, agreement, sympathy, analogy, resemblance.
مواقت *mawâqit*, pl. of *mauqit*; — ة *muwâqata-t*, appointment of a time, fixing a term (s.).
مواقذ *mawâqiẓ*, pl. of موقذ *mauqiẓ*.
مواقر *mawâqir*, pl. of موقر *mûqar*.
مواقع *mawâqi'*, pl. of موقع *mauqi'*, and ميقعة *mîqa'a-t*; — ة *muwâqa'at*, attack, combat.
مواقة *mawâqa-t*, stupidity; ruin, destruction.
مواقيت *mawâqît*, pl. of ميقات *mîqât*.
مواقير *mawâqîr*, pl. of ميقار *mîqâr*.
مواكب *mawâkib*, pl. of موكب *maukib*.
مواكل *mu'âkil*, table-companion.
مواكمة *mu'âkama-t*, having thick hips (woman).
موال *muwwâl*, pl. *mawâwîl*, song, romance of the Bedouins.
موالاة *muwâlât*, mutual friendship, love; patronage, clientship.
موالج *mawâlij*, pl. of مولج *maulij*.
موالد *mawâlid*, pl. of مولد *maulad*.
موالف *mu'âlif*, familiar; —*muwâlif*, who arranges, adjusts, re-establishes concord; — ة *mu'âlafa-t*, *muwâlafa-t*, familiarity, close friendship.
موألة *mau'ala-t*, place of refuge.
موالى *mawâlî*, pl. of مولى *maula*; — *muwâlî*, pl. *muwâlûn*, helper; — *muwâliy-an*, in unbroken succession.
مواليد *mawâlîd*, pl. of مولد *mûlid*, مولود *maulûd* and ميلاد *mîlâd*.
موام *muwa''am*, big-headed, ugly; — *mu'âmm*, near; agreeable, suiting; distinct; — ة *mu'âmma-t*, approach; — *mau'ama-t*, iron cap, helmet without a point.
مواماة *muwâma'a-t*, consent.
موامرة *mu'âmara-t*, consultation.
موامى *mawâmiyy*, pl. of موما *maumâ'*.
مواميس *mawâmîs*, pl. of *mûmisa-t*.
موان *mawwân*, who procures provisions, purveyor.
موانات *muwânât*, indolence.
موانس *mu'ânis*, familiar, confidential; — ة *mu'ânisa-t*, familiarity, social intercourse.
موانى *mawânî*, pl. of مينا *mîna*, *mînâ'*.
مواهب *mawâhib*, pl. of موهبة *mauhaba-t*.

مواهطة *muwâhaṭa-t*, foolhardiness.
مواهة *muwâha-t*, beauty of face.
مواهيب *mawâhîb*, pl. of موهوب *mauhûb*.
مواويل *mawâwîl*, pl. of *muwwâl*.
موائد *mawâ'id*, pl. of مويد *mu'yid*, q.v. and مائدة *mâ'ida-t*, table, &c.
موايدة *mu'âyada-t*, invigorating, help.
موبات *mu'abât*, abominations, infamies.
موبد *maubad*, موبذ *maubaẓ*, *maubad*, *maubaẓ*, *mûbaẓ*, *mûbiẓ*, موبذان *mûbaẓân*, pl. *mawâbiẓa-t*, priest of the fire-worshippers, magian; — *mu'abbad*, everlasting.
موبر *mu'abbar*, fecundated, fructified.
موبق *maubiq*, dangerous place; valley of Gehenna; prison; ruin; — *mûbaq*, destroyed; imprisoned; — *mûbiq*, pernicious, destructive, hurtful.
موبل *maubil*, stick, cudgel; faggot.
موبن *mu'abbin*, fault-finder, censor, critic.
موبوة *maubû'a-t*, موبئة *mûbi'a-t*, plague-stricken.
(موت) *mât*, U, A, INF. *maut*, die; rest, sleep; calm down (wind); get extinguished, cease; — II. INF. *tamwît*, kill, murder; mortify one's body, one's passions; — IV. INF. *imâta-t*, id.; — VI. INF. *tamâwut*, feign death; — X. INF. *istimât*, *istimâta-t*, devote one's self to death; defy mortal danger, risk one's life; (m.) *istamwat*, feign death.
موت *maut*, death; — ة *mûta-t*, asphyxia, fainting-fit; epilepsy; insanity.
موتان *mûtân*, *mautân*, cattle-plague; *mautân*, lifeless; م الفواد *mautân al-fu'âd*, stupid; — *mawatân*, immovable goods; uncultivated land; (m.) mortality.
موتب *mu'attab*, crooked, curved, distorted.
. . موة *mu'ta* . ., to be looked for under (. . ا VIII.), as—
موتجر *mu'tajir*, ag. of (اجر VIII.), hired.
موتخذ *mu'taḫiẓ*=متخذ *muttaḫiẓ*, who takes for himself, &c.
موتر *mûtar*, stringed (bow).
موتزر *mu'tazar*, place where the belt is put, waist; — *mu'tazir*, wearing trowsers.
موتفك *mu'tafik*, destroyed by an earthquake; liar; — ات *al-mu'tafikât*, destructive tempests, fecundating winds.
موتك *mu'takk*, boiling, hot; raving mad.
موتكل *mu'takil*, corroded; infuriated, enraged.
موتلف *mu'talif*, familiar.
موتم *mûtim*, pl. *mayâtîm*, mother of fatherless children; — *mu'tamm*, taken as a model; — *mu'timm*, taking as a model or leader, follower, disciple.
موتمن *mu'taman*, he in whom trust is put (God); curator, trustee; — *mu'tamin*, trustful.
موتنب *mu'tanib*, having no appetite.
موتنف *mu'tanaf*, not yet grazed upon; untouched; ة *mu'tanafa-t*, on the point of getting marriageable; — *; — *mu'tanif*, beginner; coming, future.
موتور *mautûr*, who does not avenge the death of a friend or is unable to do so; vengeful.
موتوى *mu'tawî*, compassionate, affectionate, fond; receiving or received hospitably.
موتى *mauta*, pl. of ميت *mayyit*; — *mu'tî* (موت *mu't-in*), who leads up, brings.
(موث) *mâs̱*, U, INF. *maus̱*, *mawas̱*, *mawas̱ân*, mix up; dissolve in water, macerate.
موثبان *maus̱abân*, who stays always at home, undertakes nothing (prince).
. . مو *mu'* . ., . . موّ *mu'a* . ., to be looked for under (. . ا IV. and II.), as—
موثر *mu's̱ir*, ag. of (اثر IV.), who

prefers, closes; — *mu'assar*, pat. of (اثر II.), who has been influenced, what has received an impression; — *mu'assir*, what leaves traces, makes an impression, influences; effective, impressive.

موثق *mausiq*, pl. *mawâsiq*, compact, treaty; also ة *mausaqa-t*, confidence, trust; — *mûsaq*, firmly united; — *muwassaq*, who is trusted in; firm; of a strong body.

موثل *mu'assal*, firmly rooted; of noble origin; مال م *mâl mu'assal*, original capital.

موثوق *mausûq*, firmly tied, strapped; firm, persevering; thoroughly trustworthy.

موثوءة *mausu'a-t*, *mausuwwa-t*, موثى *mausiyy*, sprained.

(موج) *mâj*, U, INF. *mauj*, be violently agitated, throw up high billows; flow together, fluctuate (crowd); deviate from what is right; — *ma'uj*, INF. *mu'uja-t*, be bitter, salt (water); — V. INF. *tamawwuj*, VI. INF. *tamâwuj*, be agitated.

موج *mauj*, ة, pl. *amwâj*, wave, billow; gust; caprice; — ة *mu'uja-t*, saltness, see the previous.

موجب *mûjab*, what is required, necessaries; task; affirmative; — *mûjib*, necessitating, causing; cause, reason; first cause (God); worthy of; who holds binding; who listens to, receives petitions; — ة *mûjiba-t*, what is not indifferent, what entails reward or punishment, eternal rewards or chastisements.

موجد *mûjid*, who calls into existence, originator, author; inventor; — *mu'jad*, ة, strong, firm; compact, solid, solidly built; — ة *maujida-t*, INF. of (وجد).

موجر *mu'jir*, who lends, hires out, lets; prostitute; — *mu'ajjir*, who makes bricks or tiles; who rewards, pays the wages, &c.

موجز *mûjaz*, summed up, short; compendium, epitome; — * .

موجعة *mûji'a-t*, pain.

موجف *mûjaf*, excited, agitated.

موجل *maujal*, fear; — *maujil*, dangerous place (also ة *maujila-t*); pond of stagnant water; — *mu'ajjal*, having a fixed term; delayed, adjourned; — *mu'ajjil*, fixing a term.

موجن *muwajjan*, having strong protruding cheeks.

موجه *muwajjah*, approved, suitable, acceptable; of great authority; given, entrusted (office).

موجود *maujûd*, found, existing; at hand; review; — ات *maujûdât*, all things in existence, creation; ready money, merchandise, goods, stock in trade.

موجوع *maujû'*, suffering, ill.

موحد *mauhad*, single, one after the other; — *muwahhad*, ة, pointed with one dot (letter); — *muwahhid*, professing the unity of God, Unitarian.

موحل *mauhil*, mud.

موحوش *mauhûś*, inhabited by wild beasts.

(موخ) *mâh*, U, INF. *mauh*, calm down (n.).

موخذ *mu'ahhaz*, seized, taken away drawn to account; leavened.

موخر *mu'har*, *mu'hir*, ة *mu'hara-t*, back part of the saddle; stern; outer corner (of the eye); — *mu'ahhar*, put back, delayed, adjourned; back part; outer corner (of the eye); — ة *mu'ahhara-t*, consequence, conclusion, end, epilogue.

موخف *mauhaf*, dish of cheese, butter, and dates; a carpet as substratum.

موخمة *mauhama-t*, indigestible food; unwholesome country.

موخوط *mauhût*, deeply wounded.

مود *miwadd*, who loves violently; — ة *mawadda-t*, *miwadda-t*, love, friendship, good-will, benevolence; desire, wish; letter, book.

موداءة *muwadda'a-t*, dangerous tract.
مودب *mu'addab*, well-educated; punished; — *mu'addib*, educator, teacher, tutor; who punishes (children).
مودّدة *maudida-t*, love, friendship.
مودع *mûda'*, obedient, docile.
مودن *mu'dan*, *mûdan*, short, dwarfish.
مودوع *maudû'*, deposited, &c.; left alone; obedient; modesty, polite manners; — ة *maudû'a-t*, egg placed in the empty nest to cause the hen to lay others with it.
مودی *mûdî* (مود *mûd-in*), perishing; lion; kind;—*mu'dî*, promoting; helper, assistant; strong, powerful, capable; — *mu'addā*, paid; sense, meaning; *mu'addî*, paying; bringing on, causing; cause; — *muwaddî*, sending, dispatching; leading to.
موذر *mauẓar*, foul, putrid.
موذن *mu'aẓẓin*, who calls to prayer, Muazzin.
موذی *mu'ẓî* (موذ *mû'ẓ-in*), hurtful, pernicious; offending; paining; — *.
(مور) *mâr*, U, INF. *maur*, oscillate, swing from side to side; be moved by the wind; wave, be agitated; flow; run about, roam, rove; come to a higher country, to Najd; pick wool; pull out hair; — IV. INF. *imâra-t*, raise dust; — V. INF. *tamawwur*, swing to and fro, oscillate; roam about; — VII. INF. *imtiyâr*, be pulled out, fall out (hair); draw from the scabbard.
مور *maur*, walking to and fro, roaming (s.); wave, billow; agitation, emotion; path, road; — *mûr*, flying dust; — ة *mûra-t*, dropping wool; Morea, Peloponnesus.
موراق *mûrâqq*, beginning to colour (ripening date, &c.).
موراك *miwrâk*, front piece of a camel-saddle.
مورث *mûraṣ*, made a legatee; heirloom, inherited property; — *.
مورج *mauraj*, threshing-sledge; — INF. ة, move violently (n.); — *mu'arraj*, easily excited, lion; — *.
مورخ *mu'arraḥ*, dated; — *mu'arriḥ*, chronicler, historian.
مورد *maurid*, pl. *mawârid*, road to the water, to the watering-place; coming; access, entrance; place of embarking, of entering; place of appearance, of arrival, of alighting; station; مصادر و موارد *maṣâdir wa mawârid*, places where people go frequently in and out, where scholars meet; ة *maurida-t*, high-road; watering-place; — *muwarrad*, rose-coloured; painted red (face).
مورط *maurat*, precipice, abyss; — *.
مورع *mûri'*, separating.
مورق *mauraq*, Maurice; — *mûriq*, pushing forth leaves; rich; — *mu'riq*, *mu'arriq*, what awakens, renders sleepless;—ة *mauraqa-t*, what increases wealth; stationary.
مورك *maurik*, ة *maurika-t*, *miwraka-t*=موراك *miwrâk*.
مورنب *mu'arnab*, interwoven with hare's-hair.
موروd *maurûd*, arrived, &c.; handed down by tradition, related; place of arrival; shaken by the fever.
(موز) *mauz*, *mûz*, Banana (tree and fruit); large Syrian grapes; — ة *muwazza-t*, place abounding with geese.
موزج *mauzaj*, pl. *mawâzij*, *mawâzija-t*, boot, shoe (Pers.).
موزر *mu'azzar*, wearing trowsers; invigorated, strong.
موزن *mauzan*, place where anything is weighed.
موزورة *mauzûra-t*, crime.
موزون *mauzûn*, weighed, &c., of full weight; correctly scanned; harmonic, harmonious; correctly balanced (account); moderate, good, pleasant.

(موس) *mâs*, U, INF. *maus*, shave (the head).
موس *mûs*, pl. *amwâs*, razor; pen-knife; scalpel.
موسر *mûsir*, pl. *-ûn*, *mayâsîr*, well-to-do, rich, in affluence; — *mausar*, INF. ة, reel.
موسط *mûsaṭ*, middle of the house.
موسع *mûsa'*, rich, powerful; — * .
موسم *mausim*, pl. *mawâsim*, time or season appointed for the pilgrimage, for fasting, for harvest, for a fair or market; fair, annual market; harvest; place of assembly; camp.
موسوم *mausûm*, marked, &c.; qualified, denominated.
موسون *mausûn*, sleepy, lazy.
موسوى *mûsawiyy*, Mosaic; — ة *al-mûsawiyya-t*, the Mosaic law.
موسى *mûsa*, Moses; (m. f.) pl. *mawâsî*, (m.) *amwâs*, razor; point of a helmet's crest; — *mûsiyy*, Mosaic.
موسيقا *mûsîqâ*, موسيقى *musîqî*, music.
موسيقار *mûsîqâr*, a musical instrument; musician.
(موش) *mâś*, U, INF. *mauś*, glean grapes after the gathering; (m.) wash to the shore earth, sand, &c.; — also II. INF. *tamwîś*, be formed by alluvium
موش *mauś*, alluvium.
موشح *muwaśśaḥ*, adorned with a sash, &c.; adorned, ornate; acrostic.
موشر *mu'aśśar*, indented like a saw.
موشم *mûśim*, beginning to grow grass; — *muwaśśam*, covered with grass.
موشور *mauśûr*, sawn; prism.
(موص) *mâṣ*, U, INF. *mauṣ*, wash slightly; rub with the hand; — ة *mauṣa-t*, ablution.
موصد *mu'ṣad*, *mûṣad*, closed; covered; — *muwaṣṣad*, curtain behind which the women sit; — ة *muwaṣṣada-t*, girl's chemise.
موصل *mauṣil*, pl. *mawâṣil*, place where one thing joins another, articulation, commissure, suture; also du. *al-mauṣilân*, Mosul; pl. *mawâṣil*, ligaments; — *mûṣil*, bearer; — *; — *muwaṣṣal*, happily arrived; reached; — *muwaṣṣil*, who causes to arrive at the destination, guide; — *; — *mu'aṣṣal*, rooted firmly; اصل م *aṣl mu'aṣṣal*, old noble descent.
موصوف *mauṣûf*, described, &c.; اسم م *ism mauṣûf*, substantive; — ية *mauṣûfiyya-t*, description; qualification, qualifiedness.
موصول *mauṣûl*, united, &c.; attended; reached; collected, collection; tax, custom, duty; relative pronoun.
موصى *mûṣî* (موص *mûṣ-in*), who leaves or orders by will, testator (f. ة *mûṣiya-t*); who orders, commissions, recommends; — *; — *muwaṣṣa*, appointed as a guardian by will.
موضحة *mûḍiḥa-t*, large wound which lays bare the bone.
موضع *mauḍi'*, *mauḍa'*, pl. *mawâḍi'*, place where anything is put down; place, spot; locality; site, situation, position; village; district; opportunity; — *muwaḍḍa'*, brought low, weakened.
موضوع *mauḍû'*, put down, &c.; deposited, preserved; founded, established; destined for; damaged, meeting with a loss; position; pl. *mawâḍi'*, object of a speech, a book, a science; pl. *mauḍû'ât*, scientific axioms; م قابل *mauḍû' qâbil*, object capable of oratorical or scientific treatment; child with talents worthy of cultivation.
موضونة *mauḍûna-t*, double armour.
موطا *mauṭa'*, موطى *mauṭi'*, pl. *mawâṭi'*, place where the foot steps, footstep, track; socks; — *muwaṭṭa'*, kicked, trodden under foot; flat, level; abused, humiliated; م الاكناف *muwaṭṭa' al-aknâf*, influential and much-visited person, very hospitable man.

موطن *mauṭin,* pl. *mawâṭin,* fixed abode, domicile, house; native country, home; camp; battle-field where martyrs fell; martyrdom.

موطوءة *mauṭû'a-t,* tracks of travellers.

موطى *mauṭi',* see موطا *mauṭa'.*

موظف *muwazzaf,* official, dignitary; — *.

(موع), II. *mawwa',* INF. *tamwî',* cause to flow, to spread (fluids); push back occurring thoughts; — ة, موعة الشباب *mau'a-t aś-śabâb,* early youth.

موعد *mau'id,* ة *mau'ida-t,* pl. *mawâ'id,* promise; prediction; place and time of a promise or prediction; agreement; appointment, rendezvous.

موعظة *mau'iẓa-t,* pl. *mawâ'iẓ, mawâ'îẓ,* exhortation, admonition, sermon; good advice, warning.

موعلة *mau'ila-t,* mountain-goat.

موعود *mau'ûd,* promised, predicted, pre-ordained, &c.; also ة *mau'ûda-t,* pl. *mawâ'îd,* promise, prediction.

موعوظ *mau'ûẓ,* who is preached to, catechumen.

موعى *mau'iyy,* filled, comprising; well-formed, neat (ankle).

موفل *mu'affal,* weak.

موفور *maufûr,* abundant, enough and above; complete, perfect, great.

موفى *mûfî* (موف *mûf-in*), who keeps his word; — *maufiyy,* fully paid, completely satisfied.

(موق) *mâq,* U, INF. *mûq, mu'ûq, mu'ûqa-t, mawâqa-t,* be thoughtless and stupid;—INF. *mauq,* be cheap;—INF. *mauq, mûq, mu'ûq, mawâqa-t,* perish.

موق *mûq,* thoughtlessness, stupidity; pl. *amwâq,* large over-boot; a winged kind of ant; dust; — *mu'q, mûq,* pl. *am'âq, âmâq,* inner corner of the eye, low ground.

موقت *mauqit,* pl. *mawâqit,* appointed time, term or place, rendezvous; pl. sun-dials, watches; — *muwaqqat,* fixed for an appointed time or hour; appointed; temporary, provisory; — *muwaqqit,* who tells the hour; — *.

موقد *mauqid,* ة *mauqida-t,* pl. *mawâqid,* fire-place, hearth, stove; — *.

موقذ *mauqiẕ,* pl. *mawâqiẕ,* projecting part (of the elbow, &c., where a blow is particularly painful).

موقر *mauqir,* plain at the foot of a mountain; — *mûqar,* ة, pl. *mawâqir,* burdened; loaded with fruit; pregnant; — *muwaqqar,* honoured, venerable; dignified, grave; experienced in worldly matters.

موقع *mauqi',* pl. *mawâqi',* place where anything falls, alights, happens; event, accident; case of war; fit, the right man in the right place; — *mûqi',* disastrous; — *muwaqqa',* sharpened; broken by a hammer; much trodden, frequent (road); calamity-stricken; decree; — *muwaqqi',* who executes the signature of the sovereign, signs a patent, &c.; sharpening; stepping lightly; — *; — ة *mauqa'a-t, mauqi'a-t,* pl. *mawâqi',* place where a drop falls, where a bird alights or nestles; battle-field, battle, combat; — ى *mauqi'iyy,* local.

موقف *mauqif,* pl. *mawâqif,* place where one stops, station; — *.

موقن *mûqin,* knowing for certain; surmising (adj.).

موقوذ *mauqûẕ,* on the point of death, dangerously ill.

موقوف *mauqûf,* delayed, &c.; legacy; founded upon, referring to, bound up with, dependent on (على *'ala*); vowelless, quiescent (letter); — ات *mauqûfât,* mortmain, inalienable estates.

مولع *mûla',* passionate, in love,

addicted to, fond of (ب *bi*); — *muwalla'*, id.; shining, bright; intermixed.

مولف *mu'allaf*, composed; book; pl. *mu'allafât*, compositions, writings; — *mu'allif*, uniting, &c.; compiler, composer, author.

مولة *mûla-t*, pl. *mûl*, spider.

مولود *maulûd*, born, &c.; المولود له *al-maulûd la-hu*, father, المولود لها *al-maulûd la-hâ*, mother; birth, birthday; pl. *mawâlid*, son; pl. the three natural kingdoms.

مولوى *maulawiyy*, ة, referring to a grandee, judge, person in authority; law-scholar; dervish; — ة *maulawiyya-t*, quality of the afore-mentioned.

مولى, مولا *maula*, pl. *mawâlî*, lord, master, God, prince, judge, magistrate; patron, protector, benefactor; client, freed-man, slave, servant; friend; lover; neighbour; guest; — *mu'lî*, who takes an oath; — ة *mauliyya-t*, repeatedly rained upon.

(موم) *mûm*, pleurisy, small-pox (pass. *mîm*, suffer from pleurisy or small-pox); wax.

موما *mauman*, *mauma*, *maumâ'*, ة *maumât*, pl. *mawâmiyy*, desert, wilderness; — *mûma'* (عليه *'alai-hi*), previously mentioned.

مومد *mu'ammad*, ended, terminated.

مومسة *mûmisa-t*, pl. *mawâmîs*, unchaste woman.

مومل *mu'ammil*, hoping; giving hope, trusty patron.

مومن *mu'min*, ة, faithful, true believer.

مومى *mauma*=موما *mauman*, &c.

موميا *mûmiyâ*, ة *mûmiyya-t*, mummy; bitumen.

(مون) *mân*, U, INF. *maun*, take care of one's family, feed them; victual; (m.) be proxy for; — II. INF. *tamwîn*, provision one's house; victual; give to a day-labourer his food as well as wages; — V. INF. *tamawwun*, lay in provisions, provide one's self with victuals; — ة *ma'ûna-t*, *mu'na-t*, *mauna-t*, provender, victuals; — *ma'ûna-t*, provision-bag; saddle-bag; burden, molestation.

مونى *mu'nî*, hesitating, tarrying, slow.

(موه) *mâh*, U, I, A, INF. *mauh*, *maih*, *mu'ûh*, *mâha-t*, *maiha-t* (also VI.), abound in water; (also VI.) be full of sap; draw water (ship); — U, INF. *mauh*, mix; — U, I, give water to drink; — II. INF. *tamwîh*, put much water into the pot; gild, plate, glaze; give an improper answer to a question; adorn a tale, falsify news, equivocate; colour, illuminate (a picture); crack the teeth, eat; keep off or put away a thought; — IV. INF. *imâha-t*, abound in water; rain plenteously; give water to drink; meet with water in digging; — VI. INF. *tamâwuh*, see I.; — ة *mûha-t*, beauty and brightness of the face.

موهب *mauhib*, ة *mauhaba-t*, *mauhiba-t*, pl. *mawâhib*, gift, bounty; favour; — ة *mauhaba-t*, hole for water, small pond.

موهن *mauhin*, midnight or time soon after; — *mûhin*, *muwahhin*, weakening.

موهوب *mauhûb*, pl. *mawâhîb*, *mawâhib*, granted, given as a present; presented with (له *la-hu*).

موهول *mauhûl*, frightened; timorous.

موهوم *mauhûm*, imagined, &c.; imaginary.

موهى *mauhiyy*, torn.

مووجة *mu'ûja-t*, saltness.

موود *mau'ûd*, buried alive.

موول *mu'ûl*, ة *mu'ûla-t*, see (مول) and (مال); — *mu'awwil*, explaining, commenting upon; commentator.

موؤم *mu'wam*, *mu'awwam*, big-headed.
موون *mu'ûn*, pl. of مأنة *ma'na-t*, abdomen;—ة *ma'ûna-t*, provender, victuals; burden.
موى *muwayy*=مويه *muwaih*.
موئبة *mau'iba-t*, disgrace.
مويد *mu'yad*, assisted, victorious;—*mu'yid*, pl. *ma'âyid*, helper; pl. *mawâ'id*, heavy, evil, calamity;—*mu'ayyad*, strengthened, supported, authorised;—*mu'ayyid*, who strengthens, helps.
مويل *mau'il*, refuge, asylum;—*muwail*, *muwayyil*, small property, a few cattle.
مويه *muwaih*, ة *muwaiha-t*, a little water.
مى *mayy*, name of the mistress of the poet *Gailân*.
مياتيم *mayâtîm*, pl. of موتم *mûtim*.
مياثق *mayâsiq*, مياثيق *mayâsîq*, pl. of ميثاق *mîsâq*.
مياح *mayyâḥ*, ة, walking elegantly.
مياد *mayyâd*, ة, walking with a proud swing; tottering, tossed about (ship).
مياداة *muyâdât*, requital; handing over.
ميادين *mayâdîn*, pl. of ميدان *maidân*.
ميإذين *mayâẓîn*, pl. of مئذنة *mi'ẓana-t*.
ميار *mayyâr*, who imports corn;—*muyyâr*, pl. of مائر *mâ'ir*, who travels about, importer, &c.
ميازيب *mayâzîb*, pl. of ميزاب *mîzâb*.
مياس *mayyâs*, walking pompously; lion; wolf.
مياسر *mayâsir*, left side;—*muyâsara-t*, kindness, benevolence.
مياسير *mayâsîr*, pl. of ميسور *maisûr*.
مياسيق *mayâsîq*, pl. of ميساق *mîsâq*.
مياسين *mayâsîn*, pl. of ميسان *maisân*.
مياط *miyâṭ*, rebuke, rebuff;—*mayyâṭ*, inactive, trifling, toying.
مياطين *mayâṭîn*, pl. of ميطان *mîṭân*.
مياعة *miyâ'a-t*, fluidity.
مياكيد *mayâkîd*, girths of a camel-saddle.
مئال *mi'âl*, pl. of مألة *ma'la-t*, meadow;—*mayyâl*, bending, inclining; prepossessed, well-disposed, inclined towards.
ميامن *mayâmin*, right side; pl. of يمن *yumn*, good fortune, &c.
ميامين *mayâmîn*, pl. of ميمون *maimûn*.
ميان *mayyân*, arch-liar.
مياه *miyâh*, pl. of ما *mâ'*, water.
مئبر *mi'bar*, pl. *ma'âbir*, *mayâbir*, large thick needle; also ة *mi'bara-t* (same pl.), needle-case; sting; grudge; calumny.
ميبل *mîbal*, ة *mîbala-t*, plaited whip;—*mîbal*, *mi'bal*, thick stick.
(ميت) *mât*, I, die.
ميت *mait*, ة *mayyit*, pl. *-ûn*, *amwât*, *mauta*, dead;—ة *maita-t*, corpse, carcass.
مئتا *mi'tâ'*, boundary, sign-post; goal in a race; confining, (s.) contiguity; high-road; meeting of roads.
ميتخة *mîtaḥa-t*, cudgel, club; palm-branch; stalk of a date-branch.
ميتد *mîtad*, ة *mîtada-t*, hammer for ramming in pegs.
ميتم *muyattim*, making orphans;—ة *maitama-t*, pl. of يتيم *yatîm*, orphaned, &c.
ميتى *maitiyy*, referring or belonging to the dead.
(ميث) *mâs*, I, INF. *mais*, dip into water, soften, dissolve, macerate.
ميث *mayyis*, soft, mild, gentle.
ميثا *maisâ'*, pl. *mîs*, soft ground;—*mîsâ'*, ة *mîsâ'a-t*, club, flail; anvil.
ميثاق *mîsâq*, pl. *mawâsîq*, *mayâsiq*, *mayâsîq*, contract, treaty of peace; bargain; promise; testament; alliance, confederacy.
مئشب *mi'sab*, pl. *ma'âsib*, short sword; also *mîsab*, hilly ground.
ميثرة *mîsara-t*, pl. *mawâsir*, *mayâsir*, saddle-cloth; wrapper; skin of game.
ميثم *mîsam*, striking or breaking forcibly.
(ميج) *mâj*, I, INF. *maij*, be mixed.

ميج *maij*, mixture, confusion, hurly-burly.

ميجار *mîjâr*, pl. *mawâjîr*, crosier.

ميجاز *mîjâz*, concise, compendious; laconic.

ميجر *maijar*, ة *maijara-t*, little horn or tube for taking medicines.

ميجمة *mîjama-t*, girdle, belt; flail; hammer; anvil.

مئجن *mi'jan*, *mîjan*, ة *mi'jana-t*, *mîjana-t*, pl. *mawâjin*, flail, hammer.

(ميح) *mâḥ*, I, INF. *maiḥ*, descend into the well to draw water; give alms; — INF. *maiḥ*, *maiḥû-ḥa-t*, walk elegantly; waddle; — VIII. INF. *imtiyâḥ*, give, dole out; — X. INF. *istimâḥa-t*, ask for a present or favour; beg alms.

ميح *maiḥ*, gain, advantage.

ميحاد *mîḥâd*, pl. *mawâḥîd*, unit.

(ميخ) *mâḫ*, I, INF. *maiḫ*, walk along proudly.

مئخار *mi'ḫâr*, who delays for a long time; palm which keeps its fruit to the end of winter.

(ميد) *mâd*, I, INF. *maid*, *mayadân*, be moved, undulate, oscillate; thrill; bend (n.); walk with a proud swing; be giddy; increase, grow (n.).

ميد *maid*, boundary, boundary-post; — *maid-a*, except, on account of, considering that; — ة *maida-t*, dressed table.

ميدا (ميدى) *maida*, on account of, considering that; opposite; — *maidâ'*, measure, quantity; space, distance; end; opposite.

ميداعة *mîdâ'a-t*, every-day dress.

ميدان *maidân*, *mîdân*, pl. *mayâdîn*, vast plain, open place; race-course, hippodrome; battle-field; combat.

ميدع *mîda'*, cloth bag, wardrobe; sufficient living; also ة *mîda'a-t*, pl. *mawâdi'*, every-day dress.

ميدن *maidan*, INF. ة, *maidân*, gallop over a race-course, through a hippodrome; put a horse into gallop (m.).

ميدى *mîda*, end.

مئذنة *mi'ẕana-t*, pl. *ma'âẕin*, tower, minaret.

(مير) *mâr*, I, INF. *mair*, provide one's family with food, especially corn; import corn; — VIII. INF. *imtiyâr*, procure bread for one's family.

مير *mîr* (m. for امير *amîr*), commander, governor; ميرالاى *mîrâ-lâi*, colonel; — مئر *ma'ir*, v. see (مار), conceive hatred against, &c.; *ma'ir*, disastrous, mischievous; also *mi'ar*, mischievous person; — *mi'arr*, addicted to sexual intercourse; — ة *mîra-t*, pl. *mîr*, *miyar*, imported corn, corn; (m.) fisc, tax; — *mi'ra-t*, pl. *mi'ar*, *miyar*, hostility; calumny.

ميراث *mîrâs̱*, pl. *mawâris̱*, inheritance; — ى *mîrâs̱iyy*, hereditary.

ميراخور *mîrâḫûr*, chief equerry.

مئران *mi'rân*, pl. *ma'ârîn*, hiding-place of the game.

ميركة *mîraka-t* = موركة *miwraka-t*.

ميروق *mairûq*, seized with mildew; jaundiced.

ميرون *mairûn*, *mîrûn*, holy oil, chrism.

ميرى *mîriyy*, ة princely; fisc, taxation (m.)

(ميز) *mâz*, I, INF. *maiz*, separate, sever, distinguish, understand, comprehend; give the preference, prefer; wander from place to place; — II. INF. *tamyîz*, separate, distinguish; understand, comprehend; — V. INF. *tamayyuz*, be separated, distinguished, distinguish one's self, have the preference; burst (n.); — VII. INF. *inmiyâz*, *immiyâz*, be separated, distinguished; be broken; — VIII. INF. *imtiyâz*, distinguish; draw apart; — X. INF. *istimâza-t* be distinguished.

مئزاب *mi'zâb*, *mîzâb*, pl. *ma'âzîb*, *mayâzîb*, *mawâzîb*, aqueduct;

canal; gutter; waterfall, cataract.

ميزان *mîzân*, pl. *mawâzîn*, balance; measure, metre, prosody; form of a verb; rule, method; arithmetical proof; object of comparison, counterpart; conclusion, syllogism; quantity, bulk; intelligence, prudence.

ميزر *mi'zar*, pl. *ma'âzir*, veil; apron, pinafore; trowsers; dress; mantle, cloak.

(ميس) *mâs*, I, INF, *mais*, *mayasân*, balance one's self proudly in walking; talk and act thoughtlessly; — v. INF. *tamayyus*, walk proudly.

ميس *ma'is*, tree of whose wood saddles are made; (m.) tinsel; —*ma'is*, v. see (ماس) gape.

ميساق *mîsâq*, pl. *mayâsîq*, bird flapping its wings in flying.

ميسان *maisân*, pl. *mayâsîn*, walking proudly; glittering, shining, sparkling; — *mîsân*, sleepy; — *mayasân*, INF. of (ميس).

ميسر *maisir*, lottery by arrows for portions of a camel; game of chance; — *muyassar*, made easy, &c.; attainable, easy to be got; ready, at hand; — *muyassir*, facilitating, &c.; who grants success (God); — ة *maisara-t*, pl. *mayâsir*, left side; left wing of an army; also *maisira-t*, *maisura-t*, comfort and ease, competence, wealth; ease of manners, affability, sociability, gentleness.

ميسق *muyassaq*, imprisoned, sequestrated; covered with clouds; — جى *muyassaq-jiyy*, who keeps in confinement, turn-key, jailer.

ميسم *mîsam*, pl. *mayâsim*, *mawâsim*, iron for branding animals; mark by branding, mark, sign; beauty-spot; countenance; character; stamp; origin.

ميسور *maisûr*, pl. *mayâsîr*, made easy; successful, fortunate; easy to be done; friendly, kind; — ات *maisûrât*, flourishing affairs, good business.

ميسون *maisûn*, handsome.

(ميش) *mâś*, I, INF. *maiś*, mix; — INF. *maiśa-t*, travel over.

مئشار *mi'śâr*, pl. *ma'âśîr*, also *mîśâr*, pl. *mawâśîr*, saw.

ميشوم *maiśûm*, foreboding evil ill-omened, disastrous; cursed.

مئشير *mi'śîr*, lively, brisk.

ميضاء *mîḍâ'*, basin for ablutions; — ة *mîḍâ'a-t*, id.; place for making ablutions.

ميضانة *mîḍâna-t*, ميضنة *mîḍana-t*, pl. *mawâḍîn*, a bag or basket of palm-leaves.

(ميط) *mâṭ*, I, INF. *maiṭ*, push back, drive away, throw away, rebuke violently; —INF. *maiṭ*, *mayaṭân*, be far, withdraw, desist, forsake, leave in the lurch; doff; —INF. *maiṭ*, deviate from what is right; be unjust in one's judgment; oppress; — IV. INF. *imâṭa-t*, desist, leave off, leave; avert; take away; remove obstacles; — VI. INF. *tamâyuṭ*, get estranged, throw off one another.

ميط *maiṭ*, power; also *mayyiṭ*, increase, surplus.

ميطا *mîṭâ'*, low ground between hills.

ميطان *mîṭân*, pl. *mayâṭîn*, end, termination, boundary; starting-post in a race-course; = ميدان; — *mayaṭân*, INF. of (ميط).

ميطدة *mîṭada-t*, flail; rammer.

ميظب *mîẓab*, sharp stone.

(ميع) *mâ'*, I, INF. *mai'*, flow slowly over a surface; melt (n.); run fast; — IV. INF. *imâ'a-t*, make to flow; make fluid, melt (a.); — V. INF. *tamayyu'*, be made fluid, flow; — ة *mai'a-t*, flowing of what is poured out; storax; perfume, frankincense; balsam, oil of myrrh; bloom of youth; early morning; cheerfulness, joyousness.

ميعاس *mî'âs*, soft ground or road.

ميغار *mîgâr*, ة *mîgâra-t*, fixed term.

ميفا *mîfâ'*, stove for drying, brick-kiln, oven; also ة *mîfât*, high ground.

ميفاق *mîfâq*, favourable opportunity, suitable time.

مئفر *mi'far*, nimble, ready to serve, serviceable.

مئق *ma'iq*, breathing heavily; slow; — *ma'iq*, v. see (ماق), sob, sigh.

ميقات *mîqât*, pl. *mawâqît*, appointed time and place; season.

ميقاد *mîqâd*, materials for striking fire, steel.

ميقار *mîqâr*, pl. *maqâqîr*, heavily laden.

ميقان *mîqân*, credulous.

ميقب *mîqab*, shell used as money.

ميقعة *mîqa'a-t*, pl. *mawâqi'*, sledge-hammer; fuller's flail; grindstone; file; hawk's nest.

مئكال *mi'kâl*, eating-implement, fork, spoon; — *mîkâl*, pl. *mayâkîl*, Michael.

ميكع *mîka'*, ة plough-share.

مئكلة *mi'kala-t*, small kettle or dish.

(ميل) *mâl*, I, INF. *mail*, *mayalân*, *mailûla-t*, *tamyâl*, *mamâl*, *mamîl*, bend (n.), incline to; be friendly-inclined; hang down; sink; move towards (not in a straight line); decline, deviate; sympathise with (الى *ila*), have an antipathy against (على *'ala*); INF. *muyûl*, turn towards setting; friendly-disposed towards (acc. or الى *ila*); — *mayil*, A, INF. *mayal*, have one side of the body inclined; — II. INF. *tamyîl* (also IV.) bend (a.), cause to incline, to turn towards, inspire with sympathy for; II. curve, fold; waver undecidedly between two things; turn aside from the road to alight at (عند *'ind*); — III. INF. *mumâyala-t*, share in one's inclination for; — IV. INF. *imâla-t*, see I.; — VI. INF. *tamâyul*, balance proudly in walking; get loose and be on the point of falling (saddle); — X. INF. *isti-mâla-t*, incline towards, be favourably disposed; dispose one kindly towards another; try to gain one's favour or inclination.

ميل *mail*, pl. *amyâl*, inclination, goodwill, sympathy; taste, disposition, a mind for; setting; side; — *mîl*, pl. *amyâl*, *muyûl*, reach of the eye; mile; milestone, column, obelisk, boundary-stone; hand of a sun-dial; axle-tree; probe; instrument for applying collyrium; iron for blinding; pl. of أميل *amyal*, leaning to one side; — *ma'il*, corpulent, fat; — *mayyil*, rich; — *muyyal*, pl. of مائل *mâ'il*, bending, &c.; — *mi'all*, swift, fleet; — ة *mîla-t*, pl. *miyal*, time.

ميلا *mailâ'*, f. of أميل *amyal*, leaning to one side; — ة *mi'lât*, pl. *ma'âlî*, cloth with which mourning women gird themselves.

ميلاد *mîlâd*, pl. *mawâlîd*, birth; birthday; م عيسى *mîlâd 'îsa*, Christmas; — ى *mîlâdiyy*, ة, referring to the birthday; سنة ميلادية *sana-t mîlâdiyya-t*, year after Christ.

ميلان *mayalân*, inclination, INF. of (ميل).

ميلاه *mîlâh*, seized with violent grief; rutting.

ميلغة *mîlaga-t*, dog-trough.

مئلق *mi'laq*, stupid, imbecile.

ميلة *mîlah*, waste plain.

ميلولة *mailûla-t*=ميلان *mayalân*.

ميلى *mailiyy*, willingly.

ميم *mîm*, pass. see (موم); name of the letter م; pure (wine); well; — *mi'amm*, guide, leader.

ميماس *mîmâs*, river Orontes.

ميمن *muyamman*, blessed; fertile; — ة *maimana-t*, pl. *mayâmin*, right side or hand; right wing; luck; lucky disposition.

ميموم *maimûm*, sunk in the sea; over-flooded.

ميمون *maimûn*, pl. *mayâmîn*, lucky, fortunate, auspicious; large ape.

(مين) *mân*, I, INF. *main*, tell lies, lie; till the ground for the seed.
مين *main*, pl. *muyûn*, lie, falsehood, deceit; — *mîn*, m.=من *man*, who? — *miyan*, pl. of مينا *mîna'*; — ة *mîna-t*, see مينا *mînâ'*; — *ma'inna-t*, sign, mark; worthy, fit.
مينا *mîna'*, *mînâ'*, ة *mîna-t*, pl. *mawânî*, *miyan*, harbour, anchorage; — *mînâ'*, glass bead.
مئناث *mi'nâs*, bearing or begetting only girls; effeminate; blunt; abounding in grass.
مئناف *mi'nâf*, travelling at the beginning of night; untouched, not grazed off; leading to such pasture-ground (herdsman).
مينى *mîna*, harbour; glass bead.
(ميه) *mâh*, I, INF. *maih*, *maiha-t*, give water to drink; abound in water; draw in water; gild, plate.
ميه *mayyih*, full of water.
ميوس *mayûs*, balancing one's self proudly in walking; — *mai'ûs*, despairing; — ية *mai'ûsiyya-t*, despair.
ميول *muyûl*, pl. of ميل *mail*; also ة *muyûla-t*, INF. of (ميل).
ميون *mayûn*, liar; pl. of مين *main*; — *mi'ûn*, pl. of مائة *mi'a-t*, a hundred.
ميووس *mai'ûs*=ميوس *mayûs*.
مئوى *mi'awiyy*, centigrade.
مئيد *ma'îd*, soft, delicate.
مئير *ma'îr*, covered (woman); — *mi'yar*, addicted to sexual intercourse.
مئيف *ma'îf*, mildewed.

ن

ن *n*, as a numeral sign=50; in almanacs abbreviation for the conjunction of stars.
نا *nâ*, affix of the 1st person plural, possessive with nouns, objective with verbs; — *nâ'*, see (نى , نو).
نآت *na''ât*, who sighs or groans frequently; lion.
نآج *na''âj*, lion.
ناب *nâb*, pl. *anyub*, *anyâb*, *nuyûb*, *anâyîb*, dog-tooth, tusk, molar tooth; ivory; pl. *anyâb*, *nuyûb*, *nîb*, old she-camel; chieftain, prince, leader.
نابتة *nâbita-t*, pl. *nawâbit*, anything sprouting, growing, plant, young of an animal, child.
نابجة *nâbija-t*, calamity.
نابح *nâbiḥ*, barking.
نابض *nâbiḍ*, beating, throbbing; anger; twanger of the bow.
نابغ *nâbig*, gushing forth; — *nâbiga-t*, pl. *nawâbig*, rising unexpectedly in greatness, eminent man; brilliant passage in a poem; eminent, excellent; of quick understanding; name of a poet; — ى *nâbigiyy*, ة, of Nâbiga, as described by Nâbiga.
نابك *nâbik*, ة, pl. *nawâbik*, high, placed on high.
نابل *nâbil*, pl. *nubbal*, arrow-shooter; archer; maker of arrows; skilful, clever; woof; — *nâbul*, a proper name.
نابلس *nâbulus*, town in Palestine.
نابه *nâbih*, pl. *nabh*, celebrated, illustrious; important.
نابى *nâbî* (ناب *nâb-in*), pl. *nubiyy*, high ground; — *nâbi'*, bossed, convex; coming from the opposite side; — ة *nâbiya-t*, strongly-bent bow.
نات *nât*=ناس *nâs*, men.
(نات) *na'at*, A, I, INF. *na't*, *na'ît*, sigh, groan; envy.
ناتق *nâtiq*, shaking, &c.; rising, stepping forward, projecting; advancing too far.
ناتى *nâtî* (نات *nât-in*), *nâti'*, swell-

ing, swollen, projecting, in relief; advancing too far.

(ناث) *na'as̱*, INF. *na's̱*, be far; INF. *na's̱*, *man'as̱*, exert one's self, make efforts, be industrious.

ناثر *nâs̱ir*, writer of prose.

(ناج) *na'aj*, INF. *nu'uj*, travel; INF. *na'j*, groan; bellow; scream, shriek; INF. *na'ij*, be agitated, blow violently; pass. *nu'ij*, come during a violent storm; — *na'ij*, A, INF. *na'aj*, eat slowly and slightly masticating.

ناجح *nâjiḥ*, roaring (sea).

ناجذ *nâjiẓ*, pl. *nawâjiẓ*, molar tooth; wisdom tooth.

ناجر *nâjir*, hot.

ناجز *nâjiz*, ready, at hand; ready money, cash.

ناجس *nâjis*, dirty, unclean, impure; incurable.

ناجع *nâji'*, nourishing, quenching thirst, wholesome; effective; — ة *nâji'a-t*, foragers, who look out for food.

ناجل *nâjil*, generator; du. parents; thoroughbred (horse).

ناجود *nâjûd*, wine; wine-vessel, large cup.

ناجور *nâjûr*, turn-pike, toll-bar; bolt; buttress.

ناجى *nâjî* (ناج *nâj-in*), who escapes, &c.; rescued; swift; elected, predestinate to the grace of God.

ناحاة *nâḥât*, side, direction, region.

ناحر *nâḥir*, du. *nâḥirân*, two veins in the throat; — ة *nâḥira-t*, pl. *nawâḥir*, last day and night of a lunar month.

ناحس *nâḥis*, ill-omened, disastrous.

ناحل *nâḥil*, pl. *naḥla*, emaciated; thin, slender.

ناحى *nâḥî* (ناح *nâḥ-in*), inclined; pl. *nuḥât*, grammarian; — ة *nâḥiya-t*, pl. *nawâḥî*, side, coast, tract, neighbouring land, district, canton; *nâḥiyat-an*, separately, by one's self.

ناخذا *nâḫuẕâ*, ناخذاه *nâḫuẕâh*, pl. *nawâḫiẕa-t*, captain of a ship, supercargo; sailor.

ناخر *nâḫir*, worn-out, carious, &c.; somebody, لا ن *lâ nâḫir*, nobody.

ناخس *nâḫis*, mange in a camel's tail.

ناخوز *nâḫûz*, ة *naḫûza-t*, sting.

(ناد) *na'ad*, INF. *na'd*, envy; befall; exude water.

ناد *nâd*, ground abounding in water;—*nâdd*, fleeing, escaping; necessaries of life;—ة *nâddat-an*, fleeing in all directions.

نادب *nâdib*, ة, pl. *nawâdib*, lamenting the dead; pl. mourning women.

نادر *nâdir*, rare, extraordinary; eminent, precious; — ة *nâdira-t*, pl. *nawâdir*, rare thing, apparition or word, rarity; ن الزمان *nâdirat az-zamân*, phœnix of the age.

نادف *nâdif*, cotton-carder.

نادم *nâdim*, pl. *nuddâm*, *nidâm*, repenting, penitent, abashed; who announces, proclaims.

نادى *nâdî* (ناد *nâd-in*), who calls, invites; public crier; place of assembly, place of concourse, hall; assembly, council; abode; — *na'âda*, *na'âdî*, calamities; — ة *nâdiya-t*, beginning.

ناذر *nâẕir*, who makes a vow; bound by a vow; Mecca.

(نار) *na'ar*, grow agitated.

نار *nâr*, pl. *anwâr*, *nîrân*, *nûr*, *niyâr*, *anwira-t*, *niyara-t*, fire; hell fire (اهل النار *ahl an-nâr*, the damned); intelligence; advice.

نارجيل *na'rijîl*, *nârjîl*, cocoa-nut; also ة *nârjîla-t*, Persian pipe for smoking through water.

ناردين *nârdîn*, spikenard.

نارسة *nârisa-t*, best kind of dates.

نارنج *nâranj*, orange.

نارى *nâriyy*, ة, fiery; glowing, ardent; passionate, irritable; hellish, infernal; — ة *nâriyya-t*, nature of fire.

نازع *nâzi'*, taking away, pulling out, destroying, &c.; Satan; pl. *nuzza'*, foreigner, stranger; — ات *an-nâzi'ât*, angels who carry off the souls of the damned.

نازل *nâzil*, alighting, &c.; precipitous; precipice; heaven-sent; — ة *nâzila-t*, pl. *nawâzil*, calamity; cold, rheum.

نازه *nâzih*, pl. *nizâh*, *nuzahâ'*, retired from the world, secluded; pure, chaste.

نازية *nâziya-t*, deep dish; heat, passion, fit of anger.

ناس *nâs*, men, people, pl. of انسان *insân*; — *nâs-in*, see ناسى *nâsî*; — *nâss*, dry; thirsty; a species of monkey; — ة *nâssa-t*, dry bread; Mecca.

ناسج *nâsij*, weaver; author.

ناسك *nâsik*, pl. *nussâk*, pious, devout; devotee, hermit, ascetic; — ة *nâsika-t*, ground rained upon and flourishing.

ناسم *nâsim*, fetching the last gasps, dangerously ill.

ناسوت *nâsût*, humanity; — ى *nâsûtiyy*, human.

ناسور *nâsûr*, pl. *nawâsîr*, wound which continually opens again, fistula.

ناسى *nâsî* (ناس *nâs-in*), forgetting, forgetful; dilatory.

(ناش) *na'aś*, INF. *na'ś*, take, seize by force, snatch from; delay, adjourn; rise; leap upon, assail, attack; — VIII. INF. *inti'âś*, snatch away; be put off; urge to haste.

ناشب *nâśib*, adhering, &c.; who has arrows.

ناشرة *nâśira-t*, pl. *nawâśir*, vein or sinew of the arm.

ناشز *nâśiz*, agitated; — ة *nâśiza-t*, refractory wife.

ناشط *nâśiṭ*, lively, brisk, vigorous, &c.; pl. *nawâśiṭ*, irrelevant questions.

ناشع *nâśi'*, high, projecting.

ناشف *nâśif*, dry, &c.; austere, severe.

ناشوف *nâśûf*, pole for hanging up washed linen.

ناشى *nâśî'*, growing; pl. *naśâ*, نشو *naś'*, *anśâ'*, youth, girl; pl. *nâśi'a-t*, what has grown or happened during the night; — ة *nâśi'a-t*, pl. *nawâśi'*, growing-up girl; germ; first hour (of day, night, &c.), beginning, commencement.

ناص *nâṣṣ*, who dictates; who tells, narrates, reports.

ناصاة *nâṣât*, forelocks.

ناصب *nâṣib*, who sets up, plants, &c.; grieving; toilsome; tired, weary; pl. *nawâṣib*, words which put nouns in the accusative and verbs in the subjunctive; the adversaries of Ali.

ناصت *nâṣit*, silent; taciturn.

ناصح *nâṣiḥ*, pl. *nuṣṣaḥ*, *nuṣṣâḥ*, who gives good advice; sincere; pure; (m.) fat, stout, corpulent; also ى *nâṣiḥiyy*, tailor.

ناصر *nâṣir*, pl. *nâṣira-t*, *nuṣṣâr*, *naṣr*, *nuṣar*, *anṣâr*, helper; God; pl. *nawâṣir*, canal, channel, gutter; — ة *nâṣira-t*, Nazareth; — ى *nâṣiriyy*, of Nazareth.

ناصع *nâṣi'*, pure.

ناصف *nâṣif*, pl. *naṣaf*, servant; — ة *nâṣifa-t*, pl. *nawâṣif*, gutter, canal.

ناصية *nâṣiya-t*, pl. *nawâṣî*, forelock; personal appearance, gait; appearance, semblance.

ناض *nâḍḍ*, easily executed; money.

ناضب *nâḍib*, disappearing in the ground; vast.

ناضح *nâḍiḥ*, ة *nâḍiḥa-t*, pl. *nawâḍiḥ*, camel which draws water, which is used for irrigating.

ناضل *nâḍil*, pl. *nuḍḍâl*, superior archer, champion.

(ناط) *na'aṭ*, INF. *na'îṭ*, cry out, scream; breathe heavily.

ناطب *nâṭib*, strainer.

ناطح *nâṭiḥ*, butting; game, hunting-prey; pl. *nawâṭiḥ*, calamity.

ناطر *nâṭir*, pl. *-ûn*, *nuṭṭâr*, *nuṭarâ'*,

naṭara-t, *nawâṭir*, keeper, guardian, watchman.

ناطف *nâṭif*, a kind of sweetmeat; — ى *nâṭifiyy*, seller of it.

ناطق *nâṭiq*, speaking, &c.; rational; distinct, clear; living possessions, slaves, cattle; also ة *nâṭiqa-t*, hypochondres; waist; *nâṭiqa-t*, gift of speech.

ناطل *nâṭil*, what remains in a measure; draught; also *nâṭal*, pl. *nayâṭil*, a measure for wine, wine-cup; wine, liquor.

ناطور *nâṭûr*, pl. *nawâṭîr*, watchman, keeper (ن الحرش *nâṭûr al-ḥarś*, game-keeper, forester); who looks out from the mast.

ناطى *nâṭî* (ناط *nâṭ-in*), moist.

ناظر *nâẕir*, who sees, looks at, &c.; pl. *nawâẕir*, overseer, inspector, director, minister; image in the eye; du. *nâẕirân*, the two lachrymal ducts; also ة *nâẕira-t*, pl. *nawâẕir*, eye; sight; aspect, appearance, face; *nâẕira-t*, reading.

ناظم *nâẕim*, who arranges well, regulates, &c.; governor; composer of verses.

ناظور *nâẕûr*=ناطور; — ة *nâẕûra-t*, looked at and respected before others; president.

ناعصة *nâ'iṣa-t*, helpers, assistants.

ناعل *nâ'il*, shoed, soled; hard; wild ass, onager.

ناعم *nâ'im*, soft, tender, delicate, fond; thin, fine; in powder (sugar); — ة *nâ'ima-t*, tenderly-reared (woman); meadow, garden.

ناعور *nâ'ûr*, bleeding vein which cannot be staunched; also ة *nâ'ûra-t*, pl. *nawâ'îr*, water-wheel, hydraulic machine for irrigation, mill; — ة *na'ûra-t*, large cistern; bucket; nose, septum of the nose.

ناعى *nâ'î* (ناع *nâ'-in*), pl. *nu'ât*, *nâ'iya-t*, who announces one's death, death-message.

(ناف) *na'af*, INF. *na'f*, exert one's self; — *na'if*, A, INF. *na'af*, eat; drink one's fill.

نافجة *nâfija-t*, pl. *nawâfij*, beginning of a storm; short false rib; daughter; bladder of the musk-cat; vessel with perfumes; abounding in water.

نافخ *nâfiḥ*, blowing, &c.; trumpeter; ن الصور *nâfiḥ aṣ-ṣûr*, who sounds the trumpet of the last judgment.

نافذ *nâfiẕ*, penetrating, piercing through; executing; meeting with obedience (ن الكلمتين *nâfiẕ al-kalimataini*, who is strictly obeyed in what he commands or forbids, absolute ruler); quicksilver; — ة *nâfiẕa-t*, pl. *nawâfiẕ*, opening, loop-hole, window; ن روحية *nâfiẕa-t rûḥiyya-t*, ejaculatory prayer.

نافر *nâfir*, pl. *nafr*, who flees, saves himself; pl. *nuffar*, *nawâfir*, timid, timorous, shy; feeling aversion; victor, conqueror; commander; (m.) swollen; — ة *nâfira-t*, close relations.

نافطة *nâfiṭa-t*, sheep; goat.

نافق *nâfiq*, selling well; — ة *nâfiqa-t*, bladder of the musk-cat.

نافقا *nâfiqâ'*, pl. *nawâfiq*, hole of the field-mouse.

نافلة *nâfila-t*, pl. *nawâfil*, voluntary good work, alms, prayer, &c.; present; anything useless; booty; grandchild.

نافوخ *nâfûḥ*, liquorice-root; crown of the head.

نافور *nâfûr*, pall; liturgy.

ناقرة *nâqira-t*, calamity; demonstration, proof; subject of controversy, thesis.

ناقز *nâqiz*, leaping, jumping; lively, brisk; paltry.

ناقس *nâqis*, sour.

ناقص *nâqiṣ*, decreasing, diminishing, &c.; defective, verb with و or ى as a third radical; less; (m.) paederast.

ناقع *nâqi'*, macerating, &c.; poison

which pervades the body; fresh, freshly shed (blood).

ناقل *nâqil*, pl. *naqala-t*, transporting, &c.; bearer; narrator; translator; copyist, draughtsman, painter; — ة *nâqila-t*, pl. *nawâqil*, fickle, unstable; vicissitude of fortune; not settled, nomad; fluctuating population; translation; copy.

ناقه *nâqih*, pl. *nuqqah*, still weak, only beginning to recover.

ناقة *nâqa-t*, pl. *nâq*, *nûq*, *nâqât*, *anwuq*, *an'uq*, *ainuq*, *anyuq*, *niyâq*, *anwâq*, she-camel; pustule.

ناقود *nâqûd*=نقاد *naqqâd*.

ناقود *nâqûd*, trumpet, trombone.

ناقوس *nâqûs*, pl. *nawâqîs*, rattle used by Christians instead of a bell; bell.

ناقى *nâqî* (ناق *nâq-in*), pure, clear, serene; cheerful.

ناكح *nâkiḥ*, ة *nâkiḥa-t*, married woman; — *.

ناكوزة *nâkûza-t*, sting, goad; horsewhip (m.).

(نال) *na'al*, INF. *na'l*, *na'al*, *na'îl*, *na'alân*, walk in jerks and raising one's head.

نال *nâl*, pl. *anwâl*, gift; anything received, acquired, earned; liberal; — ة *nâla-t*, obtaining, reaching (s.); courtyard; open inclosure of the sanctuary in Mecca.

(نام) *na'am*, I, A, INF. *na'îm*, breathe heavily, sigh, moan; roar; bleat; shriek; sound; — ة *na'ma-t*, *nâmma-t*, song, voice.

نامرة *nâmira-t*, trap for wolves.

(نامل) *na'mal*, INF. ة, walk like one fettered.

نامور *nâmûr*, blood; also ة *nâmûra-t*, trap for wolves.

ناموس *nâmûs*, pl. *nawâmîs*, law, law code; decree of God, God's will; good name, honour and estimation; who shares in a secret (*an-nâmûs*, الن الاكبر *an-nâmûs al-akbar*, Gabriel); master of the house; roll of an army; clamour and combat; stratagem and fraud; cunning (adj.); flatterer; slanderer; hiding-place of a hunter; hunting-net; trap for game; lair; cell, hermitage; (m.) coffin; also ة *nâmûsa-t*, lion's den; gnat, mosquito; — ى *nâmûsiyy*, legal, legitimate; — ية *nâmûsiyya-t*, gauze curtain for protection from mosquitoes, &c.; mosquito-net.

نامية *nâmiya-t*, creature, being; stalk, pedicle; plant; growth.

(نانا) *na'na'*, INF. ة, *muna'na-t* (also II.), be of weak intellect and ill advised; act slowly, hinder, prevent; (also II.) be unequal to the task, do too little; — II. INF. *tana'nu'*, see I.

نانا *na'na'*, *na'nâ'*, weak, imbecile; timid, timorous.

ناهت *nâhit*, roaring; throat.

ناهج *nâhij*, path-finder, who opens a road; out of breath.

ناهد *nâhid*, swelling; also ة *nâhida-t*, girl with a high bosom; *nâhida-t*, planet Venus.

ناهق *nâhiq*, braying, neighing; pl. *nawâhiq*, place in the throat where a sound is formed.

ناهك *nâhik*, very zealous.

ناهل *nâhil*, pl. *nihâl*, *nawâhil*, *nahal*, *nuhûl*, drink the first draught; thirsty; — ة *nâhila-t*, people thronging to the water.

ناهور *nâhûr*, cloud.

ناهى *nâhî* (ناه *nâh-in*), ة, pl. *nuhât*, forbidding, prohibiting; sufficing for to the exclusion of anything else; — ة *nâhiya-t*, pl. *nawâhî*, prohibition, interdiction; anything forbidden.

(ناو)=(نای).

ناوس *nâwus*=ناووس *nâwûs*.

ناوق *nâwaq*, boat.

ناووس *nâwûs*, pl. *nawâwîs*, fire-temple; burial-place of the

Parsees; sepulchre, tomb; sarcophagus, coffin.

ناوى *nâwî* (ناو *nâw-in*), purposing, intending; (m.) paraphrases the future: ن تمطر *nâwî tamṭur*, it is going to rain.

(نأى) *na'a*, INF. *na'y*, depart, remove (n.), leave; be far; make a water-ditch round a tent;— IV. INF. *in'â'*, remove (a.), send to foreign lands; make water-ditches round the tent;—VI. INF. *tanâu'*, remove or be far from one another; be far distant from one another;—VIII. INF. *intî'â'*, be far from (عن *'an*).

نأى *nây*, pl. *nâyât*, flute;—*na'y*, نوى *nu'y*, *nu'a*, نئى *ni'y*, pl. *nuwiyy*, *ni'iyy*, *an'â'*, *ânâ'*, water-ditch round a tent;—*na'y*, remoteness from one's people.

نائب *nâ'ib*, pl. *naub*, *nuwwâb*, substitute, vicar, deputy, lieutenant; pl. *nuwwâb*, soldiers of the guard; pl. *nûb*, bee; event; much, many, in abundance;—ة *nâ'iba-t*, pl. *nawâ'ib*, vicissitudes, calamity.

نائح *nâ'iḥ*, pl. *nauḥ*, who mourns, bewails;—ة *nâ'iḥa-t*, pl. *-ât*, *nawâ'iḥ*, *nauḥ*, *anwâḥ*, *nuwwaḥ*, mourning-woman.

نائرة *nâ'ira-t*, pl. *nawâ'ir*, fire, flame, conflagration, inflammation, heat; fire-place; charcoal; hatred, hostility.

نائع *nâ'i'*, pl. *niyâ'*, thirsty; جائع نائع *jâ'i' nâ'i'*, famished, starved.

نائف *nâ'if*, exceeding (the proper number).

نائل *nâ'il*, who obtains, &c.; liberality; gift, bounty, favour;—ة *nâ'ila-t*, a female idol.

نائم *nâ'im*, pl. *niyâm*, *nuwwâm*, *nuyyâm*, *naum*, sleeping, in bed; quiet;—ة *nâ'ima-t*, pl. *nuwwam*, *nuyyam*, sleeping woman; death; a snake.

نائى *nâ'î* (ناء *nâ-in*), far from one's people.

(نب) *nabb*, I, INF. *nabb*, *nubâb*, *nabîb*, bleat from rut; be haughty;—II. INF. *tambîb*, form knots (plant).

نب *nab'*, superiority, victory, success;—ة *nabba-t*, bad smell.

(نبا) *naba'*, INF. *nab'*, *nubû'*, be high, tower over; be desolate; come upon from above; conquer, surpass; consider, ponder; produce;—INF. *nab'a-t*, produce a low sound, bark; announce, make known;—II. INF. *tambi'a-t*, *tambî'*, announce, bring the news of;—III. INF. *munâba'a-t*, *nibâ'*, communicate to one another;—IV. INF. *imbâ'*, make known to, communicate;—V. INF. *tanabbu'*, declare one's self or pretend to be a prophet; prophecy, prèdict;—X. INF. *istimbâ'*, beg for information, inquire.

نبا *naba'*, pl. *ambâ'*, news, information, tidings, message; report;—*nibâ'*, INF. of (نبا III.);—*nuba'â'*, pl. of نبى *nabiyy*;—ة *naba'a-t*, faint sound; bark.

نبابيت *nabâbît*, pl. of نبوت *nabbût*.

نبات *nabât*, sprouting, growing, INF. of (نبت); pl. *nabâtât*, plant, shrub, grass, vegetation; down, hair; (m.) سكر نبات *sakkar nabât*, sugar-candy; *nabâtât*, sweets;—ة *nabâta-t*, *nubâta-t*, plant, grass;—ى *nabâtiyy*, ة, referring to plants, vegetable; botanist;—ية *nabâtiyya-t*, plants.

نباج *nabâj*, pl. of نبجة *nabja-t*;—*nubâj*, rough bark; rumbling in the bowels; breaking wind;—*nabbâj*, ى *nubâjiyy*, barking roughly, rough-voiced;—ة *nabbâja-t*, anus.

نباح *nubâḥ*, *nibâḥ*, barking, roaring, (s.);—*nabbâḥ*, always barking, boisterous;—*nubbâḥ*, hoopoe;—*nabbûḥa-t*, pl. *nabbâḥ*, Mecca-shell (for necklaces).

نباخ *nabbâḫ*, sour.

نباديد *nabâdîd*, dispersed, scattered (pl.).
نباذ *nabbâẓ*, wine-seller, liquor-seller.
نبار *nabbâr*, who speaks in a commanding tone; screamer.
نباريس *nabârîs*, pl. of نبراس *nibrâs*.
نباش *nabbâś*, digger, who digs for treasures, grave-digger; spoliator of dead bodies.
نباض *nabbâḍ*, physician; mobile.
نباطى *nabâṭiyy*, Nabathean.
نباعة *nabbâ'a-t*, anus.
نباغ *nubâg*, ة *nubâga-t*, flour-dust, flour; — *; — *nabbâg*, ة *nubâga-t*, scurf; — *nabbâga-t*, anus.
نبال *nabâl*, ة *nabâla-t*, intelligence and skill; outfit, equipment; being prepared or in readiness; *nabâla-t*, higher merit or skill, superiority; — *nibâl*, pl. of نبل *nabl* and نبيل *nabîl*; — *nabbâl*, maker of arrows; good archer; skilful and intelligent; — ة *nibâla-t*, art of making arrows.
نباه *nabâh*, illustrious, of high rank; — ة *nabâha-t*, celebrity, glory, nobility; presence of mind.
نباوة *nibâwa-t*, office of a prophet, prophecy.
(نبت) *nabat*, U, INF. *nabt*, *nabât*, germinate, sprout, grow; produce plants; — II. INF. *tambît*, cause to grow; (m.) quilt; — IV. INF. *imbât*, produce plants; cause to grow; make to grow and thrive; grow the hair of puberty; — X. INF. *istimbât*, transplant, accustom to a climate.
نبت *nabt*, ة, germ, plant, vegetable grass, herb; — ة *nabta-t*, (m.) abscess; — *nibta-t*, growth of plants.
(نبث) *nabas̱*, U, INF. *nabs̱*, dig out with one's hand; clean a well; lay open; uproot; be angry; — VIII. INF. *intibâs̱*, dig out, excavate; reach for a thing, take it.
نبث *nabs̱*, anger; — *nabas̱*, trace, token, sign, mark.
(نبج) *nabaj*, U, INF. *nabj*, creep out of the egg; break forth, flow.
نبج *nabj*, oakum for caulking ships; — *nubuj*, corn-sacks; — ة *nabja-t*, pl. *nabâj*, hill.
(نبح) *nabaḥ*, A, I, INF. *nabḥ*, *nubâḥ*, *nibâḥ*, *nabîḥ*, *tambâḥ*, bark; bellow; hiss; — IV. INF. *imbâḥ*, X. INF. *istimbâḥ*, incite to barking, rouse the dogs (by imitating a bark).
نبح *nabḥ*, barking (s.).
نبحا *nubḥâ'*, bellowing (adj. f.).
(نبخ) *nabaḫ*, INF. *nubûḫ*, turn sour, deteriorate; — IV. INF. *imbâḫ*, eat the root of the papyrus.
نبخ *nabḫ*, eatable root of the papyrus; blisters on the hand; also *nabaḫ*, pocks, small-pox; — ة *nabḫa-t*, thread dipped in sulphur; also *nabaḫa-t*, oakum for caulking ships.
(نبذ) *nabaẓ*, I, INF. *nabẓ*, fling out of one's hand, cast, reject, let go; INF. *nabẓ*, *nabaẓân*, beat, throb; press grapes; brew beer; (m.) show one's self; — III. INF. *munâbaẓa-t*, withdraw from the enemy, desist from the combat; combat openly, fight with; fling towards; — IV. INF. *imbâẓ*, press grapes; — VIII. INF. *intibâẓ*=IV.; go aside, set one's self aside, depart; give over fighting.
نبذ *nabẓ*, pl. *ambâẓ*, a little of, a small quantity; — ة *nabẓa-t*, *nubẓa-t*, pl. *nubaẓ*, id.; short sketch, paper not exhausting a subject; number of a work; side, direction; *nabzat-an*, aside, separately.
نبذان *nabaẓân*, throbbing, INF. of (نبذ).
(نبذر) *nabẓar*, INF. ة, scatter thoughtlessly, squander.
(نبر) *nabar*, I, INF. *nabr*, raise, elevate; grow, thrive; shout to, drive away by cries or shouts, prevent; pierce through and draw the lance quickly back; mark with *hamza-t*; (m.) rummage, search, turn over the

leaves of a book; — IV. INF. *imbâr*, build a store-house, a barn; — V. INF. *tanabbur*, speak to in a haughty or commanding tone, shout to, address gruffly (على *'ala*); —VIII. INF. *intibâr*, swell.

نبر *nabr*, sudden, unexpected; impudent, haughty, abrupt, gruff; — *nibr*, pl. *ambâr*, pl. pl. *ambârât*, *anâbîr*, store-house, barn, loft, corn-magazine, warehouse; pl. *ambâr*, *nibâr*, short and ugly; camel-louse, tick, cattle-fly; a beast of prey; — ة *nabra-t*, rising, swelling; transition from bass to treble; the sign *hamza-t*.

نبراس *nibrâs*, pl. *nabârîs*, lantern, lamp; head of a spear, spear.

نبريج *nibrîj*, pl. *nabârîj*, leather tube of the Nargilah.

(نبز) *nabaz*, I, INF. *nabz*, give one a nickname; revile, dishonour;— VI. INF. *tanâbuz*, give nicknames to one another, revile one another.

نبز *nabz*, reviling, abuse; — *nabaz*, pl. *ambâz*, mock-name, nickname; — *nabiz*, contemptible;— ة *nubaza-t*, who is fond of giving nicknames to others.

(نبس) *nabas*, I, INF. *nabs*, *nubsa-t*, speak; move, stir, speed (n.).

(نبش) *nabaś*, U, INF. *nabś*, uncover; dig out; dig; (m.) search, rummage, turn over the leaves of a book, look out in books or documents; bring to light; try to earn for one's family; — II. INF. *tambîś*, dig out, lay open, bring to light; rummage, search; — VI. INF. *tanâbuś*, disclose one another's secrets; — X. INF. *istimbâś*, try to discover or bring to light.

نبش *nabś*, excavation, investigation, discovery, disclosure; — *nibś*, a fir-tree with very hard wood.

(نبص) *nabaṣ*, I, INF. *nabṣ*, speak; be on the point of sprouting; INF. *naṣîb*, peep, chirp; — ة *nabṣa-t*, word.

(نبض) *nabaḍ*, I, INF. *nabḍ*, *nabaḍân*, beat, throb, quiver; twang the string of a bow; flash lightly; INF. *nubûḍ*, sink in the ground (water).

نبض *nabḍ*, ة pl. *ambâḍ*, beating of the pulse, pulsation, pulse.

(نبط) *nabaṭ*, I, U, INF. *nabṭ*, *nubûṭ*, gush forth from the spring, well, flow; — INF. *nabṭ*, draw water from the well; — II. INF. *tambîṭ*, IV. INF. *imbâṭ*, V. INF. *tanabbuṭ*, dig until one meets with water; IV. draw water; — X. INF. *istimbâṭ*, id.; meet with, obtain; invent; derive from the source, draw forth, elicit.

نبط *nabaṭ*, deep thought; depth; Nabatheans; (m.) pulse; also ة *nubṭa-t*, first water which one meets with in digging; — *nabaṭ*, *nubṭ*, ة *nubṭa-t*, white hair on the chest or belly of a horse.

نبطا *nabṭâ'*, white-bellied (sheep).

نبطي *nabaṭiyy*, Nabathean.

(نبع) *naba'*, A, I, U, INF. *nab'*, *nubû'*, gush forth from the spring; — II. INF. *tambî'*, gush forth violently; — IV. INF. *imbâ'*, cause to gush forth; — V. INF. *tanabbu'*, flow out slowly; — X. INF. *istimbâ'*=IV.

نبع *nab'*, source, origin; n. u. ة, a mountain-tree and its wood, of which arrows and bows are made; white poplar; pole of a carriage: — ة *nab'a-t*, weak source.

(نبغ) *nabag*, A, U, I, INF. *nabg*, appear, come to light, get known; break forth; come forward as an innovator, heretic, &c.; emerge from obscurity, as a poet, &c.; grow wise, clever, skilful; spread abroad; fly off; — IV. INF. *imbâg*, frequent a town.

(نبق) *nabaq*, U, INF. *nabq*, write; break wind lightly; spurt out of a wound (blood, pus);— II. INF. *tambîq*, write; break wind;

make blood to spurt out ;— VIII. INF. *intibâq*, elicit a speech, cause one to speak.

نبق *nabq*, sweet farina in the heart of a palm-tree ; a small tree ; also *nibq*, *nabiq*, ة *nabiqa-t*, fruit of the lotus-tree.

(نبك) — VIII. *intabak*, INF. *intibâk*, be high, sublime, elevated ; — ة *nabka-t*, *nabaka-t*, pl. *nabk*, *nabak*, *nibâk*, *nubûk*, pointed hill ; hilly tract.

(نبل) *nabal*, U, INF. *nabl*, shoot arrows, throw spears ; take as a mark, shoot at ; (also IV.) provide with arrows ; surpass in shooting arrows ; surpass in any skill ; — *nabul*, INF. *nabâla-t*, be noble, of high birth or rank ; be possessed of intelligence, genius, skill, merit, distinguish one's self ; — IV. INF. *imbâl*, see I. ; — V. INF. *tanabbul* = *nabul* ; show one's skill ; — VIII. INF. *intibâl*, be equipped ; die ; kill ; — X. INF. *istimbâl*, ask one for arrows ; take the best.

نبل *nabl*, pl. *nibâl*, *nublân*, *ambâl*, arrow ; javelin ; outfit, equipment ; — *nubl*, excellent or perfect condition ; talents, capabilities, merits ; nobility ; equipment ; — *nabâl*, ة, noble ; of high rank or birth ; intelligent and clever, distinguished ; pl. of نبيل *nabîl* ; — *nubbal*, pl. of نابل *nâbil*, archer ; — ة *nabla-t*, arrow ; present ; white ivy ; pl. of نبيل *nabîl* ; also *nubla-t*, pl. *nubal*, matter of great importance ; — *nubla-t*, pl. *nubal*, reward ; present ; intelligence and skill ; little stone for cleaning one's self after satisfying a natural want.

نبلا *nubalâ'*, pl. of نبيل *nabîl*.

نبلان *nublân*, pl. of نبل *nabl*.

(نبنب) *nabnab*, INF. ة, bellow from rut ; perform anything slowly but well.

(نبه) *nabah*, INF. *nubh*, awake (n.) ; = *nabuh* ; — *nabih*, A, INF. *nabah*, recollect, heed, attend to, be attentive ; — *nabuh*, INF. *nabâha-t*, be of high rank or birth, celebrated, generally known ; — II. INF. *tanbîh*, awake (a.), rouse ; bid one to be on his guard, warn, call one's attention to, give one a hint or advice ; make one celebrated ; — IV. INF. *imbâh*, awake (a.) ; — V. INF. *tanabbuh*, awake (n.) ; attend to, rouse one's self to ; — VIII. INF. *intibâh*, awake (n.) ; recover, collect one's self, take courage ; recollect suddenly ; follow a hint and direct one's attention to ; be cautious, on one's guard.

نبه *nabh*, pl. of نابه *nâbih*, illustrious, &c. ; — *nubh*, awakening (s.), vigilance, attention ; intelligence ; — *nabah*, what is suddenly found ; *nabah-an*, unexpectedly ; also *nabih*, known, renowned, celebrated.

(نبو) *nabâ*, U, INF. *nabw*, *nubuww*, *nabwa-t*, remove (n.), withdraw, desist ; be ugly ; be disagreeable, inconvenient, irksome ; miss the aim, miss one's place, be restless ; — INF. *nabw*, *nabwa-t*, rebound and become blunt ;— INF. *nubuww*, *nubiyy*, *nabwa-t*, grow dim, be unable to see.

نبو *nubu'*, being high, superiority ; — ة *nabwa-t*, height ; rising ground ; rebound of a blade ; — *nubuwwa-t*, office of a prophet.

نبوت *nabbût*, pl. *nabâbît*, cudgel, club ; — *nubût*, INF. of (نبت).

نبوح *nubûḥ*, clamour ; barking ; boisterous crowd ; glory ; INF. of (نبح).

نبور *nabûr*, anus.

نبوغ *nubûg*, coming forward, appearance.

نبوى *nubawiyy*, prophetic.

نبى *nabiyy*, pl. -*ûn*, *anbiyâ'*, *ambâ'*, *nuba'â'*, prophet ; also *nabî'*, high point ; open path ; — *nubayy*, little prophet ; — *nubiyy*, INF. of

(نبو); pl. of نابى *nâbî*, high ground; — ة *nabiyya-t*, table-board; table-cloth of palm-leaves; prophetess.

نبيب *nabîb*, INF. of (نب).

نبيثة *nabîsa-t*, mud of a river or well.

نبيح *nabîḥ*, barking (s.), bark.

نبيخة *nabîḫa-t*, thread dipped in sulphur.

نبيذ *nabîẕ*, flung; pl. *ambiẕa-t*, wine (of grapes, dates, &c.).

نبيص *nabîṣ*, peeping, chirping (s.).

نبيط *nabîṭ*, pl. *ambâṭ*, Nabathean.

نبيل *nabîl*, pl. *nibâl*, *nabal*, *nabla-t*, *nubalâ'*, talented and skilful; noble, of high rank or birth; excellent, handsome; good archer; standard, flag.

نبيه *nabîh*, renowned, celebrated.

نبيى *nabî'* = نبى *nabiyy*; —*nubayyi'*, little prophet; — ة *nubayya-t*, little prophecy.

(نت) *natt*, INF. *natt*, *natît*, swell or blow with rage (nostrils); INF. *natît*, boil, bubble; ferment; — ة *nutta-t*, small cavity in a stone.

(نتا) *nata'*, INF. *nat'*, *nutû'*, swell and protrude, project, jut; leave one's place; appear suddenly; be produced; grow up and become marriageable; — ة *na-t'a-t*, hill; ascent, acclivity.

نتاج *nitâj*, birth, time of parturition; new-born young of an animal.

نتاش *nattâś*, who pulls out or snatches away with violence; — *nuttâś*, pl. jugglers, impostors, rabble.

نتاف *nutâf*, ة *nutâfa-t*, offal in picking anything; pulled-out hair.

نتاق *nitâq*, opposite; (m.) vomiting.

نتانة *natâna-t*, offensive smell, stench.

(نتج) *nataj*, I, INF. *natj*, *natâj*, *nitâj*, support the she-camel in parturition; pass. INF. *nitâj* (m. act.), give birth, bring forth, produce; result, follow as a conclusion or consequence; grow; make progress; draw advantage; — II. INF. *tantîj*, conclude, make a conclusion, draw an inference; — IV. INF. *intâj*, support the she-camel in parturition; be on the point of parturition; pass. give birth, bring forth; have for a result or consequence; — V. INF. *tanattuj*, result, follow; — X. INF. *istintâj*, draw an inference, conclude, derive an advantage; yield offspring.

(نتح) *nataḥ*, I, U, INF. *natḥ*, *nutûḥ*, ooze out, sweat out; cause one to perspire; evaporate.

نتح *natḥ*, sweat, perspiration; damp, moist.

(نتخ) *nataḫ*, I, INF. *natḫ*, draw out, pull out; tear; weave.

(نتر) *natar*, U, INF. *natr*, take by force, snatch, rob; tear with hands or teeth; pierce; — *natir*, A, INF. *natar*, perish; — VIII. INF. *intitâr*, be drawn or pulled away.

نتر *natr*, harshness, violence; — *natar*, ruin, perdition; — ة *natra-t*, pl. *natarât*, a piercing thrust; hurting speech.

(نتش) *nataś*, I, INF. *natś*, pull out; deprive of the hair; tear away and try to carry off; extort; seek or earn sustenance for one's family; slander; beat; — IV. INF. *intâś*, germinate.

نتش *natś*, snatching away violently; earnings, gain; — *nataś*, first germ.

(نتض) *nataḍ*, U, INF. *nutûḍ*, be diseased and peel off in strips (skin).

(نتع) *nata'*, I, U, INF. *nutû'*, drop slowly; break forth, spring, gush forth; (m.) tear away by force; carry off on one's shoulders; — IV. INF. *intâ'*, perspire violently.

(نتغ) *natag*, I, U, INF. *natg*, slander,

calumniate ; — IV. INF. *intâg*, laugh secretly, laugh at.

(نتف) *nataf*, I, INF. *natf*, pull out; deprive of the hair, pluck; draw the bow slightly ; — II. INF. *tantîf*, pull out much hair or pull it out violently; — VI. INF. *tanâtuf*, VIII. INF. *intitâf*, be pulled out.

نتف *natf*, pulling out, plucking (s.); — ة *nutfa-t*, pl. *nutaf*, as much as can be pulled out or plucked by the hand at one time; over-subtle remark, hair-splitting; رجل نتفة *rajul nutfa-t*, hair-splitter.

(نتق) *nataq*, U, INF. *natq*, shake; draw the bucket out of the well; (m.) seize violently and carry off; (m.) vomit; have many children; speak; INF. *nutûq*, be very fat; — II. INF. *tantîq*, make to vomit ; — V. INF. *tanattuq*, assault one furiously (m.); — ة *natqa-t*, m. for نتأة *nat'at*, hill, acclivity.

(نتك) *natak*, I, INF. *natk*, snatch violently and break; pull out.

(نتل) *natal*, I, INF. *natl*, draw to one's self; speak gruffly to, drive away with abuse; INF. *natl*, *nutûl*, *natalân*, step forward from amongst one's companions and walk in advance (also X.); — VI. INF. *tanâtul*, have grown crookedly (plant); — X. INF. *istintâl*, see I.

(نتم), VIII. *intatam*, INF. *intitâm*, talk ribaldry.

(نتن) *natan*, I, INF. *natn*, smell offensively; — *natun*, INF. *natâna-t*, id.; — II. INF. *tantîn*, make to smell offensively; — IV. INF. *intân*, smell offensively.

نتن *natn*, offensive smell; stench; — *natin*, smelling offensively, putrid.

(نتو) *natâ*, U, INF. *nutuww*, swell; — IV. INF. *intâ'*, lag behind; break one's nose so as to make it swell; — V. INF. *tanattî*, cover (stallion); assault furiously; — X. INF. *istintâ'*, swell with pus.

نتو *nutû'*, INF. of (نتا).

نتوج *natûj*, on the point of parturition.

نتيت *natît*, boiling, bubbling, INF. of (نت).

نتيجة *natîja-t*, pl. *natâ'ij*, breed of one year, new offspring; result, produce; sum; corollary; consequence, conclusion (*bi'-n-natîja-t*, consequently); gain, profit; reward; ن الكلام *natîjat al-kalâm*, in short.

نتيجى *natîjiyy*, to be inferred, resulting from, consequential.

نتيلة *natîla-t*, cause, reason; means, ways.

(نث) *nas̱s̱*, I, INF. *nas̱îs̱*, leak, let ooze; put ointment to a wound; — U, I, INF. *nas̱s̱*, publish, communicate; speak; — VI. INF. *tanâs̱us̱*, spread about one another's words.

نث *nas̱s̱*, damp wall.

نثاث *nis̱âs̱*, wound-salve; oil for anointing; — *nus̱s̱âs̱*, pl. tale-bearers, tell-tales.

نثار *nis̱âr*, spreading, scattering (s.); offering, sacrifice;—*nus̱âr*, ة *nus̱âra-t*, what is scattered, crumbs from the table, small coin at weddings, &c.

(نثت) *nas̱it*, A, INF. *nas̱as̱*, smell offensively, be putrid.

(نثج) *nas̱aj*, I, INF. *nas̱j*, pierce, stab; — X. INF. *istins̱âj*, hang loosely.

(نثد) *nas̱id*, A, INF. *nas̱ad*, stand quiet, rest; grow.

(نثر) *nas̱ar*, U, I, INF. *nas̱r*, *nis̱âr*, spread, scatter; be prolix; write in prose; have many children; be spread, scattered; fall off (leaves); fall in rags; — INF. *nas̱îr*, sneeze; (also VIII. and X.) draw in water by the nose and blow it out again ; — II. INF. *tans̱îr*, spread abundantly; cause leaves to fall; — IV. INF

inṣâr, wound so as to make the blood run; — VI. INF. *ta-nâṣur*, be scattered, spread (n.); fall off; — VIII. INF. *intiṣâr*, id.; get loose (string of pearls); also X. INF. *istinṣâr*, see I.

نثر *naṣr*, prose; eloquence; بياع ن *bayyâ' naṣr*, retail dealer; — *naṣar*, what falls off in small pieces, crumbs, &c.; — *naṣir*, prolix in speech; — ة *naṣra-t*, sneezing of animals; also نثلة *naṣla-t*, place between the moustachios and the adjoining parts of the nose (especially of a lion); lion's nose (constellation); commodious armour; (m.) painted or embroidered flowers on stuffs; (m.).

(نثط) *naṣaṭ*, I, INF. *naṣṭ*, press one to the ground and keep him quiet; burden, weigh down; sprout, grow; — INF. *naṣṭ*, *nuṣûṭ*, be quiet, rest; — II. INF. *tanṣîṭ*, quiet.

(نثع), IV. *anṣa'*, INF. *inṣâ'*, vomit violently; bleed from the nose; gush forth.

(نثل) *naṣal*, I, INF. *naṣal*, clear earth out of a well, clean it; empty a quiver, or a provision-bag; pull off the armour and throw it away; clothe one in a coat of mail or armour; put meat into the pot; — U, INF. *maṣl*, drop excrement; — VI. INF. *tanâṣul*, rush against, assail; — VIII. INF. *intiṣâl*, clean a well; — X. INF. *istinṣâl*, empty the quiver.

نثل *naṣal*, pit out of which earth is taken; — ة *naṣla-t*, see نثرة *naṣra-t*.

(نثم) *naṣam*, I, *naṣm*, also VIII. INF. *intiṣâm*, talk ribaldry.

نثنث *naṣnaṣ*, INF. ة, perspire abundantly; wipe; ooze, leak; cry, weep.

(نثو) *naṣâ*, U, INF. *naṣw*, spread, scatter; publish, make known.

نثور *naṣûr*, having many children (woman).

(نثى) *naṣa*, I, INF. *naṣy*, publish, make known; — IV. INF. *inṣâ'*, slander; scorn, disdain (عن *'an*).

نثيث *naṣîṣ*, ة *naṣîṣa-t*, oozing, leaking (s.).

نثير *niṣîr*, sneezing of animals.

(نج) *najj*, I, INF. *najj*, *najîj*, bleed, suppurate; hasten, hurry (n.).

(نجا) *naja'*, INF. *naj'*, harm by the evil eye; — V. INF. *tanajju'*, VIII. INF. *intijâ'*, id.

نجا *najan*, *naja*, skinning (s.); skin; wood, branch, stick; high ground; — *najâ'*, rescue, escape, flight, speed (*an-najâ'a-ka an-najâ'a-ka*, save yourself! flee in haste!) refuge, asylum; — *nijâ'*, pl. of نجو *najw*; — ة *najât*, rescue, escape; salvation, everlasting happiness; pl. نجا *najan*, *naja*, greed; envy; high ground; branch; mushroom; — *naj'a-t*, evil eye.

نجابة *najâba-t*, nobility, generosity, magnanimity, liberality; distinguished conduct; noble breed (of a horse).

نجاث *najjâṣ*, who examines, investigates.

نجاح *najâḥ*, success, victory; progress; — ة *najâḥa-t*, patience.

نجاد *nijâd*, sabretache, sword-belt; — *; — *najjâd*, who makes or beats mattresses, cushions, &c.; apt, clever, up to a thing; — ة *najâda-t*, bravery, magnanimity; combat; misfortune.

نجار *nijâr*, *nujâr*, origin, descent, race, nature; colour; estimation; — *najjâr*, carpenter, joiner, cabinet-maker; — ة *nijâra-t*, trade of such; — *nujâra-t*, chips, shavings.

نجاز *najâz*, execution, performance, completion; — ة *najâza-t*, gift.

نجاسة *najâsa-t*, dirt, filth, uncleanliness; profanation.

نجاش *nijâś*, strap, wedge-like piece

of leather ;—*najjâś*, game-driver, hunter ;— ى *najjâśiyy*, id. ; title of the kings of Ethiopia ; — ة *nijâśa-t*, nimbleness, agility.

نجاف *nijâf*, short woollen vest ; bolt ; hinge of a door, joint of a lid ; — *.

نجال *nijâl*, pl. of انجل *anjal*, having large well-slit eyes, &c.

نجام *najjâm*, astronomer, astrologer ; — ة *nijâma-t*, astronomy, astrology.

نجاوة *najâwa-t*, far-stretching country.

نجاوى *najâwî*, pl. of نجوى *najwa*.

نجاية *najâya-t*, rescue, escape.

(نجب) *najab*, I, U, INF. *najb*, bark a tree ;—*najub*, INF. *najâba-t*, be noble, of high rank or birth, magnanimous, liberal, distinguished ;— II. INF. *tanjîb*, bark ; — IV. INF. *injâb*=*najab* ; beget an excellent son ; — VIII. INF. *intijâb*, bark ; elect, select.

نجب *najb*, high-born, noble, magnanimous, liberal ;— *najab*, bark of a tree ; lower part of the trunk of a tree ; — *nujub*, نجبا *nujabâ'*, pl. of نجيب *najîb* ; — ة *nujaba-t*, pl. *anjâb*=*najb* ; hero ; the most noble of the people.

(نجث) *najaṡ*, I, INF. *najṡ*, cry for help ; examine, test, investigate ; bring on mischief ; — V. INF. *tanajjuṡ*, examine, investigate ; — VIII. INF. *intijâṡ*, X. INF. *istinjâṡ*, pull out, draw out, bring out.

نجث *nujṡ*, *nujuṡ*, pl. *anjâṡ*, breastplate, armour ; pericardium ; — *najiṡ*, who examines, tests, investigates.

(نجح) *najaḥ*, INF. *najḥ*, succeed well ; be fortunate, lucky ; make progress ; — II. INF. *tanjîḥ*, facilitate, help to secure success ; promote one's prosperity or progress ; — IV. INF. *injâḥ*, succeed, have luck, obtain one's end ; help one to success, promote one's good fortune ; carry on successfully ; grant success and prosperity ; — V. INF. *tanajjuḥ*, carry out easily and successfully ; — X. INF. *istinjâḥ* =V.

نجح *nujḥ*, success ; prosperity, good fortune ; victory, triumph.

(نجخ) *najaḫ*, INF. *najḫ*, boast ; dig ; bring wind and rain ; rage ; carry off part of a precipice (torrent) ; — VI. INF. *tanâjuḫ*, clash against and tear off some land ; clash against one another ; — VIII. INF. *intijâḫ*, rumble (bowels).

(نجد) *najad*, I, INF. *najd*, conquer ; help, assist, favour ; drip with perspiration ; INF. *nujûd*, be clear and evident ; — *najid*, A, INF. *najad*, perspire ; be grieved, in anxiety, weary, languid, dull ; — *najud*, INF. *najda-t*, *najâda-t*, be bold, brave, heroic ; — II. INF. *tanjîd*, run ; render skilled and experienced ; furnish a house with carpets, divans, &c. ; (m.) beat mattresses ; — III. INF. *munâjada-t*, help, assist, defend ; — IV. INF. *injâd*, help, favour ; rise, be high ; come to Najd ; — V. INF. *tanajjud*, be high ; — X. INF. *istinjâd*, ask for one's help or protection.

نجد *najd*, help, assistance ; victory ; pl. *nujud*, *nijâd*, *anjâd*, *nujûd*, *anjud*, pl. pl. *anjida-t*, high ground ; (also *najud*), highlands of Arabia, Najd ; distinct elevated road ; طلاع النجاد *tallâ'-u 'n-nijâd-i*, who plans great things ; pl. *nujûd*, *nijâd*, carpet, cushion and similar furniture ; clever, agile, nimble ; bold, courageous ;—*najad*, sweat, perspiration ; anxiety, sorrow, weariness ; dulness, obtuseness ; — *najid*, *najud*, pl. *anjâd*, bold, courageous ; — *nujud*, pl. of نجود *najûd*, نجيد *najîd* ; — ة *najda-t*, boldness, bravery ; magnanimity ; vigour, strength, en-

ergy; help, assistance, succour, battle; pl. *najadât*, calamity; — ى *najdiyy*, bold, courageous; of Najd.

(نجذ) *najaẓ*, I, INF. *najẓ*, seize or bite violently with the molar teeth; utter biting words; molest, importune; — II. INF. *tanjîẓ*, make one wise, experienced.

(نجر) *najar*, U, I, INF. *najr*, cut or plane wood; make a roof entirely of wood; bolt the door with a wooden bar; beat; prepare the dish نجيرة *najîra-t*; INF. *najar*, be seized with violent thirst; — II. INF. *tanjîr*, hew wood; carry on the trade of a carpenter or joiner; — IV. INF. *injâr*, feed one on the dish نجيرة *najîra-t*; — V. INF. *tanajjur*, be hewn, planed.

نجر *najr*, root, origin, nature; descent; form, shape; authority, renown; estimation; colour; intention; neat; precincts of Mecca and Medina; — *najar*, violent thirst from eating bitter seeds or drinking sour milk; — ة *najira-t*, ى *najra*, thirsty camels.

نجران *najrân*, horizontal sill on which a door turns; thirsty; name of a country.

(نجز) *najaz*, U, INF. *najz*, carry out, complete, fulfil a promise; — also *najiz*, A, INF. *najaz*, be carried out, completed, fulfilled; — II. INF. *tanjîz*, carry out, complete; — III. INF. *munâjaza-t*, make ready for combat, enter the lists, the arena, &c.; fight against (acc.); — IV. INF. *injâz*, carry out successfully, perform, fulfil one's promise; — V. INF. *tanajjuz*, complete speedily and successfully; — VI. INF. *tanâjuz*, fight against one another; — X. INF. *istinjâz*=V.; demand, require, urge the fulfilment.

نجز *najz*, execution, performance, completion, fulfilment.

(نجس) *najis*, A, INF. *najas*, be dirty, contaminated, impure; — *najus*, INF. *najâsa-t*, id.; — II. INF. *tanjîs*, dirty, contaminate, pollute; profane; — IV. INF. *injâs*, id.; — V. INF. *tanajjus*, dirty one's self, pollute one's self; be profaned; — X. INF. *istinjâs*, find dirty, unclean, impure.

نجس *najs*, *nijs*, *najis*, *najas*, *najus*, pl. *anjâs*, dirty, contaminated, polluted; — *najas*, dirt, pollution, impurity; profanation.

(نجش) *najaś*, U, INF. *najś*, *najâśa-t*, hunt up the game; excite, agitate, irritate; drive together the scattered camels; kindle; hasten (n.); entice to come out, bring out; examine, investigate, test; — X. INF. *istinjâś*, try to decoy or entice out.

(نجع) *naja'*, INF. *nujû'*, do good, have a wholesome effect; turn to a good purpose; digest well; prosper; give a camel the drink نجوع *najû'*; — II. INF. *tanjî'*, produce a good effect; — IV. INF. *injâ'*=II.; make an impression; feel well and thrive, prosper; — VIII. INF. *intijâ'*, go after good food; forage; try to profit from; — X. INF. *istinjâ'*, grow fat by good or well-digested food; — ة *nuj'a-t*, pl. *nuju'*, going after good food, foraging; good pasture.

(نجف) *najaf*, INF. *najf*, shave or polish an arrow; milk a sheep well; cut down, pull out; — INF. *nijâf*, also IV. INF. *injâf*, prevent a he-goat or stallion from covering by tying up the genital.

نجف *najaf*, ة *najafa-t*, pl. *nijâf*, rising ground not reached by the water; hill; sand-heap; dam; *najaf*, glass, crystal; — *najif*, prevented from covering

(see (نجف)); —*nujuf*, pl. of نجيف *najîf*; — ة *nuffa-t*, a little, small quantity, trifle.

(نجل) ***najal*, I, INF. *najl*, throw away, fling; kick; — U, beget; produce, bring to light, publish, make known; beat, push; split; pierce; blot out, erase, wipe the writing-tablet; cover itself with grass; abound with springs of water; — *najil*, A, INF. *najal*, have large eyes; — IV. INF. *injâl*, let an animal graze on the plant نجيل *najîl*; — VI. INF. *tanâjul*, combat, fight; beget, produce; — VIII. INF. *intijâl*,** show one's self, appear; — X. INF. *istinjâl*, abound with springs.

نجل *najl*, pl. *anjâl*, offspring, son, progeny, family; young (of an animal); generator, father; outflowing water, spring; broad road; — *nujl*, pl. of نجيل *najîl*, q.v., and انجل *anjal*, having large eyes, &c.

(نجم) *najam*, U, INF. *nujûm*, appear; rise; break forth, grow; come forward; (also II.) pay punctually at appointed terms; — II. INF. *tanjîm*, fix according to the course of stars; (also V.) observe the stars; be an astrologer or astronomer; see I.; — IV. INF. *injâm*, appear, rise; cease; — V. INF. *tanajjum*=see II.; — VIII. INF. *intijâm*, cease.

نجم *najm*, pl. *nujum*, *nujûm*, *anjum*, *anjâm*, heavenly body, luminary, star, constellation (علم النجوم *'ilm an-nujûm*, astronomy, اهل الن *ahl an-nujûm*, astronomers); star of nativity, nati..ty, horoscope, prediction; appointed time, term; pay, wages; certain origin; stalkless plant, herb, grass; — ة *najma-t*, *najama-t*, grass; —(m.) *nijma-t*, white spot on a horse's forehead (blaze).

(نجنج) *najnaj*, INF. ة, prevent, hinder; consider a thing indolently and treat it lazily; move, shake (a.); — II. INF. *tanajnuj*, be shaken; get confused.

(نجه) ***najah*, INF. *najh*, deter, turn off with contempt; receive haughtily; come suddenly upon; — V. INF. *tanajjuh*, refuse, repel, turn off; — VIII. INF. *intijâh*, id.**

(نجو) *najâ*, U, INF. *najw*, *najâ'*, *najât*, *najâya-t*, escape, save one's self, be rescued; hurry, hasten (n.); be dropped, drop (n.); ease the bowels; skin a camel; cut down a tree and strip off its branches; INF. *najiyy*, impart a secret; — II. INF. *tajniya-t*, cause to escape, rescue, liberate, bring to a place of safety; escape, save one's self; — III. INF. *nijâ'*, *munâjât*, impart secrets to, whisper to, talk to; — IV. INF. *injâ'*, rescue, save, relieve; bring to a higher place; — V. INF. *tanajjî*, save one's self, escape, be rescued; look for a higher place; — VI. INF. *tanâjî*, impart secrets to one another; whisper; suggest; — VIII. INF. *intijâ'*=VI.; act with a secret understanding; — X. INF. *istinjâ'*, save one's self, escape; hasten (n.); clean a part of the body polluted by excrement; uproot a tree.

نجو *najw*, pl. *nijâ'*, pouring cloud; pulled-off skin; excrement, wind (of the body); secret between two persons; — *naju'*, *najû'*, who injures by the evil eye; — ة *najwa-t*, higher place, hill; secret; worst kind of dates.

نجوج *najûj*, swift, nimble, agile.

نجوخ *najûḥ*, infuriated, roaring.

نجود *najûd*, pl. *nujud*, swift and strong; handsome and intelligent (woman); — *nujûd*, pl. of نجد *najd*.

نجوع *najû'*, wholesome, healthy; ن الصبى *najû' aṣ-ṣabiyy*, milk;

water with flour as a drink for camels; — *nujû'*, INF. of (نجع).

نجوم *nujûm*, pl. of نجم *najm*; — ى *nujûmiyy*, astronomical; astronomer, astrologer.

نجوى *najwa*, pl. *najâwî*, secret communication; secret; talk; interview; pl. *anjiya-t*, who shares in a secret; — *najiyy*, secret communication; pl. *anjiya-t*, sharer in a secret, confidant; who talks with, communer; — *naji'*, *najî'* = نجو *naju'*, *najû'*; — ة *najiyya-t*, swift camels.

نجيب *najîb*, pl. *nujub*, *nujabâ'*, *anjâb*, noble, of high descent; generous, excellent; hero; good steed; fleet camel; volunteer; — ة *najîba-t*, pl. *najâ'ib*, best part of anything; finest passages; generous camels or horses.

نجيث *najîs*, secret; — ة *najîsa-t*, earth cleared out of a well; what becomes generally known; (evil) report; aim, end, intention.

نجيج *najîj*, flowing (s.).

نجيح *najîh*, successful; correct.

نجيد *najîd*, pl. *nujud*, *nujadâ'*, bold, brave; lion; grieved, sad, sorrowful.

نجير *najîr*, trellissed balcony with cushions for resting in; paste used by a weaver; — ة *najîra-t*, reward; a mixture of butter, milk and flour; hot stone for boiling milk; wooden roof.

نجيز *najîz*, ready.

نجيس *najîs*, dirty, polluted, unclean, impure; incurable.

نجيش *najîś*, hunter; game-driver.

نجيع *najî'*, wholesome, nourishing; effective; blackish blood; fresh blood.

نجيف *najîf*, pl. *nujuf*, old leathern flask; broad-headed (arrow).

نجيل *najîl*, pl. *nujl*, a plant and its leaves used as green food.

(نح) *nahh*, U, INF. *nahh*, urge to haste, goad on; INF. *nahîh*, repeat a tone in the chest; INF. *nahah*, *nuhha-t*, have a deep firm voice; — ة *nuhha-t*, hoarseness.

نحا *nihâ'*, pl. of نحي *nahy*, &c.

نحات *nahât*, nature; — *nahhât*, stone-carver, sculptor; — ة *nuhâta-t*, splinters; chips, shavings.

نحاحة *nahâha-t*, patience; liberality; avarice.

نحاز *nahâz*, far-stretching country; — *nuhâz*, violent cough of a camel.

نحاس *nuhâs*, brass (ن اصفر *nuhâs asfar*), copper (ن احمر *nuhâs ahmar*); sparks of a smithy; flame without smoke; also *nihâs*, origin; natural disposition; — *nahhâs*, copper-smith, brazier, kettle-maker; — ى *nuhâsiyy*, of copper.

نحاشة *nihâśa-t*, burnt bread.

نحاض *nihâd*, pl. of نحضة *nahda-t*; — ة *nihâda-t*, fleshiness.

نحاط *nuhât*, sigh; — *nahhât*, proud.

نحاف *nihâf*, pl. of نحيف *nahîf*; — ة *nahâfa-t*, leanness, thinness, slimness.

نحام *nahhâm*, who sighs frequently and deeply; lion; also *nuhâm*, a red water-bird; goose.

نحانحة *nahâniha-t*, misers.

(نحب) *nahab*, U, INF. *nahb*, make a vow, devote, consecrate; go, travel; be zealous and careful; — A, INF. *nahb*, *nahîb*, sob and cry aloud, lament, wail; die; bet against stakes; play at dice; — II. INF. *tanhîb*, be zealous and careful; — III. INF. *munâhaba-t*, bring an adversary before court; bet with; — VI. INF. *tanâhub*, appoint a time between one another; — VIII. INF. *intihâb*, sob or cry aloud, wail.

نحب *nahb*, sobbing, crying, tears, sighs; grief; great danger; important matter; necessity;

space, time, space of time; last gasp, death; sleep; soul; vow; intention; — ة *nuḥba-t*, cast lot.

نحباة *naḥbât*, lamentation for the dead.

(نحت) *naḥat*, I, U, A, INF. *naḥt*, shave, plane, smooth; scratch; saw off; carve wood or stone; excavate a rock; lie with; emaciate a camel (toilsome journey).

نحت *naḥt*, sharp, cold; nature.

(نحر) *naḥar*, U, INF. *naḥr*, *tanḥâr*, slaughter a camel (by a stab above the collar-bone); wound at the collar-bone, or the throat; stand opposite; stand upright towards the Kibla placing the right hand on the left in praying (بالصلوة *bi'ṣ-ṣalât*); — III. INF. *munâḥara-t*, injure at the throat; — VI. INF. *tanâḥur*, seize one another by the throat, come to blows; stand opposite one another; — VIII. INF. *intiḥâr*, stab one's self, commit suicide.

نحر *naḥr*, slaughtering, sacrificing (يوم الن *yaum an-naḥr*, day of sacrifice, 10th of *ẕû 'l-ḥijja-t*); pl. *nuḥûr*, collar-bone; throat, neck; beginning; pl. accesses, approaches, boundary places, frontiers; — ة *naḥra-t*, first (or last) day of the new moon.

نحرا *nuḥarâ'*, نحرى *nuḥra*, pl. of نحير *naḥîr*.

نحرير *niḥrîr*, pl. *naḥârîr*, sharp, intelligent, the knowing one; zealous and industrious; practised, clever, skilful.

(نحز) *naḥaz*, INF. *naḥz*, push, push away; drive off; pound in a mortar; — IV. *inḥâz*, suffer from a violent cough; — *naḥiz*, coughing violently.

(نحس) *naḥas*, INF. *naḥs*, treat harshly; torment, render miserable; tire the rider; pass. *nuḥis*, also — *naḥis*, A, INF. *naḥas*, and — *naḥus*, INF. *nuḥûsa-t*, be ill-omened, disastrous, bring calamity; — II. INF. *tanḥîs*, inquire, question, explore; (m.) grow hard; — IV. INF. *inḥâs*, render disastrous, calamitous, unfortunate; — V. INF. *tanaḥḥus*, X. INF. *istinḥâs*, inquire.

نحس *naḥs*, pl. *naḥûs*, disaster, calamity, evil omen, fore-token of evil; also *naḥis*, ة, ill-omened, disastrous, bringing calamity, unfortunate; du. *an-naḥsân*, Saturn (اكبر *akbar*) and Mars (اصغر *aṣgar*).

(نحص) *naḥaṣ*, INF. *nuḥûṣ*, be very fat; INF. *naḥṣ*, pay off a debt.

نحص *naḥṣ*, wild she-ass one year old; — *nuḥṣ*, foot of a mountain.

(نحض) *naḥaḍ*, A, I, INF. *naḥḍ* (also VIII.), loosen the flesh from the bone; lay the bone open; ask obtrusively; make thin and sharp; — A, INF. *nuḥûḍ*, fall off, grow thin, emaciate (n.); — *naḥuḍ*, INF. *naḥâḍa-t*, be very fleshy, have compact muscles.

نحض *naḥḍ*, compact flesh; — ة *naḥḍa-t*, pl. *niḥâḍ*, *nuḥûḍ*, large masses of flesh.

(نحط) *naḥaṭ*, I, INF. *naḥṭ*, *naḥîṭ*, breathe heavily, pant, fetch deep sighs; — INF. *naḥṭ*, speak harshly to and turn off.

(نحف) *naḥif*, A, INF. *naḥaf*, also — *naḥuf*, INF. *naḥâfa-t*, be naturally thin; — IV. INF. *inḥâf*, make thin or still thinner.

نحفا *nuḥafâ'*, pl. of نحيف *naḥîf*.

(نحل) *naḥal*, INF. *nuḥl*, *nuḥla-t*, present, reward; give the morning-gift to a wife, secure her jointure; (m.) take out a beehive; — A, INF. *naḥl*, provoke by abuse, revile; trace a saying to its author; (also VIII.) arrogate another's verses, commit plagiarism; — A, INF. *nuḥûl*, be emaciated by illness, &c.; — *naḥil*, A, *naḥul*, INF. *naḥal*, id.; — II. INF. *tanḥîl*, heat the room for silk-worms; — IV. INF.

inḥâl, emaciate (a.); — VIII. INF. *intiḥâl*, see I.; profess the creed of a sect.

نحل *naḥl* (m. f.), ة, bee (راس ن *ra's naḥl*, swarm of bees); thin; also *nuḥl*, نحلان *nuḥlân*, gift; — ة *niḥla-t*, *nuḥla-t*, present, gift; part of the morning-gift; jointure; claim; law-suit; plagiarism; religious sect; *niḥlat-an*, of free will; — ى *naḥla*, pl. ناحل *nâḥil* and نحيل *naḥîl*; — *nuḥla*, gift; — *naḥliyy*, rearer of bees.

(نحم) *naḥam*, I, INF. *naḥm*, *naḥîm*, *naḥamân*, breathe deeply and violently, sigh, groan, cough, hawk, roar; — VIII. INF. *intiḥâm*, sigh, groan; purpose, intend, resolve upon, undertake.

نحم *niḥamm* = نحام *naḥḥâm*; — ة *naḥma-t*, cough.

نحن *naḥnu*, *naḥn*, we.

(نحنح) *naḥnaḥ*, INF. ة, also II. INF. *tanaḥnuḥ*, cough as in a whooping cough; hawk; rumble (bowels).

(نحو) *naḥâ*, U, A, INF. *naḥw* (also VIII.), turn and move in a certain direction; go aside, across, come upon one's flank; direct the eyes to (الى *ila*); turn from (عن *'an*); — INF. *tanḥiya-t*, push or put aside; take from the place, remove; observe the rules of grammar; — IV. INF. *inḥâ'*, turn from; assail with a whip; — V. INF. *tanaḥḥî*, go aside, depart; — VIII. INF. *intiḥâ'*, see I.; step forward against, advance towards; intend, aim at; lean upon; depend upon; rely; devote pains and zeal to (فى *fî*).

نحو *naḥw*, pl. *nuḥuww*, *anḥâ'*, side, direction; region, tract; road; intention, purpose, tendency; kind, sort, manner; pl. *nuḥuww*, *nuḥiyy*, grammar, particularly syntax; *naḥw-a*, in the direction of, after, in accordance with; like, like as, as for instance (declinable); about.

نحوس *naḥûs*, forboding evil, ill-omened, disastrous; — ة *nuḥûsa-t*, evil omen, bad augury; power of hurting; calamity.

نحوص *naḥûṣ*, pl. *naḥâ'iṣ*, without milk and foal; — *nuḥûṣ*, fatness.

نحول *naḥûl*, leanness, thinness.

نحوى *naḥwiyy*, ة, grammatical, grammatically correct; syntactical; pl. *naḥwiyyûn*, grammarian; pedant.

(نحى) *naḥa*, I, A, INF. *naḥy*, shake the milk for making butter; push aside, remove, cause to cease; direct the eyes towards (الى *ila*); — II. INF. *tanḥiya-t*, push aside, remove, cause to cease; — IV. INF. *inḥâ'*, shoot at, pierce; — VIII. INF. *intiḥâ'*, devote pains and zeal to (فى *fî*); lean upon; rely upon.

نحى *naḥy*, *niḥy*, *naḥa*, pl. *anḥâ'*, *naḥiyy*, *niḥâ'*, earthen milk-vessel for making butter; bag for making butter; — *nuḥiyy*, pl. of نحو *naḥw*; — ة *naḥiyya-t* (القوارع *al-qawâri'*), threatened with calamity.

نحيب *naḥîb*, loud sobbing and crying; lamentation, bewailing of the dead.

نحيت *naḥît*, smoothly carved; cut in stone; emaciated; comb; also ة *naḥîta-t*, cry, complaint, lamentation; sigh; nature; dysentery.

نحيح *naḥîḥ*, rumbling in the bowels.

نحير *naḥîr*, pl. *naḥra*, *nuharâ'*, *naḥâ'ir*, slaughtered camel; also ة *naḥîra-t*, first or last day (or night) of a month.

نحيزة *naḥîza-t*, nature; manner, custom; narrow path or tract; strip of cloth.

نحيس *naḥîs*, ill-omened, disastrous; year of famine.

نحيض *naḥîḍ*, firm of flesh; fleshless; thin and sharp.

نحيط *naḥîṭ*, groaning (s.).

نحيف *naḥîf*, pl. *niḥâf*, *nuḥafâ'*, thin, weak, delicate.

نحيل *naḥîl*, lean, thin; (m.) swarm of bees.

نحيم *naḥîm*, groaning, hawking (s.).

(نخ) *naḫḫ*, U, INF. *naḫḫ*, stride along; walk fast; urge on violently; (also II.) bid a camel to kneel down by the cry *iḫ iḫ!* (m.) kneel down; (m.) bow; — II. INF. *tanḫîḫ*, see I.

نخ *naḫḫ*, an oblong carpet; — *nuḫḫ*, marrow; — ة *naḫḫa-t*, inclination of the head, the body; slave; gold *dînâr*; also *niḫḫa-t*, *nuḫḫa-t*, wine.

نخاخة *nuḫâḫa-t*, marrow.

نخاريب *naḫârîb*, pl. of نخروب *nuḫrûb*.

نخاس *niḫâs*, a round hollow piece of wood placed between the axle-tree and the nave of a wheel which has grown too wide; — *naḫḫâs*, cattle-dealer or slave-trader; — ة *niḫâsa-t*, such trade.

نخاع *naḫâ'*, *niḫâ'*, *nuḫâ'*, pl. *nuḫu'*, spinal marrow; brain; — ة *nuḫâ'a-t*, mucus, phlegm; the white of an egg.

نخاف *niḫâf*, pl. *anḫifa-t*, boot.

نخالة *nuḫâla-t*, anything sifted; what remains in a sieve; bran.

نخامة *nuḫâma-t*, mucus, phlegm.

نخانيق *naḫânîq*, pl. of نخنوق *nuḫnûq*.

نخاورة *naḫâwira-t*, pl. of نخوار *niḫwâr*.

(نخب) *naḫab*, U, INF. *naḫb*, pull out; select, choose; separate, sever; bite; — A, U, lie with; — IV. INF. *inḫâb*, have a timorous son; — VIII. INF. *intiḫâb*, select, choose; predestinate; give one's vote to; — X. INF. *istinḫâb*, id.

نخب *naḫb*, selection, choice; the most exquisite part, cream of; also ة *nuḫba-t*, a full draught (especially to one's health); *naḫb*, ة *naḫba-t*, buttocks; *naḫb*, *naḫab*, *naḫib*, *niḫabb*, *niḫibb*, pl. *nuḫub*, timorous, cowardly; — ة *nuḫba-t*, *nuḫaba-t*, pl. *nuḫab*, selected, chosen, selection; anything better, anything choice, the best of, choice phrases, &c.; timorous, cowardly.

(نخت) *naḫat*, U, INF. *naḫt*, pick up with the beak; take out singly; pull out; go to the bottom of a speech.

(نخج) *naḫaj*, INF. *naḫj*, shake the bucket in the water so as to fill it; break wind; dash against the banks, &c. (torrent).

نخج *naḫj*, stream, torrent; its murmuring.

(نخر) *naḫar*, U, I, INF. *naḫr*, *naḫîr*, blow the air noisily from the nose, snort, snore, snuffle; (m.) gnaw at; — *naḫir*, A, INF. *naḫar*, be worn out and ragged; be carious, putrid; be bored through.

نخر *naḫir*, ة, old and worn out, ragged; bored through; carious, mouldering; hollow, blown through by the wind; worm-eaten; — ة *nuḫra-t*, gust of wind; storm; also *nuḫara-t*, nostril; tip of the nose; muzzle, snout.

نخروب *nuḫrûb*, pl. *naḫârîb*, split; cavity; cell of a honey-comb.

(نخز) *naḫaz*, INF. *naḫz*, pierce, prick; goad, goad on; hurt by words.

نخز *naḫz*, pricking, piercing (s.); — ة *naḫza-t*, prick, puncture; pleurisy; — *nuḫza-t*, id.; hole.

(نخس) *naḫas*, A, U, INF. *naḫs*, pierce, prick, goad, goad on; drive.

نخس *naḫs*, ة *naḫsa-t*=نخز *naḫz*, ة *naḫza-t*; — ابن نخسة *ibn niḫsa-t*, bastard.

(نخش) *naḫaś*, INF. *naḫś*, spur, urge on violently; move, shake (a.); hurt, injure, damage; — *naḫiś*, A, INF. *naḫaś*, grow old

and get worn out underneath (cloth).

(نحص) *naḥaṣ*, A, U, INF. *naḥṣ*, be emaciated and shrivelled; emaciate and weaken (old age); — *naḥiṣ*, A, INF. *naḥaṣ*, also VIII. INF. *intiḥâṣ*, waste away.

(نحط) *naḥaṭ*, U, INF. *naḥṭ*, fall upon suddenly; (also VIII.) blow the nose; — I, INF. *naḥîṭ*, scold, abuse, revile; behave haughtily towards; — VIII. INF. *intiḥâṭ*, see I.

نحط *nuḥṭ*, spinal marrow; also *naḥṭ*, men.

(نحع) *naḥa'*, INF. *naḥ'*, have true affection for, give sincere advice; acknowledge a debt; cut in slaughtering as far as the spinal marrow; (m.) push the dam with the head in sucking; — *naḥi'*, A, INF. *naḥa'*, grow full of sap; — V. INF. *tanaḥḥu'*, expectorate phlegm or mucus; — VIII. INF. *intiḥâ'*, pour down (n.).

(نحف) *naḥaf*, A, U, INF. *naḥf*, breathe through the nose, snort; fetch a deep breath.

(نحل) *naḥal*, U, INF. *naḥl*, sift, bolt; filter, strain; choose the best, select; rain, snow; — V. INF. *tanaḥḥul*, VIII. INF. *intiḥâl*, select, choose the best.

نحل *naḥl*, ة pl. *naḥîl*, date-palm; palm-tree (ذو نحلة *zû naḥla-t*, Jesus); young tree, plant; woman's ornament; wreath of flowers, garland; — ة *naḥla-t*, stick, staff (of a dervish, &c.).

(نحم) *naḥam*, U, INF. *naḥm*, play or sing well; — *naḥim*, A, INF. *naḥm*, *naḥam*, secrete phlegm or mucus; hawk, blow one's nose; INF. *naḥam*, be tired; — II. INF. *tanḥîm*, bring forth a secretion of phlegm; — V. INF. *tanaḥḥum* = *naḥim*; — ة *naḥma-t*, beauty; phlegm, mucus.

(نحنح) *naḥnaḥ*, INF. ة make a camel kneel down; remove, put away; (m.) speak through the nose; — II. INF. *tanaḥnuḥ*, kneel down.

نحنوق *nuḥnûq*, pl. *naḥâniq*, low wall round a well.

(نحو) *naḥâ*, U, INF. *naḥwa-t*, be proud, inflated, vain; boast; pass. id.; praise, glorify; — II. INF. *tanḥiya-t*, fill one with self-confidence and courage, instigate one to risk everything; — VIII. INF. *intiḥâ'*, affect a mien of proud superiority towards; show courage against, defy, threaten; — X. INF. *istinḥâ'* = II.; — ة *naḥwa-t*, high self-confidence, pride, haughtiness; courage, fearlessness; splendour, magnificence, pomp.

نحوار *niḥwâr*, pl. نحاورة *naḥâwira-t*, self-confident, self-relying, proud; mean, cowardly.

نحوص *naḥûs*, young mountain-goat.

(نحى) = (نحو).

نحيب *naḥîb*, timid, timorous.

نحير *naḥîr*, snoring (s.).

نحيط *naḥîṭ*, calumny, slander.

نحيف *naḥîf*, blowing the nose (s.).

نحيل *naḥîl*, palm-tree; palm-grove; — *.

(ند) *nadd*, I, INF. *nadd*, *nadad*, *nidâd*, *nudûd*, *nadîd*, run away, take to flight, escape, run astray; desert; also — II. INF. *tandîd*, make known, talk over publicly; disgrace, dishonour; — III. INF. *munâdda-t*, oppose one in a hostile manner; — IV. INF. *indâd*, disperse, separate (a.); — VI. INF. *tanâdd*, separate and disperse in all directions (n.).

(ندا) *nada'*, INF. *nad'*, put on coals or in the hot ashes; stir up the ashes; feel aversion, loathe.

ندا *nidâ'*, call, outcry, exclamation; voice, sound; public proclamation; vocative; particle; INF. of (ندو III.); — ة *nadât*, inside of a horse's thigh; — *nad'a-t*, *nud'a-t*, plenty, abundance; also *nuda'a-t*, rainbow, halo round sun or moon; — *nud'a-t*, *nu-*

da'a-t, pl. *nadâ'*, stray parts of plants.

ندارة *nadâwa-t*, moisture of the ground.

(ندب) *nadab*, U, INF. *nadb*, eulogize the dead in a poem, bewail, lament; call up, invite, summon; encourage, incite, instigate; choose one for a particular purpose in preference to others; — *nadib*, A, INF. *nadab*, be healed to a scar, be cicatrized; INF. *nadab*, *nudûb*, *nudûba-t*, be covered with scars, with scurf; — *nadub*, INF. *nadâba-t*, be clever, nimble, and pretty; — VIII. INF. *intidâb*, call up, summon, invite, choose in preference; be easily induced, comply with, grant a request; be skilful, apt.

ندب *nadb*, lamentation for the dead, elegy; complaint; pl. *nudabâ*, *nudûb*, clever and nimble; intelligent, noble, liberal; generous, mettled, fleet; — *nadab*, healing of a wound to a scar; danger, bet for stakes; archery; — ة *nadba-t*, pl. *nadab*, *andâb*, *nudûb*, crust of a healing wound; scar; — *nudba-t*, elegy in honour of the dead, lamentation; crying and wailing.

(ندح) *nadaḥ*, A, INF. *nadḥ*, widen, extend; — VIII. INF. *intidâḥ*, be free of, unincumbered with.

ندح *nadḥ*, *nudḥ*, pl. *andâḥ*, vast open tract (also ة *nadḥa-t*, *nudḥa-t*); plenty, affluence.

(ندخ) *nadaḫ*, INF. *nadḫ*, push, thrust, knock; strike against the shore, land (ship); — IV. INF. *indâḫ*, make the ship to land.

ندخ *nadḫ*, landing, arrival.

ندد *nadad*, dispersed (pl.)

ندداء *nudadâ'*, pl. of نديد *nadîd*.

(ندر) *nadar*, U, INF. *nadr*, *nudûr*, fall or step out one by one, be isolated, single, unique, rare; fall from (speech); put forth leaves.

ندر *nadr*, isolated, single, rare; — ة *nadra-t*, particles (of gold, &c.); *nadrat-an*, accidentally; — *nudra-t*, rareness, rarity.

(ندس) *nadas*, U, INF. *nads*, pierce; kick; throw down; revile; lead out of the road; — *nadis*, A. INF. *nadas*, be intelligent, comprehend easily; — III. INF. *munâdasa-t*, abuse, revile.

ندس *nads*, *nadis*, *nadus*, quick of understanding, very intelligent; — *nadas*, intelligence, prudence; cunning, stratagem.

(ندش) *nadaś*, U, INF. *nadś*, *nadaś*, examine, investigate; card cotton.

(ندص) *nadaṣ*, U, INF. *nadṣ*, *nudûṣ*, come out; come forward; jut out, project; protrude; INF. *nadaṣ*, break open and discharge pus.

(ندع) *nad'*, wild marjoram; — IV. *anda'*, INF. *indâ'*, imitate bad manners; — I. and V. INF. *tanaddu'*, m. for the following:

(ندغ) *nadag*, INF. *nadg*, poke with the finger; sting, pierce; sting with words; — III. INF. *munâdaga-t*, coax, cajole, quiet by cajoling; — IV. INF. *indâg*, hurt, injure; — VIII. INF. *intidâg*, smile stealthily.

ندغ *nadg*, *nidg*, wild marjoram; best honey; — ة *nudga-t*, white spots on the nails.

(ندف) *nadaf*, I, INF. *nadf*, card cotton; drop rain, snow; play the cithern, play on an instrument; — INF. *nadf*, *nadafân*, move the fore-feet quickly drink by draughts; eat; — II. INF. *tandîf*, have cotton carded; — ة *nudfa-t*, pl. *nudaf*, a small quantity, little of; fleak.

(ندل) *nadal*, U, INF. *nadl*, take from the place and transfer; take dates from the table or bread out of the basket; draw out; select, choose; rob; drop excrement; — *nadil*, A, INF.

nadal, be dirtied; — v. INF. *tanaddul*, wipe one's self; cover the head with a cloth or veil.

ندل *nadl*, dirt, mud;—*nudul*, pl. waiters at table.

(ندم) *nadim*, A, INF. *nadm*, *nadam*, *nadâma-t*, repent, feel remorse; — II. INF. *tandîm*, exhort to repentance; — III. INF. *nidâm*, *munâdama-t*, keep one company at table or in pleasures; be one's boon companion; — IV. INF. *indâm*=II.; —lead to repentance; — V. INF. *tanaddum*, repent; — VI. INF. *tanâdum*, revel, have a drinking-bout.

ندم *nadm*, ingenious, witty; — *nadam*, repentance, remorse, contrition.

ندما *nudamâ'*, pl. of نديم *nadîm*.

ندمان *nadmân*, pl. *nadâma*, *nidâm*, table-companion, boon-companion; ة pl. *nudâma*, repentant; (m.) who cries out, announces, proclaims; — *nudmân*, pl. of نديم *nadîm*.

(ندة) *nadah*, INF. *nadh*, urge on camels, drive them away, bring them to a stand by cries; drive the camels together; (m.) call; — VIII. INF. *intidâḥ*, X. INF. *istindâḥ*, be well managed, flourish (business); — ة *nadha-t*, *nudha-t*, plenty, great quantity.

(ندو) *nadâ*, U, INF. *nadw*, call, call out, call upon or to; call together, invite; assemble (n.); be present at an assembly; hold a number of persons, be sufficiently spacious for them; — ندى *nadî*, A, INF. *nadan*, be moist, damp, wet; be fresh and green; come from a distance; — II. INF. *tandiya-t*, moisten, wet; expose to the dew; produce plenty of dew; — III. INF. *nidâ'*, *munâdât*, call upon, invoke, summon; keep company; blab out another's secrets; cry out publicly, proclaim; — IV. INF. *indâ'*, moisten, wet; be liberal; have a fine voice; — V. INF. *tanaddî*, be covered with dew, be moist; sweat, perspire; show one's self liberal; = VIII.; — VI. INF. *tanâdî*, call to one another; assemble in consequence of a summons or invitation; sit together and converse; —VIII. INF. *intidâ'*, assemble (n.) sit together; — ة *nadwa-t*, assembly; court; — *nudwa-t*, watering-place for camels; — *nuduwwa-t*, moisture.

ندوب *nudûb*, healing of a wound, scarring.

ندى *nada*, pl. *andâ'*, *andiya-t*, moisture, dampness; dew; rain; fresh food; fat; liberality; rich gift, largess, bounty; reach of hearing; space of time; end, limit; — *nadî*, v. see (ندو); — *nadî* (ند *nad-in*), ة, moist, wet; fresh and green; liberal; — *nadiyy*, pl. *andiya-t*, moist, fresh, juicy; liberal; calling aloud; assembly, company; — *nadî'* = ندي *nadî'*; — ة *nadiya-t*, moist ground.

نديان *nadyân*, juicy.

نديب *nadîb*, scarred, cicatrized; covered with a crust or scurf.

نديد *nadîd*, pl. *nudadâ'*, f. ة pl. *nadâ'id*, equal; rival.

نديف *nadîf*, carded.

نديم *nadîm*, ة *nadîma-t*, pl. *nudamâ'*, *nidâm*, *nudmân*, boon companion, sharer in another's pleasures; confidant; courtier; court jester.

نديى *nadî'*, placed at the fire, in the hot ashes; redness of the clouds; rainbow.

(نذ) *naẓẓ*, U, INF. *naẓîẓ*, make water.

نذارة *naẓâra-t*, *niẓârat*, admonition, warning, threat; fright.

نذال *nuẓẓâl*, pl. of نذيل *naẓîl*.

(نذخ) *naẓaḥ*, INF. *naẓḥ*, run fast.

(نذر) *naẓar*, U, I, INF. *naẓr*, *nuẓûr*, make a vow, devote one's son to the service of God; doom to death, place in front in a com-

bat; warn, threaten; — *naẓir*, A, INF. *naẓar*, see the danger, see through the intentions of an enemy and be on one's guard; — II. INF. *tanẓîr*, make a vow to, profess before, profess a belief; — IV. INF. *inẓâr*, warn, call attention to the consequences; predict; threaten; preach the true belief, sermon on morals; — VI. INF. *tanâẓur*, warn one another, bid one another to be on one's guard; — VIII. INF. *intiẓâr*, impose a vow upon one's self.

نذر *naẓr*, pl. *nuẓûr*, *nuẓur*, vow; anything consecrated to God; pious gift; present to superiors; a mulct for wounds; — *naẓr*, *nuẓr*, *nuẓur*, نذری *nuẓra*, warning, admonition, threat; — *nuẓur*, *nuẓra*, fear, fright; also—

نذرا *nuẓarâ'*, pl. of نذير *naẓîr*.

(نذع) *naẓa'*, INF. *naẓ'*, break forth, flow, run; — V. INF. *tanaẓẓu'*, fall in drops.

(نذل) *naẓul*, INF. *naẓâla-t*, *nuẓûla-t*, be vile, mean, despised, reprobate.

نذل *naẓl*, pl. *anẓâl*, *nuẓûl*, mean, vile, abject, despised.

نذلا *nuẓalâ'*, pl. of نذيل *naẓîl*.

نذول *nuẓûl*, pl. of نذل *naẓl*, and نذيل *naẓîl*; — ة *nuẓûla-t*, INF. of (نذل).

نذيذ *naẓîẓ*, spittle; INF. of (نذ).

نذير *naẓîr*, pl. *nuẓur*, *nuẓarâ'*, consecrated to God; Nazarite; warner; prophet, apostle, preacher; warning, threat; frightened; naked, stripped; — ة *naẓîra-t*, thing or person consecrated to God; foremost line of battle, forlorn hope.

نذيل *naẓîl*, pl. *nuẓalâ'*, *nuẓẓâl*, vile, despised, abject.

نراد *narrâd*, chess-player, &c.

نربيج *narbîj* = نبريج *nabrîj*.

نرجس *nirjis*, *narjis*, *narjas*, narcissus, daffodil.

نرد *nard*, game at chess, or at draughts; game at dice; sack of palm-leaves for dates.

نردين *nardîn*, spikenard.

(نرز) *naraz*, U, INF. *narz*, hide one's self from fear.

نرسی *narsiyy*, of Nars (cloth).

(نرش) *naraś*, INF. *narś*, reach for, take in one's hand.

(نز) *nazz*, I, INF. *nazîz*, run; tremble, oscillate; also INF. *nazz*, exude water, abound with springs; leak; (m.) suppurate; — III. INF. *munâzza-t*, dispute with; — IV. INF. *inzâz*, exude water.

نز *nazz*, *nizz*, pl. *nuzûz*, water exuding from the earth, spring-water; — *nazz*, ة nimble, agile, active, always on the move; witty; liberal; — ة *nizza-t*, desire.

(نزا) *naza'*, INF. *naz'*, *nuzû'*, stir up discord; assail, rush against; — INF. *naz'*, urge to, compel; prevent.

نزا *nazâ'*, leap, leap at; — *nizâ'*, covering (of a male animal); — *nazzâ'*, ready for mischief; given to attacking others.

نزار *nizâr*, name of the first ancestor of an Arab tribe; — *; — ة *nazâra-t*, paltriness.

نزاز *nizâz*, prone to evil; — ة *nazâza-t*, walk, march; — ة *nazzâza-t*, water oozing out of the ground, spring-water (m.).

نزاع *nizâ'*, quarrel, dispute, lawsuit, agony, INF. (نزع III.); *nazzâ'*, dwarf; — *nuzzâ'*, pl. of نازع *nâzi'*, foreigner, stranger.

نزاغ *nazzâg*, malicious slanderer.

نزاق *nizâq*, scolding; — ة *nazâqa-t*, swiftness, nimbleness; flying into a passion (s.).

نزاك *nazzâk*, slanderer, reviler; — ة *nazâka-t*, delicacy, refinement, elegance.

نزال *nizâl*, fight, combat, skirmish; *nazâl-i*, come forth for combat!; — *nuzzâl*, pl. of نازل *nâzil*, ag. of (نزل); — ة *nizâla-t*, day's march; — ة *nuzâla-t*, discharged human

sperm; what falls from the sieve; chaff.

نزاه *nizâh*, pl. of *nâzih*, retired from the world, &c.; — ة *nazâha-t*, ية *nazâhiya-t*, spotless purity, chastity, honesty; healthy situation and pleasantness of a country; recreation; INF. of (نزه).

(نزب) *nazab*, I, INF. *nazb*, *nuzâb*, *nazîb*, bellow, low.

نزب *nazab*, nickname, mock-name.

(نزج) *nazaj*, U, INF. *nazj*, dance.

(نزح) *nazaḥ*, A, I, INF. *nazḥ*, nearly exhaust a well; be nearly exhausted; have the wells far distant or almost exhausted; pass. be far from home, depart and disappear; — A, I, INF. *nazḥ*, *nuzûḥ*, be distant; — II. INF. *tanzîḥ*, drive from house and home, compel to emigrate; —IV. INF. *inzâḥ* = II.; nearly exhaust a well; — VIII. INF. *intizâḥ*, leave house and home, emigrate, live in exile; be far distant.

(نزر) *nazar*, U, INF. *nazr*, importune with requests or questions; command; urge to haste; make little of, disdain; find little; be swift, nimble; be excited;— *nazur*, INF. *nazr*, *nazar*, *nuzûr*, *nazâra-t*, *nuzûra-t*, be little, paltry, insignificant, of small value;—II. INF. *tanzîr* = IV.; — IV. INF. *inzâr*, make small; — V. INF. *tanazzur*, grow little, small.

نزر *nazr*, pl. *nizâr*, little, paltry, insignificant, of small value; tasteless, insipid; *nazr-an*, slowly, late; — *nuzur*, spectre, phantom; — عن نزر *'an nuzur-in*, face to face; — ة *nazira-t*, poor in milk, unprolific.

نزع *naza'*, I, INF. *naz'*, take away, snatch from the place, tear off, pull out; draw up (the bucket); draw wide (the bow); rob one of his clothes, strip; (m.) depose, deprive of office, cashier; (m.) spoil;—INF. *nizâ'*, *nazâ'a-t*, *nuzû'*, long for one's people, be home-sick; INF. *nuzû'*, recede, desist, draw off; be restive; — *nazi'*, A, INF. *naza'*, be bald on the temples; — III. INF. *nizâ'* *munâza'a-t*, begin a quarrel with, dispute, have a law-suit against; try to tear from, dispute a thing; pull out; be in agony, in a death-struggle; long for one's home and people; — IV. INF. *inzâ'*, take from the place; — VI. INF. *tanâzu'*, quarrel with one another; take the cup out of one another's hand;— VIII. take from the place, pull out; be taken away, pulled out; (m.) get spoiled; abstain, be unwilling to (عن *'an*).

نزع *naz'*, taking away, pulling out (s.); death-struggle, agony; deposition, degradation;—*naza'*, baldness about the temples; — ة *naz'a-t*, *naza'a-t*, bald spot about the temples;—*naza'a-t*, mountain-path; pl. of نازع *nâzi'*, drawing the bow, shooting.

(نزغ) *nazag*, A, I, INF. *nazg*, sting by words, revile, abuse; slander; stir up discord; urge to evil;— ة *nazga-t*, pl. *nazagât*, inciting to do evil; mischief.

(نزف) *nazaf*, I, U, INF. *nazf*, exhaust a well entirely; be entirely exhausted; pass. lose a great deal of blood; — I, INF. *nazf*, grow weak from loss of blood; pass. lose one's clear senses, get intoxicated; pass. have exhausted one's arguments and give over disputing; — *nazif*, A, INF. *nazaf*, be exhausted, fail; — *nazuf*, be entirely exhausted; — IV. INF. *inzâf*, be drunk; also—X. INF. *istinzâf*, exhaust one's tears.

نزف *nazf*, *nazaf*, *nuzf*, hemorrhage, loss of blood;—*nuzf*, exhaustion of water; — *nazif*, weakened by loss of blood; — *nuzzaf*, veins no longer bleeding; — ة *nuzfa-t*, pl. *nuzaf*, a few drops.

(نزق) *nazaq*, U, I, INF. *nazq*, *nuzûq*,

also *naziq*, A, INF. *nazaq*, be swift and get the lead of others (horse); cover the mare; — *nazaq*, I, *naziq*, A, INF. *nazq*, *nazaq*, *nuzûq*, get easily angry and pacified again; — *naziq*, A, INF. *nazaq*, be brimful; — III. INF. *nizâq*, *munâzaqa-t*, scold in anger, abuse; be closely related; —IV. INF. *inzâq*, urge the horse to haste, so as to overtake the others; make the stallion to cover; laugh immoderately; — VI. INF. *tanâzuq*, be angry with one another; abuse each other in anger.

نزق *nazaq*, swiftness, fleetness; capriciousness, fickleness; levity; — *nazaq*, near; — *naziq*, ة, easily provoked and pacified; swift, fleet; full of levity, frivolous.

(نزك) *nazak*, U, INF. *nazk*, pierce with a spear; hurt with words; rebuke unjustly.

(نزل) *nazal*, I, INF. *nuzûl*, *manzil*, descend, alight; make a halt; put up; take quarters, live, dwell; come down; abate; come upon, hit; assail; get a cold; — *nazil*, A, INF. *nazal*, grow, thrive; have cold or rheum; — II. INF. *tanzîl* (also IV.), bid to alight and invite to put up; grant hospitality; (also IV.) send down his word by a prophet (God); let down, take down; lower, abate (a.); depose; insert, put in; — III. INF. *nizâl*, *munâzala-t*, mount from a camel upon a horse to fight; descend for combat; — IV. INF. *inzâl*, *munzal*, let down from above; carry down; take down; bid to descend; see II.; — V. INF. *tanazzul*, come slowly down; descend; resign, tender one's resignation; renounce a claim; have a cold, a rheum; be put in, inserted; — VI. INF. *tanâzul*, show one's self obliging, conciliatory, yielding, condescending; alight to fight one another; resign; — X. INF. *istinzâl*, invite one to alight, give one a lodging; demand the payment of a debt; beseech; force to leave; pass. be deposed, degraded.

نزل *nazl*, place where one halts or alights; station; relay; — *nizl*, alighting (s.); cold, rheum; also *nazil*, close, narrow; *nazil*, ة *nazila-t*, hard, impenetrable for the rain (ground); place where one frequently alights; — *nuzl*, human sperm; also *nuzul*, *nazal*, pl. *anzâl*, food and other requisites for the reception and entertainment of a guest; bread and provisions in abundance, provender; *nuzl*, *nuzul*, place of hospitable reception; *nuzul*, pl. of نزيل *nazîl*; — *nazal*, rain; gain; — ة *nazla-t*, alighting, putting up (s.); also *nuzla-t*, pl. *nazalât*, cold, rheum; — *nazalât*, *nazilât*, good arrangements and provisions.

(نزم) *nazam*, I, INF. *nazm*, bite severely.

(نزنز) *naznaz*, INF. ة, shake, nod.

(نزه) *nazah*, INF. *nazh*, *nazahân*, drive the camels far from the water; keep aloof from evil; — I, also *nazuh*, INF. *nazâha-t*, *nazâhiya-t*, be far from water, a morass or the sea; be free from unhealthiness of climate; — *nazuh*, INF. *nazâha-t*, *nazâhiya-t*, keep aloof from anything impure, from weakness or sin; also — *nazih*, be pleasant and healthy; — II. INF. *tanzîh*, keep from, liberate or exempt from anything contaminating; loose one's heart from anything earthly; distract from; — V. INF. *tanazzuh*, be far from water or pasture grounds; be free from anything impure; loose one's self from earthly things; take a pleasure-walk in a pleasant country, in gardens, in the green fields; divert and recreate one's

self; — X. INF. *istinzâh*, clean one's self from contamination by excrement, &c.

نزه *nazh*, *nizh*, free from any weakness, sin, or passion; — *nazh*, *nazih*, ة, far from water, morasses, or pasture grounds; pleasant and wholesome; ة *nazha-t*, &c., such a country; — ة *nazha-t*, distance; pleasantness and healthiness of a country; diversion, recreation in the open air, pleasure-walk; opportunity.

نزها *nuzahâ*, pl. of نازه *nâzih*, retired from the world, &c.

(نزو) *nazâ*, U, INF. *nazw*, *nuzâ'*, *nuzuww*, *nazawân*, assail, attack; skip about; resist, be averse to; boil (n.); — INF. *nizâ'*, cover the female; — INF. *nazawân*, depart, escape; — II. INF. *tanziya-t*, assail, attack; = IV; — IV. INF. *inzâ'*, make to leap upon, to assail, to cover; — V. INF. *tanazzî*, assail; — ة *nazwa-t*, assault.

نزوان *nazawân*, assault, attack; violence.

نزوح *nazûḥ*, exhausted; distant, far; — *.

نزور *nazûr*, poor in milk; not prolific; — *.

نزوز *nuzûz*, pl. of نز *nazz*.

نزول *nuzûl*, alighting; descending, putting up; arrival; befalling (of calamities); cold, rheum, apoplexy; abdication.

نزى *naziyy* = نزا *nazzâ'*; — ة *naziyya-t*, deep dish; cloud.

نزيح *nazîḥ*, far distant.

نزير *nazîr*, little, paltry, insignificant.

نزيز *nazîz*, nimble, agile, brisk; cheerful; fickle; — *.

نزيع *nazî'*, strange; stranger; — ة *nazî'a-t*, pl. *nazâ'i'*, excellent, fit for exportation.

نزيف *nazîf*, weakened by loss of blood; dried up with thirst; hæmorrhage.

نزيل *nazîl*, stranger, who arrives, alights, puts up; guest.

نزيه *nazîh*, ة = نزه *nazih*, ة.

(نس) *nass*, U, I, INF. *nass*, call to the camels, urge them on, make them to halt; be persevering and active in everything; — INF. *nass*, *nusûs*, be dry, stale; — II. INF. *tansîs*, drive; — V. INF. *tanassus*, learn, hear the news.

نس *nas'*, generous wine; thin milk; also *nis'*, *nus'*, woman who is thought to be in the family-way; نسا ن *nis' nisâ'in*, fond of women.

(نسا) *nasa'*, INF. *nas'*, call to the camels, urge them on, make them to halt; — INF. *nasâ'*, protect, guard, grant a long life to; mix, water; — INF. *nas'*, *mansa'a-t*, delay, put off; defer one's death, allow him to live much longer; prolong a debt; put off the month of *Muḥarram* to *Safar*; — INF. *nasâ'*, *nus'a-t*, give one goods on credit; — INF. *nas'a-t*, pass. cease to have the menses and be thought to be in the family-way; — II. INF. *tansi'a-t*, call to the camels; — IV. INF. *insâ'*, defer, delay, put off; prolong a debt; prolong one's life; give goods on credit; — VIII. INF. *intisâ'*, roam about; — X. INF. *istinsâ'*, ask for prolongation of a debt.

نسا *nasan*, *nasa*, du. *nasawân*, *nasayân*, pl. *ansâ'*, nerve of the hip; hip-gout, sciatica; — *nasâ'*, sale on credit; delay, prolongation, long life; — *nisâ'*, women; woman; — *nassâ'*, very forgetful; — ة *nus'a-t*, prolongation of a debt; sale on credit; — *nasa'a-t*, pl. of ناسى *nâsi'*, fat.

نساب *nisâb*, relation, relationship; — *nassâb*, ة *nassâba-t*, well-versed in genealogy, learned in heraldry.

نساج *nassâj*, weaver; inventor, composer; liar; maker of coats of mail; — ة *nisâja-t*, art of weaving; texture.

نسارية *nusâriyya-t*, an eagle.

نساسة *nassâsa-t* (ال *an-*), Mecca.

نساسيف *nasâsîf*, pl. of نساف *nussâf*.

نساطرة *nasâṭira-t*, pl. of نسطوری *nasṭuriyy*.

نساف *nisâf*, pl. of نسيفة *nasîfa-t*; — *nussâf*, pl. *nasâsîf*, a swallow-like bird; — ة *nusâfa-t*, chaff; milk-froth.

نساق *nisâq*, arrangement, ranging.

نساك *nussâk*, pl. of ناسك *nâsik*, pious, &c.; — ة *nasâka-t*, piety, devotion, devoted life.

نسال *nusâl*, ة *nusâla-t*, wool, hair, or feathers fallen off; gossamer.

نسام *nisâm*, pl. of نسيم *nasîm*.

نسانس *nusânis*, a species or the females of نسناس *nasnâs*.

نساوة *nisâwa-t*, forgetting, neglecting (s.).

نسائی *nisâ'iyy*, feminine, womanly; effeminate.

(نسب) *nasab*, U. I, INF. *nasab*, *nisba-t*, quote the pedigree of a person; ask one after his paternal descent; trace back to a certain ancestor, range into a family; ascribe, refer to; reproach with;—INF. *nasab*, *nasîb*, *mansaba-t*, celebrate by a poem, make verses on a beloved person; — III. INF. *munâsaba-t*, belong to the same family, be related to; be similar, resemble; be proportional, analogous, fitting, convenient, compatible; — IV. INF. *insâb*, blow violently, raise dust; — V. INF. *tanassub*, claim relationship with (الى *ila*); — VI. INF. *tanâsub*, be related to one another; be analogous, proportional, fit one another, agree well; — VIII. INF. *intisâb*, claim a certain descent or relationship; be called after; pass as a member of a family; be ascribed;— X. INF. *istinsâb*, trace one's origin to; ask for one's pedigree; find fit, convenient.

نسب *nasab*, pl. *ansâb*, origin, genealogy, pedigree, family; ن و حسب *nasab wa ḥasab*, descent and personal merit; — ة *nisba-t*, *nusba-t*, descent, origin, race, kindred;— *nisba-t*, reference, relation, proportionality; noun of relation in ى; logarithm; — *nasaba-t*, proportion; — تى *nisbatiyy*, relative; —ى *nasabiyy*, related by blood; kindred (adj.); referring to one's origin or descent.

نستعليق *nasta'lîq*, character between *nasḫiyy* and *ta'lîq* (m.).

(نسج) *nasaj*, I, U, INF. *nasj*, weave; invent a tissue of lies, compose artificial speeches; make verses; twist, entwine; furrow the water, the sand, &c.

نسج *nasj*, weaving (s.); texture, web; basket-work; — *nusuj*, pl. prayer-carpets.

(نسح) *nasaḥ*, INF. *nasḥ*, sweep away earth, dust, &c.; — *nasiḥ*, A, INF. *nasaḥ*, desire, crave for.

(نسخ) *nasaḫ*, INF. *nasḫ*, efface, blot out; cause to disappear; abolish, repeal, annul and replace by others (laws, verses of the Koran, &c.); copy; transform (into something ugly); — II. INF. *tansîḫ*, make one copy a book (2 acc.); — VI. INF. *tanâsuḫ*, emigrate from one body into another; — VIII. INF. *intisâḫ*, efface, cause to disappear; be effaced, blotted out, abolished, annulled; copy; be copied; — X. INF. *istinsâḫ*, copy; ask one to copy.

نسخ *nasḫ*, effacing, abolishing, annulling (s.); copy; modern Arabic character; — ة *nusḫa-t*, pl. *nusuḫ*, copy of a manuscript, copy; original, manuscript, proof-sheet, impression; prescription, recipe; written amulet; — ى *nasḫiyy*, modern Arabic character in manuscripts and print.

(نسر) *nasar*, U, INF. *nasr*, loosen and take away, tear off; U, I, tear with the beak; open a tumour; wound; blame, censure; — II. INF. *tansîr*, divide into small parts or strips; — V. INF.

tanassur, pass. of the previous; tear (n.); get untwisted; burst by the pus; — VIII. INF. *intisâr*, break open again (n.); — X. INF. *istinsâr*, resemble an eagle or vulture, be taken for an eagle, grow like a bird of prey.

نسر *nasr*, pl. *ansur*, *nusûr*, eagle, vulture; du. *an-nasrân*, the constellations of the eagle (النسر الطاير *an-nasr aṭ-ṭâ'ir*) and lyre (النسر الواقع *an-nasr al-wâqi'*); pl. *nusûr*, muscle in a horse's hoof; — ة *nasra-t*, particle of wood, splinter; strip of skin or flesh; envy; — ى *nasriyy*, aquiline.

نسرين *nasrîn*, wild rose; Jericho rose.

(نسط) *nasaṭ*, INF. *nasṭ*, wring out washed clothes or guts.

نسطور *nusṭûr*, Nestorius; — ى *nasṭûriyy*, pl. *nasâṭira-t*, Nestorian; — ية *nusṭûriyya-t*, *nasṭûriyya-t*, sect of the Nestorians.

(نسع) *nasa'*, INF. *nas'*, *nusû'*, be loose and rickety (tooth); have such teeth; travel; — INF. *nusû'*, be long; — VIII. INF. *intisâ'*, disperse on the pasture-ground.

نسع *nis'*, ة, pl. *nus'*, *nisa'*, *nusû'*, *ansu'*, *ansâ'*, broad twisted strap to fasten the load on the camel's saddle; north wind; — ية *nas'iyya-t*, north wind.

(نسغ) *nasag*, INF. *nasg*, urge on, prick, goad; hurt by words; slander; brush with feathers; be rickety; tattoo the skin; water; — II. INF. *tansîg*, be rickety; — IV. INF. *insâg*, put forth fresh shoots; — VIII. INF. *intisâg*, beat with the fore-foot towards the chest to chase away the flies.

نسغ *nasg*, flowing sap of fresh shoots of newly-pruned trees.

(نسف) *nasaf*, I, INF. *nasf* (also VIII.), destroy, pull down a building to its foundations; (also VIII.) pull out by the root; break (a.) into small pieces; scatter to dust; winnow; INF. *nasf*, *nusûf*, bite; (m.) clip a horse's hoof; (m.) draw to one's self, refer everything to one's self; also — II. INF. *tansîf*, winnow corn; — V. INF. *tanassuf*, pass. of the previous; — VI. INF. *tanâsuf*, impart secrets to one another; — VIII. INF. *intisâf*, see I.; pass. change, alter (n.); (m.) be clipped; — ة *nasfa-t*, cut with the clipping iron; also *nisfa-t*, *nusfa-t*, *nasafa-t*, a kind of pumice-stone.

نسفان *nasfân*, full to overflowing.

(نسق) *nasaq*, U, INF. *nasq*, arrange well; string pearls; water; — INF. *tansîq*=I.; — IV. INF. *insâq*, speak rhythmically or in rhymes; — V. INF. *tanassuq*, VI. INF. *tanâsuq*, VIII. INF. *intisâq*, be well arranged.

نسق *nasaq*, beautiful order, good arrangement, fine style; well-ordered speech; fine set of teeth, of pearls, of trees, &c.; succession, rank; manner, method; — *nusuq* (ال *an-*), Orion, the twins.

(نسك) *nasak*, U, I, INF. *nask*, *nisk*, *nusk*, *nusuk*, *naska-t*, *mansak*, lead a life devoted to God, practise virtue and piety; become a hermit; U, INF. *nask*, give one's self up to virtue; sacrifice to God; wash clothes; — *nasuk*, INF. *nasâka-t*, lead a life devoted to God; — V. INF. *tanassuk*, id.

نسك *nask*, *nisk*, *nusk*, *nusuk*, ة *naska-t*, pious life; life as a hermit; — *nusk*, *nusuk*, sacrifice.

(نسل) *nasal*, U, INF. *nasl*, beget, bear; moult, lose feathers or hair; pluck out; INF. *nusûl*, fall off, drop; slip from the shoulders; fall in rags; (m.) unsew; — I, INF. *nasal*, *nasl*, *nasalân*, run fast; — II. INF.

tansîl, fall in rags; get unsewn; — IV. INF. *insâl*, beget, bear; fall out; throw off the slough; — VI. INF. *tanâsul*, descend from one another in an unbroken succession; multiply by continuous generation.

نسل *nasl*, pl. *ansâl*, progeny, descent; race, family; offspring, child, grandchild, nephew; — ى *nasliyy*, referring to progeny, descent, race.

(نسم) *nasam*, I, INF. *nasm*, *nasîm*, *nasamân*, (also II.) blow gently; (also II.) spread (odour); U, INF. *nasâma-t*, exude water; I, INF. *nasm*, beat with the foot or hoof;—*nasim*, A, INF. *nasam*, deteriorate, turn offensive to the smell; — II. INF. *tansîm*, see I.; vivify, call into life; begin; — III. INF. *munâsama-t*, perceive by the smell, smell at, get a scent; stand close by one and tell him secretly; — V. INF. *tanassum*, live and breathe; smell; blow and be fragrant; inquire.

نسم *nasam*, pl. *ansâm*, gentle breeze; breath, vital spirits; — ة *nasama-t*, breathing, respiration, breath of life; pl. *nasam*, *nasamât*, breathing being; souls, men; slave.

نسناس *nasnâs*, *nisnâs*, pl. *nasânis*, large ape, orang-outang, chimpanzee; one-armed and one-legged wood-demon; قرب ن *qarab-un nasnâsun*, quick night-march towards water.

(نسنس) *nasnas*, INF. ة, urge on the camels; fly swiftly; be weak; blow cold.

نسو *nasu'*, supposed to be in the family-way;—ة *niswa-t*, *nuswa-t*, also—

نسوان *niswân*, women; — *nasawân*, du. of نسا *nasan*, *nasa*; — ى *niswâniyy*, feminine, womanly; effeminate.

نسوس *nusûs*, dryness, INF. of (نس).

نسول *nusûl*, moulting (s.).

نسون *nisûn*, women.

نسوى *niswiyy*, female, feminine; effeminate.

(نسى) *nasî*, A, INF. *nisy*, *naswa-t*, *nisâwa-t*, *nisâya-t*, *nisyân*, forget, neglect, leave undone; — *nasa*, A, INF. *nasy*, hit one and injure him at the tendon of the foot; —*nasî*, A, INF. *nasan*, have pain in this spot; suffer from sciatica; — II. INF. *tansiya-t*, cause one to forget or neglect; — III. INF. *munâsât*, forget; = II.; — IV. INF. *insâ'* = II.; — VI. INF. *tanâsî*, pretend to have forgotten; neglect wilfully; seek to forget.

نسى *nasy*, *nisy*, anything forgotten or worthy of being forgotten; what must be forgotten; — *nasiyy*, forgetful; who is counted for nothing, who is despised; intercalary day; — *nasî'* = نسيى *nasî'*; — ة *nus'a-t*, sale on credit; — *nusayya-t*, little woman.

نسيا *nasyâ'*, suffering from hip-gout or sciatica (f.).

نسيان *nasyân*, forgetful; negligent; — *nisyân*, forgetting, neglecting (s.), leaving undone; forgetfulness; lethargy, somnolency; — *nasayân*, du. of نسا *nasan*, *nasa*.

نسيب *nasîb*, love-poetry, poetical praise of a mistress; ة, pl. *ansibâ'*, belonging to the circle of a family, related by blood; fitting, corresponding, homogeneous; high-born; — ى *nasîbiyy*, composer of love-poetry; worshipper of women.

نسيج *nasîj*, woven, interwoven; weaver; ن وحده *nasîju waḥdi-hi*, unique in its kind, incomparable; — ة *nasîja-t*, pl. *nasâ'ij*, texture; tissues.

نسيس *nasîs*, last gasp or breath of life; utmost effort; violent hunger; also ة *nasîsa-t*, natural disposition; temper;—ة *nasîsa-t*,

pl. *nasâ'is*, slander, mischief caused by it.

نسيغ *nasîg*, sweat, perspiration.

نسيف *nasîf*, secret; — ة *nasîfa-t*, pl. *nisaf*, *nusuf*, *nisâf*, a kind of pumice-stone.

نسيق *nasîq*, in beautiful order, well-connected (speech).

نسيك *nasîk*, gold, silver; ة *nasîka-t*, lump or ingot of such; — ة *nasîka-t*, pl. *nusuk*, *nasâ'ik*, sacrifice.

نسيل *nasîl*, feathers or hair, &c. fallen off; also ة *nasîla-t*, honey; — ة *nasîla-t*, progeny; wick; rag.

نسيم *nasîm* (f.), pl. *nisâm*, gentle breeze, zephyr, fragrant air; breath, breathing (s.).

نسيى *nasî'*, delayed, put off; delay; sale on credit; sacred month put off; leap-day; — ة *nasî'a-t*, delay; credit.

(نش) *naśś*, I, INF. *naśîś*, dry up, be dried up; (m.) imbibe, absorb; (m.) ooze; boil, bubble; hiss; — U, INF. *naśś*, drive (slowly); mix; — VIII. INF. *intiśâś*, be long.

نش *naśś*, a weight (20 drachms); absorption; oozing (s.); — *naś'*, high cloud; pl. *naśa'*, young camel.

(نشا) *naśa'*, INF. *naś'*, *nuśû'*, *naśâ'*, *naśâ'a-t*, grow, grow up, be brought up; originate, exist, live; INF. *naś'*, *naśâ'*, *nuśû'*, rise, hover high; create; — *naśu'*, INF. *naśâ'a-t*, originate, exist, grow, grow up; — II. INF. *tanśi'a-t*, cause to grow, bring up, rear, educate; — IV. INF. *inśâ'*, create, call forth, produce; bring up; raise the cloud; devise, invent, compose verses, letters, speeches, &c., edit a newspaper; begin; — V. INF. *tanaśśu'*, rise and set to work; — VIII. INF. *intiśâ'*, grow, grow up; — X. INF. *istinśâ'*, perceive by the smell; follow up news.

نشا *naśa'*, pl. of نش *naś'* and ناهى *nâśi'*; — *naśan*, *naśa*, *naśâ'*, pleasant smell; starch; — *naśâ'*, growth, creation; — ة *naśa-t*, pl. *naś-an*, little tree; — *naś'a-t*, creation; creature; origin; growth; also *naśâ'a-t*, INF. of (نشا).

نشاب *naśśâb*, fashioner of arrows; — *nuśśâb*, ة, arrow; — ة *naśśâba-t*, pl. archers.

نشات *naśât*, what springs up, shows itself, grows; creature; du. *naśâtân*, this world and the world to come.

نشادر *nuśâdir*, *niśâdir*, sal ammoniac.

نشارة *niśâra-t*, sawing; — *nuśâra-t*, saw-dust.

نشاستج *naśâstaj*, نشاستة *niśâsta-t*, starch.

نشاش *naśśâś*, ة *naśśâśa-t*, absorbing water and devoid of vegetation.

نشاص *naśâṣ*, persons of the same age; equal flocks; also *niśâṣ*, pl. *nuśuṣ*, high mass of clouds.

نشاط *naśâṭ*, briskness, vivacity, exulting joy, fiery bravery; — *niśâṭ*, ى *naśâṭa*, pl. of نشيط *naśîṭ*.

نشاف *naśśâf*, drying up (adj.); easily dried up; ورق ن *waraq naśśâf*, blotting-paper; — ة *nuśâfa-t*, milk-froth; water in the hold of a ship.

نشاقى *naśâqa*, game caught in a noose.

نشال *naśśâl*, who snatches away quickly, robs; juggler.

نشان *niśân*=نيشان *nîśân*.

نشاوى *naśâwa*, pl. of نشوان *naśwân*; — ة *naśâwiyya-t*, dish prepared with starch.

نشائى *naśâ'iyy*, maker of starch.

(نشب) *naśib*, A, INF. *naśb*, *nuśba-t*, *nuśûb*, adhere firmly, be fastened to, stick in; be imposed as indispensable; spout or gush forth; — II. INF. *tanśîb*, fasten one thing firmly to another, insert, entwine, entangle one in a matter and leave him in the

lurch;— IV. INF. *inśâb*, fix in;— VIII. INF. *intiśâb*, adhere to, be fixed to, be entangled.

نشب *naśab*, ة *naśaba-t*, fortune, wealth; a tree; — ة *nuśba-t*, adhering firmly (s.); who clings firmly to; wolf.

نشتر *naśtar*, lancet (Pers.).

(نشج) *naśaj*, I, INF. *naśîj*, sob or cry in a subdued manner; cry out repeatedly; quack; trill; bubble.

نشج *naśaj*, pl. *anśâj*, aqueduct; canal.

(نشح) *naśaḥ*, INF. *naśḥ*, *nuśûḥ*, drink; water the horses; (m.) deteriorate, putrefy (n.).

نشح *nuśuḥ*, pl. drunkards.

(نشد) *naśad*, U, INF. *naśd*, *niśda-t*, *niśdân*, seek anything lost; indicate where anything lost is to be found; know well;=III.; — III. INF. *niśâd*, *munâśada-t*, conjure by the name of God; demand one to swear in the name of God; — IV. INF. *inśâd*, inform one where anything lost is to be found; cause to find again; recite verses; conjure by the name of God; praise, glorify; — VI. INF. *tanâśud*, recite verses to one another; praise or lampoon one another in verses; ask one to recite verses; — ة *niśda-t*, tone, voice; verses to be recited; see above.

(نشر) *naśar*, U, INF. *naśr*, spread out, unfold or unroll, exhibit; spread or hang up linen in the sun; — U, I, spread about, make publicly known, communicate, propagate; separate, disperse; be scattered; put forth leaves; grass to sprout forth; blow; cut or carve wood; saw; INF. *naśr*, *nuśûr*, raise the dead, revive; be revived, rise from the dead, live; — *naśir*, A, INF. *naśar*, have the mange; — II. INF. *tanśîr*, spread out, unfold; open a book; saw through; avert evil by an amulet; — IV. INF. *inśâr*, raise the dead; — V. INF. *tanaśśur*, be spread out; — VIII. INF. *intiśâr*, id.; be propagated; be scattered, separate, disperse (n.); be published; be erect (penis); — X. INF. *istinśâr*, seek news.

نشر *naśr*, spreading, publishing (s.); sawing (s.); life, resurrection; first germination of a plant; fragrance, odour, scent, smell; — *nuśr*, *nuśur*, pl. of نشور *naśûr*; — *naśar*, anything dispersed or scattered; — ة *naśra-t*, publication, proclamation, edict, order; — *nuśra-t*, amulet, spell against illness or madness; — ى *nuśriyy*, magic, endowed with magic power.

(نشز) *naśaz*, U, INF. *naśz*, *nuśûz*, situated or placed on high; rise high; rise from a place; be agitated, excited; INF. *nuśûz*, be refractory towards a husband; treat a wife brutally; be froward; — IV. INF. *inśâz*, take from the place, lift up; gather and pile up the bones of the dead.

نشز *naśz*, pl. *nuśûz*, also *naśaz*, pl. *niśâz*, *anśâz*, high place; high rank.

(نشص) *naśaṣ*, U, I, INF. *nuśûṣ*, be high and cumulous (clouds); be long, protrude; be excited, agitated; be scared up, chased away; pierce; pull out, take out, bring out; be froward, refractory; — IV. INF. *inśâṣ*, scare up, chase away; — VIII. INF. *intiśâṣ*, uproot a tree.

نشص *nuśuṣ*, pl. of نشاص *niśâṣ*.

(نشط) *naśaṭ*, I, INF. *naśṭ*, go out of, leave a place; drive from place to place; U, make a knot in a rope or tie it by a knot when broken; U, I, bite (snake); — *naśiṭ*, A, INF. *naśâṭ*, be brisk, lively, in high spirits, joyful; be fresh, nimble, vigorous, enter-

prising, set cheerfully to work; — II. INF *tanśîṭ*, make brisk and joyous; invigorate, encourage, render willing; — IV. INF. *inśâṭ* = II.; loose a knot in a rope, loose; bite; snatch from; fasten, tie up; — V. INF. *tanaśśuṭ*, be very lively, brisk, and cheerful; grow nimble, agile, bold, enterprising; be invigorated, encouraged; set to work zealously; speed along briskly; — VIII. INF. *intiśâṭ*, stretch a rope until it breaks; take booty on the way, carry off cattle; — X. INF. *istinśâṭ*, deem brisk and bold; be wrinkled, shrivelled.

نشط *naśṭ*, change of place; — *naśiṭ*, brisk, nimble, lively, agile, enterprising, vigorous and brave.

(نشظ) *naśaẓ*, U, INF. *naśẓ*, take quickly away, snatch from; INF. *nuśûẓ*, spring forth from the ground, sprout.

(نشع) *naśa'*, INF. *naś'*, sob, hiccough, emit a death-rattle; INF. *nuśû'*, recover from a dangerous illness; (also IV.) administer medicine by the mouth or nose; prompt a speech to, put a speech into one's mouth; INF. *naś'*, *manśa'*, take away forcibly, pull out; — IV. INF. *inśâ'*, see I.; — VIII. INF. *intiśâ'*, take away, pull out, strike off; snuff a medicine.

(نشغ) *naśag*, INF. *naśg*, flow; drink out of the hand; administer a medicine; (also IV.) sob, hiccough; — IV. INF. *inśâg*, deviate; see I.

نشغ *nuśśag*, pl. of ناشغ *nâśig*, ag. of the previous.

(نشف) *naśaf*, U, INF. *naśf*, depart, disappear, set; also — *naśif*, A, INF. *naśaf*, absorb or imbibe water, sweat, &c.; be absorbed, imbibed, disappear in the ground; be dried, dry up (n.); — II. INF. *tanśîf*, cause water, &c. to be absorbed by a sponge, cloth, &c.; wipe; dry (a.); be dry; — IV. INF. *inśâf*=II.; make drink the froth of fresh milk; — V. INF. *tanaśśuf*, absorb, imbibe; be wiped; be dry; — VIII. INF. *intiśâf*, drink off the froth of fresh milk.

نشف *naśaf*, ة *naśifa-t*, ground which absorbs water; — ة *naśfa-t*, piece of cloth to absorb water; — *naśfa-t*, *niśfa-t*, *nuśfa-t*, *naśafa-t*, pl. *naśaf*, *niśf*, *niśaf*, *nuśaf*, *niśâf*, a black pumice-stone to rub the dirty feet with; — *niśfa-t*, *nuśfa-t*, small remainder in a kettle; — *nuśfa-t*, froth of fresh milk.

(نشق) *naśiq*, A, INF. *naśaq*, snuff up, inhale; take a pinch; perceive by the smell, smell (a.); be caught in a noose; — II. INF. *tanśîq*, cause to snuff in, to inhale, to smell; — IV. INF. *inśâq*, id.; catch in a noose; — VIII. INF. *intiśâq*, be snuffed up, inhaled; — X. INF. *istinśâq*, snuff up, inhale.

نشق *naśaq*, scent, smell, odour; — *naśiq*, who gets entanged in a matter; — ة *niśqa-t*, *nuśqa-t*, pinch of snuff; — *nuśqa-t*, noose.

(نشل) *naśal*, U, INF. *naśl*, pull quickly out, draw to one's self; lift up; (m.) juggle, trick by sleight of hand; — I, U, (also VIII.) snatch meat out of the kettle with the hand; INF. *nuśûl*, have but little flesh; — II. INF. *tanśîl*, give one a breakfast or luncheon; — VIII. INF. *intiśâl*, see I.

(نشم) *naśim*, A, INF. *naśam*, be covered with black and white spots or dots; — II. INF. *tanśîm*, rot, putrefy (n.); begin; undertake anything bad; — V. INF. *tanaśśum*, begin; try to attain to knowledge.

نشم *naśim*, spotted.

نشناش *naśnâś*, nimble and skilful; void of vegetation.

(نشنش) *naśnaś*, INF. ة, boil, bubble; pull off a dress; skin quickly; swallow quickly; push and put into quick motion; drive, chase away; — II. INF. *tanaśnuś*, improve (in health), begin to recover; — ة *niśniśa-t* = شنشنة *śinśina-t*, nature, natural disposition, &c.;—ى *naśnaśiyy*, nimble and skilful.

(نشو) *naśû*, U, also نشى *naśî*, A, INF. *naśwa-t*, *niśwa-t*, *nuśwa-t*, smell (a.), have a scent of; have knowledge, information of; do a thing repeatedly; also INF. *naśw* and —*naśi*, A, INF. *naśa-n*, be giddy from wine, be slightly intoxicated; — II. INF. *tanśiya-t*, starch the linen; — V. INF. *tanaśśî* (also VIII. and X.), smell (a.), distinguish by the smell; (also VIII.) be slightly intoxicated, be tipsy; — VIII. INF. *intiśâ'*, X. INF. *istinśâ'*, see V.

نشو *naś'*, pl. of ناشى *nâśi'*, young man, girl;—*nuśu'*, *nuśû'*, growth; thriving, prospering (s.); creation; INF. of (نشا); — ة *niśwa-t*, smell, scent, perfume; also *niśwa-t*, *nuśwa-t*, slight intoxication, tipsiness; merry mood produced by some stimulant; giddiness.

نشوان *naśwân*, pl. *naśâwa*, intoxicated; giddy from watching.

نشور *naśûr*, pl. *nuśr*, *nuśur*, chasing clouds and bringing rain; — *nuśûr*, resurrection.

نشوز *nuśûz*, refractoriness of a wife; brutal treatment on the part of a husband; violation of matrimonial duties.

نشوص *nuśûṣ*=نشيص *naśîṣ*; — *.

نشوع *naśû'*, breathing heavily; also *nuśû'*, medicine administered by the mouth or nose.

نشوفات *nuśûfât*, anything dry, especially dry fruit for a dessert.

نشوق *naśûq*, medicine to be smelled at or snuffed; snuff.

نشى *naśi*, V. see (نشو); — *naśi'*= نشيى *naśî'*; — ة *naś'a-t* = نشاة *naś'a-t*; (m.)=نشوة *naśwa-t*; — *naśiyya-t*, smell, scent, fragrance.

نشيان *naśyân*, who inquires, gets the first news; slightly intoxicated, half drunk.

نشيج *naśîj*, subdued crying.

نشيد *naśîd*, ة *naśîda-t*, alternately recited verses; song, hymn; raising of the voice.

نشير *naśîr*, apron, belt.

نشيس *naśîs*, boiling, bubbling (s.).

نشيص *naśîṣ*, erect.

نشيط *naśîṭ*, pl. *niśâṭ*, *naśâṭa*, nimble, brisk, cheerful; enterprising, well disposed, ready for; bold, brave; — ة *naśîṭa-t*, booty made on the way.

نشيف *niśśîf*, easily drying up.

نشيى *naśî'*, cloud on the point of forming itself; — ة *naśî'a-t*, stone bottom of a cistern; anything beginning to grow, germ; origin, birth.

(نص) *naṣṣ*, U, INF. *naṣṣ*, announce, indicate, point out, draw one's attention to, submit to one's judgment, state explicitly; appeal to a higher authority; quote another's words; transmit a tradition or support it by authority; move; put to pace; place the bride on the bridal chair; pile up; inquire minutely, investigate; (m.) dictate a letter; — I, INF. *naṣîṣ*, swelter, stew, bubble; — II. INF. *tanṣîṣ*, make clear, evident; press a debtor, dun; — VIII. INF. *intiṣâṣ* be high, elevated, sublime; be set up, stand erect; sit in state on the bridal chair.

نص *naṣṣ*, pl. *nuṣûṣ*, (holy) text, its tenor; Koran; tradition; ordinance of law, decision of a legal authority, sanction; (m.) dictation, wording of a letter; term (of puberty); — ة *naṣṣa-t*, female sparrow; — *nuṣṣa-t*, forelock of a woman; a way of dressing the hair.

(نصا) *naṣa'*, INF. *naṣ'*, elevate, lift up; call or cry to; seize by the fore-lock.

نصا *niṣâ'*, INF. of (نصو III.).

نصاب *niṣâb*, origin, beginning, principle; principal thing; original stock, amount of a fortune or capital which imposes the duty of paying the زكاة *zakât*; proper measure or proportion, corresponding degree; position, dignity, rank; pl. *nuṣub*, handle of a knife; horn; fish-bladder; — *; — *naṣṣâb*, cunning, sly, wily; sharper, thief.

نصاح *niṣâḥ*, pl. *nuṣḥ*, *niṣâḥa-t*, thread passed through the needle; — *naṣṣâḥ*, tailor; — *nuṣṣâḥ*, pl. of ناصح *nâṣiḥ*, who gives good advice; — ة *naṣâḥa-t*, sincere advice, admonition; (m.) corpulence, plumpness; — *niṣâḥa-t*, skin, hide, leather; a rope with nooses to catch monkeys; — ية *naṣâḥiyat*=*naṣâḥa-t*, INF. of (نصح).

نصار *naṣṣâr*, strong helper; a proper name; — *nuṣṣâr*, pl. of ناصر *nâṣir*, helper, &c.; — ى *naṣâra*, Christians, pl. of نصران *naṣrân*.

نصاعة *naṣâ'a-t*, purity of colour; snowy whiteness.

نصاف *niṣâf*, *naṣâf*, ة *niṣâfa-t*, *naṣâfa-t*, service in the house; — ة *niṣâfa-t*, halving (s.).

نصال *naṣṣâl*, maker of heads of arrows or spears.

(نصب) *naṣab*, U, INF. *naṣb*, erect; lay down; set up, stick into the ground, plant; hoist a flag; pitch a tent; appoint officials; surround; tire out; be hostile to; declare war; lay traps, intrigue against; cheat out of, steal from cunningly; cede, give over to; mark a letter with ـَ, put a noun in the accusative or a verb in the subjunctive mood; continue (a journey) all day long or hasten one's travel; — I, INF. *naṣb*, pain, depress; — *naṣib*, A, INF. *naṣab*, be tired and weary; be active and zealous; — II. INF. *tanṣîb*, plant, place, erect; make to stand upright; have a field planted over; — III. INF. *munâṣaba-t*, be hostile to (acc.); oppose; declare war to (acc.); farm out a field for half of the produce; — IV. INF. *inṣâb*, pain, depress, weary, tire out; put a handle to the knife; — V. INF. *tanaṣṣub*, plant one's self; place one's self upright; rise and stand erect; be raised; be appointed; — VIII. INF. *intiṣâb*, be raised, erected, set up; be marked with ـَ, be put in the accusative or subjunctive.

نصب *naṣb*, setting up, planting, raising, erecting (s.); appointment to an office; pl. *anṣâb*, what is set up, &c.; plants; plantation; statue; mile-stone, boundary-sign; boundary, limit, end; hunting-net, noose; vowel ـَ, accusative, subjunctive; correct rhythm; soft music; — *niṣb*, portion, share, lot, luck; — *nuṣb*, *nuṣub* (also *naṣb*), pl. *anṣâb*, statue, idol; flag, standard; illness, sorrow, calamity; — *naṣab*, tiredness, weariness, depression, calamity; — *nuṣub*, mile-stone, road-sign; idol; pl. of نصاب *niṣâb*; — ة *naṣba-t*, plant; hostile opposition; — *nuṣba-t*, column; mast.

نصبا *naṣbâ'*, f. of انصب *anṣab*, having straight horns; having a high straight chest.

(نصت) *naṣat*, I, INF. *naṣt*, be silent and listen; lend one's ear; listen attentively; — II. INF. *taṣnît*, silence, make one hold his tongue; — IV. INF. *inṣât*, be silent; =II.; — V. INF. *tanaṣṣut*, VIII. INF. *intiṣât*=I.; — X. INF. *istinṣât*, bid to be silent; — ة *nuṣta-t*, silence.

نصح *naṣaḥ*, INF. *naṣḥ*, *nuṣḥ*, *naṣâḥa-t*, *naṣîḥa-t*, *naṣâḥiya-t*, advise

and admonish sincerely; mend, darn; INF. *naṣaḥ, nuṣûḥ*, be pure, unmixed; be of a pure and sincere mind; be faithful; (m.) grow corpulent, fat; INF. *nuṣûḥ*, be correct, in conformity with truth; INF. *nuṣḥ, nuṣûḥ*, drink their fill (camels); water well; — II. INF. *tanṣîḥ* (m.) fatten, batten; — III. INF. *munâṣaḥa-t*, advise and admonish as a sincere friend; — IV. INF. *inṣâḥ*, let the camels drink their fill; show one's self as a faithful friend and sincere adviser; — VIII. INF. *intiṣâḥ*, accept advice or admonition from a sincere friend; — X. INF. *istinṣâḥ*, ask for advice, consult; (m.) find fat.

نصح *nuṣḥ*, sincere advice; pl. of نصاح *niṣâḥ*; — *nuṣṣaḥ*, pl. of ناصح *nâṣiḥ*, who advises well, &c.

نصحا *nuṣaḥâ'*, pl. of نصيح *naṣîḥ*.

(نصر) *naṣar*, U, INF. *naṣr, nuṣûr*, help, assist; grant victory; rescue, save; water abundantly; conduct water into a river (tributary); — II. INF. *tanṣîr*, make one a Christian; — V. INF. *tanaṣṣur*, be anxious to help one, to assist him; become a Christian; — VI. INF. *tanâṣur*, assist one another; conclude a defensive alliance; — VIII. INF. *intiṣâr*, gain victory and power over, triumph over (على *'ala*); — X. INF. *istinṣâr*, ask for help; conquer, vanquish.

نصر *naṣr*, ة *nuṣra-t*, help, assistance; victory, triumph; *naṣr*, helper; gift, present; — *nuṣar*, pl. helpers; — ة *nuṣra-t*, support, victory.

نصرا *nuṣarâ'*, pl. of نصير *naṣîr*.

نصران *naṣrân*, f. ة, pl. *naṣâra*, Christian; — ى *naṣrâniyy*, ة, Christian (adj.); Christ; — ية *naṣrâniyya-t*, Christianity.

نصرن *naṣran*, INF. ة, make one a Christian; — II. INF. *tanaṣrun*, become a Christian.

نصرى *naṣriyy*, victorious.

(نصع) *naṣa'*, A, INF. *nuṣû'*, *naṣâ'a-t*, be pure, unmixed, unalloyed; — INF. *nuṣû'*; be snowy white; be visible, evident, clear; (also IV.) acknowledge a debt and pay it; give birth; quench one's thirst; — IV. INF. *inṣâ'*, see I.; yield to the stallion (she-camel).

نصع *naṣ', niṣ', nuṣ'*, white cloth= نطع *naṭ'*.

(نصف) *naṣaf*, U, INF. *naṣf*, come to the middle of a thing; take the half of; divide into two equal parts, halve; be in the middle of; INF. *naṣf, naṣâfa-t, niṣâfa-t*, take half of one's property; divide equitably, be just and equitable; — I, U, INF. *naṣf, naṣâf, niṣâf, naṣâfa-t, niṣâfa-t, naṣafân, niṣafân*, serve one, be one's servant (acc.); — II. INF. *tanṣîf*, come to the middle; halve; divide justly; be just and equitable; — III. INF. *munâṣafa-t*, divide with another by halves; act justly and equitably towards; — IV. INF. *inṣâf*, take half of; divide or act justly; be just and equitable; stand in the middle; serve one; — V. INF. *tanaṣṣuf*, be divided into two equal parts, or equitably; be in the middle; ask services from (acc.); submit to; be veiled; — VI. INF. *tanâṣuf*, act justly towards one another; — VIII. INF. *intiṣâf*, be or stand in the middle; keep the golden mean; act justly and equitably; claim one's right from another, right one's self; cover one's self with a veil or head-band.

نصف *niṣf*, pl. *anṣâf*, middle, half; half a denar; justice, equity; of medium height; middle-aged; *niṣf-a*, in the midst; — *naṣaf*, ة *naṣafa-t*, justice, equity; pl. *-ûn, anṣâf*, f. ة,

pl. *anṣâf*, *nuṣuf*, *nuṣf*, middle-aged; *naṣaf*, pl. of *nâṣif*, servant.

نصفان *naṣfân*, f. *naṣfa*, half full; — *naṣafân*, INF. of (نصف).

(نصل) *naṣal*, A, U, INF. *nuṣûl*, get lost, fade, waste away; clear away; leave; recover from a fever; lose its effect; escape; fall off (nail, hoof, &c.); — U, INF. come out of the head (arrow); be well fixed to the head; fix well an arrow; — II. INF. *tanṣîl*, take the head from an arrow; put a head to an arrow or spear; — III. INF. *munâṣala-t*, fight with pointed weapons; — IV. INF. *inṣâl*=II.; take out, pull out; — V. INF. *tanaṣṣul*, be acquitted, justify one's self; recover; free one; also — X. INF. *istinṣâl*, take out, pull out.

نصل *naṣl*, pl. *niṣâl*, *nuṣûl*, *anṣul*, head of an arrow or spear, point of a sword, lance, or knife; also ة *naṣla-t*, crown of the head, head; — ة *naṣla-t*, and—

نصلان *naṣlân*, head of an arrow or spear; blade of a knife or sword.

نصمة *naṣama-t*, idol.

(نصنص) *naṣnaṣ*, INF. ة, shake; move the knees in order to get up.

(نصو) *naṣâ*, U, INF. *naṣw* (also III. and IV.), seize by the fore-lock and draw towards one's self; (also III.) abut; uncover; — III. INF. *niṣâ'*, *munâṣât*, see I.; — IV. INF. *inṣâ'*, see I.; produce an abundance of thistles; — V. INF. *tanaṣṣî*, abut, adjoin, be connected; — VIII. INF. *intiṣâ'*, hang down long (hair); be far-stretching and high; select, choose.

نصوح *naṣûḥ*, faithful, true, sincere; well sown; — *naṣṣûḥ*, wasp (m.).

نصور *naṣûr*, helper; — *nuṣûr*, help.

نصوع *nuṣû'*, purity of colour; clearness.

نصى *naṣiyy*, ة, a white thistle; — ة *naṣiyya-t*, pl. *naṣiyy*, *anṣâ'*, *anâṣî*, the most exquisite, the best part of.

نصيب *naṣîb*, pl. *anṣibâ'*, *anṣiba-t*, share, lot, portion; luck, fortune, destiny; winning lot; outspread net; — ة *naṣîba-t*, pl. *naṣâ'ib*, what is raised as a signal; stones round a well.

نصيبون *naṣîbûn*, نصيبين *naṣîbîn*, Nisibis.

نصيح *naṣîḥ*, pl. *nuṣaḥâ'*, sincere adviser, counsellor; faithful, true; — ة *naṣîḥa-t*, pl. *naṣâ'iḥ*, sincere advice, admonition.

نصير *naṣîr*, pl. *anṣâr*, *nuṣarâ'*, helper, defender, assistant, ally; — ى *nuṣairiyy*, believer in the divinity of Ali.

نصيص *naṣîṣ*, quick, swift; INF. of (نص).

نصيع *naṣî'*, pure; unmixed; clear.

نصيف *naṣîf*, halved, half; veil; head-band, turban; a measure.

نصيل *naṣîl*, crown of the head; beak, muzzle, snout; arrow; axe, hatchet.

(نض) *naḍḍ*, I, INF. *naḍḍ*, *naḍîḍ*, ooze out, exude, flow out slowly; be doled out; burst; make known, publish; INF. *naḍḍ*, flap the wings; become possible; — IV. INF. *inḍâḍ*, perform, carry out, execute, accomplish; — V. INF. *tanaḍḍud*, id.; incite, spur on; =X; — X. INF. *istinḍâḍ*, receive a debt by small instalments, draw payment.

نض *naḍḍ*, money; a little (of water); — ة *naḍḍa-t*, gold or silver coin.

نضاح *naḍḍâḥ*, watering abundantly, pouring everywhere.

نضاخ *naḍḍâḫ*, ة, abundant; — ة *naḍḍâḫa-t*, an engine for irrigating.

نضار *nuḍâr*, *naḍâr*, pure fossil gold, bright gold; the purest and best, purity; — *nuḍâr*, tamarisk; also *niḍâr*, a kind of wood; — *; — ة *naḍâra-t*, brightness, freshness, verdure, beauty; tamarisk.

نضاض *niḍâḍ*, what falls in drops; small gift, dole; pl. of نضيض

naḍîḍ; — *nuḍâḍ*, choice of the best; — *naḍḍâḍ*, ة *naḍḍâḍa-t*, a snake; — ة *nuḍâḍa-t*, rest, remainder; ن الولد *nuḍâḍat al-walad*, nestling, youngest child.

نضافة *naḍâfa-t*, impurity; (m.) purity, cleanliness.

نضال *niḍâl*, combat, skirmish, conflict, INF. of (نضل III.);—*nuḍḍâl*, pl. of ناضل *nâḍil*, superior archer, champion.

(نضب) *naḍab*, U, INF. *nuḍûb* (also II.), dry up, get absorbed; die; be scanty, fail (crops); — U, INF. *naḍb*, flow, run;—II. INF. *tanḍîb*, see I.; — IV. INF. *inḍâb*, draw and twang the bow-string.

(نضج) *naḍij*, A, INF. *naḍj*, *nuḍj*, be fully ripe, well done (meat); suppurate; — *naḍaj*, sweat, perspire (m.); — II. INF. *tanḍîj*, ripen, maturate (a.); cork well; digest well; — IV. INF. *inḍâj*= II.; promote digestion.

(نضح) *naḍaḥ*, I, INF. *naḍḥ*, sprinkle with water, water; overwhelm with arrows; quench the thirst; only half quench one's thirst; avert; (also IV.) begin to fill; open its buds (tree); shed tears; — A, INF. *naḍḥ*, *tanḍâḥ*, ooze, leak; sweat, perspire;— IV. INF. *inḍâḥ*, see I.; — V. INF. *tanaḍḍuḥ*, shed tears; get out of a difficulty, justify one's self; — VIII. INF. *intiḍâḥ*, shed tears; be watered, sprinkled over; (m.) be baptized; — X. INF. *istinḍâḥ*, sprinkle water over the pudenda.

نضح *naḍaḥ*, pl. *anḍâḥ*, reservoir, cistern; — *nuḍuḥ*, pl. of نضيح *naḍîḥ*.

(نضخ) *naḍaḫ*, INF. *naḍḫ*, sprinkle with water, &c.; gush forth, boil or bubble up; — III. INF. *niḍâḫ*, *munâḍaḫa-t*, sprinkle over or pour water over one another; — VIII. INF. *intiḍâḫ*, be sprinkled over.

نضخ *naḍḫ*, trace of a perfume; — ة *naḍḫa-t*, gush of water.

(نضد) *naḍad*, I, INF. *naḍd*, pile up, lay one on the top of another (carpets, &c.), string;—II. INF. *tanḍîd*, id.; bed up; set jewels.

نضد *naḍad*, pl. *anḍâd*, piled up carpets, &c.; stand or place in a house where they are piled up; covered seat, bed, &c.; distinguished, of high rank or birth, illustrious; nobility, high rank or birth; fat (adj.).

(نضر) *naḍar*, U, INF. *naḍr* (also II. and IV.), endow with splendour and beauty; brighten (a.); INF. *naḍra-t*, *nuḍûr*, also — *naḍir*, A, INF. *naḍar*, and — *naḍur*, INF. *naḍâra-t*, shine in beauty and freshness, be resplendent, bright, fresh; — II. INF. *tanḍîr*, IV. INF. *inḍâr*, see I.; — X. INF. *istinḍâr*, find bright, resplendent, beautiful.

نضر *naḍr*, pl. *niḍâr*, *anḍur*, gold, silver; verdant, blooming; — *niḍr*, woman; — *naḍar*, ة *naḍra-t*, splendour, brightness, freshness, beauty, elegance; — *naḍir*, ة, fresh, brilliant, beautiful; — ة *naḍra-t*, riches, wealth; good fortune, happiness, pleasure.

(نضف) *naḍaf*, U, I, INF. *naḍf* (also VIII.), suck out the udder; serve one; break wind; — *naḍif*, A, INF. *naḍaf*, suck out the udder; be unclean, impure; (m.) be clean, cleanly; — IV. INF. *inḍâf*, make to break wind.

نضف *naḍif*, unclean, stained.

(نضل) *naḍal*, U, INF. *naḍl*, shoot the arrow, be superior in shooting; —*naḍil*, be emaciated and weak; — III. INF. *niḍâl*, *munâḍala-t*, *tanḍâl*, vie in shooting with, shoot against; defend, protect, excuse; — IV. INF. *inḍâl*, emaciate and weaken, jade; — VI. INF. *tanâḍul*, vie (in shooting), contest; — VIII. INF. *intiḍâl*, id.; select, choose, pick out.

نضم *naḍm*, ة, rich wheat.

نضناض *naḍnâḍ*, ة *naḍnâḍa-t*, a snake

with ever-darting tongue whose bite kills instantaneously.

(نضنض) *naḍnaḍ*, INF. ة, move the tongue, dart.

(نضو) *naḍâ*, U, INF. *naḍw*, pull out, unsheath, strip, put off; undress (n.); dry up; travel through; INF. *naḍw*, *nuḍiyy*, break forth and get the lead (horse in a race); INF. *naḍw*, *nuḍuww*, get lost, fade, disappear; — IV. INF. *inḍâ'*, emaciate (a.), jade; put off; — VIII. INF. *intiḍâ'*, draw the sword.

نضو *niḍw*, ة, pl. *anḍâ'*, emaciated and weak, jaded; lean beast; worn out garment; iron part of a bridle; — ة *naḍwa-t*, horse-shoe (m.).

نضوح *naḍûḥ*, a perfume.

نضور *naḍûr*, bright, brilliant, fresh, verdant, blooming; — *nuḍûr*, brightness, brilliancy, freshness, beauty.

(نضى) *naḍa*, I, INF. *naḍy*, draw the sword; also:—VIII. INF. *intiḍâ'*, wear out a garment.

نضى *naḍiyy*, jaded; pl. *anḍiya-t*, arrow without head and feathering; head of an arrow or spear; neck from the shoulders to the ears; — *nuḍiyy*, INF. of (نضو).

نضيج *naḍîj*, fully ripe; well done (meat); well digested; mature (of judgment).

نضيح *naḍîḥ*, pl. *nuḍuḥ*, reservoir, cistern; — ة *naḍîḥa-t*, a perfume.

نضيد *naḍîd*, piled up; — ة *naḍîda-t*, cushion, bolster.

نضير *naḍîr*, bright, fresh, verdant, blooming; gold, silver.

نضيض *naḍîḍ*, pl. *niḍâḍ*, but little, a trifle; thin, lean; — ة *naḍîḍa-t*, pl. *aniḍḍa-t*, *naḍâ'iḍ*, a little rain; thirst; troop.

نضيف *naḍîf*, unclean, impure, stained; (m.) clean, cleanly.

(نط) *naṭṭ*, U, INF. *naṭṭ*, stretch, extend; fasten, tie up; (m.) leap; (m.) be agitated, excited, tremble; — I, travel, travel over; dote, delirate;— INF. *naṭîṭ*, flee; — II. INF. *tanṭîṭ*, make to leap, let jump.

نط *naṭṭ*, leap, jump; — ة *naṭṭa-t*, leap; excitement, agitation.

نطا *naṭṭâ'*, f. of انط *anaṭṭ*, long, far distant; — ة *naṭṭât*, pl. *anṭâ'*, pedicle of a date.

نطاح *naṭṭâḥ*, given to butting.

نطار *nuṭṭâr*, scare-crow; pl. of ناطر *nâṭir*, keeper, watch-man; — ة *naṭâra-t*, (m.) expectation; — *niṭâra-t*, office of a guard-keeper in a vineyard.

نطاسى *niṭâsiyy*, *naṭâsiyy*, very intelligent and clever; pl. *nuṭus*, physician.

نطاط *naṭṭâṭ*, who jumps well, jumper; doting, delirating.

نطاف *niṭâf*, pl. of نطفة *nuṭfa-t*; — ة *nuṭâfa-t*, rest of water in a bottle; — *.

نطاق *niṭâq*, pl. *nuṭuq*, girdle, belt; apron, skirt; — *naṭṭâq*, who talks much.

نطاوة *naṭâwa-t*, moisture (m.); — INF. of (نطو).

(نطب) *naṭab*, U, INF. *naṭb*, give a fillip on the ear; — III. INF. *munâṭabat*, incite against.

نطثر *naṭṡar*, inf. ة = طنثر *tanṡar*, bring on indigestion by eating fat.

نطح *naṭaḥ*, A, INF. *naṭḥ*, butt with the horns; — II. INF. *tanṭîḥ*, id.; VI. *tanâṭuḥ*, fight one another with the horns; — VIII. INF. *intiṭâḥ*, id.

نطح *naṭḥ*, butting (s.); star in the horn of the Ram; — ة *naṭḥat*, butt.

نطح شر *niṭḥ-u śarr-in*, mischief-maker.

(نطر) *naṭar*, U, INF. *naṭr*, *niṭâra-t*, keep guard in a vine-yard or palm-garden; (m.) wait for, expect; — II. INF. *tanṭîr*, make one a guard-keeper, have guarded by.

نطر *naṭr*, keeping guard, guarding

(s.); — ة *naṭra-t*, expectation;— *naṭara-t*, and—

نطرا *nuṭarâ'*, pl. of ناطر *nâṭir*, who keeps guard.

نطرون *natrûn*, natron; borax.

(نطس) *naṭis*, A, inf. *naṭas*, excel, be intelligent and skilful; be practised in an art; — V. INF. *tanaṭṭus*, id.

نطس *naṭs*, *naṭis*, *naṭus*, intelligent, clever, skilful; scrupulously accurate, painfully conscientious; — *nuṭus*, pl. persons of such description, physicians; — ة *nuṭasa-t*, painfully accurate and clean.

نطش *naṭś*, strong bodily constitution.

نطط *nuṭuṭ*, pl. of انط *anaṭṭ*, long, far distant.

(نطع) pass. *nuṭi'*, change, alter (n.); — V. INF. *tanaṭṭu'*, enter deep into a matter in speaking; show intelligence and skill.

نطع *naṭ'*, *niṭ'*, *naṭa'*, *niṭa'*, pl. *nuṭû'*, *anṭâ'*, piece of leather used as a table-cloth or game-board, or on which a criminal is placed for execution; leathern bag; — *niṭ'*, *niṭa'*, front part of the palate; hence ية *niṭ'iyya-t*, the letters ث, د, ط.

(نطف) *naṭaf*, U, I, INF. *naṭf*, *naṭâf*, *naṭafân*, *niṭâfa-t*, *tanṭâf*, drop, drip, trickle; pour down upon; pour out; accuse one of infamous things; (m.) snuff a candle; — *naṭif*, A, INF. *naṭaf*, *naṭâfa-t*, *nuṭûfa-t*, be stained with vices or crimes, be guilty or suspected of such; be spoiled; suffer from indigestion; — II. INF. *tanṭîf*, accuse, declare suspicious; — V. INF. *tanaṭṭuf*, be stained, disgraced; be suspected of a crime; adorn one's self with ear-rings.

نطف *naṭaf*, vice, crime, corruption; irreptitious evil;— *naṭif*, ة, pl. -*ûn*, corrupt, suspicious, unclean; impure; — ة *nuṭfa-t*, pl. *nuṭuf*, *niṭâf*, drop; drop of sperm; a little, trifle; water (du. *an-nuṭfatân*, Mediterranean and Red Sea; Persian Gulf and Pacific Ocean); pl. *nuṭaf*, human sperm; — *naṭafa-t*, *nuṭafa-t*, pl. *nuṭaf*, ear-ring; small pearl; — ى *nuṭfiyy*, referring to human sperm, spermatic, seminal.

(نطق) *naṭaq*, I, INF. *nuṭq*, *nuṭûq*, *manṭiq*, utter articulate and rational speech, speak logically, speak; be endowed with reason; — II. INF. *tanṭîq*, gird; — III. INF. *munâṭaqa-t*, endow with reason and speech; — IV. INF. *inṭâq*, id.; make one to speak articulately and rationally; — V. INF. *tanaṭṭuq*, gird one's self; — VI. INF. *tanâṭuq*, id.; gird one's self or tuck one's garments up for work; — X. INF. *istinṭâq* = IV.; cause to give utterance.

نطق *nuṭq*, rational speech; human language; word, speech; edict, decree; — *nuṭuq*, pl. of نطاق *niṭâq*.

(نطل) *naṭal*, U, INF. *naṭl*, press (wine, &c.); (also II.) wash (the head or limbs of a sick person) with an aromatic decoction; — II. INF. *tanṭîl*, see I.; — VIII. INF. *intiṭâl*, let flow out but a little.

نطل *naṭl*, *niṭl*, dregs, lees, sediment; — ة *nuṭla-t*, a draught.

نطلا *naṭlâ'*, evil, calamity.

نطناط *naṭnâṭ*, نطنط *naṭnaṭ*, *niṭniṭ*, pl. *naṭâniṭ*, long, very tall.

(نطنط) *naṭnaṭ*, INF. ة, stretch, extend; be long (journey); undertake a long journey; be far distant.

(نطو) *naṭâ*, U, INF. *naṭw*, stretch, extend; be silent about (عن *'an*); be distant; (m.) INF. *naṭâwa-t*, be moist, be damp.

نطوف *naṭûf*, rainy.

نطوق *naṭûq*, who speaks fluently and distinctly; — *nuṭûq*, human speech; girdle, apron.

نطول *naṭûl*, lotion with an aromatic decoction.

نطيح *naṭîḥ*, ة, gored to death.

نطيس *naṭîs*, very intelligent and clever; — *niṭṭîs*, id.; physician.

نطيش *naṭîś*, strongly made, vigorous; motion, movement.

نطيط *naṭîṭ*, distant, far; flight.

نظار *niẕâr*, sharp-sightedness, sagacity, penetration; physiognomy; *naẕâr-i*, wait! stop! — *naẕẕâr*, who looks sharply at, sees through, examines; generous, mettled; — *nuẕẕâr*, ة *naẕẕâra-t*, pl. spectators; — ة *naẕâra-t*, supervision, inspection, superintendence, direction, management; ministry; look, aspect; spectacle; view, scenery; — *naẕẕâra-t*, spectacles, telescope.

نظاف *niẕâf*, pl. of نظيف *naẕîf*; — ة *naẕâfa-t*, cleanness, purity, cleanliness.

نظام *niẕâm*, good order, arrangement, organisation; pl. *nuẕum*, *anẕima-t*, *anâẕîm*, foundation of order, constitution; order or rule of life, conduct; custom, habit, manner; right road; method; regular troop, soldier of the line; pl. *nuẕum*, string of pearls; line; poetry; ن الملك *niẕâm al-mulk*, grand vizier; — *naẕẕâm*, who strings pearls; — ة *niẕâma-t*, administration of justice, government, order; — ى *niẕâmiyy*, soldier of the line.

نظائر *naẕâ'ir*, pl. of نظيرة *naẕîra-t* and نظورة *naẕûra-t*.

(نظح), IV. *anẕaḥ*, INF. *inẕâḥ*, form into grains (ear of corn).

(نظر) *naẕar*, U, I, INF. *naẕar*, *naẕarân*, *tanẕâr*, *manẕar*, *manẕara-t*, fix the look upon, look at, contemplate; consider, ponder over; judge, decide; observe, watch, spy out; expect, wait for; predict, prophesy, foretell; regard, pay regard to; give a hearing to (acc.); be fondly inclined towards, solicitous for, assist, help; have supervision or superintendence over, be an inspector, director, manager, &c.; grant indulgence or respite; sell on credit; pass. have a fault or vice, be pale and haggard, be frail; — *naẕir*, A, INF. *naẕar*, look at, regard; stand opposite; — II. INF. *tanẕîr*, look at attentively, contemplate, consider; sell on credit, grant a delay of payment; keep waiting; — III. INF. *munâẕara-t*, be like, resemble; make alike, make similar, compare; dispute; have the supervision, be inspector, &c. (see I.); — IV. INF. *inẕâr*, delay, put off, adjourn; grant indulgence or a respite; make alike, equalize, compare; — V. INF. *tanaẕẕur*, contemplate; expect; — VI. INF. *tanâẕur*, look at one another; be opposite, in front of one another; dispute; — VIII. INF. *intiẕâr*, wait, wait for, expect; watch, spy out; — X. INF. *istinẕâr*, id.; ask for a respite.

نظر *niẕr*, similar, alike; — *naẕar*, pl. *anẕâr*, look; outlook, view; synopsis; aspect, appearance, face; consideration, contemplation (ديوان الن *dîwân an-naẕar*, a consultative body, اهل ن *ahl naẕar*, penetrating, keen-sighted); metaphysical speculation; favourable look, kind regard, sympathy, benevolence, kindness; the evil eye; supervision, superintendence, surveillance; auspices; review; embarrassment; doubt; section, paragraph; insight; — ا *nuẕarâ'*, pl. of نظير *naẕîr*; — ة *naẕra-t*, pl. *naẕarât*, look; aspect, appearance, phantom, ghost; evil eye; frailness, weakness, ugliness; fault, error, vice; respect, fear, awe; fainting-fit, swoon; also — *naẕira-t*, respite, indulgence,

credit; — ى nazariyy, ة, visible, evident; contemplative, speculative, metaphysical; dogmatical; — ية nazariyya-t, discernment, sound judgment.

(نظف) nazuf, INF. nazâfa-t, be clean, pure, cleanly; — II. INF. tanzîf, clean, cleanse; — V. INF. tanazzuf, be cleaned, clean one's self; — X. INF. istinzâf, make a clean dish of it, take all; take the whole of taxes at once or demand their payment; find clean, pure; select the purest, the best.

(نظم) nazam, I, INF. nazm, join one thing to another; — INF. nazm, nizâm, bring into good order, range, string pearls; make verses, compose poetry; compose, word; adorn, embellish; — II. INF. tanzîm, put into order, arrange; string pearls; compose verses; organise, constitute; (m.) make one a soldier of the line, levy regular troops; — V. INF. tanazzum, be put into order, ranged; be embellished; become a soldier; — VIII. INF. intizâm, be put into order, ranged; be well organised.

نظم nazm, in good order, ranged; pl. manâzim, order, good organisation, orderly conduct; string of pearls, chaplet; metrical speech, poetry, verses; —nuzum, pl. of نظام nizâm.

نظور nazûr, ة nazûra-t, pl. nazâ'ir, looked at before others, honoured above all; — ة nazûra-t, first line of battle, vanguard.

نظير nazîr, pl. nuzarâ', similar, alike; corresponding; opposite, in front of, parallel; in the same manner, as; an-nazîr, ن السمت nazîr as-samt, zenith; — ة nazîra-t, pl. nazâ'ir=نظور nazûr and نظورة nazûra-t; similitude, simile, comparison; imitation; model, example, parallel, counterpart; anecdote.

نظيف nazîf, ة, pl. nizâf, clean, pure, cleanly; ن السراويل nazîf as-sarâwîl, chaste.

نظيم nazîm, well ordered, ranged; (m.) handsome, pretty.

نع na'', weak, without strength.

نعا nu'â', mewing; — na'â'-i, announce his death! — ة nu'ât, pl. of ناعى nâ'î, who announces one's death, death-message.

نعاب nu'âb, croaking; — na''âb, raven, young raven; — ة na'âba-t, swift, fleet (she-camel).

نعاتة na'âta-t, fleetness of a generous horse.

نعار nu'âr, rough nasal sound; — na''âr, a kind of green finch; flowing vein; ة, refractory, clamorous, given to screaming; — ة nu'âra-t, earthen vessel with a narrow neck and two handles.

نعاس nu'âs, sleepiness, drowsiness, lethargy; — na''âs, very sleepy, drowsy; lethargic.

نعاق nu'âq, croaking (s.).

نعال na''âl, farrier; — ى ni'âliyy, shoe-maker.

نعام na'âm (coll. and n.u.), ostrich; — ة na'âma-t, pl. na'â'im, ostrich; name of a celebrated horse; cross-beam over a well from which the bucket is suspended; crane for lifting loads; road-sign in the desert; desert; brain; membrane of the brain; soul, self; — ابن الن ibn an-na'âma-t, road; horse; — ى nu'âma, south wind, south-east wind; نعاماك nu'âmâka, according to your power.

نعائم na'â'im, pl. of نعامة na'âma-t.

(نعب) na'ab, A, I, INF. na'b, nu'âb, na'îb, na'abân, tan'âb, croak and augur evil; crow; call out the hour for prayer; — A, INF. na'b, run fast and move the head (camel).

نعب na'b, violent; — nu'ub, pl. of نعوب na'ûb.

(نعت) *na'at*, A, INF. *na't* (also IV. and VIII.), describe, qualify; give an attribute to a substantive and make it agree with the same; — *na'it*, A, INF. *na'at*, cope, vie with; — *na'ut*, INF. *na'âta-t*, be naturally generous and fleet; — IV. INF. *in'ât*, VIII. INF. *inti'ât*, see I.

نعت *na't*, description, qualification; praise, commendation, fame; pl. *nu'ût*, adjective, attribute; also ة *na'ta-t*, fleet winning race-horse;—ة *nu'ta-t*, highest degree (of beauty, &c.).

(نعث) *na'as̱*, A, INF. *na's̱*, take with the hand; — IV. INF. *in'âs̱*, make ready for a journey; dissipate, squander.

نعثل *na's̱al*, male hyena; decrepit man; — INF. ة, gather, grasp; walk with the feet turned inwards (like one weak from old age or proud).

(نعج) *na'aj*, A, U, INF. *na'j*, pace vigorously along;—U, INF. *na'aj*, *nu'ûj*, be pure, be entirely white and bright;—*na'ij*, A, INF. *na'aj*, be fat; have indigestion from eating mutton; — ة *na'ja-t*, pl. *na'ajât*, *ni'âj*, sheep; white doe.

(نعر) *na'ar*, A, I, INF. *nu'âr*, *na'îr*, cry out, scream; utter a rough nasal sound; bellow; — A, INF. *na'r*, *na'îr*, making the blood to spurt out with a noise; oppose, refuse; assemble in excitement (n.); rise and set zealously to work; sting; (m.) say stinging words to (acc.); — *na'ir*, A, INF. *na'ar*, be molested by flies (see below); — ة *na'ra-t*, nasal sound or tone; clamour, noise, roaring; woeful cry, lamentation; battle-cry, vociferation of combatants; wind and heat; — *nu'ra-t*, *nu'a-ra-t*, inside of the nose; — *nu'a-ra-t*, pl. *nu'ar*, a large blue fly; — نعرى *na'ra*, clamorous woman.

(نعس) *na'as*, A, INF. *na's*, be weak (in body and mind); be dull; INF. *na's*, *nu'âs*, be sleepy, drowsy, lethargic; — II. INF. *tan'îs*, make sleepy, cause to sleep; operate as a narcotic; — VI. INF. *tanâ'us*, feign to sleep; set one's self to slumber; — ة *na'sa-t*, sleep, slumber.

نعسان *na'sân*, sleepy, drowsy, lethargic.

(نعش) *na'aś*, A, INF. *na'ś*, elevate; make one rich after being poor; raise the fallen; place the dead on the bier; — II. INF. *tan'îś*, raise, elevate; praise the dead; — IV. INF. *in'âś*, place the dead on a bier; — VIII. INF. *inti'âś*, rise from a fall, get up; recover.

نعش *na'ś*, bier, coffin, catafalco; funeral procession; duration; بنات ن *banât-u na'ś-in*, the constellation Ursa.

(نعص) *na'aṣ*, A, INF. *na'ṣ*, eat the ground bare (locusts); (m.) also نعوص *na'waṣ*, INF. ة, howl woefully (dog); — *na'iṣ*, A, INF. *na'aṣ*, walk with a swing to the left and right, be bent, curved; — VIII. INF. *inti'âṣ*, be angry; rise from a fall, get up again.

نعص *na'ṣ*, woeful cry or howl (m.); marshy ground; — *na'aṣ*, bend, curve; — ة *na'ṣa-t*, morass.

(نعض) *na'aḍ*, A, INF. *na'ḍ*, receive, obtain.

نعض *nu'ḍ*, a thorn-tree.

(نعط) — IV. *an'aṭ*, INF. *in'âṭ*, cut a morsel in two.

(نعظ) *na'aẓ*, A, INF. *na'ẓ*, *na'aẓ*, *nu'ûẓ*, have an erection (penis); — IV. INF. *in'âẓ*, rut.

(نعف) *na'f*, pl. *ni'âf*, slope; نعاف نعف *ni'âf-un nu''af-un*, precipices, declivities; — III. *nâ'af*, INF. *munâ'afa-t*, step into one's way and try to get in advance of him; resist, oppose; — VIII. INF. *inti'âf*, ascend a declivity; appear, show one's self; leave a thing to another; — ة *na'fa-t*, *na'afa-t*, strap, feathers, &c. hanging down.

(نعق) *na'aq*, A, I, INF. *na'q*, *nu'âq*, *na'iq*, *na'aqân*, croak; bleat; call to.

(نعل) *na'l*, (f.) ة, *ni'âl*, sole, sandal, shoe, slipper; horse-shoe; hoof; hard shiny pebbly ground; woman, wife.

نعل *na'al*, give one shoes, shoe; sole shoes; (m.) curse; — *na'il*, A, INF. *na'al*, be soled or shoed; — II. INF. *tan'îl*=I.; — IV. INF. *in'âl*, shoe a horse or camel; — V. INF. *tana''ul*, VIII. INF. *inti'âl*, put on shoes, be shoed.

نعلبند *na'lband*, farrier (Pers.).

نعلى *na'liyy*, in shape of a horse-shoe.

نعلين *na'len*, m. du. pair of shoes.

(نعم) *na'am*, U, I, INF. *na'îm*, live in ease and affluence, enjoy life; be comfortable and pleasant for (acc.); INF. *na'm* (also IV.) come bare-footed to (acc.); — *na'im*, A, I, INF. *na'am*, live in affluence and enjoyment; be fresh and tender; also — *na'um*, INF. *nu'm*, be soft and delicate, juicy and sweet, good, precious; be fine and thin; be complied with, be answered with Yes; — II. INF. *tan'îm*, procure affluence and an enjoyable life for (acc.); overwhelm with riches; answer one with نعم *na'am*, yes; make thin and fine, reduce to powder; — III. INF. *munâ'ama-t*, live in affluence and enjoyment; procure one such a life; — IV. INF. *in'âm*, overwhelm with benefits, be bountiful towards, present with, grant, rejoice (a.); say Yes; attend diligently to (فى *fî*), go far in; make comfortable and pleasant; be comfortable; enjoy; see I.; — V. INF. *tana''um*, lead an enjoyable and luxurious life, be comfortable, suitable, well-situated, wholesome for (acc.); go barefooted; be made thin and fine, be pounded minutely, reduced to powder; — VI. INF. *tanâ'um*, live in ease and enjoyment; — X. INF. *istin'âm*, find thin and fine, choose the finest.

نعم *nu'm*, pl. *an'um*, enjoyable and luxurious life, ease, happiness, enjoyment, pleasure; — *na'ma*, *ni'ma*, *na'ima*, *ni'ima*, well! well done! go on! courage! how excellent! (followed by a noun in the nominative); — *na'am*, *na'im*, *ni'am-u*, yes, so it is; — *na'am*, *na'm*, pl. *an'âm*, *anâ'îm*, herd of cattle, pasturing cattle, cattle (esp. sheep and camels); — *na'îm*, comfortable and pleasant, enjoyable; soft, tender, delicate; — ة *na'ma-t*, pleasant and comfortable life; riches, wealth; delicacy; — *ni'ma-t*, pl. *ni'am*, *an'um*, id.; pl. *ni'am*, *an'um*, *ni'amât*, *ni'imât*, benefit, bounty, favour, mercy, kindness; helping hand; hand; (m.) privilege; ن عين *ni'mat-a* (*na'mat-a*, *nu'mat-a*) *'ain-in*, for the sake of; — ى *nu'mā*, ease, affluence, riches; enjoyment of life, pleasure; benefit, bounty, favour; helping hand; pleasant to the eye.

نعما *ni'immâ*, *ni'ammâ*=نعم *na'ma*, &c.; — *na'mâ'*, benefit, bounty, favour, mercy; helping hand.

نعمان *nu'mân*, blood; name of the kings of Hira; شقائق الن *śaqâ'iq an-nu'mân*, anemone.

نعناع *na'nâ'*, mint (plant).

(نعنع) *na'na'*, INF. ة, become relaxed again (after erection, genital of a horse); stammer; pronounce *na* for *la*; — II. INF. *tana'nu'*, be far, remove to a distance; be agitated and totter.

نعنع *na'na'*, mint (plant); — *nu'nu'*, long and flaccid; — ة *nu'nu'a-t*, crop of a bird.

(نعو) *na'â*, INF. *nu'â'*, mew.

نعو *na'w*, dimple under the nose; groove in the upper lip of a camel, in the hoof of a horse;

fresh dates; — ة *na'wa-t*, death-message.

نعوب *na'ûb*, pl. *nu'ub*, swift.

نعور *na'ûr*, spurting out blood (vein).

نعوص *na'waṣ*, INF. ة, howl (m.).

نعومة *na'ûma-t*, softness, gentleness; pleasantness, pleasure.

(نعى) *na'a*, I, INF. *na'y*, *na'iyy*, *nu'yân*, announce one's (acc.) death to (ل *li* or الى *ila*), report one as dead; wail, lament; reproach with; make one's faults public;—IV. INF. *in'â'*, announce one's death; — VI. INF. *tanâ'î*, call out the names of the fallen to one another so as to excite to combat; — X. INF. *istin'â'*, run away with the rider.

نعى *na'iyy*, messenger of death; death-message.

نعيب *na'îb*, croaking (s.); — ة *na'îba-t*, tax on treasures found.

نعيث *na'îs*, ة *na'îsa-t*, winning race-horse.

نعير *na'îr*, rough nasal sound or tone, clamour, noise, vociferation of fighting men; ن الهم *na'îr al-hamm*, far-thinking.

نعيف ضعيف *na'îf ḍa'îf*, weak.

نعيق *na'îq*, croaking (s.).

نعيلة *nu'aila-t*, little shoe.

نعيم *na'îm*, pleasant, comfortable life; enjoyment, pleasure; satisfaction; delightful place of sojourn, paradise; good things, bounty; — *na'îm-an*, excellent! may it do you good! to your health! ن عين *na'îm-a 'ain-in*, for the sake of.

نغار *naggâr*, bleeding.

نغاز *naggâz*, mischief-maker.

نغاش *nugâś*, ى *nugâsiyy*, very small dwarf, pigmy, Lilliputian.

(نغب) *nagab*, A, I, U, INF. *nagb*, imbibe, absorb, swallow down; sip water; —ة *nagba-t*, sip, draught; *nugba-t*, pl. *nugab*, id.

نغبق *nagbaq*, INF. ة, rumble (bowels of a horse); — *nugbuq*, stupid.

(نغث) *nagas*, A, INF. *nags*, pull, pull out (hair).

نغث *nags*, lasting and violent evil.

(نغر) *nagar*, A, INF. *nagr*, *nagarân*, boil, bubble; be internally enraged against (على *'ala*);—*nagir*, A. INF. *nagar*, id.; drink much water; abound; — II. INF. *tangîr*, cry out to the camel; tickle; — V. INF. *tanaggur*, be angry, averse.

نغر *nagir*, angry, in a passion, passionate; ة, jealous; — ة *nugara-t*, pl. *nugar*, *nigrân*, nightingale; young sparrow.

نغز *nagaz*, INF. *nagz*, tickle; make mischief.

(نغش) *nagaś*, INF. *nagś*, *nagaśân*, be unstable, totter, shake (n.); move restlessly; bend (n.); nod one's head; spur; — III. INF. *munâyaśa-t*, flatter, coax; sing, chirp, twitter; reckon closely with; — V. INF. *tanagguś*, be unstable, nod, totter; — VIII. INF. *intigâś*, id.

(نغص) *nagiṣ*, A, INF. *nagaṣ*, miss one's wish or aim; be troubled, made unpleasant; trouble (n.); stop drinking; drive camels from the water to make room for others; — II. INF. *tangîṣ*, trouble or embitter one's life; disturb one's pleasure; — IV. INF. *ingâṣ* =II.; — V. INF. *tanaggus*, be troubled, embittered, unbearable;—X. INF. *istingâṣ*, be moved with pity at another's misery;— ة *nagṣa-t*, pitiable calamity.

(نغض) *nagaḍ*, U, I, INF. *nagḍ*, *nagaḍ*, *nugûḍ*, *nagaḍân*, totter, nod, be rickety, move (n.); be many, numerous; be dense and crowd together (clouds); move, shake (a.);—II. INF. *tangîṣ*, move (a.); embitter one's life; — III. INF. *munâgaḍa-t*, press one another in a narrow place; — IV. INF. move (n.), be rickety, totter; move, shake (a.); — V. INF. *ta-*

naggud, move, shake (n.), be rickety.

نغض *nagd*, trembling movement; also *nigd*, male ostrich; — *nagd*, *nugd*, cartilage of the shoulder-blades; — *nuggad*, large pulley of a well.

(نغضل) *nagdal*, heavy, clumsy.

نغط *nugut*, pl. tall men.

نغف *nagaf*, ة, worm in the nose of a camel or sheep; — *nagif*, A, INF. *nagaf*, have many of such; — ة *nagafa-t*, mucus, snot; du. the extremities of the upper jaw.

(نغق) *nagaq*, I, INF. *nagîq*, croak and augur well.

(نغل) *nagil*, A, INF. *nagal*, get spoiled in tanning; get or be spoiled; suppurate, become malignant, poisonous; be angry with, irritated against (على *'ala*); be malicious; sow discord; — *nagul*, INF. *nugûla-t*, be unhealthy, sickly.

نغل *nagl*, *nagil*, spoiled, corrupted; bastard; vile person; malicious, full of wicked intentions; — *nagal*, spoiled or corrupted condition; malice; discord; — ة *nugla-t*, getting (s.) spoiled in tanning; — ة *nagila-t*, rotten nut.

(نغم) *nagam*, I, U, INF. *nagm*, *nagma-t*, read in a subdued voice and modulating, sing; hum a song; INF. *nagm*, sip, swallow; — *nagim*, A, INF. *nagam*, sing in a subdued voice and melodiously; — II. INF. *tangîm*, id.; — III. INF. *munâgama-t*, address in a low voice; — V. INF. *tanaggum* = II.

نغم *nagm*, *nagam*, low voice; pl. *angâm*, low melodious song; — ة *nagma-t*, *nagama-t*, pl. *nagamât*, subdued tone; song, air, melody; — *nugama-t*, pl. *nugam*, draught, sip.

(نغمش) *nagmaś*, INF. ة, tickle (m.).

(نغنغ) *nugnug*, pl. *nagânig*, partition between the alimentary canal and the wind-pipe; — *nagnag*, INF. ة, suffer from a disease in this spot.

(نغو) *nagâ*, A, INF. *nagw* = (نغى); — ة *nagwa-t*, musical tone.

(نغى) *naga*, I, INF. *nagy*, speak intelligibly; — III. INF. *munâgât*, speak tenderly to, coax; (m.) stammer; (m.) twitter, chirp; — IV. INF. *ingâ'* = I.; — VI. INF. *tanâgî*, speak intelligibly to one another; speak coaxingly; — ة *nagya-t*, musical tone; first rumour.

نغيق *nagîq*, (auspicious) croaking (s.).

نغيل *nagîl*, f. ة, bastard, illegitimate; spoiled.

(نف) *naff*, U, INF. *naff*, sow the ground.

نفا *nafâ'*, ة *nafât* = نفاية *nufâya-t*, *nafâya-t*; — ة *nuf'a-t*, pl. *nufa'*, scattered particles of plants.

نفاث *naffâs*, ة, blowing; نفاثة فى العقد *nafâssa-t fî 'l-'uqad*, she who blows on magic knots, sorceress; pl. *nafâssât*, sorceries; — ة *nufâsa-t*, what is spat out of the mouth, especially in cleaning the teeth.

نفاج *naffâj*, inflated, boasting; — ة *nifaja-t*, *nuffâja-t*, wedge-like piece of cloth, &c.

نفاح *nufâh*, odour, fragrance; — *naffâh*, fragrant, odoriferous; beneficent, bountiful; who blows; breathes into, suggests, prompter; — *nuffâh*, tumour; — ة *naffâha-t*, blister, pustule; — *naffâha-t*, water-bubble; fish-bladder.

نفاد *nafâd*, wasting away, getting exhausted, ceasing (s.); destruction, death.

نفاذ *nafâz*, piercing (s.); execution or effectiveness of an order; escape; safe arrival of a letter, &c.; name of the ـِ under the pronominal ه preceded by ـِ; — *naffâz*, what pierces, penetrates; effective.

نفار *nifâr*, running away (s.), flight;

aversion, disaffection, loathing; — ة *nufâra-t*, carried off booty; sequestrated property; dominion, power.

نفاس *nifâs*, throes of child-birth, confinement; hæmorrhage after parturition; confined woman (during 40 days); pl. of نفسا *nafsâ'*; also ة *nafâsa-t*, anything precious; costliness, great value, goodness.

نفاش *naffâś*, camels or sheep which pasture only at night without a herdsman.

نفاص *nufâṣ*, fatal urinary flux of sheep.

نفاض *nafâḍ*, shiver of a fever, ague; also *nufâḍ*, exhaustion of provisions; want, famine; — *nifâḍ*, pl. *nufaḍ*, trowsers; also *nufâḍ* and — ة *nufâḍa-t*, *nifâḍa-t*, what falls off by shaking; shaking (s.); *nufâḍa-t*=نفاثة *nufâsa-t*.

نـفـاط *nafâṭ*, bitumen, naphtha; torch, candle, lamp; — *naffâṭ*, who prepares naphtha; also ة *nafaṭa-t*, naphtha-cannon, bomb filled with naphtha; —ات *nafâṭât*, blisters, pustules.

نفاع *nafâ'*, use, profit, advantage; — *naffâ'*, who makes himself very useful.

نفافى *nafâfî*, pl. of نفى *naffa*.

نفاق *nafâq*, good sale, good market; —*nifâq*, hypocrisy, falseness, lie; discord; sacrilege; — *.

نفاوش *nafâwiś*=نفاش *naffâś*.

نفاوة *nufâwa-t*, نفاية *nufâya-t*, *nafâya-t*, anything rejected, refuse, offal.

(نفت) *nafat*, I, INF. *naft*, *nafatân*, boil violently, seethe; foam with rage.

نفت *naft* (m.), for نفط *nafṭ*, naphtha.

(نفث) *nafas*, I, U, INF. *nafs*, blow upon (as a conjurer); spit out, spurt out; pronounce, utter; — III. INF. *munâfasa-t*, breathe upon, whisper into one's ear, converse.

نفث *nafs*, ة, blowing, breathing, spitting (s.); *nafs*, speech; ن الشيطان *nafs aś-śaiṭân*, devilry (poetry).

(نفج) *nafaj*, INF. *nafj*, *nafajân*, creep out of the egg; jump up; blow violently; INF. *nafj*, raise; increase; — V. INF. *tanaffuj*, be inflated, boast; — VIII. INF. *intifâj*, be inflated; protrude; — X. INF. *istinfâj*, excite anger; — ة *nufja-t*, wedge-like piece of cloth, &c.; — *nuffaja-t*=نافجة *nâfija-t*, q.v.

(نفح) *nafaḥ*, (m.) *nafiḥ*, A, INF. *nafḥ*, *nufûḥ*, *nafaḥân*, spread odour, be fragrant; INF. *nafḥ*, blow; move (a.); kick; strike at with a sword; gently toss to, give, make a present; bleed; — III. INF. *manâfaḥa-t*, dispute, contend; — VIII. INF. *intifâḥ*, resist, oppose.

نفح *nafḥ*, blowing (s.), breeze, breath; — *nafaḥ*, remote; — ة *nafḥa-t*, pl. *nafaḥât*, blast, breeze, breath, wave of air; spreading odour, fragrance; authority, consideration, renown; gift, present.

(نفخ) *nafaḫ*, INF. *nafḫ*, blow; breathe in air, inflate; blow upon; blow the horn; break wind; make one inflated, proud; — II. INF. *tanfîḫ*, inflate vigorously (a skin bag, &c.); — INF. *intifâḫ*, be inflated, swollen; be inflated with pride, give one's self airs.

نفخ *nafḫ*, blowing, inflating (s.); breeze, breath; tumour, swelling; rupture, hernia; pride, inflation; — ة *nafḫa-t*, breeze, breath; blast of a trumpet; also *nifḫa-t*, *nufḫa-t*, tumour, swelling.

(نفد) *nafid*, A, INF. *nafad*, *nafâd*, *nafadân*, waste (n.), be consumed, get exhausted, fail; be dried up; lose the means of subsistence; — III. INF. *munâfada-t*, contend with, summon

before a court of justice; — IV. INF. *infâd*, exhaust one's means, have nothing left; — VIII. INF. *intifâd*, claim and receive the whole of a debt; — X. INF. *istinfâd*, squander one's property, exhaust.

(نفذ) *nafaẓ*, U, INF. *nafâẓ*, *nufûẓ*, pierce through; come forth, show one's self, appear, arrive, reach; pass by, overtake; be heard and taken into consideration; — *nafuẓ*, get fulfilled, be effective and executed (order); —II. INF. *tanfîẓ*, pierce through; come forth, appear; transmit; have executed, make effective, enforce; — IV. INF. *infâẓ*, pierce through or make to pierce through; transmit (a message, &c.); send a messenger; execute, carry out; — VI. INF. *tanâfuẓ*, bring their case before a judge.

نفذ *nafaẓ*, penetrating power; free course.

(نفر) *nafar*, U, I, INF. *nifâr*, *nufâr*, shy and run away; INF. *nafr*, *nafarân*, flee and disperse, run away; INF. *nufûr*, feel disaffection, aversion; INF. *nufûr*, be inflamed and swollen; be swollen; — I, INF. *nafr*, *nufûr*, return from the valley of Mina to Mecca; — I, INF. *nifâr*, *nufûr*, *nafîr*, set out, go to work, to combat; — U, INF. *nafr*, conquer, vanquish; —II. INF. *tanfîr*, scare away, put to flight; inspire with disaffection, with aversion; (also IV.) declare one to be a victor over others; — III. INF. *nifâr*, *munâfara-t*, dispute glory, honour, merit to another, contend in honour; contend; — IV. INF. *infâr*, put to flight; see II.; — VI. INF. *tanâfur*, run away, flee; dispute glory, honour, merit to one another; refer (a dispute to); set at work; feel a mutual aversion; —X. INF. *istinfâr*, have a dislike, an aversion towards; run away; scare away; put to flight.

نفر *nafr*, number of persons belonging to one another, troop of fugitives, company; flight, dispersion, departure; also *nuffar*, pl. of نافر *nâfir*, fugitive, timid, &c.; — *nafar*, pl. *anfâr*, persons, people, followers (3 to 10); individual, private person, common soldier; servant; a piece or head; —ة *nafra-t*, fright, scare, flight; aversion, dislike, disaffection; troop of people, associates, relations; — *nafra-t*, dominion, authority; also *nufara-t*, amulet worn round the neck of a child; — ات *nafarât*, troops of soldiers.

نفراج *nifrâj*, ة, cowardly.

نفران *nafarân*, flight.

نفرج *nifrij*, ة *nifrija-t*, نفرجا *nifrijâ'*, cowardly.

نفريت *nifrît*, نفرية *nifrîyya-t*=عفريت *'ifrît*, gigantic and powerful demon, &c.

نفريج *nifrîj*, talkative.

(نفز) *nafaz*, I, INF. *nafazân*, leap, run in leaps; — II. INF. *tanfîz*, make to leap; try the arrowhead on one's nail.

(نفس) *nafas*, injure by breathing upon or by the evil eye; — *nafis*, A, INF. *nafas*, *nafâsa-t*, *nifâs*, have given birth and still lose blood, be confined, get up from child-bed; save, be sparing with; envy for (ب *bi*); — *nafis*, A, *nafus*, INF. *nafas*, *nifâs*, *nafâsa-t*, be precious, valuable; — II. INF. *tanfîs*, cheer, comfort, relieve, quiet; refresh; have a hole and let out air; — III. INF. *nifâs*, *munâfasa-t*, long for a thing together with another; prize: envy and dispute anything with another; contend, dispute; — IV. INF. *infâs*, make one to desire; —V. INF. *tanaffus*, fetch a deep breath, breathe;

fetch a sigh; appear, shine;— VI. INF. *tanâfus*, long passionately for; dispute any desired thing with each other.

نفس *nafs* (f.), pl. *nufûs*, *anfus*, breath of life, vital spirit, soul; self (takes the pronominal affixes and governs other nouns in the oblique case); person, individual; essence, substance, reality; desire, wish, passion; pride; vice, infamy; punishment; blood, sperm; *nafs-an*, willingly;— *nafas*, pl. *anfâs*, breath, breathing; draught, sip; desire, wish, inclination, mind for; long-winded speech; style or spirit of an author; full freedom, one's own pleasure or will;— *nufus*, *nufs*, pl. of نفسا *nafsâ'*;— ة *nafsa-t*, duration of a breathing; respite, short delay;— ى *nafsiyy*, ة, desirous, libidinous, carnal, sensual, vital.

نفساء *nafsâ'*, *nufasâ'*, *nafasâ'*, pl. *nufasawât*, *nifâs*, *nufâs*, *nufus*, *nufs*, *nafâwis*, (m.) *manâfis*, woman giving birth, confined woman.

نفسان *nafsân*, selfish, partial; also ى *nafsâniyy*, libidinous, sensual, carnal;—ية *nafsâniyya-t*, selfishness, partiality; libidinousness, sensuality, voluptuousness; pride, pomp.

(نفش) *nafaś*, U, INF. *nafś* (also II.), pick wool or cotton; pluck; I, U, INF. *nafaś*, *nufûś*, also—*nafiś*, A, INF. *nafaś*, (also V.), pasture at night without a herdsman;— m. (also II.) open (n.), expand, swell in the water;— II. INF. *tanfîś*, see I.;— IV. INF. *infâś*, allow to pasture at night without a herdsman;— V. INF. *tanaffuś*, ruffle the feathers, (also VIII.) bristle up the hair or tail; be picked, plucked; (m.) swell in the water; see I.;— VIII. INF. *intifâś*, be swollen; see V.

نفش *nafś*, small household things or furniture (m.);—*nafaś*, wool; rich produce; = نفاش *naffâś*;— ية *nafśiyya-t*, confection of almonds.

(نفص) *nafaṣ*, INF. *nafṣ*, emit urine forcibly; deliver one's speech quickly;— IV. INF. *infâṣ*, make water frequently; suffer from the disease نفاص *nufâṣ*;— ة *nufṣa-t*, violent hæmorrhage.

(نفض) *nafaḍ*, U, INF. *nafḍ*, shake (a.), shake off; drop a foal; be fertile; put forth ears; form into grapes; have consumed the provisions; (also V. and X.) examine a place for safety, reconnoitre; INF. *nufûḍ*, recover; (m.) get unloaded (ship);— II. INF. *tanfîḍ*, shake violently; dust; exhaust one's provisions; deprive one of all his means; (m.) repair a roof, the terrace of a roof;— IV. INF. *infâḍ*, drop a foal; have exhausted one's resources, consumed one's store, suffer want;— V. INF. *tanaffuḍ*, be shaken, dusted; see I.;— VIII. INF. *intifâḍ*=V.;— X. INF. *istinfâḍ*, see I.

نفض *nafaḍ*, what is shaken or falls off a tree;— *nufuḍ*, pl. of نفاض *nifâḍ*;— ة *nafaḍa-t*, pl. spies, scouts;— *nufḍa-t*, *nufaḍa-t*, also نفضا *nufaḍâ'*, shiver of a fever, ague;— ى *nafaḍû*, *nifiḍḍa*, concussion, agitation, emotion, trembling.

(نفط) *nafaṭ*, I, INF. *nafîṭ*, sneeze; boil, bubble; boil with rage;— *nafiṭ*, A, INF. *nafṭ*, *nafaṭ*, *nafîṭ*, be covered with blisters or pustules;— II INF. *tanfîṭ*, IV. INF. *infâṭ*, call forth blisters or pustules.

نفط *nafṭ*, *nifṭ*, bitumen, naphtha; gunpowder; phosphor-matches;— ة *nafṭa-t*, *nifṭa-t*, *nafiṭa-t*, blisters, pustules; *nafiṭa-t*, covered with blisters;—*nufaṭa-t*, who is easily provoked to anger, irritable;— ى *nafṭiyy*, ة, of

naphtha, impregnated with it; naphtha-coloured, brownish-yellow; — ـيّة naftiyya-t, pl. fire-workers.

(نفع) nafa', INF. naf', be useful, advantageous, profit (a.); be conducive to health; be effective as an antidote; — II. INF. tanfî', allow one to profit by, to draw advantage from; promote one's interests, be useful to; — V. INF. tanaffu', VIII. INF. intifâ', draw advantage from, gain or profit by (ب bi), draw a rent from.

نفع naf', advantage, profit, gain; — nuf', pl. of نفوع nafû'; — ة na-f'a-t, pl. nafa'ât, rod, stick; — nif'a-t, pl. nif', nifa', leathern trimming of a travelling-bag.

(نفغ) nafag, A, INF. nafg, nufûg, get covered with blisters (n.); — V. INF. tanaffug, id.

(نفق) nafaq, U, INF. nafâq, sell well, be lively (market); = nafiq; INF. nufûq, lose its crust (wound); die; — nafiq, A, INF. nafaq, grow less, draw to an end, be exhausted; creep out of its hole (mouse); — II. INF. tanfîq, make merchandise to sell well, sell quickly, dispose of readily; — III. INF. nifâq, munâfaqa-t, creep into the hole; commit religious hypocrisy; change one's creed, one's opinion; lie; blaspheme, commit sacrilege; — IV. INF. infâq, spend much money for a thing or person; give alms; dispose quickly of one's merchandise; — V. INF. tanaffuq, chase out of the hole; make one's self valuable in the market; — VI. INF. tanâfuq, dissemble, lie, deceive; — VIII. INF. intifâq, creep into or out of the hole; — X. INF. istinfâq, spend money.

نفق nafaq, ة nufaqa-t, hole of a field-mouse, or a mole; hole in the wall for the water; — nafiq, soon exhausted by running (horse); — ة nafaqa-t, pl. -ât, nifâq, expenses, costs, spending (s.), sustenance; small coin for daily expenditure.

نفكة nafaka-t, base of the nether jaw.

(نفل) nafal, U, I, INF. nafl (also II.), leave the whole booty to the soldiers; give one his share of the booty; make a present; — II. INF. tanfîl, see I.; favour one in distributing the booty or presents; prefer, give preference to; — V. INF. tanafful, do more than one is bound to do by duty; claim or take beforehand a larger part of the booty; — X. INF. istinfâl, pray more than is prescribed.

نفل nafl, pl. nufûl, supererogation, what is optional, prayer of free will; present; grandson, grandchild; — nafal, pl. anfâl, nifâl, nufûl, booty (also ة nafla-t); present; also (m.) nafl, a kind of fragrant clover; — nufal, second three nights of a month.

نفناف nafnâf, valley between mountains; (m.) snow-flake.

(نفنف) nafnaf, INF. ة, be careful in one's toilet, trim in one's dress; ripple; — II. INF. tanafnuf, be dressed up.

نفنف nafnaf, pl. nafânif, deep valley between mountains; steep mountain-slope; wall; desert; atmosphere.

(نفه) nafah, INF. nufûh, grow obedient, docile; — nafih, A, INF. nafah, grow sullen and despondent; — II. INF. tanfîh, jade; — IV. INF. infâh, id.; — X. INF. istinfâh, find rest, rest.

نفه nuffah, pl. of نافه nâfih, ag. of the previous.

(نفو) nafâ, U, INF. nafw, drive away, chase off; — ة nafwa-t, nifwa-t, anything bad, abject; — nifwa-t, outcast.

نفوت nafût, foaming over (adj.).

نفوذ nafûẓ, who penetrates, prevails, carries out; — nufûẓ, penetra-

tion, success, efficacy, influence; long sandy tracts in northern Arabia.

نفور *nafûr*, running away, fleeing (adj.); feeling aversion, abhorrence, loathing; — *nufûr*, running away (s.), flight; setting out (s.), departure, start; aversion, abhorrence; swelling (s.); — ة *nufûra-t*, dominion, chief command; relationship.

نفوز *nafûz*, leaping (adj.).

نفوض *nafûḍ*, fertile; — *nufûḍ*, recovery.

نفوع *nafû'*, pl. *nuf'*, useful, beneficial, bountiful.

(نفى) *nafa*, I, INF. *nafy*, also نفو *nafâ*, U, INF. *nafw*, expel, drive away, banish, exile, repudiate; be driven away, repudiated, cast out; deny, refuse, hinder; carry off, remove; pour out its water (cloud);—II. INF. *tanfiya-t*, drive far away, expel, banish, cast out, excommunicate; — III. INF. *munâfât*, try to remove, to expel; exclude, abrogate, be inconsistent with; clear one's self; — VI. INF. *tanâfî*, try to remove, to expel, to exclude from a possession or advantage; be inconsistent with, abrogate one another; — VIII. INF. *intifâ'*, be expelled, banished, an outcast.

نفى *nafy*, expulsion, banishment, excommunication; denying (s.); negation, prohibition;–*nufa*, also *naffa*, pl. *tanâfî*=*nafya-t*, *nufya-t* (see below); — *nafiyy*, expelled, banished, exiled, outcast, excommunicated, denied; what is separated as bad, rejected; fallen leaves round the trunk of a tree; pebbles, &c. thrown up by a horse's hoof; sprinkled over (by the rain); negative; — ة *nafya-t*, *nufya-t*, round table made of palm-leaves;—*nifya-t*, banished, outcast.

نفيذ *nafîẓ*, penetrating; effective; — *niffîẓ*, very effective.

نفير *nafîr*, small troop (three to ten, esp. of fugitives); levy or mobilisation of an army; return of the pilgrims from the valley of Mina to Mecca; pipe, flute, hautboy, trumpet, and their sound (Pers.); scream, shout;— *nufair*, a very small number of people.

نفيس *nafîs*, ة, precious, costly, valuable, good; — ة *nafîsa-t*, pl. *nafâ'is*, anything precious, great wealth.

نفيش *nafîś*, stray small objects, household stuff.

نفيضة *nafîḍa-t*, pl. *nafâ'iḍ*, scouts.

نفيضى *niffîḍā*, concussion, agitation, emotion, trembling (s.).

نفيط *nafîṭ*, INF. of (نفط); — ة *nafîṭa-t*, covered with blisters.

نفيع *niffî'*=نفاع *naffâ'*; — ة *nafî'a-t*, use, profit, advantage.

نفيلة *nafîla-t* = نافلة *nâfila-t*, supererogatory work, &c.

نفيف *nafîf*, girth of a camel.

(نق) *naqq*, I, INF. *naqîq*, croak; mew; (m.) contradict continually.

نق *naqq*, croaking.

نقا *naqan*, *naqa*, pl. *anqâ'*, *nuqiyy*, sand-heap; marrowy bone; bone of the arm; — *nuqa*, pl. of نقاوة *naqâwa-t*; — *naqâ'*, purity, innocence; untroubled serenity; pure; — *niqâ'*, pl. of نقى *naqiyy*; — *nuqâ'*, pl. of نقاوة *naqâwa-t* and نقاية *nuqâya-t*; — ة *naqât*, best and purest part; — *nuqât*, what is thrown away in selecting, weeds, darnel, tare, shells, husks, &c.; — ة *naqâ'a-t*, purity.

نقاب *niqâb*, pl. *nuqub*, veil covering the upper part of the face; sign, mark; rugged path; — *naqqâb*, miner; who examines, investigates; — ة *niqâba-t*, magistracy, prefecture, tribunal, presidency.

نقاخ *nuqâḥ*, cold, pure and sweet; refreshing; — *nuqqâḥ*, back part of the head, occiput.

نقاد *naqqâd*, who separates the good

from the bad; money-changer; observer, examiner, critic; — *.

نقار *niqâr*, provocation, challenge, quarrel, dispute; — *; — *naqqâr*, hitting or tearing with the beak; who whets the mill-stones; (m.) sharp pebbles; — ة *nuqâra-t*, beakful; — *naqqâra-t*, small kettle-drum, cymbal; — ى *naqqâriyy*, drummer.

نقاز *nuqâz*, a disease which makes the cattle to leap until they die; — *naqqâz, nuqqâz*, a bird.

نقاسة *niqâsa-t*, mockery; mock-name.

نقاش *naqqâś*, painter; gilder; sculptor; engraver, chiseller; embroiderer; whitewasher; — ة *niqâśa-t*, art of painting, sculpture, &c.

نقاصة *naqâṣa-t*, purity and sweetness of the water; — *nuqâṣa-t*, deficiency, defective condition, default, decrease.

نقاض *naqqâḍ*, breaking the back (load).

نقاط *naqqâṭ*, who dots, points.

نقاع *naqqâ'*, infatuated, vain, boasting; — *; — ة *nuqâ'a-t*, fluid in which anything is dissolved or decocted.

نقاف *niqâf*, manslaughter, murder; also *naqqâf*, asking intelligently and with a wish to acquire knowledge; — *naqqâf*, murderer.

نقاق *naqqâq*, f. ة, frog; who always contradicts.

نقال *naqqâl*, pacing fast; who removes, porter; — *; — ة *naqqâla-t*, cart.

نقام *naqâm, niqâm*, muddy.

نقاهة *naqâha-t*, recovery; weakness.

نقاوة *naqâwa-t, nuqâwa-t*, purity; pl. *nuq-an, nuqa, nuqâ'*, best and most refined part, selection; — *nuqâwa-t*, an alkaline plant serving for washing.

نقاية *naqâya-t*, purity; — *nuqâya-t*, pl. *naqâyâ, nuqâ'*, best and most refined part; what is thrown away in selecting, refuse.

(نقب) *naqab*, U, INF. *naqb*, pierce or break through; hollow out, excavate, mine, dig a tunnel; tap a dropsical person; till or cultivate the ground; mend; inquire for news; bring news, report; travel, travel over; — *naqib*, A, INF. *naqab*, be torn, have holes; have the hoofs worn out; — *naqub*, INF. *naqâba-t*, be chosen as a chieftain, leader, &c.; — II. INF. *tanqîb*, examine minutely; criticise; travel, travel over; — III. INF. *niqâb*, meet unexpectedly; — IV. INF. *inqâb*, travel through or over; — V. INF. *tanaqqub*, veil one's self; — VIII. INF. *intiqâb*, be pierced through, cribbled; be tilled, cultivated; be veiled, veil one's self.

نقب *naqb*, hole in a wall or in the earth; passage, mine, tunnel; digging, tilling, cultivation of the ground; mange; tumour in the side; — *nuqb*, pl. *anqâb, niqâb*, mange, scab; — *nuqub*, pl. of نقاب *niqâb*; — ة *naqba-t*, tilled or cultivated ground; — *niqba-t*, way of veiling one's self; — *nuqba-t*, hole; mange, scab; trowsers; colour; rust; face.

نقبا *nuqabâ'*, pl. of نقيب *naqîb*.

(نقت) *naqat*, U, INF. *naqt*, suck the marrow out of a bone.

(نقث) *naqaṯ*, U, INF. *naqṯ* (also VIII.), suck the marrow out of a bone; (also VIII.) excavate and lay bare; examine; confuse; hurt by words; also — II. INF. *tanqîṯ*, hasten (n.), speed; — V. INF. *tanaqquṯ*, win the love of a woman; — VIII. INF. *intiqâṯ*, see I.; hasten (n.).

(نقثل) *naqṯal*, ة, walk with a heavy step and raise the dust.

(نقح) *naqaḥ*, A, INF. *naqḥ* (also II., IV., and VIII.), suck the marrow out of a bone; shell, peel; (also II.) prune a palm-tree; be stained; — II. INF. *tanqîḥ*, see I.; (also IV.) compose a speech or

poem according to all rules of the art; select; make precise, speak with precision; (m., also IV.) revise carefully and correct; — IV. INF. *inqâḥ*, see I. and II.); — V. INF. *tanaqquḥ*, diminish (n.).

نقح *naqḥ*, white summer cloud; — *naqaḥ*, clean sand; — ة *naqḥa-t*, stain in a dress.

(نقخ) *naqaḫ*, A, INF. *naqḫ*, pierce, hit, beat; break the skull and injure the brain; — VIII. INF. *intiqâḫ*, suck the marrow out of a bone.

(نقد) *naqad*, U, INF. *naqd* (also VIII.), cast a stealthy glance upon; INF. *naqd*, *tanqâd* (also VIII.), separate the good from the bad, test coins; (also VIII.) hollow or peck a nut with the beak; peck through a net; pay in cash, in ready money; — *naqid*, A, INF. *naqad*, be peeled off (hoof); be broken or decayed (tooth); — II. INF. *tanqîd*, pay in ready money; — III. INF. *munâqada-t*, dispute with; — V. INF. *tanaqqud*, separate the good coin from the bad; — VIII. INF. *intiqâd*, see I.; criticise; be paid in ready money.

نقد *naqd*, payment in cash; readiness; pl. *nuqûd*, ready money, cash (pl. pieces of money presented to a bride); good coin; dowry; — *naqad*, ة, pl. *niqâd*, *niqâda-t*, an inferior short-legged kind of sheep; — *naqid*, peeled off (hoof); — ة *naqda-t*, يّة *naqdiyya-t*, ready money, cash, good coin; — *niqda-t*, cummin, caraway; — ى *naqdiyy*, ready (money); rich in money.

(نقذ) *naqaẕ*, U, INF. *naqẕ*, free, rescue, save from danger; — *naqiẕ*, A, INF. *naqaẕ*, save one's self, escape; — II. INF. *tanqîẕ*, IV. INF. *inqâẕ*, V. INF. *tanaqquẕ*, VIII. INF. *intiqâẕ*, X. INF. *istinqâẕ*, rescue, free, liberate.

نقذ *naqẕ*, rescue, delivery, salvation, escape; security; — *naqaẕ*, rescued, liberated.

(نقر) *naqar*, U, INF. *naqr*, pierce through, excavate; carve or engrave in stone, pick, pick open, make a way for the young; pick up grain; whet the mill-stones; beat, hit; hurt by words, revile, slander; smack with the lips or tongue, snap the fingers; strike two things against one another; blow (the trumpet); invite specially; — *naqir*, A, INF. *naqar*, get angry; suffer from the disease نقرة *nuqra-t*; — II. INF. *tanqîr*, pick open; examine, test; — III. INF. *niqâr*, *munâqara-t*, quarrel, dispute with; scold, rebuke, reproach; contradict; vex, wrangle with; — IV. INF. *inqâr*, spare, abstain from; — V. INF. *tanaqqur*, examine, test; — VI. INF. *tanâqur*, dispute with one another, quarrel; — VIII. INF. *intiqâr*, be excavated.

نقر *naqr*, excavation, cavity; — *naqar*, anger; loss, calamity; — *naqir*, angry; — ة *niqra-t*, quarrel, dispute; — *nuqra-t*, pl. *nuqar*, *niqâr*, cavity, pit; dimple; socket; hollow of the neck; neck; pl. *niqâr*, molten gold or silver, molten ore, gold or silver coin; also *nuqara-t*, stiffness of the legs.

نقران *nuqrân*, pl. of نقير *naqîr*.

(نقرد) *naqrad*, INF. ة, remain always in the same place.

(نقرس) *niqris*, rheumatics with swelling, arthritic pains, gout; calamity; = نقريس *niqrîs*.

نقرى *naqrā*, personal invitation; calumny.

نقريس *niqrîs*, very clever.

(نقز) *naqaz*, U, INF. *naqz*, *naqazân*, leap; tremble with fear; (m.) INF. *naqîz*, sting, pain, ache; — II. INF. *tanqîz*, make to leap;

— VIII. INF. *intiqâz*, suffer from the disease نقاز *niqâz*.

نقز *niqz*, *naqaz*, *naqiz*, worst kind of cattle; — *nuqz*, well; — *naqaz*, *naqiz*, nick-name, mock-name; — *naqiz*, pure and sweet water; — ة *naqza-t*, leap; trembling (s.).

(نقس) *naqas*, U, INF. *naqs*, strike the ناقوس *nâqûs*, ring the bell; revile, abuse; — II. INF. *tanqîs*, give one a nick-name.

نقس *naqs*, fault, vice; abuse; mange, scab; — *niqs*, pl. *anqus*, *anqâs*, ink.

(نقش) *naqaś*, INF. *naqś*, paint with two or more colours, paint, imprint; make parti-coloured; embroider, engrave, chisel, carve in stone, &c.; coin; do carefully; pull out a thorn or sting; pull out hair; investigate; lie with; publish, make known; — II. INF. *tanqîś*, colour, paint, enamel; — III. INF. *munâqaśa-t*, reckon minutely with; (also VI.) dispute in joke; — IV. INF. *inqâś*, press a debtor, dun; — VI. INF. *tanâquś*, dispute with one another in joke; — VIII. INF. *intiqâś*, be painted, carved, &c.: be spotted or piebald; have painted, engraved, &c.; pull out a thorn or sting.

نقش *naqś*, coinage, engraving (of a seal, &c.); — *niqś*, *naqś*, pl. *nuqûś*, figure, picture, image; painting, drawing, coinage; pigment, colour; — ة *niqśa-t*, image, likeness, portrait, draught of a plan, vignette.

(نقص) *naqaṣ*, U, INF. *naqṣ*, *nuqṣân*, *tanqâṣ*, decrease, diminish (n.), become defective; be defective, damaged; diminish, lessen (a.); (m.) be wanting to, fail; — *naquṣ*, INF. *naqâṣa-t*, be sweet; — II. INF. *tanqîṣ*, diminish, lessen (a.); injure, damage; — V. INF. *tanaqquṣ*, diminish; blame, revile; also — VIII. *intiqâṣ*, diminish, lessen (n.); become defective, get damaged; — X. INF. *istinqâṣ*, ask or wish for a diminution, an abatement; find diminished, defective, damaged.

نقص *naqṣ*, نقصان *nuqṣân*, decrease, diminution, defect, loss, damage; want, defectiveness, defective condition; vice; rendering quiescent the fourth letter of a foot, when it has a vowel, and suppressing the seventh when it is quiescent (concurrence of *'aṣb* and *kaff*); — ة *naqṣa-t*, diminution; want, defect, shortcoming; vice.

(نقض) *naqaḍ*, U, I, INF. *naqḍ*, destroy, demolish, pull down; tear (a.), disjoin, loose; break a compact; crack, creak; scream, cry out; (m.) copy a book; — III. INF. *munâqaḍa-t*, contradict, disagree; — IV. INF. *inqâḍ*, crack, creak; weigh heavy upon; — V. INF. *tanaqquḍ* = VIII.; — VI. INF. *tanâquḍ*, be destroyed, demolished, pulled down; contradict one another, oppose, exclude one another (logically); — VIII. INF. *intiqâḍ*, dissolve (n.), fall in, be destroyed, demolished; be broken; break open (n.); (m.) be copied.

نقض *naqḍ*, dissolution, destruction, ruin, breach, rupture; state of dissolution, &c.; logical exclusion, contradiction; — *niqḍ*, ة, pl. *anqâḍ*, dissolved, destroyed; quite emaciated; — *nuqḍ*, pl. *anqâḍ*, ruins, rubbish; destruction, ruin; — ة *naqḍa-t*, beam (m.).

(نقط) *naqaṭ*, U, INF. *naqṭ*, dot, point; fall in drops; — II. INF. *tanqîṭ*, dot, mark with dots; (m.) make to fall in drops; present a bride with coin; — V. INF. *tanaqquṭ*, pass. of II.

نقط *naqṭ*, dot, point; — ة *nuqṭa-t*, pl. *nuqaṭ*, *niqâṭ*, dot, spot; drop; *niqâṭ*, particles; داء الن *dâ' an-nuqṭa-t*, epilepsy.

(نقع) *naqa'*, INF. *naq'*, macerate; quench one's thirst; kill; tear

(a.); rend; shout; (also VIII.) slaughter; irritate by reproaches and abuse; (m.) keep waiting; — INF. naq‘, nuqû‘, (also X.) stagnate; gather in the pond (n.); (m., also X.) wait for; — IV. INF. inqâ‘, macerate; (m.) keep waiting; — VIII. INF. intiqâ‘, see I.; be macerated; be quenched; pass. change colour; — X. INF. istinqâ‘, see I.

نقع naq‘, maceration; pl. niqâ‘, nuqû‘, dust raised by the wind; pl. anqu‘, stagnating water; pl. niqâ‘, anqu‘, place with stagnant water; rent; killing (s.), murder.

نقعاء naq‘â’, flat country.

(نقف) naqaf, U, INF. naqf, break one's skull, lay the brain bare; break the egg; (m.) fillip; strain (wine); water; — II. INF. tanqîf, fillip repeatedly; inflect a word; — III. INF. niqâf, munâqafa-t, break one's skull; — IV. INF. inqâf, split; break to pieces; — VIII. INF. intiqâ‘, id.; pull out, take out.

نقف naqf, pallor (m.); — niqf, naqf, young bird creeping out of the egg; — nuqf, pl. of نقيف naqîf; — ة naqfa-t, fillip.

(نقل) naqal, U, INF. naql, bring from one place to another, transport; (m.) remove (n.), emigrate; make a move (in a game of chess, &c.); translate; copy, copy out; report, hand down a tradition of, tell with reference to an authority; imitate, personate; mend, patch up; protect the hoof of a camel; — II. INF. tanqîl, remove or transport frequently or a great quantity; have removed or transported; cause one to change place; (m.) arm; (m.) serve or offer the dessert; — III. INF. munâqala-t, niqâl, bring to, report to, communicate to; run fast; — IV. INF. inqâl, mend, patch up; — V. INF. tanaqqul, be removed, transferred, transported; change place; eat dessert; — VI. INF. tanâqul, relate to one another; (m.) alternate with one another; — VIII. INF. intiqâl, be removed, transported, translated, copied; depart, remove (n.), emigrate; (m.) decease, die.

نقل naql, removal, transfer, transport; translation; report, relation, tradition, anecdote, proverb (naql-an according to tradition, ن كلام naql kalâm, tale-bearing, denunciation); copy; what is removed, load; transitive meaning; also niql, naqal, pl. anqâl, niqâl, torn and mended; (m.) also nuql, dried fruit, confections, &c., as dessert; — nuql, emigration; presents of the bridegroom carried in pomp to the bride's house; also ة nuqla-t, tale-bearing, denunciation; sport and jest; — naqal, pl. anqâl, glibness of tongue, ready repartee; — ة naqla-t, pl. -ât, also nuqla-t, pl. nuqal, transfer, transport; removal, emigration; — naqala-t, murmuring of running water; also نقلا nuqalâ’, pl. of ناقل nâqil, relator; — ى naqliyy, ة copied; traditional; imitated, counterfeit; feigned, invented, seller of dried fruit; — ية naqliyya-t, costs of transport, carriage, porterage, postage, &c.; pl. naqliyyât, tales.

(نقم) naqam, INF. naqm, eat greedily; I, INF. naqm, tiniqqâm, revenge one's self upon, punish, chastise; hate, abhor, loathe; revile, overwhelm with reproaches; — naqim, A, INF. naqam, revenge one's self; — III. INF. munâqama-t, vex, torment (m.); — VIII. INF. intiqâm, take revenge upon, punish, chastise; bear a grudge to (على ‘ala); — X. INF. istinqâm, id.

نقم *naqm*, revenge, punishment; grudge, hatred, malice; anger; — *naqam*, middle of the road; — ة *naqma-t*, *niqma-t*, *naqima-t*, pl. *niqam*, *naqim*, *naqimât*, revenge, chastisement, punishment; anger, hatred; torment, pain; — *niqma-t*, violence; harshness.

(نقنق) *naqnaq*, INF. ة croak continually (frog); cluck; be deeply set (eye); (m.) scold; contradict always.

نقنق *niqniq*, pl. *naqâniq*, ostrich; timid; fugitive; light.

(نقه) *naqah*, INF. *naqh*, *nuqûh*, begin to recover, be still weak; INF. *naqh*, comprehend, understand; — *naqih*, A, INF. *naqah*, begin to recover; understand; — IV. INF. *inqâh*, make one to recover, give one back health; — VIII. INF. *intiqâh*, recover; receive comfort; — X. INF. *istinqâh*, comprehend, understand.

نقه *naqh*, recovery, convalescence; — *nuqqah*, pl. of ناقه *nâqih*, still weak, but recovering.

نقوع *naqû'*, dissolved in water, macerated; (m.) dried apricot.

نقوة *naqwa-t*, selection.

(نقى) *naqa*, INF. *naqy*, suck the marrow out of a bone; INF. *niqy*, meet; — *naqî*, A, INF. *naqâ'*, *naqâ'a-t*, *naqâwa-t*, *nuqâwa-t*, be pure, be spotless; — II. INF. *tanqiya-t*, cleanse, purify; select the best; prune a vine-tree; pluck the ripest figs; — IV. INF. *inqâ'* = II; — V. INF. *tanaqqî*, select; be cleansed, pruned, selected; — VIII. INF. *intiqâ'* = V.

نقى *niqy*, pl. *anqâ'*, marrow; fat in the eye; — *naqiyy*, ة pl. *niqâ'*, *naqwâ'*, *anqiyâ'*, pure, spotless; holy; clear, serene; marrow; brain; finest flour; — *nuqiyy*, pl. of نقا *naqan*, *naqa*; — ة *naqiyya-t*, word, speech.

نقيب *naqîb*, pl. *nuqabâ'*, leader, chief; magistrate, head of a community; prefect, governor; corporal; intelligent man; who introduces, master of ceremonies; tongue of a balance; pipe, flute; — ة *naqîba-t*, soul, mind, natural disposition, character; advice, instruction; success.

نقيذة *naqîzat*, pl. *naqâ'iz*, a horse rescued from the enemy.

نقير *naqîr*, pl. *nuqur*, hollowed, excavated, deep; pl. *anqira-t*, cavity, pit, canal; trough; (m. pl. *nuqrân*), tub for clay; nature, natural disposition, character, manner; split in a date-stone, hence paltry, worthless; ن و قطمير *naqîr wa qiṭmîr*, to the smallest detail, quite minutely; — ة *niqqîra-t*, hand-drum, cymbal.

نقيز *naqîz*, acute pain.

نقيش *naqîś*, image, simile, symbol, similarity; similar, alike; companion.

نقيص *naqîṣ*, wanting (adj.), defective, bad, worthless; miserly; pure and sweet water; aroma, perfume; — ة *naqîṣa-t*, want, defect, shortcoming, fault, vice; disgrace.

نقيض *naqîḍ*, reversed, opposite, contrary; contrast; hostile; adversary; demolition, ruin, destruction, cracking, creaking or whizzing sound; cry of an eagle; — ة *naqîḍa-t*, response in a poetical contest; counter-assertion, contradiction.

نقيع *naqî'*, wholesome, fresh and quenching the thirst; dissolved in water, macerated; decoction; stagnant water; raisin or date wine; pl. *anqi'at*, overflowing well; scream, cry; — ة *naqî'a-t*, slaughtered animal and other preparations for the entertainment of guests.

نقيف *naqîf*, pl. *nuqf*, worm-eaten; split.

نقيق *naqîq*, croaking, clucking, quacking.

نقيل *naqîl*, ة foreign, strange; traveller (ابن نقيلة *ibn naqîla-t*, stranger); vagabond, vagrant; nomad; water-stream; a pace of the horse; road;— ة *naqîla-t*, pl. *naqîl*, *naqâ'il*, strip of leather used as a patch to protect a camel's hoof, patch.

نقيمة *naqîma-t*, nature, natural, character.

نقيه *naqîh*, weak.

(نكا) *naka'*, INF. *nak'*, take the crust off a wound not yet healed; hurt, wound, kill; pay one's debt to, fulfil one's obligations towards (2 acc.);— VIII. INF. *intikâ'*, receive payment of a debt.

نكات *nakkât*, slanderer; critic, censurer; disturber of peace or pleasure.

نكاثة *nukâṡat*, loosened end of a rope, parts separated into fibres.

نكاح *nikâḥ*, pl. *ankiḥa-t*, sexual intercourse, connection between married people; matrimony, marriage; dowry; — *nakkâḥ*, who has frequent sexual intercourse; who possesses many wives.

نكارة *nakâra-t*, difficulty; prudence, cunning.

نكاز *nakkâz*, pl. *-ât*, *nakâkîz*, a seemingly headless poisonous snake.

نكاس *nukâs*, relapse.

نكاش *nikâś*, digging up (s.).

نكاف *nukâf*, tumour on a camel's throat.

نكاكيز *nakâkîz*, pl. of نكاز *nakkâz*.

نكال *nakâl*, ة *nakâla-t*, pl. *ankâl*, exemplary punishment, exhibition in the pillory; warning, example.

نكاية *nikâya-t*, wounding, killing (s.); slaughter, massacre.

(نكب) *nakab*, U, INF. *nakb*, *nukûb*, deviate; INF. *nakb*, upturn and empty; throw away; hurt, injure; INF. *nakb*, *nukb*, make unhappy, render miserable; INF. *nukûb*, blow from a lateral direction; INF. *nukûb*, *nikâba-t*, be a prefect, superior, or helper;— *nakib*, A, INF. *nakab*, deviate; limp in consequence of a disease of the shoulders; — II. INF. *tankîb*, cause to turn aside from the road and to alight; — IV. INF. *inkâb*, render miserable;— V. INF. *tanakkub*, swerve; hang over the shoulder; — VIII. INF. *intikâb*, take upon or hang over one's shoulder.

نكب *nakab*, pain in the shoulder and limping (s.) in consequence; inclination; — ة *nakba-t*, pl. *-ât*, sore on the foot caused by stones; calamity, adversity, misery, distress; national calamity, plague; illness; disgrace, infamy.

نكبا *nakbâ'*, f. of انكب *ankab*, limping as above, see (نكب); — lateral wind.

نكبتى *nakbatiyy*, unhappy, miserable; wicked, vile (m.).

(نكت) *nakat*, U, INF. *nakt*, poke the ground with a stick or finger; stir up the ground with a piece of wood; throw one on his head; leap high in running; — II. INF. *tankît*, cavil at, censure, criticise; contradict always; seek a quarrel; give a good answer, crack a joke, say something witty; — VIII. INF. be thrown or fall on one's head; — ة *nukta-t*, pl. *nikât*, *nuka-t*, point, dot, tittle; spot; pl. *nukat*, finesse, witty saying, witticism, anecdote; artificial equivocal answer, conceit; (m.) odd person; (m.) merry-andrew.

(نكث) *nakaṡ*, U, I, INF. *nakṡ*, untwist; break an oath or compact; — VI. INF. *tanâkuṡ*, break mutually one's word or compact; —VIII. INF. *intikâṡ*, be dissolved; turn from one business to another.

نكث *nakṡ*, breach of a compact;— *nikṡ*, pl. *ankâṡ*, anything torn or spoiled.

(نكح) *nakaḥ*, A, I, INF. *nikâḥ*, lie

with, have connection, marry, visit one's wife; be married; — II. INF. *tankîḥ*, flee from the place where it (an animal) has been beaten (m.); — III. INF. *munâkaḥa-t*, have connection, lie with; — IV. INF. *inkâḥ*, give one a woman in marriage (2 acc.); marry (a.); — VI. INF. *tanâkuḥ*, ask from one another a woman in marriage; lie with one another; — X. INF. *istinkâḥ*, ask in marriage, marry (n.).

نكح *nakḥ*, pudenda of a woman; sexual intercourse; married woman; — *nukaḥ*, ة *nukaḥa-t*= نكاح *nakkâḥ*.

(نكخ) *nakah*, INF. *nakh*, hit or injure one at the throat.

(نكد) *nakad*, U, INF. *nakd*, cry out or croak with all its might (raven); prevent, hinder; refuse, withhold from, give but scantily; — *nakid*, U, INF. *nakad*, be hard and difficult to bear; be hard and without any good quality; be useless; contain but little water; — II. INF. *tankîd*, make one's life hard to; molest, torment; — III. INF. *munâkada-t*, place difficulties in one's way; — V. INF. *tanakkud*, suffer, endure; be difficult to bear; — X. INF. *istinkâd*, find hard and toilsome; feel aversion, disinclination.

نكد *nakd*, *nukd*, little, a trifle; — *nakad*, hard life, adversities; — *nakid*, *nakad*, pl. *ankâd*, *anâkîd*, hard towards others, who refuses every service, unaccommodating; hard and miserable (life).

(نكر) *nakir*, A, INF. *nakr*, *nukr*, *nakar*, *nukur*, *nukûr*, *nakîr*, ignore; mistake, misjudge; deny, disapprove, reject, condemn, protest against; refuse, decline; — *nakur*, INF. *nakâra-t*, be hard and difficult; be unknown, unaccustomed; be of a sharp intellect, prudent, cunning; — II. INF. *tankîr*, render unrecognizable, disfigure; leave a word indefinite, without the article; generalize; — III. INF. *munâkara-t*, contend, fight, dispute; wage war against; — IV. INF. *inkâr*, ignore; deny, abjure, disapprove, reject; — V. INF. *tanakkur*, become unrecognizable, disfigured, change countenance; disguise one's self, guard an incognito; estrange one's self from (ل *li*); — VI. INF. *tanâkur*, ignore; pretend to ignore; treat one another as unknown, a stranger, or hostile; quarrel, brawl, dispute; — X. INF. *istinkâr*, ignore; ask after what one does not know; disapprove of, abhor; disbelieve.

نكر *nakr*, *nikr*, *nukr*, also *nakra-t*, sharpness of intellect, prudence; cunning; deceit; — *nukr*, *nukur*, sharp, prudent, cunning; anything unknown, unwonted, unaccustomed; anything disagreeable, to be disapproved of, rejectable; incognito, disguise; — *nakir*, *nakur*, pl. *ankâr*, very sagacious, prudent, cunning; *nakir*, ة, indefinite, without article; — ة *nakra-t*, entertaining comical story; — *nakara-t*, نكران *nakarân*, ignorance; denial, abjuration; disapproval, rejection; refusal; — *nakira-t*, misfortune, calamity; blood, pus, &c. issuing from the body.

(نكز) *nakaz*, U, INF. *nakz* (m. also نكوز *nakwaz*), prick with anything pointed, goad; put to the spit; bite, sting; push with the elbow; beat; chase away, turn off; desist; INF. *nukûz*, disappear in the ground (water); — *nakiz*, A, INF. *nakaz*, be waterless, empty.

نكز *nakz*, putting in, pricking, goading (s.); — *nikz*, bad, worthless; — *nukuz*, pl. of نكوز *nakûz*; — ة *nakza-t*, prick, puncture.

(نكس) *nakas*, U, INF. *naks*, turn upside down; hang down one's

head; do anything in reversed order (as reading, &c.); be perverse; bring on a relapse; pass. *nukis*, the illness returns; (m.) bend one's head forward; (m.) lower the flag; — II. INF. *tankîs*, turn upside down; — V. INF. *tanakkus*, be turned upside down; hang down one's head; — VIII. INF. *intikâs*=V.; have a relapse.

نكس *niks*, pl. *ankâs*, weak, powerless; mean, niggardly; broken in the notch; — *nuks*, relapse.

(نكش) *nakaś*, I, U, INF. *nakś* (also VIII.), clean the well from mud, &c.; consume entirely, graze off; bring to an end, have done with (من *min*); dig up; — II. INF. *tankîś*, make one to dig up (m.); — VIII. INF. *intikâś*, see I.

(نكص) *nakaṣ*, I, INF. *nakṣ*, *nukûṣ*, *mankaṣ*, withdraw from, desist.

(نكظ) *nakaẕ*, INF. *nakẕ*, suffer from violent hunger, be famished; urge to haste; (also II.) make a thing difficult for; — *nakiẕ*, A, INF. *nakaẕ*, hasten (n.);—II. INF. *tankîẕ*, see I.;=IV; — IV. INF. *inkâẕ*, urge to haste; — V. INF. *tanakkuẕ*, turn (n.); be miserly; suffer hardship in travelling.

(نكع) *naka'*, INF. *nak'*, hurry (a.) from, chase away, make to desist in haste from, to give up in disgust; desist; refuse or withhold the payment of a debt; make payment; kick one's buttocks; — *naki'*, A, INF. *naka'*, have a red nose, be reddish; — IV. INF. *inkâ'*, urge to haste, make desist from; weaken, tire out, jade.

نكع *nuka'*, red colour; — ة *nak'a-t*, kick on the buttocks, blow in the ribs, buffet;—*naka'a-t*, red dye; — *naki'a-t*, red (f.).

(نكف) *nakaf*, U, INF. *nakf*, endure; (also X.) find again the lost track of a camel; wipe away; desist; scorn; — *nakif*, A, INF. *nakaf*, scorn, reject; be exempt from (من *min*); pain (n.), ache; —III. INF. *munâkafa-t*, vex, tease, torment (m.); — IV. INF. *inkâf*, keep off anything disagreeable or adverse; — VI. INF. *tanâkuf*, quarrel; — VIII. INF. *intikâf*, endure; desist; — X. INF. *istinkâf*, feel aversion, scorn, reject; desist, abstain from; be haughty, arrogant; think one (ل *li*) free from (عن *'an*); see I.; — ة *nakfa-t*, *nukfa-t*, *nakafa-t*, pl. *nakafât*, base of the chin-bone.

(نكل) *nakal*, U, I, INF. *nukûl*, shrink, desist, shirk; — *nakil*, A, INF. *nakal*, id.; take a warning from; — II. INF. *tankîl*, make one a warning example; — IV. INF. *inkâl*, prevent, repel; — V. INF. *tanakkul*, make an example of.

نكل *nikl*, pl. *ankâl*, fetter, chain, bracelet, necklace; a kind of bridle; also ة *nukla-t*, bulwark; *nukl*, ة *nukla-t*, punishment as warning example; what brings on punishment; — *nakal*, brave man; generous horse.

(نكنك) *naknak*, INF. ة, press a debtor hard; do a thing well.

(نكه) *nakah*, I, A. INF. *nakh*, breathe into another's nose; glow; *nakah*, A, also—*nakih*, A, INF. *nakh*, smell another's breath (to know what he has been eating or drinking); — X. INF. *istinkâh*, id.; — ة *nakha-t*, smell of the breath.

نكوز *nakûz*, pl. *nukuz*, well with water; — *nakwaz*, see نكز *nakaz*.

(نكى) *naka*, I, INF. *nikâya-t* (also IV.), hurt, injure, wound, kill; take the crust from a wound; (also IV.) vex, torment, anger, enrage; — IV. INF. *inkâ'*, see I.; —VIII. INF. *intikâ'*, be angry and abuse.

نكيبا *nukaibâ'*, dimin. of نكبا *nakbâ'*.

نكيثة *nakîṯa-t*, serious business; strength, power, might; utmost effort; soul, mind, spirit; natural disposition, temper; breach of promise.

نكير *nakîr*, denial, disapproval, refusal, rejection, INF. of (نكر); distasteful, disagreeable, objectionable, rejectable; change, alteration; degenerated, fallen off, decayed; impregnable; one of the two angels of death.

نكيف *nakîf*, gland.

(نلك) *nulk*, *nilk*, ة, plane-tree; medlar-tree.

(نم) *namm*, U, I, INF. *namm*, spread about what another has said to make mischief; distort and disfigure a speech with lies; slander; emit an odour, smell (n.); disclose; — III. INF. *munâma-t*, try to injure one by spreading about and distorting what he has said.

نم *namm*, breath, breeze; movement, motion; pl. *-ûn*, *animmâ'*, tale-bearer, slanderer; — *numm*, pl. slanderers;—ة *namma-t*, slanderess;—*nimma-t*, ant, louse.

(نما) *nam'*, *nama'*, small lice, nits; — *namâ'*, growth, increase; — ة *namât*, pl. *namā*, a small kind of ant; — *nummât*, n. u. of نمى *nummā*.

نماس *nammâs*, tale-bearer, informer, slanderer.

نماص *nimâṣ*, thread passed through a needle; — *numâṣ*, pl. *numuṣ*, *anmiṣa-t*, month.

نمال *nammâl*, tale-bearer, slanderer; — *.

نمام *nammâm*, tale-bearer, slanderer; betrayer; wild thyme;— ة *namâma-t*, mint (plant); — ى *namâma*, pl. of نمى *nummā*.

(نمر) *namar*, U, INF. *namr*, ascend, mount; — *namir*, A, INF. *namar*, be spotted, dotted; be angry, be malicious; — II. INF. *tanmîr*, get angry; be malicious; (m.) number, count; — IV. INF. *inmâr*, meet with good water; — V. INF. *tanammur*, resemble a panther or tiger; be angry with; be malicious; (m.) be numbered, counted.

نمر *nimr*, *namir*, pl. *numr*, *nimâr*, *numûr*, *nimâra-t*, *anmur*, *anmâr*, panther, leopard; (m.) tiger; good, wholesome; sincere; much, many; first ancestor of an Arab tribe; — ة *numra-t*, pl. *numar*, spot on a ground of different colour; (m.) number, sort, kind (of goods); — *namira-t*, female panther; tigress; pl. *namir*, small part of a cloud; a striped stuff; trap for wolves.

نمرا *namrâ'*, f. of انمر *anmar*, spotted, &c.

نمرق *namraq*, *nimriq*, *numruq*, ة *namraqa-t*, &c., pl. *namâriq*, saddle-cushion.

نمرود *namrûd*, *numrûd*, pl. *namârida-t*, Nimrod.

نمرى *namariyy*, like a panther or tiger; belonging to the tribe of Namir.

(نمس) *namas*, I, INF. *nams*, keep secret, be silent about, conceal; (also III.) make one sharer in a secret, one's confidant; — *namis*, A, INF. *namas*, be spoiled, corrupted; — III. INF. *munâmasa-t*, see I.; go to one's hiding-place; — IV. INF. *inmâs*, bring about discontent or discord;—VII. INF. *innimâs*, conceal one's self, hide (m.).

نمس *nims*, ة, pl. *numûs*, ichneumon; ferret; weasel; — نمس *nums*, the Qaṭa-birds, pl. انمس *anmas*, dark-grey.

(نمش) *namaś*, U, INF. *namś* (also IV.), slander; lie; (also II.) whisper to; eat the ground bare; pick up;—*namiś*, A, INF. *namaś*, be spotted or dotted; be marked by a disease; be freckled; — II. INF. *tanmîś*, see I.; wet the grain; — IV. INF. *inmâś*, see I.

نمش *namś*, *namaś*, ة, red spots, freckles; — *namiś*, spotted; striped.

(نمص) *namaṣ*, U, INF. *namṣ*, pull out hair; — II. INF. *tanmîṣ*, *tanmâṣ*, id.; — IV. INF. *inmâṣ*,

sprout, spring forth; — V. INF. *tanammuṣ*, pull out the eyebrows.

نمص *namaṣ*, fine hair or down; also *nimṣ*, a plant; — *numuṣ*, pl. of نماص *numâṣ*.

(نمط) — II. *nammaṭ*, INF. *tanmîṭ*, show, indicate, point out, lead.

نمط *namaṭ*, pl. *nimâṭ*, *anmâṭ*, manner, way, fashion, calibre, class; woollen covering; hand-basket; company of men;— ى *namaṭiyy*, maker of woollen coverings.

(نمغ) — II. *nammag*, INF. *tanmîg*, be striped white, black, and red; be fickle; — ة *namaga-t*, mountain-ridge, summit; crown of the head; middle-class.

(نمق) *namaq*, U, INF. *namq*, strike one with the palm of the hand on the eye; (also II.) write with a fine and bold hand, write; (also II.) adorn; — II. INF. *tanmîq*, see I.; — IV. INF. *inmâq*, bear stoneless dates; — ة *namaqa-t*, ready sale of goods.

(نمل) *namal*, U, INF. *naml* (also IV.), slander; climb; — *namil*, A, INF. *namal*, be benumbed, feel as if crept over by ants;—III. INF. *munâmala-t*, walk like one fettered;— IV. INF. *inmâl*, see I.;— V. INF. *tanammul*, swarm like ants.

نمل *naml*, ة (*numl*, *namul*, *numal*, *numul*), pl. *nimâl*, ant; small pustules or blisters; — *namil*, ة, active, always on the move, restless; abounding with ants; pl. *anmâl*, given to slander; — ة *namla-t*, calumny, slander; — ى *namlā*, f. restlessly active.

نمنم *nimnim* (also نمنيم *nimnîm*), trace of the wind in sand; also ة *nimnima-t*, white spot on the nail; *nimnima-t*, wren; — *namnam*, INF. ة, make furrows in the sand; adorn, paint, imprint, embroider; write beautifully; embellish with lies.

(نمه) *namih*, A, INF. *namah*, be perplexed, confused.

(نمو) *namâ*, U, INF. *numuww*, grow, increase; rise; prosper, thrive, gain; make progress; grow deeper, more intense (colour); — IV. INF. *inmâ'*, make to grow, multiply; make to prosper, to make progress, to gain.

نمو *numuww*, growth, increase, thriving (s.), prosperity, progress; gain; rising of the water.

نمودج *numûdaj*, model.

نموم *namûm*, slanderer, liar, traitor.

(نمى) *nama*, I, INF. *namy*, *namâ'*, *numiyy*, *namiyya-t*, grow, increase (n.), sprout; rise; raise, elevate; stir the fire; grow fat; reach, be reported to; (also II.) report, ascribe a saying to; lift a thing up and place it on the top of another; — II. INF. *tanmiya-t*, grow, increase (n.); see I.; — IV. INF. *inmâ'*, grow, increase (n.), rise; make to grow, increase (a.); put upon; slander; — V. INF. *tanammî*, rise and fly elsewhere; — VIII. INF. *intimâ*, id.; descend from, claim relationship to.

نمى *nummā*, *nummiyy*, somebody, anybody; *nummā*, n.u. نماة *nummât*, pl. *namâma*, coin, piece of money; scale (of a balance); hostility; stratagem, deceit; treachery; fault, vice; substance, essence; nature, character, genius; — ة *nammiya-t*, growth;— *nummiyya-t*, female ring-dove.

نمير *namîr*, wholesome; sincere; much, many.

نميص *namîṣ*, pulled out.

نميقة *namîqa-t*, pl. *namâ'iq*, letter.

نميلة *namîla-t*, slander.

نميمة *namîma-t*, slander; whisper; twang of a bow; scratching of a pen.

نميمى *namîmiyy*, slanderous.

نن *nann*, thin hair; food.

(نندل) *nandul*, *nindul*, *nindal*, نندلان

nindulân, nightmare; du. *nandalân*, two teats.

(نها) *naha'*, INF. *nah'*, be full, crammed; — INF. *nah'*, *nuh'*, *nuhû'*, be partly raw, underdone; — *nahi'*, A, id.; — *nahu'*, INF. *nahâ'a-t*, *nuhâ'a-t*, id.; — IV. INF. *inhâ'*, let the meat be underdone.

نها *nihâ'*, rain-pit; pond; end, limit, extreme; (also *nihan*, *niha*) pl. *nuhât*, glass, vial; pl. of نهى *nahy*; — *nihâ'*, *nuhâ'*, number, troop; — ة *nuhât*, pl. of ناهى *nâhî*, forbidding, &c.; — ةء *nahâ'a-t*, the being underdone of meat.

نهاب *nahhâb*, plunderer, robber; lion.

نهابير *nahâbîr*, pl. of نهبورة *nuhbûra-t*.

نهات *nuhât*, bellowing, roaring (s.); — *nahhât*, bellowing, roaring, groaning (adj.).

نهاد *nuhâd*, number of men, troop (100).

نهار *nahâr*, pl. *anhur*, *nuhur*, (m.) *nahârât*, day; daylight, brightness of light; pl. *anhira-t*, *nuhur*, young bustard.

نهاز *nuhâz*, ة *nuhâza-t*, measure, quantity.

نهاس *nahhâs*, lion; sparrow-hawk.

نهاض *nihâḍ*, *nuhâḍ*, steep mountain-paths; — *nahhâḍ*, swift.

نهاق *nuhâq*, braying (s.).

نهاكة *nahâka-t*, INF. of (نهك).

نهال *nihâl*, pl. of ناهل *nâhil*, thirsty, &c.

نهام *nahâm*, *nihâm*, *nuhâm*, ى *nahâmiyy*, *nihâmiyy*, *nuhâmiyy*, smith; carpenter; — *nuhâm*, owl; also ى *nuhâmiyy*, monk, abbot; — *nahhâm*, lion; middle of the road; ى *nihâmiyy*, open road; — ة *nahâma-t*, greed, voracity; lion.

نهاوش *nahâwiś*, pl. calamity, distress; injury, wrong, violence.

نهاوة *nahâwa-t*, intellect, prudence; =نهاءة *nahâ'a-t*.

نهاية *nahâya-t*, intellect, prudence; — *nihâya-t*, extreme limit, extreme; end, conclusion; aim, purpose; excess; anything very striking; *nihâyat-an*, after all, nevertheless.

(نهب) *nahab*, A, U, INF. *nahb*, seize and carry away, rob, plunder; revile, abuse, scold; seize by the heel; — *nahib*, A, INF. *nahab*, rob, plunder; — III. INF. *munâhaba-t*, take away, rob; dispute; contend, vie; talk about, revile; — IV. INF. *inhâb*, allow to plunder, leave to plunder or as booty; — VI. INF. *tanâhub*, rob one another; — VIII. INF. *intihâb*, take away, rob, plunder, be plundered or robbed.

نهب *nahb*, ة *nahba-t*, robbery, plunder; *nahb*, pl. *nihâb*, *nuhûb*, plunder, booty; — ة *nuhba-t*, pl. *nuhab*, booty.

نهبرة *nahbara-t*, long and thin; on the point of death (woman); — *nuhbura-t*, pl. *nahâbir*, pit between sand-hills; dangerous place; precipice, abyss; hell; danger.

(نهبل) *nahbal*, ة, old; — INF. ة, grow old; walk with difficulty.

نهبور *nuhbûr*, sand-hill; ة *nuhbûra-t*, pl. *nahâbir*=نهبرة *nuhbura-t*.

نهبوغ *nuhbûġ*, long and fast-sailing ships; a bird; a kind of beans.

نهبى *nuhbā*, left to plunder; booty.

(نهت) *nahat*, I, INF. *nuhât*, *nahît*, roar; snort; groan.

(نهتر) *nahtar*, INF. ة, tell lies against (على *'ala*).

(نهج) *nahaj*, INF. *nahj*, open a road, trace out; be distinct and open; follow a road; — *nahij*, A, INF. *nahaj*, be out of breath, pant; (also *nahaj*, *nahuj*) be used up, worn out; — II. INF. *tanhîj*, encourage, stimulate; — IV. INF. *inhâj*, open or trace out a road for; be or become open and distinctly visible; make to get out of breath; — VIII. INF.

intihâj, walk in, strike in, enter on; — X. INF. *istinhâj*, be open and distinct; follow another's way, follow, imitate.

نهج *nahj*, open road; path; manner, ways; — *nahaj*, breathlessness; asthma; — ة *nahja-t*, heavy breathing.

(نهد) *nahad*, A, U, INF. *nahd*, *nahad*, rise and rush against; INF. *nuhûd*, grow round and rise, swell, be high (bosom); be high-bosomed; — *nahud*, INF. *nuhûda-t*, be tall and fleshy; — II. INF. *tanhîd*, have large breasts; — III. INF. *munâhada-t*, draw or cast lots with; share in expenses with; come to close quarters with; — IV. INF. *inhâd*, make a present large; fill or almost fill up a vessel; — V. INF. *tanahhud*, sigh, groan; — VI. INF. *tanâhud*, draw equal lots, divide equally between each other; share in the expenses.

نهد *nahd*, equal division; anything high, elevated, sublime; high bosom; handsome and full in flesh; good steed; generous and aspiring; lion.

نهدا *nahdâ'*, pl. *nuhd*, high-bosomed.

نهدان *nahdân*, nearly full.

(نهر) *nahar*, INF. *nahr*, cause to flow; flow abundantly; dig until one meets with water; scare away by shouting; (m.) call up, summon; — *nahir*, A, INF. *nahar*, dig until one meets with water; — IV. INF. *inhâr* = *nahir*; enlarge the bed of a river; — VIII. INF. *intihâr*, scare away by shouting; (m.) scold; — X. INF. *istinhâr*, spread far (n.); enlarge its bed (river).

نهر *nahr*, *nahar*, pl. *anhur*, *anhâr*, *nuhûr*, *nuhur*, *nuhr*, river, stream, running water; ن السلام *nahr as-salâm*, Tigris; — *nahir*, broad; clear; doing anything in open daylight; — *nuhur*, pl. of نهار *nahâr*; — ة *nahra-t*, invitation; plunder, robbery.

(نهرج) *nahraj*, broad, wide; — INF. ة, lie with.

نهری *nahriyy*, referring or belonging to rivers.

(نهز) *nahaz*, INF. *nahz*, thrust, beat; push back, keep off, prevent; be near; goad on, urge; shake; butt; — III. INF. *munâhaza-t*, approach, be near to; come in advance of the game; — VIII. INF. *intihâz*, seize the opportunity.

نهز *nahz*, number, quantity; — *nahiz*, lion; — ة *nahza-t*, shaking (s.), push, thrust; — *nuhza-t*, opportunity.

(نهس) *nahas*, INF. *nahs* (also VIII.), seize the flesh with the front teeth and tear it off; bite; — *nahis*, A, INF. *nahas*, id.; — VIII. INF. *intihâs*, see I.; revile, abuse.

نهس *nuhas*, pl. *nihsân*, sparrow-hawk.

(نهسر) *nahsar*, voracious; wolf; cross between a wolf and a hyena; swift; — INF. ة, cut meat; consume, swallow.

(نهش) *nahaś*, INF. *nahś*, sting, bite, bite with the front or molar teeth; throw into poverty; pass. be thin, lean; — *nahiś*, A, be out of breath; — VI. INF. *tanâhuś*, bite one another.

(نهشل) *nahśal*, wolf; hawk; trembling with old age; — INF. ة, be very old; bite; eat very greedily.

(نهض) *nahaḍ*, INF. *nahḍ*, *nuhûḍ*, rise; sprout, spring forth, grow; lift up, carry (ب *bi*); spread the wings for flying; — III. INF. *munâhaḍa-t*, rise against, oppose, contend with; — IV. INF. *inhâḍ*, bid to rise; incite, stimulate; — VI. INF. *tanâhuḍ*, rise against one another; — VIII. INF. *intihâḍ*, be awakened, bid to rise, put on one's feet; rise, get up; be instigated,

stimulated ; — X. INF. *istinhâḍ*, bid to rise ; instigate, stimulate ; bid to set to work.

نهض *nahḍ*, pl. *anhuḍ*, middle part of a camel's shoulder ; wrong, act of violence ; — ة *nahḍa-t*, rising (s.) ; departure, start.

(نهضل) *nahḍal*, old.

(نهط) *nahaṭ*, INF. *nahṭ*, pierce.

(نهع) *naha'*, INF. *nuhû'*, belch.

(نهف) *nahaf*, INF. *nahf*, be astonished, perplexed.

(نهق) *nahaq*, *nahiq*, A, INF. *nuhâq*, *nahîq*, bray, cry out.

نهق *nahq*, a bird ; a kind of cress.

(نهك) *nahak*, INF. *nahk*, suck out the breast ; drink out ; torture, put to torture ; punish cruelly ; weaken, unnerve ; (also INF. *nahâka-t*) emaciate and exhaust ; INF. *nahâka-t*, conquer, get the better of, overpower ; wear out a dress ; be excessive in (من *min*) ; damage one's honour and good name ; also — *nahuk*, INF. *nahâka-t*, attend to zealously ; pass. *nuhik*, and — *nahik*, A, INF. *nahak*, suffer from a chronic disease, grow thin and weak ; — IV. INF. *inhâk*, punish cruelly, torture ; — VIII. INF. *intihâk*, emaciate and exhaust ; damage one's honour ; diminish the value of a thing ; violate ; — ة *nahka-t*, pain, torture, cruel punishment ; emaciation and exhaustion by illness.

(نهل) *nahil*, A, INF. *nahal*, *manhal*, take the first draught ; quench one's thirst ; (m.) be exhausted and tired ; — IV. INF. *inhâl*, make the camels take their first draught, water them early in the morning.

نهل *nahal*, first draught ; — ة *nahla-t*, draught, also ى *nahla*, camels taking the first draught.

نهلان *nahlân*, taking the first draught ; suffering from thirst ; (m.) exhausted, tired.

(نهم) *naham*, A, I, INF. *nahm*, *nahma-t*, *nahîm*, shout to the camels and urge them to greater speed ; address violently, threaten ; groan deeply, roar ; cry out ; — *nahim*, groan deeply, roar ; INF. *naham*, *nahâma-t*, also pass. *nuhim*, have ravenous hunger, be insatiable, eat greedily or too much.

نهم *naham*, ravenous hunger ; insatiable greed ; gluttony ; — *nahim*, voracious, insatiable ; glutton ; — *nuhm*, Satan, servants of Satan ; — ة *nahma-t*, greed, voracity ; want, need ; roaring, screaming, shouting (s.).

(نهنه) *nahnah*, INF. ة, push back, thrust aside, repel, refrain from (a.) ; scare away by shouting ; overwhelm with blows, beat fiercely ; — II. INF. *tanahnuh*, abstain, refrain from (n.) ; (m.) be fiercely beaten ; (m.) be emaciated and exhausted.

نهو *nah'*, *nuhû'*, see (نها).

نهود *nuhûd*, rising (s.), advancing against the enemy.

نهوس *nahûs*, lion.

نهوض *nahûḍ*, rising, getting up (adj.) ; — *nuhûḍ*, rising (s.).

نهوك *nahûk*, strong, bold.

(نهى) *naha*, A, I, INF. *nahy*, forbid, prohibit ; desist, give up ; (m.) INF. *nahw*, carry out, perform ; pass. *nuhî*, be finally brought to, arrive at, extend to ; — *nahû*, INF. *nahâwa-t*, *nahâya-t*, be intelligent, wise, prudent ; — II. INF. *tanhiya-t*, come, attain to ; — IV. INF. *inhâ'*, make to attain to, lead to a certain point ; bring to an end, accomplish, complete ; decide ; bring news ; — VI. INF. *tanâhî*, reach ; arrive ; come to the utmost limits, reach one's aim ; be extreme ; be brought to a conclusion, carried out, accomplished, perfect ; be limited, restricted ; restrain one another

from what is bad; — VIII. INF. *intihâ'*, arrive finally at, extend to; finish by; be brought to an end, be at an end, be perfect; abstain from.

نهى *nahy*, pl. *nawâhî*, prohibition; negation; prudence; نهيك *nahyuka*=ناهيك *nâhîka*, see ناهى *nâhî*; — *nahy*, *nihy*, pl. *anh-in*, *anhî*, *anhâ'*, *nuhiyy*, *nihâ'*, rain-pit, pond, pool; — *nahî*, intelligent, prudent; — *nahiyy*, pl. *anhiyâ'*, id.; forbidden, prohibited; — *nahi'*, half raw, underdone; — ة *nuhya-t*, pl. *nuha-n*, *nuha*, prohibition; anything forbidden, prohibited; prudence, intelligence; extreme, limit, end; — *nihya-t*, *nahiyya-t*, fat.

نهيبى *nuhaibâ*, *nuhhaibâ*, robbery, plunder.

نهيت *nahît*, roaring, cry, outcry.

نهيدة *nahîda-t*, a dish made of flour and the marrow of colocynth.

نهير *nahîr*, abundant, plentiful.

نهيق *nahîq*, braying (s.).

نهيك *nahîk*, strong, bold; bloodthirsty; sharp; generous and handsome; also *nuhaik*, a fly.

نهيم *nahîm*, roaring, screaming, shouting; insatiable; glutton.

نهيى *nahî'*, half raw, underdone.

(نو) *nâ'*, U, INF. *nau'*, *tanwâ'*, rise with difficulty (under a load); — INF. *nau'*, press heavily upon; break down; set in the west, while another luminary is rising in the east; remove to a distance; desist; — III. INF. *niwâ'*, *munâwa'a-t*, oppose, contend, vie with; — IV. INF. *inâ'a-t*, press upon; — X. INF. *istinâ'a-t*, ask for a present.

نو *nau'*, gift, present; pl. *anwâ'*, *nû'ân*, star or its setting in the west, while another (رقيب, *raqîb*) is rising in the east, which forebodes rain and storm, hence rain, tempest, hurricane.

نوا *niwâ'*, dispute, contest, INF. (نو III.); pl. of ناوى, fat; — ة *nawât*, intention, purpose; pl. *nawa*, *niwiyy*, *nuwiyy*, *anwâ'*, date-stone; a weight (three to five drachms); ounce of gold; a number (ten, twenty).

نواب *nawwâb*, guard; — *nuwwâb*, pl. of نائب *nâ'ib*, substitute, &c.

نوابت *nawâbit*, pl. inexperienced youths.

نوابع *nawâbi'*, pores.

نواتى *nawâtî*, pl. of نوتاة *nautât*; — *nawâtiyy*, pl. of نوتى *nûtiyy*.

نواجب *nawâjib*, pl. pure, unmixed; noblemen.

نواح *nawâḥ*, bewailing of the dead; — *nuwwâḥ*, tract, coast; — ة *nawwâḥa-t*, mourning woman.

نواخذة *nawâḫiza-t*, pl. of *naḫizâ*, sea-captain, &c.

نوادى *nawâdî*, pl. events.

نوار *nawâr*, flight; pl. *nûr*, avoiding even appearances, innocent; — *nuwwâr*, ة, pl. *nawâwîr*, blossom, flower; tinsel; (m.) month of May.

نواس *nuwâs*, waving curl; — *nawwâs*, moved, oscillating.

نواسير *nawâsîr*, pl. of ناسور *nâsûr*.

نواشغ *nawâšig*, gutters, channels.

نواصب *nawâṣib*, the opponents of Ali.

نواطير *nawâṭîr*, pl. of ناطور *nâṭûr*.

نواعير *nawâ'îr*, pl. of ناعور *nâ'ûr*.

نوافس *nawâfis*, pl. of نفسا *nafsâ'*.

نوافق *nawâfiq*, pl. of نافقا *nâfiqâ'*, hole of the field-mouse.

نواق *nawwâq*, experienced, apt; camel-driver, trainer.

نواقر *nawâqir*, forcible proofs; revilings, abuses; calamities.

نواقيس *nawâqîs*, pl. of ناقوس *nâqûs*.

نواكة *nawâka-t*, stupidity.

نوال *nawâl*, gift, present, bounty, favour; liberality; portion, lot; measure, weight; anything beseeming, duty, right; — ة *nawâla-t*, gift, present; mat; hut, cottage; brothel.

نوام *nuwâm*, sleepiness; — *nawwâm*,

who sleeps much, lie-a-bed; — *nuwwâm*, pl. of نائم *nâ'im*, sleeping, &c.

نواميس *nawâmîs*, pl. of ناموس *nâmûs*.

نوان *nu'ân*, pl. of نو *nau'*.

نواهة *nawwâha-t*, mourning-woman.

نواهى *nawâhî*, pl. of ناهية *nâhiya-t* and نهى *nahy*, prohibition, &c.

نواوير *nawâwîr*, pl. of نوار *nuwwâr*.

نواويس *nawâwîs*, pl. of ناووس *nâwûs*, fire-temple, &c.

نوای *nû'â*, water-ditch round a tent.

نوايا *nawâyâ*, pl. of نية *niyya-t*.

(نوب) *nâb*, U, INF. *naub*, *manâb*, supply one's place, substitute, be one's vicegerent or lieutenant; INF. *naub*, *nauba-t*, come upon, befall; be near; INF. *naub*, return from time to time; visit; return to God in repentance, repent, attend to religious duties; — III. INF. *munâwaba-t*, follow on one's heels, come behind; — IV. INF. *inâba-t*, make one to supply another's place, appoint as a substitute, &c.; return repentingly to God; grant; come from time to time; — VI. INF. *tanâwub*, approach in turns; — VIII. INF. *intiyâb*, observe mutually one's turn; befall; visit from time to time; — X. INF. *istinâba-t*, wish one for or appoint one as a substitute, &c.; ask for a substitute.

نوب *naub*, event, case, turn; success, result; cause, reason; strength, power, might; (m.) بنوب *bi-naub*, entirely, altogether; also *nûb*, pl. of نائب *nâ'ib*, substitute, &c.; — *nûb*, Nubian, Ethiopian; — ة *nauba-t*, *nûba-t*, pl. *nuwab*, returning period, turn; what happens in turns or alternately; case, opportunity; time (once, &c.); befalling, calamity; — *nauba-t*, degree, rank; guard, post, sentinel; music, concert, orchestra; (m.) musical clock or box; *naubât*, pl. drums, &c. which are beaten from time to time in front of a great man's residence; — *nûba-t*, Nubia.

نوبتجى *naubatjî*, musician (m.).

نوبتى *naubatiyy*, musician; — ة *naubatiyya-t*, orchestra.

(نوبع) *nauba'*, INF. ة, gush forth from the ground.

نوبى *nûbiyy*, Nubian.

(نوت) *nât*, U, INF. *naut*, totter in walking.

نوتاة *nautât*, pl. *nawâtî*, small, dwarfish.

نوتى *nûtiyy*, pl. *nawâtiyy*, (m.) *nûtiyya-t*, sailor, seafaring man; (m.) miser; — ة *nûtiyya-t*, navigation; navy.

(نوج) *nâj*, U, INF. *nauj*, dissemble, behave as a hypocrite.

نوج *na'uj*, violent; — *nu'uj*, journey; — ة *nauja-t*, storm, tempest, hurricane.

نوجر *naujar*, wooden frame of a plough.

(نوح) *nâḥ*, U, INF. *nauḥ*, *nuwâḥ*, *niyâḥ*, *niyâḥa-t*, *manâḥ*, bewail the dead; lament, sigh, cry, weep; — INF. *nauḥ*, coo; utter a rhythmic speech; — II. INF. *tanwîḥ*, bewail the dead in company; — III. INF. *munâwaḥa-t*, turn to, set one's self to; — V. INF. *tanawwuḥ*, oscillate, swing to and fro; — VI. INF. *tanâwuḥ*, lie opposite to one another; — X. INF. *istinâḥa-t*, bewail, lament, weep; howl; cause one to weep, touch.

نوح *nauḥ*, ة *nauḥa-t*, bewailing of the dead; *nauḥ*, rhythmical speech; cooing; pl. of نائحة *nâ'iḥa-t*, mourning woman; — *nûḥ*, Noah.

(نوخ) *nâḫ*, kneel down (camel); — II. INF. *tanwîḫ*, make to kneel down; encamp; — IV. INF. *inâḫa-t*=II.; — V. INF. *tanawwuḫ*, kneel down; make the she-camel kneel down to admit the stallion; — X. INF. *istinâḫa-t*, kneel down;

— ة *nauḥa-t*, standstill, stand, stop, halt.

نوحعة *nauḥa'a-t*, neck.

(نود) *nâd*, U, INF. *naud*, *nuwâd*, *nawadân*, totter; nod the head (as praying Jews); — V. INF. *tanawwud*, be moved, wave (branch).

نود *na'ud*, misfortune, calamity.

(نودا) *nauda'*, INF. ة, run.

نودل *naudal*, (female) breast; — INF. ة, wave, swing to and fro, oscillate, totter; hang flabbily down.

نوذخ *nauẕaḥ*, coward.

(نور) *nâr*, U, *naur*, shine; see fire in the distance; brand an animal; take fright and flee; — II. INF. *tanwîr*, bloom, blossom; shine; light up, illuminate; enlighten; mark by branding; tattoo; — III. INF. *munâwara-t*, revile, inveigh against; — IV. INF. *inâra-t*, shine, light, light up, illuminate; — V. INF. *tanawwur*, shine, be brilliant; see fire in the distance; be lit up, illuminated; be enlightened by God; rub one's self with نورة *nûra-t*, q.v.; — VIII. INF. *intiyâr*, *intiwâr*, rub one's self with هنا *hinâ*; — X. INF. *istinâra-t*, ask for light or fire; seek light, enlightenment; be lit up, illuminated.

نور *naur*, ة, pl. *anwâr*, blossom of a tree, blossom; — *nûr*, pl. *nîrân*, *anwâr*, light, ray of light, brightness; enlightenment, truth; luminary; du. sun and moon; the eyes; pl. of نار *nâr*, *nuwâr*, and نوور *na'ûr*; —*na'ur*=نوور *na'ûr*; —*nawar*, pl. of نورى *nawariyy*; — ة *nûra-t*, pl. *nûr*, mark by branding, brand; pitch to smear the camels with for the mange; an ointment to take away the hair or for tatooing; (m.) lime, chalk.

نوروز *naurûz*, festival of the new year in the spring equinox (Pers.).

نورى *nûriyy*, ة, shining, resplendent, brilliant; illuminating, lighting up; lit up, illuminated; ة *nûriyya-t*, lighting up of a church; money for church candles; — *nawariyy*, pl. *nawar*, gipsy.

(نوز), II. *nawwaz*, INF. *tanwîz*, diminish.

(نوس) *nâs*, U, INF. *naus*, *nawasân*, wave, oscillate; fall down the neck (hair); urge on; — II. INF. *tanwîs*, remain, abide.

(نوش) *nâś*, U, INF. *nauś*, seize, grasp; (m.) touch, feel, grope; seek, demand; go, advance; rise quickly; — II. INF. *tanwîś*, prepare a meal for (acc.), invite to a meal; — III. INF. *munâwaśa-t*, attack and fight with; — VI. INF. *tanâwuś*, reach for, seize, take; (m.) feel; — VIII. INF. *intiyâś*=VI.

نوشادر *nûśâdir*, ammoniac.

(نوص) *nâṣ*, U, INF. *nauṣ*, recede, remain behind; flee from, shun, avoid; take refuge; rise, set one's self to; — INF. *nauṣ*, *nawîṣ*, *nawaṣân*, *manâṣ*, move (n.); — III. INF. *munâwaṣa-t*, attack, combat; set one's self to, undertake, carry on; — X. INF. *istinâṣa-t*, recede, remain behind; move (a.); begin to run; despise and use one for one's own purposes.

نوص *nauṣ*, wild ass; — ة *nauṣa-t*, lotion, ablution.

(نوض) *nâḍ*, U, INF. *nauḍ*, travel over or through; shake (a.); draw or drain water; move, swing (n.); shine, flash; — II. INF. *tanwîḍ*, dye.

نوض *nauḍ*, pl. *anwâḍ*, base of the tail; also pl. *anâwîḍ*, place where water runs out, high ground.

(نوط) *nâṭ*, U, INF. *nauṭ*, *niyâṭ*, tie and suspend one thing to another; don; pass. attack; (m.) be tied to, belong to, depend on; be far distant; (also VIII.)

undertake anything of one's own accord, without consulting others; — IV. INF. *inâṭa-t*, transmit, deliver, hand over; (m.) ascribe to; — VIII. INF. *intiyâṭ*, be tied to; hang from, be suspended at; be distant; see I.

نوط *nauṭ*, pl. *anwâṭ*, *niyâṭ*, what is tied up and suspended; also ة *nauṭa-t*, a basket for the transport of dates; store; base of the tail; —*nûṭ*, pl. of نياط *niyâṭ*; — ة *nauṭa-t*, hatred, malice; plague-blister of a camel; crop of a bird; dense shrub of acacias or tamarisks.

(نوع) *nâ'*, U, INF. *nau'*, seek for, long for, demand; move, wave (n.); spread the wings to pounce upon the prey; — II. INF. *tanwî'*, move (a.); specify, classify; — V. INF. *tanawwu'*, be moved, agitated; (also X.) ramify (n.), be specified, classified; be of many kinds, manifold.

نوع *nau'*, pl. *anwâ'*, kind, sort, species, genus; manner, way, fashion; *nau'-an*, in a certain manner, in a certain measure, to a certain degree; — *nû'*, thirst; — ة *nau'a-t*, fresh fruit; — ى *nau'iyy*, referring to kind or species, specific.

(نوف) *nâf*, U, INF. *nauf*, tower over, hang over, dominate; surpass, surmount; be long and high; suck the breast; — II. INF. *tanyîf*, surpass; — IV. INF. *inâfa-t*, tower over.

نوفل *naufal*, sea; liberal man; gift, present, bounty; very handsome young man; — ة *naufala-t*, salt-works, saline; woollen veil.

(نوق) *nâq*, U, INF. *nauq*, clean the flesh from fat; — II. INF. *tanwîq*, break in camels; — V. INF. *tanawwuq*, perform anything well and neatly; INF. also *tanayyuq*, be dainty in food and dress; — VIII. INF. *intiyâq*, select.

نوق *nûq*, pl. of ناقة *nâqa-t*, she-camel, &c.; — *nawaq*, reddish white; — ة *nûqa-t*, skill; — *nawaqa-t*, Jewish butcher.

(نوك) *nawik*, A, INF. *nawak*, *nawâk*, *nawâka-t*, be stupid; — IV. INF. *inwâk*, find stupid; — X. INF. *istinwâk*=I.

نوك *nûk*, *nauk*, *nawak*, stupidity; *nûk*, نوكى *nauka*, pl. and نوكا *naukâ'*, f. of انوك *anwak*, stupid.

(نول) *nâl*, U, INF. *naul*, offer, give, present with; INF. *naul*, *nail*, reach, obtain, receive, get; be the time for; — A, INF. *nail*, *nâ'il*, be liberal; attend zealously to (ب *bi*); — II. INF. *tanwîl*, procure, offer, give, present with, help to; — III. INF. *munâwala-t*, reach to; give one the holy communion; take an oath; — IV. INF. *inâla-t*=II.; — V. INF. *tanawwul*, reach, obtain, get; — VI. INF. *tanâwul*, reach for, seize, take, obtain, receive; receive holy communion.

نول *naul*, pl. *anwâl*, gift, present; manner, way; duty; loom; workroom of a weaver; load, freight, cargo; carriage (costs of); — ة *naula-t*, *nûla-t*, present; something; kiss; area of the temple of Mecca.

نولون *naulûn*, load, cargo, freight; freightage, carriage.

(نوم) *nâm*, A, INF. *naum*, *niyâm*, *manâm*, fall asleep, sleep, slumber; go to sleep; rest; be dull (market); submit quietly; INF. *naum*, surpass in sleeping; — II. INF. *tanwîm*, (also IV.) bid to sleep; make sleep; operate as a narcotic; INF. *tanyîm*, lull to sleep; spread on the floor; — III. INF. *munâwama-t*, vie in sleeping; — IV. INF. *inâma-t*, see I.; — V. INF. *tanawwum*, dream; — VI. INF. *tanwâum*, pretend to sleep; — X. INF. *istinâma-t*, give one's self over to sleep; nap, dream.

نوم *naum,* sleep, slumber; also *nuwwam,* pl. of نائم *nâ'im,* sleeping, &c.; — *nuwam,* sleepy, drowsy, lethargic; — ة *nauma-t,* sleep; — *nuwama-t,* who sleeps much, lie-a-bed.

نومان *nûmân,* sleepy; a plant.

(نومس) *naumas,* INF. ة, make one respected and honoured, bring into good renown; — II. INF. *tanaumus,* enjoy respect and honour (m.).

نون *nûn,* pl. *-ât,* name of the letter ن; pl. *nînân, anwân,* large fish (ذو النون *zû 'n-nûn,* Jonas); edge of a sword, sword (ذو النون *zû 'n-nûn,* name of a celebrated sword); riches, wealth; ink-bottle; — ة *nûna-t,* a fish; dimple in the chin of a child; — II. *nawwan,* INF. *tanwîn,* pronounce a vowel with final *n,* nunate.

نونو *nûnû,* eel (m.); — *nu'nu',* weak, cowardly.

(نوه) *nâh,* U, INF. *nauh,* be high, elevated, sublime; tower above, be eminent; be firm, courageous; lift the head and scream or screech; fill without satiating; — U, A, INF. *nauh,* abstain from, refuse; — II. INF. *tanwîh,* raise, elevate; praise up to the clouds; mention with praise; call aloud; — V. INF. *tanawwuh,* be high, elevated, sublime; be exalted, praised, mentioned with praise.

نووج *na'ûj,* blowing; — *nu'ûj,* INF. of (ناج).

نوود *na'ûd,* misfortune, calamity.

نوور *na'ûr,* woad for dyeing, indigo; soot as a dye; a powder for the gums; pl. *nûr,* avoiding even appearances (woman).

نووم *na'ûm,* sleepy; who sleeps much, slumberer, lie-a-bed.

(نوى) *nawa,* I, INF. *niya-t, niyya-t,* intend, resolve upon, purpose; guard, heed, preserve; throw away date-stones; — INF. *nawa-n, niyya-t,* be far, remove to a distance (n.); desist, abstain from; wander from one place to another; — II. INF. *tanwiya-t,* carry out one's purpose; form its stone (date); (m.) mew; — III. INF. *munâwât,* rise against, oppose, be adverse; — IV. INF. *inwâ'* (also X.), throw away; form its stone; be far; travel much and far; — V. INF. *tanawwî,* resolve upon, purpose, intend; — VIII. INF. *intiwâ',* intend; — X. INF. *istinwâ',* see IV.

نوى *nawa,* intention, purpose; destination; departure, journey; absence, separation; manner, way; also *nuwiyy,* pl. of نواة *nawât,* date-stone; — *nu'y, nu'a,* pl. *nuwiyy* = نای *nâ'y,* water-ditch round a tent; — *nawiyy,* of the same mind, congenial.

نويان *nûyân,* son of a king, prince; leader of ten thousand; wicker basket.

نويب *nuwaib,* little tooth.

نويرة *nuwaira-t,* little fire.

نويم *nawîm,* sleepy; negligent.

نى *nayy,* fat; — *niyy,* id.; also *ni',* half-cooked, underdone, almost raw; — ة *niyya-t,* pl. *-ât, nawâya,* intention, purpose, resolution; will, tendency, inclination, wish, object of investigation; distance; — also *niya-t,* INF. of (نوى).

(نى) *nâ',* aor. *yani',* INF. *nay', nuyû',* *nuyû'a-t,* be underdone; — II. INF. *tani'a-t,* cook but half; treat any matter not thoroughly.

نيابة *niyâba-t,* period, turn; vicegerency, representation, vicariate, office of a deputy; succession.

نياح *niyâḥ,* tranquillity of mind; death; also ة *niyâḥa-t,* bewailing of the dead, lamentation.

نيار *niyâr,* pl. of نار *nâr,* fire, etc.

نيازك *nayâziq,* pl. of نيزك *naizak.*

نياشين *nayâśîn,* pl. of نيشان *nîśân.*

نياضة *niyâḍa-t,* motion, movement.

نياط *niyâṭ,* pl. *anwiṭa-t, anwâṭ, nûṭ,*

far-stretching desert; string; vital vein; artery of the back; (m.) having long fibres.

نياطل *nayâṭil*, pl. of ناطل *nâṭil*, a wine-measure, cup, &c.

نياع *niyâ'*, pl. of نائع thirsty, and نيع *ni'*, jaw.

نياف *niyâf*, high, elevated, towering above others, dominating; ة *ni-yâfa-t*, eminence, excellency (titles);—*nayyâf*, having a high hump.

نياق *niyâq*, delight; pl. of ناقة *nâ-qa-t*, she-camel, and نيق *nîq*, mountain-top.

نياك *nayyâk*, who has frequent sexual intercourse.

نيام *niyâm*, sleep; pl. of نائم *nâ'im*, sleeping, &c.

(نيب) *nâb*, I, INF. *naib*, injure with the dog-teeth; (also II.) bite with them; fix teeth in;—II. INF. *tanyîb*, see I.; be very old; also—V. INF. *tanayyub*, sprout.

نيب *nîb*, pl. of ناب *nâb*, old she-camel, &c.; — (m.) *naib*, dog-tooth.

(نيت) *nât*, I, INF. *nait*, bend in walking, totter (from weakness).

نيثران *naiṡurân*, talkative.

نئج *na'ij*, see (ناج).

(نيح) *nâḥ*, I, INF. *naiḥ*, turn hard; harden (n.); INF. *naiḥ*, *naiḥân*, move (m.), wave;—II. INF. *tan-yîḥ*, harden (a.); give one eternal rest; procure one quiet from;—V. INF. *tanayyuḥ*, find quiet or rest from, get rid of, go to rest, die.

نيح *nayyiḥ*, hard; — ة *nayyiḥa-t*, wind blowing contrary to another.

نئدل *ni'dil*, calamity; — ة *nîdul*, *ni'dil*, نئدلان *nîdulân*, *ni'dulân*, nightmare.

(نير) *nâr*, I, INF. *nair*, put to cloth a border of a different colour; —II. INF. *tanyîr*, IV. INF. *inâra-t*, id.; weave stripes into cloth.

نير *nîr*, pl. *anyâr*, border or hem of a different colour (ذو نيرين *ẕû nîrain*, with two hems; having the strength of two men); woof; connected threads; bulrush; road; (m., also ة *nîra-t*) gums; pl. *anyâr*, *nîrân*, yoke of oxen; luminary, star; — *nayyir*, ة, shining, bright; light; lit up, illuminated; du. sun and moon; — ة *niyara-t*, pl. of نار *nâr*, fire, &c.; — *nayyira-t*, sorceress, witch; visible blow, shot.

نيران *nîrân*, pl. نار *nâr*, نور *nûr*, نير *nîr*; — ى *nîrâniyy*, fiery, glowing, ardent, passionate.

نيرب *nairab*, INF. ة, slander; utter lies; weave; furrow the sand, or the water; — *nairab*, slander, calumny, malice; — ى *nairabā*, misfortune, calamity.

نيرج *nairaj*, implement for threshing corn, harrow, ploughshare; slanderer; — INF. ة, slander; lie with; waver in one's opinion.

نيرز *nairaz*, INF. ة, bring a new year's gift.

نيرانجات *nîrânjât*, conjurations (Pers.).

نيروز *nairûz*=نوروز *naurûz*.

نيزب *naizab*, he-goat; ox.

نيزك *naizak*, pl. *nayâzik*, short lance (Pers.).

نيسان *nîsân*, *naisân*, month of April.

نيسب *naisab*, INF. ة, play the part of go-between or tale-bearer; — *naisab*, traces; also—

نيسبان *naisabân*, road.

نيسون *nîsûn*, anise.

نيش *nîś*, apricot (m.).

نيشان *nîśân*, pl. *nayâsîn*, sign; mark; decoration, star; aim, target.

(نيص) *nâṣ*, I, INF. *naiṣ*, move gently.

(نيض) *nâḍ*, I, INF. *naiḍ*, beat (n.), throb, pulsate.

(نيط) *nâṭ*, I, INF. *naiṭ*, be far distant.

نيط *naiṭ*, vein to which the heart is suspended; last gasp, death; burial; (m.) having long fibres.

نيطرون *naiṭarûn*, borax.

نيطل *naiṭal*, large bucket; a wine-

measure; wine; also *nîṭâl*, *ni'ṭal*, heavy calamity; *naiṭal*, *ni'ṭal*, cunning fellow.

(نيع) *nâ'*, I, INF. *nai'*, bend, wave.

نيع *nî'*, pl. *niyâ'*, Jew.

نئف *na'if*, see (ناف) eat, &c.; — *nayyif*, *naif*, excessive; surplus; appendix; upwards (of a given number).

نيق *nîq*, astonishing, delighting (s.); pleasure; pl. *niyâq*, *anyâq*, *nuyûq*, mountain-top, mountain-chain;—*nayyiq*, dainty in eating; ة, *nîqa-t*, dainty taste; tidiness, neatness, elegance; skill, practice; — V. INF. *tanayyuq*, see (نوق).

(نيك) *nâk*, I, INF. *naik*, lie with;— VI. INF. *tanâyuk*, be overcome by sleep, close (n.).

(نيل) *nâl*, I, A, INF. *nâl*, *nail*, *nâla-t*, reach, obtain, get; also—IV. INF. *inâla-t*, procure, offer, give.

نيل *nail*, obtaining (s.); also ة *naila-t*, that which one obtains or possesses; advantage, gift, present;—*nîl*, indigo (also ة *nîla-t*); indigo-blue; river Nile.

نيلج *nîlaj*, dried indigo juice; indigo.

نيلنج *nîlanj*, green-dyeing soot (for tattooing).

نيلوفر *nailûfar*, water-lily, nenuphar.

نيلى *nîliyy*, indigo-blue; bluish black; referring to the Nile.

نيم *nîm*, anything pleasant or comfortable; soft garment, coat of mail, velvet, night-dress; good friend; — *nuyyam*, pl. of نائم *nâ'im*, sleeping, &c.; — ة *nîma-t*, sleep; sloth; night-quarters.

نينان *nînân*, pl. of نون *nûn*.

نينوفر *nainûfar*=نيلوفر *nailûfar*.

نينوى *nînawa*, Niniveh.

(نيه) *nâh*, be high, elevated, sublime; astonish, please.

نيو *nuyû'*, ة *nuyû'a-t*, half raw or underdone state of the meat.

نيوب *nuyûb*, pl. of ناب *nâb*, dog-tooth, &c.; — *nayyûb*, very old; head of a family; chieftain.

نيى *nî'*, half raw, underdone; — *ni'y*, water-ditch; — *na'iyy*, distant, far.

نييب *nuyaib*, little chief.

نئيت *na'ît*, roar; envy.

نئيج *na'îj*, whistling of the wind.

نئيشا *na'îsan*, finally, in the end.

نئيط *na'îṭ*, screaming; groaning (s.).

نئيل *na'îl*, INF. of (نال), walk in jerks.

نئيم *na'îm*, soft tone; groaning (s.), complaint.

ه

ه *h*, as a numerical sign=5; abbreviation for Thursday, Venus, Virgo, and moon-light; — *ha*, interrogative particle for أ; sometimes, especially in poetry, pleonastically added to the end of a word; — ه *hi*, for هى *hiya*, she; — ه *hu* (after ـِ or ى turning into *hi*), pron. affix of the 3rd pers. masc., him, his.

ها *hâ*, lo! behold! there!; placed before the demonstrative pronoun ذا; — suffix of the 3rd pers. fem. sing., she, her;—*ha'*, imperative of (هيا); — *hâ'*, pl. *hâ'at*, name of the letter ه; — *hâ-'a*, fem. *hâ-'i*, du. *hâ'umâ*, pl. m. *hâ'um*, f. *hâ'unna*, well! there! take!

هاب *hâb*, snake; — *hâb hâb*, call of a camel-driver; — *hâb-in*, see هابى *hâbî*.

هابشة *hâbiśa-t*, assembled crowd.
هابط *hâbiṭ*, falling, alighting; condescending; putting up (in an inn, &c.).
هابى *hâbî* (هاب *hâb-in*), covered or filled with dust; grave-dust.
هابيل *hâbîl*, Abel.
هات *hât*, f. هاتى *hâtî*, du. هاتيا *hâtiyâ*, pl. m. هاتوا *hâtû*, f. هاتين *hâtîna*, give here! bring here! come! have done!
هاتا *hâtâ*, du. *hatân-i*, she, this one (f.); — هاتاك *hâtâka*, that one (f.).
هاتف *hâtif*, ag. of (هتف), calling, &c., caller (ة الغيب *hâtif al-gaib*, voice from heaven); caller in the desert, well intentioned demon who leads the wanderer on the right road; good angel, genius.
هاتل *hâtil*, pl. *huttal*, also هاتن *hâtin*, pl. *huttan*, raining gently and continuously.
هاتيك *hâtîka*, she, this one (f.).
هاجر *hâjar*, Hagar; — *hâjir*, abandoning, forsaking, emigrating, excellent, beautiful; delirious, doting; *hâjir*, ة *hâjira-t*, pl. *hawâjir*, hot mid-day; — ة *hâjira-t*, pl. *-ât*, *hawâjira-t*, idle or obscene talk; — ى *hâjiriyy*, excellent, handsome, beautiful; architect; inhabitant of a town, citizen.
هاجس *hâjis*, ة *hâjisa-t*, pl. *hawâjis*, occurring thought, thought.
هاجشة *hâjiśa-t*, assembled crowd.
هاجع *hâji'*, pl. *hujja'*, *hujû'*, slee p ing; quiet.
هاجنة *hâjina-t*, palm-tree which produces at first but small fruit.
هاجة *hâja-t*, female frog; — *hâjja-t*, deeply sunk or set (eye).
هاجى *hâjî* (هاج *hâj-in*), spelling; satirist; satirical.
هاد *hâdd*, roaring of the sea; — ة *hâdda-t*, thunder.
هادر *hadir*, roaring; who allows blood to be shed with impunity; contemptible.
هادف *hâdif*, who approaches or enters as a guest; stranger; — ة *hâdifa-t*, crowd.
هادل *hâdil*, hanging, having hanging lips.
هادى *hâdî* (هاد *had-in*), pl. *hâdûn*, *hudât*, who leads on the right road, guide, leader; God; leading ram; foremost part; handpiece; also ة *hâdiya-t*, leading ram, leading animal; the middle ox in threshing; pl. *hawâdî*, neck; — *hâdi'*, quieting, tranquillizing; — ة *hâdiya-t*, stick, staff; cliff above the water.
هاذ *hâz*, ة a tree.
هاذا *hâzâ*, this, this one (m.).
هاذر *hâẓir*, oppressively hot.
هاذل *hâẓil*, midnight; beginning or remainder of the night.
هاذى *hâẓî*, this, this one (f.)
هار *hâr*, weak from old age, decrepit; weakened; = هائر *hâ'ir*; — هار *hârr*, cry of the cat.
هارب *hârib*, pl. *hurrâb*, fugitive.
هارج *hârij*, jester.
هاروت *hârût*, companion of ماروت *mârût*, two angels seduced by women and suspended for punishment in a well near Babylon.
هاز *hâzz*, shaking; glittering.
هازبا *hâzibâ'*, هازبى *hâziba*, *hâzibî*, *hâzibiyy*, ة *hâẓibiyya-t*, a fish.
هازبانية *hâzubâniya-t*, feeler of an insect.
هازل *hâzil*, jesting, buffoon; playful.
هازمة *hâzima-t*, calamity.
هازى *hâzi'*, who laughs at, scoffs; mocker, scoffer.
هاشل *hâśil*, vagrant, vagabond.
هاشمة *hâśima-t*, wound which breaks a bone.
هاصر *hâṣir*, tearing to pieces; — *.
هاضب *hâḍib*, falling in large drops, watering abundantly.
هاضم *hâḍim*, soft; loose; bearing a grudge, resentful; also—
هاضوم *hâḍûm*, promoting digestion; *hâḍûm*, liberal; lion.
هاطل *hâṭil* = هاتل *hâtil*.

هاع *hâ'*, greedy; avarice, meanness; cowardice; هاع لاع *hâ' lâ'*, cowardly.

هاف *hâf-in*, هافى *hâfî*, poor; famished.

هاك *hâka*, pl. *hâkum*, f. *hâki*, pl. *hâkunna*, there! take!

هال *hâl*, progeny, family; mirage; — ة *hâla-t*, halo of the moon.

هالع *hâli'*, excessively impatient; — *.

هالك *hâlik*, pl. *halkâ*, *hullak*, *hullâk*, *hawâlik*, perishing, &c.; reprobate, damned; destroying; — ى *hâlikiyy*, smith; polisher, furbisher.

هام *hâm*, thirsty; — ة *hâma-t*, pl. *-ât*, *hâm*, head; chief; pl. *hâm*, owl; horse; — *hâmma-t*, pl. *hawâmm*, *hamîm*, dangerous reptile, reptile, worm; cattle; نعم الهامة *ni'm-u 'l-hâmmat-i*, horse.

هامج *hâmij*, violent; margin of a book.

هامد *hâmid*, extinguished; getting extinguished, going out; calming down; old, worn out, weather-beaten; without vegetation, barren.

هامز *hâmiz*, m. f. slanderer.

هامش *hâmiś*, margin of a book.

هامل *hâmil*, ة pl. *hawâmil*, *humûla-t*, *hummal*, *himâl*, *hamla*, pasturing at large.

هاموم *hâmûm*, melted fat of a camel's hump.

هانذا *hânazâ*, lo! look there! behold!

هانع *hâni'*, pl. *hunna'*, submissive, humble.

هانى *hâni'*, domestic servant.

(هاها) *ha'ha'*, INF. *hi'hâ'*, *ha'hâ*, ة *ha'ha'at*, urge the camels by the cry هاها *ha'ha'*, or call them to their food with the cry هى هى *hi' hi'*; laugh aloud.

هاها *ha'ha'*, *ha'hâ'*, laugher;—*hahâ'*, ة *ha'hâ'a-t*, laughter.

هاهنا *hâhuna*, *hâhannâ*, here; hither; هاهناك *hâhunâk*, *hâhannâk*, there; thither.

هاوم *hâ'um*, pl. m., هاوما *hâ'umâ*, du., هاون *hâ'unna*, pl. f. of ها *hâ'*; *hâwun*, *hâwan*, and—

هاوون *hâwûn*, pl. *hawâwîn*, mortar (for pounding).

هاوى *hâwî* (هاو, *hâw-in*), ة falling head over heels; thrown down; in love, loving; pl. ة *hâwiya-t*, locust; — ة *hâwiya-t*, lowest hell; deep black abyss; mother deprived of her children.

هائج *hâ'ij*, agitated, &c.; rutting; agitation, excitement, rage; dried up, withered.

هائد *hâ'id*, repenting, atoning.

هائر *hâ'ir*, carried off by water, washed away; in ruins; come down in the world.

هائع *hâ'i'*, fluid, molten; هائع لائع *hâ'i' lâ'i'*, cowardly;— ة *hâ'i'a-t*, terrible noise.

هائل *hâ'il*, terrible, awful.

هايهات *hâyahât*, هايهان *hâyahân* = هيهات *haihât*.

هب *hab*, supposing, let us suppose, imp. of (وهب);— ة *hiba-t*, giving, making a present, pardoning (s.), INF. of (وهب); pl. *hibât*, gift, present;— *huba-t*, preparations for war, armaments;— *habba-t*, gust of wind; *habba-t*, *hibba-t*, hour, while, year, moment, remaining time;—*hibba-t*, cutting power of a sword; pl. *hibab*, rags, tatters; moment of ecstacy, ecstacy.

(هب) *habb*, U, INF. *habb*, *hubûb*, *habîb*, blow violently; rouse itself; awake (n.); — I, U, INF. *hibâb*, *hibba-t*, *hubûb*, *habîb* (also VIII.) groan from rut; — INF. *habb*, *hibâb*, pace along briskly; come; depart; be absent; be brandished; be beaten, flee; begin, set one's self to; — V. INF. *tahabbub*, be torn, used up; — VIII. INF. *ihtibâb*, cut or tear off; see I.

هبا *habâ'*, pl. *ahbâ'*, motes in the sunlight; blockhead.

هباب *habâb*, fine dust; — *; — *habbâb*, blowing violently.

هبار *habbâr*, sharp; a very hairy monkey; du. *al-habbârân*, the two months كانون *kânûn*, December and January; — ة *habâriya-t*, refuse of wool, feathers, &c.

هباش *habbâś*, who grasps, earns;— ة *hubâśa-t*, crowd, herd.

هبال *habbâl*, who tries to deceive, catch, lays traps or snares; — ة *habâla-t*, perseverance in seeking or demanding.

هبانق *hubâniq*, pl. *habâniq*, boy, lad, young fellow, servant.

هبائب *habâ'ib*, garment (in rags).

هباية *hubâya-t*, bark of a tree.

هبب *hibab*, pl. of هبة *hibba-t*.

(هبت) *habat*, I, INF. *habt*, beat, strike down; make to alight, let down, throw down; remove one from his office, break one's power; alight; fall; pass., also *habit*, A, be confused, agitated, lose courage; — ة *habta-t*, blow; weakness; discouragement.

هبتر *habtar*, dwarfish, small, short.

(هبج) *habaj*, A, INF. *habj*, beat, cudgel; (m.) scratch so that blood flows; — II. INF. *tahbîj* = I.; make a limb to swell; — V. INF. *tahabbuj*, be swollen, have a tumour; (m.) be scratched so that blood flows.

هبج *habj*, canings; — ة *habja-t*, blow.

(هبد) *habad*, I, INF. *habd*, gather, pound, boil or present for food the seed of colocynth; — VIII. INF. *ihtibâd*, prepare a dish of colocynth for one's self.

هبد *habd*, wild pumpkin; colocynth and its seed.

(هبذ) *habaẕ*, I, INF. *habẕ*, hurry (n.), run, fly swiftly.

(هبر) *habar*, U, INF. *habr*, cut flesh in large pieces, cut off a piece of it, cut off; — *habir*, A, INF. *habar*, be very fleshy;— IV. INF. *ihbâr*, grow fat; — VIII. INF. *ihtibâr*, cut off entirely.

هبر *habr*, flesh (without fat); cutting off, severing; pl. *hubûr*, *hubr*, flat sandy ground;— *hubr*, refuse of flax; grape-stone; — *habir*, very fleshy and fat; — *hibbir*, cut off; — *hubur*, pl. of هبير *habîr*; — ة *habra-t*, piece of flesh without bones and fat, the lean; an amulet.

(هبرج) *habraj*, INF. ة, embroider or colour stuff with figures; walk on an even road as if pushed on; step along proudly; (m.) tear (a.).

هبرج *habraj*, garments embroidered or painted with figures; bull; also *hibrij*, big and fat.

هبرزى *hibrîziyy*, pure gold; new gold coin; handsome, elegant; lion.

(هبرس) — II. INF. *tahabrus*, step along proudly.

هبرقى *habraqiyy*, *hibriqiyy*, smith, goldsmith, artist; wild bull.

هبرك *habrak*, ة, full-grown.

(هبرم) *habram*, INF. ة, eat much; talk much, chatter.

هبرية *hibriya-t*, dandruff; refuse of wool, feathers, &c.

(هبز) *habaz*, I, INF. *hubûz*, *habazân*, die (suddenly); cut in pieces, cut off.

(هبس) *habas*, violet; wild thyme; mallows; ox-eye (plant).

(هبش) *habaś*, I, INF. *habś*, grasp together, gather; earn for one's family and bring home; reach, obtain, find; beat; — II. INF. *tahbîś*, gather;—V. INF. *tahabbuś*, acquire, gain, earn; — VIII. INF. *ihtibâś*, earn, obtain, get.

(هبص) *habiṣ*, A, INF. *habaṣ*, be brisk, nimble; lie in ambush for game; eat greedily; — VII. INF. *inhibâṣ*, indulge in immoderate laughter; — VIII. INF. *ihtibâṣ*, laugh immoderately; hasten (n.).

هبص *habaṣ*, briskness, nimbleness; haste; — *habiṣ*, brisk, nimble, agile; — ى *habaṣa*, quick pace.

(هبط) *habaṭ*, I, U, INF. *hubûṭ*, fall

down, descend, alight; fall in; depart; abate (n.); pounce upon; alight and put up;—U, INF. *habṭ*, let down, throw down, precipitate; enter a country or cause to do so; INF. *habṭ*, *hubûṭ*, abate (a.); beat; emaciate and weaken;—II. INF. *tahbîṭ*, make to fall; throw down; abate (a. and n.); —IV. INF. *ihbâṭ*=II.;—V. INF. *tahabbuṭ*, fall in, fall in ruins; —VII. INF. *inhibâṭ*, let one's self down; be let or thrown down;—ة *habṭa-t*, low ground; calamity.

(هبع) *haba'*, A, INF. *hubû'*, *haba'ân*, come suddenly up from all sides, fall upon; stretch out the neck; —X. INF. *istihbâ'*, urge to haste.

هبع *huba'*, f. ة, last-dropped camel-foal, or one born in autumn or too early.

(هبغ) *habag*, A, INF. *habg*, *hubûg*, sleep.

(هبك), VII. *inhabak*, INF. *inhibâk*, yield under one's feet (ground); —ة *hubaka-t*, blockhead.

(هبل) *habil*, A, INF. *habal*, lose a son by death;—II. INF. *tahbîl*, be heavy upon; (m.) make one take a steam-bath; foment; (also V. and VIII.) earn for one's family;—IV. INF. *ihbâl*, deprive one of his children;—V. INF. *tahabbul*, see I.; (m.) take a steam-bath; be fomented;—VIII. INF. *ihtibâl*, see II.; make one's son an orphan; surround the game; put in opportunely (a word); اهتبل هبلك *ihtabala habaluka*, it beseems you.

هبل *habal*, bereavement; see the previous;—*habil*, watching for prey;—*hibil*, *hiball*, *hibill*, stout and old;—*hubal*, name of an idol in Mecca;—ة *habla-t*, hot steam, steam-bath.

هبلع *hibla'*, chained-up dog, dog; also *haballa'*, هبلاع *hiblâ'*, voracious eater, glutton.

(هبنق) *habnaq*, INF. ة, sit on the inner side of the thigh.

هبنق *hubnuq* = هبنوق *hubnûq*;—*habannaq*, dwarf; stupid (also هبنك *habannak*).

هبنوق *hubnûq*, هبنيق *hibnîq*, pl. *habânîq*, young fellow, servant; —ة *hubnûqa-t*, flute.

هبهاب *habhâb*, mirage; a game; swift, nimble.

(هبهب) *habhab*, INF. ة, groan from rut.

هبهب *habhab*, swift, nimble;—ى *habhabiyy*, ة, id.; clever camel-driver.

(هبو) *habâ*, U, INF. *hubuww*, rise and fly in the air (dust); flee; run away; die;—IV. INF. *ihbâ'*, raise dust;—V. INF. *tahabbî*, shake one's hands;—ة *habwa-t*, dust; whirling dust-cloud; dust-colour; darkness.

هبوب *habûb*, ة *habûba-t*, blowing violently and raising dust;—*.

هبور *habûr*, spider;—*;—*habbûr*, a small kind of ants.

هبوط *habûṭ*, precipitous place; precipice;—*hubûṭ*, sliding down, falling (s.), fall; decrease, abatement; precipice.

هبول *habûl*, bereft of her children.

هبون *habûn*, spider.

هبى *habayy*, f. ة, innocent boy, or girl.

هبيت *habît*, *hibbît*, quite discouraged; utterly agitated and confused.

هبيج *habayyaj*, هبيخ *habayyaḥ*, ة, exuberant with strength and health.

هبيد *habîd*, colocynth and its seed.

هبير *habîr*, severing; pl. *hubur*, *ahbira-t*, low ground, sands;—ة *hubaira-t*, hyena; ابو (ام) ه *abû (umm) hubaira-t*, frog; *hubairat-an*, never.

هبيط *habîṭ*, emaciated.

هبيل *habîl*, Abel.

(هت) *hatt*, U, INF. *hatt*, deliver one's speech fluently and well-

connectedly, report well; break (a.), crumble; tear (a.); dishonour, depose, destroy one's position; strip off the leaves; pour out.
هت *hatt*, breach, rent.
(هتا) *hata'*, INF. *hat'*, beat; eat; tear, rend; injure one's honour; — هتى *hati'*, A, INF. *hata'*, be bent; — IV. INF. *ihtâ'*, be worn-out and torn.
هتات *hattât*, glib.
هتار *hitâr*, reviling (s.), abuse.
هتاف *hutâf*, cry, outcry, call; — ة *hattâfa-t*, twanging (adj. n.).
هتاك *hattâk*, who tears the veil, dishonours, profanes.
هتامة *hutâma-t*, morsel, bit.
هتان *hâtân*, these two (f.);—*hattân*, glib, ready of speech.
(هتر) *hatar*, I, INF. *hatr*, tear, break (a.); injure one's character, dishonour; weaken the intellect; — II. INF. *tahtîr*, dishonour, disgrace; — III. INF. *hitâr*, *muhâtara-t*, abuse in a frivolous and lying way; — IV. INF. *ihtâr*, be weak of intellect, dote; — V. INF. *tahattur*, *tahtâr*, be ignorant and stupid; — VI. INF. *tahâtur*, be arrogant towards one another; — X. INF. *istihtâr*, be given to frivolities; (m.) be negligent, careless.
هتر *hitr*, pl. *ahtâr*, lie, idle frivolous talk; error of speech; anything extraordinary, wonder; first half of the night; — *hutr*, confusion of mind, weakness of intellect; — ة *hatra-t*, silliness, stupidity.
هترك *hatrak*, lion.
(هتش) *hataś*, I, INF. *hatś*, irritate, tease; pass. and — VIII. INF. *ihtitâś*, be irritated.
(هتع) *hata'*, INF. *hat'*, approach quickly.
(هتف) *hataf*, I, INF. *hatf*, coo; INF. *hatf*, *hutûf*, call, call to (ب *bi*); praise; congratulate a woman on her beauty.
(هتك) *hatak*, I, INF. *hatk*, rend the veil and disclose anything hidden; expose, disgrace, dishonour; commit rape; deflower; desecrate, profane; — III. INF. *muhâtaka-t*, travel in a dark night; — V. INF. *tahattuk*, be rent, broken; be dishonoured, deflowered; — VII. INF. *inhitâk*, be rent.
هتك *hatk*, rending (s.), injury; disgrace, exposure; — *hutk*, midnight; — *hatik*, want of respect, damaging one's honour (s.); — *hitak*, scalp of a new-born child; — ة *hutka-t*, rent in a veil, torn-off piece; reviling, dishonouring (s.); hour of night.
(هتل) *hatal*, I, INF. *hatl*, *hutûl*, *hatalân*, *tahtâl*=هطل *haṭal*, rain, &c.
هتل *hatil*, pl. *huttal*=هاتل *hâtil*.
هتلان *hatalân*, continuous fine rain.
(هتم) *hatam*, I, INF. *hatm* (also IV.), strike on the mouth and beat out one's front teeth; — *hatim*, A, INF. *hatam*, have the front teeth broken off; — II. INF. *tahtîm*, disgrace and weaken by beating; — V. INF. *tahattum*, be broken.
هتم *hutm*, pl., هتما *hatmâ'*, f. of اهتم *ahtam*, have the front teeth broken out.
(هتمر) *hatmar*, INF. ة, be talkative.
(هتمل) *hatmal*, INF. ة, murmur to one's self.
(هتمن) *hatman*, INF. ة=هتمر *hatmar*.
(هتن) *hatan*, I, INF. *hatn*, *hutûn*, *hatanân*, *tahtân*=هطل *haṭal*, rain, &c.
هتهات *hathât*, glib, ready of speech.
(هتهت) *hathat*, INF. ة, break (a.), crush; speak fast and fluently; call the camel with the cry *hat hat* to be watered.
(هتو) *hatâ*, U, INF. *hatw*, crush with the foot; — III. INF. *muhâtât*, give, grant.
هتي *hati'*, see (هتا).
هتيكة *hatîka-t*, exposure, disgrace.
(هث) *has̱s̱*, U, INF. *has̱s̱*, lie, tell lies.
هثاث *has̱s̱âs̱*, liar.

(هثم) *hasam*, I, INF. *hasm*, pound minutely, grind to powder; give liberally of one's own.
هثملة *hasmala-t*, confusion and disaster.
هثمن *hasman*=هتمن *hatman*.
هثهاث *hashâs*, quick, nimble; confused, entangled; dusty; liar.
(هثهث) *hashas*, pour down rain or snow (cloud); tread violently under feet; be unjust, tyrannical; be confused, entangled, mixed up.
هثى *hasa*, INF. *hasayân*, scatter.
(هج) *hajj*, U, INF. *hajj*, *hajîj*, be deep set or sunk (eye); pull down, demolish; (m.) leave one's country, emigrate; — II. INF. *tahjîj*, force one to emigrate (m.); — VIII. INF. *ihtijâj*, go far in a matter, push a thing far; — X. INF. *istihjâj*, act headstrongly.
هج *hujj*, yoke.
(هجا) *haja'*, INF. *haj'*, *hujû'*, subside, cease; eat; fill one's stomach; — هجى *haji'*, A, INF. *haja'*, have intense hunger; — IV. INF. *ihjâ'*, appease one's hunger.
هجا *hijâ'*, m. *hajâ'*, satire, lampoon; biting remark; form, figure, manner, way; spelling (s.), alphabet; — ة *hajât*, frog; — *huja'a-t*, blockhead.
هجاج *hajâj*, fast walk; also ة *hajâja-t*, obstinate blockhead.
هجار *hijâr*, bow-string; chain; rope; diadem; ring used as an aim.
هجاس *hajjâs*, lion watching for his prey.
هجال *hijâl*, pl. of هجل *hajl* and هجيل *hajîl*; — ة *hajjâla-t*, widow.
هجان *hijân*, noble and excellent; bad, mean, vile; (m. and f., sing. & pl., pl. also *hajâ'in*) white generous camels; pl. of هجينة *hajîna-t*; —*hajjân*, pl. *hajjâna-t*, riders on dromedaries; —*hujjân*, pl. of هجيج *hajîj*; — ة *hajâna-t*, noble birth; excellence; low extraction and conduct.
هجاوة *hajâwa-t*, sultriness, closeness.

هجائن *hajâ'in*, pl. of هجان *hijân* and هجينة *hajîna-t*.
هجائى *hijâ'iyy*, ة, referring to the alphabet.
(هجب) *hajab*, I, INF. *hajb*, urge, urge on; hasten (n.); beat, thrash.
(هجد) *hajad*, U, INF. *hujûd*, sleep, sleep a short time; be awake and pray; press the neck to the ground (camel); — II. INF. *tahjîd*, put to sleep; — IV. INF. *ihjâd*, id.; find one asleep; sleep; —V. INF. *tahajjud*, sleep; be awake; pray the night through.
هجد *hujjad*, pl. of هجود *hajûd*.
(هجر) *hajar*, U, INF. *hajr*, *hijrân*, break with, leave, forsake; leave undone, renounce; INF. *hujr*, *hujûr*, tie up the foot of the camel with the rope هجار *hijâr*; INF. *hujr*, *hijjîrā*, *ihjîrā*, delirate, dote; — II. INF. *tahjîr* (also IV., V.), travel in the heat of mid-day; — III. INF. *muhâjara-t*, leave one's people or country, emigrate, flee; — IV. INF. *ihjâr*, abandon, leave undone, renounce; dote, talk at random; see II.; — V. INF. *tahajjur*, see II.; emigrate; — VI. INF. *tahâjur*, break with one another, separate (n.); — VII. INF. *inhijâr*, be abandoned, deserted; — VIII. INF. *ihtijâr*=VI.
هجر *hajr*, abandoning, forsaking (s.); separation; mid-day; hottest time of the day; good, excellent, noble, handsome (also *hajir*); bridle, halter; pl. *ahjâr*, fertile; *hijr*, most excellent, first-rate; — *hujr*, dotage, foolish talk, folly; —*hajar*, canton, town; — *hujur*, pl. of هجير *hajîr*; — ة *hajra-t*, year; —*hijra-t*, *hujra-t*, breaking off friendly relations, rupture, abandoning (s.), separation; emigration, flight; *al-hijra-t*, Mohammed's flight from Mecca to Medina 622 A.D.; — ى *hijj-*

riyy, ة, referring to Mohammed's flight; after the *hijra-t*.

هجريا *hijriyyâ*, custom, habit.

(هجز) *hajz*, what occurs to or passes through one's mind; anything spoken unintelligibly; — III. *hâjaz*, INF. *muhâjaza-t*, make a secret communication to (acc.).

(هجس) *hajas*, I, INF. *hajs*, occur, fall into; murmur to one's self; repel, prevent; — V. INF. *tahajjus*, think of, care for; — VII. INF. *inhijâs*, be refused and desist.

هجس *hajs*, occurring thought, thought; unintelligible murmur.

(هجش) *hajaś*, U, INF. *hajś*, drive slowly; give one a hint; bring about mischief, discord; desire, long for; — ة *hajśa-t*, departure, start.

(هجع) *haja'*, INF. *hujû'*, *tahjâ'*, sleep quietly; subside, calm down; — INF. *haj'*, cease, be appeased; appease; — II. INF. *tahjî'*, let one sleep; quiet, calm (a.); also — IV. INF. *ihjâ'*, appease one's hunger.

هجع *hij'*, *haji'*, *huja'*, ة *hij'a-t*, *huja'a-t*, thoughtless, careless; — *hujja'*, pl. of هاجع *hâji'*; — ة *haj'a-t*, light sleep in the first hours of the night, slumber; part of the night, night-watch; — *hij'a-t*, way of sleeping.

(هجف) *hajif*, INF. *hajaf*, be hungry and have a flaccid belly.

هجف *hijaff*, old; lazy and stupid; paunch-bellied; — ة *hijfa-t*, moist ground; meadow.

هجفان *hajfân*, thirsty.

(هجل) *hajal*, U, INF. *hajl*, fling, throw; give a side-glance and wink to (woman); — II. INF. *tahjîl*, revile, abuse; slander; — III. INF. *muhâjala-t*, vie with; — IV. INF. *ihjâl*, let the camels go at large; lose; widen (a.); — VIII. INF. *ihtijâl*, invent.

هجل *hajl*, pl. *hajalât*, *ahjâl*, *hijâl*, *hujûl*, broad valley or wood between mountains; — *hujul*, pathless, untrodden.

(هجم) *hajam*, I, INF. *hujûm*, rush suddenly upon, attack; surprise, enter suddenly and without permission; cause to surprise or enter; overthrow, pull down; fall in; — INF. *hajam*, *hujûm*, be deeply set or sunk; keep quiet (n.); — INF. *hajm*, drive away, expel; make perspire; = VIII.; — III. INF. *muhâjama-t*, rush suddenly upon; — IV. INF. *ihjâm*, introduce suddenly and without announcement; — V. INF. *tahajjum*, rush headlong into; — VII. INF. *inhijâm*, fall, tumble down; — VIII. INF. *ihtijâm*, milk so as to empty the udder entirely.

هجم *hajm*, sweat, perspiration; also *hajam*, pl. *ahjâm*, large cup; — ة *hajma-t*, surprise, sudden attack; violence; herd of camels (forty to a hundred).

(هجن) *hajan*, U, INF. *hujna-t*, *hajâna-t*, *hujûna-t*, be low, vile, of a mean race; be quick, nimble, excellent; — I, U, INF. *hajn*, be married too early, bear fruit for the first time, produce at first but small fruit; give no fire; — II. INF. *tahjîn*, deem or call one mean, of low birth, son of a female slave; revile, damage one's honour or character; — IV. INF. *ihjân*, have many generous camels; — VIII. INF. *ihtijân*, pass. be known by a man before maturity; — X. INF. *istihjân*, find a speech or action mean, disgraceful, abominable, improper.

هجن *hujn*, هجنا *hujanâ'*, هجنان *hujnân*, pl. of هجين *hajîn*; — ة *hujna-t*, meanness; vice; fault; faulty expression; INF. of (هجن).

(هجهج) *hajhaj*, INF. ة, scare away by shouting; urge on the camel by the cry هيج *hîj*.

(هجو) *hajâ*, U, INF. *hajw*, *hijâ'*,

tahjâ', persecute with satires, lampoon, ridicule; criticise, censure; — INF. *hajw*, join sounds in syllables, spell; — *hajû*, INF. *hajâwa-t*, be oppressively hot, sultry; be satirical; — II. INF. *tahjiya-t*, spell; — III. INF. *muhâjât*, direct a satire against, lampoon; — IV. INF. *ihjâ'*, find a poem satirical; — V. INF. *tahajjî*, spell; — VI. INF. *tahâjî*, VIII. INF. *ihtijâ'*, lampoon one another.

هجو *hajw*, satire, lampoon; biting speech; mockery, irony; — *hujû'*, INF. of (هجا).

هجود *hajûd*, pl. *hujûd*, *hujjad*, who remains awake the night through in prayer; — *hujûd*, sleep, slumber; pl. of هاجد *hâjid*, sleeping.

هجورى *hajûriyy*, slight meal, lunch.

هجوع *hujû'*, sleep; sleepers.

هجوم *hajûm*, suddenly falling upon; blowing down houses; — *hujûm*, surprise, sudden attack; vehemence, impetuosity.

هجونة *hujûna-t*, meanness, vileness.

هجوى *hajwiyy*, satirical, ironical; pl. ات *hajwiyyâ-t*, satirical poems.

(هجى) *haja*, spell; — *haji'*, A, INF. *hajy*, be open (tent); be deeply set or sunk (eye).

هجى *hajiyy*, satirical; satirist.

هجيج *hajîj*, intensity of heat; far-stretching deep valley; — *; pl. *hujjân*, *ahâjîj*, lines drawn on the ground by a sorcerer.

هجير *hajîr*, ة, a bitter plant; *hajîr*, pl. *hujur*, large cistern, cup; also ة *hajîra-t*, hottest mid-day; — *hujaira-t*, a little year; — *hijjîra-t*=

هجيرى *hajjîrâ*, custom, manner, habit.

هجيع *hajî'*, part of the night.

هجيل *hajîl*, pl. *hijâl*, flat ground.

هجين *hajîn*, pl. *hujn*, *hujanâ*, *hujnân*, *mahâjin*, *mahâjina-t*, f. ة, pl. *hujun*, *hajâ'in*, *hijân*, child of a free man and a female slave; mongrel; of low extraction, ignoble blood; mean, vile; swift, nimble, excellent; (m.) dromedary (pl. *hujun*).

(هد) *hadd*, U, INF. *hadd*, *hudûd*, break (a.) with a loud crack, pull down, demolish; make powerless, ruin; INF. *hadîd*, fall with a crash (house); — I, A, INF. *hadd*, suffer from great weakness; I, roar; be excellent, praised as a brave man; — II. INF. *tahdîd*, frighten, intimidate, threaten; — V. INF. *tahaddud* = II.; — VII. INF. *inhidâd*, be pulled down, fall in ruins.

هد *hadd*, destruction, demolition, annihilation; weakness from old age, weakness; roar; liberal, generous, magnanimous; — *hadd*, *hidd*, pl. *-ûn*, weak; هدك من رجل *haddaka* (*haddika*) *min rajul-in*, that is your man! — ة *hadda-t*, *hudda-t*, crash of ruin.

(هدا) *hada'*, INF. *had'*, *hudû'*, rest, calm down (n.), subside; keep quiet (n.); halt; stop, abide; die; — هدى *hadi'*, A, INF. *hada'*, be hump-backed; — II. INF. *tahdi'a-t*, calm (a.), quiet, appease, moderate; (m.) hold water; (m.) stop, halt; — IV. INF. *ihdâ'*, let rest; pacify, calm (a.); — V. INF. *tahaddu'*, rest, calm down (n.); feel relieved; abate (n.).

هدا *had'*, *hud'*, part of the night (up to a third); — *had'*, state, condition, way of living; — *hada'*, bend; — ة *hadât*, tool, instrument; — *hudât*, pl. of هادى *hâdî*, guide, &c.; — *had'a-t*, part of the night; — *hada'a-t*, a kind of trot; — ة *huddâ'a-t*, slender horse.

هداب *huddâb*, weak, impotent; fringed; separated into fibres at the edge; n. u. ة, fine leaf; palm-branches; fringes; — *.

هداج *haddâj*, having a trembling walk, tottering (adj.).

هدادة *hadâda-t*, timorous.

هداديك *hadâdaika*, gently! patience!

هدار *haddâr*, gang of robbers and murderers.

هدارس *hadâris*, calamities.

هدافة *hudâfat*, corpulence.

هدال *hadâl*, hanging branches; — ة *hadâla-t*, pl. *hidâl*, crowd, troop.

هدام *hudâm*, sea-sickness.

هدان *hidân*, idle, lazy, stupid, timid; — ة *hudâna-t*, rest, peace, truce.

هداهد *hadâhid*, politeness, courtesy; — *; — *hudâhid*, pl. *hadâhid*, *hadâhîd*, hoopoe.

هداهيد *hadâhîd*, pl. of the previous and of هدهد *hudhud*.

هداوة *hadâwa-t*, rest, quiet, tranquillity; peacefulness, peaceableness.

هداوى *hadâwa*, هدايا *hadâya*, pl. of هدية *hadiyya-t*.

هداية *hidâya-t*, right guidance; title of a legal book.

(هدب) *hadab*, I, INF. *hadb*, milk; cut off; pluck, cull; — *hadib*, A, INF. *hadab*, have long eye-lashes; (also IV.) have long hanging branches; — IV. INF. *ihdâb*, see I.

هدب *hudb*, *hudub*, ة, pl. *ahdâb*, eyelashes; hem, fringes; skirt; — *hadab*, ة, pl. *ahdâb*, *hidâb*, branches with very fine hair-like leaves; ه العين *hadab al-'ain*, eyelashes; — *hadib*, lion; — *hudubb*, weak, impotent; — ة *hudaba-t*, a bird.

هدبا *hadbâ'*, f. of اهدب *ahdab*, having long eye-lashes.

هدبد *hudabid*, very thick milk; a kind of gum; weakness of the eyes.

هدبس *hadabbas*, male tiger.

(هدج) *hadaj*, I, INF. *hadajân*, *hudâj*, walk with a tremble, totter; — V. INF. *tahadduj*, be fond of the foal; tremble; — ة *hadaja-t*, cry of a fond she-camel for her foal.

هدد *hadad*, rough hoarse voice.

(هدر) *hadar*, I, U, INF. *hadr*, *hadar*, be spent uselessly; be shed with impunity; INF. *hadr*, spend money or pains to no purpose; lavish, squander; shed blood or allow it to be shed with impunity; — I, INF. *hadr*, *hadîr*, *tahdâr*, roar, give utterance; be agitated, infuriated (sea); bray; coo; stand high and luxuriant; INF. *hadr*, *tahdâr*, ferment; — II. INF. *tahdîr*, roar; coo; — IV. INF. *ihdâr*, allow blood to be shed with impunity; — VI. *tahâdur*, shed blood with impunity or to no purpose; — VII. INF. *inhidâr*, be spent uselessly; be shed with impunity; — XII. *ihdaudar*, INF. *ihdîdâr*, pour down abundantly.

هدر *hadr*, *hadar*, impunity in a case of bloodshed; useless expenditure; — *hidr*, heavy, clumsy; — *hadar*, ة *hadra-t*, crash of a fall; — ة *hadara-t*, *hidara-t*, *hudara-t*, worthless person, wretch.

(هدس) *hadas*, myrtle.

(هدش), pass. *hudiś*, also VII. INF. *inhidâś*, get irritated.

(هدغ) *hadag*, INF. *hadg*, break into pieces; — VII. INF. *inhidâg*, get soft, burst (date).

(هدف) *hadaf*, I, INF. *hadf*, appear, enter; approach; — I, be heavy, clumsy, weary and lazy; — IV. INF. *ihdâf*, approach, be near; tower over, look down from above; take refuge with (الى *ila*); — X. INF. *istihdâf*, rise and appear, serve as an aim or target; expose one's self.

هدف *hadaf*, pl. *ahdâf*, anything rising above the ground and visible from a distance; aim, target; heavy, clumsy; sleepy; — *hidf*, corpulent; — ة *hidfa-t*, troop; group of houses; — *hadafa-t*, visor (m.).

(هدك) *hadak*, I, INF. *hadk*, pull down, demolish; — V. INF. *tahadduk*, attack and hurt by words.

هدكر *hudakir*, thick milk.

(هدل) *hadal*, I, INF. *hadîl*, coo; INF. *hadl*, let hang down loosely; — *hadil*, A, INF. *hadal*, hang down; — V. INF. *tahaddul*, id.

هدل *hidl*, thick milk; — *hadil*, with a hanging lip.

هدلا *hadlâ'*, هدلى *hadla*, hanging down, f. of اهدل *ahdal*.

(هدم) *hadam*, I, INF. *hadm*, pull down, demolish, level with the ground; break one's back; — *hadim*, A, INF. *hadam*, *hadama-t* (also IV. and V.), be hot, rutting; — II. INF. *tahdîm*, destroy from the foundations; — IV. INF. *ihdâm*, see *hadim*; — V. INF. *tahaddum* (also VII.), be pulled down, destroyed, fall in ruins; fall upon angrily and threaten; see *hadim*; — VII. INF. *inhidâm*, = V.

هدم *hadm*, *hadam*, blood shed with impunity; — *hidm*, pl. *ahdâm*, *hidam*, *hudûm*, torn and patched-up garment, rags, tatters; (m.) trowsers, drawers; old boot; — *hadim*, destroyer; — ة *hadma-t*, light rain; — *hadima-t*, pl. *hadâma*, *hidama-t*, rut, rutting.

(هدمل) *hadmal*, INF. ة tear one's clothes.

هدن *hadan*, I, INF. *hudûn*, calm down (n.), rest; — INF. *hadn*, calm (a.), appease; bury; — II. INF. *tahdîn*, calm (a.), appease, set at rest; — III. INF. *muhâdana-t*, make a truce with; — VI. INF. *tahâdun*, make a truce with one another; be settled amicably, flourish; — VII. INF. *inhidân*, allow one's self to be turned from one's purpose, yield, relent.

هدن *hidn*, abundance, affluence; — ة *hadna-t*, gentle rain; — *hudna-t*, truce, peace; quiet, rest.

(هدهد) *hadhad*, INF. ة, coo; rock a child in one's arms and quiet it; roar; thunder violently.

هدهد *hadhad*, pl. *hadâhîd*, voices, calls of the demons; — *hudhud*, *hudahid*, pl. *hadâhid*, *hadâhîd*, hoopoe; bird which coos or calls much; wood-pigeon; — *hudu'*, part of the night; — *haduww*, guide, leader; — *hudû'*, *huduww*, quieting (s.), quiet, rest; night-rest; — ة *hadhada-t*, pl. *hadâhid*, cooing; murmur; roar of a camel; lullaby.

هدود *hadûd*, plain; steep precipice; — *hudûd*, breach, demolition, destruction.

هدون *hudûn*, rest, comfort; quietude, quieting, appeasing (s.).

(هدى) *hada*, I, INF. *hady*, *huda*, *hidya-t*, *hidâya-t*, lead on the right path, guide; (also IV. and VIII.) conduct the bride to the bridegroom; be rightly guided; find the right way; lead a good life; follow, imitate; — II. INF. *tahdiya-t*, offer a present; — III. INF. *muhâdât*, id.; present with; — IV. INF. *ihdâ'*, send, bring or offer a present; lead, guide; conduct (see I.), lead animals to Mecca to be sacrificed; — V. INF. *tahaddî*, be well guided; find one's way; — VI. INF. *tahâdî*, make presents to one another; balance one's self in walking, swagger; — VII. INF. *inhidâ'*, be offered, given as a present; — VIII. INF. *ihtidâ'*, be rightly guided, keep in the right way; find one's way; allow one's self to be guided; reach one's goal; see I.; — X. INF. *istihdâ'*, ask for guidance, for a guide, for the right way; reach one's goal or destination; gain as a gift.

هدى *hady*, conduct, way of life, habit, natural disposition, man-

ner, way; — *hady, hadiyy*, sacrifice for Mecca; bride conducted to the bridegroom; *hadiyy*, captive; anything venerable or precious; — *hudan, huda*, right guidance; leading in the right way; *al-huda*, the right way, way of salvation, true religion; — *hadi'*, part of the night; — ة *hadya-t*, sacrifice for Mecca; also *hidya-t*, pl. *hady*, institution, custom, manner; also *hudya-t*, way of life, conduct, acting according to circumstances; purpose, aim; — *hadiyya-t*, pl. *hâdâyâ, hadâwa, hadâwî, hadâw-in*, present; beast of sacrifice; bride.

هديد *hadîd*, crash of a downfall; rough hoarse voice.

هدير *hadîr*, roaring, cooing (s.); dove.

(هذ) *hazz*, U, INF. *hazz, hazaz, hazâz*, cut, sever; INF. *hazz, hazâz*, (m.) *hazîz*, read fast and fluently; read aloud to; meditate, ponder over, study; — VIII. INF. *ihtizâz*, cut.

هذ *hazz*, sharp, cutting.

(هذا) *haza'*, INF. *haz'*, cut off quickly; strike down, destroy; — هذى *hazi'*, A, INF. *haza'*, perish, freeze to death; — V. INF. *tahazzu'*, become malignant and break open (tumour).

هذا *hâzâ*, this, this one; — *huzâ'*, delirium, dotage, foolish talk; — *hazzâ'*, ةء *hazzâ'a-t*, delirating, doting, talking foolishly (adj.); — ة *haz'a-t*, spade, mattock; pick-axe.

هذابة *hazâba-t*, haste, swiftness, nimbleness.

هذاذ *hazâz*, INF. of (هذ); — *hazzâz*, cutting quickly, sharp.

هذاذيك *hazâzaika*, give over! leave off!

هذار *hizâr*, jest; — *hazzâr*, who delirates, dotes; idle talker.

هذاف *hazzâf*, swift, nimble; sharp.

هذاك *hâzâka*, that.

هذاليل *hazâlîl*, pl. of هذلول *huzlûl*.

هذام *huzâm*, sharp; bold.

(هذب) *hazab*, I, INF. *hazb*, cut off what is superfluous, prune, cut wood, adapt, adjust; (m.) bring up a child; (m.) polish one's style; flow; INF. *hazb, hazâba-t*, hasten (n.), be swift, nimble; — II. INF. *tahzîb*, hasten (n.); cut and adjust; perfect; refine; educate; work out neatly; — III. INF. *muhâzaba-t*, hasten, do quickly; — IV. INF. *ihzâb*, hasten, hurry (n.); — V. INF. *tahazzub*, be cut and adjusted; be put in order; be well educated, refined, polite.

هذب *hazab*, sincerity of friendship; purity, brilliancy.

(هذخر) *hazhar*, INF. ة, walk proudly and rejoicing in victory.

(هذر) *hazar*, U, I, INF. *hazr, tahzâr*, delirate, dote, talk foolishly; be talkative; be very hot; — *hazir*, A, INF. *hazr*, be false, idle, foolish; — IV. INF. *ihzâr*, delirate, dote, talk foolishly.

هذر *hazr*, delirious talk, foolishness, nonsense; idle talk; — *hazir, hazur*, ة, delirating, doting (adj.); — ة *huzara-t, huzura-t*, foolish talker.

هذرب *hazrab*, INF. ة, speak very fast, be glib of tongue.

هذربان *huzrubân*, glib of tongue; nimble.

هذرف *hazraf*, be swift, nimble.

هذرم *hazram*, INF. ة, speak or read fast.

هذرمى *hazramā*, screaming woman.

هذروف *huzrûf*, pl. *hazârîf*, swift, nimble.

هذريان *hizriyân*, delirating, doting; glib; nimble.

(هذف) *hazaf*, I, INF. *huzûf*, be swift, nimble.

هذف *hazif*, swift, nimble; sharp.

(هذلب) *hazlab*, هذلم *hazlam*, INF. ة, hasten (n.), be swift, nimble.

هذلة *hazla-t*, quick short pace.

هذلول *huzlûl*, pl. *hazâlîl*, small hill,

sand-heap; thin cloud or fine rain; mildew; light, swift.
(هذم) *hażam*, I, INF. *hażm*, cut off quickly; eat fast.
(هذمل) *hażmal*, INF. ة, walk with short steps.
هذه *hâżihi*, this, this one (f.).
هذهاذ *hażhâż*, sharp.
(هذو) *hażâ*, U, INF. *hażw*, delirate, dote, talk foolishly; brandish the sword over and strike.
(هذى) *haża*, I, INF. *haży*, *hażayân*, delirate, dote, talk foolishly.
هذى *hâżî*, this, this one (f.).
هذيان *hażayân*, foolish talk, nonsense, INF. of (هذى).
هذيذ *hażîż*, meditation on what has been read; study.
(هر) *harr*, U, I, INF. *harr*, *harîr*, abhor, detest; I, INF. *harîr*, (also IV.) whine, yelp; make to whine; twang (n.); pass. INF. *hurr*, *harâr*, suffer from dysentery or the tumour *hurâr*; die of the former; bring on diarrhœa; (m.) leak; (m.) pour out; — *harir*, A, be malicious; — III. INF. *muhârra-t*, whine to; — IV. INF. *ihrâr*, see I.; make to whine; — VII. INF. *in-hirâr*, be poured out.
هر *hirr*, pl. *hirara-t*, f. ة *hirra-t*, pl. *hirar*, cat; — *hurr*, diarrhœa.
(هرا) *hara'*, INF. *har'*, use faulty, coarse or obscene expressions; INF. *har'*, *harâ'a-t*, injure greatly, kill; be exceedingly cold; cook the meat until it separates into fibres; deteriorate (a.), spoil; — هرى *hari'*, A, INF. *har'*, *hur'*, *hurû'*, *hara'*, (also V.) cook as above; — II. INF. *tahri'a-t*, (also IV.) cook as above; (also IV.) injure, make to suffer; deteriorate (a.), spoil; (m.) wear out a garment; — IV. INF. *ihrâ'*, see II.; — V. INF. *taharru'*, see *hari'*; — VIII. INF. *ihtirâ'*, be separated into fibres by cooking; (m.) rot, get putrid; (m.) be entirely worn out.
هرا *hirâ'*, young palm-shoot; (m.) putrefaction, decay, destruction; — *hurâ'*, prolix foolish talk; — ة *harâ'a-t*, icy cold (s.).
هراب *hurrâb*, pl. of هارب *hârib*, fugitive.
هرات *harrât*, lion.
هراثم *hurâsim*, lion.
هراج *harrâj*, swift, fleet; public cry, auction.
هرار *hirâr*, abhorrence; — *hurâr*, violent diarrhœa, dysentery; tumour between the flesh and skin; — *harrâr*, noisy, clamorous; du. *al-harrârân*, two months (December and January), two stars; — ة *harrâra-t*, overflowing.
هراس *harâs*, a thorn-tree; — *hurâs*, *harrâs*, voracious; — *harrâs*, seller of the dish هريسة *harîsa-t*.
هراش *hirâś*, exciting one against another (s.); jesting, toying.
هراطقة *harâṭiqa-t*, pl. of هرطوقى *harṭûqiyy*.
هراق *harâq*, be poured out; — ة *hirâqa-t*, pouring out (s.).
هراكل *hurâkil*, thick, massy; — ة *harâkila-t*, large sea-fishes, seals, &c.; flux of the sea.
هرام *harrâm*, who cuts tobacco.
هرامس *hurâmis*, grim lion.
هراميل *harâmîl*, pl. of هرمول *hurmûl*.
هراوة *hirâwa-t*, pl. *harâwa*, *hiriyy*, *huriyy*, large stick, staff, cudgel, club.
(هرب) *harab*, U, INF. *harab*, *harabân*, *mahrab*, flee, run away, escape; sink in the ground; — *harib*, A, be weak from old age, decrepit; — II. INF. *tahrîb*, put to flight; (m.) هرب الكمرك *harrab al-kumruk*, smuggle; — IV. INF. *ihrâb*, see II.; depart hurriedly, scamper away.
هرب *harab*, flight, escape; emigration.

هربان *harbân*, fugitive ; — *harabân*, flight.

هربذ *hirbiẕ*, pl. *harâbiẕa-t*, worshipper of fire, Magian.

(هرت) *harat*, I, U, INF. *hart*, pierce ; tear, rend ; injure one's honour ; over-cook the meat ; — *harit*, A, INF. *harat*, have large corners of the mouth.

هرت *harit*, lion.

هرتك *hartak*, pl. *harâtik*, things, chattels, luggage.

هرث *hirs̱*, worn-out garment.

هرثم *hars̱am*, lion ; — ة *hars̱ama-t*, id. ; tip of the nose, snout, muzzle ; dimple in the upper lip.

(هرج) *haraj*, I, INF. *harj*, overdo anything, be prolix and confused in one's speech ; get into discord, rebellion, bloodshed ; (m.) jest, joke, toy ; — *harij*, A, INF. *haraj*, suffer from heat, &c., be excited ; — II. INF. *tahrîj* (also IV.), excite the camel by urging it on ; make giddy, intoxicate ; (m.) jest, joke, mimic ;—IV. INF. *ihrâj*, see II. ; — VII. INF. *inhirâj*, be giddy from wine.

هرج *harj*, excitement, agitation, tumult, bloodshed, war ; هرج ومرج *harj wa marj*, great confusion, chaos, anarchy ; (m.) jesting, toying, sporting (s.) ;—*hirj*, stupid, incapable.

هرجان *harjân*, wild almond.

(هرجل) *harjal*, INF. ة ; walk with unequal steps.

(هرد) *harad*, I, INF. *hard*, tear, rend, unsew, split, spoil ; damage one's character ; (also II.) overcook the meat.

هرد *hard*, tumult, riot ; — *hurd*, saffron ; a root for dyeing ; red clay.

هرر *harar*, INF. of (هر) ; — *hirar*, pl. of هرة *hirra-t* ; — ة *hirara-t*, pl. of هر *hirr*.

(هردب) *hardab*, INF. ة , walk with short steps ; run heavily.

هردج *hardaj*, INF. ة , walk fast.

هردى *hurdiyy*, dyed with هرد *hurd* ; — ة *hurdiyya-t*, fence of bulrush.

(هرز) *haraz*, U, INF. *harz*, beckon to one, press with the hand, pinch ; beat, thrash ; — *hariz*, A, INF. *haraz*, perish, die ; — II. INF. *tahrîz*, thrash, maltreat (m.).

هرزوقى *hurzûqā*, prison.

(هرس) *haras*, U, INF. *hars*, eat greedily ; (also II.) crush violently, pound minutely ;—*haris*, A, INF. *haras*, be voracious, gluttonous ; — II. INF. *tahrîs*, see I. ; — V. INF. *taharrus*, be entirely crushed.

هرس *hars*, crushing, pounding (s.) ; violent push or thrust ; cat ; — *haris*, voracious ; lion ; cat ; worn-out.

(هرش) *haraś*, I, U, INF. *harś*, be adverse ; — *hariś*, A, INF. *haraś*, be malicious ; — II. INF. *tahrîś*, set against one another ; grow old, decrepit ; — III. INF. *hirâś*, *muhâraśa-t*, set or incite against one another ; jest, sport, toy with ; — V. INF. *taharruś*, dissolve (n.) ; — VI. INF. *tahâruś* (also VIII.), be set or incited against one another ; (m.) jest or sport with one another ; — VIII. INF. *inhirâś*, see VI.

(هرشف) *harśaf*, INF. ة , drink slowly ; dry up ; — III. INF. *ihriśfâf*, id. ; — ة *hirśaffa-t*, cotton steeped in ink ; cloth intercepting rain-water to be wrung out afterwards ; old woman.

(هرص) *hariṣ*, A, INF. *haraṣ*, be afflicted with dry scab, with the mange.

هرص *haraṣ*, mange, dry scab.

(هرض) *haraḍ*, U, INF. *harḍ*, tear one's garment.

هرض *haraḍ*, mange, dry scab.

(هرط) *haraṭ*, I, INF. *harṭ*, tear one's garment ; damage one's character.

هرط *hirṭ*, ة , pl. *hiraṭ*, *ahrâṭ*, *hurûṭ*, old sheep ; rich man.

هرطق *harṭaq*, INF. ة, become a heretic; — ة *harṭaqa-t*, heresy.

هرطمان *hurṭumân, harṭumân*, a kind of oats.

هرطوقى *harṭûqiyy*, pl. *harâṭiqa-t*, heretic.

(هرع) *hari'*, A, INF. *hara'*, flow fast; hurry excitedly; *hara'*, INF. *har'*, drive fast; — II. INF. *tahrî'* (also V.), advance against the enemy with lowered lances; — IV. INF. *ihrâ'*, hasten, hurry (n.); pass. tremble with rage; — V. INF. *taharru'*=II.; — VIII. INF. *ihtirâ'*, break (a.).

هرع *hara'*, swiftness, haste; rapid flow; — *hari'*, flowing fast, hot; ة *hari'a-t*, unchaste, lewd (f.);— ة *har'a-t, hara'a-t*, small louse.

(هرف) *haraf*, I, INF. *harf*, praise immoderately; also — II. INF. *tahrîf* (and IV. INF. *ihrâf*) mature the dates quickly; hurry over one's prayer.

(هرق) — II. *harraq*, INF. *tahrîq*, pour out entirely or forcibly, shed much; — IV. *harâq* (for اراق IV. of (روق), *ahraq*, aor. *yuhrîq*, INF. *hirâqa-t*, pour out, shed.

(هرق) *hirq*, worn-out and ragged garment.

هرقاهة *harqâha-t*, large black tent.

هرقل *hirqil*, sieve, strainer; also *hiraql*, Heraclius.

(هركل) *harkal*, INF. ة, swagger; (m.) grow old and decrepit; — ة *harkala-t, hirakla-t, hurakila-t*, also—

هركولة *hirkaula-t*, هركيل *hirkîl*, noble beautiful woman with a proud walk.

هركمة *harkama-t*, pl. *harâkim*, head and feet of a slaughtered sheep.

(هرم) *harim*, A, INF. *haram, mahram, mahrama-t*, be very old, weak from old age, decrepit; — (m.) *haram*, U, INF. *harm*, cut tobacco minutely; — II. INF. *tahrîm* (also IV.), render old and weak; (m.) cut tobacco or have it cut minutely; cut in pieces, hash; — IV. INF. *ihrâm*, see II.; — V. INF. *taharrum*, be cut minutely; — VI. INF. *tahârum*, feign to be old and weak; — VII. INF. *inhirâm*=V.

هرم *harm*, ة, a plant; (m.) cutting into small pieces, hashing (s.); — *haram*, weakness from old age; decrepitude; pl. *hirâm, ahrâm*, pyramid; old Himyaritic buildings in Yemen; — *harim*, (m.) *harm, hirm*, pl. *-ûn* (f. ة, pl. *-ât*), *harmā*, weak with age, decrepit; mind, intellect; ة *harima-t*, lioness; — ة *harma-t*, a small slice of tobacco.

هرمان *hurmân*, mind, intellect.

(هرمز) *harmaz*, INF. ة, be extinguished; masticate and roll the morsels slowly in the mouth.

هرمز *hurmuz* (ال *al*), هرمزان *hurmuzân*, designation of the Shah of Persia.

(هرمس) *harmas*, INF. ة, be austere, severe-looking.

(هرمط) *harmaṭ*, INF. ة, damage one's character.

(هرمع) *haramma'*, who cries easily; swiftness; — *ihramma'*, INF. *ihrimmâ'*, be swift, nimble; be prolix; be easily induced to cry.

(هرمل) *harmal*, INF. ة, pull out hair; bungle, slur over; be decrepit.

هرمل *hirmil*, old she-camel; old woman.

هرمول *hurmûl*, pl. *harâmîl*, stubble of hair.

هرميش *hirmîś*, grim lion; rhinoceros; buffalo.

(هرنص) *harnaṣ*, bore holes, eat the wood (as a worm).

هرنصانة *harnaṣâna-t*, worm in a ship.

(هرنف) *harnaf*, INF. ة, laugh low or in one's sleeve.

هرنوة *harnuwa-t*, هرنوى *harnuwiyy*, *harnawa*, fruit of the aloes-tree, a plant growing in the sand.

(هرهر) *harhar*, INF. ة, call or lead the sheep to the watering-place; move, shake (a.); use violence against, wrong; bleat; — ة *har-*

hara-t, bleating, bellowing (s.); murmuring of the water.

هرهور *hurhûr*, murmuring stream; a kind of ship.

(هرو) *harâ*, U, INF. *harw*, also هرى *hara*, INF. *hary*, beat with a stick, cudgel, thrash; — III. INF. *muhârât*, make fun of, mock at; — V. INF. *taharrî*, thrash.

هرو *hurû'*, INF. of هرى *hari'*, see (هرا).

هروت *harût*, lion.

هروز *harwaz*, INF. ة, perish, die; — II. INF. *taharwuz*, id.

هرول *harwal*, INF. ة, trot moderately, amble, walk fast.

هروى *harawiyy*, of or from Herat.

هرى *hury*, pl. *ahrâ'*, public corn-magazine, store-house, granary; — *hara*, see (هرو); — *hari'*, over-cooked; see (هرا); — *huriyy*, pl. of *harâwa-t*; — ة *hariyya-t*, deathly cold.

هرياع *hiryâ'*, stray leaf.

هريان *harayân*, putrefaction, decay.

هريبة *harîba-t*, flight.

هريت *harît*, having broad corners of the mouth; who blabs out everything; lion.

هرير *harîr*, abhorrence; whining, yelping (s.); — ة *huraira-t*, kitten, pussy.

هريس *harîs*, ة, entirely crushed, pounded minutely, ground into powder; — ة *harîsa-t*, pl. *harîs*, *harâ'is*, a paste made of pounded wheat, butter, meat, and spices.

هريصة *harîṣa-t*, pond, sheet of water.

هريى *harî'*, deadly.

(هز) *hazz*, U, I, INF. *hazz*, shake (a.); (m.) rock a child; (m.) totter; — INF. *hazîz*, urge on the camels by singing; — II. INF. *tahzîz*, shake, move (a.); — V. INF. *tahazzuz*, be moved, move (n.); totter; — VII. INF. *inhizâz*, VIII. INF. *ihtizâz*, id.

هز *hazz*, shaking (s.); rocking (s.); — *huz'*, mockery, scoffing (s.); — ة *hazza-t*, motion, commotion, concussion, shock; earthquake; — *hizza-t*, briskness, cheerfulness; murmuring (s.); echo of thunder.

(هزا) *haza'*, INF. *haz'*, break (a.); allow to freeze or to freeze to death; put in motion, urge on; die; — INF. *huz'*, *huzû'*, *mahza'a-t*, mock at, make sport of; — هزى *hazi'*, A, INF. *haza'*, id.; die; — IV. INF. *ihzâ'*, allow to freeze, to freeze to death; — V. INF. laugh at, make an object of derision.

هزا *haza'*, mockery, persiflage; death; — ة *huza'-t*, laughed at by everybody; — *huza'a-t*, who always laughs at, scoffs, derides.

هزابر *huzâbir*, lion; — *.

هزار *hazâr*, nightingale (Pers.); — ة *hazâra-t*, thrashing (s.), ill-treatment.

هزارف *huzârif*, swift.

هزاز *hazzâz*, plover.

هزاع *hazzâ'*, lion.

هزال *hazâl*, *huzâl*, emaciation, thinness; *huzâl*, thin, emaciated; — *hazzâl*, jester, buffoon; — ة *huzâla-t*, jest, jocularity.

(هزبر) *hazbar*, INF. ة, cut off.

هزبر *hizbar*, *hizabr*, pl. *hazâbir*, lion.

(هزبل) *hazbal*, INF. ة, fall into utter poverty.

(هزج) *hazij*, A, INF. *hazaj*, modulate one's voice, trill, quiver; also II. INF. *tahzîj*, IV. INF. *ihzâj*, use the metre هزج *hazaj*.

هزج *hazaj*, trill, quiver; rhythm, rhythmical speech; name of a metre (مفاعيلن *mafâ'îlun* ⏑ — — — six times repeated); — *hazij*, modulating; ه العشى *hazij al-'aśiyy*, wild cat.

(هزر) *hazar*, I, INF. *hazr*, thrash; pinch violently; ill-treat; slander badly; expel, exile, banish; sell dearly, cheat; buy inconsiderately; — II. INF. *tahzîr*=I.; — V. INF. *tahazzur*, be ill-treated; — ة *hazra-t*, *hazara-t*, blow with a stick; ذو هزرات *ẕû hazarât-in*, cheated.

(هزرف) *hazraf*, INF. ة, hasten, hurry (n.).

هرزوقى *huzrûqa*, prison.
(هرع) *haza'*, INF. *haz'*, (also VIII.) hasten (n.); be quick; — II. INF. *tahzî'*, break (a.), crush; — VII. INF. *inhizâ'*, be broken, crushed; — VIII. INF. *ihtizâ'*=I.; be brandished.
هزع *huza'*, lion.
(هزف) *hazaf*, I, INF. *hazf*, carry or blow away.
(هزق) *hazaq*, briskness, nimbleness, vivacity; — IV. *ahzaq*, INF. *ihzâq*, laugh immoderately.
(هزل) *hazal*, I, INF. *hazl*, *huzl*, emaciate (a.); U, be thin, emaciated; grow poor; pass. *huzil*, INF. *huzâl*, be emaciated; (m.) be little esteemed, despised; I, INF. *hazl*, also — *hazil*, A, INF. *hazal*, jest, speak or act in joke, not in earnest; play buffoon; — II. INF. *tahzîl*, emaciate; III. INF. *muhâzala-t*, jest; — IV. INF. *ihzâl*=II.; have lean cattle; make little of, disdain; — VII. INF. *inhizâl*, be emaciated, without strength; — X. INF. *istihzâl*, make little of, disdain.
هزل *hazl*, jest, joke, sport; obscene talk or action; also *huzl*, leanness, emaciation; — *hazil*, who does everything in joke, who is always jesting; — ى *hazla*, pl. of هزيل *hazîl*; — يات *hazliyyât*, jests, jokes; obscene verses.
(هزم) *hazam*, I, INF. *hazm*, press with the hand so as to leave an impression; pass. *huzim*, feel inclination towards (على *'ala*); — INF. *hazm*, *hazîma-t*, beat and put to flight; — INF. *hazîm*, (also V.) twang (n.); — II. INF. *tahzîm*, put to flight, rout; — V. INF. *tahazzum*, see I.; also VII. INF. *inhizâm*, break with a crack; be routed; — VIII. INF. *ihtizâm*, burst with a crash and pour down rain; set quickly to work.
هزم *hazm*, defeat and flight, rout; hollow of the stomach; n. u. ة, pl. *hazm*, *huzûm*, impression made by the hand; — *hazam*, twang of a bow; — *hazim*, like a water-spout.
(هزمج) *hazmaj*, INF. ة, talk without interruption, sound confusedly.
هزمر *hazmar*, INF. ة, shake violently (a.); molest, vex, torment; compel.
هزنبر *hazambar*, هزنبران *hazambarân*, cunning, sly, malicious.
نزنبز *hazambaz*, هزنبزان *hazambazân*= the previous; springer, dancer.
هزهاز *hazhâz*, flashing; flowing abundantly.
(هزهز) *hazhaz*, INF. ة, push, move (a.), swing (a.), brandish, rock, cause to vibrate or oscillate; render contemptible, humiliate; — II. INF. *tahazhuz*, move to and fro, swing (n.), vibrate, oscillate; be restless from impatience or exultation, beat joyfully towards (heart); — ة *hazhaza-t*, pl. *hazâhiz*, tumult, commotion, sedition, civil war; swing; oscillation.
(هزو) *hazâ*, U, INF. *hazw*, travel, depart.
هزو *huz'*, *huzû'*, mockery, persiflage.
هزوم *hazûm*, twanging, sounding (adj.); — *huzûm*, last part of the night; pl. of هزمة *hazma-t*.
هزيز *hazîz*, rustling of the wind in the trees; sound of thunder.
هزيع *hazî'*, part of the night; stupid.
هزيل *hazîl*, pl. *hazla*, emaciated.
هزيم *hazîm*, sound, INF. of (هزم); — ة *hazîma-t*, pl. *hazâ'im*, defeat, flight, rout (also هزيمى *hazîmâ*); pl. *hazâ'im*, well abounding with water.
(هس) *hass*, U, INF. *hass*, pound or break minutely; — I, talk to one's self; whisper to.
هسرة *husra-t*, relations, uncles.
هساهس *hasâhis*, whisper.
(هسع) *hasa'*, INF. *has'*, hasten (n.).
(هسم) *hasam*, I, INF. *hasm*, break (a.), crush.

هسهاس *hashâs*, who works or tends cattle the night through; swift; butcher.

(**هسهس**) *hashas*, INF. ة, whisper; sound, twang (n.), rattle, rustle, clatter; flow like a chain.

هسيس *hasîs*, crumbled; whisper.

(**هش**) *haśś*, U, I, INF. *haśś*, beat off with a stick; INF. *huśûśa-t*, be soft; I, also — *haśiś*, A, INF. *haśś*, *haśâś*, *haśâśa-t*, be in good humour, cheerful, friendly, talkative, obliging; — II. INF. *tahśîś*, render cheerful, &c.;—VIII. INF. *ihtiśâś*, show one's self friendly, obliging to, be joyful; — X. INF. *istihśâś*, find joyous and cheerful.

هش *haśś*, fresh and soft; reduced to powder; joyous, cheerful (هش بش ب *haśś baśś bi*, very glad of); friendly; in great perspiration.

هشاش *haśâś*, soft; also ة *haśâśa-t*, merriment, cheerfulness, friendly advances, obligingness;—*haśśâś*, joyous, cheerful, friendly and obliging; — ة *haśâśa-t*, softness.

هشام *hiśâm*, liberality.

(**هشر**) *haśar*, U, INF. *haśr*, milk the camels to the last drop.

هشر *haśr*, thinness, softness, lightness, weakness;—ة *haśra-t*, pertness, haughtiness, ingratitude.

(**هشل**) *haśal*, U=VIII.; (m.) emigrate; (m.) roam about, be vagabond; — II. INF. *tahśîl*, leave some milk in the udder; (m.) expel from one's home, force to emigrate; — IV. INF. *ihśâl*, give one a هشيلة *haśîla-t*; — VIII. INF. *ihtiśâl*, use a beast of burden without the owner's permission, but with the intention of giving it back;—ة *haśla-t*, roaming about, vagabondage.

(**هشم**) *haśam*, I, INF. *haśm*, break (a.), crush; — II. INF. *tahśîm*, break or crush entirely; wound in many places; (also V.) respect and honour; — V. INF. *tahaśśum*, be broken, crushed, go to pieces; be reduced to powder; be wounded in many places, badly injured; see II.; — VII. INF. *inhiśâm*, be weak, broken down; — VIII. INF. *ihtiśâm*, be broken, crushed.

هشم *haśim*, liberal; — ة *haśama-t*, mountain-goat.

هشمشمة *haśamśama-t*, lion.

هشهاش *haśhâś*, obliging, liberal.

هشهش *haśhaś*, INF. ة, push on, put in motion, shake (a.).

(**هشو**), III. *hâśa*, INF. *muhâśât*, sport with, toy with.

هشيش *haśîś*, joyous, cheerful, friendly, obliging; soft; relaxed, weak.

هشيلة *haśîla-t*, beast of burden of which one makes use without the owner's permission.

هشيم *haśîm*, broken, crushed; dry and brittle; dry stalk; dry hay, stubble; — ة *haśîma-t*, pl. *haśîm*, withered tree, piece of dry wood; ه الكرم *haśîma-t al-karam*, liberal.

(**هص**) *haṣṣ*, U, INF. *haṣṣ*, press with the hand so as to leave a trace; break (a.), crush, crush with the foot.

هصار *haṣṣâr*, lion.

هصام *haṣṣâm*, lion.

(**هصب**) *haṣab*, I, INF. *haṣb*, flee, run away.

(**هصر**) *haṣar*, I, INF. *haṣr*, push back, repel, drive off; (also II.) draw and bend towards one's self; break (a.); bend and break without severing; — II. INF. *tahṣîr*, see I.; — VII. INF. *inhiṣâr*, be bent, broken; — VIII. INF. *ihtiṣâr*, break (n.); be broken.

هصر *haṣir*, *huṣar*, ة *huṣara-t*, lion;— ة *haṣra-t*, *haṣara-t*, enchanted potion, philter.

(**هصم**) *haṣam*, I, INF. *haṣm*, break (a.), crush.

هصم *huṣam*, lion.

(**هصهص**) *haṣhaṣ*, INF. ة, press with the hand so as to leave a trace; accuse, slander.

(**هصو**) *haṣâ*, U, INF. *haṣw*, be very old.

هصور *hasûr*, *haṣwar*, ة *haṣwara-t*, lion.

هصيص *haṣîṣ*, broken, crushed, crushed with the foot; flickering of the fire.

(هض) *hadd*, U, INF. *hadd*, break (a.), pound; cut off; instigate, urge on; go a good pace, hurry (n.); — VII. INF. *inhiḍâḍ*, be broken; — VIII. INF. *ihtiḍâḍ*, break (a.), pound.

هضا *haḍḍâ'*, troop, squadron; — ة *hiḍât*, fore-locks; she-ass.

هضاضة *haḍâḍa-t*, anything broken.

هضام *haḍḍâm*, conducive to digestion; easily digesting; liberal; who diminishes or increases at will; lion.

(هضب) *haḍab*, I, INF. *haḍb*, rain continuously; (also IV. INF. *ihḍâb*) make too many words; walk lazily; sulkily.

هضب *hiḍabb*, in great perspiration; strong; — ة *haḍba-t*, pl. *hiḍab*, *hiḍâb*, *haḍabât*, *ahâḍib*, shower of rain in large drops; high massy isolated mountains.

(هضج) — II. *haḍḍaj*, INF. *tahḍîj*, tend the cattle not well.

(هضل) *haḍal*, U, INF. *haḍl*, flow abundantly in speech or verses; — IV. INF. *ihḍâl*, rain abundantly.

هضل *haḍl*, abundant, plentiful.

هضلا *haḍlâ'*, having long teats.

(هضم) *haḍam*, I, INF. *haḍm*, break (a.); digest well; make to digest well, promote digestion; suffer patiently; fall upon suddenly, attack; (also V. and VIII.) wrong; take from forcibly (2 acc.);—*haḍim*, A, INF. *haḍam*, have a slender waist; be sunk; — II. INF. *tahḍîm*, digest very well; promote digestion greatly; pass. have thin flanks; — V. INF. *tahaḍḍum*, see I.; — VII. INF. *inhiḍâm*, be digested; — VIII. INF. *ihtiḍâm* = V.

هضم *haḍm*, digestion; patience, long-suffering (s.); violence, wrong, injury; سوق الهضم *sûq al-haḍm*, losing market; also — *hiḍm*, pl. *ahḍâm*, *huḍûm*, low plain, ground in a valley; canal, lake; —*haḍam*, slimness of waist; also *haḍm*, pl. *ahḍâm*, an aroma; — *huḍum*, pl. of هضوم *haḍûm*.

هضما *haḍmâ'*, f. of اهضم *ahḍam*, having thin flanks, &c.

(هضهض) *haḍhaḍ*, INF. ة break (a.); pound.

(هضو) — III. *hâḍa*, INF. *muhâḍât*, deem stupid, think little of.

هضوبة *huḍûba-t*, sufficient rain.

هضوم *haḍûm*, promoting digestion (adj.); digesting well; liberal; pl. *huḍum*, hands; — *

هضيض *haḍîḍ*, broken, pounded.

هضيم *haḍîm*, injured, wronged; having thin flanks; sunk; pipe, flute; — ة *haḍîmat*, wrong, injury, violence, outrage; pl. *haḍâ'im*, mourning entertainment.

هطال *haṭṭâl*, raining continuously.

(هطر) *haṭar*, I, INF. *haṭr*, beat, thrash; — V. INF. *tahaṭṭur*, fall in ruins; cringe, humble one's self; — ة *haṭra-t*, humility of a beggar.

(هطرس) — II. INF. *tahaṭrus*, walk with a proud swing, swagger.

(هطع) *haṭa'*, INF. *haṭ'*, *huṭû'*, run away frightened with one's eyes fixed on the object of fear; — IV. INF. *ihṭâ'*, stretch the neck and lift the head in running; run fast.

(هطف) *haṭaf*, I, INF. *haṭf*, milk; rain.

هطف *haṭif*, heavy rain.

(هطق) *haṭaq*, swift walk.

(هطل) *haṭal*, I, INF. *haṭl*, *haṭalân*, *tahṭâl*, rain continuously; rain in large drops, but interruptedly; send down a shower; flow in torrents; flow over, cry; — I, repeatedly cause the horse to perspire.

هطل *haṭl*, *huṭl*, continuous rain; — *hiṭl*, wolf; robber; — *haṭil*, pl. *huṭṭal*, raining continuously

(adj.); — *huttal*, pl. of هاطل *hâṭil*, id.
هطلا *haṭlâ'*, continuous, lasting.
(هطلس) *haṭlas*, *haṭallas*, robber; wolf; — II. INF. *tahaṭlus*, rob cunningly; recover.
هطلع *haṭalla'*, numerous; big, corpulent.
(هطهط) *haṭhaṭ*, INF. ة neigh; walk apace, hasten (n.).
(هطو) *haṭâ*, U, INF. *haṭw*, throw.
هطيع *haṭî'*, broad high-road.
(هع) *ha''*, U, INF. *ha''a-t*, vomit.
(هف) *haff*, I, INF. *haff*, *hafîf*, blow noisily, whistle, rustle; (m.) spread (n.); INF. *hafîf*, walk apace; shine, flash; (m.) feel fondness for; — ة *hiffa-t*, little fish; tadpole.
هفا *hafan*, *hufa*, ة slight rain; — ة *hafât*, custom, habit, usage.
هفات *hafât*, stupid, foolish; — *.
هفاف *haffâf*, ة light, nimble; flighty; thin, transparent; bright.
(جاء على) هفانه *jâ'a 'ala*) *hiffâni-hi*, he followed upon his heels, came behind him.
(هفت) *hafat*, I, INF. *haft*, *hufât*, fly to and fro, hover, flit; be pressed down; sink, fall, slip (land); be worn, thin; talk at random; — VI. INF. *tahâfut*, rush upon one another; rush headlong into danger; throw one's self on a woman's neck; hasten after; totter; fly into the flame; — VII. INF. *inhifât*, sink, fall.
هفهف *hafhaf*, INF. ة, be tall and slender.
(هفو) *hafâ*, U, INF. *hafw*, *hafwa-t*, *hafawân*, step swiftly along, hurry on in mad course; beat the wings in flying; slip, trip; get on a slippery road; commit a fault; be hungry; — INF. *hafw*, *hufuww*, fly through the air; chase about; dart after; ponder over; follow up passionately; have a fond affection for; rejoice, exult; — ة *hafwa-t*, pl. *hafawât*, slip, fault, transgression, sin.
هفيف *hafîf*, whistling, rustling (s.); lightness, nimbleness, swiftness; brightness, brilliancy.
هفية *hafiyya-t*, superintendence of a temple.
(هق) *haqq*, U, INF. exhaust a woman by sexual intercourse.
هقاع *huqâ'*, insensibility, apathy, indifference, indolence.
(هقب) *haqb*, width, breadth; — *hiqabb*, corpulent, heavy; having a large gullet.
(هقط) *haqaṭ*, swiftness.
(هقع) *haqa'*, INF. *haq'*, mark a horse by branding; — *haqi'*, A, INF. *haqa'*, fall down from rut; — VII. INF. *inhiqâ'*, be hungry; — VIII. INF. *ihtiqâ'*, delay, prevent, hinder, keep aloof (a.) from what is good.
هقع *haqi'*, ة, unable to rise; — ة *haq'a-t*, a circle of hair at the side of a horse's upper chest (fault); three stars in the head of Orion; — *huqa'a-t*, who always crouches down.
(هقغ) *haqag*, INF. *huqûg*, be weak.
(هقف) *haqaf*, slight appetite.
(هقل) *hiql*, ة, young ostrich.
(هقلس) *haqallas*, pl. *haqâlis*, famished and vicious.
(هقم) *haqim*, A, INF. *haqam*, have a ravenous appetite; — V. INF. *tahaqqum*, tame, subdue.
هقم *haqim*, having a ravenous appetite, famished; — *hiqamm*, insatiable; the sea.
هقهاق *haqhâq*, expeditious, swift.
هقهق *haqhaq*, INF. ة, walk apace vigorously.
(هقو) *haqâ*, U, INF. *haqw*, also — هقى *haqa*, I, INF. *haqy*, delirate, revile; — IV. INF. *ihqâ'*, corrupt one's manners.
(هك) *hakk*, U, INF. *hakk*, beat, strike; make giddy, intoxicate; wear out, use up; have frequent sexual intercourse; pierce repeatedly, wound; drop excre-

ment; break wind slightly; pass. be thrown down; —VII. *inhikâk*, be made giddy, intoxicated; kneel down.

هك *hakk*, violent rain; pl. *hakaka-t*, *ahkâk*, depressed, suffering; excrement of a bird.

هكاع *hukâ'*, cough; rest, quiet; slumber; voluptuousness, sensuality; — ى *hukâ'iyy*, voluptuous, sensual.

(هكب) *hakab*, I, INF. *hakb*, laugh at, mock at, deride.

(هكد), II. *hakkad*, INF. *tahkîd*, press a debtor hard.

هكذا *hâkazâ*, thus, in such a manner.

(هكر) *hakar*, I, INF. *hakr*, (also V.) admire or wonder greatly; — *hakir*, A, INF. *hakar*, id.; be sleepy or in deep sleep; — V. INF. *tahakkur*, see I.

هكر *hakr*, *hakar*, admiration, astonishment; slumber;—*hakir*, wondering (adj.); also *hakur*, sleepy.

(هكع) *haka'*, INF. *hukû'*, rest, be quieted, keep quiet (n.); stretch one's self down; stop, abide; put up at night; cough;—*haki'*, A, INF. *haka'*, be impatient, grieved, submissive, humble; — ة *huka'a-t*, blockhead.

(هكف) *hakif*, A, INF. *hakaf*, walk fast, run.

هككة *hakaka-t*, pl. of هك *hakk*.

(هكل), VI. *tahâkal*, INF. *tahâkul*, dispute with one another.

(هكم), II. *hakkam*, INF. *tahkîm*, sing a mocking song upon (ل *li*); — V. INF. *tahakkum*, deride, mock at, speak ironically about; tumble in.

(هكن), V. *tahakkan*, INF. *tahakkun*, repent of (على *'ala*).

(هكهك) *hakhak*, INF. ة, have frequent connection.

(هكو), III. *hâka*, INF. *muhâkât*, deem one stupid.

هكوك *hakûk*, *hakawwak*, impudent; precipitate, hasty.

هكيك *hakîk*, worn out, diminished; effeminate; dishonourable.

(هل) *hall*, U, INF. *hall*, (m.) I, INF. *halâl*, appear in the sky; begin with a new moon; pour down violently; shout for joy, exult, cry out; rejoice; — II. INF. *tahlîl*, praise God, profess the unity of God, pronounce the words لا اله الا الله *lâ ilâha illâ 'l-lâhu*;—III. INF. *hilâl*, *muhâlla-t*, conclude a contract or agreement for a month; — IV. INF. *ihlâl*, watch the appearance of the new moon; act. and pass. be on the point of showing itself (also X.) begin to cry or scream;—V. INF. *tahallul*, shout for joy; (also VIII.) flash, shine, be bright; weep; = VII.; — VII. INF. *inhilâl*, pour down; — VIII. INF. *ihtilâl*, see V.; — X. INF. *istihlâl*, begin to appear; perceive the new moon; beam with joy; begin one's speech, make an exordium; see IV.

هل *hal*, particle of interrogation; see حى *hayya*; — *hill*, appearance of the new moon; — ة *halla-t*, pl. *halal*, shower of rain; — *hilla-t*, beginning of a moon; beginning.

هلا *halâ*, come! come here; see حى *hayya*;—*hallâ*, why not? is not? has not? well then! come here!

هلاب *hallâb*, rainy; also ة *hallâba-t*, cold wind with rain;—ة *hulâba-t*, water of the placenta.

هلاث *hulâs̱*, weariness, languor, weakness.

هلاس *hulâs*, consumption.

هلاع *hulâ'*, discouragement, impatience.

هلاك *halâk*, ة *halâka-t*, ruin, perdition; annihilation, death; eternal damnation; — *hullâk*, pl. of هالك *hâlik*, perishing, &c.

هلال *hilâl*, pl. *ahilla-t*, *ahâlîl*, new moon on the point of appearance, first quarter; in the shape of a half-moon, crescent (ه من ريش *halâl min rîś*, plume); point of a lance; hunting-spear

pointed at both ends; first shower of rain; (m.) parenthesis; — *.

هلام *hulâm*, veal-jelly.

هلاهل *halâhil*, *halâhal*, *halâhul*, deadly; *halâhil*, pl. of هلهل *halhal*; — *hulâhil*, abundant and clear.

هلب *halab*, I, INF. *halb*, pull out the long hairs of a horse's tail or the bristles of a pig; moisten (a.) by lasting rain or dew; I, scold, revile, lampoon; (also IV.) continue running; — *halib*, A, INF. *halab*, be hairy; — V. INF. *tahallub*, be plucked, have hair or bristles pulled out.

هلب *hulb*, ة, long or thick hair (esp. in a horse's tail); bristles; — *halab*, hairiness; — ة *hulba-t*, *hulabba-t*, severity of winter.

هلبا *halbâ'*, f. of اهلب *ahlab*, hairy, &c.

(هلت) *halat*, U, INF. *halt*, bark, peel; uproot; — VII. INF. *inhilât*, escape.

هلت *halt*, bark of a tree.

(هلثا) *halsâ*, *hilsâ*, ةه *halsâ'a-t*, *hilsâ'a-t*, also هلثة *hulsa-t*, هلثى *halsa*, tumultuous crowd; — ةه *halsâ'a-t*, *hilsâ'a-t*, weakness.

(هلج) *halaj*, I, INF. *halj*, tell incredible things; — IV. INF. *ihlâj*, hide, conceal (a.).

هلج *hulj*, confused dreams.

هلجاب *hiljâb*, large kettle.

(هلد) *halad*, U, INF. *hald*, befall.

هلد *hald*, access of fever.

هلدم *hildim*, saddle-cloth; rags.

(هلز), V. *tahallaz*, INF. *tahalluz*, gird one's self and set to work.

(هلس) *halas*, I, INF. *hals*, emaciate and make consumptive; pass. be emaciated, consumptive; (m.) laugh, jest, crack jokes; (m.) refine; (m.) pound minutely, reduce to powder; — II. INF. *tahlîs*, emaciate (n.), grow thin; make a mash of peas; — III. INF. *muhâlasa-t*, communicate a secret; — IV. INF. *ihlâs*, keep secret; smile faintly.

هلس *hals*, emaciation, consumption; — *hulus*, weakly persons.

(هلض) *halaḍ*, I, INF. *halḍ*, draw or pull out.

هلطة *halṭa-t*, uncertain rumours.

(هلع) *hali'*, A, INF. *hala'*, be agitated, restless, be seized with an abject discouragement; be struck with terror.

هلع *hala'*, restlessness and discouragement; — *hali'*, ة *hula'a-t*, very impatient, restless; — *hula'*, greedy; — *hilla'*, f. ة, kid.

هلفوف *hulfûf*, very hairy.

(هلق) *halaq*, I, INF. *halq*, hasten (n.); — V. INF. *tahalluq*, id.

هلقامة *hilqâma-t*, having large corners of the mouth; gluttonous.

(هلقم) *halqam*, INF. ة, swallow, gulp; eat much.

هلقم *hulaqim*, *hilqamm*, voracious eater, glutton; very corpulent.

(هلك) *halak*, I, A, INF. *hulk*, *halâk*, *hulûk*, *tuhlûk*, *tahlaka-t*, *tahlika-t*, *tahluka-t*, *mahlika-t*, perish, die; I, INF. *halk*, ruin, annihilate, destroy; I, INF. *halâk*, be avaricious, greedy; — *halik*, A, INF. *halak*, perish, die; be eternally damned; — II. INF. *tahlîk*, ruin, destroy, annihilate; — IV. INF. *ihlâk*, id.; allow to perish miserably; jade; damn; — VI. INF. *tahâluk*, throw one's self upon anything with too much greed and impatience; throw one's self upon; — VII. INF. *inhilâk*, rush into deadly danger, into perdition; — VIII. INF. *ihtilâk*, id.; — X. INF. *istihlâk*, perish; annihilate; devote to destruction; squander, dissipate.

هلك *hulk*, ruin, perdition, destruction; shipwreck; — *halak*, precipitous place; interval; carcass of an animal; — *hullak*, pl. of هالك *hâlik*, perishing, &c.; — ة *hilka-t*, pl. *hilak*, fallen being; — *halaka-t*, هلكا *halkâ'*, ruin, annihilation, calamity, perdition; *halaka-t*, pl. *-ât*, *halak*, year of

famine ; — ى *halka*, pl. of هالك *hâlik*.

هلل *halal*, pl. of هلة *halla-t* ; INF. of (هل).

هلم *halumma*, here! come here! well! give! bring! up with! هلم جرا *halluma jarran*, and so on, etcetera ; — *hilamm*, weak ; — IV. INF. *ihlâm*, call to one with *halluma* ; — VIII. INF. *ihtilâm*, take away.

(هلمط) *halmat*, INF. ة , take, gather.

(هلمم) *halmam*, INF. ة , address one with هلم *halumma*.

هلهال *halhâl*, loose texture ; sieve with large holes.

(هلهل) *halhal*, INF. ة , weave loosely ; sift meal through a loose tissue ; repeat a voice, or raise and lower it alternately ; bewail the dead at the grave ; (m.) threaten to turn Mohammedan by pronouncing the words لا اله الا الله *lâ ilâha illâ 'l-lâhu*.

هلهل *halhal*, deadly ; pl. *halâhil*, loose tissue ; sieve with large holes ; — *hulhul*, snow.

هلوس *halûs*, spider.

(هلوع) *halwa'*, INF. ة , hasten (n.).

هلوع *halû'*, impatient ; always in anxiety and trembling.

هلوك *halûk*, strumpet, prostitute.

(هلى) — III. *hâla*, INF. *muhâlât*, frighten ; — V. *tahalla*, INF. *tahallî*, pace swiftly.

هليون *hilyaun*, asparagus.

هم *hum*, they (m.) ; as an affix after a noun, their ; after a verb or preposition, them ; — *hamm*, pl. *humûm*, care, sorrow ; intention, purpose ; important matter ; — *himm*, pl. *ahmâm*, weak with age, decrepit ; large ; — *him'*, pl. *ahmâ'*, worn-out garment ; — ة *himma-t*, *hamma-t*, pl. *himam* (also *hamâ'im*), intention, wish, plan, concern ; care, solicitude ; favour, predilection ; higher aspiration, magnanimity, courage ; power ; — *himma-t*, pl. *hamâ'im*, decrepit man or woman.

(هم) *hamm*, U, INF. *hamm*, be concerned at, solicitous about, purpose, intend, strive after ; INF. *hamm*, *mahamma-t*, preoccupy, engross ; melt fat ; INF. *hamîm*, creep, crawl ; — for *hamum*, INF. *hamâma-t*, *humûma-t*, be decrepit ; — IV. INF. *ihmâm*, cause sorrow, fill with care, engross ; — VII. INF. *inhimâm*, be full of cares, anxious ; get sorrowful ; grow decrepit ; — VIII. INF. *ihtimâm*, be anxious about, concerned at, solicitous ; take pains in a matter (ب *bi*) for another's sake (ل *li*) ; — X. INF. *istihmâm*, be solicitous for one's family ; instigate zeal and efforts.

(هما) *hama'*, INF. *ham'*, use up or tear a garment ; — IV. INF. *ihmâ'*, id. ; — V. INF. *tahammu'*, be used up, torn.

هما *hamâ*, truly! verily! — *humâ*, both of them (m. and f.) ; as an affix after a verb or prep., id. ; after a noun, both their.

همار *hammâr*, talkative, garrulous ; raining.

هماز *hammâz*, slanderer.

هماس *hammâs*, lion.

همال *himâl*, camels left at large ; — *hummâl*, land left uncultivated (in time of war).

هماليج *hamâlîj*, pl. of هملاج *himlâj*.

همام *hamâm* : لا همام *lâ hamâmi*, it does not matter ; — *hammâm*, who is greatly solicitous about others ; tale-bearer, informer ; — *humâm*, pl. *himâm*, magnanimous, noble, generous ; hero, prince ; lion ; — ة *hamâma-t*, growing old.

هماهم *hamâhim*, pl. sorrows, cares.

همائم *hamâ'im*, pl. of همة *himma-t* and هميمة *hamîma-t*.

(همت) *hamat*, U, INF. *hamt*, disappear ; — IV. INF. *ihmât*, speak or smile stealthily.

(همج) *hamaj*, U, INF. *hamj*, drink its fill at once (camel) ; (m.) dispatch (well or badly) ; — IV. INF.

ihmâj, strain the nerves in running ; — VIII. INF. *ihtimâj*, be weakened, unnerved ; be thin, emaciated.

همج *hamaj*, ة, small flies penetrating into the mouths and eyes of cattle ; stupid, rough, uncultivated men, barbarians ; rough manners ; hunger ; — ى *hamajiyy*, ة, uncultivated, barbarous ; — ية *hamajiyya-t*, barbarity, barbarous state.

(همد) *hamad*, U, INF. *humûd*, go out (fire) ; die ; subside, calm down (n.) ; INF. *hamd*, *humd*, be worn out, rent ; — II. INF. *tahmîd*, extinguish ; calm down (a.) ; — IV. INF. *ihmâd*=II. ; remain, abide ; — V. INF. *tahammud*, be extinguished, calmed ; — ة *hamda-t*, calming (s.), calm ; apoplexy ; resting in the grave (between death and resurrection).

(همر) *hamar*, I, U, INF. *hamr*, pour out, shed ; be poured out, shed ; milk the udder empty ; make many words, be prolix ; give part of one's property to another ; (also VIII.) paw the ground violently ; (m.) neigh ; — VII. INF. *inhimâr*, be poured out ; flow ; — VIII. INF. *ihtimâr*, see I. ; run.

همر *hamr*, neighing (s.) ; — *hamir*, stout, fat ; large sandhill ; — ة *hamra-t*, shower of rain ; burst of passion ; spell, enchantment.

(همرج) *hamraj*, INF. ة, be complicated, entangled, confused ; talk confusedly ; — ة *hamraja-t*, confusion ; confused noise ; nimbleness, swiftness, haste.

(همرشة) *hamraśa-t*, motion, emotion.

(همز) *hamaz*, I, U, INF. *hamz*, press in the hands, in the claws, press down ; urge on, spur on, goad ; beat ; push back with a blow ; throw down ; sting, bite ; break (a.) ; slander ; provide a vowel with *hamza-t* ; wink ; — II. INF. *tamhîz*, (m.) threaten to beat, threaten.

(همس) *hamas*, I, INF. *hams*, chew without opening the mouth ; mumble ; break (a.) ; press out ; travel without interruption ; (m.) give one a blow, a thrust.

همس *hams*, mumbling (s.) ; indistinctness of sound.

(همش) *hamaś*, U, INF. *hamś*, gather ; milk in a certain way ; shake (a.) ; bite ; I, also — *hamiś*, A, INF. *hamaś*, be prolix ; — III. INF. *muhâmaśa-t*, hurry on a thing together with another ; — VIII. INF. *ihtimâś*, move to and fro without order (crowd) ; walk slowly ; creep.

همش *hamiś*, skilful ; — ة *hamśa-t*, confused noise.

(همص) *hamaṣ*, U, INF. *hamṣ*, eat ; throw down ; overpower and kill.

(همط) *hamaṭ*, I, INF. *hamṭ*, wrong, oppress ; beat violently, kick ; take all ; swallow all ; talk at random ; (also V. and VIII.) take forcibly, plunder ; — V. INF. *tahammuṭ*, see I. ; — VIII. INF. *ihtimâṭ*, see I. ; damage one's character or honour.

(همع) *hama'*, U, A, INF. *ham'*, *humû'*, *hama'ân*, *tahmâ'*, shed tears, cry ; flow, drop ; — V. INF. *tahammu*, pretend to cry ; — VIII. INF. *ihtimâ'*, change.

همع *hami'*, raining.

(همغ) *hamag*, INF. *hamg*, break one's skull ; — VII. INF. *inhimâg*, be broken.

(همق) *hamiq*, be soft and tender ; — *himmiq*, bewildered, confused in mind, stupid.

همقاق *hamqâq*, *humqâq*, a grain which is roasted and used as a stimulant.

همقع *humaqi'*, *hummaqi'*, ة, stupid ; — ة *humaqi'a-t*, *hummaqi'a-t*, a fruit.

(همك) *hamak*, U, INF. *hamk*, press, urge on ; pass. engage in, merge in ; — V. INF. *tahammuk*, VII. INF. *inhimâk*, give one's self over

to, indulge in; — XI. INF. *ihmîkâk*, be full of anger.

(همل) *hamal*, U, I, INF. *haml*, *humûl*, *hamalân*, be bathed in tears, shed tears in profusion; flow; rain steadily and uniformly; — I, INF. *haml*, pasture at large day and night; (m.) leave undone, neglect, forget; — IV. INF. *ihmâl*, allow the camels to pasture at large; allow things to go on as they may; leave people to themselves; neglect, omit, forget; leave the consonant without a vowel sign; suspend the government of a word; — VI. INF. *tahâmul*, be careless, negligent, lazy; — VII. INF. *inhimâl*, be left to one's self; be neglected, left undone, omitted, forgotten; shed tears.

همل *himl*, coarse garment; tent of hair; — *hamal*, cattle left to pasture at large; men in state of nature; — *hummal* and—

هملاج *himlâj*, pl. *hamâlij*, gently and steadily-going horse.

هملج *hamlaj*, INF. ة, go steadily and gently.

هملط *hamlaṭ*, INF. ة=(هلمط).

هملع *hamalla'*, stepping along vigorously and with long strides.

(هملق) *hamlaq*, INF. ة, step apace, hasten (n.).

هملى *hamla*, pl. of هامل *hâmil*, pasturing at large.

همم *himam*, pl. of همة *himma-t*.

(همن) — II. *hamman*, INF. *tahmîn*, put in a side-pocket or purse.

همهام *hamhâm*, generous and powerful prince, hero; lion; — ة *hamhâma-t*, large troop.

(همهم) *hamham*, INF. ة, murmur in a low voice, mumble; groan; bellow; lull to sleep by humming.

همهم *himkim*, همهيم *himhîm*, braying (adj.); also همهوم *humhûm*, lion; — ة *hamhama-t*, pl. *hamâhim*, hoarse rattling in the throat.

(همو) *hamâ*, U, INF. *hamw*, flow.

همود *humûd*, getting extinguished (s.); calming down (s.); death.

هموس *hamûs*, tearing lion; producing a sound in walking.

هموع *hamû'*, flowing (adj.); — *humû'*, INF. of (همع).

همول *humûl*, INF. of (همل); — ة *humûla-t*, pl. of هامل *hâmil*, pasturing at large, &c.

هموم *hamûm*, abounding in water.

(همى) *hama*, I, INF. *hamy*, *humiyy*, *hamayân*, *himyân*, flow, run; shed tears, overflow; fall; lower.

هميان *himyân*, *hamyân*, pl. *hamâyîn*, purse, pocket; belt serving as a purse; game-bag; trowser-belt; — *hamayân*, INF. of (همى).

هميد *hamîd*, tax, impost, duty.

هميز *hamîz*, bold, energetic.

هميم *hamîm*, pl. of هامة *hâmma-t*; also ة *hamîma-t*, thin rain; — ة *hamîma-t*, pl. *hamâ'im*, object of sorrow or solicitude.

(هن) *hann*, I, A, INF. *hann*, *hanîn*, sigh aloud, weep; groan from fondness (camel for her foal).

هن *han*, du. *hanân*, *hanawân*, pl. *hanûn*, ة *hana-t*, pl. *hanât*, *hanawât*, thing, something, particularly in a bad sense; something paltry or trifling; *han*, somebody, a person; يا هن *yâ han*, halloo! you there! — *hunn-a* (after ـِ *hinna*), they (f.); as an affix after a noun, their (f.); after a verb or preposition, them (f.); — *han'*, INF. of (هنا).

(هنا) *hana'*, A, U, I, INF. *han'*, smear a camel with pitch; say to one "May it do you good!" wish health to one, congratulate; make the food wholesome; A, I, INF. *han'*, *hin'*, do good, promote health; help, assist, sustain, feed; give, present with; — هنى *hani'*, A, INF. *han'*, *hana'*, be wholesome, do one good; derive health from good food, relish it; come to pass happily, succeed well and easily; rejoice; (m.) be in a

good state; (m.) be pleasant; fortunate, auspicious; lack sufficient food on meagre pasture-ground; — هنو *hanu'*, INF. *han'*, *hana'a-t*, *hanâ'a-t*, do one good, be wholesome; INF. *hanâ'a-t*, succeed easily; — II. INF. *tanhî'*, *tanhî'a-t*, rejoice (a.); make grateful; gain one's favour; congratulate, wish joy or health to (acc.); — IV. INF. *inhâ'*, give, present with; — V. INF. *tahannu'*, find the food good, feel well and strengthened after it, relish it; enjoy; be happy, prosper, have success; be congratulated; — X. INF. *istihnâ'*, ask for one's help, for a present.

هنا *hunâ*, *hone*, *hannâ*, *henne*, here; من هنا و هنا *min hunâ wa hunâ*, &c., from here and there; — *hanâ'*, congratulation, wishing joy (s.); — *hinâ'*, pitch in a fluid state; — ة *hanât*, pl. *hanawât*, calamity; — *hana'a-t*, ةه *hanâ'a-t*, digestiveness and wholesomeness of food.

هناب *hunâb*, wooden plate (m.).

هنابير *hanâbîr*, pl. high sand-hills; hell; ruins.

هنادسة *hanâdisa-t*, pl. of هندس *hindis* and هندوس *hundûs*.

هنادك *hanâdik*, ة *hanâdika-t*, pl. of هندكى *hindikiyy*.

هناف *hinâf*, ironical smile; — *.

هناك *hunâka*, *hannâka*, هنالك *hunâlika*, there.

هنانة *hunâna-t*, fat, marrow; vigour, strength.

هناه (يا) *yâ*) *hanâha*, halloo!

(هنب) *hanab*, simplicity, stupidity.

هنبا *hambâ'*, *hunnabâ'*, هنبى *hunnabâ*, simple, stupid, silly (f.).

(هنبت) *hamba-t*, INF. ة, slacken and hesitate or delay.

هنبثة *hambaṡa-t*, هنبذة *hambaẓa-t*, pl. *hanâbiẓ*, important and difficult affair; confusion.

هنبر *hinabr*, *hinnabr*, *himbir*, hyena; horse; bull; — ة *himbara-t*, she-ass.

(هنبس) *hambas*, INF. ة, investigate a matter, spy out; — II. INF. *tahambus*, id.

(هنبص) *hambaṣ*, INF. ة, smile stealthily.

(هنبغ) *hambag*, INF. ة, *himbâg*, have a ravenous appetite; be plentiful and fly about (dust); —*humbug*, ة *hambaqa-t*, ravenous hunger; flying dust.

(هنبل) *hambal*, INF. ة, walk with a limp like a hyena.

(هنج), V. *tahannuj*, INF. *tahannuj*, come to life and move (fœtus).

(هند) *hind*, (about) a hundred camels; pl. *hindât*, *hinidât*, *hunûd*, a female proper name; pl. *hunûd*, *ahânîd*, Indian, Hindoo; — II. *hannad*, INF. *tahnîd*, tarry, hesitate and do little, fall short; revile; win one by coquetry; make of Indian or excellent steel; sharpen, whet.

هنداز *hindâz*, *handâz*, ة *hindâza-t*, *handâza-t*, a measure; geometry; architecture (Pers.).

هندام *handâm*, symmetry; handsome form (Pers.).

(هندب) *hindab*, هندبا *hindabâ*, *hindibâ'*, هندبى *hindiba*, n. u. هندباة *hindibât*, wild chicory, endive.

(هندس) *hindis*, grim; pl. *hanâdisa-t*, intelligent and skilful; — *handas*, INF. ة, be clever; be a geometrician, an architect, engineer; draw up a plan; — ة *handasa-t*, geometry, architecture, profession of an engineer; — ى *handasiyy*, ة, geometrical, architectural.

هندكى *hindikiyy*, pl. *hanâdik*, ة *hanâdika-t*, Indian, Hindoo.

(هندم) *handam*, INF. ة, arrange symmetrically, adjust; — II. INF. *tahandum*, be symmetrically arranged or formed; — ة *handama-t*, symmetry, proportion, elegance.

هندوانى *hindawâniyy, hundawâniyy*, Indian (adj.); Indian steel or made of it.

هندوس *hundûs*, pl. *hanâdisa-t*, intelligent and skilful, clever.

هندى *hindiyy*, ة, Indian (adj.); pl. *hunûd*, Indian (s.); also علم الهـ *'ilm al-hindiyy*, arithmetic.

هنذا *hanazâ*, here I am!

(هنع) *hana'*, INF. *han'*, bend together (a.); submit; — *hani'*, A, INF. *hana'*, be bent; have a crooked neck; — ة *han'a-t*, mark by branding on the lower part of a camel's neck; name of several constellations; sixth station of the moon.

(هنغ), III. *hânag*, INF. *muhânaga-t*, sport amorously with one's wife.

(هنف), II. *hannaf*, INF. *tahnîf*, hasten (n.); — III. INF. *hinâf*, *muhânafa-t*, laugh ironically, laugh at; toy with; be on the point of crying; — VI. INF. *tahânuf*=III.

(هنق) *hanaq*, anxiety, anguish.

(هنقب) *hanqab*, dwarf; dwarfish.

(هنم) *hanam*, a kind of dates.

هنو *hanû*, in construction for هن *han*; — *hinw*, time, season.

هنوات *hanawât*, pl. of هنة *hana-t* and هناة *hanât*.

هنود *hunûd*, pl. of هند *hind* and هندى *hindiyy*.

(يا) هنوك *yâ hanûka*, halloo! you there! (sing.).

(يا) هنون *yâ hanûna*, halloo! you there! (pl.); pl. of هن *han*.

(هنى) *hana*, do, make; =(هنا).

هنى *hani'*, v. see (هنا); adj. f. ة, wholesome; pleasant; coming off easily and happily; — يا هنى *yâ hanyi*, du. *hanayya*, pl. *haniyya*, Ho, my son! halloo! come here! — ة *hunayya-t*=هنيهة *hunaiha-t*.

هنيدة *hunaida-t*, one hundred.

هنيزة *haníza-t*, sorrow, grief.

هنيع *hanî*, having a crooked neck.

هنين *hanîn*, groaning.

هنيهة *hunaiha-t*, little thing, trifle; little while.

هنيى *hanî'*, ة = هنى *hani'*; هنيئا مريئا *hanî'an marî'an*, may it do you good! — *hunai'a-t* = هنيهة *hunaiha-t*.

(هه) *hahh*, INF. *hahh*, *hahha-t*, have a heavy tongue, an impediment, stammer.

ههنا *hâhunâ*, here.

هو *huwa, hû*, he, it; God; — *haww*, side; window; — *hau'*, intention, aim, purpose; بعيد الهو *ba'îd al-hau'*, far-thinking, aspiring for high things; also *hû'*, thought, opinion; — ة *huwwa-t*, deep valley; valley; precipice, cave, cavern; air, atmosphere; rising (s.), ascent.

(هوا) *hâ'*, U, INF. *hau*, set one's thoughts (on high things); rejoice (n.); come to, reach; come with, bring; — هوى *hawi'*, A, INF. *hawa'*, purpose, intend.

هوا=هوى *hawa*; — *hawâ'*, pl. *ahwiya-t*, air; ether; atmosphere; empty space between heaven and earth; breeze; tone, voice, song, tune; — *hiwâ'*, INF. of (هوى III.); — ة *hawât*, air, atmosphere; — ة *huwwâ'a-t*, deep valley; abyss, precipice.

هواجم *hawâjim*, attacks.

هوادة *hawâda-t*, friendly yielding, compliance; conclusion of peace; inclination; indulgence, permission.

هوادج *hawâdij*, pl. of هودج *haudaj*.

هوادى *hawâdî*, troop, crowd; pl. of هادى *hâdî*, neck.

هوارة *hawâra-t*, destruction, annihilation, ruin; fall from on high; — *hawwâra-t*, pl. of هورى *hawwariyy*, Albanian soldier; garrison-soldier; volunteer.

هواس *hiwâs*, desire; rut; sexual intercourse.

هواشة *huwâsa-t*, confused crowd.

هواع *huwâ'*, vomiting (s.); what has been vomited; pl. *-ât*, *ah-*

wi'a-t, a month (ذو القعدة *zû 'l-qa'da-t*).

هواك *hawwâk*, confused, perplexed; — ة *hawwâka-t*, offensive smell.

هوام *huwâm*, excessive thirst; madness; — *hawwâm*, lion; — *hawâmm*, pl. of هامّة *hâmma-t*, reptile.

هوان *hawân*, contemptibleness; shame; insignificance; contempt; mildness, kindness.

هواهى *hawâhî*, silly things, stupidities, follies; — ة *hawâhiya-t*, very deep well.

هواوين *hawâwîn*, pl. of هاوون, mortar for pounding.

هوائى *hawâ'iyy*, ة, airy; aerial, ethereal, atmospheric; windy, breezy; imaginary, like castles in the air.

(هوب) *haub*, heat of fire; also *hûb*, distance; — IV. INF. *ihâba-t*, cry to, call to; bid, invite.

هوبجة *haubaja-t*, low ground where water collects; pond.

(هوبر) *haubar*, a very hairy ape; hunting-panther; purple lily; — INF. ة, hum to one's self a merry tune.

(هوبل) *haubal*, INF. ة, do a thing in a hurry and badly; cheat; — ة *haubala-t*, what is done in a hurry and badly; deceit, fraud.

(هوت) — II. *hawwat*, INF. *tahwît*, cry out, call to; — ة *hûta-t*, *hauta-t*, pl. *huwat*, low ground; deep valley; precipice, ravine, abyss.

هوثة *hausa-t*, thirst.

(هوج) *hawij*, A, INF. *hawaj*, be foolish, thoughtless and precipitate; blow violently.

هوج *hawaj*, utmost levity, thoughtlessness, foolishness; precipitation; — *hûj*, pl. and—

هوجا *haujâ'*, f. of اهوج, far-stretching, &c.; tempest, hurricane.

(هود) *hâd*, U, INF. *haud*, return to one's duty, become converted; INF. *tahwâd* (also II.), produce a low sound; speak quietly and gently; — II. INF. *tahwîd*, see I.; walk slowly; (m.) walk fast, hasten, speed; make one a Jew; — III. INF. *muhâwada-t*, have affection, kindness for, be indulgent; be regardful, deal honestly with; reconcile one's self with; — V. INF. *tahawwud*, be quiet and gentle in one's speech; be related to or a client of; become a Jew; — VI. INF. *tahâwud*, abate (n.).

هود *hûd*, Jews; name of a prophet; pl. of هائد *hâ'id*, repenting; — ة *hawada-t*, pl. *hawad*, camel's hump.

(هودج) *haudaj*, pl. *hawâdij*, camel's litter for women; travelling-litter.

(هودع) *hauda'*, ostrich.

(هوذل) *hauzal*, INF. ة, be swift; be shaken, swing to and fro, totter.

(هور) *hâr*, U, INF. *haur*, *huwûr*, be demolished, fall; be carried off, washed away; INF. *haur*, pull down, destroy; throw down; kill in heaps and throw one above another; surmise, suspect of; turn from (a.); cause, incite; — II. INF. *tahwîr*, throw down; demolish; make to roll down, to fall; — V. INF. *tahawwur*, fall (in ruins); fall down, roll down; rush headlong into (danger, &c.); — VII. INF. *inhiyâr*, be destroyed, demolished; fall, crumble in; — VIII. INF. *ihtiyâr*, perish.

هور *haur*, pl. *ahwâr*, pond, morass, marshes; herd of sheep; — ة *haura-t*, dangerous place; pl. dangers, anything threatening to fall in; — *hûra-t*, surmise, suspicion.

هوز *hûz*, creatures; men; — II. *hawwaz*, INF. *tahwîz*, die.

هوزب *hauzab*, vulture; strong camel.

(هوس) *hâs*, U, INF. *haus*, pound minutely; break; go or drive slowly; eat greedily; — INF. *haus*, *hawasân*, walk about at

night-time; step vigorously; rage in a herd; walk round; — II. INF. *tahwîs*, excite a keen desire, give one pleasure, cheer up; — V. INF. *tahawwus*, have a great wish for; give one's self over to pleasure, amuse one's self.

هوس *hawas*, *haus*, passionate desire, passion; mania; ambition; mind, pleasure, amusement; folly; (m.) levity, dryness; — *hawis*, ة, rutting; — ة *hausa-t*, pleasure, amusement; — ى *hausa*, greedy eaters, gluttons, pl. of اهوس *ahwas*.

(هوش) *hâś*, U, INF. *hauś*, also—*hawiś*, A, INF. *hawaś*, be excited, agitated; be tumultuous; have a small belly; — II. INF. *tahwîś*, confuse, agitate (a.); set dogs against one another; — III. INF. *muhâwaśa-t*, mix with others; quarrel, scuffle with; — V. INF. *tahawwuś*, quarrel, scuffle; assemble; — VI. INF. *tahâwuś*, be mixed up; be set against.

هوش *hauś*, great crowd; excitement, agitation, tumult; هوش بوش *hauś bauś*, topsy-turvy, in confusion; — ة *hauśa-t*, crowd, throng; confusion, tumult, turmoil, combat, battle.

(هوع) *hâ'*, U, INF. *hau'*, be light and mobile; be easily excited, disquieted, frightened; be about to attack one another; — A, U, INF. *hau'*, also—V. INF. *tahawwu'*, vomit.

هوع *hau'*, vomiting; disorderly desire; also *hû'*, enmity, hatred.

(هوغ) *haug*, much, many, numerous.

(هوف) *hûf*, idle good-for-nothing fellow.

(هوك) *hawik*, A, INF. *hawak*, be half-mad; — II. INF. *tahwîk*, dig; — V. INF. *tahawwuk*, get perplexed; get into trouble by carelessness; rush into danger.

هوك *hauk*, *hiwakk*, half-mad; — ة *hûka-t*, ditch, hole; — *hawika-t*, saline, salt (adj.).

(هول) *hâl*, U, INF. *haul*, frighten, inspire with terror; pass. *hil*, believe one sees phantoms, &c., have hallucinations; — II. INF. *tahwîl*, frighten, inspire with terror; represent to one as terrible; (m.) wave the fan, the handkerchief; — V. INF. *tahawwul*, be frightful, terrible; — VIII. INF. *ihtiyâl*, be frightened, terrified.

هول *haul*, pl. *ahwâl*, *huwûl*, fright, terror; anything fearful (also ة *haula-t*); sphinx; — ة *hûla-t*, sacred fire by which an oath was taken; woman enchanting by beauty; self-complacency.

هولا *hâ'ulâ'i*, these.

هولع *haula'*, swift.

هولى *hûla*, f. of اهول, more frightful; ابو هولى *abû hûla*, sphinx); a talisman against vermin.

(هوم) *haum*, low grounds; — II. *hawwam*, INF. *tahwîm*, nod from sleepiness; — V. INF. *tahawwum*, id.; — ة *hauma-t*, desert.

(هون) *hûn*, U, INF. *haun*, be light, be easy to do or to suffer; be slow and deliberate; — INF. *hûn*, *hawân*, *mahâna-t*, be or seem contemptible; be lowly, humble; remain quiet, rest; — II. INF. *tahwîn*, facilitate, make bearable, alleviate; take a thing easy; — III. INF. *muhâwana-t*, be self-indulgent; — IV. INF. *ihâna-t*, despise; (m.) offend; — VI. INF. *tahâwun*, be negligent, neglect, despise; — VII. INF. *inhiyân*, be despised; (m.) be offended; — X. INF. *istihâna-t*, consider easy; make light of.

هون *haun*, rest; ease; contentment; deliberateness, slowness; modesty; kindness, gentleness; contemptibleness, contempt; contemptible; — *hûn*, contemptibleness; the things created,

creation ;— ة hauna-t, hûna-t, rested ; quiet, gentle, kind.

هوة hûh, ة hûha-t, timorous, cowardly ;— huwah, he ;— hiwah, mallows.

هوهاة hauhât, hûhât, ة hauhâ'a-t, blockhead.

هوول huwûl, pl. of هول haul.

(هوى) hawa, I, INF. huwiyy, fall ; die ; blow ; pounce upon ; INF. hawiyy, huwiyy, hawayân, fall down ; descend into the well ; INF. huwwa-t, ascend ; — hawî, A, INF. hawa, love, like ; — II. INF. tahwiya-t, blow ; expose to the wind, to the air ; — III. INF. muhâwât, love tenderly ; show one's love to, caress, cajole, flatter ; — IV. INF. ihwâ', fall down ; come upon, rush against with, destroy ; strive for ; reach or lift the hand for ;— V. INF. tahawwî, air one's self ; deteriorate in the air ; — VI. INF. tahâwî, fall one after another ; — VII. INF. inhiwâ', fall down, be thrown down ; — VIII. INF. ihtiwâ', id. ; — X. INF. istihwâ', inspire with passionate love, madden with love, fascinate ; seduce ; be passionately in love.

هوى hawa, pl. ahwâ', passionate desire, craving for ; love, amorousness ; inclination, wish, liking, pleasure, enjoyment ; anything loved or desired ; pl. passions ; — hawiyy, who desires, longs for, loves ; who falls down ; low tone or sound ; tingling in the ear ; part of the night ; also huwiyy, INF. of (هوى) ; — ة hawiyya-t, desire, longing (s.) ; anything desired, longed for ; deep well ; — huwiyya-t, substance, essence, existence ; divine substance.

هويس hawîs, thought, wish.

هويشة hawîsa-t, confused crowd.

هوينا , هوينى huwaina, gentleness, mildness ; modest bearing ; slow walk ; deliberateness.

هى hiya, hiyya, she ; she is ; — يا ه yâ hayya, oh ! ; — hayyi', of handsome appearance ; considerable, dignified ;— هى بن بى hayy bnu bayy (also هيان بن بيان hayyânu bnu bayyânin), one unknown, son of one unknown ; — ة hi'a-t = هيئة hai'a-t.

(هيا) hâ', pret. hi'tu, I, A, INF. hai'a-t, be prepared, ready, in readiness ; A, INF. hî'a-t, be seized with a longing for, desire, crave ; A, I, also — هيو hayu', be of handsome appearance or figure, be fair, beautiful ; — II. INF. tahyî', tahyi'a-t, prepare, make ready, fit out, arrange well ; — V. INF. tahayyu', be put in readiness, be ready ; prepare one's self, make ready ; become possible ; — VI. INF. tahâyu', agree between one another.

هيا hayâ, (m.) hayyâ, halloo ! well ! quick ! come !— ة hai'a-t, pl. -ât, hî'a-t, manner, way, fashion, style ; astronomy ; readiness ;— hayyât, affair, matter.

هياب hayyâb, ة hayyâba-t, timid, timorous ; frightful, terrible.

هياج hiyâj, excitement, agitation ; combat, slaughter ; stir of ill.

هيار hayâr, fallen, destroyed ; — hayyâr, weak.

هياط hiyâṭ, screaming, shouting, clamour ; approach, proximity ; هياط و مياط hiyâṭ wa miyâṭ, coming and going.

هياطل hayâṭil, ة hayaṭila-t, a Scythian tribe.

هياف hiyâf, intense thirst.

هيام hayâm, huyâm, pl. huyum, finest drifting sand ; huyum, hiyâm, intense thirst or passion ; mad love ; — * ; — hiyâm, pl. of هيما haimâ', and هيمان haimân ; — huyyâm, pl. of هائم hâ'im, crazed, &c.

(هيب) hâb, INF. haib, mahâba-t,

fear; honour, respect, revere; — II. INF. *tahyîb*, render terrible, make to appear terrible; — IV. INF. *ihâba-t*, id.; — V. INF. *tahayyub*, fear; honour, revere; frighten; — VIII. INF. *ihtiyâb*, fear; honour, revere; — X. INF. *istihâba-t* = VIII.

هيب *hayyib*, timorous; — ة *haiba-t*, fear; awe, reverence, respect; severity, earnestness, dignity, majesty; modesty; (m.) bearing and aspect of a person.

هيبان *haibân*, terrible; also *hayabân*, *hayyibân*, very timorous, cowardly; very respectful, reverential.

هيبلى *haibaliyy*, Christian monk.

هيت *hît*, low ground; — هـ لك *haitu* (*haita*, *haiti*) *laka*, come! come here! — II. *hayyat*, INF. *tahyît*, call to, call up; (m.) scold, rebuke.

هيتم *haitam*, a bitter plant.

(هيث) *hâs*, I, INF. *hais*, *hayasân*, give but little; waste, squander, ruin; INF. *hais*, be moved, shaken.

هيثم *haisam*, young eagle or vulture, reddish and soft sandy ground.

(هيج) *hâj*, I, INF. *haij*, *hiyâj*, *hayajân*, be moved, agitated, roused; be moved with a violent passion; be thirsty; wither, fade; rush against and attack; excite, rouse; — III. INF. *hiyûj*, *muhâjaja-t*, excite, rouse, spur on, goad; fight against; — IV. INF. *ihâja-t*, wither, dry up (a.); — V. INF. *tahayyuj*, be moved, agitated, roused; — VI. INF. *tahâyuj*, be roused against one another and come to close quarters, fight; — VIII. INF. *ihtiyâj* = V.

هيج *haij*, stormy weather; day of combat; — *hayyij*, excited, roused.

هيجا *haijâ*, *haijâ'*, combat, strife, battle, close fight.

هيجان *hayajân*, excitement, agitation, passionate emotion; anger, violence.

هيجمان *haijumân*, ة *haijumâna-t*, large pearl; — ة *haijumâna-t*, spider.

(هيخ) *hîḥ*, cry by which a camel is bid to kneel down; — II. *hayyaḥ*, INF. *tahyîḥ*, put much fat to the broth; entice the he-goat to cover.

(هيد) *hâd*, I, INF. *hâd*, *haid*, inspire with fear, frighten, terrify; grieve (a.), depress; move, rouse, scare up; chase away; mend; put on the roof; — II. INF. *tahyîd*, frighten; grieve (a.); move (a.).

هيدب *haidab*, weak, relaxed, slack; fringed edge; fringes.

هيدكر *haidakur*, هيدكور *haidakûr*, ة corpulent, heavy; strong.

هيذار *haizâr*, ة *haizâra-t*, idle talker, babbler.

هيذام *haizâm*, bold.

هيذلى *haizula*, swift pace.

هيذم *haizam*, swift.

(هير) — II. *hayyar*, INF. *tahyîr*, destroy, demolish; throw down from on high; — V. INF. *tahayyur*, fall in; be thrown down.

هير *hair*, *hîr*, *hayyir*, north wind; part of the night; — *hayyir*, who engages inconsiderately in; — ة *haira-t*, level ground.

هيرع *haira'*, fickle.

هيزب *haizab* (هيزم *haizam*), strong and grim.

هيزعة *haiza'a-t*, tumult; vociferations of a combat.

(هيس) *hâs*, I, INF. *hais*, take or give in great quantity; walk, step; throw down, tread down.

هيس *hais*, plough; — *haisi*, bravo! well done! go on like that!

(هيش) *hâś*, I, INF. *haiś*, be excited, agitated; be garrulous, wordy; plunder, devastate; collect, hoard up; — II. INF. *tahyîś*, incite to sedition, raise an insurrection; (m.) be densely-leaved; be curly-haired.

هيش *haiś, hîś,* ة *haiśa-t,* crowd; tumult, sedition, insurrection; (m.) thicket, shrubbery.

(هيص) *hâṣ,* I, INF. *haiṣ,* treat with violence; break one's neck; drop excrement.

هيصار *haiṣâr,* هيصر *haiṣar,* هيصم *haiṣam,* هيصور *haiṣûr,* lion.

(هيض) *hâḍ,* I, INF. *haiḍ,* (also VII., VIII.) break a healed bone again; make a wound raw again; render a cured person ill again; ache, vex; drop excrement; — V. INF. *tahayyuḍ,* get broken again; — VII. INF. *inhiyâḍ,* VIII. INF. *ihtiyâḍ,* see I.; — ة *haiḍa-t,* relapse into illness; diarrhœa with vomiting; cholera.

هيضل *haiḍal,* large army, host; — ة *haiḍala-t,* id.; vociferations of a combat.

هيضمان *haiḍamân,* horse-radish.

(هيط) *hâṭ,* I, A, INF. *haiṭ,* scream, shout, clamour, be tumultuous; — III. INF. *hiyâṭ, muhâyaṭa-t,* scream, shout, cry out; — VI. INF. *tahâyuṭ,* come together for a conference and mend matters.

هيطل *haiṭal,* fox; — ة *haiṭala-t,* copper-kettle.

(هيع) *hâ',* I, A, INF. *hai',* be spread out on the ground; become fluid, melt (n.); INF. *hai'û'a-t,* vomit; INF. *hai', haya'ân, huyû',* long for a thing but want courage, be cowardly, fear; — A, be grieved; — V. INF. *tahayyu',* be spread; — VII. INF. *inhiyâ',* flow, spread (n.); dissolve (n.); — ة *hai'a-t,* flowing, dissolution; vileness; weakness, cowardice, terrible voice or sound.

هيعر *hai'ar,* INF. ة, be restless; be reckless and frivolous; — II. INF. *tahai'ur,* id.; — ة *hai'ara-t,* fickleness, levity; a fickle and flighty woman; a monster, demon.

هيعوعة *hai'û'a-t,* vomiting (s.).

(هيغ), II. *hayyag,* INF. *tahyîg,* grease much; wet the ground.

(هيف) *hâf,* A, INF. *haif,* run away; also — *hayif,* A, INF. *hayaf,* have a sunken belly and thin hypochondres; — IV. INF. *ihâfa-t,* have thirsty camels.

هيف *hîf,* pl., هيفا *haifâ',* f. of اهيف *ahyaf,* slender, slim; — *haif,* intense thirst; hot and dry south-west wind; — *hayaf,* slenderness.

هيفان *haifân,* very thirsty.

(هيق) *haiq,* also (m.) *hîq,* long-bodied and thin of flanks; male ostrich; (f. ة); (m.) clumsy churl; — II. *hayyaq,* INF. *tahyîq,* become clumsy and churly; stand idle.

هيقعة *haiqa'a-t,* clash of swords; clatter, rattle.

هيقم *haiqam,* male ostrich; sea, agitation of the sea.

(هيك), II. *hayyak,* INF. *tahyîk,* hasten, hurry (n.); dig.

هيكل *haikal,* ة, pl. *hayâkil,* strong and big; gigantic form, giant; huge building, palace, temple; altar, choir; convent.

هيكوك *haikûk,* stupid and cunning.

(هيل) *hâl,* I, INF. *hail,* pour out without measuring; heap up; — IV. INF. *ihâla-t,* id.; — V. INF. *tahayyul,* VII. INF. *inhiyâl,* be poured out, pour (n.).

هيل *hail,* anything pouring; plenty, abundance; wind; an inferior sort of cardamom; — ة *hîla-t,* anything terrible, fright.

هيلع *haila',* weak and timid.

هيلل *hailal,* INF. ة, pronounce the words لا اله الا الله *lâ ilâha illâ 'l-lâhu.*

هيلمان *hailamân, hailumân,* wealth, abundance.

(هيم) *hâm,* I, INF. *haim, hayamân,* love passionately; be astonished; feel inclination or sympathy for; wander about in a craze; — X. INF. *istihâma-t,* be in love; make one to fall in love.

هيم *huyum,* pl. of هيام *hayâm.*

هيما *haimâ',* pl. *hîm,* thirsty and

wandering; pl. *hiyâm*, waterless desert.
هيمان *haimân*, f. *haimā*, pl. *hiyâm*, thirsty; amorous; crazed, mad.
هيمع *haima'*, sudden.
هيمن *haiman*, INF. ة, say Amen; cover the young ones with the wings; guard, protect.
هين *hayyin*, *hain*, pl. *ahwinâ'*, *ahyinâ'*, *hainûn*, easy to do or to bear, easy; insignificant, contemptible; modest, quiet; — ة *hîna-t*, *haina-t*, ease, comfort.
هينغ *hainag*, shameless woman.
هينام *hainâm*, unintelligible speech.
(هينم) *hainam*, INF. ة, speak or read in a low voice, mumble.
هينم *hainam*, low tone.
هينوم *hainûm*=هينام *hainâm*.
(هيه) *haih*, dirty fellow; — *hîh hîh*, be gone! avaunt! well done! bis! — *hiyah*=هى *hiya*, she.
هيهات *haihât*, vast desert; — *haihâtu*, *haihâti*, *haihâta*, also—
هيهان *haihân*, هيهاه *haihâh*, off with it! away! be gone! far from it.
هيو *hayu'*, see (هيا).

هيوب *hayûb*, ة *hayûba-t*, timid, shy; to be feared, venerable.
هيوف *hayûf*, very thirsty; who gets thirsty soon.
هيول *hayûl*, mote in a sunbeam; — ى *hayûla*, *hayyulā*, raw matter; first principle; first rough sketch or draught; cotton; — *hayûliyy*, and—
هيولانى *hayyûlâniyy*, material, referring to matter.
هيوم *hayûm*, confused, crazed; perplexed.
هيى *hayyi'* (also هيئى *hai'iyy*), handsome, pleasant, considerable, dignified; — ة *hai'a-t*, pl. *hai'ât*, also *hî'a-t*, pl. *hî'ât*, exterior, aspect, appearance; handsome form, pleasant appearance; mien, physiognomy; bearing, behaviour; circumstances, situation, position; manner, way, fashion, style; heavenly aspect (علم الـ *'ilm al-hî'a-t*, astronomy); — *hai'a-t*, readiness; — *hî'a-t*, longing (s.), desire.

و

و *w*, as a numerical sign=6; abbreviation for Friday and Libra; — *wa*, and, also; then, while, during; at the same time, together with; but, however;=رب *rubba*, frequently, sometimes, perhaps; particle of swearing, by.
وا *wâ*, halloo! oh! وا حرزى *wâ ḥarazā*, stop! enough!—ة *wa'a-t*, pl. *wa'ât*, wild she-ass.
(واب) *wa'ab*, aor. *ya'ib*, INF. *iba-t*, *wa'b*, shrink; be ashamed, blush; — *wa'ib*, A, INF. *wa'ab*, be angry; — IV. *au'ab*, *at'ab*, INF. *î'âb*, abash; provoke to anger;—VIII. INF. *itti'âb*, blush, be ashamed.
واب *wâb*, blushing (s.), shame; large cup; strong;— ة *wa'ba-t*, hole in a rock with water in it.
وابر *wâbir*, someone, somebody.
وابصة *wâbiṣa-t*, fire; credulous.
وابط *wâbiṭ*, weak, cowardly.
وابل *wâbil*, pl. *wubbal*, rain in large drops, rain-flood; — ة *wâbila-t*, top of the shoulder-blade; head of the hip-bone.
واتن *wâtin*, واثن *wâṯin*, lasting; permanently settled; always flowing.
واجب *wâjib*, ة, necessary, obligatory, according to duty, beseeming, equitable; proper, fit; affirmative; wages (monthly); — ة *wâjiba-t*, anything necessary, indispensable; pl. *wâjibât*,

duties of good breeding; requisites.

واجد *wâjid*, inventor; — *.

واجز *wâjiz*, abbreviated, short.

واجس *wâjis*, what occurs to the mind.

واجل *wâjil*, timid, bashful.

واحد *wâḥid*, ة, pl. *-ûn*, one; single, unique; pl. *wuḥdân*, *uḥdân*, unique, incomparable; — ية *wâḥidiyya-t*, doctrine or sect of the Unitarians.

واحف *wâḥif*, luxuriant.

(واد) *wa'ad*, aor. *ya'id*, INF. *wa'd*, bury alive; — V. INF. *tawa''ud*, VIII. INF. *itti'âd*, be heavy and slow; tarry, hesitate, linger.

واد *wa'd*, loud voice, roaring (s.).

وادع *wâdi'*, quiet, gentle, mild.

وادق *wâdiq*, sharp; hot (she-ass).

وادك *wâdik*, fat, corpulent.

وادى *wâdî* (واد, *wâd-in*), pl. *audiya-t*, *audâ'*, *audât*, *audâya-t*, valley; low ground; river; reedy bank; oasis, desert; style of writing, &c.; who pays blood-money.

(وار) *wa'ar*, aor. *ya'ir*, INF. *wa'r*, frighten; (also II.) throw into calamity; make the fire to flare; — II. INF. *taw'îr*=I.; — IV. INF. *î'âr*, frighten and put to flight; inform.

وار *wu'âr*, pl. of وورة *wu'ra-t*, fire, hearth.

وارب *wârib*, awry, oblique; insincere.

وارث *wâris̱*, pl. *waras̱a-t*, *wurrâs̱*, who inherits, heir; possessor, lord, master.

وارد *wârid*, ة, pl. *-ûn*, *wurrâd*, who descends, particularly to the water; who arrives, new-comer, guest, one present; coming to knowledge; appropriate; hanging down; long-haired; success, result, issue; also ة, road; — ات *wâridât*, revenues, rents; events; real circumstances.

وارس *wâris*, yellowish.

وارش *wâriś*, who comes uninvited to a meal.

وارف *wârif*, far-stretched; spacious, roomy, wide.

وارق *wâriq*, forming into leaves, verdant, blooming; having a dense foliage.

وارك *wârik*, ة *wârika-t*, part of a camel's saddle on which the rider places his foot.

وارم *wârim*, swelling, swollen.

وارهة *wâriha-t*, spacious, roomy.

وارى *wârî* (وار, *wâr-in*), ة, giving fire; having a subtle and sharp smell; fat; — ة *wâriya-t*, disease of the lungs.

وازر *wâzir*, burdened; criminal.

وازع *wâzi'*, pl. *waza'a-t*, preventing, hindering; prince, governor, prefect; leader; attendant; watch-dog.

وازن *wâzin*, who weighs; of full weight.

واسط *wâsiṭ*, ة, what is in the middle, middle, medium; mediator; — ة *wâsiṭa-t*, pl. *wasâ'iṭ*, mediator; means, expedient; mediation; reason, cause; prime minister; pl. *awâsiṭ*, large middle pearl of a necklace.

واسع *wâsi'*, wide, &c.; comprehensive; free-thinking, liberal; generous.

واسق *wâsiq*, pl. *wisâq*, *mawâsiq*, *mawâsîq*, big with young.

واسل *wâsil*, necessary, beseeming, according to duty; desiring, longing (adj.); pious, devout; — ة *wâsila-t*, relationship; favour and influence with the king.

واشج *wâśij*, intricate, complicated; — ة *wâśija-t*, complicated relationship.

واشرة *wâśira-t*, woman who sharpens ladies' teeth.

واشمة *wâśima-t*, woman who tattoos.

واشى *wâśî* (واش *wâś-in*), pl. *wuśât*, tale-bearer, slanderer; miner, sapper; mint-master; weaver; — ة *wâśiya-t*, having many children.

(واص) *wa'aṣ*, aor. *ya'iṣ*, INF. *wa'ṣ*,

throw on the ground; —VI. INF. *tawâ'uṣ*, throng (n.).
واصب *wâṣib*, eternal; indispensable; — ة *wâṣiba-t*, vast, extended.
واصف *wâṣif*, who describes, pictures, praises; descriptive.
واصل *wâṣil*, what or who comes, &c.; frequent comer, clinging guest; arrived, received; united, joined; — ة *wâṣila-t*, woman who mingles false hair with her own.
واصى *wâṣî* (واص *wâṣ-in*), testator.
واضح *wâḍiḥ*, clear, evident, &c.; white; *al-wâḍiḥ*, morning-star; — ات *wâḍiḥât*, evident truths, truisms; front teeth.
واضع *wâḍi'*, who puts down, &c.; inventor, author, creator.
واضى *wâḍî*, pure, bright.
(واط) *wa'aṭ*, aor. *ya'iṭ*, INF. *wa'ṭ*, visit; excite, be excited.
واطد *wâṭid*, firm, solid.
واطى *wâṭi'*, treading under foot; mean; contemptible; low (voice); — ة *wâṭi'a-t*, pedestrians, wanderers; trodden path.
واعد *wâ'id*, promising; — ة *wâ'ida-t*, ground which promises a rich harvest.
واعر *wâ'ir*, rough, rugged.
واعظ *wâ'iẕ*, pl. *wu''âẕ*, preacher; — *.
واعى *wâ'î* (واع *wâ'-in*), ة, remembering; awake, attentive; upon one's guard, cautious; guardian, watcher; — ة *wâ'iya-t*, clamour; bewailing of the dead.
واغر *wâgir*, furious, enraged.
واغل *wâgil*, who comes uninvited to an entertainment.
وافد *wâfid*, pl. *wufûd*, *aufâd*, *wafd*, *wuffad*, arriving, reaching (adj.); comer; envoy, ambassador; contagious; pl. *wâfidûn*, grandees, lords, peers; du. *al-wâfidân*, the cheeks.
وافر *wâfir*, ة, abundant, plentiful, numerous; rich; wide, ample; name of a metre (*mufâ'alatun* ◡ — ◡ ◡ — six times repeated); — ة *wâfira-t*, this world.
وافه *wâfih*, sacristan.
وافى *wâfî* (واف *wâf-in*), ة, who keeps his promise, &c.; full, complete, of full weight; (*al-wâfî*, drachm); abundant; — ة *al-wâfiya-t*, full weight or measure.
واقح *wâqiḥ*, hard.
واقع *wâqi'*, ة, pl. *wuqqa'*, falling, &c.; real; necessary; transitive; reality; — ة *wâqi'a-t*, event; news; accident, calamity; combat, battle; vision in a dream; *al-wâqi'a-t*, day of the last judgment; — ى *wâqi'iyy*, real, true; perfect, proper; the essential thing; — ية *wâqi'iyya-t*, reality.
واقف *wâqif*, pl. *wuqûf*, stopping, standing upright, &c.; bystander; informed; experienced; who bequeaths by will, maker of a pious foundation; — ية *wâqifiyya-t*, knowledge, information, comprehension, experience.
واقم *wâqim*, citadel of Medina.
واقى *wâqî* (واق *wâq-in*), ة, guarding, protecting, &c.; cautious; — ة *wâqiya-t*, guard, protection, safeguard; pl. *awâq-in*, *awâqî*, ounce (weight); protectress.
(وال) *wa'al*, aor. *ya'il*, INF. *wa'l*, *wu'ûl*, *wa'il*, take refuge with (الى *ila*), try to escape, escape; hasten to; — III. INF. *wi'âl*, *muwâ'ala-t*, take refuge with, flee; — IV. INF. *î'âl*, pollute a place by excrement or urine, be polluted thereby; — X. INF. *istî'âl*, be assembled; — ة *wa'la-t*, excrement, dung; dung-hill.
والبة *wâliba-t*, shoot of corn; young (of an animal), young ones, children.
والث *wâliṯ*, pressing, oppressive; — *.

والجة *wâlija-t*, internal injury or pain; grief; calamity; abscess.

والد *wâlid*, giving birth, pregnant; father, mother; *al-wâlidân*, both parents; *al-walidûn*, paternal relations; — ة *walida-t*, mother, dam; — ى *wâlidiyy*, paternal.

والع *wâli'*, pl. *wala'a-t*, liar.

واله *wâlih*, ة, perplexed, dumbfounded, confused; made desperate; love-crazed; blockhead.

والى *wâlî* (وال *wâl-in*), pl. *wulât*, regent, governor, prefect of a province.

(وام) *wa'm*, very warm, hot; — II. *wa''am*, INF. *tau'îm*, render ugly, disfigure; — III. INF. *wi'âm*, *muwâ'ama-t*, agree; try to surpass in beauty; — IV. INF. *î'âm*, bear twins; — ة *wa'ama-t*, an equal, companion, fellow; imitator.

وامق *wâmiq*, lover.

وامئة *wâmi'a-t*, calamity, ruin.

(وان) *wa'n*, ة, short and thick-set, broad.

وان *wa'in*, and if, although; — *wân-in*, وانى *wânî*, slow, tired, faint; cowardly.

واه *wah*, واها *wâh-an*, *wâhâ*, oh! ah! well done! — *wâh-in*, see واهى *wâhî*.

واهف *wâhif*, sacristan.

واهلة *wâhilat-an*, before all things.

واهن *wâhin*, ة, pl. *wuhn*, weak, enervated; incapable.

واهى *wâhî* (واه *wâh-in*), ة, weak, perishable, brittle; broken, rent; without foundation; absurd, silly (*wâhiyât*, follies); (m.) abundant, plentiful, important, great.

واو *wâw*, pl. *-ât*, name of the letter و; water-colour.

واوا *wa'wa'*, cry of the jackal.

واويلا *wâ-wailâ*, woe!

(وأى) *wa'a*, aor. *ya'î*, INF. *wa'y*, promise, warrant; vow; stand security; — VIII. INF. *itti'â'*, receive a promise; — X. INF. *isti'â'*, ask for a promise.

واى *wa'y*, promise; opinion, notion; great number, troop, crowd; — *wa'a*, wild ass; — ة *wa'ya-t*, large pot.

واياواى *wâyâwây*, vociferations of a combat.

وائر *wâ'ir*, timorous, frightened.

وائية *wa'iya-t*, large bowl, pot.

(وب) *wabb*, U, INF. *wabb*, prepare for attack and battle.

(وبا) *waba'*, INF. *wab'*, point with the fingers to; range, make ready; spread the plague; — وبى *wabi'*, aor. *tauba'*, *taiba'*, be visited by the plague; — وبو *wabu'*, INF. *wabâ'*, *wabâ'a-t*, *abâ'*, *abâ'a-t*, also pass. *wubi'*, INF. *wab'*, id. — IV. INF. *îbâ'*, id.; — X. INF. *istîbâ'*, find or believe a country to be visited by the plague.

(وبا) *waba'*, pl. *aubâ'*, also *wabâ'*, pl. *aubi'a-t*, contagious disease, epidemic, plague, cholera.

وباص *wabbâṣ*, shining, resplendent; moon.

وباطة *wabâṭa-t*, cowardice.

وباعة *wabbâ'a-t*, وباغة *wabbâga-t*, anus.

وبال *wabâl*, unhealthiness of the air or climate (also ة *wabâla-t*); injury, damage; harshness, anything oppressive, vexation; crime, sin, punishment.

وبائى *wabâ'iyy*, contagious, epidemic, pestiferous.

(وبت) *wabat*, aor. *yabit*, INF. *wabt*, *bita-t*, remain, stay, abide.

(وبح) — II. *wabbaḥ*, INF. *taubîḥ*, scold, rebuke, threaten, terrify; — ة *wabḥa-t*, rebuke, scolding (s.).

(وبد) *wabid*, A, INF. *wabad*, be angry with, enraged against (على *'ala*); have a large family and small means, live in misery; be hot, sultry; be unwell; be worn out; — IV. INF. *îbâd*, isolate, separate, single out.

وبد *wabad*, pl. *aubâd*, poverty with a numerous family, misery, distress; anger, rage, fury; heat;

shame; vice, fault; — *wabid*, famished.

(وبر) *wabar*, aor. *yabir*, INF. *wabr* (also II.), stay, abide; — *wabir*, A, INF. *wabar*, have plenty of hair or wool; — II. INF. *taubîr*, see I.; grow the first hair, down, or wool; shun company and keep at home.

وبر *wabr*, ة, pl. *wibâr*, *wubûr*, *wibâra-t*, a dust-coloured tail-less quadruped, smaller than a cat; — *wabar*, ة, pl. *aubâr*, soft hair of camels, goats, hares, &c. (for tents); اهل الو *ahl al-wabar*, inhabitants of hair-tents, nomads; — *wabir*, ة, hairy; having soft hair.

(وبش) *wabiś*, A, INF. *wabaś*, have white spots; — II. INF. *taubîś*, come together from various places for an affair.

وبش *wabś*, *wabaś*, white spots on the nails; — *wabaś*, pl. *aubâś*, gathered people, rabble, dregs of the populace; — *wabiś*, having white spots from the scab.

(وبص) *wabaṣ*, aor. *yabiṣ*, INF. *wabṣ*, *wabîṣ*, flash; open the eyes; (also IV.) be luxuriantly grown over; — *wabiṣ*, A, INF. *wabaṣ*, be brisk, be nimble; — II. INF. *taubîṣ*, give, present with; — IV. INF. *îbâṣ*, see I.; begin to burn and blaze.

وبص *wabiṣ*, fresh, brisk.

وبصان *wabṣân*, the month ربيع الاخر *rabî' al-âḥir*.

(وبط) *wabaṭ*, aor. *yabiṭ*, INF. *wabṭ*, prevent, hinder; render contemptible; *wubûṭ*, be weak, cowardly, irresolute, wavering, mean, contemptible; — *wabiṭ*, A, INF. *wabaṭ*, also — *wabuṭ*, INF. *wabâṭa-t*, id.; — IV. INF. *îbâṭ*, weaken, render powerless, impotent.

(وبع) — II. *wabba'*, INF. *taubî'*, break wind.

(وبغ) *wabag*, aor. *yabig*, INF. *wabg*, rebuke, revile; — II. INF. *taubîg*, id.

وبغ *wabag*, dandruff; — *wabig*, scurvy; — ة *wabaga-t*, crowd.

(وبق) *wabaq*, aor. *yabiq*, also — *wabiq*, A, INF. *wubûq*, *maubiq*, perish; — IV. INF. *îbâq*, throw into prison; destroy, annihilate; — X. INF. *istîbâq*=I.

(وبل) *wabal*, aor. *yabil*, INF. *wabl*, pour down rain in large drops; chase; beat, thrash; — *wabul*, INF. *wabâl*, *wubûl*, *wabâla-t*, be unhealthy; — III. INF. *muwâbala-t*, attend to zealously and perseveringly.

وبل *wabl*, rain in large drops, rainflood; — *wubul*, pl. of وبيل *wabîl*; *wubbal*, pl. of وابل *wâbil*; — ة *wabala-t*, unhealthiness.

وبنة *wabna-t*, hunger; injury, damage.

(وبه) *wabah*, A, INF. *wabh*, be haughty, arrogant, proud; think of, be concerned at, have regard to; — *wabih*, A, INF. *wabh*, id.; — IV. INF. *îbâh*, id.

وبه *wabh*, intelligence, prudence; pride, haughtiness, splendour, pomp.

(وبوب) *wabwab*, INF. ة=(وب).

وبى *wabi'*, v. see (وبا); — *wabi'*, *wabî'*, ة, visited by the plague; — ة *wabi'a-t*, country visited by the plague.

وبيصة *wabîṣa-t*, fire, flame.

وبيل *wabîl*, f. ة, pl. *wubul*, unhealthy, dangerous, pernicious; violent; also ة *wabîla-t*, pl. *wubul*, thick cudgel, flail, club; a fuller's hammer; bundle of rods; ابيل على وبيل *abîl 'ala wabîl*, old man leaning on a staff.

وبيى *wabî'*, ة=وبى *wabi'*.

(وت) *watt*, *wutt*, ة *wutta-t*, cooing of a dove.

(وتا) *wata'*, aor. *yata'*, INF. *wat'*, step along slowly and heavily.

وتاحة *watâḥa-t*, cheapness.

وتاوت *watâwit*, pl. evil counsels.

(وتب) *watab*, aor. *yatib*, INF. *watb*, remain motionless.

(وتح) *wataḥ*, aor. *yatiḥ*, INF. *watḥ*, give but little, dole; — *watuḥ*, INF. *watâḥa-t*, *wutûḥa-t*, be paltry, of little value, cheap; — IV. INF. *îtâḥ*, make the gift small; possess but little, live in straightened circumstances; press hard; — V. INF. *tawattuḥ*, drink but little.

وتح *watḥ*, *wataḥ*, *watiḥ*, but little; of small value, paltry, cheap; of little use; — ة *wataḥa-t*, a little, trifle.

(وتخ) *wataḫ*, aor. *yatiḫ*, INF. *watḫ*, beat, thrash; — IV. INF. *îtâḫ*, press hard; — ة *wataḫa-t*, mud, mire; fear; something.

(وتد) *watad*, aor. *yatid*, INF. *watd*, *tida-t*, ram in a peg or pole; be rammed in; — II. INF. *taudîd*, ram in; — IV. INF. *îtâd*, id.

وتد *watad*, *watid*, pl. *autâd*, pole, peg, wooden nail; foot of a short and long syllable (مجموع و *watad majmû'* = ⏑ —, مفروق و *watad mafrûq* = — ⏑).

(وتر) *watar*, aor. *yatir*, INF. *watr*, *tira-t*, hate and persecute, bring calamity, enmity upon, frighten; — INF. *watr*, cheat, deprive one of part of his fortune, injure, wrong; (also IV.) do everything separately; make an even number odd; (also II. and IV.) string or draw a bow; (also II. and IV.) perform prayers of free will; — II. INF. *tautîr*, see I.; — III. INF. *witâr*, *muwâtara-t*, do anything in intervals, with interruptions; write one (book or letter) after another; — IV. INF. *îtâr*, see I. and II.; — V. INF. *tawattur*, be strained and hard; — VI. INF. *tawâtur*, follow one another in short intervals; repeat itself continually.

وتر *watr*, *witr*, single, separate; unity; odd number; hatred, feud, grudge, revengefulness; — *witr*, prayers of free will; *al-witr*, day of the procession to Mount Arafat; single, separate; *witr-an witr-an*, one after another, each separately; — *watar*, pl. *autâr*, string of a bow, of a musical instrument; sinew; bow; diameter, hypothenuse, side of an angle; — ة *watara-t*, pl. *watar*, partition wall of the nose, septum; ligament of the tongue, of the prepuce, &c.; — ى *watra*, single, separate, one after another.

(وتش) *watś*, little, few; — *wataś*, rabble; — ة *wataśa-t*, down in the world and miserable.

(وتغ) *watig*, aor. *yatig*, INF. *watag*, commit a crime; be guilty of such; be blameworthy; be profligate in secret (woman); be malicious, speak maliciously; aor. *yautag*, perish; feel pain, suffer; — IV. INF. *îtâg*, destroy, give over to perdition; bring pain or calamity upon; imprison; contaminate one's conscience with a crime.

وتغ *watag*, crime; corruption; vice; disgrace; fault; stupidity; pain; — ة *watiga-t*, profligate (f.).

وتل *wutul*, pl. of اوتل *autal*, who fills himself with food and drink.

(وتن) *watan*, aor. *yatin*, INF. *watn*, wound one's aorta; INF. *wutûn*, *tina-t*, *watna-t*, endure, flow perennially; — III. INF. *muwâtana-t*, attend to with untiring zeal; — X. INF. *istîtân*, grow fat.

وتن *watun*, pl. of وتين *watîn*; — ة *watna-t*, duration, lastingness, perennial flow.

وتوحة *watûḥa-t*, cheapness.

(وتى) *waty*, ة, stagnant water, pool.

وتيح *watiḥ*, little and cheap.

وتيرة *watîra-t*, pl. *watâ'ir*, *watîr*, road, path, mountain-path; manner, way, custom, style; grudge, vindicativeness; interruption, pause, delay, procras-

tination, slowness; envelope, case; septum; ligament of the tongue; nerve; notch of a bow to place the arrow upon; a white rose.

وتين *watîn*, pl. *wutun*, *autina-t*, the great artery, aorta.

(وثأ) *wasa'*, aor. *yasa'*, INF. *was'*, bruise or wound the flesh without injuring the bone; deaden; injure or sprain a bone without breaking it; sprain one's wrist; — وثى, f. *wasi'a-t*, *tausa'*, also pass. f. *wusi'at*, *tûsa'*, INF. *was'*, *wasa'*, be bruised, injured, sprained (hand); — IV. INF. *îsâ'* = *wasa'*.

وثأ *was'*, bruise, injury, sprain; — ة *was'a-t*, blow which leaves a bruise without breaking a bone; sprain.

وثاب *wisâb*, leap, rush against, attack; habitations, dwelling-places; seat, throne, couch; — *wassâb*, given to leaping; fierce in attack; — ة *wasaba-t*, leap against, attack.

وثاجة *wasâja-t*, thickness, fleshiness.

وثار *wasâr*, *wisâr*, anything soft; *wisâr*, pl. of وثيرة *wasîra-t*; — ة *wasâra-t*, softness, woolliness; fatness.

وثاق *wasâq*, *wisâq*, tie, string, rope, fetter, chain; tent-rope; — *wisâq*, compact, alliance, covenant; captivity; pl. of وثيق *wasîq*; — ة *wasâqa-t*, firmness, solidity; self-reliance.

وثامة *wasâma-t*, fleshiness.

(وثب) *wasab*, aor. *yasib*, INF. *wasb*, *wisâb*, *wusûb*, *wasîb*, *wasabân*, leap, leap upon, attack, rush against impetuously; — INF. *wasb*, *wusûb*, sit down; — II. INF. *tausîb*, bid to sit down on a cushion, place a cushion beneath one; (m.) have spasms, suffer from neuralgia; — III. INF. *muwâsaba-t*, leap against, attack, assault; — IV. INF. *îsâb*, make one to leap, to assault, to attack; — V. INF. *tawassub*, take forcible possession of another's property; — VI. INF. *tawâsub*, leap against one another, assault or attack one another; — ة *wasba-t*, pl. *wasabât*, leap, jump; assault, attack, charge; boldness; magnanimity; departure.

(وثج) *wasuj*, INF. *wasâja-t*, be thick; — X. INF. *istîsâj*, be densely grown together; be numerous, in abundance.

وثخة *wasaha-t*, mud, mire.

(وثر) *wasar*, aor. *yasir*, INF. *wasr*, beat or tread soft; cover repeatedly but without success (stallion); — *wasur*, INF. *wasâra-t*, be soft; be abundant; — II. INF. *tausîr*, tread soft; — X. INF. *istîsâr*, demand or wish for much.

وثر *wasr*, *wasir*, unstiffened, trodden or beaten soft; *wasr*, soft garment, a kind of apron for girls made of strips of leather; — *wisr*, soft carpet, bed or saddle-cloth.

(وثغ) *wasag*, A, INF. *wasg*, beat in one's skull; — ة *wasga-t*, a little.

(وثف) *wasaf*, aor. *yasif*, prop a kettle or tripod.

(وثق) *wasiq*, aor. *yasiq*, INF. *siqa-t*, *mausiq*, trust in, rely upon; — *wasuq*, INF. *wasâqa-t*, be firm, solid; be of a firm mind, act with self-reliance; — II. INF. *tausîq*, make firm, consolidate; deem or declare one to be trustworthy; — III. INF. *wisâq*, *muwâsaqa-t*, make a covenant with, bind one by contract; — IV. INF. *îsâq*, make firm; strengthen; fetter, tie fast, strap together; — V. INF. *tawassuq*, have self-reliance and act resolutely; — VI. INF. *tawâsuq*, bind one another by contract; — X. INF. *istîsâq*, secure one's self by contract, documents, &c.; rely upon.

وثق *wasq*, confidence, reliance; —

ى **wusqa**, f. of اوثق *ausaq*, trustworthy, firm.

(وثل) *wasal*, rope of bast; — II. *wassal*, INF. *tausîl*, set firmly, fix; gather, hoard up.

(وثم) *wasam*, aor. *yasim*, INF. *wasm*, run, speed along; break, pound, grind, crush; paw the ground; INF. *wasm*, *wisâm*, scratch the foot so as to make it bleed; INF. *wasm*, *wasîma-t*, gather into a heap; — *wasim*, A, INF. *wasam*, produce but little grass or food; — *wasum*, INF. *wasâma-t*, be fleshy, muscular; — III. INF. *muwâsama-t*, leap with joined feet, throw one's self onward in running

(وثن), IV. *ausan*, INF. *îsân*, spend liberally, make rich presents; multiply, increase (a.); — X. INF. *istisân*, be fat; demand much.

وثن *wasan*, pl. *wusun*, *ausân*, idol; — ى *wasaniyy*, pl. *-ûn*, idolater.

وثوق *wusûq*, confidence; self-reliance, firmness.

(وثى), pass. f. *wusiyat*, aor. *tûsa*, INF. *wasy*, be sprained, bruised, injured (hand); — IV. INF. *îsâ'*, suffer shipwreck or a break-down of one's beast or carriage.

وثى *wasy*, pl. *wusa-n*, hurt, injury, pain; — ة *wasî'a-t*, sprained.

وثيج *wasîj*, dense, firm of flesh.

وثيخة *wasîha-t*, bunch of fresh herbs; loam, clay; thick milk.

وثير *wasîr*, soft (by beating, treading, &c.); soft garment, skin or couch; saddle-cloth; cloth for covering; — ة *wasîra-t*, pl. *wasâ'ir*, *wisâr*, fleshy, soft.

وثيغة *wasîga-t*, a little.

وثيق *wasîq*, ة, pl. *wisâq*, firm, solid; full of self-reliance, persevering, not to be shaken; of legal force; — ة *wasîqa-t*, pl. *wasâ'iq*, self-reliance; firmness, perseverance; covenant, contract, written obligation; document, deed, claim on a pledge or mortgage; pl. proofs, guarantees.

وثيل *wasîl*, fibres of the trunk of a palm; also ة *wasîla-t*, rope made of such, weak rope; weak, relaxed.

وثيم *wasîm*, fleshy, muscular; — ة *wasîma-t*, stack of corn or grass; pebbles.

وثيئة *wasî'a-t*, sprained.

(وج) *wajj*, U, INF. *wajj*, be quick, hasten (n.).

وج *wajj*, haste; yoke; a plant; bird Qata.

(وجا) *waja'*, aor. *yauja'*, INF. *waj'*, (also V.) beat, thrust; decapitate; lie with; INF. *waj'*, *wijâ'*, castrate, geld; sink, dry up; — II. INF. *tauji'*, find (a well) waterless; — IV. INF. *îjâ'*, prevent, hinder; be disappointed; — V. INF. *tawajju'*, see I.; — VIII. INF. *ittijâ'*, be gathered, heaped up.

وجا *wajan*, *waja*, soreness of the feet; — *waja'*, bad (water); — *wijâ'*, pl. *anjiya-t*, bundle of clothes; portmanteau; INF. of (وجا); — ة *waj'a-t*, waterless well.

وجاب *wajâb*, consent; adjudication; — *; — *wajjâb*, ة *wajjâba-t*, timorous, cowardly.

وجاح *wajâh*, smooth stones; also *wijâh*, *wajâh*, veil, covering; ادنى وجاح *adna wajâh-in*, what comes first in view, at first sight.

وجار *wajâr*, *wijâr*, pl. *aujira-t*, *wujur*, den, lair; troop of hyenas.

وجازة *wajâza-t*, readiness, nimbleness; glibness, quickness of repartee and precision of speech.

وجاق *wajâq*, fire-place, hearth, stove, chimney; family, corps; barracks; protection.

وجالة *wajâla-t*, great old age.

وجاه *wijâh*, confronting, meeting face to face; measure, sum, approximate amount; — ة *wajâha-t*, consideration in which

one is held, dignity, high rank; aspect, appearance, presence; sightliness, beauty; decency, good manners.

(وجب) *wajab*, aor. *yajib*, INF. *jiba-t*, *wujûb*, be incumbent, necessary, a duty; have to do or to suffer necessarily; be deserved; INF. *wajb*, *wajîb*, *wajabân*, beat, throb; INF. *wajba-t*, fall with a noise; INF. *wajb*, *wujûb*, set (sun); be sunk, deep-set; die; turn off, refuse; (also II. and IV.) eat but once a day; — *wajub*, INF. *wujûba-t*, be timorous, cowardly; — II. INF. *taujîb*, see I.; make incumbent upon, declare indispensable; treat one according to his dignity and merits, observe the duties of good breeding towards; — III. INF. *wijâb*, *muwâjaba-t*, accept a price offered, adjudge the merchandise; — IV. INF. *îjâb*, make incumbent upon, impose as a duty; hold binding; bring on, cause; oblige, compel; commit an action which brings on a reward or punishment in the future life; make the heart to beat; — X. INF. *istîjâb*, deem necessary, incumbent, obligatory, decent; be worthy of, deserve.

وجب *wajb*, pledge, stake, bet; timid, timorous, cowardly; stupid; pl. *wijâb*, bag of goat-skin; — ة *wajba-t*, noise made in falling; a certain quantity of; a single meal a-day.

وجبان *wajabân*, throbbing of the heart.

(وجح) — II. *wajjaḥ*, INF. *taujîḥ*, appear, become visible, be evident; — IV. INF. *îjâḥ*, id.; force one to take refuge with, compel; let down the curtain of a tent.

وجح *wajaḥ*, refuge, loop-hole.

(وجد) *wajad*, aor. *yajid*, INF. *jida-t*, *wujd*, *wujûd*, *wijdân*, *ijdân*, find; INF. *wajd*, *wijdân*, find what was lost; pass. *wujid*, aor. *yûjad*, INF. *wujûd*, be to be found, exist, be in readiness; — aor. *yajid*, INF. *jida-t*, *wajd*, *wijd*, *wujd*, have plenty of, have enough and be contented; — aor. *yajid*, *yajud*, INF. *jida-t*, *wajd*, *maujida-t*, *wijdân*, be angry with (على *'ala*); INF. *wajd*, be passionately in love with; also *wajud*, grieve for (ب *bi*); — IV. INF. *îjâd*, call into existence, create, produce; imagine, invent; cause one to feel, to perceive, to find, to obtain his wish; enrich; force, compel to (على *'ala*); — V. INF. *tawajjud*, suffer by, complain of; — VII. INF. *inwijâd*, (m.) = VIII. INF. *ittijâd*, be found, find, or find one another again, meet.

وجد *wajd*, pl. *wujûd*, strong emotion, violent joy or grief, love-pain; passionate love; ecstasy of love, of a saint; also *wijd*, *wujd*, and — ة *wijda-t*, pl. *wujûd*, riches, wealth.

وجدان *wajdân*, violent emotion; ecstasy; — *wijdân*, INF. of (وجد); — *wujdân*, pl. of وجيد *wajîd*.

(وجذ) *wajẓ*, pl. *wijâẓ*, *wijẓân*, pond in a mountain, cistern; — *wajiẓ*, abounding with ponds; — IV. *aujaẓ*, INF. *îjâẓ*, force, compel.

(وجر) *wajar*, aor. *yajir*, INF. *wajr*, give one unpleasant things to hear; (also IV.) instil medicine into a child's mouth; — IV. INF. *îjâr*, see I.; — V. INF. *tawajjur*, swallow the medicine (little by little); — VIII. INF. *ittijâr*, take physic.

وجر *wajr*, ة *wajra-t*, *wajara-t*, pl. *aujâr*, mountain-cave, cave, grotto; pitfall; — *wajir*, ة, timid, timorous; — *wujur*, pl. of وجار *wajâr*.

وجرا *wajrâ'*, f. of اوجر *aujar*, very cautious, timorous.

(وجز) *wajaz*, aor. *yajiz*, INF. *wajz*, *wujûz*, be swift and ready; also

— *wajuz*, INF. *wajâza-t*, be short and precise in one's speech; — INF. *îjâz*, be brief, abbreviate; —V. INF. *tawajjuz*, ask one to do a thing.

وجز *wajz*, ة *wajza-t*, ready, swift, nimble; prone to give; prompt, quickly done; brief, short and precise; abbreviated, compendium.

(وجس) *wajas*, aor. *yajis*, INF. *wajs*, *wajasân*, be seized with fear, take fright at; — IV. INF. *îjâs*, conceive a thought, take an idea into one's head, imagine; — V. *tawajjus*, hear a noise, listen to it; perceive.

وجس *wajs*, low and indistinct noise; whisper; also—

وجسان *wajasân*, fright at a noise.

(وجع) *waji'*, aor. *yauja'*, *yaija'*, *yâja'*, *yîja'*, also (less good) *waja'*, aor. *yaji'*, INF. *waj'*, ache, suffer pain; — II. INF. *taujî'*, IV. INF. *îjâ'*, cause pain; — V. INF. *tawajju'*, mourn for; feel compassion; — VII. INF. *inwijâ'* (m.) = VIII. INF. *ittijâ'*, feel pain; suffer from a bodily complaint.

وجع *waja'*, ة, pl. *wijâ*, *aujâ'*, pain, ache, bodily complaint; complaint; — *waji'*, ة, pl. (m.) *waji'ûn*, *waj'ā*, *wujâ'ā*, (f.) *waji'ât*, *wujâ'ā*, aching, suffering pain.

وجعا *waj'â'*, back.

(وجف) *wajaf*, aor. *yajif*, INF. *wajf*, *wujûf*, *wajîf*, be moved, totter; beat, throb; INF. *wajf*, *wajîf*, run fast and with leaps; — IV. INF. *îjâf*, make the beast run as above, put to a gallop; — X. INF. *istîjâf*, captivate the heart.

وجف *wajf*, a kind of gallop.

(وجل) *wajal*, aor. *yaujul*, INF. *wajl*, (also III.) surpass in fear; — *wajil*, aor. *yaujal*, *yaijal*, *yâjal*, *yîjal*, imp. *îjal*, INF. *wajl*, *maujal*, fear, be afraid; — *wajul*, aor. *yaujul*, INF. *wajâla-t*, be advanced in years, be an old man; — III. INF. *muwâjala-t*, see I. — IV. INF. *îjâl*, frighten.

وجل *wajal*, pl. *aujâl*, fear; — *wajil*, ة, pl. -*ûn*, *wijâl*, timorous, cowardly.

وجلا *wajlâ'*, f. of اوجل *aujal*, timid.

(وجم) *wajam*, aor. *jajim*, INF. *wajm*, *wujûm*, be silent, fix the eyes on the ground in silence; grow sullen; feel aversion, abhorrence; INF. *wajm*, strike with the fist.

وجم *wajm*, face; وجم سو *wajm-u sau'-in*, bad man, scamp; — *wajam*, pl. *aujâm*, large heap of stones, road-sign in the desert; — *wajim*, silent with grief or rage, sullen; — ة *wajama-t*, disgrace, ignominy.

(وجن) *wajan*, aor. *yajin*, INF. *wajn*, beat the cloth or linen, full; throw to the ground; throw; — V. INF. *tawajjun*, humble one's self.

وجن *wajn*, blow, thrust; — ة *wajna-t*, *wijna-t*, *wujna-t*, *wajana-t*, pl. -*ât*, *aujân*, cheek.

وجنا *wajnâ'*, having strong cheeks (strong she-camel).

(وجه) *wajah*, aor. *yajih*, INF. *wajh*, strike on the face and push back; surpass in dignity or rank; — *wajuh*, aor. *yaujuh*, INF. *wajâha-t*, enjoy respect and consideration; be handsome of face; — II. INF. *taujîh*, give a fine aspect to, polish, smooth; make one honoured and respected; turn the face of a person or the front of a thing towards (الى *ila*); direct, send; bring to an end; invest with a dignity, entrust with an office; — III. INF. *wijâh*, *muwâjaha-t*, meet face to face, confer; flatter; — IV. INF. *îjâh*, make or find one honoured and respected; exalt, elevate; — V. INF. *tawajjuh*, direct one's self towards, repair to, depart, travel; — VI. INF. *tawâjuh*, meet face to face, have an interview

or conference ; — VIII. INF. *ittijah*, turn towards, repair to ; be directed or referred to ; occur ; appear conclusive.

وجه *wajh*, pl. *ujûh*, *wujûh*, *aujuh*, front, face, physiognomy ; outer side of a stuff ; exterior ; aspect, appearance, image ; surface ; layer ; place of honour ; precedence, preference, pre-eminence ; personal satisfaction ; (pl. *wujûh*) prominent personage, prince, grandee, worthy ; beginning ; intention, aim, tendency, thrift ; reason, cause ; respect, regard, concern, sake ; manner, ways, style, means ; salary, wages, rent, rental ; essence, substance, individuality ; also *wajah*, a little water ; — *wijh*, *wujh*, side ; — *wajah*, considered, respected ; — ة *wijha-t*, *wujha-t*, side, direction.

وجها *wajh-an*, according to appearance, seemingly ; — *wujahâ'*, pl. of وجيه *wajîh*.

وجوب *wujûb*, necessity, incumbency, duty, propriety ; obligation (debt) ; death ; — ة *wujûba-t*, timidity, timorousness.

وجود *wujûd*, ية *wujûdiyya-t*, being found (s.), existence ; essence, substance ; individuality ; invention ; *wujûd*, person, personality ; consciousness ; penis ; trunk of a tree ; pl. of وجد *wajd*.

وجور *wajûr*, what is unpleasant to hear ; also *wujûr*, a medicine administered through the mouth.

وجوز *wujûz*, quickness, promptitude ; precision of speech.

وجول *wujûl*, pl. old men.

(وجى) *waja*, aor. *yajî*, INF. *wajy* ; see IV. ; — *wajî*, aor. *yauja*, INF. *waja-n* (also V.), have the hoofs worn out, suffer in the hoofs, be foot-sore ; — IV. INF. *îjâ'*, make hoof-sore ; (also I.) find utterly heartless and miserly ; be niggardly towards, stint, give nothing ; give ; abstain, desist ; come home without prey ; — V. INF. *tawajjî*, see I.

وجى *waja*, soreness of the hoof or foot ; — *wajî*, hoof-sore ; — *wajiyy*, id. ; miserly, avaricious ; — ة *waji'at*, waterless.

وجيا *wajyâ'*, hoof-sore (f.).

وجيب *wajîb*, palpitation ; — * ; — ة *wajîba-t*, pay, wages, pension ; purchase-money to be paid by instalments ; purchase.

وجيح *wajîḥ*, thick, strong.

وجيز *wajîz*, brief, precise ; abbreviated ; compendious ; short.

وجيع *wajî'*, painful ; suffering.

وجيف *wajîf*, palpitation ; a short gallop.

وجيل *wajîl*, pond.

وجيم *wajîm*, hot, sultry ;—ة, mildewed.

وجين *wajîn*, rugged ground ; mountain-slope ; river-bank.

وجيه *wajîh*, pl. *wujahâ'*, distinguished and highly respected ; prince, leader, person of quality ; sightly, pretty, handsome of face ; decorous, beseeming ; to be worn on both sides ; also ة *wajîha-t*, pearls, &c. used as an amulet.

وجيى *wajî'*, gelded ; — ة *wajî'a-t*, cow ; dish of pounded locusts or date-stones with butter.

وح abbreviation for وحينئذ *wa-ḥaina'iz-in*, and then ; — *waḥḥ*, tent-peg ; proverbial name of a very poor man ; — *waḥḥ-i*, cry to oxen.

وحا *waḥâ'*, haste ; — ة *waḥât*, n. u. of وحى *waḥa*.

وحاد *wuḥâd*, one at a time ; *wuḥâd-a*, one by one, one after the other ; — ة *waḥâda-t*, singleness, being unique (s.), incomparability.

وحاشى *waḥâśa*, pl. of وحشان *waḥśân*.

وحام *wiḥâm*, *waḥâm*, desire of a pregnant woman, violent longing ; also *waḥâma*, pl. of وحمى *waḥmâ*.

(وحج) *waḥij*, A, INF. *waḥaj*, flee, seek refuge ; — IV. INF. *îḥâj*, compel to seek refuge, force.

وحج *waḥaj*, refuge, asylum; — ة *waḥaja-t*, pl. *auḥâj*, loop-hole.

(وحد) *waḥad*, *waḥid*, aor. *yaḥid*, INF. *ḥida-t*, *waḥd*, *waḥdat*, *wuḥûd*, also *waḥud*, aor. *yaḥid*, INF. *waḥâda-t*, *wuḥûda-t*, be single, by one's self, unique, incomparable; — II. INF. *tauḥîd*, reduce to one, consider as single or unique, profess the unity of; — IV. INF. *îḥâd*, make single, unique, incomparable; leave alone, forsake; — V. INF. *tawaḥḥud*, be one, single, alone; be reduced to one; isolate one's self, live in solitude, become an original; — VIII. INF. *ittiḥâd*, be united, unite (n.); make an agreement with.

وحد *waḥd*, single, alone, unique; by one's self (takes the pron. affixes); solitary; solitude; — ة *waḥda-t*, isolation; unity; INF. of (وحد).

وحدان *wuḥdân*, pl. of واحد *wâḥid*; — ى *waḥdâniyy*, ة, single, isolated; — ية *waḥdâniyya-t*, unity; being unique (s.), incomparability.

(وحر) *waḥir*, A, INF. *waḥar*, be poisoned by a venomous lizard (food), or eat of such food; — *waḥir*, aor. *yaḥir*, *yauḥir*, *yaiḥir*, be filled with rage against, bear a secret grudge to (على *'ala*).

وحر *waḥr*, anger, grudge; — *waḥir*, angry, bearing a grudge; — ة *waḥra-t*, *waḥara-t*, pl. *waḥar*, a poisonous lizard.

(وحش) *waḥaś*, aor. *yaḥiś*, INF. *waḥś* (also II.), throw away one's clothes and arms in fleeing; — *waḥuś*, INF. *waḥâśa-t*, *wuḥûśa-t*, fall into poverty and contempt; grow savage and brute-like; be devastated and unpeopled; — II. INF. *tauḥîś*, devastate and depopulate; turn a land into a wilderness; allow one to grow savage and brute-like; make wild; leave one in solitude, in sorrow; see I.; — IV. INF. *îḥâś*, devastate and depopulate; grieve by absence or departure; be devastated and depopulated; find a country so; suffer from hunger; — V. INF. *tawaḥḥuś*, be devastated and depopulated; grow savage, brute-like, malicious; be famished; — X. INF. *istîḥâś*, be grieved at a friend's absence; find one's solitude unbearable; be afraid.

وحش *waḥś*, waste and depopulated; desert; savageness, natural wildness; grief, melancholy, disturbed mind; pl. *auḥâś*, famished; insipid, tasteless; pl. *wuḥûś*, *wuḥśân*, wild beast; wild, savage; — ة *waḥśa-t*, solitude, abandonment; grief, melancholy on account of the absence of a friend; fear, fright; savageness, brutishness, brutality; waste and deserted.

وحشان *waḥśân*, pl. *waḥâśa*, grieved, sorrowful, melancholy; — *wuḥśân*, pl. of وحش *waḥś*.

وحشى *waḥśiyy*, ة, wild, grown wild or savage; barbarous, cruel; timid, shy; outside; — ة *waḥśiyya-t*, wild state, savageness, cruelty.

(وحص) *waḥas*, aor. *yaḥiṣ*, INF. *waḥṣ*, drag on the ground, trail.

(وحف) *waḥaf*, aor. *yaḥif*, INF. *waḥf*, throw one's self on the ground, lie down; approach, come and put up; hasten up, hurry (n.); — *waḥif*, A, INF. *waḥaf* and — *waḥuf*, INF. *waḥûfa-t*, *wuḥûfa-t*, have grown luxuriant and densely entwined; be dense and black; — II. INF. *tauḥîf*, throw one's self down; beat, thrash; hasten (n.); — IV. INF. *îḥâf*, hasten (n.).

وحف *waḥf*, luxuriant; dense and black; densely feathered; — ة *waḥfa-t*, pl. *wiḥâf*, sound, noise; black stone.

وحفا *waḥfâ'*, pl. *waḥâfa*, covered with black stones.

(وحل) *waḥal*, aor. *yaḥil*, INF. *waḥl*, fall deeper into the mud than

another; — *waḥil*, A, INF. *waḥal*, *mauḥal* (also V.), fall into the mud; stick in the mud; dirty one's self with mud; — II. INF. *tauḥîl* (m.), see — IV. INF. *îḥâl*, throw into the mud, dirty with mud; (also II.) get muddy; — V. INF. *tawaḥḥul*, be muddy; see *waḥil* above.

وحل *waḥal*, *waḥl*, pl. *wuḥûl*, *auḥâl*, thin mud, mire; — *waḥil*, وحلان *waḥlân*, muddy; — ة *waḥla-t*, miry pool, puddle.

(وحم) *waḥam*, INF. *waḥm*, go towards a place, try to get there; — *waḥim*, aor. *yaḥim*, *yauḥam*, resist the stallion; (also V.) long for some particular dish or food (pregnant woman); desire intensely; — II. INF. *tauḥîm*, slaughter an animal to give a woman the food she is longing for; — V. INF. *tawaḥḥum*, see I.; long for violently.

وحم *waḥam*, desire of a pregnant woman; violent craving for; what is longed for; rustling of a wing; — ى *waḥma*, pl. *wiḥâm*, *waḥâma*, longing for (pregnant woman).

(وحن) *waḥin*, aor. *yaḥin*, *yauḥan*, be angry, hate, bear a grudge; — V. INF. *tawaḥḥun*, be paunch-bellied; fall into misery, perish.

وحواح *waḥwâḥ*, nimble and active; strong and courageous; howling, barking.

(وحوح) *waḥwaḥ* = the previous; a bird; — INF. ة, utter a rough sound, cry out; blow into one's hands.

وحود *wuḥûd*, ة *wuḥûda-t*, singleness, being unique (s.).

(وحى) *waḥa*, aor. *yaḥî*, INF. *waḥy*, inform, insinuate, suggest; tell in secret; inspire, reveal; send a messenger to; write; hasten (n.); — II. INF. *tauḥiya-t*, urge to haste, bid to make haste; — IV. INF. *îḥâ'*, send; inspire, reveal to (الى *ila*); hint; be seized with fear; — V. INF. *tawaḥḥî*, hasten (n.); — X. INF. *istîwâ'*, beg for information, for explanation, inquire.

وحى *waḥy*, pl. *wuḥiyy*, sound, noise; letter, book; (also pl. *auḥiya-t*) divine inspiration, revelation; امين الوحى *amîn-u 'l-waḥy-i*, the archangel Gabriel; — *waḥa*, n.u. وحاة *waḥât*, sound, noise; powerful prince, king; haste; falcon; — *waḥiyy*, swift, nimble.

وحيد *waḥîd*, ة, alone, single, isolated, unique, incomparable; وحيد دهره *waḥîd-u dahri-hi*, the phœnix of his age.

وحيش *waḥîś*, wild; beast; malicious, vicious; horrible, ugly, abominable; disgraceful, infamous.

وحيم *waḥîm*, hot, sultry.

(وخ) *waḥḥ*, intention; pain, grief.

وخاء *wiḥâ'*, ة *wiḥâ'a-t*, brotherhood. INF. of (اخو III.).

وخاد *waḥḥâd*, wide-stepping (adj.).

وخاشة *waḥâśa-t*, badness, worthlessness.

وخام *waḥâm*, unwholesome; — *wiḥâm*, ى *waḥâma*, pl. of وخم *waḥm*, *waḥim*, وخوم *waḥûm*, وخيم *waḥîm*; — ة *waḥâma-t*, surfeit, indigestion; unhealthiness, hurtfulness.

(وخد) *waḥad*, aor. *yaḥid*, INF. *waḥd*, *waḥîd*, *waḥadân*, stride along (like an ostrich).

(وخز) *waḥaz*, aor *yaḥiz*, INF. *waḥz*, wound slightly; prick with a lancet or needle, bleed; make gradually grey.

وخز *waḥz*, a little; *waḥz-an waḥz-an*, by fours.

(وخش) *waḥuś*, INF. *waḥâśa-t*, *wuḥûśa-t*, be bad and worthless; be good for nothing, be despised.

وخش *waḥś* (m. f., sing. pl.), pl. also *wiḥâś*, *auḥâś*, bad, worthless, good-for-nothing; rabble.

(وخص) *waḥaṣ*, INF. *wuḥûṣ*, be moved, stir.

(وحض) *waḥaḍ*, aor. *yaḥiḍ*, INF. *waḥḍ*, stab, wound; make gradually grey.
(وحط) *waḥaṭ*, aor. *yaḥiṭ*, INF. *waḥṭ*, make gradually grey; step apace, run; enter, introduce one's self; wound; creak.
(وحف) *waḥaf*, aor. *yaḥif*, INF. *waḥf*, revile, abuse, insult.
وحف *waḥf*, stupid; — ة *waḥfa-t*, leathern purse.
(وحم) *waḥim*, aor. *yaḥim* (also VIII.), suffer from surfeit or indigestion; be difficult to deal with, clumsy, a bore; (m.) be dirty; — *waḥum*, INF. *waḥâma-t*, *wuḥûma-t*, *wuḥûm*, id.; be injurious to the health; — VIII. INF. *ittiḥâm*, see I.; — X. INF. *istîḥâm*, find the food indigestible.
وحم *waḥm*, indigestion; also *waḥim*, pl. *auḥâm*, suffering from indigestion; ة, indigestible, injurious to the health; ة *waḥima-t*, unhealthy tract; *waḥm*, pl. *auḥâm*, *wiḥâm*, also *waḥim*, pl. *waḥâma*, difficult to deal with, disagreeable; clumsy; a bore; (m.) dirty; — (m.) *waḥam*, pl. *auḥâm*, uncleanliness, dirt.
وحنة *waḥna-t*, damage, corruption, calamity; — V. *tawaḥḥan*, INF. *tawaḥḥun*, intend, purpose.
وحواح *waḥwâḥ*, lax, relaxed.
وحوحة *waḥwaḥa-t*, cry of a certain bird.
وحوصة *wuḥûṣa-t*=وحاصة *waḥâṣa-t*.
وحوم *waḥûm*, ة, pl. *wiḥâm*, *waḥâma*, *auḥâm*, suffering from indigestion; unhealthy; disagreeable, difficult to deal with, a bore; clumsy; also ة *wuḥûma-t*, indigestion; being indigestible (s.).
(وحى) *waḥa*, aor. *yaḥî*, INF. *waḥy*, advance straight forward, intend, purpose; study diligently; — III. INF. *muwâḥât*, be one's brother; fraternise with; — V. INF. *tawaḥḥî*, purpose, try to bring about, to realise; — X. INF. *istîḥâ'*, question, inquire from.
وحى *waḥy*, *waḥa*, pl. *waḥiyy*, *wuḥiyy*, resolution, intention, purpose; right road, way; journey; traveller; messenger, express.
وحيز *waḥîz*, honey-cake; stabbed, wounded by a stab.
وحيم *waḥîm*, ة=وحوم *waḥûm*.
(ود) *wadd*, pret. *wadad-tu*, *wadid-tu*, aor. *yawaddu*, INF. *wadd*, *widd*, *wudd*, *waddâd*, *widdâd*, *wuddâd*, *wadâda-t*, *mawadda-t*, *miwadda-t*, *maudûda-t*, love, like; INF. *wadd*, *wudd*, *wadâda-t*, wish for, like to see or to do; — III. INF. *muwâdda-t*, love, like; — V. INF. *tawaddud*, show love and affection to; gain one's love (acc.); — VI. INF. *tawâdd*, love one another.
ود *wadd*, *wudd*, *widd*, love, affection, friendship; desire, wish; بودى لو *bi-wuddî lau*, (m.) بدى *biddî*, it is in my wish that (hence the m. paraphrase of the future: بدى اكتب *biddî aktub*, I shall write, &c.); — *wadd*, *wudd*, *widd*, pl. *awidd*, *awudd*, lover, friend; — *wadd*, tent-peg; — *wudd*, name of an idol.
(ودا) *wada'*, aor. *yada'*, INF. *wad'*, level, plane; wrong or do one evil in every way; — ودى *wadi'*, A, INF. *wada'*, be intercepted, fail to arrive; — II. INF. *taudî'*, level the ground over, bury (على *'ala*); — V. INF. *tawaddu'*, get buried, be dead.
وداج *widâj*, vein of the throat.
وداد *wadâd*, *widâd*, *wudâd*, ة *wadâda-t*, love, friendship.
وداس *widâs*, first grass.
وداع *wadâ'*, *widâ'*, giving or taking leave (s.), leave, adieu, farewell; — ة *wadâ'a-t*, mildness, gentleness, peaceableness; rest, quiet, ease; entrusted goods, deposit.
وداق *widâq*, rut; sharp.
(ودب) *wadb*, evil condition.

(ودج) *wadaj*, aor. *yadij*, INF. *wadj*, bleed a horse at the jugular vein; make peace between, settle a dispute in a friendly way.

ودج *wadaj*, pl. *audâj*, jugular vein (du. *wadajân*, also two brothers, equals, fellows); means, mediator, mediation.

(ودح), IV. *audaḥ*, INF. *îdâḥ*, submit, obey; — ة *wadaḥa-t*, something, anything.

ودداء *wudadâ'*, pl. of وديد *wadîd*.

(ودر) *wadar*, aor. *yadir*, INF. *wadr*, be drunk to insensibility; — II. INF. *taudîr*, (also V.) drive into danger or perdition; — V. INF. *tawaddur*, squander, dissipate; throw one's self into danger or perdition; = II.; be squandered.

(ودس) *wadas*, aor. *yadis*, INF. *wads*, (also II.) be concealed; depart; (also II.) put forth at first isolated shoots or blades; throw out half a word to; — II. INF. *taudîs*, see I.; — V. INF. *tawaddus*, graze off the first blades.

ودس *wads*, first grass.

ودش *wadś*, corruption, corruptedness.

(ودص) *wadaṣ*, aor. *yadiṣ*, INF. *wadṣ*, throw out half a word to.

(ودع) *wada'*, aor. *yada'*, INF. *wad'*, put down; deposit; leave behind; take leave of and wish a good journey to; abandon, forsake; let alone, let be done, admit, allow (IMP. *da'*, permit! let! give over!); leave undone; preserve, spare (a garment, &c.); also — *wadu'*, INF. *wadâ'a-t*, be quiet, mild, gentle, peaceable; stand firm and quiet; — II. INF. *taudî'*, put down, deposit; (also III.) say farewell to, take leave; abandon, forsake; — III. INF. *widâ'*, *muwâda'a-t*, see II.; reconcile one's self with; — IV. INF. *îdâ'*, put down; deposit with, give into one's keeping (2 acc.); endow; impart a secret; bid farewell to; — V. INF. *tawaddu'*, be deposited, given into keeping; be left alone, left quiet; deposit; preserve, keep in a pocket or chest; receive one's farewell; — VI. INF. *tawâdu'*, treat one another gently, get reconciled; — VIII. INF. *ittidâ'*, be left alone, be at rest; — X. INF. *istîdâ'*, beg to accept as a deposit, to take into one's keeping, recommend to one's care; recommend one's self to (الى *ila*).

ودع *wad'*, grave, inclosure of a grave; also *wada'*, jerboa; ذات الودع *ẕât al-wada'*, Noah's ark; temple in Mecca; — ة *wad'a-t*, *wada'a-t*, pl. *wada'*, *wada'ât*, Venus-shell (used for polishing); small white shell worn as an amulet.

ودعا *wid'â'*, pl. of وديع *wadî'*.

(ودف) *wadaf*, aor. *yadif*, INF. *wadf*, melt and drip, melt; trickle, let the water out in drops; give but little; — V. INF. *tawadduf*, tower over; (also X.) inquire, investigate; — X. INF. *istîdâf*, melt fat; be grown high; see V.; — ة *wadfa-t*, green meadow.

(ودق) *wadaq*, aor. *yadiq*, INF. *wadq*, drip, drop; be sharp; become tame, submissive, docile; swell; relax, purge [(n.); — INF. *wadq*, *wudûq*, approach, be near, be within reach of, be possible; — INF. *wadq*, *wadâq*, *wadaqân*, desire the stallion; — *wadiq*, A, INF. *wadaq*, have red pustules on the eye; — IV. *îdâq*, rain; — X. INF. *istîdâq*, see I.

ودق *wadq*, rain; side, front; ذات ودقين *ẕât-u wadqain*, double calamity; also *wadaq*, red pustules on the eye; — ة *wadiqa-t*, afflicted with such.

(ودك) *wadik*, A, INF. *wadak*, be fat; — II. INF. *taudîk*, put into fat or grease.

ودك *wadak*, fat, grease; stickiness of the eye-lids.

(ودل) *wadal*, aor. *yadil*, INF. *wadl*, shake the skin bag for making butter.

(ودن) *wadan*, aor. *yadin*, INF. *wadn*, *widân*, wet, moisten, put into water, macerate (a.); make everything comfortable for a bride; INF. *wadn*, abbreviate, shorten; beat, thrash; — *wadin*, A, INF. *wadan*, give birth to a small and weak child.

(وده) *wadah*, aor. *yadih*, prevent, hinder; — *wadih*, A, INF. *wadah*, be hindered, desist; — IV. INF. *îdâh*, cry out to, shout to; X. *istaudah*, INF. *istîdâh*, be driven together, assemble (n.); submit (n.).

ودها *wadhâ'*, handsome, pretty (f.).

ودود *wadûd*, loving; friend; beloved one; God.

ودوق *wadûq*, hot, rutting; — *.

ودوك *wadûk*, fat.

(ودى) *wada*, aor. *yadî*, IMP. د *di*, INF. *diya-t*, atone for a murder by paying blood-money; INF. *wady*, protrude the penis (stallion); let come up, bring near; — II. INF. *taudiya-t*, carry one off; (m.) send, bring, lead to; — IV. INF. *îdâ'*, perish; — X. INF. *istîdâ'*, acknowledge a debt or another's legal claim.

ودى *wadî'*, v. see (ودا); — *wada*, death, ruin; murder; destruction; — *wadiyy*, ة, young palm-shoot.

وديد *wadîd*, pl. *wudadâ'*, *awiddâ'*, lover, friend, beloved one.

وديس *wadîs*, dry, withered.

وديع *wadî'*, pl. *widâ'*, quiet, mild, gentle, peaceable; modest; — pl. *wadâ'i'*, contract; — *wadî'a-t*, pl. *wadâ'i'*, deposit; subjects.

وديفة *wadîfa-t*, green meadow.

وديق *wadîq*, hot, rutting; — ة *wadîqa-t*, rut; heat.

وديك *wadîk*, ة, fat.

ودين *wadîn*, wetted, steeped.

(وذا) *waẓa'*, aor. *yaẓî*, INF. *ẓi'a-t*, *waẓ'*, accuse, rebuke, scold, put to scorn, despise; scare away by shouting at; — VIII. INF. *ittiẓâ'*, be accused, scolded, despised.

وذا *waẓ'*, invective (s.); — ة *waẓ'a-t*, *waẓât*, wrong, insult; calamity.

وذاب *wiẓâb*, paunch, stomach.

وذام *wiẓâm*, tripes.

(وذح) *waẓaḥ*, aor. *yaẓiḥ*, INF. *waẓḥ*, walk with an impetuous and vigorous step; — *waẓiḥ*, aor. *yauẓaḥ*, *yaiẓaḥ*, INF. *waẓaḥ*, have excrement and urine sticking to the fleece.

وذح *waẓaḥ*, ة, pl. *wuẓḥ*, excrement, urine, sweat, dirt, &c. sticking to the fleece or wool.

وذر *waẓar*, aor. *yaẓir*, INF. *waẓr*, cut; wound; cut meat into pieces or slices; — aor. *yaẓar*, IMP. *ẓar*, leave, leave behind, let go, let alone; — ة *waẓra-t*, pl. *waẓr*, *waẓar*, clitoris; gland of the penis; also *waẓara-t*, piece or slice of meat without bone; du. *al-waẓratan*, the lips.

(وذع) *waẓa'*, aor. *yaẓi'*, INF. *waẓ'*, flow, run.

(وذف) *waẓaf*, aor. *yaẓif*, INF. *waẓf*, dissolve (n.), melt; — II. INF. *tauẓîf*, walk with short steps and in jerks; — V. INF. *tawaẓẓuf*, id.

وذفان *waẓfân*, hastening (adj.), in a hurry.

وذلة *waẓala-t*, *waẓila-t*, nimble, agile, active; nimble servant girl.

(وذم) *waẓim*, A, INF. *waẓam*, have the strap وذم *waẓam* broken; — II. INF. *tauẓîm*, cut entirely into pieces; — IV. INF. *îẓâm*, put a *waẓam* to a bucket.

وذم *waẓam*, pl. *auẓâm*, strap or rope running through the handles of a bucket; fleshy excrescence, wart; — ة *waẓama-t*, tripes.

وذما *waẓmâ'*, barren (woman).

(وذن) — V. *tawaẓẓan*, INF. *tawaẓẓun*, change, alter, exchange; please.

وذواذ *waẓwâẓ*, quick, hasty.

وذوذ *waẓwaẓ*, INF. ة, hasten (n.), speed; glide by swiftly.

(ودى) *waḍa*, aor. *yaḍî*, INF. *waḍy*, scratch with the nails.
ودى *waḍy*, scratch; — ة *waḍya-t*, pain, suffering; fault, defect.
وذيلة *waḍîla-t*, pl. *waḍîl*, *waḍâ'il*, polished silver; mirror; slice of fat; nimble maid-servant.
وذيمة *waḍîma-t*, pl. *waḍâ'im*, beast of sacrifice, sacrifice in Mecca.
(ور) *warr*, hip-bone, hip (also ة *warra-t*); rich harvest; — (m.) *warr*, INF. *warr*, throw, throw away, reject.
(ورأ) *wara'*, aor. *yara'*, *yaura'*, INF. *war'*, turn off, refuse, hinder; surfeit (n.); suffer from indigestion.
وراء *warâ'*, what is behind, on the other side (also what is in front, on this side); what is out of sight; back-part; buttocks; grandson, progeny; *warâ'a*, behind, beyond, on the other side (in front, on this side).
وراث *wurrâs*, pl. of وارث *wâris*, who inherits, &c.; — ة *wirâsa-t*, inheriting (s.); inheritance.
وراد *wirâd*, pl. of ورد *ward*; — *warrâd*, grower of roses; gardener; —*wurrâd*, pl. of وارد *wârid*, who descends, &c.; — ة *warâda-t*, a reddish-brown, bay-colour.
وراشين *warâšin*, pl. of ورشان *warašân*.
وراط *wirâṭ*, deception, fraud; pl. of ورطة *warṭa-t*.
وراع *warâ'*, ة *warâ'a-t*, timidity, cautiousness, fear of sin.
وراف *warrâf*, of fresh green.
وراق *warâq*, verdant plain;— *wirâq*, time of verdure; — * ; — *warrâq*, copyist; paper-maker, stationer; rich in money;—*wirâqa-t*, trade of a paper-maker or stationer; — ة *warrâqa-t*, paper in place of window-panes; — ى *waraqî*, pl. of ورقا *warqâ'*.
وراك *wirâk*, pl. *wurk*, *wuruk*, front part of a camel's saddle, where the rider places his feet; cushion or saddle, cloth upon it.
ورانى *warâniyy*, ة behind, ulterior, on the other side; — ة *warâniyya-t*, back side, hind-part.
ورايا *warâya*, created things.
(ورب) *warib*, A, INF. *warab*, be degenerated, corrupted; perish; be awry, aslant, oblique, diagonal, transverse; (also II.) go crooked ways; — II. INF. *taurîb*, talk equivocally; make transverse, oblique; see I.; — III. INF. *muwâraba-t*, try to deceive, to outwit; — VII. INF. *inwirâb* = I. (m.).
ورب *warb*, pl. *aurâb*, obliqueness, obliquity; diagonal; crooked ways, tricks, cunning, stratagem; lair, loop-hole; mouth of a field-mouse's hole; membrane, interstice between the fingers, ribs, &c.; limb; hips, buttocks; — *wirb*, cunning, stratagem; — *warab*, degeneration, corruption; — *warib*, degenerated; hanging, suspended; — ة *warba-t*, headband, turban; limb; buttocks.
(ورث) *waris*, aor. *yaris*, INF. *irs*, *risa-t*, *wirâsa-t*, be heir, inherit; — II. INF. *tauris*, make one a heir, leave as a legacy to; — IV. INF. *îrâs* = II.; bring upon; — VI. INF. *tawârus*, inherit, possess by inheritance.
ورث *wars*, anything new or fresh; — *wirs*, inheritance, heir-loom; — ة *warasa-t*, pl. of وارث *wâris*, heir, &c.
(ورخ) *wariḥ*, A, INF. *waraḥ* (also V.), be thin; — INF. *taurîḥ*, add the date, date; — V. INF. *tawarruḥ*, see I; be wetted, moistened, be damp; — X. INF. *istirâḥ*, id.
ورخ *warḥ*, a tree; — ة *wariḥa-t*, densely grown over.
(ورد) *warad*, aor. *yarid*, INF. *wurûd*, come, descend to the watering-place; arrive, come in, appear, present one's self; accrue;—*warud*, aor. *yaurud*, INF. *wurûda-t*, be red, tawny;—II. INF. *taurîd*, paint one's self red, rouge; bloom,

bear blossoms; — III. INF. *muwârada-t*, come to the watering-place at the same time with another; — IV. INF. *îrâd*, lead to the watering-place; cause to arrive, lead up, bring; offer, present; send, dispatch; expound, explain; yield a rent, an advantage, produce; — V. INF. *tawarrud*, come to the watering-place, resort to, arrive; be rosy; — VI. INF. *tawârud*, come together to the watering-place; come in a lump, all at once; — VIII. INF. *inwirâd*, accrue, come in; arrive; — X. INF. *istîrâd*, draw advantage from, derive profit.

ورد *ward*, ة pl. *wurûd*, blossom; flower; rose; flower-leaf; saffron; warlike, brave; ابو الورد *abû-'l-ward*, penis; f. ة, pl. *wurd*, *wirâd*, red, carroty, tawny; lion; rose-coloured, rosy; *wurd*, roses; — *wird*, pl. *aurâd*, access; watering (s.), time or place of watering, resting-place, station; troop (of people or cattle) coming to a watering-place, troop, cohort, detachment; flock of birds; section of the Koran; daily fever; continual motion, activity, exercise, practice, task, business; — ة *wurda-t*, red or tawny colour; — ى *wardiyy*, ة rose-coloured, rosy; slave; — ية *wardiyya-t*, rosary; smell of roses.

(ورز) *waraẓ*, aor. *yariẓ*, INF. *warẓ*, be slow, tarry, hesitate.

(ورس) *waris*, A, INF. *waras*, be covered with moss or sea-weed; — III. INF. *muwârasa-t*, dye yellow.

ورس *wars*, a yellow plant from which a wash for freckles, a yellow dye, &c. are made; saffron.

(ورش) *waraś*, aor. *yariś*, INF. *warś*, *wurûś*, snatch up the food and swallow it rapidly; eat; be greedy, covet; come to a meal uninvited; incite; attend to the smallest detail; — *wariś*, A, INF. *waraś*, be brisk and swift; — II. INF. *taurîś*, set up one's timber-yard, dock-yard, workshop, &c.

ورش *warś*, a milk-dish; — *waraś*, briskness; colic; — *wariś*, ة, brisk, swift; — ة *warśa-t*, timber-yard; dock-yard; workshop.

ورشان *waraśân*, pl. *wirśân*, *warâsîn*, wood-pigeon, turtle-dove.

(ورص) *waraṣ*, aor. *yariṣ*, INF. *warṣ*, lay an egg with one effort.

(ورض) *waraḍ*, aor. *yariḍ*, INF. *warḍ*, = the previous; drop excrement with one effort.

(ورط) — II. *warraṭ*, INF. *taurîṭ*, throw down; throw into an abyss, into perdition; — IV. INF. *îrâṭ*, id.; — V. INF. *tawarruṭ*, fall into an abyss, into danger, ruin, &c.; sink in the mud; — X. INF. *istîrâṭ*, entangle one's self in difficulties and dangers; — ة *warṭa-t*, pl. *wirâṭ*, depth, abyss, whirlpool; labyrinth; danger, perdition, ruin, annihilation; low ground; mud; well; anus.

(ورع) *wari'*, aor. *yari'*, *yaura'*, also *wara'*, aor. *yara'*, and *waru'*, aor. *yauru'*, INF. *warâ'a-t*, *war'*, *warâ'*, *warû'*, *wurû'*, abstain from what is unlawful; lead an abstemious, pious, modest life; be timid, timorous, cowardly; be weak and useless; INF. *wur'*, *wuru'*, *war'a-t*, *wur'a-t*, *warâ'*, *wurû'*, graze, pasture; — II. INF. *taurî'*, prevent from doing wrong; send one's cattle to the pasture; — III. INF. *muwâra'a-t*, converse, confer; — V. INF. *tawarru'*, abstain from evil through piety.

ورع *wara'*, abstinence from what is unlawful, abstemiousness, chastity, self-restraint; piety; conscientiousness; timidity, cowardice; pl. *aurâ'* small, weak, useless; — *wari'*, id.; abste-

mious, chaste, pious, conscientious; timorous; — ة war'a-t, wur'a-t, timidity; scrupulosity.

(ورف) *waraf*, aor. *yarif*, INF. *warf*, *wurûf*, *warîf* (also II. and IV.), extend (n.) in length and breadth; be luxuriantly verdant; — II. INF. *taurîf*, IV. INF. *îrâf*, see I.

ورف *warf*, edge of the liver.

(ورق) *waraq*, aor. *yariq*, INF. *warq*, get leaves; ramify, branch out; (also II.) strip off the leaves; — II. INF. *tauriq*, see I.; (m.) cover the wall with a layer of mortar; — V. INF. *tawarruq*, eat leaves.

ورق *warq*, *wirq*, *wurq*, *waraq*, *wariq*, (coll. sing. and pl.) pl. *wirâq*, and *aurâq*, coined money, coinage; — *wurq*, pl. of أورق *auraq*, dark grey, &c.; — *waraq*, ة pl. *aurâq*, branch; leaf of a tree, foliage; leaf of paper, of a book, scroll; slice; disk; sheet of metal; gold-beater's skin; card (for playing); coined money; fortune, wealth; sail; dropping blood or pus; beauty of this world; men in their bloom; — *wariq*, leafy, of dense foliage; ة, mean, low, miserly; — ة *warqa-t*, fault in a bow; — *wurqa-t*, grey colour, ash colour; —*waraqa-t*, leaf, note, letter; sheet of metal, thin layer.

ورقا *warqâ'*, dove; she-wolf; soul of the world; f. of أورق *auraq*, dark grey.

ورقاوى *warqâwiyy*, dark-grey, ash-coloured.

(ورك) *warak*, aor. *yarik*, INF. *wark*, *wurûk* (also V.), lean on the hip to rest, lie on the hip; INF. *wark*, strike on the hip; (also II.) put on the hip; INF. *wurûk*, stay, abide; (also II.) be equal to and succeed in; — *warik*, A, INF. *warak*, have large hips; — II. INF. *taurîk*, see I.; impute to; necessitate, cause; — V. INF. *tawakkur*, see I.; sit on one buttock; mount; — VI. INF. *tawâkur*, sit or lean upon one buttock.

(ورك) *wark*, *wirk*, *warak*, *warik* (f.), pl. *aurâk*, hip-bone, hip, buttock; knotty part of a branch; — *wark*, *warik*, crowd, troop; — *wurk*, pl. of وراك *wirâk*; — ى *warka*, *wirka*, root, origin.

(ورل) *waral*, (f.) pl. *wirlân*, *aurâl*, *ar'ul*, a large venomous lizard.

(ورم) *warim*, aor. *yarim*, INF. *waram*, (also V.) swell, be swollen; swell with anger; grow high; —II. INF. *taurîm*, cause to swell, bring on a tumour; provoke to anger; — III. INF. *îrâm*, have swelling udders; — V. INF. *tawarrum*, see I.

ورم *waram*, pl. *aurâm*, swelling, tumour; tubercle.

(ورن) *waran*, ة, lizard; — V. *tawarran*, INF. *tawarrun*, anoint one's self frequently and live effeminately; — ة *warna-t*, the month ذو القعدة *ẕû 'l-qa'da-t*.

(ورة) *warih*, A, INF. *warah*, be stupid; blow violently; aor. *yarih*, be very fat; — V. INF. *tawarruh*, be very stupid and clumsy.

ورود *wurûd*, going to the watering-place, arrival, appearance; access of fever; pl. of وريد *warîd*; — ة *wurûda-t*, tawny colour.

(وروز) *warwar*, INF. ة, sharpen one's look, look sharply at; speak fast; —*warwar*, a bird;—ى *warwariyy*, dim-sighted.

(ورى) *wara*, aor. *yarî*, INF. *wary*, corrode the inner parts of the body (pus); injure in the lungs; INF. *riya-t*, *wary*, burn, blaze; be fat; INF. *riya-t*, *wary*, *wuriyy*, yield fire; — *warî*, aor. *yara*, id.; be firm; be corroded internally; — II. INF. *tauriya-t*, strike fire; conceal, disguise, dissemble; cause to disappear, change by sleight of hand; point at by a figure or

metaphor; (m.) show; — III. INF. *muwârât*, try to conceal, to keep secret, hide (a.); — IV. INF. *îrâ'*, strike fire; show; — V. INF. *tawarrî*, conceal one's self, hide (n.), flee; — VI. INF. *tawârî*, hide (n.), be concealed; (m.) remain behind and disappear out of sight; — X. INF. *istîrâ'*, strike fire.

ورى *wary*, corroding pus; abscess; fat meat; — *wara*, disease of the lungs; the mortals, men; — *wariyy*, yielding fire; fire-stick; f. ة, fleshy, fat; — *wuriyy*, INF. of (ورى); — ة *warya-t*, materials for striking fire, match.

وريخة *warîḫa-t*, thin dough; wet ground.

وريد *warîd*, pl. *aurida-t*, *wurûd*, *warâ'id*, jugular vein.

وريزة *warîza-t*, vein between stomach and liver (vena portarum).

وريس *warîs*, ة, dyed yellow.

وريع *warî'*, abstemious, pious, conscientious.

وريف *warîf*, far-extended, wide, roomy, spacious; long, broad.

وريق *warîq*, ة, leafy, of dense foliage; — *wuraiq*, greyish.

وريهة *warîha-t*, fat.

وريئة *wurayyi'a-t*, a little farther behind, a little more on the other side.

(وز) *wazz*, INF. *wazz*, incite against another.

وز *wazz*, ة, goose; و عراقى *wazz 'irâqiyy*, crane; — *waz'*, strongly built, vigorous.

(وزأ) *waza'*, aor. *yaza'*, INF. *waz'*, dry meat; drive asunder, disperse; — *wazi'*, A, INF. *waz'*, be strongly built and vigorous; — II. INF. *tauzî'*, *tauzi'a-t*, throw off the rider; fill.

وزاب *wazzâb*, cunning, sly.

وزارة *wizâra-t*, *wazâra-t*, dignity of a minister, a vizier, viziership.

وزال *wazâl*, broom, furze.

وزان *wizân*, opposite and corresponding; — *wazzân*, who weighs; — ة *wazâna-t*, prudence, pondering (s.); consideration.

وزاوزة *wuzâwiza-t*, fickle, changeable.

(وزب) *wazab*, aor. *yazib*, INF. *wazb*, *wuzûb*, flow; — IV. INF. *îzâb*, wander through, travel over.

(وزر) *wazar*, aor. *yazir*, INF. *wizr*, take a heavy burden upon one's self and carry it; fill up, stop up; conquer, vanquish; take office as a minister, be a vizier; INF. *wizr*, *zira-t*, (also VIII.) burden one's conscience, commit a crime; — *wazir*, A, INF. *wazar*, be burdened with or accused of a crime; — II. INF. *tauzîr*, make one a vizier; — III. INF. *muwâzara-t*, share the burden of government with, be one's vizier; assist in business affairs; — IV. INF. *îzâr*, preserve, guard, watch; carry off, take away; — V. INF. *tawazzur*, get appointed as a minister or vizier; — VIII. INF. *ittizâr*, see I.; — X. INF. *istîzâr*, make one's minister.

وزر *wizr*, pl. *auzâr*, heavy burden, load; heaviness; packet, bundle; crime, sin; — *wazar*, place of refuge; — ة *wazra-t*, cloth to cover the loins in a bath, apron.

وزرا *wuzarâ'*, pl. of وزير *wazîr*.

(وزع) *waza'*, aor. *yaza'*, INF. *waz'*, restrain, keep back, hinder; incite, goad on, urge; — II. INF. *tauzî'*, distribute, assign, divide a work between; send soldiers on furlough; — IV. INF. *îzâ'*, urge on, spur on; inspire with, give reason for, help; — V. INF. *tawazzu'*, be divided, distributed, divide between themselves or several persons; — VIII. INF. *ittizâ'*, be prevented, hindered; abstain; — X. INF. *istîzâ'*, ask God for enlightenment or inspiration; — ة *waza'a-t*, pl. of وازع *wâzi'*, prevented, &c.

(وزغ) *wazag*, aor. *yazig* (also IV.),

make water in jets; — II. INF. *tauzî'*, pass. *wuzzig*, be formed in the womb; — IV. INF. *îzâg*, see I.

وزغ *wazag*, nimbleness; shower; a good-for-nothing fellow; — ة *wazaga-t*; pl. *wazag*, *wizâg*, *auzâg*, *wizgân*, *izgân*, a venomous lizard.

(وزف) *wazaf*, aor. *yazif*, INF. *wazf*, *wazîf*, hasten (n.), walk fast; urge to haste; — II. INF. *tauzîf*, hasten; — III. INF. *muwâzafa-t*, divide the costs equally with another; — IV. INF. *îzâf*=II.; — VI. INF. *tawâzuf*=III.

(وزك) *wazak*, INF. *wazk*, walk fast or in an ungraceful manner.

(وزم) *wazam*, aor. *yazim*, INF. *wazm*, pay one's debt; eat but once a day; blunt; — II. INF. *tauzîm*, be satisfied with one meal a day.

وزم *wazm*, bunch of herbs; also ة *wazma-t*, a certain quantity of.

(وزن) *wazan*, aor. *yazin*, INF. *wazn*, *zina-t*, weigh; ponder over, examine; weigh out to; pay; INF. *wazn*, compose verses in the proper measure; estimate as to weight or measure; — *wazun*, INF. *wazâna-t*, be highly valued; be wise, prudent; — II. INF. *tauzîn*, have weighed; — III. INF. *ziwân*, *muwâzana-t*, be equal to another in weight, measure or value, counterbalance; be opposite, in front of; retaliate, requite; — IV. INF. *îzân*, fix one's mind upon, ponder, examine the pros and cons; — VI. INF. *tawâzun*, be equal to one another in weight, measure or value, counterbalance; — VII. INF. *inwizân*, be weighed; — VIII. INF. *ittizân*, id.; have anything weighed out to one's self; have the same weight.

وزن *wazn*, pl. *auzân*, weight; full weight or measure; a certain weight (shekel); proper form and proportion; metre; paradigm, measure of a word; consideration, examination; esteem, respect; ebb; pl. *wuzûn*, heavy load; of full weight; *wazn-u*, *wazn-a*, opposite and corresponding; — ة *wazna-t*, pl. *wazanât*, a weight; talent (of silver), shekel; present, favour; gravity; (m.) balance; (m.) powder-horn; — *wizna-t*, manner of weighing; — ى *wazniyy*, weighty, heavy.

وزواز *wazwâz*, full of levity, frivolous, fickle; nimble, alert, agile.

وزوز *wazwaz*, INF. ة, walk with a strong movement of the hips; leap fast; (m.) hum, buzz; — ة *wazwaza-t*, nimbleness, agility; fickleness, frivolity, levity.

(وزى) *waza*, aor. *yazî*, INF. *wazy*, be gathered, heaped up; — III. INF. *muwâzât*, correspond, be equal, parallel, a counterpart to, counterbalance, be equivalent; put into equilibrium; — IV. INF. *îzâ'*, lean upon or against; coat a house with lime; — VI. INF. *tawâzî*, correspond to one another, &c., as III.; — X. INF. *istîzâ'*, ascend a mountain.

وزى *waza*, short and thick-set; strong.

وزير *wazîr*, pl. *wuzarâ'*, *auzâr*, vizier, minister; assistant, helper.

وزيف *wazîf*, haste.

وزيم *wazîm*, bunch of herbs.

وزين *wazîn*, weighty, heavy; وزين الراى *wazîn ar-ra'î*, wise, prudent.

(وس) *wass*, U, INF. *wass*, reward, recompense.

وساج عساج *wassaj 'assâj*, swift.

وساد *wisâd*, *wasâd*, *wusâd*, ة *wisâda-t*, &c., pl. *wusud*, *wasâ'id*, cushion, pillow, couch; throne.

وساطة *wasâṭa-t*, mediation, intercession; means; mediocrity; office of prime minister.

وساع *wasâ'*, fleet and wide-stepping generous horse; — *wisâ'*, pl. of

وسيع *wasî'* ; — *wassâ'*, wide-stepping ;— ة *wasâ'a-t*, INF. of (وسع).

وساق *wisâq*, pl. of واسق *wâsiq*, big with young.

وسالة *wasâla-t*, means, mediation ; canal.

وسام *wasâm*, ة *wasâma-t*, beauty ; — *wisâm*, mark by branding, sign.

وساوس *wasâwis*, pl. of وسواس *waswâs* and وسوسة *waswasa-t*.

وسائد *wasâ'id*, pl. of وساد *wisâd*.

(وسب) *wasab*, aor. *yasib*, INF. *wasb* (also IV.), abound in grass and herbs ; — *wasib*, A, INF. *wasab*, be dirty, soiled ; — IV. INF. *îsâb*, see I. ; be very woolly.

وسب *wasb*, pl. *wusûb*, board to protect a well from the sand ; — *wisb*, grass and herbs ; — *wasab*, dirt.

(وسج) *wasaj*, aor. *yasij*, INF. *wasîj*, go at a quick pace.

(وسخ) *wasiḥ*, aor. *yausaḥ*, *yaisaḥ*, *yâsaḥ*, INF. *wasaḥ*, be dirty, soiled, uncleanly ; — II. INF. *tausîḥ*, dirty, contaminate ; — IV. INF. *îsâḥ*, id. ; — V. INF. *tawassuḥ*, be dirty, uncleanly ; — VIII. INF. *ittisâḥ*, id.

وسخ *wasaḥ*, pl. *ausâḥ*, dirt, uncleanliness ; ear-wax ; و الكوارير *wasaḥ al-kawârîr*, bees-wax ; — *wasiḥ*, dirty, soiled, uncleanly.

(وسد) *wusud*, pl. of وساد *wisâd* ; — II. *wassad*, INF. *tausîd*, place a cushion beneath one, give for a pillow (2 acc.) ; — V. INF. *tawassud*, lean on a cushion, use as a pillow.

(وسط) *wasaṭ*, aor. *yasiṭ*, INF. *wasṭ*, *siṭa-t*, be in the middle, penetrate into the middle ; — *wasuṭ*, id. ; enjoy authority ; — II. INF. *tausîṭ*, place or put in the middle ; divide in the middle ; halve ; — III. INF. *muwâsaṭa-t*, mediate between ; — V. INF. *tawassuṭ*, place or keep one's self in the middle ; live in middling circumstances ; mediate between ; — VI. INF. *tawâsuṭ*, mediate.

وسط *wasṭ*, middle ; — *wasaṭ*, pl. *ausâṭ*, middle, centre ; waist ; the golden mean ; central ; medial, moderate, middling ; just and equitable ; mediocre, of medium quality.

وسطا *wusaṭâ'*, pl. of وسيط *wasîṭ*.

وسطانى *wusṭâniyy*, central, keeping the middle, mediocre.

وسطى *wusṭa*, middle finger ; the middle one of the five prayers of the day ; medial term ; anything central, middling, moderate.

(وسع) *wasi'*, aor. *yasa'*, INF. *sa'a-t*, be wide, spacious, be spacious enough, hold ; INF. *sa'a-t*, *si'a-t*, *wus'*, be possible, be in one's power ; INF. *sa'a-t*, give one an opportunity for, authorise to ; —*wasu'*, INF. *sa'a-t*, *wusâ'a-t*, be wide and spacious ; go with wide steps ; — II. INF. *tausî'*, (also IV.) widen, enlarge, amplify, make room, give an opportunity, authorise ; enrich, make wealthy ; — IV. INF. *îsâ'*, see II. ; be rich, powerful ; penetrate deeply into ; — V. INF. *tawassu'*, be widened, enlarged, amplified ; have room enough, be at ease, make one's self comfortable ; make room for one another ; — VIII. INF. *ittisâ'* (also X.), be wide and roomy ; extend far ; widen (n.) ; hold (n.) ; — X. INF. *istîsâ'*, see VIII.

وسع *wus'*, *was'*, *wis'*, width, capacity, extent, faculty of comprehension, amount ; plenteousness, wealth ; opportunity, authority, eloquence ; — ة *wus'a-t*, width, roominess ; reach, range ; ease, comfort ; opportunity ; widened part of a road.

وسف *wasf*, rent in the skin of a camel which grows fat ; — V. *tawassaf*, INF. *tawassuf*, get such rents.

(وسق) *wasaq*, aor. *yasiq*, INF. *wasq*, gather and heap up ; carry ; load a ship, freight ; gather tears, be

moist with tears (eye); veil in darkness; conceive, get in the family way; — INF. *wasîq*, drive together;—III. INF. *muwâsaqa-t*, oppose, show one's self another's equal; — IV. INF. *îsâq*, load, freight;—VII. INF. *inwisâq*, pass. of the previous; be gathered, heaped up, assembled; — VIII. INF. *ittisâq*, be in good order; be complete, perfect, whole; — X. INF. *istîsâq*, be driven together.

وسق *wasq*, *wisq*, pl. *wusûq*, *ausuq*, load of a camel, freight of a ship, cargo; load of corn (sixty صاع *ṣâʻ*); import, export; — ة *wasqa-t*, a load, cargo.

(وسل) — II. *wassal*, INF. *tausîl*, V. INF. *tawassul*, try to get a hearing, beg, implore; apply to.

(وسم) *wasam*, aor. *yasim*, INF. *wasm*, *sima-t*, mark by branding, brand, impress a sign; impart a lasting mark or impression (sacrament); describe; INF. *wasm*, surpass in beauty;—*wasum*, INF. *wasâm*, *wasâma-t*, be handsome of face or figure; — II. INF. *tausîm*, attend the pilgrimage, or a fair; — III. INF. *muwâsama-t*, vie in beauty with; — V. INF. *tawassum*, recognise by an external sign; guess at the character by the features; examine; look out for the first spring food; — VII. INF. *inwisâm*, be marked by branding; — VIII. INF. *ittisâm*, id.; stigmatise one's self; be distinguished by a particular mark or sign.

وسم *wasm*, pl. *wusûm*, mark by branding, stigma, mark, sign; indelible character imparted by a sacrament; — ة *wasma-t*, mark by branding, stigma; also *wasima-t*, leaves of dyer's weed or indigo for dyeing.

وسما *wusamâʼ*, pl. of وسيم *wasîm*.

وسمى *wasmiyy*, vernal; spring rain; spring grass.

(وسن) *wasin*, A, IMP. *iwsan*, INF. *wasan*, *wasna-t*, *wasana-t*, *sina-t*, lie in the first or in deep sleep, sleep, slumber; be stifled by the air of a well; — IV. INF. *îsân*, bring on such a condition; sleep, slumber.

وسن *wasan*, ة *wasna-t*, *wasana-t*, deep (first) sleep, slumber, nap; sleepiness, drowsiness; — *wasin*, ة, sleepy, drowsy; stifled by the air of a well.

وسنان *wasnân*, f. *wasna*, in deep sleep; slumbering (adj.); sleepy, lazy.

وسواس *waswâs*, *wiswâs*, pl. *wasâwis*, diabolical suggestion, temptation of the devil; fantasy; scruple; rustling (s.); *al-waswâs*, Satan, the tempter.

(وسوس) *waswas*, INF. ة, suggest wicked or foolish things; disquiet, cause scruples; whisper; clatter; — II. INF. *tawassus*, feel inquietude, alarm, scruples; be scrupulous; — ة *waswasa-t*, pl. *wasâwis*, suggestion of the devil, temptation; disquietude, trouble of mind, scruple.

وسوط *wasûṭ*, hair tent; camel.

(وسى) — III. *wâsa*, INF. *muwâsât*, console for (ب *bi*); share; (m.) for ساوى *sâwa*; — IV. INF. *îsâʼ*, shave; cut.

وسيج *wasîj*, quick pace.

وسيط *wasîṭ*, pl. *wusaṭâʼ*, in the middle, anything central; mediator; respected, the highest in rank, first of the people.

وسيع *wasîʻ*, pl. *wisâʻ*, wide, extended, spacious; with great mental capacity; wide-stepping generous horse.

وسيق *wasîq*, rain; INF. of (وسق);— ة *wasîqa-t*, camels driven together.

وسيلة *wasîla-t*, pl. *wasîl*, *wasâʼil*, relationship; means of approach, of gaining one's favour; conciliation; ways and means; reasons, pretexts; opportunity, occasion;

influence, credit, authority; protection; support, help.

وسيم *wasîm*, pl. *wusamâ'*, *wisâm*, f. ة, pl. *wisâm*, handsome of face, pretty, goodly, elegant; marked; sign, mark.

وشا *waśâ'*, riches, wealth; — *wiśâ'*, pl. of وشى *waśy*; — *wuśât*, pl. of واشى *wâśî*, slanderer.

وشاح *wiśâḥ*, *wuśâḥ*, pl. *wuśḥ*, *wuśuḥ*, *auśiḥa-t*, *waśâ'iḥ*, lady's girdle set with jewels, sash, scarf; wide, precious mantle; sword-belt; — ة *wiśâḥa-t*, sword.

وشاية *wiśâya-t*, slander, tale-bearing.

(وشب) *waśb*, coarse and bad; — *wiśb*, pl. *auśâb*, mixed crowd; — II. *waśśab*, INF. *tauśîb*, urge on, goad on.

(وشج) *waśaj*, aor. *yaśij*, INF. *waśj*, be densely grown together, be divided into many branches, greatly ramified (relationship); tie fast; — II. INF. *tauśîb*, unite in firm relationship.

وشج *wuśj*, gum of a plant.

(وشح)—II. *waśśaḥ*, INF. *tauśîḥ*, gird with the وشاح *wiśâḥ*; deck out, adorn; (m.) paraphrase a text; — V. INF. *tawaśśuḥ*, gird one's self; put on a cloak; provide one's self with; be adorned, decked out.

وشح *wuśḥ*, *wuśuḥ*, pl. of وشاح *wiśâḥ*.

(وشخ) *waśḫ*, weak, stupid, bad; date-basket; — ة *waśaḫa-t*, basket-work of palm-leaves.

(وشر) *waśar*, INF. *waśr*, saw; sharpen the teeth.

وشر *wuśur*, pl. sharp teeth.

(وشز) *waśiz*, aor. *yaśiz*, INF. *waśz*, hasten (n.); — V. INF. *tawaśśuz*, prepare one's self for evil.

وشز *waśz*, *waśaz*, high place, refuge; calamity, poverty; haste, hurry.

(وشظ) *waśaẓ*, aor. *yaśiẓ*, INF. *waśẓ*, break loose a piece of a bone; fix the iron of an axe with a wedge.

(وشع) *waśa'*, aor. *yaśa'*, INF. *waś'*, *śi'a-t*, mix; grow; ascend, climb; — II. INF. *tauśî'*, wind thread or wool; mark, impress; befall, come upon; — IV. INF. *îśâ'*, blossom; — V. INF. *tawaśśu'*, climb up a mountain.

وشع *waś'*, blossoms; balsam-tree; — *wuśu'*, spider-web.

(وشغ) *waśag*, aor. *yaśig*, INF. *waśg* (also IV.), make water in jets; — II. INF. *tauśîg*, soil in stripes; — IV. INF. *îśâg*, administer medicine by the mouth; make the gift small; see I.; — V. INF. *tawaśśug*, contaminate one's self (by sin); — X. INF. *istîśâg*, draw water with a leaking bucket.

(وشق) *waśaq*, aor. *yaśiq*, INF. *waśq* (also VIII.), cut meat into long strips to dry it; pierce; hasten (n.); — VIII. INF. *ittiśâq*, see I.

وشق *wuśśaq*, ammoniac.

(وشك) *waśuk*, INF. *waśk*, *waśâka-t*, be quickly dispatched (business); — II. INF. *tauśîk*, id.; — III. INF. *wiśâk*, *muwâśaka-t*, be quick, swift accelerate; — IV. INF. *îśâk*, walk fast, accelerate one's march; be about, on the point of, going to (followed by ان *an*).

وشك *waśk*, *wuśk*, haste, hurry.

وشكان *waśkân*, *wiśkân*, *wuśkân*, quickly dispatched; haste, hurry; *waśkân-a*, in great hurry, how quick you are!

(وشل) *waśal*, aor. *yaśil*, INF. *waśl*, *waśalân*, fall or flow in drops, trickle; — also INF. *wuśûl*, be poor and weak; humble one's self before, supplicate; — IV. INF. *îśâl*, find but little trickling water.

(وشم) *waśam*, aor. *yaśim*, INF. *waśm*, tattoo the skin; — II. INF. *tauśîm*, id.; — IV. INF. *îśâm*, flash slightly; begin to colour or ripen, to turn grey, to get breasts; begin; — X. INF. *istîśâm*, ask to be tattooed.

وشم *waśm*, pl. *wiśâm*, *wuśûm*, tattooing with a needle and dyer's weed or indigo; tattooed figures;

first sprouting grass; — ة waśma-t, rain-drop; word.
وهن waśn, elevated ground, height; stout and strong; — V. INF. tawaśśun, be but little, be scarce; — ة wiśna-t, cherry.
وهواش waśwâś, thin and nimble.
(وهوش) waśwaś, INF. ة, give but little, stint; whisper into one's ear; — II. INF. tawaśwuś, whisper to one another; stir and murmur to each other (crowd); — waśwaśa-t, agility, nimbleness; whisper.
وهوغ waśûg, medicine.
وهول waśûl, yielding milk (adj.), milch; — wuśûl, weakness, poverty.
وهوى waśawiyy, marked, signed, imprinted with colours.
(وهى) waśa, aor. yaśî, IMP. هه śih, INF. waśy, śiya-t, give a design to a material, imprint colours on it, variegate, embroider; embellish at the expense of truth; tinsel; — INF. waśy, wiśâya-t, bear tales, slander; — II. INF. tauśiya-t, paint, colour, adorn, embellish; imprint on a stuff; embroider a dress; — IV. INF. îśâ', slander; put forth the first grass; pull out, bring out; (also X.) spur on a horse to test its running power; — V. INF. tawaśśî, be coloured, embroidered, imprinted upon, adorned; — X. INF. istîśâ', see IV.
وهى waśy, pl. wiśâ', colouring, adornment, embroidery; imprinted silk-stuff; brilliancy of metal or a blade; eloquence.
وهيج waśîj, ramification of relationship; ash-tree; — ة waśîja-t, pl. waśâ'ij, root of a tree, fibre of a root; crowd of people.
وهيظ waśîẓ, pl. auśâẓ, mixed crowd, followers of a camp, attendance; also ة waśîẓa-t, pl. waśâ'iẓ, splinter of a bone.
وهيع waśî', mat; tent of the chief; thorn-hedge; embroidered hem; board at a well to stand upon; ة waśî'a-t, pl. waśâ'i', spool; clew, hank; strip.
وهيق waśîq, ة waśîqa-t, pl. waśâ'iq, meat cut into strips to be dried; such shreds.
وهيك waśîk, swift, in a hurry.
وهيمة waśîma-t, malicious information; malice; grudge.
(وص) waṣṣ, U, INF. waṣṣ, carry out well.
(وصا) waṣi', A. INF. waṣa', be dirty.
وصا waṣâ', ة٥ waṣâ'a-t, INF. of (وصى); — ة waṣât, will, testament; commission; order; advice, admonition; recommendation; pl. waṣa, palm-branch used as a rope.
وصاب wiṣâb, ى waṣâba, pl. of وصب waṣab.
وصاد waṣṣâd, weaver.
وصاف waṣṣâf, who describes well; who praises; eulogist; who prescribes medicine, clever physician; — ة waṣâfa-t, serviceableness.
وصال wiṣâl, union; tête-à-tête; connection, sexual intercourse; —*; — ة waṣṣâla-t, strip attached to a tent-cloth.
وصايا waṣâya, pl. of وصية waṣiyya-t.
وصاية waṣâya-t=وصاة waṣât; — wiṣâya-t, wuṣâya-t, guardianship, office of a manager.
(وصب) waṣab, aor. yaṣib, INF. wuṣûb, last; be zealous and diligent; — waṣib, A, INF. waṣab, be ill, have a head-ache; — II. INF. tauṣib, id.; — IV. INF. îṣâb, id.; render ill; — V. INF. tawaṣṣub, be ill.
وصب waṣab, pl. auṣâb, illness; head-ache; pain; — waṣib, pl. wiṣâb, waṣâba, ill, suffering.
(وصح) waṣaḥ, dirt.
(وصد) waṣad, aor. yaṣid, INF. waṣad, weave; — INF. wuṣûd, last, stand firm, remain, abide; — IV. INF. îṣâd, shut the door; stop up the mouth; consolidate; set on a sporting dog; =X.; — X. INF. istîṣâd, raise an enclosure of stone.

وصد *wuṣud*, pl. of وصيد *waṣîd*.

وصر *wiṣr*, ة *waṣarra-t*, *waṣira-t*, covenant, compact, contract, legal titles, claims, documents; testimonial, testimony, certificate.

(وصع) *waṣa'*, INF. *waṣ'*, cover, inclose; chirp.

وصع *waṣ'*, *waṣa'*, ة, pl. *wiṣ'ân*, a small bird; — *waṣ'*, chirping (s.).

(وصف) *waṣaf*, aor. *yaṣif*, INF. *waṣf*, *ṣifa-t*, describe, picture; praise, eulogise; give one a character; prescribe a medicine; — *waṣuf*, INF. *waṣâfa-t*, be old enough and apt for service; — VI. INF. *tawâṣuf*, describe to one another, tell to one another; be rude to one another; — VIII. INF. *ittiṣâf*, be described; be distinguished by peculiar qualities or manners; — X. INF. *istîṣâf*, ask for a description, demand a prescription from a doctor; prescribe a medicine.

وصف *waṣf*, description; praise, eulogy; pl. *auṣâf*, quality; laudatory epithet; virtue, merit; adjective, attribute; prescription.

وصفا *wuṣafâ'*, pl. of وصيف *waṣîf*.

وصفى *waṣfiyy*, ة, descriptive, graphic; attributive, adjective; — ة *waṣfiyya-t*, descriptive quality, qualification.

(وصل) *waṣal*, aor. *yaṣil*, INF. *waṣl*, *ṣila-t*, *ṣula-t*, unite one thing with another, join, combine; — INF. *ṣila-t*, *waṣla-t*, *wuṣûl*, reach a place, arrive, come to hand; — INF. *waṣl*, *ṣila-t*, (also III.) be united by an alliance, friendship, intercourse; show affection; have connection; give, present with; — II. INF. *tauṣîl*, join well, unite (a.); = IV.; — III. INF. *wiṣâl*, *muwâṣala-t*, do without interruption, persevere in, persist in; be united with; see I.; — IV. INF. *îṣâl*, lead or bring to; join, unite (a.); — V. INF. *tawaṣṣul*, be united by friendship, &c.; be joined, coupled; get to, reach; obtain access by friendliness; obtain by stratagem; — VI. INF. *tawâṣul*, be united by friendship; follow one another in unbroken succession, be connected, concatinated; come at the same time; — VIII. INF. *ittiṣâl*, come to the point that; be united in friendship with; trace one's descent to; confine; abut, be adjacent; cohere, adhere; last without interruption.

وصل *waṣl*, union, connection; intercourse, friendship; union with the beloved object, amorous enjoyment; liberality; pl. *auṣâl*, connecting link, articulation, joint; appurtenance, counterpart; — *wiṣl*, *wuṣl*, pl. *auṣâl*, joint, link; limb; — ة *waṣla-t*, union; link; the sign ـٓ; (m.) small beam, rafter; — *wuṣla-t*, pl. *wuṣal*, union; meeting (s.); tête-à-tête between lovers, sexual intercourse; link, hinge, joint, articulation, seam; — ى *waṣliyy*, connecting (adj.), copulative.

(وصم) *waṣam*, aor. *yaṣim*, INF. *waṣm*, break (a.); unite quickly; ruin, destroy, spoil; treat contemptuously, slight, scoff at, accuse, disgrace; — II. INF. *tauṣîm*, do a great deal of harm; — V. INF. *tawaṣṣum*, be greatly harmed, suffered.

وصم *waṣm*, ة *waṣma-t*, pl. *wuṣûm*, breach, rupture, rent, jag; defect; knot in the wood; fault, crime, ill-fame, stigma; — *waṣam*, illness; — ة *wuṣma-t*, faintness, weakness.

وصواص *waṣwâṣ*, وصوص *waṣwaṣ*, pl. *waṣâwiṣ*, opening in a veil for the eyes; small veil for a girl.

(وصوص) *waṣwaṣ*, INF. ة, look through the opening in the veil; look with the eyes almost closed, blink; open the eyes.

وصول *wuṣûl*, arrival; union; obtaining (s.); pl. *-ât*, receipt; و باقی *wuṣûl bâqî*, money which has not come in.

(وصی) *waṣa*, aor. *yaṣî*, INF. *waṣy*, join one thing to another, unite; be closely united; be humbled; — II. INF. *tauṣiya-t*, make a will, bequeath by will; recommend; give a commission with regard to (especially in dying), commission; — IV. INF. *îṣâ'* = II.; recommend in dying to the guardianship of; recommend; give orders, prescriptions; bequeath; choose as curator of one's fortune; — V. INF. *tawaṣṣî*, be commissioned; be trusted with the care of; accept a recommendation, a commission with regard to; — VI. INF. *tawâṣî*, give one another commissions, admonitions; — X. INF. *istîṣâ'*, leave a legacy to.

وصی *waṣi'*, v. see (وصا); — *waṣiyy*, pl. *auṣiyâ*, who makes a will, testator; who gives commissions, mandatory, proxy; executor of a will; appointed guardian, manager, administrator; regent, lord protector; — ة *waṣiyya-t*, pl. *waṣiyy*, palm-branch used as a rope; pl. *waṣâya*, *wiṣiyy*, will, testament; what is stipulated by such; commission, recommendation, prescription, exhortation; pl. the ten commandments.

وصيب *waṣîb*, ill, suffering.

وصيد *waṣîd*, pl. *wuṣud*, threshold; portico; locked; narrow; cave; also ة *waṣîda-t*, inclosure of stones.

وصيرة *waṣîra-t* = وصر *wiṣr*.

وصيع *waṣî'*, chirping (s.).

وصيف *waṣîf*, pl. *wuṣafâ'*, be old and skilful enough for service; young servant, servant girl; — ة *waṣîfa-t*, pl. *waṣâ'if*, female servant.

(وصيل) *waṣîl*, uninterrupted, continuous; inseparable friend, confidant; police-sergeant; — ة *waṣîla-t*, pl. *waṣâ'il*, what joins two things: link, tie, joint; occasion, cause; rich produce; abundance, affluence; cultivated state; society; politeness; she-camel (or sheep) set free after ten (six) consecutive parturitions; pious foundation; a striped material; clew.

(وض) *waḍḍ*, U, INF. *waḍḍ*, be without means, poor, miserable.

(وضا) *waḍa'*, aor. *yaḍu'*, INF. *waḍ'*, surpass in cleanliness, tidiness, brightness; — *waḍu'*, INF. *waḍâ'a-t*, *wuḍû'*, *wuḍuww*, shine from cleanliness, be bright and handsome of face; — II. INF. *tauḍi'a-t*, wash (a.); — V. INF. *tawaḍḍu'*, wash (n.); perform religious ablutions; attain to puberty.

وضا *wiḍâ'*, pl. of وضیی *waḍî'*; — *wuḍḍâ'*, pl. *wuḍḍâ'ûn*, *waḍâḍi'*, cleanly, tidy, neat; — ة *waḍâ'a-t*, cleanliness, tidiness, neatness; whiteness, brightness.

وضاح *waḍâḥ*, evident, distinct, clear; — *waḍḍâh*, very clear and distinct; resplendent with beauty; exceedingly handsome of face; bright day; marked by leprosy.

وضاضی *waḍâḍi'*, pl. of وضا *wuḍḍâ'*.

وضاع *waḍḍâ'*, collector, compiler; — ة *waḍâ'a-t*, humility, humiliation; lowliness.

(وضح) *waḍaḥ*, aor. *yaḍiḥ*, INF. *ḍaḥa-t*, *ḍiḥa-t*, *wuḍûḥ*, be evident, clear and distinct, plain; be distinctly visible; yield milk of a bright whiteness; — II. INF. *tauḍîḥ*, make evident, explain distinctly, clear up, show, reveal, make known; — IV. INF. *îḍâḥ*, id.; — V. INF. *tawaḍḍuḥ*, be evident, clear, distinct, or be made so; be distinctly visible; be explained, cleared up; — VIII. INF. *ittiḍâḥ* = V.; — X. INF. *istiḍâḥ*, ask for an explanation, an

elucidation; wish to know distinctly, to investigate thoroughly; see clearly through.

وضح *waḍaḥ*, pl. *auḍâḥ*, brightness, clearness; good money; bracelet, necklace (of silver); white spot, white hair; milk; open part of a road; merit, virtue; leprosy; وضح الفم *waḍaḥ al-fam*, the teeth; — ة *waḍaḥa-t*, she-ass.

(وضخ) *waḍaḫ*, aor. *yaḍiḫ*, INF. *waḍḫ*, half-fill the bucket; — III. INF. *wiḍâḫ*, *muwâḍaḫa-t*, vie in drawing water, running, dancing, &c. with (acc.).

(وضر) *waḍir*, A, INF. *waḍar*, be soiled with fat, be greasy; be soiled with saffron.

وضر *waḍar*, pl. *auḍâr*, dirt, spot, stain; dirty water; smell of corrupted meat; — *waḍir*, f. ة, *waḍra*, stained, dirty.

وضرا *waḍrâ'*, وضرى *waḍra*, large projecting rock.

(وضع) *waḍa'*, aor. *yaḍa'*, INF. *waḍ'*, *mauḍa'*, *mauḍi'*, *mauḍû'*, put down, put, set; abate from the price; take a burden or anything unpleasant from (عن *'an*); degrade, lower one's position, humble, render contemptible; lower the head and step apace; give birth, miscarry; compose; — *waḍi'*, aor. *yauḍa'*, also pass. *wuḍi'*, INF. *ḍa'a-t*, *ḍi'a-t*, *waḍî'a-t*, suffer a loss; — *waḍu'*, INF. *ḍa'a-t*, *ḍi'a-t*, *waḍâ'a-t*, also pass. *wuḍi'*, be abased, degraded, deposed; become contemptible; humble one's self; — II. INF. *tauḍî'*, abase, render contemptible; — III. INF. *muwâḍa'a-t*, try to abase, humble; give a pledge to, bet against a stake with; make peace, come to an agreement with; — IV. INF. *îḍâ'*, speed; urge to a quicker pace; pass. *ûḍî*, suffer loss in trade; — VI. INF. *tawâḍu'*, behave humbly and modestly; — VIII. INF. *ittiḍâ'*, humble one's self; be humbled, fall into contempt; — X. INF. *istîḍâ'*, ask for relief, for an abatement of price, for an allowance.

وضع *waḍ'*, pl. *auḍâ'*, putting down, putting, setting (s.); humiliation, deposition; parturition; miscarriage; creating, inventing, composing (s.); position, site; attitude, behaviour, manners; proceeding, way of acting; case; plan, intention; external form, figure, shape; institute, establishment; literary composition, work; subtraction, abatement; وضعا و قولا *waḍ'an wa qaul-an*, in deeds and words; — *wuḍ'*, birth; fœtus, embryo; — ة *waḍ'a-t*, *wiḍ'a-t*, position, site; erection.

وضعا *wuḍa'â'*, pl. of وضيع *waḍî'*.

وضعى *waḍ'iyy*, referring to form, site, position; positive, affirmative.

(وضف) *waḍaf*, aor. *yaḍif*, INF. *waḍf*, go apace, hasten (n.); — IV. INF. *îḍâf*, id.; urge to a quick pace.

(وضم) *waḍam*, aor. *yaḍim*, INF. *waḍm*, put the meat on the shambles; — IV. INF. *îḍâm*, set up shambles; = I.

وضم *waḍam*, pl. *auḍâm*, *auḍima-t*, bench, board or mat to place meat upon, tray, shambles; — ة *waḍma-t*, troop (200 to 300).

(وضن) *waḍan*, aor. *yaḍin*, INF. *waḍn*, lay close upon one another, double, fold; twist, entwine; — V. INF. *tawaḍḍun*, humble one's self before (ل *li*).

وضن *wuḍun*, pl. of وضين *waḍîn*.

وضو *wuḍû'*, *waḍû'*, *wuḍûww*, religious ablution; *waḍû'*, water for it.

وضوح *wuḍûḥ*, clearness, distinctness, evidence; demonstration, proof.

وضى *waḍî'* = وضيى *waḍî'*.

وضيح *waḍîḥ*, ة, evident, clear, distinct; — ة *waḍîḥa-t*, pl. *waḍâ'iḥ*, pasturing cattle.

وضيع *waḍî'*, pl. *wuḍa'â'*, mean, low,

plebeian; small, paltry; deposit, pledge; — ة *wadî'a-t*, pl. *wadâ'i'*, what is put down, deposed; load, luggage; loss in trade; allowance, abatement of price, discount; military colony, boundary post, garrison; spurious, bastard, adopted; duty, tax, toll; entry-book, scrap-book; a bitter plant; abuse, offence; patch.

وضيمة *wadîma-t*, troop (200 to 300); heap of green food; mourning-entertainment.

وضين *wadîn*, pl. *wudun*, put upon one another, doubled, folded; plaited, entwined; girth, girdle.

وضيى *wadî'*, pl. *audiyâ'*, *widâ*, *wuddâ'*, bright with cleanliness and whiteness; clean, tidy, neat; handsome of face.

(وط) *waṭṭ*, U, INF. *waṭṭ*, creak; chirp.

(وطا) *waṭa'*, وطی *waṭi'*, aor. *yaṭa'*, INF. وطا, وطی *waṭ'*, tread upon, tread under feet, pass over; put the foot on the ground and impress a trace; lie with; mount a horse; level, plane by treading upon, beating, &c.; range, put in order, prepare; take under one's arm; — *wuṭu'*, INF. *waṭâ'a-t*, *wuṭû'a-t*, be level, even, smooth (by treading, &c.); be low; be lowered, humbled; — II. INF. *tauṭi'a-t*, tread, tread upon; level, plane; make the bed smooth and soft; make low, humiliate, depreciate; — III. INF. *wiṭâ'*, *muwâṭa'a-t*, vie with, rival with; agree upon; make fit for (acc.); — IV. INF. *îṭâ'*, have trodden down; oppress, humiliate, depreciate; agree upon; cause one to undertake what he does not understand; — V. INF. *tawaṭṭu'*, tread upon, kick; be trodden upon, humiliated; — VI. INF. *tawâṭu'*, agree with one another, make an agreement; humble one's self; — VIII. INF. *îtiṭâ'*, *ittiṭâ'*, get levelled; be put in readiness; be well conducted and successful; — X. INF. *istîṭâ'*, deem a smooth bed, find the beast commodious for riding; find low, mean, vile.

وطا *waṭâ'*, low ground, low place, low part; anything low; also *wiṭâ'*, disclosure, unveiling (s.); — *wiṭâ'*, agreement; — ة *waṭ'a-t*, treading down, treading upon; place where one puts the foot, footprint; violence, force; violent attack, access; — *waṭa'a-t*, pedestrians, travellers on foot; trodden path; — ءة *waṭâ'at*, evenness and smoothness of the ground, of a bed, &c.

وطاس *waṭṭâs*, shepherd, herdsman.

وطاق *waṭâq*, pl. *-ât*, tent (m. Turk).

وطاوط *waṭâwiṭ*, وطاويط *waṭâwîṭ*, pl. of وطواط *waṭwâṭ*.

(وطب) *waṭb*, pl. *auṭub*, *wiṭâb*, *auṭâb*, *awâṭib*, leathern bag for milk; wallet; harsh, blunt, rude; large breast of a woman.

وطبا *waṭbâ'*, woman with hanging breasts.

(وطث) *waṭaṣ*, aor. *yaṭiṣ*, INF. *waṭṣ*, stamp the foot.

(وطح) *waṭaḥ*, aor. *yaṭiḥ*, INF. *waṭḥ*, push violently back; — VI. INF. *tawâṭuḥ*, throng together round the cistern; also تواطخ *tawâṭuḥ*, intend mischief against one another, combat with one another.

وطح *waṭḥ*, mud on the feet of animals.

(وطخ) — VI. INF. *tawâṭuḥ*, see (وطح VI.).

(وطد) *waṭad*, aor. *yaṭid*, INF. *waṭd*, *ṭida-t*, fix, make firm, consolidate; make heavy, weigh upon; fix one thing to another, insert; plant in the ground; stand firm; tread down; tread under feet, trample upon; tread the ground firm, ram; — II. INF. *tauṭîd*, fix, make firm, consolidate; — V. INF. *tawaṭṭud*, pass. of the previous.

وطد *waṭid*, ة, firm, solid; — ة *waṭda-t*, tread, foot-step.

(وطر) *waṭar*, pl. *auṭâr*, necessary or important matter, need; anything indispensable; concern, intention.

(وطس) *waṭas*, aor. *yaṭis*, INF. *waṭs*, tread upon with a shoe or boot; break (a.); — *wuṭus*, pl. of وطيس *waṭîs*.

(وطش) *waṭaś*, aor. *yaṭiś*, INF. *waṭś* (also II.) communicate only partly; speak indistinctly or obscurely; repel, turn off; beat; — II. INF. *tauṭîś*, see I.; give but little.

(وطف) *waṭif*, A, INF. *waṭaf*, have much hair on the eye-lids or eye-brows; pour abundantly; — *waṭaf*, INF. *waṭf*, hang low.

وطفا *waṭfâ'*, raining abundantly (cloud).

(وطق) — II. *waṭṭaq*, INF. *tauṭîq*, pitch a tent (m.).

(وطم) *waṭam*, aor. *yaṭim*, INF. *waṭm*, tread upon, trample; lower a curtain or veil.

(وطن) *waṭan*, aor. *yaṭin*, INF. *waṭn*, be accustomed to a place, stay there permanently, abide, dwell; — II. INF. *tauṭîn* (also IV. and X.), select a place for a dwelling; accustom one's self to; — IV. INF. *îṭân*, see II.; dwell, abide; — V. INF. *tawaṭṭun*, id.; be accustomed to, addicted to (على *'ala*); — X. INF. *istîṭân*, see II.

وطن *waṭn*, *waṭan*, pl. *auṭân*, permanent dwelling, residence; home; place where the cattle lie down or are tied up, stable; *al-auṭân*, places between which nomads alternate; — ى *waṭaniyy*, native, homely.

وطو *waṭu'*, V. see (وطا); — *waṭû'*, humiliation, lowliness; — ة *wuṭû'a-t*, INF. of وطو *waṭu'* (وطا).

وطواط *waṭwâṭ*, pl. *waṭâwiṭ*, *waṭâwîṭ*, bat; mountain-swallow; frog; و البحر *waṭwâṭ al-bahr*, flying fish; also ى *waṭwâṭiyy*, talkative, garrulous; noisy; cowardly.

(وطوط) *waṭwaṭ*, INF. ة, be weak and cowardly; chirp; speak fast.

وطى *waṭi'*, V. see (وطا); — *waṭiyy*, trotten upon; well-trained.

وطيد *waṭîd*, ة, fixed, consolidated, firm, unshakable; — (ة *waṭîda-t*), pl. *waṭâ'id*, foundations; tripods.

وطيرة *waṭîra-t*, custom, usage.

وطيس *waṭîs*, pl. *wuṭus*, iron stove, furnace; also ة *waṭîsa-t*, importance.

وطيى *waṭî'*, ة, trodden upon; level, even and soft; — ة *waṭî'a-t*, bread-bag.

(وظب) *waẓab*, aor. *yaẓib*, INF. *wuẓûb* (also III.), practice without interruption, attend zealously to; continue; — INF. *waẓb*, tread upon; — III. INF. *muwâẓaba-t*, see I.; persist in; — ة *waẓba-t*, vagina of hoofed animals.

(وظر) *waẓir*, A, INF. *waẓar*, be fat and fleshy.

وظر *waẓir*, fat and fleshy.

وظف *waẓaf*, aor. *yaẓif*, INF. *waẓf* shorten a camel's tether; strike the camel on the thin part of the thigh; join, follow; — II. INF. *tauẓîf*, fix the rations of food for the day; assign to one his ration or pay; give an office to, raise to a dignity; — III. INF. *muwâẓafa-t*, agree; attend to; assist, conduct one's affairs, be one's official; — V. INF. *tawaẓẓuf*, be entrusted with an office, raised to a dignity.

وظف *wuẓuf*, pl. of وظيف *waẓîf*.

وظوب *wuẓûb*, perseverance, assiduity.

وظيف *waẓîf*, pl. *wuẓuf*, *auẓifa-t*, thinnest place of a camel's or horse's thigh; على و *'ala waẓîf-in*, coming one behind another; — ة *waẓîfa-t*, pl. *waẓâ'if*, *wuẓuf*, daily ration of food; pay, salary, pension; office, dignity (ارباب وظائف *arbâb waẓâ'if*, officials, pensioners); task, duty; destina-

tion, employment; aim; business; agreement.

(وع) *wa'*, jackal.

وعا *wi'â'*, *wu'â'*, pl. *au'iya-t*, *au'ât*, vessel, vase, bottle, sheath, case, receptacle, drawer, pigeon-hole; wallet; (m.) a piece of clothing.

وعارة *wa'âra-t*, ruggedness, roughness, difficulty.

وعاط *wa'âṭ*, rose.

وعاظ *wu''âẕ*, pl. of واعظ *wâ'iẕ*, preacher, &c.

وعاق *wu'âq*, rumbling noise in a horse's belly.

(وعب) *wa'ab*, aor. *ya'ib*, INF. *wa'b* (also IV. and X.), take hold of all; — IV. INF. *î'âb*, id.; cut off, cut out; gather, hoard up; put one thing entirely into another; fill; — X. INF. *istî'âb*=I.; gather the whole at once; inquire into all details of news (acc.).

وعب *wa'b*, pl. *wi'âb*, large streets, extended grounds.

(وعث) *wa'is̱*, A, INF. *wa'as̱*, be broken; also—*wa'us̱'* INF. *wu'ûs̱a-t*, be difficult; — IV. INF. *î'âs̱*, come upon soft ground and sink.

وعث *wa's̱*, soft ground or sand where one sinks; broken bone; also *wa'is̱*, difficult; — ة *wa'is̱a-t*, fat, plump (woman).

وعثا *wa's̱â'*, difficulty, hardship.

(وعد) *wa'ad*, aor. *ya'id*, INF. *wa'd*, *'ida-t*, *mau'id*, *mau'ida-t*, *mau'ûd*, *mau'ûda-t*, promise, promise good to, announce, give hope for, inspire with fear of, threaten with; INF. *wa'd*, *wa'îd*, surpass in promises; INF. *wa'îd*, threaten; — III. INF. *muwâ'ada-t*, promise one, give one's word to; bind one's self to fulfil a promise at an appointed place or time, to appear personally; promise for a certain term; — IV. INF. *î'âd*, promise firmly, promise good to; threaten with; — V. INF. *tawa''ud*, threaten, frighten by threats; — VI. INF. *tawâ'ud*, promise one another; — VII. INF. *inwi'âd* (m.) = VIII.; — VIII. INF. *itti'âd*, *i'ti'âd*, exact or accept a promise, have received a promise.

وعد *wa'd*, pl. *wu'ûd*, promise; threat, menace; anything promised or threatened; — ة *wa'da-t*, promise, vow; promised term; transaction, business, affair.

(وعر) *wa'ar*, aor. *ya'ir*, INF. *wa'r*, *wu'ûr*, *wu'ûra-t*, be rugged; hinder, obstruct, prevent; — *wa'ir*, A, INF. *wa'ar*, also—*wa'ur*, INF. *wa'âra-t*, be rugged; be hard, difficult; — II. INF. *tau'îr*, make rugged, difficult; — V. INF. *tawa''ur*, become so; — X. INF. *istî'âr*, find so.

وعر *wa'r*, ة, pl. *au'ur*, *wu'ûr*, *au'âr*, rugged, difficult; وعر المعروف *wa'r al-ma'rûf*, disobliging; — *wa'ir*, rugged; inaccessible; *wa'ir wa'ir*, obscure (verse, &c.).

(وعز) *wa'az*, aor. *ya'iz*, INF. *wa'z*, (also II.) set an example (to be followed or avoided), precede in; give a sign, a hint, order; — II. INF. *tau'îz*, see I.; — IV. INF. *î'âz*, make sign, order, prescribe, recommend.

(وعس) *wa'as*, aor. *ya'is*, INF. *wa's*, tread upon, tread down; — III. INF. *muwâ'asa-t*, make wide steps with outstretched neck (camel); — IV. INF. *îw'âs*, drive such camels.

وعس *wa's*, footprint; a tree; sandy plain; — *wu's*, pl. and—

وعسا *wa'sâ'*, f. of اوعس *au'as*, q.v.; a sand-hill abounding with eatable herbs.

(وعظ) *wa'aẕ*, aor. *ya'iẕ*, INF. *wa'ẕ*, *'iẕa-t*, *mau'iẕa-t*, announce future reward or punishment, warn; preach; — VIII. INF. *itti'âẕ*, listen to warnings, to sermons, &c.; take warning and obey.

وعظ *wa'ẕ*, ة *wa'ẕa-t*, warning, admonition, sermon.

(وعف) *wa'af*, U, INF. *wu'ûf*, be weak, dim.

وعف *wa'f*, pl. *wi'âf*, hard ground with water.

(وعق) *wa'aq*, aor. *ya'iq*, INF. *wa'q*, *wu'âq*, *wa'îq*, produce a rumbling noise in the belly when going; — *wa'iq*, A, INF. *wa'aq*, be swift, hasten (n.); — II. INF. *tau'îq*, hinder, place difficulties in one's way; — IV. INF. *î'âq*, urge to haste.

وعق *wa'q*, *wa'iq*, ة, ill-tempered, peevish, refractory; — ة *wa'qa-t*, peevishness, moroseness.

(وعك) *wa'ak*, aor. *ya'ik*, INF. *wa'k*, *wa'ka-t*, be very intense with calm air (heat); emaciate and weaken; (also IV.) roll on the ground, in the dust (a.); — IV. INF. *î'âk*, see I.; throng round the water.

وعك *wa'k*, intense heat, sultriness; weakness from fever; also *wa'ik*, weakened by the fever; — ة *wa'ka-t*, sultriness; great throng, turmoil; battle; battle-field.

(وعل) *wa'al*, aor. *ya'il*, INF. *wa'l*, tower, stand high, be of high rank; — V. INF. *tawa''ul*, ascend a mountain; — X. INF. *istî'âl*, flee into the mountains, seek refuge.

وعل *wa'l*, pl. *au'âl*, *wu'ûl*, refuge, asylum; also *wa'il*, pl. *au'âl*, *wi'lân*, noble, powerful; grandee, prince; month of شعبان *śa'bân*, — *wa'l*, *wa'il*, f. ة, pl. *wu'ul*, *wa'ila-t*, *wu'ûl*, *au'âl*, *mau'ila-t*, mountain-goat, chamois, argali, steinbock; — ة *wa'la-t*, handle of a jar; button-hole; mountain-crag, rock.

(وعم) *wa'am*, aor. *ya'im*, also — *wa'im*, aor. *yau'am*, INF. *wa'm*, greet a house with the word: انعمى *in'amî*, grant a favour!

وعم *wa'm*, pl. *wi'âm*, coloured vein of stone in a mountain.

(وعن) *wa'n*, ة *wa'na-t*, hard white and bare ground; refuge, asylum; — V. INF. *tawa''un*, grow very fat; take all; — ة *wa'na-t*, pl. *wi'ân*=وعم *wa'm*.

وعواع *wa'wâ'*, noise, tumult; howl; noise, crowd; screamer.

وعوثة *wu'ûsa-t*, softness of the ground.

وعور *wu'ûr*, ة *wu'ûra-t*, ruggedness.

(وعوع) *wa'wa'*, INF. ة, *wa'wâ'*, stir up, excite, agitate; scream, bark, yelp, howl; (m.) cry (child).

وعوع *wa'wa'*, eloquent; fox, jackal; desert; guard; weak; — ة *wa'wa'a-t*, barking, howling (s.); — ى *wa'wa'iyy*, witty.

(وعى) *wa'a*, aor. *ya'î*, INF. *wa'y*, gather and preserve in one place; grasp together and put into a vessel, a receptacle; preserve in the memory, remember, know; learn; gather (n. as pus); (m.) awake (n.); (m.) heed, be on one's guard, restrain one's self; heal; — II. INF. *tau'iya-t*, awake (a.); — IV. INF. *î'â'*, put into a vessel, receptacle, bag; pocket; hoard; keep to one's self, keep secret; — V. INF. *tawa''î*, be awake; be on one's guard; consider, think over; — X. INF. *istî'â'*, uproot or cut off entirely; do a thing considerately, take one's time over.

وعى *wa'y*, pus; flight; refuge; asylum; also *wa'a*, shouting, barking, howling (s.); — *wa'iyy*, strong.

وعيب *wa'îb*, roomy, spacious; extended.

وعيد *wa'îd*, threats.

وعير *wa'îr*, rugged.

وعيق *wa'îq*, rumbling noise in the belly.

وغا *wagâ*, noise, turmoil.

وغادة *wagâda-t*, stupidity.

(وغب) *wagub*, INF. *wugûba-t*, be big and strong.

وغب *wagb*, pl. *wigâb*, *augâb*, large bag; big and strong camel; small furniture, utensils, &c.;

f. ة (also m. ة *wagaba-t*) stupid and weak.

(وغد) *wagad*, aor. *yagid*, INF. *wagd*, serve; — *wagud*, INF. *wagâda-t*, *wugûda-t*, be stupid, weak, servile, contemptible; — III. INF. *muwâgada-t*, imitate, ape.

وغد *wagd*, pl. *wigdân*, *wugdân*, *augâd*, servant, errand-boy; stupid, weak, servile; contemptible, despised; an Indian fruit.

(وغر) *wagar*, aor. *yagir*, INF. *wagr*, be very hot and sultry; — INF. *wagr*, and—*wagir*, A, INF. *wagar*, burn with anger, bear a grudge; — IV. INF. *îgâr*, boil the milk by means of a hot stone, make water to boil; provoke to anger, incense; meet with the heat of the afternoon; — V. INF. *tawaggur*, burn with anger, be furious, rage.

وغر *wagr*, *wagar*, ة *wagra-t*, *wagara-t*, anger, hatred, grudge; din of arms, turmoil, tumult; *wagar*, ة *wagra-t*, heat, sultriness.

(وغص), II. *waggaṣ*, INF. *taugîṣ*, fill entirely.

(وغف) *wagaf*, aor. *yagif*, INF. *wagf*, step apace, run; — INF. *wagf*, *wugûf*, be dim; — IV. INF. *îgâf*, run.

(وغل) *wagal*, aor. *yagil*, INF. *wugûl*, enter, enter and hide one's self; go far in; depart; — INF. *wagl*, come (uninvited) to a drinking-bout, intrude; — IV. INF. *îgâl*, walk fast and enter suddenly, penetrate; urge on, push on, press on; force one to enter and hide one's self; = V.; — V. INF. *tawaggul*, penetrate, sneak in; break into the middle of; go far in; fathom knowledge, sink deep into sin.

وغل *wagl*, good-for-nothing fellow, scamp, vagabond; thick foliage; flight, refuge, asylum.

(وغم) *wagam*, aor. *yagim*, INF. *wagm*, impart uncertain news; treat violently, subdue; — *wagim*, A, INF. *wagam*, bear a deep grudge; — V. INF. *tawaggum*, id.

وغم *wagm*, pl. *augâm*, deep hatred, grudge; violence; combat, war; soul.

(وغن), V. *tawaggan*, INF. *tawaggun*, be bold;—ة *wagna-t*, large wine-jar.

وغى *waga*, *wiga*, turmoil, tumult; combat, war; — ة *wagya-t*, a little.

وغير *wagîr*, heated, cooked; also ة *wagîra-t*, dish of milk.

وفا *wafâ'*, fulfilment of a promise or duty, full payment of a debt, satisfaction; due; sincerity, honesty, conscientiousness, excellence, security, bail; fulfilment, completion, end; long life; — ة *wafât*, pl. *wafayât*, death, decease.

وفادة *wifâda-t*, arrival.

وفارة *wafâra-t*, abundance, affluence, completeness.

وفاع *wifâ'*, stopper.

وفاق *wifâq*, assent, consent, agreement; concord, harmony; conspiracy.

وفاهة *wifâha-t*, office of a Christian churchwarden.

(وفد) *wafad*, aor. *yafid*, INF. *wafd*, *wufûd*, *wifâda-t*, *ifâda-t*, come, arrive; — II. INF. *taufîd*, send, despatch; — IV. INF. *îfâd*, id.

وفد *wafd*, arrival; pl. *wufûd*, *aufâd*, a troop of new-comers; top of a sand-hill; — *wuffad*, *wafd*, pl. of وافد *wâfid*, arriving, &c.

(وفر) *wafar*, aor. *yafir*, INF. *wafr*, *fira-t*, *wufûr*, be abundant, plentiful; be full, complete; INF. *wafar*, *fira-t*, make abundant, increase, multiply, make full; INF. *wafr*, spare one's good name, abstain from scolding; reciprocate one's gift; — *wafur*, INF. *wafâra-t*, be abundant, plentiful; — II. INF. *taufîr*, make more abundant, more numerous, increase; save, econo-

mise; pay the whole debt, give the whole; — V. INF. *tawaffur*, respect one's good name, honour, pay regard to; be saved, economised; — VI. INF. *tawâfur*, multiply, increase (n.); be abundant; —VIII. INF. *ittifâr*, be abundant; — X. INF. *istîfâr*, exact payment of the whole debt, take the whole of.

وفر *wafr*, pl. *wufûr*, abundance, affluence, wealth; abundant; comprehensive, general; (m.) saving (s.); مخزن الو *maḥzan al-wafr*, savings-bank; — ة *wafra-t*, pl. *wifâr*, great quantity, plenty, abundance (also *wafira-t*); rich hair; lock of hair.

وفرا *wafrâ'*, f. of اوفر *aufar*, very spacious, &c.

(وفز) *wafz*, *wafaz*, pl. *aufâz*, *wifâz*, haste, hurry; — IV. INF. *îfâz*, urge to haste; hasten (n.); — X. INF. *istîfâz*, sit so as to be ready to break forth at the first sign; be ready to profit by the first opportunity.

(وفض) *wafaḍ*, aor. *yafiḍ*, INF. *wafḍ*, run, hurry (n.); — IV. INF. *îfâḍ*, id.; — X. INF. *istîfâḍ*, id.; urge to haste.

وفض *wafḍ*, *wafaḍ*, pl. *aufâḍ*, haste, hurry; *wafaḍ*, pl. *aufâḍ*, board to cut meat upon; *aufâḍ*, several groups, sects, companies; — ة *wafḍa-t*, pl. *wifâḍ*, leathern quiver; bread-bag, travelling-bag, wallet; حاوى الوفاض *ḥâwî al-wifâḍ*, with empty pockets.

وفع *waf'*, high building; cloud which promises rain; — *wafa'*, ة *wafa'a-t*, pl. *wif'ân*, lad up to 20 years of age; — ة *waf'a-t*= وفيعة *wafî'a-t*.

(وفق) *wafiq*, aor. *yafiq*, INF. *wafq*, find fit; fit, please; be useful, profitable; assist; — II. INF. *taufîq*, make fit; fit one thing to another; make the circumstances to fit, to be favourable to, assist, grant success; bring about an agreement between two parties; — III. INF. *wiqâf*, *muwâfaqa-t*, put one's self in accordance with, agree with, yield to; fit (n.), be in accordance with one's wishes or interests, befit; bring about an agreement between (بين *bain*, *ben*); — IV. INF. *îfâq*, fit well (acc.); — V. INF. *tawaffuq*, enjoy the assistance of God and be successful, prosper; — VI. INF. *tawâquf*, come to an agreement with one another, agree; live in concord; join harmoniously; assist one another; — VIII. INF. *ittifâq*, make an agreement with, agree; happen, occur; — X. INF. *istîfâq*, pray to God for assistance or success.

وفق *wafq*, *wufq*, fitting, corresponding, promoting (adj.), advantageous; sufficiency; sufficient quantity; proper time or opportunity, season; accordance, concord, harmony; a written amulet; logarithm.

(وفل) *wafal*, aor. *yafil*, INF. *wafl*, peel, shell; — II. INF. *taufîl*, increase (a.).

وفل *wafl*, a little, trifle.

وفنة *wafna-t*, small quantity.

(وفه) *wafah*, A, INF. *wafh*, be a Christian churchwarden.

وفهية *wafhiyya-t*, office of a churchwarden; superintendence; church discipline.

وفود *wufûd*, arrival.

وفور *wufûr*, abundance, affluence; great quantity; savings.

(وفى) *wafa*, aor. *yafî'*, INF. *wafâ'*, keep one's promise, fulfil one's engagements; pay the whole of a debt; do penance, atone, conciliate God; be or last long; — INF. *wufiyy*, be perfect, complete, abundant; — II. INF. *taufiya-t*, give, do or pay the whole at once; — III. INF. *muwâfât*, id.; arrive, come to (acc.); show true friendship to; — IV. INF.

îfâ', keep one's promise, fulfil a compact; give all, pay the whole of; accomplish, complete; tower over and afford a view or insight; come to; — V. INF. *tawaffî*, demand or receive the whole at once, receive full payment; take or call to one's self (pass. توفى *tuwuffî*, die); exhaust, carry out completely; — VI. INF. *tawâfî*, be perfect, complete, full in number; — X. INF. *istîfâ'*, demand or take the whole at once; exhaust a matter; (m.) recover one's self, take one's revenge.

وفى *wafa*, high ground; — *wafiyy*, ة, whole, complete, perfect; full; numerous; who keeps his word; sincere and faithful, trustworthy; — *wuffiyy*, INF. of (وفى).

وفيات *wafayât*, pl. of وفاة *wafât*.

وفيعة *wafî'a-t*, fleak of wool or piece of cloth to wipe with, &c.; cotton in the ink-bottle; stopper; basket of palm-leaves.

وفيق *wafîq*, companion, friend.

وقا *waqâ'*, *wiqâ'*, protection, guard.

وقاح *waqâḥ*, pl. *wuquḥ*, hard; brazen, impudent, daring, rash; — ة *waqâḥa-t*, hardness; impudence.

وقاد *wiqâd*, material for burning, fuel; — *waqqâd*, who kindles; burning, shining; fiery, ardent; intelligent, clever, skilful.

وقار *waqâr*, steady, grave, earnest, demure, mild and prudent; also ة *waqâra-t*, staidness, demureness, modesty, mildness and earnestness, patience, magnanimity; dignified bearing, gravity of manners; esteem, respect; majesty.

وقاط *wiqâṭ*, pl. of وقيط *waqîṭ*.

وقاع *wiqâ'*, INF. of (وقع); pl. of وقيعة *waqî'a-t*; — *waqqâ'*, ة *waqqâ'a-t*, pl. *wuqqâ'*, malicious and slandering.

وقاف *wiqâf*, assistance; resistance; INF. of (وقف III.); — *waqqâf*, hesitating, tarrying.

وقام *wiqâm*, sword; whip; cudgel; rope; — ة *waqâma-t*, submission; rough refusal.

وقاه *wuqâh*, Christian church-warden; — ية *waqâhiyya-t*, office of such.

وقايا *waqâya*, pl. of وقية *waqiyya-t*.

وقائذ *waqâ'iẓ*, paving-stones in a row.

وقاية *wiqâya-t*, protection, guard, preservation, care, solicitude; also *waqâya-t*, *wuqâya-t*, that by which anything is protected; — *waqâya-t*, *wiqâya-t*, kerchief.

(وقب) *waqab*, aor. *yaqib*, INF. *waqb*, enter a cavern; come, approach, set in; be dark; INF. *waqb*, *wuqûb*, disappear, be absent, set; be eclipsed.

وقب *waqb*, pl. *auqâb*, cave in a rock with stagnant water, cavern, cavity, socket, &c.; — ة *waqba-t*, niche in a wall; hole in a cake, pudding, &c.; cavity of the ear.

(وقت) *waqat*, aor. *yaqit*, INF. *waqt*, fix for a certain time, time; — II. INF. *tauqît*, appoint a time or term; — III. INF. *muwâqata-t*, appoint a term to (acc.).

وقت *waqt*, pl. *auqât*, space of time, time, season, term; opportunity; accident, calamity; *waqt-an*, once, once upon a time; *auqât-an auqât-an*, from time to time; لوقته *li-waqti-hi*, in (its proper) time; بوقته *bi-waqti-hi*, at once, immediately; — ى *waqtiyy*, referring to time, timely, temporal, perishable, provisional.

وقتئذ *waqta'iẓ-in*, at that very time.

(وقح) *waqaḥ*, aor. *yaqiḥ*, also—*waqiḥ*, A, and—*waquḥ*, INF. *waqâḥa-t*, *wuqûḥa-t*, *qiḥa-t*, *qaḥa-t*, *waqḥ*, be hard; be impudent, daring, brazen; — II. INF. *tanqîḥ*, harden (a.); lose all sense of shame; — IV. INF. *îqâḥ*, be

hard; — VI. INF. *tawâquḥ*, be brazen, behave impudently; — VIII. INF. *ittiqâḥ*, id.; — X. INF. *istîqâḥ*=IV.

(وقد) *waqad*, aor. *yaqid*, INF. *waqd*, *wuqûd*, *qida-t*, *waqadân*, ignite and burn; kindle (n.) — IV. INF. *îqâd*, kindle (a.), light; burn; — V. INF. *tawaqqud*, VIII. INF. *ittiqâd*=I.;— X. INF. *istîqâd*, id.; kindle (a.).

وقد *waqd*, burning (s.), cremation; heat of the fire; — *waqad*, fire; — ة *waqda-t*, a fire; heat of the fire; middle of the month.

(وقذ) *waqaẕ*, aor. *yaqiẕ*, INF. *waqẕ*, crush, tread, beat fiercely; throw down; vex; overpower, overwhelm; (also II. and IV.) leave in miserable condition; — II. INF. *tauqîẕ*, IV. INF. *îqâẕ*, see I.

(وقر) *waqar*, aor. *yaqir*, INF. *waqr*, burden, load, weigh upon; make one deaf; INF. *waqr*, split, break (a.); INF. *waqr*, *wuqûra-t*, sit; INF. *waqâr*, *qira-t*, be heavy, weighty; be grave, steady, firm, dignified; be patient, gentle, demure; — *waqir*, A, INF. *waqr*, also pass. *wuqir*, be deaf; — *waqur*, INF. *waqâra-t*, be heavy; be grave, dignified, venerable; be patient and gentle;— II. INF. *tauqîr*, deem one a grave and dignified man, honour, respect; make one venerable, respectable; — IV. INF. *îqâr*, load, burden, freight; press, straiten; be laden with fruit; — V. INF. *tawaqqur*, be grave, steady, dignified; be honoured, respected.

وقر *waqr*, deafness; hatred, grudge; cavity;—*wiqr*, pl. *auqâr*, weight, load, burden; heaviness of a load; — ة *waqra-t*, lameness; pl. *waqarât*, cavity; impression, track;— ى *waqra*, laden; — *waqariyy*, herdsman; rich in flocks; owner of asses.

(وقس) *waqas*, aor. *yaqis*, INF. *waqs*, skin, take the skin or crust off a wound;—utter vulgar or obscene talk; (m.) eat of a dead body, eat greedily; seize; — II. INF. *tauqîs*, render mangy.

وقس *waqs*, mange, dry scab, scurf; vulgar or obscene talk, ribaldry.

(وقش) *waqaś*, aor. *yaqiś*, INF. *waqś*, be effaced; — V. INF. *tawaqquś*, be moved, agitated.

(وقش) *waqś*, *waqaś*, ة *waqśa-t*, *waqaśa-t*, motion, emotion, commotion, tumult; chips for firing.

(وقص) *waqaṣ*, aor. *yaqiṣ*, INF. *waqṣ*, break one's neck; throw one off so as to break his neck; crush; be broken; — *waqiṣ*, aor. A, INF. *waqaṣ*, have a short neck; — II. INF. *tauqîṣ*, break (a.); — IV. INF. *îqâṣ*, make short-necked.

وقص *waqṣ*, fault, want, lack, defect; suppression of the second letter of a foot with its vowel; — *waqaṣ*, chips for firing; shortness of the neck.

وقصا *waqṣâʼ*, f. of اوقص *auqaṣ*, short-necked, &c.

(وقط) *waqaṭ*, aor. *yaqiṭ*, INF. *waqṭ*, beat fiercely and get the better of; tread (as a cock); cause indigestion.

وقط *waqṭ*, hole with water in a stone.

وقطان *wiqṭân*, pl. of وقيط *waqîṭ*.

(وقظ) *waqaẓ*, aor. *yaqiẓ*, INF. *waqẓ*, beat fiercely; persevere, endure.

(وقع) *waqaʻ*, aor. *yaqaʻ*, INF. *wuqûʻ*, fall down, fall, fall upon; occur to the mind; alight; kneel down; lie down; happen, occur; befall; be firm, solid, fortified; be necessary, incumbent, indispensable; INF. *waqʻ*, hurry away, depart; rush upon, attack and fight; desist; slander, blacken one's character, insult; (also VI.) intercede in favour of, ask for one's intercession; sharpen; — *waqiʻ*, A, INF. *waqaʻ*, be bare-footed; be hurt in the foot or hoof; — II. INF. *tauqîʻ*, cause to fall, bring to fall, drop;

apply; adjust, arrange; put the royal seal or signature to; enter or register a royal edict or sentence, register; write down, put into writing; — III. INF. *wiqâ'*, *muwâqa'a-t*, rush upon, attack, come to close quarters; undertake anything difficult; lie with; — IV. INF. *îqâ'*, make fall, bring to fall; throw into danger or calamity; rush upon, attack and throw down or beat, fall foul of, assail; tune; — V. INF. *tawaqqu'*, expect, look for, prepare one's self for, hope; meet with one's wish accidentally; (m.) request; — VI. INF. *tawâqu'*, see I.; rush full upon; encounter, come to close quarters; — X. INF. *istîqâ'*, expect.

وقع *waq'*, falling (s.), fall, blow, stroke; event; gravity of bearing or manners; — *wuqqa'*, pl. of واقع *wâqi'*, falling, &c.; — ة *waq'a-t*, pl. *waqa'ât*, fall, push, blow; event; calamity, catastrophe; vision in a dream; encounter, skirmish, battle; *al-waq'at-a*, all at once; — *wiq'a-t*, way of falling.

(وقف) *waqaf*, aor. *yaqif*, INF. *waqf*, *wuqûf*, stop, stand still; stand upright; make a pause in reading; delay; cost; — INF. *waqf*, stop one's beast, pull up; retain, delay; make cease to boil by pouring cold water to; give to consider, draw one's attention to, instruct, put in view; consecrate to a pious purpose or foundation; — INF. *wuqûf*, give one's time or attention to, occupy one's self with, inquire after; superintend workmen; — INF. *wiqqîfa*, serve in a church; — II. INF. *tauqîf*, stop (a.), bring to a standstill; make to stand upright, set up; make to halt; cause one to remain, keep back; delay, put off, procrastinate; (m.) stop (n.) to wait for; — III. INF. *wiqâf*, *muwâqafa-t*, stand by one in a combat, assist; make a stand against, oppose; array one's self in front of the adversary; — IV. INF. *îqâf*, stop (a.), bring to a standstill, retain, cause a delay; consecrate to a pious purpose; — V. INF. *tawaqquf*, stop (n.), halt; delay, put off; abstain, desist, keep aloof from, renounce; consist in, rest on; — VI. INF. *tawâquf*, array one's self in front of another, make a stand against one another; appear before the judge; — X. INF. *istîqâf*, bid to stop.

وقف *waqf*, stopping, making a halt (s.), pause; making the last letter of a *watad mafrûq* quiescent; restraint, abstemiousness; calmness, firmness, perseverance; confinement, arresting (s.); bracelet of ivory; edge of horn or metal to a shield; pl. *auqâf*, *wuqûf*, pious foundation, mortmain; — ة *waqfa-t*, delay; standing upright (s.), array, stoppage; sinew wound round a bow; — ى *waqfiyy*, ة, referring to a pious foundation; — ية *waqfiyya-t*, register of pious foundations; foundation-deed.

(وقل) *waqal*, aor. *yaqil*, INF. *wuqûl* (also V.), ascend a mountain; lift one foot while the other is standing; — V. INF. *tawaqqul*, see I.

وقل *waql*, pl. *auqâl*, n.u. ة, pl. *wuqûl*, dwarf palm and its dried fruit; — *waqal*, rock, stone; stump of a palm-branch; — *waqil*, *waqul*, good mountain-stepper (horse).

(وقم) *waqam*, aor. *yaqim*, INF. *waqm* (also IV.), treat violently, subdue; (also IV.) turn off ignominiously, treat with contempt; pull up; keep back, prevent; pass. be trodden down and grazed off; — IV. INF. *îqâm*, see I.; — V. INF. *tawaqqum*, kill the prey (hunter); threaten; intend.

(وقن) — IV. *auqan*, INF. *îqân*, hunt pigeons or catch them out of their nests ; — ة *wuqna-t*, nest or hiding-place of a bird ; small cavity.

(وقه) *waqih*, aor. *yaqih*, INF. *waqah*, obey ; — VIII. INF. *ittiqâh*, id. ; bring to an end, finish, complete ; — ة *waqha-t*, obedience ; fulfilment of one's duties.

وقواق *waqwâq*, cowardly ; a tree in hell ;— ة , talkative, garrulous.

وقوب *wuqûb*, setting (s.) ; eclipse ; disappearance, absence.

وقوحة *wuqûḥa-t*, hardness ; impudence, insolence.

وقود *waqûd*, fuel, wood ; also *wuqûd*, heat of the fire ; — *wuqûd*, burning (s.) ; burnt-offering.

وقور *waqûr*, earnest, grave, steady, dignified ; gentle and wise ; demure ; honoured, respected, venerable ; — ة *wuqûra-t*, INF. of (وقر).

وقوع *wuqû'*, falling (s.), fall ; happening (s.) ; event, occurrence ; reality, evidence ; destruction, death.

وقوف *wuqûf*, stopping, standing upright (s.) ; standstill, pause, stoppage, block ; attention to a matter, wish to understand it ; understanding, knowledge, experience ; pl. of واقف *wâqif* and وقف *waqf* ; — ية *wuqûfiyya-t*, understanding, comprehension ; knowledge, experience.

(وقوق) *waqwaq*, INF. ة , bark ; scream, screech, cry out.

(وقى) *waqa*, aor. *yaqî*, INF. *waqy*, *wiqâya-t*, *wâqiya-t*, guard, preserve, protect ; be on one's guard ; keep one's self pure ; INF. *waqy*, *wuqiyy*, put into good working order, arrange well ; INF. *wuqiyy*, also—*waqî*, INF. *waqa-n*, hurt the hoof ; — II. INF. *tauqiya-t*, guard, preserve, protect ; watch over ; — V. INF. *tawaqqî*, fear and be on one's guard ; protect one's self ; — VIII. INF. *ittiqâ'*, be on one's guard ; fear and honour God, be pious ; protect one's self.

وقى *waqiyy*, guarded, protected ; protecting ; — *wuqiyy*, protection ; abstinence, abstemiousness, chastity ; INF. of (وقى) ; — ة *waqiyya-t*, Tırkish pound (2¾ English) ; — *wuqiyya-t*, pl. *wuqiyy*, *waqâya*, ounce (weight).

وقيب *waqîb*, rumbling noise in a horse's belly.

وقيح *waqîḥ*, impudent, brazen.

وقيد *waqîd*, fuel, wood for burning ; heat of the fire.

وقيذ *waqîẕ*, thrown down ; utterly exhausted, on the point of death ; lazy.

وقير *waqîr*, hole with water in a rock (also ة *waqîra-t*) ; herd ; grave, steady and prudent ; in debt, poor.

وقيسة *waqîsa-t*, pl. *waqâ'is*, carcass, corpse, dead body.

وقيط *waqîṭ*, pl. *wiqṭân*, *wiqâṭ*, *iqâṭ*, large cavern with water, water-ditch in a mountain ; afflicted, grieved.

وقيع *waqî'*, sharpened ; worn-out (hoof) ; having holes with water ; — ة *waqî'a-t*, pl. *waqâ'i'*, occurrence, event ; calamity ; encounter, shock in a combat, skirmish, battle ; calumny, slander ; hatred, grudge ; pen-wiper ; basket of palm-leaves ; pl. *wiqâ'*, *waqâ'i'*, small hole with water.

(وك) *wakk*, INF. *wakk*, impel, repel.

(وكا) *waka'*, INF. *wak'*, lean upon ; — IV. INF. *îkâ'*, id. ; make one to lean upon, prepare a seat or a support for (acc.) ; — V. INF. *tawakku'*, lean upon ; lie at table ; — VIII. INF. *ittikâ'*=V.

وكا *wikâ'*, pl. *aukiya-t*, string to tie up a bag, wallet-string ; closed vessel ; miser.

وكاب *wakkâb*, who mourns much.

وكاث *wikâs̱*, *wukâs̱*, hurriedly prepared food, hasty meal.

وكاد *wikâd*, pl. *wakâ'id*, *aukida-t*, leathern belt ; saddle-strap.

وكار *wakkâr*, horse who likes to caracole, parade-horse.
وكاعة *wakâ'a-t*, hardness.
وكاف *wikâf*, *wukâf*, stuffing of a saddle.
وكال *wikâl*, confidence (وكل, III.); also *wakâl*, slowness; — ة *wakâla-t*, *wikâla-t*, vicariate, office of a substitute, an advocate, an agent, a deputy, a manager; agency, superintendence, delegation, proxy, trusteeship, guardianship; (m.) inn, hotel.
وكائد *wakâ'id*, pl. of وكاد *wikâd*.
وكاية *wikâya-t*, support, walking-stick.
(وكب) *wakab*, aor. *yakib*, IFF. *wakb*, *wukûb*, *wakabân*, go step by step, trot; (also III.) attend zealously to; INF. *wakb*, rise, stand up;— *wakib*, A, INF. *wakab*, be unclean, dirty, stained; grow black; — III. INF. *muwâkaba-t*, ride at the side of others and try to get in advance of them; see I.; — IV. INF. *îkâb*, keep in a cavalcade.
(وكت) *wakat*, aor. *yakit*, INF. *wakt*, make an impression upon, leave a trace; fill; walk in short steps; — II. INF. *taukît*, be dotted, get spots.
وكت *wakt*, anything insignificant; calumny, slander; — ة *wakta-t*, spot, dot; white spot in the eye; — *wakta-t*, part of the material where fire is struck.
(وكث) — X. INF. *istîkâs̱*, prepare food in a hurry, take a hasty meal.
(وكح) *wakaḥ*, aor. *yakiḥ*, INF. *wakḥ*, tread violently upon; — IV. INF. *îkâḥ*, jade, tire out; meet with stones in digging; desist; — X. INF. *istîkâḥ*, be miserly, give nothing; grow fat.
وكح *wukuḥ*, fat chickens.
(وكد) *wakad*, aor. *yakid*, INF. *wukûd*, stop (n.), halt; (m.) be firm, solid; — INF. *wakd*, intend, purpose, undertake; meet with, reach, obtain; fasten, tie fast;— II. INF. *taukîd*, fix, fasten, consolidate; tie fast; put emphasis upon, emphasise, confirm, affirm; look attentively at, fix one's looks upon; — V. INF. *tawakkud*, be fixed, made firm, consolidated; be confirmed, affirmed, assured.
وكد (*wakd*) *wukd*, intention, purpose, undertaking; zeal, attention, effort; strength, power.
(وكر) *wakar*, aor. *yakir*, INF. *wakr*, *wukûr*, go to the nest; enter a new house, give an entertainment at the completion of a house; leap; INF. *wakr*, go in leaps, rear and prance, caracole; run fast;—II. INF. *taukîr*, build a nest; fill;—IV. INF. *îkâr*, fill;— V. INF. *tawakkur*, fill one's stomach; — VIII. INF. *ittikâr*, build a nest, nestle.
وكر *wakr*, pl. *wukar*, *wukûr*, *aukur*, *aukâr*, nest; night's lodging, abode; — *wakr*, ى *wakra*, short and thick-set; — *wakr*, *wakar*, ى *wakra*, caracoling; — ة *wakra-t*, nest; also *wakara-t*, entertainment at the completion of a house;—*wukra-t*, cistern.
(وكز) *wakaz*, aor. *yakiz*, INF. *wakz*, strike with the fist, crush, bruise; drive away, keep off; push, urge, spur on; pierce; thrust into the ground; fill;—V. INF. *tawakkuz*, fill one's self with food; lean upon.
(وكس) *wakas*, aor. *yakis*, INF. *waks*, be diminished, lessen (n.), decrease; (also II.) diminish (a.), damage; lose in value, lower (n.) in price; (also IV.) waste away, get lost; pass. suffer a loss; — II. INF. *taukîs*, see I.;— IV. INF. *îkâs*, see I.
وكس *waks*, defect, loss, damage, diminution of value or price; entrance of the moon into an inauspicious constellation, eclipse.
(وكظ) *wakaz̤*, aor. *yakiz̤*, INF. *wakz̤*, push back, drive away; (also IV.) attend zealously and perseveringly to; — III. INF. *muwâkaza-t*, see I.

(وكع) **waka'**, aor. *yaka'*, INF. *wak'*, sting, bite; break (a.), crush; scold, silence; fall down from pain; — *waki'*, A, INF. *waka'*, have one toe protruding over another; — *waku'*, INF. *wakâ'a-t* (also IV., VIII., and X.), be hard, be firm and strong; be mean, vile; — IV. INF. *îkâ'*, see I.; bring about anything hard, unpleasant, adverse; — VIII. INF. *ittikâ'*, see I.; show hardness; — X. INF. *istîkâ'*, see I.

(وكف) *wakaf*, aor. *yakif*, INF. *wakf*, *wakîf*, *taukâf*, drop, drip, shower; have eaves, a gutter; — *wakif*, A, INF. *wakaf*, bend aside (n.), incline, deviate; be unjust, guilty, criminal, have weaknesses or faults; — III. INF. *muwâkafa-t*, resist, combat against; — IV. INF. *îkâf*, drip; throw one into guilt, into crime; — V. INF. *tawakkuf*, expect news; — X. INF. *istîkâf*, let drop, drip; beg for a dole.

وكف *wakf*, event, issue, result, consequence; piece of leather used as a table-cloth, a chess-board, &c.; — *wakaf*, pl. *aukâf*, injustice, guilt, crime, weakness; heaviness, weight; difficulty; projection, eaves, gutter, balcony over the door of a house or tent; mountain-slope; sweat, perspiration; vein.

(وكل) *wakal*, aor. *yakil*, INF. *wakl*, *wukûl*, entrust another with the management of one's affairs, consign; leave one to himself; trust, rely upon; be faint, tired jaded; — II. INF. *taukîl*, appoint as a substitute, agent, deputy, curator, advocate, manager, &c.; authorise, commission, delegate; — III. INF. *wikâl*, *muwâkala-t*, rely upon, give one's confidence to; — IV. INF. *îkâl*, trust in God; — V. INF. *tawakkul*, rely upon another, confide one's affairs to, trust entirely in (على *'ala*); be appointed as a substitute, &c.; — VI. INF. *tawâkul*, confide in one another; — VIII. INF. *ittikâl*, rely entirely upon, commit one's self to.

وكل *wakal*, ة *wukala-t*, not equal to one's own affairs, too weak and relying upon others.

وكلا *wukalâ'*, pl. of وكيل *wakîl*.

(وكم) *wakam*, aor, *yakim*, INF. *wakm*, put to anxiety, grieve (a.); subdue; tame; pass. *wukim*, be trodden down and grazed off by the cattle; — *wakim*, A, INF. *wakam*, be in anxiety, grieved, sorrowful.

وكم *wakam*, anxiety; grief.

(وكن) *wakan*, aor. *yakin*, INF. *wakn*, sit; pace along vigorously, get along, advance; — INF. *wukûn*, sit upon the nest, brood.

وكن *wakn*, pl. *wukûn*, *aukun*, nest, hole; — ة *wakna-t*, *wikna-t*, *wukna-t*, pl. *wukn*, *wuknât*, *wukunât*, id.

وكواك *wakwâk*, cowardly; trotting.

وكوع لكوع *wakû' lakû'*, vile and good-for-nothing.

(وكوك) *wakwak*, INF. ة, trot; take to flight; coo.

(وكى) *waka*, aor. *yakî*, INF. *waky*, tie up a skin bag, stop up a vessel; — IV. INF. *îkâ'*, id.; make one to sit, let one lean upon or against; — VIII. INF. *ittikâ'*, lean upon; — X. INF. *istîkâ'*, be very fat.

وكيت *wakît*, calumny, slander, lie.

وكيد *wakîd*, firm, strong, solid.

وكير *wakîr*, ة *wakîra-t*, entertainment at the completion of a house.

وكيع *wakî'*, hard, firm, strong; leading sheep; وكيع لكيع *wakî' lakî'* = وكوع لكوع *wakû' lakû'*.

وكيل *wakîl*, pl. *wukalâ*, substitute, agent, proxy, curator, advocate, deputy, envoy; lieutenant; manager, steward; governor; protector.

ولا *walâ'*, relationship, relatives; clientship; assistance, help, friendship, love; helpers,

friends; power of government, government, kingdom; right of inheritance to the property of a freed slave; liberty; proximity; — *wilâ'*, unbroken succession, continuation; — ة *wulât*, pl. of والي *wâlî*, regent, &c.; — ة *walâ'a-t*, authority, power of government, government; friendship; love.

ولاد *wilâd*, ة *wilâda-t*, parturition, birth, confinement.

ولاذ *wallâz*, swift; liar.

ولاس *wallâs*, wolf.

ولاف *wilâf*, intimate intercourse, familiarity, friendship.

ولاول *walâwil*, pl. of ولوال *wilwâl* and ولولة *walwala-t*.

ولايا *walâya*, pl. of ولية *waliyya-t*.

ولاية *wilâya-t*, *walâya-t*, pl. *-ât*=ولاءة *walâ'a-t*; empire, country, province, district; seat of government; guardianship; favour with God, holiness; *walâya-t*, help, assistance.

(ولب) *walab*, aor. *yalib*, INF. *wulûb*, enter; come to, arrive at; hasten (n.).

(ولت) *walat*, aor. *yalit*, INF. *walt*, wrong, cheat.

(ولث) *walas*, aor. *yalis*, INF. *wals*, beat, thrash; give one a faint promise.

ولث *wals*, blow; faint promise; promise of freedom to a slave after one's own death; remains; weak, mean, vile.

(ولج) *walaj*, aor. *yalij*, INF. *lija-t*, *walûj* (also V. and VIII.), enter; creep or slip in; engage in; join; pass. be seized with pain or grief; — II. INF. *taulîj*, IV. INF. *îlâj*, cause or allow to enter; put one thing into another; let follow; — V. INF. *tawalluj*, VIII. INF. *ittilâj*, see I.

ولج *walaj*, path in the sand; — *wulaj*, eaglet; — *wuluj*, pl. quarters of a town, streets; shores, coasts; — ة *walaja-t*, pl. *-ât*, *walaj*, *aulâj*, cave, grotto where one takes shelter from the rain; bend of a valley; — ، خرجة *walaja-t ḥuraja-t*, one who goes continually in and out, restless.

(ولح) *walaḥ*, aor *yaliḥ*, INF. *walḥ*, overburden a camel.

(ولخ) ة *waliḫa-t*, well-watered, rich in vegetation; — X. INF. *istîlâḫ*, be well-watered.

(ولد) *walad*, aor. *yalid*, INF. *lida-t*, *wilâd*, *wilâda-t*, *ilâda-t*, *maulid*, give birth, beget; — II. INF. *taulîd*, assist a woman in giving birth, act as a midwife; give birth; make children to; derive (a word); — IV. INF. *îlâd*, give birth; be on the point of confinement, or parturition; have a child from; derive, deduce; — V. INF. *tawallud*, be born, originate; be derived, deduced, result from; be created, come to light; — VI. INF. *tawâlud*, multiply by generation; — VIII. INF. *ittilâd* =V.; — X. INF. *istîlâd*, wish to have children from a woman, make her a mother.

ولد *walad*, *wald*, *wild*, *wuld*, pl. *aulâd*, *wilda-t*, *ilda-t*, *wild*, *wuld*, child, offspring, descendant; son, boy; lad, youngster; young of an animal; — *wuld*, pl. of ولود *walûd*, وليد *walîd*; — ة *wilda-t*, see above; also—

ولدان *wildân*, pl. of وليد *walîd*.

ولدنة *waldana-t*, childhood, childlike manners, childishness; — II. INF. *tawaldun*, play childish tricks, behave childishly.

(ولذ) *walaz*, aor. *yaliz*, INF. *walz*, walk apace; move quickly.

(ولس) *walas*, aor. *yalis*, INF. *walas*, *walasân*, stride along swiftly with outstretched neck; — INF. *wals*, falsify news, deceive, cheat; — III. INF. *muwâlasa-t*, (also IV.) represent without clearness, with reticence or falsification; deceive, cheat; — IV. INF. *îlâs*, see III.; — VI. INF. *tawâlus*, assist

one another in cheating or deceiving.

(ولع) *wala'*, aor. *yala'*, INF. *wal'*, *wala'ân*, grow frivolous; lie; take another's property, wrong; hinder, prevent; — *wali'*, A, INF. *wala'*, *walû'*, be intent upon, greedy for; — II. INF. *taulî'*, make one eager, greedy, enamoured; kindle, light; — IV. INF. *îlâ'*, make eager, greedy for, goad on, instigate; pass. be greedy after; — V. INF. *tawallu'*, be passionately addicted, violently in love; long for ardently.

ولع *wal'*, lie; — *wala'*, violent desire, passion, love; — ة *wala'a-t*, material to light with, match; — *wula'a-t*, very greedy, covetous (for other people's property).

(ولغ) *walag*, aor. *yalig*, *yâlag*, INF. *walg*, *wulûg*, *walagân*, lap; suck; — IV. INF. *îlâg*, make to lap, give to drink, water; — ة *walga-t*, small bucket.

(ولف) *walaf*, aor. *yalif*, INF. *walf*, *wilâf*, *ilâf*, *walîf*, flash continuously; INF. *walîf*, come at the same time; come one behind another; — II. INF. *taulîf*, prepare, equip, arrange; make ready for departure, pack one's bundle; — III. INF. *wilâf*, *muwâlafa-t*, have familiar intercourse with, be intimate, joined in close friendship; arrange, adjust; re-establish concord, bring about a reconciliation.

(ولق) *walaq*, aor. *yaliq*, INF. *walq*, be nimble, agile, active; hasten (n.); be ready for deceit and fraud; persevere, continue; stab, wound, strike slightly; — IV. pass. *ûliq*, INF. *îlâq*, be seized with madness, be half crazed; — ة *walaqa-t*, pl. *-ât*, blow; — ى *walaqa*, swift run in leaps; — *walqa*, swift.

ولكن *wa-lâkin*, but, however.

(ولم) *walm*, *walam*, girth, girth-leather, saddle-strap; fetter, tether, rope; — IV. *aulam*, INF. *îlâm*, give an entertainment to; — ة *walma-t*, the whole, all of.

(وله) *walah*, aor. *yalih*, also—*walih*, aor. *yalih*, *yaulah*, INF. *walah*, *walahân* (also V. and VIII.), be confused, deeply moved, agitated, terrified by grief; be afraid, fear; be passionately in love; — IV. INF. *îlâh*, fill with fear; — V. INF. *tawalluh*, see I.; — VIII. INF. *ittilâh*, see I.; confuse, make giddy, inebriate.

وله *walah*, confusion of the mind, trouble, fright, astonishment; painful emotion, grief; love-passion.

ولهان *walhân*, f. *walha*, confused in mind, terrified, astonished, stunned, painfully moved, seized with love-passion; *al-walhân*, a demon who induces to use up much water in washing; — *walahân*, INF. of (وله).

ولو *wa-law*, and even if, although.

ولوال *walwâl*, anxiety, anguish; male owl; also *wilwâl*, pl. *walâwil*, wailing, lamentation for the dead.

ولوج *wulûj*, entrance.

ولود *walûd*, pl. *wuld*, giving birth to many, fertile; — ة *wulûda-t*, generation, birth; — ية *walûdiyya-t*, *wulûdiyya-t*, tender age, childhood; childishness; childish tricks, ill-bred manners, churlishness.

ولوع *walû'*, greedy; greed, greediness; love.

ولوغ *walûg*, what is sipped or lapped up; — *wulûg*, INF. of (ولغ).

ولوف *walûf*, lightening without interruption.

(ولول) *walwal*, INF. ة, *walwâl*, *wilwâl*, bewail, lament; call imploringly on God; curse aloud; twang (n.); — ة *walwala-t*, pl. *walâwil*, bewailing, lamentation for the dead; noise, turmoil, tumult.

(ولى) *wala*, aor. *yalî*, INF. *waly*, be close to, stand immediately by, be neighbouring, follow close upon, confine with, depend, appertain; — *walî*, aor. *yalî*, INF. *waly*, id.; be a friend, assistant, helper; INF. *wilâya-t*, *walâya-t*, be placed at the head of, govern, administer; wet continuously; — II. INF. *tauliya-t*, turn the back, move away, yield, take to flight; prepose, make one a governor, regent, prefect, entrust with affairs; — III. INF. *wilâ'*, *muwâlât*, continue without interruption, be constant, carry on two things at the same time; befriend, be an assistant to, help, protect, make a covenant with; — IV. INF. *îlâ'*, prepose, place at the head of, entrust with an affair or office; confer, bestow, benefit; cause one to be near; — V. INF. *tawallî*, be invested with power (by a superior), govern, administer; be nominated, appointed; turn the back, yield, take to flight, turn away; remove to a distance, desist, give up; — VI. INF. *tawâlî*, follow one another in unbroken succession; — VIII. INF. *ittilâ'*, have under one's management or direction; — X. INF. *istîlâ'*, make one's self master of, take possession of; become master, lord it.

ولى *waly*, nearness, proximity, contiguity; friendship; government of a province; shower after shower; — *wula*, pl. of وليا; — *waliyy*, ة, near, close, neighbouring, contiguous, adjacent; pl. *auliyâ'*, relative, neighbour, friend, beloved one; helper, protector, benefactor, patron, master; who administers, bestows; client, slave; favourite (with God, with a prince); prophet, saint; و لعهد *waliyy al-'ahd*, heir apparent; pl. *auliya-t*, shower after shower; — ة *waliyya-t*, pl. *walâyâ*, power of government, sovereignty, jurisdiction; government, province; saddle-cloth, cushion-saddle, cushion.

وليا *wulyâ*, pl. *wula*, f. of اولى *aula*, fitter, more excellent.

وليجة *walîja-t*, intimate friend; hiding-place.

وليحة *walîha-t*, pl. *walîh*, *walâ'ih*, large corn-sack or basket.

وليح *walîḥ*, linen; — ة *walîḥa-t*=ولخة *waliḥa-t*.

وليد *walîd*, pl. *wilda-t*, *walâ'id*, *wildân*, born, in existence, created; son, boy, lad; slave; — *wulaid*, babe, little child; — ة *walîda-t*, pl. *walâ'id*, daughter, girl; maid-servant, female slave.

وليف *walîf*, lightening without interruption.

وليقة *walîqa-t*, dish of milk, flour, and butter.

وليمة *walîma-t*, pl. *walâ'im*, entertainment, wedding-banquet, dinner-party.

(وما) *wama'*, aor. *yama'*, INF. *wam'*, give a sign or hint to, beckon; — II. INF. *taumi'a-t*, id.; — III. INF. *muwâma't*, agree with, come to an agreement; — IV. INF. *îmâ'*= I.; point to.

وما *wam'*, sign, hint.

وماح *wammâḥ*, vagina.

ومحة *wamḥa-t*, spot caused by the heat of the sun.

ومخة *wamḫa-t*, stinging reproach.

(ومد) *wamid*, A, INF. *wamad*, be very sultry; burn with anger, rage.

ومد *wamad*, ة *wamada-t*, sultriness of a night; anger, rage; — *wamid*, ة, sultry and dewy; — ان *wamdân*, id.

ومذة *wamẓa-t*, pure whiteness.

(ومز) *wamaz*, aor. *yamiz*, INF. *wamz*, turn up the nose, make a sign with it.

(ومس) *wamas*, aor. *yamis*, INF. *wams*, rub off, polish, smooth.

وصعة **wamśa-t**, white spot on the face.
(ومض) **wamaḍ**, aor. *yamiḍ*, INF. *wamḍ*, *wamîḍ*, *wamaḍân*, flash slightly, lighten without thundering; — IV. INF. *îmâḍ*, id.; indicate stealthily, steal a look at.
وصطة *wamṭa-t*, falling down from fatigue (s.).
ومعة *wam'a-t*, rolling wave, surge.
ومغة *wamga-t*, long hair.
(ومق) *wamiq*, aor. *yamiq*, INF. *wamq*, *miqa-t*, love tenderly, be in love with; — IV. INF. *îmâq*, show love to (acc.).
ومق *wamq*, tender love.
ومكة *wamka-t*, spaciousness, width, freedom.
(ومه) *wamih*, aor. A, INF. *wamah*, be very hot; — ة *wamha-t*, anything made fluid, molten.
وميض *wamîḍ*, sheet - lightning; gleam, flash; lightening without thundering (adj.); breaking forth, dawning (adj.).
وميق *wamîq*, beloved, dear.
(ون) *wann*, weariness, tiredness, weakness; castanets.
ونا *wanâ*, *winâ'*, relaxedness, weakness; — ة *wanât*, tired, faint, gentle; a pearl.
(ونب) — II. *wannab*, INF. *taunîb*, overwhelm with reproaches, scold.
(ونج) *wanaj*, lute, cithern.
(ونح) — III. *wânaḥ*, INF. *muwânaḥa-t*, agree with, assent to (acc.).
(ونر) — II. *wannar*, INF. *taunîr*, lift up, raise, put on high.
(ونك) *wanak*, aor. *yanik*, INF. *wank*, dwell amongst (فى *fî*).
(ونم) *wanam*, aor. *yanim*, INF. *wanm*, *wanîm*, drop excrement; — ة *wanama-t*, excrement of flies.
(ونى) *wana*, aor. *yanî*, INF. *wanan*, *wany*, *winâ'*, *wuniyy*, *wanya-t*, *winya-t*, be weak, faint, without strength; desist from weakness; be tardy; leave, forsake; tuck up one's sleeve; — III. INF. *muwânât*, carry on languidly; — IV. INF. *înâ'*, render tired, faint, languid; weaken; — VI. INF. *tawânî*, relax, slacken, grow tired, lose courage; be tardy, neglect.
ونى *wanan*, *wana*, *wany*, *wuniyy*, languidness, weakness, faintness; — ة *wanya-t*, *winya-t*, slackness, faintness, tardiness; — *wanya-t*, string of pearls; sack, bag.
ونيم *wanîm*, excrement of flies.
(وه) *wahh*, sorrow, grief; *wahh-in*, fie! for shame!
وهاب *wahhâb*, who makes many presents, liberal, generous; God; — ى *wahhâbiyy*, f. and pl. ة, Wahabite; — ية *wahhâbiyya-t*, utmost liberality.
وهاج *wahhâj*, blazing (adj.), enraged.
وهازة *wahâza-t*, graceful walk of a modest woman.
وهاس *wahhâs*, lion.
وهافة *wihâfa-t*, *wahâfa-t*, office of a churchwarden.
وهام *wahhâm*, suspicious, distrustful; sceptic.
(وهب) *wahab*, aor. *yahab*, INF. *wahb*, *wahab*, *hiba-t*, *mauhiba-t*, give, present with, grant; forgive, pardon; admit; suppose; IMP. هب *hab*, let us suppose! aor. *yahab*, *yahib*, surpass in liberality; — III. INF. *muwâhaba-t*, vie in liberality with; — IV. INF. *îhâb*, prepare, equip; remain perpetually with; be in one's reach; — VI. INF. *tawâhub*, make presents to one another; — VII. INF. *inwihâb*, be given, presented, granted; — VIII. INF. *ittihâb*, receive for a present; — X. INF. *istîhâb*, ask for a present.
وهب *wahb*, *wahab*, ة *wahba-t*, *wahaba-t*, gift, present; — ى *wahabiyy*, given by God or nature, natural.
(وهت) *wahat*, aor. *yahit*, INF. *waht*, press, cuff, crush; — IV. INF. *îhât*, be putrid.
(وهث) *wahas̱*, aor. *yahis̱*, INF. *wahs̱*,

devote zeal and diligence to (فى *fî*); tread down violently; — V. INF. *tawahhuṣ*, make the utmost efforts in, go far in.

(وهج) *wahaj*, aor. *yahij*, INF. *wahj*, *wahajân*, also—*wahij*, A, ignite (n.), burn, blaze; — IV. INF. *ihâj*, kindle, light; — V. INF. *tawâhhuj*, be kindled, burn; glow.

وهج *wahaj*, glow, heat of fire.

وهجان *wahjân*, burning (adj.); — *wahajân*, INF. of (وهج).

(وهد) *wahd*, pl. *wihdân*, *auhud*, also ة *wahda-t*, pl. *wihâd*, low ground, deep valley; pit, precipice; — II. *wahhad*, INF. *tauhîd*, prepare a soft couch for (ل *li*).

(وهر) *wahar*, aor. *yahir*, INF. *wahr* (also II.) lead into danger, embarrassment, error, sin; deceive, cheat; (m.) frighten, terrify; — II. INF. *tauhîr*, see I.; — V. INF. *tawahhur*, render one confused in speaking.

وهر *wahar*, reflected sunbeams lying like a mist on the ground; — ة *wahra-t*, fright, fear.

(وهز) *wahaz*, aor. *yahiz*, INF. *wahz*, tread, push or kick back; incite, instigate; kill (vermin) on the nail.

وهز *wahz*, short and thick-set.

وهس *wahas*, aor. *yahis*, INF. *wahs*, tread down, trample under foot; break (a.), pound; treat haughtily, offend; walk fast; use stratagem; — III. INF. *muwâhasa-t*, walk fast and with a vigorous tread; — V. INF. *tawahhuṣ*, VI. INF. *tawâhus*, id.

وهس *wahṣ*, secret; stratagem, deceit; calumny, slander.

(وهش) — V. *tawahhaś*, INF. *tawahhuś*, walk barefooted.

(وهص) *wahaṣ*, aor. *yahiṣ*, INF. *wahṣ*, break (a.); tread or throw down violently.

(وهط) *wahaṭ*, aor. *yahiṭ*, INF. *wahṭ*, break (a.); tread down; sting, prick; be weak, faint; — IV. INF. *îhâṭ*, make weak, relax (a.); throw into adversities, throw one down so as not to rise again, kill; — V. INF. *tawahhuṭ*, sink in mud; rush rashly into.

وهط *wahṭ*, thinness, leanness; large troop, crowd; — ة *wahṭa-t*, pl. *wahṭ*, low ground; — ى *wahṭiyy*, small black grapes.

(وهف) *wahaf*, aor. *yahif*, INF. *wahf*, *wahîf*, put forth leaves, blossom, bloom; be shaken, approach; appear, happen, befall; INF. *wahf*, *wahâfa-t*, *wihâfa-t*, serve a Christian church.

وهفية *wahfiyya-t*, *wihifiyya-t*=وهافة *wihâfa-t*.

(وهق) *wahaq*, aor. *yahiq*, INF. *wahq*, prevent, hinder; — III. INF. *muwâhaqa-t*, keep equal pace with.

وهق *wahq*, *wahaq*, pl. *auhâq*, noose; rope to bind the feet with.

(وهل) *wahal*, aor. *yauhal*, *yahil*, INF. *wahl*, be of opinion, form a view, surmise; frighten; — *wahil*, A, INF. *wahal*, be weak, timid; be terrified, be struck dumb with terror; commit an error, make a mistake, be deceived; — II. INF. *tauhîl*, frighten violently; terrify; — VII. INF. *inwihâl*, form an opinion; be seized with fear.

وهل *wahal*, terror, fear; forgetfulness, error; — *wahl*, *wahil*, weak, timorous; — ة *wahla-t*, fright, terror; instant, moment; اول وهلة *awwal-a wahlat-in*, in the first moment, at once, before anything else.

(وهم) *waham*, aor. *yahim*, INF. *wahm*, form an opinion, opine, think, fancy, imagine; suppose, surmise; doubt, be afraid of making a mistake; be confused, fear; aor. *yahim*, *yauham*, forget in calculating or counting; — *wahim*, A, INF. *waham*, be of a wrong opinion, mistake, commit errors; — II. INF. *tauhîm*, inspire with an opinion, a surmise, a suspicion; make believe; (m.) frighten; — IV. INF. *ihâm*=II.;

inspire with doubt, uncertainty; be dubious, equivocal; omit in calculation; — V. INF. *tawahhum*, opine, think, suppose, surmise, suspect, imagine, conjecture; — VII. INF. *inwihâm*, (m.) be frightened, be struck dumb with terror, get confused;—VIII. INF. *ittihâm*, surmise, suspect, accuse of.

وهم *wahm*, pl. *auhâm*, opinion, surmise, idea, fancy, delusion, infatuation, suspicion; instinct; fear, terror, anguish; escape; pl. *wuhum*, *wuhûm*, high-road; big, corpulent; — ة *wahma-t*, anything terrible, dreadful difficulty, trouble; — ى *wahmiyy*, ة, imagined, imaginary, hypothetical, conjectural, false;—ية *wahmiyya-t*, pl. *-ât*, imagination, fancy, chimera, mere hypothesis, conjecture.

(وهن) *wahan*, aor. *yahin*, *yahan*, INF. *wahn*, be weak, too weak;— *wahin*, A, *wahun*, INF. *wahan*, id.; — II. INF. *tauhîn*, IV. INF. *îhân*, weaken, unnerve, damage.

وهن *wahn*, *wahan*, weakness, want of power; *wahn*, midnight; short and thick-set; — *wuhun*, pl. of واهن *wâhin*, weak, &c.

وهنانة *wahnâna-t*, lazy woman.

وهواة *wahwâh*, roaring;=وهوة *wahwah*.

وهوب *wahûb*, liberal.

(وهوة) *wahwah*, INF. ة, roar in a subdued manner; bark, snarl; lament, wail.

وهوة *wahwah*, lively, mettled; — ة *wahwaha-t*, guttural sound of a horse after neighing.

(وهى) *waha*, aor. *yahî*, INF. *wahy*, also—*wahî*, aor. *yahî*, INF. *wahan*, be weak, brittle, frail, perishable, threaten ruin, decay; be torn; break, burst (n.); rain violently; be stupid, weak-headed, useless; — IV. INF. *îhâ'*, make weak, frail; rend (n.), chap.

وهى *wahy*, pl. *wuhiyy*, *auhiya-t*, rent, split, chap; also *wahan*, *waha*, weakness, frailness, perishableness;—ة *wahya-t*, rent, split; — *wahiyya-t*, large pearl; young fat camel to be slaughtered.

وهيج *wahîj*, heat, sultriness, flame.

وهيدة *wuhaida-t*, small cavern.

وهيسة *wahîsa-t*, dish of dried and pounded locusts.

وهين *wahîn*, overseer of slaves.

وورة *wu'ra-t*, pl. *wu'âr*, fire, hearth.

وؤول *wu'ûl*, escape, INF. of (وال).

وى *wai*, woe! oh! ويك *waika*, woe to you! well done! bravo!

ويا *wayyâ*, (m.) with, together with =وايا *wa-iyyâ*.

وئال *wi'âl*, flight.

ويب *waib*, woe! (takes pron. affixes); — *wa'ib*, v. see (واب); — ة *waiba-t*, pl. *-ât*, a measure (24 مد *mudd*).

ويج *waij*, wooden sock to which the ploughshare is attached.

ويح *waih*, woe to (ل *li*); also expressing admiration.

وئر *wa'ir*, entirely dried up.

ويس *wais*, poverty; want.

ويك *waika*, see وى; also—

ويكان *waika'anna*, do you not see?

(ويل) *wail*, disaster, terrible calamity; punishment; revenge; a door of hell, valley of hell; woe! — II. *wayyal*, INF. *tauyîl*, exclaim repeatedly ويل *wail*, woe! over (acc. or ل *li*); — VI. INF. *tawâyul*, say woe! to one another; — ة *waila-t*, calamity, disgrace; woe!

ويلمه *wailummihi*=ويل لامه *wail-un li-ummi-hi*, woe to his mother! (a curse).

ويلمة *wailima-t*, *wailuma-t*, and—

ويله *wailih*, *wailuh*, cunning, wily, sly.

ويمة *waima-t*, suspicion, accusation.

وين *wain*, ة, black grapes.

ويه *waih-a*, *waih-i*, ويها *waih-an*, well then! come on! make haste!

وئيب *wa'îb*, ة, deep.
وئيد *wa'îd*, ة *wa'îda-t*, girl buried alive.
وئيصة *wa'îṣa-t*, troop, company.
وئيل *wa'îl*, escape.
وئية *wa'iyya-t*, fine pearl.

ي

ى letter *y*, as a numeral sign=10; abbreviation for Jupiter and Aquarius; — *î*, *ya* (pronominal suffix of the 1st person sing. after nouns and prepositions), my, me; in the vocative, abbreviated into ـِ: يا رب *yâ rabb-i*, O my Lord!

يا *yâ*, exclamation oh! ah! ياهو *yâhû*, he! (God); — *yâ'*, pl. *yâyât*, name of the letter ى *y*.

يائى *ya'â'î*, pl. of يويو *yu'yu'*.

يابس *yabis*, pl. *yabs*, dry, withered.

ياجوج *yâjûj*, who runs always to and fro; — *ya'jûj*, who lights a fire, incites to rebellion; Gog (the Scythians).

ياجور *yâjûr*, brick.

يارق *yâraq*, bracelet.

يارة *yârra-t*, fire.

ياروج *yârûj*, sword, spear, arrow.

(ياس) يئس *ya'is*, aor. *yai'as*, INF. *ya's*, *ya'sa-t*, give up hope, despair; — INF. *ya's*, know; — IV. INF. *î'âs*, cause one to despair, deprive of hope; — X. INF. *istî'âs*, despair.

ياس *ya's*, ة *ya'sa-t*, despair; — *ya'as*, consumption.

ياسر *yâsir*, what is easy to be done or got; soft, mild, gentle; left-handed; disastrous; pl. *aisâr*, who slaughters and divides a camel.

ياسم *yâsam*, *yâsim*, ياسمن *yâsaman*, ياسمون *yâsamûn*, ياسمين *yâsamîn*, jasmine.

ياصول *yâṣûl*, root, origin.

ياعاط *yâ'ât*=يعاط *ya'ât*.

يافث *yâfiṯ*, Yaphet.

يافع *yâfi'*, ة, pl. *-ûn*, *yafa'a-t*, *yuf'ân*, tall, long, high; young man of about 20; pl. *yâfi'ât*, high mountains, difficult matters.

يافوخ *yâfûḥ*, *ya'fûḥ*, pl. *yawâfîḥ*, *ya'âfîḥ*, middle and crown of the head; middle or principal part of the night.

يافوف *yâfûf*, timorous, weak.

ياقوت *yâqût*, ة, pl. *yawâqît*, ruby, sapphire, precious stone; ى احمر *yaqût aḥmar*, ruby; — ى *yâqûtiyy*, ruby-coloured; red grapes.

يالق *yâliq*, (m.) large bag of haircloth for the load of a mule.

يامن *yâmin*, to the right hand, auspicious.

يانع *yâni'*, pl. *yan'*, ripe; scarlet.

يانيسون *yanîsûn*, anise.

ياه *yâh*, oh! (vocative exclamation).

ياهو *yâhû*, see يا *yâ*.

ياوى *yâwiyy*, ة referring to or rhyming with the letter ى *y*.

(يايا) *ya'ya'*, INF. ة, *ya'yâ'*, treat kindly; pacify, coax, flatter; call by يا *yâ*, call, call together.

يائس *yâ'is*, ة, despairing.

ياياه *yâyâh*, take courage!

يائى *ya'â'i*, pl. of يويو *yu'yu'*; — *yâ'iyy*=ياوى *yâwiyy*.

يباب *yabâb*, wilderness; deserted, waste.

يبرق *yabraq*, rice and hashed meat, dished on vine-leaves.

يبروح *yabrûḥ*, mandrake.

(يبس) *yabis*, aor. *yaibas*, *ya'bas*, INF. *yabas*, *yubs*, dry up, wither (n.); get dry (anything wet); —II. INF. *taibîs*, dry, wither (a.); — IV. INF. *îbâs*, id.; — V. INF. *tayabbus*, dry, be dry; — VIII. INF. *ittibâs*, id.

يبس *yabs*, *yubs*, *yabas*, dryness, drought; — *yabs*, *yabas*, *yabis*,

dry, withered; *al-yabs*, the dry land; *yabas*, barren (woman); *yabs*, pl. of يابس *yâbis*.

يبوسة *yabûsa-t*, dryness; religious lukewarmness.

يبيس *yabîs*, ة, dry, withered.

يتامى *yatâma*, pl. of يتيم *yatîm*.

(يتم) *yatam*, *yatim*, aor. *yaitam*, INF. *yatm*, *yutm*, be fatherless, orphaned, forsaken and lonely; become an orphan; be unique, without an equal, incomparable; —*yatim*, A, INF. *yatam*, be not equal to an undertaking, be faint and weak; — II. INF. *taitîm*, make one an orphan; — IV. INF. *îtâm*, id.; have fatherless children; — V. INF. *tayattum*, be an orphan.

يتم *yatm*, *yutm*, *yatam*, orphanage, abandonment, loneliness; — ة *yatama-t*, pl. of يتيم *yatîm*.

يتمان *yatmân*, orphaned; under age, minor.

(يتن) *yatan*, INF. *yatn*, be born feet foremost; — II. INF. *taitîn*, give such a birth.

يتن *yatn*, child born feet foremost.

يتيم *yatîm*, ة, pl. *aitâm*, *yatâma*, *yatamd-t*, *maitama-t*, orphaned, orphan; unique, incomparable.

يثرب *yasrib*, Medina.

يثلث *yaslas*, *yaslis*, firm, solid.

يثموم *yasmûm*, a plant.

(يجر) — VI. *tayâjar*, INF. *tayâjur*, deviate.

يحبور *yaḥbûr*, cheerful, happy; pl. *yaḥâbir*, *yaḥâbîr*, young bustard.

يحمور *yaḥmûr*, red; wild ass; a species of antelope.

يحموم *yaḥmûm*, black; smoke.

يحيط *yaḥîṭ*, year of famine.

يحيا, يحيى *yaḥya*, John; ابو يحيى *abu yaḥya*, death.

يخضود *yaḥḍûd*, freshly-cut branch.

يخضور *yaḥḍûr*, pl. *yaḥâḍîr*, green plot.

يخنى *yaḥnî*, ragout, sauce (Pers.).

يد *yad*, f. (m. *yadd*, *iyad*), pl. *yadiyy*, *aid-in*, *aidî*, pl. pl. *ayâd-in*, hand; (ذو اليدين *ẕû-'l-yadain*, ambidexter; بين يديه *bain-a yadai-hi*, before him, in his presence; عن ظهر يد *'an ẓahr-i yad-in*, gratis, for nothing); fore-foot; fore-arm, wing; handle of a bow, knife, tool, &c.; winch; pl. *yadiyy*, *yidiyy*, *yudiyy*, *aidî*, benefit, bounty, favour; power, influence; assistance, help, protection; troop, host, army; possessions, wealth; promise; submission; length, duration; — ة *yada-t*, hand.

يداء *yudâ'*, pain in the hand.

(يدع) — II. *yadda'*, INF. *taidî'*, dye with saffron, brazil-wood, &c.

يدك *yadak*, reserve-horse.

يدوى *yadawiyy*, referring to the hand, manual.

(يدى) *yada*, aor. *yaidî*, INF. *yady*, touch, hit, or hurt on the hand; seize by the fore-foot; cut off the hand; benefit, do good to; — *yadî*, have a withered hand; III. INF. *muyâdât*, requite, retaliate; reach from hand to hand, pass on; — IV. INF. *îdâ'*, confer a benefit; assist, help; fix, consolidate.

يدى *yadan*, *yada*, du. *yadayân*, hand; large, wide; — *yadiyy*, referring to the hand, done by hand, manual; handy, skilful; referring to possession, possessive; wide, large; narrow, tight; comfortable; straitened; — *yudiyy*, pl. of يد *yad*; — ة *yadiyya-t*, quick-handed (woman); — *yudaiyya-t*, little hand.

يديا *yadyâ'*, quick-handed (f.)

(ير) *yarr*, aor. *yayarr*, INF. *yarar*, be hard and smooth; be hard as stone; be hot, glow.

ير *yarr*, evil, mischief, calamity; — ة *yarra-t*, fire, glow.

يرابيع *yarâbî'*, pl. of يربوع *yarbû'*.

يراع *yarâ'*, ة, glowworm; a stinging fly; reed, pen; reed-pipe; coward; block-head; — ة *yarâ'a-t*, reed-bank.

يربوع *yarbû'*, pl. *yarâbî'*, jerboa; muscle of the loin.

يرحم *yarḥum*, *yarḥam*, يرحوم *yarḥam*, male pelican.

يرر *yarar*, hardness; heat, INF. of (يرّ).

(يرع) *yari'*, A, INF. *yara'*, be timorous, cowardly.

يرع *yar'*, calf; — *yara'*, cowardice; a stinging fly.

يرقان *yaraqân*, *yarqân*, blight, mildew; jaundice; yellowness.

يرقود *yarqûd*, who sleeps much.

يرمع *yarma'*, pl. *yarâmi'*, white shingle; toy.

يرموق *yarmûq*, dim-sighted.

يرمول *yarmûl*, sandy.

يرمى *yarmiyy*, stone as a road-mark in the desert.

يرنا *yaranna'*, henna-plant; — *yaranna'a*, INF. *yarannu'*, dye with it.

يرندج *yarandaj*, black leather.

يروع *yarû'*, fear, cowardice.

يزك *yazak*, military post; — ى *yazakiyy*, soldier on watch-duty.

يزلى *yaziliyy*, unceasing, eternal.

يزيد *yazîd*, proper name of several Chalifs; founder of the sect of Yazîdîs; hence reprobate, impious; — ى *yazîdiyy*, a Yazîdî; — ية *yazîdiyya-t*, sect of the Yazîdîs.

(يس) *yass*, aor. *yayiss*, INF. *yass*, step, walk.

يسار *yasâr*, *yisâr*, *yassâr*, pl. *yusr*, *yusur*, left, left hand or side; *yasâr*, ة *yasâra-t*, mild character; ease, comfort, affluence, wealth; *yisâr*, mildness, gentleness; *yasâr-i*, a little.

يساق *yasâq*, prohibition; anything forbidden, what is confiscated, contraband.

يسر *yasar*, aor. *yaisir*, INF. *yasr*, *yusr*, throw dice or draw lots with arrows; be easy to deal with, gentle, kind, docile; — *yasur*, also pass. *yusir*, be easy to do or to get; (m.) see IV.; come or show one's self from the left side; —II. INF. *taisîr*, make easy and comfortable, facilitate; grant good luck and success; assist, favour, help to; — III. INF. *yisâr*, *muyâsara-t*, behave gently and kindly towards; show mercy; go to the left; —IV. INF. *îsâr*, (also m. I.), be able to do or procure easily; be or grow rich, live in affluence; = II.; have an easy confinement; — V. INF. *tayassur*, be facilitated, grow easy, succeed; —VI. INF. *tayâsur*, throw dice or cast lots with arrows one with another for; divide between each other by lot; work or act with ease and success; assist one another; — VIII. INF. *ittisâr*, *îtisâr*, let the dice or lot decide; — X. INF. *istîsâr*, succeed easily and well; be ready.

يسر *yasr*, *yusr*, *yasar*, *yusur*, facility of accomplishment or attainment; easy intercourse, complacency, kindness; prosperity; — *yasar*, *yusur*, ease, affluence, wealth; *yasar*, pl. *aisâr*, easy; easy to deal with, accommodating, kind, gentle, docile; ready; company who cast dice or lots; —*yusr*, *yusur*, pl. of يسار *yasâr*; ة *yasra-t*, left side; *yasrat-an*, on the left; — *yusra-t*, ease, facility; wealth; — *yasara-t*, pl. *aisâr*, lines of the hand; *yasarât*, pl. skilful hands, swift feet.

يسروع *yasrû'*, *yusrû'*, a white worm with a red head.

يسرى *yusra*, pl. *yusrayât*, left side, left hand; luck, success, wealth; — *yasriyy*, lucky, successful; — *yasariyy*, easy, comfortable.

يسف *yasaf*, a species of fly.

(يسق) — II. *yassaq*, INF. *taisîq*, take hold of and confine; — V. INF. *tayassuq*, be arrested, imprisoned.

(يسن) *yasan*, stifling air of a well; — *yasin*, aor. *yaisin*, be stifled by it.

يسور *yasûr*, gambler.

يسير **yasîr**, easy to be done or got; moderate, little, paltry.
(يش) *yaśś*, A, INF. *yaśś*, be joyous, rejoice, exult.
يشب *yaśb*, white jasper.
يشم *yaśm*, green jasper; agate.
يشمظة *yaśmaẓa-t*, flying fast.
(يص) — II. *yaṣṣaṣ*, INF. *taiṣîṣ*, open the eyes; put forth blossoms; cover itself with plants; attack.
يصب *yaṣb*, يصف *yaṣf*, jasper.
(يض)—II. *yaḍḍaḍ*, INF. *taiḍîḍ*=يصص *yaṣṣaṣ*.
يعار *yu'âr*, bleating (s.).
يعاسيب *ya'âsîb*, pl. of يعسوب *ya'sûb*.
يعاط *ya'âṭ*, *yi'âṭ*, *yu'âṭ*, watch-cry.
يعافير *ya'âfîr*, pl. of يعفور *ya'fûr*.
يعاقبة *ya'âqiba-t*, pl. of يعقوبى *ya'-qûbiyy*.
يعاقيب *ya'âqîb*, pl. of يعقوب *ya'qûb*.
يعالول *ya'âlûl*, pl. of يعلول *ya'lûl*.
يعامير *ya'âmîr*, pl. of يعمور *ya'mûr*.
يعبوب *ya'bûb*, rapid stream; cloud; big wide-stepping horse, good steed.
(يعر) *ya'ir*, aor. *yai'ir*, *yai'ar*, INF. *yu'âr*, bleat.
يعر *ya'r*, ة *ya'ra-t*, kid.
يعسوب *ya'sûb*, pl. *ya'âsîb*, queen-bee; chief, prince; a kind of partridge; white spot on a horse's forehead.
(يعط), II. *ya''aṭ*, INF. *yai'îṭ*, shout at, drive away by shouting; — INF. *muyâ'aṭa-t*, IV. INF. *î'âṭ*, id.
يعفور *ya'fûr*, pl. *ya'âfîr*, young doe, young bitch; noise, agitation, commotion.
يعقوب *ya'qûb*, pl. *ya'âqîb*, male partridge; Jacob; — ى *ya'qû-biyy*, pl. *ya'âqabit*, Jacobite.
يعقيد *ya'qîd*, honey thickened at the fire.
يعلول *ya'lûl*, pl. *ya'âlîl*, floating water-bubble; white cumulative clouds.
يعملة *ya'mala-t*, generous she-camel.
يعمور *ya'mûr*, pl. *ya'âmîr*, kid, lamb; — ة *ya'mûra-t*, a tree.
يعنى *ya'nî*, that is to say, namely.
يعور *ya'ûr*, bleating (adj.).

يفاع *yafâ'*, *yaffâ'*, hill, height.
(يفح) *yafaḥ*, aor. *yaifaḥ*, INF. *yafḥ*, hit or hurt on the crown of the head.
(يفع) *yafa'*, aor. *yaifa'*, INF. *yaf'*, ascend; grow up, be grown up, be about 20 years of age; — IV. INF. *îfâ'*, id.
يفع *yafa'*, hill; pl. *aifâ'*, full-grown, about 20 years old; — ة *yafa'a-t*, also—
يفعان *yuf'ân*, pl. of يافع *yâfi'*.
(يفن) *yafan*, pl. *yufn*, old, decrepit; four-year-old bullock; — ة *ya-fana-t*, cow.
يفوع *yufû'*, pl. hills, heights.
(يق) *yaqq*, aor. *yayaqq*, INF. *yuqû-qa-t*, be of a bright white, shine.
يقاظة *yaqâẕa-t*, being awake, awakening (s.).
يقاظى *yaqâẕa*, pl. of يقظان *yaqẕân*.
يقدومية *yaqdûmiyya-t*, going in advance, leading, leadership.
يقطين *yaqṭîn*, ة, pumpkin.
(يقظ) *yaqiẕ*, aor. *yaiqaẕ*, INF. *yaqaẕ*, be awake, awake (n.); — *yaquẕ*, INF. *yaqâẕa-t*, id.; — II. INF. *taiqîẕ*, IV. INF. *îqâẕ*, awake (a.); — V. INF. *tawaqquẕ*, be awake, wake, watch; — X. INF. *istîqâẕ*, awaken (a.); be awake, watch, be on one's guard, be attentive.
يقظ *yaqaẕ*, waking (s.); — *yaqiẕ*, *yaquẕ*, pl. *aiqâẕ*, awake, watchful, cautious;— ة *yaqaẕa-t*, night-watch; waking people, watchmen.
يقظان *yaqẕân*, f. *yaqẕa*, pl. *yaqâẕa*, awake, watchful, cautious; ابو اليقظان *abû 'l-yaqaẕân*, cock.
يقق *yaqaq*, cotton; marrow of the palm-tree; ابيض يقق *abyaḍ yaqaq* (*yaqiq*), pl. بيض يقائق *bîḍ yaqâ'iq*, snow-white.
يقلوم *yaqlûm*, hunting-hut.
(يقن) *yaqin*, aor. *yaiqan*, INF. *yaqn*, *yaqan*, know for certain; (m.) be certain, sure; be abashed, confused; — IV. INF. *îqân*, know for certain, believe firmly, make sure of; think true, surmise; — V. INF. *tayaqqun*=IV.; — VIII,

INF. *ittiqân*, know for certain, be well grounded in (acc. or ب *bi*); — X. INF. *istiqân*, id.

يقن *yaqn*, *yaqan*, certainty; anything certain, sure; — *yaqin*, *yaqun*, *yaqan*, who knows for certain; *yaqin*, greedy, addicted to (ب *bi*); — ة *yaqana-t*, who believes everything, credulous.

يقوقة *yuqûqa-t*, snowy whiteness.

يقين *yaqîn*, certainty, security, belief; certain, sure; — ى *yaqîniyy*, ة, referring to indubitable truth, scientific; pl. f. *yaqîniyyât*, certainties.

يك *yaku*, for يكن *yakun*, apocopated aor. of (كان).

يكسوم *yaksûm*, abounding with herbs.

يلا *yallâ'*, f. of ايل *ayall*, having the upper teeth turned inwards, &c.

(يلب) *yalab*, ة, skin of the back of wild beasts; shields, helmets, &c. made of such; iron, steel.

(يلق) *yalaq*, white, bright; — ة *yalaqa-t*, white goat.

يلل *yalal*, shortness and inequality of the upper teeth; smoothness.

يلمع *yalma'*, pl. *yalâmi'*, lightning; mirage; pl. anything flashing, glittering; — ى *yalma'iyy*, ingenious, witty; liar.

يلمق *yalmaq*, pl. *yalâmiq*, Tartar overcoat open at the sides.

يلنجج *yalanjaj*, يلنجوج *yalanjûj*, wood of aloes.

يلندد *yalandad*, pl. *yalâdd*, brave champion, terrible adversary.

(يم), pass. *yumm*, be thrown into the sea, be covered by the sea; — II. INF. *taimîm*, intend, purpose; perform an ablution with sand; — V. INF. *tayammum*, intend; perform one's ablutions with sand.

يم *yamm*, pl. *yumûm*, sea, ocean; large river; wood-pigeon; (m.) side.

يمام *yamâm*, ة, pl. *-ât*, *yamâ'im*, wood-pigeon; also ة *yamâma-t*, intention, purpose; — ة *yamâma-t*, proper name of a part of Arabia and of a very sagacious girl; — ى *yamâmiyy*, of or from Yamâmah.

يمان *yamân-in*, يمانى *yamâniyy*, ة, of or from Yemen; — ة *yamâniyya-t*, a red kind of oats.

يمقور *yamqûr*, bitter.

يمم *yamam*, wood-pigeon.

(يمن) *yaman*, aor. *yaiman*, *yâman*, INF. *yumn*, *yumna-t*, go to the right; A, also—*yamin*, aor. *yaiman*, appear or come from one's right; also—*yamun*, be auspicious, bring luck; pass. *yumin*, be lucky; — II. INF. *taimîn* (also VI.) go to the right; — III. INF. *muyâmana-t*, go to the right, be on the right of; — IV. INF. *îmân* (also VI.) come to Yemen or Arabia Felix; — V. INF. *tayammun*, become of Yemen, refer to Yemen; see a good omen in, become fortunate by, succeed in, prosper in; — VI. INF. *tayâmun*, see II. and IV.; bring luck to one another; — X. INF. *istîmân*, have luck, success; exact an oath from; take an oath.

يمن *yumn*, pl. *mayâmin*, luck, good fortune, prosperity, success; auspicious omen, good prospect; — *yaman*, right side or hand; — *al-yaman*, Yemen, Arabia Felix; — ة *yamna-t*, right side or hand; — *yumna-t*, luck, good fortune; a striped stuff of Yemen.

يمنا *yamnâ'*, f. of ايمن *aiman*, fortunate, &c.

يمنى *yumna*, pl. *yumnayât*, right hand; — *yamaniyy*, ة, of or from Yemen.

يموود *yam'ûd*, ة, tender, delicate.

يمين *yamîn*, pl. *aimun*, *aimân*, *ayâmin*, *ayâmîn*, right-sided; right side, hand, &c.; pl. *aimân*, auspicious, fortunate; luck, good fortune, power; pl. *aimun*, *aimân*, oath.

ينابيع *yanâbî'*, pl. of ينبوع *yambû'*.

ينبوت *yambût*, carob-tree.

ينبوع *yambû'*, pl. *yanâbî'*, spring, fountain, brook.

(ينخ) — IV. *ainaḥ*, INF. *înâḥ*, call the stallion by the cry *îniḥ îniḥ* to cover the she-camel.

(ينع) *yana'*, aor. *yaina'*, *yaini'*, INF. *yan'*, *yun'*, *yunû'*, ripen; — IV. INF. *înâ'*, id.

ينفور *yanfûr*, runaway, cowardly.

(ينق) *yanq*, rennet.

ينيع *yanî'*, ripe.

(يهر) *yahr*, spacious place; quarrelsomeness; importunity; — X. INF. *istîhâr*, insist upon, be unyielding; lose one's senses; exchange.

يهكوك *yahkûk*, blockhead.

(يهم) *yaham*, madness, folly.

يهما *yahmâ'*, f. of ايهم *aiham*, stupid, &c.; desert.

يهود *yahûd*, coll. pl. *yuhdân*, Jews; — ى *yahûdiyy*, pl. ة, Jewish; Jew; — ية *jahûdiyya-t*, Judea; Judaism.

يهير *yahyarr*, hard; hard resin of the tree طلح *ṭalḥ*; wild pumpkin; mirage; deception, snare, lie; dispute, quarrel; poison; also ى *yahyarra*, hard stone; toy.

(يهيه) *yahyah*, INF. ة, call to the camels with the cry *yâh yâh*.

يوافيخ *yawâfîḥ*, pl. of يافوخ *yâfûḥ*.

يواقيت *yawâqît*, pl. of ياقوت *yâqût*.

يوام *yiwâm*, INF. of (يوم III.).

يوح *yûḥ*, يوحى *yûḥa*, sun.

يوس *ya'us*, desperate.

يوسف *yûsuf*, sigh; Joseph.

يوصى *yawaṣiyy*, *yûṣa*, a kind of hawk.

يوك *yûk*, pl. *-ât*, lumber-room (m.).

(يوم) *yaum*, pl. *ayyâm*, pl. pl. *ayâwîm*, day (of twenty-four hours); time, season; day of battle; ذات يوم *ẕâta yaum-in*, on a certain day, once; *al-yaum*, to-day; يوم الاحد *yaum al-aḥad*, Sunday; ي الاثنين *yaum al-isnain*, Monday; ي الثلاثا *yaum as-salâsâ*, Tuesday; ي الاربعا *yaum al-arba'â'*, Wednesday; ي الخميس *yaum al-ḥamîs*, Thursday; ي الجمعة *yaum al-jum'a-t*, Friday; ي السبت *yaum assabt*, Saturday; ايام العجوز *ayyâm al-'ajûz*, seven days of mid-winter; — III. *yâwam*, INF. *yiwâm*, *muyâwama-t*, make an agreement by day, hire for a day; — ى *yaumiyy*, ة, daily; — ية *yaumiyya-t*, daily wages, daily bread, ration for the day, day's work; الاخبار اليومية *al-aḥbâr al-yaumiyya-t*, journals.

يومئذ *yauma'iẕ-in*, on that very day, just then.

يون *yûn*, *yawan*, son of Japhet; ancestor of the Greeks;—*yu'ûn*, *yûn*, skin of a leopard, &c. used as saddle-cloth.

يونان *yûnân*, the Ionians, ancient Greeks; Greece; — ى *yûnâniyy*, ة, Hellenic, Greek; Grecian; Greek language.

يووس *ya'ûs*, despairing, desperate.

يويو *yu'yu'*, pl. *ya'â'î*, common sparrow-hawk.

يئس *ya'is*, despairing, desperate.

ييعث *yai'uṡ*, an Arabic desert with shifting sands.

يين *yayan*, time between twilight and sunrise; name of a country.

ف. ستانغس

قاموس المتعلم عربي - إنكليزي

مكتبة
لبنان

مكتبة لبنان
ساحة رياض الصلح
بيروت

جميع الحقوق محفوظة
مكتبة لبنان ١٩٨٩

طبع في لبنان

قاموسُ المتعلِّم

عَرَبيٌ - إنكليزيٌ